GAMBERO ROSSO

ITALIAN
WINES
2025

ITALIAN WINES 2025

senior editors
Giuseppe Carrus
Gianni Fabrizio
Marco Sabellico

co-editor
William Pregentelli

editorial coordinator
Marzio Taccetti

special contributor
Paolo Zaccaria

contributors
Nino Aiello
Francesco Beghi
Nicola Frasson
Massimo Lanza
Gianni Ottogalli
Franco Pallini
Pierpaolo Rastelli
Antonio Stelli
Divina Vitale
Danilo Zannella

winery profile editors
Michele Bressan
Pasquale Buffa
Rosario Finocchiaro
Maria Antonietta Pioppo
Filippo Rapini
Jacopo Rossi
Moreno Rossin
Giulia Sampognaro
Daniele Siena
Sabrina Somigli
Cinzia Tosetti

other contributors
Carmelo Amorelli, Giovanni Angelucci,
Gioia Bacoccoli, Stefano Barone,
Enrico Battistella, Sergio Bonanno,
Francesca Bonatti, Claudio Cammarata,
Gabriele Casagrande, Claudio Cavani,
Enrico Ciuffa, Tommaso Crociera,
Francesco D'Angelo, Filippo Donarini,
Isacco de Porzio, Emilio Del Fante,
Fabio Ferrari, Francesca Ferrini,
Denise Franceschetti, Franco Fusco,
Ilario Giglio, Sante Guerrini, Giovanni
Lanzillo, Vittorio Le Pera, Giacomo
Lonati, Alessandro Mancuso, Salvatore
Marino, Roberto Mattozzi, Viola
Megliorin, Sara Mignone, Jacopo Minniti,
Giacomo Mojoli, Michele Muraro,
Carlotta Ozino Caligaris, Aristide
Pagani, Davide Pelucchi, Dario Piccinelli,
Nicola Piccinini, Mario Plazio, Michele
Quagliarini, Ugo Quaranta, Marianna
Rolfo, Maurizio Rossi, Marco Salomoni,
Angelo Sabadin, Carlotta Sanviti, Simona
Silvestri, Giuseppe Spina, Marcello
Striano, Luca Urbini

graphics
TB DESIGN
Via Ghibellina, 57 - 98123 Messina
tel. 3483848528
tina.berenato@gmail.com

layout
Marina Proietti

translation
Jordan De Maio

Gambero Rosso S.p.A.
via Ottavio Gasparri, 13/17
00152 Roma
tel. 06/551121 - fax 06/55112260
www.gamberorosso.it
email: gambero@gamberorosso.it

managing editor
Lorenzo Ruggeri

commercial director
Fabrizia Del Toro

publisher advertising office
Via Ottavio Gasparri, 17 – Roma
Tel. 06/55112341
email: commerciale@gamberorosso.it

advertising sales agency
Class Pubblicità SpA
Milano, Via Marco Burigozzo, 5
tel. +39 02 58219522
Per informazioni commerciali: sbianchi@class.it

distribution
USA and Canada
by ACC ART BOOKS, 6 West 18th Street, Suite 4B
New York, NY 10011
UK and Australia
by ACC ART BOOKS Sandy Lane, Old Martlesham,
Woodbridge, Suffolk IP12 4SD - United Kingdom
Italy
by Messaggerie Libri S.p.A.
via Verdi, 8 - 20090 Assago (MI)

ISBN 978-88-6641-2915

The final edit of Italian Wines was completed on
6 September 2024

**Printed in Italy for
Gambero Rosso S.p.A**
in October 2024 by
STR PRESS srl
P.zza Cola di Rienzo 85
00192 Roma

MISTO
Carta | A sostegno della
gestione forestale responsabile
FSC® C117195

SUMMARY

THE GUIDE 4
TRE BICCHIERI 2025 8
SPECIAL AWARDS 20
TRE BICCHIERI VERDI 22
TABLE OF VINTAGES 26
STARS 30
HOW TO USE THE GUIDE ... 34
THE RARE WINES COLLECTION ... 35

REGIONS

VALLE D'AOSTA 53
PIEDMONT 61
LIGURIA 231
LOMBARDY 249
TRENTINO 311
ALTO ADIGE 331
VENETO 369
FRIULI VENEZIA GIULIA 465
BRDA - SLOVENIA 545
EMILIA ROMAGNA 553
TUSCANY 593
MARCHE 771
UMBRIA 819
LAZIO 847
ABRUZZO 865
MOLISE 889
CAMPANIA 893
BASILICATA 927
PUGLIA 937
CALABRIA 967
SICILY 981
SARDINIA 1019

INDEX

WINERIES IN ALPHABETICAL ORDER ... 1047

THE GUIDE

We have spent 38 years among vineyards and wineries, talking with growers and oenologists, entrepreneurs and enthusiasts. Over these years, we've shared their stories, dreams, and the emotions stirred by tasting the fruits of their labor—across our guide and the expanding media landscape that now includes our website, TV channel, monthly magazine, and various social media platforms. Condensing all of this into a few words isn't easy. In these 38 years, we have tasted more than a million wines, and nearly 50,000 this year alone. Although the work is spread out among a team of more than 70 members, it represents an invaluable collection of notes, insights, and evaluations—perhaps unmatched anywhere else. Each wine is the product of a specific year, a terroir, and a producer's efforts. When assembled together, what do they form? An edition of the guide, with over 25,000 reviews, is like a high-resolution photograph made up of thousands upon thousands of pixels, creating a faithful image: the world of Italian wine in the year 2025. It's a world of fascinating complexity, one we explore and narrate each year, capturing its deep-rooted attachment to ancient traditions while staying open to innovation, experimentation, and constant evolution. We do this with passion, recounting stories and emotions, not passing judgment, but inviting readers and enthusiasts to do the same. Each wine reviewed here is like a dot in a post-impressionist painting—just a taste. But when you step back and see the whole picture, the landscape of Italy's vineyards in 2025 magically appears.

At the end of this long journey through vineyards and wineries, from the Aosta Valley down to the island of Pantelleria, we found Italy's wine scene—despite the complex international challenges affecting the industry—in a moment of great creative ferment. On the one hand, we see technical innovation and experimentation, with developments like resistant grape varietals, new rootstocks in vineyards, and the continued technological upgrading of wineries. On the other, there is a renewed focus on environmental sustainability and holistic growth that, with each passing year, shows a greater sensitivity to the importance of local policies. And all of this comes about in a way that is distinctive and distinctly Italian, drawing on the country's traditional grape varieties—whether it's the rediscovery of time-honored winemaking styles or the use of alternative containers, alongside more classic and well-established approaches. Like all of those around the globe who have made Italy the top exporter of wine, we seek harmony, balance, freshness, and an authentic reflection of the territory in the glass—an expression of the beauty and excellence that our country has to offer—regardless of whether it's a simple, everyday wine or one hailing from a renowned appellation. You'll find all of this encapsulated in our 498 Tre Bicchieri wines and the roughly 2,000 more that made it to our final tastings. It's a list that sees international producers and cooperatives sit alongside small winemakers and artisans. And it's to these last that a new, special section has been dedicated: our "Rare Wines". These are the rare bottles, limited in production, that capture the curiosity of collectors and disappear as soon as they appear in online marketplaces. We have selected 50 (a challenging task) to give further visibility to these intriguing expressions, which are also wonderful to drink. It's a veritable treasure trove of oenological gems, whether they are prestigious cuvées aged for 40 years on the lees, single-vineyard expressions, or meditation wines like Moscato di Saracena (one of which also received a special award). They compose our own, very personal and unconventional wine list, which we invite you to choose from for a worthy occasion or dinner. But the best way to fully understand our philosophy is to explore our special awards—those wines that moved us most during these months of travel, tastings, and retastings.

Sparkling Wine of the Year

OP Pinot Nero M. Cl. Pas Dosé Poggio dei Duca '19 - Calatroni

An extraordinary Metodo Classico with finesse and gustatory tension that is only just now beginning to reveal the complexity that it will develop in the years to come. Waves of red fruit, balsamic notes, and a vibrant, flavorful character linger with a textbook persistence. A splendid example of what pinot nero can achieve in a prime terroir like Oltrepò, here sourced from a single plot at 550 meters elevation in Rocca de' Giorgi.

White of the Year

Alto Adige Sauvignon Gran Lafóa Ris. '21 - Colterenzio

For those who thought Colterenzio had reached its peak, this wine marks yet another step forward. The Gran Lafóa originates from the vineyard that sparked this winery's quality revolution back in the 1980s. It is an extreme selection of the portion of the vineyard best suited to the variety, at 450 meters above sea level, offering a powerful, intensely elegant white wine.

Rosé of the Year

RGC Valtènesi Chiaretto Antitesi '23 - Avanzi

Seemingly delicate and subtle, Antitesi is part of the new wave of Italian oenology that has transformed the style and image of rosés in Italy. This revolution began in Valtènesi, where Avanzi crafts this delightful chiaretto from groppello: fresh, with fine fruity notes, sharp and mineral. It also has a remarkable capacity for aging.

Red of the Year

Chianti Colli Fiorentini Molino degli Innocenti Ris. '19 - Torre a Cona

Choosing this wine was challenging due to the fierce competition, but we settled on it because it perfectly embodies the paradigm of a great red—classic and modern at the same time. It's a wine with structure but not overpowering, born from a historic terroir and an indigenous grape variety, all built on depth, fine details, and elegance.

Meditation Wine of the Year

Moscato Passito al Governo di Saracena '15 - Feudo dei Sanseverino

It's not the first time Calabria, and Saracena in particular, has given us great thrills. The Bisconte brothers have created another small masterpiece: the 2015 Moscato, a bottle of spectacular depth and complexity. It's a true meditation wine to be savored slowly in all its nuances.

Solidarity Award
Lis Neris

The Pecorari family's winery, known for its high-quality wines, runs the Francesca Pecorari ONLUS Foundation, which has been supporting projects for children in Myanmar, Andhra Pradesh in India, and Uganda for years. Thanks to their support, 14 schools have been built.

Up-and-Coming Winery
Maugeri

Etna continues to spawn new spectacular wines and wineries. In just three harvests, Renato Maugeri and his daughters Carla, Michela, and Paola have established themselves as major players in the appellation, with projects ranging from single-vineyard vinifications to comprehensive guest accomodations. They have ambitious plans for the future.

Best Value for Money
Lambrusco di Grasparossa di Castelvetro 7Bio - Settecani

This award goes not only to the delicious Grasparossa 7Bio but also to a cooperative that works in an exemplary way, producing authentic wines that tell the story of their terroir and are offered at an accessible price, thanks to the dedication of its members and management team.

Sustainable Viticulture
Resistenti Nicola Biasi

The introduction of new "resistant" varieties in viticulture has sparked a wide-ranging debate that is far from over. Nicola Biasi, an oenologist with a long track record, has turned words into action, crafting and helping to create some of the most interesting and innovative wines with these new varieties under the "Resistenti Nicola Biasi" banner—a well-deserved award.

Cooperative of the Year
Belisario

Amid challenging times for Le Marche's cooperatives, we wanted to highlight the work of a solid and praiseworthy producer. Over its 50-plus years of history, Belisario has represented the territory of Matelica with carefully crafted, often unforgettable wines that stand the test of time. This is thanks to a passionate, competent team, rigorous management, and the collective commitment of all its members.

Grower of the Year
Mario Fontana

Heir to a long tradition of viticulturalists, Mario Fontana personally tends his family's vineyards, where he grew up learning the trade from his grandfather. If you pass by the Villero vineyard in Castiglione Falletto, you'll likely find him there, pruning shears in hand.

Winery of the Year

San Leonardo

For over 300 years, the Guerrieri Gonzaga family has stewarded this splendid estate, which, thanks to the passion and commitment of Carlo, an oenologist, and now his son Anselmo, has earned an international reputation for the quality of its wine. But San Leonardo is more than just a famous brand—it's a place of peace and beauty that has inspired, and continues to inspire, producers throughout the region and beyond. Visit, and you'll understand why...

We welcome Lorenzo Ruggeri to his new role as the Managing Director of our publishing house. He has been with us for over 15 years since his master's in Food and Wine Journalism, and this promotion is a testament to his hard work and excellent results.

Marco Sabellico, Gianni Fabrizio, Giuseppe Carrus

ACKNOWLEDGMENTS

We extend our gratitude to the Associazione +Freisa of Castelnuovo Don Bosco, Albugnano 549, the AproFormazione Institute of Alba, UniDOC of Corno di Rosazzo, the Wine Roads of Arezzo, the Marche Wine Protection Institute of Jesi (IMT) and VINEA of Offida, the Ente Vini Bresciani, the Valbormida Training Consortium of Carcare (SV), the Committee for the Great Cru of the Tuscan Coast, the Association of Winegrowers of Montespertoli, Umbria Top, Assovini Sicilia, the Municipality of Alcamo, the Girolamo Caruso Technical Economic and Technological Institute of Alcamo, and the following protection consortiums: Gavi, Roero, Barolo, Barbaresco, Alba, Langhe, and Dogliani, the Wines of Colli Tortonesi, the Nebbiolos of Upper Piedmont, the Hills of Monferrato Casalese, Barbera d'Asti and Wines of Monferrato, Caluso, Carema and Canavese, the Wines of Valtellina, Oltrepò Pavese, Franciacorta, Valcalepio, Valcamonica Wines, San Colombano, Lugana, Valtenesi, Conegliano Valdobbiadene, Bardolino, Valpolicella, Consorzio Colli Euganei, Consorzio Colli Berici, the Alto Adige Wine Consortium, the Trentini Wine Consortium, the TrentoDoc Institute, and the Lambrusco Protection Consortium, as well as the Romagna Wines Consortium, those of Bolgheri, Brunello di Montalcino, Chianti Classico, Valdarno Superiore, Orcia, Suvereto and Val di Cornia, Cortona, San Gimignano, Montepulciano, Chianti Colli Fiorentini, Terre di Pisa, Lucchesi Hills, Chianti Rufina, Morellino di Scansano, the Maremma Toscana Wines Consortium, Montecucco, Carmignano, the Tuscany Wine Consortium, Orvieto, Montefalco, Torgiano, the Piceno Wines Protection Consortium, the Abruzzo Wines Protection Consortium, and lastly the Sicilia DOC Wines Consortium and the Etna Wines Consortium.

We further extend our thanks to the Regional Enoteca of Nizza Monferrato, the Cantina Comunale I Sörì of Diano d'Alba, the Bottega del Vino of Dogliani, Gattolardo restaurant in Desenzano del Garda, the Città del Gusto Academy, the Basilicata Regional Enoteca of Venosa, the Western Sicily Regional Enoteca of Alcamo, and Caneva in Mogliano Veneto. Lastly, we express our heartfelt gratitude to our entire team of collaborators, who passionately supported us in the creation of this guide, from tastings in the field to drafting the profiles and the publication of the volume. We also thank all those who have collaborated with us over the years, with a special acknowledgment to Danilo Zannella, who has directed all our tastings at our Rome headquarters.

THE GUIDE

I TRE BICCHIERI 2025

VALLE D'AOSTA

Sopraquota 900 '22	Rosset Terroir	59
VdA Chambave Moscato Passito Prieuré '21	La Crotta di Vegneron	55
VdA Nebbiolo Dessus '22	Pianta Grossa	58
VdA Petite Arvine '23	Elio Ottin	57
VdA Petite Arvine Les Fréres '22	Grosjean	56

PIEMONTE

Alta Langa Extra Brut Bio Giulio Cocchi '19	Bava - Cocchi	75
Alta Langa Pas Dosé Blanc de Blancs '20	Marcalberto	150
Barbaresco Asili '21	Carlo Giacosa	138
Barbaresco Asili Ris. '19	Ca' del Baio	91
Barbaresco Giacone Lorens '21	Lodali	147
Barbaresco Mondino '21	Piero Busso	89
Barbaresco Montestefano Ris. '19	Produttori del Barbaresco	179
Barbaresco Ovello '20	Cantina del Pino	93
Barbaresco Pajè V. V. '19	Roagna	185
Barbaresco Pajoré '21	Bel Colle	76
Barbaresco Pajoré '21	Sottimano	198
Barbaresco Rabajà '20	Bruno Giacosa	137
Barbaresco Sorì Tildin '21	Gaja	134
Barbaresco Vanotu '21	Pelissero	171
Barbera d'Alba Elena La Luna '22	Roberto Sarotto	192
Barbera d'Asti Lavignone '23	Pico Maccario	173
Barbera d'Asti Sup. La Luna e i Falò '22	Vite Colte	209
Barbera d'Asti Sup. Montruc '22	Franco M. Martinetti	152
Barbera d'Asti Sup. Mysterium '19	Tenuta Montemagno	158
Barbera d'Asti Sup. Sansì '21	Scagliola - Sansì	192
Barbera del M.to Sup. Cantico della Crosia '20	Vicara	206
Barolo Arborina '20	Mauro Veglio	205
Barolo Cannubi '20	Giacomo Fenocchio	128
Barolo Castelletto '20	Fortemasso	131
Barolo del Comune di Castiglione Falletto '19	Cascina Fontana	101
Barolo Francia '20	Giacomo Conterno	117
Barolo Ginestra Ris. '16	Paolo Conterno	117
Barolo Lazzarito '20	Casa E. di Mirafiore	96
Barolo Meriame '20	Paolo Manzone	149
Barolo Monprivato '19	Giuseppe Mascarello e Figlio	153
Barolo Monvigliero '20	F.lli Alessandria	66
Barolo Mosconi '20	Pio Cesare	174
Barolo Rive '20	Negretti	162
Barolo Rüncot Ris. '16	Elio Grasso	140
Barolo Sottocastello di Novello '20	Ca' Viola	92
Barolo Vigna Rionda Ester Canale Rosso '20	Giovanni Rosso	188
Barolo Vignarionda '16	Figli Luigi Oddero - Tenuta Parà	165
Barolo Vignarionda '20	Guido Porro	177

Barolo Villero '20	Livia Fontana	130
Barolo Villero Ris. '16	Vietti	206
Boca '20	Le Piane	173
Canelli Casa di Bianca '23	Gianni Doglia	124
Canelli Sant'Ilario '23	Ca' d' Gal	90
Colli Tortonesi Timorasso Derthona Filari di Timorasso '22	Luigi Boveri	83
Colli Tortonesi Timorasso Derthona Origo '21	Vigneti Repetto	182
Colli Tortonesi Timorasso Il Montino '22	La Colombera	116
Dogliani Papà Celso '23	Abbona	62
Dolcetto di Ovada '22	Tacchino	200
Gattinara Osso San Grato Ris. '19	Antoniolo	70
Gattinara Ris. '19	Giancarlo Travaglini	203
Gavi del Comune di Gavi Rovereto Minaia '23	Nicola Bergaglio	77
Gavi del Comune di Gavi Vigne Rade '23	La Toledana	202
Gavi V. della Madonnina Ris. '21	La Raia	181
Gavi V. della Rovere Verde Ris. '21	La Mesma	155
Ghemme V. Pelizzane '17	Torraccia del Piantavigna	203
Grignolino d'Asti Monferace '19	Tenuta Santa Caterina	191
Grignolino del M.to Casalese Arbian '23	Paolo Angelini	69
Grignolino del M.to Casalese Bricco del Bosco '23	Accornero Giulio e Figli	64
Langhe Riesling Hérzu '22	Ettore Germano	137
Langhe Rosso Larigi '22	Elio Altare	68
Lessona '21	Villa Guelpa	207
M.to Rosso La Mandorla di Mauro '22	Luigi Spertino	198
Nebbiolo d'Alba Mompissano '22	Cascina Chicco	99
Nizza Cremosina '21	Bersano	78
Nizza Crivelletto '22	Cossetti 1891	122
Nizza La Court Ris. '21	Michele Chiarlo	110
Nizza Pomorosso '21	Coppo	119
Ovada Convivio '22	Gaggino	133
Piemonte Pinot Nero Bricco del Falco '20	Isolabella della Croce	144
Roero Arneis Cecu d'La Biunda '23	Monchiero Carbone	156
Roero Arneis Seminari '23	Stefanino Costa	122
Roero Ciabot San Giorgio Ris. '21	Angelo Negro	162
Roero Mompissano Ris. '21	Cascina Ca' Rossa	98
Roero Renesio Ris. '20	Malvirà	148
Roero V. di Lino '20	Cascina Val del Prete	105

LIGURIA

Colli di Luni Vermentino Boboli '23	Giacomelli	238
Colli di Luni Vermentino Lunae Et. Nera '23	Cantine Lunae Bosoni	240
Colli di Luni Vermentino Solaris '23	La Baia del Sole - Federici	234
Colline di Levanto Vermentino Luccicante '23	Cà du Ferrà	236
Dolceacqua '23	Terre Bianche	243
Riviera Ligure di Ponente Pigato U Baccan '22	Bruna	235

LOMBARDIA

Botticino Pià de la Tesa '21	Noventa Botticino	280
Capriano del Colle Fausto '23	Lazzari	273

Farfalla Dosaggio Zero M. Cl.		
Cave Privée '17	Ballabio	252
Franciacorta Brut Teatro alla Scala '19	Bellavista	253
Franciacorta Dosage Zéro		
Vintage Collection '19	Ca' del Bosco	258
Franciacorta Dosaggio Zero		
Naturae Edizione '20	Barone Pizzini	253
Franciacorta Dosaggio Zero ND	San Cristoforo	286
Franciacorta Dosaggio Zero Riserva 33 '16	Ferghettina	269
Franciacorta Extra Brut Boschedòr '19	Bosio	256
Franciacorta Extra Brut EBB '18	Mosnel	279
Franciacorta Extra Brut Rosé		
Lucrezia Ris. '11	Castello Bonomi	256
Franciacorta Nature Rosé 61 '17	Guido Berlucchi Franciacorta	254
Franciacorta Satèn	Muratori	279
Lugana Cemento '22	Marangona	275
Lugana Perla '23	Perla del Garda	283
Mattia Vezzola		
Grande Annata M. Cl. Rosé '18	Costaripa	268
OP Buttafuoco Storico V. Solenga '20	Fiamberti	270
OP Cruasé Roccapietra '18	Scuropasso - Roccapietra	288
OP M. Cl. Brut Cuvée 59	Tenuta Travaglino	291
OP Pinot Nero M. Cl. Brut		
1870 Gran Cuvée Storica '20	Giorgi	272
OP Pinot Nero M. Cl. Pas Dosé		
Poggio dei Duca '19	Calatroni	260
OP Pinot Nero M. Cl. Pas Dosé		
Vergomberra '20	Bruno Verdi	294
OP Pinot Nero Pernice '21	Conte Vistarino	266
RGC Valtènesi Chiaretto Antitesi '23	Giovanni Avanzi	251
RGC Valtènesi Chiaretto Cl.		
Fontanamora '23	F.lli Turina	292
RGC Valtènesi Chiaretto Rosagreen '23	Pasini San Giovanni	282
San Martino della Battaglia		
Campo del Soglio '23	Selva Capuzza	288
Terrazze Alte Pinot Nero '22	Tenuta Mazzolino	276
Valtellina Sforzato Corte di Cama '21	Mamete Prevostini	274
Valtellina Sfursat 5 Stelle '21	Nino Negri	280
Valtellina Sup. Grumello SO '21	I Vitari	295
Valtellina Sup. Inferno Flammante '21	Tenuta Scerscé	287
Valtellina Sup. Inferno Ris. '19	Aldo Rainoldi	285
Valtellina Sup. Sassella		
Nuova Regina Ris. '18	AR.PE.PE	251
TRENTINO		
Monogramma Müller Thurgau '21	Pojer & Sandri	324
San Leonardo '19	San Leonardo	327
Teroldego Rotaliano Sup. Ottavio Ris. '19	De Vigili	317
Teroldego Rotaliano Vigilius '21	De Vescovi Ulzbach	316
Trentino Pinot Nero V. Cantanghel '21	Maso Cantanghel	322
Trento Brut Altemasi Graal Ris. '17	Cavit	315
Trento Brut Nature '18	Moser	323
Trento Brut Rotari Flavio Ris. '16	Rotari	326
Trento Dosaggio Zero '20	Revì	326
Trento Dosaggio Zero Oro		
Rosso Cembra '18	La Vis - Cembra	319
Trento Extra Brut Cuvée N. 8 '19	Etyssa	318

Trento Extra Brut Riserva Lunelli '16	Ferrari	319
Trento Extra Brut Rosé Inkino '20	Mas dei Chini	321

ALTO ADIGE

A. A. Cabernet Sauvignon		
Freienfeld Ris. '20	Cantina Kurtatsch	345
A. A. Chardonnay		
Kreuzweg Family Reserve Ris. '20	Castelfeder	335
A. A. Chardonnay Troy Ris. '21	Cantina Tramin	359
A. A. Gewürztraminer V. Kastelaz '22	Elena Walch	362
A. A. Lago di Caldaro Cl. Sup.		
Quintessenz '23	Cantina Kaltern	342
A. A. Lagrein Ris. '21	Untermoserhof - Georg Ramoser	360
A. A. Lagrein Taber Ris. '22	Cantina Bozen	333
A. A. Lagrein V. Klosteranger Ris. '20	Muri-Gries	350
A. A. Müller Thurgau		
V. Feldmarschall von Fenner '21	Tiefenbrunner	359
A. A. Pinot Bianco Sirmian '22	Nals Margreid	350
A. A. Pinot Bianco Tyrol '22	Cantina Merano	349
A. A. Pinot Nero Matan Ris. '21	Tenuta Pfitscher	352
A. A. Pinot Nero Sanct Valentin Ris. '21	Cantina Produttori	
	San Michele Appiano	354
A. A. Pinot Nero Trattmann Ris. '21	Cantina Girlan	338
A. A. Santa Maddalena Cl.		
V. Premstallerhof '23	Tenuta Hans Rottensteiner	353
A. A. Sauvignon Gran Lafóa Ris. '21	Cantina Colterenzio	335
A. A. Sauvignon Renaissance Ris. '21	Gump Hof - Markus Prackwieser	341
A. A. Sauvignon Sàcalis Ris. '21	Tenuta Ansitz Waldgries	332
A. A. Spumante Pas Dosé		
Comitissa Ris. '20	Lorenz Martini	348
A. A. Terlano Nova Domus Ris. '21	Cantina Terlano	358
A. A. Terlano Pinot Bianco Eichhorn '22	Manincor	347
A. A. Val Venosta Riesling '22	Falkenstein - Franz Pratzner	337
A. A. Valle Isarco Riesling		
Praepositus '22	Abbazia di Novacella	332
A. A. Valle Isarco Sylvaner R '22	Köfererhof -	
	Günther Kerschbaumer	344

VENETO

Amarone della Valpolicella '20	Monte Zovo - Famiglia Cottini	414
Amarone della Valpolicella		
Campo dei Gigli '19	Tenuta Sant'Antonio	429
Amarone della Valpolicella		
Case Vecie '18	Brigaldara	379
Amarone della Valpolicella Cl. '20	Allegrini	371
Amarone della Valpolicella Cl. '15	Bertani	375
Amarone della Valpolicella Cl. '17	Giuseppe Quintarelli	424
Amarone della Valpolicella Cl.		
Cima Caponiera Ris. '17	Ca' Rugate	382
Amarone della Valpolicella Cl.		
Sant'Urbano '20	Speri	432
Amarone della Valpolicella Cl.		
Sergio Zenato Ris. '18	Zenato	448
Amarone della Valpolicella		
Mai Dire Mai '16	Pasqua	421
Amarone della Valpolicella		
Valzzane Corte Sant'Alda '17**	Camerani - Corte Sant'Alda	383

Bardolino Cl. '23	Le Tende	435
Campo Sella '20	Sutto	434
Capitel Foscarino '23	Anselmi	372
Cartizze Brut La Rivetta '23	Villa Sandi	445
Chiaretto di Bardolino Traccia di Rosa '22	Le Fraghe	400
Colli Berici Cabernet Bradisismo '21	Inama	405
Colli Euganei Cabernet Borgo delle Casette Ris. '20	Il Filò delle Vigne	399
Colli Euganei Rosso Gemola '19	Vignalta	443
Conegliano Valdobbiadene Rive di Ogliano Extra Brut '23	BiancaVigna	375
Custoza Sup. Amedeo '22	Cavalchina	388
Custoza Sup. Ca' del Magro '22	Monte del Frà	412
Custoza Sup. Summa '22	Gorgo	404
Lessini Durello Pas Dosé Nera Ris. '16	Fongaro Spumanti	399
Lugana Molceo Ris. '22	Ottella	421
Madre '22	Italo Cescon	390
Montello Asolo Rosso dell'Abazia '20	Serafini & Vidotto	432
Montello Asolo Rosso Sup. Venegazzù Capo di Stato '19	Loredan Gasparini	406
Soave Cl. Calvarino '22	Pieropan	422
Soave Cl. Campo Vulcano '23	I Campi	384
Soave Cl. Carbonare Roccolo del Durlo '22	Le Battistelle	374
Soave Cl. Monte Carbonare '22	Suavia	433
Soave Cl. Monte Grande '22	Graziano Prà	423
Soave Cl. Sup. Le Coste Verso '21	Canoso	385
Soave Sup. Il Casale '22	Agostino Vicentini	442
Soave Sup. Roncà Monte Calvarina Runcata '22	Dal Cero - Tenuta Corte Giacobbe	395
Valdadige Terra dei Forti Pinot Grigio Rìvoli '21	Roeno	426
Valdobbiadene Extra Dry Giustino B. '23	Ruggeri & C.	427
Valdobbiadene Extra Dry Molera '23	Bisol 1542	376
Valdobbiadene Rive di Col San Martino Brut del Fondatore Graziano Merotto '23	Graziano Merotto	411
Valdobbiadene Rive di Farra di Soligo Extra Brut Col Credas '23	Adami	370
Valdobbiadene Rive di Rua Brut Particella 181 '23	Sorelle Bronca	380
Valdobbiadene Rive di San Pietro di Barbozza Extra Brut Grande Cuvée del Fondatore Motus Vitae '22	Bortolomiol	379
Valdobbiadene Rive di Santo Stefano Extra Dry Dirupo Etichetta del Fondatore Nazareno Pola '23	Andreola	372
Valpolicella Cl. Sup. '21	Rubinelli Vajol	427
Valpolicella Cl. Sup. San Giorgio '20	Corte Rugolin	394

FRIULI VENEZIA GIULIA

Braide Alte '22	Livon	495
Capo Martino '22	Jermann	492
Chardonnay '19	Vigne del Malina	530
Collio Bianco Broy '22	Eugenio Collavini	479
Collio Bianco Fosarin '22	Ronco dei Tassi	513
Collio Bianco Luna di Ponca '21	Tenuta Borgo Conventi	469

Collio Bianco Stare Brajde		
Uve Autoctone '22	Muzic	499
Collio Bianco Uve Autoctone '22	Cantina Produttori Cormòns	482
Collio Chardonnay Ris. '19	Primosic	507
Collio Friulano Kaj Ris. '21	Paraschos	500
Collio Malvasia '23	Doro Princic	508
Collio Sauvignon '23	Tiare - Roberto Snidarcig	524
Collio Sauvignon Extempore '18	Venica & Venica	527
Eclisse '22	La Roncaia	511
FCO Bianco Myò I Fiori di Leonie '21	Zorzettig	535
FCO Biancosesto '22	Tunella	526
FCO Friulano Masiero Ris. '21	Torre Rosazza	525
FCO Schioppettino '21	Teresa Raiz	509
Friuli Aquileia Pinot Bianco Opimio '20	Ca' Bolani	474
Friuli Isonzo Bianco Flor di Uis '22	Vie di Romans	528
Friuli Isonzo Friulano I Ferretti '22	Tenuta Luisa	495
Friuli Isonzo Pinot Grigio Gris '22	Lis Neris	494
Friuli Pinot Bianco '23	Le Monde	497
Kronos Vitovska '18	Bajta - Fattoria Carsica	467
Rosazzo Terre Alte '21	Livio Felluga	486

BRDA -SLOVENIA

Brda Amber Gris Época '21	Ferdinand	547
Brda Bela Carolina Cosana I Classe '21	Carolina Jakončič Winery	548
Brda Chardonnay Opoka Jordano Cru '21	Domaine Marjan Simčič	549
Brda Chardonnay Tejca		
Vedrignano II Cru '21	Vini Noüe Marinič	549

EMILIA ROMAGNA

Il Pigro Dosaggio Zero M. Cl. '21	Cantine Romagnoli	575
Lambrusco di Sorbara Brut M. Cl.		
Brutrosso '23	Cantina della Volta	557
Lambrusco di Sorbara Brut		
Omaggio a Gino Friedmann '23	Cantina di Carpi e Sorbara	558
Lambrusco di Sorbara Leclisse '23	Alberto Paltrinieri	573
Lambrusco di Sorbara V. del Cristo '23	Cavicchioli	559
Lambrusco Grasparossa di Castelvetro		
7Bio '23	Cantina Settecani	578
Lambrusco Grasparossa di Castelvetro		
Monovitigno '23	Fattoria Moretto	570
Lambrusco Grasparossa di Castelvetro		
Vign. Cialdini '23	Cleto Chiarli Tenute Agricole	560
Reggiano Lambrusco Concerto '23	Medici Ermete	567
Romagna Albana Secco Codronchio '22	Fattoria Monticino Rosso	569
Romagna Albana Vitalba '23	Tre Monti	579
Romagna Sangiovese Marzeno		
Poggio Vicchio '22	Fattoria Zerbina	583
Romagna Sangiovese Modigliana		
Vigna Probi Ris. '20	Villa Papiano	582
Romagna Sangiovese Predappio		
Godenza '22	Noelia Ricci	571
Umberto '21	Umberto Cesari	560

TOSCANA

Arcanum '20	Tenuta di Arceno	723
Bolgheri Rosso Sup. Atis '21	Guado al Melo	662
Bolgheri Rosso Sup. Dedicato a Walter '20	Poggio al Tesoro	699

Bolgheri Rosso Sup. Grattamacco '21	Grattamacco	661
Bolgheri Rosso Sup. Guado de' Gemoli '21	Giovanni Chiappini	632
Bolgheri Rosso Volpolo '22	Podere Sapaio	717
Bolgheri Sassicaia '21	Tenuta San Guido	716
Bolgheri Sup. Castello di Bolgheri '21	Castello di Bolgheri	623
Brunello di Montalcino '18	Biondi - Santi Tenuta Greppo	603
Brunello di Montalcino '19	Tenuta Fanti	649
Brunello di Montalcino '19	Fattoi	650
Brunello di Montalcino '19	Fuligni	658
Brunello di Montalcino '19	Poggio Antico	699
Brunello di Montalcino '19	Poggio di Sotto	700
Brunello di Montalcino '19	Ridolfi	708
Brunello di Montalcino Campo del Drago '19	Castiglion del Bosco	629
Brunello di Montalcino Duelecci Est Ris. '18	Tenuta di Sesta	726
Brunello di Montalcino Giodo '19	Giodo	659
Brunello di Montalcino I Poggiarelli '19	Cortonesi	642
Brunello di Montalcino Paesaggio Inatteso '19	Camigliano	610
Brunello di Montalcino Tenuta Nuova '19	Casanova di Neri	617
Brunello di Montalcino V. del Suolo '19	Argiano	596
Caiarossa '21	Caiarossa	610
Caperrosso Senti Oh! '23	Fontuccia	655
Carmignano Grumarello Ris. '20	Tenuta di Artimino	723
Carmignano Ris. '21	Tenuta Le Farnete - Cantagallo	650
Carmignano Villa di Capezzana '20	Tenuta di Capezzana	724
Cepparello '21	Isole e Olena	663
Chianti Cl. '22	Castello di Monsanto	625
Chianti Cl. '22	Castello di Volpaia	627
Chianti Cl. '22	Le Miccine	674
Chianti Cl. '21	Pomona	703
Chianti Cl. '21	Tenuta di Carleone	725
Chianti Cl. '21	Val delle Corti	734
Chianti Cl. Ama '22	Castello di Ama	622
Chianti Cl. Borgo '22	San Felice	715
Chianti Cl. Gran Selezione '21	Tenuta di Lilliano	726
Chianti Cl. Gran Selezione Capraia Effe 55 '20	Rocca di Castagnoli - Tenute Calì	710
Chianti Cl. Gran Selezione Colledilà '21	Barone Ricasoli	708
Chianti Cl. Gran Selezione Giovanni Folonari '19	Tenute Ambrogio e Giovanni Folonari	654
Chianti Cl. Gran Selezione La Corte '21	Castello di Querceto	626
Chianti Cl. Gran Selezione Lapina '20	Vallepicciola	736
Chianti Cl. Gran Selezione Le Bolle '21	Castello Vicchiomaggio	628
Chianti Cl. Gran Selezione Poggiarso '20	Castello di Meleto	624
Chianti Cl. Gran Selezione Sergio Zingarelli '20	Rocca delle Macìe - Famiglia Zingarelli	710
Chianti Cl. Gran Selezione V. Istine '21	Istine	664
Chianti Cl. Gran Selezione Villa Rosa '20	Famiglia Cecchi	630
Chianti Cl. Lamole '22	I Fabbri - Susanna Grassi	647
Chianti Cl. Lareale Ris. '21	Lamole di Lamole	665
Chianti Cl. Ris. '21	L'Erta di Radda	647
Chianti Cl. Vign. La Selvanella Ris. '20	Melini - Vigneti La Selvanella	674
Chianti Classico V. Barbischio Ris. '21	Maurizio Alongi	594
Chianti Colli Fiorentini Molino degli Innocenti Ris. '19	Torre a Cona	732

14

Chianti Rufina Terraelectae V. Montesodi Ris. '21	Marchesi Frescobaldi	658
Chianti Rufina Terraelectae Vigna Le Rogaie Ris. '21	Colognole	639
Colline Lucchesi Tenuta di Valgiano '21	Tenuta di Valgiano	727
Cortona Syrah Castagnino '23	Fabrizio Dionisio	645
Cortona Syrah Serine '20	Stefano Amerighi	595
I Sodi di San Niccolò '20	Castellare di Castellina	620
La Regola '21	Podere La Regola	707
Lupicaia '19	Castello del Terriccio	621
Maremma Toscana Alicante Oltreconfine '22	Bruni	608
Maremma Toscana Ciliegiolo San Lorenzo '21	Sassotondo	718
Maremma Toscana Merlot Baffonero '21	Rocca di Frassinello	711
Mello 700 '21	Tolaini	731
Montecucco Rosso Ris. '21	ColleMassari	638
Montevertine '21	Montevertine	680
Morellino di Scansano V. Bersagliere Ris. '18	Podere 414	696
Morellino di Scansano V. I Gaggioli Ris. '22	Roccapesta	712
Nobile di Montepulciano '21	Boscarelli	606
Nobile di Montepulciano Cervognano Alto '20	Podere Le Bèrne	665
Nobile di Montepulciano I Quadri '21	Bindella - Tenuta Vallocaia	603
Nobile di Montepulciano Le Caggiole '21	Poliziano	703
Nobile di Montepulciano Pagliareto Sel. Bio '20	Lunadoro	668
Nobile di Montepulciano SorAldo '20	De' Ricci	643
Oreno '22	Tenuta Sette Ponti	720
Orpicchio '21	Dianella	644
Paleo Rosso '21	Le Macchiole	669
Pianirossi '21	Pianirossi	694
Poggio alle Gazze '22	Ornellaia	684
Poggio de' Colli '21	Piaggia	692
Riecine di Riecine '21	Riecine	709
Saletta Riccardi '20	Fattoria Villa Saletta	739
Sangioveto '20	Badia a Coltibuono	599
Solaia '21	Marchesi Antinori	595
Tinto di Spagna '21	Antonio Camillo	611
Valdarno di Sopra Sangiovese V. Bòggina C Ris. '21	Fattoria Petrolo	692
Valdarno di Sopra Sangiovese V. Polissena '20	Il Borro	606
Vernaccia di San Gimignano L'Albereta Ris. '21	Il Colombaio di Santa Chiara	640
Vernaccia di San Gimignano Ris. '20	Panizzi	689
Vernaccia di San Gimignano Sant'Elena Ris. '20	Teruzzi	730

MARCHE

Bianchello del Metauro Sup. Chiaraluce '22	Crespaia	783
Castelli di Jesi Verdicchio Cl. Ambrosia Ris. '21	Vignamato	813
Castelli di Jesi Verdicchio Cl. Franz Ris. '21	Tenuta di Frà	808
Castelli di Jesi Verdicchio Cl. Kochlos Ris. '22	Edoardo Dottori	785
Castelli di Jesi Verdicchio Cl. Lauro Ris. '21	Poderi Mattioli	794
Castelli di Jesi Verdicchio Cl. Origini Ris. '22	Fattoria Nannì	797

Castelli di Jesi Verdicchio Cl.		
Rincrocca Ris. '21	La Staffa	807
Castelli di Jesi Verdicchio Cl.		
San Paolo Ris. '21	Pievalta	800
Castelli di Jesi Verdicchio Cl.		
Selezione Cimarelli Ris. '22	Cimarelli	780
Castelli di Jesi Verdicchio Cl.		
Villa Bucci Ris. '21	Bucci	775
Conero Sassi Neri Ris. '20	Fattoria Le Terrazze	810
Falerio Pecorino Al MonteNero '22	Quntì	801
Falerio Pecorino Onirocep '23	Pantaleone	798
Kurni '22	Oasi degli Angeli	798
Offida Pecorino Artemisia '23	Tenuta Spinelli	806
Piceno Sup. '20	La Valle del Sole	811
Piceno Sup. Morellone '20	Le Caniette	777
Rosso Piceno Sup. Roggio del Filare '21	Velenosi	812
Verdicchio dei Castelli di Jesi Cl. Sup.		
V. V. Historical '19	Umani Ronchi	811
Verdicchio dei Castelli di Jesi Cl. Sup.		
Vign. del Balluccio '22	Tenuta dell'Ugolino	807
Verdicchio di Matelica Cambrugiano Ris. '21	Belisario	773
Verdicchio di Matelica Senex Ris. '18	Bisci	773
Verdicchio di Matelica Vertis '22	Borgo Paglianetto	774
Vignagiulia Rosso '19	Emanuele Dianetti	785

UMBRIA

Fiommarino Sangiovese '22	Cantina Monte Vibiano	
Montefalco Bianco Plentis '21	Terre de La Custodia	838
Montefalco Rosso Pomontino '21	Tenuta Bellafonte	822
Montefalco Rosso Ris. '20	Antonelli - San Marco	820
Montefalco Rosso Rosso Mattone Ris. '21	Briziarelli	823
Montefalco Rosso Ziggurat '22	Tenute Lunelli - Castelbuono	830
Montefalco Sagrantino '20	Scacciadiavoli	837
Montefalco Sagrantino 25 Anni '20	Arnaldo Caprai	824
Montefalco Sagrantino		
Il Bisbetico Domato '20	Giampaolo Tabarrini	838
Orvieto Cl. Sup. Mare Antico '22	Decugnano dei Barbi	828
Orvieto Cl. Sup. Panata '22	Argillae	821
Orvieto Cl. Sup. San Giovanni della Sala '23	Castello della Sala	824
Orvieto Cl. Sup. V.T. Muffa Nobile '22	Palazzone	834
Ràmici Ciliegiolo '21	Leonardo Bussoletti	823
Torgiano Bianco Torre di Giano V. Il Pino '21	Lungarotti	831
Trasimeno Gamay C'Osa '22	Madrevite	832
Trasimeno Gamay Poggio Pietroso Ris. '21	Duca della Corgna -	
	Cantina del Trasimeno	829

LAZIO

Anthium Bellone '23	Casale del Giglio	849
Biancolella '23	Antiche Cantine Migliaccio	848
Cesanese del Piglio Sup. Hernicus '22	Antonello Coletti Conti	851
Fiorano Bianco '22	Tenuta di Fiorano	857
Frascati Sup. '23	Casale Marchese	849
Habemus '22	San Giovenale	856
Montiano '21	Famiglia Cotarella	852
Poggio Triale '22	Tenuta La Pazzaglia	855
Roma Bianco '23	Poggio Le Volpi	855
Sergio Mottura Brut M. Cl. '15	Sergio Mottura	853

ABRUZZO

Abruzzo Pecorino

Giocheremo con i Fiori '23	Torre dei Beati	881
Cerasuolo d'Abruzzo '23	Cingilia	870
Cerasuolo d'Abruzzo Giusi '23	Tenuta Terraviva	880
Cerasuolo d'Abruzzo Sup.		
Terre di Chieti Fossimatto '23	Fontefico	873
Colline Teramane		
Montepulciano d'Abruzzo		
Neromoro Ris. '20	Fattoria Nicodemi	876
Montepulciano d'Abruzzo '22	Emidio Pepe	877
Montepulciano d'Abruzzo		
Alto Tirino Campo Affamato '21	Inalto Vini d'Altura	874
Montepulciano d'Abruzzo		
Capo le Vigne '19	VignaMadre - Famiglia Di Carlo	883
Montepulciano d'Abruzzo Casauria		
Podere Castorani Ris. '20	Castorani	868
Montepulciano d'Abruzzo		
Fosso Cancelli '19	Ciavolich	870
Trebbiano d'Abruzzo '22	Amorotti	866
Trebbiano d'Abruzzo		
Le Stagioni del Vino '21	Spinelli	879
Trebbiano d'Abruzzo Sup.		
Castello di Semivicoli '22	Masciarelli	875
Trebbiano d'Abruzzo Sup. Spelt '22	La Valentina	882
Tullum Pecorino Biologico '23	Feudo Antico	873
Villamagna '22	Torre Zambra	882

MOLISE

Molise Rosso Don Luigi Ris. '20	Di Majo Norante	891
Molise Tintilia 200 Metri '23	Tenimenti Grieco	891

CAMPANIA

Campi Flegrei Piedirosso '21	Contrada Salandra	902
Campi Flegrei Piedirosso V. Madre '22	La Sibilla	920
Costa d'Amalfi Furore Bianco Fiorduva '23	Marisa Cuomo	902
Falanghina del Sannio '22	Fappiano	907
Falanghina del Sannio		
Sant'Agata dei Goti V. Segreta '22	Mustilli	913
Falanghina del Sannio Svelato '23	Terre Stregate	921
Falanghina del Sannio Taburno		
BjondoRe '23	Fontanavecchia	910
Falanghina del Sannio Taburno Bonea '23	Masseria Frattasi	911
Fiano di Avellino '23	Colli di Lapio	901
Fiano di Avellino Alimata '22	Villa Raiano	922
Fiano di Avellino Ciro 906 '21	Ciro Picariello	915
Fiano di Avellino		
Colle delle Ginestre Ris. '22	Tenuta del Meriggio	920
Fiano di Avellino Le Grade '23	Vinosia	922
Fiano di Avellino Tognano Ris. '21	Rocca del Principe	916
Greco di Tufo Cutizzi Ris. '22	Feudi di San Gregorio	908
Greco di Tufo V. Serrone Ris. '22	Cantine di Marzo	905
Greco di Tufo Vittorio Ris. '10	Di Meo	905
Irpinia Aglianico Audeno '21	Masseria Della Porta	904
Taurasi '21	Donnachiara	906
Taurasi Terzotratto '19	I Favati	907
Zagreo '22	I Cacciagalli	897

BASILICATA

Aglianico del Vulture Calice '22	Donato D'Angelo di Filomena Ruppi	930
Aglianico del Vulture Il Repertorio '22	Cantine del Notaio	929
Aglianico del Vulture Nocte '20	Terra dei Re	933
Aglianico del Vulture Titolo '22	Elena Fucci	931

PUGLIA

Amativo '22	Cantele	940
Askos Verdeca '23	Masseria Li Veli	960
Bialento '23	Amastuola	938
Castel del Monte Bombino Nero Rosato Veritas '23	Torrevento	958
Es '22	Gianfranco Fino	947
Gioia del Colle Primitivo 17 Vign. Montevella '21	Polvanera	953
Gioia del Colle Primitivo Colpo di Zappa '21	Leone de Castris	948
Gioia del Colle Primitivo Fanova Ris. '20	Terrecarsiche 1939	958
Gioia del Colle Primitivo Marpione Ris. '21	Tenuta Viglione	961
Gioia del Colle Primitivo Muro Sant'Angelo Contrada Barbatto '21	Tenute Chiaromonte	943
Gioia del Colle Primitivo Ris. '19	Pietraventosa	952
Gioia del Colle Primitivo Ris. '21	Cantine Tre Pini	959
Gioia del Colle Primitivo Senatore '21	Coppi	944
Moramora Malvasia Nera '23	Cantine Paolo Leo	947
Negroamaro di Terra d'Otranto Rosso Filo Ris. '22	Menhir Salento	949
Patriglione '19	Cosimo Taurino	956
Primitivo di Manduria Collezione Privata Cosimo Varvaglione Old Vines '21	Varvaglione 1921	960
Primitivo di Manduria Mirea '22	Masseria Borgo dei Trulli	939
Primitivo di Manduria Raccontami '22	Vespa - Vignaioli per Passione	961
Primitivo di Manduria Sonetto Ris. '19	Produttori di Manduria	954
Primitivo di Manduria Terra Bianca Giravolta '20	Felline	946
Primitivo Old Vines '20	Morella	950
Salice Salentino Rosso Cantalupi Ris. '22	Conti Zecca	943
Salice Salentino Rosso Selvarossa Ris. '21	Cantine Due Palme	945
Talò Malvasia Nera '23	San Marzano Vini	955
Zacinto '23	Masseria Cuturi	949

CALABRIA

Cirò Rosso Cl. Sup. Duca Sanfelice Ris. '22	Librandi	973
Cirò Rosso Cl. Sup. Ris. 0727 '19	Brigante Vigneti & Cantina	969
Grisara Pecorello '23	Roberto Ceraudo	970
Particella 58 '23	Antonella Lombardo	974

SICILIA

Cavadiserpe Mandrarossa '22	Cantine Settesoli	1006
Cerasuolo di Vittoria '22	Planeta	1002
Etna Bianco Alta Mora '23	Alta Mora	982
Etna Bianco Muganazzi '22	Graci	996
Etna Bianco Sup. Contrada Volpare '23	Maugeri	998
Etna Rosso Contrada Monte Ilice '22	Barone di Villagrande	983
Etna Rosso Contrada Pietrarizzo '21	Francesco Tornatore	1010
Etna Rosso Contrada Zottorinoto Ris. '20	Cottanera	988

Etna Rosso Erse 1911 Contrada Moscamento '20	Tenuta di Fessina	1008
Etna Rosso Lenza di Munti 720 slm '21	Cantine Nicosia	999
Etna Rosso Mofete '21	Palmento Costanzo	1001
Etna Rosso Qubba '22	Monteleone	998
Etna Rosso V. Barbagalli '21	Pietradolce	1002
Faro '22	Le Casematte	987
Faro Palari '19	Palari	1000
Infatata '23	Caravaglio	986
Krimiso '19	Aldo Viola	1010
Marsala Vergine Secco Tino n. 8 '04	Francesco Intorcia Heritage	997
Monreale Bianco V. di Mandranova '22	Alessandro di Camporeale	982
Moro di Testa '21	Feudi del Pisciotto	992
Munjebel Rosso MC '21	Frank Cornelissen	988
Passito di Pantelleria Ben Ryé '21	Donnafugata	990
Sicilia Bianco Catarratto Buonsenso '23	Tasca d'Almerita	1007
Sicilia Hedonis Ris. '22	Feudo Arancio	992
Sicilia Nero d'Avola Duca Enrico '20	Duca di Salaparuta	991
Sicilia Nero d'Avola Saia '22	Feudo Maccari	993
Sicilia Perricone Ribeca '19	Firriato	994
Ziller 47	Tenuta Gorghi Tondi	995

SARDEGNA

Angialis '19	Argiolas	1020
Cagnulari '22	Chessa	1025
Cannonau di Sardegna Cl. Dule '21	Giuseppe Gabbas	1029
Cannonau di Sardegna Le Anfore '22	Olianas	1033
Cannonau di Sardegna Mustazzo '20	Tenute Sella & Mosca	1038
Cannonau di Sardegna Perda Rubia '21	Tenute Perda Rubia	1034
Cannonau di Sardegna Ris. '21	Antonella Corda	1027
Carignano del Sulcis 6Mura Ris. '21	Cantina Giba	1029
Carignano del Sulcis Sup. Terre Brune '20	Cantina Santadi	1037
Casesparse Ogliastra '22	Pusole	1035
Mandrolisai Fradiles '22	Fradiles	1028
Stellato Vermentino '23	Pala	1033
Su'Nico Bovale '22	Su'Entu	1039
Vermentino di Gallura Sup. Pitraia Monogram '21	Tenute Gregu	1030
Vermentino di Gallura Sup. Sciala '23	Surrau	1040
Vermentino di Gallura Sup. Sienda '23	Mura	1032
Vermentino di Sardegna Tuvaoes '23	Giovanni Maria Cherchi	1025

I TRE BICCHIERI 2025

SPECIAL AWARDS

THE BEST

RED OF THE YEAR

Chianti Colli Fiorentini Molino degli Innocenti Ris. '19
Torre a Cona

WHITE OF THE YEAR

A. A. Sauvignon Gran Lafóa Ris. '21
Colterenzio

SPARKLER OF THE YEAR

OP Pinot Nero M. Cl. Pas Dosé Poggio dei Duca '19
Calatroni

ROSÉ OF THE YEAR

RGC Valtènesi Chiaretto Antitesi '23
Avanzi

MEDITATION WINE OF THE YEAR

Moscato Passito al Governo di Saracena '15
Feudo dei Sanseverino

BEST VALUE FOR MONEY

Lambrusco Grasparossa di Castelvetro 7Bio '23
Cantina Settecani

WINERY OF THE YEAR
SAN LEONARDO

COOPERATIVE OF THE YEAR
BELISARIO

UN-AND-COMING WINERY
MAUGERI

GROWER OF THE YEAR
MARIO FONTANA

AWARD FOR SUSTAINABLE VITICULTURE
RESISTENTI NICOLA BIASI

SOLIDARITY AWARD
LIS NERIS

TRE BICCHIERI VERDI

With our Tre Bicchieri Verdi we make note of those wines that are made through certified organic or biodynamic management (which we indicate in red). This year there are 184 in all, some 37% of the wines awarded. It's a record for Italian Wines, testifying to how this positive trend is growing from vintage to vintage, from boutique wineries to large producers, all of whom have taken on the multiple challenges of achieving more sustainable and ecological production approaches.

A. A. Terlano Pinot Bianco Eichhorn '22	Manincor	Alto Adige
Abruzzo Pecorino		
Giocheremo con i Fiori '23	Torre dei Beati	Abruzzo
Aglianico del Vulture Nocte '20	Terra dei Re	Basilicata
Aglianico del Vulture Titolo '22	Elena Fucci	Basilicata
Amarone della Valpolicella '20	Monte Zovo	
	Famiglia Cottini	Veneto
Amarone della Valpolicella Cl.		
Cima Caponiera Ris. '17	Ca' Rugate	Veneto
Amarone della Valpolicella Cl.		
Sant'Urbano '20	Speri	Veneto
Amarone della Valpolicella		
Val**zzane Corte Sant'Alda '17	Camerani - Corte Sant'Alda	Veneto
Barbaresco Mondino '21	Piero Busso	Piedmont
Barbaresco Pajoré '21	Sottimano	Piedmont
Barbera d'Asti Sup. La Luna e i Falò '22	Vite Colte	Piedmont
Barbera del M.to Sup.		
Cantico della Crosia '20	Vicara	Piedmont
Bardolino Cl. '23	Le Tende	Veneto
Barolo Lazzarito '20	Casa E. di Mirafiore	Piedmont
Barolo Meriame '20	Paolo Manzone	Piedmont
Barolo Sottocastello di Novello '20	Ca' Viola	Piedmont
Barolo Villero Ris. '16	Vietti	Piedmont
Bialento '23	Amastuola	Puglia
Bianchello del Metauro Sup. Chiaraluce '22	Crespaia	Marche
Bolgheri Rosso Sup. Grattamacco '21	Grattamacco	Tuscany
Bolgheri Rosso Sup. Guado de' Gemoli '21	Giovanni Chiappini	Tuscany
Bolgheri Rosso Volpolo '22	Podere Sapaio	Tuscany
Botticino Pià de la Tesa '21	Noventa Botticino	Lombardy
Brunello di Montalcino		
Paesaggio Inatteso '19	Camigliano	Tuscany
Brunello di Montalcino '19	Poggio di Sotto	Tuscany
Brunello di Montalcino		
Campo del Drago '19	Castiglion del Bosco	Tuscany
Brunello di Montalcino Giodo '19	Giodo	Tuscany
Brunello di Montalcino V. del Suolo '19	Argiano	Tuscany
Caiarossa '21	Caiarossa	Tuscany
Cannonau di Sardegna Le Anfore '22	Olianas	Sardinia
Cannonau di Sardegna Perda Rubia '21	Tenute Perda Rubia	Sardinia
Cannonau di Sardegna Ris. '21	Antonella Corda	Sardinia
Capriano del Colle Fausto '23	Lazzari	Lombardy
Carmignano Villa di Capezzana '20	Tenuta di Capezzana	Tuscany
Castelli di Jesi Verdicchio Cl.		
Ambrosia Ris. '21	Vignamato	Marche
Castelli di Jesi Verdicchio Cl. Franz Ris. '21	Tenuta di Frà	Marche
Castelli di Jesi Verdicchio Cl. Kochlos Ris. '22	Edoardo Dottori	Marche
Castelli di Jesi Verdicchio Cl. Lauro Ris. '21	Poderi Mattioli	Marche
Castelli di Jesi Verdicchio Cl.		
Origini Ris. '22	Fattoria Nanni	Marche

Castelli di Jesi Verdicchio Cl. Rincrocca Ris. '21	La Staffa	**Marche**
Castelli di Jesi Verdicchio Cl. San Paolo Ris. '21	Pievalta	**Marche**
Castelli di Jesi Verdicchio Cl. Villa Bucci Ris. '21	Bucci	**Marche**
Cerasuolo d'Abruzzo Giusi '23	Tenuta Terraviva	**Abruzzo**
Cerasuolo d'Abruzzo Sup. Terre di Chieti Fossimatto '23	Fontefico	**Abruzzo**
Cerasuolo di Vittoria '22	Planeta	**Sicilia**
Chardonnay '19	Vigne del Malina	**Friuli Venezia Giulia**
Chianti Cl. '22	Castello di Volpaia	**Tuscany**
Chianti Cl. '22	Le Miccine	**Tuscany**
Chianti Cl. '21	Pomona	**Tuscany**
Chianti Cl. '21	Tenuta di Carleone	**Tuscany**
Chianti Cl. '21	Val delle Corti	**Tuscany**
Chianti Cl. Gran Selezione '21	Tenuta di Lilliano	**Tuscany**
Chianti Cl. Gran Selezione Capraia Effe 55 '20	Rocca di Castagnoli Tenute Calì	**Tuscany**
Chianti Cl. Gran Selezione V. Istine '21	Istine	**Tuscany**
Chianti Cl. Lamole '22	I Fabbri	**Tuscany**
Chianti Cl. Lareale Ris. '21	Lamole di Lamole	**Tuscany**
Chianti Cl. Ris. '21	L'Erta di Radda	**Tuscany**
Chianti Classico V. Barbischio Ris. '21	Maurizio Alongi	**Tuscany**
Chiaretto di Bardolino Traccia di Rosa '22	Le Fraghe	**Veneto**
Cirò Rosso Cl. Sup. Ris. 0727 '19	Brigante Vigneti & Cantina	**Calabria**
Colli Berici Cabernet Bradisismo '21	Inama	**Veneto**
Colli Tortonesi Timorasso Derthona Origo '21	Vigneti Repetto	**Piedmont**
Colline di Levanto Vermentino Luccicante '23	Cà du Ferrà	**Liguria**
Colline Lucchesi Tenuta di Valgiano '21	Tenuta di Valgiano	**Tuscany**
Colline Teramane Montepulciano d'Abruzzo Neromoro Ris. '20	Fattoria Nicodemi	**Abruzzo**
Collio Friulano Kaj Ris. '21	Paraschos	**Friuli Venezia Giulia**
Conegliano Valdobbiadene Rive di Ogliano Extra Brut '23	BiancaVigna	**Veneto**
Cortona Syrah Castagnino '23	Fabrizio Dionisio	**Tuscany**
Cortona Syrah Serine '20	Stefano Amerighi	**Tuscany**
Custoza Sup. Summa '22	Gorgo	**Veneto**
Dogliani Papà Celso '23	Abbona	**Piedmont**
Dolceacqua '23	Terre Bianche	**Liguria**
Etna Bianco Muganazzi '22	Graci	**Sicily**
Etna Bianco Sup. Contrada Volpare '23	Maugeri	**Sicily**
Etna Rosso Contrada Monte Ilice '22	Barone di Villagrande	**Sicily**
Etna Rosso Erse 1911 Contrada Moscamento '20	Tenuta di Fessina	**Sicily**
Etna Rosso Lenza di Munti 720 slm '21	Cantine Nicosia	**Sicily**
Etna Rosso Mofete '21	Palmento Costanzo	**Sicily**
Falerio Pecorino Al MonteNero '22	Quntì	**Marche**
Falerio Pecorino Onirocep '23	Pantaleone	**Marche**
Faro '22	Le Casematte	**Sicily**
Fiano di Avellino Alimata '22	Villa Raiano	**Campania**
Fiano di Avellino Le Grade '23	Vinosia	**Campania**
Fiommarino Sangiovese '22	Cantina Monte Vibiano	**Umbria**
Fiorano Bianco '22	Tenuta di Fiorano	**Lazio**
Franciacorta Dosage Zéro Vintage Collection '19	Ca' del Bosco	**Lombardy**
Franciacorta Dosaggio Zero Naturae Edizione '20	Barone Pizzini	**Lombardy**

Franciacorta Dosaggio Zero Riserva 33 '16	Ferghettina	**Lombardy**
Franciacorta Extra Brut Boschedòr '19	Bosio	**Lombardy**
Franciacorta Extra Brut EBB '18	Mosnel	**Lombardy**
Franciacorta Nature Rosé 61 '17	Guido Berlucchi Franciacorta	**Lombardy**
Franciacorta Satèn	Villa Crespia - Muratori	**Lombardy**
Gavi V. della Madonnina Ris. '21	La Raia	**Piedmont**
Gavi V. della Rovere Verde Ris. '21	La Mesma	**Piedmont**
Gioia del Colle Primitivo 17 Vign. Montevella '21	Polvanera	**Puglia**
Gioia del Colle Primitivo Marpione Ris. '21	Tenuta Viglione	**Puglia**
Gioia del Colle Primitivo Muro Sant'Angelo Contrada Barbatto '21	Tenute Chiaromonte	**Puglia**
Gioia del Colle Primitivo Ris. '19	Pietraventosa	**Puglia**
Gioia del Colle Primitivo Ris. '21	Cantine Tre Pini	**Puglia**
Gioia del Colle Primitivo Senatore '21	Coppi	**Puglia**
Greco di Tufo Cutizzi Ris. '22	Feudi di San Gregorio	**Campania**
Grisara Pecorello '23	Roberto Ceraudo	**Calabria**
Habemus '22	San Giovenale	**Lazio**
Il Pigro Dosaggio Zero M. Cl. '21	Cantine Romagnoli	**Emilia Romagna**
Infatata '23	Caravaglio	**Sicily**
La Regola '21	Podere La Regola	**Tuscany**
Lambrusco di Sorbara Leclisse '23	Alberto Paltrinieri	**Emilia Romagna**
Lambrusco Grasparossa di Castelvetro Monovitigno '23	Fattoria Moretto	**Emilia Romagna**
Lessini Durello Pas Dosé Nera Ris. '16	Fongaro Spumanti	**Veneto**
Lugana Perla '23	Perla del Garda	**Lombardy**
Madre '22	Italo Cescon	**Veneto**
Maremma Toscana Ciliegiolo San Lorenzo '21	Sassotondo	**Tuscany**
Mello 700 '21	Tolaini	**Tuscany**
Molise Rosso Don Luigi Ris. '20	Di Majo Norante	**Molise**
Monogramma Müller Thurgau '21	Pojer & Sandri	**Trentino**
Monreale Bianco V. di Mandranova '22	Alessandro di Camporeale	**Sicily**
Montecucco Rosso Ris. '21	ColleMassari	**Tuscany**
Montefalco Rosso Ris. '20	Antonelli - San Marco	**Umbria**
Montefalco Rosso Ziggurat '22	Tenute Lunelli - Castelbuono	**Umbria**
Montepulciano d'Abruzzo '22	Emidio Pepe	**Abruzzo**
Montepulciano d'Abruzzo Capo le Vigne '19	VignaMadre Famiglia Di Carlo	**Abruzzo**
Montepulciano d'Abruzzo Casauria Podere Castorani Ris. '20	Castorani	**Abruzzo**
Moramora Malvasia Nera '23	Cantine Paolo Leo	**Puglia**
Morellino di Scansano V. Bersagliere Ris. '18	Podere 414	**Tuscany**
Munjebel Rosso MC '21	Frank Cornelissen	**Sicily**
Nobile di Montepulciano Le Caggiole '21	Poliziano	**Tuscany**
OP Pinot Nero M. Cl. Pas Dosé Poggio dei Duca '19	Calatroni	**Lombardy**
Oreno '22	Tenuta Sette Ponti	**Tuscany**
Orpicchio '21	Dianella	**Tuscany**
Piceno Sup. '20	La Valle del Sole	**Marche**
Piceno Sup. Morellone '20	Le Caniette	**Marche**
Primitivo di Manduria Terra Bianca Giravolta '20	Felline	**Puglia**
Primitivo Old Vines '20	Morella	**Puglia**
Ràmici Ciliegiolo '21	Leonardo Bussoletti	**Umbria**
Reggiano Lambrusco Concerto '23	Medici Ermete	**Emilia Romagna**
RGC Valtènesi Chiaretto Rosagreen '23	Pasini San Giovanni	**Lombardy**
Riecine di Riecine '21	Riecine	**Tuscany**

Riviera Ligure di Ponente Pigato		
U Baccan '22	Bruna	**Liguria**
Roero Mompissano Ris. '21	Cascina Ca' Rossa	**Piedmont**
Roero Renesio Ris. '20	Malvirà	**Piedmont**
Roero V. di Lino '20	Cascina Val del Prete	**Piedmont**
Romagna Albana Vitalba '23	Tre Monti	**Emilia Romagna**
Romagna Sangiovese Marzeno Sup.		
Poggio Vicchio '22	Fattoria Zerbina	**Emilia Romagna**
Romagna Sangiovese Modigliana		
Vigna Probi Ris. '20	Villa Papiano	**Emilia Romagna**
Romagna Sangiovese Predappio		
Godenza '22	Noelia Ricci	**Emilia Romagna**
Salice Salentino Rosso Selvarossa Ris. '21	Cantine Due Palme	**Puglia**
San Leonardo '19	San Leonardo	**Trentino**
Sangioveto '20	Badia a Coltibuono	**Tuscany**
Sergio Mottura Brut M. Cl. '15	Sergio Mottura	**Lazio**
Sicilia Nero d'Avola Saia '22	Feudo Maccari	**Sicily**
Sicilia Perricone Ribeca '19	Firriato	**Sicily**
Soave Cl. Calvarino '22	Pieropan	**Veneto**
Soave Cl. Monte Carbonare '22	Suavia	**Veneto**
Soave Cl. Monte Grande '22	Graziano Prà	**Veneto**
Talò Malvasia Nera '23	San Marzano Vini	**Puglia**
Taurasi '21	Donnachiara	**Campania**
Terrazze Alte Pinot Nero '22	Tenuta Mazzolino	**Lombardy**
Tinto di Spagna '21	Antonio Camillo	**Tuscany**
Trebbiano d'Abruzzo '22	Amorotti	**Abruzzo**
Trebbiano d'Abruzzo Sup. Spelt '22	La Valentina	**Abruzzo**
Trentino Pinot Nero V. Cantanghel '21	Maso Cantanghel	**Trentino**
Trento Brut Altemasi Graal Ris. '17	Cavit	**Trentino**
Trento Dosaggio Zero '20	Revì	**Trentino**
Trento Dosaggio Zero Oro Rosso		
Cembra '18	La Vis - Cembra	**Trentino**
Tullum Pecorino Biologico '23	Feudo Antico	**Abruzzo**
Umberto '21	Umberto Cesari	**Emilia Romagna**
Valdarno di Sopra Sangiovese		
V. Bòggina C Ris. '21	Fattoria Petrolo	**Tuscany**
Valdarno di Sopra Sangiovese		
V. Polissena '20	Il Borro	**Tuscany**
Valdobbiadene		
Rive di San Pietro di Barbozza		
Extra Brut Grande Cuvée		
del Fondatore Motus Vitae '22	Bortolomiol	**Veneto**
VdA Petite Arvine Les Fréres '22	Grosjean	**Valle d'Aosta**
Verdicchio dei Castelli di Jesi Cl. Sup.		
V. V. Historical '19	Umani Ronchi	**Marche**
Verdicchio dei Castelli di Jesi Cl. Sup.		
Vign. del Balluccio '22	Tenuta dell'Ugolino	**Marche**
Verdicchio di Matelica Senex Ris. '18	Bisci	**Marche**
Verdicchio di Matelica Vertis '22	Borgo Paglianetto	**Marche**
Vernaccia di San Gimignano		
L'Albereta Ris. '21	Il Colombaio di Santa Chiara	**Tuscany**
Vernaccia di San Gimignano Ris. '20	Panizzi	**Tuscany**
Vernaccia di San Gimignano		
Sant'Elena Ris. '20	Teruzzi	**Tuscany**
Villamagna '22	Torre Zambra	**Abruzzo**
Zacinto '23	Masseria Cuturi	**Puglia**
Zagreo '22	I Cacciagalli	**Campania**
Ziller 47	Tenuta Gorghi Tondi	**Sicily**

TABLE OF VINTAGES FROM 1995 TO 2023

	ALTO ADIGE BIANCO	LUGANA/ SOAVE	FRIULI BIANCO
2006	🍾🍾🍾	🍾🍾🍾	🍾🍾🍾🍾🍾
2007	🍾🍾🍾	🍾🍾🍾🍾	🍾🍾🍾🍾🍾
2008	🍾🍾🍾	🍾🍾🍾🍾	🍾🍾🍾
2009	🍾🍾🍾🍾	🍾🍾🍾🍾🍾	🍾🍾🍾🍾
2010	🍾🍾🍾🍾🍾	🍾🍾🍾🍾	🍾🍾
2011	🍾🍾🍾	🍾🍾🍾	🍾🍾🍾
2012	🍾🍾🍾🍾	🍾🍾🍾	🍾🍾🍾🍾
2013	🍾🍾🍾🍾	🍾🍾🍾🍾	🍾🍾🍾🍾🍾
2014	🍾🍾	🍾🍾🍾	🍾🍾🍾
2015	🍾🍾🍾🍾	🍾🍾🍾🍾	🍾🍾🍾🍾🍾
2016	🍾🍾🍾🍾🍾	🍾🍾🍾🍾🍾	🍾🍾🍾🍾🍾
2017	🍾🍾🍾	🍾🍾🍾🍾	🍾🍾🍾🍾
2018	🍾🍾🍾🍾🍾	🍾🍾🍾🍾🍾	🍾🍾🍾🍾🍾
2019	🍾🍾🍾🍾🍾	🍾🍾🍾🍾	🍾🍾🍾🍾🍾
2020	🍾🍾🍾🍾	🍾🍾🍾	🍾🍾🍾🍾
2021	🍾🍾🍾🍾🍾	🍾🍾🍾🍾🍾	🍾🍾🍾🍾
2022	🍾🍾🍾🍾	🍾🍾🍾	🍾🍾🍾🍾
2023	🍾🍾🍾	🍾🍾🍾	🍾🍾🍾🍾

VERDICCHIO DEI CASTELLI DI JESI	FIANO DI AVELLINO	GRECO DI TUFO	FRANCIACORTA
🍾🍾🍾🍾🍾	🍾🍾🍾🍾	🍾🍾🍾🍾	🍾🍾🍾🍾
🍾🍾	🍾🍾🍾	🍾🍾	🍾🍾🍾
🍾🍾🍾🍾	🍾🍾🍾	🍾🍾🍾🍾🍾	🍾🍾🍾🍾🍾
🍾🍾🍾🍾	🍾🍾🍾	🍾🍾🍾🍾	🍾🍾🍾
🍾🍾🍾🍾🍾	🍾🍾🍾🍾🍾	🍾🍾🍾🍾🍾	🍾🍾🍾
🍾	🍾🍾🍾	🍾🍾	🍾🍾🍾🍾🍾
🍾🍾🍾🍾	🍾🍾🍾🍾	🍾🍾🍾🍾	🍾🍾🍾🍾
🍾🍾🍾🍾🍾	🍾🍾🍾🍾🍾	🍾🍾🍾	🍾🍾🍾🍾🍾
🍾🍾🍾	🍾🍾🍾	🍾🍾🍾	🍾🍾🍾
🍾🍾🍾	🍾🍾🍾🍾	🍾🍾🍾	🍾🍾🍾
🍾🍾🍾🍾🍾	🍾🍾🍾🍾🍾	🍾🍾🍾🍾	🍾🍾🍾🍾🍾
🍾🍾	🍾🍾🍾	🍾🍾🍾	🍾🍾
🍾🍾🍾🍾	🍾🍾🍾🍾🍾	🍾🍾🍾🍾	🍾🍾🍾🍾🍾
🍾🍾🍾🍾🍾	🍾🍾🍾🍾	🍾🍾🍾🍾	🍾🍾🍾🍾
🍾🍾🍾🍾	🍾🍾🍾	🍾🍾🍾🍾	🍾🍾🍾🍾
🍾🍾🍾	🍾🍾🍾🍾	🍾🍾🍾	
🍾🍾	🍾🍾🍾🍾	🍾🍾🍾	
🍾🍾	🍾🍾🍾🍾	🍾🍾🍾🍾	

	BARBARESCO	BAROLO	AMARONE	CHIANTI CLASSICO
1995	3	3	5	5
1996	5	5	3	4
1997	3	3	4	4
1998	3	4	3	3
1999	5	4	3	5
2000	3	3	4	4
2001	5	5	5	5
2002	2	1	3	2
2003	2	1	3	2
2004	4	4	4	4
2005	3	3	4	3
2006	3	4	3	3
2007	3	3	5	4
2008	4	4	3	4
2009	2	2	3	3
2010	5	5	4	5
2011	4	4	4	3
2012	3	3	3	3
2013	5	5	4	4
2014	3	2	2	3
2015	4	4	4	4
2016	5	5	5	5
2017	3	4	4	3
2018	4	3	3	4
2019	5	5	4	5
2020	4	3		4
2021	5			5
2022				3

BRUNELLO DI MONTALCINO	BOLGHERI	TAURASI	MONTEPULCIANO D'ABRUZZO	ETNA ROSSO
🍾🍾🍾🍾🍾	🍾🍾🍾🍾	🍾🍾🍾	🍾🍾🍾🍾🍾	🍾🍾🍾
🍾🍾	🍾🍾🍾	🍾🍾🍾	🍾🍾🍾🍾	🍾🍾
🍾🍾🍾🍾	🍾🍾🍾🍾	🍾🍾🍾🍾	🍾🍾🍾🍾	🍾🍾🍾
🍾🍾🍾🍾	🍾🍾🍾🍾🍾	🍾🍾	🍾🍾🍾🍾	🍾🍾🍾
🍾🍾🍾🍾🍾	🍾🍾🍾🍾🍾	🍾🍾🍾🍾🍾	🍾🍾	🍾🍾🍾🍾
🍾🍾🍾	🍾🍾🍾	🍾🍾	🍾🍾🍾🍾	🍾🍾🍾
🍾🍾🍾🍾🍾	🍾🍾🍾🍾🍾	🍾🍾🍾	🍾🍾🍾🍾🍾	🍾🍾🍾
🍾🍾	🍾🍾	🍾🍾🍾	🍾🍾	🍾🍾
🍾🍾🍾	🍾🍾	🍾🍾🍾🍾	🍾🍾🍾	🍾🍾🍾
🍾🍾🍾	🍾🍾🍾	🍾🍾🍾🍾	🍾🍾🍾🍾	🍾🍾🍾
🍾🍾🍾	🍾🍾🍾	🍾🍾🍾	🍾🍾🍾🍾	🍾🍾🍾🍾
🍾🍾🍾	🍾🍾🍾🍾	🍾🍾🍾	🍾🍾🍾	🍾🍾🍾🍾
🍾🍾🍾	🍾🍾🍾🍾	🍾🍾🍾	🍾🍾🍾	🍾🍾🍾🍾🍾
🍾🍾🍾	🍾🍾🍾🍾	🍾🍾🍾🍾🍾	🍾🍾🍾	🍾🍾🍾🍾🍾
🍾🍾	🍾🍾🍾🍾🍾	🍾🍾🍾	🍾🍾	🍾🍾🍾
🍾🍾🍾🍾	🍾🍾🍾	🍾🍾🍾🍾	🍾🍾🍾	🍾🍾🍾🍾
🍾🍾🍾	🍾🍾🍾🍾	🍾🍾	🍾🍾🍾🍾	🍾🍾🍾🍾
🍾🍾🍾	🍾🍾🍾🍾	🍾🍾🍾	🍾🍾🍾	🍾🍾🍾🍾
🍾🍾🍾🍾	🍾🍾🍾🍾🍾	🍾🍾🍾🍾	🍾🍾🍾🍾	🍾🍾
🍾🍾	🍾🍾	🍾🍾🍾	🍾🍾🍾	🍾🍾🍾🍾🍾
🍾🍾🍾🍾	🍾🍾🍾🍾	🍾🍾🍾	🍾🍾🍾🍾	🍾🍾🍾
🍾🍾🍾🍾🍾	🍾🍾🍾🍾	🍾🍾🍾	🍾🍾🍾	🍾🍾🍾🍾🍾
🍾🍾	🍾🍾🍾🍾	🍾🍾🍾	🍾🍾🍾🍾	🍾🍾
🍾🍾🍾	🍾🍾🍾🍾	🍾🍾🍾	🍾🍾🍾🍾	🍾🍾🍾🍾
🍾🍾🍾	🍾🍾🍾🍾🍾	🍾🍾🍾🍾	🍾🍾🍾	🍾🍾🍾🍾
	🍾🍾🍾🍾	🍾🍾🍾🍾	🍾🍾🍾	🍾🍾🍾🍾
			🍾🍾🍾	🍾🍾🍾🍾
				🍾🍾🍾🍾

STARS

★★★★★★
61
Gaja (Piedmont)

★★★★
49
Ca' del Bosco (Lombardy)

43
Elio Altare (Piedmont)

40
Allegrini (Veneto)

★★★
39
Valentini (Abruzzo)

38
La Spinetta (Piedmont)

36
Bellavista (Lombardy)
Castello di Fonterutoli (Tuscany)
Jermann (Friuli Venezia Giulia)
Tenuta San Guido (Tuscany)
Cantina Produttori San Michele Appiano
(Trentino)

35
Giacomo Conterno (Piedmont)
Ferrari (Trentino Alto Adige)
Masciarelli (Abruzzo)

34
Castello della Sala (Umbria)

33
Planeta (Sicily)
Tasca d'Almerita (Sicily)
Cantina Tramin (Trentino)
Vie di Romans (Friuli Venezia Giulia)

32
Marchesi Antinori (Tuscany)
Bruno Giacosa (Piedmont)
Pieropan (Veneto)
Poliziano (Tuscany)

31
Ornellaia (Tuscany)

30
Argiolas (Sardinia)
Cantina Bozen (Alto Adige)
Arnaldo Caprai (Umbria)
Livio Felluga (Friuli Venezia Giulia)
Feudi di San Gregorio (Campania)
Nino Negri (Lombardy)

★★
29
Famiglia Cotarella (Lazio)
Schiopetto (Friuli Venezia Giulia)
Tenute Sella & Mosca (Sardinia)
Cantina Terlano (Alto Adige)

28
Ca' Viola (Piedmont)
Cantina Colterenzio (Alto Adige)
Fèlsina (Tuscany)
Vietti (Piedmont)

27
Castello di Ama (Tuscany)
Michele Chiarlo (Piedmont)
Isole e Olena (Tuscany)
Barone Ricasoli (Tuscany)
San Leonardo (Trentino)
Paolo Scavino (Piedmont)
Elena Walch (Alto Adige)

26
Ca' Rugate (Veneto)
Castellare di Castellina (Tuscany)
Les Crêtes (Valle d'Aosta)
Fontodi (Tuscany)
Cantina Kaltern (Alto Adige)
Le Macchiole (Tuscany)
Montevertine (Tuscany)
Villa Russiz (Friuli Venezia Giulia)

25
Antoniolo (Piedmont)
Donnafugata (Sicily)
Montevetrano (Campania)
Serafini & Vidotto (Veneto)
Sottimano (Piedmont)
Volpe Pasini (Friuli Venezia Giulia)

24
Castello del Terriccio (Tuscany)
Cataldi Madonna (Abruzzo)
Cusumano (Sicily)

Firriato (Sicily)
Gravner (Friuli Venezia Giulia)
Muri-Gries (Trentino Alto Adige)
Ronco dei Tassi (Friuli Venezia Giulia)
Ruffino (Tuscany)
Cantina Santadi (Sardinia)
Umani Ronchi (Marche)

23

Abbazia di Novacella (Alto Adige)
Anselmi (Veneto)
Casanova di Neri (Tuscany)
Domenico Clerico (Piedmont)
Coppo (Piedmont)
Lis Neris (Friuli Venezia Giulia)
Doro Princic (Friuli Venezia Giulia)
Giuseppe Quintarelli (Veneto)
Velenosi (Marche)
Venica & Venica (Friuli Venezia Giulia)

22

Bertani (Veneto)
Cascina La Barbatella (Piedmont)
Livon (Friuli Venezia Giulia)
Massolino - Vigna Rionda (Piedmont)
Monsupello (Lombardy)
Fiorenzo Nada (Piedmont)
Fattoria Zerbina (Emilia Romagna)

21

Abbona (Piedmont)
Bucci (Marche)
Cavit (Trentino Alto Adige)
Di Majo Norante (Molise)
Gioacchino Garofoli (Marche)
Elio Grasso (Piedmont)
Grattamacco (Tuscany)
Librandi (Calabria)
Lungarotti (Umbria)
Fattoria Petrolo (Tuscany)
Bruno Rocca (Piedmont)
Rocca di Frassinello (Tuscany)
Tenuta Sant'Antonio (Veneto)

20

Lorenzo Begali (Veneto)
Dorigo (Friuli Venezia Giulia)
Ferghettina (Lombardy)
Malvirà (Piedmont)
Palari (Sicily)
Piaggia (Tuscany)
Pietracupa (Campania)
San Felice (Tuscany)
Luciano Sandrone (Piedmont)
Speri (Veneto)
Suavia (Veneto)
Franco Toros (Friuli Venezia Giulia)
Vignalta (Veneto)
Le Vigne di Zamò (Friuli Venezia Giulia)

STARS

19

Giulio Accornero Giulio e Figli (Piedmont)
Biondi - Santi Tenuta Greppo (Tuscany)
Boscarelli (Tuscany)
Ca' del Baio (Piedmont)
Cavalchina (Veneto)
Eugenio Collavini (Friuli Venezia Giulia)
Matteo Correggia (Piedmont)
Tenute Ambrogio e Giovanni Folonari (Tuscany)
Marchesi Frescobaldi (Tuscany)
Elena Fucci (Basilicata)
Köfererhof - Günther Kerschbaumer (Alto Adige)
Leone de Castris (Puglia)
Mamete Prevostini (Lombardy)
Masi (Veneto)
Monchiero Carbone (Piedmont)
Sergio Mottura (Lazio)
Nals Margreid (Trentino Alto Adige)
Russiz Superiore (Friuli Venezia Giulia)
San Patrignano (Emilia Romagna)
Tenuta Unterortl - Castel Juval (Alto Adige)
Valle Reale (Abruzzo)

18

Brancaia (Tuscany)
Cascina Ca' Rossa (Piedmont)
Castello Banfi (Tuscany)
Castello di Volpaia (Tuscany)
Elvio Cogno (Piedmont)
Conterno Fantino (Piedmont)
Cantine Due Palme (Puglia)
Ettore Germano (Piedmont)
Cantina Girlan (Alto Adige)
Dino Illuminati (Abruzzo)
Kuenhof - Peter Pliger (Alto Adige)
Cantina Kurtatsch (Trentino Alto Adige)
Bartolo Mascarello (Piedmont)
Mastroberardino (Campania)
Graziano Prà (Veneto)
Aldo Rainoldi (Lombardy)
Albino Rocca (Piedmont)
Tenuta di Valgiano (Tuscany)
Viviani (Veneto)

17

F.lli Alessandria (Piedmont)
Brigaldara (Veneto)
Castello di Albola (Tuscany)
ColleMassari (Tuscany)
Falkenstein - Franz Pratzner (Alto Adige)
Poggio di Sotto (Tuscany)
Querciabella (Tuscany)
Giampaolo Tabarrini (Umbria)
Tenuta di Ghizzano (Tuscany)
Torrevento (Puglia)
Zenato (Veneto)

Maison Anselmet (Valle d'Aosta)
Guido Berlucchi Franciacorta (Lombardy)
Piero Busso (Piedmont)
Tenute Chiaromonte (Puglia)
Aldo Conterno (Piedmont)
Cottanera (Sicily)
Marisa Cuomo (Campania)
Romano Dal Forno (Veneto)
Poderi Luigi Einaudi (Piedmont)
Feudi del Pisciotto (Sicily)
Feudo Maccari (Sicily)
Giuseppe Gabbas (Sardinia)
Giorgi (Lombardy)
Cantine Lunae Bosoni (Liguria)
Medici Ermete (Emilia Romagna)
Miani (Friuli Venezia Giulia)
La Monacesca (Marche)
Oasi degli Angeli (Marche)
Ottella (Veneto)
Pio Cesare (Piedmont)
Produttori del Barbaresco (Piedmont)
Tenute Rubino (Puglia)
Luigi Spertino (Piedmont)
Tiefenbrunner (Alto Adige)
Torraccia del Piantavigna (Piedmont)
Uberti (Lombardy)
G. D. Vajra (Piedmont)
Villa Medoro (Abruzzo)

15

Brovia (Piedmont)
I Campi (Veneto)
Cleto Chiarli Tenute Agricole (Emilia Romagna)
Tenute Cisa Asinari dei Marchesi di Grésy (Piedmont)
Paolo Conterno (Piedmont)
Gump Hof - Markus Prackwieser (Alto Adige)
Lo Triolet (Valle d'Aosta)
Franco M. Martinetti (Piedmont)
Monte del Frà (Veneto)
Pietradolce (Sicily)
Poggio Le Volpi (Lazio)
Polvanera (Puglia)
Ruggeri & C. (Veneto)
Tenuta Sette Ponti (Tuscany)
Tenute del Cerro (Tuscany)
Villa Sandi (Veneto)
Roberto Voerzio (Piedmont)

14

Avignonesi (Tuscany)
Belisario (Marche)
Braida (Piedmont)
Bricco Rocche - Bricco Asili (Piedmont)
Fattoria Carpineta Fontalpino (Tuscany)
Castorani (Abruzzo)
Famiglia Cecchi (Tuscany)
Tenuta Col d'Orcia (Tuscany)
Colli di Lapio (Campania)
Gini (Veneto)
Edi Keber (Friuli Venezia Giulia)

Letrari (Trentino)
Vigneti Massa (Piedmont)
Graziano Merotto (Veneto)
Angelo Negro (Piedmont)
Orma (Tuscany)
Elio Ottin (Valle d'Aosta)
Fattoria Le Pupille (Tuscany)
Re Manfredi (Basilicata)
Riecine (Tuscany)
Rocca delle Macìe - Famiglia Zingarelli (Tuscany)
Ronco del Gelso (Friuli Venezia Giulia)
Giovanni Rosso (Piedmont)
Tenute San Sisto (Marche)
Podere Sapaio (Tuscany)
Tacchino (Piedmont)
F.lli Tedeschi (Veneto)
Tenuta di Capezzana (Tuscany)
Tenuta di Lilliano (Tuscany)
Villa Sparina (Piedmont)

13

Abate Nero (Trentino)
Tenuta Ansitz Waldgries (Alto Adige)
Benanti (Sicily)
Cà Maiol (Lombardy)
Camerani - Corte Sant'Alda (Veneto)
Cantine del Notaio (Basilicata)
Castello di Monsanto (Tuscany)
Cavalleri (Lombardy)
Cavallotto - Tenuta Bricco Boschis (Piedmont)
Decugnano dei Barbi (Umbria)
Dorigati (Trentino)
Le Due Terre (Friuli Venezia Giulia)
Foradori (Trentino Alto Adige)
Galardi (Campania)
Inama (Veneto)
Maculan (Veneto)
Marchesi di Barolo (Piedmont)
Giuseppe Mascarello e Figlio (Piedmont)
Cantina Merano (Alto Adige)
Le Monde (Friuli Venezia Giulia)
Montenidoli (Tuscany)
Palazzone (Umbria)
Pecchenino (Piedmont)
Le Piane (Piedmont)
Roagna (Piedmont)
Rocca del Principe (Campania)
Salvioni (Tuscany)
Enrico Serafino (Piedmont)
Surrau (Sardinia)
Tenuta di Fessina (Sicily)
Tormaresca (Puglia)
Torre dei Beati (Abruzzo)
Tua Rita (Tuscany)
Agostino Vicentini (Veneto)
Villa Papiano (Emilia Romagna)

12

Gianfranco Alessandria (Piedmont)
Azelia (Piedmont)
Badia a Coltibuono (Tuscany)

Nicola Balter (Trentino)
Barone Pizzini (Lombardy)
Nicola Bergaglio (Piedmont)
Giacomo Borgogno & Figli (Piedmont)
Bruna (Liguria)
Carvinea (Puglia)
Castello dei Rampolla (Tuscany)
Castello di Spessa (Friuli Venezia Giulia)
Cavicchioli (Emilia Romagna)
Roberto Ceraudo (Calabria)
Collestefano (Marche)
Còlpetrone (Umbria)
Conti Zecca (Puglia)
Felline (Puglia)
Fontanavecchia (Campania)
Graci (Sicily)
Guerrieri Rizzardi (Veneto)
Franz Haas (Alto Adige)
Lamole di Lamole (Tuscany)
Manincor (Alto Adige)
Masseto (Tuscany)
Mastrojanni (Tuscany)
Pala (Sardinia)
Dario Raccaro (Friuli Venezia Giulia)
Rocca di Castagnoli - Tenute Calì
(Tuscany)
Rocche dei Manzoni (Piedmont)
Roeno (Veneto)
Girolamo Russo (Sicily)
Cantine Settesoli (Sicily)
Tenuta Spinelli (Marche)
Tenuta di Fiorano (Lazio)
Terenzi (Tuscany)
Torre Rosazza (Friuli Venezia Giulia)
Tunella (Friuli Venezia Giulia)

11

Giovanni Almondo (Piedmont)
Antonelli - San Marco (Umbria)
AR.PE.PE (Lombardy)
Baricci (Tuscany)
Bel Colle (Piedmont)
Enzo Boglietti (Piedmont)
Borgo San Daniele (Friuli Venezia Giulia)
Sorelle Bronca (Veneto)
Le Caniette (Marche)
Capichera (Sardinia)
Ceretto (Piedmont)
F.lli Cigliuti (Piedmont)
Il Colombaio di Santa Chiara (Tuscany)
Stefanino Costa (Piedmont)
Duca di Salaparuta (Sicily)
Duemani (Tuscany)
I Favati (Campania)
Andrea Felici (Marche)
Tenuta Luisa (Friuli Venezia Giulia)
Claudio Mariotto (Piedmont)
La Massa (Tuscany)
Poderi e Cantine Oddero (Piedmont)
Poggio Antico (Tuscany)
Prunotto (Piedmont)
Giuseppe Rinaldi (Piedmont)

Rotari (Trentino)
Salcheto (Tuscany)
San Salvatore 1988 (Campania)
Fattoria Le Terrazze (Marche)
Terre Stregate (Campania)
Tiare - Roberto Snidarcig
(Friuli Venezia Giulia)
Cantina Tollo (Abruzzo)
Val delle Corti (Tuscany)
Mauro Veglio (Piedmont)
Villa Matilde Avallone (Campania)
Luigi Viola (Calabria)
La Vrille (Valle d'Aosta)

10

Stefano Amerighi (Tuscany)
Barberani (Umbria)
Tenuta Bellafonte (Umbria)
Bisci (Marche)
Brezza Giacomo e Figli (Piedmont)
Casale del Giglio (Lazio)
Le Casematte (Sicily)
Castello di Bolgheri (Tuscany)
Castello di Cigognola (Lombardy)
Castello di Radda (Tuscany)
Giovanni Corino (Piedmont)
Giuseppe Cortese (Piedmont)
Tenimenti Luigi D'Alessandro (Tuscany)
Gianni Doglia (Piedmont)
Tenuta Fanti (Tuscany)
Gianfranco Fino (Puglia)
Enrico Gatti (Lombardy)
La Guardiense - Janare (Campania)
Hilberg - Pasquero (Piedmont)
Tenuta J. Hofstätter (Alto Adige)
Alois Lageder (Alto Adige)
Poderi Mattioli (Marche)
Monte Rossa (Lombardy)
Fattoria Nicolucci (Emilia Romagna)
Tenuta Olim Bauda (Piedmont)
Orsolani (Piedmont)
Alberto Paltrinieri (Emilia Romagna)
Pasqua (Veneto)
Paternoster (Basilicata)
Pelissero (Piedmont)
Pojer & Sandri (Trentino)
Guido Porro (Piedmont)
Primosic (Friuli Venezia Giulia)
Ricci Curbastro (Lombardy)
Tenuta Ritterhof (Alto Adige)
Roccapesta (Tuscany)
Rosset Terroir (Valle d'Aosta)
Skerk (Friuli Venezia Giulia)
Lo Sparviere (Lombardy)
Tenuta delle Terre Nere (Sicily)
Tenuta di Tavignano (Marche)
La Valentina (Abruzzo)
Vespa - Vignaioli per Passione (Puglia)
Zorzettig (Friuli Venezia Giulia)

HOW TO USE THE GUIDE

WINERY INFORMATION

CELLAR SALES
PRE-BOOK VISITS
ACCOMODATION
RESTAURANT SERVICE

ANNUAL PRODUCTION
HECTARES UNDER VINE
SUSTAINABLE WINERY

VITICULTURE METHOD
- certified biodynamic
- certified organic

N.B. The figures related here are provided annually by the producers.
The publisher is not responsible for eventual errors or inconsistencies.

SYMBOLS

○ WHITE WINE
⊙ ROSÉ
● RED WINE

RATINGS

moderately good to good wines in their respective categories
very good to excellent wines in their respective categories
very good to excellent wines that went forward to the final tastings
excellent wines in their respective categories

WINES RATED IN PREVIOUS EDITIONS OF THE GUIDE ARE INDICATED BY WHITE GLASSES (♀, ♀♀, ♀♀♀), PROVIDED THEY ARE STILL DRINKING AT THE LEVEL FOR WHICH THE ORIGINAL AWARD WAS MADE.

STAR ★

indicates wineries that have won ten tre bicchieri awards for each star

PRICE RANGES

I up to 5 euro
3 from € 10,01 to € 15,00
5 from € 20,01 to € 30,00
7 from € 40,01 to € 50,00

2 from € 5,01 to € 10,00
4 from € 15,01 to € 20,00
6 from € 30,01 to € 40,00
8 more than € 50,01

prices indicated refer to average prices in wine stores

L'ASTERISK *

indicates especially good value wines

ABBREVIATIONS

A. A.	Alto Adige	P.R.	Peduncolo Rosso
C.	Colli		(red bunchstem)
Cl.	Classico	P.	Prosecco
C.S.	Cantina Sociale	RDG	Riviera del Garda
	(co-operative winery)	Ris.	Riserva
Cons.	Consorzio	Sel.	Selezione
Coop.Agr.	Cooperativa Agricola	Sup.	Superiore
	(farming co-operative)	V.	Vigna (vineyard)
C. B.	Colli Bolognesi	VdA	Valle d'Aosta
C. P.	Colli Piacentini	Vign.	Vigneto (vineyard)
Et.	Etichetta	V. T.	Vendemmia Tardiva
FCO	Friuli Colli Orientali		(late harvest)
M.	Metodo (Method)	V. V.	Vecchia Vigna/Vecchie Vigne
M.to	Monferrato		(old vine/old vines)
OP	Oltrepò Pavese		

THE
RARE WINES
COLLECTION
Few bottles plenty of character

The following is a selection of
exceptional wines, produced
in limited quantities. These
are distinctive expressions
that tell a unique story—
whether it be a single
vineyard wine, the result of
long aging, or crafted through
an unconventional approach.
We've categorized the list by
type so as to make it easy to
explore at your leisure.

SPARKLERS

Franciacorta Dosaggio Zero Annamaria Clementi R.S. Ris. 1980
Ca' del Bosco - LOMBARDY

98/100

ANNUAL PRODUCTION **4,000 bottles**
PRICE **€ 700.00**

André Dubois (then cellar master) and Maurizio Zanella set aside a few thousand bottles from the excellent 1980 vintage, just now disgorged after 42 years. This wine reveals extreme elegance and equally extreme complexity and depth: hazelnut, candied citrus, and oyster hints on both the nose and palate, supported by a bead of unparalleled finesse and persistence.

Alta Langa Pas Dosè 140 Mesi Zero 2011
Enrico Serafino - PIEDMONT

95/100

ANNUAL PRODUCTION **3,000 bottles**
PRICE **€ 135.00**

A truly refined sparkling wine, both deep and sapid. It's incredible how, thirteen years after the harvest, this wine still shows such vitality and energy. The nose is a kaleidoscope of aromas: it starts with dried fruit and nuts, followed by spicy tones, pastry, peach, and wildflowers. The palate is pervasive, with creamy bubbles and acidity supporting a long finish.

Franciacorta Brut Nature Orfano Terre Rosse Ris. 2016
Corte Fusia - LOMBARDY

95/100

ANNUAL PRODUCTION **1,200 bottles**
PRICE **€ 80.00**

This Blanc de Noirs from Franciacorta is made with select grapes cultivated on the slopes of Monte Orfano. Only a few bottles are produced, but they convey their origins well. It opens with aromas of toasted bread and hazelnut, followed by anise and almond. The palate is creamy and pervasive, with an intriguing attack marked by mineral notes. Alluringly drinkable.

Franciacorta Extra Brut Supèi 2017
Uberti - LOMBARDY

95/100

ANNUAL PRODUCTION **318 bottles**
PRICE **€ 64.00**

From a parcel in the Salem vineyard in Erbusco, the Supèi Extra Brut 2017 impresses with its ability to balance breadth of flavor and freshness. Made from chardonnay grapes vinified in barriques, it opens on the nose with notes of yellow peach, tropical fruit, and toasted hazelnuts. This richness is mirrored on the palate, all refreshed by a sapid finish.

Trento Brut Madame Martis Ris. 2013
Maso Martis - TRENTINO

94/100

ANNUAL PRODUCTION **1,000 bottles**
PRICE **€ 115.00**

Production is tiny for this cuvée dedicated to Roberta, the "madame" of the house. A classic blend of pinot noir, chardonnay, and pinot meunier, it spends nine long years on the lees. The result is incredible. The complexity on the nose is astounding, but even more impressive is the finesse of its aromas. On the palate, it's slender, linear, alternating sapid sensations with crisp acidity.

Lambrusco di Sorbara Brut Nature M. Cl. Ring Adora 2021
Podere Il Saliceto - EMILIA ROMAGNA

93/100

ANNUAL PRODUCTION **600 bottles**
PRICE **€ 24.00**

The dedication of Podere Il Saliceto in working with sorbara grapes is clear when you taste the Ring Adora. A Metodo Classico Lambrusco di Sorbara produced in just a few hundred bottles, it stands out for its fine perlage, pronounced acidity, and textbook depth, making it one of the most interesting wines in its category.

WHITES

Cupo Fiano 2020
Pietracupa - CAMPANIA

98/100

ANNUAL PRODUCTION **4,000 bottles**
PRICE **€ 48.00**

It opens slowly, but finishes in glory. Its incomparable purity of aromas blends anise, citron, and flint. On the palate, it's creamy, delicate, with a flavorful, sapid depth. It has a poised, harmonious character, and a long finish with enormous aging potential. Truly one of Italy's greatest white wines, without question.

Etna Bianco Sup. Kudos 2019
Curtaz - SICILY

98/100

ANNUAL PRODUCTION **3,600 bottles**
PRICE **€ 50.00**

A truly unique wine that brings together elegance, depth, complexity, and fullness. It's produced by Federico Curtaz on Etna, a terroir that the winemaker knows well and expresses masterfully. White fruit, a subtle touch of anise, mountain flowers, and a broad palate that fills the mouth without weighing it down. Oak is impeccably calibrated. The high elevation of the vineyard and the Mediterranean influence are unmistakable—it's all here.

Vitovska Solo MM 2020
Vodopivec - FRIULI VENEZIA GIULIA

98/100

ANNUAL PRODUCTION **3,000 bottles**
PRICE **€ 65.00**

Serve at no less than 13-14°C. This is one of Italy's greatest white wines, crafted from a single parcel in Carso Triestino. The wine is aged in amphorae, in contact with the skins for about six months before moving to large barrels. Exuberant aromas of oyster, almond, and strawflower emerge. On the palate, it's sense-stimulating: marine, spicy, and flavorful, with endless persistence.

Etna Bianco Palmento Caselle 2020
I Vigneri - SICILY

97/100

ANNUAL PRODUCTION **1,277 bottles**
PRICE **€ 140.00**

I Vigneri is the project of Salvo Foti, a seasoned oenologist and above all, a great connoisseur of Etna and its vineyards. The Vigna di Milo hails from the vineyard of the same name on Etna's eastern slope, at 750 meters elevation. Briny, flavorful, and incredibly fresh, it immediately evokes a "volcanic" wine, with its complex and multifaceted nose.

Friuli Isonzo Chardonnay Glesie 2018
Vie di Romans - FRIULI VENEZIA GIULIA

97/100

ANNUAL PRODUCTION **1,800 bottles**
PRICE **€ 65.00**

In their deep exploration of their estate's various crus, the Gallo family has developed the Climat project: six wines from six parcels, vinified separately but using the same technique. The Chardonnay Glesie '18 from the Vie di Romans vineyard matures 18 months on the lees and two years in the bottle. It's an exceptionally elegant white, where the fruit-wood combination expresses itself with unmatched finesse.

Greco di Tufo Le Arcaie di San Pio 2022
Passo delle Tortore - CAMPANIA

97/100

ANNUAL PRODUCTION **1,000 bottles**
PRICE **€ 48.00**

A Greco di Tufo Riserva produced in very limited quantities, but captivating for the clarity of its aromas and flavors. The Arcaie di San Pio '22 opens with smoky sensations, white flowers, and subtle fruit whiffs, all within an elegant and refined profile. These sensations culminate in a palate of incredible tension and freshness, highlighted by a juicy interplay of acidity and sapidity.

Poggio del Crine Sauvignon 2021
Montauto - TUSCANY

96/100

ANNUAL PRODUCTION **880 bottles**
PRICE **€ 90.00**

A truly exceptional Sauvignon from central Italy? Absolutely, when the producer is Montauto. The Poggio del Crine is the result of rigorous grape selection, expertly crafted to yield a complex nose with notes of white fruit and anise, and a subtle herbaceous touch that precedes a refined, elegant, and impeccably clean palate.

Trebbiano d'Abruzzo Di-Vèrto 2022
Torre dei Beati - ABRUZZO

96/100

ANNUAL PRODUCTION **2,500 bottles**
PRICE **€ 20.00**

The Diverto is born in a 25-year-old, half-hectare vineyard in Francavilla al Mare, on steep slopes surrounded by woods. A multifaceted trebbiano with mineral, briny, and Mediterranean notes, what stands out most about the wine is the palate, full of tension and vitality, unlike most other trebbianos in the region.

Vin de la Neu 2022
Resistenti Nicola Biasi - TRENTINO

96/100

ANNUAL PRODUCTION **1,000 bottles**
PRICE **€ 110.00**

The Vin della Neu marks Nicola Biasi's first step in his efforts to cultivate disease-resistant grapes in the Trentino Dolomites. Its name refers to a vineyard that lies at 1,000 meters elevation, planted with johanniter. On the nose it offers a multifaceted aromatic profile of rosemary, wisteria, eucalyptus, and mountain herbs, which, combined with an intense, energetic, and sapid palate, highlights the potential of these varieties.

Campo delle Oche Integrale (Magnum) 2018
Fattoria San Lorenzo - MARCHE

95/100

ANNUAL PRODUCTION **500 bottles**
PRICE **€ 75.00**

This wine differs from its namesake Campo delle Oche because the Integrale is aged for 48 months and bottled with the fine lees, exclusively in magnums. The 2018 embodies all the brightness, energy, and vitality of Natalino Crognaletti's style: veiled, with hints of straw, almond, and ripe apple, bound by a touch of volatility. On the palate, it's full-bodied and rich in alcohol. Boundless.

Pian di Stio Evoluzione 2019
San Salvatore 1988 - CAMPANIA

95/100

ANNUAL PRODUCTION **2,800 bottles**
PRICE **€ 35.00**

The fiano grapes used for the Evoluzione are meticulously selected from the Stio vineyard. Fermentation and maturation are carried out in barriques, resulting in a white with an intricate aromatic profile. Varietal citrus notes are complemented by spicy and faintly smoky sensations. The palate is firm, harmonious, and shows superb acidic-sapid tension.

WHITES

Kamen Vitovska 2020
Zidarich - FRIULI VENEZIA GIULIA

94/100

ANNUAL PRODUCTION **1,900 bottles**
PRICE **€ 45.00**

In his underground cellar, Beniamino Zidarich has installed a tank made of local stone so as to vinify a single wine. The result is the Vitovska Kamen (stone in Slovenian), sourced from the vineyards surrounding the estate. It's sapid and taut, with briny, sea-like aromas and hints of Mediterranean scrub. On the palate, it shows flesh, skin, and citrus zest. A deep wine with an unforgettable, radiant character.

Roero Arneis Giuan Da Pas 2015
Pace - PIEDMONT

94/100

ANNUAL PRODUCTION **600 bottles**
PRICE **€ 42.00**

Roero Arneis Giuan da Pas is fermented and aged on the fine lees in stainless steel for several months, but is released only after ten years of bottle aging. The 2015 is rich on the nose, with notes of yellow peach, candied citron, and white pepper. The palate is well-structured, pervasive and pleasant, with a long finish that closes on citrus notes.

Sicut Erat Vermentino 2022
La Contralta - SARDINIA

94/100

ANNUAL PRODUCTION **2,000 bottles**
PRICE **€ 38.00**

Roberto Gariup, a seasoned Friulian-born winemaker who has long made Sardinia his home, brings his expertise to bear in crafting vermentino through carefully balanced maceration. The result is Sicut Erat, a wine of great allure—complex and persistent, with a sapid, textured palate that's never bitter or tight, but rather offers long-lasting depth and progression.

AV 01 Catarratto Orange 2022
Rallo - SICILY

93/100

ANNUAL PRODUCTION **3,000 bottles**
PRICE **€ 26.00**

The AV 01 is made with select catarrato grapes that, as its name suggests, undergo skin maceration. This year's production is even smaller than in the past, but given the wine's quality, we had to include it. Notes of orange blossom, beeswax, and hints of field daisies converge with a flavorful palate, marked by a light but well-integrated tannic sensation, fading into a subtle bitter note.

Carso Malvasia Dileo Ris. 2022
Castelvecchio - FRIULI VENEZIA GIULIA

93/100

ANNUAL PRODUCTION **2,500 bottles**
PRICE **€ 20.00**

The Dileo is the result of a rigorous selection of malvasia grapes from a small plot that perfectly expresses the Karst terroir. On the nose it's vibrant, with the grape's aromatic profile evoking hints of yellow-fleshed fruit, herbs, wildflowers, and a faint touch of sweet spices. The palate is expansive, with noticeable volume, but it's sapidity that dominates, leading to a clean, deep finish.

Collio Friulano Miklus Francesco 2019
Draga - Miklus - FRIULI VENEZIA GIULIA

93/100

ANNUAL PRODUCTION **2,000 bottles**
PRICE **€ 37.00**

A very limited number of bottles are produced from old friulano vineyards (60+ years old) planted in San Floriano del Collio. The Francesco '19 Collio perfectly expresses the terroir's soil and climate. A broad nose with fruity, floral, and spicy aromas introduces a full, fresh palate with remarkable persistence, where impeccable skin maceration adds rhythm and flavor.

WHITES

REDS

Etna Rosso San Lorenzo Piano delle Colombe 2021
Girolamo Russo - SICILIA

99/100

ANNUAL PRODUCTION **750 bottles**
PRICE **€ 160.00**

One of the best wines tasted this year. Piano delle Colombe is a small parcel set within the San Lorenzo cru, on the northern slopes of the volcano. The nerello mascalese cultivated here gives rise to a truly world-class pour. Haematic notes and iron merge with whiffs of underbrush and pepper, the prelude to a graceful, flowing, incredibly fresh and deep palate. A masterpiece.

Cannonau di Sardegna Franzisca Ris. 2021
Giovanni Montisci - SARDEGNA

98/100

ANNUAL PRODUCTION **2,666 bottles**
PRICE **€ 90.00**

Giovanni Montisci is a master winemaker from Mamoiada, and the Franzisca is made with cannonau grapes from the oldest of his small vineyards. Onlt a few bottles are produced, but this is one of the best wines of its kind. Its aromas are distinctly Mediterranean, with prominent notes of wild brush and myrtle. The palate is supple and fluid, yet not lacking in complexity or depth.

Cinabro 2020
Le Caniette - MARCHE

98/100

ANNUAL PRODUCTION **1,000 bottles**
PRICE **€ 92.00**

The Cinabro '20, a monovarietal grenache, is a magnetic blend of sour cherry aromas, pepper, herbs, and Mediterranean scrub. Over time, new nuances emerge: smoky traces, a hint of cocoa, and dry hay. On the palate, it moves gracefully, unveiling silky tannins, and precisely conveying its vibrant aromatic complexity.

Chianti Classico Gran Selezione Bragantino 2019
Monteraponi - TOSCANA

97/100

ANNUAL PRODUCTION **1,333 bottles**
PRICE **€ 300.00**

The Bragantino doesn't disappoint with this new vintage, unveiling a magical lightness. Produced in very limited quantities, it matures for 42 months in 1000-liter barrels, making for extraordinary elegance and drinkability. Its stylistic precision and clarity of fruit are incredible, all topped off by a fresh, vibrant finish that embodies the spirit of Radda.

Etna Rosso Signum Aetnae 2015
Firriato - SICILIA

97/100

ANNUAL PRODUCTION **2,436 bottles**
PRICE **€ 135.00**

After several years, this great red expresses elegant balsamic notes of root, cocoa, and potpourri, which then evolve into fig jam, carob, and mulberry. On the palate, it's pervasive, with soft tannins, concluding with a sapid, warm finish, like the black sands where this age-old, pre-phylloxera vineyard of nerello mascalese has its roots.

Habemus Cabernet Et. Rossa 2021
San Giovenale - LAZIO

97/100

ANNUAL PRODUCTION **1,200 bottles**
PRICE **€ 110.00**

The Habemus Cabernet '21, from cabernet franc grapes grown in a vineyard of just under a hectare (planted at a density of over 13,000 vines), shows great aromatic breadth, passing from black fruit to rhubarb, graphite, and coffee scents. A full, balanced palate follows, making for a pervasive and long drink, with a sapid note and robust acidity.

Valtellina Sup. Inferno V. Guast 2021
Dirupi - LOMBARDY

97/100

ANNUAL PRODUCTION **1,000 bottles**
PRICE **€ 36.00**

The terraced vineyards of chiavennasca in the Inferno part of Valtellina are emblematic of heroic viticulture. The Guast '21 conjures up vibrant notes of fresh raspberry, licorice, and tobacco on the nose. The palate shows incredible flesh and freshness, with elegant, refined tannins adding weight to a long finish.

REDS

Barolo Bussia Briccotto 2020
Domenico Clerico - PIEDMONT

96/100

ANNUAL PRODUCTION **950 bottles**
PRICE **€ 135.00**

Just nine rows of vines produce this exceptional red from the Briccotto parcel in the Bussia Soprana cru. First produced in 1978, the wine is only made in the best vintages. The 2020 showcases gorgeous red fruit, with notes of tobacco and licorice adding complexity and character. The palate is fleshy, and the finish extraordinarily long. Not to be missed.

Eleuteria Special Edition in Anfora 2020
Tenuta del Travale - CALABRIA

96/100

ANNUAL PRODUCTION **600 bottles**
PRICE **€ 150.00**

A true gem. Here in Rovito, in Sila,, they cultivate nerello mascalese grapes at over 500 meters above sea level. After whole bunch fermentation, the wine ages for over 20 months in cocciopesto. The nose proves ethereal, ever-changing, with pronounced floral aromas and orange peel that makes for bold flavor. Light on weight yet with refined tannins, it closes on playful notes of black tea and gentian.

Langhe Rosso Seifile 2020
Fiorenzo Nada - PIEDMONT

96/100

ANNUAL PRODUCTION **3,000 bottles**
PRICE **€ 80.00**

The austerity of nebbiolo meets the lively vibrance of barbera cultivated in old vineyards. An enticing nose summons notes of raspberry, currant, and underbrush, transitioning into sensations of licorice, tobacco, and smoky tones. The palate is equally impressive: a rich and velvety expression where freshness and measured sapidity deliver a deep, persistent finish.

A. A. Santa Maddalena Cl. V. Rondell R 2022
Glögglhof - Franz Gojer - ALTO ADIGE

95/100

ANNUAL PRODUCTION **666 bottles**
PRICE **€ 48.00**

More than a new Santa Maddalena from Gojer, this represents a new vision of this South Tyrolean appellation. Without sacrificing its signature light and sapid drinkability, it offers a refined aromatic profile, where red fruit is accompanied by intense herbal and spicy inflections. The palate is dynamic and long.

Barbaresco Roncaglie 2021
Mura Mura - PIEMONTE

95/100

ANNUAL PRODUCTION **1,394 bottles**
PRICE **€ 73.00**

Hailing from a cru in the Barbaresco area, the wine reveals a nose of superb finesse and complexity. Floral and fruity notes, highlighted by blueberry, currant, and violet, blend with nuances of anise. An elegant nose combines with a fleshy palate, dense yet balanced by a vibrant freshness. It finishes with rarefied spicy notes of great persistence.

Cannonau di Sardegna Ghirada Zi'Spanu 2022
Giuseppe Sedilesu - SARDINIA

95/100

ANNUAL PRODUCTION **1,200 bottles**
PRICE **€ 26.00**

The first vintage of this remarkable cru perfectly embodies the mamoiadino terroir. Just a thousand bottles are produced, but they're full of character: aromas span from red fruit to spices, from petrichor to a touch of wood resin. The palate is broad and warm, with significant volume, yet sapidity and acidity perfectly balance the immense depth.

Amarone della Valpolicella Cl. La Fabriseria Ris. 2016
F.lli Tedeschi - VENETO

94/100

ANNUAL PRODUCTION **1,400 bottles**
PRICE **€ 227.00**

The Fabriseria vineyard unfolds at elevations spanning 430-500 meters. From here, during the best vintages, the Tedeschi brothers produce a limited quantity of Amarone, noted for its extraordinary richness and depth. Sweet red fruit finds balance in briny and spicy tones, while on the palate, its traditional exuberance is kept in check by a close-knit tannic structure that provides precision and energy.

Barbaresco Gallina Ris. 2019
Ugo Lequio - PIEDMONT

94/100

ANNUAL PRODUCTION **1,536 bottles**
PRICE **€ 73.00**

Only a few bottles are produced, drawing on carefully selected grapes from the historic cru in the municipality of Neive. The nose is delicate yet intense, with elegant notes of red berries and fresh roses intertwining with subtle spices. The palate is harmonious and balanced, with gentle, well-integrated tannins providing depth to a long finish.

REDS

Barolo Bussia V. Colonnello 2017
Bussia Soprana - PIEDMONT

94/100

ANNUAL PRODUCTION **3,000 bottles**
PRICE **€ 90.00**

Vigna Colonello is a half-hectare plot planted with old vines (70+ years old). No beating around the bush here: the 2017 is stunning. On the nose, it manifests a shimmering, multifaceted profile of rose, licorice, and tobacco aromas. The palate is elegant and full-bodied, with sweet tannins and a seemingly endless finish.

Be Luna 2022
Bentu Luna - SARDEGNA

94/100

ANNUAL PRODUCTION **1,300 bottles**
PRICE **€ 110.00**

Bentu Luna has focused entirely on old vines, and the Be Luna encapsulates the essence of these time-honored plots, planted decades ago. The vineyard follows Mandrolisai tradition, predominantly bovale and cannonau with a touch of monica. The result is a wine that offers up aromas of ripe red fruit, accented by a hint of spice. On the palate, it's creamy, pervasive, and expansive, with a warmth that's perfectly balanced by remarkable sapidity.

Romagna Sangiovese Modigliana Acereta 2021
Mutiliana - EMILIA ROMAGNA

94/100

ANNUAL PRODUCTION **2,600 bottles**
PRICE **€ 22.00**

Giorgio Melandri's Mutiliana is aimed at producing great wines that truly interpret the terroir of Modigliana. Three Romagna sangiovese wines are produced, each named after a different valley. The Acereta is an exceptional red, light-footed, elegant, juicy, and complex on the nose, with a linear flavor development. Its fine tannins are well-integrated, accompanied by exemplary freshness.

VdA Pinot Noir Pierre 2021
Cave Gargantua - VALLE D'AOSTA

94/100

ANNUAL PRODUCTION **1,500 bottles**
PRICE **€ 42.00**

Here we have a great wine from a small, Aosta Valley-based producer. The Pierre is a Pinot Nero made with grapes cultivated at 550-750 meters above sea level. On the nose it reveals all the fragrances you'd expect from the mountains: delightful fruity notes, whiffs of wild strawberry, flowery and spicy nuances. In the mouth it showcases notable structure, though it's aptly balanced by elegant tannins. And it's all topped off by a long, pleasant finish.

Romagna Sangiovese Modigliana Area 66 2022
Menta e Rosmarino - EMILIA ROMAGNA

93/100

ANNUAL PRODUCTION **1,125 bottles**
PRICE **€ 21.00**

This small but promising Romagna-based winery made its debut in the guide last year, and now their Area 66 has entered the elite circle of our "Rare Wines". It's an elegant red, featuring notes of red fruit, subtle spices, and a faint underbrush perfume. The palate is fine, its rhythm lively, and the finish impeccably clean and long.

REDS

SWEET AND MEDITATION WINES

Moscato Passito al Governo di Saracena 2015
Feudo dei Sanseverino - CALABRIA

98/100

ANNUAL PRODUCTION **2,800 bottles**
PRICE **€ 34.00**

We've already described it in detail in the winery's notes, but it's worth adding a few more words about our Sweet Wine of the Year. There's not just aromatic complexity and a perfect palate here; this is about rediscovering an ancient wine, the pleasure of savoring it slowly, and the excitement of watching it evolve minute by minute. It's not a wine to be confined to the end of a meal, with dessert, but a bottle to open for all of life's great occasions.

Malvasia di Bosa Ris. 2017
Columbu - SARDINIA

96/100

ANNUAL PRODUCTION **3,000 bottles**
PRICE **€ 51.00**

Columbu is an absolute benchmark for malvasia, and the estate has benefited from the visionary ideas of its founder, Giovanni Battista (the winery is today run by his son Gian Michele and Gian Michele's wife Vanna Mazzon). The 2017 Riserva is truly exceptional: complex on the nose with notes of dried fruit, nuts and sponge cake, and incredible on the palate for its sapidity and textbook saline freshness.

Vin Santo di Carmignano 2015
Fattoria Ambra - TUSCANY

96/100

ANNUAL PRODUCTION **1,200 bottles**
PRICE **€ 25.00**

Beppe Rigoli gathers ripe trebbiano and San Colombano grapes from old vines and lets them wither until January. The wine ferments slowly and matures for six years in small oak barrels, followed by another year in the bottle. The result? Sweet, velvety magic, redolent of dried fruits, nuts, rancio, spices, and candied citrus, offering extraordinarily complex depth. A taste of the infinite.

Moscato di Saracena Passito 2021
Luigi Viola - CALABRIA

95/100

ANNUAL PRODUCTION **3,000 bottles**
PRICE **€ 45.00**

It's our Sweet Wine of the Year. A broad, nuanced nose surprises with its aromas of candied fruit, citron, nuts, jasmine, orange blossom, aromatic herbs, and then croissant and sweet spices. On the palate, it's fresh and harmonious, aptly balancing acidity and fruit, with an incredibly long aromatic persistence.

VdA Chambave Muscat Flétri 2022
La Vrille - VALLE D'AOSTA

95/100

ANNUAL PRODUCTION **900 bottles**
PRICE **€ 41.00**

Only 900 bottles are produced, but this Muscat Flétri delivers pure pleasure, opening on aromas of raisins, dried apricots, and acacia honey, joined by floral hints and a touch of herbs. On the palate, its structure is present, but its acidity makes the difference—it's never cloying, its fluidity is balanced, the finish clean, lightly sweet, flavorful, but above all, deep.

Vernaccia di Oristano Antico Gregori Ris. 1979
Attilio Contini - SARDEGNA

95/100

ANNUAL PRODUCTION **2,000 bottles**
PRICE **€ 84.00**

Tasting a wine nearly fifty years old is always exciting, especially when you realize it still has a long life ahead. That's the case with Vernaccia, particularly the remarkable Antico Gregori Riserva. Its aromas are abundant, ranging from iodized notes to nuts, from wildflowers to incense and spices.

Verdicchio dei Castelli di Jesi Passito Lina 2022
Santa Barbara - MARCHE

94/100

ANNUAL PRODUCTION **1,110 bottles**
PRICE **€ 30.00**

The Lina '22, a passito, pours an intense golden hue. In the glass, the wine reveals a glycerine-rich texture, confirmed upon tasting by its densely concentrated sweetness. On the palate, a captivating, long note of honey is accompanied by hints of candied orange peel, toasted almonds, and anise, all adorned by subtle whiffs of thyme and saffron.

VALLE D'AOSTA

Wine production in Valle d'Aosta is relatively limited, which, fortunately, allows prices to remain sufficiently profitable. This ensures that the entire supply chain can not only sustain itself but also invest in improving quality, from vineyard to bottle. With tourism driving high demand, regional production no longer suffices to meet internal consumption needs. Thankfully, in recent years, healthy competition and the arrival of a new generation of young winemakers have led to a notable increase in quality. Today, it's safe to say that Valle d'Aosta is drinking quite well. The first real push for quality came in the 1990s, led by Costantino Charrère, to whom the region owes much of its viticultural success. His vision emphasized international grape varieties, particularly chardonnay, which he believed would allow the region to compete with the world's top producers. During this time, many small wineries sprang up, and chardonnay spread rapidly across the valley. However, in recent years, interest in the variety has waned—if not in terms of hectares planted, at least in the minds of producers. The focus has shifted dramatically toward indigenous grapes. The first to really shine a light on Valle d'Aosta's potential was fumin, a recently rediscovered varietal. Fumin is perhaps the only native red grape with a truly international appeal, producing powerful, deeply colored wines that stand in stark contrast to the region's typical reds.

But the real turning point in regional winemaking came with the decision to stop competing with the rest of Italy—and the world—on heavy, concentrated wines, and instead embrace the unique character imparted by the local climate and terroirs. In other words, producers had the courage to offer lighter, more drinkable wines. Since then, interest in petit rouge and nebbiolo has reignited, while petite arvine is slowly replacing chardonnay. Pinot nero, with its fruity, fresh, and angular profile, is undeniably easy to drink and perfectly reflects the region's character. With a bit more knowledge and daring, syrah could follow suit; its potential in Valle d'Aosta is clear, especially if producers focus on creating lighter wines that highlight pepper and violet aromas over ripe plum.

Finally, the region's long-standing talent for producing passito wines shouldn't be overlooked. Exceptional examples like La Vrille's Chambave Muscat Flétri '22 have earned their place in our prestigious new section, the Rare Wine List.

VALLE D'AOSTA

★Maison Anselmet

fraz. Vereytaz, 30
11018 Villeneuve [AO]
☎ +39 0165904851
🌐 www.maisonanselmet.it

CELLAR SALES
PRE-BOOKED VISITS
ANNUAL PRODUCTION 100,000 bottles
HECTARES UNDER VINE 15.00

Giorgio Anselmet continues the tradition of his father, Renato, embodying generations deeply rooted in the land, customs, and traditions of their community, but who have also come to embrace innovation. The wines from this estate fully express the rugged character of the mountains and those who produce here, yet a soft elegance emerges after the first sip, captivating the palate. The production area is ideally suited for viticulture, and Giorgio expertly harnesses its full potential. Today, Maison Anselmet is a global benchmark, recognized worldwide. The Semel Pater impresses with its intense red berry aromas and a subtle note of alcohol that slightly impacts its freshness, resulting in a refined and complex wine. The palate is powerful and rich, with delicate tannins. Plum notes emerge from a Petite Arvine in full evolution; the palate is rich and powerful, balanced with a long finish destined to evolve. The Mains et Cœur lives up to its reputation, offering rich aromas of plum and acacia flowers, enhanced by sweet spices and a hint of toast against a backdrop of cotton candy. The palate is balanced and rich. Don't forget the family gem: the Prisonnier.

○ VdA Chardonnay Mains et Cœur '22	♟♟	8
○ VdA Petite Arvine '22	♟♟	7
● VdA Pinot Nero Semel Pater '22	♟♟	8
● Le Prisonnier	♟♟	8
○ Mathieu Nix Nivis	♟♟	5
● VdA Fumin Aron '19	♟♟	7
○ VdA Pinot Gris '23	♟♟	5
● VdA Syrah Henri '22	♟♟	6
○ VdA Chardonnay Mains et Cœur '21	♟♟♟	8
○ VdA Chardonnay Mains et Cœur '20	♟♟♟	6
○ VdA Chardonnay Mains et Cœur '18	♟♟♟	6
○ VdA Chardonnay Mains et Cœur '16	♟♟♟	6
● VdA Pinot Noir Semel Pater '19	♟♟♟	8
● VdA Pinot Noir Semel Pater '17	♟♟♟	7
● VdA Pinot Noir Semel Pater '13	♟♟♟	8

★★Les Crêtes

s.da regionale 20, 50
11010 Aymavilles [AO]
☎ +39 0165902274
🌐 www.lescretes.it

CELLAR SALES
PRE-BOOKED VISITS
ANNUAL PRODUCTION 250,000 bottles
HECTARES UNDER VINE 35.00
SUSTAINABLE WINERY

Led by visionary winemaker Costantino Charrere, Les Crêtes is synonymous with the history of Valdostan viticulture. What he accomplished in the 1990s seemed impossible at the time, but would go on to become a model for the region. Costantino has since passed the reins to his family. Giulio, the next generation, leads the estate to national and international recognition with great enthusiasm. While noteworthy results have been achieved with international varietals, indigenous grapes are also cultivated. This modern winery is always exploring new ways to welcome guests and tourists in the best possible manner. The Cuvée Bois is fine, with sweet spice notes adding complexity to the fruit, accompanied by a slightly toasty finish. The palate is a bit closed and compact, but with a long, lightly tannic finish. The Petite Arvine Fleur presents a delicate sweet spice on the nose, very balanced, though still evolving on the palate with a firm sensation. The Pinot Nero Revei reveals intense notes of dried herbs and tobacco, with delicate tannins on the palate and a fruity finish.

○ VdA Chardonnay Cuvée Bois '22	♟♟	8
○ VdA Petite Arvine Fleur V. Devi Ros '22	♟♟	5
○ VdA Bianco Neige d'Or '20	♟♟	8
○ VdA Chardonnay '23	♟♟	5
● VdA Fumin '22	♟♟	5
● VdA Nebbiolo Sommet '21	♟♟	6
○ VdA Petite Arvine '23	♟♟	4
● VdA Pinot Nero '23	♟♟	4
● VdA Pinot Nero Revei '21	♟♟	6
○ VdA Chardonnay Cuvée Bois '21	♟♟♟	7
○ VdA Chardonnay Cuvée Bois '20	♟♟♟	7
○ VdA Chardonnay Cuvée Bois '19	♟♟♟	7
○ VdA Chardonnay Cuvée Bois '18	♟♟♟	7
○ VdA Chardonnay Cuvée Bois '17	♟♟♟	7
○ VdA Chardonnay Cuvée Bois '16	♟♟♟	7
● VdA Nebbiolo Sommet '15	♟♟♟	6

La Crotta di Vegneron

p.zza Roncas, 2
11023 Chambave [AO]
☏ +39 016646670
✉ www.lacrotta.it

Cave Gargantua

fraz. Clos Chatel, 1
11020 Gressan [AO]
☏ +39 3299271999
✉ www.cavegargantua.it

VALLE D'AOSTA

CELLAR SALES
PRE-BOOKED VISITS
RESTAURANT SERVICE
ANNUAL PRODUCTION 200,000 bottles
HECTARES UNDER VINE 31.00

CELLAR SALES
PRE-BOOKED VISITS
ANNUAL PRODUCTION 30,000 bottles
HECTARES UNDER VINE 6.50

A large number of producers contribute the fruits of their labor to this cooperative, the largest in the Aosta Valley. The deep connection to the land and its winemaking traditions is evident, as every member takes turns lending a hand. Despite working with international grapes, the primary focus remains native varietals. The Chambave Muscat has become a regional symbol. While it's never easy to find consensus among so many members, this coop remains committed to innovative projects, the latest being the aging of certain bottles in a mine. Originally conceived by the marketing department, the idea has proven to be an inspired decision with a strong focus on quality. The passito Moscato showcases aromas of citrus peels and dried apricots, followed by a saffron undertone, with an elegant and harmonious palate. The Esprit Follet is intense and refined, with signature vegetal notes, and a velvety, sapid palate.

The Cunéaz brothers continue their family's legacy, carrying on a legacy rooted in the customs and traditions of the Valdostan community, but they do so with a modern twist. Their wines are known for their structure and elegance, yet they retain the freshness and character that can only come from the mountains. Laurent and André are deeply passionate about their work, investing in their products and facilities. They experiment with different materials for aging and, after acquiring new vineyards, have worked to expand their cellar space. The Gamaret proves fresh and bold, with hints of blackberry coulis on the nose and a palate full of flesh, supported by still-evolving tannins. The Torrette Supérieur Labié stands out for its fine alcohol balance and good structure. The Pinot Gris is a highly characterful pour, revealing ripe fruit on the nose and a rich, fresh palate. The Sauvignon Mon Dadà is varietal in its profile, showcasing white currant sensations alongside vegetal nuances. The complex, flowery, balanced, and persistent Gamay also performed well.

○ VdA Chambave Moscato Passito Prieuré '21	♟♟♟ 5
● VdA Fumin Esprit Follet '21	♟♟ 5
● VdA Fumin Mines '19	♟♟ 6
○ VdA Chambave Muscat '23	♟♟ 4
○ VdA Chambave Muscat Attente '21	♟♟ 4
○ VdA Chambave Muscat Mines '22	♟♟ 5
○ VdA Nus Malvoisie '23	♟♟ 4
○ VdA Petite Arvine '23	♟ 4
○ VdA Chambave Moscato Passito Prieuré '15	♕♕♕ 5
○ VdA Chambave Moscato Passito Prieuré '13	♕♕♕ 5
○ VdA Chambave Moscato Passito Prieuré '12	♕♕♕ 5
○ VdA Chambave Moscato Passito Prieuré '11	♕♕♕ 5

● VdA Gamaret '22	♟♟ 5
○ Mon Dadà '22	♟♟ 5
○ VdA Blanc Daphne '22	♟♟ 5
● VdA Gamay '23	♟♟ 4
○ VdA Pinot Gris '23	♟♟ 5
● VdA Rosso Impasse '21	♟♟ 6
● VdA Torrette Sup. Labié '22	♟♟ 5
● VdA Pinot Noir Pierre '20	♕♕♕ 6
○ VdA Blanc Daphne '19	♕♕ 5
● VdA Gamaret '21	♕♕ 5
○ VdA Gamaret '20	♕♕ 4
● VdA Pinot Noir Pierre '18	♕♕ 5
● VdA Torrette Sup. Labié '20	♕♕ 4
● VdA Torrette Sup. Labié '19	♕♕ 4

Grosjean

fraz. Ollignan, 2
11020 Quart [AO]
☎ +39 0165775791
⊛ www.grosjeanvins.it

CELLAR SALES
PRE-BOOKED VISITS
ANNUAL PRODUCTION 150,000 bottles
HECTARES UNDER VINE 16.30
VITICULTURE METHOD Certified Organic

When writing about this winery, one can't help but be struck not only by the quality of the wines but also by the constant evolution and commitment to environmental sustainability. For years, their organic farming practices have been certified. Solar power now provides a significant portion of their energy needs, and they've constructed a reservoir for rainwater collection, which also serves as a watering hole for their livestock. The winery remains firmly anchored in tradition while marketing itself in a modern way. Their communication strategy through social media is highly effective, as are their expertly organized events and tastings. We were struck by the pleasantness of the Petite Arvine Les Frères, an exuberant style typical of the Valais school, with notes of mandarin meeting grapefruit, white fruit, and mineral nuances. Very balanced on its long finish. The Fumin stands out for its typicity and exceptional structure, playing on vegetal and fruity olfactory notes. A well-balanced drink. The Pinot Nero features an ethereal nose with lovely fruit reminiscent of jam. Balanced tannins.

Wine	Rating
○ VdA Petite Arvine Les Fréres '22	6
● VdA Fumin V. Rovettaz '22	6
○ VdA Chardonnay '22	6
● VdA Donnas Le Roncdevaccaz '21	6
● VdA Pinot Noir V. Tzeriat '22	5
● VdA Fumin '06	4
● VdA Fumin V. Rovettaz '07	5
○ VdA Petite Arvine V. Rovettaz '09	4
○ VdA Chardonnay '19	4
○ VdA Chardonnay Le Vin de Michel '19	5
● VdA Fumin V. Rovettaz '21	6
● VdA Fumin V. Rovettaz '19	5
○ VdA Petite Arvine V. Rovettaz '20	4
○ VdA Petite Arvine V. Rovettaz '19	4
● VdA Pinot Noir V. Tzeriat '19	5
● VdA Torrette Sup. V. Rovettaz '20	5

★Lo Triolet

loc. Junod, 7
11010 Introd [AO]
☎ +39 016595437
⊛ www.lotriolet.vievini.it

CELLAR SALES
PRE-BOOKED VISITS
ANNUAL PRODUCTION 60,000 bottles
HECTARES UNDER VINE 6.00

For over 30 years, this winery has delighted us with a masterful interpretation of a grape variety often considered humble: pinot grigio. The results Marco Martin has achieved with his pinot gris have garnered global attention, allowing enthusiasts to reassess a grape that has historically received little recognition. But Triolet is more than this; it's about preserving the culture of the land, respecting the past while embracing the future with a modern approach. This estate is a must-visit, not only for its tourism facilities but also for its stunning tasting room, carefully crafted from a former stable. The Pinot Gris highlights fresh vegetal notes on the nose, followed by local apples and Abate pears, with great gustatory balance. The Coteau Barrage reveals an intense and fruity nose with pleasant peppery nuances, leading to a sapid, long palate. The Petite Arvine opens on citrus notes harmonized by a very fresh vegetal background dominated by ferns. The palate is marked by pronounced freshness.

Wine	Rating
○ VdA Pinot Gris '23	5
● VdA Rosso Coteau Barrage '22	6
○ VdA Petite Arvine '23	4
○ VdA Pinot Gris Choeur '22	5
● VdA Pinot Noir '22	5
● VdA Torrette '22	5
● VdA Fumin '16	5
○ VdA Pinot Gris '22	5
○ VdA Pinot Gris '20	4*
○ VdA Pinot Gris '19	4*
○ VdA Pinot Gris '18	4*
○ VdA Pinot Gris '16	5
○ VdA Pinot Gris '15	5
○ VdA Pinot Gris '14	3*
○ VdA Pinot Gris '13	3*
● VdA Rosso Coteau Barrage '20	5

★Elio Ottin

fraz. Porossan Neyves, 209
11100 Aosta
☎ +39 3474071331
✎ www.ottinvini.it

CELLAR SALES
PRE-BOOKED VISITS
ANNUAL PRODUCTION 60,000 bottles
HECTARES UNDER VINE 9.00
SUSTAINABLE WINERY

If you find yourself in the Aosta Valley, are passionate about wine, and want to learn about the history of apples—a symbol of the region's agriculture—then Elio Ottin's estate is the perfect place to visit. It doesn't matter which family member greets you; hospitality is at the heart of their philosophy. In Porossan, a hamlet along the main road of the city, the winery's gems await. Don't worry about what to taste—every wine upholds the highest quality standards. The Petite Arvine is intense, with superb character and remarkable complexity, revealing a refined fruit profile where mandarin and plum aromas stand out. The palate is powerful and rich, yet supported by vibrant acidity and a lively sapidity, resulting in a long, youthful finish. The Emerico offers powerful, rich fruit on the nose, sensations balanced on the palate by velvety tannins. The Fumin stands out for its typicity. Don't miss the wines mentioned.

Wine	Rating
○ VdA Petite Arvine '23	♟♟♟ 5
● VdA Fumin '22	♟♟ 5
○ VdA Petite Arvine Nuances '22	♟♟ 6
● VdA Pinot Noir '22	♟♟ 6
● VdA Pinot Noir L'Emerico '21	♟♟ 6
● VdA Syrah Non Expedit '22	♟♟ 5
○ VdA Chardonnay Canto X '22	♟♟ 5
● VdA Torrette Sup. '22	♟♟ 5
○ VdA Petite Arvine '22	♟♟♟ 5
○ VdA Petite Arvine '20	♟♟♟ 4*
○ VdA Petite Arvine '19	♟♟♟ 4*
○ VdA Petite Arvine '17	♟♟♟ 4*
○ VdA Petite Arvine '16	♟♟♟ 5
○ VdA Petite Arvine '15	♟♟♟ 5
● VdA Pinot Noir L'Emerico '19	♟♟♟ 6
● VdA Pinot Noir L'Emerico '16	♟♟♟ 6

André Pellissier

fraz. Bussan Dessous, 17
11010 Saint Pierre [AO]
☎ +39 3405704029
✎ www.pellissierwine.it

CELLAR SALES
PRE-BOOKED VISITS
ANNUAL PRODUCTION 14,000 bottles
HECTARES UNDER VINE 2.50

In one of the Aosta Valley's most prestigious areas, a young producer is dedicated exclusively to red wines, with deep respect for the environment and local traditions. All the work is done manually, and the constant breeze in the central valley allows for the production of healthy grapes, allowing for minimal intervention in the vineyard. The use of barriques is a recent development, and while the methods are rooted in tradition, they are applied with a modern twist. The resulting wines are characterized by their structure, but also freshness and elegance, a quality only the mountains can impart. In the Syrah, spicy aromas harmonize with the fruity notes of blackberries. The palate is well-structured, with a strong encore of fruitiness leading to a very long finish. The Torrette Supérieur stands out for its typicity, with red fruits emerging both on the nose and palate, culminating in a remarkable finish. The Fumin, with its inky color and spiced nose of cocoa, clove, pepper, and licorice, offers a full and smooth palate with a long finish. The Pinot Nero and blends are excellent as well.

Wine	Rating
● VdA Syrah '22	♟♟ 5
● VdA Torrette Sup. '21	♟♟ 5
● Sancto Petro MMXXI	♟♟ 6
● VdA Fumin '21	♟♟ 5
● VdA Pinot Nero '22	♟♟ 5
● Neyr MMXXI	♟ 5
● VdA Fumin '18	♟♟ 5
● VdA Fumin '17	♟♟ 4
● VdA Syrah '21	♟♟ 6
● VdA Syrah '19	♟♟ 5
● VdA Syrah '18	♟♟ 4
● VdA Syrah '17	♟♟ 4
● VdA Torrette Sup. '20	♟♟ 6
● VdA Torrette Sup. '19	♟♟ 5
● VdA Torrette Sup. '18	♟♟ 4
● VdA Torrette Sup. '17	♟♟ 4

Pianta Grossa

via Roma, 213
11020 Donnas [AO]
📞 +39 3480077404
🌐 www.piantagrossadonnas.it

La Plantze

fraz. Vereytaz, 30
11018 Villeneuve [AO]
📞 +39 0165904851
🌐 www.laplantze.it

CELLAR SALES
PRE-BOOKED VISITS
ANNUAL PRODUCTION 25,000 bottles
HECTARES UNDER VINE 4.50

CELLAR SALES
PRE-BOOKED VISITS
ANNUAL PRODUCTION 30,000 bottles
HECTARES UNDER VINE 6.50

In the lower Aosta Valley, the principal grape variety is picotendro, an Italianized version of picutenner, a unique clone of nebbiolo shared with the nearby Carema region in Piedmont. Luciano Zoppo of Azienda Piantagrossa is a master of the variety, producing wines that rival the nobility of those from Piedmont. A reserved character, Zoppo's eyes light up at the mention of nebbiolo, and he closely follows the work of the Piedmontese masters, humbly learning and incorporating the best of their techniques. This year, the Dessus is even better, a wine of superb harmony. It's intense and refined on the nose, with pleasing fruity and spicy notes, where tobacco and licorice stand out. The palate is rich and well-structured, with tannins that are already integrated. Its balance is exceptional, making this an outstanding wine. The Georgos displays great personality, with strawberry fruitiness immediately pleasing the nose, followed by hints of mountain herbs harmonized by tobacco notes. The body is firm, with close-knit tannins and magnificent fruity flesh.

We still think of La Plantze as a new winery, but it's now been over 10 years since it started operating in Villeneuve, a village at the heart of one of the region's most prized vineyard areas. Henri Anselmet's philosophy is to interpret the terroir with appropriate grape varieties, which is why he hasn't hesitated to experiment with less-known varieties in the region, such as viognier. With great skill, he blends the tradition of indigenous grapes with the modernity of international varieties, resulting in wines that are robust, fresh, and easy to drink. The signature wild aromatic notes of the sauvignon grape are brought out in La Copine, a wine that sees hints of tomato leaves accompany a fine and harmonious persistence on the palate. El Teemp opts for vibrant forest fruit aromas, accented by spice and pepper, with good structure. The Nagot proves intense on the nose, revealing plum jam and rosehip, while on the palate, it stands out for its notable structure, fruity richness, tension, and nice persistence. The Pinot Gris is still evolving.

● VdA Nebbiolo Dessus '22	♟♟♟ 6
● VdA Donnas Georgos '21	♟♟ 7
● VdA Nebbiolo 396 Aesculus Hippocastanum '22	♟♟ 4
○ BiancOne '22	♟ 6
◉ VdA Rosato Rose Tendre '23	♟ 4
● VdA Donnas Georgos '20	♈ 7
● VdA Donnas Georgos '19	♈ 7
● VdA Donnas Georgos '18	♈ 7
● VdA Donnas Georgos '17	♈ 7
● VdA Donnas Georgos '15	♈ 6
● VdA Nebbiolo 396 Aesculus Hippocastanum '21	♈ 4
● VdA Nebbiolo 396 Aesculus Hippocastanum '20	♈ 4
● VdA Nebbiolo Dessus '21	♈ 5

○ La Copine '23	♟♟ 3
● Nagòt '22	♟♟ 6
○ Pas Toi '23	♟♟ 6
○ VdA Pinot Gris Trii Rundin '23	♟♟ 4
● VdA Rosso El Teemp '23	♟♟ 4
● VdA Syrah L'Avenir pur Mathieu '22	♟♟ 6
● Cornalin Vioux '22	♈ 5
● Nagòt '21	♈ 6
○ Trii Rundin Pinot Gris '19	♈ 4
○ VdA Pinot Gris Trii Rundin '22	♈ 4
○ VdA Pinot Gris Trii Rundin '21	♈ 4
● VdA Rosso El Teemp '22	♈ 4
● VdA Syrah L'Avenir '21	♈ 6
● VdA Syrah L'Avenir '20	♈ 6
● VdA Torrette Sup. '19	♈ 5
● Vda Torrette Sup. '18	♈ 5

★Rosset Terroir

loc. Torrent de Maillod, 4
11020 Quart [AO]
☎ +39 0165774111
@ www.rosseterroir.it

CELLAR SALES
ANNUAL PRODUCTION 60,000 bottles
HECTARES UNDER VINE 12.00

Nicola Rosset is an entrepreneur renowned worldwide for his achievements in the spirits and liqueurs industry. Rosseterroir, his family-run winery, is a highly modern estate that embraces green practices, drawing on an off-the-grid energy system and an unparalleled commitment to the land. The family has deep roots in the Aosta Valley, and their connection to the region's history is evident in every aspect of their work. Thanks to major investments in technology and materials, their high-quality range keeps getting better. Their flagship remains the Sopraquota, an unblended Petite Arvine. While the nose is still slightly closed, it releases aromas of dried mountain herbs, then quince. The palate is rich, aiming for a powerful style, somewhat neglecting the elegant, refined typicity that we'd expect from the grape. The Syrah reveals fine, complex black berry notes, with a finish that evokes black pepper, and velvety tannins that add personality and balance to the palate.

o Sopraquota 900 '22	♟♟♟ 7
● VdA Syrah 870 '22	♟♟ 6
o VdA Chardonnay 770 '22	♟♟ 6
● VdA Cornalin '23	♟♟ 5
● VdA Nebbiolo '23	♟♟ 5
● VdA Petite Arvine '22	♟♟ 5
● VdA Pinot Noir '22	♟♟ 6
o VdA Blanc Prémisse '23	♟ 4
o VdA Chambave Muscat '22	♟ 5
o Sopraquota 900 '21	♟♟♟ 7
o Sopraquota 900 '20	♟♟♟ 7
o Sopraquota 900 '19	♟♟♟ 4*
o Sopraquota 900 '18	♟♟♟ 4*
o Sopraquota 900	♟♟♟ 4*
o VdA Chardonnay 770 '19	♟♟♟ 6
● VdA Cornalin '16	♟♟♟ 4*

★La Vrille

loc. Grangeon, 1
11020 Verrayes [AO]
☎ +39 3332393695
@ www.lavrille.it

CELLAR SALES
PRE-BOOKED VISITS
ANNUAL PRODUCTION 18,000 bottles
HECTARES UNDER VINE 3.00
SUSTAINABLE WINERY

La Vrille operates organically (though uncertified) with total respect for the environment and nature. The hollow where the estate is located perfectly aligns with Hervè's philosophy; a gentle breeze from Mont Blanc aids the healthy ripening of grapes, allowing for low intervention in the vineyard. Before dedicating himself to wine-growing, Hervè was a sailor, but now he is fully committed to nature, without forgetting the customs upheld by his ancestors. He prefers to work with native grape varieties, consistently producing high-quality wines for the market. The Muscat Flétrì is the pinnacle expression of moscato bianco, showcasing aromas of candied fruit, particularly orange. The palate is broad, fresh, and seemingly endless. True to type in its vegetal notes, the Fumin reveals tannins that still need to soften. The Clairet, a new addition, plays on notes of wilted rose petals, wild strawberries, and sweet spices, with balanced tannins on the palate.

● VdA Cornalin '22	♟♟ 4
● Clairetz '21	♟♟ 6
o VdA Chambave Muscat '22	♟♟ 4
● VdA Fumin '20	♟♟ 5
● VdA Pinot Noir '20	♟♟ 5
● VdA Vuillermin '21	♟♟ 4
o VdA Chambave Muscat '19	♟♟♟ 4*
o VdA Chambave Muscat '12	♟♟♟ 4*
o VdA Chambave Muscat Flétri '20	♟♟♟ 6
o VdA Chambave Muscat Flétri '18	♟♟♟ 7
o VdA Chambave Muscat Flétri '17	♟♟♟ 7
o VdA Chambave Muscat Flétri '16	♟♟♟ 7
o VdA Chambave Muscat Flétri '15	♟♟♟ 7
o VdA Chambave Muscat Flétri '14	♟♟♟ 7
o VdA Chambave Muscat Flétri '11	♟♟♟ 6

VALLE D'AOSTA

Château Feuillet

loc. Château Feuillet, 12
11010 Saint Pierre
📞 +39 3287673880
🌐 www.chateaufeuillet.it

CELLAR SALES
ACCOMMODATION AND RESTAURANT SERVICE
ANNUAL PRODUCTION 45,000 bottles
HECTARES UNDER VINE 8.00
VITICULTURE METHOD Certified Biodynamic

○ VdA Petite Arvine '23	♟	5
● VdA Torrette Sup. '21	♟	5

Di Barrò

loc. Château Feuillet, 8
11010 Saint Pierre
📞 +39 0165903671
🌐 www.dibarro.vievini.it

CELLAR SALES
PRE-BOOKED VISITS
ANNUAL PRODUCTION 20,000 bottles
HECTARES UNDER VINE 4.00

○ VdA Petite Arvine '23	♟	5
● VdA Fumin '22	♟	5
● VdA Torrette Sup. Ostro '20	♟	6

Caves de Donnas

via Roma, 97
11020 Donnas [AO]
📞 +39 0125807096
🌐 www.donnasvini.it

CELLAR SALES
PRE-BOOKED VISITS
ANNUAL PRODUCTION 140,000 bottles
HECTARES UNDER VINE 25.00

● VdA Donnas '20	♟	5
● VdA Donnas Napoléon '20	♟	4
● Vda Nebbiolo Barmet '23	♟	4

Cave Monaja

loc. Amérique, 8
11020 Quart [AO]
📞 +39 3339538849
🌐 www.cavemonaja.it

ANNUAL PRODUCTION 8,000 bottles
HECTARES UNDER VINE 3.00
SUSTAINABLE WINERY

○ Prêt a Boire '23	♟	5
● VdA Rouge Foehn '21	♟	6
● VdA Ruoge Djoué '21	♟	8
○ VdA Blanc Stau '22	♟	6

Cave Mont Blanc de Morgex et La Salle

fraz. La Ruine
Chemin des Iles, 31
11017 Morgex [AO]
📞 +39 0165800331
🌐 www.cavemontblanc.com

CELLAR SALES
PRE-BOOKED VISITS
ANNUAL PRODUCTION 140,000 bottles
HECTARES UNDER VINE 18.30

○ VdA Blanc de Morgex et de La Salle Cuvée du Prince '18	♟	7
○ VdA Blanc de Morgex et de La Salle Miniera '22	♟	5

Noussan

loc. Maillod, 41
11020 Saint Christophe [AO]
📞 +39 3355630909
🌐 www.noussanvini.it

CELLAR SALES
ANNUAL PRODUCTION 10,000 bottles
HECTARES UNDER VINE 2.50

○ VdA Petite Arvine Toules '23	♟	4
● VdA Torrette Sup. V. de la Prieure '21	♟	5
○ Câline '22	♟	4

PIEDMONT

As this guide is about to go to press, in early September 2024, the current state of Piedmont wine production resembles a flat, windy stage of the Tour de France. No one is out of the race completely, though some participants find themselves several hundred meters from the leaders. This pretty much sums up regional winemaking, with one key distinction: here, merit isn't the only factor—luck plays a significant role, too. The luck of being born and running your winery in certain parts of the region. Take, for example, the producers of Barolo and Barbaresco. In truth, we should include all wines made from nebbiolo grapes—they have the wind at their backs. But there's another distinction to be made: if you have a long-established history or a sharp marketing team supporting you, perhaps one that can ignite social media buzz, you can sell Barolo year after year, even on allocation, and at sky-high prices. If not, you'll still sell your Barolo, but you'll have to settle for market prices. In the world of red wines, it seems fair to say that Grignolino is enjoying a bit of a renaissance, especially among younger enthusiasts.

However, the overall trend in wine consumption seems to be shifting towards whites. Timorasso, in particular, is having its moment in the sun. Its growth has been rapid, even somewhat chaotic, despite the consortium's efforts to keep a close eye on things. Fortunately, this surge of interest hasn't undermined its prestige or the price of its grapes. Arneis, too, is in a positive phase, with slower but steady growth. This trend will likely play out over a longer period, as it involves a larger number of producers.

In Roero, there's a general sense of progress, aimed at including as many players as possible. Gavi, on the other hand, is making quiet strides forward, with much less fanfare and publicity, yet still showing positive signs. Finally, we must once again sing the praises of Alta Langa. In just a short time, it has gone from near obscurity to experiencing a rapid rise in both fame and sales. In any case, let's not forget that Piedmont remains above all a land of great winemakers, as underscored by this year's special Grower of the Year Award, which we've given to Mario Fontana of Cascina Fontana in Perno di Monforte. This year, 75 wines, representing terroirs from across the region, received Tre Bicchieri. Additionally, seven new wines have been added to our prestigious Rare Wines list.

★★Abbona

b.go San Luigi, 40
12063 Dogliani [CN]
(») +39 0173721317
@ www.abbona.com

Anna Maria Abbona

fraz. Moncucco, 21
12060 Farigliano [CN]
(») +39 0173797228
@ annamariabbona.it

CELLAR SALES
PRE-BOOKED VISITS
ACCOMMODATION
ANNUAL PRODUCTION 350,000 bottles
HECTARES UNDER VINE 50.00
VITICULTURE METHOD Certified Organic

CELLAR SALES
PRE-BOOKED VISITS
ANNUAL PRODUCTION 130,000 bottles
HECTARES UNDER VINE 22.00

Celso Abbona has always prioritized Dogliani, developing and promoting Dolcetto. Today, the producer is supported by Marziano and his two daughters, Mara and Chiara. For over 20 years, their vineyards have been organically farmed, and the Abbona family's commitment to the environment is a true way of life. Indeed, theirs is a philosophy that permeates production, with an emphasis on maximizing sustainability. The Dogliani Papà Celso offers incredible drinkability, with aromas of blackberry and bitter almond. In the mouth, vibrant acidity invites you to take another sip, complemented by a well-balanced structure and an exceptionally long finish. The Barolo Pressenda '20 proves vibrant, with notes of tobacco and licorice, adorned by raspberry and pomegranate. The palate is remarkable for its close-knit and delicate tannins, which, along with its fleshiness and a sapid finish, bring great harmony. The Barbera is also excellent—more mature, with a beautiful, opulent palate and a fresh, lengthy finish.

Since 1995, Anna Maria Abbona and Franco Schellino, today joined by their sons Federico and Lorenzo, have successfully managed the winery inherited from Anna Maria's father, Giuseppe. Their approach has always been artisanal, inspired by classical tradition. The family directly oversees work both in the vineyard and the cellar, aiming to create balanced, enjoyable wines. Deep in color, the Dogliani San Bernardo opens on the nose with bold, still-fresh fruit; in the mouth, it has good flesh and a long finish that will soften with time. The Bricco San Pietro '20 also impressed, standing out for its intensity and fullness. Unmistakable whiffs of sweet and spicy oak are nicely balanced by notes of fresh red fruit. The palate is dense and rich, with a razor-sharp balance between fruit and oak. A finish with modest acidity lends freshness.

● Dogliani Papà Celso '23	♥♥♥ 4*
● Barolo Pressenda '20	♥♥ 8
● Barolo Ravera '20	♥♥ 7
● Barbera d'Alba Rinaldi '22	♥♥ 4
● Barolo Cerviano-Merli '20	♥♥ 8
● Dogliani San Luigi '23	♥♥ 3
● Barolo Cerviano '10	♥♥♥ 7
● Barolo Cerviano-Merli '17	♥♥♥ 8
● Barolo Pressenda '16	♥♥♥ 7
● Dogliani Papà Celso '22	♥♥♥ 4*
● Dogliani Papà Celso '21	♥♥♥ 4*
● Dogliani Papà Celso '18	♥♥♥ 4*
● Dogliani Papà Celso '17	♥♥♥ 4*
● Dogliani Papà Celso '16	♥♥♥ 4*
● Dogliani Papà Celso '15	♥♥♥ 4*
● Dogliani Papà Celso '13	♥♥♥ 4*

● Barolo Bricco San Pietro '20	♥♥ 7
● Dogliani Superiore San Bernardo '20	♥♥ 5
● Barolo Bricco San Pietro Ris. '16	♥♥ 8
● Dogliani Sorí dij But '23	♥♥ 3
● Langhe Nebbiolo '21	♥ 4
○ Langhe Riesling L'Alman '22	♥ 4
● Dogliani Sorì Dij But '19	♥♥♥ 3*
● Dogliani Sup. Maioli '19	♥♥♥ 3*
● Dogliani Sup. San Bernardo '19	♥♥♥ 5
● Dogliani Sup. San Bernardo '18	♥♥♥ 4*
● Dogliani Sup. San Bernardo '12	♥♥♥ 4*
● Dogliani Sup. San Bernardo '11	♥♥♥ 4*
● Barolo Bricco San Pietro '19	♥♥ 7
● Barolo del Comune di Castiglione Falletto '19	♥♥ 6
● Dogliani Sorì Dij But '21	♥♥ 3*

F.lli Abrigo

loc. Berfi
via Moglia Gerlotto, 2
12055 Diano d'Alba [CN]
( ) +39 017369104
@ abrigofratelli.it

CELLAR SALES
PRE-BOOKED VISITS
ANNUAL PRODUCTION 60,000 bottles
HECTARES UNDER VINE 25.00

The Abrigo family's history in the Langhe region dates back to 1935. Their most notable wines draw on Dolcetto di Diano d'Alba, but as the winery has grown, they've also begun producing other local varietals, including barbera, nebbiolo, arneis, and favorita, and even Alta Langa sparkling wines. The estate is led by Ernesto, his sister Mariarita, his son Walter, and his brother-in-law, winemaker Emanuele Antona. The Diano d'Alba La Voghera '22 opens on aromas of red cherries and violets, with a balsamic whiff reminiscent of wild mint, leading to a juicy, deep, and long-lasting palate. Simpler but equally enjoyable, the Diano d'Alba Sorì Cascina Carbone '22 proves grapey, juicy, and fleshy—a perfect companion at the dinner table. The Langhe Bianco Lumiè '22, a blend of favorita and arneis, reveals a lovely bouquet reminiscent of jasmine and lemon, with a smooth, pleasant palate. The other wines tasted are also on point.

Giovanni Abrigo

via Santa Croce, 9
12055 Diano d'Alba [CN]
( ) +39 017369345
@ www.abrigo.it

CELLAR SALES
PRE-BOOKED VISITS
ANNUAL PRODUCTION 40,000 bottles
HECTARES UNDER VINE 15.00
SUSTAINABLE WINERY

Giulio and Sergio Abrigo, both graduates of the Alba School of Oenology, quickly made their mark in the family winery, taking charge of all stages of production, from vineyard to cellar, and managing the new technology introduced during the estate's modernization. The Garabei, their Dolcetto Superiore, is the winery's flagship, made from vines over 50 years old, cultivated at 350 meters elevation. The Garabei was a pleasant surprise for our tasting panel, impressing with its complexity on the nose, depth on the palate, and overall fullness—all expressed with elegance. Cherry, raspberry, and subtle spices stand out, while the palate is fresh, thanks to integrated acidity, and flavorful, with a faint mineral vein that enhances its drinkability. The Ravera, a Barolo of great finesse, is another outstanding wine, with caressing tannins and incredible sapidity. The rest of their range is also of excellent quality.

● Barolo Ravera '20	♛♛ 7
● Diano d'Alba La Voghera '22	♛♛ 5
○ Alta Langa Brut Sivà '19	♛♛ 5
● Diano d'Alba Sorì Cascina Carbone '22	♛♛ 5
● Diano d'Alba Sorì del Fossà '22	♛♛ 5
○ Langhe Bianco Lumié '22	♛♛ 3
○ Alta Langa Brut Sivà Ris. '18	♛ 7
● Langhe Nebbiolo '22	♛ 3
○ Alta Langa Brut Sivà '17	♛♛ 5
● Barbera d'Alba Sup. '21	♛♛ 3
● Barbera d'Alba Sup. '20	♛♛ 3
● Barolo Ravera '19	♛♛ 7
● Barolo Ravera '16	♛♛ 7
● Diano d'Alba '22	♛♛ 3*
● Diano d'Alba '21	♛♛ 2*
● Nebbiolo d'Alba '21	♛♛ 3
● Nebbiolo d'Alba '20	♛♛ 3

● Barolo Ravera '20	♛♛ 7
● Dolcetto di Diano d'Alba Sup. Garabei '22	♛♛ 4
● Nebbiolo d'Alba '22	♛♛ 5
● Barbera d'Alba Marminela '21	♛♛ 3
● Barbera d'Alba Marminela '19	♛♛ 2*
● Barbera d'Alba Sup. Rocche dei Frisu '20	♛♛ 5
● Barolo Ravera '19	♛♛ 7
● Barolo Ravera '18	♛♛ 7
● Barolo Ravera '17	♛♛ 6
● Dolcetto di Diano d'Alba Sorì dei Crava '22	♛♛ 3*
● Dolcetto di Diano d'Alba Sorì dei Crava '21	♛♛ 3
● Dolcetto di Diano d'Alba Sup. Garabei '21	♛♛ 4
● Dolcetto di Diano d'Alba Sup. Garabei '20	♛♛ 4
● Nebbiolo d'Alba '21	♛♛ 5

Orlando Abrigo

via Cappelletto, 5
12050 Treiso [CN]
(+39 0173630533
www.orlandoabrigo.com

★Accornero Giulio e Figli

via Ca' Cima, I
15049 Vignale Monferrato [AL]
(+39 0142933317
www.accornerovini.it

CELLAR SALES
PRE-BOOKED VISITS
ACCOMMODATION
ANNUAL PRODUCTION 100,000 bottles
HECTARES UNDER VINE 23.00
SUSTAINABLE WINERY

CELLAR SALES
PRE-BOOKED VISITS
ACCOMMODATION
ANNUAL PRODUCTION 150,000 bottles
HECTARES UNDER VINE 30.00
SUSTAINABLE WINERY

Giovanni Abrigo inherited his father Orlando's production legacy, focusing on Barbaresco while also producing other local classics like Barbera and Dolcetto d'Alba. In recent years, he's paid special attention to the Barbaresco Crus, Montersino and Meruzzano, yielding compact, vigorous, and fragrant wines from grapes grown in the appellation's highest vineyards. The 2020 Barbaresco Montersino is well-crafted, with an intensely fruity nose touched by notes of cinchona and tobacco. The palate is tightly woven with a multifaceted and firm tannic structure, delivering a vigorous mouthfeel and a long, persistent finish. The Barbaresco Meruzzano '21 also boasts aromatic intensity, while the palate proves austere, with a compact development and a deep finish. The Barbaresco Rongalio Riserva '19 is a pure, no-frills type of wine, elegant in its restraint.

The Accornero family's agricultural roots stretch back more than a century, but the real turning point came in 1957 when Giulio Accornero decided to vinify his own grapes. Today, his sons Ermanno and Massimo continue to run the winery, pursuing excellence and honoring their land. The estate's soils, rich in limestone and marl, lend the wines a distinctive depth and strong aging potential. The star varietals here are barbera and grignolino, which thrive in this unique terroir. The Accornero family once again proves to be one of the finest interpreters of the region, presenting a line of consistently high-quality wines. The Grignolino del Monferrato Casalese Bricco del Bosco '23 pours an enticing, brilliant ruby color, with aromas of red fruit and pepper rising from the glass. The palate is decisive, with refined tannins and a sapid finish. The Barbera Superiore Bricco Battista '20 is more mature, characterized by brandied fruit. While it lacks freshness, it makes up for it with complexity, offering a powerful, dense palate with great length.

● Barbaresco Montersino '20	¶¶ 7
● Barbaresco Rongalio Ris. '19	¶¶ 8
○ Langhe Très Plus '22	¶¶ 4
● Barbaresco Meruzzano '21	¶¶ 6
● Barbaresco Cn Centoundici '20	¶ 8
● Barbaresco Meruzzano '20	♀♀ 6
● Barbaresco Meruzzano '18	♀♀ 6
● Barbaresco Meruzzano '15	♀♀ 5
● Barbaresco Montersino '19	♀♀ 7
● Barbaresco Montersino '18	♀♀ 7
● Barbaresco Montersino '13	♀♀ 7
● Barbaresco Montersino '12	♀♀ 7
● Barbaresco Rongalio Ris. '15	♀♀ 8
● Barbaresco Rongalio Ris. '12	♀♀ 8
● Barbaresco Rongalio Ris. '11	♀♀ 8
● Barbera d'Alba Sup. Mervisano '20	♀♀ 4
○ Langhe Bianco Très Plus '13	♀♀ 3*

● Grignolino del M.to Casalese Bricco del Bosco '23	¶¶¶ 3*
● Barbera del Monferrato Sup. Bricco Battista '20	¶¶ 6
● Grignolino del M.to Casalese Bricco del Bosco V.V. Ris. '20	¶¶ 7
○ Accornero Extra Brut Blanc de Blancs M.Cl. '20	¶¶ 7
● Barbera del Monferrato Sup. Giulin '22	¶¶ 3
● Monferrato Freisa La Bernardina '23	¶¶ 3
● Monferrato Rosso Girotondo '21	¶¶ 4
● Piemonte Barbera Campomoro '23	¶¶ 3
● Ruché di Castagnole M.to Viarì '23	¶¶ 4
● Malvasia di Casorzo Brigantino '23	¶ 3
● Grignolino del M.to Casalese Bricco del Bosco V.V. Ris. '19	♀♀♀ 7

Adriano Marco e Vittorio

fraz. San Rocco Seno d'Elvio, 13a
12051 Alba [CN]
☎ +39 0173362294
✉ adrianovini.it

Claudio Alario

via Santa Croce, 23
12055 Diano d'Alba [CN]
☎ +39 0173231808
✉ www.alarioclaudio.it

CELLAR SALES
PRE-BOOKED VISITS
ACCOMMODATION
ANNUAL PRODUCTION 160,000 bottles
HECTARES UNDER VINE 30.00
SUSTAINABLE WINERY

CELLAR SALES
PRE-BOOKED VISITS
ANNUAL PRODUCTION 46,000 bottles
HECTARES UNDER VINE 10.00

Founded in the early 20th century, the Adriano family winery cultivates Langhe's most important varieties in a landscape dedicated to biodiversity, maintaining vineyards alongside several hectares of forest and hazelnut groves. Since 1994, their Barbaresco has been produced according to eco-sustainable principles, including the use of renewable energy and water purification processes. The Barbaresco Sanadaive '21 opens with an intense and fragrant fruity attack, evolving into notes of cinchona. The palate is powerful and multifaceted, with energetic tannins that are still maturing. Fresh red fruits also characterize the Barbaresco Basarin '21, with some vegetal nuances preceding a well-defined and persistent palate. The Langhe Sauvignon Basaricò '22 proves sapid and juicy, with aromatic hints of white peach.

Claudio Alario began revitalizing his family's winery in Diano d'Alba in the late 1980s. Initially focusing on Dolcetto, he later added Barbera and Barolo. Their vineyards in Diano d'Alba, Serralunga d'Alba, and Verduno go back anywhere from 20 to 50 years, with their Barolo Riva Rocca cultivated in Verduno, while their Barolo Sorano hails from Serralunga d'Alba. The Barolo Sorano '20 stands out for its well-defined and flavorful palate, with prominent fruity aromas and a delicate hint of spice. The Dolcetto di Diano d'Alba Sorì Montagrillo '23 offers raspberry aromas and balsamic hints that give way to blackberry tones. It's a juicy, smooth, and flavorful drink. The Barolo Riva Rocca '20 is pleasant on the palate, though very tannic and leaning toward sweetness, with an intense flavor profile.

● Barbaresco Sanadaive '21	♟♟ 5
● Barbaresco Basarin '21	♟♟ 6
● Barbera d'Alba Sup. '21	♟♟ 3
○ Langhe Sauvignon Basaricò '22	♟♟ 3
● Langhe Nebbiolo Cainassa '22	♟ 3
● Barbaresco Basarin '18	♟♟ 5
● Barbaresco Basarin '16	♟♟ 5
● Barbaresco Basarin Ris. '13	♟♟ 6
● Barbaresco Basarin Ris. '12	♟♟ 6
● Barbaresco Basarin Ris. '11	♟♟ 6
● Barbaresco Sanadaive '20	♟♟ 5
● Barbaresco Sanadaive '19	♟♟ 5
● Barbaresco Sanadaive '18	♟♟ 5
● Barbaresco Sanadaive '17	♟♟ 5
● Barbaresco Sanadaive '15	♟♟ 5

● Barolo Sorano '20	♟♟ 7
● Dolcetto di Diano d'Alba Sup. Sorì Pradurent '22	♟♟ 4
● Barolo Riva Rocca '20	♟♟ 6
● Dolcetto di Diano d'Alba Sorì Montagrillo '23	♟♟ 2*
● Dolcetto di Diano d'Alba Sorì Costa Fiore '23	♟ 3
● Nebbiolo d'Alba Cascinotto '22	♟ 4
● Barolo Sorano '05	♟♟♟ 7
● Barolo Riva Rocca '19	♟♟ 5
● Barolo Riva Rocca '16	♟♟ 5
● Barolo Sorano '19	♟♟ 6
● Barolo Sorano '18	♟♟ 6
● Barolo Sorano '17	♟♟ 6
● Dolcetto di Diano d'Alba Sorì Costa Fiore '22	♟♟ 3*

★F.lli Alessandria

via B. Valfré, 59
12060 Verduno [CN]
(») +39 0172470113
⊛ www.fratellialessandria.it

★Gianfranco Alessandria

loc. Manzoni, 13
12065 Monforte d'Alba [CN]
(») +39 017378576
⊛ www.gianfrancoalessandria.com

CELLAR SALES
PRE-BOOKED VISITS
ACCOMMODATION
ANNUAL PRODUCTION 90,000 bottles
HECTARES UNDER VINE 15.00

CELLAR SALES
PRE-BOOKED VISITS
ANNUAL PRODUCTION 55,000 bottles
HECTARES UNDER VINE 7.00

Founded in 1870, Fratelli Alessandria is one of the oldest wineries in Verduno. Today, the producer is run by Gian Battista, his wife Flavia, his brother Alessandro, and his son Vittore, who continue the family's winemaking legacy drawing on solid, time-honored methods. Alongside nebbiolo, their vineyards host dolcetto, barbera, freisa, and pelaverga, with favorita being the only white grape variety cultivated. The Barolo Monvigliero '20 possesses focused aromas of bright fruity and balsamic tones, while in the mouth it's broad, gratifying, and beautifully tense. A well calibrated and flavorful drink. The Barolo del Comune di Verduno '19 is also excellent, offering dark, deep aromas and a fleshy, sweet, and tasty palate. The aromatic Barolo Gramolere '20 is highly enjoyable, with beautiful length on the palate.

Gianfranco Alessandria runs this small, family-operated winery together with his wife Bruna and daughters Vittoria and Marta. Their vines are cultivated in a single plot in the Bussia-San Giovanni valley in Monforte. Their most important wines undergo short maceration before aging in small, new and second-use barrels, resulting in a range characterized by solid structure, aromatic fragrance, and good longevity. This year, the winery presented another solid pair of Barolos. The San Giovanni '20 proves vibrant on the nose, blending sweet spices from the oak with lovely red fruit and a slight hint of tobacco. The palate is fine, juicy, with good structure and a long finish. The Barolo '20 also performs very well; here, fruit balances tertiary notes, with a tidy tannic structure, focusing more on drinkability than complexity.

● Barolo Monvigliero '20	♟♟♟ 8
● Barolo del Comune di Verduno '20	♟♟ 6
● Barolo Gramolere '20	♟♟ 8
● Barbera d'Alba Sup. La Priòra '21	♟♟ 4
● Barolo San Lorenzo di Verduno '20	♟♟ 8
● Verduno Pelaverga Speziale '23	♟♟ 4
● Barolo Gramolere '11	♟♟♟ 6
● Barolo Gramolere '10	♟♟♟ 6
● Barolo Monvigliero '16	♟♟♟ 6
● Barolo Monvigliero '15	♟♟♟ 6
● Barolo Monvigliero '14	♟♟♟ 6
● Barolo Monvigliero '13	♟♟♟ 6
● Barolo Monvigliero '12	♟♟♟ 6
● Barolo Monvigliero '09	♟♟♟ 6
● Barolo Monvigliero '06	♟♟♟ 6
● Barolo S. Lorenzo '08	♟♟♟ 6

● Barolo San Giovanni '20	♟♟ 8
● Barbera d'Alba Vittoria '21	♟♟ 6
● Barolo '20	♟♟ 7
● Barbera d'Alba Vittoria '15	♟♟♟ 5
● Barbera d'Alba Vittoria '11	♟♟♟ 5
● Barbera d'Alba Vittoria '98	♟♟♟ 5
● Barbera d'Alba Vittoria '97	♟♟♟ 4*
● Barbera d'Alba Vittoria '96	♟♟♟ 6
● Barolo '93	♟♟♟ 6
● Barolo S. Giovanni '04	♟♟♟ 7
● Barolo S. Giovanni '01	♟♟♟ 7
● Barolo S. Giovanni '00	♟♟♟ 7
● Barolo S. Giovanni '99	♟♟♟ 8
● Barolo S. Giovanni '98	♟♟♟ 7
● Barolo S. Giovanni '97	♟♟♟ 7
● Barolo '19	♟♟ 7
● Barolo San Giovanni '19	♟♟ 8

Marchesi Alfieri

p.zza Alfieri, 28
14010 San Martino Alfieri [AT]
☎ +39 0141976015
🖰 www.marchesialfieri.it

Cantina Alice Bel Colle

reg. Stazione, 9
15010 Alice Bel Colle [AL]
☎ +39 014474103
🖰 www.cantinaalicebc.it

CELLAR SALES
PRE-BOOKED VISITS
ACCOMMODATION
ANNUAL PRODUCTION 120,000 bottles
HECTARES UNDER VINE 20.00
SUSTAINABLE WINERY

CELLAR SALES
PRE-BOOKED VISITS
ACCOMMODATION
ANNUAL PRODUCTION 150,000 bottles
HECTARES UNDER VINE 350.00
SUSTAINABLE WINERY

Located in San Martino Alfiero, and headquartered in the historic castle of the Marquis Alfieri family, this winery is led by sisters Emanuela, Antonella, and Giovanna, though it has benefited from the technical direction of Mario Olivero since the late 1990s. For more than 30 years, barbera has been the primary grape cultivated here, alongside other regional varieties such as grignolino and nebbiolo, and international grapes like pinot noir (the star of their Metodo Classico), making for a range of strong territorial identity and character. The Barbera d'Asti Superiore Alfiera '21 highlights notes of black fruits, spices, and petrichor, followed by a balanced, fresh, and fruit-forward palate. The Terre Alfieri Nebbiolo Costa Quaglia '21 also impressed, with its aromas of violet, raspberry, licorice, and aromatic herbs. The palate is elegant and delicate, yet long, vibrant, and deep. The Piemonte Grignolino Sansoero '23 is well-crafted, showcasing tones of pepper and rose, unfolding smooth and balanced.

The "Viticoltori Insieme" cooperative may have reached its 70th anniversary, but under the leadership of the tireless duo, Claudio Negrino and Bruno Roffredo, it's as vibrant as ever. Indeed, the cooperative has established a dynamic group of young members to foster new ideas and training for the next generation. A key focus is to boost wine tourism tied to the iconic "Belvedere" in the town's main square, an attraction that also graces the cooperative's colorful wine labels. A refined and complex Barbera, the Alix boasts aromas of bright cherry and plum fruit with a powerful, lingering palate, lifted by a vibrant vein of acidity. The Barbera Al Casò, aged entirely in stainless steel, pours an inky ruby hue, releasing aromas rich in red and black berries. On the palate, it offers substance and flesh. The Brachetto Le Casette proves fresh and flavorful, striking a harmonious balance between sweetness and acidity. The Alta Langa Tresessanta Pas Dosé opens on notes of bread crust, followed by floral hints and citrus peel.

● Barbera d'Asti Sup. Alfiera '21	♟♟ 6
● Terre Alfieri Nebbiolo Costa Quaglia '21	♟♟ 5
● Piemonte Barbera-Pinot Nero Sostegno '23	♟♟ 3
● Piemonte Grignolino Sansoero '23	♟♟ 3
● Barbera d'Asti La Tota '22	♟ 4
● Barbera d'Asti Sup. Alfiera '07	♟♟♟ 5
● Barbera d'Asti Sup. Alfiera '05	♟♟♟ 5
● Barbera d'Asti Sup. Alfiera '01	♟♟♟ 5
● Barbera d'Asti Sup. Alfiera '00	♟♟♟ 5
● Barbera d'Asti Sup. Alfiera '99	♟♟♟ 5
● Barbera d'Asti La Tota '20	♟♟ 3*
● Barbera d'Asti La Tota '19	♟♟ 3*
● Barbera d'Asti Sup. Alfiera '20	♟♟ 6
● Barbera d'Asti Sup. Alfiera '19	♟♟ 5
● Barbera d'Asti Sup. Alfiera '18	♟♟ 5
○ Blanc de Noir Extra Brut M. Cl. '17	♟♟ 5

● Barbera d'Asti Al Casò Collezione 360° '22	♟♟ 3*
● Barbera d'Asti Sup. Alix '21	♟♟ 4
○ Alta Langa Pas Dosé Cuvée Tresessanta	♟♟ 5
● Brachetto d'Acqui Le Casette di Alice '23	♟♟ 2*
● Dolcetto d'Acqui Coste di Muiran Collezione 360° '22	♟♟ 3
○ Moscato d'Asti Le Casette di Alice '23	♟♟ 2*
○ Asti M. Cl. Cuvée Tresessanta '20	♟ 4
○ Moscato d'Asti Strevi Paiè '23	♟ 3
○ Piemonte Moscato Secco Filarej Collezione 360° '23	♟ 2
● Acqui Secco Monteridolfo '22	♟♟ 3*
○ Alta Langa Pas Dosé Tresessanta Ris. '18	♟♟ 5
● Barbera d'Asti Collezione 360° Al Casò '20	♟♟ 3*
● Barbera d'Asti Sup. Alix '19	♟♟ 4
○ Moscato d'Asti Strevi Paiè '22	♟♟ 3*

★Giovanni Almondo

via San Rocco, 26
12046 Montà [CN]
📞 +39 0173975256
🌐 www.giovannialmondo.com

★★★★Elio Altare

fraz. Annunziata, 51
12064 La Morra [CN]
📞 +39 017350835
🌐 www.elioaltare.com

PRE-BOOKED VISITS
ANNUAL PRODUCTION 130,000 bottles
HECTARES UNDER VINE 22.00
VITICULTURE METHOD Certified Organic
SUSTAINABLE WINERY

CELLAR SALES
PRE-BOOKED VISITS
ANNUAL PRODUCTION 70,000 bottles
HECTARES UNDER VINE 11.00

Situated in the northernmost part of Roero, the Almondo family's winery relies on vineyards within the municipal boundaries of Montà d'Alba. The white grape varieties, arneis and riesling, are grown in the higher, sandier areas, while the red varieties, nebbiolo, barbera, and freisa, thrive in the lower areas, where sand is accompanied by the presence of limestone. Almondo offers about 10 wines, producing elegant and characterful wines with a distinctly recognizable style. This year, we were particularly impressed by the producer's red wines. The Roero Bric Valdiana '21 showcases tones of black currant, violet, and licorice, with a juicy, sapid, and smooth palate. The Roero '22 features floral notes, cherry, and rosemary, delivering a pleasant, long finish. We found two wines less brilliant compared to previous years: the Roero Arneis Le Rive del Bricco delle Ciliegie '22, which opts for flavors of white currant and pear, and the Roero Arneis Bricco delle Ciliegie '23, which is soft, with sweet citrus tones and moderate length.

Since the 2000s, Silvia has proudly and respectfully led the winery to success, following in the footsteps of her father, Elio Altare. The vineyards can be found in some of Langhe's most prestigious growing areas, including La Morra, Barolo, Castiglione Falletto, Monforte, and Serralunga d'Alba. The producer's wines are characterized by clarity, elegance, balance, and personality, fully embracing the concept of "modern tradition." The Langhe Rosso Larigi '22 exemplifies finesse and elegance, with a nose that perfectly balances cherry and sweet spices. The palate is rich and pervasive, with a silky texture. A final touch of acidity balances this wonderfully drinkable wine. The Barolo Arborina '20 proves exceptional, more intense than the previous vintage, yet equally refined, offering tobacco and licorice aromas, alongside notes of strawberry and raspberry. Masterfully balanced sweet spices and finely sculpted tannins lend this Barolo infinite length.

● Roero '22	🍷🍷 5
● Roero Bric Valdiana '21	🍷🍷 6
○ Roero Arneis Le rive Del Bricco delle Ciliegie '22	🍷🍷 5
○ Roero Arneis Bricco delle Ciliegie '23	🍷 5
○ Roero Arneis Le Rive del Bricco delle Ciliegie '20	🍷🍷🍷 4*
○ Roero Arneis Le Rive del Bricco delle Ciliegie '16	🍷🍷🍷 4*
● Roero Bric Valdiana '20	🍷🍷🍷 5
● Roero Bric Valdiana '11	🍷🍷🍷 5
● Roero Bric Valdiana '07	🍷🍷🍷 5
● Roero Bric Valdiana '03	🍷🍷🍷 5
● Roero Bric Valdiana '01	🍷🍷🍷 4
● Roero Giovanni Almondo Ris. '13	🍷🍷🍷 5
● Roero Giovanni Almondo Ris. '11	🍷🍷🍷 5
● Roero Giovanni Almondo Ris. '09	🍷🍷🍷 5

● Langhe Rosso Larigi '22	🍷🍷🍷 8
● Barolo Arborina '20	🍷🍷 8
● Langhe Rosso Giàrborina '22	🍷🍷 8
● Barolo Cerretta V. Bricco Ris. '18	🍷🍷 8
● Langhe Rosso La Villa '22	🍷🍷 8
● Barolo Arborina '17	🍷🍷🍷 8
● Barolo Arborina '16	🍷🍷🍷 8
● Barolo Cerretta V. Bricco '11	🍷🍷🍷 8
● Barolo Cerretta V. Bricco '10	🍷🍷🍷 8
● Barolo Cerretta V. Bricco Ris. '16	🍷🍷🍷 8
● Barolo Cerretta V. Bricco Ris. '13	🍷🍷🍷 8
● Langhe Larigi '13	🍷🍷🍷 8
● Langhe Larigi '12	🍷🍷🍷 8
● Langhe Rosso Giàrborina '16	🍷🍷🍷 8
● Langhe Rosso Larigi '21	🍷🍷🍷 8

Amalia Cascina in Langa

loc. Sant'Anna, 85
12065 Monforte d'Alba [CN]
📞 +39 0173789013
🌐 www.cascinaamalia.it

CELLAR SALES
PRE-BOOKED VISITS
ACCOMMODATION
ANNUAL PRODUCTION 35,000 bottles
HECTARES UNDER VINE 8.00
VITICULTURE METHOD Certified Organic

The winery took its first steps in 2003 when the Boffa family acquired the estate, renovating the 20th-century farmhouse and establishing a modern cellar. The vineyards, initially planted with dolcetto and barbera, were expanded to include renowned Crus like Bussia and Le Coste di Monforte. Today, this organic winery adheres to a classic production style, using traditional winemaking methods with the utmost respect for the land. Fragrant and appetizing, the Barolo Bussia Vigna Fantini unfolds with a supple, slender, and flavorful palate, recalling crunchy forest fruits and spices. Briny hints and citrus whiffs characterize the Langhe Rossese Bianco '22, which delivers a penetrating, sapid, and persistent palate. The Langhe Nebbiolo '22 is juicy and smooth, with wild strawberry aromas and herbaceous notes.

Paolo Angelini

Cascina Cairo, 10
15039 Ozzano Monferrato [AL]
📞 +39 3468549015
🌐 www.angelinipaolo.it

CELLAR SALES
PRE-BOOKED VISITS
ANNUAL PRODUCTION 100,000 bottles
HECTARES UNDER VINE 40.00
SUSTAINABLE WINERY

With over a century of history, the Angelini family's winery continues to evolve. Perhaps it's the firm foundations laid by past generations that has allowed Paolo and Franco Angelini, the current (fourth) generation, to breathe new life into the winery without sacrificing its core identity. The estate spans 42 hectares of vineyards, divided into four distinct parcels, giving the winery the ability to fully express the nuances of its territory. Two wines caught our attention this year: the Grignolino del Monferrato Casalese Arbian '23 stands out for its typicity, with a broad nose of rose petals and pepper, and a powerful palate with firm yet fleshy tannins. The Barbera del Monferrato First '23 is also noteworthy, offering rich fruit and a dense mouthfeel, with a nose of cherries, plums, and subtle chocolate. The palate is equally rich and refined, finishing warm and full.

● Barolo Bussia V. Fantini '20	🍷🍷 7
● Langhe Nebbiolo '22	🍷🍷 4
○ Langhe Rossese Bianco '22	🍷🍷 4
● Barbera d'Alba '22	🍷 3
● Dolcetto d'Alba '22	🍷 3
● Barolo '11	🍷🍷 6
● Barolo Bussia '17	🍷🍷 6
● Barolo Bussia '16	🍷🍷 6
● Barolo Bussia '15	🍷🍷 6
● Barolo Bussia '13	🍷🍷 6
● Barolo Bussia V. Fantini '18	🍷🍷 6
● Barolo Le Coste di Monforte '19	🍷🍷 7
● Barolo Le Coste di Monforte '17	🍷🍷 6
● Barolo Le Coste di Monforte '16	🍷🍷 6
● Barolo Le Coste di Monforte '13	🍷🍷 6
● Barolo Le Coste di Monforte '11	🍷🍷 6

● Grignolino del M.to Casalese Arbian '23	🍷🍷🍷 3*
● Barbera del M.to First '23	🍷🍷 2*
● Barbera del M.to Jenerosa '20	🍷🍷 3
● Grignolino del M.to Casalese Monferace Golden Arbian '19	🍷 5
● Barbera del M.to First '22	🍷🍷 2*
● Barbera del M.to First '21	🍷🍷 2*
● Barbera del M.to Jenerosa '19	🍷🍷 2*
● Barbera del M.to Jenerosa '18	🍷🍷 2*
● Barbera del M.to Jenerosa '17	🍷🍷 2*
● Barbera del M.to Sup. Adamant '19	🍷🍷 3
● Grignolino del M.to Casalese Arbian '22	🍷🍷 2*
● Grignolino del M.to Casalese Monferace Golden Arbian '18	🍷🍷 5
● Grignolino del M.to Casalese Monferace Golden Arbian '16	🍷🍷 6

Antichi Vigneti di Cantalupo

via Michelangelo Buonarroti, 5
28074 Ghemme [NO]
☎ +39 0163840041
⊛ www.cantalupo.net

CELLAR SALES
PRE-BOOKED VISITS
ANNUAL PRODUCTION 180,000 bottles
HECTARES UNDER VINE 35.00

The Alunno family has been tied to the territory of Ghemme for two centuries. In 1981, Alberto Alunno took the reins, driven by a deep belief in the area's winemaking potential. The family's vineyards are spread across two hillsides of Monte Rosa's glacial terraces, ranging between 250 and 310 meters in elevation with southern and southwestern exposures. All cultivation and harvesting are carried out by hand. While the entire range is of high quality, it's the Collis Breclemae '17, a symbol of the estate since 1979, that stands out most. It expresses power and charm with aromas of blood orange, black plum, licorice, and tobacco, and a focused, flavorful palate with harmonious tannins and a smooth finish. The Agamium '22 proves fresh and lively, with notes of black cherry, spiced cherries, and licorice, offering a dynamic, spicy palate.

★★Antoniolo

c.so Valsesia, 277
13045 Gattinara [VC]
☎ +39 0163833612
antoniolovini@bmm.it

CELLAR SALES
PRE-BOOKED VISITS
ANNUAL PRODUCTION 60,000 bottles
HECTARES UNDER VINE 12.00

Lorella and Alberto Antoniolo's wines are marked by their character and typicity, revealing a style that balances depth with elegance. Founded by Lorella's grandfather Mario in 1948, the winery is a cornerstone of Gattinara. Their 14 hectares of vineyards, primarily dedicated to nebbiolo, feature three estate crus: Osso San Grato (five hectares of south-facing, volcanic soils), San Francesco (3.5 hectares, with a west-facing exposure), and Castelle (a 1.3-hectare site whose soils are deeper and richer). The Osso San Grato '19 offers continuously evolving flavors and aromas, with balsamic notes enhancing citrus, tobacco, and licorice sensations, alongside a ferrous, meaty nuance. The palate is dense and voluminous, with a long finish. The Riserva '20 is more reserved and deep, blending blackberry, wood tar, and underbrush with mineral undertones, delivering a taut, sapid, and rhythmically structured palate, finishing rich and flavorful.

Wine	Rating
● Colline Novaresi Nebbiolo Agamium '22	♟♟ 3*
● Ghemme Collis Breclemae '17	♟♟ 7
● Ghemme Cantalupo Anno Primo '17	♟♟ 5
● Ghemme Collis Carellae '17	♟♟ 6
● Ghemme Signore di Bayard '17	♟♟ 6
○ Carolus '23	♟ 2
⊙ Colline Novaresi Nebbiolo Rosato Il Mimo '23	♟ 2
⊙ Mia Ida Brut	♟ 3
● Ghemme '05	♟♟♟ 4
● Ghemme Collis Breclemae '00	♟♟♟ 6
● Colline Novaresi Abate di Cluny '16	♟♟ 6
● Ghemme Collis Breclemae '16	♟♟ 7
● Ghemme Collis Breclemae '15	♟♟ 7
● Ghemme Collis Carellae '15	♟♟ 6

Wine	Rating
● Gattinara Osso San Grato Ris. '19	♟♟♟ 8
● Coste della Sesia Nebbiolo Juvenia '22	♟♟ 4
● Gattinara Ris. '20	♟♟ 6
● Gattinara Osso S. Grato '11	♟♟♟ 8
● Gattinara Osso S. Grato '10	♟♟♟ 8
● Gattinara Osso S. Grato '09	♟♟♟ 8
● Gattinara Osso San Grato '15	♟♟♟ 8
● Gattinara Osso San Grato '14	♟♟♟ 8
● Gattinara Osso San Grato '13	♟♟♟ 8
● Gattinara Osso San Grato '12	♟♟♟ 8
● Gattinara Osso San Grato Ris. '18	♟♟♟ 8
● Gattinara Osso San Grato Ris. '17	♟♟♟ 8
● Gattinara Osso San Grato Ris. '16	♟♟♟ 8
● Gattinara S. Francesco '08	♟♟♟ 7
● Gattinara S. Francesco '07	♟♟♟ 5
● Gattinara San Francesco Ris. '19	♟♟♟ 8

Odilio Antoniotti

fraz. Casa del Bosco
v.lo Antoniotti, 5
13868 Sostegno [BI]
📞 +39 0163860309
antoniottiodilio@libero.it

CELLAR SALES
PRE-BOOKED VISITS
ANNUAL PRODUCTION 16,000 bottles
HECTARES UNDER VINE 5.50

The Antoniotti family has been a fixture in Bramaterra for over 150 years. Since 1997, Odilio Antoniotti and his son Mattia (the seventh generation) run the winery, which consists of five and a half hectares of vineyards. The soils here are volcanic, acidic, and rocky, rich in porphyry and minerals like iron and manganese, while the vineyards lie at elevations spanning 400-450 meters, in a position that benefits from notable day-night temperature swings. The estate follows sustainable farming practices, avoiding the use of herbicides. The Bramaterra '20 always stands out for its typicity and elegance. This vintage is marked by character, power, and austerity, with a nose of Asian spices, black pepper, ripe red fruit, rhubarb, and cinchona bark. The palate is rich, energetic, and vigorous, with a long, refined finish.

● Bramaterra '20	🍷🍷 6
● Bramaterra '10	🍷🍷🍷 3*
● Coste della Sesia Nebbiolo '15	🍷🍷🍷 3*
● Bramaterra '19	🍷🍷 6
● Bramaterra '18	🍷🍷 6
● Bramaterra '17	🍷🍷 6
● Bramaterra '16	🍷🍷 6
● Bramaterra '15	🍷🍷 6
● Coste della Sesia Nebbiolo '19	🍷🍷 5
● Coste della Sesia Nebbiolo '18	🍷🍷 4
● Coste della Sesia Nebbiolo '17	🍷🍷 4
● Coste della Sesia Nebbiolo '16	🍷🍷 4

F.lli Aresca

via Pontetto, 8a
14047 Mombercelli [AT]
📞 +39 0141955128
⊕ www.arescavini.it

CELLAR SALES
PRE-BOOKED VISITS
ANNUAL PRODUCTION 230,000 bottles
HECTARES UNDER VINE 12.00
SUSTAINABLE WINERY

Founded 70 years ago by the Aresca family and now in its 3rd generation, this producer is based between Langhe and Monferrato, on the hills of Mombercelli. It's an area historically well suited to barbera, which indeed is their flagship product, but the cellar also offers other wines from different territories, both reds, like Barolo and Dolcetto di Ovada, and whites, like Roero Arneis and Gavi. Their production style, marked by minimal intervention, results in modern and precise wines. The Nizza Riserva '20 is one of the best of its kind, rich in fruit and complex spices, with a structured, full palate that's also long and balanced. Other well-crafted wines include the Nizza San Luigi '21, powerful and close-knit with notes of ripe cherry and clove, the juicy and harmonious Barbera d'Asti Superiore La Rossa '21, with its herbal and black plum aromas, and the Grignolino d'Asti Testa Balorda '23, a pleasant and soft pour with floral and red fruit tones.

● Nizza Ris. '20	🍷🍷 5
● Barbera d'Asti Sup. La Rossa '21	🍷🍷 2*
● Grignolino d'Asti Testa Balorda '23	🍷🍷 2*
● Nizza San Luigi '21	🍷🍷 4
● Barbera d'Asti La Moretta '20	🍷🍷 2*
● Barbera d'Asti Sup. La Rossa '20	🍷🍷 2*
● Barbera d'Asti Sup. La Rossa '19	🍷🍷 2*
● Barbera d'Asti Sup. La Rossa '18	🍷🍷 3
● Grignolino d'Asti Testa Balorda '22	🍷🍷 2*
● Grignolino d'Asti Testa Balorda '20	🍷🍷 2*
● Nizza Barbera San Luigi '17	🍷🍷 5
● Nizza Ris. '19	🍷🍷 5
● Nizza Ris. '16	🍷🍷 5
● Nizza San Luigi '20	🍷🍷 4
● Nizza San Luigi '18	🍷🍷 5
● Nizza San Luigi '16	🍷🍷 5

PIEDMONT

L'Armangia

fraz. reg. San Giovanni 122
14053 Canelli [AT]
📞 +39 3665644575
🌐 www.armangia.it

CELLAR SALES
PRE-BOOKED VISITS
ACCOMMODATION
ANNUAL PRODUCTION 95,000 bottles
HECTARES UNDER VINE 11.00
SUSTAINABLE WINERY

L'Armangia, which means "revenge" in Piedmontese, is just over 30 years old, though the Giovine family has been involved in winemaking since the mid-19th century. Today, Ignazio, along with his wife Giuliana, continues the historic tradition of moscato planted around their estate in Canelli, while also cultivating various red grapes—primarily barbera—in their vineyards in Moasca, San Marzano Oliveto, and Castel Boglione. The Nizza Titon '21 opens on notes of wild blackberries and blood orange, with a backdrop of spices and tobacco. The palate is fresh, sapid, and balanced. The Barbera d'Asti Sopra Berruti '22 showcases tones of Mediterranean scrub and black cherry, with a juicy, fruit-forward palate that's rich, enjoyable, and well-structured. The well-crafted Nizza Vignali Riserva '20 offers aromas of blackberry and porcini mushrooms, with nice sapidity and pluck, while the Canelli Spaccavento '23 plays on classic hints of candied fruit and raisins.

Arnaldo Rivera

via Alba-Barolo, 8
12060 Castiglione Falletto [CN]
📞 +39 0173262053
🌐 www.arnaldorivera.com

PRE-BOOKED VISITS
ANNUAL PRODUCTION 100,000 bottles
HECTARES UNDER VINE 18.00

Terre di Barolo is the most important cooperative winery in Langa. Established in 1958 by the then-mayor of Castiglione Falletto, Arnaldo Rivera, it now offers a range named after its founder. This premium line is the result of specific production protocols and the identification of prestigious vineyards in areas such as Castello, Monvigliero, Ravera, Bussia, Rocche dell'Annunziata, Vignarionda, Villero, and Rocche di Castiglione. The Barolo Ravera '20 impresses with its vibrant, focused, and fragrant fruit on the nose, accompanied by subtle field herbs and spices. On the palate, it's firm and flavorful, with clean tannins and a long, compact finish. The Barolo Bussia '20 is more austere but still well-made, while the Barolo Monvigliero '20 is powerful, with oak more prominent. The Barolo Villero '20 is also well-crafted.

● Barbera d'Asti Sopra Berruti '22	🍷🍷 2*
● Nizza Titon '21	🍷🍷 4
○ Canelli Spaccavento '23	🍷🍷 2*
● Nizza Vignali Riserva '20	🍷🍷 5
○ Moscato d'Asti Canelli '18	🍷 4
○ Piemonte Chardonnay Robi&Robi '21	🍷 4
● Barbera d'Asti Sopra Berruti '21	🍷🍷 2*
○ Moscato d'Asti Canelli '20	🍷🍷 2*
● Nizza Titon '17	🍷🍷 4

● Barolo Ravera '20	🍷🍷 8
● Barolo Undicicomuni '20	🍷🍷 6
● Barolo Bussia '20	🍷🍷 8
● Barolo Cannubi '20	🍷🍷 8
● Barolo Castelletto '20	🍷🍷 8
● Barolo Monvigliero '20	🍷🍷 8
● Barolo Rocche dell'Annunziata '20	🍷🍷 8
● Barolo Villero '20	🍷🍷 8
● Barolo Vignarionda Arnaldo Rivera '13	🍷🍷🍷 7
● Barolo Bussia '15	🍷🍷 7
● Barolo Monvigliero '18	🍷🍷 8
● Barolo Monvigliero '17	🍷🍷 7
● Barolo Vignarionda '19	🍷🍷 8
● Barolo Vignarionda '17	🍷🍷 8
● Barolo Vignarionda '16	🍷🍷 7
● Barolo Villero '18	🍷🍷 8

Vinicola Arno

via Nizza, 1090
14047 Mombercelli [AT]
📞 +39 0141959327
🌐 www.vinicolaarno.com

CELLAR SALES
PRE-BOOKED VISITS
ANNUAL PRODUCTION 40,000 bottles
SUSTAINABLE WINERY

Founded in 2017 by Mara and Michael Arno, she
from Portugal and he from Emilia (though born
in England), this winery has quickly taken
advantage of the beautiful terroir of Mombercelli.
On their two main estates, one in Mombercelli
and the other in Castelnuovo Calcea, barbera is
the primary grape, including vines that go back
over 75 years, but they also grow nascetta and
sauvignon. The range is small but well crafted.
The Barbera d'Asti Superiore Maria Augusta '21
reveals notes of blood orange on the nose,
accompanied by spicy hints and cherry jam. The
palate is dense, with great structure and alcohol
volume, leading to a very persistent finish. The
Nizza Leone Riserva '20 proves full, rich, and
long, featuring tones of black fruits and balsamic
notes. The Monferrato Bianco Bilotto '22, a
balanced blend of nascetta and sauvignon, stands
out for its good structure and richness,
complemented by fair energy and pleasantness.

★Azelia

via Alba Barolo, 143
12060 Castiglione Falletto [CN]
📞 +39 017362859
🌐 www.azelia.it

CELLAR SALES
PRE-BOOKED VISITS
ANNUAL PRODUCTION 80,000 bottles
HECTARES UNDER VINE 16.00
SUSTAINABLE WINERY

Based in Castiglione Falletto, Azelia is run by
Luigi Scavino and his son Lorenzo. The vineyards
include nebbiolo vines planted in the 1940s. The
winery's style combines the finesse of nebbiolo
with the pursuit of its power, achieved through
rigorous vineyard work and generous extraction
in the cellar, where they use various sizes of
barrels for aging. The Barolo Cerretta '20 proves
elegant right from the outset, with its finely
spiced, fruity, and balsamic notes, opening the
way to a juicy palate with solid tannic grip and a
broad, fragrant finish. The Barolo Margheria '20
is darker, opting for aromas of coffee grounds,
aromatic herbs, and earth, which precede a
fleshy, multifaceted palate. The well-made Barolo
Bricco Fiasco '20 is supple, decisive, and sapid,
with a nicely focused aromatic bouquet.

● Barbera d'Asti Sup. Maria Augusta '21	♀♀ 4
○ M.to Bianco Bilotto '22	♀♀ 2*
● Nizza Leone Ris. '20	♀♀ 6
● Barbera d'Asti Desolina '23	♀ 3
● Barbera d'Asti Desolina '21	♀♀ 3
● Barbera d'Asti Desolina '20	♀♀ 3*
● Barbera d'Asti Desolina '19	♀♀ 3
● Barbera d'Asti Sup. Agosta '19	♀♀ 4
● Barbera d'Asti Sup. Agosta '18	♀♀ 3
● Barbera d'Asti Sup. Maria Augusta '19	♀♀ 4
● Nizza Leone Ris. '19	♀♀ 6
● Nizza Lorella '19	♀♀ 5
● Nizza Lorella '18	♀♀ 4
● Nizza Ris. '19	♀♀ 5

● Barolo Bricco Fiasco '20	♀♀ 8
● Barolo Cerretta '20	♀♀ 8
● Barolo Margheria '20	♀♀ 8
● Barolo '20	♀♀ 6
● Barolo San Rocco '20	♀♀ 8
◐ Dolcetto d'Alba Bricco dell'Oriolo '23	♀♀ 3
● Barbera d'Alba Punta '22	♀ 5
● Barolo Bricco Fiasco '12	♀♀♀ 8
● Barolo Bricco Fiasco '09	♀♀♀ 8
● Barolo Bricco Fiasco '01	♀♀♀ 7
● Barolo Bricco Fiasco '95	♀♀♀ 7
● Barolo Margheria '06	♀♀♀ 7
● Barolo S. Rocco '11	♀♀♀ 8
● Barolo S. Rocco '08	♀♀♀ 8
● Barolo S. Rocco '99	♀♀♀ 7
● Barolo Voghera Brea Ris. '01	♀♀♀ 8

Batasiolo

fraz. Annunziata, 87
12064 La Morra [CN]
☎ +39 017350130
☞ www.batasiolo.com

CELLAR SALES
PRE-BOOKED VISITS
ANNUAL PRODUCTION 2,500,000 bottles
HECTARES UNDER VINE 130.00

Fabrizio Battaglino

loc. Borgonuovo
via Montaldo Roero, 44
12040 Vezza d'Alba [CN]
☎ +39 0173658156
☞ www.battaglino.com

CELLAR SALES
PRE-BOOKED VISITS
ANNUAL PRODUCTION 30,000 bottles
HECTARES UNDER VINE 5.00

Located in La Morra, Batasiolo was founded in 1978 when the Fininc group acquired Kiola. The producers chose to work with nebbiolo, allowing it to mature for extended periods in various sizes of barrels. The estate cultivates nine plots, including five crus in the Barolo appellation: Cerequio, Bussia, Brunate, Briccolina, and Boscareto. The result is a well-crafted range characterized by nice overall clarity. The Chardonnay del Vigneto Morino proves rich and multifaceted, with a bouquet centered on generous aromas of tropical fruits like mango and pineapple. Fragrant sensations pave the way for a fresh, pleasant palate, completed by excellent overall sapidity. The Barbera d'Alba Sovrana '22 is characteristic for its richness, with a nose of ripe cherry and a backdrop of sweet spices. The palate is full and velvety, making for a wine of great appeal and pervasiveness.

Fabrizio Battaglino's winery boasts several estate vineyards on the predominantly sandy-limestone soils common to Roero, in the municipalities of Canale, Guarene, and Vezza d'Alba. Among these, the MGA Colla vineyard, owned by the family for generations, is particularly noteworthy, with arneis and nebbiolo planted there. The wines aim to express the characteristics of their terroir while maintaining aromatic clarity. All the proposed wines performed admirably during our tastings. The Roero Colla Riserva '20 stands out for its aromas of cinchona, nutmeg, and blackcurrant, followed by a well-structured, juicy, and energetic palate. The well-made Roero Arneis San Michele '23 highlights notes of flat peach and citrus on the nose, with a smooth and immediately expressive palate. The Roero Colla '21 features violet notes, with shades of red fruits and Mediterranean scrub, offering good structure and length, while the Barbera d'Alba Superiore Munbèl '22 proves fruity, with a pleasant spiciness.

● Barbera d'Alba Sovrana '22	♟♟4
● Barolo Beni '20	♟♟6
○ Langhe Chardonnay Vign. Morino '22	♟♟5
● Barbera d'Alba Sovrana '20	♟♟♟4*
● Barolo Boscareto '05	♟♟♟7
● Barolo Briccolina '15	♟♟♟8
● Barolo Corda della Briccolina '90	♟♟♟7
● Barolo Corda della Briccolina '89	♟♟♟7
● Barolo Corda della Briccolina '88	♟♟♟7
● Barbera d'Alba Sovrana '21	♟♟4
● Barolo '17	♟♟6
● Barolo Brunate '16	♟♟7
● Barolo Cerequio '16	♟♟7
● Barolo Ris. '13	♟♟6
○ Langhe Chardonnay Vign. Morino '21	♟♟5
○ Langhe Chardonnay Vign. Morino '20	♟♟5

● Roero Colla Ris. '20	♟♟5
● Barbera d'Alba Sup. Munbèl '22	♟♟4
○ Roero Arneis San Michele '23	♟♟3
● Roero Colla '21	♟♟4
○ Roero Arneis Bastia '23	♟3
○ Spumante M. Cl. Brut Nature Nebula '20	♟5
● Nebbiolo d'Alba V. Colla '07	♟♟♟3*
○ Roero Arneis San Michele '19	♟♟3*
○ Roero Arneis Bastia '22	♟♟3
○ Roero Arneis San Michele '22	♟♟3*
○ Roero Arneis San Michele '21	♟♟3*
● Roero Colla '20	♟♟4
● Roero Colla '19	♟♟5
● Roero Colla Ris. '19	♟♟5
● Roero Colla Ris. '18	♟♟5

Vignaioli Battegazzore

fraz. Mombisaggio
via del Popolo, 13
15057 Tortona [AL]
(») +39 3392974853
info@vignaiolibattegazzore.it

CELLAR SALES
PRE-BOOKED VISITS
ANNUAL PRODUCTION 6,000 bottles
HECTARES UNDER VINE 1.50
SUSTAINABLE WINERY

This small family-run producer is making its debut in the guide with a lineup of surprisingly bold wines. In 2016, Bruno Battegazzore and his partner Elisa decided to reopen the family winery where Bruno's grandfather had once made wine. Three wines are produced: two Derthona Timorasso and one Monleale. The first two are vinified entirely in stainless steel, while the red is aged for a year in barriques, followed by 12 months in steel and another 12 months in the bottle. The Colli Tortonesi Monleale '20 opens on distinct dark fruit, complemented by sweet spices from well-calibrated oak. The palate is rich and dense, balanced by refreshing acidity. The Derthona Maggiora '21 reveals a complex and intriguing nose, ranging from citrus to tobacco, and even naphthalene. The palate is structured, with a slight tannic vein and a long finish.

● Colli Tortonesi Monleale '20	♟♟ 4
○ Colli Tortonesi Timorasso Derthona Maggiora '21	♟♟ 6
○ Colli Tortonesi Timorasso Derthona '20	♟♟ 5

Bava - Cocchi

s.da Monferrato, 2
14023 Cocconato [AT]
(») +39 0141907083
☞ www.bava.com

CELLAR SALES
PRE-BOOKED VISITS
ACCOMMODATION
ANNUAL PRODUCTION 490,000 bottles
HECTARES UNDER VINE 50.00

This winery includes three properties located in some of Piedmont's classic wine-growing regions: Monferrato, Langa, and Astigiano. Naturally, the primary grapes are barbera, nebbiolo, and moscato, but significant work is also done with other aromatic varieties like ruchè and malvasia. Although the winery itself is over a century old, the Bava family has a history in the field that spans over four centuries. Leading the winer's range is the Alta Langa Extra Brut Vino Biologico '19, a wine redolent of white fruit and Mediterranean scrub, with fine bubbles and a pleasant, fresh palate that's also creamy and deep. The Alta Langa Bianc 'd Bianc Brut '18 expresses citrusy tones, golden apple, and bread crust, with a long and harmonious palate. The well-made Nizza Piano Alto '20 showcases red-orange and sweet spice notes, with a structured, full-bodied palate. The Monferrato Nebbiolo Superiore Serre di San Pietro '21 proves austere, with tannins still prominent but offering good tension and length.

○ Alta Langa Extra Brut Bio Giulio Cocchi '19	♟♟♟ 5
○ Alta Langa Brut Bianc 'd Bianc Giulio Cocchi '18	♟♟ 6
○ Alta Langa Brut Totocorde Giulio Cocchi '18	♟♟ 5
○ Alta Langa Extra Brut Giulio Cocchi '19	♟♟ 5
○ Alta Langa Pas Dosé Giulio Cocchi '18	♟♟ 6
● Barbera d'Asti Libera '22	♟♟ 3
● Monferrato Nebbiolo Sup. Serre di San Pietro '21	♟♟ 4
● Langhe Nebbiolo '22	♟ 4
○ Alta Langa Brut Bianc 'd Bianc Giulio Cocchi '16	♕♕ 6
○ Alta Langa Brut Bianc 'd Bianc Giulio Cocchi '17	♕♕ 6

★Bel Colle

fraz. Castagni, 56
12060 Verduno [CN]
+39 0172470196
www.belcolle.eu

CELLAR SALES
PRE-BOOKED VISITS
ANNUAL PRODUCTION 180,000 bottles
HECTARES UNDER VINE 14.00

Located in the Verduno subzone, Bel Colle was founded over 40 years ago by brothers Franco and Carlo Pontiglione along with Giuseppe Priola. In 2015, it became part of the Bosio Family Estate, led by Valter and Luca Bosio, father and son. The winery's range exhibits nice balance and precise craftsmanship, with measured extractions and a generally restrained use of wood for aging. The Barbaresco Pajoré '20 is truly a complete wine, refined and fragrant, with floral, spicy, and balsamic aromas. Its dynamic and juicy palate is structured, with polished tannins. The Barolo Bussia '20 is deep and balsamic on the nose, with a solid and persistent palate. The Barbaresco Convivio '21 proves generous in its fruit aromas, with touches of medicinal herbs, while the palate is fleshy and broad.

● Barbaresco Pajoré '21	🍷🍷🍷 5
● Barolo Bussia '20	🍷🍷 6
○ Alta Langa Brut Cuvée Valentina '20	🍷🍷 5
⊙ Alta Langa Extra Brut Pas Dosé Rosé Cuvée Valentina '20	🍷🍷 5
● Barbaresco Convivio '21	🍷🍷 5
● Barbaresco Gallina '21	🍷🍷 6
● Barolo 10 Anni Ris. '15	🍷🍷 7
● Barolo Monvigliero '20	🍷🍷 6
● Barolo Simposio '20	🍷 6
● Verduno Pelaverga '23	🍷 3
● Barbaresco Pajoré '18	🍷🍷🍷 5
● Barbaresco Pajoré '16	🍷🍷🍷 5
● Barolo 10 Anni Ris. '13	🍷🍷🍷 7
● Barolo Monvigliero '19	🍷🍷🍷 6
● Barolo Monvigliero '16	🍷🍷🍷 6

Bera

via Castellero, 12
12050 Neviglie [CN]
+39 0173630500
www.bera.it

CELLAR SALES
PRE-BOOKED VISITS
ANNUAL PRODUCTION 210,000 bottles
HECTARES UNDER VINE 30.00
VITICULTURE METHOD Certified Organic

The Beras have overseen this decidedly "family-run" winery since the late 1970s, with Valter and Alida's sons, Riccardo and Umberto, now on board. The vineyards are located on the road that leads from Neive to Neviglie in the heart of Barbaresco. And it's thanks to this particular territory that the Beras have stood out, especially, with their Rabaja, Basarin, and Serraboella crus. Their Moscato d'Asti wines are excellent. The 2023 offers aromas of medicinal herbs on a base of lime and candied orange peel, followed by a balanced palate made possible by vibrant acidity that supports its richness and sweetness. The Su Reimond highlights tones of Williams pear, pastry, and sage, with nice structure, persistence, and the right amount of sweetness, enhanced by bright acidity and freshness on the finish. The Barbaresco Rabajà Riserva '17 plays on aromas of dates, Mediterranean scrub, and violet. It's a fresh and harmonious drink, with velvety tannins and a long, structured finish.

● Barbaresco Rabajà Ris. '17	🍷🍷 8
○ Moscato d'Asti '23	🍷🍷 3*
○ Moscato d'Asti Su Reimond '23	🍷🍷 3*
○ Alta Langa Bera Brut '19	🍷🍷 6
● Barbaresco '21	🍷🍷 5
● Barbaresco Serraboella '21	🍷🍷 6
● Langhe Nebbiolo Alladio '21	🍷🍷 5
⊙ Alta Langa Bera Extra Brut Rosé '20	🍷 5
○ Alta Langa Blanc De Blancs Bera Extra Brut '20	🍷 5
● Barbaresco Rabajà Ris. '16	🍷🍷 8
● Barbaresco Serraboella '19	🍷🍷 6
● Barbaresco Serraboella '16	🍷🍷 8
○ Moscato d'Asti Canelli '20	🍷🍷 4
○ Moscato d'Asti Su Reimond '22	🍷🍷 3*
○ Moscato d'Asti Su Reimond '19	🍷🍷 4

Cinzia Bergaglio

via Gavi, 29
15060 Tassarolo [AL]
+39 0143342203
cinziabergagliovini.it

CELLAR SALES
PRE-BOOKED VISITS
ANNUAL PRODUCTION 30,000 bottles
HECTARES UNDER VINE 9.00

Cinzia Bergaglio has been bottling her own wine since 2002. This family-run operation, managed with her husband and two children, practices environmentally sustainable viticulture. The vineyards, predominantly planted with cortese grapes, are spread out across the municipalities of Gavi and Tassarolo. Their wines are characterized by a fresh and sapid profile, complemented by intense aromas. The Gavi del Comune di Rovereto Modesto '22 features a vibrant aromatic profile with lovely hints of mint and flint. The palate is balanced by vibrant acidity and a long, characterful finish. The Gavi Grifone delle Roveri '23 also boasts a rich and well-defined aromatic profile, playing on a blend of white fruit and fresh herbs. On the palate, it's both flavorful and remarkably smooth.

○ Gavi del Comune di Rovereto Modesto '22	🍷🍷 3*
○ Gavi del Comune di Gavi Grifone delle Roveri '23	🍷🍷 4
○ Gavi La Fornace '23	🍷🍷 3
○ Gavi del Comune di Gavi Grifone delle Roveri '20	🍷🍷 2*
○ Gavi del Comune di Gavi Grifone delle Roveri '19	🍷🍷 2*
○ Gavi del Comune di Gavi Grifone delle Roveri '18	🍷🍷 2*
○ Gavi del Comune di Gavi Grifone delle Roveri '15	🍷🍷 2*
○ Gavi del Comune di Gavi Grifone delle Roveri '14	🍷🍷 2*
○ Gavi La Fornace '21	🍷🍷 3*
○ Gavi La Fornace '13	🍷🍷 2*

★Nicola Bergaglio

fraz. Rovereto
loc. Pedaggeri, 59
15066 Gavi [AL]
+39 0143682195
nicolabergaglio@alice.it

CELLAR SALES
PRE-BOOKED VISITS
ANNUAL PRODUCTION 140,000 bottles
HECTARES UNDER VINE 17.00
SUSTAINABLE WINERY

Bergaglio's first harvest dates back to 1970, marking the start of a successful journey that has made it a key player in the Gavi appellation. Today, this family-run winery is led by Gianluigi Bergaglio and his children Diego and Ilaria, who continue to produce well-structured wines, with Minaia and Rovereto standing as their flagship bottles. The Gavi del Comune di Gavi Minaia '23 unveils a refined aromatic spectrum, with notes of white flowers, lightly toasted almond, and aromatic herbs. The palate is rich and powerful, featuring lively acidity that extends its juicy and sapid mouthfeel, leading to a long, vibrant finish. The Gavi del Comune di Gavi Rovereto '23, with its balsamic tones, proves delicate and well-proportioned on the palate.

○ Gavi del Comune di Gavi Rovereto Minaia '23	🍷🍷🍷 4*
○ Gavi del Comune di Gavi Rovereto '23	🍷🍷 3*
○ Gavi del Comune di Gavi Minaia '22	🍷🍷🍷 4*
○ Gavi del Comune di Gavi Minaia '21	🍷🍷🍷 4*
○ Gavi del Comune di Gavi Minaia '20	🍷🍷🍷 4*
○ Gavi del Comune di Gavi Minaia '19	🍷🍷🍷 4*
○ Gavi del Comune di Gavi Minaia '18	🍷🍷🍷 4*
○ Gavi del Comune di Gavi Minaia '17	🍷🍷🍷 4*
○ Gavi del Comune di Gavi Minaia '15	🍷🍷🍷 4*
○ Gavi del Comune di Gavi Minaia '14	🍷🍷🍷 4*
○ Gavi del Comune di Gavi Minaia '11	🍷🍷🍷 4*
○ Gavi del Comune di Gavi Minaia '10	🍷🍷🍷 4
○ Gavi del Comune di Gavi Minaia '09	🍷🍷🍷 4
○ Gavi del Comune di Gavi '22	🍷🍷 3*
○ Gavi del Comune di Gavi '21	🍷🍷 3*
○ Gavi del Comune di Gavi '20	🍷🍷 3*

Bersano

p.zza Dante, 21
14049 Nizza Monferrato [AT]
(+39 0141720211
www.bersano.it

CELLAR SALES
PRE-BOOKED VISITS
ACCOMMODATION
ANNUAL PRODUCTION 1,000,000 bottles
HECTARES UNDER VINE 230.00

Bersano, a key player in the Asti region and beyond, has been owned by the Massimelli and Soave families for 30 years. The winery manages eleven estates across Asti, Alto Monferrato, and the Langhe, producing a wide range that represents some of the region's most important appellations. The wines aim to showcase the unique qualities of the various grape varieties used and the territories they come from. The Nizza Cremosina '21 showcases classic aromas of petrichor, tobacco, and cherry, followed by a powerful and dense palate, which also carries a sapid quality, finishing long and drinkable. The Barbera d'Asti Superiore Costalunga '22 is excellent, unveiling floral notes, black forest fruits, and aromatic herbs, while the palate is fresh, smooth, and juicy. The Ruché di Castagnole Monferrato San Pietro Realto '23, with its aromas of red berries, rose, and plum, delivers an austere yet fleshy palate. Similarly, the Barbera d'Asti 4 Sorelle '23 showcases solid fruit and structure.

● Nizza Cremosina '21	♥♥♥ 4*
● Barbera d'Asti Sup. Costalunga '22	♥♥ 3*
● Barbera d'Asti 4 Sorelle '23	♥♥ 3
● Barolo Nirvasco '20	♥♥ 5
● Nizza Generala Ris. '20	♥♥ 5
● Ruché di Castagnole M.to San Pietro Realto '23	♥♥ 4
○ Arturo Pas Dosè M. Cl. '16	♥ 4
● Nebbiolo d'Alba Paisan '22	♥ 3
○ Roero Arneis Eroe '23	♥ 3
● Barbera d'Asti Sup. Generala '97	♥♥♥ 5
● Nizza Generala Ris. '16	♥♥♥ 5
● Barbera d'Asti Sup. Costalunga '20	♥♥ 3*
● Barolo Badarina '15	♥♥ 7
● Barolo Cannubi Ris. '17	♥♥ 8
● Nizza Generala Ris. '18	♥♥ 5
● Nizza La Generala Ris. '19	♥♥ 6

Boasso - Gabutti

b.ta Gabutti, 3a
12050 Serralunga d'Alba [CN]
(+39 0173613165
www.gabuttiboasso.com

CELLAR SALES
PRE-BOOKED VISITS
ACCOMMODATION
ANNUAL PRODUCTION 25,000 bottles
HECTARES UNDER VINE 7.00

Boasso was founded in the 1950s by Giuseppe Boasso, however it was his son Franco who, during the 1970s and 1980s, helped the producer break out and began bottling their own wines. The estate is headquartered in Serralunga, in the Gabutti area, at the center of the geographical indication. Today, Franco's sons, Ezio and Claudio, continue the family tradition. This year the Boasso family presented a solid lineup for tasting. The top contenders for the title of best wine are the Gabutti '20 and the Lazzarito '20. The Gabutti displays great character with tobacco, pepper, and underbrush, while fruit takes a secondary role. On the palate, it's powerful and close-knit, but its tannins are offset by balanced fruit progression. The Lazzarito is more spicy and fruity, with light floral hints; on the palate, it offers captivating cocoa notes framed by a solid tannic structure. The austere Margheria Riserva '18 is also noteworthy.

● Barolo Gabutti '20	♥♥ 7
● Barolo Lazzarito '20	♥♥ 7
● Barolo del Comune di Serralunga d'Alba '20	♥♥ 6
● Barolo Margheria Ris. '18	♥♥ 8
● Langhe Nebbiolo '22	♥♥ 4
● Barbera d'Alba Sup. '22	♥ 3
● Barolo Gabutti '13	♥♥♥ 6
● Barolo Margheria '05	♥♥♥ 5*
● Barbera d'Alba Sup. '21	♥♥ 3
● Barolo del Comune di Serralunga d'Alba '19	♥♥ 6
● Barolo Gabutti '18	♥♥ 6
● Barolo Margheria '19	♥♥ 7
● Barolo Margheria '18	♥♥ 6
● Barolo Margheria Ris. '16	♥♥ 7
● Langhe Nebbiolo '21	♥♥ 4

★Enzo Boglietti

via Fontane, 18a
12064 La Morra [CN]
📞 +39 017350330
🌐 www.enzoboglietti.com

CELLAR SALES
PRE-BOOKED VISITS
ANNUAL PRODUCTION 100,000 bottles
HECTARES UNDER VINE 22.00
VITICULTURE METHOD Certified Organic
SUSTAINABLE WINERY

Enzo Boglietti, along with his children Linda and Matteo, runs this winery based in La Morra. Their vineyards are situated in Barolo, Monforte, Roddino, Serralunga, and Sinio. The approach to winemaking is mixed, drawing on both stainless steel and oak, with maturation mainly in concrete, tonneaux, and large barrels. Recently, barrel aging times have been reduced, resulting in leaner, fresher wines. The Barolo Fossati '20 opens with violet and licorice, then moves towards fruitier and spicier tones. The palate is well-structured, with a dense, focused tannic texture that supports a fragrant fruit core through to a long, sapid finish. The Barolo Brunate '20 is equally impressive, with a more fruit-forward aroma and a seductive smoky touch. On the palate, it's juicy and flavorful. The rest of the winery's lineup also fares well.

La Bollina

loc. Monterotondo, 58
15069 Serravalle Scrivia [AL]
📞 +39 014361984
🌐 labollina.it

CELLAR SALES
PRE-BOOKED VISITS
ACCOMMODATION
ANNUAL PRODUCTION 245,000 bottles
HECTARES UNDER VINE 33.00
SUSTAINABLE WINERY

La Bollina is nestled in the hills of Serravalle Scrivia, in the province of Alessandria, southern Piedmont, near Lombardy, Liguria, and Emilia Romagna. Here, whites of consistent quality are produced, with cortese grapes as the main star, although chardonnay, sauvignon, barbera, and nebbiolo are also cultivated in the estate's vineyards. The winery also features well-developed guest accommodations and a golf course. The Gavi '23 features fresh white fruit aromas, with light floral whiffs. The palate shows volume and a certain richness, with a slight sweetness. The Gavi Ventola '21 exhibits intense aromas of honey and dried flowers, adorned with spicy notes. On the palate, it maintains its balance and fragrance. The Monferrato Chiaretto Tinetta '23 offers aromas of sage and peach, with a fresh, pleasant palate.

● Barolo Arione '20	🍷🍷 7
● Barolo Brunate '20	🍷🍷 8
● Barolo Fossati '20	🍷🍷 8
● Barolo Brandini '20	🍷🍷 8
● Barolo Case Nere '20	🍷🍷 8
● Barolo del Comune di La Morra '20	🍷🍷 6
● Barolo Boiolo '20	🍷 7
● Barolo Arione '06	🍷🍷🍷 8
● Barolo Arione '05	🍷🍷🍷 8
● Barolo Brunate '17	🍷🍷🍷 8
● Barolo Brunate '13	🍷🍷🍷 8
● Barolo Brunate '01	🍷🍷🍷 8
● Barolo Case Nere '04	🍷🍷🍷 8
● Barolo V. Arione '07	🍷🍷🍷 8

○ Gavi Ventola '21	🍷🍷 4
○ Gavi '23	🍷🍷 3
◉ M.to Chiaretto Tinetta '23	🍷🍷 3
○ Piemonte Chardonnay Beneficio '23	🍷🍷 3
● M.to Nebbiolo Nêuve '22	🍷 4
○ Gavi '22	🍷🍷 3
○ Gavi '21	🍷🍷 3*
○ Gavi '20	🍷🍷 3
○ Gavi '18	🍷🍷 3*
○ Gavi Ventola '20	🍷🍷 3*
○ Gavi Ventola '19	🍷🍷 3*
○ M.to Bianco Armason '21	🍷🍷 3
◉ M.to Bianco Beneficio '21	🍷🍷 2*
◉ M.to Chiaretto Tinetta '22	🍷🍷 3
◉ M.to Chiaretto Tinetta '21	🍷🍷 3
● M.to Rosso Bricchetta '19	🍷🍷 3

Marco Bonfante

s.da Vaglio Serra, 72
14049 Nizza Monferrato [AT]
📞 +39 0141725012
🌐 www.marcobonfante.com

Gilberto Boniperti

via Vittorio Emanuele, 43/45
28010 Barengo [NO]
📞 +39 0321997123
🌐 www.bonipertivignaioli.com

CELLAR SALES
PRE-BOOKED VISITS
ANNUAL PRODUCTION 250,000 bottles
HECTARES UNDER VINE 13.00
SUSTAINABLE WINERY

CELLAR SALES
ANNUAL PRODUCTION 12,000 bottles
HECTARES UNDER VINE 3.50

Marco Bonfante and his sister Micaela oversee the family winery, which has its roots in the early 2000s, supported by eight generations of winemaking experience in Montferrato Astigiano. In addition to estate vineyards, they rely on a network of growers and managed vineyards, which enables them to produce wines from some of Piedmont's most prestigious appellations. Their offerings focus on modern expressions of barbera and nebbiolo. The Barolo Bussia Riserva remains a standout among the winery's offerings. The 2018 conjures up notes of black forest fruit and aromatic herbs, with balsamic hints, and a firm, elegant palate that's both clear and pleasant. The Nizza Bricco Bonfante Riserva '19, with its hints of ripe black cherry and rain-soaked earth, is compact and full-bodied. The Barbera d'Asti Superiore La Stella '21 offers up aromas of stone fruit and a mature, pervasive palate. The Barbaresco '20 proves pleasant and immediately expressive.

"When you don't know what to do, go to the vineyard—there's always something to be done there." These words, spoken countless times by his grandfather, are now the foundation of Gilberto Boniperti's work philosophy. In 2003, with the replanting of the Barton vineyard, Boniperti established the winery, driven by a commitment to quality. The estate consists of 3.5 hectares, spread out across four vineyards at 250 meters elevation, each with distinct soils and exposures. The Fara Bartön '21 is an icon of typicity and tradition, showcasing delicate notes of sour cherry and pomegranate, floral aromas, and hints of minerality and spice. The palate is harmonious, with a soft, silky tannic texture. The Carlin '22 is also impressive, with balsamic notes complemented by blackberry jam and underbrush alongside iron accents. The palate is dynamic and multifaceted, with a taut, flavorful finish.

● Barolo Bussia Ris. '18	🍷🍷 8
● Barbaresco '20	🍷🍷 6
● Nizza Bricco Bonfante Ris. '19	🍷🍷 6
● Barbera D'asti Sup. Anniversario Menego '20	🍷 5
● Langhe Nebbiolo Imma '22	🍷 4
● Barbera d'Asti Sup. La Stella '20	🍷🍷 2*
● Barbera d'Asti Sup. La Stella '19	🍷🍷 2*
● Barbera d'Asti Sup. Menego '19	🍷🍷 8
● Barolo Bussia Ris. '17	🍷🍷 7
○ Gavi del Comune di Gavi I Ronchetti '22	🍷🍷 3
○ Moscato d'Asti '22	🍷🍷 2*
● Nizza Bricco Bonfante Ris. '16	🍷🍷 5

● Fara Bartön '21	🍷🍷 5
● Colline Novaresi Nebbiolo Carlin '22	🍷🍷 4
● Fara Bartön '15	🍷🍷🍷 5
● Colline Novaresi Nebbiolo Carlin '21	🍷🍷 4
● Colline Novaresi Nebbiolo Carlin '19	🍷🍷 4
● Colline Novaresi Nebbiolo Carlin '18	🍷🍷 4
● Colline Novaresi Vespolina Favolalunga '20	🍷🍷 3
● Colline Novaresi Vespolina Favolalunga '19	🍷🍷 3
● Colline Novaresi Vespolina Favolalunga '18	🍷🍷 3
● Fara Bartön '20	🍷🍷 5
● Fara Bartön '19	🍷🍷 5
● Fara Bartön '18	🍷🍷 5
● Fara Bartön '17	🍷🍷 5
● Fara Bartön '16	🍷🍷 5

Borgo Maragliano

via San Sebastiano, 2
14051 Loazzolo [AT]
+39 014487132
www.borgomaragliano.it

CELLAR SALES
PRE-BOOKED VISITS
ANNUAL PRODUCTION 385,000 bottles
HECTARES UNDER VINE 44.00
SUSTAINABLE WINERY

Situated in the hills of Loazzolo in southern Piedmont, at an elevation of 450 meters, on sandy soils rich in tuff and limestone, this winery has a 35-year history. Founded by Carlo Galliano and Silvia Quirico, it looks ahead to the next 35 years with their children Giovanni, Francesco, and Federico. They primarily produce Metodo Classico sparkling wine from chardonnay and pinot noir, but also cultivate moscato, riesling, and brachetto. An outstanding line of Metodo Classicos were presented. The Alta Langa Blanc de Blancs Brut Francesco Galliano '20 features a fine, persistent perlage, with floral notes, white fruit, and bread crust on the nose. The palate is marked by lively acidity and character, making for a rich, multifaceted wine. The Giuseppe Galliano Brut Nature '19 offers vibrant aromas of plum and spices, with a fine, complex profile. The palate is austere yet long and fascinating.

○ Alta Langa Blanc De Blancs Brut Francesco Galliano '20	ΨΨ 5
○ Giuseppe Galliano Brut Nature M. Cl. '19	ΨΨ 5
○ Cuvée Germana Beltrame Brut Nature Editione V M. Cl.	ΨΨ 6
○ Dogma Blanc de Noirs Brut Nature M. Cl. '19	ΨΨ 6
○ Federico Galliano Brut Nature M. Cl. '19	ΨΨ 6
○ Piemonte Chardonnay Crevoglio '23	ΨΨ 3
⊙ Alta Langa Brut Rosé Giovanni Galliano '20	Ψ 5
○ Moscato d'Asti La Caliera '23	Ψ 3
○ Giuseppe Galliano Ris. Brut M. Cl. '01	ΥΥΥ 4*
⊙ Giovanni Galliano Brut Rosé M. Cl. '15	ΥΥΥ 5
○ Giuseppe Galliano Brut Nature M. Cl. '13	ΥΥΥ 5

★Giacomo Borgogno & Figli

via Gioberti, 1
12060 Barolo [CN]
+39 017356108
www.borgogno.com

CELLAR SALES
PRE-BOOKED VISITS
ANNUAL PRODUCTION 250,000 bottles
HECTARES UNDER VINE 52.00
VITICULTURE METHOD Certified Organic
SUSTAINABLE WINERY

The winery, based in Barolo, became part of the Farinetti family's "oenological orbit" in 2008. Today the estate is led by Andrea, Oscar's son. Despite some changes in production, such as returning to fermentation in concrete and earning organic certification, the stylistic foundation remains rooted in the tradition of one of the Langhe's oldest brands. These changes have had an overall positive effect on the expressiveness of the wines. The Barolo Cannubi '20 convinces with its intense aromas of toasted notes, spices, wilted flowers, tobacco, and licorice. On the palate, lively acidity and energetic tannins drive it towards an airy finish with smoky undertones. The Barolo Fossati '20 focuses more on fruit in its nose, while the palate has good structure with layered tannins and a vibrant fruit core.

● Barolo Cannubi '20	ΨΨ 8
● Barolo Fossati '20	ΨΨ 8
● Barolo Liste '20	ΨΨ 8
● Langhe Bartomè '22	ΨΨ 5
● Barolo '20	Ψ 8
● Barolo Ris. '17	Ψ 8
● Langhe Barbera Bompè '22	Ψ 5
● Langhe Dolcetto Ancum '23	Ψ 4
● Barolo Liste '16	ΥΥΥ 8
● Barolo Liste '15	ΥΥΥ 8
● Barolo Liste '11	ΥΥΥ 8
● Barolo Liste '10	ΥΥΥ 8
● Barolo Liste '08	ΥΥΥ 8
● Barolo Ris. '15	ΥΥΥ 8
● Barolo Ris. '11	ΥΥΥ 8
● Barolo Ris. '10	ΥΥΥ 8

Boroli

via Brunella, 4
12060 Castiglione Falletto [CN]
(📞) +39 017362927
🌐 boroli.it

CELLAR SALES
PRE-BOOKED VISITS
ACCOMMODATION AND RESTAURANT SERVICE
ANNUAL PRODUCTION 40,000 bottles
HECTARES UNDER VINE 8.20
SUSTAINABLE WINERY

A family that has shaped the entrepreneurial history of Piedmont since the 19th century, first in textiles and later in publishing, began its wine journey in the final decade of the 20th century. The Boroli family's adventure in Langhe is now led by Achille, who has shifted the focus to their estate crus: Brunella in the municipality of Castiglione Falletto and Cerequio in Barolo. This year, we tasted only of the Boroli family's wines. The well-crafted Barolo '20 stands out for its floral aromas, followed by hints of raspberry and tobacco against a spicy background. In the mouth, the palate is rich and fleshy, with firm tannins and a focused structure, culminating in a long, persistent finish.

Giacomo Boveri

fraz. Montale Celli
via Costa Vescovato
15050 Costa Vescovato [AL]
(📞) +39 3441305126
🌐 www.vignetigiacomoboveri.it

CELLAR SALES
PRE-BOOKED VISITS
ANNUAL PRODUCTION 25,000 bottles
HECTARES UNDER VINE 9.00

For five generations, this family has dedicated itself to agriculture and developing the resources that the territory has to offer. In 1988, Giacomo Boveri chose to continue the family traditions by focusing on timorasso, a bet that has paid off. In addition to four wines made with the grape, he also produces reds with barbera, croatina, and freisa. The winery follows the "DTP Passione & Ragione - Sustainable Viticulture" protocol, with vineyards located in Costa Vescovado and Montegioco. The various versions of Derthona submitted for tasting reveal the nuances and potential of timorasso. The Munta lè Ruma '21 (named after an old farming proverb) has a powerful yet graceful drive. Its complex aromas of lime, grapefruit, mimosa, and broom lead to a bold and dense palate. The Piazzera '19 is bright and fresh, with citrus and fresh herb notes, while the Lacrime del Bricco '21 proves deep and complex. The Barbera 19 marzo 1878 is a fine, elegant wine.

● Barolo '20	🍷🍷 7
● Barolo Villero '01	🍷🍷🍷 6
● Barolo Villero '00	🍷🍷🍷 4*
● Barolo '19	🍷🍷 7
● Barolo '18	🍷🍷 6
● Barolo Brunella '19	🍷🍷 8
● Barolo Brunella '18	🍷🍷 8
● Barolo Brunella '17	🍷🍷 8
● Barolo Brunella '16	🍷🍷 8
● Barolo Brunella '15	🍷🍷 8
● Barolo Cerequio '19	🍷🍷 8
● Barolo Cerequio '17	🍷🍷 8
● Barolo del Comune di Castiglion Falletto '19	🍷🍷 7
● Barolo Villero '19	🍷🍷 8
● Barolo Villero '18	🍷🍷 8
● Barolo Villero '17	🍷🍷 8

● Colli Tortonesi Barbera 19 Marzo 1878 '23	🍷🍷 3*
○ Colli Tortonesi Timorasso Derthona Lacrime del Bricco '21	🍷🍷🍷 5
○ Colli Tortonesi Timorasso Munta l'è Ruma '21	🍷🍷🍷 5
○ Colli Tortonesi Timorasso Derthona Piazzera '19	🍷🍷🍷 5
○ Colli Tortonesi Timorasso Derthona Lacrime del Bricco '20	🍷🍷🍷 5
● Colli Tortonesi Barbera Sup. Bricco della Ginestra '16	🍷🍷 3*
● Colli Tortonesi Barbera Sup. Bricco della Ginestra '15	🍷🍷 3*
○ Colli Tortonesi Timorasso Derthona Lacrime del Bricco '19	🍷🍷 5
○ Colli Tortonesi Timorasso Munta l'è Ruma '20	🍷🍷 5

Luigi Boveri

loc. Montale Celli
via XX Settembre, 6
15050 Costa Vescovato [AL]
📞 +39 0131838165
🌐 www.boveriluigi.com

CELLAR SALES
PRE-BOOKED VISITS
ANNUAL PRODUCTION 80,000 bottles
HECTARES UNDER VINE 22.00

In 1992, Luigi Boveri, driven by tradition, passion, and courage, believed in the richness of the terroir and the strength of timorasso. Alongside his wife Germana and now their children Francesco, Matteo, and Sara, he has maintained their vineyards in Costa Vescovado. They manage five vineyards—Boccanera, Borgo, Casassa, Montesoro, and della Croatina—on clay-limestone and marl-limestone soils. An ability to live the land and express its attributes is evident in the dynamism and quality of their wines. The refined and elegant Filari di Timorasso '21 showcases delicate notes of tropical fruit, white peach, and minerals, sensations that amplify on the palate, revealing continuity and richness. The excellent Derthona '21 proves flowery and harmonious, with a fresh, sapid palate. The Barbera Boccanera '23 delivers power and dynamism, playing on hints of tobacco and licorice.

Gianfranco Bovio

fraz. Annunziata
b.ta Ciotto, 63
12064 La Morra [CN]
📞 +39 017350667
🌐 www.cantinabovio.it

CELLAR SALES
PRE-BOOKED VISITS
ANNUAL PRODUCTION 65,000 bottles
HECTARES UNDER VINE 9.50

With the arrival of Elisa, daughter of Alessandra Bovio and Marco, the path forged by founder Gianfranco Bovio in the 1970s continues. In the cellar, macerations are medium to long, and aging is carried out in large wooden barrels. In the vineyard, the pride of the winery are the crus of Castiglione Falletto and La Morra: Rocchettevino, Annunziata, Arborina, Gattera, and Parussi. The Barolo Rocchettevino '20 offers up pleasant citrus aromas before a supple, flavorful, and energetic palate, with a relaxed structure and a pervasive finish. The well-crafted Barolo Arborina '20 features more fruity aromas, accompanied by a smooth yet firm palate. The Barolo Gattera '20 is aromatically more mature, with tighter tannins and a compact, sapid finish.

○ Colli Tortonesi Timorasso Derthona Filari di Timorasso '22	🍷🍷🍷 7
○ Colli Tortonesi Timorasso Derthona '22	🍷🍷 5
● Colli Tortonesi Barbera Boccanera '23	🍷🍷 4
● Colli Tortonesi Barbera Poggio delle Amarene '22	🍷 5
○ Colli Tortonesi Cortese Terre del Prete '23	🍷 4
● Colli Tortonesi Croatina Sensazioni '21	🍷 5
○ Colli Tortonesi Timorasso Derthona '11	🍷🍷🍷 4*
○ Colli Tortonesi Timorasso Derthona Filari di Timorasso '20	🍷🍷🍷 6
○ Colli Tortonesi Timorasso Filari di Timorasso '12	🍷🍷🍷 5
○ Colli Tortonesi Timorasso Filari di Timorasso '07	🍷🍷🍷 3

● Barolo Arborina '20	🍷🍷 8
● Barolo Rocchettevino '20	🍷🍷 7
● Barbera d'Alba Sup. Regiaveja '21	🍷🍷 5
● Barolo Gattera '20	🍷🍷 8
● Barolo Parussi '20	🍷🍷 8
● Langhe Nebbiolo Firagnetti '22	🍷🍷 4
○ Langhe Chardonnay Alessandro '22	🍷 4
● Barolo Bricco Parussi Ris. '01	🍷🍷🍷 6
● Barolo Gattera '11	🍷🍷🍷 6
● Barolo Rocchettevino '06	🍷🍷🍷 5*
● Barolo V. Arborina '90	🍷🍷🍷 6
● Barolo Arborina '19	🍷🍷 8
● Barolo Arborina '18	🍷🍷 8
● Barolo De-Rieumes Ris. '17	🍷🍷 8
● Barolo De-Rieumes Ris. '15	🍷🍷 8
● Barolo Parussi '18	🍷🍷 8

★Braida

loc. Ciappellette
s.da prov.le 27, 9
14030 Rocchetta Tanaro [AT]
☎ +39 0141644113
⊕ www.braida.it

CELLAR SALES
PRE-BOOKED VISITS
ACCOMMODATION
ANNUAL PRODUCTION 700,000 bottles
HECTARES UNDER VINE 70.00
SUSTAINABLE WINERY

Founded by Braida, also known as Giuseppe Bologna, this legendary winery has gifted Italian oenology with two of the most famous Barbera wines ever created: Bricco dell'Uccellone and Bricco della Bigotta. Both are produced in the Rocchetta Tanaro area, but the estate's vineyards also extend to Costigliole d'Asti, Trezzo Tinella, Castelnuovo Calcea, and Mango d'Alba. Today, the third generation, Giuseppe and Raffaella, continues the tradition with a high-quality line of barbera, grignolino, and moscato. The Barbera d'Asti Bricco dell'Uccellone '21 conjures up a vibrant nose, with lovely notes of stone fruit and sweet spices, followed by a sapid palate with prominent tannins, notable body, and endurance. The Grignolino d'Asti Limonte GB '16 plays on notes of tobacco, pepper, cinchona, and licorice, with a deep palate and long finish. The Barbera d'Asti Bricco della Bigotta '20 opts for tones of black fruits and underbrush, with a palate marked by sweet, ripe fruit. The flowery, long, and pleasant Langhe Nascetta La Regina '23 also caught our attention.

● Barbera d'Asti Bricco Dell'Uccellone '21	❦❦ 8
● Barbera d'Asti Bricco della Bigotta '20	❦❦ 8
● Grignolino d'Asti Limonte GB '16	❦❦ 3
○ Langhe Nascetta La Regina '23	❦❦ 3
● Monferrato Rosso Il Bacialè '20	❦❦ 5
● Barbera d'Asti Ai Suma '21	❦ 8
● Barbera d'Asti Curej Cascina San Bernardo '23	❦ 3
● Barbera d'Asti Montebruna '21	❦ 4
● Grignolino d'Asti Limonte '23	❦ 3
○ Langhe Bianco Il Fiore '23	❦ 3
○ Langhe Chardonnay Asso di Fiori '22	❦ 5
○ Moscato d'Asti Vigna Senza Nome '23	❦ 3

★Brezza Giacomo e Figli

via Lomondo, 4
12060 Barolo [CN]
☎ +39 0173560921
⊕ www.brezza.it

CELLAR SALES
PRE-BOOKED VISITS
ACCOMMODATION AND RESTAURANT SERVICE
ANNUAL PRODUCTION 100,000 bottles
HECTARES UNDER VINE 20.00
VITICULTURE METHOD Certified Organic
SUSTAINABLE WINERY

The Brezza family has been at the forefront of regional winemaking since the late 19th century, intertwining its journey with the Marchesi di Barolo, from whom they acquired important plots in 1880. The first bottles date back to 1910, and their winemaking philosophy has remained consistent ever since, passed down from father to son. There's practically no concession to fleeting trends, all in the name of preserving a time-honored style and tradition. The Barolo Castellero '20 is a wine of great personality, showcasing aromas ranging from flowers to fruit on a spicy base. The palate is rich, compact, and sapid, leading to a long, persistent finish. The Barolo Cannubi '20 offers up notes of cinchona, licorice, and tobacco, with a nicely structured palate of vibrant, fruity pulp that extends into a deep, flavorful finish. The Nebbiolo Santa Rosalia '22 is juicy, balsamic, and fragrant. The Barbera d'Alba Superiore '21 is also well-made.

● Barolo Cannubi '20	❦❦ 7
● Barolo Castellero '20	❦❦ 8
● Barbera d'Alba Sup. '21	❦❦ 4
● Barolo Sarmassa '20	❦❦ 7
● Nebbiolo d'Alba V. Santa Rosalia '22	❦❦ 4
● Langhe Freisa '23	❦ 3
● Barolo Bricco Sarmassa '08	❦❦❦ 7
● Barolo Bricco Sarmassa '07	❦❦❦ 7
● Barolo Cannubi '01	❦❦❦ 6
● Barolo Sarmassa '11	❦❦❦ 6
● Barolo Sarmassa '05	❦❦❦ 6
● Barolo Sarmassa '04	❦❦❦ 6
● Barolo Sarmassa '03	❦❦❦ 6
● Barolo Sarmassa V. Bricco Ris. '15	❦❦❦ 8
● Barolo Sarmassa V. Bricco Ris. '11	❦❦❦ 7

Bric Castelvej
Gallino Domenico

via Castelvecchio, 70
12043 Canale [CN]
(☎) +39 017398108
@ www.briccastelvej.com

Bric Cenciurio

via Roma, 24
12060 Barolo [CN]
(☎) +39 01731950404
@ www.briccenciurio.com

CELLAR SALES
PRE-BOOKED VISITS
ANNUAL PRODUCTION 100,000 bottles
HECTARES UNDER VINE 16.00
SUSTAINABLE WINERY

CELLAR SALES
PRE-BOOKED VISITS
ANNUAL PRODUCTION 70,000 bottles
HECTARES UNDER VINE 15.00
SUSTAINABLE WINERY

Founded by Domenico Gallino in 1956, and now managed by his son-in-law Mario Repellino and grandson Cristiano, Bric Castelvej boasts vineyards on sandy soils interlaced with bands of loam and calcareous clay in the municipality of Canale. Here they cultivate local grapes like arneis, barbera, and nebbiolo, along with small quantities of other native and international varieties, producing traditional wines characterized by a smooth drinkability. The Barbera d'Alba '23 features aromas of wild black fruits and rain-soaked earth, while the palate is juicy, with nice fruit and a long, well-sustained finish made possible by good acidic tension. The Roero '21 is well-crafted, with floral, underbrush, and red cherry tones, good structure, and depth. The Nebbiolo d'Alba Il Pilone Anfora '23, aged in amphora for a year (after oak), unveils aromas of black fruits and aromatic herbs, with a fresh, smooth palate and nice tension and sapidity.

In 1990, Franco Pittatore and his brother-in-law Carlo Sacchetto decided to combine their lands in Barolo and Roero to create a genuine wine enterprise. Today, Bric Cenciurio is managed by Franco's sons, Alessandro and Alberto, who produce Barolo in Coste di Rose and Monrobiolo di Bussia. Since 1994, arneis has been cultivated on the hill that gives the estate its name, near Castellinaldo. The grapes for their Barbera d'Alba, meanwhile, are cultivated in Magliano Alfieri. The Barolo Coste di Rose Riserva '17 is a wine of character and flavor, with nicely expressed, vibrant tannins. The nose reveals aromas of red fruit jam, cocoa, and spices. The lively and flavorful Barolo Coste di Rose '20 has delicate, focused aromas and a firm, persistent palate. The Barolo del Comune di Barolo '20 is also well-crafted.

● Barbera d'Alba '23	♉♉ 4
● Barbera d'Alba Sup. V. Monpissano '22	♉♉ 5
● Nebbiolo d'Alba Il Pilone Anfora '23	♉♉ 5
● Roero '21	♉♉ 5
○ Langhe Bianco San Vittore Anfora '23	♉ 5
○ Langhe Favorita '23	♉ 3
◉ Langhe Rosato Il Nini Anfora '23	♉ 4
● Nebbiolo D'alba '23	♉ 4
○ Roero Arneis '23	♉ 4
○ Roero Arneis V. Bricco Novara '23	♉ 4
● Roero Panera Alta Ris. '21	♉ 6
○ Roero Arneis V. Bricco Novara '22	♉♉ 4
● Roero Panera Alta Ris. '20	♉♉ 6
● Roero Panera Alta Ris. '19	♉♉ 6
● Roero Panera Alta Ris. '18	♉♉ 6
● Roero Panera Alta Ris. '17	♉♉ 6
● Roero Panera Alta Ris. '16	♉♉ 6

● Barolo Coste di Rose '20	♉♉ 8
● Barbera d'Alba Sup. Naunda '22	♉♉ 5
● Barolo Coste di Rose Ris. '17	♉♉ 8
● Barolo del Comune di Barolo Pittatore '20	♉♉ 7
○ Roero Arneis Sito dei Fossili '23	♉♉ 4
● Barolo Monrobiolo di Bussia '20	♉ 8
● Barolo '16	♉♉ 6
● Barolo Coste di Rose '19	♉♉ 7
● Barolo Coste di Rose '18	♉♉ 7
● Barolo Coste di Rose '16	♉♉ 7
● Barolo Coste di Rose Ris. '13	♉♉ 7
● Barolo Coste di Rose Ris. '11	♉♉ 7
● Barolo Coste di Rose Ris. '09	♉♉ 7
● Barolo del Comune di Barolo Pittatore '19	♉♉ 6
● Barolo Monrobiolo di Bussia '17	♉♉ 6
● Barolo Monrobiolo di Bussia '15	♉♉ 6

PIEDMONT

Bricco dei Guazzi

via Vittorio Veneto, 23
15030 Olivola [AL]
☎ +39 0422864511
✉ www.briccodeiguazzi.it

ANNUAL PRODUCTION 150,000 bottles
HECTARES UNDER VINE 33.00
SUSTAINABLE WINERY

The story of the Bricco dei Guazzi estate, founded in the 16th century and now part of Le Tenute di Monte Alto (under the Generali Group), stretches back more than 500 years. At the heart of the project is a focus on the region's identity and its traditional grape varieties, though international grapes such as merlot, chardonnay, and pinot nero also find a home in the estate's vineyards. This year's tastings didn't yield a standout, but we noted solid quality overall. The Gavi del Comune di Gavi '23 has a broad nose of white flowers and citrus zest. On the palate, it shows excellent freshness and sapidity in a linear, pleasant profile. The Barbera d'Asti Superiore '21 leans on freshness, with a nose hinting at red fruit and a palate of fine acidity and good balance. The Chiaretto Funtanin '23 is simple but delightful, with floral aromas and a sapid finish.

Bricco Maiolica

fraz. Ricca
via Bolangino, 7
12055 Diano d'Alba [CN]
☎ +39 0173612049
✉ www.briccomaiolica.it

CELLAR SALES
PRE-BOOKED VISITS
ACCOMMODATION
ANNUAL PRODUCTION 100,000 bottles
HECTARES UNDER VINE 24.00
SUSTAINABLE WINERY

In 2013, Beppe Accomo and Claudia Castella joined forces, merging Bricco Maiolica and Casa Castella, and establishing a shared oenological path capable of enhancing and streamlining management. Today the producer's range revolves around Barolo from the municipality of Diano d'Alba, as well as a rich portfolio that spans everything from dolcetto to nebbiolo, pinot nero and chardonnay, all marked by a modern stylistic approach. Refined in its delicate fruit tones, the nose of the Barolo del Comune di Diano d'Alba Contadin '20 gains freshness with citrus and spice notes. On the palate, it's powerful and rich, with a compact, persistent structure and a nice, long finish. The Nebbiolo d'Alba Sup. Cumot '21 is also very good, revealing vibrant aromas and a sapid, powerful, and multifaceted palate. The juicy and vibrant Langhe Chardonnay Pensiero Infinito '20 also proves well-crafted.

● Barbera d'Asti Sup. '21	♥♥ 5
○ Gavi del Comune di Gavi '23	♥♥ 4
◉ M.to Chiaretto Funtanin '23	♥♥ 4
● Piemonte Pinot Nero Funtanin '21	♥♥ 5
● Barbera d'Asti '21	♥♥ 3
● Barbera d'Asti '19	♥♥ 2*
● Barbera d'Asti '18	♥♥ 2*
● Barbera d'Asti Sup. '20	♥♥ 4
○ Gavi del Comune di Gavi '22	♥♥ 4
○ Gavi del Comune di Gavi '20	♥♥ 3
○ Gavi del Comune di Gavi '19	♥♥ 3
◉ M.to Chiaretto Funtanin '22	♥♥ 4
● M.to Rosso La Presidenta '21	♥♥ 3
● M.to Rosso La Presidenta '20	♥♥ 3
● Piemonte Albarossa '18	♥♥ 5
● Piemonte Albarossa '16	♥♥ 5

● Barolo del Comune di Diano d'Alba Contadin '20	♥♥ 7
○ Langhe Chardonnay Pensiero Infinito '20	♥♥ 7
● Nebbiolo d'Alba Sup. Cumot '21	♥♥ 5
● Barbera d'Alba Sup. V. Vigia '21	♥♥ 5
● Pinot Nero Perlei '21	♥♥ 5
● Dolcetto di Diano d'Alba '23	♥ 3
● Barbera d'Alba V. Vigia '98	♥♥♥ 4*
● Diano d'Alba Sup. Sörì Bricco Maiolica '07	♥♥♥ 3*
● Nebbiolo d'Alba Cumot '11	♥♥♥ 5
● Nebbiolo d'Alba Cumot '10	♥♥♥ 4*
● Nebbiolo d'Alba Cumot '09	♥♥♥ 4*
● Nebbiolo d'Alba Sup. Cumot '20	♥♥♥ 5
● Nebbiolo d'Alba Sup. Cumot '13	♥♥♥ 5
● Barolo del Comune di Diano d'Alba Contadin '19	♥♥ 7

Francesco Brigatti

via Olmi, 31
28019 Suno [NO]
☏ +39 032285037
✉ www.vinibrigatti.it

CELLAR SALES
PRE-BOOKED VISITS
ANNUAL PRODUCTION 25,000 bottles
HECTARES UNDER VINE 6.50

Brigatti is a family-run producer whose origins go back to the early 1900s. It all began with grandfather Alessandro, who passed the baton to his son Lucian. Today the founder's grandson, also named Alessandro, remains deeply committed to the vineyard. Their six hectares of vines are divided across three hills: MötZiflon, with its clay soil and southwest exposure; Mötfrei, facing south with silty-sandy soil; and Campazzi, which has a higher sand content and a western exposure. The Mötfrei '20 expresses class and elegance, with an aromatic bouquet centered on ripe red fruit and floral potpourri, followed by hints of Kentucky tobacco, graphite, and balsamic nuances. The palate is rich and full, with a close-knit and progressively unfolding tannic structure. The MötZiflon '20 is consistently precise and well-structured—a deep, powerful wine. The succulent and floral Oltre il Bosco '20 offers up aromas of violet and rose petals, along with plum and black prune, while the palate unfolds rich and flavorful.

Broccardo

loc. Manzoni, 22
12065 Monforte d'Alba [CN]
☏ +39 017378180
✉ www.broccardo.it

CELLAR SALES
PRE-BOOKED VISITS
ANNUAL PRODUCTION 95,000 bottles
HECTARES UNDER VINE 13.00
SUSTAINABLE WINERY

At the winery in Monforte d'Alba, siblings Filippo, Laura, and Federico Broccardo have benefited from the teachings of their grandparents and parents. Their Barolos, from the crus of San Giovanni and Bricco San Pietro in Monforte d'Alba, Barolo Paiagallo, and Ravera in Novello, are well-structured, encapsulating refined and complex characteristics. They also produce wines with barbera, dolcetto, and arneis grapes. Fragrant floral notes and aromatic herbs open the nose of the Barolo San Giovanni '20, which then shifts to smoky and spicy hints. In the mouth, the palate is juicy and taut, with a focused tannic weave, finishing with a persistent finale. Also excellent, the Barolo Bricco San Pietro '20 displays aromas of red fruit and licorice. On the palate, its flavor development is balanced, resulting in a fine, well-proportioned wine. The Langhe Nebbiolo Il Giò Pì '22 stands out for its pleasantly flavorful drinkability.

● Colline Novaresi Nebbiolo Mötfrei '20	♟♟ 5
● Colline Novaresi Nebbbiolo MötZiflon '20	♟♟ 5
● Ghemme Oltre Il Bosco '20	♟♟ 6
● Colline Novaresi Barbera Campazzi '23	♟ 3
● Colline Novaresi Uva Rara Selvalunga '23	♟ 4
● Colline Novaresi Vespolina Maria '23	♟ 4
● Colline Novaresi Barbera Campazzi '21	♟♟ 3
● Colline Novaresi Nebbiolo Mötziflon '19	♟♟ 5
● Colline Novaresi Nebbiolo MötZiflon '18	♟♟ 3
● Colline Novaresi Nebbiolo V. Mötfrei '19	♟♟ 3*
● Colline Novaresi Nebbiolo V. Mötfrei '18	♟♟ 3*
● Colline Novaresi Nebbiolo V. Mötfrei '17	♟♟ 3*
● Colline Novaresi Vespolina Maria '22	♟♟ 4
● Colline Novaresi Vespolina Maria '21	♟♟ 3
● Ghemme Oltre Il Bosco '19	♟♟ 6
● Ghemme Oltre il Bosco '18	♟♟ 5
● Ghemme Oltre il Bosco '17	♟♟ 5

● Barolo Bricco San Pietro '20	♟♟ 6
● Barolo San Giovanni '20	♟♟ 8
● Barbera d'Alba La Martinella '23	♟♟ 2*
● Barbera d'Alba Sup. La Tina '22	♟♟ 3
● Barolo I Tre Pais '20	♟♟ 5
● Dolcetto d'Alba Le Campanelle '23	♟♟ 2*
● Langhe Nebbiolo Il Giò Pì '22	♟♟ 3
● Barolo Ravera '20	♟ 8
○ Langhe Arneis Langhèt '23	♟ 2
● Barolo Bricco San Pietro '16	♟♟ 6
● Barolo I Tre Pais '17	♟♟ 5
● Barolo Paiagallo '19	♟♟ 7
● Barolo Paiagallo '16	♟♟ 7
● Barolo Ravera '19	♟♟ 8
● Barolo Ravera '17	♟♟ 7
● Barolo San Giovanni '18	♟♟ 7
● Langhe Nebbiolo Il Gio Pì '19	♟♟ 3*

Broglia - Tenuta La Meirana

loc. Lomellina, 22
15066 Gavi [AL]
📞 +39 0143642998
🌐 broglia.it

PIEDMONT

CELLAR SALES
PRE-BOOKED VISITS
ACCOMMODATION
ANNUAL PRODUCTION 480,000 bottles
HECTARES UNDER VINE 65.00

Tenuta La Meirana was purchased in 1972 by textile entrepreneur Bruno Broglia. In 1974, Broglia leased the property to his son Piero, who released the first wine under the Broglia label the same year. By the late 1990s, the winery had taken on its current form. Today, managed by Roberto and Filippo Broglia, it's a leading name in the Gavi Docg production zone, crafting some of the area's most intriguing bottles. The Gavi La Meirana '23, a Gavi del comune di Gavi, is a wine of great complexity, starting with elegant aromas of wildflowers and white-fleshed fruit, followed by lightly spiced whiffs. The palate is broad and fleshy, with a persistent, focused progression, ending on a firm, flavorful finish with fruity echoes. The nose of the Gavi Bruno Broglia '20 from the same appellation has evolved beautifully, combining hints of citrus and freshly wilted flowers to its bouquet. On the palate, it's energetic and compact, with a lively acidity that drives a long, sapid finish.

★Brovia

via Alba Barolo, 145
12060 Castiglione Falletto [CN]
📞 +39 017362852
🌐 www.brovia.net

PRE-BOOKED VISITS
ANNUAL PRODUCTION 80,000 bottles
HECTARES UNDER VINE 16.00
VITICULTURE METHOD Certified Organic

The Brovia family winery boasts vines in some of the most renowned crus of the appellation: Rocche, Villero, and Garblèt Sue' (Castiglione Falletto), Ca' Mia and Brea (Serralunga d'Alba). Managed by sisters Elena and Cristina (along with Elena's husband Alex), who carry on the work of their father Giacinto, Brovia's wines are devoid of unnecessary embellishments, showcasing a clear, almost whispered elegance. The Barolo '20 is fragrant, racy, and lively, with a vibrant, flavorful drinkability. The nose, too, possesses a nice overall freshness with citrus and spice accents, culminating in a refreshing balsamic note. The Barolo Rocche di Castiglione '20 is also excellent, playing on aromas dominated by fruit, spices, and balsamic nuances, leading to a properly austere palate. The Barolo Brea Vigna Ca' Mia '20 unveils focused, red fruit and smoky accents on the nose, with a subtle, multifaceted palate to follow.

○ Gavi del Comune di Gavi Bruno Broglia '20	🍷🍷 5
○ Gavi del Comune di Gavi La Meirana '23	🍷🍷 4
○ Gavi del Comune di Gavi Bruno Broglia '19	🍷🍷🍷 5
○ Gavi del Comune di Gavi Bruno Broglia '12	🍷🍷🍷 5
○ Gavi del Comune di Gavi Bruno Broglia '08	🍷🍷🍷 5
○ Gavi del Comune di Gavi Bruno Broglia '07	🍷🍷🍷 5
○ Colli Tortonesi Timorasso Derthona '20	🍷🍷 5
○ Gavi del Comune di Gavi Vecchia Annata '15	🍷🍷 8

● Barolo '20	🍷🍷 8
● Barolo Brea Vigna Ca' Mia '20	🍷🍷 8
● Barolo Rocche di Castiglione '20	🍷🍷 8
● Barbera d'Alba Sorì del Drago '22	🍷🍷 5
● Barolo Garblèt Sue' '20	🍷🍷 8
● Barolo Villero '20	🍷🍷 8
● Dolcetto d'Alba Vignavillej '22	🍷🍷 4
● Barolo Brea V. Ca' Mia '10	🍷🍷🍷 8
● Barolo Brea Vigna Ca' Mia '15	🍷🍷🍷 8
● Barolo Ca' Mia '09	🍷🍷🍷 8
● Barolo Rocche di Castiglione '19	🍷🍷🍷 8
● Barolo Rocche di Castiglione '12	🍷🍷🍷 8
● Barolo Villero '16	🍷🍷🍷 8
● Barolo Villero '13	🍷🍷🍷 8
● Barolo Villero '11	🍷🍷🍷 8
● Barolo Villero '10	🍷🍷🍷 8

G. B. Burlotto

via Vittorio Emanuele, 28
12060 Verduno [CN]
(·) +39 0172470122
⊕ www.burlotto.com

CELLAR SALES
PRE-BOOKED VISITS
ACCOMMODATION
ANNUAL PRODUCTION 60,000 bottles
HECTARES UNDER VINE 15.00

The prized vineyards of this historic Verduno winery—located in noteworthy crus such as Monvigliero, Cannubi, and Castelletto—highlight the expressive capabilities and quality of its wines. Fabio Alessandria has crafted Barolo with a particularly refined stylistic touch, characterized by grace and elegance. The winery also cultivates other local varieties: pelaverga, barbera, dolcetto, freisa, and a small amount of sauvignon. The Barolo Cannubi '20 is a wine of great breadth, starting with its aromas of small red fruits, spices, and balsamic notes. In the mouth, its tannic expression is impeccable, with an energetic progression that finishes on airy nuances. The Barolo Castelletto '20 offers a pervasive, persistent development of flavor, with fresh, citrus aromas. The alluring Monvigliero '20 and the lively, enjoyable Pelaverga '23, with its crisp and flavorful palate, both stand out.

★Piero Busso

via Albesani
12052 Neive [CN]
(·) +39 017367156
⊕ bussopiero.com

CELLAR SALES
PRE-BOOKED VISITS
ACCOMMODATION
ANNUAL PRODUCTION 45,000 bottles
HECTARES UNDER VINE 11.50
VITICULTURE METHOD Certified Organic
SUSTAINABLE WINERY

The Busso family' deep historical roots begin with the Borgese vineyard in Albesani, planted in 1948, and the first bottles of Barbaresco, which hit the market back in 1982. Today, the winery is run by Piero and Lucia Busso, along with their children Pierguido and Emanuela. Most of their vineyards are located in the municipality of Neive, with a small plot in Treiso, which gives rise to their San Stunet Cru. Benefiting from holdings in some of the best subzones of eastern part of the appellation, the Busso family offers a classic lineup of Barbaresco wines. This year, we faced a fortunate dilemma. Among the four splendid Barbarescos, the Mondino '21 stands out for its immediate pleasantness, with fruity and floral emanations that pleasantly envelop the nose and a velvety pulp that caresses the palate. The others, led by the Gallina '20, comes across as more serious and austere, with extremely refined tannins and a complex, multifaceted nose—Barbarescos built for long aging.

● Barolo Cannubi '20	♟♟ 8
● Barolo Castelletto '20	♟♟ 8
● Barolo Monvigliero '20	♟♟ 8
● Barbera d'Alba Aves '22	♟♟ 5
○ Langhe Sauvignon Dives '22	♟♟ 4
● Verduno Pelaverga '23	♟♟ 4
● Barolo Acclivi '11	♟♟♟ 6
● Barolo Acclivi '07	♟♟♟ 6
● Barolo Cannubi '17	♟♟♟ 8
● Barolo Cannubi '16	♟♟♟ 7
● Barolo Cannubi '12	♟♟♟ 7
● Barolo Monvigliero '18	♟♟♟ 7
● Barolo Monvigliero '10	♟♟♟ 7
● Barolo '17	♟♟ 8
● Barolo Cannubi '19	♟♟ 8
● Barolo Castelletto '18	♟♟ 8
● Barolo Monvigliero '17	♟♟ 8

● Barbaresco Mondino '21	♟♟♟ 6
● Barbaresco Gallina '20	♟♟ 8
● Barbaresco Albesani V. Borgese '20	♟♟♟ 7
● Barbaresco S. Stunet '20	♟♟ 8
● Barbaresco Albesani V. Borgese '15	♟♟♟ 7
● Barbaresco Borgese '09	♟♟♟ 6
● Barbaresco Borgese '08	♟♟♟ 6
● Barbaresco Gallina '18	♟♟♟ 8
● Barbaresco Gallina '12	♟♟♟ 8
● Barbaresco Gallina '11	♟♟♟ 8
● Barbaresco Gallina '09	♟♟♟ 8
● Barbaresco Gallina '05	♟♟♟ 7
● Barbaresco S. Stefanetto '07	♟♟♟ 7
● Barbaresco S. Stefanetto '04	♟♟♟ 7
● Barbaresco S. Stefanetto '03	♟♟♟ 7
● Barbaresco S. Stunet '11	♟♟♟ 7

Ca' Bianca

reg. Spagna, 58
15010 Alice Bel Colle [AL]
📞 +39 0144745420
🌐 cantinacabianca.it

CELLAR SALES
PRE-BOOKED VISITS
ANNUAL PRODUCTION 308,000 bottles
HECTARES UNDER VINE 24.00

Founded in 1952 just a few kilometers from Acqui Terme, this winery is now part of the Italian Wine Group. Its atmospheric cellar is surrounded by 24 hectares of vineyards planted on sandy soils. Winemakers Giandomenico Longo and Matteo Marchisio produce an extensive range, focusing on the historic grape varieties of the region. Recently, the addition of the Alta Langa appellation (with their Marchio Calissano selection) has further expanded their offerings. The wines presented this year are characterized by a fresh drinkability. The Dolcetto D'Acqui '22, for example, offers elegant spice and floral aromas, with a pleasant and persistent palate. The Barbera d'Asti Superiore '22 follows a similar path, featuring tobacco and spices on the nose and continuing with a full-bodied yet fresh palate. The Moscato d'Asti '23 also delivers, with its rich straw-yellow color. Its aromas recall aromatic herbs and yellow peach, and the palate strikes an excellent balance between sweetness and freshness.

Ca' d' Gal

fraz. Valdivilla
s.da Vecchia di Valdivilla, 1
12058 Santo Stefano Belbo [CN]
📞 +39 0141847103
🌐 www.cadgal.com

CELLAR SALES
PRE-BOOKED VISITS
ACCOMMODATION
ANNUAL PRODUCTION 85,000 bottles
HECTARES UNDER VINE 15.00

Ca' d' Gal has long been focused on moscato d'asti, despite also producing barbera, freisa, sauvignon, chardonnay, and pinot noir. Located in Santo Stefano Belbo, in the heart of the appellation, its light and sandy soils impart elegance and drinkability. The Boido family is so dedicated to the grape that they've zoned vineyards over 70 years old in pursuit of consistently enthralling wines. Ca' d' Gal has delivered a series of high-level Moscato d'Asti wines. The Vigna Vecchia '19 is vibrant and complex on the nose, with notes of sage, citrus, and tropical fruit, while the palate is simultaneously rich and fresh. The Canelli Sant'Ilario '23 follows with aromas of anise and sage, complemented by floral, peach, and white fruit hints, leading to a palate of great harmony and balance. The Lumine '23 showcases aromas of apricot and canned peach alongside nuances of medicinal herbs, and a deep yet fresh palate.

● Barbera d'Asti Sup. '22	♟♟ 3
● Brachetto d'Acqui '23	♟♟ 3
● Dolcetto d'Acqui '22	♟♟ 3
○ Moscato d'Asti '23	♟♟ 3
○ Alta Langa Pas Dosé Calissano '19	♟♟ 5
● Barbera d'Asti Sup. '21	♟♟ 3
● Barbera d'Asti Sup. '18	♟♟ 2*
● Barbera d'Asti Sup. Chersì '20	♟♟ 4
● Barbera d'Asti Sup. Chersì '18	♟♟ 4
● Barbera d'Asti Sup. Chersì '16	♟♟ 4
● Barbera d'Asti Sup. Chersì '15	♟♟ 5
● Brachetto d'Acqui '22	♟♟ 3
● Dolcetto d'Acqui '21	♟♟ 3
○ Gavi '22	♟♟ 3
○ Moscato d'Asti '22	♟♟ 3

○ Canelli Sant'Ilario '23	♟♟♟ 5
○ Moscato d'Asti Lumine '23	♟♟ 4
○ Moscato d'Asti V. Vecchia '19	♟♟ 4
● Barbera d'Asti Fabè '22	♟ 3
○ Moscato d'Asti Canelli Sant'Ilario '20	♟♟♟ 4*
○ Moscato d'Asti Canelli Sant'Ilario '19	♟♟♟ 4*
○ Moscato d'Asti Canelli Sant'Ilario '16	♟♟♟ 4*
○ Moscato d'Asti Canelli Sant'Ilario '15	♟♟♟ 3*
○ Moscato d'Asti V.V. '11	♟♟♟ 3*
○ Moscato d'Asti Canelli Sant'Ilario '21	♟♟ 4
○ Moscato d'Asti Lumine '22	♟♟ 4
○ Moscato d'Asti Lumine '21	♟♟ 3*
○ Moscato d'Asti Vite Vecchia '18	♟♟ 8
○ Moscato d'Asti Vite Vecchia '16	♟♟ 7

★Ca' del Baio

via Ferrere Sottano, 33
12050 Treiso [CN]
℡ +39 0173638219
✉ www.cadelbaio.com

CELLAR SALES
PRE-BOOKED VISITS
ANNUAL PRODUCTION 150,000 bottles
HECTARES UNDER VINE 25.00
SUSTAINABLE WINERY

For four generations, the Grasso family—now led by Giulio and Luciana, along with their daughters Paola, Valentina, and Federica—has managed this solid winery. The vineyards surrounding the farmhouse near Treiso, which form an almost single, contiguous tract, give rise to their Vallegrande and Marcarini Crus. They're accompanied by Barbaresco, Asili, and Pora, as well as wines made from international grape varieties, such as chardonnay and riesling. A trio of well-crafted Barbaresco wines were submitted for tasting. The Autinbej '20 opens with aromas of black cherry and spices, coupled with a vigorous, racy palate. The Asili '20 possesses notable stuffing, with refined tannins that mark its delicious palate. The Vallegrande Viti Vecchie Riserva '19 showcases finely fruity aromas with an elegant balsamic streak, leading to an authoritative, focused progression of flavor. The true champion of the Grasso family is the Asili Riserva '19, a wine that's complex and elegant on the nose, with a fresh, structured, and persistent palate.

Wine	Rating	Score
● Barbaresco Asili Ris. '19	🍷🍷🍷	8
● Barbaresco Asili '21	🍷🍷	8
● Barbaresco Autinbej '21	🍷🍷	6
● Barbaresco Vallegrande V.V. Ris. '19	🍷🍷	8
● Barbaresco Pora '20	🍷🍷	8
● Barbaresco Vallegrande '21	🍷	6
● Barbaresco Asili '19	🍷🍷🍷	6
● Barbaresco Asili '15	🍷🍷🍷	6
● Barbaresco Asili '12	🍷🍷🍷	6
● Barbaresco Asili Ris. '16	🍷🍷🍷	8
● Barbaresco Asili Ris. '11	🍷🍷🍷	8
● Barbaresco Pora '10	🍷🍷🍷	6
● Barbaresco Vallegrande '17	🍷🍷🍷	5
● Barbaresco Vallegrande '16	🍷🍷🍷	5
● Barbaresco Vallegrande '14	🍷🍷🍷	5
● Barbaresco Vallegrande V.V. Ris. '18	🍷🍷🍷	5

Ca' Romé

s.da Rabajà, 86
12050 Barbaresco [CN]
℡ +39 0173635126
✉ www.carome.com

CELLAR SALES
PRE-BOOKED VISITS
ANNUAL PRODUCTION 30,000 bottles
HECTARES UNDER VINE 5.00

Ca' Romé is a small winery founded in 1980 by Romano Marengo, who, together with his wife Olimpia, embarked on a decidedly successful journey into the world of wine production. This family-run estate now also involves their children, Paola, Maria, and Giuseppe. The vineyards are located in the Barbaresco area, with the Cru Rio Sordo, and in Serralunga d'Alba, with the Cru Cerretta. The Barolo Cerretta '20 impresses with its exuberant, fragrant fruitiness. On the nose touches of anise merge with balsamic echoes, while its progression of flavor is equally focused, balancing tannins and fruit pulp, closing with a finish that builds in intensity. The Barbaresco Maria di Brün '20, which also caught our attention, showcases clearly-defined aromas and a dense, sapid, and long palate. The Barbaresco Rio Sordo '21 and Chiaramanti '21 are also both well-made.

Wine	Rating	Score
● Barbaresco Maria di Brün '20	🍷🍷	8
● Barolo Cerretta '20	🍷🍷	8
● Barbaresco Chiaramanti '21	🍷🍷	8
● Barbaresco Rio Sordo '21	🍷🍷	8
● Barolo Rapet '20	🍷	8
● Barbaresco Maria di Brün '13	🍷🍷🍷	8
● Barbaresco Sorì Rio Sordo '06	🍷🍷🍷	6
● Barolo Rapet '14	🍷🍷🍷	7
● Barolo Rapet '11	🍷🍷🍷	7
● Barolo Rapet '08	🍷🍷🍷	7
● Barolo V. Cerretta '09	🍷🍷🍷	7
● Barbaresco Chiaramanti '20	🍷🍷	8
● Barbaresco Maria di Brün '18	🍷🍷	8
● Barolo Cerretta '18	🍷🍷	8
● Barolo Cerretta '17	🍷🍷	8
● Barolo Rapet '19	🍷🍷	8

★★Ca' Viola

b.ta San Luigi, 11
12063 Dogliani [CN]
(+39 017370547
⊕ www.caviola.com

CELLAR SALES
PRE-BOOKED VISITS
ACCOMMODATION AND RESTAURANT SERVICE
ANNUAL PRODUCTION 80,000 bottles
HECTARES UNDER VINE 10.00
VITICULTURE METHOD Certified Organic

Giuseppe Caviola is a renowned oenological
consultant who, early in his career, also became a
producer of his own. In 1991, near his
hometown of Montelupo, he spotted a small
vineyard called Barturot, which he rented,
vinifying the grapes in his home garage. Much has
changed since then, and today Ca' Viola is among
Langhe's leading wineries, producing a
well-crafted range with impeccable style. Once
again, this year saw a series of impeccable
tastings, with the standout being the ever-reliable
Barolo Sottocastello di Novello. The 2020 opens
with intense aromas of medicinal herbs and
rose, followed by notes of tobacco and
raspberry. The palate is refined and deep,
perfectly balancing structure and freshness. The
Barbera d'Alba Bric du Luv '22 also delivered.
Despite their differences, both wines impress for
their clear aromatic suite, superb harmony and
endless length.

Fabrizia Caldera

fraz. Portacomaro Stazione,53
14100 Asti
(+39 0141296154
⊕ www.vinicaldera.it

CELLAR SALES
PRE-BOOKED VISITS
ACCOMMODATION
ANNUAL PRODUCTION 95,000 bottles
HECTARES UNDER VINE 22.00

Four generations have led this winery in
Portacomaro Stazione, just a few kilometers
from Asti. Today, Fabrizia Caldera, with her
husband Roberto and son Fabio, upholds a
philosophy of terroir and consistency, primarily
using native grapes that reflect their soils. Here
they produce wines from barbera, moscato,
cortese, and grignolino, with special attention to
ruchè. The Ruché di Castagnole Monferrato
Prevost '23 is one of the best of its kind,
summoning aromas of rose, ripe dark fruit, and
licorice, while the palate offers good substance,
with close-knit, pervasive tannins and a long
finish. The other Ruché di Castagnole Monferrato
2023 wines are also well-crafted. The Xenio
proves approachable with floral tones and red
fruit, while the full-bodied Genìt shows nice
balance. The Piemonte Viognier Viò '23 plays on
aromas of ripe apricots and white pepper before
a sapid, long palate. The juicy and enjoyable
Barbera d'Asti Harmonius '22 opts for notes of
plum and aromatic herbs.

Wine	Rating
● Barolo Sottocastello di Novello '20	♆♆♆ 8
● Barbera d'Alba Bric du Luv '22	♆♆ 5
● Langhe Nebbiolo Rangone '23	♆♆ 5
● Barbaresco Matthias '21	♆♆ 5
● Barbera d'Alba Brichet '23	♆♆ 4
● Barolo Caviot '20	♆♆ 7
● Dolcetto d'Alba Vilot '23	♆♆ 3
○ Langhe Arneis Sirena '23	♆♆ 3
○ Langhe Riesling Clem '23	♆♆ 5
⊙ Langhe Rosato Rita '23	♆♆ 4
● Barolo Sottocastello di Novello '19	♆♆♆ 8
● Barolo Sottocastello di Novello '17	♆♆♆ 8
● Barolo Sottocastello di Novello Ris. '16	♆♆♆ 8
● Ruché di Castagnole M.to Prevost '23	♆♆ 4
● Barbera d'Asti Harmonius '22	♆♆ 3
○ Piemonte Viognier Viò '23	♆♆ 3
● Ruché di Castagnole Monferrato Genìt '23	♆♆ 3
● Ruché di Castagnole Monferrato Xenio '23	♆♆ 3
● Barbera d'Asti Sup. Balmét '21	♆ 5
● Grignolino d'Asti Le Serre '23	♆ 3
● Ruché di Castagnole M.to Prevost '22	♆♆♆ 4*
● Barbera d'Asti Sup. Balmèt '18	♆♆ 4
● Grignolino d'Asti Le Serre '22	♆♆ 3*
● Grignolino d'Asti Leserre '21	♆♆ 3*
● Grignolino d'Asti Leserre '19	♆♆ 3*
● Ruché di Castagnole M.to Prevost '21	♆♆ 4
● Ruché di Castagnole M.to Xenio '19	♆♆ 3*

Cantina del Nebbiolo

via Torino, 17
12050 Vezza d'Alba [CN]
(+39 017365040
www.cantinadelnebbiolo.com

CELLAR SALES
PRE-BOOKED VISITS
ANNUAL PRODUCTION 350,000 bottles
HECTARES UNDER VINE 350.00
VITICULTURE METHOD Certified Organic

Cantina del Nebbiolo relies on 170 members who cultivate a large area under vines across 18 municipalities in Langhe and Roero, covering prestigious appellations such as Barbaresco, Barolo, and Roero. In addition to nebbiolo, they grow various grapes, primarily native varietals, crafting traditional wines that express the region's signature characteristics and terroir. As always, the winery's range is solid and reliable. In terms of Langhe, the two Barbaresco Meruzzano wines stand out. The Riserva '19, with its intense floral notes, fresh red fruit, and tobacco, offers a beautifully structured palate that is harmonious and balanced, with tannins already showing softness. The 2021 showcases lovely complexity and finesse, with tones of fresh fruit and licorice. In the Roero region, the Roero Arneis Arenarium '23 is worth mentioning, with its aromas of aromatic herbs, almond, and white currant, offering a spirited, well-structured palate with nice volume and sapidity. Also of note is the Langhe Favorita '23, a fresh, juicy, and pleasant sip.

Cantina del Pino

s.da Ovello, 31
12050 Barbaresco [CN]
(+39 0173635147
www.cantinadelpino.com

ANNUAL PRODUCTION 48,000 bottles
HECTARES UNDER VINE 10.00

PIEDMONT

Franca Miretti's Cantina del Pino can be found to the north of Barbaresco, in Ovello, one of the appellation's most important crus. The estate also includes plots in the geographical indications of Albesani and Gallina, in the municipality of Neive. Franca's wines are characterized by a modern production style, showcasing superb aromatic delicacy, with aging predominantly carried out in large oak barrels. The Barbaresco Ovello '20 is a complete, focused wine, with an aromatic profile redolent of spices, hints of citrus flowers, and balsamic nuances. In the mouth, the palate is expansive, with abundant, yet elegant, tannic texture, extending into a long finish on licorice notes. The vibrant Barbaresco '20 is also noteworthy, releasing aromas of strawberry, pomegranate, and nutmeg, while offering a firm, persistent palate. The well-crafted Barbaresco Albesani '20 is austere, though nicely balanced.

● Barbaresco '21	♟♟ 5
● Barbera d'Alba '23	♟♟ 2*
● Barolo '20	♟♟ 5
● Barolo del comune di Serralunga d'Alba '20	♟♟ 6
○ Langhe Favorita '23	♟♟ 2*
● Nebbiolo d'Alba '22	♟♟ 3
○ Roero Arneis Arenarium '23	♟♟ 3
● Barolo del Comune di Barolo '18	♟ 7
● Dolcetto d'Alba '23	♟ 2
○ Langhe Arneis '23	♟ 2
○ Moscato d'Asti '23	♟ 3
○ Roero Arneis '23	♟ 3
● Barbaresco '20	♟♟ 4
● Barbaresco Meruzzano '20	♟♟ 5
● Barbaresco Meruzzano '17	♟♟ 5
● Barolo '17	♟♟ 5

● Barbaresco Ovello '20	♟♟♟ 8
● Barbaresco '20	♟♟ 6
● Barbaresco Albesani '20	♟♟ 8
● Barbera d'Alba Sup. '22	♟ 5
● Barbaresco '04	♟♟♟ 5*
● Barbaresco '03	♟♟♟ 4*
● Barbaresco Albesani '14	♟♟♟ 7
● Barbaresco Albesani '05	♟♟♟ 6
● Barbaresco Ovello '13	♟♟♟ 7
● Barbaresco Ovello '07	♟♟♟ 6
● Barbaresco Ovello '99	♟♟♟ 5
● Barbaresco Albesani '19	♟♟ 8
● Barbaresco Albesani '18	♟♟ 7
● Barbaresco Albesani '17	♟♟ 7
● Barbaresco Ovello '18	♟♟ 7
● Barbaresco Ovello '17	♟♟ 7

Cantina di Tortona

via Muraglie Rosse, 5
15057 Tortona [AL]
(☎) +39 0131861265
⊛ cantinatortona.it

La Caplana

via Circonvallazione, 4
15060 Bosio [AL]
(☎) +39 0143684182
⊛ www.lacaplana.com

ANNUAL PRODUCTION 500,000 bottles
HECTARES UNDER VINE 280.00
VITICULTURE METHOD Certified Organic

CELLAR SALES
PRE-BOOKED VISITS
ANNUAL PRODUCTION 120,000 bottles
HECTARES UNDER VINE 5.00

Founded in 1931 so as to curb rural exodus, combat the decline of vineyard areas, and offer new sales opportunities to producers, this cooperative was pivotal in the establishment of the region's appellations in the 1960s. Today, it has 160 members, exemplifying high-level cooperation. There are two production lines: Collezione Pellizza and Selezione Fiumana, showcasing the full potential of the Tortonese territory. The richness and depth of the Aemilia Scauri Riserva '20 is striking, with its intricate and captivating aromatic dynamism—a note of hydrocarbons intensifies along with hints of citron and grapefruit peel, Mediterranean herbs, and dried flowers. The palate is lively and vibrant, with outstanding acidity and a long, flavorful finish. The Derthona '22 is no less impressive, opting for notes of fresh herbs and flint before a juicy, fresh palate. The Monleale '20, a Barbera with vibrant acidity and good fruit is right up there as well.

Since 1994, the Guido family—siblings Natalino and Carmen, along with Carmen's husband Luca and daughter Alice—has managed this winery in the Bosio district. They produce well-crafted Gavis, drawing in part on amphorae so as to preserve the fruitiness and fragrance of the grapes. Besides the predominantly grown white varieties cortese and chardonnay, they also cultivate dolcetto and barbera. The Gavi Villavecchia '22 offers an intense, focused aromatic profile dominated by fresh notes of ferns and wildflowers, underpinned by flint. The palate is austere yet full of character, with a vivid acidic freshness that extends the palate and leads to a crisp finish. The Gavi '23 sees aromas of field herbs combined with hints of apple, white flowers, and nuts, leading to a bold, full, and long palate.

○ Colli Tortonesi Timorasso Derthona '22	♟♟ 3*
○ Colli Tortonesi Timorasso Derthona Aemilia Scauri '20	♟♟ 4
● Colli Tortonesi Monleale '20	♟♟ 4
○ Colli Tortonesi Favorita Delre '22	♟ 2
● Vino Rosso Ossonella '23	♟ 2
● Colli Tortonesi Monleale '18	♟♟ 4
○ Colli Tortonesi Timorasso Derthona '21	♟♟ 3*
○ Colli Tortonesi Timorasso Derthona Aemilia Scauri '19	♟♟ 4
○ Colli Tortonesi Timorasso Piccolo Derthona '21	♟♟ 2*

○ Gavi Villavecchia '22	♟♟ 2*
● Barbera d'Asti Rubis '19	♟♟ 3
● Dolcetto di Ovada '23	♟♟ 2*
○ Gavi '23	♟♟ 2*
○ Gavi del Comune di Gavi '23	♟ 3
● Dolcetto di Ovada Narcys '17	♟♟ 3*
● Dolcetto di Ovada Narcys '15	♟♟ 3*
● Dolcetto di Ovada Narcys '13	♟♟ 3*
○ Gavi '19	♟♟ 2*
○ Gavi del Comune di Gavi '22	♟♟ 3*
○ Gavi del Comune di Gavi '20	♟♟ 2*
○ Gavi del Comune di Gavi '18	♟♟ 2*
○ Gavi del Comune di Gavi '17	♟♟ 2*
○ Gavi del Comune di Gavi '16	♟♟ 2*
○ Gavi Villavecchia '21	♟♟ 2*
○ Gavi Villavecchia '20	♟♟ 2*

Pierangelo Careglio

loc. Aprato, 15
12040 Baldissero d'Alba [CN]
☎ +39 3339905448
⊛ www.cantinacareglio.it

Davide Carlone

via Monsignor Sagliaschi, 8
28075 Grignasco [NO]
☎ +39 3290987672
⊛ davidecarlone.com

PIEDMONT

CELLAR SALES
PRE-BOOKED VISITS
ANNUAL PRODUCTION 35,000 bottles
HECTARES UNDER VINE 9.00
SUSTAINABLE WINERY

CELLAR SALES
PRE-BOOKED VISITS
ANNUAL PRODUCTION 35,000 bottles
HECTARES UNDER VINE 7.00
SUSTAINABLE WINERY

The Careglio family's winery has become one of the most interesting in the Roero landscape in recent years. Their vineyards are located on both the sandy marine soils for which the area is known and areas with more calcareous clay, with arneis, barbera, and nebbiolo cultivated alongside a small vineyard of pinot noir. Their technically well-crafted wines aim to express the attributes of the varietal and terroir. This year, the Roero Arneis Savij Riserva takes center stage in the winery's lineup. The 2020 unveils aromas of fresh citrus, ginger, and rosemary, followed by a fresh, energetic palate with nice flesh and juiciness, extending into a long, pleasant finish. The Roero Valmezzana Riserva '20, with its good softness and volume, is still marked by oak, finishing on tones of sweet fruit. The Roero Arneis '23, on the other hand, plays on aromas of jasmine and almond, with nice citrus freshness and sapidity.

In 1991, Davide Carlone, with the help of his sister Michela, revived the family business, whose roots go all the way back to 1880. Their project centers on highlighting the potential of the territory, growing local varieties with sustainable, eco-friendly methods. In the cellar, the emphasis is on craftsmanship and authenticity, an approach that results in wines that reflect the region's unique characteristics. This year's tastings feature two standout Boca wines, distinguished by characteristics typical of the appellation, making them intriguing to taste. The Boca Adele '20, with its notes of cinchona and rhubarb, features a structured palate, slightly restrained by its close-knit tannins, though well-balanced by a rich texture that lends volume to the palate. The Boca '20 also sees notes of rhubarb and a hint of olives, while showcasing a complex and refined palate with a well-knit tannic weave.

○ Roero Arneis Savij Ris. '20	♟♟ 6
○ Roero Arneis '23	♟♟ 3
● Roero Valmezzana Ris. '20	♟♟ 5
● Langhe Nebbiolo '22	♟ 2
● Barbera d'Alba '21	♟♟ 4
● Barbera d'Alba '20	♟♟ 4
○ Langhe Favorita '22	♟♟ 3
○ Langhe Favorita '21	♟♟ 2*
○ Langhe Favorita '20	♟♟ 2*
● Langhe Nebbiolo '21	♟♟ 2*
● Roero '18	♟♟ 5
○ Roero Arneis '22	♟♟ 3
○ Roero Arneis '21	♟♟ 3
○ Roero Arneis Savij Ris. '19	♟♟ 6
○ Roero Arneis Savij Ris. '18	♟♟ 6
● Roero Ris. '18	♟♟ 5
● Roero Valmezzana Ris. '19	♟♟ 5

● Boca Adele '20	♟♟ 6
● Boca '20	♟♟ 5
○ Colline Novaresi Bianco Maria Pia '23	♟ 3
● Colline Novaresi Croatina '20	♟ 3
● Colline Novaresi Nebbiolo '22	♟ 4
⊙ Colline Novaresi Nebbiolo Rosato Albarossa '23	♟ 2
● Boca '17	♟♟ 5
● Boca '16	♟♟ 5
● Boca Adele '19	♟♟ 6
● Boca Adele '17	♟♟ 6
● Boca Adele '16	♟♟ 6
○ Colline Novaresi Bianco Maria Pia '22	♟♟ 3
● Colline Novaresi Nebbiolo '20	♟♟ 4
● Colline Novaresi Nebbiolo '19	♟♟ 4
● Coste della Sesia Nebbiolo '18	♟♟ 3

PIEDMONT

Tenuta Carretta

loc. Carretta, 2
12040 Piobesi d'Alba [CN]
📞 +39 0173619119
🌐 www.tenutacarretta.it

CELLAR SALES
PRE-BOOKED VISITS
ACCOMMODATION AND RESTAURANT SERVICE
ANNUAL PRODUCTION 550,000 bottles
HECTARES UNDER VINE 85.00
SUSTAINABLE WINERY

For 40 years, the Miroglio family has managed this historic estate, mentioned since the 15th century for its vineyards. Today, the winery boasts a single 35-hectare plot surrounding the cellar and several vineyards in prestigious Piedmont appellations, from Cannubi in Barolo to Treiso in Barbaresco, Alta Langa (for Metodo Classico) and Asti. The wines offered exhibit a modern style and clear territorial expression. The Roero Arneis Alteno della Fontana Riserva '19 opens on aromas of Mediterranean scrub and grapefruit, followed by a sapid palate with nice structure and a pleasant, almost spicy finish. The Roero Bric Paradiso Riserva '20 reveals notes of ripe black fruits, truffle, and aromatic herbs, with a rich, juicy, long palate of excellent fullness. The wines from their Langhe estates are equally well-crafted, particularly the Barolo Cannubi Collezione Rag. Franco Miroglio Riserva '18, with its balanced tannins and notes of red berries and pencil lead.

○ Roero Arneis Riserva Alteno della Fontana Ris. '19	🍷🍷	7
● Roero Bric Paradiso Ris. '20	🍷🍷	8
○ Alta Langa Pas Dosè Airali '20	🍷🍷	7
● Barbaresco Cascina Bordino '21	🍷🍷	8
● Barbaresco Cascina Bordino Ris. '19	🍷🍷	8
● Barolo Cannubi Collezione Rag. Franco Miroglio Ris. '18	🍷🍷	8
○ Roero Arneis Canorei Ris. '22	🍷🍷	6
○ Roero Arneis Cayega '23	🍷🍷	5
○ Alta Langa Brut Airali '20	🍷	7
● Dolcetto d'Alba Sup. Il Palazzo Madonna Di Como '22	🍷	5
● Barolo Vign. in Cannubi '00	🍷🍷🍷	7
● Barolo Cannubi Collezione Franco Miroglio Ris. '16	🍷🍷	8

Casa E. di Mirafiore

via Alba, 15
12050 Serralunga d'Alba [CN]
📞 +39 0173626111
🌐 www.mirafiore.it

CELLAR SALES
PRE-BOOKED VISITS
ACCOMMODATION AND RESTAURANT SERVICE
ANNUAL PRODUCTION 200,000 bottles
HECTARES UNDER VINE 25.00
VITICULTURE METHOD Certified Organic
SUSTAINABLE WINERY

It was Emanuele Alberto Guerrieri, Count of Mirafiore, son of the first King of Italy, who founded Casa E. di Mirafiore in 1878. In 1900, after his death, the winery reached its peak commercial expansion, but under the management of his son Gastone, things began to decline until its closure in 1931. In 2008, the brand and winery were revived to their former glory by the Farinetti family, as part of a project that also includes Fontanafredda and Borgogno. The Barolo Riserva '17 features a delicate fruitiness on the nose, alongside hints of underbrush and licorice root. On the palate, the wine is fragrant, showing good flesh and a focused finish. The Barolo '20 has nice body, accompanied by clean, intense aromas. However, this year, our preference goes to the Lazzarito '20, a splendid Barolo with an elegant nose, where notes of blood orange alternate with balsamic hints. The palate is rich and juicy, with especially long persistence.

● Barolo Lazzarito '20	🍷🍷🍷	8
● Barolo Ris. '17	🍷🍷	8
○ Alta Langa Brut Blanc de Noir '20	🍷🍷	5
● Barolo '20	🍷🍷	7
● Langhe Rosso Pietra Magica '21	🍷🍷	5
● Barolo Meriame '20	🍷	6
● Barolo Paiagallo '20	🍷	8
● Barolo Lazzarito '16	🍷🍷🍷	8
● Barolo Paiagallo '13	🍷🍷🍷	7
● Barolo Paiagallo '12	🍷🍷🍷	7
● Barolo Ris. '04	🍷🍷🍷	8
○ Alta Langa Blanc de Noir '19	🍷🍷	6
● Barbera d'Alba Sup. '19	🍷🍷	5
● Barolo Lazzarito '18	🍷🍷	8
● Barolo Lazzarito '17	🍷🍷	8
● Barolo Paiagallo '19	🍷🍷	8
● Barolo Ris. '13	🍷🍷	8

Profumo di casa
Sfumature di generazioni
Sapore di famiglia

LUISA

EDDI, MICHELE
E DAVIDE
LUISA

Pinot Nero
ITALIA

CAMPAGNA FINANZIATA AI SENSI DEL REG.
UE N. 2021/2115
CAMPAIGN FINANCED ACCORDING TO EU
REG. N. 2021/2115

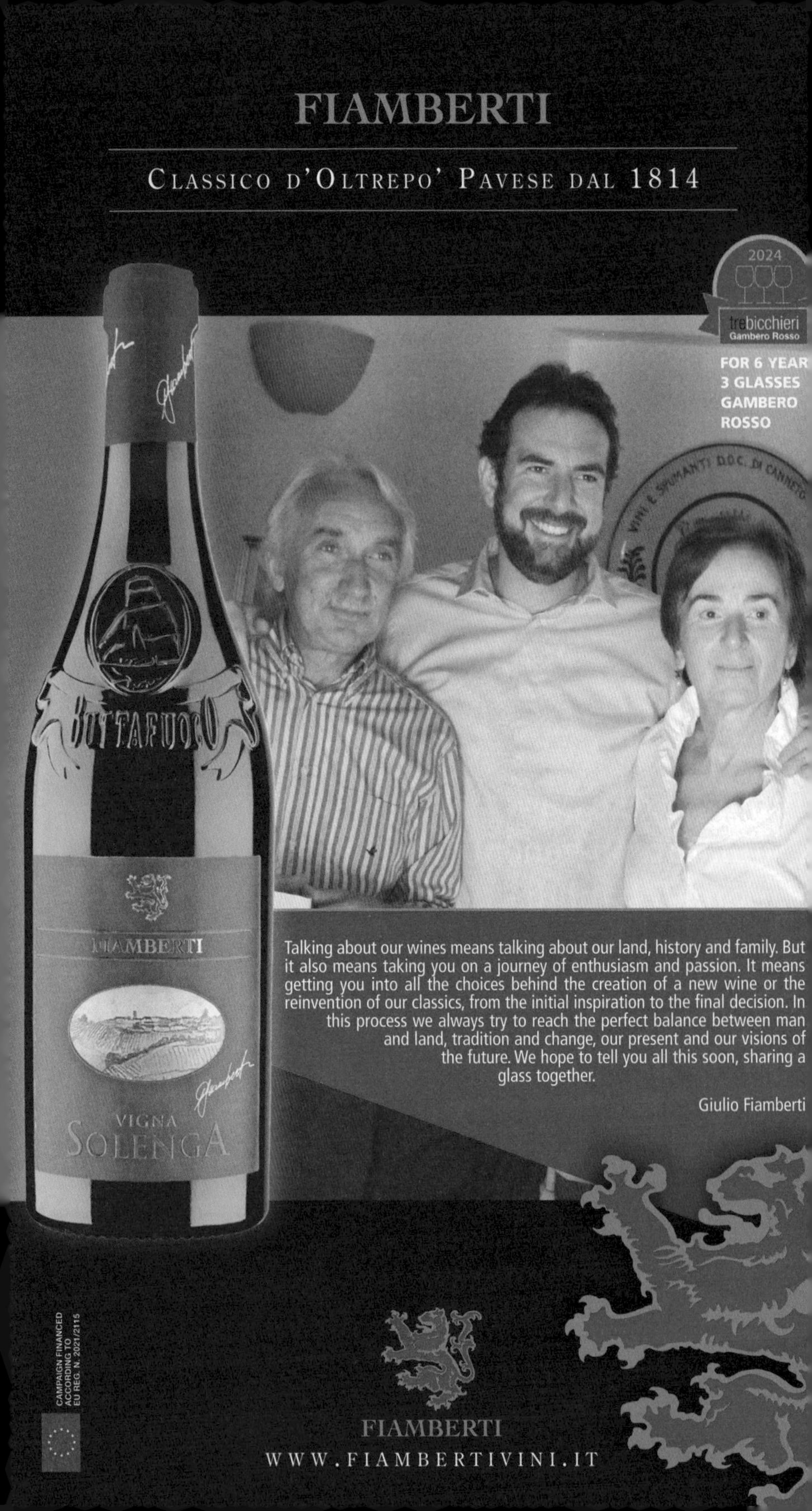

FIAMBERTI

CLASSICO D'OLTREPO' PAVESE DAL 1814

Talking about our wines means talking about our land, history and family. But it also means taking you on a journey of enthusiasm and passion. It means getting you into all the choices behind the creation of a new wine or the reinvention of our classics, from the initial inspiration to the final decision. In this process we always try to reach the perfect balance between man and land, tradition and change, our present and our visions of the future. We hope to tell you all this soon, sharing a glass together.

Giulio Fiamberti

CAMPAIGN FINANCED
ACCORDING TO
EU REG. N. 2021/2115

FIAMBERTI

WWW.FIAMBERTIVINI.IT

THE BEST AND SAFEST WAY FOR INDIVIDUALS TO SHIP WINE TO THEIR HOME

WE SHIP YOUR WINE WORLWIDE

Discover our premium wine shipping service, dedicated to privite customers, that brings your favorite wines directly from renowned producers to your doorstep. Our global network ensures safe and reliable delivery, maintaining the highest standards of care and quality. Whether you're a collector or a casual enthusiast, enjoy the convenience of having exquisite wines from Italian producers delivered straight to your home. Trust IWS for the ultimate wine shipping experience.

SCAN THE QR CODE AND
SHIP YOUR WINE WITH IWS

IWS SRL - LA MORRA (CN) - ITALY - WWW.LOGISTICAIWS.COM - MAIL@LOGISTICAIWS.COM

La Casaccia

via D. Barbano, 10
15034 Cella Monte [AL]
☎ +39 0142489986
🌐 www.lacasaccia.biz

CELLAR SALES
PRE-BOOKED VISITS
ANNUAL PRODUCTION 25,000 bottles
HECTARES UNDER VINE 6.70
VITICULTURE METHOD Certified Organic

Elena and Giovanni's passion for farming has been a constant throughout their lives, from their agricultural studies to their decision, at 40, to move to Cella Monte and continue their grandparents' work at Casaccia. Today, alongside Margherita and Marcello, they manage the winery in harmony with nature, employing organic farming practices, while drawing on renewable energy and rainwater collection. Their project is rounded out by a charming agriturismo that offers overnight stays. The wines presented at our tasting tables this year were a bit less convincing than in the past. However, the Barbera del Monferrato Giuanìn '22 performed well, offering notes of fruit and pepper, with a warm and mouthfilling palate. On the other hand, the Barbera del Monferrato Bricco dei Boschi '19 reveals distant fruit beneath its toasty and spicy notes. On the palate, it gets back some pulp so as to balance its abundant texture.

Cascina Barisél

reg. San Giovanni, 30
14053 Canelli [AT]
☎ +39 3394165913
🌐 www.barisel.it

CELLAR SALES
PRE-BOOKED VISITS
ANNUAL PRODUCTION 35,000 bottles
HECTARES UNDER VINE 4.50
SUSTAINABLE WINERY

For some 40 years, the Penna family has been dedicated to developing and promoting the splendid territory of Canelli and its steep, calcareous soils, which confer freshness and sapidity to the wines. They focus on local grape varieties, starting with moscato, dolcetto, barbera, and favorita, but also cultivate chardonnay and pinot nero for Metodo Classico sparklers. An artisanal production approach and family management do the rest. The delightful Barbera d'Asti Barisel '23 stands out with its cherry aromas and whiffs of forest floor, alongside a rich and fleshy palate that boasts great freshness and a very long finish. The Nizza Vigna dei Pilati Riserva '20 is also excellent—juicy and pleasant, with nice energy and persistence in its red berry and spicy notes. The well-crafted Barbera d'Asti Superiore Listoria '22 showcases fine stuffing, along with tones of black stone fruit and Mediterranean scrub. The Nizza La Cappelletta '21, meanwhile, offers a balsamic, fruity profile and a notable body.

● Barbera del M.to Giuanìn '22	🍷🍷 2*
● Dulcinea	🍷🍷 2*
● M.to Freisa Monfiorenza '22	🍷🍷 3
○ Piemonte Chardonnay Charnò '23	🍷🍷 3
● Barbera del M.to Bricco dei Boschi '19	🍷 3
● Grignolino del M.to Casalese Ernesto '16	🍷 5
● Barbera del M.to Bricco dei Boschi '18	🍷🍷 3
● Barbera del M.to Calichè '18	🍷🍷 3
● Barbera del M.to Calichè '17	🍷🍷 3*
● Barbera del M.to Giuanìn '20	🍷🍷 3*
● Grignolino del M.to Casalese Poggeto '22	🍷🍷 3*
● Grignolino del M.to Casalese Poggeto '21	🍷🍷 3*
○ La Casaccia Brut M.Cl. '16	🍷🍷 4
● M.to Freisa Monfiorenza '20	🍷🍷 3
○ Piemonte Chardonnay Charnò '22	🍷🍷 3

● Barbera d'Asti '23	🍷🍷 3*
● Nizza V. dei Pilati Ris. '20	🍷🍷 6
● Barbera d'Asti Sup. Listoria '22	🍷🍷 3
● Nizza La Cappelletta '21	🍷🍷 5
○ Canelli '23	🍷 2
● Nizza La Cappelletta '20	🍷🍷🍷 5
● Barbera d'Asti '22	🍷🍷 3
● Barbera d'Asti '21	🍷🍷 2*
● Barbera d'Asti Sup. Listoria '21	🍷🍷 3
● Barbera d'Asti Sup. Listoria '20	🍷🍷 3*
○ Moscato d'Asti Canelli '22	🍷🍷 2*
● Nizza La Cappelletta '18	🍷🍷 3*
● Nizza V. dei Pilati Ris. '19	🍷🍷 6
● Nizza V. dei Pilati Ris. '16	🍷🍷 6

Cascina Bongiovanni

loc. Uccellaccio
via Alba Barolo, 3
12060 Castiglione Falletto [CN]
(+39 0173262184
 cascinabongiovanni.it

CELLAR SALES
PRE-BOOKED VISITS
ACCOMMODATION
ANNUAL PRODUCTION 50,000 bottles
HECTARES UNDER VINE 7.20
SUSTAINABLE WINERY

Cascina Bongiovanni, which takes its name from the family who founded the winery in 1950, is led by Davide Mozzone. Davide avails himself of vineyards spread out across the municipalities of Castiglione Falletto, Serralunga, Diano, Roddino, and Monforte, cultivating the area's classic grapes, from nebbiolo to arneis, dolcetto and barbera, with Barolo taking center stage. Here it's crafted in a straightforward, convincing style. The Barolo Pernanno '20 finds its strength in its focused and fresh aromas of fruit, enriched with spicy and balsamic touches. In the mouth, the palate is sapid, lively, and racy, with dynamic development and an energetic finish. The Langhe Arneis '23 offers scents of white flowers and citrus, with a rich and sapid palate that flows with easy drinkability. The well-crafted Barolo '20 opens on red fruit and spice aromas, leading to a pleasant palate with nicely resolved tannins and good acidic fragrance.

● Barolo Pernanno '20	🍷🍷 7
● Barolo '20	🍷🍷 6
○ Langhe Arneis '23	🍷🍷 3
● Barolo Pernanno '01	🍷🍷🍷 6
● Barolo '19	🍷🍷 6
● Barolo '13	🍷🍷 6
● Barolo Pernanno '18	🍷🍷 7
● Barolo Pernanno '17	🍷🍷 7
● Barolo Pernanno '16	🍷🍷 7
● Barolo Pernanno '14	🍷🍷 7
● Barolo Pernanno '13	🍷🍷 7
● Barolo Pernanno '12	🍷🍷 7
● Barolo Pernanno '11	🍷🍷 6
● Barolo Ris. '13	🍷🍷 8
● Dolcetto di Diano d'Alba '15	🍷🍷 3*
● Langhe Rosso Faletto '17	🍷🍷 4

★Cascina Ca' Rossa

loc. Cascina Ca' Rossa, 56
12043 Canale [CN]
(+39 017398348
 www.cascinacarossa.com

CELLAR SALES
PRE-BOOKED VISITS
ANNUAL PRODUCTION 90,000 bottles
HECTARES UNDER VINE 16.00
VITICULTURE METHOD Certified Organic

Angelo Ferrio's winery offers some of the most representative and expressive wines in the Roero area, characterized by their typicity, charm, tension, and pronounced elegance. The vineyards are located in prestigious crus, from Mompissano to Valmaggiore, and Le Coste. The grape varieties cultivated include those classic to the left bank of the Tanaro River, from nebbiolo to arneis and barbera. The splendid Roero Mompissano Riserva '21 sees red berry notes combine with aromatic herbs and violet, as well as smoky undertones. Its palate is fresh, juicy, and sapid, with elegant tannins and a long finish. The Roero Le Coste Riserva '22, an Arneis, is also excellent—aromas of white fruit, jasmine and almond make for a wine of pleasant freshness. The rest of the range is well-crafted, particularly the Roero Le Coste Riserva '21, with its black forest fruit tones and notable structure, and the Roero Valmaggiore Audinaggio '22, which features notes of blood orange, anise, and turmeric, showing finesse and good persistence on the palate.

● Roero Mompissano Ris. '21	🍷🍷🍷 5
● Roero Le Coste Ris. '22	🍷🍷 7
● Barbera d'Alba Mulassa '22	🍷🍷 5
○ Roero Arneis Merica '23	🍷🍷 3
● Roero Le Coste Ris. '21	🍷🍷 7
● Roero Valmaggiore V. Audinaggio '22	🍷🍷 5
● Roero Le Coste '19	🍷🍷🍷 7
● Roero Le Coste Ris. '20	🍷🍷🍷 7
● Roero Mompissano Ris. '18	🍷🍷🍷 5
● Roero Mompissano Ris. '17	🍷🍷🍷 5
● Roero Mompissano Ris. '13	🍷🍷🍷 5
● Roero Mompissano Ris. '12	🍷🍷🍷 5
● Roero Mompissano Ris. '10	🍷🍷🍷 5
● Roero Mompissano Ris. '07	🍷🍷🍷 6
● Roero Valmaggiore V. Audinaggio '17	🍷🍷🍷 5
● Roero Valmaggiore V. Audinaggio '16	🍷🍷🍷 5
● Roero Valmaggiore V. Audinaggio '15	🍷🍷🍷 5

Cascina Chicco

via Valentino, 14
12043 Canale [CN]
☎ +39 0173979411
✉ www.cascinachicco.com

CELLAR SALES
PRE-BOOKED VISITS
ANNUAL PRODUCTION 435,000 bottles
HECTARES UNDER VINE 50.00

The Faccenda family's winery covers a large area, from historic Roero estates in Canale, Vezza d'Alba, Castellinaldo, and Castagnito, planted with traditional local grapes like arneis, barbera, and nebbiolo, to an eight-hectare plot in Monforte d'Alba dedicated to Barolo production. The wines offered are technically well-crafted, attentive to the expression of their various origins. The brilliant Roero Arneis Renesio Incisa Riserva '22 summons aromas of Mediterranean scrub, plum, and cinnamon, with a rich, sapid, and long-lasting palate. The Nebbiolo d'Alba Mompissano '22 is particularly impressive, with its spicy and black fruit scents leading to an elegant yet structured and clear palate, with fine tannins. The Cuvée Zero Brut '20 is floral, with white fruit notes giving way to a soft and pleasant palate. The Barolo Ginestra Riserva '18 is sapid and rich, showing fine elegance, while the Roero Valmaggiore Riserva '21 features black fruit and cardamom aromas before a persistent, long, and energetic palate.

● Nebbiolo d'Alba Mompissano '22	♟♟♟ 4*
○ Roero Arneis Renesio Incisa Ris. '22	♟♟ 5
● Barbaresco Noce Grande '21	♟♟ 5
● Barbera d'Alba Bric Loira '22	♟♟ 5
● Barolo Ginestra Ris. '18	♟♟ 8
● Barolo Rocche di Castelletto '20	♟♟ 6
⊙ Cuvée Dosaggio Zero M. Cl. Rosé '20	♟♟ 5
○ Cuvée Zero Brut M. Cl. '20	♟♟ 5
○ Extra Brut Dosage Zero Cuvée Zero '19	♟♟ 5
⊙ Extra Brut Dosage Zero Cuvée Zero Rosé '20	♟♟ 5
○ Roero Arneis Anterisio '23	♟♟ 3
● Roero Valmaggiore Ris. '21	♟♟ 5
● Barolo Ginestra Ris. '11	♟♟♟ 8
● Barolo Rocche di Castelletto '16	♟♟♟ 5
● Roero Valmaggiore Ris. '12	♟♟♟ 4*

Cascina Corte

fraz. San Luigi
b.ta Valdiberti, 33
12063 Dogliani [CN]
☎ +39 0173743539
✉ www.cascinacorte.it

CELLAR SALES
PRE-BOOKED VISITS
ACCOMMODATION
ANNUAL PRODUCTION 30,000 bottles
HECTARES UNDER VINE 5.00
VITICULTURE METHOD Certified Organic
SUSTAINABLE WINERY

Based in San Luigi, in Dogliani and Monforte, Cascina Corte is managed by Sandro Barosi and his wife Amalia. The couple restructured the estate, aiming to preserve the old vines, cultivated with dolcetto, nebbiolo, and barbera, dating back to the immediate post-war period. In 2015, traditional winemaking methods were complemented by the introduction of amphorae, resulting in more immediately expressive wines. Once again, Sandro Barosi presents a highly convincing lineup, with wines rich in personality. The Dogliani Superiore Pirochetta Amphorae '21 reveals vibrant and elegant aromas of blackberries, with subtle hints of petrichor adding complexity. On the palate, it offers commendable structure, brightened by good acidity and an unexpected saline vein. The first vintage of the Barolo Amalia '20 bursts with intense red berry aromas, accompanied by hints of incense and soot, while the palate reveals mellow tannins, offering a silky sensation.

● Dogliani Sup. Pirochetta Amphorae '21	♟♟ 5
● Barolo Amalia '19	♟♟ 8
○ Langhe Nascetta '23	♟♟ 3
○ Langhe Riesling '23	♟♟ 3
● Langhe Nebbiolo Amphorae '21	♟ 4
● Dogliani San Luigi '22	♟♟ 3*
● Dogliani San Luigi '21	♟♟ 3
● Dogliani Sup. Pirochetta '21	♟♟ 3
● Dogliani Sup. Pirochetta Amphorae '20	♟♟ 4
● Langhe Barbera '21	♟♟ 3
● Langhe Freisa '21	♟♟ 4
○ Langhe Nascetta '22	♟♟ 3*
● Langhe Nebbiolo '21	♟♟ 4
● Langhe Nebbiolo '20	♟♟ 4
● Langhe Nebbiolo Amphorae '20	♟♟ 4
⊙ Matilde	♟♟ 3

Cascina delle Rose

fraz. Tre Stelle
s.da Rio Sordo, 58
12050 Barbaresco [CN]
(☎) +39 0173638292
⊕ www.cascinadellerose.it

CELLAR SALES
PRE-BOOKED VISITS
ACCOMMODATION
ANNUAL PRODUCTION 32,000 bottles
HECTARES UNDER VINE 5.50
VITICULTURE METHOD Certified Organic

Giovanna Rizzolio and Italo Sorbino, today
accompanied by their sons Riccardo and Davide,
have been running their winery since 1974.
Based in the Rio Sordo valley in Barbaresco, in
the town of Tre Stelle, the vineyards are
cultivated organically. Naturally, Barbaresco takes
center stage. Here it's made with grapes from
the three estate crus: Tre Stelle, Rio Sordo, and
Marcorino. Their portfolio also includes
Dolcetto and Barbera d'Alba. The Barbaresco
Marcorino '21 possesses a generous and vibrant
fruit-driven bouquet, with hints of leather
meeting licorice and tobacco. Its tannic structure
is evenly proportioned, and the palate is rich and
energetic, closing with a sapid, persistent finish.
The Barbaresco Rio Sordo '21 is also good, fresh
and fruity on the nose, with a citrus-forward and
assertive palate. The Barbera d'Alba Superiore
Vigna Elena '20 proves highly enjoyable.

Cascina Faletta

reg. Mandoletta, 81
15033 Casale Monferrato [AL]
(☎) +39 0142670068
⊕ www.faletta.it

CELLAR SALES
PRE-BOOKED VISITS
ACCOMMODATION AND RESTAURANT SERVICE
ANNUAL PRODUCTION 25,000 bottles
HECTARES UNDER VINE 10.50
VITICULTURE METHOD Certified Organic
SUSTAINABLE WINERY

A historic farmhouse, restored to its former
glory in 2014 by Elena Novarino and Giovanni
Rosso with their son Lorenzo, this family-run
estate focuses on promoting the local terroir
through a hospitality experience reminiscent of
a French Relais Chateaux. The cellar remains
rooted in the region's winemaking traditions, but
international varieties such as syrah, chardonnay,
and pinot noir are also featured. The estate's
offerings include a well-regarded restaurant and
eight meticulously maintained guest rooms. The
Barbera del Monferrato Braja '21 stands out for
its freshness and finesse, offering fresh fruit
aromas reminiscent of crunchy red cherries. The
palate has good structure and acidity, with a long
and refreshing finish. The Piemonte Chardonnay
Myricae '22 offers great pleasure, with its notes
of pear and apple followed by wafts of acacia
flower towards the end. The palate is rich and
structured, with a touch of elegance, and the
finish reveals a slight hint of almond.

● Barbaresco Marcorino '21	♛♛ 8
● Barbaresco Rio Sordo '21	♛♛ 8
● Barbaresco Tre Stelle '21	♛♛ 8
● Langhe Nebbiolo '23	♛♛ 5
○ Dolcetto d'Alba A Elizabeth '23	♛ 4
● Barbaresco Rio Sordo '18	♛♛♛ 7
● Barbaresco Rio Sordo '16	♛♛♛ 7
● Barbaresco Rio Sordo '17	♛♛ 7
● Barbaresco Rio Sordo '15	♛♛ 5
● Barbaresco Tre Stelle '20	♛♛ 8
● Barbaresco Tre Stelle '19	♛♛ 7
● Barbaresco Tre Stelle '18	♛♛ 7
● Barbaresco Tre Stelle '17	♛♛ 7
● Barbaresco Tre Stelle '15	♛♛ 5
● Langhe Nebbiolo '16	♛♛ 4

● Barbera del M.to Braja '21	♛♛ 4
○ Piemonte Chardonnay Myricae '22	♛♛ 4
○ Piemonte Chardonnay Primo Bianco '21	♛♛ 3
● Piemonte Pinot Nero 3 Fucili '22	♛♛ 4
● Vino Rosso Rosso di Rosso	♛♛ 3
○ Crucànt Brut	♛ 3
● Grignolino del M.to Casalese Baudolino '22	♛ 4
● Grignolino del M.to Casalese Indelebile '19	♛ 5
● Barbera del M.to Sup. La Pignola '20	♛♛ 4
● Barbera del Monferrato Braja '16	♛♛ 3
○ M.to Bianco Primo Grigio '21	♛♛ 3*
● M.to Rosso di Rosso '18	♛♛ 3
○ Piemonte Chardonnay Myricae '21	♛♛ 4
● Piemonte Pinot Nero 3 Fucili '19	♛♛ 4
○ Piemonte Pinot Nero Brut M. Cl. Marchesa Virginia '14	♛♛ 4

Cascina Fonda

via Spessa, 29
12052 Mango [CN]
(☎) +39 0173677877
☞ www.cascinafonda.com

CELLAR SALES
PRE-BOOKED VISITS
ACCOMMODATION
ANNUAL PRODUCTION 110,000 bottles
HECTARES UNDER VINE 12.00

Cascina Fonda traces its origins to the early 1960s, but it wasn't until 1988 that brothers Massimo and Marco Barbero began bottling wines from their family's estate. In 2002, they expanded by building a new winery. Their vineyards are located in two towns: Mango, where moscato dominates, and Neive, where nebbiolo reigns. Their wines offer a modern take while staying true to the region's character. The Canelli Moscato Bel Fiore '23 is truly brilliant, emanating enticing aromas of candied orange peel and panettone, leading to a palate of great richness and length, nicely supported by vibrant acidity. The rest of the range is well-crafted, particularly the Alta Langa Extra Brut '19, which offers plum and bread crust aromas and a balanced, pervasive palate, as well as the classic Moscato d'Asti Bel Piano '23, a vibrant wine, rich with notes of pear, peach, and sage, showing great character thanks to its acidity, which balances the wine's sweet vein.

○ Canelli Moscato Bel Fiore '23	♥♥ 3*
○ Alta Langa Blanc de Blancs Extra Brut '20	♥♥ 5
○ Alta Langa Extra Brut '19	♥♥ 5
○ Asti Bel Piasì '20	♥♥ 2*
● Barbaresco '21	♥♥ 5
○ Moscato d'Asti Bel Piano '23	♥♥ 3
● Piemonte Brachetto Bel Roseto '23	♥♥ 3
○ Asti Spumante Bel Piasì '22	♀♀ 2*
○ Asti Spumante Bel Piasì '21	♀♀ 2*
○ Moscato d'Asti Bel Piano '22	♀♀ 3
○ Moscato d'Asti Bel Piano '21	♀♀ 3
○ Moscato d'Asti Canelli '21	♀♀ 2*

Cascina Fontana

loc. Perno
v.lo della Chiesa, 2
12065 Monforte d'Alba [CN]
(☎) +39 0173789005
☞ www.cascinafontana.com

PRE-BOOKED VISITS
ANNUAL PRODUCTION 30,000 bottles
HECTARES UNDER VINE 5.50
SUSTAINABLE WINERY

Mario Fontana founded his winery in 1994, in Monforte d'Alba (the most important plots are located in Castiglione Falletto, with the crus Mariondino, Villero, and Giachini), respecting tradition while simultaneously expressing his unique vision. The result is a fascinating and decidedly personal range of wines, capable of capturing the truest nuances of the different vintages. The extraordinary Barolo del Comune di Castiglione Falletto '19 opens on clear red fruit and licorice aromas, which give way to notes of tobacco and violet petals. The palate displays disarming balance, with elegant tannins and a very long finish. The Barolo '19 also shows superb typicity, with its dark fruit and tobacco aromas, and a serious, austere palate that promises a radiant future. Such creations are the work of a true artisan, and so we've decided to name Mario Fontana our Winegrower of the Year. Bravo!

● Barolo del Comune di Castiglione Falletto '19	♥♥♥ 8
● Barolo '19	♥♥ 7
● Barolo '18	♀♀♀ 7
● Barolo '12	♀♀♀ 6
● Barolo '10	♀♀♀ 7
● Barolo del Comune di Castiglione Falletto V.V. '15	♀♀♀ 7
● Barolo '17	♀♀ 7
● Barolo '15	♀♀ 6
● Barolo '13	♀♀ 6
● Barolo '11	♀♀ 6
● Barolo '09	♀♀ 7
● Barolo del Comune di Castiglione Falletto '17	♀♀ 8
● Barolo del Comune di Castiglione Falletto '16	♀♀ 8

PIEDMONT

101

Cascina Gilli

fraz. Nevissano, 36
14022 Castelnuovo Don Bosco [AT]
☎ +39 0119876984
✉ www.cascinagilli.it

CELLAR SALES
PRE-BOOKED VISITS
ANNUAL PRODUCTION 100,000 bottles
HECTARES UNDER VINE 10.00
SUSTAINABLE WINERY

In Castelnuovo Don Bosco, in Monferrato, the terroir is rich in clay marl that not only gives body and suppleness to the wines but is also perfect for a long-forgotten local grape variety, malvasia di Schierano. Paolo Vergnano, son of the founder Gianni, continues the path of safeguarding the value of classic local varieties, like malvasia, freisa, barbera, bonarda, and nebbiolo, drawing on vineyards planted in the best soils. At the top we find the Barbera d'Asti Le More '22, with its aromas of black cherry and rain-soaked earth, and a palate that plays on fruit—fresh with a juicy, pleasant finish. The Freisa d'Asti Il Forno '22 is vibrant in its notes of spices and wild black fruits, powerful, with a close-knit tannic structure and a long, energetic finish. The Albugnano Superiore Neuv '21 proves well-crafted, offering fine fruit on the nose and an austere yet harmonious palate. The soft and enjoyable Piemonte Chardonnay Rafé '23 plays on tones of banana and white peach. The Malvasia di Castelnuovo Don Bosco '23 stands out for its typicity and immediate appeal.

● Barbera d'Asti Le More '22	♟♟ 3*
● Freisa d'Asti Il Forno '22	♟♟ 3*
● Albugnano Sup. Neuv '21	♟♟ 5
● Malvasia di Castelnuovo Don Bosco '23	♟♟ 3
○ Piemonte Chardonnay Rafé '23	♟♟ 3
● Albugnano Sup. Notturno '21	♟♟ 4
● Barbera d'Asti Le More '21	♟♟ 3
● Barbera d'Asti Sup. Dedica '20	♟♟ 4
● Freisa d'Asti Il Forno '20	♟♟ 3
● Freisa d'Asti Il Forno '18	♟♟ 2*
● Malvasia di Castelnuovo Don Bosco '22	♟♟ 3
● Malvasia di Castelnuovo Don Bosco '21	♟♟ 2*
● Malvasia di Castelnuovo Don Bosco '20	♟♟ 2*

Cascina Guido Berta

loc. Saline, 63
14050 San Marzano Oliveto [AT]
☎ +39 0141856731
✉ www.cascinaguidoberta.com

CELLAR SALES
PRE-BOOKED VISITS
ANNUAL PRODUCTION 68,000 bottles
HECTARES UNDER VINE 20.00

The estate's vineyards are primarily situated in San Marzano Oliveto, in the small village of Saline. The soils here are rich in aquifers, thanks to the clay, but also traversed by calcareous veins that lend freshness to the wines. For over a quarter of a century, Guido Berta has managed the family farm, focusing on local grape varieties, especially barbera, but also chardonnay and pinot nero. This year, the highlight of the winery's range is the Nizza '21, which showcases fresh red forest fruits, cinchona, and underbrush on the nose, with a well-structured, juicy palate that exhibits remarkable length and persistence. The well-crafted Moscato d'Asti '23 plays on signature aromas of gingerbread, cinnamon, and candied orange, while the palate is classic, offering delicate sweetness, a pervasive freshness, and a long finish. The Piemonte Chardonnay Le Rondini '22 stands out for its vibrant vegetal tones, nice stuffing and tension.

● Nizza '21	♟♟ 5
○ Moscato d'Asti '23	♟♟ 3
○ Piemonte Chardonnay Le Rondini '22	♟♟ 4
● Barbera d'Asti '22	♟ 3
● Barbera d'Asti '19	♟♟ 3
● Barbera d'Asti Sup. '18	♟♟ 4
○ Moscato d'Asti '22	♟♟ 3*
○ Moscato d'Asti '21	♟♟ 3
○ Moscato d'Asti '20	♟♟ 3
● Nizza '20	♟♟ 5
● Nizza '19	♟♟ 5
● Nizza Canto di Luna '18	♟♟ 5
● Nizza Canto di Luna Ris. '19	♟♟ 5
○ Piemonte Chardonnay '20	♟♟ 4
○ Piemonte Chardonnay Le Rondini '20	♟♟ 4
● Piemonte Pinot Nero '20	♟♟ 4

★★Cascina La Barbatella

s.da Annunziata, 55
14049 Nizza Monferrato [AT]
📞 +39 0141701434
🖥 labarbatella.com

CELLAR SALES
PRE-BOOKED VISITS
ANNUAL PRODUCTION 25,000 bottles
HECTARES UNDER VINE 4.00

For nearly 15 years, Lorenzo and Cinzia Perego have passionately and attentively managed this farm, founded in 1982 by Angelo Sonvico. Drawing on just a few hectares of vineyards, the winery produces complex wines with great character, starting with its flagship barbera-based wines. Other grape varieties are also present, from cabernet sauvignon, used in blends, to sauvignon, chardonnay and pinot nero (the latter two for the estate's Metodo Classico). The Nizza La Vigna dell'Angelo '21 features scents of Mediterranean scrub, cinnamon, and cherry, followed by a juicy palate centered on fruit, balanced by tannins. Other impressive wines include the Monferrato Rosso Ruanera '22, with its vibrant aromas of blackcurrant and sweet spices, and a powerful, fleshy palate that's both pleasant and harmonious, and the Monferrato Rosso Sonvico '19, which showcases notes of plum, cocoa, and spices. Here the palate aptly balances the tannins of cabernet and the richness of barbera, leading to a long, spice-laden finish.

● M.to Rosso Ruanera '22	🍷🍷 3*
● M.to Rosso Sonvico '19	🍷🍷 6
● Nizza La V. dell'Angelo '21	🍷🍷 5
○ M.to Bianco Noè '22	🍷🍷 3
● Nizza La V. dell'Angelo Ris. '20	🍷🍷 5
○ Piemonte Chardonnay Non È '22	🍷🍷 3
● Barbera d'Asti Sup. Nizza V. dell'Angelo '11	🍷🍷🍷 5
● Barbera d'Asti Sup. Nizza V. dell'Angelo '07	🍷🍷🍷 5
● M.to Rosso Sonvico '09	🍷🍷🍷 6
● M.to Rosso Sonvico '06	🍷🍷🍷 5
● M.to Rosso Sonvico '04	🍷🍷🍷 5
● Nizza La V. dell'Angelo '17	🍷🍷🍷 5
● Nizza La V. dell'Angelo '14	🍷🍷🍷 5

Cascina Lanzarotti

fraz. Sant'Anna - Ferreri, 18
12040 Monteu Roero [CN]
📞 +39 0173978127
🖥 www.cascinalanzarotti.it

ANNUAL PRODUCTION 70,000 bottles
HECTARES UNDER VINE 10.00

Established in the late 19th century as a fully integrated farm, Cascina Lanzarotti originally produced fruit, corn, fodder, and wine, as well as raising livestock. The winery began bottling its own wines in the early 1990s, and 20 years ago, the decision was made to focus solely on winemaking. A complete renovation of the cellar in 2020 has since led to a marked improvement in quality. The Roero Arneis '23 is excellent, conjuring up signature aromas of white currant, almond, and jasmine, while presenting a sapid, fresh, and fluid palate. The Roero Bin Fait '21 follows with notes of aromatic herbs and plum on the nose, leading to a fruit-forward, consistent palate with a juicy and pleasant finish. The Roero Arneis Sant'Anna Sette Gennaio Riserva '18 opts for spicy tones with notes of white fruit on the nose, and a palate marked by grittiness and sapidity. The Roero Arneis Brut Soeli' '20, a Metodo Classico, features hints of sweet citrus and pastry, with a fine, pleasant, and lengthy finish.

○ Roero Arneis '23	🍷🍷 3*
● Roero Bin Fait '21	🍷🍷 5
○ Roero Arneis Brut Soeli' '20	🍷🍷 5
○ Roero Arneis Sant'Anna Sette Gennaio Ris. '18	🍷🍷 5
● Langhe Nebbiolo Arbuté '22	🍷 4
○ Roero Arneis Arlass Ris. '22	🍷 4
● Barbera d'Alba Sup. Püjina '21	🍷🍷 3
● Barbera d'Alba Sup. Püjina '18	🍷🍷 3
● Roero '18	🍷🍷 3
○ Roero Arneis Sant'Anna Ris. '20	🍷🍷 2*
● Roero Bin Fait '19	🍷🍷 3
● Roero Carlinöt Ris. '17	🍷🍷 4
● Roero Sru Carlinöt Ris. '19	🍷🍷 4
● Roero Sru Carlinöt Ris. '18	🍷🍷 4

Cascina Luisin

s.da Rabajà, 34
12050 Barbaresco [CN]
+39 0173635154
cascinaluisin@gmail.com

Cascina Morassino

s.da Bernino, 10
12050 Barbaresco [CN]
+39 3471210223
morassino@gmail.com

PRE-BOOKED VISITS
ANNUAL PRODUCTION 30,000 bottles
HECTARES UNDER VINE 8.00

CELLAR SALES
PRE-BOOKED VISITS
ANNUAL PRODUCTION 20,000 bottles
HECTARES UNDER VINE 4.50
SUSTAINABLE WINERY

Founded in 1913 by Luigi Minuto, great-grandfather of the winery's current owner Roberto, Cascina Luisin draws on some of Barbaresco's most import crus, names such as Asili, Rabajà, and Basarini. The Minuto family champions a discreet style, characterized by long macerations and patient aging, delivering delicate wines that avoid extractive shortcuts and superficial embellishments. The Barbaresco Paolin Vecchie Viti '21 intrigues with its multifaceted aromatic profile, combining red fruit and finely spiced touches. In the mouth, it delivers a fleshy structure and a dynamic tannic weave, making for a vibrant, fragrant palate with an impressively long finish. The Barbaresco Asili Vecchie Viti '21 is also well-crafted, conjuring clear aromas and a persistent, fresh, and juicy palate. The Barbera d'Alba Axilium '22 is marked by blackberry and underbrush aromas, with a supple and flavorful palate.

Roberto Bianco, son of the founder Mauro, now runs Cascina Morassino, a winery with a strong focus on Barbaresco. The Ovello Cru dominates production, reflecting its importance within the estate's total vineyard area, though they also draw on a small plot in the Cottà Cru of Neive. While nebbiolo is the star, the winery's Merlot stands out as a unique outlier among the vineyards. The Barbaresco Ovello '21 showcases aromas of tobacco and raspberry, with touches of licorice over a balsamic background. In the mouth, it stands out for its tannic drive, complemented by full, fleshy fruit, finishing with length and persistence. The Barbaresco Morassino '21 shows more mature tones, with ripe fruit on the nose, accented by hints of tobacco and licorice, and toasty notes. On the palate, it's slender but evenly proportioned.

● Barbaresco Asili V.V. '21	♟♟ 8
● Barbaresco Paolin V.V. '21	♟♟ 7
● Barbaresco Rabajà '21	♟♟ 7
● Barbaresco Rabajà-Bas '21	♟♟ 7
● Barbaresco Ris. '19	♟♟ 8
● Barbera d'Alba Axilium '22	♟♟ 5
● Langhe Nebbiolo Maggiur '22	♟♟ 5
● Barbera d'Alba Maggiur '22	♟ 4
● Dolcetto d'Alba Trifula '23	♟ 3
○ Roero Arneis Ave '23	♟ 3
● Barbaresco Asili '19	♟♟♟ 7
● Barbera d'Alba Asili '00	♟♟♟ 5
● Barbera d'Alba Asili '99	♟♟♟ 5
● Barbaresco Basarin '20	♟♟ 8
● Barbaresco Paolin V.V. '20	♟♟ 6
● Barbaresco Rabajà V.V. '20	♟♟ 6

● Barbaresco Ovello '21	♟♟ 7
● Barbaresco Morassino '21	♟♟ 6
● Barbaresco Morassino '09	♟♟♟ 5
● Barbaresco Ovello '14	♟♟♟ 6
● Barbaresco Morassino '20	♟♟ 6
● Barbaresco Morassino '19	♟♟ 5
● Barbaresco Morassino '18	♟♟ 5
● Barbaresco Morassino '17	♟♟ 5
● Barbaresco Morassino '16	♟♟ 5
● Barbaresco Morassino '15	♟♟ 5
● Barbaresco Morassino '14	♟♟ 5
● Barbaresco Ovello '20	♟♟ 7
● Barbaresco Ovello '19	♟♟ 6
● Barbaresco Ovello '18	♟♟ 6
● Barbaresco Ovello '16	♟♟ 6
● Barbaresco Ovello '15	♟♟ 6

PIEDMONT

Cascina Salicetti

via Cascina Salicetti, 2
15050 Montegioco [AL]
☏ +39 0131875192
✉ www.cascinasalicetti.it

CELLAR SALES
PRE-BOOKED VISITS
ANNUAL PRODUCTION 25,000 bottles
HECTARES UNDER VINE 16.00

Pietro Franzosi leaves behind an important legacy, a 30-year effort aimed at growing and honing the family's vineyards. It's a heritage that winemaker Anselmo has stewarded with passion and attention, bringing out the quality and typicity of the territory. The winery, located atop a hill, was named 2019's "Unesco slope", an award given to those vintners who safeguard picturesque vineyards on high. The Ombra di Luna '22 is a fresh and approachable expression of timorasso, with aromas of pear, peach, and a hint of minerality. The palate is sapid, dynamic, and expressive, ending with a juicy and fruity finish. The Cortese Montarlino '23 reveals vibrant notes of apple and yellow flowers on the nose, followed by a fine, balanced palate with a flavorful and persistent finish.

Cascina Val del Prete

s.da Santuario, 2
12040 Priocca [CN]
☏ +39 0173616534
✉ www.valdelprete.com

CELLAR SALES
PRE-BOOKED VISITS
ANNUAL PRODUCTION 55,000 bottles
HECTARES UNDER VINE 10.00
VITICULTURE METHOD Certified Organic

Giovanni Roagna and Lodovica Tedeschi continue the path set out 20 years ago by Mario Roagna. Their natural approach to viticulture involves exclusively manual work in the vineyard and minimal intervention in the cellar. The estate's vineyards mostly unfold around the cellar, where local varieties—arneis, barbera, and nebbiolo—are cultivated in pursuit of an authentic expression of the terroir. The 2020 is perhaps the best version yet of the Roero Vigna di Lino yet tasted. The nose is rich with notes of violet, truffle, white pepper, and orange peel, while the palate proves full-bodied, sapid, finishing long with spicy notes. We were also impressed with the Barbera d'Alba Serra de' Gatti '23, where whiffs of stone fruits and aromatic herbs are followed by a juicy, nicely integrated, and pleasant palate. The cherry- and cinnamon-scented Barbera d'Alba Superiore Carolina '21 is well-crafted, standing out for its firm structure and freshness.

○ Colli Tortonesi Timorasso Ombra di Luna '22	♟♟ 4
○ Colli Tortonesi Cortese Montarlino '23	♟ 4
● Colli Tortonesi Dolcetto Mont'Effe '21	♟ 2
● Colli Tortonesi Rosso Il Seguito '21	♟ 2
○ Colli Tortonesi Timorasso Ombra di Luna '15	♟♟♟ 4*
● Colli Tortonesi Barbera Morganti '13	♟♟ 4
○ Colli Tortonesi Timorasso Ombra di Luna '20	♟♟ 4
○ Colli Tortonesi Timorasso Ombra di Luna '18	♟♟ 4
○ Colli Tortonesi Timorasso Ombra di Luna '16	♟♟ 4
○ Colli Tortonesi Timorasso Ombra di Luna '13	♟♟ 4

● Roero V. di Lino '20	♟♟♟ 5
● Barbera d'Alba Serra de' Gatti '23	♟♟ 3*
● Barbera d'Alba Sup. Carolina '21	♟♟ 5
○ Roero Arneis Luèt '23	♟ 3
● Roero Bricco Medica '21	♟ 4
● Nebbiolo d'Alba V. di Lino '00	♟♟♟ 5
● Roero '04	♟♟♟ 6
● Roero '03	♟♟♟ 6
● Roero '01	♟♟♟ 6
● Roero '00	♟♟♟ 6
● Barbera d'Alba Serra de' Gatti '22	♟♟ 3
● Barbera d'Alba Sup. Carolina '20	♟♟ 5
○ Roero Arneis Luèt '21	♟♟ 3*
● Roero Bricco Medica '20	♟♟ 4
● Roero Bricco Medica '19	♟♟ 3
● Roero V. di Lino '19	♟♟ 5
● Roero V. di Lino '18	♟♟ 5

Castellari Bergaglio

fraz. Rovereto, 136r
15066 Gavi [AL]
📞 +39 0143644000
🌐 castellaribergaglio.it

CELLAR SALES
PRE-BOOKED VISITS
ANNUAL PRODUCTION 90,000 bottles
HECTARES UNDER VINE 11.00

Currently the winery Castellari Bergaglio (or rather the "brand" Castellari Bergaglio, as it includes the production of La Polastra) stands out as one of the most representative producers operating in the Gavi appellation, thanks to its major work on the cortese grape, which is considered excellent for its capacity for aging. Bergaglio's strengths lie in the wines cultivated in its estate crus: Fornaci, Rolona, and Rovereto. The Gavi del Comune di Tassarolo Fornaci '23 impresses with its aromas of apple, nuts, aromatic herbs, and mint. The palate is full and harmonious, led by lively acidity, making it a vibrant and dynamic drink. The Gavi del Comune di Gavi Rolona '23 is also delicious, opting for aromas of ferns and fresh herbs accented by flinty notes. In the mouth, the palate is powerful but nicely supported by fragrant acidity, ensuring it flows smoothly and remains flavorful.

Castello di Gabiano

via San Defendente, 2
15020 Gabiano [AL]
📞 +39 0142945004945004
🌐 www.castellodigabianowine.it

CELLAR SALES
PRE-BOOKED VISITS
ACCOMMODATION AND RESTAURANT SERVICE
ANNUAL PRODUCTION 130,000 bottles
HECTARES UNDER VINE 24.00

This estate spans 260 hectares, 22 of which are under vines, in the town of Gabiano (from which it takes its name). Giacomo Cattaneo Adorno, the last marquis of Gabiano, now manages the property, which has been in operation for more than 400 years. Their diverse range of wines caters to both lovers of local varieties and fans of international grapes. Visitors can enjoy tastings in a stunning setting, complete with elegantly appointed guest rooms and a restaurant dedicated to seasonal, local cuisine—all housed within the estate's castle. The Grignolino del Monferrato Casalese Il Ruvo '22 stands out among the wines tasted this year. Its intense ruby-garnet color is reflected in an elegant nose with clear notes of pepper and rose petals. The palate is juicy and fleshy, accompanied by a fresh and silky vein—a wine of real class. The Gabiano Riserva A Matilde Giustiniani '19 proved slightly underwhelming this year; while the nose is rich, oak dominates its fruit, while the palate is extracted but somewhat restrained.

○ Gavi del Comune di Tassarolo Fornaci '23	♟♟ 3*
○ Gavi del Comune di Gavi Rolona '23	♟♟ 4
○ Gavi M. Cl. Ardè	♟♟ 5
○ Gavi Pilin '21	♟♟ 5
○ Gavi Pilin '14	♟♟♟ 5
○ Gavi del Comune di Gavi Pilin '15	♟♟ 5
○ Gavi del Comune di Gavi Rolona '21	♟♟ 3*
○ Gavi del Comune di Gavi Rolona '20	♟♟ 3*
○ Gavi del Comune di Gavi Rolona '19	♟♟ 3
○ Gavi del Comune di Gavi Rolona '17	♟♟ 3*
○ Gavi del Comune di Gavi Rovereto Vignavecchia '16	♟♟ 3*
○ Gavi del Comune di Tassarolo Fornaci '21	♟♟ 2*
○ Gavi del Comune di Tassarolo Fornaci '18	♟♟ 2*

● Gabiano A Matilde Giustiniani Ris. '19	♟♟ 7
● Grignolino del M.to Casalese Il Ruvo '22	♟♟ 3*
◉ M.to Chiaretto Castelvere '23	♟♟ 3
● Piemonte Pinot Nero '22	♟♟ 3
● Barbera d'Asti La Braja '21	♟ 2
● Gabiano A Matilde Giustiniani Ris. '17	♟♟ 7
● Gabiano A Matilde Giustiniani Ris. '16	♟♟ 8
● Gabiano A Matilde Giustiniani Ris. '15	♟♟ 8
● Gabiano A Matilde Giustiniani Ris. '12	♟♟ 8
● Grignolino del M.to Casalese Il Ruvo '20	♟♟ 4
○ Piemonte Chardonnay Castello '19	♟♟ 8

Castello di Verduno

via Umberto I, 9
12060 Verduno [CN]
☎ +39 0172470284
● www.cantinecastellodiverduno.it

CELLAR SALES
PRE-BOOKED VISITS
ACCOMMODATION AND RESTAURANT SERVICE
ANNUAL PRODUCTION 80,000 bottles
HECTARES UNDER VINE 12.00
SUSTAINABLE WINERY

Owned by Gabriella Burlotto and Franco Bianco, the Castello di Verduno name brings with it a touch of Savoyard history, along with an impressive range of wines, from Barolo to Barbaresco. The wines are known for their traditional style, with aging in large oak barrels. The estate also stands out for its commitment to the pelaverga grape, which they were among the first to plant, producing one of Italy's most distinctive and enjoyable wines. The expansive Barolo Monvigliero Riserva '19 offers airy aromas of raspberry, tobacco, and graphite, accented by balsamic and spicy hints. On the palate, it's dynamic and juicy, concluding with a focused, persistent finale. The Barbaresco Rabajà Riserva '19 is equally impressive, with finely fruity aromas complemented by tobacco and violets. In the mouth, the palate is solid, sustained, and precise. As always, the Pelaverga Basadone '23 makes for an engaging and lively sip.

● Barbaresco Rabajà Ris. '19	♈♈ 8
● Barolo Monvigliero '19	♈♈ 8
● Verduno Pelaverga Basadone '23	♈♈ 4
● Barbaresco Rabajà '21	♈♈ 8
● Barolo Massara '20	♈♈ 8
● Barbaresco Rabajà '20	♈♈♈ 6
● Barbaresco Rabajà '04	♈♈♈ 6
● Barolo Massara '08	♈♈♈ 6
● Barolo Massara '01	♈♈♈ 6
● Barolo Monvigliero Ris. '08	♈♈♈ 7
● Barolo Monvigliero Ris. '04	♈♈♈ 7
● Verduno Pelaverga Basadone '21	♈♈♈ 4*
● Barbaresco Rabajà '19	♈♈ 6
● Barbera d'Alba Bricco del Cuculo '21	♈♈ 4
● Barolo Massara '19	♈♈ 6
● Barolo Massara '17	♈♈ 6

Caudrina

via Valle Bera, 10
12053 Castiglione Tinella [CN]
☎ +39 0141855126
● www.caudrina.it

CELLAR SALES
PRE-BOOKED VISITS
ANNUAL PRODUCTION 200,000 bottles
HECTARES UNDER VINE 25.00

Operating in Castiglione Tinella, on soils rich in marl and limestone, Romano Dogliotti harnesses the terroir to produce wines that exude elegance, freshness, and minerality. Various vineyards, including many going back more than 40 years, contribute to this distinctive profile. The estate grows a diverse mix of grapes, including barbera and nebbiolo (in the areas between Alba and Nizza Monferrato), as well as dolcetto, moscato, and chardonnay, the only international variety cultivated, in Ottiglio Monferrato. Romano Dogliotti's range remains solid and reliable. The Moscato d'Asti La Galeisa '23 features notes of grapefruit, candied orange peel, anise, and sage, followed by a palate that's sweet yet fresh and pleasant. The Piemonte Moscato Passito Redento '20 showcases lovely varietal notes of raisins, leading to a smooth, well-sustained palate balanced by acidity. The Monferrato Nebbiolo Superiore Sfacciato '22 focuses more on richness and tannic power, while the Moscato d'Asti La Caudrina '23 combines dried fig flavors with a citrusy, immediate palate of good persistence.

● M.to Nebbiolo Sup. Sfacciato '22	♈♈ 3
○ Moscato d'Asti La Caudrina '23	♈♈ 3
○ Moscato d'Asti La Galeisa '23	♈♈ 3
○ Piemonte Chardonnay Mej '23	♈♈ 3
○ Piemonte Moscato Passito Redento '20	♈♈ 3
● Barbera d'Asti La Solista '21	♈♈ 2*
● Barbera d'Asti La Solista '19	♈♈ 2*
● M.to Nebbiolo Sup. Sfacciato '19	♈♈ 3
● M.to Nebbiolo Sup. Sfacciato Facia d'Tola '21	♈♈ 3
○ Moscato d'Asti La Galeisa '20	♈♈ 3*
○ Moscato d'Asti La Galeisa '19	♈♈ 3*
● Nizza Montevenere '19	♈♈ 3
● Nizza Montevenere '16	♈♈ 3*
● Piemonte Barbera La Guerriera '22	♈♈ 2*
○ Piemonte Chardonnay Mej '22	♈♈ 3

★Cavallotto
Tenuta Bricco Boschis

loc. Bricco Boschis
via Alba-Monforte
12060 Castiglione Falletto [CN]
(☎ +39 017362814
✉ www.cavallotto.com

CELLAR SALES
PRE-BOOKED VISITS
ANNUAL PRODUCTION 110,000 bottles
HECTARES UNDER VINE 25.00
VITICULTURE METHOD Certified Organic

Davide Cavelli

via Provinciale, 77
15010 Prasco [AL]
(☎ +39 0144375706
✉ www.cavellivini.com

ANNUAL PRODUCTION 60,000 bottles
HECTARES UNDER VINE 10.50

The Cavallotto family, represented by siblings Alfio, Giuseppe, and Laura, manages their family winery near Castiglione Falletto. Established in the early 1970s, the winery's vineyards are almost entirely located in the Bricco Boschis Cru. Their range, which spans the region's most important appellations, is marked by a strong, classic personality, characterized by a consistent and rigorous approach. The Barolo Bricco Boschis '20 is a wine of substance, with refined aromas of blackberries, ripe red fruits, spices, and licorice. The palate is rich, well-structured, with lively development and an airy finish. Close behind is the Barolo Riserva Bricco Boschis Vigna San Giuseppe '18, which plays on more balsamic notes and hints of aromatic herbs on the nose. It offers great length and breadth on the palate. The vibrant and juicy Freisa '22 brings wild blackberry flavors and Mediterranean scrubland to the table.

Given its consistent level of quality, it was only a matter of time before the Cavelli family's winery earned a place in our main section. Their more than century-old winemaking tradition—which began in 1904—is now expertly maintained by Davide, the fourth generation of family to lead the estate. Their philosophy is as simple as it is effective: hands-on vineyard management, low yields, and a careful balance between modernity and tradition in the cellar. The Ovada Riserva Bricco Le Zerbe '21 stands out among the wines tasted for its richness and depth, with blackberry and cocoa notes. The palate opens sweet but is immediately tempered by close-knit tannins and a long finish. The Dolcetto di Ovada Le Zerbe '23 is equally characterful, with immediate aromas of crisp red fruit and a beautifully sapid, fresh, and taut palate. The Barbera del Monferrato Paian '22 is simpler but marked by enjoyable richness and intensity.

● Barolo Bricco Boschis '20	▼▼ 8
● Barolo Bricco Boschis V. San Giuseppe Ris. '18	▼▼ 8
● Barolo Vignolo Ris. '18	▼▼ 8
● Barbera d'Alba Sup. V. Cuculo '22	▼▼ 6
● Langhe Freisa '22	▼▼ 5
● Langhe Nebbiolo '22	▼▼ 6
● Barolo Bricco Boschis '19	▼▼▼ 8
● Barolo Bricco Boschis '12	▼▼▼ 8
● Barolo Bricco Boschis V. S. Giuseppe Ris. '05	▼▼▼ 8
● Barolo Bricco Boschis V. San Giuseppe Ris. '16	▼▼▼ 8
● Barolo Bricco Boschis V. San Giuseppe Ris. '15	▼▼▼ 8
● Barolo Vignolo Ris. '06	▼▼▼ 8

● Ovada Bricco Le Zerbe Ris. '21	▼▼ 3*
● Barbera del M.to Sup. Le Muraglie '20	▼▼ 3
● Barbera del Monferrato Paian '22	▼▼ 3
● Dolcetto di Ovada Le Zerbe '23	▼▼ 3
● Barbera del M.to Sup. Le Muraglie '19	♈♈ 3*
● Barbera del M.to Sup. Le Muraglie '15	♈♈ 3
● Dolcetto di Ovada Bricco Le Zerbe '17	♈♈ 2*
● Dolcetto di Ovada Le Zerbe '22	♈♈ 2*
● Dolcetto di Ovada Le Zerbe '20	♈♈ 2*
● Dolcetto di Ovada Le Zerbe '19	♈♈ 2*
● M.to Nebbiolo Sup. Cris '19	♈♈ 3
● Ovada Bricco Le Zerbe '17	♈♈ 3*
● Ovada Bricco Le Zerbe '16	♈♈ 3*
● Ovada Bricco Le Zerbe '15	♈♈ 3
● Ovada Bricco Le Zerbe Ris. '20	♈♈ 3
● Ovada Bricco Le Zerbe Ris. '19	♈♈ 3

★Ceretto

loc. San Cassiano, 34
12051 Alba [CN]
☏ +39 0173282582
✉ www.ceretto.com

CELLAR SALES
PRE-BOOKED VISITS
RESTAURANT SERVICE
ANNUAL PRODUCTION 950,000 bottles
HECTARES UNDER VINE 180.00
VITICULTURE METHOD Certified Organic
SUSTAINABLE WINERY

The Ceretto family, one of Piedmont's most prominent winemaking dynasties, traces its roots back to the 1930s. It all began with Riccardo, then came Bruno and Marcello, who purchased vineyards and began bottling individual crus. Today the family's legacy continues with Alessandro. Production focuses on the region's main DOCG wines, with Barolo (from the Cannubi San Lorenzo, Bricco Rocche, Brunate, and Prapò Crus) and Barbaresco (from the Asili and Bernadot Crus) representing the pinnacle of their offerings. The focused Barolo Rocche di Castiglione '20 boasts a complete and subtle aromatic profile, with red fruits meeting spices, and balsamic tones. In the mouth, its fleshy palate contrasts with firm, multifaceted tannins, concluding vibrant and airy. Assertive and persistent, the Barolo Brunate '20 is more powerful. Fresh roses and sweet spices define the aromas of the Barbaresco '21, whose palate is rich, broad, and slightly austere.

Cerutti

via Canelli, 205
14050 Cassinasco [AT]
☏ +39 0141851286
✉ www.cascinacerutti.it

CELLAR SALES
PRE-BOOKED VISITS
ANNUAL PRODUCTION 30,000 bottles
HECTARES UNDER VINE 8.00
SUSTAINABLE WINERY

The Cerutti family, today represented by Gianmario (the fourth generation), has been cultivating and producing wine since the 1930s. The grapes grown range from the region's classics, predominantly barbera and moscato (and also cortese), to international varietals like chardonnay and pinot nero. The wines are traditionally crafted, highlighting the unique terroirs of Cassinasco, where the winery is based, along with Canelli and Agliano. The excellent Alta Langa Brut Enrico Cerutti '20 displays fine, harmonious beading, with intense aromas of apple and plum over a backdrop of citrus and toasted bread. Complex and multifaceted on the palate, it has a power that imparts great character and personality, finishing persistent and captivating. The Piemonte Chardonnay Riva Granda '20 is well-crafted, with intense notes of butter, vanilla, toasted hazelnuts, and acacia flowers, followed by a fresh and harmonious palate with a long finish. Similarly, the Canelli Surì Sandrinet '23 is broad on the nose, with great richness and sweetness on the palate.

● Barolo Brunate '20	♟♟ 8
● Barolo Rocche di Castiglione '20	♟♟ 8
● Barbaresco '21	♟♟ 8
● Barbaresco Bernadot '21	♟♟ 8
● Barolo Bricco Rocche '20	♟♟ 8
● Barolo Bussia '20	♟♟ 8
● Barolo Prapò '20	♟♟ 8
● Langhe Nebbiolo Bernardina '22	♟♟ 5
● Barbaresco Asili '21	♟ 8
● Barbaresco Gallina '21	♟ 8
○ Langhe Arneis Blangé '23	♟ 5
● Barbaresco Asili '19	♟♟♟ 8
● Barbaresco Asili '16	♟♟♟ 8
● Barbaresco Asili '15	♟♟♟ 8
● Barbaresco Asili '13	♟♟♟ 8
● Barolo Bricco Rocche '13	♟♟♟ 8

○ Alta Langa Brut Enrico Cerutti '20	♟♟ 5
○ Canelli Surì Sandrinet '23	♟♟ 3
○ Piemonte Chardonnay Riva Granda '20	♟♟ 4
○ Alta Langa Brut Cuvée Enrico Cerutti '19	♟♟ 5
○ Alta Langa Brut Cuvée Enrico Cerutti '18	♟♟ 5
○ Alta Langa Brut Cuvée Enrico Cerutti '17	♟♟ 5
● Barbera d'Asti '22	♟♟ 3
● Barbera d'Asti '21	♟♟ 3
○ Moscato d'Asti Canelli Surì Sandrinet '22	♟♟ 3*
○ Moscato d'Asti Canelli Surì Sandrinet '21	♟♟ 3*
● Nizza Nizza Föje Rùsse '19	♟♟ 5
○ Piemonte Chardonnay Riva Granda '19	♟♟ 3*

La Chiara

loc. Vallegge, 24/2
15066 Gavi [AL]
☎ +39 0143642293
🌐 www.lachiara.it

CELLAR SALES
PRE-BOOKED VISITS
ANNUAL PRODUCTION 190,000 bottles
HECTARES UNDER VINE 28.00

For three generations, the Bergaglio family has been producing wine in Gavi. La Chiara was founded in 1912 by Ferdinando and later carried forward by his son Roberto and his wife, Silvana Figini. Today, the estate is run by their children, Simona and Dario. Primarily Gavi is produced, drawing on traditional methods, while striving to align with the natural characteristics of the land, with a constant focus on environmental sustainability. They also produce sparkling wines, Monferrato reds, grappa, and a dessert wine. The Gavi del Comune is a beautiful interpretation, displaying vibrant aromas alongside balsamic nuances, ferns, and mountain herbs. The palate is refined and elegant, opening with harmonious fleshiness, balanced by vibrant, fresh acidity. The Gavi Groppella also impressed, with its pleasant notes of white flowers and a broad, juicy palate.

○ Gavi del Comune di Gavi '23	🍷🍷 2*
○ Gavi del Comune di Gavi Groppella '23	🍷🍷 3
○ Gavi del Comune di Gavi '20	♀♀ 2*
○ Gavi del Comune di Gavi '19	♀♀ 2*
○ Gavi del Comune di Gavi '18	♀♀ 2*
○ Gavi del Comune di Gavi Et. Nera '22	♀♀ 3
○ Gavi del Comune di Gavi Et. Nera '18	♀♀ 3
○ Gavi del Comune di Gavi Et. Nera '17	♀♀ 3
○ Gavi del Comune di Gavi Et. Verde '22	♀♀ 2*
○ Gavi del Comune di Gavi Groppella '20	♀♀ 3
○ Gavi del Comune di Gavi Groppella '19	♀♀ 3
○ Gavi del Comune di Gavi Groppella '18	♀♀ 2*
○ Gavi del Comune di Gavi Groppella '17	♀♀ 2*
○ Gavi del Comune di Gavi La Chiara '11	♀♀ 2*
○ Gavi del Comune di Gavi La Chiara '10	♀♀ 2*
● M.to Rosso Nabari '09	♀♀ 2

★★Michele Chiarlo

s.da Nizza-Canelli, 99
14042 Calamandrana [AT]
☎ +39 0141769030
🌐 www.michelechiarlo.it

CELLAR SALES
PRE-BOOKED VISITS
ACCOMMODATION
ANNUAL PRODUCTION 1,100,000 bottles
HECTARES UNDER VINE 150.00
SUSTAINABLE WINERY

Michele Chiarlo, who founded the winery that bears his name in 1956, passed away in 2024, but his vision lives on through the work of his sons, Alberto and Stefano, who have been deeply involved in the business for years, along with the rest of the family. The winery, based in Calamandrana, is known for its innovative, unconventional approach. Their portfolio is vast, ranging from Barolo and Barbaresco to Gavi and Moscato d'Asti, with a special emphasis always given to Nizza Barbera. The Nizza La Court Riserva '21 offers red forest fruit and spicy notes, leading to a close-knit, juicy palate with good length and persistence. The Barbaresco Faset '21 features tobacco and graphite tones over red fruit, with a rich, sapid palate. The Barbaresco Asili '21 delivers notes of quinine and porcini mushrooms, with a dense tannic structure and a long, austere finish. The Barolo Cerequio '20 combines sweet spices and fresh fruit, harmonious tannins, and a characterful finish. The Nizza La Court Vigna Veja Riserva '19 proves sapid, energetic, and highly complex.

● Nizza La Court Ris. '21	🍷🍷🍷 8
● Barbaresco Asili '21	🍷🍷 8
● Barbaresco Faset '21	🍷🍷 8
● Barolo Cerequio '20	🍷🍷 8
● Barbaresco Montestefano Ris. '19	🍷🍷 8
● Barolo Cannubi '20	🍷🍷 8
○ Gavi del Comune di Gavi Rovereto '23	🍷🍷 3
○ Gavi Fornaci '23	🍷🍷 4
● Nizza Cipressi '22	🍷🍷 4
● Nizza La Court Vignaveja Ris. '19	🍷🍷 7
● Nizza Montemareto '21	🍷🍷 5
● Barolo Cerequio '18	♀♀♀ 8
● Barolo Cerequio '16	♀♀♀ 8
● Nizza Cipressi '21	♀♀♀ 4*
● Nizza La Court '18	♀♀♀ 6
● Nizza La Court Ris. '15	♀♀♀ 6

Chionetti

fraz. San Luigi
b.ta Valdiberti, 44
12063 Dogliani [CN]
☎ +39 017371179
✉ www.chionetti.com

CELLAR SALES
PRE-BOOKED VISITS
ANNUAL PRODUCTION 80,000 bottles
HECTARES UNDER VINE 16.00
VITICULTURE METHOD Certified Organic

Quinto Chionetti expanded his family's winery from its founding in the mid-1950s until 2013, when he handed over the reins to his grandson Nicola. The Chionetti family, among the first to bring renewed attention to Dolcetto di Dogliani, remains one of the most important producers in the appellation. However, since 2015, their focus has shifted towards Barolo, with the acquisition of vineyards in the Parussi, Roncaglie, and Bussia crus. Red fruits and quinine over a background of anise and fresh flowers—these are the well-etched aromas of the Barolo Parussi '20. Its dense and solid palate features structured tannins and fleshy fruit, making it enjoyable and refined. Black currant and medicinal herbs characterize the aromas of the Dogliani San Luigi Vigna La Costa '22, with comes through juicy, sapid, on the palate—a relaxed drink. We also appreciated the Langhe Nebbiolo La Chiusa '22, in its pure simplicity.

Ciabot Berton

fraz. Santa Maria, 1
12064 La Morra [CN]
☎ +39 017350217
✉ www.ciabotberton.it

CELLAR SALES
PRE-BOOKED VISITS
ANNUAL PRODUCTION 75,000 bottles
HECTARES UNDER VINE 14.00

La Morra's Oberto family bottled their first Barolo in 1961, establishing the winery as it is known today in the 1980s. The name refers to a small building ("ciabot" in Piedmontese) on the property, once owned by a certain Berton. Today, the winery is run by Marco, along with his wife Federica and Paola Oberto. The vineyards, most of which can be found in the vicinity of their production spaces, also include the Rocchettevino cru. We were won over by the fruity verve of the Barolo Roggeri '20, a wine reminiscent of ripe raspberries and cherries, accompanied by a subtle spice that transforms into a sapid, elegantly deep palate. Black pepper and ripe red fruit appear in the Barolo del Comune di La Morra '20, a wine with a dense tannic structure and an austere character. The Barbera d'Alba Fisetta '22 showcases plum aromas and a simple yet deliciously juicy palate, recalling ripe black fruits. The other wines are also well-crafted.

● Barolo Parussi '20	♟♟ 7
● Dogliani San Luigi V. La Costa '22	♟♟ 5
● Barbera d'Alba V. San Sebastiano '22	♟♟ 4
● Langhe Nebbiolo La Chiusa '22	♟♟ 4
○ Langhe Riesling '22	♟♟ 5
● Barolo Bussia V. Pianpolvere '20	♟ 8
● Dolcetto di Dogliani Briccolero '07	♟♟♟ 3*
● Dolcetto di Dogliani Briccolero '04	♟♟♟ 3*
● Barolo Bussia V. Pianpolvere '19	♟♟ 8
● Barolo Bussia V. Pianpolvere '18	♟♟ 8
● Barolo Bussia V. Pianpolvere '17	♟♟ 8
● Barolo Parussi '16	♟♟ 7
● Dogliani Briccolero '22	♟♟ 3*
● Dogliani Briccolero '21	♟♟ 3*
● Dogliani Briccolero '20	♟♟ 3*
● Dogliani Briccolero '19	♟♟ 3*

● Barbera d'Alba Fisetta '22	♟♟ 3
● Barolo del Comune di La Morra '20	♟♟ 5
● Barolo Rocchettevino '19	♟♟ 6
● Barolo Roggeri '18	♟♟ 6
● Barbera d'Alba Sup. V. Bricco San Biagio '21	♟ 4
● Barolo 1961 '19	♟ 7
● Barolo '18	♟♟ 5
● Barolo '17	♟♟ 5
● Barolo '16	♟♟ 5
● Barolo del Comune di La Morra '17	♟♟ 5
● Barolo Rocchettevino '18	♟♟ 6
● Barolo Roggeri '18	♟♟ 6
● Barolo Roggeri '17	♟♟ 6

Cieck

Cascina Castagnola, 2
10090 San Giorgio Canavese [TO]
(☎ +39 0124330522
✆ www.cieck.it

★F.lli Cigliuti

via Serraboella, 17
12052 Neive [CN]
(☎ +39 0173677185
✆ www.cigliuti.it

CELLAR SALES
PRE-BOOKED VISITS
ANNUAL PRODUCTION 70,000 bottles
HECTARES UNDER VINE 13.00
SUSTAINABLE WINERY

CELLAR SALES
PRE-BOOKED VISITS
ANNUAL PRODUCTION 35,000 bottles
HECTARES UNDER VINE 8.50

Remo Falconieri and his daughter Lia run this San Giorgio Canavese-based winery, a key player in the Caluso production zone. The pair are dedicated to preserving tradition, while also being mindful of market trends. Most of their energy centers on erbaluce (experiments with sparkling wine production date back to 1951), but their vineyards (mainly pergola trained) also host nebbiolo, barbera, neretto, and freisa g rapes. The Erbaluce di Caluso Spumante San Giorgio '20 opens with a fine, continuous bead and aromas of citrus and bread crust. On the palate, it's soft, fresh, and sapid, with a pleasantly dynamic drinkability. The Erbaluce di Caluso Vigna Misobolo '22 is well-crafted, offering floral and fruity aromas that develop into a full, round palate with a nearly brackish finish. The Erbaluce di Caluso Calliope '19 is more fleshy, delivering energy, intensity, and persistence on the palate.

Fratelli Cigliuti, named for brothers Leone and Romualdo Cigliuti, who originally sold grapes and bulk wine, is now led by Leone's son Renato, together with his wife Dina and daughters Claudia and Silvia. The highest expression of the Cigliuti family's line of Barbarescos is undoubtedly the Serraboella cru, whose name has graced their labels since the 1970s, as well as Bricco di Neive. At Cigliuti, the new generation, though entirely female, hasn't changed a thing about the slightly rustic yet gratifying style of Renato's wines. Claudia and Silvia, delaying the release of their wines by a year to allow them to soften, present two excellent 2020 Barbarescos. Both exhibit deep, intense noses where fruit aromas take a backseat, giving way to notes of Tuscan tobacco and cinchona, though they differ on the palate: the Serraboella is powerful and potent, while the Bricco di Neive is less robust but equally austere.

○ Erbaluce di Caluso Brut San Giorgio '20	♀♀ 5
○ Erbaluce di Caluso V. Misobolo '22	♀♀ 4
○ Erbaluce di Caluso '23	♀♀ 3
○ Erbaluce di Caluso Brut Calliope '19	♀♀ 4
○ Erbaluce di Caluso Pas Dosé Nature '19	♀♀ 5
○ Erbaluce di Caluso Passito Alladium '18	♀♀ 5
○ Erbaluce di Caluso T '21	♀♀ 4
○ Erbaluce di Caluso Passito Alladium '06	♀♀♀ 5
○ Erbaluce di Caluso '22	♀♀ 3
○ Erbaluce di Caluso Passito Alladium '15	♀♀ 5
○ Erbaluce di Caluso Passito Alladium '14	♀♀ 5
○ Erbaluce di Caluso Passito Alladium '10	♀♀ 5
○ Erbaluce di Caluso V. Misobolo '21	♀♀ 4
○ Erbaluce di Caluso V. Misobolo '20	♀♀ 3*

● Barbaresco Serraboella '20	♀♀ 8
● Barbaresco Bricco di Neive Vie Erte '20	♀♀ 7
● Barbera d'Alba V. Serraboella '20	♀♀ 4
● Barbaresco Serraboella '13	♀♀♀ 8
● Barbaresco Serraboella '11	♀♀♀ 7
● Barbaresco Serraboella '10	♀♀♀ 7
● Barbaresco Serraboella '09	♀♀♀ 7
● Barbaresco V. Erte '04	♀♀♀ 6
● Barbaresco Bricco di Neive Vie Erte '19	♀♀ 7
● Barbaresco Bricco di Neive Vie Erte '18	♀♀ 6
● Barbaresco Bricco di Neive Vie Erte '17	♀♀ 6
● Barbaresco Serraboella '19	♀♀ 8
● Barbaresco Serraboella '17	♀♀ 8
● Barbaresco Serraboella '16	♀♀ 8
● Barbaresco Vie Erte '16	♀♀ 6
● Barbaresco Vie Erte '15	♀♀ 6
● Barbera d'Alba V. Serraboella '19	♀♀ 4

★Tenute Cisa Asinari dei Marchesi di Grésy

loc. Martinenga
s.da della Stazione, 21
12050 Barbaresco [CN]
☏ +39 0173635222
⊕ marchesidigresy.com

CELLAR SALES
PRE-BOOKED VISITS
ACCOMMODATION
ANNUAL PRODUCTION 200,000 bottles
HECTARES UNDER VINE 35.00
SUSTAINABLE WINERY

Four wineries set between Treiso and Cassine (in Monferrato) make up the mosaic of the Tenute Cisa Asinari dei Marchesi di Grésy: La Serra, Monte Colombo, Monte Aribaldo, and Martinenga. This last can be found at the center of the cru of the same name, which virtually encircles their production spaces. Here, some of Barbaresco's most important wines are produced, a selection characterized by impeccable style and flawless craftsmanship. Delicate floral and small red fruit aromas introduce the enticing, decisive palate of the Barbaresco Martinega Gaiun Riserva '19, a wine marked by a close-knit, multifaceted tannic texture, well-supported by persistent fruit flesh, culminating in a solid and sapid finish. Ripe red fruits and hints of tobacco define the Camp Gros '19, which also boasts a rich, fleshy palate with silky tannins. An intriguing balsamic vein runs through the Dolcetto d'Alba Monte Aribaldo '22, which features a supple and flavorful palate. The well-crafted Barbaresco Martinenga '21 also stands out.

Aldo Clerico

loc. Manzoni, 69
12065 Monforte d'Alba [CN]
☏ +39 0173209981
⊕ www.aldoclerico.it

CELLAR SALES
PRE-BOOKED VISITS
ANNUAL PRODUCTION 40,000 bottles
HECTARES UNDER VINE 6.00

Aldo Clerico embarked on his winemaking adventure in 2004 with the founding of his winery in Monforte d'Alba. His vineyards are mainly located in this part of Barolo, where he also produces a Cru Ginestra, with a few plots extending into the Dogliani area near Monchiero. His wines exhibit a strong sense of place, with maturation taking place in both large and small wooden barrels. Ripe red fruits, tobacco, and spices characterize the Barolo Ginestra '20, which delivers a powerful, rich, and sustained palate, with a close-knit tannic texture and a long, persistent finish. The well-crafted Barolo '20 also shines. The intriguing Langhe Nebbiolo '22 features a nose marked by a pleasant smoky note over small red fruits, while the palate is deep and pervasive. The juicy Dolcetto d'Alba '23 is pleasantly flavorful.

● Barbaresco Camp Gros Ris. '19	🍷🍷 8
● Barbaresco Martinenga Gaiun Ris. '19	🍷🍷 8
● Barbaresco Martinenga '21	🍷🍷 8
● Barbera d'Asti Monte Colombo '16	🍷🍷 5
● Dolcetto d'Alba Monte Aribaldo '22	🍷🍷 3
○ Langhe Chardonnay Grésy '22	🍷🍷 5
● Barbaresco Camp Gros '06	🍷🍷🍷 8
● Barbaresco Camp Gros '05	🍷🍷🍷 8
● Barbaresco Camp Gros Martinenga '09	🍷🍷🍷 8
● Barbaresco Camp Gros Martinenga '08	🍷🍷🍷 8
● Barbaresco Camp Gros Martinenga Ris. '13	🍷🍷🍷 8
● Barbaresco Martinenga Camp Gros Ris. '15	🍷🍷🍷 8
● Barbaresco Martinenga Camp Gros Ris. '12	🍷🍷🍷 8

● Barolo Ginestra '20	🍷🍷 8
● Barolo '20	🍷🍷 6
● Barolo del Comune di Serralunga d'Alba '20	🍷🍷 7
● Dogliani '23	🍷🍷 3
● Dolcetto d'Alba '23	🍷🍷 2*
● Langhe Nebbiolo '22	🍷🍷 3
● Barbera d'Alba '22	🍷 3
● Barolo '19	🍷🍷 6
● Barolo del Comune di Serralunga d'Alba '19	🍷🍷 7
● Barolo del Comune di Serralunga d'Alba '18	🍷🍷 7
● Barolo Ginestra '19	🍷🍷 8
● Barolo Ginestra '18	🍷🍷 8
● Dogliani '21	🍷🍷 3*

PIEDMONT

★★Domenico Clerico

loc. Manzoni, 67
12065 Monforte d'Alba [CN]
☎ +39 017378171
🌐 www.domenicoclerico.com

CELLAR SALES
PRE-BOOKED VISITS
ANNUAL PRODUCTION 120,000 bottles
HECTARES UNDER VINE 26.00
SUSTAINABLE WINERY

The story of this Monforte d'Alba winery is intertwined with that of a man, Domenico Clerico, who revolutionized viticulture here in Langhe. Starting in 1976, when he took over the family business, Clerico introduced new principles to the winemaking process. Domenico Clerico passed away in 2017, leaving his legacy in the hands of his wife, Giuliana Viberti, who, together with a determined team, continues to uphold the innovative and uncompromising spirit of its founder. The Barolo Aeroplanservaj '20 is an absolutely refined and vibrant wine, with an aromatic profile that recalls red berries, licorice, and tobacco over a backdrop of graphite and balsam. The palate has a close-knit yet delicate tannic structure, developing into a multifaceted profile that finishes with a lingering balsamic touch. Also noteworthy is the Barolo Ginestra Ciabot Mentin '20, which opens with fragrant and airy aromas, leading to a slender, supple, and flavorful palate. You'll find the refined, fleshy Barolo Bussia Briccotto '20 in our "Rare Wines" section.

● Barolo del Comune di Serralunga d'Alba Aeroplanservaj '20	♙♙ 8
● Barolo Ginestra Ciabot Mentin '20	♙♙ 8
● Barolo Ginestra Pajana '20	♙♙ 8
● Barbera d'Alba Trevigne '22	♙♙ 4
● Barolo del Comune di Monforte d'Alba '20	♙ 8
● Barolo Percristina '14	♙♙ 8
● Langhe Dolcetto Visadì '23	♙♙ 3
● Barolo Ciabot Mentin '08	♙♙♙ 8
● Barolo Ciabot Mentin Ginestra '05	♙♙♙ 8
● Barolo Ciabot Mentin Ginestra '04	♙♙♙ 8
● Barolo Ciabot Mentin Ginestra '92	♙♙♙ 8
● Barolo Ciabot Mentin Ginestra '86	♙♙♙ 8
● Barolo Ginestra Ciabot Mentin '17	♙♙♙ 8
● Barolo Percristina '01	♙♙♙ 8

★Elvio Cogno

via Ravera, 2
12060 Novello [CN]
☎ +39 0173744006
🌐 www.elviocogno.com

CELLAR SALES
PRE-BOOKED VISITS
ANNUAL PRODUCTION 120,000 bottles
HECTARES UNDER VINE 16.00
SUSTAINABLE WINERY

The winery in Novello, today owned by Valter Fissore and Nadia Cogno, remains closely tied to the vision of its founder, Elvio Cogno, who revived the estate in 1990. Cogno's Barolos stand out for their lengthy fermentation times and the restrained use of oak, offering a classic style that never feels excessive. Production centers around the cru Rivera, home to the prized estate parcels of Bricco Pernice, Vigna Elena, and Cascina Nuova. The well-crafted Barolo Cascina Nuova '20 reveals fragrant, intense fruit with smoky nuances and subtle balsamic tones. The palate is round, solid, with lively, balanced progression, ending on a fruity note. The Barolo Ravera Bricco Pernice '19 is also good, offering a fleshy and dynamic palate. The stunning Vigna Elena '18 is less structured but infinitely elegant. The lighter Barolo Ravera '20 focuses on drinkability. The fresh, flavorful Barbera d'Alba Bricco dei Merli '22 and Dolcetto d'Alba Mandorlo '22 are both delightful.

● Barolo Cascina Nuova '20	♙♙ 7
● Barolo Ravera Bricco Pernice '19	♙♙ 8
● Barolo Ravera V. Elena Ris. '18	♙♙ 8
● Barbaresco Bordini '21	♙♙ 7
● Barbera d'Alba Bricco dei Merli '22	♙♙ 5
● Barolo Ravera '20	♙♙ 8
● Dolcetto d'Alba Mandorlo '23	♙♙ 3
● Langhe Nebbiolo Montegrilli '23	♙♙ 5
● Barolo Ravera '19	♙♙♙ 8
● Barolo Ravera Bricco Pernice '16	♙♙♙ 8
● Barolo Ravera Bricco Pernice '13	♙♙♙ 8
● Barolo Ravera Bricco Pernice '12	♙♙♙ 8
● Barolo Ravera V. Elena Ris. '16	♙♙♙ 8
● Barolo Ravera V. Elena Ris. '13	♙♙♙ 8

Poderi Colla

fraz. San Rocco Seno d'Elvio, 82
12051 Alba [CN]
☎ +39 0173290148
@ www.podericolla.it

CELLAR SALES
PRE-BOOKED VISITS
ANNUAL PRODUCTION 150,000 bottles
HECTARES UNDER VINE 26.00

Initially, the Colla family's history intertwined with that of the Prunotto winery. In 1956, Beppe Colla took over, introducing the separate vinification of grapes from individual crus. His brother Tino Colla joined him in the Prunotto venture, and later became the key figure in the new Poderi Colla winery, established in 1994 through the merger of properties owned by Federica Colla (Beppe's niece) and Pietro Colla (his son). The nose of the Barbaresco Roncaglie Tenuta Roncaglia '21 is vibrant, defined by berry notes, with hints of roasted coffee and licorice. The palate is easygoing, smooth, fragrant, and refined. The Barolo Bussia Dardi Le Rose '20 is also good, with dominant red fruit aromas and a solid, multifaceted tannic structure that guides its progression of flavors.

Collina Serragrilli

via Serragrilli, 30
12052 Neive [CN]
☎ +39 0173677010
@ www.serragrilli.it

CELLAR SALES
PRE-BOOKED VISITS
ANNUAL PRODUCTION 100,000 bottles
HECTARES UNDER VINE 15.00
SUSTAINABLE WINERY

In Neive, the Lequio family continues a longstanding winemaking tradition that has evolved from selling grapes and wines to third parties to bottling under their own label. The vineyards are primarily located in the Sorì Serragrilli cru, where the winery is also situated. In addition to Barbaresco Serragrilli, they also produce a version from the Starderi cru. The winery's portfolio includes Barolo, Barbera, and Dolcetto d'Alba. Mature black berries and cocoa notes weave through the aromatic bouquet of the Barbaresco Serragrilli '21, which offers a powerful, multifaceted, and solid palate, finishing long on fruit, with a pleasant balsamic touch. Yellow peach and hay aromas mark the Langhe Grillobianco '23, which delivers a rich, sapid palate. The Starderi '21 showcases an elegant nose of raspberry, wild strawberry, and sweet tobacco, with a powerful yet delicately tannic palate.

PIEDMONT

● Barbaresco Roncaglie Tenuta Roncaglia '21	♟♟ 6
● Barolo Bussia Dardi Le Rose '20	♟♟ 6
○ Nebbiolo d'Alba Drago '22	♟♟ 4
● Barbaresco Roncaglie '14	♟♟♟ 6
● Barolo Bussia Dardi Le Rose '09	♟♟♟ 6
● Barolo Bussia Dardi Le Rose '99	♟♟♟ 6
● Barbaresco Roncaglie '18	♟♟ 6
● Barbaresco Roncaglie '17	♟♟ 6
● Barbaresco Roncaglie '16	♟♟ 6
● Barbaresco Roncaglie '15	♟♟ 6
● Barbaresco Roncaglie Tenuta Roncaglia '20	♟♟ 6
● Barbaresco Roncaglie Tenuta Roncaglia '19	♟♟ 6
● Barolo Bussia Dardi Le Rose '17	♟♟ 6
● Barolo Bussia Dardi Le Rose '16	♟♟ 6
● Barolo Bussia Dardi Le Rose '15	♟♟ 6

● Barbaresco Starderi '21	♟♟ 7
● Barbaresco Serragrilli '21	♟♟ 6
○ Langhe Bianco Grillobianco '23	♟♟ 3
● Langhe Nebbiolo Bailè '21	♟ 4
● Barbaresco Serragrilli '20	♟♟ 6
● Barbaresco Serragrilli '19	♟♟ 6
● Barbaresco Serragrilli '18	♟♟ 6
● Barbaresco Serragrilli '13	♟♟ 5
● Barbaresco Serragrilli '09	♟♟ 5
● Barbaresco Serragrilli '07	♟♟ 5
● Barbaresco Serragrilli '05	♟♟ 5
● Barbaresco Serragrilli '04	♟♟ 5
● Barbaresco Starderi '20	♟♟ 7
● Barbera d'Alba Grillaia '20	♟♟ 4
● Barbera d'Alba Serraia '20	♟♟ 3
● Langhe Nebbiolo Bailè '19	♟♟ 4

La Colombera

loc. Vho
s.da comunale per Vho, 7
15057 Tortona [AL]
☎ +39 0131867795
✉ lacolomberavini.it

CELLAR SALES
PRE-BOOKED VISITS
ANNUAL PRODUCTION 80,000 bottles
HECTARES UNDER VINE 24.00
SUSTAINABLE WINERY

Elisa Semino's enthusiasm and passion are not only evident in her commitment but also reflected in the charm and quality of her wines. Together with her father Piercarlo and brother Lorenzo, she is dedicated to exploring the vast potential of the timorasso grape. The winery boasts two crus: Montino, on the hills of Vho, and the new Santa Croce, in the Sarezzano area. La Colombera also produces barbera, cortese, dolcetto, and croatina. The richness of both Il Montino '22 and Santa Croce '22 is remarkable, a contest between two standouts where elegance, power, and nobility come to the fore. The Montino is richer and more refined, while the Santa Croce is more powerful and juicy. Both offer a complex and rich aromatic suite, with the Santa Croce alternating notes of hydrocarbons and flint with grapefruit and lime, while the Montino plays on citron zest, chamomile, and aromatic herbs, finishing fresh and vibrant.

○ Colli Tortonesi Timorasso Il Montino '22	♈♈♈ 5
○ Colli Tortonesi Timorasso Santa Croce '22	♈♈ 5
● Colli Tortonesi Barbera Elisa '22	♈♈ 4
● Colli Tortonesi Monleale '21	♈♈ 4
● Colli Tortonesi Rosso Vegia Rampana '23	♈♈ 3
○ Colli Tortonesi Timorasso Derthona '22	♈♈ 4
○ Colli Tortonesi Cortese Bricco Bartolomeo '23	♈ 2
● Colli Tortonesi Croatina Arché '22	♈ 4
● Nibiò Suciaja '22	♈ 3
○ Colli Tortonesi Timorasso Il Montino '18	♈♈♈ 5
○ Colli Tortonesi Timorasso Il Montino '17	♈♈♈ 5
○ Colli Tortonesi Timorasso Il Montino '16	♈♈♈ 5

Colombo

Reg. Cafra, 172b
14051 Bubbio [AT]
☎ +39 3338877225
✉ www.colombovino.it

CELLAR SALES
PRE-BOOKED VISITS
ANNUAL PRODUCTION 70,000 bottles
HECTARES UNDER VINE 10.00

Cascina Pastori, the brainchild of Antonio Colombo, a renowned cardiologist, recently celebrated its 20th anniversary. Nestled in a green oasis near Bubbio, in the heart of historic Alta Langa, the estate sits in a region where some of the first vines of pinot nero were planted (which later led to the establishment of the Alta Langa appellation). Today, the winery, led by Antonio's son Andrea, focuses on two categories: Metodo Classico sparkling wines and still pinot nero. In the sparkling wine category, the two Alta Langa wines dominate. The Blanc de Blancs Brut '20 is a small wonder of finesse and harmony, with aromas of brioche and plum, and a fresh, creamy palate. The Brut Rosé '20 stands out for its decisive character, though it loses a bit of elegance. Between the two pinot neros, we preferred the fresher aromas and flavors of the Apertura, which reveals clear, appealing small red fruit aromas. In this 2020 vintage, the top selection, Maxima, appears more evolved, weighed down by alcohol.

○ Alta Langa Brut Blanc de Blancs '20	♈♈ 5
⊙ Alta Langa Brut Rosé Ris. '20	♈♈ 5
● Piemonte Pinot Nero Apertura '20	♈♈ 4
● Piemonte Pinot Nero Maxima '20	♈♈ 5
○ Piemonte Spumante Brut M. Cl. Natusia '21	♈♈ 5
○ Piemonte Spumante Brut M. Cl. Pentaris '20	♈ 5
○ Alta Langa Brut Blanc de Blancs '18	♈♈♈ 5
⊙ Alta Langa Brut Rosé 60 Mesi Ris. '13	♈♈♈ 5
⊙ Alta Langa Brut Rosé Ris. '15	♈♈♈ 5
● Piemonte Pinot Nero Apertura '16	♈♈♈ 4*
● Piemonte Pinot Nero Apertura '15	♈♈♈ 3*
○ Piemonte Chardonnay Blanc de Blancs 60 Mesi M. Cl. '14	♈♈ 4
● Piemonte Pinot Nero Apertura '18	♈♈ 5
● Piemonte Pinot Nero Apertura '17	♈♈ 4
● Piemonte Pinot Nero Apertura '14	♈♈ 3*

★★★Giacomo Conterno

loc. Ornati, 2
12065 Monforte d'Alba [CN]
+39 017378221
conterno.it

PRE-BOOKED VISITS
ANNUAL PRODUCTION 60,000 bottles
HECTARES UNDER VINE 23.00

The winery based in Monforte d'Alba was founded a century ago, when Giacomo Conterno created Monfortino. In 1974, his son Giovanni purchased the Francia vineyard, which became the sole source of grapes for the winery's celebrated masterpiece. Giovanni's son, Roberto Conterno, expanded the estate further in 2015 with the acquisition of the Cerretta cru and the Arione vineyard in Serralunga d'Alba, followed by the 2018 acquisition of Cantine Nervi in Gattinara. Once again, since taking the reins from his father Roberto, he presents a flawless selection. Leading the pack this year is the exceptional Francia, which, thanks to the vintage, embodies the archetype of Serralunga Barolo. Complex aromas, slow to reveal, showcase licorice and rose alongside fruit, while on the palate, the tannins, still slightly rough, benefit from the wine's excellent structure. In the same vein is the Barbera Francia: full of blackberry sensations and petrichor, it's restrained, with a stern and almost tannic character, yet full of hidden fruit pulp.

● Barolo Francia '20	🍷🍷🍷 8
● Barbera d'Alba V. Francia '22	🍷🍷 8
● Barolo Cerretta '20	🍷🍷 8
● Barbera d'Alba V. Cerretta '22	🍷🍷 5
● Barolo Arione '20	🍷🍷 8
● Nebbiolo d'Alba V. Arione '21	🍷🍷 8
● Barbera d'Alba V. Francia '20	YYY 5
● Barolo Cerretta '14	YYY 8
● Barolo Francia '12	YYY 8
● Barolo Francia '10	YYY 8
● Barolo Monfortino Ris. '15	YYY 8
● Barolo Monfortino Ris. '14	YYY 8
● Barolo Monfortino Ris. '13	YYY 8
● Barolo Monfortino Ris. '10	YYY 8
● Barolo Monfortino Ris. '08	YYY 8
● Barolo Monfortino Ris. '06	YYY 8
● Barolo Monfortino Ris. '05	YYY 8

★Paolo Conterno

loc. Ginestra, 34
12065 Monforte d'Alba [CN]
+39 017378415
www.paoloconterno.com

CELLAR SALES
PRE-BOOKED VISITS
ACCOMMODATION
ANNUAL PRODUCTION 180,000 bottles
HECTARES UNDER VINE 37.00
SUSTAINABLE WINERY

Today this Monforte d'Alba-based winery is managed by the fourth generation of the Conterno family, led by Giorgio Conterno. Production centers around the Ginestra cru, one of Barol's most important vineyards. Over time, the winery has embraced new challenges, such as the 2015 acquisition of the Antico Podere del Sant'Uffizio in Cioccaro di Penango, Monferrato, and the Tenuta Ortaglia in the hills of Fiesole, Tuscany. One wonders how Giorgio Conterno has managed to handle the family business with such steady leadership and impressive results in recent years. Between renting vineyards in Piedmont and Tuscany for producing both wine and extra virgin olive oil, he's rarely found at home in Ginestra. Yet, the results are evident. Hailing from a legendary vintage, the 2016 Riserva confirms both the greatness of the terroir and the skill of the winemaker. The signature of Ginestra marks the wine, as few other crus do: alongside raspberry, there's an explosion of balsamic and minty aromas, leading to a powerful and sleek palate. The Ginestra '20 is good but still very young and austere.

● Barolo Ginestra Ris. '16	🍷🍷🍷 8
● Barolo Ginestra '20	🍷🍷 8
● Barbera d'Alba La Ginestra '20	🍷🍷 4
● Barolo Riva del Bric '20	🍷🍷 7
● Langhe Nebbiolo A Mont '22	🍷🍷 4
● Barbera d'Asti Bricco '22	🍷 3
○ Piemonte Chardonnay Divers '22	🍷 6
● Barolo Ginestra '10	YYY 8
● Barolo Ginestra Ris. '15	YYY 8
● Barolo Ginestra Ris. '14	YYY 8
● Barolo Ginestra Ris. '13	YYY 8
● Barolo Ginestra Ris. '12	YYY 8
● Barolo Ginestra Ris. '11	YYY 8
● Barolo Ginestra Ris. '10	YYY 8
● Barolo Ginestra Ris. '09	YYY 8
● Barolo Ginestra Ris. '08	YYY 8
● Barolo Ginestra Ris. '06	YYY 8

Convento Cappuccini - B8

reg. Balascera, 8
15010 Ricaldone [AL]
(☎ +39 3335328471
☞ www.bottovini.com

Vigne Marina Coppi

via Sant'Andrea, 5
15051 Castellania [AL]
(☎ +39 0131837089
☞ www.vignemarinacoppi.com

HECTARES UNDER VINE 20.00

CELLAR SALES
PRE-BOOKED VISITS
ANNUAL PRODUCTION 25,000 bottles
HECTARES UNDER VINE 4.50

The Botto family's winery continues to shine, earning a spot in this edition's main section. In 1994 a long tradition of viticulture led to Pier Luigi making and selling his own wine. Today, his sons Andrea and Stefano carry on the work in their new, state-of-the-art facility, inaugurated in 2018. The vineyards, spread across three different villages in the area, benefit from varied terroirs, allowing the wines to express their full potential in distinct ways. The Barbera d'Asti Convento Cappuccini is dense, offering aromas of blackberries and quinine. On the palate, it's rich and warm, unfolding into a long and elegant finish, with great harmony. The Barbera d'Asti Superiore Convento Cappuccini '22 follows a similar line, with quinine scents alternating with pronounced, though not excessive, oak; a full-bodied palate with nice length follows. The Piemonte Albarossa Convento Cappuccini '22 is also good, featuring fruit and spices on the nose, with a sapid finish.

Francesco Bellocchio's sensitivity emerged in his tribute to his grandfather, the great Fausto Coppi, when he set out to revitalize the winery in Castellania. That was back in 2000, and since then Francesco's passion for the vineyard, the land, and tradition has only deepened. His production style is artisanal, blending respect for time-honored practices with new agronomic knowledge and a commitment to the natural environment. What a wine! The Colli Tortonesi Timorasso Fausto '22 opens with vibrant mineral notes, combined with hints of incense and grains, lending it great complexity and finesse. The palate is rich and concentrated, yet remains light thanks to its remarkable acidity, leading to a seemingly endless finish. In a similar vein, the Colli Tortonesi Timorasso Francesca '23 displays its characteristic minerality on the nose, accompanied by citrus and tropical fruit aromas. The palate is structured and exuberantly acidic, promising great aging potential.

● Barbera d'Asti Convento Cappuccini '22	♟♟ 3*
● Barbera d'Asti Sup. Convento Cappuccini '22	♟♟ 5
● Piemonte Albarossa '20	♟♟ 4
● Brachetto D'Acqui Convento Cappuccini '23	♟ 3
● Acqui '21	♟♟ 3
● Barbera d'Asti '21	♟♟ 3
● Piemonte Albarossa '19	♟♟ 4
○ Piemonte Sauvignon '22	♟♟ 3

○ Colli Tortonesi Timorasso Fausto '22	♟♟ 6
○ Colli Tortonesi Timorasso Francesca '23	♟♟ 4
● Colli Tortonesi Barbera Sant'Andrea '23	♟♟ 3
● Colli Tortonesi Rosso Lindin '20	♟♟ 5
○ Colli Tortonesi Timorasso Fausto '15	♟♟♟ 6
○ Colli Tortonesi Timorasso Fausto '12	♟♟♟ 6
○ Colli Tortonesi Timorasso Fausto '11	♟♟♟ 6
○ Colli Tortonesi Timorasso Fausto '10	♟♟♟ 6
○ Colli Tortonesi Timorasso Fausto '09	♟♟♟ 6
● Colli Tortonesi Barbera Sant'Andrea '22	♟♟ 3*
● Colli Tortonesi Barbera Sant'Andrea '21	♟♟ 3*
○ Colli Tortonesi Timorasso Fausto '21	♟♟ 6
○ Colli Tortonesi Timorasso Fausto '19	♟♟ 6

★★Coppo

via Alba, 68
14053 Canelli [AT]
☎ +39 0141823146
✉ www.coppo.com

CELLAR SALES
PRE-BOOKED VISITS
ANNUAL PRODUCTION 420,000 bottles
HECTARES UNDER VINE 60.00
SUSTAINABLE WINERY

Founded in Canelli in 1892 by Piero Coppo, this winery has long been recognized as one of the most important producers of Barbera d'Asti and Nizza. Recently, the producer has also focused on the Metodo Classico sparkling wines of Alta Langa, following the 2021 transition of ownership from the Coppo family to Gianfranco Lanci (President of Lenovo), who also owns the Barolo producer Dosio. Beyond their sparkling wines and chardonnay, the future of Coppo also lies in the language of Barolo and its finest subzones. Yet, their Barbera still regularly stands out, especially the Pomorosso. The 2021 plays heavily on smoky notes of roasted coffee and cocoa, which enrich the classic cherry aromas. Its richness of flavor, well-supported by its vibrant acidity, plays an important role as well. The Monteriolo once again proves to be one of Italy's best chardonnays, with rich aromas of hazelnut and fresh butter and a persistent, classy palate.

Gabriele Cordero

s.da Moriondo, 40
12040 Priocca [CN]
☎ +39 3349440947
✉ www.gabrielecordero.com

A small family-run business founded in 2016, this winery operates vineyards primarily in Priocca, with one exception in Vezza d'Alba, on the sandy soils that are a hallmark of Roero. The vineyards are planted with the classic varieties of the left bank of the Tanaro River: arneis, barbera, and nebbiolo, with the recent addition of timorasso, riesling, and bianver as well. The wines, which are crafted according to a modern approach, aim to express the character of the land and grapes used. The Roero '21 impresses with its sweet spice and cherry aromas and a palate full of juicy, long-lasting fruit. The Barbera d'Alba '21 follows with hints of black forest fruits and aromatic herbs, leading to a well-balanced, fresh, and pleasant palate. The entire range is well-crafted. The Barbera d'Alba Superiore Hica '21 is spicy and energetic, while the Roero Arneis Innav '23 features sweet tropical fruit on the nose, with a palate marked by sapidity and finesse. The Langhe Nebbiolo Foschìa '22 reveals pomegranate notes and a juicy, smooth finish.

● Nizza Pomorosso '21	♥♥♥ 8
● Barbera d'Asti Camp du Rouss '22	♥♥ 4
○ Piemonte Chardonnay Monteriolo '22	♥♥ 6
○ Alta Langa Brut Luigi Coppo '21	♥♥ 5
○ Alta Langa Extra Brut Coppo Ris. '19	♥♥ 6
● Barbera d'Asti L'Avvocata '23	♥♥ 3
◉ Clelia Coppo Brut Rosé M. Cl. '21	♥♥ 6
○ Moscato d'Asti Canelli Moncalvina '23	♥♥ 3
● Nizza Bric del Marchese '20	♥♥ 8
● Nizza Pontiselli '20	♥♥ 8
○ Piemonte Chardonnay Riserva della Famiglia '19	♥♥ 8
○ Alta Langa Extra Brut Ris. '15	♥♥♥ 6
● Barbera d'Asti Camp du Rouss '19	♥♥♥ 4*
● Nizza Pomorosso '20	♥♥♥ 8
● Nizza Pomorosso '19	♥♥♥ 8
● Nizza Pomorosso '17	♥♥♥ 7

● Barbera d'Alba '21	♥♥ 3*
● Roero '21	♥♥ 3*
● Barbera d'Alba Sup. Hica '21	♥♥ 5
● Langhe Nebbiolo Fuschia '22	♥♥ 4
○ Roero Arneis Innav '23	♥♥ 4
● Barbera d'Alba '20	♥♥ 3
○ Roero Arneis Innav '21	♥♥ 4

★Giovanni Corino

fraz. Annunziata, 25b
12064 La Morra [CN]
☎ +39 0173509452
✈ www.corino.it

Renato Corino

fraz. Annunziata
b.go Pozzo, 49a
12064 La Morra [CN]
☎ +39 0173500349
✈ renatocorino.it

CELLAR SALES
PRE-BOOKED VISITS
ANNUAL PRODUCTION 50,000 bottles
HECTARES UNDER VINE 9.50

CELLAR SALES
PRE-BOOKED VISITS
ANNUAL PRODUCTION 45,000 bottles
HECTARES UNDER VINE 8.00

The winery based in La Morra, which began selling its first bottles of Barolo in the mid-1980s, is run by Giuliano Corino, his wife Stefania, and their children Veronica and Andrea. The estate's vineyards include coveted plots in the Arborina and Giachini crus, and their production style is subtly modern, with aging primarily carried out in small oak barrels. The Barolo Arborina '20 is full of tension and youth, with fragrant red fruits and green spice on the nose. The palate plays on finesse and elegance, leading to a finish of nice depth. Slightly too prominent tannins do detract from overall harmony, but these will soften with time. The Barolo Giachini '20 is richer and more ready, opening with aromas of ripe red fruits accompanied by sweet spices. The palate is full-bodied and dense.

Renato Corino has managed his own winery in La Morra, where he works alongside his children Chiara and Stefano, since 2005. The estate's vineyards feature plots in the Arborina and Rocche dell'Annunziata crus. Complementing this Barolo production is a Barolo Riserva, made from a selection of grapes sourced from 50-year-old vines in the Rocche dell'Annunziata area. The wines, rooted in tradition, exhibit personality and depth. The Barolo Rocche dell'Annunziata '20 is incredibly clean, revealing red fruit aromas that guide the nose toward elegance and class. The palate is perfectly framed by silky tannins and excellent freshness—a Barolo built on finesse. The modern style adopted for the Barolo Roncaglie '20 also stands out. Red berries alternate with floral notes, underscored by a touch of licorice; the palate is finely calibrated with excellent acidity, making for a highly drinkable wine.

● Barolo Giachini '20	♀♀8
● Barolo Arborina '20	♀♀8
● Barolo Bricco Manescotto '20	♀♀7
● Barolo Ris. '18	♀♀8
● Barolo del Comune di La Morra '20	♀6
● Barbera d'Alba Ciabot dù Re '17	♀♀♀5
● Barolo Giachini '12	♀♀♀7
● Barolo Giachini '11	♀♀♀7
● Barolo Rocche '01	♀♀♀7
● Barbera d'Alba Ciabot dù Re '20	♀♀5
● Barolo Arborina '19	♀♀8
● Barolo Arborina '18	♀♀8
● Barolo Bricco Manescotto '18	♀♀7
● Barolo Giachini '19	♀♀8
● Barolo Ris. '17	♀♀8
● Barolo Ris. '16	♀♀8

● Barolo Rocche dell'Annunziata '20	♀♀8
● Barolo Roncaglie '20	♀♀8
● Barbera d'Alba Pozzo '22	♀♀5
● Barolo Arborina '20	♀♀8
● Barolo del Comune di La Morra '20	♀♀6
● Barolo Rocche dell'Annunziata '16	♀♀♀8
● Barolo Rocche dell'Annunziata '14	♀♀♀8
● Barolo Rocche dell'Annunziata '11	♀♀♀8
● Barolo Rocche dell'Annunziata '10	♀♀♀7
● Barolo Rocche dell'Annunziata '09	♀♀♀7
● Barolo Vign. Rocche '06	♀♀♀7
● Barolo Vign. Rocche '04	♀♀♀8
● Barolo Vign. Rocche '03	♀♀♀8
● Barolo Arborina '19	♀♀8
● Barolo del Comune di La Morra '19	♀♀6
● Barolo Rocche dell'Annunziata '19	♀♀8

il vino di Firenze

On the rolling hills around the city of Florence lie the vineyards and olive groves of Chianti Colli Fiorentini, this small but surprising area is full of beauty, history, good food and above all, excellent wines.

The authors of this unique landscape and the products it can offer are the Winemakers and Farmers who for generations have carefully taken care of preserving a landscape and a culture of living and drinking well that is admired throughout the world.

The winemakers of Chianti Colli Fiorentini have always focused on superior quality products, directing their philosophy towards a strong territoriality and authenticity, creating Wine, Extra Virgin Olive Oil and Vin Santo with a proudly Tuscan character.

It is possible to experience first-hand the uniqueness of these companies, almost all family-run, small and mostly organic, through tastings, cellar tours and above all by staying in their Agriturismo and first-class accommodation facilities.

The Chianti Colli Fiorentini Wineries know how to offer truly unforgettable food and wine experiences, tailor-made for people who want to get lost in the countryside around Florence and appreciate the slow passage of time, listening to stories, meeting people and savoring the true essence of Florence's wine.

chianti-collifiorentini.it

REALIZZATO NELL'AMBITO DELL'INTERVENTO SRG10 ANNO 2023 "PROMOZIONE DEI PRODOTTI DI QUALITÀ"
DEL COMPLEMENTO PER LO SVILUPPO RURALE DELLA TOSCANA 2023/2027, COFINANZIATO CON IL FONDO EUROPEO AGRICOLO PER LO SVILUPPO RURALE (FEASR)

CENTO ANNI DI GALLO NERO.
INSIEME.

IL PRIMO CONSORZIO DI VINO
dal 1924

BEVI RESPONSABILMENTE

VINO NOBILE DI MONTEPULCIANO, TOSCANA.
THE HISTORY-TELLER.

It is in the noble region of Tuscany, the cradle of the Renaissance, that the production of Vino Nobile di Montepulciano has taken place year after year for centuries. It is here, on ancient lands, that expert winemakers have cultivated its Sangiovese grapes for generations. It is here that Vino Nobile di Montepulciano ages for 24 months, acquiring its ruby red colour, intense aroma, and floral and fruity notes. And it is always here that it acquires its unique character, in a perfect balance between passion and quality, know-how and respect for the environment, history and future.

**CONSORZIO
DI TUTELA**

TOSCANA

   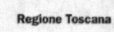

INTERVENTO REALIZZATO CON IL COFINANZIAMENTO FEASR
DEL PIANO SI SVILUPPO RURALE 2014-2020
DELLA REGIONE TOSCANA SOTTOMISURA 3.2

Cornarea

via Valentino, 150
12043 Canale [CN]
☎ +39 017365636
✎ www.cornarea.com

CELLAR SALES
PRE-BOOKED VISITS
ACCOMMODATION
ANNUAL PRODUCTION 90,000 bottles
HECTARES UNDER VINE 14.00

On the Cornarea hill, just outside Canale, the Bovone family tends a contiguous block of vineyards planted between 1975 and 1978 on calcareous-clay soils rich in magnesium. Here, they cultivate the region's two most important varietals: arneis, which makes up 80% of the vineyard area, and nebbiolo. The wines are traditionally crafted in pursuit of typicity and aromatic precision. The splendid Tarasco '20, a passito made from arneis grapes, offers great complexity with lush aromas of nuts, dates, dried figs, cinnamon, cloves, and dried apricot. The palate is rich and elegant, with a balanced, taut, and beautifully long finish. The Roero Santa Margherita '21 impresses with its black fruit and pepper aromas and a juicy, substantial palate. The Nebbiolo d'Alba '22 reveals hints of aromatic herbs, with a smooth and fruity finish, while the Roero Arneis Enritard Riserva '19 proves sapid and energetic.

★Giuseppe Cortese

s.da Rabajà, 80
12050 Barbaresco [CN]
☎ +39 0173635131
✎ www.cortesegiuseppe.it

CELLAR SALES
PRE-BOOKED VISITS
ACCOMMODATION
ANNUAL PRODUCTION 68,000 bottles
HECTARES UNDER VINE 9.00
SUSTAINABLE WINERY

Giuseppe Cortese first bet on Barbaresco in 1971, in times when such a decision was far from obvious. Today, Giuseppe and his wife Rosella are joined by their children Tiziana, Pier Carlo, and son-in-law Gabriele in working the vineyards, some of which go back as many as 70 years, located on one of the historic "Sorì" of the area, the Rabajà, which has defined the identity of this producer. The Barbaresco Rabajà '21 reaffirms its status as the estate's flagship wine, with a generous nose of ripe red and black fruits, spices, and balsamic notes. On the palate, it's sapid and lively, progressing with a firm, taut development toward a long finish, accented by refined nuances of licorice. The Barbaresco '21 displays darker tones, with a well-paced palate and a broad, pleasant progression. Floral and spicy, the Langhe Nebbiolo '22 stands out for its solid, focused profile.

○ Tarasco Passito '20	♥♥ 5
● Nebbiolo d'Alba '22	♥♥ 3
○ Roero Arneis Enritard Ris. '19	♥♥ 4
● Roero Santa Margherita '21	♥♥ 5
○ Roero Arneis '23	♥ 3
● Barbera d'Alba '19	♀♀ 4
● Roero '20	♀♀ 5
● Roero '18	♀♀ 4
○ Roero Arneis '21	♀♀ 3*
○ Roero Arneis '20	♀♀ 3*
○ Roero Arneis En Ritard Ris. '18	♀♀ 4
○ Roero Arneis Enritard '18	♀♀ 3*
○ Tarasco Passito '19	♀♀ 5

● Barbaresco Rabajà '21	♥♥ 8
● Barbaresco '21	♥♥ 6
● Barbera d'Alba Morassina '20	♥♥ 4
● Langhe Nebbiolo '22	♥♥ 5
● Barbera d'Alba '23	♥ 3
● Langhe Dolcetto '23	♥ 3
● Barbaresco Rabaja '19	♀♀♀ 8
● Barbaresco Rabajà '18	♀♀♀ 7
● Barbaresco Rabajà '16	♀♀♀ 6
● Barbaresco Rabajà '15	♀♀♀ 6
● Barbaresco Rabajà '11	♀♀♀ 5
● Barbaresco Rabajà '10	♀♀♀ 5
● Barbaresco Rabajà '08	♀♀♀ 5
● Barbaresco Rabajà Ris. '16	♀♀♀ 8
● Barbaresco Rabajà Ris. '13	♀♀♀ 8
● Barbaresco Rabajà Ris. '96	♀♀♀ 8

PIEDMONT

Cossetti 1891

via Guardie, 1
14043 Castelnuovo Belbo [AT]
📞 +39 0141799803
🖥 www.cossetti.it

CELLAR SALES
PRE-BOOKED VISITS
ACCOMMODATION AND RESTAURANT SERVICE
ANNUAL PRODUCTION 350,000 bottles
HECTARES UNDER VINE 35.00
SUSTAINABLE WINERY

For over a century, the Cossetti name has been synonymous with wine, beginning with Giovanni's founding of the estate. Today, the fourth generation, led by sisters Clementina and Giulia, passionately manage this historic Castelnuovo Belbo property's 30 hectares, focusing on traditional varietals, including red barbera, dolcetto, albarossa, and brachetto, as well as white moscato and cortese. The Nizza Criveletto '22 continues to impress, with its intense aromas of black cherry, underbrush, and aromatic herbs. On the palate, it's both substantial and juicy, with a smooth flow and vibrant acidity supporting the finish. The Piemonte Viognier Lo Zucca '22 is also well-crafted, offering apricot and white fruit notes with a spicy undertone on the nose. The palate is fleshy and structured, sapid and long. The Nizza Lo Zucca '22 plays on tones of ripe black cherry, with a fresh and easy-drinking character.

★Stefanino Costa

b.ta Benna, 5
12046 Montà [CN]
📞 +39 0173976336
ninocostawine@gmail.com

CELLAR SALES
PRE-BOOKED VISITS
ANNUAL PRODUCTION 50,000 bottles
HECTARES UNDER VINE 9.50

The Costa family's winery features estate vineyards located on predominantly sandy soils in the municipalities of Canale, Montà, and Santo Stefano Roero. Here they grow Roero's classic varietals, from arneis to nebbiolo, barbera and brachetto. Their wines are traditionally crafted, emphasizing typicity and precise aromatic expression. A solid showing from the Roero Arneis Seminari. The 2023 reveals a rich and complex nose, with aromas of kaiser pear, spices, and aromatic herbs, followed by a palate marked by good sapidity and smoothness, finishing with a long citrus note. The Roero Arneis Sarun '23, on the other hand, highlights notes of verbena, ginger, and tangerine, offering a pleasant palate of medium length and persistence. The Roero Gepin '20, with its balsamic and floral tones, and the Barbera d'Alba Bardot '23, which features sweet spices and juicy black plum, both show excellent craftsmanship and structure.

● Nizza Crivelletto '22	♀♀♀ 5
● Nizza Lo Zucca '22	♀♀ 6
○ Piemonte Viognier Lo Zucca '22	♀♀ 5
● Barbera d'Asti Sup. La Vigna Vecchia '22	♀ 3
● Barbera d'Asti Gelsomora '21	♀♀ 2*
● Barbera d'Asti Sup. La Vigna Vecchia '21	♀♀ 3
● Barbera d'Asti Sup. La Vigna Vecchia '20	♀♀ 2*
● Barbera d'Asti Sup. La Vigna Vecchia '18	♀♀ 2*
● Barbera d'Asti Venti di Marzo '20	♀♀ 3
● Grignolino d'Asti Gelsomora '21	♀♀ 2*
○ Moscato d'Asti Gelsomora '22	♀♀ 3
○ Moscato d'Asti Gelsomora '21	♀♀ 3*
● Nizza Crivelletto '21	♀♀ 5
● Nizza Crivelletto '19	♀♀ 4
● Nizza Lo Zucca '21	♀♀ 6
○ Piemonte Viognier Lo Zucca '21	♀♀ 5

○ Roero Arneis Seminari '23	♀♀♀ 4*
○ Roero Arneis Sarun '23	♀♀ 4
● Barbera d'Alba Barbot '23	♀♀ 3
● Roero Gepin '20	♀♀ 5
○ Roero Arneis Sarun '21	♀♀♀ 3*
○ Roero Arneis Sarun '20	♀♀♀ 3*
○ Roero Arneis Sarun '19	♀♀♀ 3*
○ Roero Arneis Sarun '18	♀♀♀ 3*
○ Roero Arneis Sarun '17	♀♀♀ 3*
○ Roero Arneis Seminari '22	♀♀♀ 3*
● Roero Gepin '13	♀♀♀ 4*
● Roero Gepin '12	♀♀♀ 4*
● Roero Gepin '11	♀♀♀ 4*
● Roero Gepin '10	♀♀♀ 4*
○ Roero Arneis Seminari '21	♀♀ 3*
○ Roero Arneis Seminari '20	♀♀ 3*
● Roero Gepin '17	♀♀ 5

Giovanni Daglio

via Montale Celli, 10
15050 Costa Vescovato [AL]
(℘ +39 0131838262
✉ www.vignetidaglio.com

CELLAR SALES
ANNUAL PRODUCTION 15,000 bottles
HECTARES UNDER VINE 10.00

The Giovanni Daglio winery deserves special recognition this year for its excellent range of wines. Born into a family of farmers, Giovanni pursued studies in Genoa before realizing his true calling was agriculture. In the 1980s, he returned to his roots, steering the estate toward viticulture. His deep connection to the land is evident in the wines, which are made with the goal of faithfully capturing the essence of the grapes and the region. This year, the two Derthona wines captivate with their structure and finesse. The Colli Tortonesi Timorasso Derthona Cantico '20 enchants with its rich and dynamic profile, revealing notes of grapefruit, citron, chalk, benzine, and tobacco. The palate is flavorful and powerful, balanced by a beautiful sapid note. Nearly as refined, the Colli Tortonesi Timorasso Derthona '22 opens with mustard seed, fresh herbs, and citrus. Though the palate's structure is still tight in its youth, this is a wine with excellent potential.

○ Colli Tortonesi Timorasso Derthona Cantico '20	♟♟ 4
● Colli Tortonesi Barbera Basinas '18	♟♟ 4
● Colli Tortonesi Barbera Pias '22	♟♟ 3
○ Colli Tortonesi Timorasso Derthona '22	♟♟ 4
● Colli Tortonesi Barbera Basinas '17	♟♟ 4
● Colli Tortonesi Barbera Pias '21	♟♟ 3
● Colli Tortonesi Dolcetto Nibiö '17	♟♟ 3
○ Colli Tortonesi Timorasso Cantico '19	♟♟ 4
○ Colli Tortonesi Timorasso Cantico '18	♟♟ 4
○ Colli Tortonesi Timorasso Cantico '17	♟♟ 4
○ Colli Tortonesi Timorasso Derthona '21	♟♟ 4
○ Colli Tortonesi Timorasso Derthona '19	♟♟ 4
○ Colli Tortonesi Timorasso Derthona '18	♟♟ 4
○ Colli Tortonesi Timorasso Derthona '17	♟♟ 4

Deltetto 1953

c.so Alba, 43
12043 Canale [CN]
(℘ +39 0173979383
✉ www.deltetto.com

CELLAR SALES
PRE-BOOKED VISITS
ANNUAL PRODUCTION 190,000 bottles
HECTARES UNDER VINE 30.00
VITICULTURE METHOD Certified Organic
SUSTAINABLE WINERY

The Deltetto family winery, a prominent player in the Roero landscape, produces a wide range. In recent years, they have expanded from a focus on Roero so as to include sparkling Alta Langa, utilizing chardonnay and pinot nero vineyards in Roddino, as well as prestigious appellations such as Barolo and Gavi. Their production approach is modern, with a particular focus on expressing the terroir. Standing out among the winery's range are the Roero Roncaglie Riserva '19, with its aromas of black fruits and sweet spices, and a fresh, long, and energetic palate, and the Barbera d'Alba Superiore Rocca delle Marasche '21, which offers red forest fruits and white pepper on the nose, while the palate is rich, juicy, and pleasant. The Roero Arneis 2023, San Michele, showcases sweet citrus and aromatic herbs, with good energy and tension. The Daivej, with its pear and almond aromas, follows with a palate of nice sapidity and persistence.

● Barbera d'Alba Sup. Rocca delle Marasche '21	♟♟ 5
● Roero Roncaglia Ris. '19	♟♟ 6
● Langhe Pinot Nero 777 '21	♟♟ 4
⊙ Nebbiolo d'Alba Spumante Rosé Brut M. Cl. '20	♟♟ 5
○ Roero Arneis Daivej '23	♟♟ 3
○ Roero Arneis San Michele '23	♟♟ 3
● Roero Gorrini Ris. '20	♟♟ 5
○ Alat Langa Brut '20	♟ 5
○ Alta Langa Brut Nature Blanc De Blancs Ris. '19	♟ 6
○ Alta Langa Brut Nature Blanc de Noirs Ris. '19	♟ 6
○ Roero Arneis San Defendente Ris '21	♟ 5
● Roero Braja Ris. '09	♟♟♟ 4*
● Roero Braja Ris. '08	♟♟♟ 4

Dezzani

c.so Pinin Giachino, 140
14023 Cocconato [AT]
📞 +39 0141907236
🌐 www.dezzani.it

CELLAR SALES
PRE-BOOKED VISITS
ANNUAL PRODUCTION 1,200,000 bottles
HECTARES UNDER VINE 20.00
VITICULTURE METHOD Certified Organic
SUSTAINABLE WINERY

Founded in 1934 by Luigi Dezzani, the winery has seen renewed energy over the past 15 years under the Rocca family, which has been involved in the wine world for five generations. Around 100 wine-growing families across Langhe, Roero, and Monferrato supply the grapes for their range, which is crafted with a modern touch, emphasizing the characteristics of the varietals used and their origin. The Barbera d'Asti Superiore 80 Anni '20 is outstanding, with its characteristic aromas of rain-soaked earth and black forest fruits, leading to a taut palate rich in fruit, with a long and pleasant finish. Also well-crafted, the Barbera d'Asti Superiore La Luna e Le Stelle '21, offers up ginger, rhubarb, and underbrush on the nose, while the palate is juicy, sapid, fresh, and drinkable. We also appreciated the Ruché di Castagnole Monferrato '23, with its vibrant nose where spicy notes stand out, and a slightly tannic but soft and pervasive finish on the palate.

★Gianni Doglia

via Annunziata, 56
14054 Castagnole delle Lanze [AT]
📞 +39 0141878359
🌐 www.giannidoglia.it

CELLAR SALES
PRE-BOOKED VISITS
ANNUAL PRODUCTION 110,000 bottles
HECTARES UNDER VINE 16.00
SUSTAINABLE WINERY

Nestled in a corner of paradise in the Annunziata hamlet of Castagnole delle Lanze, this family-run winery is led by the talented duo Paola and Gianni Doglia. One of Moscato d'Asti's leading producers, the winery also excels with its barbera, delivering impeccable interpretations. With a now internationally recognized reputation for quality, every visit here offers new insights. Take, for example, the elegant and pure Casa di Bianca, a wine that has become a standard-bearer for the grape and region. The producer's style favors freshness and drinkability, which can also be found in their more complex and structured wines. The Grignolino, with its rare charm and harmony, sets the stage for the barbera-based reds, which once again impress with their varietal clarity, led by the Nizza Vecchie Viti '22, a wine in great form. The Casa di Bianca '23, despite hailing from a scorching vintage, reveals energy and exceptional expressive dynamism.

● Barbera d'Asti Sup. 80 Anni '20	4
● Barbera d'Asti Sup. La Luna e le Stelle '21	3
● Ruchè di Castagnole M.to '23	3
● Barbera d'Asti Sup. 80 Anni '18	4
● Barbera d'Asti Sup. Gli Scaglioni '13	7
● Barbera d'Asti Sup. La Luna e le Stelle '20	3*
● Barbera d'Asti Sup. La Luna e Le Stelle '19	3*
○ Gavi '22	3
● Piemonte Doc Albarossa '20	3

○ Canelli Casa di Bianca '23	5
● Barbera d'Asti Sup. Genio '22	5
● Nizza Vecchie Viti '22	5
● Barbera d'Asti Bosco Donne '23	4
● Grignolino d'Asti Il Grignolino '23	3
○ Moscato d'Asti '23	3
● Barbera d'Asti Bosco Donne '20	3*
● Barbera d'Asti Sup. Genio '12	4*
○ Canelli Casa di Bianca '22	4*
○ Moscato d'Asti Casa di Bianca '21	4*
○ Moscato d'Asti Casa di Bianca '19	3*
○ Moscato d'Asti Casa di Bianca '17	5
○ Moscato d'Asti Casa di Bianca '16	3*
○ Moscato d'Asti Casa di Bianca '15	3*
○ Moscato d'Asti Casa di Bianca '18	3*

Dosio Vigneti

reg. Serradenari, 6
12064 La Morra [CN]
☎ +39 017350677
🖰 www.dosiovigneti.com

CELLAR SALES
PRE-BOOKED VISITS
ACCOMMODATION
ANNUAL PRODUCTION 100,000 bottles
HECTARES UNDER VINE 17.00
SUSTAINABLE WINERY

Based in the Serradenari area near La Morra, Dosio operated on the fringes of Barolo's rising success when Giuseppe Dosio was the owner. For the past decade, however, the winery has been owned by manager Gianfranco Lanci (president of Lenovo and a former executive of Acer and Texas Instruments), who also owns Coppo in Canelli. Lanci has been slowly but surely guiding the winery along a successful path. The Barolo del Comune di La Morra '20 is decisively well-crafted, offering intense aromas of red fruits intertwined with citrus hints and touches of pomegranate. A sharp, acidic freshness drives the palate, ensuring rhythm and a rising finish. The Langhe Sauvignon Olivia '23 features a delightful aromatic profile, with notes of tomato leaf and yellow fruit. The palate is rich, juicy, and sapid. The Barbaresco '21, too, is focused and well-crafted, with a fleshy, persistent character.

Durio

Reg. Montà n.9
14041 Agliano Terme [AT]
☎ +39 3311591587
🖰 www.duriowines.com

Alessandro and Alberto Durio represent the third generation of family to manage the winery, which was founded in the 1950s. The estate's vineyards, situated on clay-limestone soils and, at higher elevations, sandy marl, are predominantly planted with barbera, though nebbiolo, grignolino, dolcetto, arneis, and cortese are also grown. Their wines are modern in style and technically well-crafted. At the top of the winery's lineup is the Barbera d'Asti Per Berto '23, with its vibrant aromas of black fruit, petrichor, Mediterranean scrub, and tobacco. The palate is rich with fruit, fleshy yet taut, long, and highly drinkable. The Grignolino d'Asti '22 offers characteristic floral notes and white pepper on the nose, followed by hints of candied orange peel and a tightly knit, tannic palate, with good energy and freshness. Other well-crafted wines include the Barbera d'Asti L'Armatore '23, with its fine structure and fleshiness, and the sapid, easy-drinking Nizza Pragerolamo '21.

Wine	Score
● Barolo del Comune di La Morra '20	♔♔ 6
● Barbaresco '21	♔♔ 5
● Barolo Fossati '20	♔♔ 8
○ Langhe Sauvignon Olivia '23	♔♔ 3
● Barbera d'Alba Sup. '21	♔ 4
● Barolo Serradenari '20	♔ 8
● Langhe Nebbiolo '22	♔ 3
● Barolo del Comune di La Morra '19	♕♕ 6
● Barolo Fossati '18	♕♕ 7
● Barolo Fossati '16	♕♕ 7
● Barolo Fossati Ris. '12	♕♕ 8
● Barolo Serradenari '19	♕♕ 8
● Barolo Serradenari '18	♕♕ 7
● Barolo Serradenari '17	♕♕ 7
● Barolo Serradenari '15	♕♕ 7
● Langhe Momenti '16	♕♕ 5

Wine	Score
● Barbera d'Asti Per Berto '23	♔♔ 2*
● Grignolino d'Asti '22	♔♔ 4
● Barbera d'Asti L'Armatore '23	♔♔ 4
● Nizza Pragerolamo '21	♔♔ 3
● Barbera d'Asti L'Armatore '22	♕♕ 4
● Nizza Pragerolamo '20	♕♕ 3*

★Poderi Luigi Einaudi

loc. Cascina Tecc
b.ta Gombe, 31/32
12063 Dogliani [CN]
📞 +39 017370191
🌐 www.poderieinaudi.com

CELLAR SALES
PRE-BOOKED VISITS
ACCOMMODATION
ANNUAL PRODUCTION 350,000 bottles
HECTARES UNDER VINE 70.00
SUSTAINABLE WINERY

The story of Poderi Luigi Einaudi begins in 1897, when Luigi Einaudi purchased Cascina San Giacomo, not far from the center of Dogliani. Despite his academic and political career, Einaudi never missed a harvest, even when serving as President of the Republic, bequeathing Langhe with a model winery. This legacy continued through his son Roberto and persists today under the guidance of his grandson Matteo Sardagna. The excellent Barolo Cannubi '20 showcases clearly defined aromas of small red fruits and spices, with touches of licorice. On the palate, its texture is fleshy and well-structured, juicy and fragrant, moving with supple, flavorful ease. The Barolo Monvigliero '20 is also outstanding, with its citrusy aromatic tones and solid, austere progression of flavor. The Barolo Ludo '20 places red fruit at the forefront, with nice tension in the mouth and hints of tobacco and licorice refining the finish. The Barolo Villero '20 is particularly fine, with its powerful and decisive character.

● Barolo Cannubi '20	♟♟ 8
● Barolo Monvigliero '20	♟♟ 8
● Barolo Villero '20	♟♟ 8
● Barolo Bussia '20	♟♟ 8
● Barolo Ludo '20	♟♟ 6
● Dogliani Sup. V. Tecc '22	♟♟ 4
● Verduno Pelaverga '23	♟♟ 3
● Barbaresco Bric Micca '21	♟ 6
● Barolo Terlo V. Costa Grimaldi '20	♟ 7
● Langhe Nebbiolo '23	♟ 4
● Barolo Cannubi '16	♟♟♟ 8
● Barolo Cannubi '15	♟♟♟ 8
● Barolo Cannubi '11	♟♟♟ 8
● Barolo Cannubi '10	♟♟♟ 8
● Barolo Terlo V. Costa Grimaldi '19	♟♟♟ 7
● Dogliani Sup. V. Tecc '10	♟♟♟ 3*

F.lli Facchino

loc. Val del Prato, 210
15078 Rocca Grimalda [AL]
📞 +39 014385401
🌐 www.vinifacchino.it

CELLAR SALES
PRE-BOOKED VISITS
RESTAURANT SERVICE
ANNUAL PRODUCTION 80,000 bottles
HECTARES UNDER VINE 31.00

The Facchino family's roots run deep in the hills of Rocca Grimalda, where Giorgio, together with his wife Rosaria, decided to open their winery in 1958. Today, the couple's children, Carmine and Teresa, alongside Giorgio and Diego, continue the tradition. The grapes, cultivated exclusively in their own vineyards, are vinified using the latest winemaking techniques while maintaining a respect for tradition—an approach they've honed over the years. The Barbera del Monferrato '22 offers extraordinary drinkability, opening with notes of blackcurrant syrup, raspberry, and spices. On the palate, it displays a finely polished elegance, with a progressive, lengthy finish. The Apostrofo 58 '20 has a more herbaceous nose, with green spice notes. This ensures a fresh, energaletic palate that brings balance to the wine. The Dolcetto di Ovada '22 also performs well, with intense blackberry and currant sensations on the nose, finishing slightly warm. The palate is rich, with a rather long finish. The Poggiobello '19 shows great concentration, still a bit stern but already rich with fruit and featuring dense, fine tannins.

● Barbera del M.to '22	♟♟ 2*
● Ovada Poggiobello '19	♟♟ 3*
● Dolcetto di Ovada '22	♟♟ 2*
● M.to Rosso Apostrofo 58 '20	♟♟ 4
● Barbera del M.to Terre del Re '21	♟ 3
● Barbera del M.to '16	♟♟♟ 2*
● Barbera del M.to Terre del Re '20	♟♟ 2*
○ Cortese dell'Alto M.to Pacialan '22	♟♟ 2*
● Dolcetto di Ovada '17	♟♟ 2*
● Dolcetto di Ovada '16	♟♟ 2*
● Dolcetto di Ovada Poggiobello '16	♟♟ 2*
● Dolcetto di Ovada Poggiobello '15	♟♟ 2*
● Ovada Carasöi '18	♟♟ 4
● Ovada Poggiobello '18	♟♟ 2*
○ Piemonte Chardonnay '22	♟♟ 2*

Tenuta Il Falchetto

fraz. Ciombi
via Valle Tinella, 16
12058 Santo Stefano Belbo [CN]
+39 0141840344
www.ilfalchetto.com

CELLAR SALES
PRE-BOOKED VISITS
ANNUAL PRODUCTION 280,000 bottles
HECTARES UNDER VINE 52.00
SUSTAINABLE WINERY

The Forno brothers, Giorgio, Fabrizio, and Adriano, produce a diverse range of wines, both in terms of grapes and growing areas. The varieties cultivated, primarily barbera and moscato from the Nizza and Canelli appellations, as well as chardonnay, cabernet sauvignon, merlot, pinot nero, and dolcetto, hail from some six different properties across the provinces of Cuneo and Asti. Their goal is to highlight the unique characteristics of each varietal as well as the essence of the terroir. The Canelli Tenuta del Fant '23 offers elegant floral and fruity notes, with a touch of candied orange zest. The palate is harmonious, with a masterful balance of sweetness and acidity, finishing long and vibrant. The Nizza Bricco Roche Riserva '18 impresses with its red berry and damp earth aromas, followed by a juicy, smooth palate marked by finesse and pleasure. The Moscato d'Asti Ciombo '23, always well-crafted, plays on tones of medicinal herbs, honey, and peach, with notable sweetness balanced by fresh acidity on the finish.

○ Canelli Tenuta del Fant '23	🍷🍷 3*
● Nizza Bricco Roche Ris. '18	🍷🍷 6
○ Moscato d'Asti Ciombo '23	🍷🍷 3
○ Moscato d'Asti Canelli Ciombo '17	YYY 2*
○ Moscato d'Asti Canelli Tenuta del Fant '22	YYY 2*
○ Moscato d'Asti Canelli Tenuta del Fant '21	YYY 2*
○ Moscato d'Asti Ciombo '15	YYY 2*
○ Moscato d'Asti Tenuta del Fant '11	YYY 2*
○ Moscato d'Asti Tenuta del Fant '09	YYY 2*
● Barbera d'Asti Pian Scorrone '22	YY 2*
● Barbera d'Asti Pian Scorrone '21	YY 2*
● Barbera d'Asti Sup. Bricco Paradiso '18	YY 4
● Barbera d'Asti Superiore Lurëi '21	YY 3*
● M.to Nebbiolo Sup. Barbarossa '20	YY 4

Benito Favaro

s.da Chiusure, 1bis
10010 Piverone [TO]
+39 012572606
www.cantinafavaro.it

CELLAR SALES
PRE-BOOKED VISITS
ANNUAL PRODUCTION 20,000 bottles
HECTARES UNDER VINE 3.50
VITICULTURE METHOD Certified Organic

The Favaro family are artisans of the vineyard, custodians of a cultural heritage represented by the unique erbaluce grape. Today, Camillo, son of Benito, leads the winery, continuing the meticulous work of this small producer both in the vineyard and the cellar, always with a focus on erbaluce di Caluso. The wines that emerge from their Piverone cellar are crafted with a conscious and rigorous approach, resulting in a range of great charm and energy. The Canavese Nebbiolo Pies '22 is a well-crafted wine, showcasing berry aromas with touches of licorice bark. On the palate, it's supple, with a rhythmic progression and refined contrasts. The Canavese Nebbiolo Ros '22 is just as good, offering clear and fragrant fruit aromas, with a flavorful, dynamic, and persistent palate. Shining as always, the Erbaluce Tredicimesi skillfully combines structure and freshness on the palate with a mineral, elegant finish.

● Canavese Nebbiolo Pies '22	🍷🍷 6
● Canavese Nebbiolo Ros '22	🍷🍷 5
○ Erbaluce di Caluso Tredicimesi '22	🍷🍷 5
● Cavanese Rosso F2 '22	🍷🍷 5
○ Erbaluce di Caluso Le Chiusure '22	🍷🍷 5
● Rossomeraviglia '22	🍷🍷 5
○ Erbaluce di Caluso Le Chiusure '20	YYY 4*
○ Erbaluce di Caluso Le Chiusure '16	YYY 2*
○ Erbaluce di Caluso Le Chiusure '13	YYY 2*
○ Erbaluce di Caluso Le Chiusure '12	YYY 2*
○ Erbaluce di Caluso Le Chiusure '11	YYY 2*
○ Erbaluce di Caluso Le Chiusure '10	YYY 2*
○ Erbaluce di Caluso Tredicimesi '17	YYY 4*
○ Erbaluce di Caluso Tredicimesi '16	YYY 3*

Giacomo Fenocchio

loc. Bussia, 72
12065 Monforte d'Alba [CN]
(+39 017378675
www.giacomofenocchio.com

CELLAR SALES
PRE-BOOKED VISITS
ACCOMMODATION
ANNUAL PRODUCTION 95,000 bottles
HECTARES UNDER VINE 16.00
SUSTAINABLE WINERY

Monforte's Fenocchio family embarked on their successful winemaking journey in 1989 with Claudio Fenocchio, after his father Giacomo had been developing the wine business since the 1950s as a grape supplier. Today, the estate's wines—born in the crus Bussia (owned by the Fenocchio family since 1972), Cannubi, Villero, and Castellero—maintain an authentic, traditional style, free from any forced interventions. The 2020 version of the Barolo Cannubi is particularly noteworthy, with its refined nose of citrus, floral hints, and traces of anise. In the mouth, the palate is notably sapid and dynamic, with sustained development and a broad, lively finish. Not far behind is the Barolo Villero '20, with its focused aromas and a lively, dynamic palate. The Barolo Bussia 90 Dì Ris. '18 is fine and spicy, a more compact wine with a complex tannic weave.

● Barolo Cannubi '20	❦❦❦	8
● Barolo Villero '20	❦❦	8
● Barolo Bussia '20	❦❦	8
● Barolo Bussia 90 Dì Ris. '18	❦❦	8
● Barolo Castellero '20	❦❦	8
● Barolo Bussia '11	❦❦❦	6
● Barolo Bussia '09	❦❦❦	6
● Barolo Bussia 90 Dì Ris. '12	❦❦❦	8
● Barolo Bussia 90 Dì Ris. '10	❦❦❦	8
● Barolo Castellero '18	❦❦❦	6
● Barolo Bussia '19	❦❦	6
● Barolo Bussia '18	❦❦	6
● Barolo Bussia '17	❦❦	6
● Barolo Bussia 90 Dì Ris. '16	❦❦	8
● Barolo Cannubi '19	❦❦	7
● Barolo Villero '17	❦❦	7

Ferrando

via Torino, 599
10015 Ivrea [TO]
(+39 0125633550
www.ferrandovini.it

CELLAR SALES
PRE-BOOKED VISITS
ANNUAL PRODUCTION 50,000 bottles
HECTARES UNDER VINE 5.00

The Ferrando family has been producing Carema—a wine made from nebbiolo grapes and nicknamed the "Barolo of the mountains"— since the late 1950s, a full decade before it was recognized as an appellation. Today, Roberto and Andrea Ferrando continue to elevate this variety, which has become the winery's flagship. Over time, they've expanded to produce the entire range of Canavese wines, with Erbaluce di Caluso, in both sparkling and passito styles, leading the charge. The 2020 Carema Etichetta Bianca is a beautiful rendition, redolent of red flowers and spices like cloves. The palate is sweet, with intriguing softness and mellow tannins, offering length, elegance, and persistence. The Etichetta Nera is marked by deep notes of iron, tobacco, and licorice, delivering great finesse and delicate aromas. Both versions of Erbaluce are commendable, with the Etichetta Bianca offering subtly whispered exotic notes, rich and mature, while the Verde is more Mediterranean, harmonious, and taut.

● Carema Et. Nera '20	❦❦	7
● Carema Et. Bianca '20	❦❦	5
○ Erbaluce di Caluso Et. Bianca '23	❦❦	3
○ Erbaluce di Caluso Et. Verde '23	❦❦	3
● Carema Et. Bianca '12	❦❦❦	5
● Carema Et. Nera '11	❦❦❦	7
● Carema Et. Nera '09	❦❦❦	6
● Carema Et. Nera '08	❦❦❦	6
● Carema Et. Nera '07	❦❦❦	6
● Carema Et. Nera '06	❦❦❦	6
● Carema Et. Nera '05	❦❦❦	6
● Carema Et. Nera '01	❦❦❦	5
● Carema Et. Bianca '19	❦❦	5
● Carema Et. Nera '19	❦❦	7

Roberto Ferraris

fraz. Dogliano, 33
14041 Agliano Terme [AT]
(» +39 3200950639
www.robertoferraris.com

CELLAR SALES
PRE-BOOKED VISITS
ANNUAL PRODUCTION 70,000 bottles
HECTARES UNDER VINE 12.00
SUSTAINABLE WINERY

Barbera is undoubtedly the star here at Ferraris. Founded in the 1920s by Stefano Ferraris and now led by the third and fourth generations, Roberto and Marco, the winery is based in Agliano Terme, where the primarily silty-limestone soils with low clay content give rise to a fresh and vibrant Barbera del Monferrato Astigiano that stands out for its typicity. Five different versions are produced, each with its own nuances. The Barbera d'Asti Superiore Bisavolo '22 shines with its tones of rain-soaked earth and red berries, juicy, sapid, and energetic, finishing with energy. The Piemonte Pinot Nero Valmanella '22 offers vibrant fresh fruity and smoky notes on the nose, with a palate of good harmony and finesse. The fleshy and fresh Nizza Liberta '21 reveals black fruit and undergrowth flavors. The juicy and substantive Barbera d'Asti Superiore La Cricca '22 is also well-crafted, as is the Barbera d'Asti Nobbio '22, which plays on sweet fruit, cinchona, and chocolate tones.

Ferraris Agricola

loc. Rivi, 7
s.da prov.le 14
14030 Castagnole Monferrato [AT]
(» +39 0141292202
www.ferrarisagricola.com

CELLAR SALES
PRE-BOOKED VISITS
ACCOMMODATION
ANNUAL PRODUCTION 300,000 bottles
HECTARES UNDER VINE 36.00
SUSTAINABLE WINERY

The winery's story is deeply intertwined with the USA. Initially, the savings of great-grandfather Luigi, who emigrated to America, provided the initial funds, and more recently, Californian Randall Grahm significantly contributed to the creation of the Ruchè line. It was Luigi Ferraris, the namesake grandson, who completely renovated the old cellar in 1999, breathing new life into this century-old establishment. Their Ruché di Castagnole Monferrato wines are among the best of the appellation. The Riserva Castelletto di Montemagno '21 shines with its bright notes of rose, citrus, and berries, with a rich palate and a tannic structure that maintains the right austerity through a long finish. The Sant'Eufemia '23 is harmonious, with delicate tannins and floral and red fruit tones. The Riserva Opera Prima '21 combines rose and cocoa aromas with a dense, almost chewy palate, while the Clàsic '23 proves smooth and immediately approachable.

Wine	Rating
● Barbera d'Asti Sup. Bisavolo '22	♀♀ 3*
● Piemonte Pinot Nero Valmanella '21	♀♀ 5
● Barbera d'Asti Nobbio '22	♀♀ 3
● Nizza Liberta '21	♀♀ 5
● M.to Nebbiolo Grixa '22	♀ 4
● Nizza Liberta '15	♀♀♀ 5
● Barbera d'Asti Nobbio '20	♀♀ 3*
● Barbera d'Asti Nobbio '19	♀♀ 3*
● Barbera d'Asti Sup. Bisavolo '21	♀♀ 3
● Barbera d'Asti Sup. Bisavolo '19	♀♀ 3*
● Barbera d'Asti Sup. La Cricca '21	♀♀ 4
● M.to Nebbiolo Grixa '21	♀♀ 4
● Nizza Liberta '20	♀♀ 5
● Nizza Liberta '18	♀♀ 5
● Piemonte Pinot Nero Valmanella '21	♀♀ 5

Wine	Rating
● Ruché di Castagnole Monferrato Castelletto di Montemagno Ris. '21	♀♀ 5
● Ruché di Castagnole Monferrato Sant'Eufemia '23	♀♀ 3*
○ Piemonte Viognier Bisou '21	♀♀ 5
○ Piemonte Viognier Sensazioni '23	♀♀ 3
● Ruché di Castagnole Monferrato Clàsic '23	♀♀ 4
● Ruché di Castagnole Monferrato Opera Prima Ris. '21	♀♀ 6
● Ruché di Castagnole M.to Clàsic '21	♀♀♀ 4*
● Ruché di Castagnole M.to Clàsic '20	♀♀♀ 3*
● Ruchè di Castagnole M.to Clàsic '19	♀♀♀ 3*
● Barbera d'Asti Superiore Ca' Mongròss La Regina '21	♀♀ 4
● Ruché di Castagnole M.to Clàsic '22	♀♀ 4
● Ruché di Castagnole M.to V. del Parroco '22	♀♀ 5

Livia Fontana

via Fontana, 1
12060 Castiglione Falletto [CN]
(+39 017362844
@ www.liviafontana.it

Fontanabianca

loc. Bordini, 15
12057 Neive [CN]
(+39 017367195
@ www.fontanabianca.it

CELLAR SALES
PRE-BOOKED VISITS
ACCOMMODATION
ANNUAL PRODUCTION 60,000 bottles
HECTARES UNDER VINE 10.00
SUSTAINABLE WINERY

CELLAR SALES
PRE-BOOKED VISITS
ANNUAL PRODUCTION 110,000 bottles
HECTARES UNDER VINE 17.00
SUSTAINABLE WINERY

Livia made a smart move by involving her sons, Lorenzo and Michele, in repositioning this historic winery (an ancient municipal document confirms that the Fontana family has been cultivating vines on these hills since 1643). In just a few short years, the winery has flourished. Half a hectare of Villero has been replanted through massal selection to eliminate gaps, and investments in the cellar have led to improvements, including the installation of large Stockinger barrels. The Villero impresses once again with its refined elegance, featuring notes of citrus, violet, and sweet spices, with a delicately balsamic finish and a bright ruby color. The Fontanin, named after the family's old name, is finer and more approachable, opting for undergrowth aromas, dried flowers, and licorice. The Barbera stands out with a palate of excellent structure and depth, featuring lovely blackberry notes. Mint and mineral hints characterize the fragrant, sapid and crisp Arneis, with its flavors of white fruit. The Nebbiolo offers a juicy palate with floral aromas.

Aldo Pola, along with his family, has invested considerable energy in their winery in Neive, continuing the work started by his father, Franco, in 1969. The most important Barbaresco crus produced are Bordini and Serraboella, which deeply express their connection to their native territory. In addition to nebbiolo, they also cultivate dolcetto, barbera, and arneis, enriching their portfolio with the most important appellations from the region. The Barbaresco '21 is a refined pour, releasing aromas of small red fruits, citrus, and spices. On the palate, the wine is firm, with compact tannins and a focused finish. Red fruit and licorice characterize the Barbaresco Bordini '21, a wine with a strong palate and a tight tannic structure, but also greater length. The Langhe Arneis Sommo '23 sees aromas of white peach combine with tomato leaf, with a rich, clearly defined palate.

● Barolo Villero '20	♟♟♟8
● Barbera d'Alba Sup. '21	♟♟6
● Barolo Fontanin '20	♟♟8
● Langhe Nebbiolo '22	♟♟6
○ Roero Arneis '23	♟♟5
● Barolo Villero '19	♟♟♟8
● Barbera d'Alba Sup. '20	♟♟6
● Barolo Bussia Ris. '17	♟♟8
● Barolo Bussia Ris. '16	♟♟8
● Barolo Fontanin '19	♟♟8
● Barolo Fontanin '17	♟♟5
● Barolo Fontanin '16	♟♟5
● Barolo Villero '18	♟♟8
● Barolo Villero '17	♟♟8
○ Roero Arneis '22	♟♟5
● Roero Arneis '21	♟♟3

● Barbaresco Bordini '21	♟♟6
● Barbaresco '21	♟♟5
○ Langhe Arneis Sommo '23	♟♟3
● Barbaresco Serraboella '21	♟6
● Barbera d'Alba Sup. '22	♟4
● Barolo del Comune di Serralunga d'Alba Ris. '18	♟8
● Barbaresco Serraboella '06	♟♟♟6
● Barbaresco Sorì Burdin '05	♟♟♟6
● Barbaresco Sorì Burdin '04	♟♟♟6
● Barbaresco Sorì Burdin '01	♟♟♟6
● Barbaresco Sorì Burdin '98	♟♟♟7
● Barbaresco Bordini '18	♟♟6
● Barbaresco Bordini '13	♟♟6
● Barbaresco Serraboella '20	♟♟6
● Barbaresco Serraboella '16	♟♟6

Fontanafredda

loc. Fontanafredda
via Alba, 15
12050 Serralunga d'Alba [CN]
(☏) +39 0173626111
✆ www.fontanafredda.it

CELLAR SALES
PRE-BOOKED VISITS
ACCOMMODATION AND RESTAURANT SERVICE
ANNUAL PRODUCTION 7,000,000 bottles
HECTARES UNDER VINE 120.00
VITICULTURE METHOD Certified Organic
SUSTAINABLE WINERY

Fontanafredda is steeped in history. Located in Serralunga d'Alba, it was once owned by King Vittorio Emanuele II, who gifted it to Rosa Vercellana, known as "Bela Rusin," his mistress for many years. Their son, Emanuele Guerrieri, started the winery in 1878, adopting a highly modern approach, making Fontanafredda a pioneer in the industry. In recent years, after a series of changes, the estate was acquired by Oscar Farinetti, who has restored it to its former glory. The Barolo Paiagallo Vigna La Villa '20 possesses a fruity nose adorned by hints of tobacco and cinchona, along with some ethereal nuances. In the mouth, the palate is flavorful, with a compact finish. Red fruit is more defined in the Barolo del Comune di Serralunga d'Alba '20, a medium-bodied and evenly proportioned wine that finishes clean and still fruity. The nose of the Riserva '17 proves complex and multifaceted, delivering weight and structure as well on the palate, all balanced by beautiful harmony.

Fortemasso

loc. Castelletto, 21
12065 Monforte d'Alba [CN]
(☏) +39 0173328148
✆ www.fortemasso.it

CELLAR SALES
PRE-BOOKED VISITS
ANNUAL PRODUCTION 61,000 bottles
HECTARES UNDER VINE 13.50

In 2013, the Gussalli Beretta family entered the Langhe by acquiring plots in Castelletto, including one in the prestigious Pressenda vineyard, and in San Sebastiano of Monforte d'Alba. Fortemasso, a winery that quickly established itself as one of the most solid in the area, produces not only Barolo but also Langhe Nebbiolo and Barbera d'Alba. Their wines are well-crafted and consistently reliable in quality. The Barolo Castelletto '20 is a focused wine, with red and black ripe fruit, spices, and balsamic notes characterizing its aromatic suite. In the mouth it's decisive and sapid, with firm development and a back palate that stands out for its mellow tannins and a fruity encore. Licorice and small red fruits characterize the aromas of the Barbera d'Alba Superiore '22, a wine with nice richness on the palate. The Dolcetto d'Alba '23 offers delicate floral aromas, with a fragrant, flavorful, and enjoyable palate.

● Barolo Ris. '17	♛♛ 8
● Barolo del Comune di Serralunga d'Alba '20	♛♛ 7
● Barolo V. La Villa Paiagallo '20	♛♛ 8
○ Alta Langa Blanc de Blancs '20	♛ 5
● Barolo Proprietà in Fontanafredda '20	♛ 8
○ Langhe Chardonnay Ampelio '22	♛ 5
● Nebbiolo d'Alba Marne Brune '20	♛ 5
● Barolo Fontanafredda V. La Rosa '07	♛♛♛ 7
● Barolo Lazzarito V. La Delizia '04	♛♛♛ 8
● Barolo Lazzarito V. La Delizia '01	♛♛♛ 7
● Barolo Lazzarito V. La Delizia '99	♛♛♛ 7
● Barolo Ris. '16	♛♛♛ 8
● Barolo V. La Rosa '04	♛♛♛ 7
● Barolo V. La Rosa '00	♛♛♛ 7
● Barolo Paiagallo V. La Villa '19	♛♛ 8

● Barolo Castelletto '20	♛♛♛ 8
● Barbera d'Alba Sup. '22	♛♛ 5
● Dolcetto d'Alba '23	♛♛ 3
● Langhe Nebbiolo '23	♛♛ 4
● Barolo Castelletto '16	♛♛♛ 6
● Barolo Castelletto Ris. '17	♛♛♛ 8
● Barolo Castelletto Ris. '16	♛♛♛ 8
● Barolo Castelletto Ris. '15	♛♛♛ 8
● Barolo Castelletto Ris. '13	♛♛♛ 8
● Barbera d'Alba Sup. '21	♛♛ 5
● Barolo Castelletto '19	♛♛ 8
● Barolo Castelletto '18	♛♛ 7
● Barolo Castelletto '17	♛♛ 7
● Barolo Castelletto '15	♛♛ 6
● Barolo Castelletto '14	♛♛ 6
● Barolo Castelletto '13	♛♛ 6

Frasca - La Guaragna

s.da Antica Fornace, 31
14051 Canelli [AT]
☎ +39 3404270939
🌐 www.frascawine.com

Davide Fregonese

via Roddino, 10/1
12050 Serralunga d'Alba [CN]
☎ +39 3409643637
🌐 www.davidefregonese.com

CELLAR SALES
PRE-BOOKED VISITS
ANNUAL PRODUCTION 80,000 bottles
HECTARES UNDER VINE 22.00

ANNUAL PRODUCTION 5,000 bottles
HECTARES UNDER VINE 1.00

Even if it's less than 10 years old, Frasca - La Guaragna already has a clear vision. Founded in 2017 by American Curt Frasca, the winery now boasts over 20 hectares of vineyards, primarily in Nizza Monferrato, but also in Agliano Terme and Moasca. 7 wines are produced here, both whites and reds, mainly drawing on barbera and moscato. Small amounts of grignolino, freisa, arneis, and riesling are cultivated as well. The excellent Nizza '21 features vibrant notes of red fruit and spices, with a rich palate balanced by freshness and drinkability, leading to a harmonious and persistent finish full of character and personality. Other well-crafted wines include the Monferrato Bianco Sèj '23 (arneis and 15% riesling), with its fine aromas of white fruit, well-rounded palate, and nice balance of fullness and freshness, and the Grignolino d'Asti '23, which stands out for its signature aromas of black pepper, nice structure and enjoyable drinkability.

Named after its founder, former finance manager Davide Fregonese, this estate is located in Serralunga d'Alba. For this new venture, Fregonese brought in friends and wine professionals like Luigi Vico and Davide Rosso. In 2014, he purchased several vineyard plots, including portions of two famous crus: Cerretta and Prapò. Fregonese, in partnership with Davide Rosso, is also involved in another wine project on Mount Etna. Fregonese submitted some convincing Barolos for tasting, including the Cerretta '20. It pours a brilliant ruby-garnet hue, releasing lovely notes of red fruit and elegant spices, accompanied by refined hints of licorice and rose petals. In the mouth, it offers good structure and a firm, fleshy core that balances close-knit tannins and a classic, austere profile. Red fruit dominates in the Prapò, a wine enriched by sweet tobacco and dried flower accents, while the palate is substantial and harmonious.

● Nizza '21	♟♟ 5
● Grignolino d'Asti '23	♟♟ 3
○ M.to Bianco Sèj '23	♟♟ 3
● Barbera d'Asti '21	♟ 3
○ Piemonte Riesling "Tardoché" '22	♟ 5
● Barbera d'Asti '20	♟♟ 4
● Freisa d'Asti '21	♟♟ 3
● Grignolino d'Asti '21	♟♟ 3
○ M.to Bianco Sèj '22	♟♟ 4
● Nizza '20	♟♟ 5
● Nizza '19	♟♟ 5
● Nizza La Veja '20	♟♟ 5
○ Piemonte Riesling Tardochè '21	♟♟ 3

● Barolo Cerretta '20	♟♟ 7
● Barolo Prapò '20	♟♟ 7
● Barolo Cerretta '19	♟♟ 7
● Barolo Cerretta '18	♟♟ 7
● Barolo Cerretta '17	♟♟ 7
● Barolo Cerretta '16	♟♟ 7
● Barolo Cerretta '15	♟♟ 7
● Barolo Prapò '19	♟♟ 7
● Barolo Prapò '18	♟♟ 7
● Barolo Prapò '17	♟♟ 7
● Barolo Prapò '16	♟♟ 7
● Barolo Prapò '15	♟♟ 7
○ Etna Bianco '21	♟♟ 4
● Etna Rosso '21	♟♟ 4
● Etna Rosso Ris. '16	♟♟ 6
● Langhe Nebbiolo '19	♟♟ 5

La Fusina

fraz. Santa Lucia, 33
12063 Dogliani [CN]
📞 +39 017370488
🖥 www.lafusina.com

CELLAR SALES
PRE-BOOKED VISITS
ANNUAL PRODUCTION 80,000 bottles
HECTARES UNDER VINE 20.00
SUSTAINABLE WINERY

La Fusina, a winery in Dogliani owned by Luigi Abbona, is fully managed by his family. The vineyard holdings extend from Dogliani to Monforte d'Alba and the Perno hamlet, where the winery produces Barolo. Their production style is generally well-focused, particularly with the dolcetto grape, where they emphasize aromatic freshness and an approachable drinkability. The Dogliani Santa Lucia '23 impresses with its great finesse and character. A striking ruby red color anticipates vibrant aromas of blackberries, followed by delicate notes of chocolate. The palate stands out for its power and superb typicity, with close-knit tannins and a deep finish. The Barolo Perno '20 is also excellent, more evolved and complex, with mature blood orange on the nose, followed by tobacco. The palate is rich, with present but nicely integrated tannins.

● Dogliani Santa Lucia '23	♟♟ 4
○ Alta Langa Extra Brut '20	♟♟ 5
● Barbera d'Alba Sup. La Castella '20	♟♟ 4
● Barolo Perno '20	♟♟ 6
● Dogliani Sup. San Luigi Cavagnè '22	♟♟ 4
● Langhe Pinot Nero '21	♟♟ 4
○ Langhe Chardonnay '23	♟ 3
● Langhe Nebbiolo '22	♟ 3
○ Langhe Sauvignon Il Futuro Nelle Mani '23	♟ 3
● Barolo '14	♟♟ 5
● Barolo '10	♟♟ 5
● Barolo Perno '19	♟♟ 6
● Barolo Perno '17	♟♟ 6
● Barolo Perno '15	♟♟ 6
● Dogliani Santa Lucia '22	♟♟ 4
● Dogliani Sup. San Luigi Cavagnè '20	♟♟ 3*

Gaggino

s.da Sant'Evasio, 29
15076 Ovada [AL]
📞 +39 0143822345
🖥 www.gaggino.it

CELLAR SALES
PRE-BOOKED VISITS
ACCOMMODATION
ANNUAL PRODUCTION 150,000 bottles
HECTARES UNDER VINE 70.00
SUSTAINABLE WINERY

It's been 100 years since Tommaso Gaggino founded this successful winery. Much credit goes to Gabriele Gaggino, who now runs the estate and has given both the wines and the winery their distinctive identities. Production is in the capable hands of Roberto Olivieri, a winemaker who masterfully balances a range that focuses on classic Piedmontese varieties, while still making room for international grapes. Once again, this year's best taste is the Ovada Convivio '22, thanks to its fragrant black fruit aromas and subtle hints of cocoa. The palate is marked by a well-structured tannic frame and a fleshy core, finishing long. The Dolcetto di Ovada Sedici '23 is simpler but enjoyable nonetheless, delivering delightful drinkability. It stands out for its red fruit aromas and a final sapidity that invites the next sip.

● Ovada Convivio '22	♟♟♟ 3*
● Dolcetto di Ovada Sedici '23	♟♟ 3
○ Gavi '23	♟♟ 3
● Piemonte Barbera Lazzarina '23	♟♟ 2*
◎ Piemonte Rosato Sedici Rosé '23	♟♟ 3
◎ Barbera del M.to Sup. Ticco '21	♟ 5
○ Piemonte Bianco Pagliuzza '23	♟ 2
○ Piemonte Cortese Spumante Brut Courteisa	♟ 2
● Ovada Convivio '21	♟♟♟ 3*
● Ovada Convivio '20	♟♟♟ 3*
● Ovada Convivio '19	♟♟♟ 3*
● Ovada Convivio '18	♟♟♟ 3*
● Ovada Convivio '17	♟♟♟ 3*
● Ovada Convivio '16	♟♟♟ 3*
● Ovada Convivio '13	♟♟♟ 2*

PIEDMONT

Poderi Gianni Gagliardo

fraz. Santa Maria
b.go Serra dei Turchi, 88
12064 La Morra [CN]
☎ +39 017350829
⊕ www.gagliardo.it

CELLAR SALES
PRE-BOOKED VISITS
ANNUAL PRODUCTION 180,000 bottles
HECTARES UNDER VINE 25.00

Monvigliero in Verduno, Santa Maria and Serra dei Turchi in La Morra, Fossati in Barolo, Lazzarito in Serralunga d'Alba, Castelletto, Bricco San Pietro, and Mosconi in Monforte d'Alba: these are the crus that Gianni Gagliardo draws on. Managed by the founder alongside his sons Stefano, Alberto, and Paolo, the La Morra-based winery focuses on Barolo, though Roero and Nizza wines are also produced with the Garetto estate. The Barolo Monvigliero '20 possesses fruity, spicy, and toasted aromas, finding a pleasant fragrance on the palate. It flows nicely and finishes with sapid touches and an encore of toasty notes. The Barolo Fossati reveals a lush and fragrant fruity nose, which translates into freshness and rhythm on the palate, finishing with good length. The Barolo Lazzarito Vigna Preve '20 is warmer and more compact, with oak still prominent.

● Barolo Castelletto '20	♥♥ 8
● Barolo Fossati '20	♥♥ 8
● Barolo Lazzarito V. Preve '20	♥♥ 8
● Barolo Monvigliero '20	♥♥ 8
● Barolo del Comune di La Morra '20	♥ 7
● Barolo Mosconi '20	♥ 8
● Barolo Castelletto '18	♀♀ 8
● Barolo Castelletto '17	♀♀ 8
● Barolo Fossati '18	♀♀ 8
● Barolo Lazzarito V. Preve '19	♀♀ 8
● Barolo Lazzarito V. Preve '18	♀♀ 8
● Barolo Lazzarito V. Preve '16	♀♀ 8
● Barolo Mosconi '19	♀♀ 8
● Barolo Mosconi '18	♀♀ 8
● Barolo Serra Dei Turchi '18	♀♀ 5

★★★★★Gaja

via Torino, 18
12050 Barbaresco [CN]
☎ +39 0173635158
info@gaja.com

ANNUAL PRODUCTION 350,000 bottles
HECTARES UNDER VINE 92.00

Wines bearing the Gaja label are now considered among the world's finest, and Angelo Gaja's pioneering work is universally recognized. He dared to innovate traditional Piedmontese winemaking with practices that are commonplace today—such as yield reduction, temperature-controlled fermentation, the use of oversized corks, and aging in barriques—but were nothing short of revolutionary in the 1960s. In doing so, he reshaped the way wine is conceived in Italy. As always, Gaja's wines exhibit perfect form and refined character, though they remain quite distinct from each other. The gap between the measured structure and delicate tannins of the Conteisa and the more robust body and slightly rough tannins of the Sperss is significant. This year, our favorite is the Sorì Tildin, whose innate freshness and slight tannic firmness pair beautifully with the warm, fully mature 2021 vintage, compared to the greater softness and juiciness of the Sorì San Lorenzo. However, the always-excellent Barbaresco, a blend of different sites, remains the truest testament to the vintage.

● Barbaresco Sorì Tildin '21	♥♥♥ 8
● Barbaresco Sorì San Lorenzo '21	♥♥ 8
● Barolo Sperss '20	♥♥ 8
● Barbaresco '21	♥♥ 8
● Barbaresco Costa Russi '21	♥♥ 8
● Barolo Conteisa '20	♥♥ 8
● Barbaresco '08	♀♀♀ 8
● Barbaresco Costa Russi '13	♀♀♀ 8
● Barbaresco Sorì Tildin '20	♀♀♀ 8
● Barbaresco Sorì Tildin '16	♀♀♀ 8
● Barbaresco Sorì Tildin '15	♀♀♀ 8
● Barbaresco Sorì Tildin '14	♀♀♀ 8
● Barolo Sperss '18	♀♀♀ 8
● Barolo Sperss '16	♀♀♀ 8
● Langhe Nebbiolo Costa Russi '10	♀♀♀ 8
● Langhe Nebbiolo Sorì Tildin '11	♀♀♀ 8
● Langhe Nebbiolo Sperss '11	♀♀♀ 8

Filippo Gallino

fraz. Valle del Pozzo, 63
12043 Canale [CN]
☎ +39 017398112
✉ www.filippogallino.com

CELLAR SALES
PRE-BOOKED VISITS
ACCOMMODATION
ANNUAL PRODUCTION 100,000 bottles
HECTARES UNDER VINE 14.00
SUSTAINABLE WINERY

The Gallino family winery relies on various vineyards, all located in the municipality of Canale, including some of Roero's most renowned crus, from Briccola to Renesio to Mompissano. The vineyards, which mostly grow in clay-sandy soils, host the varietals most common to the left bank of the Tanaro, from arneis to nebbiolo, barbera, and brachetto. The wines produced here are characterized by a traditional approach that emphasizes fruitiness and richness. The Roero Arneis 4 Luglio Riserva '22 stands out with its aromas of Kaiser pear, plum, and white pepper, followed by a flavorful, energetic palate with nice length and persistence. The Roero Licin '21 reveals aromas of violet and wild red berries, with spicy nuances on the nose, while the palate is rich and full-bodied, with prominent but well-textured tannins and a long, juicy finish. The Roero Arneis '23 is well-crafted, sapid, and enjoyable, while the Barbera d'Alba Superiore Elaine '21 proves fresh and approachable with its notes of black forest fruits.

○ Roero Arneis 4 Luglio Ris. '22	♛♛ 5
● Roero Licin '21	♛♛ 5
● Barbera d'Alba Sup. Elaine '21	♛♛ 4
○ Roero Arneis '23	♛♛ 2*
● Barbera d'Alba '22	♛ 3
● Langhe Nebbiolo '22	♛ 2
● Barbera d'Alba Sup. '05	♛♛♛ 4*
● Barbera d'Alba Sup. '04	♛♛♛ 4*
● Barbera d'Alba Sup. '97	♛♛♛ 3
● Roero '06	♛♛♛ 4*
● Roero Sup. '03	♛♛♛ 3
● Roero Sup. '01	♛♛♛ 5
● Roero Sup. '99	♛♛♛ 5
● Roero Sup. '98	♛♛♛ 5
● Barbera d'Alba Sup. Elaine '18	♛♛ 5
○ Roero Arneis '22	♛♛ 2*
○ Roero Arneis 4 Luglio Ris. '20	♛♛ 5

Garesio

loc. Sordo, 1
12050 Serralunga d'Alba [CN]
☎ +39 3667076775
✉ www.garesiovini.it

CELLAR SALES
PRE-BOOKED VISITS
ACCOMMODATION
ANNUAL PRODUCTION 85,000 bottles
HECTARES UNDER VINE 25.00
VITICULTURE METHOD Certified Organic
SUSTAINABLE WINERY

Based in Serralunga d'Alba, the Garesio family offers a diverse range of wines, from Barolo Crus like Cerretta and Gianetto to barbera (for two versions of Nizza, produced in Incisa Scapaccino and Castelnuovo Calcea), and an Alta Langa sparkling wine from Perletto. Their portfolio is classically styled, with their premium wines aged in large wooden barrels. The Barolo del comune Serralunga d'Alba '20 is very good, offering up aromas of cinchona and nuances of rhubarb against a fruity and spicy backdrop. The palate is austere but lively and compact, providing persistence right through the finish. The Barolo Gianetto '20 proves well-crafted, with delicate, clean aromas and a juicy progression of flavor, finishing with good length. The Langhe Nebbiolo '22 is sapid, with lovely fruity structure.

● Barolo del Comune di Serralunga d'Alba '20	♛♛ 6
● Barbera d'Asti Glug '23	♛♛ 3
● Barolo Cerretta '20	♛♛ 8
● Barolo Gianetto '20	♛♛ 8
○ Alta Langa M. Cl. Pas Dosé '20	♛ 5
● Langhe Nebbiolo '22	♛ 4
● Barolo Cerretta '15	♛♛♛ 7
○ Alta Langa M. Cl. Pas Dosé '19	♛♛ 5
● Barolo Cerretta '18	♛♛ 8
● Barolo Cerretta Ris. '16	♛♛ 8
● Barolo del Comune di Serralunga d'Alba '19	♛♛ 6
● Barolo del Comune di Serralunga d'Alba '17	♛♛ 6
● Barolo Gianetto '17	♛♛ 8
● Nizza Ris. '17	♛♛ 5
● Nizza Ris. '16	♛♛ 5

Cantine Garrone

via Scapaccino, 36
28845 Domodossola [VB]
📞 +39 0324242990
🌐 www.cantinegarrone.it

CELLAR SALES
PRE-BOOKED VISITS
ACCOMMODATION
ANNUAL PRODUCTION 45,000 bottles
HECTARES UNDER VINE 14.00

The Garrone family has been a living testament to Val d'Ossola's time-honored winemaking traditions since 1920. Their vineyards, some over a century old and planted on their original rootstock, are nestled in small terraced plots supported by stone walls. This is an exceptional example of traditional viticulture, where everything from pruning to harvesting is carried out by hand. At the top of the winery's range are two Prünents, which aptly express the austere, authentic character of mountain-grown nebbiolo. The Vigna La Fornace '22 reveals aromas of blueberry juice, rhubarb candy, and licorice root, with an intense and varied aromatic profile, followed by a slender palate of aristocratic elegance. The Diecibrente '21, by contrast, is more immediately expressive, concentrated, and direct, with notes of spices, cinchona, and tobacco, and a supple, energetic palate.

• Valli Ossolane Nebbiolo Prünent V. La Fornace '22	🍷🍷 5
• Valli Ossolane Nebbiolo Sup. Prünent Diecibrente '21	🍷🍷 6
• Valli Ossolane Nebbiolo Sup. Prünent '22	🍷🍷 5
• Munaloss '23	🍷 2
○ Valli Ossolane Bianco La Gera '22	🍷 4
• Valli Ossolane Nebbiolo Sup. Prünent '20	🍷🍷 5
• Valli Ossolane Nebbiolo Sup. Prünent '19	🍷🍷 5
• Valli Ossolane Nebbiolo Sup. Prünent Diecibrente '20	🍷🍷 6
• Valli Ossolane Nebbiolo Sup. Prünent Diecibrente '19	🍷🍷 6
• Valli Ossolane Nebbiolo Sup. Prünent Diecibrente '17	🍷🍷 6
• Valli Ossolane Rosso Cà d'Maté '19	🍷🍷 4
• Valli Ossolane Rosso Tarlap '21	🍷🍷 3
• Valli Ossolane Rosso Tarlap '20	🍷🍷 3
• Valli Ossolane Rosso Tarlap '19	🍷🍷 3

Pierfrancesco Gatto

via Vittorio Emanuele II, 13
14030 Castagnole Monferrato [AT]
📞 +39 0141292149
🌐 www.gattopierfrancesco.it

CELLAR SALES
PRE-BOOKED VISITS
ANNUAL PRODUCTION 60,000 bottles
HECTARES UNDER VINE 8.00

Pierfrancesco Gatto has been leading this winery for over thirty years, representing a family whose roots in winemaking go back centuries. Despite the passage of time and changes, the core values remain: territory and tradition. The main grape varieties grown are barbera, ruchè, and grignolino, making for a range that reflects the diverse terroirs of Castagnole Monferrato and Montemagno. The Ruché di Castagnole Monferrato San Vittore Riserva '21 conjures up notes of rose, plum, tobacco, and licorice. In the mouth it's dense, with close-knit tannins, but also full-bodied and long. The Grignolino d'Asti Montalto '23 shows a lovely floral note accompanied by peppery accents, perfectly in line with its typicity. It's a juicy drink, long, and has fine tannins. Other notable wines include the smooth and persistent Monferrato Nebbiolo Gatto Matto '22, with its tones of raspberry and violet, and the Ruché di Castagnole Monferrato Caresana '23, with its close-knit tannins, rich flesh, and pleasant drinkability.

• Grignolino d'Asti Montalto '23	🍷🍷 3*
• Ruché di Castagnole M.to San Vittore Ris. '21	🍷🍷 5
• Barbera d'Asti Robiano '23	🍷🍷 3
• M.to Nebbiolo Gatto Matto '22	🍷🍷 2*
• Ruché di Castagnole M.to Caresana '23	🍷🍷 3
○ Piemonte Viognier Gatto Bianco '22	🍷 2
• Barbera d'Asti Sup. Iolanda '17	🍷🍷 3*
• Barbera d'Asti Sup. Jolanda '19	🍷🍷 3*
• Grignolino d'Asti Montalto '22	🍷🍷 3*
• M.to Nebbiolo Gatto Matto '21	🍷🍷 2*
• Ruché di Castagnole M.to Caresana '22	🍷🍷 3*
• Ruché di Castagnole M.to Caresana '21	🍷🍷 3*
• Ruché di Castagnole M.to Caresana '20	🍷🍷 3*

★Ettore Germano

loc. Cerretta, 1
12050 Serralunga d'Alba [CN]
☎ +39 0173613528
✉ www.ettoregermano.com

CELLAR SALES
PRE-BOOKED VISITS
ANNUAL PRODUCTION 170,000 bottles
HECTARES UNDER VINE 20.00
SUSTAINABLE WINERY

Cerretta, Lazzarito, Vignarionda, and Prapò are the crus produced by Serralunga d'Alba's Ettore Germano. The sale of grapes to third parties ended in the 1960s when Ettore renovated the vineyards and acquired new plots. The first time that their entire production of grapes was bottled was in 1993, though the winery took on its current form with the arrival of Ettore's son Sergio, who's today helped by the new generation, Elia and Maria. The elegant Barolo Lazzarito Riserva '18 features nuances of mint candy, spices, and underbrush. On the palate, it's compact and multifaceted, with juicy development and a balsamic finish. The intensely aromatic Langhe Riesling Hérzu '22 showcases tropical fruit fragrances with flinty accents, leading to a rich, flavorful, and deep palate. The Alta Langa Extra Brut '20 is also well-crafted. The darker and more restrained Barolo Prapò '20 rounds out the lineup.

○ Langhe Riesling Hérzu '22	♥♥♥ 5
○ Alta Langa Extra Brut '20	♥♥ 6
● Barolo Lazzarito Ris. '18	♥♥ 8
● Barolo del Comune di Serralunga d'Alba '20	♥♥ 7
● Barolo Prapò '20	♥♥ 8
● Barolo Vignarionda '19	♥ 8
○ Langhe Nascetta '22	♥ 5
○ Alta Langa Blanc de Blanc Pas Dosé Sessantacinquemesi Ris. '16	♥♥♥ 8
● Barolo Lazzarito Ris. '16	♥♥♥ 8
● Barolo Lazzarito Ris. '15	♥♥♥ 8
● Barolo Lazzarito Ris. '13	♥♥♥ 8
● Barolo Lazzarito Ris. '12	♥♥♥ 8
● Barolo Lazzarito Ris. '11	♥♥♥ 8
● Barolo Lazzarito Ris. '10	♥♥♥ 8
● Barolo Prapò '11	♥♥♥ 7

★★★Bruno Giacosa

via XX Settembre, 52
12052 Neive [CN]
☎ +39 0173367027
✉ brunogiacosa.it

ANNUAL PRODUCTION 300,000 bottles
HECTARES UNDER VINE 20.00
SUSTAINABLE WINERY

Bruno Giacosa joined the family business shortly after World War II. It wouldn't be an exaggeration to say that he may have been one of the world's greatest producers, and certainly the most accomplished Italian négociant of all time. Few knew the Langhe crus as intimately as he did, and no one else managed to create such oenological masterpieces. Following his death in 2018, his daughter Bruna continues his legacy with wines that, unsurprisingly, shine on the global stage, cementing the producer's worldwide success. While awaiting the highly sought-after Etichette Rosse Reserves, which were not produced in 2018 and 2019, we sampled two outstanding 2020s, wines of exceptional quality. The Barolo Falletto '20, with its aromas of raspberry, anise, licorice, and sweet tobacco, possesses excellent structure and harmony, as well as that appealing austerity that we'd expect of Barolo. Giacosa's Barbaresco Rabajà '20, which could easily mislead experts in a blind tasting, shares a similar structure to the Falletto, with refined aromas.

● Barbaresco Rabajà '20	♥♥♥ 8
● Barolo Falletto '20	♥♥ 8
● Nebbiolo d'Alba V. Valmaggiore '22	♥♥ 6
○ Roero Arneis '23	♥♥ 5
● Barbaresco Asili '12	♥♥♥ 8
● Barbaresco Asili Ris. '16	♥♥♥ 8
● Barbaresco Asili Ris. '14	♥♥♥ 8
● Barbaresco Asili Ris. '11	♥♥♥ 8
● Barbaresco Asili Ris. '07	♥♥♥ 8
● Barolo Falletto '07	♥♥♥ 8
● Barolo Falletto V. Le Rocche Ris. '17	♥♥♥ 8
● Barolo Falletto V. Le Rocche Ris. '16	♥♥♥ 8
● Barolo Falletto V. Le Rocche Ris. '14	♥♥♥ 8
● Barolo Falletto V. Le Rocche Ris. '12	♥♥♥ 8
● Barolo Falletto V. Le Rocche Ris. '11	♥♥♥ 8
● Barolo Le Rocche del Falletto Ris. '08	♥♥♥ 8
● Barolo Le Rocche del Falletto Ris. '07	♥♥♥ 8

PIEDMONT

Carlo Giacosa

s.da Ovello, 9
12050 Barbaresco [CN]
☎ +39 0173635116
🌐 www.carlogiacosa.it

CELLAR SALES
PRE-BOOKED VISITS
ANNUAL PRODUCTION 42,000 bottles
HECTARES UNDER VINE 5.50
SUSTAINABLE WINERY

Founded by Carlo Giacosa and now run by his daughter Maria Grazia and son Luca, this Barbaresco winery boasts a diverse array of vineyards, cultivating not only dolcetto, barbera, arneis, and pinot nero but also several plots in the Ovello, Asili, and Montefico crus. The estate's wines are known for their stylistic finesse, combining robust structure with a sophisticated touch and remarkable aromatic intensity. The Barbaresco Asili '21 shows nice overall definition, standing out for its dazzling aromas of ripe red berries, licorice, and tobacco, with accents of anise. On the palate, its tannic structure is close-knit but well-calibrated, leading to a long, flavorful finish. Similarly well-defined aromas characterize the Barbaresco Montefico '21, a wine that, on the palate, is slightly restrained by tannins. The Barbaresco '21 is simpler but still enjoyable.

Wine	Rating
● Barbaresco Asili '21	♈♈♈ 8
● Barbaresco Montefico '21	♈♈ 7
● Barbaresco '21	♈♈ 6
● Barbaresco Ovello '21	♈♈ 7
● Langhe Pinot Nero '22	♈♈ 5
● Langhe Nebbiolo Maria Grazia '22	♈ 5
● Barbaresco Asili '20	♈♈♈ 8
● Barbaresco Montefico '15	♈♈♈ 6
● Barbaresco Montefico '08	♈♈♈ 5*
● Barbaresco Asili '19	♈♈ 8
● Barbaresco Asili '18	♈♈ 8
● Barbaresco Luca Ris. '16	♈♈ 8
● Barbaresco Montefico '20	♈♈ 7
● Barbaresco Montefico '19	♈♈ 7
● Barbaresco Ovello '20	♈♈ 7
● Barbaresco Ovello '19	♈♈ 6

F.lli Giacosa

via XX Settembre, 64
12052 Neive [CN]
☎ +39 017367013
🌐 www.giacosa.it

CELLAR SALES
PRE-BOOKED VISITS
ANNUAL PRODUCTION 1,000,000 bottles
HECTARES UNDER VINE 51.00
VITICULTURE METHOD Certified Organic
SUSTAINABLE WINERY

The pride of this Neive-based winery is the Vigna Mandorlo, located in the Scarrone area within the Castiglione Falletto appellation. However, Vigna Mandorlo is just a small part of the vineyard holdings, which are mainly concentrated in Barbaresco. The estate, currently managed by Maurizio and Paolo Giacosa, expanded significantly during the 1990s, though its roots trace back to 1895 when Giuseppe Giacosa purchased the land with winnings from a lottery. The well-crafted Barolo Scarrone Vigna Mandorlo Riserva '16 reveals focused aromas and intense fruit with smoky and balsamic nuances. On the palate, it's fleshy, with a balanced tannic structure and a broad, persistent finish. The Barbaresco Basarin Vigna Gianmaté Riserva '18 is equally well-crafted with an enticing, spicy, and fragrant aromatic profile. The palate is soft, dense, and multifaceted. The fragrant Langhe Chardonnay Rorea '22 plays on peach and mint aromas.

Wine	Rating
● Barbaresco Basarin Vigna Gianmaté Ris. '18	♈♈ 8
● Barolo Scarrone Vigna Mandorlo Ris. '16	♈♈ 8
● Barolo Bussia '20	♈ 8
○ Langhe Chardonnay Rorea '23	♈ 5
● Barbaresco Basarin '20	♈♈ 8
● Barbaresco Basarin '18	♈♈ 8
● Barbaresco Basarin V. Gianmatè '14	♈♈ 7
● Barbaresco Basarin V. Gianmatè '12	♈♈ 6
● Barbaresco Basarin V. Gianmatè '11	♈♈ 6
● Barbera d'Alba Maria Gioana '11	♈♈ 4
● Barolo Scarrone V. Mandorlo '14	♈♈ 8
● Barolo Scarrone V. Mandorlo '11	♈♈ 8
● Barolo Scarrone V. Mandorlo '10	♈♈ 7
● Barolo Scarrone V. Mandorlo Ris. '15	♈♈ 8
● Barolo Scarrone V. Mandorlo Ris. '14	♈♈ 8
● Barolo V. Mandorlo '08	♈♈ 7

La Gironda

s.da Bricco, 12
14049 Nizza Monferrato [AT]
☎ +39 0141701013
✉ www.lagironda.com

CELLAR SALES
PRE-BOOKED VISITS
ANNUAL PRODUCTION 75,000 bottles
HECTARES UNDER VINE 10.00
VITICULTURE METHOD Certified Organic
SUSTAINABLE WINERY

Although the winery has existed for around 20
years, its owners, Susanna Galandrino and
Alberto Adamo, were no strangers to the world
of wine before its founding. Indeed, La Gironda
came out of their previous business, producing
oenological machinery. The vineyards are
primarily planted with local varieties, with
barbera (from historic crus) leading the way,
alongside plots of chardonnay and pinot nero,
which are used to produce the estate's Metodo
Classico. A strong overall showing from La
Gironda's wines. The Nizza Ago Riserva '19
highlights pleasant notes of rosemary, thyme, and
black olive tapenade on the nose, while the
palate is juicy and long. The Barbera d'Asti La
Lippa '23 reveals tones of red fruit and
rain-soaked earth, followed by a palate rich in
fruit. The Nizza Le Nicchie '21 is spicy, with notes
of black forest fruits, offering a clear profile and
vibrant acidity. The Moscato d'Asti '23 features
fine, delicate aromas of medicinal herbs and lime,
with a fresh, juicy palate to follow.

Tenuta La Giustiniana

fraz. Rovereto, 5
15066 Gavi [AL]
☎ +39 0143682132
✉ lagiustiniana.it

CELLAR SALES
PRE-BOOKED VISITS
ANNUAL PRODUCTION 200,000 bottles
HECTARES UNDER VINE 39.00

Magda Pedrini and Stefano Massone have been
overseeing this estate, which features the
splendid villa of La Giustiniana, since 2016. This
winery was the first in the area to develop the
concept of a Gavi cru, bottling wines from
different plots separately. Their range has
character, and the producers faithfully represent
the region's classic style, resulting in rich, juicy,
and persistent wines. The Gavi del Comune di
Gavi Lugarara '23 displays an aromatic bouquet
that combines freshly cut grass and wildflowers
with a backdrop of nuts. The palate is compact
and structured, with a sapid development and a
long, focused finish. The Gavi del Comune di
Gavi Montessora '23 is more pungent, with its
citrus aromas and a dynamic, crisp palate, though
the finish leans slightly raw.

● Nizza Ago Ris. '19	🍷🍷 6
● Barbera d'Asti La Lippa '23	🍷🍷 3
● Barbera d'Asti Sup. La Gena '22	🍷🍷 4
○ Moscato d'Asti '23	🍷🍷 3
● Nizza Le Nicchie '21	🍷🍷 5
● Barbera d'Asti Sup. Nizza Le Nicchie '11	🍷🍷🍷 5
● Barbera d'Asti La Lippa '22	🍷🍷 3
● Barbera d'Asti La Lippa '21	🍷🍷 3
● Barbera d'Asti Sup. La Gena '21	🍷🍷 4
● Barbera d'Asti Sup. La Gena '20	🍷🍷 4
● M.to Rosso Chiesavecchia '19	🍷🍷 5
● M.to Rosso Chiesavecchia '17	🍷🍷 5
○ Moscato d'Asti '22	🍷🍷 3*
○ Moscato d'Asti '21	🍷🍷 3*
● Nizza Ago Ris. '17	🍷🍷 7
● Nizza Le Nicchie '20	🍷🍷 5
● Nizza Le Nicchie '19	🍷🍷 5

○ Gavi del Comune di Gavi Lugarara '23	🍷 3*
○ Gavi del Comune di Gavi Montessora '23	🍷🍷 4
○ Gavi del Comune di Gavi Il Nostro Gavi '07	🍷🍷🍷 4
○ Gavi del Comune di Gavi Lugarara '22	🍷🍷 3*
○ Gavi del Comune di Gavi Lugarara '21	🍷🍷 3*
○ Gavi del Comune di Gavi Lugarara '20	🍷🍷 3*
○ Gavi del Comune di Gavi Lugarara '18	🍷🍷 3*
○ Gavi del Comune di Gavi Montessora '21	🍷🍷 4
○ Gavi del Comune di Gavi Montessora '19	🍷🍷 4
○ Gavi del Comune di Gavi Montessora '18	🍷🍷 4
○ Gavi del Comune di Gavi Montessora '17	🍷🍷 4

PIEDMONT

Gozzelino

s.da Bricco Lù, 7
14055 Costigliole d'Asti [AT]
📞 +39 0141966134
🌐 www.gozzelinovini.com

CELLAR SALES
PRE-BOOKED VISITS
ANNUAL PRODUCTION 150,000 bottles
HECTARES UNDER VINE 30.00

For over a century, the Gozzelino family has called Bricco Lù home. It's a hill that offers stunning views, stretching from Monferrato to the Langhe, Roero, and the Ligurian Apennines. Barbera is the star of their vineyards here, but the range of wines produced is extensive, with each crafted in a classic style that aptly expresses the characteristics of the grapes and the terroirs in which they're cultivated. The delightful Barbera d'Asti Ciabot d'la Mandorla '21 opens on aromas of black forest fruits and Mediterranean brush, followed by a fresh, energetic, and easy-drinking palate. The Grignolino d'Asti wines are all well-made. The Bric d'La Riva '23 sees notes of spices and tobacco meet harmonious tannins, which are slightly austere but fine, all before a long finish. The Luigi '22 showcases classic aromas of pepper and rosemary, pleasant and rich in fruit. The Barbera d'Asti Superiore 2019, including the Sergio, is close-knit and rich in fruit, while the Gozzelino Lorenzo features cherry and underbrush aromas, with good structure and length.

★★Elio Grasso

loc. Ginestra, 40
12065 Monforte d'Alba [CN]
📞 +39 017378491
🌐 www.eliograsso.it

PRE-BOOKED VISITS
ANNUAL PRODUCTION 90,000 bottles
HECTARES UNDER VINE 18.00
SUSTAINABLE WINERY

Since the early 1980s, the Grasso family has shifted the focus of their agricultural business to wine, restructuring their vineyards, which are planted with nebbiolo, dolcetto, and barbera, and bottling their first Barolos. Today, Gianluca Grasso leads the Monforte d'Alba estate, producing wines that maintain a strong connection to their origins, drawing primarily on large oak barrels for aging. The Barolo Rüncot Riserva '16 is a vibrant, well-crafted wine with focused, generously fruity aromas. The powerful and nearly opulent palate develops compactly, leading to a long, persistent finish with an encore of fruit. The still youthful Barolo Gavarini Chiniera '20 reveals aromas of tobacco and violet with spicy touches. On the palate, it's densely structured, with fleshy substance and a full, satisfying finish.

● Barbera d'Asti Sup. Ciabot d'la Mandorla '21	▼▼ 3*
● Barbera d'Asti Sup. Sergio '19	▼▼ 3
● Barbera d'Asti Sup. Gozzelino Lorenzo '19	▼▼ 8
● Grignolino d'Asti Bric d'la Riva '23	▼▼ 2*
● Grignolino d'Asti Luigi '22	▼▼ 3
● M.to Nebbiolo Sup. San Goslino '20	▼ 3
○ Moscato d'Asti Bruna '23	▼ 3
● Barbera d'Asti Sup. Ciabot d'la Mandorla '19	♈ 3*
● Barbera d'Asti Sup. Sergio '18	♈ 3
● Grignolino d'Asti Bric d'la Riva '22	♈ 2*
● Grignolino d'Asti Bric d'la Riva '20	♈ 2*
● Grignolino d'Asti Luigi '21	♈ 3
○ Moscato d'Asti Bruna '22	♈ 3

● Barolo Rüncot Ris. '16	▼▼▼ 8
● Barolo Gavarini Chiniera '20	▼▼ 8
● Barolo Ginestra Casa Matè '20	▼▼ 8
● Barolo Gavarini Chiniera '09	♈ 8
● Barolo Gavarini V. Chiniera '06	♈ 8
● Barolo Gavarini V. Chiniera '01	♈ 7
● Barolo Gavarini V. Chiniera '00	♈ 7
● Barolo Ginestra Casa Maté '15	♈ 8
● Barolo Ginestra Casa Maté '12	♈ 8
● Barolo Ginestra Casa Maté '07	♈ 8
● Barolo Ginestra V. Casa Maté '05	♈ 8
● Barolo Ginestra V. Casa Maté '04	♈ 8
● Barolo Ginestra V. Casa Maté '03	♈ 7
● Barolo Rüncot '01	♈ 8
● Barolo Rüncot '00	♈ 8
● Barolo Ginestra Casa Maté '19	♈ 8

Silvio Grasso

fraz. Annunziata, 112
12064 La Morra [CN]
📞 +39 3516703545
🌐 www.silviograsso.com

CELLAR SALES
PRE-BOOKED VISITS
ANNUAL PRODUCTION 80,000 bottles
HECTARES UNDER VINE 12.00

Located in La Morra, this winery began selling its
Barolos in the early 1980s, during a period of
major transformation for the appellation. Under
the leadership of Alessio Federico, son of Silvio,
the winery carved out a notable presence in the
competitive Langhe wine scene. The estate
continues to attract enthusiasts, particularly
those who appreciate a modern style of Barolo
that doesn't shy away from power and intensity.
The Barolo Bricco Luciani '20 unveils aromas of
ripe red fruit and spices alongside smoky and
toasted accents. The palate is powerful, with a
multifaceted tannic structure and fleshy texture,
developing broadly and sapidly, ending with a
fruity, toasted finish. The tannins in the other
Barolo wines are firmer, though they remain
generally well-made.

Bruna Grimaldi

via Parea, 7
12060 Grinzane Cavour [CN]
📞 +39 0173262094
🌐 grimaldibruna.it

CELLAR SALES
PRE-BOOKED VISITS
ANNUAL PRODUCTION 85,000 bottles
HECTARES UNDER VINE 15.00
VITICULTURE METHOD Certified Organic
SUSTAINABLE WINERY

The family-run Bruna Grimaldi winery has been
producing and selling its wines from its base in
Serralunga d'Alba since 1999. Bruna, together
with her husband Franco Fiorino and their
children Simone and Martina, manages an estate
primarily located in Grinzane Cavour, with
additional plots in Serralunga d'Alba, including
the La Badarina vineyard, as well as a few
hectares in Roddi and Diano d'Alba. The refined
and complex Barolo Badarina Vigna Regnola '20
delivers, opening with delicately whispered hints
of flowers and fine-spiced aromas. The palate is
equally graceful, revealing a taut and persistent
structure, with a sapid, lingering finish. Fragrant
and slightly sweeter, the Barolo Badarina '20
offers a lively and focused palate. The Barolo
Bricco Ambrogio '20, however, is a bit more
restrained by its firm tannins.

● Barolo Bricco Luciani '20	♀♀ 7
● Barolo Turnè '20	♀♀ 7
● Barolo Annunziata V. Plicotti '20	♀ 7
● Barolo Bricco Manzoni '20	♀ 8
● Barolo Bricco Luciani '04	♀♀♀ 7
● Barolo Bricco Luciani '01	♀♀♀ 6
● Barolo Bricco Luciani '96	♀♀♀ 6
● Barolo Bricco Luciani '95	♀♀♀ 6
● Barolo Bricco Luciani '90	♀♀♀ 6
● Barolo Bricco Manzoni '10	♀♀♀ 7
● Barolo Annunziata V. Plicotti '18	♀♀ 7
● Barolo Bricco Manzoni '19	♀♀ 8
● Barolo Bricco Manzoni '18	♀♀ 8
● Barolo Bricco Manzoni '16	♀♀ 8
● Barolo Turnè '18	♀♀ 7
● Barolo Turnè '16	♀♀ 7

● Barolo Badarina '20	♀♀ 7
● Barolo Badarina V. Regnola '20	♀♀ 8
● Barbera d'Alba Sup. Scassa '22	♀♀ 4
● Barolo Bricco Ambrogio '20	♀♀ 7
● Barolo Camilla '20	♀♀ 6
● Dolcetto d'Alba San Martino '22	♀ 3
● Nebbiolo d'Alba Bonurei '22	♀ 4
● Barolo Badarina '19	♀♀♀ 6
● Barolo Badarina '17	♀♀ 6
● Barolo Badarina '16	♀♀ 6
● Barolo Badarina '15	♀♀ 6
● Barolo Bricco Ambrogio '19	♀♀ 6
● Barolo Bricco Ambrogio '18	♀♀ 6
● Barolo Bricco Ambrogio '17	♀♀ 6
● Barolo Camilla '19	♀♀ 5
● Barolo Camilla '18	♀♀ 5

Giacomo Grimaldi
via Luigi Einaudi, 8
12060 Barolo [CN]
(» +39 0173560536
⊛ www.giacomogrimaldi.com

CELLAR SALES
PRE-BOOKED VISITS
ANNUAL PRODUCTION 70,000 bottles
HECTARES UNDER VINE 16.00

Three generations of Grimaldi family—Ernesto, Giacomo, and Ferruccio—have devoted themselves to viticulture. Today, Ferruccio continues this legacy, producing Barolo from the Le Coste, Sottocastello di Novello, and Ravera crus, alongside Barbera and Dolcetto d'Alba. The wines from their Barolo estate are aged in a mix of large oak barrels and barriques, showcasing a style that is deeply rooted in the local terroir. Delicate hints of rose, anise, and balsamic notes emanate from the nose of the Barolo Sotto Castello di Novello '20, a wine with a firm body and mellow, multifaceted tannins. A persistent, extended finish tops things off. The Barolo Ravera '20 shows a fruitier and spicier aromatic profile, with a compact and focused palate, though it loses a bit of rhythm on the finish.

Fratelli Grimaldi
Ca' du Sindic
loc. San Grato, 15
12058 Santo Stefano Belbo [CN]
(» +39 0141840341
⊛ www.fratelligrimaldi.it

CELLAR SALES
PRE-BOOKED VISITS
ANNUAL PRODUCTION 100,000 bottles
HECTARES UNDER VINE 16.00
SUSTAINABLE WINERY

The Grimaldi family winery was reborn in 1989 with the renovation of the historic family cellar. Sergio, helped by his parents, decided to dedicate himself entirely to viticulture. Today, with the support of his wife and children, he continues to drive this family business towards the future, cultivating local varietals like barbera, moscato, brachetto, and dolcetto, as well as pinot nero for their Alta Langa. The Grimaldi family's wines put in a strong overall performance. The Moscato d'Asti Vigna San Maurizio '23 stands out for its classic notes of orange and aromatic herbs, followed by candied ginger and acacia honey, delivering a harmonious and refreshingly vibrant palate. The Moscato d'Asti Canelli Vigna Moncucco '22 reveals candied citrus aromas, leading to a rich, sweet-toned palate, while the Moscato d'Asti '23 focuses more on finesse, with sage and cinnamon aromas, and a balanced, fresh palate. The Alta Langa Brut '20 boasts a fine, persistent bead—pleasantly drinkable.

● Barolo Sotto Castello di Novello '20	♀♀ 8
● Barolo Ravera '20	♀♀ 8
● Barolo '20	♀ 6
● Barolo Sotto Castello di Novello '05	♀♀♀ 6
● Barolo Le Coste '15	♀♀ 7
● Barolo Le Coste '14	♀♀ 7
● Barolo Le Coste '13	♀♀ 7
● Barolo Le Coste Ris. '16	♀♀ 8
● Barolo Ravera '17	♀♀ 7
● Barolo Ravera '16	♀♀ 7
● Barolo Sotto Castello di Novello '19	♀♀ 8
● Barolo Sotto Castello di Novello '18	♀♀ 8
● Barolo Sotto Castello di Novello '17	♀♀ 6
● Barolo Sotto Castello di Novello '14	♀♀ 6
● Barolo Sotto Castello di Novello '13	♀♀ 6
● Nebbiolo d'Alba V. Valmaggiore '17	♀♀ 4

○ Alta Langa Brut Ca' du Sindic '20	♀♀ 8
○ Moscato d'Asti '23	♀♀ 5
○ Moscato d'Asti Canelli V. San Maurizio '22	♀♀ 6
○ Moscato d'Asti V. Moncucco '22	♀♀ 3
○ Alta Langa Brut Ca' du Sindic '19	♀♀ 8
○ Alta Langa Brut Ca' du Sindic '18	♀♀ 8
○ Langhe Chardonnay '20	♀♀ 4
○ Moscato d'Asti '21	♀♀ 5
○ Moscato d'Asti Canelli V. San Maurizio '22	♀♀ 6
○ Moscato d'Asti Canelli V. San Maurizio '21	♀♀ 6
○ Moscato d'Asti Et. Argento '22	♀♀ 3
○ Moscato d'Asti V. Moncucco '19	♀♀ 3*
○ Moscato d'Asti V. San Maurizio '20	♀♀ 6

★Hilberg - Pasquero

via Bricco Gatti, 16
12040 Priocca [CN]
+39 3756269611
www.hilberg-pasquero.com

CELLAR SALES
PRE-BOOKED VISITS
ANNUAL PRODUCTION 25,000 bottles
HECTARES UNDER VINE 12.00
VITICULTURE METHOD Certified Organic
SUSTAINABLE WINERY

Based on a hill over Priocca called Bricco Gatti, Miclo Pasquero and Annette Hilberg's winery relies on vineyards surrounding the cellar, on silty and marly soils, and in the Monteforche and Bricco Stella areas. Only Roero's classic red grape varieties are cultivated, including barbera, nebbiolo, brachetto, and a bit of dolcetto. The wines produced are notable for their typicity, balance and structure. Overall, their wines put in a commendable performance. The Roero Mon Surí Riserva '21 opens with notes of black stone fruits and Mediterranean herbs, leading to a juicy and approachable palate. The Roero Val Martin '20 pairs herbal whiffs and black plum tones with a palate of nice volume and appeal. The Vareij '23, made from Roero brachetto grapes, charms with its blood orange, rosemary, and mint aromas, offering a dry, aromatic, and fresh palate. The Barbera d'Alba Superiore Mon Seij '21 proves juicy and nicely textured.

● Barbera d'Alba Sup. Mon Seij '21	🍷🍷 7
● Roero Mon Surí Ris. '21	🍷🍷 8
● Roero Val Martin '20	🍷🍷 8
● Vareij '23	🍷🍷 5
● Barbera d'Alba Sup. Sulla Stella '22	🍷 5
● Barbera d'Alba Sup. '09	🍷🍷🍷 5
● Barbera d'Alba Sup. '98	🍷🍷🍷 5
● Barbera d'Alba Sup. '97	🍷🍷🍷 5
● Nebbiolo d'Alba '06	🍷🍷🍷 5
● Nebbiolo d'Alba '05	🍷🍷🍷 5
● Nebbiolo d'Alba '04	🍷🍷🍷 5
● Nebbiolo d'Alba '03	🍷🍷🍷 5
● Nebbiolo d'Alba '01	🍷🍷🍷 5
● Nebbiolo d'Alba '00	🍷🍷🍷 4
● Nebbiolo d'Alba '99	🍷🍷🍷 4*
● Nebbiolo d'Alba Sup. Mon Surì '20	🍷🍷 8
● Roero Val Martin '18	🍷🍷 8

Marchesi Incisa della Rocchetta

via Roma, 66
14030 Rocchetta Tanaro [AT]
+39 0141644647
www.marchesiincisawines.it

CELLAR SALES
PRE-BOOKED VISITS
ACCOMMODATION AND RESTAURANT SERVICE
ANNUAL PRODUCTION 120,000 bottles
HECTARES UNDER VINE 20.00
SUSTAINABLE WINERY

About 50 years ago, Barbara Incisa revitalized the family winery, which is now run by her children Filiberto and Francesca. The Marchesi Incisa family has been linked to Monferrato since the year 1000. The vineyards in Rocchetta Tanaro, where the cellars are located today, feature sandy and clay-rich soil, an ancient seabed ideal for cultivating barbera, but also suitable for grignolino, merlot, and pinot nero. The latest plots acquired host nebbiolo, arneis, and moscato. This year's selection truly impressed. The Piemonte Pinot Nero Marchese Leopoldo '20 conjures up lovely notes of red fruit, tobacco, and spices, followed by a well-structured palate that aptly balances fruit and tannins, finishing long and juicy. The Barbera d'Asti Valmorena '22 opts for tones of raspberry and rain-soaked earth, with notable substance and a refreshing acidity. The Barbera d'Asti Superiore Sant'Emiliano '20 sees whiffs of underbrush combine with aromatic herbs, offering a juicy, taut, and immensely enjoyable palate.

● Barbera d'Asti Sup. Sant'Emiliano '20	🍷🍷 5
● Barbera d'Asti Valmorena '22	🍷🍷 4
● Piemonte Pinot Nero Marchese Leopoldo '20	🍷🍷 5
● Grignolino d'Asti '23	🍷🍷 3
● Barbera d'Asti Sup. Sant' Emiliano '15	🍷🍷🍷 5
● Barbera d'Asti Sup. Sant' Emiliano '17	🍷🍷 5
● Barbera d'Asti Sup. Sant'Emiliano '19	🍷🍷 5
● Barbera d'Asti Valmorena '21	🍷🍷 4
● Barbera d'Asti Valmorena '19	🍷🍷 3*
● Grignolino d'Asti '19	🍷🍷 3*
● Grignolino d'Asti La Corte Chiusa '20	🍷🍷 3
● Piemonte Pinot Nero Barbera Rollone '19	🍷🍷 3
● Piemonte Pinot Nero Marchese Leopoldo '19	🍷🍷 5
● Piemonte Pinot Nero Marchese Leopoldo '18	🍷🍷 5

Ioppa

fraz. Mauletta
via delle Pallotte, 10
28078 Romagnano Sesia [NO]
☎ +39 0163833079
✉ www.viniioppa.it

CELLAR SALES
PRE-BOOKED VISITS
ANNUAL PRODUCTION 400,000 bottles
HECTARES UNDER VINE 31.00

This winery's story is a family journey that traces the evolution of Piedmontese viticulture, from 1852 onward, when Michelangelo Ioppa first purchased several estates in the town of Romagnano Sesia. Today, the seventh generation—Andrea, Marco, and Luca Ioppa—runs the estate. Their vineyards, which range in age from three to 45 years, are situated both on the fluvial-alluvial ridges of the Novara Hills, and on southwest-facing slopes, where the soil is mostly clay and sand mixed with stones. Special attention is given to eco-friendly viticulture. The Santa Fé '19 delivers concentrated power and opulence, yet maintains its elegance and finesse. On the nose, it expresses a nice sense of place—minty hints blended with red fruit, iron, and Tuscan cigar aromas. A characterful and complex palate follows. The Ghemme '19 is even darker and deeper, with blackberry jam, quinine, rhubarb, and underbrush tones, alongside a dense, powerful palate that finishes sapid and mineral. The Balsina '19 is a balsamic, juicy and fresh pour.

● Ghemme '19	♟♟ 4
● Ghemme Santa Fé '19	♟♟ 6
● Ghemme Balsina '19	♟♟ 6
☉ Colline Novaresi Nebbiolo Rosato Rusin '23	♟ 2
● Colline Novaresi Vespolina Coda Rossa '23	♟ 3
● Ghemme Balsina '13	♟♟♟ 6
● Ghemme Santa Fé '17	♟♟♟ 6
● Ghemme Santa Fé '16	♟♟♟ 6
● Colline Novaresi Vespolina Mauletta '16	♟♟ 3*
● Ghemme '18	♟♟ 4
● Ghemme '16	♟♟ 4
● Ghemme Balsina '18	♟♟ 6
● Ghemme Balsina '17	♟♟ 6
● Ghemme Santa Fé '18	♟♟ 6

Isolabella della Croce

loc. Saracchi
Regione Caffi, 3
14051 Loazzolo [AT]
☎ +39 014487166
✉ www.isolabelladellacroce.it

CELLAR SALES
PRE-BOOKED VISITS
ANNUAL PRODUCTION 90,000 bottles
HECTARES UNDER VINE 15.00
SUSTAINABLE WINERY

Following major renovations, Isolabella della Croce is now ready to host vertical tastings of its exclusive single-vineyard wines. The estate recently opened a vault for older vintages, along with a tasting veranda and guest rooms, where wine tourists can stay and enjoy views of a pristine nature reserve. Andrea Elegir is the driving force behind this small winery, whose range is growing in terms of structure, personality, and quality. Sweet spice, delicate tannins, and an elegant yet full-bodied finish characterize the Bricco del Falco, a wine that reaffirms its excellence. The Solum opens with acacia flowers and vanilla, with a pleasant backdrop of apple, all rounded out by a touch of richness. Their Barberas shine with their juicy pulp and dark fruit. The Augusta is fresh and pleasing, the while Serena features great structure and a long finish. The Ginevra offers a fine bead, with fruit and floral notes that harmonize with buttery accents, making for a broad and well-rounded drink.

● Piemonte Pinot Nero Bricco del Falco '20	♟♟♟ 6
● Nizza Agusta '20	♟♟ 5
☉ Piemonte Chardonnay Solum '22	♟♟ 5
☉ Alta Langa Brut Nature Ginevra '19	♟♟ 5
● Barbera d'Asti Sup. Serena '21	♟♟ 5
☉ Piemonte Sauvignon Blanc '23	♟♟ 5
☉ Canelli Valdiserre '23	♟ 3
● Nizza Augusta '14	♟♟♟ 4*
● Piemonte Pinot Nero Bricco del Falco '19	♟♟♟ 6
● Piemonte Pinot Nero Bricco del Falco '17	♟♟♟ 5
● Piemonte Pinot Nero Bricco del Falco '16	♟♟♟ 5
● Piemonte Pinot Nero Fra '16	♟♟♟ 7

Franco Ivaldi

s.da Caranzano, 211
15016 Cassine [AL]
(» +39 348 7492231
@ www.francoivaldivini.com

PRE-BOOKED VISITS
ANNUAL PRODUCTION 40,000 bottles
HECTARES UNDER VINE 7.00
SUSTAINABLE WINERY

Franco Ivaldi, a Liguria native, developed a passion for wine and the area after spending his youth at his family's farm in Caranzano di Cassine. In 1995, he began producing wine and, in 2003, moved to his current property. Today, his son Giorgio, who graduated with a degree in oenology in 2014, manages production, imprinting each wine with a distinct personality. The grapes from their various plots are vinified separately, and oak is used in the reds but never overwhelms. The Barbera d'Asti La Guerinotta '23 is textbook perfect, with its fleshy red fruit aromas, hints of plum, cherry, and underbrush for complexity. In the mouth, it's full of typicity: rich and dense, with a long, vibrant finish. The Piemonte Albarossa '20 leans greener, with balsamic and broom flower aromas, yet still delivers a full and deep palate. The Monferrato Bianco Ca' d'Nucent '23 is more about minerality and finesse, with a sapid, persistent palate.

● Barbera d'Asti La Guerinotta '23	🍷🍷	3*
● Piemonte Albarossa '20	🍷🍷	4
⊙ Acqui '23	🍷🍷	3
● Barbera d'Asti Sup. La Balzana '21	🍷🍷	4
● Dolcetto d'Acqui Sup. La Uèca '22	🍷🍷	3
○ M.to bianco Cà d'Nucent '23	🍷🍷	3
● M.to Freisa La Gilarda '22	🍷🍷	3
● Acqui '22	🍷🍷	2*
● Barbera d'Asti La Guerinotta '22	🍷🍷	4
● Barbera d'Asti Sup. La Balzana '20	🍷🍷	4
● Dolcetto d'Acqui La Moschina '22	🍷🍷	2*
● Dolcetto d'Acqui Sup. La Uèca '21	🍷🍷	3*
● Dolcetto d'Acqui Sup. La Uèca '20	🍷🍷	3*
● Dolcetto d'Acqui Sup. La Uèca '18	🍷🍷	3*
○ M.to Bianco Ca' d'Nucent '22	🍷🍷	3
● Piemonte Albarossa '19	🍷🍷	4

Tenuta Langasco

fraz. Madonna di Como, 10
12051 Alba [CN]
(» +39 0173286972
@ tenutalangasco.it

CELLAR SALES
PRE-BOOKED VISITS
ANNUAL PRODUCTION 60,000 bottles
HECTARES UNDER VINE 22.00

Tenuta Langasco has been cultivating the region's classic varieties—favorita, dolcetto, barbera, and nebbiolo—since its founding in 1979 by Valerio Sacco, drawing on vineyards spread across the hills of Mango in the Moscato d'Asti production area and in Madonna di Como, Alba. Now under the management of his son Claudio, the winery's offerings (including an Alta Langa sparkling wine) are generally well-crafted, with a particularly noteworthy aromatic profile. The lineup felt solid as always, although it's lacking a standout this year. The task may fall to the Dolcetto Vigna Madonna di Como, which is fresh with notes of cherry, spices, and violets, offering a pleasantly sapid, rounded, and approachable palate. The eponymous Barbera, too, displays unusual aromatic elegance—sensations of currant, riper dark fruits, and sweet spices. Here, a briny trace on the palate helps the wine unfold with ease. The Moscato d'Asti proves well-made. The other wines tasted are also on point.

● Barbera d'Alba Sup. V. Madonna di Como '22	🍷🍷	3
● Dolcetto d'Alba V. Madonna di Como '23	🍷🍷	3
○ Moscato d'Asti '23	🍷🍷	3
○ Alta Langa Extra Brut Gredo '20	🍷	5
● Nebbiolo d'Alba Sorì Coppa '22	🍷	4
● Barbera d'Alba Sorì '21	🍷🍷	3
● Barbera d'Alba Sorì '20	🍷🍷	3
● Barbera d'Alba Sup. V. Madonna di Como '21	🍷🍷	2*
● Barbera d'Alba Sup. V. Madonna di Como '20	🍷🍷	2*
● Dolcetto d'Alba Madonna di Como V. Miclet '19	🍷🍷	3
● Dolcetto d'Alba V. Miclet '22	🍷🍷	3*
● Dolcetto d'Alba V. Miclet '21	🍷🍷	3*

Ugo Lequio

via del Molino, 10
12057 Neive [CN]
☎ +39 0173677224
⊕ www.ugolequio.it

CELLAR SALES
ANNUAL PRODUCTION 30,000 bottles

The first bottles of Barbaresco bearing Ugo Lequio's name hit the market in the early 1980s, with the Gallina cru representing the winery's flagship. The Neive estate also produces Barbera d'Alba and Langhe Arneis. Ugo Lequio's wines are known for their classic style, favoring long macerations and lengthy aging in large oak barrels. The Barbaresco Gallina '20 exudes aromas of rose, currant, raspberry, and spices, setting the stage for a evenly proportioned progression of flavor, with gentle tannins that lead to a long, persistent finish. The Barbaresco '21 has a more subdued aromatic profile, offering herbal and licorice notes. In the mouth, the palate is focused, with nice tannic structure and a pleasurable finish, accented by a fruity aftertaste. In our Rare Wines section, you'll find the magnificent Barbaresco Gallina Riserva '19, produced in extremely limited quantities.

Cascina Lo Zoccolaio

loc. Boschetti, 4
12060 Barolo [CN]
☎ +39 0141837211
⊕ www.cascinalozoccolaio.it

CELLAR SALES
ANNUAL PRODUCTION 128,000 bottles
HECTARES UNDER VINE 22.00

Cascina Lo Zoccolaio, named after the town in Bricco di Barolo, belongs to the Martini family, already owners of Villa Lanata, La Toledana, and Cascina La Doria. In addition to their Barolo vineyards, their holdings include properties in Ornate (Monforte d'Alba), Verduno, and the Cru Ravera in Novello. Currently, their stylistic approach has returned to more classical tones, utilizing large oak barrels for aging. The Barbera d'Alba Superiore Suculè '21 proves highly enjoyable overall, with minty aromas mixed with the sweetness of black cherries, and a decisive, deep palate marked by a fresh, lively profile. The Barolo Ravera Riserva '18 is more austere, with red fruit, anise, and licorice notes, followed by a full-bodied, close-knit tannic palate, and a long, lingering finish. The Barolo '20 is slightly less exciting.

● Barbaresco Gallina '20	♟♟ 7
● Barbaresco '21	♟♟ 6
● Langhe Nebbiolo '23	♟♟ 5
○ Langhe Arneis '23	♟ 3
● Barbaresco Cascina Növa '20	♟♟ 6
● Barbaresco Gallina '19	♟♟ 7
● Barbaresco Gallina '18	♟♟ 6
● Barbaresco Gallina '17	♟♟ 6
● Barbaresco Gallina '16	♟♟ 6
● Barbaresco Gallina Ris. '16	♟♟ 7
● Barbera d'Alba Sup. V. Gallina '20	♟♟ 5
● Barbera d'Alba Sup. V. Gallina '18	♟♟ 4
● Barbera d'Alba Sup. V. Gallina '17	♟♟ 4
○ Langhe Arneis '22	♟♟ 3
● Langhe Nebbiolo '20	♟♟ 4
● Langhe Nebbiolo '19	♟♟ 4
● Langhe Nebbiolo '18	♟♟ 4

● Barbera d'Alba Sup. Suculè '21	♟♟ 3*
● Barolo Ravera Ris. '18	♟♟ 6
○ Chardonnay Re Noir La Rusa du Scurun '22	♟♟ 5
● Langhe Rosso Baccanera '21	♟♟ 3
● Piemonte Pinot Nero Re Noir '20	♟♟ 4
● Barolo Ravera Ris. '17	♟♟♟ 6
● Barolo Ravera Ris. '16	♟♟♟ 6
● Barolo Ravera Ris. '15	♟♟♟ 6
● Barbera d'Alba Sup. Suculè '20	♟♟ 3
● Barbera d'Alba Sup. Suculè '19	♟♟ 3
● Barolo '19	♟♟ 5
● Barolo '18	♟♟ 5
● Barolo '17	♟♟ 5
● Barolo '16	♟♟ 5
● Langhe Rosso Baccanera '19	♟♟ 3
● Piemonte Pinot Nero Re Noir '18	♟♟ 3

Lodali

v.le Rimembranza, 5
12050 Treiso [CN]
(+39 0173638109
@ www.lodali.it

CELLAR SALES
PRE-BOOKED VISITS
ACCOMMODATION
ANNUAL PRODUCTION 110,000 bottles
HECTARES UNDER VINE 18.00
SUSTAINABLE WINERY

The year began on a somber note with a final farewell to the legendary Rita, who, before passing away, saw the completion of the new cellar, a project years in the making beneath the historic estate. In this grotto, where tuff and limestone crystals emerge from the walls, the large Stockinger barrels now rest. The microclimate here is ideal for aging nebbiolo, destined to become Barbaresco and Barolo. Walter Lodali works tirelessly to highlight the distinctiveness of his vineyards while also focusing on sustainability, with Equalitas certification as proof of his efforts. Aamong Lodali's line of Barbaresco, the Lorens (from the renowned Giacone cru in Treiso) represents the most sophisticated expression. The Giacone '21 opens on aromas of plum, violet, and rose, leading to a velvety and persistent palate. The Bricco Ambrogio Lorens unveils rich, fleshy fruit and spice notes, while the classic version boasts lovely hints of red berries and sweet spices, making for a very pleasant finish. The Rocche dei 7 Fratelli, from a vineyard that overlooks a striking precipice, reveals tobacco notes, a deep palate, and a harmonious structure.

● Barbaresco Giacone Lorens '21	♥♥♥ 8
● Barbaresco Rocche dei 7 Fratelli '21	♥♥ 5
● Barolo Bricco Ambrogio '20	♥♥ 6
● Barolo Bricco Ambrogio Lorens '20	♥♥ 8
● Barbera d'Alba Lorens '22	♥♥ 5
○ Langhe Chardonnay Lorens '22	♥♥ 5
● Langhe Nebbiolo Lorens '22	♥♥ 4
● Nebbiolo d'Alba '22	♥ 3
● Barbaresco Giacone Lorens '20	♥♥♥ 8
● Barbaresco Lorens '19	♥♥♥ 7
● Barbera d'Alba Lorens '21	♥♥ 5
● Barolo Bricco Ambrogio Lorens '19	♥♥ 8
● Barolo Lorens '18	♥♥ 7
○ Langhe Chardonnay Lorens '21	♥♥ 5
○ Langhe Chardonnay Lorens '20	♥♥ 5
○ Langhe Chardonnay Lorens '19	♥♥ 5

Malabaila di Canale

via Madonna dei Cavalli, 93
12043 Canale [CN]
(+39 017398381
@ www.malabaila.com

CELLAR SALES
PRE-BOOKED VISITS
ANNUAL PRODUCTION 100,000 bottles
HECTARES UNDER VINE 22.00
SUSTAINABLE WINERY

The Malabaila family has been linked to viticulture and wine commerce since the 16th century. Founded in the late 1980s, today the winery relies on vineyards located in a single 90-hectare estate on loose, marly, and sandy soils. Roero's classic varietals are cultivated, such as arneis, nebbiolo, favorita, brachetto, and dolcetto, with some plots going back 60 years. The wines are crafted in a modern style, attentive to the terroir and drinkability. The excellent Roero Arneis Le Tre '23 stands out for its vibrant nose of pear, wisteria, and almond, leading to a nicely textured, lengthy palate. The rest of the lineup is well-crafted, starting with the Barbera d'Alba Superiore Mezzavilla '20, with its hints of blood orange and rosemary, nice concentration of fruit, and a sapid, juicy finish. The Roero Bric Volta '21, with its tones of black fruit and field herbs, proves clean and smooth. The citrusy and pleasant Roero Arneis Pradvaj '23 completes the range.

○ Roero Arneis Le Tre '23	♥♥ 2*
● Barbera d'Alba Sup. Mezzavilla '20	♥♥ 3
○ Roero Arneis Pradvaj '23	♥♥ 3
● Roero Bric Volta '21	♥♥ 3
○ Langhe Favorita Maredentro '23	♥ 3
⊙ Nebbiolo d'Alba Spumante Rosé Pas Dosé '18	♥ 5
● Roero Castelletto Ris. '20	♥ 5
○ Spumante Pas Dosé M. Cl. '18	♥ 5
● Barbera d'Alba Sup. Mezzavilla '18	♥♥ 3*
○ Roero Arneis Le Tre '22	♥♥ 2*
○ Roero Arneis Pradvaj '21	♥♥ 3*
● Roero Bric Volta '20	♥♥ 3
● Roero Bric Volta '19	♥♥ 3*
● Roero Castelletto Ris. '19	♥♥ 5
● Roero Castelletto Ris. '18	♥♥ 5
● Roero Castelletto Ris. '17	♥♥ 5

★★Malvirà

loc. Canova
via Case Sparse, 144
12043 Canale [CN]
☎ +39 0173978145
⊛ www.malvira.com

CELLAR SALES
PRE-BOOKED VISITS
ACCOMMODATION AND RESTAURANT SERVICE
ANNUAL PRODUCTION 300,000 bottles
HECTARES UNDER VINE 43.00
VITICULTURE METHOD Certified Organic

The Damonte brothers' winery has been a benchmark in the Roero production scene for several years. Their vineyards are located in some of the area's most renowned crus, including Mombeltramo, Renesio, and Trinità, among others. Here, the grape varieties common to the left bank of the Tanaro river are cultivated: arneis, barbera and nebbiolo. There is also a vineyard in La Morra for producing Barolo. Longevity and a strong sense of terroir are the hallmarks of their range. The Roero Renesio Riserva '20 opens on aromas of herbs, black forest fruits, and hints of truffle and violet, followed by a rich, full-bodied palate with elegant tannins and a long, sapid finish. The appealing Roero S.S. Trinità Riserva '20, with its tones of quinine, blueberry, and Mediterranean scrub, offers up rich fruit and softness. The fresh, sapid, long, and juicy Roero Arneis Renesio '23 opts for notes of flat peach, citrus, and white pepper. But the entire range is crafted well.

● Roero Renesio Ris. '20	▼▼▼ 6
○ Roero Arneis Renesio '23	▼▼ 4
● Roero S.S. Trinità Ris. '20	▼▼ 6
● Barolo Boiolo '20	▼▼ 8
○ Roero Arneis '23	▼▼ 3
○ Roero Arneis S. S. Trinità '23	▼▼ 4
○ Roero Arneis V. Saglietto Ris. '22	▼▼ 5
● Roero Mombeltramo Ris. '20	▼▼ 6
● Barbera d'Alba Sup. V. San Michele '20	▼ 3
○ Roero Arneis Renesio '19	♈♈♈ 3*
○ Roero Arneis Renesio '18	♈♈♈ 3*
○ Roero Arneis V. Saglietto Ris. '20	♈♈♈ 5
● Roero Renesio Ris. '19	♈♈♈ 6
● Roero V. Mombeltramo Ris. '17	♈♈♈ 6
● Roero V. Mombeltramo Ris. '12	♈♈♈ 5

Mandirola

via Roma, 29
15050 Casasco [AL]
☎ +39 3485931889
⊛ www.mandirolavini.it

CELLAR SALES
PRE-BOOKED VISITS
ANNUAL PRODUCTION 25,000 bottles
HECTARES UNDER VINE 10.00
SUSTAINABLE WINERY

Enrico Mandirola has a clear vision of how to produce quality products. Indeed, the producer hails from four generations of family who've dedicated themselves to preserving the uniqueness of the territory and adhering to environmental sustainability. The vineyards are located along the ridge connecting Casasco to Magrassi, at elevations spanning 300-350 meters, with a southwest exposure. Barbera, croatina and especially timorasso are cultivated, with this last offered in three versions, including a Metodo Classico sparkling wine. The 2022 Derthona Timorasso and Tantèi Riserva '21 showcase their potential for evolution and rich expression. The former is dynamic and radiant, with scents of broom, medicinal herbs, and white peach, and a taut, citrusy palate that finishes on floral notes. The Riserva is austere, with notes of citrus peel, hydrocarbons, and flint, a balanced palate, and a long, flavorful finish. The Barbera Praie '22, with its aromas of cherries, pomegranates, and black plums, reveals a compact and juicy palate.

○ Colli Tortonesi Timorasso Derthona '22	▼▼ 5
○ Colli Tortonesi Timorasso Tantéi Ris. '21	▼▼ 5
● Colli Tortonesi Barbera Praie '22	▼ 2
○ Colli Tortonesi Barbera Sarsé '20	♈♈ 5
○ Colli Tortonesi Croatina Lù della Costa '20	♈♈ 5
○ Colli Tortonesi Timorasso Derthona '21	♈♈ 5
○ Colli Tortonesi Timorasso Tantéi '20	♈♈ 5

Giovanni Manzone
via Castelletto, 9
12065 Monforte d'Alba [CN]
(+39 017378114
@ www.manzonegiovanni.com

Paolo Manzone
loc. Meriame, 1
12050 Serralunga d'Alba [CN]
(+39 0173613113
@ www.barolomeriame.com

CELLAR SALES
PRE-BOOKED VISITS
ANNUAL PRODUCTION 50,000 bottles
HECTARES UNDER VINE 8.00
SUSTAINABLE WINERY

CELLAR SALES
PRE-BOOKED VISITS
ACCOMMODATION
ANNUAL PRODUCTION 85,000 bottles
HECTARES UNDER VINE 12.00
VITICULTURE METHOD Certified Organic

The Manzone family, who've been in the business since 1925, produce wines that are both consistent in style and deeply connected to their home territory. The Barolos from their Monforte d'Alba property are expressive and personal, with a clear nod to tradition. Giovanni, now supported by his children Patrizia, Mirella, and Mauro, is also credited with saving the ancient rossese white grape variety from extinction. The Barolo Bricat '20 makes for a convincing interpretation, harmonious and vibrant, with intense notes of tobacco and licorice that add complexity to its subtle red fruit. It has nice structure, a fine finish, and evolving tannins. The Gramolere Riserva '17 features notable hints of sweet spices from oak, with a close-knit and dense palate. The Barolo Castelletto focuses on the pleasure of red fruit, accented by vegetal notes and whiffs of field herb—an enjoyable drink.

Gian Paolo Manzone and his wife Luisella Corino have been dedicated to producing Barolo, Dolcetto d'Alba, and Barbera d'Alba since 1999, operating near Serralunga, in the Meriame area, where the winery's most important cru lies. Their range exhibits a classic style, with aging carried out in large wooden casks and tonneaux. Additional vineyards, for the production of Roero, are cultivated in Sinio and Canale. The 2020 Meriame opens on refined aromas of tobacco, red fruits, and spices, all adorned by pleasant balsamic nuances. On the palate, it favors pleasure over power, offering a juicy mouthfeel with a balanced tannic counterpart. The Riserva '18 is equally impressive, blending red fruit sensations with accents of autumn undergrowth. Though less complex than other vintages, its tightly-knit tannins lead to a long and harmonious finish. The Barbera Fiorenza, Ruja, and Dolcetto Magna are also well-crafted.

● Barolo Bricat '20	♟♟ 6
● Barolo Castelletto '20	♟♟ 7
● Barolo Gramolere '20	♟♟ 7
● Barolo Gramolere Ris. '17	♟♟ 8
● Barolo Bricat '05	♟♟♟ 6
● Barolo Castelletto '09	♟♟♟ 5
● Barolo Gramolere Ris. '05	♟♟♟ 7
● Barolo Le Gramolere '04	♟♟♟ 6
● Barolo Le Gramolere Ris. '01	♟♟♟ 7
● Barolo Le Gramolere Ris. '00	♟♟♟ 7
● Barolo Le Gramolere Ris. '99	♟♟♟ 7
● Barolo Castelletto '19	♟♟ 7
● Barolo Gramolere '19	♟♟ 7
● Barolo Gramolere '18	♟♟ 7
● Barolo Gramolere Ris. '16	♟♟ 8
● Barolo Gramolere Ris. '15	♟♟ 8

● Barolo Meriame '20	♟♟♟ 7
● Barolo Ris. '18	♟♟ 8
● Barbaresco San Giuliano '21	♟♟ 6
● Barbera d'Alba Ruja '23	♟♟ 3
● Barbera d'Alba Sup. Fiorenza '22	♟♟ 3
● Barolo del Comune di Serralunga d'Alba '20	♟♟ 6
○ Blanc De Noir Brut M. Cl.	♟♟ 5
● Dolcetto d'Alba Magna '22	♟♟ 2*
○ Roero Arneis Reysù '23	♟♟ 3
● Langhe Rosso Luvi '22	♟ 4
● Barolo Meriame '19	♟♟♟ 7
● Barolo Meriame '17	♟♟♟ 7
● Barolo Meriame '16	♟♟♟ 7
● Barolo Ris. '16	♟♟♟ 8
● Barolo Ris. '13	♟♟♟ 7
● Barolo Ris. '11	♟♟♟ 7

Marcalberto

via Porta Sottana, 9
12058 Santo Stefano Belbo [CN]
☎ +39 0141844022
⊛ www.marcalberto.it

Poderi Marcarini

p.zza Martiri, 2
12064 La Morra [CN]
☎ +39 017350222
⊛ www.marcarini.it

CELLAR SALES
PRE-BOOKED VISITS
ANNUAL PRODUCTION 40,000 bottles
HECTARES UNDER VINE 6.50

CELLAR SALES
PRE-BOOKED VISITS
ACCOMMODATION
ANNUAL PRODUCTION 125,000 bottles
HECTARES UNDER VINE 20.00

Marco and Alberto Cane are confidently steering their charming, small estate toward increasingly ambitious goals. With valuable contributions from their mother, Marina, and expert guidance from their father, Piero, they represent a rare example of a fully family-driven operation. From meticulous vineyard management to the delicate cellar work required for crafting top-tier Metodo Classico wines, their dedication is evident in every step. Spring 2025 will mark the debut of two new versions, produced in very limited quantities and set to become the pinnacle of the estate's offerings. This year's tastings confirmed the high quality of all the wines presented. The Sansannée, with its expressive clarity and character, is an authentic showcase of the Marcalberto style. The 2020 Alta Langa, a blend of mostly pinot nero, makes for energetic and solid drinking. Highly ageworthy. The kaleidoscopic and electric Blanc de Blancs Pas Dosè '20—taut, juicy, and persistent—is a true champion of the style.

The Marcarini family, one of the oldest in La Morra, is now in its sixth generation, with siblings Elisa (in charge of production) and Andrea (who handles the commercial side) leading the winery. A new cellar will soon be completed, while the historic space will be dedicated to aging their Barolo. The family's meticulous vineyard care is epitomized by Boschi di Berri, a pre-phylloxera Dolcetto vineyard where propagation techniques are employed, making it a favorite destination for wine lovers. Spices and blackberries on the nose make this a complex and convincing version of Dolcetto, honoring the ancient grape and earning it a place in the spotlight. Marcarini's signature wine, however, remains the Barolo Brunate, from an iconic vineyard that delivers elegant notes of sweet spicess, tobacco, and mountain hay. La Serra, from a vineyard that ripens slightly later than Brunate, showcases tobacco, licorice, and fresh red fruit, with a sapid, delicate finish. The Lasarin makes for a precise, fresh, and enjoyable expression of nebbiolo.

○ Alta Langa Pas Dosé Blanc de Blancs '20	♀♀♀ 5
○ Alta Langa Extra Brut '20	♀♀ 5
○ Marcalberto Brut Sansannée M. Cl.	♀♀ 5
◉ Marcalberto Brut Rosé M. Cl.	♀♀ 4
○ Marcalberto Nature M. Cl. Senza Aggiunta di Solfiti	♀♀ 6
○ Alta Langa Extra Brut Millesimo 2Mila19 '19	♀♀♀ 5
○ Alta Langa Extra Brut Millesimo2Mila15 '15	♀♀♀ 5
○ Alta Langa Extra Brut Millesimo2Mila18 '18	♀♀♀ 5
○ Marcalberto Extra Brut Millesimo2Mila13 M. Cl. '13	♀♀♀ 5

● Barolo Brunate '19	♀♀ 8
● Barolo La Serra '20	♀♀ 7
● Barolo del Comune di La Morra '20	♀♀ 6
● Dolcetto d'Alba Boschi di Berri Pre-Fillossera '22	♀♀ 4
● Langhe Nebbiolo Lasarin '23	♀♀ 4
○ Roero Arneis '23	♀ 3
● Barolo Brunate '05	♀♀♀ 6
● Barolo Brunate '03	♀♀♀ 6
● Barolo Brunate '01	♀♀♀ 6
● Barolo Brunate '99	♀♀♀ 6
● Barolo Brunate '96	♀♀♀ 6
● Barolo Brunate Ris. '85	♀♀♀ 6
● Dolcetto d'Alba Boschi di Berri '96	♀♀♀ 4*
● Barolo Brunate '16	♀♀ 8
● Barolo del Comune di La Morra '18	♀♀ 6
● Barolo La Serra '16	♀♀ 7

★Marchesi di Barolo

via Roma, 1
12060 Barolo [CN]
☎ +39 0173564419
🌐 www.marchesibarolo.com

CELLAR SALES
PRE-BOOKED VISITS
RESTAURANT SERVICE
ANNUAL PRODUCTION 1,300,000 bottles
HECTARES UNDER VINE 200.00
SUSTAINABLE WINERY

With Ernesto and Anna, and their children Valentina and Davide, the Abbona family has reached its sixth generation in the world of wine. In recent years, Marchesi di Barolo has taken steps to rejuvenate the winery, giving Valentina and Davide more responsibilities. Valentina, despite just becoming a mother, continues to uphold the brand's prestige internationally, while Davide is gradually taking over the production side, overseeing both vineyard management and winemaking. The youthful vigor introduced by Davide is beginning to show in his 2020 Barolo and Barbaresco wines, where we find more juiciness and flesh compared to previous years. Without detracting from the famous Barolos, this year we were particularly impressed by the magnificent Rio Sordo '20, probably the best produced since the acquisition of Cascina Bruciata in 2016. Its aromatic profile offers clear raspberry aromas, echoed by complex hints of sweet tobacco and licorice, while a refined and progressively unfolding tannic structure leads to a long, sapid finish.

● Barbaresco Rio Sordo Cascina Bruciata '20	♟♟ 7
● Barolo Cannubi '20	♟♟ 8
● Barolo Sarmassa '20	♟♟ 8
● Barbaresco Rio Sordo Cascina Bruciata Ris. '19	♟♟ 8
● Barolo Coste di Rose '20	♟♟ 8
● Barolo del Comune di Barolo Composizione Parcellare '20	♟♟ 8
● Barolo Cannubi '14	♟♟♟ 8
● Barolo Cannubi '12	♟♟♟ 8
● Barolo Cannubi '11	♟♟♟ 8
● Barolo Cannubi '10	♟♟♟ 8
● Barolo Sarmassa '09	♟♟♟ 8
● Barolo Sarmassa '08	♟♟♟ 7
● Barolo Sarmassa '07	♟♟♟ 7

Mario Marengo

loc. Serradenari, 2a
12064 La Morra [CN]
☎ +39 017350115
🌐 www.cantinamarengo.it

CELLAR SALES
PRE-BOOKED VISITS
ANNUAL PRODUCTION 38,000 bottles
HECTARES UNDER VINE 7.50
SUSTAINABLE WINERY

The Marengo family winery, now managed by Marco, his wife Jenny, and their son Stefano, is located in Serradenari, in the La Morra production zone. The producer boasts a small but prized patrimony that includes plots in Valmaggiore in Roero and, most notably, portions of the Brunate Cru in La Morra and Bricco delle Viole in Barolo. The style of their wines has a contemporary flair, with aging mostly carried out in barriques. The Barolo Brunate '20 has an aromatic profile featuring hints of meadow herbs and smoky accents on a fruity base, opening the way to a well-structured progression of flavor, with deep tannins balanced by fleshiness. The Barolo Bricco delle Viole '20, with its subtle aromas of small red fruits, quinine, and licorice, proves austere, broad, and compact on the palate.

● Barolo Bricco delle Viole '20	♟♟ 7
● Barolo Brunate '20	♟♟ 8
● Barolo '20	♟♟ 6
● Nebbiolo d'Alba V. Valmaggiore '21	♟♟ 5
● Barbera d'Alba Vigna Pugnane '22	♟ 4
● Langhe Nebbiolo '22	♟ 3
● Barolo Brunate '12	♟♟♟ 7
● Barolo Brunate '11	♟♟♟ 7
● Barolo Brunate '09	♟♟♟ 6
● Barolo Brunate '07	♟♟♟ 6
● Barolo Brunate '06	♟♟♟ 6
● Barolo Brunate '05	♟♟♟ 6
● Barolo Brunate '04	♟♟♟ 6
● Barolo Bricco delle Viole '19	♟♟ 6
● Barolo Bricco delle Viole '18	♟♟ 6
● Barolo Brunate '17	♟♟ 7

★Claudio Mariotto

s.da per Sarezzano, 29
15057 Tortona [AL]
☎ +39 0131868500
⊛ www.claudiomariotto.it

CELLAR SALES
PRE-BOOKED VISITS
ANNUAL PRODUCTION 100,000 bottles
HECTARES UNDER VINE 24.00

In the 1990s, Claudio was among the few winemakers who believed in reviving timorasso. Founded in 1921 by his great-grandfather Bepi, the winery cultivates vineyards between Vho and Sarezzano, at the foothills of the Apennines overlooking the Po Valley, at elevations spanning 250-300 meters. Production focuses on barbera, croatina and, especially, timorasso, the winery's flagship, with some five different versions offered, including the "Imbevibile", aged in amphora. Precise and impeccable, Claudio is as unique as his wines. The various versions of Timorasso submitted for tasting are all of remarkable quality, each incredibly distinct. The Derthona '22 is the most complete, a fusion of freshness and depth, with notes of lime, grapefruit, citron, flint, and saffron, and a bright, rhythmic palate. The Cavallina '22 is fresh and juicy, offering tones of citrus juice, broom, and orange blossom. The Pitasso '22 is more concentrated and mineral, with a close-knit and pervasive character. The Bricco San Michele proves vibrant and versatile.

○ Colli Tortonesi Timorasso Derthona '22	🍷🍷 5
○ Colli Tortonesi Timorasso Derthona Pitasso '22	🍷🍷 6
○ Colli Tortonesi Timorasso Derthona Cavallina '22	🍷🍷 5
○ Colli Tortonesi Timorasso Derthona Bricco San Michele '22	🍷 5
○ Colli Tortonesi Timorasso Cavallina '19	🍷🍷🍷 5
○ Colli Tortonesi Timorasso Derthona Pitasso '21	🍷🍷🍷 6
○ Colli Tortonesi Timorasso Derthona Pitasso '17	🍷🍷🍷 6
○ Colli Tortonesi Timorasso Pitasso '20	🍷🍷🍷 6
○ Colli Tortonesi Timorasso Pitasso '18	🍷🍷🍷 6
○ Colli Tortonesi Timorasso Pitasso '13	🍷🍷🍷 6

★Franco M. Martinetti

via San Francesco da Paola, 18
10123 Torino
☎ +39 0118395937
⊛ www.francomartinetti.it

PRE-BOOKED VISITS
ANNUAL PRODUCTION 120,000 bottles
HECTARES UNDER VINE 5.00
SUSTAINABLE WINERY

What do you do when, as a young boy, you're passionate about haute cuisine and fine French wines, but your expertise lies only in your knowledge of terroirs and the best producers? You become a small négociant. For over 50 years, Franco has been selecting vineyards and winemakers of high quality, purchasing batches of grapes every year, and vinifying them according to his methods. The results have often been astonishing, with his innovative ideas and vision for wine setting him apart. Over the years, Franco has worked in all the key wine regions of Piedmont, from Asti and Alba to Gavi and Tortona. This year feels like a return to the early 1990s when we first discovered Martinetti's Barbera Montruc '90. With the Montruc '22, nothing seems to have changed: the nose features cherry and spices, while the palate is balanced by light tannins and fleshiness. The Martin '23 is also splendid, playing on aromatic and gustatory finesse with tension on the palate, marking a distinct shift from the richness of past vintages.

● Barbera d'Asti Sup. Montruc '22	🍷🍷🍷 7
○ Colli Tortonesi Timorasso Martin '23	🍷🍷 7
● Barbera d'Asti Sup. Bric dei Banditi '22	🍷🍷 5
● Barolo Marasco '20	🍷🍷 8
○ Colli Tortonesi Timorasso Biancofranco '23	🍷🍷 5
○ Gavi del Comune di Gavi '23	🍷🍷 5
○ Gavi Minaia '23	🍷🍷 6
● M.to Rosso sul Bric '22	🍷🍷 7
● Barbera d'Asti Sup. Montruc '06	🍷🍷🍷 5
● Barolo Marasco '01	🍷🍷🍷 7
● Barolo Marasco '00	🍷🍷🍷 7
○ Colli Tortonesi Timorasso Martin '12	🍷🍷🍷 6
○ Gavi Minaia '14	🍷🍷🍷 5
● M.to Rosso Sul Bric '10	🍷🍷🍷 6
● M.to Rosso Sul Bric '09	🍷🍷🍷 6

★Giuseppe Mascarello e Figlio

via Borgonuovo, 108
12060 Monchiero [CN]
(℘ +39 0173792126
www.mascarello1881.com

CELLAR SALES
PRE-BOOKED VISITS
ANNUAL PRODUCTION 60,000 bottles
HECTARES UNDER VINE 13.50

The Mascarello family winery is behind some of the most prestigious wines in the Barolo appellation—a range that's always refined and unmistakably styled. The Monprivato, the estate's flagship, is produced from one of the most important crus in Barolo, located in the hills of Castiglione Falletto, a vineyard known for its luminous, timeless wines. Giuseppe Mascarello e Figlio, which owns nearly the whole parcel, is renowned as the cru's most prominent producer. At the Mascarello estate, every change, even a minor one, is carefully considered; labels and vines remain largely unchanged, except for natural fluctuations in climate. Looking back, it's clear that Monprivato carries fifty years of unwavering prestige. However, we feel the 2019 version will be remembered for years to come. Hailing from a rather warm vintage, it has shed some of its youthful austerity to reveal crystalline class in its aromas, with a measured, delicate tannic structure and a long trail of flavor.

★Vigneti Massa

p.zza G. Capsoni, 10
15059 Monleale [AL]
(℘ +39 013180302
massa@vignetimassa.com

CELLAR SALES
PRE-BOOKED VISITS
ANNUAL PRODUCTION 120,000 bottles
HECTARES UNDER VINE 25.00
SUSTAINABLE WINERY

Calling Walter Massa the father and pioneer of timorasso seems like an understatement, because he is so much more. He is not only the face of the success of Colli Tortonesi, but also a passionate vinedresser, a dynamic artist, and a volcano of ideas constantly seeking new projects and goals with energy and determination. Alongside timorasso, he also cultivates barbera, freisa, and croatina. Today Walter is joined by his grandsons, Filippo and Edoardo. The Derthona '22 stands out for its masterful quality, representing a multisensory fusion of fragrances, density, and volume. Aromas of citrus, yellow plum, ripe apple, and broom unfold along with mineral notes of chalk, creating an ever-shifting interplay of sensations. The palate is dynamic, with nice tension, both glyceric and taut, finishing with a velvety and balanced texture. The Barbera Monleale '20 proves fresh, juicy, and flavorful, with blueberry and spicy notes and a satisfying, thirst-quenching palate.

● Barolo Monprivato '19	♟♟♟ 8
● Dolcetto d'Alba Bricco Mirasole '22	♟♟ 3
● Barolo Monprivato '17	♟♟♟ 8
● Barolo Monprivato '15	♟♟♟ 8
● Barolo Monprivato '13	♟♟♟ 8
● Barolo Monprivato '12	♟♟♟ 8
● Barolo Monprivato '11	♟♟♟ 8
● Barolo Monprivato '10	♟♟♟ 8
● Barolo Monprivato '09	♟♟♟ 8
● Barolo Monprivato '08	♟♟♟ 8
● Barolo Monprivato '01	♟♟♟ 8
● Babera D'Alba Scudetto '18	♟♟ 6
● Barolo Monprivato '18	♟♟ 8
● Barolo Monprivato '16	♟♟ 8
● Barolo Monprivato '14	♟♟ 8
● Barolo Villero '14	♟♟ 8
● Langhe Nebbiolo '18	♟♟ 7

● Colli Tortonesi Monleale '20	♟♟ 5
○ Derthona '22	♟♟ 5
○ Colli Tortonesi Bianco Costa del Vento '05	♟♟♟ 7
○ Colli Tortonesi Bianco Sterpi '04	♟♟♟ 6
○ Colli Tortonesi Timorasso Derthona '06	♟♟♟ 5
○ Colli Tortonesi Timorasso Sterpi '08	♟♟♟ 7
○ Colli Tortonesi Timorasso Sterpi '07	♟♟♟ 7
○ Costa del Vento '15	♟♟♟ 6
○ Costa del Vento '12	♟♟♟ 6
○ Derthona '09	♟♟♟ 5
○ Derthona Montecitorio '19	♟♟♟ 6
○ Derthona Sterpi '16	♟♟♟ 6
○ Montecitorio '11	♟♟♟ 6
○ Montecitorio '10	♟♟♟ 6
○ Sterpi '13	♟♟♟ 6

★★Massolino Vigna Rionda

p.zza Cappellano, 8
12050 Serralunga d'Alba [CN]
📞 +39 0173613138
✉ www.massolino.it

CELLAR SALES
PRE-BOOKED VISITS
ANNUAL PRODUCTION 460,000 bottles
HECTARES UNDER VINE 57.00

The Massolino family winery is closely associated with Vigna Rionda, a vineyard known since the 19th century and made famous in the late 1960s by Bruno Giacosa. The Massolinos purchased their first plots in 1956, transforming the wine produced there into their "brand." Today, the Serralunga d'Alba producer has further refined its approach to individual vineyards, raising the bar with Barolo Parafada, Margheria, Parussi, and Albesani. The Barolo Parafada '20 impresses with its depth and richness, transitioning from fruity hints to aromatic herbs on a balsamic and smoky background. The palate is rich, almost opulent, with a close-knit, complex tannic texture and a long, vibrant finish. The Barbaresco '21 is also excellent, offering violet aromas with light citrus and licorice accents that lead to a juicy, solid, and powerful palate with an expansive finish and lingering citrus notes.

● Barbaresco '21	♥♥	6
● Barolo Margheria '20	♥♥	8
● Barolo Parafada '20	♥♥	8
● Barolo '20	♥♥	6
● Barolo Parussi '20	♥♥	8
● Langhe Nebbiolo '22	♥♥	4
● Barbaresco Albesani '21	♥	8
● Barbera d'Alba '23	♥	3
● Dolcetto d'Alba '23	♥	3
● Barolo Parafada '19	♥♥♥	8
● Barolo Parafada '16	♥♥♥	8
● Barolo Vigna Rionda Ris. '16	♥♥♥	8
● Barolo Vigna Rionda Ris. '15	♥♥♥	8
● Barolo Vigna Rionda Ris. '11	♥♥♥	8
● Barolo Vigna Rionda Ris. '10	♥♥♥	8

Tiziano Mazzoni

via Roma, 73
28010 Cavaglio d'Agogna [NO]
📞 +39 3488200635
✉ www.vinimazzoni.it

CELLAR SALES
PRE-BOOKED VISITS
ANNUAL PRODUCTION 25,000 bottles
HECTARES UNDER VINE 4.50
SUSTAINABLE WINERY

Everything started with Tiziano's passion, which he inherited from his father Natalino, along with a vineyard in the Franconi area of Cavaglio d'Agogna. He later expanded with the purchase of historic vineyards in the Livelli area of Ghemme. Since 2005, his son Gilles has worked alongside him throughout all phases of production. This winery exemplifies passion, dedication, and respect for tradition. Their vineyards are planted in morainic and clay soils, at elevations spanning 280-300 meters, with a south/southwest exposure. Made from the oldest vines, the Nebbiolo Ai Livelli '19 is expressive and distinctive, with aromas of blackberry and plum accompanied by balsamic, mineral, and spicy undertones. The palate is concentrated and flavorful, with mature, silky tannins and a sapid, powerful finish. The Dei Mazzoni '20 proves balanced and delicate, alternating citrus and Indian spice aromas before a rich, dense palate, featuring mature, silky tannins and a long, flavorful finish.

● Ghemme ai Livelli '19	♥♥	7
● Ghemme dei Mazzoni '20	♥♥	6
● Colline Novaresi Nebbiolo del Monteregio '22	♥	4
● Colline Novaresi Vespolina Il Ricetto '23	♥	4
○ Iris '23	♥	3
● Ghemme dei Mazzoni '12	♥♥♥	5
● Colline Novaresi Nebbiolo del Monteregio '21	♥♥	4
● Colline Novaresi Vespolina Il Ricetto '22	♥♥	4
● Ghemme ai Livelli '18	♥♥	6
● Ghemme Ai Livelli '17	♥♥	6
● Ghemme Ai Livelli '16	♥♥	6
● Ghemme Ai Livelli '15	♥♥	6
● Ghemme dei Mazzoni '19	♥♥	5
● Ghemme dei Mazzoni '17	♥♥	5

La Mesma

s.da Tassarolo, 26
15067 Novi Ligure [AL]
☏ +39 0143342012
🖳 lamesma.it

CELLAR SALES
PRE-BOOKED VISITS
ACCOMMODATION
ANNUAL PRODUCTION 60,000 bottles
HECTARES UNDER VINE 28.00
VITICULTURE METHOD Certified Organic

Dedicated to Gavi DOCG and cortese grapes, La Mesma has been run by the Rosina sisters, Paola, Francesca, and Anna, since 2001. The three left their jobs in Genoa to become producers, starting with 2 hectares and then expanding by purchasing plots from neighbors. In 2004, they acquired the Bella Alleanza estate: 10 hectares of vineyards in Novi Ligure and Tassarolo, and an already operational cellar. The Gavi Vigna della Rovere Verde Riserva '21 offers a nose dominated by a lovely balsamic vein, with citrus whiffs and fruity tones as a finishing touch. The palate is lively and flavorful, with a crisp, fragrant, and precise development. The Gavi Monterotondo Etichetta Nera '22 delivers nuances of field herbs and white fruit aromas, progressing with a fresh, linear palate that flows smoothly into a sapid, well-sustained finish.

Mauro Molino

fraz. Annunziata Gancia, 111a
12064 La Morra [CN]
☏ +39 0173500035
🖳 www.mauromolino.com

CELLAR SALES
PRE-BOOKED VISITS
ANNUAL PRODUCTION 95,000 bottles
HECTARES UNDER VINE 20.00
SUSTAINABLE WINERY

After working as a winemaker in Emilia Romagna, Mauro Molino inherited a piece of land in his native Langhe. The Vigna Conca was the first Barolo he produced in Annunziata di La Morra. It was 1982, and since then, his work has been dedicated not only to the crus of La Morra (Conca was joined by Gallinotto, in the geographical indication of Berri, La Serra, and Bricco Luciani in Annunziata), but also to barbera, dolcetto, chardonnay, and arneis. Delicate spicy notes, with hints of licorice and cinchona, accompany a raspberry-based aromatic core in the Barolo Conca '20. The palate develops with a complex, close-knit tannic texture and a broad, persistent finish. The Barolo La Serra '20 is also good, with less precise but intense aromas introducing a firm and lively palate.

○ Gavi V. della Rovere Verde Ris. '21	♈♈♈ 6
○ Gavi del Comune di Gavi Monterotondo Et. Nera '22	♈♈ 4
○ Gavi Pas Dosé M. Cl. '16	♈♈ 5
○ Gavi del Comune di Gavi Monterotondo Indi '23	♈♈ 5
○ Gavi Le Rose '23	♈♈ 3
○ Gavi del comune di Gavi Et. Gialla '23	♈ 4
○ Gavi del Comune di Gavi Et. Gialla '20	♈♈♈ 3*
○ Gavi del Comune di Gavi Monterotondo Et. Nera '21	♈♈♈ 4*
○ Gavi del Comune di Gavi Monterotondo Et. Nera '20	♈♈♈ 3*
○ Gavi V. della Rovere Verde Ris. '17	♈♈♈ 5
○ Gavi V. della Rovere Verde Ris. '15	♈♈♈ 5
○ Gavi del Comune di Gavi Et. Gialla '22	♈♈ 4
○ Gavi V. della Rovere Verde Ris. '20	♈♈ 5

● Barolo Conca '20	♈♈ 8
● Barolo La Serra '20	♈♈ 8
● Barbera d'Alba V. Gattere '00	♈♈♈ 5
● Barbera d'Alba V. Gattere '97	♈♈♈ 7
● Barbera d'Alba V. Gattere '96	♈♈♈ 7
● Barolo Gallinotto '11	♈♈♈ 6
● Barolo Gallinotto '03	♈♈♈ 6
● Barolo Gallinotto '01	♈♈♈ 6
● Barolo V. Conca '00	♈♈♈ 7
● Barolo V. Conca '97	♈♈♈ 7
● Barolo V. Conca '96	♈♈♈ 7
● Barolo '18	♈♈ 5
● Barolo Bricco Luciani '18	♈♈ 6
● Barolo Bricco Luciani '17	♈♈ 6
● Barolo La Serra '17	♈♈ 7
● Barolo La Serra '16	♈♈ 7

PIEDMONT

F.lli Monchiero

via Alba Monforte, 49
12060 Castiglione Falletto [CN]
(☎ +39 017362820
⊛ www.monchierovini.it

CELLAR SALES
PRE-BOOKED VISITS
ANNUAL PRODUCTION 40,000 bottles
HECTARES UNDER VINE 12.00
SUSTAINABLE WINERY

The Monchiero family has been producing
Barolo for generations. The grandparents of the
winery's current owner, Vittorio Monchiero,
were farmers and owned just over a hectare in
Roere di Santa Maria before the war. In the
1980s, Vittorio completely restructured the
family vineyards and began his production
journey. Today, the family's vineyards can be
found across the municipalities of Castiglione
Falletto, La Morra, Alba, and Treiso. Raspberry,
wild strawberries, and smoky, citrus tones
dominate the aromatic bouquet of the Barolo
del Comune di Castiglion Falletto '20, which
develops with nice body and delicate but
present tannins, concluding with a long,
persistent finish. The Barolo Montanello '19
offers a sapid palate with clearly defined aromas.
The pleasantly drinkable Langhe Nebbiolo '22 is
fragrant and enjoyable.

● Barolo del Comune di Castiglione Falletto '20	♟♟ 6
● Barbera d'Alba Sup. '22	♟♟ 3
● Barolo del Comune di La Morra '20	♟♟ 6
● Barolo Montanello '19	♟♟ 7
● Langhe Nebbiolo '22	♟♟ 4
● Barolo Rocche di Castiglione '17	♟♟♟ 6
● Barolo del Comune di Castiglione Falletto '19	♟♟ 6
● Barolo del Comune di Castiglione Falletto '16	♟♟ 8
● Barolo Montanello '16	♟♟ 5
● Barolo Pernanno Ris. '16	♟♟ 6
● Barolo Rocche di Castiglione '19	♟♟ 8
● Barolo Rocche di Castiglione '18	♟♟ 6
● Barolo Rocche di Castiglione '15	♟♟ 5
● Barolo Rocche di Castiglione Ris. '15	♟♟ 6
● Barolo Rocche di Castiglione Ris. '13	♟♟ 7

★Monchiero Carbone

via Santo Stefano Roero, 2
12043 Canale [CN]
(☎ +39 017395568
⊛ www.monchierocarbone.com

CELLAR SALES
PRE-BOOKED VISITS
ANNUAL PRODUCTION 200,000 bottles
HECTARES UNDER VINE 30.00
SUSTAINABLE WINERY

The Monchiero family offers a range of wines
that are stylistic and qualitative benchmarks for
Roero. The estate vineyards are located in the
municipalities of Canale, Vezza d'Alba, Monteu
Roero, and Priocca, in some of the district's most
famous crus. Roero's classic grapes are cultivated
from arneis to nebbiolo and barbera. Their
production approach is modern, characterized by
great clarity, aromatic complexity, and typicity.
Francesco and Lucrezia have decided to keep the
Arneis Renesio Incisa in the cellar for another
year, but their range of wines leaves no shortage
of excellent choices. The Roero Arneis Cecu d'la
Biunda '23 highlights citrus, pepper, and white
currant aromas before a fresh, savory, almost
salty palate, finishing long with beautiful tension.
The Roero Printi Riserva '20 is also excellent,
playing on aromas of rain-soaked earth,
underbrush, and black stone fruits, offering
impressive volume and structure, while the
Barbera d'Alba Monbirone '20 stands out for its
intense Mediterranean herb notes, juicy fruit,
and richness.

○ Roero Arneis Cecu d'La Biunda '23	♟♟♟ 4
● Barbera d'Alba Monbirone '20	♟♟ 5
○ Roero Printi Ris. '20	♟♟ 6
● Barbera d'Alba Pelisa '23	♟♟ 3
○ Langhe Bianco Tamardi '23	♟♟ 4
○ Roero Arneis Recit '23	♟♟ 3
● Roero Srü '21	♟♟ 5
○ Roero Arneis Cecu d'La Biunda '20	♟♟♟ 3
○ Roero Arneis Cecu d'La Biunda '19	♟♟♟ 3
○ Roero Arneis Cecu d'la Biunda '17	♟♟♟ 3
○ Roero Arneis Cecu d'la Biunda '16	♟♟♟ 3
○ Roero Arneis Renesio Incisa Ris. '19	♟♟♟ 6
○ Roero Arneis Renesio Incisa Ris. '18	♟♟♟ 6
● Roero Printi Ris. '15	♟♟♟ 6
● Roero Printi Ris. '12	♟♟♟ 5
● Roero Printi Ris. '11	♟♟♟ 5
● Roero Printi Ris. '10	♟♟♟ 5

La Montagnetta

fraz. Bricco Cappello, 4
14018 Roatto [AT]
☎ +39 335309361
✉ www.lamontagnetta.com

CELLAR SALES
PRE-BOOKED VISITS
ANNUAL PRODUCTION 50,000 bottles
HECTARES UNDER VINE 10.00

La Montagnetta cultivates many different grapes, from natives like barbera and bonarda to international varieties like chardonnay, viognier, and sauvignon. Domenico Capello's favorite, however, remains freisa. He has always championed this often-overlooked variety, and is now rightly considered its standard-bearer. The winery's range includes five different types, including a rosé, a spumante, and a version aged in amphorae, all emphasizing clarity and varietal stamping. The Barbera d'Asti P-Tic '23 stands out with its nose of wild blackberries, cocoa, cardamom, and cloves. On the palate, it's fresh and juicy, with a sapid, pleasant finish that lingers on fruit. The balanced and energetic Freisa d'Asti Superiore Bugianen '19 impresses with its great finesse, offering aromas of red fruit and anise, with good harmony in the finish. The well-crafted Barbera d'Asti Superiore Piovà '21 reveals cherry and tobacco on the nose, with a notably structured palate and an austere finish.

Montalbera

via Montalbera, 1
14030 Castagnole Monferrato [AT]
☎ +39 0141292125
✉ www.montalbera.it

CELLAR SALES
PRE-BOOKED VISITS
ACCOMMODATION
ANNUAL PRODUCTION 650,000 bottles
HECTARES UNDER VINE 130.00
SUSTAINABLE WINERY

The Morando family, now in its third generation of producers, has long been linked to a little-known and distinctive Piedmontese variety: ruchè. This semi-aromatic red finds an excellent terroir in the territory of Castiglione, where it is produced in three different versions. More than half of the ruchè from the Castagnole Monferrato appellation belongs to Montalbera, which has always work to express its attributes. Moscato, barbera, chardonnay, viognier and grignolino are also cultivated. The Ruché di Castagnole Monferrato wines continue to be among the appellation's best. The Laccento '23 opens with intense aromas of plum, rose, and licorice, while the palate is full, soft, and persistent. The Riserva del Fondatore '21 showcases floral aromas with sweet spicy undertones, offering a rich, juicy palate and a long finish. The Tradizione '23 is pleasantly aromatic and easy to drink, while the Grignolino d'Asti Grignè '23 displays tobacco and black fruit tones. The Nizza Nuda '22 proves full and complex.

● Barbera d'Asti Pi Cit '23	🍷🍷 2*
● Freisa d'Asti Sup. Bugianen '19	🍷🍷 4
● Barbera d'Asti Sup. Piovà '21	🍷🍷 4
○ Piemonte Viognier A-Stim '22	🍷 3
● Barbera d'Asti Pi Cit '22	🍷🍷 2*
● Barbera d'Asti Pi Cit '21	🍷🍷 2*
● Barbera d'Asti Pi Cit '20	🍷🍷 2*
● Barbera d'Asti Sup. Piovà '20	🍷🍷 4
● Barbera d'Asti Sup. Piovà '19	🍷🍷 4
● Barbera d'Asti Sup. Piovà '18	🍷🍷 4
● Freisa d'Asti L'Altra '22	🍷🍷 2*
● Freisa d'Asti L'Altra '20	🍷🍷 3*
● Freisa d'Asti Sup. Bugianen '17	🍷🍷 4
● Piemonte Freisa Anphora '20	🍷🍷 2*
● Piemonte Freisa Anphora '18	🍷🍷 2*

● Ruchè di Castagnole M.to Laccento '23	🍷🍷 4
● Ruchè di Castagnole M.to Riserva del Fondatore '21	🍷🍷 5
○ Colli Tortonesi Timorasso Derthona Calypsos '22	🍷🍷 5
○ Langhe Chardonnay Il Mio Nudo '22	🍷🍷 4
● Monferrato Nebbiolo Superiore Il Don '22	🍷🍷 4
○ Piemonte Viognier Calypsos '23	🍷🍷 3
● Ruchè di Castagnole M.to La Tradizione '23	🍷🍷 3
● Barbera d'Asti La Ribelle '23	🍷 3
● Grignolino D'Asti Lanfora '23	🍷 4
● Ruché di Castagnole M.to Laccento '21	🍷🍷🍷 4*
● Ruché di Castagnole M.to Laccento '20	🍷🍷🍷 4*
● Ruché di Castagnole M.to Laccento '19	🍷🍷🍷 4*
● Ruché di Castagnole M.to Laccento '18	🍷🍷🍷 4*

Montaribaldi

fraz. Tre Stelle
s.da Nicolini Alto, 12
12050 Barbaresco [CN]
☎ +39 0173638220
✉ www.montaribaldi.com

CELLAR SALES
PRE-BOOKED VISITS
ANNUAL PRODUCTION 200,000 bottles
HECTARES UNDER VINE 30.00
SUSTAINABLE WINERY

The Taliano brothers, Luciano and Roberto, lead the family winery, which focuses on Barbaresco. Given the increasing attention toward the vineyards with the highest potential (from Pajorè to Tre Stelle, Rio Sordo to Marcarini, Starderi to Canova), the estate's most well-known Barbarescos (Sorì Motaribaldi, Palazzina, and Ricü) will soon be joined by single-vineyard wines in a new initiative focused on quality. The Barbaresco Sorì Montaribaldi offers up classic aromas of fresh red berries, with floral accents and spice adding complexity. The palate is austere and still a bit tight in its tannic development but will evolve beautifully over time, thanks to its pulpy, ripe texture. The Rio Sordo '20 reveals a beautifully complex nose, with mature red fruit and tobacco. On the palate, the cru's power and juiciness shine through, concluding in a very long finish. The Starderi is simpler, with crisp fruit, but it's still a pleasing, fine, and persistent drink.

● Barbaresco Rio Sordo '20	♟♟ 5
● Barbaresco Sorì Montaribaldi '21	♟♟ 5
● Barbaresco Palazzina '21	♟♟ 5
● Barbaresco Starderi '21	♟♟ 8
● Barbaresco Palazzina '20	♟♟ 5
● Barbaresco Ricü '19	♟♟ 6
● Barbaresco Ricü '15	♟♟ 6
● Barbaresco Ricü '09	♟♟ 6
● Barbaresco Rio Sordo '19	♟♟ 5
● Barbaresco Sorì Montaribaldi '20	♟♟ 5
● Barbaresco Sorì Montaribaldi '16	♟♟ 5
● Barbera d'Alba Dü Gir '20	♟♟ 4
● Barolo Borzoni '09	♟♟ 6
● Barolo Sàrz '19	♟♟ 7
● Dolcetto d'Alba Vagnona '19	♟♟ 2*

Tenuta Montemagno

via Cascina Valfossato, 9
14030 Montemagno [AT]
☎ +39 014163624
✉ www.tenutamontemagno.it

CELLAR SALES
PRE-BOOKED VISITS
ACCOMMODATION AND RESTAURANT SERVICE
ANNUAL PRODUCTION 140,000 bottles
HECTARES UNDER VINE 15.00
SUSTAINABLE WINERY

Surrounded by vineyards, the charming Tenuta Montemagno estate also hosts a splendid Relais & Châteaux hotel and an elegant restaurant. Owned by the Barea family, the estate benefits from the expertise of winemaker Gianfranco Cordero. Thanks to the southwest exposure of the vineyards, an excellent microclimate, and clay-limestone soils, Montemagno has consistently achieved remarkable results over the years. The tasting room, with its spectacular westward view, is also worth mentioning. Once again, the Barbera d'Asti Superiore Mysterium '19 captures our attention. The nose reveals the beginnings of a well-controlled, fascinating evolution, with notes of brandied dark fruit merging with blood orange. On the palate, it offers density without excess, supported by balanced acidity. Among the white wines tasted, the Monferrato Bianco Solis Vis stands out for its refined, complex nose— aromas of white fruit, citrus, and hydrocarbon. The palate is rich and pervasive, balanced by nice freshness.

● Barbera d'Asti Sup. Mysterium '19	♟♟♟ 5
○ M.to Bianco Solis Vis '23	♟♟ 4
● Barolo Soranus '19	♟♟ 6
● Grignolino d'Asti Ruber '23	♟♟ 3
● Ruchè di Castagnole Monferrato Invictus '22	♟♟ 5
⊙ TM 24 Brut M.Cl.	♟♟ 5
⊙ TM 36 Brut M.Cl.	♟♟ 6
○ M.to Bianco Musae '23	♟ 3
● Ruchè di Castagnole M.to Nobilis '22	♟ 4
● Barbera d'Asti Sup. Mysterium '18	♟♟ 4
● Grignolino d'Asti Ruber '21	♟♟ 3*
● Ruché di Castagnole M.to Invictus '21	♟♟ 4
● Ruché di Castagnole M.to Invictus '20	♟♟ 3*

La Morandina

loc. Morandini, 11
12053 Castiglione Tinella [CN]
☎ +39 0141855261
✉ www.lamorandina.com

CELLAR SALES
PRE-BOOKED VISITS
ANNUAL PRODUCTION 100,000 bottles
HECTARES UNDER VINE 20.00

The four main estates, starting with Castiglione Tinella, are all situated between 280-400 meters above sea level around the historic cellar. Moscato is a focus, with some plots going back more than 40 years. They also grow nebbiolo in Bricco Spessa, Neive, for the production of Barbaresco, and barbera in the two estates of Varmat (where some vineyards are more than a century old) and Zucchetto, both in Montegrosso d'Asti. Their range is aimed at expressing the union between territory and grape variety as best possible. The Moscato d'Asti '23 is excellent, conjuring up vibrant aromas of sage, apple, candied ginger, and aromatic herbs. The palate is rich yet fresh and harmonious, with acidity perfectly balancing sugar, giving the wine length and character. The Langhe Chardonnay '23 is also well-crafted, playing on acacia flower, white and tropical fruit tones, showing nice structure and energy, finishing long and balanced. Slightly austere but with good substance, the Barbera d'Asti 5 Vignés '22 offers blueberry and black olive aromas.

◐ Moscato d'Asti '23	♟♟ 3*
● Barbera d'Asti 5 Vignés '22	♟♟ 3
◐ Langhe Chardonnay '23	♟♟ 3
● Barbera d'Asti Zucchetto '22	♟ 4
● Barbaresco '19	♟♟ 6
● Barbaresco '18	♟♟ 6
● Barbaresco '17	♟♟ 6
● Barbera d'Asti 5 Vignés '21	♟♟ 3
● Barbera d'Asti 5 Vignés '20	♟♟ 3
● Barbera d'Asti Sup. Varmat '19	♟♟ 6
● Barbera d'Asti Zucchetto '20	♟♟ 4
● Barbera d'Asti Zucchetto '19	♟♟ 4
◐ Langhe Chardonnay '22	♟♟ 3
◐ Moscato d'Asti '22	♟♟ 3*
◐ Moscato d'Asti Canelli '21	♟♟ 3*
◐ Moscato d'Asti Canelli '20	♟♟ 2*

Diego Morra

via Cascina Mosca, 37
12060 Verduno [CN]
☎ +39 3279398609
✉ www.morrawines.com

CELLAR SALES
PRE-BOOKED VISITS
ANNUAL PRODUCTION 80,000 bottles
HECTARES UNDER VINE 34.00
SUSTAINABLE WINERY

Domenico, Antonio, and now Diego Morra have been building their family winery in Verduno, cultivating vineyards in some of the most prestigious terroirs of Barolo, including La Morra and Roddi. In addition to Barolo (with the Monvigliero Cru as their flagship), they also produce Pelaverga, Barbera, and Dolcetto d'Alba. The family began bottling their wines in 2006, though since 2018 they've been making improvements aimed at modernizing the estate, including investments in wine tourism. Tobacco, wilted flowers, small red fruits, and spices characterize the nose of the Barolo Zinzasco '20, a measured wine on the palate, with well-resolved tannins and a multifaceted development, finishing long and focused. The Barolo San Lorenzo di Verduno '20 also delivers, combining nuanced fruity aromas with a sapid and juicy palate. The Verduno Pelaverga '22 proves pleasantly fragrant, with easy-drinking appeal.

● Barbera d'Alba Sup. Le Schiene '21	♟♟ 5
● Barolo Monvigliero '20	♟♟ 8
● Barolo San Lorenzo di Verduno '20	♟♟ 8
● Barolo Zinzasco '20	♟♟ 6
● Barolo del Comune di Verduno '20	♟ 7
○ Langhe Chardonnay '23	♟ 4
● Langhe Nebbiolo Il Sarto '22	♟ 4
● Verduno Pelaverga '23	♟ 4
● Barolo Monvigliero '18	♟♟ 8
● Barolo Monvigliero '17	♟♟ 7
● Barolo Monvigliero '16	♟♟ 7
● Barolo Monvigliero '15	♟♟ 7
● Barolo San Lorenzo di Verduno '19	♟♟ 6
● Barolo Zinzasco '16	♟♟ 6

Morra Stefanino

loc. San Pietro
via Castagnito, 50
12050 Castellinaldo [CN]
(») +39 0173213489
⊛ www.morravini.it

CELLAR SALES
PRE-BOOKED VISITS
ANNUAL PRODUCTION 80,000 bottles
HECTARES UNDER VINE 15.00
SUSTAINABLE WINERY

This year the Morra family are celebrating the centennial of their winery, which was founded in 1925. Most of the vineyards are situated in Castellinaldo, near the cellar, though they also stretch across other parts of Roero, from Canale to Castagnito, Priocca, and Vezza d'Alba. The grapes grown here—arneis, barbera, and nebbiolo—express the character of the territory through wines that emphasize typicity and vibrant fruit expression with a classic style. The Roero Arneis Vigna San Pietro '22 is excellent. Aromas of white fruit and green citrus rise from the glass, with a fresh, juicy palate to follow. The Roero Sräi Riserva '20 highlights fig, pepper, and aromatic herb aromas, with a well-structured palate, fine tannins, and a long, fruity finish. The Roero '21 is well-crafted, releasing bright, appealing red forest fruit aromas and hints of bay leaf. The Barbera d'Alba Superiore '21 offers tones of porcini mushrooms and petrichor, with a rich, juicy, fruit-driven palate.

Mura Mura

reg. Vianoce, 1
14048 Montegrosso d'Asti [AT]
(») +39 01411852673
⊛ www.muramura.it

After selling their gelato chain, Grom, in 2015, Federico Grom and Guido Martinetti turned their attention to winemaking—though they were no novices. Guido is the son of Franco, a well-known wine merchant. Their estate is based in Montegrosso d'Asti and focuses on barbera and grignolino, as well as ruchè and moscato. They also own four hectares in Barbaresco, featuring the Roncaglie, Starderi, Currà, and Serragrilli crus, along with a vineyard in Serralunga d'Alba within the Sorano cru. The winery presented an impressive range. The Barolo Sorano '20 stands out with its aromas of red fruit, tobacco, and spices, offering a powerful, dense palate with exuberant fruit. The Barbera d'Asti Superiore Miolera '21 sees aromas of berries merge with Mediterranean scrub, and cinchona, with a fresh, well-structured, juicy, and pleasant palate. The Grignolino d'Asti Garibaldi '22 offers classic notes of pepper and tobacco, while in the mouth, tannins accompany the palate rather than drying it, making for a long and energetic drink. You'll find the Barbaresco Roncaglie '21 listed in our Rare Wines section.

○ Roero Arneis V. San Pietro '22	♥♥ 4
● Roero Sräi Ris. '20	♥♥ 5
● Barbera d'Alba Sup. '21	♥♥ 4
● Roero '21	♥♥ 4
● Barbera d'Alba '21	♥ 4
○ Roero Arneis '23	♥ 3
● Barbera d'Alba '20	♥♥ 3
● Barbera d'Alba '18	♥♥ 3
● Barbera d'Alba Sup. '20	♥♥ 4
● Roero '19	♥♥ 3
○ Roero Arneis V. San Pietro '21	♥♥ 3
○ Roero Arneis V. San Pietro '19	♥♥ 3
● Roero Sräi Ris. '19	♥♥ 5

● Barbera d'Asti Miolera '21	♥♥ 6
● Barolo Sorano '20	♥♥ 8
● Grignolino d'Asti Garibaldi '22	♥♥ 6
● Barbaresco Faset '20	♥♥ 5
● Barbaresco Faset '19	♥♥ 5
● Barbaresco Serragrilli '20	♥♥ 5
● Barbaresco Serragrilli '19	♥♥ 5
● Barbaresco Starderi '20	♥♥ 5
● Barbaresco Starderi '19	♥♥ 5
● Barbera d'Asti Miolera '20	♥♥ 6
○ Derthona Beatrice '21	♥♥ 6

Ada Nada

loc. Rombone
via Ausario, 12
12050 Treiso [CN]
(+39 0173638127
www.adanada.it

CELLAR SALES
PRE-BOOKED VISITS
ACCOMMODATION
ANNUAL PRODUCTION 45,000 bottles
HECTARES UNDER VINE 9.00

This Treiso-based winery boasts vineyards that go back, on average, 40 years. Since 1989, Gian Carlo Nada and his wife Ada have been the driving force behind the estate, which unfolds in the subzones of Valeirano and Rombone, though today the property is managed by their son Elvio and his wife Anna Lisa. Together they produce wines with a distinctive style, drawing primarily on large oak barrels and barriques for aging, resulting in drinkable yet characterful range. The Barbaresco Valeirano '21 has a distinctive personality, with raspberry and wild strawberry aromas enhanced by tobacco, spices, and refreshing minty tones. On the palate, the wine is refined and pulpy, with measured tannins and a broad, minty finish. The Barbaresco Rombone Cichin Ris. '19 is also delicious, a richer, more complex wine that plays the intensity card with success. The pleasantly flavorful Dolcetto d'Alba Autinot '23 opts for more flowery aromas.

★★Fiorenzo Nada

via Ausario, 12c
12050 Treiso [CN]
(+39 0173638254
www.nada.it

CELLAR SALES
PRE-BOOKED VISITS
ANNUAL PRODUCTION 40,000 bottles
HECTARES UNDER VINE 9.00
VITICULTURE METHOD Certified Organic
SUSTAINABLE WINERY

In 1982, an estate based in Treiso began bottling its own wines, moving away from selling grapes and bulk wine to third parties. Founded by Fiorenzo and later revitalized by his son Bruno, the winery is now run by Bruno's son Danilo. He has reinterpreted his father's vision with a more contemporary approach, starting with an agronomic overhaul of their prized vineyards in Treiso—Rombone and Manzola—and Montaribaldi in Barbaresco. A fragrant aromatic profile of raspberry, licorice, and spices characterizes the Barbaresco Rombone '20, which offers a rich palate with rhythm and contrast, culminating in a broad, persistent, and focused finish. The Langhe Nebbiolo '22 proves pleasantly fragrant, with berry and violet aromas accented by mint. A juicy, fresh palate with good depth follows. The Barbaresco Monzola '20 is also well-crafted. Another of this historic winery's standouts is the Langhe Seifile '20, featured among our Rare Wines.

● Barbaresco Rombone Cichin Ris. '19	♟♟ 7
● Barbaresco Valeirano '21	♟♟ 6
● Barbaresco Rombone Elisa '20	♟♟ 6
● Barbera d'Alba Sup. Salgae '21	♟♟ 3
● Dolcetto d'Alba Autinot '23	♟♟ 3
● Langhe Nebbiolo Serena '23	♟ 3
● Barbaresco Rombone Elisa '16	♟♟♟ 5
● Barbaresco Cichin Ris. '15	♟♟ 6
● Barbaresco Rombone Chichin Ris. '17	♟♟ 7
● Barbaresco Rombone Chichin Ris. '16	♟♟ 7
● Barbaresco Rombone Elisa '19	♟♟ 5
● Barbaresco Rombone Elisa '15	♟♟ 5
● Barbaresco Valeirano '20	♟♟ 6
● Barbaresco Valeirano '19	♟♟ 6
● Barbaresco Valeirano '17	♟♟ 5
● Barbaresco Valeirano '15	♟♟ 5

● Barbaresco Rombone '20	♟♟ 8
● Barbaresco Manzola '20	♟♟ 8
● Langhe Nebbiolo '22	♟♟ 5
● Barbaresco Manzola '19	♟♟♟ 7
● Barbaresco Manzola '18	♟♟♟ 7
● Barbaresco Manzola '08	♟♟♟ 6
● Barbaresco Manzola '06	♟♟♟ 6
● Barbaresco Montaribaldi '15	♟♟♟ 7
● Barbaresco Montaribaldi '14	♟♟♟ 7
● Barbaresco Montaribaldi '13	♟♟♟ 7
● Barbaresco Rombone '16	♟♟♟ 8
● Barbaresco Rombone '12	♟♟♟ 7
● Barbaresco Rombone '10	♟♟♟ 7
● Barbaresco Rombone '09	♟♟♟ 7
● Barbaresco Rombone '07	♟♟♟ 7
● Barbaresco Rombone '06	♟♟♟ 7

Negretti

fraz. Santa Maria, 53
12064 La Morra [CN]
☎ +39 3923321177
⊕ www.negrettivini.com

CELLAR SALES
PRE-BOOKED VISITS
ANNUAL PRODUCTION 60,000 bottles
HECTARES UNDER VINE 13.00

In 2002, brothers Ezio and Massimo founded the winery that bears their surname in the Santa Maria hamlet of La Morra. Both winemakers, the Negretti brothers produce Barolo from three vineyard plots—one in Roddi's Bricco Ambrogio and two others, Rive and Bettolotti, in La Morra. The winery also works with barbera and chardonnay. Their range tends towards a modern production style, with maturation carried out predominantly in tonneaux and barriques. The Barolo Rive '20 gracefully reveals a refined and airy bouquet, ranging from floral nuances to small red fruits, with spices and balsamic tones completing the circle. In the mouth, the palate is light and linear, enlivened by well-measured tannins, all topped off by a persistent and dynamic finish. Darker in its aromatic tones, the Barolo Bricco Ambrogio '20 is just as well-focused in its development of flavor. The Langhe Chardonnay Dinoi '22 proves sapid, fragrant and aromatic.

★Angelo Negro

fraz. Sant'Anna, 1
12040 Monteu Roero [CN]
☎ +39 017390252
⊕ www.angelonegro.it

CELLAR SALES
PRE-BOOKED VISITS
ANNUAL PRODUCTION 430,000 bottles
HECTARES UNDER VINE 65.00
SUSTAINABLE WINERY

In recent years, the Negro family's winery has expanded production to the historic appellations of the Langhe, from Barbaresco, with the Basarin vineyard in Neive, to Barolo, with the Baudana vineyard in Serralunga d'Alba, while maintaining its core vineyards and production base in Roero. Traditional grape varieties are cultivated, making for a range characterized by classic structure and notable typicity and sense of place. Standing out among a high-level lineup is the Roero Ciabot San Giorgio Riserva '21. Forest floor aromas and small red fruits emerge alongside balsamic hints. The palate is juicy, rich in fruit, with silky tannins and a balanced, energetic finish. The fresh and sapid Roero Sudisfà Riserva '21 opts for tones of black fruits, with a pleasant drinkability. The Roero Arneis Sette Anni '17 reveals aromas of almonds, lemon zest, and dried herbs, followed by a charming palate with nice structure, length, and complexity.

● Barolo Rive '20	♟♟♟ 8
● Barolo Bricco Ambrogio '20	♟♟ 8
○ Langhe Chardonnay Dinoi '22	♟♟ 8
● Barbera d'Alba Sup. '22	♟♟ 4
● Barolo '20	♟♟ 7
● Barolo Mirau '20	♟♟ 7
● Barolo Bricco Ambrogio '18	♟♟♟ 8
● Barolo Bricco Ambrogio '14	♟♟♟ 6
● Barolo Bricco Ambrogio Indio Ris. '17	♟♟♟ 8
● Barolo Rive '17	♟♟♟ 7
● Barolo Rive '16	♟♟♟ 7
● Barolo Rive '15	♟♟♟ 6
● Barolo Bricco Ambrogio '19	♟♟ 8
● Barolo Mirau '18	♟♟ 7
○ Langhe Chardonnay Indio '21	♟♟ 8

○ Roero Ciabot San Giorgio Ris. '21	♟♟♟ 5
○ Roero Arneis Sette Anni '17	♟♟ 7
● Roero Sudisfà Ris. '21	♟♟ 6
● Barbaresco Basarin '21	♟♟ 6
● Barolo Baudana '20	♟♟ 8
● Barolo del Comune di Serralunga d'Alba '20	♟♟ 7
○ Roero Arneis Perdaudin Ris. '22	♟♟ 4
○ Roero Arneis Serra Lupini '23	♟♟ 3
● Roero Prachiosso '22	♟♟ 4
● Barbaresco Basarin '19	♟♟♟ 6
● Roero Sudisfà Ris. '20	♟♟♟ 6
● Roero Sudisfà Ris. '19	♟♟♟ 6
● Roero Sudisfà Ris. '18	♟♟♟ 6
● Roero Sudisfà Ris. '17	♟♟♟ 6
● Roero Sudisfà Ris. '16	♟♟♟ 6
● Roero Sudisfà Ris. '13	♟♟♟ 6

Lorenzo Negro

fraz. Sant'Anna, 55
12040 Monteu Roero [CN]
+39 3392278337
www.lorenzonegro.com

CELLAR SALES
PRE-BOOKED VISITS
ANNUAL PRODUCTION 35,000 bottles
HECTARES UNDER VINE 8.00
SUSTAINABLE WINERY

Lorenzo Negro avails himself of a single, contiguous tract of vineyards around the cellar on Serra Lupini hill, an estate characterized by Roero's classic sandy soils interlaced with loam and clay. Arneis, barbera, nebbiolo, and small quantities of albarossa are cultivated, making for a modern range in which aromatic clarity and sense of place are key aims. This year, their Roero Arneis wines particularly impressed us. The 2023 version showcases notes of aromatic herbs and white currants on the nose, with a fruit-rich, citrusy, sapid, and juicy palate. The long and pleasant Riserva Sant'Anna '22 displays lovely complexity, with tones of sweet citrus, yellow-fleshed fruits, and Mediterranean scrub. Nice body and acidity on the palate. The rest of the range is also well-crafted. Highlights include the nicely-textured, delicate Roero Prachiosso '21, where whiffs of aromatic herbs combine with cherry, and rhubarb, and the vibrant, close-knit Roero S. Francesco Riserva '20.

○ Roero Arneis '23	🍷🍷 2*
○ Roero Arneis S. Anna Ris. '22	🍷🍷 3*
○ Roero Arneis M. Cl. Pas Dosé Riserva 10 Anni '13	🍷🍷 5
● Roero Prachiosso '21	🍷🍷 3
● Roero S. Francesco Ris. '20	🍷🍷 4
● Barbera d'Alba '21	🍷 2
● Barbera d'Alba Sup. La Nanda '21	🍷 4
● Langhe Nebbiolo '21	🍷 2
● Langhe Rosso Arbesca '20	🍷 4
● Barbera d'Alba '20	🍷🍷 3*
○ Roero Arneis Extra Brut M. Cl. '16	🍷🍷 5
○ Roero Arneis S. Anna Ris. '21	🍷🍷 3
○ Roero Arneis S. Anna Ris. '20	🍷🍷 3*
● Roero Prachiosso '20	🍷🍷 3
● Roero S. Francesco Ris. '19	🍷🍷 4
● Roero S. Francesco Ris. '18	🍷🍷 4

Nervi Conterno

c.so Vercelli, 117
13045 Gattinara [VC]
+39 0163833228
www.nervicantine.it

CELLAR SALES
PRE-BOOKED VISITS
ANNUAL PRODUCTION 120,000 bottles
HECTARES UNDER VINE 27.00

Founded in 1905 by Luigi Nervi, the winery now spans 27 hectares in Valsesia, at the foot of Monte Rosa, where the volcanic soils are rich in quartz and porphyry. The vines, over 30 years old, grow at elevations between 290 and 425 meters. In 2018, renowned Barolo producer Roberto Conterno acquired the estate. His influence has added new depth and elegance to the wines, while staying true to the traditional character of Gattinara and Alto Piemonte nebbiolo. The Vigna Molsino '20 is an austere pour. Dark fruits and tobacco meet the nose. As it opens, clear notes of blackberries and cinchona emerge, making for a powerful yet elegant aromatic suite. The palate is full-bodied, structured, and rich, with a depth that time will only enhance. The Gattinara Vigna Valferana '20, with its pomegranate and raspberry notes, followed by a touch of tobacco, is more ready to uncork. The palate strikes a perfect balance between fruit and acidity, with a long, fresh finish.

● Gattinara V. Molsino '20	🍷🍷 8
● Gattinara V. Valferana '20	🍷🍷 8
● Gattinara '21	🍷🍷 8
⊙ Jefferson Dosaggio Zero Rosé M. Cl. '19	🍷🍷 8
● Gattinara Podere dei Ginepri '01	🍷🍷🍷 5
● Gattinara Vign. Molsino '00	🍷🍷🍷 5
● Gattinara '20	🍷🍷 8
● Gattinara '19	🍷🍷 5
● Gattinara '18	🍷🍷 5
● Gattinara '17	🍷🍷 5
● Gattinara V. Molsino '19	🍷🍷 8
● Gattinara V. Molsino '18	🍷🍷 8
● Gattinara V. Molsino '16	🍷🍷 8
● Gattinara V. Valferana '19	🍷🍷 8
● Gattinara V. Valferana '18	🍷🍷 6
● Gattinara V. Valferana '16	🍷🍷 6

Silvano Nizza

fraz. Balla Lora 29a
12040 Santo Stefano Roero [CN]
☎ +39 017390516
✉ www.nizzasilvano.it

CELLAR SALES
PRE-BOOKED VISITS
ANNUAL PRODUCTION 65,000 bottles
HECTARES UNDER VINE 8.00

The Nizza family's winery is located at Ca'
Boscarone, one of the best growing areas in
Santo Stefano Roero. Arneis, barbera, brachetto,
and nebbiolo are the grape varieties cultivated in
the vineyards around the manor and in the
municipalities of Canale and Montà. The wines
offered are characterized by a modern approach,
crafted so as to express the characteristics of
the grapes and their origins as best possible. The
Roero Ca' Boscarone Riserva '20 maintains its
position at the top of the winery's range. On the
nose, it highlights aromas of wild black fruits and
anise, with a fresh palate and nice fruit—a juicy
and sapid drink. The Nebbiolo d'Alba Bric del
Gross '22, with its tones of rain-soaked earth,
rhubarb, and plum, proves pleasant and
well-structured. The Barbera d'Alba Superiore
Crua '22 sees aromas of blood orange and
underbrush followed by a juicy, approachable
palate. The Roero S. Stefano Roero '21, with its
lovely citrus notes, needs time, as oak is still
somewhat prominent.

Noah

via Libertà, 59
13862 Brusnengo [BI]
☎ +39 3201510906
info@noah.wine

CELLAR SALES
PRE-BOOKED VISITS
ANNUAL PRODUCTION 15,000 bottles
HECTARES UNDER VINE 5.00
SUSTAINABLE WINERY

Established in 2010 by Andrea Mosca and his
wife Giovanna Pepe Diaz, Noah Winery is named
after their first son, Francesco Noah. The
couple's desire for a lifestyle change led them to
acquire their first vineyard in Brusnengo. Today,
they own seven hectares of vineyards at
elevations spanning 250- 300 meters, in an area
whose soils are of volcanic origin. The winery
focuses on light-handed techniques: spontaneous
fermentation and the careful use of wood, all in
pursuit of typicity, tradition, and quality. The
Salero '20 showcases character, typicity, and
vitality— vibrant notes of red fruits alternating
with blackberry jam, spices, tobacco, and mineral
accents, making for a fine, austere, and rigorous
palate with an authoritative and elegant finish.
The Noah Rosso proves harmonious and
pleasant, playing on floral hints, pomegranate, and
plum, with a harmonious and enjoyable palate.
The glyceric, delicate Della Mesola '22 also
caught our attention.

● Roero Ca' Boscarone Ris. '20	♟♟ 6
● Barbera d'Alba Sup. Crua '22	♟♟ 4
● Nebbiolo d'Alba Bric del Gross '22	♟♟ 4
● Roero del Comune di S. Stefano Roero '20	♟♟ 4
○ Roero Arneis Jemel '23	♟ 4
● Barbera d'Alba Sup. Crua '20	♟♟ 4
● Nebbiolo d'Alba '20	♟♟ 4
● Nebbiolo d'Alba Bric del Gross '21	♟♟ 4
○ Roero Arneis '21	♟♟ 3
○ Roero Arneis Jemel '22	♟♟ 4
● Roero Ca' Boscarone Ris. '19	♟♟ 6
● Roero Ca' Boscarone Ris. '18	♟♟ 6
● Roero Ca' Boscarone Ris. '17	♟♟ 6
● Roero del Comune di S. Stefano '19	♟♟ 4
● Roero del Comune di S. Stefano Roero '20	♟♟ 4

● Bramaterra Salero '20	♟♟ 5
● Coste della Sesia Rosso '23	♟♟ 4
● Coste della Sesia Rosso Dellamesola '22	♟ 3
● Bramaterra '12	♟♟♟ 5
● Bramaterra '19	♟♟ 5
● Bramaterra '17	♟♟ 5
● Bramaterra Rocce di Lucce '19	♟♟ 5
● Bramaterra Rocce di Luce '18	♟♟ 6
● Bramaterra Salero '18	♟♟ 5
● Coste della Sesia Rosso '21	♟♟ 4
● Coste della Sesia Rosso Dellamesola '20	♟♟ 3
● Coste della Sesia Rosso Dellamesola '19	♟♟ 3
● Lessona '19	♟♟ 6
● Lessona '18	♟♟ 6

★Poderi e Cantine Oddero

fraz. Santa Maria
via Tetti, 28
12064 La Morra [CN]
(☎ +39 017350618
@ www.oddero.it

CELLAR SALES
PRE-BOOKED VISITS
ANNUAL PRODUCTION 150,000 bottles
HECTARES UNDER VINE 35.00
VITICULTURE METHOD Certified Organic

Founded in the late 19th century, in La Morra, this historic producer got its start when Giacomo Oddero bottled the first wines under the family name. The winery's modern history was forged by Giacomo's grandson (another Giacomo), whose daughter Mariacristina and grandchildren Isabella and Pietro manage the business today. Here modern production spaces combine with an approach rooted in tradition and the territory for a range in which premium crus like Villero, Rocche di Castiglione, Monvigliero, and Bussia Vigna Mondoca stand out. The Barolo Brunate '20 presents an intriguing layering of aromas, combining clear raspberry notes with aromatic herbs, tobacco, and refreshing balsamic hints. The palate is vibrant and fleshy, with a progressive tannic texture and a long, fruity finish. The well-crafted Barolo Rocche di Castiglione '20 hints at brandied fruit and forest floor on the nose, with a refined, multifaceted palate that balances the sweetness of the fruit with spirited tannins. The Barbaresco Gallina '21 is also enjoyable.

● Barolo Brunate '20	♈♈ 8
● Barolo Rocche di Castiglione '20	♈♈ 8
● Barbaresco Gallina '21	♈♈ 7
● Barolo '20	♈ 6
● Barolo Vignarionda Ris. '18	♈ 8
● Barolo Villero '20	♈ 8
● Barbaresco Gallina '04	♈♈♈ 6
● Barolo Bussia V. Mondoca Ris. '12	♈♈♈ 8
● Barolo Bussia V. Mondoca Ris. '10	♈♈♈ 8
● Barolo Bussia V. Mondoca Ris. '08	♈♈♈ 8
● Barolo Mondoca di Bussia Soprana '04	♈♈♈ 7
● Barolo Mondoca di Bussia Soprana '97	♈♈♈ 7
● Barolo Rocche di Castiglione '09	♈♈♈ 7
● Barolo V. Rionda '01	♈♈♈ 8
● Barolo V. Rionda '00	♈♈♈ 8
● Barolo V. Rionda '98	♈♈♈ 8

Figli Luigi Oddero Tenuta Parà

fraz. Santa Maria
Tenuta Parà, 95
12604 La Morra [CN]
(☎ +39 0173500386
@ www.figliluigioddero.it

CELLAR SALES
PRE-BOOKED VISITS
ANNUAL PRODUCTION 90,000 bottles
HECTARES UNDER VINE 32.00
SUSTAINABLE WINERY

The founder of this La Morra-based winery appears in the pages of "Vino al Vino," where Mario Soldati portrays him as a man capable of blending the energy of the past with a forward-looking vision. This philosophy has remained intact since his passing in 2010, passed down to his wife Lena and their children Maria and Giovanni, who now lead the estate. Their vineyards are located in La Morra, Castiglione Falletto, and Serralunga, within the Rive, Santa Maria, Scarrone, and Vigna Rionda crus, as well as in Treiso, in the Rombone cru. The Barolo Vigna Specola '20, with its aromas of small red fruits, spices, and aromatic herbs, along with spicy and minty accents, is a wine of great breadth. In the mouth, the palate possesses flesh and drive, with a rhythmic progression rich in contrast, culminating in an airy, balsamic finish. Equally excellent, the Barolo Vignarionda '16 offers a broad palate, distinguished by progressively unfolding tannins and a dynamic finish with fragrant length—it's a red of extraordinary power and harmony. The Barolo Vigne Rocca Rivera '20 is just as well-crafted.

● Barolo Vignarionda '16	♈♈♈ 8
● Barolo V. Rocche Rivera '20	♈♈ 8
● Barolo V. Specola '20	♈♈ 8
● Barolo '20	♈♈ 7
● Barbaresco Rombone '21	♈ 6
● Barolo Vigna Rionda '15	♈♈♈ 8
● Barolo Vigna Rionda '13	♈♈♈ 8
● Barolo Vigna Rionda '10	♈♈♈ 8
● Barolo Vignarionda '18	♈♈♈ 8
● Barbaresco Rombone '20	♈♈ 6
● Barbaresco Rombone '19	♈♈ 7
● Barbaresco Rombone '17	♈♈ 6
● Barolo '17	♈♈ 6
● Barolo Rocche Rivera '18	♈♈ 8
● Barolo Rocche Rivera '16	♈♈ 8
● Barolo Specola '19	♈♈ 8

★Tenuta Olim Bauda

via Prata, 50
14045 Incisa Scapaccino [AT]
☎ +39 0141702171
✉ www.tenutaolimbauda.it

CELLAR SALES
PRE-BOOKED VISITS
ANNUAL PRODUCTION 200,000 bottles
HECTARES UNDER VINE 30.00
VITICULTURE METHOD Certified Organic
SUSTAINABLE WINERY

With over 60 years of history, Olim Bauda is one of Monferrato's most prominent wineries. Led by the Bertolino family, with siblings Dino, Diana, and Giovanni at the helm, the producer has made barbera its flagship, thanks in part to a territory that's particularly well suited to its cultivation. Indeed, the Nizza Monferrato-based estate enjoys soils of marine origins, marly clay but rich in sand, limestone, and gypsum, a mix that confers great elegance to the grapes. The Barbera d'Asti Superiore Le Rocchette '21 showcases blackberry, cinchona, and plum notes on the nose, with a juicy palate that drives forward to a long, energetic finish. The Nizza Riserva '21 sees balsamic, blood orange, and Mediterranean scrub aromas followed by a well-structured palate, finishing on a long, sapid note. The rest of the range is also well-crafted, including the Piemonte Moscato Passito SanGiovanni '07, with its dried fig notes and a sweetness well-supported by acidity, the fruity and enjoyable Barbera d'Asti La Villa '23, and the fresh, juicy Grignolino d'Asti Isolavilla '23.

● Barbera d'Asti Sup. Le Rocchette '21	♟♟ 5
● Nizza Ris. '21	♟♟ 6
● Barbera d'Asti La Villa '23	♟♟ 3
● Grignolino d'Asti Isolavilla '23	♟♟ 3
○ Piemonte Moscato Passito San Giovanni '07	♟♟ 7
○ Brut Nature Quarantadue Mesi M. Cl. '19	♟ 6
○ Moscato d'Asti Centive '23	♟ 3
● Nebbiolo d'Alba '20	♟ 4
● Barbera d'Asti La Villa '21	♟♟♟ 3*
● Barbera d'Asti Sup. Nizza '13	♟♟♟ 5
● Barbera d'Asti Sup. Nizza '12	♟♟♟ 5
● Barbera d'Asti Sup. Nizza '11	♟♟♟ 5
● Nizza '15	♟♟♟ 5
● Nizza Ris. '17	♟♟♟ 5
● Nizza Ris. '16	♟♟♟ 5

★Orsolani

via Michele Chiesa, 12
10090 San Giorgio Canavese [TO]
☎ +39 012432386
✉ www.orsolani.it

CELLAR SALES
PRE-BOOKED VISITS
ANNUAL PRODUCTION 140,000 bottles
HECTARES UNDER VINE 19.00

This century-old winery in Canavese, run by the Orsolani family, has long championed the erbaluce grape. Almost all the vineyards are devoted to the variety, making for a range that includes dry whites, passitos and Metodo Classico sparkling wines. Located mainly on the hills between Mazzè and Caluso, the vineyards are cultivated with a low environmental impact approach. The result is consistently high-quality wines characterized by a focused stylistic profile. The sparkling Caluso Cuvée Tradizione 1968 '18 boasts a fine and persistent effervescence, accompanied by delicate aromas with almond nuances. In the mouth, the palate is refined, beautifully balancing sweetness and fresh acidity. The Brut, with its citrusy aromatic hints, is also good, offering a fresh and dynamic palate. The Erbaluce La Rustia '23 shows delicate floral aromas, leading to a flavorful, well-paced progression of flavor.

○ Caluso Extra Brut Cuvée Tradizione 1968 '18	♟♟ 5
○ Caluso Spumante Brut	♟♟ 5
○ Erbaluce di Caluso La Rustia '23	♟♟ 4
○ Caluso Passito Sulé '19	♟♟ 5
○ Caluso Spumante Extra Brut Cuvée Tradizione '19	♟♟ 5
○ Caluso Vintage '19	♟♟ 5
○ Erbaluce di Caluso La Rustia '20	♟♟♟ 3*
○ Erbaluce di Caluso La Rustia '19	♟♟♟ 3*
○ Erbaluce di Caluso La Rustia '15	♟♟♟ 3*
○ Erbaluce di Caluso La Rustia '13	♟♟♟ 3*
○ Erbaluce di Caluso La Rustia '12	♟♟♟ 3*
○ Erbaluce di Caluso La Rustia '11	♟♟♟ 3*
○ Erbaluce di Caluso La Rustia '10	♟♟♟ 3*
○ Erbaluce di Caluso La Rustia '09	♟♟♟ 3*
○ Erbaluce di Caluso La Rustia '22	♟♟ 4

Pace

fraz. Madonna di Loreto
loc. Cascina Pace, 52
12043 Canale [CN]
📞 +39 3384323245
🌐 www.pacevini.it

CELLAR SALES
PRE-BOOKED VISITS
ACCOMMODATION
ANNUAL PRODUCTION 90,000 bottles
HECTARES UNDER VINE 28.00

For four generations, the Negro family has cultivated vineyards on a hill overlooking Canale, in a district called Pace, one of the territory's most wooded and cool areas, on sandy, medium-textured soils. Roero's classic varieties—arneis, barbera, favorita, and nebbiolo—are grown, while winemaking draws on a traditional approach that's attentive to expressing characteristics of the grapes and their origins as best possible. The Roero '20 opens on tones of violet with nuances of truffle and aromatic herbs. Pleasant and fruity, it has a juicy, fresh finish. Two well-crafted Roero Arneis stand out. The 2023, which plays on aromas of white fruit and navel orange, is your classic, approachable, standard-label wine. The Riserva Mompellini '22 combines aromas of peach and white pepper on the nose with a palate of vibrant energy and freshness. Despite the limited number of bottles produced, the Roero Arneis Giuan da Pas '15 is extraordinary. You can read about it in the Rare Wines section.

● Roero '20	♟♟ 4
○ Roero Arneis '23	♟♟ 2*
○ Roero Arneis Mompellini Ris. '22	♟♟ 4
● Barbera d'Alba '22	♟ 2
● Langhe Nebbiolo '22	♟ 3
● Barbera d'Alba '20	♟♟ 2*
● Barbera d'Alba Sup. '19	♟♟ 5
● Roero '19	♟♟ 3
○ Roero Arneis '22	♟♟ 2*
○ Roero Arneis '21	♟♟ 2*
○ Roero Arneis Giuan da Pas '13	♟♟ 7
○ Roero Arneis Mompellini Ris. '21	♟♟ 4
○ Roero Arneis Mompellini Ris. '20	♟♟ 5
● Roero Ris. '18	♟♟ 5
● Roero Ris. '16	♟♟ 5
● Roero Ris. '15	♟♟ 5

Paitin

fraz. Bricco di Neive
via Serraboella, 20
12052 Neive [CN]
📞 +39 017367343
🌐 www.paitin.it

PIEDMONT

CELLAR SALES
PRE-BOOKED VISITS
ACCOMMODATION
ANNUAL PRODUCTION 90,000 bottles
HECTARES UNDER VINE 18.00
VITICULTURE METHOD Certified Organic
SUSTAINABLE WINERY

In 1796, the "sorì" (a southfacing hillslope) on Bricco di Neive (now Serraboella) took the name Sorì 'd Paitin, referring to the the Elia family's vineyards. After Giuseppe's death in 1938, his son Alessandro chose to not continue his father's path. Giovanni, husband of Elisa Pasquero-Elia, attempted to carry on, but died prematurely. It was then up to their son Secondo to continue the family's winemaking journey. Today, this tradition is upheld by Secondo's sons and grandson—Giovanni, Silvano, and Luca—who continue the historic vineyard's legacy. The refined and focused Barbaresco Faset '21 reveals vibrant aromas of small red fruits, aromatic herbs, balsamic notes, and spices. In the mouth, the palate is fleshy, crisp and well-balanced, with precise tannins and a long, persistent finish. The nose of the Barbaresco Albesani '21 offers clear whiffs of raspberry and tobacco, leading to a palate where tannins unfold gradually towards an elegant finish. The Barbaresco Serraboella Sorì Paitin Vecchie Vigne '19 also put in an impressive showing.

● Barbaresco Albesani '21	♟♟ 7
● Barbaresco Faset '21	♟♟ 7
● Barbaresco Sorì Paitin V.V. Ris. '19	♟♟ 8
● Barbaresco Sorì Paitin '07	♟♟♟ 5
● Barbaresco Sorì Paitin '04	♟♟♟ 5
● Barbaresco Sorì Paitin '97	♟♟♟ 5
● Barbaresco Sorì Paitin '95	♟♟♟ 7
● Barbaresco Sorì Paitin V.V. '04	♟♟♟ 7
● Barbaresco Sorì Paitin V.V. '01	♟♟♟ 7
● Barbaresco Sorì Paitin V.V. '99	♟♟♟ 8
● Barbaresco Sorì Paitin V.V. Ris. '16	♟♟♟ 8
● Langhe Paitin '97	♟♟♟ 5
● Barbaresco Basarin '20	♟♟ 6
● Barbaresco Basarin '19	♟♟ 7
● Barbaresco Serraboella '20	♟♟ 6

Palladino

p.zza Cappellano, 9
12050 Serralunga d'Alba [CN]
(☎) +39 0173613108
⊕ www.palladinovini.com

CELLAR SALES
ACCOMMODATION
ANNUAL PRODUCTION 180,000 bottles
HECTARES UNDER VINE 11.00
SUSTAINABLE WINERY

Founded in 1974, the Palladino family's winery is located in Serralunga d'Alba. Here, Piero Palladino, a textile entrepreneur with a passion for wine, entrusted the viticultural business to his cousin Maurilio. Today, the winery continues its successful journey under the guidance of the next generation. While the vineyards span several of Langhe's appellations, the standout plots are in Barolo, specifically within the San Bernardo, Parafada, and Ornato crus. The Barolo Ornato '20 exudes red berries and spicy undertones against a backdrop of tobacco. In the mouth, its well-structured tannins and vibrant acidity come together for a deep, rhythmic, and sapid finish. Aromas of brandied cherries and balsamic accents characterize the Barbera d'Alba Bricco delle Olive '21, which on the palate reveals density, flavor, and persistence.

Parusso

loc. Bussia, 55
12065 Monforte d'Alba [CN]
(☎) +39 017378257
⊕ www.parusso.com

CELLAR SALES
ANNUAL PRODUCTION 150,000 bottles
HECTARES UNDER VINE 26.00
SUSTAINABLE WINERY

The Parusso brothers, who draw on vineyards in Monforte d'Alba and Castiglione Falletto, belong to a family of winemakers spanning four generations. In 1971, Armando Parusso, father of Marco and Tiziana, introduced the family's first Barolo. Since then, the producer has expanded, offering a wide range based on dolcetto, barbera, and nebbiolo grapes, including Barolos sourced from the Bussia, Mosconi, and Mariondino crus. Echoes of underbrush, ripe red fruits, smoky and toasted nuances characterize the Bussia Vigna Le Rocche '15. In the mouth, the palate is fleshy and dense, thanks to a multifaceted tannic structure that melds beautifully with its fruity pulp, leading to a long, persistent finish. The Mariondino '20 reveals aromas influenced by aging in oak, with notes of roasted coffee and spices. On the palate, it proves complex, with tannins taking center stage. The Rovella, an atypical but fascinating sauvignon, opts for structure and more complex aromas over the typical herbal profile and sharp acidity.

● Barolo Ornato '20	♟♟ 8
● Barbera d'Alba Sup. Bricco delle Olive '21	♟♟ 5
● Barolo del Comune di Serralunga d'Alba '20	♟ 7
● Barolo Parafada '20	♟ 8
● Nebbiolo d'Alba '22	♟ 5
● Barolo San Bernardo Ris. '13	♟♟♟ 8
● Barolo San Bernardo Ris. '10	♟♟♟ 6
● Barolo Ornato '17	♟♟ 7
● Barolo Ornato '16	♟♟ 6
● Barolo Ornato '15	♟♟ 6
● Barolo Parafada '19	♟♟ 7
● Barolo Parafada '18	♟♟ 7
● Barolo Parafada '17	♟♟ 7
● Barolo Parafada '16	♟♟ 6
● Barolo Parafada '15	♟♟ 6
● Barolo San Bernardo Ris. '16	♟♟ 8

● Barolo Bussia V. Rocche Ris. '15	♟♟ 8
○ Langhe Sauvignon Rovella 30 Vendemmie '21	♟♟ 7
● Barolo Mariondino '20	♟♟ 8
● Barolo Bussia '20	♟ 8
● Barolo Mosconi '20	♟ 8
● Barbera d'Alba Sup. '00	♟♟♟ 5
● Barolo Bussia V. Munie '99	♟♟♟ 8
● Barolo Bussia V. Munie '97	♟♟♟ 8
● Barolo Bussia V. Munie '96	♟♟♟ 8
● Barolo V.V. in Mariondino Ris. '99	♟♟♟ 8
● Langhe Rosso Bricco Rovella '96	♟♟♟ 8
● Barolo Bussia Riserva Oro '12	♟♟ 8
● Barolo Mariondino '19	♟♟ 8
● Barolo Perarmando '17	♟♟ 7
○ Langhe Bianco 30 Vendemmie '20	♟♟ 7

Agostino Pavia e Figli

loc. Molizzo, 3
14041 Agliano Terme [AT]
℡ +39 0141954125
☙ www.agostinopavia.it

CELLAR SALES
PRE-BOOKED VISITS
ACCOMMODATION
ANNUAL PRODUCTION 75,000 bottles
HECTARES UNDER VINE 9.00

Agostino Pavia e Figli is one of Monferrato's historic estates. Giuseppe and Mauro Pavia's vineyards, all situated in the town of Agliano Terme (except for a small plot in Montegrosso), are dedicated primarily to barbera, though other varieties like grignolino, dolcetto, syrah, and albarossa are also grown. The wines are traditionally styled and are technically well-crafted. On the nose, the Barbera d'Asti Superiore Moliss '21 reveals ginger, nutmeg, pomegranate, and cinchona. The palate is both grippy and harmonious, nicely balancing sweetness of fruit and the austerity of the whole, finishing long. Other highlights include the Grignolino d'Asti '23, bursting with red forest fruit, juicy and vibrant; the Monferrato Nebbiolo Gustën '21, intense and complex, with hints of tobacco, licorice, and cinchona, structured with slightly austere but long tannins; and the Barbera d'Asti Blina '21, which offers aromas of verbena and red cherry. It's a fresh, juicy wine, rich in fruit.

★Pecchenino

b.ta Valdiberti, 59
12063 Dogliani [CN]
℡ +39 017370686
☙ www.pecchenino.com

CELLAR SALES
PRE-BOOKED VISITS
ACCOMMODATION
ANNUAL PRODUCTION 150,000 bottles
HECTARES UNDER VINE 31.00
SUSTAINABLE WINERY

Orlando Pecchenino stepped onto the Langhe wine scene in the mid-1980s, a time when rich, concentrated wines were in vogue, produced using low vineyard yields and generous oak in the cellar. Today, the winery has refined its style, smoothing out some of the excesses in both its Dolcetto di Dogliani and Barolos, focusing on the expression of its vineyards and maturing the wines in barrels of varying sizes. Pecchenino submitted a well-crafted roster of wines for tasting. The Barolo San Giuseppe unveils red berry aromas with a lovely backdrop of violet and licorice. The palate is very harmonious, with medium structure and perfectly integrated tannins—a fine wine. The Dogliani Sirì d'Jermu is also excellent: mature, with accents of cocoa and spices; fleshy, fresh, and persistent. The Bussia proves vibrant, with ethereal and tobacco notes, leading to a persistent and powerful palate.

● Barbera d'Asti Sup. Moliss '21	♟♟ 3*
● Barbera d'Asti Blina '21	♟♟ 5
● Grignolino d'Asti '23	♟♟ 2*
● M.to Nebbiolo Gustën '21	♟♟ 3
● Barbera d'Asti Casareggio '23	♟ 2
● Barbera d'Asti Sup. La Marescialla '21	♟ 4
● Barbera d'Asti Blina '20	♟♟ 5
● Barbera d'Asti Blina '19	♟♟ 5
● Barbera d'Asti Blina '18	♟♟ 2*
● Barbera d'Asti Casareggio '22	♟♟ 2*
● Barbera d'Asti Casareggio '20	♟♟ 2*
● Barbera d'Asti Sup. La Marescialla '20	♟♟ 4
● Barbera d'Asti Sup. La Marescialla '17	♟♟ 4
● Barbera d'Asti Sup. Moliss '20	♟♟ 3
● Barbera d'Asti Sup. Moliss '19	♟♟ 3
● Grignolino d'Asti '21	♟♟ 2*

● Barolo San Giuseppe '20	♟♟ 7
● Dogliani Sup. Sirì d'Jermu '22	♟♟ 4
● Barolo Bussia '20	♟♟ 8
● Barolo Le Coste di Monforte '20	♟♟ 8
● Langhe Nebbiolo Bricco Ravera '20	♟ 3
● Barolo Le Coste '05	♟♟♟ 8
● Dogliani Bricco Botti '07	♟♟♟ 4
● Dogliani Sirì d'Jermu '09	♟♟♟ 3*
● Dogliani Sirì d'Jermu '06	♟♟♟ 4
● Dogliani Sup. Bricco Botti '10	♟♟♟ 4*
● Dolcetto di Dogliani S. Luigi '00	♟♟♟ 4*
● Dolcetto di Dogliani Sirì d'Jermu '03	♟♟♟ 3
● Dolcetto di Dogliani Sirì d'Jermu '01	♟♟♟ 3*
● Dolcetto di Dogliani Sirì d'Jermu '99	♟♟♟ 3*
● Dolcetto di Dogliani Sup. Bricco Botti '04	♟♟♟ 4

Pedemontis

s.da Valfenera, 6
12040 Priocca [CN]
📞 +39 3284188889
🌐 www.pedemontis.it

PRE-BOOKED VISITS
ANNUAL PRODUCTION 25,000 bottles
HECTARES UNDER VINE 13.00
SUSTAINABLE WINERY

Pedemontis is a multifaceted agricultural operation, ranging from forestry to truffle and hazelnut production to viticulture. The estate vineyards are located on sandy soils in the municipalities of Magliano Alfieri, Castellinaldo, Priocca, and Govone. Roero's classic grape varieties are cultivated, from arneis to barbera, favorita and nebbiolo, while the production style is modern, with great clarity and aromatic precision serving as key elements. Although lacking that standout star, Pedemontis presented a solid and convincing range. The Roero '21 features balsamic, floral, and red fruit notes; a juicy, fresh wine that's easy to drink. The Barbera d'Alba Superiore Betlem '22 opens on darker tones of bark, petrichor, and porcini mushrooms, delivering a full, well-structured palate. The Roero Arneis Arajs '22 plays on white fruit and almond notes, with accents of citron; in the mouth it's energetic and taut. The Nebbiolo d'Alba Djun '22 has aromas of black forest fruits and refined tannins that are still prominent but polished.

● Barbera d'Alba Superiore Betlem '22	🍷🍷 5
● Nebbiolo d'Alba Djun '22	🍷🍷 5
● Roero '21	🍷🍷 3
○ Roero Arneis Arajs '22	🍷🍷 3
● Barbera d'Alba Bajet '22	🍷 4
○ Langhe Favorita Jaiet '22	🍷 3
● Barbera d'Alba Bajet '21	🍸 4
● Barbera d'Alba Superiore Betlem '21	🍸 5
○ Roero Arneis Arajs '21	🍸 3*

Magda Pedrini

loc. Ca' da' Meo
via Pratolungo, 163
15066 Gavi [AL]
📞 +39 0143667923
🌐 www.magdapedrini.it

CELLAR SALES
PRE-BOOKED VISITS
ANNUAL PRODUCTION 90,000 bottles
HECTARES UNDER VINE 11.50
SUSTAINABLE WINERY

There was a time when Pratolongo's Tenuta Ca' da Meo was in a state of complete disrepair. But in 2006, the property was restored to its former glory by Magda Pedrini, who purchased and completely renovated the estate, reviving old vineyards and planting new ones, primarily cortese, while also building a new, modern cellar. Their Gavi wines are well crafted, showcasing nice aromatic clarity and a fine, balanced drinkability. The Gavi del Comune di Gavi Magda '23 offers up aromas of fresh hay and green apple, with chalky and flint-like nuances. In the mouth, the palate is supple and focused, finishing long and sapid. The Gavi del Comune di Gavi Ad Lunam '23 opts for more herbal and citrusy tones on the nose, while the palate showcases richness and depth, concluding with a pleasantly fragrant, persistent finish.

○ Gavi del Comune di Gavi Magda '23	🍷🍷 3*
○ Gavi del Comune di Gavi Ad Lunam '23	🍷🍷 3
○ Gavi del Comune di Gavi '22	🍸 3
○ Gavi del Comune di Gavi Ad Lunam '21	🍸 3
○ Gavi del Comune di Gavi Ad Lunam '20	🍸 3
○ Gavi del Comune di Gavi ad Lunam '19	🍸 3
○ Gavi del Comune di Gavi ad Lunam '18	🍸 3*
○ Gavi del Comune di Gavi E' '16	🍸 3*
○ Gavi del Comune di Gavi La Piacentina '17	🍸 3*
○ Gavi del Comune di Gavi Magda '21	🍸 3
○ Gavi del Comune di Gavi Magda '20	🍸 3
○ Gavi del Comune di Gavi Magda '19	🍸 3*
○ Gavi del Comune di Gavi Magda '18	🍸 3*

Pelassa

b.go Tucci, 43
12046 Montà [CN]
☎ +39 0173971312
🌐 www.pelassa.com

CELLAR SALES
ANNUAL PRODUCTION 80,000 bottles
HECTARES UNDER VINE 14.00

The Pelassa family has been a key player in the Roero winemaking scene for several years. Their vineyards are located in the northern part of Montà d'Alba, an area known for its cooler climate, and in Verduno, where the grapes for their Barolo are cultivated. The region's classic varietals are grown—arneis, barbera, and nebbiolo—making for a range that highlights both the distinctiveness of the terroir and the grapes themselves. The Roero S.......i Riserva '21 conjures up aromas of black fruits and sweet spices, while the palate is full and fruit-driven. The Roero Arneis Tucci '22 features notes of citrus and Mediterranean scrub, coming through fresh, juicy, and pleasant in the mouth. Other highlights include the black fruit- and herb-scented Barolo San Lorenzo di Verduno '20, with its substantive palate and elegant tannins, and the close-knit, long Barbera d'Alba Superiore San Pancrazio '22, which opts for aromas of black plum and balsamic nuances.

○ Roero Arneis Tucci '22	♟♟ 4
● Roero S.......i Ris. '21	♟♟ 5
● Barbera d'Alba Sup. San Pancrazio '22	♟♟ 3
● Barolo '19	♟♟ 6
● Barolo San Lorenzo di Verduno '20	♟♟ 6
● Nebbiolo d'Alba Sot '22	♟♟ 3
● Piemonte Rosso Oltre '22	♟♟ 5
○ Roero Arneis San Vito '23	♟♟ 3
● Barbera d'Alba Sup. San Pancrazio '21	♙♙ 3
● Barolo '18	♙♙ 6
● Barolo San Lorenzo di Verduno '19	♙♙ 6
● Nebbiolo d'Alba Sot '21	♙♙ 3
● Roero Antaniolo Ris. '17	♙♙ 4
○ Roero Arneis San Vito '22	♙♙ 3
○ Roero Arneis San Vito '20	♙♙ 3*
○ Roero Arneis Tucci '21	♙♙ 4
● Roero S.......i Ris. '20	♙♙ 5

★Pelissero

via Ferrere, 10
12050 Treiso [CN]
☎ +39 0173638430
🌐 www.pelissero.com

CELLAR SALES
PRE-BOOKED VISITS
ANNUAL PRODUCTION 250,000 bottles
HECTARES UNDER VINE 42.00
SUSTAINABLE WINERY

The Pelissero family is deeply rooted in Treiso. The first bottles bearing the family name were released in 1960. Since then, the winery has embarked on a compelling journey, focusing on quality and establishing itself among the ranks of the area's most notable producers. Production centers around the territory's three traditional red varietals: nebbiolo, barbera, and dolcetto. However, the portfolio also includes whites made from moscato, favorita, and riesling. The overindulgence in concentrated, oaky wines that began around the turn of the millennium (and in which Giorgio Pelissero and many Italian producers participated) has gradually faded. But two good things came out of that period: an emphasis on cleanness and structure. The Vanotu remains a superb example of the DOCG production area's potential, with its clear fruit aromas enriched by a restrained spiciness. On the palate, the wine offers plenty of substance and structure, with just a hint of austerity. Santo Stefanetto confirms its versatility with an elegant Barbaresco Tulin and a powerful, fresh Barbera Tulin.

● Barbaresco Vanotu '21	♟♟♟ 8
● Barbaresco Tulin '21	♟♟ 8
● Barbera d'Alba Tulin '22	♟♟ 5
● Barbaresco Nubiola '21	♟♟ 6
● Barbera d'Alba Piani '22	♟♟ 3
● Dolcetto d'Alba Augenta '23	♟♟ 3
● Langhe Nebbiolo '22	♟♟ 4
● Langhe Rosso Long Now '21	♟♟ 5
● Dolcetto d'Alba Munfrina '23	♟ 2
○ Langhe Bianco Le Nature '23	♟ 3
○ Moscato d'Asti '23	♟ 2
● Barbaresco Vanotu '20	♙♙♙ 8
● Barbaresco Vanotu '19	♙♙♙ 8
● Barbaresco Vanotu '08	♙♙♙ 8
● Barbaresco Vanotu '07	♙♙♙ 8
● Barbaresco Vanotu '06	♙♙♙ 8
● Barbaresco Vanotu '01	♙♙♙ 7

Pertinace

loc. Pertinace, 2/5
12050 Treiso [CN]
☏ +39 0173442238
⊕ www.pertinace.com

CELLAR SALES
PRE-BOOKED VISITS
ANNUAL PRODUCTION 700,000 bottles
HECTARES UNDER VINE 100.00

Founded in 1973 by Mario Barbero, this Treiso-based cooperative has only 20 members but produces a range of wines, including Langhe, Dolcetto d'Alba, Barbera d'Alba, Barbera d'Asti, and Moscato d'Asti. Naturally, the top tier of the portfolio is occupied by Barbaresco, drawing on the three crus of Castellizzano, Marcarini, and Nervo, all matured in large oak barrels. The wines are generally clean and well-defined, representing commendable value for the money. The Barbaresco Marcarini '21 is a skillfully made wine. A focused aromatic profile with generous fruit opens the way to a refined progression of flavor, accompanied by predominantly soft tannins, and a long finish. The Barbaresco Nervo '21 is more evolved, with aromas of dried flowers and underbrush—it finds its strength in a firm and sapid palate, where it reveals a solid structure. The Langhe Arneis '23 proves fragrant and pleasantly aromatic. The austere Barbaresco Castellizzano Riserva '19 also caught our attention

● Barbaresco Marcarini '21	▼▼ 7
● Barbaresco Nervo '21	▼▼ 6
○ Langhe Arneis '23	▼▼ 3
● Barbaresco '21	▼ 5
● Barbaresco Castellizzano Ris. '19	▼ 7
● Dolcetto d'Alba '23	▼ 3
● Langhe Nebbiolo '22	▼ 4
● Barbaresco Castellizzano '17	♈♈ 5
● Barbaresco Castellizzano '12	♈♈ 5
● Barbaresco Marcarini '18	♈♈ 5
● Barbaresco Marcarini '16	♈♈ 5
● Barbaresco Marcarini '14	♈♈ 5
● Barbaresco Marcarini '13	♈♈ 5
● Barbaresco Nervo '20	♈♈ 6
● Barbaresco Nervo '15	♈♈ 5
● Barbaresco Vign. Castellizzano '11	♈♈ 5

Pescaja

fraz. San Matteo, 59
14010 Cisterna d'Asti [AT]
☏ +39 0141979711
⊕ www.pescaja.com

CELLAR SALES
PRE-BOOKED VISITS
ANNUAL PRODUCTION 200,000 bottles
HECTARES UNDER VINE 30.00

Beppe Guido's winery relies on two privately-owned estates, straddling the Roero and Terre Alfieri appellations: one in Cisterna d'Asti, on predominantly sandy soils, and the other in Nizza Monferrato, on calcareous soils. Many grapes are cultivated, both traditional varieties, such as arneis, barbera, nebbiolo, bonarda, and international ones, like chardonnay. The result is a pleasant and modern range characterized by nice aromatic clarity. Pescaja presented a lineup of solid, reliable wines this year. The Monferrato Rosso Solis '21 opens with intense aromas of black stone fruit, while the palate is close-knit, full, and of notable length and clarity. The Piemonte Sauvignon Celestine '22 offers aromas of currant and nuances of tomato leaf, showing nice harmony and structure, with a long, fresh finish. The Terre Alfieri Nebbiolo Tuké '22 unveils notes of red berries, wood, and alcohol on the nose, followed by a dense and tannic palate. The result is an austere, full-bodied Nebbiolo with great persistence.

● Monferrato Rosso Solis '21	▼▼ 6
○ Piemonte Sauvignon Celestine '22	▼▼ 4
● Terre Alfieri Nebbiolo Tuké '22	▼▼ 8
● Nizza Solneri '21	▼ 6
● Barbera d'Asti Soliter '21	♈♈ 3
● M.to Rosso Solis '20	♈♈ 5
● Monferrato Rosso Solis '19	♈♈ 6
● Nizza Solneri '19	♈♈ 6
○ Roero Arneis Stella '22	♈♈ 3
○ Roero Arneis Stella '21	♈♈ 3
○ Terre Alfieri Arneis Solei '22	♈♈ 5
○ Terre Alfieri Arneis Solo Luna '20	♈♈ 6
● Terre Alfieri Nebbiolo Tuké '21	♈♈ 3
● Terre Alfieri Nebbiolo Tuké '20	♈♈ 3

★Le Piane

p.zza Matteotti, 2
28010 Boca [NO]
📞 +39 3483354185
🌐 www.bocapiane.com

Pico Maccario

via Cordara, 87
14046 Mombaruzzo [AT]
📞 +39 0141774522
🌐 www.picomaccario.com

PIEDMONT

CELLAR SALES
PRE-BOOKED VISITS
ANNUAL PRODUCTION 80,000 bottles
HECTARES UNDER VINE 10.00
SUSTAINABLE WINERY

CELLAR SALES
PRE-BOOKED VISITS
ANNUAL PRODUCTION 650,000 bottles
HECTARES UNDER VINE 100.00

Nestled in the Monte Fenera Natural Park, this winery has become a model for the revival of northern Piedmontese viticulture. The passion and dedication of Christofer Kunzli, who drives the estate, are at its heart. In 1998, his love for the region, shared with friend Alexandr Trolf, led to the purchase of the Campo alle Piane vineyard from Antonio Cerri. With their southern exposure and significant temperature swings, the porphyry- and gravel-rich soils offer ideal conditions for viticulture. The Boca '20 opens with fruit and tobacco notes, continuing with a fine iron-like nuance. The palate is austere, with tannins that are well-integrated, balanced by the richness and depth of a great wine. The Nebbiolo delle Colline Novaresi '23 follows in the same vein: rose petals and red fruit lend elegance to the nose, while firm tannins and broad pulp ensure an elegant yet structured palate.

Pico Maccario began its journey in Mombaruzzo in the mid-1990s. Over time, the winery has expanded both its vineyard area and production range. Now, Gavi and Langhe are part of their portfolio, and consequently vineyards of cortese and nebbiolo grapes (for their Barolos and Barbarescos). Pico and Vitaliano Maccario have also integrated international varietals like cabernet, sauvignon, viognier, merlot, and chardonnay into their multifaceted portfolio. Their Nizza wines put in a good showing. The Riserva Epico '21 boasts vibrant aromas of blood orange, aromatic herbs, and rain-soaked earth, with a full-bodied, lively palate that finishes fresh, persistent, and fine. The Tre Roveri '22 sees spicy notes of clove and pepper combine with fruity whiffs of plum and cherry; it's all followed by a palate of volume and rich fruit, balanced by tannins and acidity that provide length and harmony. As always, the Barbera d'Asti Lavignone '23 is superb—a classic, fresh, juicy Barbera with great pleasure in its tones of wild berries—an outstanding example of the variety's versatile character.

Wine	Rating		Wine	Rating
Boca '20	♦♦♦ 8		Barbera d'Asti Lavignone '23	♦♦♦ 4*
Bianko '23	♦♦ 4		Nizza Epico Ris. '21	♦♦ 8
Colline Novaresi Nebbiolo '23	♦♦ 4		Nizza Tre Roveri '22	♦♦ 5
Boca '18	♦♦♦ 8		Barbera d'Asti Lavignone '22	♦♦♦ 4*
Boca '17	♦♦♦ 8		Barbera d'Asti Lavignone '18	♦♦♦ 3*
Boca '16	♦♦♦ 8		Barbera d'Asti Lavignone '17	♦♦♦ 3*
Boca '15	♦♦♦ 8		Barbera d'Asti Sup. Epico '15	♦♦♦ 5
Boca '12	♦♦♦ 8		Nizza Epico Ris. '19	♦♦♦ 6
Boca '11	♦♦♦ 8		Nizza Tre Roveri '19	♦♦♦ 4*
Boca '10	♦♦♦ 7		Nizza Tre Roveri '18	♦♦♦ 4*
Boca '08	♦♦♦ 7		Barbera d'Asti Lavignone '21	♦♦ 3
Boca '06	♦♦♦ 6		Barbera d'Asti Lavignone '20	♦♦ 3*
Boca '05	♦♦♦ 6		Barbera d'Asti Lavignone '19	♦♦ 3*
Boca '04	♦♦♦ 6		Nizza Epico Ris. '20	♦♦ 6
Boca '03	♦♦♦ 6		Nizza Tre Roveri '21	♦♦ 4
			Nizza Tre Roveri '20	♦♦ 4

★Pio Cesare

via Cesare Balbo, 6
12051 Alba [CN]
(☎) +39 0173440386
⊕ www.piocesare.it

PRE-BOOKED VISITS
ANNUAL PRODUCTION 420,000 bottles
HECTARES UNDER VINE 80.00
SUSTAINABLE WINERY

The Boffa family now represents this pivotal
Alba-based winery, with Augusto, Cesare
Benvenuto, and Federica Rosy at the helm.
Barolo and Barbaresco serve as the pillars of
production, though the winery's range includes
nearly every other Langhe appellation, and more.
Their wines consistently demonstrate a high
level of quality, with expressions that resonate
with the terroir, often reaching the heights of
excellence. Once again, the Barolo Mosconi
2020 stands out for its refined aromatic
bouquet, blending fruit notes with rich spices.
The palate is also well-orchestrated, with fine,
soft tannins, compact development, and a long
finish, rounded out by a pleasant balsamic touch.
Equally well-crafted, the Barbera d'Alba Vigna
Mosconi Fides '21 proves juicy, fragrant, and
precise. The intense Barbaresco '20 impresses
with its aromas of raspberry and tobacco,
accented by hints of rose, and a multifaceted,
rich palate.

Luigi Pira

via XX Settembre, 9
12050 Serralunga d'Alba [CN]
(☎) +39 0173613106
⊕ www.piraluigi.it

CELLAR SALES
PRE-BOOKED VISITS
ANNUAL PRODUCTION 65,000 bottles
HECTARES UNDER VINE 13.00

This Serralunga d'Alba-based producer
transitioned to viticulture in the 1950s, thanks to
the efforts of Luigi Pira. However, the decisive
turning point came in the 1990s, when his son
Gianpaolo began bottling wine himself. Today, the
winery is also run by his brothers Romolo and
Claudio, alongside Gianpaolo's daughters
Annalisa and Elena, who work to maintain its
important place in the Langhe wine scene. The
Barolo del Comune di Serralunga '20 is taut and
sapid, with focused aromas and a juicy, fragrant,
and multifaceted progression, featuring
well-managed tannins and a persistent finish. Red
and black fruit contrasted by spices dominate
the nose of the Barolo Vignarionda '20, which on
the palate showcases structure and density, with
particularly invigorating tannins still in
development, and a long, compact finish. The
fleshy and powerful Barolo Marenca '20 also
caught our attention.

Wine	Rating
● Barolo Mosconi '20	♥♥♥ 8
● Barbaresco Bricco di Treiso Il Bricco '20	♥♥ 8
● Barbera d'Alba Sup. Fides V. Mosconi '22	♥♥ 6
● Barbaresco Pio '20	♥♥ 8
● Barolo Ornato '20	♥♥ 8
● Barolo Pio '20	♥♥ 8
○ Langhe Sauvignon Blanc '23	♥♥ 5
● Barolo Ornato '19	♀♀♀ 8
● Barolo Ornato '18	♀♀♀ 8
● Barolo Ornato '17	♀♀♀ 8
● Barolo Ornato '16	♀♀♀ 8
● Barolo Ornato '13	♀♀♀ 8
● Barolo Ornato '12	♀♀♀ 8
● Barolo Ornato '11	♀♀♀ 8
● Barolo Ornato '10	♀♀♀ 8

Wine	Rating
● Barolo Marenca '20	♥♥ 8
● Barolo Vignarionda '20	♥♥ 8
● Barolo del Comune di Serralunga d'Alba '20	♥♥ 6
● Barolo Margheria '20	♥ 8
● Barolo Marenca '11	♀♀♀ 7
● Barolo Marenca '09	♀♀♀ 7
● Barolo Marenca '08	♀♀♀ 7
● Barolo V. Marenca '01	♀♀♀ 7
● Barolo V. Marenca '97	♀♀♀ 8
● Barolo Vignarionda '12	♀♀♀ 8
● Barolo Vignarionda '06	♀♀♀ 8
● Barolo Vignarionda '04	♀♀♀ 8
● Barolo Vignarionda '00	♀♀♀ 8
● Barolo del Comune di Serralunga d'Alba '19	♥♥ 6
● Barolo Marenca '19	♥♥ 8
● Barolo Vignarionda '19	♥♥ 8

Guido Platinetti

via Roma, 60
28074 Ghemme [NO]
(》 +39 3389945783
⊛ www.platinettivini.com

CELLAR SALES
PRE-BOOKED VISITS
ANNUAL PRODUCTION 25,000 bottles
HECTARES UNDER VINE 8.00

Four generations of farmers and winemakers
have cultivated the land here in Alto Piemonte.
Experience, tradition, care, and technique form
the foundation of the Fontana family's
philosophy, which is carried on by the current
generation: Stefano, Maria, and Andrea. The
vineyards, located in Ronco Maso, sit on a stony,
iron-rich terrace, with two plots of 40 and 30
years old, facing southwest. Another hectare and
a half is located in Barragiola, south of Ghemme,
facing southeast. The Nebbiolo '22 is excellent,
rich in vibrant aromas of fresh red fruit, with a
bouquet of violet, underbrush, graphite, and
mineral and iron-like nuances. The palate is rich
and fleshy, with a delicate, silky tannic texture
and a persistent, authoritative finish. Classic and
terroir-driven, the Ronco al Maso '20 showcases
aromas of rhubarb and iodine, red fruit, and hints
of underbrush, with a powerful and dense palate
of great class and complexity.

Poderi Vaiot

s.da Borgata Laione, 43
12046 Montà [CN]
(》 +39 0173976283
⊛ www.poderivaiot.it

PRE-BOOKED VISITS
ANNUAL PRODUCTION 45,000 bottles
HECTARES UNDER VINE 8.00

The Casetta family founded Poderi Vaiot about
30 years ago. Their vineyards are spread out
across Montà and Santo Stefano Roero, on sandy
soils, and host the area's classic grape varieties,
particularly arneis, barbera, and nebbiolo. The
wines are crafted with precision and clarity, in a
traditional style that seeks to fully express the
character of the grapes and the vineyards in
which they're cultivated. The Barbera d'Alba
Lupestre remains their flagship. The 2022
highlights herbal, blueberry, and cinchona notes
on the nose, with a well-structured, austere
palate supported by firm acidity. The Roero
Pierin Riserva '20 is well-crafted, offering aromas
of rhubarb and black plum on the nose, while
the palate is juicy and flowing, with well-
integrated tannins. The Roero Arneis Franco '23
plays on citrus notes of bergamot, with a sapid,
taut palate of fine length. The Nebbiolo d'Alba
Sesanta Dì '22 is spicy and energetic.

● Colline Novaresi Nebbiolo '22	♙♙ 3*
● Ghemme V. Ronco al Maso '20	♙♙ 5
⊙ Colline Novaresi Rosato Luisa '23	♙♙ 4
● Colline Novaresi Vespolina '23	♙ 3
● Ghemme V. Ronco al Maso '15	♙♙♙ 4*
● Colline Novaresi Barbera Pieleo '19	♙♙ 3
● Colline Novaresi Nebbiolo '21	♙♙ 3
● Colline Novaresi Nebbiolo '20	♙♙ 3
● Colline Novaresi Nebbiolo '19	♙♙ 3
● Colline Novaresi Nebbiolo '18	♙♙ 3
● Colline Novaresi Vespolina '22	♙♙ 3
● Colline Novaresi Vespolina '19	♙♙ 3
● Ghemme V. Ronco al Maso '18	♙♙ 5
● Ghemme V. Ronco al Maso '17	♙♙ 5
● Ghemme V. Ronco al Maso '16	♙♙ 5

● Barbera d'Alba Lupestre '22	♙♙ 3*
● Nebbiolo d'Alba Sesanta Dì '22	♙♙ 3
⊙ Roero Arneis Franco '23	♙♙ 2*
● Roero Pierin Ris. '20	♙♙ 4
⊙ Langhe Rosato N-Rose '23	♙ 2
⊙ Nebbiolo d'Alba Spumante Rosé M. Cl. Dosaggio Zero '21	♙ 5
● Barbera d'Alba Lupestre '21	♙♙ 3*
● Barbera d'Alba Lupestre '20	♙♙ 2*
⊙ Nebbiolo d'Alba Dosaggio Zero M. Cl. Rosé '19	♙♙ 4
● Nebbiolo d'Alba Sesanta Dì '20	♙♙ 3
⊙ Roero Arneis Franco '22	♙♙ 2*
⊙ Roero Arneis Franco '21	♙♙ 2*
● Roero Pierin '19	♙♙ 4

Ezio Poggio

loc. Colombaie
15060 Vignole Borbera [AL]
☎ +39 014367106
✉ eziopoggio.com

PRE-BOOKED VISITS
ANNUAL PRODUCTION 35,000 bottles
HECTARES UNDER VINE 8.00

Ezio Poggio is today led by the third generation of family, siblings Ezio and Mary. The pair have shown notable commitment to gaining recognition for the "Terre di Libarna" subzone of the Colli Tortonesi appellation, highlighting the Val Borbera and Valle Spinti growing districts in particular. Production focuses mainly on timorasso, which comes in four versions, including two sparkling wines (one Metodo Martinotti and one Metodo Classico). Both versions of Timorasso are commendable. The Archetipo '21 showcases citrus aromas, flint, chalky notes, tea, and Mediterranean herbs, with a taut, sapid palate and a slightly glyceric finish. The nose of the Caespes '22 is more multifaceted and intense, with notes of grapefruit and lemon zest that give way to mineral and spicy sensations, while the palate is playful and citrusy, with a finish recalling freshness and sapidity.

Marco Porello

c.so Alba, 71
12043 Canale [CN]
☎ +39 0173979324
✉ www.porellovini.it

CELLAR SALES
PRE-BOOKED VISITS
ANNUAL PRODUCTION 130,000 bottles
HECTARES UNDER VINE 15.00

For thirty years, Marco Porello has led his family winery, which operates from two locations: one in Canale for vinification and bottling, and another in Guarene for aging. Their vineyards in Vezza d'Alba and Canale, where both sandy and calcareous-clay soils dominate, give rise to modern wines with clear aromatic profiles, drawing on arneis, barbera and nebbiolo grapes. The Roero Torretta returns to the spotlight. The 2022 opens with notes of wild red berries, licorice, and a light spiciness on the nose, while the palate is rich in fruit, with fine tannins, unfolding fresh and energetic. Other highlights include the floral- and black fruit-scented Roero San Michele Riserva '21, a juicy drink of good structure, the sapid and enjoyable Nebbiolo d'Alba Vigna Valmaggiore '22, the Barbera d'Alba Mommiano '23, which is true to type in its notes of petrichor and cherry, and the Roero Arneis Camestrì '23, a flowing and approachable wine redolent of flowers and white currant.

○ Colli Tortonesi Terre di Libarna Timorasso Archetipo '21	♟♟ 4
○ Colli Tortonesi Terre di Libarna Timorasso Caespes '22	♟♟ 4
● Colli Tortonesi Terre di Libarna Rosso Caespes '22	♟ 3
○ Colli Tortonesi Terre di Libarna Bianco Extra Brut M. Cl. '19	♟♟ 6
○ Colli Tortonesi Terre di Libarna Extra Brut M. Cl. '18	♟♟ 4
● Colli Tortonesi Terre di Libarna Rosso Caespes '21	♟♟ 3
○ Colli Tortonesi Terre di Libarna Timorasso Archetipo '20	♟♟ 4
○ Colli Tortonesi Terre di Libarna Timorasso Archetipo '19	♟♟ 4
○ Colli Tortonesi Terre di Libarna Timorasso Caespes '21	♟♟ 4

● Roero Torretta '22	♟♟ 4
● Barbera d'Alba Mommiano '23	♟♟ 3
● Nebbiolo d'Alba V. Valmaggiore '22	♟♟ 5
○ Roero Arneis Camestrì '23	♟♟ 3
● Roero San Michele Ris. '21	♟♟ 5
○ Roero Arneis '23	♟ 3
○ Roero Arneis Camestrì '20	♟♟♟ 3*
● Roero Torretta '06	♟♟♟ 3*
● Roero Torretta '04	♟♟♟ 3*
● Barbera d'Alba Mommiano '22	♟♟ 3
○ Langhe Favorita '22	♟♟ 2*
● Nebbiolo d'Alba V. Valmaggiore '21	♟♟ 5
○ Roero Arneis '22	♟♟ 3
○ Roero Arneis Camestrì '21	♟♟ 4
● Roero San Michele Ris. '20	♟♟ 5
● Roero San Michele Ris. '19	♟♟ 5
● Roero Torretta '20	♟♟ 4

★Guido Porro

via Alba, I
12050 Serralunga d'Alba [CN]
(») +39 0173613306
⊜ www.guidoporro.com

CELLAR SALES
PRE-BOOKED VISITS
ACCOMMODATION
ANNUAL PRODUCTION 45,000 bottles
HECTARES UNDER VINE 8.00

This Serralunga d'Alba winery is best known for its Barolo, produced from the Lazzairasco vineyard, but it also owns parcels in the Santa Caterina and Vigna Rionda crus. In recent years, the Porro family's wines have gained prominence in the Langhe wine scene, thanks to a precise, classical style that is very much in tune with their home territory, with maturation carried out in large oak barrels and a restrained production approach. The Barolo Vignarionda '20, unsurprisingly, opens elegantly, right from the nose, where fragrant wild berries meet a backdrop of graphite sensations. On the palate, the wine is focused and persistente, with progressive tannins and juicy fruit, concluding with an evenly proportioned finish. Red fruit and tobacco emerge in the Barolo Lazzairasco '20, a wine marked by a firm tannic structure. The Barolo Giannetto '20 proves supple and subtle.

Post dal Vin
Terre del Barbera

fraz. Possavina
via Salie, 19
14030 Rocchetta Tanaro [AT]
(») +39 0141644143
⊜ www.postdalvin.it

CELLAR SALES
PRE-BOOKED VISITS
ANNUAL PRODUCTION 80,000 bottles
HECTARES UNDER VINE 100.00

The winery's name immediately evokes its signature grape: barbera, offered here in seven versions, including a unique Barbera Chinata. Located in Rocchetta Tanaro, with vineyards in Cortiglione and Masio, this cooperative winery has a 75-year history and now includes about 200 contributing members. All their wines reflect the territory's essence, as well as various approaches to aging. Both the Barbera d'Asti Superiore Castagnassa '22 and the Maricca '23 stand out. The Castagnassa reveals notes of blackcurrant and Mediterranean scrub, with an approachable, juicy palate full of good texture. Meanwhile, the Maricca '23, a classic, standard-label Barbera d'Asti, showcases fresh fruit, a rich and fleshy profile, with immediate appeal and a long, flavorful finish. The Grignolino d'Asti '23 features classic pepper and bark notes, with a slightly tannic yet balanced character, while the Barbera d'Asti Superiore BriccoFiore '21 plays on clear and pleasant tones of wild berries.

● Barolo Vignarionda '20	▼▼▼ 8
● Barolo V. Lazzairasco '20	▼▼ 6
● Barolo V. Santa Caterina '20	▼▼ 6
● Barbera d'Alba V. Santa Caterina '23	▼▼ 3
● Barolo Gianetto '20	▼▼ 6
● Dolcetto d'Alba V. Pari '23	▼▼ 3
● Lange Nebbiolo Camilu '23	▼ 4
● Barolo V. Lazzairasco '13	♡♡♡ 5
● Barolo V. Lazzairasco '12	♡♡♡ 5
● Barolo V. Lazzairasco '11	♡♡♡ 5
● Barolo Vigna Rionda '18	♡♡♡ 8
● Barolo Vigna Rionda '16	♡♡♡ 8
● Barolo Vigna Rionda '15	♡♡♡ 8
● Barolo Vignarionda '19	♡♡♡ 8

● Barbera d'Asti Maricca '23	▼▼ 2*
● Barbera d'Asti Sup. Castagnassa '22	▼▼ 4
● Grignolino d'Asti '23	▼▼ 2*
● Barbera d'Asti Rebarba '21	▼ 4
● Barbera d'Asti Castagnassa '20	♡♡ 3
● Barbera d'Asti Maricca '22	♡♡ 2*
● Barbera d'Asti Maricca '21	♡♡ 2*
● Barbera d'Asti Rebarba '20	♡♡ 3
● Barbera d'Asti Rebarba '18	♡♡ 3
● Barbera d'Asti Sup. Briccofiore '20	♡♡ 2*
● Barbera d'Asti Sup. Briccofiore '19	♡♡ 2*
● Barbera d'Asti Sup. Castagnassa '21	♡♡ 3
● Grignolino d'Asti '22	♡♡ 2*
● Grignolino d'Asti '21	♡♡ 2*

Prediomagno

via Professor Garrone, 43
14031 Grana [AT]
+39 0141924243
www.prediomagno.com

CELLAR SALES
PRE-BOOKED VISITS
ANNUAL PRODUCTION 100,000 bottles
HECTARES UNDER VINE 25.00
SUSTAINABLE WINERY

Emanuela Novello runs this spectacular winery in Grana with great determination. After a period of uncertainty, the estate is making a strong comeback, regaining attention in the wine scene thanks to careful craftsmanship. The estate itself is worth a visit, with its stunning palazzo and elegantly furnished tasting room. Emanuela and her husband Giovanni, who also produces olive oil, warmly welcome visitors as they present their original wines. In the cellar, young winemaker Pietro Simondi is making significant strides. The Ruché Vigna del Castello, a historic cru dressed in a new label from the Falconidi collection, impresses with both the beauty of the vineyard and the quality of the wine. This Ruché expresses broad notes of spice, florals, and fruit, harmoniously blended, with a soft and persistent palate of great pleasure. The Barbera Vlù offers bracing and long-lasting balsamic and spicy notes. The ruby-red Pinot Nero Regalis, with its garnet highlights, reveals whiffs of mocha, raspberry, and pink pepper.

● Ruchè di Castagnole M.to V. Del Castello '22	ΨΨ 4
● Barbera d'Asti Sup. Vlu '21	ΨΨ 5
○ Piemonte Chardonnay Le Sime '21	ΨΨ 6
● Piemonte Pinot Nero Regalis '21	ΨΨ 5
● Ruchè di Castagnole M.to Nisus '22	Ψ 5
● Barbera d'Asti Sup. Vlu '19	ΥΥ 5
⊙ Brut Rosé M. Cl. '16	ΥΥ 5
● Grignolino d'Asti Splé '21	ΥΥ 4
⊙ Neonà '20	ΥΥ 3
○ Piemonte Chardonnay Piumago '20	ΥΥ 4
○ Piemonte Sauvignon Suitas '21	ΥΥ 4
○ Piemonte Sauvignon Suitas '20	ΥΥ 4
● Ruchè di Castagnole M.to Nisus '21	ΥΥ 5

Diego Pressenda

loc. Sant'Anna, 98
12065 Monforte d'Alba [CN]
+39 017378327
www.diegopressenda.it

CELLAR SALES
PRE-BOOKED VISITS
ACCOMMODATION AND RESTAURANT SERVICE
ANNUAL PRODUCTION 85,000 bottles
HECTARES UNDER VINE 15.00
SUSTAINABLE WINERY

Rosanna and Diego Pressenda began their winemaking journey in 2004, among the hills of Monforte d'Alba and Roddino. Since then their children Silvia and Oscar have come on board. The varietals grown include the region's classics—dolcetto, barbera, and nebbiolo—while white wine production centers on the international grapes chardonnay and riesling. Both of the two Barolo Bricco San Pietro wines sampled this year are excellent. The 2019 features fragrant streaks of raspberry, spices, and tobacco, which lend complexity. The palate is rich, with soft, well-integrated tannins and a long, austere finish. The 2020 showcases a lovely, fruity profile, with hints of violet and licorice. Its palate is fine, with pervasive tannins and a pleasant fleshiness. The other two Barolos are also well-crafted, both the austere Le Coste di Monforte and the Barbadelchi.

● Barolo Bricco San Pietro '20	ΨΨ 8
● Barolo Bricco San Pietro '19	ΨΨ 8
● Barolo Barbadelchi '20	ΨΨ 7
● Barolo Le Coste di Monforte '20	ΨΨ 8
● Dolcetto d'Alba Dosso '23	ΨΨ 3
● Nebbiolo d'Alba Il Donato '21	ΨΨ 5
● Barbera d'Alba Sup. Ariota '20	ΥΥ 4
● Barolo Barbadelchi '18	ΥΥ 6
● Barolo Barbadelchi '17	ΥΥ 6
● Barolo Barbadelchi '16	ΥΥ 6
● Barolo Bricco San Pietro '18	ΥΥ 7
● Barolo Le Coste di Monforte '19	ΥΥ 7
● Barolo Le Coste di Monforte '18	ΥΥ 7
● Dolcetto d'Alba Dosso '22	ΥΥ 2*
○ Langhe Chardonnay '22	ΥΥ 3
● Nebbiolo d'Alba Il Donato '19	ΥΥ 4

Prinsi

via Gaia, 5
12052 Neive [CN]
(☎ +39 017367192
🖳 www.prinsi.it

CELLAR SALES
PRE-BOOKED VISITS
ANNUAL PRODUCTION 60,000 bottles
HECTARES UNDER VINE 25.00

Prinsi is a family-owned winery based in Neive. Franco Lequio started bottling wine in 1967, while his son Daniele has been working alongside him since 1999. The heart of production lies with Barbaresco, with crus including Gaia Principe, Gallina, Fausoni, and Basarin. Their winemaking style, which combines classic and modern approaches, calls for aging in a mix of barriques, tonneaux, and large wooden casks. The Barbaresco Gallina Viti Vecchie '20 displays a fine and multifaceted aromatic interplay of spices and balsamic accents. The wine is expansive and occasionally austere on the palate, with a compact development and decisive finish. The Camp d'Pietru '23, a monovarietal sauvignon, bursts with citrus and aromatic herb fragrances, with a rich, fragrant, and persistent palate. The Langhe Nebbiolo Sandrina '22 proves highly enjoyable.

● Barbaresco Gallina Viti Vecchie '20	♀♀ 8
○ Camp'd Pietru Sauvignon '23	♀♀ 4
● Langhe Nebbiolo Sandrina '22	♀♀ 4
○ Alta Langa Extra Brut '20	♀♀ 5
● Barbaresco Gaia Principe '21	♀♀ 5
○ Langhe Arneis Il Nespolo '23	♀♀ 4
● Barbaresco Fausoni Ris. '16	♀♀ 6
● Barbaresco Fausoni Ris. '11	♀♀ 5
● Barbaresco Gaia Principe '20	♀♀ 5
● Barbaresco Gaia Principe '17	♀♀ 5
● Barbaresco Gaia Principe '15	♀♀ 5
● Barbaresco Gaia Principe '14	♀♀ 5
● Barbaresco Gaia Principe '13	♀♀ 5
● Barbaresco Gallina '19	♀♀ 6
● Barbaresco Gallina '17	♀♀ 5
● Barbaresco Gallina '12	♀♀ 5

★Produttori del Barbaresco

via Torino, 54
12050 Barbaresco [CN]
(☎ +39 0173635139
🖳 produttoridelbarbaresco.com

CELLAR SALES
PRE-BOOKED VISITS
ACCOMMODATION
ANNUAL PRODUCTION 540,000 bottles
HECTARES UNDER VINE 105.00

The Produttori del Barbaresco cooperative was founded in 1894 by Domizio Cavazza, then head of the Alba School of Oenology. Cavazza died in 1913, and the cooperative was shut down during the rise of fascism, in the 1920s. In 1958, together with 19 members, Don Fiorino Marengo revived the producer. Today, Produttori del Barbaresco counts 50 growers among its ranks and is regarded as one of the most important players in the Langhe. This year's lineup of 2019 Barbaresco Riserva is outstanding, starting with the Muncagota '19, where gorgeous, fresh fruit notes and layers of violet and licorice shine through. The palate is focused, revealing texture and complexity. The Montestefano is a vibrant pour, with lovely notes of ripe red berries and licorice adding character and complexity, alongside fine nuances. The palate is firm and powerful, with fine tannins and nice flesh. The elegant and velvety Asili also delivers.

● Barbaresco Montestefano Ris. '19	♀♀♀ 6
● Barbaresco Asili Ris. '19	♀♀ 6
● Barbaresco Muncagota Ris. '19	♀♀ 6
● Barbaresco Ovello Ris. '19	♀♀ 6
● Barbaresco Pajè Ris. '19	♀♀ 6
● Barbaresco Pora Ris. '19	♀♀ 6
● Barbaresco Rabajà Ris. '19	♀♀ 6
● Barbaresco Asili Ris. '13	♀♀♀ 6
● Barbaresco Ovello Ris. '09	♀♀♀ 6
● Barbaresco Vign. in Montestefano Ris. '05	♀♀♀ 6
● Barbaresco Vign. in Montestefano Ris. '04	♀♀♀ 6
● Barbaresco Vign. in Ovello Ris. '08	♀♀♀ 6
● Barbaresco Vign. in Pora Ris. '07	♀♀♀ 6
● Barbaresco '19	♀♀ 5

Cantina Produttori del Gavi

via Cavalieri di Vittorio Veneto, 45
15066 Gavi [AL]
+39 0143642786
cantinaproduttoridelgavi.it

CELLAR SALES
PRE-BOOKED VISITS
ANNUAL PRODUCTION 300,000 bottles
HECTARES UNDER VINE 220.00

Cantina Produttori del Gavi boasts 80 current members. Established in 1951, the cooperative brought together the region's pioneering growers. Their first bottles of Gavi were produced when the appellation was established in 1974. Today, the winery's extensive portfolio includes nine Gavis and a selection of reds that features Dolcetto d'Ovada, Barbera del Monferrato, and Barbera d'Asti. The Gavi Il Forte '23 offers up pleasant aromas of field herbs and white-fleshed fruits alongside nuances of fresh almond. On the palate it's refined, with a sleek and supple texture, concluding with a flavorful and fleshy finish. The Gavi del Comune di Gavi GG '21 is redolent of exotic fruits and white flowers, with a fragrant, sapid, and long-lasting palate. The Gavi Primi Grappoli '23 proves vibrant and approachable.

○ Gavi del Comune di Gavi GG '21	🍷🍷 3*
○ Gavi Il Forte '23	🍷🍷 2*
○ Gavi del Comune di Gavi Maddalena '23	🍷🍷 2*
○ Gavi G '21	🍷🍷 3
○ Gavi Primi Grappoli '23	🍷🍷 3
○ Gavi del Comune di Gavi '23	🍷 3
○ Gavi del Comune di Gavi Mille951 '23	🍷 2
○ Gavi del Comune di Gavi GG '15	🍷🍷🍷 3*
○ Gavi del Comune di Gavi Bio '20	🍷🍷 3*
○ Gavi del Comune di Gavi GG '19	🍷🍷 3*
○ Gavi del Comune di Gavi Mille951 '21	🍷🍷 2*
○ Gavi Il Forte '22	🍷🍷 2*
○ Gavi Primi Grappoli '22	🍷🍷 3*
○ Gavi Primi Grappoli '20	🍷🍷 3*

★Prunotto

c.so Barolo, 14
12051 Alba [CN]
+39 0173280017
www.prunotto.it

CELLAR SALES
PRE-BOOKED VISITS
ACCOMMODATION
ANNUAL PRODUCTION 800,000 bottles
HECTARES UNDER VINE 74.00

Founded by Alfred Prunotto in 1922, Prunotto was sold to Beppe and Tino Colla in 1956. In 1989, the Antinori family acquired the producer, initially focusing solely on distribution before taking over technical management as well in 1994. The estate now spans Langhe and Monferrato, with notable crus like Bric Turot, Costamiòle, Bussia and Bricco Colma, where the albarossa grape (a cross between nebbiolo and barbera) is cultivated. The Barolo Mosconi '20 showcases nice gustatory structure before a long, persistent finish, with aromas of ripe red fruit, spices, and toasty accents emerging on the nose. The Barbaresco Secondine '21 exudes whiffs of small red fruits and spices, with a precise and measured palate, guided by gentle tannins towards a focused finish. The Barolo Bussia Vigna Colonnello Riserva '18 proves mature and austere.

● Barbaresco Secondine '21	🍷🍷 8
● Barolo Mosconi '20	🍷🍷 8
● Barbaresco Bric Turot '21	🍷🍷 7
● Barolo Bussia V. Colonnello Ris. '18	🍷🍷 8
● Barolo Cerretta '20	🍷🍷 8
● Barbaresco '21	🍷 6
● Barolo '20	🍷 7
● Barolo Bussia '20	🍷 8
● Barbera d'Asti Costamiòle '99	🍷🍷🍷 4*
● Barbera d'Asti Costamiòle '97	🍷🍷🍷 6
● Barbera d'Asti Costamiòle '96	🍷🍷🍷 6
● Barolo Bussia '01	🍷🍷🍷 8
● Barolo Bussia '99	🍷🍷🍷 8
● Barolo Bussia '98	🍷🍷🍷 8
● Barolo Bussia '96	🍷🍷🍷 8
● Barolo Bussia '85	🍷🍷🍷 8

La Raia

s.da Monterotondo, 79
15067 Novi Ligure [AL]
☎ +39 0143743685
✉ www.la-raia.it

CELLAR SALES
PRE-BOOKED VISITS
ACCOMMODATION
ANNUAL PRODUCTION 350,000 bottles
HECTARES UNDER VINE 50.00
VITICULTURE METHOD Certified Biodynamic
SUSTAINABLE WINERY

Nestled in the Gavi hills of Alessandria province, La Raia has been owned by the Rossi Cairo family since 2003. The winery adheres to biodynamic principles, with minimal human and chemical intervention in the vineyards. Their wine range primarily features Gavi DOCG, along with a small selection of Barberas, as well as notable offerings from important crus like Pisé and La Madonnina. The Gavi Vigna della Madonnina Riserva '21 carries an aromatic profile dominated by flinty notes, complemented by herbaceous and floral hints. The palate is powerful and rich, with a spirited development and a lively finish that's both airy and crisp. The Gavi Pisè '20 is redolent of freshly cut grass, wildflowers, and white-fleshed fruits—a sapid, rich, and fragrant palate follows, finishing long and focused.

Raineri

loc. Panerole, 24
12060 Novello [CN]
☎ +39 3396009289
✉ www.rainerivini.com

CELLAR SALES
PRE-BOOKED VISITS
ANNUAL PRODUCTION 40,000 bottles
HECTARES UNDER VINE 6.00
SUSTAINABLE WINERY

Gianmatteo Raineri, Fabrizio Giraudo, and Luciano Racca were still in school when, in 2004, the three friends decided to rent a vineyard. The first year, they sold the grapes; the second year, they produced their first Dogliani; and by the third year, they were vinifying their first Barolo, using the cellars of the wineries where, in the meantime, they had begun working. They've kept their day jobs, but today they own a number of hectares, producing eight wines, half of which are Barolos. Aromatically, the Barolo Castelletto '20 sees fresh flowers interlace with pencil lead, red fruits, and licorice, leading to a firm palate with close-knit tannins and a deep finish. The Barolo Perno '20 is well-crafted, while the Langhe Pinot Nero '22 reveals a clearly defined, varietal character. The Barbera d'Alba Superiore Sagrin '22 proves fresh and spicy, offering extreme pleasure on the palate.

○ Gavi V. della Madonnina Ris. '21	♟♟♟ 5
○ Gavi Pisé '20	♟♟ 6
○ Gavi Pleo '23	♟♟ 3
○ Piemonte Bianco Passito '22	♟♟ 5
○ Gavi V. della Madonnina Ris. '16	♟♟♟ 3*
○ Gavi '21	♟♟ 3*
○ Gavi '20	♟♟ 3*
○ Gavi Pisé '19	♟♟ 5
○ Gavi Pisé '18	♟♟ 5
○ Gavi Pisé '17	♟♟ 5
○ Gavi V. della Madonnina Ris. '19	♟♟ 4
○ Gavi V. della Madonnina Ris. '18	♟♟ 3*
○ Gavi V. della Madonnina Ris. '17	♟♟ 3*
○ Gavi V. Madonnina Ris. '20	♟♟ 5

● Barolo Castelletto '20	♟♟ 8
● Barbera d'Alba Sup. Sagrin '22	♟♟ 3
● Barolo Perno '20	♟♟ 8
● Langhe Nebbiolo Snart '22	♟♟ 4
● Langhe Pinot Nero '22	♟♟ 4
⊙ Langhe Rosato '23	♟♟ 3
● Barbera d'Alba Sagrin '13	♟♟ 5
● Barolo '19	♟♟ 6
● Barolo '18	♟♟ 6
● Barolo Castelletto '18	♟♟ 8
● Barolo Castelletto '17	♟♟ 8
● Barolo Monserra '14	♟♟ 7
● Barolo Perno '18	♟♟ 8
● Dogliani Cornole '13	♟♟ 3*
● Dogliani Zovetto '19	♟♟ 2*
○ Langhe Bianco Elfobianco '22	♟♟ 3*

PIEDMONT

Renato Ratti

fraz. Annunziata, 7
12064 La Morra [CN]
(») +39 017350185
⊕ www.renatoratti.com

Vigneti Repetto

loc. Mongualdone
s.da Mombisaggio
15050 Sarezzano [AL]
(») +39 01311936041
⊕ www.vignetirepetto.it

CELLAR SALES
PRE-BOOKED VISITS
ACCOMMODATION
ANNUAL PRODUCTION 350,000 bottles
HECTARES UNDER VINE 35.00

CELLAR SALES
PRE-BOOKED VISITS
ANNUAL PRODUCTION 60,000 bottles
HECTARES UNDER VINE 27.00
VITICULTURE METHOD Certified Organic
SUSTAINABLE WINERY

Renato Ratti founded his winery in 1965, becoming a pivotal figure in Langhe's wine culture. He also established the "Ratti Museum of Barolo and Alba Wines," where he created a map of historic vintages and subzones, highlighting their impact. Today, the winery is run by his son Pietro, who maintains the family's philosophy, emphasizing the perfect marriage of nebbiolo and the local terroir. The skillfully made Barolo Rocche dell'Annunziata '20 opens with aromas of raspberry, tobacco, and spices. On the palate, it shows fine tannins and a long, persistent finish. The well-crafted Langhe Nebbiolo Reggimento '21 is right up there as well. The Barbera d'Asti Superiore Villa Pattono '21 impresses with its blackberry and pomegranate notes, leading to a dynamic, firm, and sapid palate.

"Ancient Methods, Modern Technology" is Vigneti Repetto's motto, a philosophy that reflects a balance of tradition and innovation, as well as a deep respect for nature. Gian Paolo and Marina Repetto embody this approach through their sunny dispositions and professionalism, blending passion and precision into their daily work. Their 18-hectare vineyard, located in the hills of Sarezzano in the heart of Colli Tortonesi, benefits from excellent exposure and elevations spanning 240-320 meters. The Timorasso Origo '21 pours a bright, straw-yellow and greenish hue. On the nose it's harmonious and refined, with a complex suite in which mineral notes join grapefruit juice, and citron peel, all followed by a faint hint of hydrocarbons. The palate is extraordinary in its density and close-knit structure, balanced by freshness and a very long finish. The citrusy, taut, and sapid Timorasso Quadro '22 is excellent as well. We also appreicate the fresh Piccolo Derthona '22.

● Barolo Rocche dell'Annunziata '20	♥♥ 8
● Barbera d'Asti Sup. Villa Pattono '21	♥♥ 5
● Langhe Nebbiolo Reggimento '21	♥♥ 5
● Barolo Marcenasco '20	♥ 7
● Barolo Serradenari '20	♥ 7
○ Langhe Chardonnay Brigata '22	♥ 3
● Langhe Nebbiolo Ochetti '22	♥ 4
● Barolo Rocche '06	♥♥♥ 8
● Barolo Rocche Marcenasco '84	♥♥♥ 6
● Barolo Rocche Marcenasco '83	♥♥♥ 6
● Barolo Conca '18	♥♥ 8
● Barolo Marcenasco '18	♥♥ 6
● Barolo Marcenasco '17	♥♥ 6
● Barolo Rocche dell'Annunziata '19	♥♥ 8
● Barolo Rocche dell'Annunziata '17	♥♥ 8
● Barolo Serradenari '19	♥♥ 6

○ Colli Tortonesi Timorasso Derthona Origo '21	♥♥♥ 5
○ Colli Tortonesi Timorasso Derthona Quadro '22	♥♥ 4
○ Colli Tortonesi Timorasso Piccolo Derthona '22	♥ 3
⊙ Rosato '23	♥ 3
○ Colli Tortonesi Timorasso Derthona Origo '20	♥♥ 5
○ Colli Tortonesi Timorasso Derthona Origo '19	♥♥ 4
○ Colli Tortonesi Timorasso Derthona Quadro '18	♥♥ 4
○ Colli Tortonesi Timorasso Piccolo Derthona '19	♥♥ 3*

Réva

loc. Gallinotto, 128
12064 La Morra [CN]
+39 0173789269
www.revawinery.com

CELLAR SALES
PRE-BOOKED VISITS
ACCOMMODATION AND RESTAURANT SERVICE
ANNUAL PRODUCTION 85,000 bottles
HECTARES UNDER VINE 35.00
VITICULTURE METHOD Certified Organic
SUSTAINABLE WINERY

Since 2011, this Monforte d'Alba-based winery has been owned by Czech entrepreneur Miroslav Lekes and managed by Daniele Scaglia. Réva, which stands out as one of the area's most important, recently acquired producers, focuses on the territory's classic wines, well-represented by the Ravera, Cannubi, and Lazzarito crus, interpreted here with a stylishly modern touch. They also place considerable emphasis on Alta Langa sparkling wines. The Barolo Ravera '20 still offers youthful aromas, with oak prevailing over fruit, though it's still clearly defined on the nosed. The palate is firm, with a sure and multifaceted progression, and a focused finish. The dark and spicy Barolo Cannubi '20 possesses energy, flavor, and pleasure on the palate. The Barolo '20 also impresses with its clean, fruity aromas and a supple, easy-drinking palate.

● Barolo Cannubi '20	▼▼ 8
● Barolo Ravera '20	▼▼ 8
● Barolo '20	▼▼ 6
○ Langhe Bianco Grey '22	▼▼ 4
● Barolo Cannubi '17	▽▽▽ 8
● Barolo Lazzarito Ris. '16	▽▽▽ 8
● Barolo '18	▽▽ 6
● Barolo '17	▽▽ 6
● Barolo '16	▽▽ 5
● Barolo '15	▽▽ 5
● Barolo '13	▽▽ 5
● Barolo '12	▽▽ 5
● Barolo Cannubi '19	▽▽ 8
● Barolo Cannubi '18	▽▽ 8
● Barolo Lazzarito Ris. '17	▽▽ 8
● Barolo Ravera '16	▽▽ 8

Carlo & Figli Revello

fraz. Santa Maria
12064 La Morra [CN]
+39 3356765021
www.carlorevello.com

PRE-BOOKED VISITS
ANNUAL PRODUCTION 25,000 bottles
HECTARES UNDER VINE 7.00

Carlo Revello has been running his winery in La Morra since 2016, together with his wife Paola and sons Erik and Niklas. This small artisanal operation offers wines that are generally direct, well-defined, and classically styled, with aging carried out in oak barrels of various sizes. In addition to Barolo—produced from the Rocche dell'Annunziata, Boiolo, and Giachini crus—the winery also makes Barbera and Dolcetto d'Alba. The Barolo '20 shows nice intensity and austerity, with red fruit meeting abundant licorice, all further enriched by graphite and tobacco, adding complexity and finesse. On the palate, it displays great juiciness, with a well-structured tannic weave and a very long finish. The Barolo Boiolo features fresh fruit, a touch of green, and a very straightforward finish, with a subtle green sensation on the palate.

● Barolo '20	▼▼ 5
● Barolo Boiolo '20	▼▼ 6
● Barolo Giachini '20	▼▼ 7
● Dolcetto d'Alba '23	▼ 2
● Langhe Nebbiolo '23	▼ 4
● Barolo '19	▽▽ 5
● Barolo '18	▽▽ 5
● Barolo Boiolo '19	▽▽ 6
● Barolo Boiolo '18	▽▽ 6
● Barolo Giachini '19	▽▽ 7
● Barolo Giachini '18	▽▽ 7
● Barolo Rocche dell'Annunziata Ris. '17	▽▽ 8
● Barolo Rocche dell'Annunziata Ris. '16	▽▽ 8

F.lli Revello

fraz. Annunziata, 103
12064 La Morra [CN]
📞 +39 017350276
🌐 www.revello.wine

CELLAR SALES
PRE-BOOKED VISITS
ACCOMMODATION
ANNUAL PRODUCTION 55,000 bottles
HECTARES UNDER VINE 12.00
SUSTAINABLE WINERY

In 1967, the Revello family began vinifying some of their grapes, producing their first bottle of Barolo. In 1990, the winery was passed on to brothers Carlo and Lorenzo, who decided in 2016 to split the estate to allow their children to join the business. The vineyards, predominantly planted with nebbiolo, cover portions of the Giachini, Rocche dell'Annunziata, Coca, and Gattera crus. The Barolo Giachini '20 stands out for its aromatic intensity—toasty and spicy notes that accompany lush, ripe fruit. This same character defines its generous, juicy, and flavorful palate. The Barolo '20 proves bright and lively, with highly sapid flavor. The Barolo Conca '20 opens on red fruit and smoky, spicy accents, though its focused palate is slightly one-dimensional. The Barolo Gattera '20 features whiffs of small red fruits and oaky hints on the nose, with a powerful and warm palate to follow.

Michele Reverdito

fraz. Rivalta
b.ta Garassini, 74a
12064 La Morra [CN]
📞 +39 017350336
🌐 www.reverdito.it

CELLAR SALES
PRE-BOOKED VISITS
ANNUAL PRODUCTION 100,000 bottles
HECTARES UNDER VINE 26.00
SUSTAINABLE WINERY

Founded in 2000, this La Morra-based winery is the work of Silvano and his children, Michele and Sabina Reverdito. The family has been gradually acquiring vineyards since 1967, including the crus Bricco Cogni (La Morra), Ascheri (La Morra), Badarina (Serralunga d'Alba), Riva Rocca (Verduno), Bricco San Pietro (Monforte d'Alba), La Serra, Castagni, and Berri (La Morra). The wines mature in oak and amphorae, offering a distinctive interpretation full of character. The Barolo '20 makes an intense aromatic impact dominated by citrus and spices, with a lively, sustained, and persistent progression on the palate. The well-crafted Barolo Riserva La Serra '17 is more concentrated and mature. The Nascetta '22 features aromas of jasmine and sage, with a full-bodied, sapid, and long palate to follow.

● Barolo Giachini '20	🍷🍷 7
● Barbera d'Alba Ciabot du Re '22	🍷🍷 5
● Barolo '20	🍷🍷 6
● Barolo Conca '20	🍷🍷 8
● Barolo Gattera '20	🍷🍷 7
● Barolo Cerretta '20	🍷 8
● Barbera d'Alba Ciabot du Re '05	🍷🍷🍷 5
● Barbera d'Alba Ciabot du Re '00	🍷🍷🍷 5
● Barolo '93	🍷🍷🍷 5
● Barolo Rocche dell'Annunziata '01	🍷🍷🍷 8
● Barolo Rocche dell'Annunziata '00	🍷🍷🍷 8
● Barolo Rocche dell'Annunziata '97	🍷🍷🍷 8
● Barolo V. Conca '99	🍷🍷🍷 7
● Barolo Conca '18	🍷🍷 8
● Barolo Giachini '19	🍷🍷 7
● Barolo Giachini '18	🍷🍷 7

● Barolo '20	🍷🍷 5
● Barolo La Serra Ris. '17	🍷🍷 5
○ Langhe Nascetta '23	🍷🍷 3
● Barolo Ascheri '20	🍷 6
● Verduno Pelaverga '23	🍷 4
● Barolo Bricco Cogni '04	🍷🍷🍷 6
● Barolo Badarina '17	🍷🍷 8
● Barolo Badarina '16	🍷🍷 8
● Barolo Badarina '15	🍷🍷 7
● Barolo Badarina '12	🍷🍷 6
● Barolo Bricco Cogni '17	🍷🍷 8
● Barolo Bricco Cogni '15	🍷🍷 6
● Barolo Castagni '19	🍷🍷 6
● Barolo La Serra '16	🍷🍷 8
● Barolo Ris. '17	🍷🍷 8
● Barolo Ris. '16	🍷🍷 8

Rizzi

via Rizzi, 15
12050 Treiso [CN]
📞 +39 0173638161
🌐 www.cantinarizzi.it

CELLAR SALES
PRE-BOOKED VISITS
ANNUAL PRODUCTION 90,000 bottles
HECTARES UNDER VINE 40.00
SUSTAINABLE WINERY

Established in 1974 by Ernesto Della Piana and now run by his children, Jole and Enrico, the winery finds its heart on the Rizzi di Treiso hill, a prized vineyard location. However, the estate also offers wines from the Pajorè, Giacone and Bricco di Neive crus, drawing on a classic and clearly discernible production style that calls for aging in mostly large oak barrels. Their vineyards are rich with nebbiolo da Barbaresco, alongside barbera, dolcetto, and chardonnay grapes. The Barbaresco Pajoré '21 showcases aromas of red fruit, herbs, cinchona, and spices, with a fragrant, evenly proportioned palate. The Barbaresco Rizzi Vigna Boito Ris. '19 is notable for its vibrant aromatic profile and racy, energetic progression on the palate. The Barbaresco Rizzi '21 stands out for its nice overall focus, while the Langhe Nebbiolo '22 is citrusy, sapid, and dynamic.

● Barbaresco Pajorè '21	♟♟ 7
● Barbaresco Rizzi '21	♟♟ 5
● Barbaresco Rizzi V. Boito Ris. '19	♟♟ 8
● Langhe Nebbiolo '22	♟♟ 4
○ Alta Langa Pas Dosé '20	♟ 5
● Barbaresco Boito Ris. '10	♟♟♟ 6
● Barbaresco Nervo '14	♟♟♟ 6
● Barbaresco Nervo '19	♟♟ 7
● Barbaresco Nervo '18	♟♟ 7
● Barbaresco Pajorè '20	♟♟ 7
● Barbaresco Pajorè '19	♟♟ 7
● Barbaresco Pajorè '18	♟♟ 7
● Barbaresco Pajorè '17	♟♟ 6
● Barbaresco Rizzi V. Boito Ris. '16	♟♟ 8
● Barbaresco Rizzi V. Boito Ris. '15	♟♟ 8

★Roagna

loc. Pajé
s.da Paglieri, 7
12050 Barbaresco [CN]
📞 +39 0173635109
🌐 roagna.com

CELLAR SALES
PRE-BOOKED VISITS
ANNUAL PRODUCTION 50,000 bottles
HECTARES UNDER VINE 15.00

Roagna has been around since 1929, but its success is a much more recent story. Once almost forgotten, the winery has managed to stay true to its roots. Today, Alfredo and his son Luca have vaulted the estate into the Langhe winemaking elite, where it belongs, drawing on Barbaresco crus, Asili, Montefico, and Pajé, as well as ventures in Castiglione Falletto (Barolo Pira) and their vineyards of Derthona Timorasso. They also produce Barolo Chinato, a type that is becoming increasingly rare. The Pajè Vecchie Viti '19 exemplifies finesse and elegance, with delicate aromas of small red fruits and balsamic notes emerging on the nose. The palate shows character and clarity, unfolding through a harmonious structure and an endless finish. The Asili Vecchie Viti '19 proves multifaceted and progressive, while the Montefico Vecchie Viti '19 is fresh and finely tannic. The Barolo Pira Vecchie Viti '19 is an intriguing and dynamic drink, while the Rocche di Castiglione '19 stands out for its energy and balance

● Barbaresco Pajè V.V. '19	♟♟♟ 8
● Barbaresco Asili V.V. '19	♟♟ 8
● Barbaresco Montefico V.V. '19	♟♟ 8
● Barolo Pira V.V. '19	♟♟ 8
● Barolo Rocche di Castiglione '19	♟♟ 8
● Barbaresco Albesani '19	♟♟ 8
● Barbaresco Crichët Pajé '16	♟♟ 8
● Barbaresco Gallina '19	♟♟ 8
● Barbaresco Pajè '18	♟♟ 8
● Barbaresco Asili V.V. '18	♟♟♟ 8
● Barbaresco Asili V.V. '17	♟♟♟ 8
● Barbaresco Asili V.Viti '13	♟♟♟ 8
● Barbaresco Crichët Pajé '13	♟♟♟ 8
● Barbaresco Crichët Pajé '12	♟♟♟ 8
● Barbaresco Crichët Pajé '11	♟♟♟ 8
● Barbaresco Crichët Pajé '08	♟♟♟ 8
● Barbaresco Pajé '11	♟♟♟ 8

★Albino Rocca

s.da Ronchi, 18
12050 Barbaresco [CN]
📞 +39 0173635145
🌐 www.albinorocca.com

CELLAR SALES
PRE-BOOKED VISITS
ANNUAL PRODUCTION 100,000 bottles
HECTARES UNDER VINE 18.00
SUSTAINABLE WINERY

Daniela, Monica, and Paola Rocca (assisted by Paola's husband, Carlo Castellengo) have been managing the winery in Barbaresco since their father Angelo passed away in 2012. Giacomo Rocca began vinifying his own grapes in 1956, but the breakthrough took place in the 1980s, when Angelo, Albino's son, changed the winery's philosophy and dynamics. The vineyards feature not only nebbiolo, with the Ovello and Ronchi crus leading the way, but also cortese, moscato, and barbera. The Barbaresco Ovello Vigna Loreto '21 conjures up an elegant nose, blending red berries, roses, spices, and tobacco. In the mouth, the wine is fleshy, with a continuous, focused tannic grip and a broad, persistent finish. The rich and powerful Barbaresco Ronchi '21 is similarly vibrant, juicy, and deep.

★★Bruno Rocca

s.da Rabajà, 60
12050 Barbaresco [CN]
📞 +39 0173635112
🌐 www.brunorocca.it

ANNUAL PRODUCTION 80,000 bottles
HECTARES UNDER VINE 15.00

Founded in 1978 and led by Bruno Rocca (now with the help of his children Francesco and Luisa), this Barbaresco winery is a cornerstone of the appellation. Their range of wines features Dolcetto d'Alba, Langhe Nebbiolo, Barbera d'Alba and d'Asti, and most notably, the highly acclaimed Barbaresco Rabajà and Currà. There's also a single white based on chardonnay. The Barbaresco Maria Adelaide '19 convinces with its intensity, blending balsamic herbs and light graphite touches over a focused base of fruit. On the palate, the wine is generous and persistent, with a powerful, juicy development and a broad, lingering finish. The Barbaresco Rabajà '20 is also delicious, playing on aromas of small red fruits and balsamic hints before a focused, flavorful palate with a long finish.

● Barbaresco Ovello V. Loreto '21	♥♥	7
● Barbaresco Ronchi '21	♥♥	7
● Barbaresco Ronchi Ris. '19	♥♥	8
● Barbaresco Cottà '21	♥♥	6
● Barbaresco Angelo '19	♥♥♥	5
● Barbaresco Angelo '13	♥♥♥	5
● Barbaresco Ovello V. Loreto '16	♥♥♥	6
● Barbaresco Ovello V. Loreto '11	♥♥♥	6
● Barbaresco Ovello V. Loreto '09	♥♥♥	6
● Barbaresco Ovello V. Loreto '07	♥♥♥	6
● Barbaresco Ronchi '10	♥♥♥	6
● Barbaresco Vign. Brich Ronchi '05	♥♥♥	6
● Barbaresco Vign. Brich Ronchi '03	♥♥♥	6
● Barbaresco Vign. Brich Ronchi '00	♥♥♥	6
● Barbaresco Vign. Brich Ronchi Ris. '06	♥♥♥	8
● Barbaresco Vign. Brich Ronchi Ris. '04	♥♥♥	8
● Barbaresco Vign. Loreto '04	♥♥♥	6

● Barbaresco Maria Adelaide '19	♥♥	8
● Barbaresco Rabajà '20	♥♥	8
● Barbaresco Currà '20	♥♥	8
● Barbaresco Coparossa '04	♥♥♥	8
● Barbaresco Currà Ris. '13	♥♥♥	8
● Barbaresco Currà Ris. '12	♥♥♥	8
● Barbaresco Maria Adelaide '07	♥♥♥	8
● Barbaresco Maria Adelaide '04	♥♥♥	8
● Barbaresco Maria Adelaide '01	♥♥♥	8
● Barbaresco Rabajà '16	♥♥♥	8
● Barbaresco Rabajà '13	♥♥♥	8
● Barbaresco Rabajà '12	♥♥♥	8
● Barbaresco Rabajà '11	♥♥♥	8
● Barbaresco Rabajà '10	♥♥♥	8
● Barbaresco Rabajà '09	♥♥♥	8
● Barbaresco Rabajà Ris. '15	♥♥♥	8

Rocche Costamagna

via Vittorio Emanuele, 8
12064 La Morra [CN]
+39 0173509225
www.roccheCostamagna.it

CELLAR SALES
PRE-BOOKED VISITS
ACCOMMODATION
ANNUAL PRODUCTION 95,000 bottles
HECTARES UNDER VINE 15.80

Rocche Costamagna is one of the oldest wineries in Barolo, recognized as a major producer in the area since 1841. Today, Alessandro Locatelli, who has been with the winery since the 1980s, is at the helm, maintaining a style that adheres to a healthy tradition. Undoubtedly, both now and in the past, the La Morra-based estate's success can be traced back to the Rocche dell'Annunziata cru, which produces their flagship. The Barolo Rocche dell'Annunziata '20 features a focused aromatic profile with notes of ripe red fruit, tobacco, licorice, and spices. On the palate, it's clearly defined, with a firm structure, making for a persistent, sapid, and pervasive drink. The Barbera d'Alba Sup. Rocche delle Rocche '20 goes all in on a pleasantly approachable, easy-drinking profile.

● Barolo Rocche dell'Annunziata '20	TT 7
● Barbera d'Alba Sup. Rocche delle Rocche '20	T 4
● Barolo '20	T 7
● Barolo Rocche dell'Annunziata '04	YYY 5
● Barbera d'Alba Sup. Rocche delle Rocche '17	YY 4
● Barolo Rocche dell'Annunziata '19	YY 6
● Barolo Rocche dell'Annunziata '18	YY 6
● Barolo Rocche dell'Annunziata '17	YY 6
● Barolo Rocche dell'Annunziata '16	YY 6
● Barolo Rocche dell'Annunziata Bricco Francesco Ris. '15	YY 8
● Barolo Rocche dell'Annunziata Bricco Francesco Ris. '13	YY 8

Il Rocchin

loc. Vallemme, 39
15066 Gavi [AL]
+39 0143642228
www.ilrocchin.it

CELLAR SALES
PRE-BOOKED VISITS
ANNUAL PRODUCTION 50,000 bottles
HECTARES UNDER VINE 20.00

Founded by the Zerbo family, this winery has long aimed to highlight the attributes of the terroir, focusing on native varietals such as cortese, dolcetto, and barbera. In recent years, the estate has expanded its hospitality and wine tourism offerings, promoting outdoor activities and events in the vineyard. Based in an 18th-century farmhouse, the winery employs modern, environmentally respectful production methods. Their wines are deeply tied to the land, striving for precision and clarity of fruit. The 2023 version of the Gavi Il Bosco is lively, vibrant and sunny. It pours a bright straw-yellow color, releasing notes of flowers and white fruit over an elegant mineral base. On the palate, it's powerful, showing great character with a long, sapid finish. The Gavi del Comune di Gavi is also delicious (and already fairly complex), offering aromas of fresh herbs, ferns, wildflowers, and almonds. Full and fleshy on the palate, it showcases a steady persistence.

○ Gavi del Comune di Gavi Il Bosco '22	TT 3*
○ Gavi del Comune di Gavi '23	TT 3
○ Gavi '23	T 2
● Barbera del M.to Il Basacco '17	YY 3*
● Dolcetto di Ovada '19	YY 2*
● Dolcetto di Ovada '18	YY 2*
○ Gavi '22	YY 2*
○ Gavi '21	YY 2*
○ Gavi del Comune di Gavi '22	YY 3
○ Gavi del Comune di Gavi '21	YY 2*
○ Gavi del Comune di Gavi '20	YY 2*
○ Gavi del Comune di Gavi '19	YY 2*
○ Gavi del Comune di Gavi '17	YY 2*
○ Gavi del Comune di Gavi Il Bosco '20	YY 3*
○ Gavi del Comune di Gavi Il Bosco '17	YY 3*
● Piemonte Barbera '20	YY 2*

★Giovanni Rosso

via Roddino, 10/1
12050 Serralunga d'Alba [CN]
☎ +39 0173613340
✉ www.giovannirosso.com

CELLAR SALES
PRE-BOOKED VISITS
ANNUAL PRODUCTION 130,000 bottles
HECTARES UNDER VINE 18.00

Under the direction of Davide Rosso, this winery has achieved a notable level of stylistic precision, skillfully interpreting nebbiolo with traditional wisdom and impeccable craftsmanship. The Barolo Vigna Rionda Ester Canale, their flagship, is produced in limited quantities, but it encapsulates the quintessence of a celebrated vineyard—one of the legendary sites for enthusiasts of Langhe's great wines, and a true altar in the Barolo sanctuary that is Serralunga. When it seemed impossible to repeat last year's incredible performance, Davide Rosso and his capable young team prove otherwise. The Vigna Rionda '20 may not have the exuberance of the 2019, but it compensates with an extremely delicate and precise tannic structure, delivering the same magic in the end. The Nebbiolo Ester Canale Rosso '21 is richer than the Barolo but lacks its class. Between the Serra and the Cerretta, this year we favor the latter, which is fuller and more immediately enjoyable than the Serra.

● Barolo Vigna Rionda Ester Canale Rosso '20	♟♟♟ 8
● Barolo Cerretta '20	♟♟ 8
● Langhe Nebbiolo Ester Canale Rosso '21	♟♟ 8
● Barolo Serra '20	♟♟ 8
● Barolo Serra '15	♟♟♟ 8
● Barolo Vigna Rionda Ester Canale Rosso '19	♟♟♟ 8
● Barolo Vigna Rionda Ester Canale Rosso '18	♟♟♟ 8
● Barolo Vigna Rionda Ester Canale Rosso '17	♟♟♟ 8
● Barolo Vigna Rionda Ester Canale Rosso '16	♟♟♟ 8
● Barolo Vigna Rionda Ester Canale Rosso '14	♟♟♟ 8

Poderi Rosso Giovanni

p.zza Roma, 36/37
14041 Agliano Terme [AT]
☎ +39 0141954006
✉ www.rossowines.it

CELLAR SALES
PRE-BOOKED VISITS
ANNUAL PRODUCTION 67,000 bottles
HECTARES UNDER VINE 12.00
SUSTAINABLE WINERY

The Rosso family, now in its third generation with Lionello, manages this Agliano Terme winery. About 12 hectares of vineyards are cultivated in the heart of Monferrato, in Cascina Perno and Cascina San Sebastiano. The marl and calcareous soils are predominantly planted with barbera. Indeed they produce some 4 versions, divided by vineyard and age. There's also a bit of cabernet sauvignon used in blends. This year saw a splendid performance from their wines. The Barbera d'Asti Superiore Cascina Perno '22 summons aromas of cherry and blackberry, with a grippy, well-structured, and long palate—juicy and flavorful. The Nizza Riserva Gioco dell'Oca '21 proves vibrant, with fresh and pleasant fruity and spicy aromas, a rich and fruit-filled palate, and a fine overall balance. The Barbera d'Asti San Bastian '23, with its tones of ripe red fruit and hints of rain-soaked earth, comes through fleshy and full on the palate, finishing long with a tension and clarity that verge on austerity.

● Barbera d'Asti San Bastian '23	♟♟ 2*
● Barbera d'Asti Sup. Cascina Perno '22	♟♟ 3*
● Nizza Gioco dell'Oca Ris. '21	♟♟ 6
● Barbera d'Asti Sup. Carlinet '21	♟♟ 4
● Barbera d'Asti San Bastian '22	♟♟ 2*
● Barbera d'Asti San Bastian '21	♟♟ 2*
● Barbera d'Asti San Bastian '20	♟♟ 2*
● Barbera d'Asti Sup. Carlinet '20	♟♟ 4
● Barbera d'Asti Sup. Carlinet '19	♟♟ 4
● Barbera d'Asti Sup. Carlinet '18	♟♟ 4
● Barbera d'Asti Sup. Cascina Perno '21	♟♟ 3
● Barbera d'Asti Sup. Cascina Perno '20	♟♟ 3
● Barbera d'Asti Sup. Cascina Perno '19	♟♟ 3*
● Nizza Gioco dell'Oca Ris. '20	♟♟ 6
● Nizza Gioco dell'Oca Ris. '19	♟♟ 6
● Nizza Gioco dell'Oca Ris. '17	♟♟ 6

Josetta Saffirio

loc. Castelletto, 39
12065 Monforte d'Alba [CN]
☎ +39 0173787278
✉ jwww.osettasaffirio.com

CELLAR SALES
PRE-BOOKED VISITS
ANNUAL PRODUCTION 30,000 bottles
HECTARES UNDER VINE 5.00
VITICULTURE METHOD Certified Organic
SUSTAINABLE WINERY

Wines under the Josetta Saffirio label have been produced since the 1980s. Today the Monforte d'Alba producer is run by Sara Vezza who, over the years, has merged her personal brand with that of the winery—she's also partnered with fashion entrepreneur Renzo Rosso. Alongside all this, she produces sparkling wines and other selections carried over from the original winery, drawing on barbera, nebbiolo, and rossese grapes. The Barolo Persiera '20 has a flavorful and mature profile, recalling strawberry preserves, with nice grip on the palate. It's a supple wine, with decent length and tannic harmony. The Riserva Millenovecento48 leans more toward tones of cinchona and sweet spices. The Saffirio, concentrated in its aromas of red fruits, is fine and energetic on the palate, though marked by tannins with a fairly long finish. Darker with more prominent sweet-spice notes, the Barolo Perno sees a slightly less relaxed progression on the palate.

San Fereolo

loc. San Fereolo
b.ta Valdibà, 59
12063 Dogliani [CN]
☎ +39 0173742075
✉ www.sanfereolo.com

PRE-BOOKED VISITS
ANNUAL PRODUCTION 46,000 bottles
HECTARES UNDER VINE 12.00

Nicoletta Bocca founded her winery in 1992 in Rocca Cigliè, a small town in Mondovì. Nicoletta, who used to work in the fashion industry, has opted for an environmentally conscious approach to production, and some of her vineyards are quite old, lending her wines a complexity not always found in Dogliano. The plots are scattered across various parts of the municipality, including Austri, Cerri, Costabella, San Fereolo, and Le Coste di Riavolo. The Dogliani Superiore San Fereolo '17 stands out for its focused aromatic profile and rare fruit richness, calling up blackberries on the nose. On the palate, it's equally full and generous, yet never heavy, with a dynamic structure that concludes in a broad finish where fruit makes an encore. The Dogliani Vigne Dolci '22 is well-crafted, opting for black fruit aromas and an enjoyable palate.

Barolo Persiera '20	♥♥ 8
Barolo Millenovecento48 Ris. '18	♥♥ 8
Barolo Saffirio '20	♥♥ 6
Barolo Perno '19	♥ 8
Barolo Ravera '20	♥ 8
Langhe Rossese Bianco '22	♥ 3
Barolo '89	♥♥♥ 6
Barolo '88	♥♥♥ 6
Barolo Millenovecento48 Ris. '16	♥♥ 8
Barolo Perno '18	♥♥ 8
Barolo Ravera '19	♥♥ 8
Barolo Ravera '18	♥♥ 8

● Dogliani Sup. San Fereolo '17	♥♥ 5
● Dogliani Sup. Valdibà '22	♥♥ 4
● Dogliani Sup. Vigne Dolci '22	♥♥ 5
● Langhe Nebbiolo Il Provinciale '19	♥♥ 5
⊙ Langhe Rosato La Lupa '23	♥♥ 5
○ Coste di Valanche '22	♥ 6
● Langhe Rosso Austri '19	♥ 6
○ Terra Celeste '21	♥ 6
● Dogliani Sup. Vigneti Dolci '17	♥♥♥ 3*
● Dolcetto di Dogliani S. Fereolo '99	♥♥♥ 2*
● Dolcetto di Dogliani S. Fereolo '97	♥♥♥ 2*
● Langhe Rosso Austri '03	♥♥♥ 5
● Langhe Rosso Brumaio '97	♥♥♥ 4*
● Dogliani Sup. Valdibà '21	♥♥ 3*
● Dogliani Sup. Vigne Dolci '21	♥♥ 3*
● Langhe Nebbiolo Il Provinciale '20	♥♥ 5

Tenuta San Sebastiano

Cascina San Sebastiano, 41
15040 Lu [AL]
☎ +39 0131741353
✆ www.dealessi.it

★★Luciano Sandrone

via Pugnane, 4
12060 Barolo [CN]
☎ +39 0173560023
✆ www.sandroneluciano.com

CELLAR SALES
PRE-BOOKED VISITS
ANNUAL PRODUCTION 70,000 bottles
HECTARES UNDER VINE 9.00

PRE-BOOKED VISITS
ANNUAL PRODUCTION 110,000 bottles
HECTARES UNDER VINE 27.00
SUSTAINABLE WINERY

Tenuta San Sebastiano is renowned for the passion and dedication Roberto De Alessi brings to running the estate, following a long family tradition. The winery is known for producing an authentic and refined range, with a focus on native varietals like barbera and grignolino. At the same time, they embrace innovation, incorporating modern technology in the cellar while also experimenting with international grapes, such as cabernet franc, pinot nero, and chardonnay. Always a sure bet, this year the Grignolino Monfiorato '19 pours a vibrant, brilliant color. The nose is bursting with pepper and tobacco, followed by licorice and violet. Majestic on the palate, delicate tannins and a nice fleshiness emerge, finishing incredibly long. The Barbera del Monferrato '22 also sports a bright ruby hue. It's a highly refined and complex wine, lacking some depth but compensated by a fresh acidity that ensures its appeal.

Luciano Sandrone revolutionized the way Barolo was conceived in 1979, paving the way for the "Barolo Boys" and a healthy stylistic debate. His wines are a benchmark of excellence, known for their impeccable craftsmanship and crystal-clear technical skill, marking the most recent chapter in Langa's wine history. Following Luciano's recent passing in 2023, the estate is run by Luciano Sandrone's brother Luca and his daughter Barbara. Vitality and elegance characterize the Barolo Le Vigne '20, with raspberry, tobacco, licorice, and smoky hints emerging on the nose. On the palate, it's fleshy and dynamic, with a vibrant, fragrant palate that never loses its intensity, leading to a broad, lingering finish. Ripe, lush fruit with toasty and spicy nuances feature in the Barolo Aleste '20; a firm and clearly defined development of flavor follows.

● Piemonte Grignolino Monfiorato '19	♟♟ 4
● Barbera del M.to '22	♟♟ 4
○ M.to Bianco Disneuf '19	♟♟ 4
● Barbera del M.to Sup. Mepari '21	♟ 4
○ Piemonte Viognier Sperilium '22	♟ 3
● Barbera del M.to '20	♟♟ 4
● Barbera del M.to Sup. Mepari '20	♟♟ 4
● Barbera del M.to Sup. Mepari '19	♟♟ 4
● M.to Nebbiolo Capolinea '20	♟♟ 2*
● M.to Nebbiolo Capolinea '19	♟♟ 3
● M.to Rosso Daler '20	♟♟ 3
● Piemonte Grignolino Monfiorato '18	♟♟ 5
● Piemonte Grignolino Monfiorato '16	♟♟ 4
○ Piemonte Viognier Sperilium '21	♟♟ 3

● Barolo Aleste '20	♟♟ 8
● Barolo Le Vigne '20	♟♟ 8
● Nebbiolo d'Alba Valmaggiore '22	♟♟ 5
● Barolo Aleste '17	♟♟♟ 8
● Barolo Aleste '15	♟♟♟ 8
● Barolo Cannubi Boschis '11	♟♟♟ 8
● Barolo Cannubi Boschis '10	♟♟♟ 8
● Barolo Cannubi Boschis '08	♟♟♟ 8
● Barolo Cannubi Boschis '07	♟♟♟ 8
● Barolo Cannubi Boschis '06	♟♟♟ 8
● Barolo Cannubi Boschis '05	♟♟♟ 8
● Barolo Cannubi Boschis '04	♟♟♟ 8
● Barolo Cannubi Boschis '03	♟♟♟ 8
● Barolo Cannubi Boschis '01	♟♟♟ 8
● Barolo Cannubi Boschis '00	♟♟♟ 8
● Barolo Le Vigne '99	♟♟♟ 8

Cantine Sant'Agata

fraz. Regione Mezzena, 19
14030 Scurzolengo [AT]
☎ +39 041203186
🌐 www.tenimentifamigliacavallero.com

CELLAR SALES
PRE-BOOKED VISITS
RESTAURANT SERVICE
ANNUAL PRODUCTION 60,000 bottles
HECTARES UNDER VINE 12.00
SUSTAINABLE WINERY

The Cavallero family winery, established in the early 19th century, is one of the leading producers of wines made from ruché, with several versions offered. The estate's vineyards, spread out across various municipalities and appellations, from Portacomaro to Gavi to Monforte d'Alba, also host barbera, cortese, and nebbiolo. Their production methods are modern, making for wines characterized by a clean, technically precise profile. The Ruché di Castagnole Monferrato 'Na Vota '23 opens with classic, refined notes of rose and plum. A notably structured palate follows, where pervasive tannins provide length and density without sacrificing balance. Both their Ruché di Castagnole Monferrato Riserva wines are well-crafted. The enveloping and full Hereditarium '20 features aromas of licorice and red fruits, while the Pro Nobis '21, with its floral tones, showcases nice body, freshness and length. The Monferrato Nebbiolo Superiore Il Cavaliere '22 is a dense, tannic, and energetic drink.

Tenuta Santa Caterina

via Guglielmo Marconi, 17
14035 Grazzano Badoglio [AT]
☎ +39 0141925108
🌐 www.tenuta-santa-caterina.it

CELLAR SALES
PRE-BOOKED VISITS
ACCOMMODATION
ANNUAL PRODUCTION 50,000 bottles
HECTARES UNDER VINE 23.00

Guido Alleva and Luciana Biondo are a well-established winemaking duo, known for planting new vineyards of grignolino, including plots in the Casale area. One of the hallmarks of this beautiful Piedmont winery is its deep connection to this noble, rebellious varietal, of which they are proud champions. Conversion to organic farming is nearly complete, and the cellar remains steadfast in its adherence to tradition. They've also recently published their first Sustainability Report. Tenuta Santa Caterina submitted a high-quality lineup this year. The Grignolino d'Asti Monferace '19 is excellent, emanating intriguing notes of dried flowers, white truffle, pepper, and licorice, making for a complex and elegant nose. The palate is powerful and close-knit, with a tannic structure that carries its aromas and flavors far. The Barbera d'Asti Superiore Vignalina '21 is also outstanding, rich but endowed with a balsamic touch and lively acidity that refreshes the palate.

Ruché di Castagnole M.to 'Na Vota '23	♟♟ 3*
M.to Nebbiolo Sup. Il Cavaliere '22	♟♟ 5
Ruché di Castagnole M.to Hereditarium Ris. '20	♟♟ 5
Ruché di Castagnole M.to Pro Nobis Ris. '21	♟♟ 4
Barbera d'Asti Sup. Altea '22	♟ 3
Barbera d'Asti Sup. Altea '20	♟♟ 3
Barbera d'Asti Sup. Altea '19	♟♟ 3*
Barbera d'Asti Sup. Cavalé '20	♟♟ 5
Barolo La Fenice '19	♟♟ 6
Ruché di Castagnole M.to 'Na Vota '22	♟♟ 3*
Ruché di Castagnole M.to 'Na Vota '21	♟♟ 3
Ruché di Castagnole M.to 'Na Vota '20	♟♟ 3
Ruché di Castagnole M.to 'Na Vota '19	♟♟ 3
Ruché di Castagnole M.to Il Cavaliere '21	♟♟ 2*
Ruché di Castagnole M.to Il Cavaliere '19	♟♟ 2*

● Grignolino d'Asti Monferace '19	♟♟♟ 6
● Barbera d'Asti Sup. Vignalina '21	♟♟ 4
○ M.to Bianco Silente delle Marne '20	♟♟ 6
● M.to Nebbiolo Sup. Illegale '21	♟♟ 5
● Barbera d'Asti Sup. Setecàpita '19	♟♟ 5
● Grignolino d'Asti Arlandino '22	♟♟ 3
○ Guido Carlo Extra Brut M. Cl. '19	♟♟ 7
● Grignolino d'Asti Monferace '18	♟♟♟ 6
● Grignolino d'Asti Monferace '17	♟♟♟ 6
● Grignolino d'Asti Monferace '16	♟♟♟ 6
● Grignolino d'Asti Monferace '15	♟♟♟ 5
● Barbera d'Asti Sup. Setecàpita '18	♟♟ 5
● Grignolino d'Asti Arlandino '21	♟♟ 3*
● Grignolino d'Asti Arlandino '20	♟♟ 3*
○ M.to Bianco Silente delle Marne '17	♟♟ 5

Roberto Sarotto

via Ronconuovo, 13
12050 Neviglie [CN]
(☏ +39 0173630228
✆ www.robertosarotto.com

CELLAR SALES
PRE-BOOKED VISITS
ANNUAL PRODUCTION 900,000 bottles
HECTARES UNDER VINE 90.00
SUSTAINABLE WINERY

Roberto Sarotto's Barolo vineyards are split between Barolo and San Ponzio Novello (the Bergera-Pezzole and Pallaretta production zones). In the 1990s, Sarotto brought about a pivotal change to the family winery, expanding the estate with vineyards in Barbaresco and later in Gavi. He also introduced a wider range of varietals, from arneis and chardonnay to brachetto and cabernet sauvignon. Significant progress has been made in the many wine-growing areas overseen by Roberto Sarotto, starting with the Alba region, where the producer's Barolo and Barbaresco reflect a more restrained use of oak and extraction, resulting in greater finesse compared to the past. This buoyant style, which we'd expect more from a Barbera d'Alba, makes for a splendid version of the Elena e La Luna, rich with aromas of plum preserves and hints of clove, featuring a dense and vigorous structure. As always, both Gavi are excellent.

● Barbera d'Alba Elena La Luna '22	▼▼▼ 4*
○ Gavi del Comune di Gavi Bric Sassi Tenuta Manenti '23	▼▼ 2*
○ Alta Langa Dosaggio Zero '18	▼▼ 5
● Barbaresco Currà Ris. '19	▼▼ 5
● Barolo ai Fondatori Ris. '16	▼▼ 6
● Barolo Bergera-Pezzole Audace '20	▼▼ 6
● Barolo Bergera-Pezzole Briccobergera '20	▼▼ 5
○ Gavi del Comune di Parodi Aurora '23	▼▼ 3
○ Langhe Arneis Srej '23	▼▼ 2*
● Langhe Nebbiolo Nativo '22	▼▼ 3
● Langhe Rosso Enrico I '22	▼▼ 7
○ Moscato d'Asti Solatìo '23	▼▼ 2*
● Barbaresco Gaia Principe '21	▼ 6
○ Langhe Arneis Runcneuv '23	▼ 2
● Langhe Rosso Lautus '22	▼ 3

Scagliola - Sansì

via San Siro, 42
14052 Calosso [AT]
(☏ +39 0141853183
✆ www.scagliolavini.com

CELLAR SALES
PRE-BOOKED VISITS
ANNUAL PRODUCTION 350,000 bottles
HECTARES UNDER VINE 40.00

The Scagliola family's historic winery, now in its fifth generation with Martina and Federica, has nearly 90 years of history behind it. Their barbera highlights the area's rich tufa and sandy soils interlaced with bands of limestone, a mix that provides body and freshness to the wines. Their moscato, on the other hand, reflects Canelli's layers of fine sand and marl. The estate is based in San Siro di Calosso, at about 400 meters elevation, on a hill between Monferrato and Langhe. The Barbera d'Asti Superiore Sansì '21 opens on aromas of black fruit and tobacco, while the palate is close-knit and dense, leading to a harmonious and characterful finish. The Nizza Forvia '21 reveals notes of petrichor and black stone fruits, with spicy nuances; it's a well-structured, lengthy wine, and taut. The Moscato d'Asti Volo di Farfalle '23, on the other hand, showcases aromas of herbs and candied orange peel, leading to a harmonious palate with a lingering finish, where varietal tones of sage and mandarin emerge.

● Barbera d'Asti Sup. Sansì '21	▼▼▼ 6
○ Moscato d'Asti Volo di Farfalle '23	▼▼ 4
● Nizza Forvia '21	▼▼ 6
● Barbera d'Asti Frem '22	▼▼ 4
● Monferrato Rosso Azörd '21	▼▼ 6
● Barbera d'Asti Frem '20	▼▼▼ 4
● Barbera d'Asti Sup. SanSì Sel. '01	▼▼▼ 6
● Barbera d'Asti Sup. SanSì Sel. '00	▼▼▼ 6
● Barbera d'Asti Sup. SanSì Sel. '99	▼▼▼ 5
○ Moscato d'Asti Volo di Farfalle '20	▼▼▼ 3
● Barbera d'Asti Frem '21	▼▼ 4
● Barbera d'Asti Frem '18	▼▼ 4
○ Moscato d'Asti Volo di Farfalle '21	▼▼ 4
○ Moscato d'Asti Volo di Farfalle '19	▼▼ 3
● Nizza Foravia '19	▼▼ 5
● Nizza Forvia '20	▼▼ 6

Scarpa

via Montegrappa, 6
14049 Nizza Monferrato [AT]
☎ +39 3407730621721331
✉ www.scarpawine.com

CELLAR SALES
PRE-BOOKED VISITS
ANNUAL PRODUCTION 150,000 bottles
HECTARES UNDER VINE 30.00
SUSTAINABLE WINERY

In recent years, the winery has been working to recapture the success of its past, refreshing its winemaking style without abandoning traditional techniques. Their aim is to produce wines that reflect the terroir while showcasing aromatic clarity. The grapes are cultivated in Monferrato (in Castel Rocchero and Acqui Terme, where the La Bogliona vineyard is situated) and Langhe (in Neive, La Morra, and Verduno). The historic Barbera d'Asti Superiore La Bogliona shines. The 2019 vintage exudes aromas of wild blackberries and Mediterranean scrub—a juicy and sapid palate follows with good structure. The rest of the lineup is well-crafted, particularly the soft yet powerful Barbaresco Tettineive '20, a vibrant pour redolent of dried herbs and underbrush, the Barolo Monvigliero '19, where tannins are still a bit prominent but balanced by good fruit and fullness, and the Barbera d'Asti Casascarpa '22, whose aromas of tapenade and plum give way to a juicy, fruit-rich, approachable and enjoyable palate.

Giorgio Scarzello e Figli

via Alba, 29
12060 Barolo [CN]
☎ +39 017356170
✉ www.scarzellobarolo.com

CELLAR SALES
PRE-BOOKED VISITS
ANNUAL PRODUCTION 45,000 bottles
HECTARES UNDER VINE 6.50

Giorgio Scarzello, who passed away in 2023, left his winemaking legacy in good hands. His son, Federico, continues his work with renewed consistency, producing wines with a classic and compelling style that remains deeply connected to their place of origin. Their Barolos hail from renowned vineyards such as Sarmassa, Boschetti, and Terlo, while the barbera is sourced from the Paiagallo cru. The Barolo del Comune di Barolo '20 impresses with its generous, vibrant fruit on the nose, alongside spicy, balsamic, and smoky whiffs. In the mouth, resolved tannins are well integrated with the fruit's flesh, making for a juicy, focused palate with an airy, evenly-proportioned finish. The Barolo Sarmassa Vigna Merenda '20 proves well-crafted, with aromas of small red fruits and quinine adorning an austere and still quite young flavor profile.

Barbera d'Asti Sup. La Bogliona '19	♟♟ 7
Barbaresco Tettineive '20	♟♟ 7
Barbera d'Asti CasaScarpa '22	♟♟ 3
Barolo Monvigliero '19	♟♟ 8
M.to Rosso Rouchet '20	♟♟ 5
Nebbiolo Bric Du Nota '22	♟♟ 5
Verduno Pelaverga '23	♟ 4
Rouchet Briccorosa '90	♟♟♟ 5
Barbaresco Tettineive '19	♟♟ 7
Barbera d'Asti Sup. La Bogliona '17	♟♟ 6
Barbera d'Asti Sup. La Bogliona '16	♟♟ 6
Barbera d'Asti Sup. La Bogliona '15	♟♟ 5
Barolo Monvigliero '18	♟♟ 8
Barolo Tettimorra '19	♟♟ 7
Barolo Tettimorra '18	♟♟ 7
M.to Rosso Rouchet '19	♟♟ 5

● Barolo del Comune di Barolo '20	♟♟ 7
● Barolo Sarmassa V. Merenda '20	♟♟ 8
● Barbera d'Alba Sup. '21	♟ 5
● Langhe Nebbiolo '22	♟ 4
● Barolo Sarmassa V. Merenda '17	♟♟♟ 8
● Barolo Sarmassa V. Merenda '10	♟♟♟ 6
● Barolo V. Merenda '99	♟♟♟ 5
● Barolo Boschetti '19	♟♟ 8
● Barolo Boschetti '18	♟♟ 8
● Barolo Boschetti '17	♟♟ 8
● Barolo del Comune di Barolo '16	♟♟ 7
● Barolo del Comune di Barolo '15	♟♟ 7
● Barolo del Comune di Barolo '13	♟♟ 5
● Barolo Sarmassa V. Merenda '19	♟♟ 8
● Barolo Sarmassa V. Merenda '18	♟♟ 8
● Barolo Sarmassa V. Merenda '15	♟♟ 8

★★Paolo Scavino

fraz. Garbelletto
via Alba-Barolo, 157
12060 Castiglione Falletto [CN]
📞 +39 017362850
🌐 www.paoloscavino.com

CELLAR SALES
PRE-BOOKED VISITS
ANNUAL PRODUCTION 130,000 bottles
HECTARES UNDER VINE 29.00

Enrico Scavino, along with his daughters Enrica and Elisa, runs the family winery in Castiglione Falletto. The estate's vineyards form a prized mosaic, reaching into many of the Barolo appellation's most important areas, including Castiglione Falletto, Barolo, La Morra, Novello, Serralunga d'Alba, Verduno, Roddi, and Monforte d'Alba. Their flagship, the Bric del Fiasc, which they've been producing since 1978, hails from the hills of Castiglione Falletto. The Barolo Bric dël Fiasc '20 captivates with its fragrant nose, interweaving lush fruit, spices, and balsamic tones. The palate is powerful, sapid, and dense, with a multifaceted development and a very long finish that returns to fruit and balsamic touches. The intense Barolo Monvigliero '20 features focused aromas of fruit and licorice, accompanying a flavorful, juicy, and deep palate. The mouthfilling and pervasive Barolo Paolo Scavino Riserva '16, still showing youthful elements, stands out as well.

● Barolo Bric dël Fiasc '20	🍷🍷	8
● Barolo Monvigliero '20	🍷🍷	8
● Barolo Bricco Ambrogio '20	🍷🍷	8
● Barolo Paolo Scavino Ris. '16	🍷🍷	8
● Barolo Enrico Scavino '20	🍷	7
● Barolo Prapò '20	🍷	8
● Barolo Ravera '20	🍷	8
● Barolo Bric dël Fiasc '18	🍷🍷🍷	8
● Barolo Bric dël Fiasc '16	🍷🍷🍷	8
● Barolo Bric dël Fiasc '12	🍷🍷🍷	8
● Barolo Bric dël Fiasc '11	🍷🍷🍷	8
● Barolo Bric dël Fiasc '09	🍷🍷🍷	8
● Barolo Monvigliero '08	🍷🍷🍷	8
● Barolo Novantesimo Ris. '11	🍷🍷🍷	8
● Barolo Rocche dell'Annunziata Ris. '11	🍷🍷🍷	8
● Barolo Rocche dell'Annunziata Ris. '08	🍷🍷🍷	8

Mauro Sebaste

fraz. Gallo d'Alba
via Garibaldi, 222bis
12051 Alba [CN]
📞 +39 0173262148
🌐 www.maurosebaste.it

CELLAR SALES
PRE-BOOKED VISITS
ANNUAL PRODUCTION 120,000 bottles
HECTARES UNDER VINE 30.00
SUSTAINABLE WINERY

Mauro Sebaste established his winery in 1991, in Alba, after leaving his family's estate, which was led by his mother, Sylla (known as "La Dama di Langa"). Today, he runs the winery with his wife Maria Teresa and their daughters, Sylla and Angelica. The grapes for their Barolos come from Serralunga d'Alba, La Morra, Verduno, and Monforte d'Alba; their Dolcetto and Barbera d'Alba plots lie in Diano d'Alba and Grinzane Cavour; their Nizzas hail from Vinchio and Nizza Monferrato; and their Alta Langas are sourced from Mango, Montelupo, and Diano d'Alba. The Barolo Ghè Riserva '18 opens with vibrant fruity notes on a spicy and balsamic background. On the palate, it unfolds light yet multifaceted, with firm, focused tannins that add rhythm and energy to its progression, culminating in a broad, flavorful finish. The sapid and rich Alta Langa Dosaggio Zero Avremo '20 passes from aromas of small red fruits to bread crust and light citrus tones. In the mouth, its bubbles are nicely calibrated, making for a lively and evenly proportioned palate.

○ Alta Langa Dosaggio Zero Avremo '20	🍷🍷	5
● Barolo Ghè Ris. '18	🍷🍷	8
● Barolo Cerretta '20	🍷	8
● Barolo Tresüri '20	🍷	6
○ Alta Langa Dosaggio Zero Avremo '18	🍷🍷	5
● Barbera d'Alba Sup. Centobricchi '22	🍷🍷	5
● Barbera d'Alba Sup. Centobricchi '20	🍷🍷	5
● Barolo Cerretta '18	🍷🍷	8
● Barolo Cerretta '17	🍷🍷	8
● Barolo Cerretta '15	🍷🍷	6
● Barolo Ghe Ris. '14	🍷🍷	8
● Barolo Ghè Ris. '12	🍷🍷	8
● Barolo Prapò '11	🍷🍷	7
● Barolo Tresüri '19	🍷🍷	6
○ Langhe Bianco Centobricchi '22	🍷🍷	5
● Nebbiolo d'Alba Parigi '22	🍷🍷	5

Tenute Sella

via IV Novembre, 130
13060 Lessona [BI]
(+39 01599455
www.tenutesella.it

CELLAR SALES
PRE-BOOKED VISITS
ANNUAL PRODUCTION 70,000 bottles
HECTARES UNDER VINE 23.00
SUSTAINABLE WINERY

This historic estate was founded by Cosimo Sella, who in 1671 acquired a vineyard in Lessona, in the province of Biella. For over 350 years, the family has preserved and passed down the culture and values of quality winemaking, honoring the traditions of the region. Their vineyards are located in Lessona, where the soil consists of acidic marine sands, and in the heavily wooded Bramaterra to the east, where the land is characterized by red volcanic porphyry alongside sands of marine origin and clays. The dynamic and characterful Lessona '19 features a nose of floral and fruity notes of black plum and pomegranate, with spicy and mineral nuances and balsamic hints. The palate is juicy and flavorful, with silky, integrated tannins and a persistent, extremely pleasant finish. The Quintino Sella '15 is darker and more floral, while the San Sebastiano allo Zoppo '15 proves ethereal and evolved.

★Enrico Serafino

c.so Asti, 5
12043 Canale [CN]
(+39 0173970474
www.enricoserafino.it

CELLAR SALES
PRE-BOOKED VISITS
ANNUAL PRODUCTION 360,000 bottles
HECTARES UNDER VINE 60.00
SUSTAINABLE WINERY

Enrico Serafino is increasingly focused on Alta Langa spumante and wines from their Langa vineyards, including Barolo and Barbaresco. The area's classic varietals are cultivated, along with chardonnay and pinot nero for the production of Metodo Classico. Theirs is a modern range characterized by superb technical rigor and aromatic precision. Their Alta Langa sparkling wines are always first rate. The Rosé de Saignée Zero Riserva '18 opens with floral notes, wild red berries, and custard, while the palate is harmonious, flavorful, with nice structure and energy, and a long finish. The Pas Dosé Zero Sboccatura Tardiva Riserva '18 reveals aromas of herbs, raspberry, and red currant, with good body and depth, while the Extra Brut M+M 18 Perpetuelle Sbagliato 15 20 '18 proves austere, taut, and well-structured. The Barolo '20 is also well-crafted: rich in fruit, with notes of licorice, tobacco, and anise. A balanced wine with well-managed tannins.

Lessona '19	♟♟ 5
Lessona Omaggio a Quintino Sella '15	♟♟ 7
Lessona S. Sebastiano allo Zoppo '15	♟ 8
Bramaterra I Porfidi '07	♟♟♟ 5
Bramaterra I Porfidi '05	♟♟♟ 5
Bramaterra I Porfidi '03	♟♟♟ 5
Lessona Omaggio a Quintino Sella '06	♟♟♟ 7
Lessona Omaggio a Quintino Sella '05	♟♟♟ 6
Lessona S. Sebastiano allo Zoppo '04	♟♟♟ 5
Lessona S. Sebastiano allo Zoppo '01	♟♟♟ 5
Bramaterra '12	♟♟ 5
Bramaterra I Porfidi '13	♟♟ 8
Bramaterra I Porfidi '10	♟♟ 5
Coste della Sesia Rosso Orbello '18	♟♟ 3*
Lessona '13	♟♟ 5
Lessona S. Sebastiano allo Zoppo '12	♟♟ 8
Lessona S. Sebastiano allo Zoppo '10	♟♟ 6

○ Alta langa Extra Brut M+M 18 Perpetuelle Sbagliato 15 20 '18	♟♟ 8
○ Alta Langa Pas Dosé Zero Sboccatura Tardiva Ris. '18	♟♟ 8
⊘ Alta Langa Rosé de Saignée Zero Ris. '18	♟♟ 8
○ Alta Langa Brut Oudeis '20	♟♟ 5
⊘ Alta Langa Brut Rosé Oudeis Rosé De Saignée '20	♟♟ 6
● Barbaresco Bricco Di Neive '21	♟ 8
○ Gavi del Comune Di Gavi Grifo del Quartaro '23	♟ 5
○ Gavi del Comune di Gavi Maneo Poggio della Rupe '18	♟ 7
○ Alta Langa Pas Dosé Zero Ris. '15	♟♟♟ 7
○ Alta Langa Pas Dosé Zero Sboccatura Tardiva '17	♟♟♟ 6
○ Alta Langa Zero Pas Dosé '16	♟♟♟ 7

La Smilla

via Garibaldi, 7
15060 Bosio [AL]
☎ +39 0143684245
🌐 www.lasmilla.it

CELLAR SALES
ANNUAL PRODUCTION 100,000 bottles
HECTARES UNDER VINE 5.00

A traditional producer guided by Danilo and Matteo Guido, this winery focuses on the area's time-honored varietals: cortese, barbera, and dolcetto. Located in the historic center of Bosio, the winery draws on concrete, stainless steel, and small oak barrels during the wine maturation process. Their range is well-crafted and diverse, faithfully reflecting their region of origin. The Barbera d'Asti Calicanto '20 is well-crafted, unveiling a complex aromatic suite where vegetal aromas are accented by tobacco and leather. On the palate, the wine is rich and compact, with well-sustained development and a warm, persistent finish. The fragrant Gavi '23 proves immediately aromatic and has an easy-to-drink quality. The intriguing Monferrato Bianco I Bergi '21 opts for whiffs of aromatic herbs, citrus, and exotic fruit, with a soft, deep palate.

Francesco Sobrero

via Pugnane, 5
12060 Castiglione Falletto [CN]
☎ +39 017362864
🌐 www.sobrerofrancesco.it

CELLAR SALES
PRE-BOOKED VISITS
ACCOMMODATION
ANNUAL PRODUCTION 90,000 bottles
HECTARES UNDER VINE 16.00

Parussi is a historic vineyard here in Castiglione Falletto, the area in which the winery was founded in 1940 (the first bottles came in 1964). But Parussi is only one of three Barolo crus produced by the Sobrero family. There's also Villero and Pernanno. In 2008, they added three hectares in Canelli, a cradle of the moscato grape. Flavio, representing the third generation, has been leading the winery since 2000, continuing nearly a century-old legacy. With its focused aromatic profile (red fruit, spices, and licorice), the Barolo Parussi '20 stands out for its smooth progression on the palate, with delicate tannins accompanying a pleasantly soft and sweet profile, finishing long and pervasive. The fruit aromas of the Barolo Ciabot Tanasio '20 are less focused, with hints of hay and slightly wilted flowers dominating the nose, and the palate feeling somewhat less fresh and dynamic. The sapid and fresh Dolcetto d'Alba Selection '23 is well-crafted.

○ Gavi '23	♟♟ 2*
● Barbera D'Asti Calicanto '20	♟♟ 3
● Dolcetto di Ovada '23	♟♟ 3
○ M.to Bianco Bergi '21	♟♟ 3
● M.to Nebbiolo '20	♟♟ 3
○ Gavi del Comune di Gavi '23	♟ 4
○ Gavi M. Cl. '19	♟ 4
● Dolcetto di Ovada '20	♟♟ 2*
● Dolcetto di Ovada '13	♟♟ 2*
○ Gavi '15	♟♟ 2*
○ Gavi Brut M. Cl. '18	♟♟ 4
○ Gavi del Comune di Gavi '20	♟♟ 2*
○ Gavi del Comune di Gavi '17	♟♟ 2*
○ Gavi del Comune di Gavi '15	♟♟ 2*
○ Gavi del Comune di Gavi '13	♟♟ 2*
○ Gavi I Bergi '15	♟♟ 3*

● Barolo Ciabot Tanasio '20	♟♟ 7
● Barolo Parussi '20	♟♟ 8
● Dolcetto d'Alba Selectio '23	♟♟ 3
● Langhe Nebbiolo '22	♟ 4
● Barbera d'Alba La Pichetera '19	♟♟ 3
● Barbera d'Alba La Pichetera '18	♟♟ 3
● Barolo Ciabot Tanasio '18	♟♟ 6
● Barolo Ciabot Tanasio '17	♟♟ 6
● Barolo Ciabot Tanasio '16	♟♟ 6
● Barolo Ciabot Tanasio '10	♟♟ 6
● Barolo Parussi '18	♟♟ 8
● Barolo Parussi '17	♟♟ 7
● Barolo Parussi '16	♟♟ 7
● Barolo Pernanno Ris. '15	♟♟ 8
● Barolo Villero Ris. '16	♟♟ 8
● Barolo Villero Ris. '15	♟♟ 8

Socré

s.da Terzolo, 7
12050 Barbaresco [CN]
☏ +39 3487121685
🌐 www.socre.it

CELLAR SALES
PRE-BOOKED VISITS
ANNUAL PRODUCTION 35,000 bottles
HECTARES UNDER VINE 12.00

This Barbaresco winery began its journey in 1958, when Benedetto Piacentino reorganized the estate. With the arrival of his son Marco in the early 1990s, supported today by his sons Giulio and Lorenzo, the winery took on its current form. Some of the their vineyards are located in prestigious areas of the appellation, such as Roncaglie and Pajoré. In addition to nebbiolo, they also cultivate barbera, freisa, and chardonnay. The Barbaresco Pajorè '20 offers a generously fruity aromatic profile, with refreshing hints of cinchona and licorice lending airiness and finesse. In the mouth, the palate is relatively slender, flavorful and multifaceted, closing with a long and persistent finish. We also appreciated the Langhe Freisa '21, with its woodland aromas and minty nuances, and its tasty, rhythmic palate. Finally, as always, the splendid Paint It Black combines the complexity of buttery and spicy notes with the freshness of fruit-driven sensations.

● Barbaresco Pajoré '20	♟♟ 8
○ Langhe Chardonnay Paint it Black '22	♟♟ 6
● Barbaresco '21	♟♟ 6
● Barbaresco Roncaglie '20	♟♟ 8
● Langhe Freisa '21	♟♟ 5
● Barbera d'Alba Sup. '22	♟ 5
● Langhe Nebbiolo '21	♟ 5
● Barbaresco Pajoré '19	♟♟♟ 8
● Barbaresco Roncaglie Ris. '15	♟♟♟ 8
○ Alta Langa Brut Nature Terseux '19	♟♟ 5
● Barbaresco Roncaglie '19	♟♟ 8
● Barbaresco Roncaglie '18	♟♟ 7
● Barbaresco Roncaglie '17	♟♟ 7
● Barbaresco Roncaglie Ris. '16	♟♟ 8
○ Langhe Chardonnay Paint it Black '20	♟♟ 5
○ Langhe Chardonnay Paint it Black '19	♟♟ 5

Giovanni Sordo

fraz. Garbelletto
via Alba Barolo, 175
12060 Castiglione Falletto [CN]
☏ +39 017362853
🌐 www.sordogiovanni.it

CELLAR SALES
PRE-BOOKED VISITS
ACCOMMODATION
ANNUAL PRODUCTION 350,000 bottles
HECTARES UNDER VINE 53.00

Based in Castiglione Falletto, the family-run winery is today led by Giorgio Sordo and his daughter Luisa. It was founded in 1912 by Giuseppe Sordo, with the major breakthrough coming in the 1950s, when Giovanni Sordo acquired numerous vineyards in key areas, including Castiglione Falletto, Serralunga d'Alba, Monforte d'Alba, Barolo, La Morra, Verduno, and Grinzane Cavour. This expansion guaranteed eight crus across five different municipalities. The Barolo Perno '20 impresses with its intense, multifaceted nose, summoning notes of mulberry, tobacco, licorice, and aromatic herbs. On the palate, it's supple, with still-spirited tannins shaping its multifaceted development and a firm, crisp finish. The Barolo '20 is also well-crafted, offering a simpler aromatic profile and a slender palate, but with a nice progression of flavor.

● Barolo Perno '20	♟♟ 7
● Barolo '20	♟♟ 6
● Barolo Monprivato '20	♟ 8
● Barolo Rocche di Castiglione '20	♟ 7
● Nebbiolo d'Alba V. Valmaggiore '20	♟ 5
● Barolo Gabutti '16	♟♟ 7
● Barolo Monprivato '19	♟♟ 8
● Barolo Monvigliero '14	♟♟ 7
● Barolo Monvigliero '13	♟♟ 7
● Barolo Parussi '14	♟♟ 7
● Barolo Ravera '19	♟♟ 7
● Barolo Ravera '18	♟♟ 7
● Barolo Ravera '17	♟♟ 7
● Barolo Ravera '13	♟♟ 7
● Barolo Rocche di Castiglione '19	♟♟ 7
● Barolo Rocche di Castiglione '16	♟♟ 7

★★Sottimano

loc. Cottà, 21
12052 Neive [CN]
+39 0173635186
www.sottimano.it

CELLAR SALES
PRE-BOOKED VISITS
ANNUAL PRODUCTION 85,000 bottles
HECTARES UNDER VINE 18.00
VITICULTURE METHOD Certified Organic

The Sottimano family's winery is one of the best-established producers in Barbaresco, thanks to its founder, Rino, who is now joined by his children Andrea, Elena, and Claudia. Founded in the late 1960s, the estate owes much of its success to its vineyards, particularly the Cottà, Currà, and Pajoré crus, which often give rise to wines of absolute excellence. Sottimano's production style is solid, with their range benefiting from long maceration times and aging in large oak barrels. The convincing Barbaresco Pajorè '21 reveals an aromatic profile that elegantly blends notes of small red fruits with licorice, spices, and balsamic notes, all of which precede a refined, fragrant, and rhythmic palate. The Barbaresco Cottà '21 sees fleshy fruit and hints of cinchona combine with woodland sensations. A harmonious, tannic progression of flavor follows, all topped off by a long, relaxed finish.

● Barbaresco Pajoré '21	ΨΨΨ 8
● Barbaresco Cottà '21	ΨΨ 7
● Barbaresco Fausoni '21	ΨΨ 7
● Barbaresco Basarin '21	ΨΨ 8
● Barbaresco Basarin '19	ΥΥΥ 8
● Barbaresco Cottà '15	ΥΥΥ 7
● Barbaresco Currà '19	ΥΥΥ 8
● Barbaresco Currà '15	ΥΥΥ 8
● Barbaresco Currà '12	ΥΥΥ 8
● Barbaresco Currà '10	ΥΥΥ 8
● Barbaresco Currà '08	ΥΥΥ 7
● Barbaresco Pajoré '18	ΥΥΥ 8
● Barbaresco Pajoré '16	ΥΥΥ 7
● Barbaresco Pajoré '14	ΥΥΥ 7
● Barbaresco Pajoré '10	ΥΥΥ 7
● Barbaresco Ris. '10	ΥΥΥ 8

★Luigi Spertino

via Lea, 505
14047 Mombercelli [AT]
+39 0141959098
luigi.spertino@libero.it

CELLAR SALES
PRE-BOOKED VISITS
ANNUAL PRODUCTION 40,000 bottles
HECTARES UNDER VINE 9.00

Like his grandfather Luigi and father Mauro before him, Andrea Spertino shows an immense love for his land and the wine it produces. His grandfather had the courage to bottle his grignolino at a time when wine was still sold in bulk in the taverns of Turin, and personally took on the challenge of selling it himself. His father, in turn, left a prestigious job at Ramazzotti to devote himself to the winery. Now, Andrea deserves applause for his work in challenging times—personally tending the steep, manual vineyards despite the devastation caused by flavescence dorée and labor shortages. Among a commendable roster of wines, the Grignolino '23 caught our attention for its captivating aromas of pepper, rose, and licorice, along with a harmonious, smooth palate. We were especially impressed with La Mandorla, a Monferrato Rosso made from slightly raisined barbera grapes. Its nose is pervasive, with hints of cocoa and plum jam, and the palate is powerful and voluptuous, yet enlivened by sharp acidity and a welcome tannic roughness. The rest of the lineup is equally excellent.

● M.to Rosso La Mandorla di Mauro '22	ΨΨΨ 7
● Barbera d'Asti La Bigia '22	ΨΨ 5
● Grignolino d'Asti '23	ΨΨ 4
○ Brut Nature M. Cl. '21	ΨΨ 5
● Grignolino d'Asti Margherita Barbero '23	ΨΨ 3
● Barbera d'Asti Sup. La Mandorla '13	ΥΥΥ 8
● Barbera d'Asti Sup. V. La Mandorla '19	ΥΥΥ 8
● Barbera d'Asti Sup. V. La Mandorla '18	ΥΥΥ 8
● Barbera d'Asti Sup. V. La Mandorla '16	ΥΥΥ 8
● Barbera d'Asti Sup. V. La Mandorla '15	ΥΥΥ 8
● Barbera d'Asti Sup. V. La Mandorla '12	ΥΥΥ 8
● Barbera d'Asti Sup. V. La Mandorla Edizione La Grisa '14	ΥΥΥ 8
● Grignolino d'Asti '21	ΥΥΥ 4*
● Grignolino d'Asti '18	ΥΥΥ 3*
● M.to Rosso La Mandorla di Mauro '21	ΥΥΥ 7

Giuseppe Stella

s.da Bossola, 8
14055 Costigliole d'Asti [AT]
📞 +39 0141966142
🌐 www.stellavini.com

CELLAR SALES
PRE-BOOKED VISITS
ANNUAL PRODUCTION 50,000 bottles
HECTARES UNDER VINE 12.00

Giuseppe and his sons, Massimo and Paolo, currently represent the Stella family, heirs to the winery founded by Domenico in 1920. Situated in Costigliole d'Asti, in the heart of Monferrato, barbera naturally takes center stage with three different versions. Other native varietals like cortese, grignolino, freisa, and moscato are also present, along with the internationally known chardonnay, which has a historical presence in the winery. The Barbera d'Asti Stravisan '22 opens with notes of tapenade and cherries, leading to a rich, juicy palate. Other highlights include the sapid and tannic Grignolino d'Asti Sufragio '23, a classic and refined wine on the nose, with hints of tobacco and licorice, and the Barbera d'Asti Superiore Il Maestro '21, with its strongly spiced nose and red fruit notes preceding an energetic, fresh, and enjoyable palate. The Barbera d'Asti Superiore Giaiet '21 proves vibrant, redolent of fruit and sweet spices, while the palate stands out for its good body and structure.

Le Strette

via Le Strette, 1f
12060 Novello [CN]
📞 +39 0173744002
🌐 lestrette.com

CELLAR SALES
PRE-BOOKED VISITS
ANNUAL PRODUCTION 23,000 bottles
HECTARES UNDER VINE 6.50
VITICULTURE METHOD Certified Organic
SUSTAINABLE WINERY

Run by Mauro and Savio Daniele, sons of Giuliana and Giulio Lagorio, Le Strette was founded in 1997 in Novello, one of Barolo's most important production areas. The vineyards are spread across various plots between the villages of Novello and Barolo. In addition to producing Barolo, the estate also cultivates Barbera and Dolcetto d'Alba. However, the winery is particularly renowned for its dedication to reviving nascetta, an ancient white grape variety. The Barolo Corini-Pallaretta '20 shows nice overall freshness, with a nose of cinchona, woodland, and floral accents. The palate is full-bodied and focused, featuring a sustained and flavorful finish. The Nebbiolo d'Alba Pasinot '21 is juicy and fruity, playing on woodland and raspberry aromas. The Barbera d'Alba Persole '22 is a spicy, enjoyable drink where vegetal whiffs adorn a fresh, multifaceted palate.

PIEDMONT

● Barbera d'Asti Stravisan '22	🍷🍷 3*
● Barbera d'Asti Sup. Giaiet '21	🍷🍷 5
● Barbera d'Asti Sup. Il Maestro '21	🍷🍷 5
● Barbera d'Asti Giaiet '23	🍷 5
● Barbera d'Asti Stravisan '21	🍷🍷 3
● Barbera d'Asti Stravisan '20	🍷🍷 5
● Barbera d'Asti Stravisan '19	🍷🍷 3*
● Barbera d'Asti Sup. Giaiet '19	🍷🍷 5
● Barbera d'Asti Sup. Giaiet '17	🍷🍷 4
● Barbera d'Asti Sup. Il Maestro '20	🍷🍷 5
● Barbera d'Asti Sup. Il Maestro '19	🍷🍷 6
● Barbera d'Asti Sup. Il Maestro '18	🍷🍷 5
● Barbera d'Asti Sup. Il Maestro '17	🍷🍷 5
● Freisa d'Asti Convento '19	🍷🍷 3
● Grignolino d'Asti Sufragio '22	🍷🍷 3
● Grignolino d'Asti Sufragio '21	🍷🍷 5
● Grignolino d'Asti Sufragio '20	🍷🍷 5

● Barbera d'Alba Sup. Persole '22	🍷🍷 3
● Barolo Corini-Pallaretta '20	🍷🍷 7
● Barolo del Comune di Novello '20	🍷🍷 6
● Nebbiolo d'Alba Pasinot '21	🍷🍷 5
○ Langhe Nas-cëtta del Comune di Novello Pasinot '22	🍷 5
● Barolo Bergeisa '19	🍷🍷 6
● Barolo Bergeisa '18	🍷🍷 6
● Barolo Bergera-Pezzole '19	🍷🍷 7
● Barolo Bergera-Pezzole '17	🍷🍷 7
● Barolo Bergera-Pezzole '13	🍷🍷 6
○ Langhe Nas-cëtta del Comune di Novello Pasinot '20	🍷🍷 5
○ Langhe Nas-cëtta del Comune di Novello Pasinot '19	🍷🍷 5
○ Langhe Nas-Cëtta del Comune di Novello Pasinot '17	🍷🍷 4

Sulin

v.le Pininfarina, 14
14035 Grazzano Badoglio [AT]
(+39 3331254988
@ www.sulin.it

CELLAR SALES
PRE-BOOKED VISITS
ANNUAL PRODUCTION 220,000 bottles
HECTARES UNDER VINE 19.50

The Sulin winery is perched on Madonna dei
Monti hill, which offers breathtaking views of
Piedmont, Lombardy, and the Alpine peaks.
Mauro and Fabio Fracchia continue the family's
winemaking tradition, which has spanned more
than a century. Their vineyards are spread across
different zones, allowing them to explore the
unique nuances of the land through both
indigenous and international grape varieties. The
Centum '22 is an exciting expression of Barbera
del Monferrato, starting with its deep ruby color.
Morello cherry and pleasant cocoa notes
emerge on the nose, and despite its warmth, it
retains elegance and drinkability thanks to
vibrant acidity. We also enjoyed the Monferrato
Bianco Balon '22, with its layered nose of fresh
herbs and citrus, and hints of almonds and nuts.
The palate is complex and rich, though slightly
tightened by tannins that need a bit more time
to integrate.

● Barbera del Monferrato Centum '22	♟♟	3*
○ M.to Bianco Balon '22	♟♟	3*
● Casorzo '23	♟♟	2*
● Grignolino Del Monferrato Casalese Arillus '23	♟♟	3
● M.to Rosso Tambàss '21	♟♟	3
○ Piemonte Chardonnay Robinia '23	♟♟	3
● Barbera del M.to Sup. Ornella '21	♟	5
● Barbera del M.to Centum '18	♟♟	3*
● Barbera del M.to Sup. Ornella '17	♟♟	5
● Barbera del M.to Sup. Ornella '15	♟♟	5
● Grignolino del M.to Casalese '21	♟♟	4
● Grignolino del M.to Casalese Monferace Brasal '17	♟♟	5
● Piemonte Grignolino Monferace Brasal '16	♟♟	5

★Tacchino

via Martiri della Benedicta, 26
15060 Castelletto d'Orba [AL]
(+39 0143830115
@ www.luigitacchino.it

CELLAR SALES
PRE-BOOKED VISITS
ANNUAL PRODUCTION 120,000 bottles
HECTARES UNDER VINE 12.00

This family-owned winery is now in its third
generation, led by Alessio and Romina, who
follow the path laid by their grandfather Carletto
and father Luigi, with a strong commitment to
preserving their land and tradition. The estate
covers 25 hectares of white soil, half of which is
under vine (facing south-southeast). Here, classic
wines like Barbera and Dolcetto are produced,
but the winery is also looking toward modernity,
employing cutting-edge technologies and getting
external consultants involved. As usual, Dolcetto
remains Tacchino's flagship wine, with the
Dolcetto d'Ovada '22 standing out among this
year's tastings. Its captivating nose spans
everything from blackberry and cocoa to bitter
almond and a touch of camphor for added
complexity. A wine with great structure and
close-knit tannins, it culminates in a long,
character-filled finish that only time will tame.
The Monferrato Rosso Di Fatto '20 is also
excellent, with its inky color and notes of red
fruit and blackberry, followed by sweet spices on
the finish. In the mouth, its full palate boasts
lovely acidity.

● Dolcetto di Ovada '22	♟♟♟	3*
● M.to Rosso Di Fatto '20	♟♟	4
○ Gavi del Comune di Gavi '23	♟♟	3
● Piemonte Rosso Buongiorno '19	♟♟	2*
○ Piemonte Cortese Frizzante Frivolì '23	♟	3
● Barbera del M.to Albarola '16	♟♟♟	5
● Barbera del M.to Sup. Albarola '17	♟♟♟	5
● Dolcetto di Ovada '16	♟♟♟	2*
● Dolcetto di Ovada '15	♟♟♟	2*
● Dolcetto di Ovada Sup. Du Riva '19	♟♟♟	4*
● Dolcetto di Ovada Sup. Du Riva '18	♟♟♟	4*
● Dolcetto di Ovada Sup. Du Riva '15	♟♟♟	4*
● Dolcetto di Ovada Sup. Du Riva '13	♟♟♟	4*
● Dolcetto di Ovada Sup. Du Riva '12	♟♟♟	5
● Dolcetto di Ovada Sup. Du Riva '11	♟♟♟	5
● Dolcetto di Ovada Sup. Du Riva '10	♟♟♟	4*

Tenuta Tenaglia

s.da Santuario di Crea, 5
15020 Serralunga di Crea [AL]
+39 0142940252
www.tenutatenaglia.it

CELLAR SALES
PRE-BOOKED VISITS
ACCOMMODATION
ANNUAL PRODUCTION 100,000 bottles
HECTARES UNDER VINE 17.00
SUSTAINABLE WINERY

Tenuta Tenaglia's history dates back to the 18th century. Today, after several changes of ownership, it is run by Sabine Hermann and her children. The focus here is on quality: the 16 hectares of vineyards rest on clay soil and have a very low yield, producing no more than 7,000 kg per hectare. The project centers around native grape varieties like grignolino and barbera, though some international varieties, including chardonnay, syrah, and merlot, are also grown. This year, however, the winery's lineup is less consistent than usual. The Barbera del Monferrato Superiore 1930 Una Buona Annata '19 opens with warm notes and toasted wood, slightly overshadowing ripe cherry fruit; the palate is soft and pervasive. The Barbera d'Asti Giorgio Tenaglia '20 shows intriguing complexity and a firm palate with signs of good evolution. The Grignolino del Monferrato Casalese '23 offers greater drinkability, though it lacks a bit of depth.

● Barbera d'Asti Giorgio Tenaglia '20	🍷🍷 4
● Barbera d'Asti Sup Emozioni '19	🍷🍷 6
● Barbera del M.to Sup. 1930 Una Buona Annnata '19	🍷🍷 6
● Grignolino del M.to Casalese '23	🍷🍷 3
● Barbera d'Asti Emozioni '99	🍷🍷🍷 4*
● Grignolino del M.to Casalese '17	🍷🍷🍷 2*
● Barbera d'Asti Emozioni '10	🍷🍷 5
● Barbera d'Asti Sup. Emozioni '15	🍷🍷 6
● Barbera del M.to Sup. 1930 Una Buona Annata '13	🍷🍷 5
● Grignolino del M.to Casalese '22	🍷🍷 3*
● Grignolino del M.to Casalese '20	🍷🍷 2*
● Grignolino del M.to Casalese '18	🍷🍷 2*
● Grignolino del M.to Casalese '16	🍷🍷 2*
● Grignolino del M.to Casalese Monferace '15	🍷🍷 6

Tenute RaDe

fraz. Saline, 13
14050 San Marzano Oliveto [AT]
+39 0141769091
www.tenuterade.it

CELLAR SALES
PRE-BOOKED VISITS
ANNUAL PRODUCTION 40,000 bottles
HECTARES UNDER VINE 45.00

Daniele Cusmano, along with his wife Ilaria, manages the estate founded in 1988 with his father Raimondo (hence the name Tenute RaDe). Their vineyards can be found in Castel Boglione, Canelli, Cassinasco, Momperone, and Nizza Monferrato. In addition to barbera, they cultivate merlot, syrah, timorasso, sauvignon, moscato, and for Metodo Classico, chardonnay and pinot nero. A modern production approach is aimed at expressing the characteristics of the respective terroirs as best possible. The Moscato d'Asti Bele Fije '23 conjures up herbal and gingerbread scents on the nose, while the palate is taut and long, with a pronounced sweetness that's nicely balanced by acidity. The Alta Langa Pas Dosé '16, with its fine, persistent bead and minerally, citrusy tones, delivers a long, powerful, and very fresh palate. The Monferrato Bianco Lunatico '23, a sauvignon, is also well-crafted, playing on notes of sage, and a fresh, vibrant palate, long and fleshy.

○ Alta Langa Pas Dosé '16	🍷🍷 6
○ Moscato d'Asti Bele Fije '23	🍷🍷 4
○ Alta Langa Pas Dosé '17	🍷🍷 6
● Barbera d'Asti La Prüma '22	🍷🍷 3
○ Monferrato Bianco Lunatico '23	🍷🍷 3
○ Colli Tortonesi Timorasso Derthona '20	🍷 5
● Barbera d'Asti Sup. La Grissa '20	🍷🍷 5
● Barbera d'Asti La Prüma '21	🍷🍷 3

Terre Astesane

via Marconi, 42
14047 Mombercelli [AT]
☎ +39 0141959155
✺ www.terreastesane.it

CELLAR SALES
PRE-BOOKED VISITS
ANNUAL PRODUCTION 230,000 bottles
HECTARES UNDER VINE 300.00

130 members contribute to this historic cooperative winery, founded in 1901. The grapes come from vineyards in the towns of Mombercelli, Vinchio, Agliano, Belveglio, and Montaldo Scarampi. Barbera makes up the lion share, accounting for about 70% of the plantings, though brachetto, chardonnay, cortese, freisa, and grignolino are cultivated as well. The wines themselves are traditionally styled, crafted to showcase both the grape varieties and the distinct terroirs in which they're grown. The producer's range put in a strong overall performance. The Barbera d'Asti Superiore Savej '21 shines brilliantly with its aromas of blueberries and Asian spices, followed by a flavorful, fruit-rich, long, and spirited palate. The Grignolino d'Asti Ganassa '23 is a superb expression of classical style. Flowery aromas are enriched by hints of pepper, while the palate is both fine and caressing in its tannins, finishing taut and bitter. Meanwhile, the Nizza Mumbersè '21 showcases tones of cherry and cinchona, with a fruit-rich palate.

Wine	Rating
● Barbera d'Asti Sup. Savej '21	♟♟ 2*
● Grignolino d'Asti Ganassa '23	♟♟ 2*
● Nizza Mumbersè '21	♟♟ 4
● Nizza Rèis Ris. '19	♟♟ 6
○ Piemonte Chardonnay Cirivè '23	♟ 2
● Barbera d'Asti Sup. Savej '20	♟♟ 2*
● Barbera d'Asti Sup. Savej '19	♟♟ 2*
● Barbera d'Asti Sup. Savej '18	♟♟ 2*
● Grignolino d'Asti Ganassa '22	♟♟ 2*
● Grignolino d'Asti Ganassa '21	♟♟ 2*
● Grignolino d'Asti Ganassa '20	♟♟ 2*
● Grignolino d'Asti Ganassa '19	♟♟ 2*
● Nizza Mumbersè '20	♟♟ 4
● Nizza Mumbersè '19	♟♟ 3*
● Nizza Mumbersè '18	♟♟ 3*
● Nizza Mumbersé '17	♟♟ 3

La Toledana

loc. Sermoira, 5
15066 Gavi [AL]
☎ +39 0141837211
✺ www. latoledana.it

CELLAR SALES
PRE-BOOKED VISITS
ANNUAL PRODUCTION 160,000 bottles
HECTARES UNDER VINE 28.00

La Toledana is owned by the Martini family, who began their agricultural activities in 1947. The winery is part of a small group that includes Villa Lanata in Cossano Belbo, Cascina Lo Zoccolaio in Bricco Barolo, and Cascina La Doria in San Cristoforo. In Gavi, the vineyards are clustered around an ancient 16th-century villa, making for a diverse range that highlights the potential of the local terroir. The Gavi del Comune di Gavi Vigne Rade '23 possesses a focused nose dominated by notes of white fruit, accented by hints of freshly cut grass and bark. In the mouth, the palate is generally austere and pared down, remaining taut and precise in its persistent, flavorful development. A clean, long, and compact finish hints at excellent future prospects.

Wine	Rating
○ Gavi del Comune di Gavi Vigne Rade '23	♟♟♟ 3*
○ Gavi del Comune di Gavi Vigne Rade '22	♟♟♟ 3*
○ Gavi del Comune di Gavi Vigne Rade '21	♟♟♟ 3*
○ Gavi del Comune di Gavi Vigne Rade '20	♟♟♟ 5
○ Gavi del Comune di Gavi Vigne Rade '19	♟♟♟ 5
● Barolo Lo Zoccolaio '15	♟♟ 5
○ Gavi del Comune di Gavi La Toledana '18	♟♟ 5
○ Gavi del Comune di Gavi La Toledana '17	♟♟ 5
○ Gavi del Comune di Gavi La Toledana '11	♟♟ 4
○ Gavi del Comune di Gavi La Toledana '10	♟♟ 3
○ Gavi del Comune di Gavi La Toledana '09	♟♟ 3
○ Gavi del Comune di Gavi V.Rade Foglio 46 '18	♟♟ 5
○ Gavi La Doria '20	♟♟ 3*
○ Gavi La Doria San Cristoforo '21	♟♟ 3
○ Gavi La Doria San Cristoforo '19	♟♟ 3*
● Langhe Baccanera Lo Zoccolaio '16	♟♟ 3

★Torraccia del Piantavigna

via Romagnano, 20
28074 Ghemme [NO]
☎ +39 0163840040
⊛ www.torracciadelpiantavigna.it

PRE-BOOKED VISITS
ANNUAL PRODUCTION 190,000 bottles
HECTARES UNDER VINE 40.00
SUSTAINABLE WINERY

The presence of Monte Rosa and a supervolcano help explain the uniqueness of Torraccia's grapes, which are cultivated in Ghemme and Gattinara. Winemaker and director Mattia Donna is steadily taming the austere nebbiolos of this corner of northern Piedmont, particularly the iconic Vigna Pelizzane cru, which lies in front of the winery. The site is known for its finesse and specific character, producing wines with notes of rust, iodine, and a convincing, long, sapid finish. The powerful and radiant Vigna Pellizzane '17 offers up a rich balsamic note that intensifies its dynamic flavor profile, where hints of fruit jam and dried flowers alternate with whiffs of iodine; an austere palate marked by great tannic strength concludes with a finish of pronounced personality. The Gattinara '18 proves decisive and powerful, characterized by aromas of red citrus zest, minerals, sanguine sensations and spices; its compact and structured palate is topped off by an elegant finish.

Giancarlo Travaglini

via delle Vigne, 36
13045 Gattinara [VC]
☎ +39 0163833588
⊛ www.travaglinigattinara.it

CELLAR SALES
PRE-BOOKED VISITS
ANNUAL PRODUCTION 250,000 bottles
HECTARES UNDER VINE 55.00
SUSTAINABLE WINERY

When thinking of the Gattinara region, one of the historic names that comes to mind is Travaglini. Now in its fourth generation, the winery is led by Cinzia Travaglini and Massimo Collauto, who are flanked by their daughters Alessia and Carolina. Their traditional winemaking style and meticulous work in the vineyard ensure that their interpretation of this area, rich in volcanic soil, is consistently authentic and of high quality. Our tastings confirm these impressions, thanks to a highly convincing lineup. The Gattinara Riserva '19 stands out with a nose reminiscent of tobacco and dried herbs; the palate is layered and powerful, with evident tannins and a long finish. We also appreciated the Gattinara Tre Vigne '20, which is less full-bodied but highly elegant: it features aromas of red fruits and Peruvian bark before an elegant, lengthy palate.

● Ghemme V. Pelizzane '17	♟♟♟ 6
● Gattinara '18	♟♟ 6
⊙ Colline Novaresi Nebbiolo Rosato Barlàn '23	♟♟ 3
● Colline Novaresi Vespolina La Mostella '21	♟♟ 3
○ Colline Novaresi Bianco Erba Voglio '23	♟ 3
○ Erbavoglio Blanc de Blancs Doasggio Zero M. Cl.	♟ 7
● Gattinara '15	♟♟♟ 6
● Ghemme '13	♟♟♟ 6
● Ghemme '11	♟♟♟ 6
● Ghemme '10	♟♟♟ 5
● Ghemme V. Pelizzane '16	♟♟♟ 6
● Ghemme V. Pelizzane '15	♟♟♟ 6
● Ghemme V. Pelizzane '11	♟♟♟ 6
● Ghemme V. Pelizzane '10	♟♟♟ 6

● Gattinara Ris. '19	♟♟♟ 7
● Gattinara Tre Vigne '20	♟♟ 7
● Coste della Sesia Nebbiolo '23	♟♟ 4
● Gattinara '21	♟♟ 6
○ Nebolè Dosaggio Zero M. Cl. '19	♟♟ 7
● Gattinara Ris. '15	♟♟♟ 6
● Gattinara Ris. '13	♟♟♟ 7
● Gattinara Ris. '12	♟♟♟ 7
● Gattinara Ris. '06	♟♟♟ 6
● Gattinara Ris. '04	♟♟♟ 5
● Gattinara Ris. '01	♟♟♟ 5
● Gattinara Tre Vigne '04	♟♟♟ 5
● Gattinara Ris. '17	♟♟ 7
● Gattinara Tre Vigne '17	♟♟ 6
● Gattinara Tre Vigne '15	♟♟ 6

★G. D. Vajra

fraz. Vergne
via delle Viole, 25
12060 Barolo [CN]
+39 017356257
www.gdvajra.it

PRE-BOOKED VISITS
ACCOMMODATION
ANNUAL PRODUCTION 500,000 bottles
HECTARES UNDER VINE 80.00
VITICULTURE METHOD Certified Organic
SUSTAINABLE WINERY

Giuseppe, Francesca, and Isidoro work alongside their parents, Aldo and Milena, in managing the family winery. With unwavering consistency, the estate continues to produce a range known for its strong character and refined style. Their flagship is the Cru Bricco delle Viole, located on the western ridge of Barolo, cultivated with nebbiolo from the Lampia and Michet clones planted in 1949, 1963, and 1968. The Barolo Baudana Luigi Baudana '20 is a wine of great breadth, summoning dazzling aromas of red berries, tobacco and licorice, all complemented by smoky nuances on the finish. In the mouth, the palate is multifaceted, with a dynamic tannic structure and a long, airy finish. We also appreciated the Barolo Cerretta Luigi Baudana '20, which is more mature in its aromas, with a fleshy, austere, and highly persistent progression of flavor. The Barolo Coste di Rose '20 also proves well-crafted.

● Barolo Baudana Luigi Baudana '20	🍷🍷 8
● Barolo Cerretta Luigi Baudana '20	🍷🍷 8
● Barolo Coste di Rose '20	🍷🍷 8
● Barbera d'Alba Sup. Viola della Viole '22	🍷🍷 5
● Barolo Albe '20	🍷🍷 6
● Barolo Bricco delle Viole '20	🍷🍷 8
● Dolcetto d'Alba Coste & Fossati '23	🍷🍷 4
● Barolo Ravera '20	🍷 8
○ Langhe Riesling Pétracine '23	🍷 5
● Barolo Baudana Luigi Baudana '19	🍷🍷🍷 6
● Barolo Bricco delle Viole '18	🍷🍷🍷 8
● Barolo Bricco delle Viole '17	🍷🍷🍷 8
● Barolo Bricco delle Viole '15	🍷🍷🍷 8
● Barolo Bricco delle Viole '12	🍷🍷🍷 8
● Barolo Bricco delle Viole '10	🍷🍷🍷 8
● Barolo Cerretta Luigi Baudana '16	🍷🍷🍷 6

Valfaccenda

fraz. Madonna Loreto
loc. Val Faccenda, 43
12043 Canale [CN]
+39 3397303837
www.valfaccenda.it

CELLAR SALES
PRE-BOOKED VISITS
ACCOMMODATION
ANNUAL PRODUCTION 25,000 bottles
HECTARES UNDER VINE 5.00
VITICULTURE METHOD Certified Organic
SUSTAINABLE WINERY

Carolina Roggero and Luca Faccenda's winery draws on a set of privately-owned vineyards on the hills bordering Rocche, as well as rented plots in Santo Stefano Roero and Vezza d'Alba. Only arneis and nebbiolo are cultivated, with the aim being to create traditional wines through minimally invasive practices, thus expressing the characteristics of the territory as best possible. The producer's small range of wines remains consistently solid and convincing. On the nose, the Roero Valmaggiore Riserva '21 highlights notes of violet, plum, and cinnamon, offering a palate of remarkable fullness and complexity. The Roero '22 leans more towards red fruit sensations, with spicy nuances and a smooth, pleasantly flowing palate. The Roero '23, a white from arneis grapes, features notes of maceration on the nose and a palate of good substance, marked by tones of orange zest. It's slightly tannic in the mouth, but juicy on the finish.

○ Roero '23	🍷🍷 3
○ Roero '22	🍷🍷 3
● Roero V. Valmaggiore Ris. '21	🍷🍷 6
○ Roero Bianco '22	🍷🍷 5
● Roero Loreto Ris. '19	🍷🍷 5
● Roero Rosso '21	🍷🍷 5
● Roero Rosso '20	🍷🍷 5
● Roero V. Valmaggiore Ris. '20	🍷🍷 6
● Roero V. Valmaggiore Ris. '19	🍷🍷 6
● Roero V. Valmaggiore Ris. '18	🍷🍷 6
● Roero V. Valmaggiore Ris. '17	🍷🍷 6

★Mauro Veglio

fraz. Annunziata
loc. Cascina Nuova, 50
12064 La Morra [CN]
☎ +39 0173509212
✉ www.mauroveglio.com

CELLAR SALES
PRE-BOOKED VISITS
ANNUAL PRODUCTION 115,000 bottles
HECTARES UNDER VINE 22.00
SUSTAINABLE WINERY

Mauro Veglio took over the family winery in 1986 and began bottling his own wines in 1992. Later, his nephew Alessandro came on board, having already established his own production line in 2008. In 2017, the two branches of the Veglio family merged into a single producer. The estate's vineyards include prominent Crus in La Morra—Gattera, Arborina, and Rocche dell'Annunziata—as well as Castelletto in Monforte d'Alba. The Barolo Arborina '20 boasts a dazzling aromatic profile: nuances of citrus open the way to small red fruits, spices, and balsamic tones. In the mouth, the palate is full-bodied, flavorful, and evenly proportioned, with dynamic development and an airy, balsamic finish. The Barolo Castelletto '20 is also very good, showcasing finesse both on the nose, with subtle and fragrant aromas, and in the mouth, where it's flavorful and linear. The Barolo Paiagallo '20 is just as good, as is the Barolo Gattera '20, which is more mature yet very lively.

● Barolo Arborina '20	♟♟♟ 7
● Barolo Castelletto '20	♟♟ 7
● Barolo Paiagallo '20	♟♟ 8
● Barolo '20	♟♟ 6
● Barolo del Comune di Serralunga d'Alba '20	♟♟ 8
● Barolo Gattera '20	♟♟ 7
● Barolo Arborina '19	♟♟♟ 7
● Barolo Arborina '18	♟♟♟ 7
● Barolo Arborina '10	♟♟♟ 6
● Barolo Rocche dell'Annunziata '12	♟♟♟ 8
● Barolo Vign. Arborina '01	♟♟♟ 6
● Barolo Vign. Gattera '05	♟♟♟ 6

Viberti

fraz. Vergne
via delle Viole, 30
12060 Barolo [CN]
☎ +39 017356192
✉ www.viberti-barolo.com

CELLAR SALES
PRE-BOOKED VISITS
RESTAURANT SERVICE
ANNUAL PRODUCTION 205,000 bottles
HECTARES UNDER VINE 23.00
SUSTAINABLE WINERY

The history of Giovanni Viberti's winery, now run with his wife Maria and son Claudio, dates back to 1923. It all began with Cavalier Antonio Viberti's purchase of the Locanda del Buon Padre in Barolo, where wine was made in the cellar for the inn's guests. It wasn't until the 1980s that the winery began bottling its own. Today, the estate produces Barolo from the Bricco delle Viole, San Pietro, and La Volta crus. The 2018 Riserva wines are excellent, starting with La Volta, which highlights beautiful, crisp fruit, a legacy of the vintage, mixed with violet. Superb finesse here. The palate is medium-bodied but masterfully balanced, with delicate tannins and a long, multifaceted finish. The San Pietro is darker in color and flavor, structured by a very long, savoury finish, while the other San Pietro proves young and austere.

● Barolo Bricco delle Viole Ris. '18	♟♟ 8
● Barolo La Volta Ris. '18	♟♟ 8
● Barolo San Pietro Ris. '18	♟♟ 8
● Barolo Monvigliero '20	♟♟ 8
● Barolo Buon Padre '20	♟ 7
● Barolo Bricco delle Viole Ris. '17	♔♔ 7
● Barolo Bricco delle Viole Ris. '16	♔♔ 7
● Barolo Bricco delle Viole Ris. '15	♔♔ 7
● Barolo Buon Padre '19	♔♔ 6
● Barolo Buon Padre '18	♔♔ 6
● Barolo Buon Padre '16	♔♔ 6
● Barolo La Volta Ris. '16	♔♔ 8
● Barolo Monvigliero '19	♔♔ 8
● Barolo Monvigliero '18	♔♔ 8
● Barolo Ravera Ris. '15	♔♔ 8

Vicara

s.da Madonna delle Grazie, 5
15030 Rosignano Monferrato [AL]
☎ +39 0142488054
🌐 www.vicara.it

CELLAR SALES
PRE-BOOKED VISITS
ANNUAL PRODUCTION 65,000 bottles
HECTARES UNDER VINE 35.00
VITICULTURE METHOD Certified Biodynamic

This young and dynamic winery has been striving to elevate the Monferrato area and revolutionize Piedmontese winemaking since 1992. As of 2022, Giuseppe and Emanuele Visconti carry on the family philosophy. The 33 hectares are divided into three main subzones: Vadmon, Crosia, and Bricco Uccelletta, where biodiversity and sustainability are priorities. Respect for the land is reflected in their product range, which focuses exclusively on native grape varieties. The Barbera del Monferrato Superiore Cantico della Crosia '20 once again proves excellent. It features vibrant and clear aromas of morello cherry, with a palate of great structure, yet perfectly balanced, offering a velvety sensation and a very long finish. Other highlights include the Barbera Volpuva '23, a very rich and warm wine, and the Barbera 33 Cascina Rocca '21, where lovely aromatic nuances endowed by oak are supported on the palate by a lovely freshness that promises a brilliant future.

● Barbera del M.to Sup. Cantico della Crosia '20	♥♥♥ 4*
● Barbera del M.to Volpuva '23	♥♥ 3*
● Barbera del M.to Comune di Treville 33 Cascina Rocca '21	♥♥ 5
● Grignolino del M.to Casalese G '23	♥♥ 3
● Grignolino del M.to Casalese Monferace Uccelletta '20	♥♥ 7
● Barbera del M.to Sup. Cantico della Crosia '17	♥♥♥ 4*
● Grignolino del M.to Casalese '16	♥♥♥ 3*
● Grignolino del M.to Casalese G '15	♥♥♥ 4*
● Barbera del M.to Sup. Cantico della Crosia '19	♥♥ 4
● Barbera del M.to Volpuva '21	♥♥ 3*
● Grignolino del M.to Casalese G '22	♥♥ 3*
● Grignolino del M.to Casalese Monferace Uccelletta '18	♥♥ 6

★★Vietti

p.zza Vittorio Veneto, 5
12060 Castiglione Falletto [CN]
☎ +39 017362825
🌐 www.vietti.com

CELLAR SALES
PRE-BOOKED VISITS
ACCOMMODATION
ANNUAL PRODUCTION 600,000 bottles
HECTARES UNDER VINE 70.00
VITICULTURE METHOD Certified Organic
SUSTAINABLE WINERY

Vietti stands out as a benchmark in the Langhe, producing wines that have marked the area's history, drawing on some of Barolo and Barbaresco's most important crus. Based in Castiglione Falletto, the estate made headlines in 2016 when it was sold to the American Krause family, owners of Krause Holdings Inc. Despite the sale, the producer's organizational structure has remained largely unchanged. The Barolo Villero Riserva '16 possesses elegant aromas of fragrant red fruit and barely whispered hints of pepper and rose, with balsamic accents on the finish. In the mouth, the palate is fine, with a lively and focused progression, leading to a broad finish with fruity echoes and a pleasant note of licorice to top things off. The Barbera 'Alba Vigna Vecchia Scarrone '22 is decidedly flavorful, unveiling aromas of plum and pleasant, refreshing balsamic nuances. The Barolo Ravera and Brunate '20 also deliver.

● Barolo Villero Ris. '16	♥♥♥ 8
● Barbera d'Alba V. Vecchia Scarrone '22	♥♥ 8
● Barolo Brunate '20	♥♥ 8
● Barolo Ravera '20	♥♥ 8
● Barbaresco Rabajà Ris. '19	♥♥ 8
● Barbaresco Roncaglie '20	♥♥ 8
● Barbera d'Alba Vigna Scarrone '22	♥♥ 7
● Barolo Cerequio '20	♥♥ 8
● Barolo Lazzarito '20	♥♥ 8
● Barolo Rocche di Castiglione '20	♥♥ 8
● Barbera d'Alba Tre Vie '22	♥ 5
● Barolo Castiglione '20	♥ 8
● Barolo Monvigliero '20	♥ 8
○ Colli Tortonesi Timorasso Derthona '22	♥ 5
● Langhe Nebbiolo Perbacco '21	♥ 5
○ Roero Arneis '23	♥ 4

Villa Guelpa

via Francesco Cesone, 52
13853 Lessona [BI]
(» +39 3403850385
@ www.villaguelpa.it

CELLAR SALES
ACCOMMODATION
ANNUAL PRODUCTION 35,000 bottles
HECTARES UNDER VINE 8.00

Drawing on extensive experience in the industry, Daniele Dinoia began renovating his cellar and 19th-century Villa Guelpa in 2015. The property is situated adjacent to the hillside vineyard and the banks of the Strona river in Lessona, while the vineyards are spread out across different areas, each with distinct characteristics: alluvial stone soils in the hills of Roppolo, siliceous sands in Mottalciata, sandy soils in Lessona and Sizzano, and clay and porphyry in Bocal. It's an area that benefits from a mild climate and notable day-night temperature swings. The Lessona '21 stands as a clear example. Intense and elegant, it opens with beautiful aromas of medicinal herbs and licorice, complemented by notes of red fruit. In the mouth, it exhibits character and elegance, lightly restrained by dense tannins, yet nicely balanced by its flesh and a long finish. We also appreciated the Boca '21, a wine characterized by vibrant aromas of raspberry and pepper. The palate is fine and exceptionally deep. The Sizzano approaches similar standards with its character and tannic strength.

● Lessona '21	♥♥♥ 8
● Boca '21	♥♥ 7
○ Colline Novaresi Bianco Longitudine 8.10 '23	♥♥ 3
● Colline Novaresi Nebbiolo Longitudine 8.26 '21	♥♥ 4
● Sizzano '20	♥♥ 7
● Lessona '18	♥♥♥ 8
● Sizzano '20	♥♥♥ 7
● Boca '20	♥♥ 7
● Boca '19	♥♥ 7
● Colline Novaresi Nebbiolo Longitudine 8.26 '20	♥♥ 4
● Lessona '20	♥♥ 8
● Lessona '19	♥♥ 8
● Sizzano '19	♥♥ 6

★Villa Sparina

fraz. Monterotondo, 56
15066 Gavi [AL]
(» +39 0143633835
@ villasparina.it

PRE-BOOKED VISITS
ACCOMMODATION AND RESTAURANT SERVICE
ANNUAL PRODUCTION 550,000 bottles
HECTARES UNDER VINE 73.00

Villa Sparina has been managed by the Moccagatta family since the 1970s, with Stefano and Massimo now at the helm, while Tiziana oversees the hospitality side of the business. The estate, which is quite extensive, is dedicated primarily to the production of Gavi (from cortese grapes) and Barbera. Designed by Giacomo Bersanetti, the winery's bottles are notable for their rounded shape, which allows them to stand out on the shelf. The Piemonte Barbera '22 features aromas of ripe red fruits alongside hints of leather and spices. In the mouth, it possesses good acidity, extending the palate towards a persistent and warm finish. The Gavi del Comune Gavi Monterotondo 10 Anni '12 boasts an aromatic profile dominated by toasted nuances and a powerful, mouthfilling progression of flavor. Meanwhile, the Gavi del Comune di Gavi '23 showcases mostly floral tones with a pleasantly sapid and fresh flavor profile.

○ Gavi del Comune di Gavi '23	♥♥ 3*
○ Gavi del Comune di Gavi Monterotondo 10 Anni '12	♥♥ 8
○ Gavi del Comune di Gavi Monterotondo '21	♥♥ 6
● Piemonte Barbera '22	♥♥ 4
⊙ Piemonte Rosato Villa Sparina Rosé '23	♥ 4
○ Gavi del Comune di Gavi Monterotondo '14	♥♥♥ 6
○ Gavi del Comune di Gavi Monterotondo '12	♥♥♥ 6
○ Gavi del Comune di Gavi Monterotondo '11	♥♥♥ 6
○ Gavi del Comune di Gavi Monterotondo '16	♥♥♥ 6
○ Gavi del Comune di Gavi Monterotondo '15	♥♥♥ 6

Vinchio Vaglio

fraz. reg. San Pancrazio, 1
s.da prov.le 40, km. 3,75
14040 Vinchio [AT]
+39 0141950903
www.vinchio.com

CELLAR SALES
PRE-BOOKED VISITS
ANNUAL PRODUCTION 1,000,000 bottles
HECTARES UNDER VINE 500.00
VITICULTURE METHOD Certified Organic
SUSTAINABLE WINERY

This large cooperative winery has shown a consistent dedication to quality, despite large production volumes. Indeed, 200 grower members produce around 50 different wines. Barbera is undoubtedly the key varietal, offered in various styles. Vinchio and Vaglio Serra, two Monferrato towns known for their past rivalry, have partly overcome their differences through the winery, which, as a nod to history, mandates in its statute that the two most important positions are divided between the two districts. The Barbera d'Asti Vigne Vecchie 50 '22 opens with an intense, refined nose: notes of plum, cherry, cinchona and petrichor. On the palate, it's powerful and rich in flesh, nicely supported by pleasing sapidity and a notable acidic thrust. Other highlights include the long, fresh, flavorful and fruit-rich Nizza Laudana '21, with its spicy and earthy aromas alongside notes of red berries, and the sapid, juicy Barbera d'Asti Superiore I Tre Vescovi '22, with its fruity flavors and hints of Mediterranean scrub.

● Barbera d'Asti Sup. I Tre Vescovi '22	🍷🍷 3*
● Barbera d'Asti Vigne Vecchie 50 '22	🍷🍷 4
● Nizza Laudana '21	🍷🍷 4
● Barbera d'Asti Sorì dei Mori '23	🍷🍷 2*
● Barbera d'Asti Sup. Vigne Vecchie '20	🍷🍷 5
● Nizza Sei Vigne Insinthesis Ris. '19	🍷🍷 7
● Barbera d'Asti Sup. Sei Vigne Insynthesis '01	🍷🍷🍷 6
● Barbera d'Asti '21	🍷🍷 3
● Barbera d'Asti La Leggenda '22	🍷🍷 2*
● Barbera d'Asti Sup. I Tre Vescovi '21	🍷🍷 3
● Barbera d'Asti Sup. I Tre Vescovi '20	🍷🍷 3*
● Barbera d'Asti Sup. I Tre Vescovi '19	🍷🍷 3
● Barbera d'Asti Sup. V.V. '19	🍷🍷 5
● Barbera d'Asti V.V. 50 '21	🍷🍷 4
● Barbera d'Asti V.V. 50° '19	🍷🍷 3
● Nizza Laudana '20	🍷🍷 4
● Nizza Laudana Ris. '17	🍷🍷 4

Virna Borgogno

via Alba, 24/73
12060 Barolo [CN]
+39 017356120
www.virnabarolo.com

CELLAR SALES
PRE-BOOKED VISITS
ACCOMMODATION
ANNUAL PRODUCTION 75,000 bottles
HECTARES UNDER VINE 12.00
SUSTAINABLE WINERY

Virna Borgogno, a notable name in Langhe winemaking, gradually took on a leading role alongside her father Lodovico, managing the producer with her sister Ivana. The vineyards are located in key production areas, including some of Virna Borgogno's most important crus, like Cannubi, Sarmassa, and Preda. The winery also owns plots in Monforte and La Morra. The Barolo del Comune di Barolo '20 offers up whiffs of strawberries, spices, and smoky tones on the nose. On the palate, it's a decisive, rich wine with a docile tannic structure and a long finish accented by a pleasant spiciness. The Barolo Sarmassa '20 reveals a sapid and juicy palate with a solid aromatic profile. The Barolo Cannubi Boschis '14 is a bit more evolved, but nevertheless maintains its overall fragrance, especially on the palate.

● Barolo del Comune di Barolo '20	🍷🍷 7
● Barolo Noi '20	🍷🍷 6
● Barolo Sarmassa '20	🍷🍷 8
● Barbera d'Alba La '22	🍷 3
● Barbera d'Alba Sup. San Giovanni '21	🍷 5
● Barolo Cannubi '20	🍷 8
○ Langhe Bianco Stofuori '23	🍷 4
● Barbaresco Montersino '20	🍷🍷 7
● Barolo Cannubi '18	🍷🍷 8
● Barolo Cannubi Boschis '12	🍷🍷 6
● Barolo del Comune di Barolo '16	🍷🍷 6
● Barolo Ris. '16	🍷🍷 8
● Barolo Ris. '13	🍷🍷 5
● Barolo Sarmassa '19	🍷🍷 8
● Barolo Sarmassa '17	🍷🍷 8
● Barolo Sarmassa '16	🍷🍷 8

Vite Colte
via Bergesia, 6
12060 Barolo [CN]
☏ +39 0173564611
⊕ www.vitecolte.it

CELLAR SALES
PRE-BOOKED VISITS
ANNUAL PRODUCTION 1,200,000 bottles
HECTARES UNDER VINE 300.00
VITICULTURE METHOD Certified Organic
SUSTAINABLE WINERY

Vite Colte was established in 2010 as a sort of spin-off from Barolo Terre da Vino, selected from the cooperative producer's 4,000 hectares of vineyards and 2,000 growers. In the end, 316 hectares cultivated by 194 members were chosen, and strict production protocols were implemented. The first bottling took place in 2016. Vite Colte now offers a portfolio of over 30 wines. The Barbaresco Riserva Spezie '16 is a refined wine. Subtle aromas of small red fruits give way to spices, smoky whiffs, and balsamic tones. On the palate, it's vibrant, generous, and multifaceted, with a beautifully long and flavorful finish. The Barbera d'Asti Superiore La Luna e i Falò '22 showcases aromas of roses and spices, with a pleasantly sapid and deep development of flavor. The Timorasso '22 evokes strawflower, coming through dense and flavorful on the palate. The Barolo Essenze '20 is also well-crafted.

Voerzio Martini
s.da Loreto, 1
12064 La Morra [CN]
☏ +39 0173509194
⊕ www.voerziomartini.com

CELLAR SALES
ANNUAL PRODUCTION 70,000 bottles
HECTARES UNDER VINE 12.50
SUSTAINABLE WINERY

Owned by the Martini family, Voerzio Martini (formerly known as Gianni Voerzio di La Morra) is today led by Federica and Mirko. The estate's vineyards have expanded over time and now include notable parcels within the Cerequio, La Serra, and Monvigliero crus. In addition to nebbiolo, the area's classic grapes, from barbera to dolcetto, freisa, and arneis, are cultivated. The wines reflect a modern stylistic approach and are aged using a mix of different sized barrels. The skillfully crafted Langhe Nebbiolo Ciabot della Luna '21 showcases aromas of small red fruits and spices, sensations that anticipate a firm and flavorful palate. The Barolo '20 opts for flowery aromas on the nose, unfolding taut and decisive on the palate. Aromatically, the Barolo La Serra '20 sees whiffs of brandied berries dominate on the nose, while the palate plays more on pleasantness than volume. The Barolo Cerequio '19 also proves well-crafted, standing out for its persistent sapidity.

● Barbera d'Asti Sup. La Luna e i Falò '22	♟♟♟ 5
● Barbaresco Spezie Ris. '16	♟♟ 8
○ Piemonte Moscato Passito La Bella Estate '22	♟♟ 5
● Barolo del Comune di Barolo Essenze '20	♟♟ 8
○ Colli Tortonesi Derthona Timorasso '22	♟♟ 5
● Barbera d'Asti Sup. La Luna e i Falò '21	♟♟♟ 4*
● Barbera d'Asti Sup. La Luna e i Falò '19	♟♟♟ 3
● Barbera d'Asti Sup. La Luna e i Falò '18	♟♟♟ 3

● Barolo Cerequio '19	♟♟ 8
● Barolo '20	♟♟ 6
● Barolo La Serra '20	♟♟ 7
● Barolo Monvigliero '19	♟ 8
● Barolo La Serra '98	♟♟♟ 6
● Barolo La Serra '97	♟♟♟ 8
● Barolo La Serra '96	♟♟♟ 8
● Barbera d'Alba Ciabot della Luna '18	♟♟ 5
● Barbera d'Alba Ciabot della Luna '16	♟♟ 4
● Barolo '17	♟♟ 6
● Barolo Cerequio '18	♟♟ 8
● Barolo La Serra '17	♟♟ 8
● Barolo La Serra '16	♟♟ 8
● Barolo La Serra '15	♟♟ 8
● Barolo La Serra '13	♟♟ 8
● Barolo Monvigliero '18	♟♟ 8

499

fraz. Camo
via Roma, 3
12058 Santo Stefano Belbo [CN]
📞 +39 3397848846
🌐 www.499vino.it

CELLAR SALES
PRE-BOOKED VISITS
ANNUAL PRODUCTION 30,000 bottles
HECTARES UNDER VINE 12.00
SUSTAINABLE WINERY

● Langhe Freisa Coste dei Fre '22	🍷🍷 4
○ Blanc de Blancs Dosaggio Zero M. Cl. '20	🍷🍷 5
● Langhe Pinot Nero San Giorgio '22	🍷🍷 4
● Langhe Nebbiolo Sorì del Mattino '22	🍷 5

All'Insù

via San Giovanni, 53
14022 Castelnuovo Don Bosco [AT]
📞 +39 3792092202
🌐 www.allinsuvini.com

ANNUAL PRODUCTION 18,000 bottles
HECTARES UNDER VINE 2.50

● Albugnano Berenices '22	🍷🍷 3*
● Barbera d'Asti Sup. Cygnus '23	🍷🍷 3
● Barbera d'Asti Sup. Pegasus '22	🍷 3

Anzivino

c.so Valsesia, 162
13045 Gattinara [VC]
📞 +39 0163827172
🌐 anzivino.it

CELLAR SALES
PRE-BOOKED VISITS
ACCOMMODATION
ANNUAL PRODUCTION 35,000 bottles
HECTARES UNDER VINE 8.00
SUSTAINABLE WINERY

● Gattinara Ris. '19	🍷🍷 6
● Gattinara '21	🍷🍷 5
● Bramaterra '20	🍷 4

Alemat

via Giardini, 19
15020 Ponzano Monferrato [AL]
📞 +39 335268464
🌐 www.alemat.it

CELLAR SALES
PRE-BOOKED VISITS
ANNUAL PRODUCTION 20,000 bottles
HECTARES UNDER VINE 5.50
VITICULTURE METHOD Certified Organic
SUSTAINABLE WINERY

● Grignolino del M.to Casalese Monferace '20	🍷🍷 6
● M.to Rosso Brunaldo '19	🍷🍷 4
○ Piemonte Riesling Savium '22	🍷🍷 4

Antica Cascina dei Conti di Roero

loc. Val Rubiagno, 2
12040 Vezza d'Alba [CN]
📞 +39 017365459
🌐 www.anticacascinacontidiroero.it

CELLAR SALES
PRE-BOOKED VISITS
ANNUAL PRODUCTION 90,000 bottles
HECTARES UNDER VINE 13.50
SUSTAINABLE WINERY

○ Roero Arneis '23	🍷🍷 3*
● Barbera d'Alba '21	🍷 3
⊙ Nebbiolo d'Alba Spumante Rosé Brut M. Cl. Maria Teresa '21	🍷 5

L'Astemia Pentita

via Crosia, 40
12060 Barolo [CN]
📞 +39 0173560501
🌐 www.astemiapentita.it

CELLAR SALES
PRE-BOOKED VISITS
ANNUAL PRODUCTION 70,000 bottles
HECTARES UNDER VINE 20.00
VITICULTURE METHOD Certified Organic
SUSTAINABLE WINERY

● Barbera d'Alba Sup. '22	🍷🍷 4
● Barolo Terlo '19	🍷🍷 8

OTHER WINERIES

Baldissero
via Roma, 29
12050 Treiso [CN]
📞 +39 3334420201
🌐 www.baldisserovini.it

CELLAR SALES
PRE-BOOKED VISITS
ANNUAL PRODUCTION 20,000 bottles
HECTARES UNDER VINE 7.00

● Barbaresco '21	🍷🍷 6
● Barbaresco Ancò '21	🍷🍷 8

Cantina Sociale Barbera dei Sei Castelli
via Opessina, 41
14040 Castelnuovo Calcea [AT]
📞 +39 0141957137
🌐 www.barberaseicastelli.it

CELLAR SALES
PRE-BOOKED VISITS
ANNUAL PRODUCTION 80,000 bottles
HECTARES UNDER VINE 800.00

● Barbera d'Asti 50 Anni di Barbera '22	🍷🍷 2*
● Nizza Le Vignole '21	🍷🍷 3
● Barbera d'Asti Venti Forti '23	🍷 2
● Nizza Riserva Angelo Brofferio Ris. '20	🍷 5

Battaglio - Briccogrilli
loc. Borbore
via Salerio, 15
12040 Vezza d'Alba [CN]
📞 +39 017365423
🌐 www.battaglio.com

CELLAR SALES
PRE-BOOKED VISITS
ANNUAL PRODUCTION 36,000 bottles
HECTARES UNDER VINE 5.00

● Barbaresco '21	🍷🍷 7
● Barbaresco Serragrilli Ris. '18	🍷🍷 8
● Roero del Comune di Vezza d'Alba Ris. '19	🍷🍷 7
○ Roero Arneis Piasì '23	🍷 4

Barbaglia
via Dante, 54
28010 Cavallirio [NO]
📞 +39 016380115
🌐 www.vinibarbaglia.it

CELLAR SALES
PRE-BOOKED VISITS
ANNUAL PRODUCTION 25,000 bottles
HECTARES UNDER VINE 4.50

● Boca '20	🍷🍷 5
○ Colline Novaresi Bianco Lucino '23	🍷🍷 3
● Colline Novaresi Rosso Cascina del Buonumore '22	🍷 6

Osvaldo Barberis
b.ta Valdibà, 42
12063 Dogliani [CN]
📞 +39 017370054
🌐 www.osvaldobarberis.com

CELLAR SALES
PRE-BOOKED VISITS
ANNUAL PRODUCTION 20,000 bottles
HECTARES UNDER VINE 10.00
VITICULTURE METHOD Certified Organic

● Dogliani Valdibà '23	🍷🍷 4
● Dogliani Puncin '23	🍷🍷 3
● Langhe Barbera Brichat '23	🍷🍷 3
○ Langhe Nascetta Anì '23	🍷🍷 4

Davide Beccaria
via Giovanni Bianco, 3
15039 Ozzano Monferrato [AL]
📞 +39 0142487321
🌐 www.beccaria-vini.it

CELLAR SALES
ANNUAL PRODUCTION 25,000 bottles
HECTARES UNDER VINE 10.00
SUSTAINABLE WINERY

● Grignolino del M.to Casalese Grignò '22	🍷🍷 3*
○ M.to Bianco Garbello '23	🍷🍷 3
● Barbera del M.to Evoè '22	🍷 2
● M.to Freisa Lilàn '22	🍷 3

OTHER WINERIES

Antonio Bellicoso
fraz. Molisso, 5a
14048 Montegrosso d'Asti [AT]
(☎ +39 0141953233
antonio.bellicoso@alice.it

CELLAR SALES
PRE-BOOKED VISITS
ANNUAL PRODUCTION 17,000 bottles
HECTARES UNDER VINE 4.80
SUSTAINABLE WINERY

● Barbera d'Asti Amormio '23	♥♥ 2*
● Barbera d'Asti Merum '22	♥♥ 4
● Grignolino d'Asti Domine Vites '23	♥ 3

Paolo Berta
s.da San Michele, 42
14049 Nizza Monferrato [AT]
(☎ +39 3483536205
info@viniberta.com

● M.to Nebbiolo Baticheur '21	♥♥ 3
● Nizza La Berta '20	♥♥ 4
● Barbera d'Asti Belmon '22	♥ 2
● Barbera d'Asti Evolution '22	♥ 3

Bondi
s.da Cappellette, 73
15076 Ovada [AL]
(☎ +39 0131299186
⊕ www.bondivini.it

CELLAR SALES
PRE-BOOKED VISITS
ANNUAL PRODUCTION 20,000 bottles
HECTARES UNDER VINE 5.00

● Barbera del M.to Sup. Ruvrin '22	♥♥ 4
● M.to Rosso Ansensò '21	♥♥ 5
● M.to Rosso Le Guie '22	♥♥ 3
● Ovada D'Uien '22	♥♥ 3

Benotti Rosavica
via Magliano, 14
12040 Priocca [CN]
(☎ +39 3385331451
azagrbenotti@gmail.com

CELLAR SALES
PRE-BOOKED VISITS
ANNUAL PRODUCTION 15,000 bottles
HECTARES UNDER VINE 2.80

● Barbera d'Alba '23	♥♥ 3
● Roero '21	♥♥ 5
● Langhe Dolcetto '23	♥ 3
● Nebbiolo d'Alba '23	♥ 4

Cascina Biné
via Gavi, 101
15067 Novi Ligure [AL]
(☎ +39 +393318585720
⊕ www.bine.wine

○ Gavi V. Gambarotta Ris. '20	♥♥ 5
○ Gavi 11 '22	♥♥ 3
○ Gavi '23	♥ 3

Bonzano Vini
loc. Castello di Uviglie, 73
15030 Rosignano Monferrato [AL]
(☎ +39 3371250397
⊕ www.bonzanovini.it

CELLAR SALES
PRE-BOOKED VISITS
ANNUAL PRODUCTION 120,000 bottles
HECTARES UNDER VINE 46.00
SUSTAINABLE WINERY

● Barbera del Monferrato Sup. Bruno Bonzano '20	♥♥ 8
⊙ M.to Chiaretto Meridiana '22	♥ 3
○ Piemonte M. Cl. '19	♥ 5

OTHER WINERIES

F.lli Serio & Battista Borgogno

loc. Cannubi
via Crosia, 12
12060 Barolo [CN]
+39 017356107
www.borgognoseriobattista.it

CELLAR SALES
PRE-BOOKED VISITS
ANNUAL PRODUCTION 90,000 bottles
HECTARES UNDER VINE 10.00
SUSTAINABLE WINERY

● Barolo Albarella '20	♟♟ 8
● Barolo Cannubi '20	♟♟ 7
● Barbera d'Alba Sup. '23	♟ 3
● Barolo '20	♟ 6

Brema

via Pozzomagna, 9
14045 Incisa Scapaccino [AT]
+39 014174019
www.vinibrema.com

CELLAR SALES
PRE-BOOKED VISITS
ANNUAL PRODUCTION 150,000 bottles
HECTARES UNDER VINE 25.00
SUSTAINABLE WINERY

● Barbera d'Asti Sup. La Volpettona '21	♟♟ 5

Bussia Soprana

loc. Bussia, 88a
12065 Monforte d'Alba [CN]
+39 039305182
www.bussiasoprana.it

CELLAR SALES
PRE-BOOKED VISITS
ANNUAL PRODUCTION 40,000 bottles
HECTARES UNDER VINE 14.00

● Langhe Nebbiolo Navai '20	♟♟ 6

Francesco Boschis

b.ta Pianezzo, 57
12063 Dogliani [CN]
+39 017370574
www.boschisfrancesco.it

CELLAR SALES
PRE-BOOKED VISITS
ANNUAL PRODUCTION 35,000 bottles
HECTARES UNDER VINE 10.00

● Barbera d'Alba Sup. V. Le Masserie '21	♟♟ 5
● Dogliani Sup. Pianezzo V. dei Prey '22	♟♟ 4
● Dogliani Sup. Pianezzo V. del Ciliegio '21	♟♟ 5

Bricco Carlina

via Valle Talloria, 35
12060 Grinzane Cavour [CN]
+39 0173217294
www.lacarlina.com

CELLAR SALES
ACCOMMODATION
ANNUAL PRODUCTION 70,000 bottles
HECTARES UNDER VINE 15.00
VITICULTURE METHOD Certified Organic

● Barolo Castello '20	♟♟ 7
● Barolo Raviole '20	♟♟ 7
● Barolo del Comune di Grinzane Cavour '20	♟ 7

Cà Bensi

loc. Cascina Bensi, 31a
15070 Tagliolo Monferrato [AL]
+39 014389194
www.ca-bensi.it

CELLAR SALES
PRE-BOOKED VISITS
ACCOMMODATION AND RESTAURANT SERVICE
ANNUAL PRODUCTION 30,000 bottles
HECTARES UNDER VINE 8.50

● Ovada Moongiardin Ris. '20	♟♟ 4
● Ovada Poggio '22	♟♟ 3
○ Piemonte Cortese Intruso '23	♟♟ 2*

PIEDMONT

Cagliero
via Monforte, 34
12060 Barolo [CN]
☏ +39 017356172
⊛ www.cagliero.com

Luca Canevaro
fraz. Mereta, 10
15050 Avolasca [AL]
☏ +39 3394568485
⊛ canevarovini.it

● Barolo Terlo '20	♟♟ 5
● Barolo Ravera '20	♟ 5

● Colli Tortonesi Monleale '19	♟♟ 3
○ Colli Tortonesi Timorasso Derthona Ca' degli Olmi '22	♟ 3

La Capuccina
s.da Capuccina
28060 Cureggio [NO]
☏ +39 0322839930
⊛ www.lacapuccina.it

CELLAR SALES
ANNUAL PRODUCTION 330,000 bottles
HECTARES UNDER VINE 42.00
VITICULTURE METHOD Certified Organic

Carlin De Paolo
fraz. Gorzano, 238a
14015 San Damiano d'Asti [AT]
☏ +39 0141983833
⊛ www.carlindepaolo.com

CELLAR SALES
PRE-BOOKED VISITS
ANNUAL PRODUCTION 200,000 bottles
HECTARES UNDER VINE 40.00

● Colline Novaresi Nebbiolo Faren '21	♟♟ 3
● Colline Novaresi Nebbiolo Opera 32 '20	♟♟ 5
● Colline Novaresi Vespolina Novarina '22	♟♟ 3
☉ Colline Novaresi Nebbiolo Rosato Rouse '23	♟ 3

● Barbera d'Asti Sup. Ad Libitvm '21	♟♟ 4
● Barbera d'Asti Cursus Vitae '22	♟♟ 3
○ Terre Alfieri Arneis '23	♟ 3

Cascina Ballarin
fraz. Annunziata, 115
12064 La Morra [CN]
☏ +39 017350365
⊛ www.cascinaballarin.it

CELLAR SALES
PRE-BOOKED VISITS
ACCOMMODATION
ANNUAL PRODUCTION 60,000 bottles
HECTARES UNDER VINE 9.00
VITICULTURE METHOD Certified Organic
SUSTAINABLE WINERY

Cascina Castlet
s.da Cascinotto, 6
14055 Costigliole d'Asti [AT]
☏ +39 0141966651
⊛ www.cascinacastlet.com

CELLAR SALES
PRE-BOOKED VISITS
ANNUAL PRODUCTION 240,000 bottles
HECTARES UNDER VINE 30.00
SUSTAINABLE WINERY

● Barolo Bricco Rocca '20	♟♟ 7
● Barolo Bussia Ris. '18	♟♟ 8
● Barolo Boiolo '20	♟ 7
● Barolo Bussia '20	♟ 7

● Barbera d'Asti '23	♟♟ 3
● Barbera d'Asti Sup. Litina '21	♟♟ 3
● Monferrato Rosso Policalpo '19	♟ 4
○ Moscato d'Asti '23	♟ 3

OTHER WINERIES

Cascina Gentile

s.da prov.le per San Cristoforo, 11
15060 Capriata d'Orba [AL]
📞 +39 0143468975
🌐 www.cascinagentile.com

CELLAR SALES
PRE-BOOKED VISITS
ANNUAL PRODUCTION 35,000 bottles
HECTARES UNDER VINE 10.00
VITICULTURE METHOD Certified Organic

● Ovada Tre Passi Avanti '21	♟♟ 4
● Cascina Gentile M. Cl. Brut '19	♟ 5
● Piemonte Barbera Mat '21	♟ 4

Cascina Massara
Gian Carlo Burlotto

via Capitano Laneri, 6
12060 Verduno [CN]
📞 +39 0172470152
🌐 www.cantinamassara.it

CELLAR SALES
PRE-BOOKED VISITS
ANNUAL PRODUCTION 80,000 bottles
HECTARES UNDER VINE 10.00

● Barolo '20	♟♟ 6
● Barolo Massara '20	♟♟ 8
● Barolo Monvigliero '20	♟♟ 7
● Barbera d'Alba '21	♟ 3

Cascina Monpissan
Gallino Antonio

Cascina Boera, 75
12043 Canale [CN]
📞 +39 3498733527
🌐 www.cantinamonpissan.com

CELLAR SALES
PRE-BOOKED VISITS
ACCOMMODATION
ANNUAL PRODUCTION 80,000 bottles
HECTARES UNDER VINE 11.00
SUSTAINABLE WINERY

● Roero Arneis '23	♟♟ 2*
● Nebbiolo d'Alba Sup. Duble Karma '18	♟♟ 5
● Roero Arneis Toni Bel Ris. '21	♟ 3

Cascina Penna-Currado

via Alba, 7
12050 Serralunga d'Alba [CN]
📞 +39 3486607603
🌐 www.cascinapennacurrado.com

● Dolcetto d'Alba Bricco Lago '23	♟♟ 4
● Langhe Nebbiolo Bricco Lago '23	♟♟ 5

Cascina Rabaglio

s.da Rabajà, 8
12050 Barbaresco [CN]
📞 +39 3388885031
🌐 www.cascinarabaglio.com

● Barbaresco Gaia Principe '21	♟♟ 5
● Nebbiolo d'Alba Sup. '19	♟♟ 3
● Barbaresco Meruzzano '21	♟ 5

Cascina Sòt

loc. Bussia S. Pietro, 27a
12065 Monforte d'Alba [CN]
📞 +39 3346105267
🌐 www.cascinasot.com

CELLAR SALES
PRE-BOOKED VISITS
ANNUAL PRODUCTION 60,000 bottles
HECTARES UNDER VINE 19.00
SUSTAINABLE WINERY

● Barolo Bricco San Pietro '19	♟♟ 8
● Barolo del Comune di Monforte d'Alba '20	♟♟ 6

215

OTHER WINERIES

Carlo Casetta

b.ta Caretta, 2
12046 Montà [CN]
✆ +39 3382264844
✉ www.carlocasettawines.com

CELLAR SALES
PRE-BOOKED VISITS
ANNUAL PRODUCTION 25,000 bottles
HECTARES UNDER VINE 5.00
SUSTAINABLE WINERY

○ Roero Arneis Bel '23	♟♟ 3
● Roero Fil '21	♟♟ 5

Renzo Castella

via Alba, 15
12055 Diano d'Alba [CN]
✆ +39 017369203
✉ www.renzocastella.it

CELLAR SALES
PRE-BOOKED VISITS
ANNUAL PRODUCTION 35,000 bottles
HECTARES UNDER VINE 8.00

● Barbera d'Alba Sarcat '22	♟♟ 3
● Langhe Nebbiolo Madonnina '22	♟♟ 3

Castello di Perno

loc. Castelletto, 33
12065 Monforte d'Alba [CN]
✆ +39 3345648263
✉ www.castellodiperno.it

CELLAR SALES
PRE-BOOKED VISITS
ANNUAL PRODUCTION 55,000 bottles
HECTARES UNDER VINE 14.50
VITICULTURE METHOD Certified Organic

● Barolo Perno Ris. '18	♟♟ 8
● Barolo Castelletto '19	♟ 7

Francesca Castaldi

via Novembre, 6
28072 Briona [NO]
✆ +39 0321826045
✉ www.cantinacastaldi.it

CELLAR SALES
PRE-BOOKED VISITS
ANNUAL PRODUCTION 20,000 bottles
HECTARES UNDER VINE 6.30
SUSTAINABLE WINERY

● Fara '20	♟♟ 5
● Colline Novaresi Nebbiolo Bigin '22	♟♟ 3
● Colline Novaresi Vespolina Nina '23	♟♟ 3
⊙ Colline Novaresi Rosato Rosa Alba '23	♟ 3

Castello di Neive

c.so Romano Scagliola, 205
12052 Neive [CN]
✆ +39 017367171
✉ www.castellodineive.it

CELLAR SALES
PRE-BOOKED VISITS
ACCOMMODATION
ANNUAL PRODUCTION 150,000 bottles
HECTARES UNDER VINE 27.00
SUSTAINABLE WINERY

● Barbaresco Gallina '21	♟♟ 8
● Barbaresco Albesani V. Santo Stefano '21	♟♟ 8
● Barbaresco Albesani V. Santo Stefano Ris. '19	♟♟ 8

Castello di Tassarolo

loc. Alborina, 1
15060 Tassarolo [AL]
✆ +39 0143342248
✉ www.castelloditassarolo.it

CELLAR SALES
PRE-BOOKED VISITS
RESTAURANT SERVICE
ANNUAL PRODUCTION 130,000 bottles
HECTARES UNDER VINE 20.00
VITICULTURE METHOD Certified Biodynamic
SUSTAINABLE WINERY

○ Gavi del Comune di Tassarolo Il Castello '23	♟♟ 3
○ Gavi del comune di Tassarolo M. Cl. '20	♟♟ 5
● Piemonte Barbera Titouan '23	♟♟ 4

216 | PIEDMONT

OTHER WINERIES

Castello di Uviglie
via Castello di Uviglie, 73
15030 Rosignano Monferrato [AL]
+39 0142488132
www.castellodiuviglie.com

CELLAR SALES
PRE-BOOKED VISITS
ACCOMMODATION
ANNUAL PRODUCTION 130,000 bottles
HECTARES UNDER VINE 45.00
SUSTAINABLE WINERY

● Grignolino del M.to Casalese Monferace San Bastiano Terre Bianche '16	♟♟ 5
○ Le Cave Blanc de Blancs Extra Brut M. Cl. '17	♟♟ 6

Il Chiosso
v.le Guglielmo Marconi 45-47a
13045 Gattinara [VC]
+39 0163826739
www.ilchiosso.it

CELLAR SALES
PRE-BOOKED VISITS
ANNUAL PRODUCTION 80,000 bottles
HECTARES UNDER VINE 12.00
SUSTAINABLE WINERY

● Ghemme '20	♟♟ 5
● Colline Novaresi Spanna '23	♟♟ 4
● Gattinara Galizja '18	♟♟ 6
● Colline Novaresi Nebbiolo '22	♟ 4

Col dei Venti
s.da San Lazzaro, 14
12053 Castiglione Tinella [CN]
+39 0141793071
www.coldeiventi.com

PRE-BOOKED VISITS
ANNUAL PRODUCTION 35,000 bottles
HECTARES UNDER VINE 10.00

● Barbaresco Túfoblu '21	♟♟ 7
● Barolo Debútto '20	♟♟ 8
● Barbera d'Asti Petraia '23	♟ 3
● Langhe Nebbiolo Lampio '22	♟ 4

Colle Manora
loc. Colle Manora
s.da Bozzola, 5
15044 Quargnento [AL]
+39 0131219252
www.collemanora.it

CELLAR SALES
PRE-BOOKED VISITS
ACCOMMODATION
ANNUAL PRODUCTION 100,000 bottles
HECTARES UNDER VINE 21.00
SUSTAINABLE WINERY

● Barbera d'Asti Sup. Manora '21	♟♟ 3
○ M.to Bianco Mimosa '23	♟♟ 3
○ M.to Bianco Mila '21	♟ 4

Colué
via San Sebastiano, 1
12055 Diano d'Alba [CN]
+39 3395268378
www.colue.it

CELLAR SALES
PRE-BOOKED VISITS

Cortino
Produttori Dianesi
via S. Croce, 1/bis
12055 Diano d'Alba [CN]
+39 017369221
www.produttoridianesi.com

○ Piemonte Chardonnay Remondà '22	♟♟ 3
● Barbera d'Alba Sup. Carbea '22	♟ 4
● Barolo Notary '20	♟ 5

○ Alta Langa Brut '20	♟♟ 4
● Barbera d'Alba Sup. Luisella '21	♟♟ 3

OTHER WINERIES

Mario Costa

via Torino, 153
12043 Canale [CN]
📞 +39 0173979486
🌐 www.cantinamariocosta.it

○ Roero Arneis '23	🍷🍷	4
● Roero Morinaldo Ris. '20	🍷🍷	3
● Roero Pecetto Ris. '20	🍷🍷	7
● Barbera d'Alba Sup. '21	🍷	3

Cantine Crosio

via Roma, 75
10010 Candia Canavese [TO]
📞 +39 3398636004
🌐 www.robertocrosio.it

CELLAR SALES
PRE-BOOKED VISITS
ANNUAL PRODUCTION 45,000 bottles
HECTARES UNDER VINE 9.50

● Canavese Barbera Goccianera '21	🍷🍷	3
● Canavese Nebbiolo Gemini '21	🍷🍷	3
○ Erbaluce di Caluso Erbalus '23	🍷🍷	2*
○ Erbaluce di Caluso Incanto Brut Nature '15	🍷🍷	5

Daniele Dabbene

loc. Case Nuove - Gottino, 9/2
12069 Santa Vittoria d'Alba [CN]
📞 +39 3246325112
🌐 www.dabbenedaniele.com

● Barbera d'Alba Valentino '18	🍷🍷	7
● Nebbiolo d'Alba Genta '18	🍷🍷	7
○ Roero Arneis Il Pedrino '20	🍷🍷	6

Mario Cozzo

b.go Gombe, 68 - Madonna delle Grazie
12063 Dogliani [CN]
📞 +39 017370571
🌐 www.cozzomario.it

● Dogliani Pregliasco '19	🍷🍷	4
● Dogliani Sup. Dusin '21	🍷🍷	2*

Piercarlo Culasso

loc. Faset, 5
12050 Barbaresco [CN]
📞 +39 3347216383
🌐 piercarloculasso.it

● Barbaresco Faset '21	🍷🍷	5
● Barbaresco Faset Duesoli '20	🍷🍷	6

Dacapo

s.da Asti Mare, 4
14041 Agliano Terme [AT]
📞 +39 0141964921
🌐 www.dacapovini.com

CELLAR SALES
PRE-BOOKED VISITS
ACCOMMODATION
ANNUAL PRODUCTION 45,000 bottles
HECTARES UNDER VINE 7.00
VITICULTURE METHOD Certified Organic
SUSTAINABLE WINERY

● Barbera d'Asti Sanbastian '22	🍷🍷	3
● Barbera d'Asti Superiore Valrionda '21	🍷🍷	4
● Nizza Vigna Dacapo Ris. '20	🍷🍷	5
○ Moscato d'Asti Cà ed Balos '23	🍷	3

OTHER WINERIES

Duilio Dacasto

fraz. Vianoce, 26
14041 Agliano Terme [AT]
(+39 3339828612
www.dacastoduilio.com

ANNUAL PRODUCTION 24,000 bottles
HECTARES UNDER VINE 8.00

○ Alta Langa Extra Brut Millesimo 2mila20 '20	🍷🍷 5
● Barbera d'Asti Sup. Camp Riond '21	🍷🍷 3
● Nizza Moncucco '21	🍷🍷 5
○ Piemonte Chardonnay Bourg '22	🍷🍷 3

Dei Cavallini

via G. Marconi, 10
28073 Fara Novarese [NO]
(+39 3472724913
damiano.cavallini.eno@gmail.com

CELLAR SALES
PRE-BOOKED VISITS

● Colline Novaresi Nebbiolo Altro '21	🍷🍷 4
● Fara Motto del Lupo '21	🍷🍷 4

Cantina Delsignore

c.so Vercelli, 88
13045 Gattinara [VC]
(+39 0163833777
www.cantinadelsignore.com

PRE-BOOKED VISITS
ANNUAL PRODUCTION 19,500 bottles
HECTARES UNDER VINE 3.00

● Gattinara Borgofranco Ris. '19	🍷🍷 6
● Coste della Sesia Spanna La Crotta '19	🍷🍷 3
● Gattinara Il Putto '20	🍷🍷 5

Destefanis

via Mortizzo, 8
12050 Montelupo Albese [CN]
(+39 0173617189
www.cantinadestefanis.com

CELLAR SALES
PRE-BOOKED VISITS
ANNUAL PRODUCTION 60,000 bottles
HECTARES UNDER VINE 12.00

● Roero Nevis Ris. '20	🍷🍷 5
○ Roero Arneis Radius '23	🍷🍷 3
● Langhe Nebbiolo Nebias '22	🍷 3

Dof Mati

via Cesare Battisti, 19
28073 Fara Novarese [NO]
(+39 3920722767
www.idofmati.it

● Colline Novaresi Nebbiolo Trama '22	🍷🍷 4
● Ghemme Il Matto '19	🍷🍷 6
○ Colline Novaresi Bianco Eresia '23	🍷 4
● Tornato Merlot '21	🍷 5

Giuseppe Ellena

b.ta Ascheri Sottani, 62
12064 La Morra [CN]
(+39 0173500405
www.ellenagiuseppe.it

PRE-BOOKED VISITS
ANNUAL PRODUCTION 35,000 bottles
HECTARES UNDER VINE 6.00
VITICULTURE METHOD Certified Organic

● Barolo del Comune di La Morra '20	🍷🍷 5
● Barbera d'Alba '23	🍷 2
● Barolo Ascheri '20	🍷 6
○ Langhe Nascetta '23	🍷 2

OTHER WINERIES

Cooperativa Produttori Erbaluce di Caluso

piazza Mazzini, 4
10014 Caluso [TO]
📞 +39 0119831447
🌐 www.canavese.it/cpec

CELLAR SALES
PRE-BOOKED VISITS
ANNUAL PRODUCTION 200,000 bottles

○ Erbaluce di Caluso Fiordighiaccio '23	🍷🍷 2*
○ Erbaluce di Caluso Punto 75 '20	🍷🍷 2*

Ferro

fraz. Salere, 41
14041 Agliano Terme [AT]
📞 +39 3282818967
🌐 ferrovini.com

CELLAR SALES
PRE-BOOKED VISITS
ANNUAL PRODUCTION 40,000 bottles
HECTARES UNDER VINE 15.00

● Barbera d'Asti Giulia '22	🍷🍷 3
● M.to Rosso Paolo '20	🍷🍷 5
● Barbera d'Asti Sup. Notturno '21	🍷 3
● Barbera d'Asti Sup. Roche '21	🍷 4

Fogliati

via Pugnane, 8
12060 Castiglione Falletto [CN]
📞 +39 3333230410
🌐 www.poderifogliati.it

ANNUAL PRODUCTION 6,800 bottles
HECTARES UNDER VINE 3.00

● Barolo Bussia '20	🍷🍷 8
● Barolo Treturne '20	🍷🍷 7
● Dolcetto d'Alba '23	🍷 4
● Langhe Nebbiolo '22	🍷 4

Gaggiano

via Rovasenda, 10/12
13045 Gattinara [VC]
📞 +39 3899328825
🌐 www.cantinagaggiano.it

● Bramaterra Gervasio '19	🍷🍷 5
○ Coste della Sesia Rosato '23	🍷🍷 3
● Coste della Sesia Rosso Leandro '21	🍷 3

Gagliasso

b.ta Torriglione, 7
12064 La Morra [CN]
📞 +39 017350180
🌐 www.gagliassovini.it

CELLAR SALES
PRE-BOOKED VISITS
RESTAURANT SERVICE
ANNUAL PRODUCTION 50,000 bottles
HECTARES UNDER VINE 12.50

● Barolo Torriglione '20	🍷🍷 6
● Barolo Rocche dell'Annunziata '20	🍷🍷 6
● Barolo Tre Utin '20	🍷🍷 6
○ Langhe Chardonnay Ultinot '23	🍷🍷 3

Gambino

s.da San Martino, 3
14055 Costigliole d'Asti [AT]
📞 +39 3349756577
🌐 www.emanuelegambino.com

● Barbera d'Asti Sup. '21	🍷🍷 4
○ Piemonte Sauvignon '22	🍷🍷 3
● Barbera d'Asti '22	🍷 4

OTHER WINERIES

Generaj

B.ta Tucci, 4
12046 Montà [CN]
☏ +39 0173976142
🌐 www.generaj.it

CELLAR SALES
PRE-BOOKED VISITS
ANNUAL PRODUCTION 75,000 bottles
HECTARES UNDER VINE 13.00
SUSTAINABLE WINERY

○ Roero Arneis Bric Varomaldo Ris. '20	♟♟ 3
● Roero Bric Aût '21	♟♟ 5
● Roero Bric Aût Ris. '19	♟♟ 5
○ Roero Arneis Quindicilune Ris. '22	♟ 3

Guasti Clemente

c.so IV Novembre, 80
14049 Nizza Monferrato [AT]
☏ +39 3358025368
🌐 www.guasti.it

CELLAR SALES
PRE-BOOKED VISITS
ACCOMMODATION
ANNUAL PRODUCTION 100,000 bottles
HECTARES UNDER VINE 25.00

Barbaresco Sàn Giuliano '21	♟♟ 5
Barbera d'Asti Desideria '23	♟♟ 3
Barbera d'Asti Sup. Boschetto Vecchio '20	♟♟ 4
Barolo Ginestra '19	♟ 7

Paride Iaretti

via Pietro Micca, 23b
13045 Gattinara [VC]
☏ +39 0163826899
🌐 www.parideiaretti.it

CELLAR SALES
PRE-BOOKED VISITS
ANNUAL PRODUCTION 15,000 bottles
HECTARES UNDER VINE 4.00

Gattinara Pietro '20	♟♟ 5
Gattinara V. Valferana '20	♟♟ 7
Gattinara Ris. '19	♟ 6

La Ghibellina

fraz. Monterotondo, 61
15066 Gavi [AL]
☏ +39 0143686257
🌐 www.laghibellina.it

CELLAR SALES
PRE-BOOKED VISITS
ACCOMMODATION
ANNUAL PRODUCTION 60,000 bottles
HECTARES UNDER VINE 9.00
VITICULTURE METHOD Certified Organic

○ Gavi del Comune di Gavi Altius '22	♟♟ 4
○ Gavi del Comune di Gavi Mainìn '23	♟ 3

Hic et Nunc

loc. Cà Milano, 7
15049 Vignale Monferrato [AL]
☏ +39 3480007551
🌐 www.cantina-hicetnunc.it

CELLAR SALES
PRE-BOOKED VISITS
ACCOMMODATION
ANNUAL PRODUCTION 70,000 bottles
HECTARES UNDER VINE 20.00

● Barbera del M.to Sup. Monumento '20	♟♟ 6
○ Felem '21	♟♟ 6
● Grignolino del M.to Casalese Altromondo '22	♟♟ 3

Liedholm

loc. Villa Boemia, 41a
via Per Cuccaro
15043 Lu e Cuccaro Monferrato
☏ +39 0332798836
🌐 www.liedholm.com

CELLAR SALES
PRE-BOOKED VISITS
ACCOMMODATION
ANNUAL PRODUCTION 60,000 bottles
HECTARES UNDER VINE 10.00

● Grignolino del M.to Casalese '21	♟♟ 6
● Grignolino del M.to Casalese Monferace '20	♟♟ 5
○ M.to Bianco Grenoli '23	♟♟ 3
● Barbera d'Asti Sup. '20	♟ 4

OTHER WINERIES

La Lomellina di Gavi

via Lomellina, 31
15066 Gavi [AL]
+39 0143642994
lalomellinadigavi@studiobuzio.it

ANNUAL PRODUCTION 15,000 bottles
HECTARES UNDER VINE 15.00

○ Gavi del Comune di Gavi Marchese Raggio Old Année '17	♥♥ 7
○ Gavi del Comune di Gavi Marchese Raggio '22	♥♥ 3

Podere Macellio

via Roma, 18
10014 Caluso [TO]
+39 0119833511
www.erbaluce-bianco.it

CELLAR SALES
PRE-BOOKED VISITS
ANNUAL PRODUCTION 25,000 bottles
HECTARES UNDER VINE 3.50

○ Erbaluce di Caluso '23	♥♥ 2
○ Erbaluce di Caluso Extra Brut	♥♥ 3

Marenco

p.zza Vittorio Emanuele II, 10
15019 Strevi [AL]
+39 0144363133
marencovini.com

CELLAR SALES
PRE-BOOKED VISITS
ACCOMMODATION
ANNUAL PRODUCTION 250,000 bottles
HECTARES UNDER VINE 80.00
VITICULTURE METHOD Certified Organic
SUSTAINABLE WINERY

● Nizza Zana Ris. '20	♥♥ 6
○ Moscato d'Asti Scrapona '23	♥♥ 4
○ Moscato d'Asti Strev '21	♥♥ 3
● Piemonte Albarossa '21	♥♥ 5

Marrone

fraz. Annunziata, 13
12064 La Morra [CN]
+39 0173509288
denise@agricolamarrone.com

● Barolo Pichemej '20	♥♥ 7
● Barolo Bussia '20	♥♥ 6
○ Langhe Arneis Tre Fie '23	♥♥ 6
● Langhe Nebbiolo '22	♥♥ 4

Marsaglia

via Madama Mussone, 2
12050 Castellinaldo [CN]
+39 0173213048
www.cantinamarsaglia.it

CELLAR SALES
PRE-BOOKED VISITS
ANNUAL PRODUCTION 80,000 bottles
HECTARES UNDER VINE 15.00

⊙ Langhe Rosato Rustichel '23	♥♥ 4
○ Roero Arneis Serramiana '23	♥♥ 3
● Barbera d'Alba S. Cristoforo '22	♥ 3
● Nebbiolo d'Alba San Pietro '21	♥ 3

La Masera

s.da San Pietro, 32
10010 Piverone [TO]
+39 0113164161
www.lamasera.it

CELLAR SALES
PRE-BOOKED VISITS
ANNUAL PRODUCTION 25,000 bottles
HECTARES UNDER VINE 5.00
SUSTAINABLE WINERY

○ Erbaluce di Caluso Anima '22	♥♥ 4
○ Erbaluce di Caluso Anima dAnnata '21	♥♥ 4
○ Erbaluce di Caluso Macaria '21	♥♥ 4

PIEDMONT

OTHER WINERIES

F.lli Massucco
fraz. San Giuseppe
via Serra, 21c
12050 Castagnito [CN]
(+39 0173211121
www.massuccovini.com

CELLAR SALES
PRE-BOOKED VISITS
RESTAURANT SERVICE
ANNUAL PRODUCTION 180,000 bottles
HECTARES UNDER VINE 20.00

● Barbera d'Alba Sup. '21	♈♈ 3
● Nebbiolo d'Alba Sup. '21	♈♈ 4
○ Roero Arneis '23	♈♈ 2*
● Roero Ris. '16	♈ 5

Tenuta Montanello
via Alba Monforte, 88
12060 Castiglione Falletto [CN]
(+39 3488828370
www.tenutamontanello.com

● Barolo del Comune di Castiglione Falletto '20	♈♈ 5
● Barolo Montanello '20	♈♈ 5
● Langhe Nebbiolo '22	♈ 5

F.lli Mossio
fraz. Cascina Caramelli
via Montà, 12
12050 Rodello [CN]
(+39 0173617149
www.mossio.com

CELLAR SALES
PRE-BOOKED VISITS
ACCOMMODATION
ANNUAL PRODUCTION 50,000 bottles
HECTARES UNDER VINE 10.00

Dolcetto d'Alba Bricco Caramelli '22	♈♈ 3
Dolcetto d'Alba Sup. Gamus '21	♈♈ 4
Langhe Nebbiolo Luen '20	♈♈ 4
Dolcetto d'Alba Piano delli Perdoni '21	♈ 2

Tenuta La Meridiana
via Tana Bassa, 5
14048 Montegrosso d'Asti [AT]
(+39 0141956172
tenutalameridiana.com

CELLAR SALES
PRE-BOOKED VISITS
ACCOMMODATION
ANNUAL PRODUCTION 100,000 bottles
HECTARES UNDER VINE 14.00
SUSTAINABLE WINERY

● Barbera d'Asti Sup. Bricco Sereno '21	♈♈ 4
○ Piemonte Chardonnay Puntet '23	♈♈ 3
● Barbera d'Asti Le Gagie '22	♈ 3
● Barbera d'Asti Sup. Tra la Terra e il Cielo '21	♈ 5

Cecilia Monte
via Serracapelli, 17
12052 Neive [CN]
(+39 017367454
www.ceciliamonte.it

CELLAR SALES
ANNUAL PRODUCTION 19,000 bottles
HECTARES UNDER VINE 3.50

● Barbaresco San Giuliano '20	♈♈ 6
● Barbaresco Serracapelli '19	♈♈ 6
○ Colli Tortonesi Timorasso Campogatto '22	♈♈ 5
○ Piemonte Viognier Lume '22	♈♈ 4

Musso
via D. Cavazza, 5
12050 Barbaresco [CN]
(+39 0173635129
www.mussobarbaresco.it

CELLAR SALES
PRE-BOOKED VISITS
ANNUAL PRODUCTION 80,000 bottles
HECTARES UNDER VINE 10.00

● Barbaresco Pora Ris. '19	♈♈ 8
● Barbaresco Pora '21	♈♈ 6
● Barbaresco Rio Sordo '21	♈♈ 6
● Barbaresco '21	♈ 5

OTHER WINERIES

Cantina dei Produttori Nebbiolo di Carema

via Nazionale, 32
10010 Carema [TO]
(☎) +39 0125811160
⊛ www.caremadoc.it

CELLAR SALES
PRE-BOOKED VISITS
RESTAURANT SERVICE
ANNUAL PRODUCTION 65,000 bottles
HECTARES UNDER VINE 20.00

● Carema Et. Bianca Ris. '19	♟♟ 5
☉ Lunaneuva Brut M. Cl. Rosé	♟♟ 4

I Parcellari

via Valcastellana, 18
14037 Portacomaro [AT]
(☎) +39 3288891794
⊛ www.iparcellari.com

CELLAR SALES
PRE-BOOKED VISITS
ANNUAL PRODUCTION 13,000 bottles
HECTARES UNDER VINE 7.40

● Grignolino d'Asti Parcella 505 '21	♟♟ 5
● Nebbiolo d'Alba Sup. Parcella 21 '20	♟♟ 5
○ Piemonte Chardonnay Parcella 146 '21	♟♟ 5

Piazzo Comm. Armando

fraz. San Rocco di Seno d'Elvio, 31
12051 Alba [CN]
(☎) +39 0173286798
⊛ www.piazzo.it

CELLAR SALES
PRE-BOOKED VISITS
ANNUAL PRODUCTION 450,000 bottles
HECTARES UNDER VINE 70.00
SUSTAINABLE WINERY

● Barbaresco Pajoré '21	♟♟ 5
● Barolo Sottocastello di Novello '20	♟ 7
● Barolo Valente '20	♟ 5

Federico Nicola

s.da deglia Alberoni, 10
14023 Cocconato [AT]
(☎) +39 3333906436
⊛ www.nicolavini.com

CELLAR SALES
PRE-BOOKED VISITS
RESTAURANT SERVICE
ANNUAL PRODUCTION 20,000 bottles
HECTARES UNDER VINE 4.50

● Albugnano Sup. '20	♟♟ 3
● Barbera d'Asti '22	♟♟ 2
● Barbera d'Asti Sup. Ruasin '19	♟♟ 3
● Piemonte Grignolino '23	♟ 2

Pasquale Pelissero

via Cascina Crosa, 2
12052 Neive [CN]
(☎) +39 017367376
⊛ www.pasqualepelissero.com

CELLAR SALES
PRE-BOOKED VISITS
ANNUAL PRODUCTION 35,000 bottles
HECTARES UNDER VINE 8.00

● Dolcetto d'Alba Cascina Crosa '23	♟♟ 2
● Langhe Nebbiolo Pasqualin '22	♟♟ 3

Paolo Poggio

via Roma, 67
15050 Brignano Frascata [AL]
(☎) +39 0131784929
⊛ www.cantinapoggiobrignano.com

CELLAR SALES
PRE-BOOKED VISITS
ANNUAL PRODUCTION 17,000 bottles
HECTARES UNDER VINE 4.20

● Colli Tortonesi Barbera Derio '21	♟♟
○ Colli Tortonesi Timorasso Derthona '22	♟
○ Colli Tortonesi Timorasso Derthona Ronchetto '22	♟

OTHER WINERIES

Il Poggio di Gavi
fraz. Rovereto, 171r
15066 Gavi [AL]
☎ +39 3383970590
✉ www.ilpoggiodigavi.com

○ Gavi Nuvole sul Poggio '23	♥♥ 2*
○ Gavi del Comune di Gavi Luna sul Poggio '23	♥♥ 3

Pqlin
s.da Vietta 2
12050 Castagnito [CN]
☎ +39 339 6988587
✉ www.pqlin.it

● Roero '21	♥♥ 4
○ Roero Arneis '23	♥♥ 2*
● Barbera d'Alba '23	♥ 3

Eraldo Revelli
loc. Pianbosco, 29
12060 Farigliano [CN]
☎ +39 0173797154
✉ www.eraldorevelli.com

CELLAR SALES
PRE-BOOKED VISITS
ANNUAL PRODUCTION 35,000 bottles
HECTARES UNDER VINE 7.00
VITICULTURE METHOD Certified Organic
SUSTAINABLE WINERY

● Dogliani Autin Lungh '23	♥♥ 4
● Dogliani Superiore San Matteo '22	♥♥ 4
○ Langhe Rosato Ròsset '23	♥ 4

Maurizio Ponchione
via R. Sacco, 9a
12040 Govone [CN]
☎ +39 017358149
✉ www.ponchionemaurizio.com

CELLAR SALES
PRE-BOOKED VISITS
ANNUAL PRODUCTION 35,000 bottles
HECTARES UNDER VINE 11.00

● Barbera d'Alba Donia '21	♥♥ 3
○ Roero Arneis Monfrini '23	♥♥ 3
● Nebbiolo d'Alba Albazzi '20	♥ 3

Giovanni Prandi
fraz. Cascina Colombè
via Farinetti, 5
12055 Diano d'Alba [CN]
☎ +39 017369248
✉ www.prandigiovanni.it

CELLAR SALES
PRE-BOOKED VISITS
ANNUAL PRODUCTION 20,000 bottles
HECTARES UNDER VINE 5.00
SUSTAINABLE WINERY

● Dolcetto di Diano d'Alba Sörì Colombè '23	♥♥ 2*
● Dolcetto di Diano d'Alba Sörì Cristina '23	♥♥ 2*
● Barbera d'Alba '23	♥ 3
○ Langhe Arneis '23	♥ 2

Ribote - Bruno Porro
loc. San Luigi
b.ta Valdiberti, 24
12063 Dogliani [CN]
☎ +39 017370371
✉ www.ribote.it

CELLAR SALES
PRE-BOOKED VISITS
ANNUAL PRODUCTION 40,000 bottles
HECTARES UNDER VINE 15.00

● Dogliani San Luigi '23	♥♥ 2*
○ Langhe Bianco '23	♥♥ 3
○ Alta Langa Extra Brut Ribote '19	♥ 5
● Dogliani Ribote '22	♥ 3

225

OTHER WINERIES

Ridaroca

fraz. Valdoisa, 66
14015 San Damiano d'Asti [AT]
📞 +39 0141983897
🌐 www.ridaroca.it

CELLAR SALES
PRE-BOOKED VISITS
ANNUAL PRODUCTION 50,000 bottles
HECTARES UNDER VINE 10.00
VITICULTURE METHOD Certified Organic

● Roero '20	🍷🍷 4
● Roero Testum Ris. '18	🍷🍷 5
● Barbera d'Alba Sup. Magna '20	🍷 4
○ Roero Arneis Cerea Ris. '21	🍷 6

Dante Rivetti

loc. Bricco di Neive, 12
12052 Neive [CN]
📞 +39 017367125
🌐 www.danterivetti.com

CELLAR SALES
PRE-BOOKED VISITS
ANNUAL PRODUCTION 110,000 bottles
HECTARES UNDER VINE 50.00

● Barbaresco Rivetti '21	🍷🍷 5
● Barbaresco Bric Micca '21	🍷🍷 5
● Barbaresco Bricco di Neive Ris. '19	🍷 6

Rizieri

via S. Calocero, 7
12055 Diano d'Alba [CN]
📞 +39 017369183
🌐 www.rizieri.com

CELLAR SALES
PRE-BOOKED VISITS
ANNUAL PRODUCTION 40,000 bottles
HECTARES UNDER VINE 6.50

● Barolo Silio Ris. '18	🍷🍷 6
● Dolcetto di Diano d'Alba Sorì del Ricchino '23	🍷🍷 3
○ Langhe Arneis Arvià '23	🍷🍷 3

Pietro Rinaldi

fraz. Madonna di Como
12051 Alba [CN]
📞 +39 0173360090
🌐 www.pietrorinaldi.com

CELLAR SALES
PRE-BOOKED VISITS
ACCOMMODATION
ANNUAL PRODUCTION 70,000 bottles
HECTARES UNDER VINE 10.00

● Barolo '20	🍷🍷 6
● Barbaresco San Cristoforo '21	🍷🍷 5
○ Langhe Arneis Hortensia '23	🍷 2

Massimo Rivetti

via Rivetti, 22
12052 Neive [CN]
📞 +39 017367505
🌐 www.rivettimassimo.it

CELLAR SALES
PRE-BOOKED VISITS
ANNUAL PRODUCTION 70,000 bottles
HECTARES UNDER VINE 25.00

● Barbaresco Serraboella Ris. '19	🍷🍷 6
● Barbaresco '21	🍷 5
● Barbaresco Froi '21	🍷 6

Francesco Rosso

fraz. Madonna delle Grazie, 27
12040 Santo Stefano Roero [CN]
📞 +39 3356482188
🌐 www.francescorosso.org

● Roero Ris. '15	🍷🍷 5
○ Roero Arneis Madonna delle Grazie '23	🍷🍷 3
● Roero 'Nciarmà '16	🍷 5

OTHER WINERIES

Gigi Rosso

strada Alba-Barolo, 34
12060 Castiglione Falletto [CN]
(☏ +39 0173262369
✉ www.gigirosso.com

CELLAR SALES
PRE-BOOKED VISITS
ANNUAL PRODUCTION 196,000 bottles
HECTARES UNDER VINE 25.00

● Barolo Bricco San Pietro '20	♟♟ 6
● Barolo Ris. '18	♟ 7

F.lli Rovero

loc. Valdonata
fraz. San Marzanotto, 218
14100 Asti
(☏ +39 0141592460
✉ www.rovero.it

CELLAR SALES
PRE-BOOKED VISITS
ANNUAL PRODUCTION 90,000 bottles
HECTARES UNDER VINE 20.00

● Barbera d'Asti Sup. Rouvè '22	♟♟ 4
● Barbera d'Asti Sanpansè '23	♟♟ 3
● Grignolino d'Asti Casalina '23	♟♟ 2*

San Biagio

fraz. Santa Maria
San Biagio, 98
12064 La Morra [CN]
(☏ +39 017350214
✉ www.barolosanbiagio.com

CELLAR SALES
PRE-BOOKED VISITS
ANNUAL PRODUCTION 45,000 bottles
HECTARES UNDER VINE 20.00

● Barbaresco Montersino '21	♟♟ 5
● Barolo Capalot '20	♟♟ 5
● Verduno Pelaverga '23	♟♟ 3

Sassi - San Cristoforo

via Pastura, 10
12052 Neive [CN]
(☏ +39 0173677122
✉ www.sassisancristoforo.com

CELLAR SALES
PRE-BOOKED VISITS
ANNUAL PRODUCTION 14,000 bottles
HECTARES UNDER VINE 3.00

● Barbaresco San Cristoforo '20	♟♟ 5
● Barbaresco San Cristoforo Ris. '19	♟♟ 7
● Dolcetto d'Alba '23	♟♟ 3
● Barbaresco '21	♟ 5

Giacomo Scagliola

reg. Santa Libera, 20
14053 Canelli [AT]
(☏ +39 0141831146
✉ www.scagliola-canelli.it

CELLAR SALES
ANNUAL PRODUCTION 70,000 bottles
HECTARES UNDER VINE 15.00

○ Alta Langa Blanc de Blancs Brut Cuvée Alessandro '20	♟♟ 5
● Barbera d'Asti Camp d'la Bela '22	♟♟ 2*
○ Moscato d'Asti Canelli SiFaSol '23	♟♟ 2*

Simone Scaletta

loc. Manzoni, 61
12065 Monforte d'Alba [CN]
(☏ +39 3484912733
✉ www.simonescaletta.it

CELLAR SALES
PRE-BOOKED VISITS
ANNUAL PRODUCTION 40,000 bottles
HECTARES UNDER VINE 7.00
VITICULTURE METHOD Certified Organic
SUSTAINABLE WINERY

● Barbera d'Alba Sup. Sarsera '22	♟♟ 5
● Barolo Bricco San Pietro Chirlet '20	♟♟ 7
● Barolo Bussia '20	♟♟ 8

OTHER WINERIES

Schiavenza

via Mazzini, 4
12050 Serralunga d'Alba [CN]
(+39 0173613115
@ www.schiavenza.com

CELLAR SALES
PRE-BOOKED VISITS
RESTAURANT SERVICE
ANNUAL PRODUCTION 55,000 bottles
HECTARES UNDER VINE 11.50
SUSTAINABLE WINERY

● Barolo del Comune di Serralunga d'Alba '20	♟♟ 6
● Barolo Broglio '20	♟ 6
● Barolo Cerretta '20	♟ 8

Vini Silva

Cascine Rogge, 1b
10011 Agliè [TO]
(+39 3473075648
@ www.silvavini.com

CELLAR SALES
PRE-BOOKED VISITS
ANNUAL PRODUCTION 50,000 bottles
HECTARES UNDER VINE 12.00

○ Erbaluce di Caluso Dry Ice '23	♟♟ 2*
○ Erbaluce di Caluso Tre Ciochè '23	♟♟ 2*

Cantina Stroppiana

fraz. Rivalta San Giacomo, 6
12064 La Morra [CN]
(+39 0173509419
@ www.stroppianawines.com

CELLAR SALES
PRE-BOOKED VISITS
ANNUAL PRODUCTION 45,000 bottles
HECTARES UNDER VINE 8.00

● Barolo Bussia Ris. '16	♟♟ 8
● Barolo Bricco Cogni '19	♟♟ 6
● Barolo Bussia '19	♟♟ 7
● Barolo San Giacomo '20	♟♟ 7

Serra Domenico

s.da Fornaci Stazione, 18
14041 Agliano Terme [AT]
(+39 3475542447
@ www.serradomenicovini.it

CELLAR SALES
PRE-BOOKED VISITS
ANNUAL PRODUCTION 30,000 bottles
HECTARES UNDER VINE 13.00
SUSTAINABLE WINERY

● Barbera d'Asti Costacasareggio '22	♟♟ 3
● Barbera d'Asti La Padrona '22	♟♟ 2*
● Nizza Vialta '21	♟♟ 5

Marchese Luca Spinola

fraz. Rovereto
loc. Cascina Massimiliana, 97
15066 Gavi [AL]
(+39 3355634941
@ www.marcheselucaspinola.it

CELLAR SALES
PRE-BOOKED VISITS
ANNUAL PRODUCTION 30,000 bottles
HECTARES UNDER VINE 15.00
VITICULTURE METHOD Certified Organic

○ Gavi del Comune di Gavi Extra Brut M. Cl. '18	♟♟ 7
○ Gavi del Comune di Tassarolo '23	♟♟ 3
○ Gavi del Comune di Gavi Carlo '23	♟ 3

Michele Taliano

c.so A. Manzoni, 24
12046 Montà [CN]
(+39 0173975658
@ www.talianomichele.com

CELLAR SALES
PRE-BOOKED VISITS
ANNUAL PRODUCTION 60,000 bottles
HECTARES UNDER VINE 12.00

○ Roero Arneis Ris. '20	♟♟ 2*
● Roero Bric Bossola Ris. '20	♟♟ 4
● Barbera d'Alba A Bon Rendre '23	♟ 3
○ Roero Arneis Serni '23	♟ 2

OTHER WINERIES

Terre dei Santi

via San Giovanni, 6
14022 Castelnuovo Don Bosco [AT]
📞 +39 0119876117
🌐 www.terredeisanti.it

CELLAR SALES
PRE-BOOKED VISITS
ANNUAL PRODUCTION 350,000 bottles
HECTARES UNDER VINE 300.00

● Freisa d'Asti Zaffo '20	🍷🍷 3
● Freisa di Chieri Frizzante '23	🍷🍷 2*
● Albugnano Ultimum '19	🍷 4
● Piemonte Freisa Finibus Terrae '19	🍷 5

Tre Secoli

via Stazione, 15
14046 Mombaruzzo [AT]
📞 +39 014177019
🌐 www.tresecoli.com

CELLAR SALES
PRE-BOOKED VISITS
ANNUAL PRODUCTION 400,000 bottles
HECTARES UNDER VINE 1200.00
VITICULTURE METHOD Certified Organic

● Barbera d'Asti Sup. Sorangela '21	🍷🍷 3*
● Barbera d'Asti CostaMezzane '23	🍷🍷 2*
● Dolcetto d'Ovada I Torci '23	🍷🍷 2*
● Nizza '19	🍷🍷 4

Guido Vada

via Osasca, 21
14050 Coazzolo [AT]
📞 +39 3286973637
🌐 www.guidovada.it

○ Piemonte Moscato Secco Mosca Bianca '23	🍷🍷 4
● Barbera d'Asti Sup. Cà del Mura '21	🍷🍷 7
● Barbera d'Asti Tanguera '21	🍷🍷 4
○ Moscato d'Asti Florentino '23	🍷 3

Tibaldi

s.da San Giacomo, 49
12060 Pocapaglia [CN]
📞 +39 0172421221
🌐 www.cantinatibaldi.com

CELLAR SALES
ANNUAL PRODUCTION 35,000 bottles
HECTARES UNDER VINE 7.00

○ Langhe Favorita '23	🍷🍷 3
● Roero Roccapalea '20	🍷🍷 5
○ Roero Arneis '23	🍷 3
○ Roero Arneis Bricco delle Passere Ris. '22	🍷 4

Trediberri

b.ta Torriglione, 4
12064 La Morra [CN]
📞 +39 0173509302
🌐 www.trediberri.com

CELLAR SALES
PRE-BOOKED VISITS
ANNUAL PRODUCTION 50,000 bottles
HECTARES UNDER VINE 8.00
VITICULTURE METHOD Certified Organic

● Barbera d'Alba '22	🍷🍷 4
● Barolo Berri '20	🍷🍷 7
● Barolo Rocche dell'Annunziata '20	🍷🍷 8
● Langhe Nebbiolo '22	🍷🍷 4

Valdinera

via Cavour, 1
12040 Corneliano d'Alba [CN]
📞 +39 0173619881
🌐 www.valdinera.com

CELLAR SALES
PRE-BOOKED VISITS
ANNUAL PRODUCTION 160,000 bottles
HECTARES UNDER VINE 20.00

● Barbera d'Alba Sup. '21	🍷🍷 3
○ Roero Arneis '23	🍷🍷 3
● Roero San Carlo Ris. '20	🍷🍷 5
● Nebbiolo d'Alba Sontuoso '20	🍷 4

Vallebelbo

via Cossano, 2a
12058 Santo Stefano Belbo [CN]
(+39 0141844190
www.vallebelbo.it

CELLAR SALES
ANNUAL PRODUCTION 3,500,000 bottles
HECTARES UNDER VINE 500.00
VITICULTURE METHOD Certified Organic

○ Alta Langa Extra Brut Collezione '56 '20	♟♟ 5
● Barbera d'Asti Sup. Collezione '56 '22	♟♟ 3

Eraldo Viberti

fraz. Santa Maria
b.ta Tetti, 53
12064 La Morra [CN]
(+39 017350308
www.eraldoviberti.com

CELLAR SALES
PRE-BOOKED VISITS
ANNUAL PRODUCTION 27,000 bottles
HECTARES UNDER VINE 5.00

● Barolo Ris. '05	♟♟ 8

Villa Giada

reg. Ceirole, 10
14053 Canelli [AT]
(+39 0141831100
www.villagiada.wine

CELLAR SALES
PRE-BOOKED VISITS
ANNUAL PRODUCTION 180,000 bottles
HECTARES UNDER VINE 25.00
SUSTAINABLE WINERY

● Moscato d'Asti Surì '23	♟♟ 3
● Nizza Riserva Dedicato a... '20	♟♟ 6
● Nizza Dani '21	♟ 5
○ Piemonte Chardonnay Mané '23	♟ 3

Alberto Voerzio

b.go Brandini, 1a
12064 La Morra [CN]
(+39 3333927654
www.albertovoerzio.com

CELLAR SALES
ANNUAL PRODUCTION 13,000 bottles
HECTARES UNDER VINE 6.00
SUSTAINABLE WINERY

● Barbera d'Alba '21	♟♟ 4
● Barolo '20	♟♟ 6
● Barolo La Serra '20	♟♟ 7

Cantine Volpi

s.s. 10, n.72
15057 Tortona [AL]
(+39 0131861072
www.cantinevolpi.it

CELLAR SALES
ANNUAL PRODUCTION 3,000,000 bottles
HECTARES UNDER VINE 15.00
VITICULTURE METHOD Certified Organic
SUSTAINABLE WINERY

● Colli Tortonesi Barbera Sup. '21	♟♟ 5
○ Colli Tortonesi Timorasso Derthona '22	♟♟ 5
○ Colli Tortonesi Timorasso Derthona Cascina La Zerba di Volpedo '22	♟♟ 5

La Zerba

loc. Zerba, 1
15060 Tassarolo [AL]
(+39 0143342259
www.la-zerba.it

CELLAR SALES
PRE-BOOKED VISITS
ANNUAL PRODUCTION 70,000 bottles
HECTARES UNDER VINE 12.00
VITICULTURE METHOD Certified Organic

○ Gavi del Comune di Tassarolo Terrarossa '23	♟♟ 3*
○ Gavi del Comune di Tassarolo Anfora '22	♟♟ 5
○ Gavi del Comune di Tassarolo '23	♟ 2

LIGURIA

The unique and captivating landscape of Liguria seems to mirror the character of its wines. Stretching for 350 kilometers, this narrow strip of land is characterized by steep slopes and towering Apennine peaks rising from the sea. It's on these rugged hillsides that you'll find small patches where traditional grape varieties are cultivated. If there's a place that embodies the term "heroic viticulture," it's here. Vintners in Liguria work almost entirely by hand, true artisans of the vine, with little opportunity to use machinery or tractors.

The total vineyard area is modest, about 1,500 hectares, but the quality is remarkably high, spanning diverse styles and numerous grape varieties. 65% of production is focused on white wines, thanks to several grape varieties grown across various zones. Among them, vermentino stands out as the quintessential Mediterranean variety, nowhere expressing its sunny, distinctly Ligurian aromas quite like it does here. We've awarded four vermentino wines—three from Colli di Luni and one from the Colline di Levanto—but you'll find over 50 across the region, and regardless of accolades, they are all complex and captivating, with the right balance of aromatics, sapidity, and a hint of iodine. Another significant white is pigato, a close relative of vermentino found exclusively in the Riviera Ligure di Ponente. After several years, we're pleased to once again award an outstanding example of the variety: Bruna's U Baccan '22. As for the reds, the most intriguing variety, also found in Ponente, is rossese, which finds its perfect home in Dolceacqua. We've awarded Terre Bianche's Dolceacqua '23, but you'll discover many other excellent examples in the following pages.

Finally, we conclude with one of Italy's most stunning territories: the Cinque Terre. Its wines are equally famous, starting with the Sciacchetrà—raisin wines bottled in very limited quantities—and dry whites made from native varieties like bosco, albarola, and the already widely mentioned vermentino. This year, we reviewed 11 of these wines—just a handful—but they're worth seeking out. Try them, and you'll see.

Massimo Alessandri

via Costa Parrocchia, 42
18020 Ranzo [IM]
(*) +39 018253458
◈ www.massimoalessandri.it

CELLAR SALES
PRE-BOOKED VISITS
RESTAURANT SERVICE
ANNUAL PRODUCTION 35,000 bottles
HECTARES UNDER VINE 7.00

Massimo Alessandri primarily cultivates local grape varieties, bottling them under the "Costa de Vigne" label. These include the whites, pigato and vermentino, and the reds, granaccia (which is gaining increasing recognition) and rossese (western Liguria's premier wine). One pigato stands out, the "Vigne Veggie," produced from vines over 35 years old. He also works with international varieties often vinified unblended, such as the syrah-based red "Pittapummi." The strikingly harmonious Granaccia '22 offers up blackberry, plum, and a hint of underbrush, captivating the palate with its pervasive, structured body. The whites also exhibit elegance and a fresh character: the Pigato '23 opens with broad Mediterranean aromas of rosemary, thyme, and sage on a youthful, clean body, while the Vermentino '23 stands out with its intense floral and fruity aromas, and nice structure.

Tenuta Anfosso

c.so Verbone, 175
18036 Soldano [IM]
(*) +39 0184289906
◈ www.tenutaanfosso.it

CELLAR SALES
PRE-BOOKED VISITS
ACCOMMODATION
ANNUAL PRODUCTION 25,000 bottles
HECTARES UNDER VINE 4.50

Alessandro Anfosso manages about 5 hectares of vineyards in a beautiful but rugged and fragmented terrain. Finding skilled labor for the vineyards is challenging, but during harvest, cooperatives supplement the workforce with outside support. His now-grown children have joined him to support the operation. The 2022 vintage features cru wines produced from a sparse harvest, reflecting years of drought and water-stressed vines. The line of 2022 Dolceacqua Superiores impress with their aromatic and gustatory impact. The Luvaira delivers red fruit notes, nice character, and a lingering finish. The Poggio Pini offers ripe fruit alongside black pepper and spices, set in a powerful body of great intensity and persistence. Youthful energy enhances and elevates the blackberry and cherry notes of the E Prie '23, with its enveloping, well-expressed and lengthy body.

● Riviera Ligure di Ponente Granaccia '22	▼▼ 4
○ Riviera Ligure di Ponente Pigato Costa de Vigne '23	▼▼ 4
○ Riviera Ligure di Ponente Vermentino Costa de Vigne '23	▼▼ 3
○ Riviera Ligure di Ponente Pigato Vigne Vëggie '22	▼ 4
● Riviera Ligure di Ponente Rossese Costa de Vigne '18	▼▼▼ 4*
● Ligustico '19	▼▼ 6
● Riviera Ligure di Ponente Granaccia '20	▼▼ 4
○ Riviera Ligure di Ponente Pigato Vigne Vëggie '21	▼▼ 4
○ Riviera Ligure di Ponente Pigato Vigne Vëggie '19	▼▼ 4

● Dolceacqua E Prie '23	▼▼ 4
● Dolceacqua Sup. Luvaira '22	▼▼ 5
● Dolceacqua Sup. Poggio Pini '22	▼▼ 5
● Dolceacqua Sup. '20	▼ 4
● Dolceacqua Sup. '20	▼▼ 4
● Dolceacqua Sup. '18	▼▼ 4
● Dolceacqua Sup. '17	▼▼ 4
● Dolceacqua Sup. Fulavin '20	▼▼ 5
● Dolceacqua Sup. Fulavin '19	▼▼ 5
● Dolceacqua Sup. Fulavin '18	▼▼ 5
● Dolceacqua Sup. Luvaira '21	▼▼ 5
● Dolceacqua Sup. Luvaira '20	▼▼ 5
● Dolceacqua Sup. Luvaira '18	▼▼ 5
● Dolceacqua Sup. Poggio Pini '21	▼▼ 5
● Dolceacqua Sup. Poggio Pini '19	▼▼ 5
● Dolceacqua Sup. Poggio Pini '18	▼▼ 5

Arrigoni

via Sarzana, 224
19126 La Spezia
☎ +39 0187504060
✆ www.arrigoni1913.it

CELLAR SALES
PRE-BOOKED VISITS
ACCOMMODATION AND RESTAURANT SERVICE
ANNUAL PRODUCTION 150,000 bottles
HECTARES UNDER VINE 18.00
SUSTAINABLE WINERY

The winery is always bustling. In the countryside, resources are mainly focused on the vineyards of the Cinque Terre, particularly on the restoration of dry stone walls, which require constant and expensive work, often performed by helicopter. This year's vintage boasts excellent aromas and a good concentration of freshness, paving the way for experimenting with new products in the future. The Cinque Terre cellar has been expanded to accommodate more visitors. From Cinque Terre, the Pipato '23 enchants with an enveloping body and incisive structure, showcasing great balance with an enticing freshness and velvety harmony. The Prefetto '23 delivers herbaceous notes of thyme and rosemary, combining an engaging elegance with pleasing sapidity. The Cinque Terre Tra i Monti '23 sees Mediterranean notes bring harmony and balance to a deliberately youthful body.

Laura Aschero

p.zza Vittorio Emanuele, 7
18027 Pontedassio [IM]
☎ +39 3485174690
✆ www.lauraaschero.it

CELLAR SALES
PRE-BOOKED VISITS
ANNUAL PRODUCTION 70,000 bottles
HECTARES UNDER VINE 7.00

Laura Aschero's winery, now run by her granddaughter Bianca Rizzo with vineyard support from her father Marco and cellar management by her mother Carla, has planted a new vineyard to increase the production of vermentino. This expansion became necessary after several years of drought reduced yields. This year, the good harvest has restored optimal quantities, and the beautiful cellar, closed last year due to lack of product, will once again be operational for wine tourists. Pleasant hints of cherry, blackberry, and distant pink pepper emerge in the Rossese '23, which combines good character with harmony in a simple yet intriguing body. The Vermentino '23 also impresses with its vibrant harmony, featuring youthful, sapid, and Mediterranean notes that enrich the palate. Fresh notes characterize the Pigato '23, elevating its delicate extract, leaving a finish on light almond flavors.

LIGURIA

○ Cinque Terre Pipato '23	♔♔ 6
○ Colli di Luni Vermentino Il Prefetto '23	♔♔ 5
○ Cinque Terre Tra i Monti '23	♔♔ 5
○ Blanche M. Cl.	♔ 5
○ Cinque Terre Pipato '22	♕♕ 6
○ Cinque Terre Pipato '21	♕♕ 6
○ Cinque Terre Sciacchetrà Tra i Monti '19	♕♕ 8
○ Cinque Terre Sciacchetrà Tra i Monti '17	♕♕ 8
Cinque Terre Tra i Monti '22	♕♕ 5
○ Cinque Terre Tra I Monti '19	♕♕ 3
○ Colli di Luni Vermentino Il Prefetto '20	♕♕ 3
○ Colli di Luni Vermentino Il Prefetto '19	♕♕ 3*
○ Colli di Luni Vermentino La Cascina dei Peri '19	♕♕ 3*
○ Colli di Luni Vermentino Sup. Il Prefetto '21	♕♕ 5

● Riviera Ligure di Ponente Rossese '23	♔♔ 4
○ Riviera Ligure di Ponente Vermentino '23	♔♔ 4
○ Riviera Ligurre di Ponente Pigato '23	♔ 5
○ Riviera Ligure di Ponente Vermentino '10	♕♕♕ 3*
○ Riviera Ligure di Ponente Pigato '21	♕♕ 4
○ Riviera Ligure di Ponente Pigato '20	♕♕ 4
○ Riviera Ligure di Ponente Pigato '19	♕♕ 4
○ Riviera Ligure di Ponente Pigato '18	♕♕ 3*
○ Riviera Ligure di Ponente Pigato '17	♕♕ 3
● Riviera Ligure di Ponente Rossese '22	♕♕ 4
○ Riviera Ligure di Ponente Vermentino '22	♕♕ 4
○ Riviera Ligure di Ponente Vermentino '21	♕♕ 4
○ Riviera Ligure di Ponente Vermentino '20	♕♕ 4
○ Riviera Ligure di Ponente Vermentino '18	♕♕ 3
○ Riviera Ligurre di Ponente Pigato '22	♕♕ 5

La Baia del Sole - Federici

via Forlino, 3
19034 Luni [SP]
+39 0187661821
www.cantinefederici.com

CELLAR SALES
PRE-BOOKED VISITS
ANNUAL PRODUCTION 220,000 bottles
HECTARES UNDER VINE 33.00

The cellar is located just a few dozen meters from the ruins of the ancient city of Luni. Among the artifacts, authorities found very heavy and porous "cocciopesto" amphorae. Luca and Andrea Federici decided to produce their vermentino "Sol de Lun" organically, using traditional methods with long maceration on the skins and a year of aging in a 1500-liter amphorae. Currently, they produce only a few bottles, but they plan to increase production in the coming years with new organic vineyards. The winery stands out for its Vermentino, notably the Solaris '23, which opens with intoxicating aromas and a well-structured, lengthy body. The Oro d'Isée '23 appeals with vibrant white fruit over a bed of Mediterranean notes, balancing harmony and sapidity. Evolved in color and enticing in its mature fruit aromas, the Sol D Lun '22 makes an interesting first impression, leaving a clearly distinct identity in its wake.

○ Colli di Luni Vermentino Solaris '23	🍷🍷🍷 3*
○ Colli di Luni Vermentino Oro d'Isée '23	🍷🍷 5
○ Colli di Luni Vermentino Sarticola '23	🍷🍷 5
○ Colli di Luni Vermentino Sol D Lun '22	🍷🍷 5
● Colli di Luni Rosso Eutichiano '21	🍷 3
○ Colli di Luni Vermentino Sarticola '22	🍷🍷🍷 5
○ Colli di Luni Vermentino Sarticola '20	🍷🍷🍷 5
○ Colli di Luni Vermentino Sarticola '19	🍷🍷🍷 5
○ Colli di Luni Vermentino Sarticola '15	🍷🍷🍷 4*
○ Colli di Luni Bianco Gladius '21	🍷🍷 3
● Colli di Luni Terre d'Oriente Ris. '17	🍷🍷 5
○ Colli di Luni Vermentino Oro d'Isée '22	🍷🍷 5
○ Colli di Luni Vermentino Oro d'Isée '21	🍷🍷 4
○ Colli di Luni Vermentino Oro d'Isée '20	🍷🍷 4
○ Colli di Luni Vermentino Sarticola '21	🍷🍷 5
○ Colli di Luni Vermentino Solaris '21	🍷🍷 3*

Maria Donata Bianchi

via Merea, 101
18013 Diano Arentino [IM]
+39 0183498233
www.aziendaagricolabianchi.it

CELLAR SALES
PRE-BOOKED VISITS
ACCOMMODATION
ANNUAL PRODUCTION 30,000 bottles
HECTARES UNDER VINE 4.00
VITICULTURE METHOD Certified Organic

A new product is enriching the winery's range: a monovarietal Pigato, derived from a selection of grapes from a specific organic vineyard located in Diano Arentino, about 300 meters above sea level. This vineyard, with its south-west exposure and calcareous soil, imparts particular characteristics to the wine, further enhanced by a light, pre-fermentation cold maceration. Marta Trevia wanted a new wine dedicated to the commitment and skill of the women helping her in the cellar. With its Mediterranean scents and aromas of jasmine and acacia, the Pigato '23 captivates the palate with its rich and persistent body. The Antico Sfizio '23 pleases with its intense color, warm notes, and distant Mediterranean character, standing out for its sapidity and original craftsmanship. The Diana '23 put in a good debut, delivering fresh sapidity and long persistence.

○ Riviera Ligure di Ponente Pigato '23	🍷🍷 5
○ Riviera Ligure di Ponente Vermentino Antico Sfizio '23	🍷🍷 4
○ Riviera Ligure di Ponente Vermentino '23	🍷🍷 5
○ Riviera Ligure di Ponente Pigato Diana '23	🍷 5
○ Riviera Ligure di Ponente Pigato '12	🍷🍷🍷 3*
○ Riviera Ligure di Ponente Vermentino '09	🍷🍷🍷 3
○ Riviera Ligure di Ponente Vermentino '07	🍷🍷🍷 3*
○ Riviera Ligure di Ponente Pigato '22	🍷🍷 3*
○ Riviera Ligure di Ponente Pigato '20	🍷🍷 3*
○ Riviera Ligure di Ponente Pigato '19	🍷🍷 3*
○ Riviera Ligure di Ponente Pigato '14	🍷🍷 3*
○ Riviera Ligure di Ponente Pigato '13	🍷🍷 3*
○ Riviera Ligure di Ponente Vermentino '21	🍷🍷 3*
○ Riviera Ligure di Ponente Vermentino '18	🍷🍷 3*

BioVio

fraz. Bastia
via Crociata, 24
17031 Albenga [SV]
☎ +39 018220776
⊛ www.biovio.it

CELLAR SALES
PRE-BOOKED VISITS
ACCOMMODATION
ANNUAL PRODUCTION 60,000 bottles
HECTARES UNDER VINE 9.00
VITICULTURE METHOD Certified Organic

The winery cultivates pigato and vermentino on just nine hectares across three main areas. In Albenga, the vineyards are in the Marige and Salea zones—here the red, clayey soil gives the wines more sapidity, structure, and alcohol content. In Ranzo, at about 250 meters, the temperature variation and calcareous soil ensure greater aromas. These small plots help preserve and enhance the region's biodiversity. We begin our overview of Caterina and Vincenzo's wines with the Grand Père '22, a wine whose intense, marked color anticipates mature aromas, strong character, and an excellent finish. The Vermentino Aimone '23 also impresses with its hints of yellow flowers and dandelion, offering harmony, sapidity, and roundness. The Ma René '23 delivers intense aromas of mature flowers, broom, and elder, resulting in a wine with a decisive, harmonious temperament and warm finish.

★Bruna

fraz. Borgo
via Umberto I, 81
18020 Ranzo [IM]
☎ +39 3497214868
⊛ www.brunapigato.it

CELLAR SALES
PRE-BOOKED VISITS
ANNUAL PRODUCTION 33,000 bottles
HECTARES UNDER VINE 8.50
VITICULTURE METHOD Certified Organic

This year's harvest is finally regular, with the right amount of grapes allowing the winery to explore new markets that had been dormant due to product shortages. For 26 years, the winery has sold in the US through a reliable American importer, growing sales to nearly 50% of production. The remaining production, bolstered by new small vineyards, is reserved for Italy, where the wine is in demand and not oversaturated. Their whites gratify, starting with the U Baccan '22, which offers up yellow flowers on an herbaceous and Mediterranean profile that enriches the palate with substance, extract, and nice harmony. Warm and pervasive, the Majé '23 expresses abundant Mediterranean character in a harmonious body. The Vermentino '23 presents youthful aromas in a round, silky, and sapid body, set against a backdrop of fruits and Mediterranean nuances.

○ Riviera Ligure di Ponente Pigato Bon in da Bon '23	♟♟ 5
○ Riviera Ligure di Ponente Pigato Grand Père '22	♟♟ 5
○ Riviera Ligure di Ponente Pigato Ma René '23	♟♟ 4
○ Riviera Ligure di Ponente Vermentino Aimone '23	♟♟ 4
○ 4C Rossese Rosato '21	♟ 4
○ Riviera Ligure di Ponente Pigato Bon in da Bon '17	♟♟♟ 5
○ Riviera Ligure di Ponente Pigato Bon in da Bon '16	♟♟♟ 5
○ Riviera Ligure di Ponente Pigato Bon in da Bon '15	♟♟♟ 2*
○ Riviera Ligure di Ponente Vermentino Aimone '11	♟♟♟ 2*

○ Riviera Ligure di Ponente Pigato U Baccan '22	♟♟♟ 6
○ Riviera Ligure di Ponente Pigato Majé '23	♟♟ 4
○ Riviera Ligure di Ponente Vermentino '23	♟♟ 4
○ Riviera Ligure di Ponente Pigato Le Russeghine '22	♟ 5
○ Riviera Ligure di Ponente Pigato U Baccan '18	♟♟♟ 6
○ Riviera Ligure di Ponente Pigato U Baccan '16	♟♟♟ 5
○ Riviera Ligure di Ponente Pigato U Baccan '15	♟♟♟ 5
○ Riviera Ligure di Ponente Pigato U Baccan '13	♟♟♟ 5

LIGURIA

Cà du Ferrà

via Nuova per San Giorgio, 27Bis
19011 Bonassola [SP]
℡ +39 3280369500
🌐 www.caduferra.wine

CELLAR SALES
PRE-BOOKED VISITS
ACCOMMODATION
ANNUAL PRODUCTION 25,000 bottles
HECTARES UNDER VINE 4.00
VITICULTURE METHOD Certified Organic
SUSTAINABLE WINERY

At Cà du Ferrà the work is growing, with numerous objectives ranging from production to communication. The meticulous and innovative approach adopted by Davide Zoppi and Giuseppe Luciano Aieta, the two young owners behind the project, is dedicated to exploring new sensory qualities. Their futuristic vision of emotional perception has led to a new project dedicated to wine tourists, who have the chance to experience a rich sensory journey. The Luccicante '23 thrills the senses. With its strong olfactory impact, jasmine notes open to white fruit—a wine of superb complexity and pleasing harmony. The Intraprendente '22 surprises on the palate with its beautiful golden color and notes of ripe apricot, elevating to a bold freshness. The Bonazolae '23 shines with its brilliant color and vibrant structure.

○ Colline di Levanto Vermentino Luccicante '23	♔♔♔ 5
○ L'Intraprendente Passito '22	♔♔ 8
○ Colline di Levanto Bianco Bonazolae '23	♔♔ 5
◉ Magia di Rosa '23	♔ 5
○ Colline di Levanto Vermentino Luccicante '22	♕♕♕ 5
○ Colline di Levanto Bianco Bonazolae '22	♕♕ 5
○ Colline di Levanto Bianco Bonazolae '21	♕♕ 5
● Colline di Levanto Rosso 'Ngilù '19	♕♕ 4
○ Colline di Levanto Vermentino Luccicante '21	♕♕ 5
○ Diciassettemaggio '20	♕♕ 8
◉ Magia di Rosa '21	♕♕ 5
◉ Magia di Rosa '20	♕♕ 3

Cantine Calleri

loc. Salea
reg. Frati, 2
17031 Albenga [SV]
℡ +39 018220085
cantinecalleri@gmail.com

ANNUAL PRODUCTION 45,000 bottles
HECTARES UNDER VINE 6.00

The harvest has been very good, and the use of cryomaceration at 3.5 degrees, introduced by Marcello Calleri in recent years, has enhanced the quality of the wines. Here they employ conventional methods, and the owner's meticulous attention to the grapes and vineyard work is remarkable. Indeed, he's one of the few local vintners to advocate for the Albenganese subzone, with vineyards in Cisano sul Neva, Salea, and other areas inland from Albenga, at altitudes spanning 80-100 meters above sea level. We appreciated the Mediterranean Saleasco '23 from this subzone, a wine of superb balance and complex craftsmanship, where a pleasing freshness reigns. The Pigato '23 also delights with its herbal notes, nice body, pleasant extract, intense sapidity, and harmony. The I Muzazzi '23 expresses pleasant youthfulness among its pronounced aromas, with a broad aromatic profile and a complex body.

○ Riviera Ligure di Ponente Pigato di Albenga Saleasco '23	♔♔ 5
○ Riviera Ligure di Ponente Vermentino I Müzazzi '23	♔♔ 4
○ Riviera Ligure di Ponente Pigato di Albenga '23	♔♔ 5
○ Riviera Ligure di Ponente Vermentino '23	♔ 4
○ Riviera Ligure di Ponente Pigato di Albenga Saleasco '20	♕♕♕ 3*
○ Riviera Ligure di Ponente Pigato di Albenga Saleasco '19	♕♕♕ 3*
○ Riviera Ligure di Ponente Pigato di Albenga Saleasco '22	♕♕ 3*
○ Riviera Ligure di Ponente Pigato di Albenga Saleasco '21	♕♕ 3*
○ Riviera Ligure di Ponente Vermentino I Müzazzi '21	♕♕ 3*

236

Cheo

loc. Vernazza
via Brigate Partigiane, 1
19018 Vernazza [SP]
☎ +39 0187821189
⊕ www.cheo.it

CELLAR SALES
PRE-BOOKED VISITS
ANNUAL PRODUCTION 13,000 bottles
HECTARES UNDER VINE 2.00
SUSTAINABLE WINERY

The entry of Kirsi, daughter of Bartolo and Lise Lercari, into the winery has spurred new investments, with four new small plots set to increase production by about 10%. After several years of strong winds and bad weather that damaged recent harvests, this year production has returned to normal. Looking ahead, aware of the stony and rocky soil they cultivate, they plan to add drip irrigation to compensate for potential droughts. The Cinqueterre '23 features wildflower aromas, with a fresh yet warm, harmonious, and intense body. The Perciò '23 offers prominent notes of rosemary and medicinal herbs against a backdrop of pronounced sapidity and freshness. The Sciacchetrà '21 opens with an enticing palate, revealing a burst of delightful flavors ranging from ripe apricot to honey, candied orange, and date, finishing with a sweet hint of caramel.

Cantina Cinque Terre

fraz. Manarola
loc. Groppo
19010 Riomaggiore [SP]
☎ +39 0187920435
⊕ www.cantinacinqueterre.com

PRE-BOOKED VISITS
ANNUAL PRODUCTION 200,000 bottles
HECTARES UNDER VINE 45.00

A wine has changed its name: Vigne Alte is now called "Cian Auti" (in dialect), but the product remains the same, with albarola grapes (which prefer higher elevations) combined with bosco and vermentino. In other wines, where the vineyards lie at lower elevations, the primary grape is bosco, which makes up at least 50% of the area cultivated. The historical parceling of the vineyards was essential for mitigating damage from weather and the sea's whims, ensuring adequate harvests. From these vineyards perched by the sea, we appreciated the Pergole Sparse '23 with its vibrant color and aromas of apricot and ripe peach, offering a rich body and a sapid hint of the sea. The Sciacchetrà Riserva '20, a delicate treasure, proves elegant and brilliant, enveloping the senses with its intense notes of honey, ripe apricot, and candied orange. The Costa de Campu '23 releases youthful hints of white flowers.

○ Cinque Terre '23	♟♟ 5
● Cheo Rosso '22	♟♟ 5
○ Cinque Terre Perciò '23	♟♟ 5
○ Cinque Terre Sciacchetrà '20	♟♟♟ 8
● Cheo Rosso '21	♟♟ 5
○ Cinque Terre '22	♟♟ 5
○ Cinque Terre Bianco '21	♟♟ 4
○ Cinque Terre Bianco '20	♟♟ 4
○ Cinque Terre Perciò '22	♟♟ 5
○ Cinque Terre Perciò '21	♟♟ 4
○ Cinque Terre Perciò '20	♟♟ 4
○ Cinque Terre Perciò '19	♟♟ 4
○ Cinque Terre Perciò '18	♟♟ 4
○ Cinque Terre Sciacchetrà '18	♟♟ 8
○ Cinque Terre Sciacchetrà '17	♟♟ 8

○ Cinque Terre Pergole Sparse '23	♟♟ 4
○ Cinque Terre Sciacchetrà Ris. '20	♟♟ 8
○ Cinque Terre Costa de Campu '23	♟♟ 4
○ Cinque Terre '23	♟ 3
○ Cinque Terre Cian Auti '23	♟ 3
○ Cinque Terre '22	♟♟ 3
○ Cinque Terre '21	♟♟ 3*
○ Cinque Terre 50esimo Anniversario '22	♟♟ 5
○ Cinque Terre Costa da' Posa '21	♟♟ 3
○ Cinque Terre Costa de Campu '22	♟♟ 3
○ Cinque Terre Costa de Campu '21	♟♟ 3
○ Cinque Terre Costa de Campu '19	♟♟ 3*
○ Cinque Terre Sciacchetrà Ris. '21	♟♟ 6
○ Cinque Terre Sciacchetrà Ris. '18	♟♟ 6
○ Cinque Terre Vigne Alte '21	♟♟ 3
○ Cinque Terre Vigne Alte '20	♟♟ 3*

Fontanacota

fraz. Ponti
via Provinciale, 137
18024 Pornassio [IM]
📞 +39 3339807442
✉ www.fontanacota.it

CELLAR SALES
PRE-BOOKED VISITS
ANNUAL PRODUCTION 40,000 bottles
HECTARES UNDER VINE 6.00
SUSTAINABLE WINERY

There are no structural changes at the winery run by Marina Berta, assisted by her brother Fabio and the new recruits Ludovico and Andreas. In the vineyard, there's a new replanting of vermentino, while in the cellar, a new label enriches the range. It's called "Libellulablu," a Brut Rosé sparkling wine made entirely from ormeasco grapes. It originates from the vineyards of Pornassio, located at over 500 meters above sea level, where the climate and soil, combined with an early harvest, preserve acidity and aromatic profile. Their traditional whites are a delight, starting with the Vermentino '23, which entices with its yellow flower aromas and whiffs of peach pulp, set in a sapid and elegantly balanced body. The Pigato '23 excites with its fresh pine and eucalyptus aromas, evolving into peach and tropical fruit. The Libellulablu '23, with its intense color and rich perlage, offers a delicate, fresh body.

○ Riviera Ligure di Ponente Vermentino '23	🍷🍷 4
◉ Libellulablu Pas Dosé M. Cl.	🍷🍷 6
○ Riviera Ligure di Ponente Pigato '23	🍷🍷 4
◉ Ormeasco di Pornassio Sciac-trà '23	🍷 4
○ Riviera Ligure di Ponente Moscato Secco Lamantide '23	🍷 5
○ Riviera Ligure di Ponente Pigato '11	🍷🍷🍷 3*
○ Riviera Ligure di Ponente Vermentino '18	🍷🍷🍷 3*
● Pornassio '22	🍷🍷 3
● Riviera Ligure di Ponente Granaccia San Giorgio '22	🍷🍷 4
○ Riviera Ligure di Ponente Pigato '22	🍷🍷 4
○ Riviera Ligure di Ponente Pigato '20	🍷🍷 3
○ Riviera Ligure di Ponente Vermentino '21	🍷🍷 3*
○ Riviera Ligure di Ponente Vermentino '20	🍷🍷 3*

Giacomelli

via Palvotrisia, 134
19030 Castelnuovo Magra [SP]
📞 +39 3496301516
✉ www.azagricolagiacomelli.com

CELLAR SALES
PRE-BOOKED VISITS
ANNUAL PRODUCTION 100,000 bottles
HECTARES UNDER VINE 12.00
SUSTAINABLE WINERY

The work continues, with new energy brought by her son Tommaso, who is the inspiration behind the new label "TaoMa" (the name in Aramaic). This wine is made from pure vermentino grapes from a vineyard in the municipality of Luni. It's a structured wine, created through a 10-hour maceration in the press and aging on the lees with repeated batonnage. The wine is bottled with a screw cap, a modern idea for a wine that can be tasted in the new tasting room. We begin with the winery's traditional offerings. The Boboli '23 satisfies with varietal aromas and fresh Mediterranean notes, delivering a body of great complexity and balance. The Pianacce '23, more subdued in fragrance, reveals a pleasing minerality with a Mediterranean profile, marked by extended extraction and complex harmony. The TaOma '23, with its youthful green color and rosemary hints, bestows elegant freshness.

○ Colli di Luni Vermentino Boboli '23	🍷🍷🍷 4*
○ Colli di Luni Vermentino Pianacce '23	🍷🍷 3*
○ Colli di Luni Vermentino TaOma '23	🍷 4
○ Colli di Luni Vermentino Boboli '21	🍷🍷🍷 4*
○ Colli di Luni Vermentino Boboli '20	🍷🍷🍷 4*
○ Colli di Luni Vermentino Boboli '17	🍷🍷🍷 4*
○ Colli di Luni Vermentino Pianacce '19	🍷🍷🍷 3*
○ Colli di Luni Vermentino Pianacce '18	🍷🍷🍷 3*
○ Colli di Luni Vermentino Boboli '22	🍷🍷 4
○ Colli di Luni Vermentino Giardino dei Vescovi '21	🍷🍷 5
○ Colli di Luni Vermentino Giardino dei Vescovi '19	🍷🍷 5
○ Colli di Luni Vermentino Pianacce '22	🍷🍷 3
○ Colli di Luni Vermentino Pianacce '21	🍷🍷 3*

La Ginestraia

via Steria
18100 Cervo [IM]
+39 3482613723
www.laginestraia.com

ANNUAL PRODUCTION 70,000 bottles
HECTARES UNDER VINE 7.00

After the structural investment in the new cellar, Marco Brangero and Mauro Leporieri are focusing on production. This year has compensated for previous shortages, allowing them to satisfy established clients and enter new markets. The owners are committed to working only with native white grape varieties that have found an ideal microclimate in the area. They have grown to about 70,000 bottles, with an undisputed quality. Focusing on Pigato, the Via Maestra '23 stands out with its broad Mediterranean aromas of rosemary, sage, and distant eucalyptus; in the mouth it's sheer nectar, with an intense structure and a sapid, harmonious body. Le Marige '23, warm and intense, proves rich in extract, with mature fruit. On the palate, it's full and rounded, with a long aftertaste. The Vermentino '23 exhibits a youthful profile, intense sapidity, and pleasing simplicity.

○ Riviera Ligure di Ponente Pigato Via Maestra '23	🍷🍷 5
○ Riviera Ligure di Ponente Pigato Le Marige '23	🍷🍷 5
○ Riviera Ligure di Ponente Pigato '23	🍷 5
○ Riviera Ligure di Ponente Vermentino '23	🍷 5
○ Riviera Ligure di Ponente Pigato Le Marige '18	ΥΥΥ 5
○ Riviera Ligure di Ponente Pigato Le Marige '15	ΥΥΥ 3*
○ Riviera Ligure di Ponente Pigato Via Maestra '16	ΥΥΥ 5
○ Riviera Ligure di Ponente Pigato '22	ΥΥ 3*
○ Riviera Ligure di Ponente Pigato Via Maestra '22	ΥΥ 5

Ka' Manciné

fraz. San Martino
via Maciurina, 7
18036 Soldano [IM]
+39 339 3965477
www.kamancine.it

CELLAR SALES
PRE-BOOKED VISITS
ANNUAL PRODUCTION 20,000 bottles
HECTARES UNDER VINE 3.00

Maurizio Anfosso has requested additional planting rights, granted proportionally to the existing vineyards. Only 1,700 meters, a small amount given the constant annual demands. This limits production growth but not the quality, which consistently receives high praise. The 2023 harvest was good, finally aligning with the needed quantity to enter new markets, currently almost evenly split between Italy and abroad, mainly in America. Only two Dolceacquas were tasted, both of high quality. The Galeae '23 is rich in extract, dominated by red fruit with hints of spice and black pepper, offering a warm, velvety body that's both intense and complex, finishing long. Following is the Beragna '23, which pairs red fruit notes with exotic hints of nutmeg and cinnamon. Rich in extract, it delights the palate with its harmony and well-balanced alcohol.

● Dolceacqua Beragna '23	🍷🍷 4
● Dolceacqua Galeae '23	🍷🍷 4
● Dolceacqua Beragna '17	ΥΥΥ 3*
● Dolceacqua Beragna '16	ΥΥΥ 3*
● Dolceacqua Galeae '21	ΥΥΥ 4*
● Dolceacqua Galeae '13	ΥΥΥ 3*
● Dolceacqua Beragna '22	ΥΥ 3
● Dolceacqua Beragna '20	ΥΥ 3*
● Dolceacqua Bugiardino '21	ΥΥ 4
● Dolceacqua Bugiardino '20	ΥΥ 4
● Dolceacqua Galeae '22	ΥΥ 4
● Dolceacqua Galeae '20	ΥΥ 3*
● Dolceacqua Galeae Angé '21	ΥΥ 4
● Dolceacqua Galeae Angé Ris. '20	ΥΥ 4
● Dolceacqua Galeae Angè Ris. '19	ΥΥ 3
● Dolceacqua Galeae Angé Ris. '18	ΥΥ 3*

Ottaviano Lambruschi

via Olmarello, 28
19030 Castelnuovo Magra [SP]
☎ +39 0187674261
✉ www.ottavianolambruschi.com

CELLAR SALES
PRE-BOOKED VISITS
ANNUAL PRODUCTION 45,000 bottles
HECTARES UNDER VINE 7.00

The wines are the stars of the small changes at the winery: the traditional Costa Marina and Vermentino Superiore are now joined by Il Casale, produced from the younger vineyards, about 10 years old. Approximately 45,000 bottles of white vermentino wine underscore the territory's vocation, which has grown significantly in recent years. The red Maniero, produced in a limited quantity of 3,500 bottles, is a DOC wine made from canaiolo, sangiovese, and merlot, a valuable blend. An excellent debut for Il Casale '23, a Vermentino with broad aromas of ripe fruits, featuring a well-structured body that exudes harmony and finishes with lasting intensity. The Costa Marina '23 offers youthful notes and a bouquet of Mediterranean herbs, with a palate that's rounded, intriguing, and pleasantly sapid. The Superiore '23, with its youthful, brilliant color and Mediterranean herb aromas, presents a harmonious, refined body—a drink with some character.

○ Colli di Luni Vermentino Il Casale '23	♥♥ 5	
● Colli di Luni Rosso Maniero '23	♥♥ 3	
○ Colli di Luni Vermentino Costa Marina '23	♥♥ 5	
○ Colli di Luni Vermentino Sup. '23	♥♥ 6	
○ Colli di Luni Vermentino Costa Marina '16	♥♥♥ 4*	
○ Colli di Luni Vermentino Costa Marina '11	♥♥♥ 4*	
○ Colli di Luni Vermentino Costa Marina '09	♥♥♥ 3	
○ Colli di Luni Vermentino Il Maggiore '15	♥♥♥ 5	
○ Colli di Luni Vermentino Il Maggiore '14	♥♥♥ 5	
○ Colli di Luni Vermentino Il Maggiore '13	♥♥♥ 5	
○ Colli di Luni Vermentino Il Maggiore '12	♥♥♥ 4*	

★Cantine Lunae Bosoni

via Bozzi, 63
19034 Luni [SP]
☎ +39 0187669222
✉ www.cantinelunae.com

CELLAR SALES
PRE-BOOKED VISITS
ANNUAL PRODUCTION 600,000 bottles
HECTARES UNDER VINE 85.00

The Bosoni family is always on the move. Following the inauguration of the cellar, new plantings highlight their continuous growth. The restoration of old terraces has transformed into a beautiful new vineyard at about 500 meters above sea level, in a highly dedicated area in Sarticola. In a spectacular natural amphitheater, a new vermentino vineyard has become productive. The soil, rich in skeleton, aided by the cool winds from the Apuan Alps, creates the ideal environment for the grapes. The Etichetta Nera '23 thrills, with its vibrant, almost brilliant color, herbaceous and Mediterranean aromas, and a pervasive palate that offers good harmony and an enticing drinkability. The Cavagino '23, with its intense broom and elderflower notes, is a wine with a clear identity, radiating endless elegance. The Niccolò V '20 impresses with its pleasant complexity and distinguished character.

○ Colli di Luni Vermentino Lunae Et. Nera '23	♥♥♥ 5	
○ Colli di Luni Albarola '23	♥♥ 5	
○ Colli di Luni Vermentino Cavagino '23	♥♥ 6	
● Colli di Luni Rosso Niccolò V '20	♥♥ 4	
○ Labianca '23	♥♥ 3	
○ Colli di Luni Vermentino Lunae Et. Nera '22	♥♥♥ 5	
○ Colli di Luni Vermentino Lunae Et. Nera '21	♥♥♥ 4*	
○ Colli di Luni Vermentino Lunae Et. Nera '20	♥♥♥ 4*	
○ Colli di Luni Vermentino Lunae Et. Nera '19	♥♥♥ 4*	
○ Colli di Luni Vermentino Lunae Et. Nera '18	♥♥♥ 4*	

Maccario Dringenberg

via Torre, 3
18036 San Biagio della Cima [IM]
(" +39 0184289947
maccariodringenberg@icloud.com

CELLAR SALES
PRE-BOOKED VISITS
ANNUAL PRODUCTION 23,000 bottles
HECTARES UNDER VINE 7.00

Giovanna Maccario and Goetz Dringernberg work seven hectares of vineyard, with a modest annual increase. This year, due to past production shortages, we have the classic Dolceacqua for tasting, but not the 2023 crus, except for the Settecammini '23. This wine is named after seven paths that cross the Alps leading to France. The vineyard is 200 meters from the state border, at an altitude of 550 meters in a specific area within the municipality of Ventimiglia, separate from the rest of the appellation. The Settecammini '23 combines pleasant, broad red fruit notes with exotic hints of nutmeg and clove, all integrated with great harmony. On the palate, its rounded tannins create a unique and satisfying complexity. The F.lli Maccario '22, dry and tannic, yields a clean and pleasant body where licorice and spice notes are evident. The Dolceacqua San Biagio della Cima '23 proves rounded and elegant in character.

Maixei

reg. Porto
18035 Dolceacqua [IM]
(" +39 0184205015
www.maixei.it

CELLAR SALES
PRE-BOOKED VISITS
ANNUAL PRODUCTION 45,000 bottles
HECTARES UNDER VINE 12.00

No changes in terms of vineyard expansion or new labels. Structurally, Gianfranco Croese remains the president, while Fabio Corradi and Pasquale Restuccia are the two technicians covering the viticultural, olive-growing, and floral sectors. The 2023 production has returned to normal quantities after two years of contraction, with about 45,000 bottles sold mainly in Italy, thanks to a national distributor ensuring coverage. Among the various samples tasted, the Barbadirame '22 stands out with its ruby red color and distant orange reflections—a dry drink, with a dusty, expressive body, rich in abundant fruit, with lovely balsamic notes and superb character. The Superiore '22 is also notable for its good fruit, with a broad and velvety body that satisfies with its harmonious structure and long finish. The Vermentino '23 stands out for its enticing and fresh elegance.

● Rossese di Dolceacqua F.lli Maccario 1922 '22	▾▾ 5
● Rossese di Dolceacqua Settecamini '23	▾▾ 5
● Rossese di Dolceacqua San Biagio della Cima '23	▾▾ 5
● Dolceacqua Sup. Vign. Posaú '13	▾▾▾ 3*
● Rossese di Dolceacqua Posaú '21	▾▾▾ 5
● Rossese di Dolceacqua Posaú '20	▾▾▾ 5
● Rossese di Dolceacqua Posaú '19	▾▾▾ 3*
● Rossese di Dolceacqua Posaú Biamonti '17	▾▾▾ 5
● Rossese di Dolceacqua Sup. Luvaira '18	▾▾▾ 4*
● Rossese di Dolceacqua Sup. Vign. Luvaira '07	▾▾▾ 4*
● Rossese di Dolceacqua Sup. Vign. Posaú '10	▾▾▾ 3*
● Rossese di Dolceacqua Sup. Vign. Posaù '08	▾▾▾ 3

● Dolceacqua Sup. Barbadirame '22	▾▾ 5
● Dolceacqua Sup. '22	▾▾ 5
○ Riviera Ligure di Ponente Vermentino '23	▾▾ 4
● Dolceacqua '21	▾▾ 4
● Dolceacqua '18	▾▾ 3*
● Dolceacqua Sup. '21	▾▾ 4
● Dolceacqua Sup. '19	▾▾ 4
● Dolceacqua Sup. '18	▾▾ 4
● Dolceacqua Sup. '16	▾▾ 4
● Dolceacqua Sup. Barbadirame '21	▾▾ 5
● Dolceacqua Sup. Barbadirame '20	▾▾ 4
● Dolceacqua Sup. Barbadirame '19	▾▾ 4
● Dolceacqua Sup. Barbadirame '17	▾▾ 4
○ Lucrezia	▾▾ 5
● Mistral '21	▾▾ 4
○ Riviera Ligure di Ponente Riviera dei Fiori Vermentino '17	▾▾ 3

Peq Agri

s.da Castello, 20
17051 Andora [SV]
☏ +39 018336973
⊛ www.peqagri.it

CELLAR SALES
PRE-BOOKED VISITS
ANNUAL PRODUCTION 160,000 bottles
HECTARES UNDER VINE 23.00

A relatively new operation, in just a few years
Pec Agri has carved out a presence in western
Liguria. Led by two young entrepreneurs who
chose to invest in the land of their childhood, it's
absorbed several key properties in the area.
These include the "Lupi" winery in Pieve di Teco,
where they honored the Pigato "Vignamare" by
naming their on-site restaurant after it;
"Guglierame" in Pornassio, known for its
Pornassio DOC; "Berry & Berry," from which
they brought their current winemaker; and
"Cascina Praiè," the producer's main location,
which offers a stunning landscape overlooking
the Gulf of Diano Marina. The winery focuses on
the region's flagship grape, pigato, and this year,
the Vignamare '21 delivers a spectrum of
intensity—in its color, in the many aromas of
fresh and ripe yellow fruit, and in its harmonious,
richly extracted body with an impressively long
finish. We also appreciated the well crafted Il
Canneto '23, enticing in its color, with nice
extraction that evolves into a warm structure
and a full, persistent body.

○ Riviera Ligure di Ponente Pigato Il Canneto '23	♀♀ 4
○ Riviera Ligure di Ponente Pigato Vignamare '21	♀♀ 6
○ Riviera Ligure di Ponente Pigato Petraie '23	♀♀ 5
○ Riviera Ligure di Ponente Pigato '23	♀ 4
● Pornassio '21	♀♀ 3

La Pietra del Focolare

via Isola, 76
19034 Luni [SP]
☏ +39 0187662129
⊛ www.lapietradelfocolare.it

CELLAR SALES
PRE-BOOKED VISITS
ANNUAL PRODUCTION 35,000 bottles
HECTARES UNDER VINE 5.00
SUSTAINABLE WINERY

Stefano Salvetti and Laura Angelini have
embarked on a path increasingly focused on
eco-sustainable viticulture, with total respect for
both product and land. In the winery, where
grapes like vermentino, albarola, trebbiano,
malvasia, sangiovese, canaiolo, and other local
varieties from around 15 different plots come
together, their focus is on maturing their whites
through extended maceration periods and
micro-oxygenation (achieved through the use of
majolica amphorae). It's an experiment, but also
a deliberate choice to connect with traditional
winemaking methods. It's among the
Vermentinos that we find the most interesting
selections, starting with the substantial body and
broad extraction of the L'Aura di Sarticola '21, a
wine whose aromas of fruit and underbrush
enrich a palate full of flesh and marked harmony.
Young and floral, the Villa Linda '23 envelops with
its fresh sapidity. The Anfora '20 impresses with
its intense color, ample extraction, and tropical
fruit aromas.

○ Campo alle Rose '22	♀♀ 4
○ Colli di Luni Vermentino Anfora '20	♀♀ 7
○ Colli di Luni Vermentino Sup. L'Aura di Sarticola '21	♀♀ 7
○ Colli di Luni Vermentino Villa Linda '23	♀♀ 5
○ Colli di Luni Vermentino Sup. Villa Linda '20	♀♀♀ 4*
○ Colli di Luni Vermentino L'Aura Sup. di Sarticola '20	♀♀ 8
○ Colli di Luni Vermentino Sup. Solarancio '22	♀♀ 7
○ Colli di Luni Vermentino Sup. Solarancio '21	♀♀ 4
○ Colli di Luni Vermentino Sup. Solarancio '19	♀♀ 4
○ Colli di Luni Vermentino Sup. Villa Linda '22	♀♀ 6

Terenzuola

via Vercalda, 14
54035 Fosdinovo [MS]
+39 0187670387670387
www.terenzuola.it

CELLAR SALES
PRE-BOOKED VISITS
ANNUAL PRODUCTION 180,000 bottles
HECTARES UNDER VINE 20.00

Ivan Giuliani cultivates vineyards in several growing areas. Some are in the Cinque Terre appellation, a challenging and rugged coastal area. From here come his Cinque Terre Bianco and the sweet Sciacchetrà. Other vineyards are located in the Colli di Luni DOC, an area straddling the border between Liguria and Tuscany. These lands are easier to cultivate and are home to the vermentino grape, which consistently impresses with distinctive and high-quality wines. The Vigne Basse '23 enchants with its sapidity and minerality, which lend character and an elegant finish to this extract-rich wine with infinite aromas. The Fosso di Corsano '23 impresses with its notes of white flowers and Mediterranean hints; on the palate, it's fresh and offers good intensity. The Pini di Corsano '23 opens with floral tones that give way to fruit, resulting in a full-bodied and round wine with a pleasant aftertaste.

Terre Bianche

loc. Arcagna
18035 Dolceacqua [IM]
+39 018431426
www.terrebianche.com

CELLAR SALES
PRE-BOOKED VISITS
ACCOMMODATION
ANNUAL PRODUCTION 55,000 bottles
HECTARES UNDER VINE 8.50
VITICULTURE METHOD Certified Organic
SUSTAINABLE WINERY

Filippo Rondelli and Franco Locani continue to expand with new, small plantings of native grape varieties: rossese, pigato, and vermentino. In the appellation of Dolceacqua and also the Riviera Ligure di Ponente, the proximity to the Ligurian Alps gives the local whites a different interpretation, marked by finesse and elegance. However, the star wine remains the red Dolceacqua, produced in all its versions in the 2023 vintage. After a timid and reserved nose, the Dolceacqua '23 opens on the palate with a broad expression of red fruits, spices, and black pepper, with a complex body and a long finish. The Bricco Arcagna '22 makes a notable impact both on the nose and palate, with soft tannins settling in, enriched by fruit and spices that rest on a bed of licorice. Delicate and refined, the Vermentino '23 also stands out.

o Colli di Luni Vermentino V. Basse '23	♟♟ 3*
o Colli di Luni Vermentino Pini di Corsano '23	♟♟ 7
o Colli di Luni Vermentino Sup. Fosso di Corsano '23	♟♟ 4
o Cinque Terre '23	♟ 5
o Colli di Luni Vermentino Fosso di Corsano '21	♟♟♟ 4*
o Colli di Luni Vermentino Sup. Fosso di Corsano '18	♟♟♟ 4*
o Colli di Luni Vermentino Sup. Fosso di Corsano '17	♟♟♟ 3*
o Colli di Luni Vermentino Sup. Fosso di Corsano '16	♟♟♟ 3*
o Colli di Luni Vermentino Sup. Fosso di Corsano '11	♟♟♟ 3*

● Dolceacqua '23	♟♟♟ 4*
● Dolceacqua Bricco Arcagna '22	♟♟ 6
o Riviera Ligure di Ponente Pigato '23	♟♟ 4
o Riviera Ligure di Ponente Vermentino '23	♟♟ 4
● Dolceacqua Bricco Arcagna '19	♟♟♟ 6
● Dolceacqua Bricco Arcagna '17	♟♟♟ 6
● Dolceacqua Bricco Arcagna '14	♟♟♟ 5
● Dolceacqua Bricco Arcagna '12	♟♟♟ 5
● Rossese di Dolceacqua '12	♟♟♟ 3*
● Rossese di Dolceacqua Bricco Arcagna '09	♟♟♟ 4
● Rossese di Dolceacqua Bricco Arcagna '08	♟♟♟ 5
● Dolceacqua '21	♟♟ 4
● Dolceacqua Bricco Arcagna '21	♟♟ 6
● Dolceacqua Terrabianca '21	♟♟ 5

Vis Amoris

loc. Caramagna
s.da per Vasia, I
18100 Imperia
📞 +39 3483959569
🌐 www.visamoris.it

CELLAR SALES
PRE-BOOKED VISITS
ANNUAL PRODUCTION 24,000 bottles
HECTARES UNDER VINE 3.50
VITICULTURE METHOD Certified Organic
SUSTAINABLE WINERY

The 2023 harvest was marked by drought and heat, but fortunately, there was just enough rain to ensure both quality and a good yield relative to the hectares under vines. The limited bottling due to previous years' drought meant that the Sogno '22 wasn't bottled. Moreover, expansion into new markets was curbed, leading to an increased focus in Liguria. In the cellar, Simone Tozzi, the young and constantly experimenting winemaker, oversees operations. There's a different stylistic profile in the wines, starting with the Domé '23, with its delicate and elegant aromas of white fruit that envelop the palate, imparting a new and distinctive character. The Verum '23 features rich extraction, with a bold, sapid body and abundant fruit aromas. The youthful Ormeasco, the Ormè 22, showcases nice intensity, with a warm body and an elegant, restrained and well-balanced drinkability.

○ Riviera Ligure di Ponente Pigato Domè '23	♟♟	4
● Ormè '22	♟	6
○ Riviera Ligure di Ponente Pigato Verum '23	♟	4
○ Riviera Ligure di Ponente Pigato Domè '21	♟♟	4
○ Riviera Ligure di Ponente Pigato Sogno '21	♟♟	6
○ Riviera Ligure di Ponente Pigato Sogno '20	♟♟	4
○ Riviera Ligure di Ponente Pigato Sogno '19	♟♟	4
○ Riviera Ligure di Ponente Pigato Verum '21	♟♟	6
○ Verum '22	♟♟	6

Zangani

loc. Ponzano Superiore
via Gramsci, 46
19037 Santo Stefano di Magra [SP]
📞 +39 0187632406
🌐 www.zangani.it

CELLAR SALES
PRE-BOOKED VISITS
ANNUAL PRODUCTION 75,000 bottles
HECTARES UNDER VINE 10.00

Filippo Zangani, together with his family, is one of the owners of the winery. He oversees the administrative, commercial, and marketing aspects of the business. Claudio Scopsi, the vineyard coordinator, manages the fieldwork across approximately 10 hectares (divided into 7-8 plots in Santo Stefano Magra), as well as operations in the cellar. The winery is also strengthening its commitment to tourism, with a hospitality area adjacent to the production space in the hillside "Mortedo" cru, where events and activities aimed at attracting visitors are offered. Cultivated in the winery's heart, the Mortedo '23 reveals aromas of yellow flowers over Mediterranean scrub, enveloping with its enticing, youthful expression; in the mouth a slender, subtle, and sapid body wraps the palate with natural softness. Alluring and expressive, the Boceda '23 exudes harmony, thanks to its ability to balance delicacy and Mediterranean notes. The Marfi Bianco '23 is a deep, fresh, and smooth drink.

○ Colli di Luni Vermentino Sup. Boceda '23	♟♟	4
○ Colli di Luni Vermentino Mortedo '23	♟♟	3
○ Marfi Bianco '23	♟♟	3
● Gemma Vermentino Nero '23	♟	4
○ Colli di Luni Vermentino Sup. Boceda '22	♟♟♟	4*
○ Colli di Luni Vermentino Sup. Boceda '21	♟♟♟	4*
○ Colli di Luni Vermentino Sup. Boceda '19	♟♟♟	4*
○ Colli di Luni Vermentino Sup. Boceda '18	♟♟♟	4*
○ Colli di Luni Vermentino Mortedo '22	♟♟	3*
○ Colli di Luni Vermentino Sup. Boceda '20	♟♟	4

OTHER WINERIES

aMaccia
fraz. Borgo
via Umberto I, 54
18020 Ranzo [IM]
☎ +39 0183318003
✉ www.amaccia.it

CELLAR SALES
PRE-BOOKED VISITS
ACCOMMODATION
ANNUAL PRODUCTION 25,000 bottles
HECTARES UNDER VINE 3.80
SUSTAINABLE WINERY

○ Riviera Ligure di Ponente Pigato Diuna Volta '23	♀♀ 4
● Ormeasco di Pornassio '22	♀ 4
○ Riviera Ligure di Ponente Pigato '23	♀ 4

Cantine Bregante
via Unità d'Italia, 47
16039 Sestri Levante [GE]
☎ +39 018541388
✉ www.cantinebregante.it

CELLAR SALES
PRE-BOOKED VISITS
ANNUAL PRODUCTION 120,000 bottles
HECTARES UNDER VINE 1.00

○ Portofino Bianchetta Genovese Segesta '23	♀♀ 3
○ Portofino Vermentino Segesta '23	♀♀ 2*
● Portofino Ciliegiolo Oro '23	♀ 3
○ Portofino Moscato '23	♀ 3

I Cerri
via Garibotti
19012 Carro [SP]
☎ +39 3485102780
✉ www.icerrivaldivara.it

ANNUAL PRODUCTION 8,000 bottles
HECTARES UNDER VINE 1.00

○ Cian dei Seri '23	♀♀ 4
○ Poggio alle Api '23	♀♀ 3
○ Baccarosa '23	♀ 3
○ Campo Grande '23	♀ 3

Cantine Bondonor
via Isola Alta, 53
19034 Luni [SP]
☎ +39 3488713641
✉ www.cantinebondonor.it

ANNUAL PRODUCTION 15,000 bottles
HECTARES UNDER VINE 3.00

○ Colli di Luni Vermentino Aegidius I '23	♀♀ 4
○ Colli di Luni Vermentino Lunaris '23	♀♀ 4

Luca Calvini
via Solaro, 76/78a
18038 Sanremo [IM]
☎ +39 0184660242
✉ www.luigicalvini.com

CELLAR SALES
PRE-BOOKED VISITS
ANNUAL PRODUCTION 50,000 bottles
HECTARES UNDER VINE 3.50
SUSTAINABLE WINERY

○ Riviera Ligure di Ponente Vermentino V. del Poggio '23	♀♀ 5
○ Moscatello di Taggia '23	♀♀ 5
○ Riviera Ligure di Ponente Pigato '23	♀♀ 4

Il Chioso
via Mazzini, 57
19038 Sarzana [SP]
☎ +39 0187625147
✉ www.picedibenettini.it

CELLAR SALES
PRE-BOOKED VISITS
ACCOMMODATION
ANNUAL PRODUCTION 30,000 bottles
HECTARES UNDER VINE 7.00

○ Colli di Luni Vermentino Il Chioso '23	♀♀ 4
● Gran Baccano '23	♀ 4

OTHER WINERIES

LIGURIA

Colombiera

fraz. Colombiera
loc. Montecchio, 92
19033 Castelnuovo Magra [SP]
☎ +39 0187699235
✉ cantinalacolombiera.it

CELLAR SALES
PRE-BOOKED VISITS
ACCOMMODATION
ANNUAL PRODUCTION 90,000 bottles
HECTARES UNDER VINE 11.00

○ Colli di Luni Vermentino 3 Vigne '23	♟♟	3

Durin

via Roma, 202
17037 Ortovero [SV]
☎ +39 0182547007
✉ www.durin.it

CELLAR SALES
PRE-BOOKED VISITS
ACCOMMODATION
ANNUAL PRODUCTION 110,000 bottles
HECTARES UNDER VINE 18.00
SUSTAINABLE WINERY

○ Riviera Ligure di Ponente Vermentino '23	♟♟	4
● Granaccia '23	♟♟	4
○ Riviera Ligure di Ponente Pigato I Scianchi '23	♟♟	4

Tenuta La Ghiaia

via Falcinello, 127
19038 Sarzana [SP]
☎ +39 3313053842
✉ www.tenutalaghiaiawineresort.it

CELLAR SALES
PRE-BOOKED VISITS
ACCOMMODATION AND RESTAURANT SERVICE
ANNUAL PRODUCTION 30,000 bottles
HECTARES UNDER VINE 4.50
VITICULTURE METHOD Certified Organic

⊙ Atys Rosato '23	♟♟	3
○ Colli di Luni Bianco Ithaa '23	♟♟	5
○ Colli di Luni Vermentino '23	♟♟	3

Deperi

fraz. Caneto, 2
18020 Ranzo [IM]
☎ +39 3458499732
✉ www.deperi.eu

CELLAR SALES
PRE-BOOKED VISITS
RESTAURANT SERVICE
ANNUAL PRODUCTION 60,000 bottles
HECTARES UNDER VINE 9.00
SUSTAINABLE WINERY

○ Riviera Ligure di Ponente Pigato Cremen '22	♟♟	5
○ Riviera Ligure di Ponente Vermentino '23	♟♟	3¹
⊙ Ormeasco Sciac-trà '23	♟♟	3

Gajaudo

s.da prov.le 7
18035 Isolabona [IM]
☎ +39 0184208095
✉ www.gajaudo.it

CELLAR SALES
PRE-BOOKED VISITS
RESTAURANT SERVICE
ANNUAL PRODUCTION 56,000 bottles
HECTARES UNDER VINE 13.00

● Dolceacqua '23	♟♟	4
○ Riviera Ligure di Ponente Vermentino Pejuna '23	♟♟	4
○ Riviera Ligure di Ponente Vermentino '23	♟	3

Viticoltori Ingauni

via Roma, 3
17037 Ortovero [SV]
☎ +39 0182547127
✉ www.viticoltoriingauni.it

ANNUAL PRODUCTION 300,000 bottles
HECTARES UNDER VINE 84.50

⊙ Pornassio Sciac-trà '23	♟♟	3
● Pornassio Sup. '22	♟♟	4
● Pornassio '23	♟	3

OTHER WINERIES

Podere Lavandaro

via Castiglione
54035 Fosdinovo [MS]
☎ +39 018768202
🖅 www.poderelavandaro.it

CELLAR SALES
PRE-BOOKED VISITS
ANNUAL PRODUCTION 25,000 bottles
HECTARES UNDER VINE 5.00

○ Colli di Luni Vermentino '23	♓♓ 4
○ Colli di Luni Vermentino Maséro '22	♓♓ 4
● Vermentino Nero '23	♓ 4
● Vignanera '22	♓ 4

Il Monticello

via Groppolo, 7
19038 Sarzana [SP]
☎ +39 0187621432
🖅 www.ilmonticello.it

CELLAR SALES
PRE-BOOKED VISITS
ACCOMMODATION
ANNUAL PRODUCTION 120,000 bottles
HECTARES UNDER VINE 12.00

○ Colli di Luni Vermentino Argille Grigie '23	♓♓ 4
○ Colli di Luni Vermentino Groppolo '23	♓♓ 4
○ Colli di Luni Vermentino Argille Rosse '23	♓♓ 6
○ Colli di Luni Vermentino Poggio Paterno '22	♓♓ 5

Possa

via San Antonio, 72
19017 Riomaggiore [SP]
☎ +39 0187920959
🖅 www.possa.it

CELLAR SALES
PRE-BOOKED VISITS
ANNUAL PRODUCTION 7,000 bottles
HECTARES UNDER VINE 1.50

○ Cinque Terre '23	♓♓ 5
○ Principe Jacopo Frizzante '23	♓♓ 5

Tenute MFR

via Asquasciati
18010 Santo Stefano al Mare [IM]
🖅 www.tenutemfr.it

○ Riviera Ligure di Ponente Moscatello di Taggia V.T. Sansteva '19	♓♓ 5
○ Riviera Ligure di Ponente Vermentino Sansteva '23	♓♓ 4

Gino Pino

fraz. Missano
via Podestà, 31
16030 Castiglione Chiavarese [GE]
☎ +39 0185408036
🖅 www.pinogino.it

ANNUAL PRODUCTION 25,000 bottles
HECTARES UNDER VINE 3.50

⊙ Golfo del Tigullio Portofino Cerasum '23	♓♓ 4
○ Golfo del Tigullio Portofino Moscato '23	♓♓ 3
○ Golfo del Tigullio Portofino Bianchetta Genovese '23	♓ 3

Edoardo Primo

via Aurelia, 190
19030 Castelnuovo Magra [SP]
☎ +39 340 6739118
🖅 www.edoardoprimo.it

CELLAR SALES
ANNUAL PRODUCTION 30,000 bottles
HECTARES UNDER VINE 7.00

○ Colli di Luni Vermentino Cà Duà '23	♓♓ 3
● Colli di Luni Rosso Maraccio '23	♓ 3
○ Colli di Luni Vermentino Ma Teo '23	♓ 3

LIGURIA

247

OTHER WINERIES

Rocca Vinealis
via Paolo Moretto, 7
17017 Roccavignale [SV]
📞 +39 3933305772
🌐 www.roccavinealis.it

● Drü '21	♟♟ 5
⊙ La Rebecca '23	♟♟ 4
○ Terre Grigie '23	♟♟ 3

Ronco Daniele
via Roma, 17
17037 Ortovero [SV]
📞 +39 3408715596
🌐 www.aziendaagricolaronco.it

● Riviera Ligure di Ponente Granaccia '22	♟♟ 5
○ Riviera Ligure di Ponente Pigato	
Cru Rosetum '22	♟♟ 5
○ Riviera Ligure di Ponente Pigato Bio '23	♟ 4

Roberto Rondelli
fraz. Brunetti, 1
18033 Camporosso [IM]
📞 +39 3280348055
rondellivini@gmail.com

CELLAR SALES
PRE-BOOKED VISITS
ACCOMMODATION
ANNUAL PRODUCTION 15,000 bottles
HECTARES UNDER VINE 4.00

● Dolceacqua Marne Blu '22	♟♟ 4
● Dolceacqua Sup. Roja '22	♟♟ 8
○ Birbante Vermentino '23	♟ 4

Terre di Levanto
loc. San Gottardo, 1
19015 Levanto [SP]
📞 +39 3395432482
🌐 www.terredilevanto.com

CELLAR SALES
PRE-BOOKED VISITS
ANNUAL PRODUCTION 2,500 bottles
HECTARES UNDER VINE 2.50
SUSTAINABLE WINERY

● Colline di Levanto Ciliegiolo '22	♟♟ 4
○ Colline di Levanto Vermentino '22	♟♟ 4
○ Colline di Levanto Bianco Giaè '22	♟ 5

Innocenzo Turco
via Bertone, 7a
17040 Quiliano [SV]
📞 +39 0192000026
🌐 www.innocenzoturco.it

CELLAR SALES
PRE-BOOKED VISITS
ACCOMMODATION AND RESTAURANT SERVICE
ANNUAL PRODUCTION 6,000 bottles
HECTARES UNDER VINE 2.50

⊙ In Rosa '22	♟♟ 3
● Riviera Ligure di Ponente Granaccia	
Cappuccini '22	♟♟ 5
● Riviera Ligure di Ponente Granaccia '23	♟ 4

Villa Cambiaso
via privata Galla, 4
16010 Serra Riccò [GE]
📞 +39 0142945004
🌐 www.villacambiasowine.it

CELLAR SALES
PRE-BOOKED VISITS
ANNUAL PRODUCTION 60,000 bottles
HECTARES UNDER VINE 20.00

○ Pigato '23	♟♟ 3
○ Val Polcevera Bianchetta Genovese '23	♟♟ 4
○ Val Polcevera Vermentino '23	♟ 3

LOMBARDY

Lombardy is a truly comprehensive wine region. This year's tastings confirm its national leadership when it comes to Metodo Classico, with numerous Franciacorta and Oltrepò Pavese wines earning top marks. The Brescia district, in particular, has showcased ambitious efforts in terms of vineyard zoning, demonstrating a new level of production consistency, with ever more refined dosage levels and the emergence of single-vineyard wines that reflect a deepening connection to the land. The overall quality of their cuvées is high, as demonstrated by our reviews of producers along the shores of Lake Iseo. We were especially struck by the stylistic evolution of many Satèn wines, which had previously drawn criticism from us as well.

In Oltrepò Pavese, the standout producers are those fully committed to the cause of pinot nero. In fact, our Sparkling Wine of the Year hails from a single vineyard at an elevation of over 500 meters in Rocca de' Giorgi: the 2019 Poggio Dei Duca cuvée from Calatroni, a family-run winery that has seen remarkable growth in sparkling wine production. This wine offers an uncommon freshness, with a vibrant, taut, and flavorful profile. Bravo. Among the whites, there are excellent examples of Lugana and San Martino della Battaglia (made from friulano grapes), with intriguing forays into the Capriano del Colle denomination, where even the reds seem more modern and lively. For rosé lovers, Valtènesi sets a strong benchmark: it's one of the few districts that has made a dedicated effort to showcase the area's best grapes in rosé form, with an ever-expanding and increasingly diverse range of wines. Dry and fragrant, they develop their full aromatic potential after a couple of years of bottle aging. Our Rosé of the Year is the spectacular 2023 Valtènesi Chiaretto Antitesi by Avanzi.

Speaking of elegance, we turn to the slopes of Valtellina, where the region's subzones—Sassella, Inferno, Grumello—are fully asserting themselves, along with the richness of the forzato style. A special mention also goes to the marble quarries of Botticino, a fairytale-like appellation in Brescia, where some producers act as true stewards of this unique district. As for sweet wines, the rare red moscato of Scanzo, in Bergamo, or Moscato di Volpara offer excellent alternatives. Impressive results also come from the Garda and Valcalepio areas, and we close with Mantua's Lambruscos. Few regions can offer such diverse stylistic interpretations and landscapes. Lastly, we salute two wineries that have won Tre Bicchieri for the first time: San Cristoforo in Franciacorta, Marangona in Lugana, I Vitari in Valtellina and F.lli Turina in Valtènesi. This outstanding performance by Lombardy is rounded off with notable recognition in the Rare Wines section. Four exceptional expressions earned a place: three from Franciacorta and one from Valtellina.

1701

via Galileo Galiei, 44
25046 Cazzago San Martino [BS]
(☎) +39 0307750875
⊛ www.1701franciacorta.it

ANNUAL PRODUCTION 80,000 bottles
HECTARES UNDER VINE 11.00
VITICULTURE METHOD Certified Biodynamic
SUSTAINABLE WINERY

1701 is a relatively young winery in the
Franciacorta landscape, both in terms of its age
and the spirit of their production philosophy.
This is evident in the fact that Federico and
Silvia Stefini practice biodynamic farming in the
vineyards. Their commitment carries over into
the cellar, where each wine faithfully expresses
the unique terroirs and vintages. The result is a
line of wines with strong identities and
character, making tasting their Metodo Classicos
an intriguing experience. The Franciacorta
Dosaggio Zero Blanc de Noirs '19 opens with
pervasive and balsamic aromas of thyme, mint,
and peach. The palate shifts gears, starting with
fruity notes, then becoming spicier through its
long finish. The Rosé '20 is original and
commendable, offering up fragrant tones of
raspberry and hints of coffee, with a clean,
relaxed finish. The Satén '20, with its exquisitely
food-friendly character, showcases tones of
honey, pastry, and white fruit.

○ Franciacorta Dosaggio Zero Blanc de Noirs '19	♟♟ 7
⊙ Franciacorta Dosaggio Zero Rosé '20	♟♟ 7
○ Franciacorta Brut Nature	♟♟ 5
○ Franciacorta Satèn '20	♟♟ 6
○ Franciacorta Dosaggio Zero Elleessedì '20	♟ 5
○ Franciacorta Dosaggio Zero Ris. '16	♟♟♟ 8
○ Franciacorta Dosaggio Zero Blanc de Noirs '18	♟♟ 7
○ Franciacorta Dosaggio Zero Blanc de Noirs '16	♟♟ 5
○ Franciacorta Dosaggio Zero Elleessedì '16	♟♟ 5
⊙ Franciacorta Dosaggio Zero Rosé '19	♟♟ 7
⊙ Franciacorta Rosé Dosaggio Zero '17	♟♟ 6

F.lli Agnes

via Campo del Monte, 1
27040 Rovescala [PV]
(☎) +39 038575206
⊛ wwww.fratelliagnes.it

CELLAR SALES
PRE-BOOKED VISITS
ANNUAL PRODUCTION 120,000 bottles
HECTARES UNDER VINE 21.00

Brothers Cristiano and Sergio Agnes have an
unmistakable production style. They are reserved
and meticulous, working in the vineyard and
cellar on their beloved croatina, using the least
invasive methods possible to respect their family
land. They work with ancient varieties of
bonarda (in Rovescala, the name of the wine and
the grape are the same) and old vineyards in a
few crus. Their approach calls for the use of
perfectly ripe grapes, indigenous yeasts, slow
macerations, patience, care, and the ample use of
concrete in vinification. The result is a range of
distinctly regional wines. Every year, the Campo
del Monte and Cresta del Ghiffi compete for the
title of the best Bonarda Frizzante among Fratelli
Agnes' range. This year, the Cresta del Ghiffi '23
captivates with its violet and raspberry aromas, a
broad, fruit-forward palate, and notable residual
sugars balanced by abundant yet smooth tannins.
The Campo del Monte '23 is not far behind,
standing out primarily for its aromas, which lean
more toward black forest fruits.

● OP Bonarda Frizzante Cresta del Ghiffi '23	♟♟ 3
● OP Bonarda Frizzante Campo del Monte '23	♟♟ 3
● Possessione del Console '22	♟♟ 3
● Il Sole Che Ama la Terra Croatina '23	♟ 3
● Poculum '18	♟ 4
● OP Bonarda Frizzante Campo del Monte '15	♟♟♟ 2
● OP Bonarda Frizzante Campo del Monte '21	♟♟ 2
● OP Bonarda Frizzante Campo del Monte '20	♟♟ 2
● OP Bonarda Frizzante Cresta del Ghiffi '22	♟♟ 3

★AR.PE.PE

via del Buon Consiglio, 4
23100 Sondrio
℡ +39 0342214120
🌐 www.arpepe.com

CELLAR SALES
ANNUAL PRODUCTION 100,000 bottles
HECTARES UNDER VINE 15.00

The more than century-old winemaking tradition that Arturo Pelizzati Perego draws upon (he represents the fifth generation of his family to helm Ar.Pe.Pe.) is one of the core ingredients that has secured this winery a place among Italy's top producers. But it?s not just about the legacy. Arturo?s diligent work in the vineyards and his steadfast respect for tradition have been just as essential in bringing Ar.Pe.Pe.?s wines to the highest level of quality. This year's tastings reaffirm previous impressions: the entire lineup exudes great elegance, particularly the Valtellina superiore Sassella Nuova Regina Riserva '18, which blends finesse and complexity, making for superb drinkability and enjoyment. The Valtellina Superiore Sassella Riserva Ultimi Raggi '18 is steeped in classicism, with tannins that time will soften, promising greatness for this nebbiolo. The Grumello Buon Consiglio '18 brings us back to full maturity of fruit and a rich palate.

Valtellina Sup. Sassella Nuova Regina Ris. '18	▼▼▼ 8
Valtellina Sup. Grumello Buon Consiglio Ris. '18	▼▼ 8
Valtellina Sup. Sassella Ultimi Raggi Ris. '18	▼▼ 8
Rosso di Valtellina '22	▼▼ 5
Valtellina Sup. Il Pettirosso '22	▼▼ 6
Valtellina Sup. Inferno Sesto Canto Ris. '18	▼▼ 8
Valtellina Sup. Sassella Nuova Regina Ris. '16	♔♔♔ 8
Valtellina Sup. Sassella Rocce Rosse Ris. '16	♔♔♔ 8
Valtellina Sup. Sassella Stella Retica '17	♔♔♔ 6

Giovanni Avanzi

via Trevisago, 19
25080 Manerba del Garda [BS]
℡ +39 0365551013
🌐 www.avanzi.net

CELLAR SALES
PRE-BOOKED VISITS
ANNUAL PRODUCTION 500,000 bottles
HECTARES UNDER VINE 50.00
SUSTAINABLE WINERY

Avanzi is a winery with a strong local connection. Founded in 1931, it's now in its fourth generation, with Giovanni's sons, still involved in various stages of production. Divided into four estates among the towns of Sirmione, Desenzano, and Polpenazze, the winery boasts a variety of soils and microclimates, resulting in wines with distinct personalities that highlight the differences between the shores of Lake Garda and the Valtènesi area. In addition to vineyards, they also maintain olive groves, in keeping with Garda tradition. And we're pleased to announce that the Chiaretto Antitesi has been named our Rosé of the Year. The 2023 is an extraordinarily modern and dynamic version, the result of meticulous winemaking, the finest groppello grapes (with a touch of barbera) and a lengthy period on the lees. Its pale color introduces a fresh, fruit-forward nose, rich in citrus and floral tones that shift to mineral, smoky notes. On the palate, it's vibrant, slender yet deep, with a linear structure and an elegant, lively finish on fruit and fumé. The Rosavero '23, with its honed profile, performs at a similar level.

⊙ RGC Valtènesi Chiaretto Antitesi '23	▼▼▼ 6
⊙ RGC Valtènesi Chiaretto Rosavero '23	▼▼ 3*
● Garda Rosso '19	▼▼ 5
○ Lugana Borghetta Ris. '20	▼▼ 5
● RGC Cl. Groppello Predelli '22	▼▼ 3
○ Lugana Sirmione '23	▼ 4
⊙ RGC Valtènesi Chiaretto Antitesi '22	♔♔♔ 6
⊙ RGC Valtènesi Chiaretto Antitesi '21	♔♔♔ 6
○ Lugana Sirmione '22	♔♔ 4
○ Lugana Sirmione '21	♔♔ 3
⊙ RGC Valtènesi Chiaretto Rosavero '22	♔♔ 3*
⊙ RGC Valtènesi Chiaretto Rosavero '21	♔♔ 3*
⊙ RGC Valtènesi Chiaretto Rosavero '20	♔♔ 3*
○ San Martino della Battaglia Liquoroso Notorius '05	♔♔ 4

Ballabio

via San Biagio, 32
27045 Casteggio [PV]
☎ +39 0383805878
🌐 www.ballabiowinery.it

The Nevelli family has owned this renowned brand since 1987. In 2010, the family decided to focus solely on Metodo Classico. Under the expert guidance of Carlo Casavecchia, they launched the Noir Collection project, an effort characterized by uncompromising choices both in the vineyards and their modern cellar: low-impact cultivation practices, the introduction of green manure, meticulous grape selection, and cutting-edge technology. The result is a range of elegant, refined, and ageworthy sparkling wines. The Metodo Classico Cave Privée '17 confirms its pedigree year after year. This vintage stands out for its elegance, fine beading, and an expansive aromatic array spanning everything from wildflowers to saffron, with mint and balsamic sensations competing with its minerality. The palate is airy, deep, sapid, and extraordinarily long. Among their excellent offerings, the Rosé shines with its delicate opening, followed by abundant floral and berry notes, always exuding class and restraint.

○ Farfalla Dosaggio Zero M. Cl. Cave Privée '17	♟♟♟ 8
⊚ Farfalla Noir Collection M. Cl. Extra Brut Rosé Pinot Nero	♟♟ 5
○ Farfalla Noir Collection M. Cl. Extra Brut Pinot Nero	♟♟ 5
○ Farfalla Noir Collection M. Cl. Pas Dosé Pinot Nero	♟♟ 5
○ Farfalla Dosaggio Zero M. Cl. Cave Privée '16	♟♟♟ 8
⊚ Farfalla Noir Collection Extra Brut M. Cl. Rosé	♟♟ 4
⊚ Farfalla Noir Collection Extra Brut M. Cl. Rosé	♟♟ 5
○ Farfalla Noir Collection Zero Dosage M. Cl.	♟♟ 5
○ OP M. Cl. Pinot Nero Dosaggio Zero Farfalla Cave Privée '13	♟♟ 7

I Barisei

via Bellavista, 1a
25030 Erbusco [BS]
☎ +39 0307356069
🌐 www.ibarisei.it

The connection between the Bariselli family and winemaking, a legacy that began with Paolo in 1898, dates back more than 100 years. Today, the story continues with the fourth generation, represented by Gian Mario Bariselli, who crafts Franciacortas that embody his vision of the land and the historical knowledge passed down. The winery itself sits on the scenic hills of Erbusco, overlooking estate vineyards and Lake Iseo, and visitors can enjoy a warm welcome that includes a well-run agriturismo. The winery offers a solid array of high-quality wines. The Franciacorta Extra Brut Mariadri '16 boasts a fine and delicate profile, with tones of white flowers meeting citrus hints, unfolding broad and multifaceted, with a long, balsamic finish. The Satèn '20, with its caressing and persistent bead, plays on floral and spicy sensations, finishing clean and dry. The fragrant Brut Rosé '19 is delightful, offering up notes of small red fruits, particularly raspberry, making for a highly enjoyable drink.

○ Franciacorta Satèn '20	♟♟ 6
⊚ Franciacorta Brut Rosè '19	♟♟ 7
○ Franciacorta Extra Brut Mariadri '16	♟♟ 8
○ Franciacorta Extra Brut Opposè '16	♟ 8
○ Franciacorta Dosaggio Zero Francesco Battista Ris. '13	♟♟♟ 8
○ Franciacorta Dosaggio Zero Francesco Battista Ris. '12	♟♟ 8
○ Franciacorta Dosaggio Zero Francesco Battista Ris. '11	♟♟ 6
○ Franciacorta Dosaggio Zero Natura '18	♟♟ 7
⊚ Franciacorta Dosaggio Zero Natura '16	♟♟ 6
○ Franciacorta Extra Brut Mariadri '15	♟♟ 6
⊚ Franciacorta Extra Brut Mariadri '13	♟♟ 6
⊚ Franciacorta Extra Brut Mariadri '12	♟♟ 5
⊚ Franciacorta Rosé '13	♟♟ 6

★Barone Pizzini

via San Carlo, 14
25050 Provaglio d'Iseo [BS]
☎ +39 0309848311
☞ www.baronepizzini.it

CELLAR SALES
PRE-BOOKED VISITS
ACCOMMODATION
ANNUAL PRODUCTION 370,000 bottles
HECTARES UNDER VINE 58.00
VITICULTURE METHOD Certified Organic
SUSTAINABLE WINERY

In a period when sustainability is of paramount importance, it?s worth noting that Barone Pizzini earned its organic certification back in 1997. Yet, that?s only one piece of the puzzle of the winery?s success. Drawing on a holistic view of the land combined with a distinctive style of wine, Barone Pizzini has become a benchmark in Franciacorta. The Naturae Edizione '20 is complete in every aspect. Spicy notes join with whiffs of pastry and citrus tones, aromas that integrate with a vibrant, fresh palate, where a refined, perfectly balanced evolved sensation stands out. The Satèn '20 is truly intriguing, marked by delicate notes of hazelnut, butter, and white pepper, with a sapid, juicy palate to follow. The Rosé '20, made from pinot nero grapes, offers ample fruit and lively flavor.

★★★Bellavista

via Bellavista, 5
25030 Erbusco [BS]
☎ +39 0307762000
☞ www.bellavistawine.it

CELLAR SALES
PRE-BOOKED VISITS
ANNUAL PRODUCTION 1,600,000 bottles
HECTARES UNDER VINE 203.00
SUSTAINABLE WINERY

Bellavista needs little introduction, not just for sparkling wine lovers but for wine enthusiasts in general. Thanks to the visionary leadership of the Moretti family, the winery has long been at the forefront of innovation, making it one of the cornerstones of Franciacorta. The Bellavista style is iconic, from the design of its bottles to its unique interpretation of sparkling wines across its range. The Teatro alla Scala '19 brims with finesse and complexity, showcasing distinct and elegant references to pastry, citrus, and white flowers. The palate is creamy, progressive, taut, and multifaceted, with a long, satisfying finish. The Satèn '19 reveals a fresh, balanced palate, accompanied by a delicate, graceful floral profile. The Pas Operé and Alma Grande Cuvée are also excellent, the former offering sapidity and a relaxed finish, the latter more balsamic and citrusy, with nice tension on the palate.

Franciacorta Dosaggio Zero Naturae Edizione '20	♟♟♟ 6
Franciacorta Extra Brut Rosé Edizione '20	♟♟ 6
Franciacorta Satèn Edizione '20	♟♟ 6
Franciacorta Extra Brut Golf 1927 VIII Tiratura	♟♟ 5
Franciacorta Dosaggio Zero Animante XI Tiratura	♟ 5
Franciacorta Dosage Zéro Naturae '16	♟♟♟ 5
Franciacorta Dosaggio Zero Bagnadore Ris. '16	♟♟♟ 8
Franciacorta Dosaggio Zero Bagnadore Ris. '14	♟♟♟ 8
Franciacorta Dosaggio Zero Bagnadore Ris. '11	♟♟♟ 7

○ Franciacorta Brut Teatro alla Scala '19	♟♟♟ 8
○ Franciacorta Satèn '19	♟♟ 8
○ Franciacorta Brut Grande Cuvée Alma	♟♟ 7
○ Franciacorta Dosaggio Pas Operé '18	♟♟ 8
○ Franciacorta Brut Teatro alla Scala '16	♟♟♟ 7
○ Franciacorta Brut Teatro alla Scala '13	♟♟♟ 7
○ Franciacorta Extra Brut Vittorio Moretti Ris. '08	♟♟♟ 8
○ Franciacorta Non Dosato Alma	♟♟♟ 5
○ Franciacorta Pas Operé '10	♟♟♟ 7
○ Franciacorta Pas Operé '09	♟♟♟ 7
◎ Franciacorta Rosé Brut '18	♟♟♟ 8
◎ Franciacorta Rosé Brut '17	♟♟♟ 8
○ Riserva Vittorio Moretti Meraviglioso	♟♟♟ 8

★Guido Berlucchi Franciacorta

loc. Borgonato
p.zza Duranti, 4
25040 Corte Franca [BS]
☎ +39 030984381
@ www.berlucchi.it

CELLAR SALES
PRE-BOOKED VISITS
ANNUAL PRODUCTION 4,000,000 bottles
HECTARES UNDER VINE 574.00
VITICULTURE METHOD Certified Organic
SUSTAINABLE WINERY

The fact that today we can all enjoy one of Italy?s finest sparkling wines is largely thanks to the visionary Franco Ziliani and Guido Berlucchi, who were the first to believe in Franciacorta as a land of great sparkling wine. Over 60 years later, the winery is led by the next generation?Arturo, Cristina, and Paolo?who continue to be pioneers in the region. Their entire range of Metodo Classicos is of exceptional quality, with some in the 61 and Palazzo Lana lines reaching the heights of excellence. The Nature Rosé 61 '17 is truly remarkable, unveiling enticing, soft tones of raspberry, pomegranate, coffee, and brioche. The palate is pervasive and progressive, displaying depth and vibrancy, with finely crafted tactile sensations and a long, precise finish. From the same vintage, the Nature 61 impressed with its fragrant peach and pastry tones, making for a crisp, vibrant drink. The Palazzo Lana Extrême Riserva '13, made from pinot noir grapes, is more layered and rich.

Bersi Serlini

via Cereto, 7
25050 Provaglio d'Iseo [BS]
☎ +39 0309823338
@ www.bersiserlini.it

CELLAR SALES
PRE-BOOKED VISITS
ACCOMMODATION AND RESTAURANT SERVICE
ANNUAL PRODUCTION 200,000 bottles
HECTARES UNDER VINE 30.00
VITICULTURE METHOD Certified Organic

Bersi Serlini, a family-run winery deeply rooted in Franciacorta, dates back to 1886, when the family acquired a historic estate once used for winemaking by the monks of Cluny. The winery and vineyards enjoy a stunning location, overlooking the beautiful natural reserve of Torbiere. This combination of high-quality wines and a breathtaking landscape makes Bersi Serlini an inviting destination for wine lovers, who can enjoy experiences both at its restaurant and winery. A standout in this year's round of tasting is the Franciacorta Brut Rosé '16, a blend of pinot noir and chardonnay. It exudes aromas of cherries and red flowers, with a harmonious, delicately spiced palate that finishes with mint and white pepper. The Franciacorta Brut Anteprima is also excellent, meaty yet fresh, with a long, balsamic finish. Sweetness and maturity come together in a single sensation of pleasant harmony.

Wine	Rating
⊙ Franciacorta Nature Rosé 61 '17	♟♟♟ 8
○ Franciacorta Nature Blanc de Blancs 61 '17	♟♟ 8
⊙ Franciacorta Brut Rosé 61	♟♟ 5
○ Franciacorta Extra Brut 61	♟♟ 5
○ Franciacorta Extra Brut Palazzo Lana Extrême Ris. '13	♟♟ 8
○ Franciacorta Nature 61 '17	♟♟ 8
○ Franciacorta Satèn 61	♟♟ 7
○ Franciacorta Extra Brut Extrême Palazzo Lana Ris. '09	♟♟♟ 8
○ Franciacorta Nature 61 '16	♟♟♟ 8
○ Franciacorta Nature 61 '15	♟♟♟ 8
○ Franciacorta Nature 61 '14	♟♟♟ 8
○ Franciacorta Nature 61 '12	♟♟♟ 7
○ Franciacorta Nature 61 '11	♟♟♟ 7

Wine	Rating
⊙ Franciacorta Brut Rosé '16	♟♟ 5
○ Franciacorta Brut Anniversario	♟♟ 5
○ Franciacorta Brut Anteprima	♟♟ 5
○ Franciacorta Satèn	♟♟ 5
○ Franciacorta Brut Cuvée n. 4 '08	♟♟ 5
○ Franciacorta Brut Cuvée n. 4 '06	♟♟ 4
⊙ Franciacorta Brut Rosé Rosa Rosae '10	♟♟ 5
○ Franciacorta Brut Vintage Ris. '06	♟♟ 7
○ Franciacorta Brut Vintage Ris. '04	♟♟ 7
○ Franciacorta Extra Brut '12	♟♟ 6
○ Franciacorta Extra Brut '11	♟♟ 6
○ Franciacorta Extra Brut '10	♟♟ 6
○ Franciacorta Extra Brut '02	♟♟ 6
○ Franciacorta Extra Brut Solo Uva '16	♟♟ 6
⊙ Franciacorta Rosé Brut Magnum '19	♟♟

Bertè & Cordini Francesco Montagna

via Cairoli, 67
27043 Broni [PV]
+39 038551028
www.bertecordini.it

CELLAR SALES
PRE-BOOKED VISITS
ACCOMMODATION
ANNUAL PRODUCTION 700,000 bottles
HECTARES UNDER VINE 18.00

Boasting a history dating back to the late 19th century, since 1974 this winery has been in the hands of the Bert? and Cordini families, who have retained the original name. Mariella Bert? and Marzia Cordini welcome visitors to the renovated cellar in the center of Broni, while the young oenologist Luca Cordini manages a wide range of wines produced according to time-honored tradition, using both local and French-origin grapes. The range of Metodo Classico wines performed a little more quietly this year than what we're used to, with the Brut Nature standing out for its pleasant herbal notes on a fairly firm structure, featuring fine and smooth bubbles. This year, the reds fared better, particularly the Valmaga '20, which showcased broad fruit tinged with balsamic and herbal nuances. The highlight, however, was the fragrant, taut, sapid, and highly varietal Pinot Nero Viti di Luna '21. The vintage Bonarda also performed well.

OP Pinot Nero Viti di Luna '21	♥♥	3*
OP Bonarda Frizzante Viti di Luna '23	♥♥	2*
OP Rosso Valmaga '20	♥♥	5
OP Cruasé	♥	5
OP M. Cl. Brut Cuvée della Casa Pinot Nero	♥	5
OP M. Cl. Brut Nature Pinot Nero	♥	5
OP M. Cl. Brut Cuvée Tradizione '16	♀♀	5
OP M. Cl. Pinot Nero Dosage Zéro Oblio '11	♀♀	7
OP Pinot Nero Brut Cl. Cuvée della Casa Bertè & Cordini	♀♀	5
OP Pinot Nero Brut Cuvée Tradizione '10	♀♀	4
OP Pinot Nero Brut M. Cl. Cuvée Nero d'Oro	♀♀	5
OP Pinot Nero Brut Rosé Cl.	♀♀	4

Bisi

loc. Cascina San Michele
fraz. Villa Marone, 70
27040 San Damiano al Colle [PV]
+39 038575037
www.aziendagricolabisi.it

CELLAR SALES
PRE-BOOKED VISITS
ANNUAL PRODUCTION 90,000 bottles
HECTARES UNDER VINE 30.00

If you want to talk to a sincere, honest, and passionate winemaker, Claudio Bisi is the person for you. A man of few words, he prefers to let his wines speak for him, telling the story of his land and his love for it. Starting with barbera, which Claudio loves and produces in various versions, but most importantly, rooted in a profound connection with the land, he creates wines with strong personalities that should be approached calmly and "felt" deeply. The Ultrapadum, a red sparkling wine made from barbera and croatina without the addition of selected yeasts, yields aromas of chestnut, blackberry, blueberry, and raspberry. In the mouth, it offers great depth, with a long finish. The Barbera Roncolongo '21 stands out with its pulp, acidity, and clear, ripe red fruits, showing great aging potential. Among their impressive lineup of unfiltered wines, we have to mention the a highly distinctive Senz'Aiuto '21, a barbera made without added yeasts or sulfites.

● Roncolongo Barbera '21	♥♥	5
● Ultrapadum '21	♥♥	3*
○ LaGrà Riesling '23	♥♥	2*
● OP Bonarda Frizzante La Peccatrice '23	♥♥	2*
● Pramattone Croatina '22	♥♥	2*
● Senz'Aiuto Barbera '21	♥♥	3
● Pezzabianca Barbera '22	♥	3
● Calonga Pinot Nero '17	♀♀	5
● Calonga Pinot Nero '16	♀♀	5
● Roncolongo Barbera '20	♀♀	5
● Roncolongo Barbera '18	♀♀	5
● Roncolongo Barbera '17	♀♀	5
● Roncolongo Barbera '16	♀♀	5
● Ultrapadum '20	♀♀	3*
● Ultrapadum '19	♀♀	3*

Castello Bonomi

via San Pietro, 46
25030 Coccaglio [BS]
☎ +39 0307721015
🌐 www.castellobonomi.it

CELLAR SALES
PRE-BOOKED VISITS
ANNUAL PRODUCTION 200,000 bottles
HECTARES UNDER VINE 32.00
SUSTAINABLE WINERY

After acquiring the winery in 2008, the Paladin family wisely decided to continue working with cellar master Luigi Bersini, who had been with Castello Bonomi since 1985. This decision has paid off in the glass: the wines produced from the estate?s Monte Orfano vineyards exhibit a clear and distinctive identity. The style is rich and food-friendly, while maintaining a vibrant freshness, reflecting the chalky-limestone soils of the growing area. This year their lineup put in an excellent overall performance. The CruPerdu '19, a Franciacorta, impressed with its vibrant notes of apricot and a creamy, persistent perlage. The Lucrezia Riserva '11 surprised us with its charm and elegance. This captivating rosé offers a broad aromatic profile, blending notes of pomegranate and watermelon with an elegant spicy nuance. In the mouth, it's energetic, focused, and driven by vibrant, luminous freshness—a remarkable vintage, beautifully expressed in a fine cuvée.

⊙ Franciacorta Extra Brut Rosé Lucrezia Ris. '11	▼▼▼ 8
○ Franciacorta Brut CruPerdu Bio '19	▼▼ 6
○ Franciacorta Brut Cuvée 22	▼▼ 6
○ Franciacorta Brut Nature Cuvée 1564 '17	▼▼ 8
⊙ Franciacorta Brut Rosé '20	▼ 7
○ Franciacorta Brut Cru Perdu '04	♀♀♀ 7
○ Franciacorta Dosage Zéro '13	♀♀♀ 7
○ Franciacorta Dosage Zéro '11	♀♀♀ 7
○ Franciacorta Extra Brut Lucrezia Et. Nera '04	♀♀♀ 8
○ Franciacorta Brut CruPerdu '18	♀♀ 6
○ Franciacorta Extra Brut CruPerdu Grande Annata '16	♀♀ 7
⊙ Franciacorta Rosé Brut '19	♀♀ 7
○ Franciacorta Satèn '19	♀♀ 7

Bosio

fraz. Timoline
via M. Gatti, 4
25040 Corte Franca [BS]
☎ +39 0309826224
🌐 www.bosiofranciacorta.it

CELLAR SALES
PRE-BOOKED VISITS
ANNUAL PRODUCTION 150,000 bottles
HECTARES UNDER VINE 22.00
VITICULTURE METHOD Certified Organic
SUSTAINABLE WINERY

Under the leadership of siblings Cesare and Laura, Bosio is carving out a name for itself in the ever-evolving landscape of Franciacorta winemaking. While production remains small, the focus is on quality across the entire line, ensuring remarkable consistency. Through meticulous work in the vineyard and a continuous drive for innovation in the cellar, Bosio has become a reliable choice for those who appreciate food-friendly sparkling wines characterized by great tension. The Franciacorta Extra Brut Boschedòr '19 is a pour of extraordinary elegance and pleasure. Its broad and multifaceted aromatic spectrum is clear and fragrant, with pastry-like sensations and white-fleshed fruit pulp. On the palate, it shows sapid rhythms, vibrant freshness, and length. The finish is crisp, long, and vibrant. The Franciacorta Nature '20 is also surprising, creamy in its citrusy tones, with fine and progressive bubbles and a delicately spiced finish.

○ Franciacorta Extra Brut Boschedòr '19	▼▼▼
○ Franciacorta Nature '20	▼▼
○ Franciacorta Brut	▼▼
○ Franciacorta Dosaggio Zero B.C. Ris. '13	▼▼
⊙ Franciacorta Extra Brut Rosé '19	▼▼
○ Franciacorta Satèn	▼
○ Franciacorta Dosaggio Zero B.C. Ris. '11	♀♀♀
○ Franciacorta Extra Brut Boschedòr '18	♀♀♀
○ Franciacorta Extra Brut Boschedòr '16	♀♀♀
○ Franciacorta Pas Dosé Girolamo Bosio Ris. '09	♀♀♀
○ Franciacorta Dosaggio Zero '19	♀♀
○ Franciacorta Dosaggio Zero Girolamo Bosio Ris. '16	♀♀
⊙ Franciacorta Rosé Dosaggio Zero Girolamo Bosio Ris. '15	♀♀

Alessio Brandolini

fraz. Boffalora, 68
27040 San Damiano al Colle [PV]
☎ +39 038575232
🌐 www.alessiobrandolini.com

★Cà Maiol

via Colli Storici, 119
25015 Desenzano del Garda [BS]
☎ +39 0309910006
🌐 www.camaiol.it

CELLAR SALES
PRE-BOOKED VISITS
ANNUAL PRODUCTION 80,000 bottles
HECTARES UNDER VINE 11.00
SUSTAINABLE WINERY

CELLAR SALES
PRE-BOOKED VISITS
ACCOMMODATION
ANNUAL PRODUCTION 1,000,000 bottles
HECTARES UNDER VINE 118.00
SUSTAINABLE WINERY

Drawing on international experience, the young oenologist Alessio Brandolini took over the family winery after his father Costante passed away. Founded in 1873, the producer has deep roots in the border region between Oltrep? and Colli Piacentini. The area's classic grape varieties (including malvasia di Candia aromatica) are cultivated in vineyards managed using sustainable, low-impact practices. Alessio has a great passion for pinot nero, with which he has achieved significant results, especially his Metodo Classicos. Among the best of the year, the Bonarda Frizzante Il Cassino '23 stands out, conjuring up fruity notes on both the nose and palate, aptly balancing tannins and a slight residual sweetness, with a fragrant and delicious profile. The Riesling I Prà '22 is sapid, with lovely mineral tones and a precise progression towards the varietal's trademark tertiary aromas. Among their line of pinot nero Metodo Classico, the Luogo d'Agosto shines, offering peach and elegant herbal nuances, nicely sustained by a bright acidity.

C? Maiol is a symbol of Lugana, and also an important part of its history. It all began in 1967 when Milan-native Walter Contato founded the winery on the southern shore of Lake Garda. Walter, along with some local growers, established what is now the Consorzio di Tutela. Over time, the wines have grown to achieve excellence, an objective further strengthened when his children took over in 1996. Currently, the property is owned by the Marzotto family's Santa Margherita group. Cà Maiol is once again in top form this year. Two wines made it to the final round. The Lugana Riserva '21 reaffirms itself as one of the finest expressions of the appellation, with rich expression, vigorous vitality, and complex development, promising elegant things to come. The Valtènesi Chiaretto Roseri '23, with its delightful fruity tones and irresistible herbal nuances also delivered. The rest of the range is equally impressive, with a special mention for the Lugana Molin '22 and the red Groviglio from the same vintage.

● OP Bonarda Frizzante Il Cassino '23	♀♀ 2*
○ I Prà Riesling '22	♀♀ 4
● Il Beneficio '20	♀♀ 4
● Il Soffio Croatina '23	♀♀ 2*
○ OP M. Cl. Pinot Nero Extra Brut Luogo d'Agosto '20	♀♀ 5
● Al Negres Pinot Nero '22	♀ 4
○ Il Bardughino Malvasia '23	♀ 2
○ OP M. Cl. Pas Dosé I Ger	♀ 5
○ OP M. Cl. Pinot Nero Extra Brut Rosé Note d'Agosto	♀ 5
○ Note d'Agosto Extra Brut M. Cl. Rosé '17	♀♀♀ 5
○ I Prà '20	♀♀ 4
○ Note d'Agosto Extra Brut M. Cl. Rosé '18	♀♀ 5
○ OP M. Cl. Pinot Nero Extra Brut Luogo d'Agosto '19	♀♀ 5

○ Lugana Ris. '21	♀♀ 6
○ RGC Valtènesi Chiaretto Roseri '23	♀♀ 3*
○ Lugana Brut M. Cl. Cantariva '19	♀♀ 5
○ Lugana Prestige '23	♀♀ 3
○ Lugana Sup. Molin '22	♀♀ 4
● RGC Valtènesi Rosso Groviglio '22	♀♀ 4
○ Lugana Fabio Contato Ris. '18	♀♀♀ 6
○ Lugana Molin '16	♀♀♀ 3*
○ Lugana Molin '15	♀♀♀ 3*
○ Lugana Molin '14	♀♀♀ 3*
○ Lugana Molin '13	♀♀♀ 3*
○ Lugana Sel. Fabio Contato '16	♀♀♀ 5
○ Lugana Sup. Sel. Fabio Contato Ris. '19	♀♀♀ 5

Cà Tessitori

via Matteotti, 15
27043 Broni [PV]
℡ +39 038551495
🌐 www.catessitori.it

CELLAR SALES
PRE-BOOKED VISITS
ANNUAL PRODUCTION 135,000 bottles
HECTARES UNDER VINE 40.00

This winery, steeped in tradition, benefits from the expertise of Luigi Giorgi, who has over 60 harvests behind him. Today he works alongside Francesco and Giovanni, the new generation. The vineyards, located in Montecalvo Versiggia and Montalto Pavese, are managed according to sustainable viticulture practices, focusing primarily on local varieties such as croatina, barbera, and pinot nero. In the cellar, they follow a non-interventionist philosophy, using minimal sulfites, resulting in wines that strongly reflect the terroir. The LB9 repeated last year's exploit. It's a creamy, airy, sapid Pas Dosé, redolent of white fruit and pastry, with fine bubbles and a sapidity that gives great freshness to the palate. The well-crafted MV '19 is an Extra Brut with lightly oxidative tones, tropical fruit aromas, and a brilliant palate. The Oltremodo '22 stands out as one of the best vintages of this "ancestral-style", bottle-refermented croatina. It's a structured wine characterized by sour cherry and peach sensations. A taste of old-world elegance.

○ OP Pinot Nero M. Cl. Pas Dosé LB9	♈♈ 5
◉ Oltremodo '22	♈♈ 4
○ OP Pinot Nero M. Cl. Extra Brut MV '19	♈♈ 5
○ Agòlo Bianco '21	♈ 2
● Marona Barbera '21	♈ 4
● OP Bonarda Frizzante Sempà '23	♈ 3
● Oltremodo '17	♈♈ 3*
● OP Bonarda Frizzante Sempà '21	♈♈ 2*
○ OP M. Cl. Pinot Nero Dosaggio Zero LB9 '14	♈♈ 5
○ OP M. Cl. Pinot Nero Dosaggio Zero LB9	♈♈ 5
○ OP M. Cl. Pinot Nero Dosaggio Zero MV '16	♈♈ 5

★★★★Ca' del Bosco

via Albano Zanella, 13
25030 Erbusco [BS]
℡ +39 0307766111
🌐 www.cadelbosco.com

PRE-BOOKED VISITS
HECTARES UNDER VINE 259.98
VITICULTURE METHOD Certified Organic
SUSTAINABLE WINERY

There?s no doubt that Ca' del Bosco is now one of the most representative names in the Italian wine scene. A turning point was joining the Santa Margherita Group, which allowed Maurizio Zanella and his indispensable winemaker Stefano Capelli to solidify the extraordinary results already achieved, both nationally and internationally. Their achievements are also the result of ongoing technological research, unmatched in Italy. The winery?s style is unique, characterized by richness and complexity across its entire range. The Dosaggio Zero '19 from the Vintage Collection is the best of the lot this year It reaches the top for its consistency, balance, fine texture, and harmony. Aromas of strawflower and a balanced smoky note enhance a broad and cohesive palate. Next in line is the Annamaria Clementi Rosé '15, which is intensely aromatic, with notes of coffee and raspberries, a creamy perlage, complexity and fragrance. A toasty note on the finish adds allure and depth. The Annamaria Clementi '15 shows the effects of the warmer vintage.

○ Franciacorta Dosage Zéro Vintage Collection '19	♈♈♈ 8
◉ Franciacorta Extra Brut Annamaria Clementi Rosé Ris. '15	♈♈ 8
○ Franciacorta Satèn Vintage Collection '19	♈♈ 8
○ Franciacorta Dosage Zéro Annamaria Clementi Ris. '15	♈♈ 8
○ Franciacorta Dosage Zéro Cuvée Prestige RS Edizione 37	♈♈ 8
○ Franciacorta Dosage Zéro Vintage Collection Noir Ris. '15	♈♈ 8
○ Franciacorta Extra Brut Cuvée Prestige Edizione 46	♈♈ 8
○ Franciacorta Extra Brut Vintage Collection '19	♈♈ 8
◉ Franciacorta Extra Brut Rosé Cuvée Prestige Edizione 46	♈ 8

Ca' del Gè

fraz. Ca' del Gè, 3
27040 Montalto Pavese [PV]
☏ +39 0383870179
🌐 www.cadelge.com

CELLAR SALES
PRE-BOOKED VISITS
ANNUAL PRODUCTION 160,000 bottles
HECTARES UNDER VINE 45.00

Three siblings, Carlo, Sara, and Stefania Padroggi, have taken on the task of carrying forward their father's legacy. Their father, Enzo, was one of the first in Oltrep? to believe in the potential of riesling planted on white soils. As champions of biodiversity, the winery participates in the ViNO (Vineyards and Nature in Oltrep?) project. They produce a variety of wines, notably riesling (both italico and renano), along with Metodo Classico and reds. Their entire range is characterized by drinkability and reasonable prices. The Buttafuoco Fajro '21 is well-crafted, with a full-bodied and dense fruit pulp, redolent of blackberries, undergrowth, and spices. Its tannins are also well-managed. The Marinoni '22 once again proves to be a classy Riesling Renano, highlighting tropical fruit, with slightly overripe tones, without overshadowing aromas of wildflowers and a barely perceptible mineral note.

● OP Buttafuoco Fajro '21	♈♈ 4
○ OP Riesling Il Marinoni '22	♈♈ 3
○ OP Moscato '23	♈ 2
○ OP Riesling Brinà '23	♈ 2
● Costa del Vento Pinot Nero '20	♈♈ 3
○ Filagn Long Riesling '19	♈♈ 3
○ Il Marinoni Riesling '19	♈♈ 3
○ OP Brut Cà del Gé '13	♈♈ 5
○ OP M. Cl. Pinot Nero Brut '17	♈♈ 4
○ OP M. Cl. Pinot Nero Brut '15	♈♈ 5
○ OP M. Cl. Pinot Nero Pas Dosé '17	♈♈ 5
○ OP Pinot Nero Brut M. Cl. '10	♈♈ 3*
○ OP Riesling Il Marinoni '20	♈♈ 3*
○ OP Riesling Italico Brinà '20	♈♈ 2*

Ca' di Frara

via Casa Ferrari, 1
27040 Mornico Losana [PV]
☏ +39 0383892299
🌐 www.cadifrara.com

CELLAR SALES
PRE-BOOKED VISITS
ANNUAL PRODUCTION 400,000 bottles
HECTARES UNDER VINE 46.00

Over a century of history and four generations link the Bellani family to this important winery in central Oltrep?. Founded in 1905 by Giovanni, Ca' di Frara made significant progress towards quality production under his grandson Tullio, who then handed over the business to his dynamic son Luca. At this point, ideas and projects began to proliferate, resulting in excellent but inconsistent outcomes, both in terms of whites and reds. It's also worth mentioning the "Oltre il Classico" project, dedicated to pinot nero-based sparkling wines. Dominating this year are pinot nero and rhine riesling, two varietals that adapt well to the chalky white soils of this part of Oltrepò Pavese. The T4, a creamy Metodo Classico, showcases hints of field herbs emerging from an evolved and complex, pastry-like nose, with a long palate. Both 2022 versions of the Riesling Superiore prove sapid and mineral, with the Etichetta Nera leaning more towards fruity tones, while the Oliva '22 is more Alsatian in style, with a slight residual sweetness nicely balanced by acidity.

OP Pinot Nero M. Cl. Pas Dosé	
Oltre il Classico T4	♈♈ 4
○ OP Riesling Sup. Etichetta Nera '22	♈♈ 3
○ OP Riesling Sup. Oliva '22	♈♈ 4
● OP Pinot Nero 45° '22	♈ 3
● OP Pinot Nero Losana Parcella 17 '21	♈ 5
● OP Pinot Nero Mornico Parcella 4 '21	♈ 5
● OP Pinot Nero Ris.	
Oliva Parcella 18 '22	♈ 5
○ OP Riesling Oliva Ris. '16	♈♈♈ 4*
○ OP Pinot Grigio	
Selezione dei Vent'Anni '19	♈♈ 3*
● OP Pinot Nero Mornico '20	♈♈ 5
○ Pinot Grigio '18	♈♈ 3*
● Pinot Nero dell'Oltrepò Pavese	
Losana Ris. '19	♈♈ 4
● Pinot Nero dell'Oltrepò Pavese	
Mornico Ris. '19	♈♈ 5

LOMBARDY

Ca' Lojera

loc. Rovizza
via 1866, 19
25019 Sirmione [BS]
☎ +39 0457551901
🖥 www.calojera.com

CELLAR SALES
PRE-BOOKED VISITS
ANNUAL PRODUCTION 160,000 bottles
HECTARES UNDER VINE 20.00

Despite a challenging local market, in 1992 Ambra and Franco Tiraboschi had the courage and foresight to found a winery just a stone's throw from Lake Garda. Time has proven them right, and now the estate is one of the most representative in a territory that has carved out a significant place in the Italian wine scene. The estate is comprised of 18 hectares of turbiana on white clay soils that were once the lake bed, as well as 2 hectares of international varietals on the southern, morainic hills. This year one of the best Lugana wines tasted was the Superiore '21. Quintessential and no-frills, this white plays on sapidity and fruit that's never overripe. It's a linear, mineral, saline, and complex wine, with remarkable persistence. The Riserva del Lupo, slender and sapid, still needs time to evolve. The 2023 vintage of the Lugana also performs at its usual high level.

○ Lugana Sup. '21	♟♟ 5
○ Lugana Riserva del Lupo '21	♟♟ 5
○ Lugana '23	♟ 3
○ Lugana Riserva del Lupo '18	♟♟♟ 5
○ Lugana '22	♟♟ 3
○ Lugana '21	♟♟ 3
○ Lugana '20	♟♟ 3
○ Lugana '19	♟♟ 3
○ Lugana del Lupo Ris. '17	♟♟ 4
○ Lugana Riserva del Lupo '20	♟♟ 5
○ Lugana Riserva del Lupo '19	♟♟ 5
○ Lugana Riserva del Lupo '16	♟♟ 5
○ Lugana Sup. '19	♟♟ 5
○ Lugana Sup. '18	♟♟ 4
○ Lugana Sup. '17	♟♟ 4
○ Lugana Sup. '10	♟♟ 5

Calatroni

loc. Casa Grande, 7
27040 Montecalvo Versiggia [PV]
☎ +39 038599013
🖥 www.calatronivini.it

CELLAR SALES
PRE-BOOKED VISITS
RESTAURANT SERVICE
ANNUAL PRODUCTION 130,000 bottles
HECTARES UNDER VINE 30.00
VITICULTURE METHOD Certified Organic
SUSTAINABLE WINERY

As evidenced by our awards, the rapid ascent of the Calatroni family?s winery in Oltrep? Pavese hasn't gone to their heads. Christian, the winemaker, and his brother Stefano continue to strive for improvement, excelling with their Metodo Classico, while also offering a range of other interesting wines under the Mon Carul brand. Their agritourism activities, including dining and events among the vineyards, are also noteworthy. We can say without fear of contradiction that Calatroni is currently the most dynamic and interesting producer of Metodo Classico in Oltrepò. The entire lineup presented was outstanding, and unlike last year, it's the Poggio dei Duca that surpasses the Riva Rinetti. Vibrant, creamy, with notes of pastry, red citrus, and aromatic herbs, it has energy, structure, and the nose and palate of a top-drawer wine. That's why it's our Sparkler of the Year.

○ OP Pinot Nero M. Cl. Pas Dosé Poggio dei Duca '19	♟♟♟ 5
○ OP M. Cl. Pinot Nero Pas Dosé Riva Rinetti '19	♟♟ 5
○ OP M. Cl. Cruasé Extra Brut NorEma '21	♟♟ 4
○ OP M. Cl. Pinot Nero Michel '20	♟♟ 4
○ OP M. Cl. Pinot Nero Pas Dosé Cuvée Rosé '17	♟♟ 5
○ OP Riesling Campo Dottore Ris. '21	♟♟ 4
○ OP Riesling Campo Dottore '23	♟ 3
○ OP Cruasé Extra Brut NorEma '19	♟♟♟ 4*
○ OP M. Cl. Pinot Nero Pas Dosé Riva Rinetti '18	♟♟♟ 5
◎ OP Pinot Nero M. Cl. Pas Dosé Cuvée Rosé '13	♟♟♟ 5
○ Pinot Nero Brut 64 M. Cl. '11	♟♟♟ 5

Il Calepino

via Surripe, 1
24060 Castelli Calepio [BG]
📞 +39 035847178
🌐 www.ilcalepino.it

CELLAR SALES
PRE-BOOKED VISITS
ANNUAL PRODUCTION 230,000 bottles
HECTARES UNDER VINE 15.00

Without meaning any disrespect to brothers Franco and Marco Plebani, sons of founder Angelo, we might call this winery a piece of Franciacorta in Bergamasco territory. After all, it?s only the Oglio River that separates the two areas. Il Calepino, named after Ambrogio da Calepio, an Augustinian friar who lived between the 15th-16th centuries, has been making a name for itself year after year, particularly with its high-level Metodo Classico sparkling wines. At the forefront of production is, as usual, the Fra Ambrogio, the wine that spends the longest time on the lees. The 2017 displays all its complexity, with aromas of pastry, coffee beans, spices, and aromatic herbs, leading to a long, deep, full palate. The Brut '18 is slightly less complex but has plenty of structure and nerve, with creamy bead. The Non Dosato '18 is straight and linear, while the Rosé expresses small fruit tones. It's also worth mentioning the powerful and energetic Valcalepio Rosso, Riserva Surìe '19.

o M. Cl. Brut Fra Ambrogio '17	🏆🏆 5
o Il Calepino Brut M. Cl. '18	🏆🏆 4
o M. Cl. Non Dosato '18	🏆🏆 4
⊙ M. Cl. Brut Rosé Il Calepino	🏆 5
● Valcalepio Rosso Surìe Ris. '19	🏆 4
o Brut M. Cl. Fra' Ambrogio Ris. '09	🏆 4
o Brut M. Cl. Non Dosato '11	🏆 4
o Calepino Brut M. Cl. '16	🏆 4
o Calepino Non Dosato M. Cl. '15	🏆 4
o Fra Ambrogio Brut M. Cl. '11	🏆 5
o Non Dosato M. Cl.	🏆 4
⊙ Rosé Brut M. Cl.	🏆 5
o Terre del Colleoni B.D.B. Brut M. Cl.	🏆 4
o Valcalepio Bianco '19	🏆 3
● Valcalepio Rosso '17	🏆 3

Camossi

via Metelli, 5
25030 Erbusco [BS]
📞 +39 0307268022
🌐 www.camossifranciacorta.com

CELLAR SALES
PRE-BOOKED VISITS
ANNUAL PRODUCTION 60,000 bottles
HECTARES UNDER VINE 30.00

Dario and Claudio Camossi, passionate viticulturists, carry on the family business founded by their grandfather Pietro in the early 1900s. The wines produced hail from their 30 hectares of vineyards, spread out across Erbusco, where the cellar is located, Paratico, where pinot nero is grown, and Provaglio d'Iseo (particularly in the Provezze area). Since 2019, their cuv?es age in a new, fully underground cellar. This year saw an excellent lineup submitted for tasting. We were impressed by the Dosaggio Zero, an exceptional Franciacorta with a tactile quality, featuring intricate nuances of peach, mint, and curry plant. On the palate, it's broad and energetic, with a long finish that unravels on citrus tones and balsamic sensations. The Extra Brut Rosé is also excellent, crisp and elegant, with notes of raspberry meeting blood orange. The Extra Brut proves fresh and lively, while the Satèn plays on white peach tones and a soft palate.

o Franciacorta Dosaggio Zero	🏆🏆 5
o Franciacorta Brut Satèn	🏆🏆 5
o Franciacorta Extra Brut	🏆🏆 6
⊙ Franciacorta Extra Brut Rosé	🏆🏆 6
o Franciacorta Brut Satèn '11	🏆 6
o Franciacorta Dosaggio Zero CR 142 Ris. '07	🏆 8
o Franciacorta Extra Brut '14	🏆 6
o Franciacorta Extra Brut CR 149 Ris. '08	🏆 8
o Franciacorta Extra Brut Pietro Camossi Ris. '11	🏆 7
o Franciacorta Extra Brut Pietro Camossi Ris. '10	🏆 8
o Franciacorta Extra Brut Ris. '12	🏆 6
o Franciacorta Extra Brut Ris. '10	🏆 6
o Franciacorta Extra Brut Ris. '09	🏆 6

LOMBARDY

261

Cantrina

fraz. Cantrina
via Colombera, 7
25081 Bedizzole [BS]
☎ +39 3356362137
✆ www.cantrina.it

CELLAR SALES
ANNUAL PRODUCTION 35,000 bottles
HECTARES UNDER VINE 7.90
VITICULTURE METHOD Certified Organic

Founded in 1999 by Diego Lago and Cristina
Inganni, this winery has adhered to a precise
philosophy from the start: the utmost respect
for the environment, an agronomic approach
that highlights the unique characteristics of each
soil, and a production style centered on quality,
attention, and creativity. Sensitive to local
dynamics and based on organic farming since
2014, this rigorous ethic is even stricter than
certification protocols. Cristina's wines are
growing increasingly interesting. Two made it to
the finals: the delightful and fresh passito Sole di
Dario, a harmonious and elegant wine with
delicate tones of dried apricot, and the
Groppello '23, which plays on a fresh, sapid, and
airy profile, with intriguing tones of red currant
and raspberry. It's a subtle, clear, highly enjoyable,
and fragrant sip. The elegant, taut, and dynamic
Chiaretto, A Rose is a Rose '23 (from groppello),
and its counterpart, the Rosanoire '23 (from
pinot nero), confirm the stylistic maturity of
the winery.

○ Il Sole di Dario '21	🏆🏆 6
● RGC Groppello '23	🏆🏆 3*
● Nepomuceno '20	🏆🏆 6
⊙ RGC Valtènesi Chiaretto A Rose Is A Rose Is A Rose '23	🏆🏆 3
⊙ Rosanoire '23	🏆🏆 3
○ Riné '21	🏆 4
⊙ RGC Valtènesi Chiaretto '21	🏆🏆 3*
⊙ RGC Valtènesi Chiaretto A Rose Is A Rose Is A Rose '22	🏆🏆 3
○ Riné '20	🏆🏆 4
○ Riné '19	🏆🏆 3
⊙ Rosanoire '22	🏆🏆 3
● Zerdi '20	🏆🏆 4
● Zerdì '19	🏆🏆 3

CastelFaglia - Monogram

fraz. Calino
loc. Boschi, 3
25046 Cazzago San Martino [BS]
☎ +39 0307751042
✆ www.castelfaglia.it

CELLAR SALES
PRE-BOOKED VISITS
ANNUAL PRODUCTION 700,000 bottles
HECTARES UNDER VINE 23.00
SUSTAINABLE WINERY

The Cavicchioli family has been managing
CastelFaglia for about 30 years. Sandro
Cavicchioli has always overseen the production
of sparkling wines, though in recent years, he?s
been joined by his younger kin Davide, fresh
from earning his oenology degree at S. Michele
all'Adige. Claudio Cavicchioli rounds out the
family operation, managing the winery?s image
and commercial side. The two production lines,
CastelFaglia and Monogram, have long proved
reliable, with Monogram, which is aimed
exclusively at the hotel and catering industry,
showing moments of excellence. The Monogram
'18 is a wine of great elegance. A Franciacorta
with floral and citrus tones, it reveals notable
mineral depth on the palate, where it's clean and
lively, closing on a long, sapid, and gratifying finish.
The Dosaggio Zero Cuvée Monogram is
pleasant with its fruity profile of peach and apple.
Fine spices on the nose are followed by a taut
and energetic palate that finishes on fruit notes
with a hint of licorice.

○ Franciacorta Brut Monogram '18	🏆🏆 7
○ Franciacorta Dosaggio Zéro Monogram	🏆🏆 6
⊙ Franciacorta Extra Brut Rosé	🏆🏆 5
○ Franciacorta Satèn	🏆🏆 5
○ Franciacorta Satèn Monogram	🏆🏆 6
○ Franciacorta Dosage Zéro '19	🏆 6
○ Franciacorta Nature	🏆 5
⊙ Franciacorta Satèn Monogram '19	🏆 7
○ Franciacorta Brut Monogram '15	🏆🏆 7
○ Franciacorta Dosage Zero Monogram '18	🏆🏆 5
○ Franciacorta Dosage Zero Monogram '13	🏆🏆 5
○ Franciacorta Dosage Zero Monogram '12	🏆🏆 5
○ Franciacorta Monogram Zero '16	🏆🏆 5
⊙ Franciacorta Rosé Brut Monogram '15	🏆🏆 6
⊙ Franciacorta Rosé Brut Monogram '14	🏆🏆 6
○ Franciacorta Satèn Monogram '17	🏆🏆 7

★Castello di Cigognola

p.zza Castello, 1
27040 Cigognola [PV]
☎ +39 0385284828
● www.castellodicigognola.com

CELLAR SALES
PRE-BOOKED VISITS
ANNUAL PRODUCTION 75,000 bottles
HECTARES UNDER VINE 30.00

Over 40 years have passed since Gian Marco Moratti acquired the entire Castello estate. Now Gabriele Moratti, awaiting organic certification, continues to revitalize the vineyards, overseen today by Giovanni Bigot. Three winemakers handle production: Nicolas Second? is in charge of Metodo Classico, Federico Staderini handles red pinot nero, and Beppe Caviola, a true Piedmontese, manages barbera and nebbiolo. The Barbera Dodicidodici '22 proves highly fragrant, with broad red fruit—cherry and sour cherry—along with small wild berries. Harmonious and sapid, it's aptly balances oak tannins and acidity, revealing length and depth. The Pinot Nero '21 opts for varietal notes of undergrowth, sour cherry, and bark, with excellent grip on the palate—balanced and elegant, finishing with a slight hint of almond.

Castello di Gussago La Santissima

via Manica, 8
25064 Gussago [BS]
☎ +39 0302069967
● www.castellodigussago.it

CELLAR SALES
PRE-BOOKED VISITS
ANNUAL PRODUCTION 120,000 bottles
HECTARES UNDER VINE 21.00
VITICULTURE METHOD Certified Organic
SUSTAINABLE WINERY

The town of Gussago, from which the winery takes its name, marks the eastern boundary of the Franciacorta appellation. The area, set against the Alps, is characterized by steep hills and lush nature. The winery honors these territorial peculiarities by virtue of organic management of its 20 hectares. Winemaker Sabrina Gozio has skillfully crafted a distinct and identifiable style for their Franciacorta wines. Among this year's tastings, the Franciacorta Brut Noblenoir stands out. A monovarietal pinot nero, its signature coppery reflections anticipate fragrant tones of apple, small red fruits, and mountain herbs. On the palate, it's taut and flavorful, with a fine, creamy mousse. Anise and mint close the palate, along with mineral undertones. The Animapura '18 is also noteworthy: pervasive, with shades of bread crust and peach. Fresh and persistent on the palate.

● OP Barbera Dodicidodici '22	♟♟ 3*
● OP Pinot Nero '21	♟♟ 5
○ Pinot Nero M, Cl. Moratti Rosé '19	♟ 5
○ Pinot Nero M. Cl. Moratti	♟ 3
○ 'More Brut M. Cl. '11	♟♟♟ 4*
○ 'More Brut M. Cl. '10	♟♟♟ 4
● OP Barbera Castello di Cigognola '07	♟♟♟ 6
● OP Barbera Castello di Cigognola '06	♟♟♟ 6
● OP Barbera Dodicidodici '11	♟♟♟ 3*
○ OP Brut M. Cl. 'More '12	♟♟♟ 4*
○ OP M. Cl Pinot Nero Brut 'More '08	♟♟♟ 4*
○ OP M. Cl. Pinot Nero Brut 'More '13	♟♟♟ 4*

○ Franciacorta Extra Brut Noblenoir	♟♟ 5
○ Franciacorta Pas Dosé Animapura '18	♟♟ 7
○ Franciacorta Extra Brut Rosé Inganni '19	♟ 6
○ Franciacorta Satèn Club Cuvée '18	♟ 6
● Curtefranca Rosso Pomaro '17	♟♟ 4
⊙ Franciaacorta Rosé Extra Brut Operarosa Ris. '13	♟♟ 8
○ Franciacorta Brut Riserva dei Broli '14	♟♟ 8
○ Franciacorta Club Cuvée Satèn '15	♟♟ 5
○ Franciacorta Dosaggio Zero 800 '17	♟♟ 6
○ Franciacorta Dosaggio Zero Animapura '17	♟♟ 6
○ Franciacorta Pas Dosé '12	♟♟ 5
○ Franciacorta Pas Dosé Animapura '16	♟♟ 7
⊙ Franciacorta Rosé Extra Brut inganni '18	♟♟ 6
○ Franciacorta Rosé Extra Brut Inganni '15	♟♟ 5
○ Franciacorta Satèn Club Cuvée '17	♟♟ 6

Le Chiusure

fraz. Portese
via Boschette, 2
25010 San Felice del Benaco [BS]
(+39 0365626243
www.lechiusure.net

CELLAR SALES
PRE-BOOKED VISITS
ACCOMMODATION
ANNUAL PRODUCTION 24,000 bottles
HECTARES UNDER VINE 4.00

After graduating with a degree in agriculture, Alessandro Luzzago devoted himself to the family business, named after the walls that once enclosed the property. The estate includes four hectares of vineyards and two of olive groves, all carefully managed under organic practices. Integrated pest management, ground cover crops, and protection with hail nets are some of the strategies Alessandro uses to bring healthy grapes to the cellar each year, where he transforms them into a small but carefully curated range of wines that perfectly express the Valtènesi production area. The Malborghetto '20 truly impressed this year. A blend of rebo (70%) and merlot, it matures for a year in small barrels, pouring a gorgeous, deep ruby color. An intense nose rich in red fruit tones, spices, and a pleasant smoky touch rise from the glass. The palate is firm and full-bodied, supple yet intact, with a broad and persistent finish leaving a long trail of fruit on velvety tannins. The Valtenesi Chiaretto Roseti '22 is also full-bodied, sapid, fruity, and delicately smoky. One of the best of the appellation.

● Malborghetto '20	♊♊ 5
⊙ RGC Valtènesi Chiaretto '23	♊♊ 3
⊙ RGC Valtènesi Chiaretto Roseti '22	♊♊ 4
● RGC Valtènesi Rosso '21	♊♊ 3
⊙ RGC Chiaretto Roseti '20	♈♈ 4
● RGC Valtènesi '17	♈♈ 3
⊙ RGC Valtènesi Chiaretto '22	♈♈ 3*
⊙ RGC Valtènesi Chiaretto '21	♈♈ 3
⊙ RGC Valtènesi Chiaretto '20	♈♈ 3*
⊙ RGC Valtènesi Chiaretto '19	♈♈ 3
⊙ RGC Valtènesi Chiaretto Roseti '18	♈♈ 4
● RGC Valtènesi Rosso '19	♈♈ 3
● RGC Valtènesi Rosso Campei '19	♈♈ 4

Battista Cola

via Indipendenza, 3
25030 Adro [BS]
(+39 0307356195
www.colabattista.it

CELLAR SALES
PRE-BOOKED VISITS
ANNUAL PRODUCTION 50,000 bottles
HECTARES UNDER VINE 10.00
SUSTAINABLE WINERY

The story of Cola Battista begins in 1945, when Giovanni Cola decided to follow his passion and cultivate a small vineyard to reconnect with the rhythms of nature. In 1985, Battista Cola took up his father's tradition and made it his career, opening the winery in Adro that we know today. The 10 hectares are now managed by Battista and his son Stefano, whose active commitment produces wines with great character and personality, making for a distinctive and unique range. Their lineup of Franciacorta wines confirms the seriousness of the work being done. The Brut '19 has a classic, pronounced fragrance and balsamic freshness, unveiling sensations of orange peel and mint. The Extra Brut is deep and sapid, playing on tones of sage and lemon peel, with a creamy finish enhanced by fine prickle. The Dosaggio Zero '19 is energetic and lively, with almond, mint, and fresh butter aromas making for a clean and gratifying drink.

⊙ Franciacorta Brut '19	♊♊ 6
⊙ Franciacorta Dosaggio Zero '19	♊♊ 6
⊙ Franciacorta Extra Brut	♊♊ 5
⊙ Franciacorta Satèn '20	♊♊ 6
⊙ Franciacorta Brut Rosé Athena	♊ 6
⊙ Franciacorta Brut '16	♈♈ 5
⊙ Franciacorta Brut '13	♈♈ 5
⊙ Franciacorta Dosage Zéro Etichetta Storica '06	♈♈ 5
⊙ Franciacorta Dosaggio Zero '17	♈♈ 6
⊙ Franciacorta Dosaggio Zero '16	♈♈ 6
⊙ Franciacorta Non Dosato '13	♈♈ 5
⊙ Franciacorta Non Dosato '12	♈♈ 5
⊙ Franciacorta Rosé Brut Athena '19	♈♈ 6
⊙ Franciacorta Rosé Brut Athena '18	♈♈ 6
⊙ Franciacorta Rosé Brut Athena '17	♈♈ 5
⊙ Franciacorta Satèn '18	♈♈ 6
⊙ Franciacorta Satèn '17	♈♈ 5

Colline della Stella - Arici

via Forcella,70
25064 Gussago [BS]
📞 +39 3478039339
🌐 www.collinedellastella.com

CELLAR SALES
PRE-BOOKED VISITS
ANNUAL PRODUCTION 50,000 bottles
HECTARES UNDER VINE 10.00

Andrea Arici?s winery is flourishing, thanks to his patient work in restoring old terraced plots in Gussago, at the far eastern edge of the appellation. He offers an excellent range of Franciacorta cuv?es, with the distinctive feature being that production focuses exclusively on non-dosage sparkling wines. This bold choice aims to bring the territory and vintage directly into the glass, without filters, and the resulting expressions exhibit concentrated minerality and a strong sense of place. The Dosaggio Zero Nero '19 stands out among this year's tastings, reaching our final round. Its rich and creamy palate, framed by a fine and persistent bead, is accompanied by a vivid freshness that adds energy and character. It closes on tones of small red fruits and a pronounced mineral streak. The Dosaggio Zero Uno is also very good, with a fleshy and flavorful texture, featuring citrus nuances on the finish.

Contadi Castaldi

loc. Fornace Biasca
via Colzano, 32
25030 Adro [BS]
📞 +39 0307450126
🌐 www.contadicastaldi.it

CELLAR SALES
PRE-BOOKED VISITS
ANNUAL PRODUCTION 1,100,000 bottles
HECTARES UNDER VINE 174.00
SUSTAINABLE WINERY

This Adro-based winery, owned by the Moretti Group, has grown exponentially, becoming a benchmark for Franciacorta, both in terms of production volumes and quality. Much credit goes to longtime winemaker Gian Luca Uccelli, who has consistently produced wines of great personality and dynamism over the years. Today, the estate?s sparkling wines are a sure bet: refined and complex, yet uniquely drinkable and enjoyable. Among the range presented, the Satèn '19 stands out for its complex and fragrant bouquet, with tones of hazelnut and mountain butter emerging on a flowery backdrop. The palate offers crisp freshness and a persistent finish. The Zèro '19 proves well-made, with a fleshy profile marked by white fruit tones, which stand out on a lovely suite of citrus sensations. The complexity of the Pinònero Riserva '17 is also noteworthy.

○ Franciacorta Dosaggio Zero Nero '19	♟♟8
○ Franciacorta Dosaggio Zero Uno	♟♟5
○ Franciacorta Dosaggio Zero '15	♟♟5
○ Franciacorta Dosaggio Zero '09	♟♟4
○ Franciacorta Dosaggio Zero Francesco Arici Ris. '11	♟♟6
○ Franciacorta Dosaggio Zero Uno '15	♟♟5

○ Franciacorta Brut Satèn '19	♟♟6
○ Franciacorta Dosaggio Zero Pinònero Natura Ris. '17	♟♟7
○ Franciacorta Pas Dosé Zèro '19	♟♟6
○ Franciacorta Brut	♟4
☉ Franciacorta Brut Rosé	♟3
○ Franciacorta Brut Satèn Soul '11	♟♟♟6
○ Franciacorta Satèn '15	♟♟♟6
○ Franciacorta Satèn Soul '06	♟♟♟6
○ Franciacorta Satèn Soul '05	♟♟♟6
○ Franciacorta Zèro '14	♟♟♟5
○ Franciacorta Zèro '12	♟♟♟5
○ Franciacorta Zèro '09	♟♟♟5
○ Franciacorta Extra Brut Blànc '19	♟♟6
○ Franciacorta Extra Brut Blànc '18	♟♟6
○ Franciacorta Zèro '17	♟♟6

Conte Vistarino

fraz. Villa Fornace, 11
27040 Rocca de' Giorgi [PV]
📞 +39 0385241171
⊕ www.contevistarino.it

CELLAR SALES
PRE-BOOKED VISITS
ANNUAL PRODUCTION 350,000 bottles
HECTARES UNDER VINE 102.00

Given that the first pinot nero cuttings were imported to Valle Scuropasso by Count Augusto Giorgi di Vistarino in the mid-19th century, and that Luigi Veronelli praised the pinot of Pernice 60 years ago, it?s no surprise that the majority of the estate's 100-plus hectares are dedicated to this noble varietal. Today, Ottavia focuses primarily on the two classic typologies for which the grape is known: a grand cru for reds and plots for producing Metodo Classico. Pernice is Conte Vistarino's historic cru, with newer additions like Tavernetto and Bertone (different soils and exposures) yielding varied results depending on the vintage. The 2021 harvest favored Pernice, with its intense, seductive profile rich in fruity and floral whiffs, complemented by roasted coffee tones and balsamic hints. The palate is long and deep. The Tavernetto '21 showcases more citrus and spice, while the Bertone '21 offers a vibrant nose of flint and white flowers.

Cordero San Giorgio

Tenuta San Giorgio, 1
27046 Santa Giuletta [PV]
📞 +39 383398090
⊕ www.corderosangiorgio.wine

CELLAR SALES
PRE-BOOKED VISITS
ANNUAL PRODUCTION 9,000 bottles
HECTARES UNDER VINE 36.00
VITICULTURE METHOD Certified Organic

It took only a few years for the Cordero family of Castiglione Falletto to elevate this splendid estate to its rightful level (the property was purchased back in 2019). The family's know-how, combined with the passion of siblings Francesco, Lorenzo, and Caterina, enabled a swift reorganization of the vineyards: 22 hectares averaging 35 years in age, surrounded by oak and cherry woods, thus ensuring biodiversity. Combined with a streamlining of production, the results have been excellent. In this year's usual lineup of pinot nero, the Partù '22 performed particularly well. Made from grapes sourced across the estate's various plots, it evokes cherry tart and aromatic herbs with brackish hints, offering clear, juicy fruit. Sapid and easy-drinking, it's a straightforward yet satisfying wine. As for the rest of their consistently high-quality range, the V18 '21 deserves praise for its elegance, with violet and black forest fruit aromas, while the Tiamat '22 opts for autumnal notes of underbrush.

● OP Pinot Nero Pernice '21	♀♀♀ 6
● OP Pinot Nero Bertone '21	♀♀ 6
● OP Pinot Nero Tavernetto '21	♀♀ 5
○ OP Pinot Nero Pas Dosé M. Cl. 1865 '17	♀♀ 5
● Bertone Pinot Nero '15	♀♀♀ 5
● Bertone Pinot Nero '13	♀♀♀ 5
○ OP M. Cl. Pinot Nero Brut Conte Vistarino 1865 '08	♀♀♀ 4*
● OP Pinot Nero Pernice '06	♀♀♀ 4*
● Pinot Nero dell'Oltrepò Pavese Pernice '17	♀♀♀ 6
● Pinot Nero dell'Oltrepò Pavese Tavernetto '20	♀♀♀ 5
● Pinot Nero dell'Oltrepò Pavese Tavernetto '18	♀♀♀ 5
● Tavernetto Pinot Nero '16	♀♀♀ 3*

● OP Pinot Nero Tiamat '22	♀♀ 4
● OP Pinot Nero V18 '21	♀♀ 7
⊙ OP Pinot Grigio Ramé '23	♀♀ 4
● OP Pinot Nero Partù Ris. '22	♀♀ 5
● OP Barbera Ris. Fredo '21	♀ 5
○ OP Chardonnay Rivone '22	♀ 5
● OP Pinot Nero SG67 '21	♀ 7
● Pinot Nero dell'Oltrepò Pavese Tiamat '20	♀♀♀ 4*
● V18 '20	♀♀♀ 7
OP Barbera Fredo Ris. '20	♀♀ 3*
⊙ OP Pinot Grigio Ramé '22	♀♀ 4
● Pinot Nero dell'Oltrepò Pavese SG 67 '19	♀♀ 4
● Tiamat '21	♀♀ 4

Corte Fusia

via degli Orti, 2
25030 Coccaglio [BS]
☎ +39 3288471276
⊕ www.cortefusia.com

CELLAR SALES
ANNUAL PRODUCTION 38,000 bottles
HECTARES UNDER VINE 8.00

Founded in Coccaglio by two friends, Corte Fusia has since become a reference point for lovers of young, dynamic, small-scale producers. The agronomic expertise of Gigi Nembrini and the winemaking skills of Daniele Gentili, combined with vineyards on the slopes of Monte Orfano, result in a product line that is simple yet carefully crafted. Notably, the pair excel in faithfully representing the vintages and the unique terroir of this part of Franciacorta. We invite you to first try the incredible energy of the Franciacorta Orfano Terre Rosse, as described in the section dedicated to rare wines. The rest of the lineup impresses with its character and original style, starting with the complete Franciacorta Brut, which reveals notable tension and vibrant freshness. A second tasting of the Dosaggio Zero '18 surprises with its aromas of peach, mint, and almond. The palate is lively, with a decisive attack, fine bead well integrated into its structure, and a long, sapid finish.

La Costa

fraz. Costa
via Curone, 15
23888 La Valletta Brianza [LC]
☎ +39 0395312218
⊕ www.la-costa.it

CELLAR SALES
PRE-BOOKED VISITS
ACCOMMODATION AND RESTAURANT SERVICE
ANNUAL PRODUCTION 40,000 bottles
HECTARES UNDER VINE 12.00
VITICULTURE METHOD Certified Organic

Based in Perego, Brianza, just a few kilometers from Milan and near Lake Lecco, La Costa was founded in 1992 by Giordano Crippa, who restored an old farmhouse and planted the first vines. Production began in 2000, and in recent years, the winery has gained recognition for the finesse and elegance of its range, which draws on 12 hectares of vines planted on terraced plots reclaimed from the region?s morainic hills. The Solesta '21, an elegant rhine riesling, expresses clear varietal notes made more complex by acacia barrel aging and time. White fruit, white melon, citrus, and mineral notes of graphite and flint compose a complex bouquet that will evolve over the years. On the palate, it's sapid, dynamic, fruity, and very persistent. The San Giobbe '20, from the Muneda vineyard, is a well-structured monovarietal pinot nero, as is the San Giobbe '21. The other wines tasted are of high quality as well.

○ Franciacorta Brut	▼▼ 5
○ Franciacorta Rosé	▼▼ 5
○ Franciacorta Satèn	▼ 5
○ Franciacorta Dosaggio Zero '18	♊ 6
○ Franciacorta Dosaggio Zero '16	♊ 6
○ Franciacorta Dosaggio Zero Orfano Ris. '14	♊ 6

○ Solesta '21	▼▼ 5
○ Bacca '21	▼▼ 6
○ Brigante Bianco '23	▼▼ 4
○ Incrediboll Extra Brut M. Cl. '20	▼▼ 5
● San Giobbe '21	▼▼ 5
● San Giobbe Muneda '20	▼▼ 6
○ Brigante Bianco '22	♊ 3
○ Brigante Bianco '21	♊ 3
○ Brigante Bianco '20	♊ 3
● Brigante Rosso '18	♊ 3
⊙ Rosato '21	♊ 3
● San Giobbe '20	♊ 5
● San Giobbe '19	♊ 5
● San Giobbe '18	♊ 5
● Seriz '19	♊ 5
○ Solesta '20	♊ 5

Costaripa

via Costa, 1a
25080 Moniga del Garda [BS]
(*) +39 0365502010
@ www.costaripa.it

CELLAR SALES
PRE-BOOKED VISITS
ANNUAL PRODUCTION 480,000 bottles
HECTARES UNDER VINE 60.00

The Vezzola family's history in Valt?nesi began in 1928 with Mattia, who was later joined by his sons Bruno and Franco. The real breakthrough came with the founder's grandson (also Mattia), a renowned winemaker experienced in Metodo Classico in Franciacorta. Revolutionary in his methods, Mattia is particularly committed to creating a great, ageworthy ros?. This nonconformist approach, as the producer himself describes it, is continued today by his children, Gherardo and Nicole. The Vezzola family submitted an excellent lineup for tasting, despite the fact that their signature Chiaretto Molmenti is missing. The Mattia Vezzola Grande Annata Brut Rosé '18 is extraordinarily elegant—subtle, creamy, fruity, and fresh. The Chiaretto Rosamara '23 proves sapid and taut, with fragrances of small fruits and Mediterranean herbs. The Campostarne '22 delivers, with its fleshy texture and blackberry and black currant aromas, while the Maim '18 came across as more evolved.

⊙ Mattia Vezzola Grande Annata M. Cl. Rosé '18	♥♥♥ 6
⊙ RGC Valtènesi Chiaretto RosaMara '23	♥♥ 4
● RGC Valtènesi Rosso Campostarne '22	♥♥ 4
● RGC Valtènesi Rosso Maim '18	♥♥ 5
⊙ Mattia Vezzola Brut M. Cl. Rosé '22	♥ 5
⊙ RGC Valtènesi Chiaretto Molmenti '19	♡♡♡ 6
⊙ RGC Valtènesi Chiaretto Molmenti '18	♡♡♡ 6
⊙ RGC Valtènesi Chiaretto Molmenti '17	♡♡♡ 5
⊙ RGC Valtènesi Chiaretto Molmenti '16	♡♡♡ 5
⊙ RGC Valtènesi Chiaretto RosaMara '20	♡♡♡ 3*

Dirupi

loc. Madonna di Campagna
via San Carlo
23026 Ponte in Valtellina [SO]
(*) +39 3347092663
@ www.dirupi.com

CELLAR SALES
PRE-BOOKED VISITS
ANNUAL PRODUCTION 45,000 bottles
HECTARES UNDER VINE 7.50
VITICULTURE METHOD Certified Organic
SUSTAINABLE WINERY

It seems like yesterday that winemakers Pierpaolo Di Franco and Davide Fasolini began their adventure in Valtellina. In reality, it's been more than 20 years since the Dirupi winery has been producing authentic wines that perfectly express the local terroir. The success is the result of hard work both in the cellar and in the vineyard: the seven hectares of vines, planted on sandy morainic soils, unfold across steep slopes, a configuration that requires entirely manual labor. The result is a supremely elegant line of wines, such as the Valtellina Superiore Nebbiolo Grumello Riserva Vigna Dossi Salati '21, which showcases a broad aromatic range from red fruit to licorice, with a multifaceted palate of endless length. Not to be outdone, the Valtellina Superiore Grumello Vigna Gess '21 summons generous aromas of spices, a whisper of raspberry, and a palate where acidity and tannins are world-class. The Valtellina Superiore '22 continues to surprise with its delightful drinkability.

● Valtellina Sup. Grumello V. Dossi Salati Ris. '21	♥♥ 7
● Valtellina Sup. Grumello V. Gess '21	♥♥ 6
● Rosso di Valtellina Olè '23	♥♥ 4
● Sforzato di Valtellina Vino Sbagliato '22	♥♥ 6
● Valtellina Sup. Dirupi '22	♥♥ 5
● Valtellina Sup. Dirupi '16	♡♡♡ 4*
● Valtellina Sup. Dirupi Ris. '14	♡♡♡ 6
● Valtellina Sup. Dirupi Ris. '12	♡♡♡ 6
● Valtellina Sup. Dirupi Ris. '11	♡♡♡ 6
● Valtellina Sup. Dirupi Ris. '09	♡♡♡ 6
● Valtellina Sup. Grumello Dirupi Ris. '16	♡♡♡ 7
● Valtellina Sup. Grumello Ris. '17	♡♡♡ 7
● Valtellina Sup. Grumello V. Dossi Salati Ris. '19	♡♡♡ 7

LOMBARDY

Sandro Fay

loc. San Giacomo
via Pila Caselli, I
23030 Teglio [SO]
📞 +39 0342786071
🌐 www.vinifay.it

CELLAR SALES
PRE-BOOKED VISITS
ANNUAL PRODUCTION 38,000 bottles
HECTARES UNDER VINE 15.00

The winery was founded in 1973 thanks to the vision of Sandro Fay, while since 1998, his children Marco and Elena have taken the reins of the project. Their 15 hectares of terraced vineyards are mainly located in the Valgella subzone, an area characterized by sandy soils and elevations ranging from 350 to 900 meters. The focus is naturally on chiavennasca, but international varieties like chardonnay are also cultivated. This year's wines are characterized by fragrant red fruit with light green notes, as seen in the Sforzato di Valtellina Nebbiolo Ronco del Picchio '21, where sweetness is balanced by freshness. The Valtellina Superiore Nebbiolo Valgella Cà Morei '20 impresses with its spicy profile and a fleshy palate that balances evident tannins. Vegetal notes accompany red berries and licorice in the Valtellina Superiore Nebbiolo Sassella Il Glicine '21.

★★Ferghettina

via Saline, 11
25030 Adro [BS]
📞 +39 0307451212
🌐 www.ferghettina.it

CELLAR SALES
PRE-BOOKED VISITS
ANNUAL PRODUCTION 500,000 bottles
HECTARES UNDER VINE 200.00
VITICULTURE METHOD Certified Organic

In 1991, Roberto Gatti bottled his first vintage from four hectares of vineyard. Hard work, careful vineyard management, and the high quality of the entire product line have vaulted the winery to the top of the appellation. Today, the Gatti family cultivates 200 hectares across 20 municipalities in Franciacorta. This allows Roberto's children, Laura and Matteo, both winemakers, to have a comprehensive overview of the territory, enabling them to interpret its most subtle nuances from vintage to vintage. A round of applause for the lineup submitted. The Brut '16 performed well alongside the Milledì '20, the Extra Brut '16, the Brut Rosé '20, and the non-vintage Brut. But the highest praise goes to the Dosaggio Zero Riserva 33, a wine that's exemplary for its fragrance and aromatic definition—tones of almond adorned by candied ginger and lemon peel. It stands out for its finesse and overall balance, with a long, harmonious finish.

● Valtellina Sforzato Ronco del Picchio '21	🏆🏆 8
● Valtellina Sup. Sassella Il Glicine '21	🏆🏆 6
● Valtellina Sup. Valgella '21	🏆🏆 5
● Valtellina Sup. Valgella Ca' Morei '20	🏆🏆 5
● Valtellina Sup. Valgella Carterìa Ris. '19	🏆🏆 6
● Valtellina Sforzato Ronco del Picchio '16	🏆🏆🏆 6
● Valtellina Sforzato Ronco del Picchio '10	🏆🏆🏆 6
● Valtellina Sforzato Ronco del Picchio '09	🏆🏆🏆 6
● Valtellina Sforzato Ronco del Picchio '02	🏆🏆🏆 6
● Valtellina Sup. Valgella Cà Morèi '13	🏆🏆🏆 5
● Valtellina Sup. Valgella Carterìa Ris. '16	🏆🏆🏆 6
● Valtellina Sforzato Ronco del Picchio '18	🏆🏆 6
● Valtellina Sup. Valgella Carterìa Ris. '18	🏆🏆 6

○ Franciacorta Dosaggio Zero Riserva 33 '16	🏆🏆🏆 8
○ Franciacorta Satèn '20	🏆🏆 6
○ Franciacorta Brut	🏆🏆 4
○ Franciacorta Brut Milledì '20	🏆🏆 6
⊙ Franciacorta Brut Rosé '20	🏆🏆 6
○ Franciacorta Extra Brut '16	🏆🏆 6
○ Franciacorta Brut Eronero '12	🏆🏆🏆 6
○ Franciacorta Dosaggio Zero Riserva 33 '15	🏆🏆🏆 8
○ Franciacorta Dosaggio Zero Riserva 33 '13	🏆🏆🏆 7
○ Franciacorta Extra Brut Eronero '14	🏆🏆🏆 6
○ Franciacorta Pas Dosé Riserva 33 '12	🏆🏆🏆 7
○ Franciacorta Pas Dosé Riserva 33 '11	🏆🏆🏆 6

Fiamberti

via Chiesa, 17
27044 Canneto Pavese [PV]
(📞 +39 038588019
🌐 www.fiambertivini.it

CELLAR SALES
PRE-BOOKED VISITS
ANNUAL PRODUCTION 140,000 bottles
HECTARES UNDER VINE 18.00

Giulio Fiamberti, supported by his father Ambrogio, has reached a certain stage of awareness: knowing the grapes intimately and knowing how to fully express their attributes. This is especially evident in his Buttafuoco Storico, where every year the estate's two crus showcase the differences of their respective terroirs while respecting consistently high quality standards. While Ambrogio oversees his traditional reds with a steady hand, it?s in the realm of Metodo Classico that we're expecting another breakthrough. This year, the battle between Fiamberti's two Buttafuoco Storico crus was won by the Vigna Solenga '20. It opens with generous and expansive aromas, featuring notes of wild berries, spices, coffee, and the inevitable balsamic tones of mint and eucalyptus. The palate is solid, with fine, silky tannins and a long, unwavering finish. The Sacca del Prete '20 is more powerful, with notable structure and underbrush aromas. It's also worth noting the excellent Metodo Classico Caristoro, with its clear copper highlights, a trademark of pinot nero.

● OP Buttafuoco Storico V. Solenga '20	♀♀♀ 7
● OP Buttafuoco Storico V. Sacca del Prete '20	♀♀ 5
○ OP M. Cl. Pinot Nero Caristoro	♀♀ 4
● OP Bonarda Frizz. La Briccona '23	♀ 2
● OP Buttafuoco Il Cacciatore '22	♀ 3
☉ OP M. Cl. Pinot Nero Rosé Caristoro	♀ 4
● OP Buttafuoco Il Cacciatore '20	♀♀♀ 3*
● OP Buttafuoco Storico V. Sacca del Prete '17	♀♀♀ 5
● OP Buttafuoco Storico V. Sacca del Prete '15	♀♀♀ 5
● OP Buttafuoco Storico V. Solenga '19	♀♀♀ 7
● OP Buttafuoco Storico V. Solenga '16	♀♀♀ 5
● OP Buttafuoco Storico V. Sacca del Prete '19	♀♀ 5

Finigeto

loc. Cella, 27
27040 Montalto Pavese [PV]
(📞 +39 328 7095347
🌐 www.finigeto.com

CELLAR SALES
PRE-BOOKED VISITS
ACCOMMODATION
ANNUAL PRODUCTION 80,000 bottles
HECTARES UNDER VINE 42.00

Barely out of its teens (founded in 2005), Finigeto has already established itself as one of the most intriguing producers operating in Oltrep? Pavese. Founder Aldo Dellavalle, driven by determination and supported by winemaker Marco Terzoni, leads the charge. Enotourism and hospitality are part of the plan, as is a reduced environmental impact in the vineyard. The result is wines of personality and depth, with a particular focus on riesling renano and pinot nero, the latter of which is also transformed into a Metodo Classico. In the well-stocked lineup presented this year, the Cruasé Extra Brut 2005 '21 stands out. A taut Metodo Classico with clean mineral and balsamic notes reminiscent of the high mountains, it reveals alluring, creamy bubbles on the palate. The Brut from the same year offers more citrus and tropical notes, with remarkable texture on the palate. The well-made Riesling Superiore Lo Spavaldo '23 proves sapid and fragrant, playing on tropical fruit and wildflower aromas. The Bonarda Frizzante La Grintosa '23 is a balanced and fragrant drink.

☉ OP Cruasé Extra Brut 2005 '21	♀♀ 5
● OP Bonarda Frizz. La Grintosa '23	♀♀ 3
○ OP M. Cl. Pinot Nero Brut 2005 '21	♀♀ 5
○ OP Riesling Sup. Lo Spavaldo '23	♀♀ 4
○ Moscato '23	♀ 2
● OP Bonarda Il Baldo '22	♀ 3
○ OP Chardonnay Il Caroaldo '22	♀ 3
● OP Pinot Nero Il Marcovaldo '23	♀ 4
● OP Pinot Nero Il Nirò '21	♀ 5
○ Lo Spavaldo Riesling Renano '19	♀♀ 2
○ OP M. Cl. Pinot Nero Pas Dosé 2005 '18	♀♀ 5
○ OP Riesling Sup. Lo Spavaldo Ris. '20	♀♀ 4
● Pinot Nero dell'Oltrepò Pavese Il Nirò '18	♀♀ 5
● Pinot Nero dell'Oltrepò Pavese Il Nirò Ris. '19	♀♀ 5

Freccianera
F.lli Berlucchi

fraz. Borgonato
via Broletto, 2
25040 Corte Franca [BS]
☎ +39 030984451
● www.freccianera.it

CELLAR SALES
PRE-BOOKED VISITS
ANNUAL PRODUCTION 380,000 bottles
HECTARES UNDER VINE 70.00

The 16th-century Casa delle Colonne is the birthplace of Pia Donata Berlucchi and her daughter Tilli Rizzo?s stylish and distinctive Franciacorta wines, crafted from the estate?s 70 hectares of vineyards. The stunning vaulted cellars, adorned with frescoes, are well worth a visit, as are their Franciacorta wines, which are divided into two lines: Freccianera (single-vintage wines) and Casa delle Colonne (reserves). For over 20 years, the winery has adopted low-impact viticulture practices. The Extra Brut Freccianera '20, which reached the final rounds this year, stands out for its excellent quality. Floral notes and hints of ripe peach make for an enticing, precise aromatic profile. The palate is more racy and energetic, with a finish that turns to citrus notes and reveals a delightful sapid streak. We also appreciated the Freccianera Rosa '20, with its raspberry and pomegranate tones, the supple and balsamic Freccianera Satèn '20, and the crisp, energetic Freccianera Nature '20.

★Enrico Gatti

via Metelli, 9
25030 Erbusco [BS]
☎ +39 0307267999
● www.enricogatti.it

CELLAR SALES
PRE-BOOKED VISITS
ANNUAL PRODUCTION 120,000 bottles
HECTARES UNDER VINE 21.00
VITICULTURE METHOD Certified Organic
SUSTAINABLE WINERY

The historic management of the winery, once represented by Lorenzo and Paola Gatti and Paola?s husband Enzo Balzarini, has now passed down to their children Nicol? and Giulia Balzarini. Nicol? oversees the cellar and vineyards, while Giulia handles administrative tasks. The winery has steadily grown, transitioning to organic farming in 2015, while in recent years, their wines have impressed with their personality and fidelity to the terroir of Erbusco, where the winery and its vineyards are based. The winery continues to demonstrate the excellent level of production achieved, particularly with the Riserva La Casella '16. Its aromatic profile is airy and multifaceted, with mineral tones intertwining with richer notes of pastry, butter, and Mediterranean citrus sensations. On the palate, it's creamy, with lively notes of ginger and white pepper. The Satèn '20 and Nature are also well-crafted and enjoyable.

○ Franciacorta Extra Brut Freccianera '20	♥♥ 6
○ Franciacorta Brut Rosé Freccianera Rosa '20	♥♥ 8
○ Franciacorta Nature Freccianera '20	♥♥ 8
○ Franciacorta Satèn Freccianera '20	♥♥ 8
○ Franciacorta Brut Freccianera Blanc de Blancs 25	♥ 6
○ Franciacorta Brut Casa delle Colonne Ris. '13	♀♀ 8
○ Franciacorta Brut Casa delle Colonne Ris. '11	♀♀ 8
○ Franciacorta Brut Casa delle Colonne Ris. '10	♀♀ 8
○ Franciacorta Casa delle Colonne Zero Ris. '13	♀♀ 8
○ Franciacorta Casa delle Colonne Zero Ris. '12	♀♀ 8
○ Franciacorta Zero Casa delle Colonne Ris. '14	♀♀ 8

○ Franciacorta Dosaggio Zero La Casella Ris. '16	♥♥ 8
○ Franciacorta Nature	♥♥ 6
○ Franciacorta Satèn '20	♥♥ 6
○ Franciacorta Brut	♥ 5
○ Franciacorta Brut '05	♀♀♀ 6
○ Franciacorta Millesimo Nature '16	♀♀♀ 7
○ Franciacorta Nature '07	♀♀♀ 5
○ Franciacorta Satèn '05	♀♀♀ 5
○ Franciacorta Satèn '03	♀♀♀ 5
○ Franciacorta Satèn '02	♀♀♀ 4
○ Franciacorta Dosaggio Zero La Casella Ris. '15	♀♀ 8
○ Franciacorta Nature '15	♀♀ 6
○ Franciacorta Satèn '19	♀♀ 6
○ Franciacorta Satèn '18	♀♀ 6
○ Franciacorta Satèn '17	♀♀ 5

★Giorgi

fraz. Campo Noce, 39a
27044 Canneto Pavese [PV]
+39 0385262151
www.giorgi-wines.it

CELLAR SALES
PRE-BOOKED VISITS
ANNUAL PRODUCTION 1,100,000 bottles
HECTARES UNDER VINE 35.00

The Giorgi family's winery continues to see its numbers grow. The dynamic Fabiano, supported by his father Antonio, his sister Eleonora, and wife Ileana, as well as a top-notch winemaking team, has increased production of Metodo Classico to over 100,000 bottles a year, achieving consistently noteworthy results. Of course, they've also maintained their line of traditional wines from the Oltrep? region alongside Fabiano?s creations, all while keeping a watchful eye on marketing and market trends. There are always new additions to their range, especially when it comes to Metodo Classico, but a constant is the Cuvée Storica 1870, which, with the 2020 vintage, once again proves to be a sparkler of superb structure. It expresses all the energy of pinot nero, with tones of small fruits, citrus, and hints of tropical fruit. Rich and fleshy on the palate, it finishes long and lingering. The juicy and harmonious Lodola is also quite good. We also appreciated the excellent Buttafuoco Storico Vigna Casa del Corno '20, a classy drink, substantive—one of the best of its kind.

○ OP Pinot Nero M. Cl. Brut 1870 Gran Cuvée Storica '20	TTT 5
● OP Buttafuoco Storico V. Casa del Corno '20	TT 5
○ Pinot Nero M. Cl. Brut Lodola Collection	TT 5
● OP Bonarda Frizzante La Gallina '23	TT 2*
● OP Bonarda Vivace La Brughera '23	TT 2*
○ Pinot Nero M. Cl. Pas Dosé Top Zero	TT 5
● OP Barbera Regiù '23	T 2
○ OP M. Cl. Pinot Nero Extra Brut Gianfranco Giorgi	T 5
○ OP Pinot Nero M. Cl. Extra Brut 1870 Antonio Giorgi	T 5
○ OP Pinot Nero M. Cl. Extra Brut Gerry Scotti	T 3
○ OP Riesling Mesdì '23	T 3
○ M. Cl. Brut 1870 Antonio Giorgi '12	YYY 4*

Isimbarda

fraz. Castello
Cascina Isimbarda
27046 Santa Giuletta [PV]
+39 0383899256
www.isimbarda.com

CELLAR SALES
PRE-BOOKED VISITS
ANNUAL PRODUCTION 140,000 bottles
HECTARES UNDER VINE 40.00
VITICULTURE METHOD Certified Organic

The winery, directed for many years by Daniele Zangelmi with the support of Mauro Suario and Marta Borrello, is based in one of the most picturesque parts of Oltrep?, in the upper part of Santa Giuletta, where vineyards, lanes of cypress trees, and woods coexist to create a unique landscape. Thanks to its calcareous soils, this land, known for its riesling renano and pinot nero, produces wines of great elegance and longevity. The two Vigna Martina Rieslings always stand out in our tastings. While the standard-label, vintage version features a lovely aromatic profile of yellow fruit, citrus, and wildflowers, with an energetic yet delicate palate, Le Fleur '22 benefited from longer bottle aging, enhancing the mineral notes for which the varietal is known without losing tropical fruit, chamomile, and lychee aromas. On the palate, it's sapid, energetic, and racy. The Pinot Nero Costa dei Giganti '23 is also excellent, with aromas of mint and wild strawberries, unfolding airy and balsamic on the palate.

○ OP Riesling Sup. V. Martina '23	TT 3*
○ OP Riesling Sup. V. Martina Le Fleur '22	TT 4
● OP Pinot Nero Costa dei Giganti '23	TT 3
⊙ OP Cruasé	T 4
○ OP M.Cl. Pinot Nero Blanc de Noir	T 5
○ OP Riesling Renano Sup. V. Martina Le Fleur '20	YYY 3*
○ OP Riesling Le Fleur '18	YY 4
○ OP Riesling Renano Sup. V. Martina Le Fleur '21	YY 4
○ OP Riesling Renano V. Martina '21	YY 3*
○ OP Riesling Renano V. Martina '17	YY 3*
○ OP Riesling Renano V. Martina '12	YY 2*
○ OP Riesling Renano V. Martina Le Fleur '19	YY 3*

Lantieri de Paratico

loc. Capriolo
via Videtti
25031 Capriolo [BS]
(+39 030736151
⊛ www.lantierideparatico.it

CELLAR SALES
PRE-BOOKED VISITS
ACCOMMODATION AND RESTAURANT SERVICE
ANNUAL PRODUCTION 160,000 bottles
HECTARES UNDER VINE 22.00
VITICULTURE METHOD Certified Organic

The Lantieri family, a historic name in
Franciacorta, began producing Metodo Classico
in the 1970s under Giovanni Lantieri and
winemaker Cesare Ferrari. The production
space, which is housed in a 17th-century noble
palace within the village of Capriolo, has
expanded to include a well-maintained
agriturismo, operational since 2001. Their 22
hectares of vineyards are spread around the
winery and the nearby town of Adro, with
160,000 bottles (mostly Metodo Classico)
produced annually. The entire lineup confirms
the high level of quality achieved. The Satèn is
improving, with a caressing perlage, a pleasant
sapid character, and an elegant, well-paced
finish that's fresh and invigorating. The Dosaggio
Zero Origines '18 shows personality and
character, with lemon cream and peach
dominating the nose alongside mineral
sensations. On the palate, it's full and fleshy, with
great freshness and drinkability. The rest of the
lineup is equally strong.

Lazzari

via Mella, 49
25020 Capriano del Colle [BS]
(+39 0309747387
⊛ www.lazzarivini.it

CELLAR SALES
PRE-BOOKED VISITS
ANNUAL PRODUCTION 58,480 bottles
HECTARES UNDER VINE 14.00
VITICULTURE METHOD Certified Organic
SUSTAINABLE WINERY

Brothers Davide and Giordano Lazzari deserve
credit for bringing Capriano del Colle wines
back to prominence in a province dominated by
big names like Brescia. With passion and a keen
eye to protecting the environment, they cultivate
14 hectares of vineyards on Montenetto, a
plateau with red and clay soils that rises 130
meters above the Po Valley. Here you?ll find
turbiana, sangiovese, marzemino, barbera, and
international varieties, all impeccably crafted.
The Capriano Fausto '23 is a rich, full-bodied
wine with remarkable aromatic breadth,
offering tones of grapefruit and rosemary on
the nose, which carry over into a dynamic,
vibrant palate. Made from turbiana grapes, the
Fausto Origini '22, which ages an additional
year, expresses a more complex profile,
enlivened by eucalyptus and citrus nuances on
the nose. On the palate, it's sapid, vibrant,
mineral, and persistent.

○ Franciacorta Nature Origines Ris. '18	▼▼ 7
○ Franciacorta Satèn	▼▼ 5
○ Franciacorta Extra Brut	▼▼ 5
○ Franciacorta Extra Brut Arcadia '20	▼▼ 5
○ Franciacorta Brut Cuvèe	▼ 5
○ Franciacorta Rosé Brut	▼ 5
○ Franciacorta Brut Arcadia '13	♈♈♈ 5
○ Franciacorta Nature Origines Ris. '12	♈♈♈ 7
○ Franciacorta Brut Arcadia '17	♈♈ 5
○ Franciacorta Brut Arcadia '16	♈♈ 5
○ Franciacorta Brut Arcadia '15	♈♈ 5
○ Franciacorta Extra Brut Arcadia '19	♈♈ 5
○ Franciacorta Extra Brut Arcadia '18	♈♈ 5
○ Franciacorta Nature Origines Ris. '16	♈♈ 7

○ Capriano del Colle Fausto '23	▼▼▼ 3*
○ Capriano del Colle Fausto Origini '22	▼▼ 3*
● Capriano del Colle Marzemino Berzamì '23	▼▼ 3
● Capriano del Colle Riserva degli Angeli '21	▼▼ 5
● Capriano del Colle Rosso Adagio '22	▼▼ 3
○ Capriano del Colle Sup. Bastian Contrario '21	▼▼ 6
○ Capriano del Colle Bianco Fausto '21	♈♈♈ 3*
○ Capriano del Colle Fausto '22	♈♈♈ 3*
○ Capriano del Colle Fausto Origini '21	♈♈ 3*
● Capriano del Colle Rosso Riserva degli Angeli Ris. '18	♈♈ 5

★Mamete Prevostini

loc. Mese
via Don Primo Lucchinetti, 63
23020 Sondrio
(+39 034341522
www.mameteprevostini.com

CELLAR SALES
PRE-BOOKED VISITS
RESTAURANT SERVICE
ANNUAL PRODUCTION 200,000 bottles
HECTARES UNDER VINE 36.00
SUSTAINABLE WINERY

The winery?s gradual growth has made it one of the cornerstones of Valtellina today. Founded in the early 1900s as an agriturismo, it now boasts around 20 hectares of vineyards. However, it?s not just the numbers that have grown?their awareness of the importance of sustainable production has also evolved. The winery is constantly striving to achieve the fullest expression of the terroir, a goal nurtured by its long-standing bond with the land. Both the classic and "Convento" lines showcase the winery's exceptional work in the vineyard and cellar. The Sforzato Corte di Cama '21 has an intense nose of dark spices, with a crisp palate and a long finish. The Convento San Lorenzo Sforzato Ventum '19 is vibrant, emanating aromas of tobacco and red fruit, yet manages to maintain surprising balance and harmony. Another elegant wine is the Valtellina Superiore Sassella Riserva Clos Convento San Lorenzo '19, a fresh and fine sip with great elegance and appeal.

Manuelina

fraz. Ruinello di Sotto, 3a
27047 Santa Maria della Versa [PV]
(+39 0385278247
www.manuelina.com

CELLAR SALES
PRE-BOOKED VISITS
ANNUAL PRODUCTION 200,000 bottles
HECTARES UNDER VINE 24.00

In recent years, the Achilli family?s winery has made significant progress. With the involvement of Christian Calatroni and consultant Stefano Testa, they have achieved excellent results, particularly in terms of Metodo Classico. They have also embarked on an ambitious project with riesling renano, while continuing to produce traditional reds like Bonarda, both sparkling and aged. The welcoming atmosphere makes Manuelina one of the territory's most interesting estates for wine tourism. This year, the Achilli family's best Metodo Classico, in our opinion, is the Dosaggio Zero '19, a sparkling wine with aromas of nectarine and small forest berries, with floral undertones, fine and creamy bubbles, well-balanced on the palate, with a clean, lingering finish. The Brut Rosé 145 '19 is also impressive, mature with red berry and citrus notes, while the Solonero '21 proves to be a classically refined Pinot Nero, with clear fruit tones and hints of dog rose on the finish.

● Valtellina Sforzato Corte di Cama '21	♟♟♟ 8
● Valtellina Sforzato Ventum Convento San Lorenzo '19	♟♟ 8
● Valtellina Sup. Sassella Clos Convento San Lorenzo Ris. '19	♟♟ 8
● Rosso di Valtellina Vesper Convento San Lorenzo '21	♟♟ 5
● Valtellina Sforzato Albareda '21	♟♟ 8
● Valtellina Sup. Altitude Ris. '19	♟♟ 7
● Valtellina Sup. Inferno La Cruus '21	♟♟ 6
● Valtellina Sup. Sassella De Le Mur Convento San Lorenzo '20	♟♟ 6
● Valtellina Sforzato Albareda '19	♟♟♟ 6
● Valtellina Sforzato Corte di Cama '19	♟♟♟ 6
● Valtellina Sup. Sassella Clos Ris. Convento San Lorenzo '18	♟♟♟ 8

○ Pinot Nero Dosaggio Zero M. Cl. '19	♟♟ 7
● OP Pinot Nero Solonero '21	♟♟ 3
○ Pinot Nero M. Cl. Brut 137 '19	♟♟ 5
○ Pinot Nero M. Cl. Brut Rosé 145 '19	♟♟ 5
● OP Bonarda Frizzante Achillius '23	♟ 3
○ OP Riesling Filare 52 '22	♟♟ 5
○ Dosaggio Zero M. Cl. '18	♟♟ 5
○ OP M. Cl. Pinot Nero Brut 137 '13	♟♟ 4
○ OP M. Cl. Pinot Nero Brut 145 Rosé '18	♟♟ 4
○ OP M. Cl. Pinot Nero Brut 145 Rosé '16	♟♟ 4
○ OP Riesling Filare 52 '21	♟♟ 3
● Pinot Nero dell'Oltrepò Pavese Solo Nero '18	♟♟ 4
○ Pinot Nero Dosaggio Zero M. Cl. '18	♟♟ 5

Marangona

loc. Marangona 1
25010 Pozzolengo [BS]
☎ +39 030919379
🖳 www.marangona.com

CELLAR SALES
PRE-BOOKED VISITS
ANNUAL PRODUCTION 30,000 bottles
HECTARES UNDER VINE 30.00

Marangona takes its name from an old bell at the farmstead that once marked the working hours in the nearby countryside. The winery, located between Sirmione and Pozzolengo, is one of the most dynamic in the region, thanks to the dedication of siblings Laura and Alessandro Cutolo. They manage 34 hectares of organically farmed vineyards, primarily planted with turbiana vines that range from 30 to over 50 years old. Their wines are known for their mineral-driven, pure style, and all bottles use technological corks. We were particularly impressed by the three Luganas tasted this year. Our favorite is the excellent Lugana Cemento '22, from vines over 40 years old, fermented (and aged) in natural concrete with the skins. It's a wine of quintessential freshness and simplicity, with floral tones, vivid tension, and a mineral backbone that perfectly expresses the terroir. The Tre Campane '22, also from old vines and fermented in stainless steel, is equally outstanding. The Lugana '23 is simpler and more approachable, but still very enjoyable.

○ Lugana Cemento '22	▼▼▼ 5
○ Lugana '23	▼▼ 3
○ Lugana Tre Campane '22	▼▼ 4
○ Lugana '20	♈♈ 3
○ Lugana '19	♈♈ 2*
○ Lugana '18	♈♈ 2*
○ Lugana Cemento '20	♈♈ 5
○ Lugana Cemento '18	♈♈ 4
○ Lugana Marangona '22	♈♈ 3
○ Lugana Rabbiosa '15	♈♈ 3
○ Lugana Tre Campane '21	♈♈ 4
○ Lugana Tre Campane '20	♈♈ 4
○ Lugana Tre Campane '19	♈♈ 4
○ Lugana Tre Campane '18	♈♈ 3
○ Lugana Tre Campane '17	♈♈ 3
◉ RGC Valtènesi Chiaretto '20	♈♈ 2*

Le Marchesine

via Vallosa, 31
25050 Passirano [BS]
☎ +39 030657005
🖳 www.lemarchesine.it

CELLAR SALES
PRE-BOOKED VISITS
ANNUAL PRODUCTION 425,000 bottles
HECTARES UNDER VINE 48.00
SUSTAINABLE WINERY

Le Marchesine was founded in 1985 by Giovanni Biatta, who inherited his passion for winemaking from his great-grandfather Camillo, a pioneer in the wine industry. Today, the winery is run by Loris Biatta and his two children, Alice and Andrea. The wines are crafted from grapes grown across nearly 50 hectares in various Franciacorta towns. Their reserves, known for spending lengthy periods of times on the lees, reach remarkable levels of complexity and elegance. The Brigantia '20 represents an excellent example of a balanced and characterful Franciacorta Satèn. Its elegant aromatic profile combines citrus tones with almond blossom scents. Its silky, persistent bubbles add pleasure to a sapid, juicy palate. The Audens is intensely balsamic, with hints of mint and nettle, while the palate is energetic, offering nice depth of flavor. The Brut Rosé Artio and Extra Brut Nodens '17 are also very good.

○ Franciacorta Brut Satèn Brigantia '20	▼▼ 7
◉ Franciacorta Brut Rosé Artio	▼▼ 7
○ Franciacorta Dosaggio Zero Audens	▼▼ 6
○ Franciacorta Extra Brut Nodens '17	▼▼ 6
○ Franciacorta Brut Secolo Novo '15	▼ 8
○ Franciacorta Brut '04	♈♈♈ 5
○ Franciacorta Brut Blanc de Noir '09	♈♈♈ 5
○ Franciacorta Brut Secolo Novo '12	♈♈♈ 7
○ Franciacorta Brut Secolo Novo '05	♈♈♈ 7
○ Franciacorta Dosage Zero Secolo Novo Ris. '11	♈♈♈ 8
○ Franciacorta Dosage Zero Secolo Novo Ris. '08	♈♈♈ 8
○ Franciacorta Brut Esus '15	♈♈ 8
○ Franciacorta Dosaggio Zero Secolo Novo Ris. '14	♈♈ 8

Tenuta Mazzolino

via Mazzolino, 34
27050 Corvino San Quirico [PV]
☏ +39 0383876122
✎ www.tenuta-mazzolino.com

CELLAR SALES
PRE-BOOKED VISITS
ANNUAL PRODUCTION 100,000 bottles
HECTARES UNDER VINE 20.00
VITICULTURE METHOD Certified Organic
SUSTAINABLE WINERY

A trip to Oltrep? wouldn't be complete without visiting this gem overlooking the area's foothills, with its 19th-century villa, Italian garden, and splendid underground cellar. Chardonnay, pinot nero, French consultants ... It's clear where the Bragiotti family drew their inspiration in creating the estate, today led by Francesca Seralvo Bragiotti. Winemaker Stefano Malchiodi is assisted by Kyriakos Kynigopoulos for red pinot nero production and Dominique Leboeuf for Metodo Classico. Since its debut, the Terrazze Alte has been a consistently impressive Pinot Nero, and the 2022 vintage is no exception, with its alluring aromas of citrus and flowers, accompanied by herbs and sweet spices, with light vegetal notes. Other noteworthy tastes include the Blanc '22, a Chardonnay marked by clear tropical fruit notes, and the Brut Blanc de Blancs '20, an airy, well-crafted wine with aromas of hay and herbs, and a clean, mineral finish.

Mirabella

via Cantarane, 2
25050 Rodengo Saiano [BS]
☏ +39 030611197
✎ www.mirabellafranciacorta.it

CELLAR SALES
PRE-BOOKED VISITS
ACCOMMODATION
ANNUAL PRODUCTION 350,000 bottles
HECTARES UNDER VINE 45.00
SUSTAINABLE WINERY

Teresio Schiavi, now joined by his sons Alessandro and Alberto, founded Mirabella in 1979 with a clear vision: to respect both nature and humanity. Over more than 40 years, this philosophy has remained a hallmark of the wines they produce. Their sparkling wines maintain an authentic approach with minimal sulfur use, selective technology, and careful aging on the lees for all their Franciacorta wines. The Brut Nature Demetra Pinot Nero '19 stands out for its personality and originality. It offers up tones of flint, peach, and lime, with a palate that starts creamy but grows taut, linear, leaving its mark. The finish is lively and persistent. The Døm Riserva '17 is also excellent, with a more mature aromatic spectrum featuring yellow flowers and spices.

● Terrazze Alte Pinot Nero '22	♟♟♟ 4*
○ Blanc de Blancs Brut M. Cl. '20	♟♟ 4
○ Blanc Chardonnay '22	♟♟ 5
● OP Pinot Nero Noir '21	♟♟ 5
⊙ OP Cruasé '19	♟ 5
● Pinot Nero dell'Oltrepò Pavese Noir '12	♟♟♟ 5
● Pinot Nero dell'Oltrepò Pavese Noir '10	♟♟♟ 5
● Pinot Nero dell'Oltrepò Pavese Noir '09	♟♟♟ 5
● Pinot Nero dell'Oltrepò Pavese Noir '08	♟♟♟ 5
● Pinot Nero dell'Oltrepò Pavese Noir '07	♟♟♟ 5
● Pinot Nero dell'Oltrepò Pavese Noir '06	♟♟♟ 5
● Terrazze Alte '21	♟♟♟ 4*
○ Chardonnay Blanc '21	♟♟ 5
● Pinot Nero dell'Oltrepò Pavese Noir '19	♟♟ 5
● Pinot Nero dell'Oltrepò Pavese Noir '18	♟♟ 5
● Terrazze Pinot Nero '21	♟♟ 3*

○ Franciacorta Brut Nature Demetra Pinot Nero '19	♟♟ 6
○ Franciacorta Brut Nature Demetra	♟♟ 6
○ Franciacorta Brut Satèn '20	♟♟ 6
○ Franciacorta Dosaggio Zero Døm Ris. '17	♟♟ 8
○ Franciacorta Brut Edea	♟ 5
○ Franciacorta Brut Nature Demetra '19	♟ 6
⊙ Franciacorta Brut Rosé	♟ 5
○ Franciacorta Dosaggio Zero Døm Ris. '15	♟♟♟ 7
○ Franciacorta Dosaggio Zero Demetra '18	♟♟ 6
⊙ Franciacorta Rosé Dosaggio Zero '16	♟♟ 7

★★Monsupello

via San Lazzaro, 5
27050 Torricella Verzate [PV]
+39 0383896043
www.monsupello.it

CELLAR SALES
PRE-BOOKED VISITS
ANNUAL PRODUCTION 260,000 bottles
HECTARES UNDER VINE 50.00

Carlo Boatti, a key figure in Oltrep? Pavese viticulture, knew every meter of his land, the soil characteristics, and the microclimate. He knew what to plant and where, and his foresight led Monsupello to its current success, now carried on by his children Pierangelo and Laura and his granddaughter Carlotta. This year?s big news is the change in winemakers. After 18 years, Stefano Torre is replacing Marco Bertelegni, and will be tasked with maintaining the winery's high production standards. The Rosé Brut is a sapid and mineral wine, well-balanced, with aromas of berries. Among the lineup of Metodo Classicos, the Blanc de Blancs also stands out, full and creamy on the palate, expressive with tropical fruit and aromatic herbs, and racy on the finish. The award-winning Nature proves complex and evolved, with nice structure and a firm backbone. The Brut '18 pours a coppery hue (a signature of pinot nero), revealing broad flesh and substance, and fine bubbles.

○ Blanc de Blancs Extra Brut M. Cl.	🍷🍷 5
⊙ Brut Rosé M. Cl.	🍷🍷 5
○ Brut M. Cl. '18	🍷🍷 5
○ Nature M. Cl.	🍷🍷 4
○ Pinot Grigio '23	🍷🍷 3
● Barbera I Gelsi '18	🍷 3
○ Brut M. Cl.	🍷 2
○ Chardonnay Senso '20	🍷 5
○ Cuvée Ca' del Tava Brut M. Cl.	🍷 6
● Nebbiolo '17	🍷 3
● OP Bonarda Calcababio '22	🍷 3
● OP Bonarda Frizzante Vaiolet '23	🍷 2
● Podere La Borla '19	🍷 3
○ Brut M. Cl. '13	ΥΥΥ 5
○ Brut M. Cl. '11	ΥΥΥ 5
○ Riesling '21	ΥΥΥ 2*

★Monte Rossa

loc. Barco
via per Ospitaletto, 131
25046 Cazzago San Martino [BS]
+39 030725066
www.monterossa.com

CELLAR SALES
PRE-BOOKED VISITS
ANNUAL PRODUCTION 500,000 bottles
HECTARES UNDER VINE 70.00

Monte Rossa is one of Franciacorta's historic wineries. Emanuele Rabotti continues the family tradition with vision and personality, as evidenced by the cutting-edge new winery, which is set to enhance the already excellent quality of their Franciacorta wines. Additionally, the acquisition of the urban Pusterla vineyard in Brescia, where a unique white wine is produced from the indigenous invernenga grape, highlights the winery?s commitment to originality and quality. The Franciacorta Brut PR proves to be one of the best of its kind, boasting a commendable balance and drinkability. Aromas of almond and anise adorn a supple palate marked by elegant, subtle toasty notes. It finishes with sapid tones and long persistence. Other noteworthy wines include the Fuoriserie N. 025, which offers a rich aromatic profile and a vibrant, energetic palate. Equally enjoyable, the Satèn Sansevé stands out for its luscious and pleasurable hints of white peach and mint.

○ Franciacorta Brut P.R.	🍷🍷 5
○ Franciacorta Brut Cabochon Fuoriserie n. 025	🍷🍷 8
⊙ Franciacorta Rosé Brut Flamingo	🍷🍷 6
○ Franciacorta Satèn Sansevé	🍷🍷 5
○ Franciacorta Brut Cabochon Stellato '12	🍷 8
○ Franciacorta Brut Nature Coupé	🍷 5
○ Franciacorta Brut Cabochon '05	ΥΥΥ 6
○ Franciacorta Brut Cabochon '04	ΥΥΥ 6
○ Franciacorta Brut Cabochon '03	ΥΥΥ 6
○ Franciacorta Brut Cabochon '16	ΥΥ 8
○ Franciacorta Brut Nature Cabochon Doppiozero '18	ΥΥ 8
○ Franciacorta Brut Nature Cabochon Doppiozero '16	ΥΥ 8

Montina Franciacorta

via Baiana, 17
25040 Monticelli Brusati [BS]
📞 +39 030653278
🌐 www.montinafranciacorta.it

CELLAR SALES
PRE-BOOKED VISITS
RESTAURANT SERVICE
ANNUAL PRODUCTION 400,000 bottles
HECTARES UNDER VINE 70.00
SUSTAINABLE WINERY

Now in the hands of the third generation?Michele, Daniele, and Anna?La Montina is led with energy and enthusiasm. The Bozza family's estate spans 70 hectares, producing a wide and diverse range of wines. But viticulture is not the only focus here: art and gastronomy also play key roles. The winery's art gallery regularly hosts exhibitions of contemporary artists, and guests can enjoy the cuisine and pastries of Villa Baiana during special events throughout the year. A solid lineup of cuvées was presented this year, notably the Extra Brut, which expresses notes of bread crust and nuts alongside floral sensations. The palate showcases a fine and creamy bead with vivid freshness that brings an invigorating lift to the wine. The Satèn impresses with its elegance and finesse, with aromas of vanilla and white peach. Its progressive palate is pleasantly soft, leading to a finish on mineral and minty notes.

Monzio Compagnoni

via Nigoline, 98
25030 Adro [BS]
📞 +39 0307457803
🌐 www.monziocompagnoni.com

CELLAR SALES
PRE-BOOKED VISITS
ACCOMMODATION
ANNUAL PRODUCTION 250,000 bottles
HECTARES UNDER VINE 36.00

Marcello Monzio Compagnoni, who passed away in December 2021, founded his winery with a deep passion for Metodo Classico, drawing on his family's winemaking tradition in the nearby Valcalepio. Today, the winery continues to produce a consistently high-quality range, as evidenced by the impressive lineup of Franciacortas presented for this year?s tastings. Among the highlights this year is the Brut '20, which offers a vivid and clear nose, rich in fruit. Spirited on the palate, with refreshing tones of citrus peel and mint. It closes with a delightful sapid vein, inviting another sip—what a drink! We also appreciated the well-crafted Cuvée alla Moda, a rich and creamy drink, and the Blanc de Noir Riserva '18, mature in its profile, with good progression.

○ Franciacorta Extra Brut	🍷🍷 5
○ Franciacorta Brut '19	🍷🍷 5
⊙ Franciacorta Demi Sec Rosé	🍷🍷 4
○ Franciacorta Satèn	🍷🍷 5
⊙ Franciacorta Extra Brut Rosé	🍷 5
○ Franciacorta Brut '05	🍷🍷🍷 5
○ Franciacorta Extra Brut Vintage Ris. '05	🍷🍷🍷 6
○ Franciacorta Extra Brut Vintage Ris. '04	🍷🍷🍷 6
○ Franciacorta Brut '18	🍷🍷 5
○ Franciacorta Brut '15	🍷🍷 5
○ Franciacorta Brut '12	🍷🍷 5
○ Franciacorta Dosaggio Zero Baiana Ris. '12	🍷🍷 7
○ Franciacorta Dosaggio Zero La Montina Quor Nature Ris. '16	🍷🍷 8
○ Franciacorta Pas Dosé Baiana Ris. '11	🍷🍷 5

○ Franciacorta Brut '20	🍷🍷 5
○ Franciacorta Brut Cuvée alla Moda	🍷🍷 5
○ Franciacorta Dosaggio Zero Blanc de Noir Ris. '18	🍷🍷 8
⊙ Franciacorta Saten '20	🍷 6
○ Franciacorta Extra Brut '04	🍷🍷🍷 5
○ Franciacorta Extra Brut '03	🍷🍷🍷 5
○ Franciacorta Brut '18	🍷🍷 5
⊙ Franciacorta Brut Rosè '19	🍷🍷 6
○ Franciacorta Dosaggio Zero Blanc de Noir Ris. '12	🍷🍷 6
○ Franciacorta Extra Brut '19	🍷🍷 6
○ Franciacorta Extra Brut '18	🍷🍷 6
○ Franciacorta Extra Brut '12	🍷🍷 5
○ Franciacorta Nature Blanc de Noir Monti della Corte Ris. '09	🍷🍷 7
○ Franciacorta Saten '16	🍷🍷 5

Mosnel

fraz. Camignone
c.da Barboglio, 14
25050 Passirano [BS]
☏ +39 030653117
● www.mosnel.com

CELLAR SALES
PRE-BOOKED VISITS
ANNUAL PRODUCTION 250,000 bottles
HECTARES UNDER VINE 40.00
VITICULTURE METHOD Certified Organic
SUSTAINABLE WINERY

In recent years, the estate run by Lucia and Giulio Barzan?, the fifth generation of family, has become synonymous with quality. Their approximately 40 hectares of organically farmed vineyards are located in prime growing areas around Passirano, Camignone, and nearby villages. The stunning 16th-century villa that houses the winery is a must-visit. The wines are renowned for their finesse, minerality, and creaminess, delivering both elegance and complexity in every glass. The lively and balsamic Satèn proves delicate yet dynamic on the palate. Aromas of hawthorn and nuts are brightened by an undertone of mint. In the mouth it's vibrant, with a relaxed and fresh palate. The Pas Dosé Parosé '18, with its signature refined and multifaceted spice profile, makes for a subtle taste. The palate plays on tones of orange zest and pomegranate—it will reveal its best in a few years. The outstanding EBB '18, with its class and concentration, promises to drink well for many years.

Muratori

via Valli, 31
25030 Adro [BS]
☏ +39 0307451051
● www.muratoriwine.it

CELLAR SALES
PRE-BOOKED VISITS
ANNUAL PRODUCTION 401,000 bottles
HECTARES UNDER VINE 54.00
VITICULTURE METHOD Certified Organic

The historic Villa Crespia, perched on the picturesque hill of Adro, has housed the Muratori winery since 1999. Sustainability is increasingly at the heart of this estate?s efforts: in addition to organic vineyards, the producer is off the grid thanks to an agrivoltaic system, while the grapes are processed by gravity in the underground winery. Their wines, which hail from all six of Franciacorta?s growing districts, are produced in collaboration with winemaker Riccardo Cotarella. Two cuvées surprised us in this edition. The Brut Millè '20 impresses with its cohesion, integrity, and fresh flavor profile. Its fine bubbles and well-structured palate earned it a spot in the finals. However, the Satèn steals the show with its aromatic fragrance, fine bubbles, and elegant palate. Aromas of peach, almond, and apple lead to a delicious and well-paced palate, with a long, juicy finish.

○ Franciacorta Extra Brut EBB '18	♀♀♀ 8
○ Franciacorta Pas Dosé Parosé '18	♀♀ 8
○ Franciacorta Brut Nature	♀♀ 6
○ Franciacorta Brut Satèn '20	♀♀ 6
○ Franciacorta Pas Dosé	♀♀ 6
○ Franciacorta Brut Rosé	♀ 6
○ Franciacorta Extra Brut EBB '15	♀♀♀ 7
○ Franciacorta Extra Brut EBB '09	♀♀♀ 5
○ Franciacorta Pas Dosé QdE Ris. '04	♀♀♀ 6
○ Franciacorta Pas Dosé Ris. '08	♀♀♀ 8
○ Franciacorta Rosé Pas Dosé Parosé '16	♀♀♀ 8
○ Franciacorta Rosé Pas Dosé Parosé Riedizione 2023 '07	♀♀♀ 8
○ Franciacorta Satèn '15	♀♀♀ 6
○ Franciacorta Satèn '05	♀♀♀ 5
○ Franciacorta Dosaggio Zero Ris. '09	♀♀ 8

○ Franciacorta Satèn	♀♀♀ 6
○ Franciacorta Brut Millé '20	♀♀ 6
○ Franciacorta Dosaggio Zero Blanc de Noirs Cisiolo	♀♀ 6
○ Franciacorta Dosaggio Zero Riserva del Gelso '17	♀♀ 8
⊙ Franciacorta Extra Brut Rosé	♀♀ 6
○ Franciacorta Brut	♀ 5
○ Franciacorta Brut Millè Ris. '12	♀♀♀ 8
○ Franciacorta Dosaggio Zero Francesco Iacono Ris. '04	♀♀♀ 7
○ Franciacorta Dosaggio Zero Cisiolo Muratori	♀♀ 5
○ Franciacorta Dosaggio Zero Riserva del Gelso '16	♀♀ 8
⊙ Franciacorta Rosé Extra Brut	♀♀ 6

★★★Nino Negri

via Ghibellini
23030 Chiuro [SO]
📞 +39 0342485211
🌐 www.ninonegri.it

CELLAR SALES
PRE-BOOKED VISITS
RESTAURANT SERVICE
ANNUAL PRODUCTION 750,000 bottles
HECTARES UNDER VINE 160.00
SUSTAINABLE WINERY

It's nearly certain that without the contributions of Negri, Valtellina as we know it today wouldn?t exist. In 1956, Carluccio Negri, inspired by historical sources from the 1500s, invented the famous Sfursat. But that?s not the only reason the Negri winery is so vital to the region: their tremendous growth in production has never compromised quality. This has allowed the area to gain global recognition for its unique, top-quality wines. The Sfursat 5 Stelle '21 stays true to form: tobacco and spice notes, along with clear red fruit, a powerful and austere palate, and a very long finish. The Valtellina Superiore Inferno Vigna Ca' Guicciardi '21 is all about finesse, with red fruit and a lovely floral hint on the nose, and an elegant palate with finely polished tannins. In contrast, the Valtellina Superiore Grumello Vigna Sassorosso '21 bursts with aromas of raspberry and tobacco— its solid, powerful palate slightly detracts from its drinkability.

● Valtellina Sfursat 5 Stelle '21	▼▼▼ 8
● Valtellina Sup. Grumello V. Sassorosso '21	▼▼ 6
● Valtellina Sup. Inferno V. Ca' Guicciardi '21	▼▼ 6
● Valtellina Sup. Valgella V. Fracia '20	▼▼▼ 7
● Valtellina Sfursat 5 Stelle '20	♀♀♀ 8
● Valtellina Sfursat 5 Stelle '18	♀♀♀ 8
● Valtellina Sfursat 5 Stelle '17	♀♀♀ 8
● Valtellina Sfursat 5 Stelle '16	♀♀♀ 8
● Valtellina Sfursat 5 Stelle '15	♀♀♀ 8
● Valtellina Sfursat 5 Stelle '13	♀♀♀ 8
● Valtellina Sfursat 5 Stelle '11	♀♀♀ 8
● Valtellina Sfursat 5 Stelle '10	♀♀♀ 7
● Valtellina Sfursat 5 Stelle '09	♀♀♀ 7
● Valtellina Sfursat Carlo Negri '15	♀♀♀ 6
● Valtellina Sfursat Carlo Negri '11	♀♀♀ 8
● Valtellina Sup. Valgella V. Fracia '18	♀♀♀ 6

Noventa Botticino

via Merano, 28
25080 Botticino [BS]
📞 +39 0302691500
🌐 www.noventabotticino.it

CELLAR SALES
PRE-BOOKED VISITS
ANNUAL PRODUCTION 45,000 bottles
HECTARES UNDER VINE 11.00
VITICULTURE METHOD Certified Organic
SUSTAINABLE WINERY

The Noventa family has deep roots in the Botticino hills, an area known for the striking contrast between marble quarries and unspoiled nature. Indeed, the Noventas have been making wine here since the early 20th century. In recent generations, they have focused on the Botticino DOC through organic practices in the vineyards and by vinifying each terroir separately, showcasing the distinctive characteristics of each with great sensitivity. With the Pià della Tesa '21, balance is the watchword. A fresh and energetic aromatic profile, with dark spice notes alternating with balsamic hints and fragrant red fruit. In the mouth, it's full, with refined yet present tannins, finishing sapid and exceptionally elegant. The Gobbio '21 is more about power and richness, opening with notes of spice and blackberries. The palate is full-bodied and structured, refreshed by a balanced acidity that makes for a lively drink.

● Botticino Pià de la Tesa '21	▼▼▼ 5
● Botticino Gobbio '21	▼▼ 6
● Botticino Colle degli Ulivi '21	▼▼ 4
☉ L'Aura '23	▼▼ 4
● Botticino Gobbio '18	♀♀♀ 6
● Botticino Gobbio '17	♀♀♀ 5
● Botticino Gobbio '16	♀♀♀ 5
● Botticino Colle degli Ulivi '20	♀♀ 4
● Botticino Colle degli Ulivi '19	♀♀ 4
● Botticino Colle degli Ulivi '18	♀♀ 4
● Botticino Colle degli Ulivi '17	♀♀ 2*
● Botticino Gobbio '19	♀♀ 6
● Botticino Pià de la Tesa '21	♀♀ 5
● Botticino Pià de la Tesa '19	♀♀ 5
● Botticino Pià de la Tesa '18	♀♀ 5
● Botticino Pià della Tesa '17	♀♀ 3

Olivini

oc. Demesse Vecchie, 2
25015 Desenzano del Garda [BS]
+39 0309910268
www.famigliaolivini.com

CELLAR SALES
PRE-BOOKED VISITS
ANNUAL PRODUCTION 180,000 bottles
HECTARES UNDER VINE 31.00

"Agricoltura ragionata" ("Rational agriculture")
s the motto of the Olivini family, a registered
trademark since 2018. The principle was
established by founder Giuseppe in 1970 and has
since been passed down through the
generations. Today it's up to siblings Giovanni,
Giorgio, and Giordana to uphold the creed,
employing minimal interventions in the vineyard
and maximum technology in the cellar to
preserve the characteristics of the grape,
focusing especially on temperature control,
starting from the cold room where freshly
harvested grapes are stored. The Notte a San
Martino '20 earned a place in our final tastings.
An excellent Merlot, it pours a deep ruby hue,
releasing an intriguing nose of cherry and fresh
red fruits, enlivened by hints of aromatic herbs
and a well-integrated touch of vanilla. The palate
s slender, with smooth tannins and crunchy, juicy
fruit. Among the top of the vintage is the Lugana
Demesse Vecchie '22, alongside the rosés Riviera
del Garda Brut '21 and Valtènesi Chiaretto '23.

Lugana Demesse Vecchie '22	🍷🍷 4
Notte a San Martino Merlot '20	🍷🍷 5
Explorer '21	🍷🍷 4
RGC Rosé Brut M. Cl. '21	🍷🍷 5
RGC Valtènesi Chiaretto '23	🍷🍷 3
Lugana '23	🍷 3
Explorer '20	🍷🍷 4
Explorer '19	🍷🍷 4
Lugana '22	🍷🍷 3*
Lugana '13	🍷🍷 3
Lugana Brut M. Cl. '10	🍷🍷 5
Lugana Demesse Vecchie '21	🍷🍷 4
Lugana Demesse Vecchie '11	🍷🍷 4
Notte a San Martino '18	🍷🍷 5
RGC Rosé Brut M. Cl. '20	🍷🍷 5

Oltrenero

loc. Bosco
27049 Zenevredo [PV]
+39 0385245326
www.oltrenero.it

CELLAR SALES
PRE-BOOKED VISITS
ANNUAL PRODUCTION 100,000 bottles
HECTARES UNDER VINE 85.00

Oltrenero, the Zonin family's version of pinot
nero in Oltrep? Pavese, was founded in 1987.
From the outset, the idea was to pursue minimal
environmental impact. Today, alongside the area?s
traditional grape varieties, pinot nero has taken
on an increasingly prominent role. The project,
currently led by Paolo Tealdi with the support of
winemaker Cristiano Trambusti, offers various
versions of Metodo Classico, including, of late, a
notable monovarietal Pinot Meunier. Only two
wines presented this year, both Metodo
Classicos, of course. The Nature '19 stands out
immediately with its beautiful, bright golden
color, followed by an aromatic array that ranges
from rennet apple to aromatic herbs, wild
berries, and more citrusy notes. On the palate, it
has a fine and creamy bead, with substance and a
linear profile: a food-friendly and lively Pinot
Noir. The Brut is also well crafted, with its citrus
and floral notes.

○ OP M. Cl. Oltrenero Brut Nature '19	🍷🍷 6
○ OP Pinot Nero M. Cl. Brut	🍷🍷 5
○ OP M. Cl. Pinot Nero Nature Oltrenero '13	🍷🍷🍷 6
○ Oltrenero Cuvée Emme M. Cl. '17	🍷🍷 6
○ OP Brut Nature '18	🍷🍷 6
⊙ OP Cruasé Oltrenero	🍷🍷 5
⊙ OP Cruasé Oltrenero	🍷🍷 5
○ OP M. Cl. Brut	🍷🍷 5
○ OP M. Cl. Pinot Nero Brut Nature Oltrenero '16	🍷🍷 6
○ OP M. Cl. Pinot Nero Nature Oltrenero '14	🍷🍷 6
⊙ Philèo Extra Dry Rosé Martinotti	🍷🍷 2
● Pinot Nero dell'Oltrepò Pavese Poggio Pelato '17	🍷🍷 4

Opera Roses

via Caraviglia, 35
25080 Padenghe sul Garda [BS]
☎ +39 0309907005
⊕ www.operaroses.com

CELLAR SALES
PRE-BOOKED VISITS
ANNUAL PRODUCTION 50,000 bottles
HECTARES UNDER VINE 15.00

Naike and Nathan Bertola were born into a family of winemakers, so viticulture was a natural choice. However, simply collaborating with their family?s Il Pratello winery wasn?t enough for them. They decided to launch their own startup, focusing exclusively?so far the only ones in Italy to do so?on Valtenesi Chiaretto, offering it in several different expressions. The siblings cultivate seven and a half hectares of beautiful vineyards, primarily planted with groppello, the area?s signature variety. The Chiaretto Chloè '23 is made from the classic groppello, barbera, and sangiovese varietals, which macerate for a week on their skins at low temperatures after a light pressing, then ferment in stainless steel. The result is a pale, bright Chiaretto with intense and clear aromas of wild strawberry and cherry, a sapid, fruity, fresh, and vibrant palate of spectacular finesse. The Rocco '21, which ferments and ages in tonneaux, charms on re-tasting.

⊙ RGC Chiaretto Chloè '23	♥♥ 3*
⊙ RGC Chiaretto Opera '23	♥♥ 3
⊙ RGC Chiaretto Chloe '22	♥♥ 3
⊙ RGC Chiaretto Opera '22	♥♥ 3
⊙ RGC Chiaretto Rocco '21	♥♥ 4

Pasini San Giovanni

fraz. Raffa
via Videlle, 2
25080 Puegnago sul Garda [BS]
☎ +39 0365651419
⊕ www.pasinisangiovanni.it

CELLAR SALES
PRE-BOOKED VISITS
ANNUAL PRODUCTION 300,000 bottles
HECTARES UNDER VINE 36.00
VITICULTURE METHOD Certified Organic
SUSTAINABLE WINERY

Much work and passion have been passed down through the generations, ever since Andrea Pasini founded the family winery in 1958. Today, four Pasini cousins manage the estate, which spans 10 hectares of turbiana in San Benedetto, 15 hectares of Cascina San Giovanni, the historic production center, and another 12 hectares in Picedo di Polpenazze, in Valt?nesi. Different soils and exposures all respect biodiversity and sustainability, aided by a photovoltaic system installed in 2009. The Chiaretto Rosagreen '23 doesn't play second fiddle to the Lettera C, which is still maturing in the cellar. Its pale, bright color anticipates an elegant, complex, refined nose, releasing small red fruit aromas and wafts of Mediterranean scrub, sage, and rosemary. The palate is sapid, zesty, and spirited, yet rich in fruit, citrus, and minerality. It's a different take on Chiaretto, equally fascinating but perhaps more approachable. From Lugana (including sparkling versions) to their groppello reds, all their wines are truly noteworthy.

⊙ RGC Valtènesi Chiaretto Rosagreen '23	♥♥♥ 4
○ 100% Extra Brut M. Cl.	♥♥ 4
⊙ Ceppo 326 Dosaggio Zero Rosé M. Cl.	♥♥ 5
○ Lugana Brut M. Cl.	♥♥ 4
○ Lugana Il Lugana '23	♥♥ 3
● RGC Valtènesi Il Valtènesi '22	♥♥ 3
● RGC Valtènesi San Gioan I Carati Ris. '17	♥♥ 6
○ Brinat Resistenze '22	♥ 5
○ Lugana Busocaldo Ris. '20	♥ 5
⊙ RGC Valtènesi Chiaretto Lettera C '21	♥♥♥ 6
⊙ RGC Valtènesi Chiaretto Lettera C '20	♥♥♥ 6

Perla del Garda

via Fenil Vecchio, 9
25017 Lonato [BS]
📞 +39 0309103109
🌐 www.perladelgarda.it

CELLAR SALES
PRE-BOOKED VISITS
ANNUAL PRODUCTION 300,000 bottles
HECTARES UNDER VINE 40.00
VITICULTURE METHOD Certified Organic
SUSTAINABLE WINERY

A tradition dating back to the 1400s saw the family migrate from the Veronese mountains to Brescia province, on the shores of Lake Garda. After several harvests, in 2006, the first bottles were released from the cellar, built among the vineyards to allow for gravity vinification. From this production center (set near the Sanctuary of the Madonna della Scoperta), the winery expanded into Valt?nesi in 2021. Today Perla del Garda is led by Ettore and Giovanna Prandini. Extra virgin olive oil is also produced. The crystalline, sapid, and taut Lugana Perla '23 offers aromas of citrus and aromatic herbs. It's a modern, purist interpretation of the typology, coming through crisp, dynamic, and lively on the palate, enchanting with clear notes of white fruit, while finishing with a spirited touch of elegant herbal and aromatic tones. A similar profile—albeit with the obvious differences—can be found in the Brut Nature '22, which showcases creamy bubbles and a firm, clear, and pure progression on the palate. The solid Lugana Riserva '22 and Bio '23 also stood out.

○ Lugana Perla '23	♟♟♟ 3*
● Garda Merlot Leonatus '22	♟♟ 5
○ Lugana Brut Nature M. Cl. '22	♟♟ 5
○ Lugana Madre Perla Ris. '22	♟♟ 5
○ Lugana Ris. '22	♟♟ 4
○ Lugana Bio '23	♟ 3
○ RGC Valtènesi Chiaretto '23	♟ 3
○ Lugana Madre Perla Ris. '18	♟♟♟ 4
○ Lugana Sup. Madonna della Scoperta '22	♟♟♟ 5
○ Lugana Sup. Madonna della Scoperta '21	♟♟♟ 4*
○ Lugana Sup. Madonna della Scoperta '19	♟♟♟ 4*
○ Lugana Sup. Madonna della Scoperta '17	♟♟♟ 4*

Andrea Picchioni

fraz. Camponoce, 4
27044 Canneto Pavese [PV]
📞 +39 0385262139
🌐 www.picchioniandrea.it

CELLAR SALES
PRE-BOOKED VISITS
ACCOMMODATION
ANNUAL PRODUCTION 70,000 bottles
HECTARES UNDER VINE 10.00
VITICULTURE METHOD Certified Organic
SUSTAINABLE WINERY

25 years ago we wrote about Andrea Picchioni as a rising star. Now 57 years old, and with the awareness and maturity that comes from over 30 harvests, Andrea has carved out a prominent role in the Oltrep? Pavese wine scene and beyond. From reviving old, abandoned vineyards to working in the cellar with Beppe Zatti, his wines have acquired precise and distinct characteristics, including remarkable longevity. Their two most important wines—the Buttafuoco Riva Bianca '21 and Rosso d'Asia '21—were missing, as Andrea felt they weren't ready yet. However, there's still plenty to talk about when it comes to quality winemaking. The Arfena '22 is a classically elegant pinot nero, direct and refined, seemingly vinified whole cluster, as is done in pinot nero's homeland. The Buttafuoco Solinghino '23, with its brilliant notes reminiscent more of barbera than croatina (even if the latter dominates in the blend) is equally striking. The 2023 Bonarda and Sangue di Giuda are well-made and aptly represent their terroir.

● Arfena '22	♟♟ 5
● OP Bonarda Vivace Ipazia '23	♟♟ 2*
● OP Buttafuoco Solinghino '23	♟♟ 3
● OP Sangue di Giuda Fior del Vento '23	♟♟ 3
● Arfena Pinot Nero '15	♟♟♟ 4*
● OP Buttafuoco Bricco Riva Bianca '16	♟♟♟ 4*
● Arfena Pinot Nero '19	♟♟ 4
● Arfena Pinot Nero '18	♟♟ 4
● Da Cima a Fondo '17	♟♟ 3*
● Da Cima a Fondo '16	♟♟ 3*
● OP Bonarda Vivace Ipazia '17	♟♟ 2*
● OP Buttafuoco Bricco Riva Bianca '20	♟♟ 4
● OP Buttafuoco Bricco Riva Bianca '17	♟♟ 4
● Rosso d'Asia '16	♟♟ 4

Prime Alture

via Madonna, 109
27045 Casteggio [PV]
📞 +39 038383214
🌐 www.primealture.it

CELLAR SALES
PRE-BOOKED VISITS
ACCOMMODATION AND RESTAURANT SERVICE
ANNUAL PRODUCTION 40,000 bottles
HECTARES UNDER VINE 8.00

Founded by Roberto Lechiancole in 2006, this wine resort on the hills of Casteggio has significantly contributed to the revival of wine tourism in Oltrepò. It's no surprise, then, that the "Prime Alture - La cantina di Milano" communication project launched in 2022, featuring renowned Milanese chefs for themed evenings, was well-received. Production quality is ensured by a team of experts: Claudio Giorgi and Claudio Brunelli handle the vineyards, while Jean-François Coquard from Burgundy collaborates with Fausto Comotti in the cellar. The Brut Io per Te, a Metodo Classico, opens taut and clear, with fragrant mandarin orange, red citrus and mountain herb sensations, and a fine minerality that follows through on a creamy, racy palate. In the mouth it proves exceptionally well-crafted through a long finish. The French influence is evident in the Chardonnay Madame '22, with its lovely tropical notes on the nose and spices from well-integrated oak, making for a wine of depth and finesse. The Pinot Nero Monsieur '19, with its intact fruit, also delivers.

○ OP Pinot Nero M. Cl. Brut Io per Te	♟♟ 6
○ Madame Chardonnay '20	♟♟ 4
● Monsieur Pinot Noir '19	♟♟ 5
● Pinot Nero Bordo Bosco '22	♟ 4
● Centopercento Pinot Noir '15	♟♟ 5
● Centopercento Pinot Noir '14	♟♟ 5
● Centopercento Pinot Noir '13	♟♟ 5
○ Il Bianco 60&40 '17	♟♟ 4
○ Io per Te Brut M. Cl.	♟♟ 5
● Monsieur Pinot Noir '17	♟♟ 5
● Monsieur Pinot Noir '16	♟♟ 5
○ OP Pinot Nero M. Cl. Brut Io per Te	♟♟ 6
○ Sopra Riva '19	♟♟ 3
○ Sopra Riva '18	♟♟ 3

Quadra Franciacorta

via Sant'Eusebio, 1
25033 Cologne [BS]
📞 +39 0307157314
🌐 www.quadrafranciacorta.it

CELLAR SALES
PRE-BOOKED VISITS
ACCOMMODATION AND RESTAURANT SERVICE
ANNUAL PRODUCTION 170,000 bottles
HECTARES UNDER VINE 20.00
SUSTAINABLE WINERY

La Quadra sits on the southwestern slopes of Monte Orfano, in the town of Cologne. Today, the estate is run by siblings Cristina and Marco Ghezzi, children of the founder, Ugo. The winery's approximately 30 hectares of vineyards, which are organically certified, include pinot bianco and pinot nero cultivated in prime hillside growing areas, thanks to the morainic structure of the terraced plots. The result is a range of wines with structure and fine quality. The refined and elegant Qzero Nero opens on a delicate aromatic profile of strawflower, chamomile, and citrus hints. The palate is fleshy, with persistent, creamy bubbles, closing with a gentle sweet spice and more mineral notes. The Extra Brut Quvèe '16 is also excellent, with its white flowers and peach on the nose, followed by a crisp, taut palate and a finish reminiscent of lavender.

○ Franciacorta Dosaggio Zero QZero Nero Ris. '16	♟♟ 6
⊙ Franciacorta Brut QRosé '19	♟♟ 6
○ Franciacorta Extra Brut Quvée 101 Ris. '16	♟♟ 6
○ Franciacorta Brut QBlack	♟ 5
○ Franciacorta Dosaggio Zero EretiQ '18	♟ 6
○ Franciacorta Satèn QSatèn '19	♟ 6
○ Franciacorta Dosaggio Zero Eretiq '15	♟♟ 6
○ Franciacorta Extra Brut Quvée 58 Ris. '11	♟♟ 5
○ Franciacorta QSatèn '12	♟♟ 5
○ Franciacorta Quvée 72 Ris. '12	♟♟ 5
⊙ Franciacorta Rosé Brut QRosé '18	♟♟ 6
○ Franciacorta Satèn QSatèn '18	♟♟ 6
○ Franciacorta Satèn UG1941+80 Ris. '11	♟♟ 5

★Aldo Rainoldi

fraz. Casacce
via Stelvio 128
23030 Chiuro [SO]
(+39 0342482225
www.rainoldi.com

CELLAR SALES
PRE-BOOKED VISITS
ANNUAL PRODUCTION 185,000 bottles
HECTARES UNDER VINE 11.50

Aldo Rainoldi began as a wine merchant, but it wasn?t until the late 1950s, when his son Giuseppe joined the business, that they began purchasing grapes. Today, the family business is carried on by the grandson, the fourth generation, who brings his oenology studies into the mix. The winery owns 11 hectares of vineyards but also works with long-established local growers for a portion of its grapes, demonstrating a strong commitment to the land and the people who sustain it. The Valtellina Superiore Inferno Riserva '19 stood out during our tastings this year, with its layered and intense nose dominated by red fruit, refreshed by hints of licorice. The palate is fleshy yet fresh, with a persistent finish. The Valtellina Superiore Sassella Riserva '19 also delivers vibrant flavors, though its tannins are still slightly firm, balanced by rich depth. Meanwhile, the Valtellina Superiore Nebbiolo Sassella '21 proves approachable and juicy, for those seeking a delightful, easy-drinking wine.

★Ricci Curbastro

via Adro, 37
25031 Capriolo [BS]
(+39 030736094
www.riccicurbastro.it

CELLAR SALES
PRE-BOOKED VISITS
ACCOMMODATION
ANNUAL PRODUCTION 200,000 bottles
HECTARES UNDER VINE 33.00
VITICULTURE METHOD Certified Organic
SUSTAINABLE WINERY

This Franciacorta winery, one of the founding members of the local consortium, is now led by the second generation, represented by Riccardo Ricci Curbastro, the winery's agronomist. As with many Franciacorta producers, the new generation is taking its place: in this case, Gualberto Jr. (named after the founding grandfather), Daniele, and Filippo. Their influence has resulted in sparkling wines that highlight freshness and drinkability, thanks to a well-balanced use of oak and liqueur. This year the cuvée dedicated to the founder Gualberto reached our final round of tastings. The 2014 offers soft and creamy tones of peach, anise, and almond, balanced by a broad, graceful palate. The finish is persistent, lively, and refined. The mature and complex character of the two 2011 Musuem Release wines is intriguing. The Extra Brut is creamy, with toasty tones, while the Satèn plays on notes of apricot, fine bubbles, and a honey-and-white-pepper finish.

Valtellina Sup. Inferno Ris. '19	♟♟♟ 6
Valtellina Sup. Sassella Ris. '19	♟♟ 5
Valtellina Sup. Sassella '21	♟♟ 4
Valtellina Sfursat '08	♟♟♟ 5
Valtellina Sfursat Fruttaio Ca' Rizzieri '19	♟♟♟ 6
Valtellina Sfursat Fruttaio Ca' Rizzieri '15	♟♟♟ 6
Valtellina Sfursat Fruttaio Ca' Rizzieri '11	♟♟♟ 6
Valtellina Sfursat Fruttaio Ca' Rizzieri '10	♟♟♟ 6
Valtellina Sfursat Fruttaio Ca' Rizzieri '09	♟♟♟ 6
Valtellina Sup. Grumello Ris. '13	♟♟♟ 6
Valtellina Sup. Inferno Ris. '16	♟♟♟ 5
Valtellina Sup. Sassella Ris. '13	♟♟♟ 5
Valtellina Sup. Sassella Ris. '12	♟♟♟ 5

○ Franciacorta Dosaggio Zero Gualberto '14	♟♟ 7
○ Franciacorta Extra Brut '19	♟♟ 5
○ Franciacorta Extra Brut Museum Release '11	♟♟ 7
○ Franciacorta Satèn Museum Release '11	♟♟ 7
○ Franciacorta Brut	♟ 4
○ Franciacorta Demi Sec	♟ 4
○ Franciacorta Dosaggio Zero Gualberto '12	♟♟♟ 6
○ Franciacorta Extra Brut '18	♟♟♟ 5
○ Franciacorta Extra Brut '16	♟♟♟ 5
○ Franciacorta Extra Brut '15	♟♟♟ 5
○ Franciacorta Satèn '15	♟♟♟ 5
○ Franciacorta Satèn '14	♟♟♟ 5

Ronco Calino

loc. Quattro Camini
fraz. Torbiato
via Fenice, 45
25030 Adro [BS]
(+39 0307451073
www.roncocalino.it

CELLAR SALES
PRE-BOOKED VISITS
ANNUAL PRODUCTION 80,000 bottles
HECTARES UNDER VINE 13.00
VITICULTURE METHOD Certified Organic
SUSTAINABLE WINERY

Set in a stunning morainic amphitheater south of
Lake Iseo, this winery is surrounded by 13
hectares of vineyards. Lara Radici, wife of
founder Paolo Radici, runs the estate, once
owned by the famed pianist Arturo Benedetti
Michelangeli, with determination. Their wines
require extensive aging, both on the lees and in
the bottle, to fully express the complexity of the
terroir. The Pair Riserva '13 proves to be a
multifaceted and pristine Franciacorta. Aromas
of white peach and almond are enhanced by a
slight balsamic undertone. The palate is rigorous
with persistent bubbles, closing long with
mineral and sapid sensations. The Nature is also
excellent, with its whiffs of Mediterranean scrub,
lemon peel, and vanilla notes. On the palate, it's
vibrant, expansive, and harmonious, with a
pleasant saline streak that provides length and an
appealing finish.

San Cristoforo

fraz. Villa
via Villanuova, 2
25030 Erbusco [BS]
(+39 0307760482
www.sancristoforo.eu

CELLAR SALES
PRE-BOOKED VISITS
ANNUAL PRODUCTION 90,000 bottles
HECTARES UNDER VINE 11.00
SUSTAINABLE WINERY

Bruno and Claudia Dotti established this
beautiful Franciacorta winery, and in recent
years, the couple have courageously passed the
torch to their daughter, Celeste. Though young,
Celeste is making her mark on the estate?s
sparkling wines with quiet determination, aided
by long-standing cellar master Beppe and young
agronomist and enotechnician Nicol?. Their
Franciacorta wines are celebrated for their
precision and finesse, with some fine, intriguing
expressions this year as well. The winery
continues to impress with the consistent quality
and stylistic precision of its entire range. This
year, the ND, produced solely from chardonnay,
stood out. The palate is harmonious, crystalline,
sapid, and deep, with persistent and creamy
bubbles that add vitality to each sip. The nose is
intense, elegant, and multifaceted, releasing note
of white fruit alongside aromatic herbs and
honey. It closes with a long finish of sapid, highly
pleasurable sensations. Tre Bicchieri.

o Franciacorta Brut Nature Pair Ris. '13	♀♀♀ 8
o Franciacorta Brut	♀♀ 5
o Franciacorta Brut Nature '19	♀♀ 6
o Franciacorta Brut '17	♀ 6
⊙ Franciacorta Brut Rosé Radijan	♀ 6
o Franciacorta Extra Brut Centoventi Ris. '11	♀ 8
o Franciacorta Satèn	♀ 5
o Curtefranca Bianco Leànt '18	♀♀ 3
● Curtefranca Rosso Ponènt '17	♀♀ 4
o Franciacorta Brut '15	♀♀ 6
o Franciacorta Brut '14	♀♀ 6
o Franciacorta Brut '12	♀♀ 5
o Franciacorta Brut Nature '17	♀♀ 6
o Franciacorta Brut Nature '16	♀♀ 6
o Franciacorta Extra Brut Centoventi Ris. '10	♀♀ 8

o Franciacorta Dosaggio Zero ND	♀♀♀
o Franciacorta Brut	♀♀
o Franciacorta Dosaggio Zero Epta '14	♀♀
o Franciacorta Brut '19	♀
o Franciacorta Brut '18	♀♀
o Franciacorta Brut '15	♀♀
o Franciacorta Brut '14	♀♀
o Franciacorta Brut '13	♀♀
o Franciacorta Dosaggio Zero Epta '13	♀♀
o Franciacorta Pas Dosé '18	♀♀
o Franciacorta Pas Dosé '16	♀♀
o Franciacorta Pas Dosé '15	♀♀
o Franciacorta Pas Dosé '13	♀♀
o Franciacorta Pas Dosé '12	♀♀
o Franciacorta Pas Dosé Celeste '11	♀♀
o Franciacorta Pas Dosé Celeste '10	♀♀

San Michele

via Parrocchia, 57
25020 Capriano del Colle [BS]
☎ +39 0309444091
⊕ www.sanmichelevini.it

CELLAR SALES
PRE-BOOKED VISITS
ANNUAL PRODUCTION 70,000 bottles
HECTARES UNDER VINE 16.00
VITICULTURE METHOD Certified Organic

The Danesi family purchased a winery and vineyards on Montenetto back in 1982, initially to produce wine for the local market. Encouraged by their success, they invested more and expanded their range going into the early aughts. In 2011, cousins Elena and Mario took over, giving the winery a new push forward. Today, the San Michele vineyards cover 16 hectares, spread across eight plots, and are among the most notable in Capriano del Colle. Their broad lineup spans everything from whites and reds to classic sparkling wines. The Marzemino M passito pours a deep ruby color, revealing an enticing nose of dried flowers, berry jam, and chocolate, which later shifts to balsamic and resinous tones. The palate is intensely sweet but balanced by a fresh acidity, echoing its lovely fruit notes and finishing on an elegant trail of amé. Other noteworthy wines include the Capriano Rosso Carme '22, a delicately tannic and fruity drink, and the Netto '23 white, taut and mineral with notes of elderflower and fruit.

Tenuta Scerscé

via Lungo Adda V Alpini, 124
23037 Tirano [SO]
☎ +39 0342 233580
⊕ www.tenutascersce.it

CELLAR SALES
PRE-BOOKED VISITS
ANNUAL PRODUCTION 45,000 bottles
HECTARES UNDER VINE 7.00
SUSTAINABLE WINERY

Cristina Scarpellini is a dynamic and enterprising woman. After earning a law degree and spending some time in Paris, she decided in 2008 to leave behind her legal career and open her own winery in Valtellina. Her unorthodox path into the wine world has given Cristina?s approach a unique touch: meticulous study of the subtle differences in each terroir, careful analysis of her vineyards, and a keen eye for sustainability. The wines tasted this year reveal an evolving aromatic profile, as seen in the Valtellina Superiore Inferno Flammante '21, which intrigues with its hints of dry herbs, licorice, and tobacco sensations, with fruit taking a back seat. The palate is harmonious and pleasant. Similarly, the Valtellina Superiore Sassella Petrato '21 stands out for its complexity, featuring notes of cinchona and tobacco; the palate is crisp and of good length, but slightly lacking in freshness.

M Passito	♟♟ 5
Capriano del Colle Bianco Netto '23	♟♟ 3
Capriano del Colle Bianco Sup. Otten5 '20	♟♟ 5
Capriano del Colle Rosso Carme '22	♟♟ 3
Belvedere Brut M. Cl.	♟ 4
Capriano del Colle Marzemino '21	♟♟ 3
Capriano del Colle Marzemino '20	♟♟ 2*
Capriano del Colle Rosso Carme '21	♟♟ 2*
Capriano del Colle Rosso Carme '18	♟♟ 2*
Capriano del Colle Rosso Ris. 1884 '18	♟♟ 5
Gobbo '13	♟♟ 4

● Valtellina Sup. Inferno Flammante '21	♟♟♟ 6
● Valtellina Sforzato Infinito '20	♟♟ 7
● Valtellina Sup. Essenza '21	♟♟ 5
● Valtellina Sup. Sassella Petrato '21	♟♟ 6
● Valtellina Sup. Valgella Cristina Scarpellini Ris. '20	♟ 7
● Valtellina Sup. Inferno Flammante '19	♟♟♟ 6
● Valtellina Sforzato Infinito '18	♟♟ 6
● Valtellina Sup. Essenza '19	♟♟ 5
● Valtellina Sup. Essenza '18	♟♟ 5
● Valtellina Sup. Inferno Flammante '20	♟♟ 6
● Valtellina Sup. Sassella Incanto '20	♟♟ 6
● Valtellina Sup. Sassella Incanto '19	♟♟ 6
● Valtellina Sup. Sassella Incanto '18	♟♟ 5
● Valtellina Sup. Valgella Ris. Cristina Scarpellini '19	♟♟ 7

Scuropasso - Roccapietra

fraz. Scorzoletta, 40/42
27043 Pietra de' Giorgi [PV]
☎ +39 038585143
🌐 scuropasso.it

CELLAR SALES
PRE-BOOKED VISITS
ANNUAL PRODUCTION 200,000 bottles
HECTARES UNDER VINE 15.00

Driven and motivated, Fabio Marazzi and his daughter Flavia continue to pursue their diverse wine projects. At the forefront is the Metodo Classico, reflecting Fabio?s long-standing passion for Champagne. Their philosophy emphasizes long aging on the lees to achieve not only elegance but also complexity and volume. They also produce a traditional red, Buttafuoco, in several versions, including one for the Club del Buttafuoco Storico. Once again, their lineup remains impressive, with the Cruasé '18 still in the spotlight. It showcases a distinct note of granny smith intertwined with citrus and red forest fruits. In the mouth, it's rich and fleshy, with fine, buoyant bubbles and a long, lingering finish. Among the best of its kind, the Vigna Pianlong '20 is a Buttafuoco Storico with structure and elegance, redolent of small dark fruits and aromatic herbs. The Roccapietra Zero '18 proves spirited and lively.

⊙ OP Cruasé Roccapietra '18	♟♟♟ 5
○ M. Cl. Roccapietra Zero '18	♟♟ 4
● OP Buttafuoco Storico V. Pianlong '20	♟♟ 5
○ M. Cl. Brut Blanc de Noirs Roccapietra	♟♟ 5
● OP Buttafuoco Costa Barosine '20	♟ 4
○ Pienosole Riesling '20	♟ 3
⊙ OP Cruasé Roccapietra '17	♟♟♟ 5
⊙ OP Cruasé Roccapietra '15	♟♟♟ 4*
○ Roccapietra Pas Dosé M. Cl. '13	♟♟♟ 4*
○ Roccapietra Zero M. Cl. '16	♟♟♟ 4*
⊙ OP Cruasé Roccapietra '16	♟♟ 4
○ Roccapietra Zero M. Cl. '17	♟♟ 4
○ Roccapietra Zero M. Cl. '15	♟♟ 4

Selva Capuzza

fraz. San Martino della Battaglia
loc. Selva Capuzza
25010 Desenzano del Garda [BS]
☎ +39 0309910381
🌐 www.selvacapuzza.it

CELLAR SALES
PRE-BOOKED VISITS
ACCOMMODATION AND RESTAURANT SERVICE
ANNUAL PRODUCTION 300,000 bottles
HECTARES UNDER VINE 30.00
SUSTAINABLE WINERY

The winery's history began in 1917 on the morainic hills of Garda, when the Formentini family joined with the Hirundo brand. Established in 1908, Hirundo ("swallow" in local dialect) continues to represent their sparkling wines. Six grape varieties are cultivated in vineyards nestled among meadows and woods (turbiana, tuchì, groppello, marzemino, barbera, and sangiovese). These are complemented by a truffle farm, agritourism, and restaurant. The wines, which hail from three different appellations, consistently maintain high quality. The San Martino Capo del Soglio won us over with the 2023 vintage as well. Made from tuchì grapes (a local synonym for tocai friulano), its greenish straw-yellow color catches the eye, while the nose reveals clear fruit notes, delicate citrus nuances, and more complex floral and herbal hints. On the palate, it's sapid, taut, and linear, its freshness unfolding progressively towards a long, compelling finish. Other noteworthy wines include the Lugana Menasasss Riserva '20, which is elegant and linear, and the fragrant Chiaretto San Donino '23.

○ San Martino della Battaglia Campo del Soglio '23	♟♟♟
○ Lugana Menasasso Ris. '20	♟♟
⊙ RGC Chiaretto San Donino '23	♟♟
○ Lugana '23	♟
○ Nulla 222 '22	♟
○ Lugana Menasasso Ris. '19	♟♟♟
○ Lugana Menasasso Ris. '16	♟♟♟
○ Lugana Menasasso Ris. '15	♟♟♟
○ San Martino della Battaglia Campo del Soglio '22	♟♟♟
○ Lugana Selva '20	♟♟
⊙ RGC Chiaretto San Donino '22	♟♟
⊙ RGC Valtènesi Chiaretto San Donino '20	♟♟
○ San Martino della Battaglia Campo del Soglio '21	♟♟

Sincette

loc. Picedo
via Rosario, 44
25080 Polpenazze del Garda [BS]
(+39 0365651471
www.sincette.it

CELLAR SALES
PRE-BOOKED VISITS
ANNUAL PRODUCTION 40,000 bottles
HECTARES UNDER VINE 11.00
VITICULTURE METHOD Certified Biodynamic

In 1979, Giovanni Battista Brunori and his son Ruggeri renovated a rural structure named Cascina La Pertica. In the 1980s, following an encounter with Giorgio Grai, they built a new completely underground cellar. Andrea Salvetti joined in 1992, and with the support of Stefano Chioccioli and Franco Bernabei, they renovated the vineyards. In 1998, a meeting with Jacques Mell steered the winery towards biodynamic farming, leading to Demeter certification in 2011 and the adoption of the name Sincette the following year. The Brunori family submitted an excellent lineup this year, even if there wasn't a single star performer. The Groppello Foglio 9 '21 proves sapid, clean, and precise, with aromas of blackcurrant, cherry, and wild herbs. On the palate, it's lean, clear, and fluid but lacks the depth we've come to expect. The Dinamico '21, a blend of marzemino, groppello, and barbera, proves to be a sapid, smooth red with small fruit aromas and delicate vegetal notes on the nose, with a dynamic palate to follow. The Chiaretto '23 and the Bordeaux-style Le Zalte '20 are also of excellent quality.

RGC Valtènesi Groppello Foglio 9 '21	♟♟ 5
Dinamico '21	♟♟ 4
Le Zalte '20	♟♟ 6
RGC Valtènesi Chiaretto '23	♟♟ 3
RGC Groppello '20	♟♟♟ 4*
RGC Valtènesi Groppello '22	♟♟♟ 4*
RGC Valtènesi Groppello '21	♟♟♟ 4*
Dinamico '20	♟♟ 3
Il Colombaio '17	♟♟ 4
Le Zalte '18	♟♟ 6
RGC Valtènesi Chiaretto '22	♟♟ 3
RGC Valtènesi Chiaretto '21	♟♟ 3*
RGC Valtènesi Chiaretto '20	♟♟ 3*
Valtènesi Chiaretto '19	♟♟ 3*
Valtènesi Chiaretto '18	♟♟ 2*

★Lo Sparviere

via Costa
25040 Monticelli Brusati [BS]
(+39 030652382
www.losparviere.it

CELLAR SALES
ANNUAL PRODUCTION 120,000 bottles
HECTARES UNDER VINE 28.00
VITICULTURE METHOD Certified Organic

Lo Sparviere is part of a constellation of wineries owned by the historic Gussalli Beretta family from Brescia. Their vineyards, at the foot of the Lombard Pre-Alps, span the towns of Provaglio d'Iseo and Monticelli Brusati, where the terroir is characterized by limestone marl. The grapes are vinified separately by vineyard so as to emphasize their unique qualities, resulting in sparkling wines with freshness and fragrance. This year we appreciated the Brut '18, a Franciacorta that entices with its pleasing notes of sponge cake, bread crust, anise, and fresh almond. In the mouth, it's rich in fragrance and flavor, with a soft, creamy perlage that accompanies a precise and immensely pleasant palate. The Extra Brut Rosé is also very good, opting for an aromatic profile of small red fruits and a fresh, nicely expansive palate. The Extra Brut delivers tones of white peach and white flowers, with a plucky palate and a well-calibrated, clean finish.

Franciacorta Brut '18	♟♟ 7
Franciacorta Extra Brut	♟♟ 6
Franciacorta Extra Brut Rosé Monique	♟♟ 8
Franciacorta Brut '13	♟♟♟ 5
Franciacorta Brut '12	♟♟♟ 5
Franciacorta Dosaggio Zero Ris. '15	♟♟♟ 7
Franciacorta Dosaggio Zero Ris. '13	♟♟♟ 6
Franciacorta Dosaggio Zero Ris. '08	♟♟♟ 6
Franciacorta Extra Brut '14	♟♟♟ 6
Franciacorta Extra Brut '13	♟♟♟ 6
Franciacorta Extra Brut '09	♟♟♟ 5
Franciacorta Extra Brut '08	♟♟♟ 5
Franciacorta Extra Brut '07	♟♟♟ 5
Franciacorta Dosaggio Zero Ris. '07	♟♟ 6
Franciacorta Dosaggio Zero Riserva '12	♟♟ 6
Franciacorta Extra Brut Sylvò '15	♟♟ 6

Tenute del Garda

via Cesare Battisti, 37
25017 Lonato [BS]
+39 0309919000
www.tenutedelgarda.it

CELLAR SALES
PRE-BOOKED VISITS
ANNUAL PRODUCTION 50,000 bottles
HECTARES UNDER VINE 15.00

The growth of the Valt?nesi area led to the formation of a group of producers a few years ago, led by Andrea Lorenzi. Together they vinify exclusively estate-grown grapes from Barcuzzi and Campagnoli in Lonato del Garda, as well as Polpenazze and Calvagese della Riviera. Experienced farmers with old vines have teamed up with enthusiastic young people with innovative ideas and methods, thus creating an excellent range in an area historically dedicated to viticulture. Getting two wines to our final round of tastings this year illustrates the progress being made at Andrea Lorenzi's winery. The Chiaretto '23 captivates with its very pale, brilliant color, the prelude to fruity, citrus, and fresh herbal notes. On the palate, it's smooth, fruity, with a lively acidic backbone and a delicate tannic hint that makes it a very enjoyable drink. The Riesling Rie shows fruit and dynamic tension before a long, smoky finish.

○ Garda Bianco Rie '23	🍷🍷 7
⊙ RGC Valtènesi Chiaretto '23	🍷🍷 3*
○ Atmosfere Dosaggio Zero M. Cl. '17	🍷🍷 5
○ Garda Riesling '23	🍷🍷 3
● RGC Groppello Lucone '19	🍷🍷 3
○ SottoSopra M. Cl. '20	🍷🍷 4
○ Garda Riesling '19	♀♀ 3
○ Garda Riesling '18	♀♀ 3
○ Garda Riesling '17	♀♀ 2*
○ Garda Riesling '16	♀♀ 2*
⊙ RGC Valtènesi Chiaretto '22	♀♀ 3*
⊙ RGC Valtènesi Chiaretto '21	♀♀ 3*
⊙ Valtènesi Chiaretto '19	♀♀ 3
● Valtènesi Groppello Vistalago Ris. '16	♀♀ 6

Terre d'Aenòr

via Alessandro Volta, 22
25050 Provaglio d'Iseo [BS]
+39 0309830888
www.terredaenor.com

PRE-BOOKED VISITS
ANNUAL PRODUCTION 250,000 bottles
HECTARES UNDER VINE 46.00
VITICULTURE METHOD Certified Organic

After completing a law degree, Eleonora Bianchi decided to fully develop her family?s vineyards, which total 45 hectares across more than 20 plots in Franciacorta. She laid the groundwork for a solid, well-structured project. The grapes, which for years had been sold to large local houses, are now vinified according to an organic philosophy with minimal sulfur doses. The result is a lineup of wines with a strong sense of identity, deeply respectful of the land. The winery's growth continues. The Franciacorta Pas Dosé '20, which reached the final round, is a cuvée with a distinctly food-friendly character. Intense and balsamic, it offers up notes of mint, toasted bread, and white fruit. On the palate, it's creamy, energetic, with a sapid, mineral vein. We also appreciated the Satèn Ricciolina for its flora notes and citrus sensations. In the mouth, it's rich, with notable overall harmony; a creamy perlage accompanies a smooth, soft palate.

○ Franciacorta Pas Dosé '20	🍷🍷 6
○ Franciacorta Satèn Ricciolina	🍷🍷 5
○ Franciacorta Brut	🍷🍷 5
⊙ Franciacorta Extra Brut Rosé '20	🍷🍷 6
○ Franciacorta Extra Brut '20	♀♀ 5
○ Franciacorta Extra Brut '19	♀♀ 5
○ Franciacorta Extra Brut '18	♀♀ 5
⊙ Franciacorta Extra Brut Rosé '19	♀♀ 6
○ Franciacorta Pas Dosé '19	♀♀ 6

Pietro Torti

fraz. Castelrotto, 9
27047 Montecalvo Versiggia [PV]
☏ +39 038599763
🌐 www.pietrotorti.it

CELLAR SALES
PRE-BOOKED VISITS
ACCOMMODATION
ANNUAL PRODUCTION 40,000 bottles
HECTARES UNDER VINE 18.00
VITICULTURE METHOD Certified Organic

Sandro Torti, along with his daughter Chiara, a graduate in oenology, runs his small family winery with a philosophy of minimal intervention in both the vineyard and cellar. This commitment is demonstrated by their adherence to the VinNatur association in 2012 and organic certification in 2015. They cultivate traditional Oltrep? grape varieties for a diverse range, with particular attention to Metodo Classico. Their forthright wines consistently feature noteworthy highlights year after year. The Cruasé '21 proves well-crafted. It's lively right from its color, revealing brilliant aromas of berries and red citrus. On the palate, it makes an impact, with creamy and persistent bubbles, vibrant acidity, and substance right through to the finish. The Pietro Torti Brut '20 is also well-made, rich, and citrusy. It's a classic, food-friendly Metodo Classico, very typical of the old-school pinot nero style. The rest of the range proves pleasant and faithful to the varietal characteristics of the grapes used.

○ OP Cruasé '21	🏆🏆 4
○ OP Pinot Nero M. Cl. Pietro Torti Brut '20	🏆🏆 4
○ Italico '23	🏆 3
● OP Pinot Nero Terre Gobbe '22	🏆 3
● Verzello Croatina '22	🏆 3
● OP Barbera Campo Rivera '15	🏆🏆 4
● OP Barbera Campo Rivera '12	🏆🏆 4
○ OP Cruasé '19	🏆🏆 4
○ OP M. Cl. Pinot Nero Brut '15	🏆🏆 4
○ OP M. Cl. Pinot Nero Pas Dosé '20	🏆🏆 5
○ OP M. Cl. Pinot Nero Pas Dosé '18	🏆🏆 5
○ OP Pinot Nero Brut M. Cl. Torti '09	🏆🏆 3*
○ OP Riesling '22	🏆🏆 3
● Uvarara '22	🏆🏆 3

Tenuta Travaglino

loc. Travaglino
27040 Calvignano [PV]
☏ +39 0383872222
🌐 www.travaglino.it

CELLAR SALES
PRE-BOOKED VISITS
ACCOMMODATION AND RESTAURANT SERVICE
ANNUAL PRODUCTION 180,000 bottles
HECTARES UNDER VINE 80.00

Since the new generation, Cristina and Alessandro Comi, took over this prestigious winery a few years ago, the estate has been revitalized. The ancient medieval monastery has been transformed into a welcoming space, and the wines have regained their vibrant varietal character, thanks to an exceptional terroir and the expertise of Achille Bergami, with Donato Lanati's consultancy. Their focus on low environmental impact is noteworthy, particularly in their work with riesling and pinot nero. This year, the Riesling Riserva wasn't presented, but the current vintage version performed more than well. The Campo della Fojada '23 is a substantive Rhine Riesling, with aromas of hay, wildflowers, and ripe citrus; in the mouth it's sapid, with a lovely mineral vein. The Cuvée '59 is a high-quality Metodo Classico, airy and fragrant with floral and mineral aromas, fine and persistent bubbles, structured yet racy through to the finish. The Pinot Nero Poggio della Buttinera '21 proves aromatic and faithful to the varietal characteristics of the grape.

○ OP M. Cl. Brut Cuvée 59	🏆🏆🏆 5
○ OP Riesling Campo della Fojada '23	🏆🏆 4
● OP Pinot Nero Pernero '23	🏆🏆 4
● OP Pinot Nero Ris. Poggio della Buttinera '21	🏆🏆 6
○ OP Pinot Nero Brut M. Cl. Vincenzo Comi Riserva del Fondatore '17	🏆 8
○ OP Pinot Nero Rosé Brut M. Cl. Monteceresino '19	🏆 6
● OP Rosso Marc'Antonio '20	🏆 7
○ OP Riesling Campo della Fojada Ris. '19	🏆🏆🏆 5
○ OP Gran Cuvée Blanc de Noir	🏆🏆 5
○ OP Pinot Nero Brut Classese '05	🏆🏆 5
○ OP Riesling Campo della Fojada '17	🏆🏆 3*
○ OP Riesling Campo della Fojada Ris. '14	🏆🏆 3*
○ OP Riesling Renano Campo della Fojada Ris. '17	🏆🏆 3*

F.lli Turina

via Pergola, 68
25080 Moniga del Garda [BS]
+39 0365502103
www.turinavini.it

CELLAR SALES
PRE-BOOKED VISITS
ANNUAL PRODUCTION 300,000 bottles
HECTARES UNDER VINE 20.00

Matteo, Andrea, and Marco Turina (the winemaker), represent the fourth generation of family to produce wines. The estate, long focused on the Valt?nesi region, has modernized its facilities and revamped production of late, positioning itself at the top tier of the local wine scene. Their range spans Valt?nesi and Lugana, sourced from 21 hectares of estate vineyards. The Setamora '20, which we re-tasted this year, proves to be a new-generation Chiaretto from Valtènesi, unafraid to compete with the best in the world. The Fontanamora sports an appealing, pale-bright pink color. It's a wine of great complexity on the nose, offering small fruit sensations, spices, smoky and mineral notes, all with elegance. Poised, full, and taut on the palate, it shows incredible freshness and a textbook progression of flavor. The rest of the range is excellent.

⊙ RGC Valtènesi Chiaretto Cl. Fontanamora '23	🍷🍷🍷 3*
○ Lugana '23	🍷🍷 3
○ Lugana Fenil Boi '23	🍷🍷 3
● RGC Valtènesi Rosso Seselle '22	🍷🍷 3
○ Lugana Brut	🍷 4
○ Lugana '22	🍷🍷 3
○ Resembol '21	🍷🍷 4
⊙ RGC Chiaretto '22	🍷🍷 3
⊙ RGC Valtènesi Chiaretto '20	🍷🍷 2*
⊙ RGC Valtènesi Chiaretto Cl. Fontanamora '21	🍷🍷 3
⊙ RGC Valtènesi Chiaretto Fontanamora '20	🍷🍷 3
⊙ RGC Valtènesi Chiaretto Seta Mora '20	🍷🍷 3
⊙ RGC Valtènesi Chiaretto Seta Mora '19	🍷🍷 3*

★Uberti

loc. Salem
via E. Fermi, 2
25030 Erbusco [BS]
+39 0307267476
www.ubertivini.it

PRE-BOOKED VISITS
ANNUAL PRODUCTION 180,000 bottles
HECTARES UNDER VINE 25.00
SUSTAINABLE WINERY

Agostino and Eleonora Uberti founded their winery in Erbusco in 1980, though the family has been involved in viticulture in this area since 1793. Today, the estate is run by their daughters: Silvia, the winemaker, and Francesca, who manages hospitality and administration. Drawing on 25 hectares of vines in some of the best growing areas in Erbusco and Adro, they craft complex and rich Franciacorta, vinifying small parcels from various vineyards. The lineup submitted confirms the originality of a highly distinctive style. The Dequinque Cuvée 15 Vendemmie has a rich profile and fine bead, delivering a creamy sensation on the palate. Its aromatic profile is no less remarkable, playing on balsamic and toasty sensations. The Francesco I offers white peach and a pleasant, delicate spiciness, with a fleshy, fruit-forward palate. Taut and well-balanced, it has a bold, energetic palate with progression and a mineral drive.

○ Franciacorta Extra Brut De Quinque Cuvée 15 Vendemmie	🍷🍷 8
○ Franciacorta Brut Francesco I	🍷🍷 5
○ Franciacorta Dosaggio Zero Sublimis Ris. '16	🍷🍷 8
○ Franciacorta Extra Brut Comarì del Salem '17	🍷🍷 7
⊙ Franciacorta Rosé Brut Francesco I	🍷🍷 6
○ Franciacorta Brut Satèn Magnificentia '18	🍷🍷🍷 7
○ Franciacorta Extra Brut Comarí del Salem '14	🍷🍷🍷 7
○ Franciacorta Extra Brut Comarì del Salem '03	🍷🍷🍷 6
○ Franciacorta Extra Brut Comarì del Salem '02	🍷🍷🍷 6
○ Franciacorta Extra Brut Comarì del Salem '01	🍷🍷🍷 6

Agricola Vallecamonica

via Fornaci, 34a
25040 Artogne [BS]
+39 3355828410
www.vinivallecamonica.com

CELLAR SALES
PRE-BOOKED VISITS
ANNUAL PRODUCTION 20,000 bottles
HECTARES UNDER VINE 4.00

Despite the small size of his estate?just four hectares?Alex Belingheri has earned a prominent place in Lombardy?s crowded winemaking landscape. His vineyards range from 250 to 800 meters in elevation, on both sides of the valley where the Camunni and Romans cultivated vines 2,000 years ago on ruk, the region's ancient terraced slopes. While his still wines are excellent, his sparkling wines made from PIWI grapes, aged in the depths of Lake Iseo or in the icy waters of Lake Aviolo at 2,000 meters, have gained significant recognition. The Irresistibile '23, made from souvignier gris, performed well in our final tastings. This is a structured, full-bodied white with citrusy, fresh aromas of grapefruit, green tea, and eucalyptus. On the palate, it's penetrating and precise, with sapidity and persistence. The Nautilus Crustorico '18, which is made with grapes from old, local red vines and ages at length on the lees, also stood out. The Bianco dell'Annunciata '21, an Incrocio Manzoni, offers superb freshness and is beginning to s how tertiary notes of hydrocarbons, spices, and sweet almonds.

○ Irresistibile '23	▼▼ 5
○ Bianco dell'Annunciata '21	▼▼ 4
○ Estremo Adamamus Zero M. Cl. '19	▼▼ 6
○ Nautilus Crustorico Pas Dosé M. Cl. '18	▼▼ 7
● Somnium '20	▼ 4
○ Bianco dell'Annunciata '20	▽▽ 4
○ Bianco dell'Annunciata '19	▽▽ 4
○ Bianco delle Colture '20	▽▽ 4
○ Bianco delle Colture '19	▽▽ 3*
○ Bianco delle Colture '18	▽▽ 3
○ Estremo Adamamus Extra Brut M. Cl. '17	▽▽ 6
○ Irresistibile '21	▽▽ 5
○ Irresistibile '20	▽▽ 4
○ Nautilus Crustorico Pas Dosé M. Cl. '16	▽▽ 7
○ Nautilus Crustorico Pas Dosé M. Cl. '15	▽▽ 6

Vanzini

fraz. Barbaleone, 7
27040 San Damiano al Colle [PV]
+39 038575019
www.vanzini-wine.com

CELLAR SALES
PRE-BOOKED VISITS
ANNUAL PRODUCTION 400,000 bottles
HECTARES UNDER VINE 26.00
SUSTAINABLE WINERY

Antonio, Michela, and Pierpaolo Vanzini run their family winery with clearly defined roles and a dedication to their work. Founded in 1890, they focus on traditional Oltrep? Pavese grape varieties, with special attention to pinot nero, now available in a Metodo Classico version. The entire range's graphic design was updated last year, but the sparkling wines and excellent value for money remain strong points. The Bonarda Frizzante Vigna Guardia '23 is beautifully crafted, with black berry and violet aromas, and well-balanced tannins. The Barbera La Desiderata '23 proves fruity and varietal, with aromas of cherry and black cherry. It's delightful on the palate, making for a full, gratifying drink. The Aiace, a taut Metodo Classico with an iodine profile, proves highly characteristic as a pinot nero sparkler, with a fleshy palate and elegant fizz. The rest of the range proves faithful to the varietal characteristics of the grapes used—simple and enjoyable.

○ Extra Dry Martinotti	▼▼ 4
● OP Barbera La Desiderata '23	▼▼ 3
● OP Bonarda Frizzante Vigna Guardia '23	▼▼ 4
○ OP M. Cl. Brut Pinot Nero Aiace	▼▼ 5
○ Assedio Moscato Secco	▼ 3
⊙ Extra Dry Martinotti Rosé	▼ 4
● OP Bonarda Frizzante Con Tatto '23	▼ 3
○ OP Pinot Grigio '23	▼ 3
○ OP Riesling '23	▼ 3
● OP Sangue di Giuda Nemo '23	▼ 3
● OP Bonarda '16	▽▽ 2*
● OP Bonarda Frizzante '18	▽▽ 2*
○ Pinot Nero Extra Dry Martinotti	▽▽ 3*
⊙ Pinot Nero Extra Dry Martinotti Rosé	▽▽ 3*

Bruno Verdi

via Vergomberra, 5
27044 Canneto Pavese [PV]
📞 +39 038588023
🌐 www.brunoverdi.it

CELLAR SALES
PRE-BOOKED VISITS
ANNUAL PRODUCTION 100,000 bottles
HECTARES UNDER VINE 12.00

Paolo Verdi, now joined by his son Jacopo, is one of the most esteemed winemakers in the Oltrep? Pavese region. Tireless and innovative, Paolo continually seeks new ways to perfect his wines, which include still reds, sparkling reds, whites, and Metodo Classico, all with a distinctive style. Recent tastings of older bottles confirm the enduring quality of his wines, and the latest addition, Buttafuoco Storico, promises to be spectacular. This year's lineup is top-notch, starting with the Vergomberra '20, which recalls the glory of 2012, full-bodied and structured yet supple, vibrant, and splendid in its evolution, with aromas ranging from berries to aromatic herbs. The Cavariola '20 remains a dependable red: fruity, rich, broad, well-balanced, powerful, and harmonious, with its hallmark touch of mint. The Riesling Vigna Costa '22 is excellent and energetic.

Vigneti Cenci

via Riccafana, 19
25033 Cologne [BS]
📞 +39 0307156386
🌐 www.vigneticenci.com

CELLAR SALES
PRE-BOOKED VISITS
ANNUAL PRODUCTION 50,000 bottles
HECTARES UNDER VINE 6.00

Situated at the foot of Monte Orfano, this winery has been producing characterful Franciacorta for over forty years. Today, Giuliana Cenci and her son Maurizio (representing the second and third generations) continue to craft authentic, distinctive sparkling wines, thanks in part to the use of endogenous sugars in both stages of fermentation. The estate?s standout wines are those made from pinot bianco, sourced from south-facing vineyards near the winery. Strong performances across the board. Lo Zero stands out for its precision and well-defined aromatic profile, with intense fruit notes of white peach meeting lemon cream, framed by a creamy bead. La Via della Seta shines for its fine texture and harmony, offering both consistency and freshness. The Nelson Cenci also impresses with its richness, vitality, and well-structured palate, finishing on a fresh mineral vein.

○ OP Pinot Nero M. Cl. Pas Dosé Vergomberra '20	♟♟♟ 5
○ OP Riesling V. Costa '22	♟♟ 3*
● OP Rosso Cavariola Ris. '20	♟♟ 6
● OP Bonarda Frizzante Possessione di Vergombera '23	♟♟ 3
● OP Barbera Campo del Marrone '22	♟ 5
● OP Buttafuoco '23	♟ 2
○ OP M. Cl. Pinot Nero Dosage Zéro Vergomberra '13	♟♟♟ 5
○ OP M. Cl. Pinot Nero Dosage Zéro Vergomberra '12	♟♟♟ 5
○ OP M. Cl. Pinot Nero Extra Brut Vergomberra '16	♟♟♟ 5
● OP Rosso Cavariola Ris. '16	♟♟♟ 5
● OP Rosso Cavariola Ris. '10	♟♟♟ 5

○ Franciacorta Pas Dosé Zero	♟♟ 7
○ Franciacorta Brut La Capinera	♟♟ 7
○ Franciacorta Extra Brut Nelson Cenci	♟♟ 8
○ Franciacorta Saten La Via della Seta	♟♟ 7
⊙ Franciacorta Brut Rosé La Capinera	♟ 7
○ Franciacorta Brut Nelson Cenci L'Insolita '11	♟♟ 6
○ Franciacorta Brut Nelson Cenci L'Insolita Annata '15	♟♟ 8
○ Franciacorta Brut Sessanta '12	♟♟ 6
○ Franciacorta Brut Sessanta '12	♟♟ 6
○ Franciacorta Brut Sessanta '09	♟♟ 6
○ Franciacorta Extra Brut Nelson Cenci '18	♟♟ 8

I Vitari

via Bettini, 70
23100 Sondrio
☎ +39 0342213546
⊛ www.cantinaivitari.it

CELLAR SALES
PRE-BOOKED VISITS
ANNUAL PRODUCTION 27,000 bottles
HECTARES UNDER VINE 3.50

Davide Bettini?s passion for wine took him across Italy and Europe, with the producer exploring different winemaking traditions before opening his own winery, I Vitari, in 2013 with the support of expert winemaker Giuseppe Gorelli. With just two and a half hectares of vines, the estate follows the principles of integrated farming, focusing on respect for the environment and the centuries-old winemaking traditions of Valtellina. With such a stellar lineup, we couldn't leave this winery out of our main section. The Valtellina Superiore Grumello SO '21 offers a bold bouquet of licorice and tobacco, refreshed by raspberry. Its structured palate features present yet finely polished tannins, with a fleshy, deep palate. The evolution of the Valtellina Superiore Grumello SO Vigna I Vitari '21 is captivating, showcasing astounding complexity on the nose. The palate is austere but balanced by just the right amount of freshness.

Chiara Ziliani

via Franciacorta, 7
25050 Provaglio d'Iseo [BS]
☎ +39 030981661
⊛ www.cantinachiaraziliani.it

PRE-BOOKED VISITS
ANNUAL PRODUCTION 500,000 bottles
HECTARES UNDER VINE 37.00

Chiara Ziliani?s winery sits on a morainic hill in the town of Provaglio d'Iseo. The estate?s international outlook led to the decision to plant only pinot nero and chardonnay for their Franciacorta, and merlot and cabernet for their Riserva reds, across 37 hectares of vineyards. The range, which is divided into five distinct lines, has been managed by Chiara Ziliani herself since the winery's founding in 2001. Two cuvées stood out among the range presented for tasting. We start with the Franciacorta Satèn Ziliani C '20: pastry and hazelnut aromas give way to citrus and floral notes. Fragrant, with creamy effervescence, the palate finishes on spices and mineral hints. The equally impressive Brut Ziliani C '20 showcases delicate toasty and ripe fruit tones. The palate is clean and nicely expansive on the finish. The rest of the wines tasted also performed well.

● Valtellina Sup. Grumello SO '21	♛♛♛ 7
● Valtellina Sup. Grumello SO V. I Vitari '21	♛♛ 8
● Valtellina Sup. '21	♛♛ 5
● Rosso di Valtellina '20	♛♛ 5
● Valtellina Sup. Grumello SO '19	♛♛ 5

○ Franciacorta Brut Ziliani C '20	♛♛ 5
○ Franciacorta Satèn Ziliani C '20	♛♛ 5
○ Franciacorta Brut Conte di Provaglio	♛♛ 4
○ Franciacorta Satèn Conte di Provaglio	♛♛ 3
○ Franciacorta Satèn Ziliani C	♛♛ 4
○ Franciacorta Brut Noir Ziliani C '15	♛♛ 4
○ Franciacorta Brut Satèn Ziliani C '17	♛♛ 5
○ Franciacorta Brut Ziliani C '19	♛♛ 4
○ Franciacorta Brut Ziliani C Noir '19	♛♛ 5
○ Franciacorta Extra Brut Ziliani C '20	♛♛ 5
○ Franciacorta Extra Brut Ziliani C '19	♛♛ 5
○ Franciacorta Extra Brut Ziliani C '16	♛♛ 4
○ Franciacorta Pas Dosé Ziliani C '09	♛♛ 4
○ Franciacorta Satèn Ziliani C '19	♛♛ 5
○ Franciacorta Satèn Ziliani C '13	♛♛ 4

OTHER WINERIES

Annibale Alziati

fraz. Scazzolino, 55
27040 Rovescala [PV]
📞 +39 3487080841
🌐 www.alziativini.com

CELLAR SALES
PRE-BOOKED VISITS
ANNUAL PRODUCTION 100,000 bottles
HECTARES UNDER VINE 22.00
VITICULTURE METHOD Certified Organic
SUSTAINABLE WINERY

● OP Bonarda Frizzante Tenuta San Francesco '23	🏆🏆 3
● OP Bonarda Gaggiarone Ris. '15	🏆 6

Antica Fratta

via Fontana, 11
25040 Monticelli Brusati [BS]
📞 +39 030652068
🌐 www.anticafratta.com

ANNUAL PRODUCTION 280,000 bottles
HECTARES UNDER VINE 37.00
SUSTAINABLE WINERY

○ Franciacorta Brut Cuvée Real	🏆🏆 5
○ Franciacorta Satèn Essence '20	🏆🏆 6

Ascesa

via Ribolatti 42
23020 Tresivio [SO]
📞 +39 340 4132048
🌐 www.ascesavini.com

● Rosso di Valtellina '22	🏆🏆 4
● Valtellina Sup. Ascesa Ris. '20	🏆🏆 6

Tenuta Ambrosini

via della Pace, 60
25046 Cazzago San Martino [BS]
📞 +39 0307254850
🌐 www.tenutambrosini.it

CELLAR SALES
PRE-BOOKED VISITS
ACCOMMODATION AND RESTAURANT SERVICE
ANNUAL PRODUCTION 70,000 bottles
HECTARES UNDER VINE 10.00
SUSTAINABLE WINERY

○ Franciacorta Brut Batudè	🏆🏆 5
○ Franciacorta Brut Rosé Ambrosé '20	🏆🏆 6
○ Franciacorta Brut Satèn '20	🏆🏆 6
○ Francciacorta Dosaggio Zero Nihil	🏆 6

Antinori
Tenuta Montenisa

fraz. Calino
via Paolo VI, 62
25046 Cazzago San Martino [BS]
📞 +39 0307750838
🌐 www.tenutamontenisa.it

CELLAR SALES
PRE-BOOKED VISITS
ANNUAL PRODUCTION 400,000 bottles
HECTARES UNDER VINE 60.00

○ Franciacorta Brut Rosé	🏆🏆 5
○ Franciacorta Satèn Donna Cora '20	🏆🏆 6
○ Franciacorta Brut Cuvée Royale	🏆 5

Francesco Averoldi

fraz. Cantrina, 1
25081 Bedizzole [BS]
📞 +39 030674451
🌐 www.averoldifrancesco.it

CELLAR SALES
PRE-BOOKED VISITS
ANNUAL PRODUCTION 70,000 bottles
HECTARES UNDER VINE 15.00

○ RGC Bianco Canterius '22	🏆🏆 3
○ RGC Brut Graziolo	🏆🏆 3
○ RGC Valtènesi Chiaretto '23	🏆 3

OTHER WINERIES

Barboglio de Gaioncelli

fraz. Colombaro
via Nazario Sauro
25040 Corte Franca [BS]
(») +39 0309826831
@ www.barbogliodegaioncelli.it

CELLAR SALES
PRE-BOOKED VISITS
RESTAURANT SERVICE
ANNUAL PRODUCTION 50,000 bottles
HECTARES UNDER VINE 60.00

○ Franciacorta Brut	♟♟ 5
○ Franciacorta Dosaggio Zero Claro '18	♟♟ 6
○ Franciacorta Extra Brut '18	♟♟ 5
○ Franciacorta Satèn '20	♟♟ 5

Biondelli

loc. Bornato
via Basso Castello, 2
25046 Cazzago San Martino [BS]
(») +39 3311314144
@ www.biondelli.com

CELLAR SALES
PRE-BOOKED VISITS
ACCOMMODATION
ANNUAL PRODUCTION 50,000 bottles
HECTARES UNDER VINE 10.00
VITICULTURE METHOD Certified Organic

○ Franciacorta Dosaggio Zero Première Dame Ris. '16	♟♟ 7
○ Franciacorta Brut Satèn	♟ 5

Borgo La Caccia

loc. Caccia, 1
25010 Pozzolengo [BS]
(») +39 0309916044
@ www.borgolacaccia.it

CELLAR SALES
PRE-BOOKED VISITS
ANNUAL PRODUCTION 100,000 bottles
HECTARES UNDER VINE 30.00

⊙ Garda Brut M. Cl. Rosé Kames	♟♟ 5
● Garda Rosso Scudiero '22	♟♟ 3
○ Lugana Inanfora '22	♟♟ 4
○ Lugana InLegno '22	♟♟ 4

Cantina Sociale Bergamasca

via Bergamo, 10
24060 San Paolo d'Argon [BG]
(») +39 035951098
@ www.cantinabergamasca.it

CELLAR SALES
PRE-BOOKED VISITS
ANNUAL PRODUCTION 650,000 bottles
HECTARES UNDER VINE 90.00

○ Terre del Colleoni Incrocio Terzi N. 1 '21	♟♟ 2*
○ Terre del Colleoni Schiava '23	♟♟ 2*
● Valcalepio Rosso Vigna del Conte Ris. '18	♟ 3

Bonfadini

fraz. Clusane
via L. di Bernardo, 87
25049 Iseo [BS]
(») +39 0309826721
@ www.bonfadini.it

CELLAR SALES
PRE-BOOKED VISITS
ANNUAL PRODUCTION 155,000 bottles
HECTARES UNDER VINE 20.00

⊙ Franciacorta Brut Rosé Aurora '15	♟♟ 8
○ Franciacorta Brut Satèn Carpe Diem	♟ 6
○ Francicorta Dosaggio Zero Veritas Nature	♟ 6

Bosco Longhino

fraz. Molino Marconi
27047 Santa Maria della Versa [PV]
(») +39 0385798049
@ www.boscolonghino.it

PRE-BOOKED VISITS
ACCOMMODATION AND RESTAURANT SERVICE
ANNUAL PRODUCTION 200,000 bottles
HECTARES UNDER VINE 29.00

○ Chardonnay 353 '21	♟♟ 3*
● Campo dei Graci Pinot Nero '21	♟♟ 3
○ Rampicone Riesling '20	♟♟ 4
⊙ Casto Pinot Nero Brut Rosé M. Cl. '20	♟ 5

OTHER WINERIES

Cantina Bottenago

via Montecanale, 6a
25080 Polpenazze del Garda [BS]
+39 03651590240
www.cantinabottenago.it

CELLAR SALES
PRE-BOOKED VISITS
ANNUAL PRODUCTION 50,000 bottles
HECTARES UNDER VINE 55.00

○ Garda Brut M. Cl. Bottinus	♟♟ 4
○ Garda Extra Brut M. Cl. Bottinus '21	♟♟ 4
○ Garda Pinot Bianco '23	♟♟ 3

Ca' Bianche

via Santo Stefano, 15
23037 Tirano [SO]
+39 3392045524
www.cabianche.it

CELLAR SALES
PRE-BOOKED VISITS
ANNUAL PRODUCTION 12,000 bottles
HECTARES UNDER VINE 3.00
SUSTAINABLE WINERY

● Valtellina Sup. La Tèna '21	♟♟ 5
● Valtellina Sup. La Tèna Ris. '19	♟♟ 5
● Sforzato di Valtellina Fasèt '21	♟ 6

Patrizia Cadore

loc. Campagna Bianca
25010 Pozzolengo [BS]
+39 0309918138
www.vinicadore.com

ANNUAL PRODUCTION 25,000 bottles
HECTARES UNDER VINE 8.50

○ Lugana Ris. '20	♟♟ 5
○ RGC Valtènesi Chiaretto '23	♟♟ 3
○ San Martino della Battaglia '23	♟♟ 3
○ Lugana '23	♟ 3

Camilucci

via Iseo, 88
25030 Erbusco [BS]
+39 0307702739
www.camilucci.it

CELLAR SALES
PRE-BOOKED VISITS
ANNUAL PRODUCTION 120,000 bottles
HECTARES UNDER VINE 25.00

○ Franciacorta Dosaggio Zero Anthologie Blanc '20	♟♟ 6
○ Franciacorta Satèn Brut Ammonites	♟♟ 5
○ Franciacorta Dosaggio Zero St.10 Ris. '10	♟ 6

Tenuta Casa Virginia

via Cascina Violo, 1
24018 Villa d'Almè [BG]
+39 3402260681
www.tenutacasavirginia.it

CELLAR SALES
PRE-BOOKED VISITS
ANNUAL PRODUCTION 10,000 bottles
HECTARES UNDER VINE 4.00

● Il Serpente con la Cresta '21	♟♟ 4
● Il Drago di Santa Brigida '20	♟ 4
○ Il Lupo e La Volpe '23	♟ 4

Cascina Clarabella

via delle Polle, 1800
25049 Iseo [BS]
+39 0309821041
www.cascinaclarabella.it

CELLAR SALES
PRE-BOOKED VISITS
ACCOMMODATION AND RESTAURANT SERVICE
ANNUAL PRODUCTION 90,000 bottles
HECTARES UNDER VINE 13.00
VITICULTURE METHOD Certified Organic

○ Franciacorta Dosaggio Zero 180 '18	♟♟ 7
○ Franciacorta Dosaggio Zero E'ssenza	♟♟ 5
○ Franciacorta Satèn	♟ 5

LOMBARDY

298

OTHER WINERIES

Cascina San Pietro

fraz. Calino
via Alessandrini, 2
25046 Cazzago San Martino [BS]
(》 +39 0306363196
@ www.cascinaspietro.it

CELLAR SALES
PRE-BOOKED VISITS
HECTARES UNDER VINE 6.00

○ Franciacorta Brut Satèn	♥♥ 5
○ Franciacorta Dosaggio Zero	
Terre dei Trici '19	♥♥ 5
○ Franciacorta Brut	♥ 4

Castello di Luzzano

loc. Luzzano, 5
27040 Rovescala [PV]
(》 +39 0523863277
@ www.castelloluzzano.com

CELLAR SALES
PRE-BOOKED VISITS
ACCOMMODATION AND RESTAURANT SERVICE
ANNUAL PRODUCTION 120,000 bottles
HECTARES UNDER VINE 76.00

● OP Bonarda Carlino '22	♥♥ 3
● OP Bonarda Frizzante Sommossa '23	♥♥ 2*

Cantine Cavallotti

via Vallescuropasso, 92
27040 Cigognola [PV]
(》 +39 0290848829
@ www.cantinecavallotti.it

CELLAR SALES
PRE-BOOKED VISITS
ANNUAL PRODUCTION 120,000 bottles
HECTARES UNDER VINE 8.00

● Nerot '22	♥♥ 2*
● Nerot Vintage '19	♥♥ 3

Castello di Grumello

via Fosse, 11
24064 Grumello del Monte [BG]
(》 +39 0354420817
@ www.castellodigrumello.it

CELLAR SALES
PRE-BOOKED VISITS
ACCOMMODATION
ANNUAL PRODUCTION 100,000 bottles
HECTARES UNDER VINE 18.00
SUSTAINABLE WINERY

○ Valcalepio Bianco VB23 '23	♥♥ 3
● Valcalepio Moscato Passito Ros '20	♥♥ 5
● Valcalepio Rosso Colle del Calvario Ris. '19	♥ 6
● Valcalepio Rosso VR19 '19	♥ 3

Castelveder

via Belvedere, 4
25040 Monticelli Brusati [BS]
(》 +39 030652308
@ www.castelveder.it

CELLAR SALES
PRE-BOOKED VISITS
ANNUAL PRODUCTION 70,000 bottles
HECTARES UNDER VINE 12.00

○ Franciacorta Pas Dosé	♥♥ 5
○ Franciacorta Brut	♥ 5
○ Franciacorta Brut Rosé	♥ 5

Centinari

via Rampaneto, 10/12
25030 Erbusco [BS]
(》 +39 07318191
@ www.centinari.it

ANNUAL PRODUCTION 26,200 bottles
HECTARES UNDER VINE 1.00

○ Franciacorta Brut	♥♥ 5
○ Franciacorta Dosage Zéro	♥♥ 6

OTHER WINERIES

Il Cipresso

fraz. Tribulina
via Cerri, 2
24020 Scanzorosciate [BG]
(+39 0354597005
www.ilcipresso.info

CELLAR SALES
PRE-BOOKED VISITS
ANNUAL PRODUCTION 35,000 bottles
HECTARES UNDER VINE 4.00
VITICULTURE METHOD Certified Organic

● Moscato di Scanzo Serafino '20	♈♈ 6
● Valcalepio Rosso Bartolomeo Ris. '17	♈♈ 5

Citari

fraz. San Martino della Battaglia
loc. Citari, 2
25015 Desenzano del Garda [BS]
(+39 0309910310
www.citari.it

CELLAR SALES
PRE-BOOKED VISITS
ANNUAL PRODUCTION 350,000 bottles
HECTARES UNDER VINE 30.00
SUSTAINABLE WINERY

○ Lugana Torre '23	♈♈ 3*
⊙ RGC Rosé 18 e Quarantacinque '23	♈ 3

Club del Buttafuoco Storico

p.tta del Buttafuoco Storico
27044 Canneto Pavese [PV]
(+39 038560154
www.buttafuocostorico.com

CELLAR SALES
PRE-BOOKED VISITS
RESTAURANT SERVICE
ANNUAL PRODUCTION 100,000 bottles
HECTARES UNDER VINE 20.00

● OP Buttafuoco Storico '19	♈♈ 4

Corte Aura

via Colzano, 13
25030 Adro [BS]
(+39 030 7357281
www.corteaura.it

CELLAR SALES
PRE-BOOKED VISITS
ANNUAL PRODUCTION 120,000 bottles
HECTARES UNDER VINE 16.00

⊙ Franciacorta Brut Rosé	♈♈ 6
○ Franciacorta Brut Satèn	♈♈ 5
○ Franciacorta Extra Brut Blau '16	♈♈ 7
○ Franciacorta Dosaggio Zero Raramè Ris. '12	♈ 8

De Toma

via Battisti, 7
24020 Scanzorosciate [BG]
(+39 035657329
www.detomawine.com

CELLAR SALES
PRE-BOOKED VISITS
ANNUAL PRODUCTION 5,000 bottles
HECTARES UNDER VINE 2.50

● Moscato di Scanzo '19	♈♈ 7

Derbusco Cives

via Provinciale, 83
25030 Erbusco [BS]
(+39 0307731164
www.derbuscocives.com

CELLAR SALES
PRE-BOOKED VISITS
ACCOMMODATION
ANNUAL PRODUCTION 80,000 bottles
HECTARES UNDER VINE 12.50

○ Franciacorta Brut Le Millésime '15	♈♈ 7
⊙ Franciacorta Brut Rosé '17	♈♈ 7
○ Franciacorta Brut Blanc de Noir Crisalis '18	♈ 7
○ Franciacorta Brut Doppio Erre Di	♈ 5

OTHER WINERIES

Dobellone
loc. Belvedere, 55
25080 Muscoline [BS]
📞 +39 3336655430
cantinadobellone@gmail.com

ANNUAL PRODUCTION 4,500 bottles
HECTARES UNDER VINE 1.50

○ San Martino della Battaglia Aiguane '22	♀♀ 5
⊙ RGC Valtènesi Chiaretto Valt '23	♀♀ 5
○ San Martino della Battaglia Dubilù '22	♀♀ 5

Facchetti
via Solferino, 11
25030 Erbusco [BS]
📞 +39 0307267283
🌐 www.aafacchetti.it

CELLAR SALES
PRE-BOOKED VISITS
ANNUAL PRODUCTION 70,000 bottles
HECTARES UNDER VINE 8.00

○ Franciacorta Brut Nature	♀♀ 4
⊙ Franciacorta Brut Rosé	♀♀ 5
○ Franciacorta Brut Satèn	♀ 5

Luca Faccinelli
via Medici, 3a
23030 Chiuro [SO]
📞 +39 3470807011
🌐 www.lucafaccinelli.it

CELLAR SALES
PRE-BOOKED VISITS
ANNUAL PRODUCTION 20,000 bottles
HECTARES UNDER VINE 3.00
SUSTAINABLE WINERY

● Valtellina Sup. Grumello Ris. '21	♀♀ 6
● Rosso di Valtellina Matteo Bandello '22	♀♀ 4
● Valtellina Sup. Grumello Ortensio Lando '21	♀♀ 5

Faccoli
via Cava, 7
25030 Coccaglio [BS]
📞 +39 0307722761
🌐 www.faccolifranciacorta.it

CELLAR SALES
PRE-BOOKED VISITS
ANNUAL PRODUCTION 55,000 bottles
HECTARES UNDER VINE 5.50

○ Franciacorta Brut	♀♀ 6
⊙ Franciacorta Brut Rosé	♀♀ 6
○ Franciacorta Extra brut	♀♀ 6

Feliciana
loc. Feliciana
25010 Pozzolengo [BS]
📞 +39 030918228
🌐 www.feliciana.it

ANNUAL PRODUCTION 220,000 bottles
HECTARES UNDER VINE 20.00

○ Lugana Sercè Ris. '21	♀♀ 4
○ Lugana Felugan '23	♀♀ 3

Marco Ferrari
via Panoramica, 2387
23020 Montagna in Valtellina [SO]
📞 +39 3491051752
marco.ferrari998@gmail.com

● Valtellina Sup. Inferno '22	♀♀ 7
● Valtellina Sup. Sassella '22	♀♀ 7
● Rosso di Valtellina '23	♀ 5

Il Feudo Nico

via San Rocco, 63
27040 Mornico Losana [PV]
☎ +39 0383892452
⊛ www.ilfeudonico.it

PRE-BOOKED VISITS
RESTAURANT SERVICE
ANNUAL PRODUCTION 40,000 bottles
HECTARES UNDER VINE 16.00
SUSTAINABLE WINERY

○ M. Cl. Pas Dosé Maria Antonietta Blanc de Blancs '19	♟♟ 6
● Edoardo '22	♟ 5

Le Fracce

fraz. Mairano
via Castel del Lupo, 5
27045 Casteggio [PV]
☎ +39 038382526
⊛ www.lefracce.com

CELLAR SALES
PRE-BOOKED VISITS
ANNUAL PRODUCTION 180,000 bottles
HECTARES UNDER VINE 40.00

○ Pinot Nero M. Cl. Brut Special Cuvée '20	♟♟ 4
⊚ Pinot Nero M. Cl. Rosé Brut Grand Rosé	♟♟ 5
○ OP Riesling Landò '23	♟ 3

Bruno Franzosi

via XXV Aprile, 6
25080 Puegnago sul Garda [BS]
☎ +39 0365651380
⊛ www.cantinefranzosi.it

CELLAR SALES
PRE-BOOKED VISITS
ANNUAL PRODUCTION 400,000 bottles
HECTARES UNDER VINE 22.00

○ 3 Sensi '23	♟♟ 4
⊚ RGC Valtènesi Chiaretto '23	♟♟ 2*

La Fiòca

fraz. Nigoline
via Villa, 13b
25040 Corte Franca [BS]
☎ +39 0309826313
⊛ lafioca.com

CELLAR SALES
PRE-BOOKED VISITS
ACCOMMODATION AND RESTAURANT SERVICE
ANNUAL PRODUCTION 40,000 bottles
HECTARES UNDER VINE 6.00
VITICULTURE METHOD Certified Organic
SUSTAINABLE WINERY

○ Franciacorta Dosaggio Zero Orazio '19	♟♟ 6
○ Franciacorta Extra Blanc de Noir Ris. '16	♟♟ 7
○ Franciacorta Extra Brut	♟♟ 6
○ Franciacorta Satèn	♟♟ 5

Franca Contea

via Valli, 30
25030 Adro [BS]
☎ +39 0307451217
⊛ www.francacontea.it

CELLAR SALES
PRE-BOOKED VISITS
ANNUAL PRODUCTION 70,000 bottles
HECTARES UNDER VINE 12.50

○ Franciacorta Brut Primus Cuvée	♟♟ 5

La Genisia

via Villa, 2
27050 Codevilla [PV]
☎ +39 0383373001
⊛ www.lagenisia.com

CELLAR SALES
PRE-BOOKED VISITS
ACCOMMODATION
ANNUAL PRODUCTION 200,000 bottles
HECTARES UNDER VINE 70.00
VITICULTURE METHOD Certified Organic
SUSTAINABLE WINERY

○ OP Pinot Nero M. Cl. Brut	♟♟ 5
● OP Pinot Nero Centodieci '21	♟♟ 6
⊚ OP Pinot Nero M. Cl. Brut Rosé La Genisia	♟♟ 5
○ OP Pinot Nero M. Cl. Nature Centodieci '20	♟ 6

OTHER WINERIES

I Gessi

fraz. Cascina Fossa, 8
27050 Oliva Gessi [PV]
📞 +39 0383896606
🌐 www.cantineigessi.it

CELLAR SALES
PRE-BOOKED VISITS
ACCOMMODATION
ANNUAL PRODUCTION 160,000 bottles
HECTARES UNDER VINE 41.00

○ Pinot Nero M. Cl. Pas Dosé Maria Cristina '18	🍷 6
● Cinc Filagn Barbera '19	🍷 6
○ Fabbio Riesling '23	🍷 3

Involt Agnelot

loc. Tresenda
via Falk
Teglio [SO]
📞 +39 0342795102
🌐 www.involt-agnelot-vini.it

CELLAR SALES
PRE-BOOKED VISITS

● Carlione Nebbiolo '16	🍷 5
● La Purscela Nebbiolo '16	🍷 5
● Li Curt Nebbiolo '16	🍷 5

Leali di Monteacuto

fraz. Monteacuto
via Dosso, 4
25080 Puegnago sul Garda [BS]
📞 +39 0365651291
🌐 www.lealidimonteacuto.it

CELLAR SALES
PRE-BOOKED VISITS
ANNUAL PRODUCTION 40,000 bottles
HECTARES UNDER VINE 3.00

● Montagü Rebo '21	🍷 4
⊙ RGC Valtènesi Chiaretto '23	🍷 3
● RGC Valtènesi Groppello '22	🍷 3

Giorgio Gianatti

via dei Portici, 82
23020 Montagna in Valtellina [SO]
📞 +39 0342380033
gianatti.giorgio@alice.it

CELLAR SALES
PRE-BOOKED VISITS
ANNUAL PRODUCTION 8,000 bottles
HECTARES UNDER VINE 2.00

● Valtellina Sup Grumello Vign. Sassina '17	🍷 5
● Rosso di Valtellina '21	🍷 4

Tenuta La Vigna

loc. Cascina La Vigna
25020 Capriano del Colle [BS]
📞 +39 3288729264
🌐 www.tenutalavigna.it

CELLAR SALES
PRE-BOOKED VISITS
ACCOMMODATION
ANNUAL PRODUCTION 40,000 bottles
HECTARES UNDER VINE 8.00
SUSTAINABLE WINERY

○ Ugo Botti Brut Nature M. Cl.	🍷 5
○ Anna Botti Blanc de Blanc Brut M. Cl.	🍷 5
● Capriano del Colle Marzemino Lamettino '22	🍷 3

Lebovitz

fraz. Governolo
v.le Rimembranze, 4
46037 Roncoferraro [MN]
📞 +39 0376668115
🌐 www.lebovitz.it

CELLAR SALES
PRE-BOOKED VISITS
ANNUAL PRODUCTION 1,000,000 bottles

● Al Scagarün	🍷 1*
● Lambrusco Mantovano Rosso dei Concari	🍷 2*
● Sedamat	🍷 2*
● Garda Cabernet '22	🍷 2

OTHER WINERIES

Locatelli Caffi

via A. Moro, 6
24060 Chiuduno [BG]
📞 +39 035838308
🌐 www.locatellicaffi.it

○ M. Cl. EffeZeta	🍷🍷 4
○ Terre del Colleoni Incrocio Manzoni 6.0.13 Ducale '23	🍷🍷 3
● Valcalepio Rosso I Pilendrì '18	🍷 4

Sereno Magri

p.zza Alberico da Rosciate
24020 Scanzorosciate [BG]
📞 +39 035664289
🌐 www.aziendaagricolamagrisereno.it

● Moscato di Scanzo '19	🍷🍷 6
● Valcalepio Rosso '22	🍷🍷 3
○ Linda '23	🍷 3
● Valcalepio Rosso Ris. '20	🍷 3

Tenuta Martinelli

via Cadamocco, 24
25033 Cologne [BS]
📞 +39 3386863987
🌐 www.martinellifranciacorta.it

CELLAR SALES
ANNUAL PRODUCTION 40,000 bottles
HECTARES UNDER VINE 10.00
SUSTAINABLE WINERY

○ Franciacorta Brut Satèn Benedetta Buizza	🍷🍷 5
○ Franciacorta Brut Benedetta Buizza	🍷 5
○ Franciacorta Rosè Benedetta Buizza	🍷 6

Tenuta Maddalena

s.da Tibassi
46049 Volta Mantovana [MN]
📞 +39 037683323
🌐 www.tenutamaddalena.it

CELLAR SALES
PRE-BOOKED VISITS
ANNUAL PRODUCTION 40,000 bottles
HECTARES UNDER VINE 9.00

○ Col Fiorì '23	🍷🍷 3
○ Fossedal '23	🍷🍷 2*
● Il Cervo '21	🍷 3
● La Pietra '20	🍷 4

Marchesi di Montalto

loc. Costa Gallotti, 5
27040 Montalto Pavese [PV]
📞 +39 0383870358
🌐 www.marchesidimontalto.it

CELLAR SALES
PRE-BOOKED VISITS
ANNUAL PRODUCTION 50,000 bottles
HECTARES UNDER VINE 100.00

○ OP Cruasé Costadelvento '17	🍷🍷 5
○ OP Riesling Se. C. '23	🍷🍷 5
○ Natura Pas Dosé M. Cl. '15	🍷 8

Marzaghe Franciacorta

fraz. Zocco
via Parlamento, 28
25030 Erbusco [BS]
📞 +39 0307267245
🌐 www.marzaghefranciacorta.it

CELLAR SALES
PRE-BOOKED VISITS
ANNUAL PRODUCTION 45,000 bottles
HECTARES UNDER VINE 9.50
VITICULTURE METHOD Certified Organic
SUSTAINABLE WINERY

○ Franciacorta Brut Treha '18	🍷🍷 5
○ Franciacorta Brut LM 1935	🍷🍷 5
○ Franciacorta Brut Nature Aureum Ris. '10	🍷🍷 8
○ Franciacorta Satèn Premier '17	🍷🍷 6

OTHER WINERIES

Medolago Albani
via Redona, 12
24069 Trescore Balneario [BG]
(› +39 035942022
@ www.medolagoalbani.it

CELLAR SALES
PRE-BOOKED VISITS
ANNUAL PRODUCTION 200,000 bottles
HECTARES UNDER VINE 23.00

○ Valcalepio Bianco '23	♟♟ 2*
● Valcalepio Rosso '22	♟ 3
● Valcalepio Rosso I Due Lauri Ris. '20	♟ 4

Il Molino di Rovescala
loc. Molino, 2
27040 Rovescala [PV]
(› +39 339 4739924
@ www.ilmolinodirovescala.it

CELLAR SALES
PRE-BOOKED VISITS
ANNUAL PRODUCTION 40,000 bottles
HECTARES UNDER VINE 23.00
SUSTAINABLE WINERY

○ Piro Extra Brut M. Cl. '19	♟♟ 4
● OP Bonarda Povrömme '22	♟ 3
○ OP Riesling Felice '23	♟ 3

Monte Alto
Via Luigi di Bernardo, 98
25049 Iseo [BS]
(› +39 3478693294
@ www.montealtofranciacorta.it

CELLAR SALES
PRE-BOOKED VISITS
ACCOMMODATION
ANNUAL PRODUCTION 150,000 bottles
HECTARES UNDER VINE 30.00

○ Franciacorta Dosaggio Zero Blanc de Noir Ris. '17	♟♟ 6

Monte Cicogna
via delle Vigne, 6
25080 Moniga del Garda [BS]
(› +39 0365503200
@ www.montecicogna.it

○ Lugana Imperiale '23	♟♟ 3
○ Lugana S.Caterina '23	♟♟ 3
⊙ RGC Chiaretto Siclì '23	♟♟ 3

Tenuta Monte Delma
via Valenzano, 23
25050 Passirano [BS]
(› +39 0306546161
@ www.montedelma.it

CELLAR SALES
PRE-BOOKED VISITS
ANNUAL PRODUCTION 100,000 bottles
HECTARES UNDER VINE 20.00

○ Franciacorta Brut Rosé	♟♟ 5
○ Franciacorta Brut Satèn	♟♟ 5
○ Franciacorta Brut	♟ 4

Montelio
via D. Mazza, 1
27050 Codevilla [PV]
(› +39 0383373090
@ www.montelio.it

CELLAR SALES
PRE-BOOKED VISITS
ACCOMMODATION AND RESTAURANT SERVICE
ANNUAL PRODUCTION 130,000 bottles
HECTARES UNDER VINE 27.00

○ Noblerot '20	♟♟ 4
● OP Rosso Solarolo Ris. '20	♟♟ 4
● OP Pinot Nero Neos '23	♟ 4

OTHER WINERIES

Montonale

loc. Conta, 4a
25015 Desenzano del Garda [BS]
(☎) +39 0309103358
⊕ www.montonale.it

ANNUAL PRODUCTION 140,000 bottles
HECTARES UNDER VINE 30.00

○ Lugana Brut M. Cl. Primessenza '20	♟♟ 5
○ Lugana Montunal '23	♟♟ 4
○ Lugana Orestilla '22	♟♟ 6
⊙ RGC Valtènesi Chiaretto Rosa di Notte '23	♟ 3

Piccolo Bacco dei Quaroni

fraz. Costamontefedele
27040 Montù Beccaria [PV]
(☎) +39 038560521
⊕ www.piccolobaccodeiquaroni.it

CELLAR SALES
PRE-BOOKED VISITS
RESTAURANT SERVICE
ANNUAL PRODUCTION 35,000 bottles
HECTARES UNDER VINE 10.00
VITICULTURE METHOD Certified Organic

● OP Buttafuoco Ca' Padroni '20	♟♟ 4
● La Fiocca '22	♟♟ 4
● Il Moreè	♟ 2
⊙ M. Cl. Pas Dosé Rosé PBQ	♟ 4

Pratello

via Pratello, 26
25080 Padenghe sul Garda [BS]
(☎) +39 0309907005
⊕ www.pratello.com

CELLAR SALES
ACCOMMODATION AND RESTAURANT SERVICE
ANNUAL PRODUCTION 600,000 bottles
HECTARES UNDER VINE 80.00
VITICULTURE METHOD Certified Organic

○ Garda Brut Donna Caterina	♟♟ 3
⊙ Garda Brut Rosé	♟♟ 3
○ Garda Riesling '22	♟♟ 3
○ Lugana 90+10 '22	♟♟ 4

Pian del Maggio

via Iseo, 108
25030 Erbusco [BS]
(☎) +39 3355638610
⊕ www.piandelmaggio.it

CELLAR SALES
PRE-BOOKED VISITS
ANNUAL PRODUCTION 50,000 bottles
HECTARES UNDER VINE 7.40

○ Franciacorta Satèn	♟♟ 5
○ Franciacorta Extra Brut Stra	♟♟ 6
⊙ Franciacorta Brut Rosé...e Anna Sorrise	♟ 5

Pilandro

fraz. San Martino della Battaglia
loc. Pilandro, 1
25015 Desenzano del Garda [BS]
(☎) +39 0309910363
⊕ www.pilandro.it

CELLAR SALES
PRE-BOOKED VISITS
ANNUAL PRODUCTION 300,000 bottles
HECTARES UNDER VINE 33.00

○ Lugana Arilica '21	♟♟ 3*
○ Lugana '23	♟♟ 2*
○ Lugana San Pietro Ris. '20	♟♟ 4
○ Lugana Terecrea '23	♟♟ 3

Priore

fraz. Calino
via Sala, 41
25046 Cazzago San Martino [BS]
(☎) +39 0307254710
⊕ www.aziendaagricolapriore.it

CELLAR SALES
PRE-BOOKED VISITS
RESTAURANT SERVICE
ANNUAL PRODUCTION 110,000 bottles
HECTARES UNDER VINE 18.00
SUSTAINABLE WINERY

○ Franciacorta Extra Brut Lihander Noir '20	♟♟ 5
○ Franciacorta Brut	♟♟ 4
○ Franciacorta Extra Brut Lihander Blanc '20	♟♟ 5
○ Franciacorta Satèn	♟♟ 4

OTHER WINERIES

Quattro Terre

fraz. Borgonato
via Risorgimento, 11
25040 Corte Franca [BS]
☏ +39 030984312
⊛ www.quattroterre.it

CELLAR SALES
PRE-BOOKED VISITS
ACCOMMODATION AND RESTAURANT SERVICE
ANNUAL PRODUCTION 50,000 bottles
HECTARES UNDER VINE 10.00
VITICULTURE METHOD Certified Organic

○ Franciacorta Dosaggio Zero '20	♟♟ 6
○ Franciacorta Extra Brut	♟♟ 6

Cantina Sociale Cooperativa di Quistello

via Roma, 46
46026 Quistello [MN]
☏ +39 0376618118
⊛ www.cantinasocialequistello.it

CELLAR SALES
PRE-BOOKED VISITS
ANNUAL PRODUCTION 1,000,000 bottles
HECTARES UNDER VINE 330.00
SUSTAINABLE WINERY

● La Ricerca dell'Infinito	♟♟ 3
● Lambrusco Mantovano Rossissimo	♟♟ 2*
⊙ Grazie dei Fior	♟ 2

Tenuta Quvestra

loc. Case Nuove, 9
27047 Santa Maria della Versa [PV]
☏ +39 3476014109
⊛ www.quvestra.it

CELLAR SALES
PRE-BOOKED VISITS
ACCOMMODATION
ANNUAL PRODUCTION 40,000 bottles
HECTARES UNDER VINE 12.00

○ Chardonnay '21	♟♟ 5
⊙ OP Pinot Nero M. Cl. Extra Brut Rosé Zephiro	♟♟ 5
● Croatina '18	♟ 5

Rebollini

loc. Sbercia, 1a
27040 Borgoratto Mormorolo [PV]
☏ +39 0383872295
⊛ www.rebollini.it

CELLAR SALES
PRE-BOOKED VISITS
ANNUAL PRODUCTION 100,000 bottles
HECTARES UNDER VINE 35.00
SUSTAINABLE WINERY

○ OP Riesling Sup. Renio '22	♟♟ 4
⊙ OP Cruasé '20	♟♟ 4
○ OP M. Cl. Pinot Nero Brut Nature '20	♟♟ 5

La Rifra

loc. Pilandro, 2
25010 Desenzano del Garda [BS]
☏ +39 0309108023
⊛ www.aziendaagricolalarifra.it

CELLAR SALES
PRE-BOOKED VISITS
ANNUAL PRODUCTION 150,000 bottles
HECTARES UNDER VINE 21.00

○ Lugana Il Bepi Ris. '21	♟♟ 3
○ Lugana Libiam '23	♟♟ 2*

La Rocchetta

via Verdi, 4
24067 Villongo [BG]
☏ +39 035936318
⊛ www.larocchetta.it

CELLAR SALES
PRE-BOOKED VISITS
ANNUAL PRODUCTION 150,000 bottles
HECTARES UNDER VINE 17.00

○ M. Cl. Brut Cretarium	♟♟ 4
○ M. Cl. Pas Dosé Brut Nature Cretarium	♟♟ 4
● Valcalepio Rosso Lapis Rubrae '21	♟♟ 4

OTHER WINERIES

Romantica

via Vallosa, 29
25050 Passirano [BS]
(📞) +39 0365551013
🌐 www.romanticafranciacorta.com

CELLAR SALES
PRE-BOOKED VISITS
ANNUAL PRODUCTION 70,000 bottles
HECTARES UNDER VINE 10.00
SUSTAINABLE WINERY

○ Franciacorta Brut '20	🍷🍷 5
⊙ Franciacorta Brut Rosé '20	🍷🍷 6
○ Franciacorta Brut Satèn '20	🍷🍷 6
○ Franciacorta Extra Brut '20	🍷🍷 6

Santa Lucia

via Verdi, 6
25030 Erbusco [BS]
(📞) +39 0307769814
🌐 www.santaluciafranciacorta.it

CELLAR SALES
PRE-BOOKED VISITS
ANNUAL PRODUCTION 150,000 bottles
HECTARES UNDER VINE 35.00
VITICULTURE METHOD Certified Organic

○ Franciacorta Dosaggio Zero '18	🍷🍷 6
○ Franciacorta Extra Brut 　Brolo dei Longhi Ris. '17	🍷🍷 8

Santus

via Case Sparse, 2
25050 Passirano [BS]
(📞) +39 0305582053
🌐 www.santus.it

CELLAR SALES
PRE-BOOKED VISITS
ACCOMMODATION
ANNUAL PRODUCTION 65,000 bottles
HECTARES UNDER VINE 10.00
VITICULTURE METHOD Certified Organic

○ Franciacorta Brut Satèn '20	🍷🍷 6
⊙ Franciacorta Dosaggio Zero Rosè	🍷🍷 6

Saottini

via Tugurio, 3
25017 Lonato [BS]
(📞) +39 0309130801
🌐 www.saottinivini.com

CELLAR SALES
PRE-BOOKED VISITS
ACCOMMODATION AND RESTAURANT SERVICE
ANNUAL PRODUCTION 70,000 bottles
HECTARES UNDER VINE 15.00

⊙ RGC Valtènesi 　Chiaretto Rosa dei Venti '23	🍷🍷 3*

Sguardi di Terra

via Centenaro
25017 Lonato [BS]
🌐 www.sguardiditerra.it

HECTARES UNDER VINE 7.00

○ Lugana Saltafoss Ris. '20	🍷🍷 4
○ Lugana Scapuscià '23	🍷🍷 3
○ Lugana Brut M. Cl. Inlari	🍷 5

La Spia

s.da Privata Carlo Buzzi, 78
23012 Castione Andevenno [SO]
(📞) +39 3513340321
🌐 www.laspia.wine

CELLAR SALES
PRE-BOOKED VISITS
ANNUAL PRODUCTION 35,000 bottles
HECTARES UNDER VINE 4.50

● Valtellina Sup. Sassella Riserva MR 72 '18	🍷🍷 8
● Valtellina Sup. PR28 '20	🍷🍷 5

LOMBARDY

OTHER WINERIES

Cantina Tàia
fraz. Casella, 14/15
27047 Montecalvo Versiggia [PV]
📞 +39 3495300982
🌐 www.cantinataia.it

Tenuta di Caseo
fraz. Caseo, 9
27040 Canevino [PV]
📞 +39 038599937
🌐 www.caseowines.com

PRE-BOOKED VISITS
ANNUAL PRODUCTION 280,000 bottles
HECTARES UNDER VINE 47.00

● OP Pinot Nero Ris. '22	🍷🍷 5
○ OP Riesling '22	🍷🍷 5
● Il Rosso	🍷 4

○ Pinot Nero M. Cl. Brut 470 '18	🍷🍷 5
○ Pinot Nero M. Cl. Rosé Brut 530 '18	🍷🍷 5

Conti Thun
via Masserino, 2
25080 Puegnago sul Garda [BS]
📞 +39 0365651757
🌐 www.contithun.com

La Torre
via San Zeno, 6
25030 Adro [BS]
📞 +39 030 7450844
🌐 www.vinidifranciacortalatorre.it

CELLAR SALES
ACCOMMODATION AND RESTAURANT SERVICE
ANNUAL PRODUCTION 25,000 bottles
HECTARES UNDER VINE 12.00

HECTARES UNDER VINE 24.00

○ Gioia '22	🍷🍷 4
○ RGC Valtènesi Chiaretto Micaela '23	🍷🍷 4
○ RGC Valtènesi Chiaretto Rosa '22	🍷🍷 4

○ Franciacorta Dosaggio Zero '17	🍷🍷 5
○ Franciacorta Brut Satèn	🍷🍷 4

Tosi
via Pianazza, 45
27040 Montescano [PV]
📞 +39 3384781752
🌐 www.vinitosi.com

La Travaglina
fraz. Castello
via Travaglina, 1
27046 Santa Giuletta [PV]
📞 +39 0383899195
🌐 www.latravaglina.it

ANNUAL PRODUCTION 50,000 bottles
HECTARES UNDER VINE 12.00

CELLAR SALES
PRE-BOOKED VISITS
ANNUAL PRODUCTION 120,000 bottles
HECTARES UNDER VINE 30.50
SUSTAINABLE WINERY

○ Marie Riesling '22	🍷🍷 3
● OP Bonarda Frizzante Violin '23	🍷🍷 2*
● Theremin Pinot Nero '22	🍷 4

● OP Bonarda Frizzante Zavola '23	🍷🍷 3
○ OP M. Cl. Pinot Nero Brut Martinburgo '18	🍷 5
● OP Pinot Nero Casaia Ris. '21	🍷 4

OTHER WINERIES

Triacca
via Nazionale, 121
23030 Villa di Tirano [SO]
📞 +39 0342701352
🌐 www.triacca.eu

CELLAR SALES
PRE-BOOKED VISITS
RESTAURANT SERVICE
ANNUAL PRODUCTION 450,000 bottles
HECTARES UNDER VINE 40.00

● Sforzato di Valtellina San Domenico '19	🍷🍷 5
● Valtellina Sup. Sassella Ris. '20	🍷🍷 5
● Valtellina Sup. Giovanni Segantini '19	🍷 4
● Valtellina Sup. Sassella '21	🍷 4

Le Vedute
via Monte Orfano
25038 Rovato [BS]
📞 +39 3339524571
🌐 www.levedutefranciacorta.it

ANNUAL PRODUCTION 75,000 bottles
HECTARES UNDER VINE 11.00
SUSTAINABLE WINERY

○ Franciacorta Dosaggio Zero Per Enea	🍷🍷 5
⊙ Franciacorta Dosaggio Zero Rosé Per Lulu	🍷🍷 5
○ Franciacorta Satèn Per Ginevra	🍷🍷 5

Villa Franciacorta
via Villa, 12
25040 Monticelli Brusati [BS]
📞 +39 030652329
🌐 www.villafranciacorta.it

CELLAR SALES
PRE-BOOKED VISITS
ACCOMMODATION AND RESTAURANT SERVICE
ANNUAL PRODUCTION 250,000 bottles
HECTARES UNDER VINE 46.00
VITICULTURE METHOD Certified Organic
SUSTAINABLE WINERY

⊙ Franciacorta Brut Rosé Bokè '20	🍷🍷 6
○ Franciacorta Brut Cuvette '19	🍷🍷 7
○ Franciacorta Brut Emozione '20	🍷🍷 6
○ Franciacorta Extra Brut RNA Ris. '07	🍷🍷 8

L'Ulif
loc. Picedo
via Montezalto, 14
25080 Polpenazze del Garda [BS]
📞 +39 0365674969
silvano.delai@tin.it

ANNUAL PRODUCTION 22,000 bottles
HECTARES UNDER VINE 3.50
VITICULTURE METHOD Certified Biodynamic

⊙ RGC Brut Rosé Valzer '23	🍷🍷 3
⊙ RGC Valtènesi Chiaretto Minuetto '23	🍷🍷 3

Vigna Dorata
fraz. Calino
via Sala, 80
25046 Cazzago San Martino [BS]
📞 +39 0307254275
🌐 www.vignadorata.it

CELLAR SALES
PRE-BOOKED VISITS
ANNUAL PRODUCTION 70,000 bottles
HECTARES UNDER VINE 8.00
VITICULTURE METHOD Certified Organic

○ Franciacorta Extra Brut Riserva del Giglio '15	🍷🍷 8
○ Franciacorta Brut Satèn '17	🍷🍷 7
○ Franciacorta Brut Satèn	🍷🍷 5

Cantine Virgili Luigi
via M. Donati, 2
46100 Mantova
📞 +39 0376322560
🌐 www.cantinevirgili.it

CELLAR SALES
PRE-BOOKED VISITS
ANNUAL PRODUCTION 315,000 bottles
HECTARES UNDER VINE 14.30
VITICULTURE METHOD Certified Organic

● Inciostar	🍷🍷 2
⊙ Pjaföc Rosé	🍷🍷 3
● Ancellotta Frizz.	🍷 3

TRENTINO

Does Trentino still rhyme with vino? It's a question we've heard often in recent years. Let's try to answer it, particularly by looking at what's in the bottle. Without a doubt, yes! The quality of the wines is unquestionable, as are their sense of place and authenticity. The issue, if there is one, stems from some local wine critics who tend to make unproductive comparisons with certain neighboring provinces.

We prefer to focus on the dynamism of this area, driven primarily—but not exclusively—by its Metodo Classico. Trento's sparkling wines have been evolving year after year, thanks to a diverse mix of cooperatives, small independent producers, and a few prestigious private wineries. Together, they shape the region's identity. This year's most notable newcomers, both awarded Tre Bicchieri, highlight this trend. Etyssa and Lavis offer two remarkable chardonnay-based cuvées: one crafted by a small start-up of four young winemakers, the other from a leading cooperative. Looking beyond the accolades, the region shows impressive consistency even in its simpler wines, while the complexity of the vintage-dated bottles and rosé versions puts Trentino's mountain bubbly at the forefront of Italy's sparkling wine production.

But the region's talents don't end there. Its still wines are equally strong, proving Trentino has plenty of arrows in its quiver. A standout variety is teroldego, which, from the Rotaliana plain, produces deeply complex reds with smooth, satisfying drinkability. Two wines in this category received awards. Moving to other reds, pinot nero is also finding excellent expression in still wines here. Among the whites, nosiola stands out, whether enjoyed young and fresh or aged for years to reveal its long-term potential. And let's not forget the region's outstanding Vino Santo, made from the same grape and a star of the Valle dei Laghi. Another grape to watch is müller thurgau, as demonstrated by Pojer & Sandri's Monogram, one of the best examples. Last but certainly not least are the so-called international varieties. These have adapted so well to Trentino that they've practically become traditional. A prime example is the San Leonardo, produced by its namesake winery. One of Italy's great reds, it's a true benchmark for its history, richness, consistent quality, and vision. Indeed, this year San Leonardo, a model for all of Trentino, earned our coveted Winery of the Year award. Another special award highlights Trentino's excellent performance in winemaking. It's our Sustainable Viticulture award, which went to Nicola Biasi for his Resistenti project.

★Abate Nero

via Sponda Trentina, 45
38121 Trento
📞 +39 0461246566
🌐 www.abatenero.it

CELLAR SALES
ANNUAL PRODUCTION 70,000 bottles
HECTARES UNDER VINE 1.00

This historic Trentino winery, which has 50 years of artisanal, mountain sparkling wine production behind it, is led by Roberta Lunelli, daughter of founder Luciano, alongside Roberto Sebastiani. The vineyards are mainly located in Lavis, north of Trento, and retain the traditional Trentino pergola training system. The winery's philosophy emphasizes long aging periods and a strong sense of place, with every phase meticulously managed by a close-knit team. Two wines made it to the final round, confirming the impressive work being done. The Domini Nero '17 reveals aromas of yellow apple and nuts, with a slightly oxidative note that doesn't overshadow the fruit, making this an intriguing drink. The Collezione Luciano Lunelli, with its red fruit, mint, and freshly cut grass aromas, and its sinuous, elegant palate, is truly outstanding. The rest of the lineup is also impressive, especially the Brut and Brut Rosé.

Cantina Aldeno

via Roma, 76
38060 Aldeno [TN]
📞 +39 0461842511
🌐 www.cantinaaldeno.com

CELLAR SALES
PRE-BOOKED VISITS
ANNUAL PRODUCTION 240,000 bottles
HECTARES UNDER VINE 340.00

A cooperative winery located on the right bank of the Adige River, Aldeno has evolved over time by embracing modern technologies while staying true to tradition. In addition to producing reds, notably merlot, which has garnered numerous accolades over the years, they also produce Trentodoc, drawing on high-altitude vineyards situated over Aldeno. Their range, which includes an entirely bio-vegan line, is sure to please. Several wines were submitted for tasting, with some standing out as among the best in their category. One is certainly the Altinum Riserva '16, a Trentodoc Dosaggio Zero that bursts with energy, thanks to its vibrant acidity and a crisp, clean finish. Another remarkable sparkler is the Altinum Pas Dosé '20. Among the still wines, the Pinot Nero '22 and the Merlot Riserva '19 are both excellent. The other wines tasted are also well-made, offering a superb price-to-quality ratio.

○ Trento Brut Domini Nero '17	♥♥ 5
◉ Trento Brut Rosé Collezione Luciano Lunelli Ris. '09	♥♥ 8
○ Trento Brut	♥♥ 5
◉ Trento Brut Rosè	♥♥ 5
○ Trento Dosaggio Zero	♥ 5
○ Trento Brut Cuvée dell'Abate Ris. '10	♥♥♥ 6
○ Trento Brut Cuvée dell'Abate Ris. '09	♥♥♥ 6
○ Trento Brut Domini '10	♥♥♥ 5
○ Trento Brut Domini '07	♥♥♥ 5
○ Trento Brut Domini '05	♥♥♥ 5
○ Trento Brut Domini Nero '10	♥♥♥ 5
○ Trento Brut Domini Nero '08	♥♥♥ 5
○ Trento Domìni Nero '09	♥♥♥ 5

○ Trento Dosaggio Zero Altinum Ris. '16	♥♥ 6
● Trentino Merlot Ris. '19	♥♥ 5
● Trentino Pinot Nero '22	♥♥ 3
○ Trento Pas Dosé Altinum '20	♥♥ 5
○ Trentino Chardonnay '23	♥ 3
○ Trentino Gewürztraminer '23	♥ 3
● Trentino Lagrein Athesim Flumen '23	♥ 2
○ Trento Brut Altinate '19	♥ 5
○ Trento Brut Altinum '20	♥ 5
◉ Trento Extra Brut Rosé Altinum	♥ 5
● Trentino Marzemino '22	♥♥ 4
● Trentino Pinot Nero '21	♥♥ 3
○ Trento Pas Dosé Altinum '19	♥♥ 5

★Nicola Balter

via Vallunga II, 24
38068 Rovereto [TN]
📞 +39 0464664792
🌐 www.balter.it

CELLAR SALES
PRE-BOOKED VISITS
ANNUAL PRODUCTION 80,000 bottles
HECTARES UNDER VINE 10.00

A lot has changed since the historic 16th-century military structure of Castelliere was transformed into the agricultural enterprise it is today. Spearheading this shift in the mid-20th century was the Balter family, who are represented today by Francesco and his children Nicola and Barbara. Their focus is on producing high-quality Trentodocs according to a production style that favors elegant, fresh, and complex sparkling wines. The range also includes some notable still wines, like the excellent Vallagarina Sauvignon. But in terms of Metodo Classico, the Dosaggio Zero Riserva and the Brut Rosé stand out at the top of their range. The former opts for a more evolved style, with toasty and coffee notes, while the latter shines with red fruit aromas, a fleshy palate, and lively acidity, finishing on a deep, sapid note. The Nature and Brut, both non-vintage, are also excellent.

Bellaveder

fraz. Faedo
loc. Maso Belvedere, I
38010 San Michele all'Adige [TN]
📞 +39 0461650171
🌐 www.bellaveder.it

CELLAR SALES
PRE-BOOKED VISITS
ANNUAL PRODUCTION 70,000 bottles
HECTARES UNDER VINE 12.00
SUSTAINABLE WINERY

Andrea and Marco, alongside their father Tranquillo, manage their winery with a deep respect for the land, practicing organic farming. These artisan vintners follow nature's rhythms meticulously, from hand-harvesting to carefully overseeing each step, from vineyard to cellar. Whites aged in stainless steel and reds matured in oak are accompanied by a notable line of Trento Docs. We start with these last, with the Brut Nature Rosé Riserva '19 proving to be a standout in its category. Fleshy and sapid, it unveils a meaty finish, yet still manages to convey elegance and finesse. At the very top, however, we find the Pinot Nero Faedi, another standard-bearer of elegance, with a pervasive and light palate. The Riesling from the same line echoes its profile, with an energetic and vibrant character. The Sauvignon Faedi and the Nature Riserva '19, a dry and complex sparkling wine, are also excellent.

Trento Brut Rosé	♟♟ 5
Trento Dosaggio Zero Ris.'17	♟♟ 7
Sauvignon '23	♟♟ 3
Trento Brut	♟♟ 5
Trento Nature	♟♟ 5
Trento Balter Ris.'06	♟♟♟ 5
Trento Balter Ris.'05	♟♟♟ 5
Trento Balter Ris.'04	♟♟♟ 5
Trento Dosaggio Zero Ris.'10	♟♟♟ 7
Trento Pas Dosé Balter Ris.'15	♟♟♟ 6
Trento Pas Dosé Balter Ris.'14	♟♟♟ 6
Trento Pas Dosé Balter Ris.'13	♟♟♟ 6
Trento Pas Dosé Balter Ris.'12	♟♟♟ 6
Trento Pas Dosé Balter Ris.'11	♟♟♟ 5
Trento Pas Dosé Balter Ris.'09	♟♟♟ 5

● Trentino Pinot Nero Faedi '21	♟♟ 5
○ Trentino Riesling Faedi '23	♟♟ 4
⊙ Trento Brut Nature Rosé Ris.'19	♟♟ 6
○ Faedi Sauvignon '23	♟♟ 4
○ Trento Nature Ris.'19	♟♟ 5
● Trentino Lagrein Mansum '21	♟ 5
○ Trentino Müller Thurgau San Lorenz '23	♟ 3
● Trentino Pinot Nero Faedi '20	♟♟♟ 5
● Trentino Lagrein Mansum '20	♟♟ 5
○ Trentino Müller Thurgau San Lorenz '22	♟♟ 5
● Trentino Pinot Nero Faedi Ris.'19	♟♟ 5
○ Trento Brut Nature '18	♟♟ 6
○ Trento Brut Nature '17	♟♟ 6
⊙ Trento Brut Nature Rosé '18	♟♟ 6

TRENTINO

Cantina d'Isera
via al Ponte, 1
38060 Isera [TN]
(· +39 0464433795
· www.cantinaisera.it

CELLAR SALES
PRE-BOOKED VISITS
ANNUAL PRODUCTION 500,000 bottles
HECTARES UNDER VINE 200.00
VITICULTURE METHOD Certified Organic

In 1907, 32 winemakers joined forces to establish
Cantina d'Isera, a cooperative born of a shared
vision that remains strong to this day. The year of
its founding is so significant that a special line of
wines commemorates it. Today, the cooperative
boasts 150 members cultivating approximately
200 hectares of vineyards. This diverse terrain
allows for a broad range of wines, from still
reds—especially Marzemino, which thrives in the
Isera subzone—to the sparkling Trentodoc, which
they've been producing since 2004. The winery
also offers local whites, such as moscato giallo
and gewürztraminer. Some highlights include the
Brut Nature '18 from the 907 line, a Metodo
Classico of finesse and depth. From the same line
comes the Pinot Nero '21, which features red
fruit aromas and a fleshy yet delicate, refined
palate. Many other wines offer great quality at
reasonable prices: the Chardonnay '23, with its
notes of yellow fruit and wildflowers, the fresh
and lively Pinot Grigio, and the Gewürztraminer,
which has just the right amount of aromatics and
is never too sweet. The other two Trentodocs
presented are also very good.

● Trentino Pinot Nero 907 '21	♥♥ 4
○ Trento Brut Nature 907 '18	♥♥ 5
○ Trentino Chardonnay '23	♥♥ 3
○ Trentino Gewürztraminer '23	♥♥ 3
● Trentino Marzemino d'Isera Sup. Et. Verde '21	♥♥ 3
○ Trentino Pinot Grigio '23	♥♥ 3
○ Trento Brut Collezione 15	♥♥ 4
○ Trento Dosaggio Zero 907 '19	♥♥ 5
⊙ Schiava Rosato '23	♥ 2
● Trentino Marzemino Bio '22	♥ 3
○ Trentino Moscato Giallo '23	♥ 3
○ Trentino Sauvignon '23	♥ 3
● Trentino Marzemino '19	♀♀ 3
● Trentino Marzemino '18	♀♀ 3
● Trentino Marzemino Sup. Corè '17	♀♀ 4

Cantina Rotaliana
via Trento, 65b
38017 Mezzolombardo [TN]
(· +39 0461601010
· www.cantinarotaliana.it

CELLAR SALES
PRE-BOOKED VISITS
ACCOMMODATION
ANNUAL PRODUCTION 800,000 bottles
HECTARES UNDER VINE 330.00
SUSTAINABLE WINERY

La Rotaliana is a vibrant and dynamic cooperative
that brings together various winemakers under
the name of the territory it calls home: the
Rotaliana plains, renowned for the teroldego
grape, which produces a distinguished red wine.
But production doesn't stop there; it extends to
several white wines from traditional varieties,
other reds, and increasingly well-crafted
Trentodoc sparkling wines. The main vineyards
are on the plains, with additional plots in Val di
Non and Valle di Cembra. A highly commendable
lineup was presented, bringing the winery back
into the main section of our guide. What
impressed our tasters the most was the Brut
Riserva '16, a Trentodoc of noble character,
complex and deep, with notes of yellow fruit and
mountain herbs, and a fresh, supple palate. The
Rosé, with its woodland fruit sensations,
fleshiness, elegance, and finesse, follows suit.
Among the still wines, all the Teroldegos
performed excellently: the Etichetta Rossa is
fresh and juicy, the Riserva '21 is more close-knit
and pervasive, while the Clesurae, the winery's
flagship, offers complexity and length.

○ Trento Brut R Ris. '16	♥♥ 6
● Teroldego Rotaliano Clesurae '20	♥♥ 6
● Teroldego Rotaliano Et. Rossa '23	♥♥ 3
● Teroldego Rotaliano Sup. Ris. '21	♥♥ 4
○ Trento Brut Rosé R '24	♥♥ 5
○ Trentino Gewürztraminer '23	♥ 3
● Trentino Lagrein '23	♥ 3
○ Trentodoc Extra Brut R	♥ 5
● Teroldego Rotaliano Clesurae '06	♀♀♀ 5
● Teroldego Rotaliano Clesurae '02	♀♀♀ 5
● Teroldego Rotaliano Clesurae '99	♀♀♀ 5
● Teroldego Rotaliano Ris. '04	♀♀♀ 3
● Teroldego Rotaliano Sup. Clesurae Ris. '19	♀♀ 4
● Teroldego Rotaliano Sup. Ris. '18	♀♀ 4
○ Trento Brut R Ris. '12	♀♀ 6

314

★★Cavit
via del Ponte, 31
38123 Trento
☎ +39 0461381711
🖥 www.cavit.it

Comai
via San Cassiano, 9
38066 Riva del Garda [TN]
☎ +39 0464553485
🖥 www.agriturcomai.com

ANNUAL PRODUCTION 65,000,000 bottles
HECTARES UNDER VINE 6350.00
VITICULTURE METHOD Certified Organic
SUSTAINABLE WINERY

ANNUAL PRODUCTION 25,000 bottles
HECTARES UNDER VINE 16.00

This historic cooperative winery in Trentino has reinvented itself over the years, emphasizing quality and promoting specialized viticulture. Over 5,000 growers work approximately 6,300 hectares, representing 60 percent of Trentino's vineyard area. Their goal is to bring out the best of prime growing areas, with a focus on the Altemasi line of Trento Docs. And when it comes to their star performer, we start with Altemasi, the Graal Riserva '17, which reaffirms its status as a superb mountain sparkling wine. Its complexity, evolution, freshness, and sapidity make for a truly rich and multifaceted palate. The Brut '20 is also excellent and among the best tasted, while among the still wines, we were impressed by the Maso Cervara, a prized Teroldego Rotaliano Riserva. The other wines are also at high levels, particularly the Brusafer (among the reds) and the Pas Dosé '19. The rest of the lineup is very well-crafted.

You'll find the vineyards, olive groves, and winery of Andrea and Marco Comai nestled in a natural basin, kissed by the wind and protected by the lush hills overlooking Lake Garda. The two young winemakers, from a family that has farmed the land for four generations, have chosen to focus solely on viticulture. After gaining experience abroad, they returned to their family farm, a rural property now transformed into a wine estate with agritourism. They cultivate about ten hectares of organic vineyards, producing artisanal wines with a distinctive character and impressive quality. The range presented this year is impressive, with some wines standing out during our tastings. One of these is undoubtedly the Trentodoc Cuvée I, an Extra Brut '18, with fine citrus and herbal aromas and a sapid, lively palate brimming with freshness. Among the whites, we particularly appreciated the Busat (a blend of chardonnay, müller thurgau, and sauvignon), a supple wine that, despite its easy drinkability, doesn't lack in character and complexity. The Chardonnay '22 is also excellent.

○ Trento Brut Altemasi Graal Ris. '17	♟♟♟ 8
● Teroldego Rotaliano Sup. Ris. Maso Cervara '21	♟♟ 5
○ Trento Brut Altemasi '20	♟♟ 5
● Trentino Pinot Nero Sup. Brusafer '22	♟♟ 5
○ Trentino Vino Santo Arele '05	♟♟ 8
○ Trento Brut Altemasi Blanc de Noirs '20	♟♟ 6
○ Trento Pas Dosé Altemasi '19	♟♟ 7
● Trentino Lagrein Kelter Ris. '21	♟ 5
○ Trentino Pinot Grigio Sup. Rulendis '22	♟ 4
○ Trento Brut Altemasi Gran Cuvée	♟ 7
○ Trento Brut Altemasi Blanc de Noirs '16	♟♟♟ 5
○ Trento Brut Altemasi Graal Ris. '16	♟♟♟ 7
○ Trento Brut Altemasi Graal Ris. '14	♟♟♟ 8

○ Trento Extra Brut Cuvée I '18	♟♟ 7
○ Busat Bianco '23	♟♟ 3
○ Trentino Chardonnay '22	♟♟ 4
● Trentino Merlot V. Piscol '20	♟ 6
○ Trentino Sauvignon '22	♟ 4
○ Busat Bianco '22	♟♟ 4
○ Busat Bianco '20	♟♟ 4
● Busat Rosso '19	♟♟ 5
● Busat Rosso '18	♟♟ 5
○ Trentino Chardonnay '21	♟♟ 5
○ Trentino Chardonnay '19	♟♟ 4
○ Trentino Chardonnay '18	♟♟ 4
● Trentino Rosso Rovereto '18	♟♟ 4
○ Trentino Sauvignon '21	♟♟ 4
○ Trentino Sauvignon '20	♟♟ 4

Corvée

loc. Bedin, 1
38034 Lisignago [TN]
📞 +39 3440260170
🌐 www.corvee.wine

CELLAR SALES
PRE-BOOKED VISITS
ANNUAL PRODUCTION 50,000 bottles
HECTARES UNDER VINE 13.60

Here in the upper Val di Cembra they produce wines from vineyards spanning 400-700 meters in elevation. Classic Dolomitic wines like müller-thurgau, pinot grigio, pinot bianco, and riesling renano are crafted, as well as reds like pinot nero, lagrein, and schiava. Their portfolio also includes an obligatory Trento sparkler. The result is a range known for its pronounced varietal expression and finesse. The range presented this year is broad, with consistently high quality across the board. Some wines stand out for their complexity and typicity, such as the Viàch, a 2023 müller thurgau redolent of anise, citrus peel, and aromatic herbs. The palate is fresh, sapid, lithe, and very elegant. The Agole, Famei, and Corvaia—respectively, a pinot nero, riesling, and pinot grigio—also performed at excellent levels, while among the sparkling wines, both the Nature and the Rosé (both non-vintage) delivered.

De Vescovi Ulzbach

p.zza Garibaldi, 12
38016 Mezzocorona [TN]
📞 +39 04611740050
🌐 www.devescoviulzbach.it

CELLAR SALES
PRE-BOOKED VISITS
ANNUAL PRODUCTION 55,000 bottles
HECTARES UNDER VINE 8.00

The winery's vineyards unfold across the Piana Rotaliana, bordered by Mount Fausior to the south and Monticello to the north. The soil, ideal for cultivating teroldego, alternates between siliceous sands, silt, and layers of calcareous and volcanic pebbles. Winemaker Giulio de Vescovi has expanded beyond Trentino to experiment with Etna viticulture, aiming for wines that reflect their terroir with maximum elegance. All the reds presented performed at very high levels, with Teroldego the undisputed star. Once again, the Vigilius shines: 2021 made for a wine of great complexity, perfectly blending elegance, drinkability, structure, and depth. The Rosso Ulzbach, a fresh, juicy, and effortlessly drinkable Teroldego, is also very good, though not without character. The 2022 vintage is excellent as well. At the time of tasting, the Le Fron '21 was still slightly weighed down by tannins.

○ Trentino Müller Thurgau Viàch '23	♔♔ 3*
○ Trentino Pinot Grigio Corvaia '23	♔♔ 3
● Trentino Pinot Nero Àgole '22	♔♔ 6
○ Trentino Riesling Famei '23	♔♔ 3
☉ Trento Brut Rosé	♔♔ 5
○ Trento Nature	♔♔ 5
○ Trentino Gewürztraminer Clongiàn '23	♔ 3
● Trentino Lagrein Passocroce '22	♔ 3
○ Trentino Sauvignon Bisù '23	♔ 3
○ Trento Brut	♔ 5
○ Trentino Müller Thurgau Viàch '20	♔♔♔ 4*
○ Trentino Müller Thurgau Viàch '19	♔♔♔ 4*
○ Trentino Müller Thurgau Viàch '18	♔♔♔ 4*
○ Trentino Müller Thurgau Viàch '17	♔♔♔ 4*
● Trentino Pinot Nero Àgole '20	♔♔♔ 5

● Teroldego Rotaliano Vigilius '21	♔♔♔ 6
● Rosso Ulzbach '23	♔♔ 3
● Teroldego Rotaliano '22	♔♔ 4
● Teroldego Rotaliano Le Fron '21	♔ 6
● Teroldego Rotaliano '15	♔♔♔ 3*
● Teroldego Rotaliano V. Le Fron '16	♔♔♔ 6
● Teroldego Rotaliano Vigilius '20	♔♔♔ 5
● Teroldego Rotaliano Vigilius '19	♔♔♔ 5
● Teroldego Rotaliano Vigilius '18	♔♔♔ 5
● Teroldego Rotaliano Vigilius '12	♔♔♔ 5
● Kino Nero '16	♔♔ 4
● Rosso Ulzbach '22	♔♔ 3
● Teroldego Rotaliano '16	♔♔ 3*
● Teroldego Rotaliano V. Le Fron '19	♔♔ 6
● Teroldego Rotaliano Vigilius '16	♔♔ 5

De Vigili

via Molini, 28
38017 Mezzolombardo [TN]
📞 +39 3407780589
🌐 www.devigili.wine

CELLAR SALES
PRE-BOOKED VISITS
ACCOMMODATION
ANNUAL PRODUCTION 40,000 bottles
HECTARES UNDER VINE 5.00

Founded in 2015, this winery is better described as "reborn," given that the family has been producing wine since the 1800s. Now under the direction of Francesco, the producer is small in scale but big on quality. From the outset, Francesco committed to crafting artisanal wines that honor the territory and traditional grape varieties. He is a member of the TeRoldeGO(R) Evolution group, and it's no surprise that the best results come from the renowned teroldego grape of the Rotaliana plain. The two Teroldego Rotaliano wines presented hit the mark. Particularly, the Riserva Ottavio, which, with its strong personality, took home a gold. It's the first time for the winery, but it's a well-deserved achievement, considering the comprehensive work done. It opens with aromas of blackberry and spice, with a touch of underbrush introducing a creamy and elegant palate. The Tonalite '21 is simpler but still cut from the same cloth, offering freshness and sapidity. Among the whites, the pinot grigio and chardonnay are noteworthy. The Art, a Metodo Classico, also performed well.

● Teroldego Rotaliano Sup. Ottavio Ris. '19	🍷🍷🍷 6
● Teroldego Rotaliano Tonalite '21	🍷🍷 4
○ Contro Corrente Pinot Grigio '23	🍷🍷 3
○ Trentino Chardonnay Terre Bianche '22	🍷🍷 4
○ Trento Brut Art	🍷🍷 5
● Contro Corrente Teroldego '22	🍷 3
● Teroldego Rotaliano Sup. Ottaviano Ris. '17	🍷🍷 5
● Teroldego Rotaliano Sup. Ottaviano Ris. '16	🍷🍷 5
● Teroldego Rotaliano Sup. Ottavio Ris. '18	🍷🍷 7
○ Trentino Chardonnay Terre Bianche '19	🍷🍷 4

Marco Donati

via Cesare Battisti, 41
38016 Mezzocorona [TN]
📞 +39 0461604141
🌐 www.cantinadonatimarco.it

CELLAR SALES
PRE-BOOKED VISITS
ANNUAL PRODUCTION 100,000 bottles
HECTARES UNDER VINE 20.00
SUSTAINABLE WINERY

The year 1863 is prominently displayed on the Donati winery's sign, marking the estate's long history as a key player in the evolution of teroldego, the signature grape of the Campo Rotaliano. Marco Donati, who possesses the wisdom of a seasoned winemaker, has recently passed the torch to his young daughter Elisabetta, who's already making her mark among the emerging producers in the TeRoldeGO(R) Evolution group. The Donati family offers numerous selections, including wines from grapes grown in areas beyond their home vineyards, though they maintain a strong focus on tradition, yielding highly impressive results. The range continues to impress, not only with Teroldego but across multiple styles. The Sangue di Drago remains the standout, and the 2021 version, while not reaching the top, proves to be a well-crafted wine. It's close-knit, fresh, and sapid, combining drinkability with textbook complexity. The pinot nero and moscato rosa, a late harvest wine with balanced sweetness, are also excellent. Don't overlook the Cuvée del Drago, an Extrabrut Riserva '19 of rare finesse.

● Centa Pinot Nero '23	🍷🍷 4
⊙ Moscato Rosa V.T. '21	🍷🍷 3
● Teroldego Rotaliano Sup. Sangue di Drago Ris. '21	🍷🍷 4
○ Trento Extra Brut Cuvée del Drago Ris. '19	🍷🍷 6
● Trentino Lagrein Rubino V.V. '22	🍷 4
○ Trentino Müller Thurgau Albeggio '22	🍷 3
● Teroldego Rotaliano Sangue del Drago '98	🍷🍷🍷 5
● Teroldego Rotaliano Sangue di Drago '20	🍷🍷🍷 5
● Teroldego Rotaliano Bagolari '21	🍷🍷 4
● Teroldego Rotaliano Bagolari '19	🍷🍷 4
● Teroldego Rotaliano Sangue di Drago '19	🍷🍷 5

Endrizzi

loc. Masetto, 2
38098 San Michele all'Adige [TN]
☎ +39 0461650129
✉ www.endrizzi.it

CELLAR SALES
PRE-BOOKED VISITS
ANNUAL PRODUCTION 700,000 bottles
HECTARES UNDER VINE 55.00
SUSTAINABLE WINERY

A historic and passionate Trentino winemaking family now relies on the new generation: Paolo, Christine, Lisa Maria, and Daniele. Their agricultural approach is rooted in principles of sustainability, and their new winery was built according to bio-architecture standards. Most of their Trentodocs are produced from vineyards in Pian di Castello, at around 400 meters elevation. It's the Trentodoc Cuvées that surprised the tasting panel the most. Two wines made it to the final round: the Basiliscus and Piancastello Rosé. The first offers up floral, citrus, and almond notes, with a hint of pastry. On the palate, it's elegant, unveiling well-balanced acidity and sapidity harmonizing with bubbles. The second features blackberry, currant, raspberry, and wild strawberry notes, with a pervasive, soft mouthfeel and a crisp finish. The other Cuvées, such as the two Teroldego Rotaliano, also performed well, as did the rest of the range.

Etyssa

loc. Moià, 4
38121 Trento
☎ +39 3938922784
✉ www.etyssaspumanti.it

ANNUAL PRODUCTION 3,500 bottles
HECTARES UNDER VINE 14.00

Etyssa is the dream of four friends whose initial aim was to create high-quality bubbly that embodies the strength and character of great mountain wines. Their dream became reality with the 2012 harvest, which marked the release of their first Etyssa, each bottle meticulously numbered and vintage-dated to reflect the unique characteristics of the year. Some bottles are left to rest in the cellar, undisgorged, which led to the creation of their Riserva. Now in its second edition, this 2013 Riserva was disgorged after 105 months on the lees. The vineyard is small, and production is limited—especially for the Riserva—but the quality is consistently exceptional. The Cuvée Numero 8 hit its maximum potential, showcasing a broad, multifaceted nose with a slight hint of evolution, though still fragrant. The bubbles are creamy, the acidity adds freshness, and the sapidity carries the palate to a long finish. Truly a great wine. The Riserva '13 is also in excellent form.

○ Trento Brut Basiliscus '18	♀♀ 5
⊙ Trento Brut Rosé Piancastello Ris. '19	♀♀ 5
● Teroldego Rotaliano Sfere Nere Ris. '19	♀♀ 5
● Teroldego Rotaliano Sup. Leocorno '20	♀♀ 5
○ Trento Dosaggio Zero Masetto Privé Ris. '14	♀♀ 8
○ Trento Dosaggio Zero Piancastello Ris. '19	♀♀ 5
● Gran Masetto '20	♀ 8
● Teroldego Rotaliano '21	♀ 3
○ Trentino Pinot Grigio '22	♀ 3
● Gran Masetto '19	♀♀ 8
○ Masetto Doré '21	♀♀ 5
○ Trentino Riesling '22	♀♀ 4
⊙ Trento Brut Rosé Piancastello Ris. '17	♀♀ 5
○ Trento Zero Piancastello Ris. '17	♀♀ 5

○ Trento Extra Brut Cuvée N. 8 '19	♀♀♀ 5
○ Trento Nature Cuvée N. 2 Ris. '13	♀♀ 7
○ Trento Extra Brut Cuvée N. 2 '14	♀♀ 5
○ Trento Extra Brut Cuvée N. 2 '13	♀♀ 7
○ Trento Extra Brut Cuvée N. 3 '14	♀♀ 5
○ Trento Extra Brut Cuvée N. 4 '15	♀♀ 5
○ Trento Extra Brut Cuvée N. 5 '16	♀♀ 5
○ Trento Extra Brut Cuvée N. 6 '17	♀♀ 5
○ Trento Extra Brut Cuvée N. 7 '18	♀♀ 5

★★★Ferrari

via del Ponte, 15
38123 Trento
☎ +39 0461972311
🖅 www.ferraritrento.com

CELLAR SALES
PRE-BOOKED VISITS
RESTAURANT SERVICE
ANNUAL PRODUCTION 5,800,000 bottles
HECTARES UNDER VINE 100.00
SUSTAINABLE WINERY

1906 was pivotal for this Trento winery, as that was the year when Ferrari's sparkling wine won the gold medal at the International Exhibition in Milan, the first of many awards. Today a closely-knit family team leads the producer, demonstrating increasing sensitivity and adherence to their home territory year after year, while also remaining committed to preserving and promoting Trentino's cultural heritage. Their extraordinary lineup left us amazed, convincing on all fronts. Four wines made it to the finals, but excellent results were also achieved by the other Trentodoc wines presented as well. The Perlé '18 is a stellar sparkling wine, with a nose where golden apple meets lemon zest, mountain herbs, and pastry hints. The palate is vibrant, with perfect acidity lending tension and energy. Giulio Ferrari remains the winery's flagship, while the Riserva Lunelli 2016 showcases incredible complexity and a drinking rhythm that balances structure and finesse. Textbook.

○ Trento Extra Brut Riserva Lunelli '16	♈♈♈ 8
○ Trento Brut Perlé '18	♈♈ 6
○ Trento Brut Perlé Rosé Ris. '18	♈♈ 7
○ Trento Dosaggio Zero Giulio Ferrari Riserva del Fondatore '15	♈♈ 8
○ Trento Dosaggio Zero Perlé Nero Ris. '17	♈♈ 8
○ Trento Perlé Zero Cuvée Zero 17	♈♈ 8
○ Trento Brut Maximum	♈ 6
○ Trento Brut Giulio Ferrari Riserva del Fondatore '10	♈♈♈ 8
○ Trento Extra Brut Giulio Ferrari Riserva del Fondatore '12	♈♈♈ 8
○ Trento Extra Brut Perlé Nero Ris. '15	♈♈♈ 8

La Vis - Cembra

via Carmine, 7
38015 Lavis [TN]
☎ +39 0461440111
🖅 www.la-vis.com

CELLAR SALES
PRE-BOOKED VISITS
ACCOMMODATION
ANNUAL PRODUCTION 2,100,000 bottles
HECTARES UNDER VINE 700.00
VITICULTURE METHOD Certified Organic
SUSTAINABLE WINERY

Lavis is a cooperative winery that has distinguished itself as a leading and independent force in the Trentino wine landscape, backed by its 700 members who collectively manage an equal number of hectares of vineyards. The organization also oversees Cembra Cantina di Montagna, another coop established in 1952. In recent years, Lavis has embarked on a new business path focused on enhancing its unique viticultural heritage. It boasts "heroic" vineyards situated between 450 and 900 meters elevation, supported by 700 kilometers of dry stone walls that weave through the entire valley like a web. A wide range was presented, with most wines proving highly commendable. Among the main cooperative's wines, we particularly appreciated the Maso Franch, a manzoni bianco released several years after vintage. The 2018 is an energetic and youthful white. A new entry from Cembra took us by surprise: the Oro Rosso, a Trentodoc Dosaggio Zero that delivers complexity, depth, and great finesse. Notes of anise and white peach are echoed by a creamy, rhythmic palate. The Zymbra '19 also shines.

○ Trento Dosaggio Zero Oro Rosso Cembra '18	♈♈♈ 6
○ Maso Franch Manzoni Bianco La Vis '18	♈♈ 5
○ Zymbra Cembra '19	♈♈ 5
○ Nosiola La Vis '23	♈♈ 3
◉ Pinot Grigio Rosé La Vis '23	♈♈ 3
○ Trentino Chardonnay La Vis '23	♈♈ 3
○ Trentino Gewürztraminer La Vis '23	♈♈ 4
○ Trentino Müller Thurgau La Vis '23	♈♈ 3
● Trentino Pinot Nero La Vis '23	♈♈ 3
○ Trentino Riesling La Vis '23	♈♈ 3
○ Trentino Sauvignon La Vis '22	♈♈ 3
● Trentino Lagrein La Vis '23	♈ 3
○ Trentino Müller Thurgau Cembra '22	♈ 5
○ Trentino Riesling Cembra '21	♈ 5

★Letrari

via Monte Baldo, 13/15
38068 Rovereto [TN]
☎ +39 0464480200
✉ www.letrari.it

CELLAR SALES
PRE-BOOKED VISITS
ANNUAL PRODUCTION 160,000 bottles
HECTARES UNDER VINE 23.00

The Letrari family's story is one of deep passion for Trentino wine. The family's winemaking tradition began with Leonello Letrari, and its growth continues today under his daughter Lucia, a, oenologist known for producing sparkling wines with great character that capture the unique beauty and sensitivity of the Dolomite highlands. It's no coincidence that the 976 Riserva del Fondatore is their most convincing wine. Over ten years after harvest, the Riserva '13 summons complexity and allure. The nose goes all in on primary aromas of citrus and yellow-fleshed fruit, with a touch of evolution adding nutty whiffs and spices. The palate is pervasive, sapid, with a slightly smoky finish. The other Trentodoc Riserva and the Cuvée Blanche are also excellent. Lastly, the Quore Pienne, a 2016 Nature, also shines.

○ Trento Brut 976 Riserva del Fondatore '13	♟♟ 8
○ Trento Brut Cuvée Blanche	♟♟ 5
○ Trento Brut Nature Quore Pienne '16	♟♟ 8
⊙ Trento Brut Rosé +4 Ris. '15	♟♟ 7
● Ballistarius '19	♟ 5
○ Trento Dosaggio Zero '21	♟ 5
○ Trento Brut 976 Riserva del Fondatore '12	♟♟♟ 8
○ Trento Brut 976 Riserva del Fondatore '11	♟♟♟ 8
⊙ Trento Brut Rosé +4 '09	♟♟♟ 6
○ Trento Dosaggio Zero Letrari Ris. '15	♟♟♟ 6
○ Trento Dosaggio Zero Letrari Ris. '14	♟♟♟ 6
○ Trento Dosaggio Zero Letrari Ris. '12	♟♟♟ 6
○ Trento Dosaggio Zero Ris. '11	♟♟♟ 6

LeVide

b.go Italia, 22
38010 Predaia [TN]
☎ +39 3356245115
✉ www.levide.it

ANNUAL PRODUCTION 30,000 bottles
HECTARES UNDER VINE 6.00

Massimo Azzolini is dedicated to growing Vide while maintaining its meticulous, refined style. The vineyards, which are located in prized growing areas, are all dedicated to Metodo Classico, following the finest Trentino tradition. Mostly chardonnay is cultivated alongside pinot nero. From the vineyard to the winery, every process is followed with extreme precision, resulting in high-quality sparkling wines that express the best of what the territory has to offer Three Cuvées were presented, two of which made it to the final round of our tastings. The standout is the Cime di Altilia, an Extra Brut from the 2018 vintage. Anise, green tea, citrus zest, and pastry notes define the nose, while the palate is expansive, with nice volume, balanced by refreshing acidity and sapidity, particularly on the finish. We also appreciated the Maso Alesiera, despite the warm 2017 vintage. This Riserva, a Nature dosage, reveals mountain herb aromas and a crisp, deep palate. The Cime di Altilia Rosé proves enjoyable but leans more toward structure.

○ Trento Brut Nature Maso Alesiera Ris. '17	♟♟ 5
○ Trento Extra Brut Cime di Altilia '18	♟♟ 5
⊙ Trento Brut Rosé Cime di Altilia	♟ 5
○ Trento Brut Cime di Altilia '16	♟♟ 5
○ Trento Brut Nature Maso Alesiera '15	♟♟ 5
○ Trento Brut Nature Maso Alesiera Ris. '17	♟♟ 5
○ Trento Brut Nature Maso Alesiera Ris. '16	♟♟ 5
○ Trento Extra Brut Cime di Altilia '17	♟♟ 5
○ Trento Extra Brut Cime di Altilia '16	♟♟ 5
○ Trento Extra Brut Cime di Altilia '15	♟♟ 5

Man Spumanti

via Boscati, 25
38030 Giovo [TN]
📞 +39 3489238968
🌐 www.manspumanti.it

CELLAR SALES
PRE-BOOKED VISITS
ANNUAL PRODUCTION 20,000 bottles
HECTARES UNDER VINE 2.50

The name Man (meaning "hand" in Italian) was chosen by Mattia Clementi, an oenologist whose expertise is reflected in the artisanal nature of his wines. After years of working in small wineries in his native Valle di Cembra, Clementi decided to craft a few exquisite cuvées of Trentodoc. Production is small, just a few thousand bottles of six different wines that range from a Brut to a Nature Reserve, a Rosé, Blanc de Noirs, and Blanc de Blancs. The common denominator is elegance, finesse, perfectly balanced bubbles, and a refreshing vibrancy. Their best Cuvée hails from the 2016 vintage. It's a Riserva with no residual sugar, standing out for its complex nose and incredible drinkability. Aromas of nuts, particularly almond, along with a touch of white peach and citrus, define the nose, while the palate is fresh with acidity, sapid, and very, very long. The rest of the range is also outstanding, as evidenced by the delightful Brut '20.

Mas dei Chini

fraz. Martignano
via Bassano, 3
38121 Trento
📞 +39 0461821513
🌐 www.cantinamasdeichini.it

CELLAR SALES
ANNUAL PRODUCTION 55,000 bottles
HECTARES UNDER VINE 30.00

The historic 19th-century house that hosts the agriturismo showcases the long-standing connection between the Chini family and the region's winemaking traditions, a bond that dates back to 1906. Their range of authentic, high-quality wines focuses primarily on Trento DOC sparklers, while also honoring the tradition of grapes like gewürztraminer and teroldego. The Inkino Rosé is undoubtedly the best of the lineup. It's an Extra Brut that fully embodies the characteristics of mountain bubbly, thanks to its complex and expansive body, balanced by a lively, fresh acidity that dominates the palate, supported by abundant sapidity. On the finish, notes of pepper and berries bring back its aromatic profile. Among the still wines, a pleasant surprise comes from Theodor, a highly authentic manzoni bianco. The other Cuvées and the gewürztraminer are also excellent.

TRENTINO

○ Trento Nature Ris. '16	🍷🍷 7
○ Trento Brut '20	🍷🍷 6
○ Trento Brut Rosé '20	🍷🍷 5
○ Trento Nature Blanc de Blancs '19	🍷🍷 6
○ Trento Brut Nature Blanc de Noir '19	🍾 5
○ Trento Brut Rosè '19	🍾 5
○ Trento Brut Rosè '18	🍾 5
○ Trento Nature Blanc de Blancs '18	🍾 6
○ Trento Nature Blanc de Blancs '17	🍾 6

○ Trento Extra Brut Rosé Inkino '20	🍷🍷🍷 5
○ Theodor '23	🍷🍷 3*
○ Trentino Gewürztraminer '23	🍷🍷 4
○ Trento Brut Inkino '20	🍷🍷 5
○ Trento Brut Inkino Carlo V Ris. '15	🍷🍷 6
○ Trento Nature Inkino '19	🍷🍷 5
● Gloriano '21	🍷 4
● Trentino Lagrein '23	🍷 3
○ Trento Extra Brut Rosè Inkino '19	🍾🍾🍾 5
○ Theodor '22	🍾 4
○ Trento Brut Inkino '19	🍾 5
○ Trento Brut Inkino '17	🍾 5
○ Trento Brut Inkino Carlo V Ris. '14	🍾 6
○ Trento Brut Inkino Carlo V Ris. '12	🍾 6
○ Trento Extra Brut Rosè Inkino '18	🍾 6
○ Trento Nature Inkino '17	🍾 6

Maso Cantanghel

via Stazione, 19
38015 Lavis [TN]
☎ +39 0461246353
✉ www.masocantanghel.eu

CELLAR SALES
PRE-BOOKED VISITS
ANNUAL PRODUCTION 45,000 bottles
HECTARES UNDER VINE 10.50
VITICULTURE METHOD Certified Organic
SUSTAINABLE WINERY

Federico Simoni and his sister Chiara, under the supervision of their father Lorenzo, have contributed year after year to the winery's growth since taking over in 2006. Since then, the siblings have dedicated themselves to the vineyards, prioritizing ecosystem health and achieving organic certification in 2012. Their wines reflect the unique character of the Trentino region. Here we review not only the wines from Maso Cantanghel but also the Monfort Cuvées. At the top of the list is the Vigna Cantanghel, a standout among their still wines. It's a remarkable pinot nero from a single vineyard, featuring tones of small red fruits and spices. The palate is light yet sapid, with great length and a clean finish that runs deep. Among the Monfort wines, the Le Générale Dallemagne, a 2017 Brut Nature, impresses with its aromas of pastry and sweet spices, candied citrus, and medlar, leading to a richly textured palate marked by perfectly balanced bubbles and refreshing acidity. The Sotsas blend of white grapes also performs well.

● Trentino Pinot Nero V. Cantanghel '21	♛♛♛	5
○ SotSàs Cuvée '22	♛♛	4
○ Trento Brut Nature Le Générale Dallemagne Casata Monfort '17	♛♛	6
○ Corylus Nosiola '22	♛♛	4
○ Trentino Gewürztraminer V. Caselle '23	♛♛	4
○ Trentino Sauvignon '23	♛♛	4
⊙ Trento Brut Rosé Casata Monfort	♛♛	5
⊙ Trento Cuvée 85 Casata Monfort	♛♛	4
○ Trento Dosaggio Zero Le Général Blanc Casata Monfort '16	♛♛	6
○ Trentino Pinot Grigio '23	♛	3
● Trentino Pinot Nero V. Cantanghel '19	♛♛♛	5
● Trentino Pinot Nero V. Cantanghel '18	♛♛♛	5
● Trentino Pinot Nero V. Cantanghel '17	♛♛♛	5

Maso Martis

loc. Martignano
via dell'Albera, 52
38121 Trento
☎ +39 0461821057
✉ www.masomartis.it

CELLAR SALES
PRE-BOOKED VISITS
ANNUAL PRODUCTION 90,000 bottles
HECTARES UNDER VINE 11.00
VITICULTURE METHOD Certified Organic

Founded in 1990 by Antonio and Roberta Stelzer, this Trentino-based sparkling wine producer quickly gained recognition, and now churns out around 100,000 bottles annually. Daughters Alessandra and Maddalena have joined the team, contributing to a successful formula based on cohesive teamwork, attention to detail, vineyard health, and environmental protection. This year, they added a new Trentodoc Brut Nature, a monovarietal chardonnay, to their range. Across the entire range, we see high quality, though it's no surprise since the winery has consistently delivered excellent Cuvées for years. We start with the previously mentioned Blanc de Blancs. The new version, a 2021, has no sugar dosage, resulting in an elegant fizz with citrus, green apple and white flower sensations, as well as hints of almond. The palate is dry, sapid, with high but well-measured acidity and bubbles. The Rosé is also superb, a pervasive, smooth, and alluring Extra Brut '20 with notes of berries, spices, and subtle smoky hints. Kudos to the Blanc de Blancs and Dosaggio Zero Riserva '19 as well.

○ Trento Brut Nature Blanc de Blancs '21	♛♛	5
⊙ Trento Extra Brut Rosé '20	♛♛	5
○ Trento Brut Blanc de Blancs	♛♛	5
○ Trento Dosaggio Zero Ris. '19	♛♛	6
○ Trento Brut Madame Martis Ris. '10	♛♛♛	8
○ Trento Brut Madame Martis Ris. '09	♛♛♛	8
○ Trento Brut Madame Martis Ris. '08	♛♛♛	8
○ Trento Dosaggio Zero Ris. '12	♛♛♛	6
⊙ Trento Dosaggio Zero Ris. '11	♛♛♛	5
⊙ Trento Extra Brut Rosé '18	♛♛♛	5
⊙ Trento Brut Madame Martis Ris. '11	♛♛	8
⊙ Trento Brut Monsieur Martis Rosé '18	♛♛	7
⊙ Trento Brut Rosé de Noir Monsieur Martis '17	♛♛	7
○ Trento Dosaggio Zero Maso Martis Ris. '17	♛♛	5
○ Trento Dosaggio Zero Maso Martis Ris. Bio '16	♛♛	5

Mezzacorona

via del Teroldego, 1e
38016 Mezzocorona [TN]
☎ +39 0461616399
✉ www.mezzacorona.it

CELLAR SALES
PRE-BOOKED VISITS
ACCOMMODATION
ANNUAL PRODUCTION 48,000,000 bottles
HECTARES UNDER VINE 2800.00
SUSTAINABLE WINERY

Cooperative producer Mezzacorona is, above all, a family of 1,600 winegrowers who manage numerous hectares in some of Trentino's best growing areas. White varieties such as chardonnay, pinot bianco, and pinot grigio are favored, with these three grapes making up about 75% of production. There is, however, also space for native red grapes like teroldego rotaliano and lagrein. Their two flagship lines are Castel Firmiam and Musivum. The former shines with the Gewürztraminer '22, a wine of superb aromatic complexity, but with an elegant, dry palate that avoids excessive sweetness. The Müller Thurgau is also excellent. Among the reds, both the Lagrein and Teroldego stood out. Their Musivum wines (the name means "mosaic" in Latin) hail from small, special plots ideally suited to producing these emblematic varieties. Tasting the outstanding Pinot Grigio and Marzemino demonstrates just what these wines are capable of.

Moser

fraz. Gardolo di Mezzo
via Castel di Gardolo, 5
38121 Trento
☎ +39 0461990786
✉ www.mosertrento.com

CELLAR SALES
PRE-BOOKED VISITS
ANNUAL PRODUCTION 120,000 bottles
HECTARES UNDER VINE 17.00

Cousins Carlo and Matteo Moser have enhanced their winery's quality and personality by developing an extensive line of wines, focusing on Trentodoc bubbly. They remain rooted in the classicism of the region's sparkling wines while also experimenting, specializing in long aging processes and recently launching a white pinot noir aged for 72 months on the lees, sourced from Maso Marth's best vineyards (which go back some 80 years). But production goes beyond sparkling wines, as shown by the Trentino Riesling Warth, a stunning, complex, aromatic, and elegant white. In terms of their Trentodocs, two bottles stand out. One is the Rosé, an Extra Brut with great balance, and the other is the Nature '18, an incredibly refined wine, linear in its progression but also wrapping the palate with perfectly fused bubbles, acidity, and flavor. The rest of the range performs at a high level.

○ Trentino Gewürztraminer Sup. Castel Firmian '22	� 4
● Nerofino Castel Firmian '20	� 5
● Teroldego Rotaliano Sup. Castel Firmian Ris. '19	� 5
● Trentino Lagrein Castel Firmian Ris. '20	� 5
● Trentino Marzemino Sup. Musivum '17	� 8
○ Trentino Müller Thurgau Castel Firmian '23	� 3
○ Trentino Pinot Grigio Castel Firmian Ris. '22	� 5
○ Trentino Pinot Grigio Sup. Musivum '18	� 8
● Teroldego Rotaliano Nòs '19	♀♀ 6
○ Trentino Müller Thurgau Castel Firmian '21	♀♀ 3*

○ Trento Brut Nature '18	♉♉♉ 7
○ Trentino Riesling Warth '22	♉♉ 4
◉ Trento Extra Brut Rosé '19	♉♉ 6
○ Trento Brut 51,151	♉♉ 5
○ Trento Extra Brut Blanc de Noirs Blauen '17	♉♉ 8
○ Warth Moscato Giallo '23	♉♉ 3
● Warth Teroldego '22	♉♉ 5
○ Trentino Sauvignon Warth '22	♉ 5
○ Trento Brut Nature '15	♀♀♀ 6
○ Trento Brut Nature '14	♀♀♀ 5
○ Trento Brut Nature '12	♀♀♀ 5
○ Trento Extra Brut Blanc de Noir '15	♀♀♀ 6
○ Trento Extra Brut Rosé '18	♀♀♀ 6
● Rubro Teroldego Maso Warth '19	♀♀ 5
○ Trento Brut Nature '17	♀♀ 7

Pisoni Spumanti

loc. Sarche
fraz. Pergolese di Lasino
via San Siro, 7a
38076 Madruzzo
( )) +39 0461564106
✆ www.pisoni.it

CELLAR SALES
PRE-BOOKED VISITS
ANNUAL PRODUCTION 23,500 bottles
HECTARES UNDER VINE 16.00

A family of winemakers since 1852, this dynasty operates in the valley that stretches toward Lake Garda. Their journey began with a distillery—still in operation today—where they craft spirits from the finest grape pomace. The rest of production focuses exclusively on Trentodoc sparkling wines (while another branch of the family handles still wines). Their range fully embodies the essence of mountain bubbly, characterized by elegance, finesse, and the energy derived from grapes cultivated on high. The range presented by Pisoni confirms their return to the main section of our guide. Leading the way is the Riserva Erminia Segalla (dedicated to one of the family's ancestors), a Brut Nature from the 2016 vintage. The aromas are a perfect blend of more evolved notes of nuts, dried fruit and spices, alongside youthful tones of white flowers and citrus. The palate is crisp, unfolding on a linear profile, with impressive freshness. The other two Bruts are also excellent, along with the distinctive Extra Brut made from 100% pinot bianco.

○ Trento Brut Nature Erminia Segalla Ris. '16	♛♛ 8
○ Trento Brut '20	♛♛ 5
⊙ Trento Brut Rosé '20	♛♛ 6
○ Trento Extra Brut Pinot Bianco '20	♛♛ 6
○ Trento Nature '20	♛♛ 5
○ Trento Extra Brut Blanc de Noirs '20	♛ 6
○ Trento Brut Nature '18	♛♛ 5
○ Trento Brut Nature '16	♛♛ 5
○ Trento Extra Brut Blanc de Noirs '16	♛♛ 5
○ Trento Extra Brut Erminia Segalla '11	♛♛ 6
○ Trento Extra Brut Erminia Segalla Ris. '13	♛♛ 7

★Pojer & Sandri

fraz. Faedo
loc. Molini, 4
38010 San Michele all'Adige [TN]
( )) +39 0461650342
✆ www.pojeresandri.it

CELLAR SALES
PRE-BOOKED VISITS
ACCOMMODATION
ANNUAL PRODUCTION 200,000 bottles
HECTARES UNDER VINE 26.00
VITICULTURE METHOD Certified Organic

Pojer & Sandri, an artisan winery with a brazen history, was founded by Fiorentino Sandri and Mario Pojer. Their vineyards span six municipalities, including Faedo, San Michele all'Adige, and Grumes. Here they grow native grape varieties like nosiola and traminer, as well as müller thurgau and pinot noir. With their sons continuing their work, they have also ventured into cultivating disease-resistant varieties like zweigelt and franconia. Three wines were presented, each with its own unique charm and authenticity. Topping the list this year is the Mongramma '21, an energetic Müller Thurgau with complex acidity and a brackish note that carries through to a long finish. The Bianco Faye '20, a blend of chardonnay and pinot bianco, is also delicious, showing no fear of aging even four years after harvest. The Molinar, a delightful Extra Brut from the 2019 vintage, also made it to the finals.

○ Monogramma Müller Thurgau '21	♛♛♛ 5
○ Molinar Extra Brut M. Cl. '19	♛♛ 7
○ Faye Bianco '20	♛♛ 5
○ Faye Bianco '08	♛♛♛ 5
○ Faye Bianco '01	♛♛♛ 5
● Faye Rosso '05	♛♛♛ 5
● Faye Rosso '00	♛♛♛ 5
● Faye Rosso '94	♛♛♛ 5
● Faye Rosso '93	♛♛♛ 5
● Rodel Pianezzi Pinot Nero '09	♛♛♛ 5
○ Trentino Riesling '22	♛♛♛ 4*
○ Trentino Riesling '19	♛♛♛ 4*
● Faye Rosso '16	♛♛ 6
● Rodel Pianezzi Pinot Nero '18	♛♛ 5
○ Trentino Riesling '21	♛♛ 4
○ Trentino Riesling '20	♛♛ 4

Pravis

loc. Le Biolche, I
38076 Lasino [TN]
☎ +39 0461564305
⊛ www.pravis.it

CELLAR SALES
PRE-BOOKED VISITS
ANNUAL PRODUCTION 200,000 bottles
HECTARES UNDER VINE 32.00

Resistenti Nicola Biasi

fraz. Coredo
via San Romedio, 8
38012 Predaia [TN]
☎ +39 3474116854
⊛ www.resistentinicolabiasi.com

ANNUAL PRODUCTION 508 bottles
HECTARES UNDER VINE 0.35

The winery's name comes from a growing district chosen in 1974 by the three founding partners, Domenico, Gianni, and Mario. Today, Alessio and Silvio manage the fields, while Giulia and Erika handle the winery and sales, representing the second generation. Their best work remains tied to the classic production of Trentino wines, although they're also exploring contemporary viticulture by experimenting with resistant grape varieties. Six wines were presented, ranging from Metodo Classico to still wines. We begin with the latter, highlighting L'Ora, a wine whose name refers to the Garda wind that sweeps through the Valle dei Laghi. It exudes aromas of loquat, mountain flowers, and bitter herbs. On the palate, it's sapid and full-bodied, but never clumsy or unrefined. Another excellent wine is the juicy and graceful Pinot Nero, with the Teramara, Sauvignon '23 shining as well. Among the sparkling wines, both the Blau Dorè and Arìal—two Extra Bruts from the 2019 vintage—are noteworthy.

Biasi's winery aims to break the mold. Located in Coredo, high in the Trentino Dolomites, this project has been developing since 2013, focusing on cultivating disease-resistant varieties known as PIWI grapes, to ensure true environmental sustainability. This approach has given rise to the Vin de la Neu. This review covers the best wines from the producers within the Resistenti Nicola Biasi network, while the Vin de La Neu can be found in our "Rare Wines" section. The Renitens boasts an intense, balsamic nose with tones of mountain flowers and mint. The palate is taut, closing on a mineral note. The 3-6-9 '22 is subtler but exhibits good energy and progression. And this year, for all their efforts, the Resistenti Nicola Biasi project wins our Sustainability Award.

○ L'Ora '22	♔♔ 4
● Pinot Nero '20	♔♔ 4
○ Teramara Sauvignon '23	♔♔ 3
○ Trento Extra Brut Arìal '19	♔♔ 5
○ Trento Extra Brut Blau Dorè '19	♔♔ 5
● Fratagranda '16	♔ 6
● Fratagranda '10	♔♔♔ 4*
● Fratagranda '09	♔♔♔ 4*
● Fratagranda '07	♔♔♔ 4
○ L'Ora '21	♔♔♔ 4*
○ L'Ora Nosiola '18	♔♔♔ 4*
○ Stravino di Stravino '99	♔♔♔ 4*
○ Trentino Vino Santo Arèle '07	♔♔♔ 6
○ Vino Santo Arèle '06	♔♔♔ 6

○ Renitens	♔♔ 8
○ 3-6-9 '22	
Cà da Roman - Romano d'Ezzelino (VI)	♔♔ 5
○ Vin de la Neu '20	♔♔♔ 8
○ Baby Renitens '22	♔♔ 6
○ Renitens '22	♔♔ 6
○ Renitens '21	♔♔ 6
○ Vin de la Neu '21	♔♔ 8
○ Vin de la Neu '19	♔♔ 8
○ Vin de la Neu '18	♔♔ 8
○ Vin de la Neu '17	♔♔ 8
○ Vin de la Neu '15	♔♔ 8
○ Vin de la Neu '13	♔♔ 8

Revì

via Florida, 10
38060 Aldeno [TN]
☎ +39 0461843155
✉ www.revispumanti.com

CELLAR SALES
PRE-BOOKED VISITS
ANNUAL PRODUCTION 160,000 bottles
HECTARES UNDER VINE 10.00
VITICULTURE METHOD Certified Organic

Founded in 1982 in Aldeno by Paolo Malfer, the winery is now run by the second generation, Stefano and Giacomo, who continue to honor their father's philosophy by intertwining craftsmanship and innovation. Their wines fully embrace the Alpine character of their region, emphasizing freshness and finesse. The finesse of these wines is especially evident in the two Dosaggio Zeros. Both are well-crafted, with the 2020 surprising for its depth and complex nose, offering ginger, candied citrus, mountain herbs, and a fine bead that keeps everything light and elegant. Despite the vintage, the Blasé '17 is also excellent. Among the rest, we appreciate the floral and fruity Paladino '18, the Brut Revì '20—a perfect everyday sparkler—and the Cavaliere Nero '17, a structured cuvée that retains its vitality and energy.

★Rotari

via del Teroldego, 1e
38016 Mezzocorona [TN]
☎ +39 0461616399
✉ www.rotari.it

CELLAR SALES
PRE-BOOKED VISITS
ANNUAL PRODUCTION 2,500,000 bottles
HECTARES UNDER VINE 2800.00

Rotari is the branch of the Mezzacorona group dedicated to producing sparkling wines under the Trento appellation. Over the years, they have invested heavily in hospitality, constructing a winery with significant architectural value featuring a distinctive "wave roof" that echoes the movement of Trentino pergolas. The group promotes an inclusive policy, offering versatile wines that appeal to a diverse audience. This year, Rotari presented a highly respectable range of wines. Two made it to the podium, with the "usual" Flavio taking the top spot. This Riserva '16 proves remarkably complex, showcasing both the evolved notes from years on the lees and the youthful vibrancy of a great sparkling wine. The Pas Dosé, another Riserva from the 2018 vintage in the AlpeRegis line, is equally impressive. We also point out the Brut '18, Extra Brut '18, and the sapid, full-bodied Rosé '19 from the same line.

○ Trento Dosaggio Zero '20	♟♟♟ 5
○ Trento Dosaggio Zero Blasé '17	♟♟ 6
○ Trento Brut '20	♟♟ 5
○ Trento Brut Paladino '18	♟♟ 7
○ Trento Extra Brut Cavaliere Nero Ris. '17	♟♟ 6
○ Trento Brut Nature Re di Revì '14	♟ 8
○ Trento Extra Brut Re di Revì Ris. '12	♟♟♟ 8
○ Trento Brut '17	♟♟ 4
○ Trento Brut Paladino Ris. '16	♟♟ 5
⊙ Trento Brut Rosé '18	♟♟ 5
○ Trento Dosaggio Zero '18	♟♟ 5
○ Trento Extra Brut Cavaliere Nero '16	♟♟ 5
○ Trento Re di Revì Extra Brut Ris. '13	♟♟ 8
○ Trento Revì Dosaggio Zero Ris. '19	♟♟ 5

○ Trento Brut Rotari Flavio Ris. '16	♟♟♟ 8
○ Trento Pas Dosé AlpeRegis Ris. '18	♟♟ 7
○ Trento Brut AlpeRegis '18	♟♟ 6
⊙ Trento Brut Rosé AlpeRegis '19	♟♟ 7
○ Trento Extra Brut AlpeRegis '18	♟♟ 6
○ Trento Cuvée 28	♟ 5
○ Trento Brut Rotari Flavio Ris. '10	♟♟♟ 8
○ Trento Brut Rotari Flavio Ris. '15	♟♟♟ 8
○ Trento Brut Rotari Flavio Ris. '14	♟♟♟ 7
○ Trento Brut Rotari Flavio Ris. '13	♟♟♟ 6
○ Trento Brut Rotari Flavio Ris. '12	♟♟♟ 8
○ Trento Brut Rotari Flavio Ris. '11	♟♟♟ 8

★★San Leonardo

loc. San Leonardo, I
38063 Avio [TN]
📞 +39 0464689004
🌐 www.sanleonardo.it

CELLAR SALES
PRE-BOOKED VISITS
ACCOMMODATION
ANNUAL PRODUCTION 350,000 bottles
HECTARES UNDER VINE 45.00
VITICULTURE METHOD Certified Organic
SUSTAINABLE WINERY

From an ancient monastery to a wine estate, for three centuries San Leonardo has remained the residence of the Marquis Guerrieri Gonzaga family, who cultivates the vast estate according to organic methods. This iconic winery is renowned globally for its prestigious reds, made from international grape varieties, foremost among them the San Leonardo. With this wine, Carlo Guerrieri Gonzaga and his son Anselmo have captured the palates of wine enthusiasts worldwide. The prestigious red bearing the winery's name hails from the magnificent 2019 vintage, and its fruits are evident in the glass. Elegance, finesse, softness, and energy characterize the wine, which combines the depth of a complex, structured red with the lightness imparted by the soils and climate of the Dolomites. Truly a masterpiece. Echoing its success is the Terre di San Leonardo, which is far from a "second-tier wine," but rather another great red whose drinkability is its greatest asset. Somewhere in between is the ever-reliable Villa Gresti, alongside a lively and carefree Rosé. Bravo!

● San Leonardo '19	♔♔♔ 8
● Terre di San Leonardo '21	♔♔ 4
◉ Trentino Lagrein Rosé Gemma di San Leonardo '23	♔♔ 4
● Villa Gresti '20	♔♔ 6
○ Vette di San Leonardo '23	♔ 3
● San Leonardo '18	♕♕♕ 8
● San Leonardo '17	♕♕♕ 8
● San Leonardo '16	♕♕♕ 8
● San Leonardo '15	♕♕♕ 8
● San Leonardo '14	♕♕♕ 8
● San Leonardo '13	♕♕♕ 8
● San Leonardo '11	♕♕♕ 8
● San Leonardo '10	♕♕♕ 7
● San Leonardo '08	♕♕♕ 7
● San Leonardo '07	♕♕♕ 7

Cantina Toblino

fraz. Sarche
via Longa, I
38076 Madruzzo
📞 +39 0461564168
🌐 www.toblino.it

CELLAR SALES
PRE-BOOKED VISITS
RESTAURANT SERVICE
ANNUAL PRODUCTION 500,000 bottles
HECTARES UNDER VINE 840.00
VITICULTURE METHOD Certified Organic

A historic cooperative based in Valle dei Laghi, Toblino encompasses a network of 600 growers. In recent years, the coop has increasingly embraced sustainable practices and organic farming. Local varieties like nosiola and rebo are symbols of pride and identity for the winery, which continues to produce bottles that are almost rare for these representative varietals. An example is their Vino Santo, produced using an exceptionally long, natural drying process. While we await the next tasting of their prestigious sweet wine, we enjoyed the L'Ora, a Nosiola from the 2020 vintage, which, four years post-harvest, still delivers youthful primary aromas. Loquat, apricot, white flowers, and mountain herbs meet a sapid, voluptuous palate driven by incredible sapidity. Even more surprising is the aging potential of the Largiller 2016. There's also room for several lively Trentodoc sparklers that certainly hold their own against the still wines. The elegant and harmonious Vent Riserva '16 and Antares Nature '19 are prime examples.

○ L'Ora Nosiola '20	♔♔ 4
○ Largiller Nosiola '16	♔♔ 5
○ Trento Brut Antares '20	♔♔ 5
○ Trento Brut Nature Antares '19	♔♔ 5
○ Trento Extra Brut Vent '20	♔♔ 5
○ Trento Nature Vent Ris. '16	♔♔ 6
● Trentino Pinot Nero Bent Baticor '20	♔ 6
● Trentino Rebo Elimarò '19	♔ 4
○ L'Ora Nosiola '15	♕♕♕ 3*
○ Trentino Nosiola Largiller '13	♕♕♕ 5
○ Trentino Vino Santo '03	♕♕♕ 6
○ L'Ora Nosiola '16	♕♕ 3*
○ Trentino Vino Santo '06	♕♕ 6
○ Trentino Vino Santo '05	♕♕ 5

OTHER WINERIES

Avio
via Dante, 14
38063 Avio [TN]
(℡ +39 0464684008
⊕ www.viticoltoriinavio.it

CELLAR SALES
PRE-BOOKED VISITS
ANNUAL PRODUCTION 50,000 bottles
HECTARES UNDER VINE 700.00

● Ager Lagari Teroldego '22	♟♟ 4
○ Trentino Gewürztraminer '23	♟♟ 3
○ Trento Brut Sarnis Bianco	♟♟ 5
● Valdadige Terra dei Forti Ager Lagari '19	♟♟ 4

Cantina Sociale di Trento
via dei Viticoltori, 2/4
38123 Trento
(℡ +39 0461920186
⊕ www.cantinasocialetrento.it

CELLAR SALES
ANNUAL PRODUCTION 750,000 bottles
HECTARES UNDER VINE 100.00
VITICULTURE METHOD Certified Organic
SUSTAINABLE WINERY

○ Trentino Gewürztraminer Goccia d'Oro '23	♟♟ 3
○ Trento Brut Nature Zèll	♟♟ 5
⊙ Trento Brut Rosé Zèll	♟♟ 5
○ Trento Brut Zèll	♟♟ 5

★Dorigati
via Dante, 5
38016 Mezzocorona [TN]
(℡ +39 0461605313
⊕ www.dorigati.it

CELLAR SALES
PRE-BOOKED VISITS
ANNUAL PRODUCTION 100,000 bottles
HECTARES UNDER VINE 10.00
SUSTAINABLE WINERY

● Teroldego Rotaliano Luigi V. Sottodossi Ris. '21	♟♟ 6
● Teroldego Rotaliano '22	♟ 3
● Teroldego Rotaliano Diedri Ris. '21	♟ 5

Bossi Fedrigotti
via Unione, 43
38068 Rovereto [TN]
(℡ +39 0456832511
⊕ www.bossifedrigotti.com

CELLAR SALES
PRE-BOOKED VISITS
ANNUAL PRODUCTION 120,000 bottles
HECTARES UNDER VINE 40.00
SUSTAINABLE WINERY

○ Trento Brut Conte Federico Ris. '20	♟♟ 6
○ Vign'Asmara Chardonnay '23	♟♟ 5
○ Valdadige Pinot Grigio Pian del Griso '23	♟ 4

Cesarini Sforza
fraz. Ravina
via Stella, 9
38123 Trento
(℡ +39 0461382200
⊕ www.cesarinisforza.com

CELLAR SALES
PRE-BOOKED VISITS
ANNUAL PRODUCTION 1,000,000 bottles
HECTARES UNDER VINE 800.00

○ Trento Dosaggio Zero Noir 1673 Ris. '16	♟♟ 5
⊙ Trento Brut Rosé	♟♟ 4
○ Trento Brut Rosé 1673 '17	♟♟ 5
○ Trento Brut	♟ 5

Gaierhof
via IV Novembre, 51
38030 Roverè della Luna [TN]
(℡ +39 0461658514
⊕ www.gaierhof.com

CELLAR SALES
PRE-BOOKED VISITS
ANNUAL PRODUCTION 800,000 bottles
HECTARES UNDER VINE 150.00
SUSTAINABLE WINERY

⊙ Trento Brut Siris Rosé	♟♟ 4
● Trentino Lagrein '23	♟♟ 3
○ Trentino Moscato Giallo Dolce '23	♟♟ 3
○ Trentino Nosiola '22	♟♟ 2*

OTHER WINERIES

Grigoletti
via Garibaldi, 12
38060 Nomi [TN]
☎ +39 0464834215
✉ www.grigoletti.com

CELLAR SALES
PRE-BOOKED VISITS
ANNUAL PRODUCTION 60,000 bottles
HECTARES UNDER VINE 7.00

○ Retiko '21	♟♟ 5
○ Trentino Chardonnay L'Opera '23	♟♟ 4
● Trentino Marzemino '23	♟ 3

Cantina Klinger
fraz. Pressano
via Clinga, 16
38015 Lavis [TN]
☎ +39 3341539034
info@klingerpilati.it

ANNUAL PRODUCTION 35,000 bottles
HECTARES UNDER VINE 5.00

○ Trentino Gewürztraminer '22	♟♟ 4
○ Nosiola '21	♟♟ 4
○ Pizpor Chardonnay '21	♟ 3

Martinelli
via Castello, 10
38016 Mezzocorona [TN]
☎ +39 3388288686
✉ www.cantinamartinelli.com

CELLAR SALES
PRE-BOOKED VISITS
ANNUAL PRODUCTION 25,000 bottles
HECTARES UNDER VINE 3.50
SUSTAINABLE WINERY

● Teroldego Rotaliano Maso Chini '21	♟♟ 5
● Teroldego Rotaliano '21	♟♟ 4
○ Trentino Chardonnay '23	♟ 4
● Trentino Lagrein '21	♟ 5

Maso Poli
loc. Masi di Pressano, 33
38015 Lavis [TN]
☎ +39 0461871519
✉ www.masopoli.com

CELLAR SALES
PRE-BOOKED VISITS
ANNUAL PRODUCTION 75,000 bottles
HECTARES UNDER VINE 13.00

○ Trentino Riesling '23	♟♟ 3*
○ Trentino Nosiola '22	♟♟ 3
○ Trentino Pinot Grigio '23	♟♟ 3
○ Trentino Gewürztraminer '23	♟ 4

Pisoni Agricola
loc. Sarche
fraz. Pergolese
via San Siro, 7a
38076 Madruzzo
☎ +39 0461563214
✉ www.pisonivini.it

CELLAR SALES
PRE-BOOKED VISITS
ANNUAL PRODUCTION 23,500 bottles
HECTARES UNDER VINE 16.00

○ Trentino Vino Santo '08	♟♟ 6
○ Annada Nosiola '22	♟♟ 5
● Reboro Rebo '19	♟♟ 7
○ Folada Nosiola '23	♟ 5

Agraria Riva del Garda
loc. San Nazzaro, 4
38066 Riva del Garda [TN]
☎ +39 0464552133
✉ www.agririva.it

CELLAR SALES
PRE-BOOKED VISITS
ANNUAL PRODUCTION 250,000 bottles
HECTARES UNDER VINE 280.00

○ Trentino Pinot Grigio Vista Lago '22	♟♟ 3
● Trentino Pinot Nero Maso Elèsi '21	♟♟ 5
○ Trentino Sauvignon Sup. Dòs de Noà '22	♟♟ 4
○ Trento Pas Dosé Brezza Ris. '19	♟♟ 6

OTHER WINERIES

Cantina Romanese

s.da prov.le 11, 52
38056 Levico Terme [TN]
(') +39 3473817590
⊕ www.cantinaromanese.com

○ Trento Dosaggio Zero Lagorai '19	♟♟ 7
● Trentino Rebo Narciso '23	♟♟ 3
○ Trento Brut Ris. '19	♟♟ 8

Armando Simoncelli

via Navesel, 7
38068 Rovereto [TN]
(') +39 0464432373
⊕ www.simoncelli.it

CELLAR SALES
PRE-BOOKED VISITS
ANNUAL PRODUCTION 90,000 bottles
HECTARES UNDER VINE 10.50

● Trentino Cabernet Franc '22	♟♟ 2*
○ Trentino Chardonnay '23	♟♟ 2*
● Trentino Lagrein '23	♟♟ 3
● Schiava '23	♟ 3

Villa Corniole

fraz. Verla
via al Grec', 23
38030 Giovo [TN]
(') +39 0461695067
⊕ www.villacorniole.com

CELLAR SALES
PRE-BOOKED VISITS
ACCOMMODATION
ANNUAL PRODUCTION 75,000 bottles
HECTARES UNDER VINE 10.00
SUSTAINABLE WINERY

○ Trento Brut Salísa '20	♟♟ 5
⊙ Trento Extra Brut Rosé Salísa '21	♟♟ 5
○ Trento Pas Dosé Salisa Zero '18	♟♟ 5
○ Trentino Müller Thurgau Sup. Petramontis '23	♟ 4

Arcangelo Sandri

loc. Faedo
via Vanegge, 4a
38010 San Michele all'Adige [TN]
(') +39 0461650935
⊕ www.arcangelosandri.it

CELLAR SALES
PRE-BOOKED VISITS
ANNUAL PRODUCTION 22,000 bottles
HECTARES UNDER VINE 3.00

○ Kerner '23	♟♟ 3
○ Trentino Gewürztraminer Razer '23	♟♟ 3
● Trentino Lagrein Capòr '20	♟♟ 4
○ Trentino Müller Thurgau Cosler '23	♟♟ 3

Terre del Lagorai

via Lagarine
38050 Scurelle [TN]
(') +39 0461762223
⊕ www.terredellagorai.it

CELLAR SALES
PRE-BOOKED VISITS
ACCOMMODATION
ANNUAL PRODUCTION 50,000 bottles
HECTARES UNDER VINE 10.00
SUSTAINABLE WINERY

○ Trento Extra Brut Karl '21	♟♟ 5
○ Trento Extra Brut Rosé Franz '21	♟♟ 5
○ Trentino Chardonnay '23	♟ 3

Roberto Zeni

fraz. Grumo
via Stretta, 2
38010 San Michele all'Adige [TN]
(') +39 0461650456
⊕ www.zeni.tn.it

CELLAR SALES
PRE-BOOKED VISITS
ANNUAL PRODUCTION 150,000 bottles
HECTARES UNDER VINE 14.00
VITICULTURE METHOD Certified Organic

● Ternet Schwarzhof Teroldego '19	♟♟ 5
● Teroldego Rotaliano Lealbere '21	♟♟ 4
○ Trento Dosaggio Zero Maso Nero '17	♟ 7

ALTO ADIGE

The vineyards of Alto Adige are nestled within a few thousand hectares that stretch across the hillsides along the Adige and Eisack rivers. What's not immediately apparent in this description is the remarkable diversity of the terrain, which ranges from 220 meters elevation in the valley floor to over 1000 meters in Bassa Atesina and Renon, where calcareous soils alternate with silt- and porphyry-rich terrain, and where the slopes shift exposures in every direction. The area is also home to a rich variety of grape varieties and an even greater diversity of vineyards. Thousands of different families interpret the land and its harvests. The result is an exceptionally high-caliber array that increasingly reflects the region's complexity. Nowadays, wineries no longer cultivate all the varieties permitted under the appellation, but instead focus on those that best express their connection to the territory. Old, struggling vines aren't replaced haphazardly, but swapped with those better suited to the environment, seeking freshness at higher elevations or taking advantage of warmer exposures with appropriate grapes.

The vines shielded from the afternoon sun in the areas of Magrè and Sella are ideal for chardonnay. In Bolzano, lagrein is the star. We already know Mazzon's reputation for pinot nero, but the pinots from the nearby Appiano Monte area are proving increasingly impressive. Pinot bianco asserts its historical importance in many areas, from Sirmian near Nalles to Tirolo in Burgraviato, while in Terlano, it shines both as a single-varietal wine and as a key player in Terlaner blends. Riesling has found its ideal home in the higher parts of the Vinschgau and Eisack valleys, just as sylvaner, kerner, and grüner veltliner are deeply connected to the region's easternmost production zones.

Schiava, while becoming less common, still reigns supreme in the best growing areas of Caldaro and Santa Maddalena. Glögglhof's limited-production Santa Maddalena Vigna Rondell R '22 earned a place among our Rare Wines. We close with the debut of Lorenz Martini among our Tre Bicchieri winners, with his Comitissa, a sparkling wine of superb tension and finesse. In an edition that sees 24 wines earning the coveted Tre Bicchieri, there is also a special award, which goes to Colterenzio's extraordinary Alto Adige Sauvignon Gran Lafóa Riserva '21. It's our pick for White of the Year.

★★Abbazia di Novacella

fraz. Novacella
via Abbazia, 1
39040 Varna/Vahrn [BZ]
☏ +39 0472836189
✉ www.abbazianovacella.it

CELLAR SALES
PRE-BOOKED VISITS
RESTAURANT SERVICE
ANNUAL PRODUCTION 900,000 bottles
HECTARES UNDER VINE 30.00
SUSTAINABLE WINERY

The Abbey of Novacella boasts vineyards spread out across two distinct areas: the cool Eisack Valley, where white grape varieties root in light morainic soil, and around the capital, where schiava and lagrein thrive on the porphyry rocks of the northern hills. Finally, pinot nero is grown on the clay-limestone soils of Cornaiano. The warm 2022 vintage endowed the Riesling Praepositus with a wide array of fruity aromas, from intense notes of exotic fruit to chamomile, intertwined with smoky and sulfurous nuances. On the palate, it reveals a juicy profile, well supported by a lively acidity. The 2022 Sylvaner of the same name appears more closed and timid on the nose, but unveils sapidity and nice richness on the palate. The 2022 Grüner Veltliner Praepositus plays on on smoky aromas, yellow fruit, and a vibrant palate, while the 2021 Kerner Passito impresses with its broad aromatic range and harmonious palate.

★Tenuta Ansitz Waldgries

via Santa Giustina, 2
39100 Bolzano/Bozen
☏ +39 0471323603
✉ www.waldgries.it

CELLAR SALES
PRE-BOOKED VISITS
ANNUAL PRODUCTION 70,000 bottles
HECTARES UNDER VINE 8.70

Christian Plattner's winery is set on the hills surrounding Bolzano towards the Eisack Valley. Sunny slopes caressed by Alpine breezes on Ritten, historically the cradle of schiava, and just below, the home of lagrein. Over the years, the estate has expanded to the Oltradige area, where pinot bianco and sauvignon are cultivated. Known and appreciated mainly for its reds, this winery consistently offers highly worthy selection of whites as well, among which the 2021 Sauvignon Sàcalis stands out. This Riserva features a broad aromatic spectrum, beginning with smoky notes and opening up to white fruit, flowers, and a curious sulfurous note. The palate is crisp, defined by tension and sapidity. In terms of their reds, the Santa Maddalena '23 stood out for its immediately expressive fruit and spices, which translate into a juicy, very sapid palate with unfaltering drinkability.

○ A.A. Valle Isarco Riesling Praepositus '22	♟♟♟ 6
○ A.A. Valle Isarco Sylvaner Praepositus '22	♟♟ 5
● A.A. Lagrein Praepositus Ris. '20	♟♟ 6
● A.A. Moscato Rosa Praepositus '21	♟♟ 6
● A.A. Pinot Nero Praepositus Ris. '20	♟♟ 6
○ A.A. Sauvignon Praepositus '22	♟♟ 5
○ A.A. Valle Isarco Gewürztraminer Praepositus '22	♟♟ 5
○ A.A. Valle Isarco Grüner Veltliner Praepositus '22	♟♟ 5
○ A.A. Valle Isarco Kerner Passito Praepositus '21	♟♟ 6
○ A.A. Valle Isarco Kerner Praepositus '22	♟♟ 5

○ A.A. Sauvignon Sàcalis Ris. '21	♟♟♟ 6
● A.A. Santa Maddalena Cl. '23	♟♟ 3+
● A.A. Lagrein Mirell Ris. '21	♟♟ 7
● A.A. Lagrein Ris. '21	♟♟ 5
● A.A. Moscato Rosa Passito '23	♟♟ 6
○ A.A. Pinot Bianco Itos Ris. '21	♟♟ 5
● A.A. Santa Maddalena Cl. Antheos '22	♟♟ 5
○ A.A. Sauvignon Myra '22	♟♟ 4
● A.A. Lagrein Mirell Ris. '15	♟♟♟ 6
● A.A. Santa Maddalena Cl. '21	♟♟♟ 3+
● A.A. Santa Maddalena Cl. '19	♟♟♟ 3+
● A.A. Santa Maddalena Cl. Antheos '16	♟♟♟ 5
● A.A. Santa Maddalena Cl. Antheos '13	♟♟♟ 4+
● A.A. Santa Maddalena Cl. Antheos '12	♟♟♟ 4+

★★★Cantina Bozen

via San Maurizio, 36
39100 Bolzano/Bozen
📞 +39 0471270909
🌐 www.cantinabolzano.com

CELLAR SALES
PRE-BOOKED VISITS
ANNUAL PRODUCTION 3,000,000 bottles
HECTARES UNDER VINE 350.00
SUSTAINABLE WINERY

This Bolzano cooperative is one of the province's most important entities, relying on a small army of members cultivating over 300 hectares of vineyards ranging from 200 meters in the valley to 1000 meters in Ritten. Each grape variety finds its ideal position, leveraging both elevations and soil composition, making for wines that combine richness and elegance. Lagrein remains the winery's crown jewel, and this year saw a performance to remember by the 2022 Taber. Its classic, dense color serves as the prelude to aromas dominated by dark fruit, with supporting roles from spices, macerated flowers, and underbrush. On the palate, the wine's compactness gains suppleness and tension thanks to an invaluable acidic drive. Both the complex and harmonious 2022 Sauvignon Greel and the immediately expressive Huck am Bach '23, a Santa Maddalena, stand out for their freshness and impressive drinkability.

A.A. Lagrein Taber Ris. '22	🍷🍷🍷	8
A.A. Santa Maddalena Cl. Huck am Bach '23	🍷🍷	4
A.A. Sauvignon Greel Ris. '22	🍷🍷	6
A.A. Chardonnay Stegher Ris. '22	🍷🍷	6
A.A. Gewürztraminer Kleinstein '23	🍷🍷	5
A.A. Lagrein Merlot Mauritius '22	🍷🍷	7
A.A. Lagrein Prestige Ris. '22	🍷🍷	6
A.A. Moscato Giallo Passito Vinalia '22	🍷🍷	7
A.A. Pinot Bianco Dellago '23	🍷🍷	4
A.A. Pinot Nero Thalman '21	🍷🍷	6
A.A. Santa Maddalena Cl. Moar '23	🍷🍷	5
A.A. Sauvignon Mock '23	🍷🍷	4
A.A. Lagrein Taber Ris. '21	🍷🍷🍷	6
A.A. Lagrein Taber Ris. '20	🍷🍷🍷	6

Josef Brigl

loc. San Michele-Appiano
via Madonna del Riposo, 3
39057 Appiano/Eppan [BZ]
📞 +39 0471662419
🌐 www.brigl.com

CELLAR SALES
PRE-BOOKED VISITS
ACCOMMODATION
ANNUAL PRODUCTION 500,000 bottles
HECTARES UNDER VINE 50.00
SUSTAINABLE WINERY

The Brigl family is among the select few that have shaped the history of Alto Adige wine, showing a consistent commitment to both the development of high-quality viticulture and the global marketing of their wines. A sizable set of vineyards are the crown jewels of their three family estates: Haselhof in Colterenzio, Rielerhof on the slopes of Renon, and Windegg on the upper reaches of Caldaro. From the beautiful Haselhof vineyard come some of their most convincing wines, with our personal favorite being the 2021 Pinot Nero. It features a delicate aromatic profile that slowly opens to notes of wild fruit and medicinal herbs. On the palate, it develops lightly but well supported by sapidity. The 2023 Gewürztraminer, sourced from Windegg, stands out for its aromatic intensity, reminiscent of candied citrus and classic rose notes. On tasting, it proves medium-bodied, stretching gracefully towards a long, crisp finish.

A.A. Pinot Nero V. Haselhof '21	🍷🍷	5
A.A. Gewürztraminer V. Windegg '23	🍷🍷	5
A.A. Lago di Caldaro Cl. V. Windegg '23	🍷🍷	4
A.A. Pinot Bianco V. Haselhof '22	🍷🍷	5
A.A. Riesling V. Rielerhof '23	🍷🍷	4
A.A. Sauvignon V. Rielerhof '23	🍷	4
A.A. Pinot Grigio Windegg '11	🍷🍷🍷	3*
A.A. Chardonnay Seduction Ris. '20	🍷🍷	5
A.A. Gewürztraminer V. Windegg '22	🍷🍷	4
A.A. Lago di Caldaro Cl. V. Windegg '22	🍷🍷	3
A.A. Pinot Bianco V. Haselhof '21	🍷🍷	4
A.A. Pinot Bianco V. Haselhof '20	🍷🍷	4
A.A. Pinot Grigio V. Windegg '22	🍷🍷	4
A.A. Pinot Nero Ris. '19	🍷🍷	3
A.A. Riesling V. Rielerhof '22	🍷🍷	4
A.A. Sauvignon V. Rielerhof '22	🍷🍷	4

ALTO ADIGE

Brunnenhof Kurt Rottensteiner

loc. Mazzon
via degli Alpini, 5
39044 Egna/Neumarkt [BZ]
℡ +39 0471820687
✉ www.brunnenhof-mazzon.it

CELLAR SALES
PRE-BOOKED VISITS
ANNUAL PRODUCTION 35,000 bottles
HECTARES UNDER VINE 5.50
VITICULTURE METHOD Certified Organic

The Rottensteiner family's winery nestles on west-facing slopes in the Mazzon area, the heart of Alto Adige pinot nero. The few hectares cultivated extend from 280 meters at Villa, where heat-loving varieties are grown, to 450 meters in higher areas dedicated primarily to pinot nero and partially to gewürztraminer. They compensate for a small range with character and depth. This character is also found in the 2021 Pinot Nero, where vibrant notes of medicinal herbs and minerals keep wild fruit in the background. On tasting, the full strength of the terroir emerges, with a palate rich and well-supported by tannins and acidity, which add vigor. The 2022 Lagrein is more approachable in its aromas—focused on dark fruit and fine herbs. But on the palate, it shifts gears, revealing the character of the Ora vineyards, more linear and supported by acidity rather than tannic rigor.

Castel Sallegg

v.lo di Sotto, 15
39052 Caldaro/Kaltern [BZ]
℡ +39 0471963132
✉ www.castelsallegg.it

CELLAR SALES
PRE-BOOKED VISITS
ANNUAL PRODUCTION 200,000 bottles
HECTARES UNDER VINE 30.00

In recent years, this Caldaro winery has raised the bar, building on the attributes of its extensive estate. They have revamped the style and packaging of their wines, and made the bold yet crucial decision to slow down their release, allowing the wines to mature at a natural pace. The vineyard's focal point is the Caldaro area, with vines stretching from the lakeside up to higher elevations. Many wines have been left to rest in the cellar, but the Bordeaux varieties hold the producer's flag high. The 2020 Merlot Nussleiten is sourced from the Seehof vineyard, with its sandy, silty soil and notable presence of calcareous gravel. This composition allows the grapes to mature perfectly and develop rich nuances. On the nose, red fruit dominates, gradually giving way to spices and medicinal herbs. The palate is sapid and perfectly supported by tannins and acidity. The 2020 Cabernet Sauvignon, more approachable and fresh on the nose, offers a lively and harmonious palate.

Wine	Rating
● A.A. Pinot Nero Mazzon Ris. '21	♟♟ 5
○ A.A. Chardonnay Mühlanger Ris. '22	♟♟ 5
● A.A. Lagrein Mühlanger '22	♟♟ 5
○ Eva Manzoni Bianco '23	♟♟ 4
○ A.A. Spumante Brut M. Cl. Brunnenhof 25 '18	♟ 5
○ A.A. Chardonnay '21	♟♟ 4
○ A.A. Chardonnay '20	♟♟ 4
● A.A. Lagrein '20	♟♟ 5
● A.A. Pinot Nero Mazzon Ris. '20	♟♟ 5
● A.A. Pinot Nero Mazzon Ris. '19	♟♟ 5
● A.A. Pinot Nero Mazzon Ris. '17	♟♟ 5
● A.A. Pinot Nero V. Zis Ris. '18	♟♟ 5
○ Eva Manzoni Bianco '22	♟♟ 4
○ Eva Manzoni Bianco '21	♟♟ 4

Wine	Rating
● A.A. Merlot Nussleiten Ris. '20	♟♟ 6
● A.A. Cabernet Sauvignon Ris. '20	♟♟ 5
● A.A. Merlot Ris. '19	♟♟ 6
● A.A. Lago di Caldaro Scelto Sup. Bischofsleiten '15	♟♟♟ 2
● A.A. Merlot Nussleiten Ris. '19	♟♟♟ 6
● A.A. Merlot Nussleiten Ris. '18	♟♟♟ 6
● A.A. Merlot Nussleiten Ris. '17	♟♟♟ 6
● A.A. Cabernet Sauvignon Ris. '19	♟♟ 5
○ A.A. Chardonnay Marei '21	♟♟ 5
● A.A. Lago di Caldaro Cl. Sup. Bischofsleiten '22	♟♟ 3
● A.A. Lago di Caldaro Cl. Sup. Bischofsleiten '21	♟♟ 3
○ A.A. Pinot Bianco Leopoldine '21	♟♟ 5
● A.A. Pinot Nero Karal Ris. '20	♟♟ 6

Castelfeder

via Portici, 11
39040 Egna/Neumarkt [BZ]
☎ +39 0471820420
🌐 www.castelfeder.it

CELLAR SALES
PRE-BOOKED VISITS
ANNUAL PRODUCTION 600,000 bottles
HECTARES UNDER VINE 70.00

The Giovannett family's winery derives its name from an ancient castle whose ruins still overlook a hill between the towns of Ora, Egna, and Montagna. Ivan and Ines, alongside their parents Günther and Sandra, have expanded the family business, increasing the area under vines, modernizing production, and linking their most ambitious wines to their best estate vineyards. An extensive range is produced here, along Via Portici, with the 2020 Chardonnay Kreuzweg leading a highly worthy lineup. Sourced from the best hillside plots in Magrè, it opens with vibrant aromas, where smoky and sulfurous notes gradually give way to yellow fruit and floral tones. In the mouth, it reveals its class through a crisp, sapid palate with great tension. The 2021 Pinot Nero and Chardonnay Burgum Novum rank among the best in the region, combining richness and suppleness.

★★Cantina Colterenzio

loc. Cornaiano/Girlan
s.da del Vino, 8
39057 Appiano/Eppan [BZ]
☎ +39 0471664246
🌐 www.colterenzio.it

CELLAR SALES
PRE-BOOKED VISITS
ANNUAL PRODUCTION 1,600,000 bottles
HECTARES UNDER VINE 300.00
SUSTAINABLE WINERY

The Colterenzio cooperative relies on the invaluable work of around 300 grape growers, most of whom manage small vineyard plots in the areas closest to the winery: Colterenzio, Cornaiano, and Appiano. The estate is further enriched by smaller parcels around the regional capital and Salorno, near the Trentino border. It's Martin Lemayr's responsibility to transform these harvests into wines of substance. The producer performed its task perfectly, as evidenced by this year's tastings, with an outstanding debut by the new 2021 Gran Lafóa. This monovarietal sauvignon exhibits superb elegance on the nose—white fruit blending seamlessly with oak, all enhanced by delicate floral and spicy touches. On the palate, it's juicy, long, closing on a lovely note of peach. The 2021 Cabernet Sauvignon is the usual classy Bordeaux blend, while the 2022 Sauvignon Lafóa proves elegant on the nose, supple and refined on the palate.

○ A.A. Chardonnay Kreuzweg Family Reserve Ris. '20	♀♀♀ 8
○ A.A. Chardonnay Burgum Novum Ris. '21	♀♀ 6
● A.A. Pinot Nero Burgum Novum Ris. '21	♀♀ 6
○ A.A. Gewürztraminer Vom Lehm '23	♀♀ 5
○ A.A. Pinot Bianco Tecum Ris. '21	♀♀ 8
○ A.A. Pinot Bianco Vom Stein '23	♀♀ 4
● A.A. Pinot Nero Buchholz '22	♀♀ 5
● A.A. Pinot Nero Mazon '22	♀♀ 6
○ Raif Sauvignon '23	♀♀ 4
○ A.A. Chardonnay Kreuzweg Family Reserve '19	♀♀♀ 8
○ A.A. Gewürztraminer Vom Lehm '15	♀♀♀ 3*

○ A.A. Sauvignon Gran Lafóa Ris. '21	♀♀♀ 5
● A.A. Cabernet Sauvignon Lafóa Ris. '21	♀♀ 7
○ A.A. Sauvignon Lafóa '22	♀♀ 5
○ A.A. Bianco LR Ris. '20	♀♀ 8
○ A.A. Chardonnay Lafóa '22	♀♀ 5
○ A.A. Chardonnay Since 83 '23	♀♀ 4
○ A.A. Gewürztraminer Lafóa '22	♀♀ 5
○ A.A. Pinot Bianco Berg Ris. '22	♀♀ 5
● A.A. Pinot Nero Lafòa Ris. '21	♀♀ 6
● A.A. Cabernet Sauvignon Lafóa '16	♀♀♀ 7
○ A.A. Chardonnay Lafóa '19	♀♀♀ 5
○ A.A. Chardonnay Lafóa '16	♀♀♀ 5
○ A.A. Chardonnay Lafóa '15	♀♀♀ 5
○ A.A. Sauvignon Lafóa '21	♀♀♀ 5
○ A.A. Sauvignon Lafóa '20	♀♀♀ 5
○ A.A. Sauvignon Lafóa '18	♀♀♀ 5

Tenuta Ebner
Florian Unterthiner

fraz. Campodazzo, 18
39054 Renon/Ritten [BZ]
(+39 0471353386
@ www.weingutebner.it

CELLAR SALES
PRE-BOOKED VISITS
RESTAURANT SERVICE
ANNUAL PRODUCTION 20,000 bottles
HECTARES UNDER VINE 4.50

The Eisack Valley is undoubtedly one of the premier regions for South Tyrolean viticulture, often evoking thoughts of slender and fragrant whites. However, Brigitte and Florian Unterthiner craft a distinctive style from their vineyards in the southern part of the valley, near the town, producing wines known for their aromatic intensity and, above all, their fullness and consistency of flavor. Their stylistic approach is perfectly reflected in the 2023 Grüner Veltliner, sourced from a southwest-facing vineyard situated at 450 meters elevation. Its vibrant, bright straw-yellow hue introduces an intense hit of sulfur, which slowly dissipates, making way for yellow fruit and dried flowers. In the mouth, the wine reveals nice richness, supported by sapid and acidic drive, leading to tension. The 2020 Pinot Nero also caught our attention, opening with complex aromas, where fruit meets underbrush notes, sensations that follow through on a long, taut palate.

Eichenstein

via Castel Gatto, 34
39012 Merano/Meran [BZ]
(+39 3442820179
@ www.eichenstein.it

ANNUAL PRODUCTION 25,000 bottles
HECTARES UNDER VINE 4.50
SUSTAINABLE WINERY

Josef Waldner's winery is situated in a picturesque spot on a large terrace overlooking the Adige Valley, surrounded by the estate's vineyards and a dense forest that provides natural seclusion. Most of the vineyards thrive at elevations of around 550 meters above sea level, with some historic plots also found in the valley floor near Marlengo. In the winery, the young winemaker Martin Pollinger crafts a limited range but one of absolute distinction. The 2022 Sauvignon Stein opens with an intense exotic and floral note that develops further on the palate, where it reveals sapidity and a well-sustained progression. The 2022 Pinot Nero Amantus is intriguing, offering up a vibrant mineral note that slowly gives way to wild fruit and a lovely hint of underbrush. On the palate, it's medium-bodied, with tannins lending rigor and energy to its flavor profile. We conclude with a a special mention for the 2023 Gloria Dei a blend of sauvignon, pinot bianco, and riesling that combines freshness and harmony.

○ A.A. Valle Isarco Grüner Veltliner '23	♟♟ 4
○ A.A. Pinot Bianco '23	♟♟ 4
● A.A. Pinot Nero '20	♟♟ 6
○ A.A. Sauvignon '23	♟♟ 4
○ A.A. Valle Isarco Gewürztraminer '23	♟♟ 4
○ A.A. Valle Isarco Kerner '23	♟♟ 4
○ A.A. Valle Isarco Grüner Veltliner '21	♟♟♟ 3*
○ A.A. Sauvignon '22	♟♟ 3
○ A.A. Sauvignon '20	♟♟ 3*
● A.A. Schiava '22	♟♟ 2*
○ A.A. Valle Isarco Gewürztraminer '22	♟♟ 4
○ A.A. Valle Isarco Grüner Veltliner '22	♟♟ 3*
○ A.A. Valle Isarco Kerner '22	♟♟ 4

○ A.A. Sauvignon Stein '22	♟♟ 5
○ A.A. Chardonnay Seppelaia Ris. '21	♟♟ 7
● A.A. Merlot Cabernet Franc Baccara Ris. '21	♟♟ 5
● A.A. Pinot Nero Amantus '22	♟♟ 5
○ A.A. Schiava Rosé Carina '23	♟♟ 3
○ Cuvée Gloria Dei '23	♟♟ 4
○ A.A. Riesling Athos '22	♟ 3
○ A.A. Chardonnay Seppelaia Ris. '20	♟♟ 7
○ A.A. Chardonnay Seppelaia Ris. '19	♟♟ 7
● A.A. Merlot Cabernet Franc Baccara Ris. '19	♟♟ 5
● A.A. Pinot Nero Amantus '21	♟♟ 4
○ A.A. Riesling Athos '21	♟♟ 5
○ A.A. Sauvignon Stein '21	♟♟ 5
○ A.A. Schiava Rosé Carina '22	♟♟ 3
○ Cuvée Gloria Dei '21	♟♟ 3

Schloss Englar

fraz. San Michele
loc. Pigeno, 42
39057 Appiano/Eppan [BZ]
☎ +39 0471662628
🌐 www.weingut-englar.com

CELLAR SALES
PRE-BOOKED VISITS
ANNUAL PRODUCTION 15,000 bottles
HECTARES UNDER VINE 12.00

The Khuen Belasi family's estate spans around 10 hectares in the Eppan Berg area, with splendid east-facing exposures at around 500 meters above sea level, sheltered by the dense forest that climbs toward the Mendola. In the cellar, production is focused on bringing out aromatic clarity and elegant flavor, drawing exclusively on the grape varieties that thrive best in the region. The Belasy Chardonnay Riserva 2021 reveals a deep and characterful aromatic profile. A hint of sulfur quickly dissipates, making way for crisp white fruit, further enhanced by a fresh, floral stroke. On the palate, it impresses not with its concentration, but with its dynamism and tension, stretching out with supple energy toward a crisp finish. The Baltasius Pinot Nero '20 is also noteworthy, offering fresh notes of wild berry and anise, characterized by a sapid and slender palate.

○ A.A. Chardonnay Belasy Ris. '21	♟♟	7
○ A.A. Pinot Bianco St. Sebastian Ris. '21	♟♟	7
● A.A. Pinot Nero '22	♟♟	6
● A.A. Pinot Nero Baltasius Ris. '20	♟♟	8
● A.A. Schiava Léon '21	♟♟	5
○ A.A. Chardonnay Belasy Ris. '20	♟♟	7
○ A.A. Chardonnay Belasy Ris. '19	♟♟	6
○ A.A. Pinot Bianco Sebastian Ris. '19	♟♟	4
○ A.A. Pinot Bianco St. Sebastian Ris. '20	♟♟	7
● A.A. Pinot Nero '20	♟♟	6
● A.A. Pinot Nero Baltasius Ris. '19	♟♟	8
● A.A. Pinot Nero Ris. '18	♟♟	6
● A.A. Schiava R Ris. '18	♟♟	4
○ Gewürztraminer Orange '21	♟♟	6

★Falkenstein
Franz Pratzner

via Castello, 19
39025 Naturno/Naturns [BZ]
☎ +39 0473666054
🌐 www.falkenstein.bz

CELLAR SALES
PRE-BOOKED VISITS
ANNUAL PRODUCTION 90,000 bottles
HECTARES UNDER VINE 12.00

Behind Naturno, climbing the slopes leading to Monte Sole, lies a vast vineyard perfectly exposed to the south, where riesling reigns supreme. This is the estate of the Pratzner family, who began gradually converting the land to viticulture in the late 1980s, quickly becoming a reference point for Alto Adige wine enthusiasts. Today, alongside Franz and Bernadette, their daughter Michaela plays an increasingly important role. The Riesling 2022 emerges as the estate's most convincing wine, thoroughly impressing our tasters. The nose reveals youthful aromas of white fruit, gooseberry, and citrus, with a subtle mineral vein in the background. In the mouth, the warmth of the region comes through in the richness of the palate, where acidity provides tension and length. The Pinot Bianco '22 stands out for its aromatic complexity and energetic flavor.

○ A.A. Val Venosta Riesling '22	♟♟♟	5
○ A.A. Val Venosta Pinot Bianco '22	♟♟	5
○ A.A. Val Venosta Pinot Bianco Phileo '19	♟♟	6
● A.A. Val Venosta Pinot Nero '21	♟♟	6
○ A.A. Val Venosta Riesling Anadûron '19	♟♟	7
○ A.A. Val Venosta Riesling '20	♟♟♟	5
○ A.A. Val Venosta Riesling '18	♟♟♟	5
○ A.A. Val Venosta Riesling '15	♟♟♟	5
○ A.A. Val Venosta Riesling '14	♟♟♟	5
○ A.A. Val Venosta Riesling '13	♟♟♟	5
○ A.A. Val Venosta Riesling '12	♟♟♟	5
○ A.A. Val Venosta Riesling '11	♟♟♟	5
○ A.A. Val Venosta Riesling '10	♟♟♟	5
○ A.A. Val Venosta Riesling '09	♟♟♟	5
○ A.A. Val Venosta Riesling '08	♟♟♟	5

Garlider
Christian Kerschbaumer

via Untrum, 20
39040 Velturno/Feldthurns [BZ]
📞 +39 0472847296
🌐 www.garlider.it

CELLAR SALES
PRE-BOOKED VISITS
ANNUAL PRODUCTION 26,000 bottles
HECTARES UNDER VINE 4.20
VITICULTURE METHOD Certified Organic

For over twenty years, Christian Kerschbaumer has managed the family winery, with a few hectares of vineyards in the heart of the Eisack Valley. These vineyards lie on the southern and southeastern slopes of the hills, at elevations spanning 550-800 meters, and have long been farmed organically. While the wines were previously appreciated for their expressive finesse, today, with the maturity of both the vines and the winemaker, they reveal a distinctive character and boldness. Pinot Grigio is often interpreted as a light, easy-drinking white, but Günther's version is far from that. This wine offers deep aromas ranging from pear to dried flowers, with significant space given to sulfurous and smoky notes. On the palate, it's solid, taut, and notably sapid. The Müller Thurgau '22 follows a similar path, emphasizing the connection to the terroir despite the often lightweight profile attributed to this grape. It's mineral-driven, with notes of ripe yellow fruit and spices, delivering an energetic and substantial palate.

○ Pinot Grigio '22	♀♀	3*
○ A.A. Valle Isarco Grüner Veltliner '22	♀♀	4
○ A.A. Valle Isarco Müller Thurgau '22	♀♀	3
○ A.A. Valle Isarco Sylvaner '22	♀♀	3
○ A.A. Valle Isarco Sylvaner '15	♀♀♀	3*
○ A.A. Valle Isarco Sylvaner '14	♀♀♀	3*
○ A.A. Valle Isarco Sylvaner '13	♀♀♀	3*
○ A.A. Valle Isarco Sylvaner '09	♀♀♀	3*
○ A.A. Valle Isarco Veltliner '08	♀♀♀	3*
○ A.A. Valle Isarco Veltliner '07	♀♀♀	3
○ A.A. Valle Isarco Veltliner '05	♀♀♀	3*
○ Grüner Veltliner '16	♀♀	4
○ Pinot Grigio '21	♀♀	3*
○ Sylvaner '20	♀♀	3*
○ Sylvaner '16	♀♀	3*

★Cantina Girlan

loc. Cornaiano/Girlan
via San Martino, 24
39057 Appiano/Eppan [BZ]
📞 +39 0471662403
🌐 www.girlan.it

CELLAR SALES
PRE-BOOKED VISITS
ANNUAL PRODUCTION 1,500,000 bottles
HECTARES UNDER VINE 220.00

The Cornaiano cooperative has been active for over a century, with the passion of the original 24 members still alive in the efforts of 200 families who manage vineyards stretching across the Oltradige and Bassa Atesina/Unterland production zones. More than 200 hectares are cultivated in all, with a focus on the varieties that perform best here: pinot nero (especially in the Cornaiano and Mazzon areas) and schiava (in the historic Gschleier zone). Once again, the Trattman 2021 leads the estate's range. A bright ruby hue introduces refined aromas where wild berry is accompanied by smoky and herbal notes, eventually giving way to underbrush. The palate features smooth tannins—a long and juicy drink. The Flora '21, from the vineyards of Girlan Pinzon, and Mazon, plays with fresher fruit notes, offering up a harmonious and approachable palate. With its character and pluck, the Gschleier '22 is a classic Schiava.

● A.A. Pinot Nero Trattmann Ris. '21	♀♀♀	6
● A.A. Pinot Nero Flora Ris. '21	♀♀	5
○ A.A. Bianco Flora Ris. '22	♀♀	4
○ A.A. Chardonnay Flora '22	♀♀	5
○ A.A. Chardonnay Marna '23	♀♀	4
○ A.A. Gewürztraminer Flora '22	♀♀	6
○ A.A. Pinot Bianco Platt&Riegl '23	♀♀	3
○ A.A. Sauvignon Flora '22	♀♀	4
○ A.A. Sauvignon Indra '23	♀♀	4
● A.A. Schiava Fass N° 9 '23	♀♀	3
● A.A. Schiava Gschleier Alte Reben '22	♀♀	4
● A.A. Pinot Nero Trattmann Ris. '20	♀♀♀	6
● A.A. Pinot Nero Trattmann Ris. '19	♀♀♀	6
● A.A. Pinot Nero Trattmann Ris. '18	♀♀♀	6
● A.A. Pinot Nero Trattmann Ris. '17	♀♀♀	8

Glögglhof - Franz Gojer

fraz. Santa Maddalena
via Rivellone, I
39100 Bolzano/Bozen
(») +39 0471978775
www.gojer.it

CELLAR SALES
PRE-BOOKED VISITS
ACCOMMODATION
ANNUAL PRODUCTION 55,000 bottles
HECTARES UNDER VINE 7.40

In a region where acquiring vineyards is nearly impossible, Franz Gojer has expanded his estate, starting with the Santa Maddalena vineyards near the city center and reaching the higher exposures of Karneid, where white grape varieties thrive. The winery is family-run, with Franz supported by his wife Maria Luise and son Florian. A strong debut for the new Santa Maddalena selection, Rondell R '22, which pushes the boundaries of the type by exploring aromatic complexity and layering without losing sight of drinkability. The result is a fascinating and refined wine. Only a very small amount is produced. As a result you'll find it among our Rare Wines. The Lagrein Riserva '22 proves redolent of dark fruit and rain-soaked earth, developing a consistent flavor profile with well-integrated, smooth, and sweet tannins. Among the whites, the Pinot Bianco Karneid '23 impresses with its tension and length.

Gottardi

loc. Mazzon
via degli Alpini, 17
39044 Egna/Neumarkt [BZ]
(») +39 0471812773
www.gottardi-mazzon.com

ANNUAL PRODUCTION 45,000 bottles
HECTARES UNDER VINE 9.00

Founded in the mid-1980s, the Gottardi family winery is now managed by Elisabeth, who continues the work begun by her grandfather Bruno and father Alexander. The estate's vineyards are entirely located in the Mazzon area, where roughly 10 hectares have been gradually converted to pinot nero, which here matures under the sun and is consistently caressed by dry winds from the south and cooler breezes descending from the mountains. The Riserva '19 pours a lovely bright ruby color, foreshadowing aromas reminiscent of wild berry and fine herbs, with a subtle note of underbrush and rain-soaked earth in the background. On the palate, the character of the terroir emerges in an energetic profile, well-supported by smooth and sweet tannins. The Pinot Nero '20 stands out with its aromatic freshness, and a juicy, elegant, dynamic palate.

A.A. Lagrein Ris. '22	♟♟ 5
A.A. Kerner Karneid '23	♟♟ 3
A.A. Pinot Bianco Karneid '23	♟♟ 4
A.A. Santa Maddalena Cl. V. Rondell '23	♟♟ 4
A.A. Sauvignon Karneid '23	♟♟ 3
Pipa XXII	♟♟ 6
A.A. Lagrein Ris. '18	♟♟♟ 4*
A.A. Santa Maddalena Cl. Rondell '18	♟♟♟ 3*
A.A. Santa Maddalena Cl. Rondell '16	♟♟♟ 3*
A.A. Santa Maddalena Cl. Rondell '15	♟♟♟ 3*

A.A. Pinot Nero Mazzon Ris. '19	♟♟ 5
A.A. Pinot Nero Mazzon '20	♟♟ 5
A.A. Pinot Nero Mazzon Alexander Gottardi '16	♟♟ 7
A.A. Pinot Nero Mazzon '11	♟♟♟ 5

ALTO ADIGE

Griesbauerhof
Georg Mumelter

via Rencio, 66
39100 Bolzano/Bozen
☎ +39 0471973090
✉ www.griesbauerhof.it

CELLAR SALES
PRE-BOOKED VISITS
ANNUAL PRODUCTION 30,000 bottles
HECTARES UNDER VINE 3.80

Gummerhof - Malojer

via Weggenstein, 36
39100 Bolzano/Bozen
☎ +39 0471972885
✉ www.malojer.it

CELLAR SALES
PRE-BOOKED VISITS
ANNUAL PRODUCTION 100,000 bottles
HECTARES UNDER VINE 18.00

The Griesbauerhof estate, owned by the Mumelter family since the late 1700s, is the heart of production. Their vineyards extend from the city outskirts towards the Eisack Valley. On this small estate, Georg and his son Lukas tend to old vines of schiava and lagrein, to which they have added merlot and cabernet sauvignon over time. The estate also includes a small plot for white grapes in Appiano. The heart of production revolves around the two local wine types, with a preference for the Santa Maddalena '23, which highlights an aromatic profile on sweet, juicy red fruit, finding freshness in herbal and spicy notes. On the palate, it becomes even more approachable and gratifying, thanks to pronounced sapidity. The Lagrein Ronc '21 offers up aromas of dark fruit and spices, echoed by a palate that impresses more for its harmony and length than for concentration.

The Malojer family winery has been active in the capital for over a century, its location just outside the city center, highlighting a historic bond between Bolzano and viticulture. Today, Urban and his wife Helena source grapes from both estate vineyards and local growers, with red varieties cultivated within the municipality and white varieties grown on the cooler slopes of Ritten. Lagrein, the varietal that most defines local production, takes center stage here. The Riserva '21 showcases perfect oak, which seems to embrace the grape's red fruit, enhancing its ripeness and nuance. In the mouth, smoky and mineral notes emerge, adding character to a palate of superb weight and stylistic precision. The Gummer zu Gries '22 plays with crisp fruit and herbal notes of cinchona and anise, coming through firm and supple on the palate.

● A.A. Santa Maddalena Cl. '23	♈♈ 4
● A.A. Cabernet Marmot Ris. '21	♈♈ 6
● A.A. Lagrein Ronc Ris. '21	♈♈ 5
○ A.A. Pinot Bianco Domus Alba '22	♈♈ 5
○ A.A. Pinot Grigio '23	♈♈ 4
● A.A. Santa Maddalena Cl. Isarcus '22	♈♈ 5
● A.A. Lagrein Ris. '09	♈♈♈ 5
● A.A. Lagrein Scuro Ris. '99	♈♈♈ 5
● A.A. Cabernet Marmot Ris. '20	♈♈ 5
● A.A. Lagrein Ronc Ris. '20	♈♈ 5
○ A.A. Pinot Grigio '22	♈♈ 4
● A.A. Santa Maddalena Cl. '22	♈♈ 4
● A.A. Santa Maddalena Cl. Isarcus '21	♈♈ 5

● A.A. Lagrein Ris. '21	♈♈ 5
● A.A. Cabernet Lagrein Bautzanum Ris. '21	♈♈ 5
● A.A. Cabernet Sauvignon Ris. '21	♈♈ 5
○ A.A. Gewürztraminer Kui '23	♈♈ 3
● A.A. Lagrein Gummer Zu Gries '22	♈♈ 4
○ A.A. Pinot Bianco Kreiter '23	♈♈ 3
● A.A. Santa Maddalena Cl. Loamer '23	♈♈ 4
○ A.A. Sauvignon Gur zur Sand '23	♈♈ 3
○ A.A. Bianco Cuvée Bautzanum '23	♈ 3
○ A.A. Chardonnay Justinus '23	♈ 3
● A.A. Pinot Nero Gstrein '23	♈ 4
● A.A. Lagrein Gries '09	♈♈♈ 2*
● A.A. Cabernet Lagrein Bautzanum Ris. '20	♈♈ 4
● A.A. Lagrein Ris. '20	♈♈ 4
○ A.A. Pinot Grigio Gur zu Sand '22	♈♈ 3
● A.A. Santa Maddalena Cl. Loamerhof '22	♈♈ 3

★Gump Hof
Markus Prackwieser

loc. Novale di Presule - s.da di Fiè, 11
39050 Fiè allo Sciliar
Völs am Schlern [BZ]
+39 0471601190
www.gumphof.it

CELLAR SALES
PRE-BOOKED VISITS
ANNUAL PRODUCTION 65,000 bottles
HECTARES UNDER VINE 7.50
SUSTAINABLE WINERY

The Prackwieser family has been dedicated to viticulture for generations, but it was with Markus's involvement that the winery took on its current form. Their vineyards span the eastern side of the lower Eisack Valley, from 400 meters elevation, which are dedicated to heat-loving varieties, up to 800 meters, where the vines are consistently refreshed by afternoon breezes from the Ora and nighttime breezes from the Sciliar. Few varietals are cultivated here, but their range knows no weaknesses. The Sauvignon Renaissance '21 reveals an aromatic profile born from an excellent vintage, with crisp fruit intertwined with floral notes, leaving a hint of oak in the background. In the mouth, its sapidity and tension stand out, making for a long and classy palate. The Sauvignon Praesulis '22, on the other hand, focuses more on varietal freshness and drinkability, winning over with its harmony, while the Pinot Nero Renaissance '20 reveals aromatic complexity and a taut, energetic, elegant palate.

A.A. Sauvignon Renaissance Ris. '21	🍷🍷🍷 7
A.A. Pinot Nero Renaissance Ris. '20	🍷🍷 8
A.A. Sauvignon Praesulis '22	🍷🍷 5
A.A. Gewürztraminer Praesulis '22	🍷🍷 5
A.A. Pinot Bianco Mediaevum '23	🍷🍷 4
A.A. Pinot Bianco Praesulis '22	🍷🍷 5
A.A. Pinot Bianco Renaissance Ris. '21	🍷🍷 6
A.A. Pinot Nero Praesulis '21	🍷🍷 6
A.A. Sauvignon Mediaevum '23	🍷🍷 4
A.A. Schiava Mediaevum '23	🍷🍷 4
A.A. Pinot Bianco Praesulis '17	🍸🍸🍸 4*
A.A. Pinot Bianco Renaissance Ris. '19	🍸🍸🍸 6
A.A. Pinot Bianco Renaissance Ris. '18	🍸🍸🍸 6
A.A. Sauvignon Renaissance '16	🍸🍸🍸 4*
A.A. Sauvignon Renaissance Ris. '20	🍸🍸🍸 7
A.A. Sauvignon Renaissance Ris. '17	🍸🍸🍸 4*

★Franz Haas

via Villa, 6
39040 Montagna/Montan [BZ]
+39 0471812280
www.franz-haas.it

CELLAR SALES
PRE-BOOKED VISITS
ANNUAL PRODUCTION 400,000 bottles
HECTARES UNDER VINE 55.00
SUSTAINABLE WINERY

Under the leadership of Luisa Manna, with the help of her children Franz Jr. and Sofia, this winery has become a key player in Alto Adige, boasting a network of vineyards along the eastern ridge of the Valdadige. The plots enjoy sunshine until late afternoon, with the heat balanced by the coolness that only higher elevations can provide. In the cellar, pinot nero is the flagship, complemented by a broad and reliable range of products. The Pinot Nero Schweizer '20 stands tall, with aromas of wild fruit giving way to rain-soaked earth, with a timid, spicy note lingering in the background. On the palate, its sapidity impresses, and the wine stretches out, well-supported by acidity, to a crisp, refined finish. The Manna '22, a blend featuring many varietals, conjures up vibrant exotic and mineral notes, giving way to floral and citrus suggestions that are echoed on a sapid palate. Superb dynamism and length.

● A.A. Pinot Nero Schweizer '20	🍷🍷 6
○ Manna '22	🍷🍷 5
○ A.A. Gewürztraminer '22	🍷🍷 4
● A.A. Moscato Rosa '22	🍷🍷 5
● A.A. Pinot Nero '21	🍷🍷 5
○ A.A. Sauvignon '22	🍷🍷 5
○ Moscato Giallo '23	🍷🍷 5
○ Petit Manseng '22	🍷🍷 5
● A.A. Moscato Rosa '12	🍸🍸🍸 5
● A.A. Moscato Rosa '11	🍸🍸🍸 5
● A.A. Pinot Nero Schweizer '13	🍸🍸🍸 6
○ A.A. Sauvignon '13	🍸🍸🍸 5
○ Manna '17	🍸🍸🍸 5
○ Manna '07	🍸🍸🍸 4
○ Manna '05	🍸🍸🍸 4
○ Manna '04	🍸🍸🍸 4

Haderburg

fraz. Pochi
via Albrecht Dürer, 3
39040 Salorno/Salurn [BZ]
📞 +39 0471889097
🌐 www.haderburg.it

CELLAR SALES
PRE-BOOKED VISITS
ANNUAL PRODUCTION 100,000 bottles
HECTARES UNDER VINE 12.00
VITICULTURE METHOD Certified Biodynamic

Nearly half a century has passed since Alois Ochsenreiter decided to convert his family's farmstead, a handful of hectares just above Salorno, to viticulture. Today, Haderburg is one of the region's most established wineries, with vineyards that have been expanded both in the South Tyrolean Unterland, where the grapes for their sparkling wines primarily come from, and in the Eisack Valley, where higher elevations give rise to the most aromatic white wines. The Pas Dosé '20 is an excellent sparkling wine made from chardonnay grapes with a touch of pinot nero. It captivates with its complex aromas of yellow fruit, brioche, and hazelnut. On the palate, it unfolds decisively, supported by a fresh vein of acidity. The Pinot Nero Hasumannhof '22 is equally impressive, highlighting the freshness of wild fruit and medicinal herbs on a juicy and very sapid palate. The harmonious and lengthy Erah '19, a Bordeaux blend, is made with grapes from lower vineyards.

Wine	Rating
○ A.A. Spumante Pas Dosé M. Cl. '20	♙♙ 6
● A.A. Cabernet Merlot Erah '19	♙♙ 6
○ A.A. Chardonnay V. Hausmannhof '23	♙♙ 4
○ A.A. Gewürztraminer '23	♙♙ 4
● A.A. Pinot Nero V. Hausmannhof '22	♙♙ 7
● A.A. Pinot Nero V. Hausmannhof Ris. '19	♙♙ 8
○ A.A. Spumante Brut M. Cl.	♙♙ 5
⊙ A.A. Spumante Brut Rosé M. Cl.	♙♙ 5
○ A.A. Pinot Grigio Pfatten '23	♙ 4
○ A.A. Spumante Hausmannhof Ris. '97	♙♙♙ 6
○ A.A. Valle Isarco Sylvaner Obermairlhof '05	♙♙♙ 3*
● A.A. Merlot Cabernet Erah '15	♙♙ 5
○ A.A. Pinot Grigio Salurn Pfatten '18	♙♙ 5
○ A.A. Valle Isarco Riesling Obermairlhof '18	♙♙ 3

★★Cantina Kaltern

via Cantine, 12
39052 Caldaro/Kaltern [BZ]
📞 +39 0471963149
🌐 www.cantinakaltern.it

CELLAR SALES
PRE-BOOKED VISITS
ANNUAL PRODUCTION 4,000,000 bottles
HECTARES UNDER VINE 440.00
SUSTAINABLE WINERY

Kaltern epitomizes South Tyrolean viticulture, a world where numerous growers cultivate small plots and where diverse philosophies coexist— from those adhering to traditional methods to those where new generations embrace organic or biodynamic practices. Under the direction of Thomas Scarizuola, the cooperative's harvests are transformed into a range of wines marked by superb stylistic precision. The Lago di Caldaro Quintessenz '23 showcases stylistic precision, perfectly expressing all the qualities expected from this fresh red wine. Its aromas range from ripe cherry to spices, underbrush, and floral notes. The palate offers richness and texture without losing its approachable nature and suppleness. The Pinot Bianco '22 from the same line takes advantage of an excellent vintage to reveal a crisp and fragrant aromatic profile, developing into a sapid, relaxed palate with admirable length.

Wine	Rating
● A.A. Lago di Caldaro Cl. Sup. Quintessenz '23	♙♙♙ 5
○ A.A. Pinot Bianco Quintessenz '22	♙♙ 5
● A.A. Cabernet Sauvignon Quintessenz Ris. '21	♙♙ 5
○ A.A. Chardonnay Saleit '23	♙♙ 3
○ A.A. Pinot Bianco Vial '23	♙♙ 3
● A.A. Pinot Nero Saltner Ris. '21	♙♙ 4
○ A.A. Sauvignon Quintessenz '22	♙♙ 5
○ A.A. Sauvignon Stern '23	♙♙ 5
○ A.A. Spumante Brut Nature M. Cl. '19	♙♙ 5
● A.A. Lago di Caldaro Cl. Sup. Quintessenz '22	♙♙♙ 4
● A.A. Lago di Caldaro Cl. Sup. Quintessenz '21	♙♙♙
● A.A. Lago di Caldaro Cl. Sup. Quintessenz '20	♙♙♙

Kettmeir

via delle Cantine, 4
39052 Caldaro/Kaltern [BZ]
☎ +39 0471963135
🌐 www.kettmeir.com

CELLAR SALES
PRE-BOOKED VISITS
ACCOMMODATION
ANNUAL PRODUCTION 419,000 bottles
HECTARES UNDER VINE 60.00
SUSTAINABLE WINERY

In an area where sparkling wines have traditionally taken a backseat to other typologies, the Kettmeir winery has taken a different path. Alongside its classic wines from Alto Adige, it has focused heavily on spumante. The first bubbly was produced in the 1960s, while in the new millennium it became a hallmark under the management of Josef Romen. The Riserva 1919, which hails from the 2018 harvest, is a blend of chardonnay, partially matured in oak, and pinot nero. It opens with complex aromas where yellow fruit accompanies notes of toasted bread and dried flowers. On the palate, it's firm, backed by vivid acidity and impressive length. On the other hand, the Brut Athesis '21 includes a bit of pinot bianco, with the base wines entirely aged in stainless steel. The nose reveals superb freshness and aromatic clarity, leading to a juicy, refined, and very long palate. Among the still wines, we appreciated the elegance of the Pinot Bianco Athesis '22.

A.A. Spumante Brut M. Cl. Athesis '21	🍷🍷 5
A.A. Spumante Extra Brut M. Cl. 1919 Ris. '18	🍷🍷 8
A.A. Chardonnay '23	🍷🍷 4
A.A. Chardonnay V. Maso Reiner '22	🍷🍷 6
A.A. Gewürztraminer '23	🍷🍷 4
A.A. Pinot Bianco '23	🍷🍷 4
A.A. Pinot Bianco Athesis '22	🍷🍷 6
A.A. Pinot Grigio '23	🍷🍷 4
A.A. Pinot Nero V. Maso Reiner Ris. '21	🍷🍷 6
A.A. Sauvignon '23	🍷🍷 4
A.A. Spumante Extra Brut M. Cl. Rosé Athesis '21	🍷🍷 5
A.A. Spumante Pas Dosé M. Cl. '19	🍷🍷 7
A.A. Spumante Brut M. Cl. Athesis '20	🍷🍷🍷 5
A.A. Spumante Brut M. Cl. Athesis '18	🍷🍷🍷 4*

Klosterhof
Oskar Andergassen

loc. Clavenz, 40
39052 Caldaro/Kaltern [BZ]
☎ +39 0471961046
🌐 www.garni-klosterhof.com

CELLAR SALES
PRE-BOOKED VISITS
ACCOMMODATION AND RESTAURANT SERVICE
ANNUAL PRODUCTION 38,000 bottles
HECTARES UNDER VINE 5.00

As often happens in these parts, the Andergassen family divides its activities between hospitality and winemaking. The latter is managed by Oskar and his son Hannes, who oversee four vineyards in the best parts of Caldaro. Each vineyard is planted with varieties best suited to its elevation and soil conditions, from the sunny vineyards around Lake Plantaditsch to the higher ones at Vial. The Pinot Bianco Acapella is made with grapes from old vines in the Trifall and Barleit areas, harvested, pressed and matured in French oak and acacia from the nearby hills. The result is refined aromas of crisp white fruit and flowers. In the mouth, the firmness of the palate is lightened and invigorated by a mineral presence and especially by its acidic thrust. The Plantaditsch '22, a schiava, also convinces with its vibrant wild fruit sensations and pepper aromas, delivering a fresh, juicy, and irresistibly drinkable palate.

● A.A. Lago di Caldaro Cl. Sup. Plantaditsch '22	🍷🍷 4
○ A.A. Pinot Bianco Acapella '22	🍷🍷 4
● A.A. Pinot Nero Schwarze Madonna '21	🍷🍷 5
⊙ A.A. Pinot Nero Rosé Summer '23	🍷 4
● A.A. Lago di Caldaro Cl. Sup. Plantaditsch '21	🍷🍷 3
○ A.A. Pinot Bianco Acapella '21	🍷🍷 4
○ A.A. Pinot Bianco Acapella '20	🍷🍷 4
○ A.A. Pinot Bianco Acapella '19	🍷🍷 4
○ A.A. Pinot Bianco Acapella Ris. '20	🍷🍷 4
○ A.A. Pinot Bianco Acapella Ris. '19	🍷🍷 4
● A.A. Pinot Nero Schwarze Madonna '20	🍷🍷 5
● A.A. Pinot Nero Schwarze Madonna '19	🍷🍷 5
● A.A. Pinot Nero Schwarze Madonna '18	🍷🍷 5
● A.A. Pinot Nero Schwarze Madonna Ris. '20	🍷🍷 5

★Köfererhof Günther Kerschbaumer

fraz. Novacella
via Pusteria, 3
39040 Varna/Vahrn [BZ]
📞 +39 3474778009
🌐 www.koefererhof.it

CELLAR SALES
PRE-BOOKED VISITS
RESTAURANT SERVICE
ANNUAL PRODUCTION 80,000 bottles
HECTARES UNDER VINE 10.00

Günther Kerschbaumer runs the family winery near Varna, a small town renowned for the impressive Abbey of Novacella. Here, the vineyards rise from 600 meters upwards, where the grapes capture extraordinary aromas and freshness. These plots are dedicated entirely to white grape varieties, which Günther crafts into rich, vibrant wines. The Sylvaner R '22 is fantastic, debuting with an intense smoky note that slowly dissipates, letting through ripe yellow fruit, dried flowers, and a timid mineral note that's just waiting to take center stage. In the mouth, the strength of the terroir and Günther's interpretation shine through in an energetic, crisp, and taut palate that seems to never end. The Grüner Veltliner R '22 plays on the maturity of yellow fruit that develops into a juicy and refined palate. The Pinot Grigio '23 is also delicious, combining the richness of the grape variety with the tension of the Eisack Valley.

Wine	Rating	
○ A.A. Valle Isarco Sylvaner R '22	🍷🍷🍷	5
○ A.A. Valle Isarco Grüner Veltliner R '22	🍷🍷	5
○ A.A. Valle Isarco Gewürztraminer '23	🍷🍷	4
○ A.A. Valle Isarco Kerner '23	🍷🍷	4
○ A.A. Valle Isarco Pinot Grigio '23	🍷🍷	4
○ A.A. Valle Isarco Riesling R '22	🍷🍷	5
○ A.A. Valle Isarco Sylvaner '23	🍷🍷	4
○ A.A. Valle Isarco Riesling '20	🏆🏆🏆	5
○ A.A. Valle Isarco Sylvaner R '21	🏆🏆🏆	5
○ A.A. Valle Isarco Sylvaner R '19	🏆🏆🏆	5
○ A.A. Valle Isarco Sylvaner R '18	🏆🏆🏆	5
○ A.A. Valle Isarco Sylvaner R '17	🏆🏆🏆	5

Tenuta Kornell

fraz. Settequerce
via Cosma e Damiano, 6
39018 Terlano/Terlan [BZ]
📞 +39 0471917507
🌐 www.kornell.it

CELLAR SALES
PRE-BOOKED VISITS
ANNUAL PRODUCTION 250,000 bottles
HECTARES UNDER VINE 15.00

Settequerce is a tiny wine village set between Bolzano and Terlano, where apple orchards and vineyards vie for the best sun exposure on the hillsides. Here, Florian Brigl has developed the family winery into one of the region's most intriguing producers. The vineyards unfold along these slopes and in the Appiano area, making for a range that blends the Mediterranean richness of reds with the refined elegance of Alto Adige whites. This year, there's a wealth of choices among the wines produced by Florian, with the Merlot Kressfeld '19 and Aichberg '21 taking the spotlight. The former opens with classic aromas, with plum complemented by a characteristic vegetal note, introducing a firm and dense palate supported and accompanied through a long finish by tannins and acidity. The latter, a blend of pinot bianco, chardonnay, and sauvignon from the vineyards of Appiano, showcases complex aromas and a juicy, very elegant palate. Their line of standard-vintage, annata wines aptly expresses the varietal characteristics of the grapes.

Wine	Rating	
○ A.A. Bianco Aichberg '21	🍷🍷	
● A.A. Merlot Kressfeld Ris. '19	🍷🍷	
● A.A. Cabernet Sauvignon Staffes '21	🍷🍷	
○ A.A. Gewürztraminer Damian '23	🍷🍷	
● A.A. Lagrein Greif '23	🍷🍷	
● A.A. Lagrein Staffes '21	🍷🍷	
● A.A. Merlot Staffes '21	🍷🍷	
○ A.A. Pinot Bianco Eich '23	🍷🍷	
○ A.A. Pinot Grigio Gris '23	🍷🍷	
● A.A. Pinot Nero Marith '23	🍷🍷	
○ A.A. Sauvignon Cosmas '23	🍷🍷	
○ A.A. Sauvignon Oberberg '22	🍷🍷	
● A.A. Lagrein Staffes Ris. '16	🏆🏆🏆	
● A.A. Lagrein Staves Ris. '14	🏆🏆🏆	
● A.A. Merlot V. Kressfeld Ris. '16	🏆🏆🏆	

★Kuenhof - Peter Pliger

via Lahner, 12
39042 Bressanone/Brixen [BZ]
+39 0472850546
www.kuenhof.com

CELLAR SALES
PRE-BOOKED VISITS
ANNUAL PRODUCTION 42,000 bottles
HECTARES UNDER VINE 6.80
SUSTAINABLE WINERY

Peter Pliger is among those producers who have put the Eisack Valley on the oenological map. His meticulous work began with the revival of old vineyard slopes and an environmentally respectful approach to viticulture. On the terraced hills behind the winery, traditional valley grape varieties are cultivated, which Peter, his wife Brigitte, and their son Simon turn into highly elegant wines. The Sylvaner and Riesling Kaiton '23 are two refined whites, focusing more on aromatic finesse and harmony than concentration. The Sylvaner pours a delicate color, anticipating lightly smoked aromas of white fruit and flowers, perfectly expressed on a crisp, juicy, and dynamic palate. The Riesling, on the other hand, plays more on exotic notes, leaving the mineral vein in the background. On the palate, it's racy, supported by a valuable acidity, finding length and energy.

A.A. Valle Isarco Riesling Kaiton '23	♟♟ 5
A.A. Valle Isarco Sylvaner '23	♟♟ 4
A.A. Valle Isarco Gewürztraminer '23	♟♟ 4
A.A. Valle Isarco Grüner Veltliner '23	♟♟ 4
A.A. Valle Isarco Grüner Veltliner '15	♟♟♟ 3*
A.A. Valle Isarco Riesling Kaiton '16	♟♟♟ 3*
A.A. Valle Isarco Riesling Kaiton '12	♟♟♟ 4*
A.A. Valle Isarco Riesling Kaiton '11	♟♟♟ 4*
A.A. Valle Isarco Sylvaner '18	♟♟♟ 3*
A.A. Valle Isarco Sylvaner '14	♟♟♟ 3*
A.A. Valle Isarco Sylvaner '13	♟♟♟ 3*

★Cantina Kurtatsch

s.da del Vino, 23
39040 Cortaccia/Kurtatsch [BZ]
+39 0471880115
www.cantina-kurtatsch.it

CELLAR SALES
PRE-BOOKED VISITS
ANNUAL PRODUCTION 1,600,000 bottles
HECTARES UNDER VINE 190.00
SUSTAINABLE WINERY

The Cortaccia cooperative manages its vineyards in the South Tyrolean Unterland at elevations spanning 220 meters (in the valley floor) to 900 meters (in the higher zones), allowing each grape variety to mature in ideal conditions in terms of altitude, exposure, and soil. The rest is up to Erwin Carli and his team, who transform the grapes harvested into a range of wines that knows no weak points, highlighting the connection between the varietal and the best vineyards. The Cabernet Freienfeld '20, made from grapes harvested in the lower part of Cortaccia, offers up intense dark fruit suggestions on the nose, enriched by hints of graphite and spices. On the palate, it's full-bodied, invigorated by notes of anise, finishing crisp and energetic. The aromatic expression of the Gewürztraminer Brenntal '22 proves equally warm, with exotic notes of candied fruit meeting sweet spices before a sapid and harmonious palate. The Spumante 600 '18, from the vineyards of Penon, impresses with its vigorous palate.

● A.A. Cabernet Sauvignon Freienfeld Ris. '20	♟♟♟ 8
○ A.A. Gewürztraminer Brenntal Ris. '22	♟♟ 6
○ A.A. Spumante Extra Brut M. Cl. Blanc de Blancs 600 Ris. '18	♟♟ 7
○ A.A. Bianco Amos '22	♟♟ 5
○ A.A. Chardonnay Freienfeld Ris. '21	♟♟ 7
● A.A. Merlot Brenntal Ris. '21	♟♟ 8
● A.A. Merlot Cabernet Soma '22	♟♟ 6
○ A.A. Pinot Bianco Hofstatt '22	♟♟ 4
○ A.A. Pinot Grigio Penon '22	♟♟ 5
● A.A. Pinot Nero Mazon Ris. '21	♟♟ 5
○ A.A. Sauvignon Kofl '22	♟♟ 5
● A.A. Schiava Sonntaler Alte Reben '23	♟♟ 4
○ A.A. Gewürztraminer Brenntal Ris. '21	♟♟♟ 6

Laimburg

loc. Laimburg, 6
39040 Vadena/Pfatten [BZ]
+39 0471969590
www.laimburg.bz.it

CELLAR SALES
PRE-BOOKED VISITS
ANNUAL PRODUCTION 100,000 bottles
HECTARES UNDER VINE 20.00
SUSTAINABLE WINERY

Few provinces can boast a comprehensive viticulture research center that works with all production areas and supports local agriculture. The Laimburg Institute does more than this; it also operates an interesting winery. Drawing on vineyards scattered throughout the region, it produces both straightforward, varietal wines and more ambitious selections. The Gewürztraminer Elyònd is produced from grapes grown in an area extremely well suited to the variety. Söll is a small, southeast-facing vineyard situated at 350 meters elevation, whose soils are clay-limestone. The nose opens with an intense smoky note that gradually gives way to exotic fruit and spices, sensations also found on the palate, where the wine reveals its fullness and harmony. The Lagrein Barbagòl '21 is also convincing, with its vibrant dark fruit and underbrush suggestions, offering a palate of superb weight, tension, and length.

○ A.A. Gewürztraminer Elyònd Ris. '21	▼▼ 5
● A.A. Cabernet Sauvignon Sass Roà Ris. '21	▼▼ 5
● A.A. Lago di Caldaro Cl. Sup. Vernacius Solemnis '22	▼▼ 4
● A.A. Lagrein Barbagòl Ris. '21	▼▼ 5
● A.A. Moscato Rosa Passito '22	▼▼ 6
○ A.A. Pinot Bianco Musis '22	▼▼ 4
○ A.A. Riesling '22	▼▼ 4
○ A.A. Sauvignon Oyèll Ris. '21	▼▼ 5
● Col de Réy '20	▼▼ 6
○ A.A. Gewürztraminer '94	▽▽▽ 5
● A.A. Lagrein Scuro Barbagòl Ris. '00	▽▽▽ 5
○ A.A. Gewürztraminer Elyònd Ris. '20	▽▽ 4
● A.A. Lago di Caldaro Cl. Sup. Vernacius Solemnis '21	▽▽ 3*
● A.A. Moscato Rosa Passito '20	▽▽ 6
○ A.A. Riesling '21	▽▽ 4

Klaus Lentsch

s.da Reinsperg, 18a
39057 Appiano/Eppan [BZ]
+39 0471967263
www.klauslentsch.eu

CELLAR SALES
PRE-BOOKED VISITS
ANNUAL PRODUCTION 50,000 bottles
HECTARES UNDER VINE 6.00

Klaus Lentsch's winery opened in 2008, but his family's roots in viticulture run much deeper. Today, in the modern, well-equipped winery nestled among the vineyards of Oltradige, grapes from various plots are brought together. Each grape enjoys the best possible growing conditions, with the Eisack Valley, Oltradige, and Bassa Atesina forming the basis of production. The Grüner Veltliner Eichberg '22 is made from grapes harvested on a terraced vineyard that climbs from 400 to 600 meters in search of light and freshness. The nose unveils clear smoky nuances that encircle ripe white fruit, accompanied by floral and flint notes. On the palate, it reveals an unexpected firmness, lengthening decisively to a crisp and persistent finish. Among the reds, we appreciated the Lagrein Laianus Riserva '19, which showcases a highly concentrated, supple, taut profile.

○ A.A. Valle Isarco Grüner Veltliner Eichberg '22	▼▼ 5
● A.A. Lagrein Amperg Ris. '21	▼▼ 5
● A.A. Lagrein Laianus Ris. '19	▼▼ 6
○ A.A. Pinot Bianco Weissberg Ris. '22	▼▼ 5
● A.A. Pinot Nero Bachgart Ris. '21	▼▼ 4
○ A.A. Moscato Giallo '23	▼ 3
● A.A. Pinot Nero Bachgart '13	▽▽▽ 4
● A.A. Lagrein Amperg Ris. '20	▽▽ 4
● A.A. Lagrein Amperg Ris. '19	▽▽ 4
● A.A. Lagrein Laianus Ris. '18	▽▽ 6
○ A.A. Moscato Giallo '22	▽▽ 2
○ A.A. Pinot Bianco '22	▽▽ 3
○ A.A. Pinot Bianco Weissberg Ris. '19	▽▽ 4
● A.A. Pinot Nero Bachgart Ris. '20	▽▽ 4
● A.A. Pinot Nero Hemberg Ris. '17	▽▽ 6

Loacker Schwarhof

loc. Santa Giustina, 3
39100 Bolzano/Bozen
☎ +39 0471365125
🖷 www.loacker.bio

CELLAR SALES
PRE-BOOKED VISITS
ANNUAL PRODUCTION 60,000 bottles
HECTARES UNDER VINE 7.00
VITICULTURE METHOD Certified Organic
SUSTAINABLE WINERY

The Loacker family holds a prominent place among those producers who pioneered organic winemaking in Alto Adige. Active on the hillsides behind Bolzano for nearly half a century, they embraced organic practices early on, and then biodynamics. Today, Hayo, son of founder Rainer, and his brothers Franz Josef and Hannes, manage the winery with the same passion and vision, producing characterful wines, with Lagrein as their signature. This year, the standout is the Santa Maddalena Ihlderhof '22, a wine that amazes with its aromatic profile, dominated by a sulfur note that gives way to extraordinarily intact and juicy fruit, enhanced by an intriguing floral touch. On the palate, sapidity takes center stage, and the wine is supple, with a compelling drinkability. In contrast, the Gran Lareyn Riserva '21 offers deeper, more brooding aromas, with dark fruit framed by notes of spices and undergrowth. The palate is full-bodied, with smooth tannins and perfectly integrated acidity.

★Manincor

loc. San Giuseppe al Lago, 4
39052 Caldaro/Kaltern [BZ]
☎ +39 0471960230
🖷 www.manincor.com

CELLAR SALES
PRE-BOOKED VISITS
ANNUAL PRODUCTION 350,000 bottles
HECTARES UNDER VINE 50.00
VITICULTURE METHOD Certified Biodynamic
SUSTAINABLE WINERY

The agricultural landscape of Bolzano is marked by a patchwork of smallholding producers, with many wineries cultivating less than one hectare each. The Goëss Enzemberg estate is an exception, managing an extensive viticultural patrimony stretching from the shores of Lake Caldaro to Terlano and the hills overlooking Merano. This San Giuseppe al Lago producer put in an impressive performance, with many wines that thoroughly convinced our panels. We were particularly intrigued by the comparison between the two 2022 Sauvignons: the Tannenberg, which plays on aromatic intensity and a dynamic palate, and the Lieben Aich, which offers deeper, more recondite aromas, leading palate a sip of great elegance and consistency. The Eichhorn '22 is the usual top-class pinot bianco, outlined by white fruit and invigorating herbal notes, which carry through on a sapid, juicy, and notably long palate.

● A.A. Santa Maddalena Ihlderhof '22	♈♈ 4
● A.A. Lagrein Gran Lareyn Ris. '21	♈♈ 5
○ Atagis Gewürztraminer '23	♈♈ 4
● Gran Lareyn Lagrein '22	♈♈ 5
● Kastlet Cabernet '21	♈♈ 5
○ A.A. Sauvignon Tasnim '23	♈ 4
○ Souvignier Gris '23	♈ 5
● A.A. Merlot Ywain '04	♈♈♈ 4*
● A.A. Lagrein Gran Lareyn Ris. '20	♈♈ 5
○ Atagis '22	♈♈ 4
● Gran Lareyn '21	♈♈ 4
● Gran Lareyn '20	♈♈ 4
● Kastlet '20	♈♈ 5
○ Tasnim Sauvignon '22	♈♈ 4
● Ywain Merlot '19	♈♈ 4

○ A.A. Terlano Pinot Bianco Eichhorn '22	♈♈♈ 6
○ A.A. Terlano Sauvignon Lieben Aich '22	♈♈ 8
○ A.A. Terlano Sauvignon Tannenberg '22	♈♈ 6
● A.A. Pinot Nero Mason '22	♈♈ 6
● A.A. Pinot Nero Mason di Mason '21	♈♈ 8
○ A.A. Terlano Chardonnay Sophie '22	♈♈ 7
○ A.A. Terlano La Contessa '23	♈♈ 5
● Castel Campan '21	♈♈ 8
○ A.A. Terlano Pinot Bianco Eichhorn '19	♈♈♈ 5
○ A.A. Terlano Sauvignon Lieben Aich '20	♈♈♈ 8

ALTO ADIGE

Lorenz Martini

loc. Cornaiano/Girlan
via Pranzoll, 2d
39057 Appiano/Eppan [BZ]
(☎ +39 0471664136
✆ www.lorenzmartini.com

CELLAR SALES
PRE-BOOKED VISITS
ANNUAL PRODUCTION 20,000 bottles
HECTARES UNDER VINE 3.00

Considered one of the pioneers of Alto Adige's sparkling wine industry, Lorenz Martini has been producing spumante since the mid-1980s. Today, in his small cellar in Cornaiano, he focuses exclusively on bubbly made from chardonnay, pinot bianco, and pinot nero grapes, harvested in areas where cooler temperatures allow the fruit to develop elegance and gustatory tension. The Comitissa '20 perfectly embodies the concept of a sparkling wine produced in an area characterized by its light and day-night temperature swings, with grapes that ripen to perfection while retaining their acidity. The result is a pale, luminous hue and aromas of remarkable finesse, where white fruit and flowers are accompanied by a delicate hint of minerality and breakfast pastries. In the mouth, don't expect concentration; instead, expect great sapidity and a citric acid streak that lengthens and energizes the palate.

K. Martini & Sohn

loc. Cornaiano
via Lamm, 28
39057 Appiano/Eppan [BZ]
(☎ +39 0471663156
✆ www.martini-sohn.it

CELLAR SALES
PRE-BOOKED VISITS
ANNUAL PRODUCTION 230,000 bottles
HECTARES UNDER VINE 30.00

The historic winery on Via Lamm is a prominent figure in the Oltradige area, with an extensive vineyard portfolio that includes both estate-owned plots and others cultivated by local growers. It's a makeup that enables Martini & Sohn to produce excellent wines, divided between selections that focus on varietal expression and the Palladium line, which involves the careful selection of grapes. The Maturum, which hails from the best plots, represents their flagship. A wide range of wines was presented, including some that impressed our panels. The most interesting results came from their reds, such as the Lagrein Maturum '21, a Riserva redolent of dark fruit and invigorating herbal notes, sensations echoed on a firm, tense palate. The Pinot Nero '21 of the same name plays on simple aromas on the nose, while on the palate it favors elegance and suppleness over concentration. The Pinot Bianco Palladium '23 also performed well, highlighting the variety's trademark finesse.

○ A.A. Spumante Pas Dosé Comitissa Ris. '20	▼▼▼ 6
○ A.A. Spumante Brut Comitissa Gold Gran Riserva '11	♈♈ 8
○ A.A. Spumante Brut Comitissa Gold Gran Riserva '06	♈♈ 5
○ A.A. Spumante Pas Dosé Comitissa Ris. '19	♈♈ 6
○ A.A. Spumante Pas Dosé Comitissa Ris. '18	♈♈ 6
○ A.A. Spumante Pas Dosé Comitissa Ris. '17	♈♈ 6
○ A.A. Spumante Pas Dosé Comitissa Ris. '15	♈♈ 5
○ A.A. Spumante Pas Dosé Comitissa Ris. '13	♈♈ 5

○ A.A. Chardonnay Maturum Ris. '21	▼▼ 4
○ A.A. Kerner Palladium '23	▼▼ 4
● A.A. Lagrein Maturum Ris. '21	▼▼ 5
● A.A. Lagrein Pure Origin '23	▼▼ 3
○ A.A. Moscato Giallo '23	▼▼ 4
○ A.A. Pinot Bianco Alte Reben '21	▼▼ 5
○ A.A. Pinot Bianco Palladium '22	▼▼ 4
○ A.A. Pinot Grigio Palladium '23	▼▼ 4
● A.A. Pinot Nero Maturum Ris. '21	▼▼ 5
● A.A. Pinot Nero Palladium '22	▼▼ 4
○ A.A. Sauvignon Alte Reben '21	▼▼ 5
○ A.A. Sauvignon Palladium '23	▼▼ 4
○ A.A. Sauvignon Palladium '04	♈♈♈ 2
○ A.A. Chardonnay Maturum '16	♈♈ 4
○ A.A. Pinot Bianco Palladium '15	♈♈ 2
○ A.A. Sauvignon Palladium '16	♈♈ 3

★Cantina Merano

via Cantina, 9
39020 Marlengo/Marling [BZ]
☎ +39 0473447137
⊛ www.cantinamerano.it

CELLAR SALES
PRE-BOOKED VISITS
ANNUAL PRODUCTION 1,400,000 bottles
HECTARES UNDER VINE 245.00

The Merano cooperative is characterized by a highly fragmented patchwork of plots cultivated by a large number of members, each of whom often owns just over half a hectare. The vineyards, however, are meticulously cared for, in close collaboration with the technical team led by Stefan Kapfinger. This extreme level of attention ensures a range that highlights both the area around Merano and the more remote Vinschgau Valley. The cooperative produces a Pinot Bianco '22 of rare finesse, drawing on vineyards near Castel Tirolo. Aromas of ripe white fruit are accompanied by floral notes and a hint of oak in the background. On the palate, the wine follows the character of the grapes, revealing elegance, harmony, and length. The V Years '18, on the other hand, explores complexity and fruit maturity, which find their ideal complement in a mineral presence of flint. Tasting reveals a rich, juicy, and very long palate. The energetic and deep Lagrein Segen '21 is also excellent.

Tenuta Moser

Pianizza di Sotto, 13/a
39052 Caldaro/Kaltern [BZ]
☎ +39 04711551861
⊛ www.weingutmoser.it

CELLAR SALES
ANNUAL PRODUCTION 55,000 bottles
HECTARES UNDER VINE 10.00
SUSTAINABLE WINERY

Even if their winery is relatively young, the Moser family has been deeply involved in the viticulture of Oltradige for nearly half a century. Their estate stretches near Caldaro and Monticolo, where vineyards blend into the forests surrounding the small lake. In the cellar, their collaboration with winemaker Gerhard Sanin produces a high-quality range. The Pinot Grigio '23 draws on grapes harvested from a porphyry-rich vineyard in Monticolo, situated at nearly 500 meters elevation, and undergoes oak aging. The result is aromas of pear and yellow fruit, but it truly shines on the palate, where it displays freshness, sapidity, and dynamism. The Lagrein '21 is also excellent, with dark fruit followed by deeper notes of undergrowth and graphite, which reverberate on a palate of superb weight and length. The Sauvignon Gold '22 opts for sulfuric aromas and yellow fruit on an energetic and harmonious palate.

○ A.A. Pinot Bianco Tyrol '22	♟♟♟	6
○ A.A. Pinot Bianco V Years Ris. '18	♟♟	8
● A.A. Pinot Nero Zeno Ris. '21	♟♟	6
○ A.A. Cabernet Graf Ris. '20	♟♟	5
○ A.A. Chardonnay Goldegg '22	♟♟	6
● A.A. Lagrein Segen Ris. '21	♟♟	6
○ A.A. Meranese Schickenburg '23	♟♟	4
○ A.A. Merlot Freiherr Ris. '21	♟♟	6
○ A.A. Riesling Graf '23	♟♟	4
○ A.A. Sauvignon Mervin Ris. '21	♟♟	6
○ A.A. Spumante Brut M. Cl. 36 Ris. '19	♟♟	6
○ A.A. Sauvignon Graf '23	♟	4
○ A.A. Chardonnay Goldegg Ris. '19	♟♟♟	5
○ A.A. Pinot Bianco Tyrol '18	♟♟♟	4
○ A.A. Pinot Bianco Tyrol '16	♟♟♟	4*

○ A.A. Chardonnay '23	♟♟	3
● A.A. Lagrein '21	♟♟	5
● A.A. Merlot Cabernet Ris. '21	♟♟	5
○ A.A. Pinot Grigio '23	♟♟	4
○ A.A. Sauvignon '23	♟♟	3
○ A.A. Sauvignon Gold '22	♟♟	4
● A.A. Lago di Caldaro Cl. Sup. '23	♟	4
⊙ A.A. Lagrein Rosé '23	♟	3
○ A.A. Chardonnay '22	♟♟	3
● A.A. Lagrein Ris. '20	♟♟	3
○ A.A. Pinot Grigio '22	♟♟	3
○ A.A. Sauvignon '22	♟♟	3

★★Muri-Gries

p.zza Gries, 21
39100 Bolzano/Bozen
📞 +39 0471282287
🌐 www.muri-gries.com

CELLAR SALES
ANNUAL PRODUCTION 650,000 bottles
HECTARES UNDER VINE 60.00

Bolzano is the third largest wine-growing municipality in Alto Adige, with over 700 hectares unfolding around the city center. It's choice growing country for two important native grapes: schiava and lagrein. The city's standout winery is Muri Gries, which still boasts the area's most famous "clos", Klosteranger. Dedicated to lagrein, this 3-hectare plot is the producer's crown jewel. Muri Gries also draws on a vast property in Oltradige. It's hard to choose the most convincing wine from the rich array presented this year, but a skillful production approach and access to some of the best vineyards of lagrein have made for two wines of great depth. The Abtei Muri '21 conjures up dark fruit and spice aromas on a palate of great energy and tension. The Klosteranger '20 is slower, deeper, and more layered, conquering the palate with its decisiveness, harmony, and vigor. The Pinot Nero Abtei Muri '21, diametrically opposed in style, stands out for its length and elegance.

★Nals Margreid

via Heiligenberg, 2
39010 Nalles/Nals [BZ]
📞 +39 0471678626
🌐 www.nalsmargreid.com

CELLAR SALES
PRE-BOOKED VISITS
ANNUAL PRODUCTION 1,000,000 bottles
HECTARES UNDER VINE 160.00
SUSTAINABLE WINERY

Over time, cooperatives often feel the need to join forces and create larger entities. The uniqueness of Nalles lies in bringing together two very distant territories: Nalles and Magrè in the extreme south of the province. This allows Harald Schraffl and his technical team to work with grapes that mature under very different conditions, bringing character and originality to their wines. The range produced here on Via Heiligenberg is flawless. Interpretations closely tied to the varietal are flanked by selections that emphasize the bond between varietal and territory. This is the case with the Sirmian '22, a pinot bianco made from grapes harvested at 500-700 meters elevation, then pressed and matured in large barrels. The result highlights the variety's signature finesse and tension. The Pinot Grigio Punggl '22 proves to be an energetic, taut drink, while the Sauvignon Mantele '22 stands out for its suppleness and length.

● A.A. Lagrein V. Klosteranger Ris. '20	🍷🍷🍷 8
● A.A. Lagrein Abtei Muri Ris. '21	🍷🍷 6
● A.A. Pinot Nero Abtei Muri Ris. '21	🍷🍷 6
○ A.A. Lagrein Rosé '23	🍷🍷 3
● A.A. Moscato Rosa V.T. Abtei Muri '22	🍷🍷 5
● A.A. Santa Maddalena Cl. '23	🍷🍷 3
○ A.A. Terlano Pinot Bianco '23	🍷🍷 3
○ A.A. Terlano Pinot Bianco Abtei Muri Ris. '21	🍷🍷 6
● A.A. Lagrein V. Klosteranger Ris. '17	🍷🍷🍷 8
● A.A. Lagrein V. Klosteranger Ris. '16	🍷🍷🍷 8
○ A.A. Terlano Pinot Bianco Abtei Muri Ris. '20	🍷🍷🍷 6

○ A.A. Pinot Bianco Sirmian '22	🍷🍷🍷 5
○ A.A. Pinot Grigio Punggl '22	🍷🍷 5
○ A.A. Sauvignon Mantele '22	🍷🍷 5
○ A.A. Chardonnay Baron Salvadori Ris. '21	🍷🍷 6
○ A.A. Chardonnay Magred '23	🍷🍷 4
● A.A. Lagrein Gries Ris. '21	🍷🍷 4
○ A.A. Moscato Giallo Passito Baronesse '22	🍷🍷 7
○ A.A. Pinot Bianco Penon '23	🍷🍷 4
● A.A. Pinot Nero Jura Ris. '21	🍷🍷 5
● A.A. Schiava Galea '23	🍷🍷 4
● A.A. Merlot Cabernet Anticus Ris. '21	🍷 7
○ A.A. Pinot Bianco Sirmian '21	🍷🍷🍷 5
○ A.A. Sauvignon Mantele '20	🍷🍷🍷 5

Tenuta Nicolussi-Leck

via Kreith, 2
39051 Caldaro/Kaltern [BZ]
📞 +39 3382963793
🌐 www.wein.kaltern.com

ANNUAL PRODUCTION 32,000 bottles
HECTARES UNDER VINE 5.00

Between Lake Caldaro and the Adige Valley lies Monte di Mezzo, a large wooded ridge protected by the ruins of Leuchtenburg. At the area's lower elevations, vineyards flourish—and it's here, just above Campi a Lago, that we find the estate of Jakob Nicolussi Leck. The vineyards stretch between the two mountains, offering glacial soil rich in gravel and silt. The production style is characterized by aromatic clarity and gustatory tension. Jakob's wines impress more and more with each passing year, with many that made believers of our tasters. The Merlot Georg '20 is a Riserva that initially appears closed, almost reticent, then releases ripe and fleshy fruit. On the palate, the wine expresses all the warmth of the area, unfolding energetic and juicy. The Pinot Bianco Verena '22 also caught our attention, passing from intense fruity notes to an elegant and taut palate.

Niklaserhof - Dieter Sölva

loc. San Nicolò
via delle Fontane, 31a
39052 Caldaro/Kaltern [BZ]
📞 +39 0471963434
🌐 www.niklaserhof.it

CELLAR SALES
PRE-BOOKED VISITS
ANNUAL PRODUCTION 50,000 bottles
HECTARES UNDER VINE 7.00

ALTO ADIGE

The Sölva family has been based around Lake Caldaro for generations, in one of Alto Adige's most well-known wine-growing districts. The vineyards closest to the lake benefit from warmth and sunlight, while those climbing up toward the Mendola seek cooler temperatures. Their estate is divided into numerous parcels, each carefully selected to suit specific grape varieties. The grapes for the Pinot Bianco Klaser '21, a Riserva, are harvested from the Kardatsch area, situated at over 500 meters elevation, then pressed and matured in oak. Vibrant notes of ripe yellow fruit and dried flowers prove even more distinct on the palate, where the wine reveals its richness and sapidity. The Bianco DJJ '21, a multifaceted blend (the result of different vineyards), conjures up complex aromas where white fruit meets flint notes; a palate of rare precision and elegance follows. Among the reds, from vineyards closer to the lake, the juicy Klaser Hecht '23 caught our attention.

○ A.A. Gewürztraminer Stephanie '22	🍷🍷 4
○ A.A. Lago di Caldaro Cl. Sup. Alexander '22	🍷🍷 4
● A.A. Merlot 1950 Georg Ris. '20	🍷🍷 5
○ A.A. Pinot Bianco Verena '22	🍷🍷 4
○ A.A. Sauvignon Karolina '22	🍷🍷 4
○ A.A. Sauvignon Ris. '21	🍷🍷 5
○ A.A. Chardonnay Magdalena Ris. '21	🍷 4
● A.A. Cabernet Franc Ris. '20	🍷🍷 5
● A.A. Cabernet Franc Ris. '19	🍷🍷 5
○ A.A. Chardonnay Magdalena '21	🍷🍷 4
○ A.A. Gewürztraminer Stephanie '21	🍷🍷 4
○ A.A. Pinot Bianco Verena '21	🍷🍷 4
○ A.A. Pinot Bianco Verena '20	🍷🍷 4
○ A.A. Sauvignon Karolina '21	🍷🍷 4

○ A.A. Pinot Bianco Klaser Salamander Ris. '21	🍷🍷 4
○ A.A. Bianco DJJ '21	🍷🍷 6
○ A.A. Kerner Libellula Mondevinum Ris. '21	🍷🍷 4
○ A.A. Kerner Luxs '23	🍷🍷 3
● A.A. Lago di Caldaro Cl. Sup. Klaser Hecht '23	🍷🍷 4
● A.A. Lagrein Bos Taurus Mondevinum Ris. '21	🍷🍷 6
● A.A. Lagrein Cabernet Klaser Stoanadler '21	🍷🍷 5
● A.A. Merlot DJJ Ris. '21	🍷🍷 7
○ A.A. Pinot Bianco Hos '23	🍷🍷 3
○ A.A. Sauvignon Doxs '23	🍷🍷 3
○ A.A. Pinot Bianco Klaser Ris. '15	🍷🍷🍷 4*

Pfannenstielhof
Johannes Pfeifer
via Pfannestiel, 9
39100 Bolzano/Bozen
☎ +39 0471970884
● www.pfannenstielhof.it

CELLAR SALES
PRE-BOOKED VISITS
ANNUAL PRODUCTION 43,000 bottles
HECTARES UNDER VINE 4.00

The Pfeifer family's winery perfectly represents the microcosm of Santa Maddalena. This family, settled in the area for generations, cultivates their vineyards with passion and a strong connection to tradition. Johannes, his wife Margareth, and their daughters Anna and Veronika manage the estate. The porphyry-rich foothills are dedicated to schiava while the lower areas, which are characterized by river deposits, host lagrein. The excellent 2021 vintage allowed the grapes to reach perfect ripeness, and the results are evident in both the Lagrein Riserva and the Annver. The former opens with vibrant notes of dark fruit intertwined with mineral and underbrush nuances. The palate is firm, juicy, lengthening decisively toward an energetic finish. The latter, on the other hand, delves into the more hidden character of schiava: its richness of fruit on the nose is followed by a refined and consistent palate that closes with a lovely herbal note.

Tenuta Pfitscher
via Dolomiti, 17
39040 Montagna/Montan [BZ]
☎ +39 04711681317
● www.pfitscher.it

CELLAR SALES
PRE-BOOKED VISITS
ACCOMMODATION
ANNUAL PRODUCTION 180,000 bottles
HECTARES UNDER VINE 25.00
SUSTAINABLE WINERY

The Pfitscher family's winery is nestled among the vineyards in the Montagna area, where pinot nero has found superb growing conditions. The vineyards span both sides of the valley, alternating between warm, sunny areas and cooler, breezier spots. This allows for a range where each grape variety is grown in the territory to which it is best suited. The role of the Burgundian red grape variety is increasingly central at Pfitscher, with several wines exploring its connection to the area's vineyards. The Matan '21 offers up deep aromas, with wild fruit quickly giving way to notes of underbrush, wet earth, and cyclamen. On the palate, the characteristic richness of the production area emerges, with tannins and acidity providing structure and tension. The Sauvignon Mathias '22 plays on exotic fruit and sulfurous notes before delivering a refined and remarkably long palate. The Lagrein Rivus '22 is also delicious—rich and juicy.

● A.A. Lagrein Ris. '21	▼▼ 6
● A.A. Santa Maddalena Cl. Annver '21	▼▼ 5
⊙ A.A. Lagrein Rosé '23	▼▼ 3
● A.A. Lagrein vom Boden '23	▼▼ 5
● A.A. Santa Maddalena Cl. '23	▼▼ 4
● A.A. Santa Maddalena Der Pfannenstielhof '18	▼▼ 7
● A.A. Santa Maddalena Cl. '22	▼▼▼ 4*
● A.A. Santa Maddalena Cl. '14	▼▼▼ 3*
● A.A. Santa Maddalena Cl. '09	▼▼▼ 2*
● A.A. Lagrein Ris. '20	♈♈ 5
● A.A. Lagrein Ris. '19	♈♈ 5
● A.A. Santa Maddalena Cl. Annver '19	♈♈ 3
● A.A. Santa Maddalena Der Pfannenstiel '16	♈♈ 5

● A.A. Pinot Nero Matan Ris. '21	▼▼▼ 7
○ A.A. Sauvignon Mathias Ris. '22	▼▼ 6
○ A.A. Chardonnay Arvum '23	▼▼ 4
○ A.A. Gewürztraminer Stoass '23	▼▼ 4
● A.A. Lagrein Griesfeld Ris. '21	▼▼ 5
● A.A. Lagrein Rivus '22	▼▼ 4
● A.A. Merlot Cabernet Cortazo Ris. '21	▼▼ 6
○ A.A. Pinot Bianco Longarei '23	▼▼ 4
● A.A. Pinot Nero Fuxleiten '22	▼▼ 6
● A.A. Pinot Nero V. das Langefeld Ris. '20	▼▼ 7
○ A.A. Sauvignon Saxum '23	▼▼ 5
● A.A. Lagrein Griesfeld Ris. '20	♈♈ 5
● A.A. Pinot Nero V. das Langefeld Ris. '19	♈♈ 6

★Tenuta Ritterhof

s.da del Vino , I
39052 Caldaro/Kaltern [BZ]
☏ +39 0471963298
🖥 www.ritterhof.it

CELLAR SALES
PRE-BOOKED VISITS
RESTAURANT SERVICE
ANNUAL PRODUCTION 330,000 bottles
HECTARES UNDER VINE 40.00
SUSTAINABLE WINERY

The Roner family winery is set just a stone's throw from the center of Caldaro and offers a splendid view of the large vineyard sloping towards the lake. The heart of the property lies in Oltradige, but it also extends towards Bassa Atesina and the city basin, where the vineyards along the valley floor are planted with lagrein. On the slopes of Ritten, pinot bianco and sauvignon are cultivated. The standout, however, remains gewürztraminer, a variety for which the winery offers several interpretations, with the Auratus '23 being the flagship. The nose reveals clear notes of exotic fruit and spices, with a subtle citrus nuance adding freshness. On the palate, the variety's richness is perfectly expressed, with a full and persistent finish. The passito version, Sonus '21, is an explosion of candied citrus, enriched by the presence of botrytis, which captivates the palate with its measured sweetness and excellent sapidity.

○ A.A. Gewürztraminer Auratus '23	♟♟ 6
● A.A. Lago di Caldaro Cl. Sup. Novis '23	♟♟ 4
● A.A. Lagrein Latus '22	♟♟ 5
● A.A. Lagrein Manus Ris. '21	♟♟ 7
● A.A. Merlot Mollis '20	♟♟ 5
○ A.A. Pinot Bianco Venus '23	♟♟ 4
○ A.A. Pinot Grigio Opes '22	♟♟ 5
● A.A. Pinot Nero Dignus '19	♟♟ 6
○ A.A. Sauvignon Paratus '22	♟♟ 5
○ Natus Souvignier Gris '22	♟♟ 5
○ Sonus Gewürztraminer Passito '21	♟♟ 7
● Perlhofer '22	♟ 4
○ A.A. Gewürztraminer Auratus '22	♟♟♟ 6
○ A.A. Gewürztraminer Auratus '21	♟♟♟ 5
○ A.A. Gewürztraminer Auratus '20	♟♟♟ 5

Tenuta Hans Rottensteiner

fraz. Gries
via Sarentino, Ia
39100 Bolzano/Bozen
☏ +39 0471282015
🖥 www.rottensteiner.wine

CELLAR SALES
PRE-BOOKED VISITS
ANNUAL PRODUCTION 450,000 bottles
HECTARES UNDER VINE 60.50

The Rottensteiner family has been active in Alto Adige for almost 70 years. Initially, they produced wine for bulk export, mainly to Switzerland. Later, they began bottling production for the global market. For the past 20 years, Hannes has managed the family business, solidifying its historic collaboration with numerous local growers and establishing it as a reference point for enthusiasts. Their wines demonstrate superb stylistic precision, with our preferences going to the Lagrein Select '21, a Riserva that opens on aromas of dark fruit and spices, echoed on the palate where nice weight gives way to an energetic, tannic finish. The Santa Maddalena '23, from their Premstallerhof vineyard, takes a different approach, highlighting the aromatic freshness of schiava and offering a dynamic, gratifying palate. The elegant and long Pinot Bianco Carnol consistently impresses.

● A.A. Santa Maddalena Cl. V. Premstallerhof '23	♟♟♟ 4*
● A.A. Lagrein Select Ris. '21	♟♟ 5
● A.A. Cabernet Select Ris. '19	♟♟ 5
○ A.A. Gewürztraminer Cancenai '23	♟♟ 5
○ A.A. Gewürztraminer Passito Cresta '21	♟♟ 7
○ A.A. Pinot Bianco Carnol '23	♟♟ 4
○ A.A. Pinot Grigio '23	♟♟ 3
● A.A. Pinot Nero Select Ris. '21	♟♟ 5
○ A.A. Sauvignon '23	♟♟ 4
○ A.A. Sylvaner '23	♟♟ 3
⊙ A.A. Lagrein Rosé '23	♟ 3
● A.A. Schiava V. Kristplonerhof '23	♟ 3
● A.A. Santa Maddalena Cl. V. Premstallerhof '22	♟♟ 4

ALTO ADIGE

353

★★★Cantina Produttori San Michele Appiano

via Circonvallazione, 17/19
39057 Appiano/Eppan [BZ]
☎ +39 0471664466
🌐 www.stmichael.it

CELLAR SALES
PRE-BOOKED VISITS
ANNUAL PRODUCTION 2,800,000 bottles
HECTARES UNDER VINE 390.00

After many years leading the cooperative in Appiano, Hans Terzer took a step back, maintaining a consulting role while handing the reins over to the young Jakob Gasser. Indeed, starting this year, Gasser will oversee all production phases. The extensive estate spans some of the best parts of Oltradige, resulting in wines that have established themselves among Italy's finest over the decades. Many wines are convincing, starting with the Pinot Nero Sanct Valentin '21, which consistently ranks as one of the best in Italy. Its brilliant ruby color introduces aromas of great finesse, with wild fruit set against a backdrop of iris and rain-soaked earth, sensations reverberate on a firm palate, with polished tannins and notable length. The Pinot Grigio Sanct Valentin '22 proves true to type in its smoky and ripe pear notes, captivating the palate with its elegant profile. The excellent Comtess' 22, a passito, reveals a juicy and perfectly balanced palate.

Cantina San Paolo

loc. San Paolo
via Castel Guardia, 21
39057 Appiano/Eppan [BZ]
☎ +39 0471 1807700
🌐 www.stpauls.wine

CELLAR SALES
PRE-BOOKED VISITS
ANNUAL PRODUCTION 1,500,000 bottles
HECTARES UNDER VINE 185.00

The history of the San Paolo cooperative, which began over a century ago, has been marked by steady growth, with gradual expansion of its member base accompanied by improved production facilities and an increasing focus on sustainability, territorial identity, and community. The past year has seen major changes made to the commercial team, now led by Tobias Leimgruber, and the production team, headed by kellermeister Philipp Zublasing. The results didn't disappoint, and the wines presented this year thoroughly convinced our tasters. The Pinot Nero Lehmont '21 proves excellent, opening with smoky notes that gradually give way to wild fruit and herbal nuances. On the palate, it's sapid and expansive—a wine of great elegance. The Kalkberg '22 is a Pinot Bianco of remarkable freshness, sapidity, and tension. We conclude with the excellent Sauvignon Schliff '22, a wine that stands out for its suppleness and harmony on the palate.

● A.A. Pinot Nero Sanct Valentin Ris. '21	♟♟♟ 7
○ A.A. Pinot Grigio Sanct Valentin '22	♟♟ 6
○ A.A. Chardonnay Fallwind '23	♟♟ 4
○ A.A. Chardonnay Sanct Valentin '22	♟♟ 6
○ A.A. Gewürztraminer Fallwind '23	♟♟ 5
○ A.A. Gewürztraminer Passito Comtess Sanct Valentin '22	♟♟ 7
○ A.A. Gewürztraminer Sanct Valentin '23	♟♟ 6
○ A.A. Pinot Bianco Sanct Valentin '22	♟♟ 6
○ A.A. Pinot Bianco Schulthaus '23	♟♟ 4
○ A.A. Pinot Grigio Fallwind '23	♟♟ 4
○ A.A. Sauvignon Sanct Valentin '23	♟♟ 6
○ A.A. Bianco Appius '17	♟♟♟ 8
○ A.A. Pinot Bianco Sanct Valentin '21	♟♟♟ 5

○ A.A. Pinot Bianco Kalkberg '22	♟♟ 5
● A.A. Pinot Nero Lehmont Ris. '21	♟♟ 6
○ A.A. Chardonnay Fuxberg '23	♟♟ 4
○ A.A. Gewürztraminer Justina '23	♟♟ 4
● A.A. Lagrein Lagröll Ris. '21	♟♟ 6
○ A.A. Pinot Bianco Plötzner '23	♟♟ 4
○ A.A. Pinot Grigio Löss '23	♟♟ 4
● A.A. Pinot Nero Luzia '22	♟♟ 4
○ A.A. Sauvignon Gfill '23	♟♟ 4
○ A.A. Sauvignon Schliff '22	♟♟ 5
○ A.A. Spumante Brut M. Cl. Praeclarus	♟♟ 5
○ A.A. Spumante Pas Dosé M. Cl. Praeclarus '18	♟♟ 6
○ A.A. Pinot Bianco Passion Ris. '11	♟♟♟

Tenuta Seeperle

loc. San Giuseppe al Lago, 28
39052 Caldaro/Kaltern [BZ]
☎ +39 0471960158
✉ www.seeperle.it

ANNUAL PRODUCTION 25,000 bottles
HECTARES UNDER VINE 2.00

Even if the Rainer family has long been involved in viticulture, it was only in 2013 that Arthur Rainer founded the winery, named after the family's hotel just steps from the shores of Lake Caldaro. The vineyards, which span a few hectares in the area, benefit from warm days followed by cool breezes from the surrounding mountains, allowing the grapes to mature with rich aromas. Although the range is limited in numbers, it's quite extensive, with the Arthur Rainer line representing its pinnacle. The Chardonnay '22 immediately reveals the connection between ripe yellow fruit and oak, which plays a supporting role in the aromatic phase. On the palate, it's rich and juicy—nice length. The Sauvignon Arthur Rainer '22, on the other hand, plays on more pronounced fruit, revealing exotic, mineral, and dried flower notes, sensations echoed on an elegant and racy palate. On the red wine front, the fragrant Lago di Caldaro Arthur Rainer '23 proves noteworthy.

○ A.A. Chardonnay Arthur Rainer '22	♟♟ 5
● A.A. Cabernet '22	♟♟ 4
● A.A. Lago di Caldaro Cl. Sup. Arthur Rainer '23	♟♟ 5
○ A.A. Pinot Bianco Leidenschaft '23	♟♟ 4
○ A.A. Sauvignon Arthur Rainer '22	♟♟ 5
○ A.A. Sauvignon Echt Geil '23	♟♟ 4
● A.A. Lago di Caldaro Cl. Sup. Scheinheilig '23	♟ 3
● A.A. Cabernet Sauvignon Idea '20	♟♟ 4
● A.A. Lago di Caldaro Cl. Sup. Scheinheilig '22	♟♟ 3
○ A.A. Pinot Bianco Leidenschaft '21	♟♟ 3
○ A.A. Sauvignon Arthur Rainer '21	♟♟ 5
○ A.A. Sauvignon Echt Geil '22	♟♟ 4
○ A.A. Sauvignon Echt Geil '21	♟♟ 4

Peter Sölva & Söhne

via dell'Oro, 33
39052 Caldaro/Kaltern [BZ]
☎ +39 0471964650
✉ www.soelva.com

CELLAR SALES
PRE-BOOKED VISITS
ANNUAL PRODUCTION 75,000 bottles
HECTARES UNDER VINE 12.00

The Sölva family winery is located in the heart of Caldaro, just a few steps from the main square. Although unassuming from the outside, once inside, you are enveloped in an atmosphere of tradition and history. The vineyards, stretching across about a dozen hectares between Oltradige and Bassa Atesina, yield a rich and mature profile. Given the warmth of the area, great attention is given to Bordeaux red varieties, resulting in wines of depth and fullness. The Cabernet Franc Amistar '21 takes advantage of the excellent vintage to offer up intense impressions of ripe, crunchy fruit, interspersed with animal whiffs and pepper, which add character and depth. On the palate, the wine is highly consistent and tense. The profile of the Peterleiten, a Lago di Caldaro, is diametrically opposed, opting for fresh, fruity aromas, and captivating the palate with its sapidity and dynamism.

● A.A. Cabernet Franc Amistar Ris. '21	♟♟ 8
● A.A. Lago di Caldaro Cl. Sup. DeSilva Peterleiten '22	♟♟ 5
● A.A. Cabernet Sauvignon Amistar Ris. '21	♟♟ 8
○ A.A. Sauvignon DeSilva '22	♟♟ 5
● Amistar Cuvée Rosso '21	♟♟ 5
○ Amistar Cuvée Bianco '22	♟ 6
○ A.A. Terlano Pinot Bianco DeSilva '10	♟♟♟ 3
○ A.A. Terlano Pinot Bianco DeSilva '09	♟♟♟ 3
● A.A. Cabernet Franc Amistar '20	♟♟ 5
○ A.A. Sauvignon DeSilva '21	♟♟ 4
○ Amistar Cuvée Bianco '21	♟♟ 6
● Amistar Cuvée Rosso '20	♟♟ 5

St. Quirinus - Robert Sinn
via Pianizza di Sopra, 4b
39052 Caldaro/Kaltern [BZ]
📞 +39 3298085003
🌐 www.st-quirinus.it

Steinhaus
via Pochi, 11
39040 Salorno/Salurn [BZ]
📞 +39 388 640 6913
🌐 www.wsteinhaus.com

CELLAR SALES
PRE-BOOKED VISITS
ACCOMMODATION
ANNUAL PRODUCTION 30,000 bottles
HECTARES UNDER VINE 2.50
VITICULTURE METHOD Certified Organic

ANNUAL PRODUCTION 30,000 bottles
HECTARES UNDER VINE 9.00
SUSTAINABLE WINERY

The Sinn family winery has a recent history, but the passion and care invested in every stage of production reveal a deep connection to viticulture and winemaking. The modern winery, built about a dozen years ago, is designed to minimize energy and water consumption. This allows Robert and his son Michael to produce wines that combine organoleptic quality with environmental sustainability. The Pianizza di Sopra-based producer offers a wide range, with many wines impressing our panel. The Sauvignon Quirinus '23, which comes from vines cultivated at 450 meters elevation, showcases a broad, fresh aromatic profile, where white fruit emerges alongside sulfurous and balsamic hints. On the palate, it impresses with its sapidity and tension, proving long and very persistent. The Merlot Riserva '21 reveals all the warmth of the vineyards that border the lake in its aromas of sweet, fleshy fruit, sensations that grow even clearer on an energetic, juicy palate.

In Pochi, the area cultivated with vines overlooks the Adige Valley. A vast vineyard terrace, sheltered by forests and mountains, it benefits from sunlight until late afternoon. Here, the Gussalli Beretta family acquired a nine-hectare estate at approximately 600 meters elevation. The property is home to pinot noir, chardonnay, gewürztraminer, and sauvignon grapes, which are crafted into a range of exceptional wines. The Gewürztraminer '23 introduces a new style for this traditional Alto Adige grape, foregoing explosive aromatics in favor of greater finesse and delicacy, resulting in a harmonious and gradual taste. The Pinot Nero Hirsch '21 is very interesting, playing on the clarity of wild fruit and herbal notes before offering a crisp, dynamic, and refined palate. The Pinot Nero '23 in its Rosé version, intrigues, standing out for the delicacy of its aromas, while on the palate, it proves sapid, supple, and gratifying.

○ A.A. Chardonnay Ris. '21	♟♟ 5
● A.A. Lagrein Badl '22	♟♟ 5
● A.A. Merlot Ris. '21	♟♟ 6
○ A.A. Pinot Bianco Solt '23	♟♟ 4
● A.A. Pinot Nero Quirinus '22	♟♟ 5
○ A.A. Sauvignon Quirinus '23	♟♟ 4
● MMXXII '22	♟♟ 5
⊙ Planties Rosé '23	♟♟ 4
● A.A. Merlot Quirinus '22	♟ 6
○ Planties Weiss '23	♟ 4
○ A.A. Bianco MMXXI '21	♟♟ 6
● A.A. Lagrein Ris. '19	♟♟ 6
● A.A. Pinot Nero Quirinus '21	♟♟ 4
○ A.A. Sauvignon Quirinus '22	♟♟ 4
○ A.A. Terlano Cl. Bergwerk '21	♟♟ 6
○ Planties Weiss '22	♟♟ 4

○ A.A. Gewürztraminer '23	♟♟ 5
● A.A. Pinot Nero Hirsch '21	♟♟ 6
⊙ A.A. Pinot Nero Rosé '23	♟♟ 4
○ A.A. Sauvignon '22	♟♟ 5
○ A.A. Chardonnay '22	♟ 4
○ A.A. Gewürztraminer '22	♟♟ 5

Strasserhof
Hannes Baumgartner
fraz. Novacella
loc. Unterrain, 8
39040 Varna/Vahrn [BZ]
📞 +39 0472830804
🌐 www.strasserhof.info

CELLAR SALES
PRE-BOOKED VISITS
ACCOMMODATION
ANNUAL PRODUCTION 45,000 bottles
HECTARES UNDER VINE 5.50

Stroblhof
loc. San Michele
via Piganò, 25
39057 Appiano/Eppan [BZ]
📞 +39 0471662250
🌐 www.stroblhof.it

CELLAR SALES
PRE-BOOKED VISITS
ANNUAL PRODUCTION 40,000 bottles
HECTARES UNDER VINE 5.20

Summer in the Eisack Valley is characterized by warm, sunny days followed by much cooler nights. Here, Hannes Baumgartner runs the family winery, a few hectares of southwest-facing plots ranging from 680 to 750 meters above sea level. The vineyards are dedicated to the valley's traditional white grape varieties, resulting in wines that stand out for their tension and finesse. Hannes' wines exhibit superb stylistic precision, with a Sylvaner that stands out as one of the finest whites in the valley. The nose is intense, passing from exotic fruit to smoky and citrus notes, adding an element of unpredictability. On the palate, its freshness translates into a dynamic profile supported by a sapid vein, giving the wine additional depth. The Riesling from the same vintage opens with a pronounced sulfur note that dissipates, revealing white-fleshed fruit. In the mouth, acidity takes center stage, guiding each sip.

The Nicolussi-Leck family winery cultivates a small area that skirts the forest at the foot of Mendola, where evening breezes descend down from the mountain. In their beautifully integrated cellar, they bring to life a range marked by aromatic finesse and tension, focusing on the grape varieties that thrive in the territory. A remarkable debut for the new Pinot Nero Riserva, the Sepp Hanni '19, crafted from the oldest vines nestled just below Stroblhof, near the forest. The nose unfolds slowly, beginning with a hint of oak, then transitioning to wild berries and smoky notes, finally revealing herbal undertones. The palate is firm, perfectly balancing acidity and smooth tannins. The Chardonnay Schwarzhaus '23 is just as good. Aged in large barrels, its focus is on aromatic freshness and an elegant palate.

○ A.A. Valle Isarco Riesling '23	♈♈	4
○ A.A. Valle Isarco Sylvaner '23	♈♈	4
○ A.A. Sauvignon '23	♈♈	4
○ A.A. Valle Isarco Grüner Veltliner '23	♈♈	4
○ A.A. Valle Isarco Kerner '23	♈♈	4
○ A.A. Valle Isarco Pinot Grigio '23	♈♈	4
○ A.A. Valle Isarco Riesling '12	♈♈♈	3*
○ A.A. Valle Isarco Riesling '11	♈♈♈	3*
○ A.A. Valle Isarco Sylvaner '19	♈♈♈	3*
○ A.A. Valle Isarco Veltliner '10	♈♈♈	3*
○ A.A. Valle Isarco Veltliner '09	♈♈♈	3*
○ A.A. Valle Isarco Kerner '22	♈♈	3*
○ A.A. Valle Isarco Riesling '22	♈♈	4
○ A.A. Valle Isarco Riesling '21	♈♈	4
○ A.A. Valle Isarco Sylvaner '22	♈♈	3*

● A.A. Pinot Nero Seppi Hanni Ris. '19	♈♈	8
● A.A. Cabernet Merlot Valbion '21	♈♈	5
○ A.A. Chardonnay Schwarzhaus '23	♈♈	4
● A.A. Pinot Bianco Strahler '23	♈♈	4
● A.A. Pinot Nero P!geno '21	♈♈	5
● A.A. Pinot Nero Ris. '20	♈♈	6
○ A.A. Sauvignon Nico '23	♈♈	4
○ A.A. Pinot Bianco Strahler '09	♈♈♈	3*
● A.A. Pinot Nero Ris. '15	♈♈♈	6
● A.A. Pinot Nero Ris. '05	♈♈♈	5
● A.A. Cabernet Merlot Valbion '20	♈♈	5
○ A.A. Pinot Bianco Strahler '22	♈♈	4
● A.A. Pinot Nero Pigeno '20	♈♈	5
● A.A. Pinot Nero Ris. '19	♈♈	6
○ A.A. Sauvignon Nico '22	♈♈	4

Taschlerhof Peter Wachtler

loc. Mara, 107
39042 Bressanone/Brixen [BZ]
+39 0472851091
www.taschlerhof.com

CELLAR SALES
PRE-BOOKED VISITS
ANNUAL PRODUCTION 30,000 bottles
HECTARES UNDER VINE 4.20

On the right bank of the Eisack, just before Bressanone, a network of dry stone walls supports small vineyard plots that range from 530 to 730 meters above sea level with southeast exposure. Many of these are owned by Peter Wachtler, who cultivates his grapes among meadows and small woodland patches. Production centers on the valley's traditional white grape varieties, making for refined wines with great tension. The Sylvaner '23 generously offers up its aromas, with immediately pleasant, juicy white fruit complemented by a floral and citrus-driven freshness. In the mouth, the wine follows a similar stylistic path, relying on its acidic drive to extend and tighten the palate. The Lahner Riserva '22, on the other hand, reflects the warmth of the vintage, with sweeter fruit and dried floral notes giving way to a palate defined by its harmony. The Riesling '23 proves fresh, juicy, and dynamic.

○ A.A. Valle Isarco Sylvaner '23	YY 4
○ A.A. Valle Isarco Kerner '23	YY 4
○ A.A. Valle Isarco Riesling '23	YY 4
○ A.A. Valle Isarco Riesling Lahner '22	YY 4
○ A.A. Valle Isarco Sylvaner Lahner Ris. '22	YY 5
○ A.A. Valle Isarco Riesling '14	YYY 4*
○ A.A. Valle Isarco Sylvaner '15	YYY 3*
○ A.A. Valle Isarco Sylvaner Lahner '16	YYY 5
○ A.A. Valle Isarco Riesling '22	YY 4
○ A.A. Valle Isarco Riesling '21	YY 4
○ A.A. Valle Isarco Riesling '20	YY 4
○ A.A. Valle Isarco Sylvaner '22	YY 3*
○ A.A. Valle Isarco Sylvaner '21	YY 3*

★★Cantina Terlano

via Silberleiten, 7
39018 Terlano/Terlan [BZ]
+39 0471257135
www.cantina-terlano.com

CELLAR SALES
PRE-BOOKED VISITS
ANNUAL PRODUCTION 1,500,000 bottles
HECTARES UNDER VINE 190.00
SUSTAINABLE WINERY

Among the wineries that have played a crucial role in promoting the quality of South Tyrolean wines over the past few decades, the cooperative led by Rudi Kofler stands out. Nearly 200 hectares of vineyards stretch along the calcareous alluvial fan of Andriano and the red slopes of Terlano, where porphyry predominates. The grapes are carefully cultivated by the cooperative's numerous members and transformed into wine by Rudi and his team. Once again, it was challenging to single out the most interesting wines, as many impressed our panels. The Quarz '22 is the usual Sauvignon, combining richness and elegance, though this year it's marked by a particularly sapid palate. The Vorberg '21 plays on more subtle fruit, with a dynamic flavor profile rich in tension. Complexity, elegance, and length characteristic the fantastic Rarity '11, while the Nova Domus '21 takes advantage of an excellent harvest to highlight a profile of rare elegance and length.

○ A.A. Terlano Nova Domus Ris. '21	YYY 7
○ A.A. Terlano Pinot Bianco Rarity Ris. '11	YY 8
○ A.A. Terlano Pinot Bianco Vorberg Ris. '21	YY 8
○ A.A. Terlano Sauvignon Quarz '22	YY 8
○ A.A. Chardonnay Doran Andriano Ris. '21	YY 6
○ A.A. Gewürztraminer Lunare '22	YY 6
○ A.A. Gewürztraminer Passito Juvelo Andriano '22	YY 6
● A.A. Lagrein Porphyr Ris. '21	YY 8
● A.A. Lagrein Tor di Lupo Andriano Ris. '21	YY 6
● A.A. Merlot Gant Ris. '21	YY 6
● A.A. Pinot Nero Anrar Andriano Ris. '21	YY 7
○ A.A. Sauvignon Andrius Andriano '22	YY 5
○ A.A. Terlano Chardonnay Kreuth '22	YY 5
○ A.A. Terlano Cuvée '23	YY 5
○ A.A. Terlano Sauvignon Winkl '23	YY 4

★Tiefenbrunner

fraz. Niclara
via Castello, 4
39040 Cortaccia/Kurtatsch [BZ]
(☏) +39 0471880122
✉ www.tiefenbrunner.com

CELLAR SALES
PRE-BOOKED VISITS
RESTAURANT SERVICE
ANNUAL PRODUCTION 650,000 bottles
HECTARES UNDER VINE 88.00

Set close to the province of Trento, the South Tyrolean Unterland boasts vineyards that rise from 220 meters in the valley floor to over 1000 meters on steep slopes. Here, the Tiefenbrunner family has been operating for generations, relying on a sizable estate and collaborating with many local growers to produce consistently high-quality wines. An impeccable lineup was presented this year, led by a fantastic 2021 version of the Feldmarschall, which, with an additional year of aging, has gained depth and aromatic complexity (in addition to its usual class). The Vigna Au '20 is a Chardonnay with a multifaceted aromatic profile, offering an energetic, taut, and notably rich palate. The intriguing Sauvignon Vigna Rachtl '21 capitalizes on the excellent harvest to deliver vibrant, layered aromas that lead to a juicy and lengthy palate. We conclude with a Cabernet Sauvignon Toren '20 of excellent concentration and harmony.

○ A.A. Müller Thurgau V. Feldmarschall von Fenner '21	🍷🍷🍷 7
● A.A. Cabernet Sauvignon V. Toren Ris. '20	🍷🍷 8
○ A.A. Chardonnay V. Au Ris. '20	🍷🍷 8
○ A.A. Sauvignon V. Rachtl Ris. '21	🍷🍷 8
● A.A. Cabernet Merlot Linticlarus Cuvée Ris. '21	🍷🍷 6
○ A.A. Chardonnay Turmhof '22	🍷🍷 5
○ A.A. Gewürztraminer V. T. Tardus '20	🍷🍷 6
● A.A. Lagrein Linticlarus Ris. '21	🍷🍷 6
○ A.A. Pinot Bianco Anna '22	🍷🍷 5
○ A.A. Pinot Grigio Turmhof '22	🍷🍷 5
● A.A. Pinot Nero Linticlarus Ris. '21	🍷🍷 7
○ A.A. Sauvignon Turmhof '22	🍷🍷 5

★★★Cantina Tramin

s.da del Vino, 144
39040 Termeno/Tramin [BZ]
(☏) +39 0471096633
✉ www.cantinatramin.it

CELLAR SALES
PRE-BOOKED VISITS
ANNUAL PRODUCTION 1,500,000 bottles
HECTARES UNDER VINE 270.00
SUSTAINABLE WINERY

The historic cooperative of Termeno is undergoing an expansion aimed not at increasing production but at optimizing the production stages, thereby respecting the quality of the grapes supplied by its numerous members. While gewürztraminer has long been Tramin's flagship variety, increasing attention is now being given to chardonnay and pinot nero. Chardonnay made the best impression, with a Troy '21 that drew on an excellent harvest for its noteworthy aromatic finesse—a wine of extraordinary tension and length. Their line of Gewürztraminer is also convincing, from the complex Terminum, where sweetness is perfectly balanced by sapidity, to the Nussbaumer '22, which sees intense aromatic expression followed by an elegant, long palate. The Pinot Nero Maglen, sourced from the Glen and Mazon vineyards, proves clear in its aromatic expression, with a solid palate well-supported by acidity.

○ A.A. Chardonnay Troy Ris. '21	🍷🍷🍷 8
○ A.A. Gewürztraminer Nussbaumer '22	🍷🍷 6
○ A.A. Gewürztraminer V. T. Terminum '22	🍷🍷 8
○ A.A. Bianco Stoan '22	🍷🍷 6
● A.A. Cabernet Merlot Loam Ris. '22	🍷🍷 8
○ A.A. Chardonnay Glarea '22	🍷🍷 4
○ A.A. Gewürztraminer Selida '23	🍷🍷 4
○ A.A. Gewürztraminer V. T. Roen '23	🍷🍷 6
● A.A. Lagrein Urban Ris. '22	🍷🍷 7
○ A.A. Pinot Grigio Unterebner '22	🍷🍷 6
● A.A. Pinot Nero Maglen Ris. '21	🍷🍷 7
○ A.A. Sauvignon Pepi '23	🍷🍷 4
○ A.A. Chardonnay Troy Ris. '19	🍷🍷🍷 8
○ A.A. Gewürztraminer Nussbaumer '21	🍷🍷🍷 5

Erbhof Unterganzner
Josephus Mayr

fraz. Cardano
via Campiglio, 15
39053 Bolzano/Bozen
☎ +39 0471365582
✉ www.mayr-unterganzner.it

CELLAR SALES
PRE-BOOKED VISITS
ANNUAL PRODUCTION 65,000 bottles
HECTARES UNDER VINE 9.00

Over almost 400 years of history, ten generations of the Mayr family have managed Unterganznerhof, a historic estate set in the eastern part of the city basin, where it joins the Eisack valley. Here, the vineyards, constantly caressed by breezes, extend from 250 meters in the valley floor to 450 meters at the Pignat farm, where white grape varieties are cultivated. The winery focuses on schiava and lagrein but also explores other varieties. Once again, the Lagrein takes the lead, with a Riserva from the 2021 harvest that starts off closed on the nose, but after a few moments of oxygenation, reveals intense dark fruit and spice notes, accompanied by a deep mineral nuance. The palate is rich and dense, supported by close-knit tannins and a valuable acidic drive. The Cabernet Riserva '21 follows a similar tasting dynamic, offering fresher, more immediate aromas, while the Chardonnay '23 proves approachable and harmonious.

● A.A. Lagrein Ris. '21	♉♉ 5
● A.A. Cabernet Ris. '21	♉♉ 5
○ A.A. Chardonnay Platt & Pignat '23	♉♉ 3
● A.A. Santa Maddalena Cl. Heilmann '22	♉♉ 5
○ A.A. Sauvignon Platt & Pignat '23	♉♉ 3
● Composition Reif '21	♉♉ 6
● Lamarein '21	♉♉ 6
● A.A. Santa Maddalena Unterganzner '22	♉ 3
● A.A. Lagrein Ris. '13	♉♉♉ 5
● A.A. Lagrein Ris. '11	♉♉♉ 5
● A.A. Lagrein Scuro Ris. '05	♉♉♉ 4
● A.A. Lagrein Scuro Ris. '01	♉♉♉ 4
● A.A. Lagrein Scuro Ris. '00	♉♉♉ 4
● A.A. Lagrein Scuro Ris. '99	♉♉♉ 4
● A.A. Lagrein Scuro Ris. '98	♉♉♉ 4*
● Lamarein '05	♉♉♉ 6

Untermoserhof
Georg Ramoser

via Santa Maddalena di Sotto, 36
39100 Bolzano/Bozen
☎ +39 0471975481
✉ www.untermoserhof.com

CELLAR SALES
PRE-BOOKED VISITS
ACCOMMODATION
ANNUAL PRODUCTION 40,000 bottles
HECTARES UNDER VINE 4.50

The Ramoser family's winery is literally nestled among the vineyards covering the Santa Maddalena hill, where the vines reach up to the very walls of the houses. Their estate extends across these slopes to the hilltop, where a single, solitary tree has stood for as long as anyone can remember. The range produced, now overseen by Florian with the invaluable help of his father, Georg, focuses almost exclusively on schiava and lagrein. This last variety is interpreted in various styles, and we particularly appreciated the Riserva '21. Its thick and dark color, typical of the variety, foreshadows an aromatic profile of great maturity, with dark fruit accompanied by intense smoky and spicy notes that reappear on an energetic, close-knit, and perfectly harmonious palate. We also found the Santa Maddalena Hub & Leith '22 excellent, with its complex aromas of fruit and spices, and a palate that impresses with its tension and drinkability,

● A.A. Lagrein Ris. '21	♉♉♉ 5
● A.A. Santa Maddalena Cl. V. Hub & Leith '22	♉♉ 5
● A.A. Merlot Cabernet Lehm & Kies Ris. '21	♉♉ 5
A.A. Pinot Bianco Kardatsch '22	♉♉ 4
● A.A. Lagrein Ris. '20	♉♉♉ 5
● A.A. Lagrein Scuro Ris. '03	♉♉♉ 4*
● A.A. Lagrein Scuro Ris. '97	♉♉♉ 4*
● A.A. Santa Maddalena Cl. Hueb '16	♉♉♉ 3*
○ A.A. Chardonnay Moraine Ris. '20	♉♉ 4
● A.A. Lagrein Hofacker Ris. '18	♉♉ 3
● A.A. Merlot Cabernet Lehm & Kies '20	♉♉ 5
A.A. Pinot Bianco Kardatsch '21	♉♉ 4
● A.A. Santa Maddalena Cl. V. Hub '21	♉♉ 3*

★Tenuta Unterortl Castel Juval

loc. Juval, 1b
39020 Castelbello Ciardes/Kastelbell Tschars [BZ]
+39 0473667580
www.unterortl.it

CELLAR SALES
PRE-BOOKED VISITS
ANNUAL PRODUCTION 33,000 bottles
HECTARES UNDER VINE 4.00

In the case of the Unterortl estate, rather than vineyards, one might describe it as a viticultural puzzle: tiny plots carved from the mountain, following its contours, skirting rocks, and with roots sunk into the thin soil. While riesling dominates, pinot noir and pinot bianco are gradually gaining ground, with the winery's stylistic approach characterized by aromatic finesse and a taut, vibrant spectrum of flavor. The grapes for the Riesling Windbichel '22 ripen on a vineyard over 700 meters above sea level, where the wind caresses the vines and day-night temperature swings are significant, contributing to an aromatic profile of great finesse. Exotic fruit accompanies citrus notes, with chamomile lingering in the background. On the palate, the wine's sapidity complements a taut and supple mouthfeel. The subsequent vintage's Unterortl expresses even more citrusy notes, while on the palate, it unfolds with penetrating, energetic acidity.

○ A. A. Val Venosta Riesling Unterortl '23	🍷🍷 5
○ A. A. Val Venosta Riesling V. Windbichel '22	🍷🍷 6
○ A. A. Val Venosta Pinot Bianco '23	🍷🍷 4
○ A. A. Val Venosta Pinot Bianco Himmelsleiter '22	🍷🍷 6
● A. A. Val Venosta Pinot Nero Ris. '21	🍷🍷 6
○ A. A. Val Venosta Riesling Gletscherschliff '23	🍷🍷 4
○ A. A. Val Venosta Riesling V. Windbichel '19	🍷🍷🍷 6
○ A. A. Val Venosta Riesling Weingarten Windbichel '16	🍷🍷🍷 5
○ A. A. Val Venosta Riesling Windbichel '17	🍷🍷🍷 5
○ A. A. Val Venosta Riesling Windbichel '15	🍷🍷🍷 5

Cantina Produttori Valle Isarco

via Coste, 50
39043 Chiusa/Klausen [BZ]
+39 0472847553
www.cantinavalleisarco.it

CELLAR SALES
PRE-BOOKED VISITS
ANNUAL PRODUCTION 950,000 bottles
HECTARES UNDER VINE 150.00
SUSTAINABLE WINERY

Following the Eisack River from Bolzano, the valley alternates between narrow, forested stretches and wider areas where viticulture suddenly takes over the hills, often with small vineyards supported by dry stone walls climbing skyward. The cooperative of Chiusa is the most important producer in the area, mainly dedicated to the territory's native white grape varieties. This year's lineup was minimal but still highly commendable. Once again, the Kerner Aristos leads the cooperative's range, with the 2023 harvest bringing intense citrus notes, mandarin intertwining with floral nuances and a curious smoky hint. On tasting, the wine reveals the strength of the terroir, showcasing richness but above all an intense and vibrant acidity that extends and tightens the palate. The Grüner Veltliner '23 is characterized by intense aromatic expression and harmony of flavor.

○ A. A. Valle Isarco Grüner Veltliner Aristos '23	🍷🍷 5
○ A. A. Valle Isarco Kerner Aristos '23	🍷🍷 5
○ A. A. Valle Isarco Pinot Grigio Aristos '23	🍷🍷 4
○ A. A. Valle Isarco Riesling Aristos '23	🍷🍷 5
○ A. A. Valle Isarco Sylvaner Aristos '23	🍷🍷 5
○ A. A. Valle Isarco Kerner Aristos '22	🍷🍷🍷 5
○ A. A. Valle Isarco Kerner Aristos '21	🍷🍷🍷 4*
○ A. A. Valle Isarco Kerner Aristos '20	🍷🍷🍷 4*
○ A. A. Valle Isarco Kerner Aristos '05	🍷🍷🍷 3*
○ A. A. Valle Isarco Sylvaner Aristos '16	🍷🍷🍷 4*
○ A. A. Valle Isarco Sylvaner Aristos '15	🍷🍷🍷 4*
○ A. A. Valle Isarco Veltliner Aristos '03	🍷🍷🍷 3*
○ A. A. Valle Isarco Grüner Veltliner Aristos '21	🍷🍷 3*
○ A. A. Valle Isarco Grüner Veltliner Aristos '20	🍷🍷 3*
○ A. A. Valle Isarco Sylvaner Aristos '22	🍷🍷 4

Von Blumen

fraz. Pochi, 18/Bulcholz, 18
39040 Salorno/Salurn [BZ]
(+39 0457230110
www.vonblumenwine.com

CELLAR SALES
PRE-BOOKED VISITS
ANNUAL PRODUCTION 70,000 bottles
HECTARES UNDER VINE 11.00
SUSTAINABLE WINERY

The Fugatti brothers have started renovating their Pochi headquarters, a charming structure nestled among vineyards and close to the forest. About a dozen hectares are cultivated in the area, with different elevations occupied, allowing the producer to match each grape with its ideal location. Their range includes a varietal line and their "Flowers" selections, which are dedicated to the best vineyards. The Pinot Bianco '21 ages for about a year in oak before bottling. The result is a complex bouquet, where ripe white fruit is enriched by floral notes with a hint of oak in the background. On the palate, it's crisp, with remarkable length and tension. The Gewürztraminer 502 '23 is also excellent, playing on explosive aromas reminiscent of exotic fruits, candied citrus, and rose petals. In the mouth, its characteristic opulence is perfectly managed, revealing great sapidity and harmony.

★★Elena Walch

via A. Hofer, 1
39040 Termeno/Tramin [BZ]
(+39 0471860172
www.elenawalch.com

CELLAR SALES
PRE-BOOKED VISITS
RESTAURANT SERVICE
ANNUAL PRODUCTION 800,000 bottles
HECTARES UNDER VINE 90.00
SUSTAINABLE WINERY

Julia and Karoline Walch have taken over the winery founded by their mother Elena in the 1980s, confidently steering it towards new challenges. Few wineries manage vineyards in locations as prestigious as Castel Ringberg and Kastelaz, slopes where each grape variety finds its perfect growing conditions. Their modern cellar on via Hofer produces wines that exhibit no weaknesses. A year spent maturing in the cellar has allowed the Gewürztraminer Kastelaz '22 to gain depth and complexity. Today, its aromatic profile passes from rose to spices, exotic fruit to notes of toasted hazelnut. On tasting, it reveals rare harmony, with a juicy and elegant finish. Beyond the Clouds '21 is a textbook prized white, built on texture and tension. After last year's success, the Pinot Nero Aton reaffirms its class, highlighting the 2019 vintage with refined aromas and a firm palate that promises great evolution.

○ A.A. Pinot Bianco Flowers Ris. '21	♟♟ 5
○ A.A. Gewurztraminer 502 '23	♟♟ 4
○ A.A. Pinot Bianco 511 '23	♟♟ 4
● A.A. Pinot Nero 514 '22	♟♟ 4
○ A.A. Sauvignon 505 '23	♟♟ 4
○ A.A. Sauvignon Flowers '21	♟♟ 5
○ A.A. Gewurztraminer 502 '22	♟♟ 4
○ A.A. Gewurztraminer 502 '21	♟♟ 4
○ A.A. Pinot Bianco 510 '22	♟♟ 4
○ A.A. Pinot Bianco Flowers Ris. '20	♟♟ 5
● A.A. Pinot Nero 514 '21	♟♟ 4
● A.A. Pinot Nero 514 '20	♟♟ 4
● A.A. Pinot Nero Flowers Ris. '20	♟♟ 6
○ A.A. Sauvignon 505 '22	♟♟ 4
○ A.A. Sauvignon 505 '21	♟♟ 3
○ A.A. Sauvignon Flowers Ris. '20	♟♟ 5

○ A.A. Gewürztraminer V. Kastelaz '22	♟♟♟ 7
○ A.A. Bianco Grande Cuvée Beyond the Clouds '21	♟♟ 8
● A.A. Pinot Nero Aton Ris. '19	♟♟ 8
○ A.A. Chardonnay V. Castel Ringberg Ris. '21	♟♟ 8
● A.A. Lagrein V. Castel Ringberg Ris. '21	♟♟ 7
● A.A. Pinot Nero Ludwig '21	♟♟ 7
● Grande Cuvée Kermesse '21	♟ 8
○ A.A. Bianco Grande Cuvée Beyond the Clouds '19	♟♟♟ 8
○ A.A. Bianco Grande Cuvée Beyond the Clouds '18	♟♟♟ 7
○ A.A. Gewürztraminer V. Kastelaz '20	♟♟♟ 6
● A.A. Pinot Nero Aton Ris. '18	♟♟♟ 8

Wassererhof

loc. Novale di Fiè, 21
39050 Fiè allo Sciliar
Völs am Schlern [BZ]
☏ +39 0471724114
⊛ www.wasssererhof.com

CELLAR SALES
PRE-BOOKED VISITS
RESTAURANT SERVICE
ANNUAL PRODUCTION 35,000 bottles
HECTARES UNDER VINE 4.00

The Moch brothers' winery is discreetly located in Campodazzo, where the vines climb the mountain slopes in search of light and sun, benefiting from the daytime warmth and the nighttime breezes descending from higher elevations. The modern cellar is part of a major restoration project of a 14th-century farmhouse, seamlessly integrated into a small courtyard among the vineyards. Their wines get more convincing with each passing year, with a lineup that shows no weak points. The standout is the Pinot Bianco '21, which captured the finesse of this excellent harvest. On the nose, white fruit stands out clearly against a backdrop of spices and dried flowers, with fruit echoed on the palate, where harmony and tension take center stage. The Sauvignon Riserva '21, aged in oak, is also delicious. Mineral and exotic fruit aromas are followed by a palate characterized by length and suppleness.

Peter Zemmer

s.da del Vino, 24
39040 Cortina Sulla Strada del Vino
Kurtinig [BZ]
☏ +39 0471817143
⊛ www.peterzemmer.com

CELLAR SALES
PRE-BOOKED VISITS
ANNUAL PRODUCTION 500,000 bottles
HECTARES UNDER VINE 65.00

Cortina sulla strada del vino is the smallest municipality in Alto Adige, a territory perfectly nestled in the plains crossed by the Adige River. It is also home to the Peter Zemmer winery, whose vineyards benefits from the warm climate and the continuous breezes that ensure the health of the grapes. The estate includes plots on the surrounding hillsides, reaching up to 800 meters in elevation. The Pinot Grigio Giatl '21 is the quintessence of the marriage between grape and terroir: its warmth manifests in an explosive fruitiness, with pear embracing dried flowers and smoky nuances before giving way to an energetic, powerful palate well-supported by acidity. The Chardonnay '21, from the Crivelli vineyard, features aromas of ripe fruit accompanied by smoky and oak notes, which reappear on a juicy, sapid, long palate. The Pinot Bianco '23 is splendid in its immediacy and fragrance, dynamic, and irresistibly drinkable.

ALTO ADIGE

○ A.A. Pinot Bianco '21	♥♥ 5
● A.A. Cabernet Ris. '21	♥♥ 5
○ A.A. Chardonnay Ryed Ris. '21	♥♥ 5
○ A.A. Pinot Grigio '22	♥♥ 4
● A.A. Santa Maddalena Cl. '22	♥♥ 4
○ A.A. Sauvignon '22	♥♥ 4
○ A.A. Sauvignon Ris. '21	♥♥ 5
● A.A. Cabernet Ris. '19	♀♀ 3
○ A.A. Pinot Bianco '20	♀♀ 3
○ A.A. Pinot Grigio '21	♀♀ 3
○ A.A. Pinot Grigio '20	♀♀ 3
● A.A. Santa Maddalena Cl. '21	♀♀ 3
● A.A. Santa Maddalena Cl. '20	♀♀ 3
○ A.A. Sauvignon '21	♀♀ 3*
○ A.A. Sauvignon Ris. '19	♀♀ 4
● Mumbolt '20	♀♀ 4

○ A.A. Chardonnay V. Crivelli Ris. '21	♥♥ 5
○ A.A. Pinot Grigio Giatl Ris. '21	♥♥ 5
○ A.A. Chardonnay '23	♥♥ 3
○ A.A. Chardonnay Bucholz '22	♥♥ 5
○ A.A. Gewürztraminer Frauenrigl '23	♥♥ 3
● A.A. Lagrein Fruggl Ris. '21	♥♥ 5
○ A.A. Müller Thurgau '23	♥♥ 3
○ A.A. Pinot Bianco '23	♥♥ 3
○ A.A. Pinot Grigio '23	♥♥ 3
● A.A. Pinot Nero V. Kofl Ris. '21	♥♥ 6
○ A.A. Sauvignon '23	♥♥ 3
● A.A. Pinot Nero '23	♥ 5
○ A.A. Pinot Grigio Giatl Ris. '20	♀♀♀ 5

OTHER WINERIES

Arunda
via Prof. Josef-Schwarz, 18
39010 Meltina/Mölten [BZ]
📞 +39 0471668033
🌐 www.arundavivaldi.it

CELLAR SALES
PRE-BOOKED VISITS
ANNUAL PRODUCTION 90,000 bottles
HECTARES UNDER VINE 12.00

○ A.A. Spumante Brut M. Cl.	🍷🍷 5
○ A.A. Spumante Extra Brut M. Cl. Cuvée Marianna	🍷🍷 5
○ A.A. Spumante Extra Brut M. Cl. Ris. '18	🍷🍷 7

Baron Longo
via Val di Fiemme, 30
39044 Egna/Neumarkt [BZ]
📞 +39 0471 820007
🌐 www.baronlongo.com

ANNUAL PRODUCTION 30,000 bottles
HECTARES UNDER VINE 17.00

● A.A. Lagrein Friedberg '22	🍷🍷 5
● Felix Anton '21	🍷🍷 4
○ Schlossberg Pinot Bianco '22	🍷🍷 4
○ Urgestein Sauvignon '23	🍷🍷 4

Bessererhof - Otmar Mair
loc. Novale di Presule, 10
39050 Fiè allo Sciliar
Völs am Schlern [BZ]
📞 +39 0471601011
🌐 www.bessererhof.it

CELLAR SALES
PRE-BOOKED VISITS
ANNUAL PRODUCTION 40,000 bottles
HECTARES UNDER VINE 4.50

○ A.A. Pinot Bianco '23	🍷🍷 4
○ A.A. Valle Isarco Sylvaner '23	🍷🍷 5

Hartmann Donà
via Raffein, 8
39010 Cermes/Tscherms [BZ]
📞 +39 3292610628
hartmann.dona@rolmail.net

ANNUAL PRODUCTION 35,000 bottles
HECTARES UNDER VINE 4.65

○ A.A. Pinot Bianco Donà Lisl '14	🍷🍷 7
● Donà Rouge '18	🍷🍷 5
● Liquid Stone Granit '22	🍷🍷 5
● Liquid Stone Phyllit '22	🍷🍷 5

Tenuta Donà
fraz. Riva di Sotto
39057 Appiano/Eppan [BZ]
📞 +39 0473221866
🌐 www.weingut-dona.com

CELLAR SALES
PRE-BOOKED VISITS
ACCOMMODATION
ANNUAL PRODUCTION 30,000 bottles
HECTARES UNDER VINE 6.00

○ A.A. Sauvignon '23	🍷🍷 5
● A.A. Schiava '23	🍷🍷 3
● Merlot Lagrein '21	🍷🍷 5
○ A.A. Terlano Chardonnay '23	🍷 4

Weingut Thomas Dorfmann
Untrum, 8
39040 Velturno/Feldthurns [BZ]
📞 +39 3357667278
🌐 www.thomas-dorfmann.it

● A.A. Pinot Nero '22	🍷🍷 5
○ A.A. Valle Isarco Grüner Veltliner '22	🍷🍷 5
○ A.A. Valle Isarco Riesling '22	🍷🍷 5
○ A.A. Valle Isarco Sylvaner '22	🍷🍷 5

OTHER WINERIES

Fliederhof
Stefan Ramoser
loc. Santa Maddalena di Sotto, 33
39100 Bolzano/Bozen
☎ +39 0471979048
✉ www.fliederhof.it

CELLAR SALES
PRE-BOOKED VISITS
ANNUAL PRODUCTION 25,000 bottles
HECTARES UNDER VINE 2.40

● A.A. Lagrein Gran Helen Ris. '20	♟♟ 5
● A.A. Santa Maddalena Cl. Gran Marie '22	♟♟ 4
○ A.A. Sauvignon Stella '21	♟ 5

Grosskemat
Wehrburgweg, 17
39010 Tesimo/Tisens [BZ]
☎ +39 3398422920
✉ www.grosskemat.it

○ A.A. Pinot Bianco Pichl '23	♟♟ 3
○ A.A. Pinot Bianco Serenum '23	♟♟ 3

Hof Gandberg
Thomas Niedermayr
s.da Castel Palú, 1
39057 Appiano/Eppan [BZ]
☎ +39 0471664152
✉ www.thomas-niedermayr.com

CELLAR SALES
PRE-BOOKED VISITS
ANNUAL PRODUCTION 10,000 bottles
HECTARES UNDER VINE 1.50
VITICULTURE METHOD Certified Organic

○ Bronner '19	♟♟ 5
○ S.Alt '19	♟♟ 6
○ Sonnrein '19	♟♟ 5

Griesserhof
v.lo Griess, 5
39040 Varna/Vahrn [BZ]
☎ +39 0472834805
✉ www.griesserhof.it

○ A.A. Valle Isarco Gewürztraminer Gols '22	♟♟ 5
○ A.A. Valle Isarco Grüner Veltliner Rigger '22	♟♟ 5
○ A.A. Valle Isarco Müller Thurgau Gols '22	♟♟ 5
○ A.A. Valle Isarco Sylvaner Gols '22	♟♟ 5

Himmelreichhof
via Convento, 15a
39020 Castelbello Ciardes
Kastelbell Tschars [BZ]
☎ +39 0473624417
✉ www.himmelreich-hof.info

ANNUAL PRODUCTION 20,000 bottles
HECTARES UNDER VINE 3.50

○ A.A. Val Venosta Pinot Bianco Claudia Augusta '21	♟♟ 4
● A.A. Val Venosta Pinot Nero Claudia Augusta '21	♟♟ 5

Josmoar Hof
Sebastian Tonner
via Romana, 18
39020 Castelbello Ciardes
Kastelbell Tschars [BZ]
☎ +39 3331848407
✉ www.josmoar.it

● A.A. Val Venosta Pinot Nero '22	♟♟ 5
● A.A. Val Venosta Pinot Nero Ris. '21	♟♟ 6
○ Pfannegg Chardonnay '19	♟♟ 5
○ Pfannegg Sauvignon '23	♟ 4

OTHER WINERIES

Tenuta Kränzelhof
Graf Franz Pfeil
via Palade, I
39010 Cermes/Tscherms [BZ]
✆ +39 0473564549
✉ www.kraenzelhof.it

CELLAR SALES
PRE-BOOKED VISITS
ANNUAL PRODUCTION 35,000 bottles
HECTARES UNDER VINE 6.00

○ A.A. Pinot Bianco Helios Ris. '18	🏆🏆 6
● A.A. Pinot Nero Libra Ris. '21	🏆🏆 6
○ A.A. Sauvignon Aries '22	🏆🏆 5

Larcherhof - Spögler
via Rencio, 82
39100 Bolzano/Bozen
✆ +39 0471365034
larcherhof@yahoo.de

CELLAR SALES
PRE-BOOKED VISITS
ANNUAL PRODUCTION 30,000 bottles
HECTARES UNDER VINE 5.00

● A.A. Lagrein Rivelaun Ris. '20	🏆🏆 4
○ A.A. Pinot Grigio '23	🏆🏆 3
● A.A. Santa Maddalena Cl. '23	🏆🏆 4
● A.A. Merlot '22	🏆 3

Lehengut
fraz. Colsano/Galsaun
via delle Fonti, 2
39020 Castelbello Ciardes
Kastelbell Tschars [BZ]
✆ +39 3487562676
✉ www.lehengut.it

ANNUAL PRODUCTION 10,000 bottles
HECTARES UNDER VINE 3.00
VITICULTURE METHOD Certified Organic

○ A.A. Val Venosta Pinot Bianco '23	🏆🏆 4
○ A.A. Val Venosta Riesling '23	🏆🏆 4

Tenuta H. Lentsch
via Nazionale, 71
39051 Bronzolo/Branzoll [BZ]
✆ +39 0471596017
weingut_lentsch@dnet.it

CELLAR SALES
PRE-BOOKED VISITS
ANNUAL PRODUCTION 70,000 bottles
HECTARES UNDER VINE 14.50

● A.A. Cabernet Franc Ris. '18	🏆🏆 5
● A.A. Lagrein '20	🏆🏆 5
● A.A. Lagrein Morris Ris. '20	🏆🏆 5
● A.A. Merlot Ris. '20	🏆🏆 5

Oberstein
via Leiten, 6
39010 Cermes/Tscherms [BZ]
✆ +39 3386169514
✉ www.oberstein.it

○ Kerner '23	🏆🏆 5
○ Salis Sauvignon '19	🏆🏆 5
○ Kontur '21	🏆 5
○ Stein Riesling '22	🏆 5

Weingut Pföstl
s.da Vecchia, 14
39017 Scena/Schenna [BZ]
✆ +39 0473230760
✉ www.weingut-pfoestl.com

○ A.A. Chardonnay Valpitan '21	🏆🏆 4
● A.A. Pinot Nero Valpitan Ris. '20	🏆🏆 5
○ A.A. Sauvignon Valpitan '22	🏆🏆 4
○ A.A. Spumante Brut M. Cl. Valpitan '18	🏆🏆 5

OTHER WINERIES

Thomas Pichler

fraz. Villa di Mezzo
via delle Vigne, 4a
39052 Caldaro/Kaltern [BZ]
℡ +39 3403540480
✉ www.thomas-pichler.it

CELLAR SALES
PRE-BOOKED VISITS
ANNUAL PRODUCTION 20,000 bottles
HECTARES UNDER VINE 2.50

● A.A. Lago di Caldaro Cl. Sup. Olte Reben '23	♟ 3
● A.A. Lagrein Sond Ris. '21	♟ 6
● Echo der Erde '22	♟ 8
○ Olls oder Nik Sauvignon '22	♟ 7

Michael Puff

via Ronco, 16b
39057 Cornaiano/Girlan [BZ]
℡ +39 3336883837
✉ www.weingutmichaelpuff.com

● Lacuna Pinot Nero '21	♟ 6
● Pinot Nero '22	♟ 5

Weingut Rohregger

fraz. Pianizza di Sotto, 15a
39052 Caldaro/Kaltern [BZ]
℡ +39 3394610483
✉ www.rohregger.it

ANNUAL PRODUCTION 6,000 bottles
HECTARES UNDER VINE 3.50

○ A.A. Pinot Bianco Vom Berg '22	♟ 6
○ A.A. Pinot Grigio Vom Kies '22	♟ 6
● A.A. Pinot Nero Vom Lehm Ris. '21	♟ 7
○ A.A. Sauvignon Vom Kalk '22	♟ 6

Prackfolerhof

via Spiegelweg, 9
39050 Fiè allo Sciliar
Völs am Schlern [BZ]
℡ +39 0471601532
✉ www.prackfolerhof.it

ANNUAL PRODUCTION 18,000 bottles
HECTARES UNDER VINE 4.50

○ A.A. Pinot Bianco '22	♟ 5
○ A.A. Pinot Bianco Sandl Ris. '20	♟ 6
● A.A. Pinot Nero Ris. '21	♟ 6
○ A.A. Sauvignon '22	♟ 4

Rametz

loc. Maia Alta
via Labers, 4
39012 Merano/Meran [BZ]
℡ +39 0473211011
✉ www.rametz.com

CELLAR SALES
PRE-BOOKED VISITS
RESTAURANT SERVICE
ANNUAL PRODUCTION 400,000 bottles
HECTARES UNDER VINE 8.00

● A.A. Cabernet Pflannzacker Ris. '19	♟ 5
○ A.A. Gewürztraminer Donata '23	♟ 4
● A.A. Pinot Nero Windschnur '21	♟ 5
○ Césuret Chardonnay '19	♟ 5

Tenuta Romen

via Massaccio, 14a
39057 Appiano/Eppan [BZ]
℡ +39 3757774614
✉ www.weingutromen.it

○ A.A. Pinot Bianco Luma '22	♟ 5
○ A.A. Pinot Bianco Nova '23	♟ 4
● A.A. Pinot Nero Luma '21	♟ 5
○ A.A. Sauvignon Luma '23	♟ 4

OTHER WINERIES

Tenuta Spitalerhof
Günther Oberpertinger

via Leitach, 46
39043 Chiusa/Klausen [BZ]
☎ +39 0472847612
🌐 www.spitalerhof.it

ANNUAL PRODUCTION 10,000 bottles
HECTARES UNDER VINE 1.60

○ Grüner Veltliner '23	♟♟ 4
○ Muga Grüner Veltliner Selection '22	♟♟ 5
○ Sepp Sylvaner Alte Reben '23	♟♟ 4

Thomas Unterhofer

loc. Pianizza di Sopra, 5
39052 Caldaro/Kaltern [BZ]
☎ +39 0471669133
🌐 www.weingut-unterhofer.com

CELLAR SALES
PRE-BOOKED VISITS
ANNUAL PRODUCTION 12,000 bottles
HECTARES UNDER VINE 3.00

○ A.A. Chardonnay Finesse Ris. '20	♟♟ 5
● A.A. Santa Maddalena Artis '22	♟♟ 4
○ A.A. Sauvignon Mirum '23	♟♟ 4

Josef Weger

loc. Cornaiano/Girlan
via Casa del Gesù, 17
39057 Appiano/Eppan [BZ]
☎ +39 0471662416
🌐 www.wegerhof.it

CELLAR SALES
PRE-BOOKED VISITS
ACCOMMODATION AND RESTAURANT SERVICE
ANNUAL PRODUCTION 80,000 bottles
HECTARES UNDER VINE 8.00

○ A.A. Pinot Bianco Auswahl '21	♟♟ 5
● A.A. Merlot Auswahl '20	♟♟ 5
○ A.A. Sauvignon Auswahl '22	♟♟ 5
○ A.A. Sauvignon Myron '23	♟♟ 4

Thurnhof - Andreas Berger

loc. Aslago
via Castel Flavon, 7
39100 Bolzano/Bozen
☎ +39 0471288460
🌐 www.thurnhof.com

CELLAR SALES
PRE-BOOKED VISITS
ANNUAL PRODUCTION 25,000 bottles
HECTARES UNDER VINE 3.50

● A.A. Cabernet Sauvignon V. Weinegg Ris. '21	♟♟ 5
● A.A. Lagrein Ris. '21	♟♟ 5
○ A.A. Sauvignon 800 '22	♟♟ 4

Villscheiderhof
Florian Hilpold

Pian di Sotto, 13
39042 Bressanone/Brixen [BZ]
☎ +39 0472832037
villscheider@akfree.it

CELLAR SALES
PRE-BOOKED VISITS
ANNUAL PRODUCTION 4,500 bottles
HECTARES UNDER VINE 1.50

○ A.A. Valle Isarco Kerner '23	♟♟ 3
○ A.A. Valle Isarco Riesling '23	♟♟ 4
○ A.A. Valle Isarco Sylvaner '23	♟♟ 3

Weinberghof
Christian Bellutti

In der Au, 4a
39040 Termeno/Tramin [BZ]
☎ +39 0471863224
🌐 www.weinberg-hof.com

ANNUAL PRODUCTION 20,000 bottles
HECTARES UNDER VINE 2.80

○ A.A. Gewürztraminer Clos '21	♟♟ 5
● A.A. Pinot Nero Ris. '21	♟♟ 6

VENETO

The extreme weather events that characterized the 2023 growing season ultimately left less of a mark than anticipated, thanks to the awareness and sensitivity that winemakers have developed in managing their vineyards and the challenges of climate-driven harvests. While production declines can be attributed to fungal diseases and hailstorms, the results exceeded even the most optimistic expectations.

In the Valdobbiadene area, where 2023 most shone during our tastings, the wines revealed a sharper, more spirited profile than usual. Yet, in the best expressions, this translated into finesse, suppleness, and lingering flavors. Notable examples include Col Credas from the Adami family in Farra di Soligo and Particella 181 from Sorelle Bronca in Rua di Feletto. Both leverage acidic precision to highlight the salinity and elegance that the glera grape can offer when sourced from the best vineyards. Stefano Pola, drawing on grapes from Santo Stefano, has crafted a Prosecco Superiore with an alluring character and rare harmony. Heading south, we find the appellations most influenced by the nearby Adriatic. Here, standout whites like Cescon's Madre '22 shine alongside the refined Merlot '20 from Campo Sella, a wine the Sutto brothers have brought to impressive heights. As we continue westward, Montello, Colli Euganei, and Colli Berici demonstrate year after year how Bordeaux varietals have truly found a home in Veneto, producing wines that deepen in concentration and complexity with each vintage.

In Verona province, it's Soave garganega and Valpolicella corvina that take center stage. The former, especially in the sunny 2022 vintage, gave rise to numerous outstanding wines, even spilling over into the nearby Custoza appellation, where it became a backbone for robust, characterful whites. In Valpolicella, we see increasingly refined and drier Amarones, and Valpolicella Superiore wines that, harvest after harvest, showcase with greater precision the extraordinary aromatic finesse that fresh grapes can deliver. We close this brief review with two wines that go beyond mere expressive quality, seeming to push the envelope in terms of interpretative originality: Le Tende's Bardolino '23 and Canoso's Soave Verso '21 from the Le Coste area.

Stefano Accordini

fraz. Cavalo
loc. Camparol, 10
37022 Fumane [VR]
(C» +39 0457760138
⊛ www.accordinistefano.it

CELLAR SALES
PRE-BOOKED VISITS
ACCOMMODATION AND RESTAURANT SERVICE
ANNUAL PRODUCTION 207,000 bottles
HECTARES UNDER VINE 27.00
VITICULTURE METHOD Certified Organic
SUSTAINABLE WINERY

For over 20 years, the Accordini family winery has shifted its production focus from the valley floor of Pedemonte to the higher areas of Valpolicella Classica, near Cavalo, where new vineyards were first planted and later the winery was built. Today, Accordini operates in some of the area's highest vineyards, with about 30 hectares dedicated almost entirely to the territory's traditional grapes, producing wines known for their energetic style and great tension. The Amarone Bio '19 is an exemplary drink, opening on overripe and sweet red fruit, expanding through toasted and spicy layers that frame its profile. On the palate, it impresses with its richness and decisiveness, supported by a vigorous, close-knit tannic structure. The Amarone Acinatico '20 presents a more refined aromatic expression, with a clearer rendering of red fruit and a dynamic flavor profile driven by acidity and sapidity, trademarks of tradition.

Adami

fraz. Colbertaldo
via Rovede, 27
31020 Vidor [TV]
(C» +39 0423982110
⊛ www.adamiprosecco.it

CELLAR SALES
PRE-BOOKED VISITS
ANNUAL PRODUCTION 850,000 bottles
HECTARES UNDER VINE 50.00
SUSTAINABLE WINERY

The Adami family draws on grapes from 34 districts within the Conegliano Valdobbiadene area, partly from their own vineyards and partly from trusted suppliers. The most prized are undoubtedly the expansive hillside plots of the historic Giardino vineyard, which they've owned for over a century, and those of the Torri di Credazzo area, which embodies the ruggedness of the highest slopes. From these two zones come their most ambitious and expressive wines, the extra Brut Col Credas and the crisp Vigneto Giardino. The former explores the hidden, fresh side of Trevigiana, with aromas reminiscent of granny smith apples and a palate that captivates with its decisive acidic tension. The latter, however, follows a more delicate path, highlighting the gentleness of fruit—a broad array of flavors unfolding with measured sweetness, resting on the gentle support of the bubbles.

● Amarone della Valpolicella Cl. Acinatico '20	♛♛ 7
● Amarone della Valpolicella Cl. Bio '19	♛♛ 7
● Valpolicella Cl. '23	♛♛ 3
● Valpolicella Cl. Sup. Ripasso Acinatico '22	♛♛ 3
● Valpolicella Cl. Sup. Ripasso Il Fornetto '19	♛♛ 6
● Valpolicella Sup. Stefano '22	♛♛ 3
● Paxxo '21	♛ 4
● Amarone della Valpolicella Cl. Vign. Il Fornetto '95	♛♛♛ 5
● Recioto della Valpolicella Cl. Acinatico '04	♛♛♛ 6
● Recioto della Valpolicella Cl. Acinatico '00	♛♛♛ 8

○ Valdobbiadene Rive di Farra di Soligo Extra Brut Col Credas '23	♛♛♛ 4*
○ Valdobbiadene Rive di Colbertaldo Asciutto Vig. Giardino '23	♛♛ 4
○ Cartizze	♛♛ 6
○ Valdobbiadene Brut Bosco di Gica	♛♛ 4
○ Valdobbiadene Col Fondo Brut Nature	♛♛ 3
○ Valdobbiadene Extra Dry dei Casel	♛♛ 4
○ Prosecco di Treviso Brut Garbèl	♛ 3
○ Valdobbiadene Rive di Colbertaldo Asciutto Vign. Giardino '22	♛♛♛ 4*
○ Valdobbiadene Rive di Colbertaldo Asciutto Vign. Giardino '16	♛♛♛ 3*
○ Valdobbiadene Rive di Farra di Soligo Brut Col Credas '13	♛♛♛ 3*
○ Valdobbiadene Rive di Farra di Soligo Brut Col Credas '20	♛♛ 3*

Ida Agnoletti

loc. Selva del Montello
via Saccardo, 55
31040 Volpago del Montello [TV]
📞 +39 0423621555
✉ www.idaagnoletti.it

CELLAR SALES
PRE-BOOKED VISITS
ANNUAL PRODUCTION 50,000 bottles
HECTARES UNDER VINE 7.00

The Prosecco boom that has swept through the hills of Treviso hasn't shaken the convictions of Ida Agnoletti, a determined producer from Selva del Montello. For decades, she has championed the area with the grapes that best represent it—Bordeaux varieties. On her small estate on Via Saccardo, she produces wines that see classic interpretations, which express a deep connection to the land and its traditions, alternate with more original offerings that highlight her distinct personality. Fitting into the first category is the Seneca '21, a Bordeaux blend that focuses on depth rather than fruit explosiveness, with aromas intertwining herbal and underbrush notes, sensations even more clearly defined across its dry, dynamic, and impressively long palate. The Merlot La Ida '22, on the other hand, opts for the sunny character of its origin and vintage with sweet, fleshy fruit, supported by a hint of thyme for a fresher lift, crowned by a dry and supple flavor profile.

● Montello Asolo Merlot La Ida '22	♟♟	4
● Montello Rosso Seneca '21	♟♟	4
● Vita Life is Red '21	♟♟	5
○ PSL Always Frizzante '22	♟	3
○ Asolo Prosecco Il Tranquillo '21	♟♟	2*
● Montello Asolo Merlot La Ida '21	♟♟	4
● Montello Asolo Recantina '21	♟♟	3
● Montello e Colli Asolani Cabernet Sauvignon Love Is... '20	♟♟	3
● Montello e Colli Asolani Cabernet Sauvignon Love Is... '19	♟♟	3
● Montello e Colli Asolani Merlot La Ida '20	♟♟	3
● Montello e Colli Asolani Recantina '20	♟♟	3
● Montello e Colli Asolani Rosso Seneca '18	♟♟	3*
● Montello Rosso Seneca '19	♟♟	4
● Vita Life is Red '20	♟♟	5

★★★★Allegrini

via Giare, 5
37022 Fumane [VR]
📞 +39 0456832011
✉ www.allegrini.it

CELLAR SALES
PRE-BOOKED VISITS
ACCOMMODATION
ANNUAL PRODUCTION 1,000,000 bottles
HECTARES UNDER VINE 150.00
SUSTAINABLE WINERY

Last winter saw the separation of the two branches of the Allegrini family. Now, siblings Francesco, Giovanni, and Matteo, along with their cousin Silvia, firmly lead the historic Fumane estate. The vineyards remain intact, with the most esteemed parcels still in use, allowing production to slowly uncover subtler, more refined nuances in the style established by Franco. And it is precisely this greater complexity that truly hits the mark: the 2020 version of the Amarone reveals spicier and fresher notes compared to the past, keeping fruit as the protagonist but enhancing it with herbal nuances that add lightness and dynamism. On the palate, it's full-bodied yet supple, spirited, and perfectly supported by the usual sapidity—a true hallmark of Allegrini. The Recioto '18, on the other hand, presents a more complex and mature aromatic profile, where sweetness plays the leading role in captivating the palate.

● Amarone della Valpolicella Cl. '20	♟♟♟	8
● Recioto della Valpolicella Cl. Giovanni Allegrini '18	♟♟	7
● La Grola '21	♟♟	5
○ Lugana Oasi Mantellina '23	♟♟	4
● Palazzo della Torre '21	♟♟	5
● Valpolicella Cl. '23	♟♟	3
● Amarone della Valpolicella Cl. '19	♟♟♟	8
● Amarone della Valpolicella Cl. '18	♟♟♟	8
● Amarone della Valpolicella Cl. '17	♟♟♟	8
● Amarone della Valpolicella Cl. '16	♟♟♟	8
● Amarone della Valpolicella Cl. '15	♟♟♟	8
● Amarone della Valpolicella Cl. '14	♟♟♟	8
● Amarone della Valpolicella Cl. '13	♟♟♟	8
● Amarone della Valpolicella Cl. '12	♟♟♟	8
● Amarone della Valpolicella Cl. '11	♟♟♟	8

VENETO

Andreola

fraz. Col San Martino
via Via Cavre, 19
31010 Farra di Soligo [TV]
+39 0438989379
www.andreola.eu

CELLAR SALES
PRE-BOOKED VISITS
ANNUAL PRODUCTION 950,000 bottles
HECTARES UNDER VINE 110.00
SUSTAINABLE WINERY

Things are always bustling at Stefano Pola's winery, of late one of the most vibrant estates in Prosecco Superiore. The area cultivated is quite extensive—estate vineyards combine with wide-ranging collaborations with local growers, who must adhere the technical team's guidelines. The best vineyards produce grapes for their more ambitious and territorially distinctive wines. Their most successful sparkling wines come from the territory's best parcels, starting with the one dedicated to founder Nazzareno Pola. It's an extra dry '23 that opens on intense impressions of ripe and sweet fruit, refreshed by more rarefied floral nuances. Despite residual sugar, the palate is dry, extending decisively towards a finish on fresh almonds. The Extra Dry Mas de Fer '23, on the other hand, expresses a sweeter and more immediate fruity cadence, standing out for its tension and smoothness.

○ Valdobbiadene Rive di Santo Stefano Extra Dry Dirupo Etichetta del Fondatore Nazareno Pola '23	TTT 7
○ Valdobbiadene Rive di Soligo Extra Dry Mas de Fer '23	TT 4
○ Cartizze '23	TT 6
○ Valdobbiadene Brut Dirupo '23	TT 4
○ Valdobbiadene Extra Dry Dirupo '23	TT 4
○ Valdobbiadene Rive di Col San Martino Extra Brut 26° I° '23	TT 4
○ Valdobbiadene Rive di Guia Extra Brut Aldaina al Mas '23	TT 3
○ Valdobbiadene Rive di Refrontolo Brut '23	TT 4
○ Riesling Stefano Pola '22	T 4
○ Traminer Aromatico Stefano Pola '22	T 4

★★Anselmi

via San Carlo, 46
37032 Monteforte d'Alpone [VR]
+39 0457611488
www.anselmi.eu

CELLAR SALES
PRE-BOOKED VISITS
RESTAURANT SERVICE
ANNUAL PRODUCTION 750,000 bottles
HECTARES UNDER VINE 80.00

Roberto Anselmi, one of the most esteemed producers in the Soave area, has long since abandoned the appellation to create wines that tell the story of the territory beyond any single grape variety. The highest part of Monte Foscarino has been densely planted with PIWI varieties in recent years, allowing the winery to drastically reduce the environmental impact of their treatments. The San Vincenzo '23 offers a multifaceted and intense aromatic bouquet, with exotic fruit finding freshness in citrus and floral notes, enlivened by sudden vegetal bursts that add a lively touch. On the palate, it's medium-bodied, characterized by a supple and juicy drinkability. The Capitel Foscarino from the same vintage opts for a deeper and more complex profile enriched by mineral nuances intertwining ripe yellow fruit and flowers. The palate impresses with its sapidity and length, leaving a clear hazelnut note on the finish.

○ Capitel Foscarino '23	TTT 5
○ San Vincenzo '23	TT 3
○ Capitel Croce '22	YYY 5
○ Capitel Croce '21	YYY 5
○ Capitel Croce '20	YYY 5
○ Capitel Croce '19	YYY 3*
○ Capitel Croce '18	YYY 3*
○ Capitel Croce '17	YYY 3*
○ Capitel Croce '15	YYY 3*
○ Capitel Croce '09	YYY 3*
○ Capitel Croce '06	YYY 3
○ Capitel Croce '05	YYY 3
○ Capitel Croce '04	YYY 3
○ Capitel Croce '03	YYY 3
○ Capitel Croce '02	YYY 3*
○ Capitel Croce '01	YYY 3

Balestri Valda

via Monti, 44
37038 Soave [VR]
+39 0457675393
www.vinibalestrivalda.com

CELLAR SALES
PRE-BOOKED VISITS
ACCOMMODATION
ANNUAL PRODUCTION 65,000 bottles
HECTARES UNDER VINE 16.00
VITICULTURE METHOD Certified Organic
SUSTAINABLE WINERY

The road from Soave to Castelcerino climbs up the hillsides and, after two curves through a grove, opens onto perfectly manicured vineyards. Here lies the heart of Laura Rizzotto's estate, whose winery rests just beyond, surrounded by rows of garganega grapes. The utmost respect for the environment characterizes a range that blends classicism and character. This year's lineup shows no weaknesses, with the Soave Sengialta, the result of an excellent 2021 vintage, leading the way. On the nose, it reveals subtle and almost hidden aromas that quickly release whiffs of golden apple, dried flowers, and a faint hint of mint. The palate follows the same path, starting delicately and finishing with great intensity. The Lunalonga '21, a more mature and complex Soave, plays with garganega's sweeter and more mature notes, offering a seductive palate that closes with a lovely almond note.

Soave Cl. Sengialta '21	▼▼ 4
Libertate '21	▼▼ 3
Soave Cl. '23	▼▼ 3
Soave Cl. Lunalonga '21	▼▼ 3
Libertate '20	▽▽ 3*
Libertate '19	▽▽ 3*
Libertate '18	▽▽ 3
Soave Cl. '22	▽▽ 3
Soave Cl. '21	▽▽ 2*
Soave Cl. '20	▽▽ 2*
Soave Cl. '19	▽▽ 2*
Soave Cl. Lunalonga '19	▽▽ 3
Soave Cl. Lunalonga '18	▽▽ 3
Soave Cl. Sengialta '20	▽▽ 4
Soave Cl. Sengialta '19	▽▽ 4
Soave Cl. Sengialta '18	▽▽ 4
Soave Cl. Sengialta '17	▽▽ 4

Barollo

via Rio Serva, 4b
31022 Preganziol [TV]
+39 0422633014
www.barollo.com

CELLAR SALES
PRE-BOOKED VISITS
ANNUAL PRODUCTION 88,000 bottles
HECTARES UNDER VINE 45.00
SUSTAINABLE WINERY

Marco and Nicola Barollo's winery is one of the most interesting in eastern Veneto, boasting a sizable set of vineyards extending between the provinces of Venice and Treviso. Despite Prosecco's great success, the Barollo brothers have assigned only a marginal role to Treviso's beloved bubbly, focusing instead on still wines that express finesse and suppleness. This year saw the debut of the Pinot Nero '20, Barollo's latest addition, a glass that plays more with balsamic components than with fruit, winning over the palate with its sweet tannins and an acidic drive that lengthens and streamlines its profile. The house champion, however, remains the Frank ! '21, a classic cabernet franc that showcases a broad aromatic spectrum, where ripe fruit finds freshness in herbal and spicy notes. The palate impresses not with its power but with harmony, revealing length and elegance.

● Frank! '21	▼▼ 5
○ Alfredo Barollo Brut M. Cl. '18	▼▼ 5
● Pinot Nero '20	▼▼ 6
○ Venezia Chardonnay '22	▼▼ 4
○ Venezia Chardonnay Frater '23	▼▼ 3
○ Prosecco di Treviso Brut '23	▼ 2
⊙ Prosecco di Treviso Rosé Brut '23	▼ 3
● Venezia Merlot Frater '23	▼ 3
● Frank! '19	▽▽▽ 5
● Frank! '18	▽▽▽ 5
● Frank! '17	▽▽▽ 4*
○ Venezia Chardonnay '18	▽▽▽ 4*
○ Alfredo Barollo Brut M. Cl. '16	▽▽ 4
● Frank! '20	▽▽ 5
○ Venezia Chardonnay '21	▽▽ 4
○ Venezia Chardonnay '19	▽▽ 4

Le Battistelle

fraz. Brognoligo
via Sambuco, 110
37032 Monteforte d'Alpone [VR]
+39 0456175621
www.lebattistelle.it

CELLAR SALES
PRE-BOOKED VISITS
ANNUAL PRODUCTION 90,000 bottles
HECTARES UNDER VINE 13.00
SUSTAINABLE WINERY

Gelmino and Cristina Dal Bosco run this small family winery, nestled amidst the hills of Soave. A dozen hectares of dark basalt soil are dedicated exclusively to garganega, the territory's queen grape, producing authentic and characterful wines that prioritize a vigorous, deep expression of the appellation over stylistic perfection. By virtue of a sunny 2022 vintage, their premium wines put in a performance marked by consistency and class. The Roccolo del Durlo, outlined by smoky and yellow fruit notes, combines approachability with complexity—it's an energetic and dense drink. Le Battistelle, on the other hand, plays with fresher fruit, while the palate highlights a satisfying sapidity that accompanies it throughout. Finally, I Rasoli, made with grapes from a vineyard with ungrafted vines, captivates with its lightness and length on the palate, finishing on a delightful almond note.

○ Soave Cl. Carbonare Roccolo del Durlo '22	🍷🍷🍷 4*
○ Soave Cl. Battistelle '22	🍷🍷 3*
○ Soave Cl. I Rasoli '22	🍷🍷 6
○ Soave Cl. Montesei '23	🍷🍷 3
○ Soave Brut Settembrino '23	🍷 3
○ Soave Cl. Le Battistelle '21	🍸🍸🍸 3*
○ Soave Cl. Roccolo del Durlo '20	🍸🍸🍸 4*
○ Soave Cl. Roccolo del Durlo '19	🍸🍸🍸 3*
○ Soave Cl. Carbonare I Rasoli '21	🍸🍸 5
○ Soave Cl. Carbonare I Rasoli '20	🍸🍸 5
○ Soave Cl. Montesei '22	🍸🍸 3
○ Soave Cl. Montesei '21	🍸🍸 2*
○ Soave Cl. Montesei '20	🍸🍸 2*
○ Soave Cl. Roccolo del Durlo '21	🍸🍸 4

★★Lorenzo Begali

via Cengia, 10
37020 San Pietro in Cariano [VR]
+39 0457725148
www.begaliwine.it

CELLAR SALES
PRE-BOOKED VISITS
ANNUAL PRODUCTION 90,000 bottles
HECTARES UNDER VINE 15.00

Last spring, Cengia's winery took a major step forward by acquiring neighboring vineyards on Ca' Bianca, creating what might be considered a small monopole. These additional three hectares round out an estate dedicated to the area's historic wines. The team consists of father Lorenzo in the fields, Giordano in the cellar, and sister Tiliana in administration. Together the three form a skilled and cohesive unit. The Siora '21 shines. It's a Valpolicella Superiore that accomplishes the difficult task of finding a perfect balance between the aromatic and spicy freshness of traditional grapes and rich flavors. The Amarone '20, on the other hand, plays on more mature and complex tones, reflected in an enveloping and sapid profile. We conclude with a superb Recioto '21, a passito defined by intense, youthful aromas that transform into a palate where acidity contrasts with sweetness.

● Amarone della Valpolicella Cl. '20	🍷🍷 7
● Recioto della Valpolicella Cl. '21	🍷🍷 6
● Valpolicella Cl. Sup. Siora '21	🍷🍷 4
● Valpolicella Cl. '23	🍷🍷 3
● Valpolicella Cl. Sup. Ripasso La Cengia '22	🍷🍷 5
● Amarone della Valpolicella Cl. Monte Ca' Bianca '13	🍸🍸🍸 8
● Amarone della Valpolicella Cl. Monte Ca' Bianca '12	🍸🍸🍸 8
● Amarone della Valpolicella Cl. Monte Ca' Bianca Ris. '17	🍸🍸🍸 8
● Amarone della Valpolicella Cl. Monte Ca' Bianca Ris. '16	🍸🍸🍸 8
● Amarone della Valpolicella Cl. Monte Ca' Bianca Ris. '15	🍸🍸🍸 8

★★Bertani

via Asiago, I
37023 Grezzana [VR]
☎ +39 0458658444
🌐 www.bertani.net

CELLAR SALES
PRE-BOOKED VISITS
ANNUAL PRODUCTION 1,500,000 bottles
HECTARES UNDER VINE 200.00
SUSTAINABLE WINERY

A cornerstone of Amarone, this Grezzana-based winery is the only producer in the region that can offer a true archive of past vintages, including a number of bottles dating back to the post-World War II era, when Verona's celebrated red officially came into being. The estate's vineyards reach into both the Valpolicella classica zone and nearby Valpantena, making for a range deeply rooted in history, though with a keen eye to the future. L'Amarone '15 reveals a complex aromatic profile, where overripe fruit seeks momentum through notes of herbs and spices, gradually unfurling as oxygen awakens its finer expressions. The palate is rich, well-supported by close-knit and energetic tannins. In contrast, the Ognisanti '22 proves to be a fresh, multifaceted drink that highlights the spiciness of traditional grapes. On the palate, it's supple, juicy, and unexpectedly long.

BiancaVigna

loc. Ogliano
via Monte Nero, 8
31015 Conegliano [TV]
☎ +39 0438788403
🌐 www.biancavigna.it

CELLAR SALES
PRE-BOOKED VISITS
ANNUAL PRODUCTION 600,000 bottles
HECTARES UNDER VINE 32.00
VITICULTURE METHOD Certified Organic
SUSTAINABLE WINERY

Founded just 20 years ago, the winery led by siblings Elena and Enrico Moschetta has quickly gained major recognition from both the market and peers. An interpreter of the eastern Conegliano Valdobbiadene area, the producer manages more than 30 hectares of vineyards dedicated exclusively to glera, all organic. The wines themselves are decidedly dry and food friendly, with the subzones of Ogliano and Soligo providing the highest quality grapes. The most intriguing results come from Ogliano, where the Extra Brut '23 achieves the challenging task of maintaining the immediately gratifying appeal of prosecco while highlighting its finesse and tension. The Rive di Soligo '23 plays on a more assertive profile—it's slower and more reserved in offering its aromas, but capable of captivating the palate with an unexpected vigor. The Conegliano Valdobbiadene Bio is diametrically opposed, standing out for its exotic aromas and harmonious palate.

Amarone della Valpolicella Cl. '15	♟♟♟ 8
Valpolicella Cl. Sup. Ognisanti '22	♟♟ 5
Soave Cl. Vintage '23	♟♟ 3
Valpolicella Cl. Le Miniere '23	♟♟ 5
Amarone della Valpolicella Cl. '13	♟♟♟ 8
Amarone della Valpolicella Cl. '12	♟♟♟ 8
Amarone della Valpolicella Cl. '11	♟♟♟ 8
Amarone della Valpolicella Cl. '10	♟♟♟ 8
Amarone della Valpolicella Cl. '09	♟♟♟ 8
Amarone della Valpolicella Cl. '08	♟♟♟ 8
Amarone della Valpolicella Cl. '07	♟♟♟ 8
Amarone della Valpolicella Cl. '06	♟♟♟ 8
Amarone della Valpolicella Cl. '05	♟♟♟ 8
Amarone della Valpolicella Cl. '04	♟♟♟ 8
Valpolicella Cl. Sup. Ognisanti '18	♟♟♟ 5

○ Conegliano Valdobbiadene Rive di Ogliano Extra Brut '23	♟♟♟ 4*
○ Conegliano Valdobbiadene Rive di Soligo Extra Brut '23	♟♟ 4
○ Conegliano Valdobbiadene Brut '23	♟♟ 3
○ Conegliano Valdobbiadene Brut Bio '23	♟♟ 4
○ Conegliano Valdobbiadene Extra Dry '23	♟♟ 3
○ Conegliano Valdobbiadene Rive di Collalto Extra Dry '22	♟♟ 4
⊙ Prosecco Rosé Brut Spumante Rosa '23	♟♟ 3
○ Conegliano Valdobbiadene Brut Nature Sui Lieviti SL '23	♟ 4
○ Prosecco Brut	♟ 3
○ Prosecco Frizzante	♟ 2
○ Conegliano Valdobbiadene Rive di Ogliano Extra Brut '22	♟♟♟ 3*

Bisol 1542

fraz. Santo Stefano
via Follo, 33
31049 Valdobbiadene [TV]
☎ +39 0423900138
⊕ www.bisol.it

CELLAR SALES
PRE-BOOKED VISITS
ANNUAL PRODUCTION 2,000,000 bottles
HECTARES UNDER VINE 100.00
SUSTAINABLE WINERY

Bisol 1542 is among the pioneers who brought Prosecco to the world. Today, the Lunelli group's winery has honed its product range by focusing on vineyards best suited to each wine type. Only sparkling wines are produced, with softness, acidity, and bubbles blending perfectly. Recent years have seen significant changes at Bisol, including a shift in production style and the restructuring of cru spaces to keep batches separate. A collaboration with Mattia Filippi and Umberto Marchiori has enabled the producer to transform high-caliber grapes into increasingly focused and reliable wines. A prime example is the Molera '23, an Extra Dry that sees ripe fruit and sweeter, delicate, floral and confectionery nuances alternate before giving way to a sapid palate that perfectly balances sweetness, acidity, and bubbles. The Relio '23, sourced from the steepest vineyards of Guia, reveals the more spirited and hidden side of their style, showcasing fresh aromas and a nervy, taut palate with outstanding length.

○ Valdobbiadene Extra Dry Molera '23	♥♥♥ 3*
○ Valdobbiadene Rive di Guia Extra Brut Relio '23	♥♥ 4
○ Cartizze '23	♥♥ 7
○ Valdobbiadene Brut Ed. I Gondolieri '23	♥♥ 3
○ P. di Valdobbiadene Dry Garnei '95	♥♥♥ 2*
○ Valdobbiadene Brut Crede '22	♀♀ 5
○ Valdobbiadene Brut Edizione I Gondolieri '22	♀♀ 5
○ Valdobbiadene Extra Dry Molera '22	♀♀ 5
○ Valdobbiadene Rive di Campea Dry '22	♀♀ 5
○ Valdobbiadene Rive di Gua Extra Brut Relio '22	♀♀ 5
○ Valdobbiadene Rive di Guia Extra Brut Relio '21	♀♀ 5

Bolla

fraz. Pedemonte
via A. Bolla, 3
37029 San Pietro in Cariano [VR]
☎ +39 0456836555
⊕ www.bolla.it

CELLAR SALES
PRE-BOOKED VISITS
ANNUAL PRODUCTION 3,700,000 bottles
HECTARES UNDER VINE 312.00

At Bolla, Christian Zulian is firmly in control, steering one of Valpolicella's most important wineries. The area cultivated extends across the entire Classica production zone, where some truly prized plots can be found, like those in the enchanting Gnirega area, a vineyard basin in the Marano valley that's perfectly exposed to the sun. The selection carried out for their more ambitious wines draws on a deep knowledge of the territory and the character of its grapes. Bolla produced two highly sophisticated Amarones this year, both 2018s. Le Origini reflects a connection to tradition, melding fruit with notes of herbs and underbrush. A full yet settled palate finds harmony in sapidity and a vibrant acidity. The Rhetico, on the other hand, comes across as darker on the nose, with fruity whiffs bolstered by mineral and tar notes, sensations that we also find across an energetic and spirited palate.

● Amarone della Valpolicella Cl. Le Origini Ris. '18	♥♥ 7
● Amarone della Valpolicella Cl. Rhetico '18	♥♥ 6
○ Soave Cl. '23	♥♥ 2
○ Soave Cl. Sup. Castellaro Tufaie '22	♥♥ 3
● Valpolicella Cl. '23	♥♥ 3
● Amarone della Valpolicella Cl. Le Origini Ris. '17	♀♀ 7
● Amarone della Valpolicella Cl. Le Origini Ris. '16	♀♀ 7
● Amarone della Valpolicella Cl. Rhetico '17	♀♀ 6
● Amarone della Valpolicella Cl. Rhetico '16	♀♀ 5
● Valpolicella Cl. Il Calice '22	♀♀ 3

Bonotto delle Tezze

fraz. Tezze di Piave
via Duca d'Aosta, 36
31028 Vazzola [TV]
+39 0438488323
www.bonottodelletezze.it

CELLAR SALES
PRE-BOOKED VISITS
ANNUAL PRODUCTION 150,000 bottles
HECTARES UNDER VINE 48.00

Upon entering Antonio Bonotto's winery, one immediately senses a connection to the history and traditions of Piave, a bond that goes beyond the usual display of dusty old tools often found in wine shops. There's a palpable sense of belonging and a firm commitment to keeping the villages alive through viticulture, an activity that has shaped their rhythms for centuries. Only a small portion of the grapes cultivated on their vast estate end up in the bottle. Raboso, undoubtedly the winery's flagship grape, is expressed both in the Piave Malanotte '19 and the Piave Raboso Potestà '21, wines that recount two faces of this late-ripening and austere varietal, known for its acidity, fruit, tannins, and softness. The first incorporates a portion of dried grapes, playing with fullness and sunny flavors, while the second highlights the spirited and elegant aspects of raboso on a crisp, taut, and long palate.

Borgo Stajnbech

fraz. Belfiore
via Belfiore, 109
30020 Pramaggiore [VE]
+39 0421799929
www.borgostajnbech.com

CELLAR SALES
PRE-BOOKED VISITS
ANNUAL PRODUCTION 90,000 bottles
HECTARES UNDER VINE 15.00
SUSTAINABLE WINERY

Clayey soils interspersed with layers of gravel characterize the Venetian plains, an area long home to vineyards. Despite the invasion of glera, the territory has maintained an unbreakable bond with tai, a varietal that thrives here and has found a masterful interpreter in the Valent family. Giuliano and his wife Adriana lead the estate, with their daughters Rebecca and Medea taking on increasingly important roles. The estate's most convincing wine is the Lison 150 a 2022 white that doesn't offer explosive fruit but rather an elegant interplay between white fruit and flowers, with notes of Mediterranean scrub and spicy echoes. On the palate, it's medium-bodied, stretching out gracefully with suppleness. The Stajnbech Bianco '22 is also excellent—it's a monovarietal chardonnay with ripe tones, delicate and harmoniously balanced on the palate. L'Enologa '22, a blend of tai and chardonnay aged in stainless steel and oak, stands out for its sapidity.

VENETO

Carménère Barbane '22	♥♥ 3
Conegliano Valdobbiadene Rive di Collalbrigo e Costa Brut Col Real '23	♥♥ 3
Manzoni Bianco Novalis '23	♥♥ 3
Piave Malanotte '19	♥♥ 6
Piave Raboso Potestà '21	♥♥ 4
Merlot Spezza '22	♥ 3
Piave Carmenere Barabane '19	♀♀ 3
Piave Carmenere Barabane '17	♀♀ 3
Piave Malanotte '17	♀♀ 6
Piave Malanotte '15	♀♀ 6
Piave Raboso Potestà '20	♀♀ 4
Piave Raboso Potestà '19	♀♀ 4
Piave Raboso Potestà '18	♀♀ 4
Piave Raboso Potestà '17	♀♀ 3

○ Lison Cl. 150 '22	♥♥ 4
○ L'Enologa '22	♥♥ 3
● Malbech '22	♥♥ 3
● Pinot Nero '21	♥♥ 3
○ Sauvignon Bosco della Donna '23	♥♥ 3
○ Sauvignon Evo '21	♥♥ 5
○ Stajnbech Bianco '22	♥♥ 4
○ Delle Venzia Pinot Grigio '23	♥ 3
○ Merlot '21	♥ 3
● Stajnbech Rosso '21	♥ 4
○ Bosco della Donna Sauvignon '21	♀♀ 4
○ L'Enologa '21	♀♀ 3
○ Lison Cl. 150 '21	♀♀ 4
○ Sauvignon Evo '20	♀♀ 5
● Stajnbech Rosso '20	♀♀ 4

Borgoluce

loc. Musile, 2
31058 Susegana [TV]
📞 +39 0438435287
🌐 www.borgoluce.it

CELLAR SALES
PRE-BOOKED VISITS
ACCOMMODATION AND RESTAURANT SERVICE
ANNUAL PRODUCTION 500,000 bottles
HECTARES UNDER VINE 106.00

Borgoluce represents a new vision of the agricultural estate, a kind of return to the past enhanced by contemporary knowledge and care. The large property spans multiple agricultural fronts, with viticulture serving as a key focus. Glera is the star of the hills behind the modern winery, celebrated for the fruity richness that the eastern Conegliano Valdobbiadene area can offer. The grapes for the winery's most ambitious sparkling wines, the Prosecco Superiore Extra Brut and the Extra Dry (both 2023s), both hail from their best vineyards, in Collato. The former highlights the weightier side of Treviso, leveraging the fruity richness of these hills without relying on sweetness, while the latter offers greater aromatic intensity that develops into a rich, softer, more enveloping palate.

Borin Vini & Vigne

fraz. Monticelli
via dei Colli, 5
35043 Monselice [PD]
📞 +39 042974384
🌐 www.viniborin.it

CELLAR SALES
PRE-BOOKED VISITS
ANNUAL PRODUCTION 105,000 bottles
HECTARES UNDER VINE 28.00

Monticelli is one of the eastern gateways to the Euganean hills, those intricate volcanic slopes that rise rapidly from the plains below. Only some of Borin's vineyards can be found here; for their best plots, one must climb into the folds of Arquà, where mostly Bordeaux red varietals are cultivated. Francesco and Gianpaolo, with the invaluable help of their parents Gianni and Teresa, confidently manage the family estate. It's no surprise that the Euganean Hills are prime cabernet wine country, and the success of the Coldivalle '20 confirms this once again. Sweet, ripe red fruit is accompanied by balsamic and graphite notes, with oak manifesting only in the background. On the palate, the wine moves with suppleness, despite its good concentration, extending with support from a sweet, polished tannic texture. The Corte Borin '22, a Manzoni Bianco, relies less on aromatic explosiveness and more on the firmness of the palate.

○ Valdobbiadene Rive di Collalto Extra Brut '23	🍷🍷 4
● Capifosso '21	🍷🍷 5
⊙ Rosariflesso Extra Brut	🍷🍷 3
○ Valdobbiadene Brut	🍷🍷 3
○ Valdobbiadene Extra Dry	🍷🍷 3
○ Valdobbiadene Rive di Collalto Extra Dry '23	🍷🍷 4
○ Fotonico Frizzante Sui Lieviti	🍷 3
○ Valdobbiadene Brut Nature sui Lieviti '22	🍷 4
○ Valdobbiadene Rive di Collalto Extra Brut '20	🍷🍷🍷 3*
○ Valdobbiadene Rive di Collalto Extra Brut '19	🍷🍷🍷 3
⊙ Rosariflesso Extra Brut	🍷🍷 3

● Colli Euganei Cabernet Sauvignon Coldivalle '20	🍷🍷 5
○ Chardonnay V. Bianca '22	🍷🍷 3
● Colli Euganei Cabernet Sauvignon V. Costa '22	🍷🍷 3
○ Colli Euganei Manzoni Bianco Corte Borin '22	🍷🍷 3
● Colli Euganei Merlot Foscolo '22	🍷🍷 3
○ Mandorli Signature '22	🍷🍷 2
○ Colli Euganei Fior d'Arancio Fiore di Gaia '23	🍷 3
○ Colli Euganei Pinot Bianco Archino '23	🍷 2
○ Sauvignon Blanc '23	🍷 3
○ Colli Euganei Chardonnay V. Bianca '21	🍷🍷 3
● Colli Euganei Merlot Rocca Chiara Ris. '20	🍷🍷 4

Bortolomiol

via Garibaldi, 142
31049 Valdobbiadene [TV]
☏ +39 04239749
☞ www.bortolomiol.com

CELLAR SALES
PRE-BOOKED VISITS
ACCOMMODATION
ANNUAL PRODUCTION 2,300,000 bottles
HECTARES UNDER VINE 5.00
VITICULTURE METHOD Certified Organic
SUSTAINABLE WINERY

The Prosecco Superiore appellation is renowned for its breathtaking landscapes and highly prized vineyards, cultivated by a dense network of small, sometimes tiny farms. The grapes are then delivered to the wineries themselves, where they are transformed into Treviso's beloved bubbly. Bortolomiol is one of the most recognized and appreciated of these wineries, boasting a historical connection with local growers and outstanding technical expertise. A wide range of Prosecco Superiores are offered by this Valdobbiadene producer, with two standing out: the Extra Brut 70th Anniversary and the Motus Vitae, both from the 2022 harvest and both of which age for more than in a year in the cellar before being released. The former hails from the vineyards of Col San Martino and stands out for its firm, taut profile, while the latter, from the steep slopes of San Pietro di Barbozza, plays more on ripe yellow fruit and a creamy palate.

★Brigaldara

fraz. San Floriano
via Brigaldara, 20
37029 San Pietro in Cariano [VR]
☏ +39 0457701055
☞ www.brigaldara.it

CELLAR SALES
PRE-BOOKED VISITS
ANNUAL PRODUCTION 350,000 bottles
HECTARES UNDER VINE 47.00
SUSTAINABLE WINERY

Few wineries in Valpolicella can boast vineyards in both the Classica and eastern part of the territory, with a range that highlights the different territories while respecting regional tradition. Brigaldara in San Floriano, Case Vecie nestled in the woods between Grezzana and Negrar, and Cavolo in the milder Grezzana district are the basis for Brigaldara's Valpolicellas. The whites, on the other hand, are produced in Marcellise. An impeccable lineup was presented this year, with many wines ranking among the best in their respective categories. The Amarone Case Vecie '18 stands out, offering mature and complex aromas where fruit meets notes of underbrush and macerated leaves, followed by a palate of superb vitality, with the power and alcohol of Amarone perfectly balanced by a vibrant acidity. The Valpolicella Superiore Case Vecie '22 is a fresh, dynamic, and gratifying drink.

VENETO

○ Valdobbiadene
Rive di San Pietro di Barbozza Extra Brut
Grande Cuvée del Fondatore
Motus Vitae '22 · ♟♟♟ 4*
○ Valdobbiadene Rive di Col San Martino
Extra Brut 70th Anniversary '22 · ♟♟ 5
○ Valdobbiadene Brut Ius Naturae '23 · ♟♟ 5
○ Valdobbiadene Brut Prior '23 · ♟♟ 4
○ Valdobbiadene Extra Dry Bandarossa
Special Edition V. di Collagù '23 · ♟♟ 4
○ Valdobbiadene Extra Dry
Banda Rossa '23 · ♟ 3
○ Valdobbiadene Brut Ius Naturae '20 · ♟♟♟ 4*
○ Valdobbiadene Brut Ius Naturae '19 · ♟♟♟ 5
○ Valdobbiadene Brut Ius Naturae '18 · ♟♟♟ 3*
○ Valdobbiadene Rive di Col San Martino
70th Anniversary '20 · ♟♟♟ 5

● Amarone della Valpolicella
Case Vecie '18 · ♟♟♟ 8
● Amarone della Valpolicella Ris. '15 · ♟♟ 8
● Valpolicella Sup. Case Vecie '22 · ♟♟ 4
● Amarone della Valpolicella Cavolo '19 · ♟♟ 6
● Amarone della Valpolicella Cl. '19 · ♟♟ 7
● Recioto della Valpolicella '17 · ♟♟ 7
○ Soave '23 · ♟♟ 3
● Valpolicella '23 · ♟♟ 3
● Valpolicella Sup. Ripasso Il Vegro '23 · ♟♟ 4
● Amarone della Valpolicella
Case Vecie '16 · ♟♟♟ 8
● Amarone della Valpolicella
Case Vecie '15 · ♟♟♟ 8
● Amarone della Valpolicella Cl. '16 · ♟♟♟ 7
● Valpolicella Sup. Case Vecie '21 · ♟♟♟ 4*

★Sorelle Bronca

fraz. Colbertaldo
via Martiri, 20
31020 Vidor [TV]
(☎ +39 0423987201
🌐 www.sorellebronca.com

CELLAR SALES
PRE-BOOKED VISITS
ACCOMMODATION
ANNUAL PRODUCTION 350,000 bottles
HECTARES UNDER VINE 24.00

In the world of Prosecco Superiore, sisters Ersiliana and Antonella Bronca are forging an original path. Without sacrificing the unmistakable light and enticing style of Treviso prosecco, they've highlighted the wine's most distinctive territorial expressions. The eastern vineyards produce richer grapes destined for Brut, while the western plots give rise to their Extra Dry. It all culminates in their three, most expressive wines, the Particella line. East and west, in their own way, highlight the immediate expressiveness of the style. Grapes from the Farrò vineyards yield a sparkling wine that embodies all the energy and tension of the Particella 232 '23 Prosecco Superiore, while the perfectly east-facing plots of Rua produce the refined and sapid Particella 181 '23. Unfortunately, the Particella 68 wasn't produced due to a severe hailstorm that devastated the vineyard.

Luigi Brunelli

via Cariano, 10
37029 San Pietro in Cariano [VR]
(☎ +39 0457701118
🌐 www.brunelliwine.com

CELLAR SALES
PRE-BOOKED VISITS
ACCOMMODATION
ANNUAL PRODUCTION 150,000 bottles
HECTARES UNDER VINE 18.00

The Brunelli family winery might not be widely known, but their work year after year has contributed significantly to the solidity of the appellation. Just under 20 hectares of vineyards are cultivated in the Classica zone, from the valley floor around the beautiful winery to the higher areas. The result is a range of superb stylistic precision and vigor. It's a solidity that we find not only in their production style, but in the consistent quality of their entire range, led this year by a superb Amarone Campo del Titari '17. The nose is immediately struck by its rich fruit, surrounded by herbal, spicy, and underbrush notes. On the palate, it's powerful, with a rigorous tannic structure and a decisive, energetic finish. The Recioto Armenzago '22 also impresses, revealing a seductive profile with explosive fruit flavors and delightful drinkability.

○ Valdobbiadene Rive di Rua Brut Particella 181 '23	♟♟♟ 5
○ Valdobbiadene Rive di Farrò Extra Brut Particella 232 '23	♟♟ 5
● Colli di Conegliano Rosso Ser Bele '19	♟♟ 5
○ Valdobbiadene Brut L'Est	♟♟ 3
○ Valdobbiadene Extra Dry L' Ovest	♟♟ 3
● Colli di Conegliano Rosso Ser Bele '05	♟♟♟ 5
○ Valdobbiadene Rive di Farrò Extra Brut Particella 232 '22	♟♟♟ 5
○ Valdobbiadene Rive di Rua Brut Particella 181 '21	♟♟♟ 4*
○ Valdobbiadene Rive di Rua Brut Particella 181 '20	♟♟♟ 4*

● Amarone della Valpolicella Cl. Campo del Titari Ris. '17	♟♟ 8
● Amarone della Valpolicella Cl. '20	♟♟ 7
● Corte Cariano '21	♟♟ 5
● Recioto della Valpolicella Cl. Armenzago '22	♟♟ 8
● Valpolicella Cl. Sup. Ripasso Pariondo '21	♟♟ 4
● Valpolicella Classico Sup. '21	♟♟ 6
○ Carianum '22	♟ 6
● Amarone della Valpolicella Cl. Campo del Titari '97	♟♟♟ 8
● Amarone della Valpolicella Cl. Campo del Titari '96	♟♟♟ 8
● Amarone della Valpolicella Cl. Campo del Titari Ris. '16	♟♟ 8
● Amarone della Valpolicella Cl. Campo Inferi Ris. '17	♟♟ 8

VENETO

Buglioni

fraz. Corrubbio
via Campagnole, 55
37029 San Pietro in Cariano [VR]
☏ +39 0456760681
🌐 www.buglioni.it

CELLAR SALES
PRE-BOOKED VISITS
ACCOMMODATION AND RESTAURANT SERVICE
ANNUAL PRODUCTION 200,000 bottles
HECTARES UNDER VINE 60.00

Mariano Buglioni avails himself of an estate that
spans several hectares in the Valpolicella Classica
production zone, specifically in the municipalities
of San Pietro in Cariano and Sant'Ambrogio.
These are dedicated entirely to Verona's
traditional grapes, with both appellation wines
and more original interpretations produced.
Mariano's keen ability to capture the character
that the grapes develop in their interaction with
the vineyard results in a highly reliable range.
Recent years have seen a focus on Valpolicella
Superiore, with Mariano offering two highly
distinctive interpretations: L'(Im)perfetto '22 and
44 verticale '21. The first remains bound up with
the spiciness of the corvina grape. It's a supple,
juicy wine with nice length. The second is more
visionary, delivering an aromatic profile where
fruit intertwines with smoky and peppery
notes—an experience of great finesse that opens
a new stylistic possibility for Valpolicella.

Valpolicella Cl. Sup. 44 Verticale '21	🍷🍷 6
Valpolicella Cl. Sup. L'(Im)perfetto '22	🍷🍷 4
Amarone della Valpolicella Cl. Il Lussurioso '20	🍷🍷 7
Valpolicella Cl. Sup. Ripasso Il Bugiardo '22	🍷🍷 5
Valpolicella Cl. Sup. 44 Verticale '20	🍷🍷🍷 5
Amarone della Valpolicella Cl. Il Lussurioso '19	🍷🍷 7
Amarone della Valpolicella Cl. Il Lussurioso '18	🍷🍷 7
Amarone della Valpolicella Cl. Il Lussurioso '17	🍷🍷 7
Amarone della Valpolicella Cl. Teste Dure Amphora Ris. '15	🍷🍷 8
Valpolicella Cl. Sup. 44 Verticale '19	🍷🍷 3
Valpolicella Cl. Sup. L'(Im)perfetto '19	🍷🍷 4

Ca' La Bionda

via Bionda, 4
37020 Marano di Valpolicella [VR]
☏ +39 0456801198
🌐 www.calabionda.it

CELLAR SALES
PRE-BOOKED VISITS
ACCOMMODATION
ANNUAL PRODUCTION 150,000 bottles
HECTARES UNDER VINE 29.00
VITICULTURE METHOD Certified Organic

Among the wineries that have not hitched their
wagon to the success of Amarone, and have
continued to experiment and deepen their
knowledge of the territory and its grapes, the
Castellani brothers' Ca' La Bionda plays a leading
role. Alessandro and Nicola extract great
character from their vineyards, whether it's for
their premium Amarone or the simpler
Valpolicella, resulting in a contemporary range
rooted in tradition. The Valpolicella Casal Vegri '21
is an exemplary drink, avoiding the trend of
hyper-concentrated, fruit-forward wines. Instead,
it offers a subtle yet refined aromatic profile,
where wild cherry intertwines with rose and
pepper notes. The palate is supple, supported by
pronounced acidity that legthens and tightens the
palate. In contrast, the Amarone Ravazzol '18
takes on a richer and deeper tone, with mature,
fleshy fruit balanced between density and tension.
The Recioto Le Tordare '15 perfectly blends
sweetness and acidic drive.

● Amarone della Valpolicella Cl. Ravazzol '18	🍷🍷 8
● Valpolicella Cl. Sup. Casal Vegri '21	🍷🍷 6
● Recioto della Valpolicella Cl. Le Tordare '15	🍷🍷 8
● Valpolicella Cl. Sup. Casal Vegri '23	🍷🍷 6
● Valpolicella Cl. Sup. Ripasso Malavoglia '21	🍷🍷 6
● Amarone della Valpolicella Cl. Ravazzol Ris. '13	🍷🍷🍷 8
● Amarone della Valpolicella Cl. V. di Ravazzol '17	🍷🍷🍷 8
● Amarone della Valpolicella Cl. Vign. di Ravazzol '16	🍷🍷🍷 8
● Valpolicella Cl. Sup. Campo Casal Vegri '17	🍷🍷🍷 6

Ca' Lustra - Zanovello

loc. Faedo
via San Pietro, 50
35030 Cinto Euganeo [PD]
☏ +39 042994128
⊛ www.calustra.it

CELLAR SALES
PRE-BOOKED VISITS
ANNUAL PRODUCTION 160,000 bottles
HECTARES UNDER VINE 25.50
VITICULTURE METHOD Certified Organic
SUSTAINABLE WINERY

The Euganean Hills are one of Italy's most important areas for producing Bordeaux blends, a dense cluster of volcanic slopes that rise from the Po Valley, just a stone's throw from Padua. Ca' Lustra has been operating here for almost half a century, today with siblings Marco and Linda Zanovello at the helm. The pair cultivate over 20 hectares scattered across the southern ridges, producing wines rich in character and nuance. Tasting the Fior d'Arancio Passito '20 is like exploring the sunniest side of the Euganean Hills. Dense, ripe fruit surrounded by brackish notes and Mediterranean scrub are echoed on a palate of exuberant sweetness, all balanced by sapidity. The Merlot Sassonero '20, however, reveals its aromas sparingly, initially closed by dark and indistinct notes before opening to fruit and herbal nuances. The palate proves sapid, nicely balanced by acidity.

★★Ca' Rugate

via Pergola, 36
37030 Montecchia di Crosara [VR]
☏ +39 0456176328
⊛ www.carugate.it

CELLAR SALES
PRE-BOOKED VISITS
ACCOMMODATION
ANNUAL PRODUCTION 750,000 bottles
HECTARES UNDER VINE 90.00
VITICULTURE METHOD Certified Organic
SUSTAINABLE WINERY

Michele Tessari and his winery Ca' Rugate seem to thrive on challenges. No harvest passes without a new project, often a starting point for making improvements in viticulture or production, and frequently resulting in the birth of new wines. Their Corte Durlo, Amedeo, and Studio di Studio have all aimed to explore tradition, places, and grapes, resulting in a range that has no weak points. A spectacular debut for the new Amarone Cima Caponiera '17, a Riserva from a small plot on the western edge of the appellation's classic heart. It showcases a refined aromatic array where fruit, flowers, and spices blend into a note of freshness, echoed on a crisp, racy, and dynamic palate. Its eastern sibling, Punt' 470 '20, proves darker and denser, while the Soave Monte Fiorentine '22 is the usual prized white. Finally, an outstanding performance by the Amedeo '18, a bottle that puts Lessinia on the national sparkling wine map. Duly noted.

○ Colli Euganei Fior d'Arancio Passito '20	♀♀ 4
● Colli Euganei Merlot Sassonero '20	♀♀ 4
○ Colli Euganei Bianco '23	♀♀ 3
● Colli Euganei Rosso Moro Polo '21	♀♀ 3
○ Manzoni Bianco '21	♀♀ 3
● Nero Musqué	♀♀ 4
○ Roverello '19	♀♀ 4
⊙ Rosato '21	♀ 4
● Colli Euganei Cabernet Girapoggio '05	♀♀♀ 3
○ Colli Euganei Fior d'Arancio Passito '07	♀♀♀ 4
● Colli Euganei Merlot Sassonero Villa Alessi '05	♀♀♀ 3
○ Colli Euganei Fior d'Arancio Spumante Dolce '19	♀♀ 3
● Colli Euganei Rosso Moro Polo '20	♀♀ 3

● Amarone della Valpolicella Cl. Cima Caponiera Ris. '17	♀♀♀ 8
● Amarone della Valpolicella Punta 470 '20	♀♀ 7
○ Lessini Durello Pas Dosé Amedeo Ris. '18	♀♀ 6
○ Soave Cl. Monte Fiorentine '22	♀♀ 4
● Recioto della Valpolicella L'Eremita '20	♀♀ 5
○ Recioto di Soave La Perlara '20	♀♀ 5
○ Soave Cl. Monte Alto '21	♀♀ 4
○ Soave Cl. San Michele '23	♀♀ 3
○ Soave Cl. Sup. Bucciato '22	♀♀ 5
● Valpolicella Rio Albo '23	♀♀ 3
● Valpolicella Sup. Campo Lavei '21	♀♀ 5
○ Soave Cl. Monte Alto '19	♀♀♀
○ Soave Cl. Monte Fiorentine '21	♀♀♀
○ Soave Cl. Monte Fiorentine '19	♀♀♀ 3

★Camerani Corte Sant'Alda

loc. Fioi
via Capovilla, 28
37030 Mezzane di Sotto [VR]
(+39 0458880006
www.cortesantalda.it

CELLAR SALES
PRE-BOOKED VISITS
ACCOMMODATION
ANNUAL PRODUCTION 90,000 bottles
HECTARES UNDER VINE 19.00
VITICULTURE METHOD Certified Biodynamic

Established in the mid-1980s by Marinella Camerani, Camerani - Corte Sant'Alda is today one of the most noteworthy wineries operating in Verona. The vineyards around the house and cellar have gradually expanded to include the five-hectare Adalia estate in Molinetto and, finally, the Castagnè farm on the other side of the valley. The entire estate is managed biodynamically, resulting in a range that expresses terroir, tradition and dreams. The Amarone Valzzane '17 pours a luminous, intense ruby hue, unveiling its aromas gradually: first sweet fruit, then underbrush, and finally that signature pepper note of traditional grapes. The palate doesn't pursue concentration and power but rather harmony and tension, resulting in a long, juicy finish. In contrast, the Valpolicella Podere Castagne '19 explores the more restless side of the appellation, with aromas that burst into herbal and spicy notes, leaving fruit in the background. The palate is crisp, supported by pronounced acidity.

Giuseppe Campagnola

fraz. Valgatara
via Agnella, 9
37020 Marano di Valpolicella [VR]
(+39 0457703900
www.campagnola.com

CELLAR SALES
PRE-BOOKED VISITS
ANNUAL PRODUCTION 5,000,000 bottles
HECTARES UNDER VINE 140.00

The Campagnola family has been making wines for more than a century, but it was only with Giuseppe in the late 1990s that the winery took on the form we know today. Now, sons Paolo and Andrea manage the producer alongside their father. In addition to valuable collaborations with numerous local growers, they rely on estate vineyards, most notably Missoj in Mizzole. The house's most interesting wine, the Amarone Riserva '17, hails from Mizzole. Classic aromas of sweet, overripe fruit are accompanied by spices and a hint of macerated leaves. On the palate, however, it shifts gears, revealing vigor, fullness, and tension, underscored by a notable tannic structure that renders it austere, energetic. The Amarone Caterina Zardini '19 features a more straightforward profile, one focused on dense, mature fruit and firm, juicy mouthfeel. The Recioto Casotto del Merlo '21 intrigues, perfectly balancing sweetness and acidity.

Amarone della Valpolicella Val**zzane Corte Sant'Alda '17	♟♟♟ 8
Valpolicella Sup. Podere Castagne '19	♟♟ 5
Amarone della Valpolicella Ruvaln Adalia '19	♟♟ 8
Soave Fienile Corte Sant'Alda '23	♟♟ 3
Valpolicella Ca' Fiui Corte Sant'Alda '22	♟♟ 3
Valpolicella Laute Adalia '23	♟♟ 3
Valpolicella Sup. Ripasso Balt Adalia '22	♟♟ 5
Valpolicella Sup. Ripasso Campi Magri Corte Sant'Alda '20	♟♟ 5
Inti Corte Sant'Alda '22	♟ 3
Amarone della Valpolicella '10	♟♟♟ 8
Amarone della Valpolicella Val**zzane Corte Sant'Alda '16	♟♟♟ 8
Valpolicella Ca' Fiui '18	♟♟♟ 3*
Valpolicella Sup. Mithas '12	♟♟♟ 8

● Amarone della Valpolicella Tenuta di Missoj Ris. '17	♟♟ 8
● Amarone della Valpolicella Cl. Caterina Zardini Ris. '19	♟♟ 7
● Amarone della Valpolicella Cl. Giuseppe Campagnola '20	♟♟ 6
● Recioto della Valpolicella Cl. Casotto del Merlo '21	♟♟ 5
● Valpolicella Cl. Sup. Caterina Zardini '22	♟♟ 4
● Valpolicella Cl. Sup. Ripasso '22	♟♟ 4
○ Soave Cl. Vigneti di Foscarino Le Bine '23	♟ 3
● Valpolicella Cl. Le Bine '23	♟ 3
● Amarone della Valpolicella Cl. Caterina Zardini '04	♟♟♟ 6
● Amarone della Valpolicella Cl. Caterina Zardini '01	♟♟♟ 6

★I Campi

loc. Allodola
fraz. Cellore d'Illasi
via delle Pezzole, 3
37032 Illasi [VR]
📞 +39 0456175915
🌐 www.icampi.it

CELLAR SALES
PRE-BOOKED VISITS
ANNUAL PRODUCTION 80,000 bottles
HECTARES UNDER VINE 12.00

Founded in 2006, I Campi might seem young, but Flavio Prà has been exploring the hills of Soave and Valpolicella for much longer, having performed major consulting work in the area. A dozen hectares in the highest parts of both regions are the basis for a prized estate—one whose wines express the elegance and sophistication of their respective appellations. A perfect example of the style is the Soave Campo Vulcano '23, which opens on aromas of fresh fruit and flowers, still dominated by a youthful expressiveness that borders on simplicity. The palate wins you over with its lightness and tension, highlighting the suppleness and drinkability that characterize the best interpretations of the appellation. Red fruit meets oak in the Amarone Campi Lunghi '20, a wine that we appreciated for its dynamic profile and delicate tannins. The Campo delle Rocce '22, a long and energetic Valpolicella, also caught our attention.

Canevel Spumanti

fraz. Saccol
via Roccat e Ferrari, 17
31049 Valdobbiadene [TV]
📞 +39 0423975940
🌐 www.canevel.it

CELLAR SALES
PRE-BOOKED VISITS
ANNUAL PRODUCTION 1,300,000 bottles
HECTARES UNDER VINE 26.00
VITICULTURE METHOD Certified Organic
SUSTAINABLE WINERY

Founded by Mario Caramel in the late 1970s, the winery has seen significant development since 2016 thanks to a collaboration with Gargagnago's Masi group, who have brought extensive market knowledge and dynamism. Technical management has shifted towards sustainability, drawing on an extensive, organically farmed estate in the heart of the historic prosecco Superiore region. The Terre de Faè '23, a Prosecco Superiore hailing from a single vineyard surrounded by patches of woodland, opens on aromas of ripe yellow fruit with flowers playing a supporting role. On the palate, the perfect fusion of bubbles, acidity, and delicate structure makes for a highly enjoyable drink, all while maintaining a crisp, racy profile. The Millesimato '23, with its greater focus on fruit, is a true classic of the appellation—a harmonious sparkler characterized by outstanding stylistic precision.

○ Soave Cl. Campo Vulcano '23	♟♟♟ 4*
● Amarone della Valpolicella Campi Lunghi '20	♟♟ 6
○ Delle Venezie Pinot Grigio '23	♟♟ 3
○ Lugana Campo Argilla '23	♟♟ 3
○ Soave Campo Base '23	♟♟ 2*
● Valpolicella Sup. Campo delle Rocce '22	♟♟ 5
● Valpolicella Sup. Ripasso Campo Ciotoli '21	♟♟ 4
○ Soave Cl. Campo Vulcano '22	♟♟♟ 3*
○ Soave Cl. Campo Vulcano '19	♟♟♟ 3*
○ Soave Cl. Campo Vulcano '18	♟♟♟ 3*
○ Soave Cl. Campo Vulcano '15	♟♟♟ 3*
○ Soave Cl. Campo Vulcano '13	♟♟♟ 3*
○ Soave Cl. Campo Vulcano '12	♟♟♟ 3*
● Valpolicella Sup. Ripasso Campo Ciotoli '16	♟♟♟ 3*

○ Valdobbiadene Extra Brut Terre del Faè '23	♟♟ 4
○ Valdobbiadene Brut Setàge '23	♟♟ 4
○ Valdobbiadene Extra Dry Il Millesimato '23	♟♟ 5
○ Valdobbiadene Brut Campofalco '23	♟ 4
○ Valdobbiadene Brut Campofalco Vign. Monfalcon '17	♟♟♟ 5
○ Valdobbiadene Dosaggio Zero Vign. Del Faè '18	♟♟♟ 3
○ Valdobbiadene Brut Campofalco '22	♟♟ 3
○ Valdobbiadene Brut Campofalco '21	♟♟ 4
○ Valdobbiadene Brut Campofalco '20	♟♟ 3
○ Valdobbiadene Brut Campofalco '19	♟♟ 3
○ Valdobbiadene Brut Setage '22	♟♟ 3
○ Valdobbiadene Extra Brut Terre Del Faè '21	♟♟ 4

Canoso

via Roma, 97
37032 Monteforte d'Alpone [VR]
☎ +39 0456101981
🖙 www.canoso.it

CELLAR SALES
PRE-BOOKED VISITS
ANNUAL PRODUCTION 73,000 bottles
HECTARES UNDER VINE 12.00

Less than ten years ago, Giovanni Bartucci acquired the Monteforte winery, quickly transforming it into one of Soave's most highly regarded producers. Thanks to support from highly competent technicians deeply connected to the territory, their line of Soaves has achieved a high level of quality. However, there are ongoing experiments in nearby territories, starting with Lessinia and its most representative grape, durella. Their most intriguing wines come from Soave, particularly from the Le Coste area, where the Soave Verso '21 is produced. This white, aged at length in the cellar before bottling, now showcases its ability to balance complexity with immediate appeal. Aromatically it spans everything from ripe yellow fruit to dried flowers, licorice root, and smoky nuances, culminating in a rich and sapid palate. The Riserva '19, on the other hand, is more poised, standing out for its complex aromas and a full, pervasive palate.

Soave Cl. Sup. Le Coste Verso '21	▼▼▼ 4*
Soave Cl. Fonte '22	▼▼ 2*
Soave Cl. Sup. Verso Ris. '19	▼▼ 4
Amarone della Valpolicella Corpo '15	♀♀ 6
Oltre '21	♀♀ 4
Soave Cl. Fonte '20	♀♀ 2*
Soave Cl. Fonte '19	♀♀ 2*
Soave Cl. Fonte '18	♀♀ 2*
Soave Cl. Fonte '17	♀♀ 2*
Soave Cl. Sup. Verso '20	♀♀ 3
Soave Cl. Sup. Verso '18	♀♀ 3
Soave Cl. Sup. Verso '17	♀♀ 3
Soave Cl. Sup. Verso '16	♀♀ 3
Soave Cl. Sup. Verso Ris. '18	♀♀ 4

Cantine di Verona

via Colonia Orfani di Guerra, 5b
37142 Verona
☎ +39 045550032
🖙 wwww.cantinediverona.it

CELLAR SALES
PRE-BOOKED VISITS
ANNUAL PRODUCTION 20,000,000 bottles
HECTARES UNDER VINE 1000.00
SUSTAINABLE WINERY

As the Verona group has expanded its production area, it has also adjusted its approach in the cellar. Without abandoning the qualities of immediacy and simplicity, they are producing wines with character and a strong bond with the territory. It's all been made possible thanks to a close-knit technical team with a deep knowledge of various regions, starting from Valpolicella and moving westward to the morainic hills of Garda and Custoza. Their most striking wines hail from Custoza, in particular the Custoza Brolo dei Giusti, which, in its second release, confirms its status as one of the appellation's most interesting wines. The 2021 takes advantage of an excellent year, offering an aromatic profile of great intensity and freshness, ranging from white fruit to citrus. On the palate, its solid structure is matched perfectly by acidity and the sapidity we'd expect from lower Garda. Among the reds, the Amarone Collector's Edition '18 impressed with its depth and richness.

○ Custoza Sup. Brolo dei Giusti '21	▼▼ 5
● Amarone della Valpolicella Collector's Edition Ris. '18	▼▼ 8
● Bardolino Cl. Val dei Molini '23	▼▼ 2*
○ Custoza Sup. Torre del Falasco '22	▼▼ 3
○ Garda Brut '19	▼▼ 4
○ Lugana Torre del Falasco '23	▼▼ 3
● Valpolicella Ripasso Torre del Falasco '21	▼▼ 4
● Valpolicella Sup. Ripasso Torre del Falasco '21	▼▼ 5
● Valpolicella Sup. Torre del Falasco '22	▼▼ 3
⊙ Chiaretto di Bardolino Val dei Molini '23	▼ 2
○ Custoza Val dei Molini '23	▼ 3
● Garda Merlot '19	▼ 2
● Valpolicella Sup. Brolo dei Giusti '15	♀♀♀ 6
● Valpolicella Valpantena Ripasso Ritocco '21	♀♀ 4

La Cappuccina

fraz. Costalunga
via San Brizio, 125
37032 Monteforte d'Alpone [VR]
📞 +39 0456175036
🌐 www.lacappuccina.it

CELLAR SALES
PRE-BOOKED VISITS
ANNUAL PRODUCTION 350,000 bottles
HECTARES UNDER VINE 42.00
VITICULTURE METHOD Certified Organic
SUSTAINABLE WINERY

Today, concepts like sustainability, organic
farming, and environmental respect are widely
discussed, but it's important to recognize the
pioneering wineries that first adopted such
principles, convinced that good wine can only
come from a healthy environment. The Tessari
brothers oversee one such winery, a family-run
estate located on the eastern side of the Soave
appellation, nestled between the hills of the
Classica zone and those on the outskirts of
Lessinia. Their sizable estate provides the grapes
for a range that is noteworthy both in terms of
quantity and quality. Leading this year's lineup is
the Soave San Brizio '22, with its broad and
energetic aromatic expression, where smoky
notes gradually give way to dried flowers and
ripe, sweet yellow fruit. The palate is sapid, crisp,
and impressively long. The Recioto Arzimo '20 is
even more complex and alluring, a sweet wine
characterized by aromas of toasted hazelnuts
and candied apricots, offering a bold sweetness
balanced by a brackish note that lends harmony.

Le Carline

via Carline, 24
30020 Pramaggiore [VE]
📞 +39 0421799741
🌐 www.lecarline.com

CELLAR SALES
PRE-BOOKED VISITS
ANNUAL PRODUCTION 500,000 bottles
HECTARES UNDER VINE 35.00
VITICULTURE METHOD Certified Organic
SUSTAINABLE WINERY

Daniele Piccinin, now joined by his son
Alessandro, has created one of the most notable
wineries operating in the vast area between the
provinces of Venice, Treviso, and Pordenone.
Together they oversee a large, organically
managed estate spanning several hectares on
soils where gravel and clay alternate
continuously. Here the region's historic varieties
endure, despite glera's meteoric rise, while the
production style favors tension over power. The
tai grape is undoubtedly the emblem of the area.
Here it gives rise to a Lison redolent of white
fruit and almond, complemented by a subtle
floral vein that refreshes the overall profile. The
2022 exhibits a full, juicy palate that stands out
for its length. The Dogale, a late-harvest
verduzzo, captivates with its broad aromatic
range, where dried fruit and notes of
caramelized hazelnuts give way to herbal
nuances. On the palate, its sweetness is perfectly
balanced by a pronounced sapidity.

○ Recioto di Soave Arzimo '20	♟♟♟ 6
○ Soave San Brizio '22	♟♟♟ 5
○ Sauvignon Basaltik '23	♟♟ 4
○ Soave '23	♟♟ 3
○ Soave Cl. Monte Stelle '23	♟♟ 4
○ Soave Fontègo '23	♟♟ 4
○ Villa Buri M. Cl. Brut '12	♟♟ 5
○ Filòs brut	♟ 4
● Madègo '21	♟ 4
● Camp Buri Cabernet Sauvignon '95	♟♟♟ 5
○ Recioto di Soave Arzimo '19	♟♟ 6
○ Recioto di Soave Arzimo '18	♟♟ 6
○ Soave Cl. Monte Stelle '21	♟♟ 4
○ Soave Cl. Monte Stelle '20	♟♟ 3*
○ Soave Cl. Monte Stelle '19	♟♟ 4
○ Soave San Brizio '21	♟♟ 5

○ Lison Cl. '22	♟♟
● Carline Rosso '21	♟♟ -
○ Chardonnay '22	♟♟
○ Diana M.Cl. Brut	♟♟
○ Dogale V.T.	♟♟
● Prior Resiliens '22	♟♟
○ Venezia Pinot Grigio '23	♟♟
○ Bianco Resiliens '23	♟
● Rosso Resiliens '23	♟
● Carline Rosso '20	♟♟
○ Lison Cl. '21	♟♟
○ Lison-Pramaggiore Chardonnay '21	♟♟
● Lison-Pramaggiore Refosco P. R. '21	♟♟
○ Resiliens Bianco '22	♟♟
○ Sauvignon Nepis Resiliens '22	♟♟
○ Venezia Pinot Grigio '22	♟♟

Casa Cecchin

via Agugliana, 11
36054 Montebello Vicentino [VI]
(") +39 0444649610
@ www.casacecchin.it

CELLAR SALES
PRE-BOOKED VISITS
ANNUAL PRODUCTION 30,000 bottles
HECTARES UNDER VINE 7.00
SUSTAINABLE WINERY

The hills separating the Alpone valley from that of Chiampo constitute the cradle of durella, a grape that produces bold and challenging fruit. It's here that we find the winery established by Renato Cecchin, and now led by his daughter Roberta. A few hectares situated in an area of enchanting beauty, the estate has elevated the status of Lessinia and its wines, thanks primarily to a focus on Metodo Classico spumante. If the world is beginning to appreciate Durello, much credit goes to the winery on Via Agugliana, which continues to demonstrate its class. The Dosaggio Zero Riserva '17 opens with a sulfur note that conceals its fruit, which later emerges, settling on a mineral backdrop. On the palate, the wine impresses with its solid structure, supported by its characteristic acidic drive. The Nostrum '19 offers up fresher and more immediate aromas, coming through dry and lean on the palate.

Case Paolin

via Madonna Mercede, 55
31040 Volpago del Montello [TV]
(") +39 0423871433
@ www.casepaolin.it

CELLAR SALES
PRE-BOOKED VISITS
ANNUAL PRODUCTION 180,000 bottles
HECTARES UNDER VINE 18.00
VITICULTURE METHOD Certified Organic

The Pozzobon brothers have transformed the winery founded by their father, Emilio, into one of the most intriguing operations in the Treviso area. They boast an estate that spans two distinct viticultural zones. One part of the vineyards thrives on the gravelly soils of the Piave River, which give rise to fresh and dynamic wines, while the other benefits from the clayey slopes of Montello, the basis for their more ambitious selections. The grapes for the San Carlo '21, a Bordeaux blend, come from the vineyards on Montello. Ripe, juicy red fruit meets intense herbal notes that add freshness and lightness. The palate is marked by harmony, with a sapid dynamic perfectly supported by acidity. The broad range of Proseccos includes the standout Asolo Pietra Fine '22, a dry spumante that's nicely sustained in its progression of flavor.

Lessini Durello Dosaggio Zero M. Cl. Ris. '17	♀♀ 6
Lessini Durello Extra Brut M. Cl. Nostrum '19	♀♀ 5
Lessini Durello Dosaggio Zero M. Cl. Ris. '14	♀♀♀ 5
Lessini Durello Dosaggio Zero M. Cl. Ris. '15	♀♀ 5
Lessini Durello Dosaggio Zero Ris. '16	♀♀ 6
Lessini Durello Extra Brut M. Cl. Nostrum '17	♀♀ 5
Lessini Durello Extra Brut M. Cl. Nostrum '16	♀♀ 5
Lessini Durello Extra Brut M. Cl. Nostrum '15	♀♀ 5
Lessini Durello Pietralava '14	♀♀ 2*

● Montello Asolo Rosso San Carlo '21	♀♀ 6
○ Asolo Brut	♀♀ 3
○ Asolo Extra Brut Pietra Fine '22	♀♀ 4
○ Manzoni Bianco Costa degli Angeli '23	♀♀ 3
● Montello Asolo Recantina Majo Rosso '22	♀♀ 4
● Rosso del Milio '22	♀♀ 4
○ Asolo Prosecco Sui Lieviti Brut Nature Col Fondo '23	♀ 3
● Campo dei Morer '23	♀ 3
○ Prosecco di Treviso Extra Dry Campo dei Sass	♀ 3
● Montello Asolo Rosso San Carlo '19	♀♀ 5
● Montello Colli Asolani Rosso San Carlo '20	♀♀ 5
● Montello e Colli Asolani Rosso San Carlo '17	♀♀ 5

Michele Castellani

fraz. Valgatara
via Granda, 1
37020 Marano di Valpolicella [VR]
☎ +39 0457701253
🌐 www.castellanimichele.it

CELLAR SALES
PRE-BOOKED VISITS
ANNUAL PRODUCTION 300,000 bottles
HECTARES UNDER VINE 50.00

The Castellani family's winery is located in Valgatara, the broadest part of the Marano valley floor, surrounded by vineyards that gradually climb the valley slopes in search of freshness. The estate covers many hectares in Valpolicella classica, including the parcels of I Castei, Ca' del Pipa, Monte Fasenara, and Costamaran, which provide the grapes for a range closely tied to local traditions. The Recioto '22 remains one of the most interesting sweet wines of the appellation. It pours an intense ruby color, the prelude to a deep, complex aromatic profile. Sweet stewed fruit is echoed by vegetal and balsamic notes, with a subtle, sanguine nuance in the background. On the palate, its sweetness is measured, resulting in a solid, well-structured wine. The 2020 Amarones, however, are less convincing, relying on mature fruit tones that come off as evolved on the palate.

Wine	Rating
● Recioto della Valpolicella Cl. I Castei '22	♟♟ 6
● Amarone della Valpolicella Cl. Campo Casalin I Castei '20	♟ 6
● Amarone della Valpolicella Cl. Cinquestelle Collezione Ca' del Pipa '20	♟ 7
● Valpolicella Cl. Sup. Ripasso I Castei '21	♟ 4
● Recioto della Valpolicella Cl. Le Vigne Ca' del Pipa '99	♟♟♟ 6
● Amarone della Valpolicella Cl. Campo Casalin I Castei '19	♟♟ 6
● Recioto della Valpolicella Cl. I Castei '21	♟♟ 5
● Recioto della Valpolicella Cl. I Castei '19	♟♟ 5
● Recioto della Valpolicella Cl. Monte Fasenara I Castei '19	♟♟ 5
● Valpolicella Cl. I Castei '22	♟♟ 2*

★Cavalchina

loc. Cavalchina
fraz. Custoza
via Sommacampagna, 7
37066 Sommacampagna [VR]
☎ +39 045516002
🌐 www.tenutedifamiglia.com

CELLAR SALES
PRE-BOOKED VISITS
ANNUAL PRODUCTION 385,000 bottles
HECTARES UNDER VINE 40.00
SUSTAINABLE WINERY

What started as a passion, almost a hobby, by the Piona family in the post-war era, has now become a full-fledged winery that extends into the major territories around Lake Garda. Today Cavalchina is led by Franco Piona and his grandchildren Francesco and Giulia, who together cultivate an area that stretches from the morainic hills of the Prendina estate to those of Custoza, from the clayey vineyards near Lake Frassino in Lugana to the calcareous soils of Torre d'Orti. Each wine in their extensive range has its place, perfectly showcasing the various terroirs and grape varieties cultivated. This is true for the Amedeo '22, a Custoza that highlights the aromatic breadth and dynamic, sapid quality of the vineyards surrounding the winery, as well as the Brolo Camozzini '17, an Amarone that draws its exuberant character from the acidity of Marcellise. We finish with an excellent Chiaretto di Bardolino '23, a wine whose aromatic freshness and pronounced sapidity derive from corvina cultivated on the hills of Garda.

Wine	Rating
○ Custoza Sup. Amedeo '22	♟♟♟ 3
⊙ Chiaretto di Bardolino '23	♟♟ 2
● Amarone della Valpolicella Brolo Camozzini Torre d'Orti Ris. '17	♟♟ 8
● Amarone della Valpolicella Torre d'Orti '20	♟♟ 6
● Bardolino '23	♟♟ 2
● Bardolino Sup. Santa Lucia '22	♟♟ 3
○ Custoza '23	♟♟ 2
● Garda Merlot Faial Prendina '21	♟♟ 6
○ Garda Riesling Paroni Prendina '23	♟♟ 2
● Valpolicella Sup. Ripasso Torre d'Orti '22	♟♟ 4
● Bardolino Casella '21	♟ 5
○ Lugana 'L Lac '23	♟ 3
○ Custoza Sup. Amedeo '21	♟♟♟ 3
○ Custoza Sup. Amedeo '20	♟♟♟ 3
○ Custoza Sup. Amedeo '19	♟♟♟ 3

Cavazza

c.da Selva, 22
36054 Montebello Vicentino [VI]
📞 +39 0444649166
🌐 www.cavazzawine.com

CELLAR SALES
PRE-BOOKED VISITS
ANNUAL PRODUCTION 620,000 bottles
HECTARES UNDER VINE 135.00
SUSTAINABLE WINERY

Founded during the interwar period, the Cavazza family's winery expanded in the late 1980s from the volcanic hills of Gambellara to the nearby slopes of Berici, creating a viticultural estate with specific goals. The first territory is almost exclusively dedicated to garganega, while the second is reserved for Bordeaux varieties. Today, the winery is managed by the fourth generation: Elisa, Andrea, Mattia, and Stefano, who oversee all production phases. Cavazza's wines delivered a flawless performance, not only winning over our tasters but also proving to be perfect expressions of their respective terroirs. The Cabernet Cicogna '20 captures the sunny character of Berici, with aromas of ripe plum and spices accompanied by a balsamic note that brings freshness. The palate is juicy, supple, and satisfying. From the Gambellara territory comes an excellent Bocara '23, a glass of great freshness that combines approachability with solidity.

Giorgio Cecchetto

fraz. Tezze di Piave
via Piave, 67
31028 Vazzola [TV]
📞 +39 043828598
🌐 www.rabosopiave.com

CELLAR SALES
PRE-BOOKED VISITS
ANNUAL PRODUCTION 250,000 bottles
HECTARES UNDER VINE 103.00
SUSTAINABLE WINERY

A year after Giorgio Cecchetto's untimely passing, Cristina, along with her children Marco, Sara, and Alberto, has taken the helm of the family winery, continuing the journey started in the latter part of the 20th century. The extensive estate, structured across the vineyards of Tezze di Piave, Cornuda, and Motta di Livenza, provides a vast quantity of grapes, but only the best plots contribute to the winery's range. The Sante Rosso '21 is a monovarietal merlot made from grapes harvested in a state of over-ripeness in the Largoni vineyard in Motta di Licenza. The result is aromas of sweet, fleshy red fruit refreshed by delicate notes of oak and herbal hints. The palate is full and juicy, supported by sweet, polished tannins. The Malanotte Gelsaia '20, rich, full, and powerful, contrasts sensations of dried fruit with a long, energetic palate. The Manzoni Bianco '23 also caught our attention. A gratifying drink.

● Colli Berici Cabernet Cicogna '20	🍷🍷 6
● Colli Berici Merlot Cicogna '20	🍷🍷 6
● Colli Berici Tai Rosso '23	🍷🍷 3
● Colli Berici Tai Rosso Corallo '21	🍷🍷 5
● Fornetto '22	🍷🍷 4
○ Gambellara Cl. Bocara '23	🍷🍷 3
○ Recioto di Gambellara Cl. Capitel '20	🍷🍷 5
● Syrha Cicogna '20	🍷🍷 4
● Colli Berici Cabernet Cicogna '19	🍷🍷 5
● Colli Berici Cabernet Cicogna '18	🍷🍷 5
● Colli Berici Merlot Cicogna '19	🍷🍷 5
● Colli Berici Merlot Cicogna '18	🍷🍷 5
● Colli Berici Tai Rosso Corallo '20	🍷🍷 4
○ Gambellara Cl. Bocara '22	🍷🍷 3
○ Gambellara Cl. Creari '20	🍷🍷 3
○ Gambellara Creari '19	🍷🍷 3

○ Manzoni Bianco '23	🍷🍷 3
● Piave Malanotte Gelsaia '20	🍷🍷 6
● Piave Raboso '21	🍷🍷 4
● Sante Rosso '21	🍷🍷 5
● Carménère '23	🍷 2
● Gelsaia '17	🍷🍷 6
● Piave Raboso '20	🍷🍷 4
● Piave Raboso '18	🍷🍷 3
● Piave Raboso '17	🍷🍷 3
● Raboso Passito RP	🍷🍷 4
● Raboso Passito RP	🍷🍷 5
● RP Passito di Raboso	🍷🍷 4
● Sante '19	🍷🍷 4
● Sante Rosso '20	🍷🍷 5
● Sante Rosso '18	🍷🍷 4

Gerardo Cesari

loc. Sorsei, 3
37010 Cavaion Veronese [VR]
(☎) +39 0456260928
⊕ www.cesariverona.it

CELLAR SALES
PRE-BOOKED VISITS
ANNUAL PRODUCTION 1,500,000 bottles
HECTARES UNDER VINE 120.00
SUSTAINABLE WINERY

One of Verona's prominent wineries, Gerardo Cesari joined the Caviro group several years ago. In recent years, in particular, there has been a noticeable shift in quality, most evident in their Valpolicellas. The winery operates in 3 main zones: about 10 hectares in Sant'Ambrogio, another 10 in Corrubbio di Negarine, and 5 in Castelrotto. The Amarone della Valpolicella '19 impresses with its aromas of mint, dark chocolate, sour cherries, and tobacco. The palate is dense, characterized by a balsamic touch, finishing particularly fresh. The Valpolicella '22 offers a crisp, joyful fruitiness, making it highly drinkable and ideal for its category. The Valpolicella Superiore Bosan '21 is more close-knit, with a nose marked by hints of underbrush and spices. Lastly, the Lugana '23 stands out among the reds with its exceptional appeal as a white. The other wines tasted are also well crafted.

Italo Cescon

fraz. Roncadelle
p.zza dei Caduti, 3
31024 Ormelle [TV]
(☎) +39 0422851033
⊕ www.cesconitalo.it

CELLAR SALES
PRE-BOOKED VISITS
ANNUAL PRODUCTION 950,000 bottles
HECTARES UNDER VINE 124.00
VITICULTURE METHOD Certified Organic
SUSTAINABLE WINERY

The vast growing area northeast of Treviso has seen a surge in glera over the past decade. However, the Cescon siblings—Gloria, Graziella, and Domenico—have resisted the allure of Prosecco, and continue to be the area's most important winery. They believe that a wine's greatness is achieved only by respecting the environment and valuing the bond between vineyard and varietal. Year after year, Madre continues to establish itself as one of Italy's great white wines. This monovarietal Manzoni Bianco from the 2022 vintage upholds its class with distinction. Sourced from the vineyards of Fagarè and San Polo di Piave, it matures first in oak and then in the bottle, making for aromas of citrus, exotic fruits, and spices over a smoky, mineral backdrop. The palate is energetic and rich, marked by superb tension. The Biancogrigio '22, on the other hand, explores a new concept of pinot grigio, starting with a sulfury note and opening into exotic nuances before giving way to a long, juicy finish.

● Amarone della Valpolicella Cl. '19	♟♟ 6
● Valpolicella Cl. '22	♟♟ 3*
○ Lugana Cento Filari '23	♟♟ 2*
● Valpolicella Cl. Sup. Bosan '21	♟♟ 5
● Valpolicella Sup. Ripasso '21	♟♟ 4
● Amarone della Valpolicella Cl. '17	♟♟ 6
● Amarone della Valpolicella Cl. Bosan Ris. '13	♟♟ 8
● Amarone della Valpolicella Cl. Il Bosco '17	♟♟ 7
● Amarone della Valpolicella Cl. Il Bosco '16	♟♟ 7
● Jèma '16	♟♟ 5
○ Lugana Cento Filari '22	♟♟ 2*
○ Lugana Cento Filari '21	♟♟ 2*
● Valpolicella Cl. Sup. Ràjo '20	♟♟ 3
● Valpolicella Cl. Sup. Ràjo '19	♟♟ 3
● Valpolicella Sup. Ripasso Mara '20	♟♟ 3

○ Madre '22	♟♟♟ 6
○ Delle Venezie Pinot Grigio Biancogrigio Integro Tesirare '22	♟♟ 5
○ Delle Venezie Pinot Grigio Grigioramato Macerato Tesirare '21	♟♟ 5
○ Delle Venezie Pinot Grigio Tralcetto '23	♟♟ 3
● Merlot Rompicapo Tulipe Tesirare '22	♟♟ 5
● Pinot Nero '23	♟♟ 3
○ Madre '21	♟♟♟ 6
○ Madre '20	♟♟♟ 6
○ Madre '19	♟♟♟ 5
○ Madre '18	♟♟♟ 5
○ Madre '17	♟♟♟ 5
○ Madre '16	♟♟♟ 5
○ Madre '14	♟♟♟ 4*
○ Pinot Grigio delle Venezie Biancogrigio Integro Tesirare '21	♟♟ 4

Coffele

via Roma, 5
37038 Soave [VR]
(☎) +39 0457680007
⊛ www.coffele.it

CELLAR SALES
PRE-BOOKED VISITS
ANNUAL PRODUCTION 120,000 bottles
HECTARES UNDER VINE 25.00
VITICULTURE METHOD Certified Organic
SUSTAINABLE WINERY

With just over half a century of history behind it and one of the most important wineries in the Soave area, Coffele spans two dozen hectares in Castelcerino, a small village perched on calcareous rocks with basaltic insertions. Here, Alberto and his sister Chiara focus on producing the region's most important white wine, emphasizing its finer, more elegant side. The grapes for the estate's most intriguing Soave, the Ca' Visco '23, come from vineyards surrounding the historic 18th-century farmhouse. Garganega cultivated in limestone soils and trebbiano di Soave from basaltic terrain creates a marriage of aromatic finesse and vibrant tension, resulting in a wine of superb pleasure and dynamism. The Alzari '22, a monovarietal garganega aged in large casks, reveals a riper and more seductive aromatic profile. On the palate, it impresses with its delicate texture, finishing with a lovely almond note. The Recioto Le Sponde '22 proves exuberant and juicy, weighty.

Conte Collalto

via XXIV Maggio, 1
31058 Susegana [TV]
(☎) +39 0438435811
⊛ www.cantine-collalto.it

CELLAR SALES
PRE-BOOKED VISITS
ACCOMMODATION
ANNUAL PRODUCTION 650,000 bottles
HECTARES UNDER VINE 146.00

Beyond the left bank of the Piave River, the Treviso plains begin to ripple, forming the complex hill system that is the realm of glera. The Conti Collalto winery, based in Susegana for over a century, is one of Prosecco Superiore's most important producers, boasting many hectares of vineyards on the eastern side of the appellation, where both native and international varieties grow alongside glera. However, the Susegana winery most impresses when it comes to glera, with a sumptuous version of the Ponte Rosso '23, a Prosecco Superiore named after the brick bridge near the vineyard. The nose offers crisp, clear white fruit, accented by delicate floral hints and vanilla bean. The palate is dry, defined by the characteristic firmness of the area's wines, all perfectly complemented by bubbles and acidity. The Isabella '23 is finer, dominated by white fruit, and finishing on a dry almond note.

○ Soave Cl. Ca' Visco '23	♟♟ 3*
○ Recioto di Soave Cl. Le Sponde '22	♟♟ 5
○ Soave Cl. Alzari '22	♟♟ 3
○ Soave Cl. Castel Cerino '23	♟♟ 3
○ Recioto di Soave Cl. Le Sponde '09	♟♟♟ 5
○ Soave Cl. Ca' Visco '14	♟♟♟ 3*
○ Soave Cl. Ca' Visco '05	♟♟♟ 3*
○ Soave Cl. Ca' Visco '04	♟♟♟ 2
○ Soave Cl. Ca' Visco '03	♟♟♟ 2
○ Recioto di Soave Cl. Le Sponde '21	♟♟ 5
○ Recioto di Soave Cl. Le Sponde '20	♟♟ 5
○ Soave Cl. Alzari '21	♟♟ 3
○ Soave Cl. Ca' Visco '22	♟♟ 3*
○ Soave Cl. Ca' Visco '21	♟♟ 3*
○ Soave Cl. Castel Cerino '22	♟♟ 3
○ Soave Cl. Castel Cerino '21	♟♟ 3

○ Conegliano Valdobbiadene Extra Brut Ponte Rosso '23	♟♟ 3*
○ Conegliano Valdobbiadene Brut San Salvatore '23	♟♟ 3
○ Conegliano Valdobbiadene Rive di Collalto Brut Isabella '23	♟♟ 4
○ Pinot Grigio delle Venezie '23	♟♟ 2*
● Wildbacher '20	♟♟ 3
○ Conegliano Valdobbiadene Extra Dry Gaio '23	♟ 3
● Incrocio Manzoni Rosso 2.15 '21	♟ 3
○ Rosabianco '22	♟ 2
◉ Violette Extra Dry	♟ 3
○ Conegliano Valdobbiadene Rive di Collalto Brut Isabella '21	♟♟ 4
● Piave Cabernet Torrai Ris. '18	♟♟ 5

La Collina dei Ciliegi

fraz. Romagnano
loc. Erbin, 36
37023 Grezzana [VR]
☏ +39 0459814900
✉ www.lacollinadeiciliegi.it

CELLAR SALES
PRE-BOOKED VISITS
ACCOMMODATION AND RESTAURANT SERVICE
ANNUAL PRODUCTION 100,000 bottles
HECTARES UNDER VINE 30.00

Even with fewer than 20 harvests under its belt, Collina dei Ciliegi is already standing out for its adherence to the territory and the character of its grapes. The many hectares of hillside vineyards benefit from the fresh breezes descending from Lessinia, conferring finesse and aromatic freshness to the grapes. In the cellar, production is divided between appellation wines and those interpreted more freely. The Prea makes an impressive debut. It's an original blend of garganega, pinot bianco, and chardonnay sourced from the vineyard of the same name at around 600 meters elevation. First produced in the 2021 vintage, the wine matures in concrete and ceramic Clayver tanks. The result is intense white fruit impressions intertwined with flinty nuances, while on the palate, acidity takes the lead in a brisk, lengthy progression of flavor. The Valpolicella Peratara '20, which follows a similar stylistic approach, with grapes grown at over 500 meters above sea level, stands out for its elegant aromas and a palate marked by vibrant tension.

Le Colture

loc. Santo Stefano
via Follo, 5
31049 Valdobbiadene [TV]
☏ +39 0423900192
✉ www.lecolture.com

CELLAR SALES
PRE-BOOKED VISITS
ACCOMMODATION
ANNUAL PRODUCTION 750,000 bottles
HECTARES UNDER VINE 40.00

Silvia, Alberto, and Veronica Ruggeri have taken the reins of the family winery. Founded by their father, Cesare, in the mid-1980s, the winery is based in Santo Stefano, in the heart of the UNESCO heritage hills. 16 different parcels are cultivated, from the steep hills of Valdobbiadene to the gentler slopes of Conegliano and finally Montello, where the winery has also established a charming B&B. The most ambitious wine from the estate, the Gerardo '23, is an Extra Brut made from the best-exposed vineyards in the Santa Stefano area, at the heart of Prosecco di Valdobbiadene. This sparkling wine delivers fruit with great delicacy, framed by floral notes that gradually give way to hints of dried fruit. The palate is dry, perfectly balanced by a backbone of acidity and creamy bubbles. The Fagher, a Brut, is also very good, following its subtle aromas with a palate of great sapidity and harmony.

○ Prea '21	♥♥ 7
● Valpolicella Sup. Peratara '20	♥♥ 7
● Amarone della Valpolicella Ciliegio '19	♥♥ 8
● Amarone della Valpolicella '19	♀♀ 7
● Amarone della Valpolicella '17	♀♀ 7
● Amarone della Valpolicella Ciliegio '18	♀♀ 8
● Amarone della Valpolicella Ciliegio '15	♀♀ 8
● Amarone della Valpolicella Ciliegio Armando Gianolli Ris. '15	♀♀ 8
● Valpolicella Sup. Peratara '19	♀♀ 7
● Valpolicella Sup. Ripasso Macion '17	♀♀ 5

○ Valdobbiadene Rive di Santo Stefano Extra Brut Gerardo '23	♥♥ 3*
○ Cartizze	♥♥ 5
○ Valdobbiadene Brut Fagher	♥♥ 3
○ Valdobbiadene Dry Cruner	♥♥ 3
○ Valdobbiadene Extra Dry Pianer	♥ 3
○ Valdobbiadene Brut Rive di Santo Stefano Gerardo '16	♀♀ 3
○ Valdobbiadene Rive di Santo Stefano Brut Gerardo '20	♀♀ 3*
○ Valdobbiadene Rive di Santo Stefano Brut Gerardo '19	♀♀ 3*
○ Valdobbiadene Rive di Santo Stefano Brut Gerardo '18	♀♀ 3*
○ Valdobbiadene Rive di Santo Stefano Extra Brut Gerardo '21	♀♀ 3*

Corte Gardoni
loc. Gardoni, 5
37067 Valeggio sul Mincio [VR]
☏ +39 0456370270
⊛ www.cortegardoni.it

Corte Moschina
via Moschina, 1
37030 Roncà [VR]
☏ +39 0457460788
⊛ www.cortemoschina.it

CELLAR SALES
PRE-BOOKED VISITS
ANNUAL PRODUCTION 180,000 bottles
HECTARES UNDER VINE 25.00

CELLAR SALES
PRE-BOOKED VISITS
ANNUAL PRODUCTION 140,000 bottles
HECTARES UNDER VINE 35.00
SUSTAINABLE WINERY

The expansive Bardolino area stretches from the cooler lands near Garda and the Adige valley to the morainic hills that surround the southern shore of the lake. For over four decades, the Piccoli family has operated here, establishing a beautiful family-run winery. At Corte Gardoni, the grapes reflect the climatic conditions of each harvest, producing soft and enveloping wines in warmer years and vibrant, spirited wines in cooler vintages. The Bardolino Pradicà '22 leveraged the warm vintage to deliver an aromatic profile dominated by ripe cherry, complemented by fresher, vegetal notes, before giving way to its characteristic spiciness. The palate is dry, extending gracefully, defined by pleasantly rough tannins. Le Fontane '23 leans more heavily on fruity richness, offering an approachable glass where red fruit melds with earthy and underbrush notes. On the palate, it's medium-bodied and closes on an intriguing hint of incense.

The eastern extremity of the Soave appellation, represented by the slopes of the Duello, Crocetta, and Calvarina mountains, represents a new frontier. Here, the grapes mature while maintaining a pronounced acidic tension, allowing careful producers to craft wines that combine immediate expressiveness and character. Patrizia Niero, along with her sons Giacomo and Alessandro, is among the most skilled interpreters of the territory. Durella and garganega vie for the best exposures in Corte Moschina, with our preference leaning toward the latter, which results in an excellent territorial expression in the Soave I Tarai '22. While the nose is characterized by exotic notes enhanced by floral nuances and a delicate touch of oak, it's on the palate where the wine shifts gears, revealing fullness and the characteristic tension of wines from this region. Among the Durello wines, the Extra Brut '18 stands out for its aromatic complexity, with a palate that highlights the spirited nature of the grape.

● Bardolino Le Fontane '23	♛♛ 3
● Bardolino Sup. Pràdicà '22	♛♛ 3
○ Custoza Mael '21	♛♛ 3
○ Chiaretto di Bardolino Nichesole '23	♛ 2
○ Custoza Greoto '23	♛ 2
● Bardolino Sup. Pràdicà '18	♛♛♛ 3*
● Bardolino Sup. Pràdicà '16	♛♛♛ 3*
○ Bianco di Custoza Mael '09	♛♛♛ 2*
○ Bianco di Custoza Mael '08	♛♛♛ 2*
○ Custoza Mael '13	♛♛♛ 3*
○ Custoza Mael '11	♛♛♛ 3*
● Bardolino Le Fontane '22	♛♛ 3
● Bardolino Le Fontane '21	♛♛ 2*
● Bardolino Sup. Pràdicà '21	♛♛ 3
● Bardolino Sup. Pràdicà '20	♛♛ 3*
● Bardolino Sup. Pràdicà '19	♛♛ 3*

○ Soave Sup. Roncà Monte Calvarina I Tarai '22	♛♛ 5
○ Lessini Durello Dosaggio Zero Ris. '17	♛♛ 6
○ Lessini Durello Extra Brut Ris. '18	♛♛ 5
○ Soave Roncà Monte Calvarina Roncathe '23	♛♛ 3
○ Purocaso Sui Lieviti Frizzante	♛ 4
○ Soave Roncà Monte Calvarina Evaos '22	♛ 4
● Colli Berici Carmenere Calcareo '19	♛♛ 5
○ Lessini Durello Dosaggio Zero Ris. '16	♛♛ 6
○ Soave Roncà Monte Calvarina Evaos '21	♛♛ 4
○ Soave Roncà Monte Calvarina Evaos '20	♛♛ 4
○ Soave Roncà Monte Calvarina Roncathe '22	♛♛ 3
○ Soave Superiore. Roncà Monte Calvarina I Tarai '21	♛♛ 5

Corte Rugolin

fraz. Valgatara
loc. Rugolin, 1
37020 Marano di Valpolicella [VR]
📞 +39 0457702153
🌐 www.corterugolin.it

CELLAR SALES
PRE-BOOKED VISITS
ANNUAL PRODUCTION 80,000 bottles
HECTARES UNDER VINE 13.00

It would have been easy to lose sight of tradition in pursuit of commercial success in a region whose fame came quite suddenly in the mid-1990s. However, Elena Coati and her brother Federico managed to navigate the period while developing their family winery, emphasizing the bond with the land and its traditions. They restored their historic vineyards and focused production solely on designated appellation wines. Patience is required with the Amarone Monte Danieli, a wine that demands a full 8 years before its dark cherry and spice notes, alongside underbrush and damp earth, can be fully appreciated. The 2016 vintage brought with it a dynamic flavor profile, rich in sapidity and defined by a spirited tannic structure. The Valpolicella San Giorgio '20 is also intriguing, exploring a new facet of the style by emphasizing fruity freshness and delivering a palate that prioritizes precision and length over sheer power.

● Valpolicella Cl. Sup. San Giorgio '20	♟♟♟ 5
● Amarone della Valpolicella Monte Danieli Ris. '16	♟♟ 8
● Amarone della Valpolicella Cl. Crosara de le Strie '17	♟♟ 7
● Valpolicella Cl. Rugolin '23	♟♟ 3
● Valpolicella Cl. Sup. Ripasso '21	♟♟ 5
● Amarone della Valpolicella Monte Danieli Ris. '13	♟♟♟ 8
● Amarone della Valpolicella Cl. Crosara de le Strie '16	♟♟ 7
● Amarone della Valpolicella Cl. Crosara de le Strie '15	♟♟ 7
● Valpolicella Cl. Sup. Ripasso '20	♟♟ 5
● Valpolicella Cl. Sup. San Giorgio '19	♟♟ 5
● Valpolicella Cl. Sup. San Giorgio '16	♟♟ 5

Corte Scaletta

fraz. Marcellise
via Cao di Sopra, 19
37036 San Martino Buon Albergo [VR]
📞 +39 0458740269
🌐 www.cortescaletta.it

CELLAR SALES
PRE-BOOKED VISITS
ANNUAL PRODUCTION 25,000 bottles
HECTARES UNDER VINE 12.00
SUSTAINABLE WINERY

The Cavedini family's winery lies in the northeastern part of Verona, with around 12 hectares cultivated with the utmost respect for the environment. The uniformity of the vineyards is occasionally interrupted by small patches of woodland and olive groves. The vineyard area is almost exclusively dedicated to Valpolicella's historic varietals, except for a small parcel reserved for cabernet sauvignon, which is vinified separately and not included among their appellation wines. These wines exhibit a style that doesn't overreach in richness, as demonstrated by the Amarone '16. Its intense ruby hue is the prelude to an aromatic bouquet dominated by red fruit, which is given a fresher lift by spicy and balsamic notes. In the mouth, fullness is well-managed by a vital acidic drive that lengthens the wine and and refines the palate. The Valpolicella Superiore '17, with its mature nose, showcases sweet fruit interwoven with herbal and mineral notes, all of which reappear on a dry, taut palate.

● Amarone della Valpolicella Ris. '16	♟♟ 7
● Valpolicella Sup. '17	♟♟ 4
● Valpolicella '21	♟ 3
● Valpolicella Sup. Ripasso '20	♟ 5
● Valpolicella Sup. Ripasso '19	♟♟ 5
● Amarone della Valpolicella '16	♟♟ 7
● Amarone della Valpolicella '15	♟♟ 7
● Valpolicella '20	♟♟ 3
● Valpolicella '18	♟♟ 3
● Valpolicella Sup. '16	♟♟ 5
● Valpolicella Sup. '15	♟♟ 5
● Valpolicella Sup. '14	♟♟ 5
● Valpolicella Sup. Ripasso '18	♟♟ 5
● Valpolicella Sup. Ripasso '15	♟♟ 5

VENETO

Costa Arente

loc. Costa, 86
37023 Grezzana [VR]
📞 +39 0422864511
🌐 www.costarente.it

CELLAR SALES
PRE-BOOKED VISITS
ANNUAL PRODUCTION 110,000 bottles
HECTARES UNDER VINE 17.00
SUSTAINABLE WINERY

The winery managed by the Generali group is
set in a charming location in the heart of
Valpantena. The beautiful cellar and hospitality
structure lie on a small plateau at 250 meters
elevation, surrounded on three sides by
vineyards and protected by the Lessinia hills.
Here, the grapes mature slowly, caressed by
mountain breezes that ensure healthy conditions,
allowing for the development of an elegant
aromatic profile. The Amarone Valpantena '19
delivers an impressive showing, opening with
characteristic dried fruit notes, where cherry
seeks freshness in herbal nuances and gains
personality in earthy and spicy tones. On the
palate, the wine shifts gears, moving away from
classicism to embrace a more energetic and vital
profile, where savoriness, texture, and a firm
tannic structure take center stage. We
appreciated the traditionally-styled Ripasso '20
for its aromatic breadth and a delicate palate.

Dal Cero
Tenuta Corte Giacobbe

via Moschina, 11
37030 Roncà [VR]
📞 +39 0457460110
🌐 www.dalcerofamily.it

CELLAR SALES
PRE-BOOKED VISITS
ANNUAL PRODUCTION 300,000 bottles
HECTARES UNDER VINE 40.00

Based in the eastern hills of the Soave
appellation, the Dal Cero family's Tenuta Corte
Giacobbe is among those leading the area's new
wave. Here on the slopes of the ancient
Calvarina and Crocetta volcanoes, they cultivate
grapes that maintain a pronounced acidity, which
endows their whites with an unmistakable
character. It's hard to pick Dal Cero's standout
wine this year, with two true champions
presented: the Soave Runcata '22 and the
Durello Augusto '18. The former captivates with
its clear aromas of white fruit intertwined with
mineral and oak notes, sensations that grow
even more expressive on a dynamic, long-lasting
palate. The latter, a sparkling wine, boasts a
complex aromatic profile where fruit whiffs
merge with the varietal's characteristic mineral
notes, making for a full, energetic palate with
lovely progression.

● Amarone della Valpolicella Valpantena '19	🍷🍷 8
○ Molinara Brut Rosé	🍷🍷 3
● Valpolicella Sup. Valpantena Ripasso '20	🍷🍷 6
● Amarone della Valpolicella Ris. '17	🍷🍷 8
● Amarone della Valpolicella Ris. '16	🍷🍷 7
● Amarone della Valpolicella Valpantena '18	🍷🍷 8
● Amarone della Valpolicella Valpantena '17	🍷🍷 8
● Amarone della Valpolicella Valpantena '16	🍷🍷 8
● Valpolicella Ripasso Sup. Valpantena '19	🍷🍷 5
● Valpolicella Valpantena Sup. Ripasso '18	🍷🍷 4

○ Soave Sup. Roncà Monte Calvarina Runcata '22	🍷🍷🍷 5
○ Lessini Durello Brut Cuvée Augusto Ris. '18	🍷🍷 6
○ Lessini Durello Brut Cuvée Augusto 10-10 Ris. '21	🍷🍷 6
● Monti Lessini Pinot Nero Niconero '20	🍷🍷 6
○ Soave Roncà Monte Calvarina '23	🍷🍷 3
● Valpolicella '22	🍷🍷 3
● Valpolicella Sup. Ripasso '21	🍷🍷 5
○ Lessini Durello Extra Brut M. Cl. Cuvée Augusto Ris. '16	🍷🍷🍷 5
○ Lessini Durello Extra Brut M. Cl. Cuvée Augusto Ris. '14	🍷🍷🍷 5
○ Soave Sup. Roncà Monte Calvarina Runcata '21	🍷🍷🍷 5
○ Soave Sup. Runcata '18	🍷🍷🍷 5
○ Soave Sup. Runcata '17	🍷🍷🍷 3*

Dal Maso

c.da Selva, 62
36054 Montebello Vicentino [VI]
☎ +39 0444649104
✆ www.dalmasovini.com

CELLAR SALES
PRE-BOOKED VISITS
ACCOMMODATION
ANNUAL PRODUCTION 300,000 bottles
HECTARES UNDER VINE 30.00
SUSTAINABLE WINERY

Founded in the volcanic territory of the
Gambellara hills in the early 20th century, the
Dal Maso brothers' winery has expanded its
reach to the Berico area, creating an estate
where each grape variety finds its ideal location.
The white durella and garganega grapes thrive in
the basalt soils of Lessinia, while tai rosso and
Bordeaux varieties are cultivated in the red clays
of the Berici hills. Dal Maso's range shows no
weaknesses this year, with several convincing
wines presented. We have a preference for the
Merlot 25° Anniversario and the Cabernet
Casara Roveri '21, while the Durello Serafino
takes us back to the 2017 vintage. The Merlot is
rich with fruity and spicy suggestions, enhancing
a full-bodied and powerful palate, perfectly
supported by clearly discernible, polished
tannins. The Cabernet follows a similar aromatic
path but reveals more pluck and firmness on the
palate. We conclude with a sparkling wine of
great aromatic finesse—one characterized by a
slender and long profile.

● Colli Berici Cabernet Casara Roveri '21	♀♀ 6
● Colli Berici Merlot 25° Anniversario '21	♀♀ 8
○ Lessini Durello Pas Dosé M. Cl. Cuvée Serafino Ris. '17	♀♀ 7
● Cabernet Montebelvedere '22	♀♀ 3
● Colli Berici Merlot Casara Roveri '21	♀♀ 6
● Colli Berici Tai Rosso Colpizzarda '21	♀♀ 5
○ Gambellara Ca' Fischele '23	♀♀ 3
○ Gambellara Riva del Molino '22	♀♀ 4
○ Lessini Durello Pas Dosé M. Cl. Ris. '20	♀♀ 5
● Colli Berici Merlot Casara Roveri '15	♀♀♀ 5
● Colli Berici Merlot Casara Roveri 25° Anniversario '19	♀♀♀ 5
○ Gambellara Cl. Riva del Molino '07	♀♀♀ 2*
○ Lessini Durello Pas Dosé M. Cl. Cuvée Serafino Ris. '16	♀♀♀ 7

La Dama

fraz. San Vito
via Giovanni Quintarelli, 39
37024 Negrar [VR]
☎ +39 0456000728
✆ www.ladamavini.com

ANNUAL PRODUCTION 50,000 bottles
HECTARES UNDER VINE 10.00
VITICULTURE METHOD Certified Organic

Gabriele and Miriam Dalcanale's winery spans
about ten hectares divided into two distinct
areas. The older vineyards in the Negrar valley
rest on alluvial clay soils, while the Colombarino
vineyards in Sant'Ambrogio grow in clay-
limestone terrain. The climate also varies
significantly, with Colombarino benefiting from
an extraordinary amount of light and beneficial
day-night temperature swings. Some of the most
intriguing results hail from the vineyards
ascending the western slope of the Negrar
valley, like the Valpolicella Ca' Besi '21. A superb
vintage endowed the wine with aromas ranging
from ripe cherry to sudden bursts of
underbrush, rain-soaked earth, and cyclamen. On
the palate, the wine is full, yet retains a vital
suppleness that lengthens and sharpens its
profile. The Recioto '20 is equally enthralling,
with simple aromas of dried and sweet fruit
followed by a gustatory dynamic where
sweetness is balanced by sapidity.

● Valpolicella Cl. Sup. Ca' Besi '21	♀♀ 5
● Recioto della Valpolicella Cl. '20	♀♀ 6
● Valpolicella Cl. '23	♀♀ 3
● Valpolicella Cl. Sup. Ripasso '21	♀♀ 5
● Valpolicella Cl. Sup. Vign. Colombarino '20	♀♀ 5
● Amarone della Valpolicella Cl. '19	♀♀ 7
● Amarone della Valpolicella Cl. '18	♀♀ 7
● Amarone della Valpolicella Cl. '17	♀♀ 7
● Recioto della Valpolicella Cl. '19	♀♀ 6
● Valpolicella Cl. '22	♀♀ 3
● Valpolicella Cl. Sup. Ca' Besi '20	♀♀ 5
● Valpolicella Cl. Sup. Ca' Besi '18	♀♀ 5
● Valpolicella Cl. Sup. Ripasso '20	♀♀ 5
● Valpolicella Cl. Sup. Vign. Colombarino '19	♀♀ 5

De Stefani

via Cadorna, 92
30020 Fossalta di Piave [VE]
(☎) +39 042167502
⊕ www.de-stefani.it

CELLAR SALES
PRE-BOOKED VISITS
ANNUAL PRODUCTION 500,000 bottles
HECTARES UNDER VINE 80.00
SUSTAINABLE WINERY

With the arrival of Marco, who works alongside his father Alessandro, the De Stefani family has now seen five generations guide the family winery, one of the most important in the growing area that unfolds between the provinces of Venice and Treviso. Their extensive vineyard acreage stretches across the plains of Venice, rich in compacted silt and sand (known locally as "caranto"), and the Prosecco Superiore hills. The Olmèra '22 is a blend of tai (dried for about a month and matured in oak) and sauvignon (matured in concrete until blending). On the nose, it offers up vibrant fruity suggestions, with the exotic component invigorated by vegetal and almond nuances that bring freshness and unpredictability. On the palate, tai's fullness finds the right support in sauvignon's tension and dynamism, resulting in an energetic and juicy drink. Among the reds, we appreciated the harmony that the Kreda '21, taut, well-textured, delivers.

○ Olmèra '22	♈♈ 6
○ Chardonnay Vitàlys '23	♈♈ 3
● Colli di Conegliano Rosso Refrontolo Stèfen 1624 '21	♈♈ 8
● Piave Malanotte '19	♈♈ 8
● Solèr '21	♈♈ 5
○ Valdobbiadene Sup. Rive di Refrontolo Extra Brut '23	♈♈ 4
● Venezia Cabernet Sauvignon Ris. '21	♈♈ 3
● Venezia Refosco P.R. Kreda Ris. '21	♈♈ 5
○ Venezia Pinot Grigio '23	♈ 3
○ Venezia Sauvignon Vènis '23	♈ 4
● Colli di Conegliano Refrontolo Stèfen 1624 '18	♈♈ 8
○ Valdobbiadene Sup. Rive di Refrontolo Extra Brut '22	♈♈ 4

Drusian

fraz. Bigolino
via Anche, 1
31049 Valdobbiadene [TV]
(☎) +39 0423982151
⊕ www.drusian.it

CELLAR SALES
PRE-BOOKED VISITS
ANNUAL PRODUCTION 1,500,000 bottles
HECTARES UNDER VINE 80.00

Few wineries in the Conegliano Valdobbiadene area can boast an estate as vast as that managed by Francesco Drusian. His vineyards extend from Bigolino to Colfosco, from Collalto to Santo Stefano, where the grapes develop aromatic and gustatory nuances that are then brought out during the winemaking process. Glera is the undisputed star of a range that combines immediate expressiveness and character. Their higher-volume wines from Drusian, a Brut and an Extra Dry sourced from vineyards scattered throughout the appellation, truly impressed this year. The Extra Dry offers up fresh fruit and floral aromas, with a subtle exotic vein pushing from the background. It's even more pronounced on the palate, where the wine reveals a fine harmony, achieving a balance of sweetness, acidity, and bubbles. The Brut, on the other hand, moves with more tension and clout. The Rive di Santo Stefano expresses superb richness of ripe yellow fruit, sensations echoed by a smooth mouthfeel that caresses the palate.

○ Valdobbiadene Brùt	♈♈ 3
○ Valdobbiadene Extra Brut 30 Raccolti	♈♈ 3
○ Valdobbiadene Extra Dry	♈♈ 3
○ Valdobbiadene Rive di Santo Stefano Extra Dry '23	♈♈ 3
○ Cartizze	♈ 4
○ Valdobbiadene Brut Nature Sui Lieviti '22	♈ 3
○ Valdobbiadene Rive di Bigolino Brut '23	♈ 3
○ Cartizze	♈♈ 4
○ Valdobbiadene 30 Raccolti Extra Brut	♈♈ 3
○ Valdobbiadene Brut Nature Sui Lieviti '21	♈♈ 3
○ Valdobbiadene Dry '20	♈♈ 3
○ Valdobbiadene Extra Brut 30 Raccolti '21	♈♈ 3
○ Valdobbiadene Extra Brut 30 Raccolti	♈♈ 3
○ Valdobbiadene Rive di Colfosco Brut '22	♈♈ 3
○ Valdobbiadene Rive di Collalto Brut '21	♈♈ 3

Conte Emo Capodilista La Montecchia

via Montecchia, 16
35030 Selvazzano Dentro [PD]
☏ +39 049637294
⊕ www.lamontecchia.it

CELLAR SALES
PRE-BOOKED VISITS
ACCOMMODATION
ANNUAL PRODUCTION 144,000 bottles
HECTARES UNDER VINE 30.00
SUSTAINABLE WINERY

The Euganean hills stretch north to south for just about 20 kilometers, but the climate can vary significantly across this small area. Indeed, Giordano Emo Capodilista's winery is divided into two different growing areas: the first in Selvazzano, at the northern end of the appellation, where merlot, carmenere, and white grape varieties dominate; the second in Baone, where cabernet sauvignon reigns supreme. Cuore di Donna Daria is a blend of 10 vintages of Fior d'Arancio Passito. It pours a dark amber color, releasing aromas of candied fruit, caramelized hazelnuts, Mediterranean scrub, and dates. On the palate, it impresses with its density and power, closing with an almost endless finish. The Ireneo '19, a Cabernet Sauvignon, expresses all the warmth of the Baone area in its dark fruit and spice notes, which find freshness in an herbal vein. On the palate, it's rich, juicy, and nicely supported by a weighty tannic structure.

Farina

loc. Pedemonte
via Bolla, 11
37029 San Pietro in Cariano [VR]
☏ +39 0457701349
⊕ www.farinawines.com

CELLAR SALES
PRE-BOOKED VISITS
ANNUAL PRODUCTION 800,000 bottles
HECTARES UNDER VINE 65.00

Despite the Farina family's connection to viticulture in Valpolicella dating back to the early 1900s, it took a century and the full-time involvement of cousins Elena and Claudio for the winery to make a decisive breakthrough. The estate comprises about ten hectares, with a sizable area also managed by local growers, who follow the technical group's precise guidelines. The result is a range centered on classic Veronese wines. We've noticed that Pedemonte has been stepping up its game for a few years, but this year's lineup leaves no doubt. The Amarone Mezzadro alla Fontana '15 is one of the most intriguing wines of the year, revealing deep aromas where overripe cherry intertwines with mineral and spice notes, all of which are echoed on a palate of great density—yet it lengthens with lightness and harmony. The Amarone Famiglia Farina '20 is also delicious, opting for more approachable fruit and a pervasive palate.

● Colli Euganei Cabernet Sauvignon Ireneo '19	♟♟ 5
○ Cuore di Donna Daria	♟♟ 8
● Ca' Emo '21	♟♟ 3
● Cabernet Franc Godimondo '22	♟♟ 3
● Carménère Progetto Recupero '21	♟♟ 4
○ Colli Euganei Fior d'Arancio Spumante Dolce	♟♟ 2*
● Forzaté '20	♟ 3
○ Piùchebello '23	♟ 3
● Baon '15	♟♟♟ 7
● Colli Euganei Cabernet Sauvignon Ireneo '12	♟♟♟ 4*
○ Colli Euganei Fior d'Arancio Passito Donna Daria '06	♟♟♟ 5
● Baon '19	♟♟ 7
● Colli Euganei Merlot Carlotto '19	♟♟ 4

● Amarone della Valpolicella Cl. Mezzadro alla Fontana Ris. '15	♟♟ 8
● Amarone della Valpolicella Cl. Famiglia Farina '20	♟♟ 7
● Valpolicella Cl. Ripasso Sup. Montecorna '22	♟♟ 3
● Valpolicella Cl. Sup. Alessandro '21	♟♟ 5
● Valpolicella Cl. Sup. Ripasso '22	♟♟ 3
● Amarone della Valpolicella Cl. '21	♟ 6
● Amarone della Valpolicella Cl. Famiglia Farina '18	♟♟ 5
● Amarone della Valpolicella Cl. Famiglia Farina '17	♟♟ 5
● Amarone della Valpolicella Cl. Mezzadro alla Fontana '11	♟♟ 7
● Amarone della Valpolicella Cl. Montefante Ris. '17	♟♟ 8

Il Filò delle Vigne

via Terralba, 14
35030 Baone [PD]
☎ +39 042956243
🌐 www.ilfilodellevigne.it

CELLAR SALES
PRE-BOOKED VISITS
ANNUAL PRODUCTION 50,000 bottles
HECTARES UNDER VINE 22.00

Although the Euganean Hills complex is just a few kilometers from Padua, its climate has a Mediterranean character, highlighted by the presence of broom, prickly pear, and strawberry trees, which become more evident as one moves south. At the southernmost tip lies Filò delle Vigne, a winery that has skillfully interpreted this climate with a production of great character and maturity. The Cabernet Borgo delle Casette is consistently one of the appellation's most interesting reds, and this year, with the 2020 vintage, it doesn't disappoint in showcasing its class. Its intense ruby color anticipates an aromatic profile that unfolds gradually, starting with ripe red fruit, then herbal notes, and finally hints of pencil lead. On the palate, it approaches almost brazenly, rich and perfectly supported by a significant tannic structure before a dry, very long finish. The Casa del Merlo '21 is more relaxed and supple, a Merlot of finesse and depth.

● Colli Euganei Cabernet Borgo delle Casette Ris. '20	▼▼▼ 5
● Colli Euganei Merlot Casa del Merlo '21	▼▼ 5
○ Calto delle Fate '22	▼▼ 5
● Colli Euganei Cabernet Cecilia di Baone Ris. '21	▼▼ 4
● Io di Baone '20	▼▼ 5
○ Terralba di Baone '23	▼ 3
● Colli Euganei Cabernet Borgo delle Casette Ris. '19	♈♈♈ 5
● Colli Euganei Cabernet Borgo delle Casette Ris. '18	♈♈♈ 5
● Colli Euganei Cabernet Borgo delle Casette Ris. '16	♈♈♈ 5
● Colli Euganei Merlot Casa del Merlo '18	♈♈♈ 5

Fongaro Spumanti

via Motto Piane, 12
37030 Roncà [VR]
☎ +39 0457460240
🌐 www.fongarospumanti.it

CELLAR SALES
PRE-BOOKED VISITS
ANNUAL PRODUCTION 70,000 bottles
HECTARES UNDER VINE 12.00
VITICULTURE METHOD Certified Organic

Tanita Danese's winery is located in the Val d'Alpone valley, the easternmost part of Lessinia, at the foot of the reserve. Here viticulture blends with wooded areas, creating a landscape of enchanting beauty. The dozen hectares at Tanita's disposal are almost entirely dedicated to durella, except for small plots of chardonnay and Manzoni bianco intended for simpler cuvées. Roncà's range is dedicated entirely to sparkling wines made with the Metodo Classico, led by the Riserva '16 Pas Dosé Nera. This sparkling wine expresses the full character of durella from the first whiff, with fruit remaining in the background as the mineral vein takes center stage. In the mouth, its aromatic complexity becomes more evident— the palate lengthens, stretching along the varietal's signature acidity. The Verde '19, on the other hand, moves on more integrated tones, veiled by a slight smoky note, while the palate is slimmer and more dynamic.

○ Lessini Durello Pas Dosé Nera Ris. '16	▼▼▼ 7
○ Cuvée Extra Brut M. Cl. '21	▼▼ 5
○ Lessini Durello Brut Viola Ris. '19	▼▼ 5
○ Monti Lessini Durello Brut Nera Ris. '16	▼▼ 6
○ Monti Lessini Durello M.Cl. Pas Dosé Verde Ris. '19	▼▼ 5
○ Lessini Durello Brut Nera Ris. '15	♈♈♈ 6
○ Lessini Durello Brut M. Cl. Ris. '10	♈♈ 5
○ Lessini Durello Brut Ris. '09	♈♈ 4
○ Lessini Durello M. Cl. Brut Guerrino Ris. '13	♈♈ 6
○ Lessini Durello M. Cl. Brut Nera Ris. '14	♈♈ 6
○ Lessini Durello M. Cl. Brut Viola Ris. '17	♈♈ 5
○ Lessini Durello M.Cl. Pas Dosé Verde Ris. '17	♈♈ 5
○ Lessini Durello Pas Dosé M. Cl. '10	♈♈ 5

VENETO

399

Le Fraghe

loc. Colombara, 3
37010 Cavaion Veronese [VR]
(☏ +39 0457236832
⊛ www.fraghe.it

CELLAR SALES
PRE-BOOKED VISITS
ACCOMMODATION
ANNUAL PRODUCTION 150,000 bottles
HECTARES UNDER VINE 32.00
VITICULTURE METHOD Certified Organic

When aptly interpreted, Bardolino can highlight the climatic conditions and soils of the terroir, producing either mature and fruity wines or more aromatic and lively expressions. With great skill, Matilde Poggi has understood the territory of Cavaion, building on the attributes of the glacial-origin soils and exploiting the cool breezes descending from Baldo and the Adige Valley, making for a range of great personality. If last year's Traccia di Rosa was a delightful surprise, this year's version is an even more welcome affirmation. The 2022 pours a pale hue, leading into aromas that captivate with their continuous interplay between sulfur notes, wild berries, flowers, and wild cherry, culminating in a palate of superb tension and sapidity. The aromatic profile of the Brol Grande '21 is equally complex, with fruit that remains hidden behind herbal and earthy notes, only to emerge more distinctly on the palate, where the wine shows its savory, energetic side.

Franchetto

fraz. Terrossa
via Binelli, 2
37030 Roncà [VR]
(☏ +39 0457460287
⊛ www.cantinafranchetto.com

ANNUAL PRODUCTION 35,000 bottles
HECTARES UNDER VINE 15.00

Today led by Giulia, who's supported by her parents Mara and Antonio, Franchetto is located in the Val d'Alpone valley, at the foot of the Lessinia hills. Here, garganega and durella (further to the north) take root in volcanic soils. The extensive estate allows Giulia to select the best vineyards for production, focusing primarily on Soave and Lessini Durello. Giulia Franchetto's wines get more convincing with each passing year, offering both pleasure and a strong connection to their terroir. La Capelina '23, a Soave, opens on simple and fragrant fruit on the nose, immediately expressive. However, on the palate, the wine takes on a different character, abandoning simplicity to embrace the power of the terroir, revealing an unmistakable, sapid, energetic acidic streak. The Recorbian '21, on the other hand, draws on garganega grapes harvested at overripeness but is well-balanced on the palate by its acidic tension.

⊙ Chiaretto di Bardolino Traccia di Rosa '22	♟♟♟ 5
● Bardolino Monte Grande Brol Grande '21	♟♟ 4
● Bardolino '23	♟♟ 3
○ Camporengo Garganega '23	♟♟ 3
⊙ Chiaretto di Bardolino Rodon '23	♟♟ 3
● Montalto Cabernet Franc '21	♟♟ 6
● Bardolino Cl. Brol Grande '15	♟♟♟ 3*
● Bardolino Cl. Brol Grande '12	♟♟♟ 3*
● Bardolino Cl. Brol Grande '11	♟♟♟ 3*
⊙ Chiaretto di Bardolino Traccia di Rosa '21	♟♟♟ 5
● Bardolino '22	♟ 3*
⊙ Chiaretto di Bardolino Traccia di Rosa '20	♟ 4
⊙ Chiaretto di Bardolino Traccia di Rosa '19	♟ 4
○ Traccia di Bianco '20	♟ 4

○ Soave Roncà Monte Calvarina La Capelina '23	♟♟ 3*
○ Soave Sup. Roncà Monte Calvarina Recorbian '21	♟♟ 4
○ Lessini Durello Brut '17	♟♟ 4
○ Lessini Durello Brut Borgoletto '22	♟♟ 5
○ Pinot Grigio delle Venezie Val Serina '23	♟♟ 3
○ Soave La Capelina '21	♟ 3*
○ Soave La Capelina '20	♟ 3*
○ Soave La Capelina '19	♟ 3
○ Soave La Capelina '18	♟ 3
○ Soave Recorbian '18	♟ 3
○ Soave Recorbian '16	♟ 3
○ Soave Roncà Monte Calvarina La Capelina '22	♟ 3*
○ Soave Recorbian '17	♟ 3

Gamba

loc. Valgatara
via Gnirega, 19
37020 Marano di Valpolicella [VR]
(+39 0456801714
www.vinigamba.it

CELLAR SALES
PRE-BOOKED VISITS
ANNUAL PRODUCTION 90,000 bottles
HECTARES UNDER VINE 15.00
VITICULTURE METHOD Certified Organic
SUSTAINABLE WINERY

Among the valleys of Valpolicella Classica,
Marano offers glimpses of rare beauty, with
viticulture perfectly integrated into the territory
and more developed areas coming across as
rural enclaves. Established just 20 years ago in
the Gnirega basin, the Aldrighetti brothers'
winery has already gained appreciation for the
quality of its wines. Only traditional grapes are
used, making for a reliable and characterful
range. The Amarone Campedel '17 Riserva is at
the top of its game, revealing its aromas
gradually, starting with a veil of reduction that
quickly dissipates to reveal dense and overripe
fruit, refreshed by spicy and thyme notes. On the
palate, it impresses with its fullness and warmth,
leaving it up to tannins and acidity to bring the
palate back to a more rigorous and composed
path. The nose of the Valpolicella Superiore '19,
from the same line, is darker and more
compressed, playing with the fullness and
generosity of its flavors.

Gentili

loc. Pesina
via S. Antonio, 271
37013 Caprino Veronese [VR]
(+39 3391651823
www.cantinagentili.com

CELLAR SALES
PRE-BOOKED VISITS
ANNUAL PRODUCTION 20,000 bottles
HECTARES UNDER VINE 40.00
SUSTAINABLE WINERY

Traveling through the Bardolino appellation from
south to north, one senses that the wines
gradually become more focused and longer,
perhaps losing some of the immediacy that we
associate with the area, but gaining in character
and dynamism. Enrico and Elisa have access to an
extensive set of vineyards and select the best
batches of grapes to create wines of marked
personality. With the Montebaldo San Verolo still
resting in the cellar, our attention was captured
by the Barbagliante '22, a Chiaretto di Bardolino
that forgoes immediate simplicity in favor of
aromatic breadth and a sapid, energetic profile.
The intriguing Metodo Classico '21 stands out
for its aromatic clarity and tension on the palate,
lengthening supple and brisk towards a crisp
finish. We also appreciated the Bardolino '22, a
juicy glass and highly drinkable.

VENETO

● Amarone della Valpolicella Cl. Campedel Ris. '17	▼▼ 8
● Recioto della Valpolicella Cl. Le Quare '20	▼▼ 7
● Valpolicella Cl. '23	▼▼ 3
● Valpolicella Cl. Sup. Campedel '19	▼▼ 5
● Valpolicella Cl. Sup. Ripasso Campedel '19	▼▼ 6
● Valpolicella Cl. Sup. Ripasso Le Quare '20	▼▼ 4
● Amarone della Valpolicella Cl. Campedel '18	♀♀ 8
● Amarone della Valpolicella Cl. Campedel '17	♀♀ 8
● Amarone della Valpolicella Cl. Campedel Ris. '16	♀♀ 8
● Amarone della Valpolicella Cl. Le Quare '18	♀♀ 8
● Amarone della Valpolicella Cl. Le Quare '17	♀♀ 7
● Recioto della Valpolicella Cl. Le Quare '18	♀♀ 7
● Valpolicella Cl. Campedel '21	♀♀ 3
● Valpolicella Cl. Campedel '20	♀♀ 4

⊙ Chiaretto di Bardolino Barbagliante '22	▼▼ 2*
● Bardolino Cl. '22	▼▼ 3
⊙ Chiaretto di Bardolino '23	▼▼ 2*
⊙ Chiaretto di Bardolino Dosaggio Zero M. Cl. '21	▼▼ 5
○ Souvignier Gris '22	▼▼ 4
● Bardolino Montebaldo San Verolo '21	♀♀ 4
● Bardolino Montebaldo San Verolo '20	♀♀ 4
● Bardolino San Verolo '19	♀♀ 4
● Bardolino San Verolo '18	♀♀ 3
⊙ Chiaretto di Bardolino '20	♀♀ 2*
⊙ Chiaretto di Bardolino Barbagliante '21	♀♀ 2*
⊙ Chiaretto di Bardolino Dosaggio Zero M. Cl. '20	♀♀ 5
⊙ Chiaretto di Bardolino Dosaggio Zero M. Cl. '19	♀♀ 5

Giannitessari

via Prandi, 10
37030 Roncà [VR]
(») +39 0457460070
⊕ www.giannitessari.wine

CELLAR SALES
PRE-BOOKED VISITS
ANNUAL PRODUCTION 350,000 bottles
HECTARES UNDER VINE 35.00
VITICULTURE METHOD Certified Organic
SUSTAINABLE WINERY

Gianni Tessari is an eclectic producer who has navigated through the appellations of Soave, Valpolicella, Lessinia, and Colli Berici. Today, his venture at the borders of the provinces of Verona and Vicenza is centered on the Lessini hills, with a production focused on Metodo Classico sparkling wines. The main ingredients are durella, volcanic hills, and time. More than 10 years after harvest, the Riserva '13 opens on aromas dominated by trademark mineral notes, leaving a background echo of fruit and dried flowers. The palate moves with suppleness, supported by the grape's signature acidity, lending fullness through its pronounced sapidity. In terms of the Soaves, we appreciated the energy and dynamism expressed by the Soave Pigno '22, while the Tai Rosso '22, made with grapes from vineyards on the Berici hills, features a smoky, juicy profile that accompanies a long and satisfying progression of flavor.

★Gini

via Giacomo Matteotti, 42
37032 Monteforte d'Alpone [VR]
(») +39 0457611908
⊕ www.ginivini.com

CELLAR SALES
PRE-BOOKED VISITS
ANNUAL PRODUCTION 200,000 bottles
HECTARES UNDER VINE 60.00
VITICULTURE METHOD Certified Organic

Claudio and Sandro Gini's winery is one of the most renowned in the Soave area, and the two brothers are often regarded as custodians of the identity of this Veronese white. However, they have also embraced major challenges in terms of innovation, taking on international varieties in the upper Val Tramigna and, in recent years, moving into Valpolicella, always while maintaining high quality standards. The Campo alle More '20 exemplifies this innovative spirit. A pinot nero, it sees signature fruity suggestions of wild berries and herbal notes followed by a sunny, flavorful palate. The Salvarenza '22 is the usual high-class Soave, outlined by ripe fruit made complete by notes of dried flowers and flint, revealing energy and a sapid, juicy palate. La Froscà '23, on the other hand, goes all in on elegance. It's a Soave with white fruit aromas, captivating with its dynamic flavor and remarkable length.

○ Lessini Durello Dosaggio Zero Ris. '13	♈♈ 7
● Colli Berici Rosso Pian Alto '20	♈♈ 4
● Colli Berici Tai Rosso '22	♈♈ 3
○ Lessini Durello Extra Brut Ris. '17	♈♈ 5
○ Soave '23	♈♈ 2*
○ Soave Cl. Perinato Pigno '22	♈♈ 3
○ Due Bianco	♈ 2
● Due Rosso '22	♈ 2
● Pinot Nero '23	♈ 2
○ Soave Cl. Tenda Scalete '23	♈ 3
○ Soave Cl. Pigno Gianni Tessari '13	♈♈♈ 3*
○ Lessini Durello Extra Brut M. Cl. Ris. '14	♈♈ 6
○ Soave '22	♈♈ 2*
○ Soave Cl. Perinato V. Pigno '21	♈♈ 3

○ Soave Cl. Contrada Salvarenza V.V. '22	♈♈ 5
○ Soave Cl. La Froscà '23	♈♈ 5
● Campo alle More '20	♈♈ 6
○ Soave Cl. '23	♈♈ 3
○ Soave Cl. Contrada Salvarenza V.V. '14	♈♈♈ 5
○ Soave Cl. Contrada Salvarenza V.V. '09	♈♈♈ 5
○ Soave Cl. Contrada Salvarenza V.V. '08	♈♈♈ 5
○ Soave Cl. Contrada Salvarenza V.V. '07	♈♈♈ 5
○ Soave Cl. La Froscà '18	♈♈♈ 4*
○ Soave Cl. La Froscà '11	♈♈♈ 4*
○ Soave Cl. La Froscà '06	♈♈♈ 4*
○ Soave Cl. La Froscà '05	♈♈♈ 4*
○ Soave Cl. Sup. Contrada Salvarenza V.V. '00	♈♈♈ 5

Giusti Wine

via Arditi, 14a
31040 Nervesa della Battaglia [TV]
📞 +39 0422720198
🌐 www.giustiwine.com

CELLAR SALES
PRE-BOOKED VISITS
ACCOMMODATION
ANNUAL PRODUCTION 650,000 bottles
HECTARES UNDER VINE 120.00
SUSTAINABLE WINERY

At the foot of Montello lies a new, large winery whose undulating profile seems to blend with the folds of the nearby hills, allowing it to integrate perfectly with the landscape. This is the production facility built by Giusti Wine, one of the most interesting producers to have emerged in Treviso in recent years. The vineyards unfold across many hectares in the area, alternating flat zones with more secluded areas nestled among the Montello dolines. This year, the winery on Via Arditi presented a highly commendable lineup, led by the impressive Asolo Extra Brut and Montello Rosso Superiore. The first is the Oro '22, a Prosecco Superiore that, after over a year of maturation, offers up an aromatic bouquet of flowers and white fruit, sensations that we also find on a crisp palate with a pronounced sapid streak. The second is the Umberto I° '21, a Bordeaux blend that's still timid in its aromatic expression but reveals character and energy on the palate, managing its rich and long palate with precision.

La Giuva

via Trezzolano, 20c
37141 Verona
📞 +39 3421117089
🌐 www.lagiuva.com

CELLAR SALES
PRE-BOOKED VISITS
ANNUAL PRODUCTION 20,000 bottles
HECTARES UNDER VINE 9.50
VITICULTURE METHOD Certified Organic

The winery led by Sandro Veronesi is located in the highest part of Val Squaranto, around the small village of Trezzolano, a still largely unexplored area of Valpolicella that offers intriguing opportunities, especially due to the freshness that permeates the vineyards. This is particularly true their La Giuva holdings, which also benefit from a north-facing exposure in some cases. The modern, beautifully designed cellar produces wines that are closely aligned with the appellation. The Amarone L'Aristide perfectly expresses all the warmth that raisining imparts to the grapes. Its jammy red fruit is surrounded by notes of sweet spices and olives in brine. On the palate, the wine proves dense, full, and juicy. The Amarone '19 follows the same aromatic path but moves on a different track in the mouth. Its impact is decisive, supremely concentrated—it's left up to acidity and tannins to provide the rigor.

○ Asolo Extra Brut Oro '22	♈♈ 4
● Montello Rosso Sup. Umberto I° '21	♈♈ 8
● Amarone della Valpolicella Cl. '19	♈♈ 8
○ Asolo Brut	♈♈ 2*
● Asolo Montello Recantina Anfora Tenuta Aria Valentina Mateociei '21	♈♈ 4
○ Chardonnay dei Carni '22	♈♈ 3
● Asolo Montello Rosso Tenuta Aria Valentina Antonio '21	♈ 5
○ Delle Venezie Pinot Grigio Longheri '23	♈ 3
○ Prosecco Brut Rosalia	♈ 3
○ Sauvignon Nepis Sant'Eustachio '22	♈ 3
● Amarone della Valpolicella Cl. '18	♈♈ 8
● Montello e Colli Asolani Recantina Augusto '20	♈♈ 5
● Montello e Colli Asolani Rosso Antonio '20	♈♈ 5

● Amarone della Valpolicella '19	♈♈ 8
● Amarone della Valpolicella L'Aristide '17	♈♈ 8
● Valpolicella Sup. Il Rientro '20	♈♈ 5
● Recioto della Valpolicella '21	♈ 7
● Valpolicella Il Valpo '23	♈ 4
● Amarone della Valpolicella '18	♈♈ 8
● Amarone della Valpolicella '16	♈♈ 8
● Amarone della Valpolicella L'Aristide '15	♈♈ 8
● Recioto della Valpolicella '18	♈♈ 6
● Recioto della Valpolicella '17	♈♈ 6
● Valpolicella '21	♈♈ 4
● Valpolicella Sup. Il Rientro '19	♈♈ 5
● Valpolicella Sup. Il Rientro '18	♈♈ 5
● Valpolicella Sup. Il Rientro '17	♈♈ 5
● Valpolicello Il Valpo '22	♈♈ 4
● Valpolicello Il Valpo '19	♈♈ 4

Gorgo

fraz. Custoza
loc. Gorgo, 15
37066 Sommacampagna [VR]
☎ +39 0455160063
✇ www.cantinagorgo.com

CELLAR SALES
PRE-BOOKED VISITS
ANNUAL PRODUCTION 600,000 bottles
HECTARES UNDER VINE 53.00
VITICULTURE METHOD Certified Organic
SUSTAINABLE WINERY

Roberta Bricolo took over the family winery less than 10 years ago, driving a decisive shift in its direction. Today, Gorgo stands as one of southern Garda's most intriguing producers, with an extensive vineyard acreage largely dedicated to Verona's traditional grapes. A young team of collaborators oversees viticulture and production, making wines that honor Garda by favoring elegance over power. The style is perfectly expressed in the San Michelin '23, the producer's historic Custoza. Here the fernanda grape (a local name for cortese) transmits its aromatic character right from the outset. Redolent of flowers and citrus, white fruit sensations slowly emerge from the background. On the palate, it's crisp, dynamic, and accompanied by a highly fresh acidic streak. The Summa '22, on the other hand, explores the richer and deeper side of the appellation, offering aromas ranging from ripe fruit to mineral notes, culminating in a palate of superb solidity and harmony.

○ Custoza Sup. Summa '22	♀♀♀ 4*
○ Custoza San Michelin '23	♀♀ 3*
● Bardolino '23	♀♀ 2*
● Bardolino Sup. Monte Maggiore '22	♀♀ 3
● Ca' Nova '22	♀♀ 3
⊙ Chiaretto di Bardolino '23	♀♀ 2*
○ Custoza '23	♀♀ 2*
⊙ Chiaretto di Bardolino Brut Perlato Rosa	♀ 3
○ Custoza San Michelin '20	♀♀♀ 2*
○ Custoza Sup. Summa '21	♀♀♀ 4*
○ Custoza Sup. Summa '20	♀♀♀ 3*
● Bardolino '22	♀♀ 2*
● Bardolino Sommacampagna '20	♀♀ 5
⊙ Chiaretto di Bardolino '22	♀♀ 2*
○ Custoza San Michelin '22	♀♀ 3*
○ Custoza San Michelin '21	♀♀ 2*

Gregoletto

fraz. Premaor
via San Martino, 83
31050 Miane [TV]
☎ +39 0438970463
✇ gregoletto.com

CELLAR SALES
PRE-BOOKED VISITS
ANNUAL PRODUCTION 200,000 bottles
HECTARES UNDER VINE 18.00

As you travel the Prosecco Superiore area from west to east, you'll notice that viticulture has occupied nearly all the cultivable space. However, near Miane, the landscape offers new vistas, where vineyards remain predominant, yet woods start to reappear. It is here, in Premaor, that the Gregoletto family's winery is located. For over 70 years, they have been served as one of the territory's most intriguing interpreters. The Gregoletto family offers a wide range. Glera is the focus, but there are also Bordeaux varieties and lesser-known grapes, like boschera. The Merlot '22 is a perfect example of how an everyday wine can possess personality and depth, with a multifaceted aromatic profile and a crisp, brisk palate—irresistibly drinkable. Great attention is paid to the world of sparklers refermented in the bottle, a deeply rooted tradition at Gregoletto, with the harmonious and sapid Prosecco and the more spirited Boschera standing out.

○ Boschera Frizzante Sui Lieviti '23	♀♀ 3
○ Conegliano Valdobbiadene Extra Dry	♀♀ 3
○ Conegliano Valdobbiadene Prosecco '23	♀♀ 3
● Merlot '22	♀♀ 3
○ Prosecco di Treviso Frizzante sui Lieviti '23	♀♀ 3
○ Verdiso Frizzante Sui Lieviti '23	♀♀ 3
● Cabernet '22	♀ 3
○ Conegliano Valdobbiadene Brut Nature Sui Lieviti '22	♀ 4
⊙ Le Rosé Frizzante Sui Lieviti	♀ 3
○ Conegliano Valdobbiadene Prosecco '22	♀♀ 3
○ Conegliano Valdobbiadene Prosecco '21	♀♀ 3
○ Conegliano Valdobbiadene Sui Lieviti Brut Nature '21	♀♀ 4
○ Conegliano Valdobbiadene Sui Lieviti Brut Nature '20	♀♀ 4

★Guerrieri Rizzardi

s.da Campazzi, 2
37011 Bardolino [VR]
📞 +39 0457210028
🌐 www.guerrieri-rizzardi.it

CELLAR SALES
PRE-BOOKED VISITS
ANNUAL PRODUCTION 950,000 bottles
HECTARES UNDER VINE 100.00
SUSTAINABLE WINERY

Only 14 Italian businesses are members of the 'Hénokiens," an association of family businesses with at least two centuries of history, and Guerrieri Rizzardi is the sole member dedicated to wine production. Today, brothers Giuseppe and Agostino are at the helm, managing an estate that spans all the main Veronese appellations, producing wines of exceptional quality. The Amarone Villa Rizzardi, a Riserva from the excellent 2019 vintage, opens on dark aromas dominated by a sulfur note that overlays its sweet, fleshy fruit. As you dig deeper, you'll find medicinal herbs, underbrush, and a captivating spiciness that becomes even more pronounced on the palate, where significant power is elegantly managed by acidity and tannins. The Bardolino Delara '22 makes an excellent debut. Sourced from vineyards in the Montebaldo area, it showcases elegant aromas and a crisp, sapid palate that finishes on a lovely whiff of rose.

★Inama

loc. Biacche, 50
37047 San Bonifacio [VR]
📞 +39 0456104343
🌐 www.inama.wine

CELLAR SALES
PRE-BOOKED VISITS
ANNUAL PRODUCTION 650,000 bottles
HECTARES UNDER VINE 80.00
VITICULTURE METHOD Certified Organic

More than half a century has passed since the first vineyards were acquired in Soave Classico and nearly 30 years since the property in the Berico district. Today, the Inama family's winery is undoubtedly among these two territories' most important interpreters. The extensive estate is inseparably linked to the grape varieties that reign in these lands: garganega in the Soave area and Bordeaux varieties, particularly carménère, in Vicenza. Bradisismo was the first red produced by Inama in the Berici hills, and with the 2021 vintage, it reasserts its leadership role. This blend of cabernet sauvignon, franc, and carménère reveals vibrant red fruit aromas, with oak subtly pushing spices from the background, leading to a well-structured palate where tannins and acidity guide the wine across its long progression. On the Soave front, I Palchi, made from garganega vines on Monte Foscarino, proves to be a prized white through and through, delivering rich flavors in an elegant and harmonious profile.

Amarone della Valpolicella Cl. Villa Rizzardi Ris. '19	🍷🍷 8
Bardolino Montebaldo Delara '22	🍷🍷 4
Amarone della Valpolicella Cl. 3 Cru '19	🍷🍷 7
Chiaretto di Bardolino Cl. Keya '23	🍷🍷 3
Clos Roareti '21	🍷🍷 5
Munus '22	🍷🍷 4
Soave Cl. Costeggiola '23	🍷🍷 3
Soave Cl. Ferra '22	🍷🍷 3
Valpolicella Cl. Sup. Ripasso Pojega '21	🍷🍷 4
Bardolino Cl. Cuvée XV '23	🍷 3
Amarone della Valpolicella Cl. Calcarole '11	🍷🍷🍷 8
Amarone della Valpolicella Cl. Villa Rizzardi '13	🍷🍷🍷 7
Amarone della Valpolicella Cl. Villa Rizzardi Ris. '15	🍷🍷🍷 8

● Colli Berici Cabernet Bradisismo '21	🍷🍷🍷 7
○ Soave Cl. Foscarino I Palchi '21	🍷🍷 7
○ Soave Cl. Foscarino '22	🍷🍷 7
○ Vulcaia Fumé '22	🍷🍷 7
● Bradisismo '08	🍷🍷🍷 5
● Colli Berici Cabernet Bradisismo '20	🍷🍷🍷 7
● Colli Berici Cabernet Bradisismo '19	🍷🍷🍷 6
● Colli Berici Carménère Carminium '16	🍷🍷🍷 5
● Colli Berici Carménère Oratorio di San Lorenzo Ris. '09	🍷🍷🍷 6
○ Sauvignon Vulcaia Fumé '96	🍷🍷🍷 4*
○ Soave Cl. Vign. di Foscarino '08	🍷🍷🍷 4
○ Soave Cl. Vign. Du Lot '05	🍷🍷🍷 2*
○ Soave Cl. Vign. Du Lot '01	🍷🍷🍷 4
○ Soave Cl. Vign. Du Lot '00	🍷🍷🍷 4*
○ Soave Cl. Vign. Du Lot '99	🍷🍷🍷 4*

Loredan Gasparini

fraz. Venegazzù
via Martignago Alto, 23
31040 Volpago del Montello [TV]
(+39 0423870024
⊛ www.loredangasparini.it

CELLAR SALES
PRE-BOOKED VISITS
ANNUAL PRODUCTION 400,000 bottles
HECTARES UNDER VINE 60.00
SUSTAINABLE WINERY

The Palla family winery manages their holdings in the Montello area with great acumen. 30 hectares are dedicated entirely to Bordeaux varieties in Venegazzù, where the red soil is characterized by a strong presence of iron, and an area of equal size in Giavera, where glera, Manzoni bianco and chardonnay are cultivated. Their wines favor the influence of the territory over mere varietal expression. The Capo di Stato '19, a traditional Bordeaux blend from the estate's best old vines, exudes aromas of plum and wild blackberry, echoed by fresher herbal nuances. On the palate, it's rich and full-bodied, tapering off with a sapid note and, thanks to the tannins, a spirited finish. Its younger sibling, the Venegazzù della Casa '19, leans more towards fruit, with acidity lending the suppleness for which Montello is known. The Brut, a monovarietal chardonnay, proves elegant on the nose—supple and racy.

● Montello Asolo Rosso Sup. Venegazzù Capo di Stato '19	♟♟♟ 8
○ Asolo Brut	♟♟ 3
○ Brut M. Cl.	♟♟ 4
● Montello Asolo Cabernet Sauvignon '21	♟♟ 3
● Montello Asolo Rosso Venegazzù Della Casa '19	♟♟ 5
● Montello e Colli Asolani Venegazzù Sup. Capo di Stato '17	♟♟♟ 8
● Montello Asolo Venegazzù Sup. Capo di Stato '18	♟ 8
● Montello e Colli Asolani Venegazzù Sup. Capo di Stato '16	♟ 8
● Montello e Colli Asolani Venegazzù Sup. Capo di Stato '15	♟ 6

★Maculan

via Castelletto, 3
36042 Breganze [VI]
(+39 0445873733
⊛ www.maculan.net

CELLAR SALES
PRE-BOOKED VISITS
ANNUAL PRODUCTION 600,000 bottles
HECTARES UNDER VINE 35.00
SUSTAINABLE WINERY

More than half a century has passed since Fausto made his debut in the family winery, and still today, he supports his daughters Angela (who handles the commercial side) and Maria Vittoria (who focuses on production). Knowing their father, it is safe to say that both have followed in his footsteps, dedicating themselves passionately and competently to the winery without ever forgetting the importance of the market. The Fratta '19 put in a high-profile performance this year. A blend of cabernet sauvignon and merlot, it has shed some of the exuberance of recent vintages in favor of finesse and depth. Dark fruit emerges clearly against a backdrop of spices and balsamic notes, culminating in an energetic palate, nicely contoured by tannins and acidity, which provide tension and length. The Palazzotto '20, by contrast, proves fresher, with its more immediately expressive aromatic profile, and a more dynamic, spirited palate. The Torcolato shines with its harmonious character, a defining trait for this passito.

● Fratta '19	♟♟ 8
● Bregante Cabernet Sauvignon Palazzotto '20	♟♟ 5
○ Breganze Torcolato '22	♟♟ 7
● Brentino '22	♟♟ 3
○ Chardonnay Ferrata '22	♟♟ 5
○ Dindarello '23	♟♟ 5
● Marzemino Cornorotto '21	♟♟ 3
○ Breganze Vespaiolo '23	♟ 3
○ Breganze Vespaiolo Valvolpara '23	♟ 5
● Pinot Nero '22	♟ 3
● Breganze Cabernet Sauvignon Palazzotto '05	♟♟♟ 4
● Breganze Cabernet Sauvignon Palazzotto '04	♟♟♟ 4
● Fratta '01	♟♟♟ 8

Manara

loc. San Floriano
via Don Cesare Biasi, 53
37029 San Pietro in Cariano [VR]
(» +39 0457701086
⊕ www.manaravini.it

CELLAR SALES
PRE-BOOKED VISITS
ANNUAL PRODUCTION 170,000 bottles
HECTARES UNDER VINE 12.00
SUSTAINABLE WINERY

Changes in the agricultural world happen slowly, and similarly, the fourth generation of the Manara family is beginning to make its mark. They work alongside their parents, managing activities and contributing to a stylistic renewal. The strength of this small producer undoubtedly lies in its estate, which boasts some of the most beautiful vineyards in Valpolicella Classica. This year the San Floriano brothers fielded almost entirely traditional wines, with the Amarone Corte Manara standing out as our favorite. Overripe cherry dominates the nose, set against a background of spices and aromatic herbs, sensations that introduce a palate where power is present but not overpowering. The perfect balance of its signature warmth of alcohol, acidity, and smooth tannins gives the wine harmony and length. The Postera '17, on the other hand, leans more into its power, revealing aromatic complexity and flavorful compactness.

Amarone della Valpolicella Cl. Corte Manara '19	♥♥ 5
Amarone della Valpolicella Cl. Postera '17	♥♥ 6
Recioto della Valpolicella Cl. El Rocolo '21	♥♥ 5
Valpolicella Ripasso Cl. Sup. Le Morete '22	♥♥ 3
Vlpolicella Cl. Sup. Vecio Belo '22	♥♥ 3
Guido Manara '18	♥ 6
Amarone della Valpolicella Cl. '00	♥♥♥ 5
Amarone della Valpolicella Cl. Corte Manara '18	♡♡ 5
Amarone della Valpolicella Cl. Corte Manara '17	♡♡ 6
Amarone della Valpolicella Cl. Postera '16	♡♡ 6
Amarone della Valpolicella Cl. Postera '15	♡♡ 6
Amarone della Valpolicella Cl. Postera '14	♡♡ 6

Le Marognole

loc. Valgatara
via Marognole, 7
37020 Marano di Valpolicella [VR]
(» +39 3492569347
⊕ www.lemarognole.it

CELLAR SALES
PRE-BOOKED VISITS
ANNUAL PRODUCTION 15,000 bottles
HECTARES UNDER VINE 5.50

VENETO

If there were a classification of vineyards in Valpolicella, like in some of the most renowned wine regions abroad, Gnirega would certainly be among the most important. This sun-kissed, expansive basin allows grapes to mature healthily, caressed by evening breezes. Fabio Corsi is celebrating his 20th harvest this year, and what once seemed an uncertain adventure has become a winery of great qualitative consistency and adherence to tradition. The Amarone CampoRocco '15, a Riserva that ages at length before being released, takes its time revealing its aromas, starting out closed and almost reluctant to reveal hints of cherry compote, rain-soaked earth, and spices, sensations that express themselves more clearly on the palate. Here, the wine moves richly and powerfully, nicely supported by a vibrant acidity. The Valpolicella '22 intrigues with its fresh fruit accompanied by an intense balsamic note, which follows through a crisp palate that's perfectly balanced by acidity.

Amarone della Valpolicella Cl. CampoRocco Ris. '15	♥♥ 7
Valpolicella Cl. '22	♥♥ 3
Valpolicella Cl. Sup. Ripasso '19	♥♥ 3
⊙ El Marascar '23	♥ 3
Amarone della Valpolicella Cl. CampoRocco '18	♡♡ 5
Amarone della Valpolicella Cl. CampoRocco '17	♡♡ 5
Amarone della Valpolicella Cl. CampoRocco '16	♡♡ 5
Amarone della Valpolicella Cl. CampoRocco Ris. '13	♡♡ 5
Amarone della Valpolicella Cl. CampoRocco Ris. '11	♡♡ 5
Valpolicella Cl. Sup. Ripasso '18	♡♡ 3

Masari

loc. Maglio di Sopra
c.da Bevilacqua, 2a
36078 Valdagno [VI]
📞 +39 0445410780
🌐 www.masari.it

CELLAR SALES
PRE-BOOKED VISITS
ANNUAL PRODUCTION 55,000 bottles
HECTARES UNDER VINE 10.00
VITICULTURE METHOD Certified Organic
SUSTAINABLE WINERY

It is difficult to speak of Massimo Dal Lago and Arianna Tessari's winery without mentioning the Agno Valley, an unspoiled area whose viticultural value is being rediscovered thanks to Masari's efforts. A few small plots of land have grown into ten hectares that reach into both sides of the valley, where the calcareous soil to the east and the volcanic soil to the west impart character and distinctiveness to their wines. The grapes for their Masari '19 are sourced from the eastern slopes at about 450 meters above sea level. A blend of cabernet sauvignon and merlot, it conjures intense aromas of ripe, sweet red fruit alongside spices and then a fresh balsamic vein. A firm palate follows, with acidity, tannins, and richness blending perfectly. The San Martino '20, from the opposite slope, stands out for its fresh aromatic profile and dynamic flavors, which lengthen and tighten the palate.

★Masi

fraz. Gargagnago
via Monteleone, 26
37015 Sant'Ambrogio di Valpolicella [VR]
📞 +39 0456832511
🌐 www.masi.it

CELLAR SALES
PRE-BOOKED VISITS
ACCOMMODATION AND RESTAURANT SERVICE
ANNUAL PRODUCTION 3,950,000 bottles
HECTARES UNDER VINE 550.00
SUSTAINABLE WINERY

Active since time immemorial in the heart of Valpolicella Classica, the Boscaini family winery is now an absolute touchstone for knowing and appreciating the wines of this part of Veneto. Alongside Valpolicella, they've also made inroads in the main appellations of the territory, with collaborations and parcels that draw on Bardolino, Lugana, and Soave, all interpreted with a clear and distinctive style. From four small old-vine plots around the village of Torbe, at about 400 meters altitude, come the grapes for one of Masi's flagship wines, the Campolongo di Torbe '15. The deep color introduces intense and profound aromas dominated by stewed red fruit, echoed by herbal and spicy notes that carry through to an energetic sip, perfectly supported by a close-knit tannic structure. The Amarone Costasera '18, by contrast, plays on explosive fruitiness that reverberates in a compact palate.

● Masari '19	🍷🍷 6
○ Agnobianco '22	🍷🍷 3
○ Leon Dosaggio Zero M. Cl.	🍷🍷 5
● Pinot Nero Costa Nera '22	🍷🍷 4
● San Martino '20	🍷🍷 4
○ Agnobianco '21	🍷🍷 3
○ Antico Pasquale '11	🍷🍷 8
● Costa Nera '19	🍷🍷 4
○ Leon Dosaggio Zero M. Cl.	🍷🍷 5
● Masari '18	🍷🍷 6
● Masari '17	🍷🍷 6
● Masari '16	🍷🍷 6
● Masari '15	🍷🍷 6
● Monte Pulgo '15	🍷🍷 8
● Monte Pulgo '13	🍷🍷 8
● San Martino '19	🍷🍷 4

● Amarone della Valpolicella Cl. Campolongo di Torbe '15	🍷🍷 8
● Amarone della Valpolicella Cl. Costasera Ris. '18	🍷🍷 8
● Recioto della Valpolicella Amandorlato Cl. Mezzanella '17	🍷🍷 8
○ Rosa dei Masi '23	🍷🍷 3
● Amarone della Valpolicella Cl. Campolongo di Torbe '13	🍷🍷🍷 8
● Amarone della Valpolicella Cl. Campolongo di Torbe '12	🍷🍷🍷 8
● Amarone della Valpolicella Cl. Costasera Ris. '16	🍷🍷🍷 8
● Amarone della Valpolicella Cl. Costasera Ris. '13	🍷🍷🍷 8
● Amarone della Valpolicella Cl. Mazzano '12	🍷🍷🍷 8

Masottina

via Via Custoza, 2
31015 Conegliano [TV]
☏ +39 0438400775
✉ www.masottina.it

CELLAR SALES
ANNUAL PRODUCTION 1,500,000 bottles
HECTARES UNDER VINE 280.00
SUSTAINABLE WINERY

Masottina's cellar, a large structure nestled on the ridge of the Ogliano hill, almost seems to rise from the glera vineyards. Architecturally, it's perfectly integrated with the surrounding landscape, while inside it's equipped with all the technology that Treviso's sparkling wines require. A large estate allows Federico and Filippo Dal Bianco to produce wines of absolute value, drawing from the UNESCO heritage hills and the neighboring plains. However, Ogliano is where the heart of Masottina beats, a vast hilly area where vineyards stretch as far as the eye can see on glacial soils. The R.D.O. Levante '23, an Extra Dry made from vineyards facing east, smells of white fruit and flowers and delights the palate with the delicate charm that glera cultivated in its historic cradle possesses. The sip is supple, sapid, and irresistibly drinkable. Its sibling, the R.D.O. Ponente '23, benefits from the west-facing vineyards, where the richer grapes allow for lower sugar dosage, resulting in a Brut of great finesse and tension.

Conegliano Valdobbiadene Rive di Ogliano Extra Dry R.D.O. Levante '23	♙♙ 4
Conegliano Valdobbiadene Brut ContradaGranda	♙♙ 3
Conegliano Valdobbiadene Extra Dry ContradaGranda	♙♙ 3
Conegliano Valdobbiadene Rive di Ogliano Brut R.D.O. Ponente '23	♙♙ 4
Merlot Ai Palazzi '19	♙ 4
Prosecco di Treviso Extra Brut ViaVenti	♙ 2
Prosecco di Treviso Rosé Brut Viaventi '23	♙ 3
Conegliano Valdobbiadene Rive di Ogliano Brut R.D.O. Ponente '22	♙♙ 3*
Conegliano Valdobbiadene Rive di Ogliano Brut R.D.O. Ponente '21	♙♙ 3*
Conegliano Valdobbiadene Rive di Ogliano Extra Dry R.D.O. Levante '22	♙♙ 3*

Massimago

via Giare, 11
37030 Mezzane di Sotto [VR]
☏ +39 3426604566
✉ www.massimago.com

CELLAR SALES
PRE-BOOKED VISITS
ACCOMMODATION AND RESTAURANT SERVICE
ANNUAL PRODUCTION 80,000 bottles
HECTARES UNDER VINE 12.00
VITICULTURE METHOD Certified Organic
SUSTAINABLE WINERY

Camilla Rossi Chauvenet's winery comprises about 12 organically farmed hectares, set within a larger estate that stretches across the hills of Val di Mezzane, surrounded by woods and olive groves. The property is divided into 13 parcels, which are vinified separately, resulting in a broad range of Amarone that reflects the different characteristics of the grapes. Crafted from a selection of estate vineyards, the the Amarone Conte Gastone 2019 aims to highlight the immediacy and gentleness of this style, with delicate yet lively acidity highlighting elegant fruit. The Amarone SVM 400 Macie, made from grapes ripened at 400 meters altitude, follows a more energetic register, with fruit well-framed by spicy and herbal notes, offering a crisp sip, pleasantly rough and with good length. The Duchessa Allegra '23, a monovarietal garganega, stands out for its good aromatic intensity and a supple, racy profile.

● Amarone della Valpolicella Conte Gastone '19	♙♙ 7
● Amarone della Valpolicella '18	♙♙ 8
● Amarone della Valpolicella SVM 400 Macie '18	♙♙ 8
● Amarone della Valpolicella SVT 300 Terrazze '18	♙♙ 8
○ Duchessa Allegra Gargenega '23	♙♙ 3
● Valpolicella Duca Fedele '23	♙ 3
● Valpolicella Sup. Ripasso Marchesa MariaBella '22	♙ 5
● Amarone della Valpolicella SVM400 '16	♙♙ 8
● Amarone della Valpolicella SVT300 Terrazze '17	♙♙ 8
● Valpolicella Duca Fedele '22	♙♙ 3
● Valpolicella Sup. Ripasso Marchesa Mariabella '18	♙♙ 4

Roberto Mazzi e Figli

loc. San Peretto
via Crosetta, 8
37024 Negrar [VR]
📞 +39 0457502072
🖥 www.robertomazzi.it

CELLAR SALES
PRE-BOOKED VISITS
ACCOMMODATION AND RESTAURANT SERVICE
ANNUAL PRODUCTION 50,000 bottles
HECTARES UNDER VINE 8.00

The winery run by brothers Antonio and Stefano Mazzi is nestled in the almost hidden valley of Negrar, in the small village of San Peretto, where the vineyards quickly climb the eastern slope of the valley, seemingly in search of freshness. Next to the historic cellar, a new building has been constructed to optimize bottle management. Interpreted with a clear, rich fruitiness, their wines adhere strongly to tradition. The selection from the Negrar brothers, highlighted by the Amarone Punta di Villa '19, impresses with its intense wild fruit notes on the nose. Herbal and peppery hints emerge alongside, with a deep undertone of underbrush that subtly refreshes the palate. On the palate, the wine is rich, with good density and well-supported sapidity. The Castel '18 follows a similar aromatic path, while displaying greater agility and tension on the palate.

Menegotti

loc. Acquaroli, 7
37069 Villafranca di Verona [VR]
📞 +39 0457902611
🖥 www.menegotticantina.com

CELLAR SALES
PRE-BOOKED VISITS
ACCOMMODATION
ANNUAL PRODUCTION 250,000 bottles
HECTARES UNDER VINE 30.00
SUSTAINABLE WINERY

The Menegotti family winery is nestled among the hills surrounding the southern shore of Lake Garda—gently rolling, glacially formed slopes that stretch southward. In the appellations of Bardolino and Custoza, the Menegottis have, for decades, complemented their offerings with a noteworthy line of Metodo Classico sparkling wines. Often, traditional grape varieties are utilized, taking advantage of their acidic and aromatic profiles. The Elianto '21 is an intriguing blend of traditional grapes, aged extensively in the cellar before release. It offers intense aroma of fresh flowers and white-fleshed fruit, characteristics echoed on the palate, where the wine unfolds gracefully, resulting in a long and juicy finish. Among the sparkling wines, the Extra Brut, a monovarietal garganega, stood out for its discreet display of yellow fruit, bread crust, and dried mushrooms. On the palate, the fullness finds tension as it tapers around the acidity.

Wine	Rating
● Amarone della Valpolicella Cl. Punta di Villa '19	♟♟ 8
● Amarone della Valpolicella Cl. Castel '18	♟♟ 8
● Valpolicella Cl. Sup. Poiega '20	♟♟ 5
● Valpolicella Cl. Sup. Sanperetto '21	♟♟ 5
● Amarone della Valpolicella Cl. Punta di Villa '11	♟♟♟ 7
● Valpolicella Cl. Sup. Sanperetto '11	♟♟♟ 3*
● Amarone della Valpolicella Cl. Castel '17	♟♟ 7
● Amarone della Valpolicella Cl. Castel '16	♟♟ 7
● Amarone della Valpolicella Cl. Punta di Villa '18	♟♟ 7
● Valpolicella Cl. Sup. Poiega '19	♟♟ 4
● Valpolicella Cl. Sup. Poiega '18	♟♟ 4

Wine	Rating
○ Brut M. Cl. '18	♟♟ 5
○ Brut M. Cl.	♟♟ 5
○ Custoza '23	♟♟ 2
○ Elianto '21	♟♟ 4
○ Extra Brut M. Cl.	♟♟ 3
● Bardolino '23	♟ 2
⊙ Chiaretto di Bardolino Cl. '23	♟ 2
● Geodoro '19	♟ 5
● Bardolino '22	♟♟ 2
○ Brut M. Cl. '17	♟♟ 4
○ Custoza Sup. Elianto '20	♟♟ 3
○ Custoza Sup. Elianto '19	♟♟ 3
○ Custoza Sup. Elianto '18	♟♟ 3
○ Custoza Sup. Elianto '17	♟♟ 3
○ Custoza Sup. Elianto '16	♟♟ 3
○ Extra Brut M. Cl.	♟♟ 3

VENETO

★Graziano Merotto

fraz. Col San Martino
via Scandolera, 21
31010 Farra di Soligo [TV]
📞 +39 0438989000
🌐 www.merotto.it

CELLAR SALES
PRE-BOOKED VISITS
ACCOMMODATION
ANNUAL PRODUCTION 610,000 bottles
HECTARES UNDER VINE 45.00

Graziano Merotto stands among those enlightened producers who have skillfully combined rural wisdom with cellar expertise, improving every stage of production year after year, from vineyard to bottle, without falling prey to commercial whims. The extensive area under vines, largely managed directly by the winery, allows for the production of a refined range of sparkling wines that closely reflect their terroir. The Extra Dry Castè '23 showcases all the delicate fruitiness of glera grown on the best-exposed slopes, with aromas of apple, pear, linden flowers, and wisteria, leading to a generous palate where sweetness is balanced by acidity and sapidity. More refined and slow to reveal itself is the Graziano Merotto '23, where white fruit takes center stage, with floral notes and a subtle green vein emerging gradually. The palate is crisp, perfectly complemented by the bubbles, and of notable length.

Ornella Molon

fraz. Campodipietra
via Risorgimento, 40
31040 Salgareda [TV]
📞 +39 0422804807
🌐 www.ornellamolon.it

CELLAR SALES
PRE-BOOKED VISITS
RESTAURANT SERVICE
ANNUAL PRODUCTION 500,000 bottles
HECTARES UNDER VINE 42.00
SUSTAINABLE WINERY

Enclosed between the Adriatic coast and the hills, the wide plain that stretches between the provinces of Venice and Treviso has been a land of viticulture for as long as anyone can remember, and responded over time to the production needs of the area's wineries. If in the 1990s it was the land of pinot grigio, today it is the domain of glera. However, some wineries, like Ornella Molon's, remain stubbornly attached to their roots and character, making it one of the most appreciated in the region. The estate's flagship wine, the Rosso di Villa '17, is a monovarietal merlot that matures extensively in the cellar before offering aromas of plum and spices, with a subtle balsamic vein adding a touch of freshness. On the palate, it impresses with power and warmth, highlighting a dense, enveloping taste profile. The Malanotte '16 utilizes a small percentage of dried raboso to enhance the notes of sweet, fleshy dark fruit, which reverberate on the palate, where the wine moves powerfully, well-supported by typical acidity and tannic structure.

○ Valdobbiadene Rive di Col San Martino Brut Cuvée del Fondatore Graziano Merotto '23	♈♈♈ 5	
○ Valdobbiadene Extra Dry Castè '23	♈♈ 4	
○ Cartizze	♈♈ 5	
● Grani Rosa di Pinot Nero Brut	♈♈ 4	
○ Pinot Bianco B. Giussin '22	♈♈ 3	
● Rosso Dogato '20	♈♈ 5	
○ Valdobbiadene Brut Bareta	♈♈ 4	
○ Valdobbiadene Dry La Primavera di Barbara '23	♈♈ 4	
○ Valdobbiadene Extra Brut Integral '23	♈♈ 4	
○ Valdobbiadene Extra Dry Colbelo	♈♈ 4	
○ Valdobbiadene R ive di Col San Martino Brut Cuvée del Fondatore Graziano Merotto '21	♈♈♈ 5	

○ Bianco di Ornella '20	♈♈ 5	
● Piave Malanotte '16	♈♈ 8	
● Piave Merlot Rosso di Villa '17	♈♈ 5	
○ Vite Bianca '22	♈♈ 4	
○ Èros '22	♈ 4	
○ Traminer '23	♈ 3	
○ Bianco di Ornella '18	♈♈ 5	
○ Bianco di Ornella Passito '17	♈♈ 5	
● Piave Malanotte '15	♈♈ 8	
● Piave Merlot Rosso di Villa '15	♈♈ 6	
● Piave Merlot Rosso di Villa Ris. '16	♈♈ 6	
● Piave Raboso Ris. '16	♈♈ 5	
● Venezia Merlot Ris. '18	♈♈ 4	
○ Vite Bianca '20	♈♈ 3	
○ Vite Bianca '19	♈♈ 3	
● Vite Rossa '17	♈♈ 5	

Monte dall'Ora

loc. Castelrotto
via Monte dall'Ora, 5
37029 San Pietro in Cariano [VR]
📞 +39 0457704462
🌐 www.montedallora.com

CELLAR SALES
PRE-BOOKED VISITS
ACCOMMODATION
ANNUAL PRODUCTION 50,000 bottles
HECTARES UNDER VINE 12.50
VITICULTURE METHOD Certified Biodynamic
SUSTAINABLE WINERY

Carlo Venturini and his wife Alessandra run their small family winery on the slopes of Castelrotto. Since its inception in the mid-1990s, the winery has embraced a synergistic relationship with the environment, focusing solely on traditional grape varieties and wines. Unique choices are made in the vineyard, while maintaining an unbreakable bond between each parcel of land and the wine type being produced. It's hard to choose the most convincing wine this year, with labels that skillfully blend quality with a vision of wine that goes beyond mere pleasantness. The Amarone Stropa '15 reveals its complex and layered aromas gradually, starting with overripe red fruit, followed by spice, underbrush, and finally, a medicinal note. On the palate, the fullness finds the right balance with sapidity and delicate tannins. The San Giorgio Alto '19, on the other hand, explores a new concept of Valpolicella Superiore, emphasizing elegance and tension.

● Amarone della Valpolicella Cl. Stropa '15	♟♟	8
● Valpolicella Cl. Sup. San Giorgio Alto '19	♟♟	5
● Valpolicella Cl. Saseti '23	♟♟	4
● Valpolicella Cl. Sup. Camporenzo '21	♟♟	5
● Valpolicella Cl. Sup. Camporenzo '15	♟♟♟	4*
● Valpolicella Cl. Sup. Camporenzo '13	♟♟♟	4*
● Valpolicella Cl. Sup. Camporenzo '11	♟♟♟	4*
● Valpolicella Cl. Sup. Camporenzo '10	♟♟♟	4*
● Valpolicella Cl. Sup. Ripasso Saustò '07	♟♟♟	5
● Valpolicella Cl. Sup. San Giorgio Alto '17	♟♟♟	5
● Amarone della Valpolicella Cl. Stropa '12	♟♟	8
● Recioto della Valpolicella Cl. Sant'Ulderico '15	♟♟	8
● Valpolicella Cl. Sup. Camporenzo '20	♟♟	5
● Valpolicella Cl. Sup. Camporenzo '19	♟♟	4

★Monte del Frà

s.da per Custoza, 35
37066 Sommacampagna [VR]
📞 +39 045510490
🌐 www.montedelfra.it

CELLAR SALES
PRE-BOOKED VISITS
ANNUAL PRODUCTION 1,000,000 bottles
HECTARES UNDER VINE 197.00

The Bonomo family winery has been part of the agricultural fabric of the Custoza hills since the mid-20th century. With the entry of the third generation in the 2000s, the winery took a definitive step forward. Today, the few vineyards around the original cellar have become an impressive estate reaching into the area's most important appellations, from Bardolino to Custoza, Lugana and Valpolicella, naturally. The most interesting wines from the estate hail from the Custoza area, with Ca' del Magro '22 and Bonomo Sexaginta '21 leading the way. The former has become a classic of the appellation, a white that captivates with the breadth and fragrance of its aromas, followed by a classy palate where the fullness finds harmony in acidity and sapid push. The latter explores a lesser-known side of Custoza, where ripe yellow fruit melds with nuances of oak and spices, also found on the palate, where the wine reveals elegance and great consistency.

○ Custoza Sup. Ca' del Magro '22	♟♟♟	4
● Amarone della Valpolicella Cl. Scarnocchio Lena di Mezzo Ris. '18	♟♟	8
○ Custoza Sup. Bonomo Sexaginta '21	♟♟	6
● Bardolino '23	♟♟	2
⊙ Chiaretto di Bardolino '23	♟♟	2
○ Custoza '23	♟♟	2
● Valpolicella Cl. Lena di Mezzo '23	♟♟	3
● Valpolicella Cl. Sup. Lena di Mezzo '22	♟♟	4
● Valpolicella Cl. Sup. Ripasso Lena di Mezzo '22	♟♟	4
○ Custoza Sup. Ca' del Magro '21	♟♟♟	3
○ Custoza Sup. Ca' del Magro '20	♟♟♟	3
○ Custoza Sup. Ca' del Magro '19	♟♟♟	3
○ Custoza Sup. Ca' del Magro '18	♟♟♟	3
○ Custoza Sup. Ca' del Magro '17	♟♟♟	3

Monte Santoccio

loc. Santoccio, 6
37022 Fumane [VR]
☎ +39 3496461223
⊕ www.montesantoccio.it

CELLAR SALES
PRE-BOOKED VISITS
ANNUAL PRODUCTION 55,000 bottles
HECTARES UNDER VINE 7.50

Although Nicola Ferrari founded Monte Santoccio just 15 years ago, his connection to Valpolicella viticulture and winemaking dates back much further. The historical core of the vineyards is located on the limestone hill near Santa Maria Valverde, with additional plots in the more secluded area of the Fumane valley. His wines and grape varieties are tied to tradition, favoring complexity over power. Vintage after vintage, the wines are becoming increasingly focused, combining organoleptic appeal with a deep connection to the land and its traditions. The Amarone '19 is still slightly closed on the nose, but quickly reveals notes of overripe red fruit, medicinal herbs, and spices, which precede a full palate balanced by acidity-driven tension. The Valpolicella Superiore '21 is also excellent, with aromas of wild fruit and pepper that develop into a palate defined by agility.

Monte Tondo

loc. Monte Tondo
via San Lorenzo, 89
37038 Soave [VR]
☎ +39 0457680347
⊕ www.montetondo.it

CELLAR SALES
PRE-BOOKED VISITS
ACCOMMODATION
ANNUAL PRODUCTION 200,000 bottles
HECTARES UNDER VINE 32.00

The Magnabosco family's winery spans both the Soave Classico zone and nearby Valpolicella, with over 30 hectares of vineyards primarily dedicated to the traditional varieties of these two appellations (pinot grigio and Bordeaux varieties are also present). The winery, situated between the towns of Soave and Monteforte d'Alpone, draws on a production style that pursues fullness and pervasiveness of flavor. Among the Soave wines, the standout is Vigna Casette '22, a traditional blend of garganega with a splash of trebbiano di Soave, aged in small wood barrels. It impresses with aromas of ripe yellow fruit and dried flowers. On the palate, the wine showcases great richness, with the acidity-driven push bringing harmony and tension. On the red front, we appreciated the immediacy and clarity of the aromas of the Valpolicella San Pietro '22, with ripe cherry intersected by subtle hints of flowers and pepper, which are mirrored on a palate of good tension and agility.

Wine	Rating
Amarone della Valpolicella Cl. '19	♆♆ 6
Valpolicella Cl. '23	♆♆ 3
Valpolicella Cl. Sup. '21	♆♆ 4
Valpolicella Cl. Sup. Ripasso '21	♆ 4
Amarone della Valpolicella Cl. '18	♆♆ 6
Amarone della Valpolicella Cl. '17	♆♆ 6
Amarone della Valpolicella Cl. '16	♆♆ 6
Amarone della Valpolicella Cl. '15	♆♆ 7
Amarone della Valpolicella Cl. Nicola Ferrari '13	♆♆ 8
Amarone della Valpolicella Cl. Ris. '15	♆♆ 6
Recioto della Valpolicella Cl. '17	♆♆ 5
Valpolicella Cl. Sup. '19	♆♆ 2*
Valpolicella Cl. Sup. '18	♆♆ 2*
Valpolicella Cl. Sup. Ripasso '19	♆♆ 4
Valpolicella Cl. Sup. Ripasso '18	♆♆ 4

Wine	Rating
○ Soave Cl. Foscarino V. Casette '22	♆♆ 4
○ Soave Cl. Monte Tondo '23	♆♆ 2*
● Valpolicella Sup. San Pietro '22	♆♆ 3
○ Soave Brut '23	♆ 3
● Valpolicella Sup. Ripasso Campo Grande '21	♆ 4
○ Soave Cl. Monte Tondo '06	♆♆♆ 2*
○ Soave Cl. Sup. Foscarin Slavinus '20	♆♆ 4
○ Soave Cl. Sup. Foscarin Slavinus '19	♆♆ 4
○ Soave Cl. Sup. Foscarin Slavinus '18	♆♆ 4
○ Soave Cl. Sup. Foscarin Slavinus '17	♆♆ 4

Monte Zovo
Famiglia Cottini

loc. Zovo, 23a
37013 Caprino Veronese [VR]
(☏) +39 0457281301
⊛ www.montezovo.com

CELLAR SALES
PRE-BOOKED VISITS
ACCOMMODATION AND RESTAURANT SERVICE
ANNUAL PRODUCTION 1,000,000 bottles
HECTARES UNDER VINE 170.00
VITICULTURE METHOD Certified Organic
SUSTAINABLE WINERY

Diego Cottini has managed to transform his small family business into a much larger operation that now presides over a large estate, reaching into the Bardolino and Lugana productions zones, as well as Valpolicella, naturally. Alongside Diego are his wife Annalberta and their sons, Michele, who handles the technical management of the cellar, and Mattia, who takes care of hospitality and communications. The Amarone '20 comes from the Tregnago estate, a vast property that rises from 300 to 600 meters in altitude, allowing the grapes to mature while retaining fresh aromas and a good acidic backbone. The nose reveals ripe cherry intertwined with balsamic and peppery notes, echoed on a rich, harmonious palate with a racy finish. From the Civaie estate, situated on clay soils south of Lake Garda, comes a Lugana with fresh fruit and floral aromas that captivate the palate with sapidity and tension.

Cantina Sociale di
Monteforte d'Alpone

via XX Settembre, 24
37032 Monteforte d'Alpone [VR]
(☏) +39 0457610110
⊛ www.cantinadimonteforte.it

CELLAR SALES
PRE-BOOKED VISITS
ANNUAL PRODUCTION 3,000,000 bottles
HECTARES UNDER VINE 1300.00

In recent years, the large cooperative of Monteforte has embarked on a journey to develop its best vineyards, getting the most attentive grower members involved and creating a new range of wines tied to the individual UGA production area of Soave. The vast area cultivated is managed by over 600 members spread throughout the Verona appellation, with only a small part of the grapes ending up in the bottle. The Soave from the Tremenalto vineyards in the northern part of the classic zone excels, utilizing the 2023 harvest to deliver aromas reminiscent of fresh fruit and flowers. On the palate, it reveals its essence, moving with lightness and sapidity, creating a profile that highlights elegance and harmony. The Soave Foscarino '22, on the other hand, presents a complex and evolving aromatic profile, introducing a palate centered around sapidity. The Valpolicella Superiore Clivus is intriguing, a fresh and lively glass.

Wine	Rating
● Amarone della Valpolicella '20	♟♟♟ 8
● Bardolino Montebaldo '20	♟♟ 3
● Calinverno '20	♟♟ 5
○ Lugana Le Civaie Terralbe '23	♟♟ 4
● Amarone della Valpolicella '19	♟♟♟ 8
● Amarone della Valpolicella '18	♟♟♟ 8
● Amarone della Valpolicella '17	♟♟♟ 8
● Amarone della Valpolicella '16	♟♟♟ 8
● Amarone della Valpolicella '15	♟♟♟ 8
● Amarone della Valpolicella '14	♟♟♟ 8
● Amarone della Valpolicella '13	♟♟ 7
● Ca' Linverno '14	♟♟ 4
● Calinverno '15	♟♟ 5
○ Lugana Le Civaie Terralbe '22	♟♟ 4
○ Lugana Le Civaie Terralbe Ris. '19	♟♟ 5
● Valpolicella Sup. Ripasso '21	♟♟ 5

Wine	Rating
○ Soave Cl. Tremenalto '23	♟♟
○ Soave Cl. Foscarino '22	♟♟
● Valpolicella Sup. Clivus '22	♟♟
● Valpolicella Ripasso Clivus '21	♟
○ Soave Cl. Sup. Vign. di Castellaro '15	♟♟♟
○ Soave Cl. Clivus '20	♟♟
○ Soave Cl. Foscarino '21	♟♟
○ Soave Cl. Foscarino '19	♟♟
○ Soave Cl. Il Vicario '20	♟♟
○ Soave Cl. Il Vicario '19	♟♟
○ Soave Cl. Sup. Castellaro '21	♟♟
○ Soave Cl. Sup. Castellaro '20	♟♟
○ Soave Cl. Sup. Castellaro '19	♟♟
○ Soave Cl. Sup. Monte Grande '21	♟♟
○ Soave Cl. Sup. Tremenalto '22	♟♟
○ Soave Cl. Sup. Tremenalto '21	♟♟

Montegrande - Cristofanon

via Torre, 2
35030 Rovolon [PD]
☎ +39 0495226276
🌐 www.vinimontegrande.it

CELLAR SALES
PRE-BOOKED VISITS
ANNUAL PRODUCTION 250,000 bottles
HECTARES UNDER VINE 35.00

The Euganean Hills, which span 19,000 hectares south of Padua, are a dense cluster of slopes formed by underwater volcanic activity. Within the namesake regional park, viticulture and olive growing are widespread, in a landscape where forests and natural vegetation still play a leading role. Raffaele and Paola Cristofanon manage the family winery with the valuable help of the new generation. The Ottomano is a classic Bordeaux blend made from grapes grown in the Rovolon area, on the northwestern slope of the appellation. It opens with intense aromas ranging from sweet fruit to spices, but it's on the palate that it truly reveals its personality. The impact is rich and powerful, supported by a close-knit tannic structure that gives the wine rigor and energy. In contrast, the profile of the Borgomoro, a blend of cabernet sauvignon and cabernet franc, is appreciated for its clear fruitiness and the dynamic palate, driven by a lively acidity.

Colli Euganei Cabernet Borgomoro '22	🍷🍷 2*
Colli Euganei Merlot Corterocco '22	🍷🍷 2*
Colli Euganei Merlot Luigi Cristofanon Ris. '18	🍷🍷 5
Colli Euganei Rosso Momi '22	🍷🍷 2*
Colli Euganei Rosso Ottomano Ris. '18	🍷🍷 5
Colli Euganei Bianco Erto '23	🍷 2
Colli Euganei Fior d'Arancio Spumante Dolce '23	🍷 2
Colli Euganei Serprino Extra Dry	🍷 2
Colli Euganei Cabernet Borgomoro '21	🍷🍷 2*
Colli Euganei Cabernet Sereo Ris. '18	🍷🍷 4
Colli Euganei Merlot Corterocco '21	🍷🍷 2*
Colli Euganei Rosso Momi '21	🍷🍷 2*
Colli Euganei Rosso V. delle Roche Ris. '18	🍷🍷 5

Montelvini

fraz. Venegazzù
via Cal Trevigiana, 51
31040 Volpago del Montello [TV]
☎ +39 04238777
🌐 www.montelvini.it

CELLAR SALES
ANNUAL PRODUCTION 6,000,000 bottles
HECTARES UNDER VINE 35.00
SUSTAINABLE WINERY

The success that has swept through the world of Prosecco has seen many wineries chasing the market, often more concerned with numbers and prices than quality. Sarah and Alberto Serena, on the other hand, have used this moment to consolidate their market presence while adapting their production approach so that quality is closely linked to the Asolo terroir. Hence the decision to strengthen their ties with a large group of independent growers. The Brut FM333 confirms its status as a thoroughbred, a sparkling wine that doesn't rely on explosive aromas but rather on their breadth, revealing itself little by little: first with white fruit, then with floral memories, and finally a subtle green note that adds freshness and unpredictability. The palate is crisp, caressed by the bubbles, and reveals all the sapidity and acidic energy typical of the Asolo area. The Manzoni Bianco Zuitèr '22 is very good, with a seductive expression of citrus and floral notes, developing into a juicy palate with an irresistible drinkability.

○ Asolo Brut Serenitatis FM333 '23	🍷🍷 4
○ Asolo Brut Serenitatis	🍷🍷 3
○ Asolo Extra Brut Serenitatis '23	🍷🍷 3
○ Asolo Extra Dry Serenitatis	🍷🍷 3
○ Montello Asolo Manzoni Bianco Zuitér '22	🍷🍷 3
○ Asolo Brut Nature Sui Lieviti Il Brutto '22	🍷 3
○ Delle Venezie Pinot Grigio S. Osvaldo '23	🍷 2
○ Lison S. Osvaldo '23	🍷 2
⊙ Prosecco di Treviso Brut Rosè '23	🍷 3
○ Asolo Brut	🍷🍷 3
○ Asolo Brut FM333 '22	🍷🍷 4
○ Asolo Brut Serenitatis FM 333 '21	🍷🍷 4
○ Asolo Extra Brut '22	🍷🍷 3
○ Asolo Extra Dry	🍷🍷 3

Monteversa
via Monte Versa, 1024
35030 Vo' [PD]
(☎) +39 0499941092
⊛ www.monteversa.it

Giacomo Montresor
via Ca' di Cozzi, 16
37124 Verona
(☎) +39 045913399
⊛ www.vinimontresor.it

CELLAR SALES
PRE-BOOKED VISITS
ANNUAL PRODUCTION 23,000 bottles
HECTARES UNDER VINE 17.00
VITICULTURE METHOD Certified Organic

PRE-BOOKED VISITS
ANNUAL PRODUCTION 2,500,000 bottles
HECTARES UNDER VINE 150.00

Monte Versa is a gentle ridge extending westward in the southernmost part of the Euganean Hills. The area, densely planted with vines, benefits from a particularly warm climate that ensures optimal ripening of Bordeaux varieties. The Voltazza family's winery is located here, with vineyards carefully structured to place the heat-loving varieties on the south-facing slope and the white grapes facing north. The Cabernet Sauvignon '20 debuts with sweet, crunchy dark fruit that highlights the youthfulness of the wine, followed by an intense note of graphite and gradually by hints of underbrush and damp earth. The palate is energetic, compact with tannins, but relaxes on the backbone of acidity that accompanies the finish. The Animaversa '23, a Manzoni Bianco, showcases an intense note of ripe yellow-fleshed fruit that carries through to the palate, where the wine reveals fullness and great harmony.

With the entry of the Cevico group in 2018, this historic Veronese winery underwent a profound transformation, further tying itself to the Valpolicella region. After renovating the cellar and establishing an enchanting wine museum, Montresor focused on viticulture, developing a collaboration with a prominent estate in the Classica zone, which brought a vast area under vines. The Valpolicella Capitel della Crosara '23 represents the new stylistic direction of the Ca' di Cozzi winery, a glass that enhances the character of traditional grapes by elevating their aromatic expression, where cherry notes are echoed by spicy and herbal suggestions. On the palate, it is crisp, highlighting the acidic tension that extends and tightens the sip. The Amarone '21 plays a different game, linking its appeal to the richness of overripe fruit, which is clearly discernible on the nose, and the generosity of the palate.

● Colli Euganei Cabernet Sauvignon '20	♟♟ 4
○ Animaversa '23	♟♟ 5
● Colli Euganei Rosso Versacinto '21	♟♟ 3
○ Versavò '23	♟♟ 2*
● Vo'lare '23	♟♟ 3
○ Tai '21	♟ 4
● Colli Euganei Cabernet Animaversa '12	♟♟ 4
● Colli Euganei Cabernet Sauvignon '19	♟♟ 4
● Colli Euganei Cabernet Sauvignon Animaversa '18	♟♟ 4
○ Colli Euganei Manzoni Bianco Animaversa '17	♟♟ 3
● Colli Euganei Rosso Animaversa '16	♟♟ 4
● Colli Euganei Rosso Animaversa '13	♟♟ 4
● Colli Euganei Rosso Animaversa '11	♟♟ 4
● Colli Euganei Rosso Versacinto '19	♟♟ 3
● Colli Euganei Rosso Versacinto '18	♟♟ 3

● Amarone della Valpolicella '21	♟♟ 5
● Valpolicella Cl. Capitel della Crosara '23	♟♟ 2
● Valpolicella Ripasso Capitel della Crosara '21	♟♟
● Amarone della Valpolicella '19	♟♟
● Amarone della Valpolicella Cl. Capitel della Crosara '16	♟♟
● Amarone della Valpolicella Cl. Capitel della Crosara '09	♟♟
● Amarone della Valpolicella Cl. Capitel della Crosara '08	♟♟
● Amarone della Valpolicella Cl. Castelliere delle Guaite '07	♟♟
● Amarone della Valpolicella Fondatore Giacomo Montresor '09	♟♟
● Amarone della Valpolicella Il Fondatore '08	♟♟

Le Morette

fraz. San Benedetto di Lugana
v.le Indipendenza, 19d
37019 Peschiera del Garda [VR]
(+39 0457552724
www.lemorette.it

CELLAR SALES
PRE-BOOKED VISITS
ANNUAL PRODUCTION 450,000 bottles
HECTARES UNDER VINE 40.00
SUSTAINABLE WINERY

The Zenato brothers lead one of the most important wineries in the southern Garda area, with around 40 hectares mostly dedicated to Lugana. Their deep knowledge of the territory and even deeper understanding of the varietal, thanks to their historic nursery activities, have allowed Paolo and Fabio to produce wines of great qualitative consistency, with lugana as the star, followed by smaller quantities of bardolino. The wines from Le Mandolare continue to impress, focusing on the production of white wines from the lake area while not neglecting the Bardolino appellation. However, it's the Riserva Valerio Zenato '21 that takes the lead, a Lugana of absolute value, offering subtle aromas of white fruit and flint, gradually opening to more mature and inviting tones. On the palate, it impresses with how it combines richness, elegance, and tension, resulting in great pleasure. The Mandolara '23, more immediately expressive and fragrant, is appreciated for its dynamism and juiciness.

Lugana Valerio Zenato Ris. '21	♟♟ 4
Bardolino Cl. '23	♟♟ 2*
Brut M. Cl. Trentaseimesi	♟♟ 5
Chiaretto di Bardolino Cl. '23	♟♟ 2*
Lugana Benedictus '22	♟♟ 3
Lugana Mandolara '23	♟♟ 3
Chiaretto di Bardolino Brut Cépage	♟ 2
Lugana Benedictus '19	♟♟♟ 3*
Bardolino Cl. '22	♟♟ 2*
Chiaretto di Bardolino Cl. '22	♟♟ 2*
Lugana Benedictus '21	♟♟ 3*
Lugana Benedictus '20	♟♟ 3*
Lugana Mandolara '22	♟♟ 3
Lugana Mandolara '21	♟♟ 3
Lugana Ris. '20	♟♟ 4
Lugana Ris. '19	♟♟ 4

Marco Mosconi

via Paradiso, 5
37031 Illasi [VR]
(+39 0456529109
www.marcomosconi.it

CELLAR SALES
PRE-BOOKED VISITS
ANNUAL PRODUCTION 25,000 bottles
HECTARES UNDER VINE 10.00

Marco Mosconi's winery lies in the heart of Val d'Illasi, where the vineyards gradually climb from the valley floor toward the nearby hills. Here, the Valpolicella and Soave appellations vie for the best exposures. With around 10 hectares dedicated almost exclusively to the area's classic grapes, the winery has, over the years, adopted an increasingly delicate and non-invasive approach to viticulture and production, resulting in wines of great character. The Amarone '17 is the result of a careful selection of grapes for drying, harvested from estate vineyards located between 250 and 300 meters above sea level. After spontaneous fermentation, it undergoes a long maturation in large oak barrels, allowing the wine to express itself with tones of sweet, overripe fruit, spices, and a lovely balsamic nuance. The palate is full and generous, accompanied by a vital acidic drive. A fresher and more intact fruit characterizes the Valpolicella Montecurto '23, juicy and with irresistible drinkability.

● Amarone della Valpolicella '17	♟♟ 8
○ Bucce '23	♟♟ 4
● Valpolicella Montecurto '23	♟♟ 3
● Valpolicella Sup. '19	♟♟ 5
○ Soave Paradiso '23	♟ 2
● Valpolicella Sup. '13	♟♟♟ 5
● Valpolicella Sup. '12	♟♟♟ 5
● Amarone della Valpolicella '16	♟♟ 8
● Amarone della Valpolicella '15	♟♟ 8
● Amarone della Valpolicella '13	♟♟ 8
● Amarone della Valpolicella '12	♟♟ 8
● Valpolicella Montecurto '22	♟♟ 3
● Valpolicella Sup. '17	♟♟ 5
● Valpolicella Sup. '15	♟♟ 5
● Valpolicella Sup. '14	♟♟ 5
● Valpolicella Sup. '11	♟♟ 5

Mosole

loc. Corbolone
via Annone Veneto, 60
30029 Santo Stino di Livenza [VE]
☎ +39 0421310404
www.mosole.com

CELLAR SALES
PRE-BOOKED VISITS
ANNUAL PRODUCTION 250,000 bottles
HECTARES UNDER VINE 30.00
SUSTAINABLE WINERY

Over more than 30 harvests, Lucio Mosole has developed a profound understanding of his territory, with clays stretching between the Adriatic coast to the south and the pre-Alps to the north. Here, international varieties have found a home for over a century, and Lucio interprets them, favoring elegance over fullness, with wines that now emphasize varietal freshness, now the complexity and connection between vineyard and varietal. The Merlot Ad Nonam '20 is still resting in the cellar, but the lineup presented this year didn't make us miss it. Hora Prima '22 is a noble white, the result of a blend of chardonnay, which matures in oak, and tai with a splash of sauvignon, both aged in steel. The result offers aromas of fresh fruits and flowers with a subtle iodine and citrus vein in the background, even more evident on the palate, where the wine reveals extraordinary elegance and length. The Cabernet Hora Sexta '19, on the other hand, alternates fruit notes with spices and offers a dynamic, energetic sip.

○ Hora Prima '22	▼▼ 7
● Venezia Cabernet Hora Sexta '19	▼▼ 4
○ Ad Nonam Passito '20	▼▼ 6
○ Venezia Bianco Eleo '21	▼▼ 3
○ Venezia Chardonnay '23	▼▼ 3
○ Venezia Pinot Grigio '23	▼▼ 3
● Venezia Refosco P.R. '22	▼▼ 3
○ Venezia Tai '23	▼▼ 3
○ Ribolla Gialla '23	▼ 3
● Venezia Cabernet Franc '22	▼ 3
● Venezia Merlot '22	▼ 3
○ Venezia Sauvignon '23	▼ 3
○ Hora Prima '18	▽▽▽ 5
○ Hora Prima '21	▽▽ 5
● Venezia Merlot Ad Nonam '19	▽▽ 6
● Venezia Refosco P.R. '21	▽▽ 3

Il Mottolo

loc. Le Contarine
via Comezzara, 13
35030 Baone [PD]
☎ +39 3479456155
www.ilmottolo.it

CELLAR SALES
PRE-BOOKED VISITS
ANNUAL PRODUCTION 35,000 bottles
HECTARES UNDER VINE 8.50

The southern part of the Euganean Hills is characterized by a warm and dry climate, significantly different from the surrounding areas Here, red Bordeaux grapes ripen consistently, and the most astute producers create wines of great character. Among them are certainly Sergio Fortin and Roberto Dalla Libera, who, with Mottolo, have established one of the region's most intriguing wineries. The Serro '21 is a Bordeaux blend dominated by merlot, captivating with its broad aromas where fruit takes the lead but also leaves room for herbal notes, graphite, and an intriguing hint of macerated leaves. The palate is full, juicy, and satisfying. The Baciorosso '21 follows a similar interpretation but appears more youthful, while the Costalupa '20, a blend of cabernet sauvignon and cabernet franc with a slight predominance of the former, follows its intensely fruity and balsamic aromas with a sip that is almost gruff in its tannic structure yet full of character, finding harmony and length through its acidic drive.

● Colli euganei Cabernet Costalupa '20	▼▼ 6
● Colli Euganei Rosso Baciorosso '21	▼▼ 3
● Colli Euganei Rosso Serro '21	▼▼ 4
● A Marè Cabernet '22	▼▼ 3
● Colli Euganei Carménère Vinànima '21	▼▼ 5
● Colli Euganei Merlot '22	▼▼ 3
○ Le Contarine '22	▼▼ 2
● Pinot Nero '21	▼▼ 4
● Colli Euganei Rosso Serro '16	▽▽▽ 4
● Colli Euganei Rosso Serro '11	▽▽▽ 3
● Colli Euganei Rosso Serro '10	▽▽▽ 3
● Colli Euganei Rosso Serro '09	▽▽▽ 3
● Colli Euganei Cabernet Costalupa '19	▽▽ 6
● Colli Euganei Carménère Vinànima '20	▽▽ 5
● Colli Euganei Merlot '21	▽▽ 3
● Colli Euganei Rosso Serro '20	▽▽ 4

Tenuta Mulin di Mezzo

via Molin di Mezzo, 16
30020 Annone Veneto [VE]
(☏) +39 0422 769398
⊛ www.mulindimezzo.com

PRE-BOOKED VISITS
ANNUAL PRODUCTION 40,000 bottles
HECTARES UNDER VINE 6.00

Paolo Lazzarin's winery covers just a few hectares on the Venetian plains, a stone's throw from the Friuli border. The soil here is a mix of gravel, clay, and ancient limestone. The Adriatic Sea lies just a few kilometers to the south, with the Pre-Alps to the north, creating a territory that has fostered quality viticulture for decades. A meticulous focus on grape ripening, combined with a production approach that respects the character of the fruit, results in a rich style of wine. The proximity to the Friuli region influences both the choice of grape varieties and the wine style, as evidenced by the Lison '23 tasting, with its intense notes of yellow fruit intersecting with Mediterranean scrub and an intriguing iodine hint. On the palate, it is rich, full, and supported by a vigorous acidic presence that gives the drink a lively character. The Chardonnay '23, on the other hand, offers a more elegant and clear fruit expression, delivering a sip of good concentration and tension.

Nardello

via IV Novembre, 56
37032 Monteforte d'Alpone [VR]
(☏) +39 0457612116
⊛ www.nardellovini.it

CELLAR SALES
PRE-BOOKED VISITS
ANNUAL PRODUCTION 80,000 bottles
HECTARES UNDER VINE 14.00
SUSTAINABLE WINERY

Often, agricultural estates were once farms that over time gained in importance and size. In the case of Nardello, Federica and Daniele Nardello were the main architects of this transformation, which began at the turn of the new millennium with the construction of the cellar. The vineyards, all of old planting, lie on the southern hills of the Soave Classica zone. From the vineyards on Monte Zoppega come the grapes for the winery's most ambitious wine, the eponymous Soave '21, which matures in oak before offering its aromas of ripe yellow fruit and dried flowers. On the palate, the sunny, Mediterranean character of the region emerges, and the wine reveals a rich and enveloping profile. The Turbian from the following harvest, on the other hand, benefits from the presence of trebbiano di Soave in the blend and the maturation entirely in steel, enhancing the fresher and more floral notes and developing a more streamlined and supple gustatory dynamic.

○ Lison Cl. '23	♟♟ 4
● Lison Pramaggiore Merlot '21	♟♟ 4
● Rosso Molino '21	♟♟ 5
● Venezia Cabernet Sauvignon '20	♟♟ 3
○ Venezia Chardonnay '23	♟♟ 3
● Il Priore '19	♟ 6
○ Sauvignon '23	♟ 4
● Venezia Cabernet Franc '22	♟ 3
○ Lison Cl. '22	♟♟ 4
○ Lison Cl. '21	♟♟ 3
● Lison Pramaggiore Cabernet Franc '20	♟♟ 4
○ Lison Pramaggiore Chardonnay '20	♟♟ 2*
● Lison Pramaggiore Merlot '19	♟♟ 3
● Lison Pramaggiore Merlot '18	♟♟ 3
● Lison Pramaggiore Merlot '16	♟♟ 2*

○ Soave Cl. Monte Zoppega '21	♟♟ 5
○ Recioto di Soave Suavissimus '19	♟♟ 4
○ Soave Cl. Meridies '23	♟♟ 3
○ Soave Cl. Turbian '22	♟♟ 4
○ Soave Cl. Meridies '22	♟♟ 3*
○ Soave Cl. Meridies '21	♟♟ 3
○ Soave Cl. Meridies '20	♟♟ 3
○ Soave Cl. Monte Zoppega '20	♟♟ 5
○ Soave Cl. Monte Zoppega '19	♟♟ 5
○ Soave Cl. Monte Zoppega '18	♟♟ 4
○ Soave Cl. Monte Zoppega '17	♟♟ 4
○ Soave Cl. Monte Zoppega '16	♟♟ 4
○ Soave Cl. Turbian '21	♟♟ 4
○ Soave Cl. Turbian '20	♟♟ 4
○ Soave Cl. Turbian '19	♟♟ 3
○ Soave Cl. V. Turbian '17	♟♟ 3*

Nicolis

via Villa Girardi, 29
37029 San Pietro in Cariano [VR]
☎ +39 0457701261
✸ www.vininicolis.com

CELLAR SALES
PRE-BOOKED VISITS
ANNUAL PRODUCTION 220,000 bottles
HECTARES UNDER VINE 49.00
SUSTAINABLE WINERY

For more than 70 years, the Nicolis family has dedicated itself to viticulture. Today, alongside Giuseppe, we find his children Angelo and Sofia managing the winery. The extensive estate extends into the Valpolicella Classic zone, enabling a range closely tied to tradition. The cellar, which is located along the valley floor of San Pietro in Cariano, allows for lengthy aging of the wines, which are only released after an adequate period of time. The Amarone Ambrosan Riserva 2017 is a wine produced only in the finest vintages. After lengthy maturation in large barrels and barriques, it offers a subtle, reserved aromatic profile, with sweet, ripe fruit echoed by balsamic notes, signature pepper tones, and a lovely mineral note. All this carries over on the palate, which opens full and weighty, but gains tension and suppleness thanks to a pronounced acidity. In contrast, the Amarone '19 impresses with its solid structure and harmonious balance, dominated by herbal notes.

● Amarone della Valpolicella Cl. Ambrosan Ris. '17	♟♟ 8
● Amarone della Valpolicella Cl. '19	♟♟ 7
○ Lugana '23	♟♟ 3
● Valpolicella Cl. '23	♟♟ 3
● Amarone della Valpolicella Cl. Ambrosan '06	♟♟♟ 7
● Amarone della Valpolicella Cl. Ambrosan '98	♟♟♟ 7
● Amarone della Valpolicella Cl. Ambrosan '93	♟♟♟ 6
● Amarone della Valpolicella Cl. '17	♟♟ 7
● Amarone della Valpolicella Cl. Ambrosan '11	♟♟ 8
● Amarone della Valpolicella Cl. Ambrosan '09	♟♟ 7

Novaia

via Novaia, 1
37020 Marano di Valpolicella [VR]
☎ +39 0457755129
✸ www.novaia.it

CELLAR SALES
PRE-BOOKED VISITS
ANNUAL PRODUCTION 50,000 bottles
HECTARES UNDER VINE 8.00
VITICULTURE METHOD Certified Organic
SUSTAINABLE WINERY

The Vaona family's winery, a beautiful 15th-century villa surrounded by vineyards, is somewhat secluded in the highest part of the Marano valley. The new cellar, built about 10 years ago a few meters from the historic site, hosts all phases of production, allowing cousins Cristina and Marcello to produce according to a traditional approach. The utmost care is given to the vineyards, as evidenced by their premium wines. This year the Vaona family's wines impressed across the board, even if there's no standout star. The Recioto Le Novaje '22 generously reveals intense aromas of sweet, ripe fruit, enhanced by balsamic accents that lend freshness. On the palate, its sweetness is prominent, but the grape's trademark acidity adds lightness and tension. The Amarone Corte Vaona '19 summons complex aromas of red fruit preserves and spices, followed by a dry, energetic palate that concludes with a pleasing tobacco note.

● Amarone della Valpolicella Cl. Corte Vaona '19	♟♟ 7
● Fapulito '23	♟♟ 3
● Recioto della Valpolicella Cl. Le Novaje '22	♟♟ 6
● Valpolicella Cl. '23	♟♟ 3
● Valpolicella Cl. Sup. I Cantoni '21	♟♟ 5
● Valpolicella Cl. Sup. Ripasso '21	♟♟ 4
● Amarone della Valpolicella Cl. '17	♟♟ 5
● Amarone della Valpolicella Cl. '16	♟♟ 5
● Amarone della Valpolicella Cl. Corte Vaona '18	♟♟ 7
● Amarone della Valpolicella Cl. Corte Vaona '15	♟♟ 6
● Valpolicella Cl. '22	♟♟ 3
● Valpolicella Cl. Fapulito '22	♟♟ 3

★Ottella

fraz. San Benedetto di Lugana
loc. Ottella
37019 Peschiera del Garda [VR]
📞 +39 0457551950
🌐 www.ottella.it

CELLAR SALES
PRE-BOOKED VISITS
ACCOMMODATION
ANNUAL PRODUCTION 600,000 bottles
HECTARES UNDER VINE 90.00

Francesco and Michele Montresor have realized their dream of giving their winery a true home: a cellar built from an old storage space, now one of the region's most beautiful wine structures to visit. The attention given to the construction and furnishing of the cellar reflects the emphasis on quality here, both in terms of cultivation of the grapes and production itself. The focus is primarily on lugana but nearby territories are also referenced in their range. The Molceo Lugana Riserva has established a signature style over the years—one characterized by aromatic depth, richness, and tension on the palate. The 2022 emphasizes the warmth of the vintage with a swirl of fruit that gives way to fresher floral and citrus notes. On the palate, it reveals an extraordinary youthfulness, moving with suppleness, perfectly supported by its sapidity. The Le Creete '23 plays on intense vegetal and exotic notes, sensations that are also vividly present on a dry, juicy palate.

○ Lugana Molceo Ris. '22	▼▼▼ 4*
○ Lugana Le Creete '23	▼▼ 4
○ Lugana '23	▼ 3
○ Lugana Molceo Ris. '21	♈♈♈ 4*
○ Lugana Molceo Ris. '20	♈♈♈ 4*
○ Lugana Molceo Ris. '19	♈♈♈ 4*
○ Lugana Molceo Ris. '18	♈♈♈ 4*
○ Lugana Molceo Ris. '17	♈♈♈ 4*
○ Lugana Molceo Ris. '16	♈♈♈ 4*
○ Lugana Molceo Ris. '15	♈♈♈ 4*
○ Lugana Molceo Ris. '14	♈♈♈ 4*
○ Lugana Molceo Ris. '13	♈♈♈ 4*
○ Lugana Molceo Ris. '12	♈♈♈ 4*
○ Lugana Sup. Molceo '11	♈♈♈ 4*
○ Lugana Sup. Molceo '10	♈♈♈ 4*
○ Lugana Sup. Molceo '09	♈♈♈ 4

★Pasqua

loc. San Felice Extra
via Belvedere, 135
37131 Verona
📞 +39 0458432111
🌐 www.pasqua.it

CELLAR SALES
PRE-BOOKED VISITS
ANNUAL PRODUCTION 12,800,000 bottles
HECTARES UNDER VINE 322.00
SUSTAINABLE WINERY

In the world of Veronese wine, Pasqua is increasingly a leading winery, a producer that has seized challenges and turned them into a springboard for its activity. Much credit goes to Riccardo Pasqua, who surrounded himself with competent and passionate collaborators who have played a crucial role in the transformation. There is a strong focus on Valpolicella classics, but you'll find more original interpretations as well. The Mai Dire Mai '16 benefited from another year in the cellar, making it one of the most intriguing interpretations of Amarone. It sees intense aromas of sweet, ripe dark fruit followed by herbal and peppery notes, sensations mirrored on the palate, where it shows compactness and tension. The Amarone Famiglia Pasqua '20 is more immediately expressive, pervasive and sapid, while Hey French, a blend of different grapes and vintages now in its fourth edition, evokes intricate aromas and a juicy, compelling profile.

● Amarone della Valpolicella Mai Dire Mai '16	▼▼▼ 8
● Amarone della Valpolicella Famiglia Pasqua '20	▼▼ 8
○ Hey French Ed.4	▼▼ 6
● Mai Dire Mai Fear No Dark '20	▼▼ 8
○ Soave Cl. Brognoligo Cecilia Beretta '23	▼▼ 3
● Valpolicella Superiore Mizzole Cecilia Beretta '19	▼▼ 5
● Amarone della Valpolicella Cascina San Vincenzo Famiglia Pasqua '18	♈♈♈ 8
● Amarone della Valpolicella Famiglia Pasqua Ris. '13	♈♈♈ 6
● Amarone della Valpolicella Mai Dire Mai '15	♈♈♈ 8
● Amarone della Valpolicella Mai Dire Mai '13	♈♈♈ 8

VENETO

★★★Pieropan

via Matteotti
37038 Soave [VR]
+39 0456190171
www.pieropan.it

CELLAR SALES
PRE-BOOKED VISITS
ANNUAL PRODUCTION 680,000 bottles
HECTARES UNDER VINE 75.00
VITICULTURE METHOD Certified Organic

Talking about Pieropan is a bit like talking about the history of Soave and Italian white wine. As early as the 1970s, the producer indicated the vineyard of origin on their labels. Today, Andrea and Dario continue the path set by their father Nino, with the same passion and attention to detail. The new cellar, perfectly integrated into the vineyard landscape behind the castle, gives rise to a first-rate range. Once again, the Calvarino and La Rocca lead Pieropan's lineup, this year with the 2022 vintage. The Calvarino, a blend that includes trebbiano di Soave, opens on intense aromas—floral and citrus notes meeting white fruit—before revealing a juicy, dynamic palate. La Rocca, a monovarietal garganega matured in oak, features beautifully mature fruit and spices, with a rich, juicy palate of impressive length. The Amarone Riserva '18 proves deep in its mineral and spicy expression.

○ Soave Cl. Calvarino '22	🍷🍷🍷 5
○ Soave Cl. La Rocca '22	🍷🍷 6
● Amarone della Valpolicella Ris. '18	🍷🍷 7
○ Recioto di Soave Cl. Le Colombare '20	🍷🍷 5
○ Soave Cl. '23	🍷🍷 3
● Valpolicella Sup. Ruberpan '21	🍷🍷 4
○ Soave Cl. Calvarino '21	🍷🍷🍷 5
○ Soave Cl. Calvarino '19	🍷🍷🍷 4*
○ Soave Cl. Calvarino '18	🍷🍷🍷 4*
○ Soave Cl. Calvarino '17	🍷🍷🍷 4*
○ Soave Cl. Calvarino '16	🍷🍷🍷 4*
○ Soave Cl. Calvarino '15	🍷🍷🍷 4*
○ Soave Cl. Calvarino '13	🍷🍷🍷 4*
○ Soave Cl. La Rocca '20	🍷🍷🍷 5
○ Soave Cl. La Rocca '14	🍷🍷🍷 5

Il Pignetto

loc. Pigneto
37012 Bussolengo [VR]
+39 0457151232
www.cantinailpignetto.com

CELLAR SALES
PRE-BOOKED VISITS
ACCOMMODATION
ANNUAL PRODUCTION 50,000 bottles
HECTARES UNDER VINE 8.00
SUSTAINABLE WINERY

Though the Morando family winery was officially founded in 1993, their relationship with viticulture on the morainic hills of southern Garda is far older, intertwined with the family's very way of life. Today, Adriano is joined by his daughter Silvia, a winemaker who has taken over the technical management of the cellar, while her father continues to oversee all viticultural activities. Production is closely tied to the wines of Bardolino and Custoza, interpreted here with a refined style. The estate's standout wine is the Custoza 218 (named after the parcel's registered number in the county records). The 2022 harvest endowed the wine with intense fruity sensations, with a hint of minerality that has yet to fully develop but is more pronounced on its energetic, sapid palate. From the same vintage, the Bardolino Sommacampagna, a traditional blend of corvina, rondinella, and a splash of sangiovese, offers subtle aromas but captivates with a solid, lingering palate.

○ Custoza 218 '22	🍷🍷 3*
● Bardolino Sommacampagna '22	🍷🍷 4
⊙ Chiaretto di Bardolino '23	🍷🍷 2*
○ Custoza '23	🍷🍷 2*
● Bardolino '23	🍷 2
● Bardolino '20	🍷🍷 2*
⊙ Bardolino Chiaretto '16	🍷🍷 2*
● Bardolino Sommacampagna '21	🍷🍷 4
⊙ Chiaretto di Bardolino Le Morandine '21	🍷🍷 3
⊙ Chiaretto di Bardolino Le Morandine '20	🍷🍷 2*
○ Custoza 218 '21	🍷🍷 3
○ Custoza 218 '15	🍷🍷 3

Piovene Porto Godi

fraz. Toara
via Villa, 14
36021 Villaga [VI]
(» +39 0444885142
⊕ www.piovene.com

CELLAR SALES
PRE-BOOKED VISITS
ACCOMMODATION
ANNUAL PRODUCTION 120,000 bottles
HECTARES UNDER VINE 41.00
SUSTAINABLE WINERY

Tomaso Piovene Porto Godi's winery is one of
the most intriguing in the Berico area, sprawling
across many hectares, though only part of it is
dedicated to viticulture. The best parcels allow
the grapes to mature while retaining freshness
and finesse. Tomaso, along with his children
Emanuele and Alessandra, manages the winery,
which focuses on Bordeaux varietals and tai
rosso. The Vigneto Riveselle '23, a Tai Rosso,
shows a promising path for this fragrant grape
from the Berici Hills. Without sacrificing
lightness and immediate appeal, it offers a
multifaceted aromatic profile and a juicy,
satisfying palate, leaning more on sapidity than
acidity. The Fra I Broli '21 expresses the deep
connection between this warm land and the
bordeaux varietal, highlighting its sweet, fleshy
fruit, which develops and unfolds into a dense,
close-knit palate perfectly supported by smooth,
sweet tones.

★Graziano Prà

via della Fontana, 31
37032 Monteforte d'Alpone [VR]
(» +39 0457612125
⊕ www.vinipra.it

CELLAR SALES
PRE-BOOKED VISITS
ACCOMMODATION
ANNUAL PRODUCTION 410,000 bottles
HECTARES UNDER VINE 50.00
VITICULTURE METHOD Certified Organic
SUSTAINABLE WINERY

Graziano Prà deftly navigates the Soave and
Valpolicella appellations, taking unique paths that
bring out the bond between wine and its terroir.
His whites offer aromatic breadth and density,
while his Valpolicella wines highlight the refined,
subtle characteristics that traditional grapes can
provide. This year the Soave Wild '23 made its
debut. Ponsara, a basaltic hill from which the
grapes are sourced, imparts intense aromas of
white fruit and flowers, which resonate on a
highly enjoyable palate. However, the estate's
true stars are the Monte Grande '22 and Vigna
Colle Sant'Antonio '19. The Monte Grande is a
classic of the appellation, a white with intricate
aromas where fruit, flowers, and citrus hints
blend perfectly, leading to a sapid palate of great
length. The Vigna Colle Sant'Antonio, on the
other hand, ages at length in the cellar before
revealing its yellow fruit and spice aromas,
sensations echoed on a full, pervasive palate.

VENETO

● Colli Berici Merlot Fra i Broli '21	♟♟ 4
● Colli Berici Tai Rosso Vign. Riveselle '23	♟♟ 3*
● Colli Berici Cabernet Pozzare '21	♟♟ 4
○ Colli Berici Sauvignon Fostine '23	♟♟ 3
● Colli Berici Tai Rosso Thovara '21	♟♟ 5
● Polveriera '22	♟♟ 3
○ Sauvignon Campigie '22	♟ 3
● Colli Berici Cabernet Vign. Pozzare '12	♟♟♟ 4*
● Colli Berici Cabernet Vign. Pozzare '07	♟♟♟ 3
● Colli Berici Cabernet Pozzare '20	♟♟ 4
● Colli Berici Merlot Fra i Broli '19	♟♟ 4
● Colli Berici Tai Rosso Thovara '19	♟♟ 5
● Colli Berici Tai Rosso Vign. Riveselle '22	♟♟ 3*

○ Soave Cl. Monte Grande '22	♟♟♟ 5
○ Soave Cl.V. Colle Sant'Antonio '19	♟♟ 7
○ Soave Cl. Otto '23	♟♟ 3
○ Soave Cl. Ponsara Wild '23	♟♟ 4
● Valpolicella Sup. Morandina '20	♟♟ 7
● Valpolicella Sup. Ripasso Morandina '21	♟ 5
○ Soave Cl. Monte Grande '21	♟♟♟ 5
○ Soave Cl. Monte Grande '16	♟♟♟ 4*
○ Soave Cl. Monte Grande '11	♟♟♟ 4*
○ Soave Cl. Monte Grande '08	♟♟♟ 4
○ Soave Cl. Staforte '19	♟♟♟ 3*
○ Soave Cl. Staforte '15	♟♟♟ 3*
○ Soave Cl. Staforte '14	♟♟♟ 4*
○ Soave Cl. Staforte '13	♟♟♟ 4*
○ Soave Cl. Staforte '11	♟♟♟ 4*
○ Soave Cl. Staforte '08	♟♟♟ 4

★★Giuseppe Quintarelli

via Cerè, 1
37024 Negrar [VR]
☎ +39 0457500016
vini@giuseppequintarelli.it

CELLAR SALES
PRE-BOOKED VISITS
ANNUAL PRODUCTION 60,000 bottles
HECTARES UNDER VINE 10.00

After the passing of Giuseppe Quintarelli, there were concerns about the future of the Negrar winery. However, his wife Fiorenza and their sons Francesco and Lorenzo have upheld the family tradition. They interpret the vintages and wines as they always have here at Via Cerè No. 1, utilizing the new, captivating cellar to allow the wines to mature slowly. The Amarone '17 is the quintessence of this tradition, a wine that reveals its aromas slowly. Sweet, ripe cherry gives way to notes of rain-soaked earth and underbrush, with a subtle, spicy vein emerging from the background. The palate is full and powerful, finding harmony and lightness through its sapidity and acidity. The Recioto '15 oscillates between red fruit preserves and dates, with herbal notes adding freshness. On tasting, it reveals a measured sweetness, closing with a spirited tannic presence.

• Amarone della Valpolicella Cl. '17	🍷🍷🍷	8
• Recioto della Valpolicella Cl. '15	🍷🍷	8
• Valpolicella Cl. Sup. '17	🍷🍷	7
• Amarone della Valpolicella Cl. '15	🍷🍷🍷	8
• Amarone della Valpolicella Cl. '13	🍷🍷🍷	8
• Amarone della Valpolicella Cl. '11	🍷🍷🍷	8
• Amarone della Valpolicella Cl. '09	🍷🍷🍷	8
• Amarone della Valpolicella Cl. '06	🍷🍷🍷	8
• Amarone della Valpolicella Cl. '03	🍷🍷🍷	8
• Amarone della Valpolicella Cl. Ris. '09	🍷🍷🍷	8
• Amarone della Valpolicella Cl. Ris. '07	🍷🍷🍷	8
• Amarone della Valpolicella Cl. Sup. Monte Cà Paletta '00	🍷🍷🍷	8
• Recioto della Valpolicella Cl. '01	🍷🍷🍷	8
• Recioto della Valpolicella Cl. Monte Ca' Paletta '97	🍷🍷🍷	8

Quota 101

fraz. Luvigliano
via Malterreno, 12
35038 Torreglia [PD]
☎ +39 0495211322
⊕ www.quota101.com

CELLAR SALES
PRE-BOOKED VISITS
ACCOMMODATION
ANNUAL PRODUCTION 60,000 bottles
HECTARES UNDER VINE 16.00
VITICULTURE METHOD Certified Organic
SUSTAINABLE WINERY

What began as a restful retreat has, in a dozen or so years, transformed into one of the Euganean hills' wineries to watch. Quota 101 boasts a diverse range of vineyards, taking advantage of varying climatic and soil conditions so that the varietal being cultivated is best suited to each plot. The marl and clay of Torreglia benefit white grapes, while the warmer, red shale zone of Baone is ideal for Bordeaux reds. The Gardina family presented many convincing wines this year, among which the Ortone '20, a bordeaux blend dominated by merlot, stands out. Intense aromas of ripe red fruit are enhanced by mineral nuances and macerated leaves. On the palate, it's concentrated and spirited, showcasing the warmth of the terroir. The Gelso di Lapo '19 plays on explosive fruitiness, where candied notes meet caramel, while on the palate, the wine's exuberant sweetness finds balance through its brackish presence.

• Colli Euganei Cabernet Poggio Ameno '22	🍷🍷	3
○ Colli Euganei Fior d'Arancio Passito Il Gelso di Lapo '19	🍷🍷	5
• Colli Euganei Merlot Silvano '22	🍷🍷	3
• Colli Euganei Rosso Ortone '20	🍷🍷	4
○ Tai '22	🍷🍷	3
○ Colli Euganei Manzoni Bianco '22	🍷	4
• Colli Euganei Cabernet Poggio Ameno '21	🍷🍷	3
• Colli Euganei Cabernet Poggio Ameno '20	🍷🍷	2*
○ Colli Euganei Fior d'Arancio Passito Il Gelso di Lapo '18	🍷🍷	5
○ Colli Euganei Fior d'Arancio Secco '20	🍷🍷	3
○ Colli Euganei Fior d'Arancio Spumante Dolce '22	🍷🍷	3
• Colli Euganei Rosso Ortone '19	🍷🍷	4
○ Malterreno '21	🍷🍷	2*

Le Ragose

fraz. Arbizzano
via Ragose, I
37024 Negrar [VR]
(+39 0457513241
⊕ www.leragose.com

CELLAR SALES
PRE-BOOKED VISITS
ANNUAL PRODUCTION 130,000 bottles
HECTARES UNDER VINE 18.00
SUSTAINABLE WINERY

The Galli family was among the first to recognize Valpolicella's immense potential, investing in what would become by the late 1960s one of the area's most important producers. Today, alongside Paolo and Marco, is Marta, representing the third generation with a keen focus on sustainability—environmental, economic, and social. Only Amarone was tasted this year, with two purebreds truly impressing our panels. Leading the pack was the Marta Galli '13, a wine that showcases a deep aromatic suite, slow to reveal itself, almost shy. The sweet, fleshy fruit seems to step aside, allowing space for bitter cocoa and notes of rain-soaked earth. On the palate, it strikes rich and powerful, marked by close-knit tannins and a vital acidic drive. The Amarone Riserva '13 offers even more complex aromas alongside a crisp, energetic flavor profile.

Reassi

via A. Manzoni, 9
35030 Rovolon [PD]
(+39 3475340932
⊕ www.reassi.it

CELLAR SALES
PRE-BOOKED VISITS
ACCOMMODATION
ANNUAL PRODUCTION 25,000 bottles
HECTARES UNDER VINE 6.50
VITICULTURE METHOD Certified Organic

The Bonato family has cultivated vines on the Euganean Hills for generations, but it wasn't until the early 1990s that their winery took on the shape it has today. A handful of hectares are dedicated to both viticulture and olive growing on the western slopes of the ridge, and mostly the Bordeaux varieties that have thrived here for more than a century are cultivated. Nearly forgotten native varieties like pinella and turchetta are also grown. The grapes for the OP! '20 hail from an old pinella vineyard, one whose origins go back at least a century. It's a spumante with simple aromas (fruit and mineral nuances), while on the palate, the sharp, cutting character of pinella emerges, making for a dry, taut drink. The Merlot Archè '22 performs well with its red fruit and herbal aromas, which develop depth on a dry, dynamic, and juicy palate. The Tre Frazioni '21, a Bordeaux blend of mostly cabernet sauvignon, offers nice richness and harmony.

● Amarone della Valpolicella Cl. Marta Galli Ris. '13	♟♟ 8
● Amarone della Valpolicella Cl. Ris. '13	♟♟ 7
● Amarone della Valpolicella Cl. '88	♟♟♟ 7
● Amarone della Valpolicella Cl. '86	♟♟♟ 7
● Amarone della Valpolicella Cl. Marta Galli '05	♟♟♟ 8
● Amarone della Valpolicella Cl. '10	♟♟ 7
● Amarone della Valpolicella Cl. Caloetto '10	♟♟ 7
● Amarone della Valpolicella Cl. Marta Galli '10	♟♟ 7
● Amarone della Valpolicella Cl. Marta Galli Ris. '12	♟♟ 8
● Amarone della Valpolicella Cl. Marta Galli Ris. '11	♟♟ 7
● Amarone della Valpolicella Cl. Ris. '12	♟♟ 7

● Colli Euganei Cabernet Sparviere '22	♟♟ 3
● Colli Euganei Merlot Archè '22	♟♟ 3
● Colli Euganei Rosso Tre Frazioni '21	♟♟ 4
○ OP! Opera Prima Dosaggio Zero M.Cl. '20	♟♟ 5
○ Colli Euganei Fior d' Arancio Spumante Dolce	♟ 3
○ Colli Euganei Manzoni Bianco Terre d' Argilla '23	♟ 3
● L'Antenato '22	♟ 3
● Colli Euganei Cabernet Sparviere '21	♟♟ 3
● Colli Euganei Cabernet Sparviere '20	♟♟ 3
● Colli Euganei Cabernet Sparviere '17	♟♟ 3
○ Colli Euganei Fior d' Arancio Spumante '21	♟♟ 3
● Colli Euganei Merlot Archè '21	♟♟ 3
● Colli Euganei Rosso Tre Frazioni '20	♟♟ 4
● Colli Euganei Rosso Tre Frazioni '19	♟♟ 4
● Colli Euganei Rosso Tre Frazioni '18	♟♟ 3
○ Opera Prima Dosaggio Zero M.Cl. '19	♟♟ 5

Roccolo Grassi

via San Giovanni di Dio, 19
37030 Mezzane di Sotto [VR]
(☎) +39 0458880089
⊕ www.roccolograssi.it

★Roeno

via Mama, 5
37020 Brentino Belluno [VR]
(☎) +39 0457230110
⊕ www.cantinaroeno.com

PRE-BOOKED VISITS
ANNUAL PRODUCTION 49,000 bottles
HECTARES UNDER VINE 14.00
SUSTAINABLE WINERY

CELLAR SALES
PRE-BOOKED VISITS
ACCOMMODATION AND RESTAURANT SERVICE
ANNUAL PRODUCTION 400,000 bottles
HECTARES UNDER VINE 80.00
SUSTAINABLE WINERY

The Sartori siblings, Francesca and Marco, have been pivotal in elevating Valpolicella's wines, bringing attention to a previously lesser-known territory. Meticulous vineyard care ensures perfectly ripe and healthy grapes, which are transformed in their Mezzane cellar into a handful of highly esteemed labels. Although the winery only produces a few bottles of Soave, the Broia '22 leaves a lasting impression. Its pale straw color betrays the aromatic breadth it has to offer, with white fruit interwoven with floral notes and a subtle minerality waiting to emerge. The palate is weighty and tense, finishing sapid and very long. The Valpolicella Superiore '19 expresses ripe, crunchy red fruit, sensations mirrored on a solid, energetic palate, extended by a juicy acidity.

When thinking of borders, limits and restrictions usually come to mind. The Fugatti brothers view their borderland between Veneto and Trentino as an exchange point, blending traditions and forging new paths. Their extensive vineyards stretch across Affi, Terra dei Forti, and Trentino, enabling a broad production scope. The Rivoli Pinot Grigio '21 (named for the growing region at the northern edge of Verona province) brings all the complexity and depth of the grape to the table, manifesting even more clearly in a palate of great concentration and tension. The Riesling Collezione di Famiglia '19 boasts complex aromas and a juicy, long flavor profile. The Cristina, a late-harvest white, is excellent, combining aromatic breadth with a sweet, seductive palate that finds balance in its saline presence.

○ Soave Broia '22	♟♟	4
● Valpolicella Sup. '19	♟♟	5
● Amarone della Valpolicella '19	♟♟	8
● Amarone della Valpolicella Roccolo Grassi '07	♟♟♟	8
● Amarone della Valpolicella Roccolo Grassi '00	♟♟♟	7
● Amarone della Valpolicella Roccolo Grassi '99	♟♟♟	7
○ Soave La Broia '20	♟♟♟	3*
● Valpolicella Sup. '13	♟♟♟	5
● Valpolicella Sup. '11	♟♟♟	5
● Valpolicella Sup. Roccolo Grassi '09	♟♟♟	5
● Valpolicella Sup. Roccolo Grassi '07	♟♟♟	5
● Valpolicella Sup. Roccolo Grassi '04	♟♟♟	5
● Amarone della Valpolicella '16	♟♟	8

○ Valdadige Terra dei Forti Pinot Grigio Rivoli '21	♟♟♟	5
○ Cristina V.T. '21	♟♟	5
○ Riesling Renano Collezione di Famiglia '19	♟♟	6
● Marzemino La Rua '23	♟♟	3
○ Riesling Praecipuus '22	♟♟	5
○ Valdadige Pinot Grigio Tera Alta '23	♟♟	3
○ Valdadige Terra dei Forti Enantio 1865 Pre-Fillossera Ris. '19	♟♟	6
● Valdadige Terra dei Forti Enantio Red Point '21	♟♟	5
○ Repanda Solaris '22	♟	5
○ Riesling Collezione di Famiglia '17	♟♟♟	6
○ Riesling Renano Collezione di Famiglia '16	♟♟♟	6
○ Riesling Renano Collezione di Famiglia '15	♟♟♟	6
○ Valdadige Terra dei Forti Pinot Grigio Rivoli '20	♟♟♟	5

Rubinelli Vajol

loc. Vajol
fraz. San Floriano
via Paladon, 31
37029 San Pietro in Cariano [VR]
📞 +39 0456839277
🌐 www.rubinellivajol.it

CELLAR SALES
PRE-BOOKED VISITS
ACCOMMODATION
ANNUAL PRODUCTION 70,000 bottles
HECTARES UNDER VINE 10.00

Despite its foundation date (Est. 1953), it wasn't until the 2000s that Rubinelli Vajol began taking on its current form. It was then that they decided to vinify and bottle grapes from the beautiful Vajol basin. The vineyards' roots penetrate the tuff soil, allowing grapes to mature with unexpected finesse and lightness, a characteristic that's highlighted by a skilled team of winemakers who bring out the best of traditional classics. After more than 10 years maturing in the cellar, the Amarone Destinée '11 reveals an extraordinarily youthful expression, with sweet yet still crunchy wild fruit, threaded with subtle herbal nuances. On the palate, time has brought calm and relaxation, allowing the wine to stretch out with supple sapidity, unfolding with finesse. Fresh, with intense notes of fruit and dark spices, the Valpolicella Superiore '21 capitalizes on an excellent vintage to highlight elegant aromas and a dynamic, juicy palate.

★Ruggeri & C.

via Prà Fontana, 4
31049 Valdobbiadene [TV]
📞 +39 04239092
🌐 www.ruggeri.it

CELLAR SALES
PRE-BOOKED VISITS
ANNUAL PRODUCTION 1,700,000 bottles
HECTARES UNDER VINE 28.00
SUSTAINABLE WINERY

Founded in 1950, Ruggeri has played a major role in introducing Prosecco to the world, combining technological and entrepreneurial dynamism with the wisdom and knowledge of the countryside. Today, the winery relies on a dense network of growers, while the grapes are transformed into a range of high-profile spumante by Fabio Roversi's technical team. The Giustino B. '23, now approaching its 30th edition, remains one of the most interesting Extra Drys of the appellation. It opens on fresh fruit and floral aromas, with jasmine notes standing out against a backdrop of apple and pear. In the mouth, the perfect balance of bubbles, acidity, and sweetness makes for a palate of great pleasure and finesse. The Vecchie Viti from the same vintage explores the appellation's more hidden and energetic side—a dry and racy drink.

● Valpolicella Cl. Sup. '21	🍷🍷🍷 5
● Amarone della Valpolicella Cl. Destinée Ris. '11	🍷🍷 8
● Valpolicella Cl. '23	🍷🍷 4
● Valpolicella Cl. Sup. Ripasso '19	🍷🍷 6
● Valpolicella Cl. Sup. '20	🍷🍷🍷 5
● Amarone della Valpolicella Cl. '16	🍷🍷 7
● Amarone della Valpolicella Cl. '15	🍷🍷 7
● Amarone della Valpolicella Cl. '13	🍷🍷 7
● Amarone della Valpolicella Cl. '12	🍷🍷 7
● Amarone della Valpolicella Cl. '10	🍷🍷 6
● Amarone della Valpolicella Cl. Destinée Ris. '10	🍷🍷 8
● Valpolicella Cl. Sup '18	🍷🍷 5
● Valpolicella Cl. Sup. '16	🍷🍷 4
● Valpolicella Cl. Sup. Ripasso '12	🍷🍷 5

○ Valdobbiadene Extra Dry Giustino B. '23	🍷🍷🍷 5
○ Valdobbiadene Brut V.V. '23	🍷🍷 5
○ Cartizze	🍷🍷 5
○ Valdobbiadene Brut Quartese	🍷🍷 4
○ Valdobbiadene Dry Santo Stefano	🍷🍷 4
○ Valdobbiadene Extra Brut L'Extrabrut '23	🍷🍷 5
○ Valdobbiadene Extra Brut Saltèr	🍷🍷 4
○ Valdobbiadene Extra Dry Giall'Oro	🍷🍷 4
○ Valdobbiadene Extra Dry Giustino B '20	🍷🍷🍷 5
○ Valdobbiadene Extra Dry Giustino B '19	🍷🍷🍷 5
○ Valdobbiadene Extra Dry Giustino B. '21	🍷🍷🍷 5
○ Valdobbiadene Extra Dry Giustino B. '18	🍷🍷🍷 5
○ Valdobbiadene Extra Dry Giustino B. '17	🍷🍷🍷 5
○ Valdobbiadene Extra Dry Giustino B. '16	🍷🍷🍷 4*

VENETO

VENETO

Le Salette

via Pio Brugnoli, 11c
37022 Fumane [VR]
📞 +39 0457701027
🖂 www.lesalette.it

CELLAR SALES
PRE-BOOKED VISITS
ANNUAL PRODUCTION 130,000 bottles
HECTARES UNDER VINE 20.00

Among those who have brought Amarone to
wine lists worldwide, Franco Scamperle and his
Le Salette must surely be mentioned. Over the
decades, the winery has expanded to cover
around 20 hectares in Valpolicella Classica, and
today, as in the past, it remains one of the area's
most esteemed producers. The cellar, located in
the heart of the village of Fumane, houses all
stages of production. The area cultivated is
dedicated entirely to traditional grape varieties,
with the exception of a small plot for whites.
The Recioto Pergole Vece '21 matures in
terracotta amphorae before evoking intense
hints of cherry compote and sweet spices,
sensations that resonate on a palate where
sweetness takes center stage, contrasted by a
sapid thrust and a gritty tannic finish. The
Amarone La Marega '19, on the other hand,
moves with immediate aromatic appeal, with
juicy red fruit resting on herbal notes. The palate
is rich and supple. Nice length.

● Amarone della Valpolicella Cl. La Marega '19	♟♟ 6
● Recioto della Valpolicella Cl. Pergole Vece '21	♟♟ 6
● Valpolicella Cl. '23	♟♟ 2*
● Ca' Carnocchio '19	♟ 4
● Valpolicella Cl. Sup. Ripasso I Progni '21	♟ 3
● Amarone della Valpolicella Cl. Pergole Vece '05	♟♟♟ 8
● Amarone della Valpolicella Cl. Pergole Vece '95	♟♟♟ 8
● Amarone della Valpolicella Cl. La Marega '17	♟♟ 6
● Amarone della Valpolicella Cl. Pergole Vece '16	♟♟ 8
● Amarone della Valpolicella Cl. Pergole Vece Ris. '17	♟♟ 8

Sansonina

loc. Sansonina
37019 Peschiera del Garda [VR]
📞 +39 0457551905
🖂 www.sansonina.it

CELLAR SALES
ANNUAL PRODUCTION 21,000 bottles
HECTARES UNDER VINE 13.00

The southern shore of Lake Garda and the lands
stretching southward are characterized by a high
clay content, making them ideal for cultivating
varieties like turbiana and merlot. Carla
Prospero founded this small winery a quarter of
a century ago, and today, Sansonina remains one
of the most notable producers to operate here
at the border between the provinces of Verona
and Brescia. Her range not only offers superb
organoleptic qualities but also a strong sense of
place. The Sansonina '20 offers up immediately
expressive, vibrant aromas of plum and thyme,
sensations that explode on the palate, where its
juicy richness is countered by a dense tannic
weave that lends rigor and clout. The Lugana '22
also caught our attention, evoking a multifaceted
aromatic profile where yellow fruit is
accompanied by notes of Mediterranean scrub,
with exotic hints and a subtle but promising
mineral vein that becomes even more evident
on its dry, lingering palate.

● Garda Merlot Sansonina '20	♟♟ 7
○ Lugana Fermentazione Spontanea '22	♟♟ 5
● Garda Rosso Evaluna '21	♟♟ 4
● Garda Merlot '19	♟♟ 7
● Garda Merlot '18	♟♟ 6
○ Lugana Fermentazione Spontanea '20	♟♟ 4
○ Lugana Fermentazione Spontanea '19	♟♟ 3*
○ Lugana Fermentazione Spontanea '18	♟♟ 3*
○ Lugana Fermentazione Spontanea '17	♟♟ 3
○ Lugana Fermentazione Spontanea '16	♟♟ 3*
○ Lugana Sansonina '09	♟♟ 3*
○ Lugana V. del Morano Verde '15	♟♟ 4
● Sansonina '13	♟♟ 6
● Sansonina '07	♟♟ 6
● Sansonina '06	♟♟ 6
● Sansonina '05	♟♟ 6

★★Tenuta Sant'Antonio

loc. San Zeno
via Ceriani, 23
37030 Colognola ai Colli [VR]
📞 +39 0457650383
🌐 www.tenutasantantonio.it

Santa Margherita

via Ita Marzotto, 8
30025 Fossalta di Portogruaro [VE]
📞 +39 0421246111
🌐 www.santamargherita.com

CELLAR SALES
PRE-BOOKED VISITS
ANNUAL PRODUCTION 700,000 bottles
HECTARES UNDER VINE 150.00
SUSTAINABLE WINERY

CELLAR SALES
PRE-BOOKED VISITS
ANNUAL PRODUCTION 18,100,000 bottles
HECTARES UNDER VINE 145.00

Since the founding of Tenuta Sant'Antonio in the late 20th century, the Castagnedi brothers have focused on the winery's vineyards, making constant improvements while expanding into Valpolicella Orientale and Soave. Operations are based in San Briccio and Colognola ai Colli, while the most prized plots can be found on the white limestone soil surrounding the Monti Garbi cellar. The Amarone Campo dei Gigli '19 is an explosion of fruit on the nose, with wild fruit notes intertwined with herbal and peppery nuances. On the palate, what stands out is the wine's compactness—full, tight-knit, and energetic, with alcohol playing its part. La Bandina '21 takes advantage of an excellent vintage to take another step towards tension and freshness, as seen in recent vintages, with a palate that appears more expansive, and supported more by acidity than tannins. The Soave Vecchie Vigne '21 is delicious—a complex and dynamic libation.

Founded during the interwar period as an agricultural hub, this Fossalta di Portogruaro-based winery shifted its focus towards quality wine production after WWII and quickly became a global touchstone for Italian white wine, thanks to its insights into the style of pinot grigio. Today, the producer operates across three distinct areas: the Venetian plains, the Prosecco Superiore production zone, and Alto Adige. From the finest vineyards in the Refrontolo area come the grapes for their most ambitious Prosecco Superiore, a wine that delicately reveals its aromas, first golden apple, then floral notes, showcasing all the delicacy that Treviso bubbly can offer. In the mouth, the 2023 harvest brought sapidity and tension—the palate lengthens, supported by acidity and close-knit bead. The producer's interpretation of Cartizze is also intriguing, forgoing explosive sweetness in favor of a creamy, harmonious profile.

● Amarone della Valpolicella Campo dei Gigli '19	♔♔♔ 8
● Valpolicella Sup. La Bandina '21	♔♔ 5
● Amarone della Valpolicella Antonio Castagnedi '20	♔♔ 7
○ Soave V. Monte Ceriani '22	♔♔ 4
○ Soave V.V. '21	♔♔ 5
● Valpolicella Nanfrè '23	♔♔ 3
● Valpolicella Sup. Ripasso Monti Garbi '21	♔♔ 4
○ Soave Monte di Colognola '23	♔ 3
● Amarone della Valpolicella Campo dei Gigli '18	♔♔♔ 8
● Amarone della Valpolicella Campo dei Gigli '16	♔♔♔ 8
● Valpolicella Sup. La Bandina '19	♔♔♔ 5
● Valpolicella Sup. La Bandina '18	♔♔♔ 5

○ Cartizze Extra Dry	♔♔ 5
○ Valdadige Pinot Grigio '23	♔♔ 3
○ Valdobbiadene 52 Brut '23	♔♔ 4
○ Valdobbiadene Brut	♔♔ 3
○ Valdobbiadene Rive di Refrontolo Extra Brut '23	♔♔ 4
○ Valdobbiadene Extra Dry	♔ 3
○ A.A. Pinot Grigio Impronta del Fondatore '22	♔♔ 4
○ A.A. Pinot Grigio Impronta del Fondatore '21	♔♔ 4
○ A.A. Pinot Grigio Impronta del Fondatore '20	♔♔ 4
○ Valdobbiadene Rive di Refrontolo Extra Brut '22	♔♔ 4
○ Valdobbiadene Rive di Refrontolo Extra Brut '21	♔♔ 4

Santa Sofia

fraz. Pedemonte di Valpolicella
via Ca' Dedé, 61
37029 San Pietro in Cariano [VR]
(☎) +39 0457701074
⊕ www.santasofia.com

Santi

via Ungheria, 33
37031 Illasi [VR]
(☎) +39 0456529068
⊕ www.cantinasanti.it

CELLAR SALES
PRE-BOOKED VISITS
ANNUAL PRODUCTION 750,000 bottles
HECTARES UNDER VINE 66.00

CELLAR SALES
PRE-BOOKED VISITS
ANNUAL PRODUCTION 1,200,000 bottles
HECTARES UNDER VINE 65.00

The Begnoni family has been active in Valpolicella for over half a century, initially with Giancarlo, and since the mid-1980s, under the leadership of his son Luciano, who continues to steer the winery today. Over these decades, the producer has forged strong relationships with local viticulturists while also developing its own vineyards, which are primarily located in the vaio Briago area in Valpantena. The property unfolds across several hectares at elevations spanning 400-500 meters. The Begnoni family's wines have seen a significant surge in quality in recent years, as evidenced by the Amarone Gioè '16. Its layered aromas unfold gradually, starting with sweet red fruit, then oaky notes, and finishing with a mineral, earthy undertone. The palate is compact, with tension and length driven by a vibrant acidity. The Lugana from the Pozzolengo estate is right up there as well, offering a broad aromatic profile with a supple, brackish character.

This historic Illasi-based producer is experiencing a period of revival and renewal. Renovating the cellar, improving the vineyards and updating the production style have all contributed to making this producer one of the most noteworthy in Valpolicella Orientale. Their range is dedicated to Verona's principal appellations, interpreted here with clarity and character. The Amarone Carlo Santi 1843 is crafted from grapes carefully selected from the Cellore and Valpantena vineyards, near the winery. It matures slowly in barrels of various sizes, making for aromas of stewed red fruit, complemented by intriguing hints of rain-soaked earth and macerated flowers. On the palate, its full body is balanced by a close-knit tannic structure that adds rigor and energy. The Amarone Santico '19, on the other hand, proves more approachable, showcasing centrality of fruit with a juicy and satisfying palate.

● Amarone della Valpolicella Cl. Gioè '16	♟♟ 8
● Amarone della Valpolicella Cl. '19	♟♟ 7
● Amarone della Valpolicella Cl. Ris. '17	♟♟ 7
○ Lugana '23	♟♟ 3
● Valpolicella Sup. Ripasso '21	♟♟ 4
● Amarone della Valpolicella Cl. '17	♟♟ 7
● Amarone della Valpolicella Cl. '16	♟♟ 7
● Amarone della Valpolicella Cl. '15	♟♟ 7
● Amarone della Valpolicella Cl. '13	♟♟ 7
● Amarone della Valpolicella Cl. '12	♟♟ 7
● Amarone della Valpolicella Cl. Gioé Ris. '13	♟♟ 7
● Amarone della Valpolicella Cl. Ris. '12	♟♟ 7

● Amarone della Valpolicella Carlo Santi 1843 '17	♟♟ 7
● Amarone della Valpolicella Cl. Santico '19	♟♟ 6
⊙ Chiaretto di Bardolino Infinito '23	♟♟ 2*
● Valpolicella Cl. Le Caleselle '23	♟♟ 3
○ Soave Cl. Colforte '23	♟ 2
● Amarone della Valpolicella Proemio '05	♟♟♟ 6
● Amarone della Valpolicella Proemio '03	♟♟♟ 6
● Amarone della Valpolicella Proemio '00	♟♟♟ 5
● Valpolicella Cl. Sup. Ripasso Solane '09	♟♟♟ 3*
● Amarone della Valpolicella Carlo Santi 1843 '16	♟♟ 6
● Amarone della Valpolicella Cl. Proemio '15	♟♟ 7
● Valpolicella Sup. Ventale '20	♟♟ 4
● Valpolicella Sup. Ventale '18	♟♟ 3*

Sartori

fraz. Santa Maria
via Casette, 4
37024 Negrar [VR]
(☏) +39 0456028011
◉ www.sartorinet.com

CELLAR SALES
PRE-BOOKED VISITS
ANNUAL PRODUCTION 15,000,000 bottles
HECTARES UNDER VINE 120.00
SUSTAINABLE WINERY

Pietro Sartori purchased the first vineyard of what would go on to become one of the most important wineries in Verona in the late 1800s. Over a century later, Luca and Andrea Sartori manage the estate in collaboration with the Collis group. This partnership grants access to a substantial vineyard area, allowing production across all Verona's major appellations. The Amarone Reius '19 put in an outstanding performance, focusing not on concentration or power, but on the more supple side of the appellation. The nose reveals lively suggestions of sweet, ripe fruit, accompanied by fresh balsamic and peppery notes, reflecting the traditional grape varieties used. On the palate, the wine follows the same stylistic path, highlighting a firm yet crisp body with nice tension. The Regolo '21 is a Ripasso that sees simple fruit aromas and vegetal notes followed by a juicy, immediately expressive palate.

Secondo Marco

via Campolongo, 9
37022 Fumane [VR]
(☏) +39 0456800954
◉ www.secondomarco.it

CELLAR SALES
PRE-BOOKED VISITS
ACCOMMODATION
ANNUAL PRODUCTION 85,000 bottles
HECTARES UNDER VINE 19.00
VITICULTURE METHOD Certified Organic

Founded in 2008, the winery might seem like a recent venture, but a visit reveals a deep-rooted connection to viticulture and the Valpolicella region, one that traces back to Marco Speri's father, Benedetto, and grandfather, Sante. Today, Marco crafts traditional wines characterized by complexity, patience, and elegance. The Amarone from the 2014 harvest is exemplary, a wine that needed time to find balance but now reveals an aromatic profile where fruit is immediately refreshed by bold spicy and vegetal notes—characteristics of the vintage. The palate follows a similar stylistic path, marked by a taut, spirited, and racy body. The Recioto '18 is also delicious, with aromas of alcohol-steeped cherries and medicinal herbs mirrored on a sweet palate perfectly balanced by acidity.

● Amarone della Valpolicella Cl. Reius '19	♛♛ 7
● Valpolicella Cl. Sup. Ripasso Regolo '21	♛♛ 4
○ Marani '22	♛ 4
● Recioto della Valpolicella Cl. Rerum '21	♛ 5
● Amarone della Valpolicella Cl. Corte Brà Ris. '16	♛♛ 7
● Amarone della Valpolicella Cl. Corte Brà Ris. '15	♛♛ 7
● Amarone della Valpolicella Cl. Corte Brà Ris. '13	♛♛ 7
● Amarone della Valpolicella Cl. Reius '17	♛♛ 7
● Amarone della Valpolicella Cl. Reius '16	♛♛ 7
● Amarone della Valpolicella I Saltari Ris. '15	♛♛ 7
● Valpolicella Cl. Sup. Montegradella '20	♛♛ 3
● Valpolicella Sup. I Saltari '19	♛♛ 4
● Valpolicella Sup. Ripasso Regolo '20	♛♛ 3

● Amarone della Valpolicella Cl. '14	♛♛ 8
● Recioto della Valpolicella Cl. '18	♛♛ 8
● Valpolicella Cl. Bio '21	♛♛ 5
● Valpolicella Cl. Sup. Ripasso '19	♛♛ 5
● Amarone della Valpolicella Cl. '13	♛♛♛ 8
● Amarone della Valpolicella Cl. '11	♛♛♛ 8
● Amarone della Valpolicella Cl. '15	♛♛ 8
● Amarone della Valpolicella Cl. '12	♛♛ 8
● Amarone della Valpolicella Cl. Fumetto '08 Ris. '08	♛♛ 8
● Valpolicella Cl. '20	♛♛ 4
● Valpolicella Cl. '19	♛♛ 4
● Valpolicella Cl. '18	♛♛ 3
● Valpolicella Cl. Sup. Ripasso '16	♛♛ 5
● Valpolicella Cl. Sup. Ripasso '15	♛♛ 5

VENETO

★★Serafini & Vidotto

via Luigi Carrer, 8
31040 Nervesa della Battaglia [TV]
℡ +39 0422773281
🌐 www.serafinividotto.it

CELLAR SALES
PRE-BOOKED VISITS
ANNUAL PRODUCTION 250,000 bottles
HECTARES UNDER VINE 23.00
SUSTAINABLE WINERY

Almost 40 years ago, Antonello Vidotto and Francesco Serafini, fresh out of school, joined forces to create a winery that quickly became a leader in the Italian Bordeaux-style blend. Today, Francesco's son, Matteo, has taken over production, continuing the successful path in the vineyard that has long distinguished the winery. The Rosso dell'Abbazia has long been one of Italy's most important Bordeaux blends. Primarily cabernet sauvignon, it has never pursued power but rather embraced the Montello region's propensity for crafting elegant and lean wines. The 2020 is redolent of wild fruit and spices, with a crisp, juicy palate of great length to follow. The Phigaia '21 follows the same stylistic path, but with added freshness and dynamism. The 2022 white version proves rich, sapid, and harmonious.

● Montello Asolo Rosso dell'Abazia '20	▼▼▼	7
○ Asolo Brut Bollicine	▼▼	3
● Montello Asolo Phigaia After The Red '21	▼▼	5
○ Phigaia After The White '22	▼▼	4
○ Manzoni Bianco '23	▼	3
● Montello Colli Asolani Il Rosso dell'Abazia '19	♀♀♀	7
● Montello e Colli Asolani Il Rosso dell'Abazia '18	♀♀♀	6
● Montello e Colli Asolani Il Rosso dell'Abazia '17	♀♀♀	6
● Montello e Colli Asolani Il Rosso dell'Abazia '16	♀♀♀	6
● Montello e Colli Asolani Phigaia '17	♀♀	4

★★Speri

fraz. Pedemonte
via Via Fontana, 14
37029 San Pietro in Cariano [VR]
℡ +39 0457701154
🌐 www.speri.com

CELLAR SALES
PRE-BOOKED VISITS
ANNUAL PRODUCTION 400,000 bottles
HECTARES UNDER VINE 60.00
VITICULTURE METHOD Certified Organic
SUSTAINABLE WINERY

The Speri family is bustling with activity, restoring their historic 16th-century residence to create new spaces for hospitality and winemaking. In the vineyard, they adhere to tradition with local varieties and pergoletta training, while in the cellar, they focus solely on appellation wines, noted for their stylistic continuity and distinctive profile. The Amarone Sant'Urbano once again proves to be one of the appellation's most interesting wines, perfectly balancing immediacy and maturity on the nose, with sweet cherry intertwined with subtle medicinal nuances—sensations that are even more distinct on the palate, where the wine reveals its fullness, juiciness, and tension. The Valpolicella Sant'Urbano '21 follows a similar approach but with greater suppleness, while La Roggia '21 plays more on immediate, clearly evident red fruit, echoed on an energetic palate, where its pronounced sweetness is nicely managed by its acidic drive.

● Amarone della Valpolicella Cl. Sant'Urbano '20	▼▼▼	7
● Recioto della Valpolicella Cl. La Roggia '21	▼▼	7
● Valpolicella Cl. '23	▼▼	3
● Valpolicella Cl. Sup. Ripasso '22	▼▼	4
● Valpolicella Cl. Sup. Sant'Urbano '21	▼▼	5
● Amarone della Valpolicella Cl. Sant'Urbano '19	♀♀♀	7
● Amarone della Valpolicella Cl. Sant'Urbano '18	♀♀♀	7
● Amarone della Valpolicella Cl. Sant'Urbano '16	♀♀♀	7
● Amarone della Valpolicella Cl. Sant'Urbano '15	♀♀♀	7
● Amarone della Valpolicella Vign. Monte Sant'Urbano '13	♀♀♀	7

David Sterza

via Casterna, 37
37022 Fumane [VR]
☎ +39 3471343121
✉ www.davidsterza.it

CELLAR SALES
PRE-BOOKED VISITS
ANNUAL PRODUCTION 40,000 bottles
HECTARES UNDER VINE 4.50

Casterna is a tiny hamlet consisting of a few houses perched on the ridge separating the lower Fumane valley from that of Marano. Here, David Sterza and his cousin Paolo Mascanzoni manage a few hectares of vineyard climbing up the hillside. Their range is distinctive, marked by integrity and clarity of fruit, delivering an energetic palate well-supported by acidity and tannins. In recent years, the producer has shifted its style, sacrificing a touch of power to highlight the finesse and suppleness that local grapes can offer. This approach is perfectly expressed in the Valpolicella Superiore '21, a wine that exudes dark cherry and spice aromas, with a subtle medicinal note adding freshness. In the mouth, it reveals compactness but also a vibrant acidity that lengthens and slims the palate. The Amarone '20, of course, shows greater maturity on the nose, making for a rich, weighty and gutsy palate.

★★Suavia

fraz. Fittà
via Centro, 14
37038 Soave [VR]
☎ +39 0457675089
✉ www.suavia.it

CELLAR SALES
PRE-BOOKED VISITS
ANNUAL PRODUCTION 200,000 bottles
HECTARES UNDER VINE 30.00
VITICULTURE METHOD Certified Organic

Suavia was founded in the early 1980s by Giovanni and Rosetta, who transitioned from grape growers to establishing their small winery. A few years later, their daughters Meri, Valentina, and Alessandra took the reins, and have since made the producer a benchmark for lovers of Verona's white wines. The initial few hectares of vineyard have expanded significantly, and their range showcases the character of the area cultivated. The Soave Monte Carbonare '22 doesn't aim for explosive aromas, opting instead for delicate, slowly unfolding fragrances—first white fruit, then floral elements, which give way to a deep mineral note, lending a smoky tone. On the palate, its juicy tension is striking, clinging to sapidity and acidity, unfolding with precision and finesse. The Massifitti '21, a monovarietal trebbiano di Soave, exudes multifaceted aromas before revealing a crisp, spirited palate. The Soave '23 combines immediacy with personality.

● Valpolicella Cl. Sup. '21	▼▼ 3*
● Amarone della Valpolicella Cl. '20	▼▼ 6
● Valpolicella Cl. '23	▼▼ 3
● Valpolicella Cl. Sup. Ripasso '22	▼▼ 3
● Amarone della Valpolicella Cl. '13	▽▽▽ 6
● Amarone della Valpolicella Cl. '12	▽▽▽ 6
● Amarone della Valpolicella Cl. '18	▽▽ 6
● Amarone della Valpolicella Cl. '17	▽▽ 6
● Amarone della Valpolicella Cl. '16	▽▽ 6
● Amarone della Valpolicella Cl. '15	▽▽ 6
● Amarone della Valpolicella Cl. '14	▽▽ 6
● Amarone della Valpolicella Cl. '11	▽▽ 6
● Valpolicella Cl. Sup. '20	▽▽ 3*
● Valpolicella Cl. Sup. '19	▽▽ 3*
● Valpolicella Cl. Sup. '18	▽▽ 3*
● Valpolicella Cl. Sup. Ripasso '13	▽▽ 3*

○ Soave Cl. Monte Carbonare '22	▼▼▼ 5
○ Massifitti '21	▼▼ 5
○ Le Rive '21	▼▼ 5
○ Soave Cl. '23	▼▼ 3
○ Soave Cl. Monte Carbonare '21	▽▽▽ 4*
○ Soave Cl. Monte Carbonare '20	▽▽▽ 4*
○ Soave Cl. Monte Carbonare '17	▽▽▽ 3*
○ Soave Cl. Monte Carbonare '16	▽▽▽ 3*
○ Soave Cl. Monte Carbonare '15	▽▽▽ 3*
○ Soave Cl. Monte Carbonare '14	▽▽▽ 3*
○ Soave Cl. Monte Carbonare '12	▽▽▽ 3*
○ Soave Cl. Monte Carbonare '11	▽▽▽ 3*
○ Soave Cl. Monte Carbonare '10	▽▽▽ 3*
○ Soave Cl. Monte Carbonare '09	▽▽▽ 3*
○ Soave Cl. Monte Carbonare '08	▽▽▽ 3*
○ Soave Cl. Monte Carbonare '07	▽▽▽ 3*

VENETO

Sutto

loc. Campo di Pietra
via Arzeri, 34/1
31040 Salgareda [TV]
📞 +39 0422744063
🌐 www.sutto.it

CELLAR SALES
PRE-BOOKED VISITS
ACCOMMODATION AND RESTAURANT SERVICE
ANNUAL PRODUCTION 600,000 bottles
HECTARES UNDER VINE 75.00

What started as a small family-run business has, over a couple of decades, become one of the region's most important wineries. Drawing on a prestigious estate spanning many hectares between the Treviso plains and the Prosecco Superiore hills, and collaborations with leading local experts, the modern Salgareda production space gives rise to wines that blend distinctiveness and character. Year after year, the Sutto brothers' range has grown increasingly precise, as evidenced by the Campo Sella '20 and even more so by the Rosso di Sutto '22. The former showcases all the fruity and medicinal maturity of merlot in a profile of elegant solidity, supported by sweet tannins and a vital acidity. The latter, a Bordeaux blend, plays on the intensity and immediacy of fruit, leaving room for intriguing hints of underbrush and rain-soaked earth. On the palate, it's full, lively, and irresistibly drinkable.

● Campo Sella '20	♟♟♟ 6
● Rosso di Sutto '22	♟♟ 3*
○ Bianco di Sutto '23	♟♟ 3
○ Conegliano Valdobbiadene Brut	♟♟ 3
○ Conegliano Valdobbiadene Extra Dry	♟♟ 3
● Dogma Rosso '21	♟♟ 4
● Piave Raboso '20	♟♟ 4
○ Ultimo Passito '21	♟♟ 4
● Campo Sella '19	♟♟♟ 6
● Campo Sella '17	♟♟♟ 5
● Campo Sella '15	♟♟♟ 5
● Campo Sella '18	♟♟ 6
● Campo Sella '16	♟♟ 5
● Dogma Rosso '20	♟♟ 4
● Dogma Rosso '19	♟♟ 4
● Dogma Rosso '17	♟♟ 4

Giovanna Tantini

loc. I Mischi
fraz. Oliosi
via Unità d'Italia, 10
37014 Castelnuovo del Garda [VR]
📞 +39 3488717577
🌐 www.giovannatantini.it

CELLAR SALES
PRE-BOOKED VISITS
ACCOMMODATION
ANNUAL PRODUCTION 42,000 bottles
HECTARES UNDER VINE 11.50

The history of the Tantini family's winery dates back about a century, but it was only with the arrival of Giovanna that it took on the profile we know today. The estate spans around 20 hectares, with more than half dedicated to vineyards nestled in the morainic folds stretching south of Lake Garda. Here, traditional grapes are cultivated alongside small plots dedicated to international varieties. The Bardolino '22 takes advantage of the sunny vintage to deliver aromas of ripe wild fruit, echoed by medicinal notes and dried flowers. On the palate, the wine opens relaxed, leaning on its acidity while leaving the tannins a secondary role. The more ambitious La Rocca '22 reveals a touch of oak on the nose intersecting with ripe cherry and spices, adding depth to its aromatic suite. The palate unfolds gracefully, finishing crisp and well-supported by sweet, polished tannins.

● Bardolino '22	♟♟ 2*
● Bardolino La Rocca '22	♟♟ 3
○ Chiaretto di Bardolino Il Rosé '23	♟ 3
○ Custoza '23	♟ 2
● Bardolino '18	♟♟ 2*
● Bardolino '17	♟♟ 2*
○ Bardolino Chiaretto '19	♟♟ 2*
● Bardolino La Rocca '21	♟♟ 3
● Bardolino La Rocca '20	♟♟ 4
○ Chiaretto di Bardolino '21	♟♟ 2*
○ Chiaretto di Bardolino '20	♟♟ 2*
○ Custoza '20	♟♟ 2*
● Ettore '15	♟♟ 4
● Ettore '14	♟♟ 4
● Garda Corvina Ma.Gi.Co. '21	♟♟ 2*
● Garda Corvina Ma.Gi.Co. '17	♟♟ 2*

★F.lli Tedeschi

fraz. Pedemonte
via G. Verdi, 4
37029 San Pietro in Cariano [VR]
☎ +39 0457701487
🌐 www.tedeschiwines.com

CELLAR SALES
PRE-BOOKED VISITS
ANNUAL PRODUCTION 500,000 bottles
HECTARES UNDER VINE 47.60
SUSTAINABLE WINERY

Among the wineries that have shaped the history of Valpolicella and its wines, F.lli Tedeschi stands out as a mainstay, skillfully navigating trends and time while remaining true to a stylistic vision that honors both tradition and the character of the grapes in their respective vineyards. Over the years, they have added the sizable Maternigo estate, a splendid biodiversity oasis in Valpolicella Orientale, to their historic vineyards in Valpolicella Classica. And it's the Maternigo property that hosts the grapes for the Valpolicella Superiore '21, a wine that pours a brilliant ruby red, releasing aromas of dark cherry, wild berries, and medicinal herbs. On the palate, it reveals impressive structure and tension, lengthening with vibrant acidity and finishing crisp and energetic. The Amarone La Fabriseria '16, sourced from vineyards between Sant'Ambrogio and Fumane, is produced in limited quantities. In fact, you'll find it in our Rare Wines section.

Le Tende

fraz. Colà
via Tende, 35
37017 Lazise [VR]
☎ +39 0457590748
🌐 www.letende.it

CELLAR SALES
PRE-BOOKED VISITS
ACCOMMODATION
ANNUAL PRODUCTION 100,000 bottles
HECTARES UNDER VINE 14.00
VITICULTURE METHOD Certified Organic

Mauro Fortuna has gradually embarked on a successful path at Le Tende, embracing organic management more than 10 years ago and moving away from the idea of Garda wines as playing solely on light and immediately gratifying sensations. Indeed, he now favors wines with greater depth and character. The area under vines spans the Bardolino Classico zone and the more northern Custoza region. The Bardolino '23 is simply fantastic, offering up vibrant impressions of wild berries, rain-soaked earth, and pepper, highlighting its youthful nature. However, the palate goes beyond mere approachability and suppleness, exploring depths of complexity, sapidity, and tension, making it a thoroughly enjoyable taste. The Chiaretto .30 '22, with its more restrained profile, plays on floral and berry notes before delivering a crisp, sapid palate characterized by commendable harmony. The Sabia Rosso '22, a blend of corvina and merlot, also impresses with its pleasing palate.

● Valpolicella Sup. Maternigo '21	♟♟ 5
● Amarone della Valpolicella Marne 180 '20	♟♟ 7
● Valpolicella Cl. Sup. La Fabriseria '21	♟♟ 5
● Valpolicella Lucchine '23	♟♟ 3
● Valpolicella Sup. Capitel Nicalò '21	♟♟ 3
● Valpolicella Sup. Ripasso Capitel San Rocco '21	♟♟ 4
● Amarone della Valpolicella Cl. Capitel Monte Olmi Ris. '17	♟♟♟ 8
● Amarone della Valpolicella Cl. Capitel Monte Olmi Ris. '16	♟♟♟ 8
● Amarone della Valpolicella Cl. Capitel Monte Olmi Ris. '15	♟♟♟ 8
● Amarone della Valpolicella Maternigo Ris. '16	♟♟♟ 8

● Bardolino Cl. '23	♟♟♟ 2*
⊙ Chiaretto di Bardolino .30 '22	♟♟ 5
● Bardolino Cl. Sup. '22	♟♟ 3
● Cicisbeo '21	♟♟ 4
⊙ Delle Venezie Pinot Grigio Lucillini '23	♟♟ 3
⊙ Sabia '22	♟♟ 3
⊙ Sabia '22	♟♟ 3
⊙ Chiaretto di Bardolino Brut Voluttà	♟ 3
⊙ Chiaretto di Bardolino Cl. '23	♟ 2
⊙ Custoza '23	♟ 2
● Bardolino Cl. '20	♟♟♟ 2*
⊙ Bardolino Chiaretto Cl. '19	♟♟ 2*
⊙ Bardolino Chiaretto Cl. '18	♟♟ 2*
● Bardolino Cl. Sup. '20	♟♟ 3*
● Bardolino Cl. Sup. '18	♟♟ 3

Terre di Leone

loc. Porta
via Valpolicella, 6b
37020 Marano di Valpolicella [VR]
(·)) +39 0456895040
@ www.terredileone.it

CELLAR SALES
PRE-BOOKED VISITS
ANNUAL PRODUCTION 36,000 bottles
HECTARES UNDER VINE 10.00

Federico Pellizzari and his wife Chiara run a small winery that hasn't capitulated to the market, producing wines that express a sense of place rather than chasing commercial trends. Great attention is paid to managing the vineyards on the high slopes of the Marano Valley, while in the cellar, they draw on the use of gravity-flow winemaking while affording plenty of time for the wines to mature. The Amarone '15 showcases its class with layered, complex aromas, opening on classic notes of cherry preserves, transitioning to tobacco, rain-soaked earth, and medicinal herbs, especially. On the palate, its tannins are resolved, and the wine unfolds with sapidity and juiciness. The Ripasso '18 offers fruit and spice aromas, which become even more pronounced on the palate, where the wine stands out for its fullness and harmony. The Ripasso Re Pazzo '21 is more approachable on the nose and dynamic on the palate.

Cornelia Tessari

fraz. Brognoligo
via Fontana Nuova, 86
37032 Monteforte d'Alpone [VR]
(·)) +39 0456176041
@ www.corneliatessari.com

CELLAR SALES
PRE-BOOKED VISITS
ACCOMMODATION
ANNUAL PRODUCTION 60,000 bottles
HECTARES UNDER VINE 13.00
VITICULTURE METHOD Certified Organic

Monteforte d'Alpone and Soave serve as the southern gateway to Verona, behind which lies a dense network of volcanic slopes that have hosted garganega grapes for centuries. In the heart of these hills we find the Tessari brothers's winery, a producer that manages about 15 hectares of estate vineyards, supplemented by a few rented plots. The area's historic varietal remains the cornerstone of production. The Soave Grisela '23 epitomizes the essence of a classic Soave: vibrant impressions of white fruit meet flowers before giving way to a subtle mineral note that's awaiting its full expression. In the mouth, it's medium-bodied, perfectly supported by vibrant acidity and sapidity, resulting in a palate of superb pleasure. The Primo Ettaro '21 (the name refers to the estate's first vineyard) is made with grapes pressed after more than a month of drying. The result is a rich, ripe white with a firm, juicy profile.

● Amarone della Valpolicella Cl. '15	♀♀ 8
● Dedicatum '19	♀♀ 6
● Valpolicella Cl. Sup. Ripasso '18	♀♀ 5
● Valpolicella Cl. Sup. Ripasso ù Il Re Pazzo '21	♀♀ 4
● Valpolicella Cl. Ripasso Il Re Pazzo '22	♀ 4
● Amarone della Valpolicella Cl. '13	♀♀ 8
● Amarone della Valpolicella Cl. '12	♀♀ 4
● Amarone della Valpolicella Cl. '10	♀♀ 4
● Amarone della Valpolicella Cl. Il Re Pazzo '17	♀♀ 6
● Amarone della Valpolicella Cl. Il Re Pazzo '15	♀♀ 8
● Amarone della Valpolicella Cl. Il Re Pazzo '15	♀♀ 8
● Amarone della Valpolicella Cl. Ris. '11	♀♀ 6

○ Soave Cl. Grisela '23	♀♀ 3
○ Soave Cl. Sup. Primo Ettaro '21	♀♀ 5
○ Arcerus Extra Brut	♀ 3
○ Soave Cl. Grisela '22	♀♀ 3
○ Soave Cl. Sup. Costalta Bine Longhe '21	♀♀ 4

Tezza

fraz. Poiano di Valpantena
stradella Maioli, 4
37142 Verona
📞 +39 045550267
🌐 www.tezzawines.it

CELLAR SALES
PRE-BOOKED VISITS
ANNUAL PRODUCTION 200,000 bottles
HECTARES UNDER VINE 27.00
VITICULTURE METHOD Certified Organic
SUSTAINABLE WINERY

The Tezza cousins' winery was established in 1960, but it only took on its current form with their arrival in the late 20th century. Their sizable estate extends across Valpantena, a territory that sees limestone soil alternate with alluvial terrain and significant day-night temperature swings (due to the currents that flow down from the nearby Lessinia). Most of their extensive range is dedicated to traditional wine types. Their flagship Brolo delle Giare line is dedicated to the best vineyards and vintages. The Valpolicella Superiore '19 benefits from a brief drying of the grapes, making for vibrant suggestions of sweet, ripe red fruit, embellished by spicy nuances reminiscent of black pepper. This is all perfectly echoed on the palate, where the wine unfolds full, juicy and long. The Ripasso Ma Roat '20, however, continues to play with very ripe fruit, while on the palate it offers greater softness and approachability.

Tenute Tomasella

via Rigole, 103
31040 Mansuè [TV]
📞 +39 0422850043
🌐 www.tenutetomasella.it

CELLAR SALES
PRE-BOOKED VISITS
ACCOMMODATION
ANNUAL PRODUCTION 120,000 bottles
HECTARES UNDER VINE 50.00
SUSTAINABLE WINERY

Paolo Tomasella's winery is located on the border between the provinces of Treviso and Pordenone, near the hills that lead to the Prealps. The vast vineyard area is primarily dedicated to international varieties, as is common in the region, along with local tai and, of course, glera. Their range includes easy-drinking wines and the Bastie selections, which age at length in the cellar before being released. The Bastie Rosso and Bianco, both 2017s, are the producer's most convincing wines. The first is a monovarietal merlot that sees fruity notes alternate with a subtle balsamic vein, flavors that follow through on a solid, sapid palate that finishes with energy. The second is a friulano that undergoes long maturation in small barrels and in the bottle before revealing aromas of yellow fruit and Mediterranean scrub. In the mouth, it showcases its full, generous palate, concluding on a signature note of almond.

VENETO

Amarone della Valpolicella Corte Majoli '20	🍷🍷 6
Valpolicella Sup. Ripasso Ma Roat '22	🍷🍷 2*
Valpolicella Valpantena Sup. Brolo delle Giare '19	🍷🍷 5
Valpolicella Valpantena Sup. Ripasso '20	🍷🍷 4
Caporal '22	🍷 2
Valpolicella Corte Majoli '22	🍷 2
Valpolicella Sup. Ripasso Corte Majoli '21	🍷 3
Amarone della Valpolicella Corte Majoli '18	🍷🍷 5
Amarone della Valpolicella Valpantena '18	🍷🍷 6
Amarone della Valpolicella Valpantena Brolo delle Giare Ris. '16	🍷🍷 8
Amarone della Valpolicella Valpantena Brolo delle Giare Ris. '15	🍷🍷 8
Valpolicella Valpantera Sup. Brolo delle Giare '18	🍷🍷 5

○ Bastie Bianco '17	🍷🍷 7
● Bastie Rosso '17	🍷🍷 7
○ Chardonnay '22	🍷🍷 2*
○ Cuvée 38 Brut M.Cl.	🍷🍷 5
○ Friuli Friulano '22	🍷🍷 3
● Rigole Rosso '21	🍷🍷 4
○ Delle Venezie Pinot Grigio '23	🍷 3
● Friuli Cabernet Franc '22	🍷 3
● Friuli Merlot '23	🍷 2
○ Prosecco di Treviso Extra Dry Prò	🍷 3
● Friuli Cabernet Franc '21	🍷🍷 3
● Friuli Cabernet Franc '20	🍷🍷 2*
○ Friuli Friulano '20	🍷🍷 2*
○ Friuli Grave Friulano Le Bastie Ris. '16	🍷🍷 6
● Friuli Grave Merlot Le Bastie Ris. '16	🍷🍷 6
● Friuli Grave Merlot Le Bastie Ris. '15	🍷🍷 5

Tommasi Viticoltori

loc. Pedemonte
via Ronchetto, 4
37029 San Pietro in Cariano [VR]
☎ +39 0457701266
⊛ www.tommasi.com

CELLAR SALES
PRE-BOOKED VISITS
ACCOMMODATION AND RESTAURANT SERVICE
ANNUAL PRODUCTION 1,500,000 bottles
HECTARES UNDER VINE 205.00
SUSTAINABLE WINERY

It's not easy to describe the Tommasi family's winery, which has expanded its horizons from Pedemonte in Valpolicella towards Lake Garda and many other Italian wine-growing areas. Today, their vineyards unfold across hundreds of hectares, reaching into all Verona's major appellations. The result is a range that spans everything from more immediately expressive wines to selections that emphasize the character of the vineyard of origin. This year Tommasi submitted two great Riservas: Le Fornaci '21 and Ca' Florian '16. The first is a Lugana defined both by its consistency and finesse, conjuring up aromas ranging from white fruit to Mediterranean scrub, with a subtle vegetal hint in the background. On the palate, the wine's trademark fullness is handled with precision and finesse, aided by vibrant acidity. The second is a classic from the Pedemonte estate, an Amarone that expresses intense dark fruit, captivating the palate with its length and sapidity.

Tonello

via Corcironda, 6
36050 Montorso Vicentino [VI]
☎ +39 0444686205
⊛ www.vinitonello.com

CELLAR SALES
PRE-BOOKED VISITS
ANNUAL PRODUCTION 30,000 bottles
HECTARES UNDER VINE 12.00

For a decade now, Diletta Tonello has been a permanent fixture in the family winery. Yet in this short time, she's already revolutionized their approach in the cellar. Today, the vineyards stretch across the Vicenza part of the Lessinia wine country, reaching into areas like Chiampo, where the grapes maintain high acidity as they ripen, and Agugliana, where they exhibit richer and more harmonious qualities. The range is entirely dedicated to durella and garganega. The Io Aura Riserva '18 excels, bringing character and depth to durello. Made from a field selection of the best grapes, it opens on multifaceted aromas—white fruit intertwining with delicately smoky notes before a subtle mineral vein that becomes even clearer on tasting. The palate showcases delicacy and harmony, suddenly invigorated by vibrant acidity. The Io Teti '19, by contrast, offers simpler, more linear aromas, while in the mouth, the grape's signature acidity dominates, resulting in a crisp, pleasantly bold palate.

● Amarone della Valpolicella Cl. Ca' Florian Ris. '16	♟♟ 8
○ Lugana Le Fornaci Ris. '21	♟♟ 5
● Amarone della Valpolicella Cl. '20	♟♟ 7
○ Lugana Le Fornaci '23	♟♟ 3
● Valpolicella Cl. Sup. De Buris '19	♟♟ 6
● Valpolicella Cl. Sup. Rafaèl '22	♟♟ 3
● Valpolicella Cl. Sup. Ripasso '21	♟♟ 4
● Amarone della Valpolicella Cl. Ca' Florian Ris. '12	♟♟♟ 8
● Amarone della Valpolicella Cl. De Buris Ris. '11	♟♟♟ 8
● Amarone della Valpolicella Cl. De Buris Ris. '10	♟♟♟ 8
● Amarone della Valpolicella Cl. De Buris Ris. '09	♟♟♟ 8

○ Lessini Durello Pas Dosé M.Cl. Io Aura Ris. '18	♟♟ 5
○ Io Eos '22	♟♟ 3
○ Lessini Durello Extra Brut M.Cl. Io Teti '20	♟♟ 5
○ Lessini Durello Pas Dosé M. Cl. Io Ulisse Ris. '19	♟♟ 5
○ Monti Lessini Durello Io Cloe	♟ 3
○ Io Eos '21	♟♟ 3
○ Io Eos '20	♟♟ 2
○ Lessini Durello Brut M.Cl. Io Teti '19	♟♟ 5
○ Lessini Durello Brut M.Cl. Io Teti '18	♟♟ 5
○ Lessini Durello M. Cl. Pas Dosé Io Aura Ris. '15	♟♟ 5
○ Lessini Durello Pas Dosé M.Cl. Io Aura Ris. '17	♟♟ 5
○ Monti Lessini Durello Io Cloe '19	♟♟ 3

La Tordera

via Alnè Bosco, 23
31020 Vidor [TV]
☏ +39 0423985362
⊛ www.latordera.it

CELLAR SALES
PRE-BOOKED VISITS
ANNUAL PRODUCTION 1,300,000 bottles
HECTARES UNDER VINE 70.00
SUSTAINABLE WINERY

The Vettoretti family's activities on the hills of
Valdobbiadene began more than a century ago,
but it was only under the direction of brothers
Renato and Paolo that the winery took on its
current form. The extensive vineyard area, which
includes some prized plots, is personally
overseen by Renato, who gets invaluable support
from his father, Pietro. Meanwhile, in the modern
winery in Vidor, Paolo takes the lead in
operations. The grapes for this 2023 sparkling
wine are sourced from what is universally
considered the appellation's grand cru, Cartizze.
Right from the outset, the nose enchants with its
exotic character. Ripe yellow fruit intersects with
exotic and fresh floral notes, while the palate
reveals a gentle sweetness supported by vibrant
acidity and creamy bubbles. The character of the
Brut Brunei '23 is diametrically opposed,
featuring white-fleshed fruit that resonates on a
palate of excellent tension. The Extra Brut
Otreval '23 is even more reserved in its aromatic
expression but energetic on the palate.

○ Cartizze '23	♟♟ 5
○ Valdobbiadene Brut Brunei '23	♟♟ 3
○ Valdobbiadene Rive di Guia	
Otreval Extra Brut '23	♟♟ 4
○ Valdobbiadene Extra Dry Serrai '23	♟ 3
○ Valdobbiadene Rive di Vidor Dry	
Tittoni '23	♟ 4
○ Cartizze Dry '22	♟♟ 5
○ Valdobbiadene Extra Dry Serrai '22	♟♟ 3
○ Valdobbiadene Rive di Guia Extra Brut	
Otreval '21	♟♟ 5
○ Valdobbiadene Rive di Guia Extra Brut	
Otreval '20	♟♟ 3*
○ Valdobbiadene Rive di Guia	
Otreval Extra Brut '22	♟♟ 4
○ Valdobbiadene Rive di Vidor Dry	
Tittoni '22	♟♟ 4
○ Valdobbiadene Rive di Vidor Dry	
Tittoni '21	♟♟ 5

Turetta Ca' Bianca

loc. Fontanafredda
via Cinto, 5
35030 Cinto Euganeo [PD]
☏ +39 042994288
⊛ www.turettacabianca.it

CELLAR SALES
RESTAURANT SERVICE
ANNUAL PRODUCTION 80,000 bottles
HECTARES UNDER VINE 20.00

The Turetta family's winery is located on a small
flat stretch nestled within the Euganean Hills,
specifically between the village of Cinto and
Mount Cucuzzola. Here, the vineyards climb up
the hillsides, alternating with patches of forest.
The result is a landscape of rare beauty—one
where human activity still doesn't dominate. The
producer's range focuses on Padua's classic wines,
with particular attention to the time needed for
the wines to reach perfect harmony. The
Cabernet Rittochino 42 relies more on tension
than power. The 2019 harvest made for fruity
aromas refreshed by vibrant balsamic accents,
sensations that follow through on the palate,
where the wine unfolds with suppleness,
concluding on a pleasant hint of anise. The
Rossura dei Briganti '18, a Bordeaux blend
dominated by merlot, conjures aromas of sweet,
ripe red fruit alongside subtle vegetal suggestions.
On the palate, it's crisp and medium-bodied,
finishing juicy.

● Colli Euganei Cabernet Rittochino 42 '19	♟♟ 3
○ Colli Euganei Chardonnay	
Passo di Santa Lucia Etichetta Bianca '23	♟♟ 3
○ Colli Euganei Chardonnay	
Passo di Santa Lucia Etichetta Nera '22	♟♟ 3
● Colli Euganei Rosso	
Rossura dei Briganti Ris. '18	♟♟ 4
○ Colli Euganei	
Fior d'Arancio Spumante Dolce	♟ 2
● Colli Euganei Merlot Bumagro '20	♟ 2
○ Colli Euganei Serprino Frizzante	♟ 2
○ Fondo Turetta Frizzante	♟ 2
● Colli Euganei Cabernet Rittochino 42 '17	♟♟ 3
○ Colli Euganei Fior d'Arancio Passito '15	♟♟ 3
● Colli Euganei Merlot Bumagro '19	♟♟ 2*
● Colli Euganei Merlot Bumagro '17	♟♟ 3
● Colli Euganei Rosso	
Rossura dei Briganti Ris. '17	♟♟ 4

Valdo Spumanti
via Foro Boario, 20
31049 Valdobbiadene [TV]
(☎) +39 04239090
🖳 www.valdo.com

CELLAR SALES
PRE-BOOKED VISITS
ANNUAL PRODUCTION 9,000,000 bottles
HECTARES UNDER VINE 155.00

This Valdobbiadene winery's strength lies in its ability to combine sizable production volumes with the quality and style of a craft winery. Credit goes to Pierluigi Bolla, an enlightened president, and Gianfranco Zanon, a highly experienced technician, who have enabled Valdo to become one of the appellation's leading players. The producer operates with the utmost respect for the grapes and the wine itself, ensuring that their premium selections spend extended time in the cellar so as to achieve the right harmony and a profile that reflects both the vintage and the terroir. The San Pietro di Barbozza Extra Brut '22, which hails from the area's finest vineyards, conjures up notes of apple and pear on the nose, unfolding rich and tense on the palate. The Cuvée del Fondatore '22, which benefits from a splash of chardonnay aged in oak, offers a mature aromatic profile and a crisp, firm palate marked by nice tension.

Cantina Valpolicella Negrar
via Ca' Salgari, 2
37024 Negrar [VR]
(☎) +39 0456014300
🖳 www.cantinanegrar.it

CELLAR SALES
PRE-BOOKED VISITS
RESTAURANT SERVICE
ANNUAL PRODUCTION 7,000,000 bottles
HECTARES UNDER VINE 700.00

This Negrar-based cooperative is a leading player in the Verona wine scene, supported by the work of 240 families operating in the Valpolicella Classica production zone, with occasional ventures into neighboring areas. The sprawling production space on Via Ca' Salgari gives rise to a wide array of wines, with the Domini Veneti line serving as its crown jewel. Under the direction of Daniele Accordini, a skilled technical team rigorously and solidly interprets the appellation's reds. To mark its 90th anniversary, the winery produced an Amarone Riserva '15 characterized by superb aromatic depth—overripe cherry accompanied by spicy notes and underbrush. In the mouth, fullness takes center stage, while tannins and acidity guide the palate onto a more structured path. The Ripasso Pruviniano '19 takes a different direction, showcasing aromatic freshness and a crisp, lively palate.

○ Valdobbiadene Brut Cuvée del Fondatore '22	♟♟ 3*
○ Valdobbiadene Rive di San Pietro di Barbozza Extra Brut '22	♟♟ 3*
○ Cartizze Cuvée Viviana	♟♟ 5
○ Valdobbiadene Brut Cuvée di Boj	♟♟ 3
○ Valdobbiadene Brut Numero 10 M. Cl. '21	♟♟ 4
⊙ Prosecco di Treviso Brut Rosé Tenuta La Maredana '23	♟ 2
⊙ Prosecco di Treviso Brut Tenuta La Maredana	♟ 2
○ Valdobbiadene Brut Amor Soli '22	♟ 3
○ Valdobbiadene Extra Dry Cuvée 1926	♟ 3
○ Valdobbiadene Rive di San Pietro di Barbozza Extra Brut '21	♟♟ 3*

● Amarone della Valpolicella Cl. Ris. '15	♟♟ 8
● Amarone della Valpolicella Cl. Domini Veneti '20	♟♟ 6
○ Soave Cl. Coste Domini Veneti '23	♟♟ 3
○ Soave Cl. Sup. Castellaro Domini Veneti '22	♟♟ 3
● Valpolicella Cl. Sup. Domini Veneti '22	♟♟ 2
● Valpolicella Cl. Sup. Ripasso Collezione Pruviniano Domini Veneti '19	♟♟ 3
● Valpolicella Cl. Sup. Ripasso Torbae Domini Veneti '21	♟♟ 3
● Valpolicella Cl. Sup. Verjago Domini Veneti '22	♟♟ 5
⊙ Damigella Blu Domini Veneti '23	♟ 3
● Amarone della Valpolicella Cl. S. Rocco Domini Veneti '08	♟♟♟ 8
● Amarone della Valpolicella Cl. Villa Domini Veneti '05	♟♟♟ 8

Odino Vaona

loc. Valgatara
via Paverno, 41
37020 Marano di Valpolicella [VR]
☎ +39 0457703710
⊜ www.vaona.it

CELLAR SALES
PRE-BOOKED VISITS
ANNUAL PRODUCTION 70,000 bottles
HECTARES UNDER VINE 10.00
VITICULTURE METHOD Certified Organic
SUSTAINABLE WINERY

The Vaona family's winery is located in the central part of the Marano Valley, where 10 hectares of vineyards, exclusively dedicated to traditional grape varieties, climb the hills. In the winery, Alberto passionately interprets the historic styles of the appellation, crafting a range where richness and immediacy are perfectly balanced. The Recioto Le Peagnè '19 is a true homage to tradition, a sweet passito redolent of cherry preserves and spices, offering a powerful sweetness tempered by tannic presence on the palate. The Amarone Paerno of the same vintage opens on notes of red fruit compote, accompanied by alcohol, which broadens its aromatic spectrum before expressing itself on a full, generous, juicy palate. The Amarone Pegrandi '16 is even more traditional in its aromatic sensations, verging on the vegetal—a Riserva with a broad and pleasantly evolved flavor profile.

● Amarone della Valpolicella Cl. Paerno '19	♛♛ 6
● Amarone della Valpolicella Cl. Pegrandi Ris. '16	♛♛ 8
● Recioto della Valpolicella Cl. Le Peagnè '19	♛♛ 5
● Valpolicella Cl. Sup. Ripasso Pegrandi '21	♛♛ 4
● Castaroto '20	♛ 4
● Valpolicella Sup. '21	♛ 3
● Amarone della Valpolicella Cl. Pegrandi '09	♛♛♛ 5
● Amarone della Valpolicella Cl. Pegrandi '08	♛♛♛ 5
● Amarone della Valpolicella Cl. Paerno '18	♛♛ 5
● Amarone della Valpolicella Cl. Pegrandi '18	♛♛ 5

Venturini

fraz. San Floriano
via Semonte, 20
37029 San Pietro in Cariano [VR]
☎ +39 3461683094
⊜ www.viniventurini.com

CELLAR SALES
PRE-BOOKED VISITS
ANNUAL PRODUCTION 160,000 bottles
HECTARES UNDER VINE 16.00
SUSTAINABLE WINERY

The Venturini brothers have been leading the family winery for decades, though the new generation is increasingly taking on an important role in managing the business. The vineyards, which host the territory's historic grape varieties, are situated in some of the best parts of Valpolicella Classica. Once harvested they will provide the foundation for a range closely tied to the appellation and rooted in tradition. It's hard to choose which of the two Amarones is more intriguing. The Classico '19 evokes aromas dominated by overripe yet still unblemished red fruit, interwoven with balsamic nuances that introduce a crisp, racy, and taut palate. The Campo Masua '18, on the other hand, expresses greater complexity in its aromas, with fruit intersected by notes of underbrush, thyme, and spices. In the mouth, concentration is supported by an acidic vein, providing length and tension to the palate. The Recioto '21 is also delicious, with explosive fruit notes and an alluring, soft sweetness.

● Amarone della Valpolicella Cl. '19	♛♛ 5
● Amarone della Valpolicella Cl. Campomasua '18	♛♛ 6
● Recioto Della Valpolicella Cl. '21	♛♛ 5
● Valpolicella Ripasso Cl. Sup. Semonte Alto '20	♛♛ 3
● Valpolicella Cl. '23	♛ 2
● Amarone della Valpolicella Cl. Campomasua '07	♛♛♛ 6
● Amarone della Valpolicella Cl. Campomasua '05	♛♛♛ 6
● Recioto della Valpolicella Cl. Le Brugnine '97	♛♛♛ 5
● Amarone della Valpolicella Cl. Campomasua '17	♛♛ 8
● Amarone della Valpolicella Cl. Ris. '11	♛♛ 8

★Agostino Vicentini

fraz. San Zeno
via C. Battisti, 62c
37030 Colognola ai Colli [VR]
📞 +39 0457650539
🖰 www.vinivicentini.com

CELLAR SALES
PRE-BOOKED VISITS
ANNUAL PRODUCTION 100,000 bottles
HECTARES UNDER VINE 20.00

A few years ago, the Vicentini family winery was just one among many seeking a place in a crowded and competitive playing field, always just a step behind the success of more well-known brands. Today, the San Zeno-based producer has secured a front-row position, boasting a range of superb character and identity. Agostino's meticulous vineyard management is complemented by his son Emanuele's work in the cellar. The Soave Il Casale '22 is a monovarietal garganega harvested at perfect ripeness, showcasing a subtle yet expansive aromatic profile where yellow fruit, flowers, and Mediterranean scrub notes emerge, revealing new facets. On the palate, fullness takes the lead, resulting in a juicy wine with good length. The Palazzo di Campiano '19, on the other hand, follows a different stylistic path, moving on a spicy and almost pungent aromatic finesse before a racy, highly supple palate.

○ Soave Sup. Il Casale '22	♟♟♟ 4*
● Valpolicella Sup. Palazzo di Campiano '19	♟♟ 5
○ Recioto di Soave '22	♟♟ 5
○ Soave Terre Lunghe '23	♟♟ 3
● Valpolicella '23	♟♟ 3
● Valpolicella Sup. Idea Bacco '19	♟♟ 5
○ Soave Sup. Il Casale '21	♟♟♟ 3*
○ Soave Sup. Il Casale '18	♟♟♟ 3*
○ Soave Sup. Il Casale '17	♟♟♟ 3*
○ Soave Sup. Il Casale '16	♟♟♟ 3*
○ Soave Sup. Il Casale '15	♟♟♟ 3*
○ Soave Sup. Il Casale '14	♟♟♟ 3*
○ Soave Sup. Il Casale '13	♟♟♟ 3*
● Valpolicella Sup. Palazzo di Campiano '17	♟♟♟ 5

Vigna Ròda

fraz. Cortelà
via Monte Versa, 1569
35030 Vo' [PD]
📞 +39 0499940228
🖰 www.vignaroda.com

CELLAR SALES
PRE-BOOKED VISITS
ANNUAL PRODUCTION 100,000 bottles
HECTARES UNDER VINE 20.00

Gianni Strazzacappa's winery, about 20 hectares where red Bordeaux varietals take center stage, unfolds across the western slopes of the Euganean Hills. Once a modest family producer with simple ambitions, Gianni has transformed Vigna Ròda into one of the most notewothy estates in the territory. The Scarlatto '19, a Bordeaux blend (mostly merlot), expresses the warmth of the western Euganean Hills without succumbing to softness. On the nose, clear suggestions of red fruit are enriched by spicy and fine herbal nuances. On the palate, its firm structure is supported by a foundation of tannins and acidity. The Damerino '21 is a monovarietal merlot that plays on fresher, more dynamic sensations, both on the nose, with aromas of fresh fruit and flowers, and in the mouth, where acidity adds tension and liveliness.

○ Colli Euganei Fior d'Arancio Spumante Dolce Praesèo '23	♟♟ 3
● Colli Euganei Rosso Scarlatto '19	♟♟ 5
● Il Damerino '21	♟♟ 3
○ Aroma 2.0 '23	♟ 3
○ Cà Zamira '23	♟ 2
○ Colli Euganei Bianco Bei Tempi '23	♟ 2
● Colli Euganei Rosso Zendal '23	♟ 2
● Colli Euganei Cabernet Èspero '21	♟♟ 2
○ Colli Euganei Fior d'Arancio Passito Petali d'Ambra '19	♟♟ 4
○ Colli Euganei Fior d'Arancio Spumante Prasèo '22	♟♟ 3
○ Colli Euganei Fior d'Arancio Passito Petali d'Ambra '20	♟♟ 4
● Colli Euganei Rosso Scarlatto '18	♟♟ 5

Vignale di Cecilia

loc. Fornaci
via Croci, 14
35030 Baone [PD]
☎ +39 042951420
🌐 www.vignaledicecilia.it

PRE-BOOKED VISITS
ANNUAL PRODUCTION 20,000 bottles
HECTARES UNDER VINE 8.00
VITICULTURE METHOD Certified Organic

Paolo Brunello, a musician turned vintner, took over his small family winery in 2000. The journey has been deliberate and unhurried, allowing time to explore, understand, experiment, and reassess, always in search of harmony not just in the glass but also in the surrounding environment, and life itself. In addition to the few hectares cultivated around the cellar, Paolo has acquired another set of small parcels, resulting in a range marked by its character and originality. El Moro '19 is a blend of cabernet franc and carménère from a vineyard over 30 years old. Sweet and juicy dark fruit aromas are broadened by vegetal notes and underbrush. The palate is full and juicy, with a long finish nicely supported by acidity. The Covolo '20, by contrast, is a classic Bordeaux blend that sees simple and immediately expressive aromas followed by a highly enjoyable palate. The Campo Nicoletta, a Prosecco produced in a warm area, also caught our attention, revealing an unexpected character dominated by ripe yellow fruit and a crisp, dense palate.

● Colli Euganei Rosso Cóvolo '20	♟♟ 4
● El Moro '19	♟♟ 4
○ Prosecco Brut Nature Campo Nicoletta	♟♟ 3
○ Val di Spin Frizzante	♟ 3
● Colli Euganei Rosso Cóvolo '19	♟♟ 3
● Colli Euganei Rosso Cóvolo '18	♟♟ 3
● Colli Euganei Rosso Cóvolo '17	♟♟ 3
● Colli Euganei Rosso Passacaglia '15	♟♟ 4
● El Moro '18	♟♟ 3*
● El Moro Cabernet '16	♟♟ 3*
● Passacaglia '18	♟♟ 4
● Passacaglia '16	♟♟ 4
○ Prosecco Brut Nature Campo Nicoletta	♟♟ 2*

★★Vignalta

via Scalette
35032 Arquà Petrarca [PD]
☎ +39 0429777305
🌐 www.vignalta.it

CELLAR SALES
PRE-BOOKED VISITS
ANNUAL PRODUCTION 230,000 bottles
HECTARES UNDER VINE 35.00
SUSTAINABLE WINERY

VENETO

More than 40 years have passed since the founding of this Arquà winery, and today, as then, passion drives every activity. Vignalta now oversees more than 30 hectares of vineyards scattered across the southern part of the Euganean Hills, including renowned sites like Monte Gemola. Here, alongside Bordeaux varietals, chardonnay has been thriving in recent years, delivering impressive results. Their most interesting wines come from the Gemola, including the Rosso '19 and the Chardonnay '22. The former impresses with the depth of its aromas: wild fruit, complemented by notes of spices and graphite, while the palate is rich, sapid, and supported by smooth tannins. The latter opens with a sulfurous and smoky note that gives way to ripe fruit, sensations that are even more defined on an energetic, vibrant palate. The Alpianae '20, an aromatically exuberant passito, is also excellent—alluring and dynamic.

● Colli Euganei Rosso Gemola '19	♟♟♟ 7
○ Colli Euganei Chardonnay Gemola '22	♟♟ 5
○ Colli Euganei Fior d'Arancio Alpianæ '20	♟♟ 5
● Agno Tinto '18	♟♟ 5
○ Blanc de Noirs Brut Nature M. Cl.	♟♟ 5
● Colli Euganei Cabernet Ris. '11	♟♟ 8
● Colli Euganei Carménère Ris. '21	♟♟ 5
● Colli Euganei Merlot Ris. '17	♟♟ 5
● Pinot Nero '18	♟♟ 5
○ Colli Euganei Fior d'Arancio Sirio '23	♟ 3
○ Colli Euganei Fiori d'Arancio Passito Alpianae '16	♟♟♟ 5
● Colli Euganei Merlot Ris. '15	♟♟♟ 5
● Colli Euganei Rosso Gemola '18	♟♟♟ 8
● Colli Euganei Rosso Gemola '13	♟♟♟ 6

Le Vigne di San Pietro

via San Pietro, 23
37066 Sommacampagna [VR]
📞 +39 045510016
🌐 www.levignedisanpietro.it

CELLAR SALES
PRE-BOOKED VISITS
ANNUAL PRODUCTION 70,000 bottles
HECTARES UNDER VINE 10.00

Carlo Nerozzi is the heart and soul of Le Vigne di San Pietro, a splendid estate nestled on San Pietro in Sommacampagna hill. Many of the vineyards unfold right around the winery and residence amidst trees, while a second property lies just a few kilometers away, in the Balconi Rossi area. Together, they form the estate from which all the grapes are harvested, producing wines that are unmistakably refined and deep. The Bardolino Sommacampagna '22 took advantage of the warm vintage to offer aromas dominated by red fruit, which finds sudden bursts of freshness in the presence of medicinal herbs and underbrush. On the palate, it's not just light and easy to drink but also reveals sapidity, length, and a supple, juicy profile. The Bardolino Superiore '21 is also delicious, the result of a completely different harvest that brought more tension and energy to the palate. The Custoza '23 showcases aromas of yellow fruit and flowers, delivering a sapid and penetrating profile.

Vigneto Due Santi

v.le Asiago, 174
36061 Bassano del Grappa [VI]
📞 +39 0424502074
🌐 www.vignetoduesanti.it

CELLAR SALES
PRE-BOOKED VISITS
ANNUAL PRODUCTION 100,000 bottles
HECTARES UNDER VINE 18.00
SUSTAINABLE WINERY

The Breganze appellation stretches across the hills overlooking the Vicenza plains, nestled between the Astico and Brenta rivers, bathed in sunlight, and protected to the north by the Sette Comuni plateau. Here, Adriano and Stefano Zonta manage their family winery, which has been active for over half a century. With around 20 hectares cultivated, they produce high-quality wines characterized by a solid and harmonious style. While the Cabernet Due Santi '21 continues to rest in the cellar, the Cavallare '20 has kept the winery's flag flying high. Ripe red fruit melds with floral and anise notes. On the palate, the wine shifts gears, impressing with its firmness, outlined by a close-knit tannic texture and an acidic presence that adds tension and length. The Merlot '22 also caught our attention, summoning aromas of plum refreshed by appealing vegetal notes, which reappear on a crisp, pleasantly spirited palate.

● Bardolino Sommacampagna '22	♟♟ 2*
● Bardolino Sup. '21	♟♟ 4
○ Custoza '23	♟♟ 2*
● Bardolino '14	♟♟♟ 2*
● Bardolino '11	♟♟♟ 2*
○ Custoza Sanpietro '16	♟♟♟ 4*
● Refolà Cabernet Sauvignon '04	♟♟♟ 6
● Bardolino '20	♟♟ 3
● Bardolino '19	♟♟ 3
● Bardolino '18	♟♟ 2*
● Bardolino Sup. '17	♟♟ 3*
○ Chiaretto di Bardolino CorDeRosa '20	♟♟ 3
● Come un Pino Nero '18	♟♟ 4
○ Custoza Sanpietro '19	♟♟ 4
○ Custoza Sanpietro '18	♟♟ 4
● Refolà '15	♟♟ 6

● Breganze Cabernet Cavallare '20	♟♟ 5
● Breganze Cabernet '22	♟♟ 4
● Breganze Merlot '22	♟♟ 3
○ Campo di Fiori Malvasia '23	♟♟ 3
○ Rivana '23	♟♟ 3
● Breganze Cabernet Due Santi '14	♟♟♟ 4*
● Breganze Cabernet Vign. Due Santi '12	♟♟♟ 4*
● Breganze Cabernet Vign. Due Santi '08	♟♟♟ 4*
● Breganze Cabernet Vign. Due Santi '07	♟♟♟ 4*
● Breganze Cabernet Vign. Due Santi '05	♟♟♟ 4*
● Breganze Cabernet Vign. Due Santi '04	♟♟♟ 4*
● Breganze Cabernet Vign. Due Santi '03	♟♟♟ 4*
● Breganze Cabernet Vign. Due Santi '00	♟♟♟ 4*
● Breganze Cabernet Cavallare '19	♟♟ 4
● Breganze Cabernet Due Santi '19	♟♟ 4
● Breganze Cabernet Due Santi '18	♟♟ 4
● Breganze Merlot '21	♟♟ 2*

★Villa Sandi

via Erizzo, 113a
31035 Crocetta del Montello [TV]
(+39 04238607
www.villasandi.it

CELLAR SALES
PRE-BOOKED VISITS
ACCOMMODATION AND RESTAURANT SERVICE
ANNUAL PRODUCTION 5,600,000 bottles
HECTARES UNDER VINE 560.00
SUSTAINABLE WINERY

The large estate owned by the Polegato family is one of the key players in the Valdobbiadene wine scene. Over the past few decades, it has significantly elevated both the quality and quantity of production. Established half a century ago, Villa Sandi is now expertly led by Giancarlo Moretti Polegato, who has expanded its reach to include prestigious areas such as La Rivetta, in the heart of Cartizze. Indeed, the Cartizze '23, sourced from this grand cru, conjures up exotic fruit aromas and notes of flowers. On the palate, it eschews the sweetness often found here, delivering a crisp, sapid experience instead, with remarkable length. On the estates of Valdobbiadene, Nervesa, Crocetta del Montello, and Spilimbergo, the glera grape is expertly highlighted, though international varieties also receive attention. The succulent Merlot Corpore '21 and the elegant Amalia Moretti Brut, crafted from pinot nero and chardonnay, are noteworthy examples.

Villa Spinosa

via Jago dall'Ora, 14
37024 Negrar [VR]
(+39 0457500093
www.villaspinosa.it

CELLAR SALES
PRE-BOOKED VISITS
ACCOMMODATION
ANNUAL PRODUCTION 45,000 bottles
HECTARES UNDER VINE 20.00
SUSTAINABLE WINERY

A quick glance at the numbers on Cascella's profile reveals the winery's production philosophy. With about 20 hectares of vineyards spread out across the hills that separate the Negrar and Marano valleys, only a portion of the harvest is used for in-house production, allowing for meticulous selection of the best parcels. In the winery, there is great attention to enhancing the aromatic finesse of the grapes and respecting the maturation time required for their most important selections. The Amarone Albasini '17 opens on more immediate, fruit-focused aromas than previous vintages, the result of a warm harvest that also influences the palate, where full flavors are underscored by sapidity and close-knit, polished tannins. The Figari continues to impress, utilizing the excellent 2021 harvest to offer vibrant notes of wild berries and spices, which are mirrored on the palate, where firmness and tension come together harmoniously, creating a juicy, refined elixir.

VENETO

Cartizze Brut La Rivetta '23	▼▼▼ 6
Amalia Moretti Brut M. Cl. Ris.	▼▼ 8
Asolo Brut Biodiversity Friend	▼▼ 3
Montello Asolo Merlot Corpore '21	▼▼ 6
Opere Trevigiane Brut M.Cl.	▼▼ 4
Valdobbiadene Extra Brut La Rivetta 120	▼▼ 4
Opere Trevigiane Brut M.Cl. Ris. '16	▼ 5
Prosecco Brut Rosé Il Fresco '23	▼ 3
Prosecco di Treviso Brut Il Fresco	▼ 2
Raboso '20	▼ 3
Cartizze Brut La Rivetta '22	♀♀♀ 6
Cartizze Brut La Rivetta '21	♀♀♀ 6
Cartizze Brut La Rivetta '20	♀♀♀ 6
Cartizze Brut V. La Rivetta '11	♀♀♀ 4*
Cartizze Brut V. La Rivetta '10	♀♀♀ 4
Cartizze Brut V. La Rivetta '09	♀♀♀ 4

● Amarone della Valpolicella Cl. Albasini '17	▼▼ 8
● Valpolicella Cl. Sup. Figari '21	▼▼ 4
● Recioto della Valpolicella Cl. Francesca Finato Spinosa '21	▼▼ 6
● Valpolicella Cl. '23	▼▼ 3
● Valpolicella Cl. Sup. Ripasso Jago '21	▼▼ 5
● Amarone della Valpolicella Cl. '08	♀♀♀ 7
● Amarone della Valpolicella Cl. Albasini '16	♀♀♀ 8
● Amarone della Valpolicella Cl. Albasini '15	♀♀♀ 8
● Amarone della Valpolicella Cl. Albasini '13	♀♀♀ 8
● Amarone della Valpolicella Cl. Albasini '11	♀♀♀ 7
● Amarone della Valpolicella Cl. Albasini '10	♀♀♀ 7
● Valpolicella Cl. Sup. Ripasso Jago '11	♀♀♀ 3*
● Valpolicella Cl. Sup. Ripasso Jago '18	♀♀ 3*
● Valpolicella Cl. Sup. Ripasso Jago '16	♀♀ 3*

Vigneti Villabella

fraz. Calmasino
loc. Canova, 2
37011 Bardolino [VR]
☎ +39 0457236448
🌐 www.vignetivillabella.com

CELLAR SALES
PRE-BOOKED VISITS
ACCOMMODATION
ANNUAL PRODUCTION 500,000 bottles
HECTARES UNDER VINE 220.00

The Delibori and Cristoforetti families' winery is a leading figure in Garda wine production. However, it's important to note that their vast estate extends across all of Verona's main appellations, which they interpret with stylistic precision, avoiding fleeting trends. A true gem in their portfolio is the Villa Cordevigo vineyard, which has been owned for nearly 30 years and is organically managed. The Bardolino Montebaldo Morlongo '22 once again stands out, expressing all the trademark nuances of its terroir. Wild berries linger in the background of a nose dominated by spices and a prominent herbal vein. The palate is sapid, juicy, and impressively long. Among the Chiaretti, the true focus of the estate, the Villa Cordevigo '23 shines with its aromatic freshness and a pleasing flavor. Lastly, the Lugana '23 stands out for its excellent solidity and tension.

★Viviani

via Mazzano, 8
37020 Negrar [VR]
☎ +39 0457500286
🌐 www.cantinaviviani.com

CELLAR SALES
PRE-BOOKED VISITS
ANNUAL PRODUCTION 80,000 bottles
HECTARES UNDER VINE 10.00
SUSTAINABLE WINERY

Claudio Viviani was one of the key figures in the revival of Valpolicella in the late 20th century, crafting wines that demonstrated the region's potential—its grapes, and its traditions—to the world. Today, in Mazzano, among the appellation's highest hills, he cultivates vineyards dedicated entirely to historic varietals, producing wines that marry rich flavors with aromatic elegance. The Valpolicella Campo Morar '19 reveals its aromas shyly, as if reluctant to offer itself to hast drinkers. Dark, sweet cherry is vividly framed by notes of medicinal herbs and peppery tones, sensations that become even more pronounced on the palate, where the wine emerges for its density and tension. With the Amarone Casa dei Bepi still resting in the cellar, our attention turned to the Amarone Classico '19, a bottle with deep, mineral aromas, captivating with its energetic and compact palate.

Wine	Rating
● Bardolino Montebaldo V. Morlongo '22	♟♟ 3*
☉ Chiaretto di Bardolino Cl. Villa Cordevigo '23	♟♟ 3*
● Amarone della Valpolicella Cl. '19	♟♟ 6
☉ Chiaretto di Bardolino Cl. '23	♟♟ 3
☉ Lugana '23	♟♟ 3
☉ Soave Cl. '23	♟♟ 3
☉ Custoza '23	♟ 3
● Bardolino Cl. V. Morlongo '14	♟♟♟ 2*
● Bardolino Montebaldo Morlongo Anniversario 50 Vendemmie '20	♟♟♟ 3*
● Bardolino Montebaldo V. Morlongo '21	♟♟♟ 3*
● Bardolino Montebaldo Morlongo '20	♟♟ 2*
☉ Chiaretto di Bardolino Cl. Gaudenzia Villa Cordevigo '19	♟♟ 3*
☉ Chiaretto di Bardolino Cl. Villa Cordevigo '22	♟♟ 3*

Wine	Rating
● Valpolicella Cl. Sup. Campo Morar '19	♟♟ 5
● Amarone della Valpolicella Cl. '19	♟♟ 6
● Valpolicella Cl. '22	♟♟
● Amarone della Valpolicella Cl. Casa dei Bepi '13	♟♟♟
● Amarone della Valpolicella Cl. Casa dei Bepi '12	♟♟♟
● Amarone della Valpolicella Cl. Casa dei Bepi '11	♟♟♟
● Amarone della Valpolicella Cl. Casa dei Bepi '10	♟♟♟
● Amarone della Valpolicella Cl. Casa dei Bepi '09	♟♟♟
● Recioto della Valpolicella Cl. '13	♟♟♟
● Valpolicella Cl. Sup. Campo Morar '17	♟♟♟
● Valpolicella Cl. Sup. Campo Morar '09	♟♟♟

Zambon Vulcano

via Duello, 8
37030 Roncà [VR]
+39 3484043008
www.zambonvulcano.com

CELLAR SALES
PRE-BOOKED VISITS
ANNUAL PRODUCTION 80,000 bottles
HECTARES UNDER VINE 14.00
VITICULTURE METHOD Certified Organic

Federico Zambon has taken the helm of his family's winery and, within a few years, overseen a major shift in the direction of production. The estate, located in the eastern part of Soave, centers on the Calvarina, Duello, and Crocetta hills and has increasingly adopted environmentally friendly viticulture practices, emphasizing the value of the grapes harvested. In the winery, spontaneous fermentations are favored, and the wines are only released after appropriate aging. The Soave Vulcano '22 is a characterful wine that, alongside ripe yellow fruit, evokes vibrant suggestions of flint and dried flowers, sensations that emerge even more clearly on a concentrated palate with good rapidity and taut acidity. Le Cervare '20, a monovarietal garganega harvested on Monte Crocetta, reveals mineral notes and white fruit on a crisp palate with notable acidic drive and length. The Durello '19, a sharp and energetic sparkler, also deserves praise.

Pietro Zanoni

fraz. Quinzano
via Are Zovo, 16d
37125 Verona
+39 0458343977
www.pietrozanoni.it

CELLAR SALES
PRE-BOOKED VISITS
ANNUAL PRODUCTION 25,000 bottles
HECTARES UNDER VINE 7.50

Pietro Zanoni has drawn the attention of Valpolicella wine enthusiasts to Quinzano, a beautiful vineyard-covered valley that descends from the hills to touch the city of Verona and the banks of the Adige River. His estate stretches across this hilly part of the territory, where all the vineyards are trellised, having abandoned the traditional pergola system. The approach yields wines that stand out for their rich flavors and aromatic integrity. This year, only Valpolicellas were presented, with the Campo Denari '18 leading the way. Made in part with slightly dried grapes, it opens on vibrant aromas of sweet, fleshy cherry, complemented by a hint of sweet spices. On the palate, it reveals a rich, juicy profile that expands decisively, perfectly supported by tannins and acidity. The Superiore '21, on the other hand, plays with fresher, more approachable fruit, while on the palate, it's supple. Good tension.

Soave Vulcano '22	♟♟ 4
Lessini Durello Pas Dosé M. Cl. 36 '19	♟♟ 5
Soave Le Cervare '20	♟♟ 6
Le Cime Merlot '20	♟ 4
Fidelis '17	♟♟ 6
Lessini Durello Pas Dosé M. Cl. 36 '18	♟♟ 5
Soave Le Cervare '19	♟♟ 6
Soave Vulcano '20	♟♟ 4

● Valpolicella Sup. '21	♟♟ 3
● Valpolicella Sup. Campo Denari '18	♟♟ 4
● Valpolicella Sup. Ripasso '20	♟ 4
● Amarone della Valpolicella '16	♟♟ 7
● Amarone della Valpolicella '15	♟♟ 7
● Amarone della Valpolicella '14	♟♟ 7
● Recioto della Valpolicella '18	♟♟ 7
● Valpolicella Ripasso Sup. '18	♟♟ 4
● Valpolicella Sup. '20	♟♟ 3
● Valpolicella Sup. '19	♟♟ 3*
● Valpolicella Sup. '18	♟♟ 3*
● Valpolicella Sup. '17	♟♟ 3
● Valpolicella Sup. Campo Denari '17	♟♟ 4
● Valpolicella Sup. Campo Denari '15	♟♟ 4
● Valpolicella Sup. Ripasso '19	♟♟ 4
● Valpolicella Sup. Ripasso '17	♟♟ 4

VENETO

447

Pietro Zardini
via Don P. Fantoni, 3
37029 San Pietro in Cariano [VR]
📞 +39 0456800989
🌐 www.pietrozardini.it

CELLAR SALES
PRE-BOOKED VISITS
ANNUAL PRODUCTION 60,000 bottles
HECTARES UNDER VINE 10.00

★Zenato
via San Benedetto, 8
37019 Peschiera del Garda [VR]
📞 +39 0457550300
🌐 www.zenato.it

CELLAR SALES
PRE-BOOKED VISITS
ANNUAL PRODUCTION 2,000,000 bottles
HECTARES UNDER VINE 95.00

Pietro Zardini approaches the Verona appellation in two closely linked but distinct ways: as a producer in his own right and as a consultant for prominent local wineries. This dual role has given him deep knowledge of Valpolicella and its grapes, which he channels at his Via Don Fantoni winery into a style that blends tradition with modernity. The Amarone Leone Zardini '18 strongly reflects its traditional roots, highlighted by tones of dried cherry, herbal notes, and a subtle yet persistent spicy edge. On the palate, the wine is rich, relying on its acidity for suppleness and tension. The Recioto Pietro Junior '22, equally rooted in tradition, intoxicates in its aromas—a juicy, well-balanced drink. Conversely, the Amarone '20 reveals a more contemporary profile, with a clear expression of fruit and an energetic, lively dynamic on the palate.

The historic winery in Peschiera del Garda has long pursued two distinct paths, each related to Verona's two most important appellations: Valpolicella and Lugana. The sizable estate spans two properties: Costalunga (dedicated to red grapes destined for Valpolicella wines), and Santa Cristina (where the turbiana variety reigns supreme). In their modern and well-equipped cellar on Via San Benedetto they craft a range of high-quality wines. The Reserves dedicated to the founder, the Amarone '18 and Lugana '21, are once again in the spotlight, each telling the story of the producer's connection to traditional wines in their own way. The Amarone '18 reveals itself slowly, exploring the deeper soul of the appellation, offering a palate of superb concentration, managed with lightness and tension. The Lugana '21, on the other hand, plays with wonderfully ripe fruit, with oak and a hint of minerality lingering in the background. A juicy and richly textured palate follows. We also appreciated the energetic and spirited Amarone '19.

- ● Amarone della Valpolicella Cl. Leone Zardini Ris. '18 — 8
- ● Amarone della Valpolicella Pietro Junior '20 — 6
- ● Recioto della Valpolicella Pietro Junior '22 — 5
- ● Rosignol '20 — 4
- ● Amarone della Valpolicella Cl. Leone Zardini Ris. '17 — 8
- ● Amarone della Valpolicella Cl. Leone Zardini Ris. '13 — 8
- ● Amarone della Valpolicella Cl. Leone Zardini Ris. '12 — 8
- ● Amarone della Valpolicella Cl. Leone Zardini Ris. '11 — 8
- ● Amarone della Valpolicella Cl. Leone Zardini Ris. '16 — 8

- ● Amarone della Valpolicella Cl. Sergio Zenato Ris. '18 — 8
- ● Amarone della Valpolicella Cl. '19
- ○ Lugana Sergio Zenato Ris. '21
- ○ Lugana San Benedetto '23
- ● Valpolicella Cl. Sup. '21
- ● Valpolicella Sup. Ripasso Ripassa '20
- ● Cresasso Corvina Veronese '18
- ● Amarone della Valpolicella Cl. Sergio Zenato Ris. '16
- ● Amarone della Valpolicella Cl. Sergio Zenato Ris. '11
- ● Amarone della Valpolicella Cl. Sergio Zenato Ris. '10
- ○ Lugana Sergio Zenato Ris. '17
- ○ Lugana Sergio Zenato Ris. '16
- ○ Lugana Sergio Zenato Ris. '15

Zeni 1870

via Costabella, 9
37011 Bardolino [VR]
☏ +39 0457210022
🌐 www.zeni.it

CELLAR SALES
PRE-BOOKED VISITS
ANNUAL PRODUCTION 1,000,000 bottles
HECTARES UNDER VINE 25.00

The Zeni family winery, now confidently led by siblings Elena, Federica, and Fausto, stands as a cornerstone of Verona winemaking. With over a century of history, it has successfully brought the vines of the Lake Garda region to the world. The producer's strength lies in its close collaboration with numerous growers who deliver their harvests to Via Costabella, as well as in the precise work of a highly skilled technical team. Among their Lake Garda wines, the Chiaretto di Bardolino '23 excels this year, offering vibrant aromas of wild berries and rose, and a sapid, juicy palate—enticingly drinkable. Moving on to neighboring territories, the Amarone Barriques '18 stands out: dried fruit finds added freshness and character from hints of ink, spices, and underbrush. The palate is firm, softened by alcohol, and enlivened at the finish by a vital acidic push.

Amarone della Valpolicella Barriques '18	♟♟ 7
Chiaretto di Bardolino Cl. Vigne Alte '23	♟♟ 2*
Lugana Vigne Alte '23	♟♟ 2*
Amarone della Valpolicella Cl. '21	♟♟ 6
Bardolino Cl. I Filari del Nino '23	♟♟ 5
Bardolino Cl. Vigne Alte '23	♟♟ 2*
Lugana Marogne '23	♟♟ 3
Valpolicella Sup. Ripasso Marogne '22	♟♟ 3
Bardolino Cl. Sup. Vigne Alte '22	♟ 4
Amarone della Valpolicella Barriques '17	♟♟♟ 7
Amarone della Valpolicella Barriques '16	♟♟ 7
Amarone della Valpolicella Cl. '20	♟♟ 6
Amarone della Valpolicella Cl. Nino Zeni Ris. '17	♟♟ 8
Amarone della Valpolicella Cl. Vigne Alte '17	♟♟ 6
Bardolino Cl. Vigne Alte '22	♟♟ 2*
Chiaretto di Bardolino Cl. Vigne Alte '22	♟♟ 2*

Zymè

loc. San Floriano
via Ca' del Pipa, 1
37029 San Pietro in Cariano [VR]
☏ +39 0457701108
🌐 www.zyme.it

CELLAR SALES
PRE-BOOKED VISITS
ANNUAL PRODUCTION 120,000 bottles
HECTARES UNDER VINE 30.00
SUSTAINABLE WINERY

Zymè's journey has now reached the quarter-century mark, but Celestino Gaspari's relationship with Valpolicella has a much deeper history, one shaped by the producer's experiences at prominent local wineries and by the knowledge and connections that have made him one of the region's best ambassadors. The estate covers many hectares, stretching across both Valpolicella Classica and other territories in Verona and Vicenza. Celestino interprets these lands—their grapes, traditions, and climates—with great precision and care. Two thrilling Amarones were presented this year. The Classico '18 embodies the essence of tradition: dried cherry comes together with spices and a soft palate revitalized by acidity. The Riserva La Mattonara, hailing from the distant 2011 vintage, expresses that hot summer with its richness of fruit, enhanced by oak and cocoa notes. The palate proves dense, compact, and extraordinarily youthful.

● Amarone della Valpolicella Cl. '18	♟♟ 8
● Amarone della Valpolicella Cl. La Mattonara Ris. '11	♟♟ 8
● Kairos '20	♟♟ 8
● Valpolicella Rêverie '22	♟♟ 3
○ Il Bianco From Black to White '21	♟ 3
● Amarone della Valpolicella Cl. '13	♟♟♟ 8
● Amarone della Valpolicella Cl. '06	♟♟♟ 8
● Amarone della Valpolicella Cl. La Mattonara Ris. '03	♟♟♟ 8
● Amarone della Valpolicella Cl. La Mattonara Ris. '01	♟♟♟ 8
● Amarone della Valpolicella Cl. '17	♟♟ 8
● Amarone della Valpolicella Cl. '16	♟♟ 8
● Harlequin '16	♟♟ 8
● Valpolicella Cl. Sup. '19	♟♟ 5

OTHER WINERIES

Aldo Adami

s.da Valbusa, 29
37066 Sommacampagna [VR]
☏ +39 045516105
🌐 www.cantinaaldoadami.com

CELLAR SALES
PRE-BOOKED VISITS
ANNUAL PRODUCTION 130,000 bottles
HECTARES UNDER VINE 13.00

○ Custoza '23	🍷🍷 2*
● Bardolino '23	🍷 2
○ Chiaretto di Bardolino '23	🍷 2

Almivisi

p.zza Marco Polo, 4/11
31045 Motta di Livenza [TV]
☏ +39 3282756432
🌐 www.almivisi.it

○ Moscato Passito '21	🍷🍷 6
○ Qortè '22	🍷🍷 3
● Qustò '20	🍷 4
● Sodalizio '18	🍷 6

Antolini

via Prognol, 22
37020 Marano di Valpolicella [VR]
☏ +39 0457755351
🌐 www.antolinivini.it

CELLAR SALES
PRE-BOOKED VISITS
ACCOMMODATION
ANNUAL PRODUCTION 60,000 bottles
HECTARES UNDER VINE 9.00
SUSTAINABLE WINERY

● Amarone della Valpolicella Cl. Morópio '20	🍷🍷 6
● Recioto della Valpolicella Cl. '22	🍷🍷 5
● Valpolicella Cl. '23	🍷🍷 2*
● Valpolicella Cl. Sup. Ripasso '21	🍷 4

Ai Galli

via Loredan, 28
30020 Pramaggiore [VE]
☏ +39 0421799314
🌐 www.aigalli.it

CELLAR SALES
PRE-BOOKED VISITS
ANNUAL PRODUCTION 600,000 bottles
HECTARES UNDER VINE 70.00

○ Lison Cl. '22	🍷🍷 4
○ Venezia Chardonnay '22	🍷🍷 4
● Lison-Pramaggiore Refosco P. R. '21	🍷 3
● Venezia Cabernet Franc '21	🍷 3

Tenuta Amadio

via Longon, 74
31010 Monfumo [TV]
☏ +39 0423560099
🌐 www.tenutamadio.com

CELLAR SALES
PRE-BOOKED VISITS
ACCOMMODATION AND RESTAURANT SERVICE
ANNUAL PRODUCTION 250,000 bottles
HECTARES UNDER VINE 15.00
SUSTAINABLE WINERY

○ Asolo Brut '23	🍷🍷 2
○ Asolo Extra Dry '23	🍷🍷 2
○ Asolo Dry '23	🍷 2
● Asolo Montelllo Recantina	🍷 4

Luciano Arduini

loc. Corrubbio
via Belvedere, 3
37029 San Pietro in Cariano [VR]
☏ +39 0457725880
🌐 www.arduinivini.it

CELLAR SALES
PRE-BOOKED VISITS
ANNUAL PRODUCTION 95,000 bottles
HECTARES UNDER VINE 16.00

● Amarone della Valpolicella Cl. '21	🍷🍷
● Amarone della Valpolicella Cl. Simison '19	🍷🍷
● Valpolicella Cl. Sup. Costelonghe '21	🍷🍷
● Valpolicella Cl. Fontana del Fongo '23	🍷

OTHER WINERIES

Asja Rigato Vini
via Brea, 7a
35024 Bovolenta [PD]
☏ +39 3409262454
⊛ www.asjarigato.it

CELLAR SALES
PRE-BOOKED VISITS
ACCOMMODATION
ANNUAL PRODUCTION 15,000 bottles
HECTARES UNDER VINE 5.00
SUSTAINABLE WINERY

● Bagnoli Friularo '19	♟♟ 5
○ Bianco '23	♟ 4
○ Flower Power Frizzante sui Lieviti	♟ 3
○ Rosato '22	♟ 4

Batìso
loc. Col San Martino
via Scandolera, 72
31010 Farra di Soligo [TV]
☏ +39 04381451289
⊛ www.batiso.it

○ Valdobbiadene Brut	♟♟ 3
○ Valdobbiadene Extra Dry	♟♟ 3
○ Valdobbiadene Rive di Colbertaldo Extra Brut '23	♟♟ 3

Bellenda
fraz. Carpesica
via Giardino, 90
31029 Vittorio Veneto [TV]
☏ +39 0438920025
⊛ www.bellenda.it

CELLAR SALES
PRE-BOOKED VISITS
ACCOMMODATION
ANNUAL PRODUCTION 1,000,000 bottles
HECTARES UNDER VINE 38.00

○ Conegliano Valdobbiadene Frizzante Sui Lieviti Brut Nature Così È	♟♟ 3
○ Valdobbiadene Rive di Carpesica Dry M.Cl. Lei '18	♟♟ 5

Bacio della Luna
via Rovede, 36
31020 Vidor [TV]
☏ +39 0423983111
⊛ www.baciodellaluna.it

ANNUAL PRODUCTION 2,000,000 bottles
HECTARES UNDER VINE 25.00
VITICULTURE METHOD Certified Organic

○ Valdobbiadene Brut '23	♟♟ 2*
○ Valdobbiadene Extra Dry '23	♟♟ 2*
○ Valdobbiadene Extra Brut '23	♟ 3

Cantina Beato Bartolomeo da Breganze
via Roma, 100
36042 Breganze [VI]
☏ +39 0445873112
⊛ www.cantinabreganze.it

CELLAR SALES
PRE-BOOKED VISITS
ACCOMMODATION
ANNUAL PRODUCTION 1,900,000 bottles
HECTARES UNDER VINE 450.00
SUSTAINABLE WINERY

○ Breganze Torcolato '19	♟♟ 5
○ Breganze Vespaiolo Brut M.Cl. Bosco Grande '18	♟♟ 5
● Breganze Cabernet Kilò Ris. '18	♟ 4

Ornella Bellia
via Roma, 117
30020 Pramaggiore [VE]
☏ +39 0421200679
⊛ www.ornellabellia.it

CELLAR SALES
PRE-BOOKED VISITS
ACCOMMODATION
ANNUAL PRODUCTION 500,000 bottles
HECTARES UNDER VINE 72.00
SUSTAINABLE WINERY

○ Venezia Manzoni Bianco '22	♟♟ 3
○ Lison '22	♟ 3
● Lison Pramaggiore Refosco P. R. G1928 '21	♟ 3
○ Venezia Chardonnay '23	♟ 2

451

Benazzoli

loc. Costiere, 25
37010 Pastrengo [VR]
📞 +39 0457170395
🌐 www.benazzoli.com

CELLAR SALES
PRE-BOOKED VISITS
ANNUAL PRODUCTION 60,000 bottles
HECTARES UNDER VINE 30.00

⊙ Chiaretto di Bardolino Tecla '23	🍷🍷 2*
○ Trento Dosaggio Zero Fulvio Ris. '19	🍷🍷 6
● Amarone della Valpolicella Cl. '17	🍷 7
● Bardolino Dafne '22	🍷 2

Pietro Bernardi

loc. Collalto
via Mercatelli S. Anna, 10
31058 Susegana [TV]
📞 +39 0438781022
🌐 www.bernardivini.com

CELLAR SALES
PRE-BOOKED VISITS
ANNUAL PRODUCTION 200,000 bottles
HECTARES UNDER VINE 15.00

○ Conegliano Valdobbiadene Brut Campal '23	🍷🍷 2*
○ Conegliano Valdobbiadene Extra Dry Altepiane '18	🍷🍷 3
○ Conegliano Valdobbiadene Brut Prà dei Salt	🍷 3

Carlo Boscaini

via Sengia, 15
37015 Sant'Ambrogio
di Valpolicella [VR]
📞 +39 0457731412
🌐 www.boscainicarlo.it

CELLAR SALES
PRE-BOOKED VISITS
ACCOMMODATION
ANNUAL PRODUCTION 60,000 bottles
HECTARES UNDER VINE 14.00

● Valpolicella Cl. Cà Bussin '23	🍷🍷 2*
● Valpolicella Cl. Sup. Ripasso Zane '20	🍷 5

Benedetti - Corte Antica

via Case Sparse Prunea di Sotto, 5
37015 Sant'Ambrogio
di Valpolicella [VR]
📞 +39 0456801736
🌐 www.cantine-benedetti.com

CELLAR SALES
ANNUAL PRODUCTION 70,000 bottles
HECTARES UNDER VINE 12.00
VITICULTURE METHOD Certified Organic

● Amarone della Valpolicella Cl. '18	🍷🍷 6
● Amarone della Valpolicella Cl. Croce del Gal Blue Ris. '12	🍷🍷 8
● Valpolicella Cl. Sup. '21	🍷🍷 3

Angelo Bortolin

loc. Guia
s.da di Guia, 107
31040 Valdobbiadene [TV]
📞 +39 0423900125
🌐 www.spumantibortolin.com

CELLAR SALES
PRE-BOOKED VISITS
ANNUAL PRODUCTION 230,000 bottles
HECTARES UNDER VINE 7.00

○ Valdobbiadene Dry	🍷🍷 3
○ Valdobbiadene Extra Dry Rù '23	🍷🍷 3
○ Valdobbiadene Brut	🍷 3
○ Valdobbiadene Exra Dry	🍷 3

Bottega

fraz. Bibiano
v.lo Aldo Bottega, 2
31010 Godega di Sant'Urbano [TV]
📞 +39 04384067
🌐 www.bottegaspa.com

● Amarone della Valpolicella '19	🍷🍷 6
○ Valdobbiadene Brut '23	🍷 3
○ Valdobbiadene Extra Dry '23	🍷 3

VENETO

OTHER WINERIES

Bronzato
via dei Peschi, 21
37141 Verona
📞 +39 3346184343
🌐 www.bronzatowine.it

● Amarone della Valpolicella Cl. '19	🍷🍷	6
● Valpolicella Sup. '21	🍷🍷	4
● Valpolicella Sup. Ripasso '21	🍷	5

Ca' da Roman
via De Gasperi, 42
36060 Romano d'Ezzelino [VI]
📞 +39 0424228620
🌐 www.cadaroman.bio

VITICULTURE METHOD Certified Organic

○ Gisla '22	🍷🍷	4
● Masnada Ezzelina '22	🍷🍷	4
○ 369 '22	🍷	4
○ Balbo '22	🍷	5

Carpenè Malvolti
via Antonio Carpenè, 1
31015 Conegliano [TV]
📞 +39 0438364611
🌐 www.carpene-malvolti.com

CELLAR SALES
PRE-BOOKED VISITS
ANNUAL PRODUCTION 5,300,000 bottles
SUSTAINABLE WINERY

○ Conegliano Valdobbiadene Extra Dry 1868	🍷🍷	3
○ Conegliano Valdobbiadene Brut 1868	🍷	4
○ Conegliano Valdobbiadene Brut 1924	🍷	4

Cà Rovere
via Bocara, 5
36045 Alonte [VI]
📞 +39 0444436234
🌐 www.carovere.it

CELLAR SALES
PRE-BOOKED VISITS
ANNUAL PRODUCTION 50,000 bottles
HECTARES UNDER VINE 30.00
SUSTAINABLE WINERY

○ Blanc de Blancs Brut M. Cl. '19	🍷🍷	5
○ Brut M.Cl. '19	🍷🍷	5
○ Brut Nature M. Cl. '18	🍷🍷	6

Cadis 1898
Cantina di Soave
v.le della Vittoria, 128
37038 Soave [VR]
📞 +39 0456139811
🌐 www.cadis1898.it

CELLAR SALES
PRE-BOOKED VISITS
ANNUAL PRODUCTION 3,000,000 bottles
HECTARES UNDER VINE 6000.00
VITICULTURE METHOD Certified Organic
SUSTAINABLE WINERY

● Amarone della Valpolicella Malanchino Ris. '16	🍷🍷	6
○ Soave Cl. Castelcerino '23	🍷🍷	3
● Valpolicella Sup. Polesella '21	🍷🍷	3

Casaretti
loc. Casaretti, 2a
fraz. Calmasino
37011 Bardolino [VR]
📞 +39 045 7235475
🌐 www.casaretti.it

CELLAR SALES
PRE-BOOKED VISITS
ANNUAL PRODUCTION 60,000 bottles
HECTARES UNDER VINE 14.00
VITICULTURE METHOD Certified Organic

● Bardolino Cl. Le Olte Longhe '23	🍷🍷	3
⊙ Chiaretto di Bardolino Cl. Rosa dei Casaretti '23	🍷🍷	3
● Bardolino Cl. La Nogara '23	🍷	3

OTHER WINERIES

Castello di Roncade

via Roma, 141
31056 Roncade [TV]
+39 0422708736
www.castellodironcade.com

CELLAR SALES
PRE-BOOKED VISITS
ACCOMMODATION
ANNUAL PRODUCTION 450,000 bottles
HECTARES UNDER VINE 110.00
SUSTAINABLE WINERY

○ Venezia Chardonnay Bianco dell'Arnasa '22	🍷🍷 3
● Piave Cabernet '22	🍷 2
● Piave Raboso '18	🍷 3
○ Venezia Pinot Grigio '23	🍷 2

Clementi

loc. Valgatara
fraz. Gnirega
via Gnirega, 2
37020 Marano di Valpolicella [VR]
+39 3472534456
www.vini-clementi.com

CELLAR SALES
PRE-BOOKED VISITS
ANNUAL PRODUCTION 35,000 bottles
HECTARES UNDER VINE 14.40
SUSTAINABLE WINERY

● Amarone della Valpolicella Cl. Ris. '07	🍷🍷 8
● Valpolicella Cl. Sup. Ripasso '19	🍷🍷 5

Vignaioli Contrà Soarda

s.da Soarda, 26
36061 Bassano del Grappa [VI]
+39 0424505562
www.contrasoarda.it

CELLAR SALES
PRE-BOOKED VISITS
RESTAURANT SERVICE
ANNUAL PRODUCTION 80,000 bottles
HECTARES UNDER VINE 20.00
VITICULTURE METHOD Certified Organic
SUSTAINABLE WINERY

● Breganze Rosso Terre di Lava Ris. '18	🍷🍷 5
○ Breganze Torcolato Sarson '18	🍷🍷 5
○ Breganze Vespaiolo Soarda '23	🍷 3
● Musso Botte '20	🍷 4

Contrada Palui

fraz. Trezzolano
via Caiò
37122 Verona
+39 3492139518
www.contradapalui.com

● Valpolicella Sup. Campo Selce '21	🍷🍷 5
● Valpolicella Sup. Graspo Alto '22	🍷🍷 4
● Amarone della Valpolicella '19	🍷 7

Corte Adami

circonvallazione Aldo Moro, 32
37038 Soave [VR]
+39 0456190218
www.corteadami.it

CELLAR SALES
PRE-BOOKED VISITS
ACCOMMODATION
ANNUAL PRODUCTION 170,000 bottles
HECTARES UNDER VINE 40.00
SUSTAINABLE WINERY

● Amarone della Valpolicella '19	🍷🍷 6
○ Soave Decennale '20	🍷🍷 4
○ Soave Sup. Castelcerino Vigna della Corte '21	🍷🍷 3

Corte Mainente

v.le della Vittoria, 45
37038 Soave [VR]
+39 0457680303
www.cortemainente.com

CELLAR SALES
PRE-BOOKED VISITS
ANNUAL PRODUCTION 40,000 bottles
HECTARES UNDER VINE 12.00
VITICULTURE METHOD Certified Organic
SUSTAINABLE WINERY

○ Recioto di Soave Luna Nova '21	🍷🍷 5
○ Soave Cl. Pigno '23	🍷🍷 2*
○ Soave Netrroir '22	🍷🍷 4
○ Soave Cl. Tenda '22	🍷 3

OTHER WINERIES

Corte Quaiara
via Corte Quaiara, 1
37060 Sona [VR]
☎ +39 0457190158
⊕ www.cortequaiara.it

○ Monte delle Saette '20	♟♟ 6
● Obardi '16	♟♟ 8
● Petit Verdot '21	♟♟ 8
○ Oseleta '17	♟ 6

Paolo Cottini
fraz. Castelrotto
via Belvedere, 29
37029 Verona
☎ +39 0456837293
⊕ www.paolocottini.it

CELLAR SALES
PRE-BOOKED VISITS
ANNUAL PRODUCTION 55,000 bottles
HECTARES UNDER VINE 5.50

● Scriba Passito '19	♟♟ 4
● Valpolicella Cl. Sup. Ripasso '21	♟♟ 4
● Paco '21	♟ 3
● Valpolicella Cl. '23	♟ 2

Degani
loc. Valgatara
fraz. Rugolin
via dell'Artigianato, 22
37020 Marano di Valpolicella [VR]
☎ +39 0459780193
⊕ www.deganivini.it

CELLAR SALES
PRE-BOOKED VISITS
ANNUAL PRODUCTION 90,000 bottles
HECTARES UNDER VINE 11.00

● Amarone della Valpolicella Cl. '20	♟♟ 5
● Amarone della Valpolicella Cl. La Rosta '20	♟♟ 5
● Valpolicella Cl. '23	♟♟ 2*
● Recioto della Valpolicella '21	♟ 5

Corte Sermana
loc. Sermana, 1a
37019 Peschiera del Garda [VR]
☎ +39 0457550903
⊕ www.cortesermana.it

○ Lugana Duerive '22	♟♟ 4
○ Lugana Cromalgo '23	♟ 4
○ Lugana Ris. '20	♟ 5

Valentina Cubi
via Casterna, 60
37022 Fumane [VR]
☎ +39 0457701806
⊕ www.valentinacubi.it

CELLAR SALES
PRE-BOOKED VISITS
ANNUAL PRODUCTION 40,000 bottles
HECTARES UNDER VINE 10.00
VITICULTURE METHOD Certified Organic

● Amarone della Valpolicella Cl. Ris. '15	♟♟ 8
● Recioto della Valpolicella Meliloto '21	♟♟ 6
● Valpolicella Cl. Sup. Il Tabarro '20	♟♟ 3
● Valpolicella Cl. Iperico '22	♟ 3

Del Rèbene
via Bertoldi, 25
36020 Zovencedo [VI]
☎ +39 3280555013
⊕ www.delrebene-oliovino.it

SUSTAINABLE WINERY

● Colli Berici Tai Rosso '21	♟♟ 5

OTHER WINERIES

Falezze

loc. Pigno, 1b
37031 Illasi [VR]
📞 +39 3487241477
🌐 www.falezze.it

CELLAR SALES
PRE-BOOKED VISITS
ACCOMMODATION
ANNUAL PRODUCTION 15,000 bottles
HECTARES UNDER VINE 5.00
SUSTAINABLE WINERY

● Amarone della Valpolicella Ris. '15	🍷🍷 8
● Valpolicella Sup. Ripasso '17	🍷🍷 6

FlaTìo

via Cariano, 20
37029 San Pietro in Cariano [VR]
📞 +39 3402596972
🌐 www.flatiowine.it

● Amarone della Valpolicella Cl. '17	🍷🍷 6
● Amarone della Valpolicella Cl. Mario Ris. '15	🍷🍷 8
● Valpolicella Cl. Sup. '22	🍷🍷 3
● Valpolicella Cl. Sup. Ripasso '19	🍷 3

Follador

fraz. Col San Martino
via Gravette, 42
31010 Treviso
📞 +39 0438898222
🌐 www.folladorprosecco.com

○ Valdobbiadene Brut Fosélios '23	🍷🍷 4
○ Valdobbiadene Rive di Col San Martino Brut Nani dei Berti '23	🍷🍷 3
○ Valdobbiadene Extra Brut Zero '23	🍷 4

La Frassina

loc. Marango
s.da Vallesina, 3
30021 Caorle [VE]
📞 +39 3332557529
🌐 www.frassina.it

● Venezia Cabernet Sauvignon Ciaro del Turco '18	🍷🍷 5
● Venezia Cabernet Sauvignon '20	🍷 2
● Venezia Merlot '21	🍷 2

Garbara

fraz. S. Stefano
s.da Menegazzi, 19
31049 Valdobbiadene [TV]
📞 +39 0423900155
🌐 www.garbara.it

CELLAR SALES
PRE-BOOKED VISITS
ANNUAL PRODUCTION 25,000 bottles
HECTARES UNDER VINE 2.70

○ Cartizze Brut Zero	🍷🍷 4
○ Cartizze Extra Dry	🍷🍷 4
○ Valdobbiadene Extra brut	🍷🍷 3

La Gioiosa

via Erizzo, 112
31035 Crocetta del Montello [TV]
📞 +39 0423.8607
info@lagioiosa.it

ANNUAL PRODUCTION 20,000,000 bottles
HECTARES UNDER VINE 10.00
SUSTAINABLE WINERY

○ Valdobbiadene Extra Dry	🍷🍷 2*
○ Asolo Extra Dry '23	🍷 2
○ Prosecco di Treviso Brut	🍷 2
○ Prosecco Rosé Brut '23	🍷 2

VENETO

OTHER WINERIES

Le Guaite di Noemi

via Capovilla , 10a
37030 Mezzane di Sotto [VR]
+39 045 8880396
www.sisure.it

CELLAR SALES
PRE-BOOKED VISITS
ANNUAL PRODUCTION 30,000 bottles
HECTARES UNDER VINE 2.00

● Amarone della Valpolicella '13	🍷🍷 7
● Valpolicella Sup. '14	🍷🍷 4
○ Diverso Brut M.Cl. '20	🍷 5
● Thano '18	🍷 4

Lenotti

via Santa Cristina, 1
37011 Bardolino [VR]
+39 0457210484
www.lenotti.com

CELLAR SALES
PRE-BOOKED VISITS
ANNUAL PRODUCTION 1,400,000 bottles
HECTARES UNDER VINE 110.00

● Amarone della Valpolicella Cl. di Carlo '16	🍷🍷 8
● Bardolino Cl. Superiore Le Olle '22	🍷🍷 4
● Valpolicella Cl. Sup. Ripasso Decus '20	🍷🍷 5
⊙ Chiaretto di Bardolino Cl. Decus '23	🍷 3

Le Manzane

via Maset, 47b
31020 San Pietro di Feletto [TV]
+39 0438486606
www.lemanzane.com

CELLAR SALES
PRE-BOOKED VISITS
ANNUAL PRODUCTION 1,000,000 bottles
HECTARES UNDER VINE 82.00
SUSTAINABLE WINERY

○ Cartizze Springo Gold	🍷🍷 5
○ Valdobbiadene Brut 20.10 '23	🍷🍷 4
○ Valdobbiadene Extra Dry 20.10 '23	🍷🍷 4
○ Valdobbiadene Extra Dry	🍷 3

Tenuta La Presa

loc. Zuane, 12
37013 Caprino Veronese [VR]
+39 045 7242314
www.tenutalapresa.it

CELLAR SALES
PRE-BOOKED VISITS
ACCOMMODATION AND RESTAURANT SERVICE
ANNUAL PRODUCTION 10,000 bottles
HECTARES UNDER VINE 95.00
SUSTAINABLE WINERY

● Bardolino Montebaldo '22	🍷🍷 3*
⊙ Chiaretto di Bardolino '23	🍷🍷 2*
○ Lugana '23	🍷🍷 2*

Maeli

fraz. Valle S. Giorgio
via Dietro Cero, 7
35030 Baone [PD]
+39 3313155244
www.maeliwine.com

CELLAR SALES
PRE-BOOKED VISITS
ANNUAL PRODUCTION 60,000 bottles
HECTARES UNDER VINE 18.50
VITICULTURE METHOD Certified Organic

● Colli Euganei Rosso Infinito '20	🍷🍷 4
○ Cero	🍷 6

Marchi

via Antonio Tirabosco, 1
37039 Tregnago [VR]
+39 3462257678
www.marchi.wine

CELLAR SALES
PRE-BOOKED VISITS
ACCOMMODATION
ANNUAL PRODUCTION 20,000 bottles
HECTARES UNDER VINE 20.00
SUSTAINABLE WINERY

● Amarone della Valpolicella '20	🍷🍷 7
● Valpolicella Sup. '22	🍷🍷 4
● Valpolicella Sup. Ripasso '22	🍷🍷 4

OTHER WINERIES

Marchiori

via Rialto, 3
31010 Farra di Soligo [TV]
(+39 0438801333
@ www.marchioriwines.com

Meroni

via Roma, 16a
37015 Sant'Ambrogio
di Valpolicella [VR]
(+39 3479186167
@ www.vinimeroni.com

CELLAR SALES
PRE-BOOKED VISITS
ANNUAL PRODUCTION 50,000 bottles
HECTARES UNDER VINE 11.00

○ Valdobbiadene Extra Brut Prologo	♟♟ 3
○ Valdobbiadene Rive di Farra di Soligo Extra Brut Rocciamadre '23	♟♟ 3

● Amarone della Valpolicella Cl. Carlo Meroni '18	♟♟ 7
● Amarone della Valpolicella Cl. Il Velluto '16	♟♟ 8
● Valpolicella Cl. Sup. Il Velluto '17	♟♟ 5

Firmino Miotti

via Brogliati Contro, 53
36042 Breganze [VI]
(+39 0445873006
@ www.firminomiotti.it

Mongarda

fraz. Col San Martino
via Canal Nuovo, 8
31010 Farra di Soligo [TV]
(+39 0438989168
@ www.mongarda.it

CELLAR SALES
PRE-BOOKED VISITS
ANNUAL PRODUCTION 25,000 bottles
HECTARES UNDER VINE 5.00

○ Breganze Vespaiolo Dosaggio Zero M.Cl. Anima '20	♟♟ 4
⊙ Fondo 53 Frizzante sui Lieviti	♟♟ 2*
○ Le Colombare '23	♟ 2

○ Valdobbiadene Brut '23	♟♟ 3
○ Valdobbiadene Extra Brut M.Cl. '22	♟♟ 4
○ Valdobbiadene Extra Dry '23	♟ 3

Le Muraglie

loc. Mostacci, 2
37067 Valeggio sul Mincio [VR]
(+39 0456302966
@ www.cantinalemuraglie.com

Walter Nardin

loc. Roncadelle
via Fontane, 5
31024 Ormelle [TV]
(+39 0422851622
@ www.vinwalternardin.it

CELLAR SALES
PRE-BOOKED VISITS
ANNUAL PRODUCTION 350,000 bottles
HECTARES UNDER VINE 28.00

⊙ Chiaretto di Bardolino Birò '23	♟♟ 2*
○ Custoza Sup. Remì '22	♟♟ 2*
● Bardolino '23	♟ 2
○ Custoza '23	♟ 2

● La Zerbaia Carménère '22	♟♟ 4
● Rosso della Ghiaia La Zerbaia '19	♟♟ 4
○ Lison Cl. La Zerbaia '22	♟ 3
● Venezia Cabernet Franc '23	♟ 2

OTHER WINERIES

Ongaresca
via Monte Cimone, 10
36030 Costabissara [VI]
📞 +39 3662837155
🌐 www.cantinaongaresca.it

● Menao'ro Passito '20	🍷🍷 4
○ Sessanta Pas Dosé M.Cl. '15	🍷🍷 5
○ Costa Fabrica '20	🍷 4
○ Menà Brut Rosé M.Cl. '17	🍷 5

Pian delle Vette
fraz. Vignui
via Teda, 11
32032 Feltre [BL]
📞 +39 0439302803
🌐 www.piandellevette.it

CELLAR SALES
PRE-BOOKED VISITS
ANNUAL PRODUCTION 12,000 bottles
HECTARES UNDER VINE 2.50
SUSTAINABLE WINERY

○ Extra Brut M.Cl Blanc de Noirs Mat '55 '19	🍷🍷 6
○ Extra Brut M.Cl. Mat '55 '15	🍷🍷 7
● Pinot Nero '19	🍷🍷 6

Possessioni di Serègo Alighieri
via Stazione Vecchia, 472
37015 Sant'Ambrogio
di Valpolicella [VR]
📞 +39 0457703622
serego@seregoalighieri.it

CELLAR SALES
PRE-BOOKED VISITS
ACCOMMODATION AND RESTAURANT SERVICE
ANNUAL PRODUCTION 350,000 bottles
HECTARES UNDER VINE 120.00

● Amarone della Valpolicella Cl. Vaio Armaron '17	🍷🍷 8
● Recioto della Valpolicella Cl. Casal dei Ronchi '19	🍷🍷 8

Cantina Pegoraro
via Calbin, 24
36048 Barbarano Mossano [VI]
📞 +39 0444886461
🌐 www.cantinapegoraro.it

CELLAR SALES
PRE-BOOKED VISITS
ANNUAL PRODUCTION 50,000 bottles
HECTARES UNDER VINE 8.00

● Colli Berici Tai Rosso Rovea '20	🍷🍷 4
○ Garganega Iose '21	🍷🍷 3
○ Colli Berici Tai '23	🍷 3

Albino Piona
Vignaioli dal 1893
loc. Casa Palazzina di Prabiano, 2
37069 Villafranca di Verona [VR]
📞 +39 045516055
🌐 www.albinopiona.it

CELLAR SALES
PRE-BOOKED VISITS
ANNUAL PRODUCTION 350,000 bottles
HECTARES UNDER VINE 45.00

○ Custoza '23	🍷🍷 2*
○ Custoza Sup. Campo del Selese '21	🍷🍷 3
⊙ Chiaretto di Bardolino '23	🍷 2
○ Custoza Crea '20	🍷 4

Cantina Produttori di Fregona
via Castagnola, 50
31010 Fregona [TV]
📞 +39 3402706497
🌐 www.torchiato.com

CELLAR SALES
PRE-BOOKED VISITS
ANNUAL PRODUCTION 10,000 bottles
HECTARES UNDER VINE 10.00

○ Colli di Conegliano Torchiato Di Fregona Piera Dolza '17	🍷🍷 5

OTHER WINERIES

PuntoZero

via Monte Palù, 1
36045 Lonigo [VI]
📞 +39 049659881
🌐 www.puntozerowine.it

CELLAR SALES
PRE-BOOKED VISITS
ANNUAL PRODUCTION 16,000 bottles
HECTARES UNDER VINE 11.00

● Colli Berici Rosso Marcella '22	🍷🍷	3
● Dimezzo '18	🍷🍷	5
○ Colli Berici Garganega Gargà '22	🍷	3

Ripa della Volta

loc. Tendina
fraz. Romagnano
37023 Grezzana [VR]
📞 +39 0458394630
🌐 www.ripadellavolta.it

● Amarone della Valpolicella '19	🍷🍷	6
● Valpolicella Ripasso '21	🍷🍷	5
● Valpolicella Sup. '22	🍷🍷	3

Ruki

via San Francesco, 46
37029 San Pietro in Cariano [VR]
📞 +39 3403465736
ruki.wines@gmail.com

○ Soave '21	🍷🍷	3
● Valpolicella Cl. '23	🍷🍷	4

Rechsteiner

fraz. Piavon
via Frassenè, 2
31046 Oderzo [TV]
📞 +39 0422752074
🌐 www.rechsteiner.it

CELLAR SALES
PRE-BOOKED VISITS
ACCOMMODATION AND RESTAURANT SERVICE
ANNUAL PRODUCTION 150,000 bottles
HECTARES UNDER VINE 50.00
SUSTAINABLE WINERY

○ Dominicale Dolce '22	🍷🍷	3
○ Pinot Grigio Delle Venezie '23	🍷	1
● Venezia Carmènère '22	🍷	2
○ Venezia Manzoni Bianco '23	🍷	2

Roccolo Callisto

fraz. Parona
s.da dei Monti, 17
37124 Verona
📞 +39 3481209808

CELLAR SALES
ANNUAL PRODUCTION 50,000 bottles
HECTARES UNDER VINE 11.00
VITICULTURE METHOD Certified Organic
SUSTAINABLE WINERY

● Amarone della Valpolicella '17	🍷🍷	7
● Valpolicella Ripasso '21	🍷🍷	3
● Valpolicella Sup. '22	🍷🍷	4

Sabaini

via Mormontea, 6a
37031 Illasi [VR]
📞 +39 0456529042
🌐 www.cantinasabaini.it

● Amarone della Valpolicella '19	🍷🍷	5
● Amarone della Valpolicella Ris. '15	🍷🍷	6
● Valpolicella '23	🍷🍷	3
● Valpolicella Sup. Ripasso '23	🍷	3

OTHER WINERIES

Salatin

fraz. Villa di Villa
via Doge Alvise IV Mocenigo, 57
31016 Cordignano [TV]
(+39 0438995928
www.salatinvini.com

CELLAR SALES
PRE-BOOKED VISITS
ANNUAL PRODUCTION 400,000 bottles
HECTARES UNDER VINE 53.00
VITICULTURE METHOD Certified Organic
SUSTAINABLE WINERY

o Manzoni Bianco Le Conche '22	♟♟ 4
o Prosecco Brut Carattere '23	♟ 3
o Valdobbiadene Brut '23	♟ 3
o Valdobbiadene Extra Dry '23	♟ 3

Tenuta San Giorgio

via Piave, 11
31052 Maserada sul Piave [TV]
(+39 0422743135
www.tenutasangiorgio.com

• Piave Malanotte Brumanera '18	♟♟ 4
o Arzarè '23	♟ 3
o Asolo Extra Brut Opera	♟ 2
o Focaia '23	♟ 2

Santa Colomba

via San Fermo, 17
36045 Lonigo [VI]
(+39 3494650127
www.santacolomba.webnode.it

o Gagà '23	♟♟ 3
• Il Moro '21	♟ 4

San Cassiano

via San Cassiano, 25
37030 Mezzane di Sotto [VR]
(+39 0458880665
www.cantinasancassiano.it

CELLAR SALES
PRE-BOOKED VISITS
ANNUAL PRODUCTION 50,000 bottles
HECTARES UNDER VINE 14.00
SUSTAINABLE WINERY

• Amarone della Valpolicella '19	♟♟ 8
o Brut Casal Sole	♟♟ 8
o Soave '23	♟ 3
• Valpolicella Sup. Ripasso '21	♟ 5

San Rustico

fraz. Valgatara
via Pozzo, 2
37020 Marano di Valpolicella [VR]
(+39 0457703348
www.sanrustico.it

CELLAR SALES
PRE-BOOKED VISITS
ANNUAL PRODUCTION 250,000 bottles
HECTARES UNDER VINE 22.00

• Recioto della Valpolicella Cl. Gaso '21	♟♟ 5
• Valpolicella Cl. Sup. '21	♟♟ 3
• Valpolicella Cl. Sup. Ripasso Gaso '19	♟♟ 4
• Valpolicella Cl. '23	♟ 2

Tenuta Santa Maria

loc. Novare, 1
37024 Negrar [VR]
(+39 0455709086
www.tenutasantamaria.wine

PRE-BOOKED VISITS
ANNUAL PRODUCTION 25,000 bottles
HECTARES UNDER VINE 19.00

• Amarone della Valpolicella Cl. Ris. '18	♟♟ 8
• Recioto della Valpolicella Cl. '21	♟♟ 6
• Valpolicella Cl. Sup. '22	♟♟ 4
• Valpolicella Cl. Sup. Ripasso '20	♟ 5

OTHER WINERIES

Tenuta Santa Maria Valverde
loc. Gazzo, 4
37020 Marano di Valpolicella [VR]
(☎ +39 3470908763
⊕ www.tenutasantamariavalverde.it

● Amarone della Valpolicella Cl. Ris. '15	♛♛ 8
● Valpolicella Cl. Sup. '21	♛♛ 5
● Valpolicella Cl. Sup. Ripasso '17	♛ 6

Talestri
via Fratta, 8
37030 Lavagno [VR]
(☎ +39 03417250234
⊕ www.talestri.com

● Valpolicella Sup. Determinazione '21	♛♛ 4
○ Extra Brut Istinto	♛ 5

Tamburino Sardo
loc. Custoza
via del Tamburino Sardo, 11
37060 Sommacampagna [VR]
(☎ +39 045516190
⊕ www.aziendaagricolatamburinosardo.it

CELLAR SALES
PRE-BOOKED VISITS
ANNUAL PRODUCTION 180,000 bottles
HECTARES UNDER VINE 15.00

○ Custoza Sup. La Guglia '22	♛♛ 3*
○ Custoza Adriano '21	♛♛ 4
○ Custoza '23	♛ 3

Terra Felice
via Marlunghe, 19
35032 Arquà Petrarca [PD]
(☎ +39 3477025928
⊕ www.cantinaterrafelice.it

CELLAR SALES
PRE-BOOKED VISITS
ANNUAL PRODUCTION 40,000 bottles
HECTARES UNDER VINE 9.00

● Altavia '19	♛♛ 4
● Cabernet '19	♛♛ 6
○ Chardonnay '22	♛ 3
● Pianoro '19	♛ 3

Terre di San Rocco
via A. Vivaldi, 32e
31056 Roncade [TV]
(☎ +39 389 1260990
⊕ www.terredisanrocco.it

○ Brut Nature M. Cl. '12	♛♛ 5
○ Pinot Bianco '22	♛♛ 4
● Cabernet Franc '20	♛ 5
○ Pinot Grigio delle Venezie Ramato '21	♛ 5

Trabucchi d'Illasi
loc. Monte Tenda
37031 Illasi [VR]
(☎ +39 0457833233
⊕ www.trabucchidillasi.it

CELLAR SALES
PRE-BOOKED VISITS
ANNUAL PRODUCTION 120,000 bottles
HECTARES UNDER VINE 25.00
VITICULTURE METHOD Certified Organic

● Amarone della Valpolicella '15	♛♛ 8
● Valpolicella Sup. '16	♛♛ 4

OTHER WINERIES

Tenute Ugolini
s.da di Bonamico, 11
37029 San Pietro in Cariano [VR]
☎ +39 0457703830
✹ www.tenuteugolini.it

ANNUAL PRODUCTION 50,000 bottles
HECTARES UNDER VINE 22.00

● Amarone della Valpolicella Cl. Valle Alta '15	▼▼ 8
● Valpolicella Cl. Sup. San Michele della Chiesa '15	▼▼ 5

Valetti
loc. Calmasino
via Pragrande, 8
37010 Bardolino [VR]
☎ +39 0457235075
✹ www.valetti.it

CELLAR SALES
PRE-BOOKED VISITS
ANNUAL PRODUCTION 70,000 bottles
HECTARES UNDER VINE 7.00

● Bardolino Cl. '23	▼▼ 2*
○ Lugana '23	▼▼ 3
⊙ Chiaretto di Bardolino Cl. '23	▼ 2

Le Vie Angarano
via Contrà San Michele, 4b
36061 Bassano del Grappa [VI]
☎ +39 3420903198
✹ www.levieangarano.com

CELLAR SALES
PRE-BOOKED VISITS
ANNUAL PRODUCTION 40,000 bottles
HECTARES UNDER VINE 8.00
VITICULTURE METHOD Certified Organic

● Breganze Merlot Masiero Ris. '20	▼▼ 3
○ Breganze Vespaiolo Brenta '23	▼ 3

Val d'Oca
via Per San Giovanni, 45
31049 Valdobbiadene [TV]
☎ +39 0423982070
✹ www.valdoca.com

CELLAR SALES
PRE-BOOKED VISITS
ANNUAL PRODUCTION 13,000,000 bottles
HECTARES UNDER VINE 950.00
SUSTAINABLE WINERY

○ Valdobbiadene Rive di San Pietro di Barbozza Brut '23	▼▼ 4
○ Valdobbiadene Rive di Santo Stefano Extra Brut '23	▼▼ 4

Vantorosso
fraz. Valgatara
v.lo Badin, 16
37020 Marano di Valpolicella [VR]
☎ +39 3355317496
✹ www.vantorosso.it

● Amarone della Valpolicella Cl. '18	▼▼ 8
● Amarone della Valpolicella Cl. Ris. '16	▼▼ 8
● Valpolicella Cl. '23	▼ 3
● Valpolicella Cl. Sup. Ripasso '20	▼ 4

Virgilio Vignato
via Guizza, 8
36053 Gambellara [VI]
☎ +39 0444444262
✹ www.virgiliovignato.com

CELLAR SALES
PRE-BOOKED VISITS
ACCOMMODATION
ANNUAL PRODUCTION 50,000 bottles
HECTARES UNDER VINE 15.00
VITICULTURE METHOD Certified Organic
SUSTAINABLE WINERY

○ Gambellara Cl. Capitel Vicenzi '22	▼▼ 3
○ Caliverna Garganega '22	▼ 3

OTHER WINERIES

VENETO

Vigneti di Ettore

via Casetta di Montecchio, 2
37024 Negrar [VR]
📞 +39 0457540158
🌐 www.vignetidiettore.it

CELLAR SALES
PRE-BOOKED VISITS
ACCOMMODATION
ANNUAL PRODUCTION 80,000 bottles
HECTARES UNDER VINE 20.00
VITICULTURE METHOD Certified Organic

● Amarone della Valpolicella Cl. '19	🍷🍷 7
● Valpolicella Cl. '23	🍷🍷 3
● Valpolicella Cl. Sup. Pavaio '21	🍷 4
● Valpolicella Cl. Sup. Ripasso '20	🍷 4

Villa Bellini

loc. Castelrotto di Negarine
via dei Fraccaroli, 6
37020 San Pietro in Cariano [VR]
📞 +39 0456850108
🌐 www.tenutavillabellini.com

PRE-BOOKED VISITS
ANNUAL PRODUCTION 12,000 bottles
HECTARES UNDER VINE 4.00
VITICULTURE METHOD Certified Organic

● Valpolicella Cl. Sup. Ripasso Sottolago '19	🍷🍷 5
● Valpolicella Cl. Sup. Tirele '22	🍷🍷 5
● Valpolicella Cl. Teatrino '23	🍷🍷 4
○ Blanc de Noirs Brut Nature M. Cl. '20	🍷 5

Villa Canestrari

via Dante Broglio, 2
37030 Colognola ai Colli [VR]
📞 +39 0457650074
🌐 www.villacanestrari.com

CELLAR SALES
PRE-BOOKED VISITS
ANNUAL PRODUCTION 150,000 bottles
HECTARES UNDER VINE 15.00

● Amarone della Valpolicella Dieci Anni Ris. '11	🍷🍷 8
● Amarone della Valpolicella Phanos '21	🍷🍷 6/
○ Soave Sup. Ris. '19	🍷🍷 4

Villa Medici

via Campagnol, 9
37066 Sommacampagna [VR]
📞 +39 045515147
🌐 www.cantinavillamedici.it

CELLAR SALES
ANNUAL PRODUCTION 220,000 bottles
HECTARES UNDER VINE 33.00
SUSTAINABLE WINERY

● Bardolino Sommacampagna Silerte Silvia Caprara '21	🍷🍷 4
● Bardolino '23	🍷🍷 2*
○ Chiaretto di Bardolino '23	🍷🍷 2*

Le Volpere

via Ugo Cecconi, 13.
31010 Farra di Soligo [TV]
🌐 www.levolpere.it

○ Valdobbiadene Rive di Premaor Brut Col Volpere '22	🍷🍷 4
○ Valdobbiadene Rive di Premaor Extra Brut Col Miliane '22	🍷🍷 4

Zonin

via Borgolecco, 9
36053 Gambellara [VI]
📞 +39 0444640111
🌐 www.zonin1821.it

CELLAR SALES
PRE-BOOKED VISITS
ANNUAL PRODUCTION 38,000,000 bottles
HECTARES UNDER VINE 2000.00

● Amarone della Valpolicella '21	🍷🍷 6

FRIULI VENEZIA GIULIA

Friuli Venezia Giulia is a region remarkably well suited to the production of high-quality white wines. The finest come mostly from the hills that form a stunning landscape, sheltered by the Julian Alps, stretching along the eastern border and stretching all the way to the Adriatic. However, most of the vineyards lie in the vast plains, where much of the land is now dedicated to glera for Prosecco. Despite this, pinot grigio dominates in terms of acreage—an interesting fact, given that it's the most produced wine, yet the least consumed within the region, where the beloved Friulano remains the everyday choice.

In recent years, however, the true standout has been ribolla gialla. Over the past decade, both vineyard area and production have increased tenfold. Rich in acidity, ribolla gialla produces excellent still wines, outstanding spumante, and some truly remarkable expressions when cultivated in top terroirs like Collio. In the area bordering Slovenia, it's still made using time-honored methods, undergoing long maceration on the skins. This results in wines with deep color, captivating aromas, and highly engaging flavors. When it comes to pinot grigio, many producers are returning to the traditional "coppery" hue the wine takes on after just a few hours of skin contact, giving it a distinctive and unmistakable varietal character. The production of pinot nero is also growing exponentially, largely driven by the demand from Prosecco producers for rosé versions.

As for reds, no discussion would be complete without mentioning refosco, the region's most widespread indigenous variety alongside schioppettino, which has found its ideal habitat in the Prepotto area. Pignolo and tazzelenghe are rare, precious gems, but it's still the whites that best showcase the land and win the most awards. This year, 25 wines were awarded the coveted Tre Bicchieri, with only one red among them—Teresa Raiz's excellent 2021 schioppettino from the Colli Orientali. On the prestigious list of Rare Wines, a quarter of the whites hail from Friuli. Standouts include the magnificent Chardonnay, Glesie 2018 by Vie di Romàns (from Soca), Zidarich's splendid Vitovska Kamen 2020, Vodopivec's Vitovska Solo MM 2020, Castelvecchio's Carso Malvasia Dileo Riserva 2022, and the captivating Collio Friulano Miklus 2019 by Draga-Miklus. Also, this year our special Solidarity Award goes to one of the region's producers, the Pecorari family at Lis Neris, in recognition for their impressive humanitarian efforts.

Antonutti

fraz. Colloredo
via D'Antoni, 21
33037 Pasian di Prato [UD]
📞 +39 0432662001
🌐 www.antonuttivini.it

CELLAR SALES
PRE-BOOKED VISITS
ANNUAL PRODUCTION 1,000,000 bottles
HECTARES UNDER VINE 50.00
SUSTAINABLE WINERY

Despite substantial production volumes, this distinguished player in the regional wine scene is still very much a family-run operation. Founded by Grandfather Ignazio in 1921, Antonutti is now managed by Adriana Antonutti along with Lino Durandi and their children, Caterina and Riccardo. Their vineyards stretch across the vast Friulian plains, with some on lean, gravelly soils and others on rich, clayey grounds. Their diverse offerings cater to every market need at competitive prices. The Bianco Bertrando '21, composed of sauvignon, tocai friulano, and chardonnay, delights the nose with suggestions of honey, golden apple peel, acacia flowers, and star jasmine. On the palate, it's pervasive and velvety. The Poppone '20, made from dried merlot with a touch of pignolo, evokes maraschino cherry jam and licorice, offering a full and flavorful palate. The Traminer Aromatico '23 features aromas of elderflower syrup and citronade, strongly emphasizing its varietal characteristics.

○ Friuli Bertrando '21	🍷🍷 4
● Friuli Grave Pinot Nero Ris. '21	🍷🍷 2*
○ Friuli Traminer Aromatico '23	🍷🍷 3
● Poppone '20	🍷🍷 5
○ Friuli Pinot Grigio '23	🍷 3
○ Friuli Sauvignon '23	🍷 3
○ Friuli Bianco Bertrando '20	♀♀ 4
○ Friuli Bianco Bertrando '18	♀♀ 4
● Friuli Grave Pinot Nero Pinus Nigra Ris. '17	♀♀ 5
● Friuli Grave Pinot Nero Ris. '20	♀♀ 5
● Friuli Merlot '20	♀♀ 2*
○ Friuli Pinot Grigio '22	♀♀ 3
○ Friuli Pinot Grigio Ramato '21	♀♀ 2*
○ Friuli Pinot Grigio Ramato '20	♀♀ 2*
○ Friuli Sauvignon '21	♀♀ 2*
● Poppòne '17	♀♀ 5

Aquila del Torre

fraz. Savorgnano del Torre
via Attimis, 25
33040 Povoletto [UD]
📞 +39 0432666428
🌐 www.aquiladeltorre.it

CELLAR SALES
PRE-BOOKED VISITS
ACCOMMODATION
ANNUAL PRODUCTION 60,000 bottles
HECTARES UNDER VINE 18.00
VITICULTURE METHOD Certified Biodynamic
SUSTAINABLE WINERY

Founded in the early 20th century, Aquila del Torre derives its name from the nearby Torre stream and the curious arrangement of the vineyards, which, when viewed from Udine, trace the winged profile of an eagle (aquila, in Italian). Michele Ciani, a biodynamic producer supported by a young, professional team, runs the winery, which his father Claudio purchased in 1996. The vineyards are nestled in splendid natural amphitheaters, often steep and rugged, divided into well-marked plots. The Torre Bianco '21, an elegant blend of tocai friulano and sauvignon, conjures up apple pulp, fruit trees blooming in spring, and citrus zest. It stands out for its delicate minerality and drinkable charm. The Sauvignon At '21 displays pronounced varietal traits, enhanced by pleasant smoky notes and hints of grapefruit, sage, and peppermint. Both wines reached the finals, standing out among the best in their respective categories.

○ FCO Sauvignon At '21	🍷🍷 5
○ FCO Torre Bianco '21	🍷🍷 3*
○ FCO Riesling At '20	🍷🍷 5
● FCO Merlot At '21	🍷 5
○ FCO Bianco Oasi '20	♀♀ 8
○ FCO Bianco Torre Bianco '20	♀♀ 3*
○ FCO Friulano At '21	♀♀ 4
○ FCO Friulano At '20	♀♀ 4
○ FCO Oasi Bianco '18	♀♀ 8
● FCO Refosco P.R. '16	♀♀ 6
● FCO Refosco P.R. At Ris. '19	♀♀ 5
○ FCO Riesling At '19	♀♀ 5
○ FCO Sauvignon At '20	♀♀ 4
○ FCO Sauvignon At '19	♀♀ 4
○ FCO Sauvignon Primaluce '19	♀♀ 6

FRIULI VENEZIA GIULIA

Attems

fraz. Capriva del Friuli
via Aquileia, 30
34070 Gorizia
(*) +39 0481806098
@ www.attems.it

CELLAR SALES
PRE-BOOKED VISITS
ANNUAL PRODUCTION 800,000 bottles
HECTARES UNDER VINE 44.00

Founded in the 16th century by the Attems family, this winery has written many chapters in the history of Friuli-Venezia Giulia wine, especially in the Collio area. In the second half of the last century, Count Douglas Attems played a pivotal role, having founded the Consorzio dei Vini del Collio in 1964, and serving as its president for 35 years. Since 2000, the Attems winery has formed a strong alliance with the Florentine Marchesi de' Frescobaldi family. As in previous editions, once again it's the Sauvignon Cicinis '22 that secures a place in the finals, leading a lineup that's impeccable in its appeal and craftsmanship. It excels with pronounced varietal notes reminiscent of sage, boxwood, and bergamot peel, while on the palate, its freshness and minerality enhance the wine's fragrance. The Pinot Grigio Ramato '23 reveals the elegant nuance characteristic of the grape, thanks to a brief period of skin contact.

Bajta - Fattoria Carsica

via Sales, 108
34010 Sgonico [TS]
(*) +39 0402296090
@ www.bajta.it

CELLAR SALES
PRE-BOOKED VISITS
ACCOMMODATION AND RESTAURANT SERVICE
ANNUAL PRODUCTION 30,000 bottles
HECTARES UNDER VINE 4.00

Bajta is a charming estate founded by the Skerlj family in 1999 when they left Sgonico to expand into the restaurant business, farming, rural hospitality, and, last but not least, winemaking. It's a classic Karst farm where you can dine, buy cured meats, spend a few relaxing days, and sample the excellent wines produced by Nevo and Andrej with the help of their father Slavko. Their broad and diverse range reflects their naturally cultivated estate vineyards, which host primarily local varietals. The Vitovska Kronos '18, the result of a meticulous double maturation process, truly thrills. After lengthy aging in oak and stainless steel, the wine matures in the bottle for another four years. Today, it pours an intense, vivid straw-yellow color, releasing a broad range of aromas, from citrus to ripe fruit, with accents of aromatic herbs and iodine nuances. In the mouth, its close-knit, dense palate shows great character and balance.

○ Collio Sauvignon Cicinis '22	♥♥ 7
○ Chardonnay '23	♥♥ 3
○ Friuli Pinot Grigio '23	♥♥ 3
○ Friuli Pinot Grigio Ramato '23	♥♥ 5
○ Ribolla Gialla '23	♥♥ 3
○ Collio Ribolla Gialla Trebes '21	♥♥ 4
○ Collio Ribolla Gialla Trebes '20	♥♥ 4
○ Collio Sauvignon Cicinis '17	♥♥ 5
○ Collio Sauvignon Cicins '21	♥♥ 5
○ Collio Sauvignon Cicins '20	♥♥ 5
○ Collio Sauvignon Cicins '19	♥♥ 5
○ Collio Sauvignon Cicins '18	♥♥ 5
○ Friuli Pinot Grigio Ramato '22	♥♥ 3
○ Ribolla Gialla '22	♥♥ 3

○ Kronos Vitovska '18	♥♥♥ 5
○ Malvasia '22	♥♥ 4
● Terrano '22	♥♥ 5
○ Vitovska '22	♥♥ 4
○ Kronos Vitovska '16	♥♥ 5
○ Majnik Vitovska '21	♥♥ 4
○ Majnik Vitovska '20	♥♥ 3
○ Majnik Vitovska '19	♥♥ 3
○ Majnik Vitovska Ris. '16	♥♥ 4
○ Malvasia '20	♥♥ 3
○ Malvasia '19	♥♥ 3
● Terrano '21	♥♥ 4
● Terrano '20	♥♥ 3
● Terrano '19	♥♥ 3
○ Vitovska Ragionata '15	♥♥ 4

Bastianich

loc. Gagliano
via Darnazzacco, 44/2
33043 Cividale del Friuli [UD]
📞 +39 0432700943
🌐 www.bastianich.com

CELLAR SALES
PRE-BOOKED VISITS
ACCOMMODATION AND RESTAURANT SERVICE
ANNUAL PRODUCTION 220,000 bottles
HECTARES UNDER VINE 27.00

Giuseppe "Joe" Bastianich, whose family is from Istria, decided to return to his Italian roots after a long career in the restaurant industry in the US. In 1997, he embarked on this regional adventure by founding a winery, quietly purchasing an estate on the hills of Buttrio and Premariacco. Later he expanded his investment by acquiring an already well-established winery surrounded by 20 hectares of vineyards near Cividale del Friuli. The Vespa Bianco '21, a blend of chardonnay, sauvignon, and picolit, has consistently proven to be the top of its range. This year, however, it was outscored by the Chardonnay Ape Regina '21 and a surprising Sauvignon '23, which both swept the competition and advanced to the finals. The former excels in its aromatic complexity and pervasive palate, while the latter offers intense varietal notes.

Bolzicco

via San Giovanni, 60
34071 Cormòns [GO]
📞 +39 335258608
🌐 www.bolziccovini.it

CELLAR SALES
PRE-BOOKED VISITS
ANNUAL PRODUCTION 20,000 bottles
HECTARES UNDER VINE 8.00

The Bolzicco Fausta estate is a small, family-run operation with historic vineyards, some of which were planted as far back as 1949. While they've always produced wine here, it was traditionally sold in bulk. In 2016, Michele, the son of the owners, made the bold decision—against his family's wishes—to start bottling on their own. The initial results were promising, and as both the numbers and quality steadily increased, the producer has gained significant recognition. The excellent performance of the entire range is highlighted by the Pinot Grigio Inedito '22, which intrigues right from the outset with its elegant coppery hues reminiscent of onion skin. The bouquet is noble and multifaceted, with notes of wild rose meeting peony, artemisia, dried flowers, caramel-covered fruit, and hazelnuts. The palate is full and graceful. The Collio Bianco da Uve Autoctone '22 (tocai friulano, malvasia istriana, and ribolla gialla) is also outstanding—fragrant and energetic.

○ FCO Chardonnay Ape Regina '21	♟♟ 8
○ FCO Sauvignon Orsone '23	♟♟ 4
○ FCO Friulano Orsone '23	♟♟ 4
○ Plus '20	♟♟ 7
○ Vespa Bianco '21	♟♟ 5
● Vespa Rosso '18	♟♟ 6
○ FCO Ribolla Gialla Orsone '23	♟ 4
○ COF Tocai Friulano Plus '02	♟♟♟ 3*
○ Vespa Bianco '04	♟♟♟ 4
○ Vespa Bianco '03	♟♟♟ 4
○ Vespa Bianco '01	♟♟♟ 4
○ Vespa Bianco '00	♟♟♟ 3
○ Vespa Bianco '99	♟♟♟ 3*
○ Plus '18	♟♟ 6
○ Vespa Bianco '19	♟♟ 5
○ Vespa Bianco '18	♟♟ 5

○ Friuli Pinot Grigio Inedito '22	♟♟ 3*
○ Brezàn Verduzzo '22	♟♟ 4
○ Collio Bianco da Uve Autoctone '22	♟♟ 3
○ Collio Ribolla Gialla '23	♟♟ 3
○ Collio Sauvignon '22	♟♟ 3
○ Collio Bianco '21	♟♟ 3
○ Collio Bianco Vigne Da Mont '20	♟♟ 3
○ Collio Friulano '22	♟♟ 3
○ Collio Friulano '21	♟♟ 3*
○ Collio Sauvignon '21	♟♟ 3
○ Friuli Malvasia '22	♟♟ 3
○ Friuli Pinot Grigio Inedito '21	♟♟ 3
● Gabernè Cabernet Sauvignon '21	♟♟ 3
○ Malvasia Mulin Gnôf '21	♟♟ 3
○ Malvasia Mulin Gnôf '20	♟♟ 3
● Merlot Mulin Gnôf '20	♟♟ 3

Tenuta Borgo Conventi

via Contessa Beretta, 19
34072 Farra d'Isonzo [GO]
📞 +39 0481888004
🌐 www.borgoconventi.it

CELLAR SALES
PRE-BOOKED VISITS
ACCOMMODATION
ANNUAL PRODUCTION 400,000 bottles
HECTARES UNDER VINE 30.00
SUSTAINABLE WINERY

Founded in 1975 by Gianni Vescovo, Tenuta Borgo Conventi quickly established itself as one of the region's leading producers. After several management changes, in April 2019 the winery was acquired by the Moretti Polegato family, owners of the prestigious Tenuta Villa Sandi. The decision to enlist the oenological expertise of Riccardo Cotarella was a clear signal of their commitment to excellence. The results were swift, and the brand regained its former glory. The outstanding performance of the entire range presented once again confirms the high level of quality achieved. The Collio Bianco Luna di Ponca '21 continues to lead the lineup. A well-calibrated mix of chardonnay, tocai friulano, and malvasia istriana delivers suggestions of lemon cream, quince jam, and syrupy peaches, wrapping the palate and leaving an indelible impression.

Collio Bianco Luna di Ponca '21	♟♟♟ 6
Collio Friulano '23	♟♟ 4
Collio Pinot Grigio '23	♟♟ 4
Collio Ribolla Gialla '23	♟♟ 4
Collio Sauvignon '23	♟♟ 4
Schioppettino '20	♟♟ 5
Friuli Isonzo Refosco P. R. '23	♟ 3
Collio Bianco Luna di Ponca '20	♟♟♟ 6
Collio Bianco Luna di Ponca '19	♟♟♟ 6
Collio Friulano '20	♟♟♟ 3*
Collio Sauvignon '19	♟♟♟ 3*
Braida Nuova '12	♟♟ 5
Collio Friulano '22	♟♟ 4
Collio Merlot '16	♟♟ 3*
Collio Ribolla Gialla '18	♟♟ 3*
Schioppettino '17	♟♟ 4

Borgo delle Oche

via Borgo Alpi, 5
33098 Valvasone Arzene [PN]
📞 +39 0434840640
🌐 www.borgodelleoche.it

CELLAR SALES
PRE-BOOKED VISITS
ACCOMMODATION
ANNUAL PRODUCTION 35,000 bottles
HECTARES UNDER VINE 7.00
SUSTAINABLE WINERY

Borgo delle Oche is owned by Luisa Menini, an outdoors enthusiast who personally tends to her vineyards, committed to producing perfect grapes that she then hands over to her life partner, Nicola Pittini, for winemaking. Luisa and Nicola operate in perfect harmony, exemplifying how, with low yields, it's possible to produce wines on the plains that rival those made in the hills. Composed exclusively of native varietals, the Lupi Terrae '21 is a true expression of the terroir. Tocai friulano, malvasia istriana, and verduzzo friulano combine in a blend that offers aromas of ripe yellow-fleshed fruit, acacia honey, citron peel, and almond stone. The palate is juicy, rich in aromatic nuances, with a fresh, balsamic finish. The performance of the other wines submitted confirms the strength of their range.

○ Lupi Terrae '21	♟♟ 3*
○ Friuli Malvasia '23	♟♟ 3
○ Friuli Pino Grigio Ramato Lùsigne '22	♟♟ 3
● Merlot '21	♟♟ 3
● Refosco P. R. '20	♟♟ 3
○ Traminer Aromatico '23	♟♟ 3
○ Friuli Pinot Grigio '23	♟ 3
○ Sauvignon '23	♟ 3
○ Alba Traminer Passito '20	♟♟ 5
○ Friuli Pino Grigio Ramato Lùsigne '21	♟♟ 3
● Refosco P. R. '19	♟♟ 3
● Refosco P. R. '13	♟♟ 2*
○ Traminer Aromatico '22	♟♟ 3
○ Traminer Passito Alba '19	♟♟ 5
○ Traminer Passito Alba '17	♟♟ 5

★Borgo San Daniele

via San Daniele, 28
34071 Cormòns [GO]
☎ +39 048160552
⊕ www.borgosandaniele.it

CELLAR SALES
PRE-BOOKED VISITS
ACCOMMODATION
ANNUAL PRODUCTION 60,000 bottles
HECTARES UNDER VINE 18.75
VITICULTURE METHOD Certified Organic
SUSTAINABLE WINERY

The words "I Am Mauri" now grace all the labels of this splendid winery, one of the most renowned producers operating here in Cormòns. Borgo San Daniele takes its name from the village that hosts the main property and the old house of Grandfather Antonio, who left a few hectares of vineyards to his grandchildren, Mauro and Alessandra Mauri, in 1990. The few wines in their meticulously crafted profile fully express the potential of the territory, interpreted flawlessly. The Pignolo Arbis Ròs '18 is an exuberant, structured, and energetic wine, releasing pleasant aromas of red and black berries, black pepper, tobacco, and licorice, then enveloping the palate with its glyceric richness, which contrasts the vigor of its soft, velvety tannins. The Malvasia '22 also impresses with its aromatic elegance, but especially for its balanced palate, rich in aromatic nuances and pleasant balsamic notes that enliven the finish.

○ Friuli Isonzo Malvasia '22	ΨΨ	5
● Friuli Isonzo Pignolo Arbis Ròs '18	ΨΨ	6
○ Arbis Blanc '21	ΨΨ	5
○ Friuli Isonzo Friulano '22	ΨΨ	4
○ Friuli Isonzo Pinot Grigio '22	ΨΨ	4
○ Ribolla Gialla '22	ΨΨ	4
○ Arbis Blanc '10	ΨΨΨ	4*
○ Arbis Blanc '09	ΨΨΨ	4
○ Arbis Blanc '05	ΨΨΨ	4
○ Friuli Isonzo Arbis Blanc '02	ΨΨΨ	4
○ Friuli Isonzo Friulano '08	ΨΨΨ	4*
○ Friuli Isonzo Friulano '07	ΨΨΨ	4*
○ Friuli Isonzo Pinot Grigio '04	ΨΨΨ	4
○ Friuli Isonzo Tocai Friulano '03	ΨΨΨ	3
● Gortmarin '03	ΨΨΨ	5
○ Arbis Blanc '20	ΨΨ	4

Borgo Savaian

via Savaian, 36
34071 Cormòns [GO]
☎ +39 048160725
⊕ www.borgosavaian.it

CELLAR SALES
PRE-BOOKED VISITS
ANNUAL PRODUCTION 100,000 bottles
HECTARES UNDER VINE 18.00

In 2001, a very young Stefano Bastiani found himself managing the winery inherited from his father Mario, who had passed away prematurely. Fresh out of school but already rich in experience, he began a new path, confidently tackling the challenges of winemaking and managing seasonal variations. Both their hillside wines and those cultivated on the plains express honesty and a strong sense of typicity, the result of a particular focus on preserving the organoleptic characteristics of each grape. The Aransat is an approachable orange wine with a competitive price, made from grapes from a vineyard over 40 years old, planted mainly with tocai friulano. After about 15 days of fermentation, the must remains in contact with the skins for another 3 months. The amber shades presented on tasting are a prelude to aromas of chamomile, sweet spices, anise, and licorice root. The palate expresses sapidity and balsamic freshness.

○ Aransat	ΨΨ
○ Collio Friulano '23	ΨΨ
○ Collio Pinot Grigio '23	ΨΨ
○ Collio Ribolla Gialla '23	ΨΨ
○ Friuli Malvasia '23	Ψ
○ Friuli Sauvignon '23	Ψ
○ Aransat	ΨΨ
○ Collio Pinot Grigio '22	ΨΨ
○ Collio Pinot Grigio '21	ΨΨ
○ Collio Pinot Grigio '19	ΨΨ
○ Collio Ribolla Gialla '22	ΨΨ
○ Collio Ribolla Gialla '21	ΨΨ
○ Collio Sauvignon '16	ΨΨ
○ Friuli Isonzo Malvasia '18	ΨΨ

Cav. Emiro Bortolusso

s.da Oltregorgo, 10
33050 Carlino [UD]
(») +39 043167596
@ www.bortolusso.it

CELLAR SALES
PRE-BOOKED VISITS
ACCOMMODATION
ANNUAL PRODUCTION 150,000 bottles
HECTARES UNDER VINE 45.00

Along a charming strip of land overlooking the Adriatic Sea, Sergio and Clara Bortolusso run one of the Friuli Annia appellation's most thriving and representative wineries. Building on the teachings and experiences inherited from their father Emiro, they offer a wide range. Consistent quality and reasonable prices contribute to the producer's success, supporting their visibility and growth. All their wines express a freshness and drinkability that confirm the attributes of this coastal growing area, known for its sapidity and enticing aromatic nuances. The Pinot Grigio '23 evokes Mediterranean scrub, withered white flowers, and acacia honey; the palate is smooth and velvety. The Traminer Aromatico '23 exudes notes of yellow rose and broom, exemplifying the varietal characteristics of the grape.

Friuli Pinot Grigio '23	♟♟ 3
Malvasia '23	♟♟ 2*
Sauvignon '23	♟♟ 3
Traminer Aromatico '23	♟♟ 2*
Friuli Friulano '23	♟ 3
Ribolla Gialla '23	♟ 3
Friuli Friulano '21	♟♟ 2*
Friuli Friulano '18	♟♟ 2*
Friuli Pinot Grigio '21	♟♟ 2*
Friuli Pinot Grigio '20	♟♟ 2*
Malvasia '22	♟♟ 2*
Malvasia '21	♟♟ 2*
Malvasia '20	♟♟ 2*
Sauvignon '22	♟♟ 2*
Traminer Aromatico '22	♟♟ 2*
Traminer Aromatico '21	♟♟ 2*

Bosco del Merlo

s.da di Sequals , 14
33090 Sequals [PN]
(») +39 0422768167
@ www.boscodelmerlo.it

CELLAR SALES
PRE-BOOKED VISITS
ANNUAL PRODUCTION 880,000 bottles
HECTARES UNDER VINE 70.00
SUSTAINABLE WINERY

Bosco del Merlo represents the Paladin family's Friulian branch. The vineyards stretch across northeastern Italy, where Friuli and Veneto embrace each other in a territory caressed by light sea breezes while also benefiting from the natural influence of the Carnic Alps, conditions that are perfect for wine-growing. In fact, Carlo and Roberto Paladin, who founded the winery in 1977, named it after the territory. Their entire range is certified sustainable by Equalitas. The Pinot Grigio Rosé '23 impresses with its elegant pink hue, but most notably with its delightful aroma of rose petals, pomegranate, wild strawberries, and peach blossoms. Freshness and sapidity make it a captivating and enjoyable quaff. The Traminer Aromatico Ibisco '23 evokes syrupy peach, blonde orange, bergamot, and dandelion, with a palate that's soft and creamy. The Cabernet Sauvignon Nono Miglio '23 wins over with its lively yet pervasive palate.

⊙ Pinot Grigio Delle Venezie Rosé '23	♟♟ 3*
○ Friuli Pinot Grigio Tudajo '23	♟♟ 3
○ Friuli Sauvignon Turranio '23	♟♟ 4
○ Friuli Traminer Aromatico Ibisco '23	♟♟ 4
○ Lison Pramaggiore Verduzzo Passito Soandre '21	♟♟ 5
⊙ Prosecco Rosè Brut '23	♟♟ 4
● Venezia Cabernet Sauvignon Nono Miglio '23	♟♟ 3
● Venezia Merlot Campo Camino Ris. '21	♟♟ 4
● Venezia Refosco P.R. Roggio dei Roveri Ris '21	♟♟ 5
● Vineargenti Rosso Ris. '21	♟♟ 6
○ Friuli Chardonnay Bricola '23	♟ 3
○ Prosecco Brut '23	♟ 3
○ Ribolla Gialla Iside '23	♟ 3

Branko

loc. Zegla, 20
34071 Cormòns [GO]
☎ +39 0481639826
🌐 www.brankowines.com

Livio e Claudio Buiatti

via Lippe, 25
33042 Buttrio [UD]
☎ +39 0432674317
🌐 www.buiattivini.it

CELLAR SALES
PRE-BOOKED VISITS
ANNUAL PRODUCTION 60,000 bottles
HECTARES UNDER VINE 9.00

CELLAR SALES
PRE-BOOKED VISITS
ANNUAL PRODUCTION 35,000 bottles
HECTARES UNDER VINE 8.00

Founded in 1950 by Branko Erzetic, who had the foresight to invest in the territory, this small winery has become a beacon for lovers of Collio whites. Today Branko's son Igor oversees the estate, paying meticulous attention to the vineyards surrounding the main property and producing a small range, which allows him to focus on the quality of both the grapes and winemaking. The Capo Branko '23, true to its name ("capo" means "boss") leads a series of wines exemplary for their elegance and pleasantness. Made from tocai friulano, malvasia istriana, and sauvignon, it offers rapid-fire notes of tropical fruit, melon, yellow bell pepper, bergamot, and vanilla, sensations that resonate on the palate. The Pinot Grigio '23 lives up to the best vintages, with a palate that excels in its freshness, fragrance, and linear profile.

Livio and Claudio Buiatti's winery is located in the town of Buttrio, with vineyards stretching out across the foothills of the Colli Orientali del Friuli and facing the sea. When Claudio inherited the prized plots from his father Livio, he gradually began modernizing the vineyards, enhancing planting density and reducing yields through drastic pruning. His efforts paid off, benefiting the entire range of wines. Today, Claudio is also supported by his son Matteo. The Sauvignon '22 opens on delicate smoky notes accompanied by aromatic herbs, citrus, and resin followed by a decisive, pronounced, and long finish. The Momon Ros Ris. '19, a classic Bordeaux blend of merlot and cabernet, offers up notes of wild berries followed by cinchona, licorice, cocoa powder, and coffee. It's rich in flavor with vibrant yet well-rounded tannins. All the other wines display maturity and elegance—the result of adequate bottle aging.

○ Capo Branko '23	♀♀ 5		● FCO Cabernet Franc '21	♀♀
○ Collio Pinot Grigio '23	♀♀ 4		○ FCO Friulano '22	♀♀
○ Collio Chardonnay '23	♀♀ 4		○ FCO Malvasia '22	♀♀
○ Collio Friulano '23	♀♀ 4		● FCO Refosco P.R. '20	♀♀
○ Collio Sauvignon '23	♀♀ 5		● FCO Rosso Momon Ros Ris. '19	♀♀
○ Ribolla Gialla '23	♀♀ 4		○ FCO Sauvignon '22	♀♀
○ Collio Pinot Grigio '14	♀♀♀ 4*		○ FCO Friulano '21	♀♀
○ Collio Pinot Grigio '08	♀♀♀ 3*		○ FCO Friulano '20	♀♀
○ Collio Pinot Grigio '07	♀♀♀ 3		○ FCO Friulano '17	♀♀
○ Collio Pinot Grigio '06	♀♀♀ 3		○ FCO Malvasia '20	♀♀
○ Collio Pinot Grigio '05	♀♀♀ 3		● FCO Merlot '19	♀♀
○ Capo Branko '21	♀♀ 5		○ FCO Pinot Grigio '21	♀♀
○ Collio Friulano '19	♀♀ 4		● FCO Refosco dal P.R. '18	♀♀
○ Collio Pinot Grigio '22	♀♀ 4		○ FCO Sauvignon '21	♀♀
○ Collio Sauvignon '20	♀♀ 4		○ FCO Sauvignon '20	♀♀
● Red Branko '18	♀♀ 4		○ FCO Sauvignon '16	♀♀

La Buse dal Lôf

via Ronchi, 90
33040 Prepotto [UD]
☎ +39 0432701523
🌐 www.labusedallof.com

CELLAR SALES
PRE-BOOKED VISITS
ANNUAL PRODUCTION 100,000 bottles
HECTARES UNDER VINE 25.00

La Buse dal Lôf, one of the region's most thriving producers, was founded in 1972 by Giuseppe Pavan and is today skillfully managed by his son Michele. The winery adheres to Friulian wine traditions in both grape cultivation and vinemaking methods, respecting varietal characteristics. The vineyards cover 25 hectares in Prepotto (schioppettino wine country), a sizable tract of land for the area. The Friulano '23 gratifies the nose with its intense aromas of ripe fruit, crispy bread crust, and acacia honey, all followed by a well-sustained, pervasive palate. The Schioppettino di Prepotto '21 unveils hints of black cherry jam, medicinal herbs, cinnamon, nutmeg, and vanilla; the palate is pleasant, with tidy and well-integrated tannins. All the other wines show a strong varietal correctness and excel in their drinkability.

FCO Friulano '23	♟♟ 3
FCO Ribolla Gialla '23	♟♟ 3
FCO Sauvignon '23	♟♟ 3
FCO Schioppettino di Prepotto '21	♟♟ 3
FCO Traminer Aromatico '23	♟♟ 3
COF Picolit '18	♟♟ 5
FCO Cabernet Franc '21	♟♟ 3
FCO Malvasia '22	♟♟ 4
FCO Malvasia '21	♟♟ 3
FCO Merlot '21	♟♟ 3
FCO Pinot Bianco In Bocca al Lupo '22	♟♟ 3
FCO Ribolla Gialla '22	♟♟ 3
FCO Sauvignon '22	♟♟ 3
FCO Schioppettino di Prepotto '19	♟♟ 4
FCO Schioppettino di Prepotto '18	♟♟ 4

Valentino Butussi

via Prà di Corte, 1
33040 Corno di Rosazzo [UD]
☎ +39 0432759194
🌐 www.butussi.it

CELLAR SALES
PRE-BOOKED VISITS
ACCOMMODATION
ANNUAL PRODUCTION 110,000 bottles
HECTARES UNDER VINE 20.00
VITICULTURE METHOD Certified Organic
SUSTAINABLE WINERY

Founder Valentino Butussi, who paved the way in 1910, was followed first by his son Angelo and now by the new generation: Tobia, Filippo, and Mattia. This family-run winery maintains the values of rural culture, team spirit, careful task distribution, and a strong sense of responsibility, making it a true gem in the Corno di Rosazzo area, offering a wide range of bottles catering to all market sectors. Double accolades for the Pinot Grigio, which garnered our highest praise, particularly the Ramato version. The Pinot Grigio Ramato Madonna d'Aiuto '21 stood out not only for its captivating appearance but also for the intensity and complexity of its aromas, ranging from cherry notes, raspberry juice, and pink grapefruit zest to rhubarb and dried medicinal herbs. The palate is juicy and long, while the Pinot Grigio Ramato '23 proves more slender but equally pleasant and notably dynamic.

○ FCO Pinot Grigio Ramato '23	♟♟ 4
○ FCO Pinot Grigio Ramato Madonna d'Aiuto '21	♟♟ 7
○ COF Picolit '16	♟♟ 6
○ FCO Chardonnay '23	♟♟ 4
○ FCO Friulano '23	♟♟ 4
○ FCO Malvasia '23	♟♟ 4
● FCO Merlot '21	♟♟ 4
● FCO Pignolo Dalpin Ris. '18	♟♟ 6
○ FCO Pinot Grigio '23	♟♟ 4
● FCO Refosco P.R. '21	♟♟ 3
○ FCO Ribolla Gialla '23	♟♟ 4
○ FCO Sauvignon '23	♟♟ 4
○ FCO Sauvignon Genesis '22	♟♟ 7
○ FCO Verduzzo Friulano '19	♟♟ 4
● FCO Cabernet Franc '21	♟ 4
● FCO Cabernet Sauvignon '21	♟ 4

Maurizio Buzzinelli

loc. Pradis, 20
34071 Cormòns [GO]
(☎) +39 048160902
⊕ www.buzzinelli.it

CELLAR SALES
PRE-BOOKED VISITS
ACCOMMODATION
ANNUAL PRODUCTION 120,000 bottles
HECTARES UNDER VINE 35.00

Maurizio Buzzinelli's winery, along with a group of remarkable local estates, contributes to the development of a truly special territory: the gentle slopes of the Pradis hills near Cormòns. With proven expertise, the winery showcases a variety of wines that pay homage to the renowned qualities of the Collio Goriziano, while their reds benefit from the iron-rich soils that characterize the Soca river plains. For the fourth consecutive year, the Malvasia '23 led a series of impeccable wines, confirming its place among the best in the category and reaching our final selections. The complexity of its aroma evokes fragrant fruit salad, a bouquet of wildflowers, and freshly cut mountain hay. The palate is pervasive, gratifying, and very long. The Friulano '23 is also excellent, highlighting and enhancing the varietal characteristics of the region's most beloved grape.

Ca' Bolani

loc. Ca' Bolani, 2
33052 Cervignano del Friuli [UD]
(☎) +39 043132670
⊕ www.cabolani.it

CELLAR SALES
PRE-BOOKED VISITS
ANNUAL PRODUCTION 1,820,500 bottles
HECTARES UNDER VINE 570.00
SUSTAINABLE WINERY

Situated in the heart of the Friuli Aquileia appellation, Tenuta Ca' Bolani was owned by the Bolani family until 1970, when it was acquired by the Zonin group. The estate includes extensive vineyards in Molin del Ponte and Ca' Vescovo—at 570 hectares, it's the largest area under vines in the region. In last year's guide, we noted the absence of their two most representative wines and hypothesized that they needed further bottle aging. We were right, and this year, they've returned (in great form, to say the least). The Pinot Bianco Opimio '20 stood out for its delicate acacia flower notes and fragrant citrus nuances, leading to a balsamic and minty finish. The Sauvignon Aquilis '20 is also excellent—refined, alluring, and energetic.

○ Collio Malvasia '23	♟♟ 3*
○ Collio Chardonnay '23	♟♟ 3
○ Collio Friulano '23	♟♟ 3
○ Collio Ribolla Gialla '23	♟♟ 3
○ Collio Sauvignon '23	♟♟ 3
○ Collio Pinot Grigio '23	♟ 3
○ Collio Bianco da Uve Autoctone '21	♟♟ 5
○ Collio Chardonnay '22	♟♟ 3*
○ Collio Friulano '22	♟♟ 3
○ Collio Friulano '18	♟♟ 3*
○ Collio Friulano '16	♟♟ 3*
○ Collio Malvasia '22	♟♟ 3*
○ Collio Malvasia '21	♟♟ 3*
○ Collio Malvasia '20	♟♟ 2*
○ Collio Pinot Grigio '22	♟♟ 3
○ Collio Ribolla Gialla '22	♟♟ 3

○ Friuli Aquileia Pinot Bianco Opimio '20	♟♟♟ 5
○ Friuli Aquileia Bianco Tamànis '22	♟♟ 5
● Friuli Aquileia Rosso Tamànis '22	♟♟ 5
○ Friuli Aquileia Sauvignon Aquilis '20	♟♟ 5
○ Friuli Aquileia Pinot Bianco '09	♟♟♟ 2
○ Friuli Aquileia Pinot Bianco '20	♟♟ 3
○ Friuli Aquileia Pinot Bianco '16	♟♟ 4
○ Friuli Aquileia Pinot Grigio '22	♟♟ 3
○ Friuli Aquileia Pinot Grigio '18	♟♟ 3
○ Friuli Aquileia Sauvignon '21	♟♟ 3
○ Friuli Aquileia Sauvignon Aquilis '19	♟♟ 5
○ Friuli Aquileia Sauvignon Aquilis '16	♟♟ 5
○ Friuli Aquileia Traminer Aromatico '22	♟♟ 3
○ Friuli Aquileia Traminer Aromatico '21	♟♟ 3

Ca' Tullio

via Beligna, 41
33051 Aquileia [UD]
📞 +39 0431919700
🌐 www.catullio.it

CELLAR SALES
PRE-BOOKED VISITS
ACCOMMODATION
ANNUAL PRODUCTION 300,000 bottles
HECTARES UNDER VINE 100.00

Founded by Paolo Calligaris in 1994, Ca' Tullio now has the support of Paolo's sons Giacomo and Emanuele as well. Based in Aquileia, in a large, early 20th-century building once used for drying tobacco, most of the winery's grapes are grown on the hills of Sdricca di Manzano, though other plots (including parcels of ungrafted traminer aromatico) are cultivated near the cellar on the sandy soils of Viola. The Chardonnay '23 opens on a rich and complex aromatic suite, with floral and fruity notes accompanied by aromatic herbs and delicate spices, sensations that carry the palate to a balsamic finish. The Pinot Grigio '23 is also excellent, conjuring up notes of blossoming hay, white melon, and russet pear on the nose, enriched by smoky notes that reappear on the palate. The Traminer Aromatico '23 is also noteworthy, with its broom blossom fragrance and palate-pleasing qualities.

Cadibon

loc. Casali Gallo, 1
33040 Corno di Rosazzo [UD]
📞 +39 0432759316
🌐 www.cadibon.com

CELLAR SALES
PRE-BOOKED VISITS
ACCOMMODATION
ANNUAL PRODUCTION 50,000 bottles
HECTARES UNDER VINE 14.00
VITICULTURE METHOD Certified Organic

Cadibon was established in 1977 by the Bon family, who have been growing wine grapes in Corno di Rosazzo for generations. Luca Bon, the enthusiastic young manager, is a staunch advocate for sustainability, biodiversity, and environmental preservation. He personally tends to vineyards spanning three different appellations, each with unique terroirs and microclimates, yet unified by a commitment to quality. The Ronco del Nonno '22 is a blend of sauvignon, chardonnay, and verduzzo grapes sourced from a vineyard over 70 years old. It unveils aromas of ripe fruit, particularly yellow peach and apricot, with hints of honey and sultanas; the palate is soft and captivating. Another winery blend, the Epoca '22, is composed of a well-calibrated mix of white grapes, matured in oak for about 6 months and then left to age further in the bottle. It's fragrant both on the nose and palate, playing on notes of fresh grass and green apple.

○ FCO Chardonnay '23	🍷🍷 3
○ FCO Pinot Grigio '23	🍷🍷 3
○ FCO Ribolla Gialla '23	🍷🍷 3
○ FCO Sauvignon '23	🍷🍷 3
○ Friuli Aquileia Traminer Aromatico '23	🍷🍷 3
○ FCO Friulano '23	🍷 3
● Refosco P.R. '22	🍷 2
○ FCO Chardonnay '22	🍷🍷 3
○ FCO Chardonnay '21	🍷🍷 3
● FCO Pignolo '18	🍷🍷 3
○ FCO Pinot Grigio '22	🍷🍷 3
○ FCO Ribolla Gialla '22	🍷🍷 3
○ FCO Ribolla Gialla '21	🍷🍷 3
○ FCO Sauvignon '22	🍷🍷 3
○ FCO Sauvignon '21	🍷🍷 3
○ Friuli Aquileia Traminer Aromatico '22	🍷🍷 3

○ Collio Chardonnay '23	🍷🍷 4
○ Collio Sauvignon '23	🍷🍷 4
○ Epoca '22	🍷🍷 5
○ FCO Ribolla Gialla '23	🍷🍷 4
● FCO Schioppettino '22	🍷🍷 4
○ Ronco del Nonno '22	🍷🍷 4
○ Verduzzo '22	🍷 3
○ Epoca '21	🍷🍷 5
○ Epoca '20	🍷🍷 5
○ FCO Friulano Bontaj '22	🍷🍷 4
○ FCO Friulano Bontaj '21	🍷🍷 4
○ FCO Friulano Bontaj '20	🍷🍷 4
○ FCO Malvasia '18	🍷🍷 3*
○ FCO Ribolla Gialla '22	🍷🍷 4
● FCO Schioppettino '21	🍷🍷 3
○ Ronco del Nonno '21	🍷🍷 4

Canus

loc. Casali Gallo
via Gramogliano, 21
33040 Corno di Rosazzo [UD]
☎ +39 0432759427
✉ www.canus.it

CELLAR SALES
PRE-BOOKED VISITS
ANNUAL PRODUCTION 60,000 bottles
HECTARES UNDER VINE 18.00

Perched on the Gramogliano hill in Corno di Rosazzo, Canus has been owned by Ottorino Casonato (known as Otto) since 2015. As a newcomer to the wine world, Otto returned to his roots in the countryside, driven by the desire to build something meaningful. He views his venture as a commitment to forging lasting relationships with his fans. The Chardonnay '22 reveals a multitude of sensations ranging from elderflower and jasmine to golden apple and williams pear, with spicy hints of cinnamon and vanilla that intoxicate the nose and gratify the palate. The Gramogliano '21, a blend of tocai friulano, pinot grigio, sauvignon, and ribolla gialla, opens on a pleasing floral bouquet followed by notes of exotic fruit, light honey, and medicinal herbs. A juicy, flavorful, and persistent follows.

Fernanda Cappello

s.da di Sequals, 15
33090 Sequals [PN]
☎ +39 042793291
✉ www.fernandacappello.it

CELLAR SALES
PRE-BOOKED VISITS
RESTAURANT SERVICE
ANNUAL PRODUCTION 150,000 bottles
HECTARES UNDER VINE 126.00
SUSTAINABLE WINERY

Fernanda Cappello's estate is nestled between the Cellina and Meduna rivers, just below the Sequals hills in western Friuli. In 1988, Fernanda fully committed to the winemaking venture launched by her father, diving into what she still calls "an exciting adventure." She immediately began modernizing the estate, elevating it to a regional gem in oenology with the help of a top-notch team. The Traminer Aromatico '23 opens with a floral bouquet, notes of yellow rose and broom followed by fruity aromas of yellow peach and melon, underpinned by tropical hints of avocado and passion fruit, aromas that follow through on the palate, leaving a long-lasting impression. The Pinot Nero '22, Pinot Grigio '23, and Chardonnay '23 all receive high praise, but the Ribolla Gialla '23 surprised with its fragrance and linear profile.

○ FCO Bianco Gramogliano '21	♔♔ 5
○ FCO Chardonnay '22	♔♔ 4
○ FCO Friulano '22	♔♔ 4
● FCO Merlot '18	♔♔ 5
○ FCO Pinot Grigio '22	♔♔ 4
● FCO Refosco P.R. '22	♔♔ 4
○ FCO Ribolla Gialla '22	♔♔ 4
○ FCO Bianco Gramogliano '20	♕♕ 5
○ FCO Bianco Gramogliano '19	♕♕ 4
○ FCO Friulano '21	♕♕ 4
○ FCO Pinot Grigio '21	♕♕ 4
● FCO Refosco P.R. '21	♕♕ 4
● FCO Refosco P.R. '19	♕♕ 4
○ FCO Ribolla Gialla '21	♕♕ 4
○ FCO Ribolla Gialla '20	♕♕ 4
○ FCO Ribolla Gialla '19	♕♕ 4

○ Friuli Chardonnay '23	♔♔ 2
○ Friuli Grave Pinot Grigio '23	♔♔ 2
● Friuli Grave Pinot Nero '22	♔♔ 2
○ Friuli Grave Traminer Aromatico '23	♔♔ 2
○ Ribolla Gialla '23	♔♔ 2
○ Friuli Grave Friulano '23	♔ 2
● Friuli Grave Merlot '22	♔ 2
● Friuli Grave Sauvignon '23	♔ 2
● Friuli Grave Cabernet Franc '20	♕♕ 2
○ Friuli Grave Chardonnay '21	♕♕ 2
○ Friuli Grave Friulano '22	♕♕ 2
○ Friuli Grave Friulano '21	♕♕ 2
○ Friuli Grave Pinot Grigio '22	♕♕ 2
● Friuli Grave Pinot Nero '20	♕♕ 2
● Friuli Grave Refosco P.R. '22	♕♕ 2
○ Friuli Grave Sauvignon '21	♕♕ 2
○ Friuli Grave Traminer Aromatico '22	♕♕ 2

Castello di Buttrio

via del Pozzo, 5
33042 Buttrio [UD]
☎ +39 0432673015
⊜ www.castellodibuttrio.it

CELLAR SALES
PRE-BOOKED VISITS
ACCOMMODATION AND RESTAURANT SERVICE
ANNUAL PRODUCTION 100,000 bottles
HECTARES UNDER VINE 25.00

Marco Felluga acquired Castello di Buttrio in
1994 and immediately began transforming it into
a winery, later passing the torch to his daughter
Alessandra. Through patient work, Alessandra
restored the ancient walls that now house the
cellar and main production spaces to their
former glory. The wines continue to flourish,
driven by the enthusiasm of the new generation
and the invaluable collaboration of Donato
Lanati. This year, the winery's most
representative wines were absent, as they
evidently need further aging. Consequently, only
our wines from the latest vintage were
presented. Despite the challenges of the harvest,
which many considered difficult, our tastings
revealed wines of great depth, particularly
among the whites. The Sauvignon '23 is one of
the best, marked by its freshness and fragrance,
with prominent notes of lychee and lime.

★Castello di Spessa

via Spessa, 1
34070 Capriva del Friuli [GO]
☎ +39 048160445
⊜ www.castellodispessa.it

CELLAR SALES
PRE-BOOKED VISITS
ACCOMMODATION AND RESTAURANT SERVICE
ANNUAL PRODUCTION 450,000 bottles
HECTARES UNDER VINE 98.00
SUSTAINABLE WINERY

Castello di Spessa, a magnificent manor with a
thousand-year history, exudes a subtle charm.
Within the bunker connecting the castle to the
cellars, used by occupying troops during World
War II, wines age in ideal temperatures and
humidity levels. The current owner, Loretto Pali,
is a staunch believer in Collio's potential for
producing the three pinots: bianco, grigio, and
nero, the estate's flagship wines. The Pinot
Bianco Santarosa '22 once again exemplifies the
grape's elegance and softness. It delights the
nose with delicate nuances of lily of the valley,
jasmine, pear, yellow currant, anise, and talcum
powder, then caresses the palate before finishing
with a pleasant balsamic note. The Sauvignon
Segrè '22 emphasizes strong varietal notes of
sage and tomato leaf, with an energetic palate.
The Friulano Rassauer '22 proves pleasantly
delicate on the nose, but unfolds sapid and linear
on the palate.

Wine	Rating
● FCO Sauvignon '23	♟♟ 4
● FCO Chardonnay '23	♟♟ 4
● FCO Friulano '23	♟♟ 4
FCO Ribolla Gialla '23	♟♟ 4
● FCO Bianco Torre Butria Ris. '13	♟♟ 5
● FCO Bianco Uve Carate Ris. '19	♟♟ 7
● FCO Friulano '22	♟♟ 4
● FCO Friulano '20	♟♟ 4
FCO Merlot Uve Carate Ris. '13	♟♟ 3*
FCO Rosso Uve Carate Ris. '17	♟♟ 8
FCO Rosso Uve Carate Ris. '15	♟♟ 7
FCO Sauvignon '21	♟♟ 4
FCO Sauvignon Ettaro Ris. '20	♟♟ 6
FCO Sauvignon Ettaro Ris. '18	♟♟ 6
Mon Blanc '20	♟♟ 3*

Wine	Rating
○ Collio Friulano Rassauer '22	♟♟ 5
○ Collio Pinot Bianco Santarosa '22	♟♟ 5
○ Collio Sauvignon Segrè '22	♟♟ 5
○ Amadeus Brut M. Cl. '18	♟♟ 6
● Collio Pinot Nero Casanova '21	♟♟ 5
○ Collio Friulano Rassauer '19	♟♟♟ 3*
○ Collio Pinot Bianco '14	♟♟♟ 3*
○ Collio Pinot Bianco '13	♟♟♟ 3*
○ Collio Pinot Bianco '11	♟♟♟ 3*
○ Collio Pinot Bianco '06	♟♟♟ 3*
○ Collio Pinot Bianco Santarosa '21	♟♟♟ 5
○ Collio Pinot Bianco Santarosa '18	♟♟♟ 3*
○ Collio Sauvignon Segrè '03	♟♟♟ 5
○ Collio Sauvignon Segrè '02	♟♟♟ 5
○ Collio Tocai Friulano '05	♟♟♟ 3*

Castelvecchio

via Castelnuovo, 2
34078 Sagrado [GO]
📞 +39 048199742
🌐 www.castelvecchio.com

CELLAR SALES
PRE-BOOKED VISITS
ACCOMMODATION AND RESTAURANT SERVICE
ANNUAL PRODUCTION 160,000 bottles
HECTARES UNDER VINE 35.00
VITICULTURE METHOD Certified Organic
SUSTAINABLE WINERY

Owned by the Terraneo family, Castelvecchio unfolds in the northernmost part of Gorizia's Karst plateau, atop a hill just above Sagrado. The estate's ancient origins are still evident in the Renaissance villa and the evocative park dotted with cypresses and centuries-old oak trees. The rocky subsoil, the thin layer of iron and limestone-rich red soil, the area's airiness, and the late harvest contribute to a limited but high-quality range. Aromatically, the Vitovska '23 evokes Mediterranean scrub, with floral aromas reminiscent of summer hay and hazelnut husk. These same sensations accompany the palate, which culminates in a delightful finish. But this is just the tip of an interesting and truly solid collection, both for the reds, as demonstrated by the Cabernet Franc and Sauvignon, the Terrano and the Refosco, and for their fragrant whites. This year's standout white is the Malvasia Dileo, a wine produced in small quantities and that can be found in the Rare Wines section.

○ Carso Vitovska '23	🍷🍷	4
● Carso Cabernet Sauvignon '22	🍷🍷	4
○ Carso Malvasia '23	🍷🍷	4
○ Carso Pinot Grigio '23	🍷🍷	4
○ Carso Sauvignon '23	🍷🍷	4
● Carso Terrano '22	🍷🍷	4
● Carso Cabernet Franc '22	🍷	4
● Carso Refosco P.R. '22	🍷	4
○ Carso Malvasia Dileo '21	🍷🍷🍷	5
○ Carso Malvasia Dileo '15	🍷🍷🍷	4*
○ Carso Malvasia Dileo '20	🍷🍷	4
○ Carso Malvasia Dileo '19	🍷🍷	4
○ Carso Vitovska '22	🍷🍷	4
○ Carso Vitovska '21	🍷🍷	3*

Tenimenti Civa

fraz. Bellazoia
via Subida, 16
33040 Povoletto [UD]
📞 +39 04321770382
🌐 www.tenimenticiva.com

CELLAR SALES
PRE-BOOKED VISITS
ANNUAL PRODUCTION 900,000 bottles
HECTARES UNDER VINE 75.00

In 2016, Valerio Civa decided to invest his extensive experience by acquiring a winery and a substantial number of vineyards in Bellazoia and surrounding areas, establishing Tenimenti Civa. Since 2021, a new production facility has been active in Povoletto. This highly innovative winery features a sophisticated digital management system that tracks every activity and converts the information into useful data to optimize processes. This year, Ribolla Gialla was presented in a myriad of versions, sourced both from their prized Colli Orientali del Friuli vineyards and from the plains, mostly as sparkling wines. However, as in the previous edition, the highest accolades went to the Sauvignon Vigneto Bellazoia '23 and the Chardonnay Vigneto Bellazoia '22. The former exudes aromas of boxwood, grapefruit, and lychee, with a distinctly varietal palate, while the latter conjures up quince jam and honey, offering a rich and fragrant mouthfeel.

○ FCO Chardonnay Vign. Bellazoia '22	🍷🍷	5
○ FCO Sauvignon Vign. Bellazoia '23	🍷🍷	5
○ FCO Ribolla Gialla '23	🍷🍷	3
○ FCO Ribolla Gialla Biele Zôe Cuvée '23	🍷🍷	3
○ FCO Ribolla Gialla Vign. Bellazoia '23	🍷🍷	5
○ Friuli Ribolla Gialla Cuvée Biele Zôe Brut	🍷🍷	2
○ Ribolla Gialla Cuvée 12 Dosaggio Zero	🍷🍷	3
○ Ribolla Gialla Ronc Marin Extra Dry '22	🍷🍷	5
○ Ribolla Gialla Ca' Floris Brut	🍷	
○ Ribolla Gialla Col Moniér	🍷	
○ FCO Sauvignon Vign. Bellazoia '21	🍷🍷🍷	5
○ FCO Chardonnay Vign. Bellazoia '21	🍷🍷	5
● FCO Refosco P. R. Vign. Bellazoia '19	🍷🍷	5
○ FCO Sauvignon Vign. Bellazoia '22	🍷🍷	5

★Eugenio Collavini

loc. Gramogliano
via della Ribolla Gialla, 2
33040 Corno di Rosazzo [UD]
(》 +39 0432753222
◈ www.collavini.it

CELLAR SALES
PRE-BOOKED VISITS
RESTAURANT SERVICE
ANNUAL PRODUCTION 1,100,000 bottles
HECTARES UNDER VINE 136.00
SUSTAINABLE WINERY

Manlio Collavini, who still manages the family business with the help of his sons Luigi and Giovanni, is considered a pioneer of high-quality regional viticulture. In the 1970s, he was one of the first to vinify pinot grigio as a white and later to make a sparkling ribolla gialla. The winery has grown significantly, with a trusted agronomist overseeing grape cultivation on both estate plots and parcels managed by third-party growers. The Ribolla Gialla Dosaggio Zero '19 captivates the palate with its ultra-fine effervescence, delivering an almost thirst-quenching effect. The Ribolla Gialla Brut '20, now a classic, is slightly softer but just as enjoyable and refreshing. The Bianco Broy '22 needs no introduction, as it's consistently outstanding. Made from tocai friulano, chardonnay, and sauvignon, it emanates tropical fruit, chamomile, honey, and much more, with a structured, juicy, and powerful palate.

Colle Duga

loc. Zegla, 10
34071 Cormòns [GO]
(》 +39 048161177
◈ www.colleduga.com

CELLAR SALES
PRE-BOOKED VISITS
ANNUAL PRODUCTION 50,000 bottles
HECTARES UNDER VINE 9.00

Colle Duga is a boutique operation, a fact that allows Damian Princic to oversee all stages of production. The vineyards in Zegla are divided into four plots, each with different microclimates and soil compositions. The region's potential is highlighted by Damian's meticulous care for the few, high-quality bottles produced, and his wines are characterized by exemplary typicity. Damian's children, Karin and Patrik, ensure the estate's future. This year, only three wines from the latest vintage were presented. We assume the others were given additional time to bottle age and look forward to tasting them in the next edition. The Collio Bianco '23 aptly represents the region. Like a well-crafted cocktail, the characteristics of tocai friulano, malvasia istriana, chardonnay, and sauvignon grapes blend into a delightful fusion of fragrant tropical fruit.

FRIULI VENEZIA GIULIA

Collio Bianco Broy '22	♟♟♟ 7
Ribolla Gialla Brut '20	♟♟ 5
Ribolla Gialla Dosaggio Zero '19	♟♟ 5
Collio Friulano T '23	♟♟ 4
Collio Merlot dal Pic '18	♟♟ 5
Collio Ribolla Gialla Turian '22	♟♟ 5
FCO Schioppettino Turian '21	♟♟ 5
Collio Bianco Broy '21	♟♟♟ 6
Collio Bianco Broy '20	♟♟♟ 6
Collio Bianco Broy '19	♟♟♟ 6
Collio Bianco Broy '18	♟♟♟ 6
Collio Bianco Broy '17	♟♟♟ 6
Collio Bianco Broy '15	♟♟♟ 5
Collio Bianco Broy '14	♟♟♟ 5
Ribolla Gialla Brut '13	♟♟♟ 5
Ribolla Gialla Dosaggio Zero '15	♟♟♟ 5

○ Collio Bianco '23	♟♟ 5
○ Collio Chardonnay '23	♟♟ 4
○ Collio Friulano '23	♟♟ 4
○ Collio Bianco '16	♟♟♟ 4*
○ Collio Bianco '11	♟♟♟ 4*
○ Collio Bianco '08	♟♟♟ 3*
○ Collio Bianco '07	♟♟♟ 3
○ Collio Chardonnay '20	♟♟♟ 4*
○ Collio Friulano '09	♟♟♟ 3*
○ Collio Tocai Friulano '06	♟♟♟ 3*
○ Collio Tocai Friulano '05	♟♟♟ 3*
○ Collio Bianco '21	♟♟ 4
○ Collio Chardonnay '22	♟♟ 4
○ Collio Chardonnay '21	♟♟ 4
○ Collio Friulano '22	♟♟ 4
○ Collio Sauvignon '22	♟♟ 3*

Gianpaolo Colutta

via Orsaria, 32a
33044 Manzano [UD]
☎ +39 0432510654
⊛ www.coluttagianpaolo.it

CELLAR SALES
PRE-BOOKED VISITS
ANNUAL PRODUCTION 70,000 bottles
HECTARES UNDER VINE 25.00
SUSTAINABLE WINERY

In the early 20th century the Colutta family, well-known in the field of pharmaceuticals, decided to venture into wine production. In 1999, Gianpaolo Colutta established his own winery, later passing it on to his daughter Elisabetta. Their vineyards stretch across the sunny slopes of Manzano, within the Friuli Colli Orientali appellation. The winery offers a wide range of wines, with special attention given to ancient, almost forgotten native grape varietals. The region is famously known for white wine production, but the hills around Manzano, closest to the Adriatic Sea, have always produced high-level reds. The Frassinolo '20, made exclusively from native grapes (refosco dal peduncolo rosso, schioppettino, and tazzelenghe), evokes tobacco, carob, dark chocolate, and roasted coffee on the nose, while gratifying the palate with its lively tannins.

Giorgio Colutta

via Orsaria, 32
33044 Manzano [UD]
☎ +39 0432740315
⊛ www.colutta.it

CELLAR SALES
PRE-BOOKED VISITS
ACCOMMODATION
ANNUAL PRODUCTION 140,000 bottles
HECTARES UNDER VINE 23.00
SUSTAINABLE WINERY

Giorgio Colutta's winery is located in Manzano, in an old 18th-century villa acquired by the Colutta family in the early 1900s, a property that still hosts the cellar. Their production range is characterized by exemplary precision and linearity, and in the best years, thanks to some outstanding crus, reaches peaks of excellence. Once known as Bandut, the winery has long stood out for its commitment to principles of environmental sustainability. This year, fewer wines than usual were presented, clearly indicating that the other wines needed additional bottle aging. The Merlot '22 offers an intriguing mix of tobacco, cocoa powder, coffee beans, and underbrush on the nose, with an enveloping, plump palate. Among the wines from the latest vintage, the Pinot Grigio '23 stands out, with aromas of acacia and elderflower, golden apple, and williams pear, excelling in balance and fragrance.

● FCO Rosso Frassinolo '20	♥♥ 4
○ FCO Bianco Prarion '23	♥♥ 3
○ FCO Friulano '23	♥♥ 3
⊙ FCO Pinot Grigio '23	♥♥ 3
● FCO Pinot Nero '21	♥♥ 4
○ FCO Ribolla Gialla '23	♥♥ 3
● FCO Schioppettino '22	♥♥ 3
● FCO Tazzelenghe '20	♥♥ 5
○ FCO Chardonnay '23	♥ 3
○ FCO Bianco Prarion '21	♀♀ 4
○ FCO Bianco Prarion '20	♀♀ 4
○ FCO Friulano '22	♀♀ 3
○ FCO Friulano '18	♀♀ 3*
⊙ FCO Pinot Grigio Ramato '20	♀♀ 3*
○ FCO Ribolla Gialla '22	♀♀ 4

○ FCO Pinot Grigio '23	♥♥ 4
○ FCO Friulano '23	♥♥ 4
● FCO Merlot '22	♥♥ 4
○ FCO Pinot Grigio Skin Contact '23	♥♥ 4
○ FCO Sauvignon '23	♥♥ 4
○ FCO Friulano '22	♀♀ 4
○ FCO Friulano '17	♀♀ 3
● FCO Merlot '21	♀♀ 4
● FCO Pignolo '16	♀♀ 7
○ FCO Pinot Grigio '22	♀♀ 4
○ FCO Pinot Grigio '18	♀♀ 3
○ FCO Ribolla Gialla '22	♀♀ 5
● FCO Schioppettino '16	♀♀ 5
○ Rosazzo Bianco Nojâr '20	♀♀ 5

Paolino Comelli

b.go Case Colloredo, 8
33040 Faedis [UD]
☏ +39 0432711226
✉ www.comelli.it

Dario Coos

loc. Ramandolo, 5
33045 Nimis [UD]
☏ +39 0432790320
✉ www.dariocoos.it

CELLAR SALES
PRE-BOOKED VISITS
ACCOMMODATION
ANNUAL PRODUCTION 50,000 bottles
HECTARES UNDER VINE 12.50
VITICULTURE METHOD Certified Organic
SUSTAINABLE WINERY

Paolino Comelli made a wise choice in the post-war era, purchasing the abandoned village of Case Colloredo in Faedis, which included some of the area's finest vineyards. It meant going against the grain, given that most were abandoning the countryside for the city. Pierluigi (known as Pigi) and his wife Daniela continued his legacy, creating a model winery that is a point of pride for the region. The Soffumbergo Rosso '21, a blend of merlot, refosco dal peduncolo rosso, and cabernet sauvignon, performed admirably, standing out for the intensity and complexity of its aromas, characterized by notes of morello cherry jam, sweet spices, sun-dried tomatoes, and black olive pâté. In the mouth it's pervasive, flavorful, with well-calibrated tannins. The Picolit dei Colli Orientali del Friuli '20 is right up there, unveiling aromas of candied fruit, dates, raisins, and honey, lingering on the palate with an unforgettable finish.

CELLAR SALES
PRE-BOOKED VISITS
ANNUAL PRODUCTION 80,000 bottles
HECTARES UNDER VINE 16.00

Founded in 1986 by Dario Coos, this winery gained fame for producing Picolit and Ramandolo, a sweet wine made from verduzzo giallo, a variety with small, thick-skinned clusters. Today, a dedicated group of passionate partners manages the winery, diversifying their offerings with a range based predominantly on native varietals, a choice that has increased their market presence. The wide variety of wines presented allowed for a comprehensive assessment of the producer's offerings, and the results were more than valid. The Malvasia '23, in particular, stood out as one of the best in its category, making it to the final tastings. It exudes pleasant aromas of ripe white-fleshed fruit, dandelion, and medicinal herbs, with a gratifying palate. We also appreciated the Friulano '23 among their standard-label, annata wines and the Ramandolo '21 among the sweets.

○ COF Picolit '20	♟♟ 5
● Suffumbergo Rosso '21	♟♟ 6
○ FCO Bianco Soffumbergo '20	♟♟ 5
○ FCO Friulano '23	♟♟ 3
○ FCO Malvasia '22	♟♟ 3
○ FCO Pinot Grigio Amplius '23	♟♟ 3
● Merlot Jacò '22	♟♟ 4
○ COF Sauvignon '13	♀♀ 3*
○ FCO Bianco Soffumbergo '19	♀♀ 5
○ FCO Malvasia '19	♀♀ 3*
○ FCO Malvasia '17	♀♀ 3*
○ FCO Malvasia '14	♀♀ 3*
○ FCO Sauvignon '18	♀♀ 3*
○ FCO Sauvignon '16	♀♀ 3*
● Soffumbergo Rosso '11	♀♀ 4

○ FCO Malvasia '23	♟♟ 3*
○ COF Picolit '20	♟♟ 6
○ FCO Friulano '23	♟♟ 3
○ FCO Pinot Bianco '23	♟♟ 4
○ FCO Ribolla Gialla '23	♟♟ 3
● Merlot '20	♟♟ 6
● Pignolo '19	♟♟ 5
○ Ramandolo Il Longhino '20	♟♟ 4
○ Ramandolo V.T. '21	♟♟ 5
○ FCO Sauvignon '23	♟ 3
○ Friuli Pinot Grigio '23	♟ 3
○ Ribolla Gialla Brut	♟ 4
○ COF Picolit '18	♀♀ 6
○ COF Picolit '17	♀♀ 6
○ COF Picolit '15	♀♀ 6
○ FCO Chardonnay '22	♀♀ 4

Cantina Produttori Cormòns

via Vino della Pace, 31
34071 Cormòns [GO]
(") +39 048162471
@ www.cormons.com

CELLAR SALES
PRE-BOOKED VISITS
ACCOMMODATION
ANNUAL PRODUCTION 2,250,000 bottles
HECTARES UNDER VINE 340.00
SUSTAINABLE WINERY

This esteemed winery emerged from a remarkable story of cooperation that began in the 1960s. A group of winegrowers from Cormons, unable to vinify individually, decided to join forces. The recent addition of Alessandro dal Zovo as general manager, supported by President Filippo Bregant, has significantly boosted the quality of their production. For the fifth consecutive year, the Collio Bianco Uve Autoctone '22 earned Tre Bicchieri. This wine is a blend of tocai friulano, malvasia istriana, and ribolla gialla, traditionally vinified together to highlight their varietal characteristics. On the nose, it conjures up mimosa, yellow peach, and acacia honey, with a very pleasing palate to follow. The refined and fragrant Pinot Bianco '23 and the balanced and harmonious Malvasia Harmo '22 are also excellent.

○ Collio Bianco Uve Autoctone '22	♥♥♥ 3*
○ Collio Pinot Bianco '23	♥♥ 3*
○ Friuli Malvasia Harmo '22	♥♥ 3*
○ Collio Friulano '23	♥♥ 3
○ Collio Pinot Grigio '23	♥♥ 3
● Collio Rosso Melograno '22	♥♥ 3
○ Collio Sauvignon '23	♥♥ 3
○ Friuli Malvasia '23	♥♥ 2*
○ Friuli Riesling Medegis '22	♥♥ 3
○ Friuli Sauvignon '23	♥♥ 2*
○ Collio Bianco Uve Autoctone '21	♀♀ 3*
○ Collio Bianco Uve Autoctone '20	♀♀ 3*
○ Collio Friulano '22	♀♀ 3*
○ Collio Pinot Bianco '21	♀♀ 3*
○ Collio Pinot Bianco '20	♀♀ 3*
○ Friuli Malvasia Harmo '21	♀♀ 3*

Crastin

loc. Ruttars, 33
34070 Dolegna del Collio [GO]
(") +39 0481630310
@ www.vinicrastin.it

CELLAR SALES
PRE-BOOKED VISITS
ANNUAL PRODUCTION 35,000 bottles
HECTARES UNDER VINE 6.00

In 1990, Sergio Collarig started bottling his own wine, offering it to guests of the agritourism he opened with his sister Vilma on the beautiful hills of Ruttars in Collio Goriziano. The small size of the winery allows him to personally tend to his vineyards using traditional methods passed down through generations. His wines reflect his character: exuberant, forthright, and engaging. In a series of excellent performances across their entire range, the standout was the Pinot Grigio '23, which made it to the finals thanks to its excellent aromatic impact and, above all, its delightful palate. On the nose it reveals aromas of blooming hay, golden apple, amaretto, and acacia honey, with a linear, fragrant palate that finishes on minty notes. We also appreciated the Sauvignon '22, with its vegetal notes of white asparagus and green pepper, and the Friulano '23, with its linear palate and rich citrus flavors.

○ Collio Pinot Grigio '23	♥♥ 3
● Collio Cabernet Franc '22	♥♥ 3
○ Collio Friulano '23	♥♥ 3
● Collio Merlot Ris. '21	♥♥ 4
○ Collio Ribolla Gialla '23	♥♥ 3
○ Collio Sauvignon '22	♥♥ 3
○ Collio Friulano '22	♀♀ 3
○ Collio Friulano '20	♀♀ 3
○ Collio Friulano '15	♀♀ 3
○ Collio Friulano '14	♀♀ 2
○ Collio Friulano '12	♀♀ 2
○ Collio Friulano '11	♀♀ 2
○ Collio Pinot Bianco '22	♀♀ 3
○ Collio Pinot Bianco '21	♀♀ 3
○ Collio Pinot Grigio '22	♀♀ 3
○ Collio Ribolla Gialla '22	♀♀ 3

Conte d'Attimis-Maniago

via Sottomonte, 21
33042 Buttrio [UD]
☎ +39 0432674027
⊕ www.contedattimismaniago.it

CELLAR SALES
PRE-BOOKED VISITS
ANNUAL PRODUCTION 400,000 bottles
HECTARES UNDER VINE 85.00

In 2023, the winery celebrated its 438th harvest on the hills of Buttrio. Today Alberto d'Attimis-Maniago Marchiò and his son Fabio manage this historic cellar, which has been passed down through 18 generations. The winery has always believed in replicating local biotypes and the oenological value of native varieties. The vineyards respect the natural environment, maintaining significant tracts of woodland and diversified crops. Among a varied lineup that included both whites and reds, the Sauvignon '23 stood out in particular. Intriguing smoky notes rise from the glass followed by candied fruit, citrus peel, and green pepper, with a fragrant and balsamic palate to follow. The Tazzelenghe '20, made with a rare native grape (its name means "tongue-cutter" in dialect), is excellent as well, unveiling aromas of licorice, graphite, and coffee. In the mouth it proves energetic and appropriately tannic.

di Lenardo

loc. Ontagnano
p.zza C. Battisti, 1
33050 Gonars [UD]
☎ +39 0432928633
⊕ www.dilenardo.it

FRIULI VENEZIA GIULIA

CELLAR SALES
PRE-BOOKED VISITS
ANNUAL PRODUCTION 650,000 bottles
HECTARES UNDER VINE 60.00
SUSTAINABLE WINERY

Di Lenardo is located in the small village of Ontagnano, a few kilometers from the walls of Palmanova. Although the winery dates back to 1878, its most notable achievements have come under its current owner, Massimo di Lenardo, who is now ready to hand things over to his son Vittorio. The wines are rich in nuances due to the location of the vineyards in the sunny Friulian plains, which are divided into different zones with various soils and microclimates. Once again, two wines reached our finals. For the Thanks '23, this has become customary. The wine, a blend of chardonnay, tocai friulano, malvasia istriana, verduzzo, and sauvignon, features pronounced aromas of dry hay, quince, and mango. On the palate, it's juicy, warm, sapid, and perfectly aligned with the nose. The Chardonnay Father Eyes '23 exudes intense aromas of broom, ripe pear, banana, candied citron, and ginger, with a voluminous and well-sustained palate to follow.

○ FCO Sauvignon '23	♟♟ 3*
○ FCO Bianco Ronco Broilo '23	♟♟ 5
○ FCO Malvasia '23	♟♟ 4
● FCO Pignolo '16	♟♟ 6
○ FCO Pinot Grigio '23	♟♟ 3
● FCO Rosso Vignaricco '19	♟♟ 5
● FCO Tazzelenghe '20	♟♟ 6
○ COF Ronco Broilo '09	♙♙ 5
○ COF Verduzzo Friulano Tore delle Signore '12	♙♙ 3
○ FCO Bianco Ronco Broilo '19	♙♙ 5
○ FCO Malvasia '21	♙♙ 4
● FCO Pignolo '13	♙♙ 6
○ FCO Pinot Grigio Ramato '22	♙♙ 3
● FCO Rosso Vignaricco '16	♙♙ 5
● FCO Tazzelenghe '19	♙♙ 6
● Vignaricco '09	♙♙ 5

○ Chardonnay Father's Eyes '23	♟♟ 3*
○ Thanks '23	♟♟ 4
○ Friuli Pinot Grigio '23	♟♟ 2*
○ Friuli Pinot Grigio Ramato Gossip '23	♟♟ 2*
● Just Me Merlot '21	♟♟ 4
○ Pass The Cookies! '23	♟♟ 3
○ Ribolla Gialla Brut M. Cl. '22	♟♟ 3
○ Ribolla Gialla Comemivuoi '23	♟♟ 2*
○ Ribolla Gialla One Shot Project '22	♟♟ 5
○ Chardonnay '23	♟ 2
○ Friuli Friulano Toh! '23	♟ 2
● Ronco Nolè '22	♟ 2
○ Sauvignon '23	♟ 2
○ Chardonnay '15	♙♙♙ 2*
○ Friuli Pinot Grigio Ramato Gossip '22	♙♙ 2*
○ Thanks '22	♙♙ 4

483

★★Dorigo

s.da prov.le Case Sparse Campo, I
33040 Premariacco [UD]
☎ +39 0432634161
✦ www.dorigowines.com

CELLAR SALES
PRE-BOOKED VISITS
ANNUAL PRODUCTION 120,000 bottles
HECTARES UNDER VINE 20.00
SUSTAINABLE WINERY

In 2012, Alessio Dorigo took over from Girolamo, initiating a series of structural and production changes that expanded the winery's offerings and enhanced its prestigious brand. Their sparkling wines, produced strictly using the Metodo Classico, are the cornerstone of their range. However, all the wines have reached high quality standards, showcasing the region's unique characteristics. For many years, Montsclapade was Dorigo's flagship wine. The 2019 vintage has made a comeback, reaching our final selections this year. A blend of cabernet sauvignon, cabernet franc, and merlot, it ages for 30 months in barriques and further in the bottle. The result exudes aromas of macerated red berries, herbs, and sweet spices, while the palate proves sumptuous and balanced. The Sauvignon '23, with its intriguing nose and fragrant palate, is also excellent.

Draga - Miklus

loc. Scedina, 8
34070 San Floriano del Collio [GO]
☎ +39 0481884182
✦ www.draga-miklus.com

CELLAR SALES
PRE-BOOKED VISITS
ANNUAL PRODUCTION 50,000 bottles
HECTARES UNDER VINE 13.00
VITICULTURE METHOD Certified Organic
SUSTAINABLE WINERY

In 1982, Milan Miklus took charge of the family winery, which at the time had only one hectare dedicated to grape growing. He converted the remaining lands to vineyards and began bottling his wines ten years later. His son Mitja now manages a highly respectable estate. Both father and son employ a mix of modern and ancient methods in the vineyard and cellar, always with respect for the land and a focus on sustainability. This year, we were only able to evaluate a few wines, yet they were sufficient to confirm the excellent quality level that has been achieved and maintained. The selections from the latest vintage prove impeccable in their varietal characteristics, especially the Malvasia '23, which pairs signature aromatic notes with delightful tropical nuances. However, as usual, the top spot goes to a macerated wine, the Friulano Miklus '19, which conjures up quince jam, ripe banana, and honey.

● FCO Rosso Montsclapade '19	♟♟ 6
○ FCO Sauvignon '23	♟♟ 3*
○ Blanc de Blancs Pas Dosé M. Cl.	♟♟ 5
○ Blanc de Noir Dosage Zéro M. Cl.	♟♟ 5
○ Dorigo Brut Cuvée M. Cl.	♟♟ 5
● Dorigo Rosso	♟♟ 4
○ FCO Chardonnay Ronc di Juri '22	♟♟ 5
○ FCO Friulano '23	♟♟ 3
○ FCO Friulano Ronc di Juri '22	♟♟ 5
○ FCO Pinot Grigio '23	♟♟ 3
○ FCO Ribolla Gialla '23	♟♟ 3
○ COF Chardonnay Vign. Ronc di Juri '96	♟♟♟ 5
○ COF Picolit Passito '95	♟♟♟ 5
● COF Rosso Montsclapade '06	♟♟♟ 6
● COF Rosso Montsclapade '04	♟♟♟ 6
● COF Rosso Montsclapade '98	♟♟♟ 6

○ Collio Friulano Miklus '19	♟♟ 6
○ Collio Friulano '23	♟♟ 4
○ Collio Malvasia '23	♟♟ 4
○ Collio Malvasia Miklus '18	♟♟♟ 6
○ Collio Malvasia Miklus '10	♟♟♟ 7
○ Miklus Natural Art Ribolla Gialla '18	♟♟♟ 7
○ Miklus Natural Art Ribolla Gialla '15	♟♟♟ 6
○ Collio Friulano '19	♟♟ 3*
○ Collio Malvasia '20	♟♟ 4
○ Collio Malvasia Miklus '16	♟♟ 5
○ Collio Malvasia Miklus '12	♟♟ 4
○ Collio Pinot Grigio Miklus '16	♟♟ 6
○ Collio Pinot Grigio Miklus '11	♟♟ 4
○ Collio Sauvignon Miklus '11	♟♟ 5
○ Jakot '19	♟♟ 7
○ Ribolla Gialla Miklus '12	♟♟ 6

Drius

via Filanda, 100
34071 Cormòns [GO]
☎ +39 048160998
🌐 www.drius.it

CELLAR SALES
PRE-BOOKED VISITS
ANNUAL PRODUCTION 55,000 bottles
HECTARES UNDER VINE 17.00
SUSTAINABLE WINERY

Mauro Drius is a true wine artisan, a skilled vintner who masterfully highlights the potential of his land. He belongs to a category of farmers who are proud of their trade and deeply connected to the land they cultivate. His precious vineyards span both the high plains of the Friuli Isonzo appellation and the slopes of Monte Quarin, in the heart of Collio. Mauro benefits from the active involvement of his female family members and has entrusted the work in the cellar to his young son Denis. This year, the top spot once again goes to the Friulano Sensar '22, a wine dedicated to Grandfather Sergio, known as the "Sensar" or mediator. Made from a selection of tocai friulano grapes from the oldest vineyards, it has aromas of wildflowers, sage, mint, candied fruit, and almond drupes, with a fresh and mineral-driven palate. The Sauvignon '22 is equally impressive, with citrusy nuances of lychee and lime meeting vegetal notes of nettle and pepper—a fragrant and dynamic drink.

○ Collio Sauvignon '22	♈♈	3*
○ Friuli Isonzo Friulano Sensar '22	♈♈	5
○ Collio Friulano '22	♈♈	3
○ Friuli Isonzo Bianco Vignis di Siris '21	♈♈	4
○ Friuli Isonzo Chardonnay '22	♈♈	3
○ Friuli Isonzo Malvasia '22	♈♈	3
● Friuli Isonzo Merlot '20	♈♈	4
○ Friuli Isonzo Pinot Bianco '22	♈♈	3
○ Friuli Isonzo Pinot Grigio '22	♈♈	3
○ Collio Tocai Friulano '05	♈♈♈	3*
○ Collio Tocai Friulano '02	♈♈♈	2*
○ Friuli Isonzo Bianco Vignis di Siris '02	♈♈♈	3*
○ Friuli Isonzo Friulano '07	♈♈♈	3
○ Friuli Isonzo Malvasia '08	♈♈♈	3*
○ Friuli Isonzo Pinot Bianco '09	♈♈♈	3*
○ Friuli Isonzo Pinot Bianco '00	♈♈♈	3*

Ermacora

fraz. Ipplis
via Solzaredo, 9
33040 Premariacco [UD]
☎ +39 0432716250
🌐 www.ermacora.it

CELLAR SALES
PRE-BOOKED VISITS
ANNUAL PRODUCTION 230,000 bottles
HECTARES UNDER VINE 70.00
SUSTAINABLE WINERY

With undeniable foresight in the early 20th century, the Ermacora family chose the hills of Ipplis to plant their vineyards. They recognized that the soil, composed of Eocene-origin calcareous clays—not very fertile but rich in mineral salts—was particularly well suited for producing high-quality wines. This family-run enterprise has been passed down through generations. Currently, Dario and Luciano lead the estate, but the new generation is ready to take over. The entire range of wines performed at the level of the best vintages, making it difficult to choose the finest. The Pinot Bianco '23 ultimately prevailed, repeating the performance of the previous edition and reaching the finals. It stood out for the elegance of its aroma, with subtle notes of anise and minty talc that bring out its bouquet and make an encore on the finish. The Malvasia '23 is also excellent, with its aromas of dried medicinal herbs, flowers, and fragrant fruit.

○ FCO Malvasia '23	♈♈	3*
○ FCO Pinot Bianco '23	♈♈	3*
○ COF Picolit '20	♈♈	6
○ FCO Friulano '23	♈♈	3
● FCO Pignolo '18	♈♈	5
○ FCO Pinot Grigio '23	♈♈	3
○ FCO Ribolla Gialla '23	♈♈	3
○ FCO Sauvignon '23	♈♈	3
● FCO Schioppettino '22	♈♈	3
● COF Pignolo '00	♈♈♈	5
○ COF Picolit '17	♈♈	6
○ FCO Malvasia '20	♈♈	3*
● FCO Pignolo '16	♈♈	5
● FCO Pignolo '14	♈♈	5
○ FCO Pinot Bianco '22	♈♈	3*
○ FCO Pinot Bianco '21	♈♈	3*

Fantinel

fraz. Tauriano
via Tesis, 8
33097 Spilimbergo [PN]
(☎) +39 0427591511
⊕ www.fantinel.com

CELLAR SALES
PRE-BOOKED VISITS
ANNUAL PRODUCTION 3,500,000 bottles
HECTARES UNDER VINE 300.00
SUSTAINABLE WINERY

The Fantinel family boast the largest privately-owned operation in the region, producing and distributing a significant number of bottles worldwide. The group includes Tenuta Sant'Helena in Vencò in Collio, La Roncaia in Nimis in the Colli Orientali, and Borgo Tesis in Tauriano di Spilimbergo. With the recent acquisition of another winery, an additional 30 prized hectares of vineyards in the Collio area have been added. All the Sant'Elena wines from latest vintage stood out for their high acidity, which has made them particularly fragrant, with an almost refreshing effect. The Pinot Grigio Rocciaponca '23 has delicate and highly appealing aromas, reminiscent of orange blossom, citronella, and lime, with a very fresh palate. The Sauvignon Judri '23 matches it in freshness, with rich citrus notes of grapefruit meeting bergamot and vegetal notes of green pepper and white asparagus.

★★★Livio Felluga

fraz. Brazzano
via Risorgimento, 1
34071 Cormòns [GO]
(☎) +39 048160052
⊕ www.liviofelluga.it

PRE-BOOKED VISITS
ANNUAL PRODUCTION 800,000 bottles
HECTARES UNDER VINE 187.00
SUSTAINABLE WINERY

Throughout his long life, Livio Felluga was always a benchmark for the entire regional wine sector. Today, the estate is managed by his four children and boasts an extensive set of hillside vineyards, especially in the Friuli Colli Orientali appellation. In the 1950s, along with a small group of enterprising growers, he promoted an initiative that was unthinkable in Italy at the time: producing grand whites capable of aging. It's now customary to find more than one standout wine from this renowned producer in our final round, but it's particularly pleasing when the mainstays are accompanied by an excellent Friulano '23. It honors the vintage with its refined aromas of blossoming hay, white peach, tarragon, and lime, followed by a very pleasant palate. However, the Rosazzo Terre Alte '21 remains the top of the range, delivering a complex nose, a sapid and satisfying palate, and an impressively long finish.

○ Collio Pinot Grigio Sant'Helena Rocciaponca '23	♟♟ 4
○ Collio Sauvignon Tenuta Sant'Helena Judri '23	♟♟ 4
○ Prosecco Brut One&Only '23	♟♟ 4
○ Ribolla Gialla Tenuta Sant'Helena Caterina '23	♟♟ 4
○ Ribolla Gialla Brut	♟ 3
○ Collio Friulano Sant'Helena Rijeka '22	♟♟ 4
○ Collio Pinot Bianco Sant'Helena Frontiere '21	♟♟ 4
○ Collio Pinot Grigio Sant'Helena '20	♟♟ 3*
○ Collio Pinot Grigio Sant'Helena Rocciaponca '22	♟♟ 4
● Collio Rosso Venko Sant'Helena '14	♟♟ 4
○ Collio Sauvignon Sant'Helena Judri '22	♟♟ 4
○ Sant'Helena Caterina Ribolla Gialla '22	♟♟ 4
● Sant'Helena Mario Refosco P. R. '18	♟♟ 4

○ Rosazzo Terre Alte '21	♟♟♟ 8
○ FCO Bianco Illivio '22	♟♟ 5
○ FCO Friulano '23	♟♟ 5
○ FCO Pinot Grigio '23	♟♟ 5
● FCO Refosco P. R. '20	♟♟ 5
● FCO Rosso Sossó Ris. '18	♟♟ 8
○ FCO Sauvignon '23	♟♟ 5
○ FCO Ribolla Gialla '23	♟ 5
○ COF Bianco Illivio '10	♟♟♟ 5
○ FCO Bianco Illivio '14	♟♟♟ 5
○ Rosazzo Terre Alte '20	♟♟♟ 8
○ Rosazzo Terre Alte '19	♟♟♟ 8
○ Rosazzo Terre Alte '18	♟♟♟ 7
○ Rosazzo Terre Alte '17	♟♟♟ 7
○ Rosazzo Terre Alte '16	♟♟♟ 7
○ Rosazzo Terre Alte '12	♟♟♟ 7
○ Rosazzo Terre Alte '11	♟♟♟ 7

Marco Felluga

via Gorizia, 121
34072 Gradisca d'Isonzo [GO]
℡ +39 048199164
⊛ www.marcofelluga.it

CELLAR SALES
PRE-BOOKED VISITS
ACCOMMODATION
ANNUAL PRODUCTION 600,000 bottles
HECTARES UNDER VINE 100.00
SUSTAINABLE WINERY

Marco Felluga, a patriarch of wine, passed away at 96 in his home in Gradisca d'Isonzo. The Felluga family's connection with the world of wine dates back to the second half of the 1800s, beginning in Isola d'Istria. A fortunate turn of events led the family across the gulf to Grado and then to Friuli. Recently, the winery joined the Tommasi group, but Marco's granddaughter, Ilaria Felluga, who manages the Collio brand, will remain with the business in her current managerial roles. The wines submitted for tasting are all from the latest vintage, but despite it being considered a difficult year, they all show excellent craftsmanship. Notably, the Friulano Amani '23 proved to be among the best in its category, advancing to our finals. It offers intense, enticing aromas with warm notes of wheat and bread crust, accompanied by citrusy bursts of lime and bergamot. The palate is fresh, sleek, perfectly balanced, with a balsamic finish.

Feudi di Romans

fraz. Pieris
via Cà del Bosco, 16
34075 San Canzian d'Isonzo [GO]
℡ +39 048176445
⊛ www.ifeudidiromans.it

CELLAR SALES
PRE-BOOKED VISITS
ANNUAL PRODUCTION 500,000 bottles
HECTARES UNDER VINE 70.00
VITICULTURE METHOD Certified Organic

Acquired by Enzo Lorenzon in the early 1990s, Feudi di Romans is one of the most important producers in the Friuli Isonzo appellation. Enzo, a charismatic figure, is the heart of the winery, which he still manages with his sons Davide and Nicola. The vineyards extend over calcareous-clay soils rich in red and ferreted gravels, which contribute to the aromatic qualities of the wines. Aiming for increasingly ambitious goals, Enzo benefits from the crucial oenological consultancy of Fabio Coser. This year, the impressive lineup presented received unanimous praise, demonstrating that the Soca plain is particularly well suited to producing quality wines. The Pinot Bianco '23 stood out for its delicate aromas, reminiscent of springtime orchard blossoms, embellished by hints of anise and peppermint. On the palate, it opens smoothly, showcasing impeccable balance and finishing with a burst of freshness.

○ Collio Friulano Amani '23	♟♟ 3*
○ Collio Chardonnay '23	♟♟ 3
○ Collio Pinot Grigio Mongris '23	♟♟ 4
○ Collio Ribolla Gialla Maralba '23	♟♟ 4
○ Collio Sauvignon '23	♟♟ 3
○ Collio Pinot Grigio Mongris Ris. '16	♟♟♟ 5
○ Collio Bianco Molamatta '15	♟♟ 5
○ Collio Chardonnay '22	♟♟ 5
○ Collio Friulano '16	♟♟ 3*
○ Collio Friulano Amani '22	♟♟ 5
○ Collio Pinot Grigio Mongris '22	♟♟ 5
○ Collio Pinot Grigio Mongris Ris. '19	♟♟ 6
○ Collio Pinot Grigio Mongris Ris. '17	♟♟ 5
○ Collio Pinot Grigio Mongris Ris. '13	♟♟ 5
○ Collio Ribolla Gialla Maralba '22	♟♟ 5
○ Collio Ribolla Gialla Maralba '21	♟♟ 4

○ Friuli Isonzo Pinot Bianco '23	♟♟ 3*
○ Friuli Isonzo Bianco Sontium '22	♟♟ 5
○ Friuli Isonzo Chardonnay '23	♟♟ 3
○ Friuli Isonzo Malvasia '23	♟♟ 3
● Friuli Isonzo Pinot Nero '22	♟♟ 3
○ Friuli Isonzo Sauvignon '23	♟♟ 3
○ Fysi '23	♟♟ 3
○ Ribolla Gialla Anfora '21	♟♟ 6
○ Friuli Isonzo Pinot Grigio '23	♟ 3
○ Ribolla Gialla '23	♟ 3
○ Friuli Isonzo Bianco Sontium '21	♟♟ 5
○ Friuli Isonzo Bianco Sontium '20	♟♟ 5
○ Friuli Isonzo Malvasia '22	♟♟ 3
○ Friuli Isonzo Pinot Grigio '22	♟♟ 3
● Friuli Isonzo Pinot Nero '21	♟♟ 3
○ Friuli Isonzo Sauvignon '22	♟♟ 3
○ Friuli Isonzo Sauvignon '21	♟♟ 3

Fiegl

fraz. Oslavia
loc. Lenzuolo Bianco, I
34170 Gorizia
☏ +39 0481547103
✆ www.fieglvini.com

CELLAR SALES
PRE-BOOKED VISITS
ANNUAL PRODUCTION 250,000 bottles
HECTARES UNDER VINE 35.00
SUSTAINABLE WINERY

The Gorizia hamlet of Oslavia, which borders Slovenia, hosts several prestigious wineries, the result of hardworking farmers proud of their land and vineyards. The Figelj family has lived and worked here for over two centuries. The new generation, represented by Martin, Robert, and Matej, has embraced the same philosophy, opting for low yields and the use of eco-compatible products, fully respecting nature and environmental sustainability. The rich selection received confirms the excellent quality level consistently achieved and maintained over time for both whites and reds. The Pinot Nero '21 is a wine of great class and personality, unveiling fruity aromas of ripe morello cherries and wild blackberries, enriched by spicy notes of black pepper, star anise, and cloves. The Malvasia '23 opens on delicate herbal scents, particularly bay leaf, coming through lively, pervasive, and flavorful on the palate.

○ Collio Malvasia '23	♟♟ 4
● Collio Pinot Nero '21	♟♟ 5
◉ Brut Rosé M. Cl.	♟♟ 5
○ Collio Friulano '23	♟♟ 4
● Collio Merlot Leopold '18	♟♟ 5
○ Collio Pinot Bianco '23	♟♟ 4
○ Collio Pinot Grigio '23	♟♟ 4
○ Collio Ribolla Gialla '23	♟♟ 4
● Collio Rosso Leopold Cuvée Rouge '18	♟♟ 5
○ Ribolla Gialla di Oslavia '22	♟♟ 5
○ Collio Sauvignon '23	♟ 4
○ Collio Friulano '15	♟♟♟ 3*
○ Collio Pinot Grigio '04	♟♟♟ 2*
● Collio Pinot Nero '20	♟♟ 5
○ Ribolla Gialla di Oslavia '21	♟♟ 5
○ Ribolla Gialla di Oslavia '20	♟♟ 5

Formentini

via Oslavia, 5
34070 San Floriano del Collio [GO]
☏ +39 0481884131
✆ www.gruppoitalianovini.it

CELLAR SALES
PRE-BOOKED VISITS
ANNUAL PRODUCTION 150,000 bottles
HECTARES UNDER VINE 58.00

Formentini has a rich history that has made it one of the region's leading producers for centuries. Founded in 1520 and now part of the Gruppo Italiano Vini, the estate stands out as one of the most noteworthy in Collio. Their wines are made primarily with traditional local varietals, though a few international grapes that have adapted well to the area are cultivated as well. Their limited range proves elegant, clean, and focused, all while staying true to the essence of the terroir. The Collio Bianco, made from the three main native varieties (ribolla, malvasia, and friulano), is indeed excellent. Complex on the nose, with subtle smoky notes and tones of ripe fruit, the wine opens to a broad palate marked by great sapidity and freshness. The Ribolla Gialla '23 also put in a good performance, revealing notes of hay and golden apple, and an enticing, deep drinkability. But the other wines tasted are quite impressive, too—all showcase superb finesse, particularly the Friulano, as well as the Chardonnay and Sauvignon.

○ Collio Bianco '21	♟♟ 4
○ Collio Ribolla Gialla '23	♟♟ 4
○ Collio Chardonnay '23	♟♟ 3
○ Collio Friulano '23	♟♟ 3
○ Collio Pinot Grigio '23	♟♟ 3
○ Collio Sauvignon '23	♟♟ 3
○ Collio Bianco '20	♟♟ 4
○ Collio Chardonnay '22	♟♟ 3
○ Collio Chardonnay '21	♟♟ 3
○ Collio Friulano '21	♟♟ 3
○ Collio Pinot Grigio '22	♟♟ 3
○ Collio Pinot Grigio '21	♟♟ 3
○ Collio Ribolla Gialla '22	♟♟ 4
○ Collio Sauvignon '22	♟♟ 3

Galliussi

fraz. Spessa
via Cormons
33043 Cividale del Friuli [UD]
☏ +39 389 05 10 268
✉ www.galliussi.com

CELLAR SALES
ANNUAL PRODUCTION 12,500 bottles
HECTARES UNDER VINE 8.00

Ivo Galliussi's winery is nestled in the hills of
Spessa di Cividale, specifically in the Bosco
Romagno area. This relatively new venture is the
fulfillment of a long-held dream to return to his
roots and the memories of his youth. Ivo began
this journey in 2017, enlisting the help of skilled
professionals from the outset. On the beautiful
terraced slopes, he modernized and replanted
the vineyards and launched construction of a
new cellar. The Pinot Bianco Il Chiaro '22 has
already become a regular in our finals. Fruity
aromas of golden apple and abate pear are
joined by hints of aromatic herbs and summer
hay, with bursts of citrus like grapefruit and
bergamot to follow. On the palate, it's smooth,
silky, yet vivid and persistent. The other wines
also performed superbly, showing improvement
year-by-year and making this an increasingly
impressive range.

Gigante

via Rocca Bernarda, 3
33040 Corno di Rosazzo [UD]
☏ +39 0432755835
✉ www.adrianogigante.it

CELLAR SALES
PRE-BOOKED VISITS
ACCOMMODATION
ANNUAL PRODUCTION 100,000 bottles
HECTARES UNDER VINE 25.00

Adrano Gigante's winery stands out on the
famous Rocca Bernarda, home to numerous
families dedicated to viticulture. Supported by
his wife Giuliana in management, and his cousin
Ariedo in the vineyards and cellar, he continues
the family tradition with a line of high-quality
wines. The producer's original parcel, a vineyard
named Storico, is well known and remains their
flagship. The Chardonnay Filo di Rocca Ris. '21
had already made a good impression in the last
edition, thanks to its strong debut. This year it
outshone the competition, advancing to our final
selections. Its aromatic spectrum ranges from
tropical notes of pineapple juice to fresh bursts
of mint and lime, enriched by spicy nuances of
white pepper and cinnamon. The palate is
perfectly balanced, with a harmonious blend of
softness and freshness, caressing the mouth and
lingering slowly.

○ FCO Pinot Bianco il Chiaro '22	♀♀ 3*
○ FCO Friulano Julii '23	♀♀ 3
○ FCO Malvasia Cornizza '23	♀♀ 3
● FCO Merlot Rocca '21	♀♀ 4
○ FCO Sauvignon Portis '22	♀♀ 3
● FCO Merlot Arimanni Ris. '19	♀♀ 5
● FCO Merlot Arimanni Ris. '18	♀♀ 5
○ FCO Pinot Bianco Il Chiaro '21	♀♀ 3*
○ FCO Pinot Bianco Il Chiaro '20	♀♀ 3
○ FCO Pinot Bianco Il Chiaro '19	♀♀ 3
● FCO Refosco P. R. Spitz '19	♀♀ 5
○ FCO Sauvignon Portis '21	♀♀ 3
○ FCO Sauvignon Portis '20	♀♀ 3

○ FCO Chardonnay Filo di Rocca Ris. '21	♀♀ 6
○ FCO Friulano Vign. Storico '22	♀♀ 4
○ FCO Malvasia '22	♀♀ 3
● FCO Merlot '19	♀♀ 5
● FCO Merlot Ris. '18	♀♀ 5
● FCO Pignolo Ris. '14	♀♀ 6
○ Friuli Bianco Sartoriale '22	♀♀ 4
○ COF Tocai Friulano Storico '00	♀♀♀ 4*
○ COF Tocai Friulano Vign. Storico '06	♀♀♀ 4
○ COF Tocai Friulano Vign. Storico '05	♀♀♀ 4
○ COF Tocai Friulano Vign. Storico '03	♀♀♀ 4
○ FCO Picolit '08	♀♀♀ 6
○ FCO Bianco Storico & Friends '19	♀♀ 5
○ FCO Friulano Vign. Storico '21	♀♀ 4
○ FCO Friulano Vign. Storico '20	♀♀ 4
○ Friuli Isonzo Malvasia '20	♀♀ 3*

Gori Agricola

via G.B. Gori, 14
33045 Nimis [UD]
(" +39 0432878475
⊚ www.goriagricola.it

CELLAR SALES
PRE-BOOKED VISITS
ANNUAL PRODUCTION 50,000 bottles
HECTARES UNDER VINE 18.00
VITICULTURE METHOD Certified Organic
SUSTAINABLE WINERY

This lovely winery was established by Gianpiero Gori, who, in 2009, decided to radically change sectors and build a splendid cellar in Nimis, in the westernmost part of the Friuli Colli Orientali appellation. Relying on a prestigious team, he quickly achieved notable results and Gori Agricola is now among the leading wineries in the region. Gori remains committed to enhancing native grape varieties while also paying great attention to pinot noir. Having tasted only three wines, it wasn't possible to provide a detailed overview of the winery's offerings, but it was enough to confirm previous positive reviews. The Chardonnay Ronc dal Gial '23 features aromas of blossoming hay, acacia honey, and white chocolate, and is fresh, fragrant on the palate. The Malvasia Celeste '22, a new entry, proves refined on the nose and velvety on the palate. The Sauvignon Busseben '23 stands out for its energy and ability to faithfully express the varietal characteristics of the grapes used.

○ FCO Chardonnay Ronc dal Gial '23	♟♟ 4
○ FCO Malvasia Celeste '22	♟♟ 4
○ FCO Sauvignon Busseben '23	♟♟ 3
○ FCO Chardonnay Giù Giù '22	♟♟ 4
○ FCO Chardonnay Giù Giù '21	♟♟ 4
○ FCO Friulano Bonblanc '22	♟♟ 3
○ FCO Friulano Bonblanc '21	♟♟ 3
○ FCO Friulano Bonblanc '17	♟♟ 3*
○ FCO Friulano Bonblanc '15	♟♟ 3*
● FCO Refosco P. R. Ronc dal Gjal Principe di Nimis '15	♟♟ 4
○ FCO Ribolla Gialla Blanc di Bianca '22	♟♟ 3
○ FCO Ribolla Gialla Blanc di Bianca '21	♟♟ 3
○ FCO Sauvignon Busseben '22	♟♟ 3
○ FCO Sauvignon Busseben '21	♟♟ 3
● Refosco P. R. Redelbosco '13	♟♟ 3*
● Refosco P. R. Redelbosco '12	♟♟ 4

Gradis'ciutta

loc. San Floriano del Collio
loc. Giasbana, 32a
34070 San Floriano del Collio [GO]
(" +39 0481390237
⊚ www.gradisciutta.eu

CELLAR SALES
PRE-BOOKED VISITS
ACCOMMODATION
ANNUAL PRODUCTION 200,000 bottles
HECTARES UNDER VINE 45.00
VITICULTURE METHOD Certified Organic

Gradis'ciutta was founded in 1997 by Robert Princic, who, after completing his oenology studies, decided to join his father Isidoro in managing the family business. The Princics had been producing wine in Kosana, in nearby Slovenia, since 1780, until Robert's great-grandfather Filip decided to settle in the surroundings of San Floriano del Collio. Their prized vineyards are located in different areas and at various elevations, with most going back anywhere from 50-90 years. This year, two wines from the latest vintage topped the rankings. The Friulano '23 captivates the nose with its elegant notes of exotic fruit, sun-kissed hints of Mediterranean scrub, white flowers, and lemon zest. In the mouth it unfolds with a rhythmic, linear progression, with sapid echoes that enhance the palate and entice further drinking. The Sauvignon '23 is equally gratifying, with its citrusy, dynamic, fragrant notes,, perfectly balancing acidity and fruit, with a balsamic undertone.

○ Collio Friulano '23	♟♟ 4
○ Collio Sauvignon '23	♟♟ 4
○ Collio Bianco Brátinis '20	♟♟ 5
○ Collio Bianco Ris. '19	♟♟ 5
○ Collio Chardonnay '23	♟♟ 4
○ Collio Malvasia '23	♟♟ 4
○ Collio Pinot Grigio '23	♟♟ 4
○ Collio Ribolla Gialla '23	♟♟ 4
○ Rebula Sveti Nikolaj '21	♟♟ 5
○ Collio Bianco Ris. '18	♟♟ 5
○ Collio Bianco Ris. '17	♟♟ 4
○ Collio Bianco Ris. '16	♟♟ 5
○ Collio Friulano '22	♟♟ 3*
○ Collio Malvasia '20	♟♟ 3*
○ Collio Pinot Grigio '20	♟♟ 3*
○ Collio Sauvignon '21	♟♟ 3*

Grillo Iole

via Albana, 60
33040 Prepotto [UD]
(◊ +39 3311122435
☙ www.vinigrillo.it

CELLAR SALES
PRE-BOOKED VISITS
ACCOMMODATION
ANNUAL PRODUCTION 40,000 bottles
HECTARES UNDER VINE 9.00
SUSTAINABLE WINERY

Founded in Albana di Prepotto in the 1970s, the winery owned by Iole Grillo has for some time now been managed by her daughter, Anna Muzzolini, an energetic entrepreneur and "donna del vino". Heavily focused on schioppettino, the area's flagship grape variety, the winery has developed its own oenological identity and remained open to innovation. Anna loves to personally oversee all the various stages of the production cycle, and now has the support of her children, Mattia and Giulia. Both versions of Schioppettino presented received unanimous acclaim and advanced to our final selections. The Schioppettino di Prepotto '20 calls up blueberry jam, wilted red rose, black pepper, and cocoa powder. On the palate, it's smooth, with lively yet balanced tannins. The Schioppettino di Prepotto Ris. '18 is slightly more austere, with its suggestions of dried plum, tobacco, black olive pâté, licorice, and coffee beans.

Jacùss

fraz. Montina
v.le Kennedy, 35a
33040 Torreano [UD]
(◊ +39 0432715147
☙ www.jacuss.it

CELLAR SALES
PRE-BOOKED VISITS
ANNUAL PRODUCTION 50,000 bottles
HECTARES UNDER VINE 12.00
VITICULTURE METHOD Certified Organic

"Jacùss" is Friulian dialect for the surname of Sandro and Andrea Iacuzzi, who founded the winery in 1990. The pair embraced the trend of the time, which saw many farming families converting their lands from mixed crops to wine-growing. The two brothers still work in perfect harmony, primarily managing the vineyards, while the responsibility of winemaking has been entrusted to Sandro's young daughter, Marta, with excellent results. This year, the Pinot Bianco '23 led the rankings, thanks to a stellar performance that earned it a place in our final tasting round. The nose sees intriguing citrusy bursts of mandarin alternate with more subdued notes of white peach, pear, and tropical fruit. The palate is compelling, with a perfectly measured progression. All the other wines reflect their varietal characteristics while proving balanced, free of excess, smooth, dynamic, and enjoyable to drink.

● FCO Schioppettino di Prepotto '20	♥♥ 3*
● FCO Schioppettino di Prepotto Ris. '18	♥♥ 5
● FCO Cabernet Franc '22	♥♥ 4
○ FCO Friulano '23	♥♥ 3
● FCO Merlot '21	♥♥ 4
● FCO Refosco P. R. '19	♥♥ 4
○ FCO Ribolla Gialla '23	♥♥ 3
○ FCO Sauvignon '23	♥♥ 3
○ FCO Verduzzo Friulano '22	♥ 3
○ FCO Friulano '22	♀♀ 3*
○ FCO Friulano '21	♀♀ 3*
○ FCO Il Sauvignon '21	♀♀ 4
○ FCO Il Sauvignon '20	♀♀ 4
○ FCO Il Sauvignon '19	♀♀ 4
○ FCO Il Sauvignon '18	♀♀ 4

○ FCO Pinot Bianco '23	♥♥ 3*
○ COF Picolit '22	♥♥ 6
○ FCO Friulano '23	♥♥ 3
● FCO Refosco P. R. '20	♥♥ 3
○ FCO Sauvignon '23	♥♥ 3
○ FCO Verduzzo Friulano '22	♥♥ 4
○ FCO Friulano '22	♀♀ 3
○ FCO Friulano '21	♀♀ 3
○ FCO Friulano Forment '21	♀♀ 3*
○ FCO Pinot Bianco '22	♀♀ 3
○ FCO Pinot Bianco '21	♀♀ 3
○ FCO Pinot Bianco '20	♀♀ 3*
● FCO Refosco dal P. R. '19	♀♀ 3
○ FCO Sauvignon '22	♀♀ 3
○ FCO Sauvignon '21	♀♀ 3
○ FCO Verduzzo Friulano '20	♀♀ 4

★★★Jermann

loc. Trussio
fraz. Ruttars
loc. Trussio, 11
34070 Dolegna del Collio [GO]
+39 0481888080
www.jermann.it

CELLAR SALES
ANNUAL PRODUCTION 1,500,000 bottles
HECTARES UNDER VINE 180.00
SUSTAINABLE WINERY

A few years ago, there was a stir when the Jermann brand joined the Antinori wine empire. Silvio Jermann, however, emphasizes that it wasn't a mere takeover, but rather a high-level partnership advantageous for both parties. Silvio still operates in the splendid Ruttars cellar, and his wines reflect his personality—pure, genuine, yet free from the production rules imposed by appellations. The trio that for years now has consistently impressed us in the final rounds continues to astound and garner acclaim. The Vintage Tunina '22 (chardonnay, malvasia istriana, picolit, ribolla gialla, and sauvignon) excels with its elegance and energetic palate. The ... Dreams... '22, made from chardonnay, proves creamy and pervasive. The Capo Martino '22 (tocai friulano, ribolla gialla, malvasia istriana, and picolit) highlights exotic fruit aromas—this is a crisp, taut, sublime taste.

○ Capo Martino '22	▼▼▼ 8
○ Vintage Tunina '22	▼▼ 8
○ W...Dreams... '22	▼▼ 8
○ Chardonnay '23	▼▼ 5
○ Friuli Pinot Grigio '23	▼▼ 5
● Pinot Nero Red Angel '21	▼▼ 5
○ Ribolla Gialla Vinnae '23	▼▼ 5
○ Sauvignon '23	▼▼ 5
○ Capo Martino '18	▽▽▽ 7
○ Capo Martino '16	▽▽▽ 7
○ Pinot Grigio '15	▽▽▽ 4*
○ Vintage Tunina '21	▽▽▽ 8
○ Vintage Tunina '20	▽▽▽ 8
○ Vintage Tunina '19	▽▽▽ 7
○ Vintage Tunina '17	▽▽▽ 7
○ Vintage Tunina '15	▽▽▽ 7

★Edi Keber

loc. Zegla, 17
34071 Cormòns [GO]
+39 048161184
www.edikeber.it

CELLAR SALES
PRE-BOOKED VISITS
ACCOMMODATION
ANNUAL PRODUCTION 45,000 bottles
HECTARES UNDER VINE 12.00
VITICULTURE METHOD Certified Biodynamic
SUSTAINABLE WINERY

For some time now, Kristian Keber has been following the path set by Edi over the course of nearly two decades, seeking to identify the territory with a single wine made from a blend of tocai friulano, malvasia istriana, and ribolla gialla, calling it simply Collio. This brave but successful choice has led many local producers to join the initiative, specifying "Collio from native grapes" on their labels. As the only wine produced by Keber, we once again review the Collio da Uve Autoctone '22, which remains largely consistent with previous editions but still reflects the change in vintage. It pours a bright, brilliant straw yellow, and the nose is complex and intriguing, with delicate floral nuances followed by fruity hints of lychee and blonde orange. In the mouth, vibrant mineral notes enhance and elevate the palate.

○ Collio da Uve Autoctone '22	▼▼ 5
○ Collio '18	▽▽▽ 3*
○ Collio Bianco '10	▽▽▽ 3*
○ Collio Bianco '09	▽▽▽ 3
○ Collio Bianco '08	▽▽▽ 3*
○ Collio Bianco '04	▽▽▽ 3*
○ Collio Bianco '02	▽▽▽ 3
○ Collio Tocai Friulano '07	▽▽▽ 3
○ Collio Tocai Friulano '06	▽▽▽ 3
○ Collio Tocai Friulano '05	▽▽▽ 3
○ Collio Tocai Friulano '03	▽▽▽ 3
○ Collio Tocai Friulano '01	▽▽▽ 3
○ Collio Tocai Friulano '99	▽▽▽ 3
○ Collio Tocai Friulano '97	▽▽▽ 3
○ Collio Tocai Friulano '95	▽▽▽ 3

Alessio Komjanc

loc. Giasbana, 35
34070 San Floriano del Collio [GO]
☎ +39 0481391228
✉ www.komjancalessio.com

CELLAR SALES
PRE-BOOKED VISITS
ANNUAL PRODUCTION 80,000 bottles
HECTARES UNDER VINE 24.00
SUSTAINABLE WINERY

The first bottle labeled with the Alessio Komjanc brand dates back to 1973, but it is known that his great-grandparents were producing wine as early as the late 19th century. The real turning point came in 2000, when all four of his children officially came on board, optimizing the entire production chain. The breakthrough in quality observed in recent vintages, thanks to valuable technical consulting, has elevated the family's name to prominence. This year, three wines achieved exceptionally high scores and deservedly made it to the final tastings. The Pinot Bianco '23 and Friulano '23 are repeat successes, while the delightful newcomer is the Pinot Nero '19. This wine reflects a modern stylistic approach, with refined aromas of sweet spices and red fruit dominating its aromatic profile. Cinnamon, star anise, cherry jam, and raspberry syrup flavors emerge, with lively yet velvety tannins.

Kurtin

loc. Novali, 9
34071 Cormòns [GO]
☎ +39 3442140560
✉ www.kurtin.it

CELLAR SALES
PRE-BOOKED VISITS
ANNUAL PRODUCTION 70,000 bottles
HECTARES UNDER VINE 11.00

The Kurtin family settled near Cormòns in the early 20th century and, realizing the potential of the land, began planting vines. Since then, knowledge has been passed from father to son until 2017, when, following the untimely death of Albino Kurtin, the property was acquired by Venetian entrepreneur Ulisse Bellesso. The winery has set new ambitious goals and entrusted local management to the expertise of Alberto Adami. We were accustomed to receiving a wide selection that allowed us to offer a varied assessment of the winery's offerings. However, it seems the latest vintage was given additional time to age, so this year only two wines were submitted. The Collio Bianco Opera Prima '21, a blend of chardonnay, pinot bianco, and ribolla gialla, proves highly fragrant on the nose, with vegetal and citrus notes. The Friulano '22 represents a classic expression of Tocai from times past.

○ Collio Friulano '23	♚♚ 3*
○ Collio Pinot Bianco '23	♚♚ 4
● Collio Pinot Nero Dedica '19	♚♚ 5
○ Collio Malvasia '23	♚♚ 4
● Collio Merlot Dedica '19	♚♚ 7
○ Collio Pinot Grigio '23	♚♚ 4
○ Collio Ribolla Gialla '23	♚♚ 4
○ Collio Sauvignon '23	♚♚ 4
○ Colllio Bianco Bratje '22	♚♚ 5
○ Collio Bianco Bratje '21	♚♚ 5
○ Collio Chardonnay Dedica '21	♚♚ 5
○ Collio Friulano '22	♚♚ 3*
○ Collio Malvasia '22	♚♚ 3
○ Collio Pinot Bianco '22	♚♚ 3*
○ Collio Ribolla Gialla '22	♚♚ 3
○ Collio Sauvignon '22	♚♚ 3

○ Collio Bianco Opera Prima '21	♚♚ 4
○ Collio Friulano '22	♚♚ 3
○ Collio Bianco Opera Prima '20	♚♚ 3
○ Collio Bianco Opera Prima '19	♚♚ 3
○ Collio Chardonnay '22	♚♚ 3
○ Collio Chardonnay '21	♚♚ 3
○ Collio Friulano '20	♚♚ 3
○ Collio Malvasia '22	♚♚ 3
○ Collio Malvasia '21	♚♚ 3
○ Collio Pinot Grigio '22	♚♚ 4
○ Collio Pinot Grigio '21	♚♚ 3
○ Collio Ribolla Gialla '22	♚♚ 3
○ Collio Ribolla Gialla '21	♚♚ 3
○ Collio Sauvignon '22	♚♚ 4
○ Collio Sauvignon '21	♚♚ 3

Lis Fadis

via Poianis
33043 Prepotto [UD]
☎ +39 3311480911
✉ www.lisfadis.com

CELLAR SALES
PRE-BOOKED VISITS
ACCOMMODATION
ANNUAL PRODUCTION 50,000 bottles
HECTARES UNDER VINE 24.00
SUSTAINABLE WINERY

Recently, the merger of two historic estates in Colli Orientali del Friuli—Colli di Poianis and Lis Fadis—led to the creation of DCPWinery Soc. Agricola, based in Prepotto, the heartland of schioppettino. The new owner, Nicola Cescutti, is dedicated to preserving the rich legacy of these two brands. The winery now boasts approximately 24 hectares under vines, all on hillside terrain. The brand name Lis Fadis was chosen, and the wines are now divided into two lines: tradition and premium. The Rosso Bergul '19 (refosco dal peduncolo rosso, merlot, and schioppettino) exudes elegance with its aromatic mosaic of spices, resinous and balsamic whiffs, wild berries, tobacco, and leather. On the palate, it opens with vigor and austerity, with lively tannins taking center stage. The Schioppettino di Prepotto '20, which bears the Colli di Poianis label, evokes spicy whiffs of black pepper, star anise, and juniper berries, followed by myrtle and dried plums. A juicy, engaging quaff.

● FCO Rosso Bergul '19	♟♟ 7	
● FCO Schioppettino di Prepotto Colli Di Poianis '20	♟♟ 5	
○ FCO Friulano '23	♟♟ 4	
○ FCO Friulano Sbilf '19	♟♟ 7	
● FCO Merlot '22	♟♟ 4	
● FCO Merlot Gian '19	♟♟ 8	
○ FCO Pinot Grigio '23	♟♟ 4	
● FCO Pinot Nero '22	♟♟ 5	
● FCO Refosco P.R. Pavar '18	♟♟ 8	
○ FCO Sauvignon '23	♟♟ 4	
● FCO Refosco dal P.R. '22	♟ 4	
○ FCO Ribolla Gialla '23	♟ 4	
● COF Merlot Gjan '09	♟♟ 5	
● FCO Bergul '12	♟♟ 6	
○ FCO Sbilf '13	♟♟ 5	

★★Lis Neris

via Gavinana, 5
34070 San Lorenzo Isontino [GO]
☎ +39 048180105
✉ www.lisneris.it

CELLAR SALES
PRE-BOOKED VISITS
ACCOMMODATION
ANNUAL PRODUCTION 400,000 bottles
HECTARES UNDER VINE 74.00
SUSTAINABLE WINERY

Since 1879, four generations of the Pecorari family have been working passionately here in San Lorenzo Isontino, building one of the region's most representative wineries. Alvaro took over management in 1981, and since then, growth has been exponential. His prized vineyards rest on a plateau of deep gravel between the Slovenian border and the right bank of the Soca River, spread out across four distinct sites: Gris, Picol, Jurosa, and Neris. Three wines making it to the finals has become a standard for this prestigious producer, a source of pride for the Soca Valley. The Chardonnay Jurosa '21 offers up aromas of quince, yellow flowers, and honey, with a pervasive palate that unfolds progressively. The Pinot Grigio Gris '22 is a true delight, very floral and refined on the nose, and superb on the palate. The Pinot Grigio Gris Unico '15 represents a prototype for a new project, an experiment aimed at prolonging both maturation and bottle aging. For years now, the Fondazione Francesca Pecorari has been committed to promoting humanitarian causes throughout the globe. A result worth our special Solidarity Award.

○ Friuli Isonzo Pinot Grigio Gris '22	♟♟♟ 5	
○ Friuli Isonzo Chardonnay Jurosa '21	♟♟♟ 5	
○ Friuli Isonzo Pinot Grigio Gris Unico '15	♟♟ 6	
○ Friuli Isonzo Sauvignon Picol '22	♟♟ 5	
○ Tal Lùc Cuvée .03.20.21 '22	♟♟ 8	
○ Fiore di Campo '06	♟♟♟ 3	
○ Friuli Isonzo Pinot Grigio Gris '21	♟♟♟ 5	
○ Friuli Isonzo Pinot Grigio Gris '13	♟♟♟ 4*	
○ Friuli Isonzo Pinot Grigio Gris '12	♟♟♟ 4*	
○ Friuli Isonzo Pinot Grigio Gris '11	♟♟♟ 4*	
○ Friuli Isonzo Pinot Grigio Gris '10	♟♟♟ 4*	
○ Friuli Isonzo Pinot Grigio Gris '09	♟♟♟ 4*	
○ Lis '15	♟♟♟ 5	
○ Pinot Grigio Gris '08	♟♟♟ 4*	
○ Pinot Grigio Gris '04	♟♟♟ 4*	
○ Sauvignon Picòl '06	♟♟♟ 3*	

★★Livon

fraz. Dolegnano
via Montarezza, 33
33048 San Giovanni al Natisone [UD]
☎ +39 0432757173
🖰 www.livon.it

CELLAR SALES
PRE-BOOKED VISITS
ACCOMMODATION
ANNUAL PRODUCTION 850,000 bottles
HECTARES UNDER VINE 180.00

For some time now Valneo and Tonino Livon have been managing the winery founded by their father Dorino in 1964. Demonstrating excellent entrepreneurial skills, they have expanded beyond regional borders, adding the prestigious brands of Borgo Salcetino in Radda in Chianti and Colsanto in Umbria to their portfolio. Valneo's son, Matteo, and Tonino's daughter, Francesca, represent the new generation and are already an integral part of the winery. Three wines have once again earned their place in the finals, a feat whose consistency confirms the quality of the entire range. The Pinot Bianco Cavezzo '22 captivates the nose with its delightful whiffs of tropical fruit, white chocolate, and citrus zest, leading to a forthright, lively palate. The Tiare Blù '21, a blend of merlot and cabernet sauvignon, proves pervasive and persistent. The Braide Alte '22, the winery's renowned flagship, is a fragrant pour, juicy and balanced.

○ Braide Alte '22	▼▼▼	6
○ Collio Pinot Bianco Cavezzo '22	▼▼	5
● Tiare Blù '21	▼▼	5
○ Collio Bianco Solarco '22	▼▼	4
○ Collio Friulano Manditocai '22	▼▼	5
○ Collio Malvasia Soluna '22	▼▼	4
○ Collio Ribolla Gialla RoncAlto '23	▼▼	4
○ Collio Sauvignon Valbuins '23	▼▼	4
○ Braide Alte '19	▽▽▽	6
○ Braide Alte '18	▽▽▽	6
○ Braide Alte '13	▽▽▽	5
○ COF Picolit '12	▽▽▽	6
○ Collio Bianco Solarco '17	▽▽▽	3*
○ Collio Bianco Solarco '15	▽▽▽	3*
○ Collio Friulano Manditocai '17	▽▽▽	5
○ Collio Friulano Manditocai '12	▽▽▽	5

★Tenuta Luisa

fraz. Corona
via Campo Sportivo, 13
34070 Mariano del Friuli [GO]
☎ +39 048169680
🖰 www.tenutaluisa.it

CELLAR SALES
PRE-BOOKED VISITS
ACCOMMODATION
ANNUAL PRODUCTION 350,000 bottles
HECTARES UNDER VINE 100.00
SUSTAINABLE WINERY

Tenuta Luisa is a splendid estate immersed in the greenery of vineyards extending along the right bank of the Soca River. The recent passing of Eddi Luisa, long considered an iconic figure in the regional wine scene, has left an unfillable void. Now, it's up to his sons Michele and Davide to uphold the family's prestigious brand. The soils, which are particularly rich in minerals (especially iron), inspired the name of the I Ferretti line. Another impressive performance from the winery's two flagships, which annually compete for the top spot. The Desiderium I Ferretti '22, a blend of chardonnay, tocai friulano, and sauvignon, tantalizes the nose with its varied bouquet of aromas, including apple peel, dried aromatic herbs, and blooming hay; on the palate, it's sapid and flavorful. The Friulano I Ferretti '22 embodies freshness with its energetic and captivating mineral notes and earns Tre Bicchieri.

○ Friuli Isonzo Friulano I Ferretti '22	▼▼▼	5
○ Desiderium I Ferretti '22	▼▼	5
○ Friuli Isonzo Chardonnay '23	▼▼	3
○ Friuli Isonzo Friulano '23	▼▼	4
○ Friuli Isonzo Malvasia '23	▼▼	3
○ Friuli Isonzo Pinot Bianco '23	▼▼	4
○ Friuli Isonzo Sauvignon '23	▼▼	4
● I Ferretti Cabernet Sauvignon '18	▼▼	5
○ Ribolla Gialla '23	▼▼	3
○ Desiderium I Ferretti '21	▽▽▽	5
○ Desiderium I Ferretti '19	▽▽▽	5
○ Desiderium I Ferretti '17	▽▽▽	4*
○ Desiderium I Ferretti '16	▽▽▽	4*
○ Friuli Isonzo Friulano I Ferretti '20	▽▽▽	4*
○ Friuli Isonzo Friulano I Ferretti '18	▽▽▽	4*
○ Friuli Isonzo Friulano I Ferretti '15	▽▽▽	3*

FRIULI VENEZIA GIULIA

Marinig

via Brolo, 41
33040 Prepotto [UD]
+39 0432713012
www.marinig.it

CELLAR SALES
PRE-BOOKED VISITS
ANNUAL PRODUCTION 30,000 bottles
HECTARES UNDER VINE 8.00
SUSTAINABLE WINERY

The Marinig family is a classic example of a family-run winery where the scale and workload are manageable, and there's a jack-of-all-trades handling various management tasks. This role is now held by Valerio Marinig, who draws on the time-honored experiences passed down through generations since his great-grandfather Luigi founded the winery over a century ago. The vineyards unfold across the hilly terrain of Prepotto, homeland of the schioppettino grape. The Pinot Bianco '23 matches the performance that made it a standout in last year's guide and once again secures its place in our finals. It's no coincidence that when we describe this wine, we frequently use the adjective "elegant." It's precisely the elegance of its aromas that distinguishes it—its delicate floral scents of hawthorn, lily of the valley, and acacia flowers, the fragrance of crisp and juicy white-fleshed fruit, and a consistently alluring, perfectly aligned palate.

Masùt da Rive

via Manzoni, 82
34070 Mariano del Friuli [GO]
+39 048169200
www.masutdarive.com

CELLAR SALES
PRE-BOOKED VISITS
ANNUAL PRODUCTION 130,000 bottles
HECTARES UNDER VINE 30.00
SUSTAINABLE WINERY

Masùt da Rive is the name that Silvano Gallo chose when he formally established the winery. His sons, Fabrizio and Marco, now manage the estate and have sped up growth, propelling Masùt da Rive to the higher echelons of regional producers. With the goal of producing high-quality wines, all white grapes undergo pre-fermentation maceration at low temperatures. For many years now, Masùt da Rive has been a leader in promoting pinot nero in the region, making it the producer's flagship. This year, both versions presented earned a spot in the finals. Of the two, the Pinot Nero Maurus '20 is the more austere and intriguing, especially on the nose, where notes of red fruit and dried fig alternate with milk chocolate and toasted almonds. The Pinot Nero '21 is more fragrant, highlighting the grape's varietal characteristics.

○ FCO Pinot Bianco '23	♟♟ 3*
○ FCO Friulano '23	♟♟ 3
● FCO Refosco dal P. R. '21	♟♟ 5
○ FCO Ribolla Gialla '23	♟♟ 3
● FCO Rosso Biel Cûr '21	♟♟ 6
○ FCO Sauvignon '23	♟♟ 4
● FCO Schioppettino di Prepotto '21	♟♟ 6
● FCO Pignolo '19	♟♟ 6
○ FCO Pinot Bianco '22	♟♟ 4
● FCO Refosco P. R. '20	♟♟ 5
○ FCO Ribolla Gialla '22	♟♟ 4
● FCO Rosso Biel Cûr '20	♟♟ 6
● FCO Rosso Biel Cûr '19	♟♟ 4
○ FCO Sauvignon '22	♟♟ 4
● FCO Schioppettino di Prepotto '20	♟♟ 6
● FCO Schioppettino di Prepotto '19	♟♟ 4

● Friuli Isonzo Pinot Nero '21	♟♟ 5
● Friuli Isonzo Pinot Nero Maurus '20	♟♟ 7
○ Friuli Isonzo Chardonnay '23	♟♟ 4
○ Friuli Isonzo Friulano '23	♟♟ 4
○ Friuli Isonzo Pinot Grigio '23	♟♟ 4
● Friuli Isonzo Rosso SassiRossi '22	♟♟ 4
○ Friuli Isonzo Sauvignon '23	♟♟ 4
○ Friuli Isonzo Pinot Bianco '17	♟♟♟ 5
○ Friuli Isonzo Pinot Bianco '16	♟♟♟ 5
○ Friuli Isonzo Tocai Friulano '04	♟♟♟ 3*
○ Friuli Isonzo Chardonnay '22	♟♟ 3
○ Friuli Isonzo Chardonnay Maurus '21	♟♟ 5
○ Friuli Isonzo Chardonnay Maurus '20	♟♟ 5
● Friuli Isonzo Pinot Nero '20	♟♟ 5
● Friuli Isonzo Rosso Sassirossi '21	♟♟ 4
○ Friuli Isonzo Sauvignon '22	♟♟ 3

Davino Meroi
via Stretta, 7b
33042 Buttrio [UD]
☎ +39 0432673369
✉ www.meroi.wine

CELLAR SALES
PRE-BOOKED VISITS
RESTAURANT SERVICE
ANNUAL PRODUCTION 45,000 bottles
HECTARES UNDER VINE 19.00
SUSTAINABLE WINERY

Paolo Meroi has been working in his family vineyards for many years, continuing the tradition started by his grandfather Domenico and later followed by his father Davino. His extensive experience combined with outstanding vineyards has made, and continues to make, a major difference. Old vines (some of which go back more than 40 years), extremely low yields, and meticulous selections are the foundation for healthy, rich, and concentrated grapes that allow the producer to impart a noble, personal style to his wines. In the absence of their more prestigious wines, we focused on the two estate blends. The Rosso Nèstri '21, composed of cabernet franc and merlot, opens with an austere and concentrated aromatic profile, manifesting cherry jam, sweet spices, tobacco, and cocoa, with nice structure and tannins that are still pronounced but promising. The Bianco Nèstri '22, a blend of chardonnay, tocai friulano, and sauvignon, proves pleasing on the nose, with enticing tropical sensations alongside fresh citrus and balsamic notes.

○ FCO Bianco Nèstri '22	♟♟ 5	
● FCO Rosso Nèstri '21	♟♟ 3	
○ COF Friulano '11	♟♟♟ 5	
○ COF Friulano '10	♟♟♟ 5	
○ COF Verduzzo Friulano '08	♟♟♟ 5	
● FCO Refosco P. R. V. Dominin '16	♟♟ 8	
○ FCO Chardonnay V. Dominin '16	♟♟ 5	
○ FCO Friulano '18	♟♟ 5	
○ FCO Friulano Zitelle Pesarin '19	♟♟ 5	
○ FCO Malvasia Zitelle Durì '16	♟♟ 5	
● FCO Merlot Ros di Burì '19	♟♟ 5	
● FCO Merlot Ros di Burì '18	♟♟ 5	
○ FCO Pinot Grigio '21	♟♟ 4	
○ FCO Pinot Grigio '20	♟♟ 3	
● FCO Rosso Nèstri '19	♟♟ 3*	
○ FCO Sauvignon '21	♟♟ 4	

★Le Monde
loc. Le Monde
via Garibaldi, 2
33080 Prata di Pordenone [PN]
☎ +39 0434622087
✉ www.lemondewine.com

CELLAR SALES
PRE-BOOKED VISITS
ANNUAL PRODUCTION 700,000 bottles
HECTARES UNDER VINE 93.00
SUSTAINABLE WINERY

Founded in 1970 at Villa Giustinian in Portobuffolè, Vigneti Le Monde was acquired by Alex Maccan in 2008 and has since become a leading winery in the region, a gem on the right bank of the Tagliamento River. The estate hosts a sizable expanse of vineyards in the vast Friulian plains, an area particularly well suited to wine-growing thanks to its gravelly and clay soils. The grapes hail from vines going back more than 30 years. Low yields, a rarity in plains viticulture, are among the secrets to their success. Having three wines in the final is a great pride for any winery, but it's certainly not news for Vigneti Le Monde. The Sauvignon '23 showcases classic aromas of sage, boxwood, tomato leaf, and green pepper, refreshing the palate and finishing with a minty, balsamic note. The Merlot .73 '20 stood out among the reds for its structure, personality, pervasive nature, and persistence. The Pinot Bianco '23 is on par with the best vintages, offering floral and fruity aromas alongside a soft, fresh palate and impeccable balance.

○ Friuli Pinot Bianco '23	♟♟♟ 3*	
● Friuli Merlot .73 '20	♟♟ 5	
○ Friuli Sauvignon '23	♟♟ 3*	
● Friuli Cabernet Franc '22	♟♟ 3	
○ Friuli Chardonnay '23	♟♟ 3	
○ Friuli Friulano '23	♟♟ 3	
○ Friuli Pinot Grigio '23	♟♟ 3	
● Friuli Refosco dal P. R. Inaco '20	♟♟ 5	
● Friuli Cabernet Franc '18	♟♟♟ 2*	
○ Friuli Chardonnay '17	♟♟♟ 3*	
○ Friuli Grave Pinot Bianco '15	♟♟♟ 2*	
○ Friuli Pinot Bianco '22	♟♟♟ 3*	
○ Friuli Pinot Bianco '21	♟♟♟ 3*	
○ Friuli Pinot Bianco '19	♟♟♟ 3*	
○ Friuli Pinot Bianco '18	♟♟♟ 3*	
○ Friuli Pinot Bianco '16	♟♟♟ 2*	

Monviert

fraz. Spessa
via Strada di Spessa, 8
33043 Cividale del Friuli [UD]
☎ +39 0432716172
✉ www.monviert.com

CELLAR SALES
PRE-BOOKED VISITS
ACCOMMODATION
ANNUAL PRODUCTION 400,000 bottles
HECTARES UNDER VINE 91.00
SUSTAINABLE WINERY

Known as Ronchi San Giuseppe until 2018, Monviert is still considered a newcomer in the regional wine scene. However, the producer is supported by the experience of 3 generations of winemakers who have, over 70 years of continuous growth, brought out the unique attributes of the Spessa di Cividale area. The winery's overhaul and rebranding began with the restructuring of the main property, which has been transformed into a small village reminiscent of the area's traditional rural buildings. The overall performance is excellent, but the Monviert Riserva wines truly have an edge. Selected grapes and bottle aging are key factors that the new generation has been pursuing for several years with encouraging results. The Picolit '20 continues its march at the top of the rankings, offering up aromas of dried figs, barley candy, honey, and dried apricots; it's very sweet but not at all cloying. The Rosso Tricùr Ris. '16, which is making its debut in the guide, is also excellent.

○ COF Picolit '20	♛♛ 7
● FCO Rosso Tricùr Ris. '16	♛♛ 8
○ FCO Bianco Tricùr Ris. '18	♛♛ 8
● FCO Cabernet Franc '23	♛♛ 3
○ FCO Chardonnay '23	♛♛ 3
○ FCO Friulano Ris. '21	♛♛ 5
○ FCO Pinot Grigio '23	♛♛ 3
● FCO Refosco dal P. R. Ris. '20	♛♛ 5
○ FCO Ribolla Gialla '23	♛♛ 3
○ FCO Sauvignon '23	♛♛ 3
● FCO Schioppettino Ris. '20	♛♛ 5
○ FCO Traminer Aromatico '23	♛♛ 3
● FCO Franconia '23	♛ 3
○ FCO Friulano '23	♛ 3
○ FCO Verduzzo Friulano '22	♛ 3
○ Ribolla Gialla Brut '23	♛ 3

Moschioni

loc. Gagliano
via Doria, 30
33043 Cividale del Friuli [UD]
☎ +39 0432730210
✉ www.michelemoschioni.it

CELLAR SALES
PRE-BOOKED VISITS
ANNUAL PRODUCTION 38,000 bottles
HECTARES UNDER VINE 14.00
SUSTAINABLE WINERY

For many years, we've noted that Michele Moschioni has consistently gone against the grain, producing only red wines in a region renowned for its exceptional whites. His wines are made using personalized winemaking practices that involve drying the grapes before pressing, resulting in highly concentrated flavors. But Michele never ceases to surprise us—this year, his reds are accompanied by a white that immediately caught our attention. The Schioppettino Ris. '15 exhibits a refined aromatic profile, with an excellent fusion of crème de cassis, blueberries, dark chocolate, and brandied cherries. This is followed by cloves, cinnamon, mace, and dried red rose petals. The palate is warm, soft, and powerful. The Bianco '21 is an exciting new addition, produced with tocai friulano grapes from a vineyard over 50 years old and slightly macerated. It's a juicy creation, recalling summer hay, honey, capers, and hazelnuts.

○ FCO Bianco '21	♛♛ 5
● FCO Schioppettino Ris. '15	♛♛ 8
● FCO Refosco P. R. Ris. '16	♛♛ 6
● FCO Rosso Celtico '15	♛♛ 6
● FCO Rosso Reâl Ris. '15	♛♛ 6
● COF Rosso Celtico '04	♛♛♛ 5
● COF Schioppettino '06	♛♛♛ 6
● COF Pignolo '07	♛♛ 6
● COF Refosco P. R. '06	♛♛ 4
● COF Rosso Celtico '09	♛♛ 5
● COF Rosso Celtico '06	♛♛ 5
● COF Rosso Reâl '09	♛♛ 5
● FCO Rosso Bisest '10	♛♛ 5
● FCO Schioppettino Ris. '13	♛♛ 7
● FCO Schioppettino Ris. '11	♛♛ 7
● Rosso Pit Franc '08	♛♛ 6

Murva

via Celso Macor, I
34070 Moraro [GO]
℡ +39 04811990638
● www.murva.it

CELLAR SALES
PRE-BOOKED VISITS
ANNUAL PRODUCTION 22,000 bottles
HECTARES UNDER VINE 5.00
SUSTAINABLE WINERY

Murva has risen to prominence among cutting-edge producers for its high-quality standards. Credit goes to Alberto Pelos, who, in 2009, decided to leverage his valuable experience by creating his own winery and setting a high bar right from the outset. He established vineyards in distinct sites, each chosen to best exploit the characteristics of each grape variety. Today, his wines are still identified by the vineyard of origin. A stellar performance by the entire range, which once again placed two wines in the finals. The Chardonnay Paladis '22 offers a rare elegance and personality on the nose. On a refined base of lavender and cream, it reveals notes of propolis, dried fruit, and almond stone, while the palate proves perfectly balanced. The Malvasia Melaris '22 opens on delicate echoes of yellow peach, plum, and wildflower honey, followed by hints of rosemary and resin, with a soft, sapid, and progressively unfolding palate.

Muzic

loc. Bivio, 4
34070 San Floriano del Collio [GO]
℡ +39 0481884201
● www.cantinamuzic.it

CELLAR SALES
PRE-BOOKED VISITS
ANNUAL PRODUCTION 130,000 bottles
HECTARES UNDER VINE 26.00
SUSTAINABLE WINERY

The Muzic family's journey into the world of wine production began in the early 1960s, when they had the opportunity to purchase 5 hectares of vineyards that they'd previously worked as sharecroppers. Now, the winery has grown, but not too much—it's still a family-managed operation, with Giovanni (known as Ivan to friends) supported by his sons Elija and Fabijan. Mama Orieta adds value, fostering the cohesion and mutual collaboration that makes the winery so successful. We found the same two wines in the finals as last year, confirming their quality. The Friulano Vigna Valeris '23 showcases a concentrated blend of flowers and fruit, with rare intensity and appeal. Wisteria and lily of the valley stand out, followed by citrus notes of lime and grapefruit, finishing with fresh mint notes. The Stare Brajde da Uve Autoctone '22 is simply delicious, emanating scents of honey, linden, lavender, and sea salt, alongside echoes of spices and aromatic herbs. It earns Tre Bicchieri.

Wine	Rating
○ Friuli Isonzo Chardonnay Paladis '22	♈♈ 6
○ Friuli Isonzo Malvasia Melaris '22	♈♈ 5
○ Friuli Isonzo Bianco Murva '21	♈♈ 5
○ Friuli Isonzo Sauvignon Corvatis '22	♈♈ 5
○ Friuli Isonzo Sauvignon Teolis '22	♈♈ 5
○ Friuli Isonzo Sauvignon Teolis '20	♈♈ 4
○ Friuli Isonzo Bianco Murva '20	♈♈ 5
○ Friuli Isonzo Chardonnay Monuments '20	♈♈ 4
○ Friuli Isonzo Chardonnay Paladis '21	♈♈ 5
○ Friuli Isonzo Chardonnay Paladis '20	♈♈ 5
○ Friuli Isonzo Malvasia Melaris '21	♈♈ 4
○ Friuli Isonzo Malvasia Melaris '20	♈♈ 4
○ Friuli Isonzo Sauvignon Corvatis '21	♈♈ 4
○ Friuli Isonzo Sauvignon Corvatis '20	♈♈ 4
○ Friuli Isonzo Sauvignon Teolis '21	♈♈ 5
○ Friuli Isonzo Sauvignon Teolis '19	♈♈ 4

Wine	Rating
○ Collio Bianco Stare Brajde Uve Autoctone '22	♈♈♈ 5
○ Collio Friulano V. Valeris '23	♈♈ 4
○ Collio Malvasia '23	♈♈ 4
○ Collio Pinot Grigio '23	♈♈ 4
○ Collio Ribolla Gialla '23	♈♈ 4
○ Collio Sauvignon V. Pàjze '23	♈♈ 4
○ Collio Bianco Stare Brajde da Uve Autoctone '21	♈♈ 5
○ Collio Bianco Stare Brajde Uve Autoctone '20	♈♈ 4
○ Collio Friulano V. Valeris '22	♈♈ 4
○ Collio Pinot Grigio '22	♈♈ 4
○ Collio Sauvignon Pàjze '21	♈♈ 4
○ Collio Sauvignon V. Pajze '22	♈♈ 4

Paraschos

loc. Bucuie, 13a
34070 San Floriano del Collio [GO]
(☎) +39 3468770730
⊕ www.paraschos.it

CELLAR SALES
PRE-BOOKED VISITS
ACCOMMODATION
ANNUAL PRODUCTION 30,000 bottles
HECTARES UNDER VINE 10.00
VITICULTURE METHOD Certified Organic

Evangelos Paraschos, a lover of nature and the outdoors, lives and works in San Floriano del Collio. His production approach involves macerating the grapes (including whites) for several days, with the skins, in open-top Slavonian oak vats or Greek terracotta amphorae, harking back to his homeland. Temperature control is eschewed, as is the use of selected yeast strains. These ancient practices are supported by 18th-century bibliographical sources that confirm this was how wine was traditionally made in Collio and the nearby Vipacco Valley. The Friulano Kaj Ris. '21 flaunts a beautiful, antique gold color, while on the nose, it reveals hints of iodine and peat, followed by whiffs of black tea, tobacco, malt, honey, resins, and candied fruit. The palate unravels slowly, alternating sapidity and minerality. The Ribolla Gialla '20 pours an amber color, revealing sensations of barley malt, beeswax, canned peaches, apricot jam, dried fruit, and apples baked with cinnamon. On the palate, it showcases structure and freshness, without hiding its tannins.

○ Collio Friulano Kaj Ris. '21	▼▼▼ 7
○ Ribolla Gialla '20	▼▼ 7
○ Collio Bianco Ponka Ris. '21	▼▼ 7
○ Collio Pinot Grigio Not Ris. '21	▼▼ 7
○ Orange One '20	▼▼ 7
○ Kai '19	♀♀ 7
○ Kaj '11	♀♀ 5
● Merlot '10	♀♀ 3*
● Noir '07	♀♀ 5
○ Not '19	♀♀ 7
○ Orange One '19	♀♀ 6
○ Pinot Grigio Not '13	♀♀ 5
○ Ponka '11	♀♀ 5
○ Ribolla Gialla '09	♀♀ 5
○ Ribolla Gialla Amphoreus '11	♀♀ 5
● Skala '15	♀♀ 7

Alessandro Pascolo

loc. Ruttars, 1
34070 Dolegna del Collio [GO]
(☎) +39 048161144
⊕ www.vinipascolo.com

CELLAR SALES
PRE-BOOKED VISITS
ANNUAL PRODUCTION 25,000 bottles
HECTARES UNDER VINE 7.00
SUSTAINABLE WINERY

In the 1970s, entrepreneur Angelo Pascolo decided to invest in the countryside, acquiring a farmhouse surrounded by vineyards on the sunny slopes of Ruttàrs Hill, a gem in the Dolegna del Collio area. In 2006, Alessandro realized his grandfather's insightful vision by adopting a philosophy focused on creating wines with a distinctive personality. He concentrated on the vineyard so as to produce rich grapes that ensure structure and a strong sense of place. We welcome the debut of a new wine, the Malvasia Etichetta Bianca '21, which immediately stood out for its fragrance and nose-palate symmetry. However, in the finals, we found the same two wines from the previous edition. The Friulano Etichetta Bianca '21 emanates intense aromas of dried aromatic herbs, wheat, wildflowers, and almond; on the palate, it's sapid and long. The Merlot Rosso di Ponca '20 recalls blackberries, blueberries, brandied cherries, and cloves—a wine of great structure and personality.

○ Collio Friulano Et. Bianca '21	▼▼ 4
● Collio Merlot Rosso di Ponca '20	▼▼ 5
○ Collio Bianco Agnul '21	▼▼ 4
○ Collio Malvasia Et. Bianca '21	▼▼ 4
○ Collio Pinot Bianco '23	▼▼ 4
○ Collio Sauvignon '23	▼▼ 4
○ Collio Bianco Agnul '19	♀♀ 4
○ Collio Friulano '22	♀♀ 3
○ Collio Friulano '21	♀♀ 3
○ Collio Friulano Et. Bianca '20	♀♀ 4
○ Collio Malvasia '22	♀♀ 3
○ Collio Malvasia '21	♀♀ 3
● Collio Merlot Rosso di Ponca '19	♀♀ 5
● Collio Merlot Rosso di Ponca '18	♀♀ 5
○ Collio Sauvignon '21	♀♀ 3
● Pascal Cabernet Sauvignon '20	♀♀ 4

Pierpaolo Pecorari

via Tommaseo, 52
34070 San Lorenzo Isontino [GO]
☎ +39 0481808775
✆ www.pierpaolopecorari.it

CELLAR SALES
PRE-BOOKED VISITS
ANNUAL PRODUCTION 215,000 bottles
HECTARES UNDER VINE 31.00

Pierpaolo Pecorari is rightly considered a pioneer of viticultural excellence in the region. He was just a young man when, in 1970, he showed the ambition and foresight to found his own winery, which he still runs today with his son Alessandro. His vineyards stretch along the left bank of the Soca River, between Cormòns and Gradisca, where the gravelly, well-drained soil proves rich in nitrates, sun-kissed, and cooled by sea breezes from the nearby Adriatic Sea. The Pinot Grigio Olivers '22 shimmers with golden highlights in the glass, the prelude to varied, enthralling aromas of pastry, honey, nougat, and candied citrus, then spicy hints of cardamom and nutmeg. The palate is warm, silky, sapid, and well-balanced. The Pinot Bianco '22 conjures up white flowers, lavender, and lemongrass, followed by white peach, citron, and gooseberry. The palate opens fresh and juicy, proceeding harmoniously, only to close slowly with perfect follow through.

Perusini

loc. Gramogliano
via del Torrione, 13
33040 Corno di Rosazzo [UD]
☎ +39 0432759151
✆ www.perusini.com

CELLAR SALES
PRE-BOOKED VISITS
ACCOMMODATION AND RESTAURANT SERVICE
ANNUAL PRODUCTION 130,000 bottles
HECTARES UNDER VINE 15.00
VITICULTURE METHOD Certified Organic
SUSTAINABLE WINERY

After its founding by the noble Perusini family in the 1700s, this historic Friulian winery would go on to spawn a number of figures who'd influence the course of the region's history. Teresa Perusini, the estate's current owner, has skillfully built on her ancestors' work, adeptly interpreting the land and passing on her enthusiasm to the next generation, Carlo, Tommaso, and Michele, a group that have long been an integral part of the winery and its growth. The Pinot Grigio Ramato '23 rightfully earned a place in our finals, opening with aromas of russet pear, hazelnuts, and dry, blooming hay. On the palate, it's smooth and gratifying. The Bianco Zenta Riserva '19, a blend of chardonnay and sauvignon, releases intense fruit fragrances of tangerine, melon, and golden apple alongside delicate spicy hints, while the palate proves rich and alluring. The Rosso Zenta Riserva '19, a merlot and cabernet sauvignon blend, evokes dark chocolate and licorice.

○ Friuli Pinot Grigio Olivers '22	♀♀ 5
○ Pinot Bianco '22	♀♀ 4
○ Kolàus Sauvignon '21	♀♀ 5
○ Malvasia '23	♀♀ 4
○ Sauvignon '23	♀♀ 4
○ Friuli Pinot Grigio '23	♀ 3
○ Kolàus Sauvignon '96	♀♀♀ 3*
○ Friuli Pinot Grigio '21	♀♀ 3
○ Friuli Pinot Grigio Olivers '21	♀♀ 5
○ Kolàus Sauvignon '20	♀♀ 5
○ Kolàus Sauvignon '19	♀♀ 5
○ Malvasia '22	♀♀ 4
○ Pinot Bianco '21	♀♀ 4
○ Sauvignon '22	♀♀ 4
○ Sauvignon '21	♀♀ 3

○ FCO Pinot Grigio Ramato '23	♀♀ 3*
○ Blanc de Noir Pas Dosé M. Cl.	♀♀ 5
○ FCO Bianco Zenta Ris. '18	♀♀ 6
○ FCO Ribolla Gialla '23	♀♀ 3
● FCO Rosso Zenta Ris. '19	♀♀ 6
○ COF Picolit '18	♀♀ 8
● FCO Cabernet Sauvignon '18	♀♀ 3
○ FCO Chardonnay '21	♀♀ 3
○ FCO Friulano '21	♀♀ 3
● FCO Merlot '20	♀♀ 3
● FCO Merlot '19	♀♀ 3*
○ FCO Pinot Grigio '15	♀♀ 3*
○ FCO Pinot Grigio Ramato '22	♀♀ 3
○ FCO Pinot Grigio Ramato '21	♀♀ 3
● FCO Rosso Zenta '18	♀♀ 5
○ FCO Sauvignon '21	♀♀ 3

Petrucco

via Morpurgo, 12
33042 Buttrio [UD]
(☎ +39 0432674387
⊛ www.vinipetrucco.it

CELLAR SALES
PRE-BOOKED VISITS
ANNUAL PRODUCTION 80,000 bottles
HECTARES UNDER VINE 25.00

In 1981, Lina and Paolo Petrucco had the opportunity to settle on the sunny slopes of Buttrio, where the beautiful natural amphitheater of Friuli begins, formed by hills exposed to sea breezes. The pair decided to establish a winery, relying on the oenological and agronomic skills of Flavio Cabas, who still manages the entire production process, overseeing prized, historic vineyards where grapes destined for the Ronco di Paolo Riserva mature. The Bianco Cabas Ronco del Balbo '22, composed of malvasia istriana, chardonnay, sauvignon, and tocai friulano, opens with a delicate floral breeze before moving on to scents of white peach, pear, citrus, almond, and aromatic herbs. The palate is enveloping, unfolding progressively, with well-balanced sapidity and a balsamic freshness on the finish. The Refosco dal Peduncolo Rosso Ronco di Paolo '21 conjures up blackberries, plums, blueberries, sour cherries, chestnut honey, and coffee; on the palate, it's smooth and balanced, with velvety tannins.

○ FCO Bianco Cabas Ronco del Balbo '22	♟♟	4
● FCO Refosco dal P. R. Ronco di Paolo '21	♟♟	4
○ FCO Friulano '23	♟♟	3
○ FCO Malvasia '23	♟♟	3
● FCO Merlot Ronco di Paolo '21	♟♟	4
● FCO Pignolo Ronco di Paolo '19	♟♟	6
○ FCO Pinot Bianco '23	♟♟	3
○ FCO Sauvignon '23	♟♟	3
○ FCO Bianco Cabas Ronco del Balbo '18	♟♟	4
○ FCO Friulano '22	♟♟	3*
● FCO Merlot Ronco del Balbo '19	♟♟	4
● FCO Pignolo Ronco del Balbo '16	♟♟	5
● FCO Pignolo Ronco di Paolo '18	♟♟	5
○ FCO Pinot Bianco '21	♟♟	3*

Petrussa

via Albana, 49
33040 Prepotto [UD]
(☎ +39 0432713192
⊛ www.petrussa.it

CELLAR SALES
PRE-BOOKED VISITS
ACCOMMODATION
ANNUAL PRODUCTION 45,000 bottles
HECTARES UNDER VINE 10.00

The lure of the land convinced Gianni and Paolo Petrussa to manage the family winery. Staunch advocates of simple, minimalist winemaking based on the values of their ancestors' farming roots, they still operate in perfect harmony in the microcosm of Albana di Prepotto, a narrow strip of land considered the cradle of Schioppettino. On their few hectares, they demonstrate their expertise in every aspect, producing some top-shelf whites as well. This year, the Chardonnay S. Elena '22 once again advanced to our finals, thanks to its exquisite bouquet of jasmine and acacia flowers, followed by refined notes of thyme, summer savory and tarragon, with wafts of white pepper and pine resin. On the palate, it's fresh, with good structure and sapidity. The Schioppettino di Prepotto S. Elena '21 remains a top-shelf wine with its intoxicating aromas of spices, wild berries, licorice root, and myrtle, offering a rich, flavorful, and invigorating palate.

○ FCO Chardonnay S. Elena '22	♟♟	5
● FCO Schioppettino di Prepotto S. Elena '21	♟♟	7
○ FCO Friulano '23	♟♟	4
● FCO Merlot Rosso Petrussa Ris. '21	♟♟	6
○ FCO Pinot Bianco '23	♟♟	4
○ FCO Sauvignon '23	♟♟	4
● FCO Schioppettino di Prepotto '21	♟♟	6
○ Pensiero '20	♟♟	6
● FCO Schioppettino di Prepotto '15	♟♟	5
● FCO Schioppettino di Prepotto '14	♟♟	5
● FCO Schioppettino di Prepotto S. Elena '20	♟♟	7
● FCO Schioppettino di Prepotto S. Elena '19	♟♟	7

Norina Pez

via Zorutti, 4
34070 Dolegna del Collio [GO]
(+39 345639951
@ www.norinapez.it

CELLAR SALES
PRE-BOOKED VISITS
ANNUAL PRODUCTION 40,000 bottles
HECTARES UNDER VINE 8.00
SUSTAINABLE WINERY

Based in the hills of Dolegna del Collio, the Bernardis family boasts nearly a century of winemaking tradition. The early 1980s marked a turning point, when Giuseppe Bernardis and his wife Norina Pez formally established the winery in her name. The couple successfully built a thriving business, which their son Stefano now manages comprehensively, using exclusively estate-grown grapes. This year, the Schioppettino '21, in particular, stood out. Signature aromas of blackberry and black pepper are joined by notes of cherry jam, undergrowth, tobacco, black olive pâté, and sun-dried tomatoes. The palate is smooth and pervasive. It edged out the winery's flagship, the El Neri di Norina '20, a blend of merlot and schioppettino, which we still appreciated for its elegant nose, substantive palate, and fresh, balsamic finish.

Schioppettino '21	♟♟ 3*
Collio Friulano '23	♟♟ 3
Collio Merlot '20	♟♟ 3
Collio Pinot Grigio '23	♟♟ 3
Collio Ribolla Gialla '23	♟♟ 3
El Neri di Norina '20	♟♟ 5
Aurea Divina '18	♟ 5
Collio Cabernet Franc '20	♟♟ 3
Collio Friulano '22	♟♟ 3
Collio Ribolla Gialla '22	♟♟ 3
El Neri di Norina '19	♟♟ 5
El Neri di Norina '18	♟♟ 5
El Neri di Norina '16	♟♟ 5
Schioppettino '20	♟♟ 3
Schioppettino '17	♟♟ 3*
Verduzzo '18	♟♟ 3

Roberto Picech

loc. Pradis, 11
34071 Cormòns [GO]
(+39 048160347
@ www.picech.com

CELLAR SALES
PRE-BOOKED VISITS
ACCOMMODATION
ANNUAL PRODUCTION 30,000 bottles
HECTARES UNDER VINE 7.50
VITICULTURE METHOD Certified Organic
SUSTAINABLE WINERY

Roberto Picéch is a renowned figure in Collio, a true wine artisan and an undisputed leader. The son of Egidio, known as "the rebel," he inherited not only the vineyards but also a forthright, tenacious character that has allowed him to impart a personal identity to his wines. Respectful of tradition yet innovative, he has perfected his winemaking style over time, often employing extended maceration to extract the maximum possible aromatic qualities. Given the fantastic array of wines presented, it was difficult to choose which should go on to the final round (even those excluded deserved a place). The Malvasia '22 offers sunny aromas of barley, wheat, dried aromatic herbs, and white pepper, with a harmonious and balanced palate. The Friulano Athena '20 pours a gold-leaf color, releasing intense fragrances of tangerines, apricot jam, and honey. The palate is juicy, fragrant, and full of flavor.

o Collio Friulano Athena '20	♟♟ 6
o Collio Malvasia '22	♟♟ 5
o Collio Bianco Jelka '19	♟♟ 6
o Collio Friulano '22	♟♟ 5
o Collio Pinot Bianco '22	♟♟ 5
• Collio Rosso Ruben Ris. '20	♟♟ 7
o Collio Bianco Athena '05	♟♟♟ 7
o Collio Bianco Jelka '11	♟♟♟ 4*
o Collio Bianco Jelka '99	♟♟♟ 7
o Collio Pinot Bianco '13	♟♟♟ 3*
o Collio Bianco Jelka '17	♟♟ 6
o Collio Bianco Jelka '16	♟♟ 6
o Collio Friulano Athena '19	♟♟ 6
o Collio Friulano Athena '17	♟♟ 5
o Collio Malvasia '21	♟♟ 4
o Collio Malvasia '20	♟♟ 4

FRIULI VENEZIA GIULIA

Pighin

fraz. Risano
v.le Grado, 11/1
33050 Pavia di Udine [UD]
(☏) +39 0432675444
✉ www.pighin.com

Vigneti Pittaro

via Udine, 67
33033 Codroipo [UD]
(☏) +39 0432904726
✉ www.vignetipittaro.com

CELLAR SALES
PRE-BOOKED VISITS
ANNUAL PRODUCTION 900,000 bottles
HECTARES UNDER VINE 160.00
SUSTAINABLE WINERY

CELLAR SALES
PRE-BOOKED VISITS
ACCOMMODATION
ANNUAL PRODUCTION 250,000 bottles
HECTARES UNDER VINE 30.00
SUSTAINABLE WINERY

The Pighin family likes to describe themselves as pioneers of Friulian wine on the global stage. In 1963, they settled in Risano, acquiring a vast estate, predominantly planted with vines, and a 17th-century Venetian villa surrounded by a magnificent property (now their production center). A few years later, they expanded their holdings with another estate in Spessa di Capriva, in the Gorizia Hills. Today, the dynamic duo of Roberto and Raffaela carries on the family legacy. In the absence of the winery's flagship, the Collio Bianco Soreli (which evidently has been granted additional time to bottle age), all the wines presented hail from the latest vintage. The wines from the plains stood out for their freshness, lightness, and drinkability, but the most praise went to their Collio selections. The Malvasia '23 proves notable for its pronounced varietal character, while the Friulano '23 impressed with its fragrance, both on the nose and palate, with citrus and tropical fruits taking center stage.

Piero Pittaro was a prominent figure in the regional wine scene. During his life, he garnered numerous successes and accolades, creating a brand that became a point of pride for the Friuli Grave appellation. After his passing, he surprised everyone by donating the winery and its precious vineyards to his nine employees, who suddenly found themselves the new owners, committed to honoring their former employer's grand gesture. The Pittaro Etichetta Oro Brut Metodo Classico '18 sees a close-knit, fine perlage illuminate the wine's golden hue. The nose exhibits supreme class, offering nuances of grapefruit and blonde orange, followed by gentle wafts of orange blossom, resins, and spices. A palate of rare elegance follows, with a pleasant finish on toasted hazelnuts. The Pittaro Etichetta Oro Pas Dosé Metodo Classico '16 pours an equally luminous gold color accompanied by lively, well-sustained bead, the prelude to refined, delicate hints of alpine hay, light spices, and sea salt breezes.

○ Collio Friulano '23	♟♟ 3*
○ Collio Malvasia '23	♟♟ 3*
○ Collio Chardonnay '23	♟♟ 3
○ Collio Pinot Grigio '23	♟♟ 3
○ Collio Ribolla Gialla '23	♟♟ 3
○ Collio Sauvignon '23	♟♟ 3
○ Friuli Grave Bianco Virdis '23	♟♟ 3
○ Friuli Grave Pinot Bianco '23	♟♟ 2*
○ Friuli Grave Sauvignon '23	♟♟ 2*
○ Friuli Grave Friulano '23	♟ 2
○ Friuli Grave Pinot Grigio '23	♟ 2
○ Ribolla Gialla '23	♟ 2
○ Collio Bianco Soreli '20	♟♟♟ 5
○ Collio Bianco Soreli '21	♟♟ 5
○ Collio Malvasia '22	♟♟ 3*
○ Collio Sauvignon '22	♟♟ 3*
○ Collio Sauvignon '21	♟♟ 3*

○ Pittaro Et. Oro Brut M. Cl. '18	♟♟ 6
○ Pittaro Et. Oro Pas Dosé M. Cl. '16	♟♟ 6
● FCO Refosco dal P. R. '20	♟♟ 4
○ Pittaro Et. Argento Brut M. Cl.	♟♟ 4
○ Pittaro Pink Brut Rosé M. Cl.	♟♟ 5
○ Ronco Vieri Ribolla Gialla Brut M. Cl.	♟♟ 5
○ Apicio '21	♟ 3
○ FCO Friulano Ronco Vieri '22	♟ 3

Denis Pizzulin

via Brolo, 43
33040 Prepotto [UD]
📞 +39 0432713425
🌐 www.pizzulin.com

CELLAR SALES
PRE-BOOKED VISITS
ACCOMMODATION
ANNUAL PRODUCTION 45,000 bottles
HECTARES UNDER VINE 11.00
SUSTAINABLE WINERY

Denis Pizzulin owns a charming winery in Prepotto, a narrow valley bordering Slovenia and Collio. The territory is teeming with small, family-run wineries that draw on time-honored traditions. It's also the homeland of ribolla nera, the grape used to produce Schioppettino, Pizzulin's flagship wine. With only a few hectares of vineyards and a limited number of wines, he personally oversees all production phases. The Schioppettino di Prepotto '21 leads the rankings for its pronounced typicity, conjuring up spicy notes of black pepper, cardamom, and cloves, followed by blackberry, dried plum, and coffee beans. The palate is smooth yet fresh and sapid, with well-integrated tannins. All the wines from the latest vintage are of excellent craftsmanship, while those from the Lastris line show greater depth, the result of lengthier bottle aging.

FCO Schioppettino di Prepotto '21	🍷🍷 5
FCO Friulano '23	🍷🍷 4
FCO Pinot Bianco '23	🍷🍷 4
FCO Pinot Nero Lastris '20	🍷🍷 5
FCO Refosco dal P. R. '21	🍷🍷 5
FCO Sauvignon '23	🍷🍷 3
FCO Sauvignon Lastris '22	🍷🍷 5
Ribolla Gialla '23	🍷🍷 4
FCO Bianco Rarisolchi '17	🍷🍷 3*
FCO Merlot '21	🍷🍷 5
FCO Merlot Scaglia Rossa Ris. '13	🍷🍷 4
FCO Pinot Bianco '22	🍷🍷 3
FCO Refosco P. R. '20	🍷🍷 5
FCO Sauvignon Lastris '21	🍷🍷 5
FCO Schioppettino di Prepotto '20	🍷🍷 5
FCO Schioppettino di Prepotto '13	🍷🍷 4

Damijan Podversic

via degli Eroi, 33
34170 Gorizia
📞 +39 048178217
🌐 www.damijanpodversic.com

CELLAR SALES
PRE-BOOKED VISITS
ANNUAL PRODUCTION 38,000 bottles
HECTARES UNDER VINE 15.00
VITICULTURE METHOD Certified Organic

Damijan Podversic is a genuine man, proud of his role as a farmer, driven by a love for the land and traditional winemaking practices. His methods involve long maceration times on the skins, even for whites, without any interventions that might alter the natural process of vinification. He operates on Monte Calvario, one of the highest peaks in the Collio region, enjoying a breathtaking view as he tends to his vineyards daily. The Malvasia '20 flaunts a characteristic amber color, exuding intense aromas of barley, nougat, honey, blood orange, and caramelized hazelnuts, with briny hints and balsamic notes of mint and eucalyptus to follow. The palate is sumptuous, persistent, and enduring. The Collio Bianco Kaplja '20, a blend of chardonnay, malvasia istriana, and tocai friulano, yields aromas of hibiscus, beeswax, and medicinal herbs, while the Pinot Grigio '21 evokes lavender, raspberry syrup, dates, and marron glacé.

○ Collio Bianco Kaplja '20	🍷🍷 8
○ Collio Malvasia '20	🍷🍷 8
○ Collio Pinot Grigio '21	🍷🍷 8
○ Collio Friulano Nekaj '20	🍷🍷 8
○ Collio Ribolla Gialla '20	🍷🍷 8
● Collio Rosso Prelit '20	🍷🍷 8
○ Kaplja '08	🍷🍷🍷 6
○ Malvasia '15	🍷🍷🍷 8
○ Malvasia '13	🍷🍷🍷 8
○ Malvasia '10	🍷🍷🍷 6
○ Malvasia '09	🍷🍷🍷 6
○ Nekaj '17	🍷🍷🍷 7
○ Nekaj '14	🍷🍷🍷 6
○ Ribolla Gialla '12	🍷🍷🍷 8
○ Ribolla Gialla Selezione '10	🍷🍷🍷 8

Isidoro Polencic

loc. Plessiva, 12
34071 Cormòns [GO]
☎ +39 048160655
✉ www.polencic.com

CELLAR SALES
PRE-BOOKED VISITS
ACCOMMODATION
ANNUAL PRODUCTION 120,000 bottles
HECTARES UNDER VINE 28.00

The Polencic family's roots in Collio date back to the late 1800s. With a determination that's been passed down through the generations, they have maintained a love for the land and traditional values. In 1968, Isidoro Polencic, a master winemaker, founded the estate now run by his three children, Elisabetta, Michele, and Alex. The pride of their range is Fisc, produced from a vineyard replanted with cuttings from century-old tocai friulano. The Friulano Fisc '22 lives up to expectations, advancing to our finals in grand style, with intense, refined aromas of yellow flowers, citrus, and tropical fruit, enriched by smoky notes. The palate is smooth, well-proportioned, sapid, and persistent. This year, it's accompanied by an excellent Pinot Bianco '23, which reveals a rich bouquet of wisteria and jasmine with echoes of white peach, lychee, and hints of medicinal herbs, like sage, thyme, and rosemary. Its perfect balance makes this a gratifying drink.

○ Collio Friulano Fisc '22	♀♀ 4
○ Collio Pinot Bianco '23	♀♀ 3*
○ Collio Chardonnay '23	♀♀ 3
○ Collio Friulano '23	♀♀ 3
○ Collio Pinot Grigio '23	♀♀ 3
○ Oblin Blanc '22	♀♀ 4
○ Collio Friulano Fisc '07	♀♀♀ 3*
○ Collio Pinot Bianco '07	♀♀♀ 3
○ Collio Pinot Grigio '98	♀♀♀ 3*
○ Collio Tocai Friulano '04	♀♀♀ 3*
○ Collio Friulano '21	♀♀ 3*
○ Collio Friulano Fisc '21	♀♀ 4
○ Collio Friulano Fisc '20	♀♀ 4
○ Collio Pinot Bianco '20	♀♀ 3*
○ Collio Pinot Grigio '22	♀♀ 3*
○ Collio Pinot Grigio '18	♀♀ 3*

Polje

loc. Novali, 11
34071 Cormòns [GO]
☎ +39 047160660
✉ www.polje.com

CELLAR SALES
PRE-BOOKED VISITS
ANNUAL PRODUCTION 67,300 bottles
HECTARES UNDER VINE 14.00

Polje was created by brothers Luigi and Stefano Sutto when, at the turn of the century, the two acquired a winery in Novali di Cormòns and whose origins go back to 1926. They named it after the sinkholes characteristic of the area, formed by the erosion of the Julian Prealps (known as "polje" in local dialect). In 2015, the Polje brand became part of the Sutto Wine group, who can now include Collio whites as part of their already extensive portfolio. The Lavino Pinot Grigio '22 reaffirms its status as one of the best of its kind. The nose exhibits supreme finesse, offering pronounced floral notes of broom and marigold, followed by hints of medicinal herbs, candied fruit, lemon wafer, citron zest, and resin. The palate is weighty, starting off fresh and then growing sapid and invigorating. The Lovian Sauvignon '22 opens on intriguing aromas of white peach, black cherry, lime, bergamot, and sea salt, with freshness and sapidity perfectly balancing its glyceric sensation on the palate.

○ Collio Pinot Grigio Lavino '22	♀♀ 4
○ Collio Sauvignon Lovian '22	♀♀ 4
○ Collio Friulano '23	♀♀ 3
○ Collio Friulano Valnoi '22	♀♀ 4
○ Collio Pinot Bianco '23	♀♀ 3
○ Collio Ribolla Gialla Nivola '22	♀♀ 4
○ Collio Sauvignon '23	♀♀ 3
○ Collio Pinot Grigio '19	♀♀♀ 4
○ Collio Bianco Fantazija '20	♀♀ 3
○ Collio Friulano Valnoi '21	♀♀ 4
○ Collio Pinot Grigio '21	♀♀ 3
○ Collio Pinot Grigio '20	♀♀ 4
○ Collio Pinot Grigio '18	♀♀ 4
○ Collio Pinot Grigio Lavino '21	♀♀ 4
○ Collio Sauvignon '19	♀♀ 4
○ Collio Sauvignon '17	♀♀ 3

Pradio

fraz. Felettis
via Udine, 17
33050 Bicinicco [UD]
(ʼ)) +39 0432990123
⊛ www.pradio.it

CELLAR SALES
PRE-BOOKED VISITS
ANNUAL PRODUCTION 300,000 bottles
HECTARES UNDER VINE 33.00

A thriving winery in Friuli, Pradio is owned by
the Cielo family, who have long operated in the
wine sector. Founded in 1974, the estate is
managed by cousins Luca and Pierpaolo, and
spans 33 hectares of stony, dry, and sunny land in
the Friuli Grave appellation. The vineyards are
overseen by Enrico Della Mora, who takes care
of the agricultural side, while winemaking has
long been entrusted to the undeniable expertise
of Gianni Menotti. This year, the entire set of
wines submitted for tasting earned unanimous
acclaim, with scores nearly matching those of
more renowned hillside estates. Leading the
pack is the Starz Bianco '23, made from
chardonnay and tocai friulano grapes. The nose
unveils delicate whiffs of white flowers and
refined tropical notes of coconut, papaya, mango,
and banana, all under a soft veil of vanilla. The
palate's linear profile and freshness make for
sheer enjoyment.

★Primosic

fraz. Oslavia
loc. Madonnina di Oslavia, 3
34170 Gorizia
(ʼ)) +39 0481535153
⊛ www.primosic.com

CELLAR SALES
PRE-BOOKED VISITS
ANNUAL PRODUCTION 210,000 bottles
HECTARES UNDER VINE 32.00

The Primosic family has been dealing in wine
since the 19th century, transporting their
precious product from the southern hills of the
Austro-Hungarian Empire to the capital, Vienna.
Today, Marko and Boris Primosic lead this family
business, which is experiencing a moment of
splendor. Their success is largely due to
diversification in winemaking, offering both
unique gems produced with time-honored
techniques and a wide array of modern, elegant
offerings. The Chardonnay Riserva '19, which
won last year's White Wine of the Year trophy,
once again performed at outstanding levels,
captivating with its alluring notes of dried yellow
flowers, candied orange, dried fruit, incense, and
nuts. On the palate, it's sumptuous, pervasive and
energetic, developing progressively. The Collio
Bianco Klin '19, a blend of chardonnay, sauvignon,
tocai friulano, and ribolla gialla, also shines with
its aromas of ripe fruit and myriad spices.

○ Friuli Bianco Starz '23	♟♟	5
○ Friuli Pinot Grigio Priara '23	♟♟	3
● Friuli Rosso Starz '20	♟♟	6
○ Friuli Sauvignon Sobaja '23	♟♟	3
○ Prosecco Brut Passaparola	♟♟	3
○ Rok Bianco '23	♟♟	3
● Rok Rosso '20	♟♟	5
○ Friuli Bianco Starz '21	♔♔	6
○ Friuli Bianco Starz '20	♔♔	6
○ Friuli Bianco Starz '19	♔♔	5
● Friuli Grave Rosso Starz '22	♔♔	5
○ Friuli Pinot Grigio Priara '22	♔♔	3
○ Friuli Sauvignon Sobaja '22	♔♔	3
○ Rok Bianco '22	♔♔	3
● Rok Rosso '19	♔♔	5
○ Starz Bianco '18	♔♔	5

○ Collio Chardonnay Ris. '19	♟♟♟	7
○ Collio Bianco Klin '19	♟♟	8
● Collio Rosso Metamorfosis '16	♟♟	8
○ Collio Friulano Skin Ris. '20	♟♟	7
○ Collio Pinot Grigio '22	♟♟	5
○ Think Yellow Ribolla Gialla '23	♟♟	5
○ Collio Chardonnay Gmajne '15	♔♔♔	5
○ Collio Chardonnay Ris. '18	♔♔♔	7
○ Collio Friulano Skin Ris. '19	♔♔♔	7
○ Collio Friulano Skin Ris. '17	♔♔♔	7
○ Collio Ribolla Gialla di Oslavia Ris. '16	♔♔♔	6
○ Collio Ribolla Gialla di Oslavia Ris. '13	♔♔♔	5
○ Collio Ribolla Gialla di Oslavia Ris. '12	♔♔♔	5
○ Collio Ribolla Gialla di Oslavia Ris. '11	♔♔♔	5

★★Doro Princic

loc. Pradis, 5
34071 Cormòns [GO]
📞 +39 048160723
doroprincic@virgilio.it

CELLAR SALES
PRE-BOOKED VISITS
ANNUAL PRODUCTION 60,000 bottles
HECTARES UNDER VINE 10.00

Sandro Princic is a classic wine craftsman who inherited extraordinary balance, straightforward speech, and great listening skills from his father, Doro. A sly smile peeks out from under his Austro-Hungarian style mustache. A firm believer in monovarietal wines, he brings out the best in each grape without manipulation or excess, respecting nature's rhythms. A winemaker of great class, he has passed on his knowledge to his son Carlo. Many deemed the 2023 vintage difficult, but tasting Sandro's wines would suggest otherwise—they even seem to take things up a notch. The Pinot Bianco '23 bursts with enviable energy, releasing tropical and balsamic notes. The Friulano '23 showcases elegance and minerality. The Sauvignon '23 proves refined and fragrant, while the Malvasia '23 is a concentrate of aromas that progressively bring out its flavor.

Puiatti

loc. Zuccole, 4
34076 Romans d'Isonzo [GO]
📞 +39 0481909608
🌐 www.puiatti.com

CELLAR SALES
PRE-BOOKED VISITS
ANNUAL PRODUCTION 800,000 bottles
HECTARES UNDER VINE 42.00
SUSTAINABLE WINERY

Vittorio Puiatti, a staunch advocate of not using oak, gave his wines a distinctive style in 1967 by respecting the original and natural character of each grape variety, and opting for low alcohol content so as to improve drinkability. A few years ago, the Puiatti winery became part of the Angelini Wines and Estates group, which fully embraced the founder's philosophy, strengthening the indissoluble bond between the land and human effort. Once again, both the whites from the latest harvest and their Metodo Classico sparkling wines stood out for their freshness and pleasant drinkability. The Chardonnay '23 offers an intriguing vegetal framework of ferns and verbena, followed by fruity tones of white peach and pineapple, and finishing with refreshing bursts of peppermint that echo on the palate. The Sauvignon '23 is a forthright pour, displaying nice acidity and reverberations of aromatic herbs and green pepper.

Wine	Rating
○ Collio Malvasia '23	🍷🍷🍷 5
○ Collio Friulano '23	🍷🍷 5
○ Collio Pinot Bianco '23	🍷🍷 5
○ Collio Sauvignon '23	🍷🍷 5
○ Collio Pinot Grigio '23	🍷🍷 5
○ Collio Ribolla Gialla '23	🍷🍷 5
○ Collio Friulano '15	♢♢♢ 5
○ Collio Malvasia '22	♢♢♢ 5
○ Collio Malvasia '20	♢♢♢ 5
○ Collio Malvasia '14	♢♢♢ 5
○ Collio Malvasia '13	♢♢♢ 5
○ Collio Pinot Bianco '21	♢♢♢ 5
○ Collio Pinot Bianco '19	♢♢♢ 5
○ Collio Pinot Bianco '18	♢♢♢ 5
○ Collio Pinot Bianco '17	♢♢♢ 5
○ Collio Pinot Bianco '16	♢♢♢ 5

Wine	Rating
○ Blanc de Blancs Extra Brut M. Cl.	🍷🍷 4
○ Friuli Chardonnay '23	🍷🍷 3
○ Friuli Friulano '23	🍷🍷 3
○ Friuli Pinot Grigio '23	🍷🍷 3
○ Friuli Sauvignon '23	🍷🍷 4
○ Ribolla Gialla Extra Brut M. Cl.	🍷🍷 5
◉ Rosé de Noirs Extra Brut M. Cl.	🍷🍷 5
○ Ribolla Gialla '23	🍷 3
○ Collio Sauvignon Archetipi '88	♢♢♢ 5
○ Friuli Pinot Grigio '22	♢♢ 3
○ Friuli Sauvignon '22	♢♢ 4
○ Friuli Sauvignon '21	♢♢ 3
○ Friuli Sauvignon '20	♢♢ 3
○ Ribolla Gialla '21	♢♢ 3
○ Ribolla Gialla Archètipi '18	♢♢ 5

Teresa Raiz

loc. Marsure di Sotto
via della Roggia, 22
33040 Povoletto [UD]
☎ +39 0432679556
✉ www.teresaraiz.it

CELLAR SALES
PRE-BOOKED VISITS
ANNUAL PRODUCTION 80,000 bottles
HECTARES UNDER VINE 11.50

For over 30 years, Teresa Raiz has been exporting Friulian wines worldwide. Paolo Tosolini founded this winery in 1971 during a period of great ferment in the regional wine sector. Since 2003, he's had the support of his son Alessandro. Teresa Raiz was Paolo's maternal grandmother, remembered as an incredible woman and a great wine enthusiast, who viewed the countryside as a heavenly gift and passed on the principles of her philosophy to the family. The negligible difference in scores between the hillside and plains wines certifies the quality of the entire range, even more so when considering their competitive prices. However, the Schioppettino '21 stands out, boasting refined aromas of sweet spices, tobacco leaves, and hibiscus, with a graceful palate that mirrors the nose. Both versions of the Pinot Grigio '23 do the grape justice, while the Merlot Le Marsure '22 excels in its substance and lively tannins.

La Rajade

loc. Petrus, 2
34070 Dolegna del Collio [GO]
☎ +39 0481639273
✉ www.larajade.it

CELLAR SALES
PRE-BOOKED VISITS
ANNUAL PRODUCTION 45,000 bottles
HECTARES UNDER VINE 7.50

The recent change in the technical staff managing the Campeotto and Faurlin families' winery has produced the desired effects, with improvements reflected across the entire range. The unique position of the vineyards, which extend over the upper hills protected to the north by the Julian Alps, inspired the winery's name. Indeed, "La Rajade" means "ray of sun," highlighting how the sun's arc contrasts with the low night temperatures, creating significant temperature swings. The Schioppettino '21 unveils aromas of wild blackberries, morello cherries, black pepper, and cloves, with a background of herbal notes like thyme and rosemary. On the palate, it's elegant and balanced, with tidy and integrated tannins. The Collio Bianco da Uve Autoctone '22 (a blend of tocai friulano, malvasia istriana, and ribolla gialla) proves redolent of Mediterranean herbs, acacia honey, alpine hay, bay leaf, eucalyptus, and mint tea, with a multifaceted, balanced, and gratifying palate.

● FCO Schioppettino '21	♟♟♟ 4*
● FCO Pinot Grigio '23	♟♟ 4
Friuli Merlot Le Marsure '22	♟♟ 3
● Friuli Pinot Grigio Le Marsure '23	♟♟ 3
Friuli Refosco P. R. Le Marsure '22	♟ 3
● Friuli Sauvignon Le Marsure '23	♟ 3
Decano Rosso '19	♟♟ 4
● FCO Friulano '22	♟♟ 2*
FCO Pinot Grigio '22	♟♟ 2*
FCO Pinot Grigio '21	♟♟ 2*
● FCO Ribolla Gialla '22	♟♟ 2*
Friuli Bianco Sovej '21	♟♟ 4
Friuli Decano Rosso '20	♟♟ 4
Friuli Pinot Grigio Le Marsure '21	♟♟ 2*
Friuli Pinot Grigio Le Marsure '19	♟♟ 2*

● Schioppettino '21	♟♟ 5
○ Collio Bianco da Uve Autoctone '22	♟♟ 5
○ Collio Friulano '22	♟♟ 4
○ Collio Pinot Grigio Nuje '22	♟♟ 4
● Collio Rosso '20	♟♟ 4
○ Collio Sauvignon '22	♟♟ 4
○ Collio Ribolla Gialla '22	♟ 4
○ Collio Bianco Caprizi Ris. '14	♟♟ 3*
● Collio Cabernet Sauvignon Ris. '13	♟♟ 4
● Collio Cabernet Sauvignon Ris. '12	♟♟ 4
○ Collio Friulano '21	♟♟ 4
○ Collio Pinot Grigio Nuje '19	♟♟ 4
○ Collio Ribolla Gialla '21	♟♟ 3
● Collio Rosso '19	♟♟ 3
○ Collio Sauvignon '21	♟♟ 3
● Schioppettino '20	♟♟ 3

Rocca Bernarda

fraz. Ipplis
via Rocca Bernarda, 27
33040 Premariacco [UD]
☏ +39 0432716914
⊛ www.rocca-bernarda.it

CELLAR SALES
PRE-BOOKED VISITS
ANNUAL PRODUCTION 100,000 bottles
HECTARES UNDER VINE 38.50

Rocca Bernarda is rightfully considered to be among Friuli-Venezia Giulia's historic wineries. Founded in 1559, it stands atop the namesake hill and is based in an old manor. In fact, a plaque on the enclosing walls testifies that the cellars were built even before the villa. The tradition of winemaking has been maintained over the centuries, primarily thanks to the Count Perusini family, who in 1977, donated the entire estate to the Knights of Malta. Since 2006, the winery has been managed by the Italian Viticulture Agricultural Society. The Friulano '23 evokes acacia flowers, geranium and wildflower on the nose, alongside honey, apple, pineapple, caper, and aromatic herbs. The palate is balanced, supported by fresh, sapid undertones that lead to a finish with Mediterranean echoes. The Ribolla Gialla '23 showcases delicate floral fragrance of orange blossom and jasmine, followed by citrus notes of grapefruit and lime, with a thirst-quenching effect on the palate. The Pignolo '17 proves austere on the nose, with notes of tobacco meeting carob, while the palate is rich, pervasive, and sapid.

o FCO Friulano '23	♥♥ 3
• FCO Pignolo '17	♥♥ 6
• FCO Refosco dal P. R. '22	♥♥ 3
o FCO Ribolla Gialla '23	♥♥ 3
• COF Merlot Centis '99	♥♥♥ 7
o COF Picolit '03	♥♥♥ 7
o COF Picolit '98	♥♥♥ 7
o COF Picolit '97	♥♥♥ 7
• FCO Cabernet Franc '21	♥♥ 3
o FCO Friulano Vineis '21	♥♥ 5
• FCO Merlot '21	♥♥ 3
• FCO Pignolo '16	♥♥ 5
o FCO Pinot Grigio '22	♥♥ 3
• FCO Refosco P.R. '21	♥♥ 3
o Novecento Bianco 1113-2013 '21	♥♥ 4
o Novecento Bianco 1113-2013 '20	♥♥ 3

Paolo Rodaro

loc. Spessa
via Cormòns, 60
33043 Cividale del Friuli [UD]
☏ +39 0432716066
⊛ www.rodaropaolo.it

CELLAR SALES
PRE-BOOKED VISITS
ANNUAL PRODUCTION 350,000 bottles
HECTARES UNDER VINE 67.00
SUSTAINABLE WINERY

Paolo Rodaro, an enterprising and dynamic wine craftsman, constantly seeks new challenges, enriching the already extensive and varied offerings of his winery with new proposals. He has long showcased the prestigious Romain line, which includes robust reds, and now, together with his wife Lara, he is focused on producing Pas Dosé Method sparkling wines, a new flagship for the winery. The Malvasia Fiore '22 reaffirms its status as one of their most prestigious wines, flaunting a rich aromatic palette where fruit salad, lemon zest, and almond stand out, followed by sage, thyme, delicate spices, and sea salt. On the palate, it's silky, with sapid bursts that make for an engaging quaff. The Schioppettino Romain '19, made from grapes dried in small crates, opens with intense notes of plums, chocolate, coffee, star anise, and cloves—the palate is soft and pervasive.

o Centomesi Pas Dosé Rosé M. Cl. '14	♥♥ 8
o FCO Malvasia Fiore '22	♥♥ 4
• FCO Schioppettino Romain '19	♥♥ 6
o FCO Friulano Fiore '23	♥♥ 4
• FCO Merlot Romain '17	♥♥ 6
o FCO Pinot Grigio Fiore '22	♥♥ 4
o FCO Ribolla Gialla Fiore '22	♥♥ 4
o FCO Verduzzo Friulano Pra Zenar '22	♥♥ 5
• COF Refosco P. R. Romain '03	♥♥♥ 6
o COF Sauvignon Bosc Romain '96	♥♥♥
o FCO Malvasia '16	♥♥♥
o Ronc '00	♥♥♥ 3
• FCO Pignolo Romain '13	♥♥ 6
o FCO Pinot Grigio Fiore '21	♥♥
• FCO Refosco P. R. Romain '16	♥♥
• FCO Schioppettino Romain '17	♥♥

La Roncaia

fraz. Cergneu
via Verdi, 26
33045 Nimis [UD]
(») +39 0432790280
◈ www.laroncaia.it

CELLAR SALES
PRE-BOOKED VISITS
ANNUAL PRODUCTION 60,000 bottles
HECTARES UNDER VINE 25.00

La Roncaia is based in Cergneu, a small hamlet of Nimis, an area famous for producing Ramandolo and Picolit. This commendable pair of sweet wines further enhances the already rich offerings of the Fantinel family, who purchased La Roncaia in 1998 with the aim of continuing a tradition that began over 30 years ago. Old vineyards cultivated with highly prized native and international grape varieties are entrusted to the oenological expertise of Gabriele Tami. This year, both sweet wines made it to the finals. The Ramandolo '19 features aromas of beeswax, turmeric, candied orange zest, and dried fig, while the Picolit '19 evokes dates and syrupy peaches. Their sweetness on the palate is tempered by a commendable freshness. The Eclisse '22 (sauvignon with a splash of picolit) offers up intense aromas of verbena, menthol, white peach, and green apple; on the palate, it's taut and vibrant.

Il Roncal

fraz. Colle Montebello
via Fornalis, 148
33043 Cividale del Friuli [UD]
(») +39 0432730138
◈ www.ilroncal.it

CELLAR SALES
PRE-BOOKED VISITS
ACCOMMODATION
ANNUAL PRODUCTION 80,000 bottles
HECTARES UNDER VINE 20.00

Il Roncal is a thriving winery managed by Martina Moreale. The name comes from "ronchi," which locally identifies the terraced, hillside plots. It is based in a splendid manor house perched on the hill of Montebello, a name that speaks for itself, foreshadowing the wonders that can be admired from up there. With courage and tenacity, Martina completed and developed the project launched in 1986 by her late husband Roberto Zorzettig. The extensive lineup submitted provided a comprehensive overview of the producer's offerings. The wines from the latest harvest rank among the best vintages, but the most praise went to the Merlot '20. It opens austere on the nose, with notes of tobacco followed by underbrush, leather, star anise, and nutmeg. Its perfectly integrated tannins guide the palate without overpowering, sustaining and amplifying its flavors.

⊙ Eclisse '22	♈♈♈ 5
● COF Picolit '19	♈♈ 6
● Ramandolo '19	♈♈ 5
○ FCO Friulano '22	♈♈ 5
● FCO Merlot Fusco '18	♈♈ 5
● FCO Pinot Grigio '22	♈♈ 5
● FCO Refosco dal P. R. '18	♈♈ 6
Eclisse '21	♈♈♈ 5
Eclisse '19	♈♈♈ 5
● Eclisse '18	♈♈♈ 5
Eclisse '12	♈♈♈ 4*
COF Picolit '16	♈♈ 5
Eclisse '20	♈♈ 5
FCO Pinot Grigio '18	♈♈ 5
Ramandolo '18	♈♈ 5
Ramandolo '17	♈♈ 5

● FCO Merlot '20	♈♈ 5
○ FCO Bianco Ploe di Stelis '22	♈♈ 5
● FCO Cabernet Franc '19	♈♈ 4
○ FCO Malvasia '23	♈♈ 4
○ FCO Pinot Grigio '23	♈♈ 4
● FCO Refosco dal P. R. '20	♈♈ 5
○ FCO Ribolla Gialla '23	♈♈ 4
○ FCO Sauvignon '23	♈♈ 4
○ FCO Friulano '23	♈ 4
○ FCO Bianco Ploe di Stelis '17	♈♈ 4
○ FCO Bianco Ploe di Stelis '15	♈♈ 4
○ FCO Friulano '17	♈♈ 3*
● FCO Pignolo '16	♈♈ 5
○ FCO Pinot Grigio '22	♈♈ 3
○ FCO Pinot Grigio '21	♈♈ 3*
● FCO Schioppettino '20	♈♈ 5

Il Roncat - Giovanni Dri

fraz. Ramandolo
via Pescia, 7
33045 Nimis [UD]
☎ +39 0432790260
⊛ www.drironcat.com

CELLAR SALES
PRE-BOOKED VISITS
ANNUAL PRODUCTION 40,000 bottles
HECTARES UNDER VINE 9.00

When Giovanni Dri founded his winery in 1968, he chose to name it Il Roncat, a local term identifying a steep hill with almost impassable slopes where cultivating vines is so challenging it's called "heroic". Verduzzo giallo, used to produce Ramandolo (the winery's flagship), has always been cultivated on these slopes. For many years now, Giovanni's daughter Stefania has been in charge of winemaking. The Ramandolo '21, with its golden hue, emanates delightful aromas of almond paste, orange zest, dried quince, and beeswax. In the mouth it opens softly sweet, lengthening with balanced acidity toward a finish where toasty notes emerge. The Schioppettino Monte dei Carpini '20 boasts an eclectic aromatic range, with hints of red fruits, both macerated and brandied meeting plum liqueur, rhubarb, and tobacco. On the palate, it's smooth, with well-integrated tannins.

Ronchi di Manzano

via Orsaria, 42
33044 Manzano [UD]
☎ +39 0432740718
⊛ www.ronchidimanzano.com

CELLAR SALES
PRE-BOOKED VISITS
ANNUAL PRODUCTION 150,000 bottles
HECTARES UNDER VINE 60.00

Roberta Borghese, an entrepreneur with an artisan's heart and an innate elegance, oversees every stage of production, from the vineyard to the cellar, with the help of her daughters Lisa and Nicole. This touch of femininity translates into the refinement and grace of their wines. The winery, which balances modernity and tradition, is housed in a rock-hewn building with two underground levels. Here their red wines age in large French oak barrels. This year, only a few wines were submitted, but they were enough to maintain the high praise that has characterized previous vintages. With some of their more important wines missing, the Chardonnay Fatato '22 received the most favorable reviews. It reveals a bouquet marked by pineapple sensations, abate fetel pear, plums, and aromatic herbs. The palate opens with a certain buoyancy, balanced by adequate softness and prolonged by a sustained brackishness.

○ Ramandolo '21	♟♟ 5
○ COF Picolit '20	♟♟ 7
● FCO Refosco dal P. R. '16	♟♟ 4
● FCO Rosso Il Roncat '18	♟♟ 5
● FCO Schioppettino Monte dei Carpini '20	♟♟ 5
○ Sauvignon '22	♟♟ 4
● FCO Merlot '19	♟ 4
○ COF Picolit '19	♟♟ 7
● FCO Pignolo Monte dei Carpini '18	♟♟ 5
● FCO Schioppettino Monte dei Carpini '19	♟♟ 5
○ Ramandolo '19	♟♟ 5
○ Ramandolo Il Roncat '19	♟♟ 5
○ Ramandolo Il Roncat '17	♟♟ 5
○ Ramandolo Uve Decembrine '18	♟♟ 5
○ Sauvignon '21	♟♟ 4

○ FCO Chardonnay Fatato '22	♟♟ 5
○ FCO Friulano Dedicato a Nonno Toni '23	♟♟ 4
● FCO Merlot Ronc di Subule '18	♟♟ 5
○ Ribolla Gialla '23	♟♟ 4
○ COF Ellegri '13	♟♟♟ 3
○ COF Friulano '10	♟♟♟ 3
○ COF Friulano '09	♟♟♟ 3
● COF Merlot Ronc di Subule '99	♟♟♟ 3
● COF Merlot Ronc di Subule '96	♟♟♟ 3
○ COF Rosazzo Bianco Ellégri '11	♟♟♟ 3
○ Rosazzo Bianco '13	♟♟♟ 3
○ FCO Bianco Ellègri '22	♟♟ 4
○ FCO Bianco Ellègri '21	♟♟ 4
○ FCO Bianco Ellègri '20	♟♟ 3
○ FCO Friulano '22	♟♟ 3
● FCO Pignolo '16	♟♟ 3

Ronco Blanchis

via Blanchis, 70
34070 Mossa [GO]
📞 +39 3515665924
🌐 www.roncoblanchis.it

CELLAR SALES
PRE-BOOKED VISITS
ANNUAL PRODUCTION 40,000 bottles
HECTARES UNDER VINE 12.00
VITICULTURE METHOD Certified Organic
SUSTAINABLE WINERY

Lorenzo Palla has been managing the family winery for some time now. Their current success can be attributed to his decision to rely on a highly skilled team. As the name would suggest, Ronco Blanchis produces only whites, which exhibit unique characteristics due to the particular microclimate of the Blanchis hill. In the valley below, day-night temperature swings often cause fog formation, leading to the development of botrytis cinerea. The Chardonnay '22 offers up a noble, multifaceted aromatic profile. Initially, it lingers on delicate mandarin notes, followed by accents of nectarine, mint, orange zest, yellow flowers, and alpine balsams. On the palate, it's fresh and mineral, with great symmetry and appeal. The Pinot Grigio '23 reveals a delicate smoky note, followed by floral hints of linden and broom, lemon cream, candied fruit, mandarin, and citron. The palate proves taut, silky, compact, and rich with fruity echoes.

★★Ronco dei Tassi

loc. Montona, 19
34071 Cormòns [GO]
📞 +39 048160155
🌐 www.roncodeitassi.it

CELLAR SALES
PRE-BOOKED VISITS
ANNUAL PRODUCTION 110,000 bottles
HECTARES UNDER VINE 18.00

Fabio Coser, together with his wife Daniela, founded Ronco dei Tassi in 1989 after purchasing a farm on the edge of a charming natural park in Cormòns, Montona, on the slope of Monte Quarin (facing Slovenia). The name was inspired by the badger colonies inhabiting the woods surrounding the vineyards. The new generation, Matteo and Enrico, has been an integral part of the winery for some time now. The Malvasia '23 opens on a pronounced floral tone of mimosa, broom, and sunflower, followed by hints of yellow peach and candied citrus, then whiffs of marjoram and mint. On the palate, it's creamy yet fresh and supple. The Sauvignon '23 conveys aromas of mint and fennel, while on the palate, it proves linear and fragrant. The Collio Bianco Fosarin '22, a magical blend of pinot bianco, tocai friulano, and malvasia istriana, reveals a complex nose with refined citrus and tropical notes, coming through juicy and rich on the palate.

Collio Chardonnay '22	♟♟ 5
Collio Pinot Grigio '23	♟♟ 4
Collio Friulano '23	♟♟ 4
Collio Sauvignon '23	♟♟ 4
Collio '13	♟♟♟ 3*
Collio '12	♟♟♟ 3*
Collio Bianco Blanc di Blanchis Ris. '17	♟♟♟ 5
Collio Chardonnay '17	♟♟♟ 3*
Collio Bianco Blanc di Blanchis Ris. '19	♟♟ 5
Collio Chardonnay '21	♟♟ 5
Collio Friulano '22	♟♟ 4
Collio Friulano '21	♟♟ 4
Collio Friulano '20	♟♟ 4
Collio Pinot Grigio '21	♟♟ 4
Collio Sauvignon '22	♟♟ 4
Collio Sauvignon '21	♟♟ 4

○ Collio Bianco Fosarin '22	♟♟♟ 5
○ Collio Malvasia '23	♟♟ 4
○ Collio Sauvignon '23	♟♟ 4
○ Collio Friulano '23	♟♟ 4
○ Collio Picolit '19	♟♟ 6
○ Collio Pinot Grigio '23	♟♟ 4
● Collio Rosso Cjarandon Ris. '19	♟♟ 5
○ Ribolla Gialla '23	♟♟ 4
○ Collio Bianco Fosarin '21	♟♟♟ 5
○ Collio Bianco Fosarin '19	♟♟♟ 4*
○ Collio Bianco Fosarin '18	♟♟♟ 3*
○ Collio Bianco Fosarin '17	♟♟♟ 3*
○ Collio Bianco Fosarin '16	♟♟♟ 3*
○ Collio Bianco Fosarin '15	♟♟♟ 3*
○ Collio Malvasia '21	♟♟♟ 3*
○ Collio Malvasia '15	♟♟♟ 3*

Ronco Margherita

via XX Settembre, 106a
33094 Pinzano al Tagliamento [PN]
📞 +39 0432950845
🌐 www.roncomargherita.it

CELLAR SALES
PRE-BOOKED VISITS
ACCOMMODATION
ANNUAL PRODUCTION 200,000 bottles
HECTARES UNDER VINE 36.00
VITICULTURE METHOD Certified Organic
SUSTAINABLE WINERY

Alessandro Bellio founded Ronco Margherita in 2009, driven by a great passion for wine and channeling his extensive experience in the field. In 2015, the operational headquarters were finally established in Pinzano al Tagliamento, an area renowned for its rare indigenous varieties, to which Bellio's paid special attention. In 2019, he incorporated the vineyards of the Rieppi estate in Albana di Prepotto, in the Colli Orientali. Tazzelenghe is a very rare native grape, with a name that clearly reflects its character and powerful tannins (it literally means "tongue-cutter" in the local dialect). This makes it all the more satisfying when one finds a wine with great stylistic depth. The Tazzelenghe Rieppi '20 offers up aromas of blackberry, blueberry, morello cherry jam, sun-dried tomatoes, licorice, and graphite; on the palate, it expresses its full strength in a blend of compelling, gratifying sensations.

Ronco Scagnèt

loc. Cime di Dolegna, 7
34070 Dolegna del Collio [GO]
📞 +39 3298536872
🌐 www.roncoscagnet.it

PRE-BOOKED VISITS
ANNUAL PRODUCTION 30,000 bottles
HECTARES UNDER VINE 12.00

Ronco Scagnet stands atop a hill overlooking Lonzano, near Dolegna del Collio. Owner Valter Cozzarolo and his son Dimitri form a duo of true wine artisans. The unique subsoil, known locally as ponca, composed of marl and sandstone, combined with the area's pedoclimatic conditions, allows for the production of highly structured wines, especially whites, with intense, fruity, and varietal aromas. While the white wines deserve praise, this year, it was the Cabernet Franc '22 that led an impressive lineup. The nose features the grape's trademark vegetal traits, freshly cut grass, enriched by plum jam, wilted red rose, brandied cherries, tobacco, juniper berries, and star anise. On the palate, it's smooth, with finely crafted tannins and an endless persistence. The Malvasia Raggio di Sole '21 also impressed with its complex aromas and balanced palate.

● FCO Tazzelenghe Rieppi '20	♟♟ 5
○ FCO Friulano Rieppi '22	♟♟ 3
○ FCO Ribolla Gialla Rieppi '22	♟♟ 3
● FCO Schioppettino di Prepotto Rieppi '20	♟♟ 5
● Parvus Piculit Neri '20	♟♟ 5
● FCO Refosco dal P. R. Rieppi '20	♟ 4
○ Ribolla Gialla Brut	♟ 3
○ FCO Chardonnay '21	♟♟ 3
● FCO Refosco P. R. Rieppi '20	♟♟ 3
● FCO Schioppettino di Prepotto Rieppi '19	♟♟ 5
● Ovalis '20	♟♟ 4
● Ovalis '19	♟♟ 4
● Ovalis '18	♟♟ 4
● Parvus Piculit Neri '19	♟♟ 4
○ Tiliae '19	♟♟ 4
○ Tiliae '18	♟♟ 4

● Collio Cabernet Franc '22	♟♟
○ Collio Friulano '23	♟♟
○ Collio Pinot Grigio '23	♟♟
○ Collio Ribolla Gialla '23	♟♟
○ Collio Sauvignon '22	♟♟
○ Raggio di Sole Malvasia '21	♟♟
● Collio Merlot '22	♟
○ Collio Bianco Folie Blanc '13	♟♟
○ Collio Friulano '22	♟♟
○ Collio Friulano '21	♟♟
● Collio Merlot '19	♟♟
○ Collio Pinot Grigio '22	♟♟
○ Collio Pinot Grigio '22	♟♟
○ Collio Ribolla Gialla '22	♟♟
● Collio Rosso Vignis Rossis '15	♟♟
○ Raggio di Sole Malvasia '20	♟♟

★Russiz Superiore
via Russiz, 7
34070 Capriva del Friuli [GO]
☎ +39 048180328
⊕ www.marcofelluga.it

CELLAR SALES
PRE-BOOKED VISITS
ACCOMMODATION
ANNUAL PRODUCTION 180,000 bottles
HECTARES UNDER VINE 50.00
SUSTAINABLE WINERY

Marco Felluga, who passed away at the age of 96, was a true pioneer of quality viticulture in the region. In 1966, he created Russiz Superiore, which immediately became a benchmark brand for Collio. Since 2021, after the premature death of Marco's son Roberto, the business has been led by the very young Ilaria Felluga, who continues to maintain her role even now that the producer has been absorbed into the Tommasi group. The Pinot Bianco '23 follows in the footsteps of the best vintages, displaying elegant aromas of budding flowers, white peach, and kaiser pear, with flashes of spice and a slight toastiness; on the palate, it's fragrant and vigorous. The Bianco Col Disôre '21, a blend of pinot bianco, tocai friulano, sauvignon, and ribolla gialla, releases delightful floral notes of acacia and magnolia, accompanied by mandarin, bergamot, tropical fruits, and eucalyptus honey. The palate proves balanced, symmetrical, progressive, and persistent.

○ Collio Bianco Col Disôre '21	♛♛ 5
○ Collio Pinot Bianco '23	♛♛ 5
● Collio Cabernet Franc '22	♛♛ 5
○ Collio Ribolla Gialla '23	♛♛ 5
● Collio Rosso Riserva degli Orzoni '18	♛♛ 6
● Collio Sauvignon '23	♛♛ 5
○ Collio Bianco Col Disôre '20	♛♛♛ 5
○ Collio Bianco Col Disôre '18	♛♛♛ 6
○ Collio Friulano '16	♛♛♛ 4*
○ Collio Friulano '15	♛♛♛ 4*
○ Collio Friulano '14	♛♛♛ 4*
○ Collio Pinot Bianco '18	♛♛♛ 4*
○ Collio Pinot Grigio '11	♛♛♛ 4*
○ Collio Sauvignon Ris. '17	♛♛♛ 5
○ Collio Sauvignon Ris. '16	♛♛♛ 5
○ Collio Sauvignon Ris. '13	♛♛♛ 5

Sant'Elena
via Gasparini, 1
34072 Gradisca d'Isonzo [GO]
☎ +39 048192388
⊕ www.sant-elena.com

CELLAR SALES
PRE-BOOKED VISITS
ANNUAL PRODUCTION 100,000 bottles
HECTARES UNDER VINE 33.00
VITICULTURE METHOD Certified Organic

Dominic Nocerino, a well-known importer of Italian wines overseas, acquired this historic winery in 1977. Originally founded in the 19th century by the Klodic family, the estate experienced various changes of ownership, leading to fluctuating periods of fame and obscurity. It was Cosimo Nocerino who revitalized the prestigious brand starting in 2015, enlisting Vincenzo Mercurio, who he made responsible for agronomic and winemaking practices, with a focus on organic certification. The entire range delivered a truly superb performance, with whites that express both fragrance and substance and reds that are powerful yet well-calibrated. The Pinot Grigio Rive Alte '22 offers up aromas of white flowers, abate pear, citron, and lemon wafer under a veil of delicate toast and dried fruit, while the palate proves sapid and persistent. Among the reds, the Merlot '18 stood out for its complexity on the nose, with notes of black pepper followed by anise, licorice, incense, and eucalyptus—but it was its pleasing palate that most impressed.

● Friuli Isonzo Merlot '18	♛♛ 5
○ Friuli Isonzo Pinot Grigio Rive Alte '22	♛♛ 4
● Friuli Isonzo Cabernet Franc '18	♛♛ 4
○ Friuli Isonzo Chardonnay Rive Alte '22	♛♛ 4
○ Friuli Isonzo Friulano Rive Alte '22	♛♛ 4
● Friuli Isonzo Pignolo '18	♛♛ 7
○ Friuli Isonzo Sauvignon Rive Alte '22	♛♛ 4
● Quantum Pignolo '18	♛♛ 7
● Ròs di Rôl Merlot '17	♛♛ 5
● Tato '17	♛♛ 5
● Friuli Isonzo Cabernet Sauvignon '18	♛ 4
● Cabernet Sauvignon '08	♛♛ 3*
● Friuli Isonzo Pignolo Quantum '10	♛♛ 7
● Merlot Ròs di Rôl '09	♛♛ 6
● Ròs di Rôl Merlot '16	♛♛ 5

Marco Sara

fraz. Savorgnano del Torre
via dei Monti, 3a
33040 Povoletto [UD]
☎ +39 0432666066
🖰 www.marcosara.com

CELLAR SALES
PRE-BOOKED VISITS
ANNUAL PRODUCTION 25,000 bottles
HECTARES UNDER VINE 8.00
VITICULTURE METHOD Certified Organic

Marco Sara's winery is located in Savorgnano del Torre, in the westernmost and coolest part of the Friuli Colli Orientali appellation. The vineyards, spread out across different areas, enable greater expressive richness and a marked territorial identity. Since 2000, Marco, along with his wife Sandra, has been managing this small yet thriving producer, long certified organic across its entire range of wines. The Bianco Monte della Guardia '21 is a blend of tocai friulano and verduzzo friulano (you can't get more Friulian than this!) while the Bianco Erba Alta '22 is a monovarietal tocai friulano, demonstrating that the grape is the region's most representative. However, it's the Picolit '22 that takes the spotlight, once again earning a place in our final tastings. On the nose, it conjures up apple juice, crème brûlée, ginger, dried figs, and beeswax, while the palate proves sweet yet balanced by lively freshness.

○ COF Picolit '22	▼▼ 7
○ FCO Bianco Erba Alta '22	▼▼ 5
○ FCO Bianco Monte della Guardia '21	▼▼ 6
○ FCO Friulano '23	▼▼ 4
● FCO Schioppettino '22	▼▼ 5
○ COF Picolit '21	▽▽ 7
○ COF Picolit '20	▽▽ 6
○ COF Picolit '18	▽▽ 6
○ COF Picolit '17	▽▽ 6
○ COF Picolit Mufis '17	▽▽ 6
○ FCO Bianco Erba Alta '21	▽▽ 5
○ FCO Bianco Monte della Guardia '20	▽▽ 6
○ FCO Bianco Monte della Guardia '19	▽▽ 6
○ FCO Friulano '22	▽▽ 4
○ FCO Friulano '21	▽▽ 4
● FCO Schioppettino '21	▽▽ 5

Sara & Sara

fraz. Savorgnano del Torre
via dei Monti, 5
33040 Povoletto [UD]
☎ +39 3393859042
🖰 www.saraesara.com

CELLAR SALES
PRE-BOOKED VISITS
ACCOMMODATION
ANNUAL PRODUCTION 30,000 bottles
HECTARES UNDER VINE 8.00
VITICULTURE METHOD Certified Organic
SUSTAINABLE WINERY

Alessandro and Manuele Sara, two brothers who took over the family winery at a young age, faced the challenge of honoring their father Giuliano's legacy. Giuliano had always been devoted to preserving the winemaking traditions of Savorgnano del Torre, especially those related to sweet wines. Not only did the brothers succeed in maintaining these traditions, but they also revived and enhanced the production of picolit and verduzzo friulano. Il Picolit '21 pours a beautiful antique gold hue, delighting the nose with intense aromas of custard, dates, white chocolate, dried apricot, and beeswax. On the palate, it caresses with its sweetness, all well-calibrated by balsamic acidity. We also appreciated the Friulano '21, which evokes yellow peach sensations, alongside medlar, dried white flowers, mountain hay, and almond husk. On the palate, it expresses its typicity with a slender yet flavorful and engaging profile.

○ COF Picolit '21	▼▼ 6
○ FCO Friulano '21	▼▼ 4
● FCO Refosco P.R. '21	▼▼ 5
○ Ribolla Gialla '23	▼▼ 4
○ COF Verduzzo Friulano Crei '10	▽▽▽ 5
○ COF Picolit '18	▽▽ 6
○ COF Picolit '15	▽▽ 6
○ COF Picolit '13	▽▽ 6
○ COF Picolit '12	▽▽ 6
○ FCO Friulano '20	▽▽ 4
○ FCO Friulano '18	▽▽ 4
○ FCO Friulano '17	▽▽ 6
● FCO Refosco P.R. '19	▽▽ 4
● FCO Refosco P.R. '18	▽▽ 4
○ FCO Verduzzo Friulano Crei '13	▽▽ 5
○ FCO Verduzzo Friulano Crei '12	▽▽ 5

La Sclusa

loc. Spessa
via Strada di Sant'Anna, 7/2
33043 Cividale del Friuli [UD]
+39 0432716259
www.lasclusa.it

CELLAR SALES
PRE-BOOKED VISITS
ACCOMMODATION
ANNUAL PRODUCTION 160,000 bottles
HECTARES UNDER VINE 40.00

Located south of Cividale del Friuli, the town of Spessa is synonymous with vineyards and wine. The Zorzettig family has been operating here for generations. Today it's Germano, Maurizio, and Luciano who manage the winery founded in 1971 by their father Gino. The production philosophy is deeply rooted in tradition, following the rhythms of nature and striving to achieve the best the land can offer without excess or force. The strong performance put in by their entire range reinforces the positive scores given in previous years, and marks another step towards excellence. The Schioppettino '22 placed among the best in its category, earning a spot in the finals. The nose releases refined varietal notes of spices like black pepper, juniper, and cloves, followed by hints of anise, iris, eucalyptus, dried plum, and underbrush. Its tannic structure remains vibrant but is well-balanced by soft components.

● FCO Schioppettino '22	TT 3*
○ COF Picolit '18	TT 6
○ FCO Friulano 12 Viti '23	TT 4
● FCO Refosco dal P. R. '22	TT 3
○ FCO Ribolla Gialla '23	TT 3
● FCO Rosso del Torrione '20	TT 5
○ FCO Sauvignon '23	TT 3
● Friuli Malvasia '23	TT 3
○ Friuli Ribolla Gialla Brut	T 3
○ FCO Friulano '22	YY 3
○ FCO Friulano 12 Viti '21	YY 4
○ FCO Friulano 12 Viti '19	YY 4
● FCO Refosco dal P. R. '21	YY 3
○ FCO Sauvignon '22	YY 3
● FCO Schioppettino '21	YY 3
● Friuli Malvasia '22	YY 3

Marco Scolaris

via Boschetto, 4
34070 San Lorenzo Isontino [GO]
+39 0481809920
www.scolaris.it

CELLAR SALES
PRE-BOOKED VISITS
ANNUAL PRODUCTION 1,300,000 bottles
HECTARES UNDER VINE 29.00
SUSTAINABLE WINERY

Founded in 1924 by Giovanni Scolaris, this winery is now run by the fourth generation of family, Gianmarco, who ensures continuity with the past. Gianmarco's father Marco, who passed away a few years ago, is credited with transforming the estate into a leader in the territory, while continuously striving for a balance between human effort and nature. With a century of activity behind it, Scolaris is undoubtedly one of the Collio and Friuli Isonzo appellations' historic wineries. Fragrance is a common denominator across all the wines, but in terms of appeal, the Pinot Grigio '23 stood out for going the extra mile. The nose conveys a commendable bouquet dominated by apricot, nectarine, orange, rosehip, incense, pink pepper, and citrus honey. Initially, the palate is fresh, but it progressively invigorates with sapid notes and mineral nuances.

○ Collio Pinot Grigio '23	TT 5
● Collio Cabernet Sauvignon '21	TT 5
○ Collio Friulano '23	TT 5
○ Collio Ribolla Gialla '23	TT 5
○ Collio Sauvignon '23	TT 5
● Schioppettino '23	TT 3
● Collio Cabernet Franc '22	YY 5
○ Collio Chardonnay '22	YY 3
○ Collio Friulano '21	YY 5
● Collio Merlot '22	YY 5
○ Collio Pinot Grigio '22	YY 5
○ Collio Ribolla Gialla '22	YY 5
○ Collio Sauvignon '22	YY 5
○ Friuli Pinot Grigio Blush '22	YY 2*
● Schioppettino '22	YY 3

Roberto Scubla

fraz. Ipplis
via Rocca Bernarda, 22
33040 Premariacco [UD]
☎ +39 0432716258
✉ www.scubla.com

CELLAR SALES
PRE-BOOKED VISITS
ACCOMMODATION
ANNUAL PRODUCTION 50,000 bottles
HECTARES UNDER VINE 12.00

Roberto Scubla established his beautiful winery on a foothill of Rocca Bernarda, a noteworthy historical site in the Colli Orientali del Friuli. With a highly skilled technical team behind him, he has made his brand one of the most prominent and reliable in the region. Their flagships are the Verduzzo Friulano Passito Cràtis and the Pomèdes, both of which have received several awards and are widely recognized as two of Italy's best whites. This year, their three most representative wines distinguished themselves and advanced to the finals. In the Verduzzo Friulano Passito Cràtis '21, intriguing scents of incense, English candy, cinnamon, and peach tea emerge. The palate is harmonious and delightful. The Pinot Bianco '23 relies on the elegance of its floral notes, while the Pomèdes '22 (a blend of pinot bianco, tocai friulano, and riesling renano) expresses itself in a powerful, never-ending crescendo.

○ FCO Bianco Pomèdes '22	♟♟ 5
○ FCO Pinot Bianco '23	♟♟ 4
○ FCO Verduzzo Friulano Passito Cràtis '21	♟♟ 6
● FCO Cabernet Sauvignon '22	♟♟ 4
○ FCO Friulano '23	♟♟ 4
○ FCO Malvasia Lo Speziale '23	♟♟ 4
● FCO Merlot '22	♟♟ 4
● FCO Merlot Sel. '20	♟♟ 6
○ FCO Pinot Bianco Vignis '23	♟♟ 4
● FCO Refosco dal P.R. '21	♟♟ 5
○ FCO Sauvignon '23	♟♟ 4
○ COF Verduzzo Friulano Passito Cràtis '09	♟♟♟ 5
○ FCO Bianco Pomèdes '21	♟♟♟ 5
○ FCO Bianco Pomèdes '20	♟♟♟ 5

Ferruccio Sgubin

via Mernico, 8
34070 Dolegna del Collio [GO]
☎ +39 048160452
✉ www.ferrucciosgubin.it

CELLAR SALES
PRE-BOOKED VISITS
ANNUAL PRODUCTION 100,000 bottles
HECTARES UNDER VINE 20.00

Ferruccio Sgubin founded his winery in 1960, at a time when many of the region's family-run farms began specializing in viticulture. Despite his age, Ferruccio remains actively involved, though he has passed management on to his son Gianni, who has made bold and successful decisions in recent years. Now, the new generation, Marco and Margherita, are preparing to take over. Due to the challenging 2023 harvest, the Petruss line was not produced, which allowed the traditional line to shine. The Pinot Bianco '23 showcases refined vegetal scents of aromatic herbs with delicate mint accents. The Sauvignon '23 proves highly varietal, with fragrant notes of lychee meeting green apple. The Collio Bianco Mirnik '22 (tocai friulano, pinot bianco, and sauvignon) is delicious and energetic, characterized by aromas of lemon wafer, honey, and turmeric.

○ Collio Bianco Mirnik '22	♟♟ 5
○ Collio Pinot Bianco '23	♟♟ 4
○ Collio Sauvignon '23	♟♟ 4
○ Collio Friulano '23	♟♟ 3
○ Collio Pinot Grigio '23	♟♟ 3
○ Collio Ribolla Gialla '23	♟♟ 3
○ Collio Bianco Mirnik '20	♟♟♟ 5
○ Collio Bianco Mirnik '21	♟♟ 5
○ Collio Friulano '21	♟♟ 3*
○ Collio Friulano Petruss '22	♟♟ 5
○ Collio Friulano Petruss '21	♟♟ 5
○ Collio Friulano Petruss '20	♟♟ 5
○ Collio Friulano Petruss '19	♟♟ 5
○ Collio Pinot Bianco '22	♟♟ 4
○ Collio Pinot Bianco '20	♟♟ 3*
● Collio Rosso Mirnik '19	♟♟ 5

Simon di Brazzan

fraz. Brazzano
via San Rocco, 17
34070 Cormòns [GO]
(☎) +39 048161182
@ www.simondibrazzan.com

CELLAR SALES
PRE-BOOKED VISITS
ANNUAL PRODUCTION 70,000 bottles
HECTARES UNDER VINE 13.00
VITICULTURE METHOD Certified Biodynamic

Daniele Drius is the owner and jack-of-all-trades at Simon di Brazzan, a winery created by his grandfather Enrico Veliscig, a tenacious and vigorous man who worked in the vineyard until he passed away at 102. Daniele, a skilled oenologist and staunch supporter of biodynamic viticulture, has embraced its principles by abandoning chemical treatments and introducing only natural practices for both soil treatment and vegetation. The Pinot Grigio Tradiziòn '22 repeated the performance of previous vintages, making its timely appearance in our finals. It stands out for its intriguing copper color, the prelude to a particularly original aromatic spectrum, with nuances of cherry jam giving way to blood orange, raspberry syrup, and hibiscus, complemented by a very harmonious palate. The Friulano Tradiziòn '19 also deserves praise, with its aromas of canned peach, orange zest, and custard.

○ Friuli Friulano Tradiziòn '19	♟♟ 4
○ Friuli Pinot Grigio Tradiziòn '22	♟♟ 5
○ Friuli Friulano Blanc di Simon '23	♟♟ 4
● Friuli Merlot '21	♟♟ 4
○ Friuli Pinot Grigio '23	♟♟ 4
○ Malvasia '23	♟♟ 4
○ Sauvignon '23	♟♟ 4
○ Friuli Friulano Blanc di Simon '19	♟♟ 3*
○ Friuli Pinot Grigio Tradiziòn '21	♟♟ 5
○ Friuli Pinot Grigio Tradiziòn '20	♟♟ 5
○ Friuli Pinot Grigio Tradiziòn '19	♟♟ 5
○ Malvasia '19	♟♟ 3*
○ Ri-nè Blanc '22	♟♟ 4
○ Ri.nè Blanc '19	♟♟ 3*
○ Sauvignon '21	♟♟ 3*
○ Sauvignon '18	♟♟ 3*

Sirch

via Fornalis, 277/1
33043 Cividale del Friuli [UD]
(☎) +39 0432709835
@ www.sirchwine.com

CELLAR SALES
PRE-BOOKED VISITS
ANNUAL PRODUCTION 600,000 bottles
HECTARES UNDER VINE 100.00

Luca Sirch's winery has experienced exponential growth in recent years, expanding significantly across the Friulian hills. This ambitious project was made possible by the interest of Feudi di San Gregorio, a giant in the export of Italian wine overseas, with whom Luca's brother Pierpaolo has collaborated for many years. The winery's philosophy aims for subtle complexity, producing increasingly elegant wines rich in nuance. The Pinot Grigio Ramato '23 emerged as the best of the lot. It exudes scents of lily of the valley, rose petals, wild strawberries, and pomegranate, while the palate is flavorful, harmonious, dynamic, and persistent. The Schioppettino di Prepotto '22 has a dark but pleasant aroma, reminiscent of plum jam, cinchona, rhubarb, licorice root, and coffee, with a pervasive and balanced palate. The other wines, all marked by particular freshness and immediacy in drinking, faithfully respect their varietal characteristics.

⊙ FCO Pinot Grigio Ramato '23	♟♟ 3*
○ FCO Chardonnay '23	♟♟ 3
○ FCO Friulano '23	♟♟ 3
○ FCO Pinot Grigio '23	♟♟ 3
○ FCO Sauvignon '23	♟♟ 3
● FCO Schioppettino di Prepotto '22	♟♟ 6
● FCO Refosco dal P. R. '22	♟ 2
○ FCO Ribolla Gialla '23	♟ 3
○ COF Friulano '07	♟♟♟ 2*
○ FCO Bianco Cladrecis '15	♟♟ 3*
○ FCO Chardonnay '22	♟♟ 3
○ FCO Chardonnay Cladrecis '19	♟♟ 5
○ FCO Friulano '22	♟♟ 3
○ FCO Pinot Grigio '22	♟♟ 3
⊙ FCO Pinot Grigio Ramato '22	♟♟ 3
○ FCO Ribolla Gialla '22	♟♟ 3

★Skerk

fraz. San Pelagio
loc. Prepotto, 20
34011 Duino Aurisina [TS]
(+39 040200156
 www.skerk.com

CELLAR SALES
PRE-BOOKED VISITS
RESTAURANT SERVICE
ANNUAL PRODUCTION 22,000 bottles
HECTARES UNDER VINE 7.00
VITICULTURE METHOD Certified Organic

Sandi Skerk's well-established winery is based in Trieste's Karst region—scattered vineyards standing out on sunny bends facing the sea amidst dense vegetation. Here, everything is done by hand. The cultivable spaces are limited, but the scarce red soil is rich in limestone and iron. Sandi knows how to exploit these characteristics, producing wines with marked personality, rich in flavor, and aromatic nuances, thanks in part to the beneficial effects of the Bora winds and sea breezes. The Ograde '21 sports an original amber color with rosy peach-skin highlights. Aromatically, it moves on refined scents of mandarin peel, dried apricot, peach juice, and rose water. On the palate, it's juicy, with persistent fruity flavors. The Vitovska '21 intersperses fruit and spicy notes with brackish wafts, both on the nose and palate. The Malvasia '21 proves stunning, releasing balsamic, minty, and resinous notes of rare elegance.

Edi Skok

loc. Giasbana, 15
34070 San Floriano del Collio [GO]
(+39 3408034045
 www.skok.it

CELLAR SALES
PRE-BOOKED VISITS
ANNUAL PRODUCTION 38,000 bottles
HECTARES UNDER VINE 11.00

Edi and Orietta Skok, pure-bred winemakers, are proud of their family's farming origins. While deeply attached to local traditions, they have always been open to innovation. Long maceration times, a common practice in the area, have been abandoned in favor of more modern techniques, thus preserving the wines' freshness. The pair have been operating for several years in a new, modern, well-equipped cellar that integrates perfectly with the environment. The Pe Ar due2, a blend of chardonnay, pinot grigio, and sauvignon, repeated its success and once again reached the finals. It opens on an alluring profile of honey and ginger, followed by nuances of nectarine, golden apple, rose water, myrtle, and almond paste. On the palate, it's velvety, soft, and perfectly balanced. The Merlot '21 and all the wines from the latest harvest are also excellent, marked by their varietal adherence, fragrance, suppleness, and pleasant drinkability.

○ Malvasia '21	♟♟ 6
○ Ograde '21	♟♟ 6
○ Vitovska '21	♟♟ 6
● Terrano '21	♟♟ 6
○ Carso Malvasia '08	♟♟♟ 4
○ Malvasia '20	♟♟♟ 5
○ Malvasia '13	♟♟♟ 5
○ Ograde '17	♟♟♟ 5
○ Ograde '16	♟♟♟ 5
○ Ograde '15	♟♟♟ 5
○ Ograde '12	♟♟♟ 5
○ Ograde '11	♟♟♟ 5
○ Ograde '10	♟♟♟ 4
○ Ograde '09	♟♟♟ 4*

○ Pe Ar Due2	♟♟ 5
○ Collio Chardonnay '23	♟♟ 3
○ Collio Friulano '23	♟♟ 3
● Collio Merlot '21	♟♟ 4
○ Collio Pinot Grigio '23	♟♟ 3
○ Collio Sauvignon '23	♟♟ 3
○ Collio Bianco Pe Ar '20	♟♟ 5
○ Collio Bianco Pe Ar '19	♟♟ 3*
○ Collio Bianco Pe Ar '16	♟♟ 3*
○ Collio Bianco Pe Ar '15	♟♟ 3*
○ Collio Chardonnay '20	♟♟ 2*
○ Collio Friulano Zabura '22	♟♟ 4
● Collio Merlot Villa Jasbinae '16	♟♟ 3*
● Collio Merlot Villa Jasbinae '09	♟♟ 3*
○ Collio Sauvignon '19	♟♟ 3*
○ Pe Ar	♟♟ 5

Specogna

via Rocca Bernarda, 4
33040 Corno di Rosazzo [UD]
📞 +39 0432755840
🌐 www.specogna.it

CELLAR SALES
PRE-BOOKED VISITS
ANNUAL PRODUCTION 120,000 bottles
HECTARES UNDER VINE 29.00
VITICULTURE METHOD Certified Organic
SUSTAINABLE WINERY

Michele and Cristian, who are now leading the winery founded by their grandfather Leonardo, have demonstrated great winemaking and communicative skills, bringing the Specogna brand to the forefront of renowned international markets and affirming a well-established standard of quality. By making the most of Rocca Bernarda's unique features, they produce increasingly intriguing wines characterized by fragrance and linearity, with a line of Riserva wines enhancing the prestige of their range. Identità '22 is the name chosen for the wine that best identifies the region's potential, being made exclusively from native grapes. The result is a harmonious and delightful blend of aromas, conjuring up exquisite balsams, ginger, white pepper, cream biscuits, and honey. On the palate, it's also complex, sapid, full-bodied, and rich in personality. We also appreciated the excellent Sauvignon Duality '22, which effuses notes of tropical fruit, citrus marmalade, and lemon balm, enhanced by a refreshing waft of alpine herbs.

Wine	Rating
○ FCO Bianco Identità '22	♀♀ 7
● FCO Rosso Oltre '20	♀♀ 7
○ FCO Sauvignon Duality '22	♀♀ 7
○ FCO Malvasia '23	♀♀ 3
○ FCO Pinot Grigio '23	♀♀ 3
○ FCO Pinot Grigio Ramato Ris. '21	♀♀ 7
○ FCO Sauvignon '23	♀♀ 3
○ FCO Bianco Identità '15	♀♀♀ 7
○ FCO Bianco Identità '21	♀♀ 7
○ FCO Bianco Identità '20	♀♀ 6
○ FCO Bianco Identità '19	♀♀ 6
○ FCO Friulano '22	♀♀ 3*
○ FCO Malvasia Ris. '17	♀♀ 8
● FCO Pignolo '16	♀♀ 6
● FCO Pignolo '14	♀♀ 6
● FCO Rosso Oltre '18	♀♀ 6

Tenuta Stella

loc. Scriò
via Sdencina, I
34070 Dolegna del Collio [GO]
📞 +39 3387875175
🌐 www.tenutastellacollio.it

CELLAR SALES
PRE-BOOKED VISITS
ANNUAL PRODUCTION 50,000 bottles
HECTARES UNDER VINE 13.00
VITICULTURE METHOD Certified Organic
SUSTAINABLE WINERY

Tenuta Stella has become one of the region's most representative wineries, particularly in the Dolegna del Collio area, where the steep slopes ensure ideal exposure to sunlight. The vineyards unfold across soils composed of marine marl and sandstone, locally known as "ponca". Founded in 2010 by Sergio Stevanato, the estate is now managed by Erika Barbieri and Alberto Faggiani, a highly skilled technical team. The Ribolla Gialla Ris. '21, the result of lengthy maceration on the skins, pours an amber hue, revealing an expansive range of aromas with waves of malt followed by honey, dried fruit, saffron, and dried yellow flowers. The palate makes a strong impact, opening fresh and lengthening towards a mineral finish. The Pinot Nero '21, appearing for the first time in our finals, exudes pleasant aromas of nutmeg and raspberry juice, while the palate proves smooth, with polished tannins.

Wine	Rating
● Collio Pinot Nero '21	♀♀ 6
○ Collio Ribolla Gialla Ris. '21	♀♀ 8
○ Collio Friulano '22	♀♀ 5
○ Collio Malvasia '22	♀♀ 5
○ Collio Ribolla Gialla '22	♀♀ 5
● Sdencina Rosso '21	♀♀ 5
○ Collio Friulano '19	♀♀♀ 4*
○ Collio Friulano '18	♀♀♀ 4*
○ Collio Ribolla Gialla Ris. '19	♀♀♀ 6
○ Collio Friulano '21	♀♀ 5
○ Collio Friulano '20	♀♀ 4
○ Collio Friulano '17	♀♀ 4
○ Collio Malvasia '21	♀♀ 5
○ Collio Malvasia '20	♀♀ 5
○ Collio Ribolla Gialla Ris. '20	♀♀ 8
○ Collio Ribolla Gialla Ris. '18	♀♀ 6

Stocco

via Casali Stocco, 12
33050 Bicinicco [UD]
(+39 0432934906
www.vinistocco.it

Sturm

loc. Zegla, 1
34071 Cormòns [GO]
(+39 048160720
www.sturm.it

CELLAR SALES
PRE-BOOKED VISITS
RESTAURANT SERVICE
ANNUAL PRODUCTION 250,000 bottles
HECTARES UNDER VINE 49.00

CELLAR SALES
PRE-BOOKED VISITS
ANNUAL PRODUCTION 150,000 bottles
HECTARES UNDER VINE 18.30
VITICULTURE METHOD Certified Organic
SUSTAINABLE WINERY

In the early part of the 20th century, the Stocco family settled in the vast Friulian plains near Bicinicco and dedicated themselves to agriculture in what later became known as Casali Stocco. In the 1960s, the business took a significant turn, shifting exclusively to winemaking. The patriarch, Francesco, has passed the torch to the fourth generation, with Andrea, Daniela, and Paola now upholding the family brand, offering a diverse range of high-quality wines at reasonable prices. The Pinot Bianco Calis '23 unveils pleasant floral notes of linden, accompanied by white chocolate and almond pastry; on the palate, it's soft and smooth. The Malvasia Dai Claps '23 conjures up ripe fruit and medicinal herbs, especially bay leaf, while on the palate, it proves pervasive and flavorful. The Pinot Grigio Ramato Settantacinque '23 opts for aromas of lemon cream and canned peach; the palate is soft and balanced. The Ribolla Gialla Albero del Noce '23 stands out for its commendable freshness on the palate.

Founded in 1850, the Sturm family's winery has carved out a prominent role in the regional winemaking scene thanks to Oscar Sturm, who achieved outstanding results. While Oscar remains active, particularly among the vines, his sons Denis and Patrick now lead the estate. They embrace the philosophy that "making organic wines means taking a step forward by looking back," adopting a minimalist approach. So, for example, copper and sulfur are used instead of herbicides. The Malvasia '23 emits pleasant fragrances of honeysuckle, citron, white peach, oregano, and bay leaf; on the palate, it's rich in flavor, finishing with distinct balsamic echoes. Aromatically, the Chardonnay Andritz '23 opens with rare elegance—a delicate yet refined base of lavender, yeasts, and pastry, revealing delightful hints of propolis, dried fruit, and almond husk, before a soft, balanced palate. The Collio Bianco Andritz Ris. '21, a blend of sauvignon and tocai friulano, is right up there.

● Cabernet Franc Lis Arbis '22	♟♟ 3
● Cabernet Sauvignon Dail Morar '22	♟♟ 2*
○ Chardonnay Braide '23	♟♟ 3
○ Friuli Pinot Grigio Ramato Settantacinque '23	♟♟ 4
○ Malvasia Dai Claps '23	♟♟ 2*
● Merlot Roos dai Lens '21	♟♟ 4
● Merlot Sant'Antoni '22	♟♟ 3
○ Pinot Bianco Calis '23	♟♟ 2*
○ Prosecco Brut Rosè '23	♟♟ 2*
○ Prosecco Extra Dry '23	♟♟ 2*
○ Ribolla Gialla Albero del Noce '23	♟♟ 3
○ Traminer Aromatico Dal Borc '23	♟♟ 3
○ Friuli Pinot Grigio Selvis '23	♟ 3
○ Prosecco Brut '23	♟ 2
○ Sauvignon Di Meris '23	♟ 3

○ Collio Malvasia '23	♟♟ 4
○ Friuli Chardonnay Andritz '23	♟♟ 4
○ Collio Bianco Andritz Ris. '21	♟♟ 6
○ Collio Friulano '23	♟♟ 4
○ Collio Pinot Grigio '23	♟♟ 4
○ Collio Ribolla Gialla '23	♟♟ 4
● Collio Rosso '16	♟♟ 8
○ Collio Sauvignon '23	♟♟ 4
○ Collio Sauvignon '06	♟♟♟ 3
○ Collio Tocai Friulano '05	♟♟♟ 3*
○ Chardonnay Andritz '13	♟♟ 3*
○ Collio Bianco Andritz '13	♟♟ 5
○ Collio Pinot Grigio '22	♟♟ 5
○ Collio Sauvignon '21	♟♟ 5
○ Collio Sauvignon Bio '20	♟♟ 5
● Friuli Refosco P.R. '19	♟♟ 5

Subida di Monte

via Subida, 6
34071 Cormòns [GO]
(+39 048161011
www.subidadimonte.it

CELLAR SALES
PRE-BOOKED VISITS
ANNUAL PRODUCTION 40,000 bottles
HECTARES UNDER VINE 8.00

Perched atop a hill overlooking the valley below, Subida di Monte is the brainchild of Luigi Antonutti, a pioneer of quality regional viticulture who realized his dream of becoming a full-time winemaker in 1972. Since 2020, Agrotech, a local agricultural company owned by the Scarpa family, has managed the estate. However, Andrea Antonutti, Luigi's son, still closely oversees the entire production process, focusing mainly on agronomic management. The Collio Rosso Poncaia '20, crafted from selected merlot grapes, intrigues on the nose, conveying tobacco, blackberries, blackcurrant, blood orange, cloves, and sandalwood sensations. The palate is powerful yet velvety, with well-integrated tannins. Fresh and balanced, the Friulano '22 opts for an alluring floral profile of linden, acacia, and hawthorn that intertwines with fruity notes of white peach and golden apple, with a fine smoky echo in the background.

Tenuta di Angoris

loc. Angoris, 7
34071 Cormòns [GO]
(+39 048160923
www.angoris.com

CELLAR SALES
PRE-BOOKED VISITS
RESTAURANT SERVICE
ANNUAL PRODUCTION 500,000 bottles
HECTARES UNDER VINE 85.00
SUSTAINABLE WINERY

In 1968, Luciano Locatelli acquired the historic Tenuta di Angoris, a regional winery boasting over 370 years of activity. Although Luciano recently passed away, leaving a deep void in the winemaking world and his family, Marta and Claudia now lead this magnificent estate, having further enhanced the winery's potential, guiding it to the pinnacle of regional excellence. The Collio Bianco Langor Giulio Locatelli Ris. '21, long considered their flagship wine, has been given another year of bottle aging and will be presented in the next edition of the guide. Leading the ranking this year are two notable reds. The Schioppettino '21 plays on aromas of cherry jam, raspberry syrup, and Sachertorte, while the Merlot Ravòst Ris. Giulio Locatelli '20 offers scents of cinchona, blond tobacco, and sweet spices.

● Collio Cabernet Franc '21	♟♟ 3
○ Collio Friulano '22	♟♟ 3
● Collio Merlot '21	♟♟ 3
● Collio Rosso Poncaia '16	♟♟ 4
● Collio Cabernet Franc '20	♟♟ 3
○ Collio Friulano '21	♟♟ 3
○ Collio Friulano '20	♟♟ 3
○ Collio Friulano Fuart '21	♟♟ 5
○ Collio Friulano Fuart '20	♟♟ 4
○ Collio Malvasia '21	♟♟ 4
○ Collio Malvasia '20	♟♟ 3
● Collio Merlot '20	♟♟ 3
○ Collio Pinot Grigio '22	♟♟ 3
○ Collio Pinot Grigio '21	♟♟ 3
● Collio Rosso Poncaia '16	♟♟ 4
○ Collio Sauvignon '21	♟♟ 3

● FCO Merlot Ravòst Giulio Locatelli Ris. '20	♟♟ 4
● FCO Schioppettino '21	♟♟ 4
○ Collio Pinot Grigio '23	♟♟ 4
○ Friuli Isonzo Sauvignon Villa Locatelli '23	♟♟ 3
○ FCO Ribolla Gialla '23	♟ 4
○ Friuli Isonzo Friulano Villa Locatelli '23	♟ 3
○ Collio Bianco Giulio Locatelli Ris. '17	♟♟♟ 4*
○ Collio Bianco Giulio Locatelli Ris. '16	♟♟♟ 4*
○ Collio Bianco Giulio Locatelli Ris. '15	♟♟♟ 4*
○ Collio Bianco Langor Giulio Locatelli Ris. '20	♟♟♟ 5
○ Collio Bianco Langor Giulio Locatelli Ris. '19	♟♟♟ 5

Matijaz Tercic

loc. Bucuie, 4a
34070 San Floriano del Collio [GO]
☏ +39 0481884920
✆ www.tercic.com

CELLAR SALES
PRE-BOOKED VISITS
ANNUAL PRODUCTION 30,000 bottles
HECTARES UNDER VINE 9.50

Matijaz Tercic hails from a family with a long history of viticulture and winemaking in the hills of San Floriano del Collio, one of the most captivating areas of the eastern Friulian foothills, recognized as the qualitative pinnacle of Collio Goriziano. Matijaz's first bottles dates back to 1994, and through steady growth, the winery has established itself as one of the region's top producers. The Chardonnay Planta '21 benefits on the nose from an intriguing floral interplay of linden, jasmine, and lily of the valley, with fragrant hints of pineapple and grapefruit under a veil of vanilla, accompanied by delicate smoky notes. The pleasantness of its aromas is matched by a palate that is both soft and at the same time vivid and fragrant. The Friulano '22 is right up there as well, evoking wildflowers, yellow currant, golden apple, and almond drupe, while on the palate, it excels in its freshness, sapidity, balance, and drinkability.

○ Collio Chardonnay Planta '21	♟♟	5
○ Collio Pinot Grigio Dar '21	♟♟	5
○ Friuli Isonzo Friulano '22	♟♟	5
○ Sauvignon Scemen '22	♟♟	5
○ Vino degli Orti '21	♟♟	5
○ Collio Pinot Grigio '07	♟♟♟	3*
○ Collio Chardonnay Planta '20	♟♟	5
○ Collio Pinot Grigio '18	♟♟	4
○ Dar Pinot Grigio '19	♟♟	5
○ Friuli Isonzo Friulano '20	♟♟	4
○ Friuli Isonzo Friulano '19	♟♟	4
○ Pinot Bianco '18	♟♟	3*
○ Pinot Grigio Dar '16	♟♟	5
○ Ribolla Gialla '20	♟♟	4
○ Sauvignon '21	♟♟	5
○ Vino degli Orti '20	♟♟	4

★Tiare - Roberto Snidarcig

fraz. Vencò
loc. Sant'Elena, 3a
34070 Dolegna del Collio [GO]
☏ +39 048162491
✆ www.tiaredoc.com

CELLAR SALES
PRE-BOOKED VISITS
RESTAURANT SERVICE
ANNUAL PRODUCTION 90,000 bottles
HECTARES UNDER VINE 10.00
SUSTAINABLE WINERY

For Roberto Snidarcig, expanding from just one hectare of vineyard to his current success was a significant leap. In 1991, together with his wife Sandra, he founded his winery, naming it Tiare as a tribute to the land that made his achievements possible. Today, his winery stands as one of the most prestigious in the regional winemaking landscape, showcasing the potential of the Dolegna del Collio area. The Pinot Grigio Masserè '23 flaunts an elegant, slightly coppery color, with aromas of strawberries, pomegranate, and rose-water rising from the glass. A refined and pleasant pour. It's rare to find a Ribolla Gialla '23 in the finals, but this year's version is spectacular. It's fragrant both on the nose and palate, with a complexity of aromas decidedly above average. We've heaped praise on the Sauvignon '23, and it's hard to find new adjectives to describe it, but perhaps we've never used "modern"—and that's exactly what it is.

○ Collio Sauvignon '23	♟♟♟	5
○ Collio Pinot Grigio Masserè '23	♟♟	4
○ Collio Ribolla Gialla '23	♟♟	4
● Cabernet Franc '22	♟♟	4
○ Collio Chardonnay '23	♟♟	3
○ Collio Friulano '23	♟♟	4
○ Collio Malvasia '23	♟♟	3
● Pinot Nero '22	♟♟	4
○ Rosè Remuàv Rouge Brut M. Cl.	♟♟	4
○ Sauvignon Il Tiare '23	♟♟	4
○ Collio Sauvignon '22	♟♟♟	5
○ Collio Sauvignon '21	♟♟♟	4*
○ Collio Sauvignon '20	♟♟♟	4*
○ Collio Sauvignon '19	♟♟♟	5
○ Collio Sauvignon '18	♟♟♟	5

★★Franco Toros

loc. Novali, 12
34071 Cormòns [GO]
📞 +39 048161327
🌐 www.vinitoros.com

CELLAR SALES
PRE-BOOKED VISITS
ANNUAL PRODUCTION 60,000 bottles
HECTARES UNDER VINE 11.00

Franco Toros comes from a family of farmers who settled in Novali at the beginning of the last century, near the Plessiva pass leading to Slovenia. It quickly became apparent that these lands were perfectly suited for wine-growing, and the family soon became meticulous vintners. Like all great producers, Franco credits the quality of his wines to Mother Nature, but it is well known that without the right interpreter, the results wouldn't be the same. The Friulano has always been a flagship of this prestigious estate, and the 2023 confirms its place among the best in its category. On the nose, it boasts fruity notes of yellow peach, white melon, and citron, complemented by alpine hay, dry pastry, and sweet almonds. The palate stands out for its fragrance and mineral tension. The Pinot Bianco '23 conjures up linden and jasmine flowers, tropical fruits, and mandarin, while the palate develops pervasive, velvety, and smooth.

★Torre Rosazza

fraz. Oleis
loc. Poggiobello, 12
33044 Manzano [UD]
📞 +39 0422864511
🌐 www.torrerosazza.com

CELLAR SALES
PRE-BOOKED VISITS
ANNUAL PRODUCTION 240,000 bottles
HECTARES UNDER VINE 100.00
SUSTAINABLE WINERY

Torre Rosazza stands out as one of the region's gems, a historic winery located in Manzano in the 18th-century Palazzo De Marchi. The estate sits atop a hill surrounded by vineyards arranged in two splendid, sun-drenched natural amphitheaters. Torre Rosazza is part of Genagricola, a well-established group that brings together prestigious brands from various parts of Italy, including Poggiobello, Borgo Magredo, and Tenuta Sant'Anna in Friuli. Friulano, the ambassador of this splendid estate, was presented in two versions this year: one from the vintage and the other from a new project that draws on maturation and bottle aging. The Friulano '23 excels with its elegant floral and fruity bouquet, which preludes a fresh, enticing palate. The Friulano Masiero Ris. '21 proves rich in citrus, spice, and mineral nuances, beautifully fused and exalted on the palate, making for a gratifying tasting experience.

○ Collio Friulano '23	♟♟	4
○ Collio Pinot Bianco '23	♟♟	4
○ Collio Pinot Grigio '23	♟♟	4
○ Collio Chardonnay '23	♟♟	4
● Collio Merlot '20	♟♟	4
○ Collio Sauvignon '23	♟♟	4
○ Collio Friulano '18	♟♟♟	4*
○ Collio Friulano '12	♟♟♟	4*
○ Collio Friulano '11	♟♟♟	4*
○ Collio Friulano '10	♟♟♟	4
○ Collio Friulano '09	♟♟♟	4*
○ Collio Friulano '08	♟♟♟	4*
○ Collio Pinot Bianco '17	♟♟♟	4*
○ Collio Pinot Bianco '14	♟♟♟	4*
○ Collio Pinot Bianco '13	♟♟♟	4*
○ Collio Pinot Bianco '08	♟♟♟	4*

○ FCO Friulano Masiero Ris. '21	♟♟♟	5
○ FCO Friulano '23	♟♟	4
● FCO Rosso Ronco Della Torre Ris. '21	♟♟	7
○ FCO Bianco Ronco delle Magnolie '22	♟♟	7
○ FCO Pinot Grigio '23	♟♟	4
○ FCO Pinot Grigio Bandaros Ris. '21	♟♟	5
○ FCO Ribolla Gialla '23	♟♟	4
○ FCO Sauvignon '23	♟♟	4
○ Ribolla Gialla Brut	♟	4
○ FCO Friulano '22	♟♟♟	3*
○ FCO Friulano '21	♟♟♟	3*
○ FCO Friulano '20	♟♟♟	3*
○ FCO Friulano '19	♟♟♟	3*

★Tunella

fraz. Ipplis
via del Collio, 14
33040 Premariacco [UD]
☎ +39 0432716030
✉ www.tunella.it

CELLAR SALES
PRE-BOOKED VISITS
ANNUAL PRODUCTION 430,000 bottles
HECTARES UNDER VINE 70.00
SUSTAINABLE WINERY

Brothers Massino and Marco Zorzettig, along with their mother Gabriella, are the proud owners of this splendid estate, a point of pride for the Friuli Colli Orientali appellation. From a young age, they took on the responsibility of managing the winery, leveraging the experiences handed down over three generations. They have long relied on the oenological skills of Luigino Zamparo, with whom they grew up and who has played a crucial role in creating and developing the brand. The Pinot Grigio Col Bajè '22 confirms its place as one of the best of its kind, once again reaching the finals. It opens with fruity aromas of apple, pear, kumquat, and pomegranate juice, followed by hints of rosehip. The palate is fresh and taut. The Schioppettino '21 excels with its pervasive palate and balsamic finish. The Biancosesto '22 (friulano and ribolla gialla) doesn't disappoint, delighting the nose with a multitude of aromatic herbs and tropical notes, offering magical moments on the palate.

Valchiarò

fraz. Togliano
via dei Laghi, 4c
33040 Torreano [UD]
☎ +39 0432715502
✉ www.valchiaro.it

CELLAR SALES
PRE-BOOKED VISITS
ANNUAL PRODUCTION 45,000 bottles
HECTARES UNDER VINE 14.00
SUSTAINABLE WINERY

Valchiarò is located in Torreano di Cividale, a cool and constantly breezy area, which allows for wines with notable aromatic profiles. In 1991, six small producers from different professional backgrounds decided to join forces, pooling their grapes into a single entity and founding the winery. Their journey has been marked by significant milestones, including the construction of a large, modern cellar inaugurated in 2006. The Friulano Nexus '23 has become a mainstay in our final selections and didn't disappoint this year either. It greets the nose with the fragrance of green apple, grapefruit, and white peach, accompanied by hints of alfalfa and wafts of lavender. On the palate, it displays perfect balance, with fresh and alluring notes. The Merlot Riserva '20 is also noteworthy, with its aromas of blackberries, licorice, and chocolate. The palate proves rich, pervasive, and enlivened by the fragrance of its tannins.

○ FCO Biancosesto '22	♟♟♟ 5
○ FCO Pinot Grigio Ramato Colbajè '22	♟♟ 5
● FCO Schioppettino '21	♟♟ 5
● Arcione '20	♟♟ 6
○ FCO Friulano '23	♟♟ 4
● FCO Pignolo '19	♟♟ 5
○ FCO Pinot Grigio '23	♟♟ 4
○ FCO Ribolla Gialla Coldebliss '22	♟♟ 5
○ FCO Ribolla Gialla Rjgialla '23	♟♟ 4
○ FCO Sauvignon Colmatiss '22	♟♟ 5
○ FCO Biancosesto '21	♟♟♟ 5
○ FCO Biancosesto '20	♟♟♟ 5
○ FCO Biancosesto '19	♟♟♟ 5
○ FCO Biancosesto '18	♟♟♟ 5
○ FCO Biancosesto '17	♟♟♟ 5

○ FCO Friulano Nexus '23	♟♟ 4
○ FCO Friulano '23	♟♟ 3
● FCO Merlot Ris. '20	♟♟ 3
● FCO Refosco P. R. '20	♟♟ 3
○ FCO Ribolla Gialla '23	♟♟ 4
○ FCO Sauvignon '23	♟♟ 3
○ FCO Verduzzo Friulano '22	♟♟ 4
○ COF Verduzzo Friulano '09	♟♟ 4*
○ FCO Friulano Nexus '22	♟♟ 4
○ FCO Friulano Nexus '21	♟♟ 4
○ FCO Friulano Nexus '20	♟♟ 3*
○ FCO Friulano Nexus '18	♟♟ 3*
○ FCO Friulano Nexus '17	♟♟ 3*
○ FCO Friulano Nexus '16	♟♟ 3*
● FCO Merlot Ris. '19	♟♟ 3*
○ FCO Verduzzo Friulano '17	♟♟ 4

Valpanera

loc. Fiumicello
via Adriano Olivetti, 52
33059 Villa Vicentina [UD]
☎ +39 0431970395
✉ www.vinivalpanera.it

CELLAR SALES
PRE-BOOKED VISITS
ANNUAL PRODUCTION 300,000 bottles
HECTARES UNDER VINE 50.00
SUSTAINABLE WINERY

Valpanera, part of the Friuli Aquileia appellation, stands as one of the territory's most important wineries. Founded in 1972 as "Casa del Refosco," it became known for championing the region's most representative black grape varietal, refosco dal peduncolo rosso. In 2019, Paolo and Alessandro Baccicchetto acquired the estate, expanding and diversifying its offerings. The Refosco '22 evokes mature morello cherries, wilted violets, cinnamon sticks, and eucalyptus on the nose, while the palate proves soft with lively tannins. The Chardonnay '22 releases scents of yellow peach, Stark apple, pineapple, papaya, and lemon shortbread, all in a refined blend accented by touches of resin; the palate is warm, pervasive, flavorful, and long-lasting. The Malvasia '23, Traminer Aromatico '23, and Cabernet Sauvignon '23 are also excellent, with the rest of the range proving more than satisfactory.

★★Venica & Venica

loc. Cerò, 8
34070 Dolegna del Collio [GO]
☎ +39 048161264
✉ www.venica.it

CELLAR SALES
PRE-BOOKED VISITS
ACCOMMODATION
ANNUAL PRODUCTION 350,000 bottles
HECTARES UNDER VINE 40.00
SUSTAINABLE WINERY

Venica & Venica is a well-established name in the international wine scene, renowned for showcasing the potential of the Gorizia Hills, especially for whites. Gianni Venica leads a dynamic family team where each member contributes to the success of a winery that blends agricultural spirit with entrepreneurial acumen, ensuring continuity and tradition. We were accustomed to receiving only standard-vintage, annata wines, but this year brought many surprises with projects focused on showcasing the aging potential of regional whites, particularly sauvignon. In the finals, the winery added a surprising Sauvignon Extempore '18 to its two well-known flagships. The nose reveals intriguing scents of yellow rose, lemon wafer, tropical fruits, dried flowers, and aromatic herbs, while the palate is penetrating, sapid, and energetic.

FRIULI VENEZIA GIULIA

● Friuli Aquileia Cabernet Sauvignon '23	♟♟ 2*
○ Friuli Aquileia Chardonnay '23	♟♟ 2*
○ Friuli Aquileia Chardonnay '22	♟♟ 2*
○ Friuli Aquileia Malvasia '23	♟♟ 2*
● Friuli Aquileia Refosco P. R. '22	♟♟ 2*
○ Friuli Aquileia Traminer Aromatico '23	♟♟ 3
○ Friuli Aquileia Sauvignon '23	♟ 2
○ Friuli Aquileia Sauvignon '22	♟ 2
○ Friuli Pinot Grigio '23	♟ 2
○ Ribolla Gialla '23	♟ 2
● Atrum '21	♟♟ 2*
● Friuli Aquileia Refosco P. R. '21	♟♟ 2*
● Friuli Aquileia Refosco P. R. Aquilio Ris. '20	♟♟ 4
● Friuli Aquileia Rosso Alma '20	♟♟ 4

○ Collio Sauvignon Extempore '18	♟♟♟ 8
○ Collio Friulano Ronco delle Cime '23	♟♟ 6
○ Collio Sauvignon Ronco delle Mele '23	♟♟ 7
○ Collio Bianco Tre Vignis '19	♟♟ 6
○ Collio Malvasia Petris '23	♟♟ 5
○ Collio Pinot Bianco Tàlis '23	♟♟ 5
○ Collio Ribolla Gialla l'Adelchi '23	♟♟ 5
○ Collio Sauvignon Ronco delle Mele Sel. d'Annata '13	♟♟ 8
● FCO Refosco P. R. Bottaz '20	♟♟ 6
○ Collio Friulano Ronco delle Cime '21	♟♟♟ 5
○ Collio Sauvignon Ronco delle Mele '20	♟♟♟ 6
○ Collio Sauvignon Ronco delle Mele '16	♟♟♟ 6

La Viarte

via Novacuzzo, 51
33040 Prepotto [UD]
(☎) +39 0432759458
✉ www.laviarte.it

CELLAR SALES
PRE-BOOKED VISITS
ACCOMMODATION
ANNUAL PRODUCTION 120,000 bottles
HECTARES UNDER VINE 22.00
SUSTAINABLE WINERY

Founded in the 1970s by the Ceschin family, La Viarte has earned a prestigious place in the regional wine industry. Recently acquired by Giorgio Polegato, who redirected his focus to La Viarte after selling his shares in Astoria, the winery is now managed by his young son Riccardo, who is driving improvements across all stages of production. An interesting selection of well-aged red wines accompanies the Liende line, which includes a series of whites made from carefully selected grapes aged appropriately in bottle. Among the best is the Pinot Bianco Liende '22, which opens on the nose with an alluring blend of lily of the valley, jasmine, white peach, and citrus. On the palate, it's elegant yet also direct. The Sauvignon Liende '22 is excellent as well, opting for delicate varietal aromas alongside a fresh, full-bodied, and balanced palate.

★★★Vie di Romans

loc. Vie di Romans, 1
34070 Mariano del Friuli [GO]
(☎) +39 048169600
✉ www.viediromans.it

CELLAR SALES
PRE-BOOKED VISITS
ANNUAL PRODUCTION 350,000 bottles
HECTARES UNDER VINE 67.00
SUSTAINABLE WINERY

The inauguration of a new aging cellar alongside the already esteemed Vie di Romans production facility marks a new chapter for this prestigious brand. Vie di Romans has transformed into an agricultural company, with Tommaso, Mattia, and Veronica proving integral to the business founded by their father, Gianfranco Gallo. The new structure is a splendid architectural model housing hundreds of barrels, blending modernity and functionality seamlessly. The Flors di Uis '22 is a blend of mostly of malvasia istriana, with a touch of tocai friulano and a sizable share of riesling renano, making it unique and singular. It's redolent of citrus jelly, ginger, canned peach, and honey candy, with a background of balsamic resins. The palate is smooth, soft, and unforgettable. Both Sauvignons are also excellent, with vegetal and citrus hints and a fragrant, harmonious palate, while The Chardonnay Vie di Romans '22 offers a pervasive and voluminous palate.

○ FCO Pinot Bianco Liende '22	♥♥ 5
○ FCO Sauvignon Liende '22	♥♥ 5
○ FCO Chardonnay Liende '22	♥♥ 5
○ FCO Malvasia Zija '23	♥♥ 6
● FCO Pignolo Ris. '11	♥♥ 8
○ FCO Sauvignon Liende '21	♥♥ 5
● FCO Schioppettino di Prepotto Ris. '15	♥♥ 5
● FCO Tazzelenghe Ris. '15	♥♥ 6
○ FCO Friulano Liende '17	♥♥♥ 5
○ FCO Friulano Liende '16	♥♥♥ 5
○ FCO Sauvignon Liende '18	♥♥♥ 5
○ FCO Sauvignon Liende '15	♥♥♥ 5
○ FCO Chardonnay Liende '20	♥♥ 5
○ FCO Pinot Bianco '21	♥♥ 5
○ FCO Pinot Bianco Liende '20	♥♥ 5
○ FCO Sauvignon Liende '20	♥♥ 5

○ Friuli Isonzo Bianco Flor di Uis '22	♥♥♥ 5
○ Friuli Isonzo Sauvignon Piere '22	♥♥ 6
○ Friuli Isonzo Sauvignon Vieris '22	♥♥ 6
○ Dut'Un '21	♥♥ 8
○ Friuli Isonzo Chardonnay Ciampagnis '22	♥♥ 5
○ Friuli Isonzo Chardonnay Vie di Romans '22	♥♥ 6
○ Friuli Isonzo Friulano Dolée '22	♥♥ 5
○ Friuli Isonzo Pinot Grigio Dessimis '22	♥♥ 6
○ Friuli Isonzo Bianco Flors di Uis '20	♥♥♥ 5
○ Friuli Isonzo Sauvignon Piere '18	♥♥♥ 5
○ Friuli Isonzo Sauvignon Piere '17	♥♥♥ 5
○ Friuli Isonzo Sauvignon Vieris '21	♥♥♥ 6
○ Friuli Isonzo Sauvignon Vieris '19	♥♥♥ 5

Vigna del Lauro

loc. Montona, 19
34071 Cormòns [GO]
(») +39 0481629549
◎ www.vignadellauro.it

CELLAR SALES
PRE-BOOKED VISITS
ANNUAL PRODUCTION 60,000 bottles
HECTARES UNDER VINE 10.00

In the late 20th century, Fabio Coser, already the owner of Ronco dei Tassi in the Gorizia Hills, decided to diversify production so as to cater to a market segment seeking simple, drinkable wines that maintained their typicity yet were also affordable. He found an old vineyard of tocai friulano almost entirely surrounded by ancient bay trees—thus Vigna del Lauro was born ("lauro" meaning "laurel"). Success was immediate, and the range has since expanded. In a varied lineup of wines, the Chardonnay '23 stands out, teasing the nose with rare elegance. On a delicate and refined base of lavender, notes of propolis, summer hay, yellow peach, and lemongrass emerge. The palate attacks fresh, lengthening towards soft and juicy textures. The Pinot Nero Novaj '21 gradually releases fruity notes of strawberry and blackberry jam, dried aromatic herbs, mace, and black pepper, with noble, rounded tannins accompanying the palate.

Vigna Petrussa

via Albana, 47
33040 Prepotto [UD]
(») +39 0432713021
◎ www.vignapetrussa.it

CELLAR SALES
PRE-BOOKED VISITS
ANNUAL PRODUCTION 40,000 bottles
HECTARES UNDER VINE 8.00
SUSTAINABLE WINERY

Hilde Petrussa chose a truly unique way to enjoy her retirement in 1995 by returning to Albana di Prepotto to manage the family estate, which had flourished in the early 1900s but had since fallen into neglect. She reconverted the vineyards, focusing on indigenous varieties, particularly ribolla nera, used to make Schioppettino. She is now joined by her daughter Francesca, ensuring the estate's continuity. The Schioppettino di Prepotto '20 continues to receive the highest praise. The nose is characterized by aromas of brandied cherries, blackberry jam, underbrush, olive brine, tobacco, and walnut husk. The palate is supported by a decisive tannic vein, fading into a finish with fruity hints. The Richenza '20 is a white blend of tocai friulano, malvasia istriana, riesling renano, and picolit. It proves redolent of orange, star anise, and almond, coming through dynamic and balanced on the palate.

○ Chardonnay '23	♏♏ 3*
○ Collio Friulano '23	♏♏ 3
○ Collio Pinot Grigio '23	♏♏ 3
○ Collio Sauvignon '23	♏♏ 3
● Friuli Isonzo Merlot '22	♏♏ 2*
● Pinot Nero Novaj '21	♏♏ 3
○ Ribolla Gialla '23	♏♏ 3
○ Traminer Aromatico '23	♏♏ 3
○ Collio Sauvignon '99	♏♏♏ 2*
○ Collio Friulano '10	♏♏ 2*
○ Collio Pinot Grigio '13	♏♏ 3*
○ Collio Sauvignon '22	♏♏ 3*
○ Collio Sauvignon '21	♏♏ 3*
○ Collio Sauvignon '20	♏♏ 3*
○ Collio Sauvignon '07	♏♏ 2*
● Friuli Isonzo Merlot '07	♏♏ 2*

● FCO Schioppettino di Prepotto '20	♏♏ 5
○ COF Picolit '18	♏♏ 7
○ FCO Friulano '23	♏♏ 3
● FCO Refosco P.R. '19	♏♏ 5
● Rebusson '21	♏♏ 5
○ Richenza '20	♏♏ 5
● FCO Schioppettino '19	♏♏♏ 5
○ COF Bianco Richenza '10	♏♏ 4
○ COF Bianco Richenza '09	♏♏ 4
○ COF Picolit '15	♏♏ 6
● COF Schioppettino di Prepotto '10	♏♏ 4
○ FCO Friulano '15	♏♏ 3*
○ Richenza '19	♏♏ 4
○ Richenza '18	♏♏ 4
○ Richenza '17	♏♏ 4
○ Richenza '15	♏♏ 4

Vigna Traverso

via Ronchi, 73
33040 Prepotto [UD]
☎ +39 0422804807
✆ www.vignatraverso.it

CELLAR SALES
PRE-BOOKED VISITS
RESTAURANT SERVICE
ANNUAL PRODUCTION 100,000 bottles
HECTARES UNDER VINE 22.00
SUSTAINABLE WINERY

Owned by the Molon Traverso family (who also run a famous winery in nearby Veneto), Vigna Traverso is managed by Stefano Traverso. Over time, Stefano has restructured the property, preserving old vineyards and planting new high-density plots. For several years, the winery has operated from a new cellar in Prepotto, equipped with the latest technology and concrete tanks, demonstrating that innovation and tradition can coexist. The Friulano '23 represents one of the finest expressions of tocai friulano, considered a daily drinking wine in the region. It exudes delightful aromas reminiscent of mountain meadows, russet pear, golden apple, and almond husk. The palate is fresh and soft, with balsamic touches. The Rosso Troj '21, a blend of merlot, refosco dal peduncolo rosso, and schioppettino, proves redolent of star anise, nutmeg, and medicinal herbs, with a pervasive, full-bodied palate.

Vigne del Malina

fraz. Orzano
via Pasini Vianelli, 9
33047 Remanzacco [UD]
☎ +39 0432649258
✆ www.vignedelmalina.com

CELLAR SALES
PRE-BOOKED VISITS
ANNUAL PRODUCTION 45,000 bottles
HECTARES UNDER VINE 10.00
VITICULTURE METHOD Certified Organic

In 2007, Roberto Bacchetti and Maria Luisa Trevisan decided to start a winemaking venture on their family estate, which included about 10 hectares of old vineyards within the Friuli Grave appellation. They founded Vigne del Malina (naming it after the stream that flows through the property). Roberto's philosophy, uncommon in the area, is that even in the plains, with low yields and meticulous care, it's possible to produce highly structured and long-lived wines. This year, the wines presented performed extraordinarily. They all possess great structure and personality, showcasing maturity, energy, and appeal. The Chardonnay '19 gratifies the nose with delightful aromas of exotic fruit, spices, resins, and refreshing minty accents, while the palate is balanced and harmonious. The Sauvignon '19 opens with notes of Mediterranean herbs, wisteria, citrus cocktail, summer savory, and lavender. The palate proves rich, assertive, and linear.

○ FCO Friulano '23	♟♟ 4
● FCO Rosso Troj '21	♟♟ 4
○ FCO Bianco Sottocastello Ris. '21	♟♟ 5
● FCO Cabernet Franc Ris. '20	♟♟ 5
● FCO Merlot Ris. '21	♟♟ 5
● FCO Merlot Sottocastello Rosso Ris. '17	♟♟ 6
○ FCO Pinot Grigio '23	♟♟ 4
○ FCO Sauvignon '23	♟♟ 4
○ FCO Ribolla Gialla '23	♟ 4
○ FCO Bianco Sottocastello '19	♟♟ 5
○ FCO Friulano '22	♟♟ 3*
● FCO Merlot Ris. '19	♟♟ 4
● FCO Rosso Troj '19	♟♟ 4
○ FCO Sauvignon '22	♟♟ 3*
● FCO Schioppettino di Prepotto '19	♟♟ 6

○ Chardonnay '19	♟♟♟ 5
○ Sauvignon '19	♟♟ 5
○ Friuli Pinot Grigio '19	♟♟ 5
● Merlot '16	♟♟ 5
● Refosco P. R. '16	♟♟ 5
● Cabernet Franc '16	♟♟ 4
○ Chardonnay '18	♟♟ 4
○ Friuli Pinot Grigio '18	♟♟ 4
● Merlot '13	♟♟ 5
○ Pinot Grigio '13	♟♟ 3*
○ Pinot Grigio Ram '16	♟♟ 7
● Refosco P. R. '13	♟♟ 5
⊚ Rosad Rosato '20	♟♟ 4
○ Sauvignon '18	♟♟ 5
○ Sauvignon Aur '09	♟♟ 5

★★Le Vigne di Zamò

loc. Rosazzo
via Abate Corrado, I
33044 Manzano [UD]
(» +39 0432759693
@ www.levignedizamo.com

CELLAR SALES
PRE-BOOKED VISITS
ANNUAL PRODUCTION 280,000 bottles
HECTARES UNDER VINE 43.00
VITICULTURE METHOD Certified Organic
SUSTAINABLE WINERY

Tullio Zamò, one of the patriarchs of regional
winemaking, began his journey in 1978 by
purchasing land on the slopes of Rocca Bernarda,
thus founding Vigne dal Leon. He later created
the Abbazia di Rosazzo brand and, in 1996, along
with his sons Silvano and Pierluigi, also founded
Le Vigne di Zamò. About a decade ago, the brand
joined the esteemed Fontanafredda group under
Oscar Farinetti, increasing its international
visibility. The Chardonnay Ronco delle Acacie '22
opens with evolved aromas that paint a broad
and varied picture, conjuring up apricot, acacia
honey, papaya, hay, and candied citrus, all
surrounded by hints of medicinal herbs, resinous
whiffs, and beeswax. On the palate, it's pervasive
and rich, elevated by an original balsamic streak.
The Pinot Bianco Tullio Zamò '22 reveals notes
of candied orange, apricot jelly, alpine hay,
summer flowers, and aromatic herbs, leading to
a broad, balanced, sapid, and lingering palate.

Villa de Puppi

via Roma, 5
33040 Moimacco [UD]
(» +39 0432722461
@ www.depuppi.it

CELLAR SALES
PRE-BOOKED VISITS
ANNUAL PRODUCTION 70,000 bottles
HECTARES UNDER VINE 25.00
SUSTAINABLE WINERY

In the small village of Moimacco, near Cividale
del Friuli, the Count de Puppi family have
managed agricultural activities for generations.
The family has produced notable figures in
politics, justice, and ecclesiastical hierarchies. In
1991, Luigi de Puppi founded the winery, now
run by his children Caterina and Valfredo. Most
of the vineyards surround the main villa, with
another 10 hectares spread across the hills of
Rosazzo. It's no surprise that their hillside
wines have an edge, but those bearing the Rosa
Bosco label are always a guarantee of quality.
The Sauvignon di Rosa Bosco '22 plays on
aromas of orange marmalade, yellow peach,
ginger, and exotic spices, with echoes of wafer
and lemon cream. On the palate, it reveals both
substance and suppleness. The Ribolla Gialla di
Rosa Bosco '22 conjures up a medley of fragrant
fruit, field herbs, and beeswax, with a silky and
balanced palate to follow.

○ FCO Chardonnay Ronco delle Acacie '22	♟♟ 5
○ FCO Pinot Bianco Tullio Zamò '22	♟♟ 5
○ FCO Friulano V. 50 Anni '22	♟♟ 6
● FCO Merlot V. 50 Anni '20	♟♟ 6
● FCO Rosso Ronco dei Roseti '21	♟♟ 6
○ Friuli Zamò Bianco '23	♟♟ 3
○ COF Friulano V. Cinquant'Anni '09	♟♟♟ 5
○ COF Friulano V. Cinquant'Anni '08	♟♟♟ 5
● COF Merlot V. Cinquant'Anni '09	♟♟♟ 5
● COF Merlot V. Cinquant'Anni '06	♟♟♟ 5
○ COF Tocai Friulano V. Cinquant'Anni '06	♟♟♟ 5
○ FCO Friulano No Name '15	♟♟♟ 5
○ FCO Friulano V. 50 Anni '21	♟♟♟ 6
○ Friuli Friulano No Name '16	♟♟♟ 4*
○ Ronco delle Acacie '93	♟♟♟ 5
○ Ronco di Corte '87	♟♟♟ 5

○ FCO Sauvignon di Rosa Bosco '22	♟♟ 5
○ FCO Ribolla Gialla di Rosa Bosco '22	♟♟ 4
○ Friuli Friulano '23	♟♟ 3
○ Friuli Pinot Grigio '23	♟♟ 3
● Merlot '21	♟♟ 3
● Refosco dal P. R. '21	♟♟ 3
● Cabernet '21	♟ 4
○ Chardonnay '23	♟ 3
○ Ribolla Gialla '23	♟ 3
○ Sauvignon '23	♟ 3
● FCO Il Boscorosso di Rosa Bosco Merlot '19	♟♟ 7
○ FCO Sauvignon di Rosa Bosco '17	♟♟ 5
● Il Boscorosso di Rosa Bosco Merlot '15	♟♟ 7
○ Sauvignon di Rosa Bosco '16	♟♟ 5

★★Villa Russiz

via Russiz, 4/6
34070 Capriva del Friuli [GO]
(+39 048180047
www.villarussiz.it

CELLAR SALES
PRE-BOOKED VISITS
ANNUAL PRODUCTION 220,000 bottles
HECTARES UNDER VINE 45.00
SUSTAINABLE WINERY

For some time now, Villa Russiz has been globally recognized for consistently producing wines of superb quality. It's worth noting that in the late 19th century, the Counts de La Tour family, lacking heirs, donated their assets to a public institution to support underprivileged children. The Villa Russiz Foundation, sustaining itself through its work, continues this commitment, exemplifying the union of labor and solidarity. The Chardonnay Gräfin de La Tour '19 pours an elegant golden hue, generously offering up aromas of rare elegance and charm, reminiscent of linden, candied citron, sweet spices, incense, resins, and medicinal herbs. On the palate, it is a concentrated burst of energy and density. The Sauvignon de La Tour '23 delivers impressions of white peach, rennet apple, gooseberry, and mint, with a pervasive and balanced palate. The Malvasia '23 is also excellent, with an abundance of tropical scents that enhance the palate as well.

○ Collio Chardonnay	
Gräfin de La Tour '19	▼▼ 7
○ Collio Malvasia '23	▼▼ 5
● Collio Cabernet Sauvignon	
Défi de La Tour '21	▼▼ 8
○ Collio Chardonnay '23	▼▼ 4
○ Collio Friulano '23	▼▼ 5
● Collio Merlot Gräf de La Tour '20	▼▼ 7
○ Collio Pinot Bianco '23	▼▼ 4
○ Collio Pinot Grigio '23	▼▼ 5
○ Collio Sauvignon de La Tour '23	▼▼ 6
○ Collio Chardonnay	
Gräfin de La Tour '14	▼▼▼ 7
○ Collio Friulano '09	▼▼▼ 4*
○ Collio Malvasia '18	▼▼▼ 4*
○ Collio Pinot Bianco '19	▼▼▼ 6
○ Collio Pinot Bianco '16	▼▼▼ 4*
○ Collio Sauvignon de La Tour '08	▼▼▼ 5

Tenuta Villanova

fraz. Villanova
via Contessa Beretta, 29
34072 Farra d'Isonzo [GO]
(+39 0481889311
www.tenutavillanova.com

CELLAR SALES
PRE-BOOKED VISITS
ANNUAL PRODUCTION 300,000 bottles
HECTARES UNDER VINE 100.00
SUSTAINABLE WINERY

Tenuta Villanova's roots date back to 1499. The estate's more recent history began in 1932, when it was acquired by the eclectic entrepreneur Arnaldo Bennati. After his death, the property passed to his his determined wife, Giuseppina Grossi, who recently entrusted management to their three grandchildren, Alberto, Francesca, and Stefano. The winery boasts a considerable number of vineyards extending into the neighboring Collio and Friuli Isonzo appellations. Benefiting from the favorable climate and terrain of the gentle Collio slopes, the Friulano '23 ranks among the best of its kind, securing a spot in the finals. Its elegant fusion of aromas opens with a mix of spring flowers, narcissus, and camellias, followed by hints of nectarine, pear, dried flowers, and cotton candy. The palate is supported by a vibrant freshness and coherent minerality. All the other wines stand out for their linearity and smoothness.

○ Collio Friulano '23	▼▼ 3*
○ Collio Ribolla Gialla '23	▼▼ 3
○ Friuli Isonzo Chardonnay '23	▼▼ 3
○ Friuli Isonzo Friulano '23	▼▼ 3
○ Friuli Isonzo Sauvignon '23	▼▼ 3
● Friuli Refosco dal P. R. '22	▼▼ 3
○ Friuli Isonzo Pinot Grigio '23	▼ 3
○ Collio Chardonnay Monte Cucco '97	▼▼▼ 3*
○ Collio Bianco 1499 '18	▼▼ 3
○ Collio Friulano Ronco Cucco '16	▼▼ 4
● Collio Merlot '20	▼▼ 3
○ Cucco Wine '20	▼▼ 5
● Fraia '15	▼▼ 5
● Fraia '13	▼▼ 5
○ Friuli Isonzo Pinot Grigio '22	▼▼ 3
○ Friuli Isonzo Sauvignon '22	▼▼ 3

Andrea Visintini

via Gramogliano, 27
33040 Corno di Rosazzo [UD]
℡ +39 0432755813
✉ www.vinivisintini.com

CELLAR SALES
PRE-BOOKED VISITS
ANNUAL PRODUCTION 140,000 bottles
HECTARES UNDER VINE 32.00
VITICULTURE METHOD Certified Organic
SUSTAINABLE WINERY

On the hills of Corno di Rosazzo stands a splendid, perfectly preserved circular watchtower dating back to 1560. It was part of the ancient feudal Castle of Gramogliano, whose ruins today host the winery acquired by the Visintini family in 1884. In 1973, management passed to Andrea by generational succession, and now his children, Oliviero, and the twins Cinzia and Palmira, who continue running the certified organic estate with renewed enthusiasm. Two wines from the latest harvest made it to the finals, and when considering quality relative to price, their value is even more appreciable. The Malvasia '23 proves distinctly varietal, with varied notes of medicinal herbs, blonde orange marmalade, yellow flowers, propolis, and toasted hazelnuts. The palate is balanced, with a pronounced sapidity and balsamic accents. The Pinot Bianco '23 exudes aromas of candied fruit, dried flowers, white pepper, and summer hay. The palate is velvety, harmonious, and well-balanced.

○ FCO Malvasia '23	▼▼ 2*
○ FCO Pinot Bianco '23	▼▼ 2*
○ FCO Friulano '23	▼▼ 2*
○ FCO Friulano Amphora '20	▼▼ 4
● FCO Pignolo Amphora '15	▼▼ 4
○ FCO Ribolla Gialla '23	▼▼ 2*
● Friuli Refosco dal P.R. '21	▼▼ 3
○ Friuli Pinot Grigio '23	▼ 2
○ FCO Friulano '22	♀♀ 2*
● FCO Friulano Amphora '19	♀♀ 4
● FCO Friulano Amphora '17	♀♀ 4
○ FCO Pinot Bianco '22	♀♀ 2*
○ FCO Pinot Grigio '22	♀♀ 2*
● FCO Ribolla Gialla '22	♀♀ 2*
○ FCO Sauvignon '16	♀♀ 2*
● Friuli Refosco P.R. '20	♀♀ 3*

Vistorta

loc. Sacile
via Vistorta, 82
33077 Sacile [PN]
℡ +39 043471135
✉ www.vistorta.it

CELLAR SALES
PRE-BOOKED VISITS
ANNUAL PRODUCTION 250,000 bottles
HECTARES UNDER VINE 36.00
VITICULTURE METHOD Certified Organic

Back in the 1800s, Guido Brandolini had the remarkable foresight to transform the small village of Vistorta (part of a family-owned agricultural estate in the heart of Western Friuli) into a modern, efficient farm. Since 1980, the estate has been run by Brandino Brandolini d'Adda, who, after gaining winemaking experience at the family's other estate, Château Greysac in Bordeaux, has successfully revitalized Vistorta following the French model. For a long period, the producer didn't send us any wines, but this year, we're delighted to have the chance to taste them again. The benchmark has always been the Merlot, now joined by two new standouts: Bianca '18 and Brando '18. These are two structured, powerful wines, the result of a long maceration in ceramic amphorae. But the best remains the Merlot Vistorta '18, which exudes aromas of black cherry jam, licorice, and rhubarb, wrapping the palate in gratifying layers.

○ Bianca '18	▼▼ 6
● Vistorta Merlot '18	▼▼ 6
● Brando '18	▼▼ 6
○ Friuli Chardonnay '23	▼▼ 3
● Friuli Refosco dal P.R. '20	▼▼ 4
○ Friuli Sauvignon '23	▼▼ 3
● Friuli Grave Merlot Vistorta '07	♀♀♀ 4
● Friuli Grave Merlot Vistorta '06	♀♀♀ 4
● Friuli Grave Merlot Vistorta '05	♀♀♀ 4
○ Friuli Grave Pinot Grigio '14	♀♀ 2*
○ Friuli Grave Sauvignon '14	♀♀ 2*
○ Friuli Grave Sauvignon '12	♀♀ 2*

Francesco Vosca

fraz. Brazzano
via Sottomonte, 19
34071 Cormòns [GO]
℡ +39 048162135
✆ www.voscavini.it

CELLAR SALES
PRE-BOOKED VISITS
ANNUAL PRODUCTION 60,000 bottles
HECTARES UNDER VINE 10.00
SUSTAINABLE WINERY

Francesco Vosca's winery is one of those classic family-run businesses with proud rural origins that, in the late 20th century, decided to gradually abandon mixed farming so as to focus exclusively on vineyards. This was a major step for Francesco, aware of the land's potential but also of the challenges ahead. Today, his flourishing business has taken a positive turn with the arrival of his son Gabriele. The Malvasia '23 is one of Vosca's highlights, impressing for its varietal characteristics and often reaching our finals. Its aromatic suite opens with fruity hints of golden apple, peach, medlar, and bergamot, followed by intriguing puffs of bay leaf, incense, sage, and rosemary. Pervasive and structured on the palate, it proceeds with balsamic freshness and pronounced sapidity right through the finish. The Friulano '23 is also excellent, just falling short of our finals.

○ Collio Malvasia '23	♟♟ 4
○ Collio Friulano '23	♟♟ 4
○ Friuli Isonzo Chardonnay '23	♟♟ 3
○ Friuli Isonzo Sauvignon '23	♟♟ 3
○ Collio Ribolla Gialla '23	♟ 3
○ Collio Friulano '22	♟♟ 3
○ Collio Friulano '21	♟♟ 3*
○ Collio Friulano '20	♟♟ 3
○ Collio Malvasia '22	♟♟ 4
○ Collio Malvasia '21	♟♟ 3
○ Collio Malvasia '20	♟♟ 3
○ Collio Ribolla Gialla '21	♟♟ 3
○ Collio Ribolla Gialla '20	♟♟ 3
○ Friuli Isonzo Pinot Bianco '22	♟♟ 3
○ Friuli Isonzo Pinot Bianco '20	♟♟ 3
○ Friuli Isonzo Sauvignon '22	♟♟ 3

Zidarich

loc. Prepotto, 23
34011 Duino Aurisina [TS]
℡ +39 040201223
✆ www.zidarich.it

CELLAR SALES
PRE-BOOKED VISITS
ANNUAL PRODUCTION 28,000 bottles
HECTARES UNDER VINE 8.00

Benjamin Zidarich's stunning cellar is carved into the hard rock, spanning 5 floors and reaching a depth of 20 meters. Temperature and humidity remain constant year-round. The wines, first in barrels and then in bottles, age for years without being affected by seasonal climate changes and temperature fluctuations. Respecting local tradition, the wines, even the whites, are made with maceration on the skins in the fermenting must, without temperature control. The Vitovska '21 opens on the nose with a pronounced Mediterranean scrub followed by candied citrus, orange blossom honey, chamomile, linden flower, and hay. The palate is crisp and sapid, with marked minerality. The Malvasia '21 recalls summer hay, preserved fruit, orange pulp, capers, and eucalyptus honey. The palate is full-bodied and penetrating, fresh on the attack, and supported by vigorous tension. You'll find the Vitovska Kamen '21 in our "Rare Wines" section.

○ Carso Vitovska '21	♟♟
○ Malvasia '21	♟♟
● Ruje '18	♟♟
○ Carso Malvasia '09	♟♟♟
○ Carso Malvasia '06	♟♟♟
○ Carso Vitovska V. Collection '09	♟♟♟
○ Prulke '10	♟♟♟
○ Prulke '08	♟♟♟
○ Vitovska V. Collection '16	♟♟♟
○ Kamen Vitovska '19	♟♟
○ Malvasia '19	♟♟
○ Prulke '20	♟♟
○ Prulke '19	♟♟
○ Prulke '18	♟♟
● Ruje '17	♟♟

★Zorzettig

fraz. Spessa
s.da Sant'Anna, 37
33043 Cividale del Friuli [UD]
(· +39 0432716156
· www.zorzettigvini.it

CELLAR SALES
PRE-BOOKED VISITS
ACCOMMODATION
ANNUAL PRODUCTION 800,000 bottles
HECTARES UNDER VINE 120.00
SUSTAINABLE WINERY

Annalisa and Alessandro Zorzettig manage the estate, proudly retaining the family brand that has distinguished many generations of winemakers in Spessa di Cividale. Annalisa is an innovative and dynamic producer, a whirlwind of ideas, while Alessandro prefers to focus on agronomic management. Amid the winery's continuous expansion, quality standards have never diminished, while excellence has been achieved by selecting grapes for the Myò line. The Pinot Bianco Myò '22, on par with the best vintages, offers delightful floral whiffs of elderflower and jasmine and a clear and gentle palate. The Malvasia Myò '22 exudes aromas of yellow peach and medlar, delighting the palate with its fragrant citrus notes. The Bianco Myò I Fiori di Leonie '21, a blend of pinot bianco, tocai friulano, and sauvignon, is complex and refined on the nose, with tropical nuances of banana giving way to papaya, broom, orange blossom, and mandarin; the palate is splendid, energetic, balanced, and harmonious.

Zuani

loc. Giasbana, 12
34070 San Floriano del Collio [GO]
(· +39 0481391432
· www.zuanivini.it

CELLAR SALES
PRE-BOOKED VISITS
ACCOMMODATION
ANNUAL PRODUCTION 100,000 bottles
HECTARES UNDER VINE 20.00
SUSTAINABLE WINERY

Zuani embodies Patrizia Felluga's philosophy and knowledge, which developed over years of experience (thanks to her keen entrepreneurial skills as well). Hailing from a family of producers herself, Patrizia has successfully passed on her love for the land and viticulture to her children Antonio and Caterina. For many years the Collio Bianco Zuani, which debuted date back to 2001, has been the only wine produced, albeit in two versions, steel and wood. For many years now, the winery's offerings have expanded to include Ribolla Gialla and Pinot Grigio in the Sodevo line, two wines that have long stood out for their fragrance and linearity. However, the Collio Bianco once again leads the rankings, although this year, the parts have been reversed, and it's the Zuani Riserva '21 that tops the list. It's an intriguing wine—complex, rich, juicy and energetic— progressive, taut, and persistent.

FCO Bianco Myò I Fiori di Leonie '21	♥♥♥ 7
FCO Malvasia Myò '22	♥♥ 5
FCO Pinot Bianco Myò '22	♥♥ 7
COF Picolit Myò '19	♥♥ 7
FCO Friulano Myò '22	♥♥ 5
FCO Sauvignon Myò '22	♥♥ 5
FCO Schioppettino Myò '19	♥♥ 6
Friuli Friulano '23	♥♥ 3
Friuli Pinot Grigio '23	♥♥ 3
Friuli Ribolla Gialla '23	♥♥ 3
Friuli Sauvignon '23	♥♥ 3
Friuli Verduzzo Friulano '19	♥♥ 4
Optimun Ribolla Gialla Brut '23	♥♥ 4
FCO Bianco Myò I Fiori di Leonie '20	♥♥♥ 6
FCO Pinot Bianco Myò '20	♥♥♥ 6

o Collio Bianco Zuani Ris. '21	♥♥ 6
o Collio Bianco Zuani Vigne '23	♥♥ 5
o Collio Ribolla Gialla Sodevo '23	♥♥ 4
o Friuli Pinot Grigio Sodevo '23	♥♥ 4
o Collio Bianco Zuani Vigne '10	♥♥♥ 3
o Collio Bianco Zuani Vigne '07	♥♥♥ 3
o Collio Bianco Zuani Ris. '20	♥♥ 6
o Collio Bianco Zuani Ris. '19	♥♥ 6
o Collio Bianco Zuani Vigne '22	♥♥ 5
o Collio Bianco Zuani Vigne '21	♥♥ 5
o Collio Bianco Zuani Vigne '20	♥♥ 4
o Collio Bianco Zuani Vigne '19	♥♥ 4
o Collio Bianco Zuani Vigne '18	♥♥ 4
o Collio Ribolla Gialla Sodevo '22	♥♥ 4
o Collio Ribolla Gialla Sodevo '21	♥♥ 4
o Friuli Pinot Grigio Sodevo '22	♥♥ 4

OTHER WINERIES

AD Coos

fraz. Ramandolo
via Pescia, 3
33045 Nimis [UD]
(+39 3356101320
azienda.ad.coos@gmail.com

CELLAR SALES
PRE-BOOKED VISITS
ANNUAL PRODUCTION 12,000 bottles
HECTARES UNDER VINE 2.50

○ FCO Friulano '22	♟♟ 3
● FCO Merlot '22	♟♟ 4
● Refosco P. R. '20	♟♟ 4
○ Ribolla Gialla '23	♟ 4

Amandum

via F. Petrarca, 40
34070 Moraro [GO]
(+39 335242566
⊕ www.amandum.it

ANNUAL PRODUCTION 35,000 bottles
HECTARES UNDER VINE 2.00

○ Friuli Isonzo Chardonnay '19	♟♟ 4
● Friuli Isonzo Cabernet Franc '19	♟♟ 5
○ Friuli Isonzo Sauvignon '20	♟♟ 4

Ascevi Luwa

loc. Uclanzi, 24
34070 San Floriano del Collio [GO]
(+39 0481884140
⊕ www.asceviluwa.it

CELLAR SALES
PRE-BOOKED VISITS
ANNUAL PRODUCTION 150,000 bottles
HECTARES UNDER VINE 30.00

○ Collio Chardonnay Rupis '23	♟♟ 3
○ Collio Pinot Grigio Grappoli '23	♟♟ 3
○ Collio Sauvignon Ronco dei Sassi '23	♟♟ 3
○ Collio Ribolla Gialla '23	♟ 3

Albafiorita Winery

via Crosere, 115
33053 Latisana [UD]
(+39 3408731918
⊕ www.albafiorita.com

CELLAR SALES
PRE-BOOKED VISITS
ACCOMMODATION
ANNUAL PRODUCTION 70,000 bottles
HECTARES UNDER VINE 8.00
VITICULTURE METHOD Certified Organic
SUSTAINABLE WINERY

● Friuli Cabernet Franc M'ama '21	♟♟ 3
● Friuli Merlot M'ama '21	♟♟ 5
○ M'ama '23	♟♟ 3
○ Soffio '22	♟ 5

Maurizio Arzenton

fraz. Spessa
via Cormons, 221
33043 Cividale del Friuli [UD]
(+39 0432716139
⊕ www.arzentonvini.it

CELLAR SALES
PRE-BOOKED VISITS
ANNUAL PRODUCTION 30,000 bottles
HECTARES UNDER VINE 10.00

○ FCO Pinot Bianco '23	♟♟ 3
○ FCO Chardonnay '22	♟♟ 3
● FCO Merlot '19	♟ 3
● FCO Refosco dal P. R. '22	♟ 3

Augusta Bargilli

via Cladrecis, 105a
33040 Cividale del Friuli [UD]
(+39 3342860711
⊕ www.augustabargilli.it

CELLAR SALES
PRE-BOOKED VISITS
ANNUAL PRODUCTION 10,000 bottles
HECTARES UNDER VINE 4.00

○ FCO Bianco Cûr Blanc '21	♟♟ 8
○ FCO Chardonnay '21	♟♟ 8
● FCO Refosco dal P. R. '20	♟♟ 8

OTHER WINERIES

Baroni del Mestri

salita al Monte Quarin, 22
34071 Cormòns [GO]
☎ +39 3485903070
🖙 www.baronidelmestri.it

CELLAR SALES
PRE-BOOKED VISITS
ANNUAL PRODUCTION 8,000 bottles
HECTARES UNDER VINE 2.00

○ Collio Malvasia Serica '23	♟♟ 5
○ Collio Bianco Sere d'Estate '22	♟♟ 5
● Collio Merlot Barone di Schönberg '21	♟♟ 5
● Refosco dal P. R. '21	♟♟ 5

Bidoli

fraz. Arcano Superiore
via Fornace, 19
33030 Rive d'Arcano [UD]
☎ +39 0432810796
🖙 www.bidolivini.com

CELLAR SALES
PRE-BOOKED VISITS
ACCOMMODATION
ANNUAL PRODUCTION 1,000,000 bottles
SUSTAINABLE WINERY

● Friuli Grave Merlot Briccolo Ris. '21	♟♟ 3
○ Friuli Grave Pinot Grigio '22	♟♟ 2*
○ Friuli Grave Sauvignon '23	♟♟ 2*
● Friuli Refosco dal P. R. '21	♟♟ 2*

Borgo Sant'Andrea

fraz. Brazzacco
via Sant'Andrea
33030 Moruzzo [UD]
☎ +39 0432642015
🖙 www.borgosantandrea.com

CELLAR SALES
PRE-BOOKED VISITS
RESTAURANT SERVICE
ANNUAL PRODUCTION 40,000 bottles
HECTARES UNDER VINE 21.00

○ Friuli Chardonnay '21	♟♟ 3
○ Friuli Friulano '21	♟♟ 3
● Friuli Merlot '21	♟♟ 3
○ Friuli Pinot Grigio '21	♟♟ 3

La Bellanotte

s.da della Bellanotte, 3
34072 Farra d'Isonzo [GO]
☎ +39 0481888020
🖙 www.labellanotte.it

CELLAR SALES
PRE-BOOKED VISITS
ANNUAL PRODUCTION 100,000 bottles
HECTARES UNDER VINE 16.00
VITICULTURE METHOD Certified Organic

○ Collio Pinot Grigio '23	♟♟ 4
● Friuli Isonzo Merlot Roja de Isonzo '15	♟♟ 5
○ Friuli Pinot Grigio Ramato Conte Lucio '19	♟♟ 5
● Friuli Pinot Nero Spartaco '19	♟♟ 6

Blason Wines

via Roma, 32
34072 Gradisca d'Isonzo [GO]
☎ +39 048192414
🖙 www.blasonwines.com

CELLAR SALES
PRE-BOOKED VISITS
ANNUAL PRODUCTION 50,000 bottles
HECTARES UNDER VINE 18.00

○ Friuli Isonzo Friulano '23	♟♟ 3
○ Friuli Isonzo Friulano Blasonato '22	♟♟ 4
● Friuli Isonzo Refosco dal P. R. Vilès '22	♟♟ 3
● Cabernet Sauvignon '22	♟ 3

Tenuta Bosco Albano

fraz. Cecchini
via Bosco di Cecchini, 27/b
33087 Pasiano di Pordenone [PN]
☎ +39 0434628678
🖙 www.boscoalbano.com

CELLAR SALES
PRE-BOOKED VISITS
ACCOMMODATION
ANNUAL PRODUCTION 90,000 bottles
HECTARES UNDER VINE 39.00

○ Friuli Friulano '23	♟♟ 3
○ Friuli Pinot Bianco '23	♟♟ 3
● Friuli Pinot Nero '22	♟♟ 3
○ Friuli Sauvignon '23	♟ 3

OTHER WINERIES

Brandolin

via Leonardo da Vinci, 42
34070 Mariano del Friuli [GO]
📞 +39 3280816859
🌐 www.vinibrandolin.com

CELLAR SALES
ANNUAL PRODUCTION 15,000 bottles
HECTARES UNDER VINE 15.00
VITICULTURE METHOD Certified Organic
SUSTAINABLE WINERY

○ Friuli Isonzo Friulano '22	🍷🍷 4
● Friuli Isonzo Merlot '21	🍷🍷 4
● Friuli Isonzo Cabernet Franc '21	🍷 4
○ Friuli Isonzo Malvasia '22	🍷 4

Gabriele Brumat

loc. Medea
c.so Friuli, 46
34076 Medea [GO]
📞 +39 3356299703
🌐 www.vinibrumat.com

CELLAR SALES
RESTAURANT SERVICE
ANNUAL PRODUCTION 19,000 bottles
HECTARES UNDER VINE 4.00
SUSTAINABLE WINERY

○ Chardonnay '23	🍷🍷 3
○ Friuli Isonzo Friulano Sot la Mont '23	🍷🍷 3
● Il Band Cabernet Franc '23	🍷🍷 4
○ Chàos Malvasia '23	🍷 3

Ca Modeano

fraz. Modeano
via Casali Modeano, 1
33056 Palazzolo dello Stella [UD]
📞 +39 043158244
🌐 www.modeano.it

CELLAR SALES
PRE-BOOKED VISITS
RESTAURANT SERVICE
ANNUAL PRODUCTION 50,000 bottles
HECTARES UNDER VINE 32.00
SUSTAINABLE WINERY

● Cabernet Sauvignon CS '21	🍷🍷 4
○ Friuli Malvasia '23	🍷🍷 3
○ Pinot Grigio '23	🍷🍷 3
◎ Pinot Grigio Ramato '23	🍷🍷 3

Cabert - Cantina di Bertiolo

via Madonna, 27
33032 Bertiolo [UD]
📞 +39 0432917434
🌐 www.cabert.it

CELLAR SALES
PRE-BOOKED VISITS
ANNUAL PRODUCTION 1,500,000 bottles
HECTARES UNDER VINE 280.00

● FCO Merlot Casali Roncali '22	🍷🍷 3
○ FCO Pinot Grigio Casali Roncali '23	🍷🍷 3
● FCO Schioppettino Casali Roncali '22	🍷🍷 3

I Clivi

loc. Gramogliano, 20
33040 Corno di Rosazzo [UD]
📞 +39 3287269979
🌐 www.iclivi.wine

CELLAR SALES
PRE-BOOKED VISITS
ANNUAL PRODUCTION 50,000 bottles
HECTARES UNDER VINE 12.00
VITICULTURE METHOD Certified Organic

○ Collio Friulano San Lorenzo '22	🍷🍷 4
○ Collio Malvasia V. 80 Anni '23	🍷🍷 4
○ FCO Bianco Galea '22	🍷🍷 4
● Schioppettino '22	🍷🍷 4

Cornium

via Aquileia, 79
33040 Corno di Rosazzo [UD]
📞 +39 3476010132
ariedogigante@alice.it

CELLAR SALES
PRE-BOOKED VISITS
ANNUAL PRODUCTION 20,000 bottles
HECTARES UNDER VINE 12.00

○ FCO Friulano '22	🍷🍷 3
○ FCO Ribolla Gialla '21	🍷🍷 2
○ Ribolla Gialla Brut '21	🍷 3

OTHER WINERIES

La Cricca

loc. Craoretto, 2
33040 Prepotto [UD]
☏ +39 3275618717
✉ www.vinilacricca.it

CELLAR SALES
PRE-BOOKED VISITS
ANNUAL PRODUCTION 7,500 bottles
HECTARES UNDER VINE 2.50
SUSTAINABLE WINERY

○ FCO Pinot Bianco '22	♟♟ 5
○ FCO Bianco Busart '22	♟♟ 5
○ FCO Friulano '22	♟♟ 4
● FCO Rosso Icarus '21	♟♟ 5

La Delizia

v.le Udine, 24
33072 Casarsa della Delizia [PN]
☏ +39 0434869564
✉ www.ladelizia.com

CELLAR SALES
PRE-BOOKED VISITS
ANNUAL PRODUCTION 26,000,000 bottles
HECTARES UNDER VINE 2000.00
SUSTAINABLE WINERY

● Friuli Refosco dal P. R. Sass Ter '22	♟♟ 5
○ Jadèr Cuvèe Naonis Brut	♟♟ 3
○ Valdobbiadene Prosecco Sup. Naonis Brut '23	♟♟ 6

Fedele Giacomo

loc. Gramogliano, 5
33040 Corno di Rosazzo [UD]
☏ +39 3406078929
✉ fedele.giacomo@alice.it

CELLAR SALES
PRE-BOOKED VISITS
HECTARES UNDER VINE 18.50

○ FCO Friulano '22	♟♟ 2*
● FCO Merlot '21	♟♟ 3
● FCO Refosco dal P.R. '21	♟♟ 4
○ FCO Sauvignon '22	♟♟ 2*

Marina Danieli

fraz. Caminetto
via Beltrame, 77
33042 Buttrio [UD]
☏ +39 0432674421
✉ www.marinadanieli.com

CELLAR SALES
PRE-BOOKED VISITS
ACCOMMODATION AND RESTAURANT SERVICE
ANNUAL PRODUCTION 150,000 bottles
HECTARES UNDER VINE 34.00
SUSTAINABLE WINERY

● FCO Cabernet '21	♟♟ 3
○ FCO Pinot Grigio '23	♟♟ 3
● FCO Schioppettino '22	♟♟ 3
○ FCO Friulano '23	♟ 3

Le Favole

loc. Terra Rossa
via Dietro Castello, 7
33070 Caneva [PN]
☏ +39 0434735604
✉ www.lefavole-wines.com

CELLAR SALES
PRE-BOOKED VISITS
ACCOMMODATION
ANNUAL PRODUCTION 80,000 bottles
HECTARES UNDER VINE 21.00

○ Friuli Bianco Picavèlt '21	♟♟ 3
● Friuli Merlot Noglar '20	♟♟ 4
○ Friuli Traminer Aromatico '23	♟♟ 3
○ Giallo di Roccia Brut M. Cl.	♟♟ 4

Ferlat

via Savaian, 1/2
34071 Cormòns [GO]
☏ +39 3391105324
✉ www.ferlatvini.it

CELLAR SALES
PRE-BOOKED VISITS
ANNUAL PRODUCTION 48,000 bottles
HECTARES UNDER VINE 7.00
VITICULTURE METHOD Certified Organic

● Cabernet Franc '21	♟♟ 4
○ Gramè Malvasia '22	♟♟ 5
● No Land Vineyard Merlot '21	♟♟ 4
○ PG rosa '23	♟♟ 4

OTHER WINERIES

Foffani

fraz. Clauiano
p.zza Giulia, 13
33050 Trivignano Udinese [UD]
+39 0432999584
www.foffani.it

CELLAR SALES
PRE-BOOKED VISITS
ACCOMMODATION AND RESTAURANT SERVICE
ANNUAL PRODUCTION 40,000 bottles
HECTARES UNDER VINE 8.00
SUSTAINABLE WINERY

● Friuli Aquileia Merlot Ris. '21	🍷🍷 3
● Friuli Aquileia Refosco dal P. R. '20	🍷🍷 3
⊙ Moscato Rosa Fior di Rosa '23	🍷🍷 3
○ Merlot Bianco '23	🍷 3

Isola Augusta

via Casali Isola Augusta, 4
33056 Palazzolo dello Stella [UD]
+39 043158046
www.isolaugusta.com

CELLAR SALES
PRE-BOOKED VISITS
ACCOMMODATION AND RESTAURANT SERVICE
ANNUAL PRODUCTION 270,000 bottles
HECTARES UNDER VINE 53.00
SUSTAINABLE WINERY

○ Edgardo II Brut M. Cl.	🍷🍷 5
○ Friuli Chardonnay Les Iles '21	🍷🍷 4
○ Friuli Chardonnay '23	🍷 3
● Friuli Refosco dal P. R. '22	🍷 3

La Magnolia

loc. Spessa
via Cormòns, 169
33043 Cividale del Friuli [UD]
+39 0432716262
www.vinilamagnolia.it

CELLAR SALES
PRE-BOOKED VISITS
ACCOMMODATION
ANNUAL PRODUCTION 250,000 bottles
HECTARES UNDER VINE 45.00

○ FCO Sauvignon '22	🍷🍷 2*
○ FCO Friulano '23	🍷🍷 2*
● Ubi Es '20	🍷🍷 3
○ Ubi Que '22	🍷🍷 4

Obiz

b.go Gortani, 2
33052 Cervignano del Friuli [UD]
+39 043131900
www.obiz.it

CELLAR SALES
PRE-BOOKED VISITS
ANNUAL PRODUCTION 100,000 bottles
HECTARES UNDER VINE 40.00
SUSTAINABLE WINERY

○ Friuli Malvasia '23	🍷🍷 2*
● Friuli Refosco dal P. R. '22	🍷🍷 2*
○ Natissa Bianco '19	🍷🍷 3
○ Friuli Friulano '23	🍷 3

Orzan

via G. Mazzini, 48
34070 Capriva del Friuli [GO]
+39 0481809419
www.orzanwines.com

CELLAR SALES
PRE-BOOKED VISITS
RESTAURANT SERVICE
ANNUAL PRODUCTION 25,000 bottles
HECTARES UNDER VINE 5.00
SUSTAINABLE WINERY

○ Collio Friulano Una Gnot '22	🍷🍷 3
○ Collio Ribolla Gialla Val di Mieç '23	🍷🍷 3
○ Collio Ribolla Gialla Zal Scur Ris. '20	🍷🍷 5
○ Collio Sauvignon aX '23	🍷🍷 3

Piè di Mont

loc. Piedimonte del Calvario
via Monte Calvario, 30
34170 Gorizia
+39 0481391338
www.piedimont.it

CELLAR SALES
PRE-BOOKED VISITS
ANNUAL PRODUCTION 10,000 bottles
HECTARES UNDER VINE 1.20

○ Blanc de Blanc Pas Dosé M. Cl. '18	🍷🍷 6
○ Cuvée Brut M. Cl. '20	🍷🍷 6

OTHER WINERIES

Piera 1899

via Pordenone, 33
33080 San Quirino [PN]
☏ +39 0434963100
@ www.piera1899.com

CELLAR SALES
PRE-BOOKED VISITS
ANNUAL PRODUCTION 600,000 bottles
HECTARES UNDER VINE 55.00
VITICULTURE METHOD Certified Organic
SUSTAINABLE WINERY

● Friuli Cabernet Franc Terre Magre '23	♟♟ 2*
○ Friuli Sauvignon Terre Magre '23	♟♟ 2*
⊙ Rosato '23	♟♟ 2*
○ FCO Ribolla Gialla '23	♟ 3

Pitticco

via Novacuzzo, 52a
33040 Prepotto [UD]
☏ +39 0432481609
@ www.pitticco.com

CELLAR SALES
PRE-BOOKED VISITS
ANNUAL PRODUCTION 15,000 bottles
HECTARES UNDER VINE 5.00
VITICULTURE METHOD Certified Organic

● FCO Schioppettino Minò Ris. '21	♟♟ 7
● FCO Rosso Migale Ris. '21	♟♟ 6
● FCO Schioppettino di Prepotto '21	♟♟ 6
● FCO Tazzelenghe Serika Ris. '21	♟♟ 7

Reguta

via Bassi, 16
33050 Pocenia [UD]
☏ +39 0432779157
@ www.reguta.com

CELLAR SALES
PRE-BOOKED VISITS
ACCOMMODATION AND RESTAURANT SERVICE
ANNUAL PRODUCTION 2,000,000 bottles
HECTARES UNDER VINE 270.00
SUSTAINABLE WINERY

⊙ Carant '19	♟♟ 3
○ Friuli Friulano '23	♟♟ 3
● Pignolo '19	♟♟ 2*
⊙ Prediale '23	♟♟ 3

Tenuta Pinni

via Sant'Osvaldo, 3
33098 San Martino al Tagliamento [PN]
☏ +39 3513520830
@ www.tenutapinni.com

CELLAR SALES
PRE-BOOKED VISITS
ANNUAL PRODUCTION 32,000 bottles
HECTARES UNDER VINE 27.00
SUSTAINABLE WINERY

○ Chardonnay '23	♟♟ 3
● Merlot '20	♟♟ 3
○ Traminer Aromatico '23	♟♟ 3
○ Friuli Pinot Grigio '23	♟ 3

Cantina Rauscedo

fraz. Rauscedo
via del Sile, 16
33095 San Giorgio
della Richinvelda [PN]
☏ +39 042794020
@ www.cantinarauscedo.com

CELLAR SALES
ANNUAL PRODUCTION 800,000 bottles
HECTARES UNDER VINE 1700.00

○ Friuli Chardonnay '23	♟♟ 2*
○ Friuli Sauvignon Casa Quaranta '21	♟♟ 3
● Rosso Casa Quaranta '21	♟ 3
○ Villamanin Brut M. Cl.	♟ 5

Barone Ritter de Záhony

fraz. Monastero
p.zza Pirano, 8
33051 Aquileia [UD]
☏ +39 043191037
@ www.ritterdezahony.it

CELLAR SALES
PRE-BOOKED VISITS
ANNUAL PRODUCTION 40,000 bottles
HECTARES UNDER VINE 55.00
SUSTAINABLE WINERY

⊙ Edda Cristina '22	♟♟ 3
○ Friuli Aquileia Chardonnay Elvine '22	♟♟ 3
● Friuli Aquileia Merlot Manfredo '21	♟♟ 3
⊙ Mavi Rosato '23	♟ 3

Ronco dei Pini

via Ronchi, 93
33040 Prepotto [UD]
☎ +39 0432713239
✉ www.novellowines.it

CELLAR SALES
PRE-BOOKED VISITS
ANNUAL PRODUCTION 90,000 bottles
HECTARES UNDER VINE 15.00

● FCO Cabernet Sauvignon '22	♟♟ 3*
○ FCO Ribolla Gialla '23	♟♟ 4
○ FCO Sauvignon '23	♟♟ 3
● FCO Schioppettino di Prepotto '20	♟♟ 5

San Simone

loc. Rondover
via Prata, 30
33080 Porcia [PN]
☎ +39 0434578633
✉ www.sansimone.it

CELLAR SALES
PRE-BOOKED VISITS
ANNUAL PRODUCTION 900,000 bottles
HECTARES UNDER VINE 85.00
SUSTAINABLE WINERY

● Friuli Grave Cabernet Franc Sugano '21	♟♟ 4
● Friuli Grave Merlot Evante Ris. '20	♟♟ 4
○ Friuli Grave Pinot Grigio Ramato Case Sugan '21	♟♟ 4

Solo Roberto

via Mazzini, 29
01035 Gallese [VT]
☎ +39 0761495086
✉ www.soloroberto.com

○ Friuli Grave Pinot Grigio '23	♟♟ 3
○ Friuli Grave Sauvignon '23	♟♟ 3
○ Friuli Grave Traminer Aromatico '23	♟♟ 3

Russolo

via San Rocco, 58a
33080 San Quirino [PN]
☎ +39 0434919577
✉ www.russolo.it

CELLAR SALES
PRE-BOOKED VISITS
ANNUAL PRODUCTION 160,000 bottles
HECTARES UNDER VINE 16.00
SUSTAINABLE WINERY

○ Doi Raps '22	♟♟ 4
○ FVG Chardonnay Ronco Calaj '23	♟♟ 3
○ FVG Sauvignon Ronco Calaj '23	♟♟ 3

Skerlj

via Sales, 44
34010 Sgonico [TS]
☎ +39 040229253
✉ www.skerlj.it

CELLAR SALES
PRE-BOOKED VISITS
ACCOMMODATION AND RESTAURANT SERVICE
ANNUAL PRODUCTION 5,000 bottles
HECTARES UNDER VINE 2.00
VITICULTURE METHOD Certified Organic

○ Vitovska 6/7 Ris. '21	♟♟ 7
○ Malvasia '21	♟♟ 5
○ Vitovska '21	♟♟ 5

Ivan Sosol

fraz. Oslavia
loc. Lenzuolo Bianco, 4
34070 Gorizia
☎ +39 3493433686
✉ www.sosol.it

CELLAR SALES
PRE-BOOKED VISITS
ANNUAL PRODUCTION 10,000 bottles
HECTARES UNDER VINE 10.00

○ Collio Ribolla Gialla '23	♟♟ 4
○ Collio Bianco Borjac '23	♟♟ 4
○ Collio Bianco Borjac '22	♟♟ 4
● Collio Merlot '22	♟♟ 5

OTHER WINERIES

Stanig

fraz. Albana di Prepotto
via Albana, 44
33040 Prepotto [UD]
+39 0432713234
www.stanig.it

CELLAR SALES
ACCOMMODATION AND RESTAURANT SERVICE
ANNUAL PRODUCTION 45,000 bottles
HECTARES UNDER VINE 9.00
SUSTAINABLE WINERY

● FCO Merlot '21	🍷🍷 4
○ FCO Friulano '23	🍷🍷 3
○ FCO Malvasia '23	🍷🍷 3
● FCO Schiopettino di Preopotto Ris. '18	🍷🍷 6

Talis

via Palmarina, 113/4
33048 San Giovanni al Natisone [UD]
+39 3355393920
www.taliswine.it

ANNUAL PRODUCTION 20,000 bottles
HECTARES UNDER VINE 40.00

● FCO Refosco dal P. R. '22	🍷🍷 2*
○ Friuli Friulano '23	🍷🍷 2*
● Friuli Merlot '22	🍷🍷 2*
○ Friuli Sauvignon '23	🍷🍷 2*

Tarlao

via San Zili, 50
33051 Aquileia [UD]
+39 3339478494
www.tarlao.eu

CELLAR SALES
PRE-BOOKED VISITS
RESTAURANT SERVICE
ANNUAL PRODUCTION 37,000 bottles
HECTARES UNDER VINE 7.00

○ Friuli Aquileia Chardonnay Ardea Alba '22	🍷🍷 5
○ Friuli Aquileia Friulano Albero del Noce '23	🍷🍷 3
○ Friuli Aquileia Pinot Bianco Poc ma Bon '23	🍷🍷 3
● Friuli Aquileia Refosco P. R. Mosaic Ros '20	🍷🍷 5

Tenuta della Casa

loc. Novali, 1
34071 Cormòns [GO]
+39 0039339688362

ANNUAL PRODUCTION 6,000 bottles
HECTARES UNDER VINE 4.00

○ Collio Bianco Preludio '22	🍷🍷 5
● Collio Rosso Overture '22	🍷🍷 5
○ Sinfonia '22	🍷🍷 5

Terre del Faet

fraz. Faet
v.le Roma, 82
34071 Cormòns [GO]
+39 3470103325
www.terredelfaet.it

CELLAR SALES
PRE-BOOKED VISITS
ANNUAL PRODUCTION 24,000 bottles
HECTARES UNDER VINE 4.50

○ Collio Bianco da Uve Autoctone '21	🍷🍷 3*
○ Collio Friulano '22	🍷🍷 4
○ Collio Malvasia '22	🍷🍷 3
○ Collio Pinot Bianco '22	🍷🍷 4

Valle

via Nazionale, 3
33042 Buttrio [UD]
+39 0432674289
www.valle.it

CELLAR SALES
PRE-BOOKED VISITS
ANNUAL PRODUCTION 300,000 bottles
HECTARES UNDER VINE 42.00

○ FCO Chardonnay '23	🍷🍷 3
○ FCO Pinot Grigio '23	🍷🍷 3
○ FCO Ribolla Gialla '23	🍷🍷 3
○ Quinta Terrazza '21	🍷🍷 5

OTHER WINERIES

Valvitis - C&C

fraz. Villotta
via Maestri del Lavoro, 20b
33083 Chions [PN]
+39 0434630667
www.cecsrl.eu

ANNUAL PRODUCTION 15,000,000 bottles
HECTARES UNDER VINE 20.00

○ Friuli Grave Friulano '23	🍷🍷 2*
● Friuli Grave Merlot '23	🍷🍷 2*
○ Friuli Grave Pinot Grigio '22	🍷🍷 2*
○ Friuli Grave Sauvignon '23	🍷🍷 2*

Vie d'Alt

via Craoretto, 16
33040 Prepotto [UD]
+39 0432713069
www.viedalt.it

CELLAR SALES
PRE-BOOKED VISITS
ACCOMMODATION
ANNUAL PRODUCTION 120,000 bottles
HECTARES UNDER VINE 20.00
SUSTAINABLE WINERY

○ FCO Bianco Aljere Ris. '20	🍷🍷 5
○ FCO Friulano '23	🍷🍷 3
● FCO Rosso Alsarà Ris. '20	🍷🍷 6
● FCO Schioppettino di Prepotto '21	🍷🍷 5

Villa Rubini

fraz. Spessa
via Case Rubini, 1
33043 Cividale del Friuli [UD]
+39 04321847443
www.villarubini.wine

CELLAR SALES
PRE-BOOKED VISITS
ANNUAL PRODUCTION 70,000 bottles
HECTARES UNDER VINE 15.00
VITICULTURE METHOD Certified Organic
SUSTAINABLE WINERY

○ FCO Pinot Grigio Ramato Sauvage '22	🍷🍷 3
● FCO Pinot Nero Corte del Tasso '23	🍷🍷 3
● FCO Pinot Nero Sauvage '22	🍷🍷 3
⊙ Pocalza in Rosa Pas Dosé M. Cl. '19	🍷🍷 6

Villa Vasi

loc. Villa Vasi, 15
34070 Gorizia
+39 3477800077
www.vinivillavasi.it

○ Collio Pinot Grigio Amorus '22	🍷🍷 4
○ Collio Ribolla Gialla '22	🍷🍷 4
○ Collio Sauvignon '22	🍷🍷 4
○ Friuli Isonzo Friulano '22	🍷🍷 4

Villa Vitas

loc. Strassoldo
via San Marco, 5
33052 Cervignano del Friuli [UD]
+39 043193083
www.vitas.it

CELLAR SALES
PRE-BOOKED VISITS
ACCOMMODATION
ANNUAL PRODUCTION 90,000 bottles
HECTARES UNDER VINE 16.00
SUSTAINABLE WINERY

○ Friuli Friulano '23	🍷🍷 3*
● Friuli Refosco dal P. R. '22	🍷🍷 3
○ Friuli Traminer Aromatico '23	🍷🍷 3
○ Ribolla Gialla '23	🍷🍷 3

Vinopera Bervini

loc. Villutta
via Treviso
33083 Chions [PN]
+39 0434630216
www.bervini.it

CELLAR SALES
PRE-BOOKED VISITS
ANNUAL PRODUCTION 500,000 bottles
HECTARES UNDER VINE 30.00
VITICULTURE METHOD Certified Organic

● Friuli Pinot Nero '22	🍷🍷 3
⊙ Prosecco Rosè Brut '23	🍷🍷 3
○ Ribolla Gialla Dry	🍷🍷 3
○ Sauvignon Friuli '22	🍷 3

BRDA
SLOVENIA

In the northeastern corner of Italy, where border checkpoints have long disappeared, it's easy to find yourself crossing into Slovenia's Brda region while wandering through the terraced hills of the Collio Goriziano. At first glance, the landscape looks the same, but as you venture deeper, the terrain becomes more rugged, with steeper hills and vineyards that are traditionally small, surrounded by local flora that fosters biodiversity, providing an ideal habitat for insects, birds, and other wildlife.

The terroir in Brda is shaped by a complex interaction between climate, soil, and human intervention. The sub-Mediterranean climate, influenced by the nearby Adriatic Sea and the Julian Alps, brings mild winters, hot, dry summers, and generally sufficient rainfall — the only water source for the vineyards. The soil is predominantly made up of Eocene flysch, known locally as "opoka", a mix of alternating layers of sandstone and marl rich in calcite, a remnant of the ocean that existed here hundreds of millions of years ago. When a vineyard is replanted, the soil is dug to a depth of at least 1.5 meters, creating the vital space needed for vine roots to develop and withstand long dry periods. Sustainability guides winemaking practices in Brda, with natural materials typically used for support poles, ties, and retaining walls. Most of the work, especially harvest, is done by hand due to the small size of the estates.

The most common grape is "rebula" (ribolla gialla), which covers more than 20% of the vineyard area. It thrives on the area's steep slopes, where it develops its characteristic bouquet of honey, floral, and fruity notes, underscored by the mineral and saline qualities that reflect the uniqueness of the region. Traditionally, tocai friulano is also grown here. It's used for wines known by various names, including Sauvignonasse, Sauvignon Vert, Jakot, and Zelena Sauvignon. Among international varieties, chardonnay and sauvignon dominate the whites, while the reds are led by merlot, cabernet sauvignon, and pinot nero. In the pages that follow, you'll find fascinating insights to guide your tasting.

Carga

Pristavo, 2
5212 Dobrovo
(+386 70820546
www.carga.si

ANNUAL PRODUCTION 450,000 bottles
HECTARES UNDER VINE 15.00

Once the farmhouse of the Counts of Thurn und Taxis, Čarga is now owned by Edbin Erzetič. The family's love for the earth's most precious gift—the vine—has been passed down through generations since 1767. Today, Martin manages the estate, where the focus in the vineyards is mainly on local grape varieties. However, the true pride of the Čarga winery is its Donna Regina sparkling wines, produced using the metodo classico since 1994. The entire selection consists of mature and decidedly dry wines. The Sauvignon Blanc '22 stands out among the best, revealing a captivating tropical breeze of pineapple on the nose, followed by citrus, kiwi, lychee, and later, white pepper, pine resin, and mint. On the palate, it showcases an intriguing sapidity that pairs seamlessly with a pronounced, velvety progression. The Donna Regina Brut Nature '20 also stands out, excelling in the sparkling wine category with its lively, fragrant profile.

Erzetič

Visnjevik 25a
5212 Dobrovo
(+386 051643114
www.vina-erzetic.com

CELLAR SALES
PRE-BOOKED VISITS
ANNUAL PRODUCTION 80,000 bottles
HECTARES UNDER VINE 15.00
VITICULTURE METHOD Certified Organic

In the small village of Višnjevik the Erzetič family boasts a winemaking tradition that spans three centuries. The current family team benefits from the invaluable advice of Anton and Marta, the experience and hard work of the present owners, Aleksij and Vera, the youthful enthusiasm of Andrej and Teja, and the joyful playfulness of Neja. Each generation brings its own vision, yet all remain devoted to the family values of diligence, teamwork, and continuous improvement. This year, in addition to the Rebula Classic '23, which distinguished itself for its freshness and fragrance, two versions of Crna Rebula (schioppettino) were presented. Both are from the 2020 vintage, with the difference being the production method. As indicated by its name the Crna Rebula Amfora '20 is aged in buried clay amphorae, while the Crna Rebula Classic '20 matures in oak. Both have a bright future ahead.

○ Brda Donna Regina Brut Nature M. Cl. '20	♙♙ 5
○ Brda Sauvignon Blanc '22	♙♙ 4
● Brda Cabernet Franc '18	♙♙ 4
○ Brda Donna Regina Blanc de Blancs Brut M. Cl. '21	♙♙ 5
⊙ Brda Donna Regina Rose Brut M. Cl. '19	♙♙ 5
○ Brda Malvazija '22	♙♙ 4
● Brda Merlot '20	♙♙ 3
● Brda Ta Star Rosso '17	♙♙ 5
○ Brda Malvazija '19	♟♟ 2*
○ Brda Chardonnay '20	♟♟ 4
○ Brda Donna Regina Extra Brut M. Cl. '19	♟♟ 5
⊙ Brda Donna Regina Rose Brut M. Cl '18	♟♟ 5
○ Brda Jakot '21	♟♟ 4
○ Brda Rebula Rumena '21	♟♟ 4
○ Brda Sauvignon Blanc '21	♟♟ 4

● Brda Crna Rebula Amfora '20	♙♙ 5
● Brda Crna Rebula Classic '20	♙♙ 5
○ Brda Rebula Classic '23	♙♙ 4
○ Brda Rebula Orbis '18	♟♟♟ 8
● Brda Cabernet Sauvignon Amfora '18	♟♟ 7
○ Brda Chardonnay Orbis '19	♟♟ 8
○ Brda Chardonnay Orbis '18	♟♟ 8
● Brda Rdeče Amfora '16	♟♟ 6
○ Brda Rebula Amfora '16	♟♟ 6
○ Brda Rebula Classic '22	♟♟
○ Brda Rebula Classic '21	♟♟
○ Brda Rebula Crna Rebula Classic '18	♟♟
○ Brda Rebula Orbis '19	♟♟ 6
○ Brda Sauvignon Blanc Orbis '19	♟♟
● Brda Sivi Pinot Classic '21	♟♟

Ferdinand

Kojsco 5c
5211 Kojsko
📞 +386 041510636
🌐 www.ferdinand.si

Iaquin

Vipolže, 3
5212 Dobrovo
📞 +386 41456506
🌐 www.iaquin.si

CELLAR SALES
PRE-BOOKED VISITS
ANNUAL PRODUCTION 45,000 bottles
HECTARES UNDER VINE 11.00
SUSTAINABLE WINERY

ANNUAL PRODUCTION 15,000 bottles
HECTARES UNDER VINE 2.90

This charming winery is located near the village of Kojsko, where the Brda region meets the Prealps. In 1992, Matjaž Četrtič, then still a student, began tending the vineyards once owned by his great-grandfather Ferdinand. From the start, he could rely on the full moral and material support of his father, Marjan. Now, together with his wife Jasmina, Matjaž manages this thriving estate, which benefits from a precious legacy of old vines with deep, well-developed root systems. The lineup presented also includes a notable selection of Metodo Classico sparkling wines (the Sinefinis line). The Blanc de Blancs Brut '18 impresses with its lively, extremely fine, and persistent bead, emanating citrus aromas and refreshing the palate with marked fragrance and minerality. The Amber Gris Época '21 releases intriguing aromas of mulberries, currants, dried flowers, hazelnuts, and alchermes, while on the palate, it's perfectly balanced, soft yet energetic and flavorful.

Iaquin was founded in 1997 when Uroš Jakončič decided to formalize his family's deep roots in agriculture and winemaking and embark on his own journey. The winery is still very small, but its prospects for growth are strong, especially given the excellent reception its wines are receiving. The production philosophy is straightforward, focusing on crafting wines that are mature, elegant, balanced, and complex when they leave the cellar. All the wines presented received high marks and prove particularly enjoyable, satisfying both the nose and palate with pronounced varietal notes and making a pleasant lasting impression. We were particularly struck by the Rebula '21, the most representative variety in the Brda region, which exudes intriguing vegetal notes of boxwood and nettle, aromatic herbs, and citrus. On the palate, it's energetic and harmonious, exhibiting a modern style.

○ Brda Amber Gris Época '21	♟♟♟ 5
● Brda Rdece Brutus '18	♟♟ 8
○ Brda Rebula Brutus '19	♟♟ 7
○ Sinefinis Blanc de Blancs Brut M. Cl. '18	♟♟ 5
● Brda Epoca '18	♟ 6
○ Brda Malvazija Época '21	♟ 5
○ Brda Rebula '22	♟ 4
○ Brda Rebula '21	♟ 3
○ Brda Rebula Brutus '18	♟ 7
● Brda Rebula Época '21	♟ 5
● Brda Rebula Época '20	♟ 5

○ Brda Rebula '21	♟♟ 5
○ Brda Chardonnay '20	♟♟ 6
○ Brda Dolan '18	♟♟ 5
○ Brda Malvazija '20	♟♟ 5
● Brda Merlot '18	♟♟ 5
○ Brda Chardonnay '17	♟ 4
○ Brda Dolan '18	♟ 4
● Brda Jak Rdeče '17	♟ 4
○ Brda Malvazija '19	♟ 4

Carolina Jakončič Winery

Kozana 5
5212 Dobrovo
☏ +386 31737263
✆ www.jakoncic.eu

Klet Brda

Zadružna cesta 9
5212 Dobrovo
☏ +386 53310102
✆ www.klet-brda.si

PRE-BOOKED VISITS
ANNUAL PRODUCTION 90,000 bottles
HECTARES UNDER VINE 23.00

CELLAR SALES
ANNUAL PRODUCTION 7,000,000 bottles
HECTARES UNDER VINE 1200.00
SUSTAINABLE WINERY

In 1847, Mihael and Carolina Jakončič had the inspired idea to plant their first vineyard in Kozana, consciously or not laying the foundation for their winery. Today, Aljoša and Mitja Jakončič lead Carolina Jakončič, a thriving estate that brings prestige to the Brda region, the cradle of great wines from western Slovenia. The producer's offerings are extensive, divided into four categories: Jakončič, Carolina, Mosaic, and Uvaia. The Jakončič e Carolina line is the largest, while their Mosaic line represents their Metodo Classicos. Uvaia is a fortified wine fermented in special egg-shaped barrels. The Bela Carolina Cosana I Classe '21 (chardonnay, ribolla gialla, and sauvignon) reveals refined floral notes on the nose, with hints of tropical fruit and acacia honey. A gratifying drink. The soft and compelling Chardonnay Borgo Scholaris '21 plays on intoxicating aromas of linden, mango, and vanilla.

Founded in 1957, Klet Brda is the largest producer and exporter of Slovenian wines worldwide, earning respect in 26 countries. The winery's mission is to represent the exceptional terroir of Goriška Brda through its wines and to promote their commercial success, contributing to the region's development and the well-being of its inhabitants. In the vineyards, young growers inherit the knowledge of previous generations, ensuring employment in rural areas. A blend of chardonnay and sauvignon the de Baguer Belo '19 is a white of superb structure and personality. It presents a seductive bouquet of honey and ginger, intertwined with nectarine, golden apple, myrtle, marzipan, and a delightful smoky note. On the palate, it's velvety, soft, and perfectly balanced by a fragrant sapidity. The highly aromatic Sivi Pinot Ramato Bagueri Sup. '21 stands out for its slenderness and drinkability.

○ Brda Bela Carolina Cosana I Classe '21 ♟♟♟ 6
● Brda Carolina Select '16 ♟♟ 8
○ Brda Chardonnay Borgo Scholaris '21 ♟♟ 8
○ Brda Rebula '23 ♟♟ 3
○ Brda Bela Carolina '19 ♟♟♟ 6
○ Brda Rebula Carolina '19 ♟♟♟ 8
○ Brda Bela Carolina '20 ♟♟ 6
● Brda Carolina Select '15 ♟♟ 8
○ Brda Chardonnay Borgo Scholaris '19 ♟♟ 8
○ Brda Chardonnay Borgo Scholaris '18 ♟♟ 8
○ Brda Pinot Gris Uvaia '20 ♟♟ 8
● Brda Pinot Noir Carolina '17 ♟♟ 7
○ Brda Rebula Carolina '17 ♟♟ 8

● Brda de Baguer Belo '19 ♟♟ 6
○ Brda Chardonnay Bagueri Sup. '20 ♟♟ 4
● Brda de Baguer Rdece '18 ♟♟ 5
○ Brda Rebula Bagueri Sup. '20 ♟♟ 4
○ Brda Sivi Pinot Ramato Bagueri Sup. '21 ♟♟ 3
● Brda Cabernet Sauvignon Bagueri Sup. '18 ♟♟ 5
○ Brda Chardonnay Bagueri Sup. '18 ♟♟ 4
● Brda de Baguer Merlot-Cabernet Franc '16 ♟♟ 5
○ Brda Krasno Orange '20 ♟♟ 4
● Brda Merlot - Cabernet Franc de Baguer '17 ♟♟ 6
● Brda Merlot Bagueri Sup. '18 ♟♟ 4
○ Brda Rebula Bagueri Sup. '19 ♟♟ 4
○ Brda Rebula Bagueri Sup. '18 ♟♟ 4
○ Brda Rebula Krasno '20 ♟♟ 3

Vini Noüe Marinič

Vedrijan 17
5211 Kojsko
☏ +386 3405838551
✇ www.domaine-nouemarinic.com

CELLAR SALES
PRE-BOOKED VISITS
ANNUAL PRODUCTION 200,000 bottles
HECTARES UNDER VINE 140.00

When Charles-Louis de Noüe left Burgundy for Brda, he was driven by a passion for authentic and prestigious terroirs, particularly those well suited to the cultivation of white wine grapes. With an ambitious project, he rescued and revived abandoned vineyards, preserving a rich genetic heritage through massal selection, which has added complexity to the wines. His partnership with Slovenian ally Alis Marinič led to the creation of Domaine Vicomte de Noüe-Marinič. This year, four Chardonnays were presented, each identified by the vineyard plot where the grapes were grown and the respective cru. All are of the highest quality, with the Chardonnay Tejca Vedrignano II Cru '21 standing out for its balance and fragrance, the Chardonnay Groblja Vedrignano II Cru '21 for its elegant tropical nuances, and the Chardonnay Sotto la Chiesa Bigliana II Cru '21 for its delightful fruity notes, both on the nose and palate.

Domaine Marjan Simčič

Ceglo 3b
5212 Dobrovo
☏ +386 53959200
✇ www.simcic.si

CELLAR SALES
PRE-BOOKED VISITS
ANNUAL PRODUCTION 130,000 bottles
HECTARES UNDER VINE 24.00

Representing the fifth generation of family, Marjan Simčič runs the estate founded by Jožef Simčič in 1860, drawing on the support of his wife Valerija and son Leonardo. His range, synonymous with quality, elegance, and the utmost expression of the terroir, is divided into three lines: Brda Classic includes wines with brief skin contact; the Cru Selection hails from old vines; Opoka Cru (named after the local soil type) represents their most prestigious offerings. The Rebula Opoka Medana Jama Cru '21 reveals intoxicating aromas of summer hay, Mediterranean scrub, fruit jelly, and cinnamon stick, while on the palate, it proves flavorful, sapid, and mineral. The Chardonnay Opoka Jordano Cru '21 conjures up yellow-fleshed fruit, lavender, and candied citrus, with a velvety and satisfying palate. The Sauvignon Blanc Opoka Jordano Cru '22 is redolent of green apple, white peach, and verbena, with a firm, fragrant, linear flavor profile.

○ Brda Chardonnay Tejca Vedrignano II Cru '21	♈♈♈ 8
○ Brda Chardonnay Groblja Vedrignano II Cru '21	♈♈ 8
○ Brda Chardonnay Sotto la Chiesa Bigliana II Cru '21	♈♈ 8
○ Brda Malvazija Erigone Zala Locca III Cru '21	♈♈ 5
○ Brda Chardonnay Attico San Pietro III Cru '21	♈♈ 8
● Brda Merlot Érigone San Pietro III Cru '21	♈♈ 8
● Brda Pinot Nero Érigone San Pietro III Cru '21	♈♈ 8
○ Brda Ribolla Gialla Erigone Gaugnaz I Cru '21	♈♈ 5

○ Brda Chardonnay Opoka Jordano Cru '21	♈♈♈ 8
○ Brda Rebula Opoka Medana Jama Cru '21	♈♈ 8
○ Brda Sauvignon Blanc Opoka Jordano Cru '22	♈♈ 8
● Brda Merlot Opoka Trobno Cru '18	♈♈ 8
○ Brda Pinot Grigio Ramato Cru Selection '22	♈♈ 6
● Brda Pinot Noir Opoka Breg Cru '20	♈♈ 8
○ Brda Sauvignon Vert Opoka Ronc Zegla Cru '21	♈♈ 8
○ Brda Chardonnay Opoka Jordano Cru '20	♈♈♈ 8
○ Brda Rebula Cru Selection '19	♈♈♈ 5

Valter Sirk

Visnjevik 38
5212 Dobrovo
+386 3045363
www.valtersirk.com

CELLAR SALES
PRE-BOOKED VISITS
ANNUAL PRODUCTION 40,000 bottles
HECTARES UNDER VINE 9.50

Valter Sirk founded his winery in 1991 in Višnjevik, a small village just a few kilometers from the Italian border. He cultivates his vineyards as naturally as possible, following the cycles of the sun and moon. His range is divided into three lines: "Fresh Wines," which are aged for a year (80% in stainless steel and 20% in non-new wood); "Mature Wines," which age for at least 18 months in oak; and the "ConteA line," which includes all the reserves. Only 2022 whites were presented this year. All reveal superb freshness and drinkability, and most importantly, faithfully express the varietal characteristics of the grapes used. We particularly appreciated the Malvazija '22, which exudes whiffs of fresh and balsamic medicinal herbs followed by citrus, stark apple, and white peach. The Sivi Pinot '22 is also excellent, revealing an aromatic profile reminiscent of citron peel, orange jelly, peach, and apricot.

○ Brda Malvazija '22	🍷🍷 5
○ Brda Sivi Pinot '22	🍷🍷 3*
○ Brda Beli Pinot '22	🍷🍷 5
○ Brda Chardonnay '22	🍷🍷 4
○ Brda Jakot '22	🍷🍷 4
○ Brda Rebula '22	🍷🍷 4
○ Brda Sauvignon '22	🍷🍷 5
○ Brda Beli Pinot '21	ϒϒ 5
○ Brda Beli Pinot '20	ϒϒ 4
○ Brda Contea Pinot Blanc '12	ϒϒ 8
○ Brda Malvazija '21	ϒϒ 5
○ Brda Sauvignon '21	ϒϒ 5
○ Brda Tereza Belo '17	ϒϒ 6

Zanut

Neblo 27
5212 Dobrovo
+386 31757672
www.zanut.si

CELLAR SALES
ANNUAL PRODUCTION 50,000 bottles
HECTARES UNDER VINE 8.00
SUSTAINABLE WINERY

Founded in 1976, the Zanut winery is today managed by the third generation, Borut Kocijančič, who runs the family business with the help of his wife Mateja. Their young sons, Mark and Filip, represent the future. Most of the vineyards, which are terraced and grass-covered, stretch across the hills of Brda, near the Italian border. In the cellar, only indigenous yeasts are used, with a minimal intervention approach adopted so as to preserve the typicity of each variety. This year, fewer wines were presented than in the past, but they were enough to confirm the excellent quality level achieved and maintained. The Malvazija '22 earned its place in the final tastings with its pronounced varietal profile of lemon balm, bay leaf, and rosemary, followed by mandarin, dried fruit, and wildflower honey. The palate is soft, sapid, and well-balanced. The Sivi Pinot '22, a pinot grigio, plays on aromas of hazelnuts and sponge cake.

○ Brda Malvazija '22	🍷🍷 4
● Brda Cabernet Sauvignon '21	🍷🍷 5
○ Brda Sivi Pinot '22	🍷🍷 4
○ Brda Verduc '22	🍷🍷 4
○ Brda Jama '20	ϒϒϒ 6
○ Brda Zakaj '21	ϒϒ 4
○ Brda Zakaj '20	ϒϒ 4
● Brda Augustus '16	ϒϒ 8
● Brda Cabernet Sauvignon '20	ϒϒ 5
● Brda Cabernet Sauvignon '18	ϒϒ 3
○ Brda Jama '19	ϒϒ 5
● Brda Merlot Brjac '16	ϒϒ 8
○ Brda Rebula '21	ϒϒ 4
○ Brda Rebula '19	ϒϒ 3
○ Brda Sauvignon '20	ϒϒ 5
○ Brda Sivi Pinot '21	ϒϒ 4

OTHER WINERIES

Dobuje
Snežeče, 16
5212 Dobrovo
☏ +386 41773721
✉ www.dobuje.com

● Brda Crno Selection '19	♟♟ 6
○ Brda Maria Nevea Selection '13	♟♟ 5
○ Jan Pet-Nat	♟♟ 3

Atelier Kramar
via Barbana, 12
5212 Dobrovo
☏ +386 31391575
✉ www.atelier-kramar.si

○ Brda Celeste '22	♟♟ 3
● Brda Merlot Garanza '19	♟♟ 4

Kristalvin
Višnjevik, 39
5212 Dobrovo
☏ +386 31855162
info@kristalvin.si

○ Brda Jacot Selection '21	♟♟ 5
● Brda Merlot Selection '19	♟♟ 5

Kristančič
Medana 29
5212 Dobrovo
☏ +386 41788670
✉ www.kristancic.com

○ Brda Chardonnay Pavò '22	♟♟ 6
○ Brda Rebula '23	♟♟ 3
● Brda Red Artwork '20	♟♟ 7
○ Brda Sauvignon '23	♟♟ 3

Medot
Market 25 May, 8a
5212 Dobrovo
☏ +386 59336160
✉ www.medot-wines.com

○ Brda Brut M. Cl. '15	♟♟ 5
○ Brda Rebula Journey '22	♟♟ 3

Prinčič
Kozana, 11
5212 Dobrovo
☏ +386 041721929
✉ www.princic.si

○ Brda Jakot '22	♟♟ 4
● Brda Merlot '22	♟♟ 4
○ Brda Rebula '23	♟♟ 3
○ Brda Sivi Pinot Aurei '21	♟♟ 4

OTHER WINERIES

Pulec
Plešivo, 38a
5212 Dobrovo
(☎ +386 41775958
⊕ www.pulec.com

Ronk
Vipolže, 94
5212 Dobrovo
(☎ +386 040554451
⊕ www.vinaronk.si

● Brda Cabernet Sauvignon '19	♈♈ 4
○ Brda Konrad Belo '22	♈♈ 3
○ Brda Rebula '22	♈♈ 3
○ Brda Sivi Pinot '23	♈♈ 3

○ Brda Malvazija '22	♈♈ 3
● Brda Selectus Red '18	♈♈ 4
○ Brda Selectus Sauvignon Blanc '20	♈♈ 4

Ščurek
Plesivo 44
5212 Dobrovo
(☎ +386 40604881
⊕ www.scurek.com

Silveri
Neblo, 1h
5212 Dobrovo
(☎ +386 53022562
⊕ www.silveri.si

○ Brda Malvazija '20	♈♈ 5
○ Brda Jazbine '21	♈♈ 5
○ Brda Sivi Pinot '23	♈♈ 5
○ Brda Stara Brajda '20	♈♈ 5

○ Brda Blanc de Blancs Brut M. Cl.	♈♈ 4
○ Brda Rebula '20	♈♈ 3
● Brda Tenor '18	♈♈ 4

Aljoša Sirk
Visnjevik 20
5212 Dobrovo
(☎ +386 40821704
vinarstvo.sirk@gmail.com

Zarova
Gonjate, IV
Kojsko
(☎ +386 51298729
⊕ www.zarova.si

● Brda Ivo '18	♈♈ 5
○ Brda Malvazija '22	♈♈ 3

○ Brda Rebula Class '22	♈♈ 5
○ Brda Chardonnay Class '22	♈♈ 4
○ Brda Sauvignon Blanc Class '22	♈♈ 4
○ Brda Sivi Pinot '23	♈♈ 3

EMILIA ROMAGNA

The Province of Bologna acts as a natural divide between the two halves of this large region, which are so distinct from one another that we will likely address them separately in future editions. In Emilia, it's no surprise that lambrusco dominates the scene, both in sheer volume and in the number of top-quality producers. This trend is only amplified by today's consumers, who increasingly prefer lighter, easy-drinking wines over the heavier styles that were once in fashion.

From the elegance of Sorbara—which also shines as a sparkling wine—to the bolder fruit of Grasparossa di Castelvetro and Salamino di Santa Croce, we've seen steady improvement, especially in hillside production areas and in the historically more renowned zones of Modena and Reggio Emilia. It's no coincidence that this year's Best Value for Money Award went to a lambrusco: the Grasparossa 7Bio '23 from the Settecani cooperative winery. The quality gap between this and generic Lambrusco Emilia blends—which often include less noble varieties and come at a significantly lower price point—is striking. Pignoletto is increasingly becoming identified with the Colli Bolognesi, despite some confusion over the various appellations, and is standing strong against wines made from international varietals. In contrast, Parma struggles to fully express its territorial characteristics. The story is different in Piacenza, where Metodo Classico sparkling wines, made from pinot nero and chardonnay, show great promise thanks to the area's proximity to Oltrepò Pavese, a region with a long tradition of sparkling wine production. Meanwhile, a group of producers is working hard to showcase the potential of malvasia di Candia aromatica, an indigenous grape capable of producing dry wines with remarkable personality and surprising longevity. We'll be watching closely.

Romagna, too, is having its moment of glory. We've said it before, and we'll say it again: it's on the right path, highlighting the region's diverse terroirs more and more. The undisputed star is sangiovese, cultivated in 16 subzones (the "Rocche di Romagna"). Some of these are quite large, making it difficult to find a unifying style, while others are more contained, and this is reflected in the glass. But sangiovese isn't the only story here. Though production is limited, albana is a variety we hold in high regard, excelling in various styles—from classic white vinification to skin-contact wines, from sparkling to late harvests where botrytis enhances the grapes. Finally, there's trebbiano. Especially when cultivated in the hills, we believe that it has the potential to bring out Romagna's true character.

Albinea Canali

fraz. Canali
via Tassoni, 213
42123 Reggio Emilia
+39 0522569505
www.albineacanali.com

CELLAR SALES
PRE-BOOKED VISITS
ANNUAL PRODUCTION 492,000 bottles
HECTARES UNDER VINE 150.00
VITICULTURE METHOD Certified Organic
SUSTAINABLE WINERY

Now part of the Cantine Riunite CIV group, this winery has preserved its identity and distinctive brand. Its origins date back to between 1934-1936, with the union of various local growers. Production focuses mainly on lambrusco, particularly the varieties that characterize Reggiano. However, several international grape varieties, well-adapted to the region's gravelly soils, are also cultivated. The Extra Brut AC sparkling wine once again demonstrates its delightful fruitiness, with prominent notes of strawberry and raspberry. The sapid and fragrant Ottocentonero, a dry and fruity Lambrusco, proves open and precise. The Stellato, an undosed sparkling wine made from spergola grapes, is redolent of floral and red fruit notes. The rest of the range is equally pleasant, particularly the Ottocentorosa, which represents the elegance of Sorbara as a spumante.

● Reggiano Lambrusco Spumante Extra Brut AC	🍷🍷 3*
● Ottocentonero	🍷🍷 2*
○ Spumante Pas Dosé Stellato Spergola	🍷🍷 2*
● 1936 Lambrusco Bio	🍷 2
⊙ Ottocentorosa Extra Dry Rosé	🍷 2
○ Pignoletto '22	🍷 2
● Reggiano Lambrusco Foglie Rosse	🍷 2
○ Spergola M. Cl. Dosaggio Zero '21	🍷 4
● 1936 Lambrusco Bio	🍷🍷 2*
● 1936 Lambrusco Bio	🍷🍷 2*
● 1936 Lambrusco Bio	🍷🍷 2*
● FB Lambrusco Ancestrale	🍷🍷 2*
● Mearse Lambrusco	🍷🍷 1*
● Reggiano Lambrusco Spumante AC Extra Brut	🍷🍷 3*

Assirelli

via Monte del Re, 31p
40060 Dozza [BO]
+39 0542678303
www.cantinadavittorio.com

CELLAR SALES
PRE-BOOKED VISITS
RESTAURANT SERVICE
ANNUAL PRODUCTION 45,000 bottles
HECTARES UNDER VINE 16.00
SUSTAINABLE WINERY

Founded in the early 1960s, this winery has been run by Vittorio and his sons Luca and Matteo since 2000. Their philosophy emphasizes minimal intervention in the vineyard, following integrated pest management protocols. Currently, the vineyards are divided into five estates, featuring Romagna's traditional grape varieties, with a particular focus on albana, thanks to a clone study carried out with the University of Bologna. The Albena '23 is a classic Albana, featuring ripe yet intact tropical fruit, citrus, and mineral hints that culminate in delightful sapidity on the palate. The Monte del Re '20 is a Sangiovese Riserva with beautiful fruit, aromas of red fruit jam, and tertiary notes of tobacco, leather, and forest floor, offering substantial flavor and a certain elegance. The white Gallo di Dozza, made from riesling italico grapes, is also well-made.

○ Romagna Albana Albena '23	🍷🍷 3*
● Romagna Sangiovese Sup. Monte del Re Ris. '20	🍷🍷 5
○ Gallo di Dozza	🍷🍷 2*
Colli di Imola Sup. Monte del Re '21	🍷 5
● Grifo di Dozza	🍷 2
○ Romagna Albana Passito Piccolo Fiore '19	🍷 6
○ Romagna Albana Spumante Incanto '23	🍷 4
● Romagna Sangiovese Sup. Moro di Dozza '23	🍷 4
○ Romagna Albana Passito Piccolo Fiore '18	🍷🍷 5
○ Romagna Albana Passito Piccolo Fiore '16	🍷🍷 4
○ Romagna Albana Passito Piccolo Fiore '15	🍷🍷 4
○ Romagna Albana Spumante Incanto '22	🍷🍷 4
● Romagna Sangiovese Sup. Monte del Re Ris. '19	🍷🍷 5
● Romagna Sangiovese Sup. Moro di Dozza '22	🍷🍷 3*

Francesco Bellei & C.

fraz. Cristo di Sorbara
via Nazionale, 130/132
41030 Bomporto [MO]
☎ +39 059902009
⊛ www.francescobellei.it

CELLAR SALES
PRE-BOOKED VISITS
ANNUAL PRODUCTION 40,000 bottles
HECTARES UNDER VINE 5.00

Nearly fifty years ago, Giuseppe Bellei adopted a revolutionary approach in the area, producing bottle-fermented wines by planting chardonnay and pinot noir for the Metodo Classico in the heart of Lambrusco di Sorbara. In the new millennium, the winery also embraced native varieties like pignoletto for their Metodo Ancestrale. Located in the Cristo di Sorbara area, the winery is now owned by the Cavicchioli family. The Brut Rosé proves deep and intense, with citrus and black berry aromas. The Cuvée 101, made from pinot nero, is fragrant, smooth, and well-balanced, while the Brut Nature impresses with its creamy bubbles and hints of fine pastry. The two Metodo Ancestrale wines are intriguing, with the Pignoletto '23 standing out for its vibrant fruit and nerve.

Stefano Berti

loc. Ravaldino in Monte
via La Scagna, 18
47121 Forlì
☎ +39 0543488074
⊛ www.stefanoberti.it

CELLAR SALES
PRE-BOOKED VISITS
ANNUAL PRODUCTION 25,000 bottles
HECTARES UNDER VINE 5.50
VITICULTURE METHOD Certified Organic

Berti was founded in 1963 after two estates in Ravaldino in Monte, in the Forlì municipality, merged together. Stefano, an agronomist and son of the founders, joined the winery in 1982. His arrival gave a decisive boost to viticulture, thanks to his encounters with Michele Satta, a prominent Bolgheri producer, and winemaker Attilio Pagli. The vineyards, now dominated by sangiovese, replaced arable and fruit crops. The Sangiovese Superiore Calisto Riserva '21 features pronounced notes of wild berries alongside spices and aromatic herbs. On the palate, it shows good fullness, with lively tannins that round out the finish. The Sangiovese Predappio Ravaldo '22 evokes strong aromas of black berries and forest floor, then vegetal hints of tomato leaf; in the mouth it opens with good, clearly present fruit. The Bartimeo '23 is a youthful, straightforward and enjoyable Sangiovese.

⊙ M. Cl. Brut Rosé	♟♟ 6
○ M. Cl. Brut Nature	♟♟ 6
○ M. Cl. Cuvée 101 Blanc de Noir	♟♟ 6
○ Pignoletto Ancestrale '23	♟♟ 3
● Lambrusco di Sorbara Ancestrale '23	♟ 4
○ M. Cl. Brut	♟ 5
○ Brut Nature	♟♟ 5
○ Brut Nature M. Cl. '15	♟♟ 6
○ Cuvée Blanc de Noirs Brut M. Cl. '13	♟♟ 6
○ Cuvée Brut M.Cl.	♟♟ 5
⊙ Cuvée Brut Rosé M.Cl. '12	♟♟ 5
● Cuvée Brut Rosso M. Cl. '14	♟♟ 3*
● Lambrusco di Modena Rifermentazione Ancestrale '15	♟♟ 3*
● Modena Lambrusco Rifermentazione Ancestrale '16	♟♟ 3*

● Romagna Sangiovese Sup. Calisto Ris. '21	♟♟ 4
● Bartimeo '23	♟ 3
● Romagna Sangiovese Predappio Ravaldo '22	♟ 3
● Romagna Sangiovese Predappio Calisto Ris. '16	♟♟♟ 4*
● Romagna Sangiovese Sup. Bartimeo '16	♟♟♟ 2*
● Sangiovese di Romagna Sup. Calisto '01	♟♟♟ 4
● Bartimeo '22	♟♟ 3
● Romagna Sangiovese Bartimeo '20	♟♟ 3*
● Romagna Sangiovese Predappio Calisto Ris. '18	♟♟ 4
● Romagna Sangiovese Predappio Calisto Ris. '15	♟♟ 4
● Romagna Sangiovese Predappio Ravaldo '21	♟♟ 3*

Alfredo Bertolani

via Pedemontana, 10
42019 Scandiano [RE]
📞 +39 0522857577
✉ www.bertolanialfredo.it

CELLAR SALES
PRE-BOOKED VISITS
ANNUAL PRODUCTION 400,000 bottles
HECTARES UNDER VINE 40.00
SUSTAINABLE WINERY

The winery founded by Alfredo Bertolani is
nearing the century mark. Originally, Bertolani
worked as a grape broker, but in 1920 he
decided to strike out on his own and began
constructing a cellar that would be completed
five years later. In the 1960s, his son Vincenzo
took over the business, but it was with the
arrival of his grandson Giancarlo that the winery
underwent a series of technological
improvements. By 2008, the fourth generation—
Nicola, Andrea, and Elena—established a new,
environmentally friendly headquarters. In this
year's extensive lineup, two Lambruscos stand
out: the Rosé, with its strawberry and raspberry
notes, and the Lambrusco Oro '23, which pours
brilliant red-purple hue, releasing candid aromas
of small red berries, and a subtle vegetal
undertone, all before giving way to a satisfying
palate. We preferred the Spergola Artemis '23
over the Spergolino '23 (which is nevertheless
good) for its broader and more varied aromas.

○ Colli di Scandiano e di Canossa Spergola Artemis '23	♟♟ 3
● Reggiano Lambrusco Oro '23	♟♟ 2*
○ Reggiano Lambrusco Rosé '23	♟♟ 2*
● Colli di Scandiano e Canossa Lambrusco Grasparossa Collezione Alfredo '23	♟ 3
○ Colli di Scandiano e Canossa Spergolino '23	♟ 2
● Reggiano Lambrusco Amabile '23	♟ 2
● Colli di Scandiano e Canossa Lambrusco Grasparossa Collezione Alfredo '21	♟♟ 3*
○ Colli di Scandiano e Canossa Spergola M.Cl. Brut '20	♟♟ 5
○ Colli di Scandiano e di Canossa Bianco Spergolino '21	♟♟ 2*
● Reggiano Lambrusco Oro '21	♟♟ 2*

Branchini

fraz. Toscanella di Dozza
via Marsiglia, 3
40060 Dozza [BO]
📞 +39 054253778
✉ www.branchini1858.it

CELLAR SALES
PRE-BOOKED VISITS
ACCOMMODATION
ANNUAL PRODUCTION 85,000 bottles
HECTARES UNDER VINE 28.00
VITICULTURE METHOD Certified Organic

The Branchini family winery deserves its
elevation to the top tier. Their story dates back
to 1858 when they crossed the Apennines,
moving from their native Siena to the Dozza
area. Here, they began producing wine on land
bordered by the Sillaro, Sellustra, and Sabbioso
rivers, which also feature in their stylized logo.
The soil is a mix of sand, clay, and silt, which gives
the wines their distinct character. The estate
adheres to a non-interventionist approach in the
vineyard, while using cutting-edge technology in
the winery. The Cardinala '20, a Sangiovese
Riserva, immediately impresses with its intact
and expansive fruit profile, ranging from sour
cherry to blackberry, raspberry to blackcurrant,
with a palate that expands into fullness and
substance, well-calibrated tannins, and a long
finish. The Albana Passito D'Or Luce '17 is among
the best of its kind this year, with its deep gold
color, elegance, balanced floral nose, and sapid
palate. The Dutia '23 Albana is also very
well-crafted, playing on citrus notes.

○ Romagna Albana Passito D'Or Luce '17	♟♟ 4
● Romagna Sangiovese Sup. Cardinala Ris. '20	♟♟ 4
○ Romagna Albana Secco Dutia '23	♟♟ 3
○ 1858 Brut M. Cl.	♟ 5
○ 1858 Dosaggio Zero M. Cl.	♟ 5
● Romagna Sangiovese Sup. Contragrande '23	♟ 3
○ Romagna Albana Passito D'or Luce '15	♟♟ 5
○ Romagna Albana Passito D'or Luce '14	♟♟ 5
○ Romagna Albana Secco Dutia '22	♟♟ 3
○ Romagna Albana Secco Dutia '20	♟♟ 3
● Romagna Sangiovese Sup. Contragrande '20	♟♟ 3
● Romagna Sangiovese Sup. Contragrande '19	♟♟ 3
● Romagna Sangiovese Sup. Contragrande '18	♟♟ 2*

Ca' di Sopra

loc. Marzeno
via Feligara, 15
48013 Brisighella [RA]
📞 +39 3284927073
🌐 www.cadisopra.com

CELLAR SALES
PRE-BOOKED VISITS
ANNUAL PRODUCTION 40,000 bottles
HECTARES UNDER VINE 27.00
SUSTAINABLE WINERY

Marzeno, a small area on the first Faentine hills, is characterized by clay and limestone soils, with elevations ranging from 120-240 meters above sea level. Although the winery was founded in 1967, major progress was made in the early 2000s with replanting of the vineyards and the introduction of the first bottled wines. Further changes came in 2006 with Camillo and Giacomo Montanari, who've chosen to focus on sustainability. Once again, the Vigna Ca' del Rosso Riserva '20 stands out with its aromas of plum, forest floor, small berries, and sour cherry, offering a compact, structured palate with well-managed tannins and a clean finish. The Cadisopra '21 proves fresh, sapid, and scented with dark berries, showing good length on the palate. The Vigna Montale Ris. '20 is riper and darker, with notes of coffee and grippy tannins.

Cantina della Volta

via per Modena, 82
41030 Bomporto [MO]
📞 +39 0597473312
🌐 www.cantinadellavolta.com

CELLAR SALES
PRE-BOOKED VISITS
ANNUAL PRODUCTION 130,000 bottles
HECTARES UNDER VINE 10.00
SUSTAINABLE WINERY

EMILIA ROMAGNA

In 2010, Christian Bellei started this winery with the support of some friends, leveraging the extensive experience acquired with his family, long involved in the production and sale of Lambrusco di Sorbara. His main goal was to create Lambrusco Metodo Classico at the original Bellei cellar near the 18th-century dock of the Bomporto canal, as represented by the winery's distinctive boat logo. Four wines were presented this year, all Sorbaras but very distinct from one another. The Brutrosso '23, a briefly-aged Metodo Classico, impressed us the most, expressing the full fruitiness of the variety, with an acidic backbone that supports the overall richness of the palate. The Rimosso '23, on the other hand, is a clear, clean, and well-made Metodo Ancestrale characterized by citrus and floral notes, intense on the palate and thoroughly satisfying. La Prima Volta '18 and DDR '15 benefit from long aging on the lees, with more evolved aromas.

● Romagna Sangiovese Marzeno Vigna Ca' del Rosso Ris. '20	🍷🍷 5
● Romagna Sangiovese Marzeno Cadisopra '21	🍷🍷 3
● Romagna Sangiovese Marzeno V.Montale Ris. '20	🍷🍷 4
● Remel '21	🍷 4
○ Romagna Albana '22	🍷 3
○ Trebbiano '23	🍷 3
○ Uait Pinot Bianco '23	🍷 2
● Remel '18	🍷🍷 3*
● Romagna Sangiovese Marzeno Cadisopra Ris. '20	🍷🍷 3
● Romagna Sangiovese Marzeno V.Montale Ris. '19	🍷🍷 4
● Romagna Sangiovese Marzeno Vigna Ca' del Rosso Ris. '19	🍷🍷 5

● Lambrusco di Sorbara Brut M. Cl. Brutrosso '23	🍷🍷🍷 4*
● Lambrusco di Sorbara Rimosso '23	🍷🍷 4
○ M. Cl. La Prima Volta '18	🍷🍷 4
● Lambrusco di Sorbara Brut M. Cl. DDR '15	🍷 5
⊙ Lambrusco di Modena Brut Rosé M. Cl. '13	🍷🍷🍷 5
⊙ Lambrusco di Sorbara Brut M. Cl. Rosé '17	🍷🍷🍷 5
⊙ Lambrusco di Sorbara Brut Rosé M. Cl. '18	🍷🍷🍷 5
⊙ Lambrusco di Sorbara Brut Rosé M. Cl. '16	🍷🍷🍷 5
⊙ Lambrusco di Sorbara Brut Rosé M. Cl. '15	🍷🍷🍷 5
● Lambrusco di Sorbara Rimosso '13	🍷🍷🍷 3*

Cantina di Carpi e Sorbara

via Cavata, 14
41012 Carpi [MO]
(☎) +39 059 643071
⊛ www.cantinadicarpiesorbara.it

CELLAR SALES
ANNUAL PRODUCTION 3,500,000 bottles
HECTARES UNDER VINE 2300.00

In 2012, the historic Cantine di Carpi (founded in 1903) and Sorbara (founded in 1923) decided to merge, creating a single cooperative with about 1,200 members and six facilities dedicated to winemaking, bottling, and storage, including a venture in Lombardy, in the Bassa Mantovana. In addition to Sorbara, their range of Lambrusco is explored with various typologies and methods, including sparkling wines. This winery continues to impress with its excellent flagship products. This year, the Lambrusco di Sorbara Brut Omaggio a Gino Friedmann '23 stood out during our tastings for its citrus and white flower aromas, intact fruit, and elegance. The Omaggio a Gino Friedmann '23, the other Sorbara (referemented in the bottle), has more pronounced fruit and a more rustic palate. The Salamino '23 Alfredo Molinari is also excellent, with its meaty and sapid profile.

Tenuta Casali

via della Liberazione, 32
47025 Mercato Saraceno [FC]
(☎) +39 0547690334
⊛ www.tenutacasali.it

CELLAR SALES
PRE-BOOKED VISITS
ANNUAL PRODUCTION 100,000 bottles
HECTARES UNDER VINE 23.00
VITICULTURE METHOD Certified Organic

At Casali, only 20 hectares out of a total of 80 are used for viticulture, a choice that has allowed the winery to focus on the best soils. Four areas are cultivated: Baruccia, Palazzina, Galassino, and Monte Paderno, situated on ancient fluvial terraces. The Casali brothers, Valerio and Paolo, assisted by their respective children, oversee operations, using alternating row cover crops and manual interventions to maximize the unique pedoclimatic characteristics of each vineyard. The Quartosole Riserva '21 is a robust Sangiovese, with varied aromas of berries, forest floor, bark, and cloves, offering a dense palate and great length on the finish. The Vigna Cavaliere Bianco '23 is a Trebbiano redolent of nectarine and dried herbs, pleasing and fragrant on the palate. The Sangiovese Vigna Baruccia '22 plays on a fresh, subtle profile, with citrus undertones and fine elegance. The floral-scented Famoso '23 is a lovely and straightforward drink.

● Lambrusco di Sorbara Brut Omaggio a Gino Friedmann '23	♟♟♟ 4*
● Lambrusco di Sorbara Omaggio a Gino Friedmann FB '23	♟♟ 4
● Lambrusco Salamino di Santa Croce Dedicato ad Alfredo Molinari '23	♟♟ 3
● Lambrusco di Sorbara Amabile Emma '23	♟ 3
● Lambrusco di Sorbara Omaggio a Gino Friedmann FB '21	♟♟♟ 3*
● Lambrusco di Sorbara Secco Omaggio a Gino Friedmann '16	♟♟♟ 3*
● Lambrusco di Sorbara Secco Omaggio a Gino Friedmann FB '14	♟♟♟ 3*

● Romagna Sangiovese San Vicinio Quartosole Ris. '21	♟♟ 5
○ Colli Romagna Centrale Trebbiano V. Cavaliere Bianco '23	♟♟ 3
● Romagna Sangiovese Mercato Saraceno V. Baruccia '22	♟♟ 3
● Colli Romagna Centrale Cabernet Sauvignon Damianus Ris. '21	♟ 4
○ Romagna Famoso di Mercato Saraceno '23	♟ 3
○ Colli Romagna Centrale Trebbiano V. Cavaliere Bianco '22	♟♟ 3
○ Colli Romagna Centrale Trebbiano V. Cavaliere Bianco '21	♟♟ 3
● Romagna Sangiovese Mercato Saraceno V. Baruccia '20	♟♟ 3*
● Romagna Sangiovese San Vicinio Quartosole Ris. '19	♟♟ 5

★Cavicchioli

via Canaletto, 52
41030 San Prospero [MO]
☎ +39 059812412
✉ www.cavicchioli.it

Celli

v.le Carducci, 5
47032 Bertinoro [FC]
☎ +39 0543445183
✉ www.celli-vini.com

CELLAR SALES
PRE-BOOKED VISITS
ANNUAL PRODUCTION 10,000,000 bottles
HECTARES UNDER VINE 60.00

CELLAR SALES
PRE-BOOKED VISITS
ANNUAL PRODUCTION 300,000 bottles
HECTARES UNDER VINE 35.00
VITICULTURE METHOD Certified Organic
SUSTAINABLE WINERY

On April 6, 1928, in the picturesque town of San Prospero, Umberto Cavicchioli founded what would become one of the most renowned and important estates in the world of Lambrusco winemaking. Since 2011, the producer has been part of the behemoth Giv group, but it remains firmly in the hands of the family, represented by Umberto's grandsons, Sandro and Claudio. With ten million bottles produced annually, the winery offers a wide range, with Sorbara standing out. The lineup of Sorbara wines is outstanding this year. Leading the pack are the Vigna del Cristo '23 (Martinotti) and the Rosé del Cristo '22 (Metodo Classico). The former reveals citrus aromas of pink grapefruit and clementine, with substantial breadth on the palate. The latter pours a pale color, evoking a broader bouquet that includes not only citrus but also mint and aromatic herbs, and it doesn't disappoint on the palate with its expansive and satisfying mouthfeel. The Scarlatto di Umberto is equally broad and airy.

Celli was founded in Bertinoro in 1963, thanks to the combined efforts of the Sirri and Casadei families. The vineyards span several estates, including Tenuta Maestrina, La Massa, and Campi di Bracciano. This last features the distinctive "spungone" (seabed tufa), a calcareous soil of organic origin formed when Romagna emerged from the sea, imparting unique characteristics to the wines. Alongside traditional grape varieties, they also cultivate chardonnay and cabernet sauvignon. The I Croppi '23 is an Albana characterized by a broad bouquet of very ripe fruit, ranging from melon to grapefruit, while maintaining its overall freshness thanks to its lovely sapidity and vibrant acidity. The soft and well-crafted Chardonnay Bron & Rusèval '23 proves redolent of tropical fruit, accented by hints of vanilla and aromatic herbs. The Sangiovese Le Grillaie Riserva '21 has plenty of substance, though oak still needs to fully integrate.

● Lambrusco di Sorbara V. del Cristo '23	♟♟♟ 3*
⊙ Lambrusco di Sorbara M.Cl Rosé del Cristo '22	♟♟ 5
⊙ Lambrusco di Sorbara L'Ancestrale	♟♟ 2*
● Lambrusco di Sorbara M. Cl. Lo Scarlatto di Umberto	♟♟ 3
● Lambrusco di Sorbara Tre Medaglie '23	♟♟ 2*
● Lambrusco Grasparossa di Castelvetro Tre Medaglie '23	♟♟ 3
● Fieronero	♟ 2
⊙ Lambrusco di Sorbara Antica Foresteria	♟ 2
● Lambrusco Grasparossa di Castelvetro Col Sassoso '23	♟ 2
○ Modena Pignoletto Brut	♟ 2
○ Pignoletto L'Ancestrale	♟ 3

○ Bron & Rusèval Chardonnay '23	♟♟ 3
○ Romagna Albana I Croppi '23	♟♟ 3
● Romagna Sangiovese Sup. Le Grillaie Ris. '21	♟♟ 3
○ Romagna Albana Passito Sol Ara '22	♟ 4
○ Romagna Pagadebit Campi di Fratta '23	♟ 2
● Romagna Sangiovese Sup. Le Grillaie '23	♟ 2
○ Romagna Albana Secco I Croppi '20	♟♟♟ 2*
○ Romagna Albana Secco I Croppi '17	♟♟♟ 2*
○ Romagna Albana Secco I Croppi '16	♟♟♟ 2*
○ Romagna Albana Secco I Croppi '15	♟♟♟ 2*
○ Romagna Albana I Croppi '22	♟♟ 2*
○ Romagna Albana Secco I Croppi '21	♟♟ 2*
● Romagna Sangiovese Bertinoro Bron & Rusèval Ris. '20	♟♟ 4
● Romagna Sangiovese Sup. Le Grillaie '22	♟♟ 2*
● Romagna Sangiovese Sup. Le Grillaie '21	♟♟ 2*

Umberto Cesari

via Stanzano, 1120
40024 Castel San Pietro Terme [BO]
(+39 0516947811
www.umbertocesari.com

CELLAR SALES
PRE-BOOKED VISITS
ANNUAL PRODUCTION 3,500,000 bottles
HECTARES UNDER VINE 355.00
VITICULTURE METHOD Certified Organic
SUSTAINABLE WINERY

Founded in 1964 on the hills of Castel San Pietro, this historic winery is divided into eight grassy farms managed according to sustainable principles of agriculture. Over time, in addition to cultivating local grapes, the winery has added international varieties to its portfolio. Technology serves the quality of the grapes and the integrity of the wine. Careful experiments with different aging methods and materials are also carried out. The Umberto '21 is a monovarietal merlese, a grape obtained from crossing merlot and sangiovese. It passes from black cherry aromas to hay and bell pepper, with a touch of spice. Mature and deep on the palate, it flows harmoniously with a satisfying finish. The Resultum '20, made entirely of sangiovese, is a soft, evolved red, perfumed with dried fruit, nuts and plum preserves, offering sapidity and a solid structure on the palate. The Albana Passito Colle del Re '15 is intriguing and mature, with aromas of candied fruits.

★Cleto Chiarli Tenute Agricole

via Belvedere, 8
41014 Castelvetro di Modena [MO]
(+39 0593163311
www.chiarli.it

CELLAR SALES
PRE-BOOKED VISITS
ANNUAL PRODUCTION 900,000 bottles
HECTARES UNDER VINE 100.00
SUSTAINABLE WINERY

Cleto Chiarli is a pivotal figure in the history of Modena Lambrusco. It all began in 1860 when the founder decided to revolutionize wine service in his Osteria dell'Artigliere by opting for bottles instead of selling in bulk. The wine was re-fermented in the bottle, a common practice before the invention of autoclaves. In 2000, the "new" Cleto Chiarli was born, focusing on the best grapes, particularly Sorbara and Grasparossa. Their 2023 Grasparossa wines are in great form. The Vigneto Cialdini is fragrant, fruity, and full-bodied, with a pleasant, lingering finish. Similarly, the Nivola stands out for its aromas of small black forest fruits and rewarding fleshiness on the palate. Regarding the Sorbara '23, while the Fondatore has tones of underbrush and black fruits, the Premium Mention Honorable offers up classic citrus aromas and robust acidity.

● Umberto '21	▼▼▼ 8
● Resultum '20	▼▼ 8
⊙ Costa di Rose '23	▼ 5
○ Romagna Albana Passito Colle del Re '15	▼ 5
● Sangiovese di Romagna Ris. '21	▼ 4
● Resultum '19	▽▽ 8
● Resultum '15	▽▽ 8
○ Romagna Albana Passito Colle del Re '14	▽▽ 5
○ Romagna Albana Passito Colle del Re '13	▽▽ 5
● Romagna Sangiovese Laurento Ris. '20	▽▽ 4
⊙ Romagna Sangiovese Rosé Costa di Rose '22	▽▽ 4
● Solo '19	▽▽ 8
● Solo '18	▽▽ 8
● Tauleto '17	▽▽ 8

● Lambrusco Grasparossa di Castelvetro Vign. Cialdini '23	▼▼▼ 3*
● Lambrusco Grasparossa di Castelvetro Nivola '23	▼▼ 2*
● Lambrusco di Sorbara del Fondatore '23	▼▼ 3
● Lambrusco di Sorbara Premium Mention Honorable '23	▼▼ 3
⊙ Lambrusco Grasparossa di Castelvetro Rosé de Noir Brut '23	▼ 3
● Modena Lambrusco Dry Pruno Nero '23	▼ 3
● Lambrusco di Sorbara del Fondatore '21	▽▽▽ 3*
● Lambrusco di Sorbara del Fondatore '19	▽▽▽ 2
● Lambrusco di Sorbara del Fondatore '18	▽▽▽ 3*
● Lambrusco di Sorbara del Fondatore '17	▽▽▽ 3*
● Lambrusco di Sorbara del Fondatore '16	▽▽▽ 3*
● Lambrusco di Sorbara Vecchia Modena Premium '20	▽▽▽ 3*

Floriano Cinti
via dei Gamberi, 50
40037 Sasso Marconi [BO]
☎ +39 0516751646
⊜ www.florianocinti.it

CELLAR SALES
PRE-BOOKED VISITS
RESTAURANT SERVICE
ANNUAL PRODUCTION 100,000 bottles
HECTARES UNDER VINE 26.00
VITICULTURE METHOD Certified Organic

In 1978, Floriano Cinti, along with a small group of friends in a cooperative, purchased the Isola farm. The first two hectares of vineyard were planted the following year, and the operation expanded until 1992 when, after the cooperative dissolved, Floriano continued alone. He planted an additional six hectares in the Tignano area, rented more plots, created a new cellar, and updated it with modern equipment. The winery also offers hospitality and dining services. The Pignoletto Frizzante '23 is redolent of citrus, Williams pear, and wildflowers, making for a smooth and enjoyable drink. The Pinot Bianco '22 starts out very floral, then opens up to reveal yellow-fleshed fruits with an interesting mineral note. The Cabernet Sauvignon '22 is highly varietal, with scents of summer hay meeting green bell pepper, all accented by hints of small forest fruits; a rather sustained palate follows.

Condé
loc. Fiumana
via Lucchina, 27
47016 Predappio [FC]
☎ +39 0543940860
⊜ www.conde.it

CELLAR SALES
PRE-BOOKED VISITS
ACCOMMODATION AND RESTAURANT SERVICE
ANNUAL PRODUCTION 130,000 bottles
HECTARES UNDER VINE 77.00
VITICULTURE METHOD Certified Organic
SUSTAINABLE WINERY

The winery run by Francesco Condello lies in the heart of the Predappio valley, nestled in a territory marked by the widespread presence of "spungone" (seabed tufa). This unique soil, combined with considerable day-night temperature swings, greatly contributes to the maturation of the grapes, giving the wines distinctive aromas and flavors. Borgo Condè welcomes visitors to taste the wines and enjoy various experiences, from food to guided tours of the cellar. The Raggio Brusa Riserva '21 stood out during our tastings for its broad aromatic profile of plum, sour cherry, bramble blackberry, and earthy underbrush, sensations characteristic of Predappio Sangiovese. The palate is well sustained, sapid, robust, with polished tannins and a long finish. The Sangiovese Predappio '21 features black cherry and blueberry alongside notes of medicinal herbs. It's a fragrant pour, with a pleasant, long, and flavorful palate.

○ C.B. Pignoletto Frizz. '23	♟♟ 2*
○ C.B. Pinot Bianco '22	♟♟ 3
● C.B. Cabernet Sauvignon '22	♟ 3
● C.B. Merlot Sassobacco '22	♟ 3
○ C.B. Pignoletto Cl. Sup. Sassobacco '22	♟ 3
○ C. B. Pignoletto Frizzante '19	♟♟♟ 2*
● C. B. Cabernet Sauvignon Sassobacco '18	♟♟ 3
● C. B. Merlot '19	♟♟ 2*
○ C. B. Pignoletto Cl. Sup. Sassobacco '20	♟♟ 3*
○ C. B. Pignoletto Frizzante '22	♟♟ 2*
○ C. B. Pignoletto Frizzante '09	♟♟ 2
● C.B. Bologna Rosso '16	♟♟ 3
● C.B. Cabernet Sauvignon '15	♟♟ 2*
○ C.B. Sauvignon '20	♟♟ 2*
● Pinot Nero Ronco Antico	♟♟ 4

● Romagna Sangiovese Predappio V. Raggio Brusa Ris. '21	♟♟ 8
● Romagna Sangiovese Predappio '21	♟♟ 4
● Romagna Sangiovese Predappio Ris. '18	♟ 6
● Romagna Sangiovese Sup. Al Caleri '23	♟ 3
● Romagna Sangiovese Predappio '20	♟♟ 4
● Romagna Sangiovese Predappio '19	♟♟ 4
● Romagna Sangiovese Predappio Raggio Brusa Ris. '17	♟♟ 8
● Romagna Sangiovese Predappio Raggio Brusa Ris. '16	♟♟ 8
● Romagna Sangiovese Predappio Ris. '16	♟♟ 6
● Romagna Sangiovese Predappio V. Raggio Brusa Ris. '20	♟♟ 8
● Romagna Sangiovese Sup. Al Caleri '21	♟♟ 3
● Romagna Sangiovese Sup. Al Caleri '20	♟♟ 3

Chiara Condello

loc. Fiumana
via Lucchina, 27
47016 Predappio [FC]
📞 +39 0543940860
🌐 www.chiaracondello.com

CELLAR SALES
PRE-BOOKED VISITS
ANNUAL PRODUCTION 35,000 bottles
HECTARES UNDER VINE 6.50
VITICULTURE METHOD Certified Organic
SUSTAINABLE WINERY

Chiara Condello made a bold decision: after graduating in oenology, she decided to separate from the family business to create her own venture, without leaving her beloved area of Predappio. With just a few hectares at nearly 300 meters elevation, surrounded by woods and rich in spungone (seabed tufa), the vineyards benefit from manual work and minimal intervention both in the vineyard and the cellar, resulting in highly distinctive sangioveses. The often Tre Bicchieri-awarded Le Lucciole Riserva once again shines in the 2021 vintage—it's a Sangiovese of great character, with deep and dark aromas of black forest fruits, underbrush, bark, and earthy and mineral notes. On the palate, it's robust, powerful, with muscular fruit and exuberant tannins, still youthful and in need of time to evolve and soften. The other Predappio '22 is simpler but remains robust and spirited.

Gaggioli

via F. Raibolini, 55
40069 Zola Predosa [BO]
📞 +39 051753489
🌐 www.gaggiolivini.it

CELLAR SALES
PRE-BOOKED VISITS
ACCOMMODATION AND RESTAURANT SERVICE
ANNUAL PRODUCTION 120,000 bottles
HECTARES UNDER VINE 11.00
SUSTAINABLE WINERY

Carlo Gaggioli, a veterinarian by profession with a passion for viticulture, revived a vineyard called Bagazzana in the 1970s so as to continue the area's millennia-old winemaking tradition. In the 1980s, he began producing bulk wine, and in the 1990s, he started bottling his own. Among his achievements is a belief in pignoletto, to the point of being the first to make an unblended sparkling wine with it. Now, he runs the winery and its adjacent agritourism together with his daughter, Maria Letizia. Gaggioli's Pignoletto Superiore '23 is a good still wine, redolent of apricot and nectarine, with citrusy hints, and a racy, refreshing palate. The Bologna Bianco '23, a blend of sauvignon blanc, pinot bianco, and grechetto gentile, offers up notes of yellow fruit, sage, mango, and spicy hints. The palate is sapid, with nice flesh and substance. The Bologna Rosso '20, a blend of cabernet sauvignon, merlot and syrah, features lovely fragrant fruit.

● Romagna Sangiovese Predappio Le Lucciole Ris. '21	🍷🍷 8
● Romagna Sangiovese Predappio '22	🍷🍷 5
● Romagna Sangiovese Predappio Le Lucciole Ris. '20	🍷🍷🍷 8
● Romagna Sangiovese Predappio Le Lucciole Ris. '17	🍷🍷🍷 7
● Romagna Sangiovese Predappio Le Lucciole Ris. '16	🍷🍷🍷 7
● Romagna Sangiovese Predappio '21	🍷🍷 5
● Romagna Sangiovese Predappio Chiara Condello '20	🍷🍷 4
● Romagna Sangiovese Predappio Le Lucciole Ris. '19	🍷🍷 8
● Romagna Sangiovese Predappio Le Lucciole Ris. '18	🍷🍷 8

○ C.B. Bologna Bianco '23	🍷🍷 3
○ C.B. Pignoletto Superiore '23	🍷🍷 3
● C.B. Bologna Rosso '20	🍷 4
● C.B. Cabernet Sauvignon '21	🍷 3
● C.B. Merlot '21	🍷 3
○ Colli Bolognesi Pignoletto Sup. '21	🍷🍷🍷 3
○ C. B. Bologna Bianco '22	🍷🍷 3
● C. B. Bologna Rosso '18	🍷🍷 3
○ C. B. Pignoletto Sup. P '22	🍷🍷 3
○ C.B. Pignoletto Frizzante P '20	🍷🍷 2
○ C.B. Pignoletto Sup. Fermo '21	🍷🍷 3
○ C.B. Pignoletto Sup. P '20	🍷🍷 3
○ Colli Bolognesi Bologna Bianco '21	🍷🍷 3
● Colli Bolognesi Cabernet Sauvignon '19	🍷🍷 3
● Colli Bolognesi Merlot '19	🍷🍷 3
○ Pignoletto Passito Ambrosia '15	🍷🍷 5

Gallegati

via Lugo, 182
48018 Faenza [RA]
☎ +39 0546621149
● www.aziendaagricolagallegati.it

CELLAR SALES
PRE-BOOKED VISITS
ACCOMMODATION
ANNUAL PRODUCTION 15,000 bottles
HECTARES UNDER VINE 6.00

Under the guidance of brothers Cesare and Antonio Gallegati, both graduates in Agricultural Sciences, the estate extends over 20 hectares at nearly 200 meters above sea level. The property is divided into two parts, with the flat area towards Faenza dedicated to fruit cultivation, while the hills of Brisighella host the vineyards. As of 2019, the winery has been certified organic. An agritourism also offers guest accommodations. Among the Coralli di Gallegati wines, the Corallo Nero Riserva '20 takes center stage. A Sangiovese from Brisighella, it conjures up broad aromas of forest fruits and underbrush, coming through sapid on the palate, with full fruit and lively, well-developed tannins. The Corallo Rosso '22 is lighter and more supple, still with a focus on small fruit aromas, all topped off by a beautiful final stretch. The tropical fruit-scented Albana Corallo Giallo '23 proves fresh and well-made.

Isola

fraz. Mongiorgio
via G. Bernardi, 3
40050 Monte San Pietro [BO]
☎ +39 0516768428
info@aziendaagricolaisola.it

CELLAR SALES
PRE-BOOKED VISITS
ANNUAL PRODUCTION 60,000 bottles
HECTARES UNDER VINE 12.50

Viticulture has been the main focus of the Franceschini family since the late-19th century, although the current winery was founded in 1957. Alongside the vineyard, as per tradition, part of the property is dedicated to orchards and part to arable crops. Currently, the winery is managed by Marco Franceschini, his wife Paola, and their children Gian Luca and Claudia, who have worked to identify the plots best suited to each grape variety, both whites and reds. The Pignoletto Spumante Brut Picrì '23 is aromatic, emanating citrus and floral notes, flowing pleasantly and fragrantly on the palate. The Cabernet Sauvignon Monte Gorgii '22 is highly varietal, fruity, and structured, bursting with small forest fruit sensations and a note of summer hay on the palate. The Riesling Le Vaie '23 is well-made, fresh, and youthful, with classic aromas of chamomile and wildflowers. The palate is gratifying, easy to drink, and immediately enjoyable.

○ Romagna Albana Secco Corallo Giallo '23	♀♀ 3
● Romagna Sangiovese Brisighella Corallo Nero Ris. '20	♀♀ 4
● Romagna Sangiovese Brisighella Corallo Rosso '22	♀♀ 3
○ Colli di Faenza Corallo Bianco '23	♀ 3
○ Romagna Trebbiano Brisighella Corallo Argento '23	♀ 3
○ Albana di Romagna Passito Regina di Cuori Ris. '10	♀♀♀ 4*
● Albana di Romagna Passito Regina di Cuori Ris. '09	♀♀♀ 4*
○ Romagna Albana Passito Regina di Cuori Ris. '12	♀♀♀ 4*
Romagna Sangiovese Brisighella Corallo Rosso '19	♀♀♀ 3*
Sangiovese di Romagna Sup. Corallo Nero Ris. '06	♀♀♀ 3

● C. B. Cabernet Sauvignon Monte Gorgii '22	♀♀ 3
○ C. B. Pignoletto Brut Picrì '23	♀♀ 2*
○ C. B. Riesling Le Vaie '23	♀♀ 2*
● C. B. Barbera Monte Gorgii '22	♀ 2
○ C. B. Bologna Bianco '23	♀ 2
○ C. B. Pignoletto Cl.V.V. '22	♀ 3
○ C. B. Pignoletto Frizzante '23	♀ 2
○ C.B. Sauvignon Il Dale '23	♀ 2
○ C. B. Bologna Bianco '22	♀♀ 2*
● C. B. Cabernet Sauvignon '22	♀♀ 3
● C. B. Cabernet Sauvignon Monte Gorgii '20	♀♀ 3
● C. B. Merlot '22	♀♀ 2*
○ C. B. Pignoletto Sup. '22	♀♀ 2*
○ C. B. Pignoletto Sup. '21	♀♀ 2*
○ C. B. Riesling Le Vaie '21	♀♀ 2*

Podere La Berta

via Berta, 13
48013 Brisighella [RA]
☎ +39 3491456114
🖰 www.poderelaberta.com

Lini 910

fraz. Canolo
via Vecchia Canolo, 7
42015 Correggio [RE]
☎ +39 0522690162
🖰 www.lini910.it

CELLAR SALES
PRE-BOOKED VISITS
RESTAURANT SERVICE
ANNUAL PRODUCTION 73,200 bottles
HECTARES UNDER VINE 14.00
VITICULTURE METHOD Certified Organic

CELLAR SALES
PRE-BOOKED VISITS
ANNUAL PRODUCTION 400,000 bottles
HECTARES UNDER VINE 25.00

Since 2009, the Poggiali family, represented by brothers Giovanni, Nicolò, and Domenico, has continued a journey begun in the 1970s, emphasizing biodiversity, experience, and terroir. Podere La Berta is more than a winery. Nestled among ravines and forests, the estate is situated in the Lamone Valley, in the first stretch of the Tuscan-Romagna Apennines, between Faenza and Brisighella. The property hosts a restaurant and transforms into a charming venue for private events and parties in the summer. The spectacular Albana Passito '16 sports a deep golden color, the prelude to rich and opulent aromas of brioche, candied fruit, apricot, acacia honey, and wood resin. On the palate, its sweetness is perfectly balanced by a bright acidity, making for a harmonious and elegant wine with an endless finish. The Albana '23 is also very good, offering broad and expressive aromas of citrus and tropical fruits. The Solano '22, a full-bodied and flavorful sangiovese, bursts with an abundance of wild berries.

The winery's name includes its founding year, 1910, when great-grandfather Oreste built the cellar to process grapes on his own. Now in its fourth generation, the winery has chosen over the years to vinify its grapes using the Metodo Classico, producing red sparkling wines with extended yeast aging. The winery also cultivates and vinifies pinot noir for more "conventional" spumante, while lambrusco is produced using the Metodo Italiano. Their pinot nero Metodo Classicos are of high quality, with a special mention for the Pas Dosé '18, which opens with floral and citrus notes on the nose and offers a sapid, airy palate. The Rosé from the same vintage is also very well-crafted, with a slight residual sugar that's well-balanced by fresh and lively acidity, making for a crisp and progressive drink. The Lambrusco Scuro '23, made from salamino and ancellotta grapes, reveals a racy palate, with clear and fragrant wild berry fruit. Truly delicious.

○ Romagna Albana Passito '16	♟♟ 5
○ Romagna Albana '23	♟♟ 3
● Romagna Sangiovese Sup. Solano '22	♟♟ 3
● Romagna Sangiovese Sup. Olmatello Ris. '21	♟ 5
○ Romagna Trebbiano Floresco '23	♟ 2
○ Romagna Albana Passito '15	♟♟ 5
○ Romagna Albana Passito '14	♟♟ 5
● Romagna Sangiovese Sup. '20	♟♟ 2*
● Romagna Sangiovese Sup. Olmatello Ris. '20	♟♟ 5
● Romagna Sangiovese Sup. Olmatello Ris. '17	♟♟ 4
● Romagna Sangiovese Sup. Solano '21	♟♟ 3
○ Romagna Trebbiano Floresco '20	♟♟ 3
● Sangiovese di Romagna Sup. Solano '20	♟♟ 3

○ Lini 910 Pas Dosé M. Cl. '18	♟♟ 5
● Lambrusco Scuro '23	♟♟ 2
⊙ Lini 910 M. Cl. Rosé '18	♟♟ 5
● Gran Cuvée di Lambrusco M. Cl.	♟ 4
○ In Correggio Brut M. Cl. '14	♟♟ 4
⊙ In Correggio Brut Rosé M. Cl. '14	♟♟ 4
● In Correggio Lambrusco Scuro '16	♟♟ 2
● In Correggio Pas Dosé M. Cl	♟♟ 4
● Lambrusco Spumante Rosso	♟♟ 4
⊙ Lini 910 M. Cl. Rosé '17	♟♟ 5
⊙ Lini 910 M. Cl. Rosé '15	♟♟ 5
○ M. Cl. Brut '17	♟♟ 4
○ M. Cl. Brut '16	♟♟ 4
⊙ Reggiano Lambrusco Labrusca Rosato '19	♟♟ 2
● Reggiano Lambrusco Labrusca Rosso	♟♟ 2

Cantine Lombardini

via Cavour, 15
42017 Novellara [RE]
☎ +39 0522654224
✉ www.lombardinivini.it

CELLAR SALES
PRE-BOOKED VISITS
ANNUAL PRODUCTION 600,000 bottles
HECTARES UNDER VINE 30.00

Cantine Lombardini's story is one of a century-old family tradition. Founded by patriarch Angelo at its current location in the Novellara city center, it originally included the Bar Roma with an adjoining cinema (since restored and transformed into a tasting room). Today, the winery is run by Marco Lombardini with his three daughters: Chiara, the commercial director; Cecilia, a sommelier and lab technician; and Virginia, who manages administration. The Signor Campanone '23 is a true Lambrusco, redolent of strawberry, raspberry, and aromatic herb notes. It features a fresh and open fruit profile, with a sincere, thoroughly enjoyable palate. The Rosato del Campanone '23, made from salamino with a touch of sorbara, exudes citrus scents, from mandarin to pink grapefruit, with an elegant nose and a sapid, smooth palate. The rest of the range also delivers, including a sparkling wine made from spergola grapes.

Lu.Va.

via C. A. Dalla Chiesa, 70
47015 Modigliana [FC]
☎ +39 3483986331
✉ www.luvass.it

CELLAR SALES
PRE-BOOKED VISITS
ANNUAL PRODUCTION 15,000 bottles
HECTARES UNDER VINE 7.50

Lu.Va. stands for Luciano and Valerio Ciani, who founded their winery in 2000 by merging their respective Ceretola and Cucculia estates. Although adjacent along the Tramazzo Valley, these two vineyards differ entirely in terms of elevation and exposure, allowing the owners to cultivate the grapes best suited to each area's specific conditions. Ciliegiolo, sangiovese, trebbiano, and cabernet sauvignon yield wines that express the territory's character. The Cucco Nero Riserva '20, a Sangiovese Modigliana, conjures up ripe fruit with aromas of dried plum, licorice, and underbrush. It's a wine of remarkable structure and vigorous tannins that, in its youth, slightly temper the final thrust. The Carbonaro '22, another well-made Sangiovese Modigliana, is more relaxed, with a full body and lively tannins that tease the palate. The rest of the range is also well-crafted, including the straightforward and easy-drinking Cucco Rosso '22.

● Reggiano Lambrusco Il Signor Campanone '23	♈♈ 3*
○ Reggiano Lambrusco Rosato del Campanone '23	♈♈ 2*
● Lambrusco di Sorbara Brut 1925 '23	♈ 2
○ Reggiano Lambrusco Spumante Brut Il Lombardini '22	♈ 4
○ Spergola Spumante Brut 1925 '23	♈ 2
● Lambrusco di Sorbara Brut 1925 '22	♉♉ 2*
● Lambrusco di Sorbara Brut 1925 '21	♉♉ 2*
○ Reggiano Lambrusco Il Campanone '21	♉♉ 2*

● Romagna Sangiovese Modigliana Cucco Nero Ris. '20	♈♈ 5
● Romagna Sangiovese Modigliana Il Carbonaro '22	♈♈ 4
● Il Macchiaiolo '22	♈ 4
○ Romagna Bianco Modigliana Angiulì '23	♈ 3
● Romagna Sangiovese Sup. Cucco Rosso '22	♈ 3
● Romagna Sangiovese Modigliana Cucco Nero Ris. '19	♉♉ 5
● Romagna Sangiovese Modigliana Il Carbonaro '21	♉♉ 3*
● Romagna Sangiovese Modigliana Il Carbonaro '20	♉♉ 3
● Romagna Sangiovese Sup. Cucco Rosso '21	♉♉ 3

Luretta

loc. Castello di Momeliano
29010 Gazzola [PC]
☎ +39 335437408
✉ www.luretta.com

CELLAR SALES
PRE-BOOKED VISITS
ANNUAL PRODUCTION 250,000 bottles
HECTARES UNDER VINE 50.00
VITICULTURE METHOD Certified Organic
SUSTAINABLE WINERY

Set in the evocative landscape of the Momeliano Castle, the estate, which operates under organic farming practices, spans 50 hectares with varied soils. Lucio Salamini, with the invaluable help of his mother Carla Asti (who designs the labels and names the wines), is dedicated to enhancing quality. The wines, never mundane, reflect the nuances of each harvest. Lucio focuses particularly on Malvasia di Candia. The Malvasia Boccadirosa '23 stood out during this year's tastings. Fleshy and fragrant, it showcases the varietal's still partially untapped potential. The Pantera '21, a blend of barbera, croatina, and cabernet sauvignon, is mature, with underbrush aromas accompanying a balanced palate. The On Attend Les Invités '21 is an impressive Metodo Classico Rosé, with intense aromas, fine bubbles, and a long finish. The rest of the winery's broad range is also very good.

Giovanna Madonia

loc. Villa Madonia
via de' Cappuccini, 130
47032 Bertinoro [FC]
☎ +39 0543444361
✉ www.giovannamadonia.it

CELLAR SALES
PRE-BOOKED VISITS
RESTAURANT SERVICE
ANNUAL PRODUCTION 60,000 bottles
HECTARES UNDER VINE 14.00

When Pietro Madonia purchased the vast estate known as "the balcony of Romagna" immediately after World War II, the property was known primarily for olive cultivation, with only a few hectares dedicated to vineyards. In 1992, his granddaughter Giovanna took over, reversing his priorities by replanting the vineyards and establishing new ones, while maintaining a small production of extra virgin olive oil. The production philosophy centers on minimal intervention both in the vineyard and the cellar. Despite its name, the Ombroso '21, a Sangiovese Bertinoro Riserva, offers an open and aromatic bouquet with prominent raspberry and blackcurrant notes, alongside root and underbrush nuances. On the palate, it's flowing, energetic, balanced, with a lively thrust and superbly well-managed tannins. The Trapunta '22 is a lively and mature Albana, with citrus and aromatic herb scents, a sapid palate, and nice progression.

○ C. P. Malvasia Boccadirosa '23	♥♥ 4
● Pantera '21	♥♥ 5
● C. P. Barbera Carabas '21	♥♥ 5
● Gutturnio Sup. '22	♥♥ 3
⊙ On Attend Les Invités Brut Rosé M. Cl. '21	♥♥ 5
○ C. P. Chardonnay Selin dl'Armari '21	♥ 6
○ C. P. Malvasia Passita Le Rane '19	♥ 5
○ M. Cl. Pas Dosé '20	♥ 5
○ Principessa Brut M. Cl.	♥ 4
● C. P. Cabernet Sauvignon Corbeau '00	♥♥♥ 4*
○ C. P. Malvasia Boccadirosa '10	♥♥ 2*
○ C. P. Malvasia Dolce Le Rane '08	♥♥ 2*
● Come la Pantera e i Lupi nella Sera '18	♥♥ 4
○ Principessa Blanc de Blancs Brut M. Cl.	♥♥ 4

● Romagna Sangiovese Bertinoro Ombroso Ris. '21	♥♥ 5
○ Romagna Albana Trapunta '22	♥♥ 5
● Romagna Sangiovese Sup. Fermavento '22	♥♥ 3
● Colli Romagna Centrale Rosso Barlume Ris. '19	♥ 4
○ Romagna Albana Neblina '23	♥ 3
○ Romagna Albana Secco Neblina '14	♥♥♥ 2
● Sangiovese di Romagna Sup. Ombroso Ris. '06	♥♥♥ 5
● Sangiovese di Romagna Sup. Ombroso Ris. '01	♥♥♥ 5
○ Romagna Albana Secco Neblina '22	♥♥ 3
● Romagna Sangiovese Bertinoro Ombroso Ris. '20	♥♥ 5

Tenuta Biodinamica Mara

via Ca' Bacchino, 1665
47832 San Clemente [RN]
+39 0541988870
www.tenutamara.com

CELLAR SALES
PRE-BOOKED VISITS
ACCOMMODATION AND RESTAURANT SERVICE
ANNUAL PRODUCTION 80,000 bottles
HECTARES UNDER VINE 12.00
VITICULTURE METHOD Certified Biodynamic
SUSTAINABLE WINERY

In 2000, Giordano Emendatori acquired land for a project dedicated from the start to his wife Mara. This biodynamically certified winery minimizes human intervention, letting nature take its course, following the lunar calendar and using animal and plant-based preparations instead of fertilizers. Walking among the vineyards is a unique experience, with a park featuring outdoor artworks where sangiovese reigns supreme. This year, the winery didn't present their flagship Sangiovese, MaraMia. Instead, we reviewed the Guiry '22, a younger Sangiovese that still shows a certain maturity of fruit, with a forest berry, sour cherry, and aromatic herb bouquet. The palate is pleasant, rhythmic, and generously drinkable. The Maramato '21 is a rosé Sangiovese redolent of rosehip and currant aromas. The Pinot Nero Totmà '22 proves distinctly varietal.

● Guiry Sangiovese '22	🍷🍷 3*
● MaraMato Sangiovese '21	🍷🍷 4
● Totmà '22	🍷 5
● MaraMia Sangiovese '18	🍷🍷🍷 6
● Guiry Sangiovese '21	🍷🍷 5
● Guiry Sangiovese '20	🍷🍷 4
● Guiry Sangiovese '19	🍷🍷 5
● MaraMia Sangiovese '19	🍷🍷 6
MaraMia Sangiovese '17	🍷🍷 6

★Medici Ermete

loc. Gaida
via I. Newton, 13a
42124 Reggio Emilia
+39 0522942135
www.medici.it

CELLAR SALES
PRE-BOOKED VISITS
ACCOMMODATION
ANNUAL PRODUCTION 900,000 bottles
HECTARES UNDER VINE 75.00
VITICULTURE METHOD Certified Organic
SUSTAINABLE WINERY

The history of Lambrusco Reggiano is intertwined with the Medici family. The estate was founded by Remigio in the late-19th century, though it was his son Ermete who carried the business forward, laying the foundation for the quality and character of today's Lambrusco. This commitment has been passed down through the years to the fourth generation, represented by Alberto Medici, who has implemented new planting patterns, reduced yields, and identified clones, with significant results. The Gran Concerto '21 is a Lambrusco Metodo Classico with depth, broad and fruity on the nose, offering hints of wild berries and red citrus, well-supported by acidity on a velvety palate. The Assolo and Concerto '23 are also very good, with the former being more fragrant, with strawberry and raspberry notes, and the latter leaning towards dark berry fruits. The Bocciolo '23 is a highly enjoyable Grasparossa that perfectly balances residual sugar, acidity, and tannins.

● Reggiano Lambrusco Concerto '23	🍷🍷🍷 2*
● Reggiano Lambrusco M. Cl. Gran Concerto '21	🍷🍷 4
● Colli di Scandiano e Canossa Lambrusco Grasparossa Bocciolo '23	🍷🍷 2*
● Reggiano Lambrusco Assolo	🍷🍷 2*
● Lambrusco di Sorbara I Quercioli	🍷 2
● Lambrusco di Sorbara Phermento '22	🍷 3
● Reggiano Lambrusco Unique '21	🍷 4
● Reggiano Lambrusco Concerto '22	🍷🍷🍷 2*
● Reggiano Lambrusco Concerto '21	🍷🍷🍷 2*
● Reggiano Lambrusco Concerto '20	🍷🍷🍷 2*
● Reggiano Lambrusco Concerto '19	🍷🍷🍷 2*
● Reggiano Lambrusco Concerto '18	🍷🍷🍷 2*
● Reggiano Lambrusco Concerto '17	🍷🍷🍷 2*
● Reggiano Lambrusco Concerto '16	🍷🍷🍷 2*
● Reggiano Lambrusco Concerto '15	🍷🍷🍷 2*

Menta e Rosmarino

via San Casciano
47015 Modigliana [FC]
☎ +39 3351227105
✉ www.mentaerosmarinovini.it

CELLAR SALES
PRE-BOOKED VISITS
ANNUAL PRODUCTION 12,000 bottles
HECTARES UNDER VINE 5.00

Two friends, Francesco and Luciano, along with Luciano's children, Valentina and Michele—united by a passion for wine—identified the Modigliana area as the ideal place to establish their small agricultural enterprise. The estate consists of 16 hectares, most of it wooded, with three hectares under vines at two different elevations. The vineyard includes old vines from the 1970s alongside more recent plantings from the 2000s, and they also maintain 150 olive trees for oil production. Their philosophy is as hands-off as possible. The Area 8 '22 is a fragrant Sangiovese, with mature wild berry fruit that emerges from the glass and remains vibrant on the palate, with energy, substance, and a fine tannic weave. The Area 88 '23 is a delightful white made from trebbiano, with peach and apricot aromas. The Area '58 '23, made from ciliegiolo grapes, is a fresh, vinous, violet-hued wine for drinking young. The Area 66 can be found in the guide's "Rare Wines" section.

● Romagna Sangiovese Modigliana Area 8 '22	♟♟ 5
○ Romagna Bianco Modigliana Area 88 '23	♟♟ 4
● Area 58 '23	♟ 4
● Romagna Sangiovese Modigliana Area 66 '21	♟♟ 5
● Romagna Sangiovese Modigliana Area 8 '21	♟♟ 5

Merlotta

via Merlotta, 1
40026 Imola [BO]
☎ +39 054241740
✉ www.merlotta.com

CELLAR SALES
PRE-BOOKED VISITS
ANNUAL PRODUCTION 400,000 bottles
HECTARES UNDER VINE 50.00
SUSTAINABLE WINERY

In 1962, Paolo Minzolini and his wife, Giovanna Mimmi, began working as tenant farmers at the Merlotta estate. However, it wasn't until 1983, when they purchased the property, that the modern story of this beautiful winery in the hills of Imola (near the Dozza Enoteca Regionale) began. In the early 1990s, the winery welcomed the couple's sons, Raffaele and Nerio, to the business. In the new millennium, the third generation, represented by Raffaele's sons, Fabio and Marco, came on board. During this time, the estate has expanded, and new vineyards were planted, carefully selecting the varietals best suited to each plot of land. The Albana grape stood out in our tastings, starting with the Passito Ombre di Luna '22, which features unique balsamic aromas of mint and eucalyptus, along with a floral honeysuckle note, broad and fragrant on the palate. The Albana Tridente '22 unveils a broad nose of yellow fruits and ripe fruit, while the Albana Fondatori '23 shows hints of citrus and aromatic herbs, with a lively palate.

○ Romagna Albana Passito Ombre di Luna '22	♟♟ 5
○ Romagna Albana Fondatori '23	♟♟ 3
○ Romagna Albana Tridente '22	♟♟ 5
● Colli di Imola Cabernet Sauvignon Grifaia Ris. '21	♟ 4
○ M. Cl. Dosaggio Zero Tridente	♟ 5
● Romagna Sangiovese Sup. Fondatori Ris. '21	♟ 5
● Romagna Sangiovese Sup. Tridente Ris. '21	♟ 6
○ Romagna Albana Fondatori GP '21	♟♟ 3
○ Romagna Albana Passito Ombre di Luna '18	♟♟ 5
● Romagna Sangiovese Sup. Petali di Viola '21	♟♟ 3

Monte delle Vigne

loc. Ozzano Taro
via Monticello, 22
43044 Collecchio [PR]
+39 0521309704
www.montedellevigne.it

CELLAR SALES
PRE-BOOKED VISITS
ACCOMMODATION
ANNUAL PRODUCTION 250,000 bottles
HECTARES UNDER VINE 60.00
VITICULTURE METHOD Certified Organic

Purchased by the father of the current owner, Paolo Pizzarotti, in 1963, the winery spans hundreds of hectares of woods, ravines, lakes, waterways, and vineyards. The new stunning underground cellar, powered by solar energy, was inaugurated in late 2006. Simultaneously, the vineyards were converted to organic farming, utilizing existing water resources and adopting a philosophy of minimal environmental impact. The winery has also started producing sparkling wines. The Chiuso '22 is a varietal cabernet franc with a lovely, straightforward fruitiness, expansive aromas of summer hay, and a palate that evokes wild berries. The Primavera '22, a sparkling malvasia made using the Martinotti (Charmat) method, is dry and also highly varietal, clean and crisp both on the nose and palate. The Ginestra '23, another malvasia, this time a still wine, is floral and pleasant, with hints of wildflowers.

Fattoria Monticino Rosso

via Montecatone, 7
40026 Imola [BO]
+39 054242687
www.fattoriamonticinorosso.it

CELLAR SALES
PRE-BOOKED VISITS
ANNUAL PRODUCTION 140,000 bottles
HECTARES UNDER VINE 23.00

In 1965, on the hills of Imola, at the border between Emilia and Romagna, Antonio Zeoli purchased a farm called Olmo. Acquisition of the Monticino Rosso vineyard, which gives the estate its name, came later. Antonio was then joined by his sons, Luciano and Gianni, who now lead the winery with a keen eye towards innovation. The estate spans about 24 hectares planted with traditional Romagna grape varieties, and the winery features a green roof to preserve the landscape. The Codronchio '22 confirms its status as a top-drawer wine. This is a complex, intriguing albana, offering a broad aromatic range from white flowers and citrus to brackish, mineral notes and candied fruit. In the mouth it's sapid and vibrant, with a harmonious profile that culminates in an applause-worthy finish. The Frutti Rossi '21, a riserva sangiovese, features tones of underbrush, bark, and black berries. The Sangiovese Superiore S '23 is more fragrant, simple, and immediately expressive.

Colli di Parma Cabernet Franc Il Chiuso '22	♈♈ 4
Colli di Parma Spumante Brut Malvasia Primavera '22	♈♈ 3
Colli di Parma Lambrusco I Calanchi '23	♈ 3
Colli di Parma Malvasia Callas '23	♈ 5
Colli di Parma Malvasia Ginestra '23	♈ 3
Colli di Parma Rosso Nabucco '21	♈ 5
Lambrusco Spumante Brut Riovalli '23	♈ 3
Rubina Spumante Brut '23	♈ 3
Callas Malvasia '20	♈♈♈ 5
Callas Malvasia '17	♈♈♈ 4*
Callas Malvasia '15	♈♈♈ 4*
Colli di Parma Malvasia Callas '21	♈♈♈ 5
Colli di Parma Rosso MDV '16	♈♈♈ 3*
Colli di Parma Rosso MDV '14	♈♈♈ 2*

○ Romagna Albana Secco Codronchio '22	♈♈♈ 4*
● Romagna Sangiovese Sup. Frutti Rossi Ris. '21	♈♈ 3*
○ Blanc de Blanc Pas Dosé M. Cl. '20	♈♈ 5
○ Romagna Albana Passito '20	♈♈ 4
● Romagna Sangiovese Sup. S '22	♈♈ 2*
○ Romagna Albana A '23	♈ 2
○ Albana di Romagna Secco Codronchio '08	♈♈♈ 3*
○ Romagna Albana Secco A '19	♈♈♈ 2*
○ Romagna Albana Secco Codronchio '21	♈♈♈ 4*
○ Romagna Albana Secco Codronchio '20	♈♈♈ 4*
○ Romagna Albana Secco Codronchio '19	♈♈♈ 3*
○ Romagna Albana Passito '19	♈♈ 4
● Romagna Sangiovese Sup. Frutti Rossi Ris. '20	♈♈ 3*
● Romagna Sangiovese Sup. Le Morine Ris. '18	♈♈ 4

Fattoria Moretto
via Tiberia, 13b
41014 Castelvetro di Modena [MO]
☎ +39 059790183
🖰 www.fattoriamoretto.it

CELLAR SALES
PRE-BOOKED VISITS
ACCOMMODATION
ANNUAL PRODUCTION 75,000 bottles
HECTARES UNDER VINE 10.00
VITICULTURE METHOD Certified Organic
SUSTAINABLE WINERY

The story begins with Antonio Altariva in the early 1960s, but it was in 1991 that his grandsons, Fabio and Fausto, transitioned from selling bulk wine to bottling their own. At the same time, a new, larger, semi-underground cellar was built. From the initial wines, which underwent second fermentation in the bottle, they moved to using autoclaves. Vineyard management follows organic methods, while microzoning of different parcels allows for precise selection of grapes. Five different interpretations of Lambrusco Grasparossa di Castelvetro from the 2023 vintage, each with its own style, were submitted for tasting. We start with the Monovitigno, a solid, structured Lambrusco with dark aromas of black fruits and underbrush, and balanced tannins on the palate. The Semprebon is more of a crowd-pleaser. True to its name, it reveals lovely aromas and a seductive sweetness on the palate. The Canova also offers an abundance of fruit and pulp.

Mutiliana
via Ibola, 24
47015 Modigliana [FC]
☎ +39 3295433483
🖰 www.mutiliana.it

ANNUAL PRODUCTION 12,000 bottles
HECTARES UNDER VINE 6.00
SUSTAINABLE WINERY

Giorgio Melandri, already a well-known wine writer, decided about ten years ago to switch sides and get into winemaking. This led to the creation of Mutiliana, the ancient name of Modigliana, an estate characterized by vineyards located at unusually high elevations for viticulture, on the lower foothills of the Apennines. At around 600 meters above sea level, it can be called "mountain sangiovese", which Giorgio produces in three different versions on loose soils rich in marl and sandstone. It's difficult to choose the best of the three sangiovese crus submitted—all are rich and well-crafted. The Ibbola '21 may be the most mature, with distinct notes of dried leaves, underbrush, and blueberry jam. Management of oak and tannins is excellent, giving the wine a powerful, flavorful palate that's still supple and lively, like a heavyweight boxer. The Tramazo '21 features pepper, dried plum, and underbrush, while the Acereta '21, found in our "Rare Wines" section, leans more towards black berries.

- Lambrusco Grasparossa di Castelvetro Monovitigno '23 ♟♟♟ 3*
- Lambrusco Grasparossa di Castelvetro Amabile Semprebon '23 ♟♟ 3
- Lambrusco Grasparossa di Castelvetro Canova '23 ♟♟ 3
- Lambrusco Grasparossa di Castelvetro Rosato Sbiadì '23 ♟ 3
- Lambrusco Grasparossa di Castelvetro Tasso '23 ♟ 3
- Lambrusco Grasparossa di Castelvetro Canova '19 ♟♟ 3*
- Lambrusco Grasparossa di Castelvetro Monovitigno '22 ♟♟ 3*
- Lambrusco Grasparossa di Castelvetro Rosato Sbiadì '22 ♟♟ 3*
- Lambrusco Grasparossa di Castelvetro Secco Rosato Sbiadì '21 ♟♟ 3*

- Romagna Sangiovese Modigliana Ibbola '21 ♟♟
- Romagna Sangiovese Modigliana Tramazo '21 ♟♟
- Romagna Bianco Modigliana Ecce Draco '22 ♟
- Romagna Sangiovese Modigliana Acereta '19 ♟♟♟
- Romagna Sangiovese Modigliana Tramazo '20 ♟♟♟
- Romagna Sangiovese Modigliana Acereta '20 ♟♟
- Romagna Sangiovese Modigliana Acereta '18 ♟♟

★Fattoria Nicolucci

fraz. Predappio Alta
via Umberto Primo, 21
47016 Predappio [FC]
📞 +39 0543922361
🌐 www.vininicolucci.com

CELLAR SALES
PRE-BOOKED VISITS
ANNUAL PRODUCTION 100,000 bottles
HECTARES UNDER VINE 12.00
VITICULTURE METHOD Certified Organic
SUSTAINABLE WINERY

For many years, the Nicolucci family and their sangiovese has been a benchmark in Romagna's wine landscape, in a region with millennia of tradition. The fourth generation, represented by Alessandro Nicolucci, is currently at the helm, bringing new vitality to a family business that has been operational since 1885. Recently, he initiated organic conversion, completely eliminating the use of copper and sulfur in the vineyard, and replacing them with organic products like bicarbonate. The Vigna del Generale '21, a Riserva, opens slowly, gradually revealing a diverse bouquet of blackberries, California plums are followed by spices, bark, underbrush, and dried herbs. In the mouth, it starts austere, then unfolds with a persistent palate, where tannins balance well with structure, alcohol, and acidity. The Sangiovese superiore Tre Rocche '23 is more approachable.

Noelia Ricci

loc. Fiumana
via Pandolfa, 35
47016 Predappio [FC]
📞 +39 0543940073
🌐 www.noeliaricci.it

CELLAR SALES
PRE-BOOKED VISITS
ACCOMMODATION
ANNUAL PRODUCTION 48,000 bottles
HECTARES UNDER VINE 9.00
VITICULTURE METHOD Certified Organic
SUSTAINABLE WINERY

From the Marquis Albicini family to the decorated citizen Giuseppe Ricci, the roots of Tenuta Pandolfa run deep. After World War II, Ricci planted new vineyards and began constructing the winery. In 1980, upon his passing, his daughter Noelia took over, followed by her daughter Paola Piscopo, and today, by Paola's son, Marco Cirese, the fourth generation, who started a zoning project in 2010 to select the best plots to maximize the land's potential. The Godenza '22 is a rich and lively Sangiovese from Predappio. Aromas of underbrush, blackberry, and blueberry rise from the glass. On the palate, it's sapid and flavorful, with a substantial, full-bodied character where fruit and tannin play together at a lively pace, leading to a satisfying finish. The Sangiovese '23 boasts the vivacity of youth, with fleshy, straightforward but rich fruit, easy to drink with a lingering finish. The Brò '23 proves to be a sapid and enjoyable trebbiano.

EMILIA ROMAGNA

Romagna Sangiovese Predappio di Predappio Sup. V. del Generale Ris. '21	▼▼ 6
Nero di Predappio '23	▼ 5
Romagna Sangiovese Sup. Tre Rocche '23	▼ 3
Romagna Sangiovese Sup. Predappio di Predappio V. del Generale Ris. '19	♀♀♀ 6
Romagna Sangiovese Sup. Predappio di Predappio V. del Generale Ris. '16	♀♀♀ 5
Romagna Sangiovese Sup. Predappio di Predappio V. del Generale Ris. '15	♀♀♀ 5
Romagna Sangiovese Sup. V. del Generale Ris. '13	♀♀♀ 5

● Romagna Sangiovese Predappio Godenza '22	▼▼▼ 5
● Romagna Sangiovese Sup. Il Sangiovese '23	▼▼ 3
○ Romagna Trebbiano Brò '23	▼ 3
● Romagna Sangiovese Predappio Godenza '20	♀♀♀ 5
● Romagna Sangiovese Predappio Godenza '19	♀♀♀ 4*
● Romagna Sangiovese Predappio Godenza '18	♀♀♀ 4*
● Romagna Sangiovese Predappio Godenza '16	♀♀♀ 4*
● Romagna Sangiovese Predappio Il Sangiovese '18	♀♀♀ 3*
● Romagna Sangiovese Sup. Il Sangiovese '16	♀♀♀ 3*

Enio Ottaviani

loc. Sant'Andrea in Casale
via Pian di Vaglia, 17
47832 San Clemente [RN]
☏ +39 0541952608
✉ www.enioottaviani.it

CELLAR SALES
PRE-BOOKED VISITS
ANNUAL PRODUCTION 130,000 bottles
HECTARES UNDER VINE 12.00

Situated a few steps from the Adriatic and Le Marche, and set within the 700-hectare Conca River Wildlife Oasis, this winery saw a significant turnaround when Davide (oenologist) and Massimo Lorenzi, along with their cousins Marco and Milena Tonelli, took the reins. The vineyards are located in San Clemente di Rimini, on clay soils that benefit from the sea's influence. The production style is characterized by a precise and focused profile. The Sole Rosso Riserva Sangiovese '21 comes across as a solid wine with concentrated aromas of dried plum, brandied cherry, coffee, underbrush, and cinnamon, with a long, deep palate hinting at its potential for aging. The Caciara '22 is a more immediately drinkable Sangiovese, where vegetal notes accompany the usual ripe red fruit before a nice, racy finish. The Rebola '23 proves straightforward and flavorful.

Podere Palazzo

via Orte, 120
47521 Cesena [FC]
☏ +39 340 9592725
✉ www.poderepalazzo.it

ANNUAL PRODUCTION 60,000 bottles
HECTARES UNDER VINE 10.00

On the clay-rich soils of Carpineta, between Rubicone and Cesena, lies the young winery founded by Cesare Trevisani and his children. The vineyards that surround the main property host both international grape varieties and traditional ones. The nearby Adriatic Sea, visible in the distance, influences the microclimate, which in turn affects the character of the wines, produced using modern vineyard monitoring systems. In the cellar, French oak barrels of various sizes are employed. The Augustus '20 is an opulent, mature Sangiovese Riserva, rich in aromas of ripe fruit, tobacco, spices. A muscular, energetic, intense palate follows accompanied by a slight hint of oak. The Caesena Riserva '19 also features very ripe fruit, reminiscent mainly of plum and blueberry, with hints of underbrush and walnut shell. The Ramato della Fiamma '22 is made from late-harvest trebbiano grapes from fifty-year-old vines. Its deep color anticipates a beautifully fragrant, ready-to-drink character.

● Romagna Sangiovese Sup. Sole Rosso Ris. '21	▼▼ 5
● Romagna Sangiovese Sup. Caciara '22	▼▼ 4
● Dado Sangiovese '19	▼ 7
○ Rimini Rebola '23	▼ 5
○ Romagna Pagadebit Strati '23	▼ 4
● Romagna Sangiovese Sup. Sole Rosso Ris. '20	▼▼▼ 5
○ Colli di Rimini Rebola '21	♈ 5
○ Colli di Rimini Rebola '20	♈ 4
○ Rimini Rebola Secco '22	♈ 5
● Romagna Sangiovese Dado '18	♈ 6
● Romagna Sangiovese Sup. Caciara '21	♈ 4
● Romagna Sangiovese Sup. Sole Rosso Ris. '19	♈ 5

○ Ramato della Fiamma '22	▼▼
● Romagna Sangiovese Cesena Caesena Ris. '19	▼▼
● Romagna Sangiovese Sup. Augustus Ris. '20	▼▼
● Castello '21	▼
○ M. Cl. Dosaggio Zero Terramossa N°04	▼
● Romagna Sangiovese Sup. Don Pasquale '21	▼
● Romagna Sangiovese Sup. Augustus Ris. '16	♈
● Romagna Sangiovese Sup. Don Pasquale '20	♈

★Alberto Paltrinieri

fraz. Sorbara
via Cristo, 49
41030 Bomporto [MO]
☎ +39 059902047
✦ www.cantinapaltrinieri.it

CELLAR SALES
PRE-BOOKED VISITS
ACCOMMODATION
ANNUAL PRODUCTION 160,000 bottles
HECTARES UNDER VINE 17.00
VITICULTURE METHOD Certified Organic
SUSTAINABLE WINERY

Grandfather Achille, a wine enthusiast and chemist by trade, created the oldest part of the winery in 1926, while his son Gianfranco helped to solidify its foundations. This legacy has been carried forward by Alberto Paltrinieri and his wife Barbara, who've transformed the winery into a true gem. Located in the heart of the Cristo di Sorbara area, between the alluvial soils of the Secchia and Panaro rivers, the winery produces intense and elegant sorbara. As always, Paltrinieri offers a first-rate range. The Leclisse '23 has become a classic: fragrant with berries, citrus, and aromatic herbs, it's an elegant, harmonious, textbook Sorbara. The Solco '23, 100% salamino, is very good this year, with explosive fruit that carries through to a broad, fragrant palate. Among the other Sorbaras, the Sant'Agata '23, made from organic grapes, deserves a special mention for its pure aromas, primarily of red citrus.

Pezzuoli

via Vignola, 136
41053 Maranello [MO]
☎ +39 0536948800
✦ www.pezzuoli.it

CELLAR SALES
PRE-BOOKED VISITS
ANNUAL PRODUCTION 220,000 bottles
HECTARES UNDER VINE 120.00

Founded in Carpi in 1932, the winery was moved to Maranello by the grandfather of its current owners. Initially a multi-purpose farm, the Pezzuoli family gradually focused on wine, particularly various lambrusco varieties. The estate boasts the first vineyard to have been designated within the Salamino di Santa Croce appellation. To ensure the best results, vinification and refermentation take place in spaces with strictly controlled temperatures and humidity. The Sorbara Rosé Pietrachiara '23 earned a place in the final round with a broad bouquet of orange peel and wildflowers, along with a graceful, deep palate. The Grasparossa di Castelvetro '23 is a dry Lambrusco, redolent of cherry, making a strong impression on the palate, broad and balanced, with a fine, racy finish. The Pietrarossa '23 is a very fruity Sorbara, with raspberry and blueberry aromas standing out, and a persistent, multifaceted palate.

● Lambrusco di Sorbara Leclisse '23	♟♟♟ 3*
● Solco '23	♟♟ 2*
● Lambrusco di Sorbara Lariserva '22	♟♟ 3
● Lambrusco di Sorbara Radice '23	♟♟ 3
● Lambrusco di Sorbara Sant'Agata '23	♟♟ 3
● Lambrusco di Sorbara Grosso '21	♟ 4
Lambrusco di Sorbara Piria '23	♟ 2
Lambrusco di Sorbara Leclisse '22	♟♟♟ 3*
Lambrusco di Sorbara Leclisse '21	♟♟♟ 3*
Lambrusco di Sorbara Leclisse '20	♟♟♟ 3*
Lambrusco di Sorbara Leclisse '19	♟♟♟ 3*
Lambrusco di Sorbara Leclisse '18	♟♟♟ 3*
Lambrusco di Sorbara Leclisse '17	♟♟♟ 3*
Lambrusco di Sorbara Leclisse '16	♟♟♟ 2*
Lambrusco di Sorbara Leclisse '10	♟♟♟ 3*
Lambrusco di Sorbara Radice '13	♟♟♟ 2*

⊙ Lambrusco di Sorbara Rosé Pietrachiara '23	♟♟ 2*
● Lambrusco di Sorbara Pietrarossa '23	♟♟ 2*
● Lambrusco Grasparossa di Castelvetro '23	♟♟ 2*
● Lambrusco Grasparossa di Castelvetro Pietrascura '23	♟ 2
● Lambrusco Grasparossa di Castelvetro Sudigiri '23	♟ 2
● Lambrusco di Sorbara Pietrarossa '21	♟♟ 2*
⊙ Lambrusco di Sorbara Rosé Pietrachiara '22	♟♟ 2*
● Lambrusco Grasparossa di Castelvetro Etichetta Nera '22	♟♟ 2*
● Lambrusco Grasparossa di Castelvetro Pezzuoli Morbido '21	♟♟ 1*
● Lambrusco Grasparossa di Castelvetro Pietra Scura '19	♟♟ 1*

Podere dell'Angelo

fraz. Vergiano
via Rodella, 38r
47923 Rimini
+39 3923801594
www.vinidellangelo.it

CELLAR SALES
PRE-BOOKED VISITS
ANNUAL PRODUCTION 50,000 bottles
HECTARES UNDER VINE 15.00
VITICULTURE METHOD Certified Organic
SUSTAINABLE WINERY

The Bianchi family winery, which just celebrated its centennial, is now taking on new challenges under the leadership of the third generation—Giulia and Giacomo—who work alongside Angelo and Milena, all under the watchful eye of their grandfather Luigi (born in 1929). The limestone-clay soils, which host organically cultivated vines, benefit from the influence of sea breezes. Since 2010, a photovoltaic system has allowed the estate to operate off-the-grid, while their approach in the cellar remains minimally interventionist. The Sangiovese Verucchio Luis Riserva '21 reveals lovely citrus, fruit, and brackish aromas. On the palate, it's close-knit and full-bodied, with a firm texture and a nice finish. The Ali Bianco '23 (85% pagadebit) stands out for its aromaticity, its fresh and easy-drinking profile, its sapidity and its fragrant quality—a delightful everyday wine. The Sangiovese Fulgor '23 opens on black forest fruit aromas; an approachable, fragrant palate follows, making it a firm, fragrant drink. Similarly, the Ali Rosso '23, a simpler monovarietal sangiovese, is equally quaffable, with similar aromatics.

○ Ali Bianco '23	▼▼ 2*
● Rimini Sangiovese Sup. Fulgor '23	▼▼ 3
● Romagna Sangiovese Verucchio Luis Ris. '21	▼▼ 4
● Ali Rosso '23	▼ 2
○ Aureum	▼ 4
● Colli di Rimini Rosso Cabiria '22	▼ 4
○ Fulgor '23	▼ 3
○ Rimini Rebola Giulietta '23	▼ 3
○ Rimini Rebola Landi '22	▼ 4
● Ali Rosso '21	▽▽ 2*
○ Colli di Rimini Rebola Giulietta '22	▽▽ 4
○ Colli di Rimini Rebula Giulietta '20	▽▽ 3*
● Colli di Rimini Rosso Cabiria '21	▽▽ 4
● Colli di Rimini Sangiovese Sup. Fulgor Rosso '21	▽▽ 2*

Le Rocche Malatestiane

via Emilia, 104
47900 Rimini
+39 0541743079
www.lerocchemalatestiane.it

CELLAR SALES
PRE-BOOKED VISITS
ANNUAL PRODUCTION 700,000 bottles
HECTARES UNDER VINE 800.00

The name pays homage to the Malatestas, a family with historical roots in Rimini. Production is made possible thanks to the work of 500 growers who cultivate some 800 hectares of vineyards in the hills, overlooking the sea, in an area straddling Romagna and Le Marche. Winemaking takes place in their Coriano cellar. Today, Rocche Malatestiane aptly represents the territory, with projects aimed at reviving historical native grape varieties like sangiovese, pagadebit, and biancame. The Mastino '20 is a Sangiovese Riserva bursting with fruit, featuring cherry and wild berry aromas alongside subtle herbal hints. On the palate, it reveals good structure, well-managed tannins, and a persistent finish. Among the subzone Sangioveses presented, we were particularly impressed by the Verucchio Tre Miracoli '23, which is fresh, fragrant, and filled with red berry aromas. The San Clemente I Diavoli '23 is similar, opening on notes of cherry, with a racy palate to follow.

● Romagna Sangiovese San Clemente I Diavoli '23	▼▼ 2
● Romagna Sangiovese Sup. Il Mastino Ris. '20	▼▼ 3
● Romagna Sangiovese Verucchio Tre Miracoli '23	▼▼ 2
○ Colli di Rimini Rebola Larus '23	▼ 2
● Romagna Sangiovese Coriano Sigismondo '23	▼ 3
● Romagna Sangiovese Sup. Sigismondo '17	▽▽▽ 2
● Romagna Sangiovese Sup. Sigismondo '16	▽▽▽ 2
● Romagna Sangiovese Sup. Tre Miracoli '18	▽▽▽ 2
● Romagna Sangiovese Verucchio Tre Miracoli '22	▽▽ 2

Cantine Romagnoli

loc. Villò
via Genova, 20
29020 Vigolzone [PC]
(+39 0523870904
⊕ www.cantineromagnoli.it

CELLAR SALES
PRE-BOOKED VISITS
ANNUAL PRODUCTION 300,000 bottles
HECTARES UNDER VINE 45.00
VITICULTURE METHOD Certified Organic
SUSTAINABLE WINERY

The story of this farmhouse begins in the mid-19th century when various agricultural and livestock activities were carried out. In 1926, the property passed to the Romagnoli family, who decided to focus exclusively on viticulture. Under the new ownership, the ancient courtyard was restored, with the addition of a new climate-controlled winery and an underground barrel cellar next to the original property. Alessandro Perini, director and winemaker, leads the enterprise. The Pigro Poetario Extra Brut '17 is a new Metodo Classico that matures at length on the yeasts. It features mature aromas with a slightly oxidative note, very fine and creamy bead, and an elegant palate that leads to a long finish. The Pigro Dosaggio Zero '21 is similarly linear, with an elegant bouquet of ethereal aromas and fragrant bead. The Malvasia Ape Selezione '22 proves well-crafted, showcasing lovely varietal aromas.

Ronchi di Castelluccio

loc. Poggiolo di Sotto
via Tramonto, 15
47015 Modigliana [FC]
(+39 0546942486
⊕ www.ronchidicastelluccio.com

CELLAR SALES
PRE-BOOKED VISITS
ANNUAL PRODUCTION 8,000 bottles
HECTARES UNDER VINE 10.00
VITICULTURE METHOD Certified Organic
SUSTAINABLE WINERY

Founded in 1974 by intellectual and filmmaker Gian Vittorio Baldi, a close friend of Luigi Veronelli, Ronchi di Castelluccio represents one of the earliest attempts to produce quality wines on the wooded slopes of Modigliana. Here, the Ronchi, small farms immersed in woodlands, foster biodiversity. In 2020, the producer was taken over by brothers Aldo and Paolo Rametta, who have set their sights high. The Buco del Prete di Castelluccio '21 is a warm, mature Sangiovese redolent of plum, black forest fruit, and underbrush, enriched with spices. On the palate its weighty, with exuberant tannins well-integrated with fruit. The Ronco Casone '20 also features dark plum and blackberry jam tones, though the tannins are a bit more pronounced. The Ronco della Simia '20 features pastry and plum tart notes, while Il Poggiolo '20 plays more on herbal tones.

Il Pigro Dosaggio Zero M. Cl. '21	♟♟♟ 4*
Gutturnio Sup. Ape '23	♟♟ 4
Il Pigro Poetario Extra Brut M. Cl. Ris. '17	♟♟ 6
Ape Malvasia '22	♟♟♟ 3
Il Pigro Brut M. Cl. '22	♟♟ 4
Valluna '20	♟ 5
Valnuraia Merlot '21	♟ 5
Il Pigro Dosaggio Zero M.Cl. '20	♟♟♟ 5
Ape Pinot Nero '21	♟♟ 4
Il Pigro Brut M. Cl. '20	♟♟ 4
Il Pigro Brut M.Cl. '21	♟♟ 5
Il Pigro Brut M.Cl. Rosé '19	♟♟ 5
Il Pigro Brut M.Cl. Rosé '18	♟♟ 5
Il Pigro Dosaggio Zero M. Cl. '17	♟♟ 5
Il Pigro Dosaggio Zero M.Cl. '18	♟♟ 5
Il Pigro Rosé Brut M. Cl. '17	♟♟ 5

Romagna Sangiovese Modigliana Buco del Prete di Castelluccio '21	♟♟ 5
Romagna Sangiovese Modigliana Ronco Casone '20	♟♟ 8
Colli di Faenza Rosso Il Poggiolo '20	♟ 8
Romagna Sangiovese Modigliana Ronco della Simia '20	♟ 8
Massicone '01	♟♟♟ 5
Ronco dei Ciliegi '02	♟♟♟ 5
Ronco dei Ciliegi '00	♟♟♟ 5
Ronco delle Ginestre '90	♟♟♟ 5
Romagna Sangiovese Modigliana Buco del Prete di Castelluccio '20	♟♟ 5
Romagna Sangiovese Modigliana Ronco dei Ciliegi '20	♟♟ 3
Romagna Sangiovese Sup. Le More '22	♟♟ 3
Romagna Sangiovese Sup. Le More '21	♟♟ 3

Podere Il Saliceto

via Albone, 10
41011 Campogalliano [MO]
(+39 3491459612
www.podereilsaliceto.com

ANNUAL PRODUCTION 13,000 bottles
HECTARES UNDER VINE 4.00

Based in the Campogalliano area, this agricultural estate is a small gem. Founded in 2004 by Gian Paolo Isabella and Marcello Righi, the winery achieved significant interest over the years. Meticulous and careful work in the vineyards is the foundation of their production philosophy. The property extends over about four hectares, mainly concentrated around the cellar. The varieties cultivated include malbo gentile and lambrusco salamino. The Falistra is a Lambrusco di Sorbara that evokes citrus peel and berry aromas on the nose, while the palate is supported by acidity and persistent bead. The Malbolle '22, an undosed Metodo Classico made from malbo gentile, sees berry aromas accompany a well-structured palate. The Ring Adora is a Metodo Classico produced in very limited quantities. You'll find it in the "Rare Wines" section.

★San Patrignano

loc. Coriano
via San Patrignano, 53
47853 Coriano [RN]
(+39 0541362111
www.vinisanpatrignano.com

CELLAR SALES
PRE-BOOKED VISITS
RESTAURANT SERVICE
ANNUAL PRODUCTION 500,000 bottles
HECTARES UNDER VINE 110.00

Founded by Vincenzo Muccioli on the hills of Coriano in 1978, San Patrignano needs no introduction. A recovery community rooted in farming activities, here winemaking was initially limited to a few plots of sangiovese and trebbiano, harvested by hand and crushed by foot, using an old press and a few barrels. The breakthrough came in the mid-1990s, with the planting of new vineyards, the introduction of international grape varieties, and the involvement of consultant Riccardo Cotarella (and subsequent-ly Luca d'Attoma). The Ora '21 is a Sangiovese with floral and berry aromas, fresh and well-paced on the palate, with moderate tannins and supple drinkability. The Noi '21 offers up aromas of blackberry and licorice, with more vibrant tannins and a pleasant almond finish to follow. The Prenna '23, a highly aromatic, fresh, and lively rosé made from syrah, is extremely enjoyable in its simplicity. Among the other wines, the Sauvignon Vie '23 deserves a mention for its aromatic and sapid profile.

● Lambrusco di Sorbara Falistra '23	♜♜ 3*
⊙ Malbolle Pas Dosé Rosé M. Cl. '22	♜♜ 4
⊙ Cichin Rosé	♜ 3
● Modena Lambrusco Albone '23	♜ 2
○ Bi Fri Frizzante '21	♛♛ 2*
○ Bi Fri Frizzante	♛♛ 2*
⊙ Cichin Brut Nature Rosé	♛♛ 3
⊙ Extra Brut Rosé Malbolle '22	♛♛ 4
⊙ Extra Brut Rosé Malbolle '18	♛♛ 4
● Lambrusco di Sorbara Brut Nature M. Cl. Ring Adora '19	♛♛ 3
● Lambrusco di Sorbara Brut Nature M. Cl. Ring Adora '18	♛♛ 3
● Modena Lambrusco Albone '17	♛♛ 2*

⊙ Prenna '23	♜♜ 3
● Rimini Rosso Noi '21	♜♜ 3
● Romagna Sangiovese Sup. Ora '21	♜♜ 3
● Aulente Rosso '21	♜ 2
○ Rimini Rebola Jaminia '23	♜ 3
● Romagna Sangiovese Sup. Avi Ris. '21	♜ 5
○ Vie '23	♜ 3
● Colli di Rimini Cabernet Sauvignon Montepirolo '15	♛♛♛ 4
● Colli di Rimini Cabernet Sauvignon Montepirolo '13	♛♛♛ 4
● Colli di Rimini Cabernet Sauvignon Montepirolo '12	♛♛♛ 4
● Romagna Sangiovese Sup. Avi Ris. '16	♛♛♛ 4
● Romagna Sangiovese Sup. Avi Ris. '11	♛♛♛ 5
● Sangiovese di Romagna Sup. Ora '12	♛♛♛ 3
● Sangiovese di Romagna Sup. Ora '11	♛♛♛ 3

San Valentino

fraz. San Martino in Venti
via Tomasetta, 13
47900 Rimini
(☏) +39 0541752231
⊕ www.vinisanvalentino.com

CELLAR SALES
PRE-BOOKED VISITS
ANNUAL PRODUCTION 135,000 bottles
HECTARES UNDER VINE 17.00
VITICULTURE METHOD Certified Organic

San Valentino has its roots in an old, post-war wine-growing project. In the 1990s, Giovanni Mascarin bought the entire estate from the Nanni family. Since 1997, his son Roberto Mascarin, along with his wife Valeria, has managed the estate, driven by a passion for agriculture and the belief that Colle di Covignano has the ideal climate and soil for producing great wines. By the end of 2022, Gianluca Marchetti and Giovanni Sidoli also joined the team. An association of 15 producers is working to promote rebola, a traditional grape of Rimini. Among them is San Valentino with their Rebola Scabi '23, a bright and fruity wine with peach and apricot aromas, very pleasant, fresh, and smooth on the palate. The Sangiovese Superiore Scabi '22 proves slender and supple, with plum and dark berry aromas. The Luna Nuova '19, a more complex and robust cabernet franc, stands out for its good persistence.

Cantina Santa Croce

fraz. Santa Croce
s.s. 468 di Correggio, 35
41012 Carpi [MO]
(☏) +39 059664007
⊕ www.cantinasantacroce.it

CELLAR SALES
PRE-BOOKED VISITS
ACCOMMODATION
ANNUAL PRODUCTION 400,000 bottles
HECTARES UNDER VINE 750.00
VITICULTURE METHOD Certified Organic

The cooperative's origins date back to 1907. Currently, it has 250 members who are primarily dedicated to cultivating lambrusco salamino, a variety native to this area, while also growing other varieties like sorbara. The predominantly clayey soils allow the salamino grape to be transformed into forthright, robust wines. Winemaker Maurizio Boni knows the grape's peculiarities well and interprets it in various styles, including sparkling versions. The classic red fruitiness of lambrusco salamino is powerful and fragrant in the dry 2023 version, aptly balancing tannins and residual sugar, with fruity flesh pleasantly returning on the palate. This year, the Sorbara '23 is also convincing, highly varietal in its notes of clementine and pink grapefruit aromas, and well-marked sapidity and acidity on the palate. The 100 Vendemmie, a sparkling Salamino rosé, is also well-crafted, revealing a fleshy and fruity character.

○ Colli di Rimini Rebola Scabi '23	♟♟ 2*
● Luna Nuova '19	♟♟ 8
● Rimini Sangiovese Sup. Scabi '22	♟♟ 3
○ Colli di Rimini Rebola Vivi '21	♟ 4
● Romagna Sangiovese Sup. Terra di Covignano Ris. '20	♟ 5
● ViVi Rubicone Rosso '21	♟ 4
● Sangiovese di Romagna Sup. Terra di Covignano Ris. '05	♟♟♟ 5
● Sangiovese di Romagna Sup. Terra di Covignano Ris. '03	♟♟♟ 4
● Sangiovese di Romagna Sup. Terra di Covignano Ris. '02	♟♟♟ 4
● Sangiovese di Romagna Sup. Terra di Covignano Ris. '01	♟♟♟ 4
○ Colli di Rimini Rebola Vivi '20	♟♟ 4

● Lambrusco di Sorbara '23	♟♟ 2*
● Lambrusco Salamino di Santa Croce Rosso Brut 100 Vendemmie '23	♟♟ 2*
● Lambrusco Salamino di Santa Croce Secco '23	♟♟ 2*
● Lambrusco Salamino di Santa Croce La Tradizione	♟ 2
● Lambrusco Salamino di Santa Croce V.V. '23	♟ 2
● Lambrusco di Sorbara '17	♟♟ 1*
● Lambrusco Salamino di Santa Croce Rosso Brut 100 Vendemmie	♟♟ 2
● Lambrusco Salamino di Santa Croce Tradizione	♟♟ 2
● Lambrusco Salamino di Santa Croce V.V.	♟♟ 2
● Modena Lambrusco Il Lambrusco	♟♟ 2*
○ Pignoletto Frizzante	♟♟ 2*

Tenuta Santa Lucia

via Giardino, 1400
47025 Mercato Saraceno [FC]
☎ +39 054790441
✺ www.santaluciabiodinamica.it

CELLAR SALES
PRE-BOOKED VISITS
ACCOMMODATION
ANNUAL PRODUCTION 90,000 bottles
HECTARES UNDER VINE 24.00
VITICULTURE METHOD Certified Biodynamic
SUSTAINABLE WINERY

Founded in the late 1960s as a multifunctional farm—wine, milk, grains, meat, fruit—the winery led by Paride Benedetti underwent a decisive shift in the late 1990s, abandoning other activities to focus solely on viticulture. Their philosophy is clear: only native grape varieties are cultivated—sangiovese, albana, famoso, centesimino—and the most natural methods possible are employed, including organic and biodynamic practices, with zero-impact energy and waste recycling. Like last year, the Taibo '22 stands out as a clear and warm Sangiovese with very ripe fruit, fleshy on the palate with smooth tannins. The Albana Albarara '23 is also delicious, characterized by its fleshy, ripe fruit, rich, full, creamy, and long on the finish. The Famoso Famous '23 is sapid, tropical fruit-scented, harmonious, and very pleasant to drink. The two Metodo Classicos, made from famoso and sangiovese grapes, are both enjoyable and smooth.

● Romagna Sangiovese Sup. Taibo '22	♟♟ 3*
○ Romagna Albana Albarara '23	♟♟ 3
○ Romagna Famoso Mercato Saraceno Famous '23	♟♟ 3
○ M. Cl. Extra Brut Blanc de Blancs Albarara '18	♟ 5
○ M. Cl. Extra Brut Blanc de Noirs Santa Lucia '19	♟ 5
○ Albarara M. Cl. Extra Brut '17	♟♟ 5
○ Romagna Albana Secco Albarara '22	♟♟ 3
○ Romagna Albana Secco Albarara '21	♟♟ 3
○ Romagna Mercato Saraceno Famoso Famous '22	♟♟ 3
● Romagna Sangiovese Sup. Taibo '21	♟♟ 3*
○ Santa Lucia Blanc de Noirs Extra Brut M. Cl. '17	♟♟ 4
○ Santalucia Blanc de Noir '16	♟♟ 4

Cantina Settecani

via Modena, 184
41014 Castelvetro di Modena [MO]
☎ +39 059702505
✺ www.cantinasettecani.it

CELLAR SALES
ANNUAL PRODUCTION 1,000,000 bottles
HECTARES UNDER VINE 530.00

La cantina deve il suo nome alla località di Settecani, frazione di Castelvetro di Modena nel cuore del territorio dove si produce il Lambrusco Grasparossa. Sulla facciata storica della cantina, fondata nel 1923, sono scolpiti i musi di sette cagnolini; in quell'anno 48 viticoltori si unirono per creare quella che oggi è una delle più antiche cooperative vitivinicole dell'Emilia, con 150 soci impegnati nella produzione dei vini tipici della tradizione regionale. This year, only Grasparossa in various versions was presented. While last year we awarded the Vini del Re, which in the 2023 vintage still exhibits lovely, straightforward and fragrant fruit with well-managed tannins, this year we preferred the 7Bio '23, a textbook Grasparossa in terms of its generosity of red fruit, both on the nose and palate, muscular and fragrant—a true drink and dine wine. The DiVino '23 is also very fruity, revealing floral aromas as well.

● Lambrusco Grasparossa di Castelvetro 7Bio '23	♟♟♟ 2*
● Lambrusco Grasparossa di Castelvetro Vini del Re '23	♟♟ 2*
● Lambrusco Grasparossa di Castelvetro DiVino '23	♟♟ 3
● Lambrusco Grasparossa di Castelvetro M. Cl. Brut Rosé Settimo Cielo '23	♟ 5
● Lambrusco Grasparossa di Castelvetro Tradizione '23	♟ 1*
● Lambrusco Grasparossa di Castelvetro Vini del Re '22	♟♟♟ 2*
● Lambrusco Grasparossa di Castelvetro 7Bio '22	♟♟ 2*
● Lambrusco Grasparossa di Castelvetro Secco Tradizione '22	♟♟ 1*

La Tosa

loc. La Tosa
29020 Vigolzone [PC]
📞 +39 0523870727
🌐 www.latosa.it

CELLAR SALES
PRE-BOOKED VISITS
RESTAURANT SERVICE
ANNUAL PRODUCTION 110,000 bottles
HECTARES UNDER VINE 19.00
VITICULTURE METHOD Certified Organic

In 1980, brothers Stefano and Ferruccio Pizzamiglio decided to leave Milan and their careers in medicine to return to the hills of their childhood and reinvent themselves as farmers. They bought a farmhouse with a small property, initially intended as a weekend escape from the city. Four years later, they founded the winery, which, over more than forty years of careful, committed work has established itself as a regional benchmark. Once again, the lineup presented didn't disappoint. Leading the way is the Malvasia Sorriso di Cielo '23, one of the first to showcase the potential of malvasia di Candia aromatica, with its broad aromas of wildflowers, ripe tropical fruits, and aromatic herbs. The Cabernet Sauvignon Luna Selvatica '22 is also well-crafted, varietal but with a clearly regional profile. The rest of the range is equally commendable, starting with the intense Vignamorello '22.

Tre Monti

fraz. Bergullo
via Lola, 3
40026 Imola [BO]
📞 +39 0542657116
🌐 www.tremonti.it

CELLAR SALES
PRE-BOOKED VISITS
ANNUAL PRODUCTION 200,000 bottles
HECTARES UNDER VINE 40.00
VITICULTURE METHOD Certified Organic
SUSTAINABLE WINERY

This winery's journey began in 1966 when Thea and Sergio Navacchia purchased a farm to make wine for their friends. However, they soon recognized the untapped potential of Imola. In 1974, Tre Monti was established with densely planted vineyards, experimentation with non-traditional grape varieties, and innovation both in the vineyard and the cellar. Since 1989, after the passing of Thea, Sergio has been joined by his sons David and Vittorio, who further experiment with winemaking in amphorae. A red of great class, the Petrignone Riserva '21 opens on generous aromas of morello cherry, raspberry, and currant, with hints of spice and aromatic herbs. On the palate, it's elegant and supple, unfolding with momentum, thanks to commendably well-managed tannins. The Albana Vitalba '23 is fabulous, golden and floral, rich and dynamic on the palate. The other Albana, the Vigna Rocca '23, also showcases vigour, varied aromas, and a sapid, lively character.

● C.P. Cabernet Sauvignon Luna Selvatica '22	♛♛ 5
○ C.P. Malvasia Sorriso di Cielo '23	♛♛ 5
● Gutturnio Sup. Vignamorello '22	♛♛ 5
○ L'Ora Felice Malvasia Passito '23	♛♛ 5
○ C.P. Sauvignon Ombrasenzombra '23	♛ 4
● Gutturnio Sup. Terredella Tosa '23	♛ 3
● C. P. Cabernet Sauvignon Luna Selvatica '06	♛♛♛ 5
● C. P. Cabernet Sauvignon Luna Selvatica '04	♛♛♛ 5
● C. P. Cabernet Sauvignon Luna Selvatica '97	♛♛♛ 5
○ C. P. Malvasia Sorriso di Cielo '19	♛♛ 4
● C. P. Cabernet Sauvignon Luna Selvatica '21	♛♛ 5
○ C. P. Malvasia Sorriso di Cielo '22	♛♛ 4

○ Romagna Albana Vitalba '23	♛♛♛ 5
● Romagna Sangiovese Sup. Petrignone Ris. '21	♛♛ 3*
○ Romagna Albana Vigna Rocca '23	♛♛ 3
● Romagna Sangiovese Sup. Campo di Mezzo '23	♛♛ 3
○ Classe 33 Bianco '22	♛ 4
● Romagna Sangiovese Serra Classe 33 '22	♛ 4
● Romagna Sangiovese Sup. Thea Ris. '21	♛ 4
○ Thea Bianco '22	♛ 4
○ Romagna Albana Secco Vitalba '22	♛♛♛ 4*
○ Romagna Albana Secco Vitalba '18	♛♛♛ 4*
● Sangiovese di Romagna Sup. Petrignone Ris. '08	♛♛♛ 3*
● Sangiovese di Romagna Sup. Petrignone Ris. '07	♛♛♛ 4

Trerè

loc. Monticoralli
via Casale, 19
48018 Faenza [RA]
(℡ +39 054647034
⊛ www.trere.com

CELLAR SALES
PRE-BOOKED VISITS
ACCOMMODATION AND RESTAURANT SERVICE
ANNUAL PRODUCTION 160,000 bottles
HECTARES UNDER VINE 35.00
SUSTAINABLE WINERY

This winery got its start in the late 1960s when Valeriano Trerè decided to acquire the Saccona estate on the Faenza hills, beginning to vinify sangiovese, albana, and trebbiano, the area's traditional grapes. The story continued through the generations: Valeriano's daughter Morena joined the venture, followed by her son Massimiliano. They expanded by acquiring new plots and built an underground cellar. A key decision was made to vinify only estate-grown grapes. The Amarcord d'un Ross, a sangiovese, consistently stands out in our tastings. The Riserva '21 proves straightforward and honest, unveiling aromas ranging from floral notes to black forest fruit preserves and spices. The palate is sapid and elegant, with nice length on the finish. The Albana Arlùs '23 is rich and sapid, redolent of citrus and tropical fruits, and rich and flavorful on the palate. The drinkable and fragrant Re Famoso '23 is also well-crafted.

○ Romagna Albana Secco Arlùs '23	🍷🍷 2*
● Romagna Sangiovese Sup. Amarcord d'un Ross Ris. '21	🍷🍷 3*
○ Re Famoso '23	🍷🍷 2*
○ Colli di Faenza Bianco Re Bianco '23	🍷 2
● Romagna Sangiovese Lôna Bôna '23	🍷 2
○ Colli di Faenza Bianco Re Bianco '22	🍷🍷 2*
○ Re Famoso '22	🍷🍷 2*
● Romagna Sangiovese Lôna Bôna '22	🍷🍷 2*
● Romagna Sangiovese Sup. Amarcord d'un Ross '20	🍷🍷 3*
● Romagna Sangiovese Sup. Amarcord d'un Ross '19	🍷🍷 3
● Romagna Sangiovese Sup. Amarcord d'un Ross '18	🍷🍷 3*
● Romagna Sangiovese Sup. V. dello Sperone '21	🍷🍷 2*

Cantina Valtidone

via Moretta, 58
29011 Borgonovo Val Tidone [PC]
(℡ +39 0523846411
⊛ www.cantinavaltidone.it

CELLAR SALES
PRE-BOOKED VISITS
ANNUAL PRODUCTION 6,500,000 bottles
HECTARES UNDER VINE 1100.00
VITICULTURE METHOD Certified Organic

La cantina nata nel 1966 con 16 soci, ne conta ora 220. Negli ultimi anni, sotto la presidenza di Gianpaolo Fornasari, ha dimostrato chiara volontà di migliorare l'intera gamma e di realizzare prodotti di livello, puntando sulla selezione delle migliori uve sin dal momento del conferimento, grazie ad attrezzature d'avanguardia. Questo impegno è evidente nella linea 50 Vendemmie, ottenuta da vigneti piantati negli anni Sessanta. Con l'enologo piemontese Francesco Fissore si punta al Metodo Classico. Leading the way this year is the Arvange, a Metodo Classico Pas Dosé made from pinot nero. Elegant and floral, with a slightly oxidative tendency reminiscent of noble sparkling wine regions, it has an ultra-fine, creamy perlage, with great momentum on the palate and a memorable finish. The Malvasia 50 Vendemmie '23 is also delicious, evoking aromas of flat peaches and yellow flowers, developing fragrant and intense on the palate.

○ Arvange Pas Dosé M. Cl.	🍷🍷 6
○ C.P. Malvasia Frizzante 50 Vendemmie '23	🍷🍷 3*
● Gutturnio Cl. Sup. 50 Vendemmie '23	🍷🍷 2*
● Gutturnio Cl. Sup. Bollo Rosso '20	🍷🍷 4
● C.P. Barbera Sapio '23	🍷 3
● C.P. Bonarda Frizzante Domina '23	🍷 3
○ C.P. Malvasia Spumante Venus '23	🍷 3
○ C.P. Ortrugo Frizzante 50 Vendemmie '23	🍷 3
○ C.P. Ortrugo Frizzante Armonia '23	🍷 3
○ M.Cl Brut Perlage	🍷 5
○ Arvange Pas Dosè M. Cl	🍷🍷🍷 6
○ Arvange Pas Dosé M. Cl.	🍷🍷🍷 4
○ Arvange Pas Dosé	🍷🍷 6
○ Arvange Pas Dosé M. Cl.	🍷🍷 6
● Gutturnio Ris. Bollo Rosso '19	🍷🍷 4
○ Perlage Brut M. Cl.	🍷🍷 4

Venturini Baldini

fraz. Roncolo
via Turati, 42
42020 Quattro Castella [RE]
☎ +39 0522249011
🌐 www.venturinibaldini.it

CELLAR SALES
PRE-BOOKED VISITS
RESTAURANT SERVICE
ANNUAL PRODUCTION 90,000 bottles
HECTARES UNDER VINE 35.00
VITICULTURE METHOD Certified Organic
SUSTAINABLE WINERY

An ancient estate dating back to the 16th century, it was acquired in 1976 by the Venturini Baldini family, who were the first to venture into wine production. In 2015, the Prestia family took over, introducing organic farming, shorter supply chains, sustainability at every stage, low yields per hectare, and processing entirely by hand. They also revived ancient grape varieties like malbo gentile, spergola, and montericco, which are also used in a line of sparkling wines. The deep ruby-colored Malbo Gentile from the T.E.R.S. line stands out for its lovely aromas of black forest fruits and underbrush, while on the palate it reveals fullness, with a well-balanced combination of softness and smooth tannins. The Marchese Manodori, a lambrusco that brings together marani, maestri, salamino, and grasparossa grapes, bursts with exuberant and fragrant fruit, well-defined aromas, and a sapid, weighty palate.

Villa di Corlo

loc. Baggiovara
s.da Cavezzo, 200
41126 Modena
☎ +39 059510736
🌐 www.villadicorlo.com

CELLAR SALES
PRE-BOOKED VISITS
ANNUAL PRODUCTION 120,000 bottles
HECTARES UNDER VINE 20.50
VITICULTURE METHOD Certified Organic
SUSTAINABLE WINERY

Founded in 1998, today Villa di Corlo is run by Antonia Munari, who operates in the southwest of Modena, an area particularly well suited to cultivating Grasparossa di Castelvetro. At higher elevations, over 300 meters above sea level, on slopes primarily facing south/southeast, they grow pignoletto and some international grape varieties, including chardonnay (used for producing Metodo Classico). The villa's attic houses the vinegar production facility. Two grasparossas, the Corleto and Villa di Corlo '23, proves highly representative of the grape, revealing a fruity profile redolent of berries. The differences between them are subtle: the first is more fleshy and immediately expressive, while the second sees the addition of floral notes and is more dynamic on the palate. In a similar vein, the Olimpia '23, made from organic grapes, is a vivid drink with lively fizziness. The Metodo Classico Sorbara Elettra '21 is an intriguing, varied, and smooth Brut Rosé.

● Colli di Scandiano e Canossa Malbo Gentile T.E.R.S.	♟♟ 4
● Reggiano Lambrusco Marchese Manodori	♟♟ 3
⊙ Reggiano Lambrusco Brut Cadelvento Rosé	♟ 3
⊙ Reggiano Lambrusco Brut Cadelvento Rosé '18	♟♟♟ 3*
⊙ Reggiano Lambrusco Brut Cadelvento Rosé '17	♟♟♟ 3*
● Reggiano Lambrusco Marchese Manodori '16	♟♟♟ 3*
⊙ Reggiano Lambrusco Brut Cadelvento Rosé '21	♟♟ 3*
⊙ Reggiano Lambrusco Brut Rosato Cadelvento	♟♟ 3

● Lambrusco Grasparossa di Castelvetro Corleto '23	♟♟ 3*
● Lambrusco Grasparossa di Castelvetro Villa di Corlo '23	♟♟ 2*
⊙ Lambrusco di Sorbara Brut Rosé M. Cl. Elettra '21	♟♟ 3
● Lambrusco Grasparossa di Castelvetro Olimpia '23	♟♟ 2*
⊙ Lambrusco di Sorbara Primevo '23	♟ 2
● Lambrusco Grasparossa di Castelvetro Mezzatorre '23	♟ 4
⊙ Lambrusco di Sorbara Brut Rosé M. Cl. Elettra '20	♟♟ 3*
⊙ Lambrusco di Sorbara Brut Rosé M. Cl. Elettra '19	♟♟ 2*
● Lambrusco Grasparossa di Castelvetro Corleto '21	♟♟ 2*

★Villa Papiano

via Ibola, 24
47015 Modigliana [FC]
📞 +39 3381041271
🌐 www.villapapiano.it

CELLAR SALES
PRE-BOOKED VISITS
ANNUAL PRODUCTION 40,000 bottles
HECTARES UNDER VINE 11.00
VITICULTURE METHOD Certified Biodynamic
SUSTAINABLE WINERY

Four siblings, Francesco, Maria Rosa, Giampaolo, and Enrica, each with a specific role, are the driving force behind this winery nestled in the woods near the Casentino Forests National Park, on the border between the Romagna and Tuscan Apennines. It is a place that blends ancient natural surroundings with a vision keenly aware of the great potential offered by the area's grapes, with the siblings constantly engaged in developing the resources that the territory has to offer. Though the Vigna Beccaccia wasn't submitted this year, the Vigna Probi Riserva '20 didn't disappoint. This Modigliana sangiovese features black forest fruits and plum jam, with a broad, fragrant, and intense palate, calibrated tannins, and a persistent finish. The Strada Corniolo '22 is also excellent, a captivating trebbiano redolent of spices, dried flowers, and citrus peel, while the Tregenda R! '22, a late-harvest Albana Passito, impresses as well.

Tenuta La Viola

via Colombarone, 888
47032 Bertinoro [FC]
📞 +39 0543445496
🌐 www.tenutalaviola.it

CELLAR SALES
PRE-BOOKED VISITS
ANNUAL PRODUCTION 60,000 bottles
HECTARES UNDER VINE 23.20
VITICULTURE METHOD Certified Organic
SUSTAINABLE WINERY

The story began over sixty years ago, in 1962, when the Gibellini family moved to Bertinoro and acquired some vineyards of sangiovese and albana grapes. Over time, their commitment to environmental respect grew, as evidenced by the organic certification obtained in 1999 and the adoption of biodynamic farming practices starting in 2018. Grass cover, green manure, and minimal intervention in the vineyard and cellar are key practices. We begin with the P. Honorii '20, a sangiovese Riserva with open fruit, notes of morello cherry and blueberry, all combined with hints of medicinal herbs. The palate shows character and vigour, with fruity flesh, controlled tannins, and a rising finish. The Colombarone '22 proves simpler and more approachaloe, with pronounced forest fruit sensations and a slender, pleasant, fragrant palate. The Albana Frangipane '23 is rich and sapid, evoking aromas of mint and tropical fruits.

● Romagna Sangiovese Modigliana Vigna Probi Ris. '20	♟♟♟ 5
○ Strada Corniolo '22	♟♟ 4
○ Tregenda R! '22	♟♟ 6
● Romagna Sangiovese Modigliana Papesse '23	♟ 4
○ Terra! '23	♟ 5
● Romagna Sangiovese Modigliana I Probi di Papiano Ris. '15	♟♟♟ 4*
● Romagna Sangiovese Modigliana I Probi Ris. '18	♟♟♟ 4*
● Romagna Sangiovese Modigliana I Probi Ris. '17	♟♟♟ 4*
● Romagna Sangiovese Modigliana V. Beccaccia '21	♟♟♟ 5
● Romagna Sangiovese Modigliana V. Probi Ris. '19	♟♟♟ 5

○ Romagna Albana Secco Frangipane '23	♟♟ 3
● Romagna Sangiovese Bertinoro Il Colombarone '22	♟♟ 3
● Romagna Sangiovese Bertinoro P. Honorii Ris. '20	♟♟ 5
○ Intrigo Famoso '23	♟ 3
● Romagna Sangiovese Sup. Oddone '23	♟ 3
○ Romagna Albana Secco Frangipane '21	♟♟ 3
○ Romagna Albana Secco InTerra '20	♟♟ 5
● Romagna Sangiovese Bertinoro Il Colombarone '19	♟♟ 3*
● Romagna Sangiovese Bertinoro P. Honorii Ris. '18	♟♟ 5
● Romagna Sangiovese Bertinoro P. Honorii Ris. '16	♟♟ 4
● Romagna Sangiovese Sup. Oddone '22	♟♟ 3

★★Fattoria Zerbina

fraz. Marzeno
via Via Vicchio, 11
48018 Faenza [RA]
(") +39 054640022
✉ www.zerbina.com

CELLAR SALES
PRE-BOOKED VISITS
ANNUAL PRODUCTION 180,000 bottles
HECTARES UNDER VINE 26.50
VITICULTURE METHOD Certified Organic

When Vincenzo Geminiani purchased his first vineyards in 1966 on the hills between Faenza and the Tuscan Apennines, he already had a clear intention to produce wine of superior quality compared to the standards of the time. The true turning point came in 1987 when his granddaughter Cristina Geminiani took over, implementing cutting-edge winemaking practices, clonal selections of sangiovese, and the first attempt to manage botrytis on the albana grape. The Poggio Vicchio '22 is an exemplary sangiovese from Romagna, bursting with red fruits, flowers, and golden-leaf tobacco. Ample, fragrant, and vibrant, it entices the palate thanks to its balance and fine tannic texture. The Monografia/4 Riserva '19 leans more towards plum jam—an evolved but firm wine. Only good things to say about the Bianco di Ceparano '23, an Albana that radiates aromas of tropical fruits and yellow citrus, unfolding fresh and taut on the palate.

Zucchi

loc. San Lorenzo
via Viazza, 64
41030 San Prospero [MO]
(") +39 059908934
✉ www.vinizucchi.it

CELLAR SALES
PRE-BOOKED VISITS
ACCOMMODATION
ANNUAL PRODUCTION 130,000 bottles
HECTARES UNDER VINE 10.00
SUSTAINABLE WINERY

In the 1950s, pioneer Bruno Zucchi began vinifying the family's grapes in San Prospero, a territory renowned for its Sorbara. His passion was passed on to his son Davide and wife Maura. 2010 saw the arrival of the third generation, Silvia, a graduate in oenology with considerable international experience. She's given new impetus to production with the Silvia Zucchi line, which focuses on various expressions of Sorbara, showcasing the best the grape variety has to offer. The Rosé Silvia Zucchi '23 stands out with its elegance and floral, citrusy aromas on the nose, fully expressing the qualities of sorbara, with an open, sincere palate to follow. The Marascone '23, made from 100% salamino grapes, boasts cherry aromas, with a full and tasty palate that echoes its intact fruit. The Metodo Classico Brut Silvia Zucchi '21 plays on notes of mandarin and grapefruit, with nice vigour to back it up.

● Romagna Sangiovese Marzeno Poggio Vicchio '22	♟♟♟ 3*
○ Romagna Albana Secco Bianco di Ceparano '23	♟♟ 3*
● Romagna Sangiovese Marzeno Monografia/4 Ris. '19	♟♟ 8
● Marzieno '18	♟♟ 5
● Romagna Sangiovese Marzeno Pietramora Ris. '18	♟♟ 5
● Romagna Sangiovese Sup. Torre di Ceparano Ris. '19	♟ 4
○ Tergeno '23	♟ 5
○ Romagna Albana Secco Bianco di Ceparano '21	♟♟♟ 3*
● Romagna Sangiovese Marzeno Sup. Poggio Vicchio '21	♟♟♟ 3*

○ Lambrusco di Sorbara Brut Rosè Silvia Zucchi '23	♟♟ 5
● Modena Lambrusco Marascone '23	♟♟ 3*
● Lambrusco di Sorbara Brut Etichetta Bianca '23	♟♟ 3
● Lambrusco di Sorbara M. Cl. Brut Silvia Zucchi '21	♟♟ 6
● Lambrusco di Sorbara Extra Brut Infondo Silvia Zucchi '21	♟ 5
● Lambrusco di Sorbara Purezza '23	♟ 5
○ Lambrusco di Sorbara Rito '23	♟ 3
● Lambrusco di Sorbara Brut In Purezza Silvia Zucchi '22	♟♟♟ 5
● Lambrusco di Sorbara Brut In Purezza Silvia Zucchi '21	♟♟♟ 4*
○ Lambrusco di Sorbara Brut Rosé Silvia Zucchi '20	♟♟♟ 3*
● Lambrusco di Sorbara Secco Rito '15	♟♟♟ 2*

Agrintesa
Poderi delle Rose
via G. Galilei, 15
48018 Faenza [RA]
C☏ +39 0546941195
✉ www.cantineintesa.it

CELLAR SALES
PRE-BOOKED VISITS
ANNUAL PRODUCTION 350,000 bottles
HECTARES UNDER VINE 44.00

○ Romagna Albana Passito Loveria '21		♥♥ 3*
○ Romagna Albana Poderi delle Rose '23		♥ 2
● Romagna Sangiovese '22		♥ 2

Balìa di Zola
via Casale, 11
47015 Modigliana [FC]
C☏ +39 0546940577
✉ www.baliadizola.com

CELLAR SALES
PRE-BOOKED VISITS
ANNUAL PRODUCTION 30,000 bottles
HECTARES UNDER VINE 5.00

○ Romagna Albana Isola '23		♥♥ 3
● Romagna Sangiovese Modigliana Redinoce Ris. '21		♥ 4
● Romagna Sangiovese Sup. Balitore '23		♥ 3

Botti
via Elio Roda, 19/1
40050 Monte San Pietro [BO]
C☏ +39 3474497346
✉ www.vinibotti.it

○ C. B. Pignoletto Lieto '23		♥♥ 3
○ C. B. Pignoletto Sup. D'Estro '22		♥♥ 3
○ C. B. Sauvignon D'Intenso '23		♥ 2

Tenute Bacana
via Trieste, 100
48013 Brisighella [RA]
C☏ +39 3395988464
✉ www.bacanawines.com

○ Romagna Albana Secco '23		♥♥ 3
○ Romagna Bianco Brisighella Intento '23		♥ 4
● Romagna Sangiovese Sup. '22		♥ 3

Tenuta Bonzara
via Sanchierlo, 37a
40050 Monte San Pietro [BO]
C☏ +39 0516768324
✉ www.bonzara.it

CELLAR SALES
PRE-BOOKED VISITS
ACCOMMODATION AND RESTAURANT SERVICE
ANNUAL PRODUCTION 70,000 bottles
HECTARES UNDER VINE 13.60

● C. B. Cabernet Sauvignon Bonzarone '21		♥♥ 5
○ C. B. Sauvignon Le Carrate '23		♥♥ 3
● C. B. Bologna Il Rosso '23		♥ 3

Calonga
loc. Castiglione
via Castel Leone, 8
47121 Forlì
C☏ +39 0543753044
✉ www.calonga.it

CELLAR SALES
PRE-BOOKED VISITS
ANNUAL PRODUCTION 50,000 bottles
HECTARES UNDER VINE 18.00

● Il Bruno '23		♥♥ 3
○ Romagna Pagadebit L'Azzurro '23		♥ 2

OTHER WINERIES

Casali Viticultori

fraz. Pratissolo
via delle Scuole, 7
42019 Scandiano [RE]
(+39 0522855441
www.casalivini.it

CELLAR SALES
PRE-BOOKED VISITS
ANNUAL PRODUCTION 1,500,000 bottles
HECTARES UNDER VINE 48.00

● Lambrusco Secco 1900	♀♀ 2*
● Reggiano Lambrusco Pra di Bosso Storico	♀♀ 3
○ Colli di Scandiano e di Canossa Spergola Brut 1077 '23	♀ 2

Caviro - Vigneti Romio

via Convertite, 12
48018 Faenza [RA]
(+39 0546629111
www.caviro.it

CELLAR SALES
ANNUAL PRODUCTION 75,000,000 bottles
HECTARES UNDER VINE 35.20
SUSTAINABLE WINERY

○ Romagna Trebbiano '23	♀♀ 2*
● Romagna Sangiovese Sup. Ris. '20	♀♀ 3
○ Novebolle Extra Dry	♀ 2
⊙ Novebolle Extra Dry Rosé	♀ 2

Colombarda

fraz. San Vittore
via Rio Acqua di San Vittore, 140
47522 Cesena [FC]
(+39 0547663688
www.colombarda.it

CELLAR SALES
PRE-BOOKED VISITS
ANNUAL PRODUCTION 35,000 bottles
HECTARES UNDER VINE 21.00
SUSTAINABLE WINERY

● Romagna Sangiovese Sup. Ca' Manacca '22	♀♀ 4
○ Romagna Albana '23	♀ 3
○ Romagna Pagadebit Bertinoro '23	♀ 2

Cavaliera

via Cavalliera, 1b
41014 Castelvetro di Modena [MO]
(+39 059799835
www.cavaliera.it

● Beatrice Nuvola '23	♀♀ 3
○ Caterina Pas Dosé Rosé M. Cl. '21	♀♀ 5
○ Modena Pignoletto Elena Nuvola '23	♀ 2

La Collina del Tesoro

fraz. Massa di Vecchiazzano
via del Tesoro, 18
47121 Forlì
(+39 0543179698
www.lacollinadeltesoro.com

CELLAR SALES
ANNUAL PRODUCTION 130,000 bottles
HECTARES UNDER VINE 38.00
VITICULTURE METHOD Certified Organic
SUSTAINABLE WINERY

● Romagna Sangiovese Predappio Monte Massa Ris. '21	♀♀ 5

Tenuta de' Stefenelli

fraz. Fratta Terme
via Fratta, km 1,800
47032 Bertinoro [FC]
(+39 3483997443
www.destefenelli.it

CELLAR SALES
PRE-BOOKED VISITS
ACCOMMODATION AND RESTAURANT SERVICE
ANNUAL PRODUCTION 20,000 bottles
HECTARES UNDER VINE 11.00
VITICULTURE METHOD Certified Organic

● Red Blues Cabernet Franc '20	♀♀ 5
● Romagna Sangiovese Sup. Rondò '22	♀♀ 3
● Romagna Sangiovese Sup. Be Bop '22	♀ 3

EMILIA ROMAGNA

Drei Donà
Tenuta La Palazza
fraz. Massa di Vecchiazzano
via del Tesoro, 23
47121 Forlì
☎ +39 0543769371
✉ www.dreidona.it

CELLAR SALES
PRE-BOOKED VISITS
ANNUAL PRODUCTION 130,000 bottles
HECTARES UNDER VINE 27.00
VITICULTURE METHOD Certified Organic
SUSTAINABLE WINERY

○ Il Tornese '23	🍷🍷 4
● Romagna Sangiovese Predappio Notturno '22	🍷🍷 4
● Magnificat '20	🍷 6

Cantina Sociale
Formigine Pedemontana
via Radici in piano, 228
41043 Formigine [MO]
☎ +39 059558122
✉ www.lambruscodoc.it

CELLAR SALES
PRE-BOOKED VISITS
ANNUAL PRODUCTION 960,000 bottles
HECTARES UNDER VINE 580.00
VITICULTURE METHOD Certified Organic

● Lambrusco Grasparossa di Castelvetro Passione Bio '23	🍷🍷 2*
○ Pignoletto For.Mo.Sa. '23	🍷🍷 1*
● Lambrusco Grasparossa di Castelvetro '23	🍷 2

Maria Galassi
fraz. Paderno
via Casetta, 688
47522 Cesena [FC]
☎ +39 3387230288
✉ www.galassimaria.it

CELLAR SALES
PRE-BOOKED VISITS
ACCOMMODATION
ANNUAL PRODUCTION 40,000 bottles
HECTARES UNDER VINE 29.00
VITICULTURE METHOD Certified Organic
SUSTAINABLE WINERY

● Romagna Sangiovese Sup. Smembar '22	🍷🍷 3
○ Fiaba '22	🍷 3
○ Romagna Albana La Sgnòra '23	🍷 3

Fondo Cà Vecja
loc. Ponticelli
via Montanara, 333
40020 Imola [BO]
☎ +39 0542665194
✉ www.fondocavecja.it

CELLAR SALES
PRE-BOOKED VISITS
ANNUAL PRODUCTION 25,000 bottles
HECTARES UNDER VINE 18.00

● Angiolla Sangiovese	🍷🍷 2*
● Colnero '22	🍷 3
○ Tumbaza	🍷 2

La Fornace
fraz. San Savino
via Fornace, 42
47016 Predappio [FC]
☎ +39 0543923150
✉ www.vinilafornace.it

CELLAR SALES
PRE-BOOKED VISITS
ANNUAL PRODUCTION 3,000 bottles
HECTARES UNDER VINE 3.00
VITICULTURE METHOD Certified Organic

● Romagna Sangiovese Predappio Cassiano '21	🍷🍷 3
● Romagna Sangiovese Predappio Profondo Rosso Ris. '19	🍷🍷 3

Garuti
fraz. Sorbara
via per Solara, 6
41030 Bomporto [MO]
☎ +39 059902021
✉ www.garutivini.it

ANNUAL PRODUCTION 120,000 bottles
HECTARES UNDER VINE 30.00

● Lambrusco di Sorbara Garuti '23	🍷🍷 2
● Lambrusco Grasparossa di Castelvetro Romeo '23	🍷🍷 3
● Lambrusco di Sorbara Dante '23	🍷 2

OTHER WINERIES

Giovannini

via Punta, 82
40026 Imola [BO]
☎ +39 3389763854
✉ www.vinigiovannini.it

CELLAR SALES
PRE-BOOKED VISITS
ANNUAL PRODUCTION 75,000 bottles
HECTARES UNDER VINE 15.00
VITICULTURE METHOD Certified Organic

○ Romagna Albana Secco G.G.G. '22	♀♀ 3
○ Romagna Albana Secco Gioja '23	♀♀ 2*
● Oplà Sangiovese '23	♀ 2

Tenuta La Riva

via Farnè, 430
40050 Valsamoggia [BO]
☎ +39 3356212888
✉ www.tenutalariva.it

CELLAR SALES
PRE-BOOKED VISITS
ANNUAL PRODUCTION 50,000 bottles
HECTARES UNDER VINE 12.00

○ C. B. Pignoletto Brut Nature M. Cl. Pinus Laetus '16	♀♀ 4
○ Farnè VIII Brut Nature M. Cl. '16	♀ 4

Manaresi

loc. Podere Bella Vista
via Bertoloni , 14/16
40069 Zola Predosa [BO]
☎ +39 3358032189
✉ www.manaresi.net

CELLAR SALES
PRE-BOOKED VISITS
ANNUAL PRODUCTION 50,000 bottles
HECTARES UNDER VINE 10.00
VITICULTURE METHOD Certified Organic
SUSTAINABLE WINERY

● C. B. Colli Bolognesi Bologna Rosso Controluce '21	♀♀ 5
○ C. B. Pignoletto Cl. '22	♀♀ 3
○ C. B. Bianco Duesettanta '23	♀ 3

Podere La Grotta

loc. Saiano
via Cimadori, 621
47521 Cesena [FC]
☎ +39 0547326368
✉ www.lagrottavini.it

CELLAR SALES
PRE-BOOKED VISITS
ANNUAL PRODUCTION 30,000 bottles
HECTARES UNDER VINE 12.00
VITICULTURE METHOD Certified Organic
SUSTAINABLE WINERY

○ Romagna Albana Damadora '23	♀♀ 3
● Romagna Sangiovese Sup. Mazapegul '23	♀♀ 3
● Romagna Sangiovese Sup. Cleto Ris. '21	♀ 5

Otto Logiurato

via Montebudello, 68
40053 Valsamoggia [BO]
☎ +39 3476030240
✉ www.ottologiurato.it

HECTARES UNDER VINE 10.50

● C. B. Barbera Giunco delle Creste '21	♀♀ 3
● C. B. Bologna Rosso Noah '22	♀♀ 3
○ C. B. Pignoletto Sup. Neve '23	♀ 3

La Mancina

fraz. Montebudello
via Motta, 8
40050 Monteveglio [BO]
☎ +39 051832691
✉ www.lamancina.it

CELLAR SALES
PRE-BOOKED VISITS
ANNUAL PRODUCTION 110,000 bottles
HECTARES UNDER VINE 25.00

○ Dosaggio Zero M. Cl. '18	♀♀ 4
○ C. B. Pignoletto Cl. Terre di Montebudello '22	♀ 3

587

OTHER WINERIES

EMILIA ROMAGNA

Manicardi

via Massaroni, 1
41014 Castelvetro di Modena [MO]
+39 059799000
www.manicardi.it

CELLAR SALES
PRE-BOOKED VISITS
ANNUAL PRODUCTION 100,000 bottles
HECTARES UNDER VINE 16.90

● Lambrusco Grasparossa di Castelvetro '23	♥♥ 2*
● Lambrusco Grasparossa di Castelvetro V. Ca' del Fiore '23	♥♥ 2*
○ Fabula Brut Rosé '23	♥ 3

Il Monticino

via Predosa, 72
40069 Zola Predosa [BO]
+39 051755260
www.ilmonticino.it

CELLAR SALES
PRE-BOOKED VISITS
ANNUAL PRODUCTION 40,000 bottles
HECTARES UNDER VINE 6.00
VITICULTURE METHOD Certified Organic

○ C. B. Pignoletto Frizzante del Monticino '23	♥♥ 2*
○ C. B. Bologna Bianco Bianco Bolognino '23	♥ 2
● C. B. Bologna Rosso Ris. '20	♥ 5

Tenute Nura

fraz. Villò
via Genova, 20
29020 Vigolzone [PC]
+39 0523870904
www.cantineromagnoli.it

CELLAR SALES
PRE-BOOKED VISITS
ANNUAL PRODUCTION 60,000 bottles
HECTARES UNDER VINE 45.00
VITICULTURE METHOD Certified Organic
SUSTAINABLE WINERY

○ Blanc de Blancs M. Cl. Extra Brut	♥♥ 5
● P188 Gutturnio Rls. '19	♥♥ 5
○ Blanc de Noirs M. Cl. Dosaggio Zero	♥ 5
○ P188 Malvasia '22	♥ 5

Tenuta Masselina

loc. Serrà
via Pozze, 1030
48014 Castel Bolognese [RA]
+39 0545284711
www.masselina.it

ACCOMMODATION
ANNUAL PRODUCTION 50,000 bottles
HECTARES UNDER VINE 16.00

○ Romagna Albana Secco '23	♥♥ 3
● Romagna Sangiovese Serra Ris. '21	♥♥ 4
○ Extra Brut M. Cl. '19	♥ 4
● Romagna Sangiovese Sup. 138 '22	♥ 3

Poderi Morini

loc. Oriolo dei Fichi
via Gesuita
48018 Faenza [RA]
+39 0546634257
www.poderimorini.com

ANNUAL PRODUCTION 100,000 bottles
HECTARES UNDER VINE 26.00
SUSTAINABLE WINERY

○ Romagna Albana Secco Sette Note '23	♥♥ 3
● Romagna Sangiovese Oriolo Nonno Rico Ris. '19	♥♥ 4
○ Romagna Albana Passito Innamorato '22	♥ 5

Palazzo di Varignana

fraz. Varignana
via Ca'Masino 611A
40024 Castel San Pietro Terme [BO]
+39 05119939917
www.palazzodivarignana.com

● Pinot Nero '22	♥♥ 3
○ Colli di Imola Chardonnay '23	♥ 3
● Romagna Sangiovese Sup. '22	♥ 3

OTHER WINERIES

Palazzona di Maggio

via Panzacchi, 20
40064 Ozzano dell'Emilia [BO]
☎ +39 335397030
✉ www.palazzonadimaggio.it

CELLAR SALES
PRE-BOOKED VISITS
ACCOMMODATION
ANNUAL PRODUCTION 65,000 bottles
HECTARES UNDER VINE 15.50
VITICULTURE METHOD Certified Organic

○ Maleto Chardonnay '23	🍷🍷 3
⊘ Aspro Brut Nature	🍷 3
● Colli di Imola Rosso Dracone Ris. '19	🍷 6

Piccolo - Brunelli

s.da San Zeno, 1
47010 Galeata [FC]
☎ +39 3468020206
✉ www.piccolobrunelli.it

CELLAR SALES
PRE-BOOKED VISITS
ACCOMMODATION
ANNUAL PRODUCTION 17,000 bottles
HECTARES UNDER VINE 17.00
VITICULTURE METHOD Certified Organic
SUSTAINABLE WINERY

● Romagna Sangiovese Predappio Pietro 1904 '22	🍷🍷 3*
● Romagna Sangiovese Predappio Dante 1872 Ris. '21	🍷🍷 5

Il Pratello

via Morana, 14
47015 Modigliana [FC]
☎ +39 0546942038
✉ www.ilpratello.net

CELLAR SALES
PRE-BOOKED VISITS
RESTAURANT SERVICE
ANNUAL PRODUCTION 15,000 bottles
HECTARES UNDER VINE 5.00
VITICULTURE METHOD Certified Organic

● Romagna Sangiovese Modigliana Mantignano dei Ginepri '22	🍷🍷 5
○ Le Fornaci del Re '22	🍷 5

Pandolfa

loc. Fiumana
via Pandolfa, 35
47016 Predappio [FC]
☎ +39 0543940073
✉ www.pandolfa.it

CELLAR SALES
PRE-BOOKED VISITS
ACCOMMODATION
ANNUAL PRODUCTION 120,000 bottles
HECTARES UNDER VINE 30.00
VITICULTURE METHOD Certified Organic
SUSTAINABLE WINERY

○ Battista '23	🍷🍷 2*
● Romagna Sangiovese Sup. Federico '23	🍷 2
● Romagna Sangiovese Sup. Pandolfo Ris. '21	🍷 4

Il Poggiarello

fraz. Scrivellano di Statto
loc. Il Poggiarello
29020 Travo [PC]
☎ +39 0523957241
✉ www.ilpoggiarellovini.it

CELLAR SALES
PRE-BOOKED VISITS
ANNUAL PRODUCTION 200,000 bottles
HECTARES UNDER VINE 20.00

● Gutturnio Tradizione Piacentina Gli Spaghi '23	🍷🍷 3
○ Come il Vento Sauvignon '23	🍷 3
● Gutturnio La Barbona Ris. '21	🍷 5

Cantina Puianello

fraz. Puianello
via C. Marx, 19a
42020 Quattro Castella [RE]
☎ +39 0522889120
✉ www.cantinapuianello.it

CELLAR SALES
PRE-BOOKED VISITS
ANNUAL PRODUCTION 980,000 bottles
HECTARES UNDER VINE 240.00
VITICULTURE METHOD Certified Organic

● Colli di Scandiano e Canossa Lambrusco Montericco Amarcord '23	🍷🍷 2*
● Reggiano Lambrusco Contrada Borgoleto '23	🍷🍷 2*

OTHER WINERIES

Quintopasso

loc. Sozzigalli
via Canale, 267
41019 Soliera [MO]
+39 0593163311
www.quintopasso.it

ANNUAL PRODUCTION 40,000 bottles
HECTARES UNDER VINE 12.00
SUSTAINABLE WINERY

○ Cuvée Paradiso Brut M. Cl. '17	🍷🍷 5

Randi Vini

via San Savino, 113
48034 Fusignano [RA]
+39 054558231
www.randivini.it

CELLAR SALES
PRE-BOOKED VISITS
ANNUAL PRODUCTION 150,000 bottles
HECTARES UNDER VINE 50.00
VITICULTURE METHOD Certified Organic

● Blu di Bursôn '22	🍷🍷 2*
● Randi Selezione '19	🍷🍷 4
○ Rambëla Bianca '23	🍷 2

Rinaldini

fraz. Calerno
via Andrea Rivasi, 27
42049 Sant'Ilario d'Enza [RE]
+39 0522679190
www.rinaldinivini.it

CELLAR SALES
PRE-BOOKED VISITS
ANNUAL PRODUCTION 100,000 bottles
HECTARES UNDER VINE 15.50

● Pjcol Ross Brut '23	🍷🍷 3
● Vecchio Moro '23	🍷🍷 3
⊙ R'Ose '23	🍷 2

Podere Riosto

via di Riosto, 12
40065 Pianoro [BO]
+39 051777109
www.podereriosto.it

CELLAR SALES
PRE-BOOKED VISITS
ACCOMMODATION
ANNUAL PRODUCTION 80,000 bottles
HECTARES UNDER VINE 15.80
SUSTAINABLE WINERY

● C. B. Merlot '22	🍷🍷 3
● Aquilante '15	🍷 4
○ C. B. Pignoletto Frizzante '23	🍷 3

Cantine Riunite & Civ

via G. Brodolini, 24
42040 Campegine [RE]
+39 0522905711
www.riuniteciv.com

CELLAR SALES
ANNUAL PRODUCTION 130,000,000 bottles
HECTARES UNDER VINE 3500.00
SUSTAINABLE WINERY

● Lambrusco di Sorbara Righi	🍷🍷 1*
● Modena Lambrusco Semisecco Righi	🍷🍷 1*
● Reggiano Lambrusco 1950 Secco	🍷🍷 1*
● Modena Lambrusco Notturno	🍷 1*

I Sabbioni

loc. I Sabbioni
v.le Bologna, 286a
47122 Forlì
+39 0543755711
www.isabbioni.it

CELLAR SALES
ANNUAL PRODUCTION 70,000 bottles
HECTARES UNDER VINE 9.00
VITICULTURE METHOD Certified Organic

● Romagna Sangiovese Sup. I Voli dei Gruccioni '22	🍷🍷 3
○ Romagna Albana '22	🍷 3
○ Romagna Albana Uva Flava '23	🍷 4

OTHER WINERIES

SaDiVino

loc. Trivella Sant'Agostino
via Trivella, 16a
47016 Predappio [FC]
℡ +39 3665949948
⊚ www.sadivino.com

CELLAR SALES
PRE-BOOKED VISITS
ACCOMMODATION
ANNUAL PRODUCTION 35,000 bottles
HECTARES UNDER VINE 7.00
VITICULTURE METHOD Certified Organic
SUSTAINABLE WINERY

● Romagna Sangiovese Predappio Maestroso Ris. '19	♆♆ 5
● Romagna Sangiovese Sup. Solfatare Ris. '19	♆♆ 5
○ Colli Romagna Centrale Chardonnay '22	♆ 3

Scarabelli

loc. Genepreto
29010 Nibbiano [PC]
℡ +39 32754099672

CELLAR SALES
ACCOMMODATION AND RESTAURANT SERVICE
ANNUAL PRODUCTION 40,000 bottles
HECTARES UNDER VINE 18.00
SUSTAINABLE WINERY

● Gutturnio '23	♆♆ 3
● Gutturnio Sup. '22	♆♆ 3
○ C. P. Malvasia Lus '23	♆ 2

Terre della Rocca

fraz. Isola
via Trinzano
48025 Riolo Terme [RA]
℡ +39 0510188106
⊚ www.terredellarocca.it

CELLAR SALES
ANNUAL PRODUCTION 10,000 bottles
HECTARES UNDER VINE 22.00
VITICULTURE METHOD Certified Organic
SUSTAINABLE WINERY

○ Romagna Albana Alle Dodici a Monte Tondo '23	♆♆ 4
● Romagna Sangiovese Sup. La Furha del Basino '22	♆ 4

Tenuta Santa Croce

loc. Monteveglio
via Albè, 33
40050 Valsamoggia [BO]
℡ +39 0516702069
⊚ www.tenutasantacroce.it

● C. B. Barbera Vignole '22	♆♆ 3
○ C. B. Bologna Bianco Desimo '23	♆♆ 3
○ C. B. Pignoletto Frizzante Abbazia '23	♆ 2

Terraquilia

via Marano, 583
41052 Guiglia [MO]
℡ +39 059931023
⊚ www.terraquilia.it

CELLAR SALES
PRE-BOOKED VISITS
ANNUAL PRODUCTION 75,000 bottles
HECTARES UNDER VINE 12.00
VITICULTURE METHOD Certified Organic
SUSTAINABLE WINERY

⊙ Extra Brut Rosé Metodo Ancestrale '20	♆♆ 5
○ Brut Nature Metodo Ancestrale '19	♆♆ 4
○ Conca d'Oro Zero Metodo Ancestrale '19	♆♆ 3
○ Tresassi Ancestrale '21	♆ 4

Tizzano

via Marescalchi, 13
40033 Casalecchio di Reno [BO]
℡ +39 051571208
⊚ www.tizzano.it

CELLAR SALES
PRE-BOOKED VISITS
ANNUAL PRODUCTION 140,000 bottles
HECTARES UNDER VINE 25.00

● C. B. Cabernet Sauvignon '21	♆♆ 3
○ C. B. Pignoletto Frizzante '23	♆♆ 2*
● C. B. Barbera Frizzante '23	♆ 2

OTHER WINERIES

EMILIA ROMAGNA

Tenute Tozzi

via Renzuno, 16
48032 Casola Valsenio [RA]
(+39 0544525500
www.tenutetozzi.it

CELLAR SALES
PRE-BOOKED VISITS
ANNUAL PRODUCTION 35,000 bottles
HECTARES UNDER VINE 8.00
SUSTAINABLE WINERY

○ Romagna Albana Tantalilli '21	♀♀ 4
● Vivì '22	♀♀ 5
○ Memì '22	♀ 4

Tenuta Uccellina

via Aldo Moro, 23/1
48026 Russi [RA]
(+39 0544580144
www.tenutauccellina.com

CELLAR SALES
PRE-BOOKED VISITS
ANNUAL PRODUCTION 40,000 bottles
HECTARES UNDER VINE 5.00
VITICULTURE METHOD Certified Biodynamic
SUSTAINABLE WINERY

● Bursôn '17	♀♀ 5
● Romagna Sangiovese Brisighella Ghineo Ris. '19	♀♀ 5
○ Rambëla '23	♀ 2

Ventiventi

via della Saliceta, 15
41036 Medolla [MO]
(+39 3440330771
www.ventiventi.it

CELLAR SALES
PRE-BOOKED VISITS
RESTAURANT SERVICE
ANNUAL PRODUCTION 75,000 bottles
HECTARES UNDER VINE 30.00
VITICULTURE METHOD Certified Organic
SUSTAINABLE WINERY

○ Ventiventi Brut M.Cl '20	♀♀ 5
⊙ Modena Lambrusco Brut M. Cl. Rosé '20	♀ 5
○ Ventiventi Pas Dosé M. Cl. '20	♀ 5

Villa Venti

loc. Villaventi di Roncofreddo
via Doccia, 1442
47020 Forlì
(+39 333 4645911
www.villaventi.it

CELLAR SALES
PRE-BOOKED VISITS
ACCOMMODATION
ANNUAL PRODUCTION 42,000 bottles
HECTARES UNDER VINE 7.00
VITICULTURE METHOD Certified Organic

● Romagna Sangiovese Longiano Particella 10 '21	♀♀ 5
○ Romagna Bianco Longiano Tre Albe '23	♀ 3

Zanasi

loc. Cavidole
via Settecani Cavidole, 53a
41051 Castelnuovo Rangone [MO]
(+39 059537052
www.zanasi.net

CELLAR SALES
ANNUAL PRODUCTION 200,000 bottles
HECTARES UNDER VINE 23.00
VITICULTURE METHOD Certified Organic

⊙ Lambrusco di Sorbara '23	♀♀ 3
● Lambrusco Grasparossa di Castelvetro Sassostorno '22	♀♀ 3

Stefano Zavalloni

via Madonna dell'Olivo, 2300
47521 Cesena [FC]
(+39 0547301190
www.zavallonivini.com

○ Romagna Albana Amedeo '22	♀♀ 4
● Romagna Sangiovese Sup. Solaris '22	♀ 3

TUSCANY

Tuscany, along with Piedmont, holds the top spot in Gambero Rosso's guide both in terms of the number of producers featured and the international renown of its appellations. It's been that way for years. Once again, the region leads the national rankings with 90 award-winning wines, solidifying its role as a driving force in both the domestic market and, together with Veneto, in exports. One of Italy's largest regions, Tuscany boasts terroirs and prestigious zones famous around the world. What truly sets it apart, though, is the incredible diversity of its soils and microclimates, paired with the innovation, creativity, and ambition of its producers. From the Apuan Alps to the Apennine foothills, from the Maremma coast to Bolgheri and the rolling hills of Chianti Classico, there's no shortage of choices here.

Looking at the awarded wines, Chianti Classico is the most represented appellation, and in our view, the most dynamic and forward-thinking in the entire region. With each harvest, the growth of the Gran Selezione category becomes more apparent, and this evolution gives us pause for thought. Chianti Classico producers now have the option to indicate Additional Geographical Units (AGUs) to highlight their connection to the terroir, and many are choosing to go even deeper by naming the individual vineyards. These are significant decisions that the market is recognizing and rewarding. Montepulciano's Le Pievi and Rufina's Terraelectae have successfully taken a similar path. Montalcino isn't resting on its laurels either, offering increasingly refined wines that remain true to sangiovese grosso and the local territory.

These are prestigious bottles with rising prices, much like the other stronghold of Bolgheri, which focuses on international varietals. But from Carmignano to the now entirely organic Alta Valdarno, from Montepulciano to San Gimignano, from Rufina to the Colli Fiorentini, the Maremma, and the Colline Pisane and Lucchesi, there is no shortage of memorable wines, including many that prioritize brand over appellation. Tignanello, the quintessential Super Tuscan, celebrates 50 years of international success with its 2021 vintage, and it's joined by a dazzling Solaia '21. Other standout Super Tuscans can be found in every corner of the region. Among the whites, vermentino from the coast is seeing a rapid ascent, both in terms of planted hectares and bottles produced, while the trend toward organic, biodynamic, and sustainable certification continues to grow across Tuscany. A special award recognizes this stellar performance. Our Red of the Year, the wine that moved us most, is Torre a Cona's elegant Chianti Colli Fiorentini Molino degli Innocenti Riserva '20. It's a truly memorable pour, as are the three Tuscan wines that we've included in our Rare Wines list: an extraordinary white, a red, and a meditation wine. In short, if you're looking for exceptional bottles in Tuscany, you're spoiled for choice.

Maurizio Alongi

loc. Casetta
53013 Gaiole in Chianti [SI]
(📞) +39 3389878937
(✉) www.maurizioalongi.it

ANNUAL PRODUCTION 6,000 bottles
HECTARES UNDER VINE 1.30
VITICULTURE METHOD Certified Organic

Winemaker Maurizio Alongi has taken on the
challenge of Gaiole in Chianti, a renowned but
demanding district, with a straightforward and
clear-cut project. He's registered his Barbischio
vines in the regional list of vineyards that can
claim the "Vigna" designation and maintained the
health of 40-year-old vines. The result is a
straightforward and largely indisputable wine
that, year after year, grows in prestige, having
become one of the finest contemporary
expressions of Chianti Classico. The Chianti
Classico Vigna Barbischio Riserva '21 reaffirms
its place as one of the best examples of its type.
Its well-defined, vibrant aromas of herbs, bright
fruits, flint, and spices impress, though that's to
be expected. The palate is refined, supple, yet
also multifaceted, sustained by lively acidity and
fine, precise tannins. The finish underscores both
flavor and airiness.

Fattoria Ambra

via Lombarda, 85
59015 Carmignano [PO]
(📞) +39 0558719049
(✉) www.fattoriaambra.it

CELLAR SALES
PRE-BOOKED VISITS
ANNUAL PRODUCTION 90,000 bottles
HECTARES UNDER VINE 24.00
VITICULTURE METHOD Certified Organic

Fattoria Ambra has been owned by the Romei
Rigoli family since the late 19th century and is
currently run by Giuseppe Rigoli, his wife Susan,
and young Fabio Marzotti. The vineyards,
predominantly planted with sangiovese, cabernet
sauvignon, and canaiolo, are located in some of
the best parts of the Carmignano appellation:
Montalbiolo, Elzana, Santa Cristina in Pilli,
Montefortini, and Podere Lombarda, all farmed
organically. The Carmignano Montalbiolo Riserva
'20 possesses richness and structure, while
retaining a dynamic, taut palate with impressive
breadth, accompanied by an intense and
well-focused aromatic profile. The Carmignano
Montefortini Podere Lambarda '21 offers a
vibrant progression of flavor, defined by lively
tannins and culminating in a long, balsamic finish.
The Vin Santo '15, reviewed in the Rare Wines
section, proves particularly captivating.

● Chianti Classico V. Barbischio Ris. '21	🍷🍷🍷 6
● Chianti Cl. V. Barbischio Ris. '20	🍷🍷🍷 6
● Chianti Cl. V. Barbischio Ris. '19	🍷🍷🍷 5
● Chianti Cl. V. Barbischio Ris. '18	🍷🍷🍷 5
● Chianti Cl. V. Barbischio Ris. '16	🍷🍷🍷 5
● Chianti Cl. V. Barbischio Ris. '17	🍷🍷 5
● Chianti Cl. V. Barbischio Ris. '15	🍷🍷 5

● Carmignano Montalbiolo Ris. '20	🍷🍷 5
● Barco Reale di Carmignano '23	🍷🍷 2*
● Carmignano Elzana Ris. '20	🍷🍷 5
● Carmignano Montefortini Podere Lombarda '21	🍷🍷 3
⊙ Barco Reale Rosato Vin Ruspo '23	🍷 2
● Carmignano Santa Cristina in Pilli '21	🍷 3
○ Trebbiano '23	🍷 2
○ Vermentino '23	🍷 3
● Carmignano Santa Cristina in Pilli '16	🍷🍷🍷 3*
● Carmignano Santa Cristina in Pilli '15	🍷🍷🍷 3*
● Carmignano Elzana Ris. '18	🍷🍷 5
● Carmignano Montefortini Podere Lombarda '20	🍷🍷 3*
○ Vin Santo di Carmignano '12	🍷🍷 5

★Stefano Amerighi

fraz. Farneta
loc. Poggiobello
52044 Cortona [AR]
☏ +39 0575649241
☞ www.stefanoamerighi.it

CELLAR SALES
PRE-BOOKED VISITS
ANNUAL PRODUCTION 35,000 bottles
HECTARES UNDER VINE 8.50
VITICULTURE METHOD Certified Biodynamic
SUSTAINABLE WINERY

Stefano Amerighi has enriched land traditionally
used for raising Chianina cattle with a vineyard
renowned for its uniquely expressive syrah, a
grape that seems to find its ideal home here.
Since the late 1990s, Amerighi has overseen an
estate of undisputed quality at Poggiobello di
Farneta. An eclectic vigneron and tireless
experimenter, Amerighi has also formed a
fruitful relationship with prominent Rhône
producers, from whom he continues to draw
inspiration. The Cortona Syrah '21 opens on
fragrant aromas and tasty, taut, and vibrant
flavors. The Cortona Apice '20 captivates with
its floral and black cherry aromas, introducing a
palate of dynamic, unstoppable sapidity. The
Cortona Syrah Serine '20 is also excellent,
unveiling aromas of red berries, hints of citrus,
and refined spiciness. Its impact on the palate
is unforgettable.

★★★Marchesi Antinori

fraz. Bargino
via Cassia per Siena, 133
50026 San Casciano in Val di Pesa [FI]
☏ +39 05523595
☞ www.antinori.it

CELLAR SALES
PRE-BOOKED VISITS
ACCOMMODATION AND RESTAURANT SERVICE
ANNUAL PRODUCTION 1,900,000 bottles
HECTARES UNDER VINE 391.00

In the hills of the San Casciano Val di Pesa UGA
production zone, the Antinori family has not
only built a futuristic Bargino winery, but also
consolidated their historical roots and
productive base in Tuscany. Alongside the estates
of Villa Antinori (Villa del Cigliano), Péppoli,
Tignanello, and Badia a Passignano, the recent
addition of the San Sano and Capraia vineyards
has further strengthened the family's presence in
Chianti. The Solaia '21 is a majestic, rich, and
complex red, with a fleshy texture and an
enticing, multifaceted, spicy profile. A drink of
uncommon energy and length. The Tignanello '21
also impresses with its maturity and structure,
showing great potential for evolution. The
Chianti Classico Villa Antinori Riserva '21 reveals
red and black fruit aromas with spiced, toasted
accents on the nose, while on the palate it's
flavorful and relaxed.

TUSCANY

● Cortona Syrah Serine '20	♟♟♟ 8
● Cortona Syrah '21	♟♟ 5
● Cortona Syrah Apice '20	♟♟ 7
● Cortona Syrah '18	♟♟♟ 5
● Cortona Syrah '17	♟♟♟ 5
● Cortona Syrah '16	♟♟♟ 5
● Cortona Syrah '15	♟♟♟ 5
● Cortona Syrah '14	♟♟♟ 5
● Cortona Syrah '11	♟♟♟ 5
● Cortona Syrah '10	♟♟♟ 5
● Cortona Syrah '09	♟♟♟ 5
● Cortona Syrah Apice '19	♟♟♟ 7
● Cortona Syrah '20	♟♟ 5
● Cortona Syrah Apice '16	♟♟ 6
● Cortona Syrah Apice '15	♟♟ 6
● Cortona Syrah Serine '18	♟♟ 7

● Solaia '21	♟♟♟ 8
● Chianti Cl. Villa Antinori Ris. '21	♟♟ 5
● Tignanello '21	♟♟ 8
● Villa Antinori Rosso '21	♟♟ 4
● Chianti Cl. Gran Selezione Badia a Passignano '21	♟♟ 7
● Chianti Cl. Marchese Antinori Ris. '21	♟♟ 6
● Chianti Cl. Pèppoli '22	♟ 4
● Chianti Cl. Marchese Antinori Ris. '15	♟♟♟ 5
● Chianti Cl. Villa Antinori Ris. '20	♟♟♟ 5
● Solaia '18	♟♟♟ 8
● Solaia '17	♟♟♟ 8
● Solaia '16	♟♟♟ 8
● Tignanello '19	♟♟♟ 8
● Tignanello '13	♟♟♟ 8
● Tignanello '09	♟♟♟ 8

Argentiera

loc. I Pianali
fraz. Donoratico
via Aurelia, 412a
57022 Castagneto Carducci [LI]
(+39 0565773176
@ www.argentiera.eu

CELLAR SALES
PRE-BOOKED VISITS
ACCOMMODATION
ANNUAL PRODUCTION 450,000 bottles
HECTARES UNDER VINE 85.00
SUSTAINABLE WINERY

Owned by Austrian entrepreneur Stanislaus Turnauer, who acquired the property in late 2015, Tenuta Argentiera produces impeccably executed wines with a strong Mediterranean personality. The estate is named after one of its main plots, "Podere Argentiera," historically a silver mining area in Etruscan times. Their wines consistently showcase quality and are capable of standing the test of time. The Bolgheri Superiore Argentiera '21 proves refined and elegant in its aromas, featuring sharply delineated and juicy fruit, interspersed with notes of Mediterranean shrub. Sapid and with a beautiful progression on the palate, it finishes with great persistence. The Bolgheri Rosso Villa Donoratico '22 is dark and intense, playing on aromas of small dark fruits and a continuous, pleasant balsamic vein. A fleshy and taut drink, it finishes satisfyingly.

Argiano

loc. Sant'Angelo in Colle
53024 Montalcino [SI]
(+39 0577844037
@ www.argiano.net

CELLAR SALES
PRE-BOOKED VISITS
ANNUAL PRODUCTION 300,000 bottles
HECTARES UNDER VINE 60.00
VITICULTURE METHOD Certified Organic
SUSTAINABLE WINERY

The splendid 16th-century villa with its spectacular Italian garden makes Argiano one of the most beautiful estates in all of Tuscany. Beyond the beauty of the place, we must also appreciate the efforts and investments made in recent years to reduce environmental impact and simultaneously safeguard the biodiversity of this beautiful corner of Montalcino. At Argiano, plastic is no longer used, energy comes from certified renewable sources, no chemicals are used in either the vineyard or the cellar, and all production waste is recycled. The wines that reached our finals confirm that, increasingly, sustainability and quality go hand in hand. The Brunello Vigna del Suolo '19 is complex on the nose, with tones of plum, Mediterranean scrub, and licorice, leading to an elegant, sapid palate, with tannins and fruit in perfect harmony. The Solengo '21 is monumental, opening with intense fruity and spiced notes, rich in texture and well-balanced on the palate.

● Bolgheri Rosso Sup. Argentiera '21	♥♥ 8
● Bolgheri Rosso Villa Donoratico '22	♥♥ 6
● Bolgheri Rosso Sup. '19	♥♥♥ 8
● Bolgheri Rosso Sup. '18	♥♥♥ 8
● Bolgheri Rosso Villa Donoratico '18	♥♥♥ 5
● Bolgheri Sup. '11	♥♥♥ 8
● Bolgheri Sup. '10	♥♥♥ 7
● Bolgheri Sup. '06	♥♥♥ 7
● Bolgheri Sup. '05	♥♥♥ 7
● Bolgheri Sup. '04	♥♥♥ 7
● Bolgheri Rosso Poggio ai Ginepri '20	♥♥ 4
● Bolgheri Rosso Sup. '17	♥♥ 8
● Bolgheri Rosso Sup. '16	♥♥ 8
● Bolgheri Rosso Sup. Argentiera '20	♥♥ 8
● Bolgheri Rosso Villa Donoratico '21	♥♥ 6
● Bolgheri Rosso Villa Donoratico '19	♥♥ 5

● Brunello di Montalcino V. del Suolo '19	♥♥♥ 8
● Brunello di Montalcino '19	♥♥ 8
● Solengo '21	♥♥ 8
● Non Confunditur '22	♥ 3
● Rosso di Montalcino '22	♥ 5
● Rosso di Montalcino Sella del Leccio '20	♥ 6
● Brunello di Montalcino Ris. '88	♥♥♥ 7
● Brunello di Montalcino Ris. '85	♥♥♥ 7
● Brunello di Montalcino V. del Suolo '18	♥♥♥ 8
● Brunello di Montalcino V. del Suolo '16	♥♥♥ 8
● Brunello di Montalcino V. del Suolo '15	♥♥♥ 8
● Solengo '19	♥♥♥ 8
● Solengo '97	♥♥♥ 6
● Solengo '95	♥♥♥ 6
● Rosso di Montalcino '19	♥♥ 5
● Solengo '20	♥♥ 8

Arillo in Terrabianca

loc. San Fedele a Paterno
53017 Radda in Chianti [SI]
📞 +39 057754029
🌐 www.arilloimterrabianca.com

CELLAR SALES
PRE-BOOKED VISITS
ANNUAL PRODUCTION 250,000 bottles
HECTARES UNDER VINE 49.00
VITICULTURE METHOD Certified Organic
SUSTAINABLE WINERY

Swiss couple Adriana and Urs Burkard
launched "Arillo," a name that refers to botany,
in 2019. The project consists of three distinct
properties: Terrabianca, located in the UGA
production zone of Radda in Chianti (where the
winery will draw on the talents of Mario Botta);
the Maremma estate of Il Tesoro, in Massa
Marittima; and Colle Brezza in Pienza, in the
heart of the Val d'Orcia. The wines are
well-crafted, exhibiting a modern stylistic profile,
with the Maremma wines standing out as more
intense and radiant. The Chianti Classico Gran
Selezione Vigna Terrabianca '20 features aromas
of red and black fruits with spicy notes. On the
palate, it's firm and multifaceted, with a
close-knit, fleshy development and a finish that
returns to dark fruits and spices. The Maremma
Bevorosso '22 is well-crafted, with balsamic
aromas and a generous, soft, and juicy palate.
The other Maremma wines, the Campaccio
Collezione '20 and Campaccio '20, both based
on sangiovese, cabernet sauvignon, and merlot,
are still maturing.

● Chianti Cl. Gran Selezione Vigna Terrabianca '20	♟♟ 7
● Maremma Merlot Bevorosso '22	♟♟ 3
● Campaccio '20	♟ 5
● Campaccio Collezione '20	♟ 6
● Campaccio '19	♟♟ 6
● Campaccio Collezione '19	♟♟ 6
● Chianti Cl. Poggio Croce Ris. '20	♟♟ 5
● Chianti Cl. Poggio Croce Ris. '19	♟♟ 5
● Chianti Cl. Sacello '21	♟♟ 3
● Chianti Cl. Sacello '20	♟♟ 4

Arrighi

loc. Pian del Monte, I
57036 Porto Azzurro [LI]
📞 +39 3356641793
🌐 www.arrighivigneolivi.it

CELLAR SALES
PRE-BOOKED VISITS
ANNUAL PRODUCTION 45,000 bottles
HECTARES UNDER VINE 9.00
VITICULTURE METHOD Certified Organic
SUSTAINABLE WINERY

Situated near Porto Azzurro, this small artisanal
winery is led by Antonio Arrighi. Arrighi is an
explosive and tireless experimenter, as
evidenced by his efforts to revive the ancient
production method of the island of Chios, an
initiative inspired by Attilio Scienza. In 2010, he
introduced the first amphorae in the cellar, now
a defining element of his wines. A range of
different grapes are used, from procanico to
ansonica, biancone vermentino, sangiovese,
aleatico, viognier, syrah, and sagrantino. The
Viognier Hermia '23 offers up intense aromas,
with brackish tones of herbs and ripe yellow
fruit. On the palate, it's pleasant and well-
proportioned, with persistent, well-sustained
length. The Elba Aleatico Passito Silosò '23
proves well-crafted, with an intriguing aromatic
profile of Mediterranean shrub and balsams. On
the palate, it reveals an engaging progression of
flavor, alternating sweet tones with pronounced
sapidity, finishing long and airy.

● Elba Aleatico Passito Silosò '23	♟♟ 6
○ Hermia Viognier '23	♟♟ 5
● Tresse Anfora '21	♟ 6
○ Valerius '23	♟ 5
● Elba Aleatico Passito Silosò '22	♟♟ 6
● Elba Aleatico Passito Silosò '21	♟♟ 5
● Elba Aleatico Passito Silosò '20	♟♟ 5
○ Elba Vermentino Arembapampane '20	♟♟ 4
○ Hermia '22	♟♟ 4
○ Hermia '20	♟♟ 4
● Tresse '19	♟♟ 5
● Tresse Anfora '20	♟♟ 5
○ V.I.P. '22	♟♟ 4
○ V.I.P. '21	♟♟ 4
○ Valerius '22	♟♟ 5
○ Valerius '21	♟♟ 5

★Avignonesi

fraz. Valiano
via Colonica, 1
53045 Montepulciano [SI]
📞 +39 0578707 41
🌐 www.avignonesi.it

CELLAR SALES
PRE-BOOKED VISITS
ACCOMMODATION AND RESTAURANT SERVICE
ANNUAL PRODUCTION 600,000 bottles
HECTARES UNDER VINE 169.00
VITICULTURE METHOD Certified Biodynamic
SUSTAINABLE WINERY

The Falvo family's former winery seems to have regained the "magic" that once made it a benchmark in the Montepulciano wine scene. The new Belgian ownership has steered the entire range towards excellence, with sangiovese exhibiting a refined stylistic approach, and their Vin Santo making a grand comeback. Some adore these wines passionately, while others struggle to even classify them as wines. One thing is for sure, as true classics of Montepulciano oenology, they can't be ignored. The Vin Santo Occhio di Pernice '11 is an intriguing version of this particular style. On the nose, its fruit aromas are constantly evolving, evoking fresh, preserved, and dried fruits, with a firm, iodized note in the background. On the palate, it's dense and sweet, yet dynamic, with acidity maintaining a creamy texture. The Vin Santo '11 follows the same style, though it's a bit less defined. The Nobile '20 proves fragrant, flavorful, and multifaceted.

Baciate Me

p.zza Livio Zannoni, 7
50026 San Casciano in Val di Pesa [FI]
📞 +39 3491834696
🌐 www.baciateme.it

ANNUAL PRODUCTION 12,000 bottles
HECTARES UNDER VINE 2.70

The winery, whose unusual name is a fusion of the surnames of the four friends who founded it (Battaglini, Ciarla, Tempestini, and Mechini), is the result of rigorous and constant work, starting with the revival of a 50-year-old abandoned vineyard near Montefiridolfi in the San Casciano Val di Pesa UGA production area. In the cellar, the focus is on spontaneous fermentations and maturation in stainless steel, concrete, and small used barrels. The result is a range of refined, contemporary wines that are beautifully crafted. The Chianti Classico Avenne '21 features a delicate and fragrant aromatic profile, combining light fruits, slight earthy hints, and spicy touches. On the palate, it's supple and rhythmic, with an airy development and a rising finish on fruit. The BaciateMe '21, a monovarietal canaiolo, offers fresh, straightforward aromas and a slender, flavorful palate. The Cribbio '21, a white made from trebbiano, is also well-crafted, with flinty aromas and a delicious progression.

● Nobile di Montepulciano '20	🍷🍷 5
○ Vin Santo di Montepulciano '11	🍷🍷 8
● Vin Santo di Montepulciano Occhio di Pernice '11	🍷🍷 8
● Nobile di Montepulciano Poggetto di Sopra '20	🍷🍷 8
● Rosso di Montepulciano '21	🍷🍷 3
● Nobile di Montepulciano '12	🍷🍷🍷 4*
● Nobile di Montepulciano Ris. '85	🍷🍷🍷 8
○ Vin Santo '98	🍷🍷🍷 8
○ Vin Santo '96	🍷🍷🍷 8
○ Vin Santo '95	🍷🍷🍷 8
○ Vin Santo '93	🍷🍷🍷 8
● Vin Santo Occhio di Pernice '97	🍷🍷🍷 8
● Vin Santo Occhio di Pernice '93	🍷🍷🍷 8
○ Vin Santo Occhio di Pernice '90	🍷🍷🍷 8

● Chianti Cl. Avenne '21	🍷🍷 5
● BaciateMe '21	🍷🍷 6
○ Cribbio '21	🍷🍷 6

★Badia a Coltibuono

loc. Badia a Coltibuono
53013 Gaiole in Chianti [SI]
☎ +39 057774481
✉ www.coltibuono.com

Badia di Morrona

via del Chianti, 6
56030 Terricciola [PI]
☎ +39 0587658505
✉ badiadimorrona.it

CELLAR SALES
PRE-BOOKED VISITS
ACCOMMODATION AND RESTAURANT SERVICE
ANNUAL PRODUCTION 240,000 bottles
HECTARES UNDER VINE 64.00
VITICULTURE METHOD Certified Organic
SUSTAINABLE WINERY

CELLAR SALES
PRE-BOOKED VISITS
ACCOMMODATION AND RESTAURANT SERVICE
ANNUAL PRODUCTION 500,000 bottles
HECTARES UNDER VINE 110.00

The Stucchi Prinetti family's Badia a Coltibuono is situated in Monti, in the southern part of the Gaiole in Chianti production zone. For years now, the expressive naturalness of the producer's wines, the result of a mature oenological sensitivity, has been a defining characteristic—a trait that has elevated their range to the rank of true "classics" of Chianti, with sangiovese maintaining an extraordinarily faithful character and profile. The Sangioveto '20, a monovarietal sangiovese, stands out for its depth of aromas and flavor. The wine plays on notes of small red fruits and underbrush, with a palate balancing fruit sweetness and bright acidity, highlighting its refined and profound character. This style is also characteristic of the Chianti Classico Riserva '20, where enticing aromas precede a finely layered palate. The Chianti Classico RS '22, with its lively drinkability, is delightful.

Badia di Morrona has been owned by the Gaslini Alberti family since 1939. Here an ancient medieval abbey, after which the winery was named, overlooks the vineyards, which experienced a breakthrough in the 1990s, thanks to the work of Duccio Gaslini Alberti. Today this Terricciola producer is run by his children, Filippo and Alessandra, who have, especially in recent years, managed to further improve the quality of their range. The N'Antia '21, a blend of cabernet sauvignon, cabernet franc, and merlot, proves bright and crisp on the nose, with herbal notes and toasted touches. On the palate, it offers vibrant sapidity, flavor, and a fruit-forward, expansive finish. The Terre di Pisa Vigna Alta '21 is equally well-crafted, with its dark fruit and spicy notes on the nose, and a beautiful progression of flavor on the palate. The Chianti I Sodi del Pareto Ris. '21 offers a distinct hint of blueberry, showing nice suppleness on the palate.

● Sangioveto '20	▼▼▼ 8
● Chianti Cl. Ris. '20	▼▼ 6
● Chianti Cl. RS '22	▼▼ 4
● Chianti Cetamura '22	▼▼ 3
● Chianti Cl. '22	▼▼ 4
● Chianti Cl. Cultus Ris. '19	▼ 6
● Colmaia '22	▼ 3
● Chianti Cl. '18	♈♈♈ 4*
● Chianti Cl. '15	♈♈♈ 4*
● Chianti Cl. '13	♈♈♈ 3*
● Chianti Cl. '12	♈♈♈ 3*
● Chianti Cl. '06	♈♈♈ 3*
● Chianti Cl. Cultus Boni '15	♈♈♈ 4*
● Chianti Cl. Cultus Boni '09	♈♈♈ 4*
● Chianti Cl. Ris. '09	♈♈♈ 5
● Chianti Cl. Ris. '07	♈♈♈ 5
● Chianti Cl. Ris. '04	♈♈♈ 5

● N'Antia '21	▼▼ 5
● Chianti I Sodi del Paretaio '23	▼▼ 3
● Chianti I Sodi del Paretaio Ris. '21	▼▼ 4
● Terre di Pisa Sangiovese VignaAlta '21	▼▼ 5
● Taneto '22	▼ 4
● Terre di Pisa Sangiovese VignaAlta '16	♈♈♈ 5
● Chianti I Sodi del Paretaio '22	♈♈ 2*
● Chianti I Sodi del Paretaio '20	♈♈ 2*
● Chianti I Sodi del Paretaio '19	♈♈ 2*
● Chianti I Sodi del Paretaio Ris. '20	♈♈ 4
● Chianti I Sodi del Paretaio Ris. '19	♈♈ 3*
● Chianti I Sodi del Paretaio Ris. '18	♈♈ 3*
● Taneto '20	♈♈ 3*
● Taneto '16	♈♈ 3*

Baldetti

loc. Pietraia, 71a
52044 Cortona [AR]
(☏) +39 057567077
⊕ www.baldetti.com

CELLAR SALES
PRE-BOOKED VISITS
ANNUAL PRODUCTION 50,000 bottles
HECTARES UNDER VINE 15.00
SUSTAINABLE WINERY

Daniele and Gianluca Baldetti have worked tirelessly in recent years, uncompromisingly aiming for absolute quality. Together the brothers have expanded the winery founded by their father, Alfonso, who passed away suddenly this year. Proud of his experience and having learned from it, Daniele and Gianluca are focused on producing syrah, the area's principal grape, developing a contemporary, personal style, and crafting bottles with superb aromatic impact that appeals to both traditional palates and new enthusiasts. The Cortona Syrah Crano '20 proves fragrant, with a juicy, racy palate, rich in nuances and contrasts. The Arenite '20, a monovarietal syrah, carries spicy aromas of black olives, unfolding on the palate with deep, compact development. The Cortona Syrah Spazzanido '23 is lively and bright, with immediate appeal on both the nose and its fresh, approachable palate.

● Arenite '20	♟♟ 8
● Cortona Syrah Crano '20	♟♟ 5
○ Chagrè '23	♟♟ 3
● Cortona Syrah Spazzanido '23	♟♟ 4
⊙ Piet Rosè '23	♟♟ 3
● Arenite '18	♟♟ 7
○ Chagrè '21	♟♟ 3
○ Chagrè '20	♟♟ 2*
● Cortona Sangiovese Marius '17	♟♟ 3
● Cortona Syrah Arenite '17	♟♟ 7
● Cortona Syrah Crano '18	♟♟ 5
● Cortona Syrah Crano '17	♟♟ 4
● Cortona Syrah Crano '16	♟♟ 4
● Cortona Syrah Crano '15	♟♟ 5
○ Cortona Vin Santo Leopoldo '05	♟♟ 5

Giacomo Baraldo

p.zza Matteotti, 4
53040 San Casciano dei Bagni [SI]
(☏) +39 3336844189
⊕ www.giacomobaraldo.it

CELLAR SALES
PRE-BOOKED VISITS
ACCOMMODATION AND RESTAURANT SERVICE
ANNUAL PRODUCTION 20,000 bottles
HECTARES UNDER VINE 5.00
SUSTAINABLE WINERY

Giacomo Baraldo unexpectedly fell in love with wine while tasting some exceptional ones on his 18th birthday. It was a moment that ignited a passion that led him to dedicate his life to artisanal, high-quality production. The winery was founded in the 1990s by his father, Silvestro. Almost five of the estate's 12 hectares are under vines, including some veritable crus—Bossolo, Affacciatoio, Pozzone, and Caccialupi—with various exposures and elevations spanning 300-600 meters above sea level. The dynamic Il Pergola '21, made from grechetto grapes, features enticing aromas of mandarin, citron peel, hay, and aromatic herbs. The palate is sapid, rhythmic, flavorful, and sapid, with a juicy finish. The Chardonnay Affacciatolo '22 is glyceric and smooth, with aromas of golden apple, ripe pear, and bergamot, touched lightly by vanilla. The palate is rich, silky, and pervasive, with a spicy finish. The Sangiovese Caccialupi '21, from a 50-year-old vineyard cultivated at 600 meters elevation, offers up aromas of blueberry and cherry, with lovely tannins and dynamic energy.

● Caccialupi '21	♟♟ 6
○ Il Pergola '21	♟♟ 5
○ L'Affacciatoio '22	♟♟ 5
● 0.0K Tullio '21	♟ 7
● Il Pozzone '21	♟ 6
● 0.0K '20	♟♟ 4
● 0.0K '19	♟♟ 4
● 0.0K Tullio '18	♟♟ 4
● Caccialupi '19	♟♟ 4
● Il Bossolo '20	♟♟ 5
● Il Bossolo '19	♟♟ 5
● Il Bossolotto '21	♟♟ 2*
● Il Pozzone '20	♟♟ 4
● Il Pozzone '19	♟♟ 4
○ Il Risveglio '21	♟♟ 5

★Baricci

loc. Colombaio di Montosoli, 13
53024 Montalcino [SI]
☎ +39 0577848109
🌐 www.baricci.it

CELLAR SALES
PRE-BOOKED VISITS
ANNUAL PRODUCTION 30,000 bottles
HECTARES UNDER VINE 5.00

It's been 70 years since Nello Baricci bought Podere Colombaio in Montosoli, seven kilometers from the town of Montalcino on the northwest side of the appellation, a hill of only 30 hectares (half of which are vineyards) and now considered to be among the best Brunello crus. Today, Nello's grandsons, Federico and Francesco Buffi, run the winery, which boasts five hectares of vineyards in Montosoli. The property is divided into six different plots, all vinified separately before being blended into Rosso and Brunello. Both wines that reached our final selections are well-made and deeply connected to their terroir and vintage. The Brunello Montosoli '19 promises great things, with its well-defined aromas of fruit, dry flowers, and cinchona bark. Its tannins are finely extracted and elegant, leading to a long, balsamic finish. The Rosso '22 is also pleasant: complex and elegant on the nose, taut and dynamic on the palate.

Basile

pod. Monte Mario
58044 Cinigiano [GR]
☎ +39 3355882149
🌐 www.basilessa.it

CELLAR SALES
PRE-BOOKED VISITS
ANNUAL PRODUCTION 50,000 bottles
HECTARES UNDER VINE 8.00
VITICULTURE METHOD Certified Organic
SUSTAINABLE WINERY

There are no secrets at Giovan Battista Basile's winery, just rigorous work in the vineyard, starting with organic methods and minimalist winemaking operations, with even the white wines performing well. For the reds, the focus is on sangiovese, which the winery, located at Podere Monte Mario (near Cinigiano), delivers with solid qualitative consistency and a coherent stylistic profile, often reaching peaks of absolute excellence. The Montecucco Sangiovese Adagio Riserva '20 conjures up aromas of underbrush and earth, from which a lush fruitiness with spicy touches emerges. On the palate, it's juicy, with compact development and an intense, fruit-forward finish. The Montecucco Sangiovese Cartacanta '21 reveals meaty and sanguine aromas, with a fleshy, robust palate. The Maremma Rosso Comandante '21 proves to be a smooth and sweet drink, with fresh aromas.

Brunello di Montalcino '19	♟♟ 8
Rosso di Montalcino '22	♟♟ 4
Brunello di Montalcino '16	♟♟♟ 6
Brunello di Montalcino '15	♟♟♟ 6
Brunello di Montalcino '14	♟♟♟ 6
Brunello di Montalcino '10	♟♟♟ 6
Brunello di Montalcino '09	♟♟♟ 5
Brunello di Montalcino '07	♟♟♟ 5
Brunello di Montalcino '83	♟♟♟ 5
Brunello di Montalcino Nello Ris. '16	♟♟♟ 6
Brunello di Montalcino Nello Ris. '10	♟♟♟ 6
Rosso di Montalcino '16	♟♟♟ 4*
Rosso di Montalcino '15	♟♟♟ 4*
Brunello di Montalcino '18	♟♟ 6
Brunello di Montalcino Nello Ris. '15	♟♟ 6
Rosso di Montalcino '20	♟♟ 4

Montecucco Sangiovese Ad Agio Ris. '20	♟♟ 5
Maremma Toscana Rosso Comandante '21	♟♟ 4
Montecucco Sangiovese Cartacanta '21	♟♟ 3
Montecucco Vermentino Artèteca '23	♟♟ 3
Montecucco Sangiovese Ad Agio Ris. '18	♟♟♟ 5
Montecucco Sangiovese Ad Agio Ris. '15	♟♟♟ 5
Montecucco Sangiovese Ad Agio Ris. '14	♟♟♟ 5
Montecucco Sangiovese Ad Agio Ris. '12	♟♟♟ 5
Montecucco Sangiovese Ad Agio Ris. '19	♟♟ 5

Belguardo

loc. Poggio La Mozza
strada delle Campore, 18
58100 Grosseto
☎ +39 057773571
⊕ www.mazzei.it

CELLAR SALES
PRE-BOOKED VISITS
ANNUAL PRODUCTION 250,000 bottles
HECTARES UNDER VINE 48.00
SUSTAINABLE WINERY

The history of the Mazzei family is one of the most important in the Tuscan wine scene, being bound up with the destiny of Maremma winemaking. Here, starting in the mid-1990s, the Belguardo estate was founded, a property that's now looking to expand into the Grosseto area. Francesco Mazzei, who's also president of the Consorzio Doc Maremma Toscana, continues to be enthusiastic about the territory's potential, still partially untapped. The Vermentino Belguardo V '22 opens on aromas of white-fleshed fruits and citrus touches, with slight briny and spicy notes. On the palate, it's juicy and fragrant, with a well-sustained development and a broad, balsamic finish. The Maremma Vermentino '23 is also well-crafted, though less complex. Its aromas recall linden flowers and tropical fruits, while the palate proves dynamic, with a citrusy finish.

○ Maremma Toscana Vermentino Sup. Belguardo V '22	▼▼ 5
○ Maremma Toscana Vermentino '23	▼▼ 4
● Maremma Toscana Rosso Tenuta Belguardo Ris. '20	▼ 8
● Maremma Toscana Rosso Tirrenico '20	▼ 5
● Morellino di Scansano Bronzone Ris. '21	▼ 5
● Maremma Toscana Rosso Tenuta Belguardo Ris. '19	▽▽ 8
○ Maremma Toscana Vermentino Sup. Belguardo V '21	▽▽ 6
● Morellino di Scansano Bronzone Ris. '20	▽▽ 5
● Morellino di Scansano Bronzone Ris. '18	▽▽ 4

Cantine Bellini

via Piave, 1
50068 Rufina [FI]
☎ +39 0558396025
⊕ www.bellinicantine.it

CELLAR SALES
ANNUAL PRODUCTION 900,000 bottles
HECTARES UNDER VINE 15.00

Now in its fifth generation of winemakers, Cantine Bellini is a historic winery in the Rufina area. The Bellini family, traditionally agricultural producers, draw on different production areas throughout Tuscany, including Chianti Classico. One of their estates is Podere Il Pozzo, located in Rufina, an old farm complex with about 10 hectares of mostly southeast-facing vineyards at 300 meters elevation. The Chianti Rufina Riserva '21 is balanced, precise, and well-crafted, with a silky attack that gives way to fully integrated, velvety tannins. Aromas of cherry and underbrush are echoed on the palate. The Terraelectae Vigna Il Fiorino '20 is rich, balsamic, and dense with medicinal herb aromas, though a bit less convincing on the palate due to overly sweet fruit, made even sweeter by a pronounced note of alcohol on the finish.

● Chianti Rufina Ris. '21	▼▼ 2
● Chianti '23	▼▼ 2
● Chianti Rufina Podere Il Pozzo '22	▼▼ 3
● Chianti Rufina Terraelectae Vigna Il Fiorino Ris. '20	▼▼ 5
● Chianti Ris. '21	▼ 4
● Chianti Rufina Podere Il Pozzo Ris. '21	▼ 3
● Comedia '21	▼ 2
● Le Lodole '21	▼ 2
● Chianti Rufina Ris. '15	▽▽ 2
● Mamb-o Dominante '15	▽▽ 2
○ Vin Santo del Chianti Rufina '09	▽▽ 4

Bindella - Tenuta Vallocaia

via delle Tre Berte, 10a
53045 Montepulciano [SI]
📞 +39 0578767777
🌐 www.bindella.it

CELLAR SALES
PRE-BOOKED VISITS
RESTAURANT SERVICE
ANNUAL PRODUCTION 200,000 bottles
HECTARES UNDER VINE 54.00
SUSTAINABLE WINERY

Now in its 40th year, Rudolf Bindella's winery
has consistently proven its capacity for quality,
and Vallocaia's wines now occupy a prominent
place in Nobile di Montepulciano. Their success
is due to meticulous work both in the vineyard
and in the cellar, and particularly to a stylistic
approach that emphasizes balance and elegance.
Here sangiovese, vinified with modern
techniques, retains its distinctive character and
personality. The Nobile I Quadri '21 features
aromatic notes ranging from fruity to floral and
earthy, with spices adding elegance. The structure
is precise, with flavorful tannins and sapidity
extending through to a finish marked by a lovely
iron note. The Nobile Vallocaia Ris. '20 proves
firm and clearly defined in its profile, with
chiaroscuro aromas. The Rosso di
Montepulciano Fossolupaio '22, with its lively
drinkability, is delightful.

Nobile di Montepulciano I Quadri '21	♟♟♟ 6
Nobile di Montepulciano Vallocaia Ris. '20	♟♟ 7
Rosso di Montepulciano Fossolupaio '22	♟♟ 3*
Nobile di Montepulciano '21	♟♟ 5
Nobile di Montepulciano I Quadri '20	♟♟♟ 6
Nobile di Montepulciano I Quadri '19	♟♟♟ 8
Nobile di Montepulciano I Quadri '18	♟♟♟ 5
Nobile di Montepulciano I Quadri '17	♟♟♟ 5
Nobile di Montepulciano '19	♟♟ 4

★Biondi - Santi Tenuta Greppo

loc. Villa Greppo, 183
53024 Montalcino [SI]
📞 +39 0577848023
🌐 www.biondisanti.it

HECTARES UNDER VINE 26.00

No winery in Italy is as closely tied to an
appellation as Biondi Santi is to Brunello di
Montalcino, to the point where the two are
virtually synonymous. The family boasts seven
generations of winemaking, with the first
"Brunello" dating back to 1865, and the first
bottle to be officially labeled Brunello produced
in 1888 (it's still preserved in the cellar). The
iconic Montalcino winery is now owned by the
French group EPI, who have other prestigious
holdings, such as Charles Heidsieck and Piper in
Champagne, Château La Verrerie in Côte du
Rhône, and Isole e Olena in Chianti Classico. The
outstanding work of Giampiero Bertolini's team
continues to amaze, ensuring stylistic
consistency across the Greppo wines. The
fantastic Brunello '18, with its pronounced sense
of place, exemplifies this. Dark berries, balsamic
herbs, and underbrush form a bouquet of rare
complexity and freshness, framed by cut flowers,
licorice, dark tobacco, and spices. The palate is
full, but not muscular, with elegant, close-knit
tannins that are polished yet still lively.

Brunello di Montalcino '18	♟♟♟ 8
Rosso di Montalcino '21	♟♟ 7
Brunello di Montalcino '12	♟♟♟ 8
Brunello di Montalcino '10	♟♟♟ 8
Brunello di Montalcino '09	♟♟♟ 8
Brunello di Montalcino '06	♟♟♟ 7
Brunello di Montalcino '04	♟♟♟ 8
Brunello di Montalcino '03	♟♟♟ 8
Brunello di Montalcino Ris. '16	♟♟♟ 8
Brunello di Montalcino Ris. '15	♟♟♟ 8
Brunello di Montalcino Ris. '13	♟♟♟ 8
Brunello di Montalcino Ris. '10	♟♟♟ 8
Brunello di Montalcino Ris. '07	♟♟♟ 8
Brunello di Montalcino Ris. '06	♟♟♟ 8
Brunello di Montalcino Ris. '04	♟♟♟ 8
Brunello di Montalcino Ris. '01	♟♟♟ 8

Cantine Bonacchi

loc. Quarrata
fraz. Campiglio
via Colli Mozzi 26
51039 Pistoia
📞 +39 0573735457
🌐 www.bonacchi.it

CELLAR SALES
PRE-BOOKED VISITS
ACCOMMODATION
ANNUAL PRODUCTION 3,000,000 bottles
HECTARES UNDER VINE 110.00

The Bonacchi family's story spans generations, evolving through different phases of wine commerce. Now led by Andrea Bonacchi, the third generation, they began in Montalbano with their headquarters in Quarrata, expanding into Tuscany's most important appellations. They produce Chianti Classico at Fattoria Casalino in Castelnuovo Berardenga and Brunello at Molino della Suga. Their most recent acquisition was 4.4 hectares in Bolgheri. The Bolgheri wines have certainly hit the mark, particularly the Gerbido Superiore '19, which presents complex notes of mint, red fruit, rain-soaked earth, and wood resins. On the palate, it opens with freshness, growing dense and creamy, developing depth with lovely sapidity. The Chianti Classico and Montalcino wines from the Molino della Suga estate are also very good. The other wines tasted are equally enjoyable.

Fattoria Bonsalto

fraz. Anselmo
via Bonsarto, 1
50025 Montespertoli [FI]
📞 +39 3355731699
🌐 www.fattoriabonsalto.it

PRE-BOOKED VISITS
ANNUAL PRODUCTION 25,000 bottles
HECTARES UNDER VINE 22.00

Founded in the 1970s as a winery for personal use and bulk wine sales, the Paci family's Fattoria Bonsalto took a more focused turn in 2021. Their wines have a contemporary style, emphasizing finesse and contrast, focusing on ancient grape varieties from the Montespertoli area. Aging takes place in a mix of barrel sizes, stainless steel, concrete, and terracotta. The Sopralago '22, a monovarietal sangiovese, impresses with its fragrant aromas of small red fruits and floral flashes on a flinty base. Supple and well-balanced on the palate, it concludes with a rising finish. The Declivio '22, a blend of trebbiano and malvasia, offers floral aromas with hints of honey and nuts, while the palate proves sapid and refreshing. The rest of the range is well-crafted, with a special mention for the Primomarzo '22, made from an ancient local red grape variety called boggione (curiously nicknamed "ingannacane", or "dog tricker").

● Bolgheri Rosso Sup. Gerbido '19	🍷🍷 6
● Badesco '19	🍷🍷 3
● Brunello di Montalcino Molino della Suga '19	🍷🍷 6
● Chianti Cl. '22	🍷🍷 3
● Chianti Cl. Ris. '20	🍷🍷 5
● Rosso di Montalcino Molino della Suga '20	🍷🍷 4
● Bolgheri Rosso '21	🍷 5
● Bolgheri Rosso Gerbido '21	🍷 5
● Brunello di Montalcino '19	🍷 5

○ Declivio '22	🍷🍷 3
● Sopralago '22	🍷🍷 5
● Bonsalto '22	🍷🍷 3
● Primomarzo '22	🍷🍷 4
● Sette Grazie '22	🍷🍷 4
○ Declivio '21	🍷🍷 4
● Primomarzo '21	🍷🍷 4
● Settegrazie '21	🍷🍷 4
● Sopralago '21	🍷🍷 4

Borgo Macereto

loc. Macereto
50062 Dicomano [FI]
☎ +39 333429 2316
🌐 www.borgomacereto.it

CELLAR SALES
PRE-BOOKED VISITS
ACCOMMODATION AND RESTAURANT SERVICE
ANNUAL PRODUCTION 25,000 bottles
HECTARES UNDER VINE 6.00
VITICULTURE METHOD Certified Organic

Since 2014, the Foscarini family has been managing the property (agritourism included) here in the town of Dicomano, nestled between the Mugello valley and Val di Sieve. The estate spans six hectares and hosts traditional local varieties alongside non-native ones, like pinot nero (which has found a home in the Apennines), and gamay (an unusual variety for the region). Their labels, designed by Tuscan artist Francesco Nesi, are true gems. The Chianti Rufina Riserva Musica '20 opens with a gamey hint on the nose, followed by black fruits, tanned leather, and ferns. On the palate, it shows structure and finishes with a slightly drying note. The Chianti Rufina La Fuga '22 has a more mountainous character, with spicy notes and a delicious bitter streak. The Doppio Senso '23, a blend of various white varieties including incrocio Manzoni, riesling, and moscato, proves quite pleasant, revealing both pulp and finesse. Floral notes combine with thyme and apple peel, and the palate shows good length and plenty of salinity.

Borgo Salcetino

loc. Lucarelli
53017 Radda in Chianti [SI]
☎ +39 0577733541
🌐 www.livon.it

PRE-BOOKED VISITS
ANNUAL PRODUCTION 95,000 bottles
HECTARES UNDER VINE 15.00
SUSTAINABLE WINERY

The Livon family, renowned for their white wines in Friuli, ventured into Chianti in 1996, founding Borgo Salcetino. Their vineyards, located in the heart of the Radda in Chianti production zone, are among the few that also face the neighboring Panzano area, creating a unique geological "kinship" between the two districts. Salcetino's wines are well-crafted, marked by a tendency towards finesse, combining clean execution with the careful use of oak. The Chianti Classico '21 continues to prove clearly defined in its profile, expressing not only remarkable drinkability but also a certain complexity, especially on the nose, where characteristic elements of the appellation shine through: red fruits, flowers, and light hints of underbrush. The palate is slender, dynamic, and flavorful. The Chianti Classico Lucarello Riserva '20 is a bit more austere in its tone.

⊃ Doppiosenso '23	🍷🍷 3*
● Chianti Rufina La Fuga '22	🍷🍷 3
● Chianti Rufina Musica Ris. '20	🍷🍷 5
● Incipit '20	🍷🍷 4
● Chianti Rufina La Fuga '21	♛♛ 3
● Chianti Rufina La Fuga '20	♛♛ 3
● Chianti Rufina La Fuga '19	♛♛ 3
● Chianti Rufina Musica Ris. '19	♛♛ 5
● Chianti Rufina Musica Ris. '18	♛♛ 5
● Il Borgo '19	♛♛ 5
● Incipit '18	♛♛ 4

● Chianti Cl. '21	🍷🍷 4
● Chianti Cl. Lucarello Ris. '20	🍷🍷 5
● Chianti Cl. Gran Selezione I Salci '18	🍷 7
● Rossole '22	🍷 4
● Chianti Cl. '16	♛♛♛ 3*
● Chianti Cl. '15	♛♛♛ 3*
● Chianti Cl. '14	♛♛♛ 3*
● Chianti Cl. '13	♛♛♛ 3*
● Chianti Cl. '11	♛♛♛ 3*
● Chianti Cl. Lucarello Ris. '15	♛♛♛ 4*
● Rossole '12	♛♛♛ 3*
● Chianti Cl. '20	♛♛ 3*
● Chianti Cl. Lucarello Ris. '20	♛♛ 5

Il Borro

fraz. San Giustino Valdarno
loc. Il Borro, 1
52024 Loro Ciuffenna [AR]
📞 +39 055977053
🌐 www.ilborro.it

CELLAR SALES
PRE-BOOKED VISITS
ACCOMMODATION AND RESTAURANT SERVICE
ANNUAL PRODUCTION 310,000 bottles
HECTARES UNDER VINE 87.00
VITICULTURE METHOD Certified Organic
SUSTAINABLE WINERY

Il Borro has been owned by Ferruccio Ferragamo since 1993. Today the estate, which is managed by his children, Salvatore and Vittoria, combines agriculture, hospitality, and winemaking. Initially, their wines followed the Tuscan style of the time, with international grape varieties taking center stage, while ancient cultivars remained in the background. Recently, however, the winery has rethought its approach, featuring notable expressions of sangiovese in its portfolio. The Valdarno di Sopra Vigna Polissena '20 exhibits a pleasantly nuanced nose, where touches of small red fruits, underbrush, and spices converge. On the palate, it's well-defined and proportioned, with fragrant development and a lively, sapid finish. The Pian di Nova '21, a sangiovese-syrah blend, offers fruity and spicy aromas, with a tasty progression on the palate that finishes on a spicy note.

★Boscarelli

loc. Cervognano
via di Montenero, 28
53045 Montepulciano [SI]
📞 +39 0578767277
🌐 poderiboscarelli.com

CELLAR SALES
PRE-BOOKED VISITS
ANNUAL PRODUCTION 100,000 bottles
HECTARES UNDER VINE 14.00

Boscarelli is undoubtedly a prominent name in the Nobile di Montepulciano appellation, consistently producing wines that preserve the natural and vibrant qualities of authentic sangiovese, regardless of the vintage. This is thanks to the excellent soils of Cervognano and the uncompromising decisions of the De Ferrari Corradi family, who, over 60 years of activity, have created a true classic of Tuscan winemaking. The refined and delicious Nobile '21 opens with prominent fruit, alongside subtle earthy and spicy hints, accented by aromatic herbs. In the mouth, it's juicy, sapid, and lively, with sweet-and-sour contrasts that enhance the palate. The Nobile Costagrande '20 proves aromatically precise, with a fleshy impact on the palate. The Nobile Il Nocio '20, more powerful but well-crafted, is equally notable. The Rosso di Montepulciano Prugnolo '23 continues to impress with its persistent drinkability.

● Valdarno di Sopra Sangiovese V. Polissena '20	♟♟♟ 5
● Pian di Nova '21	♟♟ 4
● Alessandro Dal Borro Syrah '16	♟♟♟ 8
● Il Borro '19	♟♟♟ 7
● Il Borro '18	♟♟♟ 7
● Il Borro '16	♟♟♟ 7
● Valdarno di Sopra Sangiovese V. Polissena '18	♟♟♟ 5
● Alessandro Dal Borro '15	♟♟ 8
● Il Borro '15	♟♟ 7
● Il Borro '13	♟♟ 7
● Pian di Nova '18	♟♟ 3*
● Polissena '15	♟♟ 5
● Valdarno di Sopra Sangiovese V. Polissena '19	♟♟ 5

● Nobile di Montepulciano '21	♟♟♟ 5
● Nobile di Montepulciano Costa Grande '20	♟♟ 8
● Nobile di Montepulciano Il Nocio '20	♟♟ 8
● Rosso di Montepulciano Prugnolo '23	♟♟ 3
○ Vin Santo di Montepulciano Occhio di Pernice Familiae '13	♟♟ 7
● Nobile di Montepulciano Ris. '20	♟ 5
● Nobile di Montepulciano Sottocasa Ris. '20	♟ 6
● Nobile di Montepulciano '16	♟♟♟ 5
● Nobile di Montepulciano Costa Grande '19	♟♟♟ 8
● Nobile di Montepulciano Il Nocio '18	♟♟♟ 8
● Nobile di Montepulciano Il Nocio '17	♟♟♟ 8
● Nobile di Montepulciano Il Nocio '16	♟♟♟ 8
● Nobile di Montepulciano Il Nocio '13	♟♟♟ 8

★Brancaia
loc. Poppi, 42
53017 Radda in Chianti [SI]
(☎) +39 0577742007
🌐 www.brancaia.it

CELLAR SALES
PRE-BOOKED VISITS
ACCOMMODATION AND RESTAURANT SERVICE
ANNUAL PRODUCTION 614,000 bottles
HECTARES UNDER VINE 90.00
VITICULTURE METHOD Certified Organic
SUSTAINABLE WINERY

For over 40 years, Brancaia, owned by the Swiss Widmer family, has produced Chianti Classico with a strong focus on overall balance, achieved through absolute precision in execution. The winery is located in the Radda in Chianti UGA production zone, but also owns vineyards in the northern part of Castellina in Chianti. Their Maremma estate, Poggio al Sasso (acquired in 1998), yields naturally sunnier and more intense wines. The Chianti Classico Gran Selezione '21 is a refined wine, with airy aromas and a dynamic, fragrant palate. The Chianti Classico '22 is also well-crafted, conveying fine and intriguing aromas. It's subtle on the palate but not insubstantial, with its strength lying in its drinkability. The Tre '22, a sangiovese, merlot, and cabernet sauvignon blend, proves rhythmic and juicy. The Blu '21, also a merlot-sangiovese-cabernet blend, is intense and well-proportioned.

Gianni Brunelli
Le Chiuse di Sotto
loc. Podernovone, 157
53024 Montalcino [SI]
(☎) +39 0577849337
🌐 www.giannibrunelli.it

CELLAR SALES
PRE-BOOKED VISITS
ACCOMMODATION AND RESTAURANT SERVICE
ANNUAL PRODUCTION 30,000 bottles
HECTARES UNDER VINE 6.50
SUSTAINABLE WINERY

Laura Vacca Brunelli's beautiful winery, along with some of its vineyards, is situated on the southeastern slope of the appellation. A woman of rare culture and artistic sensitivity, Laura has enriched her garden and winery with sculptures and paintings by renowned contemporary artists, creating a delightful blend of art and wine. The winery's other vineyards are located in Chiuse di Sotto, on the northern side of Montalcino. The Brunello '19 is complex and intense, offering impressively fresh fruit for the vintage. It opens with notes of red berries, underpinned by elegant layers of licorice and graphite. The palate is refined, with great structure, fine-knit tannins, and a long, classy, persistent finish. The Merlot Amor Costante '21 is delightful, unveiling aromas of brandied cherries and Mediterranean brush, juicy yet well-balanced by acidity on the palate.

● Chianti Cl. '22	♟♟ 4
● Chianti Cl. Gran Selezione '21	♟♟ 8
● Il Blu '21	♟♟ 8
● Tre '22	♟♟ 4
● Chianti Cl. Ris. '21	♟ 6
● Chianti Cl. '13	♟♟♟ 4*
● Chianti Cl. Ris. '14	♟♟♟ 5
● Chianti Cl. Ris. '13	♟♟♟ 5
● Chianti Cl. Ris. '11	♟♟♟ 5
● Chianti Cl. Ris. '10	♟♟♟ 4*
● Chianti Cl. Ris. '09	♟♟♟ 7
● Il Blu '08	♟♟♟ 8
● Il Blu '07	♟♟♟ 7
● Il Blu '06	♟♟♟ 6
● Il Blu '05	♟♟♟ 6
● Il Blu '04	♟♟♟ 6
● Il Blu '03	♟♟♟ 6

● Brunello di Montalcino '19	♟♟ 8
● Amor Costante '21	♟♟ 6
● Rosso di Montalcino '22	♟♟ 6
● Amor Costante '05	♟♟♟ 5
● Brunello di Montalcino '14	♟♟♟ 6
● Brunello di Montalcino '12	♟♟♟ 6
● Brunello di Montalcino '10	♟♟♟ 6
● Brunello di Montalcino '18	♟♟ 8
● Brunello di Montalcino '17	♟♟ 8
● Brunello di Montalcino '16	♟♟ 8
● Brunello di Montalcino '15	♟♟ 6
● Brunello di Montalcino '13	♟♟ 6
● Brunello di Montalcino '09	♟♟ 6
● Brunello di Montalcino Ris. '16	♟♟ 8
● Brunello di Montalcino Ris. '15	♟♟ 8
● Brunello di Montalcino Ris. '13	♟♟ 8

Bruni

fraz. Fonteblanda
s.da vic.le Migliorina, 6
58015 Orbetello [GR]
(☎ +39 0564885445
⊛ www.aziendabruni.it

CELLAR SALES
ANNUAL PRODUCTION 600,000 bottles
HECTARES UNDER VINE 48.00

The Bruni family's winery has become one of
the most interesting producers in the Maremma
wine scene, with a range that consistently
maintains high quality and a clear stylistic
identity, faithfully representing the
contemporary and Mediterranean character of
this corner of Tuscany. Marco and Moreno Bruni
have also introduced more ambitious whites and
reds that consistently rank at the top of Tuscan
wine production. The Maremma Alicante
Oltreconfine '22 stands out for its fragrant nose,
with hints of blueberries, pomegranate, and
spices, leading to a sweet, juicy, and refined
palate, with soft tannins and a broad finish. The
Perlaia '23, a monovarietal vermentino, is precise
and clean, with aromas of linden flowers and
tropical fruits. On the palate, it's pervasive
and lively. The Morellino di Scansano Laire
Riserva '21, a sangiovese inflected by
Mediterranean tones, is right up there.

● Maremma Toscana Alicante Oltreconfine '22	♟♟♟ 6
● Morellino di Scansano Laire Ris. '21	♟♟ 5
○ Perlaia '23	♟♟ 4
○ Moscato '23	♟♟ 3
○ Maremma Toscana Vermentino Plinio '23	♟ 3
● Maremma Toscana Alicante Oltreconfine '21	♟♟♟ 6
● Maremma Toscana Alicante Oltreconfine '20	♟♟♟ 6
● Maremma Toscana Alicante Oltreconfine '19	♟♟♟ 6
● Maremma Toscana Alicante Oltreconfine '18	♟♟♟ 6

Bulichella

loc. Bulichella, 131
57028 Suvereto [LI]
(☎ +39 0565829892
⊛ www.bulichella.it

CELLAR SALES
PRE-BOOKED VISITS
ACCOMMODATION AND RESTAURANT SERVICE
ANNUAL PRODUCTION 75,000 bottles
HECTARES UNDER VINE 14.00
VITICULTURE METHOD Certified Organic
SUSTAINABLE WINERY

Agricola Bulichella was founded in 1983 by four
families who wanted to live together and
produce for their own consumption. In 1999, the
Miyakawa family became the owners, focusing on
winemaking. Today, Bulichella continues to
maintain its strong connection with Val di Cornia
winemaking. Indeed, Hideyuki Miyakawa, having
served as president of the local consortium,
helped achieve recognition of the Docg Suvereto
appellation in 2012. The Hide '21, a monovarietal
syrah, is lively, with a rich, fruity, and balsamic
aromatic profile. The palate is intense and
full-bodied. The Suvereto Coldipietrerosse '21
reveals a vigorous and pervasive progression of
flavor, accompanied by intense and defined
aromas. The Rubino '21, a blend of sangiovese,
merlot, and cabernet sauvignon, is very fruity on
the nose, with a rich and generous palate.

● Hide '21	♟♟ 8
● Rubino '21	♟♟ 4
● Suvereto Rosso Coldipietrerosse '21	♟♟ 7
○ Tuscanio '23	♟ 3
● Hyde '19	♟♟ 6
● Hyde '18	♟♟ 5
● Rubino '20	♟♟ 4
● Suvereto Merlot Maria Shizuko '19	♟♟ 8
● Suvereto Montecristo Ris. '20	♟♟ 8
● Suvereto Rosso Coldipietrerosse '20	♟♟ 7
● Suvereto Rosso Coldipietrerosse '19	♟♟ 6
● Suvereto Rosso Coldipietrerosse '18	♟♟ 5
● Suvereto Rosso Montecristo '19	♟♟ 8
● Suvereto Rosso Montecristo '18	♟♟ 8
○ Tuscanio '21	♟♟ 3
○ Vermentino Tuscanio '20	♟♟ 3

Ca' Marcanda

loc. Santa Teresa, 272
57022 Castagneto Carducci [LI]
☎ +39 0565763809
info@camarcanda.com

CELLAR SALES
PRE-BOOKED VISITS
ANNUAL PRODUCTION 450,000 bottles
HECTARES UNDER VINE 120.00

One of the Gaja family's Tuscan wineries (along with Pieve Santa Restituta in Montalcino), Ca' Marcanda was purchased in 1996 after long negotiations with the previous owners (hence the name, derived from the Piedmontese word for "haggling"). Today, Angelo Gaja runs the estate with his children, Gaia, Rossana, and Giovanni, the fifth generation. The winery's architecture, designed by Giovanni Bo, is fully underground and is considered one of the most noteworthy in the region in terms of sustainability and elegance. Ca' Marcanda have reduced the presence of merlot, carved out a more prominent role for cabernet, and opted for shorter oak aging—the result is a style that opts more for freshness and finesse than in the past. The Bolgheri Superiore Ca' Marcanda '21 opens with crisp, fresh fruit aromas, leading to a vibrant, sapid, and racy palate. Similarly, the Bolgheri Magari '22 shows refined tannic structure, offering a full and well-balanced palate.

Caccia al Piano

loc. Bolgheri
via Bolgherese, 279
57022 Castagneto Carducci [LI]
☎ +39 0565763394
⊕ www.cacciaalpiano.it

CELLAR SALES
PRE-BOOKED VISITS
ANNUAL PRODUCTION 140,000 bottles
HECTARES UNDER VINE 23.00
SUSTAINABLE WINERY

In 2003, Franco Ziliani (owner of Franciacorta's Guido Berlucchi) bought and renovated an 1868 hunting estate that once belonged to the Della Gherardesca family. The purchase included the Grottine, Cantina, Le Bozze, and San Biagio vineyards, with this last located in a particularly favorable position in the hills. Currently, the producer's style is proving very interesting, drawing on reduced oak aging and focusing on expressive finesse. The Bolgheri Superiore '21 plays on aromatic finesse, with a Mediterranean character remaining the leitmotif of an expressive, expansive, and structured palate. The Bolgheri Rosso '22 is more generous in its lush fruit, pronounced yet well-defined on the palate. The Bolgheri Bianco Lungocosta '22 proves fresh and sapid, with continuous and intense tones of white fruit.

Bolgheri Sup. Camarcanda '21	♟♟ 8
Bolgheri Rosso Magari '22	♟♟ 1*
Bolgheri Camarcanda '13	♟♟♟ 8
Bolgheri Camarcanda '07	♟♟♟ 8
Bolgheri Camarcanda '01	♟♟♟ 8
Magari '03	♟♟♟ 6
Bolgheri Camarcanda '12	♟♟ 8
Bolgheri Camarcanda '11	♟♟ 8
Bolgheri Camarcanda '10	♟♟ 8
Bolgheri Camarcanda '09	♟♟ 8
Bolgheri Camarcanda '08	♟♟ 8
Bolgheri Camarcanda '06	♟♟ 8
Bolgheri Camarcanda '05	♟♟ 8
Magari '09	♟♟ 8

● Bolgheri Rosso Sup. '21	♟♟ 8
○ Bolgheri Bianco Lungocosta '22	♟♟ 5
● Bolgheri Rosso Ruit Hora '22	♟♟ 5
○ Bolgheri Bianco Lungocosta '21	♟♟ 5
● Bolgheri Rosso Ruit Hora '21	♟♟ 5
● Bolgheri Rosso Ruit Hora '20	♟♟ 5
● Bolgheri Rosso Ruit Hora '17	♟♟ 4
● Bolgheri Rosso Ruit Hora '16	♟♟ 4
● Bolgheri Rosso Sup. '20	♟♟ 8
● Bolgheri Rosso Sup. '19	♟♟ 8
● Bolgheri Rosso Sup. '18	♟♟ 5
● Bolgheri Rosso Sup. Levia Gravia '16	♟♟ 7
● Grottaia Rosso '19	♟♟ 3
● Grottaia Rosso '18	♟♟ 3*

TUSCANY

Caiarossa

loc. Serra all'Olio, 59
56046 Riparbella [PI]
☎ +39 0586699016
🖥 www.caiarossa.com

CELLAR SALES
PRE-BOOKED VISITS
ANNUAL PRODUCTION 130,000 bottles
HECTARES UNDER VINE 32.00
VITICULTURE METHOD Certified Biodynamic

Founded in 1998, Caiarossa is located near the small village of Riparbella in the Val di Cecina. Since 2004, the winery has been owned by the Dutch Albada Jelgersma family, who also own two Grands Crus Classés in Margaux: Château Giscours and Château du Tertre. The estate's biodynamic vineyards are populated with Bordeaux varieties like merlot, cabernet franc, cabernet sauvignon, and petit verdot, as well as syrah, sangiovese, and alicante. The Caiarossa '21 is deep and intense, an intricate blend of cabernet franc, syrah, cabernet sauvignon, merlot, sangiovese, petit verdot, and grenache. Its iron-rich, Mediterranean aromas open the way to a dynamic and well-focused palate. The Aria di Caiarossa '21, made from cabernet franc, merlot, cabernet sauvignon, syrah, and grenache, also impresses. The Pergolaia '21, a blend of sangiovese, merlot, and cabernet sauvignon, proves well-crafted.

Camigliano

loc. Camigliano
via d'Ingresso, 2
53024 Montalcino [SI]
☎ +39 0577844068
🖥 www.camigliano.it

CELLAR SALES
PRE-BOOKED VISITS
ANNUAL PRODUCTION 350,000 bottles
HECTARES UNDER VINE 92.00
VITICULTURE METHOD Certified Organic
SUSTAINABLE WINERY

In 1957, the Ghezzi family purchased the large Camigliano estate, a 500-hectare property then mostly dedicated to grain and olive trees. The viticultural transformation began in the 1980s when Gualtiero Ghezzi, along with his recently deceased wife Laura, planted over 100 hectares of vineyards. They also started restoring the ancient borgo and, a few years later, constructed a large, entirely underground cellar. The entire range at this year's tasting session stood out for its high quality, especially the stunning Brunello Paesaggio Inatteso '19, with its refined yet complex aromatic profile, full of red fruit, flowers, and underbrush. Expansive and fresh on the palate, it's driven by an elegant, vibrant tannic structure, with a seemingly endless finish. The Riserva Gualto '18 is also excellent, with its tones of ripe black fruit, licorice, and spices, austere and close-knit on the palate.

● Caiarossa '21	▼▼▼ 6
● Aria di Caiarossa '21	▼▼ 5
● Pergolaia '21	▼▼ 3
○ Caiarossa Bianco '22	▼ 5
● Aria di Caiarossa '16	♔♔♔ 5
● Caiarossa '18	♔♔♔ 6
● Aria di Caiarossa '19	♔♔ 5
● Aria di Caiarossa '18	♔♔ 5
● Caiarossa '19	♔♔ 6
● Caiarossa '19	♔♔ 6
● Caiarossa '17	♔♔ 6
● Caiarossa '16	♔♔ 6
● Caiarossa '13	♔♔ 6
● Caiarossa '12	♔♔ 6
● Caiarossa '08	♔♔ 6
● Caiarossa '07	♔ 7

● Brunello di Montalcino Paesaggio Inatteso '19	▼▼▼ 7
● Brunello di Montalcino Gualto Ris. '18	▼▼ 8
● Poderuccio '22	▼▼ 3
● Rosso di Montalcino '22	▼▼ 3
● Brunello di Montalcino '19	▼ 6
○ Gamal '23	▼ 3
● Brunello di Montalcino '15	♔♔♔
● Brunello di Montalcino Gualto Ris. '16	♔♔♔
● Brunello di Montalcino Gualto Ris. '12	♔♔♔
● Brunello di Montalcino Paesaggio Inatteso '18	♔♔
● Brunello di Montalcino Paesaggio Inatteso '17	♔♔
● Brunello di Montalcino Paesaggio Inatteso '16	♔♔

Antonio Camillo

loc. Pianetti di Montemerano
58014 Manciano [GR]
☎ +39 3391525224
🌐 www.antoniocamillo.it

Antonio Camillo has managed to skillfully interpret ciliegiolo, the most important variety of his range, seeking various expressions from different vineyards. A number of rented plots are cultivated, everywhere from remote areas of Maremma, to Capalbio, Manciano, Montemerano and Pitigliano. This viticultural, archaeological work, aimed at reviving and restoring these agricultural treasures, continues today with new varieties like grenache and carignano. The Tinto di Spagna '21 is a monovarietal grenache, named after the Maremma region where it's grown. Aromatically it's reminiscent of Mediterranean scrub, earth, small red fruits, and mint. The palate is flavorful and energetic, with crunchy tannins and lively acidity leading to a balsamic finish. The Ciliegiolo Vallerana Alta '22 offers blueberry and blackberry aromas, introducing a supple, vibrant, and irresistible palate.

● Tinto di Spagna '21	🍷🍷🍷 7
○ Procanico '22	🍷🍷 4
● Vallerana Alta Ciligiolo '22	🍷🍷 5
● Ciliegiolo '23	🍷🍷 3
● Grané '21	🍷🍷 7
● Mediterraneo '23	🍷🍷 3
● Maremma Toscana Ciliegiolo V. Vallerana Alta '16	🍷🍷🍷 5
● Maremma Toscana Ciliegiolo V. Vallerana Alta '15	🍷🍷🍷 6
● Maremma Toscana Ciliegiolo V. Vallerana Alta '14	🍷🍷🍷 3*
● Vallerana Alta Ciliegiolo '21	🍷🍷 5
● Vallerana Alta Ciliegiolo '20	🍷🍷 5
● Vallerana Alta Ciliegiolo '18	🍷🍷 5

Campo alla Sughera

loc. Caccia al Piano
s.da prov.le Bolgherese, 280
57020 Castagneto Carducci [LI]
☎ +39 0565766936
🌐 www.campoallasughera.com

The German Knauf family, renowned worldwide in the building materials sector, has been producing wine in Alta Maremma since 1998 with their boutique winery, Campo alla Sughera. Located between Bolgheri and Castagneto Carducci along the provincial road, the "Montenapoleone street" of the Bolgheri appellation, they continue to invest in the area, recently acquiring three more hectares of vineyards. The focus is on impeccably crafted wines with a distinctly Bordeaux style. The Bolgheri Superiore Arnione '21 showcases fine, delicate spices and a long, smooth progression of flavor on the palate. The Bolgheri Rosso Adeo '22 has a fresh, juicy palate, with balsamic aromas over a fruity base of cherry, wild strawberry, and currant. The Campo alla Sughera '20, a blend of petit verdot and cabernet franc, is rich and sapid, with aromatic nuances of scrubland and licorice.

● Bolgheri Rosso Sup. Arnione '21	🍷🍷 8
● Bolgheri Rosso Adeo '22	🍷🍷 5
● Campo alla Sughera Rosso '20	🍷🍷 8
○ Arioso '23	🍷 5
● Bolgheri Sup. Arnione '06	🍷🍷🍷 6
○ Arioso '22	🍷🍷 5
○ Arioso '21	🍷🍷 5
● Bolgheri Rosso Adeo '20	🍷🍷 5
● Bolgheri Rosso Adeo '19	🍷🍷 5
● Bolgheri Rosso Adeo '18	🍷🍷 5
● Bolgheri Rosso Sup. Arnione '20	🍷🍷 6
● Bolgheri Rosso Sup. Arnione '19	🍷🍷 6
● Bolgheri Rosso Sup. Arnione '18	🍷🍷 6
● Bolgheri Sup. Arnione '14	🍷🍷 6
● Campo alla Sughera Rosso '19	🍷🍷 8
● Campo alla Sughera Rosso '18	🍷🍷 8

Cantina Canaio

loc. La Rota - Farneta
52044 Cortona [AR]
 +39 0575604866
 www.cantinacanaio.it

CELLAR SALES
PRE-BOOKED VISITS
ACCOMMODATION AND RESTAURANT SERVICE
ANNUAL PRODUCTION 15,000 bottles
HECTARES UNDER VINE 5.00

Mirco Zappini is a modern producer with an
old-fashioned craft. Along with his wife Pamela
and in-laws Simone and Doriana, he runs the
family textile business in Camucia, a district of
the municipality of Cortona. However, wine has
been part of the family for at least 30 years,
initially by growing and selling grapes to third
parties and, since 2014, by marketing their own
bottles under the Cantina Canaio brand.
Located in La Rota Farneta, a hilly area situated
between two valleys, the estate's vineyards
host predominantly syrah and merlot. The
Cortona Syrah Villa Passerini '21, aged in both
wood and amphora, features violet and red
berry aromas. Its dynamic, focused palate carries
a continuous spicy and sapid undertone that
lingers through an elegant finish. The Cortona
Syrah Terrasolla '21 is more earthy in its aromas,
with a rich, lively progression on the palate.

● Cortona Syrah Terrasolla '21	♟♟ 5
● Cortona Syrah Villa Passerini '21	♟♟ 7
● Cortona Syrah Terrasolla '20	♟♟ 5
● Cortona Syrah Villa Passerini '20	♟♟ 7
● Cortona Syrah Il Calice '20	♟♟ 4
● Cortona Syrah Il Calice '19	♟♟ 4
● Cortona Syrah Il Calice '17	♟♟ 4
● Cortona Syrah Terra Solla '19	♟♟ 5
● Cortona Syrah Terra Solla '18	♟♟ 5
● Cortona Syrah Terra Solla '17	♟♟ 5
● Cortona Syrah Villa Passerini '19	♟♟ 6

Canalicchio di Sopra

loc. Casaccia, 73
53024 Montalcino [SI]
 +39 0577848316
 www.canalicchiodisopra.com

CELLAR SALES
PRE-BOOKED VISITS
ACCOMMODATION
ANNUAL PRODUCTION 80,000 bottles
HECTARES UNDER VINE 19.00

The Ripaccioli family, now in their third
generation of winemakers, boasts 19 hectares of
sangiovese vineyards in two of Montalcino's
most prestigious areas, Canalicchi and Montosoli,
both on the north side of the appellation. The 10
different plots, planted between 1988 and 2014,
vary significantly in terms of soil and exposure,
despite often being adjacent. These differences
necessitate separate harvesting and vinification,
with decisions as to which to bottle individually
made on an annual basis. The Brunello Vigna
Montosoli '19 lives up to expectations with its
intense, elegant aromatic expression of red fruit,
tobacco, violets, Mediterranean scrub, and a
graphite undertone. The palate is elegant, rich,
and fleshy, but lightened by a refined tannic
presence. The Brunello Vigna La Casaccia '19 is
also good, if less complex, with ripe fruit, quinine,
and tobacco aromas. A full, juicy, and sapid wine.

● Brunello di Montalcino V. Montosoli '19	♟♟ 8
● Brunello di Montalcino V. La Casaccia '19	♟♟ 8
● Brunello di Montalcino '19	♟ 8
● Rosso di Montalcino '22	♟ 5
● Brunello di Montalcino '10	♟♟♟ 6
● Brunello di Montalcino '07	♟♟♟ 6
● Brunello di Montalcino '06	♟♟♟ 6
● Brunello di Montalcino '04	♟♟♟ 6
● Brunello di Montalcino Ris. '07	♟♟♟ 7
● Brunello di Montalcino Ris. '04	♟♟♟ 7
● Brunello di Montalcino Ris. '01	♟♟♟ 7
● Brunello di Montalcino '17	♟♟ 8
● Brunello di Montalcino '16	♟♟ 8
● Brunello di Montalcino Ris. '16	♟♟ 8
● Brunello di Montalcino Ris. '13	♟♟ 8
● Brunello di Montalcino V. Montosoli '18	♟♟ 8

Capanna

loc. Capanna, 333
53024 Montalcino [SI]
☎ +39 0577848298
✉ www.capannamontalcino.com

CELLAR SALES
PRE-BOOKED VISITS
ACCOMMODATION AND RESTAURANT SERVICE
ANNUAL PRODUCTION 80,000 bottles
HECTARES UNDER VINE 23.00

Amedeo Cencioni, a fourth-generation vintner in Montalcino, produced some of the most technically well-crafted wines tasted this year, showcasing Brunello sangiovese with great accuracy while aptly expressing the terroir of northern Montalcino. Founded in 1957, the winery now has 23 hectares of vineyards, mostly planted with sangiovese grosso from massal selections of the best estate clones. There's also a lovely cellar that houses large Slavonian oak barrels (1000-3000 liters). Once again, the winery delivered an exceptional performance, with two wines reaching the final round of tastings. The Brunello Nicco '19 is marked by intense, fresh red fruit aromas, despite the vintage, along with tobacco and graphite. The palate is full-bodied and rich, beautifully supported by the acidity-tannin combination, with a long finish. The Brunello Riserva '18 promises great things, with fine fruity and floral aromas and a harmonious palate, still evolving tannically.

● Brunello di Montalcino Nicco '19	▼▼ 8
● Brunello di Montalcino Ris. '18	▼▼ 8
● Brunello di Montalcino '19	▼▼ 7
● Rosso di Montalcino '22	▼▼ 4
● Brunello di Montalcino Ris. '10	▽▽▽ 8
● Brunello di Montalcino Ris. '06	▽▽▽ 7
● Brunello di Montalcino Ris. '04	▽▽▽ 7
● Brunello di Montalcino Ris. '90	▽▽▽ 6
● Rosso di Montalcino '15	▽▽▽ 3*
● Brunello di Montalcino '16	▽▽ 7
● Brunello di Montalcino '15	▽▽ 7
● Brunello di Montalcino '10	▽▽ 6
● Brunello di Montalcino 50° Vendemmia Ris. '13	▽▽ 8
● Brunello di Montalcino Nicco '17	▽▽ 8
● Brunello di Montalcino Ris. '12	▽▽ 8

Cappellasantandrea

loc. Casale, 26
53037 San Gimignano [SI]
☎ +39 3471946103
✉ www.cappellasantandrea.it

CELLAR SALES
PRE-BOOKED VISITS
RESTAURANT SERVICE
ANNUAL PRODUCTION 45,000 bottles
HECTARES UNDER VINE 8.00
VITICULTURE METHOD Certified Organic
SUSTAINABLE WINERY

Couple Flavia Del Seta and Francesco Galgani manage the estate purchased by Flavia's grandfather in 1959. Cappella Sant'Andrea is a small, family-run organic winery where compost comes from farm animals, and vines are interplanted with apple, pear, and maple trees. Alongside vernaccia, they cultivate sangiovese, merlot, and ciliegiolo. The estate's wines are matured in amphorae, wood, and cement, depending on the type. Maceration gives a touch of tannins that enrich the palate of the Vernaccia di San Gimignano Prima Luce Riserva '21, with a fleshy yet delicate profile that finishes warm and almondy. The Vernaccia di San Gimignano Clara Stella '23 is rich and dynamic on the palate, with an aromatic profile of iodine, nuts, dried fruit and medicinal herbs. The Vernaccia di San Gimignano Rialto '22 has body and complexity, with a not-too-long but highly pleasant palate, ending on a brackish note, refreshed by eucalyptus.

○ Vernaccia di San Gimignano Clara Stella '23	▼▼ 3
○ Vernaccia di San Gimignano Prima Luce Ris. '21	▼▼ 5
○ Vernaccia di San Gimignano Rialto '22	▼▼ 5
● Serreto '19	▼ 5
● Chianti Colli Senesi Arciduca '19	▽▽ 3
○ Vernaccia di San Gimignano Clara Stella '21	▽▽ 3
○ Vernaccia di San Gimignano Prima Luce Ris. '20	▽▽ 5
○ Vernaccia di San Gimignano Prima Luce Ris. '19	▽▽ 5
○ Vernaccia di San Gimignano Rialto '21	▽▽ 3
○ Vernaccia di San Gimignano Rialto '20	▽▽ 3

Caprili

fraz. Tavernelle
loc. Caprili, 268
53024 Montalcino [SI]
☏ +39 0577848566
✉ www.caprili.it

CELLAR SALES
PRE-BOOKED VISITS
ACCOMMODATION
ANNUAL PRODUCTION 75,000 bottles
HECTARES UNDER VINE 21.00
SUSTAINABLE WINERY

The Bartollomei family's large estate spans 60 hectares, with 20 hectares, divided into 6 different plots, dedicated to sangiovese grosso. The vineyards, Ceppo Nero, Vigna Madre, Testucchiaia, Quadrucci, del Pino, and Palazzetto, are meticulously vinified and aged separately in large barrels before being blended. Despite challenges, such as the difficult 2019 vintage, their careful vineyard work consistently reveals the energetic and sunny character of Brunello from the southwest side of Montalcino. The Brunello '19 stands out with its rich and harmonious bouquet of fresh red fruit and deeper, more complex notes of tobacco and licorice. The palate is austere, with a close-knit tannic structure that amplifies the wine's fruit-driven depth and length. The Brunello Riserva '18 Ad Alberto also impresses with its intensity, though it's less complex on the nose, offering aromas of red and black berries. On the palate, it's rich and fleshy, leading to a long, pleasant finish.

★Fattoria Carpineta Fontalpino

fraz. Montaperti
loc. Carpineta
53019 Castelnuovo Berardenga [SI]
☏ +39 0577369219
✉ www.carpinetafontalpino.it

CELLAR SALES
PRE-BOOKED VISITS
ACCOMMODATION
ANNUAL PRODUCTION 100,000 bottles
HECTARES UNDER VINE 23.00
VITICULTURE METHOD Certified Organic

Owned by Gioia and Filippo Cresti, Carpineta Fontalpino was founded in 1994 near Montaperti hill, the site of the famous medieval battle between Siena and Florence. Cultivated in the southern part of the Chianti Classico appellation, in the Castelnuovo Berardenga area, their sangiovese exhibits a straightforward, generous, and sunny character. These well-executed wines are known for their modern style, with a predominant use of small wood barrels for maturation. The Chianti Classico Gran Selezione Vigna Dofana '19 offers generous aromas, with lush fruity tones, spices, toasted hints, and underbrush. In the mouth, the wine is broad and sustained, with a juicy palate that stretches into a long finish. The Chianti Classico '22 is well-crafted, with a continuous, sapid drinkability. The Do Ut Des '19, a blend of cabernet sauvignon, merlot, and petit verdot, along with the Chianti Classico Gran Selezione Vigna Montaperto '19, both opt for a more compact structure.

● Brunello di Montalcino '19	♥♥ 7
● Brunello di Montalcino AdAlberto Ris. '18	♥♥ 8
● Rosso di Montalcino '22	♥♥ 4
● Brunello di Montalcino '13	♀♀♀ 6
● Brunello di Montalcino '10	♀♀♀ 6
● Brunello di Montalcino '06	♀♀♀ 7
● Brunello di Montalcino AdAlberto Ris. '10	♀♀♀ 8
● Brunello di Montalcino Ris. '08	♀♀♀ 7
● Brunello di Montalcino Ris. '06	♀♀♀ 7
● Brunello di Montalcino Ris. '04	♀♀♀ 5
● Brunello di Montalcino '18	♀♀ 7
● Brunello di Montalcino '14	♀♀ 6
● Brunello di Montalcino '12	♀♀ 6
● Rosso di Montalcino '19	♀♀ 4
● Rosso di Montalcino '16	♀♀ 3*

● Chianti Cl. Gran Selezione V. Dofana '19	♥♥ 5
● Chianti Cl. Fontalpino '22	♥♥ 4
● Chianti Classico Gran Selezione V. Montaperto '19	♥♥ 6
● Do Ut Des '19	♥♥ 5
● Chianti Cl. Dofana '16	♀♀♀ 4*
● Chianti Cl. Fontalpino '20	♀♀♀ 4*
● Chianti Cl. Fontalpino '19	♀♀♀ 3*
● Chianti Cl. Fontalpino '17	♀♀♀ 3*
● Chianti Cl. Montaperto '17	♀♀♀ 4*
● Chianti Cl. Montaperto '15	♀♀♀ 4*
● Do ut Des '13	♀♀♀ 5
● Do ut Des '12	♀♀♀ 5
● Do ut Des '11	♀♀♀ 5
● Do ut Des '10	♀♀♀ 5
● Do ut Des '09	♀♀♀ 5
● Dofana '10	♀♀♀ 7
● Dofana '07	♀♀♀ 8

Carpineto

s.da prov.le della Chiana, 62
53042 Montepulciano [SI]
(☎ +39 0558549086
✉ www.carpineto.com

CELLAR SALES
ACCOMMODATION
ANNUAL PRODUCTION 3,500,000 bottles
HECTARES UNDER VINE 221.00
SUSTAINABLE WINERY

Giovanni Sacchet and Antonio Zaccheo were very young when they founded Carpineto in Dudda, near Greve in Chianti. It was 1967 when they started with their first 20 hectares of vineyards. Today, their estate has expanded more than tenfold to 220 hectares, spread across their Chianti headquarters, Gaville in Alta Valdarno, Montepulciano, Gavorrano in Maremma, and Montalcino. Their 50-year history is documented in the Carpineto Enolibreria, an archive of 100,000 bottles available to enthusiasts and collectors, with some wines dating as far back as 1988. The Nobile Riserva '20 offers intense aromas, blending dark fruits with spicy and oaky flashes. On the palate, the wine is fleshy with a balsamic finish. The Chianti Classico Gran Selezione '21 follows a similar stylistic path. The Dogajolo '22, a blend of sangiovese and cabernet sauvignon, reveals fragrant aromas reminiscent of lush fruit. In the mouth, its supple palate makes the wine pleasantly drinkable.

Casa alle Vacche

fraz. Pancole
loc. Lucignano, 73a
53037 San Gimignano [SI]
(☎ +39 0577955103
✉ www.casaallevacche.it

CELLAR SALES
PRE-BOOKED VISITS
ACCOMMODATION AND RESTAURANT SERVICE
ANNUAL PRODUCTION 120,000 bottles
HECTARES UNDER VINE 28.00
SUSTAINABLE WINERY

Casa alle Vacche, the Ciappi family winery, is located in Lucignano, just a stone's throw away from San Gimignano. A crucial breakthrough in winemaking came in the early 1990s, positioning the winery, now run by brothers Fernando and Lorenzo, among the most significant in the appellation. Their portfolio prominently features vernaccia, although there is also a limited range of reds as well. The Vernaccia di San Gimignano Crocus Riserva '21 delivers aromas of basil and grapefruit, with a light spiced note from oak that sculpts a fine and focused nose. The palate is marked by significant acidity, with citrus and brackish notes that linger through the finish. The Vernaccia di San Gimignano I Macchioni '23 is firm and precise, with decisive aromas of white fruit and sweet citrus, convincing in its progression with a full, creamy palate.

● Brunello di Montalcino Ris. '18	♟♟ 8
● Nobile di Montepulciano Ris. '20	♟♟ 5
● Brunello di Montalcino '18	♟♟ 7
● Chianti Cl. Gran Selezione '21	♟♟ 6
● Dogajolo Rosso '22	♟♟ 3
● Rosso di Montalcino '22	♟♟ 5
● Chianti Cl. '22	♟ 4
● Chianti Cl. Ris. '20	♟ 5
● Nobile di Montepulciano Sant'Albino '21	♟ 5
● Brunello di Montalcino '18	♟♟ 8
● Brunello di Montalcino Ris. '17	♟♟ 8
● Chianti Cl. '21	♟♟ 4
● Nobile di Montepulciano Ris. '19	♟♟ 5
● Rosso di Montalcino '21	♟♟ 5

○ Vernaccia di San Gimignano Crocus Ris. '21	♟♟ 4
● Colorino '23	♟♟ 2*
○ Vernaccia di San Gimignano '23	♟♟ 3
○ Vernaccia di San Gimignano I Macchioni '23	♟♟ 3
● Aglieno '20	♟ 2
● Chianti Colli Senesi '22	♟ 2
● Chianti Colli Senesi Cinabro Ris. '20	♟ 3
● Ciliegiolo '23	♟ 3
⊙ Raffy Rosato '23	♟ 3
○ Sangiovese B. '23	♟ 3
● Acantho '18	♟♟ 5
● Chianti Colli Senesi Cinabro Ris. '19	♟♟ 3
● Merlot '18	♟♟ 3
○ Vernaccia di San Gimignano Crocus Ris. '20	♟♟ 4

La Casaccia di Franceschi

loc. Podere la Casaccia
53024 Montalcino [SI]
📞 +39 3247335099
🌐 www.lacasacciadifranceschi.it

ANNUAL PRODUCTION 17,500 bottles
HECTARES UNDER VINE 30.00

La Casaccia, owned by Flavia and Federico Franceschi, represents the sixth generation of family vintners in Montalcino. This dynamic winery operates two different production areas: one south of the appellation, near Sant'Angelo in Colle, and the other in Cinigiano, in the Grosseto area. The Franceschis' philosophy is simple yet ambitious: to produce high-quality wines while respecting the environment. They manage their 30 hectares organically, selecting the best grapes for their elegant, modern range. Due to the challenging 2019 vintage for Brunello, it's the wines from the San Leopoldo estate in the Grosseto area that stood out in our tastings. The San Leopoldo '21, a blend of cabernet and merlot, showcases great clarity on the nose, with dark fruit, floral notes, balsamic essences, and graphite leading to a sensual, velvety palate, taut and with long-lasting persistence. The Merlot San Leopoldo '21 is solid and weighty, pervasive yet fresh on the palate, with broad and multifaceted aromas of red fruits, Mediterranean scrub, and spices.

• San Leopoldo Cabernet Merlot '21	♟♟ 6
• San Leopoldo Cabernet Franc '21	♟♟ 6
• San Leopoldo Merlot '21	♟♟ 6
• Brunello di Montalcino '19	♟ 7
• Brunello di Montalcino Ris. '16	♟♟♟ 6
• Brunello di Montalcino '18	♟♟ 7
• Brunello di Montalcino Ris. '17	♟♟ 8
• Brunello di Montalcino Ris. '15	♟♟ 8
• San Leopoldo '20	♟♟ 6
• San Leopoldo Merlot '20	♟♟ 6

Tenuta Casadei

loc. San Rocco
57028 Suvereto [LI]
📞 +39 05651933605
🌐 www.tenutacasadei.it

CELLAR SALES
PRE-BOOKED VISITS
ANNUAL PRODUCTION 130,000 bottles
HECTARES UNDER VINE 24.00
VITICULTURE METHOD Certified Biodynamic
SUSTAINABLE WINERY

Stefano Casadei, in partnership with the Cline family (already established vintners from Sonoma Valley), is the driving force behind this Suvereto producer. Founded in 1997, Casadei combines organic and biodynamic practices. The vineyards host predominantly international varieties—cabernet franc, petit verdot, grenache, syrah, mourvèdre, cabernet sauvignon, sauvignon, and semillon—along with local ansonica and moscato. In the cellar, maturation takes place in cement, barriques, and buried terracotta. The Sogno Mediterraneo '22, a blend of syrah, grenache, and mourvèdre, proves clearly defined in its profile, flaunting generous spiciness over a fruity base on the nose. In the mouth, the palate is relaxed and rhythmic, with solid, continuous progression. The cabernet franc Filare 18 '22 offers intense balsamic aromatics, while on the palate it's dense, rich, and juicy.

○ Incanto Mediterraneo '23	♟♟ 3*
• Sogno Mediterraneo '22	♟♟ 4
• Filare 18 '22	♟♟ 7
• Filare 41 '22	♟♟ 7
○ Le Anfore di Elena Casadei Ansonaco '22	♟ 5
• Le Anfore di Elena Casadei Syrah '22	♟ 5
• Filare 18 '20	♟♟♟ 6
• Filare 18 '19	♟♟♟ 6
• Filare 18 '21	♟♟ 6
• Filare 18 '16	♟♟ 6
• Filare 18 '14	♟♟ 6
○ Filare 23 '22	♟♟ 6
• Filare 41 '21	♟♟ 7
• Filare 41 '17	♟♟ 6
○ Incanto Mediterraneo '22	♟♟ 3

★★Casanova di Neri

pod. Fiesole
53024 Montalcino [SI]
📞 +39 0577834455
🌐 www.casanovadineri.com

Tenute Casenuove

loc. San Martino a Cecione, 39
50022 Panzano [FI]
📞 +39 055852009
🌐 www.tenuta-casenuove.com

PRE-BOOKED VISITS
ACCOMMODATION
ANNUAL PRODUCTION 225,000 bottles
HECTARES UNDER VINE 63.00

PRE-BOOKED VISITS
ANNUAL PRODUCTION 70,000 bottles
HECTARES UNDER VINE 30.00

Describing Giacomo Neri and his sons Giovanni and Gianlorenzo merely as skilled would be an understatement. Their winery's achievements make them one of Brunello's best interpreters. Few manage to be as successful at getting the best out of their vineyards, a feat made possible thanks to meticulous agronomic work in which only perfectly ripe and healthy grapes are harvested. The skillful use of wood—be it small, large, or new barrels—always enhances, rather than overwhelms, the varietal characteristics of sangiovese grosso. It's rare for Giacomo Neri's wines to fall short, even in hot years like 2019 when caution might suggest holding back rather than taking risks. The Brunello Tenuta Nuova '19, however, earns Tre Bicchieri, balancing ripe fruit on the nose with fresh balsamic herbs, tobacco, candied violets, dark citrus, and spices. The palate is satisfying, propelled by acidity into a long, pervasive spiral of fruit and tannins with exceptional persistence.

In 2015, French entrepreneur Philippe Austruy—already the owner of La Commanderie de Peyrassol, Château Malescasse, and Quinta Da Côrte—arrived in Tuscany, undertaking a complete renovation of Tenuta Casenuove, a Panzano-based estate that had been well-known in the 1970s and 1980s. In 2019, Austruy launched the Tenuta Isola project on Giglio, a small production site with just over a hectare of vineyards located on the island off the Argentario coast. The Chianti Classico '21 offers a beautiful nose of small red fruits and underbrush, with smoky and toasted touches and light spicy nuances. On the palate, it's flavorful, smooth, and nicely orchestrated, with a fragrant and lively finish. The Tenuta Casenuove '20, a blend of merlot and sangiovese, is also impressive—mature, intense, and generous, where the soft Bordeaux grape meets the more rustic character of Tuscany's signature varietal.

● Brunello di Montalcino Tenuta Nuova '19	♈♈♈	8
● Brunello di Montalcino Cerretalto '18	♈♈	8
● Brunello di Montalcino Giovanni Neri '19	♈♈	8
● Brunello di Montalcino '19	♈♈	8
● Pietradonice '21	♈♈	8
● Rosso di Montalcino Giovanni Neri '22	♈♈	8
● Brunello di Montalcino '09	♈♈♈	6
● Brunello di Montalcino Cerretalto '16	♈♈♈	8
● Brunello di Montalcino Cerretalto '15	♈♈♈	8
● Brunello di Montalcino Cerretalto '07	♈♈♈	8
● Brunello di Montalcino Cerretalto '06	♈♈♈	8
● Brunello di Montalcino Giovanni Neri '18	♈♈♈	8
● Brunello di Montalcino Tenuta Nuova '15	♈♈♈	8
● Brunello di Montalcino Tenuta Nuova '13	♈♈♈	8
● Brunello di Montalcino Tenuta Nuova '06	♈♈♈	8
● Brunello di Montalcino Tenuta Nuova '05	♈♈♈	7

● Chianti Cl. '21	♈♈	5
● Tenuta Casenuove '20	♈♈	6
● Chianti Cl. '20	♈♈	5
● Chianti Cl. '18	♈♈	5
● Chianti Cl. Gran Selezione '19	♈♈	5
● Chianti Cl. Ris. '19	♈♈	6
● Chianti Cl. Ris. '17	♈♈	6
● Tenuta Casenuove '17	♈♈	6

TUSCANY

Casisano

loc. Casisano
53024 Montalcino [SI]
📞 +39 0577835540
🌐 www.casisano.it

ANNUAL PRODUCTION 11,000 bottles
HECTARES UNDER VINE 22.00

Casisano is situated in one of the highest parts of Montalcino, on a hill that rises to 480 meters elevation, near the village of Sant'Angelo in Colle. Currently, the vineyard spans 22 hectares, all planted with sangiovese grosso, forming a mosaic of a dozen plots surrounding the winery. This area is ideal for producing elegant and fresh wines, thanks in part to its exposure to northern winds, which ensure excellent temperature fluctuations in summer. Additionally, the rocky schist and clay soils provide good drainage in case of rain. It seems that Tommasi has yet to fully master Montalcino, alternating between standout performances and less impressive results year after year. The wines are always technically well-made and enjoyable, but from such a prestigious producer, we expected a little more in this territory. The Brunello '19 is intense, with an opening of red fruit, cinchona bark, and tobacco. On the palate, it's full-bodied with close-knit, austere tannins, finishing fresh and with good length.

● Brunello di Montalcino '19	♟♟ 8
● Rosso di Montalcino '22	♟♟ 4
● Brunello di Montalcino '15	♟♟♟ 7
● Brunello di Montalcino Colombaiolo Ris. '15	♟♟♟ 8
● Brunello di Montalcino '16	♟♟ 7
● Brunello di Montalcino '01	♟♟ 5
● Brunello di Montalcino Colombaiolo Ris. '17	♟♟ 8
● Brunello di Montalcino Colombaiolo Ris. '16	♟♟ 8
● Brunello di Montalcino Colombaiolo Ris. '13	♟♟ 8
● Brunello di Montalcino Ris. '01	♟♟ 8
● Rosso di Montalcino '18	♟♟ 4
● Rosso di Montalcino '17	♟♟ 4

Castelfalfi

loc. Castelfalfi
50050 Montaione [FI]
📞 +39 0571891014
🌐 www.castelfalfi.com

CELLAR SALES
PRE-BOOKED VISITS
ACCOMMODATION AND RESTAURANT SERVICE
ANNUAL PRODUCTION 80,000 bottles
HECTARES UNDER VINE 25.00
VITICULTURE METHOD Certified Organic
SUSTAINABLE WINERY

Based near Montaione, Tenuta di Castelfalfi has been owned by the Lohia family (leaders of one of the world's largest chemical industry groups) since 2021. Though its core business is luxury hospitality, the estate also includes 25 hectares of vineyards, planted with sangiovese, colorino, merlot, cabernet sauvignon, syrah, alicante, and vermentino. The result is a well-defined range, particularly when it comes to red wines. The Poggio alla Fame '21, a monovarietal sangiovese, offers aromas that shift from fruit to notes of underbrush and spices. In the mouth, the palate is slim yet flavorful, with well-sustained development and a fruit-driven finish. The Cappella del Lupo '21, a blend of cabernet sauvignon and merlot, is also well-crafted, featuring darker aromatic tones and a well-structured palate. The Casiscala '22, a blend of sangiovese and syrah, presents earthy touches and graphite flashes, with lively energy.

● Poggio alla Fame '21	♟♟ 8
● Cappella del Lupo '21	♟♟ 8
● Casiscala '22	♟♟ 6
● Falecine '23	♟ 6
○ Fonterinaldo '23	♟ 8
○ Poggio I Soli '23	♟ 5
○ Castelfalfi Bianco '20	♟♟ 2*
● Castelfalfi Rosso '19	♟♟ 2*
● Chianti Cerchiaia Ris. '19	♟♟ 5
● Chianti Cerchiaia Ris. '17	♟♟ 3
○ Fonterinaldo '22	♟♟ 3
● Poggio alla Fame '19	♟♟ 6
● Poggio alla Fame '16	♟♟ 4
● Poggionero '19	♟♟ 5
● Poggionero '18	♟♟ 4
● San Piero '21	♟♟ 3

Tenuta CastelGiocondo

loc. Castelgiocondo
53024 Montalcino [SI]
+39 057784131
www.frescobaldi.com

CELLAR SALES
PRE-BOOKED VISITS
ANNUAL PRODUCTION 450,000 bottles
HECTARES UNDER VINE 274.00

The Frescobaldi family's Montalcino property boasts one of the largest tracts of land cultivated with sangiovese grosso, exceeding 200 hectares between Brunello and Rosso, all located on the southwest side of the appellation. The charming turreted village of Castelgiocondo, with its castle, was built to defend Montalcino from enemy incursions from the nearby sea. Due to the favorable microclimate, the territory has long been used for agriculture, and like all the surrounding areas, it has gradually pivoted to viticulture over the past two centuries. The Riserva Vigna Ripa al Convento '18 shows promise for the future with its vibrant and multifaceted nose, offering a harmonious blend of red fruit, Mediterranean herbs, licorice, and spices. The palate is fine, rich with fruit pulp and subtle but detectable tannins, finishing long. Simpler but still pleasant, the Brunello '19 stands out for its fruity and floral aromas, tannic structure, spicy notes, and nice persistence on the palate.

• Brunello di Montalcino '19	YY 8
• Brunello di Montalcino Ripe al Convento Ris. '18	YY 8
• Brunello di Montalcino '16	YYY 6
• Brunello di Montalcino '00	YYY 6
• Brunello di Montalcino Ripe al Convento Ris. '14	YYY 8
• Brunello di Montalcino Ris. '90	YYY 7
• Brunello di Montalcino Ris. '88	YYY 7
• Luce '94	YYY 8
• Brunello di Montalcino Ripe al Convento Ris. '17	YY 8
• Brunello di Montalcino Ripe al Convento Ris. '16	YY 8
• Brunello di Montalcino Ripe al Convento Ris. '15	YY 8

Castell'in Villa

loc. Castell'in Villa
53019 Castelnuovo Berardenga [SI]
+39 0577359074
www.castellinvilla.com

CELLAR SALES
PRE-BOOKED VISITS
ANNUAL PRODUCTION 100,000 bottles
HECTARES UNDER VINE 54.00

Castell'in Villa remains true to the great Chianti tradition, avoiding ephemeral trends. For over 50 years, Coralia Pignatelli's wines have consistently been at the pinnacle of Tuscan winemaking, faithfully interpreting the UGA production zone of Castelnuovo Berardenga. Intense yet nuanced, elegant yet robust, these wines continue to define the expressive paths of auteur-style Tuscan wines, naturally showcasing sangiovese's superb potential. After the great success of recent editions, only the Chianti Classico '20 was submitted for tasting this year, likely due to the owner's health issues, which may have slowed the release of new wines. The Chianti Classico '20 impressed with its complex and refined nose dominated by fruit and spice aromas. The palate still shows some effects from the hot year, with a close-knit but somewhat edgy tannic structure.

• Chianti Cl. '20	YY 5
• Chianti Cl. '19	YYY 5
• Chianti Cl. '11	YYY 5
• Chianti Cl. '09	YYY 5
• Chianti Cl. '08	YYY 5
• Chianti Cl. Castell'in Villa 'In Ris. '16	YYY 8
• Chianti Cl. Ris. '15	YYY 6
• Chianti Cl. Ris. '85	YYY 6
• Chianti Cl. '17	YY 5
• Chianti Cl. '14	YY 5
• Chianti Cl. '12	YY 5
• Chianti Cl. Poggio delle Rose Ris. '10	YY 8
• Chianti Cl. Ris. '13	YY 6
• Chianti Cl. Ris. '11	YY 6
• Chianti Cl. Ris. '10	YY 6

Podere Il Castellaccio

loc. Segalari, 102
57022 Castagneto Carducci [LI]
📞 +39 3358210510
🌐 www.podereilcastellaccio.it

PRE-BOOKED VISITS
ANNUAL PRODUCTION 30,000 bottles
HECTARES UNDER VINE 6.50
VITICULTURE METHOD Certified Organic

Agronomist Alessandro Scappini has chosen
to go against the grain, at least compared to
the general setup of Bolgheri winemaking. On
the hill of Castagneto Carducci, where his
vineyards are located, he has focused on
ancient Tuscan varieties—sangiovese, pugnitello,
foglia tonda, and vermentino—while still
cultivating the area's classic varieties: merlot,
syrah, and cabernet franc. This last, less than one
hectare, is grown on bush-trained vines. The
Somatico '21, a monovarietal pugnitello, is a
deep, dark red. The nose alternates between
morello cherry and blackberry jam, while the
palate is dense, rich, and multifaceted. The
Bolgheri Superiore '21 is fuller-bodied, offering
herbaceous aromas and a fine, persistent palate.
The Bolgheri Rosso Orio '22 is more
immediately expressive and fragrant.

★★Castellare di Castellina

loc. Castellare
53011 Castellina in Chianti [SI]
📞 +39 0577742903
🌐 www.castellare.it

CELLAR SALES
PRE-BOOKED VISITS
ACCOMMODATION
ANNUAL PRODUCTION 200,000 bottles
HECTARES UNDER VINE 28.00

The winery's owner is also a shareholder of
Gambero Rosso spa. To avoid any conflict of
interest, Paolo Panerai has subordinated the
possible awarding of Tre Bicchieri—which, in any
case, only occurs through a blind tasting—to the
attainment of the same rating of excellence,
upwards of 90/100, by an independent,
international panel. This was the case here. The
Sodi di San Niccolò '20, a blend of sangiovese
and malvasia nera, features an intense, focused
profile, with a flavorful and dynamic palate as its
strength. The Coniale '20, a monovarietal
cabernet sauvignon, is also well-crafted, with
clean, full aromas and a balanced, refined palate.
The Poggio ai Merli '22, a monovarietal merlot,
follows a similar stylistic path, offering warm,
nuanced aromas and a full, multifaceted palate.

● Somatico '21	♟♟ 5
● Bolgheri Rosso Orio '22	♟♟ 4
● Bolgheri Rosso Sup. '21	♟♟ 8
● Valénte '22	♟♟ 4
● Bolgheri Rosso Orio '21	♟♟ 4
● Bolgheri Rosso Orio '20	♟♟ 4
● Bolgheri Rosso Orio '19	♟♟ 4
● Bolgheri Rosso Sup. '20	♟♟ 8
● Bolgheri Rosso Sup. '19	♟♟ 8
● Dinostro '20	♟♟ 3
● Dinostro '15	♟♟ 4
● Somatico '20	♟♟ 5
● Somatico '19	♟♟ 5
● Somatico '18	♟♟ 5
● Valénte '19	♟♟ 4
● Valénte '18	♟♟ 4
● Valente '15	♟♟ 4

● I Sodi di San Niccolò '20	♟♟♟ 8
● Coniale '20	♟♟ 8
● Poggio ai Merli '22	♟♟ 8
● Chianti Cl. '22	♟ 4
● Chianti Cl. Il Poggiale Ris. '21	♟ 6
● Chianti Cl. Ris. '21	♟ 5
● I Sodi di S. Niccolò '13	♟♟♟ 8
● I Sodi di S. Niccolò '12	♟♟♟ 8
● I Sodi di S. Niccolò '11	♟♟♟ 8
● I Sodi di S. Niccolò '10	♟♟♟ 8
● I Sodi di S. Niccolò '09	♟♟♟ 8
● I Sodi di San Niccolò '19	♟♟♟ 8
● I Sodi di San Niccolò '18	♟♟♟ 8
● I Sodi di San Niccolò '17	♟♟♟ 8
● I Sodi di San Niccolò '16	♟♟♟ 8
● I Sodi di San Niccolò '15	♟♟♟ 8
● I Sodi di San Niccolò '14	♟♟♟ 8

★★Castello del Terriccio

loc. Terriccio
via Bagnoli, 16
56040 Castellina Marittima [PI]
☎ +39 050699709
⊕ www.terriccio.com

CELLAR SALES
PRE-BOOKED VISITS
RESTAURANT SERVICE
ANNUAL PRODUCTION 200,000 bottles
HECTARES UNDER VINE 60.00

Located near Castellina Marittima, il Castello del Terriccio belongs to Vittorio Piozzo di Rosignano Rossi di Madelana, who inherited the estate in 2019 after the passing of its founder, his uncle Gian Annibale. Established in the 1980s, the winery initially focused on international grape varieties such as chardonnay, sauvignon, cabernet franc, cabernet sauvignon, and merlot. In the 1990s, they added syrah and petit verdot to their repertoire. The Lupicaia '19, a blend of cabernet sauvignon and a touch of petit verdot, features aromas of bell pepper, blueberry, ivy, and bark, with balsamic and spicy hints. The palate is decidedly juicy and flavorful, finishing with blackberry tones and flashes of mint. The Tassinaia '20, a blend of merlot and cabernet sauvignon, shines with its pleasantly supple and flavorful palate. As always, Castello del Terriccio '19, a syrah with a touch of petit verdot, proves solid and refined.

Castello del Trebbio

via Santa Brigida, 9
50065 Pontassieve [FI]
☎ +39 0558304900
⊕ www.castellodeltrebbio.eu

CELLAR SALES
PRE-BOOKED VISITS
ACCOMMODATION AND RESTAURANT SERVICE
ANNUAL PRODUCTION 350,000 bottles
HECTARES UNDER VINE 60.00
VITICULTURE METHOD Certified Organic
SUSTAINABLE WINERY

Anna Baj Macario and her husband Stefano Casadei run Castello del Trebbio. They have developed a small wine group, including the Casadei estate in Maremma and a joint venture with the Olianas family in Sardinia. At their Santa Brigida winery, they grow sangiovese, trebbiano, merlot, and syrah, using oak, cement, and terracotta for aging. A "biointegral" method is employed, combining organic and biodynamic techniques. The Terraelectae Vigneto Lastricato '19 is dry and unembellished, standing out for its simple purity. The palate highlights acidity and tannins, as we'd expect of Rufina, with pleasant vegetal notes blending with plum, blood, and geranium leaf. The Chianti Rufina Riserva '19 is decidedly more balsamic, with a firm mid-palate and a nose that reveals a lovely peppery spiciness. It closes with hints of after-dinner mints and coffee.

● Lupicaia '19	♟♟♟ 8
● Castello del Terriccio '19	♟♟ 8
● Tassinaia '20	♟♟ 5
○ Con Vento '23	♟♟ 5
● Castello del Terriccio '18	♟♟♟ 8
● Castello del Terriccio '11	♟♟♟ 8
● Castello del Terriccio '07	♟♟♟ 8
● Castello del Terriccio '04	♟♟♟ 8
● Lupicaia '18	♟♟♟ 8
● Lupicaia '13	♟♟♟ 8
● Lupicaia '11	♟♟♟ 8
● Lupicaia '10	♟♟♟ 8
● Lupicaia '07	♟♟♟ 8
● Lupicaia '06	♟♟♟ 8
● Lupicaia '05	♟♟♟ 8
● Lupicaia '04	♟♟♟ 8

● Chianti Rufina Terraelectae Vign. Lastricato Ris. '19	♟♟ 6
● Chianti Rufina Ris. '19	♟♟ 4
● Chianti Sup. Trebbio '22	♟ 3
● Ciliegiolo Canaiolo '23	♟ 3
● Chianti Rufina Lastricato Ris. '11	♟♟♟ 4*
● Chianti Rufina Ris. '18	♟♟♟ 4*
● Chianti Rufina Lastricato Ris. '17	♟♟ 4
● Chianti Rufina Lastricato Ris. '16	♟♟ 5
● Chianti Rufina Lastricato Ris. '14	♟♟ 5
● Chianti Sup. '15	♟♟ 3*
● Chianti Vign. Trebbio '20	♟♟ 2*
● Ciliegiolo Canaiolo '22	♟♟ 3
● Le Anfore Sangiovese '20	♟♟ 5
● Le Anfore Sangiovese '19	♟♟ 5
○ Le Anfore Trebbiano '21	♟♟ 5
○ Le Anfore Trebbiano '20	♟♟ 5

★Castello di Albola

loc. Pian d'Albola, 31
53017 Radda in Chianti [SI]
☎ +39 0577738019
⊗ www.albola.it

★★Castello di Ama

loc. Ama
53013 Gaiole in Chianti [SI]
☎ +39 0577746031
⊗ www.castellodiama.com

CELLAR SALES
PRE-BOOKED VISITS
ACCOMMODATION AND RESTAURANT SERVICE
ANNUAL PRODUCTION 750,000 bottles
HECTARES UNDER VINE 125.00
VITICULTURE METHOD Certified Organic
SUSTAINABLE WINERY

CELLAR SALES
PRE-BOOKED VISITS
ANNUAL PRODUCTION 300,000 bottles
HECTARES UNDER VINE 90.00

As we have noted in the past, Castello d'Albola is the most important producer in the Zonin 1821 portfolio. Based in the Radda production zone, in Chianti, the winery benefits from exceptional soil and climate conditions, which the staff skillfully interprets. Albola's wines are known for their impeccable technical craftsmanship, character, and personality, ranking among the best in the Chianti Classico appellation. The Chianti Classico Gran Selezione Il Solatio '20 offers up delicate aromas of small red fruits, underbrush, aromatic herbs, and gunflint. On the palate, the wine is juicy with intriguing contrasts, finishing with a broad and persistent finale. The Acciaiolo '20, a blend of cabernet sauvignon and sangiovese, is also well-crafted, unveiling intense aromas of dark fruit and spices, and a rich, multifaceted palate.

In the early 1970s, three friends—GianVittorio Cavanna, Lionello Sebasti, and Pietro Tradico—began their winemaking adventure in Gaiole in Chianti. In 1982, Marco Pallanti, an oenologist from Florence who had just graduated from the University of Bordeaux, joined Ama. Lorenza Sebasti, Lionello's daughter, took over management in 1993 and, together with Pallanti, established Ama as one of Chianti's most important wineries. Today, the producer continues its quality journey with unwavering strength. The Chianti Classico Ama '22 possesses airy and fragrant aromas that range from hints of herbs and underbrush to fruit and floral notes. The palate is lean, juicy, and sapid, with lively acidity that gives it both drive and freshness. The Chianti Classico Montebuoni Riserva '21 is more austere and compact, while the Chianti Classico Gran Selezione San Lorenzo '20 is characterized by more intense tones. Both wines are refined and well-calibrated.

● Chianti Cl. Gran Selezione Il Solatio '20	♟♟ 8
● Acciaiolo '20	♟♟ 8
● Chianti Cl. Gran Selezione Santa Caterina '20	♟ 7
● Chianti Cl. '14	♟♟♟ 3*
● Chianti Cl. Gran Selezione '13	♟♟♟ 5
● Chianti Cl. Gran Selezione Santa Caterina '19	♟♟♟ 7
● Chianti Cl. Il Solatio Gran Selezione '11	♟♟♟ 5
● Chianti Cl. Ris. '20	♟♟♟ 8
● Chianti Cl. Ris. '18	♟♟♟ 6
● Chianti Cl. Ris. '17	♟♟♟ 6
● Chianti Cl. Ris. '16	♟♟♟ 5
● Chianti Cl. Ris. '14	♟♟♟ 4*

● Chianti Cl. Ama '22	♟♟♟ 4*
● Chianti Cl. Gran Selezione San Lorenzo '20	♟♟ 6
● Chianti Cl. Montebuoni Ris. '21	♟♟ 5
● Il Chiuso '21	♟ 5
● Chianti Cl. Ama '18	♟♟♟ 4*
● Chianti Cl. Ama '11	♟♟♟ 4*
● Chianti Cl. Bellavista '01	♟♟♟ 8
● Chianti Cl. Castello di Ama '05	♟♟♟ 5
● Chianti Cl. Castello di Ama '03	♟♟♟ 5
● Chianti Cl. Castello di Ama '01	♟♟♟ 5
● Chianti Cl. Gran Sel. San Lorenzo '13	♟♟♟ 6
● Chianti Cl. La Casuccia '04	♟♟♟ 8
● Chianti Cl. La Casuccia '01	♟♟♟ 8
● Chianti Cl. San Lorenzo '83	♟♟♟ 8
● L'Apparita '01	♟♟♟ 8

★Castello di Bolgheri

loc. Bolgheri
s.da Lauretta, 7
57020 Castagneto Carducci [LI]
📞 +39 0565762110
🌐 www.castellodibolgheri.eu

ANNUAL PRODUCTION 120,000 bottles
HECTARES UNDER VINE 61.00
SUSTAINABLE WINERY

The Zileri dal Verme family are the historical stewards of Castello di Bolgheri, the only winery within the walls of the village that gave its name to the renowned appellation of Alta Maremma. Federico Zileri leads the estate, which entered the Bolgheri wine scene in the late 1990s. He was among the first to experiment with aging cabernet in large oak barrels, an innovative practice for the region. The Bolgheri Superiore Castello di Bolgheri '21 is excellent, a wine of density and finesse, with a decidedly sapid palate that ends on a long finish, offering aromas of Mediterranean scrub and ripe fruit. The Bolgheri Rosso Varvàra '22 is more subtle, with violet and balsamic herb aromas, resulting in a fragrant and smooth palate.

★★★Castello di Fonterutoli

loc. Fonterutoli
via Ottone III di Sassonia, 5
53011 Castellina in Chianti [SI]
📞 +39 057773571
🌐 www.mazzei.it

CELLAR SALES
PRE-BOOKED VISITS
ACCOMMODATION AND RESTAURANT SERVICE
ANNUAL PRODUCTION 800,000 bottles
HECTARES UNDER VINE 110.00
SUSTAINABLE WINERY

Fonterutoli, one of Chianti's historic wineries, owes its success to a complex set of vineyards divided into seven main properties, totaling 114 parcels in all. These plots, each identified and managed separately, are located near the winery in the Castellina in Chianti UGA production zone, with additional vineyards in the UGA of Castelnuovo Berardenga and Radda in Chianti. The Chianti Classico Gran Selezione Castello di Fonterutoli '21 is a refined wine with a vibrant nose full of nuances, leading to a deep progression on the palate. Equally impressive is the Chianti Classico Gran Selezione Vico Regio 36 '21, which unveils aromas of red fruit, flowers, underbrush, and spices, all complementing a smooth but slightly more monotone palate. The Chianti Classico Gran Selezione Badiòla '21 is more assertive in its tannic structure.

• Bolgheri Sup. Castello di Bolgheri '21	▼▼▼ 6
• Bolgheri Varvàra '22	▼▼ 4
• Bolgheri Rosso Sup. '20	♀♀♀ 6
• Bolgheri Rosso Sup. '19	♀♀♀ 6
• Bolgheri Rosso Sup. '16	♀♀♀ 7
• Bolgheri Sup. Castello di Bolgheri '18	♀♀♀ 6
• Bolgheri Sup. Castello di Bolgheri '12	♀♀♀ 6
• Bolgheri Sup. Castello di Bolgheri '10	♀♀♀ 6
• Bolgheri Sup. Castello di Bolgheri '09	♀♀♀ 6
• Bolgheri Sup. Castello di Bolgheri '07	♀♀♀ 6
• Bolgheri Varvàra '18	♀♀♀ 4*
• Bolgheri Rosso Sup. '15	♀♀ 7
• Bolgheri Rosso Sup. '13	♀♀ 7
• Bolgheri Sup. Castello di Bolgheri '17	♀♀ 6
• Bolgheri Varvàra '21	♀♀ 4
• Bolgheri Varvàra '20	♀♀ 4
• Bolgheri Varvàra '19	♀♀ 4

• Chianti Cl. Gran Selezione Castello di Fonterutoli '21	▼▼ 8
• Chianti Cl. Gran Selezione Badiòla '21	▼▼ 8
• Chianti Cl. Gran Selezione Vicoregio 36 '21	▼▼ 8
• Chianti Cl. Ser Lapo Ris. '21	▼▼ 5
• Concerto '21	▼▼ 8
• Philip '21	▼▼ 6
• Siepi '21	▼▼ 8
• Chianti Cl. Fonterutoli '22	▼ 5
• Poggio Badiòla '22	▼ 5
• Mix36 '15	♀♀♀ 8
• Mix36 '11	♀♀♀ 8
• Siepi '20	♀♀♀ 8
• Siepi '19	♀♀♀ 8
• Siepi '15	♀♀♀ 8
• Siepi '13	♀♀♀ 8

Castello di Gabbiano

fraz. Mercatale Val di Pesa
via Gabbiano, 22
50020 San Casciano in Val di Pesa [FI]
☎ +39 055821053
✉ www.castellogabbiano.it

CELLAR SALES
PRE-BOOKED VISITS
ACCOMMODATION AND RESTAURANT SERVICE
ANNUAL PRODUCTION 1,000,000 bottles
HECTARES UNDER VINE 145.00

Based in San Casciano Val di Pesa, Gabbiano is one of Tuscany's oldest and most noble castles. The winery was acquired by Beringer in the early 2000s and is now part of Australia's Treasury Wine Estates, which oversees a number of brands. The technical staff remains Italian, focusing on producing a range that reflects the region's character, where vineyards thrive in clay and limestone-rich soils rich in stones. Sangiovese, the dominant grape, features in three Chianti Classico wines, though other traditional and international varieties are also grown across the estate's 150 hectares. The Bellezza Gran Selezione 2019 is a delicious pour. A full-bodied, close-knit, and pervasive wine, it also retains a certain suppleness. Even more impressive is the Riserva '20, with its vibrant drinkability, bright tones, and textbook depth. The Chianti Classico '21 proves straightforward and pleasant, while the Alleanza, a cabernet-merlot blend, is structured and slightly extracted.

● Chianti Cl. Ris. '20	♟♟ 5
● Alleanza '20	♟♟ 5
● Chianti Cl. Gran Selezione Bellezza '19	♟♟ 6
● Chianti Cl. '21	♟ 3
● Cabernet Franc '18	♙♙ 5
● Chianti Cl. '11	♙♙ 3
● Chianti Cl. Cavaliere d'Oro '18	♙♙ 3
● Chianti Cl. Cavaliere d'Oro Ris. '18	♙♙ 5
● Chianti Cl. Gran Sel. Bellezza '17	♙♙ 5
● Chianti Cl. Gran Sel. Bellezza '13	♙♙ 5
● Chianti Cl. Gran Sel. Bellezza '12	♙♙ 5
● Chianti Cl. Gran Sel. Bellezza '11	♙♙ 5
● Chianti Cl. Ris. '13	♙♙ 5
● Chianti Cl. Ris. '12	♙♙ 5
● Chianti Cl. Ris. '09	♙♙ 5

Castello di Meleto

loc. Meleto
53013 Gaiole in Chianti [SI]
☎ +39 0577749217
✉ www.castellomeleto.it

CELLAR SALES
PRE-BOOKED VISITS
ACCOMMODATION AND RESTAURANT SERVICE
ANNUAL PRODUCTION 700,000 bottles
HECTARES UNDER VINE 144.00
SUSTAINABLE WINERY

Primarily owned by the Swiss Schuler family, Vinicola Toscana manages a diverse operation that includes hospitality, olive oil production, cinta senese pig farming, beekeeping, and winemaking. Recently, Castello di Meleto has shown a deep commitment to quality, particularly with its top-tier wines, which are known for their aromatic depth and fresh flavor, making them some of the best in Gaiole in Chianti. The Chianti Classico Gran Selezione Poggiarso '20 opens with clearly defined aromas: abundant fruit, spices, and woodland and smoky tones. In the mouth, the palate is racy and expansive, with full, flavorful tannins and a finish that builds. The Chianti Classico Gran Selezione Trebbio '20 also delivered, with its subtle aromas and a solid, multifaceted development. The Camboi '20, a monovarietal malvasia nera, offers broad fruit and a juicy palate.

● Chianti Cl. Gran Selezione Poggiarso '20	♟♟♟ 7
● Camboi '20	♟♟ 6
● Chianti Cl. Castello di Meleto '20	♟♟ 5
● Chianti Cl. Gran Selezione Casi '20	♟♟ 6
● Chianti Cl. Gran Selezione Trebbio '20	♟♟ 6
● Chianti Cl. '22	♟ 4
● Chianti Cl. Gran Selezione V. Poggiarso '18	♙♙♙ 7
● Chianti Cl. Ris. '03	♙♙♙ 4
● Chianti Cl. V. Casi Ris. '11	♙♙♙ 5
● Chianti Cl. '18	♙♙ 3*
● Chianti Cl. Gran Selezione '15	♙♙ 6
● Chianti Cl. Gran Selezione Poggiarso '19	♙♙ 7
● Chianti Cl. Gran Selezione V. Casi '18	♙♙ 6
● Chianti Cl. Ris. '18	♙♙ 5

★Castello di Monsanto

via Monsanto, 8
50028 Barberino Tavarnelle [FI]
☎ +39 0558059000
● www.castellodimonsanto.it

CELLAR SALES
PRE-BOOKED VISITS
ANNUAL PRODUCTION 450,000 bottles
HECTARES UNDER VINE 72.00

Owned by the Bianchi family, Castello di Monsanto is one of the most captivating wineries in the Chianti Classico appellation. It embodies tradition and classicism in their most coherent and rigorous forms. Sangiovese dominates the vineyard, producing refined and elegant wines that age exceptionally well, aptly expressing their terroir with a contemporary flair. The Chianti Classico '22 features clearly defined aromas where red fruits and herbs alternate with smoky and flinty hints. In the mouth, perhaps its greatest strength, its progression is flavorful, balanced, and fragrant, condensed into a lively palate. The Chianti Classico Gran Selezione Il Poggio '19 shows impeccable stylistic precision, with its delicate aromas and a subtle, rhythmic development of flavor. The Nemo '19, a monovarietal cabernet sauvignon, proves well-crafted.

● Chianti Cl. '22	♟♟♟ 4*
● Chianti Cl. Gran Selezione Il Poggio '19	♟♟ 7
○ Chardonnay Collezione Fabrizio Bianchi '22	♟♟ 5
● Nemo '19	♟♟ 6
● Chianti Cl. Ris. '21	♟ 5
● Chianti Cl. '15	♟♟♟ 3*
● Chianti Cl. '11	♟♟♟ 3*
● Chianti Cl. Cinquantenario Ris. '08	♟♟♟ 6
● Chianti Cl. Gran Selezione Il Poggio '18	♟♟♟ 7
● Chianti Cl. Gran Selezione Il Poggio '15	♟♟♟ 7
● Chianti Cl. Il Poggio Ris. '13	♟♟♟ 7
● Chianti Cl. Il Poggio Ris. '10	♟♟♟ 8
● Chianti Cl. Il Poggio Ris. '06	♟♟♟ 6
● Chianti Cl. Ris. '11	♟♟♟ 5
● Nemo '01	♟♟♟ 6
● Sangioveto '10	♟♟♟ 7

Castello di Montepò

loc. Montepò
58054 Scansano [GR]
☎ +39 0577848238
● www.castellodimontepo.it

CELLAR SALES
PRE-BOOKED VISITS
ANNUAL PRODUCTION 200,000 bottles
HECTARES UNDER VINE 55.00

Montepò, with its 14th-century castle, lies in the heart of Maremma. Owned by Jacopo Biondi Santi, today assisted by his son Tancredi, the property was purchased in the early 2000s. This project is defined by the cultivation of the exclusive BBS11 sangiovese clone, registered and owned by the Biondi Santi family. It accounts for 70% of the vineyard area, while the remaining 30% is dedicated to cabernet sauvignon and merlot. The Maceone '20, a monovarietal sangiovese, reveals lush fruit with a spicy backbone on the nose. In the mouth, the palate is powerful and multifaceted, with a compact development and a finish that lingers on fruity notes and a pleasant balsamic touch. The Poggio al Ferro '20, also a monovarietal sangiovese, carries Mediterranean aromatic traits and a tightly wound development of flavor, finishing broad and pervasive. The Sassoalloro '22, with its ferrous and spicy aromas, proves well crafted, featuring a juicy, smooth palate.

● Maceone '20	♟♟ 8
● Poggio al Ferro '20	♟♟ 8
● Sassoalloro '22	♟♟ 5
● Sassoalloro Oro '20	♟♟ 5
● Fontecanese '20	♟ 8
○ JeT '23	♟ 5
● Fontecanese '19	♟♟ 8
● Maceone '19	♟♟ 8
● Morellino di Scansano '06	♟♟ 3*
● Poggio al Ferro '19	♟♟ 8
● Sassoalloro '20	♟♟ 5
● Sassoalloro 30° Anniversario '21	♟♟ 5

Castello di Monterinaldi

fraz. Lucarelli
loc. Pesanella, 75
53017 Radda in Chianti [SI]
☏ +39 0577733533
⊜ www.monterinaldi.it

CELLAR SALES
PRE-BOOKED VISITS
RESTAURANT SERVICE
ANNUAL PRODUCTION 100,000 bottles
HECTARES UNDER VINE 50.00
VITICULTURE METHOD Certified Organic
SUSTAINABLE WINERY

Based in the Radda in Chianti UGA production zone, Castello Monterinaldi boasts vineyards in some of the area's most historic locations. Recently, the producer's wines have reflected a confident, skillful level of craftsmanship, brought out through the use of diverse aging methods, including oak, terracotta, stainless steel, and concrete. The estate vineyards are primarily planted with local varieties such as sangiovese, canaiolo, and malvasia, though merlot and cabernet sauvignon are also cultivated. The Chianti Classico '21 displays nice aromatic definition, with hints of red fruit, underbrush, and spices. In the mouth, the palate is pleasing and well-sustained, with a touch of lightness, ending on a crisp finish. Both the approachable Il Gotto di Gottifredo '21, a monovarietal sangiovese with fresh aromas and a smooth palate, and the Purple Turtle '22, a sangiovese-merlot blend with clean aromas and flavor to spare, are delightful.

● Chianti Cl. '21	♟♟ 3
● Il Gotto di Gottifredo '21	♟♟ 2*
● Purple Turtle '22	♟♟ 2*
● Chianti Cl. '20	♟♟ 3
● Chianti Cl. '19	♟♟ 3*
● Chianti Cl. '18	♟♟ 3
● Chianti Cl. Carpe Testudinem '17	♟♟ 4
● Chianti Cl. Ris. '19	♟♟ 5
● Chianti Cl. Ris. '18	♟♟ 4
● Chianti Cl. Ris. '16	♟♟ 4
● Chianti Cl. Vign. Boscone '19	♟♟ 5
○ Gotto di Gottifredo '18	♟♟ 2*
● Purple Turtle '21	♟♟ 5
● Purple Turtle '19	♟♟ 3
● Purple Turtle '18	♟♟ 3

Castello di Querceto

via Alessandro Francois, 2
50022 Greve in Chianti [FI]
☏ +39 05585921
⊜ www.castellodiquerceto.it

CELLAR SALES
PRE-BOOKED VISITS
ACCOMMODATION
ANNUAL PRODUCTION 500,000 bottles
HECTARES UNDER VINE 60.00
SUSTAINABLE WINERY

Marianna Codacci François and Elvira Colombini François were among the 33 producers who founded the "Consortium for the Defense of Traditional Chianti Wine and its Brand of Origin" in 1924, the first consortium in Italian wine history. The François family has owned Castello di Querceto since 1897 and continues to run it, offering wines with a captivating style, particularly in recent years. The Chianti Classico Gran Selezione La Corte '21 emanates airy aromas, with notes of small red fruits, spices, and underbrush, all on a smoky base. In the mouth, the wine is well-balanced, with a juicy, fragrant progression, driven by pointed acidity, playing off a fruity encore. The Chianti Classico Riserva '21 is also well-crafted, with a solid, multifaceted palate. The Chianti Classico '22 proves highly drinkable.

● Chianti Cl. Gran Selezione La Corte '21	♟♟♟ 6
● Chianti Cl. Ris. '21	♟♟ 5
● Chianti Cl. '22	♟♟ 3
● Chianti Cl. Gran Selezione Il Picchio '21	♟ 6
● Cignale '20	♟ 8
● Il Sole di Alessandro '20	♟ 8
● Chianti Cl. Gran Selezione La Corte '20	♟♟♟ 6
● Chianti Cl. Gran Selezione La Corte '19	♟♟♟ 6
● Chianti Cl. '21	♟♟ 3
● Chianti Cl. '18	♟♟ 3
● Chianti Cl. Gran Selezione Il Picchio '20	♟♟ 6
● Chianti Cl. Ris. '20	♟♟ 5
● Chianti Cl. Ris. '18	♟♟ 4
● Chianti Cl. Ris. '17	♟♟ 4
● Chianti Cl. Ris. '16	♟♟ 4
● Cignale '19	♟♟ 8
● Il Querciolaia '19	♟♟ 6

★Castello di Radda

loc. Il Becco, 101a
53017 Radda in Chianti [SI]
☎ +39 0577738992
🌐 www.castellodiradda.it

CELLAR SALES
PRE-BOOKED VISITS
ANNUAL PRODUCTION 150,000 bottles
HECTARES UNDER VINE 40.00
VITICULTURE METHOD Certified Organic
SUSTAINABLE WINERY

Acquired in 2003 by the Agricola Gussalli Beretta group, Castello di Radda produces well-crafted wines with a modern profile, often aged in oak (tonneaux, in particular). Located just below Castello di Volpaia on the hill facing the village of Radda in Chianti, the winery is expanding its presence in Chianti with a nearly completed project in Gaiole in Chianti, including new vineyards and a modern winery. The Chianti Classico Riserva '19 offers a variety of aromas, including underbrush, lightly wilted flowers, freshly cut grass, and smoky tones. In the mouth, the wine is juicy, with a solid, contrasting development, ending with a broad, flavorful finish. The Chianti Classico '22, also well-crafted, goes all in on drinkability. Oak slightly tempers the intense energy of the Chianti Classico Gran Selezione Vigna Il Corno '18.

● Chianti Cl. Ris. '19	♟♟ 6	
● Chianti Cl. '22	♟♟ 4	
● Chianti Cl. Gran Selezione		
V. Il Corno '18	♟♟ 8	
● Chianti Cl. '21	♟♟♟ 4*	
● Chianti Cl. '19	♟♟♟ 3*	
● Chianti Cl. '18	♟♟♟ 3*	
● Chianti Cl. '15	♟♟♟ 3*	
● Chianti Cl. Gran Selezione		
V. Il Corno '15	♟♟♟ 3*	
● Chianti Cl. Gran Selezione		
V. Il Corno '14	♟♟♟ 6	
● Chianti Cl. Ris. '13	♟♟♟ 5	
● Chianti Cl. Ris. '12	♟♟♟ 5	
● Chianti Cl. Ris. '11	♟♟♟ 6	
● Chianti Cl. Ris. '07	♟♟♟ 5	
● Chianti Cl. Ris. '18	♟♟ 6	

★Castello di Volpaia

loc. Volpaia
via Pier Capponi, 2
53017 Radda in Chianti [SI]
☎ +39 0577738066
🌐 www.volpaia.com

CELLAR SALES
PRE-BOOKED VISITS
ACCOMMODATION AND RESTAURANT SERVICE
ANNUAL PRODUCTION 220,000 bottles
HECTARES UNDER VINE 45.00
VITICULTURE METHOD Certified Organic
SUSTAINABLE WINERY

The Mascheroni Stianti family estate expertly combines organic vineyard management with flawless winemaking. The result is an elegant range characterized by a modern stylistic approach. Their wines, aged in both large and small wooden barrels, maintain their personality and character. Castello di Volpaia has solidified its position as a leading brand in the Radda in Chianti UGA production area, consistently delivering high-quality wines. The Chianti Classico '22 boasts a brilliant aromatic profile, with fragrant fruit well-integrated with hints of herbs and smoky notes, leading to a lively, sapid, and well-paced development on the palate. The Chianti Classico Riserva '21 is also excellent, with a strong progression of flavor, revealing a juicy, sapid, and multifaceted palate. The Chianti Classico Gran Selezione Il Puro '20 and Balifico '21, both sangiovese-cabernet sauvignon blends, prove vibrant and and rich.

● Chianti Cl. '22	♟♟♟ 5	
● Chianti Cl. Ris. '21	♟♟ 7	
● Balifico '21	♟♟ 8	
● Chianti Cl. Gran Selezione		
Il Puro '20	♟♟ 8	
● Chianti Cl. Gran Selezione		
Coltassala '21	♟ 8	
● Chianti Cl. '16	♟♟♟ 4*	
● Chianti Cl. '15	♟♟♟ 4*	
● Chianti Cl. '13	♟♟♟ 3*	
● Chianti Cl. Gran Selezione		
Coltassala '20	♟♟♟ 8	
● Chianti Cl. Ris. '19	♟♟♟ 6	
● Chianti Cl. Ris. '18	♟♟♟ 6	
● Chianti Cl. Ris. '17	♟♟♟ 6	
● Chianti Cl. Ris. '16	♟♟♟ 5	
● Chianti Cl. Ris. '13	♟♟♟ 5	
● Chianti Cl. Ris. '10	♟♟♟ 5	

Castello Romitorio

loc. Romitorio, 279
53024 Montalcino [SI]
(+39 0577847212
www.castelloromitorio.com

CELLAR SALES
PRE-BOOKED VISITS
ACCOMMODATION
ANNUAL PRODUCTION 150,000 bottles
HECTARES UNDER VINE 30.00

Founded in the 1980s by renowned Italian artist Sandro Chia, this solid Montalcino estate has grown increasingly impressive under the direction of his son, Filippo. In a few years, Filippo has not only constructed a new, well-equipped winery but also expanded the area under vines. The vineyards are primarily divided between the stunning Poggio di Sopra, overlooking the Abbey of Sant'Antimo, and those around the castle. Additionally, the Chia family owns the Ghiaccio Forte estate in Maremma and a couple of hectares in Chianti. For several years, a common thread has tied together the winery's offerings: refined elegance, without the pursuit of immediate drinkability at all costs. This is evident in the Brunello Filo di Seta '19, a clear, complex, and character-driven wine, with aromas of red berries, violets, tobacco, Mediterranean underbrush, and graphite. The palate is close-knit, with tannins that slowly unfurl, giving fruit a long-lasting persistence. It's still young, but we can wait.

Castello Vicchiomaggio

loc. Le Bolle
via Vicchiomaggio, 4
50022 Greve in Chianti [FI]
(+39 055854079
www.vicchiomaggio.it

CELLAR SALES
PRE-BOOKED VISITS
ACCOMMODATION AND RESTAURANT SERVICE
ANNUAL PRODUCTION 300,000 bottles
HECTARES UNDER VINE 33.00
SUSTAINABLE WINERY

Castello Vicchiomaggio, owned by the Matta family, has carved out a niche among Chianti Classico's wine firmament. Located on the Florentine side of the appellation, in the Greve in Chianti UGA, their vineyards give rise to top-quality grapes. In the cellar, the fruit is handled with care and precision. The result is a comforting consistency in quality, showcased in a range that exhibits character and a modern stylistic profile, without being over the top. The Chianti Classico Gran Selezione Le Bolle '21 features focused and multifaceted aromas, leading to a full, juicy palate with driving freshness and energy. The FSM '20, a monovarietal merlot, is also well-crafted, with an aromatic profile where red fruits meet refreshing herbal notes, all on a spicy background. In the mouth, the palate is supple and smooth, with an airy finish. The Chianti Classico Gran Selezione La Prima '21 proves slightly influenced by the toasted notes of oak.

● Brunello di Montalcino Filo di Seta '19	♥♥ 8
● Brio '22	♥♥ 5
● Brunello di Montalcino '19	♥♥ 8
● Syrah '21	♥♥ 8
● Brunello di Montalcino '10	♥♥♥ 8
● Brunello di Montalcino '05	♥♥♥ 8
● Brunello di Montalcino Ris. '97	♥♥♥ 8
● Brunello di Montalcino '17	♥♥ 8
● Brunello di Montalcino '15	♥♥ 8
● Brunello di Montalcino '11	♥♥ 8
● Brunello di Montalcino '09	♥♥ 8
● Brunello di Montalcino Filo di Seta '17	♥♥ 8
● Brunello di Montalcino Filo di Seta '16	♥♥ 8
● Brunello di Montalcino Filo di Seta '15	♥♥ 8
● Brunello di Montalcino Ris. '13	♥♥ 8
● Rosso di Montalcino '15	♥♥ 5

● Chianti Cl. Gran Selezione Le Bolle '21	♥♥♥ 8
● FSM '20	♥♥ 8
● Chianti Cl. Agostino Petri Ris. '21	♥♥ 5
● Chianti Cl. Gran Selezione La Prima '21	♥♥ 7
● Chianti Cl. Guado Alto '22	♥ 4
● Ripa delle More '21	♥ 6
● Chianti Cl. Gran Selezione Le Bolle '19	♥♥♥ 8
● Chianti Cl. Gran Selezione V. La Prima '10	♥♥♥ 7
● FSM '18	♥♥♥ 8
● FSM '07	♥♥♥ 8
● FSM '04	♥♥♥ 5
● Ripa delle More '97	♥♥♥ 6
● Ripa delle More '94	♥♥♥ 7
● Chianti Cl. Agostino Petri Ris. '20	♥♥ 5
● Chianti Cl. Gran Selezione La Prima '17	♥♥ 7
● Chianti Cl. Gran Selezione Le Bolle '18	♥♥ 8

Castelvecchio

fraz. San Pancrazio
via Certaldese, 30
50026 San Casciano in Val di Pesa [FI]
+39 0558248032
www.castelvecchio.it

CELLAR SALES
PRE-BOOKED VISITS
ACCOMMODATION
ANNUAL PRODUCTION 80,000 bottles
HECTARES UNDER VINE 24.00
VITICULTURE METHOD Certified Organic
SUSTAINABLE WINERY

The Castelvecchio farm, located in the San Pancrazio part of San Casciano Val di Pesa, has been owned by the Rocchi family since 1962. The estate, both vineyards and cellar, underwent major renovations in the mid-1990s and is now managed by siblings Filippo and Stefania. The varieties cultivated include cabernet sauvignon, petit verdot, merlot, and, naturally, sangiovese, canaiolo, trebbiano, and malvasia, with aging carried out in barriques. The Brecciolino '21, a blend of merlot, petit verdot, and sangiovese, is a well-crafted red. Its aromas are reminiscent of ripe black and red cherries, rose, and violet, with hints of spice and smoke. On the palate, it's juicy and vibrant, with mature tannins and a compact finish refreshed by citrus whiffs. The Chianti Santa Caterina '22 proves supple, flavorful, and straightforward, while the Chianti Colli Fiorentini '22, with its balsamic-infused aromas, is smooth and well-sustained.

Il Brecciolino '21	♟♟ 6
Chianti Santa Caterina '22	♟♟ 2*
Chianti Colli Fiorentini Il Castelvecchio '22	♟ 3
Il Brecciolino '15	♟♟♟ 5
Il Brecciolino '11	♟♟♟ 5
Chianti Colli Fiorentini Il Castelvecchio '19	♟♟ 2*
Chianti Colli Fiorentini V. La Quercia '20	♟♟ 4
Colli dell'Etruria Centrale Vin Santo '03	♟♟ 8
Il Brecciolino '20	♟♟ 6
Il Brecciolino '19	♟♟ 5
Il Brecciolino '18	♟♟ 5
Numero Otto '20	♟♟ 5
Numero Otto '19	♟♟ 4
Orme in Rosso '19	♟♟ 4
Solo Uno '19	♟♟ 6
Solo Uno '18	♟♟ 5

Castiglion del Bosco

loc. Castiglion del Bosco
53024 Montalcino [SI]
+39 05771913238
www.castigliondelbosco.com

CELLAR SALES
PRE-BOOKED VISITS
ACCOMMODATION AND RESTAURANT SERVICE
ANNUAL PRODUCTION 250,000 bottles
HECTARES UNDER VINE 62.00
VITICULTURE METHOD Certified Organic

Castiglion del Bosco has a long history, having changed ownership frequently, though without ever losing its viticultural foundations. In 1967, it was among the 25 wineries that founded the Brunello Consortium. Massimo Ferragamo purchased the entire estate in 2003, transforming it into a luxurious resort with a golf course, while also planting new vineyards and building a new winery. In 2023, the entire structure was acquired by an international holding, which renewed collaborations with the existing winery staff, led by winemaker Cecilia Leoneschi. The Brunello Campo del Drago '19 is a wine of rare pleasure, with a vibrant bouquet where dark berries are complemented by tobacco and intriguing notes of red citrus. On the palate, its close-knit and elegant tannic structure matches its richness of fruit, while the finish is fresh and long. The Brunello '19, also well-made, opens with scents of currant, blueberry, medicinal herbs, and iron; its tannins are pleasantly rustic on the palate, with a long, fruity finish.

Brunello di Montalcino Campo del Drago '19	♟♟♟ 8
Brunello di Montalcino '19	♟♟ 8
Brunello di Montalcino '16	♟♟♟ 7
Brunello di Montalcino 1100 Ris. '16	♟♟♟ 6
Brunello di Montalcino Campo del Drago '18	♟♟♟ 8
Brunello di Montalcino Campo del Drago '17	♟♟ 8
Brunello di Montalcino Campo del Drago '16	♟♟ 8
Brunello di Montalcino Campo del Drago '15	♟♟ 8
Rosso di Montalcino Deimassi '20	♟♟ 4

★Famiglia Cecchi

loc. Casina dei Ponti, 56
53011 Castellina in Chianti [SI]
☎ +39 057754311
✉ www.cecchi.net

CELLAR SALES
PRE-BOOKED VISITS
RESTAURANT SERVICE
ANNUAL PRODUCTION 8,500,000 bottles
HECTARES UNDER VINE 331.00
SUSTAINABLE WINERY

The Cecchi brand is a cornerstone in the
Chianti Classico appellation. Based in the
Castellina in Chianti UGA production area, the
estate has achieved a top-quality position
through notable stylistic choices, emphasizing a
singular identity, especially with the wines from
Villa Cerna and Villa Rosa estates. The approach
has also been extended to Maremma, with the
Val delle Rose estate. The Chianti Classico Gran
Selezione Villa Rosa '20 is already highly
enjoyable. Its aromas range from red berry notes
to earthy and floral hints. In the mouth, its
structure is lean and multifaceted, with firm
tannins, vibrant acidity, and a finish marked by
contrast, flavor, and depth. We also appreciated
the Chianti Classico Gran Selezione Valore di
Famiglia '20, with its warm, intense aromas and
juicy, flavorful palate. The Chianti Classico Villa
Rosa Ribaldoni '21 also delivers.

Patrizia Cencioni

pod. Capanna, 102
53024 Montalcino [SI]
☎ +39 0577849426
✉ www.solariacencioni.com

CELLAR SALES
PRE-BOOKED VISITS
ANNUAL PRODUCTION 35,500 bottles
HECTARES UNDER VINE 9.00

Patrizia Cencioni is heir to a legacy of
winemaking. Indeed, from a young age, she
worked with her grandfather Giuseppe, who was
among the 25 pioneers who founded the
Brunello consortium, both in the vineyard and
the winery. Naturally, after this extensive
apprenticeship, she founded her own winery in
1989, at just over 18 years old, on a family farm
on the southeastern slope of Montalcino, near
the town. Now, Patrizia is joined by her
daughters, Arianna and Annalisa, who are
passionate and determined to follow in their
mother's footsteps. Character and substance
define Patrizia's style, which is fully expressed in
the Brunello Ofelio '19. It features close-knit
notes of dark berries and flowers, enriched by
hints of cinchona, ink, and well-integrated, spicy
wood. The palate is dense and vigorous, with
vibrant acidity and a long finish marked by the
youthfulness of its tannins. The Brunello '19 has
a more rustic style, focused on ripe fruit on the
nose, with a structured and juicy palate, framed
by close-knit, polished tannins.

● Chianti Cl. Gran Selezione Villa Rosa '20	♟♟♟ 6
● Chianti Cl. Gran Selezione Valore di Famiglia '20	♟♟ 8
● Chianti Cl. Storia di Famiglia '22	♟♟ 5
● Chianti Cl. Villa Rosa Ribaldoni '21	♟♟ 5
● Chianti Cl. Riserva di Famiglia Ris. '20	♟ 5
● Chianti Cl. Villa Cerna Primo Colle '21	♟ 4
● Chianti Cl. Villa Cerna Ris. '20	♟ 5
● Chianti Cl. Gran Selezione Villa Rosa '19	♟♟♟ 6
● Chianti Cl. Gran Selezione Villa Rosa '18	♟♟♟ 6
● Chianti Cl. Gran Selezione Villa Rosa '17	♟♟♟ 6
● Chianti Cl. Gran Selezione Villa Rosa '16	♟♟♟ 6
● Chianti Cl. Riserva di Famiglia '15	♟♟♟ 5
● Chianti Cl. Storia di Famiglia '19	♟♟♟ 3*
● Chianti Cl. Villa Cerna Ris. '13	♟♟♟ 5
● Chianti Cl. Villa Cerna Ris. '12	♟♟♟ 5
● Coevo '11	♟♟♟ 8

● Brunello di Montalcino '19	♟♟ 6
● Brunello di Montalcino Ofelio '19	♟♟ 8
● Rosso di Montalcino '22	♟♟ 3
● Brunello di Montalcino 123 Ris. '18	♟ 8
● Brunello di Montalcino '97	♟♟♟ 7
● Brunello di Montalcino '17	♟♟ 6
● Brunello di Montalcino '15	♟♟ 6
● Brunello di Montalcino 123 Ris. '17	♟♟ 8
● Brunello di Montalcino 123 Ris. '16	♟♟ 8
● Brunello di Montalcino 123 Ris. '15	♟♟ 8
● Brunello di Montalcino 30 Anni '15	♟♟ 8
● Brunello di Montalcino 31 Anni '16	♟♟ 8
● Brunello di Montalcino Ofelia '18	♟♟ 6
● Rosso di Montalcino '21	♟♟ 3
● Rosso di Montalcino '20	♟♟ 3
● Rosso di Montalcino '17	♟♟ 3

Centolani

loc. Friggiali
s.da Maremmana
53024 Montalcino [SI]
☎ +39 0577849454
✉ www.tenutafriggialiepietranera.it

CELLAR SALES
PRE-BOOKED VISITS
ACCOMMODATION
ANNUAL PRODUCTION 260,000 bottles
HECTARES UNDER VINE 70.00

Founded in 1975 by Neapolitan lawyer Giovanni
Peluso and now managed by his daughter Olga,
Agricola Centolani includes the Friggiali estate
on the western side of Montalcino, Pietranera
on the southern side near Sant'Antimo, and
Donna Olga to the southwest, facing Maremma.
These three estates differ in terms of exposure,
elevation, and soil type, leading to Brunellos that
are vinified and bottled separately, thus
preserving the distinct varietal expressions of
sangiovese from each terroir. The wines from all
three estates maintain a high level of quality. The
Brunello Donna Olga '19, which reached the
finals, shows pronounced aromas of ripe cherry
and underbrush, followed by tobacco and
graphite, sensations that enhance its character
and complexity. Rich and juicy on the palate, it's
supported by well-structured tannins, with a
long finish. The Brunello Pietranera '19 offers an
expansive nose with ripe red fruit meeting wild
herbs, and a delightful hint of licorice. On the
palate, it's a pervasive and persistent drink.

Vincenzo Cesani

loc. Pancole, 82d
53037 San Gimignano [SI]
☎ +39 0577955084
✉ www.cesani.it

CELLAR SALES
PRE-BOOKED VISITS
ACCOMMODATION
ANNUAL PRODUCTION 30,000 bottles
HECTARES UNDER VINE 26.00
VITICULTURE METHOD Certified Organic

Cesani's story began in 1949 when Guido and
Annunziata Cesani moved to San Gimignano
from Le Marche, buying a house and a small plot
of land in Pancole, where they practiced
subsistence farming and raised a few livestock.
Their son, Vincenzo, transformed this small
operation into a winery, bottling the first
Vernaccia in 1980. His daughters, Letizia and
Marialuisa, have been actively involved in the
business for many years. The Vernaccia di San
Gimignano Sanice Ris. '21 proves soft and
creamy, with slightly evolved tones on the nose,
leaning toward almond paste and white
chocolate. The palate shows good structure and
retains a certain finesse in its broad
development, finishing with marked brackish
notes. The Serisé '21, a firm and sapid ciliegiolo,
has fresh, crisp red fruit aromas and a silky,
fruity palate.

TUSCANY

● Brunello di Montalcino Donna Olga Tenute Donna Olga '19	♈♈ 8
● Brunello di Montalcino Pietranera '19	♈♈ 8
● Brunello di Montalcino Pietranera Ris. '18	♈♈ 8
● Brunello di Montalcino Tenuta Friggiali '19	♈♈ 8
● Brunello di Montalcino Tenute Donna Olga '19	♈♈ 7
● Sant'Antimo Tenuta Friggiali '20	♈♈ 4
● Brunello di Montalcino Poggiotondo '19	♈ 8
● Clos degli Omodeo '19	♈ 6
● Rosso di Montalcino Tenuta Friggiali '21	♈ 3
● Brunello di Montalcino Tenuta Friggiali '04	♈♈♈ 5
● Brunello di Montalcino Tenuta Friggiali Ris. '99	♈♈♈ 7

○ Vernaccia di San Gimignano Sanice Ris. '21	♈♈ 4
● Serisé Ciliegiolo '21	♈♈ 4
○ Vernaccia di San Gimignano '23	♈♈ 3
● Luenzo '17	♈ 4
⊙ Rosato '23	♈ 3
○ Vernaccia di San Gimignano Clamys '22	♈ 3
● Luenzo '99	♈♈♈ 4
● Luenzo '97	♈♈♈ 4*
○ Vernaccia di San Gimignano Sanice Ris. '15	♈♈♈ 3*
○ Vernaccia di San Gimignano Sanice Ris. '14	♈♈♈ 3*
○ Vernaccia di San Gimignano Sanice Ris. '20	♈♈ 4

Giovanni Chiappini

loc. Felciaino
via Bolgherese, 189c
57020 Castagneto Carducci [LI]
(☎) +39 0565765201
⊕ www.giovannichiappini.it

CELLAR SALES
PRE-BOOKED VISITS
ANNUAL PRODUCTION 70,000 bottles
HECTARES UNDER VINE 23.00
VITICULTURE METHOD Certified Organic
SUSTAINABLE WINERY

Giovanni Chiappini, the son of farmers from Le
Marche who moved to Bolgheri in the 1950s,
was among the first to recognize the viticultural
potential of the Bolgherese area at a time when
horticulture still prevailed. A knowledgeable
expert on the local soils—the historic vineyards,
including Le Grottine, surround the estate—he
is now joined by his daughters, Martina and Lisa,
who aim to offer a contemporary interpretation
of the estate's wines, focusing more on freshness
than power. The Bolgheri Superiore Guado de'
Gemoli '21 stands out for its character and
energy, especially in its juicy, vibrant, and focused
palate. The nose reveals dark fruit, brightened by
fresh mint. The Bolgheri Felciaino '22 is a
well-made, forthright wine, with earthier aromas
but a lively, flavorful palate. The Bolgheri
Vermentino Le Grottine '23 offers herbs and
white fruit aromas, with an incredibly drinkable
palate.

Le Chiuse

loc. Valdicava
s.da vicinale Sferracavalli
53024 Montalcino [SI]
(☎) +39 055597052
⊕ www.lechiuse.com

CELLAR SALES
PRE-BOOKED VISITS
ACCOMMODATION
ANNUAL PRODUCTION 35,000 bottles
HECTARES UNDER VINE 8.00
VITICULTURE METHOD Certified Organic

Le Chiuse is one of the oldest estates in
Montalcino and has been an integral part of the
Biondi Santi family holdings for centuries. This
single, contiguous tract of sangiovese vineyards
is located on the northern slope of the
appellation, between Montosoli and Canalicchi,
regions long esteemed for producing Brunello.
Now owned by Lorenzo Magnelli, a great-
grandson of Franco Biondi Santi, the winery
continues to produce classic, highly-regarded
wines known for their elegance and sense of
place. The Brunello '19 proves vibrant and
multifaceted on the nose, passing from red fruit
to underbrush, tobacco, cinchona, and a striking
note of red oranges. Muscular yet supple on the
palate, it boasts juicy fruit, maintaining its
balance, finishing long and fragrant. The dynamic
and racy Sangiovese Sferracavalli '22 is all about
immediate pleasure, opening with strawberry
and violet aromas and closing with a fresh,
satisfying finish.

● Bolgheri Rosso Sup. Guado de' Gemoli '21	♟♟♟ 8
● Bolgheri Rosso Felciaino '22	♟♟ 4
○ Bolgheri Vermentino Le Grottine '23	♟♟ 3
● Lienà '21	♟♟ 7
● Bolgheri Rosso Felciaino '21	♟♟ 4
● Bolgheri Rosso Felciaino '17	♟♟ 4
● Bolgheri Rosso Sup. Guado de' Gemoli '20	♟♟ 8
● Bolgheri Rosso Sup. Guado de' Gemoli '19	♟♟ 8
● Bolgheri Sup. Guado de' Gemoli '13	♟♟ 8
● Bolgheri Sup. Guado de' Gemoli '12	♟♟ 8
○ Bolgheri Vermentino Le Grottine '22	♟♟ 3
● Lienà '20	♟♟ 7
● Lienà '19	♟♟ 7
● Lienà Cabernet Franc '17	♟♟ 8
● Lienà Cabernet Franc '16	♟♟ 8
● Lienà Cabernet Franc '15	♟♟ 8
● Lienà Cabernet Sauvignon '11	♟♟ 7

● Brunello di Montalcino '19	♟♟ 8
● Sferracavalli '22	♟♟ 5
● Rosso di Montalcino '22	♟ 5
● Brunello di Montalcino '15	♟♟♟ 7
● Brunello di Montalcino '12	♟♟♟ 7
● Brunello di Montalcino '11	♟♟♟ 7
● Brunello di Montalcino '10	♟♟♟ 7
● Brunello di Montalcino Diecianni Ris. '13	♟♟♟ 8
● Brunello di Montalcino Ris. '07	♟♟♟ 8
● Brunello di Montalcino '17	♟♟ 8
● Brunello di Montalcino '16	♟♟ 8
● Brunello di Montalcino Diecianni Ris. '12	♟♟ 8
● Brunello di Montalcino Ris. '10	♟♟ 8

Tiziano Ciacci
Poggio Nardone

loc. Mocali
53024 Montalcino [SI]
☎ +39 0577849485
azpoggionardone@tiscali.it

CELLAR SALES
PRE-BOOKED VISITS
ANNUAL PRODUCTION 25,000 bottles
HECTARES UNDER VINE 3.00

Poggio Nardone may have ancient roots, but it was only in 1996 that Tiziano and Alessandra Ciacci began producing wine on land inherited from Tiziano's grandfather Dino (one of the founders of the Brunello consortium). The estate is situated on the southwestern slope of Montalcino, in an area with a particularly mild climate and soils rich in galestro and alberese, at an elevation of 350 meters. Since 2001, the Ciacci family has also cultivated a small three-hectare property in Maremma, near Montiano, where a Morellino di Scansano is produced. The Brunello '19 Poggio Nardone is a pleasant pour that plays on notes of cherries, black cherry, wild herbs, licorice, and roasted coffee. The palate is full and flavorful, with good aromatic persistence. The Brunello Mocali '19 shows great promise, with a rich fruit base on the nose leading into a dense, juicy palate— an extremely long and compact drink. The Rosso Poggio Nardone '22 goes down easy, conjuring up red fruit and spice aromas, while the palate is deliciously fresh, balanced by a sapid streak.

Ciacci Piccolomini
D'Aragona

fraz. Castelnuovo dell'Abate
loc. Molinello
53024 Montalcino [SI]
☎ +39 0577835616
✉ www.ciaccipiccolomini.com

CELLAR SALES
PRE-BOOKED VISITS
ACCOMMODATION
ANNUAL PRODUCTION 300,000 bottles
HECTARES UNDER VINE 40.00

The Bianchini family's ties to the territory are so strong that the community of Montalcino named the municipal stadium after Giuseppe Bianchini, the winery's founder and long-time president of the local soccer team. Today run by Giuseppe's children, Paolo and Laura, Ciacci Piccolomini has managed to stay ahead of the curve, consistently delivering wines that stay true to the region and its preferred grape, sangiovese grosso. Among the best Brunellos tasted this year, the Pianrosso '19 proves complex and refined, with gorgeous, warm, expansive notes of red berries, wild herbs, medicinal herbs, and flint. The palate is rich with fruit, surprising for the elegance of its dense but delicate tannic weave; the finish is long and vibrant. The Brunello '19 doesn't disappoint either, with its aromas of plums and Mediterranean herbs, followed by more refined balsamic and spicy notes. The palate is close-knit and juicy, with lively tannins that promise great aging potential.

● Brunello di Montalcino Mocali '19	♀♀ 6
● Brunello di Montalcino Poggio Nardone '19	♀♀ 6
● I Piaggioni Mocali '22	♀♀ 2*
● Rivus Poggio Nardone '22	♀♀ 2*
● Rosso di Montalcino Mocali '22	♀♀ 3
● Rosso di Montalcino Poggio Nardone '22	♀♀ 4
● Brunello di Montalcino V. delle Raunate Mocali '19	♀ 8
● I Fossetti Mocali '22	♀ 2
● Moscadello di Montalcino V.T. Mocali '16	♀ 5
● Brunello di Montalcino Mocali '17	♀♀ 6
● Brunello di Montalcino Mocali Le Raunate '18	♀♀ 8
● Brunello di Montalcino Poggio Nardone Ris. '17	♀♀ 8

● Brunello di Montalcino '19	♀♀ 6
● Brunello di Montalcino Pianrosso '19	♀♀ 8
● Brunello di Montalcino V. di Pianrosso '98	♀♀♀ 6
● Brunello di Montalcino V. di Pianrosso '90	♀♀♀ 8
● Brunello di Montalcino V. di Pianrosso '88	♀♀♀ 8
● Brunello di Montalcino V. di Pianrosso Ris. '99	♀♀♀ 8
● Brunello di Montalcino V. di Pianrosso Ris. '95	♀♀♀ 8
● Brunello di Montalcino '18	♀♀ 5
● Brunello di Montalcino '15	♀♀ 5
● Brunello di Montalcino Pianrosso '18	♀♀ 8

TUSCANY

Cincinelli

p.zza della Vittoria, 11
52010 Capolona [AR]
(☎) +39 3356913678
⊛ www.aziendaagricolacincinellimarco.it

CELLAR SALES
PRE-BOOKED VISITS
ACCOMMODATION
ANNUAL PRODUCTION 10,000 bottles
HECTARES UNDER VINE 42.00
VITICULTURE METHOD Certified Organic
SUSTAINABLE WINERY

Marco Cincinelli's winery, located near Capolona, focuses on the area's ancient grape varieties. Alongside sangiovese, mammolo, canaiolo, and foglia tonda, the estate also cultivates international varieties such as cabernet sauvignon, syrah, and merlot in its organically farmed vineyards. The wines, aged in concrete and oak barrels of various sizes, exhibit a refined style aimed at elegance and drinkability. The Legato '20, a monovarietal mammolo, is a subtle, lively, and flavorful drink, with airy aromas of pomegranate, raspberry, and spices, refined with balsamic hints. The Avanzo '21, a blend of sangiovese and mammolo, offers fragrant and delicately fruity aromas, paired with an easygoing, flavorful, and vibrant palate. The focused Botti Sangiovese '20, a monovarietal sangiovese, features cherry aromas with smoky and spicy whiffs, leading to a multifaceted and deep progression of flavor.

Le Cinciole

via Case Sparse, 83
50020 Panzano [FI]
(☎) +39 055852636
⊛ www.lecinciole.it

CELLAR SALES
PRE-BOOKED VISITS
ANNUAL PRODUCTION 45,000 bottles
HECTARES UNDER VINE 11.00
VITICULTURE METHOD Certified Organic
SUSTAINABLE WINERY

For over 30 years, Luca and Valeria Orsini have been at the helm of this small yet noteworthy winery in the UGA production zone of Panzano in Chianti. Their vineyards, situated at the highest elevations of the area, are organically farmed. The wines are aged in concrete, barriques, and large casks. The winery's style emphasizes freshness, drinkability, and balance, making for an impeccably crafted range that is not only distinctive and full of character but also stands the test of time. The Chianti Classico Gran Selezione Aluigi '20 expresses layered aromas that alternate between small red fruits, spicy hints, freshly cut grass, and underbrush. On the palate, it shows rhythm and complexity, with deep development and a particularly sapid and juicy finish. The Chianti Classico '21 is well-crafted. The Petresco '20, a monovarietal sangiovese, proves vibrant and well-balanced. The Camalaione '19, a blend of cabernet sauvignon, syrah, and merlot, opts for a Mediterranean profile.

● Il Legato '20	♉♉ 5
● Botti Sangiovese '20	♉♉ 5
● L'Avanzo '21	♉♉ 3
● Mandorli '20	♉ 5
● Botti '18	♉♉ 5
● Chianti '18	♉♉ 3
● Mandorli '18	♉♉ 5
● Mandorli '17	♉♉ 5

● Chianti Cl. Gran Selezione Aluigi '20	♉♉ 6
● Camalaione '19	♉♉ 6
● Chianti Cl. '21	♉♉ 5
● Petresco '20	♉♉ 6
● Camalaione '04	♉♉♉ 7
● Chianti Cl. '14	♉♉♉ 3
● Chianti Cl. '12	♉♉♉ 3
● Chianti Cl. Petresco Ris. '01	♉♉♉ 5
● Petresco '12	♉♉♉ 5
● Chianti Cl. '20	♉♉ 5
● Chianti Cl. '19	♉♉ 3
● Chianti Cl. '17	♉♉ 3
● Chianti Cl. Gran Selezione Aluigi '19	♉♉ 6
● Chianti Cl. Gran Selezione Aluigi '18	♉♉ 5
● Petresco '17	♉♉ 5
● Petresco '16	♉♉ 5

Donatella Cinelli Colombini

loc. Casato,17
53024 Montalcino [SI]
(☎ +39 0577662108
✉ www.cinellicolombini.it

CELLAR SALES
PRE-BOOKED VISITS
ACCOMMODATION AND RESTAURANT SERVICE
ANNUAL PRODUCTION 140,000 bottles
HECTARES UNDER VINE 34.00

It might be easier to list what Donatella Cinelli Colombini hasn't done in her life. As the founder and long-time president of the Movimento Turismo del Vino and the association Le Donne del Vino, creator of Cantine Aperte, instigator of the Casato Prime Donne literary prize, university lecturer, and Siena's former tourism commissioner, her passion for viticulture is evident. Together with her daughter Violante, Donatella runs two beautiful, all-female-managed wineries in Montalcino and Trequanda. The Brunello Progetto Prime Donne '19 stands out for its solid yet refined palate, with all the classic descriptors, like red berries, tobacco, and licorice, qualities that make it a wine of great character and personality. The Brunello '19 proves austere on the nose with captivating notes of tanned leather, cinchona, and spices over a fruity backdrop; the palate is long and full of character, though marked by youthful tannic sharpness.

● Brunello di Montalcino Prime Donne '19	♈♈ 7
● Brunello di Montalcino '19	♈♈ 6
● Rosso di Montalcino '22	♈♈ 3
● Brunello di Montalcino Ris. '18	♈ 8
● Brunello di Montalcino '15	♈♈♈ 6
● Brunello di Montalcino Prime Donne '01	♈♈♈ 6
● Brunello di Montalcino '18	♈♈ 6
● Brunello di Montalcino '17	♈♈ 6
● Brunello di Montalcino '05	♈♈ 5
● Brunello di Montalcino Prime Donne '16	♈♈ 8
● Brunello di Montalcino Ris. '13	♈♈ 8
● Brunello di Montalcino Ris. '12	♈♈ 8
● Orcia Rosso Cenerentola '18	♈♈ 5

★Tenuta Col d'Orcia

via Giuncheti
53024 Montalcino [SI]
(☎ +39 0577808091
✉ www.coldorcia.it

CELLAR SALES
PRE-BOOKED VISITS
ANNUAL PRODUCTION 800,000 bottles
HECTARES UNDER VINE 142.00
VITICULTURE METHOD Certified Organic
SUSTAINABLE WINERY

The expansive estate managed by Count Francesco Marone Cinzano and his son Santiago is located on the southern slope of Montalcino at about 450 meters elevation. This area benefits from a unique microclimate, with winters that are never too harsh and summers tempered by breezes from the nearby Tyrrhenian Sea, which increase the day-night temperature swings. The entire 540-hectare estate, including forested areas, is organically farmed. In recent years, they have begun converting the vineyards to biodynamic farming. The Brunello '19 reveals plums and blackberries on the nose, all with great breadth and complexity. Elegant hints of Mediterranean scrub blend with tobacco on a fine backdrop of graphite, opening the way to a palate of volume and density, balanced by firm, close-knit, and well-extracted tannins. The Brunello Vigna Nastagio '19 is reluctant to reveal itself on the nose but opens with fine notes of blackberries, cocoa, and sweet spices. The palate is full and fruity, with dense tannins that are still rough but will soften over time.

● Brunello di Montalcino '19	♈♈ 7
● Brunello di Montalcino V. Nastagio '19	♈♈ 8
● Rosso di Montalcino '22	♈♈ 4
● Spezieri '22	♈♈ 2*
● Brunello di Montalcino Poggio al Vento Ris. '16	♈♈♈ 8
● Brunello di Montalcino Poggio al Vento Ris. '10	♈♈♈ 8
● Brunello di Montalcino Poggio al Vento Ris. '06	♈♈♈ 8
● Brunello di Montalcino Poggio al Vento Ris. '04	♈♈♈ 8
● Brunello di Montalcino Poggio al Vento Ris. '83	♈♈♈ 7
● Olmaia '00	♈♈♈ 7

Col di Bacche

fraz. Montiano
s.da di Cupi, 65a
58051 Magliano in Toscana [GR]
+39 0564589538
www.coldibacche.com

CELLAR SALES
PRE-BOOKED VISITS
ANNUAL PRODUCTION 80,000 bottles
HECTARES UNDER VINE 13.50

The Carnasciali family's Col di Bacche, which first released its wines in 2004, offers an impeccable range characterized by a clearly defined style alongside elements of complexity and character. These solidly conceived wines have gained a reassuring authority, especially as the winery focuses more on sangiovese and the use of large casks, which add freshness and suppleness to their abundant offering, reflecting the terroir of Magliano in Toscana. The Morellino di Scansano Rovente Riserva '21 reveals generous fruit on the nose, with touches of graphite and smoky hints. On the palate, the wine is complex, with a juicy and sapid finish, marked by spicy and fruity echoes. The Vermentino '23 exudes Mediterranean character, with clean aromas and a tasty, vibrant progression of flavor. The Morellino di Scansano '23 is striking on the nose, flavorful and easy-drinking on the palate.

● Morellino di Scansano Rovente Ris. '21	🍷🍷 5
● Morellino di Scansano '23	🍷🍷 4
○ Vermentino '23	🍷🍷 3
● Cupinero '21	🍷 5
● Cupinero '09	YYY 5
● Morellino di Scansano Rovente '05	YYY 4
● Morellino di Scansano Rovente Ris. '15	YYY 5
● Poggio alle Viole '15	YYY 5
● Morellino di Scansano '20	YY 3*
● Morellino di Scansano Rovente Ris. '16	YY 5
● Poggio alle Viole '19	YY 5
● Poggio alle Viole '18	YY 5
● Poggio alle Viole '16	YY 5

Col di Lamo

pod. Grosseto 28
53024 Montalcino [SI]
+39 0577834433
www.coldilamo.me

ANNUAL PRODUCTION 28,000 bottles
HECTARES UNDER VINE 7.50
VITICULTURE METHOD Certified Organic

As often happens in the world of wine, returning to one's roots can be an irresistible pull, even for those who have sought other professional paths. This is the case for Giovanna Neri, the daughter of one of Brunello's founding figures, who left a promising academic career to return to Torrenieri and establish her own winery from scratch. She now runs it with her daughter Diletta, finding fulfillment and happiness in this venture. The wines tasted this year are elegant and lithe. The Brunello '19 shows promise, with aromas of blackberries, laurel, and licorice resting on a light bed of sweet spices, showcasing the skillful use of oak. The palate is deep and energetic, with a lovely balsamic finish. The Rosso di Montalcino '21 is jovial and enticing on the nose, with fresh red fruit, aromatic herbs, and wildflowers. It's a juicy drink, but balanced by acidity on the palate, making for great enjoyment.

● Brunello di Montalcino '19	🍷🍷 7
● Brunello di Montalcino A Diletta '19	🍷🍷 8
● Rosso di Montalcino '21	🍷🍷 4
● Brunello di Montalcino '18	YY 7
● Brunello di Montalcino '17	YY 7
● Brunello di Montalcino '13	YY 7
● Brunello di Montalcino A Diletta '16	YY 7
● Brunello di Montalcino Ris. '16	YY 8
● Brunello di Montalcino Ris. '15	YY 8
● Rosso di Montalcino '20	YY 4
● Rosso di Montalcino '19	YY 4
● Rosso di Montalcino '18	YY 4
● Rosso di Montalcino '16	YY 4

Colle di Bordocheo

loc. Segromigno in Monte
via di Piaggiori Basso, 123
55012 Capannori [LU]
📞 +39 0583929821
🌐 www.colledibordocheo.com

CELLAR SALES
PRE-BOOKED VISITS
ACCOMMODATION
ANNUAL PRODUCTION 30,000 bottles
HECTARES UNDER VINE 20.00

Aldo Chelini's passion for the land, the panoramic hills of Segromigno in Monte, and the cultivation of vines and olive trees led to the founding of this winery in the 1960s. Today, the estate has 20 hectares of vineyards and produces high-quality wines. International varieties thrive alongside local grapes such as sangiovese, trebbiano, canaiolo, and ciliegiolo. Today the estate is managed by Aldo's daughter Barbara and her son Pietro, one of the youngest members of the family. The latter, who grew up surrounded by vineyards and olive groves, is full of passion and professionalism. The Picchio '21 is complex, refined, and elegant, with aromas that mediate the austerity of sangiovese and the opulence of merlot, striking a balance that offers richness and pleasure. Notes of black cherry, raspberry, pomegranate, subtle hints of vanilla, and black pepper grace the nose; the palate is rich, taut, and flavorful. The Syrah Lanario '21 is excellent, with spicy tones of black pepper, cinnamon, and Kentucky tobacco, all complemented by blackberry jam's creaminess and a lovely smoky finish.

● Picchio '21	♟♟ 4
● Bordocheo Rosso '22	♟♟ 3
● Lanario '21	♟♟ 5
○ Bianco dell'Oca '22	♟ 3
○ Bordocheo Vermentino '23	♟ 2
○ Sestilia '23	♟ 3
4	
● Colline Lucchesi Rosso Mille968 '16	♟♟ 5
● Colline Lucchesi Sangiovese Picchio Rosso '16	♟♟ 3*
○ Colline Lucchesi Vermentino '21	♟♟ 2*
○ Colline Lucchesi Vermentino '20	♟♟ 2*
Lanario '19	♟♟ 5
● Lanario '18	♟♟ 5
Sestilia '20	♟♟ 3
Sestilia '19	♟♟ 3

Colle Santa Mustiola

via delle Torri, 86a
53043 Chiusi [SI]
📞 +39 057820525
🌐 www.poggioaichiari.it

CELLAR SALES
PRE-BOOKED VISITS
ANNUAL PRODUCTION 18,000 bottles
HECTARES UNDER VINE 5.00
SUSTAINABLE WINERY

Fabio Cenni's small estate near Chiusi is undoubtedly one of the most prized growing areas for Tuscan sangiovese. Here they produce wines with great personality and an exceptional ability to age, something not commonly found. The 2016 vintage, in particular, stands out, with a pair of sangioveses that evoke a truly captivating energy. The Sangiovese Poggio ai Chiari '16 unveils aromas of herbs, flowers, earth, and graphite. On the palate, it's multifaceted, energetic, sapid, and extremely long. The Vignaflavia '16 is no less impressive, with aromas of small red fruits combining with smoky and spicy whiffs, and a fragrant, luscious progression on the palate. The L'Oreus, debuting as a cuvée of the estate's best sangiovese vintages, is a red with generous and focused aromas, foreshadowing a dense, juicy, and persistent palate.

● Poggio ai Chiari '16	♟♟ 8
● Vignaflavia Sangiovese '16	♟♟ 6
● L'Oreus	♟♟ 8
● Poggio ai Chiari '07	♟♟♟ 6
● Poggio ai Chiari '06	♟♟♟ 6
⊙ Kernos '20	♟♟ 4
⊙ Kernos Rosato '19	♟♟ 4
● Poggio ai Chiari '15	♟♟ 8
● Poggio ai Chiari '14	♟♟ 8
● Poggio ai Chiari '13	♟♟ 8
● Poggio ai Chiari '12	♟♟ 6
● Poggio ai Chiari '11	♟♟ 6
● Vignaflavia Sangiovese '15	♟♟ 6
● Vignaflavia Sangiovese '14	♟♟ 5
● Vignaflavia Sangiovese '13	♟♟ 5

Collelceto - Elia Palazzesi

loc. Camigliano
pod. La Pisana
53024 Montalcino [SI]
(+39 0577816606
⊕ www.eliapalazzesi.it

CELLAR SALES
PRE-BOOKED VISITS
ANNUAL PRODUCTION 22,000 bottles
HECTARES UNDER VINE 7.00

Owned by Elia Palazzesi's family since the 19th century, Collelceto is situated at the southwestern edge of the appellation, at the foot of Montalcino near the Ombrone River. The estate spans over 100 hectares, with vines cultivated alongside grains and olives using organic farming practices. The vineyards, shielded and oxygenated by the surrounding forest, unfold across some 10 hectares at elevations spanning 150-180 meters, on clayey soils rich in gravel and sand. The Rosso '22 landed a place in our finals, standing out for its nice persistence and complexity on the nose, opening on notes of fresh red fruit, pomegranate, wilted rose, and wild shrubs, like oleaster. Sapid and lively, it offers a lovely encore of fruit in the mouth, and a rich, satisfying finish. Blackberries, blueberries, plums, and mulberries stand out on the nose of The Riserva '18, a wine enriched by fine notes of camphor and tobacco. The palate reveals evolving tannins, already well-harmonized with alcohol, fruit, and acidity, though it still needs more time in the bottle.

● Rosso di Montalcino '22	♟♟ 4
● Brunello di Montalcino '19	♟♟ 7
● Brunello di Montalcino Ris. '18	♟♟ 8
● Brunello di Montalcino '10	♟♟♟ 5
● Brunello di Montalcino '06	♟♟♟ 5
● Brunello di Montalcino '17	♟♟ 6
● Brunello di Montalcino '16	♟♟ 6
● Brunello di Montalcino '15	♟♟ 6
● Brunello di Montalcino '14	♟♟ 5
● Brunello di Montalcino '13	♟♟ 5
● Brunello di Montalcino Elia Palazzesi '18	♟♟ 6
● Brunello di Montalcino Ris. '16	♟♟ 6
● Brunello di Montalcino Ris. '15	♟♟ 6
● Brunello di Montalcino Ris. '13	♟♟ 6
● Brunello di Montalcino Ris. '12	♟♟ 6
● Rosso di Montalcino '19	♟♟ 4

★ColleMassari

loc. Poggi del Sasso
58044 Cinigiano [GR]
(+39 0564990496
⊕ www.collemassari.it

CELLAR SALES
PRE-BOOKED VISITS
ACCOMMODATION AND RESTAURANT SERVICE
ANNUAL PRODUCTION 500,000 bottles
HECTARES UNDER VINE 120.00
VITICULTURE METHOD Certified Organic

ColleMassari got started in 1999 in the then-little-known area of Maremma. Today, after 25 years of activity, the winery headquartered in Poggi del Sasso is a leading producer, and not only for Montecucco. Their range is exceptionally well crafted, often exhibiting a pronounced personality, and frequently reaching peaks of excellence. The vineyards are organically farmed, and the wines crafted in a modern style drawing on both small and large wooden barrels for aging. The Montecucco Rosso Riserva '21 opens with a nuanced nose, moving from lush fruit to underbrush and spices, with a distinctive iron note as a finishing touch. On the palate, it's racy and well-sustained in its sapidity. The Montecucco Rosso Rigoleto '22 proves well-crafted, with dark aromatic tones and a pleasantly flavorful palate. The Montecucco Vermentino Irisse '22 offers tropical fruit aromas, the prelude to a juicy, focused palate.

● Montecucco Rosso Ris. '21	♟♟♟ 4
● Montecucco Rosso Rigoleto '22	♟♟ 3
○ Montecucco Vermentino Irisse '22	♟♟ 4
⊙ Montecucco Rosato Grottolo '23	♟ 3
○ Montecucco Vermentino Melacce '23	♟ 3
● Montecucco Rosso Ris. '19	♟♟♟ 4
● Montecucco Rosso Ris. '18	♟♟♟ 4
● Montecucco Rosso Ris. '16	♟♟♟ 4
● Montecucco Sangiovese Poggio Lombrone Ris. '19	♟♟♟ 6
● Montecucco Sangiovese Poggio Lombrone Ris. '16	♟♟♟ 6
● Montecucco Sangiovese Poggio Lombrone Ris. '14	♟♟♟ 6
● Montecucco Sangiovese Poggio Lombrone Ris. '13	♟♟♟ 6

Colognole

loc. Colognole
via del Palagio, 15
50065 Pontassieve [FI]
(+39 0558319870
@ www.colognole.it

CELLAR SALES
PRE-BOOKED VISITS
ACCOMMODATION AND RESTAURANT SERVICE
ANNUAL PRODUCTION 90,000 bottles
HECTARES UNDER VINE 27.00

Located on the hills northeast of Florence, Colognole is one of Rufina's historic wineries, owned by the Count Spalletti Trivelli family for five generations, ever since they acquired the land and buildings in the mid-19th century. Colognole primarily vinifies sangiovese, alongside smaller quantities of colorino, merlot, chardonnay, and syrah, from vineyards climbing the right bank of the Sieve River at elevations spanning 250-520 meters above sea level. The entire range impresses with its high quality, the common denominator being an aromatic profile centered on herbal sensations. In the Terreaelectae, this takes on nuances of rosemary and sage, with cherry and black plum rounding out a refined and expressive bouquet. The palate is tenacious and persistent, with iron-like hints. In the Chianti Rufina Riserva del Don, balsamic notes of sage and mint return, with whiffs of tanned leather, smooth tannins, and a fine structure.

Colombaio di Cencio

loc. Cornia
53013 Gaiole in Chianti [SI]
(+39 0577747178
@ www.colombaiodicencio.com

CELLAR SALES
PRE-BOOKED VISITS
ACCOMMODATION
ANNUAL PRODUCTION 22,000 bottles
HECTARES UNDER VINE 25.00
SUSTAINABLE WINERY

Colombaio di Cencio has been part of the Farinetti family's wine ventures since 2017. The winery's vineyards are spread out across the UGA production area of Gaiole in Chianti, and occupy three main plots: Cornia, where they grow sangiovese, merlot, cabernet sauvignon, malvasia, trebbiano, chardonnay, sauvignon, and pinot bianco; Montelodoli, home to sangiovese, cabernet franc, petit verdot, and merlot; and Vinci, where only sangiovese is cultivated. The wines mature in a mix of small and large wooden barrels. The vivid Classico Gran Selezione Vinci '21 conjures up floral scents, small red berries, earth, and spices, all leading to a juicy and lively palate. The solid Chianti Classico Gran Selezione Lodoli '21 boasts a vibrant and evenly proportioned aromatic profile. The well-crafted Chianti Classico Gran Selezione Cornia '21 showcases more pronounced toasty notes. The Chianti Classico Monticello '22 goes all in on drinkability.

Chianti Rufina Terraelectae Vigna Le Rogaie Ris. '21	♟♟♟ 7
Chianti Rufina '22	♟♟ 3
Chianti Rufina Collezione '21	♟♟ 4
Chianti Rufina Riserva del Don '21	♟♟ 5
Quattro Chiacchiere a Oltrepoggio '22	♟♟ 4
Chianti Rufina '21	♟♟ 3
Chianti Rufina '17	♟♟ 3*
Chianti Rufina Collezione '17	♟♟ 4
Chianti Rufina Riserva del Don '18	♟♟ 5
Chianti Rufina Riserva del Don '17	♟♟ 5
Chianti Rufina Riserva del Don '15	♟♟ 5
Chianti Rufina Riserva del Don '12	♟♟ 5
Chianti Rufina Terraelectae Vign. Le Rogaie Ris. '20	♟♟ 6
Le Lastre '20	♟♟ 4
Saràsyrah '20	♟♟ 4

Chianti Cl. Gran Selezione Lodoli '21	♟♟ 6
Chianti Cl. Gran Selezione Vinci '21	♟♟ 6
Chianti Cl. Gran Selezione Cornia '21	♟ 6
Chianti Cl. Massi del Colombaio Ris. '20	♟ 5
Chianti Cl. Monticello '22	♟ 4
Chianti Cl. I Massi Ris. '03	♟♟ 5
Il Futuro '99	♟♟ 4*
Il Futuro '97	♟♟ 4*
Il Futuro '95	♟♟ 4*
Chianti Cl. Gran Selezione '18	♟♟ 6
Chianti Cl. Gran Selezione Lodoli '20	♟♟ 6
Chianti Cl. Gran Selezione Vinci '20	♟♟ 6
Chianti Cl. Massi del Colombaio Ris. '19	♟♟ 5
Chianti Cl. Massi del Colombaio Ris. '17	♟♟ 5
Chianti Cl. Monticello '20	♟♟ 4
Chianti Cl. Monticello '19	♟♟ 3

★Il Colombaio di Santa Chiara

loc. Racciano
via San Donato, 1
53037 San Gimignano [SI]
📞 +39 0577942004
🌐 www.colombaiosantachiara.it

CELLAR SALES
PRE-BOOKED VISITS
ACCOMMODATION
ANNUAL PRODUCTION 98,000 bottles
HECTARES UNDER VINE 22.00
VITICULTURE METHOD Certified Organic
SUSTAINABLE WINERY

The Logi family has, since 2002, overseen an impressive project that has rapidly brought their wines, especially Vernaccia, to the top of the San Gimignano appellation. Colombaio di Santa Chiara's wines are masterfully crafted, standing out for their clear and distinctive characteristics, resulting in an authentic, delicious, and regionally expressive range. The Vernaccia di San Gimignano L'Albereta Ris. '21 impresses with its great persistence, offering up aromas of flowers, flint, and spices. Its subtle and dynamic palate integrates wood perfectly with sharp acidity, creating a multifaceted and flavorful experience. The Vernaccia di San Gimignano Selvabianca '23 seems to anticipate its name with fresh white fruit aromas, alongside herbal and almost underbrush tones. Crispness and brisk drinkability, as always, define the palate.

Conte Guicciardini Castello di Poppiano

loc. Poppiano
via Fezzana, 45/49
50025 Montespertoli [FI]
📞 +39 05582315
🌐 www.conteguicciardini.it

CELLAR SALES
PRE-BOOKED VISITS
ANNUAL PRODUCTION 270,000 bottles
HECTARES UNDER VINE 140.00
SUSTAINABLE WINERY

The Guicciardini family oversees one of the oldest agricultural and winemaking enterprises in Tuscany, drawing on three main properties: the historic family home at Castello di Poppiano in Montespertoli (within the Chianti Colli Fiorentini appellation); Massi di Mandorlaia in Maremma near Scansano (acquired in 1998); and Belvedere Campóli (acquired in 2016) in the San Casciano Val di Pesa area, within the Chianti Classico appellation. The Syrah '22 offers up aromas of black plum, cherry, violet, and rose, with spicy and toasted undertones. In the mouth, it reveals a solid and flavorful palate, finishing with a balsamic note and a lovely hint of pepper. The Tricorno '21, a blend of sangiovese, cabernet sauvignon, and merlot, features floral scents with light minty and smoky notes. On the palate, it's dense and fleshy. The Chianti Classico Gran Selezione Tabernacolo '20 proves juicy and aromatic. The Morellino di Scansano Carbonile '23 is also enjoyable.

○ Vernaccia di San Gimignano L'Albereta Ris. '21	♟♟♟ 5
● Bacicolo '21	♟♟ 8
○ Vernaccia di San Gimignano Campo della Pieve '22	♟♟ 5
○ Vernaccia di San Gimignano Selvabianca '23	♟♟ 3
● Chianti Colli Senesi Il Priore Ris. '20	♟ 4
● Colombaio Ris. '21	♟ 5
⊙ Cremisi '23	♟ 4
○ Vernaccia di San Gimignano L'Albereta Ris. '20	♟♟♟ 5
○ Vernaccia di San Gimignano L'Albereta Ris. '19	♟♟♟ 5
○ Vernaccia di San Gimignano L'Albereta Ris. '18	♟♟♟ 5

● Syrah '22	♟♟ 4
● Chianti Cl. Gran Selezione Il Tabernacolo Belvedere Campòli '20	♟♟ 6
● Morellino di Scansano Carbonile Massi di Mandorlaia '23	♟♟ 2
● Ottosecoli E'Ssenza '23	♟♟ 3
● Tricorno '21	♟♟ 7
● Chianti Cl. Belvedere Campoli '22	♟ 4
● Chianti Cl. Belvedere Campoli Ris. '21	♟ 5
● Morellino di Scansano I Massi Massi di Mandorlaia '22	♟ 3
● Morellino di Scansano Massi di Mandorlaia Ris. '20	♟ 4
● Canaiolo '21	♟♟ 3
● Chianti Colli Fiorentini Ris. '20	♟♟ 5
● La Historia di Italia '20	♟♟ 6
● Tricorno '20	♟♟ 7

Corte dei Venti

loc. Piancornello, 35
53024 Montalcino [SI]
☎ +39 3473653718
🌐 www.lacortedeiventi.it

CELLAR SALES
PRE-BOOKED VISITS
ANNUAL PRODUCTION 20,000 bottles
HECTARES UNDER VINE 7.00

Clara Monaci, the third generation of winemakers in Montalcino, operates a small winery in Piancornello, in the sun-drenched and windy southern quadrant of the Montalcino hills, facing Maremma. Appropriately named Corte dei Venti, the winery benefits from the cool northern winds and marine breezes from the nearby Tyrrhenian Sea, which help reduce winter humidity and temper the summer heat. These climatic conditions, along with marl soils rich in limestone and iron, give the sangiovese here its minerality and freshness. Despite the hot vintage, the Brunello '19 reveals fine and complex aromas, alternating between cherry, dried dark flowers, and tobacco. On the palate, it's fresh, juicy, and rich in sweet tannins. The Poggio dei Lecci '22 is also pleasant, with dark fruit on the nose, showing good finesse and decent complexity, while the palate aptly balances pulp and tannins.

● Brunello di Montalcino '19	♟♟ 8	
● Sant'Antimo Poggio dei Lecci '22	♟♟ 3	
● Brunello di Montalcino '13	♟♟♟ 8	
● Brunello di Montalcino '12	♟♟♟ 8	
● Brunello di Montalcino '17	♟♟ 8	
Brunello di Montalcino '16	♟♟ 8	
Brunello di Montalcino '14	♟♟ 8	
Brunello di Montalcino Ris. '16	♟♟ 8	
Le Terre Rosse '20	♟♟ 2*	
Rosso di Montalcino '21	♟♟ 5	
Rosso di Montalcino '20	♟♟ 5	
Rosso di Montalcino '18	♟♟ 5	
Sant'Antimo Poggio dei Lecci '17	♟♟ 3	
Sant'Antimo Poggio dei Lecci '16	♟♟ 3*	

Corte Pavone

loc. Corte Pavone
53024 Montalcino [SI]
☎ +39 0577848110
🌐 www.loacker.net

CELLAR SALES
PRE-BOOKED VISITS
ANNUAL PRODUCTION 80,000 bottles
HECTARES UNDER VINE 19.00
VITICULTURE METHOD Certified Organic

The Loacker estate is located on the northwestern slope of Montalcino at an elevation of 450 meters. Their new three-story winery, built using bio-architecture principles, features an impressive underground barrel cellar 20 meters deep. The 20 hectares of sangiovese vines are cultivated biodynamically. After extensive studies on microclimates and soils, Haio Loacker identified seven distinct "dynamic" crus, each vinified and bottled separately. True to the estate's philosophy, Haio managed to bottle almost all the single-vineyard wines, even in a challenging year like 2019, which posed significant difficulties for many Montalcino winemakers. The standout is the Brunello Fiore del Vento '19, an elegant and vibrant wine redolent of blackberries, cinchona, and spices. The palate is juicy, rich in tannins that are still exuberant. Red and black fruit, spices, and tobacco define the elegant Riserva Anemone al Sole '18—it's a powerful drinkn but aptly balances fruit and tannins.

● Brunello di Montalcino Fiore del Vento '19	♟♟ 8	
● Brunello di Montalcino '19	♟♟ 8	
● Brunello di Montalcino Anemone al Sole Ris. '18	♟♟ 8	
● Brunello di Montalcino Campo Marzio '19	♟♟ 8	
● Brunello di montalcino Fior di Meliloto '19	♟♟ 8	
● Rosso di Montalcino '22	♟♟ 5	
● Brunello di Montalcino V. Poggio Molino al Vento Ris. '18	♟ 8	
● Brunello di Montalcino '18	♟♟ 8	
● Brunello di Montalcino Fiore del Vento '18	♟♟ 8	

Cortonesi

loc. La Mannella, 322
53024 Montalcino [SI]
(+39 0577848268
⊕ www.lamannella.it

PRE-BOOKED VISITS
ANNUAL PRODUCTION 35,000 bottles
HECTARES UNDER VINE 8.00

Tommaso Cortonesi hails from a long line of vintners. Founded by Marco, Tommaso's father, Cortonesi operates in two primary areas: the original site at La Mannella, on Montalcino's northern slope near Montosoli, characterized by clay and sandstone soils; and the Poggiarelli area on the southeastern slope, noted for its stony, galestro-rich terrain. An ability to bring together the challenging character of sangiovese with the exuberant identity of the Poggiarelli terroir makes this Brunello '19 a true top-drawer wine. Classic aromas of plum and licorice blend seamlessly with notes of herbs and tobacco. The palate is deep, ample, sapid, and endowed with refined tannins rooted in a juicy core. The finish is incredibly long. The Rosso '22 is also very good: intense fruit on the nose, solid yet fresh and pervasive on the palate.

Fattoria Corzano e Paterno

loc. Corzano
fraz. San Pancrazio
via San Vito di Sopra
50026 San Casciano in Val di Pesa [FI]
(+39 0558248179
⊕ www.corzanoepaterno.com

CELLAR SALES
PRE-BOOKED VISITS
ACCOMMODATION
ANNUAL PRODUCTION 85,000 bottles
HECTARES UNDER VINE 19.00
VITICULTURE METHOD Certified Organic

This family success story began in 1971 when Swiss architect Wendelin Gelpke purchased the Fattoria Corzano from descendants of the Niccolini family, Florentine nobility. The first vines were planted that year, six hectares in prime growing areas around Corzano, at an elevation of 300 meters in a natural amphitheater with south-west exposure and excellent soils. Today, there are 20 hectares of vineyards, and the estate is run by Aljoscha and Arianna, the founder's grandson and daughter, alongside William, Aljoscha's son. The Terre di Corzano '22 surprises with its quality and depth, yielding intense aromas of pomegranate, cherry, potpourri, and dried citrus. The palate is sapid, juicy, and dynamic, with a rich, pervasive finish. The lively Il Corzano '21 plays on notes of violet rose, and cherry, with a supple and flavorful palate. The delicate Corzanello Rosato '23 offers up aromas of rose petals, powder, and wild strawberries. The Corzanello Bianco '23 is thirst quenching and juicy, with refreshing notes of citron peel, lime, and grapefruit.

• Brunello di Montalcino I Poggiarelli '19	♛♛♛ 8
• Rosso di Montalcino '22	♛♛ 4
• Leonus '22	♛♛ 3
• Brunello di Montalcino '19	♛ 6
• Brunello di Montalcino '18	♛♛ 6
• Brunello di Montalcino '17	♛♛ 5
• Brunello di Montalcino Ris. '16	♛♛ 6
• Brunello di Montalcino I Poggiarelli '18	♛♛ 8
• Brunello di Montalcino I Poggiarelli '17	♛♛ 8
• Brunello di Montalcino I Poggiarelli '16	♛♛ 5
• Brunello di Montalcino I Poggiarelli '15	♛♛ 5
• Brunello di Montalcino La Mannella '16	♛♛ 5
• Brunello di Montalcino La Mannella '14	♛♛ 5

• Chianti Terre di Corzano '22	♛♛ 4
• Il Corzano '21	♛♛ 6
○ Il Corzanello Bianco '23	♛ 3
⊙ Il Corzanello Rosato '23	♛ 3
• Il Corzanello Rosso '23	♛ 3
• Chianti I Tre Borri Ris. '07	♛♛♛ 5
• Il Corzano '05	♛♛♛ 5
• Il Corzano '97	♛♛♛
• Chianti Terre di Corzano '21	♛♛
• I Tre Borri '21	♛♛
• I Tre Borri '19	♛♛
• I Tre Borri '18	♛♛
○ Il Corzanello '21	♛♛
• Il Corzano '20	♛♛
• Il Corzano '19	♛♛
• Il Corzano '18	♛♛

De' Ricci

fraz. S.Albino
via Fontecornino, 15
53045 Montepulciano [SI]
(☎) +39 0578798152
✎ www.dericci.it

CELLAR SALES
PRE-BOOKED VISITS
RESTAURANT SERVICE
ANNUAL PRODUCTION 90,000 bottles
HECTARES UNDER VINE 32.00
SUSTAINABLE WINERY

The Trabalzini family's De' Ricci avails itself of a historic cellar in Palazzo Ricci, Montepulciano, a must-visit for tourists and enthusiasts. The vineyards are spread out across three distinct areas: Ascianello, Nottola (Croce), and Fontecornino, which also houses their winemaking facility. Their sangioveses exhibit a modern profile, with sparkling expressiveness and a refined style, representing some of the finest examples of Nobile di Montepulciano's potential. The elegant Nobile SorAldo '20 reveals a complex aromatic weave of floral hints and fruit notes, all enhanced by spicy undertones and flinty tones. The Nobile '20 proves delightful, particularly for its floral and citrus aromas. On the palate, it has freshness and a slim, supple structure that enhances its dynamic drinkability. The firm and focused Nobile Soraldo '19 displays clearly defined aromas of fruit and underbrush.

Maria Caterina Dei

via di Martiena, 35
53045 Montepulciano [SI]
(☎) +39 0578716878
✎ www.cantinedei.it

CELLAR SALES
PRE-BOOKED VISITS
ACCOMMODATION
ANNUAL PRODUCTION 250,000 bottles
HECTARES UNDER VINE 60.00
VITICULTURE METHOD Certified Organic

Since 1991, Maria Caterina Dei has been leading the family winery, which began with the acquisition of the Bossona vineyard in 1964 and the Martiena estate in 1973 (now the central hub of operations). Their first bottles, produced in 1985, marked the start of Dei wines' gradual rise to prominence within the Nobile di Montepulciano appellation. Theirs is a generous yet balanced range capable of aging gracefully. The Nobile '21 features fragrant fruit and sweet tones of cocoa and spices on the nose, while the palate is broad, lively, and easy to drink. Intense, dark and concentrated aromatically, the full-bodied and juicy Nobile Bossona Riserva '19 unfolds with a generous development on the palate—there's just a slight excess of tannins. The powerful Sancta Catharina '18, a blend of sangiovese, cabernet sauvignon, and merlot, is darker, with slightly aged aromas.

TUSCANY

● Nobile di Montepulciano SorAldo '20	♛♛♛ 7
● Nobile di Montepulciano '20	♛♛ 5
● Nobile di Montepulciano SorAldo '19	♛♛ 7
● Rosso di Montepulciano '22	♛♛ 3*
● Nobile di Montepulciano SorAldo '18	♛♛♛ 7
● Il Vignone '17	♛♛ 5
● Nobile di Montepulciano '19	♛♛ 5
● Nobile di Montepulciano '18	♛♛ 5
● Nobile di Montepulciano '17	♛♛ 5
● Nobile di Montepulciano '16	♛♛ 5
● Nobile di Montepulciano '15	♛♛ 5
● Nobile di Montepulciano SorAldo '16	♛♛ 6
● Nobile di Montepulciano SorAldo '15	♛♛ 6
● Rosso di Montepulciano '21	♛♛ 3
● Rosso di Montepulciano '18	♛♛ 3
● Rosso di Montepulciano '17	♛♛ 3

● Nobile di Montepulciano '21	♛♛ 5
● Nobile di Montepulciano Bossona Ris. '19	♛♛ 8
● Sancta Catharina '18	♛ 8
● Nobile di Montepulciano '19	♛♛♛ 5
● Nobile di Montepulciano '14	♛♛♛ 4*
● Nobile di Montepulciano '13	♛♛♛ 4*
● Nobile di Montepulciano Bossona Ris. '13	♛♛♛ 6
● Nobile di Montepulciano Bossona Ris. '04	♛♛♛ 5
● Nobile di Montepulciano Madonna della Querce '18	♛♛♛ 8
● Nobile di Montepulciano Madonna della Querce '15	♛♛♛ 8
● Nobile di Montepulciano '20	♛♛ 5
● Nobile di Montepulciano Bossona Ris. '17	♛♛ 7

Dario Di Vaira

fraz. Bolgheri
via Bolgherese, 275a
57022 Castagneto Carducci [LI]
(+39 0565763511
www.dariodivairavini.it

CELLAR SALES
PRE-BOOKED VISITS
ACCOMMODATION
ANNUAL PRODUCTION 45,000 bottles
HECTARES UNDER VINE 10.00
SUSTAINABLE WINERY

In 2008, fresh out of oenology school, Dario Di Vaira decided to convert his family's mixed-use farm into a wine estate. After a necessary period of making adjustments so as to align with the quality standards of the Bolgheri appellation, today he stands as a major representative of Bolgheri's "nouvelle vague" movement. His wines are notable for their authority, personality, and commendable precision. Dario Di Vaira continues to produce increasingly authoritative wines, and by now his growth as a winemaker is evident. A highly precise version of his Bolgheri Superiore '21 is one example. Deep on the nose, with tones of ink and medicinal herbs, it offers vibrant sapidity on the palate with smooth tannins, finishing with a delicate persistence. The Bolgheri Superiore C.F.11 '21 is also a success, revealing herbal and spicy aromas with a fresh, bold flavor.

Dianella

via Dianella, 48
50059 Vinci [FI]
(+39 0571508166
www.villadianella.it

CELLAR SALES
PRE-BOOKED VISITS
ACCOMMODATION
ANNUAL PRODUCTION 130,000 bottles
HECTARES UNDER VINE 25.00
VITICULTURE METHOD Certified Organic
SUSTAINABLE WINERY

Borgo di Dianella consists of the oratory of S. Michaelis de Aliana (built in the 1200s), several houses, and a Medici villa from the late 16th century. The poet Renato Fucini wrote many of his works here, dedicating a short story to Dianella. Since the early 18th century, the property and the surrounding estate, which spans 90 hectares (25 of which are vineyards), have been owned by the Count Passerin d'Entrèves family. Current restoration of the property was made possible thanks to Francesco and Veronica Passerin d'Entrèves, who produce a range that expresses the local terroir with great care and respect for tradition. Made from the ancient trebbiano clone, the vitality of the Orpicchio '21 stands out. Its nose displays floral fragrances of mimosa, broom, grapefruit juice, and citron. The palate is slender, elegant, and delicate, with a pervasive, soft, and notably long finish. The Cabernet Franc '21 impresses with its notes of black plum, cherry, quinine, and black pepper. In the mouth, it's taut and austere, finishing on a spicy note.

● Bolgheri Superiore '21	♀♀ 7
● Bolgheri Superiore C.F.11 '21	♀♀ 8
● Bolgheri Rosso Clarice '22	♀ 4
○ Bolgheri Bianco Rapè '19	♀♀ 3
● Bolgheri Rosso Clarice '20	♀♀ 4
● Bolgheri Rosso Clarice '18	♀♀ 3
● Bolgheri Rosso Clarice '17	♀♀ 3*
● Bolgheri Rosso Clarice '16	♀♀ 3
● Bolgheri Rosso Sup. '20	♀♀ 7
● Bolgheri Rosso Sup. '19	♀♀ 7
● Bolgheri Rosso Sup. '18	♀♀ 6
● Bolgheri Rosso Sup. Ville Rustiche '16	♀♀ 5
● Bolgheri Rosso Sup. Ville Rustiche '15	♀♀ 5
● Bolgheri Sup. Ville Rustiche '10	♀♀ 5
○ Bolgheri Vermentino Le Pinete '18	♀♀ 3

○ Orpicchio '21	♀♀♀ 7
● Cabernet Franc '21	♀♀ 8
○ Sereno e Nuvole '23	♀♀ 3
⊙ All'Aria Aperta '23	♀ 3
● Chianti Ris. '21	♀ 4
● Il Matto delle Giuncaie '21	♀ 5
● Le Veglie di Neri '22	♀ 3
○ Orpicchio '20	♀♀♀ 7
● Chianti '22	♀♀ 2
● Chianti '21	♀♀ 2
● Il Matto delle Giuncaie '20	♀♀ 5
● Le Veglie di Neri '19	♀♀ 3
⊙ Maria Vittoria and Ottavia Brut '22	♀♀ 3
○ Orpicchio '19	♀♀ 6
○ Sereno e Nuvole '22	♀♀ 3
○ Sereno e Nuvole '21	♀♀ 3

TUSCANY

Dievole

fraz. Vagliagli
loc. Dievole, 6
53019 Castelnuovo Berardenga [SI]
☎ +39 0577322613
● www.dievole.it

CELLAR SALES
PRE-BOOKED VISITS
ACCOMMODATION AND RESTAURANT SERVICE
ANNUAL PRODUCTION 350,000 bottles
HECTARES UNDER VINE 153.00
VITICULTURE METHOD Certified Organic
SUSTAINABLE WINERY

Since 2012, Dievole has been part of the Alejandro Bulgheroni Family Vineyards group, restoring the Vagliagli winery to its former glory. The vineyards are managed organically, with optimized zoning, while the cellar predominantly uses concrete and large wooden casks for maturation. The result is a range of well-executed wines that reflect a strong connection to their territory, aligning with the finest expressions of Chianti winemaking. The Chianti Classico Casanova '21 opens with a fragrant and vibrant aromatic profile, with lush, sustained fruit preceding a juicy, well-calibrated palate, and an energetic, slightly spicy finish. The Chianti Classico Gran Selezione Vigna Sessina '20 is equally commendable, more multifaceted and complex, yet also flavorful and appealing on the palate. The Chianti Classico '22 is an easy-going, relaxed drink.

Fabrizio Dionisio

loc. Il Castagno C. S. Ossaia, 64
52040 Cortona [AR]
☎ +39 063223391
● www.fabriziodionisio.it

TUSCANY

CELLAR SALES
PRE-BOOKED VISITS
ANNUAL PRODUCTION 50,000 bottles
HECTARES UNDER VINE 15.00
VITICULTURE METHOD Certified Organic
SUSTAINABLE WINERY

Roman lawyer Fabrizio Dionisio carried forward and nurtured his father's passion for the Tuscan countryside by transforming the family farmhouse into a thriving wine estate. Together with his wife, Alessandra, and their children Isotta, Lavinia, and Niccolò, he runs a winery that has made a mark in the appellation with innovative and contemporary interpretations of syrah, such as the Linfa, vinified in amphora. The aromatic brilliance of the Cortona Syrah Castagnino '23, matured in concrete, is particularly striking, offering a juicy and fresh progression of flavor, with crisp, clear fruit that enhances its vibrant drinkability. The Cortona Syrah Linfa '22 is darker, with autumnal underbrush aromas and a dynamic, flavorful palate. The Cortona Syrah Il Castagno '21, with its complex aromas and solid structure, is a fleshy and flavorful red. Worth waiting for.

● Chianti Cl. Casanova '21	♀♀ 5
● Chianti Cl. Gran Selezione V. Sessina '20	♀♀ 7
○ Campinovi '22	♀♀ 4
● Chianti Cl. '22	♀♀ 4
● Chianti Cl. Catignano '21	♀♀ 5
● Chianti Cl. Petrignano '21	♀♀ 5
● Chianti Cl. Ris. Novecento '21	♀♀ 6
● Chianti Cl. Novecento Ris. Dievole '14	♀♀♀ 5
● Chianti Cl. Petrignano '20	♀♀♀ 5
● Chianti Cl. Petrignano '19	♀♀♀ 4*
○ Campinovi '21	♀♀ 4
● Chianti Cl. '19	♀♀ 4
● Chianti Cl. Catignano '20	♀♀ 5
● Chianti Cl. Gran Selezione V. Sessina '19	♀♀ 7
● Chianti Cl. Novecento Ris. '20	♀♀ 5

● Cortona Syrah Castagnino '23	♀♀♀ 4*
● Cortona Syrah Il Castagno '21	♀♀ 5
● Cortona Syrah Linfa '22	♀♀ 6
⊙ Rosa del Castagno '23	♀♀ 4
○ Linfa Viognier '22	♀ 4
● Cortona Syrah Cuculaia '18	♀♀♀ 8
● Cortona Syrah Il Castagno '20	♀♀♀ 5
● Cortona Syrah Il Castagno '12	♀♀♀ 5
● Cortona Syrah Il Castagno '11	♀♀♀ 5
● Cortona Syrah Il Castagno '10	♀♀♀ 5
● Cortona Syrah Castagnino '15	♀♀ 3*
● Cortona Syrah Il Castagno '18	♀♀ 5
● Cortona Syrah Il Castagno '17	♀♀ 5
● Cortona Syrah Il Castagno '16	♀♀ 5
● Cortona Syrah Il Castagno '15	♀♀ 5

Donna Olimpia 1898

fraz. Bolgheri
loc. Migliarini, 142
57020 Castagneto Carducci [LI]
📞 +39 0302279601
🌐 www.donnaolimpia1898.it

★Duemani

loc. Ortacavoli
56046 Riparbella [PI]
📞 +39 3388203886
🌐 www.duemani.eu

CELLAR SALES
ACCOMMODATION AND RESTAURANT SERVICE
ANNUAL PRODUCTION 250,000 bottles
HECTARES UNDER VINE 45.00
SUSTAINABLE WINERY

CELLAR SALES
PRE-BOOKED VISITS
ANNUAL PRODUCTION 50,000 bottles
HECTARES UNDER VINE 12.00
VITICULTURE METHOD Certified Biodynamic
SUSTAINABLE WINERY

In 2002, Guido Folonari purchased this winery from the Count Gherardesca family, who had owned the land for centuries. Today, Donna Olimpia comprises an impressive 45 hectares of vineyards, meticulously managed, and focused on international varieties, from cabernet sauvignon and franc to merlot, syrah, petit verdot, and whites such as vermentino, viognier, and petit manseng. The winery also boasts a state-of-the-art cellar designed with sustainability in mind. The result is a range of wines that stands out for its exceptional quality, even in a playing field as crowded as Bolgheri. The Bolgheri Superiore Millepassi '21 delivers a graceful aromatic profile, offering understated elegance and classic intensity. On the palate, it opens broad and fresh, with commendably managed tannins. A long, fleshy, and vibrantly dynamic drink. The Petit Verdot Orizzonte '19 is also characterful, featuring intense, ripe red fruit followed by juicier, vibrant notes of currant and blackberry. Its tannins are sweet, the palate soft.

Roman lawyer Fabrizio Dionisio has maintained and cultivated his father's passion for the Tuscan countryside, enriching it with a productive touch by transforming the family farmhouse into the headquarters of his winery. Together with his wife Alessandra and their children Isotta, Lavinia, and Niccolò, he now runs a winery that has distinguished itself in the appellation, particularly with contemporary and unique interpretations of syrah, such as the Linfa, vinified in amphora. The SuiSassi '21, a monovarietal syrah, offers up aromas of ripe red fruit refreshed by dazzling spicy tones. The palate is juicy, finishing with a lovely peppery note. The Duemani '21, a monovarietal cabernet franc, has dark aromatic traits with touches of Mediterranean scrub, leading into a tightly structured and multifaceted palate. The G. Punto '22, a monovarietal grenache, displays airy fruity aromas and a lively, smooth, flavorful palate. The Si '32, a rosé from syrah, stands out for its pomegranate aromas and a supple, immediately pleasing palate.

● Bolgheri Rosso Sup. Millepassi '21	♟♟ 7
● Bolgheri Rosso '22	♟♟ 5
● Orizzonte '19	♟♟ 7
● Tageto '22	♟♟ 2*
○ Bolgheri Bianco '22	♟ 4
⊙ Bolgheri Rosato '23	♟ 4
● Bolgheri Rosso Sup. Millepassi '15	♟♟♟ 7
● Bolgheri Rosso Sup. Millepassi '13	♟♟♟ 6
● Bolgheri Rosso Sup. Millepassi '11	♟♟♟ 8
○ Bolgheri Bianco '20	♟♟ 4
● Bolgheri Rosso '21	♟♟ 5
● Bolgheri Rosso '20	♟♟ 5
● Bolgheri Rosso Campo alla Giostra '20	♟♟ 5
● Bolgheri Rosso Sup. Millepassi '20	♟♟ 7
○ Obizzo '22	♟♟ 2*
○ Obizzo '21	♟♟ 2*

● Duemani '21	♟♟ 8
● Suisassi '21	♟♟ 8
● G. Punto '22	♟♟ 8
⊙ Si '23	♟ 6
● Altrovino '15	♟♟♟ 6
● Duemani '20	♟♟♟ 8
● Duemani '19	♟♟♟ 8
● Duemani '18	♟♟♟ 8
● Duemani '17	♟♟♟ 8
● Duemani '15	♟♟♟ 8
● Duemani '13	♟♟♟ 8
● Duemani '12	♟♟♟ 8
● Duemani '09	♟♟♟ 8
● Suisassi '16	♟♟♟ 8
● Suisassi '10	♟♟♟ 8
● G. Punto '21	♟♟ 8

L'Erta di Radda

Case Sparse Il Corno, 25
53017 Radda in Chianti [SI]
📞 +39 3284040500
🌐 www.ertadiradda.it

ANNUAL PRODUCTION 22,000 bottles
HECTARES UNDER VINE 5.00
VITICULTURE METHOD Certified Organic

In 2006, Diego Finocchi purchased some old vineyards in Radda in Chianti, beginning to develop his oenological project with his partner Elisa Arretini, who is also a winemaker. Chianti's main grape varieties, sangiovese and canaiolo, take center stage, but there's also trebbiano and malvasia, making for a charming range that exhibits clear territorial consistency, marked by pronounced aromatic fragrance and a savory, delectable progression of flavor. The Chianti Classico Riserva '21 exhibits a refined aromatic weave, evoking pomegranate and blackberry, with earthy whiffs and light spice for contrast. On the palate, it's dynamic and sapid, with a lively finish. The Chianti Classico '22, with its aromas of ripe, small red fruits, has a palate that leans slightly sweet. The Bianco '23, a blend of trebbiano and malvasia, is direct and decisive on the nose, with sapid and delicious flavor to follow. The Due & Due '22, a sangiovese and canaiolo blend, proves pleasantly fragrant and smooth.

● Chianti Cl. Ris. '21	🍷🍷🍷 5
○ Bianco '23	🍷🍷 3
● Chianti Cl. '22	🍷🍷 4
● Due & Due '22	🍷🍷 4
● Chianti Cl. '21	🍷🍷🍷 4*
● Chianti Cl. '19	🍷🍷🍷 3*
● Chianti Cl. '20	🍷🍷 3*
● Chianti Cl. Ris. '20	🍷🍷 5
● Chianti Cl. Ris. '19	🍷🍷 5
● Chianti Cl. Ris. '18	🍷🍷 5
● Chianti Cl. Ris. '16	🍷🍷 5

I Fabbri - Susanna Grassi

loc. Lamole
via Lamole, 80
50022 Greve in Chianti [FI]
📞 +39 3394122622
🌐 www.ifabbrichianticlassico.it

CELLAR SALES
PRE-BOOKED VISITS
RESTAURANT SERVICE
ANNUAL PRODUCTION 35,000 bottles
HECTARES UNDER VINE 6.50
VITICULTURE METHOD Certified Organic
SUSTAINABLE WINERY

The UGA production area of Lamole is one of the most captivating subzones in the whole of Chianti Classico, truly a world of its own. And Susanna Grassi is probably the purest interpreter of this unique terroir, with her wines representing some of the highest points in the whole Chianti appellation. Her wines exhibit a sparkling, elegant style, characterized by fragrant and well-defined aromas, and a compelling dynamism of flavor that drives a slender yet deep gustatory structure. The Chianti Classico Lamole '22 reveals a refined aromatic mix of flowers, earth, spices, and iron notes. The palate is delicious, never losing its vibrancy, thanks to flavorful tannic expression and precise acidity, concluding on bright fruit notes. The Chianti Classico Riserva '20 is equally well-crafted, with red fruit and underbrush aromas preceding a supple, juicy palate.

● Chianti Cl. Lamole '22	🍷🍷🍷 5
● Chianti Cl. Ris. '20	🍷🍷 5
○ Casole Bianco '23	🍷🍷 4
● Chianti Cl. Terra di Lamole '21	🍷🍷 5
● Chianti Cl. Gran Selezione '18	🍷🍷🍷 6
● Chianti Cl. Lamole '21	🍷🍷🍷 5
● Chianti Cl. Lamole '19	🍷🍷🍷 4*
● Chianti Cl. Lamole '18	🍷🍷🍷 4*
● Chianti Cl. Lamole '17	🍷🍷🍷 4*
● Chianti Cl. Gran Selezione '19	🍷🍷 6
● Chianti Cl. Lamole '20	🍷🍷 4
● Chianti Cl. Olinto '18	🍷🍷 4
● Chianti Cl. Ris. '16	🍷🍷 4
● Chianti Cl. Terra di Lamole '18	🍷🍷 3*

Fabbrica Pienza

loc. Borghetto
53026 Pienza [SI]
☎ +39 0578810030
🌐 www.fabbricapienza.com

CELLAR SALES
PRE-BOOKED VISITS
ANNUAL PRODUCTION 50,000 bottles
HECTARES UNDER VINE 35.00
VITICULTURE METHOD Certified Organic
SUSTAINABLE WINERY

Swiss couple Tonie and Philippe Bertherat
founded their winery in 2013 near Pienza.
Fabbrica Pienza produces contemporary wines
inspired by the Burgundian Méthode Dujac. It's
an approach that features whole-cluster
fermentation and robust pre-oxidation,
complemented by spontaneous fermentation.
Maceration begins in the baskets used to collect
the freshly harvested grapes, which facilitates
grape crushing, sometimes even by foot. The
result is a range that certainly makes an
impression. The Orcia Sangiovese Tinia Riserva
'20 offers pomegranate and fresh plum aromas,
with lightly earthy notes on the side. The palate
is slender and supple, with well-structured
tannins and a rising finish. The Prototipo Viognier
'20 is also noteworthy, with its citrus aromas and
hints of flint, followed by a sapid, sustained
palate. The sparkling Popnat '23, made from
sangiovese grapes, is inspired by Pét-Nat styles
and very enjoyable. The Newton Rosso '21, a
sangiovese, is also well-made.

● Orcia Sangiovese Tinia Ris. '21	🍷🍷 8
○ Prototipo Viognier '20	🍷🍷 8
● Popnat '23	🍷🍷 4
● Newton Rosso '21	🍷 3
○ Bianco di Fabbrica '19	🍷🍷 6
○ Bianco di Fabbrica '18	🍷🍷 6
○ Menrva '20	🍷🍷 5
● Newton Rosso '20	🍷🍷 3
● Orcia Rosso '19	🍷🍷 3
● Rosso di Fabbrica '18	🍷🍷 4
● Sangiovese di Fabbrica '19	🍷🍷 5
● Syrah '17	🍷🍷 5
● Syrah di Fabbrica '19	🍷🍷 6
● Uni '20	🍷🍷 5

Le Falene

loc. Il Fontino
58023 Gavorrano [GR]
☎ +39 3336533306
valdelbosco@gmail.com

ANNUAL PRODUCTION 4,000 bottles
HECTARES UNDER VINE 2.00

Le Falene was launched in 2016 when Vincenza
Folgheretti, a Sicilian winemaker who'd relocated
to Tuscany, and Massimo Casagrande, an
agronomist with extensive industry experience,
leased their first vineyard plot in Maremma.
Their goal was to produce artisanal wines along
the Tuscan coast, drawing on prized vineyards
that were in danger of being abandoned. The
Bianco '22, a vermentino, is expertly crafted. The
nose reveals vibrant top notes of mimosa,
broom, grapefruit, and lemon juice, while its
aromatic core centers on citron and lime zest,
culminating in a finish on iodine, sea breezes, and
Mediterranean scrub. The palate is taut, sapid,
rhythmic, and flavorful, with a fresh, sapid finish.
The Sangiovese '20 reveals aromas of cherry
liqueur and chocolate, with a spicy hint of
patchouli. The palate is taut and elegant.

○ Le Falene Bianco '22	🍷🍷 3*
● Le Falene Rosso '20	🍷🍷 5
● Le Falene Sangiovese '20	🍷🍷 6
● Cabernet Franc '20	🍷 6
● Cabernet Franc '17	🍷🍷 5
○ Le Falene Bianco '21	🍷🍷 3
○ Le Falene Bianco '18	🍷🍷 3
● Le Falene Sangiovese '19	🍷🍷 6

Emiliano Falsini

loc. le Ferruggini 162/a
57022 Castagneto Carducci [LI]
(📞 +39 3483965967
🌐 www.emilianofalsini.com

ANNUAL PRODUCTION 20,000 bottles
HECTARES UNDER VINE 6.00

★Tenuta Fanti

fraz. Castelnuovo dell'Abate
loc. Podere Palazzo, 14
53024 Montalcino [SI]
(📞 +39 0577835795
🌐 www.tenutafanti.it

CELLAR SALES
PRE-BOOKED VISITS
ANNUAL PRODUCTION 200,000 bottles
HECTARES UNDER VINE 50.00

TUSCANY

Tuscany-based winemaker and consultant Emiliano Falsini embarked on his production project in 2019. That same year, he released his first and only two wine. Both are made with cabernet franc, the difference lying in the method of maturation—one is aged in oak, the other in terracotta cocciopesto. Building on this experience, he's since turned to Etna, where he has been working as a consultant since 2005. In this volcanic region, he produces nerello mascalese at elevations of around 700 meters. Falsini's wines put in an impressive performance, considering it's the first time they're being reviewed here. Two reds stand out at the top, one from Tuscany and the other from Etna. The first is the Limite '22, made from 100% cabernet franc. Complex aromas of fruit and balsamic tones rise from the glass alongside a subtle touch of oak. The palate is delicious, showcasing textbook elegance with impeccable tannins and a freshness perfectly integrated with the wine's structure. The Etna Feudo Pignatone Davanti Casa, a small cru wine that's light yet flavorful and deep, is also delightful.

Of late the Fanti family, father Filippo and daughter Elisa, are among those investing the most in Montalcino. It was Filippo who transformed the family's 19th-century farm into a winery in the 1980s. The cellar and vineyards are located on the southeastern slope of Montalcino, along with an elegant wine resort overlooking the Abbey of Sant'Antimo. Production is consistently of a high level, featuring radiant wines that aptly describe one of the best parts of the appellation. In vintages like this, experience makes all the difference: the exemplary Brunello '19 proves multifaceted and varietal, with tones of ripe cherry, autumnal underbrush, tobacco, and a near-perfect finish highlighted by an elegant graphite note. The palate is both fleshy and austere, finishing with great persistence. The Brunello Vallocchio '19 shows lovely red fruit on a slightly spicy background, with a gentle, well-distributed palate and a long, dynamic finish.

● Etna Rosso Feudo Pignatone Davanti Casa '22	🍷🍷 8
● Limite Cabernet Franc '22	🍷🍷 7
⊙ Etna Rosato Feudo Pignatone '23	🍷🍷 5
● Il Debbio Cabernet Franc '22	🍷🍷 7

● Brunello di Montalcino '19	🍷🍷🍷 6
● Sant'Antimo Rosso Sassomagno '22	🍷🍷 3*
● Brunello di Montalcino Vallocchio '19	🍷🍷 7
● Rosso di Montalcino '21	🍷🍷 4
⊙ Toscana Rosato '23	🍷 3
● Brunello di Montalcino '16	🍷🍷🍷 6
● Brunello di Montalcino '15	🍷🍷🍷 6
● Brunello di Montalcino '07	🍷🍷🍷 5
● Brunello di Montalcino '00	🍷🍷🍷 6
● Brunello di Montalcino '97	🍷🍷🍷 5
● Brunello di Montalcino Ris. '95	🍷🍷🍷 5
● Brunello di Montalcino V. Le Macchiarelle Ris. '16	🍷🍷🍷 8
● Brunello di Montalcino Vallocchio '18	🍷🍷🍷 7
● Brunello di Montalcino Vallocchio '13	🍷🍷🍷 7
● Brunello di Montalcino '17	🍷🍷 6

Tenuta Le Farnete - Cantagallo

fraz. Comeana
via Macia
59100 Carmignano [PO]
☎ +39 0571910078
⊛ www.cantagallolefarnete.it

CELLAR SALES
PRE-BOOKED VISITS
ACCOMMODATION AND RESTAURANT SERVICE
ANNUAL PRODUCTION 180,000 bottles
HECTARES UNDER VINE 40.00
SUSTAINABLE WINERY

The Pierazzuoli family owns Tenuta Le Farnete in the Carmignano appellation and Tenuta Cantagallo in the Chianti Montalbano production area. In the former, they mainly cultivate sangiovese, cabernet sauvignon, and aleatico; in the latter, sangiovese, merlot, syrah, colorino, trebbiano, and malvasia. The style of the wines is clear and, in general, reflects a modern approach with a touch of finesse, all nicely supported by the restrained use of oak. The Carmignano Riserva '21 exudes red fruit aromas with smoky and grassy hints on a spicy base. Its palate is dense and fleshy, concluding with a long, fruity, and minty finish. The Chianti Montalbano Il Fondatore Riserva '21 proves smooth and juicy, with a lively, almost brackish finish. Its fragrant aromas play on a mix of small red fruits and spices. The Barco Reale '23 makes for a pleasant and supple drink, with iron-like notes and a touch of mint on the nose.

Fattoi

loc. Santa Restituta
pod. Capanna, 101
53024 Montalcino [SI]
☎ +39 0577848613
⊛ www.fattoi.it

CELLAR SALES
PRE-BOOKED VISITS
ANNUAL PRODUCTION 60,000 bottles
HECTARES UNDER VINE 11.50

The Fattoi family's winery is located on the southwestern slope of Montalcino, in an area of rare natural beauty, between the Orcia and Ombrone rivers. It was 1979 when Ofelio bottled his first Brunello; now, as then, the winery is family-run, with his sons Lamberto and Leonardo personally taking care of it. The Mediterranean and sunny character of Fattoi's wines, which mature in large Slavonian oak barrels, represent some of the best interpretations of the area around the Pieve di Santa Restituta. The Brunello '19 showcases an intense, focused bouquet where ripe red fruits alternate with notes of violet, tobacco, dried herbs, and spices. The palate is close-knit and dense, with acidity and tannins working together to lighten the structure; the finish reveals a delightful touch of red citrus. The Riserva '18 unveils a lively, youthful profile, with hints of dark berries and medicinal herbs, and a palate driven by vibrant acidity that fully engages the palate.

● Carmignano Ris. '21	♟♟♟ 5
● Chianti Montalbano Tenuta Cantagallo Il Fondatore Ris. '21	♟♟ 6
● Barco Reale '23	♟♟ 2*
● Chianti Montalbano Tenuta Cantagallo '23	♟♟ 3
● Chianti Montalbano Tenuta Cantagallo Ris. '21	♟♟ 4
● Carmignano '22	♟ 3
● Carmignano Ris. '20	♟♟♟ 5
● Carmignano Ris. '19	♟♟♟ 4*
● Carmignano Ris. '18	♟♟♟ 5
● Carmignano Ris. '17	♟♟♟ 4*
● Carmignano Ris. '16	♟♟♟ 4*
● Carmignano Ris. '15	♟♟♟ 4*
● Carmignano Ris. '14	♟♟♟ 4*

● Brunello di Montalcino '19	♟♟♟ 6
● Brunello di Montalcino Ris. '18	♟♟ 7
● Toscana Rosso '22	♟♟ 3
● Rosso di Montalcino '22	♟ 4
● Brunello di Montalcino '10	♟♟♟ 5
● Brunello di Montalcino Ris. '12	♟♟♟ 7
● Brunello di Montalcino '18	♟♟ 5
● Brunello di Montalcino '17	♟♟ 5
● Brunello di Montalcino '15	♟♟ 5
● Brunello di Montalcino '14	♟♟ 5
● Brunello di Montalcino '12	♟♟ 5
● Brunello di Montalcino '11	♟♟ 5
● Brunello di Montalcino '09	♟♟ 5
● Brunello di Montalcino Ris. '15	♟♟ 7
● Brunello di Montalcino Ris. '10	♟♟ 7
● Brunello di Montalcino Ris. '06	♟♟ 4

Fattoria dei Barbi

loc. Podernovi, 170
53024 Montalcino [SI]
(☎) +39 0577841111
✉ www.fattoriadeibarbi.it

Fattoria del Pino

via Osticcio, 26
53024 Montalcino [SI]
(☎) +39 3475719051
✉ www.fattoriadelpino.com

CELLAR SALES
PRE-BOOKED VISITS
ACCOMMODATION AND RESTAURANT SERVICE
ANNUAL PRODUCTION 600,000 bottles
HECTARES UNDER VINE 66.00

ANNUAL PRODUCTION 30,000 bottles
HECTARES UNDER VINE 6.00

The history of the Cinelli Colombini family and that of Montalcino have been intertwined for centuries. The noble Colombini family, bankers from Siena, have owned properties in Montalcino since 1352, and the current Fattoria dei Barbi since the 18th century. Here, as early as 1870, they produced a Brunello that the Colombini were the first to export to the USA. The winery and vineyards are located in the southern part of Montalcino, on the road to Castelnuovo dell'Abate. The Brunello di Montalcino '19 handily landed a place in our finals. Its intense and refined nose offers up dark berries alongside hints of quinine, licorice, and tobacco on a background of autumnal underbrush. The palate is rich and full-bodied, with well-balanced fruit and close-knit, harmonious tannins, finishing long and sapid. The Vigna del Fiore '19, a Brunello with lovely notes of ripe red fruits and licorice, also impressed, coming through powerful and rich on the palate, with a lovely brackish finish.

Jessica Pellegrini's winery is among the newest in Montalcino, with the first vintage produced at Fattoria del Pino in 2010. Sangiovese is sourced from vineyards planted in the Montosoli area, on Montalcino's north-facing slope, overlooking Siena, a region highly esteemed for its elevation and breezy exposure (which tempers the summer heat), as well as its galestra soils rich in clay and limestone. In the cellar, chemical additives are eschewed in favor of indigenous yeasts, and extended maturation is carried out in traditional large oak barrels. The Brunello '19 conjures up intense notes of cherry and red fruit, followed by hints of licorice, bay leaf, and spices from nicely integrated wood. The palate is elegant, though still marked by youthful and unruly tannins, but its acidity and fruit suggest good aging potential. The Rosso '21 is complex, with notes of Mediterranean scrub and fruits, and a well-structured, fragrant palate.

• Brunello di Montalcino '19	♟♟♟ 6
• Brunello di Montalcino V. del Fiore '19	♟♟ 7
• Brunello di Montalcino '16	♟♟♟ 5
• Brunello di Montalcino '18	♟♟ 6
• Brunello di Montalcino '17	♟♟ 6
• Brunello di Montalcino '15	♟♟ 5
• Brunello di Montalcino '13	♟♟ 5
• Brunello di Montalcino Ris. '13	♟♟ 7
• Brunello di Montalcino Ris. '10	♟♟ 7
• Brunello di Montalcino V. del Fiore '17	♟♟ 7
• Brunello di Montalcino V. del Fiore '16	♟♟ 7
• Brunello di Montalcino V. del Fiore '15	♟♟ 7

• Brunello di Montalcino '19	♟♟♟ 7
• Rosso di Montalcino '21	♟♟ 5
• Brunello di Montalcino '18	♟♟ 7
• Brunello di Montalcino '17	♟♟ 7
• Rosso di Montalcino '19	♟♟ 5
• Rosso di Montalcino Il Jeccardo '18	♟♟ 6

Fattoria di Magliano

loc. Sterpeti, 10
58051 Magliano in Toscana [GR]
(☎) +39 0564593040
⊛ www.fattoriadimagliano.it

★★Fèlsina

loc. Fèlsina
via del Chianti, 101
53019 Castelnuovo Berardenga [SI]
(☎) +39 0577355117
⊛ www.felsina.it

CELLAR SALES
PRE-BOOKED VISITS
ACCOMMODATION AND RESTAURANT SERVICE
ANNUAL PRODUCTION 300,000 bottles
HECTARES UNDER VINE 45.00
VITICULTURE METHOD Certified Organic

CELLAR SALES
PRE-BOOKED VISITS
ANNUAL PRODUCTION 561,000 bottles
HECTARES UNDER VINE 72.00
VITICULTURE METHOD Certified Organic

Just 20 years ago, in 2004, Agostino Lenci's winery appeared in this guide, marking itself as one of the most intriguing new entries of the time. Today, the producer, based near Magliano in Tuscany, with vineyards in the areas of Colle Sterpeti, Vigna Tizzi, and Poggio Bestiale, remains firmly one of the benchmark brands of the Maremma wine scene. Its wines aptly represent the generous character of southern Tuscan reds and the potential of the area's white wines as well. The Maremma Vermentino Pagliatura '23 stands out for its aromas of ripe white fruits and aromatic herbs, with a smooth, juicy, and sapid palate. The Maremma Ansonica Brissaia '23 is also well-made, with flinty and earthy aromas preceding a delicate palate and a smoky finish. Graphite, underbrush, and ripe red fruit aromas characterize the Maremma Cabernet Poggio Bestiale '20, a wine with a fleshy and intense palate that finishes with balsamic and spicy nuances.

Situated just a stone's throw from Castelnuovo Berardenga, Fèlsina was founded in 1966 by the Ravenna entrepreneur Domenico Poggiali, who, together with his son Giuseppe, chose to invest in one of Tuscany's most important territories for winemaking. Since the 1990s, Giuseppe's son Giovanni Poggiali has also been part of the winery, and is now leading it along an exemplary path, making Fèlsina one of Chianti's most prominent brands. Giuseppe's determined son-in-law Giuseppe Mazzocolin is also making a contribution. The Chianti Classico Pagliarese Riserva '21 features aromas of ripe plums, aromatic herbs, earth, and smoky hints. On the palate, it has a focused progression, revealing finesse, drive, and sapidity. The Chianti Classico Pagliarese '22 proves enjoyable, with fragrant aromas and a firm, well-sustained palate. The Chianti Classico Gran Selezione Pagliarese '20 is well-crafted, though perhaps with a bit of oak still needing to integrate.

Wine	Rating
○ Maremma Toscana Ansonica Brissaia '23	♟♟ 3
● Maremma Toscana Cabernet Poggio Bestiale '20	♟♟ 5
○ Maremma Toscana Vermentino Pagliatura '23	♟♟ 3
● Maremma Toscana Syrah Perenzo '20	♟ 5
● Morellino di Scansano Heba '21	♟ 3
○ Maremma Toscana Ansonica Brissaia '22	♟♟ 4
● Maremma Toscana Rosso Altizi '18	♟♟ 6
● Maremma Toscana Rosso Poggio Bestiale '19	♟♟ 5
○ Maremma Toscana Vermentino Pagliatura '22	♟♟ 4
○ Maremma Toscana Vermentino Pagliatura '21	♟♟ 4
○ Maremma Toscana Vermentino Pagliatura '20	♟♟ 3

Wine	Rating
● Chianti Cl. Pagliarese Ris. '21	♟♟ 5
● Chianti Cl. Gran Selezione Pagliarese '20	♟♟ 5
● Chianti Cl. Pagliarese '22	♟♟ 4
● Fontalloro '21	♟♟ 8
● Chianti Cl. Berardenga '22	♟ 5
● Chianti Cl. Gran Selezione Colonia '21	♟ 8
● Chianti Cl. Gran Selezione Rancia '21	♟ 8
● Maestro Raro '21	♟ 8
● Chianti Cl. Rancia Ris. '07	♟♟♟ 6
● Chianti Cl. Rancia Ris. '05	♟♟♟ 5
● Chianti Cl. Rancia Ris. '04	♟♟♟ 5
● Chianti Cl. Rancia Ris. '03	♟♟♟ 5
● Fontalloro '10	♟♟♟ 6
● Fontalloro '07	♟♟♟ 6
● Fontalloro '06	♟♟♟ 6
● Fontalloro '05	♟♟♟ 6

Guido F. Fendi

fraz. La Sgrilla
loc. Pian di Macchia
58014 Manciano [GR]
☎ +39 0668801183
✉ www.guidoffendi.com

ANNUAL PRODUCTION 40,000 bottles
HECTARES UNDER VINE 22.00

Guido and Franca Formilli Fendi, along with their children, lead this recently launched project in Tuscany. Fendi is based in the Maremma hinterland, an area yet to be fully discovered and known for its generous viticulture. Technical direction of the winery is overseen by the young consultant Andrea Pala, who mainly trained in Sardinia with vermentino. And his experience can make a difference in a territory like Maremma, which has a lot in common with the island. This Manciano-based winery presented a well-crafted pair of Vermentinos. The Idillio Maremmano '23 possesses immediately fragrant aromas of white flowers and aromatic herbs, leading to a flavorful, smooth, and well-paced palate. The Chicca '22, on the other hand, shows a more complex and mature aromatic profile, with notes of white fruit accompanied by citrus, and balsamic tones—a fleshy palate follows with fruity echoes on the finish.

Fattoria Fibbiano

via Fibbiano, 2
56030 Terricciola [PI]
☎ +39 0587635677
✉ www.fattoria-fibbiano.it

CELLAR SALES
PRE-BOOKED VISITS
RESTAURANT SERVICE
ANNUAL PRODUCTION 150,000 bottles
HECTARES UNDER VINE 25.00
VITICULTURE METHOD Certified Organic

This historic winery in Pisa, which dates back to the 18th century, is owned by the Cantoni family. Giuseppe Cantoni breathed new life into the farm upon returning to agriculture after years in the industrial sector. Today, Nicola oversees the agronomic operations while his brother Matteo manages the commercial side. The winery demonstrates a strong commitment to vineyard care and environmental stewardship, spearheading a noteworthy project to revive certain extinct grape varieties, including sanforte and colombana. Deep aromas of underbrush and ripe red fruits characterize the Igt Le Pianette, all adorned by delicate hints of spice. It has a nice progression on the palate, revealing steady fruit supported by a solid structure. A racy, dynamic, and flavorful drink. The Chianti Superiore is also good, less imposing on the nose but sapid and fragrant on the palate, revealing its full character in its long and decisive persistence.

○ Maremma Toscana Vermentino Idillio Maremmano '23	♟♟ 3*
○ Maremma Toscana Vermentino Chicca '22	♟♟ 3
● Idillio Maremmano Rosso '20	♟ 3
● Maremma Sangiovese Burattini '21	♟ 5
● Maremma Sangiovese Fendente '18	♟♟ 5
○ Maremma Toscana Vermentino Burattini '20	♟♟ 4
○ Maremma Toscana Vermentino Chicca '22	♟♟ 3
○ Maremma Toscana Vermentino Chicca '20	♟♟ 3*

● Le Pianette '21	♟♟ 3*
● Chianti Sup. Casalini '21	♟♟ 3
● L'Aspetto '20	♟ 5
● Ciliegiolo '20	♟♟ 4
● L'Aspetto '19	♟♟ 5
● Le Pianette '19	♟♟ 2*
● Sanforte '19	♟♟ 6
● Terre di Pisa Sangiovese Ceppatella '19	♟♟ 8
○ Vermentino '22	♟♟ 3
○ Vermentino '21	♟♟ 3

La Fiorita

fraz. Castelnuovo dell'Abate
Podere Bellavista
53024 Montalcino [SI]
📞 +39 0577835657
🌐 www.lafiorita.com

CELLAR SALES
PRE-BOOKED VISITS
ANNUAL PRODUCTION 35,000 bottles
HECTARES UNDER VINE 9.00

Natalie Olivares has always had a great passion for wine. In her home, there was always good wine, thanks to her Italian father, who produced Moscato, and her ex-husband, who imported Italian wines to the U.S. In 1995, Natalie found herself in Montalcino, where she met winemaker Roberto Cipresso. Together, they created a wine line called Il Sogno. She later became a partner at La Fiorita winery in Montalcino and eventually acquired full ownership in 2011. In just a few years, she's expanded the vineyard acreage and built a new, state-of-the-art underground cellar. The 2019 Brunello Fiore Di No opens with broad and warm aromas of plum and cherry, followed by dark flowers, tobacco, and licorice. The palate is full and rich without losing its aristocratic elegance, all nicely guided by close-knit, long tannins that integrate seamlessly with its fleshy fruit. The finish is long and sapid. The 2018 Riserva features a vibrant nose of red fruits, which blend with spices and return on a dynamic, energetic, and juicy palate.

● Brunello di Montalcino Fiore di No '19	🍷🍷	8
● Brunello di Montalcino '19	🍷🍷	7
● Brunello di Montalcino Ris. '18	🍷🍷	8
● Rosso di Montalcino '21	🍷🍷	5
● Brunello di Montalcino Fiore di No '18	🍷🍷🍷	8
● Brunello di Montalcino Fiore di No '16	🍷🍷🍷	8
● Brunello di Montalcino Ris. '16	🍷🍷🍷	8
● Brunello di Montalcino '18	🍷🍷	6
● Brunello di Montalcino '17	🍷🍷	6
● Brunello di Montalcino '16	🍷🍷	6
● Brunello di Montalcino '13	🍷🍷	6
● Brunello di Montalcino Ris. '15	🍷🍷	8
⊙ Ninfalia '22	🍷🍷	3
● Rosso di Montalcino '20	🍷🍷	5
● Rosso di Montalcino '19	🍷🍷	5
● Rosso di Montalcino '18	🍷🍷	5

★Tenute Ambrogio e Giovanni Folonari

loc. Passo dei Pecorai
via di Nozzole, 12
50022 Greve in Chianti [FI]
📞 +39 055859811
🌐 www.tenutefolonari.com

CELLAR SALES
PRE-BOOKED VISITS
ACCOMMODATION
ANNUAL PRODUCTION 1,400,000 bottles
HECTARES UNDER VINE 100.00

Nino Folonari, a prominent figure in Italy's postwar wine industry, acquired the Cabreo estates in 1967 and Nozzole estates in 1971, both located in Greve in Chianti. In 2000, Ambrogio and Giovanni Folonari, Nino's son and grandson, respectively, founded the Ambrogio e Giovanni Folonari winery. Today they continue the family's entrepreneurial tradition not only in the Chianti region but also throughout Tuscany, including Bolgheri (Campo al Mare), Montalcino (La Fuga), and Maremma (Vigne a Porrona). The Chianti Classico Gran Selezione Giovanni Folonari 2019 offers up lovely aromas ranging from ripe fruit to fresher mint notes, all set on a spicy foundation. A satisfying wine on the palate, its sweet attack is followed by a sapid development that creates a beautiful contrast, enhancing the wine's dynamism and depth. The 2019 Brunello di Montalcino Tenuta La Fuga also impresses with its ripe cherry aromas and a flavorful, well-sustained palate.

● Chianti Cl. Gran Selezione Giovanni Folonari '19	🍷🍷🍷	5
● Brunello di Montalcino Tenuta La Fuga '19	🍷🍷	7
● Brunello di Montalcino Le Due Sorelle Ris. Tenuta la Fuga '18	🍷🍷	8
● Cabreo Il Borgo '21	🍷🍷	6
● Chianti Cl. La Forra Ris. '20	🍷🍷	5
● Il Pareto '20	🍷	8
● Rosso di Montalcino Tenuta La Fuga '22	🍷	4
● Cabreo Il Borgo '19	🍷🍷🍷	6
● Cabreo Il Borgo '16	🍷🍷🍷	6
● Chianti Cl. '19	🍷🍷🍷	3*
● Chianti Cl. La Forra Ris. '19	🍷🍷🍷	5
● Il Pareto '17	🍷🍷🍷	8
● Il Pareto '15	🍷🍷🍷	8
● Il Pareto '09	🍷🍷🍷	7
● Il Pareto '07	🍷🍷🍷	7

★★Fontodi

fraz. Panzano in Chianti
via San Leolino, 89
50020 Greve in Chianti [FI]
📞 +39 055852005
🌐 www.fontodi.com

CELLAR SALES
PRE-BOOKED VISITS
ACCOMMODATION
ANNUAL PRODUCTION 300,000 bottles
HECTARES UNDER VINE 80.00
VITICULTURE METHOD Certified Organic

In 1981, Fontodi introduced Flaccianello della
Pieve, a monovarietal sangiovese matured in
barriques. This was followed in 1985 by a Chianti
Classico Riserva, the Vigna del Sorbo, a
single-vineyard sangiovese blended with
cabernet sauvignon (at the time), and also
matured in barriques. These two wines have
become cult classics of Chianti. Indeed, Giovanni
Manetti's winery is firmly among the appellation's
top producers and a reference point for Panzano
in Chianti. The 2021 Chianti Classico Filetta di
Lamole reveals an airy aromatic profile marked
by bright red fruit and lovely balsamic nuances.
In the mouth its progression is dynamic, with
contrasts and length that conclude with a fruity
encore. The 2021 Chianti Classico is also
well-crafted, particularly for its intense and
pronounced drinkability. The Chianti Classico
Gran Selezione Vigna del Sorbo 2021 stands out
for its intensity, power, and youthful firmness.

Fontuccia

via Provinciale, 54
58012 Isola del Giglio [GR]
📞 +39 333 4303684
🌐 www.fontuccia.it

ANNUAL PRODUCTION 10,000 bottles
HECTARES UNDER VINE 5.00

On the island of Giglio, viticulture is genuinely
heroic. Vines grow with little water and soil,
poking out of the granite. The Rossi brothers,
armed with relentless perseverance, work the
land by hand almost constantly (the only method
available) so as to at least capture the moisture
from the air. The result is a range that showcases
ansonica in one of Tuscany's finest expressions of
white wine. The 2023 Caperrosso Senti Oh!
opens with a certain Mediterranean richness:
honeyed aromas that meet balsamic flashes. In
the mouth, its fleshy palate reveals light tannins
on the finish. Truly riveting. The 2023 Da
Giovacchino offers up aromas of lentisk, juniper,
broom, and iodine. In the mouth, the palate is
sapid, almost brackish, with a supple
development and an airy, saline finish. The 2023
Senti Oh! is an easy-drinking wine, where citrus
fruit plays the leading role.

● Chianti Cl. Filetta di Lamole '21	♟♟ 5	
● Chianti Cl. '21	♟♟ 4	
● Chianti Cl. Gran Selezione V. del Sorbo '21	♟♟ 6	
● Chianti Cl. Gran Selezione Terrazze San Leolino '21	♟ 8	
● Chianti Cl. Pastrolo '20	♟ 5	
● Flaccianello della Pieve '21	♟ 8	
● Chianti Cl. '10	♟♟♟ 4*	
● Chianti Cl. Gran Sel. V. del Sorbo '14	♟♟♟ 6	
● Chianti Cl. Gran Selezione V. del Sorbo '18	♟♟♟ 6	
● Chianti Cl. Gran Selezione V. del Sorbo '16	♟♟♟ 6	
● Flaccianello della Pieve '19	♟♟♟ 8	
● Flaccianello della Pieve '12	♟♟♟ 8	

○ Caperrosso Senti Oh! '23	♟♟♟ 6
○ Da Giovacchino '23	♟♟ 7
○ Fontuccia '23	♟♟ 4
○ Senti Oh! '23	♟♟ 5
○ Caperrosso Senti Oh! '22	♀♀ 5
○ Caperrosso Senti Oh! '21	♀♀ 5
○ Caperrosso Senti Oh! '20	♀♀ 4
○ Caperrosso Senti Oh! '19	♀♀ 4
○ Caperrosso Senti Oh! '18	♀♀ 4
○ Caperrosso Senti Oh! '16	♀♀ 4
○ Cocciuto Senti Oh! '22	♀♀ 4
○ Cocciuto Senti Oh! '19	♀♀ 4
○ Da Giovacchino '22	♀♀ 7
○ N'antro Po' Ansonica Passito '22	♀♀ 6
○ Senti Oh! '20	♀♀ 4
○ Storto '21	♀♀ 7

Fornacelle

loc. Fornacelle, 232a
57022 Castagneto Carducci [LI]
((·)) +39 0565775575
⊕ www.fornacelle.it

CELLAR SALES
PRE-BOOKED VISITS
ANNUAL PRODUCTION 35,000 bottles
HECTARES UNDER VINE 9.00

Founded in 1996, Stefano Billi and Silvia Menicagli's winery focuses on classic red grape varieties of the Bolgheri area: cabernet franc, cabernet sauvignon, and merlot. For white wines, they draw on local vermentino and sémillon. Their wines, mostly matured in barriques, prove stylistically well defined and well calibrated, without excessive influence from oak. The 2020 Bolgheri Superiore Foglio 38, which is celebrating its 20th vintage, expresses a clear aromatic profile with floral notes and small red fruits. In the mouth, the palate is smooth, racy, and decisive, finishing with great energy. The 2022 Bolgheri Rosso Zizzolo also impresses with its blackberry aromas, nice density on the palate, and flavorful tannins. The 2023 Bolgheri Bianco Zizzolo plays on floral tones and Mediterranean shrub.

● Bolgheri Rosso Sup. Foglio 38 '20	♥♥ 7
● Bolgheri Rosso Sup. Guardaboschi '21	♥♥ 6
● Bolgheri Rosso Zizzolo '22	♥♥ 4
○ Bolgheri Bianco Zizzolo '23	♥ 4
○ Fornacelle '22	♥ 3
● Bolgheri Rosso Sup. Foglio 38 '15	♀♀ 7
● Bolgheri Rosso Sup. Guarda Boschi '15	♀♀ 6
● Bolgheri Rosso Sup. Guardaboschi '16	♀♀ 6
● Bolgheri Rosso Zizzolo '21	♀♀ 4
● Bolgheri Rosso Zizzolo '16	♀♀ 3
● Bolgheri Sup. Foglio 38 '14	♀♀ 7
● Bolgheri Sup. Foglio 38 '13	♀♀ 6
● Bolgheri Sup. Guarda Boschi '13	♀♀ 6
● Bolgheri Sup. Guarda Boschi '11	♀♀ 6
○ Bolgheri Vermentino Zizzolo '22	♀♀ 3
● Foglio 38 '11	♀♀ 6

Podere Forte

loc. Petrucci, 13
53023 Castiglione d'Orcia [SI]
((·)) +39 05778885100
⊕ www.podereforte.it

CELLAR SALES
PRE-BOOKED VISITS
ANNUAL PRODUCTION 50,000 bottles
HECTARES UNDER VINE 24.00
VITICULTURE METHOD Certified Biodynamic
SUSTAINABLE WINERY

Drawing on his family's deep-rooted traditions and agricultural heritage, entrepreneur Pasquale Forte embarked on a visionary and heartfelt journey. His passion and love for farming led him to establish his winery in Val d'Orcia in 1997. Forte's philosophy emphasizes continual exploration and the harmonious integration of humans, animals, and plants through biodynamic practices, fostering a self-sufficient, sustainable, and balanced environment. The estate comprises 168 hectares, including 19 hectares of vineyards and 23 hectares of olive groves. The powerful and expressive 2020 Cabernet Franc Guardiavigna showcases a rich aromatic range, from cherry jam to blackberry, transitioning to notes of quinine, black pepper, tar, and tobacco, with elegant minty and balsamic hints. The palate is rich, progressive, finishing with spices. Fresher and more delicate, the 2019 Petrucci Melo, made from sangiovese, opts for aromas of pomegranate and cherry, with notes of blood orange and hints of forest floor alongside Mediterranean scrub. On the palate, it's finely textured, dynamic, and elegant, with a harmonious and persistent finish.

● Guardiavigna '20	♥♥ 8
● Petrucci Melo '19	♥♥ 8
● Petrucci Anfiteatro '19	♥♥ 8
● Villaggio '22	♥♥ 7
● Guardiavigna '19	♀♀♀ 8
● Guardiavigna '18	♀♀♀ 8
● Guardiavigna '17	♀♀♀ 8
● Guardiavigna '16	♀♀♀ 8
● Orcia Guardiavigna '01	♀♀♀ 8
● Orcia Petruccino '16	♀♀♀ 7
● Guardiavigna '15	♀♀ 8
● Orcia Anfiteatro '16	♀♀ 8
● Orcia Anfiteatro '15	♀♀ 8
● Orcia Petrucci Melo '18	♀♀ 8
● Orcia Petrucci Melo '17	♀♀ 8
● Orcia Petruccino '18	♀♀ 7

La Fralluca

loc. Barbiconi, 153
57028 Suvereto [LI]
☎ +39 0565829076
✉ www.lafralluca.com

CELLAR SALES
PRE-BOOKED VISITS
ANNUAL PRODUCTION 40,000 bottles
HECTARES UNDER VINE 10.00
VITICULTURE METHOD Certified Organic
SUSTAINABLE WINERY

Luca Recine and Francesca Bellini started their wine journey in 2005. Located in the metalliferous hills of Maremma, at Podere dei Barbiconi in Suvereto, their vineyards are organically cultivated. They grow vermentino, viognier, sangiovese, syrah, cabernet franc, and alicante bouchet. In the cellar, they favor steel and small wooden barrels for maturation. The 2020 Fillide, a blend of sangiovese, syrah, and alicante bouschet, convinces with its spicy, balsamic aromatic profile and generous fruit. In the mouth, a juicy and easy-going palate is underpinned by a structured, sapid tannic weave and a focused finish. The 2022 Bauci, a monovarietal viognier, proves fragrant and generous in its fruity aromas, while in the mouth it's sapid and persistent. The 2020 Cabernet Franc features delicate aromas of small red fruits and spices, followed by a concentrated, vibrant palate.

Frascole

loc. Frascole, 27a
50062 Dicomano [FI]
☎ +39 0558386340
✉ www.frascole.it

CELLAR SALES
PRE-BOOKED VISITS
ACCOMMODATION
ANNUAL PRODUCTION 65,000 bottles
HECTARES UNDER VINE 16.00
VITICULTURE METHOD Certified Organic

The winery in Dicomano began its wine journey in 1992. Situated between the Mugello Valley and Valdisieve, at elevations of 400 meters (with some plots even higher), it occupies the small village of Podere Vico on Frascole hill. Here they produce distinctive wines from sangiovese, canaiolo, colorino, trebbiano, and malvasia grapes, with some experimentations with merlot, sauvignon, traminer, and recently, pinot noir. The Chianti Rufina Ris. Terraelectae Vigna alla Stele is a sapid and energetic drink. A hint of pine needles—a trait often found in Frascole's wines—emerges on the nose. Its tannins are well-dosed, and the palate harmonious. The 2021 Chianti Rufina Riserva offers nice depth, fleshy fruit, and a compact mid-palate with aromas of black pepper, blood orange, and leather. The In Albis, a Trebbiano, is precise and moderately oxidative in style, with a firm, slightly tannic, and brackish palate.

○ Bauci '22	♟♟ 4
● Fillide '20	♟♟ 3*
● Cabernet Franc '20	♟♟ 6
● Pitis '20	♟♟ 5
● Suvereto Sangiovese Ciparisso '20	♟♟ 5
○ Bauci '21	♟♟ 4
○ Bauci '20	♟♟ 4
● Cabernet Franc '19	♟♟ 6
● Cabernet Franc '18	♟♟ 6
● Cabernet Franc '16	♟♟ 6
○ Filemone '20	♟♟ 3
● Fillide '19	♟♟ 3
● Fillide '18	♟♟ 3
● Suvereto Sangiovese Ciparisso '18	♟♟ 5

● Chianti Rufina Terraelectae V. alla Stele Ris. '20	♟♟ 7
● Chianti Rufina '22	♟♟ 4
● Chianti Rufina Ris. '21	♟♟ 3
○ In Albis '21	♟♟ 3
● Chianti Rufina Ris. '18	♟♟ 3*
● Chianti Rufina Ris. '17	♟♟ 3*
● Chianti Rufina Ris. '16	♟♟ 3*
● Chianti Rufina Ris. '15	♟♟ 3*
● Chianti Rufina Terraelectae V. alla Stele Ris. '19	♟♟ 7
● Chianti Rufina Terraelectae V. alla Stele Ris. '18	♟♟ 7
● Pinot Nero '16	♟♟ 4
○ Vin Santo del Chianti Rufina '09	♟♟ 7

★Marchesi Frescobaldi

via Santo Spirito, 11
50125 Firenze
(») +39 05527141
⊛ www.frescobaldi.it

Fuligni

via Saloni, 33
53024 Montalcino [SI]
(») +39 0577848710
⊛ www.fuligni.it

CELLAR SALES
PRE-BOOKED VISITS
ANNUAL PRODUCTION 9,000,000 bottles
HECTARES UNDER VINE 1200.00

CELLAR SALES
PRE-BOOKED VISITS
ANNUAL PRODUCTION 52,000 bottles
HECTARES UNDER VINE 12.00

The Frescobaldi family boasts an enviable mosaic of estates in Tuscany. These range from Tenuta di Castiglioni in Montespertoli to Rèmole in Sieci, Castelgiocondo in Montalcino to Perano in Gaiole in Chianti, Ammiraglia in Maremma to the family's project on Gorgona island, and the prestigious Ornellaia and Masseto estates. They also own Tenuta Calimaia in Montepulciano and Castello di Nipozzano and Pomino in Rufina, representing the family's centuries-old historical roots. The Chianti Rufina Riserva Terrelectae Vigna Montesodi 2021 bursts with wild cherry, bay leaf, orange peel, and hints of chocolate. It's a vibrant and bold wine, expanding on the palate and stimulating every sense—here we find strength, elegance, and a saline note on the finish. If there's one Chardonnay to reckon with in Italy, it's surely the Pomino Bianco Benefizio Riserva, which in this vintage stands out for its freshness, plumpness, and its signature, poetic oak.

Fuligni and Montalcino have been inseparable for over a century, each embodying the other's history. In an industry where storytelling often overshadows the wine itself, Fuligni needs no such embellishments. Their wines, from the vineyards and cellar at Cottimeli on the northeastern slope of the appellation, speak for themselves. They express the refined elegance of sangiovese grosso with stylistic rigor, uninfluenced by trends. The 2019 Brunello conveys a rare aromatic finesse: notes of ripe dark berries emerge alongside tanned leather and tobacco, all enlivened by hints of rose, chinotto, and mint. The palate is fruit-forward but quickly bound by a refined, energetic tannic structure, with a long, sapid finish. The 2020 Merlot Joanni, which plays more on elegance than power, balances its ripe fruit with fresh herbal notes—the palate is sapid and taut.

● Chianti Rufina Terraelectae V. Montesodi Ris. '21	♟♟♟ 8
○ Pomino Bianco Benefizio Ris. '22	♟♟ 8
● Chianti Rufina Nipozzano Ris. '21	♟♟ 5
● Chianti Rufina Nipozzano V.V. Ris. '21	♟♟ 6
● Mormoreto '21	♟♟ 8
○ Pomino Bianco '23	♟♟ 4
○ Pomino Brut M. Cl. Leonia '20	♟♟ 7
⊙ Pomino Brut Rosé M. Cl. Leonia '19	♟♟ 8
● Chianti Rufina Nipozzano Ris. '18	♟♟♟ 4*
● Chianti Rufina Nipozzano Ris. '17	♟♟♟ 4*
● Chianti Rufina Nipozzano V.V. Ris. '16	♟♟♟ 5
● Chianti Rufina Terraelectae V. Montesodi Ris. '19	♟♟♟ 6
● Chianti Rufina Terraelectae Vign. Montesodi Ris. '20	♟♟♟ 7
● Montesodi '15	♟♟♟ 6

● Brunello di Montalcino '19	♟♟♟ 8
● Joanni '20	♟♟ 8
● Rosso di Montalcino Ginestreto '22	♟ 4
● Brunello di Montalcino '18	♟♟♟ 8
● Brunello di Montalcino '16	♟♟♟ 8
● Brunello di Montalcino '10	♟♟♟ 6
● Brunello di Montalcino Ris. '16	♟♟♟ 8
● Brunello di Montalcino Ris. '01	♟♟♟ 8
● Brunello di Montalcino Ris. '97	♟♟♟ 8
● Brunello di Montalcino '17	♟♟ 8
● Brunello di Montalcino '15	♟♟ 6
● Brunello di Montalcino '14	♟♟ 6
● Brunello di Montalcino '12	♟♟ 6
● Brunello di Montalcino Ris. '15	♟♟ 8
● Brunello di Montalcino Ris. '13	♟♟ 8

La Gerla - Aisna

loc. Canalicchio
pod. Colombaio, 5
53024 Montalcino [SI]
☎ +39 0577848599
⊕ www.lagerla.it

CELLAR SALES
PRE-BOOKED VISITS
ANNUAL PRODUCTION 95,000 bottles
HECTARES UNDER VINE 11.50

La Gerla was founded by Sergio Rossi, who in 1976 acquired Podere Colombaio along with a few hectares of vineyards from the Biondi Santi family. Today, in addition to its aging cellar (housed in the former basement of a 15th-century tower), the estate comprises some 12 ha of sangiovese grosso. Some vineyards are located in Canalicchio where the calcareous, clay-rich soils mix with significant quantities of limestone, while the remaining vineyards can be found in the Castelnuovo dell'Abate area to the southeast, where the soils, though rich in marl, are sandier. The firm and austere Riserva Gli Angeli '18 opens with aromas of red berries and plum, transitioning to licorice, aromatic herbs, and hints of iron. A close-knit and fleshy palate follows, moving elegantly with supple ease, driven by a sapid acidity and streamlined tannins. The Brunello CampoNovo '19, though slightly less complex, is full of class, with a multifaceted nose of fruit, floral notes, and spices, lightly marked by a subtle vein of blood. Its rich and sapid palate reveals a lovely progression of tannins, leading to a remarkably persistent finish.

● Brunello di Montalcino Gli Angeli Ris. '18	♥♥	8
● Brunello di Montalcino '19	♥♥	6
● Brunello di Montalcino Camponovo '19	♥♥	6
● Rosso di Montalcino '22	♥♥	5
● Toscana Poggio Gli Angeli '22	♥♥	3
● Brunello di Montalcino La Pieve '19	♥	8
● Toscana La Birba '21	♥	5
● Brunello di Montalcino '17	♀♀	6
● Brunello di Montalcino Aisna '16	♀♀	6
● Brunello di Montalcino Camponovo '16	♀♀	6
● Brunello di Montalcino Gli Angeli '16	♀♀	8
● Brunello di Montalcino La Pieve '17	♀♀	8
● Quando gli Angeli Giocano nella Vigna '18	♀♀	4
● Rosso di Montalcino Camponovo '19	♀♀	4

Giodo

fraz. Sant'Angelo in Colle
loc. Casanova
53024 Montalcino [SI]
☎ +39 3516220372
⊕ www.giodo.it

CELLAR SALES
ANNUAL PRODUCTION 20,000 bottles
HECTARES UNDER VINE 5.50
VITICULTURE METHOD Certified Organic
SUSTAINABLE WINERY

Giodo is a blend of the first syllables of Giovanna and Donatello, the beloved parents of Carlo Ferrini, to whom the Tuscan winemaker has dedicated the winery. This venture was primarily driven by the determination of Carlo's daughter Bianca to harness her inherited passion for wine. Before moving to Montalcino, Bianca didn't just work alongside her father; she sought out oenological experience worldwide. This formative journey now allows them to collaborate as equals on all vineyard and cellar activities. The Brunello Giodo '19 is certainly one of the best tastes of the year, showcasing rare aromatic finesse, with a nose marked by complexity and clarity: gorgeous notes of red berries emerge alongisde mulberry, cherries, iris, balsamic herbs, chocolate, tobacco, and hints of graphite and cocoa. Its powerful, delectable, and velvety palate is balanced and perfectly streamlined by vibrant acidity, as well as smooth, flavorful tannins, all topped off by a long, balsamic finish.

● Brunello di Montalcino Giodo '19	♥♥♥	8
● La Quinta '20	♥♥	8
● Brunello di Montalcino Giodo '18	♀♀♀	8
● Brunello di Montalcino Giodo '17	♀♀♀	8
● Brunello di Montalcino Giodo '16	♀♀♀	8
● Brunello di Montalcino Giodo '15	♀♀♀	8
● Brunello di Montalcino Giodo '13	♀♀♀	8
● Brunello di Montalcino Giodo '12	♀♀♀	8
● Brunello di Montalcino Giodo '11	♀♀♀	8
● Brunello di Montalcino Giodo '14	♀♀	8
● Giodo '17	♀♀	6
● Giodo '16	♀♀	6
● Giodo '15	♀♀	6
● La Quinta '21	♀♀	8
● La Quinta '19	♀♀	8
● La Quinta '18	♀♀	8

I Giusti & Zanza

loc. Scopicci
via dei Puntoni, 9
56043 Fauglia [PI]
☏ +39 058544354
✉ www.igiustiezanza.it

CELLAR SALES
PRE-BOOKED VISITS
ANNUAL PRODUCTION 100,000 bottles
HECTARES UNDER VINE 17.00
VITICULTURE METHOD Certified Organic

Founded in 1996, this Fauglia-based winery recently began carrying out a major overhaul of its vineyards, converting to organic farming and incorporating select biodynamic techniques. The predominant varietals grown include cabernet sauvignon, cabernet franc, merlot, petit verdot, syrah, sangiovese, trebbiano, and semillon. In the cellar, aging primarily occurs in concrete tanks and tonneaux. The Perbruno '21, a monovarietal syrah, reveals a fruity nose with iron, blood, and spicy tones emerging. In the mouth it's pleasantly sapid, ending with a lovely spicy note. The Dulcamara, a blend of cabernet sauvignon, merlot, cabernet franc, and petit verdot, offers dark, deep aromatic tones alongside a dense, persistent palate. The Nemorino Bianco '23, an blend of equal parts trebbiano and semillon, proves well-made, with clean aromas and a crisp, enjoyable taste.

Marchesi Gondi
Tenuta Bossi

loc. Bossi
via dello Stracchino, 32
50065 Pontassieve [FI]
☏ +39 0558317830
✉ www.tenutabossi.com

CELLAR SALES
PRE-BOOKED VISITS
ACCOMMODATION
ANNUAL PRODUCTION 50,000 bottles
HECTARES UNDER VINE 19.00

The Gondi family, whose roots in Florence's wine culture run deep, continues to manage Fattoria di Volmiano (also producing extra virgin olive oil) and Tenuta Bossi. Their vineyards host sangiovese, a century-old indigenous clone of colorino, merlot, cabernet sauvignon, trebbiano, chardonnay, and sauvignon. The result is a range of well-crafted and widely respected wines. The excellent work done can be seen not only in their traditional Rufina varieties but also with regard to international grapes. The Chianti Rufina Riserva Terraelectae Vigneto Poggio Diamante '20 delivers a firm and racy palate, vibrant and fresh, unfolding with mineral notes and whiffs of cherry. The Ser Amerigo boasts an exquisite tannic structure, supporting a firm yet supple frame. The Vin Santo Riserva proves highly complex, with its characteristic notes of rancio and dried fig.

● Perbruno '21	♟♟ 5
● Dulcamara '21	♟♟ 6
○ Nemorino Bianco '23	♟♟ 3
● Nemorino Rosso '22	♟♟ 3
● Belcore '22	♟ 3
● Belcore '21	♟♟ 3
● Belcore '20	♟♟ 6
● Dulcamara '20	♟♟ 6
● Dulcamara '19	♟♟ 5
○ Nemorino Bianco '22	♟♟ 3
● Nemorino Rosso '21	♟♟ 3
● Nemorino Rosso '20	♟♟ 3*
● Perbruno '20	♟♟ 5
● Perbruno '19	♟♟ 6
● Vignavecchia '20	♟♟ 8
● Vigna Vecchia '19	♟♟ 8

● Chianti Rufina Terraelectae Vign. Poggio Diamante Ris. '20	♟♟ 8
● Chianti Rufina Pian dei Sorbi Ris. '22	♟♟ 3
● Chianti Rufina Villa Bossi Ris. '19	♟♟ 4
● Mazzaferrata '19	♟♟ 5
○ Sassobianco '23	♟♟ 3
● Ser Amerigo '19	♟♟ 5
○ Vin Santo del Chianti Rufina Cardinal de Retz Ris. '10	♟♟ 5
○ Violana '23	♟♟ 3
● Chianti Rufina San Giuliano '22	♟ 3
● Fiammae '19	♟ 8
● Chianti Rufina Pian dei Sorbi Ris. '19	♟♟ 3*
● Chianti Rufina Terraelectae V. Poggio Diamante Ris. '18	♟♟ 4
● Chianti Rufina Terraelectae Vign. Poggio Diamante Ris. '19	♟♟ 8

Giuseppe Gorelli

loc. Canalicchio
Podere Cerrino, 79
53024 Montalcino [SI]
☎ +39 3483530321
giuseppe.gorelli@gmail.com

PRE-BOOKED VISITS
ANNUAL PRODUCTION 27,000 bottles
HECTARES UNDER VINE 6.30

After years of practice and training, in 2017 Giuseppe Gorelli decided to draw on his vast experience to his own project. He focuses on producing wines from sangiovese grosso, aiming to showcase the varietal's potential. His vineyards are located in the celebrated Canalicchio area of northwest Montalcino, at an elevation of 350 meters. Here, he respects biodiversity, producing organic wines from spontaneous fermentations, which are then aged in large Slavonian oak barrels. The Brunello '19 is a vibrant pour, redolent of brandied red fruit, licorice, and undergrowth. The nose is broad and complex, while on the palate, its fruit is balanced by acidity, leading to a full finish with fresh balsamic notes. The Rosso '21, though less complex, is rich in fruit, with a full, juicy palate nicely supported by an adequate tannic frame.

★★Grattamacco

loc. Lungagnano
57022 Castagneto Carducci [LI]
☎ +39 0565765069
🌐 www.collemassari.it

CELLAR SALES
PRE-BOOKED VISITS
ANNUAL PRODUCTION 120,000 bottles
HECTARES UNDER VINE 16.00
VITICULTURE METHOD Certified Organic

Grattamacco was one of Bolgheri's pioneering wineries, and Piermario Meletti Cavallari, who moved to Castagneto Carducci from Bergamo, is the man who made it happen. Since 2002, the estate has been part of the Collemassari group, which has preserved its distinctive features and maintained its top position in the appellation. Consistency in production owes much to winemaker Luca Marrone's deep understanding of the Bolgheri terroir. The historic Bolgheri Superiore Grattamacco '21 unveils delightful hints of blueberry and wild blackberry, complemented by spicy nuances. Its fleshy and sapid palate reveals fragrant fruit, closing with soft tannins and nice persistence. The Bolgheri Superiore L'Alberello '21 opts for aromas of ink, Mediterranean scrub, and plum, with a long and dynamic finish. The Bolgheri Rosso '22 features citrusy notes and remarkable freshness. The Bolgheri Vermentino '22 proves pleasantly sapid.

● Brunello di Montalcino '19	▼▼ 8
● Rosso di Montalcino '21	▼▼ 6
● Brigo Sangiovese '22	▼ 4
● Brigo '21	♀♀ 4
● Brunello di Montalcino '18	♀♀ 8

● Bolgheri Rosso Sup. Grattamacco '21	▼▼▼ 8
● Bolgheri Rosso '22	▼▼ 4
● Bolgheri Rosso Sup. L'Alberello '21	▼▼ 8
○ Bolgheri Vermentino '22	▼▼ 5
● Bolgheri Rosso Sup. Grattamacco '20	♀♀♀ 8
● Bolgheri Rosso Sup. Grattamacco '19	♀♀♀ 8
● Bolgheri Rosso Sup. Grattamacco '18	♀♀♀ 8
● Bolgheri Rosso Sup. Grattamacco '17	♀♀♀ 8
● Bolgheri Rosso Sup. Grattamacco '16	♀♀♀ 8
● Bolgheri Sup. Grattamacco '15	♀♀♀ 8
● Bolgheri Sup. Grattamacco '14	♀♀♀ 8
● Bolgheri Sup. Grattamacco '13	♀♀♀ 8
● Bolgheri Sup. Grattamacco '12	♀♀♀ 8
● Bolgheri Sup. Grattamacco '10	♀♀♀ 7
● Bolgheri Sup. Grattamacco '09	♀♀♀ 7
● Bolgheri Sup. Grattamacco '07	♀♀♀ 7
● Bolgheri Sup. L'Alberello '11	♀♀♀ 6

Guado al Melo

loc. Murrotto, 130a
57022 Castagneto Carducci [LI]
📞 +39 0565763238
🖦 www.guadoalmelo.it

CELLAR SALES
PRE-BOOKED VISITS
ANNUAL PRODUCTION 120,000 bottles
HECTARES UNDER VINE 16.00
SUSTAINABLE WINERY

Since 1998, Michele Scienza, son of renowned professor Attilio Scienza, has been cultivating vineyards in the hills of Bolgheri, drawing on the support of his wife Annalisa Motta. Their winery represents an broad oenological project, encompassing a rich variety of Mediterranean and even Caucasian grape varietals. Redolent of ripe fruit with vegetal nuances and balsamic hints, the Bolgheri Superiore Atis '21 is a full-bodied and deep drink, with volume and extremely long persistence. Generous and ripe, the Jassarte '21, a complex blend of 30 local and Mediterranean grape varieties, is a mouthfilling wine with aromas of wild herbs. Concentrated in its fruit, the Bolgheri Bianco Criseo '22 has a decidedly sapid taste.

Tenuta Guado al Tasso

loc. Bolgheri
s.da Bolgherese, km 3,9
57020 Castagneto Carducci [LI]
📞 +39 0565749735
🖦 www.guadoaltasso.it

CELLAR SALES
PRE-BOOKED VISITS
RESTAURANT SERVICE
ANNUAL PRODUCTION 1,700,000 bottles
HECTARES UNDER VINE 320.00

The Antinori family, already prominent in the wine world, managed vineyards in Bolgheri's former Tenuta Belvedere, primarily producing rosé. The transformation into Tenuta Guado al Tasso, now a key player in Bolgheri, occurred in the late 1980s. The 1990 Guado al Tasso immediately became a cornerstone of the region's global success. The Bolgheri Superiore Guado al Tasso '21 reveals ripe fruity aromas of plum and raspberry, with hints of rose and bay leaf on a spicy base. In the mouth, the palate is dense, unfolding nicely, with soft tannins and a fruity finish. The Bolgheri Rosso Cont'Ugo '22 features more delicate aromatic tones, accented by balsamic flashes. On the palate, it's sapid and fragrant.

● Bolgheri Rosso Sup. Atis '21	♟♟♟ 8
○ Bolgheri Bianco Criseo '22	♟♟ 5
● Bolgheri Rosso Rute '22	♟♟ 4
● Jassarte '21	♟♟ 6
○ Bolgheri Bianco Criseo '17	♟♟♟ 5
● Bolgheri Rosso Rute '21	♟♟♟ 4*
● Bolgheri Rosso Rute '18	♟♟♟ 4*
● Bolgheri Rosso Sup. Atis '19	♟♟♟ 7
● Bolgheri Rosso Sup. Atis '12	♟♟♟ 6
○ Bolgheri Bianco Criseo '21	♟♟ 5
○ Bolgheri Bianco Criseo '20	♟♟ 5
○ Bolgheri Bianco Criseo '19	♟♟ 5
○ Bolgheri Bianco Criseo '16	♟♟ 5
● Bolgheri Rosso Rute '20	♟♟ 4
● Bolgheri Rosso Rute '13	♟♟ 5
● Bolgheri Rosso Sup. Atis '20	♟♟ 8
● Bolgheri Rosso Sup. Atis '13	♟♟ 6

● Bolgheri Rosso Sup. Guado al Tasso '21	♟♟ 8
○ Bolgheri Bianco Vermentino '23	♟♟ 4
● Bolgheri Rosso Cont'Ugo '22	♟♟ 7
● Bolgheri Rosso Il Bruciato '22	♟♟ 5
⊙ Bolgheri Rosato Scalabrone '23	♟ 4
● Bolgheri Sup. Guado al Tasso '01	♟♟♟ 8
● Bolgheri Sup. Guado al Tasso '90	♟♟♟ 8
● Bolgheri Rosso Cont'Ugo '21	♟♟ 6
● Bolgheri Rosso Cont'Ugo '19	♟♟ 6
● Bolgheri Rosso Guado al Tasso '17	♟♟ 8
● Bolgheri Rosso Il Bruciato '19	♟♟ 5
● Bolgheri Rosso Sup. Guado al Tasso '20	♟♟ 8
● Bolgheri Rosso Sup. Guado al Tasso '19	♟♟ 8
● Bolgheri Rosso Sup. Guado al Tasso '09	♟♟ 8
● Bolgheri Rosso Sup. Guado al Tasso '08	♟♟ 8
○ Bolgheri Vermentino '22	♟♟ 3

Guicciardini Strozzi

loc. Cusona, 5
53037 San Gimignano [SI]
☏ +39 0577950028
@ www.guicciardinistrozzi.it

CELLAR SALES
PRE-BOOKED VISITS
ANNUAL PRODUCTION 400,000 bottles
HECTARES UNDER VINE 100.00

Situated near San Gimignano, Tenuta Villa Cusona is where the Guicciardini Strozzi family produces one of their flagship wines, Vernaccia. In the 1970s, Girolamo Strozzi expanded the winery's viticultural activities, now led by his daughters Natalina and Irina Jr. Since 1999, Guicciardini Strozzi has broadened its horizons to Maremma (Tenuta Poggio Moreto and Tenuta I Massi), Bolgheri, and Pantelleria (Coste di Kuddi). The Vernaccia di San Gimignano Riserva '20 features a well-structured progression of flavor, with a nose of slightly evolved dried medicinal herbs and faint earthy accents, leading to a minty and almond-like finish. The Vin Santo di San Gimignano '14 has a sweet palate that shifts to savory notes on the finish, making it supple and effortless, with a nose releasing aromas of dried apricot, honey, walnut husk, white chocolate, and vanilla.

★★Isole e Olena

loc. Isole, 1
50028 Barberino Tavarnelle [FI]
☏ +39 0558072763
@ www.isoleolena.it

CELLAR SALES
PRE-BOOKED VISITS
ANNUAL PRODUCTION 250,000 bottles
HECTARES UNDER VINE 56.00

A few years ago, the French Epi group made an excellent choice in acquiring Isole e Olena, adding it to Biondi Santi. The winery, located in San Donato in Poggio, was founded in the late 1970s by Paolo De Marchi and is now widely recognized as one of the finest in the Chianti Classico region. Their wines maintain a relentless stylistic continuity, characterized by clarity of execution and a faithful reflection of the attributes of the terroir. The historic Cepparello, a monovarietal sangiovese, has never stood out for weight or volume but rather for finesse and typicity. This stylistic consistency continues with the 2021 vintage, which offers an intriguing aromatic profile of floral and woodland scents, with touches of flint and spices accompanying a racy, sustained, and highly sapid palate, where oak has already found optimal integration. The Chianti Classico '21 is a flavorful pour—delectable and enticing.

○ Vernaccia di San Gimignano Ris. '20	♛♛ 4
○ Vin Santo di San Gimignano '14	♛♛ 5
● Chianti Colli Senesi Titolato Strozzi '23	♛ 3
● Sòdole '20	♛ 6
○ Vernaccia di San Gimignano Titolato Strozzi '23	♛ 3
○ Vernaccia di San Gimignano Villa Cusona '23	♛ 3
● Millanni '99	♛♛♛ 5
○ Vernaccia di S. Gimignano Ris. '13	♛♛ 3*
○ Vernaccia di San Gimignano Ris. '19	♛♛ 3*
○ Vernaccia di San Gimignano Ris. '18	♛♛ 3*
● Vernaccia di San Gimignano Titolato Strozzi '21	♛♛ 2*

● Cepparello '21	♛♛♛ 8
● Chianti Cl. '21	♛♛ 5
○ Collezione Privata Chardonnay '22	♛♛ 7
● Cepparello '19	♛♛♛ 8
● Cepparello '18	♛♛♛ 8
● Cepparello '17	♛♛♛ 8
● Cepparello '16	♛♛♛ 8
● Cepparello '15	♛♛♛ 8
● Cepparello '13	♛♛♛ 8
● Cepparello '12	♛♛♛ 8
● Cepparello '09	♛♛♛ 8
● Cepparello '07	♛♛♛ 8
● Cepparello '06	♛♛♛ 8
● Cepparello '05	♛♛♛ 8
● Cepparello '03	♛♛♛ 7
● Cepparello '01	♛♛♛ 6
● Cepparello '00	♛♛♛ 6

Istine

loc. Istine
53017 Radda in Chianti [SI]
📞 +39 0577733684
🌐 www.istine.it

Podere La Chiesa

via di Casanova, 66a
56030 Terricciola [PI]
📞 +39 0587635484
🌐 www.poderelachiesa.it

CELLAR SALES
PRE-BOOKED VISITS
ANNUAL PRODUCTION 45,000 bottles
HECTARES UNDER VINE 26.00
VITICULTURE METHOD Certified Organic

CELLAR SALES
PRE-BOOKED VISITS
ANNUAL PRODUCTION 50,000 bottles
HECTARES UNDER VINE 10.00
VITICULTURE METHOD Certified Organic
SUSTAINABLE WINERY

Istine debuted with its first bottles of Chianti Classico in 2009. Today, Angela Fronti's project is well-recognized, holding a prominent place in the Chianti Classico wine scene. With a rigorous focus on vineyards in Radda in Chianti and Gaiole, and new ventures in Lamole and Castelnuovo Berardenga, the producer continues to shine for the stylistic consistency, aromatic freshness, and drinkability of its wines. The fragrant and floral profile of the Chianti Classico Gran Selezione Vigna Istine '21 features earthy and smoky aromas. In the mouth, it unfolds with energy but the palate is also juicy and sapid. The Chianti Classico Gran Selezione Vigna Cavarchione '21 shares the same flavorful, enjoyable palate, while the nose leans more toward fruit and spices. The Chianti Classico Gran Selezione Vigna Casanova dell'Aia '21 is similarly tasty, though slightly darker in tone.

Owned by Maurizio Iannantuono and Palma Tonacci, Podere La Chiesa is situated in the Terricciola area of Pisa. The winery focuses on classic Tuscan varieties—sangiovese, canaiolo, and vermentino—while also incorporating well-established international grapes such as cabernet franc and merlot. The style is marked by minimal extraction and the careful use of oak, resulting in generally balanced and refined wines that reflect the nuances of each vintage. The Terre di Pisa Sabiniano di Casanova '21 is a relaxed, enjoyable wine, soft and persistent on the palate, with aromatic tones of small red fruits and spices. The well-structured Opera in Nero '21, a monovarietal merlot, offers a spicy nose of pepper with piquant hints, and a development marked by exuberant fruit, culminating in balsamic and minty tones on the finish.

● Chianti Cl. Gran Selezione V. Istine '21	♟♟♟ 6
● Chianti Cl. Gran Selezione V. Cavarchione '21	♟♟ 5
● Chianti Cl. Gran Selezione V. Casanova dell'Aia '21	♟♟ 5
● Chianti Cl. Le Vigne Ris. '21	♟♟ 6
● Chianti Cl. '22	♟ 4
● Chianti Cl. Casanova dell'Aia '19	♟♟♟ 5
● Chianti Cl. Le Vigne Ris. '13	♟♟♟ 3*
● Chianti Cl. V. Cavarchione '16	♟♟♟ 5
● Chianti Cl. V. Istine '18	♟♟♟ 5
● Chianti Cl. V. Istine '15	♟♟♟ 3*
● Chianti Cl. '19	♟♟ 3*
● Chianti Cl. Le Vigne Ris. '20	♟♟ 6
● Chianti Cl. V. Cavarchione '20	♟♟ 5
● Chianti Cl. V. Istine '20	♟♟ 5

● Opera in Nero Merlot '21	♟♟ 7
● Terre di Pisa Rosso Sabiniano di Casanova '21	♟♟ 5
● CF '20	♟♟ 8
● Terre di Pisa Sangiovese I Matti '21	♟ 6
● Opera in Nero '17	♟♟ 7
● Opera in Nero Merlot '20	♟♟ 7
○ Punto di Vista '19	♟♟ 3
○ Punto di Vista Vermentino '22	♟♟ 3
○ Taigete '17	♟♟ 2
● Terre di Pisa Rosso Le Redole di Casanova '18	♟♟ 2
● Terre di Pisa Rosso Sabiniano di Casanova '20	♟♟ 5
● Terre di Pisa Sangiovese Opera in Rosso '15	♟♟ 7

★Lamole di Lamole

loc. Lamole
50022 Greve in Chianti [FI]
📞 +39 0559331256
🌐 www.lamole.com

CELLAR SALES
PRE-BOOKED VISITS
RESTAURANT SERVICE
ANNUAL PRODUCTION 250,000 bottles
HECTARES UNDER VINE 37.00
VITICULTURE METHOD Certified Organic
SUSTAINABLE WINERY

Lamole di Lamole is likely the crown jewel of the Santa Margherita Group. Located in one of the most enchanting parts of the Chianti Classico appellation, it has benefited from a comprehensive revitalization effort led by the Marzotto family since the early 1990s. This initiative has established Lamole di Lamole as one of the territory's top producers, with a range that stands out as among the best in the appellation. The Chianti Classico Lareale Ris. '21 opens with spicy, smoky, and floral aromas, with a fleshy, sapid progression on the palate, leading to a firm, dynamic finish. The Chianti Classico Maggiolo '22 is particularly enjoyable, revealing earthy accents and hints of citrus on the nose. In the mouth, it unfolds with decisive contrasts that amplify its vibrant drinkability. The Chianti Classico Gran Selezione Vigneto di Campolungo '20 is also well-crafted.

Podere Le Bèrne

loc. Cervognano
via Poggio Golo, 7
53045 Montepulciano [SI]
📞 +39 0578767328
🌐 www.leberne.it

CELLAR SALES
ANNUAL PRODUCTION 25,000 bottles
HECTARES UNDER VINE 6.00

The Natalini family's small winery excels in the Cervognano subzone, soon to be recognized as a "Pieve" by the consortium responsible for assigning Additional Geographic Units. For at least 15 years, it has been one of Montepulciano's top producers, known for its consistently outstanding wines. Their range, with its clear stylistic features, exhibits elegance and finesse, particularly their sangiovese, which expresses an undeniable and absolute level of quality. The Nobile Cervognano Alto '20 intrigues from the start with its intertwining of fruit, floral hints, flint, and flashes of menthol. In the mouth, its structure is present, yet the palate remains supple and taut, with sapid tannins and pointed acidity that enhance a lively finish. The Nobile '21 is well-crafted, opting for an aromatic profile of small ripe red fruits and smoky nuances. On the palate, it maintains a rhythmic, dynamic pace, finishing once again with fruit.

● Chianti Cl. Lareale Ris. '21	▼▼▼ 6
● Chianti Cl. Maggiolo '22	▼▼ 5
● Chianti Cl. Gran Selezione Vigneto di Campolungo '20	▼▼ 7
● Chianti Cl. Duelame '22	▼ 4
● Lam'oro '20	▼ 8
● Chianti Cl. Gran Selezione V. Grospoli '19	♈♈♈ 7
● Chianti Cl. Gran Selezione V. Grospoli '18	♈♈♈ 7
● Chianti Cl. Gran Selezione Vign. di Campolungo '16	♈♈♈ 5
● Chianti Cl. Lamole di Lamole Et. Bianca '16	♈♈♈ 3*
Chianti Cl. Lamole di Lamole Et. Blu '15	♈♈♈ 3*

● Nobile di Montepulciano Cervognano Alto '20	▼▼▼ 7
● Nobile di Montepulciano '21	▼▼ 4
● Nobile di Montepulciano Ris. '20	▼ 5
● Nobile di Montepulciano '19	♈♈♈ 4*
● Nobile di Montepulciano '18	♈♈♈ 3*
● Nobile di Montepulciano '16	♈♈♈ 3*
● Nobile di Montepulciano '15	♈♈♈ 3*
● Nobile di Montepulciano '11	♈♈♈ 3*
● Nobile di Montepulciano '06	♈♈♈ 3
● Nobile di Montepulciano '20	♈♈ 4
● Nobile di Montepulciano '17	♈♈ 3*
● Nobile di Montepulciano Cervognano Alto '19	♈♈ 7
● Nobile di Montepulciano Ris. '17	♈♈ 5
● Rosso di Montepulciano '16	♈♈ 2*

La Leccia

loc. Botinaccio
via della Leccia, 37
50025 Montespertoli [FI]
📞 +39 3495775763
🌐 www.laleccia.it

CELLAR SALES
PRE-BOOKED VISITS
ANNUAL PRODUCTION 50,000 bottles
HECTARES UNDER VINE 23.00
VITICULTURE METHOD Certified Organic

La Leccia is situated on the hills of Val di Botte in the Montespertoli area. Owned by the Bagnoli family since the 1970s, the winery took major steps in terms of production in 2013. The vineyards, which grow in mostly loamy-clay soils, host sangiovese, syrah, merlot, trebbiano, and malvasia. In the winery, the maturation of wines combines the use of large wooden barrels and barriques. In the Gotarossa '21, a monovarietal sangiovese, eucalyptus and pine resin aromas blend with cherry jam and licorice, on a spicy and smoky base. The palate is broad and juicy, with sweet tones and a firm, persistent finish. The Chianti Riserva '21 opens with floral scents, nuances of pomegranate and cherry. In the mouth, it's certainly not lacking in flavor or structure, with a finish on oak and lingering fruity notes. The sparkling Rubedo, made from sangiovese, is fun and lively.

● Gotarossa '21	♟♟ 4
● Chianti Ris. '21	♟ 3
● Chianti Sup. '22	♟ 2
⊙ Rubedo Pas Dosé M. Cl. '19	♟ 5
○ Cantagrillo '21	♟♟ 4
○ Cantagrillo '19	♟♟ 3
○ Cantagrillo Trebbiano '18	♟♟ 3*
● Chianti Ris. '20	♟♟ 3
● Chianti Sup. La Leccia '21	♟♟ 4
● Chianti Sup. Secondo Allegria '20	♟♟ 2*
⊙ Rubedo Pas Dosé M. Cl. '18	♟♟ 5
⊙ Rubedo Pas Dosé M. Cl. '17	♟♟ 5
○ Vin Santo del Chianti Sua Santità '16	♟♟ 7

La Lecciaia

loc. Vallafrico
53024 Montalcino [SI]
📞 +39 0583928366
🌐 www.lecciaia.it

PRE-BOOKED VISITS
ANNUAL PRODUCTION 200,000 bottles
HECTARES UNDER VINE 16.00

Founded by Mauro Pacini, the winery is located just outside Montalcino, on the road to the Abbey of Sant'Antimo. Today Mauro is joined by his children, Alessandra and Riccardo, who have modernized the large cellar and begun a meticulous zoning of the existing vineyards. They have also selected about 10 clones of sangiovese for replanting and for use in new plots acquired in the higher areas of Montalcino (most recently near Passo del Lume Spento). The Riserva '18 proves classically styled on the nose, opening with notes of plum, cherry, cut flowers, and petrichor, before transitioning to more playful sensations of aromatic herbs and Mediterranean scrub. The palate is firm and persistent, with pleasant sapidity balanced by plump, juicy fruit. The Brunello '19 offers up subtle red fruit aromas, followed by licorice, roasting coffee, and pencil lead. On the palate, it's harmonious, nicely balancing fruit and tannins.

● Brunello di Montalcino Ris. '18	♟♟ 7
● Brunello di Montalcino '19	♟♟ 6
● Rosso di Montalcino '21	♟ 4
● Brunello di Montalcino V. Manapetra '09	♟♟♟ 6
● Brunello di Montalcino '18	♟♟ 7
● Brunello di Montalcino '17	♟♟ 7
● Brunello di Montalcino '16	♟♟ 6
● Brunello di Montalcino Ris. '12	♟♟ 6
● Brunello di Montalcino V. Manapetra '17	♟♟ 7
● Brunello di Montalcino V. Manapetra '13	♟♟ 6
● Brunello di Montalcino V. Manapetra '10	♟♟ 6
● Brunello di Montalcino V. Manapetra '08	♟♟ 5
● Brunello di Montalcino V. Manapetra Ris. '15	♟♟ 6
● Brunello di Montalcino V. Manapetra Ris. '13	♟♟ 6
● Rosso di Montalcino '20	♟♟ 4
● Rosso di Montalcino '18	♟♟ 3

Tenuta Lenzini

fraz. Gragnano
via della Chiesa, 44
55012 Capannori [LU]
📞 +39 0583974037
🌐 www.tenutalenzini.it

CELLAR SALES
PRE-BOOKED VISITS
ACCOMMODATION
ANNUAL PRODUCTION 60,000 bottles
HECTARES UNDER VINE 24.00
VITICULTURE METHOD Certified Biodynamic

The Lenzini family's vineyards span 24 ha, nestled within a natural amphitheater on the Lucchesi Hills. This estate, which belonged to the Arnolfini family—wealthy bankers immortalized in van Eyck's famous portrait—dates back to the Renaissance. Honoring the extensive renovation work undertaken by grandfather Franco, since 2007, the property has been led by his granddaughter Benedetta. Together with her husband, Michele Guarino, she has set in motion further changes, converting to organic farming and then biodynamic practices. The Syrah '22 is a flavorful and multifaceted pour, rich in aromas of blackberry jam, aromatic herbs and violet petals, with notes of tar and cinchona. On the palate, it's full-bodied, creamy, and balanced by excellent acidic-sapid drive, leading to a rich, flavorful finish. The freshness of the Buscè '23, made from alicante bouschet, is striking—a bouquet of freshly picked flowers and red fruits emerges. Cherry, pomegranate, black cherry, and floral tones give way to a juicy, dynamic, and refreshing palate. The red Casa e Chiesa '23 is enjoyable, with its balsamic and fruity qualities.

La Syrah '22	🍷🍷 6
Buscè '23	🍷🍷 5
Casa e Chiesa '23	🍷🍷 3
B-Side '23	🍷 5
Lenzini Franco '23	🍷 5
Poggio de' Paoli '21	🍷 5
Vermignon '23	🍷 5
Buscè '21	🍷 3
Colline Lucchesi Casa e Chiesa '19	🍷 3*
La Syrah '19	🍷 5
La Syrah '18	🍷 5
La Syrah '16	🍷 5
Lenzini Franco '22	🍷 5
Poggio de' Paoli '17	🍷 4

Tenuta Licinia

loc. Meleto
p.le Il Calcione, 129a
52046 Lucignano [AR]
📞 +39 0575836451
🌐 www.tenutalicinia.com

CELLAR SALES
PRE-BOOKED VISITS
ANNUAL PRODUCTION 15,000 bottles
HECTARES UNDER VINE 6.50
VITICULTURE METHOD Certified Organic
SUSTAINABLE WINERY

Tenuta Licinia is situated between the provinces of Siena and Arezzo, at the foot of the Apennines. In the 1970s, Jacques de Liedekerke revived the estate, an effort that culminated in the establishment of the Sasso di Fata vineyard in 2006. Today, his grandson James Marshall-Lockyer, a philosopher by training, leads the winery, having been passionate about the project from its inception. Their mission is to produce distinctive wines that reflect the unique terroirs, employing biodynamic practices. The estate encompasses 60 ha of woodland and 6.5 ha of vineyards, all planted on clay schist and layered galestro soils. The elegant and powerful Sasso di Fata '21, a Bordeaux blend, offers up vibrant aromas of brandied cherry and blackberry jam, evolving toward more complex notes of tar, licorice, and underbrush. On the palate, it has structure and fullness, with fruit of great integrity, a dynamic character, and a long, pleasantly minty finish. The merlot-based Montepolli '22 showcases a vibrant and persistent balsamic streak, along with blueberry, black plum, and boisé notes. A balanced and fresh palate follows.

Sasso di Fata '21	🍷🍷 7
Montepolli '22	🍷🍷 5
Montepolli '19	🍷 5
Sasso di Fata '19	🍷 7

Lunadoro

fraz. Valiano
via Terra Rossa
53045 Montepulciano [SI]
(+39 3482215188
@ www.nobilelunadoro.it

CELLAR SALES
PRE-BOOKED VISITS
ANNUAL PRODUCTION 75,000 bottles
HECTARES UNDER VINE 12.00

Lunadoro is part of the Schenk group, flanking
Bacio della Luna in the Prosecco region and
Masso Antico in Puglia. In Montepulciano,
Lunadoro boasts 12 hectares of exquisite
vineyards in the Valiano area. Predominantly
sangiovese is grown, and almost entirely
organically. Valiano features moderate elevations
(332 meters) and clay-rich soils, with a climate
influenced by both the Val di Chiana and the
nearby Lake Trasimeno. Excellent exposure to
breezes further contributes to healthy,
high-quality grapes, which are then crafted in the
winery's modern, fully equipped facilities. The
Nobile Pagliareto Selezione Bio '20 pours a
lovely ruby color, releasing an elegant and
complex nose where ripe red fruits give way to
Mediterranean scrub and spices, with an elegant
smoky note. The palate is both slender and
elegant, but not without depth; fruit reappears
gracefully, and its tannins are of a finely wrought
finesse, leading to a truly long finish. The
Riserva '20 displays tones of ripe fruit and
spices, with a solid, harmonious structure.

● Nobile di Montepulciano Pagliareto Sel. Bio '20	♀♀♀ 5
● Nobile di Montepulciano Pagliareto '21	♀♀ 4
● Nobile di Montepulciano Quercione Ris. '20	♀♀ 5
● Rosso di Montepulciano Prugnanello '22	♀♀ 3
● Nobile di Montepulciano Pagliareto '15	♀♀♀ 3*
● Nobile di Montepulciano Pagliareto Sel. Bio '19	♀♀♀ 5
● Nobile di Montepulciano Pagliareto '20	♀♀ 4
● Nobile di Montepulciano Quercione Ris. '19	♀♀ 5

Tenute Lunelli - Podernovo

via Podernuovo, 13
56030 Terricciola [PI]
(+39 0587655173
@ www.tenutelunelli.it

CELLAR SALES
PRE-BOOKED VISITS
ACCOMMODATION AND RESTAURANT SERVICE
ANNUAL PRODUCTION 130,000 bottles
HECTARES UNDER VINE 25.00
VITICULTURE METHOD Certified Organic
SUSTAINABLE WINERY

At the start of the new millennium, the Lunelli
family, renowned for Cantine Ferrari in Trento,
expanded their production focus to central Italy.
Thus, Tenuta Podernuovo was established in the
Pisa hills, a lesser-known area in Tuscany from a
wine perspective. The vineyards primarily grow
sangiovese, teroldego, cabernet sauvignon,
cabernet franc, merlot, and syrah. The Teuto '20,
a blend of sangiovese, merlot, and cabernet
sauvignon, opens with aromas of blackberry and
blueberry, accompanied by spicy accents and
coffee powder. In the mouth, the attack is
creamy, growing more complex as it develops,
with tannic grip always in the foreground, leading
to an intense, pervasive finish. The Aliotto '21,
also a sangiovese, cabernet sauvignon, and
merlot blend, features a powerful palate and
dark aromatic traits: nuances of bottled black
cherries, medicinal herbs, and oaky tones.

● Teuto '20	♀♀ 6
● Aliotto '21	♀♀ 5
● Auritea '18	♀♀♀ 8
● Auritea '17	♀♀♀ 8
● Auritea '16	♀♀♀ 8
● Teuto '18	♀♀♀ 5
● Aliotto '19	♀♀ 5
● Aliotto '17	♀♀ 3
● Aliotto '16	♀♀ 3
● Aliotto '15	♀♀ 3
● Auritea '17	♀♀ 8
● Auritea '15	♀♀ 8
● Teuto '19	♀♀ 6
● Teuto '17	♀♀ 5
● Teuto '16	♀♀ 5
● Teuto '15	♀♀ 5

★★Le Macchiole

loc. Bolgheri
via Bolgherese, 189a
57022 Castagneto Carducci [LI]
📞 +39 0565766092
🌐 www.lemacchiole.it

PRE-BOOKED VISITS
ANNUAL PRODUCTION 200,000 bottles
HECTARES UNDER VINE 35.00
SUSTAINABLE WINERY

The story of Le Macchiole began in 1983, making it a pioneering winery in the Bolgheri region. After the premature death of her husband, Cinzia Merli, along with her brother Massimo and now her sons Elia and Mattia, has led the winery to significant acclaim. Their range of "cult" bottles includes Paleo, Bolgheri's first unblended cabernet franc, the merlot Messorio, and the syrah Scrio. Recently, the use of small oak barrels has decreased in favor of grès and concrete amphorae. On the nose, the Paleo '21, a monovarietal cabernet franc, offers up floral tones and balsamic accents, alongside whiffs of ivy and spices. In the mouth, it possesses lively energy, underscored by crunchy tannins and a fleshy fruitiness, all followed by a vibrant, deep finish. The Messorio '21, a monovarietal merlot, is a wine of stature, revealing fresh, enticing aromas and a juicy, flavorful, almost brackish palate, closing on a refreshing, spicy note.

Le Macioche

s.da prov.le 55 di Sant'Antimo, km 4,850
53024 Montalcino [SI]
📞 +39 0577849168
🌐 www.lemacioche.it

CELLAR SALES
PRE-BOOKED VISITS
ACCOMMODATION
ANNUAL PRODUCTION 18,000 bottles
HECTARES UNDER VINE 3.00

Riccardo and Renzo Cotarella own about half a dozen estates in central Italy, spanning Lazio, Umbria, and Tuscany, managed by their daughters Dominga, Marta, and Enrica. Le Macioche, their Montalcino estate, is located on the southeast side of the hill, halfway between the town and the Abbey of Sant'Antimo. It consists of four small vineyards, totaling just over three hectares, on galestro-rich soils at about 450 meters elevation, in one of the appellation's most esteemed winemaking districts. Protected from cold winds by Monte Amiata, it enjoys a temperate climate. The still-evolving Brunello '19 is a wine of class and elegance, but needs more time in the bottle. Red fruits are prominent, followed by floral notes, earth, bay leaf, and spices on the nose, which isn't peaking yet, but has all the right elements to shine. The palate is fresh, well-defined, rich in fruit and tannins without any dryness. We're patiently optimistic.

● Paleo Rosso '21	♟♟♟ 8
● Messorio '21	♟♟ 8
● Bolgheri Rosso '22	♟♟ 5
○ Paleo Bianco '22	♟♟ 8
● Scrio '21	♟♟ 8
● Bolgheri Sup. Paleo '14	♟♟♟ 8
● Paleo Rosso '20	♟♟♟ 8
● Paleo Rosso '19	♟♟♟ 8
● Paleo Rosso '18	♟♟♟ 8
● Paleo Rosso '17	♟♟♟ 8
● Paleo Rosso '16	♟♟♟ 8
● Paleo Rosso '15	♟♟♟ 8
● Paleo Rosso '13	♟♟♟ 8
● Paleo Rosso '12	♟♟♟ 8
● Paleo Rosso '11	♟♟♟ 8
● Paleo Rosso '10	♟♟♟ 8
● Paleo Rosso '09	♟♟♟ 8

● Brunello di Montalcino '19	♟♟ 8
● Brunello di Montalcino '18	♟♟♟ 8
● Brunello di Montalcino '15	♟♟♟ 8
● Brunello di Montalcino '13	♟♟♟ 7
● Brunello di Montalcino Ris. '16	♟♟♟ 8
● Brunello di Montalcino Ris. '15	♟♟♟ 8
● Brunello di Montalcino Ris. '13	♟♟♟ 8
● Brunello di Montalcino Ris. '11	♟♟♟ 8
● Brunello di Montalcino '17	♟♟ 8
● Brunello di Montalcino '09	♟♟ 7
● Brunello di Montalcino '06	♟♟ 6
● Brunello di Montalcino '04	♟♟ 6
● Brunello di Montalcino '99	♟♟ 5
● Brunello di Montalcino Ris. '06	♟♟ 8
● Brunello di Montalcino Ris. '01	♟♟ 6
● Brunello di Montalcino Ris. '97	♟♟ 7

La Madonnina

fraz. Bolgheri
via Bolgherese, 193
57022 Castagneto Carducci [LI]
☏ +39 0565763357
⊛ www.lamadonninabolgheri.it

ANNUAL PRODUCTION 40,000 bottles
HECTARES UNDER VINE 7.00

La Magia

loc. La Magia
53024 Montalcino [SI]
☏ +39 0577835667
⊛ www.fattorialamagia.it

ANNUAL PRODUCTION 80,000 bottles
HECTARES UNDER VINE 15.00

This historic Bolgheri estate was acquired in 2014 by Konstantin Nikolaev, a Moscow entrepreneur and passionate wine enthusiast (particularly when it comes to merlot). The property, which features a manor house surrounded by vineyards, now hosts the region's main varietals, with some vines going back as many as 20 years. Olive oil is produced as well, while an additional 30 hectares are dedicated to woodlands and pine forests. The winemaking style reflects the producer's international spirit. The Bolgheri Superiore Opera Omnia '20 reveals a bouquet of black currant, thyme, and graphite, with sweet tannins, a solid structure, and a pervasive dimension in the mouth. The Carpe Vesperum '20, a monovarietal merlot, impresses with its aromas of dark fruits and an intriguing smoky vein, all carried by a vibrant palate. The Viator '20, a monovarietal syrah, stands out for its pronounced spices on the nose and a well-defined palate. La Madonnina '22, a blend of cabernet franc, syrah, merlot, cabernet sauvignon, and petit verdot, is also well-crafted.

It was in the late 1970s when Harald Schwarz, a South Tyrolean vacationing in Montalcino, fell in love with a farm—an old post station—named La Màgia. He purchased it and moved there with his entire family. Today, the property is managed by his son, Fabian, who studied winemaking at the school of oenology in San Michele all'Adige. Fabian personally oversees the cellar and the estate's 15 hectares of vineyards, all planted with sangiovese da brunello, cultivated in a single parcel at an elevation of 450 meters, overlooking the centuries-old Romanesque Abbey of Sant'Antimo on the southeast slope of the appellation. All the wines presented this year were outstanding, starting with the Brunello Vigna Ciliegio '19. A focused, intense aromatic profile of ripe red fruit is accompanied by fine notes of tobacco and citrus, adding complexity and finesse. The palate is powerful yet harmonious, well-developed around a close-knit tannic structure. The Brunello '19 offers darker, more restrained aromas, while the palate still shows some tannic hardness.

● Bolgheri Sup. Opera Omnia '20	♟♟ 8
● Carpe Vesperum '20	♟♟ 8
● La Madonnina '22	♟♟ 5
● Viator '20	♟♟ 8
● La Madonnina '17	♟♟♟ 8
● Bolgheri Sup. Opera Omnia '19	♟♟ 8
● Bolgheri Sup. Opera Omnia '17	♟♟ 8
● Bolgheri Sup. Opera Omnia '16	♟♟ 8
● La Madonnina '21	♟♟ 5
● La Madonnina '19	♟♟ 5
● Viator '18	♟♟ 8
● Viator '17	♟♟ 8

● Brunello di Montalcino V. Ciliegio '19	♟♟ 8
● Brunello di Montalcino '19	♟♟ 8
● Rosso di Montalcino '22	♟♟ 4
● Brunello di Montalcino '18	♟♟ 6
● Brunello di Montalcino '17	♟♟ 6
● Brunello di Montalcino '16	♟♟ 6
● Brunello di Montalcino '15	♟♟ 6
● Brunello di Montalcino '14	♟♟ 6
● Brunello di Montalcino Ris. '16	♟♟ 8
● Brunello di Montalcino Ris. '15	♟♟ 8
● Brunello di Montalcino Ris. '01	♟♟ 8
● Il Vispo '19	♟♟ 3
● Rosso di Montalcino '19	♟♟ 3
● Rosso di Montalcino '18	♟♟ 3
● Rosso di Montalcino '17	♟♟ 3
● Rosso di Montalcino '16	♟♟ 3
● Rosso di Montalcino '06	♟♟

Malenchini

loc. Grassina
via Lilliano e Meoli, 82
50012 Bagno a Ripoli [FI]
📞 +39 055642602
🌐 www.medicivilla.com

CELLAR SALES
PRE-BOOKED VISITS
ACCOMMODATION
ANNUAL PRODUCTION 150,000 bottles
HECTARES UNDER VINE 17.00
VITICULTURE METHOD Certified Organic
SUSTAINABLE WINERY

Situated on the hills of Grassina, the Malenchini family's winery is nestled within the Medici villa of Lilliano, which they have owned since the mid-1800s. Today, Diletta Malenchini leads the estate, steering it with a compelling oenological vision where sangiovese takes center stage, complemented by local varietals such as canaiolo. The aging process has progressively shifted from small barrels to larger casks. The Chianti Colli Fiorentini Vigna di Lapeggi Riserva '21 evokes aromas of sour cherry jam, cherry liqueur, underbrush, tobacco, and spices. The palate is fleshy, focused, and dynamic, finishing with crisp, fruit and spice-infused notes. The Chianti Colli Fiorentini '22 emphasizes immediate drinkability. The Canaiolo '23 proves slender and well-paced, with aromas of ripe red berries and slightly herbal whiffs. The Bianco '23, made from chardonnay and trebbiano, is sapid, easy to drink, though quite simple.

Fattoria Mantellassi

loc. Banditaccia, 26
58051 Magliano in Toscana [GR]
📞 +39 0564592037
🌐 www.fattoriamantellassi.it

CELLAR SALES
PRE-BOOKED VISITS
ANNUAL PRODUCTION 1,000,000 bottles
HECTARES UNDER VINE 118.00

With a history spanning over 60 years, the Fattoria Mantellassi, managed by brothers Aleardo and Giuseppe Mantellassi, is a cornerstone in the Morellino di Scansano appellation. Their extensive range consistently guarantees high quality across both white and red wines, showcasing local varietals like sangiovese, ciliegiolo, and vermentino, as well as international grapes like alicante, cabernet sauvignon, merlot, and sauvignon. An instantly enjoyable drinkability characterizes the Maremma Vermentino Lucumone '23, a wine with exotic fruit notes, linden flowers, and herbal hints on the nose. The Maremma Ciliegiolo Maestrale '23 also makes for a relaxed and pleasurable drink, with a fruity aromatic profile ranging from strawberry to blackberry and pomegranate, and smoky, balsamic accents lending elegance. In the mouth, it's full, juicy, and fragrant.

● Chianti Colli Fiorentini V. di Lappeggi Ris. '21	♛♛ 4
○ Bianco '23	♛ 3
● Bruzzico '21	♛ 5
● Canaiolo '23	♛ 3
● Chianti Colli Fiorentini '22	♛ 2
● Chianti Sup. '22	♛ 3
○ Rosato '23	♛ 3
● Baliatico '19	♛♛ 7
● Bruzzico '19	♛♛ 4
● Canaiolo '22	♛♛ 3
● Chianti Colli Fiorentini '21	♛♛ 2*
● Chianti Colli Fiorentini Ris. '19	♛♛ 4
Chianti Colli Fiorentini Ris. '18	♛♛ 3
Chianti Colli Fiorentini V. di Lappeggi Ris. '20	♛♛ 4
Vin Santo del Chianti '18	♛♛ 4
Vin Santo del Chianti '17	♛♛ 4

● Maremma Toscana Ciliegiolo Maestrale '23	♛♛ 2*
○ Maremma Toscana Vermentino Lucumone '23	♛♛ 2*
● Morellino di Scansano San Giuseppe '21	♛♛ 3
○ Maremma Toscana Vermentino Scalandrino '23	♛ 3
○ Maremma Toscana Vermentino Lucumone '22	♛♛ 2*
○ Maremma Toscana Vermentino Lucumone '21	♛♛ 2*
○ Maremma Toscana Vermentino Lucumone '20	♛♛ 2*
● Morellino di Scansano Le Sentinelle Ris. '17	♛♛ 4

Podere Martoccia

pod. Martoccia, 283
53024 Montalcino [SI]
+39 0577 848540
www.poderemartoccia.it

CELLAR SALES
PRE-BOOKED VISITS
ANNUAL PRODUCTION 85,000 bottles
HECTARES UNDER VINE 15.00
SUSTAINABLE WINERY

The winery, founded by Mauro Brunelli and his wife Anna Savini, has deep roots. Both come from families that have long lived off agriculture in Montalcino, though it wasn't until 1995 that they, along with their son Luca, decided to start producing wines under their own name. Initially they began in Montalcino, where they now manage ten hectares—six of which are classified as brunello—on both the southwest and northwest slopes. Later, they expanded to Montecucco, where they recently acquired a four-hectare vineyard. Martoccia's sangioveses are highly convincing, with a refined style that aptly reflects the region. The youthful Riserva '16 proves close-knit, with magnificent red fruit on the nose accompanied by refined floral and green notes. The palate is full of character, powerful, with fleshy fruit and streamlined tannins; an endless finish. The Rosso di Montalcino '22 is fresh and surprisingly deep, with delightful aromas of tobacco, cherry, brush, and camphor. The palate is long, sapid, and fleshy, with structured, close-knit tannins.

● Brunello di Montalcino Ris. '16	ΨΨ 8
● Rosso di Montalcino '22	ΨΨ 4
● Brunello di Montalcino '19	ΨΨ 6
● Poggio Apricale '23	ΨΨ 3
● Brunello di Montalcino '18	YY 6
● Brunello di Montalcino '17	YY 6
● Brunello di Montalcino '16	YY 6
● Brunello di Montalcino '15	YY 6
● Brunello di Montalcino '14	YY 6
● Brunello di Montalcino Ris. '15	YY 8
● Brunello di Montalcino Ris. '13	YY 7
● Luca '14	YY 6
● Rosso di Montalcino '21	YY 3
● Rosso di Montalcino '20	YY 3

★Masseto

fraz. Bolgheri
57022 Castagneto Carducci [LI]
+39 056571811
www.masseto.com

ANNUAL PRODUCTION 33,000 bottles
HECTARES UNDER VINE 11.00
SUSTAINABLE WINERY

Tenuta Masseto is iconically represented by the winery situated at the heart of a 13-hectare vineyard, historically known for its opulent merlot—a cult wine since its first vintage in 1986 (initially just an experimental 800-bottle batch). The soil's unique blue clays were famously identified by oenologist André Tchelistcheff, who declared it perfect for merlot. In 2017, they introduced Massetino, another merlot embellished with cabernet franc from younger vines. The sumptuous Masseto '21, a monovarietal merlot, sees aromas of ripe red berries join eucalyptus, spices, and floral flashes. The palate is monumental: dense, broad, and vibrant, with an endless finish. The Massetino '22, also made from merlot, is right up there, playing on aromas of dark fruits, balsamic hints, and tobacco. The palate is fleshy and compact, with a solid development where close-knit tannins contain a fragrant, fleshy fruit, finishing rich and pervasive.

● Massetino '22	ΨΨ 8
● Masseto '21	ΨΨ 8
● Masseto '11	YYY 8
● Masseto '09	YYY 8
● Masseto '06	YYY 8
● Masseto '04	YYY 8
● Masseto '01	YYY 8
● Masseto '00	YYY 8
● Masseto '99	YYY 8
● Masseto '98	YYY 8
● Masseto '97	YYY 8
● Masseto '95	YYY 8
● Masseto '94	YYY 8
● Masseto '93	YYY 8
● Massetino '21	YY 8
● Masseto '20	YY 8
● Masseto '19	YY 8

★Mastrojanni

loc. Poderi Loreto e San Pio
fraz. Castelnuovo dell'Abate
53024 Montalcino [SI]
☎ +39 0577835681
✉ www.mastrojanni.com

CELLAR SALES
PRE-BOOKED VISITS
ACCOMMODATION
ANNUAL PRODUCTION 160,000 bottles
HECTARES UNDER VINE 39.00
SUSTAINABLE WINERY

It was back in 1975 when lawyer Gabriele Mastrojanni purchased the San Pio and Loreto estates, along with over 100 hectares of nearly uncultivated land near Castelnuovo dell'Abate, on the southeast slope of Montalcino. It was he who planted the first plots of sangiovese grosso. Then, after nearly half a century, the property changed hands to Francesco Illy, an educated and enlightened businessman (and also owner of Podere Le Ripi in Montalcino). Illy has further enhanced the estate's commitment to producing high-quality wines while fully respecting nature. The Vigna Loreto Brunello '19 is always a sure bet, standing out in this vintage for its compact, sweet nose, a legacy of the harvest—tones of red fruit jam combining with cinchona, and dried flowers, lightened by a touch of aromatic herbs at the end. Tight and compact on the palate, it's quite austere at the moment, particularly in its tannic expression, though a few more years in the bottle should smooth things out. The rest of the range is also of good quality.

● Brunello di Montalcino V. Loreto '19	♥♥ 8
● Brunello di Montalcino '19	♥♥ 8
● Brunello di Montalcino V. Schiena d'Asino '18	♥♥ 8
● Ciliegiolo '21	♥♥ 6
● Rosso di Montalcino '22	♥♥ 5
● Brunello di Montalcino Schiena d'Asino '08	♀♀♀ 8
● Brunello di Montalcino V. Loreto '13	♀♀♀ 7
● Brunello di Montalcino V. Loreto '10	♀♀♀ 7
● Brunello di Montalcino V. Schiena d'Asino '15	♀♀♀ 8
● Brunello di Montalcino V. Schiena d'Asino '12	♀♀♀ 8
● Brunello di Montalcino V. Schiena d'Asino '10	♀♀♀ 8

Máté

loc. Santa Restituta
53024 Montalcino [SI]
☎ +39 0577847215
✉ www.matewine.com

CELLAR SALES
PRE-BOOKED VISITS
ACCOMMODATION
ANNUAL PRODUCTION 25,000 bottles
HECTARES UNDER VINE 6.50
VITICULTURE METHOD Certified Organic

In 1990, internationally renowned author Ferenc Máté and his wife Candice, a painter, moved from chaotic New York to Montalcino. Attracted by the area's beauty, they purchased an old abandoned farmhouse near the Pieve di Santa Restituita and the surrounding land. With neighbors like Gaia and Soldera, it was natural for Ferenc, a few years later, to plant vineyards to produce his own wines. In addition to sangiovese grosso, he also cultivates small plots of merlot, syrah, and cabernet sauvignon. Whether made from sangiovese or not, we found the producer's entire range to be good and reliable. The Brunello '19 reached our finals, with its intense nose of jammy wild berries, tobacco, and spices, while the palate is harmonious and velvety, supported by delicate but elegant tannins. The Brunello Veltha '19 is also noteworthy, with its red fruit and pomegranate aromas on the nose. The palate is minimalist, with well-balanced tannins and acidity, which, combined with fruit, provide excellent structure.

● Brunello di Montalcino '19	♥♥ 8
● Banditone Syrah '21	♥♥ 7
● Brunello di Montalcino Veltha '19	♥♥ 8
● Mania Cabernet Sauvignon '21	♥♥ 7
● Mantus Merlot '21	♥♥ 5
● Banditone Syrah '16	♀♀ 7
● Brunello di Montalcino '17	♀♀ 6
● Brunello di Montalcino '16	♀♀ 6
● Brunello di Montalcino '15	♀♀ 6
● Brunello di Montalcino '13	♀♀ 6
● Brunello di Montalcino '11	♀♀ 6
● Brunello di Montalcino Ris. '16	♀♀ 7
● Brunello di Montalcino Ris. '15	♀♀ 7
● Marinaia '16	♀♀ 6
● Rosso di Montalcino '15	♀♀ 3
● Rosso di Montalcino '14	♀♀ 3

Melini
Vigneti La Selvanella
loc. Gaggiano
53036 Poggibonsi [SI]
📞 +39 0577998511
🌐 www.cantinemelini.it

CELLAR SALES
PRE-BOOKED VISITS
ANNUAL PRODUCTION 1,500,000 bottles
HECTARES UNDER VINE 86.00

Poggibonsi's Melini represent the Gruppo Italiano Vini in the Chianti Classico appellation. Indeed, the history of the Poggibonsi-based brand mirrors that of Chianti Classico itself. In 1860, Laborel Melini was the first to adopt the durable "strapeso" bottle, which resisted the pressure of machine-applied corks and contributed significantly to Chianti's global success. One of the best recent versions is the Chianti Classico Riserva 2020 from Vigneti La Selvanella. It offers up smoky and fruity aromas, while in the mouth, the wine is lively and flavorful, thanks to a dynamic acidity and crunchy tannins, which also mark its multifaceted finish. The Chianti Classico Granaio '22 is enjoyable—fragrant and ready to be uncorked. The Bonorli '22, a blend of cabernet sauvignon, merlot, and sangiovese, has a smooth and easy-drinking palate.

Le Miccine
loc. Le Miccine
s.s. Traversa Chiantigiana
53013 Gaiole in Chianti [SI]
📞 +39 0577749526
🌐 www.lemiccine.com

CELLAR SALES
PRE-BOOKED VISITS
ACCOMMODATION
ANNUAL PRODUCTION 25,000 bottles
HECTARES UNDER VINE 7.00
VITICULTURE METHOD Certified Organic

Alle Miccine cultivates certified organic sangiovese, primarily, alongside smaller quantities of malvasia nera, merlot, colorino, and vermentino. Paula Papini Cook leads this small producer in Gaiole in Chianti, crafting wines that reflect the local terroir with aromatic precision and an elegant progression of flavor, utilizing tonneaux and large wood barrels for aging. The Chianti Classico '22 stands out for its elegance, with its clean aromas leaning toward a delicate floral character. On the palate, the wine is subtle, very long, with a pleasantly spirited finish. The Chianti Classico Riserva '21 is equally well-crafted, with a tapering, flavorful development and fresh, focused aromas. The fleshy and firm Chianti Classico Gran Selezione '20 is more intense and structured.

● Chianti Cl. Vign. La Selvanella Ris. '20	♛♛♛ 5
● Bonorli '22	♛♛ 2*
● Chianti Cl. Granaio '22	♛♛ 3
● Chianti Cl. La Selvanella Ris. '06	♕♕♕ 5
● Chianti Cl. La Selvanella Ris. '03	♕♕♕ 4
● Chianti Cl. La Selvanella Ris. '01	♕♕♕ 4
● Chianti Cl. La Selvanella Ris. '00	♕♕♕ 4
● Chianti Cl. La Selvanella Ris. '99	♕♕♕ 5
● Chianti Cl. La Selvanella Ris. '90	♕♕♕ 3*
● Chianti Cl. La Selvanella Ris. '86	♕♕♕ 4*
● Chianti Cl. Granaio '21	♕♕ 3*
● Chianti Cl. Granaio '19	♕♕ 2*
● Chianti Cl. Granaio '17	♕♕ 3*
● Chianti Cl. Machiavelli Solatìo del Tani '16	♕♕ 4
● Chianti Cl. Vign. La Selvanella Ris. '19	♕♕ 5
● Chianti Cl. Vign. La Selvanella Ris. '18	♕♕ 5

● Chianti Cl. '22	♛♛♛ 4
● Chianti Cl. Gran Selezione '20	♛♛ 6
● Chianti Cl. Ris. '21	♛♛ 5
● Chianti Cl. '16	♕♕♕ 4
● Chianti Cl. '15	♕♕♕ 4
● Chianti Cl. Ris. '10	♕♕♕ 5
● Cardus '19	♕♕ 5
● Chianti Cl. '21	♕♕ 4
● Chianti Cl. '17	♕♕ 4
● Chianti Cl. Gran Selezione '19	♕♕ 6
● Chianti Cl. Gran Selezione '17	♕♕ 4
● Chianti Cl. Ris. '20	♕♕ 5
● Chianti Cl. Ris. '19	♕♕ 5
● Chianti Cl. Ris. '17	♕♕ 5
● Chianti Cl. Ris. '16	♕♕ 5

Il Molinaccio di Montepulciano

loc. Cervognano
via Antica Chiusina, 12
53045 Montepulciano [SI]
📞 +39 3332300170
✉ www.ilmolinaccio.com

CELLAR SALES
PRE-BOOKED VISITS
ACCOMMODATION AND RESTAURANT SERVICE
ANNUAL PRODUCTION 12,000 bottles
HECTARES UNDER VINE 4.10
VITICULTURE METHOD Certified Organic
SUSTAINABLE WINERY

Founded in 2012 by Alessandro Sartini and Marco Malavasi, this small winery is set in an ancient mill known as "Molinaccio" on old Grand Duchy maps. The vineyard, managed organically, primarily features sangiovese with a small amount of merlot. Their wines exhibit a clear, successful style that emphasizes finesse over power, aligning with a modern interpretation of sangiovese. In addition to wine-growing, the estate provides guest accommodations. The Nobile La Spinosa '21 is precise and measured in its aromas, with spicy and floral tones interpenetrating in a beautiful chiaroscuro. On the palate, the wine is sapid, unfolding in a steady, rhythmic manner, always well-balanced, finishing on a fragrant fruity note. More vibrant in its aromas, with some smoky accents slowing its fruity flow, the Nobile La Poiana Riserva '20 offers a pleasantly sweet and broad palate with a solid, spicy finish.

La Montanina

loc. Monti in Chianti, 25
53020 Gaiole in Chianti [SI]
📞 +39 0577280074
✉ www.aziendaagricolalamontanina.it

CELLAR SALES
PRE-BOOKED VISITS
ACCOMMODATION
ANNUAL PRODUCTION 60,000 bottles
HECTARES UNDER VINE 12.00

Situated at the southern edge of Gaiole, near Castelnuovo Berardenga, Bruno Mazzuoli's oenological project in Monti in Chianti captures the essential traits of the appellation's wines. Yet his meticulous focus on the grapes and the use of large wood barrels for aging yields a style of sangiovese that harmonizes the primary characteristics of both terroirs, making for notable acidity and full structure. The Chianti Classico '22 is an forthright, immediately pleasant wine, with a smooth and well-paced flavor profile accompanied by aromas of ripe cherries and whiffs of wild herbs. The Nebbiano '21, a monovarietal sangiovese, faithfully expresses the grape's signature traits, combining lush and fragrant fruity aromas with a flavorful, spirited, and well-proportioned palate. We also appreciated the Chianti Classico Riserva '21.

● Nobile di Montepulciano La Spinosa '21	▼▼ 5
● Nobile di Montepulciano La Poiana Ris. '20	▼▼ 6
● Rosso di Montepulciano Il Golo Decennale '22	▼▼ 3
● Nobile di Montepulciano '13	♀♀ 4
● Nobile di Montepulciano '12	♀♀ 4
● Nobile di Montepulciano La Poiana Ris. '19	♀♀ 6
● Nobile di Montepulciano La Spinosa '20	♀♀ 5
● Nobile di Montepulciano La Spinosa '19	♀♀ 5
● Nobile di Montepulciano La Spinosa '17	♀♀ 5
● Rosso di Montepulciano Il Golo '22	♀♀ 3
● Rosso di Montepulciano Il Golo '21	♀♀ 3

● Chianti Cl. '22	▼▼ 3*
● Nebbiano '21	▼▼ 3*
● Chianti Cl. Ris. '21	▼▼ 4
● Agosto di Monti '16	♀♀ 3
● Chianti Cl. '21	♀♀ 3
● Chianti Cl. '20	♀♀ 3*
● Chianti Cl. '18	♀♀ 3
● Chianti Cl. '16	♀♀ 3*
● Chianti Cl. '15	♀♀ 3*
● Chianti Cl. Ris. '20	♀♀ 4
● Nebbiano '20	♀♀ 3
● Nebbiano '19	♀♀ 3
● Nebbiano '18	♀♀ 3
● Nebbiano '16	♀♀ 3
● Piallungo Ciliegiolo '22	♀♀ 3
● Piallungo Ciliegiolo '21	♀♀ 2*

Montauto

loc. Campigliola, Km 10
58014 Manciano [GR]
📞 +39 3383833928
🌐 www.montauto.org

CELLAR SALES
PRE-BOOKED VISITS
ACCOMMODATION
ANNUAL PRODUCTION 70,000 bottles
HECTARES UNDER VINE 11.00

Sitated near Manciano, Montauto represents a
different kind of Maremma, one where the vines
are further inland and the climate tends to be
warmer. While not diametrically opposed, the
pedoclimate and soil types make it a unique
growing area within the district. Riccardo Lepri
was ahead of the curb in championing sauvignon
and pinot noir here, alongside vermentino and
ciliegiolo, aiming for a balanced, refined, drinkable
style. For proof, seek out the Poggio del Crine in
our "Rare Wines" section. Here, we present the
Sauvignon Enos I '23, a white with rich varietal
aromas of citrus, elderflower, and gooseberry.
On the palate, it's decidedly taut, driven by
acidity; it has structure but remains slender and
remarkably persistent. The Gessaia '23 opts for
more biting, vegetal notes, while the 2022 Pinot
Nero tasted is decidedly fruity, smooth, and
captivating. The intensely fruity Ciliegiolo
Silio '22 is also excellent.

Monte Solaio

via di Venturina, 17
57021 Campiglia Marittima [LI]
📞 +39 0565843291
🌐 www.montesolaio.com

CELLAR SALES
PRE-BOOKED VISITS
ACCOMMODATION AND RESTAURANT SERVICE
ANNUAL PRODUCTION 50,000 bottles
HECTARES UNDER VINE 10.00

Based in Campiglia Marittima, Livorno, Monte
Solaio was transformed from a 17th-century
building into a resort and winery by Claudio
Guglielmucci in the early aughts. The vineyards
primarily host viognier, vermentino, ansonica,
cabernet franc, merlot, cabernet sauvignon,
petit verdot, and syrah. The wines are mainly
aged in stainless steel and barriques. The
Sassin'Oro '20, a monovarietal syrah, delivers a
nicely proportioned, sapid, deep, and visceral
palate. On the nose, it reveals spicy aromas with
smoky accents and whiffs of Mediterranean
scrub. More concentrated and still developing,
the Re del Castello '20 (100% merlot) stands
out for its rich aromatic contrasts. The white
Boccasanta '23, a blend of vermentino and
ansonica, has a flavorful and persistent palate,
with a solid overall structure.

○ Maremma Toscana Sauvignon Enos I V.V. '23	♟♟ 5
○ Maremma Toscana Sauvignon Gessaia '23	♟♟ 4
● Pinot Nero '22	♟♟ 5
● Silio Ciliegiolo '22	♟♟ 4
○ Maremma Toscana Vermentino '23	♟ 3
● Maremma Toscana Ciliegiolo Silio '21	♟♟ 4
○ Maremma Toscana Sauvignon Enos I '21	♟♟ 5
○ Maremma Toscana Sauvignon Gessaia '22	♟♟ 4
○ Maremma Toscana Sauvignon Gessaia '21	♟♟ 4
● Pinot Nero '21	♟♟ 5
● Pinot Nero '19	♟♟ 5
● Pinot Nero '18	♟♟ 5

● Sassin'Oro '20	♟♟ 6
○ Boccasanta '23	♟ 3
● Collevato '20	♟ 5
● Re del Castello '20	♟ 7
⊙ Sarosa '23	♟ 3
○ Allegro '22	♟♟ 3
● Collevato '19	♟♟ 5
● Collevato '19	♟♟ 5
● Re del Castello '18	♟♟ 7
● Sacrestano '22	♟♟ 3
● Sassin'Oro '19	♟♟ 5
● Sassin'Oro '19	♟♟ 5
● Tino Rosso '21	♟♟ 3
● Tino Rosso '19	♟♟ 3

Fattoria Montellori

via Pistoiese, I
50054 Fucecchio [FI]
☎ +39 0571260641
✉ www.fattoriamontellori.it

CELLAR SALES
PRE-BOOKED VISITS
ACCOMMODATION AND RESTAURANT SERVICE
ANNUAL PRODUCTION 250,000 bottles
HECTARES UNDER VINE 51.00
SUSTAINABLE WINERY

This year, Fattoria Montellori will celebrate its 130th anniversary, marking four generations of producers from founder Giuseppe Nieri to its current leader, Alessandro Nieri. Each generation has maintained a passion for quality, crafting wines with personality and character that highlight the attributes of the territory. The vineyards are divided into two areas: in Cerreto Guidi, Podere il Moro spans 12 hectares and Podere Montauto 14 hectares (both on calcareous clay soils); in San Miniato, Podere Le Caselle features hillside vineyards on clay soils. The two vintages of the Metodo Classico Pas Dosé sparkling wine, both made from chardonnay, prove particularly interesting: the 2020 reveals a fine and persistent bead, with aromas of pastry, bread crust, helichrysum, and peach rising from the glass, then a fresh, juicy, and taut palate. The Riserva '18 is more pervasive and creamy, with notes of citrus peel, almond, hazelnut, and white melon, and a dynamic palate with a citrusy finish. The Trebbiano '22 is delicious, with its grapefruit and citron notes and a fresh, juicy palate.

○ Montellori Pas Dosé M. Cl. '20	♟♟ 5
○ Montellori Pas Dosé M. Cl. Ris. '18	♟♟ 7
● Dicatum '20	♟ 5
● Salamartano '20	♟ 8
○ Trebbiano '22	♟ 2
Bianco dell'Empolese Vin Santo '16	♟♟ 5
● Chianti Sup. Caselle '19	♟♟ 3
● Dicatum '18	♟♟ 5
○ Mandorlo '20	♟♟ 2*
○ Montellori Pas Dosé '16	♟♟ 5
○ Montellori Pas Dosé M. Cl. '17	♟♟ 5
○ Montellori Pas Dosé M. Cl. Ris. '16	♟♟ 7
● Salamartano '19	♟♟ 8
● Salamartano '18	♟♟ 6
● Salamartano '17	♟♟ 6
○ Viti di Sessant'anni Trebbiano '20	♟♟ 2*

★Montenidoli

loc. Montenidoli
53037 San Gimignano [SI]
☎ +39 0577941565
✉ www.montenidoli.com

CELLAR SALES
ACCOMMODATION
ANNUAL PRODUCTION 100,000 bottles
HECTARES UNDER VINE 24.00
VITICULTURE METHOD Certified Organic

Elisabetta Fagiuoli stands out in the world of Italian wine for her extraordinary dedication, which has allowed the producer to craft a range of genuine and highly consistent wines. Fagiuoli's work is characterized by strict adherence to traditional methods, without making overtures to the market or taking shortcuts that could compromise the quality of the final product. We can safely say that without her efforts, and Montenidoli's splendid wines, Vernaccia di San Gimignano wouldn't be what it is today. The Vernaccia di San Gimignano Carato '21—whose name was suggested by Luigi Veronelli to emphasize both its connection to the tradition of Tuscan "caratelli" (110-litre barrels) and its status as a precious wine (carato means karat in Italian)—reveals a floral and iodine-laden aromatic profile with light touches of spice. The palate is close-knit, creamy, and guided by a pleasant bitter vein that closes on notes of amaretto. The Vernaccia di San Gimignano Fiore '22 doesn't disappoint, with its fleshy palate and aromas of broom, apple, and cider.

○ Vernaccia di San Gimignano Carato '21	♟♟ 6
○ Vernaccia di San Gimignano Fiore '22	♟♟ 5
○ Il Templare '20	♟ 5
○ Vernaccia di San Gimignano Tradizionale '22	♟ 3
○ Vernaccia di San Gimignano Carato '20	♟♟ 6
○ Vernaccia di San Gimignano Carato '19	♟♟ 6
○ Vernaccia di San Gimignano Carato '18	♟♟ 6
○ Vernaccia di San Gimignano Carato '17	♟♟ 4*
○ Vernaccia di San Gimignano Carato '16	♟♟ 4*
○ Vernaccia di San Gimignano Carato '13	♟♟ 4*
○ Vernaccia di San Gimignano Carato '12	♟♟ 4*
○ Vernaccia di San Gimignano Tradizionale '15	♟♟ 2*
○ Vernaccia di San Gimignano Tradizionale '12	♟♟ 2*

Monteraponi

loc. Monteraponi
53017 Radda in Chianti [SI]
📞 +39 0577738208
🌐 www.monteraponi.it

CELLAR SALES
PRE-BOOKED VISITS
ACCOMMODATION
ANNUAL PRODUCTION 50,000 bottles
HECTARES UNDER VINE 10.00
VITICULTURE METHOD Certified Organic

Michele Braganti took over his family's winery in the late 1990s, making a name for himself with his first Chianti Classico, released in the 2003 vintage. The wine was born from choices that were unconventional at the time—traditional grape varieties, the use of concrete tanks and large wood barrels—in an era dominated by international grape varieties and barriques. Today, those choices have proven successful, embodying a stylistic continuity rooted in the "classic" character of great wine terroirs, which reveals itself only to those willing to seek it out. The Baron'Ugo '20, a monovarietal sangiovese, impresses with its nuanced, smoky aromas, conjuring up flowers, pine needles, and aromatic herbs. On the palate, its progression is pressing: rich in contrast, broad, and sapid, with a refined tannic texture. The juicy and fragrant Chianti Classico Il Campitello Riserva '21 proves focused, with its firm and crunchy tannic structure. The Chianti Classico '22 has nice energy—it's a lively, fragrant, and invigorating pour.

● Baron'Ugo '20	♟♟♟ 8
● Chianti Cl. Il Campitello Ris. '21	♟♟♟ 8
● Chianti Cl. '22	♟♟♟ 5
● Baron'Ugo '16	♟♟♟ 5
● Baron'Ugo '13	♟♟♟ 5
● Baron'Ugo '12	♟♟♟ 8
● Chianti Cl. Baron'Ugo Ris. '10	♟♟♟ 7
● Chianti Cl. Baron'Ugo Ris. '09	♟♟♟ 7
● Chianti Cl. Baron'Ugo Ris. '07	♟♟♟ 5
● Chianti Cl. Il Campitello Ris. '20	♟♟♟ 8
● Chianti Cl. Il Campitello Ris. '16	♟♟♟ 7
● Chianti Cl. Il Campitello Ris. '15	♟♟♟ 7
● Baron'Ugo '18	♟♟ 8
● Baron'Ugo '17	♟♟ 8
● Chianti Cl. '21	♟♟ 5
● Chianti Cl. '20	♟♟ 4
● Chianti Cl. Il Campitello Ris. '18	♟♟ 7

Monterò

loc. Colle Lupo
58051 Magliano in Toscana [GR]
📞 +39 3396024802
🌐 www.monterò.com

CELLAR SALES
PRE-BOOKED VISITS
ANNUAL PRODUCTION 25,000 bottles
HECTARES UNDER VINE 10.00
VITICULTURE METHOD Certified Organic
SUSTAINABLE WINERY

In 2010, Milena Cacurri and her husband Antonio Salerno established this beautiful winery among the hills of Maremma. Monterò spans over 50 hectares in Magliano in Tuscany and cultivates its ten hectares of vineyards organically (though they're now transitioning to biodynamic practices). In the state-of-the-art cellar, you'll find concrete tanks, ceramic eggs, clayver amphorae, and French oak barrels—all designed to best express the unique characteristics of this terroir, which is particularly well suited to the cultivation of grapes and olives. This year's tastings included a brilliant Morellino di Scansano '22. It reached our finals thanks to its slim and multi-layered body, with aromas of ripe cherries and wild berries combining with Mediterranean and minty fragrances. On the palate, it's dynamic and taut, rich in soft tannins, fruit, and persistence. The Syrah Mammeglio '21 proves rich in fruit pulp, with nuances of tobacco meeting chocolate and spices, finishing long and pervasive. The Linvisibile '19 is a mature white characterized by depth, complexity, and minerality.

● Morellino di Scansano More '22	♟♟ 4
○ Maremma Toscana Bianco Linvisibile '19	♟♟ 7
● Maremma Toscana Rosso Mammeglio '21	♟♟ 4
○ Maremma Toscana Bianco Linvisibile '18	♟♟ 7
○ Maremma Toscana Bianco Linvisibile '17	♟♟ 6
● Maremma Toscana Syrah Mammeglio '19	♟♟ 3*
○ Maremma Toscana Vermentino '20	♟♟ 4
○ Maremma Toscana Vermentino '19	♟♟ 4
● Morellino di Scansano More '19	♟♟ 4
● Morellino di Scansano More '18	♟♟ 4
● Morellino di Scansano More '16	♟♟ 4
● Quercia del Serpente '17	♟♟ 8

MonteRosola

loc. Pignano
pod. La Rosola
56048 Volterra [PI]
☎ +39 058835062
✉ www.monterosola.com

ANNUAL PRODUCTION 20,000 bottles
HECTARES UNDER VINE 63.00
VITICULTURE METHOD Certified Organic

The Thomaeus family, originally from Sweden, developed a passion for Italian culture and wine, which led them to acquire Monterosola in 2013. The family then began reviving the vineyards and renovating the cellar, focusing on sustainability and respect for the environment. Located near the medieval town of Volterra, the estate now boasts 25 ha of vineyards on a hill overlooking the coast, perched above two wooded valleys and kissed by a constant sea breeze. The new and impressive winery, completed in 2019, features five floors, including a terrace, tasting room, and wine shop. All the wines submitted stand out for their personality and character. The Crescendo '21, made from sangiovese, offers up aromas of rhubarb, chinotto, blood orange, forest floor, and licorice root, with a dynamic, silky, and pervasive palate. The Indomito '21, a blend of syrah and cabernet sauvignon, delivers notes of plum, black damson and cherry, with a flavorful and balanced palate. The Primo Passo '22, a blend of grechetto, manzoni bianco, and viognier, is juicy and approachable, with fragrant notes of citron and grapefruit.

● Crescendo '21	♟♟ 5
● Indomito '21	♟♟ 8
● Canto della Civetta '21	♟ 8
● Per Terras '21	♟ 8
○ Primo Passo '22	♟ 5
● Canto della Civetta '19	♟♟ 8
● Corpo Notte '20	♟♟ 6
● Corpo Notte '19	♟♟ 6
● Crescendo '20	♟♟ 5
● Crescendo '19	♟♟ 5
● Indomito '20	♟♟ 8
● Indomito '19	♟♟ 8
● Indomito '18	♟♟ 4
● Per Terras '20	♟♟ 8
● Per Terras '19	♟♟ 8
○ Primo Passo '20	♟♟ 5

Tenuta Monteti

s.da della Sgrilla, 6
58011 Capalbio [GR]
☎ +39 0564896160
✉ www.tenutamonteti.it

CELLAR SALES
PRE-BOOKED VISITS
ANNUAL PRODUCTION 130,000 bottles
HECTARES UNDER VINE 28.00
SUSTAINABLE WINERY

Owned the Baratta family, Tenuta Monteti is located near Capalbio, in the southernmost part of Maremma wine country. In 1998, Paolo Baratta and his wife Gemma founded the estate, and in 2004 the first bottles hit the market. Since 2010, their daughter Eva and her husband Javier Pedrazzini have been leading the estate. The varietals cultivated include petit verdot, cabernet franc, cabernet sauvignon, merlot, and alicante bouschet, with the wines aging in small oak barrels. The Caburnio '20, a blend of cabernet sauvignon, alicante bouschet, and merlot, unveils aromas of aromatic herbs, ripe red fruits, and spices. On the palate, it's crisp, with a sapid development and a focused finish. The Tenuta Monteti '20, a blend of petit verdot, cabernet sauvignon, and cabernet franc, explores aromas of blueberries and raspberries, with whiffs of cinnamon and toasted hints, finishing on a pleasant balsamic note. In the mouth, its progression is powerful, sustained, and compact, with a pervasive finish.

● Caburnio '20	♟♟ 5
● Monteti '20	♟♟ 7
⊙ TM Rosé '23	♟ 4
● Caburnio '17	♟♟♟ 4*
● Caburnio '15	♟♟♟ 4*
● Caburnio '14	♟♟♟ 3*
● Monteti '19	♟♟♟ 7
● Monteti '18	♟♟♟ 7
● Monteti '16	♟♟♟ 6
● Caburnio '19	♟♟ 5
● Caburnio '18	♟♟ 5
● Caburnio '16	♟♟ 4
● Monteti '17	♟♟ 6
● Monteti '15	♟♟ 6
● Monteti '13	♟♟ 6

TUSCANY

Monteverro

s.da Aurelia Capalbio, 11
58011 Capalbio [GR]
☎ +39 0564890721
🌐 www.monteverro.com

★★Montevertine

loc. Montevertine
53017 Radda in Chianti [SI]
☎ +39 0577738009
🌐 www.montevertine.it

CELLAR SALES
PRE-BOOKED VISITS
ANNUAL PRODUCTION 200,000 bottles
HECTARES UNDER VINE 40.00
VITICULTURE METHOD Certified Organic
SUSTAINABLE WINERY

PRE-BOOKED VISITS
ANNUAL PRODUCTION 85,000 bottles
HECTARES UNDER VINE 20.00

Owned by the German Weber family, Monteverro was established in 2003. The name is inspired by "verro," the local word for wild boar (specifically the male), the unchallenged king of the area's animals. In the estate's vineyards, located between Capalbio and the sea, they cultivate cabernet sauvignon, cabernet franc, merlot, syrah, grenache, petit verdot, sangiovese, chardonnay, and vermentino. The wines are generously aged in small oak barrels. The Tinata '21, a blend of syrah and grenache, reveals aromas of blueberries and strawberries on a spicy base. On the palate, it opens soft and finishes with smoky tones. The Monteverro '21, a blend of cabernet franc, cabernet sauvignon, merlot, and petit verdot, boasts aromas of ripe red fruits with balsamic and toasty hints. In the mouth it's warm and juicy, finishing with an encore of charred oak. The Terra di Monteverro '21, another blend of cabernet franc, cabernet sauvignon, merlot, and petit verdot, is quite ripe.

Universally recognized as the most accomplished and representative producer of Chianti sangiovese, at Montevertine, wines continue to emerge with unwavering consistency. Theirs is a range known for its elegant aromas, great contrast in taste, absolute freshness, and sophisticated drinkability, long serving as a stylistic model for many producers. Martino Manetti's estate is located in the hills of Radda in Chianti, and wine maturation involves a mix of concrete, small wood barrels, and large wood casks. The Montevertine '21, a blend of sangiovese, canaiolo, and colorino, once again puts in a first-rate performance. The vintage makes for a wine with highly expressive aromas, ranging from floral hints to small red fruits and flintstone, with smoky nuances. On the palate, it's fleshy, dynamic, and multifaceted. The Pergole Torte '21, a monovarietal sangiovese, exhibits a slower overall dynamic, needing more time to fully evolve.

● Monteverro '21	♈♈	8
● Tinata '21	♈	8
○ Monteverro Chardonnay '21	♈	8
● Terra di Monteverro '21	♈	7
● Monteverro '18	♔♔♔	8
● Monteverro '20	♔♔	8
● Monteverro '19	♔♔	8
● Monteverro '17	♔♔	8
○ Monteverro Chardonnay '20	♔♔	8
○ Monteverro Chardonnay '19	♔♔	8
○ Monteverro Chardonnay '18	♔♔	8
● Terra di Monteverro '20	♔♔	7
● Terra di Monteverro '19	♔♔	7
● Terra di Monteverro '18	♔♔	7
● Tinata '20	♔♔	8
● Tinata '19	♔♔	8

● Montevertine '21	♈♈♈	8
● Le Pergole Torte '21	♈♈	8
● Pian del Ciampolo '22	♈♈	5
● Le Pergole Torte '20	♔♔♔	8
● Le Pergole Torte '17	♔♔♔	8
● Le Pergole Torte '16	♔♔♔	8
● Le Pergole Torte '15	♔♔♔	8
● Le Pergole Torte '13	♔♔♔	8
● Le Pergole Torte '12	♔♔♔	8
● Le Pergole Torte '11	♔♔♔	8
● Le Pergole Torte '10	♔♔♔	8
● Le Pergole Torte '09	♔♔♔	8
● Le Pergole Torte '07	♔♔♔	8
● Le Pergole Torte '04	♔♔♔	8
● Montevertine '19	♔♔♔	6
● Montevertine '18	♔♔♔	6
● Montevertine '14	♔♔♔	6

Morisfarms

loc. Cura Nuova
Fattoria Poggetti
58024 Massa Marittima [GR]
📞 +39 0566919135
🌐 www.morisfarms.it

CELLAR SALES
PRE-BOOKED VISITS
ACCOMMODATION
ANNUAL PRODUCTION 300,000 bottles
HECTARES UNDER VINE 72.00

Morisfarms helped put southern Tuscany on the map as one of the region's most significant terroirs. Today, the estate is managed by Ranieri Moris and Giulio Parentini, with over 70 hectares under vines spread our across two estates in the provinces of Massa Marittima and Grosseto. Fattoria Poggetti is situated in the Monteregio area, while Poggio la Mozza lies in the Morellino di Scansano production zone. The winery's style is distinctive and full of character. Everyone could agree that the standout is the Riserva di Morellino '20. This Mediterranean-style red offers up aromas of myrtle, spices, floral notes, and noble resins. The palate is smooth and pervasive, with warmth, yet it retains freshness and sapidity. The Mandriolo, a sangiovese blended with international grapes, is simple yet delicious and easy to drink. The Avvoltore, the estate's flagship wine (75% sangiovese accompanied by cabernet sauvignon and syrah), also caught our attention.

Mormoraia

loc. Sant'Andrea, 15
53037 San Gimignano [SI]
📞 +39 0577940096
🌐 www.mormoraia.it

CELLAR SALES
PRE-BOOKED VISITS
ACCOMMODATION AND RESTAURANT SERVICE
ANNUAL PRODUCTION 120,000 bottles
HECTARES UNDER VINE 40.00
VITICULTURE METHOD Certified Organic

Pino Passoni purchased the old former convent of Mormoraia in 1980 and embarked on an oenological journey over the next decade, renovating the vineyards and building the estate's winery, from which his first Vernaccia wines, destined for domestic and international markets, emerged. In 2012, his son Alessandro took over Mormoraia, which boasts a diverse portfolio, including a nice selection of reds to accompany their whites. The Vernaccia di San Gimignano Antalis Ris. '21 put in a solid and convincing performance, with floral aromas of jasmine and broom rising from the glass alongside tropical fruit. On the palate, warm spicy notes and vanilla sweetness from oak marry with a smoky finish, enhancing its persistence. The Vernaccia di San Gimignano Ostrea '22, which opts for a more vegetal and balsamic profile, is marked by a structured and flavorful progression, with barley candy notes accentuating a finish on toasted almond sensations.

● Morellino di Scansano Ris. '20	♟♟ 5
● Avvoltore '19	♟♟ 6
● Maremma Toscana Rosso Mandriolo '23	♟♟ 2*
● Morellino di Scansano '22	♟ 3
● Avvoltore '06	♟♟♟ 5
● Avvoltore '04	♟♟♟ 5
● Avvoltore '01	♟♟♟ 5
● Avvoltore '00	♟♟♟ 5
● Avvoltore '16	♟♟ 6
● Avvoltore '15	♟♟ 6
● Maremma Toscana Rosso Mandriolo '20	♟♟ 2*
● Maremma Toscana Rosso Mandriolo '18	♟♟ 2*
○ Maremma Toscana Vermentino '21	♟♟ 2*
● Morellino di Scansano '19	♟♟ 2*
● Morellino di Scansano Ris. '16	♟♟ 4

○ Vernaccia di San Gimignano Antalis Ris. '21	♟♟ 4
○ Vernaccia di San Gimignano Ostrea '22	♟♟ 3
● Chianti Colli Senesi Trochus Ris. '20	♟ 5
○ Vernaccia di San Gimignano Suavis '23	♟ 3
○ Vernaccia di San Gimignano E' ReZet Mattia Barzaghi '11	♟♟♟ 3*
○ Vernaccia di San Gimignano Ostrea '17	♟♟♟ 3*
○ Opus '21	♟♟ 6
○ Vernaccia di San Gimignano Antalis Ris. '20	♟♟ 4
○ Vernaccia di San Gimignano Antalis Ris. '19	♟♟ 3*
○ Vernaccia di San Gimignano Antalis Ris. '17	♟♟ 3*
○ Vernaccia di San Gimignano Suavis '20	♟♟ 3*

Fabio Motta

Vigna al Cavaliere, 61
57022 Castagneto Carducci [LI]
☏ +39 0565773041
✉ www.mottafabio.it

CELLAR SALES
PRE-BOOKED VISITS
ANNUAL PRODUCTION 23,000 bottles
HECTARES UNDER VINE 6.50

Drawing on experience gained in his father-in-law Michele Satta's winery, Fabio Motta became a winemaker in his own right in 2010, starting with a rented four-hectare vineyard called Le Pievi. His wines, notable for their balance and finesse, are marked by a stylistic coherence with the local area but with a distinct character, making them a "novum" and propelling the agronomist from Brianza into the ranks of Bolgheri's most promising new producers. The Bolgheri Superiore Le Gonnare '21 reveals aromas of black fruits and eucalyptus, with smoky hints. On the palate, it's juicy with compact tannins, leading to a lively development that finishes on fruit again. The Lo Scudiere '21, a monovarietal sangiovese, shines with its supple drinkability. Its aromatic profile is fragrant and well-defined, with touches of Mediterranean herbs. The Bolgheri Rosso Pievi '22, with its slender profile, proves flavorful and enjoyable. The iodized and brackish Le Gonnare '23, made from vermentino, is also notable.

● Bolgheri Rosso Sup. Le Gonnare '21	♟♟8
● Lo Scudiere '21	♟♟5
● Bolgheri Rosso Pievi '22	♟4
○ Le Gonnare Vermentino '23	♟4
● Bolgheri Rosso Sup. Le Gonnare '20	♟♟♟8
● Bolgheri Rosso Sup. Le Gonnare '17	♟♟♟8
● Bolgheri Rosso Sup. Le Gonnare '16	♟♟♟8
● Bolgheri Rosso Sup. Le Gonnare '15	♟♟♟8
● Bolgheri Sup. Le Gonnare '13	♟♟♟8
○ Bolgheri Bianco Nova '19	♟♟4
● Bolgheri Rosso Pievi '21	♟♟4
● Bolgheri Rosso Pievi '19	♟♟4
● Bolgheri Rosso Sup. Le Gonnare '19	♟♟8
● Bolgheri Rosso Sup. Le Gonnare '18	♟♟8
○ Le Gonnare Vermentino '22	♟♟4
● Lo Scudiere '19	♟♟5

Muralia

loc. Il Poggiarello
fraz. Sticciano
via del Sughereto
58036 Roccastrada [GR]
☏ +39 0564577223
✉ www.muralia.it

CELLAR SALES
PRE-BOOKED VISITS
ACCOMMODATION AND RESTAURANT SERVICE
ANNUAL PRODUCTION 65,000 bottles
HECTARES UNDER VINE 14.00
VITICULTURE METHOD Certified Organic
SUSTAINABLE WINERY

The name Muralia refers to the stone wall at the entrance of the cellar, with the company logo representing a stylized hand, the first tool of human labor. Since the the early aughts, Muralia has been producing well-profiled and pleasant wines characterized by a Mediterranean character. The estate is owned by the Milanese couple Stefano and Chiara Casali, who arrived in Maremma from other experiences, completely renovating a property purchased in the 1950s by Chiara's grandfather. The Manolibera '22, a blend of sangiovese, cabernet sauvignon, and merlot, opens with aromas of small red fruits and pepper, leading to a dynamic, flavorful, and pleasantly spicy palate. The Muralia '21, a blend of syrah, cabernet sauvignon, and sangiovese, explores aromas of ripe red fruits alongside toasted and smoky hints. On the palate, it's full and intense, with a multifaceted tannic structure and a persistent finish on fruity and oaky tones.

● Manolibera '22	♟♟3
● Muralia '21	♟♟5
● Maremma Toscana Rosso Babone '21	♟3
○ Maremma Toscana Viognier Chiaraluna '23	♟4
● Manolibera '19	♟♟3*
● Maremma Toscana Babone '17	♟♟3
● Maremma Toscana Sangiovese Altana '19	♟♟3
● Maremma Toscana Sangiovese Altana '18	♟♟3
○ Maremma Toscana Vermentino Chiaraluna '21	♟♟4
○ Maremma Toscana Viognier Chiaraluna '19	♟♟4

Tenute Silvio Nardi

loc. Casale del Bosco
53024 Montalcino [SI]
☎ +39 0577808269
🌐 www.tenutenardi.com

CELLAR SALES
PRE-BOOKED VISITS
ANNUAL PRODUCTION 250,000 bottles
HECTARES UNDER VINE 80.00

Emilia Nardi's winery is one of the largest in Montalcino, at least in terms of Brunello vineyards. The two estates are divided into eight separate plots. Five vineyards (Casale, Cerralti, Sassi, Oria, and Grancia) are located in the western part of the appellation, at Casale del Bosco, where the wines are more nuanced and elegant. On the eastern side, the second property's three vineyards (Manachiara, Colombaiolo, and Pinzale) produce wines that are richer and more full-bodied. There's no star performer, but the line of 2019 Brunellos presented proves highly reliable. The Poggio Doria '19 impresses with its intense nose of lovely black fruit, thea rose, and tobacco, all on a lovely base of sweet spices. Complex and modern, yet with great typicity on the palate, it's a powerful drink—flesh and tannins stand out, yet they're perfectly balanced. A long finish is the cherry on top. The Brunello Manachiara '19 still shows some youthful edges, with a beautiful bouquet of wild berries, red citrus, and forest floor.

● Brunello di Montalcino '19	♟♟ 7
● Brunello di Montalcino V. Manachiara '19	♟♟ 8
● Brunello di Montalcino Vign. Poggio Doria '19	♟♟ 8
● Rosso di Montalcino '22	♟♟ 4
● Brunello di Montalcino Manachiara '99	♟♟♟ 7
● Brunello di Montalcino Manachiara '97	♟♟♟ 7
● Brunello di Montalcino '16	♟♟ 6
● Brunello di Montalcino Manachiara '04	♟♟ 8
● Brunello di Montalcino V. Manachiara '12	♟♟ 8
● Brunello di Montalcino Vign. Poggio Doria '17	♟♟ 8
● Rosso di Montalcino '21	♟♟ 4
● Rosso di Montalcino '02	♟♟ 3
● Rosso di Montalcino '01	♟♟ 3
● Sant'Antimo Merlot '04	♟♟ 4

Nittardi

loc. Nittardi
53011 Castellina in Chianti [SI]
☎ +39 0577740269
🌐 www.nittardi.com

CELLAR SALES
PRE-BOOKED VISITS
ACCOMMODATION
ANNUAL PRODUCTION 120,000 bottles
HECTARES UNDER VINE 38.00
VITICULTURE METHOD Certified Organic

Based in Castellina in Chianti (with 37 hectares of vineyards also in Maremma), Nittardi produces a range defined by a modern style where sangiovese meets some international varieties, aged in small wood barrels. Since 1981, the Canali-Femfert family, owners of galleries in Italy and Germany, has enhanced their wine with an artistic touch—indeed, each year an artist is invited to create a work that becomes the label for the winery's flagship product. The Chianti Classico Vigna Doghessa '22 proves clearly defined in its profile, with alternating aromas of red fruits, floral whiffs, and Mediterranean herbs, accompanied by well-integrated toasted and spicy hints. On the palate, it's juicy and lively, with a broad, invigorating finish where fruit still comes through. The Chianti Classico Gran Selezione '21 offers vibrant, mature aromas with a fleshy, solid, and dense progression of flavor. The Chianti Classico Belcanto '22 is also well-made.

● Chianti Cl. V. Doghessa '22	♟♟ 6
● Ad Astra '22	♟♟ 3
● Chianti Cl. Gran Selezione '21	♟♟ 6
● Chianti Cl. Belcanto '22	♟ 4
● Chianti Cl. Casanuova di Nittardi '21	♟ 4
● Ad Astra '08	♟♟♟ 3
● Chianti Cl. Belcanto '15	♟♟♟ 4*
● Chianti Cl. Ris. '19	♟♟♟ 6
● Chianti Cl. Ris. '13	♟♟♟ 6
● Chianti Cl. Ris. '11	♟♟♟ 6
● Chianti Cl. Ris. '10	♟♟♟ 6
● Chianti Cl. Ris. '98	♟♟♟ 6
● Chianti Cl. Casanuova di Nittardi '21	♟♟ 4
● Chianti Cl. Casanuova di Nittardi '12	♟♟ 4
● Chianti Cl. Ris. '17	♟♟ 6
● Chianti Cl. V. Doghessa '19	♟♟ 6
● Nectar Dei '12	♟♟ 7

★Orma

via Bolgherese
57022 Castagneto Carducci [LI]
(+39 0575477857
www.ormabolgheri.it

★★★Ornellaia

fraz. Bolgheri
loc. Ornellaia, 191
57022 Castagneto Carducci [LI]
(+39 056571811
www.ornellaia.it

ANNUAL PRODUCTION 65,000 bottles
HECTARES UNDER VINE 7.50
SUSTAINABLE WINERY

PRE-BOOKED VISITS
ANNUAL PRODUCTION 1,000,000 bottles
HECTARES UNDER VINE 115.00
SUSTAINABLE WINERY

The Moretti Cuseri family arrived in Bolgheri in 2004, dedicating themselves to the project with meticulous attention to the countryside, with vineyards mainly located along the Via Bolgherese, between the vineyards of Ornellaia and Sassicaia. Classic Bordeaux grape varieties are cultivated, but they also produce a monovarietal vermentino. The latest addition is Aola di Bolgheri, 85% cabernet franc with a splash of sauvignon. Their wines are generous and well-defined, with a modern and Mediterranean stylistic profile. Always impeccable. The fragrant Orma '21 stands out for its aromatic profile, in particular, revealing notes of small red fruits, cherry, spices, fresh herbs, and generous whiffs of Mediterranean scrub. In the mouth, its clearly defined, focused palate has soft tannins, lending the wine a smooth development, leading to a deep, long finish. The more vegetal-toned Aola di Orma '21 offers a powerful and compact palate with great overall persistence.

Ornellaia's wines first appeared on shelves in 1988, and the estate entered the Frescobaldi family's orbit in 2012. It's hard to confine the fame of this winery to Bolgheri, Tuscany, or even Italy, given the extraordinary number of wine legends that have been part of its history. Suffice it to say, Ornellaia represents, with unwavering consistency, the absolute excellence of the Bolgheri DOC appellation. The Bolgheri Superiore Ornellaia '21 once again proves to be a classic red through and through. Its aromas are rich and multifaceted, mingling underbrush, black fruits, and herbs. With a close-knit tannic structure, it offers a dense palate with a long, vibrant finish. However, the Poggio alle Gazze '22 particularly impressed. A blend based on sauvignon, viognier, verdicchio, and vermentino, it summons aromas of plum and white peach, mingled with whiffs of Mediterranean herbs. A fresh, sapid palate leads to a citrusy and iodized finish—an extraordinarily fine wine.

● Orma '22	♀♀ 8	○ Poggio alle Gazze '22	♀♀♀ 7
● Bolgheri Rosso Sup. Aola di Orma '21	♀♀ 8	● Bolgheri Rosso Sup. Ornellaia '21	♀♀ 8
● Orma '20	♀♀♀ 8	○ Bolgheri Bianco Ornellaia '21	♀♀ 8
● Orma '19	♀♀♀ 8	● Le Volte '22	♀♀ 3
● Orma '18	♀♀♀ 8	○ Bolgheri Bianco Ornellaia '19	♀♀♀ 8
● Orma '17	♀♀♀ 8	● Bolgheri Rosso Sup. Ornellaia '20	♀♀♀ 8
● Orma '16	♀♀♀ 8	● Bolgheri Rosso Sup. Ornellaia '18	♀♀♀ 8
● Orma '14	♀♀♀ 8	● Bolgheri Rosso Sup. Ornellaia '17	♀♀♀ 8
● Orma '13	♀♀♀ 8	● Bolgheri Rosso Sup. Ornellaia '16	♀♀♀ 8
● Orma '12	♀♀♀ 8	● Bolgheri Sup. Ornellaia '14	♀♀♀ 8
● Orma '11	♀♀♀ 8	● Bolgheri Sup. Ornellaia '13	♀♀♀ 8
● Orma '10	♀♀♀ 7	● Bolgheri Sup. Ornellaia '12	♀♀♀ 8
● Orma '09	♀♀♀ 6	● Bolgheri Sup. Ornellaia '10	♀♀♀ 8
● Orma '08	♀♀♀ 6	● Bolgheri Sup. Ornellaia '04	♀♀♀ 8
● Orma '07	♀♀♀ 5	● Masseto '11	♀♀♀ 8
● Orma '06	♀♀♀ 6	● Masseto '09	♀♀♀ 8
○ Bianco di Orma '22	♀♀ 4	● Masseto '06	♀♀♀ 8

Siro Pacenti

loc. Pelagrilli, I
53024 Montalcino [SI]
(☏) +39 0577848662
⊚ www.siropacenti.it

Pagani de Marchi

via della Camminata, 2
56040 Casale Marittimo [PI]
(☏) +39 0586653016
⊚ www.paganidemarchi.com

PRE-BOOKED VISITS
ACCOMMODATION
ANNUAL PRODUCTION 60,000 bottles
HECTARES UNDER VINE 28.00
SUSTAINABLE WINERY

CELLAR SALES
PRE-BOOKED VISITS
ANNUAL PRODUCTION 38,000 bottles
HECTARES UNDER VINE 6.50
VITICULTURE METHOD Certified Organic

Founded by Siro Pacenti in the 1970s, the winery rose to fame in the late 1990s thanks to the vision of his son, Giancarlo. It was he who introduced a modern and original interpretation of Brunello, one that remains widely appreciated by critics and wine lovers around the globe. The estate has two main production areas: the historic site in Pelagrilli on the northern slope, where the sandy clay soils sit at an elevation of 350 meters, and Piancornello on the southern slope of Montalcino, known for its stony, mineral-rich soils. The wines tasted this year display an extremely elegant and distinctive stylistic character. The refined aromas of the Brunello Vecchie Vigne '19 transition from ripe dark berries to plum, cinchona, and rhubarb, all set against a backdrop of sweet spices and a whiff of blood. The palate is firm and energetic, with invigorating pulp meeting deep, balanced tannins. The excellent Rosso di Montalcino '22 offers fruity and floral aromas with a hint of scrubland. On the palate, it's intense and dynamic, delivering great pleasure.

Located at the foot of Casale Marittimo, between Bibbona and Cecina, Pagani de Marchi is run by mother Pia and son Matteo. The winery, which debuted its first vintage in 2001, has recently refined its style. Though international varietals dominate, they also produce sangiovese and vermentino. One of their innovations includes using amphorae for vinification, while maintaining a generous use of small oak barrels for aging. The Casa Nocera '20, a monovarietal merlot, features precise aromas, anticipating a palate that's striking both for its flavor and breadth. It offers fleshy yet fresh fruit that concludes with a lively and almost brackish finish. We also appreciated the Olmata, a blend of merlot, cabernet sauvignon, and sangiovese. On the nose, it presents varied aromas, ranging from red fruits to wildflowers, while the palate is sapid, with a multifaceted, solid progression of flavor.

● Brunello di Montalcino V.V. '19	♟♟ 8
● Rosso di Montalcino '22	♟♟ 6
● Brunello di Montalcino Pelagrilli '19	♟♟ 8
● Brunello di Montalcino '97	♟♟♟ 7
● Brunello di Montalcino '96	♟♟♟ 7
● Brunello di Montalcino '95	♟♟♟ 7
● Brunello di Montalcino '88	♟♟♟ 7
● Brunello di Montalcino PS Ris. '07	♟♟♟ 8
● Brunello di Montalcino V.V. '10	♟♟♟ 8
● Brunello di Montalcino Pelagrilli '18	♟♟ 8
● Brunello di Montalcino Pelagrilli '16	♟♟ 7
● Brunello di Montalcino Pelagrilli '12	♟♟ 6
● Brunello di Montalcino PS Ris. '16	♟♟ 8
● Brunello di Montalcino PS Ris. '10	♟♟ 8
● Brunello di Montalcino V.V. '15	♟♟ 8
● Brunello di Montalcino V.V. '14	♟♟ 8

● Casa Nocera '20	♟♟ 6
● Olmata '20	♟♟ 4
○ Blumea '23	♟♟ 3
● Montescudaio Rosso Montaleo '20	♟♟ 2*
● Principe Guerriero '21	♟♟ 5
○ Blumea '21	♟♟ 3
○ Blumea '19	♟♟ 3
● Casa Nocera '16	♟♟ 5
● Casa Nocera '15	♟♟ 5
● Casalvecchio '17	♟♟ 5
● Casalvecchio '16	♟♟ 5
● Casalvecchio Anfora '17	♟♟ 7
● Montescudaio Rosso Montaleo '19	♟♟ 2*
● Olmata '18	♟♟ 4
● Olmata '17	♟♟ 4

Tenuta Pakravan-Papi

loc. Ortacavoli Nuova, 1/2
56046 Riparbella [PI]
☏ +39 05861881228
⊗ www.pakravan-papi.it

CELLAR SALES
PRE-BOOKED VISITS
ACCOMMODATION AND RESTAURANT SERVICE
ANNUAL PRODUCTION 60,000 bottles
HECTARES UNDER VINE 21.00

In 1966, Enzo Papi, a native of Maremma, met Iranian-born Amineh Pakravan in Florence. Years later, they purchased a property on the hills of Riparbella, transforming the once-uncultivated land into a modern estate that respects the natural environment of Mediterranean woods and scrubland. Today, their two children, Chiara and Leopoldo, help run the business, with Leopoldo's partner Francesca managing the estate's newly opened restaurant. They grow chardonnay, riesling, and malvasia toscana for their white wines, and cabernet sauvignon, cabernet franc, merlot, and sangiovese for their reds. Among the reds tasted, the sangiovese-based Gabriccio '19 stood out the most. It's a red of superb elegance and finesse, despite its close-knit and pervasive structure. The nose offers up aromas of red fruit and underbrush, while the palate is marked by freshness and sapidity, which lend rhythm and depth. The Cancellaia '20, a classic Bordeaux blend, is also very good, while among the whites, the Ribellante, made from riesling, malvasia, and chardonnay, caught our attention.

● Cancellaia '20	♟♟ 5
● Gabbriccio '19	♟♟ 5
● Prunicce '22	♟♟ 4
○ Ribellante '23	♟♟ 3
○ Serra de' Cocci '22	♟♟ 3
● Cancellaia di Riparbella '18	♟♟♟ 5
● Campo del Pari '17	♟♟ 6
● Campo del Pari '16	♟♟ 6
● Cancellaia '19	♟♟ 5
● Cancellaia '16	♟♟ 5
● Gabbriccio '18	♟♟ 5
○ Malvasia di Riparbella '20	♟♟ 3
● Prunicce '18	♟♟ 3
○ Serra de' Cocci '21	♟♟ 3

Tenute Palagetto

via Monteoliveto, 46
53037 San Gimignano [SI]
☏ +39 0577943090
⊗ www.palagetto.it

CELLAR SALES
PRE-BOOKED VISITS
ACCOMMODATION
ANNUAL PRODUCTION 250,000 bottles
HECTARES UNDER VINE 44.00

The story of Palagetto is one of a winery and a family that have always belonged to San Gimignano. Luano Niccolai, after his success in the camper industry, decided to invest in his homeland, purchasing the first plots in the 1980s that would become the Tenute Niccolai. The torch was then passed to his daughter Sabrina, and today the winery is managed by the third generation, with Sabrina's children, Arianna and Niccolò. The Vernaccia di San Gimignano Ris. '21 impresses with its mouthwatering acidity, iodized touches, and perfectly calibrated oak. Its aromatic profile is flawless, and in the mouth, it offers a captivating palate with remarkable length, depth, and flavor. The San Gimignano Rosso Sottobosco '18 is a juicy drink infused with sensations of morello cherry and Mediterranean scrub. Its mature, nicely resolved tannins shape a broad and fleshy palate. The Viognier '23 proves sapid, close-knit, compact, and fruity.

○ Vernaccia di San Gimignano Ris. '21	♟♟ 3*
● San Gimignano Rosso Sottobosco '18	♟♟ 5
○ Viognier '23	♟♟ 5
● Chianti Colli Senesi Ris. '19	♟ 4
● Uno di Quattro '22	♟ 5
○ Vernaccia di San Gimignano Arianna '21	♟ 2
● Chianti Colli Senesi Ris. '18	♟♟ 4
● Uno di Quattro '21	♟♟ 5
○ Vernaccia di San Gimignano '18	♟♟ 2*
○ Vernaccia di San Gimignano Arianna '20	♟♟ 2*
○ Vernaccia di San Gimignano Ris. '20	♟♟ 3
○ Vernaccia di San Gimignano Ris. '19	♟♟ 3*
○ Vernaccia di San Gimignano Ris. '18	♟♟ 3*

Il Palagione

loc. Palagione
via per Castel San Gimignano, 36
53037 San Gimignano [SI]
📞 +39 0577953134
🌐 www.ilpalagione.com

CELLAR SALES
PRE-BOOKED VISITS
ACCOMMODATION
ANNUAL PRODUCTION 60,000 bottles
HECTARES UNDER VINE 16.00
VITICULTURE METHOD Certified Organic

In 1995, Giorgio Comotti decided to leave Milan and move to Tuscany, purchasing an abandoned farm along the road between San Gimignano and Volterra, where he planted the first vineyards and built a winery. Today, the wines produced by Il Palagione are distinguished by a clear style, where Vernaccia di San Gimignano exudes fragrant aromatic traits, exhibiting a supple, fully, and pleasantly linear profile. The multifaceted, fine nose of the Vernaccia di San Gimignano Ori Ris. '22 features hints of yellow flowers, yellow fruit, and whiffs of flint. The palate is sapid, fine, and sleek, with a flavorful development and a fragrant finish. Citrus and an acidic-sapid undertone are the hallmarks of the Vernaccia di San Gimignano Lyra '21, a wine with linear development and an ultra-taut finish. The palate of the monovarietal merlot Ares '19 is defined by fine tannins, fruity sweetness, and creaminess, making for a well-crafted and enjoyable wine.

La Palazzetta

fraz. Castelnuovo dell'Abate
pod. la Palazzetta, 1p
53024 Montalcino [SI]
📞 +39 0577835531
🌐 www.palazzettafanti.com

CELLAR SALES
PRE-BOOKED VISITS
ACCOMMODATION
ANNUAL PRODUCTION 70,000 bottles
HECTARES UNDER VINE 28.00
VITICULTURE METHOD Certified Organic
SUSTAINABLE WINERY

Until 1988, La Palazzetta was primarily a grain farm. It was Flavio Fanti who transformed the estate into a winery. Today, his children Luca and Tea have taken the reins, working hard to enhance the quality of the wines, which are increasingly faithful to the territory, while also embracing environmentally-friendly production practices. The winery is now fully eco-sustainable, organic, powered by renewable energy, and recycles all production waste. The well-made Riserva '18 opens on a vibrant nose, teeming with floral notes and Mediterranean scrub, which blend nicely with fruit. Over time, a hint of oak, still in the process of being absorbed, emerges. The palate is rich in fruit pulp and dense tannins, concluding with a finish that's still just slightly green. The Brunello '19 opens on fragrant aromas reminiscent of ripe red fruit, complemented by classic notes of cinchona and licorice. The palate is pervasive, leaving a long fruity aftertaste.

● Ares '19	♟♟ 5
○ Vernaccia di San Gimignano Lyra '21	♟♟ 3
○ Vernaccia di San Gimignano Ori Ris. '22	♟♟ 3
● Chianti Colli Senesi Caelum '22	♟ 5
● Chianti Colli Senesi Draco Ris. '20	♟ 3
○ Vernaccia di San Gimignano Hydra '23	♟ 3
● Antajr '18	♟♟ 4
● Ares '18	♟♟ 5
● Ares '17	♟♟ 5
● Chianti Colli Senesi Caelum '21	♟♟ 3
● Chianti Colli Senesi Caelum '20	♟♟ 2*
○ Vernaccia di San Gimignano Hydra '22	♟♟ 3
○ Vernaccia di San Gimignano Lyra '20	♟♟ 3
○ Vernaccia di San Gimignano Ori Ris. '21	♟♟ 3*

● Brunello di Montalcino '19	♟♟ 8
● Brunello di Montalcino Ris. '18	♟♟ 8
● Rosso di Montalcino '22	♟♟ 8
● Rosso di Montalcino Flavino '22	♟♟ 5
● Sant'Antimo '22	♟ 4
● Brunello di Montalcino Ris. '97	♟♟♟ 8
● Brunello di Montalcino '18	♟♟ 8
● Brunello di Montalcino '17	♟♟ 7
● Brunello di Montalcino '16	♟♟ 7
● Brunello di Montalcino Visconti '16	♟♟ 5
● Brunello di Montalcino Visconti '15	♟♟ 5
● I Bruciati '19	♟♟ 2*
● I Bruciati '18	♟♟ 2*
● Rosso di Montalcino '21	♟♟ 5
● Rosso di Montalcino '19	♟♟ 5
● Rosso di Montalcino Visconti '18	♟♟ 3

Il Palazzone

loc. le Due Porte, 245
53024 Montalcino [SI]
+39 0577846142
www.ilpalazzone.com

CELLAR SALES
PRE-BOOKED VISITS
ANNUAL PRODUCTION 12,000 bottles
HECTARES UNDER VINE 3.96

"Small is beautiful" is the most famous work by economist and philosopher Ernst Friedrich Schumacher, an advocate for small, ecologically sustainable businesses as an alternative to capitalism and globalization. Whether Kirsten and Peter Kern ever read Schumacher or not, their winery embodies his ideals. Their small estate comprises just four tiny vineyards, each about one hectare. Producing in line with organic farming practices, they create high-quality, terroir-driven wines while respecting biodiversity. The Brunello Le Due Porte '19 proves beautifully crafted, with harmonious aromas that balance lovely notes of cinchona and licorice with a burst of fresh red fruit, enhancing its complexity. The palate is harmonious and dense, with refined, dense tannins and lively, fresh acidity, leading to a finish of nice length. The Brunello '19 offers up dark fruits in jam and smoky notes, making for an intricate and delicious wine despite a few tannic ripples. Austere and complex, the Riserva '18 is flavorful and pleasant on the palate.

● Brunello di Montalcino '19	🍷🍷 8
● Brunello di Montalcino Le Due Porte '19	🍷🍷 8
● Brunello di Montalcino Ris. '18	🍷🍷 8
● Brunello di Montalcino '01	YYY 6
● Brunello di Montalcino Ris. '01	YYY 6
● Brunello di Montalcino Ris. '99	YYY 6
● Brunello di Montalcino '18	YY 6
● Brunello di Montalcino '17	YY 6
● Brunello di Montalcino '16	YY 6
● Brunello di Montalcino '15	YY 6
● Brunello di Montalcino '04	YY 6
● Brunello di Montalcino '00	YY 6
● Brunello di Montalcino '99	YY 6
● Brunello di Montalcino Ris. '15	YY 8
● Brunello di Montalcino Ris. '97	YY 8
● Rosso di Montalcino '00	YY 4

Marchesi Pancrazi Villa di Bagnolo

fraz. Bagnolo
via Montalese, 156
59013 Montemurlo [PO]
+39 0574652748
www.pancrazi.it

CELLAR SALES
PRE-BOOKED VISITS
ACCOMMODATION
ANNUAL PRODUCTION 15,000 bottles
HECTARES UNDER VINE 5.00
SUSTAINABLE WINERY

Sometimes, fortune favors the fortunate through small mistakes. The Marquis Pancrazi family discovered the extraordinary potential of pinot nero in Tuscany by accident, when in 1965, it was delivered instead of the traditional sangiovese. The winery, housed in a historic jewel within the Tenuta di Bagnolo (at the foot of Monte Ferrato), now dedicates five hectares to pinot nero. Indeed, the vineyards, with their mineral-rich soils and a unique microclimate, have proven ideal for the grape. The Vigna Baragazza '21 is a concentration of power and elegance, a wine of superb richness and charm. The nose is saturated with notes of blueberry, black fruits, cherry, and pomegranate, followed by underbrush, licorice, leather, and black pepper. The palate is velvety, harmonious, and mouthfilling. The delicate, pleasant, and floral Monte Ferrato '22 also caught our attention, with its scents of black plum and violet.

● V. Baragazza Pinot Nero '21	🍷🍷 8
● Monte Ferrato Pinot Nero '22	🍷🍷 4
● Villa di Bagnolo Pinot Nero '22	🍷🍷 6
⊙ Villa di Bagnolo Rosé '23	🍷🍷 3
● Monte Ferrato Pinot Nero '21	YY 4
● Monte Ferrato Pinot Nero '20	YY 3
● Monte Ferrato Pinot Nero '19	YY 3
● Monte Ferrato Pinot Nero '18	YY 3
● Pinot Nero Villa di Bagnolo '19	YY 5
● Pinot Nero Villa di Bagnolo '18	YY 5
● V. Baragazza Pinot Nero '19	YY 7
● V. Baragazza Pinot Nero '18	YY 7
● V. Bragazza Pinot Nero '20	YY 8
● Villa di Bagnolo Pinot Nero '21	YY 6
● Villa di Bagnolo Pinot Nero '20	YY 5
● Villa di Bagnolo Pinot Nero '16	YY 5

Panizzi

loc. Santa Margherita, 34
53037 San Gimignano [SI]
📞 +39 0577941576
🖰 www.panizzi.it

CELLAR SALES
PRE-BOOKED VISITS
ACCOMMODATION
ANNUAL PRODUCTION 200,000 bottles
HECTARES UNDER VINE 55.60
VITICULTURE METHOD Certified Organic

Giovanni Panizzi purchased the Santa Margherita
estate in 1979, the first nucleus of a winery
today stewarded by Simone Niccolai, a man who
champions intelligent continuity. Panizzi's first
Vernaccia di San Gimignano, released in 1990,
sparked a qualitative revolution alongside a few
other pioneers. This dynamic spirit remains the
hallmark of the San Gimignano producer, which
is currently experimenting with a pinot noir, a
unique endeavor here in the "City of Towers".
The Vernaccia di San Gimignano Riserva '20 is a
wine of excellent craftsmanship. Its aromas are
refined and focused, while the palate combines
firmness and grace, with its unmistakable smoky
tone shaping a lingering finish. The same elegance
characterizes the Ermius '20, a monovarietal
pinot noir which opts for more restrained fruit
adorned by balsamic notes, all followed by a soft
and flavorful palate. The Ceraso Rosato '23,
made from merlot and sangiovese grapes, proves
sapid and fragrant, with an enticing, persistent
drinkability.

○ Vernaccia di San Gimignano Ris. '20	♟♟♟ 5
● San Gimignano Pinot Nero Ermius '20	♟♟ 5
☉ Ceraso Rosato '23	♟♟ 2*
● San Gimignano Pinot Nero '22	♟♟ 4
○ Vernaccia di San Gimignano V. Santa Margherita '22	♟♟ 4
● Chianti Colli Senesi Vertunno Ris. '21	♟ 3
○ Vernaccia di San Gimignano '23	♟ 3
○ Vernaccia di San Gimignano Ris. '19	♟♟♟ 5
○ Vernaccia di San Gimignano Ris. '18	♟♟♟ 5
○ Vernaccia di San Gimignano Ris. '17	♟♟♟ 5
○ Vernaccia di San Gimignano Ris. '16	♟♟♟ 5
○ Vernaccia di San Gimignano Ris. '07	♟♟♟ 5
○ Vernaccia di San Gimignano Ris. '05	♟♟♟ 5
○ Vernaccia di San Gimignano Ris. '98	♟♟♟ 4*
● Celii '20	♟♟ 6
● San Gimignano Pinot Nero Ermius '19	♟♟ 5

Parmoleto

loc. Montenero d'Orcia
pod. Parmoletone, 44
58040 Castel del Piano [GR]
📞 +39 0564954131
🖰 www.parmoleto.it

CELLAR SALES
PRE-BOOKED VISITS
ACCOMMODATION AND RESTAURANT SERVICE
ANNUAL PRODUCTION 22,000 bottles
HECTARES UNDER VINE 6.00

Originally a grain farm, the Sodi family's
Parmoleto began bottling wines in 1990. This
family-run enterprise is also involved in olive
cultivation and livestock farming, as well as
offering guest accommodations. Located on
the hills of Montenero d'Orcia, near Monte
Amiata, Parmoleto produces wines that are
generally reliable and well-crafted, showcasing
a straightforward and direct character, resulting
from a blend of traditional and modern
winemaking techniques. The Montecucco
Rosso '21 opens with aromas of violet and ripe
cherry over a spicy base. On the palate, it's lively,
juicy, and full-bodied. The Montecucco
Vermentino Carabatto '23 proves to be a
fragrant white with a sapid, immediately pleasing
palate. The Syrah '20 reveals dark, mature
aromatic tones, with nice dynamism of flavor. The
Sormonno '20, a blend of sangiovese and
cabernet sauvignon, is concentrated and intense.

● Montecucco Rosso '21	♟♟ 2*
○ Montecucco Vermentino Carabatto '23	♟♟ 2*
● Maremma Toscana Syrah '20	♟ 3
● Sormonno '20	♟ 4
● Maremma Toscana Syrah '19	♟♟ 3
● Montecucco Sangiovese Ris. '18	♟♟ 3*
● Montecucco Sangiovese Ris. '15	♟♟ 3*
● Montecucco Sangiovese Ris. '13	♟♟ 3*
● Montecucco Sangiovese Ris. '11	♟♟ 3*
○ Montecucco Vermentino Carabatto '22	♟♟ 2*

Antica Fattoria La Parrina

loc. Parrina
s.da vicinale della Parrina
58015 Orbetello [GR]
+39 0564862626
www.parrina.it

CELLAR SALES
PRE-BOOKED VISITS
ACCOMMODATION AND RESTAURANT SERVICE
ANNUAL PRODUCTION 80,000 bottles
HECTARES UNDER VINE 57.00
VITICULTURE METHOD Certified Organic
SUSTAINABLE WINERY

More than just a winery, Parrina is an expansive agricultural project guided by the Spinola family since the late 19th century. This name has significantly contributed to the development of Maremma's wine industry. Parrina's wines are known for their drinkability and immediate aromatic expression, although their extensive portfolio includes more ambitious bottles that have occasionally reached exceptional quality. The Ansonica Costa dell'Argentario '23 reveals an aromatic spectrum of macerated flowers, chamomile, and aromatic herbs, while the palate is pleasantly sapid and vibrant, and rich in contrasts. The Parrina Vermentino '23 is marked by aromas of ripe yellow fruits and broom flowers, leading to a slender, enjoyable palate. The Parrina Sangiovese '22 is also well-crafted, with its precise aromas accompanied by a fragrant palate.

○ Ansonica Costa dell'Argentario '23	🍷🍷 4
● Parrina Sangiovese '22	🍷🍷 4
○ Parrina Vermentino '23	🍷🍷 3
○ Parrina Bianco Vialetto '23	🍷 3
● Parrina Merlot Radaia '21	🍷 6
● Parrina Rosso Il Muraccio '21	🍷 4
○ Poggio della Fata '23	🍷 4
○ Costa dell'Argentario Ansonica '21	ΥΥΥ 3*
○ Costa dell'Argentario Ansonica '20	ΥΥΥ 3*
○ Costa dell'Argentario Ansonica '19	ΥΥΥ 3*
○ Costa dell'Argentario Ansonica '17	ΥΥΥ 3*
● Parrina Sangiovese '18	ΥΥΥ 3*
○ Costa dell'Argentario Ansonica '18	ΥΥ 3*
○ Parrina Bianco Vialetto '20	ΥΥ 2*
● Parrina Sangiovese '19	ΥΥ 3*
● Parrina Sangiovese Ris. '20	ΥΥ 5

Tenuta Perano

s.da di San Donato in Perano
53013 Gaiole in Chianti [SI]
+39 0577749563
www.frescobaldi.com

CELLAR SALES
PRE-BOOKED VISITS
ANNUAL PRODUCTION 320,000 bottles
HECTARES UNDER VINE 92.00

Part of the Frescobaldi wine empire, Tenuta Perano is located in the Gaiole in Chianti UGA production zone. Its vineyards include notable crus like "Domini" and "Montecasi." The estate's range exhibits a modern stylistic profile, with maturation carried out in wooden barrels of various sizes, predominantly small ones. Their wines are characterized by intense aromas and complex structures, and always marked by impeccable technical craftsmanship. The Chianti Classico '21 features focused aromas of small red fruits, aromatic herbs, and light spicy whiffs. On the palate, it's juicy and fragrant, with a pleasantly flavorful and rhythmic drinkability. The Chianti Classico Riserva '20, with its slightly more marked structure, is perhaps a bit overshadowed by oak but remains well-orchestrated and flavorful on the palate. The austere Chianti Classico Gran Selezione Rialzi '20 showcases a juicy, pervasive palate.

● Chianti Cl. '21	🍷🍷 6
● Chianti Cl. Ris. '20	🍷🍷 7
● Chianti Cl. Gran Selezione Rialzi '20	🍷 8
● Chianti Cl. Gran Selezione Rialzi '15	ΥΥΥ 6
● Chianti Cl. '20	ΥΥ 4
● Chianti Cl. '19	ΥΥ 3
● Chianti Cl. '18	ΥΥ 3
● Chianti Cl. '17	ΥΥ 3
● Chianti Cl. '16	ΥΥ 3
● Chianti Cl. Gran Selezione Rialzi '19	ΥΥ 6
● Chianti Cl. Gran Selezione Rialzi '18	ΥΥ 6
● Chianti Cl. Gran Selezione Rialzi '16	ΥΥ 6
● Chianti Cl. Ris. '19	ΥΥ 5
● Chianti Cl. Ris. '18	ΥΥ 5
● Chianti Cl. Ris. '17	ΥΥ 5
● Chianti Cl. Ris. '16	ΥΥ 5

Petra

loc. San Lorenzo Alto, 131
57028 Suvereto [LI]
📞 +39 0565845308
🌐 www.petrawine.it

CELLAR SALES
PRE-BOOKED VISITS
ANNUAL PRODUCTION 350,000 bottles
HECTARES UNDER VINE 103.00
SUSTAINABLE WINERY

Designed by Swiss architect Mario Botta, the Petra winery in Suvereto doubles both as a production facility and an architectural landmark. Though the winery began operations in 1997, the structure itself was inaugurated in 2003. Today, Petra is a key producer in the area and part of the Terra Moretti Group, which also includes Teruzzi in San Gimignano and La Badiola in Castiglione della Pescaia (Maremma). The Petra '21, a blend of cabernet sauvignon, merlot, and cabernet franc, exudes aromas of Mediterranean scrub, ripe red and black fruits, coffee grounds, spices, and balsamic flashes. On the palate, it's soft, juicy, and sweet, with a rhythmic structure that finishes with a vibrant, fruity, and spicy encore. The Hebo '22, a blend of cabernet sauvignon, merlot, cabernet franc, and sangiovese, is well-crafted, standing out for its reliable, flavorful drinkability. The Quercegobbe '21, a monovarietal merlot, is darker and more austere.

Petricci e Del Pianta

loc. San Lorenzo, 20
57028 Suvereto [LI]
📞 +39 3356767271
🌐 www.petriccidelpianta.it

CELLAR SALES
PRE-BOOKED VISITS
ANNUAL PRODUCTION 40,000 bottles
HECTARES UNDER VINE 11.00

This family-run winery draws its strength from tradition. Today Petricci e Del Pianta is run by Fabio and Daniele, the sons of founder Pietro Petricci, a living testament to the estate's legacy. Alongside cabernet, the family grows sangiovese, a varietal they're especially attached to, having planted 80 different clones so as to find the perfect fit for their property. For whites, they produce vermentino in a dry style, as well as Metodo Classico and trebbiano. The passito version of their Val di Cornia ansonica, the Stilloro '22, offers up an aromatic bouquet of great pleasure, with tones of chestnut honey, dates, apricot jam, and spices rising from the glass. The palate is also excellent, with a very long finish. The Suvereto Sangiovese Buca di Cleonte '20 is a wine of nice energy, with a supple, flavorful development. The Albatrone '23, also made from sangiovese, is an energetic drink—crunchy and enticing.

● Petra '21	🍷🍷 8
● Hebo '22	🍷🍷 4
● Quercegobbe '21	🍷🍷 6
● Petra '20	🍷🍷🍷 7
● Petra '19	🍷🍷🍷 7
● Petra Rosso '16	🍷🍷🍷 8
● Petra Rosso '15	🍷🍷🍷 8
● Petra Rosso '14	🍷🍷🍷 8
● Petra Rosso '13	🍷🍷🍷 8
● Petra Rosso '12	🍷🍷🍷 8
● Petra Rosso '11	🍷🍷🍷 8
● Petra Rosso '04	🍷🍷🍷 7
● Petra '18	🍷🍷 7
● Petra '17	🍷🍷 7
● Quercegobbe '20	🍷🍷 6
● Quercegobbe '19	🍷🍷 6

○ Val di Cornia Ansonica Passito Stilloro '22	🍷🍷 5
● Albatrone '23	🍷🍷 2*
● Suvereto Sangiovese Buca di Cleonte '20	🍷🍷 4
● Val di Cornia Aleatico Passito Stillo '23	🍷🍷 5
● Cerosecco '21	🍷 4
○ Fabula '23	🍷 3
● Suvereto Cabernet Sauvignon Nubio '20	🍷 5
● Suvereto Sangiovese Buca di Cleonte '19	🍷🍷 4
● Val di Cornia Aleatico Passito Stillo '22	🍷🍷 5

★★Fattoria Petrolo

fraz. Mercatale Valdarno
loc. Petrolo, 30
52021 Bucine [AR]
☎ +39 0559911322
⊕ www.petrolo.it

CELLAR SALES
PRE-BOOKED VISITS
ACCOMMODATION
ANNUAL PRODUCTION 90,000 bottles
HECTARES UNDER VINE 31.00
VITICULTURE METHOD Certified Organic
SUSTAINABLE WINERY

Situated in Bucine, Fattoria Petrolo is managed by Luca Sanjust, the third generation of Bazzocchi-Sanjust family to operate here. Indeed, Luca took over from his pioneering mother, Lucia. Located in Val d'Arno di Sopra, at elevations spanning 250-550 meters above sea level, Petrolo has been producing quality wines since the mid-1980s. Drawing on both time-honored and international grape varieties, their range is known for its excellence and distinctive style. The Valdarno di Sopra Vigna Bòggina C Riserva '21 sees aromas of small red fruits alternating with flowers, underbrush, and earthy nuances. On the palate, it's highly sapid, developing lively and persistent, with a final note refreshed by citrus tones. The Valdarno di Sopra Vigna Bòggina A '22 stands out for its focused aromatic strokes of ripe fruit and spices, with a slender, dynamic palate.

★★Piaggia

loc. Poggetto
via Cegoli, 47
59016 Poggio a Caiano [PO]
☎ +39 0558705401
⊕ www.piaggia.com

CELLAR SALES
PRE-BOOKED VISITS
ANNUAL PRODUCTION 75,000 bottles
HECTARES UNDER VINE 15.00

Founded by Mauro Vannucci in the mid-1970s, the winery is now run by his daughter Silvia. Piaggia's first bottles of Carmignano Riserva made a significant impact in the 1990s, when the winery was still very small, contributing to the revival of the appellation. Today, the estate has grown in both size and quality, consistently ranking among the top producers not only in the region but also nationally. The Poggio de' Colli '21, a monovarietal cabernet franc, opens on vibrant aromas of red and black fruits, Mediterranean scrub, and spices. In the mouth, it's a firm, lively, and precise wine, striking for its graceful and almost disarming palate. The Carmignano Riserva '21 is no less impressive, with the same overall firmness and an intriguing gamy note on the nose that embellishes cherry and orange. The palate is focused, finishing taut and voluptuous.

● Valdarno di Sopra Sangiovese V. Bòggina C Ris. '21	♟♟♟ 6
● Valdarno di Sopra Sangiovese V. Bòggina A '22	♟♟ 8
● Valdarno di Sopra Merlot V. Galatrona '21	♟♟ 8
○ Boggina B '22	♟ 8
● Torrione '22	♟ 6
● Galatrona '12	♟♟♟ 8
● Galatrona '11	♟♟♟ 8
● Valdarno di Sopra Galatrona '14	♟♟♟ 8
● Valdarno di Sopra Galatrona '13	♟♟♟ 8
● Valdarno di Sopra Merlot Galatrona '17	♟♟♟ 8
● Valdarno di Sopra Merlot V. Galatrona '20	♟♟♟ 8
● Valdarno di Sopra Sangiovese V. Bòggina C '20	♟♟♟ 6

● Poggio de' Colli '21	♟♟♟ 8
● Carmignano Ris. '21	♟♟ 6
● Carmignano Il Sasso '22	♟♟ 5
● Carmignano Ris. '18	♟♟♟ 6
● Carmignano Ris. '17	♟♟♟ 6
● Carmignano Ris. '16	♟♟♟ 6
● Carmignano Ris. '15	♟♟♟ 6
● Carmignano Ris. '14	♟♟♟ 6
● Carmignano Ris. '13	♟♟♟ 6
● Carmignano Ris. '12	♟♟♟ 6
● Carmignano Ris. '11	♟♟♟ 6
● Carmignano Ris. '08	♟♟♟ 5
● Poggio de' Colli '20	♟♟♟ 8
● Poggio de' Colli '19	♟♟♟ 8
● Poggio de' Colli '11	♟♟♟ 7
● Poggio de' Colli '10	♟♟♟ 6

Piancornello

loc. Piancornello
53024 Montalcino [SI]
☎ +39 0577844105
@ www.piancornello.it

CELLAR SALES
PRE-BOOKED VISITS
ANNUAL PRODUCTION 50,000 bottles
HECTARES UNDER VINE 10.00

The Monaci family, a historic lineage of vintners in Montalcino, is now in its fifth generation with Claudio's daughters at the helm. Their estate in Piancornello, on Montalcino's southern slope, sits in the Sesta area, one of Brunello's most renowned terroirs. The ten-hectare property, almost entirely planted with sangiovese grosso, benefits from red soils rich in stone and minerals, ideally suited for producing structured yet elegant wines. The Brunello '19 made an outstanding impression, with a complex, multifaceted nose where vibrant notes of cherry and red fruit meet violet, tobacco, and Mediterranean scrub, lending character and evident typicity. The nuanced influence of oak contributes a spicy touch. The palate is lively and dynamic, with slightly burred tannins, but nicely supported by fine flesh that harmonizes the whole without diminishing the controlled austerity of its long finish.

Piandaccoli

loc. Travalle
via Paganelle, 7
50041 Calenzano [FI]
☎ +39 0550750005
@ www.piandaccoli.it

CELLAR SALES
PRE-BOOKED VISITS
ANNUAL PRODUCTION 90,000 bottles
HECTARES UNDER VINE 20.00
SUSTAINABLE WINERY

For Giampaolo Bruni, a dream came true through a project fueled by passion, study, and a quest for excellence. His goal was to revive Tuscany's native Renaissance varietals. Situated just a few km from Florence, his 20-hectare vineyard hosts sangiovese, foglia tonda, pugnitello, barsaglina, mammolo, colorino, and malvasia toscana at 200 meters elevation. The diverse soils—strewn with pebbles, minerals, and clay-rich sand—benefit from notable temperature fluctuations, perfect for crafting exceptional wines. The Brut Rosé Baciami, a sparkling wine made from mammolo grapes, delights with its aromas of pomegranate, wild strawberry, orange, and bread crust. The palate is taut and sapid, with fine, persistent perlage, finishing with a flavorful and creamy aftertaste. The Inprimis '21 offers intriguing notes of balsam, plum, damson, graphite, and Mediterranean scrub; the palate is sapid and balanced, with powerful yet silky tannins and great persistence.

● Brunello di Montalcino '19	♟♟ 7
● Brunello di Montalcino '13	♟♟♟ 6
● Brunello di Montalcino '10	♟♟♟ 6
● Brunello di Montalcino '06	♟♟♟ 6
● Brunello di Montalcino '99	♟♟♟ 6
● Brunello di Montalcino '17	♟♟ 7
● Brunello di Montalcino '16	♟♟ 7
● Brunello di Montalcino '15	♟♟ 7
● Brunello di Montalcino Ris. '16	♟♟ 7
● Brunello di Montalcino Ris. '15	♟♟ 7
● Brunello di Montalcino Ris. '13	♟♟ 7
● Brunello di Montalcino Ris. '12	♟♟ 7
● Rosso di Montalcino '21	♟♟ 4
● Rosso di Montalcino '20	♟♟ 4
● Rosso di Montalcino '19	♟♟ 4
● Rosso di Montalcino '18	♟♟ 4

○ Baciami Brut Rosé	♟♟ 3
● Inprimis '21	♟♟ 3
● Cosmus '21	♟ 3
● Piandaccoli '21	♟ 2
● Barsaglina del Rinascimento '16	♟♟ 6
● Chianti Cosmus Ris. '14	♟♟ 2*
● Foglia Tonda del Rinascimento '17	♟♟ 6
● Foglia Tonda del Rinascimento '15	♟♟ 6
● Foglia Tonda del Rinascimento '13	♟♟ 6
● Inprimis '16	♟♟ 3
● Mammolo del Rinascimento '16	♟♟ 6
● Pugnitello del Rinascimento '17	♟♟ 6
● Pugnitello del Rinascimento '16	♟♟ 6
● Pugnitello del Rinascimento '15	♟♟ 6
○ Vin Santo del Chianti Occhio di Pernice '14	♟♟ 6

Pianirossi

loc. Porrona
pod. Santa Genoveffa, 1
58044 Cinigiano [GR]
(☏ +39 0564990573
⊕ www.pianirossi.it

CELLAR SALES
PRE-BOOKED VISITS
ACCOMMODATION AND RESTAURANT SERVICE
ANNUAL PRODUCTION 50,000 bottles
HECTARES UNDER VINE 14.00
SUSTAINABLE WINERY

Stefano Sincini initially directed his oenological efforts in Porrona, near Cinigiano, towards a modernist approach, focusing on international grape varieties rather than local ones. This strategy led to the creation of some interesting and well-made expressions, though somewhat lacking in personality. Recently, however, even the estate's Montecucco appellation wines have started to stand out, showcasing a distinctive, earthy and sapid character. The elegant Pianirossi '21 is a blend of montepulciano, cabernet sauvignon, and petit verdot. Aged in French oak tonneaux, it's a progressive, sapid, and deep wine rich in Mediterranean nuances, endowed with velvety tannins and great persistence. The Montecucco Sangiovese La Fonte 2021 features an elegant and subtle profile with crisp fruit, supported by a lovely acidic backbone and mineral sapidity. The Rosé Sabine '23 is subtle, rhythmic, and Mediterranean; the other wines tasted are also worth taking note of.

Piccini 1882

loc. Il Piano
53031 Casole d'Elsa [SI]
(☏ +39 057754011
⊕ www.piccini1882.it

ANNUAL PRODUCTION 15,000,000 bottles
HECTARES UNDER VINE 470.00
SUSTAINABLE WINERY

The Piccini family's Tuscan estates include Valiano in Chianti, Villa al Cortile in Montalcino, and Moraia in Maremma, forming a robust group along with Chianti Geografico. Founded in 1882 by Angiolo Piccini, Tenute Piccini is now led by the family's fourth generation—Mario, Martina, and Elisa Piccini—and the fifth generation—Ginevra, Benedetta, and Michelangelo. Together they continue to achieve commercial success both nationally and internationally. The Chianti Gran Selezione 6.38 '21 features a defined aromatic profile, with red fruits and hints of aromatic herbs dominating alongside smoky and spicy accents. On the palate, it's juicy, well-sustained, and flavorful, developing in good proportion and finishing long. The Chianti Classico Poggio Teo Riserva '21 is also interesting, offering darker aromatic registers and an intense progression of flavor. The rest of the winery's range also performed well.

● Pianirossi '21	♟♟♟ 6
● Montecucco Sangiovese La Fonte '21	♟♟ 5
⊙ Sabine '23	♟♟ 3*
● Sidus '21	♟♟ 3
● Solus '21	♟♟ 4
○ Maremma Toscana Vermentino Noctua '23	♟ 3
● Montecucco Rosso Sidus '18	♟♟♟ 3*
● Montecucco Rosso Sidus '17	♟♟♟ 3*
● Solus '16	♟♟♟ 4*
● Montecucco Rosso Sidus '16	♟♟ 2*
● Montecucco Sangiovese La Fonte '20	♟♟ 5
● Montecucco Sangiovese La Fonte '18	♟♟ 5
● Montecucco Sangiovese La Fonte '16	♟♟ 5
● Pianirossi '19	♟♟ 6
● Solus '19	♟♟ 4
● Solus '18	♟♟ 4

● Chianti Gran Selezione Valiano 6.38 '21	♟♟ 5
● Chianti Cl. Contessa di Radda Chianti Geografico '22	♟♟ 3
● Chianti Cl. Valiano Poggio Teo Ris. '21	♟♟ 5
● Chianti Cl. Levante Chianti Geografico '20	♟ 5
● Chianti Gran Selezione Valiano San Lazzaro '21	♟ 6
● Chianti Cl. Gran Selezione Valiano 6.38 '18	♟♟♟ 5
● Chianti Cl. Gran Selezione Valiano 6.38 '16	♟♟♟ 5
● Chianti Cl. Gran Selezione Valiano 6.38 '15	♟♟♟ 5
● Chianti Cl. Valiano '20	♟♟♟ 3

Agostina Pieri

fraz. Sant'Angelo Scalo
loc. Piancornello
53024 Montalcino [SI]
(+39 0577844163
www.pieriagostina.it

ANNUAL PRODUCTION 45,000 bottles
HECTARES UNDER VINE 10.78

Agostina Pieri's winery was founded in 1991
with just three hectares of vineyards in
Piancornello, one of the most renowned growing
areas on the southern slope of the appellation,
where the hills gradually soften toward the
Maremma. 25 years later, the estate has grown
to 10 hectares, divided into five plots, but it
remains very much a family operation. Agostina
now works alongside her two sons, who have
split the responsibilities between them: Jacopo
manages the vineyards, while Francesco tends to
the wines in the cellar. Both the Rosso di
Montalcino '22 and the Brunello '19 reached
our final round, testifying to this winery's
excellent quality and consistency. The Rosso di
Montalcino '22 offers enticing aromas of fresh
red fruit, Mediterranean scrub, and spices, aptly
balancing tannins and fruit. The Brunello '19
reveals a vibrant nose with notes of red fruit and
citrus, with a slight herbal note adding further
complexity and character. Rich and harmonious
on the palate, it balances close-knit tannins with
fleshy fruit.

• Brunello di Montalcino '19	♟♟ 7
• Rosso di Montalcino '22	♟♟ 4
• Rosso di Montalcino '95	♟♟♟ 4
• Brunello di Montalcino '17	♟♟ 6
• Brunello di Montalcino '16	♟♟ 6
• Brunello di Montalcino '15	♟♟ 6
• Brunello di Montalcino '14	♟♟ 6
• Brunello di Montalcino '13	♟♟ 6
• Brunello di Montalcino '12	♟♟ 6
• Brunello di Montalcino '11	♟♟ 6
• Brunello di Montalcino '10	♟♟ 6
• Brunello di Montalcino Ris. '15	♟♟ 7
• Rosso di Montalcino '20	♟♟ 3
• Rosso di Montalcino '18	♟♟ 3
• Rosso di Montalcino '16	♟♟ 3
• Rosso di Montalcino '14	♟♟ 3

Pietroso

loc. Pietroso, 257
53024 Montalcino [SI]
(+39 0577848573
www.pietroso.it

CELLAR SALES
PRE-BOOKED VISITS
ANNUAL PRODUCTION 30,000 bottles
HECTARES UNDER VINE 5.00

Gianni Pignattai's winery is a tight-knit family
affair. Alongside Gianni, his wife Cecilia and their
son Andrea, who studied oenology, oversee all
stages of production, from the vineyard to the
cellar. The winery's headquarters and part of the
vineyards are located in Pietroso, just a stone's
throw from the town of Montalcino, but there
some five vineyards total, each just over a
hectare. Ventolaio and Colombaio are located
on the southern slope of the Montalcino hill,
while Pietroso, Montosoli, and Fornello lie on
the northern side. Pietroso's outstanding
Brunello 2019 captivates with its aromatic
finesse and a tension typical of Montalcino
sangiovese. Cherry and sour cherry,
complemented by underbrush, licorice, and
graphite, shape a wine that's both territorial and
modern. The palate also shows great
character—fleshy and full, never sweet thanks to
a touch of sapidity and lovely acidity that lends
rhythm and progression to its fruit. The
delightful Rosso '22 features intact fruit on the
nose and sweet, smooth tannins on the palate.

• Brunello di Montalcino '19	♟♟ 8
• Rosso di Montalcino '22	♟♟ 5
• Berni Domenico '20	♟ 8
• Brunello di Montalcino '17	♟♟♟ 8
• Brunello di Montalcino '16	♟♟♟ 6
• Brunello di Montalcino '14	♟♟♟ 6
• Brunello di Montalcino '09	♟♟♟ 6
• Brunello di Montalcino '18	♟♟ 7
• Brunello di Montalcino '13	♟♟ 6
• Brunello di Montalcino '12	♟♟ 6
• Brunello di Montalcino '10	♟♟ 6
• Brunello di Montalcino Ris. '10	♟♟ 6
• Rosso di Montalcino '20	♟♟ 4
• Rosso di Montalcino '19	♟♟ 4
• Rosso di Montalcino '17	♟♟ 4
• Rosso di Montalcino '11	♟♟ 3*

Pieve di Santo Stefano

fraz. Pieve Santo Stefano
loc. Sardini
55100 Lucca
+39 0583394115
www.pievedisantostefano.com

CELLAR SALES
PRE-BOOKED VISITS
ACCOMMODATION
ANNUAL PRODUCTION 45,000 bottles
HECTARES UNDER VINE 10.60
VITICULTURE METHOD Certified Organic
SUSTAINABLE WINERY

Located on the hills around Lucca, Pieve di Santo Stefano benefits from a unique microclimate with high rainfall and notable temperate swings, ideal for producing light and fragrant wines. This stylistic hallmark is emphasized by Francesca Bogazzi's production approach, which prioritizes balance and finesse, aided by a judicious use of both large casks and small barrels for maturation. This year's tastings saw excellent results. The Villa Sardini '22 is a concentration of richness and depth; its balsamic drive amplifies aromas of blackberry, licorice, Virginia tobacco, and a touch of eucalyptus. The palate is mouthfilling, dynamic, and pervasive, with a long and flavorful finish. The Vento dell'Ovest '21, a cabernet franc, offers up a potpourri of dried flowers—rose, violet, carnation—along with notes of quinine and rhubarb, blackberry jam, and a lovely minty trail; the palate is silky and elegant.

Podere 414

fraz. Montiano
loc. Maiano Lavacchio, 10
58051 Magliano in Toscana [GR]
+39 0564507818
www.podere414.it

CELLAR SALES
PRE-BOOKED VISITS
ANNUAL PRODUCTION 180,000 bottles
HECTARES UNDER VINE 22.00
VITICULTURE METHOD Certified Organic

The name of Simone Castelli's winery emphasizes the property's deep connection with local history. Indeed, it refers to the property number assigned by authorities in Maremma the 1960s, during the agrarian reform. Founded in 1998, the winery has been primarily focused on native varieties such as sangiovese, ciliegiolo, colorino, grechetto, trebbiano, and aleatico, along with organic practices and a solid, minimalist approach. Non-invasive winemaking and aging in large wooden barrels, tonneaux, and concrete tanks support this style. The Morellino Vigna Bersagliere Riserva '18 exudes aromas of ripe red fruits and spices, with touches of slightly dried flowers and smoky hints. On the palate, it's full-bodied and focusing, finishing with a lovely note of Mediterranean scrub. The Trebbiano '22 features chamomile, linden flowers, and hints of ripe white fruits, offering a sapid, steady, and solid development on the palate. The Costa Ovest '23, a monovarietal grechetto, is a fragrant white with effortless and fragrant drinkability.

● Vento dell'Ovest '21	♥♥ 5
● Villa Sardini '22	♥♥ 3*
● Stellina '23	♥♥ 3
● Le Galline Ciliegiolo '23	♥ 3
☉ Orizzone Rosa Syrah '23	♥ 3
● Colline Lucchesi Ludovico Sardini '18	♀♀ 4
● Colline Lucchesi Ludovico Sardini '17	♀♀ 4
● Colline Lucchesi Ludovico Sardini '16	♀♀ 4
● Colline Lucchesi Villa Sardini '18	♀♀ 2*
● Lippo '19	♀♀ 4
● Lippo '16	♀♀ 4
● Stellina '22	♀♀ 3
● Vento dell'Ovest '19	♀♀ 5
● Vento dell'Ovest '18	♀♀ 5

● Morellino di Scansano V. Bersagliere Ris. '18	♥♥♥ 8
○ Trebbiano '22	♥♥ 5
○ Costa Ovest Grechetto '23	♥♥ 3
● Badilante Sangiovese '22	♥ 3
● Morellino di Scansano '22	♥ 5
● Aleatico Passito '13	♀♀ 7
● Badilante '19	♀♀ 3*
● Badilante '16	♀♀ 3
● Badilante '15	♀♀ 3
● Badilante Sangiovese '21	♀♀ 3*
● Morellino di Scansano '21	♀♀ 5
● Morellino di Scansano '19	♀♀ 4
● Morellino di Scansano '16	♀♀ 4
☉ Rosato Flower Power '15	♀♀ 2
○ Trebbiano '21	♀♀ 5

Podere della Civettaja

via di Casina Rossa, 5a
52100 Arezzo
(+39 3397098418
www.civettaja.it

CELLAR SALES
PRE-BOOKED VISITS
ANNUAL PRODUCTION 7,000 bottles
HECTARES UNDER VINE 3.00
VITICULTURE METHOD Certified Organic

Pinot nero is produced across all latitudes and corners of Italy, often yielding less than impressive results. However, the single wine produced at Vincenzo Tommasi's small winery, established in 2006, stands out as a notable exception. Situated at 500 meters elevation in Romena di Pratovecchio in the heart of Casentino, the location may not be among the most renowned in Tuscany's wine scene, but it is particularly well-suited for cultivating this Burgundian varietal. Once again, the Civettaja monovarietal pinot nero proves to be one of the best expressions of the noble Burgundian grape in Tuscany. The 2021 version features aromas of ripe small red fruits and spices, with light earthy and balsamic nuances as finishing touches. On the palate, it's slender, fragrant, and focused, with a multifaceted, flavorful progression and a finish that pleasantly returns to fruit.

Podere Erica

loc. San Donato in Poggio
fraz. Olena
s.da prov.le Castellina, 6
50021 Barberino Tavarnelle [FI]
(+39 3289567883
www.podereerica.com

CELLAR SALES
PRE-BOOKED VISITS
ANNUAL PRODUCTION 15,000 bottles
HECTARES UNDER VINE 2.00
VITICULTURE METHOD Certified Biodynamic
SUSTAINABLE WINERY

A small operation located in the heart of the Chianti-Florentine production zone (between Barberino Val d'Elsa and San Donato in Poggio), Podere Erica has been owned by American couple Neal and Jan Dempsey since 2006. In terms of viticulture, the turning point came in 2009, when winemaker and manager Marco Giordano decided to adopt biodynamic farming methods. The result is a modern and characterful selection of wines, where sangiovese reveals its earthier and more spontaneous side. The Picchio '21, a monovarietal sangiovese, features aromas of earth and flowers, with touches of flint and light spiciness for contrast. On the palate, the wine has energy and continuous sapidity, finishing with a lovely balsamic note. The Ghiandaia '22, a blend based on canaiolo and sangiovese, offers more open and fruity aromatic nuances, with a fleshy and sweet palate. The delightful L'Erica Rosé '23, from sangiovese grapes, and the equally delectable Le Rondini '23, a macerated monovarietal malvasia, are both delicious.

● Pinot Nero '21	♛♛ 8
● Pinot Nero '20	♛♛♛ 8
● Pinot Nero '17	♛♛♛ 6
● Pinot Nero '16	♛♛♛ 6
● Pinot Nero '14	♛♛♛ 6
● Pinot Nero '13	♛♛♛ 6
● Pinot Nero '18	♛♛ 6
● Pinot Nero '15	♛♛ 6
● Pinot Nero '12	♛♛ 3
● Pinot Nero '11	♛♛ 3

● Il Picchio '21	♛♛ 5
☉ L'Erica Rosé '23	♛♛ 4
● La Ghiandaia '22	♛♛ 5
○ Le Rondini '23	♛♛ 5
● Il Picchio '19	♛♛ 5
● La Ghiandaia '21	♛♛ 5
● The Raven '22	♛♛ 3

La Poderina

**fraz. Castelnuovo dell'Abate
loc. Poderina
53020 Montalcino [SI]**
(" +39 0577835737
@ www.lapoderina.it

CELLAR SALES
PRE-BOOKED VISITS
ACCOMMODATION
ANNUAL PRODUCTION 120,000 bottles
HECTARES UNDER VINE 37.00
SUSTAINABLE WINERY

La Poderina is one of five large agricultural estates owned by Tenute del Cerro, a farming enterprise managed by the Unipol insurance group, and based in central Italy. The Montalcino estate spans 80 hectares, nearly half of which are under vines, in the area of Castelnuovo dell'Abate, on the southern slope of the appellation. The property enjoys an advantageous microclimate, with hot but breezy summers and mild winters. The soil, rich in gravelly materials, such as albarese and galestro, ensures excellent drainage during the heavy rains. Once again, the range offered is characterized by reliable, territorial wines that slowly but steadily advance in quality. The exemplary Riserva Poggio Abate '18 features classic scents of red fruit and tobacco over a pleasant licorice background, adding complexity. The palate is juicy, with well-integrated tannins and a nice finish of long aromatic persistence. The delightful Moscatello Vendemmia Tardiva '18 is redolent of orange marmalade and butter, sweet on the palate but well balanced by acidity.

● Brunello di Montalcino Poggio Abate Ris. '18	♈♈ 8
○ Moscadello di Montalcino V.T. '18	♈♈ 5
● Brunello di Montalcino '19	♈ 7
● Rosso di Montalcino '22	♈ 3
● Brunello di Montalcino Poggio Banale '97	♈♈♈ 7
● Brunello di Montalcino Ris. '88	♈♈♈ 7
● Brunello di Montalcino '18	♈♈ 7
● Brunello di Montalcino '16	♈♈ 7
● Brunello di Montalcino '15	♈♈ 7
● Brunello di Montalcino Poggio Abate Ris. '16	♈♈ 8
● Rosso di Montalcino '21	♈♈ 4
● Rosso di Montalcino '20	♈♈ 4

Podernuovo a Palazzone

**loc. Le Vigne, 203
53040 San Casciano dei Bagni [SI]**
(" +39 057856056
@ www.podernuovoapalazzone.com

CELLAR SALES
ANNUAL PRODUCTION 130,000 bottles
HECTARES UNDER VINE 25.00
SUSTAINABLE WINERY

Podernuovo was launched in 2004 by Giovanni Bulgari. Son of Paolo Bulgari, chairman of the famous luxury jeweler and fashion house, Giovanni grows primarily sangiovese, montepulciano, cabernet sauvignon, cabernet franc, petit verdot, malbec, and merlot, along with smaller quantities of chardonnay and grechetto near San Casciano dei Bagni. This part of Tuscany, while not commonly associated with winemaking today, has a noble tradition in viticulture. Their wines reflect a modern style without unnecessary intervention, especially when it comes to the careful use of oak. The Argirio '21, a monovarietal cabernet franc, features aromas of coffee powder, small red fruits, spices, and refreshing herbal whiffs, anticipating a sweet and focused palate. The Therra '22, a blend of sangiovese, cabernet sauvignon, and merlot, proves juicy and solid. The well-crafted Sotirio '20, a monovarietal sangiovese, offers slightly more evolved aromas and a sapid flavor. The immediately expressive Nicoleo '22, a blend of chardonnay and grechetto, also delivers.

● Argirio '21	♈♈ 6
● Therra '22	♈♈ 4
○ NicoLeo '22	♈ 4
● Sotirio '20	♈ 8
● Argirio '18	♈♈ 6
● Argirio '17	♈♈ 6
● Argirio '16	♈♈ 6
○ G 33 Bianco '20	♈♈ 8
● Sotirio '18	♈♈ 7
● Sotirio '17	♈♈ 7
● Sotirio '16	♈♈ 7
● Sotirio '15	♈♈ 7
● Therra '21	♈♈ 5
● Therra '19	♈♈ 5
● Therra '18	♈♈ 5
● Therra '15	♈♈ 5

Poggio al Tesoro

fraz. Donoratico
via del Fosso, 33
57022 Castagneto Carducci [LI]
☎ +39 0565773051
✉ www.poggioaltesoro.it

CELLAR SALES
PRE-BOOKED VISITS
ANNUAL PRODUCTION 500,000 bottles
HECTARES UNDER VINE 67.50

Marilisa Allegrini and her daughters Carlotta and Caterina consider Bolgheri and Tuscany their second home. Passionate producers from Veneto and advocates of sustainable practices, they have created a flourishing and promising winery. Their first bottles, which hit the market in 2005, immediately stood out as full, generous interpretations. Today their production style includes a refined finesse, resulting in impeccably crafted wines. The Bolgheri Superiore Dedicato a Walter '20 is an aromatically intense wine, brightened by a delicate balsamic note. On the palate, its multifaceted tannic structure makes for a long and satisfying drink. The Bolgheri Rosso Il Seggio '22 offers up aromas of small red fruits with spicy and oaky whiffs, with a focused palate to follow. The monovarietal viognier Sondraia '22 is a white that stands out for its aromas of peach and ripe apricot with brackish nuances, while on the palate it's sapid and flavorful.

Wine	Rating
● Bolgheri Rosso Sup. Dedicato a Walter '20	♛♛♛ 8
● Bolgheri Rosso Il Seggio '22	♛♛ 5
● Bolgheri Rosso Sup. Sondraia '21	♛♛ 8
○ Bolgheri Vermentino Solosole '23	♛♛ 4
○ Sondraia '22	♛♛ 8
● Bolgheri Rosso Sup. Sondraia '16	♛♛♛ 7
● Bolgheri Rosso Sup. Sondraia '15	♛♛♛ 7
● Bolgheri Sup. Sondraia '14	♛♛♛ 5
● Bolgheri Sup. Sondraia '13	♛♛♛ 5
● Bolgheri Sup. Sondraia '11	♛♛♛ 5
● Bolgheri Sup. Sondraia '10	♛♛♛ 5
● Dedicato a Walter '12	♛♛♛ 7
● Dedicato a Walter '09	♛♛♛ 7
○ Sondraia '20	♛♛ 8

★Poggio Antico

loc. Poggio Antico
53024 Montalcino [SI]
☎ +39 0577848044
✉ www.poggioantico.com

CELLAR SALES
PRE-BOOKED VISITS
RESTAURANT SERVICE
ANNUAL PRODUCTION 120,000 bottles
HECTARES UNDER VINE 37.00

Since Belgian entrepreneur Marcel Van Poecke bought this lovely estate in 2017, he has made major investments to modernize it. The latest development is the construction of a new winery, designed by renowned architect Marco Casamonti. The project was driven by the need for more space for parcel-specific vinification of the estate's 37 hectares of vineyards. The facility is spread out over multiple levels, thus taking advantage of gravity, allowing the movement of musts and wines without mechanical pumps, which can alter the final product. As always, their wines manage to combine elegance and a sense of place, thanks in part to the elevations of the vineyards, which approach 500 meters. The Brunello '19 displays a clear and classy aromatic spectrum, marked by lush red fruit, rosehip, tobacco, and a slight iron note. On the palate, it shows great acid-tannin structure, austere and without excessive softness for the vintage, topped off by a long finish. The Brunello Vigna i Poggi '19 put in a nice debut: clear on the nose, close-knit, and of great finesse on the palate.

Wine	Rating
● Brunello di Montalcino '19	♛♛♛ 8
● Brunello di Montalcino Ris. '18	♛♛ 8
● Brunello di Montalcino V. I Poggi '19	♛♛ 8
● Rosso di Montalcino '22	♛ 5
● Brunello di Montalcino '05	♛♛♛ 7
● Brunello di Montalcino '88	♛♛♛ 7
● Brunello di Montalcino '85	♛♛♛ 7
● Brunello di Montalcino Altero '09	♛♛♛ 7
● Brunello di Montalcino Altero '07	♛♛♛ 8
● Brunello di Montalcino Altero '06	♛♛♛ 8
● Brunello di Montalcino Altero '04	♛♛♛ 8
● Brunello di Montalcino Altero '99	♛♛♛ 8
● Brunello di Montalcino Ris. '01	♛♛♛ 7
● Brunello di Montalcino Ris. '85	♛♛♛ 7
● Brunello di Montalcino '18	♛♛ 8
● Rosso di Montalcino '21	♛♛ 5

Fattoria Poggio Capponi

via Montelupo, 184
50025 Montespertoli [FI]
📞 +39 0571671914
🌐 www.poggiocapponi.it

CELLAR SALES
PRE-BOOKED VISITS
ACCOMMODATION
ANNUAL PRODUCTION 200,000 bottles
HECTARES UNDER VINE 32.00

The Rousseau Colzi family, now in its fourth generation, continues to manage Fattoria Poggio Capponi, acquired in the 1930s and located in the Montespertoli area. The winery cultivates vermentino, chardonnay, trebbiano, malvasia, san colombano, sangiovese, syrah, merlot, and alicante bouschet. Aging is predominantly carried out in small wooden barrels, resulting in a diverse portfolio of wines. The Chianti '22 goes all in on immediate pleasantness, starting with its aromas of pomegranate, plum, and violet, anticipating a fragrant and juicy palate. The Chianti Montespertoli Petriccio Riserva '21 plays on hints of cherry jam, cinchona, underbrush, with spicy and toasted whiffs on the nose. On the palate, it's multifaceted and rich, with nice development and a finish on fruity tones. The monovarietal chardonnay Sovente '23 features aromas of tropical fruits and a dense, sapid palate.

Wine	Rating
● Chianti '22	🍷🍷 2*
● Chianti Montespertoli Petriccio Ris. '21	🍷🍷 3*
● Chianti Campo alle Ginestre Ris. '21	🍷🍷 3
● Giovanni Rousseau Colzi '21	🍷🍷 4
○ Sovente '23	🍷🍷 3
○ Binto '23	🍷 2
● Tinorso '21	🍷 3
⊙ Villa Capponi Rosé '23	🍷 3
○ Binto '22	🍷🍷 2*
● Chianti Montespertoli Petriccio Ris. '20	🍷🍷 3
● Chianti Montespertoli Petriccio Ris. '19	🍷🍷 3
● Chianti Ris. '20	🍷🍷 2*
● Chianti Ris. '19	🍷🍷 2*
○ Sovente '22	🍷🍷 3
○ Sovente '21	🍷🍷 3

★Poggio di Sotto

fraz. Castelnuovo dell'Abate
loc. Poggio di Sotto
53024 Montalcino [SI]
📞 +39 0577835502
🌐 www.collemassari.it

CELLAR SALES
PRE-BOOKED VISITS
ANNUAL PRODUCTION 58,000 bottles
HECTARES UNDER VINE 20.00
VITICULTURE METHOD Certified Organic

Founded in 1989 by Piero Palmucci, Poggio di Sotto became part of the Tipa-Bertarelli family's Colle Massari group in 2011. This iconic Montalcino winery boasts 16 hectares of vineyards in the Brunello appellation on the southeast slope, all farmed organically. The grapes, hand-harvested after rigorous selection (so as to limit yields to 3500 liters per hectare), are fermented spontaneously in 7000-liter conical wooden vats and then aged in 3000-liter Slavonian oak barrels. Recently, the group also acquired the neighboring Tenuta San Giorgio, also based in Montalcino. This year their range shines for its ability to unite the expressiveness of sangiovese with a sense of territory. The Brunello '19 took home the Tre Bicchieri: clear and free of overripe fruit, it's refined in its floral and spicy nuances, extremely fine in its tones of licorice, tobacco, and citrus. On the palate, it's close-knit and vivid, showcasing the muscle and elegance of an world-class gymnast.

Wine	Rating
● Brunello di Montalcino '19	🍷🍷🍷 8
● Brunello di Montalcino Ris. '18	🍷🍷 8
● Brunello di Montalcino Ugolforte Ris. San Giorgio '18	🍷🍷 8
● Brunello di Montalcino Ugolforte San Giorgio '19	🍷🍷 7
● Rosso di Montalcino '22	🍷🍷 8
● Rosso di Montalcino Ciampoleto San Giorgio '22	🍷🍷 4
● Brunello di Montalcino '18	🍷🍷🍷 8
● Brunello di Montalcino '15	🍷🍷🍷 8
● Brunello di Montalcino '14	🍷🍷🍷 8
● Brunello di Montalcino '12	🍷🍷🍷 8
● Brunello di Montalcino Ris. '16	🍷🍷🍷 8
● Brunello di Montalcino Ris. '15	🍷🍷🍷 8
● Brunello di Montalcino Ris. '12	🍷🍷🍷 8

Poggio Landi - Podere Brizio

loc. Podere Belvedere
fraz. Torrenieri
s.da prov.le 71
53024 Montalcino [SI]
☎ +39 0577042736
✆ www.poggiolandi.it

ANNUAL PRODUCTION 90,000 bottles
HECTARES UNDER VINE 74.00

Poggio Landi and Podere Brizio are both part of entrepreneur Alejandro Bulgheroni's ABFV group, which includes six estates across Montalcino, Chianti Classico, and Bolgheri. Podere Brizio is located on the southern slope near Camigliano, while Poggio Landi is on the opposite side, in the Torrenieri area. Together, the estates span about 80 hectares of vineyards, divided into small parcels. Bulgheroni has chosen to keep the two brands separate so as to allow the wines to fully express the distinct potential of the two very different terroirs, which vary in terms of soil composition, microclimate, and elevation. The Brunello '19 Poggio Landi delivered on its promise, flaunting a classic nose endowed with finesse and intensity; energetic and lively on the palate, it reveals velvety tannins and balanced alcohol. Intriguing hints of blackberries, aromatic herbs, and tobacco characterize the Riserva '18, a full-bodied yet invigorating drink. The Brunello Podere Brizio '19 proves complex and persistent on the nose, energetic and decisive on the palate, with a balsamic, lingering finish.

● Brunello di Montalcino Poggio Landi '19	♟♟ 7
● Brunello di Montalcino Podere Brizio '19	♟♟ 7
● Brunello di Montalcino Poggio Landi Ris. '18	♟♟ 8
● Rosso di Montalcino Podere Brizio '22	♟♟ 4
● Rosso di Montalcino Poggio Landi '22	♟ 4
● Brunello di Montalcino Chiuso del Lupo Poggio Landi '18	♟♟ 8
● Brunello di Montalcino Podere Brizio '18	♟♟ 7
● Brunello di Montalcino Podere Brizio '17	♟♟ 7
● Brunello di Montalcino Poggio Landi '17	♟♟ 7
● Brunello di Montalcino Ris. Poggio Landi '16	♟♟ 8

Tenuta Poggio Rosso

fraz. Populonia
loc. Poggio Rosso, 1
57025 Piombino [LI]
☎ +39 056529553
✆ www.tenutapoggiorosso.it

CELLAR SALES
PRE-BOOKED VISITS
ACCOMMODATION
ANNUAL PRODUCTION 38,000 bottles
HECTARES UNDER VINE 6.00
VITICULTURE METHOD Certified Organic

Since 2001, the Monelli family has been passionately running Tenuta Poggio al Rosso, an estate based in the westernmost part of Val di Cornia, near Populonia. The property covers 20 hectares, divided between pine forests, Mediterranean woodland, and vineyards. Six hectares are under vine, while two are dedicated to olive groves. Notably, the family restored the old manor house and built an artificial lake, which now provides their irrigation needs. Their multifaceted range expresses all the potential of the territory: the interesting Velthune '21, a cabernet sauvignon, offers up a balsamic, marine, minty suite of aromas along with notes of blueberry and blackberry, eucalyptus, licorice, and black pepper; in the mouth, it's rich and pervasive. The Fufluna '23, a blend of international grapes, plays on freshness, expressing aromas of black cherry, cherry, underbrush, and a bouquet of violet and rose; an energetic, dynamic, and juicy palate follows. The Feronia '23 proves sapid and citrusy, with hints of grapefruit, citron, and lime.

● Fufluna '23	♟♟ 3
● Velthune '21	♟♟ 6
○ Feronia '23	♟ 4
● Tages '21	♟ 5
○ Bianco '22	♟♟ 5
● Fefluna '21	♟♟ 3
○ Feronia '22	♟♟ 4
○ Feronia '20	♟♟ 4
● Fufluna '22	♟♟ 3
○ Phylika '22	♟♟ 3
○ Phylika '20	♟♟ 3
● Tages '20	♟♟ 5
● Tages '19	♟♟ 5
● Velthune '20	♟♟ 6
● Velthune '19	♟♟ 6
○ Vermentino Macerato '22	♟♟ 3

Villa Poggio Salvi

loc. Poggio Salvi
53024 Montalcino [SI]
(☏ +39 0577847121
⊕ www.villapoggiosalvi.it

PRE-BOOKED VISITS
ANNUAL PRODUCTION 250,000 bottles
HECTARES UNDER VINE 43.00

Pierluigi Tagliabue's beautiful estate is located on the southern slope of the Montalcino hill. Nestled amidst Mediterranean scrub, the vineyards stretch from 350 to 500 meters in elevation, an ideal habitat for sangiovese, thanks in part to temperature variations provided by cool marine breezes from the nearby Maremma during the hottest months. Today Pierluigi runs the estate together with his nephew, winemaker Luca Belingardi, who also oversees the family's other property, Casavecchia, in Chianti Senese. The Riserva '18 is a great sangiovese, elegant on the nose, where it flaunts excellent fresh cherry, dark flowers, underbrush, cocoa, and graphite. It has a sumptuous, fresh yet juicy palate with close-knit and fine tannins; a pervasive, long finish tops things off. The Brunello Pomona '19 stands out for its strong sense of place, manifesting notes of cherry and tobacco and a fresh minty reminiscence. The palate is marked by an extraordinarily close-knit structure and harmony of tannins, which find a valid ally in the fruit. The finish seems to never end.

● Brunello di Montalcino Ris. '18	♀♀8
● Brunello di Montalcino Pomona '19	♀♀8
○ Moscadello di Montalcino V.T. Aurico '16	♀♀4
● Rosso di Montalcino '22	♀♀4
● Brunello di Montalcino '19	♀7
● Brunello di Montalcino '18	♀♀7
● Brunello di Montalcino '17	♀♀7
● Brunello di Montalcino '16	♀♀7
● Brunello di Montalcino Pomona '18	♀♀8
● Brunello di Montalcino Pomona '17	♀♀8
● Brunello di Montalcino Ris. '17	♀♀8
● Brunello di Montalcino Ris. '16	♀♀8
● Brunello di Montalcino Ris. '15	♀♀8
○ Moscadello di Montalcino V.T. Aurico '06	♀♀4
● Rosso di Montalcino '21	♀♀3
● Tosco '19	♀♀2*

Tenuta Il Poggione

fraz. Sant'Angelo in Colle
loc. Monteano
53024 Montalcino [SI]
(☏ +39 0577844029
⊕ www.tenutailpoggione.it

CELLAR SALES
PRE-BOOKED VISITS
ACCOMMODATION
ANNUAL PRODUCTION 600,000 bottles
HECTARES UNDER VINE 127.00

Owned by the Franceschi family for over two centuries, Il Poggione is one of Montalcino's oldest wineries, and among the first, in the early 20th century, to bottle Brunello. Under the enlightened leadership of Leopoldo Franceschi and Fabrizio Bindocci, it has also become one of the most dynamic, adapting to the times by offering hospitality services and accommodations, essential for any modern winery—particularly in a region like Montalcino, which is so deeply tied to wine tourism. The Brunello '19 opens with delicate floral hints, which give way to more decisive notes of cherry and spices; the palate is characterful with elegant tannins, sapid freshness, and a gorgeous, deep and spicy finish. The Rosso di Montalcino '22 features a clear and varietal bouquet of wilted roses, licorice, and fresh cherries; flavorful, slender, and well-balanced on the palate. Buoyant and drinkable.

● Brunello di Montalcino '19	♀♀7
○ Moscadello Frizzante '23	♀♀4
● Rosso di Montalcino '22	♀♀4
○ Sant'Antimo Vin Santo Ris. '16	♀♀7
○ Toscana Bianco '23	♀3
● Toscana Rosso '22	♀3
● Toscana Rosso Lo Sbrancato '23	♀3
● Brunello di Montalcino Ris. '97	♀♀♀7
● Brunello di Montalcino '18	♀♀7
● Brunello di Montalcino '17	♀♀7
● Brunello di Montalcino '16	♀♀7
● Brunello di Montalcino '15	♀♀7
● Brunello di Montalcino '14	♀♀7
● Brunello di Montalcino V. Paganelli Ris. '16	♀♀7
● Brunello di Montalcino V. Paganelli Ris. '10	♀♀8

★★★Poliziano

fraz. Montepulciano Stazione
via Fontago, I
53045 Montepulciano [SI]
📞 +39 0578738171
🌐 www.carlettipoliziano.com

CELLAR SALES
PRE-BOOKED VISITS
ANNUAL PRODUCTION 750,000 bottles
HECTARES UNDER VINE 160.00
VITICULTURE METHOD Certified Organic
SUSTAINABLE WINERY

Poliziano is Montepulciano's most renowned winery. Named after humanist Angelo Ambrogini (1454-1494), also known as "Il Poliziano" (in reference to his homeland), this brilliant producer was established in 1978 by Federico Carletti. The name proved to be an apt choice, given the winery's leading role in the territory, and ability to represent the excellence of Tuscany with relentless continuity. Today Carletti is also joined by his children Maria Stella and Francesco. The Nobile Le Caggiole '21 is a brilliant rendition—a wine of great breadth, with a refined aromatic profile that anticipates an equally elegant and pleasantly dynamic palate. The Nobile Asinone '21 is also well-crafted, with aromas that take on darker tones and a denser, more pervasive development on the palate. The rest of the lineup is convincing, with a very successful Le Stanze '20 (cabernet sauvignon and merlot), standing out.

Pomona

loc. Pomona, 39
s.da Chiantigiana
53011 Castellina in Chianti [SI]
📞 +39 0577740473
🌐 www.fattoriapomona.it

CELLAR SALES
PRE-BOOKED VISITS
ACCOMMODATION
ANNUAL PRODUCTION 16,000 bottles
HECTARES UNDER VINE 4.70
VITICULTURE METHOD Certified Organic

When you think of the landscape of Chianti, in addition to vineyards, you think of olive trees and forests. This is the Chianti Classico you hope to find in your glass: aromatic with lush fruit notes, refreshed by hints of citrus and aromatic herbs; tense and vibrant on the palate, with a savory tannic finish that complements rather than overwhelms the ripeness of the fruit. All of this characterizes Pomona and its Chianti Classico, masterfully crafted by Monica Raspi. Pursuing stylistic models of winemaking never gets you far, but for once, we feel like mentioning one: the Chianti Classico '21. It's a luscious drink where pulpy fruit and acidity engage in a playful dance, while frank and forthright aromas pass from lush fruitiness to a finer floral touch on a background of earth and underbrush. The Chianti Classico l'Omino Riserva '20 is also delicious, standing out for its balsamic aromas and a juicy palate.

● Nobile di Montepulciano Le Caggiole '21	🍷🍷🍷 8
● Nobile di Montepulciano Asinone '21	🍷🍷 8
● Le Stanze '20	🍷🍷 8
● Nobile di Montepulciano '21	🍷🍷 5
● Maremma Mandrone di Lohsa '20	🍷 6
● Nobile di Montepulciano '09	🍷🍷🍷 4*
● Nobile di Montepulciano Asinone '20	🍷🍷🍷 8
● Nobile di Montepulciano Asinone '14	🍷🍷🍷 7
● Nobile di Montepulciano Asinone '12	🍷🍷🍷 7
● Nobile di Montepulciano Asinone '11	🍷🍷🍷 7
● Nobile di Montepulciano Asinone '07	🍷🍷🍷 6
● Nobile di Montepulciano Asinone '06	🍷🍷🍷 6
● Nobile di Montepulciano Le Caggiole '18	🍷🍷🍷 4*
● Nobile di Montepulciano Le Caggiole '17	🍷🍷🍷 4*
● Nobile di Montepulciano Le Caggiole '16	🍷🍷🍷 4*
● Nobile di Montepulciano Le Caggiole '15	🍷🍷🍷 4*

● Chianti Cl. '21	🍷🍷🍷 4*
● Chianti Cl. L'Omino Ris. '20	🍷🍷 5
● Chianti Cl. '13	🍷🍷🍷 3*
● Chianti Cl. '12	🍷🍷🍷 3*
● Chianti Cl. Ris. '16	🍷🍷🍷 4*
● Chianti Cl. Ris. '14	🍷🍷🍷 4*
● Cabernet Sauvignon '19	🍷🍷 3
● Chianti Cl. '20	🍷🍷 4
● Chianti Cl. '19	🍷🍷 3*
● Chianti Cl. '18	🍷🍷 3
● Chianti Cl. '17	🍷🍷 3*
● Chianti Cl. L'Omino Ris. '19	🍷🍷 5
● Chianti Cl. Ris. '18	🍷🍷 4
● Chianti Cl. Ris. '17	🍷🍷 4

Tenuta Le Potazzine

loc. Le Prata, 262
53024 Montalcino [SI]
(*) +39 0577846168
⊛ www.lepotazzine.it

Fabrizio Pratesi

loc. Seano
via Rizzelli, 9
59011 Carmignano [PO]
(*) +39 0558704108
⊛ www.fabriziopratesi.it

TUSCANY

CELLAR SALES
PRE-BOOKED VISITS
RESTAURANT SERVICE
ANNUAL PRODUCTION 50,000 bottles
HECTARES UNDER VINE 4.70

CELLAR SALES
PRE-BOOKED VISITS
RESTAURANT SERVICE
ANNUAL PRODUCTION 50,000 bottles
HECTARES UNDER VINE 10.00
VITICULTURE METHOD Certified Organic

Gigliola Giannetti runs this small family winery alongside her very young daughters, Viola and Sofia. The five-hectare estate comprises two distinct Brunello production areas, but Potazzine also includes a well-stocked shop and an excellent wine bar in the Montalcino town center. The winery and a part of the vineyards are located in Le Prata, west of Montalcino, while the rest of the property stretches south near Sant'Angelo in Colle. The intense and elegant Brunello '19 opens on fresh red fruit, dark flowers, and Mediterranean herbs, all followed by hints of quinine and well-integrated, spicy oak. The palate is complex and rich in texture, with refined tannins and fruit blending well together, finishing long on balsamic sensations. The Rosso di Montalcino '22 is delightful, with a clean nose dominated by vibrant, enticing flowers and red fruit, and a velvety, lively palate.

Fabrizio Pratesi's winery was founded in 1983 at the Lolocco estate, but the real breakthrough came in the late 1990s during a period of revitalization for the appellation. Since 2014, Fabrizio Pratesi has dedicated himself full-time to wine, personally cultivating his vineyards of sangiovese, cabernet sauvignon, cabernet franc, and merlot. The wines are exclusively aged in new and second-fill barriques. The almost opulent bouquet of the Carmignano Il Circo Rosso Riserva '21 spans everything from dried flowers to raspberries and mint, all enriched with plenty of sweet spices. In the mouth, despite its rich aromas, the palate is dynamic, with soft tannins that make their presence felt at just the right moment. The Carmignano Carmione '22 is rich from the outset, with generous, ripe fruit on the nose. Its drinkability is softened by alcohol, and the finish offers balsamic nuances.

● Brunello di Montalcino '19	♟♟ 7
● Rosso di Montalcino '22	♟♟ 4
● Le Potazzine Sangiovese '22	♟ 4
● Brunello di Montalcino '10	♟♟♟ 7
● Brunello di Montalcino '08	♟♟♟ 7
● Brunello di Montalcino Ris. '11	♟♟♟ 8
● Brunello di Montalcino Ris. '06	♟♟♟ 8
● Brunello di Montalcino '18	♟♟ 7
● Brunello di Montalcino '15	♟♟ 7
● Brunello di Montalcino '14	♟♟ 7
● Brunello di Montalcino '13	♟♟ 7
● Brunello di Montalcino '12	♟♟ 7
● Rosso di Montalcino '21	♟♟ 4
● Rosso di Montalcino '18	♟♟ 4
● Rosso di Montalcino '16	♟♟ 4
● Rosso di Montalcino '15	♟♟ 4

● Carmignano Il Circo Rosso Ris. '21	♟♟ 7
● Carmignano Carmione '22	♟♟♟ 5
● I Sassi di Lolocco '21	♟♟♟ 8
● Barco Reale di Carmignano Locorosso '17	♟♟ 3
● Carmignano Carmione '21	♟♟ 5
● Carmignano Carmione '20	♟♟ 5
● Carmignano Carmione '19	♟♟ 4
● Carmignano Carmione '17	♟♟ 4
● Carmignano Il Circo Rosso Ris. '20	♟♟ 7
● Carmignano Il Circo Rosso Ris. '19	♟♟ 6
● Carmignano Il Circo Rosso Ris. '18	♟♟ 6
● Carmignano Il Circo Rosso Ris. '17	♟♟ 6
● Carmignano Il Circo Rosso Ris. '16	♟♟ 6
● Carmignano Il Circo Rosso Ris. '15	♟♟ 6
● Carmignano Il Circo Rosso Ris. '14	♟♟ 3
● I Sassi di Lolocco '19	♟♟ 8

Primaia

via Gentilino, 33
50026 San Casciano in Val di Pesa [FI]
☎ +39 3316151911
🖅 www.poggiodiguardia.com

ANNUAL PRODUCTION 40,000 bottles
HECTARES UNDER VINE 7.00
VITICULTURE METHOD Certified Organic

In San Casciano, on the border between Chianti Senese and Valdarno Superiore, winemakers Federico Cercelli and Stefano Di Blasi have breathed new life into an estate that had been forgotten for over 40 years. Set in the high hills, once considered too cold for vineyards but now gaining attention due to climate change, the estate's old vines have been revived, and new ones planted. The pair have opted for less common varietals like viognier, cabernet sauvignon, incrocio Manzoni, and Rebo to explore the potential of this cooler terroir. While the new vintage of Poggio di Guardia rests in the cellar, we sampled an excellent Primula Veris '22, which handily made it to our final round. It opens with an elegant bouquet of white fruit, shifting to citrus notes of citron, followed by floral hints of mimosa and chamomile. The palate is sapid, mineral, full of tension, fruit, and persistence. The Ser Primo '21 is also good—a juicy red with soft tannins, fading on vanilla notes.

★Fattoria Le Pupille

fraz. Istia d'Ombrone
loc. Piagge del Maiano, 92
58100 Grosseto
☎ +39 0564409517
🖅 www.fattorialepupille.it

CELLAR SALES
PRE-BOOKED VISITS
ANNUAL PRODUCTION 450,000 bottles
HECTARES UNDER VINE 85.00
SUSTAINABLE WINERY

The continuous enological success of the Maremma region owes much to the efforts of Elisabetta Geppetti, a true pioneer of Morellino di Scansano and a key figure in the region's revitalization. Today Geppetti is joined by her children Clara and Ettore. The consistent quality of the winery in Istia d'Ombrone is evident across its portfolio, which draws on both international varieties, aged in small wooden barrels, and local varieties, aged in large wooden casks. The solid Poggio Valente '21, a monovarietal sangiovese, features earthy aromas and small red fruits, joined by smoky and balsamic tones. In the mouth, it's focused, with spirited tannins and nice acidic verve, delivering a flavorful, intense palate. The Pelofino '23, a blend of sangiovese, cabernet sauvignon, and merlot, offers persistent drinkability, while the compact and generous Saffredi '21, a blend of cabernet sauvignon, merlot, and petit verdot, also performed well.

● Primula Veris '22	♀♀ 7
● Ser Primo '21	♀♀ 4
● Poggio di Guardia '18	♀♀ 8
Poggio di Guardia '17	♀♀ 8
Primula Veris '21	♀♀ 7
Ser Primo '20	♀♀ 4
Ser Primo '19	♀♀ 4

● Pelofino '23	♀♀ 2*
● Poggio Valente '21	♀♀ 6
○ Poggio Argentato '23	♀♀ 4
● Saffredi '21	♀♀ 8
● Morellino di Scansano '23	♀ 3
● Morellino di Scansano Ris. '21	♀ 5
● Morellino di Scansano Poggio Valente '04	♀♀♀ 5
● Morellino di Scansano Ris. '15	♀♀♀ 4*
● Saffredi '14	♀♀♀ 8
● Saffredi '13	♀♀♀ 8
● Saffredi '05	♀♀♀ 8
● Saffredi '04	♀♀♀ 8
● Saffredi '03	♀♀♀ 8
● Saffredi '02	♀♀♀ 7
● Saffredi '01	♀♀♀ 7
● Saffredi '00	♀♀♀ 7

TUSCANY

La Querce

via Imprunetana per Tavarnuzze, 41
50023 Impruneta [FI]
☎ +39 0552011380
⊕ www.laquerce.com

CELLAR SALES
PRE-BOOKED VISITS
ACCOMMODATION
ANNUAL PRODUCTION 35,000 bottles
HECTARES UNDER VINE 7.60
VITICULTURE METHOD Certified Organic

La Querce, a small winery based in the
Impruneta area, has been owned by the Marchi
family since 1962. However, the true driving
force behind the winery is Marco Ferretti, who
has managed both the vineyard and the cellar for
the family since 1985. The wines are
characterized by their unpretentious style and
excellent craftsmanship, predominantly utilizing
classic Tuscan varieties such as sangiovese,
canaiolo, colorino, and a small amount of merlot.
Aging takes place in both small and large
wooden barrels, as well as terracotta. The
Chianti Colli Fiorentini Sorrettole '22 features a
fresh and deep palate with a flavorful and
dynamic progression of flavor, all accompanied
by an intense bouquet of plum, black cherry, and
morello cherry, with touches of underbrush,
licorice, and balsamic notes. The Chianti Colli
Fiorentini La Torretta Riserva '21 has a more
concentrated and powerful palate, with a dense
and compact development. Its aromas recall
blackberry jam, licorice, and quinine, on a spicy
base. The M '19, a monovarietal merlot, also
holds its own.

● Chianti Colli Fiorentini Sorrettole '22	♥♥ 2*
● Chianti Colli Fiorentini La Torretta Ris. '21	♥♥ 4
● Dama Rosa '22	♥ 5
● La Querce '20	♥ 5
● M '19	♥ 7
● Chianti Colli Fiorentini La Torretta Ris. '15	♥♥♥ 3*
● La Querce '11	♥♥♥ 5
● Belrosso '22	♥♥ 2*
● Belrosso '21	♥♥ 2*
● Chianti Colli Fiorentini La Torretta Ris. '20	♥♥ 4
● Chianti Colli Fiorentini La Torretta Ris. '19	♥♥ 3
● Chianti Colli Fiorentini Sorrettole '19	♥♥ 2*
● La Querce '19	♥♥ 5

Querceto di Castellina

loc. Querceto, 9
53011 Castellina in Chianti [SI]
☎ +39 0577733590
⊕ www.quercetodicastellina.com

CELLAR SALES
PRE-BOOKED VISITS
ACCOMMODATION AND RESTAURANT SERVICE
ANNUAL PRODUCTION 50,000 bottles
HECTARES UNDER VINE 11.50
VITICULTURE METHOD Certified Organic
SUSTAINABLE WINERY

Giorgio Di Battista and his wife Laura arrived in
Tuscany in the late 1980s and began working in
Chianti, converting their estate into an
agriturismo. The almost inevitable addition of
winemaking came in 1998, thanks to their son
Jacopo's initiative. Based in Greve in Chianti,
Querceto di Castellina produces a well-crafted,
modern range that emphasizes intensity of fruit
and solid expressive detail. The well-crafted
Chianti Classico L'Aura '22 reveals a generous
fruity profile with hints of underbrush and subtle
spicy notes. In the mouth, it reveals a solid and
pleasantly sapid palate, finishing with nice
persistence. The Sei Gran Selezione 2021, in
contrast to L'Aura, is a denser, slightly extracted
wine, with unresolved tannins and a somewhat
dry finish.

● Chianti Cl. L'Aura '22	♥♥ 3
● Chianti Cl. Gran Selezione Sei '21	♥ 6
● Chianti Cl. Gran Selezione Sei '20	♥♥ 6
● Chianti Cl. Gran Selezione Sei '19	♥♥ 5
○ Livia '19	♥♥ 5
● Podalirio '18	♥♥ 5
● Venti '20	♥♥ 8

La Rasina

loc. Rasina, 132
53024 Montalcino [SI]
☎ +39 0577848536
✉ www.larasina.it

Podere La Regola

loc. Altagrada, s.da regionale 68,
km 6+400
56046 Riparbella [PI]
☎ +39 058881363
✉ www.laregola.com

CELLAR SALES
PRE-BOOKED VISITS
ACCOMMODATION
ANNUAL PRODUCTION 60,000 bottles
HECTARES UNDER VINE 12.50

CELLAR SALES
PRE-BOOKED VISITS
ANNUAL PRODUCTION 120,000 bottles
HECTARES UNDER VINE 25.00
VITICULTURE METHOD Certified Organic
SUSTAINABLE WINERY

La Rasina sits atop the northern slope of Montalcino hill at 350 meters elevation. This family-run winery, founded by Santi Mantegoli about 50 years ago, has long been known for producing high-quality wines deeply connected to the terroir. Now in its third generation, La Rasina is managed by Marco, an enthusiastic winemaker and grower. He has converted the entire estate to organic farming, producing not only wine but also olive oil and grains. The Brunello '19 opens with a lovely aromatic profile, passing from red and black berries to sweet oak spices, adding complexity with tobacco, petrichor and quinine. A regal palate is supported by refined tannins, enhancing its full yet dynamic structure, and a long finish pleasantly marked by oak. The highly terroir-driven Brunello Piersante '19 integrates fruit with ferrous mineral notes, while the sapid palate stands out for its fine aromatic texture.

The Nuti brothers and their children manage La Regola, a winery founded in 1990 and the first to believe in the oenological potential of Riparbella. The vineyards, cultivated organically, host merlot, cabernet franc, sangiovese, cabernet sauvignon, syrah, sauvignon, chardonnay, viognier, and vermentino. The result is a diverse range of wines, including some Metodo Classico, matured in stainless steel and concrete, as well as small and large wood barrels. La Regola '21, a monovarietal cabernet franc, exhibits Mediterranean aromas of ripe fruit, spices, and aromatic herbs. In the mouth, the palate is juicy and effortless, with good sapidity and a citrus-toned finish. The Vallino '21, a blend of cabernet sauvignon, sangiovese, and cabernet franc, has a solid palate with aromatic, herbaceous tones and a refreshing, minty finish. The Strido '21, a monovarietal merlot, proves well-crafted, unveiling vibrant aromas and a generous progression on the palate.

● Brunello di Montalcino '19	♟♟ 7
● Brunello di Montalcino Persante '19	♟♟ 8
● Toscana Sangiovese '22	♟ 3
● Brunello di Montalcino '01	♟♟♟ 6
● Brunello di Montalcino '00	♟♟♟ 6
● Brunello di Montalcino Il Divasco '01	♟♟♟ 8
● Brunello di Montalcino '18	♟♟ 6
● Brunello di Montalcino '17	♟♟ 6
● Brunello di Montalcino Il Divasco Ris. '16	♟♟ 8
● Brunello di Montalcino Il Divasco Ris. '15	♟♟ 8
● Brunello di Montalcino Persante '18	♟♟ 8
● Brunello di Montalcino Persante '17	♟♟ 8
● Brunello di Montalcino Persante '16	♟♟ 8
● Rosso di Montalcino '20	♟♟ 3

● La Regola '21	♟♟♟ 8
● Vallino '21	♟♟ 6
○ La Regola Bianco '21	♟♟ 8
○ Steccaia '23	♟♟ 3
● Strido '20	♟♟ 8
● La Regola '20	♟♟♟ 8
● La Regola '19	♟♟♟ 8
● La Regola '18	♟♟♟ 8
● La Regola '17	♟♟♟ 8
● La Regola '16	♟♟♟ 8
● La Regola '15	♟♟♟ 7
● La Regola '14	♟♟ 7
● La Regola '12	♟♟ 6
● La Regola '11	♟♟ 6
● Strido '13	♟♟ 8
● Vallino '15	♟♟ 5

★★Barone Ricasoli

loc. Madonna a Brolio
53013 Gaiole in Chianti [SI]
(☏) +39 05777301
✉ www.ricasoli.com

CELLAR SALES
PRE-BOOKED VISITS
ACCOMMODATION
ANNUAL PRODUCTION 1,300,000 bottles
HECTARES UNDER VINE 240.00
SUSTAINABLE WINERY

Situated in Gaiole in Chianti, Castello di Brolio boasts all the essential elements of a great wine estate: history, prestige, family, and the fact that it invented Tuscany's most famous wine. It has its own sangiovese clone, the "Brolio," and the winery's vineyard zoning has identified three different crus — "Colledilà," "Roncicone," and "CeniPrimo" — which give rise to three wines that are consistently among the appellation's best. The Chianti Classico Gran Selezione Colledilà '21, unsurprisingly, shines with its aromas of just-ripe red berries, underbrush, spices, and light, toasty notes. In the mouth, it shows depth and dynamism, with vivid, flavorful tannins, lively acidity, and sweetness. The nervy Chianti Classico Gran Selezione Roncicone '21 performed well, while the Chianti Classico Gran Selezione Castello di Brolio '19 stood out for its accents of great finesse.

Ridolfi

loc. Mercatali, 1
53024 Montalcino [SI]
(☏) +39 3371095216
✉ www.ridolfimontalcino.it/en

ANNUAL PRODUCTION 110,000 bottles
HECTARES UNDER VINE 19.00
SUSTAINABLE WINERY

The Peretti family's estate is located in Mercatali on the northeastern slope of the appellation, at about 300 meters elevation. This beautiful estate focuses on sustainable wine and olive oil production, with a strong commitment to preserving the environment and biodiversity. The older vineyards are all trained using the cordone speronato system, while those planted after 2013 follow the guyot method. Meticulous care in the vineyard ensures healthy grapes, capable of withstanding long macerations (at least 60 days), gradually releasing polyphenols, anthocyanins, and tannins. An outstanding performance from the Brunello '19, which summons a refined aromatic interplay of cherries, mulberries, plums, thyme, other aromatic herbs, tobacco, cocoa powder, and a potpourri of sweet spices. These are all so masterfully orchestrated that they create a wine of exceptional elegance. The dynamic and delicious palate is enveloped by progressive tannins, leading to a long, fleshy finish with great character. The Brunello Donna Rebecca '19, still marked by oak, offers a palate with volume, solidity, and length.

● Chianti Cl. Gran Selezione Colledilà '21	♟♟♟ 8
● Chianti Cl. Gran Selezione CeniPrimo '21	♟♟ 8
● Chianti Cl. Gran Selezione Roncicone '21	♟♟ 8
● Casalferro '20	♟♟ 8
● Chianti Cl. Brolio '22	♟♟ 5
● Chianti Cl. Brolio Bettino '21	♟♟ 6
● Chianti Cl. Brolio Ris. '21	♟♟ 7
● Chianti Cl. Gran Selezione Castello di Brolio '21	♟♟ 8
● Chianti Cl. Rocca Guicciarda Ris. '21	♟♟ 5
● Antico Feudo della Trappola '22	♟ 3
● Historia Familiae '21	♟ 8

● Brunello di Montalcino '19	♟♟♟ 8
● Brunello di Montalcino Donna Rebecca '19	♟♟ 8
● Rosso di Montalcino '22	♟♟ 4
● Brunello di Montalcino '16	♟♟♟ 6
● Brunello di Montalcino '15	♟♟♟ 5
● Brunello di Montalcino Mercatale Ris. '17	♟♟♟ 8
● Brunello di Montalcino Mercatale Ris. '16	♟♟♟ 8
● Brunello di Montalcino '18	♟♟ 6
● Brunello di Montalcino '17	♟♟ 7
● Brunello di Montalcino Mercatale Ris. '15	♟♟ 7
● Fiero '18	♟♟ 5
● Fiero '17	♟♟ 5
● Rosso di Montalcino '21	♟♟ 4
● Rosso di Montalcino '20	♟♟ 5
● Rosso di Montalcino '19	♟♟ 4
● Rosso di Montalcino '17	♟♟ 4

★Riecine

loc. Riecine
53013 Gaiole in Chianti [SI]
☎ +39 0577749098
🖳 www.riecine.it

Rigoli

loc. Cafaggio
via degli Ulivi, 8
57021 Campiglia Marittima [LI]
☎ +39 0565843079
🖳 www.rigolivini.com

CELLAR SALES
PRE-BOOKED VISITS
ACCOMMODATION
ANNUAL PRODUCTION 80,000 bottles
HECTARES UNDER VINE 16.00
VITICULTURE METHOD Certified Organic
SUSTAINABLE WINERY

ANNUAL PRODUCTION 30,000 bottles
HECTARES UNDER VINE 5.00

Riecine has been owned by Lana Frank since 2011. Here in the heart of the Gaiole in Chianti production zone, Frank has wisely preserved the stylistic profile and production philosophy of this iconic Chianti winery, known for its history and high quality. Viticulture is organic, and the approach to maturation combines a mix suited to the characteristics of the vintages, alternating barriques, tonneaux, large wood barrels, stainless steel, and concrete. The result is a range characterized by an unmistakable sense of place. The refined and minimalist Riecine di Riecine '21, a monovarietal sangiovese, features an airy nose of small red fruits and flowers, with smoky whiffs and hints of flint. On the palate, it's supple and multifaceted, sapid, and well-balanced. La Gioia '20, also made from sangiovese, is a fuller-bodied, fleshy wine, with aromas marked by spicy undertones and vibrant, ripe fruit. The palate of the Chianti Classico '22 proves highly enjoyable.

Founded in the early 1990s, Rigoli is run by father and sons, Nelusco, Edoardo, and Niccolò Pini, and was one of Val di Cornia's first producers. A small winery located in the Campiglia Marittima area, it cultivates sangiovese, merlot, cabernet sauvignon, vermentino, and ansonica in its vineyards, producing generous wines with a Mediterranean character. The Val di Cornia Ansonica Passito Magistro '23 opens with vibrant citrus aromas alongside sweeter fruity tones. On the palate, its progression is pervasive, sweet, with a caramel-tinged finish. The Val di Cornia Sangiovese Montepitti '21, though simple, is well-crafted, with enticing aromas and a pleasantly flavorful taste. The Stradivino '23, a monovarietal vermentino, expresses clean, crisp flavors with aptly expressed aromas.

● Riecine di Riecine '21	♟♟♟ 8
● La Gioia '20	♟♟ 8
● Chianti Cl. '22	♟♟ 5
● Chianti Cl. Gran Selezione V. Gittori '21	♟♟ 8
● Chianti Cl. Ris. '21	♟♟ 7
○ Bianco di Riecine '22	♟ 8
● Chianti Cl. '17	♟♟♟ 3*
● Chianti Cl. Gran Selezione V. Gittori '20	♟♟♟ 8
● Chianti Cl. Ris. '15	♟♟♟ 5
● Chianti Cl. Ris. '99	♟♟♟ 7
● La Gioia '16	♟♟♟ 8
● La Gioia '04	♟♟♟ 6
● La Gioia '01	♟♟♟ 6
● La Gioia '98	♟♟♟ 6
● La Gioia '95	♟♟♟ 6
● Riecine '17	♟♟♟ 8
● Riecine di Riecine '19	♟♟♟ 8

○ Stradivino '23	♟♟ 3
○ Val di Cornia Ansonica Passito Magistro '23	♟♟ 5
● Val di Cornia Sangiovese Montepitti '21	♟♟ 3
○ Accordo '23	♟ 3
● L'Assiolo '20	♟ 5
● N'Etrusco '23	♟ 3
○ Accordo '22	♟♟ 3
● N'Etrusco '22	♟♟ 3
● N'Etrusco '21	♟♟ 3
○ Stradivino '22	♟♟ 3
○ Stradivino '21	♟♟ 3
○ Val di Cornia Ansonica Passito Magistro '22	♟♟ 5
● Val di Cornia Sangiovese Montepitti '20	♟♟ 3

TUSCANY

★Rocca delle Macìe Famiglia Zingarelli

fraz. Lilliano
loc. Le Macìe, 45
53011 Castellina in Chianti [SI]
☏ +39 05777321
✇ www.roccadellemacie.com

CELLAR SALES
PRE-BOOKED VISITS
ACCOMMODATION AND RESTAURANT SERVICE
ANNUAL PRODUCTION 1,800,000 bottles
HECTARES UNDER VINE 206.00
SUSTAINABLE WINERY

Rocca delle Macìe is now one of Chianti's most solid producers. The winery draws on three properties within the appellation (all in Castellina in Chianti): the original estates of Sant'Alfonso and Le Macìe (the latter, acquired in 1973, also serves as their headquarters), and Fizzano, purchased in 1984 and the heart of the Zingarelli family's hospitality work, with a relais and gourmet restaurant. Not to be forgotten are the Maremma estates of Campo Maccione, acquired in 1998, and Casa Maria, purchased in 2003. The Chianti Classico Gran Selezione Sergio Zingarelli '20 showcases a refined, focused profile, with aromas of small red fruits, violets, spices, and smoky accents. On the palate, it blends the sweetness of fruit with a precise acidic verve, finishing on a lovely minty note. The Chianti Classico Riserva '21 offers pronounced aromas and a fragrant, fleshy, flavorful palate. The Vermentino Vigna L'Aja Bruciata '22 is a pleasant surprise.

★Rocca di Castagnoli Tenute Calì

loc. Castagnoli
53013 Gaiole in Chianti [SI]
☏ +39 0577731004
✇ www.roccadicastagnoli.com

CELLAR SALES
PRE-BOOKED VISITS
ACCOMMODATION AND RESTAURANT SERVICE
ANNUAL PRODUCTION 500,000 bottles
HECTARES UNDER VINE 87.00
VITICULTURE METHOD Certified Organic
SUSTAINABLE WINERY

Based in the Gaiole in Chianti UGA production zone, Rocca di Castagnoli features a clearly defined stylistic direction, favoring the balance and elegance for which the best Chianti Classicos are known. Its wines are characterized by consistent and reliable quality, often achieving peaks of excellence within the appellation. The Calì family, owners of the Sicilian winery Graffetta and the Maremma vineyards of Poggio Maestrino, owns this estate. The Chianti Classico Gran Selezione Effe 55 '20 presents an elegant profile, with an airy, sculpted bouquet that sets the stage for a dynamic, precise, and multifaceted palate. The Chianti Classico Capraia Riserva '21 proves well-crafted, with sunny, vibrant, expansive aromas and a juicy, well-balanced palate. The Chianti Classico Capraia '22 stands out for its flavorful and persistent palate, while the Rocca di Castagnoli '22 is more crisp and lively.

● Chianti Cl. Gran Selezione Sergio Zingarelli '20	▼▼▼ 8
● Chianti Cl. Ris. '21	▼▼ 4
○ Maremma Vermentino Sup. Campo Maccione V. L'Aja Bruciata '22	▼▼ 6
● Chianti Cl. Gran Selezione Tenuta di Fizzano Il Crocino '21	▼▼ 7
○ Morellino di Scansano Campomaccione '23	▼▼ 3
● Chianti Cl. '22	▼ 3
● Chianti Cl. Tenuta Sant'Alfonso '22	▼ 5
● Chianti Cl. Famiglia Zingarelli Ris. '16	♈♈♈ 5
● Chianti Cl. Gran Selezione Riserva di Fizzano '18	♈♈♈ 6
● Chianti Cl. Gran Selezione Sergio Zingarelli '19	♈♈♈ 8
● Chianti Cl. Gran Selezione Tenuta di Fizzano '19	♈♈♈ 6

● Chianti Cl. Gran Selezione Capraia Effe 55 '20	▼▼▼ 6
● Chianti Cl. Capraia '22	▼▼ 4
● Chianti Cl. Capraia Ris. '21	▼▼ 5
● Chianti Cl. Rocca di Castagnoli '22	▼▼ 4
● Chianti Cl. Gran Selezione Stielle '21	▼ 5
● Chianti Cl. Poggio a' Frati Ris. '20	▼ 5
● Morellino di Scansano Spiaggiole Poggio Maestrino '21	▼ 2
● Chianti Cl. Capraia Ris. '18	♈♈♈ 5
● Chianti Cl. Capraia Ris. '07	♈♈♈ 4
● Chianti Cl. Gran Selezione Capraia Effe 55 '16	♈♈♈ 6
● Chianti Cl. Poggio a' Frati Ris. '18	♈♈♈ 5
● Chianti Cl. Poggio a' Frati Ris. '08	♈♈♈ 4
● Chianti Cl. Rocca di Castagnoli '17	♈♈♈ 3*
● Chianti Cl. Tenuta di Capraia Ris. '06	♈♈♈ 4*

★★Rocca di Frassinello

loc. Giuncarico
58023 Gavorrano [GR]
+39 056688400
www.roccadifrassinello.it

CELLAR SALES
PRE-BOOKED VISITS
ACCOMMODATION
ANNUAL PRODUCTION 400,000 bottles
HECTARES UNDER VINE 90.00
SUSTAINABLE WINERY

The winery's owner is also a shareholder of Gambero Rosso spa. To avoid any conflict of interest, Paolo Panerai has subordinated the possible awarding of Tre Bicchieri—which, in any case, only occurs through a blind tasting—to the attainment of the same rating of excellence, upwards of 90/100, by an independent, international panel. This was the case here. The excellent 2021 vintage made for a Baffonero that's in splendid form. This merlot expresses all the elegance and depth of the Bordeaux varietal, coupled with a distinct Mediterranean grace and personality. Structured yet supple, it's rich with fruit, sapid, and deep, featuring velvety tannins and iodine fragrances. The supertuscan San Germano '20, with its complex structure and remarkable drinkability, underscores this corner of Maremma's affinity for international grapes. We also appreciated the excellent Vermentino Rocca Bianco '22, with its fleshy fruit and sapid minerality.

● Maremma Toscana Merlot Baffonero '21	▼▼▼ 8
● Maremma Toscana San Germano '20	▼▼ 8
● Maremma Toscana Rosso Le Sughere di Frassinello '22	▼▼ 5
○ Maremma Toscana Vermentino Rocca Bianco '22	▼▼ 8
● Maremma Toscana Rosso Ornello '22	▼ 4
● Maremma Toscana Rosso Poggio alla Guardia '22	▼ 3
● Maremma Toscana Rosso Rocca di Frassinello '22	▼ 8
● Maremma Toscana Baffonero '17	▽▽▽ 8
● Maremma Toscana Merlot Baffonero '20	▽▽▽ 8
● Maremma Toscana Merlot Baffonero '19	▽▽▽ 8
● Maremma Toscana Merlot Baffonero '18	▽▽▽ 8
● Maremma Toscana Rocca di Frassinello '17	▽▽▽ 8

Rocca di Montemassi

loc. Pian del Bichi
fraz. Montemassi
s.da prov.le Sant'Anna
58036 Roccastrada [GR]
+39 0564579700
www.roccadimontemassi.it

CELLAR SALES
PRE-BOOKED VISITS
ACCOMMODATION
ANNUAL PRODUCTION 480,000 bottles
HECTARES UNDER VINE 176.00
VITICULTURE METHOD Certified Organic
SUSTAINABLE WINERY

Rocca di Montemassi is the Zonin family's Maremma winery. The producer quickly established itself as a leader in the territory, which still has untapped potential. In an environment that blends Mediterranean scrub, metalliferous hills, and sea air, it has focused production on both local varieties, primarily vermentino and sangiovese, and international ones, including cabernet sauvignon, cabernet franc, merlot, syrah, sauvignon, and viognier. The Maremma Vermentino Calasole '23 offers aromas of just-ripe white fruits alongside hints of linden flowers and eucalyptus. On the palate, it's balanced, flavorful, fragrant, and persistent. The Maremma Viognier '22 proves well-crafted, featuring vibrant tropical fruit aromas with citrus whiffs, leading to a full, compact, and gently soft palate. Perhaps a bit one-dimensional.

○ Maremma Toscana Vermentino Calasole '23	▼▼ 3
○ Maremma Toscana Viognier '22	▼▼ 5
● Rocca di Montemassi '10	▽▽▽ 5
● Rocca di Montemassi '09	▽▽▽ 5
● Maremma Toscana Rosso Rocca di Montemassi '19	▽▽ 5
● Maremma Toscana Rosso Sassabruna '18	▽▽ 5
● Maremma Toscana Rosso Sassabruna '17	▽▽ 4
○ Maremma Toscana Vermentino Calasole '21	▽▽ 4
○ Maremma Toscana Viognier '20	▽▽ 7

★Roccapesta

loc. Macereto, 9
58054 Scansano [GR]
℡ +39 0564599252
🌐 www.roccapesta.com

CELLAR SALES
PRE-BOOKED VISITS
ANNUAL PRODUCTION 100,000 bottles
HECTARES UNDER VINE 26.50

Alberto Tanzini has established a benchmark winery in the Morellino di Scansano appellation, leaning heavily on tradition. He draws exclusively on local grape varieties, respecting and developing old vineyards (though he also recently acquired plots from Morello di Sellari e Franceschini, a historic producer in Scansano). Most of his wines are aged in large wooden casks, an approach that, year after year, results in charming, highly distinctive wines. The Morellino Vigna I Gaggioli Riserva '22 reveals an airy, sparkling nose of small red fruits and underbrush, complemented by a refined, dynamic palate with ample breadth. The Morellino Vigna Liuzza Riserva '22 integrates freshness and sapidity precisely, though with some tannic roughness, while also offering remarkable aromatic breadth. The Morellino '22 presents a smooth, flavorful palate. The Morellino Ribeo '22 moves on a similar track.

★★Ruffino

p.le Ruffino, 1
50065 Pontassieve [FI]
℡ +39 05583605
🌐 www.ruffino.it

CELLAR SALES
PRE-BOOKED VISITS
ACCOMMODATION AND RESTAURANT SERVICE
ANNUAL PRODUCTION 28,000,000 bottles
HECTARES UNDER VINE 550.00
SUSTAINABLE WINERY

Owned by Constellation Brands, the American behemoth, Ruffino boasts a vast oenological mosaic in Tuscany. This includes the estates of Poggio Casciano in Grassina, Montemasso in Impruneta, Santedame and Gretole in Castellina in Chianti, Greppone Mazzi in Montalcino, and La Solatia in Monteriggioni. In producing Chianti Classico, they offer a well-crafted range, at times reaching peaks of excellence, especially in those cases where appeasing international tastes is not a primary concern. The Chianti Classico Riserva Ducale '21 features aromas of violets and plums, accented with tobacco and spices, along with a pleasing sensation of iron. On the palate, it offers volume and contrast, developing in a well-structured manner and finishing with expansive fruity notes. The Chianti Classico Gran Selezione Riserva Ducale Oro '20 is more opulent, playing on intense spicy aromas and a close-knit, pervasive structure that finishes richly.

● Morellino di Scansano V. I Gaggioli Ris. '22	♟♟♟ 8
● Morellino di Scansano '22	♟♟ 4
● Morellino di Scansano Ribeo '22	♟♟ 3
● Morellino di Scansano V. Liuzza Ris. '22	♟♟ 7
● Morellino di Scansano Ris. '21	♟ 5
● Pugnitello '21	♟ 6
● Morellino di Scansano Calestaia Ris. '16	♟♟♟ 6
● Morellino di Scansano Ribeo '15	♟♟♟ 3*
● Morellino di Scansano Ris. '18	♟♟♟ 5
● Morellino di Scansano Ris. '16	♟♟♟ 5
● Morellino di Scansano Ris. '13	♟♟♟ 4*
● Morellino di Scansano V. Liuzza Ris. '21	♟♟♟ 7

● Chianti Cl. Riserva Ducale '21	♟♟ 4
● Chianti Cl. Gran Selezione Riserva Ducale Oro '20	♟♟ 6
● Alauda '20	♟ 8
● Chianti Cl. Gran Selezione Romitorio di Santedame '20	♟ 7
● Modus '20	♟ 5
● Chianti Cl. Gran Selezione Riserva Ducale Oro '15	♟♟♟ 6
● Chianti Cl. Gran Selezione Riserva Ducale Oro '14	♟♟♟ 6
● Chianti Cl. Riserva Ducale '20	♟♟♟ 4*
● Chianti Cl. Riserva Ducale '19	♟♟♟ 4*
● Chianti Cl. Riserva Ducale '18	♟♟♟ 4*
● Chianti Cl. Riserva Ducale '17	♟♟♟ 4*
● Chianti Cl. Riserva Ducale Oro '04	♟♟♟ 5
● Modus '04	♟♟♟ 5

La Sala del Torriano

via Sorripa, 34
50026 San Casciano in Val di Pesa [FI]
☎ +39 0558240013
⊘ www.lasala.it

CELLAR SALES
PRE-BOOKED VISITS
ACCOMMODATION
ANNUAL PRODUCTION 50,000 bottles
HECTARES UNDER VINE 34.00
VITICULTURE METHOD Certified Organic
SUSTAINABLE WINERY

A charming artisanal winery, La Sala del Torriano
produces wines that reflect the noble traditions
of the Chianti region. The estate takes its name
from its two main areas: the lands of Torriano in
Monteridolfi, which also hosts a farmhouse, and
La Sala, which is adjacent to the winery. The
34-hectare estate produces about 50,000
bottles, including three different types of Chianti
Classico (Annata, Riserva, and Gran Selezione), a
Bordeaux blend called Campo all'Albero, and a
limited selection of Pugnitello under the name 5
Filari. Rounding out their portfolio is a Vin Santo
made only in certain vintages. The most
well-made wine is undoubtedly the Gran
Selezione Il Torriano. The 2020 vintage delivers a
light and elegant profile, with prominent notes of
red fruit and underbrush. On the palate, it's
energetic, with perfectly integrated tannins, a
balanced mix of freshness and sapidity, and a
long, clean finish. The Chianti Classico '21 is
also delicious, as is the previously mentioned 5
Filari, a monovarietal pugnitello. The Campo
All'Albero '20 proves compact yet harmonious.

● Chianti Cl. Gran Selezione Il Torriano '20	♟♟ 8
● 5 Filari Pugnitello '20	♟♟ 7
● Campo all'Albero '20	♟♟ 6
● Chianti Cl. '21	♟♟ 4
● Chianti Cl. Ris. '20	♟ 5
● Chianti Cl. '20	♟♟ 3*
● Chianti Cl. '19	♟♟ 3
● Chianti Cl. '11	♟♟ 3
● Chianti Cl. '10	♟♟ 6
● Chianti Cl. Gran Selezione Il Torriano '19	♟♟ 8
● Chianti Cl. Gran Selezione Il Torriano '18	♟♟ 8
● Chianti Cl. Ris. '19	♟♟ 6
● Chianti Cl. Ris. '18	♟♟ 6
● Chianti Cl. Ris. '09	♟♟ 7

★Salcheto

via di Villa Bianca, 15
53045 Montepulciano [SI]
☎ +39 0578799031
⊘ www.salcheto.it

CELLAR SALES
PRE-BOOKED VISITS
ACCOMMODATION AND RESTAURANT SERVICE
ANNUAL PRODUCTION 400,000 bottles
HECTARES UNDER VINE 58.00
VITICULTURE METHOD Certified Organic
SUSTAINABLE WINERY

Based near the "Pieve" Sant'Albino, Salcheto is a
pioneering project that captures the right
balance between man and nature in
contemporary wine production. Their first
"off-grid" harvest was in 2011, the result of 15
years of experimentation that disconnected the
winery from the energy grid, making it
self-sufficient. They also produced the first
European wine bottle with a "Carbon Footprint"
certification. The wines reflect a harmony with
their native territory, displaying character and a
touch of rusticity. The vibrant Nobile '21 opens
with aromas of ripe red fruit, earth, and
underbrush, finishing with smoky notes. On the
palate, it's broad, juicy, and smooth, with slightly
spirited tannins and a still-fruity finish. The
Nobile Vecchie Viti di Salco '21, though slightly
confined by its concentration, offers austere,
dark, and earthy aromas on a background of
toasty sensations, with a sweet yet restrained
palate. The Chianti Biskero '23 proves pleasantly
approachable.

● Nobile di Montepulciano '21	♟♟ 5
● Nobile di Montepulciano Vecchie Viti del Salco '21	♟♟ 8
● Chianti Biskero '23	♟ 3
● Nobile di Montepulciano '17	♟♟♟ 4*
● Nobile di Montepulciano '16	♟♟♟ 4*
● Nobile di Montepulciano '14	♟♟♟ 4*
● Nobile di Montepulciano '10	♟♟♟ 4*
● Nobile di Montepulciano Salco '11	♟♟♟ 6
● Nobile di Montepulciano Salco '10	♟♟♟ 5
● Nobile di Montepulciano V.V. del Salco '19	♟♟♟ 8
● Nobile di Montepulciano V.V. del Salco '18	♟♟♟ 8

★Salvioni

p.zza Cavour, 19
53024 Montalcino [SI]
📞 +39 0577848499
🌐 www.aziendasalvioni.com

PRE-BOOKED VISITS
RESTAURANT SERVICE
ANNUAL PRODUCTION 15,000 bottles
HECTARES UNDER VINE 4.00

La Cerbaiola is a small estate on the
southeastern slope of Montalcino. Here, just a
few hectares of vines have been carefully tended
by the Salvioni family for generations. The
business was founded by grandfather Umberto,
an agronomist, although he never bottled his
wines. In the 1980s, his son Giulio, along with his
wife Mirella, transformed the estate's Brunello
into one of the most celebrated of the entire
appellation. Today, their children, Alessia and
David, an agronomist like his grandfather, have
come on board. The 2019 Brunello crafted by
Giulio Salvioni, one of Motalcino's great
producers, reflects decades of experience honed
in difficult vintages. A wine characterized by rare
varietal precision and deep territorial identity, it
captivates with its complex aromas of
blackberries, iris, cardamom, licorice, red citrus,
and tobacco. Its crystal-clear acidity and fine
tannic weave extend the palate endlessly. We tip
our hats to Giulio.

● Brunello di Montalcino '19	🍷🍷 8
● Rosso di Montalcino '22	🍷🍷 8
● Brunello di Montalcino '12	🍷🍷🍷 8
● Brunello di Montalcino '09	🍷🍷🍷 8
● Brunello di Montalcino '06	🍷🍷🍷 8
● Brunello di Montalcino '04	🍷🍷🍷 8
● Brunello di Montalcino '00	🍷🍷🍷 8
● Brunello di Montalcino '99	🍷🍷🍷 8
● Brunello di Montalcino '97	🍷🍷🍷 8
● Brunello di Montalcino '90	🍷🍷🍷 8
● Brunello di Montalcino '89	🍷🍷🍷 8
● Brunello di Montalcino '88	🍷🍷🍷 8
● Brunello di Montalcino '87	🍷🍷🍷 8
● Brunello di Montalcino '85	🍷🍷🍷 8
● Rosso di Montalcino '17	🍷🍷🍷 8

Podere San Cristoforo

via Forni
58023 Gavorrano [GR]
📞 +39 3358212413
🌐 www.poderesancristoforo.it

CELLAR SALES
PRE-BOOKED VISITS
ACCOMMODATION
ANNUAL PRODUCTION 60,000 bottles
HECTARES UNDER VINE 18.00
VITICULTURE METHOD Certified Biodynamic
SUSTAINABLE WINERY

Lorenzo Zonin's winemaking project, now over
20 years old, is marked by extreme choices. His
always-memorable wines are produced using
biodynamic methods and an approach that
includes techniques like "governo alla toscana"
and underwater maturation in the open sea. The
main grape varieties in the vineyards, cultivated
near Gavorrano, are sangiovese, petit verdot,
syrah, vermentino, and trebbiano, resulting in
generous range that's full of personality. The
2023 Maremma Vermentino Luminoso offers a
smooth, sapid, and focused palate, with aromas
of linden flowers meeting ripe white fruit, and
citrus notes, all accented by hints of
Mediterranean scrub. The Amphora Maris '20, a
petit verdot aged in the sea, follows the growing
trend of underwater aging, showcasing intense
aromas and balanced flavors. The 2022 Maremma
Sangiovese Carandelle proves compact and rich.

○ Maremma Toscana Vermentino Luminoso '23	🍷🍷 4
● Amphora-Maris '20	🍷🍷 8
● Maremma Toscana Sangiovese Carandelle '22	🍷🍷 5
● Ameri Governo all'Uso Toscano '22	🍷 7
● Maremma Toscana Petit Verdot San Cristoforo '22	🍷 7
● Maremma Toscana Sangiovese Amaranto '22	🍷 4
● Ameri Governo all'Uso Toscano '15	🍷🍷🍷 6
● Maremma Toscana Podere San Cristoforo '13	🍷🍷🍷 3*
● Maremma Toscana Sangiovese Carandelle '15	🍷🍷🍷 3*
● Petit Verdot '21	🍷🍷 7

Fattoria San Donato

loc. San Donato, 6
53037 San Gimignano [SI]
☏ +39 0577941616
✉ www.sandonato.it

CELLAR SALES
PRE-BOOKED VISITS
ACCOMMODATION AND RESTAURANT SERVICE
ANNUAL PRODUCTION 70,000 bottles
HECTARES UNDER VINE 20.00
VITICULTURE METHOD Certified Organic

The Lenzi family has owned the San Donato farm since 1932. Since 2001, Umberto Lenzi has steered the winery towards a respectful approach to the land, the vines, and the workers. The undisputed star of their range is Vernaccia di San Gimignano, presented in an immediately pleasing style, complemented by a small selection of reds, predominantly sangiovese. The Vernaccia di San Gimignano Benedetta Ris. '20 reveals fresh aromas of mint and medicinal herbs adorned by notes of vanilla and iodine. The palate is firm, with a final sapid vein that lingers beautifully. Similar aromatic affinities are found in the 2023 Vernaccia di San Gimignano, which adds a lovely hint of chamomile, though its palate is simpler and more immediately expressive. The 2021 Vernaccia di San Gimignano Angelica proves pleasant, with minty and floral notes, though oak can occasionally overpower the palate.

★★San Felice

loc. San Felice
53019 Castelnuovo Berardenga [SI]
☏ +39 057739911
✉ www.sanfelice.com

CELLAR SALES
PRE-BOOKED VISITS
ACCOMMODATION AND RESTAURANT SERVICE
ANNUAL PRODUCTION 1,200,000 bottles
HECTARES UNDER VINE 188.00
SUSTAINABLE WINERY

San Felice has been writing memorable chapters in the history of Chianti Classico since the late 1960s, and today plays a leading role in the Castelnuovo Berardenga UGA production zone. Owned by the Allianz insurance group, their scope isn't limited to Chianti. They also manage Campogiovanni in Montalcino and the Bolgheri vineyards of Bell'Aja (recently expanded with the 2021 acquisition of Batzella, also in Bolgheri). The vibrant 2022 Chianti Classico Borgo reveals lively and bold fruit aromas, followed by a broad, fleshy progression that culminates in a flavorful, rising finish. The 2020 Chianti Classico Gran Selezione Poggio Rosso is a focused pour, with smoky aromas and a fleshy, flavorful progression. The 2021 Chianti Classico Gran Selezione La Pieve is good, though with a slightly more rustic and austere touch; the palate is meaty, with solid persistence.

○ Vernaccia di San Gimignano Angelica '21	♟♟ 4
○ Vernaccia di San Gimignano Benedetta Ris. '20	♟♟ 5
● Arrigo '18	♟ 6
● Chianti Colli Senesi Fiamma '20	♟ 4
○ Vernaccia di San Gimignano '23	♟ 3
● Arrigo '17	♟♟ 5
● Chianti Colli Senesi Fede Ris. '16	♟♟ 3
○ Vernaccia di S. Gimignano Benedetta Ris. '17	♟♟ 3
○ Vernaccia di San Gimignano Angelica '20	♟♟ 3
○ Vernaccia di San Gimignano Angelica '19	♟♟ 3
○ Vernaccia di San Gimignano Benedetta Ris. '19	♟♟ 3
○ Vernaccia di San Gimignano Benedetta Ris. '18	♟♟ 3

● Chianti Cl. Borgo '22	♟♟♟ 5
● Chianti Cl. Gran Selezione La Pieve '21	♟♟ 7
● Chianti Cl. Gran Selezione Poggio Rosso '20	♟♟ 8
● Vigorello '20	♟ 7
● Chianti Cl. '20	♟♟♟ 3*
● Chianti Cl. '18	♟♟♟ 3*
● Chianti Cl. '13	♟♟♟ 3*
● Chianti Cl. Gran Sel. Il Grigio da San Felice '11	♟♟♟ 5
● Chianti Cl. Gran Sel. Il Grigio da San Felice '10	♟♟♟ 5
● Chianti Cl. Gran Selezione Poggio Rosso '15	♟♟♟ 5
● Chianti Cl. Il Grigio Ris. '18	♟♟♟ 3*
● Chianti Cl. Il Grigio Ris. '15	♟♟♟ 3*
● Vigorello '13	♟♟♟ 6

★★★Tenuta San Guido

fraz. Bolgheri
loc. Le Capanne, 27
57022 Castagneto Carducci [LI]
☎ +39 0565762003
⊕ www.sassicaia.com

PRE-BOOKED VISITS
RESTAURANT SERVICE
ANNUAL PRODUCTION 780,000 bottles
HECTARES UNDER VINE 90.00

The Incisa della Rocchetta family invented a new way of thinking and making wine in Italy, creating a territory so distinctive that authorities gave it its own appellation. Their wines stand as benchmarks alongside the world's greats, maintaining an appeal that resonates with casual wine enthusiasts, critics, and industry pundits alike, leaving no one unimpressed. The 2021 Bolgheri Sassicaia affirms its unmistakable grace and aromatic complexity, balancing Mediterranean and sylvan, foresty tones. The palate doesn't hide its generous fruit, with tannins expressing their characteristic finesse. The Guidalberto '22, a blend of cabernet sauvignon and merlot, features morello cherry, plum, and aromatic herbs, with a firm, well-defined palate. Le Difese '22, a blend of cabernet sauvignon and sangiovese, proves fragrant and dynamic, with blueberry and blackberry aromas.

San Leonino

fraz. San Leonino
loc. Cipressi, 49
53011 Castellina in Chianti [SI]
☎ +39 0577804101
⊕ www.sanleonino.it

CELLAR SALES
PRE-BOOKED VISITS
ANNUAL PRODUCTION 100,000 bottles
HECTARES UNDER VINE 42.00

Angelini Wines & Estates has a solid production base in Tuscany, represented by Trerose in Montepulciano and Val di Suga in Montalcino. Since 1994, they have also managed San Leonino, located in the Castellina in Chianti UGA production area. The wines from here exhibit a well-defined style, interpreting sangiovese with an emphasis on balance and finesse rather than intensity and power, yielding highly commendable results. The refined 2020 Chianti Classico Monsenese Ris. unveils aromas of small red fruits, floral touches, and smoky hints. The palate is supple, with great energy and a clean, defined finish. The 2019 Chianti Classico Gran Selezione Salivolpe proves focused, with oak playing a dominant role in both its aromas and flavor profile. The 2022 Chianti Classico Al Limite features a pleasant, continuously sapid palate.

● Bolgheri Sassicaia '21	♟♟♟	8
● Guidalberto '22	♟♟	6
● Le Difese '22	♟♟	4
● Bolgheri Sassicaia '20	♟♟♟	8
● Bolgheri Sassicaia '19	♟♟♟	8
● Bolgheri Sassicaia '15	♟♟♟	8
● Bolgheri Sassicaia '14	♟♟♟	8
● Bolgheri Sassicaia '13	♟♟♟	8
● Bolgheri Sassicaia '12	♟♟♟	8
● Bolgheri Sassicaia '11	♟♟♟	8
● Bolgheri Sassicaia '10	♟♟♟	8
● Bolgheri Sassicaia '09	♟♟♟	8
● Bolgheri Sassicaia '08	♟♟♟	8
● Bolgheri Sup. Sassicaia '18	♟♟♟	8
● Bolgheri Sup. Sassicaia '17	♟♟♟	8
● Bolgheri Sup. Sassicaia '16	♟♟♟	8
● Guidalberto '08	♟♟♟	6

● Chianti Cl. Monsenese Ris. '20	♟♟	5
● Chianti Cl. Al Limite '22	♟♟	4
● Chianti Cl. Gran Selezione Salivolpe '19	♟♟	6
● Chianti Cl. Al Limite '21	♟♟	4
● Chianti Cl. Al Limite '19	♟♟	3
● Chianti Cl. Al Limite '18	♟♟	3
● Chianti Cl. Gran Selezione Salivolpe '18	♟♟	5
● Chianti Cl. Gran Selezione Salivolpe '17	♟♟	5
● Chianti Cl. Monsenese Ris. '19	♟♟	5
● Chianti Cl. Monsenese Ris. '18	♟♟	3
● Chianti Cl. Monsenese Ris. '17	♟♟	3
● Salivolpe '99	♟♟	5

San Polo Montalcino

loc. Podere San Polo di Podernovi, 161
53024 Montalcino [SI]
☎ +39 0577835101
✉ www.sanpolomontalcino.it

CELLAR SALES
PRE-BOOKED VISITS
ANNUAL PRODUCTION 145,000 bottles
HECTARES UNDER VINE 16.00
VITICULTURE METHOD Certified Organic
SUSTAINABLE WINERY

Tenuta San Polo in Montalcino is one of two
lovely Tuscan wineries owned by Marilisa
Allegrini and her beloved daughters Carlotta and
Caterina (the other is Poggio al Tesoro in
Bolgheri). This stunning estate is located in
Podernovi, a historic name on the southeastern
slope of the hill, not far from Montalcino as you
head towards Sant'Antimo. Many historic
Brunello estates are located in the area due to
its natural predisposition for viticulture. All the
wines produced this year were exceptional—
elegant, expressive of their terroir, and never
overstated. The 2019 Brunello Podernovi stands
out for its confident style, rooted in its
territorial identity. Complex aromas of black
mulberry, morello cherry, and plum are layered
with violet, cocoa, and yellow spices. The palate
offers firm structure, with close-knit, well-
integrated tannins. The expansive, multifaceted
aromatic profile of the 2018 Riserva features
vibrant, ripe red fruit, enriched by notes of
helichrysum, pepper, and flint. The palate is full
and juicy, with silky tannins.

★Podere Sapaio

via del Fosso, 31
57022 Castagneto Carducci [LI]
☎ +39 0438430440
✉ www.sapaio.it

CELLAR SALES
PRE-BOOKED VISITS
ANNUAL PRODUCTION 110,000 bottles
HECTARES UNDER VINE 26.00
VITICULTURE METHOD Certified Organic

Massimo Piccin, a Venetian engineer, founded
Podere Sapaio in 1999, starting with a few
hectares of vineyards that have since expanded
to include Bibbona. In recent years, he's
favored maturation in larger wooden casks,
though he's increasingly drawing on concrete
and amphorae. His passionate explorations led
him to fall in love with the island of Giglio,
where since 2015, he's been producing
unblended ansonica at Le Secche, near the
Fenaio lighthouse. The 2022 Bolgheri Volpolo
showcases an alluring nose, blending ripe red
fruits, floral nuances, and spicy accents. On the
palate, it's flavorful, with a crunchy, well-defined
tannic texture, finishing on a juicy note with a
touch of spices. Le Secche '22, an ansonica from
a small vineyard on the island of Giglio, offers
citrus and spicy aromas, with brackish notes and
a persistent finish on the palate.

● Brunello di Montalcino Podernovi '19	♟♟ 8
● Brunello di Montalcino '19	♟♟ 8
● Brunello di Montalcino Ris. '18	♟♟ 8
● Brunello di Montalcino Vignavecchia '19	♟♟ 8
● Rosso di Montalcino '22	♟ 5
● Brunello di Montalcino Vignavecchia '15	♟♟♟ 8
● Brunello di Montalcino '18	♟♟ 8
● Brunello di Montalcino '16	♟♟ 7
● Brunello di Montalcino '13	♟♟ 7
● Brunello di Montalcino Podernovi '17	♟♟ 8
● Brunello di Montalcino Podernovi '16	♟♟ 8
● Brunello di Montalcino Vignavecchia '17	♟♟ 8

● Bolgheri Rosso Volpolo '22	♟♟♟ 5
○ Le Secche Paradiso dei Conigli '22	♟♟ 8
● Bolgheri Rosso Sup. '13	♟♟♟ 7
● Bolgheri Rosso Sup. '12	♟♟♟ 7
● Bolgheri Rosso Sup. '11	♟♟♟ 7
● Bolgheri Rosso Sup. Sapaio '16	♟♟♟ 7
● Bolgheri Rosso Volpolo '19	♟♟♟ 5
● Bolgheri Rosso Volpolo '18	♟♟♟ 5
● Bolgheri Sup. Sapaio '10	♟♟♟ 6
● Bolgheri Sup. Sapaio '09	♟♟♟ 6
● Bolgheri Sup. Sapaio '08	♟♟♟ 6
● Bolgheri Sup. Sapaio '07	♟♟♟ 6
● Bolgheri Sup. Sapaio '06	♟♟♟ 6
● Sapaio '19	♟♟♟ 8
● Sapaio '15	♟♟♟ 6
● Bolgheri Rosso Volpolo '21	♟♟ 5
● Sapaio '18	♟♟ 8

Sassotondo

fraz. Sovana
loc. Pian di Conati, 52
58010 Sorano [GR]
☎ +39 0564614218
@ www.sassotondo.it

CELLAR SALES
PRE-BOOKED VISITS
ANNUAL PRODUCTION 50,000 bottles
HECTARES UNDER VINE 12.00
VITICULTURE METHOD Certified Organic

Carla Benini and Edoardo Ventimiglia made a brave and important life choice years ago, and their dedication and consistent quality have made them key figures in the Maremma Toscana wine scene. Sassotondo, which comprises 12 hectares, is a historic guardian of the ciliegiolo grape, but the producer is also a keen interpreter of the tuff-rich soils of Sorano, Pitigliano, and Sovana. The 2021 San Lorenzo doesn't disappoint. Over the years, this ciliegiolo has gained greater definition. Vibrant aromas of blueberry and blackberry jam emerge under balsamic hints, leading to notes of licorice, cardamom, and underbrush. The palate is rich, mouthfilling, and glyceric, with a sapid, spicy finish. The Numero Sei '22 impresses with its mineral aromas, orange zest, citron, dried flowers, and sensations of golden-leaf tobacco. Balsamic notes add flavor to the palate, with excellent acidic-sapid tension.

● Maremma Toscana Ciliegiolo San Lorenzo '21	♟♟♟ 6
○ Numero Sei '22	♟♟ 7
● Maremma Toscana Ciliegiolo '23	♟♟ 3
● Maremma Toscana Ciliegiolo Monte Calvo '22	♟♟ 6
● Maremma Toscana Ciliegiolo Poggio Pinzo '21	♟♟ 6
○ Lady Marmalade '23	♟ 4
○ Numero Dieci '22	♟ 6
● Maremma Toscana Ciliegiolo Monte Calvo '21	♟♟ 6
● Maremma Toscana Ciliegiolo Poggio Pinzo '20	♟♟ 6
● Maremma Toscana Ciliegiolo San Lorenzo '19	♟♟ 6

Michele Satta

loc. Vigna al Cavaliere, 61b
57022 Castagneto Carducci [LI]
☎ +39 0565773041
@ www.michelesatta.com

CELLAR SALES
PRE-BOOKED VISITS
ANNUAL PRODUCTION 150,000 bottles
HECTARES UNDER VINE 25.00

The winery founded by Michele Satta, now managed by his children Giacomo and Benedetta, is among a select few pioneering estates in Bolgheri. Under Giacomo's leadership, the production has seen significant changes: more precise harvests in the vineyard and the creation of unique wines enhanced by maturation in wood, cement, and amphorae. The 2021 Bolgheri Superiore Marianova represents a convincing interpretation of the vintage. Its aromas are fragrant and well-defined, while the palate reveals juicy, solid tannins before a succulent, sapid finish. The 2021 Bolgheri Superiore Piastraia shows more Mediterranean and generous tones. The 2021 Cavaliere, a monovarietal sangiovese, is invigorating and well-executed. The 2023 Bolgheri Bianco Costa di Giulia proves pleasantly balanced and rich in appealing contrasts.

○ Bolgheri Bianco Costa di Giulia '23	♟♟ 4
● Bolgheri Rosso Sup. Marianova '21	♟♟ 8
● Bolgheri Rosso Sup. Piastraia '21	♟♟ 6
● Cavaliere '21	♟♟ 6
● Syrah '23	♟♟ 7
● Bolgheri Rosso '22	♟ 4
○ Giovin Re '22	♟ 6
● Bolgheri Rosso Piastraia '02	♟♟♟ 6
● Bolgheri Rosso Piastraia '01	♟♟♟ 6
● Bolgheri Rosso '21	♟♟ 4
● Bolgheri Rosso Sup. Marianova '17	♟♟ 8
● Bolgheri Rosso Sup. Marianova '16	♟♟ 8
● Bolgheri Rosso Sup. Marianova '15	♟♟ 8
● Bolgheri Rosso Sup. Piastraia '20	♟♟ 6
● Bolgheri Rosso Sup. Piastraia '19	♟♟ 6
● Bolgheri Rosso Sup. Piastraia '18	♟♟ 6
● Bolgheri Rosso Sup. Piastraia '15	♟♟ 6

Fattoria Selvapiana

loc. Selvapiana, 43
50068 Rufina [FI]
📞 +39 0558369848
🌐 www.selvapiana.it

Sensi - Fattoria Calappiano

fraz. Cerbaia, 107
51035 Lamporecchio [PT]
📞 +39 057382910
🌐 www.sensivini.com

CELLAR SALES
PRE-BOOKED VISITS
ANNUAL PRODUCTION 220,000 bottles
HECTARES UNDER VINE 60.00

CELLAR SALES
PRE-BOOKED VISITS
ANNUAL PRODUCTION 2,000,000 bottles
HECTARES UNDER VINE 100.00
VITICULTURE METHOD Certified Organic
SUSTAINABLE WINERY

Selvapiana is arguably the most intriguing winery in Rufina, the most interesting of Chianti's seven subzones. Established in 1948 by the Giuntini family, it is still managed today by Silvia and Federico. The winery produces characterful wines, such as the Chianti Rufina Vigneto Bucerchiale Riserva (first vintage 1979), which rigorously express the potential of sangiovese, here endowed with a distinctive personality. The delicate yet complex Riserva Terraelectae Vigneto Erchi '20 reveals sanguine aromas alongside hints of plum and subtle notes of fur, showcasing a style that's truly unique among their Rufina wines. The tannins are sapid and tight, with a balsamic finish offering fresh tones reminiscent of the underbrush. The contemporary Chianti Rufina '22 unveils a dynamic and flavorful palate, thriving on its lively lightness, balanced by the tannins that you'd expect from the production zone.

Fattoria di Calappiano covers 200 hectares in the heart of Tuscany, on the hills that unfold between Vinci and Florence, in the Montalbano area. The property represents one of the last architectural and historical treasures left to us by the Medici family. Today, Calappiano is owned by the Sensi family, who have embarked on an ambitious project aimed at quality production, with this particular estate standing out as their crown jewel. The Lungarno '21, made from cabernet sauvignon and merlot with a touch of colorino, opens on notes of black cherry and blackberry, accompanied by floral hints of rose and violet. Tones of licorice, Mediterranean scrub, and mint follow. The palate is supple and balanced, with elegant tannins and a spicy finish. The Collegonzi Ciliegiolo '23 impresses, literally exuding aromas of cherry, pomegranate, and blueberry, while the palate is juicy and dynamic. The Collegonzi Chianti '21 is rich with fruit pulp, fresh and flowery.

● Chianti Rufina Terraelectae Vign. Erchi Ris. '20	♟♟ 6
● Chianti Rufina '22	♟♟ 3
● Fornace '20	♟♟ 5
○ Vin Santo del Chianti Rufina '15	♟♟ 4
○ Pomino Bianco Villa Petrognano '23	♟ 3
● Pomino Rosso Villa Petrognano '21	♟ 3
● Chianti Rufina Vign. Bucerchiale 40 anni Ris. '19	♟♟♟ 5
● Chianti Rufina '15	♟♟ 2*
● Chianti Rufina Bucerchiale Ris. '13	♟♟ 5
● Chianti Rufina Terraelectae Vign. Erchi Ris. '19	♟♟ 6
● Chianti Rufina Vign. Bucerchiale Ris. '18	♟♟ 5
● Chianti Rufina Vign. Bucerchiale Ris. '16	♟♟ 5
● Chianti Rufina Vign. Bucerchiale Ris. '15	♟♟ 5

● Lungarno '21	♟♟ 7
● Chianti Collegonzi V. La Sughera Ris. '21	♟♟ 5
● Collegonzi Ciliegiolo '23	♟♟ 3
● Collegonzi Sangiovese '18	♟♟♟ 6
● Bolgheri Sabbiato '19	♟♟ 5
● Chianti Campoluce '22	♟♟ 2*
● Chianti Campoluce '20	♟♟ 2*
● Chianti Vinciano '22	♟♟ 5
● Chianti Vinciano Ris. '20	♟♟ 6
● Collegonzi Ciliegiolo '22	♟♟ 3
● Collegonzi Sangiovese '19	♟♟ 6
● Collegonzi Sangiovese Fattoria Calappiano '17	♟♟ 6
● Lungarno '19	♟♟ 7
● Mantello '20	♟♟ 4

Sesti - Castello di Argiano

fraz. Sant'Angelo in Colle
loc. Castello di Argiano
53024 Montalcino [SI]
(☎ +39 0577843921
elisa@sesti.net

CELLAR SALES
PRE-BOOKED VISITS
ANNUAL PRODUCTION 61,000 bottles
HECTARES UNDER VINE 9.00

Giuseppe Sesti is an eclectic man with many passions—architect, winemaker, musicologist, painter, expert in astronomy and classical myths—undoubtedly one of the most recognized figures in Montalcino. He arrived here in 1975 as a young man with his wife, Sarah, an English noblewoman and horse breeder. They settled in the ancient village of Argiano, where he began producing Brunello in 1995. Now, he shares responsibilities with his daughter Elisa, who, after earning two degrees in London—architecture and theater—has chosen to follow in her father's footsteps, at least in the vineyard. The aromatically focused Riserva Phenomena '18 captivates with its fragrant elegance, moving from cherry, enlivened by a floral touch, to rain-soaked earth, eucalyptus, and leather, concluding on a delicate, sanguine note. Resolved tannins shape a full palate with lush fruit. The Brunello '19 is also excellent, offering classic notes of dark berries and licorice, with added hints of strawberry tree and mint. The palate is flavorful and persistent, closing long and broad.

★Tenuta Sette Ponti

via Sette Ponti, 71
52029 Castiglion Fibocchi [AR]
(☎ +39 0575477857
◈ www.tenutasetteponti.it

CELLAR SALES
PRE-BOOKED VISITS
ACCOMMODATION
ANNUAL PRODUCTION 250,000 bottles
HECTARES UNDER VINE 60.00
VITICULTURE METHOD Certified Organic
SUSTAINABLE WINERY

For over two decades, the Moretti family winery has been a significant player in the new wave of Tuscan winemaking, with a patrimony that includes the Bolgheri winery Orma and the Sicilian Feudo Maccari. Sette Ponti, named after the seven bridges over the Arno between Florence and Arezzo (with the Buriano bridge immortalized in Leonardo's Mona Lisa), is known for the modern style of its wines and impeccable craftsmanship, in keeping with Tuscany's cutting-edge vision and commercial success. The Oreno '22, a blend of cabernet sauvignon, merlot, and petit verdot, boasts a rich aromatic profile of fruity and spicy tones, with toasty and balsamic accents. In the mouth, the wine is juicy, with a multifaceted tannic structure and a peppery finale. Floral and underbrush notes characterize the Valdarno di Sopra Vigna dell'Impero '20, which sees a supple, dynamic palate finish fragrant and flavorful.

● Brunello di Montalcino Phenomena Ris. '18	▼▼8
● Brunello di Montalcino '19	▼▼8
● Rosso di Montalcino '22	▼▼5
● Grangiovese '23	▼2
⊙ Toscana Rosato '23	▼4
● Brunello di Montalcino '06	♈♈♈6
● Brunello di Montalcino Phenomena Ris. '07	♈♈♈8
● Brunello di Montalcino Phenomena Ris. '01	♈♈♈8
● Brunello di Montalcino Ris. '04	♈♈♈8
● Rosso di Montalcino '16	♈♈♈4*
● Brunello di Montalcino '18	♈♈6
● Brunello di Montalcino Phenomena Ris. '17	♈♈8

● Oreno '22	▼▼▼8
● Valdarno di Sopra Sangiovese V. dell'Impero '20	▼▼8
● Oreno '21	♈♈♈8
● Oreno '20	♈♈♈8
● Oreno '19	♈♈♈8
● Oreno '18	♈♈♈8
● Oreno '17	♈♈♈8
● Oreno '16	♈♈♈8
● Oreno '15	♈♈♈8
● Oreno '12	♈♈♈7
● Oreno '11	♈♈♈7
● Oreno '10	♈♈♈7
● Oreno '09	♈♈♈7
● Valdarno di Sopra V. dell'Impero '13	♈♈♈8

Talenti

fraz. Sant'Angelo in Colle
loc. Pian di Conte
53024 Montalcino [SI]
☏ +39 0577844064
✉ www.talentimontalcino.it

CELLAR SALES
PRE-BOOKED VISITS
ANNUAL PRODUCTION 100,000 bottles
HECTARES UNDER VINE 23.00

When Pierluigi Talenti arrived in Pian di Conte in Montalcino from Romagna, he immediately recognized the potential of the region and its signature grape, sangiovese grosso. He was among the first to experiment with selecting different clones already present on the estate, later using them to plant new vineyards. His grandson, Riccardo, who now runs the winery, has identified a dozen distinct parcels on the property. These parcels, either vinified individually or blended, give rise to a range of consistently elegant and high-quality wines. The vibrant Brunello Piero '19 is modern in style, with notes of red fruit dominating. The palate is rich and full, supported by tight-knit tannins that suit the density of the wine. The Brunello '19 is just as good—intense and multifaceted, with red fruit, tobacco, and licorice aromas adding complexity, alongside a characteristic sanguine and meaty note. It's a profile that's deeply rooted in the territory. The palate reveals elegance, emphasizing delicacy and harmony without overextracting.

● Brunello di Montalcino Piero '19	♥♥ 8
● Brunello di Montalcino '19	♥♥ 8
● Rosso di Montalcino '22	♥ 5
● Brunello di Montalcino '04	♡♡♡ 8
● Brunello di Montalcino '88	♡♡♡ 8
● Brunello di Montalcino Pian di Conte Ris. '13	♡♡♡ 7
● Brunello di Montalcino Ris. '99	♡♡♡ 6
● Brunello di Montalcino Trentennale '11	♡♡♡ 8
● Brunello di Montalcino V. del Paretaio Ris. '01	♡♡♡ 6
● Brunello di Montalcino '18	♡♡ 8
● Brunello di Montalcino '17	♡♡ 8
● Brunello di Montalcino Piero '16	♡♡ 8
● Brunello di Montalcino Piero '15	♡♡ 8
● Rosso di Montalcino '17	♡♡ 3*

Talosa

via Talosa, 8
53045 Montepulciano [SI]
☏ +39 0578758277
✉ www.talosa.it

CELLAR SALES
PRE-BOOKED VISITS
ACCOMMODATION
ANNUAL PRODUCTION 100,000 bottles
HECTARES UNDER VINE 33.00
VITICULTURE METHOD Certified Organic

Talosa, one of the pioneering wineries in Montepulciano, has been owned by Angelo Jacorossi and his family since 1972. Their vineyards, located in the Pietrose area, sit at elevations between 330 and 400 meters with a southwest exposure. The oldest aging cellar is located in the historic center of Montepulciano, beneath Palazzo Tarugi and Palazzo Sinatti (both were built in the early 1500s and are situated directly across from the Duomo). In the cellar, the winemaking style balances classic, lengthy aging with a modernist approach centered on precision and aromatic clarity. Their Nobili wines prove well-crafted in their various manifestations, starting with the Alboreto, which reveals ripe, taut fruit alongside nuances of field herbs and Mediterranean underbrush. Solid and progressively structured on the palate, it flows with ease and vibrancy. The Filai Lunghi, supple in the mouth, showcases dark fruits like blueberry and wild plum, enriched by a fine, spicy undertone. The Rosso '22 displays dynamic energy on the palate—it's pure in style yet crafted with finesse and overall harmony.

● Nobile di Montepulciano Alboreto '19	♥♥ 5
● Nobile di Montepulciano Filai Lunghi '19	♥♥ 8
● Rosso di Montepulciano '22	♥♥ 3
● Nobile di Montepulciano Ris. '19	♥ 6
● Nobile di Montepulciano '17	♡♡ 4
● Nobile di Montepulciano '15	♡♡ 4
● Nobile di Montepulciano Alboreto '18	♡♡ 4
● Nobile di Montepulciano Filai Lunghi '17	♡♡ 6
● Nobile di Montepulciano Filai Lunghi '16	♡♡ 6
● Nobile di Montepulciano Filai Lunghi '13	♡♡ 5
● Nobile di Montepulciano Ris. '18	♡♡ 6
● Nobile di Montepulciano Ris. '17	♡♡ 5
● Nobile di Montepulciano Ris. '14	♡♡ 5
● Rosso di Montepulciano '18	♡♡ 2*

Tassi

v.le P. Strozzi, 1/3
53024 Montalcino [SI]
☎ +39 0577848025
✉ www.tassimontalcino.com

ANNUAL PRODUCTION 20,000 bottles
HECTARES UNDER VINE 5.00

It's hard to say whether Fabio Tassi is more successful as an entrepreneur or as a winemaker. His long-standing role as the patron of Enoteca la Fortezza in Montalcino has certainly helped—indeed, Tassi has tried plenty of wines over the past 20 years. But based on our tastings, it's clear he excels as a winemaker, as well. All the wines sampled from his selections earned commendable scores, standing out for their poise, harmony, and strong sense of place. The Brunello Giuseppe Tassi '19 holds great promise, with a vibrant and classic nose that opens on red and black fruit notes, alongside hints of quinine and iron. Still quite youthful, the palate is firm and muscular, propelled by a lively yet refined tannic structure, leading to an exceptionally long finish. The Brunello '19 offers clear aromas of blackberry, cherry, dark tobacco, and quinine, with a vibrant palate and the satisfying varietal aromas of Montalcino sangiovese.

Tenuta delle Ripalte

loc. Ripalte
57031 Capoliveri [LI]
☎ +39 056594211
✉ www.tenutadelleripalte.it

PRE-BOOKED VISITS
ACCOMMODATION AND RESTAURANT SERVICE
ANNUAL PRODUCTION 60,000 bottles
HECTARES UNDER VINE 17.00
SUSTAINABLE WINERY

Tenuta delle Ripalte is located on Elba Island in the Punta Calamita area near Capoliveri. Spanning 420 hectares, it's the island's most important agricultural operation. Thanks to Piermario Meletti Cavallari, former owner of Grattamacco in Bolgheri, the winery now boasts noteworthy production volumes, managing organic vineyards planted with aleatico, vermentino, fiano, and grenache. The Bianco Mediterraneo '19, a blend of vermentino and fiano grapes, opens with a intense and deep aromatic profile. The palate shows sapidity, structure, and a crisp finish. The Elba Aleatico Passito Alea Ludendo '22 plays on aromatic balsamic notes, balancing its sweetness without ever becoming cloying. The Aleatico '22, in its "secco" version, carries flavors of small red fruits, violets, and spices, unfurling flavorful and pleasant on the palate.

● Brunello di Montalcino Giuseppe Tassi '19	♟♟ 7
● Brunello di Montalcino '19	♟♟ 7
● Brunò '22	♟♟ 6
● Rosso di Montalcino Greppino '19	♟♟ 7
● Brunello di Montalcino '13	♟♟ 8
● Brunello di Montalcino Franci '13	♟♟ 8
● Brunello di Montalcino Franci '12	♟♟ 8
● Brunello di Montalcino Franci '07	♟♟ 4
● Brunello di Montalcino Franci Ris. '13	♟♟ 8
● Brunello di Montalcino Franci Ris. '11	♟♟ 8
● Brunello di Montalcino Tassi '18	♟♟ 7
● Brunello di Montalcino V. Colombaiolo '18	♟♟ 8
● Rosso di Montalcino '19	♟♟ 6
● Rosso di Montalcino '16	♟♟ 4
● Rosso di Montalcino Franci '18	♟♟ 8
● Rosso di Montalcino Franci '14	♟♟ 4

○ Bianco Mediterraneo '19	♟♟ 5
● Elba Aleatico Passito Alea Laudendo '22	♟♟ 6
● Aleatico '22	♟♟ 4
● Alicante '23	♟♟ 4
○ Vermentino '23	♟♟ 4
○ Bianco Mediterraneo '18	♟♟ 3
○ Bianco Mediterraneo Le Ripalte '18	♟♟ 3
● Elba Aleatico Passito Alea Ludendo '20	♟♟ 6
● Elba Aleatico Passito Alea Ludendo '16	♟♟ 6
● Elba Aleatico Passito Alea Ludendo '15	♟♟ 6
○ Le Ripalte Vermentino '19	♟♟ 3
● Rosso Mediterraneo '19	♟♟ 5
● Rosso Mediterraneo Alicante '18	♟♟ 3
○ Vermentino '21	♟♟ 3

Tenuta di Arceno

loc. Arceno
fraz. San Gusmé
53010 Castelnuovo Berardenga [SI]
☎ +39 0577359346
✉ www.tenutadiarceno.com

CELLAR SALES
PRE-BOOKED VISITS
ANNUAL PRODUCTION 250,000 bottles
HECTARES UNDER VINE 92.00

Owned by the Kendall-Jackson Group and located in the heart of Castelnuovo Berardenga, Arceno produces an impeccably crafted range of wines characterized by a modern style, emphasizing the influence of oak, structural fullness, and fruit. Their Chianti Classico features intense aromatics and a lush, enveloping palate, while their IGT wines, primarily made from Bordeaux varieties, lean towards darker, more tannic profiles. The monovarietal Cabernet Franc Arcanum '20 reveals vibrant aromas of red and black fruits, spices, and herbal notes, introducing an incredible progression of flavor—superb rhythm and depth here. The Chianti Classico Ris. '21 is enjoyable, with its generous fruit aromas and a soft, flavorful palate. The Chianti Classico Gran Selezione Campolupi '21 is more concentrated and pervasive, firm and sustained in its tannic structure. The Chianti Classico '22 also proves pleasant.

Tenuta di Artimino

fraz. Artimino
v.le Papa Giovanni XXIII, 1
59015 Carmignano [PO]
☎ +39 0558751423
✉ www.artimino.com

CELLAR SALES
PRE-BOOKED VISITS
ACCOMMODATION AND RESTAURANT SERVICE
ANNUAL PRODUCTION 420,000 bottles
HECTARES UNDER VINE 70.00

Tenuta Artimino was acquired in the 1980s by Giuseppe Olmo, an entrepreneur with a past as a cycling champion. Today, Annabella De Pascale, the third generation of the Olmo family, leads an ambitious project combining wine tourism, gastronomy, and sustainability. This shift has also influenced wine production, which now consistently delivers high quality. The Carmignano Grumarello Riserva '20 offers up a multifaceted nose with prominent black fruit, vegetal and balsamic veins. The palate is silky, with a rising finish in which fruit makes an encore, leaving a long trail of rain-washed stones. The Marrucaia '21 is rigorous in style, with evident floral notes on the nose. Its fruit is clear, and a measured note of charred oak completes a sanguine, deeply Tuscan palate. The Chianti Montalbano '23 is a buoyant pour—young, with a penetrating acidity that tingles the tongue.

● Arcanum '20	♟♟♟ 8
● Chianti Cl. Ris. '21	♟♟ 5
● Chianti Cl. Gran Selezione Campolupi '21	♟♟ 7
● Chianti Cl. '22	♟ 4
● Chianti Cl. Gran Selezione Strada al Sasso '21	♟ 6
● Il Fauno '21	♟ 4
● Arcanum '19	♟♟♟ 8
● Chianti Cl. '17	♟♟♟ 4*
● Chianti Cl. Ris. '19	♟♟♟ 5
● Chianti Cl. Ris. '18	♟♟♟ 5
● Chianti Cl. Ris. '17	♟♟♟ 5
● Valadorna '13	♟♟♟ 8
● Chianti Cl. Gran Selezione Strada al Sasso '17	♟♟ 6
● Valadorna '19	♟♟ 8

● Carmignano Grumarello Ris. '20	♟♟♟ 5
● Marrucaia '21	♟♟ 5
● Carmignano Poggilarca '21	♟♟ 4
● Chianti Montalbano '23	♟♟ 3
○ Artumes '23	♟ 3
● Barco Reale Ser Biagio '23	♟ 3
● Carmignano Grumarello Ris. '19	♟♟♟ 5
● Carmignano Grumarello Ris. '17	♟♟♟ 5
● Carmignano Grumarello Ris. '16	♟♟♟ 5
● Carmignano Poggilarca '20	♟♟ 4
● Carmignano Poggilarca '18	♟♟ 3
● Carmignano Poggilarca '17	♟♟ 3*
● Chianti Montalbano '22	♟♟ 3
● Chianti Montalbano '21	♟♟ 2*
● Chianti Montalbano '19	♟♟ 2*
● Marrucaia '20	♟♟ 5

Tenuta di Bibbiano

via Bibbiano, 76
53011 Castellina in Chianti [SI]
☎ +39 0577743065
✉ www.bibbiano.com

CELLAR SALES
PRE-BOOKED VISITS
ACCOMMODATION
ANNUAL PRODUCTION 180,000 bottles
HECTARES UNDER VINE 34.00
VITICULTURE METHOD Certified Organic

Located in the Castellina in Chianti subzone and today led by Tommaso Marrocchesi, Tenuta di Bibbiano embodies the most authentic expressions of its appellation. The vineyards are managed organically, and in the cellar, the wines mature in both large and small barrels. The result is generous wines with character and personality, consistently demonstrating a strong connection to their terroir. The solid and eloquent Chianti Classico Gran Selezione Vigne di Montornello '21 is characterized by fruity and spicy nuances alongside toasted and minty hints. The palate is juicy and pervasive, punctuated by intricate tannins and a balsamic undertone, returning on a finish that's expansive and focused, never aggressive. The Chianti Classico '22, with its subtle aromas, makes for an easy drink. The Chianti Classico Ris. '21 is more austere, with its firm tannic structure.

★Tenuta di Capezzana

loc. Seano
via Capezzana, 100
59015 Carmignano [PO]
☎ +39 0558706005
✉ www.capezzana.it

CELLAR SALES
PRE-BOOKED VISITS
ACCOMMODATION AND RESTAURANT SERVICE
ANNUAL PRODUCTION 350,000 bottles
HECTARES UNDER VINE 72.00
VITICULTURE METHOD Certified Organic
SUSTAINABLE WINERY

A lease in the Florence State Archives proves that olives and vines for oil and wine production were being cultivated in Capezzana as early as 804 AD. In 1920, Alessandro Contini Bonacossi acquired the property, today managed by the fourth and fifth generations of family: Beatrice, Filippo, Benedetta, and the younger generation, Ettore, Gaddo, and Serena, honoring the past while investing in the future. The Carmignano Villa di Capezzana '20 reveals iris, small dark fruits, and underbrush on the nose, while the palate features youthful, slightly tight tannins, closing with a long, mineral, and balsamic finish. The Vin Santo di Carmignano Ris. '16 is magnificent, thanks to an excellent vintage—deep and complex, with varietal aromas of walnut husk, barley, and caramel emerging. The Carmignano Villa di Capezzana 10 anni '14 delivers an energetic palate followed by a still-taut finish, all brought out by refined notes of coffee powder in its nuanced aromatic profile.

● Chianti Cl. Gran Selezione V. di Montornello '21	♟♟ 7
● Chianti Cl. '22	♟♟ 4
● Chianti Cl. Ris. '21	♟♟ 6
● Chianti Cl. Gran Selezione V. del Capannino '21	♟ 7
● Chianti Cl. Gran Selezione V. del Capannino '20	♟♟♟ 7
● Chianti Cl. Gran Selezione V. del Capannino '19	♟♟♟ 7
● Chianti Cl. Gran Selezione V. del Capannino '18	♟♟♟ 5
● Chianti Cl. Ris. '17	♟♟♟ 4*
● Chianti Cl. Gran Selezione V. di Montornello '18	♟♟ 5
● Chianti Cl. Ris. '19	♟♟ 6
● Chianti Cl. Ris. '16	♟♟ 4

● Carmignano Villa di Capezzana '20	♟♟♟ 5
○ Vin Santo di Carmignano Ris. '16	♟♟ 8
● Carmignano Villa di Capezzana 10 Anni '14	♟♟ 7
● Ghiaie della Furba '20	♟♟ 7
● Ugo Contini Bonacossi '19	♟♟ 8
● Barco Reale '22	♟ 3
● Carmignano Villa di Capezzana '07	♟♟♟ 4
○ Vin Santo di Carmignano Ris. '14	♟♟♟ 8
○ Vin Santo di Carmignano Ris. '13	♟♟♟ 8
○ Vin Santo di Carmignano Ris. '12	♟♟♟ 6
○ Vin Santo di Carmignano Ris. '10	♟♟♟ 6
○ Vin Santo di Carmignano Ris. '09	♟♟♟ 6
○ Vin Santo di Carmignano Ris. '08	♟♟♟ 6
○ Vin Santo di Carmignano Ris. '07	♟♟♟ 6
○ Vin Santo di Carmignano Ris. '05	♟♟♟ 5

TUSCANY

Tenuta di Carleone

loc. Castiglioni
53017 Radda in Chianti [SI]
☎ +39 0577735613
🖱 www.tenutadicarleone.com

CELLAR SALES
PRE-BOOKED VISITS
ANNUAL PRODUCTION 35,000 bottles
HECTARES UNDER VINE 15.00
VITICULTURE METHOD Certified Organic

In 2012, Austrian entrepreneur Karl Egger founded Tenuta di Carleone in the Radda in Chianti UGA, with the crucial assistance of winemaker Sean O'Callaghan. Together, they built a winery with an artisanal approach open to natural methods, signaling a "new" productive course that is, in reality, deeply tied to traditional winemaking. The wines exhibit the finesse of Radda's sangiovese, merging depth and complexity, making for a range that is both true to the territory and ultra-modern. Lively and vibrant aromas accompany the light and flavorful Chianti Classico '21—a delectable, dynamic wine. The Uno '21, a monovarietal sangiovese, reveals ripe red fruit aromas with smoky and spicy whiffs. The palate is smooth and persistent, with full, flavorful tannins. Both the Guercio '22, also a sangiovese, and the Randagio '22, a cabernet franc and merlot blend, go all in on carefree drinking.

★Tenuta di Ghizzano

fraz. Ghizzano
via della Chiesa, 4
56037 Peccioli [PI]
☎ +39 0587630096
🖱 www.tenutadighizzano.com

CELLAR SALES
PRE-BOOKED VISITS
ACCOMMODATION
ANNUAL PRODUCTION 80,000 bottles
HECTARES UNDER VINE 20.00
VITICULTURE METHOD Certified Organic

Since the mid-1980s, Ginevra Venerosi Pesciolini's winery has represented excellence in Pisa, crafting wines with a sure-handed technical approach. In 2008, the estate converted its vineyards to organic farming, and more recently, to biodynamic practices. Ghizzano's production has shown a significant stylistic shift, maintaining its leadership while focusing on the spontaneity and character of its wines. The Terre di Pisa Veneroso '20 boasts a rich floral bouquet, with whiffs of sour cherry, wild berries, and hints of earth and underbrush. Its flavorful palate proves focused, with a well-sustained progression and a finish that unveils balsamic and smoky notes. The Nambrot '20, a blend of merlot, cabernet franc, and petit verdot, offers darker and more austere aromas. It's a firm, deep, and vibrant drink.

Wine	Rating
● Chianti Cl. '21	🍷🍷🍷 5
● Uno '21	🍷🍷 8
● Il Guercio '22	🍷 7
● Il Randagio '22	🍷 4
● Chianti Cl. '15	🍷🍷🍷 5
● Uno '20	🍷🍷🍷 8
● Uno '18	🍷🍷🍷 8
● Uno '16	🍷🍷🍷 8
● Chianti Cl. '20	🍷🍷 5
● Chianti Cl. '19	🍷🍷 5
● Chianti Cl. '18	🍷🍷 5
● Il Guercio '21	🍷🍷 7
● Il Guercio '18	🍷🍷 7
● Il Randagio '21	🍷🍷 4
● Rosato '22	🍷🍷 4
● Uno '19	🍷🍷 8
● Uno '17	🍷🍷 8

Wine	Rating
● Terre di Pisa Veneroso '20	🍷🍷 5
○ Mimesi Vermentino '23	🍷🍷 5
● Nambrot '20	🍷🍷 7
● Terre di Pisa Sangiovese Mimesi '21	🍷 8
● Nambrot '18	🍷🍷🍷 7
● Nambrot '17	🍷🍷🍷 6
● Nambrot '09	🍷🍷🍷 6
● Nambrot '08	🍷🍷🍷 6
● Nambrot '06	🍷🍷🍷 6
● Nambrot '05	🍷🍷🍷 6
● Terre di Pisa Nambrot '15	🍷🍷🍷 6
● Terre di Pisa Nambrot '13	🍷🍷🍷 6
● Terre di Pisa Nambrot '12	🍷🍷🍷 6
● Veneroso '10	🍷🍷🍷 5
● Veneroso '07	🍷🍷🍷 5
● Veneroso '04	🍷🍷🍷 5

★Tenuta di Lilliano

loc. Lilliano, 8
53011 Castellina in Chianti [SI]
☎ +39 0577743070
🖳 www.lilliano.com

CELLAR SALES
PRE-BOOKED VISITS
ACCOMMODATION
ANNUAL PRODUCTION 150,000 bottles
HECTARES UNDER VINE 40.00
VITICULTURE METHOD Certified Organic

Located in the Castellina in Chianti UGA and owned by the Ruspoli family, Tenuta di Lilliano was initially inspired by figures like Enzo Morganti and Giulio Gambelli, who shaped the history of Chianti Classico. Today, the winery incorporates modern elements without losing its Chianti sense of place. The result is a range characterized by lush fruitiness and the balanced use of both small and large barrels, making for easy drinking adorned by moments of complexity. Citrus aromas add freshness to the fruit-forward and spicy base of the fragrant Chianti Classico Gran Selezione '21. On the palate, it combines flavor, density, length, and rhythm—flawless. The dynamic and juicy Chianti Classico '22 is a flavorful, easy-drinking wine. The well-crafted Chianti Classico Ris. '21 features aromas of underbrush and flowers accompanied by toasty hints, while the palate is sweet, still quite young, and slightly leaning towards sweetness.

Wine	Rating
● Chianti Cl. Gran Selezione '21	♟♟♟ 5
● Chianti Cl. '22	♟♟ 4
● Chianti Cl. Ris. '21	♟♟ 5
● Vignacatena '20	♟ 5
● Chianti Cl. '21	♕♕♕ 4*
● Chianti Cl. '10	♕♕♕ 3*
● Chianti Cl. '09	♕♕♕ 3
● Chianti Cl. E. Ruspoli Berlingieri Ris. '85	♕♕♕ 8
● Chianti Cl. Gran Sel. '14	♕♕♕ 6
● Chianti Cl. Gran Sel. '11	♕♕♕ 5
● Chianti Cl. Gran Sel. Ris. '10	♕♕♕ 6
● Chianti Cl. Gran Selezione '18	♕♕♕ 5
● Chianti Cl. Gran Selezione '16	♕♕♕ 5
● Chianti Cl. Ris. '19	♕♕♕ 5
● Chianti Cl. Ris. '17	♕♕♕ 5
● Chianti Cl. Ris. '15	♕♕♕ 5
● Chianti Cl. Ris. '13	♕♕♕ 5

Tenuta di Sesta

fraz. Castelnuovo dell'Abate
loc. Sesta
53024 Montalcino [SI]
☎ +39 0577835612
🖳 www.tenutadisesta.it

CELLAR SALES
PRE-BOOKED VISITS
ANNUAL PRODUCTION 150,000 bottles
HECTARES UNDER VINE 30.00
SUSTAINABLE WINERY

The Sesta area has long been considered one of the most promising regions in the southern part of Montalcino. The vineyards here rise from 200 to 400 meters in elevation, benefiting during the hottest months from cool breezes blowing in from the Tyrrhenian Sea. This creates noteworthy day-night temperature swings, which, when combined with proper pruning, allows the vines to thrive. Since 1966, the Ciacci family has produced Brunellos here—intense, varietal-driven wines that are rich in fruit yet refined in elegance. Complexity and elegance define the kaleidoscopic bouquet of the Brunello Riserva Due Lecci Est '18, a wine rich in sensations of flowers and red fruits, medicinal herbs, licorice, rhubarb, and spices. Nicely integrated tannins harmonize beautifully with fruit, rendering the palate highly enjoyable, all amplified by a delicate acidity that accompanies a lingering finish. The excellent Brunello Costa di Monte '19 balances pleasantness and character on the nose, with hints of red fruit meeting scrubland, and aromatic herbs; in the mouth it's firm and wonderfully persistent.

Wine	Rating
● Brunello di Montalcino Duelecci Est Ris. '18	♟♟♟ 8
● Brunello di Montalcino Costa di Monte '19	♟♟ 8
● Brunello di Montalcino '19	♟♟ 6
● Rosso di Montalcino '22	♟♟ 4
● Toscana Rosso Poggio d'Arna '21	♟♟ 3
● Brunello di Montalcino '17	♕♕♕ 6
● Brunello di Montalcino '15	♕♕♕ 8
● Brunello di Montalcino Duelecci Est Ris. '13	♕♕♕ 8
● Brunello di Montalcino Duelecci Ovest Ris. '15	♕♕♕ 8
● Brunello di Montalcino Duelecci Ovest Ris. '12	♕♕♕ 7
● Brunello di Montalcino Ris. '10	♕♕♕

Tenuta di Trinoro

via Val d'Orcia, 15
53047 Sarteano [SI]
(» +39 0578267110
@ www.vinifranchetti.com

ANNUAL PRODUCTION 120,000 bottles
HECTARES UNDER VINE 24.00

In the early 1990s, Tenuta di Trinoro was Andrea Franchetti's first major oenological revelation, and it transformed a remote corner of southeastern Siena, in Sarteano, into a small-scale Bordeaux. Franchetti, who recently passed away, trained in Bordeaux, and his winemaking and viticultural approach reflects that influence. But his wines also possess an extraordinary, unique character, expressed with a reassuring consistency. The Tenuta di Trinoro '21, a blend of cabernet franc, merlot, cabernet sauvignon, and petit verdot, summons a lush fruity nose with earthy, spicy, and toasted touches. On the palate, it's juicy, with a balsamic finish. The nicely crafted Palazzi '22, a monovarietal merlot, manifests ripe blackberry aromas with smoky accents. The palate is delicate and sweet, only becoming slightly stern towards the end. The aromatic and enjoyable Le Cupole '22, a blend of cabernet franc, merlot, cabernet sauvignon, and petit verdot from younger vines, is fragrant and enjoyable.

★Tenuta di Valgiano

via di Valgiano, 7
55015 Lucca
(» +39 0583402271
@ www.valgiano.it

CELLAR SALES
PRE-BOOKED VISITS
ANNUAL PRODUCTION 60,000 bottles
HECTARES UNDER VINE 15.00
VITICULTURE METHOD Certified Biodynamic

Tenuta di Valgiano, managed since 1993 by Moreno Petrini and Laura Di Collobiano, is one of the cradles of biodynamic winemaking in Italy. As a pioneer in Steinerian practices, the winery has maintained its role as a leader in the Lucca area with reassuring continuity. The wines are rich in personality and character, exemplifying absolute excellence with Tenuta di Valgiano, the estate's flagship product. The Mazzapink, which hails from the nearby Marchesi Mazzarosa vineyards, represents a modern, appealing interpretation of sangiovese (with a touch of cabernet). The 2022 reveals aromas of red citrus, a floral bouquet of rose, geranium, and violet, with ferrous and balsamic notes. A supple, sapid, and silky palate finishes on a highly enjoyable balsamic note. The Tenuta di Valgiano '21 is richer, showcasing exemplary evolution and perfect nose-palate symmetry. It exudes aromas of Mediterranean scrub, mulberry jam, cinchona, and licorice, with a rich, balanced palate of great persistence and depth.

● Tenuta di Trinoro '21	♈♈ 8
● Le Cupole '22	♈♈ 6
● Palazzi '22	♈♈ 8
● Campo di Camagi Cabernet Franc '18	♈♈♈ 8
● Palazzi '20	♈♈♈ 8
● Tenuta di Trinoro '20	♈♈♈ 8
● Tenuta di Trinoro '08	♈♈♈ 8
● Tenuta di Trinoro '04	♈♈♈ 8
● Tenuta di Trinoro '03	♈♈♈ 8
● Bianco di Trinoro '21	♈♈ 8
● Bianco Trinoro '19	♈♈ 7
● Campo di Tenaglia '20	♈♈ 8
● Le Cupole '21	♈♈ 6
● Le Cupole '20	♈♈ 6
● Le Cupole '19	♈♈ 5
● Tenuta di Trinoro '18	♈♈ 8

● Colline Lucchesi Tenuta di Valgiano '21	♈♈♈ 8
● Mazzapink '22	♈♈ 4
● Palistorti Rosso '22	♈♈ 5
○ Palistorti Bianco '23	♈ 5
● Colline Lucchesi Tenuta di Valgiano '18	♈♈♈ 8
● Colline Lucchesi Tenuta di Valgiano '17	♈♈♈ 8
● Colline Lucchesi Tenuta di Valgiano '16	♈♈♈ 8
● Colline Lucchesi Tenuta di Valgiano '15	♈♈♈ 8
● Colline Lucchesi Tenuta di Valgiano '13	♈♈♈ 8
● Colline Lucchesi Tenuta di Valgiano '12	♈♈♈ 6
● Colline Lucchesi Tenuta di Valgiano '11	♈♈♈ 6
● Colline Lucchesi Tenuta di Valgiano '10	♈♈♈ 6
● Palistorti Rosso '17	♈♈♈ 5

★Tenute del Cerro

fraz. Acquaviva
via Grazianella, 5
53045 Montepulciano [SI]
☏ +39 0578767722
⊕ www.fattoriadelcerro.it

CELLAR SALES
PRE-BOOKED VISITS
ACCOMMODATION AND RESTAURANT SERVICE
ANNUAL PRODUCTION 1,300,000 bottles
HECTARES UNDER VINE 181.00
SUSTAINABLE WINERY

Owned by Tenute del Cerro Spa, the agricultural and viticultural branch of the Unipol Group, this winery is one of the most important in Montepulciano. Cerro's journey began in 1978 under different ownership. Since then, the producer has been on an upward trajectory, making wines celebrated for their reliable quality and modern, generous style at its Acquaviva di Montepulciano cellar. The Rosso di Montepulciano '23 makes for a smooth and flavorful drink, highlighting fruity sensations on the nose. The Nobile Silineo '21, on the other hand, offers darker, more mature fruit aromas, with prominent spicy and smoky notes from oak. In the mouth, the wine is supported by oak as well, with a juicy yet concentrated palate, finishing with a tight, wood-dominated close.

★Terenzi

loc. Montedonico
58054 Scansano [GR]
☏ +39 0564599601
⊕ www.terenzi.eu

CELLAR SALES
PRE-BOOKED VISITS
ACCOMMODATION
ANNUAL PRODUCTION 350,000 bottles
HECTARES UNDER VINE 60.00

Through strategic and consistent choices, the Terenzi family has secured a stable position among Morellino di Scansano's top producers. Their wines consistently deliver quality, with their premium offerings exhibiting a well-defined style characterized by balance and finesse, drawing on a contemporary approach rooted in their connection to Montedonico. It's a successful mix that serves as a model for the entire territory. The Morellino di Scansano Madrechiesa Riserva '21 features a complex, deep, and flavorful palate, matching a nose focused on ripe red berries, aromatic herbs, and spices. The well-crafted Maremma Vermentino Balbino '23 is flavorful and focused on the palate, with a floral aromatic profile highlighted by minty notes. The Petit Manseng Passito '20 is sweet but never cloying, thanks to the grape's trademark acidity.

Wine	Rating
● Nobile di Montepulciano Silineo '21	♥♥ 5
● Rosso di Montepulciano '23	♥♥ 3
● Nobile di Montepulciano '17	♥♥♥ 4*
● Nobile di Montepulciano '16	♥♥♥ 4*
● Nobile di Montepulciano '15	♥♥♥ 4*
● Nobile di Montepulciano '14	♥♥♥ 3*
● Nobile di Montepulciano '11	♥♥♥ 3*
● Nobile di Montepulciano '10	♥♥♥ 3*
● Nobile di Montepulciano Ris. '12	♥♥♥ 4*
● Nobile di Montepulciano Ris. '11	♥♥♥ 4*
● Nobile di Montepulciano Ris. '06	♥♥♥ 4
● Nobile di Montepulciano Silineo '19	♥♥♥ 4*
● Nobile di Montepulciano Silineo '18	♥♥♥ 4*
● Nobile di Montepulciano Vign. Antica Chiusina '00	♥♥♥ 6
● Nobile di Montepulciano Silineo '20	♥♥ 5

Wine	Rating
● Morellino di Scansano Madrechiesa Ris. '21	♥♥ 6
○ Maremma Toscana Vermentino Balbino '23	♥♥ 3
○ Petit Manseng Passito '20	♥♥ 7
○ Maremma Toscana Vermentino Balbinus '22	♥ 5
● Morellino di Scansano '23	♥ 3
● Morellino di Scansano Purosangue '22	♥ 4
● Francesca Romana '16	♥♥♥ 5
● Morellino di Scansano Madrechiesa Ris. '20	♥♥♥ 5
● Morellino di Scansano Madrechiesa Ris. '19	♥♥♥ 5
● Morellino di Scansano Madrechiesa Ris. '18	♥♥♥

Terradonnà

loc. Notri, 78
57028 Suvereto [LI]
☎ +39 3314026914
🌐 www.terradonna.it

CELLAR SALES
PRE-BOOKED VISITS
ANNUAL PRODUCTION 30,000 bottles
HECTARES UNDER VINE 10.00
VITICULTURE METHOD Certified Organic
SUSTAINABLE WINERY

Located in Suvereto and owned by the Rossi family, Terradonnà launched its winemaking journey in 2002, when it released its first bottles. Annalisa Rossi and her husband Mauro now manage the producer, drawing on a rich collection of grape varieties, including sangiovese, syrah, cabernet sauvignon, merlot, vermentino, trebbiano, ansonica, and clairette, a white grape from southern France. The Kalsi '23, a monovarietal vermentino, showcases aromas of sage, mint, thyme, and elderflower, leading to a sapid, well-balanced palate that builds on the finish. The Prasio '21, a blend of equal parts merlot and cabernet sauvignon, boasts a bouquet of small red fruits, Mediterranean scrub, and spices. In the mouth, the palate is nicely guided by resolved tannins, with a finish returning to fruity tones.

Fattoria Terre del Marchesato

fraz. Bolgheri
loc. Sant'Uberto, 164
57022 Castagneto Carducci [LI]
☎ +39 0565749752
🌐 www.terredelmarchesato.com

CELLAR SALES
PRE-BOOKED VISITS
ACCOMMODATION
ANNUAL PRODUCTION 120,000 bottles
HECTARES UNDER VINE 16.00

Maurizio Fuselli, along with his wife Giovanna and sons Alessandro (the winemaker), Samuele (who oversees cultivation), and young Filippo, run the family winery. Originally from Le Marche, the Fuselli family arrived in Bolgheri in 1954, buying land from Mario Incisa della Rocchetta. They started by cultivating vegetables, but Maurizio's grandfather, Emilio, decided to plant vineyards, initially for domestic consumption. That tradition was carried on by Aldo, Maurizio's father. The wines now exhibit a classic, precise style that highlights the region's potential. The Franchesato '21, a monovarietal cabernet franc, shows good complexity on the palate, alternating between sapidity and sweetness. Its focused aromas recall plum and Mediterranean scrub. The rich Aldone '21, a monovarietal merlot, delivers a flavorful palate with fine, juicy tannins. Blackberry, plum, and Mediterranean herbs dominate the aromatic profile of the Maurizio Fuselli '21, a monovarietal petit verdot that's creamy and complex in the mouth, with close-knit, well-defined tannins.

● Bixbi '23	🍷🍷 3
● Giaietto '22	🍷🍷 3
○ Kalsi '23	🍷🍷 4
● Prasio '21	🍷🍷 5
○ Faden '23	🍷 3
● Spato '21	🍷 5
● Val di Cornia Cabernet Sauvignon Okenio '20	🍷 7
● Bixbi '22	🍷🍷 3
● Bixbi '20	🍷🍷 3
● Giaietto '21	🍷🍷 3
● Giaietto '20	🍷🍷 3
● Prasio '20	🍷🍷 5
● Spato '20	🍷🍷 5

● Franchesato '21	🍷🍷 8
● Aldone '21	🍷🍷 8
○ Bolgheri Bianco Papeo '23	🍷🍷 4
● Maurizio Fuselli '21	🍷🍷 8
● Aldone '20	🍷🍷 8
● Bolgheri Marchesale Sup. '17	🍷🍷 6
● Bolgheri Rosso Emilio I '21	🍷🍷 3
● Bolgheri Rosso Sup. Marchesale '20	🍷🍷 6
● Franchesato '20	🍷🍷 8
● Inedito '22	🍷🍷 2*
● Marchesale '13	🍷🍷 6
● Marchesale '12	🍷🍷 7
● Marchesale '08	🍷🍷 7
● Marchesale '07	🍷🍷 7
● Maurizio Fuselli '20	🍷🍷 8

Terre dell'Etruria

loc. Poderone
58051 Magliano in Toscana [GR]
(" +39 0564593011
@ www.terretruria.it

CELLAR SALES
PRE-BOOKED VISITS
ANNUAL PRODUCTION 200,000 bottles
HECTARES UNDER VINE 100.00
SUSTAINABLE WINERY

The cooperative winery Terre dell'Etruria operates according to a clear, well-established approach, almost like a private producer. Only the crop from those who best know how to interpret local varieties—sangiovese, ciliegiolo, vermentino, and ansonica—finishes in the bottle. The result is a range of wines that are both pleasant and full of character, crafted with authority, able to stand out for their sense of place and a convincing, contemporary stylistic identity. With a nose that plays on small fruits, spices, and balsamic touches, the Poderone '21 (100% ciliegiolo) moves rhythmically in the mouth, contrasting sapidity with fruity echoes. The well-crafted Maremma Ciliegiolo Briglia '23 delivers clean aromas and a flavorful palate. The immediately pleasant, and dynamic Maremma Ansonica Tramaglio '23 gets the job done. The intriguing Vermentino Frizzante Brumoso '23, despite its simplicity, is a delicious and highly drinkable pour.

Teruzzi

loc. Casale, 19
53037 San Gimignano [SI]
(" +39 0577940143
@ www.teruzziwine.com

CELLAR SALES
PRE-BOOKED VISITS
ANNUAL PRODUCTION 600,000 bottles
HECTARES UNDER VINE 96.00
VITICULTURE METHOD Certified Organic
SUSTAINABLE WINERY

Teruzzi boasts the largest vineyard area among private producers in the Vernaccia di San Gimignano appellation. Founded in 1974 by Enrico Teruzzi, the winery has an important place in the history of the "City of Towers". In 2016, it found renewed energy when it joined the Terra Moretti Group, gaining new momentum and opportunities for more conscious growth and a convincing relaunch. The Vernaccia di San Gimignano Sant'Elena Riserva '20 showcases a sweet, subtle palate with great definition. It's decidedly linear and lean in its progression of flavor, adorned by aromas of tropical fruit and saline hints that amplify its fragrance. The Terre di Tufi '22 features floral and white fruit aromas, revealing a vibrant, iodized, mineral, and oaky note that adds intrigue, leading to a fresh, herbaceous palate with a sapid, persistent finish.

● Il Poderone Ciliegiolo '21	♥♥ 8
○ Brumoso Vermentino Frizzante Ancestrale '23	♥♥ 3
○ Maremma Toscana Ansonica Tramaglio '23	♥♥ 3
● Maremma Toscana Ciliegiolo Briglia '23	♥♥ 3
○ Maremma Toscana Vermentino Marmato '23	♥♥ 3
● Morellino di Scansano Giogo '23	♥ 3
○ Brumoso Vermentino Frizzante Ancestrale '22	♀♀ 3
○ Maremma Toscana Ansonica Tramaglio '22	♀♀ 3*
○ Maremma Toscana Vermentino Marmato '22	♀♀ 3
○ Maremma Toscana Vermentino Marmato '21	♀♀ 2*
● Morellino di Scansano Giogo '22	♀♀ 3
● Morellino di Scansano Giogo '18	♀♀ 2*

○ Vernaccia di San Gimignano Sant'Elena Ris. '20	♥♥♥ 5
○ Terre di Tufi '22	♥♥ 5
○ Vernaccia di San Gimignano Isola Bianca '23	♥♥ 3
○ Terre di Tufi '21	♀♀ 5
○ Terre di Tufi '20	♀♀ 5
○ Vernaccia di S. Gimignano Sant'Elena Ris. '17	♀♀ 4
○ Vernaccia di San Gimignano Isola Bianca '22	♀♀ 3
○ Vernaccia di San Gimignano Isola Bianca '18	♀♀ 2
○ Vernaccia di San Gimignano Sant'Elena Ris. '19	♀♀ 5
○ Vernaccia di San Gimignano Sant'Elena Ris. '18	♀♀ 5

La Togata

fraz. Sant'Angelo in Colle
via del Colombaio, 7b
53024 Montalcino [SI]
☎ +39 0668803000
✉ www.brunellolatogata.com

CELLAR SALES
PRE-BOOKED VISITS
ANNUAL PRODUCTION 120,000 bottles
HECTARES UNDER VINE 19.00
VITICULTURE METHOD Certified Organic
SUSTAINABLE WINERY

This family-run, all-female winery boasts five different wines: La Togata, Carillon, Jacopus, Notte di Note, and Seconda Stella a Destra. The choice reflects the different terroirs where sisters Stefania, Vanessa, and Azzurra Angel manage their vineyards, a configuration that includes Sant'Angelo in Colle, Torrenieri, and Montosoli. Each parcel is vinified separately, allowing each wine to express the specific characteristics of its unique soil, exposure, and elevation. While lacking a star performer, the broad range of sangiovese produced proves reliable and well-styled overall. The Brunello La Togata '19 offers up a lively nose of lush, fragrant fruit and a vibrant palate with nice persistence. The Brunello Carrillon '19 shows more fruit than floral notes, with a subtle contribution of spices and a spirited palate that retains some youthful hardness, which will soften with time in the bottle.

Tolaini

loc. Vallenuova
s.da prov.le 9 di Pievasciata, 28
53019 Castelnuovo Berardenga [SI]
☎ +39 0577356972
✉ www.tolaini.it

CELLAR SALES
PRE-BOOKED VISITS
ACCOMMODATION
ANNUAL PRODUCTION 300,000 bottles
HECTARES UNDER VINE 48.00
VITICULTURE METHOD Certified Organic
SUSTAINABLE WINERY

Operating between Pianella and Vagliagli, Tolaini has become a solid winery in the Castelnuovo Berardenga production area. The project was founded in the late 1990s by Pierluigi Tolaini and is today carried forward with the same determination by his daughter Lia Tolaini-Banville. She not only manages the family estate but also exports and distributes Italian wines in the U.S. under the Banville Wine Merchants brand. The monovarietal Mello 700 '21 sangiovese reveals a nuanced nose of ripe small red fruits and spices. On the palate, it's juicy and slender, with well-sustained development and an airy finish. The Chianti Classico Villanuova '22 focuses on drinkability, with an appealing, juicy, and immediately approachable palate that perfectly captures the characteristics of its type. The Chianti Classico Gran Selezione Montebello Sette '20 is clearly defined in its profile.

● Brunello di Montalcino Carillon '19	♟♟ 8
● Brunello di Montalcino Jacopus '19	♟♟ 8
● Brunello di Montalcino La Togata '19	♟♟ 8
● Brunello di Montalcino La Togata dei Togati '19	♟♟ 8
● Brunello di Montalcino Notte di Note '19	♟♟ 6
● Brunello di Montalcino Seconda Stella a Destra '19	♟♟ 8
● Rosso di Montalcino Carillon '22	♟♟ 6
● Rosso di Montalcino Jacopus '22	♟ 6
● Rosso di Montalcino Togata '22	♟ 6
● Brunello di Montalcino '06	♟♟♟ 7
● Brunello di Montalcino '97	♟♟♟ 5
● Brunello di Montalcino Carillon '17	♟♟ 7
● Brunello di Montalcino Notte di Note '18	♟♟ 6
● Brunello di Montalcino Ris. '15	♟♟ 8

● Mello 700 '21	♟♟♟ 8
● Chianti Cl. Vallenuova '22	♟♟ 4
● Al Passo '21	♟♟ 4
● Chianti Cl. Gran Selezione V. Montebello Sette '20	♟♟ 6
● Perlui '21	♟♟ 8
● Valdisanti '21	♟♟ 5
● Legit '21	♟ 5
● Picconero '20	♟ 8
● Al Passo '14	♟♟♟ 4*
● Chianti Cl. Gran Selezione V. Montebello Sette '18	♟♟♟ 5
● Chianti Cl. Vallenuova '18	♟♟♟ 3*
● Mello 700 '20	♟♟♟ 8
● Picconero '10	♟♟♟ 8
● Picconero '09	♟♟♟ 8
● Valdisanti '18	♟♟♟ 5

Torre a Cona

loc. San Donato in Collina
via Torre a Cona, 49
50067 Rignano sull'Arno [FI]
☎ +39 055699000
⊕ www.torreacona.com

CELLAR SALES
PRE-BOOKED VISITS
ACCOMMODATION
ANNUAL PRODUCTION 100,000 bottles
HECTARES UNDER VINE 21.00

The Rossi di Montelera family, owners of the famed Martini & Rossi brand, have owned Torre a Cona since 1935. Their vineyards, located southeast of Florence near the Valdarno border, are planted with sangiovese, colorino, merlot, trebbiano, malvasia, and vermentino. Here they primarily produce wines under the Chianti Colli Fiorentini appellation, maturing mostly in large oak barrels and to a lesser extent in barriques. The Chianti Colli Fiorentini Molino degli Innocenti Riserva '19, a sangiovese of stature, offers aromas of pomegranate and orange, with notes of cinchona and balsamic undertones. On the palate, it's powerful and dynamic, with steady in its persistence. The Chianti Colli Fiorentini Terre di Cino Riserva '21 also impresses with its more mature characteristics. The Chianti Colli Fiorentini Crociferro '22 is a smooth and flavorful sip.

Toscani

via Pereta, 9
56040 Casale Marittimo [PI]
☎ +39 3343603735
⊕ www.vino.toscani.com

CELLAR SALES
PRE-BOOKED VISITS
ACCOMMODATION AND RESTAURANT SERVICE
ANNUAL PRODUCTION 50,000 bottles
HECTARES UNDER VINE 16.00
VITICULTURE METHOD Certified Organic

The dynamic photographer Oliviero Toscani began viticulture on his family's land in Casale Marittimo in 1968, producing his first bottle in 2006. Since 2015, his son Rocco has fully managed the estate's activities. The vineyards are organically cultivated with cabernet franc, syrah, and greco, while the cellar uses stainless steel, amphora, tonneaux, and large oak barrels for aging. The monovarietal Lumeo '21 syrah shines with its fine floral aromas; a solid, sapid, and deep palate follows, well-paced with minty and spicy tones that emerge more intensely in a finish that builds. The well-crafted Vedomare '21, another monovarietal syrah, features more fruit-concentrated aromas and a juicy, somewhat sweet palate. The playful Lolì, also from syrah grapes, makes for compelling drinkability in the Pet-Nat style.

● Chianti Colli Fiorentini Molino degli Innocenti Ris. '19	♙♙♙ 8
● Chianti Colli Fiorentini Terre di Cino Ris. '21	♙♙ 5
● Chianti Colli Fiorentino Crociferro '22	♙♙ 3
● Chianti Colli Fiorentini Badia a Corte Ris. '20	♙♙♙ 5
● Chianti Colli Fiorentini Badia a Corte Ris. '19	♙♙♙ 5
● Chianti Colli Fiorentini Badia a Corte Ris. '16	♙♙♙ 4*
● Chianti Colli Fiorentini Badia a Corte Ris. '15	♙♙♙ 4*
● Chianti Colli Fiorentini Terre di Cino Ris. '18	♙♙♙ 4*
● Vin Santo del Chianti Occhio di Pernice Fonti e Lecceta '11	♙♙♙ 6

● Lumeo '21	♙♙ 6
● Vedomare Rosso '21	♙♙ 4
● I Toscani '23	♙♙ 3
⊙ Lolì	♙♙ 4
● Vieni via con me '21	♙♙ 6
● I Toscani '21	♙♙ 3
● I Toscani '18	♙♙ 3
● Lumeo '20	♙♙ 6
● Lumeo '19	♙♙ 5
● OT '18	♙♙ 5
● OT '17	♙♙ 6
● Vedomare Rosso '20	♙♙ 4
● Vedomare Rosso '18	♙♙ 3
● Vieni via con me '20	♙♙ 6
● Vieni Via con Me '19	♙♙ 6

Tenuta Trerose

fraz. Valiano
via della Stella, 3
53040 Montepulciano [SI]
☎ +39 0577804101
✉ www.tenutatrerose.it

CELLAR SALES
PRE-BOOKED VISITS
ANNUAL PRODUCTION 400,000 bottles
HECTARES UNDER VINE 103.00
VITICULTURE METHOD Certified Organic
SUSTAINABLE WINERY

At Tenuta Trerose, owned by Angelini Wines & Estates, sangiovese wines are crafted with minimal interference in the natural winemaking process, and primarily aged in large oak barrels. Located in the center of Valiano's "Pieve," Trerose consistently produces a stylistically defined, natural and characterful range of offerings, securing the winery a place among Montepulciano's most intriguing wineries. The Nobile Santa Caterina '21 possesses impeccable aromas of small red fruits, underbrush, and spices, leading to a vibrant and lively fruit profile that moves fragrantly and rhythmically on the palate—a juicy and easygoing drink. The well-crafted Nobile Simposio Riserva '20 shows riper and fleshier aromatic traits with hints of plum preserves. In the mouth, the wine is complex and dynamic, closing on a vibrant finish.

★Tua Rita

loc. Notri, 81
57028 Suvereto [LI]
☎ +39 0565829237
✉ www.tuarita.it

CELLAR SALES
PRE-BOOKED VISITS
ANNUAL PRODUCTION 950,000 bottles
HECTARES UNDER VINE 60.00
SUSTAINABLE WINERY

When Rita Tua and Virgilio Bisti bought what would become Tua Rita in 1984, it was meant to be a place to live and farm. However, the winery's success exceeded all expectations. Today, their daughter Simena, her husband Stefano Frascolla, and their son Giovanni run this globally renowned winery, famous for bottles like the celebrated Redigaffi, first released in 1994. The Giusto di Notri '22, a blend based on cabernet sauvignon, cabernet franc, and merlot, reveals aromas of ripe plum and blackberry, accompanied by smoky, toasty, and spicy notes. On the palate, it's soft and sweet, with a broad, focused finish. The Perlato del Bosco '22, made from sangiovese grapes, plays on vibrant aromas of small red fruits and underbrush. In the mouth, it's juicy and rich in contrasts, with an expansive finish.

Nobile di Montepulciano Santa Caterina '21	♟♟ 5
Nobile di Montepulciano Simposio Ris. '20	♟♟ 6
Nobile di Montepulciano Simposio '97	♟♟♟ 5
Nobile di Montepulciano Simposio Ris. '15	♟♟♟ 6
Nobile di Montepulciano Santa Caterina '20	♟♟ 5
Nobile di Montepulciano Santa Caterina '19	♟♟ 5
Nobile di Montepulciano Simposio Ris. '18	♟♟ 6
Nobile di Montepulciano Simposio Ris. '17	♟♟ 6

● Giusto di Notri '22	♟♟ 8
● Perlato del Bosco Sangiovese '22	♟♟ 6
● Giusto di Notri '95	♟♟♟ 7
● Giusto di Notri '94	♟♟♟ 7
● Redigaffi '08	♟♟♟ 8
● Redigaffi '07	♟♟♟ 8
● Redigaffi '06	♟♟♟ 8
● Redigaffi '04	♟♟♟ 8
● Redigaffi '03	♟♟♟ 8
● Redigaffi '02	♟♟♟ 8
● Redigaffi '01	♟♟♟ 8
● Redigaffi '00	♟♟♟ 7
● Redigaffi '99	♟♟♟ 8
● Redigaffi '98	♟♟♟ 7
● Redigaffi '96	♟♟♟ 7

TUSCANY

TUSCANY

Uccelliera - Voliero

fraz. Castelnuovo dell'Abate
pod. Uccelliera, 45
53024 Montalcino [SI]
☎ +39 0577835729
✎ www.uccelliera-montalcino.it

CELLAR SALES
PRE-BOOKED VISITS
ANNUAL PRODUCTION 60,000 bottles
HECTARES UNDER VINE 10.00

Andrea Cortonesi's path as a winemaker was a conscious life choice born out of passion. From a young age, he worked with his father on their family's sharecropping land. In 1986, after saving for years, Andrea was able to buy the historic Uccelliera estate, just a stone's throw from the Abbey of Sant'Antimo. The property included a few hectares of vineyards and some olive trees on the southern slopes of Montalcino. More recently, Andrea acquired another estate with very different soils and climate characteristics, leading him to bottle his wines under the Voliero label. The Brunello '19 from the Voliero line reached our finals, showcasing a lovely aromatic range of red berries, Mediterranean scrub, blood orange, and dark tobacco. On the palate, the wine is consistent, with vigorous fruit in the foreground, mild tannins, and a fresh, pleasant finish. The Brunello '19 Uccelliera features dark fruits and flowers, with a sapid and energetic palate, well supported by acidity.

★Val delle Corti

fraz. La Croce
loc. Val delle Corti, 141
53017 Radda in Chianti [SI]
☎ +39 0577738215
✎ www.valdellecorti.it

CELLAR SALES
PRE-BOOKED VISITS
ACCOMMODATION
ANNUAL PRODUCTION 30,000 bottles
HECTARES UNDER VINE 6.00
VITICULTURE METHOD Certified Organic

Roberto Bianchi, who has run the family winery since 1999, has earned it a place among Radda in Chianti's leading producers, all while staying true to tradition. The vineyards are managed organically, with an eye towards biodynamic practices, while in the the cellar they combine concrete tanks, small and large oak barrels for aging. The wines, deeply rooted in Chianti tradition, offer enchanting aromas and rare depth of flavor, setting a high standard even within the Chianti Classico appellation. The Chianti Classico '21 opens on delicate aromas reminiscent of fresh flowers and ripe red berries, with smoky hints and touches of flint and roots. On the palate, it's penetrating, flavorful, and long, finishing with an airy profile. The Chianti Classico Riserva '20 is nicely balanced, opting for darker tones but just as enjoyable. Lo Straniero '21, a sangiovese and merlot blend, is a lively wine, surpassed only by the invigorating character of the Rosé Scuro '23.

● Brunello di Montalcino Voliero '19	♟♟ 8
● Brunello di Montalcino '19	♟♟ 8
● Rosso di Montalcino '22	♟♟ 5
● Rosso di Montalcino Voliero '22	♟♟ 4
● Rapace '21	♟ 5
● Brunello di Montalcino '10	♟♟♟ 6
● Brunello di Montalcino '08	♟♟♟ 7
● Brunello di Montalcino Ris. '97	♟♟♟ 8
● Rosso di Montalcino '16	♟♟♟ 4*
● Rosso di Montalcino '15	♟♟♟ 4*
● Rosso di Montalcino '14	♟♟♟ 4*
● Brunello di Montalcino '18	♟♟ 8
● Brunello di Montalcino Ris. '16	♟♟ 8
● Brunello di Montalcino Ris. '15	♟♟ 8
● Brunello di Montalcino Voliero '17	♟♟ 8
● Rosso di Montalcino '19	♟♟ 5

● Chianti Cl. '21	♟♟♟ 5
● Chianti Cl. Ris. '20	♟♟ 5
● Lo Straniero '21	♟♟ 3
⊙ Rosé Scuro '23	♟♟ 3
● Chianti Cl. '20	♟♟♟ 5
● Chianti Cl. '17	♟♟♟ 4
● Chianti Cl. '13	♟♟♟ 4
● Chianti Cl. '12	♟♟♟ 4
● Chianti Cl. '11	♟♟♟ 3
● Chianti Cl. '10	♟♟♟ 3
● Chianti Cl. '09	♟♟♟ 2
● Chianti Cl. Ris. '17	♟♟♟ 5
● Chianti Cl. Ris. '16	♟♟♟ 5
● Chianti Cl. Ris. '14	♟♟♟ 5

Val di Suga

loc. Val di Cava
53024 Montalcino [SI]
☎ +39 0577804101
✉ www.valdisuga.it

CELLAR SALES
PRE-BOOKED VISITS
ANNUAL PRODUCTION 250,000 bottles
HECTARES UNDER VINE 52.00

This winery's vineyards are spread out across three different slopes in Montalcino, which is why the wines are fermented separately and aged in different types of barrels—so as to highlight the distinctions between each terroir. Vigna Spuntali, on the southwest-facing side, has sandy soils and the wines age in 2500-liter oval barrels. On the higher southeastern slopes of Poggio al Granchio, where the soils are rich in schist and marl, 6000-liter conical vats are used. Finally, Vigna del Lago, on the northeast side with clay soils, sees the wines aged in traditional 4400-liter barrels. The Brunello Vigna del Lago '19 impresses with its Mediterranean charm and elegance, featuring enjoyable, bright red fruit, followed by tobacco, spices, and a fine background of pencil lead. On the palate, it's refined and complex, with notable structure, supported by close-knit, well-defined tannins that give backbone to its rich, juicy fruit. The Brunello Poggio al Granchio '19 offer up aromas of bramble berries, cinchona, Mediterranean herbs, and tobacco, with a robust and focused tannic texture.

● Brunello di Montalcino V. del Lago '19	♥♥ 8
● Brunello di Montalcino V. Poggio al Granchio '19	♥♥ 8
● Brunello di Montalcino '19	♥♥ 6
● Rosso di Montalcino '22	♥♥ 5
● Rosso di Montalcino V. Spuntali '21	♥♥ 8
● Brunello di Montalcino V. del Lago '95	♥♥♥ 8
● Brunello di Montalcino V. del Lago '93	♥♥♥ 8
● Brunello di Montalcino V. del Lago '90	♥♥♥ 8
● Brunello di Montalcino V. Spuntali '16	♥♥♥ 8
● Brunello di Montalcino V. Spuntali '15	♥♥♥ 8
● Brunello di Montalcino V. Spuntali '95	♥♥♥ 8
● Brunello di Montalcino V. Spuntali '93	♥♥♥ 8
Brunello di Montalcino Val di Suga '07	♥♥♥ 5

Tenuta Valdipiatta

via della Ciarliana, 25a
53045 Montepulciano [SI]
☎ +39 0578757930
✉ www.valdipiatta.it

CELLAR SALES
PRE-BOOKED VISITS
ANNUAL PRODUCTION 70,000 bottles
HECTARES UNDER VINE 23.00
VITICULTURE METHOD Certified Organic
SUSTAINABLE WINERY

With its 35 years of history, Miriam Caporali's winery has followed a virtuous path of quality. The wines showcase personality, finesse, and balance rather than concentration and roundness. In the vineyard, they avoid pushing for overripe grapes, while in the cellar they use both barriques and large oak barrels for aging. This approach requires patience, as the wines often need time to reach their full potential. The Nobile '21 sees subtle aromas of flowers and spicy whiffs join with toasted and smoky hints. On the palate, it's flavorful, fluid, and persistent, showing no lack of character. The Rosso di Montepulciano '22 stands out for its prominent berry aromas, accompanied by hints of aromatic herbs and fresh flowers. In the mouth, it develops with a fragrant expression and finishes with good length.

● Nobile di Montepulciano '21	♥♥ 5
● Rosso di Montepulciano '22	♥♥ 3
● Nobile di Montepulciano Vigna d'Alfiero '21	♥ 7
● Nobile di Montepulciano Ris. '90	♥♥♥ 5
● Nobile di Montepulciano V. d'Alfiero '99	♥♥♥ 5
● Nobile di Montepulciano '20	♥♥ 5
● Nobile di Montepulciano '19	♥♥ 5
● Nobile di Montepulciano '17	♥♥ 5
● Nobile di Montepulciano Ris. '13	♥♥ 6
● Nobile di Montepulciano V. d'Alfiero '18	♥♥ 8
● Nobile di Montepulciano V. d'Alfiero '16	♥♥ 6
● Nobile di Montepulciano V. d'Alfiero '10	♥♥ 6

Vallepicciola

s.da prov.le 9 di Pievasciata, 21
53019 Castelnuovo Berardenga [SI]
(+39 05771698718
www.vallepicciola.com

CELLAR SALES
PRE-BOOKED VISITS
ANNUAL PRODUCTION 600,000 bottles
HECTARES UNDER VINE 105.00

Owned by the Bolfo family, Vallepicciola spans the UGA production areas of Castelnuovo Berardenga and Vagliagli. Established in 1999, it remains one of Chianti's most ambitious projects. The winery, which opened in 2016, draws on a diverse range of grape varieties, including sangiovese and international varieties like cabernet sauvignon, merlot, cabernet franc, pinot noir, and chardonnay. The Vallepicciola '21, a monovarietal sangiovese, brings together aromas of cherry and violet with references to tobacco and vanilla. On the palate, it's juicy, persistent, and rhythmic, with a long finish marked by a refreshing balsamic note. The Chianti Classico Gran Selezione Lapina '20 is truly exciting, featuring mature red fruits, pencil lead, spices, and smoky hints. On the palate, it's firm and juicy, concluding with a rich, fruit- and spice-laden finish.

Varramista

loc. Varramista
via Ricavo
56020 Montopoli in Val d'Arno [PI]
(+39 057144711
www.varramista.it

CELLAR SALES
PRE-BOOKED VISITS
ACCOMMODATION
ANNUAL PRODUCTION 35,000 bottles
HECTARES UNDER VINE 13.00
VITICULTURE METHOD Certified Organic

Situated near Montopoli, in Pisa, Varramista gained fame through the Piaggio and Agnelli families, who made it their country residence. In the 1990s, Giovanni Alberto Agnelli, then president of Piaggio, chose the estate as his home, having inherited it from his grandfather Enrico Piaggio. He set out to develop wine production, selecting syrah alongside sangiovese as the signature grape. The Varramista '20, 100% syrah, exudes aromas of aromatic herbs and ripe red fruits, along with touches of cinchona. On the palate, it's progressively enveloping, with integrated tannins and a broad, persistent finish. The Sterpato '21, a blend of sangiovese, merlot, and cabernet sauvignon, is more concentrated, with austere aromas and a compact, smooth palate. The Terre di Pisa Frasca '20 delights with its lively and spicy character, featuring vibrant flavors and aromas.

● Chianti Cl. Gran Selezione Lapina '20	♀♀♀	6
● Vallepicciola '21	♀♀	8
● Chianti Cl. '22	♀	4
● Chianti Cl. Ris. '20	♀	5
● Moredese '21	♀	5
● Chianti Cl. '17	♀♀♀	4*
● Chianti Cl. Ris. '19	♀♀♀	5
● Migliorè '18	♀♀♀	8
● Quercegrosse Merlot '18	♀♀♀	6
● Chianti Cl. '21	♀♀	4
● Chianti Cl. '20	♀♀	4
● Chianti Cl. Gran Selezione '15	♀♀	3*
● Chianti Cl. Gran Selezione La Pina '19	♀♀	6
● Chianti Cl. Gran Selezione La Pina '18	♀♀	6
● Chianti Cl. Gran Selezione La Pina '16	♀♀	6
● Migliorè '19	♀♀	8

● Varramista '20	♀♀	8
● Sterpato '21	♀♀	3
● Terre di Pisa Rosso Frasca '20	♀♀	5
● Varramista '00	♀♀♀	6
● Sterpato '20	♀♀	3
● Sterpato '19	♀♀	3
● Sterpato '18	♀♀	3
● Sterpato '17	♀♀	3
● Terre di Pisa Rosso Frasca '19	♀♀	5
● Terre di Pisa Rosso Frasca '18	♀♀	5
● Varramista '19	♀♀	8
● Varramista '16	♀♀	7
● Varramista '15	♀♀	7
● Varramista '08	♀♀	6
● Varramista '07	♀♀	6
● Varramista '05	♀♀	8

Vecchia Cantina di Montepulciano

via Provinciale, 7
53045 Montepulciano [SI]
☎ +39 0578716092
⊗ www.vecchiacantinadimontepulciano.com

CELLAR SALES
PRE-BOOKED VISITS
ANNUAL PRODUCTION 7,000,000 bottles
HECTARES UNDER VINE 1000.00
VITICULTURE METHOD Certified Organic
SUSTAINABLE WINERY

Founded in 1937, La Vecchia Cantina is one of Tuscany's most important cooperatives, with over 300 members cultivating vineyards in Montepulciano, Pienza, Cetona, Torrita di Siena, Sinalunga, Foiano della Chiana, Castiglion Fiorentino, Cortona, and Chiusi. Currently, the cooperative, based on the outskirts of Montepulciano, is undergoing a major shakeup, with its business structure and technical management being reorganized so as to raise quality standards. The Nobile Cantina del Redi '21 features a pressing, fragrant fruity profile, with a juicy, sweet palate and soft tannins, finishing cleanly. The Nobile '21 offers simpler aromas and a carefree, flavorful drinkability. The Nobile No.Mo.S '20 is also well-crafted, while The Nobile Briareo Cantina del Redi Riserva '19 shines with its lush fruit, both on the nose and palate.

I Veroni

via Tifariti, 5
50065 Pontassieve [FI]
☎ +39 0558368886
⊗ www.iveroni.it

CELLAR SALES
PRE-BOOKED VISITS
ACCOMMODATION
ANNUAL PRODUCTION 110,000 bottles
HECTARES UNDER VINE 20.00
VITICULTURE METHOD Certified Organic

Named after the ancient term for the loggias of Tuscan country buildings, I Veroni is located on the hills of San Martino, in Pontassieve. The winery underwent a major transformation in the 1990s, with a wholesale replanting of the vineyards. Today they host sangiovese, colorino, trebbiano, canaiolo bianco, malvasia, and vermentino, along with some international varieties, like merlot. The Terraelectae Vigneto Quona '21 is dense and intense on the nose, brimming with youthful sangiovese aromas of cherry, plum, bay leaf, and clove. Its youthful character is also evident on the palate, with tannins still taut but flavorful. Fruit leads right from the attack towards a slightly warm finish. The Vin Santo del Chianti Rufina Riserva '13 offers a persistence that doesn't wane, elevated by a bittersweet touch of chestnut honey that balances the sweetness of dried apple and date.

● Nobile di Montepulciano Cantina del Redi '21	♟♟ 4	● Chianti Rufina Terraelectae Vign. Quona Ris. '21	♟♟ 5
● Nobile di Montepulciano '21	♟♟ 4	○ Vin Santo del Chianti Rufina Ris. '13	♟♟ 5
● Nobile di Montepulciano Briareo Cantina del Redi Ris. '19	♟♟ 5	○ Alba '23	♟ 3
● Nobile di Montepulciano No.Mo.S '20	♟♟ 5	⊙ Amelia Rosé '23	♟ 4
● Nobile di Montepulciano '20	♟♟ 4	● Chianti Rufina I Domi '22	♟ 4
● Nobile di Montepulciano '19	♟♟ 4	● Chianti Rufina Vign. Quona Ris. '15	♟♟♟ 5
● Nobile di Montepulciano Cantina del Redi '20	♟♟ 4	● Chianti Rufina Terraelectae Vign. Quona Ris. '20	♟♟ 5
● Nobile di Montepulciano Cantina del Redi '18	♟♟ 5	● Chianti Rufina Terraelectae Vign. Quona Ris. '19	♟♟ 5
● Nobile di Montepulciano Poggio Stella '18	♟♟ 4	● Chianti Rufina Vign. Quona Ris. '18	♟♟ 5
Rosso di Montepulciano Cantina del Redi '22	♟♟ 4	● Chianti Rufina Vign. Quona Ris. '17	♟♟ 5
		● Chianti Rufina Vign. Quona Ris. '16	♟♟ 5
		○ Vin Santo del Chianti Rufina '11	♟♟ 5
		● Vin Santo del Chianti Rufina Occhio di Pernice '09	♟♟ 6

Vignaioli del Morellino di Scansano

loc. Saragiolo
58054 Scansano [GR]
☎ +39 0564507288
✉ www.vignaiolidiscansano.it

CELLAR SALES
PRE-BOOKED VISITS
ACCOMMODATION
ANNUAL PRODUCTION 5,400,000 bottles
HECTARES UNDER VINE 700.00
VITICULTURE METHOD Certified Organic
SUSTAINABLE WINERY

It's impossible to discuss the history of Morellino without mentioning Cantina Vignaioli di Scansano. This cooperativ winerye, which has been a cornerstone for over 50 years, has played a pivotal role in the region, even during the most challenging times. Today, they offer reliably high-quality wines that are increasingly well-crafted and worth taking note of, with a modern, coherent stylistic expression that emphasizes immediate pleasure and ease of drinking. The Morellino di Scansano Roggiano '23 has immediate aromatic appeal, with notes of ripe cherry and raspberry joining with lightly spiced hints, leading to a persistent, smooth, and juicy palate. The Bianco di Pitigliano Rasenno '23 is enjoyable, with fragrant and clean aromas and a smooth, pleasant progression on the palate. The Viognier Scantianum '23 is a well-crafted white, featuring intense aromas of exotic fruit and a solid, highly sapid palate.

Vignamaggio

via Petriolo, 5
50022 Greve in Chianti [FI]
☎ +39 055854661
✉ www.vignamaggio.com

CELLAR SALES
PRE-BOOKED VISITS
ACCOMMODATION AND RESTAURANT SERVICE
ANNUAL PRODUCTION 250,000 bottles
HECTARES UNDER VINE 65.00
VITICULTURE METHOD Certified Organic
SUSTAINABLE WINERY

Owned by French lawyer Patrice Taravella, Vignamaggio is situated in the Greve in Chianti UGA production area, on the ridge leading to the Lamole area. The vineyards, located at elevations spanning 300-450 meters, are spread out across nine distinct plots: Prenzano, Petriolo, Solatio, Orto, Poggio Asciutto, Vitignano, Il Prato, Querceto, and Poggiarelli (some also extend into the Panzano area). The wines are crafted with elegance and restraint, thanks to the judicious use of oak, combining large barrels, tonneaux, and barriques. The fragrant and pleasantly flavorful Chianti Classico Terre di Prenzano '21 opens on aromas of herbs and small red fruits. The Chianti Classico Gherardino Riserva '19 represents a beautiful blend of fruit, earth, and spice on the nose, with a well-structured, persistent palate. The Cabernet Franc '20 is well-crafted, offering herbaceous and fruity aromas with finishing touches of coffee dust, leading to a flavorful, well-sustained palate.

○ Bianco di Pitigliano Rasenno '23	♥♥ 2*
● Morellino di Scansano Roggiano '23	♥♥ 3
○ Scantianum Viognier '23	♥♥ 2*
● Maremma Toscana Ciliegiolo Capoccia '23	♥ 2
● Maremma Toscana Le Vie del Mare '22	♥ 3
● Maremma Toscana Sangiovese Vin del Fattore '23	♥ 3
○ Maremma Toscana Vermentino V. Fiorini '23	♥ 3
● Morellino di Scansano Roggiano Ris. '20	♥♥ 4
● Morellino di Scansano Roggiano Ris. '15	♥♥ 3*
● Morellino di Scansano Roggiano Ris. '14	♥♥ 3*

● Cabernet Franc '20	♥♥ 8
● Chianti Cl. Gherardino Ris. '19	♥♥ 5
● Chianti Cl. Terre di Prenzano '21	♥♥ 4
● Chianti Cl. Monna Lisa Ris. '99	♥♥♥ 5
● Chianti Cl. Monna Lisa Ris. '95	♥♥♥ 5
● Vignamaggio '06	♥♥♥ 7
● Vignamaggio '05	♥♥♥ 7
● Vignamaggio '04	♥♥♥ 6
● Vignamaggio '01	♥♥♥ 6
● Vignamaggio '00	♥♥♥ 6
● Cabernet Franc '15	♥♥ 8
● Chianti Cl. Gherardino Ris. '17	♥♥ 5
● Chianti Cl. Terre di Prenzano '20	♥♥ 4
● Chianti Cl. Terre di Prenzano '17	♥♥ 3
● Chianti Cl. Terre di Prenzano '16	♥♥ 3
● Chianti Cl. Terre di Prenzano '15	♥♥
● Vignamaggio '10	♥♥

Villa Le Corti

loc. Le Corti
via San Piero di Sotto, I
50026 San Casciano in Val di Pesa [FI]
📞 +39 055829301
🌐 www.principecorsini.com

CELLAR SALES
PRE-BOOKED VISITS
RESTAURANT SERVICE
ANNUAL PRODUCTION 100,000 bottles
HECTARES UNDER VINE 50.00
VITICULTURE METHOD Certified Organic

Based in the historic Villa le Corti, the Corsini family's winery is one of the main players in the San Casciano Val di Pesa UGA production zone. Their wines have a classical stylistic profile, interpreted through a modern lens, with sangiovese leading a vibrant and easy-to-drink range that can stand toe-to-toe with Chianti's best. The Corsinis also own the Tenuta Marsiliana in Maremma, where they produce exuberant, Mediterranean wines from international varieties. The aromatic Chianti Classico '22 is sleek, fragrant, and smooth, a wine focused entirely on pleasure and very well crafted. The Chianti Classico Cortevecchia Riserva '20 stands out for its juicy development, with crunchy tannins and lively acidity balancing its fruity echoes. Its aromas are spot-on, marked by a bright citrus note that dominates its smoky and spicy undertones. The Chianti Classico Gran Selezione Don Tommaso '20 put in a solid performance.

Fattoria Villa Saletta

loc. Montanelli
via E. Fermi, 14
56036 Palaia [PI]
📞 +39 0587628121
🌐 www.villasaletta.com

CELLAR SALES
PRE-BOOKED VISITS
ACCOMMODATION
ANNUAL PRODUCTION 90,000 bottles
HECTARES UNDER VINE 32.00

Owned by the English Hands family since 2001, Villa Saletta has seen a dramatic expansion of its winegrowing activities, starting with an increase in vineyard hectares, and gaining attention with well-crafted wines. Here in the Palaia area of Pisa, the predominant grape varieties cultivated are cabernet sauvignon, cabernet franc, merlot, and sangiovese, aged in barriques and large barrels. Their 2020 vintage wines put in an outstanding showing. The Saletta Riccardi, a remarkable red made solely from sangiovese, exudes aromas of blood orange, spice, and plum. On the palate, it's dense, yet fresh and richly sapid. Equally impressive is the Saletta Giulia, a perfectly balanced blend of 65% cabernet franc and cabernet sauvignon, with red fruit and vegetal notes on the nose, followed by a sleek, minty palate. Both the Chianti Superiore and Chiave di Saletta, a blend of the estate's various grape varieties, are also very good.

TUSCANY

● Chianti Cl. '22	♟♟ 4
● Chianti Cl. Cortevecchia Ris. '20	♟♟ 5
● Chianti Cl. Gran Selezione Don Tommaso '20	♟♟ 8
● Chianti Cl. Gran Selezione Zac '20	♟♟ 8
● Chianti Cl. '12	♟♟♟ 3*
● Chianti Cl. Cortevecchia Ris. '05	♟♟♟ 4
● Chianti Cl. Don Tommaso '99	♟♟♟ 4*
● Chianti Cl. Le Corti '10	♟♟♟ 3*
● Chianti Cl. Ris. '19	♟♟♟ 5
● Chianti Cl. '21	♟♟ 4
● Chianti Cl. '13	♟♟ 3*
● Chianti Cl. Corte Vecchia Ris. '16	♟♟ 4
● Chianti Cl. Corte Vecchia Ris. '15	♟♟ 4
● Chianti Cl. Cortevecchia Ris. '14	♟♟ 4
● Chianti Cl. Gran Selezione Zac '19	♟♟ 8
● Chianti Cl. Gran Selezione Zac '16	♟♟ 7

● Saletta Riccardi '20	♟♟♟ 8
● Saletta Giulia '20	♟♟ 8
● Chianti Superiore '20	♟♟ 5
● Chiave di Saletta '20	♟♟ 7
● Chianti Sup. '18	♟♟♟ 5
● 980 AD '19	♟♟ 8
● 980 AD '18	♟♟ 8
● Chianti Sup. '19	♟♟ 3
● Chiave di Saletta '19	♟♟ 4
● Chiave di Saletta '18	♟♟ 6
● Saletta Giulia '19	♟♟ 7
● Saletta Giulia '18	♟♟ 8
● Saletta Riccardi '19	♟♟ 7
● Saletta Riccardi '18	♟♟ 8

Villa Santo Stefano

fraz. Pieve Santo Stefano
via della Chiesa di Pieve di Santo
Stefano, 504b
55100 Lucca
(+39 0583395349
@ www.villa-santostefano.it

CELLAR SALES
PRE-BOOKED VISITS
ANNUAL PRODUCTION 35,000 bottles
HECTARES UNDER VINE 7.00
VITICULTURE METHOD Certified Organic

Owned by Wolfang Reitzle and Nina Ruge since 2001, Villa Santo Stefano (formerly Villa Bertolli) was originally purchased as a "buen retiro." However, the couple's passion for wine soon drew them into the heart of wine production and sales. Alongside their Lucca vineyards, they have added another 11 hectares in Maremma, near Manciano, where they produced their first bottles in 2022. We appreciated the richness of the Sereno '22, a blend of traditional Tuscan red varietals. Enticing aromas span everything from pomegranate to currant and plum jam, evolving into notes of quinine, licorice, and black pepper with clove spice. On the palate, it's dynamic, fresh, with a pervasive finish. We were just as impressed with the Loto '21, a Bordeaux-style blend with balsamic and minty notes, and the Nina '21, a monovarietal cabernet franc that captures the essence of Mediterranean herbs.

Vinae Montae

via dei Doccia, 26
500065 Pontassieve [FI]
(+39 3282495189
@ www.ormaevinae.com

VinæMontæ (formerly OrmæVinæ), a winemaking project launched in 2017 by Alexey Kondrashov and Ella Korop, is based on the revival of the ancient farm "Il Monte" in Valdisieve. Their organically cultivated vineyards host sangiovese, cabernet sauvignon, and merlot. Those wines hailing from international varieties, which are aged in barriques, exhibit a powerful profile, while their barrel-aged Rufinas nod to tradition with an emphasis on elegance. Under the enological guidance of Valentino Ciarla, the estate's wines are rapidly gaining in popularity. The Terraelectæ Vigneto Il Monte '21 offers a smooth, round, and extremely complex palate, the product of vines over 30 years old. It has character, depth, and a pervasive flavor that lingers enticingly. The Aellae '21, a monovarietal cabernet, also impresses, thriving in this enclave of Rufina.

● Sereno '22	♟♟ 6
● Loto '21	♟♟ 8
● Nina '21	♟♟ 8
○ Gioia '23	♟ 5
☉ Luna Rosato '23	♟ 5
● Colline Lucchesi Rosso Sereno '20	♟♟ 4
● Colline Lucchesi Sereno '19	♟♟ 3
○ Gioia '21	♟♟ 3
● Loto '20	♟♟ 8
● Loto '19	♟♟ 6
☉ Luna '21	♟♟ 3
● Nina '20	♟♟ 8
● Volo '22	♟♟ 5
● Volo '21	♟♟ 3
● Volo '20	♟♟ 3

● Chianti Rufina Terraelectae Vign. Il Monte Ris. '21	♟♟ 5
● Primae '21	♟♟ 8
● Aellae '21	♟ 8
● Aellae '20	♟♟ 8
● Aellae '19	♟♟ 8
● Chianti Rufina Terraelectae Vign. Il Monte Ris. '20	♟♟ 5
● MCMXI '19	♟♟ 5
● Primae '20	♟♟ 8
● Primae '19	♟♟ 8

OTHER WINERIES

Abbadia Ardenga

fraz. Torrenieri
via Romana, 139
53028 Montalcino [SI]
📞 +39 0577834150
🌐 www.abbadiardengapoggio.it

CELLAR SALES
PRE-BOOKED VISITS
ANNUAL PRODUCTION 40,000 bottles
HECTARES UNDER VINE 10.00

● Brunello di Montalcino '19	🍷🍷 5
● Brunello di Montalcino V. Piaggia '19	🍷🍷 5

Acquabona

loc. Acquabona, 1
57037 Portoferraio [LI]
📞 +39 0565933013
🌐 www.acquabonaelba.it

CELLAR SALES
PRE-BOOKED VISITS
ANNUAL PRODUCTION 90,000 bottles
HECTARES UNDER VINE 18.00

● Elba Aleatico Passito '19	🍷🍷 6
○ Elba Bianco '23	🍷🍷 3
○ Elba Bianco Le Cote '22	🍷🍷 3
○ Elba Vermentino '23	🍷 3

Poderi Arcangelo

loc. Capezzano
via San Benedetto, 26
53037 San Gimignano [SI]
📞 +39 0577944404
🌐 www.poderiarcangelo.it

CELLAR SALES
PRE-BOOKED VISITS
ANNUAL PRODUCTION 50,000 bottles
HECTARES UNDER VINE 23.00
VITICULTURE METHOD Certified Organic

○ Vernaccia di San Gimignano Primo Angelo '23	🍷🍷 2*
○ Vernaccia di San Gimignano Madama Doré '23	🍷 2

Argentaia

s.da Colle di Lupo
58051 Magliano in Toscana [GR]
📞 +39 3394601020
🌐 www.argentaia.com

ACCOMMODATION
ANNUAL PRODUCTION 20,000 bottles
HECTARES UNDER VINE 8.00

○ Maremma Toscana Vermentino Monnallegra '23	🍷🍷 3
● Maremma Toscana Rosso Col di Lupo '22	🍷 4

Assolati

fraz. Montenero
pod. Assolati, 47
58040 Castel del Piano [GR]
📞 +39 0564954146
🌐 www.assolati.it

CELLAR SALES
PRE-BOOKED VISITS
ACCOMMODATION
ANNUAL PRODUCTION 18,000 bottles
HECTARES UNDER VINE 5.00

○ Dionysos Vermentino '23	🍷🍷 2*
● Montecucco Rosso '21	🍷🍷 2*

Armilla

via Tavernelle, 6
53024 Montalcino [SI]
📞 +39 0577816012
🌐 www.armillawine.com

ANNUAL PRODUCTION 12,000 bottles
HECTARES UNDER VINE 3.00

● Brunello di Montalcino '19	🍷🍷 7
● Rosso di Montalcino '21	🍷 4

OTHER WINERIES

Podere L'Assunta

loc. Poggiolo, 7
53035 Monteriggioni [SI]
📞 +39 0577309009
🌐 www.lassunta.it

● Costa del Pievano '19	�♖ 7
● Costa del Pievano '18	�♖ 7

Baracchi

loc. Cegliolo, 21
52044 Cortona [AR]
📞 +39 0575612679
🌐 baracchiwinery.com

CELLAR SALES
PRE-BOOKED VISITS
ACCOMMODATION AND RESTAURANT SERVICE
ANNUAL PRODUCTION 140,000 bottles
HECTARES UNDER VINE 32.00
SUSTAINABLE WINERY

● Pinot Nero '19	♥ 5
⊙ Brut Rosé M. Cl. '19	♥ 6
● Cortona Syrah Smeriglio '22	♥ 4
○ Trebbiano Brut M. Cl. '22	♥ 5

Pietro Beconcini

fraz. La Scala
via Montorzo, 13a
56028 San Miniato [PI]
📞 +39 0571464785
🌐 www.pietrobeconcini.com

CELLAR SALES
PRE-BOOKED VISITS
ANNUAL PRODUCTION 110,000 bottles
HECTARES UNDER VINE 15.00
VITICULTURE METHOD Certified Organic

● IXE Tempranillo '22	♥♥ 4
● Terre di Pisa Rosso Maurleo '22	♥♥ 3
● Terre di Pisa Sangiovese Reciso '22	♥♥ 5

Il Balzo

via Dei Poggiolo,12 12
50068 Rufina [FI]
📞 +39 3471891311
🌐 www.ilbalzo.it

CELLAR SALES
PRE-BOOKED VISITS
ANNUAL PRODUCTION 15,000 bottles
HECTARES UNDER VINE 7.00
VITICULTURE METHOD Certified Organic

● Chianti Rufina '21	♥♥ 3
● Chianti Rufina Ris. '19	♥♥ 4
○ Pettinaringhe '23	♥ 3
⊙ Rosé '23	♥ 3

Barbicaia

via di Nottola,6
53045 Montepulciano [SI]
📞 +39 3473163269
🌐 www.barbicaia.com

ANNUAL PRODUCTION 10,000 bottles
HECTARES UNDER VINE 2.67
SUSTAINABLE WINERY

● Nobile di Montepulciano La Ripa Ris. '20	♥♥ 6
● Rosso di Montepulciano '22	♥ 3

Begnardi

loc. Monte Antico
pod. Camporosso
58045 Civitella Paganico [GR]
📞 +39 3898463164
🌐 www.begnardi.com

CELLAR SALES
PRE-BOOKED VISITS
ACCOMMODATION AND RESTAURANT SERVICE
ANNUAL PRODUCTION 35,000 bottles
HECTARES UNDER VINE 7.00
VITICULTURE METHOD Certified Organic

● Montecucco Rosso Ceneo '21	♥♥ 3
● Montecucco Sangiovese Pigna Rossa Ris. '20	♥♥ 4
● Montecucco Rosso '22	♥ 2

OTHER WINERIES

Le Bertille

via delle Colombelle, 7
53045 Montepulciano [SI]
☎ +39 0578758330
✉ www.lebertille.com

CELLAR SALES
PRE-BOOKED VISITS
ACCOMMODATION
ANNUAL PRODUCTION 65,000 bottles
HECTARES UNDER VINE 14.00
SUSTAINABLE WINERY

● Nobile di Montepulciano Ris. '20	♟♟ 6
● Rosso di Montepulciano '20	♟♟ 3
● L'Attesa '19	♟ 2
● Nobile di Montepulciano '21	♟ 4

Bertinga

loc. Le Terrazze di Adine
53013 Gaiole in Chianti [SI]
☎ +39 0577746218
✉ www.bertinga.it

ANNUAL PRODUCTION 40,000 bottles
HECTARES UNDER VINE 23.00

● Sassi Chiusi '19	♟♟ 5
● Chianti Cl. La Porta di Vertine '21	♟ 5

Cacciagrande

fraz. Tirli
loc. Ampio
58043 Castiglione della Pescaia [GR]
☎ +39 0564944168
✉ www.cacciagrande.com

CELLAR SALES
PRE-BOOKED VISITS
ANNUAL PRODUCTION 100,000 bottles
HECTARES UNDER VINE 20.00
SUSTAINABLE WINERY

○ Maremma Toscana Vermentino '23	♟♟ 2*
○ Maremma Toscana Viognier '23	♟♟ 2*
● Maremma Toscana Syrah Cortigliano '23	♟ 2

Le Calle

fraz. Poggi del Sasso
loc. La Cava
58044 Cinigiano [GR]
☎ +39 3489307565
✉ www.lecalle.it

CELLAR SALES
PRE-BOOKED VISITS
ACCOMMODATION
ANNUAL PRODUCTION 26,000 bottles
HECTARES UNDER VINE 7.00
VITICULTURE METHOD Certified Organic

○ La Treggiata Vermentino '22	♟♟ 3
● Montecucco Rosso Campo Rombolo '21	♟♟ 3

Tenuta Campo al Mare

fraz. Vallone dei Messi
via Bolgherese
57024 Castagneto Carducci [LI]
☎ +39 0558598II
✉ www.tenutefolonari.com

ANNUAL PRODUCTION 100,000 bottles
HECTARES UNDER VINE 30.00

● Bolgheri Rosso Sup. Baia al Vento '21	♟♟ 5
● Bolgheri Rosso '22	♟♟ 4
● Gallico '21	♟♟ 6
○ Bolgheri Vermentino '23	♟ 3

Campo al Noce

loc. Campo al Noce, 151
fraz. Bolgheri
57022 Castagneto Carducci [LI]
☎ +39 3802519233
✉ campoalnoce.it

● Bolgheri Rosso Assiolo '22	♟♟ 4
● Bolgheri Rosso Miterre '22	♟♟ 4
● Bolgheri Rosso Sup. Riverbero '20	♟♟ 5

Campo al Pero

fraz. Donoratico
via del Casone Ugolino, 12
57022 Castagneto Carducci [LI]
📞 +39 0565774329
🌐 www.campoalpero.it

CELLAR SALES
PRE-BOOKED VISITS
ANNUAL PRODUCTION 30,000 bottles
HECTARES UNDER VINE 8.00

● Bolgheri Rosso Sup. Dedicato a Vittorio '21	🍷🍷 7
● Bolgheri Rosso '22	🍷🍷 4
● Bolgheri Rosso Zephyro '22	🍷🍷 3
● Bolgheri Sup. Dorianae '21	🍷 5

Tenuta Campo al Signore

loc. Nocino, 259
57022 Castagneto Carducci [LI]
📞 +39 0565763200
🌐 www.tenutacampoalsignore.com

● Bolgheri Rosso Sup. Campo al Signore '21	🍷🍷 6
● Bolgheri Rosso Volante '21	🍷🍷 5

Canalicchio - Franco Pacenti

loc. Canalicchio di Sopra, 6
53024 Montalcino [SI]
📞 +39 0577849277
🌐 www.canalicchiofrancopacenti.it

CELLAR SALES
PRE-BOOKED VISITS
RESTAURANT SERVICE
ANNUAL PRODUCTION 40,000 bottles
HECTARES UNDER VINE 10.00

● Brunello di Montalcino Rosildo '19	🍷🍷 8
● Brunello di Montalcino '19	🍷🍷 7
● Rosso di Montalcino '21	🍷🍷 4

Cantalici

fraz. Castagnoli
via della Croce, 17/19
53013 Gaiole in Chianti [SI]
📞 +39 0577731038
🌐 www.cantalici.it

CELLAR SALES
PRE-BOOKED VISITS
ANNUAL PRODUCTION 46,000 bottles
HECTARES UNDER VINE 30.00

● Chianti Cl. Gran Selezione '20	🍷🍷 6
● Chianti Cl. Ris. '20	🍷🍷 5

Cantina del Giusto

fraz. Acquaviva
via E. Gaci, 14
53045 Montepulciano [SI]
📞 +39 0578767256
🌐 www.cantinadelgiusto.it

CELLAR SALES
ANNUAL PRODUCTION 60,000 bottles
HECTARES UNDER VINE 4.50

● Nobile di Montepulciano San Claudio II '21	🍷🍷 4
● Rosso di Montepulciano Fontegrande '22	🍷🍷 2*
● Fontedoccia '22	🍷 2

Cantina di Montalcino

loc. Val di Cava
53024 Montalcino [SI]
📞 +39 0577848704
🌐 www.cantinadimontalcino.it

CELLAR SALES
PRE-BOOKED VISITS
ANNUAL PRODUCTION 300,000 bottles
HECTARES UNDER VINE 90.00

● Brunello di Montalcino '19	🍷🍷 6
● Brunello di Montalcino Lorenzo Melani '19	🍷🍷 6
● Brunello di Montalcino Ris. 4 Quadranti '18	🍷🍷 7
● Rosso di Montalcino Lorenzo Melani '22	🍷🍷 4

TUSCANY

OTHER WINERIES

Cantina di Pitigliano

via N. Ciacci, 974
58017 Pitigliano [GR]
☎ +39 0564616133
✉ www.cantinadipitigliano.it

CELLAR SALES
PRE-BOOKED VISITS
ACCOMMODATION
ANNUAL PRODUCTION 2,000,000 bottles
HECTARES UNDER VINE 372.00
VITICULTURE METHOD Certified Organic
SUSTAINABLE WINERY

● Maremma Toscana Ciliegiolo Nel Tufo '22	♟♟	2*
○ Maremma Toscana Vermentino Neltufo '23	♟	2

Capannelle

loc. Capannelle, 13
53013 Gaiole in Chianti [SI]
☎ +39 057774511
✉ www.capannelle.it

CELLAR SALES
PRE-BOOKED VISITS
ACCOMMODATION
ANNUAL PRODUCTION 80,000 bottles
HECTARES UNDER VINE 16.00
SUSTAINABLE WINERY

● Chianti Cl. Gran Selezione '19	♟♟	8
● Solare '19	♟♟	8
● Chianti Cl. Ris. '20	♟	6
● Chianti Classico '20	♟	4

Fattoria il Capitano

via San Martino a Quona, 2b
50065 Pontassieve [FI]
☎ +39 0558315600
✉ www.fattoriailcapitano.com

ANNUAL PRODUCTION 10,000 bottles
HECTARES UNDER VINE 10.00

● Chianti Rufina '21	♟♟	2*

Podere Capaccia

loc. Capaccia
53017 Radda in Chianti [SI]
☎ +39 0577582426
✉ www.poderecapaccia.com

PRE-BOOKED VISITS
ANNUAL PRODUCTION 22,000 bottles
HECTARES UNDER VINE 3.50

● Chianti Cl. Ris. '18	♟♟	6
● Chianti Cl. '21	♟♟	5

Caparsa

loc. Case Sparse Caparsa, 47
53017 Radda in Chianti [SI]
☎ +39 0577738174
✉ www.caparsa.it

CELLAR SALES
PRE-BOOKED VISITS
ACCOMMODATION
ANNUAL PRODUCTION 40,000 bottles
HECTARES UNDER VINE 12.10
VITICULTURE METHOD Certified Organic
SUSTAINABLE WINERY

● Rosso di Caparsa '20	♟♟	3
● Mimma '21	♟	8

Marco Capitoni

loc. Podere Sedime, 63
53026 Pienza [SI]
☎ +39 3388981597
✉ www.capitoni.eu

CELLAR SALES
PRE-BOOKED VISITS
ANNUAL PRODUCTION 20,000 bottles
HECTARES UNDER VINE 7.00

● Orcia Capitoni Ris. '20	♟♟	4
● Orcia Sangiovese Frasi Ris. '20	♟	5

Enzo Carmignani

via di Cercatoia Alta, 13b
55015 Montecarlo [LU]
☏ +39 058322463
🌐 www.fattoriacarmignani.com

CELLAR SALES
PRE-BOOKED VISITS
ACCOMMODATION
ANNUAL PRODUCTION 1,970 bottles
HECTARES UNDER VINE 9.00
VITICULTURE METHOD Certified Organic
SUSTAINABLE WINERY

● Theorema '20	♟♟ 4
○ Urano '23	♟♟ 3
○ Intrigo '22	♟ 4
● Montecarlo Rosso '22	♟ 3

Fattoria Casa di Terra

fraz. Bolgheri
loc. Le Ferruggini, 162c
57022 Castagneto Carducci [LI]
☏ +39 0565749810
🌐 www.fattoriacasaditerra.com

CELLAR SALES
PRE-BOOKED VISITS
ACCOMMODATION
ANNUAL PRODUCTION 200,000 bottles
HECTARES UNDER VINE 55.00

● Bolgheri Rosso Sup. '21	♟♟ 8
● Bolgheri Rosso Sup. Maronea '21	♟♟ 7
● Bolgheri Rosso Mosaico '22	♟ 6

Casa Emma

loc. San Donato in Poggio
s.da prov.le di Castellina in Chianti, 3
50021 Barberino Val d'Elsa [FI]
☏ +39 0558072239
🌐 www.casaemma.com

CELLAR SALES
PRE-BOOKED VISITS
RESTAURANT SERVICE
ANNUAL PRODUCTION 90,000 bottles
HECTARES UNDER VINE 31.00
VITICULTURE METHOD Certified Organic
SUSTAINABLE WINERY

● Chianti Cl. Vignalparco Parco Ris. '20	♟♟ 5
● Chianti Cl. '22	♟♟ 4
● Chianti Cl. Gran Selezione '20	♟♟ 5
● Soloio '21	♟ 6

Casa Lucii

loc. Santa Maria a Villacastelli
53037 San Gimignano [SI]
☏ +39 0577950199
🌐 www.casalucii.it

ANNUAL PRODUCTION 120,000 bottles
HECTARES UNDER VINE 100.00

○ Vernaccia di San Gimignano Mareterra Ris. '19	♟♟ 6
○ Vernaccia di San Gimignano '23	♟ 4

Podere Casina

fraz. Istia d'Ombrone
Piagge del Maiano
58040 Grosseto
☏ +39 0564408210
🌐 www.poderecasina.com

PRE-BOOKED VISITS
ACCOMMODATION
ANNUAL PRODUCTION 55,000 bottles
HECTARES UNDER VINE 11.00

● Maremma Rosso Don Lucifero '23	♟♟ 4
● Morellino di Scansano '23	♟♟ 3
● Aione '21	♟ 5
● Syrah '22	♟ 5

La Castellina

loc. Ferrozzola, 1
53011 Castellina in Chianti [SI]
☏ +39 0577740454
🌐 www.lacastellina.it

CELLAR SALES
PRE-BOOKED VISITS
ACCOMMODATION
ANNUAL PRODUCTION 175,000 bottles
HECTARES UNDER VINE 36.00
VITICULTURE METHOD Certified Organic

● Chianti Cl. Cosimo Bojola '21	♟♟ 4
● Chianti Cl. Squarcialupi '21	♟♟ 4
● Chianti Cl. Squarcialupi Ris. '20	♟♟ 5

TUSCANY

OTHER WINERIES

Podere Castellinuzza

via Petriolo, 14
50022 Greve in Chianti [FI]
☎ +39 0558549046
⊛ www.chianticlassicocastellinuzza.it

CELLAR SALES
PRE-BOOKED VISITS
ACCOMMODATION
ANNUAL PRODUCTION 7,000 bottles
HECTARES UNDER VINE 2.00

● Chianti Cl. Gran Selezione '20	♀♀ 5
● Chianti Cl. Ris. '21	♀♀ 5
● Chianti Cl. '21	♀ 4

Castellinuzza e Piuca

via Petriolo, 21A
50022 Greve in Chianti [FI]
☎ +39 0558549033
⊛ www.castellinuzzaepiuca.it

CELLAR SALES
PRE-BOOKED VISITS
ANNUAL PRODUCTION 10,000 bottles
HECTARES UNDER VINE 2.30

● Chianti Cl. '22	♀♀ 3
● Il Vegliardo '22	♀♀ 4

Castello della Paneretta

loc. Monsanto
s.da della Paneretta, 35
50021 Barberino Val d'Elsa [FI]
☎ +39 0558059003
⊛ www.paneretta.it

CELLAR SALES
PRE-BOOKED VISITS
ACCOMMODATION
ANNUAL PRODUCTION 10,000 bottles
HECTARES UNDER VINE 22.50

● Chianti Cl. '21	♀♀ 4
● Chianti Cl. Ris. '20	♀♀ 5

Castello di Cacchiano

fraz. Monti in Chianti
loc. Cacchiano
53013 Gaiole in Chianti [SI]
☎ +39 0577747018
⊛ www.castellodicacchiano.it

CELLAR SALES
PRE-BOOKED VISITS
ACCOMMODATION
ANNUAL PRODUCTION 120,000 bottles
HECTARES UNDER VINE 31.00

● Chianti Cl. '21	♀♀ 4
● Chianti Cl. Ris. '20	♀ 5

Castello di Vicarello

fraz. Poggi del Sasso
loc. Vicarello, 1
58044 Cinigiano [GR]
☎ +39 0564990718
⊛ www.castellodivicarellovini.com

CELLAR SALES
PRE-BOOKED VISITS
ACCOMMODATION AND RESTAURANT SERVICE
ANNUAL PRODUCTION 25,000 bottles
HECTARES UNDER VINE 6.50
VITICULTURE METHOD Certified Organic

● Castello di Vicarello '19	♀♀ 8
● Poggio Vico '21	♀♀ 5
● Terre di Vico '19	♀♀ 6
● Merah '22	♀ 4

Castello La Leccia

loc. La Leccia
53011 Castellina in Chianti [SI]
☎ +39 0577743148
⊛ www.castellolaleccia.com

CELLAR SALES
PRE-BOOKED VISITS
ANNUAL PRODUCTION 30,000 bottles
HECTARES UNDER VINE 13.50

● Chianti Cl. Gran Selezione Bruciagna '20	♀♀ 4

OTHER WINERIES

Castello Sonnino
via Volterrana Nord, 6a
50025 Montespertoli [FI]
(•) +39 0571609198
⊕ www.castellosonnino.it

CELLAR SALES
PRE-BOOKED VISITS
ACCOMMODATION
ANNUAL PRODUCTION 120,000 bottles
HECTARES UNDER VINE 40.00
SUSTAINABLE WINERY

● Chianti Montespertoli Sonnino '22	♥♥	2*
● Chianti Montespertoli Castello di Montespertoli Ris. '21	♥♥	3
⊙ Pichius Rosato '23	♥	2

Castelsina
loc. Osteria, 54a
53048 Sinalunga [SI]
(•) +39 0577663595
⊕ www.castelsina.it

CELLAR SALES
PRE-BOOKED VISITS
ANNUAL PRODUCTION 2,000,000 bottles
HECTARES UNDER VINE 400.00
VITICULTURE METHOD Certified Organic

● Chianti '23	♥♥	2*
● Chianti Ris. '22	♥♥	2*
● Poggiomoro '23	♥♥	3
● Governo all'uso Toscano '23	♥	2

I Cavallini
loc. Cavallini
58014 Manciano [GR]
(•) +39 0564609008
⊕ www.icavallini.it

CELLAR SALES
ACCOMMODATION
ANNUAL PRODUCTION 25,000 bottles
HECTARES UNDER VINE 11.50

○ Maremma Toscana Vermentino Diaccio '23	♥♥	3
● Morellino di Scansano '23	♥♥	3
● Maremma Toscana Merlot Pause '22	♥	6
○ Nini Vermentino '22	♥	4

Castello Tricerchi
loc. Altesi, I
53024 Montalcino [SI]
(•) +39 34725018841912361
⊕ www.castellotricerchi.com

CELLAR SALES
PRE-BOOKED VISITS
ANNUAL PRODUCTION 60,000 bottles
HECTARES UNDER VINE 13.00

● Brunello di Montalcino '19	♥♥	7
● Brunello di Montalcino AD 1441 '19	♥♥	8

Castelvecchio
loc. Seano
via delle Mannelle, 19
59011 Carmignano [PO]
(•) +39 0558705451
⊕ www.castelvecchio.net

CELLAR SALES
PRE-BOOKED VISITS
ANNUAL PRODUCTION 40,000 bottles
HECTARES UNDER VINE 10.00

● Barco Reale '22	♥♥	2*
⊙ Barco Reale Rosato Vin Ruspo '23	♥♥	2*
● Carmignano '22	♥	4

Tenuta Ceri
loc. Comeana
via delle Ginestre, 45
59015 Carmignano [PO]
edoardo@tenutaceri.it

CELLAR SALES
PRE-BOOKED VISITS
ANNUAL PRODUCTION 50,000 bottles
HECTARES UNDER VINE 14.50
VITICULTURE METHOD Certified Organic

● Carmignano Arrendevole Ris. '20	♥♥♥	8
● Carmignano Rigoccioli '21	♥♥	6
● Carmignano Rigoccioli '20	♥♥	6

OTHER WINERIES

Cantina Chiacchiera

fraz. Cervognano
via Poggio Golo, 12
53045 Montepulciano [SI]
☎ +39 3477969531
✉ www.cantinachiacchiera.it

CELLAR SALES
PRE-BOOKED VISITS
RESTAURANT SERVICE
ANNUAL PRODUCTION 30,000 bottles
HECTARES UNDER VINE 18.00

● Nobile di Montepulciano '21	♥♥ 4
● Nobile di Montepulciano Mahti Ris. '19	♥♥ 5
● Piccola Viola '21	♥ 5

Fattoria Cigliano di Sopra

via Cigliano, 30
50026 San Casciano dei Bagni [SI]
☎ +39 055828861
✉ www.ciglianodisopra.it

● Chianti Cl. '22	♥♥ 5
● Chianti Classico Vigneto Branca Ris. '21	♥♥ 8

Colle Bereto

loc. Colle Bereto
53017 Radda in Chianti [SI]
☎ +39 0577738083
✉ www.collebereto.it

CELLAR SALES
PRE-BOOKED VISITS
ANNUAL PRODUCTION 85,000 bottles
HECTARES UNDER VINE 17.00
VITICULTURE METHOD Certified Organic
SUSTAINABLE WINERY

● Chianti Cl. '22	♥♥ 5
● Chianti Cl. Gran Selezione '20	♥ 7
● Il Tocco '20	♥ 5

Chiesina di Lacona

fraz. Lacona
via Santa Maria, 209e
57031 Capoliveri [LI]
☎ +39 0565964216
✉ www.chiesinadilacona.it

○ Elba Ansonica '23	♥♥ 5
● Elba Aleatico Passito '23	♥♥ 6
○ Elba Vermentino '23	♥♥ 4
● Elba Rosso '21	♥ 4

Cinciano

loc. Cinciano, 2
53036 Poggibonsi [SI]
☎ +39 0577936588
✉ www.cinciano.it

CELLAR SALES
PRE-BOOKED VISITS
ACCOMMODATION AND RESTAURANT SERVICE
ANNUAL PRODUCTION 140,000 bottles
HECTARES UNDER VINE 24.00

● Chianti Cl. Gran Selezione '19	♥♥ 6
● Chianti Cl. Ris. '21	♥♥ 5
● Chianti Cl. '22	♥ 4

Fattoria Colle Verde

loc. Castello
fraz. Matraia
55012 Lucca
☎ +39 0583402310
✉ www.fattoria-colleverde.it

CELLAR SALES
PRE-BOOKED VISITS
ACCOMMODATION AND RESTAURANT SERVICE
ANNUAL PRODUCTION 30,000 bottles
HECTARES UNDER VINE 8.00
VITICULTURE METHOD Certified Organic

● Terre di Matraja Rosso '22	♥♥ 4
○ Brania del Cancello '23	♥ 5
● Brania delle Ghiandaie '21	♥ 5
○ Terre di Matraja Bianco '23	♥ 4

TUSCANY

Collemattoni

fraz. Sant'Angelo in Colle
loc. Collemattoni, 100
53024 Montalcino [SI]
(℣) +39 0577844127
⊛ www.collemattoni.it

CELLAR SALES
PRE-BOOKED VISITS
ANNUAL PRODUCTION 60,000 bottles
HECTARES UNDER VINE 11.00
VITICULTURE METHOD Certified Organic
SUSTAINABLE WINERY

● Brunello di Montalcino '19	♟♟ 6
● Brunello di Montalcino Fontelontano '18	♟♟ 8
● Toscana Rosso Adone '21	♟♟ 3
● Rosso di Montalcino '22	♟ 4

Colline di Sopra

via delle Colline, 17
56040 Montescudaio [PI]
(℣) +39 3347180758
⊛ www.collinedisopra.com

CELLAR SALES
PRE-BOOKED VISITS
ANNUAL PRODUCTION 40,000 bottles
HECTARES UNDER VINE 88.00
VITICULTURE METHOD Certified Organic
SUSTAINABLE WINERY

● Sopra Petit Verdot '20	♟♟ 8
● Sopra Sangiovese '20	♟♟ 8
● Sopra Merlot '20	♟ 8

Il Conventino

fraz. Gracciano
via della Ciarliana, 25b
53040 Montepulciano [SI]
(℣) +39 0578716283
⊛ www.ilconventino.it

CELLAR SALES
PRE-BOOKED VISITS
ANNUAL PRODUCTION 80,000 bottles
HECTARES UNDER VINE 20.00
VITICULTURE METHOD Certified Organic

● Nobile di Montepulciano '21	♟♟ 4
● Nobile di Montepulciano Ris. '20	♟♟ 5
● Rosso di Montepulciano '22	♟ 3

Colline Albelle

loc. Il Palazzo
s.da Terenzana, 5
56046 Riparbella [PI]
(℣) +39 3803454664
⊛ www.collinealbelle.com

CELLAR SALES
ACCOMMODATION
ANNUAL PRODUCTION 19,000 bottles
HECTARES UNDER VINE 16.50
VITICULTURE METHOD Certified Biodynamic
SUSTAINABLE WINERY

● Inrosso '21	♟♟ 4

Contucci

via del Teatro, 1
53045 Montepulciano [SI]
(℣) +39 0578757006
⊛ www.contucci.it

CELLAR SALES
PRE-BOOKED VISITS
ACCOMMODATION
ANNUAL PRODUCTION 100,000 bottles
HECTARES UNDER VINE 21.00

● Nobile di Montepulciano Pietra Rossa '19	♟♟ 5
● Nobile di Montepulciano Palazzo Contucci '19	♟♟ 7
● Vino Nobile di Montepulciano Ris. '18	♟ 7

La Cura

loc. Cura Nuova, 12
58024 Massa Marittima [GR]
(℣) +39 0566918094
⊛ www.cantinalacura.it

CELLAR SALES
PRE-BOOKED VISITS
ANNUAL PRODUCTION 30,000 bottles
HECTARES UNDER VINE 15.00
SUSTAINABLE WINERY

● Maremma Toscana Cabernet Sauvignon Vedetta '20	♟♟ 8
○ Maremma Toscana Vermentino Falco Pescatore '23	♟♟ 3

Cantina Dainelli

via della Chiesa, I
50050 Cerreto Guidi [FI]
☎ +39 3271458405
● www.cantinadainelli.it

Diadema

via Imprunetana per Tavarnuzze, 21
50023 Impruneta [FI]
☎ +39 0559335236
● www.diadema-wine.com

CELLAR SALES
PRE-BOOKED VISITS
ACCOMMODATION AND RESTAURANT SERVICE
ANNUAL PRODUCTION 110,000 bottles
HECTARES UNDER VINE 28.00

● Intruso '22	🍷 4
● Rude '22	🍷 5
○ La Sbronza '23	🍷 5
● RE'D '22	🍷 4

● Aurum Colatum '22	🍷 6
● D'Vino '22	🍷 4
○ Damare Bianco '23	🍷 4
● Villa L'Olmo '20	🍷 7

Donne Fittipaldi

fraz. Bolgheri
via Bolgherese, 198
57022 Castagneto Carducci [LI]
☎ +39 0565762175
● www.donnefittipaldi.it

ANNUAL PRODUCTION 60,000 bottles
HECTARES UNDER VINE 9.50

Fattoria di Doccia

via di Doccia, 29
50065 Pontassieve [FI]
☎ +39 0558361356
● www.fattoriadidoccia.it

● Bolgheri Rosso Sup. '21	🍷 6
● Bolgheri Rosso '22	🍷 5
● Dieffe '21	🍷 6
○ Lady F '21	🍷 5

● Collebrusco '20	🍷 4
● Levar del Sole '19	🍷 4
● Chianti Rufina Rubinato '22	🍷 3

Fattoria di Fugnano e Bombereto

via Fugnano, 52
53037 San Gimignano [SI]
☎ +39 0577940012
● www.fattoriadifugnano.com

CELLAR SALES
PRE-BOOKED VISITS
ACCOMMODATION AND RESTAURANT SERVICE
ANNUAL PRODUCTION 100,000 bottles
HECTARES UNDER VINE 26.00

Fattoria di Montechiari

loc. Montechiari, 27
55015 Montecarlo [LU]
☎ +39 3338661458
● www.montechiari.com

CELLAR SALES
PRE-BOOKED VISITS
ACCOMMODATION
ANNUAL PRODUCTION 35,000 bottles
HECTARES UNDER VINE 12.00
VITICULTURE METHOD Certified Organic
SUSTAINABLE WINERY

● Chianti Colli Senesi Da Fugnano '23	🍷 3
● Chianti Colli Senesi Da Fugnano '22	🍷 3
● Donna Gina Colorino '20	🍷 4

● Montechiari '21	🍷 5
⊙ Donna Catherine Brut Rosé M. Cl.	🍷 6
● Montechiari Cabernet '19	🍷 8
● Montechiari Merlot '19	🍷 7

OTHER WINERIES

Il Fitto

loc. Case Sparse Chianacce, 126
52044 Cortona [AR]
(+39 0575648988
www.podereilfitto.com

CELLAR SALES
PRE-BOOKED VISITS
ACCOMMODATION
ANNUAL PRODUCTION 30,000 bottles
HECTARES UNDER VINE 8.00

● Cortona Syrah Campetone '21	♟♟ 5
● Cortona Syrah Poggilunghi '22	♟♟ 4

Le Fornacelle

loc. San Benedetto 46
53037 San Gimignano [SI]
(+39 0577944958
www.fornacelle.com

● Chianti Colli Senesi '23	♟♟ 2*
○ Vernaccia di San Gimignano Fiora Ris. '22	♟♟ 5
● Marcato '19	♟ 4
○ Vernaccia di San Gimignano '22	♟ 2

Fattoria Le Ginestre

via delle Ginestre, 18
59015 Carmignano [PO]
(+39 0558792020
www.fattorialeginestre.it

● Carmignano Ris. '16	♟♟ 4
● Vin Santo di Carmignano '07	♟♟ 5
● Carmignano '19	♟ 3

Le Fonti

fraz. Panzano
loc. Le Fonti
50022 Greve in Chianti [FI]
(+39 055852194
www.fattorialefonti.it

CELLAR SALES
PRE-BOOKED VISITS
ANNUAL PRODUCTION 45,000 bottles
HECTARES UNDER VINE 8.80
VITICULTURE METHOD Certified Organic

● Chianti Cl. '21	♟♟ 3*
● Chianti Cl. Gran Selezione '20	♟♟ 5
● Chianti Cl. Ris. '20	♟♟ 4

Tenuta La Fortuna

loc. La Fortuna, 83
53024 Montalcino [SI]
(+39 0577848308
www.tenutalafortuna.it

CELLAR SALES
PRE-BOOKED VISITS
ANNUAL PRODUCTION 60,000 bottles
HECTARES UNDER VINE 18.00

● Brunello di Montalcino '19	♟♟ 6
● Brunello di Montalcino Giobi '19	♟♟ 6

Godiolo

via dell'Acquapuzzola, 13
53045 Montepulciano [SI]
(+39 0578757251
www.godiolo.it

CELLAR SALES
PRE-BOOKED VISITS
ACCOMMODATION AND RESTAURANT SERVICE
ANNUAL PRODUCTION 25,000 bottles
HECTARES UNDER VINE 6.00

● Nobile di Montepulciano '20	♟♟ 3
● Nobile di Montepulciano Ris. '20	♟♟ 6
● Nerolignite '22	♟ 4

TUSCANY

OTHER WINERIES

Tenuta di Gracciano della Seta

fraz. Gracciano
via Umbria, 59
53045 Montepulciano [SI]
☎ +39 0578708340
✆ www.gracdanodellaseta.com

CELLAR SALES
PRE-BOOKED VISITS
ANNUAL PRODUCTION 95,000 bottles
HECTARES UNDER VINE 20.58
VITICULTURE METHOD Certified Organic
SUSTAINABLE WINERY

● Nobile di Montepulciano '21	♀♀ 4
● Nobile di Montepulciano Ris. '20	♀♀ 5
● Rosso di Montepulciano '22	♀ 3
○ Vin Santo di Montepulciano '18	♀ 7

Gualdo del Re

loc. Notri, 79
57028 Suvereto [LI]
☎ +39 0565829888
✆ www.gualdodelre.it

CELLAR SALES
PRE-BOOKED VISITS
ACCOMMODATION AND RESTAURANT SERVICE
ANNUAL PRODUCTION 100,000 bottles
HECTARES UNDER VINE 27.00
VITICULTURE METHOD Certified Organic

● Cabraia '20	♀♀ 7
○ Eliseo Bianco '23	♀ 3
● Eliseo Rosso '20	♀ 3
● Suvereto Merlot l'Rennero '21	♀ 8

Isola delle Falcole

fraz. Panzano in Chianti
loc. San Cresci, 51
50022 Greve in Chianti [FI]
☎ +39 3388405894
✆ www.isoladellefalcole.com

ANNUAL PRODUCTION 10,000 bottles
HECTARES UNDER VINE 3.00

● Chianti Cl. Gran Selezione '20	♀♀ 8
● Chianti Cl. Vecchia Vigna '21	♀♀ 7
● Aurè '20	♀ 8

Fattoria di Grignano Tenuta Inghirami

via di Grignano, 22
50065 Pontassieve [FI]
☎ +39 0558398490
✆ www.fattoriadigrignano.com

CELLAR SALES
PRE-BOOKED VISITS
ANNUAL PRODUCTION 200,000 bottles
HECTARES UNDER VINE 53.00
VITICULTURE METHOD Certified Organic
SUSTAINABLE WINERY

● Chianti Rufina Poggio Gualtieri Ris. '20	♀♀ 4
● Chianti Rufina Ritratto del Cardinale '22	♀♀ 3

Innocenti

fraz. Torrenieri
loc. Citille di Sotto, 45
53028 Montalcino [SI]
☎ +39 0577834227
✆ www.innocentivini.com

CELLAR SALES
PRE-BOOKED VISITS
ANNUAL PRODUCTION 25,000 bottles
HECTARES UNDER VINE 5.00

● Toscana Rosso Vignalsole '21	♀♀ 5
● Brunello di Montalcino '19	♀♀ 7
● Rosso di Montalcino '22	♀♀ 4

Fattoria Kappa

loc. Le Badie
via Roma, 118
56040 Castellina Marittima [PI]
☎ +39 3346619711
andreadimaio1974@gmail.com

CELLAR SALES
PRE-BOOKED VISITS
ANNUAL PRODUCTION 20,000 bottles
HECTARES UNDER VINE 6.00

● Lambda '21	♀♀ 3
○ Corniello	♀ 4
○ Etabeta '23	♀ 4

OTHER WINERIES

Maurizio Lambardi
loc. Canalicchio di Sotto, 8
53024 Montalcino [SI]
☎ +39 0577848476
✉ www.lambardimontalcino.it

CELLAR SALES
PRE-BOOKED VISITS
ANNUAL PRODUCTION 17,000 bottles
HECTARES UNDER VINE 6.50

● Brunello di Montalcino '19	♟♟ 7

Lanciola
fraz. Pozzolatico
via Imprunetana, 210
50023 Impruneta [FI]
☎ +39 055208324
✉ www.lanciola.it

CELLAR SALES
PRE-BOOKED VISITS
ANNUAL PRODUCTION 250,000 bottles
HECTARES UNDER VINE 40.00

● Chianti Cl. Le Masse di Greve '21	♟ 4
● Chianti Cl. Le Masse di Greve Gran Selezione '18	♟ 4
● Terricci '20	♟ 5

LaSelva
loc. Poderone, 10a
58051 Magliano in Toscana [GR]
☎ +39 0564593077
✉ www.laselva.wine

CELLAR SALES
PRE-BOOKED VISITS
ACCOMMODATION
ANNUAL PRODUCTION 210,000 bottles
HECTARES UNDER VINE 35.00
VITICULTURE METHOD Certified Organic

○ Maremma Toscana Vermentino '23	♟♟ 3
● Morellino di Scansano Colli dell'Uccellina Ris. '21	♟ 4
● Prima Causa '21	♟ 5

La Lastra
fraz. Santa Lucia
via R. De Grada, 9
53037 San Gimignano [SI]
☎ +39 0577941781
✉ www.lalastra.it

CELLAR SALES
PRE-BOOKED VISITS
ANNUAL PRODUCTION 58,000 bottles
HECTARES UNDER VINE 7.00
SUSTAINABLE WINERY

○ San Gimignano Rosato '23	♟♟ 4
○ Vernaccia di San Gimignano Ris. '22	♟♟ 4
● Chianti Colli Senesi '23	♟ 2
● SG '20	♟ 7

Fattoria Lavacchio
loc. Lavacchio
via di Montefiesole, 55
50065 Pontassieve [FI]
☎ +39 0558317472
✉ www.fattorialavacchio.com

CELLAR SALES
PRE-BOOKED VISITS
ACCOMMODATION AND RESTAURANT SERVICE
ANNUAL PRODUCTION 120,000 bottles
HECTARES UNDER VINE 25.00
VITICULTURE METHOD Certified Organic
SUSTAINABLE WINERY

● Chianti Rufina Il Cedro Ris. '20	♟♟ 3
○ Puro Bianco PètNat '23	♟ 4
○ Puro Rosato PétNat '23	♟ 4

Leonardo da Vinci
loc. Vinci
via Provinciale Mercatale, 291
50059 Vinci [FI]
☎ +39 0571902444
✉ www.leonardodavinci.it

CELLAR SALES
PRE-BOOKED VISITS
ACCOMMODATION
ANNUAL PRODUCTION 6,000,000 bottles
HECTARES UNDER VINE 600.00
SUSTAINABLE WINERY

○ Vermentino '23	♟♟ 2*
● Chianti '22	♟♟ 2*
● Rosso di Montalcino '22	♟♟ 4

OTHER WINERIES

Leuta

via Pietraia, 21
52044 Cortona [AR]
☎ +39 3385033560
☞ www.leuta.it

CELLAR SALES
PRE-BOOKED VISITS
ANNUAL PRODUCTION 25,000 bottles
HECTARES UNDER VINE 12.60

● 2,618 Cabernet Franc '20	♟♟ 6
● Cortona Syrah 0,618 '20	♟♟ 5
○ Cortona Vin Santo '09	♟♟ 8

Tenuta Luce

loc. Castelgiocondo
53024 Montalcino [SI]
☎ +39 0577 84131
☞ www.lucedellavite.com

CELLAR SALES
PRE-BOOKED VISITS
ACCOMMODATION AND RESTAURANT SERVICE
ANNUAL PRODUCTION 470,000 bottles
HECTARES UNDER VINE 88.00
VITICULTURE METHOD Certified Organic
SUSTAINABLE WINERY

● Brunello di Montalcino Luce '19	♟♟ 8
● Lucente '21	♟♟ 6

Macinatico

loc. Macinatico
loc. San Benedetto, 56-58
53037 San Gimignano [SI]
☎ +39 3286169636
☞ www.macinatico.com

CELLAR SALES
PRE-BOOKED VISITS
ACCOMMODATION
ANNUAL PRODUCTION 30,000 bottles
HECTARES UNDER VINE 90.00
VITICULTURE METHOD Certified Organic
SUSTAINABLE WINERY

● Fabbrecchia '23	♟♟ 2*
● Massi 1956 '22	♟♟ 3
○ San Gimignano Vin Santo '20	♟♟ 3
○ Vernaccia di San Gimignano Ris. '22	♟♟ 4

Maestà della Formica

via Provinciale 17
55030 Careggine [LU]
☎ +39 3496921806
☞ www.maestadellaformica.com

CELLAR SALES
PRE-BOOKED VISITS
ACCOMMODATION
ANNUAL PRODUCTION 14,000 bottles
HECTARES UNDER VINE 3.50
SUSTAINABLE WINERY

● Sacripante '22	♟♟ 7
● Gamo '22	♟ 5
○ Riesling '22	♟ 6

Malgiacca

loc. Gragnano
via della Chiesa, 45a
55010 Capannori [LU]
☎ +39 3331840208
☞ www.malgiacca.com

CELLAR SALES
PRE-BOOKED VISITS
ANNUAL PRODUCTION 20,000 bottles
HECTARES UNDER VINE 8.00

○ Malgiacca Bianco '23	♟♟ 4
○ Tingolli '22	♟♟ 5
● Dalitro '23	♟ 4

Podere Marcampo

loc. San Cipriano
56048 Volterra [PI]
☎ +39 058885393
☞ www.poderemarcampo.com

CELLAR SALES
PRE-BOOKED VISITS
ACCOMMODATION
ANNUAL PRODUCTION 22,000 bottles
HECTARES UNDER VINE 5.00
VITICULTURE METHOD Certified Organic
SUSTAINABLE WINERY

● Giusto alle Balze '20	♟♟ 5
● Marcampo '21	♟♟ 4
● Severus '20	♟♟ 5
○ Terrablu '23	♟ 3

OTHER WINERIES

Tenuta Mareli

fraz. Montemagno
via per Frascalino
55041 Camaiore [LU]
+39 3334585266
www.tenutamareli.it

HECTARES UNDER VINE 3.50

○ Le Morette '23	🍷🍷 4
● Nicodemo '22	🍷🍷 3
● Re Magno '21	🍷🍷 6

Giorgio Meletti Cavallari

via Casone Ugolino, 12
57022 Castagneto Carducci [LI]
+39 0565775620
www.giorgiomeletticavallari.it

CELLAR SALES
PRE-BOOKED VISITS
ACCOMMODATION
ANNUAL PRODUCTION 40,000 bottles
HECTARES UNDER VINE 10.00

○ Bolgheri Bianco Borgeri '23	🍷🍷 3*
● Bolgheri Rosso Sup. Impronte '21	🍷🍷 8
⊙ Bolgheri Rosato '23	🍷 4

Tenuta Meraviglia Tenuta Le Colonne

fraz. Donoratico
s.da st.le 1 via Aurelia, 418
57022 Castagneto Carducci [LI]
+39 0565775246
www.tenutameraviglia.it

ANNUAL PRODUCTION 170,000 bottles
HECTARES UNDER VINE 30.00
SUSTAINABLE WINERY

● Bolgheri Rosso Sup. Tenuta Le Colonne '21	🍷🍷 6
● Bolgheri Rosso Tenuta Le Colonne '22	🍷🍷 6

Podere Monastero

loc. Monastero
53011 Castellina in Chianti [SI]
+39 0577740436
www.poderemonastero.com

CELLAR SALES
PRE-BOOKED VISITS
ACCOMMODATION
ANNUAL PRODUCTION 7,000 bottles
HECTARES UNDER VINE 3.00

● La Pineta '22	🍷🍷 6
● Campanaio '22	🍷🍷 6

Monastero dei Frati Bianchi

loc. Margine
Monte dei Bianchi, 10
54013 Fivizzano [MS]
+39 3408360807
www.monasterofratibianchi.it

PRE-BOOKED VISITS
ANNUAL PRODUCTION 30,000 bottles
HECTARES UNDER VINE 7.00

● Deir '20	🍷🍷 5
● Barsaré '21	🍷 5
● Polleo '21	🍷 4

Montalbino

via Colle Montalbino, 10
50025 Montespertoli [FI]
+39 3896825334
www.montalbinovini.it

CELLAR SALES
PRE-BOOKED VISITS
ACCOMMODATION AND RESTAURANT SERVICE
ANNUAL PRODUCTION 25,000 bottles
HECTARES UNDER VINE 7.00
VITICULTURE METHOD Certified Organic

● Montalbino Rosso '22	🍷🍷 4
○ Trebbiano '23	🍷🍷 3
● Chianti Montespertoli '22	🍷 3

Fattoria Montecchio

fraz. San Donato in Poggio
via Montecchio, 4
50028 Barberino Tavarnelle [FI]
📞 +39 0558072907
🌐 www.fattoriamontecchio.it

CELLAR SALES
PRE-BOOKED VISITS
ACCOMMODATION
ANNUAL PRODUCTION 250,000 bottles
HECTARES UNDER VINE 30.00

● Chianti Cl. Ris. '21	🍷🍷 4
● Chianti Cl. '22	🍷 3

Fattoria di Montemaggio

loc. Montemaggio
53017 Radda in Chianti [SI]
📞 +39 0577738323
🌐 www.montemaggio.com

CELLAR SALES
PRE-BOOKED VISITS
ANNUAL PRODUCTION 30,000 bottles
HECTARES UNDER VINE 8.00
VITICULTURE METHOD Certified Organic

● Chianti Cl. '21	🍷🍷 5
● Chianti Cl. Gran Selezione Alberello '15	🍷🍷 8

Montepepe

via Sforza, 76
54038 Montignoso [MS]
📞 +39 05851980363
🌐 www.montepepe.com

CELLAR SALES
PRE-BOOKED VISITS
ACCOMMODATION
ANNUAL PRODUCTION 25,000 bottles
HECTARES UNDER VINE 6.00

○ Degeres '20	🍷🍷 7
○ Montepepe Bianco '23	🍷🍷 5
● Pepo '21	🍷 5
○ PM '21	🍷 6

Monterotondo

loc. Monterotondo, 12
53013 Gaiole in Chianti [SI]
📞 +39 0577 749089
🌐 www.agriturismomonterotondo.net

CELLAR SALES
PRE-BOOKED VISITS
ACCOMMODATION
ANNUAL PRODUCTION 20,000 bottles
HECTARES UNDER VINE 4.00
VITICULTURE METHOD Certified Organic

● Chianti Cl. V. Vaggiolata '21	🍷🍷 4

Giacomo Mori

fraz. Palazzone
p.zza Sandro Pertini, 8
53040 San Casciano dei Bagni [SI]
📞 +39 0578227005
🌐 www.giacomomori.it

CELLAR SALES
PRE-BOOKED VISITS
ACCOMMODATION
ANNUAL PRODUCTION 45,000 bottles
HECTARES UNDER VINE 12.00
VITICULTURE METHOD Certified Organic

● Chianti Castelrotto Ris. '21	🍷🍷 4
● I 5 Mori '20	🍷 4
○ Vin Bianco '23	🍷 4

Gianni Moscardini

fraz. Pomaia
via Macchia al Pino
56040 Santa Luce [PI]
📞 +39 3459400874
🌐 www.giannimoscardini.com

CELLAR SALES
PRE-BOOKED VISITS
ANNUAL PRODUCTION 70,000 bottles
HECTARES UNDER VINE 17.50

● Penteo Rosso '21	🍷🍷 3
● Sileno Cabernet Franc '22	🍷🍷 4
● Sileno Ciliegiolo '21	🍷🍷 4

TUSCANY

OTHER WINERIES

Mulini di Segalari
loc. Felciaino, 115a
57022 Castagneto Carducci [LI]
📞 +39 0565765202
🌐 www.mulinidisegalari.it

ANNUAL PRODUCTION 10,000 bottles
HECTARES UNDER VINE 2.50
VITICULTURE METHOD Certified Organic
SUSTAINABLE WINERY

● Bolgheri Rosso Sup. '20	♟♟ 6
● Bolgheri Rosso Ai Confini del Bosco '21	♟♟ 5
● Soloterra Sangiovese '22	♟♟ 5

Musico
pod. La Casella
53024 Montalcino [SI]
📞 +39 3482212430
🌐 www.musico.pro

● Brunello di Montalcino '19	♟♟ 7
● Rosso di Montalcino '22	♟♟ 5

La Nascosta
loc. le Rovine
53023 Castiglione d'Orcia [SI]
📞 +39 3314555447
🌐 www.lanascosta.it

PRE-BOOKED VISITS
ANNUAL PRODUCTION 35,000 bottles
HECTARES UNDER VINE 15.00

● Orcia Saltamacchia Ris. '20	♟♟ 5
● Orcia Sangiovese Il Giovesone Ris. '20	♟♟ 7
○ Chard' O' '21	♟ 6
○ Gisso '23	♟ 5

Le Novelire
loc. Campo alla Capanna, 216
57022 Castagneto Carducci [LI]
📞 +39 3479828633
🌐 www.lenovelire.it

HECTARES UNDER VINE 4.00
SUSTAINABLE WINERY

● Bolgheri Sup. Re Vignon '21	♟♟ 7
● Bolgheri Rosso Re Ludio '22	♟♟ 5
● Bolgheri Rosso Sup. Re Diale '21	♟♟ 6

Fattoria Ormanni
loc. Ormanni, 1
53036 Poggibonsi [SI]
📞 +39 0577937212
🌐 www.ormanni.it

CELLAR SALES
PRE-BOOKED VISITS
ACCOMMODATION
ANNUAL PRODUCTION 120,000 bottles
HECTARES UNDER VINE 68.00

● Chianti Cl. '22	♟♟ 3
● Chianti Cl. Borro del Diavolo Ris. '20	♟♟ 5
● Chianti Cl. Gran Selezione '20	♟ 6

Orsumella
loc. Montefiridolfi
via Collina, 52
50026 San Casciano in Val di Pesa [FI]
📞 +39 3395852557
🌐 www.orsumella.it

ANNUAL PRODUCTION 200,000 bottles
HECTARES UNDER VINE 37.00
VITICULTURE METHOD Certified Organic

● Chianti Cl. Gran Selezione '20	♟♟ 6
● Chianti Cl. Corte Rinieri Ris. '20	♟♟ 4
● Chianti Cl. '22	♟ 3

TUSCANY

OTHER WINERIES

Palazzo

loc. Palazzo, 144
53024 Montalcino [SI]
📞 +39 0577849226
🌐 www.aziendapalazzo.it

CELLAR SALES
PRE-BOOKED VISITS
ANNUAL PRODUCTION 20,000 bottles
HECTARES UNDER VINE 12.00
VITICULTURE METHOD Certified Organic

● Brunello di Montalcino '19	♟♟ 6
● Brunello di Montalcino Cosimo '19	♟♟ 6
● Toscana Rosso Alcineo '18	♟♟ 5
● Rosso di Montalcino '22	♟ 4

Palazzo Vecchio

loc. Valiano
via Terrarossa, 5
53045 Montepulciano [SI]
📞 +39 0578724170
🌐 www.vinonobile.it

CELLAR SALES
PRE-BOOKED VISITS
RESTAURANT SERVICE
ANNUAL PRODUCTION 50,000 bottles
HECTARES UNDER VINE 25.00

● Nobile di Montepulciano Maestro '20	♟♟ 4
● Nobile di Montepulciano Ris. '19	♟♟ 6
● Rosso di Montepulciano Dogana '21	♟ 3

Celestino Pecci

loc. Viti - San Carlo
53024 Montalcino [SI]
📞 +39 3881236765
🌐 www.aziendapeccicelestino.com/

● Brunello di Montalcino '19	♟♟ 8
● Brunello di Montalcino Poggio al Carro '19	♟♟ 8
● Rosso di Montalcino '21	♟♟ 4
Toscana Rosso You Can '21	♟ 5

Il Palazzo

fraz. Antria
via del Moro, 6
52100 Arezzo
📞 +39 0575 361338
🌐 www.ilpalazzo.eu

CELLAR SALES
PRE-BOOKED VISITS
ANNUAL PRODUCTION 300,000 bottles
HECTARES UNDER VINE 42.00

● Maspino Syrah '21	♟♟ 3
○ Vermentino '23	♟♟ 2*
● Chianti Ris. '21	♟ 3

Paradiso di Cacuci

loc. Paradiso, 323
53020 Montalcino [SI]
📞 +39 3519892059
🌐 www.paradisodicacuci.com

ANNUAL PRODUCTION 25,000 bottles
HECTARES UNDER VINE 5.00

● Brunello di Montalcino Ris. '18	♟♟ 8
● Brunello di Montalcino '19	♟♟ 7
● Brunello di Montalcino IX Cielo '19	♟♟ 8

Pepi Lignana
Fattoria Il Casalone

fraz. Orbetello Scalo
via Aurelia, 18a, km 140,5
58016 Orbetello [GR]
📞 +39 0564 862160
🌐 www.pepilignanawine.com

CELLAR SALES
PRE-BOOKED VISITS
ACCOMMODATION
ANNUAL PRODUCTION 70,000 bottles
HECTARES UNDER VINE 16.00
SUSTAINABLE WINERY

● Maremma Toscana Cabernet Franc Don José '21	♟♟ 5
● Maremma Toscana Cabernet Poggio Colombi '21	♟♟ 4

OTHER WINERIES

Peteglia

loc. Montenero d'Orcia
Podere Peteglia
58033 Castel del Piano [GR]
☏ +39 3498335438
✉ www.peteglia.com

CELLAR SALES
PRE-BOOKED VISITS
ACCOMMODATION AND RESTAURANT SERVICE
ANNUAL PRODUCTION 35,000 bottles
HECTARES UNDER VINE 8.00
VITICULTURE METHOD Certified Organic

● Montecucco Sangiovese Ris. '19	🍷🍷 5
● Montecucco Sangiovese '20	🍷🍷 3
● Maremma Toscana Sangiovese Mezzodì '23	🍷 3
○ Montecucco Vermentino '23	🍷 3

Le Pianore

fraz. Monticello Amiata
loc. Podere Maladina, 1
58044 Cinigiano [GR]
☏ +39 3917118621
✉ www.lepianore.it

CELLAR SALES
PRE-BOOKED VISITS
ACCOMMODATION AND RESTAURANT SERVICE
ANNUAL PRODUCTION 16,000 bottles
HECTARES UNDER VINE 3.00
VITICULTURE METHOD Certified Organic
SUSTAINABLE WINERY

● Maremma Toscana Merlot Periodico '22	🍷🍷 5
○ Zancona '22	🍷🍷 4

Pietraserena

via Casale, 5
53037 San Gimignano [SI]
☏ +39 0577940083
✉ www.arrigoni1913.it

CELLAR SALES
PRE-BOOKED VISITS
ACCOMMODATION AND RESTAURANT SERVICE
ANNUAL PRODUCTION 200,000 bottles
HECTARES UNDER VINE 35.00

● Chianti Colli Senesi Caulio Ris. '21	🍷🍷 3
● Chianti Colli Senesi Poggio al Vento '22	🍷🍷 2*
● In Nero '23	🍷🍷 5
○ Vernaccia di San Gimignano V. del Sole '23	🍷🍷 3

Pian delle Querci

via Giacomo Leopardi, 10
53024 Montalcino [SI]
☏ +39 0577834174
✉ www.piandellequerci.it

CELLAR SALES
PRE-BOOKED VISITS
ANNUAL PRODUCTION 53,000 bottles
HECTARES UNDER VINE 8.50

● Brunello di Montalcino '19	🍷🍷 5
● Brunello di Montalcino Ris. '18	🍷🍷 5
● Rosso di Montalcino '21	🍷🍷 3
○ Toscana Bianco La Pergola a Le Coste '22	🍷🍷 3

Piemaggio

loc. Fioraie
53011 Castellina in Chianti [SI]
☏ +39 0577740658

CELLAR SALES
ANNUAL PRODUCTION 40,000 bottles
HECTARES UNDER VINE 11.50
SUSTAINABLE WINERY

● Chianti Cl. Le Fioraie '20	🍷🍷 4
● Chianti Cl. Le Fioraie Ris. '19	🍷🍷 5

Pieve Santa Restituta

loc. Chiesa di Santa Restituta
53024 Montalcino [SI]
☏ +39 0577848610
info@pievesantarestituta.com

ANNUAL PRODUCTION 75,000 bottles
HECTARES UNDER VINE 27.00

● Brunello di Montalcino Sugarille '19	🍷🍷 8
● Brunello di Montalcino Rennina '19	🍷🍷 8

OTHER WINERIES

Pinino

loc. Pinino, 327
53024 Montalcino [SI]
☎ +39 0577849381
⊛ www.pinino.com

CELLAR SALES
PRE-BOOKED VISITS
ANNUAL PRODUCTION 90,000 bottles
HECTARES UNDER VINE 16.00

● Brunello di Montalcino '19	♟♟ 6
● Brunello di Montalcino V. Pinino '19	♟♟ 6

Podere Le Poggiarelle

loc. Seano
via Le Volte, 2
59011 Carmignano [PO]
☎ +39 0558712343
⊛ www.lepoggiarelle.it

CELLAR SALES
PRE-BOOKED VISITS
ANNUAL PRODUCTION 1,500 bottles
HECTARES UNDER VINE 1.00

● Carmignano Ris. '19	♟♟ 4
● Carmignano Ris. '18	♟ 4

Tenuta Poggio alla Sala

via delle Chiane, 3
53045 Montepulciano [SI]
☎ +39 0578767224
⊛ www.toppetta.it

CELLAR SALES
PRE-BOOKED VISITS
RESTAURANT SERVICE
ANNUAL PRODUCTION 150,000 bottles
HECTARES UNDER VINE 25.00

● Nobile di Montepulciano '20	♟♟ 4
● Nobile di Montepulciano Ris. '19	♟♟ 5
● Rosso di Montepulciano '23	♟ 3

Poggio Brigante

loc. Colle di Lupo, 13
58051 Magliano in Toscana [GR]
☎ +39 0564592507
⊛ www.poggiobrigante.it

CELLAR SALES
ANNUAL PRODUCTION 80,000 bottles
HECTARES UNDER VINE 20.00
VITICULTURE METHOD Certified Organic
SUSTAINABLE WINERY

● Scampoli Ciliegiolo '22	♟♟ 3*
● Morellino di Scansano '23	♟♟ 3
○ L'oro di Giacomo '23	♟ 3
● Morellino di Scansano Arsura '21	♟ 5

Poggio Grande

loc. Poggio Grande, 11
53023 Castiglione d'Orcia [SI]
☎ +39 3388677637
www.aziendapoggiogrande.it

CELLAR SALES
PRE-BOOKED VISITS
ANNUAL PRODUCTION 22,000 bottles
HECTARES UNDER VINE 6.50

Orcia Scorbutico '21	♟♟ 3
Piano '23	♟♟ 2*
Orcia Sangiovese Sesterzo '20	♟ 5
Tagete '23	♟ 4

Poggio Il Castellare

fraz. Torrenieri
loc. Castel Verdelli
53024 Montalcino [SI]
☎ +39 3888315037
⊛ www.tenutapoggioilcastellare.com

PRE-BOOKED VISITS
ANNUAL PRODUCTION 46,000 bottles
HECTARES UNDER VINE 7.50

● Rosso di Montalcino '21	♟♟ 5
● Brunello di Montalcino '19	♟♟ 7
● Toscana Rosso Passo dei Caprioli '21	♟ 2

OTHER WINERIES

Poggio La Noce

loc. Ontignano
via Paiatici, 29
50014 Fiesole [FI]
📞 +39 0556549120
🌐 www.poggiolanoce.com

CELLAR SALES
PRE-BOOKED VISITS
ANNUAL PRODUCTION 20,000 bottles
HECTARES UNDER VINE 4.00
VITICULTURE METHOD Certified Organic

● Gigino '21	♟♟ 5
● Gigiò '20	♟♟ 6
⊙ Pinko Pallino '23	♟ 3

Poggio Sorbello

fraz. Centoia
loc. Case Sparse, 168
52044 Cortona [AR]
📞 +39 3395447059
🌐 www.poggiosorbello.it

CELLAR SALES
ANNUAL PRODUCTION 10,000 bottles
HECTARES UNDER VINE 9.00
SUSTAINABLE WINERY

● Cortona Syrah Ris. '19	♟♟ 5
● Cortona Cabernet Sauvignon Fossa Granaia '21	♟♟ 4
● Cortona Syrah Gortinaia '21	♟ 5

PrimaLuce

loc. Santa Lucia
53037 San Gimignano [SI]
📞 +39 3348646742
🌐 www.agricolaprimaluce.com

○ PuntoZero '23	♟♟ 5

Podere Poggio Scalette

fraz. Ruffoli
via Barbiano, 7
50022 Greve in Chianti [FI]
📞 +39 0558546108
🌐 www.poggioscalette.it

CELLAR SALES
PRE-BOOKED VISITS
ACCOMMODATION
ANNUAL PRODUCTION 65,000 bottles
HECTARES UNDER VINE 15.00
SUSTAINABLE WINERY

● Capogatto '21	♟♟ 7
● Chianti Cl. '22	♟♟ 4
● Il Carbonaione '21	♟ 7
● Piantonaia '21	♟ 8

Il Poggiolino

loc. Sambuca Val di Pesa
via Chiantigiana, 32
50020 Tavarnelle Val di Pesa [FI]
📞 +39 0558071635
🌐 www.ilpoggiolino.com

CELLAR SALES
PRE-BOOKED VISITS
ANNUAL PRODUCTION 30,000 bottles
HECTARES UNDER VINE 5.56

● Chianti Cl. '21	♟♟ 5
● Chianti Cl. Ris. '20	♟♟ 5

Priorino

via Martiri della Libertà, 16
53045 Montepulciano [SI]
📞 +39 0578707841
🌐 www.cantinapriorino.com

ANNUAL PRODUCTION 18,000 bottles
HECTARES UNDER VINE 6.00

● Nobile di Montepulciano Ris. '19	♟♟
● Umore e Luce '20	♟♟

OTHER WINERIES

Provveditore

loc. Salaiolo, 174
58054 Scansano [GR]
℡ +39 3487018670
◉ www.provveditore.net

CELLAR SALES
PRE-BOOKED VISITS
ACCOMMODATION
ANNUAL PRODUCTION 150,000 bottles
HECTARES UNDER VINE 40.00

○ Maremma Toscana Vermentino Il Bargaglino '23	🍷🍷 3
● Morellino di Scansano Sassato '23	🍷🍷 3
○ Maremma Toscana Trebbiano Piperino '23	🍷 3

Quercia al Poggio

fraz. Monsanto
s.da Quercia al Poggio, 4
50021 Barberino Val d'Elsa [FI]
℡ +39 0558075278
◉ www.quercialpoggio.com

CELLAR SALES
PRE-BOOKED VISITS
ACCOMMODATION
ANNUAL PRODUCTION 70,000 bottles
HECTARES UNDER VINE 15.00
VITICULTURE METHOD Certified Organic

● Chianti Cl. Ris. '20	🍷🍷 5
● Chianti Cl. '22	🍷🍷 3

Tenuta Querciamatta

via Bogi, 1236
50129 Monsummano Terme [PT]
℡ +39 05721790971
◉ www.querciamatta.it

CELLAR SALES
PRE-BOOKED VISITS
RESTAURANT SERVICE
ANNUAL PRODUCTION 10,000 bottles
HECTARES UNDER VINE 6.00
VITICULTURE METHOD Certified Organic
SUSTAINABLE WINERY

● Querciamatta D '21	🍷🍷 5
● Querciamatta Rosé '23	🍷 5
○ Vaiassa '22	🍷 6

Rabissi

loc. Castelnuovo dell'Abate
via dell'Olmo, 49
53024 Montalcino [SI]
℡ +39 3334864313
aziendarabissi@gmail.com

CELLAR SALES
PRE-BOOKED VISITS
ANNUAL PRODUCTION 4,000 bottles
HECTARES UNDER VINE 4.50

● Brunello di Montalcino '19	🍷🍷 7
● Rosso di Montalcino '22	🍷🍷 4

Rascioni e Cecconello

loc. Fonteblanda
s.da prov.le San Donato, 73
58010 Orbetello [GR]
℡ +39 3472915038
◉ www.rascioniececconello.it

CELLAR SALES
PRE-BOOKED VISITS
ACCOMMODATION AND RESTAURANT SERVICE
ANNUAL PRODUCTION 9,000 bottles
HECTARES UNDER VINE 4.00
VITICULTURE METHOD Certified Organic
SUSTAINABLE WINERY

Il Poggio Ciliegiolo '22	🍷🍷 7
Rotulaia Ciliegiolo '23	🍷 5

Rocca di Montegrossi

fraz. Monti in Chianti
53010 Gaiole in Chianti [SI]
℡ +39 0577747977
◉ www.roccadimontegrossi.it

CELLAR SALES
PRE-BOOKED VISITS
ANNUAL PRODUCTION 80,000 bottles
HECTARES UNDER VINE 18.00
VITICULTURE METHOD Certified Organic

● Chianti Cl. '22	🍷🍷 4
● Chianti Cl. Gran Selezione Vign. S. Marcellino '19	🍷 5
● Geremia '19	🍷 6

OTHER WINERIES

Marina Romin

fraz. Morrona
via del Chianti, 34
56030 Terricciola [PI]
📞 +39 3913506315
🌐 www.marinaromin.it

CELLAR SALES
PRE-BOOKED VISITS
ACCOMMODATION
ANNUAL PRODUCTION 30,000 bottles
HECTARES UNDER VINE 10.00
VITICULTURE METHOD Certified Organic
SUSTAINABLE WINERY

○ Aura Vermentino '23	🍷🍷 3
● Pomerio '21	🍷🍷 2*
○ Vin Santo del Chianti Sorelle Palazzi 1973 Ris. '15	🍷🍷 5

Tenute San Fabiano

via San Fabiano, 33
52100 Arezzo
📞 +39 057524566
🌐 www.tenutesanfabiano.it

CELLAR SALES
PRE-BOOKED VISITS
ACCOMMODATION
ANNUAL PRODUCTION 1,000,000 bottles
HECTARES UNDER VINE 300.00

● Chianti Putto '23	🍷🍷 2*
● Chianti Sup. Etichetta Nera '22	🍷🍷 3

San Filippo

loc. San Filippo, 134
53024 Montalcino [SI]
📞 +39 0577847176
🌐 www.sanfilippomontalcino.com

ANNUAL PRODUCTION 50,000 bottles
HECTARES UNDER VINE 10.50

● Brunello di Montalcino dei Comunali '19	🍷🍷 8
● Brunello di Montalcino Le Lucére Ris. '18	🍷🍷 7
● Rosso di Montalcino Lo Scorno '22	🍷🍷 5
● Brunello di Montalcino Le Lucére '19	🍷 6

San Benedetto

loc. San Benedetto, 4a
53037 San Gimignano [SI]
📞 +39 3386958705
🌐 www.agrisanbenedetto.com

CELLAR SALES
PRE-BOOKED VISITS
ACCOMMODATION
ANNUAL PRODUCTION 40,000 bottles
HECTARES UNDER VINE 25.00

○ Vernaccia di San Gimignano Ris. '22	🍷🍷 4
○ Vermentino '23	🍷 3
○ Vernaccia di San Gimignano '23	🍷 3

Fattoria San Felo

loc. Pagliatelli di Sotto
58051 Magliano in Toscana [GR]
📞 +39 05641950121
🌐 www.fattoriasanfelo.it

CELLAR SALES
ACCOMMODATION
ANNUAL PRODUCTION 150,000 bottles
HECTARES UNDER VINE 53.00

○ Maremma Toscana Vermentino Le Stoppie '23	🍷🍷 3
● Pinot Nero '20	🍷🍷 5
● Morellino di Scansano Lampo '22	🍷 3

San Guglielmo

loc. Il Chiesino
53024 Montalcino [SI]
📞 +39 3332114040
🌐 www.cantinasanguglielmo.it

● Brunello di Montalcino '19	🍷🍷
● Rosso di Montalcino '21	🍷🍷
● Toscana Rosso Merlot Resistentia '22	🍷🍷

OTHER WINERIES

Tenuta San Jacopo in Castiglioni

loc. Castiglioncelli, 151
52022 Cavriglia [AR]
📞 +39 055966003
🌐 www.tenutasanjacopo.it

CELLAR SALES
PRE-BOOKED VISITS
ACCOMMODATION
ANNUAL PRODUCTION 70,000 bottles
HECTARES UNDER VINE 130.00
VITICULTURE METHOD Certified Organic
SUSTAINABLE WINERY

○ Erboli '22	🍷🍷 6
● Valdarno di Sopra Orma del Diavolo '20	🍷🍷 7
○ Quarto di Luna '23	🍷 3

Tenuta San Vito in Fior di Selva

via San Vito, 59
50056 Montelupo Fiorentino [FI]
📞 +39 057151411
🌐 www.san-vito.com

CELLAR SALES
PRE-BOOKED VISITS
ACCOMMODATION AND RESTAURANT SERVICE
ANNUAL PRODUCTION 150,000 bottles
HECTARES UNDER VINE 29.00
VITICULTURE METHOD Certified Organic
SUSTAINABLE WINERY

○ Vin Santo del Chianti Malmantico '17	🍷🍷 6
○ Amantiglio Chardonnay '23	🍷 3
○ Chianti Colli Fiorentini Darno '22	🍷 3

Sant'Agnese

loc. Campo alle Fave, 1
57025 Piombino [LI]
📞 +39 0565277069
🌐 www.santagnesefarm.it

CELLAR SALES
PRE-BOOKED VISITS
ANNUAL PRODUCTION 20,000 bottles
HECTARES UNDER VINE 6.00
SUSTAINABLE WINERY

L'Etrange '22	🍷🍷 5
A Rose is a Rose '23	🍷 3
Fiori Blu '19	🍷 7

Fattoria San Michele a Torri

via San Michele, 36
50018 Scandicci [FI]
📞 +39 055769111
🌐 www.fattoriasanmichele.it

CELLAR SALES
PRE-BOOKED VISITS
RESTAURANT SERVICE
ANNUAL PRODUCTION 400,000 bottles
HECTARES UNDER VINE 138.00
VITICULTURE METHOD Certified Organic

● Chianti Colli Fiorentini '22	🍷 2
● Chianti Colli Fiorentini San Giovanni Novantasette Ris. '20	🍷 4
● V. della Luna '23	🍷 5

Tenuta Sanoner

loc. Sant'Anna
fraz. Bagno Vignoni
53027 San Quirico d'Orcia [SI]
📞 +39 05771698707
🌐 www.tenuta-sanoner.it

CELLAR SALES
PRE-BOOKED VISITS
ANNUAL PRODUCTION 36,000 bottles
HECTARES UNDER VINE 13.50
VITICULTURE METHOD Certified Organic

● Orcia Sangiovese Aetos '22	🍷🍷 5
○ Aetos Bianco '23	🍷🍷 5
⊙ Aetos Brut Rosé	🍷 4
○ Aetos Extra Brut M. Cl.	🍷 6

Santa Lucia

loc. Collecchio
s.da stat.le Aurelia, km 163.5
58051 Magliano in Toscana [GR]
📞 +39 3929506975
🌐 www.azsantalucia.com

CELLAR SALES
PRE-BOOKED VISITS
ACCOMMODATION
ANNUAL PRODUCTION 160,000 bottles
HECTARES UNDER VINE 40.00
SUSTAINABLE WINERY

● Maremma Toscana Ciliegiolo Canapone '22	🍷🍷 3
○ Maremma Toscana Vermentino Brigante '22	🍷🍷 2*
○ Maremma Toscana Viognier Dueseiquattro '23	🍷 3

OTHER WINERIES

Fattoria Santo Stefano

loc. Greti
via di Collegalle, 3
50022 Greve in Chianti [FI]
📞 +39 0558572298
🌐 www.fattoriasantostefano.it

CELLAR SALES
PRE-BOOKED VISITS
ACCOMMODATION
ANNUAL PRODUCTION 20,000 bottles
HECTARES UNDER VINE 19.00
VITICULTURE METHOD Certified Organic

● Chianti Cl. '22	🍷🍷 5
● Chianti Cl. Drugo Ris. '21	🍷🍷 6

Il Sassolo

via Citerna, 5
59015 Carmignano [PO]
📞 +39 0558706488
🌐 www.ilsassolo.it

ANNUAL PRODUCTION 9,000 bottles
HECTARES UNDER VINE 5.50

● Carmignano Santa Cristina '21	🍷🍷 3
● Barco Reale '22	🍷 3
⊙ Barco Reale Rosato Vin Ruspo '23	🍷 3

Tenuta Sette Cieli

fraz. La California
via Sandro Pertini
57020 Bibbona [LI]
📞 +39 0586677435
🌐 www.settecieli.com

ANNUAL PRODUCTION 77,000 bottles
HECTARES UNDER VINE 18.00
VITICULTURE METHOD Certified Organic
SUSTAINABLE WINERY

● Indaco '20	🍷🍷 7
● Scipio '20	🍷🍷 8

SassodiSole

fraz. Torrenieri
loc. Sasso di Sole, 85
53024 Montalcino [SI]
📞 +39 0577834303
🌐 www.sassodisole.it

CELLAR SALES
PRE-BOOKED VISITS
ANNUAL PRODUCTION 50,000 bottles
HECTARES UNDER VINE 10.00
SUSTAINABLE WINERY

● Brunello di Montalcino '19	🍷🍷 7
● Brunello di Montalcino Sasso di Luna '19	🍷🍷 7
● Rosso di Montalcino '22	🍷🍷 5
● Rosso di Montalcino Sasso di Luna '22	🍷🍷 5

Sequerciani

loc. Sequerciani
58023 Gavorrano [GR]
📞 +39 0566028053
🌐 www.sequerciani.it

CELLAR SALES
PRE-BOOKED VISITS
ACCOMMODATION
ANNUAL PRODUCTION 50,000 bottles
HECTARES UNDER VINE 14.00
VITICULTURE METHOD Certified Biodynamic
SUSTAINABLE WINERY

● Maremma Toscana Ciliegiolo '21	🍷🍷 4
● Maremma Toscana Pugnitello '21	🍷 5

Borgo La Stella

loc. Vagliagli
b.go La Stella, 60
53017 Radda in Chianti [SI]
📞 +39 0577740699
🌐 www.borgolastella.com

ANNUAL PRODUCTION 21,000 bottles
HECTARES UNDER VINE 4.50

● Chianti Cl. '21	🍷🍷
● Chianti Cl. Gran Selezione '20	🍷🍷
● Chianti Cl. '20	🍷

OTHER WINERIES

Stomennano

b.go Stomennano
53035 Monteriggioni [SI]
☎ +39 0577304033
🖱 www.stomennano.it

CELLAR SALES
ACCOMMODATION
ANNUAL PRODUCTION 50,000 bottles
HECTARES UNDER VINE 20.00
SUSTAINABLE WINERY

● Chianti Cl. Ris. '21	🍷🍷 5

Fattoria Svetoni

fraz. Gracciano
via Umbria, 63
53045 Montepulciano [SI]
☎ +39 3293030848
🖱 www.fattoriasvetoni.it

CELLAR SALES
PRE-BOOKED VISITS
ACCOMMODATION AND RESTAURANT SERVICE
ANNUAL PRODUCTION 100,000 bottles
HECTARES UNDER VINE 26.00
SUSTAINABLE WINERY

● Nobile di Montepulciano '21	🍷🍷 5
● Nobile di Montepulciano La Croce '19	🍷🍷 7

Tenuta del Buonamico

loc. Cercatoia
via Provinciale di Montecarlo, 43
55015 Montecarlo [LU]
☎ +39 058322038
🖱 www.buonamico.it

CELLAR SALES
PRE-BOOKED VISITS
ACCOMMODATION AND RESTAURANT SERVICE
ANNUAL PRODUCTION 350,000 bottles
HECTARES UNDER VINE 43.00
SUSTAINABLE WINERY

○ M.I.O. '23	🍷🍷 3
○ Particolare Brut	🍷🍷 3
○ Particolare Brut Rosé	🍷🍷 3
○ Vivi Vermentino '23	🍷 3

Terre di Sovernaja

loc. Casale, 36
53037 San Gimignano [SI]
info@terredisovernaja.com

○ Vernaccia di San Gimignano Assola Ris. '21	🍷🍷 5
○ Vernaccia di San Gimignano Viti Sparse '22	🍷🍷 4
● 9 Anime '20	🍷 5

Terre Nere

loc. Castelnuovo dell'Abate
3024 Montalcino [SI]
☎ +39 3490971713
www.terreneremontalcino.it

CELLAR SALES
PRE-BOOKED VISITS
ACCOMMODATION
ANNUAL PRODUCTION 50,000 bottles
HECTARES UNDER VINE 10.00

Brunello di Montalcino '19	🍷🍷 7
Brunello di Montalcino Capriolo '19	🍷🍷 8
Rosso di Montalcino '21	🍷🍷 4

Terreno

fraz. Greti
via Citille, 4
50022 Greve in Chianti [FI]
☎ +39 3351536335
🖱 www.terreno.eu

CELLAR SALES
PRE-BOOKED VISITS
ANNUAL PRODUCTION 100,000 bottles
HECTARES UNDER VINE 14.00

● Chianti Cl. '21	🍷🍷 4
● Chianti Cl. Gran Selezione A Sofia '20	🍷🍷 7
● Chianti Cl. Le Bonille di Sopra Ris. '20	🍷 5

OTHER WINERIES

Podere Terreno alla Via della Volpaia
via della Volpaia
53017 Radda in Chianti [SI]
📞 +39 0577738312
🌐 www.podereterreno.it

CELLAR SALES
PRE-BOOKED VISITS
ANNUAL PRODUCTION 30,000 bottles
HECTARES UNDER VINE 4.50
VITICULTURE METHOD Certified Organic

● Chianti Cl. Ris. '21	🍷🍷 5
● Chianti Cl. '22	🍷🍷 4

Tiberini
via delle Caggiole 9
53045 Montepulciano [SI]
📞 +39 0578716112
🌐 www.tiberiniwine.com

● Nobile di Montepulciano Podere Le Caggiole '19	🍷🍷 5
● Rosso di Montepulciano Sabreo '22	🍷🍷 3

Tiberio
fraz. Penna, 116a
52028 Terranuova Bracciolini [AR]
📞 +39 0559172781
🌐 www.tiberiowine.com

CELLAR SALES
PRE-BOOKED VISITS
HECTARES UNDER VINE 5.00

● Nocens '20	🍷🍷 3
● Canaiolo '20	🍷 3
● Malvasia Nera '20	🍷 3
○ Vin Santo del Chianti '20	🍷 5

Tiezzi
loc. Podere Soccorso, 199
53024 Montalcino [SI]
📞 +39 3479565201
🌐 www.tiezzivini.it

CELLAR SALES
PRE-BOOKED VISITS
ACCOMMODATION
ANNUAL PRODUCTION 30,000 bottles
HECTARES UNDER VINE 6.00
SUSTAINABLE WINERY

● Brunello di Montalcino V. Soccorso Ris. '18	🍷🍷 8
● Brunello di Montalcino V. Soccorso '19	🍷🍷 6
● Rosso di Montalcino V. Poggio Cerrino '22	🍷🍷 4
● Brunello di Montalcino V. Poggio Cerrino '19	🍷 7

Tollena
via San Giovanni, 69
53037 San Gimignano [SI]
📞 +39 0577907178
🌐 www.tollena.it

CELLAR SALES
ACCOMMODATION
ANNUAL PRODUCTION 50,000 bottles
HECTARES UNDER VINE 22.00

● San Gimignano Merlot Bernardo '18	🍷🍷 2*
● Sciccheria '23	🍷🍷 2*
○ Vernaccia di San Gimignano Signorina Vittoria Ris. '20	🍷🍷 5

Fattoria La Torre
s.da prov.le di Montecarlo, 7
55015 Montecarlo [LU]
📞 +39 058322981
🌐 www.latorrewineresort.it

CELLAR SALES
PRE-BOOKED VISITS
ACCOMMODATION AND RESTAURANT SERVICE
ANNUAL PRODUCTION 45,000 bottles
HECTARES UNDER VINE 6.50
VITICULTURE METHOD Certified Organic

● Stringaio '22	🍷🍷
● Cabernet Franc '21	🍷
● ESSE '21	🍷

OTHER WINERIES

Fattoria La Torre

loc. La Villa
53037 San Gimignano [SI]
(» +39 05771341037
⊕ www.latorrefattoria.it

○ Vernaccia di San Gimignano Il Carrobacco '22	♈♈ 5
● Chianti Colli Senesi Stradina '23	♈♈ 4
○ Vernaccia di San Gimignano Acquaiole '23	♈♈ 4

F.lli Vagnoni

loc. Pancole, 82
53037 San Gimignano [SI]
(» +39 0577955077
⊕ www.fratellivagnoni.com

CELLAR SALES
PRE-BOOKED VISITS
ACCOMMODATION
ANNUAL PRODUCTION 120,000 bottles
HECTARES UNDER VINE 17.00
VITICULTURE METHOD Certified Organic

○ Vernaccia di San Gimignano I Mocali Ris. '21	♈♈ 3*
● Chianti Colli Senesi Capanneto '19	♈ 3
● Sodi Lunghi '20	♈ 4
○ Vernaccia di San Gimignano Fontabuccio '22	♈ 3

Tenuta La Vigna

via Fugnano, 31/B C
53037 San Gimignano [SI]
(» +39 0577950045
⊕ www.tenutalavigna.com

○ Vernaccia di San Gimignano Ris. '22	♈♈ 3*
● Chianti '23	♈♈ 2*
○ Vernaccia di San Gimignano '23	♈♈ 2*

Usiglian Del Vescovo

via Usigliano, 26
56036 Palaia [PI]
(» +39 0587468000
⊕ www.usigliandelvescovo.it

CELLAR SALES
PRE-BOOKED VISITS
ANNUAL PRODUCTION 90,000 bottles
HECTARES UNDER VINE 19.00
VITICULTURE METHOD Certified Organic
SUSTAINABLE WINERY

● Terre di Pisa Rosso Il Barbiglione '22	♈♈ 6
● Chianti Sup. '19	♈ 3
● Il Grullaio '22	♈ 4

Ventolaio

loc. Ventolaio, 51
53024 Montalcino [SI]
(» +39 0577835779
⊕ www.ventolaio.it

CELLAR SALES
PRE-BOOKED VISITS
ANNUAL PRODUCTION 70,000 bottles
HECTARES UNDER VINE 14.00

● Brunello di Montalcino '19	♈♈ 6
● Brunello di Montalcino Campo dei Colti '19	♈♈ 8
● Toscana Rosso Sentiero del Fante '21	♈♈ 2*
● Rosso di Montalcino '22	♈ 4

Villa a Sesta

loc. Villa a Sesta
p.zza del Popolo, 1
53019 Castelnuovo Berardenga [SI]
(» +39 0577359014
⊕ www.villasesta.com

CELLAR SALES
PRE-BOOKED VISITS
ACCOMMODATION AND RESTAURANT SERVICE
ANNUAL PRODUCTION 150,000 bottles
HECTARES UNDER VINE 65.00

● Chianti Cl. Gran Selezione Sorleone '20	♈♈ 5
● Chianti Cl. Ris. '21	♈♈ 4
● Chianti Cl. '22	♈ 3

TUSCANY

769

OTHER WINERIES

Villa Cafaggio

fraz. Panzano in Chianti
via San Martino in Cecione, 5
50022 Greve in Chianti [FI]
(☎) +39 0558549094
⊕ www.villacafaggio.it

CELLAR SALES
PRE-BOOKED VISITS
ANNUAL PRODUCTION 220,000 bottles
HECTARES UNDER VINE 30.00
SUSTAINABLE WINERY

● Chianti Cl. Ris. '21	♟♟ 5
● Basilica del Pruneto '20	♟♟ 6
● Chianti Classico Gran Selezione Basilica Solatio '20	♟ 6

Villa La Ripa

loc. Antria, 38
52100 Arezzo
(☎) +39 3351003351
⊕ www.villalaripa.it

CELLAR SALES
PRE-BOOKED VISITS
ANNUAL PRODUCTION 25,000 bottles
HECTARES UNDER VINE 10.00
SUSTAINABLE WINERY

● Psyco '20	♟♟ 8
● Syrah '20	♟ 8
● Tiratari '20	♟ 7

Villa Vallacchio

fraz. Mercatale
via Vallacchio, 3
50026 San Casciano in Val di Pesa [FI]
(☎) +39 3353355614842
fattoriavallacchio@gmail.com

● Chianti Classico Gran Selezione Cristiano '20	♟♟ 6
● Chianti Cl. Alberta Ris. '21	♟ 5

Villa Calcinaia
Conti Capponi

fraz. Greti
via Citille, 84
50022 Greve in Chianti [FI]
(☎) +39 055853715
⊕ www.conticapponi.it

CELLAR SALES
PRE-BOOKED VISITS
ACCOMMODATION
ANNUAL PRODUCTION 100,000 bottles
HECTARES UNDER VINE 32.00
VITICULTURE METHOD Certified Organic

● Chianti Cl. Gran Selezione V. Bastignano '20	♟♟ 7
● Chianti Cl. Ris. '20	♟♟ 5
● Chianti Cl. '21	♟ 3
● Chianti Cl. Gran Selezione V. La Fornace '20	♟ 5

Villa Patrizia

loc. Cana
pod. Villa Patrizia
58053 Roccalbegna [GR]
(☎) +39 0564982028
⊕ www.villa-patrizia.com

CELLAR SALES
PRE-BOOKED VISITS
ANNUAL PRODUCTION 50,000 bottles
HECTARES UNDER VINE 10.00
VITICULTURE METHOD Certified Organic

● Montecucco Sangiovese Istrico '20	♟♟ 4
● Montecucco Sangiovese Orto di Boccio Ris. '19	♟♟ 5
● Maremma Toscana Ciliegiolo Albatraia '21	♟ 4

Villanoviana

loc. Sant'Uberto
fraz. Bolgheri
via Santa Maddalena, 172b
57022 Castagneto Carducci [LI]
(☎) +39 05861881227
⊕ www.villanoviana.it

CELLAR SALES
PRE-BOOKED VISITS
ACCOMMODATION
ANNUAL PRODUCTION 30,000 bottles
HECTARES UNDER VINE 4.00
VITICULTURE METHOD Certified Organic

● Bolgheri Rosso Sup. Ferrugo '21	♟♟ 6
● Bolgheri Rosso Sup. Sant' Uberto '21	♟♟ 7

MARCHE

Last year, we raised concerns about the tangible risks facing Le Marche's winemaking industry, and the 2023 vintage, ravaged by downy mildew, has indeed had a significant impact on producers' decisions. Some have managed to vinify what little they had, others turned to the grape market, while those hardest hit gave up entirely, skipping the vintage. Fortunately, many had a solid reserve from the abundant 2022 harvest, and there's hope for a fruitful 2024, despite a dry summer and water reserves running low after a winter and spring with scant snow and rain.

Adding to the worries about the global market slowdown, there was the collapse of Terre Cortesi Moncaro. Marche's largest cooperative, which operates across key regional production areas, spiraled into an economic and leadership crisis at the beginning of 2024, with unpredictable outcomes that are sure to affect the entire sector. The situation is so alarming that it has prompted intervention from the highest levels of government. There's hope for a quick resolution to give relief to the coop's hundreds of members and secure the future of thousands of specialized vineyards.

But now, let's move on to some good news. Le Marche's network of wineries remains resilient. Many are small-scale, family-run, and benefit from the region's deep-rooted rural culture, which naturally leans toward avoiding waste and excess. This approach has brought steady, if gradual, improvements in quality. In this vein, top recognition has been awarded to a Bianchello del Metauro, a historic DOC that spans numerous vineyards in Pesaro province. We're also celebrating the debut in the esteemed Tre Bicchieri club of Edoardo Dottori and Cimarelli in Jesi, as well as La Valle del Sole and Quinto "Quntì" Alfonsi in Piceno. Additionally, two wines have made a stellar comeback: Fattoria Nanni's Verdicchio Origini Riserva and Oasi degli Angeli's Kurni. Lastly, a well-deserved special award goes to our Cooperative of the Year: Matelica's Belisario. Le Marche keeps moving forward!

Maria Letizia Allevi

c.da Pescolla, 28
63081 Castorano [AP]
📞 +39 3494063412
🌐 www.vinimida.it

Aurora

loc. Santa Maria in Carro
c.da Ciafone, 98
63073 Offida [AP]
📞 +39 0736810007
🌐 www.viniaurora.it

CELLAR SALES
PRE-BOOKED VISITS
ANNUAL PRODUCTION 12,000 bottles
HECTARES UNDER VINE 5.50
VITICULTURE METHOD Certified Organic

CELLAR SALES
PRE-BOOKED VISITS
ACCOMMODATION
ANNUAL PRODUCTION 52,000 bottles
HECTARES UNDER VINE 10.50
VITICULTURE METHOD Certified Organic

Roberto Corradetti and Maria Letizia Allevi have a clear vision: meticulous vineyard care, production methods that respect varietal characteristics, and a well-rounded portfolio with wines that exhibit strong character and high craftsmanship. Their pecorino offers drinkability and freshness, while the reds reflect the generous, sun-soaked vineyards. Grenache gives rise to the Isra '21, a wine that combines delicacy and structural rigor, with a fascinating saline and spicy finish. It's a shame that the winery produces so few bottles. Montepulciano stars in the full-bodied and fleshy Mida Rosso '21. We also appreciated the Offida Pecorino Mida 2023, which sees a subtle herbal touch emerging amidst citrusy sensations, echoed on the palate. There's also a new red, which is equally rare: the Zampa '22 (a blend of merlot, petit verdot, grenache, and syrah). Here vegetal nuances emerge over a soft, fruity, and slightly alcohol-dominated background.

In the late 1970s, a group of friends pursued a desire to live in the countryside, practice environmentally friendly agriculture, and follow lifestyle removed from the industrialization and urbanization of the time. It was a countercultural path, not without its risks, requiring a strong collective commitment. Today, the second generation lends a hand, but little has changed in the spirit of those who launched the project. The wines are made from traditional Piceni grape varieties and have a strong sense of identity. The robust Barricadiero '21 is an extractive red full of energy. It needs a bit more time in the bottle to soften its dense tannin structure. The Rosso Piceno Superiore '21 is more ready and enjoyable now, showcasing signature notes of sour cherry and a lively, flavorful palate. Slightly rustic, the Rosso Piceno '23 boasts a full, food-friendly character. The Fiobbo '22, a Pecorino, opts for notes of black tea, canned peach, and straw, an authentically rustic drink with a saline finish.

● Isra '21	♟♟ 8
● Offida Rosso Mida '21	♟♟ 5
○ Offida Pecorino Mida '23	♟♟ 4
● Zampa '22	♟ 8
○ Offida Pecorino Mida '16	♟♟♟ 3*
● Arsi '18	♟♟ 8
● Arsi '17	♟♟ 8
● Isra '20	♟♟ 8
● Isra '19	♟♟ 8
○ Offida Pecorino Mida '22	♟♟ 3*
○ Offida Pecorino Mida '21	♟♟ 3*
○ Offida Pecorino Mida '20	♟♟ 3*
○ Offida Pecorino Mida '19	♟♟ 3*
● Offida Rosso Mida '20	♟♟ 4
● Offida Rosso Mida '19	♟♟ 4
● Offida Rosso Mida '18	♟♟ 4

○ Offida Pecorino Fiobbo '22	♟♟ 3
● Offida Rosso Barricadiero '21	♟♟ 5
● Rosso Piceno Sup. '21	♟♟ 3
● Rosso Piceno '23	♟ 3
● Barricadiero '10	♟♟♟ 4
● Barricadiero '09	♟♟♟ 4
● Barricadiero '06	♟♟♟ 4
● Barricadiero '04	♟♟♟ 3
● Barricadiero '03	♟♟♟ 3*
● Barricadiero '02	♟♟♟ 3
● Barricadiero '01	♟♟♟ 3*
● Offida Rosso Barricadiero '11	♟♟♟ 4*
● Offida Rosso Barricadiero '19	♟♟ 4
● Offida Rosso Barricadiero '18	♟♟ 4
● Rosso Piceno Sup. '20	♟♟ 3
● Rosso Piceno Sup. '19	♟♟ 3

★Belisario

via Aristide Merloni, 12
62024 Matelica [MC]
📞 +39 0737787247
🌐 www.belisario.it

CELLAR SALES
PRE-BOOKED VISITS
ANNUAL PRODUCTION 1,200,000 bottles
HECTARES UNDER VINE 300.00

With over 50 years of experience, Belisario is a pillar of viticulture in the upper Esino Valley, providing dedicated support to its members and anyone in need of expert technical advice. The estate boasts extensive facilities for vinification and aging. The range is particularly strong in the verdicchio category, offering wines that satisfy discerning tasters and other, more accessible versions intended for everyday consumption. Among these last, the Del Cerro '23 stands out with its citrusy and saline profile, as does the Vigneti B.'23, with its soft, well-sustained drinkability and pleasantly citrusy finish. The real standout, as always, is the captivating Cambrugiano '21, which conjures up whiffs of citrus, stones, and white flowers, all tied together with a subtle balsamic streak that echoes on an elegant, cohesive palate full of complex nuances. Don't overlook the flavorful and fruity Meridia '22.

o Verdicchio di Matelica Cambrugiano Ris. '21	♟♟♟ 4*
o Verdicchio di Matelica Del Cerro '23	♟♟ 3*
o Verdicchio di Matelica Meridia '22	♟♟ 4
o Verdicchio di Matelica Vign. B. '23	♟♟ 3*
● Colli Maceratesi Rosso San Leopardo Ris. '21	♟♟ 3
● Colli Maceratesi Rosso Vign. B. '21	♟♟ 3
o Verdicchio di Matelica Noi 150 Ris. '20	♟♟ 6
o Verdicchio di Matelica Valbona '23	♟♟ 2*
o Verdicchio di Matelica Extra Brut Nadir '22	♟ 2
o Verdicchio di Matelica Cambrugiano Ris. '20	♟♟♟ 4*
o Verdicchio di Matelica Cambrugiano Ris. '19	♟♟♟ 4*

★Bisci

via Fogliano, 120
62024 Matelica [MC]
📞 +39 0737787490
🌐 www.bisci.it

CELLAR SALES
PRE-BOOKED VISITS
ANNUAL PRODUCTION 130,000 bottles
HECTARES UNDER VINE 20.00
VITICULTURE METHOD Certified Organic

When Andrea Ferretti or winery owners Mauro and Tito Bisci talk about the 2023 vintage, it's unlikely to be with fondness. Despite efforts to combat the spread of downy mildew while maintaining organic practices, its severity significantly affected both the quantity and quality of the harvest. As a result, there's no vintage Matelica on offer, with the few bottles produced quickly selling out. The new Vigneto Fogliano was given more time for aging and isn't available. However, the Senex '18 made up with a shining performance. Aged in concrete for three years, this Riserva highlights Verdicchio's longevity, unveiling an alluring finesse in its notes of almond, anise, aromatic herbs, and balsamic hints on the nose. The palate unfurls with refined energy, growing in sapidity toward a long, lingering finish. The two reds are well-made, with a preference for the Villa Castiglioni '19, made from sangiovese.

o Verdicchio di Matelica Senex Ris. '18	♟♟♟ 7
● Merlot '20	♟♟ 3
● Villa Castiglioni '19	♟♟ 4
o Verdicchio di Matelica '18	♟♟♟ 3*
o Verdicchio di Matelica Senex Ris. '15	♟♟♟ 6
o Verdicchio di Matelica Vign. Fogliano '20	♟♟♟ 5
o Verdicchio di Matelica Vign. Fogliano '19	♟♟♟ 5
o Verdicchio di Matelica Vign. Fogliano '18	♟♟♟ 4*
o Verdicchio di Matelica Vign. Fogliano '15	♟♟♟ 4*
o Verdicchio di Matelica Vign. Fogliano '13	♟♟♟ 3*
o Verdicchio di Matelica Vign. Fogliano '10	♟♟♟ 3*
o Verdicchio di Matelica Vign. Fogliano '08	♟♟♟ 3*
o Verdicchio di Matelica '22	♟♟ 3*
o Verdicchio di Matelica '21	♟♟ 3*
o Verdicchio di Matelica '20	♟♟ 3*
o Verdicchio di Matelica '19	♟♟ 3*

Borgo Paglianetto

loc. Pagliano, 393
62024 Matelica [MC]
☎ +39 073785465
✺ www.borgopaglianetto.com

CELLAR SALES
PRE-BOOKED VISITS
ANNUAL PRODUCTION 120,000 bottles
HECTARES UNDER VINE 29.00
VITICULTURE METHOD Certified Organic
SUSTAINABLE WINERY

A focus on the natural disposition of the growing area and the varietal characteristics of the verdicchio grape make Borgo Paglianetto's range a kind of snapshot of the Matelica appellation. There are no forced choices here; it's the harvest that determines the stylistic direction, from the very fresh style of their standard-label, annata wines to the layered complexities of their more ambitious selections. The marvelous Vertis '22 offers up a nose of citrus and stones, while the palate is poised and elegant, with a juicy, saline touch and exceptional persistence. The Jera '19 reveals a powerful palate, soft at its core and progressive toward the finish, with an alluring balsamic nuance. The young Terravignata '23 makes for an excellent and refreshing drink, on par with the deeper and more complex Petrara '23. The distinctively territorial Matesis '19, an original montepulciano, is charming in its own right. The Spumante Brut, now from the 2019 vintage, is always a sure bet.

Brunori

v.le della Vittoria, 103
60035 Jesi [AN]
☎ +39 0731207213
✺ www.brunori.it

CELLAR SALES
PRE-BOOKED VISITS
ANNUAL PRODUCTION 50,000 bottles
HECTARES UNDER VINE 7.00

Recent renovations of the cellar in San Paolo di Jesi has introduced a spacious panoramic terrace overlooking the olive grove and the San Nicolò vineyard, one of the historic crus of Castelli di Jesi. All the wines presented by Giorgio and Carlo Brunori, the father-and-son duo at the helm, are vinified and aged in fibreglass-lined concrete tanks. The difference lies in the timing of the harvest. Le Gemme '23 represents a simpler, citrusy, easy-drinking version with a touch of sapidity and trademark aromatic notes. The San Nicolò '23, the Classico Superiore, shows its characteristic almond and white flower aromas, revealing a fairly intense palate with lively energy. There's also a Riserva version of the San Nicolò, now in its 2022 vintage, which adds complexity and structure without losing its playful fruitiness, all reflected on a soft palate where rich notes of ripe apple and sweet almond emerge.

○ Verdicchio di Matelica Vertis '22	♛♛♛ 5
● Matesis '19	♛♛ 4
○ Verdicchio di Matelica Jera Ris. '19	♛♛ 7
○ Verdicchio di Matelica Petrara '23	♛♛ 4
○ Verdicchio di Matelica Terravignata '23	♛♛ 3*
○ Verdicchio di Matelica Brut M. Cl. '19	♛♛ 6
○ Verdicchio di Matelica Jera Ris. '15	♛♛♛ 4*
○ Verdicchio di Matelica Jera Ris. '10	♛♛♛ 4*
○ Verdicchio di Matelica Petrara '22	♛♛♛ 3*
○ Verdicchio di Matelica Petrara '16	♛♛♛ 2*
○ Verdicchio di Matelica Vertis '20	♛♛♛ 4*
○ Verdicchio di Matelica Vertis '19	♛♛♛ 4*
○ Verdicchio di Matelica Vertis '16	♛♛♛ 3*
○ Verdicchio di Matelica Vertis '09	♛♛♛ 3*
○ Verdicchio di Matelica Jera Ris. '18	♛♛ 6
○ Verdicchio di Matelica Jera Ris. '17	♛♛ 4

○ Castelli di Jesi Verdicchio Cl. San Nicolò Ris. '22	♛♛ 4
○ Verdicchio dei Castelli di Jesi Cl. Le Gemme '23	♛♛ 2*
○ Verdicchio dei Castelli di Jesi Cl. Sup. San Nicolò '23	♛♛ 3
○ Castelli di Jesi Verdicchio Cl. San Nicolò Ris. '21	♛♛ 3*
○ Castelli di Jesi Verdicchio Cl. San Nicolò Ris. '20	♛♛ 3
○ Castelli di Jesi Verdicchio Cl. San Nicolò Ris. '19	♛♛ 3*
○ Castelli di Jesi Verdicchio Cl. San Nicolò Ris. '18	♛♛ 3*
○ Verdicchio dei Castelli di Jesi Cl. Sup. San Nicolò '22	♛♛ 3
○ Verdicchio dei Castelli di Jesi Cl. Sup. San Nicolò '21	♛♛ 2*

★★Bucci

fraz. Pongelli
via Cona
60010 Ostra Vetere [AN]
📞 +39 071964179
🌐 www.villabucci.com

CELLAR SALES
PRE-BOOKED VISITS
ANNUAL PRODUCTION 150,000 bottles
HECTARES UNDER VINE 31.00
VITICULTURE METHOD Certified Organic
SUSTAINABLE WINERY

In July 2024, headlines followed the sale of the
winery founded and directed by Ampelio Bucci
to the Veronesi family, fashion entrepreneurs
with growing ambitions in the wine sector. From
a technical standpoint, no major changes are
expected: the 2024 harvest will continue to be
overseen by Gabriele Tànfani and Gianni
Gasperi, the same professionals who have
managed the vineyard and cellar in recent years.
Together, they've created the splendor that is
Villa Bucci '21: the nose reveals varietal
sensations of almond, linden, anise, and
chamomile in a play of nuances that carry
through to a palate of remarkable gustatory
suppleness—an exceptional drink that remains
steady and consistent. Smoother and more
delicate, the Classico '23 leans more into citrus
tones, with a saline finish. The Tenuta Pongelli '21
shows its usual temperamental character, with
slightly mature fruit, relaxed drinkability, and
controlled tannins.

○ Castelli di Jesi Verdicchio Cl. Villa Bucci Ris. '21	♟♟♟ 8
○ Verdicchio dei Castelli di Jesi Cl. Sup. '23	♟♟ 5
● Rosso Piceno Tenuta Pongelli '21	♟♟ 4
○ Castelli di Jesi Verdicchio Cl. Villa Bucci Ris. '20	♟♟♟ 8
○ Castelli di Jesi Verdicchio Cl. Villa Bucci Ris. '19	♟♟♟ 7
○ Castelli di Jesi Verdicchio Cl. Villa Bucci Ris. '18	♟♟♟ 7
○ Castelli di Jesi Verdicchio Cl. Villa Bucci Ris. '17	♟♟♟ 7
○ Castelli di Jesi Verdicchio Cl. Villa Bucci Ris. '14	♟♟♟ 6
○ Verdicchio dei Castelli di Jesi Cl. Sup. '16	♟♟♟ 3*

Ca' Liptra

c.da San Michele, 21
60034 Cupramontana [AN]
📞 +39 3491321442
🌐 www.caliptra.it

CELLAR SALES
PRE-BOOKED VISITS
ANNUAL PRODUCTION 30,000 bottles
HECTARES UNDER VINE 8.80
VITICULTURE METHOD Certified Organic

Ca' Liptra openly draws inspiration from
traditional practices, managing small plots of old
vines, with hand-harvesting and minimal
intervention during fermentation. Agostino
Pisani oversees the agricultural side, while
Roberto Alfieri and Giovanni "The Inseminator"
Loberto handle the cellar. The wine for their
Riserva, which hails from Contrada San Michele,
is aged in used barriques. This year, it's also
divided according to the vineyard site. The
Torcolaccio '21 is made from grapes grown on
south-east facing, clay-limestone soil. It pours a
golden hue, releasing an intense, ripe nose,
slightly marked by lift, leading to a full, brackish,
and engaging palate. The Massaccese '21, from
lower vineyards in clay-gypsum soil with an
eastern exposure, offers almond, aromatic
herbs, and lemon notes on a saline, varietally-
faithful palate. Don't miss the Arancio '23,
with its enticing chinotto notes, and supple,
light mouthfeel.

○ Castelli di Jesi Verdicchio Cl. San Michele 21 Massaccese Ris. '21	♟♟ 5
○ Castelli di Jesi Verdicchio Cl. San Michele 21 Torcolaccio Ris. '21	♟♟ 5
○ Arancio '23	♟♟ 4
○ Le Lute Dosaggio Zero M. Cl.	♟ 5
● Amistà '22	♟♟ 4
● Amistà '20	♟♟ 4
○ Castelli di Jesi Verdicchio Cl. S. Michele 21 Ris. '20	♟♟ 5
○ Castelli di Jesi Verdicchio Cl. S. Michele 21 Ris. '19	♟♟ 4
○ Verdicchio dei Castelli di Jesi Cl. Sup. Kypra '22	♟♟ 3
○ Verdicchio dei Castelli di Jesi Cl. Sup. Kypra '20	♟♟ 3
○ Verdicchio dei Castelli di Jesi Cl. Sup. Kypra '17	♟♟ 3

La Calcinara

fraz. Candia
via Calcinara, 102a
60131 Ancona
(☎) +39 3933565044
⊕ www.lacalcinara.it

CELLAR SALES
PRE-BOOKED VISITS
ANNUAL PRODUCTION 60,000 bottles
HECTARES UNDER VINE 11.50
VITICULTURE METHOD Certified Biodynamic
SUSTAINABLE WINERY

Siblings Paolo and Eleonora Berluti are the heart, hands, and face of this small estate on the Candia hills. Both winemakers, they advocate for biodynamic agriculture and a handcrafted production style, personally overseeing every step. The result is a range with personality—unconventional, but capable of revealing a genuine sense of place. Their most important wine is the Folle '20, made from a single vineyard on chalky soil. It features intense sensations of sour cherries, burnt wood, haematic nuances, and light woodland echoes. The palate is meaty, slightly rustic, but full of energy and tenacity. Il Cacciatore di Sogni '22 is also excellent—it's a simpler wine but deep in capturing the softer side of Conero montepulciano: full of fruit, with whiffs of sour cherry and plum, the palate is fleshy and textured, yet not heavy, stretching into graphite notes for a fragrant, delightful finish. The Terra Calcinara '20 proves crisper and more evolved, the Clochard '23 (verdicchio) ripe and disordered.

Campanelli

via Scappia, 14
60038 San Paolo di Jesi [AN]
(☎) +39 3356044594
⊕ www.campanellivini.it

CELLAR SALES
PRE-BOOKED VISITS
ANNUAL PRODUCTION 13,000 bottles
HECTARES UNDER VINE 7.00
VITICULTURE METHOD Certified Organic

Francesco Campanelli's idea is to vinify separately the verdicchio grapes from different vineyards using the same production protocol, developed in collaboration with agronomist Luca Mercadante and winemaker Marco Gozzi. The vineyards are managed organically (some already certified, others in the process of being converted), with spontaneous fermentation and aging in concrete tanks. The unusual 2023 vintage, marked by a severe attack of downy mildew, disrupted their plan to release the three crus—San Michele (from Cupramontana), Palombare (from Serra San Quirico), and San Nicolò (from San Paolo di Jesi)—simultaneously. Francesco only presented the latter, with excellent results: an intimately varietal nose shows hints of almond and citron, leading to a palate that balances acidity and salinity, offering freshness, good flavor, and a tenacious sapidity on the finish. In the future, new crus are expected to come from San Paolo di Jesi.

● Conero Folle Ris. '20	♟♟ 6
● Rosso Conero Il Cacciatore di Sogni '22	♟♟ 4
○ Clochard '23	♟ 4
● Conero Terra Calcinara Ris. '20	♟ 5
● Conero Folle Ris. '19	♟♟ 6
● Conero Folle Ris. '18	♟♟ 6
● Conero Folle Ris. '15	♟♟ 5
● Conero Terra Calcinara Ris. '19	♟♟ 5
● Conero Terra Calcinara Ris. '18	♟♟ 5
● Conero Terra Calcinara Ris. '17	♟♟ 3
⊙ Mun '22	♟♟ 4
⊙ Mun '21	♟♟ 3*
⊙ Mun '20	♟♟ 3
● Rosso Conero Il Cacciatore di Sogni '21	♟♟ 4
● Rosso Conero Il Cacciatore di Sogni '20	♟♟ 3
● Rosso Conero Il Cacciatore di Sogni '18	♟♟ 3

○ Verdicchio dei Castelli di Jesi Cl. Sup. San Nicolò '23	♟♟ 4
○ Verdicchio dei Castelli di Jesi Cl. Sup. Palombare '22	♟♟ 4
○ Verdicchio dei Castelli di Jesi Cl. Sup. San Michele '22	♟♟ 4
○ Verdicchio dei Castelli di Jesi Cl. Sup. San Nicolò '22	♟♟ 4

Le Canà

via Molino Vecchio, 4
63063 Carassai [AP]
☏ +39 0734930054
⊛ www.lecana.it

★Le Caniette

c.da Canali, 23
63065 Ripatransone [AP]
☏ +39 07359200
⊛ www.lecaniette.it

CELLAR SALES
PRE-BOOKED VISITS
ANNUAL PRODUCTION 40,000 bottles
HECTARES UNDER VINE 25.00
VITICULTURE METHOD Certified Organic

CELLAR SALES
PRE-BOOKED VISITS
ANNUAL PRODUCTION 140,000 bottles
HECTARES UNDER VINE 16.00
VITICULTURE METHOD Certified Organic

The name Tornavento ("Return of the wind"), the agritourism run by siblings Paola, Alessandra, and Luca Polini, perfectly embodies the freshness of the wines produced here. Even on the hottest days, a constant breeze tempers the summer heat, offering a natural coolness that defines their range. North-facing exposures enhance the freshness of their Pecorino, which reveals hints of freshly cut grass and lemon, and a dynamic palate that's both supple and sapid. An irresistible drinkability is also evident in the flavorful Doravera Rosato '23 and the Infernaccio '23, a Rosso Piceno that's light in both color and tannins, yet endowed with a delicate and seductive fruity fragrance. We also appreciated the more structured Davore '20 and the powerful Vincè '20, a creamy and full-bodied red crafted from late-harvested montepulciano. For a more casual sip, there's the citrusy and floral Quies '23, made from passerina. The Retemura '22 offers woody sensations with a slightly closed palate.

Everything is running smoothly at the estate of Giovanni "Johnny" Vagnoni, and this success is no accident. It's the result of long-term planning, anchored by a few key decisions made years ago: strict adherence to organic farming practices, careful use of small oak barrels even for whites like the structured Veronica '22 or the still-aging Iosonogaia, and a focus on well-rounded aromatic profiles without sacrificing drinkability or the softness of tannins. All takes place in a winery that combines functionality with architectural and scenic beauty. The Morellone '20 exudes graceful aromas, elegantly blending fruit and spice with a juicy, fragrant, and balanced palate, resulting in an irresistible drinkability. Although the Nero di Vite was absent, one can take solace in one of the finest versions of Cinabro ever produced (you'll find it in the Rare Wines section).

⊙ Doravera '23	🍷🍷 2*
○ Offida Pecorino Tornavento '23	🍷🍷 3
● Rosso Piceno Infernaccio '23	🍷🍷 3
● Rosso Piceno Sup. Davore '20	🍷🍷 4
● Vincè '20	🍷🍷 8
○ Cretò '22	🍷 5
○ Offida Pecorino Retemura '22	🍷 4
○ Quies Passerina '23	🍷 2
○ Offida Pecorino Retemura '20	♀♀ 4
○ Offida Pecorino Tornavento '22	♀♀ 3
○ Offida Pecorino Tornavento '21	♀♀ 3
○ Quies Passerina '21	♀♀ 2*
● Rosso Piceno Infernaccio '22	♀♀ 2*
● Rosso Piceno Sup. Davore '19	♀♀ 3
● Rosso Piceno Sup. Davore '17	♀♀ 3

● Piceno Sup. Morellone '20	🍷🍷🍷 5
○ Offida Pecorino Veronica '22	🍷🍷 3*
○ Lucrezia '23	🍷🍷 3
● Piceno Rosso Bello '22	🍷🍷 3
● Cinabro '17	♀♀♀ 8
○ Offida Pecorino Iosonogaia non sono Lucrezia '10	♀♀♀ 4*
● Piceno Morellone '10	♀♀♀ 4*
● Piceno Morellone '08	♀♀♀ 4*
● Piceno Sup. Morellone '16	♀♀♀ 4*
● Piceno Sup. Morellone '15	♀♀♀ 4*
● Piceno Sup. Morellone '13	♀♀♀ 4*
● Piceno Sup. Morellone '12	♀♀♀ 4*
● Rosso Piceno Sup. Morellone '19	♀♀♀ 5
● Rosso Piceno Sup. Morellone '18	♀♀♀ 4*

Cantina dei Colli Ripani

c.da Tosciano, 28
63065 Ripatransone [AP]
☎ +39 07359505
⊕ www.colliripani.it

Podere Vito Cardinali

via Sant'Amico, 44
60030 Morro d'Alba [AN]
☎ +39 073163064
⊕ www.poderevitocardinali.com

CELLAR SALES
PRE-BOOKED VISITS
ANNUAL PRODUCTION 1,500,000 bottles
HECTARES UNDER VINE 800.00
SUSTAINABLE WINERY

ANNUAL PRODUCTION 30,000 bottles
HECTARES UNDER VINE 35.00

Colli Ripani has long been a shining example of cooperation in service of the land. Under the leadership of President Giovanni Traini and winemaker Marco Pignotti, there's a strong emphasis on organic and sustainable practices, and their efforts have yielded undeniable benefits, preserving vineyard integrity and enhancing the quality of their wines. As one might expect from a cooperative managing 800 hectares, their range is extensive and diverse, catering to all tastes and budgets. Their best whites come from pecorino grapes, but are distinctly different: the Mercantino '23 showcases its youthful verve with a pleasant palate of white fruit and aromatic herbs; in contrast, the Condivio '18 highlights the grape's aging potential, combining vegetal notes with hints of hazelnut and citrus peel on a soft, caressing, and pervasive palate. Among the reds, the standout is the "flagship" Leo Ripano '20, a wine characterized by red fruits, spicy notes, and smoky nuances, with a dynamic and robust tannic structure. The Castellano '21 is more restrained—a fragrant drink.

Love for Morro d'Alba drove Vito Cardinali to invest in his homeland. After a successful career in the steel industry, he decided to build his own winery, recently inaugurated, marking the culmination of a journey that began in the 1970s with the purchase of his first plots. Today, the vineyard spans 35 hectares, exclusively verdicchio and lacrima grapes. The wines immediately revealed a distinctive style, with a contemporary profile: no sugary or overripe embellishments, marked drinkability, and captivating aromatic clarity. In addition to the classic almond notes, the Vito '23 offers a lovely array of flavors, ranging from aromatic herbs to lemon peel and floral sensations. On the palate, it's flavorful with exceptional smoothness. The Costa Lisiano '23, a monovarietal lacrima, is even more original. Pale in color, it has floral aromas and a captivating mineral vein that shapes a supple, juicy palate, enlivened by a brackish finish. The future of Morro d'Alba is (also) moving in this direction.

○ Offida Pecorino Mercantino '23	♟♟ 3*
● Diavolo e Vento '19	♟♟ 5
○ Offida Pecorino Condivio '18	♟♟ 5
● Offida Rosso Leo Ripano '20	♟♟ 4
● Rosso Piceno Sup. Castellano '21	♟♟ 3
○ Grotte di Santità Ancestrale '20	♟ 5
○ Il Vicolo '23	♟ 3
○ Offida Passerina Lajella '23	♟ 2
○ Falerio Pecorino '21	♟♟ 2*
○ Il Vicolo '21	♟♟ 2*
○ Offida Passerina Lajella '22	♟♟ 2*
○ Offida Pecorino Mercantino '22	♟♟ 2*
○ Offida Pecorino Mercantino '21	♟♟ 2*
● Offida Rosso Leo Ripano '19	♟♟ 3
● Rosso Piceno Sup. Castellano '20	♟♟ 2*

○ Verdicchio dei Castelli di Jesi Cl. Sup. Vito '23	♟♟ 3*
● Costa Lisiano '23	♟♟ 3

CasalFarneto

via Farneto, 12
60030 Serra de' Conti [AN]
+39 0731889001
www.casalfarneto.it

CELLAR SALES
PRE-BOOKED VISITS
ANNUAL PRODUCTION 800,000 bottles
HECTARES UNDER VINE 43.00
VITICULTURE METHOD Certified Organic
SUSTAINABLE WINERY

Paolo Togni has spared no expense in developing his winery, investing heavily in both the vineyards and state-of-the-art equipment. Recently, new materials like ceramic, cocciopesto, and terracotta have been introduced for aging. These resources are at the disposal of the technical team, led by consulting winemaker Stefano Chioccioli and agronomist and director Danilo Solustri. A modern shop and tasting room with vineyard views have also been in operation for a few years now. Verdicchio remains the most important variety. It's behind the refined Riserva Crisio '21, with half the wine aged in tonneaux and the other half in stainless steel. Whiffs of citrus blend with toasted almond and lemon balm; in the mouth it's soft, with a full palate leading to a round, flavorful finish with good persistence. The Grancasale '22 also has a soft, relaxed palate—more horizontal than deep. The Fontevecchia '23 offers citrus echoes and some herbaceous overtones on a broad, long palate.

○ Castelli di Jesi Verdicchio Cl. Crisio Ris. '21	🍷🍷 5
○ Verdicchio dei Castelli di Jesi Cl. Sup. Fontevecchia '23	🍷🍷 3
○ Verdicchio dei Castelli di Jesi Cl. Sup. Grancasale '22	🍷🍷 4
● Otto Borghi '22	🍷 5
○ Paò '23	🍷 6
● Rosso Piceno Luigiprimo '21	🍷 5
○ Castelli di Jesi Verdicchio Cl. Crisio Ris. '13	🍷🍷🍷 3*
○ Castelli di Jesi Verdicchio Cl. Crisio Ris. '12	🍷🍷🍷 3*
○ Verdicchio dei Castelli di Jesi Cl. Sup. Grancasale '16	🍷🍷🍷 3*
○ Verdicchio dei Castelli di Jesi Cl. Sup. Grancasale '13	🍷🍷🍷 3*

Castignano Cantine dal 1960

c.da San Venanzo, 31
63072 Castignano [AP]
+39 0736822216
www.cantinedicastignano.com

CELLAR SALES
PRE-BOOKED VISITS
ANNUAL PRODUCTION 600,000 bottles
HECTARES UNDER VINE 450.00
VITICULTURE METHOD Certified Organic

The cooperative in Castignano is a model of successful collaboration. Founded over sixty years ago, it supports and unites many of the small winegrowers from the more inland areas of Piceno. Over the years, it has earned a solid reputation for producing well-crafted wines that offer excellent value, with freshness and drinkability serving as their hallmarks. President Omar Traini benefits from the expertise of agronomist Andrea Vannicola and winemaker Andrea Gasparroni. This year's tastings reflect a rise in quality for the Gran Maestro '19: intense morello cherry notes are softened by spicy whiffs and toasted nuances; in the mouth it's firm, flavorful, with close-knit yet sweet tannins for a robust palate. The Rosso Piceno Superiore Destriero '22 has a more rustic touch but conveys a traditional sense of expression. Moving to the whites, the Montemisio '23 remains a sure bet, moving on citrus and field herb notes on a full palate that expands appreciably.

○ Offida Pecorino Montemisio '23	🍷🍷 2*
● Offida Rosso Gran Maestro '19	🍷🍷 4
○ Falerio Pecorino Destriero '23	🍷🍷 2*
○ Notturno Moscato Spumante Dolce	🍷🍷 2
○ Offida Pecorino Bio '23	🍷🍷 3
● Rosso Piceno Sup. Destriero '22	🍷🍷 2*
● Templaria '22	🍷🍷 2*
○ Offida Passerina Bio '23	🍷 3
○ Passerina '23	🍷 2
● Rosso Piceno '23	🍷 2
● Rosso Piceno Sup. Bio '22	🍷 3
○ Terre di Offida Passerina Brut '23	🍷 2
○ Offida Pecorino Montemisio '20	🍷🍷🍷 2*
○ Offida Pecorino Montemisio '22	🍷🍷 2*
○ Offida Pecorino Montemisio '21	🍷🍷 2*

Cimarelli

via San Francesco, 1/a
60039 Staffolo [AN]
+39 3391328627
www.lucacimarelli.it

CELLAR SALES
PRE-BOOKED VISITS
ANNUAL PRODUCTION 50,000 bottles
HECTARES UNDER VINE 10.00

Luca Cimarelli and Tommaso Aquilanti's winery spans 10 hectares of vineyards, divided into two parcels: one near the cellar, planted with younger vines, and another in the Coste area, on the opposite hill, home to older vines. The winery uses no oak, not even for aging their young Rosso Piceno Grizio. Everything is done in stainless steel and fibreglass-lined concrete tanks. Technical direction has been in the hands of Giuseppe Morelli for several years now. A great team effort has led the winery to new heights in its 65-year history. A prime example is the excellent Selezione Cimarelli '22, a Riserva with an aromatic profile firmly anchored to Jesi's grapes: almond, ripe apple, linden flowers with hints of anise and aromatic herbs. The palate is fragrant, flavorful, vibrant, with a rising finish. The Cimarelli '23, a vintage Verdicchio, is also well-crafted, with its citrus notes clearly evident both on the nose and on a flavorful palate. The Due Stille '21 is elegant and brackish.

○ Castelli di Jesi Verdicchio Cl. Selezione Cimarelli Ris. '22	▼▼▼ 5
○ Verdicchio dei Castelli di Jesi Cl. Sup. Due Stille '21	▼▼ 5
⊙ Rosato '23	▼▼ 2*
○ Verdicchio dei Castelli di Jesi Cl. Sup. Cimarelli '23	▼▼ 2*
● Rosso Piceno Grizio '23	▼ 3
○ Verdicchio dei Castelli di Jesi Cl. Sup. Fra' Moriale '22	▼ 3
○ Castelli di Jesi Verdicchio Cl. Selezione Cimarelli Ris. '20	▽▽ 4
○ Verdicchio dei Castelli di Jesi Cl. Sup. Cimarelli '22	▽▽ 2*
○ Verdicchio dei Castelli di Jesi Cl. Sup. Fra' Moriale '21	▽▽ 3

Tenuta Cocci Grifoni

loc. San Savino
c.da Messieri, 12
63038 Ripatransone [AP]
+39 073590143
www.tenutacoccigrifoni.it

CELLAR SALES
PRE-BOOKED VISITS
RESTAURANT SERVICE
ANNUAL PRODUCTION 550,000 bottles
HECTARES UNDER VINE 50.00
SUSTAINABLE WINERY

Cocci Grifoni has evolved into an integrated system of wine production and tourism. The agricultural spirit passed down by the late Guido has blended with the modern ideas of his granddaughters, Marta and Camilla Capriotti. Marta oversees the magnificent resort and hospitality services, while Camilla works in the winery with the support of consulting winemaker Nicola Biasi. Overseeing everything are their mother Marilena and the experienced Valeria Cesari. The winery's reds also perform well: Il Grifone '20 (a monovarietal montepulciano) and the San Basso '21 (more authentic in character, with a strong sense of place) prove vibrant, vivid, and multifaceted. The two Pecorinos, a house specialty, remain strong: the Colle Vecchio '23 has a citrusy timbre, nice sapidity, and excellent prospects. The Tarà '23 is more approachable, flavorful, and fleshy. The Notturna '23 ranks among the best annata Passerinas in the region: elegant and harmonious, redolent of lemon and spices. The San Basso '23 is simpler and more immediately expressive.

● Offida Rosso Il Grifone '20	▼▼ 4
● Rosso Piceno Sup. San Basso '21	▼▼ 3*
○ Falerio Pecorino Tarà '23	▼▼ 3
○ Offida Passerina Notturna '23	▼▼ 3
○ Offida Pecorino Colle Vecchio '23	▼▼ 3
○ San Basso Passerina '23	▼ 3
○ Offida Pecorino Guido Cocci Grifoni '14	▽▽▽ 6
○ Offida Pecorino Guido Cocci Grifoni '13	▽▽▽ 4
○ Falerio Pecorino Tarà '22	▽▽ 3
○ Falerio Pecorino Tarà '21	▽▽ 2
○ Offida Passerina Notturna '22	▽▽ 3
○ Offida Pecorino Colle Vecchio '22	▽▽ 3
○ Offida Pecorino Guido Cocci Grifoni '20	▽▽ 6
● Offida Rosso Il Grifone '16	▽▽ 5
● Rosso Piceno Sup. San Basso '18	▽▽ 2
● Rosso Piceno Sup. V. Messieri '20	▽▽ 4

Col di Corte

via San Pietro, 19a
60036 Montecarotto [AN]
☎ +39 073189435
✉ www.coldicorte.it

★Collestefano

loc. Colle Stefano, 3
62022 Castelraimondo [MC]
☎ +39 0737640439
✉ www.collestefano.com

CELLAR SALES
PRE-BOOKED VISITS
ANNUAL PRODUCTION 45,000 bottles
HECTARES UNDER VINE 12.50
VITICULTURE METHOD Certified Organic
SUSTAINABLE WINERY

CELLAR SALES
PRE-BOOKED VISITS
ACCOMMODATION
ANNUAL PRODUCTION 165,000 bottles
HECTARES UNDER VINE 16.00
VITICULTURE METHOD Certified Organic

Col di Corte was founded in 2011 from the purchase of the Laurentina winery by three Roman partners. In a decade, Giacomo Rossi, with the help of winemaker Claudio Caldaroni, has propelled the producer to the forefront of the new wave of verdicchio producers. Their style is relaxed, inspired by biodynamic principles, with a respectful approach to varietal identity and slow aging processes aimed at finding the ideal expressive balance. The 2024 harvest will be managed by a new technical director, but the wines presented continue the established trajectory. The Verdicchio Riserva and the important Vigneto di Tobia were absent this year, but the brilliant Anno Uno '23 stands out: fresh, citrusy, and highly sapid, with that smoothness that leads to an unstoppable drinkability. Always keep another bottle chilled. A similar profile is found in the Lacestrale, a montepulciano sparkling wine that hasn't been disgorged.

A severe attack of downy mildew in the spring of 2023 made for an extremely challenging vintage, with widespread crop loss. Those committed to organic practices faced a nearly unmanageable crisis, but the experience and agronomic focus of Fabio Marchionni helped salvage what could be saved. Unfortunately, there will be far fewer bottles available to the many fans of the mountain style of Verdicchio Collestefano. The 2023 sports the usual, clear color conjuring up an aromatic blend of bergamot, rain-washed pebbles, white flowers, almond, and anise; the palate is well-defined, lacking some of the sapid depth of other versions but still offering excellent drinkability, which is a hallmark, especially in warmer vintages. We also appreciated the two Metodo Classico Vigna Le Pratas (also made with verdicchio): the 30 Mesi '20 is more brackish, mobile, and refined, while the 2021 proves delicate, citrusy, and remarkably fresh.

MARCHE

○ Verdicchio dei Castelli di Jesi Cl. Sup. Anno Uno '23	▼▼ 3*
○ Lancestrale	▼▼ 4
○ Verdicchio dei Castelli di Jesi Cl. Sup. Vign. di Tobia '21	▽▽▽ 4*
○ Castelli di Jesi Verdicchio Cl. Sant'Ansovino Ris. '16	▽▽ 5
● Esino Rosso '20	▽▽ 3
○ Sant'Ansovino '20	▽▽ 5
○ Verdicchio dei Castelli di Jesi Cl. Sup. Anno Uno '22	▽▽ 3*
○ Verdicchio dei Castelli di Jesi Cl. Sup. Anno Uno '21	▽▽ 3
○ Verdicchio dei Castelli di Jesi Cl. Sup. Vign. di Tobia '20	▽▽ 4

○ V. Le Prata Dosaggio Zero 30 Mesi '20	▼▼ 5
○ Verdicchio di Matelica Collestefano '23	▼▼ 3*
○ V. Le Prata Dosaggio Zero '21	▼▼ 4
○ Verdicchio di Matelica Collestefano '22	▽▽▽ 3*
○ Verdicchio di Matelica Collestefano '21	▽▽▽ 2*
○ Verdicchio di Matelica Collestefano '20	▽▽▽ 2*
○ Verdicchio di Matelica Collestefano '19	▽▽▽ 2*
○ Verdicchio di Matelica Collestefano '18	▽▽▽ 2*
○ Verdicchio di Matelica Collestefano '15	▽▽▽ 2*
○ Verdicchio di Matelica Collestefano '14	▽▽▽ 2*
○ Verdicchio di Matelica Collestefano '13	▽▽▽ 2*
○ Verdicchio di Matelica Collestefano '12	▽▽▽ 2*
○ Verdicchio di Matelica Collestefano '10	▽▽▽ 2*
○ Verdicchio di Matelica Collestefano '07	▽▽▽ 2*
○ Verdicchio di Matelica Collestefano '06	▽▽▽ 2*

Collevite

via Valle Cecchina, 9
63077 Monsampolo del Tronto [AP]
☎ +39 0735767050
⊕ www.collevite.com

CELLAR SALES
PRE-BOOKED VISITS
ANNUAL PRODUCTION 310,000 bottles
HECTARES UNDER VINE 170.00
VITICULTURE METHOD Certified Organic
SUSTAINABLE WINERY

Collevite is a consortium of 15 winemakers who joined forces to streamline production processes and agricultural practices. The vineyards are spread across multiple municipalities in the Piceno area, while vinification and aging of the whites take place in the large winery in Monsampolo del Tronto. The estate at Ripatransone, known as Villa Piatti, houses the barrel room dedicated to maturing the reds, two of which stood out out this year. Il Caimano '21 reveals enticing notes of red fruit and peach, clearly expressed on a full-bodied palate with well-controlled tannins. The more complex and layered Klausura '20 (montepulciano with 10% petit verdot) offers floral aromas, graphite, and cherries, with a palate of marked alcohol intensity, balanced by a mature tannic structure. Among the offerings, the tonic and brackish Trufo '23, a montepulciano, stands out. The Geko '23 is the most intriguing white: citrusy with good sapidity. The more straightforward and drinkable Armsante '23 completes the lineup.

● Offida Rosso Klausura Ripawine '20	♟♟ 5
● Rosso Piceno Sup. Il Caimano '21	♟♟ 3*
○ Falerio Pecorino Armsante '23	♟♟ 3
○ Offida Pecorino Geko Ripawine '23	♟♟ 5
● Trufo '23	♟♟ 2*
○ Falerio Pecorino Naturae '23	♟ 3
● Moromatto Ripawine '22	♟ 5
○ Offida Passerina Kreta Ripawine '23	♟ 4
● Rosso Piceno Carpino Nero '23	♟ 2
⊙ Ruflano '23	♟ 2
○ Salaria '23	♟ 2
○ Falerio Pecorino Armsante '21	♟♟ 3*
○ Offida Pecorino Villa Piatti '21	♟♟ 3*
○ Offida Pecorino Villa Piatti '20	♟♟ 2*
● Offida Rosso Klausura Ripawine '19	♟♟ 5
● Offida Rosso Klausura Ripawine '17	♟♟ 5

Colonnara

via Mandriole, 2
60034 Cupramontana [AN]
☎ +39 0731780273
⊕ www.colonnara.it

CELLAR SALES
PRE-BOOKED VISITS
ANNUAL PRODUCTION 700,000 bottles
HECTARES UNDER VINE 70.00

As of 2024, the Colonnara winery in Montecarotto is managed by the Boccafosca cooperative of Pianello di Ostra, which has taken over its lease. Little has changed in the management of the brands, a deep knowledge of verdicchio, or the sparkling wine techniques in which the producer has excelled for many years. The project is led by winemaker Giulio Piazzini, supported by the experience of Daniela Sorana, a prominent figure in the Marche wine scene. Our tastings confirm the quality of their sparkling wines. This year, alongside the already impressive Luigi Ghislieri Brut (non-vintage, identifiable by its gold label), the first vintage edition was released: the Luigi Ghislieri Dosaggio Zero '18 is balsamic, sapid, and energetic, yet maintains its composure—a fine debut. The other star, the Riserva Ubaldo Rosi Brut '17, also caught our attention, showcasing great aromatic elegance and a creamy palate. Among the still wines, the straightforward yet varietally faithful Cuprese '22 deserves notice.

○ Verdicchio dei Castelli di Jesi Brut M. Cl. Ubaldo Rosi '17	♟♟ 5
○ Verdicchio dei Castelli di Jesi Brut M. Cl. Luigi Ghislieri	♟♟ 5
○ Verdicchio dei Castelli di Jesi Cl. Sup. Cuprese '22	♟♟ 3
○ Verdicchio dei Castelli di Jesi Dosaggio Zero M.Cl. Luigi Ghislieri '18	♟♟ 5
○ Verdicchio dei Castelli di Jesi Brut Cuvée Tradition	♟ 3
○ Verdicchio dei Castelli di Jesi Cl. Lyricus '23	♟ 2
○ Verdicchio dei Castelli di Jesi M. Cl. Brut Ubaldo Rosi Ris. '06	♟♟♟ 5
○ Verdicchio dei Castelli di Jesi Brut M. Cl. Ubaldo Rosi '16	♟♟ 5

Il Conte Villa Prandone

c.da Colle Navicchio, 28
63033 Monteprandone [AP]
(+39 073562593
www.ilcontevini.it

CELLAR SALES
PRE-BOOKED VISITS
ANNUAL PRODUCTION 380,000 bottles
HECTARES UNDER VINE 50.00

Emmanuel de Angelis recognized from the start that international markets could be a significant asset. Over the years, he has built a portfolio that captures the generous climate of the slopes from Monteprandone down to the Tronto River valley, producing wines that are intense, polished, modern in style, and characterized by international appeal. In a rich lineup, the Lu Kont '21, a montepulciano, prevails, offering ripe red fruit and balsamic hints on the nose, which carry over to a fleshy, powerful, and persistent palate, though slightly lacking in nuance. A similar dynamic is found in the Marinus '22, with notes of black cherry and vanilla, and a coherent, enticing palate, with measured tannin extraction. A touch of over-ripeness is noticeable in the Conte Rosso '23, though it ultimately translates into pleasant drinkability. The Belva di Terra '23, a sauvignon in the New Zealand style, delights the palate with hints of tomato leaf and white peach. The Navicchio '23 is brackish and citrusy, while the Ceppo '23, made from passerina grapes, proves refreshing.

o Belva Di Terra '23	♟♟5
o Ceppo Passerina '23	♟♟3
● Lu Kont '21	♟♟6
o Offida Pecorino Navicchio '23	♟♟4
● Rosso Piceno Conte Rosso '23	♟♟3
● Rosso Piceno Sup. Marinus '22	♟♟5
● Donello '23	♟3
o Falerio Pecorino Aurato '23	♟3
● IX Prandone '21	♟8
o Offida Passerina Cavaceppo '23	♟3
● Rocciamara '22	♟4
◑ Rosé & Rose '23	♟3
● Zipolo '21	♟5
● Lu Kont '20	♟♟6
● Lu Kont '18	♟♟6
● Zipolo '20	♟♟5

Crespaia

loc. Prelato, 8
61032 Fano [PU]
(+39 0721862383
www.crespaia.it

CELLAR SALES
PRE-BOOKED VISITS
ANNUAL PRODUCTION 43,000 bottles
HECTARES UNDER VINE 10.00
VITICULTURE METHOD Certified Organic

Rossano Sgammini didn't start out as a winemaker, but in 2011, he invested in the beautiful estate of Prelato, where he planted 10 hectares, mostly dedicated to bianchello grapes. With the support of a skilled team, including agronomist Luca Severini and winemakers Aroldo Bellelli and Shayle Lambie-Shaw, he quickly distinguished himself with a range known for its elegant character, seamlessly blending aromatic clarity with a strong sense of place. The Bianchello Chiaraluce exemplifies the house style. It was one of the first to break away from the idea of a wine to be drunk within months of harvest and the first Bianchello to earn Tre Bicchieri (with its 2022 vintage). Elegant notes of anise, white fruits, and river stones lead to a forceful, refined progression with a persistent, delightful finish. The current-vintage Bianchello offers pleasant palate sensations. Though it's aromatically simpler, it exhibits the same production style. The winery's skill is also evident in a good, fruity, and delicious spumante, the Crespaia Brut.

o Bianchello del Metauro Sup. Chiaraluce '22	♟♟♟3*
o Bianchello del Metauro '23	♟♟2*
o Crespaia Brut '23	♟3
o Bianchello del Metauro '22	♟♟2*
o Bianchello del Metauro '18	♟♟2*
o Bianchello del Metauro '17	♟♟2*
o Bianchello del Metauro Chiaraluce '21	♟♟3*
o Bianchello del Metauro Sup. Chiaraluce '18	♟♟3
o Bianchello del Metauro Sup. Chiaraluce '17	♟♟3
o Bianchello del Metauro Sup. Chiaraluce '16	♟♟3*
● Colli Pesaresi Sangiovese Nerognolo '17	♟♟3
● Colli Pesaresi Sangiovese Nerognolo '16	♟♟3

Tenuta De Angelis

via San Francesco, 10
63082 Castel di Lama [AP]
☎ +39 073687429
✇ www.tenutadeangelis.it

CELLAR SALES
PRE-BOOKED VISITS
ANNUAL PRODUCTION 550,000 bottles
HECTARES UNDER VINE 50.00
VITICULTURE METHOD Certified Organic

Alighiero, the son of Elide De Angelis and
Quinto Fausti—prominent figures in Piceno
viticulture—now leads one of the most
important wineries in the region. With the help
of winemaker Roberto Potentini and agronomist
Nicola Bellone, he manages 50 hectares of
vineyards in prime growing areas between
Castel di Lama and Offida, including the
spectacular vineyard at the foot of Santa Maria
della Rocca. The result is a range that's
consistently high in quality, and excellent value
for the money. Among the reds, the Anghelos '21
comes highly recommended, with its aromas of
black cherry, plum, a hint of spice, and light
toasty notes. The palate is lively, with a fine,
brackish finish. The Rosso Piceno Superiore Oro
'21, is even fruitier, with a sustained palate.
Among the whites, the Pecorino Campo di
Marte '23 impresses with its flavorful, citrusy
notes, as does its unfiltered version, the Quiete
'23, which is juicy and substantial. The Oro
Bianco '21 is somewhat evolved on the nose but
remains rich on the palate.

● Offida Rosso Anghelos '21	♟♟ 4
○ Offida Pecorino Campo di Marte '23	♟♟ 2*
○ Offida Pecorino Quiete '23	♟♟ 3
● Rosso Piceno Sup. Oro '21	♟♟ 4
○ Offida Pecorino Oro Bianco '21	♟ 4
● Anghelos '01	♟♟♟ 4
● Anghelos '99	♟♟♟ 4*
● Rosso Piceno Sup. Oro '15	♟♟♟ 3*
○ Offida Pecorino Campo di Marte '21	♟♟ 2*
○ Offida Pecorino Oro Bianco '20	♟♟ 4
○ Offida Pecorino Quiete '22	♟♟ 3*
○ Offida Pecorino Quiete '21	♟♟ 3
● Offida Rosso Anghelos '20	♟♟ 4
● Offida Rosso Anghelos '19	♟♟ 4
● Rosso Piceno Sup. Campo di Marte '21	♟♟ 2*
● Rosso Piceno Sup. Oro '20	♟♟ 3

Fattoria Dezi

c.da Fontemaggio, 14
63839 Servigliano [FM]
☎ +39 0734710090
✇ www.fattoriadezi.com

CELLAR SALES
PRE-BOOKED VISITS
ANNUAL PRODUCTION 45,000 bottles
HECTARES UNDER VINE 15.00

Founded in 1975 by brothers Romolo and Remo,
Dezi is today managed by brothers Davide and
Stefano (Romolo's sons), with Davide overseeing
the vineyards and Stefano managing the cellar.
The wine dedicated to the founders (100%
grenache) is as full-bodied and extractive as ever,
with an almost impenetrable color and a nose of
dark fruit and charred wood, echoed on a
close-knit, powerful, and polished palate,
supported by notable alcohol. Similar
characteristics are found in the fleshy and sapid
Regina del Bosco '21, made from unblended
montepulciano, and its 48-month-aged version
from 2017, which is slightly evolved and shows
oaky notes. The Solo '21 (sangiovese) has less
concentration but offers good layering, with a
supple tannic palate and a racy finish. The
well-structured P. '22, a pecorino, features a solid
acidic backbone, fruity tones, and a savory,
smooth, and enduring palate.

○ Falerio Pecorino P. '22	♟♟ 4
● Regina del Bosco '21	♟♟ 6
● Romolo & Remo '21	♟♟ 7
● Solo '21	♟♟ 6
● Regina del Bosco 48 Mesi '17	♟ 8
● Regina del Bosco '06	♟♟♟ 6
● Regina del Bosco '05	♟♟♟ 6
● Regina del Bosco '03	♟♟♟ 6
● Solo Sangiovese '05	♟♟♟ 6
● Solo Sangiovese '01	♟♟♟ 5
● Solo Sangiovese '00	♟♟♟ 6
○ Falerio Pecorino P. '21	♟♟ 4
○ Falerio Pecorino P. '20	♟♟ 4
○ Falerio Pecorino P. '19	♟♟ 3*
● Regina del Bosco '18	♟♟ 6
○ Solagne '20	♟♟ 4

Emanuele Dianetti

c.da Vallerosa, 25
63063 Carassai [AP]
☎ +39 3383928439
✉ www.dianettivini.it

CELLAR SALES
PRE-BOOKED VISITS
ANNUAL PRODUCTION 20,000 bottles
HECTARES UNDER VINE 5.00

Emanuele Dianetti has quickly earned a reputation as a meticulous winemaker with a distinctive style that highlights the cool climate of the Val Menocchia. His constant pursuit of improvement drives him to experiment with new solutions and carefully consider factors such as harvest timing, grape blends, and the size and toasting of oak barrels. This dedication is reflected in a brilliant, contemporary range of wines. Pecorino Vignagiulia, which has been given an extra year of aging, is missing from their lineup. It's replaced by the brilliant Luciano Campo Vallerosa '21, an elegant wine with citrus peel aromas and delicate smoky nuances intertwined with a vibrant, sustained, and long-lasting palate. Emanuele also introduced a new red: the Vignagiulia '19 (montepulciano with 10% grenache) a fleshy drink, with intense fruit, spice notes, and toasted sensations, balanced within an impressive aromatic equilibrium and firm tannic structure.

● Vignagiulia Rosso '19	♟♟♟ 6
○ Offida Pecorino Luciano Campo Vallerosa '21	♟♟ 8
● Piceno '22	♟♟ 4
○ Offida Pecorino Vignagiulia '20	♟♟♟ 3*
○ Offida Pecorino Vignagiulia '19	♟♟♟ 3*
● Offida Rosso Vignagiulia '18	♟♟♟ 6
● Offida Rosso Vignagiulia '16	♟♟♟ 5
● Offida Rosso Vignagiulia '14	♟♟♟ 5
● Offida Rosso Vignagiulia '13	♟♟♟ 5
● Michelangelo '18	♟♟ 8
● Michelangelo '17	♟♟ 8
● Michelangelo '16	♟♟ 8
○ Offida Pecorino Luciano Campo Vallerosa '20	♟♟ 8
○ Offida Pecorino Luciano Campo Vallerosa '19	♟♟ 8

Edoardo Dottori

via Morella, 2a
60034 Cupramontana [AN]
☎ +39 3342853962
✉ www.aziendadottori.it

ANNUAL PRODUCTION 10,000 bottles
HECTARES UNDER VINE 8.00
VITICULTURE METHOD Certified Organic
SUSTAINABLE WINERY

The new Cupramontana winery began operations with the 2024 harvest. Before that, Edoardo was based at Riccardo Baldi's Staffa estate. Despite this, he has made a name for himself as one of the most talented winemakers of the latest generation, thanks to his clear vision, strict adherence to organic practices, and solid technical expertise. The Nardì '23 hails from a small vineyard in Contrada San Michele and is deliberately vinified in a traditional style, with small amounts of trebbiano and malvasia for a rustic touch, enhancing its gastronomic appeal. The other two wines draw on grapes from San Paolo di Jesi, an area known as Acquasalata. The lower part of the vineyard produces the Colle Bianco '23: aromas of citrus and grain give way to a palate full of fiber and briny energy. The upper part, rich in marine fossils, gives rise to the powerful Kochlos Riserva '22: lemon, anise, almond, and captivating mineral echoes emerge on a complex, penetrating palate with sublime drinkability and unstoppable force.

○ Castelli di Jesi Verdicchio Cl. Kochlos Ris. '22	♟♟♟ 5
○ Verdicchio dei Castelli di Jesi Cl. Nardì '23	♟♟ 4
○ Verdicchio dei Castelli di Jesi Cl. Sup. Colle Bianco '23	♟♟ 4
○ Castelli di Jesi Verdicchio Cl. Kochlos Ris. '21	♟♟ 4
○ Castelli di Jesi Verdicchio Cl. Kochlos Ris. '20	♟♟ 4
○ Verdicchio dei Castelli di Jesi Cl. Nardì '22	♟♟ 3
○ Verdicchio dei Castelli di Jesi Cl. Sup. Colle Bianco '22	♟♟ 4
○ Verdicchio dei Castelli di Jesi Cl. Sup. Colle Bianco '21	♟♟ 3

★Andrea Felici

c.da Sant'Isidoro, 28
62021 Apiro [MC]
☎ +39 0733611431
⊕ www.andreafelici.it

CELLAR SALES
PRE-BOOKED VISITS
ANNUAL PRODUCTION 106,000 bottles
HECTARES UNDER VINE 12.00
VITICULTURE METHOD Certified Organic

The severe outbreak of downy mildew that affected much of Le Marche hit those like Leo Felici, who work in cooler areas and avoid synthetic chemicals, especially hard. However, skilled hands like his managed to turn adversity into opportunity and the producer defended his crops as best he could. Leo is known as a champion of the more linear, "Appenine" style of the Jesi appellation, thanks to vineyards that benefit from the cool microclimate of the nearby Monte San Vicino. In the cellar, you'll find no trace of wood—only stainless steel and concrete. The famous Riserva Vigna il Cantico della Figura, whose 2021 vintage was given additional time to age (to highlight its longevity), was missing from the lineup. All attention shifted, therefore, to an excellent version of the Andrea Felici, a verdicchio that offers its usual bouquet of citrus, anise, and river stones, with a flowing, vibrant palate.

○ Verdicchio dei Castelli di Jesi Cl. Sup. Andrea Felici '23	♟♟ 4
○ Castelli di Jesi Verdicchio Cl. V. Il Cantico della Figura Ris. '20	♟♟♟ 8
○ Castelli di Jesi Verdicchio Cl. V. Il Cantico della Figura Ris. '19	♟♟♟ 8
○ Castelli di Jesi Verdicchio Cl. V. Il Cantico della Figura Ris. '18	♟♟♟ 8
○ Castelli di Jesi Verdicchio Cl. V. Il Cantico della Figura Ris. '17	♟♟♟ 6
○ Castelli di Jesi Verdicchio Cl. V. Il Cantico della Figura Ris. '16	♟♟♟ 6
○ Castelli di Jesi Verdicchio Cl. V. Il Cantico della Figura Ris. '15	♟♟♟ 6
○ Castelli di Jesi Verdicchio Cl. V. Il Cantico della Figura Ris. '13	♟♟♟ 6

Filodivino

via Serra, 46
60030 San Marcello [AN]
☎ +39 0731026139
⊕ www.filodivino.it

CELLAR SALES
PRE-BOOKED VISITS
ACCOMMODATION AND RESTAURANT SERVICE
ANNUAL PRODUCTION 70,000 bottles
HECTARES UNDER VINE 19.50
VITICULTURE METHOD Certified Organic
SUSTAINABLE WINERY

Stainless steel, terracotta, oak barrels of various sizes, and egg-shaped, concrete vats: nothing is missing from Alberto Gandolfi's winery. The efficiency of the equipment made available to expert consultant Luca D'Attoma blends with the space's architectural beauty, furnishings, and a magnificent resort set among vineyards of verdicchio and lacrima grapes. In addition to these two cornerstones, a few international grapes are also cultivated. The spotlight is on two versions of Lacrima: the Soara '22 delivers its best performance yet, with floral and spicy notes, a sapid, progressive palate, and a rising finish. The Diana '22 features precise rose notes, softened by a hint of nutmeg, with a well-toned and dynamic palate. The Coro '21 (syrah, cabernet franc, and merlot) confirms the winery's expertise with international varietals. Among their verdicchio wines, the Matto '22 impresses with its mature, mouthfilling style, while the orange wine Coccio '22, fermented in terracotta amphorae, proves original and distinctive.

● Lacrima di Morro d'Alba Sup. Soara '22	♟♟ 4
○ Coccio '22	♟♟ 6
● Coro '21	♟♟ 4
● Lacrima di Morro d'Alba Diana '22	♟♟ 3
○ Verdicchio dei Castelli di Jesi Cl. Sup. Matto '22	♟♟ 3
⊚ Albae '23	♟ 3
○ Perturbato '23	♟ 3
○ Verdicchio dei Castelli di Jesi Cl. Serra 46 '23	♟ 3
⊚ Albae '22	♟♟ 3
○ Castelli di Jesi Verdicchio Cl. Dino Ris. '20	♟♟ 5
○ Coccio '21	♟♟ 5
● Coro '20	♟♟ 4
○ Verdicchio dei Castelli di Jesi Cl. Serra46 '21	♟♟ 2*
○ Verdicchio dei Castelli di Jesi Cl. Sup. Matto '21	♟♟ 3

Fiorano

c.da Fiorano, 19
63067 Cossignano [AP]
☎ +39 073598247
✉ www.agrifiorano.it

CELLAR SALES
PRE-BOOKED VISITS
ACCOMMODATION
ANNUAL PRODUCTION 50,000 bottles
HECTARES UNDER VINE 9.00
VITICULTURE METHOD Certified Organic
SUSTAINABLE WINERY

Paolo Beretta and Paola Massi, the couple behind
I Paoli, have practiced organic farming for many
years, infusing every aspect of their winery and
charming agritourism venture with this
philosophy. Every step they take is rooted in the
ethic of preserving the land from synthetic
chemicals, a commitment that demands both
significant physical effort and financial resources.
However, the results speak for themselves: their
wines exhibit vitality, energy, crystalline style, and
refined pleasure, even in their younger
expressions. Dominating, as usual, is the firm and
energetic Donna Orgilla '23, a pecorino aged in
stainless steel, with a dynamic, supple profile
marked by citrusy and brackish nuances. The
Giulia Erminia '22 (pecorino) reveals more
pronounced oak maturation than in past
vintages, though delivers a vibrant palate. The
Terre di Giobbe '20 offers rich fruit and flesh,
supported by a close-knit tannic structure. The
Gallo Otto '19, a blend of syrah and
montepulciano vinified in amphora, has a
smooth, powerful, and warm palate, making it
more muscular.

○ Offida Pecorino Donna Orgilla '23	♈♈ 4
● Gallo Otto '19	♈♈ 6
○ Giulia Erminia '22	♈♈ 5
● I Paoli Sangiovese '23	♈♈ 3
● Piceno Sup. Terre di Giobbe '20	♈♈ 4
⊙ Kami '23	♈ 3
○ Offida Pecorino Donna Orgilla '14	♈♈♈ 3*
○ Giulia Erminia '21	♈♈ 5
○ Giuly '22	♈♈ 5
● I Paoli '22	♈♈ 3
⊙ Kami '22	♈♈ 3
○ Offida Pecorino Donna Orgilla '22	♈♈ 3*
○ Offida Pecorino Donna Orgilla '21	♈♈ 3*
○ Offida Pecorino Giulia Erminia '20	♈♈ 5
● Rosso Piceno Sup. Terre di Giobbe '19	♈♈ 3*
● Ser Balduzio '18	♈♈ 5

Fontezoppa

c.da San Domenico, 38
62012 Civitanova Marche [MC]
☎ +39 0733790504
✉ www.cantinefontezoppa.com

CELLAR SALES
PRE-BOOKED VISITS
ACCOMMODATION AND RESTAURANT SERVICE
ANNUAL PRODUCTION 380,000 bottles
HECTARES UNDER VINE 47.00
VITICULTURE METHOD Certified Organic

The Luzi family operates their winery on two
fronts. There are their holdings in the
Serrapetrona foothills in Macerata, where
vernaccia and pinot nero are cultivated. Then
there are their vineyards in the lower hills
behind Civitanova Marche, many of which
surround the winery and the adjacent inn (which
shares the same name). These plots are
dedicated primarily to maceratino and a wide
array of other varietals. Sardinian winemaker
Andrea Pala leads the technical team. As is often
the case, the Ribona appellation delivers the best
results. The Altabella '23 is the younger version,
with green almond notes, light herbaceous hints,
and a palate of good consistency, ending slightly
astringent. The Asola '21, aged for 18 months in
oak, proves complex and multifaceted, featuring
smoky sensations, lemon cream, and aromatic
herbs. The Iodio '20 spends six months on the
skins in stainless steel before aging a year in
terracotta, offering nutty aromas, a full palate,
and a brackish, tannic finish.

○ Colli Maceratesi Ribona Altabella '23	♈♈ 5
○ Colli Maceratesi Ribona Asola '20	♈♈ 8
○ Iodio '20	♈♈ 8
● Vernaccia di Serrapetrona Secco Selezione Fabrini	♈♈ 4
○ Colli Maceratesi Ribona Dosaggio Zero M. Cl.	♈ 6
● Colli Maceratesi Rosso Vardò Ris. '21	♈ 5
○ Falerio Pecorino Joco '23	♈ 4
● Serrapetrona Morò '21	♈ 8
● Serrapetrona Pepato '22	♈ 4
● Vernaccia di Serrapetrona Dolce Selezione Fabrini	♈ 4
○ Colli Maceratesi Ribona Altabella '22	♈♈ 5
○ Colli Maceratesi Ribona Asola '19	♈♈ 8
● Serrapetrona Morò '20	♈♈ 8

★★Gioacchino Garofoli

via Carlo Marx, 123
60022 Castelfidardo [AN]
📞 +39 0717820162
🌐 www.garofolivini.it

CELLAR SALES
PRE-BOOKED VISITS
ANNUAL PRODUCTION 1,300,000 bottles
HECTARES UNDER VINE 50.00

With 124 years of history and 5 generations at the helm, the Garofoli family winery is today managed under the leadership of Gianluca and Caterina Garofoli, children of Gianfranco, who still co-owns the winery with his brother Carlo, the winemaker. Carlo crafts a broad range that caters to both the export market and distribution in more developed markets, focusing primarily on verdicchio and montepulciano. Their line of Metodo Classicos is well-developed. The Brut Riserva '20 features lemon peel aromas and abundant, fine bubbles, while the Pas Dosé '19 showcases toasted notes and an elegant, balsamic palate. The Brut Rosé '21 is delicately sapid and well-crafted. Among the still wines, the fruity and fleshy Piancarda '21 proves decidedly enjoyable, as does the pleasantly drinkable Kòmaros '23, a rosé made from conero grapes. Less convincing is the new rosé K-Volve '22 (30% matured in barriques). The Podium '21 features fine notes of camphor and toasted almond on a powerful, slightly alcohol-dominated palate.

⊚ Brut Rosé M. Cl. '21	▼▼	5
⊚ K-Volve '22	▼▼	4
⊚ Kòmaros '23	▼▼	3
● Rosso Conero Piancarda '21	▼▼	3
○ Verdicchio dei Castelli di Jesi Brut M. Cl. Ris. '20	▼▼	5
○ Verdicchio dei Castelli di Jesi Cl. Sup. Podium '21	▼▼	5
○ Verdicchio dei Castelli di Jesi Cl. Sup. Serra Fiorese '21	▼▼	5
○ Verdicchio dei Castelli di Jesi Pas Dosé M. Cl. '19	▼▼	6
● Conero Grosso Agontano Ris. '20	▼	5
○ Verdicchio dei Castelli di Jesi Cl. Sup. Podium '19	♈♈♈	4*
○ Verdicchio dei Castelli di Jesi Cl. Sup. Podium '16	♈♈♈	4*

Marco Gatti

via Lagua e San Martino, 2
60043 Cerreto d'Esi [AN]
📞 +39 0732677012
🌐 www.cantinagattimarco.it

CELLAR SALES
PRE-BOOKED VISITS
ANNUAL PRODUCTION 30,000 bottles
HECTARES UNDER VINE 7.50

If you're seeking white wines produced with a genuine artisan spirit, you're in the right place. Marco Gatti is an accomplished agronomist specializing in horticulture. His expertise allows him to personally manage the various plots located within the small quadrant of the appellation in Ancona. At the same time, he also serves as the winemaker, relying solely on his own skills without external consultants. He favors a style that delivers clean aromas and a certain richness of flavor, with grape ripening playing a fundamental role. Notes of candied citron blend with gunpowder, anise, and yellow fruit—it's clear that the Millo Riserva '21 was made from overripe grapes. Its intensely flavorful palate, with a touch of sweetness at the core, confirms the theory, while sapidity and bright acidity provide contrast and a long finish. A wine of alluring intensity. The Villa Marilla '23 has clearer aromas of almond, anise, and flowers, though it remains rich and persistent on the finish.

○ Verdicchio di Matelica Millo Ris. '21	▼▼	5
○ Verdicchio di Matelica Villa Marilla '23	▼▼	3
○ Verdicchio di Matelica Villa Marilla '19	♈♈♈	2*
○ Verdicchio di Matelica Casale Venza '21	♈♈	2*
○ Verdicchio di Matelica Casale Venza '19	♈♈	2*
○ Verdicchio di Matelica Casale Venza '16	♈♈	2*
○ Verdicchio di Matelica Casale Venza '15	♈♈	2*
○ Verdicchio di Matelica Millo Ris. '20	♈♈	5
○ Verdicchio di Matelica Millo Ris. '19	♈♈	5
○ Verdicchio di Matelica Millo Ris. '16	♈♈	3*
○ Verdicchio di Matelica Villa Marilla '22	♈♈	3
○ Verdicchio di Matelica Villa Marilla '21	♈♈	3*
○ Verdicchio di Matelica Villa Marilla '18	♈♈	2*
○ Verdicchio di Matelica Villa Marilla '17	♈♈	2*
○ Verdicchio di Matelica Villa Marilla '16	♈♈	2*
○ Verdicchio di Matelica Villa Marilla '15	♈♈	2*

Luigi Giusti

loc. Montignano
s.da del Castellaro, 97
60019 Senigallia [AN]
(») +39 071918031
⊚ www.cantinaluigigiusti.it

CELLAR SALES
PRE-BOOKED VISITS
ANNUAL PRODUCTION 40,000 bottles
HECTARES UNDER VINE 13.50

After a few years of absence, Piergiovanni Giusti's winery is back in the guide. Known for crafting exceptional Lacrima in the early aughts, today, the producer continues to focus on the morro d'alba grape, cultivated in vineyards on the foothills overlooking Senigallia and the Adriatic sea. The range, which is divided into various types, is produced with the support of consulting winemaker David Soverchia. The best choice is undoubtedly the Rubbjano '20: a spicy and floral aromatic profile gives way to a delicate, complex palate, expansive in its development, with a poised, sapid finish. The Lacrima d'annata offers vegetal inflections intertwined with sensations of black fruits and dried rose, leading to a serious, direct palate that echoes its aromatic profile. The Vincè, a sparkling rosé, proves carefree with its delicate raspberry and almond nuances and light effervescence. The Bolla Rosa is sweeter and more playful. Le Rose di Settembre '23 is slim yet graceful.

Podere L'Infinito

c.da San Martino, 1a
60039 Staffolo [AN]
(») +39 3391068724
⊚ www.poderelinfinito.it

CELLAR SALES
PRE-BOOKED VISITS
ANNUAL PRODUCTION 31,500 bottles
HECTARES UNDER VINE 9.50
VITICULTURE METHOD Certified Organic

The yellow building in the southeast quadrant of Staffolo, where the landscape slopes towards the Musone River valley, doesn't go unnoticed. The lower floor houses the winery of Marco Simonetti and Gianni Ceci, while the upper floor is reserved for receiving guests. Marco personally tends to the vineyards, which are situated at about 400 meters elevation, following the advice of agronomist Luca Severini. The grapes are then entrusted to the expertise of consultant Pierluigi Lorenzetti, who aims to achieve a clean, smooth style balanced by substantial depth. The Eclissi di Luglio '23 impresses with its citrusy, fresh, and juicy profile, finishing racy and brackish. The Ca' di Cerere '23 is simpler but performs well, opting for notes of anise, lemon, and a slight minty undertone; its palate is a bit simple but enjoyable for its smooth, laid-back style. The Marte in Assalto '21, a monovarietal montepulciano, boasts aromas of flowers and ripe cherries, with a fleshy, energetic palate and plenty of substance.

● Lacrima di Morro d'Alba Sup. Rubbjano '20	♟♟ 5
● Lacrima di Morro d'Alba '23	♟♟ 3
⊙ Le Rose di Settembre '23	♟♟ 2*
⊙ Bolla Rosa Brut	♟ 3
● Vincè Frizzante	♟ 3
⊙ Anima Rosa '17	♟♟ 3
● L'Intruso '11	♟♟ 7
● Lacrima di Morro d'Alba '17	♟♟ 3
● Lacrima di Morro d'Alba '11	♟♟ 2*
● Lacrima di Morro d'Alba Sup. Luigino '09	♟♟ 4

○ Verdicchio dei Castelli di Jesi Cl. Sup. Eclissi di Luglio '23	♟♟ 3*
● Marte in Assalto '21	♟♟ 4
○ Verdicchio dei Castelli di Jesi Cl. Cà di Cerere '23	♟♟ 2*
● Cavalier Spron d'Oro '23	♟ 2
● Marte in Assalto '20	♟♟ 4
● Marte in Assalto '19	♟♟ 4
○ Verdicchio dei Castelli di Jesi Cl. Sup. Cor de Leone '20	♟♟ 4
○ Verdicchio dei Castelli di Jesi Cl. Sup. Eclissi di Luglio '22	♟♟ 3
○ Verdicchio dei Castelli di Jesi Cl. Sup. Eclissi di Luglio '21	♟♟ 3
○ Verdicchio dei Castelli di Jesi Cl. Sup. Eclissi di Luglio '20	♟♟ 2*

Roberto Lucarelli

loc. Ripalta
via Piana, 20
61030 Cartoceto [PU]
📞 +39 0721893019
✉ www.roberto-lucarelli.com

CELLAR SALES
PRE-BOOKED VISITS
ANNUAL PRODUCTION 250,000 bottles
HECTARES UNDER VINE 46.00
VITICULTURE METHOD Certified Organic

Roberto Lucarelli divides his time between vineyards next to the winery, where he cultivates both traditional and international varietals, and the rows dedicated to pinot nero in the Pesaro area. The grape gives rise to the Focara Pinot Nero '21, a wine redolent of blueberry, leather, and smoky, woodland accents. The juicy, elegant palate is free-flowing despite some tannic interweaving, with subtle tertiaries on the finish. The Blanc de Noir '22 pours a coppery hue, revealing light fruity notes, and a sweet, fruity palate, lacking suppleness. The opposite is true for the Giulio '37 '19, a sparkler made from noir and 30% chardonnay, with a saline bite and raspberry undertones. Returning to more traditional styles, their Bianchellos don't disappoint: the Rocho '22 is subtle, elegant on the nose, with notes of anise and white fruits; the palate is consistent, delicate, yet racy and deep. The deliberately more carefree and vegetal La Ripe '23 is also pleasant. La Ripe Sangiovese '22 delights with its precise hints of sour cherry.

○ Bianchello del Metauro Sup. Rocho '22	♟♟ 3*
○ Bianchello del Metauro La Ripe '23	♟♟ 2*
● Colli Pesaresi Focara Pinot Nero '21	♟♟ 4
○ Giulio 37 Brut Nature M. Cl. '19	♟♟ 6
○ Colli Pesaresi Focara Pinot Nero Blanc de Noir '22	♟ 3
● Colli Pesaresi Sangiovese La Ripe '22	♟ 3
○ Bianchello del Metauro Sup. Rocho '21	♟♟ 3
○ Bianchello del Metauro Sup. Rocho '20	♟♟ 3
○ Bianchello del Metauro Sup. Rocho '19	♟♟ 2*
● Colli Pesaresi Focara Pinot Nero '19	♟♟ 4
○ Colli Pesaresi Focara Pinot Nero Blanc de Noir '20	♟♟ 3
● Colli Pesaresi Sangiovese Goccione '19	♟♟ 4
● Colli Pesaresi Sangiovese Insieme Ris. '18	♟♟ 5
● Colli Pesaresi Sangiovese RL Ris. '19	♟♟ 6

Mario Lucchetti

via Santa Maria del Fiore, 17
60030 Morro d'Alba [AN]
📞 +39 073163314
✉ www.mariolucchetti.it

CELLAR SALES
PRE-BOOKED VISITS
ANNUAL PRODUCTION 180,000 bottles
HECTARES UNDER VINE 30.00
VITICULTURE METHOD Certified Organic

Mario Lucchetti is a prominent name in the world of Lacrima di Morro d'Alba. A meticulous vintner, he began his work in 1991 without much fanfare but with plenty of dedication to both the vineyard and the winery. Today, he's passed the torch to his son Paolo, who's supported by consultants Pierluigi Donna in the vineyards and Alberto Mazzoni in the winery. And two convincing Lacrimas were presented: the more compact, fruity, and spicy Guardengo '22, aged for a year in concrete, contrasts with the stainless steel-aged Fiore '23, which focuses more on floral and fruity characteristics, with a sinuous, sapid palate, well-controlled in its final astringent grip. A new addition this year is the Syria, a zero dosage Metodo Classico that faithfully expresses verdicchio's almond and citrus notes, which reappear on a well-modulated, fragrant, though not overly complex, palate. The Birbacciò '23 and Special '22, both sparkling rosés made from lacrima grapes, offer fragrance and free-flowing drinkability, with the latter remaining undisgorged.

● Lacrima di Morro d'Alba Fiore '23	♟♟ 2*
● Lacrima di Morro d'Alba Sup. Guardengo '22	♟♟ 3
○ Syria Dosaggio Zero M. Cl. '20	♟♟ 6
○ Verdicchio dei Castelli di Jesi Cl. Birbacciò '23	♟♟ 2*
⊙ Rosato Special Frizzante '22	♟ 2
● Lacrima di Morro d'Alba Fiore '21	♟♟ 2*
● Lacrima di Morro d'Alba Sup. Guardengo '20	♟♟ 3*
● Lacrima di Morro d'Alba Sup. Mariasole '20	♟♟ 6
○ Verdicchio dei Castelli di Jesi Cl. Sup. V. Vittoria '20	♟♟ 3
○ Verdicchio dei Castelli di Jesi Cl. Sup. Vittoria '21	♟♟ 3

Madonnabruna

c.da Camera, 100
63900 Fermo
+39 3273617577
www.madonnabruna.it

CELLAR SALES
PRE-BOOKED VISITS
ACCOMMODATION
ANNUAL PRODUCTION 70,000 bottles
HECTARES UNDER VINE 14.50
VITICULTURE METHOD Certified Organic
SUSTAINABLE WINERY

Paolo Petracci founded his winery in 2002 in the inland area of Fermo, in a sunlit, gently sloping valley that benefits from the thermal effect of the Adriatic Sea, visible at the horizon of the hill where the agritourism and winery are located. Today, his work is shared with his son Carlo, a graduate in oenology. For several years now, Madonna Bruna has been working with consultant Aroldo Bellelli, and in the last three vintages, their Pecorino Maree has been among the best whites in the region. Aged in stainless steel, it offers precise notes of lemon, peach, and echoes of wild herbs and anise. The palate is fruity, flavorful, irresistibly drinkable, with a long finish. The Rivafiorita '23, made from passerina grapes, follows a similar track but with less intensity and greater softness on the palate. Among the reds, the Cugnolo '21 stands out for its fruity integrity and polished palate, while the more intense and dark Portese '21, a blend of montepulciano and Bordeaux varietals, delivers power and depth.

○ Falerio Pecorino Maree '23	▼▼ 2*
○ Rivafiorita '23	▼▼ 2*
● Rosso Piceno Cugnolo '21	▼▼ 2*
● Portese '21	▼ 4
○ Falerio Pecorino Maree '22	▽▽▽ 2*
○ Falerio Pecorino Maree '21	▽▽ 2*
○ Falerio Pecorino Maree '18	▽▽ 3
● Moresco '16	▽▽ 5
● Moresco '15	▽▽ 5
○ Rivafiorita '21	▽▽ 2*
● Rosso Piceno Cugnolo '20	▽▽ 2*

Mancini

fraz. Moie
via Pianello, 5
60030 Maiolati Spontini [AN]
+39 0731702975
www.manciniwines.it

CELLAR SALES
PRE-BOOKED VISITS
ANNUAL PRODUCTION 120,000 bottles
HECTARES UNDER VINE 20.00

Emanuela, Massimo, and Sergio Mancini continue the work of their father Benito with meticulous care, shunning media attention. They cultivate about 20 hectares of mixed clay and sand soils between Moie di Maiolati Spontini and Castelbellino. In the winery, they're guided by the experienced Sergio Paolucci, who oversees a classically-styled range that varies according to the approach to maturation. Their Verdicchio Riserva '20 is excellent. It pours a bright, greenish hue, releasing precise, intense notes of anise, almond, and thyme. The palate is refined, with controlled, consistent energy that guides a sense-stimulating finish. The Santa Lucia '23 is quite flavorful, with a pronounced fruity vein of peach and pineapple, while the more herbaceous and floral Talliano '23, despite its more substantial nature, offers effective almond-flavored drinkability. The Panicale '21 doesn't disappoint, playing on the sour cherry notes we'd expect from montepulciano and a compact palate.

○ Castelli di Jesi Verdicchio Cl. Ris. '20	▼▼ 5
○ Verdicchio dei Castelli di Jesi Cl. Santa Lucia '23	▼▼ 2*
○ Verdicchio dei Castelli di Jesi Cl. Sup. Talliano '23	▼▼ 3
○ Brut	▼ 2
● Rosso Piceno Panicale '21	▼ 3
○ Castelli di Jesi Verdicchio Cl. Ris. '19	▽▽ 5
○ Castelli di Jesi Verdicchio Cl. Ris. '18	▽▽ 5
○ Verdicchio dei Castelli di Jesi Cl. Sup. Talliano '22	▽▽ 3
○ Verdicchio dei Castelli di Jesi Cl. Sup. Talliano '21	▽▽ 3*
○ Verdicchio dei Castelli di Jesi Cl. Sup. Talliano '19	▽▽ 3*

Fattoria Mancini

s.da dei Colli, 35
61100 Pesaro
📞 +39 072151828
🌐 www.fattoriamancini.com

CELLAR SALES
PRE-BOOKED VISITS
ANNUAL PRODUCTION 100,000 bottles
HECTARES UNDER VINE 22.00

Luigi Mancini's specialization in pinot nero isn't just a passing trend. The grape has been present in Pesaro for two centuries, and Mancini, representing the fifth generation of his family, considers it a local variety. The winery operates from two main sites: the spectacular Rive di Focara vineyard, located within the San Bartolo Park, features multiple plots perched on the cliffs above the sea but facing north. The Tenuta Quarta is further inland, on the highest hill in the area. The winery also cultivates albanella, ancellotta, and sangiovese. Their style is modern, with noticeable use of barriques in their more ambitious wines, which generally age very well. The Focara '21 reveals Mediterranean tones and delightful tannins, while the JNoir '22 offers a light, easygoing palate. The Terrazzi '20 impresses with its delicate balsamic complexity. The Rive '21 proves elegantly oaked. The Impero '22, a fascinating white from pinot noir, delivers a relaxed yet complex palate with smoky nuances. The Roncaja '23, made from albanella, is also noteworthy for its drinkability.

● Colli Pesaresi Focara Pinot Nero '21	🍷🍷 5
● Colli Pesaresi Focara Pinot Nero I Terrazzi di Focara '20	🍷🍷 7
● Blu '21	🍷🍷 7
● Colli Pesaresi Focara Pinot Nero Jnoir '22	🍷🍷 4
● Colli Pesaresi Focara Pinot Nero Rive di Focara '21	🍷🍷 6
○ Colli Pesaresi Roncaglia Roncaja '23	🍷🍷 3
○ Impero Blanc de Pinot Noir '22	🍷🍷 5
● Rive Sangiovese '19	🍷🍷 5
○ Tenute Quarta Blanc de Pinot Noir '22	🍷🍷 7
● Colli Pesaresi Focara Pinot Nero '06	🍷🍷 5
● Colli Pesaresi Focara Pinot Noir '07	🍷🍷 5
○ Colli Pesaresi Roncaglia '08	🍷🍷 2*
○ Colli Pesaresi Roncaglia '07	🍷🍷 2*
● Colli Pesaresi Sangiovese '06	🍷🍷 5

Clara Marcelli

c.da Pescolla
63081 Castorano [AP]
📞 +39 073687289
🌐 www.claramarcelli.it

PRE-BOOKED VISITS
ANNUAL PRODUCTION 40,000 bottles
HECTARES UNDER VINE 10.00
VITICULTURE METHOD Certified Organic

The wines produced by the Colletta brothers, sons of Clara Marcelli, aren't for everyone and don't aim to be. They focus on originality, deeply tied to the sun-drenched land of Castorano and the traditional practices of Piceno, even when made with international grape varieties. These are true terroir-driven wines, full of character, sometimes brooding in their aromas, but never dull. Leading the pack is the Ruggine '19. It's at its best, graceful in its blend of aromatic herbs, orange peel, and balsamic hints—it unveils an elegant saline progression on the palate with finely embroidered tannins. Its composed nature is echoed by the Marke '21, a pecorino aged in barriques for 20 months, with citrus, oak, and sage notes melded into a full-bodied, salty palate. More assertive are the Batatè '21, a brackish and sharp syrah; the evolved, decisive Corbù '20, made from montepulciano and 20% cabernet sauvignon; and the K'Un '20, a robust montepulciano featuring black fruits and toasty accents, with a sturdy, warm palate.

● Ruggine '19	🍷🍷 8
● Batatè '21	🍷🍷 6
● Corbù '20	🍷🍷 3
● K'un '20	🍷🍷 5
○ Marke '21	🍷🍷 6
● Rosso Piceno Sup. '19	🍷🍷 3
○ Offida Pecorino Irata '22	🍷 3
○ Raffa '22	🍷 3
● Batatè '19	🍷🍷 6
○ Marke '20	🍷🍷 6
○ Offida Pecorino Irata '21	🍷🍷 3
○ Offida Pecorino Irata '20	🍷🍷 3
● Ruggine '18	🍷🍷 8
● Ruggine '14	🍷🍷 8
● Ruggine '13	🍷🍷 8
● Ruggine '11	🍷🍷 8

Maurizio Marchetti

fraz. Pinocchio
via di Pontelungo, 166
60131 Ancona
📞 +39 071897386
🌐 www.marchettiwines.it

CELLAR SALES
PRE-BOOKED VISITS
ANNUAL PRODUCTION 60,000 bottles
HECTARES UNDER VINE 16.00

The Marchetti family founded their farm in 1890, and this century-old legacy is now managed by Maurizio Marchetti, son of Mario Marchetti, who was among those producers who first established the Rosso Conero appellation back in 1967. Today, their winery remains a pillar of the DOC, thanks in part to the consistent quality achieved through the agronomic support of Alessio Macchia and the oenological expertise of Lorenzo Landi. The star of the lineup is the Riserva Villa Bonomi '20, aged in large barrels and made from the best grapes of the Pontelungo vineyard. It boasts a refined, seductively spicy nose and a fleshy yet structurally sound, tannic palate. The Castro di San Silvestro is simpler and more energetic. A current-vintage Rosso Conero, it's slightly rough but still a tasty drink with plum and sour cherry notes. The two Verdicchios and the Filari Sparsi, a rosé also made from montepulciano, proves aromatic and irresistibly flavorful.

● Conero Villa Bonomi Ris. '20	♥♥ 5
● Rosso Conero Castro di San Silvestro '22	♥♥ 3
○ Verdicchio dei Castelli di Jesi Cl. '23	♥♥ 2*
○ Filari Sparsi '23	♥ 2
○ Verdicchio dei Castelli di Jesi Cl. Sup. Tenuta del Cavaliere '22	♥ 3
● Conero Villa Bonomi Ris. '19	♡♡ 5
● Conero Villa Bonomi Ris. '18	♡♡ 5
● Rosso Conero Castro di San Silvestro '21	♡♡ 2*
○ Verdicchio dei Castelli di Jesi Cl. '20	♡♡ 2*
○ Verdicchio dei Castelli di Jesi Cl. Sup. Tenuta del Cavaliere '21	♡♡ 3
○ Verdicchio dei Castelli di Jesi Cl. Sup. Tenuta del Cavaliere '20	♡♡ 3
○ Verdicchio dei Castelli di Jesi Cl. Sup. Tenuta del Cavaliere '19	♡♡ 3

Marotti Campi

via Sant'Amico, 14
60030 Morro d'Alba [AN]
📞 +39 0731618027
🌐 www.marotticampi.it

CELLAR SALES
PRE-BOOKED VISITS
ACCOMMODATION
ANNUAL PRODUCTION 300,000 bottles
HECTARES UNDER VINE 70.00

Lorenzo Marotti Campi's range is nearly complete—only a Metodo Classico is missing, though it's been aptly substituted by a Brut Rosé Charmat. All types of wines are represented using just two grape varieties: lacrima and verdicchio. The former gives us the Orgiolo, of late consistently among the top wines in the appellation. The 2022 is elegant and spicy, with a well-structured palate, aided by well-extracted tannins. The Rubico, from the same year, is livelier, showing signature floral aromas and a crisp, no-frills palate. The opposite is true of the Xyris, a fragrant, fruity, sweet sparkling wine. Among the Verdicchio-based wines, the Salmariano Riserva '21 stands out with its blend of ripe apple, floral sensations, anise, and a clear almond finish that echoes on its weighty palate. The Luzano '23 offers a pleasant texture on the palate, with hints of anise and sweet almond on the nose. The Onyr '21 proves commendable, a voluptuous passito with long persistence, featuring smoky and nutty sensations.

○ Castelli di Jesi Verdicchio Cl. Salmariano Ris. '21	♥♥ 4
● Lacrima di Morro d'Alba Sup. Orgiolo '22	♥♥ 4
○ Brut Rosé	♥♥ 3
● Lacrima di Morro d'Alba Rubico '23	♥♥ 2*
○ Verdicchio dei Castelli di Jesi Cl. Sup. Luzano '23	♥♥ 2*
○ Verdicchio dei Castelli di Jesi Passito Onyr '21	♥♥ 3
● Xyris	♥♥ 3
○ Regina d'Inverno '23	♥ 5
○ Rosato '23	♥ 4
○ Verdicchio dei Castelli di Jesi Cl. Albiano '23	♥ 2
○ Verdicchio dei Castelli di Jesi Cl. Sup. Volo d'Autunno '23	♥ 5

MARCHE

★Poderi Mattioli

via Farneto, 17a
60030 Serra de' Conti [AN]
📞 +39 0731878676
🌐 www.poderimattioli.it

Valter Mattoni

via Pescolla, 1
63081 Castorano [AP]
📞 +39 3473319401
🌐 www.valtermattoni.it

CELLAR SALES
PRE-BOOKED VISITS
ANNUAL PRODUCTION 50,000 bottles
HECTARES UNDER VINE 7.00
VITICULTURE METHOD Certified Organic

CELLAR SALES
PRE-BOOKED VISITS
ANNUAL PRODUCTION 10,000 bottles
HECTARES UNDER VINE 3.50

At the Mattioli estate, they rarely miss the mark. The reason isn't hard to see: old vines cultivated in a renowned growing area, obsessive care of the vineyard and harvest, and extensive cellar experience. Their style is modern and elegant, balancing drinkability with integrity of fruit. The winery's manageable size allows for personal oversight and a bespoke approach to production. The two Verdicchios engage in a fierce battle each year for the top spot. However, even the one that doesn't win remains among the finest expressions of the entire appellation. The victory once again goes to the Riserva Lauro '21. This wine is sumptuous in its crystal-clear aromatic expression, blending pleasure and complexity with a dynamic palate and a three-dimensional finish. It earns its place among the best whites in Italy. The Ylice '22 has clean aromas, a fruity character, and an a compelling palate.

Valter Mattoni has optimized the space and modernized his small winery—better described as a "studio," given its artisanal approach, which appeals to those who appreciate wines with great character, even if that means a bit of rusticity. Supported by the work of his nephew Andrea Bernabè, he's also introduced a new wine: the Quiss '21, a pecorino aged 18 months in barriques, with notes of candied lemon and hazelnut on a full, saline palate, managing to retain its suppleness despite its heft. However, the emblem of Valter and his style remains the Arshura '21, a densely fruited and meaty montepulciano with a slight hint of volatile acidity that adds authenticity, energy, and refreshes the palate. But don't underestimate the rustic spirit of the Trebbien '22, an irresistibly food-friendly trebbiano. You'll know it's a crowd-pleaser when you find the bottle empty after you go to pour more.

○ Castelli di Jesi Verdicchio Cl. Lauro Ris. '21	♟♟♟ 5
○ Verdicchio dei Castelli di Jesi Cl. Sup. Ylice '22	♟♟ 4
○ Dosaggio Zero M. Cl. '18	♟♟ 5
○ Castelli di Jesi Verdicchio Cl. Lauro Ris. '20	♟♟♟ 5
○ Castelli di Jesi Verdicchio Cl. Lauro Ris. '19	♟♟♟ 4*
○ Castelli di Jesi Verdicchio Cl. Lauro Ris. '16	♟♟♟ 4*
○ Verdicchio dei Castelli di Jesi Cl. Sup. Ylice '19	♟♟♟ 3*
○ Verdicchio dei Castelli di Jesi Cl. Sup. Ylice '18	♟♟♟ 3*
○ Verdicchio dei Castelli di Jesi Cl. Sup. Ylice '16	♟♟♟ 3*

● Arshura '21	♟♟ 6
○ Trebbien '22	♟♟ 5
○ Quiss '21	♟♟ 7
● Cosecose '23	♟ 4
● Arshura '17	♟♟♟ 5
● Arshura '16	♟♟♟ 5
● Arshura '11	♟♟♟ 3*
● Arshura '20	♟♟ 5
● Arshura '19	♟♟ 5
● Arshura '18	♟♟ 5
● Rossobordò '16	♟♟ 8
● Rossomatò '19	♟♟ 8
● Rossomatò '18	♟♟ 8
○ Trebbien '21	♟♟ 4
○ Trebbien '20	♟♟ 4
○ Trebbien '18	♟♟ 4

★La Monacesca

c.da Monacesca
62024 Matelica [MC]
📞 +39 0733672641
🌐 www.monacesca.it

CELLAR SALES
PRE-BOOKED VISITS
ANNUAL PRODUCTION 160,000 bottles
HECTARES UNDER VINE 33.00

In 2021, 75% of the company founded by the Cifola family changed hands, bringing improvements and small changes to Matelica's most renowned winery. These include revisions to the vineyards with investments aimed at enhancing agricultural yields, new labels, and a review of the winery's range. Their chardonnay grapes are now dedicated exclusively to a Metodo Classico, which displays broad aromas of ripe yellow fruits and a vigorous palate with a brackish, captivating finish. The Monaco Ribelle '23, now in its second vintage, aims to interpret Matelica with a more immediate appeal, yet in line with the estate's style, which favors a pervasive touch and a broad fruitiness, a profile that's even more evident in the Matelica '22 and especially in their flagship wine: the Mirum. The 2022 vintage pours a golden hue, releasing toasted almond sensations, licorice powder, and light black tea notes on a mature, substantial palate.

○ Ecclesia Brut Nature M. Cl.	♟♟ 5
○ Verdicchio di Matelica '22	♟♟ 3
○ Verdicchio di Matelica Mirum Ris. '22	♟♟ 5
○ Verdicchio di Matelica Monaco Ribelle '23	♟♟ 3
○ Verdicchio di Matelica Mirum Ris. '16	♟♟♟ 5
○ Verdicchio di Matelica Mirum Ris. '15	♟♟♟ 5
○ Verdicchio di Matelica Mirum Ris. '14	♟♟♟ 5
○ Verdicchio di Matelica Mirum Ris. '12	♟♟♟ 5
○ Verdicchio di Matelica Mirum Ris. '11	♟♟♟ 5
○ Verdicchio di Matelica Mirum Ris. '10	♟♟♟ 4*
○ Verdicchio di Matelica Mirum Ris. '09	♟♟♟ 4
○ Verdicchio di Matelica Mirum Ris. '08	♟♟♟ 4
○ Verdicchio di Matelica Mirum Ris. '07	♟♟♟ 4*
○ Verdicchio di Matelica Mirum Ris. '06	♟♟♟ 4
○ Verdicchio di Matelica Mirum Ris. '04	♟♟♟ 4
○ Verdicchio di Matelica Mirum Ris. '02	♟♟♟ 3

Montecappone - Mirizzi

via Colle Olivo, 2
60035 Jesi [AN]
📞 +39 0731205761
🌐 www.montecappone.com

CELLAR SALES
PRE-BOOKED VISITS
ANNUAL PRODUCTION 186,000 bottles
HECTARES UNDER VINE 53.00

The Montecappone and Mirizzi wineries share the same cellar and expertise of Lorenzo Landi, but they have different owners and vineyards. Montecappone was founded in 1968 and is owned by the Bomprezzi/Mirizzi family, while the latter is Gianluca Mirizzi's recent solo project. The wines produced by each estate are complementary, reflecting two different styles. Montecappone offers fresher profiles, with clean citrus notes and drinkability that, while straightforward in the younger versions, becomes exceptional in the Utopia '20. The elegance of its anise notes, smoky traits, and white fruit flavors come together in a racy, sapid, and cohesive drink. Similar styles are found in the Federico II '23, with its clear almond tones and a juicy palate. The Verdicchio Maesa '23 is fruitier, with a hint of peach, while its Rosso Piceno counterpart, the Maesa '22, proves light and easy to drink. The wines labeled Mirizzi are more exuberant, rich, and flavorful, such as the smooth Ergo '22 or the tasty and playful Cogito A. '23.

○ Castelli di Jesi Verdicchio Cl. Utopia Ris. '20	♟♟ 6
○ Verdicchio dei Castelli di Jesi Cl. Sup. Cogito A. Mirizzi '23	♟♟ 3
○ Verdicchio dei Castelli di Jesi Cl. Sup. Ergo Mirizzi '22	♟♟ 6
○ Verdicchio dei Castelli di Jesi Cl. Sup. Federico II AD 1194 '23	♟♟ 3
● Rosso Piceno Maesa '22	♟ 2
○ Verdicchio dei Castelli di Jesi Cl. Sup. Maesa '23	♟ 3
○ Castelli di Jesi Verdicchio Cl. Ergo Sum Ris. Mirizzi '16	♟♟♟ 8
○ Castelli di Jesi Verdicchio Cl. Utopia Ris. '19	♟♟♟ 6
○ Verdicchio dei Castelli di Jesi Cl. Sup. Ergo Mirizzi '19	♟♟♟ 5

Alessandro Moroder

via Montacuto, 112
60129 Ancona
📞 +39 071898232
🖰 www.moroder.wine

Tenuta Musone

loc. Colognola, 22a bis
62011 Cingoli [MC]
📞 +39 0733616438
🖰 www.tenutamusone.it

CELLAR SALES
PRE-BOOKED VISITS
ACCOMMODATION AND RESTAURANT SERVICE
ANNUAL PRODUCTION 140,000 bottles
HECTARES UNDER VINE 38.00
VITICULTURE METHOD Certified Organic
SUSTAINABLE WINERY

CELLAR SALES
PRE-BOOKED VISITS
ANNUAL PRODUCTION 150,000 bottles
HECTARES UNDER VINE 33.00
VITICULTURE METHOD Certified Organic

Moroder is synonymous with Conero. The Montacuto-based producer has a long history bound up with the limestone promontory that juts out into the sea just behind Ancona and the appellation that represents its wines. Today, Mattia Moroder, son of Alessandro, is at the helm, supported in the vineyard and cellar by external consultants Marco Gozzi and Luca Mercadante. Absent from the lineup is the new vintage of the famous Riserva Dorico, leaving the stage to the other Riserva, the Etere '19, aged in barrels of varying sizes. It features a multifaceted profile, dark with fruit and graphite minerality, and a powerful, layered palate full of old-world charm, ending on an elegantly austere note. The Notte '20 features leather and plum aromas, with a lively, alcohol-wrapped palate and a solid tannic structure. The Aìon '23 is more playful, plump and relaxed on the palate, but still vibrant and gripping with its sapid tension. The Emera '23, made from malvasia, offers herbaceous scents and an easy palate.

Located in Cingoli on paper, but actually situated just a stone's throw from Staffolo, the Darini family estate spans multiple vineyard plots with various exposures. The extensive area under vines, predominantly verdicchio and to a lesser extent montepulciano, allows for a wide range of harvest options, which is reflected in a portfolio that shows a particular interest in sparkling wines. This segment, overseen for several years by oenologist and manager Gabriele Villani, presents decidedly interesting products, such as the Musa Extra Brut '18, with its alluring citrus profile and perfectly modulated balsamic nuances, offering a consistent, saline palate. There's also the complex, creamy, and mature Walter Darini Riserva '14. Among the still wines, our preferences are with the original, grape-skin sensations of the Incauto '22, a wine aged in amphora for a year. The flavorful Ghiffa '22, with its slightly vegetal aromatic profile, also holds its own.

● Conero Etere Ris. '19	♙♙ 4
● Rosso Conero Aìon '23	♙♙ 2*
● Rosso Conero Notte '20	♙♙ 3
○ Emera '23	♙ 3
⊙ Rosa di Montacuto '23	♙ 3
● Rosso Conero Zero '23	♙ 3
● Conero Dorico Ris. '15	♙♙♙ 5
● Conero Dorico Ris. '05	♙♙♙ 5
● Rosso Conero Dorico '93	♙♙♙ 5
● Rosso Conero Dorico '90	♙♙♙ 5
● Rosso Conero Dorico '88	♙♙♙ 5
● Conero Dorico Ris. '18	♙♙ 6
● Conero Dorico Ris. '16	♙♙ 5
● Conero Ris. '16	♙♙ 5
● Conero Ris. '13	♙♙ 5

○ Verdicchio dei Castelli di Jesi Cl. Sup. Incauto '22	♙ 4
○ Verdicchio dei Castelli di Jesi Extra Brut M. Cl. '18	♙♙ 5
⊙ Musa Brut Rosé M. Cl.	♙♙ 4
○ Verdicchio dei Castelli di Jesi Brut M. Cl. Musa	♙♙ 4
○ Verdicchio dei Castelli di Jesi Cl. Sup. Ghiffa '22	♙♙ 3
○ Verdicchio dei Castelli di Jesi Cl. Sup. Via Condotto '23	♙♙ 3
○ Verdicchio dei Castelli di Jesi Dosaggio Zero M. Cl. Walter Darini Ris. '14	♙♙ 6
○ Verdicchio dei Castelli di Jesi Cl. Sup. Ghiffa '18	♙♙♙ 3

Fattoria Nannì

c.da Arsicci
62021 Apiro [MC]
☎ +39 3406225930
✎ www.fattoriananni.it

CELLAR SALES
PRE-BOOKED VISITS
ANNUAL PRODUCTION 40,000 bottles
HECTARES UNDER VINE 8.50
VITICULTURE METHOD Certified Organic

It's impossible not to fall in love with the breathtaking views from Roberto Cantori's winery, where the landscape opens up to Monte San Vicino and the sparsely populated surrounding countryside. Here, Roberto purchased two plots of old vines, situated at elevations spanning 380-450 meters, along with a small derelict building that he transformed into a well-functioning winery. The cool positioning of the land and the notable temperature swings, induced by the nearby massif, endow the wines with distinctive Appennine profiles. The Origini '22 is a true marvel. The hot vintage was expertly managed, resulting in a wine that's crystal-clear in color, with refined aromas of anise, citron peel, sweet almond, and river stones, all perfectly defined across a sapid, juicy palate that offers both depth and suppleness. Marvelous. Its younger sibling, the Arsicci '23, is subtler, citrusy, with light herbal inflections. Its greatest strength lies in its smoothness. Despite drawing on a different grape, the Ribona Madrerata '23 exhibits a similarly vivid acidic backbone, opting for a taut and brackish profile.

	Wine	Rating
○	Castelli di Jesi Verdicchio Cl. Origini Ris. '22	▾▾▾ 4*
○	Colli Maceratesi Ribona Madrerata '23	▾▾ 3*
○	Verdicchio dei Castelli di Jesi Cl. Sup. Arsicci '23	▾▾ 3
○	Verdicchio dei Castelli di Jesi Cl. Sup. Origini '18	♀♀♀ 3*
○	Castelli di Jesi Verdicchio Cl. Origini Ris. '21	♀♀ 4
○	Castelli di Jesi Verdicchio Cl. Origini Ris. '20	♀♀ 4
○	Colli Maceratesi Ribona Madrerata '22	♀♀ 3
○	Colli Maceratesi Ribona Madrerata '21	♀♀ 3
○	Verdicchio dei Castelli di Jesi Cl. Sup. Arsicci '22	♀♀ 3*
○	Verdicchio dei Castelli di Jesi Cl. Sup. Cantore John '22	♀♀ 5
○	Verdicchio dei Castelli di Jesi Cl. Sup. Cantore John '20	♀♀ 5

Numa

c.da San Michele
63065 Ripatransone [AP]
☎ +39 3347751831
✎ www.cantinanuma.it

CELLAR SALES
PRE-BOOKED VISITS
ANNUAL PRODUCTION 28,000 bottles
HECTARES UNDER VINE 15.00
VITICULTURE METHOD Certified Organic
SUSTAINABLE WINERY

Pierfrancesco Liberi began his project in 2016, planting new vines to complement those already in place since 1997. The time between then and the first harvest in 2019 was spent constructing a large, well-equipped winery. Various plots with different exposures are cultivated organically, growing varietals such as alicante, garofanata, passerina, sangiovese, and small quantities of international varieties. However, the heart of production focuses on pecorino and montepulciano. The style is modern, utilizing barriques and tonneaux, and taking advantage of attentively ripened grapes to create flavorful and intense wines. The Pecorino '22 offers a personal, well-crafted interpretation, blending notes of anise, subtle smoky hints, and lemon peel into a cohesive palate that's almost creamy yet invigorating. The Rosso Piceno Superiore '22 was a bit effected by the hot vintage, showing some overripe tones and a distinctly fruity character. The Numa Rosso '20, made from montepulciano, is powerful but lacks suppleness.

	Wine	Rating
○	Offida Pecorino '22	▾▾ 4
●	Rosso Piceno Sup. '22	▾▾ 4
●	Numa Rosso '20	▾ 7
○	Passerina '23	▾ 3
●	Rosso Piceno Sup. '20	♀♀♀ 4*
●	Numa Rosso '19	♀♀ 7
○	Offida Pecorino '21	♀♀ 4
○	Offida Pecorino '20	♀♀ 4
○	Offida Pecorino '19	♀♀ 4
○	Passerina '22	♀♀ 3
○	Passerina '21	♀♀ 3
●	Rosso Piceno Sup. '19	♀♀ 4

★Oasi degli Angeli

c.da Sant'Egidio, 50
63012 Cupra Marittima [AP]
☎ +39 0735778569
✉ www.kurni.it

CELLAR SALES
PRE-BOOKED VISITS
ANNUAL PRODUCTION 7,500 bottles
HECTARES UNDER VINE 16.00

The Kurni is an unrivaled milestone in the history of Piceno winemaking. Despite an unchanging production philosophy, each vintage is unique, bringing together the mood of the montepulciano grapes in the vineyards, the microclimate, and the hand of its creator, Marco Casolanetti. Indeed, those who taste it know that behind its powerful flavor, fruity intensity, and remarkable aging potential, there are subtle vibrations that change each year, making a difference. These might include a more pronounced sweetness, rougher tannins, or a noticeable presence of volatile acidity. When tasting the Kurni, you mustn't bring your own prejudices. The 2022 vintage is magnificent: black fruit, balsamic traces, and slight toasted and smoky whiffs open the way to a dense, pervasive palate with noticeable sweetness, balanced by a tannic structure of exceptional purity and elegance, ending on an endless finish. The Kupra '21 (grenache) offers fruit and Mediterranean scrub on the nose, while the palate is full-flavored and rich in contrast.

Pantaleone

via Colonnata Alta, 118
63100 Ascoli Piceno
☎ +39 3478757476
✉ www.pantaleonewine.com

PRE-BOOKED VISITS
ANNUAL PRODUCTION 80,000 bottles
HECTARES UNDER VINE 20.00
VITICULTURE METHOD Certified Organic

Sisters Federica and Francesca, their father Nazzareno (who manages the vineyards), and Francesca's husband, Peppe Infriccioli (an experienced cellar master), constitute a close-knit team. A clear division of roles and a deep understanding of the territory allow the Pantaloni family to create a range of high-value wines, stylistically harmonized with the cool microclimate induced by Monte Ascensione. The crystalline Onirocep '23 is the perfect emblem, with its intense notes of freshly cut grass, anise, and lemon peel, leading to a direct, coherent, saline, and refreshing palate. A wine with backbone and deep flavor. La Ribalta '20, a compelling red from grenache, is no less impressive, with its Mediterranean scrub sensations, black olives, and aromatic herbs on the nose, and a spirited, rhythmic palate with a long, spicy finish. The Sipario '20 (montepulciano) also delivers, with a subtle, briny palate and hints of cola and rhubarb. The Chicca '23 (passerina) and Pivuàn '23 (a rosé from sangiovese) both prove irresistibly drinkable.

● Kurni '22	♟♟♟ 8
● Kupra '21	♟♟ 8
● Kupra '17	♟♟♟ 8
● Kupra '13	♟♟♟ 8
● Kupra '12	♟♟♟ 8
● Kupra '10	♟♟♟ 8
● Kurni '10	♟♟♟ 8
● Kurni '09	♟♟♟ 8
● Kurni '08	♟♟♟ 8
● Kurni '07	♟♟♟ 8
● Kurni '04	♟♟♟ 8
● Kurni '03	♟♟♟ 8
● Kurni '02	♟♟♟ 8
● Kurni '01	♟♟♟ 8
● Kurni '00	♟♟♟ 8
● Kurni '98	♟♟♟ 8

○ Falerio Pecorino Onirocep '23	♟♟♟ 4*
● La Ribalta '20	♟♟ 8
● Sipario '20	♟♟ 4
○ Chicca '23	♟♟ 3
⊙ Pivuàn '23	♟♟ 3
○ Falerio Pecorino Onirocep '21	♟♟♟ 4*
○ Falerio Pecorino Onirocep '19	♟♟♟ 3*
○ Falerio Pecorino Onirocep '18	♟♟♟ 3*
● Sipario '19	♟♟♟ 4*
● Boccascena '18	♟♟ 3
○ Falerio Pecorino Aspralama '19	♟♟ 6
○ Falerio Pecorino Onirocep '22	♟♟ 4
○ Falerio Pecorino Onirocep '20	♟♟ 3
● La Ribalta '19	♟♟ 8
● La Ribalta '18	♟♟ 8
● La Ribalta '16	♟♟ 8

Tenuta Piano di Rustano

via Giovanni XXII, I
62022 Castelraimondo [MC]
☎ +39 3393217530
☞ www.pianodirustano.it

ANNUAL PRODUCTION 20,000 bottles
HECTARES UNDER VINE 9.00

Although the winery has been producing wine since 1920, it wasn't until 2016 that Francesco Lebboroni and Rosanna Tortolini formally organized their vineyards in Rustano, a sunny area still affected by the cool air of the Apennines. Significant efforts were also made to renovate the winery. Winemaker Marco Gozzi shows his talent for sparklers with the Cavalier Vincenzo '20, which blends whiffs of lemon, white peach, bread crust, and aromatic herbs with great precision. The palate is energetic, with creamy effervescence and a well-balanced finish, playing on the contrast between salt and liqueur d'expédition. Carefully calculated dosage avoids any bitter or herbal drift, leaving you wanting another sip. Their still Matelica wines also reveal a linear profile, with the acidic backbone more balanced in the citrusy Torre del Parco '22, while the Brondoleto '21 proves slightly grassy, with almond notes. The Monte Primo '21, a red from sangiovese (plus 15% merlot), is a pleasant surprise, floral with pronounced drinkability.

○ Verdicchio di Matelica Brut M. Cl. Cavalier Vincenzo '20	♥♥ 5
● Monte Primo '21	♥♥ 4
○ Verdicchio di Matelica Torre del Parco '22	♥♥ 3
○ Il Covone '23	♥ 2
○ Verdicchio di Matelica Brondoleto '21	♥ 4
○ Verdicchio di Matelica Brondoleto '19	♥♥ 4
○ Verdicchio di Matelica Torre del Parco '20	♥♥ 3
○ Verdicchio di Matelica Torre del Parco '19	♥♥ 3*

Tenute Pieralisi

fraz. Monteschiavo
via Vivaio
60030 Maiolati Spontini [AN]
☎ +39 0731700385
☞ www.monteschiavo.it

CELLAR SALES
PRE-BOOKED VISITS
ANNUAL PRODUCTION 710,000 bottles
HECTARES UNDER VINE 103.00
SUSTAINABLE WINERY

The Pieralisi family owns a sizable set of vineyards across several municipalities. The most important are those near the winery in Scorcelletti, known as "Colle del Sole," in Tassanare di Rosora, Poggio San Marcello, and Arcevia. Technical management is entrusted to Paolo Bucci and winemaker Simone Schiaffino, who craft a solid and diverse range. This year, Le Giuncare '21 shines. It's a vibrant Riserva perfectly in tune with its varietal profile, juicy and enveloping, delivering full satisfaction on the palate. The Pallio di San Floriano '23 features a signature almond-inflected profile and good structure, while the Coste del Molino '23 offers a more restrained body and pleasantly smooth drinkability. Aging on the fine lees gives Villaia '22 volume and density on the palate but holds back its dynamism. The Metodo Classico 1622 shows good complexity with notes of nuts and anise. Among the reds, the Re di Ras '21 stands out for its relaxed, enticing profile, with a fleshy, fruit-forward dimension.

○ Castelli di Jesi Verdicchio Cl. Le Giuncare Ris. '21	♥♥ 5
● Rosso Piceno Caccialepre '21	♥♥ 3
● Rosso Piceno Re di Ras '21	♥♥ 5
● Rosso Piceno Sassaiolo '21	♥♥ 3
○ Verdicchio dei Castelli di Jesi Cl. Sup. Pallio di S. Floriano '23	♥♥ 3
○ Verdicchio dei Castelli di Jesi Dosaggio Zero M. Cl. 1622 '17	♥♥ 5
○ Verdicchio dei Castelli di Jesi Cl. Sup. Coste del Molino '23	♥ 3
○ Verdicchio dei Castelli di Jesi Cl. Sup. Villaia '22	♥ 4
○ Verdicchio dei Castelli di Jesi Cl. Sup. Pallio di S. Floriano '11	♥♥♥ 2*

Pietro 17

c.da San Pietro, 17
60039 Staffolo [AN]
+39 3314638269
www.pietro17.com

ANNUAL PRODUCTION 6,000 bottles
HECTARES UNDER VINE 3.20
VITICULTURE METHOD Certified Organic

Alexander Rocca came to Italy from his home in the USA 22 years ago, initially following his brother, a professional basketball player for Jesi. What was meant to be a brief stop to see the world and gain some experience turned into a permanent stay in Jesi, partly because he fell in love with Laura Giuliani and partly because he found stable work. First came the children, and then an all-consuming passion for verdicchio. Together with his wife, he acquired a vineyard and a farmhouse in 2020, located on the road from Staffolo to Apiro, with the goal of fulfilling a dream to become wine producers. The first two wines from the oldest vines (50 years) were released, made according to a "supernatural" production style, but well-controlled. The Verdicchio Riserva '22 offers up notes of trail mix, apple, and a hint of anise. On the palate, it's incisive, with an old-school charm that multiplies its flavor into countless briny rivulets. The Pietro 17 Bianco '22 is actually an orange wine from trebbiano and malvasia. Bold and textured, it plays on a crisp, daring, tactile profile.

○ Castelli di Jesi Verdicchio Cl. Pietro 17 Ris. '22	TT 5
○ Pietro 17 Bianco '22	TT 5

Pievalta

via Monteschiavo, 18
60030 Maiolati Spontini [AN]
+39 0731705199
www.pievalta.it

CELLAR SALES
PRE-BOOKED VISITS
ACCOMMODATION
ANNUAL PRODUCTION 120,000 bottles
HECTARES UNDER VINE 30.50
VITICULTURE METHOD Certified Organic
SUSTAINABLE WINERY

Pievalta is a constantly evolving project: as soon as work on the guesthouse was completed, new vineyards in prime growing areas came into production. At the same time, the wines reflect a style that is thoughtfully considered each year, born from meticulous attention in the vineyards following biodynamic-inspired practices, and from a production approach that draws on the use of stainless steel containers, small and medium-sized wooden barrels, and concrete. These aspects come together magnificently in the San Paolo '21, a wine that offers a complex aromatic profile of herbs, almonds, citrus peel, and subtle balsamic hints. The palate is a refined fusion of all these sensations, with a harmonious, racy profile and a kaleidoscopic finish. The hot vintage lends a mature and voluminous tone to the Dominé '22, with its notes of yellow fruit. In contrast, the citrusy Tre Ripe '23 proves lively, drinkable, and has a pleasant saline vein. The Perlugo is a reliable sparkling wine made from 100% verdicchio.

○ Castelli di Jesi Verdicchio Cl. San Paolo Ris. '21	TTT 5
○ Perlugo Dosage Zéro M. Cl.	TT 4
○ Verdicchio dei Castelli di Jesi Cl. Sup. Dominè '22	TT 4
○ Verdicchio dei Castelli di Jesi Cl. Sup. Tre Ripe '23	TT 3
○ Castelli di Jesi Verdicchio Cl. San Paolo Ris. '19	YYY 5
○ Castelli di Jesi Verdicchio Cl. San Paolo Ris. '16	YYY 3
○ Castelli di Jesi Verdicchio Cl. San Paolo Ris. '15	YYY 3
○ Castelli di Jesi Verdicchio Cl. San Paolo Ris. '13	YYY 3
○ Verdicchio dei Castelli di Jesi Cl. Sup. Dominè '19	YYY 3

Quntì

c.da Torbidello
63071 Rotella [AP]
📞 +39 3383334787
🌐 www.qunti.it

ANNUAL PRODUCTION 6,000 bottles
HECTARES UNDER VINE 1.64
VITICULTURE METHOD Certified Organic

Don't be confused by the tricky typography: the name is pronounced "Koon-TEE" and is inspired by Quinto Alfonsi, a young winemaker and owner of this new—but not entirely unfamiliar—winery. The vineyards are cultivated at 500 meters elevation on a massif also known as "Monte Nero", situated midway between the Sibillini and the Adriatic coast. Its bulk and forests heavily influence the climate of this inland territory. Here Quinto and his consultant Giuseppe Camilli produce a pecorino that ages for six months in stainless steel on its fine lees, followed by a year in the bottle. The 2022 conjures up vibrant aromas of freshly cut grass, citron peel, and green anise, along with fascinating mineral whiffs and delicate smoky inflections. The palate is impressive for the way it expresses energy, dynamism, and a vibrant salty tone that echoes long on the finish. A rugged, mountain wine of great character, faithful to its varietal identity.

Sabbionare

via Sabbionare, 10
60036 Montecarotto [AN]
📞 +39 0731889004
🌐 www.sabbionare.it

CELLAR SALES
PRE-BOOKED VISITS
ANNUAL PRODUCTION 70,000 bottles
HECTARES UNDER VINE 24.00

Sabbionare's history may not run as deep as others, having launched in 1998, but from the very beginning, it was clear that the winery was serious about its craft. In part credit goes to the expertise of winemaker Sergio Paolucci (no relation to the owning family), who recognized the great potential of the vineyards here. Stretching from Montecarotto down toward Serra de' Conti, the plots are characterized by an extensive sandy layer that yields ripe, healthy grapes, capable of transforming into powerful, varietal wines. The iconic Sabbionare '22 is beloved by those who seek almond-like notes, vivid alcohol, and a persistent, sapid finish. The Filetto '23 is fresher, with an appealing smoothness that resolves on a final note of lemon, herbs, and fresh almond, perfectly coherent aromatically. The 2019 version of the always-reliable Dune, a Metodo Classico Pas Dosé, offers fruit fragrance, a hint of anise, and a flavorful palate.

○ Falerio Pecorino Al MonteNero '22	♟♟♟ 4*
○ Falerio Pecorino Al MonteNero '21	♟♟ 3*
○ Falerio Pecorino In Primis '20	♟♟ 3*

○ Verdicchio dei Castelli di Jesi Cl. Sup. Sabbionare '22	♟♟ 3*
○ Verdicchio dei Castelli di Jesi Cl. Il Filetto '23	♟♟ 2*
○ Verdicchio dei Castelli di Jesi Pas Dosé M. Cl. Dune '19	♟♟ 5
○ Verdicchio dei Castelli di Jesi Cl. Sup. Sabbionare '15	♟♟♟ 2*
○ Verdicchio dei Castelli di Jesi Cl. Sup. Sabbionare '21	♟♟ 3*
○ Verdicchio dei Castelli di Jesi Cl. Sup. Sabbionare '20	♟♟ 3*
○ Verdicchio dei Castelli di Jesi Cl. Sup. Sabbionare '19	♟♟ 3*
○ Verdicchio dei Castelli di Jesi Cl. Sup. Sabbionare '16	♟♟ 3*

Saladini Pilastri

via Saladini, 5
63078 Spinetoli [AP]
☏ +39 0736899534
⊕ www.saladinipilastri.it

CELLAR SALES
PRE-BOOKED VISITS
ANNUAL PRODUCTION 650,000 bottles
HECTARES UNDER VINE 150.00
VITICULTURE METHOD Certified Organic

Saladino Saladini Pilastri's winery boasts deep roots in Piceno, its name intertwined with the history of the area since the Middle Ages. Under the guidance of winemaker Fabio Felicioni and agronomist Graziano Celani, the estate's extensive vineyards host a number of different grapes, though the focus remains on local varieties. Their production approach, carried out in a well-equipped cellar, pays honor to tradition while also embracing modern techniques. The most distinctive wine is the Vigna Monteprandone '21, with its notes of black cherries and aromatic herbs that introduce a somewhat fibrous and vegetal character on the palate, though still dynamic. The Pecorino Comes '23 is simpler in its flavor profile, offering a palate that's more broad than deep, yet well-balanced. The Montetinello '21 features notes of overripe fruit and an authentic touch. The Pregio del Conte '22 is more complex, with smoky notes and dark fruit flavors on a serious, crisp, spicy palate.

o Offida Pecorino Comes '23	♥♥	3
• Pregio del Conte '22	♥♥	4
• Rosso Piceno Sup. Montetinello '21	♥♥	4
• Rosso Piceno Sup. V. Monteprandone '21	♥♥	5
o Falerio '23	♥	2
o Offida Passerina Bonaria '23	♥	3
• Rosso Piceno Piediprato '22	♥	3
• Rosso Piceno Sup. V. Monteprandone '00	♥♥♥	3
• Pregio del Conte '20	♥♥	4
• Rosso Piceno '22	♥♥	2*
• Rosso Piceno Piediprato '21	♥♥	3
• Rosso Piceno Piediprato '20	♥♥	3
• Rosso Piceno Piediprato '19	♥♥	3
• Rosso Piceno Sup. Montetinello '19	♥♥	4
• Rosso Piceno Sup. V. Monteprandone '20	♥♥	5
• Rosso Piceno Sup. V. Monteprandone '18	♥♥	5

San Filippo

loc. Borgo Miriam
c.da Ciafone, 17a
63073 Offida [AP]
☏ +39 0736889828
⊕ www.vinisanfilippo.it

CELLAR SALES
PRE-BOOKED VISITS
ANNUAL PRODUCTION 100,000 bottles
HECTARES UNDER VINE 74.00
VITICULTURE METHOD Certified Organic

The Stracci brothers oversee a sizable estate that includes plots in some of Piceno's prime wine-growing areas, while production is supervised by consultant Pierluigi Lorenzetti. Their portfolio is composed exclusively of traditional varietals, making for a range characterized by intense aromas and flavor, all achieved without resorting to excessive technical intervention. The standout this year is the Lupo del Ciafone '20, a vigorous monovarietal Montepulciano with slightly evolved notes of underbrush, cherries in syrup, and a hint of toastiness. The palate is fleshy, quite expressive, textured, and fully showcases its varietal expression. A touch of overripeness is noticeable in the Kàtharsis '21, which is dark in fruit and voluminous on the palate, thanks to a warm, alcohol-rich embrace. Among the whites, the Principe del Fosso '23 has a marked sapid streak but lacks length. Il Piuma '22, partially aged in barriques, offers a more colorful and refined aromatic palette, with a balanced pace and a nice sense of substance and structure.

o Offida Passerina Corona del Colle '23	♥♥	2
o Offida Pecorino Il Piuma '22	♥♥	4
o Offida Pecorino Il Principe del Fosso '23	♥♥	3
• Offida Rosso Il Lupo del Ciafone '20	♥♥	4
• Rosso Piceno Sup. Kátharsis '21	♥	2
o Offida Pecorino '20	♥♥	3
o Offida Pecorino '19	♥♥	3
o Offida Pecorino Il Piuma '21	♥♥	6
o Offida Pecorino Il Principe del Fosso '22	♥♥	3
• Offida Rosso Il Lupo del Ciafone '19	♥♥	4
• Offida Rosso Lupo del Ciafone '18	♥♥	4
• Offida Rosso Lupo del Ciafone '17	♥♥	4
• Rosso Piceno Sup. Kátharsis '20	♥♥	2
• Rosso Piceno Sup. Kátharsis '18	♥♥	2

Poderi San Lazzaro

fraz. Borgo Miriam
c.da San Lazzaro, 88
63073 Offida [AP]
(℡ +39 0736889189
☞ www.poderisanlazzaro.it

CELLAR SALES
PRE-BOOKED VISITS
ANNUAL PRODUCTION 50,000 bottles
HECTARES UNDER VINE 11.00
VITICULTURE METHOD Certified Organic

Paolo Capriotti, though unable to manage his 11 hectares alone, tirelessly supervises every aspect of production. His approach emphasizes full ripening of Piceno's traditional grapes, along with a touch of grenache, which usually contributes to the Pistò (a wine absent this year due to additional aging). The range is invariably rich and flavorful, and Capriotti's commitment to organic farming and meticulous winemaking without shortcuts results in bottles that are sincere, spirited, and free of any artifice. The Grifola '19 is particularly intense, gradually shedding its reduction in favor of briny notes, topsoil, and ripe black cherries. The palate is pervasive, with a firm, compact finish. Similar characteristics are found in the Podere 72 '21, also aged in used barriques, though with less structure and strength. The Pistillo '23 is well-defined, offering fresh sensations of cut grass and anise, with pleasant fruit pulp and a slightly vegetal finish.

○ Offida Pecorino Pistillo '23	♥♥ 3
● Offida Rosso Grifola '19	♥♥ 5
● Piceno Sup. Podere 72 '21	♥♥ 4
○ Elisetta '23	♥ 3
● Piceno Polesio '23	♥ 3
● Offida Rosso Grifola '11	♥♥♥ 4*
● Alicante '17	♥♥ 7
○ Elisetta '21	♥♥ 3
○ Offida Pecorino Colle San Giusto '21	♥♥ 5
○ Offida Pecorino Pistillo '22	♥♥ 3
○ Offida Pecorino Pistillo '21	♥♥ 3
● Offida Rosso Grifola '18	♥♥ 5
● Piceno Polesio '20	♥♥ 2*
● Piceno Sup. Podere 72 '18	♥♥ 4
Pistò '19	♥♥ 7
● Renzo '20	♥♥ 3

Fattoria San Lorenzo

via San Lorenzo, 6
60036 Montecarotto [AN]
(℡ +39 073189656
☞ www.fattoriasanlorenzo.com

CELLAR SALES
PRE-BOOKED VISITS
ANNUAL PRODUCTION 80,000 bottles
HECTARES UNDER VINE 24.00
VITICULTURE METHOD Certified Biodynamic

Natalino Crognaletti is well known for his infectious personality and exceptional winemaking skills, having developed a distinctive, recognizable, and inimitable style. Those who choose his wines can expect an authentic, rustic spirit, generous texture, and, for those patient enough to wait, the complexity that comes with time. His vines are grown biodynamically, while his production approach draws on spontaneous fermentation and a deep respect for nature's cycles. Beyond masterpieces like the Campo delle Oche Integrale '18 (see the Rare Wines section), their verdicchio gives rise to compelling wines like the Di Gino '23, the almondy, energetic Le Oche '22, and the fruit-rich Campo alle Oche '20. Among the reds, La Gattara '19 proves deliciously meaty, while Il Solleone '18, Burello '20, and Artù '20 are characterized by their broad personalities and vigor. The Frigidus '15, a complex and seductive icewine made from verdicchio harvested in December and aged for 100 months on the lees, is a rare gem.

○ Frigidus '15	♥♥ 5
● La Gattara '19	♥♥ 4
● Artù '19	♥♥ 3
○ Bianco di Gino '23	♥♥ 3
● Burello '20	♥♥ 3
○ Campo delle Oche '20	♥♥ 4
● Il Solleone '18	♥♥ 5
○ Le Oche '22	♥♥ 3
● Paradiso '17	♥ 5
○ Il San Lorenzo Bianco '09	♥♥♥ 8
○ Il San Lorenzo Bianco '08	♥♥♥ 8
○ Verdicchio dei Castelli di Jesi Cl. Vign. delle Oche Ris. '01	♥♥♥ 3
○ Bianco di Gino '22	♥♥ 3*
○ Campo delle Oche '19	♥♥ 4
○ Campo delle Oche Integrale '16	♥♥ 8

MARCHE

★Tenute San Sisto

via San Sisto
60031 Maiolati Spontini [AN]
☎ +39 073181591
✉ www.tenutesansisto.com

CELLAR SALES
PRE-BOOKED VISITS
ANNUAL PRODUCTION 100,000 bottles
HECTARES UNDER VINE 54.00

When Angelini Wine Estates acquired the renowned Fazi Battaglia winery in 2015, they chose to separate the more commercially-driven amphora wines from a new premium line, renamed Tenimenti San Sisto in honor of the estate's finest vineyard. The namesake Riserva, produced from this parcel, ferments and ages for one year in large, 2500-liter French oak barrels, followed by an additional year in the bottle before being released to the market. The 2021 vintage expresses its usual elegance with slightly smoky hints of anise and aromatic herbs. Its entry on the palate is slender and soft, with a refined progression, though just shy of depth. The south-facing vineyards of Maiolati provide the ripe grapes that give life to the Massaccio, which ages in concrete on the fine lees for six months, followed by another six months in the bottle. The warm 2022 vintage reveals a captivating nose of ripe fruit, candied orange peel, and a hint of hydrocarbons, with a mouthfeel that's seductively soft and flavorful.

○ Castelli di Jesi Verdicchio Cl. San Sisto Ris. '21	♥♥ 4
○ Verdicchio dei Castelli di Jesi Cl. Sup. Massaccio '22	♥♥ 4
○ Castelli di Jesi Verdicchio Cl. San Sisto Ris. '19	♥♥♥ 6
○ Castelli di Jesi Verdicchio Cl. San Sisto Ris. '18	♥♥♥ 5
○ Castelli di Jesi Verdicchio Cl. San Sisto Ris. '17	♥♥♥ 5
○ Castelli di Jesi Verdicchio Cl. San Sisto Ris. '16	♥♥♥ 5
○ Castelli di Jesi Verdicchio Cl. San Sisto Ris. '15	♥♥♥ 5
○ Verdicchio dei Castelli di Jesi Cl. Sup. Massaccio '18	♥♥♥ 4*

Santa Barbara

b.go Mazzini, 35
60010 Barbara [AN]
☎ +39 0719674249
✉ www.santabarbara.it

CELLAR SALES
PRE-BOOKED VISITS
ANNUAL PRODUCTION 900,000 bottles
HECTARES UNDER VINE 40.00

Stefano Antonucci is a highly capable entrepreneur who has closely tied his image to that of his winery. However, this shouldn't overshadow the talents of his team, led by his niece Elena Lorenzetti and the Rotatori brothers, Roberto and Daniele. Together, they craft a range that is profoundly contemporary in style. There are easy-drinking whites, like the citrusy Le Vaglie '23, the fruity Back to Basics '23, the soft and elegant Stefano Antonucci '22, and the flavorful, persistent Tardivo ma non Tardo '22, each showing increasing complexity, especially with the Moss Blanc '21, aged in barriques. The reds are more structured and initially a bit stern but soften over time. This is the fate of the Stefano Antonucci Rosso '22, Pathos '22, and Il Maschio da Monte '22. The Animale Celeste '23 is a Sauvignon redolent of citrus and bell pepper, making for an irresistible drink. The Passito Lina is unforgettable and worth seeking out among our Rare Wines.

○ Castelli di Jesi Verdicchio Cl. Tardivo ma non Tardo Ris. '22	♥♥ 6
○ Verdicchio dei Castelli di Jesi Cl. Le Vaglie '23	♥♥ 4
○ Animale Celeste '23	♥♥ 4
● Pathos '22	♥♥ 6
● Stefano Antonucci Rosso '22	♥♥ 5
○ Verdicchio dei Castelli di Jesi Back to Basics '23	♥♥ 4
○ Verdicchio dei Castelli di Jesi Cl. Sup. Moss Blanc '21	♥♥ 8
○ Verdicchio dei Castelli di Jesi Cl. Sup. Stefano Antonucci '22	♥♥ 5
● Rosso Piceno Il Maschio da Monte '22	♥ 5
● Rosso Piceno Stè '23	♥ 2
⊙ Sensuade '23	♥ 4
○ Verdicchio dei Castelli di Jesi Stè '23	♥ 2

Tenuta Santori

c.da Montebove, 14
63065 Ripatransone [AP]
☎ +39 3469559465
✆ www.tenutasantori.it

CELLAR SALES
PRE-BOOKED VISITS
ACCOMMODATION
ANNUAL PRODUCTION 75,000 bottles
HECTARES UNDER VINE 18.00
VITICULTURE METHOD Certified Organic

It's been 12 years since Marco Santori began his journey, and in measured steps, he has come a long way. Alongside the spacious, well-structured winery, a renovated farmhouse now serves as a tasting room and vacation home, and the vineyard area has been progressively expanded, again without excess, focusing primarily on traditional grape varieties. A new development is the Entroterra line, which will represent their premium offerings in the future. While we await its full expression, we tasted the Sangiovese '21, which unveils a nose of dark fruit and toasty notes; the palate is powerful and structured but still needs more time in the bottle to harmonize. At this stage, the Rosso Piceno Superiore '21 is more expressive, with its seductive spicy vein and pleasant palate, as is the Pecorino '23, with its notes of white peach, anise, and vegetal accents on a palate marked by brisk acidity and saltiness. The Offida Rosso '20 is a bit too marked by oak.

○ Offida Pecorino '23	♥♥ 3*
● Rosso Piceno Sup. '21	♥♥ 3*
● Entroterra Sangiovese '21	♥♥ 6
● Offida Rosso '20	♥♥ 5
○ Offida Passerina '23	♥ 3
○ Offida Pecorino '22	♥♥♥ 3*
○ Offida Pecorino '21	♥♥♥ 3*
○ Offida Pecorino '20	♥♥♥ 3*
○ Offida Pecorino '19	♥♥♥ 3*
○ Offida Pecorino '18	♥♥♥ 3*
○ Offida Pecorino '17	♥♥♥ 3*
○ Offida Pecorino '16	♥♥♥ 3*
● Rosso Piceno Sup. '20	♥♥ 3*
● Rosso Piceno Sup. '19	♥♥ 3*
● Rosso Piceno Sup. '18	♥♥ 3*
● Rosso Piceno Sup. '16	♥♥ 3*

Sartarelli

via Coste del Molino, 24
60030 Poggio San Marcello [AN]
☎ +39 073189732
✆ www.sartarelli.it

CELLAR SALES
PRE-BOOKED VISITS
ANNUAL PRODUCTION 300,000 bottles
HECTARES UNDER VINE 55.00
SUSTAINABLE WINERY

Only verdicchio is cultivated at Chiacchiarini Sartarelli, in vineyards free from synthetic chemical residues and harvested exclusively by hand, with multiple passes taking place (despite the sizable area cultivated). In the cellar, there's no trace of oak or alternative containers—only stainless steel tanks are used. The most notable change, though not drastic, is the switch to the Riserva category for the Balciana, their most famous wine. Made with late-harvested grapes from the namesake cru, the 2022 features notes of candied orange peel, thyme, and anise with light balsamic undertones. The palate is creamy, leading to a warm, almondy finish. The Milletta '22, another Riserva, offers up sensations of toasted almond and baked apple, with an old-school palate that combines structure, sapid tension, and a pleasantly bitter finish. The Tralivio '22 shows slightly overripe fruit on the nose, followed by a dry, earthy, and slightly rustic palate. The Sartarelli Classico '23 is fresher but somewhat thin on the palate.

○ Castelli di Jesi Verdicchio Cl. Balciana Ris. '22	♥♥ 6
○ Castelli di Jesi Verdicchio Cl. Milletta Ris. '22	♥♥ 5
○ Verdicchio dei Castelli di Jesi Cl. '23	♥ 3
○ Verdicchio dei Castelli di Jesi Cl. Sup. Tralivio '22	♥ 4
○ Verdicchio dei Castelli di Jesi Passito '22	♥ 5
○ Verdicchio dei Castelli di Jesi Cl. Sup. Balciana '09	♥♥♥ 5
○ Verdicchio dei Castelli di Jesi Cl. Sup. Balciana '04	♥♥♥ 5
○ Verdicchio dei Castelli di Jesi Cl. Sup. Contrada Balciana '98	♥♥♥ 5
○ Verdicchio dei Castelli di Jesi Cl. Sup. Contrada Balciana '97	♥♥♥ 5

Sparapani - Frati Bianchi

via Barchio, 12
60034 Cupramontana [AN]
☎ +39 0731781216
✉ www.fratibianchi.it

CELLAR SALES
PRE-BOOKED VISITS
RESTAURANT SERVICE
ANNUAL PRODUCTION 60,000 bottles
HECTARES UNDER VINE 20.00
SUSTAINABLE WINERY

The winery, with its red walls and grand, branded gate was completed in 2014, but the Sparapani family's history dates back to the mid-1950s. The hard work of Settimio has been carried on by his children, Giuseppe (known as Pino), Paolo, and Francesca, who manage the winery's vital functions. For many years, consultation has been entrusted to expert Sergio Paolucci. Across the various plots that make up the family's vineyards, verdicchio dominates, benefiting here from diverse elevations and exposures. From the Poggio Cupro vineyard comes Il Priore, their most distinctive wine. The 2022 is highly varietal, with aromas of sweet almond meeting apple, and white flowers, underpinned by a vegetal note. The palate has a significant structure, supported by broad sapidity and alcohol. The Donna Cloe '21, aged for 16 months in 1000-liter oak barrels, features complex notes of lemon peel, toasted almond, and smoky echoes on a rich palate.

★Tenuta Spinelli

via Lago, 2
63032 Castignano [AP]
☎ +39 0736821489
✉ www.tenutaspinelli.it

CELLAR SALES
PRE-BOOKED VISITS
ACCOMMODATION
ANNUAL PRODUCTION 89,000 bottles
HECTARES UNDER VINE 20.50
SUSTAINABLE WINERY

Simone Spinelli had a brilliant insight when he decided to plant pecorino in Castel di Croce. Despite the "mountain" character of this Piceno white varietal, significant elevations and the cooling influence of Monte Ascensione posed a challenge. However, a succession of warm vintages has ensured perfect fruit ripeness while preserving the grape's natural acidity. The Artemisia, initially produced solely from the plot near the Santuario di Montemisio, has gained even more vigor. The 2023 boldly displays explosive citrus aromas and a supple, vibrant, highly sapid palate. The Metodo Classico Meroè '20, made entirely from a new vineyard cultivated on high, reveals a briny, spirited palate with a vegetal accent of tomato leaf. More mature and elegant traits pervade the Pinot Nero Simone Spinelli '21, a wine that's delicate in color, with hints of cola and orange peel on a palate of nice complexity.

○ Castelli di Jesi Verdicchio Cl. Donna Cloe Ris. '21	♥♥ 5
○ Verdicchio dei Castelli di Jesi Cl. Sup. Il Priore '22	♥♥ 4
○ Verdicchio dei Castelli di Jesi Cl. Sup. Salerna '23	♥♥ 8
○ Verdicchio dei Castelli di Jesi Cl. Sup. Il Priore '20	♀♀♀ 4*
○ Verdicchio dei Castelli di Jesi Cl. Sup. Il Priore '16	♀♀♀ 3*
○ Verdicchio dei Castelli di Jesi Cl. Sup. Il Priore '14	♀♀♀ 2*
○ Verdicchio dei Castelli di Jesi Cl. Sup. Il Priore '13	♀♀♀ 2*
○ Verdicchio dei Castelli di Jesi Cl. Sup. Il Priore '12	♀♀♀ 2*

○ Offida Pecorino Artemisia '23	♥♥♥ 3*
○ Mèroe Pas Dosé M. Cl. '20	♥♥ 5
● Simone Spinelli Pinot Nero '21	♥♥ 6
○ Eden '23	♥ 3
○ Offida Pecorino Artemisia '22	♀♀♀ 3*
○ Offida Pecorino Artemisia '21	♀♀♀ 3*
○ Offida Pecorino Artemisia '20	♀♀♀ 3*
○ Offida Pecorino Artemisia '19	♀♀♀ 3*
○ Offida Pecorino Artemisia '18	♀♀♀ 3*
○ Offida Pecorino Artemisia '17	♀♀♀ 2*
○ Offida Pecorino Artemisia '16	♀♀♀ 2*
○ Offida Pecorino Artemisia '15	♀♀♀ 2*
○ Offida Pecorino Artemisia '14	♀♀♀ 2*
○ Offida Pecorino Artemisia '13	♀♀♀ 2*
○ Offida Pecorino Artemisia '12	♀♀♀ 2*

La Staffa

via Castellaretta, 19
60039 Staffolo [AN]
☎ +39 0731779810
✉ www.vinilastaffa.it

CELLAR SALES
PRE-BOOKED VISITS
ANNUAL PRODUCTION 50,000 bottles
HECTARES UNDER VINE 12.00
VITICULTURE METHOD Certified Organic

Riccardo Baldi has new vineyards to oversee, in addition to the great effort that he puts into forging a dynamic, contemporary style for his wines. He's also been actively promoting his winery in more advanced markets, pouring plenty of energy into his work and reaping substantial rewards from a well-focused range of wines. This year's tastings didn't include the new vintages of the Selva di Sotto, an important Verdicchio Riserva, nor the red Rubinia. But the Rincrocca Riserva '21 more than makes up for their absence: refined aromas of lemon peel, anise, and almond precede a palate where a whip of acidity make for a taut drink, full of energy and vitality, leaving a striking salty stroke on the finish. A similar progression awaits those who open a bottle of La Staffa '23, a wine with less structure and more pronounced acidity. Fragrant and citrusy, Mai Sentito! is an undisgorged sparkling wine made from verdicchio and trebbiano grapes—a pleasant and refreshing sip.

○ Castelli di Jesi Verdicchio Cl. Rincrocca Ris. '21	♟♟♟ 6
○ Verdicchio dei Castelli di Jesi Cl. Sup. La Staffa '23	♟♟ 3*
○ Mai Sentito!	♟♟ 3
⊙ Euphoria '23	♟ 3
○ Castelli di Jesi Verdicchio Cl. Rincrocca Ris. '20	♟♟♟ 5
○ Castelli di Jesi Verdicchio Cl. Rincrocca Ris. '19	♟♟♟ 5
○ Castelli di Jesi Verdicchio Cl. Rincrocca Ris. '18	♟♟♟ 5
○ Castelli di Jesi Verdicchio Cl. Rincrocca Ris. '17	♟♟♟ 4*
○ Castelli di Jesi Verdicchio Cl. Selva di Sotto Ris. '19	♟♟ 8

Tenuta dell'Ugolino

via Copparoni, 32
60031 Castelplanio [AN]
☎ +39 0731812569
✉ www.tenutaugolino.it

CELLAR SALES
PRE-BOOKED VISITS
ANNUAL PRODUCTION 70,000 bottles
HECTARES UNDER VINE 14.00
VITICULTURE METHOD Certified Organic
SUSTAINABLE WINERY

For several years now, Andrea Petrini, now joined by Matteo Foroni, has been crafting wines of remarkable quality. What began as a family hobby has since become a full-time job, with Aroldo Bellelli providing consulting expertise. The most representative wine is the Vigneto del Balluccio, a cru facing south/southwest on rich, fresh, and clayey soil. The 2022 vintage, as always aged in stainless steel, is a marvel: despite the hot year, it boasts a bright filigree of citrus aromas, white fruit, and almond, melting into a juicy, full-bodied palate that's deeply gratifying, yet stretches into a powerful, saline, and enchanting finish. Le Piaole '23 offers a varietal nose of fresh almond and linden flowers with herbaceous touches; on the palate, it opens with nice attack before flowing easily with light notes of field herbs and celery. The well-made Maltempo, a floral Spumante Metodo Martinotti, has a delicate, graceful, saline drinkability.

○ Verdicchio dei Castelli di Jesi Cl. Sup. Vign. del Balluccio '22	♟♟♟ 4*
○ Verdicchio dei Castelli di Jesi Cl. Sup. Le Piaole '23	♟♟ 2*
○ Verdicchio dei Castelli di Jesi Pas Dosé Maltempo	♟♟ 3
○ Verdicchio dei Castelli di Jesi Cl. Sup. Vign. del Balluccio '17	♟♟♟ 4*
○ Verdicchio dei Castelli di Jesi Cl. Sup. Vign. del Balluccio '21	♟♟♟ 4*
○ Verdicchio dei Castelli di Jesi Cl. Sup. Vign. del Balluccio '20	♟♟ 4
○ Verdicchio dei Castelli di Jesi Cl. Sup. Vign. del Balluccio '18	♟♟ 4
○ Verdicchio dei Castelli di Jesi Cl. Sup. Vign. del Balluccio '16	♟♟ 3*

Tenuta di Frà

via Marciano, 10b
60030 Morro d'Alba [AN]
☎ +39 3397229846
🖰 www.tenutadifra.com

★Tenuta di Tavignano

loc. Tavignano
62011 Cingoli [MC]
☎ +39 0733617303
🖰 www.tenutaditavignano.it

CELLAR SALES
PRE-BOOKED VISITS
ANNUAL PRODUCTION 45,000 bottles
HECTARES UNDER VINE 10.00
VITICULTURE METHOD Certified Organic

CELLAR SALES
PRE-BOOKED VISITS
ANNUAL PRODUCTION 150,000 bottles
HECTARES UNDER VINE 33.00
VITICULTURE METHOD Certified Organic
SUSTAINABLE WINERY

Franziska Waldner and Hansjörg Ganthaler, seasoned restaurateurs from Alto Adige, have long been passionate about Le Marche. They decided to invest in the Villa Uliveto estate in San Vittore and Poggio Antico in Monte San Vito, and later had the opportunity to acquire a winery in Morro d'Alba as well. Gianluca Bartolucci, a seasoned expert in the local area, manages the agricultural side, while oenologist Pierluigi Lorenzetti oversees production. Their wines exhibit a crystalline, modern character. Shining among them is the Franz '21: finely citrusy, it gradually unveils layered sensations of anise, almond, and linden flowers; in the mouth, it's complex yet superbly smooth, with a long, salty tension. The Lorenzo '22 is less impactful, though characterized by a pervasive herbaceous note of tomato leaf and sage, which returns on a fresh, sapid palate. Dark and compact, the Don Giovanni '22 is a Montepulciano with a firm tannic structure and a smoky finish.

Founded in 1973 by Stefano Aymerich and Beatrice Lucangeli, this beautifully restored estate is meticulously maintained in every aspect. The spectacular amphitheater of vineyards is dedicated to verdicchio, while the red grape varieties are cultivated near the hilltop farmhouse, which serves as both a barrel room and a tasting area. Below, the cellar houses the machinery for winemaking and the stainless steel tanks used for aging their whites. Among these, the Villa Torre '23 stands out with its aromas of fruit and herbs, and a fibrous, flavorful palate with a vegetal finish; the Misco '22 reveals a nose of linden flowers, apple, and almond, which carry through to a medium-structured palate, more broad than deep. The Riserva '21 of the same name was not presented to allow for further aging. The reds impress as well, with the Libenter '20 (70% montepulciano and Bordeaux varietals) showing graphite notes, an austere, compact palate, and dark minerality. The Cervidoni '22 is more open and fruity, though somewhat predictable.

○ Castelli di Jesi Verdicchio Cl. Franz Ris. '21	♈♈♈ 8
● Don Giovanni '22	♈♈ 6
○ Verdicchio dei Castelli di Jesi Cl. Sup. Lorenzo '22	♈♈ 5
● Lacrima di Morro d'Alba Joy '23	♈ 4
⊙ Ros'Anna '23	♈ 4
○ Castelli di Jesi Verdicchio Cl. Franz Ris. '20	♈♈♈ 6
○ Castelli di Jesi Verdicchio Cl. Franz Ris. '19	♈♈♈ 6
○ Verdicchio dei Castelli di Jesi Cl. Sup. Lorenzo '21	♈♈ 5
○ Verdicchio dei Castelli di Jesi Cl. Sup. Lorenzo '20	♈♈ 5

● Libenter '20	♈♈ 5
○ Verdicchio dei Castelli di Jesi Cl. Sup. Misco '22	♈♈ 4
○ Verdicchio dei Castelli di Jesi Cl. Sup. Villa Torre '23	♈♈ 3
● Rosso Piceno Cervidoni '22	♈ 3
○ Castelli di Jesi Verdicchio Cl. Misco Ris. '19	♈♈♈ 5
○ Verdicchio dei Castelli di Jesi Cl. Sup. Misco '17	♈♈♈ 3*
○ Verdicchio dei Castelli di Jesi Cl. Sup. Misco '16	♈♈♈ 3*
○ Verdicchio dei Castelli di Jesi Cl. Sup. Misco '15	♈♈♈ 3*
○ Verdicchio dei Castelli di Jesi Cl. Sup. Misco '14	♈♈♈ 3*
○ Verdicchio dei Castelli di Jesi Cl. Sup. Misco '13	♈♈♈ 3*

Terra Fageto

via Valdaso, 52
63827 Pedaso [FM]
☎ +39 0734931784
✆ www.terrafageto.it

CELLAR SALES
PRE-BOOKED VISITS
ANNUAL PRODUCTION 150,000 bottles
HECTARES UNDER VINE 40.00
VITICULTURE METHOD Certified Organic
SUSTAINABLE WINERY

The Di Ruscio family's winery is among the most well-structured in the Fermo area. Today, it's led by the third generation: brothers Angelo (who oversees the vineyards and winemaking) and Michele (who handles administration). Their father, Claudio, a man of great experience, still plays a major role in managing the fully organic agricultural operations. The estate includes several plots, among them the panoramic Altidona parcel overlooking the sea, where red grapes grow in iron-rich soil. The pecorino and other white varietals are cultivated in cooler, north-facing, and consistently breezy areas like Campofilone. The freshness of the Salsedine '22 and Fenèsia '23 is partly explained by the decision to preserve citrus sensations and acidity. The Salsedine '22 is rich and intensely salty, with great aromatic integrity; the Fenèsia '23 exudes hints of anise and white peach on a tasty, progressive, and supple palate. We also very much enjoyed the Cuvée P41 '20, with its creamy, fragrant bubbles.

Terrapremiata

c.da Colle
63833 Montegiorgio [FM]
☎ +39 3930866736
✆ www.terrapremiata.it

ANNUAL PRODUCTION 15,000 bottles
HECTARES UNDER VINE 10.00

Terrapremiata may seem like a new name, but its Monteverde vineyards have been in production for several years, focusing on simple, Charmat-method sparkling wines. What sets the winery apart now is the commitment of footwear entrepreneur Graziano Mazza to creating a serious, robust project. This vision led to the construction of a modern, well-functioning winery among the vineyards, a structure notable for its architectural appeal. Pinot noir gives life to the elegant Lamorosa de Monteverde '21, with delicate aromas of small fruits, orange zest, flowers, and a hint of coffee powder; the palate is lively, flavorful, and brackish, with a finish of finely woven tannins and echoes of Asian spices. Of the two Gia'mimanchi, we prefer the white 2022, made from pecorino and 15% incrocio Bruni: it offers notes of anise, hazelnut, and subtle toasted accents; the palate reveals a supple, no-frills profile of commendable complexity.

Offida Pecorino Salsedine '22	♀♀5
Offida Pecorino Fenèsia '23	♀♀4
P41 M. Cl. '20	♀♀6
Serrone '21	♀♀5
Rosso Piceno Sup. Rusus '22	♀5
Offida Pecorino Fenèsia '22	♀♀4
Offida Pecorino Fenèsia '21	♀♀3*
Offida Pecorino Fenèsia '20	♀♀3*
Offida Pecorino Salsedine '21	♀♀4
Offida Pecorino Salsedine '20	♀♀4
Offida Pecorino Salsedine '19	♀♀4
Offida Pecorino Salsedine '18	♀♀4
Rosso Piceno Colle del Buffo '18	♀♀3
Rosso Piceno Rusus '21	♀♀3
Rosso Piceno Rusus '18	♀♀3
Serrone '18	♀♀5

Lamorosa de Monteverde '21	♀♀5
Gia'mimanchi Bianco '22	♀♀4
Gia'mimanchi Rosso '21	♀5
Montevè '21	♀3

★Fattoria Le Terrazze

via Musone, 4
60026 Numana [AN]
(+39 0717390352
⊛ www.fattorialeterrazze.it

Tomassetti

s.da della Marina, 18
60019 Senigallia [AN]
(+39 3294909660
⊛ www.tomassetti.bio

CELLAR SALES
PRE-BOOKED VISITS
ANNUAL PRODUCTION 90,000 bottles
HECTARES UNDER VINE 18.00

ANNUAL PRODUCTION 12,000 bottles
HECTARES UNDER VINE 6.00
VITICULTURE METHOD Certified Organic

The winery of Antonio and Giorgina Terni is among the most renowned in the region, partly due to a history dating back to 1882 and the activism of Paolo, Antonio's father, who was at the forefront of founding the Conero DOC in the late 1960s. The winery achieved recognition in the mid-1990s when the reds produced on the hills of Numana became known for their modern style and elegance. Today, the wines once again embody a contemporary style, with well-extracted tannins and a nice balance of complexity and drinkability, all while avoiding excessive alcohol and overripe notes. In this lineup, the Sassi Neri Riserva '20 is a standout: morello cherry remains central to a nose edged with spices, burnt wood, and light plum; on the palate, it's energetic and remarkably supple within a solid structure. Also very good—and a true bargain for the price—the Rosso Conero '21 echoes some of these characteristics but with greater simplicity.

Brothers Andrea and Matteo Tommassetti have already made a name for themselves in recent years with artisanal wines that, while full of character, can sometimes be challenging, with a rougher aromatic profile. Our final tastings reveal a lineup that has lightened its profile without losing authenticity, instead making for some compelling drinkability. The Pescatore '22 (montepulciano), aged in stainless steel, is one example, a bright cerasuolo, with notes of cherries, hay, and aromatic herbs on a relaxed, fragrant palate free of tannic edges. A similar dynamic is found in the Renudo '22 (sangiovese), where floral tones, along with laurel, thyme, and orange peel, mark a flavorful profile. The Mietitore '22 (biancame) is equally well-crafted, with citrus, yellow plum, and subtle herbaceous echoes on a full-bodied, well-structured palate. The Cercanome '21 (verdicchio) is somewhat simple, with its sweet almond sensations. The pleasantly evolved Corno '16 proves relaxed, conjuring up complex notes of graphite and underbrush.

● Conero Sassi Neri Ris. '20	♙♙♙ 6
● Rosso Conero Le Terrazze '21	♙♙ 3*
○ Pink Fluid '23	♙♙ 3
○ Le Cave Chardonnay '23	♙ 3
● Chaos '04	♛♛♛ 5
● Chaos '01	♛♛♛ 6
● Chaos '97	♛♛♛ 6
● Conero Sassi Neri Ris. '19	♛♛♛ 5
● Conero Sassi Neri Ris. '04	♛♛♛ 5
● Rosso Conero Sassi Neri '02	♛♛♛ 5
● Rosso Conero Sassi Neri '99	♛♛♛ 5
● Rosso Conero Sassi Neri '98	♛♛♛ 5
● Rosso Conero Visions of J '01	♛♛♛ 7
● Rosso Conero Visions of J '97	♛♛♛ 7

● Corno '16	♙♙ 3
○ Mietitore '22	♙♙ 3
● Pescatore '22	♙♙ 3
● Renudo '22	♙♙ 3
○ Cercanome '21	♙ 4
○ Fricò '22	♙ 3

★★Umani Ronchi

via Adriatica, 12
60027 Osimo [AN]
☏ +39 0717108019
✉ www.umanironchi.com

CELLAR SALES
PRE-BOOKED VISITS
ACCOMMODATION AND RESTAURANT SERVICE
ANNUAL PRODUCTION 3,450,000 bottles
HECTARES UNDER VINE 240.00
VITICULTURE METHOD Certified Organic
SUSTAINABLE WINERY

The Winery of the Year award given in last year's edition of this guide didn't come as a bolt from the blue. For many years, the Bernetti family's winery has been presenting a series of wines of impressive quality, making it difficult to choose the best. It all stems from meticulous planning: vineyards situated in prime growing areas, careful selection of the grapes, a state-of-the-art winery (recently renovated), and a top-notch technical team. Tre Bicchieri for the Historical '19, which benefits from an exceptional year for Verdicchio: elegant on the nose with balsamic nuances, anise, almonds, and white fruits, it reveals an alluring harmony on the palate, leading to a luminous, long finish. However, don't miss the tasty Vecchie Vigne '22, the powerful Campo San Giorgio '20, the fruity Cùmaro '20, or the refined Plenio '22. The alluring Maximo '22 and the vibrant bubbles of La Hoz Rosé round out a splendid lineup.

○ Verdicchio dei Castelli di Jesi Cl. Sup. V.V. Historical '19	♟♟♟ 7	
● Conero Campo San Giorgio Ris. '20	♟♟ 8	
● Conero Cùmaro Ris. '20	♟♟ 5	
○ Verdicchio dei Castelli di Jesi Cl. Sup. V.V. '22	♟♟ 5	
○ Castelli di Jesi Verdicchio Cl. Plenio Ris. '22	♟♟ 5	
○ Centovie Pecorino '22	♟♟ 5	
⊙ La Hoz Nature M. Cl. Rosé	♟♟ 5	
○ LH2 Version 14 Extra Brut M. Cl.	♟♟ 5	
○ Maximo '22	♟♟ 5	
● Pelago '20	♟♟ 7	
● Rosso Conero Serrano '23	♟♟ 2*	
○ Verdicchio dei Castelli di Jesi Cl. Sup. Casal di Serra '23	♟♟ 3	
● Rosso Conero San Lorenzo '22	♟ 3	

La Valle del Sole

via San Lazzaro, 46
63035 Offida [AP]
☏ +39 0736889658
✉ www.lavalledelsoleoffida.com

PRE-BOOKED VISITS
ACCOMMODATION AND RESTAURANT SERVICE
ANNUAL PRODUCTION 40,000 bottles
HECTARES UNDER VINE 9.00
VITICULTURE METHOD Certified Organic

Silvano Di Nicolò founded his winery in 1989. Over the years, the producer has involved his entire family in the project, which also includes guest rooms. The vineyards, which he tends to personally, feature traditional Piceno varietals like pecorino, passerina, montepulciano, and sangiovese. The cellar is equipped with stainless steel tanks, concrete vats, and large oak barrels. Alessandro D'Angelo and winemaker Matteo Lucciarini de Vincenzi are responsible for operations. By a twist of fate, the winery presented only one wine this year, though their range is much broader. Nonetheless, the Piceno Superiore '20 is magnificent: delicate spices introduce intense yet soft fruity aromas and light toasted notes that melt into a weighty palate, harmoniously combining contrast and sapid drive with great effectiveness. This structural harmony owes much to its measured alcohol content and flavorful tannins; on the finish, it gains acquires floral tones. All at an eye-popping price.

● Piceno Sup. '20	♟♟♟ 3*
○ Offida Passerina '21	♟♟ 2*
○ Offida Pecorino '22	♟♟ 3*
○ Offida Pecorino '21	♟♟ 3
○ Offida Pecorino '20	♟♟ 3
○ Offida Pecorino '19	♟♟ 3
○ Offida Pecorino '18	♟♟ 3*
○ Offida Pecorino '17	♟♟ 3
● Offida Rosso '15	♟♟ 4
⊙ Rosato '22	♟♟ 2*
⊙ Rosato '19	♟♟ 3
⊙ Rosato '18	♟♟ 2*
● Rosso Piceno Sup. '19	♟♟ 3
● Rosso Piceno Sup. '18	♟♟ 3
● Rosso Piceno Sup. '17	♟♟ 3
● Rosso Piceno Sup. '16	♟♟ 3*

★★Velenosi

via dei Biancospini, 11
63100 Ascoli Piceno
📞 +39 0736341218
🌐 www.velenosivini.com

CELLAR SALES
PRE-BOOKED VISITS
ANNUAL PRODUCTION 2,500,000 bottles
HECTARES UNDER VINE 192.00

In recent years, Velenosi has expanded beyond the borders of Le Marche by adding wines from the Controguerra estate in Abruzzo. This decision has allowed the producer to broaden its territorial portfolio as it continues to expand its presence in global markets. The catalog is extensive but thoughtfully curated, with an appropriate number of bottles produced and options for every budget, including organic selections. The Roggio del Filare once again dominates: the 2021 vintage stands out for its brilliant fusion of fruity, spicy, and lightly smoky nuances. The palate offers an international style, with solid tannic structure and harmonious geometry. Also worth noting are the powerful Ludi '21 and The Rose '18, a Metodo Classico rosé based on pinot nero. From the neighboring region, the citrus-driven Pecorino '23 and the fruity Montepulciano d'Abruzzo '22 make a strong impression. The Brecciarolo '22 and the soft, fragrant Lacrima Quercia Antica '23 are also solid.

Wine	Rating
● Rosso Piceno Sup. Roggio del Filare '21	♥♥♥ 6
● Lacrima di Morro d'Alba Sup. Querciantica '23	♥♥ 3
● Montepulciano d'Abruzzo Prope '22	♥♥ 3
○ Offida Pecorino Bio '23	♥♥ 3
● Offida Rosso Ludi '21	♥♥ 6
○ Prope Pecorino '23	♥♥ 3
● Rosso Piceno Sup. Brecciarolo '22	♥♥ 3
⊙ The Rose Brut M. Cl. '18	♥♥ 5
⊙ Cerasuolo d'Abruzzo Prope '23	♥ 3
○ Offida Passerina Villa Angela '23	♥ 3
○ Offida Pecorino Rêve '22	♥ 5
○ Offida Pecorino Villa Angela '23	♥ 3
● Rosso Piceno Sup. Bio '22	♥ 4
● Rosso Piceno Sup. Solestà '22	♥ 4
○ Trebbiano d'Abruzzo Prope '23	♥ 2

Roberto Venturi

via Case Nuove, 1a
60010 Castelleone di Suasa [AN]
📞 +39 3381855566
🌐 www.viniventuri.it

CELLAR SALES
PRE-BOOKED VISITS
ANNUAL PRODUCTION 60,000 bottles
HECTARES UNDER VINE 8.00

Roberto Venturi's Verdicchio wines have had a mixed showing. For several years, he has accustomed us to a style that's in line with the classic traits of the Jesi grape, presenting some top-of-the-shelf wines, often among the best in the region. There is a noticeable shift in the approach at the well-equipped, modern winery near Castelleone di Suasa, as both the Qudì Classico Superiore '22 and the Qudì Riserva '20 convey distinctly vegetal and herbaceous sensations: sage, grapefruit, green pepper, and tomato leaf, all perfectly mirrored on a pleasantly approachable palate (with more weight in the 2020 version). Is this a new style or an experiment gone too far? Time will tell. For now, we can say that we enjoyed the intense citrus vein of the Donnamata '23 (moscato) and the cherry and aromatic herb notes of the Balsamino '23 (aleatico), both highly drinkable.

Wine	Rating
● Balsamino '23	♥♥ 3
○ Castelli di Jesi Verdicchio Qudì Ris. '20	♥♥♥ 5
⊙ Donnamata '23	♥♥ 3
⊙ La Rosetta '23	♥ 3
○ Verdicchio dei Castelli di Jesi Cl. Sup. Qudì '22	♥ 3
○ Castelli di Jesi Verdicchio Cl. Qudì Ris. '19	♥♥♥ 5
○ Verdicchio dei Castelli di Jesi Cl. Sup. Qudì '18	♥♥♥ 3*
○ Verdicchio dei Castelli di Jesi Cl. Sup. Qudì '15	♥♥♥ 3*
○ Verdicchio dei Castelli di Jesi Cl. Sup. Qudì '13	♥♥♥ 2*
○ Verdicchio dei Castelli di Jesi Cl. Sup. Qudì '21	♥♥ 3*

Vicari

via Pozzo Buono, 3
60030 Morro d'Alba [AN]
☎ +39 073163164
✉ www.vicarivini.it

CELLAR SALES
PRE-BOOKED VISITS
ANNUAL PRODUCTION 150,000 bottles
HECTARES UNDER VINE 40.00

Winemaking in Morro d'Alba inevitably involves dealing with verdicchio and lacrima nera. These complementary varietals, though differing in temperament, are quite adaptable, with the ability to absorb the style of whoever cultivates and vinifies them. Vicari has long favored a certain ripeness, especially for lacrima, aiming to produce tannins that are crunchy yet gentle in their astringency. Another hallmark of the Vicari style is the absence of wood, even the Passito and the powerful Lacrima Superiore '21, made from ripe grapes that provide a rich fruity core and a creamy, well-sustained palate with persistent length. The less intense but highly pleasant Dasempre '23 offers a full whiff of cherries. The L'Insolito '22 impresses with its varietal nose and a straight, powerful, and savory palate, finishing with a long citrus echo. The youthful Capofila '23 and the soft-palated Oltretempo Riserva '20 both provide tasty drinking experiences.

Vignamato

via Battinebbia, 4
60038 San Paolo di Jesi [AN]
☎ +39 0731779197
✉ www.vignamato.com

CELLAR SALES
PRE-BOOKED VISITS
ACCOMMODATION
ANNUAL PRODUCTION 150,000 bottles
HECTARES UNDER VINE 26.00
VITICULTURE METHOD Certified Organic

The winery was founded by Amato Ceci, while Maurizio and his wife Serenella would later solidify its structure before passing it on to the third generation: Andrea and Francesco. Andrea manages the vineyard and cellar, while Francesco oversees sales. This transition, which coincided with the involvement of consultant Pierluigi Lorenzetti, has marked a turning point for the wines, with a diverse range that has since gained in consistency, aromatic clarity and harmony. The sixth consecutive Tre Bicchieri award only reaffirms this, making the Ambrosia a modern classic of Verdicchio. The 2021 reveals sweet almond, anise, and both fresh and candied citrus peel, perfectly blending mature and fresh qualities. The palate balances creamy textures with sapid length, creating a crackling effect. A pronounced vegetal vein characterizes the Versus '23, a wine that's not afraid to sport a spirited, brackish profile.

○ Verdicchio dei Castelli di Jesi Cl. Sup. L'Insolito del Pozzo Buono '22	♟♟ 4
○ Castelli di Jesi Verdicchio Cl. Oltretempo del Pozzo Buono '20	♟♟ 5
● Lacrima di Morro d'Alba Dasempre del Pozzo Buono '23	♟♟ 3
● Lacrima di Morro d'Alba Sup. Lacrima del Pozzo Buono '21	♟♟ 5
○ Verdicchio dei Castelli di Jesi Cl. Capofila del Pozzo Buono '23	♟♟ 2*
● Lacrima di Morro d'Alba Passito Amaranto del Pozzo Buono '21	♟ 5
○ Verdicchio dei Castelli di Jesi Cl. Sup. Insolito del Pozzo Buono '15	♟♟♟ 3*
○ Verdicchio dei Castelli di Jesi Cl. Sup. L'Insolito del Pozzo Buono '21	♟♟ 4

○ Castelli di Jesi Verdicchio Cl. Ambrosia Ris. '21	♟♟♟ 5
○ Verdicchio dei Castelli di Jesi Cl. Sup. Versiano '23	♟♟ 3
○ Versus '23	♟♟ 3
● Campalliano '21	♟ 4
○ Verdicchio dei Castelli di Jesi Passito Antares '20	♟ 5
○ Castelli di Jesi Verdicchio Cl. Ambrosia Ris. '20	♟♟♟ 5
○ Castelli di Jesi Verdicchio Cl. Ambrosia Ris. '19	♟♟♟ 4*
○ Castelli di Jesi Verdicchio Cl. Ambrosia Ris. '18	♟♟♟ 4*
○ Castelli di Jesi Verdicchio Cl. Ambrosia Ris. '17	♟♟♟ 4*

OTHER WINERIES

Boccadigabbia

loc. Fontespina
c.da Castelletta, 56
62012 Civitanova Marche [MC]
☏ +39 073370728
✆ www.boccadigabbia.com

CELLAR SALES
PRE-BOOKED VISITS
ANNUAL PRODUCTION 100,000 bottles
HECTARES UNDER VINE 23.00
SUSTAINABLE WINERY

○ Colli Maceratesi Ribona Le Grane '22	♟♟ 3
○ Colli Maceratesi Ribona '23	♟ 3
● Rosso Piceno '20	♟ 3
● Saltapicchio '21	♟ 5

Buscareto

fraz. Pianello
via San Gregorio, 66
60010 Ostra [AN]
☏ +39 0717988020
✆ www.buscareto.com

CELLAR SALES
PRE-BOOKED VISITS
ANNUAL PRODUCTION 150,000 bottles
HECTARES UNDER VINE 36.40
SUSTAINABLE WINERY

● Lacrima di Morro d'Alba '23	♟♟ 3
● Rosso Piceno '23	♟♟ 3
○ Verdicchio dei Castelli di Jesi '23	♟♟ 3
● Bisaccione '21	♟ 4

La Canosa

c.da San Pietro, 6
63071 Rotella [AP]
☏ +39 0736374556
✆ www.lacanosaagricola.it

CELLAR SALES
PRE-BOOKED VISITS
ACCOMMODATION
ANNUAL PRODUCTION 150,000 bottles
HECTARES UNDER VINE 28.00

● Tesino	♟♟ 5
○ Verdicchio dei Castelli di Jesi Cl. Sup. Picus Viridis '22	♟♟ 3
○ Offida Passerina Servator '23	♟ 3

Broccanera

fraz. Montale
via Costa, 111
60011 Arcevia [AN]
☏ +39 3398194859
✆ www.broccanera.it

CELLAR SALES
PRE-BOOKED VISITS
ANNUAL PRODUCTION 28,000 bottles
HECTARES UNDER VINE 5.50
VITICULTURE METHOD Certified Organic

⊙ Broccanera Dosaggio Zero Rosé M. Cl. '20	♟♟ 5
○ Verdicchio dei Castelli di Jesi Guzzo '22	♟♟ 3
⊙ Scossa '23	♟ 3
○ Scosso '23	♟ 3

Irene Cameli

c.da Gaico, 19
63030 Castorano [AP]
☏ +39 073687435
✆ www.vinorossomarche.it

CELLAR SALES
PRE-BOOKED VISITS
ANNUAL PRODUCTION 15,000 bottles
HECTARES UNDER VINE 2.40

● Red '19	♟♟ 8
● Ozio '20	♟♟ 4
○ Offida Pecorino Gaico '22	♟ 3

Carminucci

via San Leonardo, 39
63013 Grottammare [AP]
☏ +39 0735735869
✆ www.carminucci.com

CELLAR SALES
ANNUAL PRODUCTION 350,000 bottles
HECTARES UNDER VINE 53.00
VITICULTURE METHOD Certified Organic

● Paccaosso '18	♟♟ 5
● Rosso Piceno Sup. Naumakos '20	♟♟ 3
○ Naumakos Chardonnay '22	♟ 3
○ Offida Pecorino Belato '23	♟ 3

OTHER WINERIES

Centanni

via Aso, 159
63062 Montefiore dell'Aso [AP]
📞 +39 0734938530
🌐 www.vinicentanni.it

CELLAR SALES
PRE-BOOKED VISITS
ANNUAL PRODUCTION 250,000 bottles
HECTARES UNDER VINE 50.00
VITICULTURE METHOD Certified Organic
SUSTAINABLE WINERY

⊙ Floralia '23	🍷🍷 3
○ Offida Pecorino Santa Maria '22	🍷🍷 5
● Montefloris '22	🍷 3
● Rosso Piceno Sup. Renarie V.T. '21	🍷 3

Colle Jano

via Rovejano, 15
60034 Cupramontana [AN]
📞 +39 3491965659
🌐 www.collejano.com

ANNUAL PRODUCTION 6,500 bottles
HECTARES UNDER VINE 3.10
VITICULTURE METHOD Certified Organic
SUSTAINABLE WINERY

○ Verdicchio dei Castelli di Jesi Cl. Sup. Jano '22	🍷🍷 3*
○ Verdicchio dei Castelli di Jesi Cl. Sup. Titillo '23	🍷🍷 4

Croce del Moro

via Tassanare, 4
60030 Rosora [AN]
📞 +39 0731814158
🌐 www.tassanare.it

PRE-BOOKED VISITS
ANNUAL PRODUCTION 50,000 bottles
HECTARES UNDER VINE 8.00

○ Verdicchio dei Castelli di Jesi Cl. Sup. Moro della Genga '23	🍷🍷 4

Cerbero

via San Silvestro, 145a
63064 Cupra Marittima [AP]
📞 +39 3458399558
🌐 www.cantina-cerbero.com

ANNUAL PRODUCTION 10,000 bottles
HECTARES UNDER VINE 2.00

○ Caronte '21	🍷🍷 7
● Dante '20	🍷🍷 8
○ Beatrice '22	🍷 4
● Virgilio '20	🍷 8

Cossignani L. E. Tempo

c.da San Pietro, 5A
63061 Massignano [AP]
📞 +39 3392162832
🌐 www.letempo.it

⊙ Brut Rosé M. Cl. '21	🍷🍷 6
○ Blanc de Blancs Pas Dosé M. Cl. '20	🍷🍷 6

Fioretti Brera

via della Stazione, 48
60022 Castelfidardo [AN]
📞 +39 335373896
🌐 www.fiorettibrera.it

ANNUAL PRODUCTION 10,000 bottles
HECTARES UNDER VINE 3.50
VITICULTURE METHOD Certified Organic

● Conero Rigo 23 Ris. '20	🍷🍷 5
● Rosso Conero Fausti '21	🍷🍷 3

OTHER WINERIES

Andrea Giorgetti

c.da Montepriori, 3
62018 Potenza Picena [MC]
📞 +39 3351401942
🌐 www.andreagiorgetti.it

CELLAR SALES
PRE-BOOKED VISITS
ANNUAL PRODUCTION 15,000 bottles
HECTARES UNDER VINE 3.00
VITICULTURE METHOD Certified Organic

⊙ Aganita '23	🍷🍷 3
⊙ Giulia Brut Rosé '23	🍷🍷 3
○ Colli Maceratesi Ribona Flosis '23	🍷 3

Tenuta Grimaldi

loc. Terricoli, 270
62024 Matelica [MC]
📞 +39 0737685616
🌐 www.tenutagrimaldi.com

ANNUAL PRODUCTION 11,000 bottles
HECTARES UNDER VINE 8.50
VITICULTURE METHOD Certified Organic
SUSTAINABLE WINERY

○ Verdicchio di Matelica '23	🍷🍷 4

Valerio Lucarelli

c.da San Costanzo, 43
62026 San Ginesio [MC]
📞 +39 3661131022
🌐 www.cantinalucarelli.com

ANNUAL PRODUCTION 5,000 bottles
HECTARES UNDER VINE 2.00

● Lenòs '21	🍷🍷 6

Claudio Morelli

v.le Romagna, 47b
61032 Fano [PU]
📞 +39 0721823352
🌐 www.claudiomorelli.it

CELLAR SALES
PRE-BOOKED VISITS
ANNUAL PRODUCTION 110,000 bottles
HECTARES UNDER VINE 40.00

○ Bianchello del Metauro Sup. Borgo Torre '23	🍷🍷 3*
○ Bianchello del Metauro San Cesareo '23	🍷🍷 2*
○ Bianchello del Metauro La V. delle Terrazze '23	🍷 2

Perseveranza

via Montoro, 17
63848 Petritoli [FM]
📞 +39 +31650267667
🌐 www.perseveranza-it.com

ANNUAL PRODUCTION 40,000 bottles
HECTARES UNDER VINE 8.00

● Rosso Piceno Sangiovese Leonardo '22	🍷🍷 5
● Rosso Piceno Sangiovese Michelangelo '22	🍷🍷 5
○ Falerio Pecorino Antonio '23	🍷 5
○ Giuseppe '23	🍷 5

Piersanti

zona ind.le Pontemagno
60034 Cupramontana [AN]
📞 +39 0731703214
🌐 www.piersantivini.com

CELLAR SALES
ANNUAL PRODUCTION 3,500,000 bottles
HECTARES UNDER VINE 23.00
VITICULTURE METHOD Certified Organic
SUSTAINABLE WINERY

○ Verdicchio dei Castelli di Jesi Cl. Quota 311 '23	🍷🍷 1*
○ Verdicchio dei Castelli di Jesi Cl. Sup. Bacareto '22	🍷🍷 2*

OTHER WINERIES

Produttori di Matelica 1932
via Raffaello, 1c
62024 Matelica [MC]
📞 +39 073784013
🌐 www.cantineprovima.it

CELLAR SALES
PRE-BOOKED VISITS
ANNUAL PRODUCTION 160,000 bottles
HECTARES UNDER VINE 130.00
VITICULTURE METHOD Certified Organic

○ Verdicchio di Matelica Egos '23	♟♟ 3
○ Verdicchio di Matelica Materga Ris. '22	♟♟ 3
○ Verdicchio di Matelica Soleiano '23	♟ 2
○ Verdicchio di Matelica Terramonte '23	♟ 3

Cantina Sant'Isidoro
fraz. Colbuccaro
c.da Colle Sant'Isidoro, 5
62014 Corridonia [MC]
📞 +39 0733770565
🌐 www.cantinasantisidoro.it

CELLAR SALES
PRE-BOOKED VISITS
ANNUAL PRODUCTION 30,000 bottles
HECTARES UNDER VINE 14.50

○ Colli Maceratesi Ribona Paucis '22	♟♟ 4
○ Colli Maceratesi Ribona Pausula '23	♟♟ 2*
○ Colli Maceratesi Ribona Dosaggio Zero M. Cl. '21	♟ 4

Terralibera
via San Paterniano
60030 Serra de' Conti [AN]
📞 +39 3460664255
🌐 www.terraliberavini.com

PRE-BOOKED VISITS
ANNUAL PRODUCTION 12,000 bottles
HECTARES UNDER VINE 7.00
SUSTAINABLE WINERY

○ Verdicchio dei Castelli di Jesi Cl. Sup. Insieme '23	♟♟ 3

Fabrizio Quaresima
via Acquaticcio, 15
60035 Jesi [AN]
📞 +39 3487729447
🌐 www.aziendaquaresima.it

CELLAR SALES
ANNUAL PRODUCTION 7,500 bottles
HECTARES UNDER VINE 1.00

○ Verdicchio dei Castelli di Jesi Cl. Sup. Diamante '23	♟♟ 4
○ Verdicchio dei Castelli di Jesi Cl. Sup. Il Filello '23	♟♟ 2*

Saputi
c.da Fiastra, 1
62020 Colmurano [MC]
📞 +39 0733508137
🌐 www.saputi.it

CELLAR SALES
PRE-BOOKED VISITS
ACCOMMODATION AND RESTAURANT SERVICE
ANNUAL PRODUCTION 80,000 bottles
HECTARES UNDER VINE 25.00
VITICULTURE METHOD Certified Organic

○ Colli Maceratesi Ribona Camurena '21	♟♟ 4
○ Colli Maceratesi Ribona R '23	♟♟ 3
● Abate Pallia '19	♟ 4

Terre di Serrapetrona
Tenuta Stefano Graidi
via Colli, 7/8
62020 Serrapetrona [MC]
📞 +39 0733908329
🌐 www.terrediserrapetrona.it

CELLAR SALES
PRE-BOOKED VISITS
RESTAURANT SERVICE
ANNUAL PRODUCTION 50,000 bottles
HECTARES UNDER VINE 17.50
VITICULTURE METHOD Certified Organic
SUSTAINABLE WINERY

● Vernaccia di Serrapetrona Vernaccianera Dolce	♟♟ 3
● Vernaccia di Serrapetrona Vernaccianera Secca	♟♟ 3

MARCHE

OTHER WINERIES

Vallerosa Bonci

via Torre, 15
60034 Cupramontana [AN]
(') +39 0731789129
⊛ www.vallerosa-bonci.com

CELLAR SALES
PRE-BOOKED VISITS
ANNUAL PRODUCTION 80,000 bottles
HECTARES UNDER VINE 13.00

○ Verdicchio dei Castelli di Jesi Cl. Sup. San Michele '22	♟♟ 4
○ Castelli di Jesi Verdicchio Cl. Pietrone Ris. '20	♟ 6

Verser

loc. Carpignano, 114
62027 San Severino Marche [MC]
(') +39 3317884283
⊛ www.agricolaverser.it

○ Rebòl '22	♟♟ 3
● Serrapetrona Clemè '22	♟♟ 4
○ Dumì '22	♟ 4

Fattoria Villa Ligi

via Zoccolanti, 25a
61045 Pergola [PU]
(') +39 0721734351
⊛ www.villaligi.it

CELLAR SALES
PRE-BOOKED VISITS
ANNUAL PRODUCTION 50,000 bottles
HECTARES UNDER VINE 28.00
VITICULTURE METHOD Certified Organic

● Pergola Aleatico Sup. Grifoglietto '22	♟♟ 4
● Skiants '22	♟♟ 4
○ Bianchello del Metauro Albaspino '23	♟ 2
○ Pergola Rosato Fiori '23	♟ 2

Vigneti Vallorani

c.da La Rocca, 28
63079 Colli del Tronto [AP]
(') +39 3534195388
⊛ www.vignetivallorani.com

CELLAR SALES
PRE-BOOKED VISITS
ACCOMMODATION
ANNUAL PRODUCTION 40,000 bottles
HECTARES UNDER VINE 9.00
VITICULTURE METHOD Certified Organic
SUSTAINABLE WINERY

○ Lefric '22	♟♟ 4
● Polisia '21	♟♟ 3
○ Avora '23	♟ 3
⊙ Octavum '23	♟ 3

Villa Forano

c.da Forano, 40
62010 Appignano [MC]
(') +39 073357102
⊛ www.fattoriaforano.it

CELLAR SALES
PRE-BOOKED VISITS
ACCOMMODATION
ANNUAL PRODUCTION 30,000 bottles
HECTARES UNDER VINE 21.00

○ Colli Maceratesi Ribona Monteferro '22	♟♟ 3*
○ Colli Maceratesi Ribona Le Piagge '23	♟ 2
⊙ Occhio di Gallo '23	♟ 2
● Rosso Piceno '22	♟ 2

Zaccagnini

via Salmagina, 9/10
60039 Staffolo [AN]
(') +39 0731779892
⊛ www.zaccagnini.it

CELLAR SALES
PRE-BOOKED VISITS
ACCOMMODATION AND RESTAURANT SERVICE
ANNUAL PRODUCTION 180,000 bottles
HECTARES UNDER VINE 35.00
VITICULTURE METHOD Certified Organic

○ Castelli di Jesi Verdicchio Cl. Maestro di Staffolo Ris. '20	♟♟ 5
○ Verdicchio dei Castelli di Jesi Cl. Sup. Argonauta '23	♟♟ 2*

UMBRIA

This year's edition of the guide sees Umbria in top form. The 17 Tre Bicchieri awarded, a record for the region, already tell part of the story, but the most compelling takeaway is the distinct style of the wines across its various territories. Though small in size, Umbria's diverse grape varieties, soils, microclimates, and the skill of its many winemakers make it a region of remarkable breadth. It's also not a region that focuses on just one type or varietal; from north to south, you find a wide range of reds and whites, each with its own character.

Montefalco is undoubtedly the region's engine. Numerous wines were awarded, starting with its prestigious Sagrantino (which, as we've often pointed out, has finally found a clear direction, one we believe is the right path) and extending to the other local standout, Montefalco Rosso, where sangiovese takes center stage. Let's not forget Montefalco Bianco, produced by only a few wineries but noteworthy for its use of trebbiano spoletino, a grape that truly comes into its own here, especially in the DOC Spoleto production zone. Speaking of sangiovese, one highlight this year is Monte Vibiano's Fiommarino, a delightful red produced southwest of Perugia—it's been a welcome addition in recent years. Staying in the realm of reds, and underscoring the region's biodiversity, we must mention the excellent Trasimeno Gamay (which, despite its name, is actually grenache, a misnomer that's stuck over time), known for being fresh, light, and juicy. Then there's Ciliegiolo di Narni, which defines the viticulture of the south.

As we continue south, we arrive at Orvieto and its renowned whites. The area's revival began several years ago, and the results are now clearly visible. Four wines were awarded (including a lovely muffa nobile), but more importantly, these wines have achieved a stylistic clarity that highlights the characteristics of each vineyard and sets them on a path for aging alongside Italy's finest wines. We close by mentioning the small DOC Torgiano appellation. Though it covers just a few hectares and involves only a handful of wineries, the valuable work Lungarotti did decades ago has paid off. Every wine from this area near Perugia is impressive, starting with the Torgiano Bianco, which also earned Tre Bicchieri this year.

Adanti

loc. Arquata
via Belvedere, 2
06031 Bevagna [PG]
☎ +39 0742360295
⊛ www.cantineadanti.com

CELLAR SALES
PRE-BOOKED VISITS
ANNUAL PRODUCTION 130,000 bottles
HECTARES UNDER VINE 30.00
SUSTAINABLE WINERY

One of the historic wineries in the Montefalco area, Adanti was founded in the 1960s by Domenico Adanti. The estate's vineyards are located on the hills of Arquata and Colcimino, with Villa Arquata serving as the heart of operations. It's a place steeped in tradition, producing classic, austere wines known for their longevity. Today, the producer is run by Daniela Adanti and her daughter Stella, who are committed to continuing the philosophy of its founder, aiming to maintain its status as a symbol of the region. Released nearly ten years after harvest, confirming the longevity that is a hallmark of the winery's offerings, the Domenico '15 remains energetic and vibrant despite its age. It reveals clean primary aromas of red fruits and spices. The tannins are soft, and the wine has a pervasive quality, but it's sapidity that gives the palate rhythm, driving it to a beautiful finish. The Arquata, another Sagrantino from 2016, is also very good. The Montefalco Rosso '20 proves pleasantly simple in its fine simplicity.

● Montefalco Sagrantino Il Domenico '15	♟♟6
○ Arquata Bianco '23	♟♟2*
● Montefalco Rosso '20	♟♟3
● Montefalco Sagrantino Arquata '16	♟♟5
○ Montefalco Grechetto '23	♟3
● Montefalco Sagrantino Passito '20	♟6
● Montefalco Sagrantino Arquata '08	♟♟♟6
● Montefalco Sagrantino Arquata '06	♟♟♟5
● Montefalco Sagrantino Arquata '05	♟♟♟5
○ Montefalco Grechetto '20	♟♟2*
● Montefalco Rosso Arquata '17	♟♟4
● Montefalco Rosso Ris. '16	♟♟4
● Montefalco Sagrantino '14	♟♟5
● Montefalco Sagrantino Il Domenico '10	♟♟6
● Montefalco Sagrantino Passito '11	♟♟6

★Antonelli - San Marco

loc. San Marco, 60
06036 Montefalco [PG]
☎ +39 0742379158
⊛ www.antonellisanmarco.it

CELLAR SALES
PRE-BOOKED VISITS
ACCOMMODATION AND RESTAURANT SERVICE
ANNUAL PRODUCTION 420,000 bottles
HECTARES UNDER VINE 60.00
VITICULTURE METHOD Certified Organic
SUSTAINABLE WINERY

The Antonelli family's roots in Umbrian viticulture run deep, having cultivated vines here in one of Montefalco's most renowned growing areas since 1881. Today, the estate boasts 60 ha under vine, primarily focusing on native varieties such as sagrantino, trebbiano spoletino, sangiovese, and grechetto, all of which have been organically farmed since 2009. The producer's portfolio offers a nuanced interpretation of the territory, delivering wines that are both characterful and long-lasting. The lineup submitted for tasting exceeded all expectations, with four wines reaching the finals. Elegance, finesse, complexity, and balance define the Montefalco Rosso Riserva '20, which we consider the best ever made. Floral notes of violet and plum are followed by a palate with measured tannins, achieving great harmony between acidity and sapidity. It's followed by two superb whites, both Trebbiano Spoletinos: the fresher and more fragrant Trebium, and the Vigna Tonda, a cru vinified in amphorae. Last but not least, we find the Molino dell'Attone, also a cru (this time a Sagrantino). A small range, but outstanding.

● Montefalco Rosso Ris. '20	♟♟♟5
● Montefalco Sagrantino Molino dell'Attone '19	♟♟8
○ Spoleto Trebbiano Spoletino Trebium '23	♟♟3*
○ Spoleto Trebbiano Spoletino V. Tonda '21	♟♟5
● Baiocco Sangiovese '23	♟♟2*
● Montefalco Rosso '21	♟♟3
● Montefalco Sagrantino '19	♟♟5
● Montefalco Sagrantino Chiusa di Pannone '19	♟♟7
● Montefalco Sagrantino Passito '20	♟♟5
● Contrario '20	♟4
○ Montefalco Grechetto '23	♟2
○ Spoleto Trebbiano Spoletino Dosaggio Zero M. Cl. '20	♟5

Argillae

voc. Pomarro, 45
05010 Allerona [TR]
☎ +39 0763624604
⊕ www.argillae.eu

CELLAR SALES
PRE-BOOKED VISITS
ANNUAL PRODUCTION 80,000 bottles
HECTARES UNDER VINE 14.00

The estate's vineyards stretch across the verdant hills between Ficulle and Allerona, north of Orvieto. The varieties cultivated fall under the Orvieto appellation and thrive on clay and limestone soils. The wines produced here have a modern edge while still reflecting their terroir. The range also includes interesting and successful experiments with amphora aging. Environmental sustainability is a key focus, with organic farming practices and the use of renewable energy being integral to their operations. At the heart of it all is Giulia Di Cosimo, a talented producer who presented a first-rate lineup this year. Tasting of the new vintage of the Primo d'Anfora has been postponed to next year, but we delighted our palates with an Orvieto Classico Superiore that's among the best in its category. It features white fruit, mountain flowers, and a fresh, invigorating, vibrant palate. The Grechetto is also delicious, boasting bolder structure while retaining a lovely acidity. The Sinuoso and the Orvieto '23 prove simple but well-crafted.

○ Orvieto Cl. Sup. Panata '22	▼▼▼ 5
○ Grechetto '23	▼▼ 4
○ Orvieto Sup. '23	▼▼ 4
● Sinuoso '23	▼▼ 4
⊙ Rosetum '23	▼ 4
○ Primo d'Anfora '20	♈♈♈ 6
○ Grechetto '22	♈♈ 3
○ Grechetto '20	♈♈ 3
○ Orvieto Cl. Sup. Panata '21	♈♈ 4
○ Orvieto Cl. Sup. Panata '20	♈♈ 4
○ Orvieto Cl. Sup. Panata '18	♈♈ 4
○ Orvieto Sup. '21	♈♈ 3
○ Orvieto Sup. '20	♈♈ 3*
○ Primo d'Anfora '19	♈♈ 6
○ Primo d'Anfora '18	♈♈ 6
● Sinuoso '22	♈♈ 3

★Barberani

fraz. Cerreto
voc. Mignattaro, 26
05023 Baschi [TR]
☎ +39 0763341820
⊕ www.barberani.it

CELLAR SALES
PRE-BOOKED VISITS
ACCOMMODATION
ANNUAL PRODUCTION 300,000 bottles
HECTARES UNDER VINE 55.00
VITICULTURE METHOD Certified Organic
SUSTAINABLE WINERY

Bernardo and Niccolò skillfully manage the family business, dividing responsibilities between marketing and production, and continually refreshing the image of this solid winemaking family. Their shared goal is to highlight the qualities and virtues of the Orvieto area through wines that strongly express their regional identity. The vineyards are organically cultivated, underscoring the importance of environmental protection. Barberani offers a broad and diverse range, including reds, whites, and sweet wines. The Luigi e Giovanna continues to prove exquisite, a superb white from Orvieto, with a percentage of grapes affected by noble rot, making it unique and highly captivating. It has a complex nose, passing from nuts to citrus zest, and acacia honey, all followed by an expansive, pervasive palate, marked by a lovely sapidity. The Polvento '20, a red from sangiovese, cabernet, and merlot, is also delicious. It's dense and multifaceted, and yet easy to drink. The Castagnolo, another Orvieto from the 2023 vintage, proves simple but not trivial, suitable for daily consumption. The other wines tasted are also well-made.

○ Orvieto Cl. Sup. Luigi e Giovanna '21	▼▼ 5
○ Orvieto Cl. Sup. Castagnolo '23	▼▼ 3
● Polvento '20	▼▼ 5
⊙ Amore '23	▼ 3
● Foresco '21	▼ 5
○ Orvieto Cl. Sup. Luigi e Giovanna '20	♈♈♈ 5
○ Orvieto Cl. Sup. Luigi e Giovanna '19	♈♈♈ 5
○ Orvieto Cl. Sup. Luigi e Giovanna '18	♈♈♈ 5
○ Orvieto Cl. Sup. Luigi e Giovanna '17	♈♈♈ 5
○ Orvieto Cl. Sup. Luigi e Giovanna '16	♈♈♈ 5

★Tenuta Bellafonte

loc. Torre del Colle
via Colle Nottolo, 2
06031 Bevagna [PG]
(+39 0742710019
@ www.tenutabellafonte.it

CELLAR SALES
PRE-BOOKED VISITS
ACCOMMODATION
ANNUAL PRODUCTION 50,000 bottles
HECTARES UNDER VINE 8.00
SUSTAINABLE WINERY

In just over a decade, this winery has proven its worth, securing a prominent position among Montefalco's producers. Credit goes to Peter Heilbron, an entrepreneur and winemaker who has successfully propelled Bellafonte to international acclaim, significantly enhancing the region's reputation. Their portfolio consists of four wines—two whites and two reds—showcasing the potential of native grape varieties. Their production philosophy emphasizes sustainability and minimally interventionist winemaking techniques. At the top of their range are two Montefalco reds. The Sagrantino Collenottolo combines structure with an elegance of drinkability, thanks to careful vinification. The Pomontino, where sangiovese offers sensations of small forest fruits, spicy touches, and a hint of underbrush on the nose, has a juicy, fresh, and deep palate. A note on the whites, given their quality: the Sperella leans more on freshness and vitality, while the Arneto is a white with long aging potential.

● Montefalco Rosso Pomontino '21	♥♥♥	4*
● Montefalco Sagrantino Collenottolo '19	♥♥	7
○ Arnèto '21	♥♥	5
○ Montefalco Bianco Sperella '23	♥♥	4
● Montefalco Rosso Pomontino '18	♥♥♥	6
● Montefalco Rosso Pomontino '17	♥♥♥	6
● Montefalco Sagrantino Collenottolo '18	♥♥♥	6
● Montefalco Sagrantino Collenottolo '16	♥♥♥	6
● Montefalco Sagrantino Collenottolo '14	♥♥♥	6
● Montefalco Sagrantino Collenottolo '13	♥♥♥	6
● Montefalco Sagrantino Collenottolo '11	♥♥♥	6

Bocale

via Fratta Alzatura
06036 Montefalco [PG]
(+39 0742399233
@ www.bocale.wine

CELLAR SALES
PRE-BOOKED VISITS
ANNUAL PRODUCTION 40,000 bottles
HECTARES UNDER VINE 6.00
VITICULTURE METHOD Certified Organic

The name Bocale comes from dialect for an old two-liter glass once commonly used in the region. Founded in 2002 by the Valentini family, which has a long tradition of winemaking, the producer, though small in both vineyard and production size, offers wines of high quality. Their success is the result of a modern approach to tradition, focusing on highlighting the attributes of the grape varieties both in the vineyard and in the cellar. Despite the quality of the two Sagrantinos, it's the Trebbiano Spoletino that shines, having reached our final tastings. The 2023 vintage reveals clean aromas with hints of white fruit, lemon zest, and a note of aromatic herbs. The palate is energetic and vibrant, with well-integrated acidity and a sapid finish. As mentioned, the two Sagrantinos don't disappoint. The Ennio, a meticulous selection of grapes, hails from the outstanding 2019 vintage, and the results are evident. The 2020, though simpler, still has great character. The Montefalco Rosso is also enjoyable.

○ Spoleto Trebbiano Spoletino '23	♥♥	3*
● Montefalco Sagrantino '20	♥♥	5
● Montefalco Sagrantino Ennio '19	♥♥	7
● Montefalco Rosso '22	♥	3
● Montefalco Rosso '21	♥♥	3
● Montefalco Rosso '20	♥♥	3
● Montefalco Rosso '19	♥♥	3
● Montefalco Rosso '18	♥♥	3
● Montefalco Sagrantino '19	♥♥	5
● Montefalco Sagrantino '17	♥♥	5
● Montefalco Sagrantino Ennio '18	♥♥	6
● Montefalco Sagrantino Ennio '17	♥♥	6
● Montefalco Sagrantino Ennio '16	♥♥	6
○ Spoleto Trebbiano Spoletino '21	♥♥	3
○ Spoleto Trebbiano Spoletino '20	♥♥	3
○ Spoleto Trebbiano Spoletino '19	♥♥	3

Briziarelli

via Colle Allodole, 10
06031 Bevagna [PG]
(+39 0742360036
www.cantinebriziarelli.it

CELLAR SALES
PRE-BOOKED VISITS
ANNUAL PRODUCTION 150,000 bottles
HECTARES UNDER VINE 25.00

The Briziarelli name has been associated with agricultural production since at least 1906. However, the family's wine project is more recent; in the 2000s, they decided to invest in the Montefalco area, starting with the planting of a vineyard and the construction of the current production space. Briziarelli's wines convey the varietal and territorial character of the grapes, blending precision and technique with a contemporary vision. Recent vintages have shifted towards drinkability and elegance rather than power and structure. This is evident in the Montefalco Rosso Riserva '21: while it certainly has a dense and pervasive quality, the wine flows beautifully on the palate, supported by lovely acidity and a sapid finish. Its aromas are captivating, ranging from forest fruits to hints of wood resins. Among the Sagrantinos, we preferred the Vitruvio, a selection from the 2018 vintage. The 2020 is still very young. The Sua Signoria Trebbiano '23 proves pleasant and well-made.

Leonardo Bussoletti

loc. Pianello, 175a
05029 San Gemini [TR]
(+39 0744715687
www.leonardobussoletti.it

CELLAR SALES
PRE-BOOKED VISITS
ACCOMMODATION AND RESTAURANT SERVICE
ANNUAL PRODUCTION 70,000 bottles
HECTARES UNDER VINE 10.00
VITICULTURE METHOD Certified Organic

Leonardo Bussoletti has brought prestige to the Narni area through his work with grechetto, trebbiano, and especially ciliegiolo, with this last a standout among local varieties. An innovative producer, Bussoletti has elevated Umbria's winemaking tradition without succumbing to nostalgia, instead crafting elegant wines with character, flavor, and persistence. Their success is due to a perfect combination of technique, skill, and the winemaker's passion. All these qualities are reflected in the glass. Two wines stand out at the top of production, both Ciliegiolos. The 05035 is a strikingly drinkable red, juicy and lively, with a flavorful and very clean finish. The Ràmici is the true top pick: complex, deep, and elegant, with aromas of blackberry, pepper, and a hint of mushroom. The palate is sapid, with well-integrated acidity, maintaining a smooth flow. The Brecciaro '22 is also excellent, while among the whites, we appreciated the Colle Murello '23, a monovarietal trebbiano.

● Montefalco Rosso Rosso Mattone Ris. '21	▼▼▼ 5
● Montefalco Sagrantino '20	▼▼ 6
● Montefalco Sagrantino Vitruvio '18	▼▼ 7
○ Sua Signoria Trebbiano '23	▼ 4
○ Mattone Bianco Trebbiano '19	♀♀♀ 3*
● Montefalco Rosso '18	♀♀♀ 3*
● Montefalco Rosso Mattone Ris. '16	♀♀♀ 5
○ Sua Signoria Trebbiano '22	♀♀♀ 4*
○ Anthaia '20	♀♀ 3
● Montefalco Rosso '20	♀♀ 3
● Montefalco Rosso Dunarobba '18	♀♀ 3*
● Montefalco Sagrantino '18	♀♀ 6
● Montefalco Sagrantino Vitruvio '15	♀♀ 6
○ Sua Signoria Trebbiano '21	♀♀ 3*
○ Sua Signoria Trebbiano '20	♀♀ 3

● Ràmici Ciliegiolo '21	▼▼▼ 5
● 05035 Ciliegiolo '23	▼▼ 3*
● Brecciaro Ciliegiolo '22	▼▼ 4
○ Colle Murello '23	▼▼ 4
○ 05035 Ciliegiolo Rosato '23	▼ 3
○ Colle Ozio Grechetto '23	▼ 4
● 05035 Rosso '16	♀♀♀ 2
● Brecciaro Ciliegiolo '18	♀♀♀ 3*
● Brecciaro Ciliegiolo '14	♀♀♀ 3*
○ Colle Ozio Grechetto '12	♀♀♀ 3*
● Ràmici Ciliegiolo '20	♀♀♀ 5
● Ràmici Ciliegiolo '19	♀♀♀ 5
● Ràmici Ciliegiolo '18	♀♀♀ 5
● Ràmici Ciliegiolo '16	♀♀♀ 5

★★★Arnaldo Caprai

loc. Torre
06036 Montefalco [PG]
☎ +39 0742378802
🌐 www.arnaldocaprai.it

CELLAR SALES
PRE-BOOKED VISITS
ACCOMMODATION
ANNUAL PRODUCTION 1,000,000 bottles
HECTARES UNDER VINE 186.00
SUSTAINABLE WINERY

Thanks to the vision and teachings of his father Arnaldo, Marco Caprai has catapulted the family winery to national and international prominence. His achievement lies in bringing about a decisive shift by betting on Montefalco's traditions and the potential of the Umbrian terroir. The winery's extensive range is marked by character and technical precision, displaying both a contemporary approach and a strong regional identity. In recent years, their wines have been produced with a clear focus on drinkability and finesse rather than structure and power. This is demonstrated by the three Sagrantinos presented. The Valdimaggio offers tones of red fruit and spices, while the Collepiano shines with freshness and sapidity. The 25 Anni is undoubtedly their flagship, combining complexity and persistence with an elegant, pervasive, never heavy drinkability. Tannins are present but don't tighten the palate, and its aromatic profile shines with red fruits, spices, and wood resins. The Montefalco Rosso Riserva '21 is also delicious. The Montefalco Rosso proves pleasant and suitable for everyday enjoyment.

● Montefalco Sagrantino 25 Anni '20	▼▼▼ 8
● Montefalco Rosso Ris. '21	▼▼ 6
● Montefalco Sagrantino Collepiano '20	▼▼ 6
● Montefalco Rosso '22	▼▼ 4
● Montefalco Sagrantino Valdimaggio '20	▼▼ 7
○ Colli Martani Grechetto Grecante '23	▼ 4
● Montefalco Rosso V. Flaminia Maremmana '22	▼ 5
● Montefalco Sagrantino 25 Anni '19	♈♈♈ 8
● Montefalco Sagrantino 25 Anni '18	♈♈♈ 8
● Montefalco Sagrantino 25 Anni '16	♈♈♈ 8
● Montefalco Sagrantino 25 Anni '15	♈♈♈ 8
● Montefalco Sagrantino 25 Anni '14	♈♈♈ 8
● Montefalco Sagrantino Collepiano '16	♈♈♈ 7

★★★Castello della Sala

loc. Sala
05016 Ficulle [TR]
☎ +39 076386127
🌐 www.antinori.it

CELLAR SALES
ANNUAL PRODUCTION 850,000 bottles
HECTARES UNDER VINE 229.00

It's no coincidence that the Antinori family chose to invest in the Umbrian region at a time when its potential still hadn't been widely recognized. Their goal was to bet on an area capable of producing long-lived, high-quality whites, and they settled on Orvieto. Thus Castello della Sala was born, the brand under which the now-famous Cervaro della Sala emerged. Over time, the producer has maintained consistent quality, expanding its range and focusing increasingly on the Orvieto appellation. The Cervaro once again stands out in our tastings, but it's not the only wine. The producer's flagship certainly lives up to expectations, offering a complex nose where attractive oak is accompanied by hints of ripe yellow fruit, honey, and almonds. Alongside it, the San Giovanni, an Orvieto Classico Superiore, confirms that here, too, the focus is on the appellation: the 2023 delivers aromas of white flowers, lemon leaf, and aromatic herbs, with a sleek, elegant, sapid palate, and a freshness that's especially noticeable on the finish. The other wines tasted are also well-made.

○ Orvieto Cl. Sup. San Giovanni della Sala '23	▼▼▼ 4*
○ Cervaro della Sala '22	▼▼ 8
○ Bramìto della Sala '23	▼ 5
○ Conte della Vipera '23	▼ 5
● Pinot Nero della Sala '21	▼ 8
○ Cervaro della Sala '21	♈♈♈ 7
○ Cervaro della Sala '19	♈♈♈ 7
○ Cervaro della Sala '18	♈♈♈ 7
○ Cervaro della Sala '17	♈♈♈ 7
○ Cervaro della Sala '16	♈♈♈ 6
○ Cervaro della Sala '15	♈♈♈ 6
○ Cervaro della Sala '14	♈♈♈ 6
○ Cervaro della Sala '13	♈♈♈ 6
○ Cervaro della Sala '12	♈♈♈ 6
○ Cervaro della Sala '11	♈♈♈ 6

Castello di Corbara

loc. Corbara, 7
05018 Orvieto [TR]
📞 +39 0763304035
🌐 www.castellodicorbara.it

CELLAR SALES
PRE-BOOKED VISITS
ANNUAL PRODUCTION 200,000 bottles
HECTARES UNDER VINE 100.00

The history of the winery began in 1997 when the Patrizi family acquired an estate that had been owned by Banca Romana since the late 19th century. The property spans 1,000 hectares, with about 100 under vines, resting on a variety of soils. Among the rows, you'll find several traditional grape varieties. While reds dominate, the estate also dedicates various plots to white wine production, including a notable clone of grechetto identified through massal selection. One Grechetto truly shone during tastings: the Orzalume is a complex and structured white. It opens on yellow peach and medlar, accompanied by hints of wildflowers. On the palate, it's broad and deep. Of comparable quality is a red: the Il Caio, also a 2023. A blend of sangiovese and merlot from its namesake estate, it proves fresh, dynamic, and fragrant, with a juicy palate and a sapid finish. We also appreciated the Calistri, from the Lago di Corbara appellation, made from sangiovese sourced from one of the estate's oldest vineyards. The other wines tasted are also well-crafted.

Wine	Rating
○ Orzalume '23	🍷🍷 4
● Podere Il Caio '23	🍷🍷 2*
○ Grechetto '23	🍷🍷 3
● Lago di Corbara Merlot De Coronis '20	🍷🍷 5
● Lago di Corbara Sangiovese Calistri '20	🍷🍷 6
● Lago di Corbara Cabernet Sauvignon Pallianum '21	🍷 5
● Lago di Corbara Thybris '21	🍷 4
○ Maria Grazia '23	🍷 3
○ Orvieto Cl. Sup. Piana Grande '23	🍷 3
● Lago di Corbara De Coronis '19	🍷🍷 4
○ Maria Grazia '22	🍷🍷 3
○ Orvieto Cl. Sup. Piana Grande '22	🍷🍷 3
● Podere Il Caio '22	🍷🍷 4

Le Cimate

fraz. Casale
loc. Cecapecore, 41
06036 Montefalco [PG]
📞 +39 0742290136
🌐 www.lecimate.it

CELLAR SALES
PRE-BOOKED VISITS
RESTAURANT SERVICE
ANNUAL PRODUCTION 900,000 bottles
HECTARES UNDER VINE 23.00
SUSTAINABLE WINERY

UMBRIA

Founded in 2011 by Paolo Bartoloni, this estate ties together a long family tradition of farming that dates back to the 1800s. The name Le Cimate refers to its location atop a hill looking out over the Monti Martani and the town of Montefalco. The vineyards, which are planted in clay-rich soils with a high percentage of limestone, host both traditional and international grape varieties. The entire range consistently impresses, especially their Trebbiano Spoletino, a wine the estate has always championed. The 2023 vintage of this white stands out for its complex, multi-layered nose, marked by notes of yellow fruit and wildflowers. On the palate, it's fresh and sapid, showing excellent progression. The Donna Giulia is a 2015 Sagrantino that we revisited after reviewing it last year. Meanwhile, the Montefalco Sagrantino '17, despite the challenging vintage, proves to be a broad, pervasive wine that drinks beautifully.

Wine	Rating
○ Spoleto Trebbiano Spoletino '23	🍷🍷 3*
● Montefalco Sagrantino '17	🍷🍷 5
● Montefalco Rosso '20	🍷🍷 3
● Montefalco Rosso '17	🍷🍷 3
● Montefalco Rosso '15	🍷🍷 3
● Montefalco Sagrantino '16	🍷🍷 5
● Montefalco Sagrantino '14	🍷🍷 5
● Montefalco Sagrantino '13	🍷🍷 5
● Montefalco Sagrantino Donna Giulia '15	🍷🍷 8
○ Spoleto Trebbiano Spoletino '20	🍷🍷 3
○ Spoleto Trebbiano Spoletino Sup. Riserva del Cavalier Bartoloni '18	🍷🍷 4
○ Trebbiano Spoletino '19	🍷🍷 3*
○ Trebbiano Spoletino '18	🍷🍷 3
○ Trebbiano Spoletino '17	🍷🍷 3

Cocco

loc. Poggetto, 6c
06036 Montefalco [PG]
☎ +39 3471916207
⊕ www.coccomontefalco.it

Colle Ciocco

via Pietrauta
06036 Montefalco [PG]
☎ +39 0742379859
⊕ www.colleciocco.it

CELLAR SALES
PRE-BOOKED VISITS
ANNUAL PRODUCTION 12,000 bottles
HECTARES UNDER VINE 3.50

CELLAR SALES
PRE-BOOKED VISITS
ANNUAL PRODUCTION 40,000 bottles
HECTARES UNDER VINE 12.00
SUSTAINABLE WINERY

Just over three hectares. That's the extent of the beautiful Montefalco estate where Ilaria Cocco has been operating since 2008. Her family's agricultural roots date back centuries, and Ilaria sought to revive this legacy, the goal being to highlight Montefalco through products and grape varieties native to the area. This is achieved with four wines that aptly represent sagrantino, sangiovese, and trebbiano spoletino. The focus is on finesse, elegance, and drinkability, without compromising the character and distinctiveness of each variety. The lineup this year is more focused compared to previous years, elevating Cocco among the region's most important producers. Two wines reached the final round: the first is the Phonsano '19, a distinguished sagrantino—close-knit and pervasive, with soft, non-astringent tannins, and a depth that comes from its sapidity and substance. The Avventata is also exceptional, a Trebbiano Spoletino released a year after harvest, confirming that Umbrian whites have aging potential. The Passito and Montefalco Rosso are also excellent.

The winery's name refers to the hill of Montefalco, where it's located. The project began in the 1930s when Settimio Spacchetti started a farm to produce wine, olive oil, and crops. Today, Eliseo and Lamberto manage the property's 20 hectares, mostly vineyards. Sagrantino, sangiovese, and trebbiano spoletino fuel a range that blends the potential of Umbria with a philosophy rooted in Montefalco tradition. The range presented this year is impressive, starting with a Montefalco Sagrantino of remarkable craftsmanship that surprises with its ability to combine density and texture with drinkability and finesse. Aromatically it evokes blackberry, blueberry, underbrush, and spices. In the mouth, its enveloping tannins don't constrict the palate but instead add rhythm, thanks to nice sapidity. We also appreciated the Montefalco Rosso '20, a juicy, everyday drinker, and the Clarignano, a Grechetto '23 with its hints of medlar and wildflowers, as well as the pleasant Tempestivo '22.

● Montefalco Sagrantino Phonsano '19	♟♟ 5
○ Spoleto Trebbiano Spoletino Avventata '22	♟♟ 3*
● Montefalco Rosso Camorata '20	♟♟ 3
● Montefalco Sagrantino Passito Fontiola '19	♟♟ 6
● Montefalco Rosso Camorata '19	♟♟ 3*
● Montefalco Rosso Camorata '17	♟♟ 3
● Montefalco Sagrantino Passito Fontiola '16	♟♟ 5
● Montefalco Sagrantino Phonsano '18	♟♟ 5
● Montefalco Sagrantino Phonsano '17	♟♟ 5
● Montefalco Sagrantino Phonsano '16	♟♟ 5
○ Spoleto Trebbiano Spoletino Avventata '21	♟♟ 3

● Montefalco Sagrantino '19	♟♟ 5
○ Montefalco Grechetto Clarignano '23	♟♟ 3
● Montefalco Rosso '20	♟♟ 3
○ Spoleto Trebbiano Spoletino Tempestivo '22	♟ 3
● Montefalco Sagrantino '18	♟♟ 5
● Montefalco Sagrantino '17	♟♟ 5
● Montefalco Sagrantino '16	♟♟ 5
● Montefalco Sagrantino Passito '16	♟♟ 6
● Montefalco Sagrantino Passito '15	♟♟ 6
● Montefalco Sagrantino Passito '14	♟♟ 5
○ Spoleto Trebbiano Spoletino Tempestivo '21	♟♟ 3
○ Spoleto Trebbiano Spoletino Tempestivo '20	♟♟ 3
○ Spoleto Trebbiano Spoletino Tempestivo '19	♟♟ 3

Fattoria ColSanto

fraz. Cantalupo
via Montarone
06031 Bevagna [PG]
📞 +39 0742360412
🌐 www.livon.it

CELLAR SALES
PRE-BOOKED VISITS
ACCOMMODATION
ANNUAL PRODUCTION 40,000 bottles
HECTARES UNDER VINE 20.00

Situated atop a hill in the heart of Montefalco, this estate serves as the Umbrian outpost for the Livon family, long-standing winemakers from Friuli. Over the years, their offerings have become consistently impressive across the board. In the vineyard, the focus is on traditional local varieties, while in the cellar, large barrels, terracotta amphorae, and meticulous extraction and aging techniques result in elegant and refined wines. A limited but distinctive range for the area. Leading the way is the Montefalco Rosso '20, a wine of superb drinkability, featuring a nose of red fruits and a palate with soft tannins and remarkable freshness. The CantaRosa, a 2023 rosé aged in amphora, is also delicious, with its distinctive and flavorful character. The Cantaluce '21, a white that certainly has no fear of aging, is delightful. The warm vintage is evident in the Sagrantino '17, a structured but slightly astringent wine, with tannins that still need to integrate.

Custodi

loc. Canale
v.le Venere
05018 Orvieto [TR]
📞 +39 076329053
🌐 www.cantinacustodi.com

CELLAR SALES
PRE-BOOKED VISITS
ANNUAL PRODUCTION 65,000 bottles
HECTARES UNDER VINE 44.00
SUSTAINABLE WINERY

The Custodi winery is based in Canale, a renowned area for those seeking authentic interpretations of Orvieto's traditional wines, with particular emphasis on the whites of this historic Italian wine-growing area. The estate covers around 70 hectares, half of which are vineyards. Among these, the classic appellations are given significant importance. The wines themselves are well-crafted, displaying expressive density and delicacy while maintaining good drinkability. This is demonstrated by two wines, the Vigna del Prete and the Belloro. The first, a true cru, is released a year after the harvest. The result is a sapid and vibrant profile with aromas of white peach and lime, and a lean, fresh palate with acidity. The Belloro, from the 2023 vintage, proves simpler, playing on the primacy of fruit. Among the reds, we appreciated the Piancoleto '23, a blend of sangiovese and merlot that's fragrant, juicy and flavorful— excellent depth.

● Montefalco Rosso '20	♀♀ 3*
○ Cantaluce '21	♀♀ 5
◎ Cantarosa Anfora '23	♀♀ 5
● Montefalco Sagrantino '17	♀ 5
○ Cantaluce '19	♀♀ 5
○ Cantaluce '18	♀♀ 5
○ CantaLuce '17	♀♀ 5
● Montefalco Rosso '19	♀♀ 3
● Montefalco Rosso '18	♀♀ 3
● Montefalco Rosso '14	♀♀ 3
● Montefalco Rosso '13	♀♀ 3
● Montefalco Sagrantino '15	♀♀ 5
● Montefalco Sagrantino '14	♀♀ 5
● Montefalco Sagrantino Montarone Ris. '12	♀♀ 6
● Ruris '20	♀♀ 3
● Ruris '14	♀♀ 2*

○ Orvieto Cl. Belloro '23	♀♀ 2*
○ Orvieto Cl. Sup. V. del Prete '22	♀♀ 3*
● Piancoleto '23	♀♀ 2*
● Austero '20	♀♀ 3
○ Orvieto Cl. Belloro '21	♀♀ 2*
○ Orvieto Cl. Belloro '20	♀♀ 2*
○ Orvieto Cl. Sup. V. del Prete '20	♀♀ 3
○ Orvieto Cl. Sup. V. del Prete '19	♀♀ 3
○ Orvieto Cl. Sup. V. T. Pertusa '21	♀♀ 5

★Decugnano dei Barbi

loc. Fossatello, 50
05018 Orvieto [TR]
☎ +39 0763308255
🌐 www.decugnano.it

CELLAR SALES
PRE-BOOKED VISITS
ANNUAL PRODUCTION 130,000 bottles
HECTARES UNDER VINE 34.00

The winery's name originates from an ancient area known for its viticulture, with written records dating back to 1212. The Barbi family purchased the property in 1973, marking the beginning of a business that has since established itself in the Umbrian winemaking scene. The vines grow in sandy and clayey soils of marine origin, which impart a mineral character to the wine—not only distinctive whites, reds, and rosés, but also an exceptional sweet wine made from noble rot and a Metodo Classico, which has a long tradition in the region. The Mare Antico is an outstanding Orvieto and the 2022 version met expectations. It passes from aromas of white flowers to citrus, with a delightful touch of anise. The palate is fresh, elegant, and lively, with sapidity that offers a long finish. The Frammento, another Orvieto, proves simpler but still full of character, demonstrating the aging potential of the area's whites. The two Metodo Classicos, both from the 2019 vintage (one a Dosaggio Zero), are also excellent.

Di Filippo

voc. Conversino, 153
06033 Cannara [PG]
☎ +39 0742731242
🌐 www.vinidifilippo.com

CELLAR SALES
PRE-BOOKED VISITS
ANNUAL PRODUCTION 250,000 bottles
HECTARES UNDER VINE 35.00
VITICULTURE METHOD Certified Organic
SUSTAINABLE WINERY

This winery was among the first in Umbria to embrace organic farming, doing so long before it became fashionable. Located in Cannara, on the hills overlooking the city of Assisi, between Torgiano and Montefalco, the Di Filippo family's estate is driven by sustainability and diversity. Their wines, which draw on sagrantino, sangiovese, and grechetto, along with the rare and precious vernaccia di Cannara, are authentic, genuine, and technically well-made. However, the entire range impresses. Thanks to a great vintage, the Montefalco Sagrantino '19 is truly excellent, embodying what we expect from this wine today: close-knit, full, pervasive, but also smooth and rhythmic in its drinkability. Its aromas evoke red fruit, while acidity and sapidity go hand in hand. The Etnico is also excellent, more full-bodied and structured, with tannins that still need to settle. The Terre di San Nicola is an excellent blend of sangiovese and merlot. The Montefalco Rosso proves pleasant and easy to drink.

○ Orvieto Cl. Sup. Mare Antico '22	▼▼▼ 4*
○ Brut M. Cl. '19	▼▼ 5
○ Dosaggio Zero M. Cl. '19	▼▼ 5
○ Orvieto Cl. Frammento '22	▼▼ 3
● Battito '21	▼ 4
○ L'Inquisitore '22	▼ 5
⊙ Tramonto d'Estate '23	▼ 3
○ Orvieto Cl. Sup. Il Bianco '17	♀♀♀ 4*
○ Orvieto Cl. Sup. Il Bianco '16	♀♀♀ 4*
○ Orvieto Cl. Sup. Il Bianco '15	♀♀♀ 4*
○ Orvieto Cl. Sup. Il Bianco '12	♀♀♀ 3*
○ Orvieto Cl. Sup. Mare Antico '21	♀♀♀ 4*
○ Orvieto Cl. Sup. Mare Antico '19	♀♀♀ 4*
○ Orvieto Cl. Sup. Muffa Nobile Pourriture Noble '20	♀♀♀ 6
○ Orvieto Cl. Villa Barbi '19	♀♀♀ 3*

● Montefalco Sagrantino '19	▼▼ 6
● Colli Martani Vernaccia di Cannara '22	▼▼ 5
○ Farandola '22	▼▼ 4
● Montefalco Rosso '22	▼▼ 3
● Montefalco Sagrantino Etnico '19	▼▼ 5
● Terre San Nicola '20	▼▼ 3
● Colli Martani Sangiovese Properzio Ris. '20	▼ 4
● Montefalco Rosso Sallustio Ris. '21	▼ 4
○ Sassi d'Arenaria '21	▼ 5
● Colli Martani Vernaccia di Cannara '21	♀♀ 4
○ Grechetto '22	♀♀ 2*
● Montefalco Rosso '20	♀♀ 3
● Montefalco Sagrantino Etnico '18	♀♀ 5
○ NonSo2 Grechetto '21	♀♀ 3
⊙ Terre San Nicola Rosato '21	♀♀ 3

Duca della Corgna
Cantina del Trasimeno
via Roma, 236
06061 Castiglione del Lago [PG]
📞 +39 0759652493
🌐 www.ducadellacorgna.it

CELLAR SALES
PRE-BOOKED VISITS
ANNUAL PRODUCTION 280,000 bottles
HECTARES UNDER VINE 55.00

Duca della Corgna, which takes its name from the founder of the Duchy of Castiglione del Lago (Ascanio Della Corgna), is a major cooperative operating in the Transimeno area. The production facility is located in Castiglione del Lago, where great efforts are made to enhance Trasimeno gamay, a grape variety that has proven its worth in the area. The lineup also includes other wines, primarily reds from sangiovese and whites from grechetto, providing a faithful oenological snapshot of the region. The Poggio Pietroso represents the pinnacle of the producer's gamay. Hailing from the namesake cru, it conjures up aromas of red fruit, with a hint of spice and a touch of dried rose. The palate is broad and voluminous, with a beautiful acidity that makes the wine highly drinkable, deep, and rhythmic. The youthful, standard-vintage version is also very good—juicy and lively with tones of currant and raspberry. The Riserva '21, however, is a bit more restrained. Among the whites, we appreciated the Trasimeno Baccio del Bianco '23. Overall, the rest of the production shows good quality.

● Trasimeno Gamay Poggio Pietroso Ris. '21	♟♟♟ 5
● Trasimeno Gamay Divina Villa '23	♟♟ 2*
● Colli del Trasimeno Rosso Baccio del Rosso '23	♟♟ 2*
○ Trasimeno Bianco Baccio del Bianco '23	♟♟ 2*
● Trasimeno Rosso Corniolo '21	♟♟ 3
⊙ Martavello '23	♟ 2
● Trasimeno Gamay Divina Villa Ris. '21	♟ 3
○ Trasimeno Grechetto Ascanio '23	♟ 2
○ Trasimeno Grechetto Nuricante '23	♟ 2
● Trasimeno Gamay Poggio Pietroso Ris. '20	♟♟♟ 4*
● Colli del Trasimeno Gamay Poggio Pietroso Ris. '19	♟♟ 4
● Trasimeno Gamay Divina Villa '21	♟♟ 2*

Goretti
fraz. Pila
s.da del Pino, 4
06132 Perugia
📞 +39 075607316
🌐 www.vinigoretti.com

PRE-BOOKED VISITS
ANNUAL PRODUCTION 300,000 bottles
HECTARES UNDER VINE 50.00

Passed down from parents to children, this winery has been in the same family for four generations. The story begins in the early 20th century, and the passion that has long distinguished the winery at the gates of Perugia continues to drive production today. The vineyards, which feature both indigenous and international varieties, are divided into two areas: one around the historic winery near Perugia, called Tenuta di Pila, and the other in the hilly terrain around Montefalco, where the Le Mura Saracene line is produced. Eight wines were presented, all of high quality. At the top of the tastings are undoubtedly the Montefalco Rosso and the Montefalco Sagrantino. The first is an everyday wine, smooth in its drinkability with delicate aromas of red fruits. The second, as expected from the variety, is a full-bodied and close-knit red, but never heavy or constrained. The nose reveals black fruit and a hit of pepper, while the palate is marked by tannins that are present but nicely integrated with the wine's structure. From the Colli Perugini, we particularly enjoyed the Grechetto '23.

● Montefalco Sagrantino Le Mura Saracene '20	♟♟ 5
○ Colli Perugini Grechetto '23	♟♟ 3
● Fontanella '23	♟♟ 2*
○ Il Trebbio '23	♟♟ 3
● Montefalco Rosso Le Mura Saracene '22	♟♟ 3
● Colli Perugini Rosso L'Arringatore '21	♟ 5
○ Il Moggio '23	♟ 3
● La Torre '23	♟ 3
○ Colli Perugini Grechetto '21	♟♟ 2*
● Colli Perugini Rosso L'Arringatore '17	♟♟ 5
● Montefalco Sagrantino '19	♟♟ 5
● Montefalco Sagrantino Le Mura Saracene '18	♟♟ 3*

UMBRIA

Lapone

s.da del Lapone, 8
05018 Orvieto [TR]
(+39 347 5472898
cantinalapone@gmail.com

CELLAR SALES
PRE-BOOKED VISITS
ACCOMMODATION
ANNUAL PRODUCTION 30,000 bottles
HECTARES UNDER VINE 16.00
SUSTAINABLE WINERY

The Cantarelli family invested in Umbria when they purchased Podere Caiano, an estate near Orvieto, in 1999. A few years later, in 2011, new vineyards were planted, and a winery was built, named Lapone after the area where the estate is located. The wines produced here draw on traditional varieties that fall under the Orvieto appellation as well as non-native varieties that have found an ideal environment here. In addition to winemaking, the estate offers hospitality, thanks to a few restored farmhouses. The Escluso stood our during our tastings. This Orvieto Classico Superiore reveals aromas of field daisies and citrus zest. The palate is elegant, sleek, refreshingly crisp, and marked by a subtle sapidity. The Caiano, a chardonnay from the 2023 vintage, and Me, from the same vintage but made from verdicchio (a curious choice for this area), are also delicious. Among the reds, La Macchia '22, a Bordeaux blend, caught our attention with its red fruit aromas and notable spiciness.

Tenute Lunelli - Castelbuono

voc. Castellaccio, 9
06031 Bevagna [PG]
(+39 0742361670
⊕ www.tenutelunelli.it

CELLAR SALES
PRE-BOOKED VISITS
ANNUAL PRODUCTION 130,000 bottles
HECTARES UNDER VINE 37.00
VITICULTURE METHOD Certified Organic
SUSTAINABLE WINERY

More than 20 years ago, the Lunelli family invested in Umbria, acquiring around 30 hectares in the Montefalco area. The vineyards, which are organically cultivated, host local varieties like sangiovese and sagrantino—the basis of a range that has evolved consistently in terms of quality and style, with recent years seeing an emphasis on drinkability and finesse. The estate is also worth a visit for its production space (called "Carapace"), an extraordinary architectural project designed by Arnaldo Pomodoro. Apropos drinkability, the Ziggurat gives you a perfect idea of what we're talking about. It's a smooth and juicy Montefalco Rosso, with flesh that's evident but never excessive. Its complexity unfolds in a linear way, enhanced by freshness and sapidity. The two Sagrantinos are also excellent, with the Carapace '19, the child of a truly harmonious vintage, standing out. The 2017, meanwhile, still shows prominent tannins and bold structure.

○ Orvieto Cl. Sup. L'Escluso '23	♟♟ 4
○ Caiano '23	♟♟ 3
● La Macchia '22	♟♟ 3
○ Me '23	♟♟ 3
● L'Incluso '22	♟ 4
○ Ramato '23	♟ 3
○ Caiano Chardonnay '21	♟♟ 3*
● L'Incluso '21	♟♟ 4
● L'incluso '20	♟♟ 3
○ Orvieto Cl. Sup. L'Escluso '22	♟♟ 4
○ Orvieto Cl. Sup. L'Escluso '21	♟♟ 3
○ Orvieto Cl. Sup. L'Escluso '20	♟♟ 3*
○ Ramato '21	♟♟ 3
● Umbria Rosso '21	♟♟ 3
● Umbria Rosso '19	♟♟ 3

● Montefalco Rosso Ziggurat '22	♟♟♟ 5
● Montefalco Sagrantino Carapace '19	♟♟ 8
● Montefalco Sagrantino Carapace Lunga Attesa '17	♟♟ 8
● Montefalco Rosso Lampante Ris. '21	♟ 6
● Montefalco Rosso Lampante Ris. '17	♟♟♟ 5
● Montefalco Rosso Ziggurat '17	♟♟♟ 4*
● Montefalco Rosso Ziggurat '16	♟♟♟ 4*
● Montefalco Sagrantino Carapace '17	♟♟♟ 8
● Montefalco Rosso Ziggurat '19	♟♟ 3*
● Montefalco Sagrantino Carapace '18	♟♟ 6
● Montefalco Sagrantino Carapace '16	♟♟ 6

★★Lungarotti

v.le G. Lungarotti, 2
06089 Torgiano [PG]
☎ +39 075988661
✉ www.lungarotti.it

CELLAR SALES
PRE-BOOKED VISITS
ACCOMMODATION AND RESTAURANT SERVICE
ANNUAL PRODUCTION 2,500,000 bottles
HECTARES UNDER VINE 250.00
SUSTAINABLE WINERY

The Lungarotti family has played a crucial role in boosting the image and popularity of Umbria and its wine production worldwide. Over decades of activity, a journey began in the 1960s has seen the producer manage to adapt without betraying its original goals. Today, the estate's vineyards span 250 hectares across the Torgiano and Montefalco areas. The wines are precise and elegant, reflecting the characteristics of the terroir with clarity and finesse. This year, several of their Torgianos, including the renowned Vigna Monticchio, were absent from our tastings; the winery decided to give them a few more months in the cellar. We sampled an excellent version of another red, though it hails from Montefalco. The Sagrantino boasts excellent structure, complexity, and freshness, with an uncompromised drinkability. On the white front, Torgiano did offer some good news: the Torre di Giano Vigna Il Pino is a remarkable wine, released three years after vintage—complex, multifaceted, intensely fresh, with a delightful vein of sapidity.

La Madeleine

fraz. Schifanoia
s.da Montini, 38
05035 Narni [TR]
☎ +39 0744040427
✉ www.cantinalamadeleine.it

CELLAR SALES
PRE-BOOKED VISITS
ANNUAL PRODUCTION 40,000 bottles
HECTARES UNDER VINE 7.50
SUSTAINABLE WINERY

Giulia and Francesco now lead the estate acquired by their parents, Linda and Massimo d'Alema. The winery was established in 2008 after the purchase of an old farm property. Just over seven hectares of vineyards host a mix of traditional local and international varieties, while production is marked by an international style, offering a diverse range that includes whites, reds, rosés, and two sparkling wines made using the Metodo Classico. Four wines were presented for tasting, with two recent additions standing out. The most convincing is undoubtedly the Flo. This lively and joyful Ciliegiolo highlights the best of what the native varietal has to offer: the 2022 is vibrant and joyful, with fresh and sapid drinkability, aromas of blackberries and raspberries, and a clean finish. Juli, a singular Pinot Nero vinified as a rosé, is also very good.

○ Torgiano Bianco Torre di Giano V. Il Pino '21	♟♟♟ 5
● Montefalco Sagrantino '21	♟♟ 6
● Il Bio '21	♟ 3
○ Torgiano Bianco Torre di Giano '23	♟ 3
○ Torgiano Bianco Torre di Giano V. Il Pino '18	♟♟♟ 5
● Torgiano Rosso Rubesco V. Monticchio Ris. '19	♟♟♟ 7
● Torgiano Rosso Rubesco V. Monticchio Ris. '16	♟♟♟ 6
● Torgiano Rosso Rubesco V. Monticchio Ris. '15	♟♟♟ 6
● Torgiano Rosso Rubesco V. Monticchio Ris. '13	♟♟♟ 6
● Torgiano Rosso V. Monticchio Ris. '18	♟♟♟ 7

● Flo Ciliegiolo '22	♟♟ 4
☉ Juli '23	♟♟ 3
● NarnOt '20	♟ 6
● Pinot Nero '22	♟ 6
☉ Juli '22	♟♟ 3
● NarnOt '15	♟♟ 6
● Pinot Nero '18	♟♟ 6
● Pinot Nero '17	♟♟ 6
● Pinot Nero '16	♟♟ 6
● Pinot Nero '15	♟♟ 6
● Sfide '20	♟♟ 3*
● Sfide '18	♟♟ 3
● Sfide '17	♟♟ 3

Madonna del Latte

loc. Sugano, 11
05018 Orvieto [TR]
(+39 3356490956
www.madonnadellatte.it

CELLAR SALES
PRE-BOOKED VISITS
ANNUAL PRODUCTION 20,000 bottles
HECTARES UNDER VINE 4.00
VITICULTURE METHOD Certified Organic

Nestled between Lake Bolsena and Orvieto, the winery has an Italian heart with a German influence. Founded by Manuela Sardo and Hellmuth Zwecker, who shifted to winemaking after careers in gastronomic journalism, the estate has followed an organic path from the start. Today, their son Leon continues their work, producing expressive wines that blend modern and classic sensibilities. Viognier seems to have found fertile ground here, as the winery produces two versions, both excellent. The difference lies in the production approach: one ferments and ages in stainless steel, the other in barriques. The former is fresh, vibrant, and highlights primary aromas, while the latter is denser and more structured, with a slight oaky touch that doesn't interfere with the grape's signature fruity and floral scents. The two reds are also pleasant and well-crafted, with a slight preference for the Sucàno due to its fleshiness and drinkability.

○ Viognier '23	♟♟ 4
○ Viognier Barrique '23	♟♟ 5
● Sucàno '22	♟♟ 5
● Montelandro Syrah '20	♟ 7
● Montelandro Syrah '19	♟♟ 7
● Pinot Nero '19	♟♟ 5
● Sucàno '19	♟♟ 5
○ Viognier '20	♟♟ 4
○ Viognier '19	♟♟ 4
○ Viognier Barrique '19	♟♟ 5
○ Viognier Et. Bianca '22	♟♟ 5
○ Viognier Et. Verde '22	♟♟ 4

Madrevite

fraz. Vaiano
via Cimbano, 36
06061 Castiglione del Lago [PG]
(+39 0759527220
www.madrevite.com

CELLAR SALES
PRE-BOOKED VISITS
ACCOMMODATION AND RESTAURANT SERVICE
ANNUAL PRODUCTION 35,000 bottles
HECTARES UNDER VINE 11.00
SUSTAINABLE WINERY

The winery owns 11 ha of vineyards scattered across the hills of Trasimeno, in Castiglione del Lago. An artisanal approach and a focus on terroir are the central pillars of the project. Their diverse range includes interpretations of various wine styles, with a strong emphasis on gamay (part of the grenache family). The estate also cultivates sangiovese, montepulciano, syrah, trebbiano spoletino, and grechetto, producing characterful reds, rosés, and whites that stay true to the quality of the region. Two Trasimeno Gamays stood out in our tastings. The drinkability and lightness of the Opra '23, with its blueberry aromas and lively palate, are impressive. C'Osa, from the 2022 vintage, is more complex, with intriguing brackish and spicy notes. It maintains drinkability while offering flesh, depth, flavor, and a very fine, elegant complexity. The rest of the range is also excellent, starting with the Elvé, a delightful Grechetto. We also appreciated the Bisbetica Rosé, a bottle-refermented wine that's fun but also hits the marks technically, and the invigorating Reminore '23.

● Trasimeno Gamay C'Osa '22	♟♟♟ 6
● Trasimeno Gamay Opra '23	♟♟ 4
○ Il Reminore '23	♟♟ 4
⊙ La Bisbetica Rosé '23	♟♟ 4
○ Trasimeno Grechetto Elvé '23	♟♟ 4
● Trasimeno Gamay C'Osa Ris. '19	♟♟♟ 5
○ Il Reminore '18	♟♟ 3
● Trasimeno Gamay '19	♟♟ 5
● Trasimeno Gamay C'Osa '18	♟♟ 5
● Trasimeno Gamay C'Osa '17	♟♟ 5
● Trasimeno Gamay C'Osa '16	♟♟ 5
● Trasimeno Gamay C'Osa Ris. '21	♟♟ 5
● Trasimeno Gamay C'Osa Ris. '20	♟♟ 5
● Trasimeno Gamay Opra '22	♟♟ 4
● Trasimeno Gamay Opra '21	♟♟ 3
● Trasimeno Gamay Opra '20	♟♟ 3

Cantine Monrubio

fraz. Monterubiaglio
loc. Le Prese, 22
05014 Castel Viscardo [TR]
☎ +39 0763626064
🌐 www.monrubio.it

CELLAR SALES
PRE-BOOKED VISITS
ANNUAL PRODUCTION 200,000 bottles
HECTARES UNDER VINE 800.00

Founded in the late 1950s and based in Castel Viscardo, near Orvieto, the Monrubio cooperative boasts a significant number of members who cultivate an equally impressive area. Many of the grapes hail from the Orvieto and Orvieto Classico appellations, but over the years, the winery has also proven adept with red varieties, crafting noteworthy wines from both local and international grapes. The wines presented were extremely well received. Both a white and a red aptly represent the production area. The first is the Soana, a well-crafted Orvieto Classico Superiore: clean, complex, and persistent, offering aromas of white flowers and fresh almonds, while the palate is sapid. The Palaia, made from a selection of sangiovese grapes from various estates, is also delicious, guaranteeing drinkability and pleasure while also conveying the character of a great red.

○ Orvieto Cl. Soana '23	♟♟	3*
● Palaia '21	♟♟	3*
○ Orvieto Cl. Soana '22	♟♟	2*
○ Orvieto Cl. Soana '20	♟♟	2*
○ Orvieto Cl. Soana '18	♟♟	2*
○ Orvieto Cl. Sup. Papabile '21	♟♟	3
○ Orvieto Cl. Sup. Papabile '20	♟♟	2*
○ Orvieto Cl. Sup. Soana '16	♟♟	2*
● Palaia '20	♟♟	3

Cantina Monte Vibiano

fraz. Mercatello
v.lo Palombaro, 22
06072 Marsciano [PG]
☎ +39 0758783386
🌐 www.montevibiano.it

CELLAR SALES
PRE-BOOKED VISITS
ANNUAL PRODUCTION 100,000 bottles
HECTARES UNDER VINE 27.00
VITICULTURE METHOD Certified Organic

Monte Vibiano Castle, a residence dating back to the 1st century BC, overlooks hundreds of hectares of farmland in the hills of Perugia. Since the late 1800s, the estate has been owned by the Fasola Bologna family, and by the early 1900s, it was producing wine and olive oil. In the late 1990s, with the opening of a new winery, the family launched a plan to produce high-quality wines made sustainably, with a focus on highlighting the local terroir in unique ways. Most of the wines are made from indigenous varieties. The Fiommarino, a sangiovese, is one of the region's best expressions of the grape, offering savory, fresh flavors with clean, intriguing aromas of red fruit, spices, and underbrush. The wine enters the palate with finesse and lightness, unfolding with a rhythmic elegance. The Campo delle Api, a white made from grechetto, also delivers, conjuring up aromas of wildflowers, hay, loquat, and everlasting flowers. The palate is rich yet smooth. The Bocca di Rigo '23 is delightful as well.

● Fiommarino Sangiovese '22	♟♟♟	4*
○ Campo delle Api '23	♟♟	5
○ Bocca di Rigo '23	♟♟	3
○ Fonte del Bosco '22	♟	5
● Colli Perugini Rosso L'Andrea '08	♟♟♟	5
○ Campo delle Api '22	♟♟	5
● Colli Perugini Rosso L'Andrea '13	♟♟	5
● Colli Perugini Rosso L'Andrea '12	♟♟	5
● Colli Perugini Rosso Monvì '14	♟♟	2*
● Colli Perugini Rosso San Giovanni '15	♟♟	4
● Fiommarino '21	♟♟	3
○ Maria Camilla '19	♟♟	3
○ Maria Camilla '17	♟♟	4
○ Maria Camilla '15	♟♟	3
○ Vigna Luisa '18	♟♟	8
● Villa Monte Vibiano Rosso '15	♟♟	1*

UMBRIA

Moretti Omero

loc. San Sabino, 20
06030 Giano dell'Umbria [PG]
📞 +39 331 5802280
🌐 www.morettiomero.it

CELLAR SALES
PRE-BOOKED VISITS
ACCOMMODATION
ANNUAL PRODUCTION 65,000 bottles
HECTARES UNDER VINE 16.00
VITICULTURE METHOD Certified Organic

In 1992, the Moretti family estate transitioned to organic farming, a decision made by founder Omero, who gave the winery its name and set the direction for production. Today, the wines, crafted from sagrantino, grechetto, and trebbiano spoletino, still bear the personal touch of honest, expressive quality, consciously avoiding industrial standardization. Their traditional Montefalcos express themselves well, starting with the Montefalco Sagrantino Vignalunga, a true cru that finds a lovely expression in the 2019 vintage, with its density, but also drinkability and aromatic complexity. The Montefalco Bianco '23, a blend dominated by trebbiano spoletino, performed even better, offering up notes of yellow-fleshed fruit, hints of ginger, and field herbs. The palate is sapid, energetic, and impressively deep. In its simplicity, the Montefalco Rosso '22 is also delicious.

★Palazzone

loc. Rocca Ripesena, 68
05019 Orvieto [TR]
📞 +39 0763344921
🌐 www.palazzone.com

CELLAR SALES
PRE-BOOKED VISITS
ACCOMMODATION AND RESTAURANT SERVICE
ANNUAL PRODUCTION 130,000 bottles
HECTARES UNDER VINE 24.00
SUSTAINABLE WINERY

Giovanni Dubini, a passionate and knowledgeable winemaker, currently leads one of the most authentic and distinctive producers in Orvieto. Great attention is paid to using traditional grapes, considered ideal for highlighting the attributes of the Umbrian terroir. A focus on whites is a given, and over many years, Palazzone has demonstrated Orvieto's enormous potential in terms of quality and longevity, as well as the producer's skill. An outstanding range of whites was presented. The Campo del Guardiano delivers—it's still full of vitality over three years after the harvest. The Musco is unique, charming, and not afraid of aging. The Terre Vineate is simple but very pleasant, and representative of the appellation. This year's masterpiece is the Muffa Nobile, complex on the nose with aromas of apricot jam and acacia honey, broad and voluminous on the palate, with sweetness tempered by a delightful vein of sapidity. One of Italy's great sweet wines.

○ Montefalco Bianco '23	♟♟ 3*
● Montefalco Rosso '22	♟♟ 3
● Montefalco Sagrantino Vignalunga '19	♟♟ 7
○ Brut M. Cl. '19	♟ 5
● Montefalco Sagrantino '19	♟ 5
● Montefalco Rosso '19	♟♟♟ 3*
○ Montefalco Bianco '21	♟♟ 3
● Montefalco Rosso Faccia Tosta Ris. '17	♟♟ 4
● Montefalco Sagrantino '18	♟♟ 5
● Montefalco Sagrantino '17	♟♟ 5
● Montefalco Sagrantino '16	♟♟ 5
● Montefalco Sagrantino Vignalunga '16	♟♟ 7
○ Nessuno '20	♟♟ 3
○ Trebbiano Spoletino '22	♟♟ 4

○ Orvieto Cl. Sup. V.T. Muffa Nobile '22	♟♟♟ 5
○ Musco '21	♟♟ 6
○ Orvieto Cl. Sup. Campo del Guardiano '21	♟♟ 5
○ Orvieto Cl. Sup. Terre Vineate '23	♟♟ 3
● Armaleo '21	♟ 5
○ Orvieto Cl. Sup. Campo del Guardiano '20	♟♟♟ 5
○ Orvieto Cl. Sup. Campo del Guardiano '19	♟♟♟ 4*
○ Orvieto Cl. Sup. Campo del Guardiano '14	♟♟♟ 3*
○ Orvieto Cl. Sup. Campo del Guardiano '11	♟♟♟ 2*
○ Orvieto Cl. Sup. Terre Vineate '11	♟♟♟ 2*
○ Orvieto Cl. Sup. V.T. '18	♟♟♟ 4*

F.lli Pardi

via G. Pascoli, 7/9
06036 Montefalco [PG]
☎ +39 0742379023
✉ www.cantinapardi.it

CELLAR SALES
PRE-BOOKED VISITS
ANNUAL PRODUCTION 55,000 bottles
HECTARES UNDER VINE 11.00

The name Pardi carries a century-old history closely intertwined with Umbria and its traditions. On one side is the fine local craftsmanship of precious textiles, and on the other is viticulture. The latter experienced a turning point in 2003, driven by the involvement of the new generation of family. The winery is located just a stone's throw from the Montefalco town center, while the vineyards are spread out across several plots in the surrounding areas. Particularly of note is the work done with sagrantino, identifying specific crus and vinifying parcels separately. This year the producer submitted a record-breaking lineup, with all the wines demonstrating superb qualities. More importantly, they very clearly express the Montefalco terroir. At the top is the Montefalco Sagrantino '20, a structured wine that also exhibits drinkability and elegance. It features blackberry aromas with a hint of underbrush, while the palate is close-knit and fresh in its acidity. The Trebbiano Spoletino '23 is among the best in its category—a vibrant and deep wine with clear notes of wildflowers.

● Montefalco Sagrantino '20	♟♟	5
○ Spoleto Trebbiano Spoletino '23	♟♟	3*
○ Clorinda Brut	♟♟	3
○ Colle di Giove '23	♟♟	2*
○ Montefalco Grechetto '23	♟♟	2*
● Montefalco Rosso '22	♟♟	3
● Montefalco Sagrantino Passito '19	♟♟	5
● Montefalco Rosso Ris. '19	♟♟♟	4*
● Montefalco Sagrantino '17	♟♟♟	6
● Montefalco Sagrantino '13	♟♟♟	5
● Montefalco Sagrantino '12	♟♟♟	5
● Montefalco Sagrantino Sacrantino '15	♟♟♟	6
● Montefalco Sagrantino Sacrantino '14	♟♟♟	6

Cantina Peppucci

loc. Sant'Antimo
fraz. Petroro, 4
06059 Todi [PG]
☎ +39 0758947439
✉ www.cantinapeppucci.com

CELLAR SALES
PRE-BOOKED VISITS
ACCOMMODATION
ANNUAL PRODUCTION 70,000 bottles
HECTARES UNDER VINE 12.50

The winery's story began in the late 1980s when Piero Peppucci and Luisa Giontella decided to settle in Sant'Antimo, an ancient abandoned Benedictine monastery in the Todi countryside. They restored the site, began acquiring the surrounding lands, and started planting vineyards: foremost grechetto, but also sagrantino, sangiovese, and cabernet sauvignon. This marked the birth of their family winery, now managed by Filippo with the support of his sisters Elisabetta and Agnese. The wines presented this year didn't disappoint either: clean, precise, and highly drinkable, but above all, they truly represent the Todi area, regardless of the varietal used. The Rovi, a selection of Grechetto di Todi, is a wine of superb aromatic complexity, with notes of loquat accompanied by a hint of hay, while the palate proves quite sapid. We also appreciated the Petroro 4, made from sangiovese grapes, and the Giovanni, a red blend of Bordeaux varietals that ages for several years before being released.

○ Todi Grechetto Sup. I Rovi '22	♟♟	5
● Giovanni '18	♟♟	4
● Todi Rosso Petroro 4 '23	♟♟	2*
○ Todi Grechetto Montorsolo '23	♟	3
○ Todi Grechetto I Rovi '19	♟♟♟	4*
○ Todi Grechetto I Rovi '16	♟♟♟	5
● Giovanni '16	♟♟	4
● Giovanni '13	♟♟	4
○ Todi Grechetto I Rovi '18	♟♟	5
○ Todi Grechetto Montorsolo '21	♟♟	3
○ Todi Grechetto Montorsolo '19	♟♟	3
○ Todi Grechetto Sup. I Rovi '17	♟♟	5
● Todi Rosso Petroro 4 '22	♟♟	2*
● Todi Rosso Petroro 4 '20	♟♟	2*
● Todi Rosso Petroro 4 '18	♟♟	2*

Pomario

loc. Pomario, 10
06066 Piegaro [PG]
☎ +39 0758358579
● www.pomario.it

CELLAR SALES
PRE-BOOKED VISITS
RESTAURANT SERVICE
ANNUAL PRODUCTION 35,000 bottles
HECTARES UNDER VINE 9.00
VITICULTURE METHOD Certified Organic
SUSTAINABLE WINERY

A beautifully restored old farmhouse, framed by woods, olive groves, and, of course, vineyards, is home to the Spalletti Trivelli family's winery. It's located in the enchanting town of Piegaro, where Umbria and Tuscany almost merge into one. Restoration of the property coincided with the revival of an old vineyard, from which a massal selection was carried out to expand the vineyard area. In addition to sangiovese, trebbiano, and malvasia, the organically farmed estate also hosts merlot, sauvignon, and riesling. Several wines stood out during the tastings, starting with a truly delicious Ciliegiolo. Aromas of blackberry, currant, and raspberry are complemented by spices and wood resins. On the palate, it's not just drinkable but also rich and flavorful. It's flanked by the Radura, another red, crafted from an intriguing blend of local varieties long present in the area: alicante, foglia tonda, malvasia nera, colorino, and sangiovese, resulting in a wine that is both traditional and charming. The Sariano, a monovarietal sangiovese, also performed at high levels.

● Ciliegiolo '22	♟♟ 3
● Radura '21	♟♟ 7
● Sariano '21	♟♟ 5
○ Arale '22	♟ 4
● Rubicola '22	♟ 2
○ Arale '19	♟♟ 4
○ Batticoda '20	♟♟ 2*
○ Batticoda '18	♟♟ 2*
○ Muffato delle Streghe '20	♟♟ 7
● Rubicola '21	♟♟ 2*
● Rubicola '19	♟♟ 2*
● Rubicola '18	♟♟ 2*
● Sariano '20	♟♟ 4
● Sariano '19	♟♟ 4
● Sariano '18	♟♟ 4
● Sariano '17	♟♟ 4

Roccafiore

fraz. Chioano
voc. Collina, 110a
06059 Todi [PG]
☎ +39 0758942746
● www.cantinaroccafiore.it

CELLAR SALES
PRE-BOOKED VISITS
ACCOMMODATION AND RESTAURANT SERVICE
ANNUAL PRODUCTION 120,000 bottles
HECTARES UNDER VINE 15.00
SUSTAINABLE WINERY

When the Baccarelli family decided to invest in Umbria in the late 1990s, they did so with clear intentions: to respect both the grapes and the traditions of Todi, as well as the surrounding territory and nature. In just over two decades, the producer has become a cornerstone of Umbrian viticulture, crafting wines that are elegant and true to their origins, with a range that gets more convincing with each passing year. Two whites and one red topped our preferences. Both whites are made from grechetto, which thrives in this area. Fiordaliso is the standard-vintage, annata version, simpler and more straightforward, with white flowers and lemon leaf on the nose, and sapidity and energy on the palate. The FiorFiore, on the other hand, is a selection released more than a year after harvest. It shows greater complexity, with primary aromas giving way to herbal notes and chamomile. The palate is deep, with acidity that harmonizes the wine's volume. Among the reds, we appreciated the Roccafiore, a standout sangiovese.

○ FiorFiore Grechetto '22	♟♟ 4
○ Fiordaliso Grechetto '23	♟♟ 3
● Il Roccafiore '21	♟♟ 4
● Melograno Sangiovese '22	♟ 3
● Prova d'autore '21	♟ 5
⊙ Rosato '23	♟ 3
○ FiorFiore Grechetto '20	♟♟♟ 4*
○ FiorFiore Grechetto '19	♟♟♟ 4*
○ FiorFiore Grechetto '18	♟♟♟ 4*
○ FiorFiore Grechetto '16	♟♟♟ 4*
● Il Roccafiore '16	♟♟♟ 3*
○ Todi Grechetto Sup. FiorFiore '14	♟♟♟ 3*
○ Collina d'Oro '19	♟♟ 5
○ FiorFiore '17	♟♟ 4
○ FiorFiore Grechetto '21	♟♟ 4
● Il Roccafiore '20	♟♟ 4

Romanelli

loc. Colle San Clemente, 129a
06036 Montefalco [PG]
📞 +39 0742378531
🌐 www.romanelli.wine

CELLAR SALES
PRE-BOOKED VISITS
ANNUAL PRODUCTION 48,000 bottles
HECTARES UNDER VINE 8.00
VITICULTURE METHOD Certified Organic

The Romanelli family's winery, which dates back to the 1970s, lies a few kilometers north of Montefalco, in the town of San Clemente. Surrounded by a majestic olive grove, their eight-hectare vineyard thrives on clayey and silty soils—home to the area's main grape varieties. The estate's wines are characterized by a style that favors harmony and balance, achieved through carefully calibrated extraction and attention to aromatic expression. A stellar example of the region's potential is the Terra Cupa, an exceptional Montefalco Sagrantino that stays true to the varietal's characteristics while delivering an engaging drinking experience through its sapidity and freshness. The nose offers up a kaleidoscope of aromas, from red fruit to spices, rain-soaked earth and pine bark. Among the whites, both the Fonte Perna and Le Tese prove outstanding: the former is a Grechetto from the Colli Martani, while the latter is a Trebbiano Spoletino with great energy and finesse.

● Montefalco Sagrantino Terra Cupa '20	♟♟ 6
○ Colli Martani Grechetto Fonte Perna '23	♟♟ 3
○ Spoleto Trebbiano Spoletino Le Tese '22	♟♟ 5
● Montefalco Rosso Molinetta Ris. '19	♟ 5
● Montefalco Sagrantino '11	♟♟♟ 5
● Montefalco Sagrantino '10	♟♟♟ 5
● Montefalco Sagrantino Medeo '16	♟♟♟ 8
● Montefalco Sagrantino Medeo '19	♟♟ 8
● Montefalco Sagrantino Terra Cupa '18	♟♟ 6
● Montefalco Sagrantino Terra Cupa '17	♟♟ 6

Scacciadiavoli

loc. Cantinone, 31
06036 Montefalco [PG]
📞 +39 0742371210
🌐 www.scacciadiavoli.it

CELLAR SALES
PRE-BOOKED VISITS
ANNUAL PRODUCTION 250,000 bottles
HECTARES UNDER VINE 39.00
SUSTAINABLE WINERY

To trace the history of Scacciadiavoli, one must go back to 1884, when Prince Ugo Boncompagni Ludovisi founded this eminent estate. Its more recent history sees the Pambuffetti family, who took over the property in the 1950s, in the spotlight. The vineyards, which span nearly 40 hectares, are set on clayey hills at around 400 meters elevation in the municipalities of Montefalco, Gualdo Cattaneo, and Giano dell'Umbria. We've already praised the 2019 Sagrantino, and the 2020 vintage didn't disappoint. This great Montefalco red exudes aromas of blackberries and licorice, with a sapid and fresh palate, soft tannins that are never bitter or astringent, and a clean, flavorful finish. The Montefalco Rosso is also delicious—simple yet gratifying. There's room for other wines as well. The energetic and aromatic Trebbiano Spoletino '22 is one, the Brut Spumante, which impresses with its elegant beading, is another.

● Montefalco Sagrantino '20	♟♟♟ 5
○ Brut M. Cl.	♟♟ 5
● Montefalco Rosso '22	♟♟ 3
○ Spoleto Trebbiano Spoletino '22	♟♟ 4
○ Brut Pas Dosé M. Cl.	♟ 5
● Montefalco Sagrantino '19	♟♟♟ 5
● Montefalco Sagrantino '10	♟♟♟ 5
● Montefalco Rosso '21	♟♟ 3*
● Montefalco Rosso '20	♟♟ 3*
● Montefalco Rosso '18	♟♟ 3
● Montefalco Sagrantino '18	♟♟ 5
● Montefalco Sagrantino Passito '19	♟♟ 5
● Montefalco Sagrantino Passito '17	♟♟ 5
○ Spoleto Trebbiano Spoletino '20	♟♟ 4
○ Spoleto Trebbiano Spoletino '19	♟♟ 4
○ Trebbiano Spoletino '21	♟♟ 4

★Giampaolo Tabarrini

fraz. Turrita
06036 Montefalco [PG]
📞 +39 0742379351
🌐 www.tabarrini.com

CELLAR SALES
PRE-BOOKED VISITS
ANNUAL PRODUCTION 70,000 bottles
HECTARES UNDER VINE 22.00
SUSTAINABLE WINERY

The Tabarrini family has been producing wine in Montefalco, on the hills of the Turrita district, for four generations. In the late 1990s, Giampaolo brought a fresh and visionary approach to production, focusing entirely on quality, bottling the wines and creating a modern cellar (one of the most beautiful in the area). The estate's vineyards yield wines that aptly represent the territory, though through a contemporary lens. Sagrantino is the flagship grape, offered in various expressions depending on the vineyard, but a white wine based on trebbiano spoletino is also part of the portfolio. Their latest creation is the Il Bisbetico Domato, a whimsical name that captures the character of Sagrantino. Tabarrini has indeed managed to tame it, as the wine reveals grace, elegance, and finesse—qualities that make it stand out among other Sagrantinos, which also achieve high levels of quality. The Adarmando once again caught our attention—a fascinating and long-lived white.

● Montefalco Sagrantino Il Bisbetico Domato '20	♥♥♥ 8
● Montefalco Sagrantino Colle alle Macchie '20	♥♥ 7
● Montefalco Sagrantino Colle Grimaldesco '20	♥♥ 6
○ Adarmando '22	♥♥ 5
● Montefalco Sagrantino Campo alla Cerqua '20	♥♥ 7
⊙ Bocca di Rosa '23	♥ 4
● Montefalco Rosso Boccatone '21	♥ 4
○ Adarmando '19	♥♥♥ 4*
● Montefalco Sagrantino Campo alla Cerqua '18	♥♥♥ 7
● Montefalco Sagrantino Colle alle Macchie '19	♥♥♥ 7

Terre de La Custodia

loc. Palombara
06035 Gualdo Cattaneo [PG]
📞 +39 0742929586
🌐 www.terredelacustodia.com

CELLAR SALES
PRE-BOOKED VISITS
RESTAURANT SERVICE
ANNUAL PRODUCTION 1,800,000 bottles
HECTARES UNDER VINE 180.00
SUSTAINABLE WINERY

The Farchioni family is well-known for its diverse portfolio of agri-food products, but Terre de La Custodia, their wine brand, holds a prominent place within the business. The vineyards feature grape varieties indigenous to Montefalco and Colli Martani, while their production approach can be said to be efficient and modern. Their sagrantino, sangiovese, and grechetto grapes give rise to reds and whites with distinct character. The range also includes experiments with Metodo Classico and Martinotti-Charmat sparkling wines, along with a merlot from an old vineyard. We'll start with their Colli Martani red, the Vigna San Martino, which hits the market after long aging. 2017 made for a close-knit wine where structure is nicely balanced by textbook sapidity. In terms of their Montefalcos, the Exubera, the winery's flagship Sagrantino, has been postponed until next year to allow for further aging. The Montefalco Bianco Plentis, released three years after harvest, is outstanding: complex on the nose, deep on the palate, with elegant aromas and a broad, refined palate. The Passito Melanto is also delicious.

○ Montefalco Bianco Plentis '21	♥♥♥ 3*
● Colli Martani Merlot V. San Martino Ris. '17	♥♥ 5
● Montefalco Sagrantino Passito Melanto '19	♥♥ 5
● Montefalco Sagrantino '15	♥♥♥ 6
● Montefalco Sagrantino Exubera '17	♥♥♥ 6
● Montefalco Sagrantino Exubera Rock '16	♥♥♥ 7
● Maior '18	♥♥ 5
○ Montefalco Bianco Plentis '20	♥♥ 3
● Montefalco Rosso '18	♥♥ 4
● Montefalco Sagrantino '16	♥♥ 6
● Montefalco Sagrantino Passito Melanto '18	♥♥ 4

Terre Margaritelli

loc. Miralduolo
06089 Torgiano [PG]
+39 0757824668
www.terremargaritelli.com

CELLAR SALES
PRE-BOOKED VISITS
ACCOMMODATION
ANNUAL PRODUCTION 120,000 bottles
HECTARES UNDER VINE 52.00
VITICULTURE METHOD Certified Organic
SUSTAINABLE WINERY

The Margaritelli family has been closely bound to the Torgiano area ever since 1870. The shift toward viticulture, a more recent development, began in 2000 when Giuseppe expanded the estate and launched high-quality wine production. The wines are full of character, crafted from traditional local grapes like sangiovese and grechetto, though the portfolio also features various international varieties that have acclimated well here. The winery also owns a cooperage in France, where it selects oak from the best forests to produce barrels tailored for aging each wine. The producer's best wines will rest for another year in the cellar, so we only tasted three for this edition: two 2023s, which prove youthful, fresh, and energetic, and a 2021. The latter is an excellent Torgiano Rosso that made it to our final tastings. It exudes blackberry and tobacco aromas, with a slender, fleshy palate, and sapidity that makes for deep drinking. The Costellato and Venturosa are also very enjoyable.

● Torgiano Rosso Miràntico '21	🍷🍷 3*
○ Torgiano Bianco Costellato '23	🍷🍷 3
⊙ Torgiano Rosato Venturosa '23	🍷🍷 3
● Torgiano Rosso Freccia degli Scacchi Ris. '20	🍷🍷🍷 6
● Torgiano Rosso Freccia degli Scacchi Ris. '19	🍷🍷🍷 6
● Torgiano Rosso Pinturicchio Ris. '16	🍷🍷🍷 5
● Malot '17	🍷🍷 4
● Torgiano Rosso Freccia degli Scacchi Ris. '18	🍷🍷 6
● Torgiano Rosso Freccia degli Scacchi Ris. '16	🍷🍷 5
● Torgiano Rosso Pictoricius Ris. '17	🍷🍷 8
● Torgiano Rosso Pictorius Ris. '18	🍷🍷 8

Todini

loc. Rosceto
voc. Collina, 29/1
06059 Todi [PG]
+39 075887122
www.wearetodini.com

CELLAR SALES
PRE-BOOKED VISITS
ACCOMMODATION AND RESTAURANT SERVICE
ANNUAL PRODUCTION 100,000 bottles
HECTARES UNDER VINE 40.00

Founded in the 1960s by the Todini family, this winery brings together diverse operations under one roof. In addition to wine production, the estate boasts a boutique hotel with a spa and restaurant, as well as tracts of arable land. On the wine front, the family has focused on indigenous grapes like sangiovese and grechetto but there are also experiments with non-native varieties such as merlot, viognier, and cabernet franc. The area's two traditional grapes provide the most gratifying results. Both hail from the Todi appellation. One is a 2021 Sangiovese, and the other is a 2023 Grechetto. The latter is truly excellent, showcasing complexity and masterful balance. It's redolent of loquat and candied citrus peel, with an herbal touch that leads into a sapid palate, defined by a vein of acidity that lightens its profile. The Sangiovese has blackberry and plum aromas, with a dense palate and soft tannins, while the Rubro, Consolare, and Laudato all prove to be pleasant wines of good overall quality.

○ Todi Grechetto '23	🍷🍷 2*
○ Todi Sangiovese '21	🍷🍷 2*
● Consolare '21	🍷 5
○ Laudato '21	🍷 5
● Rubro '21	🍷 5
○ Bianco del Cavaliere '22	🍷🍷 3*
○ Bianco del Cavaliere '21	🍷🍷 4
○ Bianco del Cavaliere '19	🍷🍷 3*
○ Bianco del Cavaliere '18	🍷🍷 3
● Consolare '16	🍷🍷 6
○ Laudato '19	🍷🍷 5
○ Laudato '18	🍷🍷 5
○ Laudato '17	🍷🍷 3*
● Rubro '19	🍷🍷 4
● Rubro '16	🍷🍷 3
● Todi Sangiovese '19	🍷🍷 2*

Tudernum

loc. Pian di Porto, 146
06059 Todi [PG]
📞 +39 0758989403
🌐 www.tudernum.it

CELLAR SALES
PRE-BOOKED VISITS
ACCOMMODATION
ANNUAL PRODUCTION 1,000,000 bottles
HECTARES UNDER VINE 180.00

Tudernum exemplifies how a well-run cooperative can craft noteworthy wines. The producer has invested wisely, resulting in a solid structure that follows a clear vision and grows year after year, thanks in part to outstanding organization. A first-rate team of technicians and consultants ensures that their wines capture the distinct identities and characteristics of the local varieties used, with grechetto taking the lead alongside sagrantino and sangiovese. Two wines stood out at the top of our tastings, both of which reached our final round thanks to their excellence. One is a white and the other a red, made from grechetto and sagrantino grapes, respectively. The first is the Colle Nobile, a careful selection released a year after harvest. It has aromas of wildflowers and herbs, with a sapid and incredibly elegant palate; the second is the Sagrantino Fidenzio, a great red from Montefalco, which, with the help of the exceptional 2019 vintage, displays both depth and substance.

Villa Mongalli

via della Cima, 52
06031 Bevagna [PG]
📞 +39 0742360703
🌐 www.villamongalli.com

CELLAR SALES
ACCOMMODATION
ANNUAL PRODUCTION 80,000 bottles
HECTARES UNDER VINE 16.50

Located on one of the region's most picturesque hills, at the border between Montefalco and Bevagna, this winery has been dedicated from the start to producing harmonious and long-lived wines using only indigenous yeasts. As reflected in a varied range of authentic and distinctive reds, rosés, and whites, the family's goal has been achieved. While sangiovese is the leading grape in their vineyards, cabernet sauvignon, trebbiano spoletino, and sangiovese are also cultivated. The Della Cima is the Sagrantino that struck us as the most harmonious and easy-drinking. It releases tobacco and underbrush aromas, while on the palate, the tannins, though present, are never bitter or overpowering. The Pozzo del Curato is denser and more structured. Among the whites, the Minganna, made from trebbiano spoletino grapes, is highly appreciated—The 2022 is redolent of yellow fruits and flowers, with a sapid and energetic palate. The other wines are also well-crafted.

● Montefalco Sagrantino Fidenzio '19	♀♀ 5
○ Todi Grechetto Sup. Colle Nobile '22	♀♀ 3*
○ Todi Grechetto '23	♀♀ 2*
● Todi Rosso Sup. Rojano '21	♀♀ 3
● Todi Sangiovese '22	♀♀ 2*
○ TS. 396 Trebbiano '22	♀♀ 2*
● Montefalco Rosso Fidenzio '22	♀ 3
● Montefalco Sagrantino Fidenzio '18	♀♀♀ 5
● Montefalco Sagrantino Fidenzio '12	♀♀♀ 4*
○ Todi Grechetto Sup. Colle Nobile '20	♀♀♀ 3*
○ Todi Grechetto Sup. Colle Nobile '18	♀♀♀ 2*
○ Todi Grechetto Sup. Colle Nobile '21	♀♀ 3*

○ Minganna '22	♀♀ 6
● Montefalco Sagrantino Della Cima '20	♀♀ 8
● Montefalco Sagrantino Pozzo del Curato '20	♀♀ 8
○ Calicanto '23	♀ 5
● Montefalco Rosso Le Grazie '22	♀ 5
● Montefalco Sagrantino Colcimino '08	♀♀♀ 3*
● Montefalco Sagrantino Della Cima '10	♀♀♀ 8
● Montefalco Sagrantino Della Cima '06	♀♀♀ 6
● Montefalco Sagrantino Pozzo del Curato '09	♀♀♀ 6

OTHER WINERIES

Cantina Altarocca

loc. Rocca Ripesena, 62
05018 Orvieto [TR]
(☎ +39 0763344210
⊗ www.cantinaaltarocca.com

CELLAR SALES
PRE-BOOKED VISITS
ACCOMMODATION AND RESTAURANT SERVICE
ANNUAL PRODUCTION 35,000 bottles
HECTARES UNDER VINE 11.00
VITICULTURE METHOD Certified Organic
SUSTAINABLE WINERY

○ Orvieto Cl. Sup. Albaco '22	♼♼ 4
● Rosso d'Altarocca '20	♼♼ 6
● Lavico '20	♼ 5
● Rosso Orvietano Librato '22	♼ 3

Baldassarri

voc. Pianelli, 1
06050 Collazzone [PG]
(☎ +39 0758707299
⊗ www.cantinabaldassarri.it

CELLAR SALES
PRE-BOOKED VISITS
ANNUAL PRODUCTION 300,000 bottles
HECTARES UNDER VINE 40.00

○ Colle Dorato Viognier '23	♼♼ 2*
● Lucardo '20	♼♼ 3
○ Archetto Dorato Grechetto '23	♼ 2
○ Grande Alone '21	♼ 3

Tenuta Baroni Campanino

loc. Santa Maria Lignano
06081 Assisi [PG]
(☎ +39 0759698046
⊗ www.campanino.it

● Intenso Sangiovese '21	♼♼ 4
● Gamay '19	♼♼ 5
● Assolo '20	♼ 8
○ Subasio Bianco '22	♼ 4

Tenuta Alzatura

loc. Fratta Alzatura, 108
06036 Montefalco [PG]
(☎ +39 0742399435
⊗ www.tenuta-alzatura.it

CELLAR SALES
PRE-BOOKED VISITS
ANNUAL PRODUCTION 40,000 bottles
HECTARES UNDER VINE 29.00

○ Montefalco Bianco Cortili '23	♼♼ 3
○ Montefalco Bianco Aria di Casa '22	♼ 5
● Montefalco Sagrantino '18	♼ 5

Tenute Baldo

via degli Olmi, 9
06083 Bastia Umbra [PG]
(☎ +39 0758010621
⊗ www.tenutebaldo.com

CELLAR SALES
PRE-BOOKED VISITS
ACCOMMODATION AND RESTAURANT SERVICE
ANNUAL PRODUCTION 700,000 bottles
HECTARES UNDER VINE 60.00

● Montefalco Rosso ReMigrante Ris. '19	♼♼ 4
● Montefalco Sagrantino Preda del Falco '20	♼♼ 5
● Montefalco Rosso Volo del Falco '21	♼ 3
● Torgiano Rosso Auravitae '22	♼ 3

Benedetti & Grigi

loc. Polzella
06036 Montefalco [PG]
(☎ +39 0759886990
⊗ www.benedettiegrigi.it

CELLAR SALES
PRE-BOOKED VISITS
ANNUAL PRODUCTION 450,000 bottles
HECTARES UNDER VINE 70.00

○ Montefalco Grechetto Eros '22	♼♼ 3
○ Montefalco Grechetto Falco Pecchiaiolo '22	♼♼ 2*
● Montefalco Rosso Attunis '21	♼♼ 4
● Montefalco Sagrantino Dioniso '18	♼ 6

OTHER WINERIES

UMBRIA

Bigi

loc. Ponte Giulio
05018 Orvieto [TR]
☎ +39 0763315888
● www.cantinebigi.it

PRE-BOOKED VISITS
ANNUAL PRODUCTION 3,500,000 bottles
HECTARES UNDER VINE 145.00

○ Orvieto Cl. Vign. Torricella '23	🍷🍷 2*
● Sartiano '21	🍷 3

La Carraia

loc. Tordimonte, 56
05018 Orvieto [TR]
☎ +39 0763304013
● www.lacarraia.it

CELLAR SALES
PRE-BOOKED VISITS
ANNUAL PRODUCTION 700,000 bottles
HECTARES UNDER VINE 119.00

● La Divina '20	🍷🍷 3
● Solcato '19	🍷🍷 3
○ Conte Marzio '23	🍷 4
● Tizzonero '20	🍷 3

Chiorri

loc. Sant'Enea
via Todi, 100
06132 Perugia
☎ +39 075607141
● www.chiorri.it

CELLAR SALES
PRE-BOOKED VISITS
ANNUAL PRODUCTION 100,000 bottles
HECTARES UNDER VINE 25.00
SUSTAINABLE WINERY

● La Cava Sangiovese '22	🍷🍷 2*
● Saliato '22	🍷🍷 3
○ Colli Perugini Grechetto Sel. Antonio Chiorri '22	🍷 4

Blasi

loc. San Benedetto
06019 Umbertide [PG]
☎ +39 3661428973
● www.blasicantina.it

CELLAR SALES
PRE-BOOKED VISITS
ACCOMMODATION AND RESTAURANT SERVICE
ANNUAL PRODUCTION 80,000 bottles
HECTARES UNDER VINE 29.00
VITICULTURE METHOD Certified Organic
SUSTAINABLE WINERY

● Cabernet Franc '22	🍷🍷 4
○ Chardonnay + Sauvignon '23	🍷🍷 3
● Syrah '22	🍷🍷 3
● Impronta '20	🍷 4

Castello di Magione

v.le Cavalieri di Malta, 31
06063 Magione [PG]
☎ +39 0755057319
● www.sagrivit.it

CELLAR SALES
PRE-BOOKED VISITS
ANNUAL PRODUCTION 200,000 bottles
HECTARES UNDER VINE 42.00

● Sangiovese '23	🍷🍷 2*
○ Artirè '22	🍷🍷 4
● Morcinaia '21	🍷🍷 5
○ Grechetto '23	🍷 2

Tenuta ColFalco

loc. Belvedere
via Valle Cupa
06036 Montefalco [PG]
☎ +39 0742379679
● www.tenutacolfalco.it

CELLAR SALES
PRE-BOOKED VISITS
ACCOMMODATION
ANNUAL PRODUCTION 20,000 bottles
HECTARES UNDER VINE 6.00
SUSTAINABLE WINERY

○ Montefalco Grechetto '23	🍷🍷 2*
● Montefalco Sagrantino Passito '19	🍷 5
⊘ Rosa del Falco '23	🍷 2

OTHER WINERIES

★Còlpetrone

fraz. Marcellano
via Ponte la Mandria, 8/1
06035 Gualdo Cattaneo [PG]
☎ +39 074299827
✉ www.colpetrone.it

CELLAR SALES
PRE-BOOKED VISITS
ANNUAL PRODUCTION 200,000 bottles
HECTARES UNDER VINE 63.00
SUSTAINABLE WINERY

○ Grechetto '23	🍷🍷 3
● Montefalco Sagrantino Memoira '16	🍷🍷 5
● Montefalco Sagrantino Ò '18	🍷🍷 8
● Montefalco Rosso '21	🍷 3

Donini

fraz. Verna
via Nestoro, 59
06019 Umbertide [PG]
☎ +39 3382878450
✉ www.vinidonini.it

CELLAR SALES
PRE-BOOKED VISITS
ANNUAL PRODUCTION 40,000 bottles
HECTARES UNDER VINE 14.00
SUSTAINABLE WINERY

● Paliotto Barbera '21	🍷🍷 3
● Settegrappoli Rigovernato '20	🍷🍷 5
● San Giovanni in Comunaglia '20	🍷 4
○ Vernino '22	🍷 3

Feudi Spada

fraz. Viceno
via Della Mola, 79
05014 Castel Viscardo [TR]
☎ +39 3493532424
✉ www.feudispada.it

CELLAR SALES
PRE-BOOKED VISITS
ACCOMMODATION
ANNUAL PRODUCTION 50,000 bottles
HECTARES UNDER VINE 7.00
SUSTAINABLE WINERY

● Peppone '23	🍷🍷 3
○ La Marchesa '23	🍷 3
● Orazio '21	🍷 5

Cantina Dionigi

voc. Madonna della Pia, 92
06031 Bevagna [PG]
☎ +39 0742360395
✉ www.cantinadionigi.it

CELLAR SALES
PRE-BOOKED VISITS
ACCOMMODATION
ANNUAL PRODUCTION 40,000 bottles
HECTARES UNDER VINE 6.00

● Montefalco Sagrantino Passito '19	🍷🍷 6
○ Scialo Moscato Passito '22	🍷🍷 7
○ Sestum Moscato Secco '23	🍷🍷 3
● Montefalco Rosso '20	🍷 3

Fattoria di Monticello

fraz. Ripalvella
voc. Ponetro
05010 San Venanzo [TR]
☎ +39 0758749606
✉ www.fattoriadimonticello.it

CELLAR SALES
PRE-BOOKED VISITS
ACCOMMODATION AND RESTAURANT SERVICE
ANNUAL PRODUCTION 70,000 bottles
HECTARES UNDER VINE 20.00

○ Ginestrello Grechetto '23	🍷🍷 3
○ Marièl Pinot Grigio '23	🍷🍷 3
● Ponetro Pinot Nero '22	🍷🍷 5
○ Giacchio '23	🍷 2

Fongoli

loc. San Marco, 67
06036 Montefalco [PG]
☎ +39 3923193233
✉ www.fongoli.com

CELLAR SALES
PRE-BOOKED VISITS
ACCOMMODATION
ANNUAL PRODUCTION 70,000 bottles
HECTARES UNDER VINE 23.00
VITICULTURE METHOD Certified Organic
SUSTAINABLE WINERY

● Montefalco Rosso Serpullo Ris. '19	🍷🍷 6
● Rossofongoli '21	🍷🍷 3
○ Biancofongoli Trebbiano '23	🍷 3
● Montefalco Sagrantino '16	🍷 6

Podere Marella

loc. Ferretto, 32
06061 Castiglione del Lago [PG]
☎ +39 0759659028
✆ www.poderemarella.com

CELLAR SALES
PRE-BOOKED VISITS
ACCOMMODATION
ANNUAL PRODUCTION 30,000 bottles
HECTARES UNDER VINE 7.50
VITICULTURE METHOD Certified Organic
SUSTAINABLE WINERY

● Cinquanta '22	♟♟ 8
○ Fiammetta Bianco '23	♟♟ 3
● Godot Sangiovese '20	♟ 5
● Trasimeno Rosso Caluna '21	♟ 3

Montioni

v.le della Vittoria, 34
06036 Montefalco [PG]
☎ +39 0742379214
✆ www.gabrielemontioni.it

CELLAR SALES
PRE-BOOKED VISITS
ANNUAL PRODUCTION 50,000 bottles
HECTARES UNDER VINE 9.00
VITICULTURE METHOD Certified Organic
SUSTAINABLE WINERY

● Montefalco Rosso '21	♟♟ 3
● Montefalco Sagrantino Passito '20	♟♟ 6
○ Grechetto '23	♟ 3
● Montefalco Sagrantino '20	♟ 6

Enrico Neri

loc. Bardano, 28
05018 Orvieto [TR]
☎ +39 3933313844
✆ www.neri-vini.it

CELLAR SALES
PRE-BOOKED VISITS
ACCOMMODATION
ANNUAL PRODUCTION 65,000 bottles
HECTARES UNDER VINE 50.00
SUSTAINABLE WINERY

○ Barrage Extra Brut M. Cl. '17	♟♟ 5
○ Orvieto Cl. Sup. Ca' Viti '23	♟♟ 3
● Rosso Orvietano Rosso dei Neri '22	♟♟ 3
○ Vardano '22	♟ 5

Mevante

via Madonna della neve 1
06031 Bevagna [PG]
☎ +39 3498057501
info@agricolamevante.com

CELLAR SALES
PRE-BOOKED VISITS
ANNUAL PRODUCTION 45,000 bottles
HECTARES UNDER VINE 20.00

○ Birbanteo '23	♟♟ 3
● Montefalco Sagrantino '20	♟♟ 5
⊙ Rosato '23	♟♟ 3
● Montefalco Rosso '21	♟ 3

Mario Napolini

loc. Gallo
fraz. Turrita
via Gallo, 71
06036 Montefalco [PG]
☎ +39 0742379362
✆ www.napolini.it

CELLAR SALES
PRE-BOOKED VISITS
ANNUAL PRODUCTION 50,000 bottles
HECTARES UNDER VINE 18.00

● Montefalco Rosso '21	♟♟ 3
● Montefalco Sagrantino '17	♟♟ 5

Plani Arche

loc. Sant'Enea
s.da Fontenuovo Piano Tevere, 7
06132 Perugia
☎ +39 3356389537
✆ www.planiarche.it

CELLAR SALES
ACCOMMODATION
ANNUAL PRODUCTION 35,000 bottles
HECTARES UNDER VINE 6.00
VITICULTURE METHOD Certified Organic
SUSTAINABLE WINERY

● Apoca '19	♟♟ 6
○ Gordito Grechetto '22	♟♟ 4
● Montefalco Rosso '22	♟♟ 3
● Troncafuga Sangiovese '22	♟ 2

OTHER WINERIES

Pucciarella

loc. Villa
v.le Perugia, 32
06063 Magione [PG]
📞 +39 0758409147
🌐 www.pucciarella.it

CELLAR SALES
PRE-BOOKED VISITS
ACCOMMODATION
ANNUAL PRODUCTION 250,000 bottles
HECTARES UNDER VINE 90.00
SUSTAINABLE WINERY

○ Trasimeno Bianco Agnolo '23	🍷🍷 1*
● Trasimeno Gamay '23	🍷🍷 2*
● Trasimeno Rosso Berlingero '23	🍷🍷 1*
● Trasimeno Rosso Sant'Anna Ris. '21	🍷 2

Saio Assisi

via Campiglione 94a
06081 Assisi [PG]
📞 +39 3358374784
🌐 www.saioassisi.it

CELLAR SALES
PRE-BOOKED VISITS
RESTAURANT SERVICE
ANNUAL PRODUCTION 40,000 bottles
HECTARES UNDER VINE 13.50
SUSTAINABLE WINERY

● Campo delle Grazie '21	🍷🍷 3
● Legenda Maior '19	🍷🍷 5
○ Colderba '23	🍷 2

Sasso dei Lupi

via Carlo Faina, 18
06055 Marsciano [PG]
📞 +39 0758749523
🌐 www.sassodeilupi.it

CELLAR SALES
PRE-BOOKED VISITS
ANNUAL PRODUCTION 150,000 bottles
HECTARES UNDER VINE 150.00

● Colli Perugini Rosso Secondoatto '21	🍷🍷 2*
● L'Intruso Cabernet Sauvignon '22	🍷 2
○ Terzastrada Grechetto '23	🍷 2

Marchesi Ruffo della Scaletta

via della Luna, 8
05035 Narni [TR]
📞 +39 0744715227
🌐 www.ruffodellascaletta.com

CELLAR SALES
PRE-BOOKED VISITS
ANNUAL PRODUCTION 80,000 bottles
HECTARES UNDER VINE 30.00
SUSTAINABLE WINERY

● Amelia Merlot Camminata '23	🍷🍷 2*
● Ciliegiolo '22	🍷🍷 3
○ Nar '23	🍷 2
● Podere Montini Ciliegiolo '21	🍷 3

Sandonna

loc. Selve
s.da della Stella Polare
05024 Giove [TR]
📞 +39 07441926176
🌐 www.cantinasandonna.com

CELLAR SALES
PRE-BOOKED VISITS
ANNUAL PRODUCTION 28,000 bottles
HECTARES UNDER VINE 6.20

● Ciliegiolo '23	🍷🍷 3
⊙ Rosaltea '23	🍷🍷 3
○ Amelia Grechetto '23	🍷 2
● Jovio '21	🍷 3

Sportoletti

via Lombardia, 1
06038 Spello [PG]
📞 +39 0742651461
🌐 www.sportoletti.com

CELLAR SALES
PRE-BOOKED VISITS
ANNUAL PRODUCTION 200,000 bottles
HECTARES UNDER VINE 30.00
SUSTAINABLE WINERY

○ Villa Fidelia Bianco '22	🍷🍷 3
● Villa Fidelia Rosso '22	🍷🍷 4
○ Assisi Grechetto '23	🍷 2
● Assisi Rosso '23	🍷 2

Terre di San Felice

via Antiluzzo, 26
06044 Castel Ritaldi [PG]
(») +39 3386798326
⊕ www.terredisanfelice.it

CELLAR SALES
PRE-BOOKED VISITS
ANNUAL PRODUCTION 13,000 bottles
HECTARES UNDER VINE 30.80

● Montefalco Rosso Ris. '20	♀♀ 5
● Montefalco Sagrantino Vinum Dei '20	♀♀ 6
● Montefalco Sagrantino '20	♀ 5
○ Spoleto Trebbiano Spoletino '23	♀ 4

Vetunna

fraz. Passaggio
via Assisi, 81
06084 Bettona [PG]
(») +39 0759885048
⊕ www.vetunna.com

CELLAR SALES
PRE-BOOKED VISITS
ANNUAL PRODUCTION 300,000 bottles
HECTARES UNDER VINE 180.00
SUSTAINABLE WINERY

⊙ R Rosato '23	♀♀ 1*
○ Viognier '23	♀♀ 2*
○ Colli Martani Grechetto Betonica '23	♀ 2
● Notabile '22	♀ 2

Casale Villachiara - Rossi

via del Colle, 57
06089 Torgiano [PG]
(») +39 0759880142
⊕ www.casalevillachiara.com

CELLAR SALES
PRE-BOOKED VISITS
ACCOMMODATION
ANNUAL PRODUCTION 10,000 bottles
HECTARES UNDER VINE 4.00

● Torgiano Rosso Amdarò '22	♀♀ 3
● Montescosso '20	♀ 4
○ Namirò '23	♀ 3

Valdangius

loc. S. Marco
via Case Sparse, 84
06036 Montefalco [PG]
(») +39 3334953595
⊕ www.cantinavaldangius.it

CELLAR SALES
PRE-BOOKED VISITS
ACCOMMODATION AND RESTAURANT SERVICE
ANNUAL PRODUCTION 20,000 bottles
HECTARES UNDER VINE 7.00
SUSTAINABLE WINERY

● Montefalco Rosso Pippinello '23	♀♀ 5
○ Spoleto Trebbiano Spoletino Campo de Pico '23	♀♀ 5
○ Bianco '23	♀ 4

Viandante del Cielo

loc. Passignano Campagna, 22
06065 Passignano sul Trasimeno [PG]
winery@viandantedelcielo.com

● Pristinum di Viandante '20	♀♀ 8
○ Lungolago di Viandante '22	♀♀ 7

Zanchi

s.da prov.le Amelia-Orte, km 4,610
05022 Amelia [TR]
(») +39 0744970011
⊕ www.cantinezanchi.it

CELLAR SALES
PRE-BOOKED VISITS
ANNUAL PRODUCTION 63,740 bottles
HECTARES UNDER VINE 35.00
VITICULTURE METHOD Certified Organic
SUSTAINABLE WINERY

○ Vignavecchia Trebbiano '18	♀♀ 5
● Amelia Ciliegiolo Antichi Cloni '23	♀♀ 3
⊙ Antichi Cloni Ciliegiolo Rosato '23	♀ 3

LAZIO

This year's guide confirms both the strengths and weaknesses of Lazio wine country. On the one hand, there's a remarkable diversity of high-quality vineyards, with our Tre Bicchieri awards scattered throughout the region, from Ponza to the Viterbo badlands. However, this also highlights an ongoing challenge: Lazio still lacks cohesive, high-quality "wine districts." Despite the existence of numerous appellations and distinct areas—from the Castelli Romani to the Terre del Cesanese, and from the stretch between Anzio and Cori to the Colli Etruschi Viterbesi—none have established a definitive influence in the region's top-tier. Lazion's diversity extends to grape varietals as well. Among the ten wines awarded Tre Bicchieri, there are no fewer than 14 different grapes, ranging from biancolella and malvasia del Lazio to grechetto and cesanese, as well as merlot, grenache, viognier, and chardonnay. This variety shows how traditional areas like Ponza and Frascati can be matched by Tuscia's hills, which have a talent for producing high-quality reds from international varieties.

However, this beauty of diversity also has its downside: it's clear that native grapes struggle to set a clear direction for the territory—more so than in most other Italian wine regions. Among the producers awarded, Casale Marchese returns to Tre Bicchieri after a 13-year drought (last winning in 2012 with the Clemens). This time, the recognition is even more significant, as it's for a Frascati Superiore, a wine historically seen as one of the region's most representative, though its appeal has waned over the years.

Another highlight is the first Tre Bicchieri awarded to a regional sparkling wine. It goes to Sergio Mottura's Metodo Classico, one of the region's most representative and historic expressions in our opinion. Finally, a standout among our Rare Wines is the splendid Cabernet Franc Habemus Etichetta Rossa '21 by San Giovenale. It goes without saying: see above.

Antiche Cantine Migliaccio

via Pizzicato
04027 Ponza [LT]
📞 +39 3392822252
🌐 www.antichecantinemigliaccio.it

CELLAR SALES
PRE-BOOKED VISITS
ANNUAL PRODUCTION 10,000 bottles
HECTARES UNDER VINE 3.00

Antiche Cantine Migliaccio's three hectares of vineyards on the island of Ponza are made up of small patches of land, nestled among rocks and stretching toward the sea. Emanuele Vittorio, heir to the Migliaccio family, cultivates indigenous grape varieties here on terraced plots, accessible only by boat or via challenging trails, which makes mechanical harvesting impossible. The only producer on the island to bottle its wines, Migliaccio offers a range characterized by a Mediterranean style, exemplary in its typicity The 2023 vintage, a difficult one for the producer, meant that only a single wine was produced and presented, the Biancolella, which nonetheless continues to impress. It mirrors the characteristics of the island, with a nose redolent of Mediterranean scrub, caper flowers, citrus, and white fruit. On the palate, it's sapid with iodized tones, offering a crisp, intact body and remarkable length that allows one to appreciate all its nuances.

○ Biancolella di Ponza '23	♟♟♟ 6
○ Biancolella di Ponza '22	♟♟♟ 6
○ Biancolella di Ponza '21	♟♟♟ 5
○ Fieno di Ponza Bianco '17	♟♟♟ 4*
○ Biancolella di Ponza '20	♟♟ 5
○ Biancolella di Ponza '19	♟♟ 5
○ Biancolella di Ponza '18	♟♟ 5
○ Biancolella di Ponza '17	♟♟ 5
○ Fieno di Ponza Bianco '22	♟♟ 5
○ Fieno di Ponza Bianco '20	♟♟ 4
○ Fieno di Ponza Bianco '19	♟♟ 4
○ Fieno di Ponza Bianco '18	♟♟ 4
⊙ Fieno di Ponza Rosato '22	♟♟ 5
⊙ Fieno di Ponza Rosato '21	♟♟ 5
● Fieno di Ponza Rosso '18	♟♟ 4

Marco Carpineti

s.da prov.le Velletri-Anzio, 3
04010 Cori [LT]
📞 +39 069679860
🌐 www.carpinetiterrae.com

CELLAR SALES
PRE-BOOKED VISITS
RESTAURANT SERVICE
ANNUAL PRODUCTION 400,000 bottles
HECTARES UNDER VINE 70.00
VITICULTURE METHOD Certified Organic

A pioneer in the region, Marco Carpineti was the first to adopt organic and later biodynamic farming. For over 40 years, he has focused on producing wines that reflect the character of his territory, Cori and the Monti Lepini. He cultivates nero buono and bellone grapes with a visionary spirit that has led him to create a three-hectare vineyard labyrinth—an architectural landscape that transforms the growing area into one meant for shared experiences. Nero buono and montepulciano form the basis of the Capolemole Rosso, a soft, juicy wine with notes of red fruits and liçorice—the white version plays on wildflowers and sweet citrus sensations. Their Metodo Classicos are well crafted: the Kius Bellone Brut stands out for its iodine profile and nice structure, with aromas of bread crust, honey, and pears, while the Nero Buono Rosé Extra Brut highlights wild strawberry and plum scents. The long, fresh, and sapid Apolide '19, a Nero Buono, also proves full-bodied and flavorful, with aromas of cherry, oregano, and licorice, while the supple with citrus Bellone Nzù opts for yellow melon tones.

● Capolemole Rosso '21	♟♟ 3*
○ Kius Bellone Brut M. Cl. '21	♟♟ 4
● Apolide '19	♟♟ 6
○ Capolemole Bianco '23	♟♟ 3
⊙ Kius Nero Buono Extra Brut Rosé M. Cl. '20	♟♟ 6
○ Nzu' Bellone '21	♟♟ 6
○ Capolemole Bianco '18	♟♟ 2*
● Capolemole Rosso '17	♟♟ 3
● Capolemole Rosso '16	♟♟ 3
○ Kius Brut '17	♟♟ 4
○ Kius Extra Brut Rosé '16	♟♟ 5
○ Moro '18	♟♟ 4
○ Moro '17	♟♟ 3*
○ Nzù Bellone '17	♟♟ 5
○ Nzù Bellone '16	♟♟ 5

★Casale del Giglio

loc. Le Ferriere
s.da Nettunense, 791
04100 Latina
☎ +39 0692902530
● www.casaledelgiglio.it

CELLAR SALES
PRE-BOOKED VISITS
ANNUAL PRODUCTION 1,707,000 bottles
HECTARES UNDER VINE 180.00

The Santarelli family's connection to wine dates back to the early 1900s when Emidio, Dino's father and the owner of the business, moved from Amatrice to Rome with his brothers to start a trading business. The Casale del Giglio project began in 1967 with the purchase of an estate in Agro Pontino, at Le Ferriere. Today, the winery is one of the region's most significant producers, with a reputation for boldness, creativity, and respect for the land. The Anthium Bellone '23 offers up ripe exotic fruit and more, with a sapid finish that highlights other sensations, like mango and aromatic herbs, resulting in a broad and persistent palate. The Faro della Guardia Biancolella '23 is fresh, intense, and citrusy, with a long finish where notes of Mediterranean scrub emerge. The Radix Bellone '20 remains flavorful, elegant, and supple, with nice energy and tension. The rest of the range is well-crafted, from the citrusy Viognier to the full-bodied Mater Matuta, the fruity Cesanese Matidia, and the sweet yet balanced Aphrodisium.

Casale Marchese

via di Vermicino, 68
00044 Frascati [RM]
☎ +39 069408932
● www.casalemarchese.it

CELLAR SALES
PRE-BOOKED VISITS
ANNUAL PRODUCTION 150,000 bottles
HECTARES UNDER VINE 50.00

The Carletti family has owned Azienda Agricola Casale Marchese for two centuries, but its history dates back to 1301. Ferdinando manages the vineyard while Alessandro handles administration, representing the seventh generation to lead the winery. Nestled at the foot of Monte Tuscolo in the Frascati appellation, the winery harmoniously blends local varieties, which have become a symbol of the territory, with international grapes. The splendid Frascati Superiore '23 is a classic expression of the territory, with aromas of yellow fruit, field herbs, and citrus. The palate is rich, flavorful, sapid, and deep, with a characteristic almond finish. The Quarto Marchese conjures up hints of citron and Mediterranean scrub, with nice freshness and structure. The Marchese de' Cavalieri, a Bordeaux blend, is vibrant and pleasant, with tones of blackberry, red currant, and spices. The Rosso Eminenza has a wild character, with cherry and plum on the nose that follow through on the palate, joined by licorice and pepper notes.

○ Anthium Bellone '23	♀♀♀ 4*
○ Faro della Guardia Biancolella '23	♀♀ 5
○ Radix Bellone '20	♀♀ 8
○ Aphrodisium '23	♀♀ 5
● Mater Matuta '20	♀♀ 8
● Matidia Cesanese '22	♀♀ 4
● Petit Verdot '22	♀♀ 3
○ Viognier '23	♀♀ 3
○ Antinoo '22	♀ 4
○ Satrico '23	♀ 3
○ Sauvignon '23	♀ 3
● Tempranijo '22	♀ 5
○ Anthium Bellone '21	♀♀♀ 3*
○ Anthium Bellone '20	♀♀♀ 3*
○ Anthium Bellone '19	♀♀♀ 3*
○ Radix Bellone '19	♀♀♀ 7

○ Frascati Sup. '23	♀♀♀ 3*
○ Frascati Sup. Quarto Marchese '23	♀♀ 3
● Marchese de' Cavalieri '22	♀♀ 4
● Rosso Eminenza '23	♀♀ 3
○ Clemens '23	♀ 3
○ Clemens '09	♀♀♀ 3
○ Clemens '22	♀♀ 3
○ Clemens '20	♀♀ 3
○ Frascati Sup. '22	♀♀ 2*
○ Frascati Sup. '21	♀♀ 3*
○ Frascati Sup. '20	♀♀ 2*
○ Frascati Sup. Quarto Marchese '21	♀♀ 3
● Marchese de 'Cavalieri '21	♀♀ 4
● Marchese de' Cavalieri '19	♀♀ 4
● Rosso Eminenza '21	♀♀ 3

849

Castel de Paolis

via Val de Paolis
00046 Grottaferrata [RM]
☏ +39 069412560
🖳 www.casteldepaolis.com

CELLAR SALES
PRE-BOOKED VISITS
RESTAURANT SERVICE
ANNUAL PRODUCTION 90,000 bottles
HECTARES UNDER VINE 11.00

Native grape varieties, a true expression of the Castelli Romani, crafted into modern wines. This was the goal of Giulio Santarelli and his wife Adriana when they founded their winery in Grottaferrata in 1985, drawing on the consultation of Professor Attilio Scienza. They aimed to revive old native varieties. Named after a medieval fortress, the estate still preserves a Roman cistern where the barrels rest. The Donna Adriana proves vibrant, sapid, with notes of aromatic herbs and yellow fruit, and a well-structured, fresh finish. The Campo Vecchio Rosso '19 opens with good substance and fruit; after a few minutes, it reveals its full potential with plum, blackberry, earthy root notes, licorice, and a spirited finish with balsamic and peppery tones. Violets and wild berries characterize the Quattro Mori, a soft and warm blend of syrah, cabernet sauvignon, merlot, and petit verdot, while the Frascati Superiore shows lovely typicity, with a pronounced minerality on the finish.

● Campo Vecchio Rosso '19	▼▼ 4
○ Donna Adriana '22	▼▼ 5
○ Frascati Sup. '23	▼▼ 5
● I Quattro Mori '19	▼▼ 6
○ Campo Vecchio Bianco '23	▼ 3
○ Donna Adriana '20	▼▼▼ 5
○ Donna Adriana '19	▼▼▼ 4*
○ Frascati Sup. '19	▼▼▼ 3*
○ Frascati Sup. '18	▼▼▼ 3*
● Campo Vecchio Rosso '18	♀♀ 4
○ Donna Adriana '21	♀♀ 5
○ Frascati Sup. '21	♀♀ 4
○ Frascati Sup. '20	♀♀ 4
○ Frascati Sup. '17	♀♀ 3*
● I Quattro Mori '14	♀♀ 5

Cincinnato

via Cori - Cisterna, km 2
04010 Cori [LT]
☏ +39 069679380
🖳 www.cincinnato.it

CELLAR SALES
PRE-BOOKED VISITS
ACCOMMODATION AND RESTAURANT SERVICE
ANNUAL PRODUCTION 950,000 bottles
HECTARES UNDER VINE 268.00
VITICULTURE METHOD Certified Organic
SUSTAINABLE WINERY

Founded in 1947, Cincinnato is now one of the region's leading wine cooperatives. The producer aims to revive and promote local grape varieties, a vision shared by its over 100 members. The focus on quality is unwavering, with the native nero buono and bellone varieties at its core. Members' vineyards are situated on the hills around Cori, an ancient town in the Monti Lepini. The cooperative's offerings are wide-ranging and of excellent quality. The Cori Bellone Enyo stands out with its tones of white fruit, citron, and aromatic herbs, leading to a supple, sapid, and long palate. The Ercole, a Nero Buono, features licorice and black fruit aromas, which return on the palate along with violet and Mediterranean scrub, concluding with a soft finish of cocoa and pink pepper notes. The Cori Nero Buono Kora is well-crafted, passing from plum to cherry and aromatic herbs, while the Quinto Bellone offers up tones of peach and wildflowers. The fruity and balsamic Pantaleo is also nice.

○ Cori Bellone Enyo '22	▼▼ 4
● Ercole Nero Buono '21	▼▼ 3*
● Cori Nero Buono Kora '20	▼▼ 5
○ Pantaleo Greco '23	▼▼ 2*
○ Quinto Bellone '23	▼▼ 2*
● Argeo '22	▼ 2
○ Korì Bellone Brut M. Cl. '20	▼ 3
○ Korì Bellone Pas Dosé M. Cl. '17	▼ 3
○ Puntinata '23	▼ 2
○ Castore Bellone '22	♀♀ 2*
○ Cori Bellone Enyo '21	♀♀ 4
○ Cori Bellone Enyo '20	♀♀ 4
● Kora Nero Buono '19	♀♀ 5
● Kora Nero Buono '18	♀♀ 5
○ Pantaleo Greco '22	♀♀ 2*

Damiano Ciolli

via del Corso
00035 Olevano Romano [RM]
(☎) +39 069563334
⊚ www.damianociolli.it

CELLAR SALES
PRE-BOOKED VISITS
ANNUAL PRODUCTION 35,000 bottles
HECTARES UNDER VINE 9.00
SUSTAINABLE WINERY

Supported by a winemaking tradition spanning three generations, Damiano Ciolli began his venture in 2001, taking over the family business in Olevano Romano and immediately imprinting it with his personal touch. Believing that cesanese could produce fine wines, he focused on quality production, seeking elegance while respecting the land, producing wines that highlight the unique characteristics of the volcanic soil at the foot of Monte Celeste. The Cesanese di Olevano Romano Riserva '20 opens with Mediterranean scrub and black cherry on the nose, with cardamom, cinchona, and rhubarb adding complexity on the palate. It shows slightly aggressive tannins, but the finish is well-structured. The Cesanese di Olevano Romano Silene '22 is less brilliant than other versions, with very ripe black fruit tones and a less fresh and spirited mid-palate, leading to a supple and somewhat simple finish.

Antonello Coletti Conti

via Vittorio Emanuele, 116
03012 Anagni [FR]
(☎) +39 0775728610
⊚ www.coletticonti.it

CELLAR SALES
PRE-BOOKED VISITS
ACCOMMODATION
ANNUAL PRODUCTION 45,000 bottles
HECTARES UNDER VINE 17.00
SUSTAINABLE WINERY

Antonello Coletti Conti owns this historic winery, which has belonged to his family since the 13th century. Located in Anagni, the city of the Popes, the first land transaction between the Conti family and Boniface VIII, Benedetto Caetani, played out here in 1200. The estate, named La Caetanella, primarily cultivates cesanese, making for wines of great character and typicity. The Hernicus displays excellent tannins, presenting aromas of bramble, laurel, cardamom, and Mediterranean scrub. The palate is consistent, spirited, well-structured, and deep, finishing with mineral and sweet spice notes. The Per Emilia, a wine that Antonello dedicates to his wife, put in a nice debut. The result of extensive vineyard research and meticulous work on an estate clone of cesanese, it's redolent of ripe black fruits, licorice, and sweet spices, consistent and deep on the palate.

● Cesanese di Olevano Romano Cirsium Ris. '20	♟♟ 5
● Cesanese di Olevano Romano Sup. Silene '22	♟♟ 4
○ Botte Ventidue '22	♟ 4
● Cesanese di Olevano Romano Silene '17	♟♟♟ 3*
● Cesanese di Olevano Romano Sup. Silene '21	♟♟♟ 4*
● Cesanese di Olevano Romano Cirsium Ris. '19	♟♟ 5
● Cesanese di Olevano Romano Silene '18	♟♟ 3*
● Cesanese di Olevano Romano Sup. Silene '20	♟♟ 4
● Cesanese di Olevano Romano Sup. Silene '19	♟♟ 3*

● Cesanese del Piglio Sup. Hernicus '22	♟♟♟ 4*
● Cesanese del Piglio Sup. Per Emilia '22	♟♟ 5
● Cesanese del Piglio Romanico '11	♟♟♟ 5
● Cesanese del Piglio Romanico '07	♟♟♟ 5
● Cesanese del Piglio Sup. Hernicus '21	♟♟♟ 3*
● Cesanese del Piglio Sup. Hernicus '14	♟♟♟ 3*
● Cesanese del Piglio Sup. Hernicus '12	♟♟♟ 3*
● Cesanese del Piglio Sup. Hernicus '18	♟♟ 3*
● Cesanese del Piglio Sup. Hernicus '17	♟♟ 3*
● Cesanese del Piglio Sup. Hernicus '15	♟♟ 3*
● Cesanese del Piglio Sup. Romanico '21	♟♟ 5
● Cesanese del Piglio Sup. Romanico '20	♟♟ 5
● Cesanese del Piglio Sup. Romanico '19	♟♟ 5
● Cesanese del Piglio Sup. Romanico '17	♟♟ 5

★★Famiglia Cotarella

s.da st.le Cassia Nord, km 94,155
01027 Montefiascone [VT]
+39 07449556
www.famigliacotarella.it

CELLAR SALES
PRE-BOOKED VISITS
ACCOMMODATION
ANNUAL PRODUCTION 1,200,000 bottles
HECTARES UNDER VINE 200.00

A virtuous example of a 'family business' that has successfully integrated the freshness of new generations with the wisdom of experience over the years. The journey began in the 1960s when Antonio and Domenico Cotarella established their first winery in the small Umbrian town of Monterubiaglio. The second step was taken by Renzo and Riccardo, who founded Falesco in 1979, leading to the current leadership by cousins Dominga, Marta, and Enrica. The juicy and silky Montiano is an elegant monovarietal merlot redolent of cherry, plum, leather, and sweet spices, finishing with balsamic and cocoa nuances. The Tellus Syrah offers black fruits and a dash of pepper, while the Poggio dei Gelsi proves balanced and pleasant, a lovely expression of the appellation with its notes of lemon, hay, and field herbs. We also tasted a nice Verdeluce (a blend of pinot bianco, sémillon, and grechetto): citrus and white fruit tones are accompanied by a taut and vibrant palate. The Tellus rosé, which opts for grapefruit and wild strawberry sensations, also performed well.

● Montiano '21	▼▼▼ 8
○ Est! Est!! Est!!! di Montefiascone Poggio dei Gelsi '23	▼▼ 3
○ Ferentano '21	▼▼ 5
● Marciliano '20	▼▼ 7
● Sodale '22	▼▼ 5
⊙ Tellus Rosé di Syrah '23	▼▼ 3
● Tellus Syrah '22	▼▼ 3
● Trentanni '22	▼▼ 5
○ Verdeluce '23	▼▼ 5
○ Tellus Chardonnay '23	▼ 3
● Montiano '20	▽▽▽ 8
● Montiano '19	▽▽▽ 8
● Montiano '18	▽▽▽ 8
● Montiano '17	▽▽▽ 8
● Sodale '18	▽▽▽ 5

Paolo e Noemia d'Amico

fraz. Vaiano
loc. Palombaro
01024 Castiglione in Teverina [VT]
+39 0684561471
www.paoloenoemiadamico.net

CELLAR SALES
PRE-BOOKED VISITS
ACCOMMODATION
ANNUAL PRODUCTION 180,000 bottles
HECTARES UNDER VINE 31.00
SUSTAINABLE WINERY

Vineyards stretch across the badlands of the upper Tiber River Valley, volcanic soils marked by the presence of tuff and peperino. It was here that Paolo and Noemia D'Amico founded their winery in 1985. Mostly international varieties are cultivated, while the wines are aged in a cellar carved into the tuff rock situated beneath their hanging garden in the heart of Tuscia. The Notturno dei Calanchi '21, a pinot nero, features blueberry and dark spice aromas, with a long and full-bodied palate supported by good acidity. The Atlante '18, a cabernet franc, is soft and plump, with black fruit, chocolate, and spice aromas against a backdrop of vegetal notes, leading to a smooth palate with well-crafted tannins. The Tuscia Grechetto Agylla '23 plays on peach, acacia honey, and almond on the nose, with a fresh and balanced palate. White plum, thyme, and sage characterize the Calanchi di Vaiano '23, which finishes on white pepper tones.

● Notturno dei Calanchi '21	▼▼ 5
● Atlante '20	▼▼ 8
○ Calanchi di Vaiano '22	▼▼ 4
○ Tuscia Grechetto Agylla '23	▼▼ 4
○ Orvieto Noe dei Calanchi '23	▼ 3
● Villa Tirrena '22	▼ 5
○ Calanchi di Vaiano '21	▽▽▽ 4*
○ Calanchi di Vaiano '20	▽▽ 4
○ Falesia '20	▽▽ 5
● Notturno dei Calanchi '20	▽▽ 5
● Notturno dei Calanchi '18	▽▽ 5
● Notturno dei Calanchi '16	▽▽ 5
○ Seiano Bianco '22	▽▽ 2*
○ Terre di Ala '20	▽▽ 3
● Villa Tirrena '18	▽▽ 4

Donato Giangirolami

fraz. Le Ferriere
via del Cavaliere, 1414
04100 Latina
+39 0773458626
www.donatogiangirolami.it

CELLAR SALES
PRE-BOOKED VISITS
ANNUAL PRODUCTION 100,000 bottles
HECTARES UNDER VINE 43.00
VITICULTURE METHOD Certified Organic
SUSTAINABLE WINERY

Five hectares of land between Aprilia and Velletri were purchased by Dante Giangirolami in 1956. In the 1990s, his son Donato expanded the estate with new plots in Doganella, Ninfa, and Borgo Montello. Around the same time, he was among the first in the area to begin the process of obtaining organic certification. In 2003, the winery took a major step, moving from grape trading to direct production. Now in its third generation, and with a female-led management team, the winery continues to grow in expression and quality. The Lepino '20, a monovarietal Nero Buono, unveils a kaleidoscope of aromas and flavors: cherry, licorice, and aromatic herbs emerge on the nose, while on the palate, it expands with notes of figs and spices, offering volume and a long-lasting finish. The Fera '22 reveals dark aromas on the nose and an expansive palate, conjuring up scents of cherry and plum with unexpected freshness. Among the whites, the standout is the Cardito, a fresh and balanced Malvasia Puntinata redolent of jasmine, pear, almonds, and rosemary.

● Lepino '20	🍷🍷 4
○ Cardito '23	🍷🍷 3
● Fera '22	🍷🍷 5
○ Nynphe Ancestrale Extra Brut '19	🍷 5
○ Cardito '20	🍷🍷 2*
○ Cardito '19	🍷🍷 2*
○ Cardito '17	🍷🍷 2*
● Lepino '17	🍷🍷 3
● Peschio Trentasei '17	🍷🍷 4
● Prodigo '16	🍷🍷 2*
○ Propizio '22	🍷🍷 3
○ Propizio '17	🍷🍷 2*
○ Propizio '16	🍷🍷 2*
○ Propizio Grechetto '20	🍷🍷 2*
○ Propizio Grechetto '19	🍷🍷 2*

★Sergio Mottura

s.da Ombricolo
01020 Civitella d'Agliano [VT]
+39 0761914533
www.sergiomottura.com

CELLAR SALES
PRE-BOOKED VISITS
ANNUAL PRODUCTION 86,000 bottles
HECTARES UNDER VINE 37.00
VITICULTURE METHOD Certified Organic

The fame of grechetto is owed to Sergio Mottura's enterprising spirit. In the 1960s, it was he who embarked on field experimentation, including DNA studies, to highlight the potential of Alta Tuscia, considered to be among the best territories for producing the grape. A challenging variety, its unusual tannic component requires careful handling to ensure depth and longevity, as demonstrated by Mottura's sustainably produced wines. We found the 2015 version of the Metodo Classico Sergio Mottura Brut to be splendid. Made from chardonnay grapes, it's fine and elegant on the nose with notes of white flowers and pear. Crisp and flavorful on the palate, it offers tones of field herbs and lemon cream, with overwhelming depth. In the absence of Poggio della Costa, La Torre a Civitella aptly represents the winery's grechetto, passing from aromas of saffron to white fruit, citrus peel, and hazelnut, leading to a smooth, full-bodied palate with a long, mineral finish. The fruity Orvieto Secco, and the Tragugnano, with its gritty, fresh, sapid, and Mediterranean finish, also impress.

○ Sergio Mottura Brut M. Cl. '15	🍷🍷🍷 7
○ La Torre a Civitella Grechetto '22	🍷🍷 5
○ Orvieto Secco '23	🍷🍷 3
○ Orvieto Tragugnano '23	🍷🍷 4
● Civitella Rosso '22	🍷 4
● Syracide Syrah '20	🍷 5
○ Latour a Civitella Grechetto '11	🍷🍷🍷 4*
○ Poggio della Costa '21	🍷🍷🍷 4*
○ Poggio della Costa '20	🍷🍷🍷 4*
○ Poggio della Costa '19	🍷🍷🍷 4*
○ Poggio della Costa '18	🍷🍷🍷 4*
○ Poggio della Costa '17	🍷🍷🍷 4*
○ Poggio della Costa '16	🍷🍷🍷 3*
○ Poggio della Costa '15	🍷🍷🍷 3*
○ Poggio della Costa '14	🍷🍷🍷 3*
○ Poggio della Costa '12	🍷🍷🍷 3*

LAZIO

Ômina Romana

via Fontana Parata, 75
00049 Velletri [RM]
📞 +39 0696430193
🌐 www.ominaromana.com

CELLAR SALES
PRE-BOOKED VISITS
ANNUAL PRODUCTION 150,000 bottles
HECTARES UNDER VINE 60.00
SUSTAINABLE WINERY

Nestled in the Velletri hills south of Rome, Ômina Romana features a vast estate that hosts both international and native grape varieties. In 2007, Bavarian entrepreneur Börner embarked on a winemaking project here, assembling a team, carrying out studies, and acquiring the tools necessary to create the best wine possible. Operating under the auspicious Latin name, the winery made bold decisions from the start, such as focusing on monovarietal selections. Among the whites, the Hermes Diactoros II stands out with its notes of white fruit and Mediterranean scrub, offering a sapid, pleasant, and lengthy finish. Among the reds, the Ceres Anesidora I emerges with its scents of cherry, cocoa, underbrush, and sweet spices, while the palate is characterized by nice length and energy. The Diana Nemorensis I reveals notes of wild berries and earthy nuances, with a sapid and fresh finish. The Merlot '21 proves soft and pervasive, playing on tones of cherry and licorice, while the Cabernet Sauvignon sees fruity notes combine with cocoa and vegetal aromas.

● Ceres Anesidora I '19	♟♟ 8
○ Hermes Diactoros II '22	♟♟ 5
● Cabernet Sauvignon '21	♟♟ 6
● Diana Nemorensis I '21	♟♟ 5
○ Chardonnay '21	♟ 7
● Merlot '21	♟ 7
○ Ars Magna Viognier '21	♟♟♟ 8
○ Ars Magna Viognier '20	♟♟♟ 8
● Ars Magna Cabernet Franc '18	♟♟ 8
● Ars Magna Cabernet Franc '17	♟♟ 8
○ Ars Magna Chardonnay '21	♟♟ 5
● Ars Magna Merlot '19	♟♟ 8
● Ars Magna Merlot '18	♟♟ 8
● Ceres Anesidora I '18	♟♟ 8
● Diana Nemorensis I '20	♟♟ 3
● Diana Nemorensis I '19	♟♟ 5

Antonella Pacchiarotti

via Roma, 14
01025 Grotte di Castro [VT]
📞 +39 0763796852
🌐 www.vinipacchiarotti.it

CELLAR SALES
PRE-BOOKED VISITS
ANNUAL PRODUCTION 8,000 bottles
HECTARES UNDER VINE 2.00
SUSTAINABLE WINERY

In 1998, Antonella Pacchiarotti founded her namesake winery with a clear and daring vision: to tell the story of her homeland, Lake Bolsena, her origins, and her family through wine. She focused particularly on the aleatico grape, exploring its full potential through various expressions. A unique approach sees this indigenous varietal take center stage among her range. The Ramatico is unique in its category. A rosé with a copper hue, it evokes the grape's signature aromas: small red fruits, juniper, dog rose, and wood resin, sensations that return on the palate supported by a robust acidic structure. The Cavarosso is a captivating, spirited wine redolent of wild strawberries and Mediterranean scrub. The Pian di Stelle reveals a sweet nose with notes of currant accompanied by honey and carob, but surprises with its fresh and pervasive palate. The crisp and sapid Matèe, a 'white' version of aleatico, exudes scents of citron and kumquat, while the Turan features black fruit fragrances, bay leaf, and spices.

● Cavarosso '22	♟♟ 5
○ Matèe '22	♟♟ 5
◉ Pian di Stelle '22	♟♟ 5
◉ Ramatico '22	♟♟ 4
● Turan '21	♟♟ 6
● Cavarosso '21	♟♟ 5
● Cavarosso '19	♟♟ 3
○ Fatì '20	♟♟ 3
○ Matèe '21	♟♟ 5
○ Matèe '19	♟♟ 3
◉ Pian di Stelle '21	♟♟ 5
◉ Ramatico '21	♟♟ 4
◉ Ramatico '20	♟♟ 4
● Turan '20	♟♟ 6

Tenuta La Pazzaglia

loc. Pazzaglia
s.da di Bagnoregio, 4
01024 Castiglione in Teverina [VT]
☎ +39 3486610038
✈ www.tenutalapazzaglia.it

CELLAR SALES
PRE-BOOKED VISITS
ACCOMMODATION
ANNUAL PRODUCTION 56,000 bottles
HECTARES UNDER VINE 12.00

The Verdecchia family's story in Castiglione in Teverina began in 1990 when Teresa followed through on a hunch, purchasing the La Pazzaglia estate, despite its neglected state, recognizing its potential. She involved her entire family, moving them from Mentana to the Tiber Valley. Their goal remains to craft wines from native varieties that highlight the distinctive qualities of the volcanic borderlands between Lazio, Umbria, and Tuscany. The Poggio Triale had an excellent vintage, showcasing the great complexity and resilience of monovarietal grechetto. It opens with aromas of sage, broom, resin, almond, sweet citrus, and white pepper, all of which follow through on the palate, which is full, crisp, and sapid, with a light and very pleasant tannic note, as the grape requires. The Montijone, a monovarietal merlot, proves velvety and elegant, with aromas of black cherry, blueberry, and coriander, complemented by a fresh and supple palate.

★Poggio Le Volpi

via Colle Pisano, 27
00078 Monte Porzio Catone [RM]
☎ +39 069426980
✈ www.poggiolevolpi.com

CELLAR SALES
PRE-BOOKED VISITS
RESTAURANT SERVICE
ANNUAL PRODUCTION 1,000,000 bottles
HECTARES UNDER VINE 210.00

Established in 1996 in Monte Porzio Catone on the Alban Hills, Poggio Le Volpi benefits from volcanic soils rich in tuff, lava rocks, and sand. While the winery's history is recent, the Mergè family's passion for winemaking dates back four generations, starting with Manlio, followed by his son Armando, and then his grandson Felice. The winery's philosophy has always been to enhance quality while maintaining authenticity. The Roma Bianco '23 opens with aromas of loquat and kumquat, sensations that evolve on the palate to reveal elderflower, acacia, sage, and grapefruit, culminating in a broad, persistent, sapid, and mineral finish. Both on the nose and palate, the Baccarossa '22 proves concentrated: initially shy, it gradually reveals notes of cherry, licorice, cinnamon, and nutmeg, offering significant volume and finishing with tones of ripe black stone fruits. The Barcaccia '22, made from bombino and malvasia, features notes of orange blossom, jasmine, and tropical fruit, with a soft, mineral finish.

	Wine	Glasses	Score
○	Poggio Triale '22	♟♟♟	5
●	Montijone '21	♟♟	5
○	Poggio Triale '21	♟♟♟	5
○	Poggio Triale '19	♟♟♟	3*
○	109 Grechetto '21	♟♟	4
○	109 Grechetto '20	♟♟	3
○	109 Grechetto '19	♟♟	3
○	109 Grechetto Anfora '18	♟♟	3
○	109 Grechetto Edizione Speciale 10 Anni '22	♟♟	4
●	Aurelius '18	♟♟	2*
○	Miadimia '22	♟♟	3
○	Miadimia '19	♟♟	3
●	Palagio '19	♟♟	2*
○	Poggio Triale '20	♟♟	3*
○	Poggio Triale '18	♟♟	3*
○	Rendu '21	♟♟	4

	Wine	Glasses	Score
○	Roma Bianco '23	♟♟♟	5
●	Baccarossa '22	♟♟	6
○	Barcaccia '22	♟♟	6
○	Donnaluce '23	♟	5
●	Baccarossa '20	♟♟♟	6
●	Baccarossa '15	♟♟♟	5
●	Baccarossa '13	♟♟♟	4*
●	Baccarossa '11	♟♟♟	4*
○	Frascati Sup. Epos '13	♟♟♟	2*
○	Frascati Sup. Epos '11	♟♟♟	2*
○	Frascati Sup. Epos Ris. '15	♟♟♟	3*
○	Roma Malvasia Puntinata '20	♟♟♟	5
●	Roma Rosso Ed. Limitata '17	♟♟♟	5
●	Roma Rosso Ed. Limitata '16	♟♟♟	5
●	Roma Rosso Ed. Limitata '15	♟♟♟	5
●	Roma Rosso Ris. '20	♟♟♟	6

San Giovenale

loc. La Macchia
01010 Blera [VT]
(* +39 066877877
www.sangiovenale.it

CELLAR SALES
PRE-BOOKED VISITS
ACCOMMODATION AND RESTAURANT SERVICE
ANNUAL PRODUCTION 9,000 bottles
HECTARES UNDER VINE 10.00
VITICULTURE METHOD Certified Organic
SUSTAINABLE WINERY

When then 20-year-old Emanuele Pangrazi discovered Tuscia, it was love at first sight. What followed was vision and study, drawing inspiration from international wine greats while experimenting in his own way. He planted grenache, carignano, syrah, and cabernet franc, all organically cultivated, to harness the land's authentic qualities. The result is a collection of excellent, complex, and highly captivating wines. The Habemus '22, a complex blend of grenache, syrah, carignan, and malvasia nera, is characterized by great structure and character. It's an authoritative, intense, deep, and harmonious wine characterized by aromas of tapenade, Mediterranean scrub, pepper, and licorice. Although produced in small quantities, the red-label Habemus achieves extraordinary results, and we review it in our Rare Wines section.

Cantina Sant'Andrea

loc. Borgo Vodice
via Renibbio, 1720
04019 Terracina [LT]
(* +39 0773755028
www.cantinasantandrea.it

CELLAR SALES
PRE-BOOKED VISITS
ACCOMMODATION AND RESTAURANT SERVICE
ANNUAL PRODUCTION 1,500,000 bottles
HECTARES UNDER VINE 120.00

From Pantelleria to Terracina via Tunisia, the journey of Cantina Sant'Andrea reflects its establishment as a key player in the Pontine archipelago. This odyssey began with Andrea Pandolfo and continued with Gabriele and his family, focusing on local grape varieties. The 70 hectares are spread across three vineyards: the historic Borgo Vodice, the Aprilia vineyard, and the Terracina vineyard, which preserves the charm of traditional manual grape harvesting. Among their broad and high-quality range, the Moscato di Terracina Hum stands out for its complex and captivating nose, with notes of aromatic herbs and citrus returning coherently on the palate, supported by vibrant acidity. The 253 giorni Vermentino proves approachable and straightforward, with notes of citrus and Saturn peach. The Incontro al Circeo offers violet, sour cherry, and pepper aromas, with good structure and sapidity. The Sogno '17, a blend of merlot and cesanese, proves juicy, playing on notes of blackberry and tobacco. The Capitolium, a passito, displays date and honey flavors balanced on the palate by lively sapidity.

● Habemus '22	♛♛♛ 8
● Habemus '21	♛♛♛ 8
● Habemus '20	♛♛♛ 8
● Habemus '19	♛♛♛ 8
● Habemus '18	♛♛♛ 8
● Habemus '16	♛♛♛ 7
● Habemus '15	♛♛♛ 7
● Habemus '14	♛♛♛ 7
● Habemus '17	♛♛ 7
● Habemus Cabernet '20	♛♛ 8
● Habemus Cabernet '19	♛♛ 8
● Habemus Cabernet '18	♛♛ 8
● Habemus Cabernet '17	♛♛ 8
● Habemus Cabernet '16	♛♛ 8
● Habemus Cabernet '15	♛♛ 8

○ 253 Giorni Vermentino '23	♛♛ 3
● Circeo Rosso Incontro al Circeo '20	♛♛ 3
○ Moscato di Terracina Passito Capitolium '21	♛♛ 4
○ Moscato di Terracina Secco V. Campo Soriano Hum '23	♛♛ 5
● Sogno '17	♛♛ 5
○ Circeo Bianco Dune '22	♛ 3
○ Moscato di Terracina Amabile Templum '23	♛ 3
○ Moscato di Terracina Secco Oppidum '23	♛ 3
○ Oppidum Brut '23	♛ 3
○ Moscato di Terracina Secco V. Campo Soriano Hum '21	♛♛ 5
○ Moscato di Terracina Secco V. Campo Soriano Hum '20	♛♛ 4

Tenuta Sant'Isidoro

loc. Portaccia
01016 Tarquinia [VT]
☎ +39 0766869716
🖳 www.santisidoro.net

CELLAR SALES
PRE-BOOKED VISITS
ANNUAL PRODUCTION 92,000 bottles
HECTARES UNDER VINE 57.00

Founded in the late 1930s, Tenuta Sant'Isidoro lies at the northernmost edge of the region, along the Maremma Laziale coast. Giovanni Palombi foresaw the area's viticultural potential, and his son Emidio, to whom the flagship wine is dedicated, developed the estate. Today, Giovanni and Antonio continue their grandfather's legacy, cultivating native varieties like montepulciano, sangiovese, and trebbiano toscano, along with international grapes. The Soremidio '22, a refined montepulciano, offers up aromas of wild berries and chocolate, leading to a juicy and full-bodied palate. The Terzolo '23 has a vegetal profile with cherry and dark spices preceding a crunchy and dynamic palate. A blend of sangiovese, montepulciano, and merlot, the Corithus '22 exudes scents of aromatic herbs and red fruits, sensations that return in the mouth alongside a balsamic vein. The Soraluisa '23, an easy-drinking pinot bianco, proves taut, sapid, flavorful, floral, and fruity. The fresh and fragrant Chardonnay Forca di Palma '23 plays on white flower aromas, sage, and banana.

Wine	Rating
● Soremidio '22	♟♟ 4
● Corithus '22	♟♟ 3
○ Forca di Palma '23	♟♟ 2*
○ Soraluisa '23	♟♟ 3
● Terzolo '23	♟♟ 2*
○ Sant'Isidoro Brut	♟ 3
○ Tarquinia Bianco Tatia '23	♟ 2
● Tarquinia Rosso Larth '23	♟ 2
● Corithus '20	♟♟ 6
○ Forca di Palma '22	♟♟ 2*
○ Soraluisa '22	♟♟ 3
○ Soraluisa '21	♟♟ 7
● Soremidio '21	♟♟ 4
● Tarquinia Rosso Larth '20	♟♟ 2*
● Tarquinia Rosso Larth '19	♟♟ 1*
● Terzolo '22	♟♟ 2*

★ Tenuta di Fiorano

via di Fioranello, 19
00134 Roma
☎ +39 0679340093
🖳 www.tenutadifiorano.it

CELLAR SALES
PRE-BOOKED VISITS
ACCOMMODATION AND RESTAURANT SERVICE
ANNUAL PRODUCTION 40,000 bottles
HECTARES UNDER VINE 12.00
VITICULTURE METHOD Certified Organic

LAZIO

The story of Tenuta di Fiorano, located along the Appian Way near Rome, is rich with mystery and visionary decisions. In the 1940s, Alberico Boncompagni Ludovisi boldly planted the vineyard. In 1998, production halted suddenly, only to resume in the early 2000s under Alessandrojacopo, who, despite lacking winemaking experience, took over the historic estate with great passion. The Fiorano Bianco once again leads the rankings. A remarkably balanced and elegant blend of grechetto and viognier grapes, it's redolent of yellow-fleshed fruit, broom, and almond, supported by an iodized base that prolongs the palate, with vanilla and sweet spices on the finish. The Fiorano Rosso, made from cabernet sauvignon and merlot, also excels, offering intriguing and sanguine notes of blackcurrant, tomato leaf, tobacco, and bay leaf, with a vibrant and fresh palate. The two Fioranellos are also pleasant: the white version features notes of lychee, flint, and cut grass, while the red offers coffee and black fruit sensations.

Wine	Rating
○ Fiorano Bianco '22	♟♟♟ 7
● Fiorano Rosso '19	♟♟ 8
○ Fioranello Bianco '23	♟♟ 4
● Fioranello Rosso '22	♟ 4
○ Fiorano Bianco '20	♟♟♟ 6
○ Fiorano Bianco '19	♟♟♟ 6
○ Fiorano Bianco '17	♟♟♟ 6
○ Fiorano Bianco '16	♟♟♟ 6
○ Fiorano Bianco '13	♟♟♟ 5
○ Fiorano Bianco '12	♟♟♟ 4*
○ Fiorano Bianco '10	♟♟♟ 5
● Fiorano Rosso '18	♟♟♟ 8
● Fiorano Rosso '15	♟♟♟ 8
● Fiorano Rosso '12	♟♟♟ 7
● Fiorano Rosso '11	♟♟♟ 7

Giovanni Terenzi

fraz. La Forma
via Forese, 13
03010 Serrone [FR]
📞 +39 0775594286
🌐 www.viniterenzi.com

Villa Simone

via Frascati Colonna, 29
00078 Monte Porzio Catone [RM]
📞 +39 069449717
🌐 www.villasimone.it

CELLAR SALES
PRE-BOOKED VISITS
ANNUAL PRODUCTION 120,000 bottles
HECTARES UNDER VINE 12.00

CELLAR SALES
PRE-BOOKED VISITS
ACCOMMODATION
ANNUAL PRODUCTION 200,000 bottles
HECTARES UNDER VINE 24.00
SUSTAINABLE WINERY

This family-run estate in northern Ciociaria dates back to the 1950s and is still managed by Giovanni and his wife, Santa, who handle the vineyards from pruning to harvest. In the cellar, their son Armando oversees winemaking, while daughters Pina and Maria manage sales and administration. The family's radical choices include focusing solely on two grape varieties, Cesanese d'Affile and Passerina, which are grown without chemical fertilizers or herbicides. The multifaceted nose of the Passerina del Frusinate Vigna Santa reveals notes of grapefruit, loquat, and white peach, all of which return on the palate along with mint and thyme, making for a fresh and captivating drink. The other Passerina, the Zerli, is softer, with ripe fruit and vanilla notes. The three versions of cesanese prove well-crafted: the Velobra stands out for its juicy tones of blackberry, cherry, and bay leaf, echoed on a palate marked by great suppleness. The Colle Forma is more robust and darker, with hints of bramble and juniper. The Vajoscuro is wild and full-bodied, with warm, soft tannins.

The story of Villa Simone began in 1982, when Piero Costantini moved from Le Marche to Rome with the aim of acquiring the cardinal Pallotta's old vineyards in Monte Porzio Catone, at the heart of the Frascati appellation. His goal was to produce high-quality wines. Today, the producer is run by Piero's nephew, Lorenzo, who continues his uncle's work, convinced of the potential of the volcanic soils here and the region's indigenous grapes. The Torraccia '21 evokes a rich aromatic profile of blackberry jam, cinchona, medicinal herbs, ink, and pepper, leading to a palate that's refreshingly full and vibrant. The Ferro e Seta impresses with its fragrant aromas of red berry fruits, followed by coffee and cocoa on the finish. Among the various versions of Frascati, we especially liked the "basic" version, which expresses great typicity in its notes of citrus, sage, and almond, showing energy and sapidity. The Superiore Villa dei Preti proves flavorful, with tones of pink grapefruit and flat peach.

● Cesanese del Piglio Sup. Colle Forma '22	▼▼ 4
● Cesanese del Piglio Sup. Vajoscuro Ris. '22	▼▼ 5
● Cesanese del Piglio Velobra '22	▼▼ 3
○ V. Santa '23	▼▼ 2*
○ Zerli '22	▼▼ 4
● Cesanese del Piglio Sup. Colle Forma '21	♀♀ 4
● Cesanese del Piglio Sup. Colle Forma '20	♀♀ 4
● Cesanese del Piglio Sup. Colle Forma '19	♀♀ 4
● Cesanese del Piglio Sup. Vajoscuro Ris. '20	♀♀ 5
● Cesanese del Piglio Velobra '20	♀♀ 3*
○ V Santa '22	♀♀ 3

○ Frascati '23	▼▼ 2*
● La Torraccia '21	▼▼ 4
● Ferro e Seta '20	▼▼ 6
○ Frascati Sup. Villa dei Preti '23	▼▼ 3
○ Frascati Sup. Vign. Filonardi Ris. '22	▼ 4
○ Frascati '22	♀♀ 2*
○ Frascati '21	♀♀ 3
○ Frascati Sup. Vign. Filonardi Ris. '20	♀♀ 5
○ Frascati Sup. Villa dei Preti '22	♀♀ 3
○ Frascati Sup. Villa dei Preti '21	♀♀ 4
● La Torraccia '20	♀♀ 3*
● La Torraccia '19	♀♀ 4

OTHER WINERIES

Brugnoli Bio

via Giovanni XXIII, 47
00036 Palestrina [RM]
☎ +39 069574324
✎ www.brugnolibio.it

CELLAR SALES
PRE-BOOKED VISITS
ANNUAL PRODUCTION 50,000 bottles
HECTARES UNDER VINE 34.00
VITICULTURE METHOD Certified Organic
SUSTAINABLE WINERY

● Grechetto Rosso '22	♟♟ 3
○ Trebbiano Giallo '22	♟♟ 3
☉ Rosato '23	♟ 3

Casale della Ioria

loc. La Gloria
s.da prov.le 118 Anagni-Paliano
03012 Anagni [FR]
☎ +39 077556031
✎ www.casaledellaioria.com

CELLAR SALES
ANNUAL PRODUCTION 100,000 bottles
HECTARES UNDER VINE 38.00
VITICULTURE METHOD Certified Organic
SUSTAINABLE WINERY

● Cesanese del Piglio Campo Novo '22	♟♟ 2*
● Cesanese del Piglio Sup. Tenuta della Ioria '22	♟♟ 3
☉ Cesanese Brut Rosé '22	♟ 4

Castello di Torre in Pietra

via di Torre in Pietra, 247
00054 Fiumicino [RM]
☎ +39 0661697070
✎ www.castelloditorreinpietra.com

CELLAR SALES
PRE-BOOKED VISITS
ANNUAL PRODUCTION 210,000 bottles
HECTARES UNDER VINE 52.00
VITICULTURE METHOD Certified Organic

● Cesanese '22	♟♟ 3
● Roma Rosso Amor '22	♟♟ 2*
○ Vermentino '23	♟♟ 2*
○ Roma Malvasia Puntinata Amor '23	♟ 2

Casa Divina Provvidenza

via dei Frati, 140
00048 Nettuno [RM]
☎ +39 069851366
✎ www.casadivinaprovvidenza.it

CELLAR SALES
PRE-BOOKED VISITS
RESTAURANT SERVICE
ANNUAL PRODUCTION 500,000 bottles
HECTARES UNDER VINE 60.00
VITICULTURE METHOD Certified Organic
SUSTAINABLE WINERY

● Cesanese '22	♟♟ 4
● Roma Rosso '20	♟♟ 3
○ Nettuno Cacchione '23	♟ 3
● Roma Rosso 200 Anni Ris. '20	♟ 8

Casata Mergè

via di Fontana Candida, 381
00132 Roma
☎ +39 0620609225
✎ www.casatamerge.it

CELLAR SALES
PRE-BOOKED VISITS
ANNUAL PRODUCTION 500,000 bottles
HECTARES UNDER VINE 30.00
VITICULTURE METHOD Certified Organic

○ Biancolella Sesto 21 '23	♟♟ 6
○ Frascati Sup. sesto 21 Ris. '22	♟♟ 4
○ Parisfal Pecorino '23	♟♟ 3
○ Spumante Brut M. Cl. Ibi Est '20	♟ 5

Colle di Maggio

via Passo dei Coresi, 25
00049 Velletri [RM]
☎ +39 0696453072
✎ www.colledimaggio.it

CELLAR SALES
RESTAURANT SERVICE
ANNUAL PRODUCTION 40,000 bottles
HECTARES UNDER VINE 10.00

● Orione '22	♟♟ 3
○ Sirio '23	♟♟ 3
● Neroparadiso '22	♟ 8
○ Vèlia '23	♟ 5

Colle Picchioni

loc. Frattocchie
via Colle Picchione, 46
00040 Marino [RM]
📞 +39 3331963261
🌐 www.collepicchioni.it

CELLAR SALES
PRE-BOOKED VISITS
ANNUAL PRODUCTION 80,000 bottles
HECTARES UNDER VINE 13.00

● Il Vassallo '21	🍷🍷 5
● Perlaia '23	🍷🍷 3
○ Le Vignole '21	🍷 3
● Mèva Rosso '23	🍷 3

Compagnia di Ermes

via San Francesco d'Assisi, 95
00035 Olevano Romano [RM]
📞 +39 069564025
compagnia-di-ermes@hotmail.it

● Olevano Romano Ris. '19	🍷🍷 5
● Olevano Romano Sup. '21	🍷🍷 4
○ Cibele '22	🍷 4
● Olevano Romano Sup. '22	🍷 4

Corte dei Papi

loc. Colletonno
03012 Anagni [FR]
📞 +39 07751860092
🌐 www.cortedeipapi.it

CELLAR SALES
PRE-BOOKED VISITS
ANNUAL PRODUCTION 60,000 bottles
HECTARES UNDER VINE 25.30

● Cesanese del Piglio Colle Ticchio '23	🍷🍷 3
● Cesanese del Piglio Sup. San Magno '22	🍷🍷 5
○ Passerina del Frusinate '23	🍷 3

Doganieri Miyazaki

fraz. Vaiano, 3
01024 Castiglione in Teverina [VT]
📞 +39 3332807985
🌐 www.doganierimiyazaki.com

CELLAR SALES
PRE-BOOKED VISITS
ANNUAL PRODUCTION 8,000 bottles
HECTARES UNDER VINE 1.30

○ Dai Dai '22	🍷🍷 4
○ Airi '23	🍷🍷 3
○ Fixus '23	🍷 4

La Ferriera

via Ferriera, 743
03042 Atina [FR]
📞 +39 0776691226
🌐 www.laferriera.it

CELLAR SALES
PRE-BOOKED VISITS
ANNUAL PRODUCTION 50,000 bottles
HECTARES UNDER VINE 15.00

● Atina Cabernet Realmagona '20	🍷🍷 4
○ Atina Semillon Semiato '21	🍷🍷 3
● Atina Cabernet Realmagona Ris. '18	🍷 5
○ Brut M. Cl. Realmagona '21	🍷 4

Emiliano Fini

via Vallelata, 141
04011 Aprilia [LT]
📞 +39 3382932111
🌐 www.emilianofini.it

CELLAR SALES
PRE-BOOKED VISITS
ANNUAL PRODUCTION 5,000 bottles
HECTARES UNDER VINE 7.00

○ Cleto '22	🍷🍷 3

OTHER WINERIES

Fontana Candida

via Fontana Candida, 11
00040 Monte Porzio Catone [RM]
☏ +39 069401881
✉ www.fontanacandida.it

CELLAR SALES
PRE-BOOKED VISITS
RESTAURANT SERVICE
ANNUAL PRODUCTION 720,000 bottles
HECTARES UNDER VINE 214.00

○ Frascati Sup. Vign. Santa Teresa '23	🍷🍷 3
○ Frascati Terre dei Grifi '23	🍷🍷 2*

Gaffino

fraz. Villaggio Ardeatino
via Ardeatina, km 24.650
00040 Ardea [RM]
☏ +39 3518071759
✉ www.cantinagaffino.it

CELLAR SALES
PRE-BOOKED VISITS
ANNUAL PRODUCTION 70,000 bottles
HECTARES UNDER VINE 28.00
VITICULTURE METHOD Certified Organic

● Opimiam Syrah '21	🍷🍷 3
● Roma Rosso '20	🍷🍷 3
● Tubbo Merlot '23	🍷🍷 3
○ Sospiro '23	🍷 2

Alberto Giacobbe

c.da Colle San Giovenale
03018 Paliano [FR]
☏ +39 3298738052
✉ www.vinigiacobbe.it

CELLAR SALES
PRE-BOOKED VISITS
ACCOMMODATION
ANNUAL PRODUCTION 60,000 bottles
HECTARES UNDER VINE 13.00

● Cesanese del Piglio Sup. Lepanto Ris. '20	🍷🍷 5
● Cesanese di Olevano Romano Sup. Giacobbe '22	🍷🍷 3
○ Duchessa W '22	🍷🍷 2*

Marcella Giuliani

loc. Gloria
s.da prov.le 118
03012 Anagni [FR]
☏ +39 3913481031
✉ www.marcellagiuliani.com

CELLAR SALES
PRE-BOOKED VISITS
ANNUAL PRODUCTION 35,000 bottles
HECTARES UNDER VINE 10.70
VITICULTURE METHOD Certified Organic

● Cesanese del Piglio Sup. Dives '21	🍷🍷 5
○ Passerina del Frusinate '23	🍷🍷 2*
● Cesanese del Piglio Dante '23	🍷 3

Cantina Imperatori

via Pietra Porzia, 14
00044 Frascati [RM]
☏ +39 3394586822
✉ www.cantinaimperatori.it

CELLAR SALES
ANNUAL PRODUCTION 35,000 bottles
HECTARES UNDER VINE 5.00

○ Frascati Flò '23	🍷🍷 3*
● Cabernet Sauvignon '22	🍷🍷 5
● Cesanese Flò '23	🍷🍷 3
○ Frascati Anfora '23	🍷 5

Antica Cantina Leonardi

via del Pino, 12
01027 Montefiascone [VT]
☏ +39 0761826028
✉ www.cantinaleonardi.it

CELLAR SALES
PRE-BOOKED VISITS
ACCOMMODATION AND RESTAURANT SERVICE
ANNUAL PRODUCTION 150,000 bottles
HECTARES UNDER VINE 30.00
VITICULTURE METHOD Certified Organic

○ Luce di Lago '23	🍷🍷 2*
○ Pensiero '23	🍷🍷 2*
● Don Carlo '20	🍷 3

OTHER WINERIES

Lotti

loc. Ascarella, 2
fraz. Italia
01010 Cellere [VT]
(+39 3342583999
www.aziendaagricolabiologicalotti.com

CELLAR SALES
PRE-BOOKED VISITS
ACCOMMODATION
ANNUAL PRODUCTION 30,000 bottles
HECTARES UNDER VINE 12.00
VITICULTURE METHOD Certified Organic

○ Crògnelo '23	♟♟ 4
○ Sterpengo '22	♟♟ 5
○ Biodiverso '23	♟ 5
○ Vionì '23	♟ 5

Antica Tenuta Palombo

via Ponte Capone
03042 Atina [FR]
(+39 3493684310
www.anticatenutapalombo.it

CELLAR SALES
PRE-BOOKED VISITS
RESTAURANT SERVICE
ANNUAL PRODUCTION 50,000 bottles
HECTARES UNDER VINE 7.00

● Atina Cabernet '20	♟♟ 4
● Atina Cabernet Duca Cantelmo Ris. '20	♟♟ 6
○ Maturano '22	♟ 2
○ Rosa Invidiata '23	♟ 3

Parvus Ager

loc. Santa Maria delle Mole
v.le della Repubblica, 10
00047 Marino [RM]
(+39 0693543162
www.parvusger.com

CELLAR SALES
PRE-BOOKED VISITS
RESTAURANT SERVICE
ANNUAL PRODUCTION 30,000 bottles
HECTARES UNDER VINE 54.00

○ Roma Malvasia Eterna '23	♟♟ 4
● Roma Rosso Eterna '22	♟♟ 4
● Essenza della Terra Cesanese '23	♟ 4
○ Essenza della Terra Vermentino '23	♟ 4

Nuova Cantina di Genazzano - Martino V

s.s. 155, km 55,500
00030 Genazzano [RM]
(+39 069579121
www.martinoquinto.it

CELLAR SALES
PRE-BOOKED VISITS
ANNUAL PRODUCTION 200,000 bottles
HECTARES UNDER VINE 35.00

○ Martino V Ottonese '20	♟♟ 3
○ Martino V Passerina '23	♟♟ 2*
● Martino V Cesanese '23	♟ 2
● Martino V Syrah '23	♟ 2

Papalino

s.da della Lega, 10
01024 Castiglione in Teverina [VT]
(+39 3405352190
www.papalino.it

CELLAR SALES
ANNUAL PRODUCTION 22,000 bottles
HECTARES UNDER VINE 5.00
SUSTAINABLE WINERY

● Senauro '21	♟♟ 5
● Tuscia Violone Solidago '21	♟♟ 4
○ Ametis '21	♟ 4
○ Lazulum '22	♟ 3

Petrucca e Vela

c.da Coce
03010 Piglio [FR]
(+39 0775501032
www.cesanese.it

CELLAR SALES
PRE-BOOKED VISITS
ANNUAL PRODUCTION 60,000 bottles
HECTARES UNDER VINE 9.50
SUSTAINABLE WINERY

● Cesanese del Piglio Sup. Tellures Ris. '19	♟♟ 5
○ Rosèsi '23	♟♟ 3
● Cesanese del Piglio Sup. Agape '21	♟ 3

OTHER WINERIES

Pietra Pinta

via Le Pastine km 20,200
04010 Cori [LT]
📞 +39 069678001
🌐 www.pietrapinta.com

CELLAR SALES
PRE-BOOKED VISITS
ACCOMMODATION AND RESTAURANT SERVICE
ANNUAL PRODUCTION 300,000 bottles
HECTARES UNDER VINE 33.00
VITICULTURE METHOD Certified Organic
SUSTAINABLE WINERY

○ Chardonnay '23	🍷🍷 3
○ Costa Vecchia Bianco '23	🍷🍷 2*
○ Sauvignon '23	🍷🍷 2*
● Nero Buono '21	🍷 2

Pileum

via Casalotto
03010 Piglio [FR]
📞 +39 3663129910
🌐 www.pileum.it

CELLAR SALES
PRE-BOOKED VISITS
ACCOMMODATION AND RESTAURANT SERVICE
ANNUAL PRODUCTION 90,000 bottles
HECTARES UNDER VINE 18.00
VITICULTURE METHOD Certified Organic
SUSTAINABLE WINERY

● Cesanese del Piglio Sup. I Cloni '22	🍷🍷 4
○ Le Fattora '23	🍷🍷 4

Proietti

loc. Campo
via Maremmana Superiore, km 2,800
00035 Olevano Romano [RM]
📞 +39 069563376
🌐 www.aziendaagricolaproietti.it

CELLAR SALES
PRE-BOOKED VISITS
ANNUAL PRODUCTION 90,000 bottles
HECTARES UNDER VINE 15.00

● Cesanese di Olevano Romano Tenuta al Campo Ris. '21	🍷🍷 6
○ Tenuta al Campo Malvasia Puntinata '23	🍷🍷 4

Tenuta Le Quinte

via delle Marmorelle Nuova, 91
00077 Montecompatri [RM]
📞 +39 069438756
🌐 www.tenutalequinte.it

CELLAR SALES
PRE-BOOKED VISITS
ANNUAL PRODUCTION 300,000 bottles
HECTARES UNDER VINE 40.00

○ Montecompatri Sup. Secco Virtù Romane '23	🍷🍷 3
● Primula Lucis '23	🍷🍷 4
○ Lucet '23	🍷 4

Ronci di Nepi

loc. Valle Ronci
via Ronci, 2072
01036 Nepi [VT]
📞 +39 0761555125
🌐 www.roncidinepi.it

CELLAR SALES
PRE-BOOKED VISITS
ANNUAL PRODUCTION 100,000 bottles
HECTARES UNDER VINE 30.00

● Ronci '19	🍷🍷 5
● Veste Porpora '22	🍷🍷 3
○ O di Ne' '23	🍷 3
● Rosso di Ne' '22	🍷 3

Cantine San Marco

loc. Vermicino
via di Mola Cavona, 26/28
00044 Frascati [RM]
📞 +39 069409403
🌐 www.sanmarcofrascati.it

CELLAR SALES
PRE-BOOKED VISITS
ANNUAL PRODUCTION 1,500,000 bottles
HECTARES UNDER VINE 42.00
VITICULTURE METHOD Certified Organic

○ De' Notari Bellone '23	🍷🍷 3
● Roma Rosso Romae '20	🍷🍷 2*
○ Frascati Sup. De' Notari Crio 12 '23	🍷 3
● Solo Cabernet Sauvignon '22	🍷 2

LAZIO

863

OTHER WINERIES

LAZIO

Stefanoni
fraz. Zepponami
via Stefanoni, 9
01027 Montefiascone [VT]
📞 +39 0761825651
🌐 www.cantinastefanoni.it

CELLAR SALES
PRE-BOOKED VISITS
ANNUAL PRODUCTION 100,000 bottles
HECTARES UNDER VINE 10.00

○ Est! Est!! Est!!! Di Montefiascone Cl. Foltone '23	♟♟ 3
○ Tuscia Roscetto Colle de' Poggeri '22	♟♟ 4
● Colle de' Poggeri Aleatico '23	♟ 3

Terre di Marfisa
loc. Le Sparme
s.da prov.le Lamone, km 7
01010 Farnese [VT]
📞 +39 0761458202
🌐 www.terredimarfisa.it

CELLAR SALES
PRE-BOOKED VISITS
ACCOMMODATION AND RESTAURANT SERVICE
ANNUAL PRODUCTION 20,000 bottles
HECTARES UNDER VINE 7.00
VITICULTURE METHOD Certified Organic

● La Cava '21	♟♟ 3
● Tesham '19	♟♟ 3
○ Zamathi Iris '22	♟ 3
○ Zamathi Vermentino '22	♟ 3

Villa Caviciana
loc. Macchia del Prete
01010 Gradoli [VT]
📞 +39 3515131307
🌐 www.villacaviciana.com

CELLAR SALES
PRE-BOOKED VISITS
ANNUAL PRODUCTION 60,000 bottles
HECTARES UNDER VINE 20.00
VITICULTURE METHOD Certified Biodynamic

○ Rasena '23	♟♟ 3
○ Valloresia '23	♟♟ 3
● Caelestio Rosso '21	♟ 3
● Montesenano Aleatico '22	♟ 3

Villa Gianna
loc. b.go San Donato
s.da Maremmana
04016 Sabaudia [LT]
📞 +39 0773250034
🌐 www.cantinavillagianna.it

CELLAR SALES
PRE-BOOKED VISITS
ACCOMMODATION
ANNUAL PRODUCTION 900,000 bottles
HECTARES UNDER VINE 75.00
SUSTAINABLE WINERY

○ Circeo Bianco Innato '23	♟♟ 4
● Rudestro '21	♟♟ 3
○ Vigne del Borgo Bellone '23	♟♟ 3
● Circeo Rosso Barriano Ris. '21	♟ 4

Vinea Domini
fraz. Frattocchie
via del Divino Amore, 347
00047 Marino [RM]
📞 +39 0693022226
🌐 www.vineadomini.it

CELLAR SALES
PRE-BOOKED VISITS
ANNUAL PRODUCTION 55,000 bottles
HECTARES UNDER VINE 75.00
SUSTAINABLE WINERY

● Cesanese del Piglio '22	♟♟ 4
○ Frascati Sup. '23	♟♟ 3
○ Roma Malvasia Puntinata '23	♟ 3
○ Sauvignon '23	♟ 3

Cantine Volpetti
via Nettunense, 21
00072 Ariccia [RM]
📞 +39 069342000
🌐 www.cantinevolpetti.it

CELLAR SALES
PRE-BOOKED VISITS
ANNUAL PRODUCTION 150,000 bottles
HECTARES UNDER VINE 20.00
VITICULTURE METHOD Certified Organic
SUSTAINABLE WINERY

● Le Piantate Sangiovese '21	♟♟ 3
● Roma Rosso '22	♟♟ 2
○ ChiaraVia '22	♟ 4
○ Frascati Sup. Le Piantate '22	♟ 2

ABRUZZO

The latest updates from Abruzzo paint a picture of a region looking toward the future. The so-called "Abruzzo Model" is reshaping local production with a clear aim: to raise quality standards and set a distinction between an increasing number of producers focused on crafting identity-driven, terroir-expressive wines and the bottlers who prioritize quantity (often at unsustainably low prices). As a result, the inclusion of sub-zones like Terre di Chieti, Terre de L'Aquila, Colline Pescaresi, and Colline Teramane on labels—specifically for Superiore and Riserva designations—will serve as a clear marker for wines bottled within their production areas and, most importantly, wines that seek to highlight the bond between grape and territory. This seems to be the right path for differentiating a region that boasts over 33,000 hectares of vineyards, stretching from the cool slopes of the Apennines, in the shadow of Gran Sasso and Majella, down to the Adriatic coast where the vineyards meet the sea. We look forward to seeing how these efforts will manifest in the bottle in the years ahead.

However, there are also some challenges. As widely reported, 2023 was a tough year due to downy mildew, which in some parts of the region led to an 80% loss in harvest. We believe this has also affected quality somewhat; we noticed it while tasting the whites (most of the reds from 2023 will reach our tasting tables in the coming years), which lacked the polish and intensity we're accustomed to. As for montepulciano, despite progress from some producers, it seems that many still cling to outdated practices, marked by excessive extraction, concentration, and the heavy use of oak. In a time when consumers are leaning toward lighter wines with lower alcohol levels, adjustments might be necessary.

That said, the high points remain impressive. This year, we awarded 16 Tre Bicchieri. Among the newcomers to the winners' circle are three producers: Cugnoli's Cingilia, which impressed us with a Cerasuolo d'Abruzzo that was as authentic as it was delicious; Spinelli, owned by the family of the same name, which has redefined its production approach to deliver an extraordinary Trebbiano d'Abruzzo; and Torre Zambra, where the enterprising Federico De Cerchio earned a prize for a Villamagna—the first ever Tre Bicchieri for this small appellation in the province of Chieti. We discuss Torre dei Beati's excellent Trebbiano d'Abruzzo Di-Vèrto '22 further in the Rare Wines section.

Agriverde

loc. Caldari
via Stortini, 32a
66026 Ortona [CH]
℡ 0859032101
⊛ www.cantineagriverde.com

CELLAR SALES
PRE-BOOKED VISITS
ANNUAL PRODUCTION 1,000,000 bottles
HECTARES UNDER VINE 65.00
VITICULTURE METHOD Certified Organic
SUSTAINABLE WINERY

The winery was established in the hills of Ortona, not far from the Adriatic coast. From the very beginning, Agriverde has been committed to organic farming, becoming one of the first producers in the region to earn certification and to incorporate bioarchitecture into the design of its cellar. The estate spans 65 hectares, predominantly planted with native grape varieties, which are crafted into a diverse range of wines, everything from everyday, easy-drinking options to more ambitious selections. The Montepulciano d'Abruzzo Natum '22 exudes aromas of ripe cherry and plum. On the palate, it unfolds its fruity sensations unwaveringly, with fine tannins and a structured yet smooth profile. The Cerasuolo Riseis '23 also caught our attention, delivering floral whiffs of rose accompanied by herbal notes on a taut palate with a pleasantly sapid undertone. Among the whites, the Pecorino Natum '22 stands out, offering up white peach, linden, and acacia before a juicy and enjoyable palate.

Amorotti

via del Baio, 31
65014 Loreto Aprutino [PE]
℡ 3494003131
⊛ www.amorotti.it

CELLAR SALES
ANNUAL PRODUCTION 23,000 bottles
HECTARES UNDER VINE 16.00
VITICULTURE METHOD Certified Organic
SUSTAINABLE WINERY

Anyone familiar with Loreto Aprutino might have noticed the recent addition of a new player in the town's winemaking scene. Amorotti, the brainchild of Gaetano Carboni, emerged about 10 years ago when he decided to revive his ancestors' old cellar, located in the historic Palazzo dei Baroni Amorotti. Here, in a space steeped in history, grapes from the estate's 16 hectares of vineyards—divided into several parcels—are processed using artisanal methods. Fermentation is strictly spontaneous, with no modern technology or stainless steel entering the cellar; instead, large wooden casks are used exclusively for both vinification and maturation. This year, the once again Trebbiano stands out among the small lineup presented. The 2022 proves to be a white with a layered and multifaceted aromatic spectrum, combining tea leaves, candied lemon, chamomile, propolis, mustard seeds, and green apricot before yielding a lively palate, infused with flavorful energy.

⊙ Cerasuolo d'Abruzzo Riseis '23	♟♟ 2*
● Montepulciano d'Abruzzo Natum '22	♟♟ 3
● Montepulciano d'Abruzzo Riseis '21	♟♟ 3
● Montepulciano d'Abruzzo Solàrea '19	♟♟ 4
○ Natum Pecorino '22	♟♟ 1*
⊙ Cerasuolo d'Abruzzo Solàrea '23	♟ 2
○ Riseis Pecorino '23	♟ 3
● Montepulciano d'Abruzzo Plateo '04	♛♛♛ 6
● Montepulciano d'Abruzzo Plateo '01	♛♛♛ 6
● Montepulciano d'Abruzzo Plateo '00	♛♛♛ 6
● Montepulciano d'Abruzzo Plateo '98	♛♛♛ 5
● Montepulciano d'Abruzzo Plateo Ris. '15	♛♛♛ 6
● Montepulciano d'Abruzzo Solàrea '03	♛♛♛ 4
○ Trebbiano d'Abruzzo Solàrea '18	♛♛♛ 4*

○ Trebbiano d'Abruzzo '22	♟♟♟ 5
⊙ Cerasuolo d'Abruzzo '22	♟♟ 5
● Montepulciano d'Abruzzo '20	♟ 5
○ Trebbiano d'Abruzzo '21	♛♛♛ 5
⊙ Cerasuolo d'Abruzzo '21	♛♛ 5
⊙ Cerasuolo d'Abruzzo '20	♛♛ 5
● Montepulciano d'Abruzzo '19	♛♛ 5
● Montepulciano d'Abruzzo '18	♛♛ 5
○ Trebbiano d'Abruzzo '20	♛♛ 5

F.lli Barba

fraz. Scerne
s.da Rotabile per Casoli
64025 Pineto [TE]
℡ 0859461020
✉ www.fratellibarba.it

CELLAR SALES
PRE-BOOKED VISITS
ACCOMMODATION
ANNUAL PRODUCTION 400,000 bottles
HECTARES UNDER VINE 62.00

Colle Morino, Casal Thaulero, and Vignafranca are the districts of the Teramo Hills where the Barba brothers cultivate their 62 hectares of vineyards. Giovanni, Domenico, and Vincenzo continue the work begun by their father, Cavalier Luigi, in the 1950s, managing not only the vineyards but also an expansive agricultural operation that encompasses nearly 700 hectares. This scale places their winery among the largest in the Abruzzo region. Their base of operations is in Scerne di Pineto, where a modern cellar produces a wide range sold worldwide. The Cerasuolo Collemorino '23 impressed us the most this year, thanks to its nose, which perfectly melds the fleshy fruitiness of cherry with black pepper and subtle smoky notes. The palate is spirited, with a pleasant acidity reminiscent of bitter citrus. The Pecorino Vignafranca '23, though less energetic, remains vibrant and flavorful, with aromas of hay meeting white fruits on a light and well-sustained palate.

Barone Cornacchia

c.da Torri, 19
64010 Torano Nuovo [TE]
℡ 0861887412
✉ www.baronecornacchia.it

CELLAR SALES
PRE-BOOKED VISITS
ACCOMMODATION
ANNUAL PRODUCTION 110,000 bottles
HECTARES UNDER VINE 60.00
VITICULTURE METHOD Certified Organic
SUSTAINABLE WINERY

The Cornacchia family has overseen the territory around the Civitella fortress since 1577, when the Viceroy of Naples granted them a noble title. On the gentle Teramane Hills, what was once a hunting reserve has been transformed into a cutting-edge winery run by siblings Caterina and Filippo. The vineyards are managed organically, with some recent biodynamic practices introduced. Naturally, Abruzzo's native grape varieties dominate. The stylistic shift undertaken by the winery is quite evident across the range, though it seems that some fine-tuning is still needed. For now, we appreciated the full-bodied nature of the Trebbiano Poggio Varano (spontaneous fermentation and maturation in amphora). It requires some exposure to oxygen before revealing an aromatic spectrum of yellow peach, broom, and beeswax, which culminate in a rather textured palate.

Wine	Rating
⊙ Cerasuolo d' Abruzzo Collemorino '23	♟♟ 2*
● Colline Teramane Montepulciano d'Abruzzo Yang '22	♟♟ 3
○ Trebbiano d' Abruzzo Collemorino '23	♟♟ 2*
○ Vignafranca Pecorino '23	♟♟ 2*
● Montepulciano d'Abruzzo I Vasari Old Vines '21	♟ 5
● Montepulciano d'Abruzzo I Vasari '10	♟♟♟ 5
● Montepulciano d'Abruzzo I Vasari '09	♟♟♟ 5
● Montepulciano d'Abruzzo I Vasari '08	♟♟♟ 5
● Montepulciano d'Abruzzo Vignafranca '07	♟♟♟ 3*
● Montepulciano d'Abruzzo Vignafranca '06	♟♟♟ 3*
○ Trebbiano d'Abruzzo '06	♟♟♟ 4*
● Colline Teramane Montepulciano d'Abruzzo Yang '20	♟♟ 2*

Wine	Rating
○ Controguerra Pecorino Casanova '23	♟♟ 3
○ Trebbiano d'Abruzzo Poggio Varano '22	♟♟ 4
⊙ Colline Teramane Cerasuolo d'Abruzzo Sup. Casanova '23	♟ 3
○ Colline Teramane Trebbiano d'Abruzzo Sup. Casanova '23	♟ 3
○ Controguerra Passerina Casanova '23	♟ 3
● Montepulciano d'Abruzzo Casanova '22	♟ 3
● Montepulciano d'Abruzzo Casanova '20	♟♟ 5
● Colline Teramane Montepulciano d'Abruzzo Vizzarro '19	♟♟ 8
● Colline Teramane Montepulciano d'Abruzzo Vizzarro Ris. '18	♟♟ 8
● Montepulciano d'Abruzzo Poggio Varano '21	♟♟ 8
○ Trebbiano d'Abruzzo Poggio Varano Macerato '21	♟♟ 8
○ Trebbiano d'Abruzzo Sup. Casanova '20	♟♟ 3

Nestore Bosco

c.da Casali, 147
65010 Nocciano [PE]
℡ 085847345
✷ www.nestorebosco.com

★Castorani

via Castorani, 5
65020 Alanno [PE]
℡ 0852012513
✷ castorani.it

CELLAR SALES
PRE-BOOKED VISITS
ANNUAL PRODUCTION 650,000 bottles
HECTARES UNDER VINE 75.00
VITICULTURE METHOD Certified Organic
SUSTAINABLE WINERY

CELLAR SALES
PRE-BOOKED VISITS
ACCOMMODATION AND RESTAURANT SERVICE
ANNUAL PRODUCTION 700,000 bottles
HECTARES UNDER VINE 150.00
VITICULTURE METHOD Certified Organic
SUSTAINABLE WINERY

Founded in Nocciano in the late 19th century by Giovanni Bosco, the winery is now run by his grandchildren, Nestore and Stefania. They oversee more than 70 hectares of vineyards on the Pescara Hills, around Nocciano, where all operations are based. The tunnels dug beneath the winery are used to age wines that require long maturation, particularly montepulciano. The portfolio is broad and varied, featuring not only more ambitious selections but also immediate, approachable options that still possess a distinct varietal character. The work done on pecorino is commendable. This is demonstrated by two wines that performed particularly well during this year's tastings. The Pecorino della Linea Storica, vintage 2023, boasts a fragrant bouquet reminiscent of citron peel and linden flowers. The palate is long, well-defined, flavorful, and deep. The same aromatic profile—citrus and white flowers, though slightly less intense— emerges in the Pecorino 1897 '23, which offers a fine and very enjoyable palate. The entire range is solid.

This historic estate, located in Alanno on the Pescara Hills, is named after its first famous owner, the surgeon Raffaele Castorani, who founded the farm in the late 1700s. After changing hands several times, the property is now owned by the Trulli and Cavuto families, who blend deep historical roots with a modern approach that balances significant production volumes with exceptional quality. The vineyards, situated at around 350 meters elevation, primarily host montepulciano, trebbiano, and pecorino grapes. The Montepulciano Podere Castorani, remains the familiar austere red we've come to expect, and that's true of the 2020 as well. Its dark aromatic profile is marked by notes of dark chocolate, toast, and graphite, lightly brushed by fruity whiffs. Its tannins are plentiful yet fine-grained, giving the palate a firm structure. The Montepulciano Amorino is simpler and more sapid. Two wines made with grapes less common to the region also caught our attention, with the citrusy character of the sangiovese and the fragrance of the pinot noir standing out.

○ 1897 Pecorino '23	♟♟ 3*
○ Pecorino Linea Storica '23	♟♟ 3*
● Montepulciano d'Abruzzo B '21	♟♟ 2*
● Montepulciano d'Abruzzo Terre dei Vestini Don Bosco Ris. '19	♟♟♟ 4
⊙ Colline Pescaresi Cerasuolo d'Abruzzo Sup. Pan '23	♟ 4
○ Colline Pescaresi Trebbiano d'Abruzzo Sup. Don Bosco '23	♟ 4
● Montepulciano d'Abruzzo Linea Classica '21	♟ 2
● Montepulciano d'Abruzzo Pan '19	♟ 5
○ Pan Chardonnay '23	♟ 4
● Montepulciano d'Abruzzo 1897 '20	♟♟ 2*
● Montepulciano d'Abruzzo 1897 '19	♟♟ 3
● Montepulciano d'Abruzzo Linea Storica '19	♟♟ 3

● Montepulciano d'Abruzzo Casauria Podere Castorani Ris. '20	♟♟♟ 6
● Montepulciano d'Abruzzo Amorino '20	♟♟ 5
○ Cadetto Pecorino '23	♟♟ 3
● Montepulciano d'Abruzzo Cadetto '22	♟♟ 3
● Montepulciano d'Abruzzo Lupaia '21	♟♟ 4
● Podere Castorani Pinot Nero '20	♟♟ 7
● Podere Castorani Sangiovese '20	♟♟ 7
○ Trebbiano d'Abruzzo Sup. Colline Pescaresi Amorino '23	♟♟ 5
○ Abruzzo Pecorino Sup. Colline Pescaresi Amorino '23	♟ 5
○ Lupaia Pecorino Orange '23	♟ 5
○ Trebbiano d'Abruzzo Cadetto '23	♟ 3
○ Trebbiano d'Abruzzo Lupaia Spontaneo '23	♟ 5
○ Lupaia Trebbiano Spontaneo '22	♟♟♟ 3

★★Cataldi Madonna

loc. Madonna del Piano
67025 Ofena [AQ]
☎ 0862708037
✉ www.cataldimadonna.com

Cerulli Spinozzi

s.da st.le 150, km 17,600
64020 Canzano [TE]
☎ 086157193
✉ www.cerullispinozzi.it

CELLAR SALES
PRE-BOOKED VISITS
ANNUAL PRODUCTION 230,000 bottles
HECTARES UNDER VINE 30.00
VITICULTURE METHOD Certified Organic
SUSTAINABLE WINERY

CELLAR SALES
PRE-BOOKED VISITS
ACCOMMODATION
ANNUAL PRODUCTION 150,000 bottles
HECTARES UNDER VINE 53.00

Ofena is commonly referred to as "The Oven of Abruzzo" due to the high summer temperatures that plunge dramatically when the Gran Sasso mountain exerts its influence. Well, Giulia Cataldi Madonna takes full advantage of these temperature fluctuations when producing her wines. Her montepulciano, trebbiano, and pecorino grapes aptly express varietal character and terroir. As widely known, pecorino is the winery's specialty, and this year, we preferred the Giulia. Aromatic sensations emerge from the glass, transporting us to mountain meadows and rocky terrain followed by citrus notes of lime and white grapefruit. The palate is taut and very sapid, with a finely flavorful finish. The Frontone '21 is even sharper and more penetrating, though it loses some flavor intensity mid-palate. Sweet spices and a captivating herbal touch define the Tonì '21, a red that successfully softens the hardness of montepulciano.

Canzano is a small town on the Teramane Hills. A few kilometers outside, in the Vomano Valley, we find the winery now managed by Enrico Cerulli Irelli. Since joining the family business, he has strived to modernize an operation dating back to the early 1900s. Grapes are sourced both from the plot surrounding the winery and another to the north in Mosciano. This year saw a good performance by the Cortalto Pecorino '22, which blends citrus and mineral nuances on a taut, energetic, and penetrating palate. Ripe cherry dominates the crisp aromatic spectrum of the Cerasuolo Cortalto '23, with a precise palate featuring a nice acidic-sapid background and a fruity encore on the finish. The Trebbiano Torre Migliori features a clean aromatic profile, with yellow fruit and freshly cut grass sensations; on the palate, it reveals a decent character and a rhythmic, pleasant profile. The other wines tasted are also on point.

○ Frontone Pecorino '21	♟♟ 8
○ Giulia Pecorino '23	♟♟ 3*
⊙ Cataldino Rosato '23	♟♟ 3
⊙ Cerasuolo d'Abruzzo Malandrino '23	♟♟ 3
● Montepulciano d'Abruzzo Malandrino '22	♟♟ 3
● Montepulciano d'Abruzzo Tonì '21	♟♟♟ 7
○ Trebbiano d'Abruzzo Malandrino '23	♟♟ 3
○ Frontone Pecorino '20	♟♟♟ 8
● Montepulciano d'Abruzzo Girovago '19	♟♟♟ 5
○ Supergiulia Pecorino '18	♟♟♟ 5
○ Supergiulia Pecorino '17	♟♟♟ 5

○ Cortalto Pecorino '22	♟♟ 3*
⊙ Colline Teramane Cerasuolo d'Abruzzo Sup. Cortalto '23	♟♟ 3
○ Trebbiano d'Abruzzo Torre Migliori '22	♟♟ 3
● Colline Teramane Montepulciano d'Abruzzo Cortalto '20	♟ 3
● Colline Teramane Montepulciano d'Abruzzo Torre Migliori '18	♟ 3
● Colline Teramane Montepulciano d'Abruzzo Torre Migliori Ris. '17	♟ 5
● Colline Teramane Montepulciano d'Abruzzo Cortalto '19	♟♟ 3
○ Cortalto Pecorino '21	♟♟ 3
○ Cortalto Pecorino '20	♟♟ 3
○ Trebbiano d'Abruzzo Torre Migliori '21	♟♟ 3
○ Trebbiano d'Abruzzo Torre Migliori '20	♟♟ 3

Ciavolich

c.da Salmacina, 11
65014 Loreto Aprutino [PE]
☏ 0858289002
⊛ www.ciavolich.com

CELLAR SALES
PRE-BOOKED VISITS
ACCOMMODATION AND RESTAURANT SERVICE
ANNUAL PRODUCTION 120,000 bottles
HECTARES UNDER VINE 35.00
SUSTAINABLE WINERY

Chiara Ciavolich, the latest heir to a long lineage of winemakers, approaches the wine world with character and determination, qualities deeply rooted in her heritage. She is the driving force behind the Fosso Cancelli line, artisanal wines with a strong identity that impressed us in our recent tastings. The vineyards are divided into two estates: 24 hectares in Loreto Aprutino, planted in the 1960s, and six hectares in Pianella, planted in 2000. Once again this year, the Fosso Cancelli line delivers a high-level performance, especially the Montepulciano and Trebbiano. The first is a characterful red, with aromas of black forest fruits, a pleasantly smoky and mineral touch, and a palate with close-knit yet fine tannins, while sapidity lengthens its flavor on t he finish. The second is a white that evokes citron, basil, and broom, with a palate focused entirely on sapid and mineral sensations. The Pecorino '21 was a bit subdued.

Cingilia

c.da Piano Carpineto, 34
65020 Cugnoli [PE]
☏ 3803474887
⊛ vinicingilia.it

CELLAR SALES
PRE-BOOKED VISITS
ANNUAL PRODUCTION 30,000 bottles
HECTARES UNDER VINE 6.00

The winery is young, as is its owner. We're talking about Cingilia and Fabio Di Donato, who began making wine about 10 years ago, aiming to put into practice what he learned while earning his degree in oenology. He works with his small vineyard, six hectares in size, located near Cugnoli on the Pescaresi Hills. In the cellar, the focus is on artisanal techniques and spontaneous fermentations, resulting in a small range with great character and a strong sense of place. The Cerasuolo impressed us greatly this year as well, once again providing a blueprint for how to produce a montepulciano rosé that reflects the varietal character of the grape. As tradition dictates, it transforms into something more like a light red—the note of graphite intertwining with fresh cherry—the palate is energetic, mineral, and lively without ever sacrificing drinkability. The rest of the range, starting with the Montepulciano '21, is equally convincing.

● Montepulciano d'Abruzzo Fosso Cancelli '19	♈♈♈ 8
○ Trebbiano d'Abruzzo Fosso Cancelli '21	♈♈ 6
○ Fosso Cancelli Pecorino '21	♈ 6
○ Trebbiano d'Abruzzo Fosso Cancelli '20	♈♈♈ 6
⊙ Cerasuolo d'Abruzzo Fosso Cancelli '22	♈♈ 6
⊙ Cerasuolo d'Abruzzo Fosso Cancelli '19	♈♈ 5
○ Fosso Cancelli Pecorino '19	♈♈ 5
○ Fosso Cancelli Pecorino '18	♈♈ 6
● Montepulciano d'Abruzzo Antrum '14	♈♈ 5
● Montepulciano d'Abruzzo Fosso Cancelli '15	♈♈ 7
○ Trebbiano d'Abruzzo Fosso Cancelli '19	♈♈ 5
○ Trebbiano d'Abruzzo Fosso Cancelli '18	♈♈ 5

⊙ Cerasuolo d'Abruzzo '23	♈♈♈ 3*
● Montepulciano d'Abruzzo '21	♈♈ 4
○ Pecorino '23	♈♈ 3
○ Trebbiano '23	♈ 3
⊙ Cerasuolo d'Abruzzo '21	♈♈ 3
● Montepulciano d'Abruzzo '19	♈♈ 3*
○ Pecorino '22	♈♈ 3
⊙ Rosato '22	♈♈ 3*
○ Trebbiano '22	♈♈ 3

Citra Vini

c.da Cucullo
66026 Ortona [CH]
℡ 0859031342
✆ www.citra.it

CELLAR SALES
PRE-BOOKED VISITS
ANNUAL PRODUCTION 24,000,000 bottles
HECTARES UNDER VINE 6000.00
VITICULTURE METHOD Certified Organic
SUSTAINABLE WINERY

Citra is a giant in the Abruzzo cooperative wine scene, bringing together nine operations from the province of Chieti: Pollutri, Rocca San Giovanni, Lanciano, Ortona, Paglieta, Crecchia, Torrevecchia Teatina, and Tollo. Founded in 1973, the company now boasts a membership base of 3,000 growers working a vast 6,000-hectare vineyard. From this massive estate come the 24 million bottles produced annually, divided across numerous commercial lines. Ferzo, a fine Pecorino Superiore, vintage 2023, is the name of one of them. On the nose, it reveals aromas of white fruits and flowers, showcasing a fragrant bouquet that nearly veers into balsamic and herbal sensations. The palate is pleasant, very clear in its progression, flavorful, finishing with a slight citrus note. The aromas of plum and black cherry that emerge from the Montepulciano Teate Ferzo '21 are equally clear, then comes a well-structured, tannic palate and a delicately herbal finish. The Spumante Trabocco Aureae Stellae, made from pecorino grapes, proves simple and enjoyable.

○ Abruzzo Pecorino Sup. Terre di Chieti Ferzo '23	♟♟ 3*
○ Abruzzo Pecorino Brut Trabocco Aureae Stellae '23	♟♟ 3
● Montepulciano d'Abruzzo Teate Ferzo '21	♟♟ 3
◉ Cerasuolo d'Abruzzo Ferzo '23	♟ 3
○ Fenaroli Dosaggio Zero M. Cl.	♟ 4
● Montepulciano d'Abruzzo Laus Vitae Ris. '20	♟ 6
○ Trebbiano d'Abruzzo Laus Vitae '21	♟ 6
○ Abruzzo Pecorino Sup. Ferzo '22	♟♟ 3*
● Montepulciano d'Abruzzo Caroso Ris. '19	♟♟ 5
● Montepulciano d'Abruzzo Caroso Ris. '18	♟♟ 5
● Montepulciano d'Abruzzo Laus Vitae Ris. '18	♟♟ 6

Contesa

s.da delle Vigne, 28
65010 Collecorvino [PE]
℡ 0858205078
✆ www.contesa.it

CELLAR SALES
PRE-BOOKED VISITS
ACCOMMODATION
ANNUAL PRODUCTION 400,000 bottles
HECTARES UNDER VINE 45.00
VITICULTURE METHOD Certified Organic
SUSTAINABLE WINERY

The winery is named after a land dispute involving Rocco Pasetti's great-grandfather during Italy's post-unification era. Located in Collecorvino, on the Pescara Hills (within the Terre dei Vestini subzone), the winery is surrounded by vineyards where local varieties like montepulciano, trebbiano, pecorino, and passerina thrive. Winemaking involves various methods, including the use of steel, barriques, and large casks. The result is a range of unique wines. The Montepulciano Riserva '20 needs a bit of time to open up and make contact with oxygen. When it does, notes of black cherry, licorice, and sweet tobacco emerge, leading to a palate with a close-knit tannic structure and a nice sapid background that mitigates its flavor. Among the whites, we enjoyed the Pecorino '23: a lively balsamic and herbal touch adds a fresh nuance to a fruity nose and a citrusy, pleasant palate. The other wines tasted were somewhat underwhelming compared to expectations.

● Montepulciano d'Abruzzo Ris. '20	♟♟ 4
○ Abruzzo Pecorino '23	♟♟ 3
○ Abruzzo Pecorino Sup. Colline Pescaresi Aspetta Primavera '23	♟♟ 4
◉ Cerasuolo d'Abruzzo '23	♟ 3
● Montepulciano d'Abruzzo Terre dei Vestini Chiedi alla Polvere Ris. '20	♟ 5
● Montepulciano d'Abruzzo Ris. '19	♟♟♟ 4*
● Montepulciano d'Abruzzo Ris. '08	♟♟♟ 3*
○ Abruzzo Pecorino Sup. Aspetta Primavera '20	♟♟ 4
◉ Cerasuolo d'Abruzzo '20	♟♟ 2*
○ Trebbiano d'Abruzzo Fermentazione Spontanea '21	♟♟ 3*
○ Trebbiano d'Abruzzo Fermentazione Spontanea '20	♟♟ 3
○ Trebbiano d'Abruzzo Fermentazione Spontanea '17	♟♟ 3*

D'Alesio - Sciarr

c.da Gaglierano, 73
65013 Città Sant'Angelo [PE]
☎ 08596713
⊕ www.dalesiovini.it

CELLAR SALES
PRE-BOOKED VISITS
RESTAURANT SERVICE
ANNUAL PRODUCTION 80,000 bottles
HECTARES UNDER VINE 17.00
VITICULTURE METHOD Certified Organic
SUSTAINABLE WINERY

In the inland area of Città Sant'Angelo, on the Pescaresi Hills, Mario and Giovanni D'Alesio decided in 2007 to revive the agricultural heritage established by their grandfather Mario by founding a new winery focused on organic farming. Their production is divided into three lines: "Sciarr," "D'Alesio," and the flagship "Tenuta del Professore." Among the rows of vines, you'll find the region's classic grapes, which form the basis for a range with a strong territorial identity. Once again this year, we were captivated by the Trebbiano Tenuta del Professore, a 2018 Riserva that exudes aromas of fresh hazelnut, ferns, propolis, and yellow flowers, all gently stroked by a slightly smoky sensation. The palate starts off rich and full-bodied but then becomes dynamic and energetic, with a lovely toasted finish. The Montepulciano Sciarr reveals notes of black fruits and pencil lead, with very close-knit tannins and a voluminous, rich palate.

● Montepulciano d'Abruzzo Sciarr '20	♟♟ 3*
○ Trebbiano d'Abruzzo Tenuta del Professore Ris. '18	♟♟ 6
○ Abruzzo Montonico Sup. '20	♟ 3
● Montepulciano d'Abruzzo Ris. '17	♟ 5
○ Abruzzo Pecorino Sup. '17	♟♟ 2*
● Montepulciano d'Abruzzo '17	♟♟ 4
● Montepulciano d'Abruzzo '15	♟♟ 4
● Montepulciano d'Abruzzo '13	♟♟ 4
● Montepulciano d'Abruzzo Tenuta del Professore Ris. '15	♟♟ 6
○ Trebbiano d'Abruzzo Tenuta del Professore '15	♟♟ 5
○ Trebbiano d'Abruzzo Tenuta del Professore '13	♟♟ 5
○ Trebbiano d'Abruzzo Tenuta del Professore Ris. '16	♟♟ 6

Tenuta I Fauri

via Foro, 8
66010 Ari [CH]
☎ 0871332627
⊕ www.tenutaifauri.it

CELLAR SALES
PRE-BOOKED VISITS
ACCOMMODATION
ANNUAL PRODUCTION 150,000 bottles
HECTARES UNDER VINE 35.00
VITICULTURE METHOD Certified Organic
SUSTAINABLE WINERY

Valentina and Luigi Di Camillo are the driving forces behind this family winery, established in the late 1970s by their father, Domenico. Valentina manages promotion and hospitality at the new guest facility, while Luigi turns the harvest into expressive, distinctive wines. The organic vineyards, which feature local grape varieties, are spread out across the municipalities of Chieti, Francavilla al Mare, Miglianico, Villamagna, Bucchianico, and Ari. Valentina and Luigi presented us with one of the most complete and solid lineups in the region. The Santa Cecilia, a Montepulciano Riserva, opens dark on sensations of gunpowder but then moves to clear black fruit. The palate is rich, but its components are in balance, its tannins flavorful and the finish balsamic. The Montepulciano Baldovino '22 is also delicious—juicy and rhythmic. The Cerasuolo Baldovino is a meaty, delectable drink, smoky and sapid. Le Belle is a Metodo Ancestrale sparkling white that we wish would never end.

⊘ Cerasuolo d'Abruzzo Baldovino '23	♟♟ 3*
● Montepulciano d'Abruzzo Baldovino '22	♟♟ 3*
● Montepulciano d'Abruzzo V. Santa Cecilia Ris. '20	♟♟ 5
○ Abruzzo Pecorino '23	♟♟ 3
○ Le Belle Frizzante '22	♟♟ 3
● Montepulciano d'Abruzzo Ottobre Rosso '22	♟♟ 3
○ Passerina '23	♟♟ 3
○ Abruzzo Pecorino '21	♟♟♟ 3*
○ Abruzzo Pecorino '18	♟♟♟ 3*
○ Abruzzo Pecorino '14	♟♟♟ 2*
○ Abruzzo Pecorino '13	♟♟♟ 2*
○ Abruzzo Pecorino '22	♟♟ 3*

Feudo Antico

c.da San Pietro, 25
66010 Tollo [CH]
📞 08719625253
🌐 www.feudoantico.it

CELLAR SALES
ACCOMMODATION
ANNUAL PRODUCTION 130,000 bottles
HECTARES UNDER VINE 20.00
VITICULTURE METHOD Certified Organic
SUSTAINABLE WINERY

Feudo Antico, a small cooperative founded in 2004, represents one of Italy's smallest appellations, the Docg Tullum production zone. The cooperative focuses on the potential of prime cultivation areas, like Pedine, Colle Secco, San Pietro, and Colle di Campli, as well as experimental projects at Niko Romito's Casadonna in Castel di Sangro (at over 800 meters elevation). With about 50 members, they meticulously cultivate 20 hectares of vineyards, paying close attention to environmental sustainability. The Tullum Pecorino Biologico is always a sure bet. This year, the 2023 captivated with its fresh notes of mountain meadow, green and yellow citrus peels, and light hints of flint. In the mouth, it dissolves into a palate of superb precision, playing on citrusy hints, coming through deep, and unfolding masterfully. The Tullum Rosso Riserva '19, a warm, toasty Montepulciano with close-knit but subtle tannins, also delivers.

○ Tullum Pecorino Biologico '23	♟♟♟ 4*
● Tullum Inanfora '22	♟♟ 5
○ Tullum Pecorino '23	♟♟ 4
● Tullum Rosso Ris. '19	♟♟ 5
○ Tullum Passerina '23	♟ 4
○ Casadonna Pecorino '15	♟♟♟ 7
● Montepulciano d'Abruzzo Organic '18	♟♟♟ 3*
○ Tullum Pecorino Bio '22	♟♟♟ 4*
○ Tullum Pecorino Biologico '21	♟♟♟ 4*
○ Tullum Pecorino Biologico '20	♟♟♟ 4*
○ Tullum Pecorino Biologico '19	♟♟♟ 3*
○ Tullum Pecorino Biologico '17	♟♟♟ 3*
● Tullum Rosso '18	♟♟ 4
● Tullum Rosso '17	♟♟ 4
● Tullum Rosso Ris. '18	♟♟ 5

Fontefico

via Difenza, 38
66054 Vasto [CH]
📞 3284113619
🌐 www.fontefico.it

CELLAR SALES
PRE-BOOKED VISITS
RESTAURANT SERVICE
ANNUAL PRODUCTION 55,000 bottles
HECTARES UNDER VINE 15.00
VITICULTURE METHOD Certified Organic
SUSTAINABLE WINERY

Led today by brothers Emanuele and Nicola Alteri, Fontefico has grown into a robust producer. The pair have taken over the winery founded by their parents Miriam and Alessandro in 1996. The beating heart of production lies in the Punta Penna promontory, home to 15 hectares of organically farmed vineyards divided into 4 parcels: Vigna Bianca (pecorino and trebbiano), Vigna del Pozzo (montepulciano), il Pàstino (also montepulciano) and Le Coste (aglianico). The Fossimatto '23 is spectacular, a true Cerasuolo where the grape's character is evident in meaty fruit, conjuring up crisp cherry and slightly smoky notes. The palate remains firm, captivating, juicy, sapid, and deep. Great work has also been done with the Cocca di Casa '21, a very dense red, yet characterized by great freshness and progression. The whites also excel, as demonstrated by the sunny Pecorino La Canaglia '23.

○ Cerasuolo d'Abruzzo Sup. Terre di Chieti Fossimatto '23	♟♟♟ 4*
○ Abruzzo Pecorino Sup. Terre di Chieti La Canaglia '23	♟♟ 4
● Montepulciano d'Abruzzo Cocca di Casa '21	♟♟ 4
○ Febbre d'A. '22	♟♟ 5
● Montepulciano d'Abruzzo Titinge Ris. '18	♟ 5
○ Abruzzo Pecorino Sup. La Canaglia '22	♟♟♟ 4*
○ Abruzzo Pecorino Sup. La Canaglia '21	♟♟ 4
○ Abruzzo Pecorino Sup. La Foia '21	♟♟ 5
○ Cerasuolo d'Abruzzo Sup. Fossimatto '21	♟♟ 4
○ Cerasuolo d'Abruzzo Sup. Fossimatto '20	♟♟ 3
● Montepulciano d'Abruzzo Cocca di Casa '20	♟♟ 4
● Montepulciano d'Abruzzo Titinge Ris. '17	♟♟ 5
○ Trebbiano d'Abruzzo Sup. Portarispetto '21	♟♟ 5

★Dino Illuminati

c.da San Biagio, 18
64010 Controguerra [TE]
☎ 0861808008
⊕ www.illuminativini.it

CELLAR SALES
PRE-BOOKED VISITS
ANNUAL PRODUCTION 1,150,000 bottles
HECTARES UNDER VINE 130.00

When it was founded more than a century ago, Illuminati was named Fattoria Nico, after its founder Nicola Illuminati. Dino, his grandson, took over in the 1950s, steering it toward modernity and success. The first bottles came in the 1970s, marking a period of consolidation and growth, with the acquisition of new vineyards and renewed commercial awareness. Today, Lorenzo and Stefano, Dino's sons, lead this historic enterprise, a stalwart of the Controguerra and Colline Teramane production zones. This year, the Illuminati brothers decided not to send us their flagship Montepulciano Zanna for tasting, letting it rest for another year in their cellar. However, we took solace in an excellent Riparosso, a young Montepulciano redolent of fresh black fruits, blueberry, and plum that offers a juicy, well-fleshed, very enjoyable palate. The Ilico, on the other hand, proves to be an austere Montepulciano, dark in its aromatic profile, with a close-knit yet dense tannic structure.

● Montepulciano d'Abruzzo Riparosso '23	▼▼ 2*
⊙ Cerasuolo d'Abruzzo Lumeggio di Rosa '23	▼▼ 3
○ Controguerra Pecorino '23	▼▼ 3
● Montepulciano d'Abruzzo Ilico '21	▼▼ 3
● Colline Teramane Montepulciano d'Abruzzo Pieluni Ris. '19	▼ 8
○ Illuminati Brut M.Cl. '18	▼ 5
● Montepulciano d'Abruzzo Lumeggio di Rosso '23	▼ 2
● Colline Teramane Montepulciano d'Abruzzo Zanna Ris. '18	♈♈♈ 5
● Colline Teramane Montepulciano d'Abruzzo Zanna Ris. '17	♈♈♈ 5
● Montepulciano d'Abruzzo Ilico '17	♈♈♈ 2*

Inalto Vini d'Altura

via del Giardino, 7
67025 Ofena [AQ]
☎ 0862956618
⊕ www.inaltovinidaltura.it

ANNUAL PRODUCTION 30,000 bottles
HECTARES UNDER VINE 12.50

The winery was founded in the mid-2010s by Adolfo De Cecco, a young man passionate about his land. He decided to create a small estate, focusing exclusively on high-elevation vineyards, as the name suggests. It began with 8 hectares in Ofena, but the estate is gradually expanding with more small plots in the Aquila area, never below 400 meters in elevation. Leading their solid lineup once again is the Montepulciano Campo Affamato. The 2021 opens on a multifaceted and complex aromatic profile, where floral sensations meet sweet spices, Mediterranean scrub, cocoa beans, and hints of blueberry. In the mouth, it proves elegant and full of tension, with a sapid undertone that lengthens the palate and balances its tannins. The Cerasuolo, a slightly aged version (also from 2021), is equally inviting, retaining the varietal and juicy luster typical of the typology. The other wines tasted are also well made.

● Montepulciano d'Abruzzo Alto Tirino Campo Affamato '21	▼▼▼ 6
● Inoltre '20	▼▼ 8
○ Le Pagliare Pecorino '21	▼▼ 6
● Montepulciano d'Abruzzo '19	▼▼ 5
○ Pecorino '22	▼▼ 5
● Montepulciano d'Abruzzo Campo Affamato '20	♈♈♈ 6
● Montepulciano d'Abruzzo Campo Affamato '19	♈♈♈ 6
○ Trebbiano d'Abruzzo Sup. '19	♈♈♈ 5
⊙ Cerasuolo d'Abruzzo Sup. '21	♈♈ 5
⊙ Cerasuolo d'Abruzzo Sup. '20	♈♈ 5
○ Le Pagliare Pecorino '19	♈♈ 6
● Montepulciano d'Abruzzo '18	♈♈ 5
● Montepulciano d'Abruzzo Campo Affamato '18	♈♈ 6

★★★Masciarelli

via Gamberale, 2
66010 San Martino
sulla Marrucina [CH]
☎ 087185241
✉ www.masciarelli.it

CELLAR SALES
PRE-BOOKED VISITS
ACCOMMODATION
ANNUAL PRODUCTION 2,500,000 bottles
HECTARES UNDER VINE 300.00

Marina Cvetic and Miriam Masciarelli helm one of the region's most important wineries, a name that has brought Abruzzo's wine to the world stage. The estate's extensive vineyards span all of Abruzzo's provinces, aiming to harness the best from each area's characteristics: from the Adriatic coast to the hills leading to Gran Sasso, passing through wine capitals like Loreto Aprutino on the Colline Pescaresi, and stretching all the way to the province of Chieti. An excellent performance from the Trebbiano Castello di Semivicoli. Lemon zest and pulp, aromatic herbs, and freshly cut hay rise from the glass, introducing a palate of great precision, light and delicate on its long finish. The Cerasuolo Villa Gemma once again stands out in its category, with raspberries and fresh strawberries emerging on the nose before a palate that proves firm and taut despite its soft attack. We also appreciated the two Montepulcianos, the Riserve Villa Gemma and Marina Cvetc, both quite dense and extractive.

○ Trebbiano d'Abruzzo Sup. Castello di Semivicoli '22	♟♟♟ 5
⊙ Cerasuolo d'Abruzzo Sup. Terre di Chieti Villa Gemma '23	♟♟ 4
● Montepulciano d'Abruzzo Marina Cvetic Ris. '20	♟♟ 5
● Montepulciano d'Abruzzo Villa Gemma Ris. '19	♟♟ 8
○ Abruzzo Pecorino Castello di Semivicoli '19	♟♟♟ 3*
⊙ Cerasuolo d'Abruzzo Sup. Villa Gemma '21	♟♟♟ 3*
⊙ Cerasuolo d'Abruzzo Villa Gemma '22	♟♟♟ 4*
○ Trebbiano d'Abruzzo Castello di Semivicoli '18	♟♟♟ 5
○ Trebbiano d'Abruzzo Sup. Castello di Semivicoli '19	♟♟♟ 5

Camillo Montori

loc. Piane Tronto, 80
64010 Controguerra [TE]
☎ 0861809900
✉ www.montorivini.it

CELLAR SALES
PRE-BOOKED VISITS
ACCOMMODATION AND RESTAURANT SERVICE
ANNUAL PRODUCTION 500,000 bottles
HECTARES UNDER VINE 50.00
SUSTAINABLE WINERY

One of Abruzzo's oldest producers, the name Montori has become synonymous with the history of winemaking in the region. Indeed, here agriculture and viticulture go back to the late-19th century, though it was only in the 1960s and 1970s that the winery solidified its position as a leading producer in the Colline Teramane. The operational base is in Controguerra, straddling Abruzzo and Marche. The vineyards, which unfold across some 50 hectares, give rise to a diverse range, with the Fontecupa line standing out. It's not the first time that the Cerasuolo Fonte Cupa has topped their lineup. The 2023 is one of the most interesting of late, thanks to a varietal profile that combines delicious fruit—ripe cherry and raspberry—with intriguing nuances of graphite and red flowers. On the palate, it proves to be juicy and well-structured, yet also supple and rhythmic. The Fonte Cupa Pecorino is also delicious: hay and meadow, yellow and green citrus sensations give way to a taut, sapid palate that unfolds masterfully.

⊙ Cerasuolo d'Abruzzo Fonte Cupa '23	♟♟ 3*
○ Fonte Cupa Pecorino '23	♟♟ 4
○ Trebbiano d'Abruzzo Fonte Cupa '23	♟♟ 3*
● Colline Teramane Montepulciano d'Abruzzo '20	♟ 5
○ Fonte Cupa Passerina '23	♟ 3
⊙ Cerasuolo d'Abruzzo Fonte Cupa '16	♟♟♟ 2*
⊙ Cerasuolo d'Abruzzo Fonte Cupa '22	♟♟ 3*
⊙ Cerasuolo d'Abruzzo Fonte Cupa '21	♟♟ 2*
● Colline Teramane Montepulciano d'Abruzzo Fonte Cupa '19	♟♟ 2*
● Colline Teramane Montepulciano d'Abruzzo Fonte Cupa Ris. '16	♟♟ 5
○ Fonte Cupa Pecorino '21	♟♟ 3*

Fattoria Nicodemi

c.da Veniglio, 8
64024 Notaresco [TE]
☎ 085895493
✉ www.nicodemi.com

CELLAR SALES
PRE-BOOKED VISITS
ANNUAL PRODUCTION 200,000 bottles
HECTARES UNDER VINE 30.00
VITICULTURE METHOD Certified Organic

Contrada Veniglio, Notaresco: if you want to visit Elena and Alessandro Nicodemi's winery, these are the names to type into your GPS. The siblings are carrying forward the work started by their father, Bruno, who began making wine in the late 1990s. The gentle Colline Teramane hills provide a picturesque backdrop to the venture: the vineyards, organically cultivated, benefit from breezes rising from the Adriatic coast, while being sheltered by the Gran Sasso. The region's classic grapes are cultivated. Among the Montepulcianos presented, it's truly difficult to choose the best. We favored the structure and full-bodied profile of the Neromoro '20, which also carries a distinctive brackish undertone. The fragrant and juicy Montepulciano Le Murate '22 features well-calibrated tannin extraction and nice progression. The Cerasuolo Le Murate '23 is also noteworthy, showcasing a straightforward, crisp character with a mineral quality. But overall, the entire lineup showed no weaknesses.

● Colline Teramane Montepulciano d'Abruzzo Neromoro Ris. '20	♟♟♟ 6
● Colline Teramane Montepulciano d'Abruzzo Le Murate '22	♟♟ 3*
⊙ Cerasuolo d'Abruzzo Sup. Colline Teramane Le Murate '23	♟♟ 3
● Colline Teramane Montepulciano d'Abruzzo Cocciopesto '21	♟♟ 5
● Colline Teramane Montepulciano d'Abruzzo Notàri '21	♟♟ 5
○ Trebbiano d'Abruzzo Sup. Colline Teramane Le Murate '23	♟♟ 3
● Montepulciano d'Abruzzo Colline Teramane Notàri '17	♟♟♟ 4*
○ Trebbiano d'Abruzzo Sup. Notàri '15	♟♟♟ 3*

Nododivino

loc. Caldari Stazione
66026 Ortona [CH]
☎ 0859031517
✉ www.nododivino.it

CELLAR SALES
PRE-BOOKED VISITS
ANNUAL PRODUCTION 120,000 bottles
HECTARES UNDER VINE 100.00
SUSTAINABLE WINERY

Meticulous zoning processes, precision viticulture, and attention to human well-being: these are the principles that guide this recent project, born within Citra, a regional pillar of wine cooperation. The producer, which has quickly established clear autonomy, is already standing out for the stylistic cleanness and gustatory breadth of its wines, both the fresher Monovarietali line and the select Oro line. The Tegèo remains a Pecorino of great substance. It opens with a broad, fragrant aromatic profile, evoking sensations of citron, fresh yellow peach, spices, and thyme. The palate is linear and compact, solid with a rich citrus character, finishing pleasantly with a hint of almond. The Trebbiano C. is also delicious, evoking a multifaceted bouquet with subtle toastiness, balsamic whiffs, and lemon zest. In the mouth it opens on a juicy palate, displaying great structure—a complex quaff, but without being complicated. The rest of the range is also commendable.

○ Abruzzo Pecorino Sup. Tegèo '22	♟♟ 6
○ Trebbiano d'Abruzzo Trebbiano C. '21	♟♟ 6
○ Abruzzo Passerina '23	♟♟ 5
○ Abruzzo Pecorino '23	♟♟ 5
⊙ Cerasuolo d'Abruzzo '23	♟♟ 5
○ Abruzzo Passerina Sup. Coda d'Oro '23	♟ 6
● Montepulciano d'Abruzzo '20	♟ 4
● Montepulciano d'Abruzzo Teate Torrepasso '20	♟ 7
○ Abruzzo Pecorino Sup. Tegèo '20	♟♟♟ 5
○ Abruzzo Pecorino Sup. Tegèo '19	♟♟♟ 4*
○ Abruzzo Pecorino Sup. Tegèo '18	♟♟♟ 4*
● Montepulciano d'Abruzzo Teate Torrepasso '19	♟♟ 6

Orlandi Contucci Ponno

loc. Piana degli Ulivi, 1
64026 Roseto degli Abruzzi [TE]
0858944049
www.orlandicontucciponno.com

CELLAR SALES
PRE-BOOKED VISITS
ANNUAL PRODUCTION 180,000 bottles
HECTARES UNDER VINE 26.00

Orlandi Contucci Ponno was a key player in the shift that took place during the 1990s, when Abruzzo wine started to break through. This is why, in 2007, the Gussalli Beretta group—already invested in Franciacorta and Chianti Classico—decided to acquire this sizable estate in Roseto. Situated on the lower slopes of the Vomano Valley, just a stone's throw from the Adriatic, the vineyards benefit from the breezes coming down from the Gran Sasso and the predominantly limestone soils. Here, you'll find local varieties like montepulciano and trebbiano growing alongside international grapes. This year, the winery decided not to submit any Montepulcianos, so the selection reviewed is somewhat reduced. The standout is the Pecorino Superiore '23, whose fragrant bouquet plays on herbaceous, almost balsamic sensations, set against a background of luscious white-fleshed fruit. The palate is light and elegant, with a well-sustained, persistent finish. The Trebbiano and Cerasuolo are also good.

⊙ Cerasuolo d'Abruzzo Sup. Colline Teramane Vermiglio '23	🍷🍷 3
○ Colline Teramane Abruzzo Pecorino Sup. '23	🍷🍷 3
○ Trebbiano d'Abruzzo Sup. Colline Teramane Colle della Corte '23	🍷🍷 3
○ Abruzzo Pecorino Sup. '22	YY 4
○ Abruzzo Pecorino Sup. '21	YY 3
⊙ Cerasuolo d'Abruzzo Sup. Vermiglio '22	YY 3
● Colline Teramane Montepulciano d'Abruzzo Podere La Regia Specula '20	YY 4
● Colline Teramane Montepulciano d'Abruzzo Podere La Regia Specula '19	YY 3
● Colline Teramane Montepulciano d'Abruzzo Podere La Regia Specula '18	YY 3

Emidio Pepe

via Chiesi, 10
64010 Torano Nuovo [TE]
0861856493
www.emidiopepe.com

CELLAR SALES
PRE-BOOKED VISITS
ACCOMMODATION AND RESTAURANT SERVICE
ANNUAL PRODUCTION 80,000 bottles
HECTARES UNDER VINE 18.00
VITICULTURE METHOD Certified Organic
SUSTAINABLE WINERY

Emidio Pepe is a venerable figure in Italian wine. His winemaking journey began in 1964, drawing on the expertise inherited from his father and grandfather, both producers. This long adventure, now successfully carried on by Emidio's daughters Daniela and Sofia, and granddaughter Chiara, unfolds in the hills of Torano Nuovo, in Teramo. And here, each year, a prestigious, artisanal range of wines comes to life. With the Montepulciano '22, it seems the winery has ventured into a new style. Even from the color—lighter and brighter than in the past—you can tell that this is a red that's grown in terms of elegance. The risk in such cases is that the wine loses its essence, but here, it's actually heightened: a sapid and mineral undertone makes it more intriguing and compelling. The palate has a driving rhythm, and a slight rusticity in both aroma and flavor creates a distinct identity rooted in tradition.

● Montepulciano d'Abruzzo '22	🍷🍷🍷 8
○ Trebbiano d'Abruzzo '22	🍷🍷 7
○ Pecorino '22	🍷🍷 7
⊙ Cerasuolo d'Abruzzo '19	YYY 5
● Montepulciano d'Abruzzo '98	YYY 8
⊙ Cerasuolo d'Abruzzo '20	YY 5
● Colline Teramane Montepulciano d'Abruzzo '21	YY 7
● Colline Teramane Montepulciano d'Abruzzo '20	YY 7
● Montepulciano d'Abruzzo '17	YY 6
○ Pecorino '20	YY 7
○ Pecorino '19	YY 7
○ Pecorino '18	YY 6
○ Trebbiano d'Abruzzo '21	YY 5
○ Trebbiano d'Abruzzo '19	YY 5
○ Trebbiano d'Abruzzo '18	YY 5
○ Trebbiano d'Abruzzo '17	YY 5

Giuliano Pettinella

via dell'Ospedale
65028 Tocco da Casauria [PE]
📞 3388279506
🌐 www.vinipettinella.com

ANNUAL PRODUCTION 5,000 bottles
HECTARES UNDER VINE 3.00
SUSTAINABLE WINERY

Going from practicing law to viticulture wouldn't seem like an easy feat. But Giuliano Pettinella, who chose to leave his career as a lawyer to dedicate himself to winemaking, didn't flinch. His roots brought him back to Abruzzo where, in Tocco di Casauria, at the foot of Monte Morrone, he established his first production hub, a small vineyard at 350 meters elevation. Later, another parcel was added, closer to the coast, in Silvi, Teramo. All attention is devoted to a single grape, montepulciano, the raw material for the producer's two wines. The Tauma, winner of last year's Rosé of the Year award, wasn't present at our tastings this year. Giuliano only submitted the Montepulciano d'Abruzzo '22. The straightforward and unadorned character of this genuine Abruzzo red stands out. On the nose, sensations of leather alternate with burnt embers, plum, and gunpowder hints, while the palate, despite its close-knit tannins, exhibits superb vitality, particularly across its juicy, sapid finish.

● Montepulciano d'Abruzzo '22	♟♟7
⊙ Cerasuolo d'Abruzzo Tauma '22	♟♟♟5
● Montepulciano d'Abruzzo '21	♟♟7

San Giacomo

c.da Novella, 51
66020 Rocca San Giovanni [CH]
📞 0872620504
🌐 www.cantinasangiacomo.it

CELLAR SALES
PRE-BOOKED VISITS
ACCOMMODATION
ANNUAL PRODUCTION 70,000 bottles
HECTARES UNDER VINE 300.00
VITICULTURE METHOD Certified Organic

San Giacomo is a Rocca San Giovanni-based cooperative, a historic operation in the province of Chieti established in the early 1970s. The vineyard spans a considerable 300 hectares across various municipalities of the Teatine Hills. Over 200 members, who are the producer's true backbone, tend to the vines. Over the years, there has been significant improvement in quality, making for a wide range that naturally focuses on the region's indigenous varieties, like montepulciano, trebbiano, and pecorino. This year, the producer didn't present any reds for tasting, but their wines still performed admirably, starting with the 2022 version of the Cerasuolo Casino Murri 14°. Fleshy red fruit and a pleasant floral and citrusy note rise from the glass. The palate is juicy but never leans into sweetness, remaining fresh and crisp despite a rather imposing structure. The Pecorino from the same line, also a 2022, also caught our attention, with linden and acacia flowers meeting nectarine peach, and aromatic herbs—a simple yet highly enjoyable white.

○ Trebbiano d'Abruzzo Casino Murri 14° '22	♟♟3*
○ Casino Murri Pecorino 14° '23	♟♟3
⊙ Cerasuolo d'Abruzzo Casino Murri '23	♟♟2*
○ Casino Murri Cococciola '23	♟2
○ Casino Murri Pecorino '23	♟2
○ Casino Murri 14° Pecorino '21	♟♟2*
○ Casino Murri 14° Pecorino '17	♟♟2*
○ Casino Murri Pecorino '22	♟♟2*
⊙ Cerasuolo d'Abruzzo Casino Murri '22	♟♟2*
⊙ Cerasuolo d'Abruzzo Casino Murri 14° '21	♟♟3
⊙ Cerasuolo d'Abruzzo Casino Murri 14° '20	♟♟3
● Montepulciano d'Abruzzo Casino Murri 14° Ris. '19	♟♟3

San Lorenzo Vini

c.da Plavignano, 2
64035 Castilenti [TE]
℡ 0861999325
✆ www.sanlorenzovini.com

CELLAR SALES
PRE-BOOKED VISITS
ACCOMMODATION
ANNUAL PRODUCTION 800,000 bottles
HECTARES UNDER VINE 173.00
SUSTAINABLE WINERY

The Galasso family leads one of Abruzzo's most prestigious and historic producers. This agricultural estate dates back to the late 19th century with the vineyards, now spanning over 170 hectares, occupying the slopes of the Colline Teramane in Castilenti (centrally located between the Adriatic coast and the foothills of Gran Sasso). The range is wide and versatile, reflecting various production choices: from ambitious selections that mature at length in wood to wines that ferment spontaneously. The lineup encountered this year is quite solid, but then again, this Castilenti producer has accustomed us to a high level of quality. Among the various Montepulcianos, we preferred the Escol, a 2019 Riserva that opens with notes of chocolate, ground coffee, plum, and blackberry. Its tannins are abundant, but the palate manages to break free from their grip, resulting in a vibrant and dynamic finish. The flavorful and elegant Pecorino '23 is also very good.

Spinelli

loc. Piazzano
via Piana La Fara, 90
66041 Atessa [CH]
℡ 0872897916
✆ www.cantinespinelli.it

CELLAR SALES
PRE-BOOKED VISITS
ANNUAL PRODUCTION 8,500,000 bottles
HECTARES UNDER VINE 100.00

Vincenzo Spinelli founded the winery bearing his name in 1973, with a clear commercial focus from the start, making Spinelli one of Abruzzo's most recognized worldwide wine brands. While in the pasat most of production was dedicated to exports, the current generation is focusing on the domestic market. In addition to their estate vineyards, Spinelli relies on trusted growers, supervised agronomically at every stage. Much of the winery's efforts are concentrated in the Le Stagioni del Vino line, and the results are excellent, starting with an outstanding Trebbiano. 2021 made for an elegant, airy smokiness, followed by sensations of aromatic herbs and pleasantly citrusy notes. The palate showcases vibrant sapidity, unfolding taut and long, with a bright finish. The wines from the Zione line are also delicious.

○ Abruzzo Pecorino '23	♟♟ 3*
● Colline Teramane Montepulciano d'Abruzzo Escol Ris. '19	♟♟ 6
⊙ Cerasuolo d'Abruzzo Casabianca Fermentazione Spontanea '23	♟♟ 2*
● Montepulciano d'Abruzzo Sirio '22	♟♟ 2*
○ Trebbiano d'Abruzzo Casabianca Fermentazione Spontanea '23	♟♟ 2*
● Colline Teramane Montepulciano d'Abruzzo Oinos '20	♟ 5
○ Trebbiano d'Abruzzo Sirio '23	♟ 2
● Colline Teramane Montepulciano d'Abruzzo Oinos '19	♟♟ 5
● Montepulciano d'Abruzzo Casabianca '20	♟♟ 2*

○ Trebbiano d'Abruzzo Le Stagioni del Vino '21	♟♟♟ 4*
⊙ Cerasuolo d'Abruzzo Zione '23	♟♟ 4
● Montepulciano d'Abruzzo Le Stagioni del Vino '22	♟♟ 4
○ Abruzzo Pecorino Sup. Terre di Chieti Le Stagioni del Vino '23	♟♟ 4
● Montepulciano d'Abruzzo Zione '21	♟♟ 4
○ Trebbiano d'Abruzzo Zione '22	♟♟ 4
⊙ Cerasuolo d'Abruzzo '19	♟♟ 2*
⊙ Cerasuolo d'Abruzzo Zione '21	♟♟ 4
● Montepulciano d'Abruzzo '18	♟♟ 2*
● Montepulciano d'Abruzzo '15	♟♟ 2*
● Montepulciano d'Abruzzo La Tessa '22	♟♟ 2*
● Montepulciano d'Abruzzo Tatone '17	♟♟ 3
● Montepulciano d'Abruzzo Zione '20	♟♟ 4
○ Trebbiano d'Abruzzo Zione '21	♟♟ 4
○ Zione Pecorino '21	♟♟ 4

Tenuta Terraviva

via del Lago, 19
64018 Tortoreto [TE]
℡ 0861786056
⊛ www.tenutaterraviva.it

CELLAR SALES
PRE-BOOKED VISITS
ACCOMMODATION
ANNUAL PRODUCTION 80,000 bottles
HECTARES UNDER VINE 22.00
VITICULTURE METHOD Certified Organic
SUSTAINABLE WINERY

In the 1970s, Gabriele Marano decided to invest in the world of wine, combining his construction business with viticulture. Though it still wasn't the Terraviva we know today. That came in 2006 when his daughter Pina and her husband, Pietro Topi, took over the winery, immediately converting it to organic agriculture. Today, thanks in part to the work of Federica, Pina and Pietro's daughter, this winery is one of the most dynamic in the Colline Teramane, offering a delightful array of artisanal wines. Giusi secures another Tre Bicchieri. The 2023 doesn't disappoint the expectations set by previous Cerasuolo releases. Notes of gunpowder, a subtle toasted hint, a delicate herbaceous sensation, followed by raspberry, redcurrant, and crunchy cherry create the profile of a fresh, smooth palate, taut and vibrant with acidity and sapidity. Among the reds, we liked the Colline Teramane '22, which balances a classic touch of graphite with fruit that leans towards plum and black cherry.

Tiberio

c.da La Vota
65020 Cugnoli [PE]
℡ 0858576744
⊛ www.tiberio.it

CELLAR SALES
PRE-BOOKED VISITS
ANNUAL PRODUCTION 90,000 bottles
HECTARES UNDER VINE 30.00

Tiberio's story begins in 2000, when Riccardo Tiberio decided to start making wine. Today, his children Cristiana and Antonio lead the producer, which has become one of the most sought-after in the region. Moving away from international grape varieties, they've focused entirely on indigenous ones, grown near Cugnoli, halfway between Gran Sasso and Majella, at about 350 meters elevation. In the cellar, only stainless steel is used to ensure that montepulciano, pecorino, and trebbiano clearly express themselves and their terroir. Despite some rustic hints, the Pecorino '23 is back at the top of its game, thanks to a nose marked by herbaceous and balsamic sensations. A slightly brackish whiff combines with notes of ripe citrus, leading to a structured and taut palate—sapid and long. The Cerasuolo also proves to be authentic and original, displaying superb vitality and a palate that's both food friendly and dynamic. Grains and hay characterize the bouquet of the Trebbiano, which tops things off with a pleasant citrus finish.

Tenuta Terraviva	Rating
⊙ Cerasuolo d'Abruzzo Giusi '23	♈♈♈ 3*
● Colline Teramane Montepulciano d'Abruzzo '22	♈♈ 3*
○ Abruzzo Passerina 12.1 '23	♈♈ 3
○ Abruzzo Pecorino '23	♈♈ 3
● Montepulciano d'Abruzzo CO2 '22	♈♈ 3
○ Trebbiano d'Abruzzo '23	♈♈ 3
● Colline Teramane Montepulciano d'Abruzzo Lui '20	♈ 4
○ Abruzzo Pecorino '21	♛♛♛ 3*
⊙ Cerasuolo d'Abruzzo Giusi '22	♛♛♛ 3*
⊙ Cerasuolo d'Abruzzo Giusi '19	♛♛♛ 2*
○ Trebbiano d'Abruzzo Sup. Mario's 44 '16	♛♛♛ 3*
○ Trebbiano d'Abruzzo Sup. Mario's 47 '19	♛♛♛ 4*

Tiberio	Rating
⊙ Cerasuolo d'Abruzzo '23	♈♈ 5
○ Pecorino '23	♈♈ 4
○ Trebbiano d'Abruzzo '23	♈♈ 4
● Montepulciano d'Abruzzo '22	♈ 4
● Montepulciano d'Abruzzo '13	♛♛♛ 2*
○ Pecorino '20	♛♛♛ 4*
○ Pecorino '16	♛♛♛ 3*
○ Pecorino '15	♛♛♛ 3*
○ Pecorino '13	♛♛♛ 3*
○ Pecorino '12	♛♛♛ 3*
○ Pecorino '11	♛♛♛ 3*
○ Pecorino '10	♛♛♛ 3
⊙ Cerasuolo d'Abruzzo '20	♛♛ 3*
● Montepulciano d'Abruzzo '19	♛♛ 3*
○ Pecorino '21	♛♛ 4

★Cantina Tollo

via Garibaldi, 68
66010 Tollo [CH]
☎ 087196251
🌐 www.cantinatollo.it

★Torre dei Beati

c.da Poggioragone, 56
65014 Loreto Aprutino [PE]
☎ 0854916069
🌐 www.torredeibeati.it

CELLAR SALES
ANNUAL PRODUCTION 18,000,000 bottles
HECTARES UNDER VINE 2500.00
VITICULTURE METHOD Certified Organic
SUSTAINABLE WINERY

CELLAR SALES
PRE-BOOKED VISITS
ANNUAL PRODUCTION 150,000 bottles
HECTARES UNDER VINE 21.00
VITICULTURE METHOD Certified Organic
SUSTAINABLE WINERY

The Chieti wine firmament is quite crowded, with a mix of both small producers and large cooperatives occupying the playing field. Among them, Cantina Tollo stands out as a giant, with 2500 hectares of vineyards (many cultivated organically) divided among 625 members. This vast area produced 18 million bottles in the last harvest. But it's not just the numbers that define this project's greatness; in recent years, there's been a notable shift in entrepreneurial and qualitative standards, progress that markets are recognizing as well. The Mo stands out as a reliable Montepulciano Riserva, produced in significant quantities but with excellent quality. It opens on medicinal herbs, then shifts toward chocolate and toasted wood before blackberry and plum sensations, the prelude to a palate with nice tannic extraction, but remaining light. The Abruzzo Pecorino '22 is also noteworthy: notes of flint, aromatic herbs like thyme and basil, and white flowers characterize this crisp and flavorful white.

In 1999, Adriana Galasso and Fausto Albanesi decided to change their lives and focus on wine production. Their adventure has played out in the hills of Loreto Aprutino, one of the most renowned territories in the Abruzzo wine scene. The couple immediately committed to combining viticulture with environmental respect, adhering to organic methods from the start. Their vineyards unfold on hills rising up to 300 meters above sea level, strategically located between Gran Sasso and the Adriatic Sea. Year after year, Adriana and Fausto continue to present remarkable wines marked by their sense of place, their character, and quality. This time, first place goes to the Pecorino Giocheremo con i Fiori '23, refined and radiant on the nose, taut, flavorful, light, and linear on the palate. Coming close is the excellent Rosa-ae '23, fragrant, spicy, and delicious. The reds also reach high peaks: the Mazzamurello gives a masterclass in combining tannic richness with a dynamic taste profile.

○ Abruzzo Pecorino '22	🍷🍷 5
● Montepulciano d'Abruzzo Mo Ris. '20	🍷🍷 3*
⊙ Cerasuolo d'Abruzzo Deivaì '22	🍷🍷 4
○ Peco Pecorino '23	🍷🍷 3
○ Trebbiano d'Abruzzo Sup. Terre di Chieti Tre '23	🍷🍷 3
⊙ Cerasuolo d'Abruzzo Hedòs '23	🍷 3
● Montepulciano d'Abruzzo Colle Secco Rubì '20	🍷 2
● Montepulciano d'Abruzzo Mo Ris. '18	🍷🍷🍷 3*
● Montepulciano d'Abruzzo Mo Ris. '17	🍷🍷🍷 3*
● Montepulciano d'Abruzzo Mo Ris. '16	🍷🍷🍷 3*
● Montepulciano d'Abruzzo Mo Ris. '15	🍷🍷🍷 3*
● Montepulciano d'Abruzzo Mo Ris. '13	🍷🍷🍷 3*
● Montepulciano d'Abruzzo Mo Ris. '12	🍷🍷🍷 2*
● Montepulciano d'Abruzzo Mo' Ris. '14	🍷🍷🍷 3*

○ Abruzzo Pecorino Giocheremo con i Fiori '23	🍷🍷🍷 4*
○ Abruzzo Pecorino Bianchi Grilli per la Testa '22	🍷🍷 5
⊙ Cerasuolo d'Abruzzo Rosa-ae '23	🍷🍷 3*
● Montepulciano d'Abruzzo Mazzamurello Ris. '21	🍷🍷 6
● Montepulciano d'Abruzzo Cocciapazza Ris. '21	🍷🍷 5
○ Trebbiano d'Abruzzo Bianchi Grilli per la Testa '22	🍷🍷 5
○ Abruzzo Pecorino Bianchi Grilli per la Testa '21	🍷🍷🍷 5
⊙ Cerasuolo d'Abruzzo Rosa-ae '21	🍷🍷🍷 3*
⊙ Cerasuolo d'Abruzzo Rosa-ae '18	🍷🍷🍷 2*
○ Trebbiano d'Abruzzo Bianchi Grilli per la Testa '18	🍷🍷🍷 4*

Torre Zambra

v.le Regina Margherita, 24
66010 Villamagna [CH]
℡ 0871300917
⊕ www.famigliadecerchio.it

CELLAR SALES
PRE-BOOKED VISITS
ANNUAL PRODUCTION 200,000 bottles
HECTARES UNDER VINE 42.00
VITICULTURE METHOD Certified Organic
SUSTAINABLE WINERY

Today, Federico De Cerchio leads a winery steeped in tradition. The group currently oversees a handful of estates in the southern part of the country. Torre Zambra, on the hills of Villamagna, a small town in the Teatine Hills, is where it all began. The vineyard covers just over 40 hectares, and from these organically farmed plots, Federico produces modern-style wines drawing on a variety of vinification and maturation techniques, including the use of concrete, stainless steel, and medium and small-sized barrels. Two reds particularly impressed us this year. Despite some slightly overpowering oak that dominates the nose, the Villamagna '22 evokes toasty notes and balsamic sensations, showcasing a rich yet vibrant palate with close-knit, flavorful, fine-grained tannins. More fruity and multifaceted, the Colle Maggio Riserva features lovely hints of Mediterranean scrub and a deep palate.

★La Valentina

via Torretta, 52
65010 Spoltore [PE]
℡ 0854478158
⊕ www.lavalentina.it

PRE-BOOKED VISITS
ANNUAL PRODUCTION 350,000 bottles
HECTARES UNDER VINE 40.00
VITICULTURE METHOD Certified Organic
SUSTAINABLE WINERY

The Di Properzio brothers' winery aims to encapsulate the two souls of Abruzzo winemaking: the Apennines and the Adriatic Sea. Their vineyards are located in Spoltore and Cavaticchi, near the coast, and in Scafa, San Valentino, and Alanno, further inland, in the heart of the Colline Pescaresi. Since the 1990s, Sabatino, Roberto, and Andrea have based their work on complete respect for the land and nature, following organic certification with increasing commitment to sustainable agricultural practices. The Montepulciano Spelt is a Riserva that opens with clear sensations of wild berries, blended with notes of cocoa beans and coffee powder. Tones of graphite and burnt embers precede a palate with close-knit yet flavorful tannins, perfectly extracted. The Trebbiano Spelt is highly appealing: a bouquet of blooming meadows and dried ginger give way to a palate that's delicious, driven by vibrant acidity, offering an impressive structure without ever feeling heavy.

● Villamagna '22	♥♥♥ 4*
● Montepulciano d'Abruzzo Colle Maggio Ris. '22	♥♥ 4
○ Poggio Salaia Pecorino '23	♥♥ 4
● Villamagna Ris. '21	♥♥ 5
⊙ Cerasuolo d'Abruzzo Passo Sacro '23	♥ 3
● Montepulciano d'Abruzzo Colle Maggio '23	♥ 3
○ Trebbiano d'Abruzzo Piana Marina '23	♥ 3
⊙ Cerasuolo d'Abruzzo Passo Sacro '21	♀♀ 3
● Montepulciano d'Abruzzo Colle Maggio Ris. '21	♀♀ 4
○ Poggio Salaia Pecorino '22	♀♀ 3*
○ Poggio Salaia Pecorino '21	♀♀ 3
● Villamagna '20	♀♀ 4
● Villamagna Ris. '19	♀♀ 5

○ Trebbiano d'Abruzzo Sup. Spelt '22	♥♥♥ 4*
● Montepulciano d'Abruzzo Docheìo '21	♥♥ 8
● Montepulciano d'Abruzzo Spelt Ris. '21	♥♥ 4
⊙ Cerasuolo d'Abruzzo Sup. Colline Pescaresi Spelt '23	♥♥ 4
● Montepulciano d'Abruzzo Binomio '20	♥♥ 6
○ Pecorino '23	♥♥ 3
● Montepulciano d'Abruzzo Terre dei Vestini Bellovedere Ris. '21	♥ 7
⊙ Cerasuolo d'Abruzzo Sup. Spelt '20	♀♀♀ 3*
● Montepulciano d'Abruzzo Spelt '08	♀♀♀ 3*
● Montepulciano d'Abruzzo Spelt Ris. '15	♀♀♀ 4*
● Montepulciano d'Abruzzo Spelt Ris. '11	♀♀♀ 4*
● Montepulciano d'Abruzzo Spelt Ris. '10	♀♀♀ 3*
● Montepulciano d'Abruzzo Terre dei Vestini Bellovedere Ris. '20	♀♀♀ 7

★Valle Reale

c.da San Calisto
65026 Popoli Terme [PE]
☏ 0859871039
✆ www.vallereale.it

CELLAR SALES
PRE-BOOKED VISITS
ACCOMMODATION
ANNUAL PRODUCTION 65,000 bottles
HECTARES UNDER VINE 46.00
VITICULTURE METHOD Certified Biodynamic
SUSTAINABLE WINERY

"Viticoltori fra i parchi" ("Vinegrowers among the parks"): the Pizzolo family chose this subtitle for their logo so as to express Valle Reale's productive spirit. Indeed, the heart of the winery lies between the provinces of Pescara and L'Aquila, in an unspoiled area where the Gran Sasso, Majella, and Sirente-Velino nature reserves converge. Nearly 50 hectares of vineyards are biodynamically certified, forming the foundation for one of the region's most exciting wine ranges. Two wines shine in this year's solid range: the Trebbiano Vigneto di Popoli and the Montepulciano Vigneto Sant'Eusanio. We slightly preferred the latter, a red with aromas of ripe black fruits that maintain a firm texture, later revealing pleasant balsamic notes and hints of soot. Juicy in the mouth, it shows well-extracted, fine-grained tannins that set the rhythm of the palate.

● Montepulciano d'Abruzzo Vign. Sant'Eusanio '22	▼▼ 6
○ Trebbiano d'Abruzzo Vign. di Popoli '21	▼▼ 7
● Montepulciano d'Abruzzo '23	▼▼ 5
○ Trebbiano d'Abruzzo '23	▼▼ 5
● Montepulciano d'Abruzzo Vign. di Sant'Eusanio '16	♈♈♈ 4*
● Montepulciano d'Abruzzo Vign. Sant'Eusanio '17	♈♈♈ 4*
● Montepulciano d'Abruzzo Vign. Sant'Eusanio '19	♈♈♈ 7
● Montepulciano d'Abruzzo Vign. Sant'Eusanio '18	♈♈♈ 6
○ Trebbiano d'Abruzzo V. del Convento di Capestrano '15	♈♈♈ 6
○ Trebbiano d'Abruzzo Vign. di Popoli '20	♈♈♈ 8
○ Trebbiano d'Abruzzo Vign. di Popoli '19	♈♈♈ 8

VignaMadre Famiglia Di Carlo

loc. Villa Caldari
via Stortini 32a
66026 Ortona [CH]
☏ 08719031500
✆ www.dicarlovini.it

PRE-BOOKED VISITS
RESTAURANT SERVICE
ANNUAL PRODUCTION 200,000 bottles
HECTARES UNDER VINE 65.00
VITICULTURE METHOD Certified Organic
SUSTAINABLE WINERY

The Di Carlo family's connection to wine dates back to the 1830s. Over this long period, there have been several commercial transformations, but the underlying idea has always been the same: to bring Abruzzo onto the prestigious wine stage. Vignamadre is the latest project by Giannicola Di Carlo and his sons Federico and Daniele. Their wines, based on classic regional varieties, are generous and technically impeccable. This is exemplified by the Montepulciano Capo Le Vigne '19. On the nose, it showcases aromas of dark chocolate and coffee powder, sensations that mask plum, ripe and sweet. On the palate, a bold tannic structure emerges, but the wine's juiciness and slight background sapidity keep it balanced; the finish highlights toasty notes of oak. The Becco Reale '20 also features a solid tannic structure, slightly stiffer, but with a finish that builds steadily. The Pecorino Nobu 1830 delivers as well, blending notes of hay, white peach, and pineapple on a flavorful, delightful palate.

● Montepulciano d'Abruzzo Capo le Vigne '19	▼▼▼ 4*
● Montepulciano d'Abruzzo Becco Reale '20	▼▼ 3
● Montepulciano d'Abruzzo Nobu 1830 Ris. '18	▼▼ 3
○ Nobu 1830 Pecorino '23	▼▼ 3
☉ Abruzzo Brut Rosé Trabocco Villa Roscià	▼ 3
○ Becco Reale Pecorino '23	▼ 3
☉ Cerasuolo d'Abruzzo Capo Le Vigne '23	▼ 3
● Montepulciano d'Abruzzo Becco Reale '19	♈♈♈ 3*
● Montepulciano d'Abruzzo Becco Reale '18	♈♈♈ 3*
● Montepulciano d'Abruzzo Capo Le Vigne '17	♈♈♈ 4*
○ Becco Reale Pecorino '21	♈♈ 3*

ABRUZZO

883

ABRUZZO

Agricosimo
c.da Santa Lucia, 11
66010 Villamagna [CH]
☎ 0871397434
⊕ www.agricosimo.it

CELLAR SALES
PRE-BOOKED VISITS
ACCOMMODATION
ANNUAL PRODUCTION 70,000 bottles
HECTARES UNDER VINE 11.00
VITICULTURE METHOD Certified Organic
SUSTAINABLE WINERY

⊙ Cerasuolo d'Abruzzo '23	♙♙ 3
● Montepulciano d'Abruzzo Scìne '22	♙♙ 2*
● Villamagna '19	♙♙ 3
○ Abruzzo Pecorino '23	♙ 3

Tenute Barone di Valforte
c.da Piomba, 11
64028 Silvi Marina [TE]
☎ 0859353432
⊕ www.baronedivalforte.it

CELLAR SALES
PRE-BOOKED VISITS
ANNUAL PRODUCTION 280,000 bottles
HECTARES UNDER VINE 50.00
SUSTAINABLE WINERY

⊙ Cerasuolo d'Abruzzo Valforte Rosè '23	♙♙ 5
● Montepulciano d'Abruzzo Ris. '19	♙♙ 6
● Colline Teramane Montepulciano d'Abruzzo Colle Sale '20	♙ 6

Bove
via Roma, 216
67051 Avezzano [AQ]
☎ 086333133
info@cantinebove.it

CELLAR SALES
PRE-BOOKED VISITS
ANNUAL PRODUCTION 1,200,000 bottles
HECTARES UNDER VINE 60.00

● Montepulciano d'Abruzzo Feudi d'Albe '22	♙♙ 1*
● Montepulciano d'Abruzzo Indio '19	♙♙ 3
○ Safari Pecorino '23	♙♙ 2*
● Montepulciano d'Abruzzo Avegiano '21	♙ 1*

Ausonia
c.da Nocella
64032 Atri [TE]
☎ 0859071026
⊕ www.ausoniawines.com

CELLAR SALES
PRE-BOOKED VISITS
ANNUAL PRODUCTION 35,000 bottles
HECTARES UNDER VINE 11.50
VITICULTURE METHOD Certified Organic
SUSTAINABLE WINERY

● Apollo Rosso '22	♙♙ 4
⊙ Cerasuolo d'Abruzzo Apollo '23	♙♙ 3
○ Trebbiano d'Abruzzo Apollo '22	♙♙ 3
○ Trebbiano d'Abruzzo San Pietro '21	♙ 5

Bossanova
c.da Pignotto, 87
64010 Controguerra [TE]
☎ 3469504581
⊕ www.vinibossanova.com

ACCOMMODATION
ANNUAL PRODUCTION 11,000 bottles
HECTARES UNDER VINE 9.00
VITICULTURE METHOD Certified Biodynamic
SUSTAINABLE WINERY

⊙ Cerasuolo d'Abruzzo '23	♙♙ 5
○ Trebbiano d'Abruzzo '23	♙♙ 5

Caprera
via Vasca
65020 Pietranico [PE]
☎ 3281913589
⊕ www.agricolacaprera.it

HECTARES UNDER VINE 3.50

⊙ Cerasuolo d'Abruzzo Le Vasche '22	♙♙ 4
⊙ Cerasuolo d'Abruzzo Sotto il Ceraso '22	♙♙ 6
● Montepulciano d'Abruzzo Le Vasche '20	♙ 4

OTHER WINERIES

Casal Thaulero

c.da Cucullo, 32
66026 Ortona [CH]
( ) 0859032533
www.casalthaulero.it

CELLAR SALES
PRE-BOOKED VISITS
ANNUAL PRODUCTION 2,000,000 bottles
SUSTAINABLE WINERY

● Montepulciano d'Abruzzo Orsetto Oro '21	♥♥ 3
○ Orsetto Oro Passerina '23	♥♥ 3
○ Orsetto Oro Pecorino '23	♥♥ 3
⊙ Cerasuolo d'Abruzzo Orsetto Oro '23	♥ 3

Cascina del Colle

via Piana, 85a
66010 Villamagna [CH]
( ) 0871301093
www.lacascinadelcolle.it

CELLAR SALES
PRE-BOOKED VISITS
ANNUAL PRODUCTION 200,000 bottles
HECTARES UNDER VINE 16.00
VITICULTURE METHOD Certified Organic

○ Abruzzo Pecorino Sup. Terre di Chieti Aimè '23	♥♥ 4
● Montepulciano d'Abruzzo Negus '19	♥♥ 6
○ Pecorino '23	♥♥ 3

Centorame

fraz. Casoli
via delle Fornaci
64032 Atri [TE]
( ) 0858709115
www.centorame.it

CELLAR SALES
PRE-BOOKED VISITS
ANNUAL PRODUCTION 110,000 bottles
HECTARES UNDER VINE 13.00
SUSTAINABLE WINERY

⊙ Cerasuolo d'Abruzzo Liberamente '23	♥♥ 3
○ Trebbiano d'Abruzzo Liberamente '23	♥♥ 3
○ Trebbiano d'Abruzzo San Michele '23	♥♥ 3
○ Tuapina Pecorino '23	♥♥ 3

Francesco Cirelli

fraz. Treciminiere
via Colle San Giovanni, 1
64032 Atri [TE]
( ) 0858700106
www.agricolacirelli.com

CELLAR SALES
PRE-BOOKED VISITS
ACCOMMODATION
ANNUAL PRODUCTION 35,000 bottles
HECTARES UNDER VINE 7.00
VITICULTURE METHOD Certified Biodynamic

● Montepulciano d'Abruzzo '23	♥♥ 3
○ Trebbiano d'Abruzzo '23	♥♥ 3
○ Trebbiano d'Abruzzo Anfora '22	♥♥ 6
⊙ Cerasuolo d'Abruzzo '23	♥ 3

Antonio Costantini - Fattoria Colline Verdi

s.da Migliori, 20
65013 Città Sant'Angelo [PE]
( ) 0859699169
www.costantinivini.it

CELLAR SALES
PRE-BOOKED VISITS
ANNUAL PRODUCTION 450,000 bottles
HECTARES UNDER VINE 50.00

○ Abruzzo Pecorino Sup. Colline Pescaresi '23	♥♥ 4
⊙ Cerasuolo d'Abruzzo Sup. Colline Pescaresi '23	♥♥ 4
○ Trebbiano d'Abruzzo Febe '23	♥♥ 3

De Angelis Corvi

c.da Pignotto
64010 Controguerra [TE]
( ) 086189475
www.deangeliscorvi.it

CELLAR SALES
PRE-BOOKED VISITS
ANNUAL PRODUCTION 30,000 bottles
HECTARES UNDER VINE 9.00
VITICULTURE METHOD Certified Biodynamic
SUSTAINABLE WINERY

⊙ Cerasuolo d'Abruzzo '23	♥♥ 4
○ Trebbiano d'Abruzzo Sup. Fonte Raviliano '22	♥♥ 4

OTHER WINERIES

Il Feuduccio di Santa Maria D'Orni

loc. Feuduccio
66036 Orsogna [CH]
☎ 0871891646
🖷 www.ilfeuduccio.it

CELLAR SALES
PRE-BOOKED VISITS
RESTAURANT SERVICE
ANNUAL PRODUCTION 250,000 bottles
HECTARES UNDER VINE 54.00
SUSTAINABLE WINERY

○ Feuduccio Pecorino '23	♟♟	3
● Montepulciano d'Abruzzo Essenza '21	♟♟	4
● Montepulciano d'Abruzzo Fonte Venna '21	♟♟	2*

Mazzarosa

c.da Borsacchio, 6
64026 Roseto degli Abruzzi [TE]
☎ 3726530062
vinimazzarosa@gmail.com

CELLAR SALES
PRE-BOOKED VISITS
ANNUAL PRODUCTION 50,000 bottles
HECTARES UNDER VINE 27.00
SUSTAINABLE WINERY

○ Abruzzo Pecorino Sup. '22	♟♟	3
⊙ Cerasuolo d'Abruzzo Sup. '22	♟♟	3
● Colline Teramane Montepulciano d'Abruzzo '21	♟♟	3

Novaripa

via Tiboni, 7
66010 Ripa Teatina [CH]
☎ 0871399001
🖷 www.novaripa.com

CELLAR SALES
ANNUAL PRODUCTION 2,000,000 bottles
HECTARES UNDER VINE 700.00
VITICULTURE METHOD Certified Organic

● Montepulciano d'Abruzzo Sotto il Cielo di Novaripa Ris. '19	♟♟	3*
● Montepulciano d'Abruzzo Dovizia '19	♟♟	3
○ Trebbiano d'Abruzzo Dovizia '21	♟♟	3

Tommaso Masciantonio

c.da Caprafico, 35
66043 Casoli [CH]
☎ 0871897457
🖷 www.trappetodicaprafico.com

PRE-BOOKED VISITS
ACCOMMODATION
ANNUAL PRODUCTION 10,000 bottles
HECTARES UNDER VINE 12.00
VITICULTURE METHOD Certified Organic

○ Abruzzo Pecorino Jernare '23	♟♟	5
○ Abruzzo Pecorino Sup. Mantica '22	♟♟	5
● Montepulciano D'Abruzzo Sciatò '20	♟♟	6
● Cerasuolo d'Abruzzo Agnès '23	♟	5

Patrizio Montali Quercia d'Arabona

via Scesa San Leonardo, 8
65024 Manoppello [PE]
☎ 3356331047
🖷 www.montalivini.it

HECTARES UNDER VINE 7.00

○ Abruzzo Pecorino '22	♟♟	4
● Montepulciano d'Abruzzo '22	♟♟	3
⊙ Cerasuolo d'Abruzzo Sup. '22	♟	4
○ Trebbiano d'Abruzzo '22	♟	4

Tommaso Olivastri

via Quercia del Corvo, 37
66038 San Vito Chietino [CH]
☎ 087261543
🖷 www.viniolivastri.com

CELLAR SALES
PRE-BOOKED VISITS
ANNUAL PRODUCTION 4,000 bottles
HECTARES UNDER VINE 12.00
SUSTAINABLE WINERY

⊙ Cerasuolo d'Abruzzo Marcantonio '23	♟♟	3
● Montepulciano d'Abruzzo La Carrata Ris. '18	♟♟	5
● Montepulciano d'Abruzzo La Grondaia '19	♟♟	4

OTHER WINERIES

Pasetti

loc. c.da Pretaro
via San Paolo, 21
66023 Francavilla al Mare [CH]
☎ 08561875
✆ www.pasettivini.it

CELLAR SALES
PRE-BOOKED VISITS
ACCOMMODATION
ANNUAL PRODUCTION 800,000 bottles
HECTARES UNDER VINE 75.00

○ Abruzzo Bianco Passito Gesmino '23	♀♀ 5
● Montepulciano d'Abruzzo Harimann '17	♀♀ 7
◎ Cerasuolo d'Abruzzo Sup.	
Terre Aquilane Testarossa '23	♀ 5

Gennaro Pigliacampo

Zona Industriale Colleranesco
64021 Giulianova [TE]
☎ 3409522942
✆ www.gennaropigliacampo.com

CELLAR SALES
PRE-BOOKED VISITS
ANNUAL PRODUCTION 30,000 bottles
HECTARES UNDER VINE 8.00
VITICULTURE METHOD Certified Organic

○ Abruzzo Pecorino '23	♀♀ 4
◎ Cerasuolo d'Abruzzo '23	♀♀ 4
● Montepulciano d'Abruzzo Fonterossa '21	♀♀ 5
○ Trebbiano d'Abruzzo '23	♀♀ 4

Strappelli

via Torri, 16
64010 Torano Nuovo [TE]
☎ 0861887402
✆ www.cantinastrappelli.it

CELLAR SALES
PRE-BOOKED VISITS
ANNUAL PRODUCTION 65,000 bottles
HECTARES UNDER VINE 10.00
VITICULTURE METHOD Certified Organic

○ Controguerra Pecorino Soprano '23	♀♀ 3*
◎ Cerasuolo d'Abruzzo Sup.	
Colline Teramane Colle Trà '23	♀♀ 3
○ Trebbiano d'Abruzzo Colle Trà '23	♀ 3

Pesolillo

via Colle Rotondo, 40
66100 Chieti
☎ 0871360245
✆ www.pesolillo.it

CELLAR SALES
PRE-BOOKED VISITS
ACCOMMODATION AND RESTAURANT SERVICE
ANNUAL PRODUCTION 50,000 bottles
HECTARES UNDER VINE 15.00
VITICULTURE METHOD Certified Organic

○ Abruzzo Pecorino Sup. '23	♀♀ 3
○ Abruzzo Pecorino Sup. Filari in Costa '22	♀♀ 3
● Montepulciano d'Abruzzo Ris. '20	♀♀ 4

Vigneti Radica

via Piana Mozzone, 4
66010 Tollo [CH]
☎ 0871962227
✆ www.vignetiradica.it

CELLAR SALES
PRE-BOOKED VISITS
ACCOMMODATION
ANNUAL PRODUCTION 120,000 bottles
HECTARES UNDER VINE 29.00
SUSTAINABLE WINERY

○ Brut M. Cl. '21	♀♀ 4
● Montepulciano d'Abruzzo '22	♀♀ 3
○ Pecorino '23	♀♀ 3
○ Trebbiano d'Abruzzo '23	♀♀ 3

Tenuta del Priore
Col del Mondo

via Masseria Flaiani, 1
65010 Collecorvino [PE]
☎ 0858207162
✆ www.tenutadelpriore.it

CELLAR SALES
PRE-BOOKED VISITS
ANNUAL PRODUCTION 230,000 bottles
HECTARES UNDER VINE 60.00
SUSTAINABLE WINERY

◎ Cerasuolo d'Abruzzo	
Fattore Col del Mondo '23	♀♀ 4
● Montepulciano d'Abruzzo Terre dei Vestini	
Fattore Col del Mondo '20	♀♀ 4

OTHER WINERIES

Tocco
p.zza Alcide De Gasperi, 9
65020 Alanno [PE]
☏ 3400558624
✉ www.toccovini.com

CELLAR SALES
PRE-BOOKED VISITS
ANNUAL PRODUCTION 55,000 bottles
HECTARES UNDER VINE 22.00
VITICULTURE METHOD Certified Organic

● Montepulciano d'Abruzzo Enisio Ris. '19	♟♟ 5
○ Trebbiano d'Abruzzo Capostazione '23	♟♟ 3
◉ Cerasuolo d'Abruzzo Capostazione '23	♟ 3

Valori
via Torquato al Salinello, 8
64027 Sant'Omero [TE]
☏ 087185241
✉ www.vinivalori.it

PRE-BOOKED VISITS
ANNUAL PRODUCTION 150,000 bottles
HECTARES UNDER VINE 26.00
VITICULTURE METHOD Certified Organic
SUSTAINABLE WINERY

◉ Cerasuolo d'Abruzzo Sup. Colline Teramane Chiamami Quando Piove '23	♟♟ 3
● Montepulciano d'Abruzzo '22	♟♟ 3

Zaccagnini
c.da Pozzo
65020 Bolognano [PE]
☏ 0858880195
✉ www.cantinazaccagnini.it

CELLAR SALES
PRE-BOOKED VISITS
ANNUAL PRODUCTION 6,000,000 bottles
HECTARES UNDER VINE 300.00

○ Abruzzo Pecorino Chronicon '23	♟♟ 3
● Montepulciano d'Abruzzo Il Vino del Tralcetto Ris. '20	♟♟ 3
○ Trebbiano d'Abruzzo San Clemente '23	♟♟ 4

Torre Raone
fraz. Passo Cordone
via Scannella, 6
65014 Loreto Aprutino [PE]
☏ 0858289699
✉ www.torreraone.com

CELLAR SALES
PRE-BOOKED VISITS
ANNUAL PRODUCTION 100,000 bottles
HECTARES UNDER VINE 30.00
VITICULTURE METHOD Certified Organic

● Montepulciano d'Abruzzo Ris. '19	♟♟ 5
● Montepulciano d'Abruzzo Terre dei Vestini San Zopito '19	♟♟ 5
○ Pecorino '23	♟♟ 3

Vinco
c.da Cucullo
66026 Ortona [CH]
☏ 0857952338
✉ www.vincoabruzzo.it

ANNUAL PRODUCTION 182,000 bottles

○ Abruzzo Bianco Brut Trabocco Venere	♟♟ 3
○ Abruzzo Pecorino Extra Dry Trabocco	♟♟ 2*
○ Abruzzo Bianco Extra Dry Trabocco Cuvée Bianca	♟ 2

Zappacosta
s.da del Tratturo, 1b
66100 Chieti
☏ 3204023266
✉ www.zappacostavini.it

CELLAR SALES
ANNUAL PRODUCTION 25,000 bottles
HECTARES UNDER VINE 4.00
VITICULTURE METHOD Certified Organic
SUSTAINABLE WINERY

○ Pecorino '23	♟♟ 4
● Montepulciano d'Abruzzo '21	♟♟ 3
○ Trebbiano d'Abruzzo '22	♟♟ 3
● Cerasuolo d'Abruzzo '23	♟ 3

MOLISE

Molise is Italy's second smallest region, but within its nearly 4,500 square kilometers, it manages to encapsulate mountains, a broad expanse of hills, and a short stretch of coast. This undulating plateau, framed by the Mainarde and Matese mountain ranges and gently sloping down to the sea, remains off the beaten tourist path. Perhaps it's precisely this isolation that preserves the area's unique charm, especially in terms of natural beauty. In this landscape, grapevines have been cultivated since ancient times, deeply intertwined with the region's rural heritage.

Like many "transitional" areas, Molise's borders have allowed grape varietals to migrate over time from neighboring regions. As a result, we find montepulciano and trebbiano from nearby (yet very different) Abruzzo, falanghina from Sannio, and aglianico from Irpinia (greco as well). However, Molise does have its own distinctive traits. This is testified to by the increasing success of its one true native grape, tintilia, which is yielding promising results more frequently. This year, we awarded Tenimenti Grieco's 200 Metri '23, a playful, lively, and delicious expression of tintilia, alongside Di Majo Norante's classic Don Luigi Riserva '20.

Yet, we must again end our introduction on a negative note: too few wineries in the region are choosing to participate in our tastings. The pages dedicated to Molise will struggle to grow as long as our dialogue with its wines remains limited to a handful of producers. Fortunately, those who do participate are proving increasingly impressive.

Catabbo

c.da Petriera
86046 San Martino in Pensilis [CB]
+39 0875604945
www.catabbo.it

CELLAR SALES
ANNUAL PRODUCTION 120,000 bottles
HECTARES UNDER VINE 40.00
VITICULTURE METHOD Certified Organic
SUSTAINABLE WINERY

In the 1990s, Vincenzo Catabbo embarked on his winemaking journey in the picturesque hills of San Martino in Pensilis, not far from the Adriatic Coast. His venture, now spread across three growing properties, began with the first tintilia vines planted at Contrada Petriera. The estate has since expanded to include the Tenute al Convento and the Tenuta al Calvario. Today, the winery boasts 40 hectares of vineyards, with 13 hectares dedicated to tintilia, the region's flagship grape variety. Vincenzo, a passionate advocate of tintilia, now works alongside his children, Sara, Carla, and Pasquale. A brilliant performance, especially for their tintilia-based wines. The amphora-aged 2022 presents fragrant notes of blueberries and wild strawberries, with a juicy, vibrant palate and subtle tannins. The Colle Cervino '21 is also delicious, playing on notes of red cherry, aromatic herbs, and a fresh, fleshy palate.

● Molise Tintilia Colle Cervino '21	🍷🍷 4
● Molise Tintilia in Anfora '22	🍷🍷 6
○ Falanghina in Anfora	🍷🍷 5
● Molise Tintilia S '21	🍷🍷 5
● Tinduce	🍷 5
○ Molise Falanghina Colle del Limone '21	YY 3
○ Molise Falanghina In Anfora '21	YY 3
● Molise Tintilia Colle Cervino '20	YY 4
● Molise Tintilia Colle Cervino '19	YY 5
● Molise Tintilia Colle Cervino '18	YY 5
● Molise Tintilia in Anfora '21	YY 6
● Molise Tintilia Ris. '14	YY 5
● Molise Tintilia S '20	YY 5
● Molise Tintilia S '19	YY 4
● Molise Tintilia Vincè Ris. '18	YY 6

Claudio Cipressi

c.da Montagna, 11b
86030 San Felice del Molise [CB]
+39 3927501578
claudiocipressi.it

CELLAR SALES
PRE-BOOKED VISITS
RESTAURANT SERVICE
ANNUAL PRODUCTION 50,000 bottles
HECTARES UNDER VINE 15.00
VITICULTURE METHOD Certified Organic
SUSTAINABLE WINERY

The name of Claudio Cipressi's winery speaks for itself. Based in Contrada Montagna, his 15 hectares of thriving certified organic vineyards unfold in the innermost hills of Campobasso province. Claudio began his winemaking career in 2000, leaving behind his previous profession to focus on promoting tintilia, the star of his estate. His vineyards also host montepulciano, falanghina, and trebbiano. This year's lineup remains solid, with a few peaks of excellence. The Tintilia '66 has never been as focused as in the 2019 version. Black olives, Mediterranean scrub, and a pleasantly spicy touch meld with notes of plum and cherry, leading to a fine tannic structure that's also quite firm. The Tintilia Macchiarossa '19 blends blueberries with a slightly ferrous sensation; on the palate, it offers nice body and volume. The other wines tasted are also well-crafted.

● Molise Tintilia 66 '19	🍷🍷 7
● Molise Tintilia Macchiarossa '19	🍷🍷 5
○ Molise Trebbiano Le Scoste '23	🍷🍷 4
○ Voira Falanghina '22	🍷🍷 5
○ Blanc de Noir Pas Dosé '17	YY 8
○ Molise Falanghina Settevigne '20	YY 4
● Molise Tintilia 66 '17	YY 7
● Molise Tintilia Macchiarossa '18	YY 5
● Molise Tintilia Macchiarossa '17	YY 5
● Molise Tintilia Macchiarossa '16	YY 5
⊙ Molise Tintilia Rosato Collequinto '22	YY 5
● Molise Tintilia Settevigne '16	YY 5
○ Molise Trebbiano Le Scoste '22	YY 4
○ Molise Trebbiano Le Scoste '20	YY 4
⊙ Pas Dosé M. Cl. Rosé '17	YY 8
○ Settevigne Falanghina '21	YY 4

★★Di Majo Norante

fraz. Nuova Cliternia
via Ramitello, 4
86042 Campomarino [CB]
📞 +39 087557208
🌐 www.dimajonorante.com

CELLAR SALES
PRE-BOOKED VISITS
ANNUAL PRODUCTION 800,000 bottles
HECTARES UNDER VINE 140.00
VITICULTURE METHOD Certified Organic

The Di Majo Norante family winery has roots that reach deep into the past. Their vineyards are located on what was once the ancient feudal estate of the Marquis Santa Caterina family, near Campomarino—a region that serves as a bridge between southern Abruzzo, Daunia, and Sannio. Today, Alessio manages the 140-hectare estate, where the grapes native to the Southern Apennines take center stage. For example, montepulciano gives life to the Don Luigi Riserva, while aglianico is the basis of the Sassius Riserva. The former, from the 2020 vintage, is an intense red characterized by toasted notes and dark chocolate on the nose, with ripe black fruit lingering in the background. The palate is full-bodied, firm, and voluminous. The latter is an Aglianico that plays on pleasant sensations of oak, with a dense and robust palate. The Ramitello '20, on the other hand, features more fleshy fruit.

● Molise Rosso Don Luigi Ris. '20	♛♛♛	6
● Molise Aglianico Sassius Ris. '17	♛♛	7
● Biferno Rosso Ramitello '20	♛♛	3
○ Molise Moscato Bianco Passito Apianae '18	♛♛	5
○ Molise Greco Bianco '23	♛	3
● Molise Aglianico Contado Ris. '19	♛♛♛	3*
● Molise Aglianico Contado Ris. '17	♛♛♛	3*
● Molise Aglianico Contado Ris. '14	♛♛♛	3*
● Molise Aglianico Sassius Ris. '16	♛♛♛	7
● Molise Rosso Don Luigi Ris. '16	♛♛♛	6
● Molise Rosso Don Luigi Ris. '15	♛♛♛	5
● Molise Rosso Don Luigi Ris. '12	♛♛♛	5
● Molise Tintilia '16	♛♛♛	3*
● Molise Tintilia '13	♛♛♛	3*

Tenimenti Grieco

c.da Difensola
86045 Portocannone [CB]
📞 +39 0875590032
🌐 www.tenimentigrieco.it

CELLAR SALES
PRE-BOOKED VISITS
ANNUAL PRODUCTION 700,000 bottles
HECTARES UNDER VINE 85.00

MOLISE

The winery that now rests on what was once known as "Masseria Flocco" is the result of a revitalization effort spearheaded over a decade ago by Antonio Grieco, a Puglian entrepreneur who ventured into the world of winemaking in nearby Molise. Located in Portocannone, not far from the Adriatic coast, the estate spans 85 hectares and cultivates both native varieties like falanghina, montepulciano, and tintilia, as well as international grapes. The result is a diverse range of wines organized into several distinct lines. The excellence of the Tintilia 200 Metri no longer comes as surprise. The 2023 tasted this year also impressed with its fragrant, fresh, and multifaceted profile, featuring nuances of red cherries, ripe raspberries, Mediterranean shrubs, and a hint of pepper. The palate is taut and crisp: a wine focused on drinkability but far from simple or banal. The Bosco delle Guardie '22 proves full-bodied and mineral, while the Triassi '21 is rich in extract and warmth.

● Molise Tintilia 200 Metri '23	♛♛♛	3*
● Biferno Rosso Bosco delle Guardie '22	♛♛	4
● Triassi '21	♛♛	6
○ Matana Chardonnay '23	♛	4
● Molise Aglianico Passo alle Tremiti '21	♛	3
○ Molise Falanghina Passo alle Tremiti '23	♛	3
● Biferno Rosso Bosco delle Guardie '21	♛♛	4
● Biferno Rosso Bosco delle Guardie '19	♛♛	4
● Biferno Rosso Bosco delle Guardie '18	♛♛	3
○ Matana Chardonnay '20	♛♛	4
● Molise Rosso I Costali Monterosso '21	♛♛	3
● Molise Rosso I Costali Monterosso '20	♛♛	2*
● Molise Tintilia 200 Metri '22	♛♛	3*
● Molise Tintilia 200 Metri '21	♛♛	3*
● Molise Tintilia 200 Metri '20	♛♛	3*

OTHER WINERIES

Borgo di Colloredo

fraz. Nuova Cliternia
via Colloredo, 15
86042 Campomarino [CB]
☎ +39 087557453
✉ www.borgodicolloredo.com

CELLAR SALES
PRE-BOOKED VISITS
ACCOMMODATION AND RESTAURANT SERVICE
ANNUAL PRODUCTION 120,000 bottles
HECTARES UNDER VINE 80.00
SUSTAINABLE WINERY

○ Biferno Rosato Gironia '23	🍷🍷 4
● Biferno Rosso Gironia Ris. '19	🍷🍷 5
● Molise Rosso Campo in Mare '22	🍷🍷 3
○ Biferno Bianco Gironia '23	🍷 4

Campi Valerio

loc. Selvotta
86075 Monteroduni [IS]
☎ +39 0865493043
✉ campi-valerio.it

CELLAR SALES
ANNUAL PRODUCTION 100,000 bottles
HECTARES UNDER VINE 10.00

○ Molise Falanghina Fannia '23	🍷🍷 2*
● Molise Rosso Calidio '22	🍷🍷 2*
● Molise Tintilia La Lana '20	🍷🍷 6
○ Molise Tintilia Rosato Per Una Rosa '23	🍷🍷 3

Tenute Martarosa

loc. Nuova Cliternia
via Madonna Grande, 11
86042 Campomarino [CB]
☎ +39 0875727757
✉ www.tenutemartarosa.com

CELLAR SALES
PRE-BOOKED VISITS
ANNUAL PRODUCTION 70,000 bottles
HECTARES UNDER VINE 20.00

● Molise Tintilia '21	🍷🍷 4
○ Molise Fiano '22	🍷🍷 3
○ Molise Moscato '23	🍷🍷 3
○ Molise Moscato Underwater '21	🍷🍷 8

Cantine Salvatore

c.da Vigne
86049 Ururi [CB]
☎ +39 0874830656
✉ www.cantinesalvatore.it

CELLAR SALES
PRE-BOOKED VISITS
ANNUAL PRODUCTION 90,000 bottles
HECTARES UNDER VINE 20.00
VITICULTURE METHOD Certified Organic
SUSTAINABLE WINERY

● Molise Rosso Biberius '20	🍷🍷 3
● Molise Rosso Don Donà '17	🍷🍷 4
○ Molise Falanghina Nysias '23	🍷 3
○ Molise Tintilia Ros is '23	🍷 3

Cantina San Zenone

c.da Piana dei Pastini
86036 Montenero di Bisaccia [CB]
☎ +39 3477998397
✉ www.cantinasanzenone.it

CELLAR SALES
PRE-BOOKED VISITS
ANNUAL PRODUCTION 150,000 bottles
HECTARES UNDER VINE 300.00
VITICULTURE METHOD Certified Organic
SUSTAINABLE WINERY

● Molise Rosso Clivia '22	🍷🍷 2*
● Molise Rosso Pluris Ris. '20	🍷🍷 5
● Nonno Matteo '21	🍷🍷 4
○ Pluris Falanghina '23	🍷 5

CAMPANIA

The latest available data indicates that Campania's vineyard area now exceeds 25,000 hectares. These vineyards span a multitude of diverse territories, each with its own production culture, different exposures, and various geological formations: volcanic areas like Roccamonfina, Vesuvius, and the Phlegraean Fields; the islands; the high-elevation vineyards of Irpinia—which reach over 700 meters above sea level; and the cliffside vines along the Amalfi Coast. It's a region with as much geographical and morphological diversity as it has variety in terms of grape cultivation. More and more, we're seeing fiano, greco, falanghina, aglianico, piedirosso, casavecchia, pallagrello (both white and red), pepella, biancolella, and many others transformed into modern wines that nearly always manage to convey a sense of place.

This year's tastings were once again impressive. We won't dwell on the obvious (the excellence of the region's whites, especially Fiano and Greco in Irpinia and Falanghina in Sannio), but we do want to highlight the reds, which struck us as a bit more refined compared to last year. The vibrancy and crispness of flegreo piedirosso is now a given, but we were pleasantly surprised by some versions of Taurasi and aglianico more broadly, which managed to tame the variety's powerful tannins. There are signs of improvement in what has been a somewhat challenging area in past editions.

This year, 21 wines received the coveted Tre Bicchieri award, 16 of them whites. Fiano di Avellino and Falanghina del Sannio lead the pack, but Greco di Tufo also secures a strong presence among the best. Rounding out the top are a return to form of Marisa Cuomo's Fiorduva and Cacciagalli's Zagreo, the latter of which proves to be one of Italy's most captivating orange wines. We also welcome Mario Fappiano, a young winemaker from Sannio, to the Tre Bicchieri club. With his debut entry in the guide, he's already won us over. Lastly, in the new Rare Wines section, you'll find three expressions of true excellence, produced in extremely limited quantities: Pietracupa's Cupo '20, Passo delle Tortore's Greco di Tufo Le Arcaie di San Pio '22, and San Salvatore's Pian di Stio Evoluzione '19.

Aia dei Colombi

c.da Sapenzie
82034 Guardia Sanframondi [BN]
(☎) +39 0824817139
⊛ www.aiadeicolombi.it

CELLAR SALES
PRE-BOOKED VISITS
ANNUAL PRODUCTION 60,000 bottles
HECTARES UNDER VINE 10.00

The Pascale family launched their winemaking
venture in 2002, reviving a long agricultural
tradition. Their estate spans about 10 hectares,
spread across Guardia Sanframondi and
Castelvenere, on calcareous-clay soils. The
vineyards primarily feature local varieties like
aglianico and falanghina, with smaller amounts of
sangiovese, fiano, merlot, and cabernet sauvignon
also cultivated. For whites, they prefer stainless
steel tanks to preserve freshness, while aglianico
matures in barriques, an approach aimed at
smoothing the grape's edges. The Falanghina
Vignasuprema once again demonstrates its
exceptional quality. A mineral and faintly smoky
note followed by hints of iodine mixed with a
signature herbaceous touch adorns this
substantive, well-structured white. The
Falanghina '23, on the other hand, proves citrusy
and fragrant, with a subtle briny hint on a
smooth, linear, and flavorful palate. The Fiano '23
is also noteworthy.

Alois

loc. Audelino
via Ragazzano
81040 Pontelatone [CE]
(☎) +39 0823876710
⊛ www.vinialois.it

CELLAR SALES
PRE-BOOKED VISITS
ANNUAL PRODUCTION 190,000 bottles
HECTARES UNDER VINE 30.00
SUSTAINABLE WINERY

The Alois family is renowned not only for their
prestigious textiles but also for their
winemaking skills. Production started in the
1990s, focusing on rediscovering and promoting
the indigenous grapes of Caserta, such as
pallagrello bianco, pallagrello nero, and
casavecchia. Their 30 hectares of vineyards are
located in Audelino, Cesone, and Morrone della
Monica, nestled in the Trebulani Mountains and
Caiatine Hills. Typically, it's Alois's whites that
make the best impression. Indeed, this year the
Morrone '22, a remarkable Pallagrello Bianco,
features smoky and herbaceous tones with a
structured, textured palate. However, their reds
have shown significant improvement. The
Murella '21, a dark Pallagrello Nero, opens on
mineral notes and ripe black fruit, with a
compact and progressively dynamic palate. The
Trebulanum, with its close-knit tannins and rich
flavor, also performs well.

○ Falanghina del Sannio Guardia Sanframondi Vignasuprema '22	♟♟ 3*
○ Falanghina del Sannio Guardia Sanframondi '23	♟♟ 2*
○ Sannio Guardia Sanframondi Fiano '23	♟♟ 3
● Sannio Barbera '23	♟ 3
○ Falanghina del Sannio Guardia Sanframondi Vignasuprema '21	♟♟♟ 3*
○ Falanghina del Sannio Guardia Sanframondi '22	♟♟ 2*
○ Falanghina del Sannio Guardia Sanframondi '21	♟♟ 2*
○ Falanghina del Sannio Guardia Sanframondi Vignasuprema '20	♟♟ 3
○ Falanghina del Sannio Guardia Sanframondi Vignasuprema '19	♟♟ 2*
● Sannio Barbera '22	♟♟ 3
○ Sannio Guardia Sanframondi Fiano '22	♟♟ 3

○ Morrone Pallagrello Bianco '22	♟♟ 7
○ Caiatì Pallagrello Bianco '23	♟♟ 4
● Casavecchia di Pontelatone Trebulanum Ris. '21	♟♟ 8
● Murella Pallagrello Nero '21	♟♟ 8
○ Ponte Pellegrino Falanghina '23	♟♟ 3
● Settimo Pallagrello Casavecchia '20	♟♟ 3
○ Caulino Falanghina '23	♟ 3
● Cunto Pallagrello Nero '20	♟ 5
○ Caiatì Pallagrello Bianco '17	♟♟♟ 4*
○ Caiatì Pallagrello Bianco '16	♟♟♟ 4*
○ Caiatì Pallagrello Bianco '15	♟♟♟ 3*
○ Caiatì Pallagrello Bianco '14	♟♟♟ 3*
○ Caiatì Pallagrello Bianco '13	♟♟♟ 2*
○ Morrone Pallagrello Bianco '20	♟♟♟ 7
○ Morrone Pallagrello Bianco '19	♟♟♟ 7
○ Morrone Pallagrello Bianco '18	♟♟♟ 6

Cantine Astroni

via Sartania, 48
80126 Napoli
☏ +39 0815884182
✉ www.cantineastroni.com

CELLAR SALES
PRE-BOOKED VISITS
RESTAURANT SERVICE
ANNUAL PRODUCTION 150,000 bottles
HECTARES UNDER VINE 25.00
SUSTAINABLE WINERY

Named after the Astroni crater, this prominent winery in the Campi Flegrei region boasts a remarkable volcanic landscape. The soils, rich in ash and lapilli, benefit from the breezes of the nearby Tyrrhenian Sea. At the moment Cristina Varchetta is at the helm, representing the estate both locally and abroad, while Gerardo Vernazzaro manages the 25 hectares of vineyards, producing a range of wines that reflect their unique terroir. The Falanghina Vigna Astroni '20 captures the volcanic essence of its region with an olfactory profile reminiscent of flint and subtle whiffs of hydrocarbon. This is followed by the grape?s classic herbaceous vein, leading to a long, deep, and sapid palate. The Colle Rotondella, a Piedirosso, is also excellent, with aromas of black pepper, ripe raspberry, and black currant. Lightly smoky, it has a coherent, smooth, and very enjoyable palate. The Falanghina Colle Imperatrice '23 also delivers.

Bambinuto

via Cerro
83030 Santa Paolina [AV]
☏ +39 0825964634
✉ www.cantinabambinuto.com

PRE-BOOKED VISITS
ANNUAL PRODUCTION 25,000 bottles
HECTARES UNDER VINE 6.00

Santa Paolina is Greco di Tufo wine country, and it's here that the Aufiero family began producing their own after years of supplying grapes to other wineries. It was Raffaele and Carmela who decided to go independent, a choice supported by their daughters Marilena and Michela. Their vineyards are located in the prime parcels of Paoloni and Picoli, at elevations of 500 meters, on clay-rich soils with layers of limestone. Recently, they also added plots in Toppole-Monteaperto, Montemiletto. Musky and sunny on the nose, the Picoli '22 features whiffs of citron peel, fresh hazelnut, kiwi, and mint as well. A mineral hint leads to a juicy palate that bursts forth with energy and flavor towards a vibrant finish. The Greco '22 proves vibrant, with notes of white fruit and iodized memories blending with aromatic herbs; lemon peel sensations make for a clean, taut, and pleasant palate.

○ Campi Flegrei Falanghina V. Astroni '20	♊♊ 5
● Campi Flegrei Piedirosso Colle Rotondella '23	♊♊ 4
○ Campi Flegrei Falanghina Colle Imperatrice '23	♊♊ 4
○ Campi Flegrei Falanghina V. Astroni '15	♊♊♊ 3*
● Campi Flegrei Piedirosso Colle Rotondella '22	♊♊♊ 4*
● Campi Flegrei Piedirosso Colle Rotondella '19	♊♊♊ 3
○ Campi Flegrei Falanghina Colle Imperatrice '22	♊♊ 3*
○ Campi Flegrei Falanghina Colle Imperatrice '21	♊♊ 3*
● Campi Flegrei Piedirosso Colle Rotondella '21	♊♊ 4
● Campi Flegrei Piedirosso Tenuta Camaldoli Ris. '16	♊♊ 3*

○ Greco di Tufo '22	♊♊ 5
○ Greco di Tufo Picoli Ris. '22	♊♊ 5
● Aglianico 212.4 Toppole '18	♊♊ 3
○ Greco di Tufo '20	♊♊ 4
○ Greco di Tufo '18	♊♊ 2*
○ Greco di Tufo '15	♊♊ 2*
○ Greco di Tufo '14	♊♊ 2*
○ Greco di Tufo Picoli '19	♊♊ 4
○ Greco di Tufo Picoli '18	♊♊ 4
○ Greco di Tufo Picoli '17	♊♊ 4
○ Greco di Tufo Picoli '16	♊♊ 4
○ Greco di Tufo Picoli '15	♊♊ 4
○ Greco di Tufo Picoli '13	♊♊ 4
○ Greco di Tufo Picoli Ris. '21	♊♊ 5
○ Greco di Tufo Rafilù Ris. '19	♊♊ 5

Bellaria

loc. Tuoro
via Fontana
83016 Roccabascerana [AV]
(") +39 3473064161
⊛ www.agricolabellaria.com

CELLAR SALES
PRE-BOOKED VISITS
ANNUAL PRODUCTION 100,000 bottles
HECTARES UNDER VINE 21.00
SUSTAINABLE WINERY

A venture initially focused on olive groves and oil, the Maffei family and Antonio Pepe decided to branch out to winemaking in 2007. They now manage 21 hectares of vineyards across various Irpinian municipalities. Their parcels in Paternopoli, Montemiletto, and Montefalcone host aglianico, while those in Candida see fiano. In Montefusco and Prata di Principato Ultra, greco is cultivated. From here come the grapes that create the Greco di Tufo Oltre '22, a whine that sees lovely smoky, briny, and mineral sensations follow through on a clear, sapid, and tension-filled palate. The Fiano '22, with its bouquet of medlar, mint, and anise, is also delicious; its palate is energetic and rhythmically vibrant. The Coda Rara '22 intrigues, with forest black fruits meeting balsamic nuances. An inky touch paves the way to a tannic, flavorful palate.

Bosco de' Medici

via Antonio Segni, 43
80045 Pompei [NA]
(") +39 3382828234
⊛ www.boscodemedici.com

CELLAR SALES
PRE-BOOKED VISITS
ACCOMMODATION AND RESTAURANT SERVICE
ANNUAL PRODUCTION 35,000 bottles
HECTARES UNDER VINE 8.00
VITICULTURE METHOD Certified Organic

The Palomba and Monaco families named their winery after the notable Medici family of Florence, who owned land near Pompeii in the 16th century, close to the current vineyards. Their estate features local vesuvian varieties, like piedirosso and aglianico for the reds, and falanghina for the whites. Additional parcels are located in Terzigno and Boscoreale. The monovarietal Piedirosso Agathos '22 proves redolent of red roses and freshly ground black pepper. Intriguing and precise on the nose, it offers a slight herbaceous sensation along with nice fruit pulp on the palate. Despite fairly close-knit tannins, the palate is supple, showcasing a pleasant, citrusy background. The dark side of aglianico emerges in the savoury and volcanic Pompeii Rosso '23. The sapid and drinkable Lavarubra '23, and the Pompeii Bianco '23 with its flavorful citrus and aromatic herb palate, also stand out.

○ Fiano di Avellino '22	♟♟ 4
○ Greco di Tufo Oltre '22	♟♟ 5
● Coda Rara '22	♟♟ 8
○ Irpinia Falanghina V. Tuoro '23	♟ 3
● Taurasi '20	♟ 7
● Aglianico '13	♟♟ 3
○ Fiano di Avellino '21	♟♟ 4
○ Greco di Tufo Oltre '21	♟♟ 5
○ Irpinia Falanghina '14	♟♟ 2*
● Taurasi '09	♟♟ 6

● Agathos '22	♟♟ 6
○ Pompeii Bianco '23	♟♟ 4
● Pompeii Rosso '23	♟♟ 4
● Vesuvio Lacryma Christi Rosso Lavarubra '23	♟♟ 3
○ Dressel 19.2 '23	♟ 6
⊙ Pompeii Rosato '23	♟ 4
○ Pompeii Bianco '18	♟♟♟ 3*
○ Dressel 19.2 '21	♟♟ 6
○ Pompeii Bianco '22	♟♟ 4
○ Pompeii Bianco '21	♟♟ 4
○ Pompeii Bianco '20	♟♟ 4
○ Pompeii Bianco '19	♟♟ 4
○ Pompeii Bianco '15	♟♟ 3*
● Pompeii Rosso '22	♟♟ 4
● Pompeii Rosso '21	♟♟ 4

I Cacciagalli

s.da prov.le 91 - Borgonuovo - Cipriani
81057 Teano [CE]
☎ +39 0823875216
🌐 www.icacciagalli.it

Antonio Caggiano

c.da Sala
83030 Taurasi [AV]
☎ +39 082774723
🌐 www.cantinecaggiano.it

CELLAR SALES
PRE-BOOKED VISITS
ACCOMMODATION AND RESTAURANT SERVICE
ANNUAL PRODUCTION 55,000 bottles
HECTARES UNDER VINE 11.00
VITICULTURE METHOD Certified Biodynamic

CELLAR SALES
PRE-BOOKED VISITS
RESTAURANT SERVICE
ANNUAL PRODUCTION 170,000 bottles
HECTARES UNDER VINE 32.00

Diana Iannaccone and Mario Basco's winery is set in a stunning 18th-century farmhouse in the picturesque Caserta region of Teano, an area known for its lush natural landscapes. Roccamonfina, a dormant volcano, has had a significant influences on the soils of their 10 hectares of biodynamic vineyards. In the cellar they draw on concrete tanks and amphorae, using indigenous yeast fermentations and macerations, for both reds and whites, resulting in a highly original range of wines. The Zagreo has lost some of its wild character but remains an intense wine with great personality. White pepper, candied ginger, green citrus, tea leaves, and pollen compose the aromatic spectrum of a textured, reactive, and full-bodied white?lively and appealing in its drinkability. The Lucno, a Piedirosso with black pepper and dried red flower notes on an energetic and fresh palate, also stood out. Overall, the entire range proves highly intriguing.

World-traveling photographer Antonio Caggiano is a prominent figure in Irpinian and Campanian wine. In the 1990s, he established his winery, constructing the cellar entirely from local stone, creating a magical and captivating structure. Today, his son Giuseppe manages the Taurasi-based estate, transforming grapes from their 30 hectares of vineyards into notable wines. From the parcel located in Contrada Macchia dei Goti comes the Taurasi of the same name. This year we tasted the 2020, which opens on ripe black cherry sensations and blueberry juice, sensations mirrored on the palate, which sees tannins and fruit pulp integrate perfectly, closing warm and enveloping. The Greco Devon '23 proves exuberant on the nose with notes of pear, apple, and white peach; very flavorful mid-palate, it finishes on a fresh herbaceous sensation. The Fiano Isca '22, while more expansive than linear, is also quite good.

○ Zagreo '22	♔♔♔ 5		○ Greco di Tufo Devon '23	♔♔ 4
○ Aorivola '23	♔♔ 4		● Taurasi V. Macchia dei Goti '20	♔♔ 6
● Lucno '22	♔♔ 5		○ Fiano di Avellino Béchar '23	♔♔ 4
○ Pellerosa '22	♔♔ 5		○ Fiano di Avellino V. Isca Ris. '22	♔♔ 5
● Phos '21	♔♔ 5		○ Mel	♔♔ 6
○ Viento 'e Mare Brut M. Cl.	♔♔ 5		○ Falanghina '23	♔ 3
● Sphaeranera '22	♔ 5		○ Fiagrè '23	♔ 3
○ Zagreo '20	♔♔♔ 5		● Irpinia Aglianico Taurì '23	♔ 3
○ Zagreo '18	♔♔♔ 4*		● Irpinia Campi Taurasini	
○ Zagreo '15	♔♔♔ 4*		Salae Domini '22	♔ 5
○ Aorivola '22	♔♔ 4		⊙ Rosa Salae '23	♔ 3
○ Aorivola '19	♔♔ 4		○ Fiano di Avellino Béchar '13	♔♔♔ 3*
● Lucno '20	♔♔ 5		● Taurasi V. Macchia dei Goti '17	♔♔♔ 6
○ Pellerosa '21	♔♔ 5		● Taurasi V. Macchia dei Goti '16	♔♔♔ 6
○ Zagreo '21	♔♔ 5		● Taurasi V. Macchia dei Goti '14	♔♔♔ 6
○ Zagreo '19	♔♔ 6		● Taurasi V. Macchia dei Goti Ris. '15	♔♔♔ 6

Cantina di Solopaca

via Bebiana, 44
82036 Solopaca [BN]
(☎) +39 0824977921
⊛ www.cantinasolopaca.it

CELLAR SALES
PRE-BOOKED VISITS
ANNUAL PRODUCTION 3,700,000 bottles
HECTARES UNDER VINE 1100.00
VITICULTURE METHOD Certified Organic

The numbers are impressive: 600 members, 1,100 hectares of vineyards cultivated across 15 municipalities, over 3 million bottles produced, and nearly 60 years of history. But Cantina di Solopaca's significance also lies in its projects. The cooperative has successfully combined these figures with concrete quality and programs focused on promoting the territory. The latest initiative, the Identitas line, aims to revitalize this behemoth of a producer. This year, there were no reds at our tasting tables. However, as usual, we found an interesting version of the Falanghina del Sannio Identitas, the 2023. An intriguing aroma of sweet spices combines with delightful sensations of ripe yellow fruit, especially peach and medlar. A classic note of freshly mown grass opens the way to a full, supple palate, marked by juicy sapidity. The other wines presented also performed well.

○ Falanghina del Sannio Identitas '23	♛♛ 3*
○ Falanghina del Sannio Brut Oro	♛♛ 3
○ Sannio Fiano Òria '23	♛♛ 3
○ Sannio Greco Fòja '23	♛♛ 3
○ Falanghina del Sannio Identitas '22	♛♛♛ 3*
○ Falanghina del Sannio '20	♛♛ 2*
○ Falanghina del Sannio Identitas '21	♛♛ 3*
○ Falanghina del Sannio Identitas '20	♛♛ 3*
○ Falanghina del Sannio Identitas '19	♛♛ 3*
● Sannio Aglianico Carrese Ris. '19	♛♛ 3
● Sannio Aglianico Carrese Ris. '18	♛♛ 3
○ Sannio Fiano '20	♛♛ 2*
○ Sannio Fiano Òria '22	♛♛ 3
○ Sannio Fiano Òria '21	♛♛ 3
○ Sannio Greco Fòja '22	♛♛ 3

Casa Setaro

c.da Bosco del Monaco, 34
80040 Trecase [NA]
(☎) +39 0818628956
⊛ www.casasetaro.it

CELLAR SALES
PRE-BOOKED VISITS
ACCOMMODATION AND RESTAURANT SERVICE
ANNUAL PRODUCTION 90,000 bottles
HECTARES UNDER VINE 16.00
VITICULTURE METHOD Certified Organic
SUSTAINABLE WINERY

Massimo Setaro and his wife Maria Rosaria's vineyards are situated on the southern slopes of Mount Vesuvius, overlooking the Gulf of Naples. Massimo cultivates 16 hectares in Trecase, in the Bosco del Monaco and Tirone della Guardia areas (some owned and others leased), at elevations spanning 200-350 meters on volcanic soils. Their diverse range includes aglianico, piedirosso, caprettone, and falanghina, with whites, reds, rosés, and a noteworthy line of Metodo Classico sparkling wines all part of their portfolio. Our annual review of the winery's portfolio starts here. The Pietrafumante Brut Nature boasts a bouquet in which fresh hazelnut blends with smoky mineral nuances on a green citrus background. The fine bubbles and a taut, supple palate give way to a long, exceptionally clean finish. Other noteworthy performances include the simpler but still good Brut '21, and the Munazei '23 a pleasant drink, precise like few other ros?s in the region.

○ Pietrafumante Brut Nature M. Cl. '19	♛♛ 8
○ Lacryma Christi del Vesuvio Rosato Munazei '23	♛♛ 3
● Lacryma Christi del Vesuvio Rosso Munazei '23	♛♛ 3
○ Pietrafumante Brut M. Cl. '21	♛♛ 6
○ Vesuvio Caprettone Aryete '22	♛♛ 4
● Vesuvio Piedirosso Fuocoallegro '22	♛♛ 4
○ Lacryma Christi del Vesuvio Bianco Munazei '23	♛ 3
○ Vesuvio Bianco Contradae 61 37 '20	♛♛♛ 4
● Lacryma Christi del Vesuvio Rosso Don Vincenzo Ris. '17	♛♛
○ Pietrafumante Brut M. Cl. '20	♛♛
○ Vesuvio Bianco Contradae 61 37 '21	♛♛

Casebianche

c.da Case Bianche, 8
84076 Torchiara [SA]
(*) +39 0974843244
@ www.casebianche.eu

CELLAR SALES
PRE-BOOKED VISITS
ANNUAL PRODUCTION 35,000 bottles
HECTARES UNDER VINE 5.50
VITICULTURE METHOD Certified Organic
SUSTAINABLE WINERY

Here at Casebianche, Betty Iurio and Pasquale Amitrano transform aglianico, barbera, piedirosso, fiano, trebbiano, and malvasia grapes into expressive wines. The pair left their work as architects in the early aughts to dedicate their lives to winemaking, reviving their family vineyards in Torchiara, Cilento, an area nestled between Monte Stella, the Acquasanta stream, and the Tyrrhenian coast. The wines produced reflect the character of the grape varietals and this unique terroir, as well as the empathetic personality of the producers. Tasting their wines is never a boring experience. Betty and Pasquale, now true experts, deserve credit for their bottle-refermented sparklers. The joyful La Matta, made from fiano grapes, lingers in our hearts with its citron, lime, and freshly cut grass notes; it's a sapid, lively, perfectly unkempt drink, fragrant, and spirited. The Dellemore '21 is also excellent, blending cherries and Mediterranean whiffs on a warm but not heavy profile.

Cautiero

c.da Arbusti
82030 Frasso Telesino [BN]
(*) +39 3387640641
@ www.cautiero.it

CELLAR SALES
ACCOMMODATION
ANNUAL PRODUCTION 18,000 bottles
HECTARES UNDER VINE 4.00
VITICULTURE METHOD Certified Organic

Fulvio Cautiero and Imma Cropano's story is a familiar one in the world of winemaking. Both pursued brilliant careers—Fulvio as an engineer and Imma as a dancer—before the allure of the land became irresistible. Rolling up their sleeves, they began restoring land and vineyards in the Taburno Regional Park. Committed to organic farming in the vineyard, their winemaking practices are as non-invasive as possible. Apple, mint, freshly cut grass, and propolis: the aromatic spectrum of the Fois proves highly original, making for a pleasantly rustic and mouthfilling white. The Fiano Erba Bianca '22 boasts aromas of blooming meadow, ferns, and medicinal herbs. On the palate, a touch of sweet citrus brings out the juicy progression of each sip. The Comm'Era Bianco stands out with its toasted hazelnut and earthy root aromas?a textured, highly food-friendly drink.

● Cilento Rosso Dellemore '21	♥♥ 4
○ La Matta Dosaggio Zero '23	♥♥ 4
● Cilento Aglianico Cupersito Ris. '21	♥♥ 5
○ Cumalè Fiano '23	♥♥ 4
◉ Il Fric '22	♥♥ 4
○ Iscadoro '22	♥♥ 5
● Pashkà '21	♥ 4
● Tondo	♥ 4
● Cilento Rosso Dellemore '20	♥♥♥ 3*
◑ Il Fric '16	♥♥♥ 3*
● Pashka' '17	♥♥♥ 4*
◑ Il Fric '21	♥♥ 4
◑ La Matta Dosaggio Zero '22	♥♥ 4
◑ La Matta Dosaggio Zero '19	♥♥ 4
◑ La Matta Dosaggio Zero '15	♥♥ 3*

○ Comm'Era Bianco	♥♥ 4
○ Erba Bianca Fiano '22	♥♥ 4
○ Fois Falanghina '22	♥♥ 3
● Fois Rosso '20	♥ 3
○ Trois Greco '22	♥ 2
○ Falanghina del Sannio Fois '13	♥♥♥ 2*
○ Eggàs Rosato Frizzante '22	♥♥ 3
○ Erba Bianca '19	♥♥ 2*
○ Fois Falanghina '21	♥♥ 3
○ Fois Falanghina '20	♥♥ 3*
● Fois Rosso '19	♥♥ 3
● Piedirosso '20	♥♥ 3
○ Trois Greco '19	♥♥ 2*
○ Venti di Frasso '20	♥♥ 3
○ Vita Nuova Rosato '22	♥♥ 3

Tenuta Cavalier Pepe

via Santa Vara
83050 Sant'Angelo all'Esca [AV]
(+39 082773766
www.tenutapepe.it

Cenatiempo

via Baldassarre Cossa, 84
80077 Ischia [NA]
(+39 081981107
www.vinicenatiempo.it

CELLAR SALES
PRE-BOOKED VISITS
ACCOMMODATION AND RESTAURANT SERVICE
ANNUAL PRODUCTION 500,000 bottles
HECTARES UNDER VINE 70.00
SUSTAINABLE WINERY

CELLAR SALES
PRE-BOOKED VISITS
ANNUAL PRODUCTION 70,000 bottles
HECTARES UNDER VINE 4.00

In 1998, President Oscar Luigi Scalfaro honored Angelo Pepe with a knighthood for promoting Italian culinary culture in Belgium, where he had opened several prestigious restaurants. Sadly, Angelo passed away last summer, leaving his daughter Milena with the responsibility and honor of running the estate they both cherished. Milena now oversees operations, managing 70 hectares of vineyards spread across the towns of Sant'Angelo all'Esca, Montefusco, Torrioni, and Luogosano. Among the wines tasted, the standout is the Brancato, a Fiano Riserva with alluring tones of white plum mixed with fragrant balsamic and yellow flower sensations. A faint smoky whiff accompanies herbal and lightly almondy notes on the palate. The 2019 Santo Stefano, earthy and driven by medicinal herbs, offers a plump, structured palate. We also appreciated the fruity verve of Grancare, a highly pleasant and sapid Greco.

This Ischian winery had slipped off our radar for a while, but with a solid performance this year, we couldn't resist featuring it in our guide. Founded in 1945 by Francesco Cenatiempo, utilizing 17th-century cellars carved into the Kalimera hillside, the winery now cultivates forastera, biancolella, and piedirosso on four hectares of vineyards. Pasquale's wines are highly expressive, striking a balance between tradition and drinkability. We start off our tastings with the excellent Rosato '23, a wine that features fresh iodized nuances amid notes of white cherry and raspberry. This minerally structured rosé proves flavorful and fragrant, rich in briny nuances and energy. The Kalimera '21, a Biancolella, bridges honey and sea aromas, releasing hints of apricot and pollen, displaying fullness without heaviness on a pleasantly textured palate. The Biancolella '22 is simpler and suppler, less complex. The Màvros, a flowery, close-knit, but juicy red, also performed well.

○ Fiano di Avellino Brancato Ris. '22	♟♟ 5
○ Greco di Tufo Grancare Ris. '22	♟♟ 5
● Irpinia Campi Taurasini Appio '18	♟♟ 8
● Irpinia Campi Taurasini Santo Stefano '19	♟♟ 5
● Taurasi La Loggia del Cavaliere Ris. '16	♟♟ 7
○ Irpinia Coda di Volpe Bianco di Bellona '23	♟ 3
○ Irpinia Falanghina V. Santa Vara '21	♟ 5
○ Fiano di Avellino Brancato Ris. '21	♟♟ 5
○ Fiano di Avellino Brancato Ris. '19	♟♟ 5
○ Greco di Tufo Grancare Ris. '21	♟♟ 5
● Irpinia Campi Taurasini Appio '17	♟♟ 8
● Taurasi La Loggia del Cavaliere Ris. '15	♟♟ 7

○ Rosato '23	♟♟ 3*
○ Ischia Bianco Sup. Lefkòs '22	♟♟ 5
○ Ischia Biancolella '22	♟♟ 4
○ Ischia Biancolella Kalimera '21	♟♟ 6
● Ischia Per' 'e Palummo '22	♟♟ 4
● Màvros '21	♟♟ 5
○ Ischia Biancolella '19	♟♟ 3*
○ Ischia Biancolella '18	♟♟ 3
○ Ischia Biancolella '16	♟♟ 3
○ Ischia Biancolella Kalimera '18	♟♟ 4
○ Ischia Biancolella Kalimera '16	♟♟ 4
○ Ischia Forastera '18	♟♟ 4
○ Ischia Forastera '17	♟♟ 4
○ Ischia Forastera '16	♟♟ 4

Colli di Castelfranci

c.da Braudiano
83040 Castelfranci [AV]
📞 +39 082772392
🌐 www.collidicastelfranci.com

CELLAR SALES
PRE-BOOKED VISITS
ACCOMMODATION AND RESTAURANT SERVICE
ANNUAL PRODUCTION 150,000 bottles
HECTARES UNDER VINE 25.00
SUSTAINABLE WINERY

Luciano Gregorio and Gerardo Colucci helm this producer, named after the village of Castelfranci where the winery is located, in the verdant Alta Irpinia. They started their venture in 2002, focusing on the region's classic wines, particularly aglianico, which they vinify using various techniques (depending on the version). Whites also play a major role in their portfolio, which stands out for its strong connection to the territory and its solid craftsmanship. Few wineries achieve such satisfying results across their entire range. The Paladino Riserva '22 plays on a floral profile of freshly cut hay before an elegant and taut palate marked by its restraint. The smoky, dark Irpinia Aglianico Vadantico '21 displays formidable structure, though its palate escapes tannic grip with its nice trail of sapidity. In the Greco Riserva Vallicelli '22 yellow fruit aromas prevail, sensations that dialog perfectly with acidity and iodized tendencies on the palate.

★Colli di Lapio

c.da Arianiello, 47
83030 Lapio [AV]
📞 +39 0825982184
🌐 www.collidilapio.it

CELLAR SALES
PRE-BOOKED VISITS
ANNUAL PRODUCTION 60,000 bottles
HECTARES UNDER VINE 12.00

Clelia Romano, her husband Angelo, and their children Carmela and Federico cultivate about a dozen hectares of vineyards in Arianiello, a district of Lapio recognized as a cru for Fiano di Avellino. Here at elevations reaching 600 meters, aglianico, greco, and, of course, fiano thrive, giving rise to a small range that directly reflect the winery's philosophy, the territory, and the character of the varietals. The Fiano di Avellino returns to form with a 2023 that sees sunny notes of medlar merge with an elegant citrus profile and flinty nuances. The palate is full, effective, laced with pleasant herbal sensations leading to a minerally accented finish. We also appreciated the Donna Chiara, an Irpinia Campi Taurasini redolent of cherry pulp and ripe strawberries, luscious without being sweet, flavorful, and warm on the finish.

○ Fiano di Avellino Paladino Ris. '22	♟♟ 4
○ Fiano di Avellino Pendino '23	♟♟ 4
○ Greco di Tufo Grotte '23	♟♟ 3
○ Greco di Tufo Vallicelli Ris. '22	♟♟ 4
● Irpinia Aglianico Vadantico '21	♟♟ 4
○ Fiano di Avellino Paladino Ris. '21	♟♟ 4
○ Fiano di Avellino Paladino Ris. '20	♟♟ 4
○ Fiano di Avellino Pendino '22	♟♟ 4
○ Greco di Tufo Grotte '22	♟♟ 3
○ Greco di Tufo Grotte '21	♟♟ 3
○ Greco di Tufo Vallicelli '20	♟♟ 4
● Irpinia Aglianico Vadantico '19	♟♟ 4
● Irpinia Campi Taurasini Vadantico '15	♟♟ 4
● Taurasi Alta Valle '18	♟♟ 7
● Taurasi Alta Valle '17	♟♟ 7

○ Fiano di Avellino '23	♟♟♟ 5
○ Greco di Tufo Alexandros '23	♟♟ 5
● Irpinia Campi Taurasini Donna Chiara '22	♟♟ 4
○ Fiano di Avellino '20	♟♟♟ 4*
○ Fiano di Avellino '19	♟♟♟ 4*
○ Fiano di Avellino '18	♟♟♟ 4*
○ Fiano di Avellino '16	♟♟♟ 4*
○ Fiano di Avellino '15	♟♟♟ 4*
○ Fiano di Avellino '14	♟♟♟ 4*
○ Fiano di Avellino '13	♟♟♟ 4*
○ Fiano di Avellino '10	♟♟♟ 4
○ Fiano di Avellino '09	♟♟♟ 4
○ Fiano di Avellino '08	♟♟♟ 4*
○ Fiano di Avellino '07	♟♟♟ 4
○ Fiano di Avellino '05	♟♟♟ 4
○ Fiano di Avellino '04	♟♟♟ 4

Contrada Salandra

fraz. Coste di Cuma
via Tre Piccioni, 40
80078 Pozzuoli [NA]
📞 +39 0815265258
🌐 www.contradasalandra.it

CELLAR SALES
PRE-BOOKED VISITS
ANNUAL PRODUCTION 20,000 bottles
HECTARES UNDER VINE 4.50

The Phlegraean Fields faces a complicated situation due to volcanic activity that has intensified in recent months. It's here in this challenging yet fascinating area, where underground heat meets the Tyrrhenian coast, that Giuseppe Fortunato operates. Among the black sands of Coste di Cuma, Monte Sant'Angelo, and Monteruscello, Giuseppe crafts wines from falanghina and piedirosso grapes, creating a range that powerfully conveys the voice of this magical terroir. The Piedirosso '21 proves intriguing on the nose, playing on a Mediterranean profile: shrubs, black olives, charcoal, red flowers, black pepper, and aromatic herbs precede a distinctive, layered palate, with subtle tannins leading to a red berry-focused finish. Slightly smoky, with yellow citrus peel and sage aromas, the Falanghina '22 proves elegant and restrained, lean-structured but harmonious.

★Marisa Cuomo

via G. B. Lama, 16/18
84010 Furore [SA]
📞 +39 089830348
🌐 www.marisacuomo.com

CELLAR SALES
PRE-BOOKED VISITS
RESTAURANT SERVICE
ANNUAL PRODUCTION 200,000 bottles
HECTARES UNDER VINE 40.00

Raffaele and Dora have joined their parents, Marisa Cuomo and Andrea Ferraioli, in running the family winery. They've inherited the same energy needed to tackle the numerous challenges of Furore, in the heart of the Amalfi Coast, where production conditions are as extreme as they are captivating. The micro-parcels of land, reclaimed from the rock, host dozens of local varieties, some of which are unknown to most, with diverse characteristics and ripening times, resulting in a diverse range with no weak points. 2023 yielded an exquisite Fiorduva. The nose unmistakably evokes its origins: lemon and citron, orange blossoms, rocks, and aromatic herbs. On the palate, it's enticing, radiant and harmonious, with a crescendo of fruity and menthol tones on the finish. We also appreciated the Furore Rosso Riserva '21, a Mediterranean drink in its black olive and caper sensations, but also fragrant, playing on blackberry and blueberry notes. The sapidity that marks the palate harmonizes nicely with a dense tannic weave.

Wine	Rating
● Campi Flegrei Piedirosso '21	♟♟♟ 5
○ Campi Flegrei Falanghina '22	♟♟ 4
○ Campi Flegrei Falanghina '20	♀♀♀ 4*
● Campi Flegrei Piedirosso '20	♀♀♀ 4*
○ Campi Flegrei Falanghina '21	♀♀ 4
○ Campi Flegrei Falanghina '19	♀♀ 3*
○ Campi Flegrei Falanghina '18	♀♀ 3*
○ Campi Flegrei Falanghina '17	♀♀ 3
○ Campi Flegrei Falanghina '16	♀♀ 3
○ Campi Flegrei Falanghina '15	♀♀ 3
● Campi Flegrei Piedirosso '19	♀♀ 4
● Campi Flegrei Piedirosso '18	♀♀ 3
● Campi Flegrei Piedirosso '17	♀♀ 3
● Campi Flegrei Piedirosso '16	♀♀ 3
● Campi Flegrei Piedirosso '15	♀♀ 3
● Campi Flegrei Piedirosso '13	♀♀ 3*

Wine	Rating
○ Costa d'Amalfi Furore Bianco Fiorduva '23	♟♟♟ 8
○ Costa d'Amalfi Furore Bianco '23	♟♟ 5
● Costa d'Amalfi Furore Rosso '23	♟♟ 5
● Costa d'Amalfi Furore Rosso Ris. '21	♟♟ 6
○ Costa d'Amalfi Ravello Bianco '23	♟♟ 5
◉ Costa d'Amalfi Rosato '23	♟ 5
○ Costa d'Amalfi Furore Bianco Fiorduva '21	♀♀♀ 8
○ Costa d'Amalfi Furore Bianco Fiorduva '20	♀♀♀ 8
○ Costa d'Amalfi Furore Bianco Fiorduva '19	♀♀♀ 7
○ Costa d'Amalfi Furore Bianco Fiorduva '18	♀♀♀ 7
○ Costa d'Amalfi Furore Bianco Fiorduva '17	♀♀♀ 7

D'Ambra - Vini d'Ischia

fraz. Panza
via Mario D'Ambra, 44
80075 Forio [NA]
(+39 081907210
⊚ www.dambravini.com

CELLAR SALES
PRE-BOOKED VISITS
ACCOMMODATION
ANNUAL PRODUCTION 450,000 bottles
HECTARES UNDER VINE 14.00

The D'Ambra family has been instrumental in preserving Ischian viticulture. The winery's history dates back to the late 1800s when Francesco d'Ambra founded it. Much has changed since then: today, Andrea, the fourth generation of the D'Ambra family, runs the estate with the help of his daughters Marina and Sara. Biancolella, forastera, piedirosso, and guarnaccia are the main grape varieties cultivated, along with aglianico and fiano. The vineyards span multiple parcels, totaling just under 15 hectares. The biancolella grapes used in the Tenuta Frassitelli hail from a vineyard at 700 meters above sea level. This white sees linden and acacia flowers overlapping with aromatic herb sensations, like thyme and sage. The palate opens with a lovely white fruit sensation, lengthening with an acidity that brings along an herbal verve. The simpler but equally enjoyable Biancolella '23 is also noteworthy. The easy-drinking Forastera opts for banana and pear aromas.

De Falco Vini

via Figliola
80040 San Sebastiano al Vesuvio [NA]
(+39 0817713755
⊚ www.defalco.it

CELLAR SALES
PRE-BOOKED VISITS
ANNUAL PRODUCTION 220,000 bottles
HECTARES UNDER VINE 58.00

Initially, after World War II, the De Falco family focused on selling bulk wine. In the 1990s, with the arrival of young Gabriele, they decided it was time to start bottling their own, aiming for high quality. Today, in addition to a dozen hectares in the San Sebastiano al Vesuvio area, the De Falcos rely on a series of leased parcels for their diverse range, which includes selections from Vesuvio and other regional areas. We focus primarily on the reds. Lahar, for instance, is a monovarietal Piedirosso characterized by nice aromatic precision, calling up ripe raspberry and red cherry streaked with clear smoky suggestions. In the mouth, silky tannins guide its flavor towards an encore of fruit. The Fiordilava '23 opens on whiffs of aromatic herbs, particularly sage, then shifts towards green citrus. The palate is linear and pleasant, unfolding smoothly. We also appreciated the fragrant Piedirosso '23, a simple but highly enjoyable wine.

○ Ischia Biancolella Tenuta Frassitelli '23	♟♟ 5
○ Ischia Biancolella '23	♟♟ 4
○ Ischia Forastera '23	♟♟ 4
○ Le Ninfe	♟♟ 3
○ Ischia Biancolella Tenuta Frassitelli '12	♟♟♟ 3*
○ Ischia Biancolella Tenuta Frassitelli '21	♟♟ 5
○ Ischia Biancolella Tenuta Frassitelli '18	♟♟ 5
○ Ischia Biancolella Tenuta Frassitelli '17	♟♟ 5
○ Ischia Biancolella Tenuta Frassitelli '14	♟♟ 3*
○ Ischia Biancolella Tenuta Frassitelli '13	♟♟ 3*
○ Ischia Biancolella Tenuta Frassitelli '11	♟♟ 3*
● Ischia Per'e Palummo La Vigna dei Mille Anni '12	♟♟ 5

○ Vesuvio Falanghina Fiordilava '23	♟♟ 4
● Vesuvio Lacryma Christi Rosso '23	♟♟ 3
● Vesuvio Lacryma Christi Rosso Sup. Lahar '23	♟♟ 5
● Vesuvio Piedirosso '23	♟♟ 3
○ Vesuvio Lacryma Christi Bianco '23	♟ 3
○ Vesuvio Lacryma Christi Bianco Sup. Ikon '23	♟ 5
● Vesuvio Piedirosso Pietranera '23	♟ 4
○ Fiano di Avellino '21	♟♟ 3
● Taurasi '19	♟♟ 5
● Vesuvio Lacryma Christi Rosso '22	♟♟ 3
○ Vesuvio Lacryma Christi Bianco Sup. Ikon '22	♟♟ 5
● Vesuvio Lacryma Christi Rosso Sup. Lahar '21	♟♟ 5

CAMPANIA

Laura De Vito

c.da Sauroni
83030 Lapio [AV]
☏ +39 3341494724
✉ www.lauradevito.it

CELLAR SALES
PRE-BOOKED VISITS
ACCOMMODATION
ANNUAL PRODUCTION 25,000 bottles
HECTARES UNDER VINE 10.00
SUSTAINABLE WINERY

We are closely following the work of Laura De Vito at her young winery. This round of tastings confirmed our admiration for the Fiano she's producing at her small Lapio-based estate. The grapes hail from a vineyard of about 10 hectares (dedicated exclusively to fiano), divided into 3 contradas of the prestigious Irpinian town: Arianiello, Verzare, and Saudoni. Each property produces its own version, while the blend of all 3 results in the Elle, a sort of oenological summary of the winery. The Li Sauruni '22 reveals aromas of freshly cut hay and fresh almond, opening to fresh bursts of yellow citrus. On the palate, it combines finesse and elegance with flavor, offering clear citrus notes that echo across a long, smoky finish? it's an energetic drink that unfolds masterfully, playing on mineral complexity and structure. The Elle is also very pleasant, fine, and rich in balsamic details. The Arian? opts for a profile on anise and fennel, coming through relaxed and harmonious on the palate.

○ Fiano di Avellino Arianè '22	♉♉ 6	
○ Fiano di Avellino Elle '22	♉♉ 5	
○ Fiano di Avellino Li Sauruni '22	♉♉ 6	
○ Fiano di Avellino Verzare '22	♉♉ 6	
○ Fiano di Avellino Araniè '19	♀♀ 4	
○ Fiano di Avellino Araniè '18	♀♀ 4	
○ Fiano di Avellino Arianè '20	♀♀ 6	
○ Fiano di Avellino Elle '20	♀♀ 5	
○ Fiano di Avellino Elle '19	♀♀ 4	
○ Fiano di Avellino Elle '18	♀♀ 4	
○ Fiano di Avellino Li Sauruni '20	♀♀ 6	
○ Fiano di Avellino Li Sauruni '19	♀♀ 4	
○ Fiano di Avellino Li Sauruni '18	♀♀ 4	
○ Fiano di Avellino Verzare '19	♀♀ 4	
○ Fiano di Avellino Verzare '18	♀♀ 4	

Masseria Della Porta

fraz. Montaperto
via Luigi della Porta, 20
83038 Montemiletto [AV]
☏ +39 3889274006
✉ www.masseriadellaporta.com

CELLAR SALES
PRE-BOOKED VISITS
ANNUAL PRODUCTION 10,000 bottles
HECTARES UNDER VINE 4.00

Achille Della Porta is as young as his winery. He planted his first hectare of aglianico while still studying Agronomy in 2003. More than 20 years have passed, and his dream of having his own estate has come true; the vineyard has since grown to about 4 hectares in the Montepaerto area, a district of Montemiletto. Achille's wines have a handcrafted style that unmistakably conveys both the character of aglianico and the terroir of this important Irpinian wine center. The Audeno is this year's new addition, replacing the usual Taurasi. This Irpinia Aglianico is crafted from grapes grown in the four estate vineyards, at elevations ranging from 380-420 meters. After aging in third-pass tonneaux and barriques for about a year, the result is a red with balsamic, forest-like nuances, notes of dark fruits, and smoky streaks. Its tannic extraction is textbook, its structure detectable but not overwhelming, all topped off by a warm, pervasive finish.

● Irpinia Aglianico Audeno '21	♉♉♉ 6	
● Taurasi Quattro Cerri '19	♀♀♀ 8	
● Irpinia Aglianico Quattro Cerri '20	♀♀ 4	
● Irpinia Aglianico Quattro Cerri '19	♀♀ 4	
● Irpinia Aglianico Quattro Cerri '18	♀♀ 4	
● Irpinia Aglianico Quattro Cerri '17	♀♀ 4	
● Taurasi Quattro Cerri '18	♀♀ 5	
● Taurasi Quattro Cerri '17	♀♀ 5	

Cantine di Marzo

s.da st.le 371
83010 Tufo [AV]
📞 +39 0825998022
🌐 www.cantinedimarzo.it

The history of Cantine di Marzo is deeply intertwined with that of Tufo and its sulfur mines, which were founded (not by coincidence) by the same family. In 1647, Scipione di Marzo arrived here to escape the plague in Nola. Today, the winery is led by siblings Ferrante and Maria Giovanna Somma, with greco at the heart of production, cultivated in some of the area's best contradas, such as Laure, Serrone, and Ortale. The grapes from these three crus are vinified separately to create three distinct wines. The Serrone Riserva '22 impressed us this year with its aromas of rain-washed stones, fresh hazelnut, and flint. On the palate, it opens with solid mineral structure and citrusy fullness, proving rich and flavorful before a lively, energetic finish. The elegant and taut Ortale '22 leans more towards herbal and green citrus peel sensations. The Laure '22 proves sapid and balsamic. The other wines presented also performed well.

○ Greco di Tufo V. Serrone Ris. '22	🍷🍷🍷	5
○ Greco di Tufo V. Laure Ris. '22	🍷🍷	5
○ Greco di Tufo V. Ortale Ris. '22	🍷🍷	5
○ 1930 Nature M. Cl. '21	🍷🍷	5
○ Fiano di Avellino '23	🍷🍷	4
○ Greco di Tufo '23	🍷🍷	4
● Irpinia Aglianico '20	🍷🍷	4
○ Greco di Tufo '16	🍷🍷🍷	2*
○ Greco di Tufo '21	🍷🍷	3*
○ Greco di Tufo V. Laure '21	🍷🍷	5
○ Greco di Tufo V. Laure Ris. '20	🍷🍷	4
○ Greco di Tufo V. Laure Ris. '19	🍷🍷	4
○ Greco di Tufo V. Ortale Ris. '21	🍷🍷	5
○ Greco di Tufo V. Serrone '21	🍷🍷	5
○ Greco di Tufo V. Serrone Ris. '19	🍷🍷	4

Di Meo

c.da Coccovoni, 1
83050 Salza Irpina [AV]
📞 +39 0825981419
🌐 www.dimeo.it

The winery managed by brothers Roberto and Generoso Di Meo is housed in a charming 18th-century farmhouse, at one time the hunting lodge of the Caracciolo Princes. Active since the 1980s, the producer has expanded from Salza Irpina, a cradle of Fiano di Avellino, to other Irpinian appellations. Hence, their aglianico hails from Montemarano while their greco is cultivated in Santa Paolina and Montefusco. The range presented this year was impeccable, with the Greco and Fiano Riserva, released many years after vintage, standing out. To describe the aromatic layering of the Vittorio Riserva as "complex" would be an understatement. Yellow peach, pollen, helichrysum, white apples, turmeric, and smoky overtones are just some of the sensations noted. All of this translates to a complete palate that harmoniously combines flavor with a fresh, dynamic acidity. The Colle dei Cerri follows the same pattern, being complex, balsamic, and energetic. The pleasantly intriguing Fiano '23 also delivers.

○ Greco di Tufo Vittorio Ris. '10	🍷🍷🍷	8
○ Fiano di Avellino '23	🍷🍷	4
○ Fiano di Avellino Colle dei Cerri Ris. '08	🍷🍷	8
● Aglianico '19	🍷🍷	4
○ Greco di Tufo '23	🍷🍷	4
○ Falanghina '23	🍷	4
○ Fiano di Avellino '22	🍷🍷🍷	4*
○ Fiano di Avellino Alessandra '12	🍷🍷🍷	3*
○ Fiano di Avellino Alessandra Ris. '13	🍷🍷🍷	7
○ Greco di Tufo G '19	🍷🍷🍷	3*
○ Greco di Tufo Vittorio Ris. '08	🍷🍷🍷	3*
● Taurasi Ris. '06	🍷🍷🍷	5
○ Fiano di Avellino '20	🍷🍷	3*
○ Fiano di Avellino F '19	🍷🍷	3*
○ Greco di Tufo '22	🍷🍷	4

Donnachiara

loc. Pietracupa
via Stazione
83030 Montefalcione [AV]
☎ +39 0825977135
⊕ www.donnachiara.com

CELLAR SALES
PRE-BOOKED VISITS
ACCOMMODATION
ANNUAL PRODUCTION 300,000 bottles
HECTARES UNDER VINE 27.00
VITICULTURE METHOD Certified Organic
SUSTAINABLE WINERY

Ilaria Petitto went from lawyer to wine producer when she took over the winery created by her father Umberto. What's more, Ilaria would go on to transform Donnachiara into a major regional player, despite the heavy competition. The grapes come from various parts of Irpinia: aglianico from Torre Le Nocelle, fiano from Montefalcione, and greco from Tufo. The range is technically precise and has improved in recent releases. The Taurasi '21 stands out for its solid structure, austere in its balsamic notes and hints of pencil lead, all complemented by a juicy sensation of fleshy dark fruits. In the mouth it shows nice concentration without losing its dynamism and drive; the tannic component is present but fine-grained, with a tasty, rich finish. The Taurasi Riserva '20 is more mature and full-bodied; the Riserva Aletheia is excellent, with notes of sweet yellow fruit blending with fresh sensations of ripe citrus. The Fiano '23 also proves well crafted.

Dryas

via Toppole, 10
83030 Montefredane [AV]
☎ +39 3472392634
⊕ www.cantinadryas.it

ANNUAL PRODUCTION 10,000 bottles
HECTARES UNDER VINE 2.00

Stefano and Rossella Loffredo started their winery in 2011 with the aim of developing and promoting an important, prestigious varietal: fiano. After all, Montefredane, the nerve center of their operations, is one of the cradles of the grape. Initially, they started with the production of still wines, but would gradually specialize in spumante, for which the winery is now among the region's best. Just a couple of hectares are cultivated, and both Loffredos handle all the operations related to both the vineyard and the winery. We tasted both a Metodo Classico and a Metodo Martinotti, both made from unblended fiano grapes. As we?ve written before, Stefano could teach many Italian sparkling wine producers, even from renowned areas, a thing or two. The Brut '18 showcases a signature note of fresh hazelnut and a vaguely smoky mineral undertone, very characteristic of the region; in the mouth, its bubbles are fine, the palate is fresh, harmonious, and extremely clean. The Brut '23 also stood out.

● Taurasi '21	♟♟♟ 6	○ Brut M. Cl. '18	♟♟ 5
○ Greco di Tufo Aletheia Ris. '23	♟♟ 5	○ Irpinia Fiano Brut '23	♟♟ 3*
● Taurasi Ris. '20	♟♟ 7	○ Brut M. Cl. '16	♟♟ 5
○ Fiano di Avellino Esoterico '23	♟♟ 5	○ Brut M. Cl. '15	♟♟ 5
● Aglianico '16	♟♟♟ 3*	○ Dosaggio Zero M. Cl. '16	♟♟ 5
○ Fiano di Avellino Empatia '18	♟♟♟ 4*	○ Et. Nera M. Cl. '15	♟♟ 5
○ Greco di Tufo '16	♟♟♟ 3*	○ Griseo '19	♟♟ 3
○ Greco di Tufo Aletheia '21	♟♟♟ 5		
○ Greco di Tufo Aletheia Ris. '19	♟♟♟ 5		
● Taurasi '16	♟♟♟ 6		
● Taurasi Ris. '19	♟♟♟ 7		
● Taurasi '19	♟♟ 6		
● Taurasi Ris. '17	♟♟ 7		
● Taurasi Ris. '07	♟♟ 6		

Fappiano

via Napoli, 4bis
82030 San Lorenzello [BN]
☎ +39 00393298241625
✆ www.fappiano.it

★I Favati

p.zza Barone di Donato
83020 Cesinali [AV]
☎ +39 0825666898
✆ www.cantineifavati.it

CELLAR SALES
ANNUAL PRODUCTION 50,000 bottles
HECTARES UNDER VINE 12.00
SUSTAINABLE WINERY

CELLAR SALES
PRE-BOOKED VISITS
ANNUAL PRODUCTION 120,000 bottles
HECTARES UNDER VINE 21.00

San Lorenzello is a small village at the foot of the Matese Massif. Here, for 4 generations, the Fappiano family has been producing wine, but it was only a few years ago that Mario, after earning a degree in Economics and now leading the winery that bears his name, decided to take it seriously. The estate, about 12 hectares, mainly hosts traditional Sannio varieties: aglianico, piedirosso, barbera (or camaiola), fiano, and, of course, falanghina. This was our first time tasting Mario's wines, and we were immediately pleasantly surprised. The entire range impressed, especially the Falanghina '22. Quite golden in color, it opens on tones of dried aromatic herbs and spices, citron peel, and a slight mineral and iodized touch. On the palate, it shows nice fullness and flavor, with a lively saline trail that extends through a finish of aromatic herbs. Two fun and delicious reds were proposed, the floral Barbera '21 and the peppery Piedirosso '21. The clear, plump, firm Fiano '22 also performed well.

In the early 2000s, Rosanna Petrozziello, together with her husband Giancarlo and brother-in-law Piersabino, decided to start a winery: over more than 20 years, I Favati has become one of the benchmark producers in Irpinia. The vineyards, just over 20 hectares, are located on the southern slopes of the Sabato River on calcareous-clay soils at about 450 meters elevation. The range, as solid as ever, is composed of wines with great expressiveness. Usually, their fiano-based wines lead the lineup, but not this year. We found the Taurasi Terzotratto '19 particularly solid, almost paradigmatic, and we couldn?t help but recognize it. Initially austere, it gradually releases mineral sensations of flint, balsamic notes, black currant, and morello cherry. In the mouth, its tannins prove well-extracted, making for a firm and compact structure that never hinders the palate, giving way to brackish sensations across a long progression of flavor. The other wines presented were also excellent.

○ Falanghina del Sannio '22	▼▼▼ 3*
● Sannio Barbera '21	▼▼ 4
○ Sannio Fiano '22	▼▼ 3
● Sannio Piedirosso '21	▼▼ 4

● Taurasi Terzotratto '19	▼▼▼ 8
○ Fiano di Avellino Pietramara '23	▼▼ 6
○ Fiano di Avellino Pietramara Et. Bianca Ris. '21	▼▼ 8
○ Greco di Tufo Terrantica Et. Bianca Ris. '22	▼▼ 5
● Irpinia Campi Taurasini Cretarossa '20	▼▼ 6
● Taurasi Terzotratto Et. Bianca Ris. '18	▼▼ 8
○ Fiano di Avellino Pietramara '21	♀♀♀ 6
○ Fiano di Avellino Pietramara '19	♀♀♀ 5
○ Fiano di Avellino Pietramara '18	♀♀♀ 5
○ Fiano di Avellino Pietramara '17	♀♀♀ 5
○ Fiano di Avellino Pietramara '16	♀♀♀ 5
○ Fiano di Avellino Pietramara Et. Bianca Ris. '18	♀♀♀ 8
○ Fiano di Avellino Pietramara Et. Bianca Ris. '20	♀♀♀ 8

Benito Ferrara

fraz. San Paolo
83010 Tufo [AV]
📞 +39 0825998194
🌐 www.benitoferrara.it

CELLAR SALES
PRE-BOOKED VISITS
ANNUAL PRODUCTION 90,000 bottles
HECTARES UNDER VINE 28.00
SUSTAINABLE WINERY

Some wineries mark the history of the regions where they were founded. When it comes to Greco di Tufo, this honor belongs to the Ferrara family, who debuted in the early 1990s by creating their own winery, after serving as grape suppliers in the past. All this happened in San Paolo, a particularly favorable production area situated in the municipality of Tufo, where most of their current 28 hectares of vineyards are located (there are also parcels in Montemiletto, where aglianico is grown). From the prestigious Vigna Cicogna, one of the first crus identified in the region, comes a Greco '23 redolent of broom, helichrysum, hay, aromatic herbs, and yellow-fleshed fruit. A delicate nuance of fresh hazelnut opens the way to a palate with nice acidic drive. The Sequenzha '23, an elegant fiano, plays on citrus and mineral hints, slightly smoky; the palate is linear and dynamic, featuring nice progression and fullness. But the whole range is solid, including the reds, with both the Taurasi and the Irpinia Aglianico performing well.

○ Fiano di Avellino Sequenzha '23	🍷🍷 5
○ Greco di Tufo V. Cicogna '23	🍷🍷 6
● Irpinia Aglianico V. Quattro Confini '21	🍷🍷 5
● Taurasi V. Quattro Confini '20	🍷🍷 7
○ Greco di Tufo V. Cicogna '15	🍷🍷🍷 4*
○ Greco di Tufo V. Cicogna '14	🍷🍷🍷 4*
○ Greco di Tufo V. Cicogna '13	🍷🍷🍷 5
○ Greco di Tufo V. Cicogna '12	🍷🍷🍷 4*
○ Greco di Tufo V. Cicogna '10	🍷🍷🍷 4
○ Greco di Tufo V. Cicogna '09	🍷🍷🍷 4
○ Fiano d'Avellino Sequenzha '22	🍷🍷 4
○ Greco di Tufo Terra d'Uva '22	🍷🍷 5
○ Greco di Tufo Terra d'Uva '21	🍷🍷 4
○ Greco di Tufo V. Cicogna '22	🍷🍷 6
○ Greco di Tufo V. Cicogna '21	🍷🍷 4
○ Greco di Tufo V. Cicogna '20	🍷🍷 4

★★★Feudi di San Gregorio

loc. Cerza Grossa
83050 Sorbo Serpico [AV]
📞 +39 0825986683
🌐 www.feudi.it

CELLAR SALES
PRE-BOOKED VISITS
RESTAURANT SERVICE
ANNUAL PRODUCTION 3,500,000 bottles
HECTARES UNDER VINE 300.00
VITICULTURE METHOD Certified Organic

When telling the story of Campanian wine, one cannot overlook Feudi di San Gregorio. Founded in 1986, the winery is now in the hands of Antonio Capaldo, who, with the collaboration of Pierpaolo Sirch, has consolidated its role as a benchmark of Italian wine. Production focuses on Irpinia but spans all the region's main appellations. Production is enriched by important parallel projects such as FeudiStudi and the sparkling wine brand Dubl. The Riserva Cutizzi '22 tops our preferences this year due to its superb aromatic precision. Light citrus and cut grass overlap on a slightly smoky background before revealing a clear, elegant palate with a decisive, enticing progression. We were struck by the quality of the Dubl Esse, a 2015 Dosaggio Zero that can go toe-to-toe with Italy's best sparkling wines. The taut and very fine Fiano Riserva Pietracalda is also noteworthy.

○ Greco di Tufo Cutizzi Ris. '22	🍷🍷🍷 4*
○ Dubl Esse Dosaggio Zero M. Cl. '15	🍷🍷 7
○ Fiano di Avellino Pietracalda Ris. '22	🍷🍷 4
○ Dubl Edition II Brut M. Cl.	🍷🍷 5
○ Greco di Tufo '23	🍷🍷 3
● Taurasi '20	🍷🍷 4
⊘ San Greg Rosato '23	🍷 4
● Taurasi Piano di Montevergine '18	🍷 7
○ Greco di Tufo Cutizzi '22	🍷🍷🍷 3*
○ Greco di Tufo Cutizzi '12	🍷🍷🍷 3*
● Taurasi '18	🍷🍷🍷 6
● Taurasi '13	🍷🍷🍷 5
● Taurasi Piano di Montevergine Ris. '14	🍷🍷🍷 6
● Taurasi Piano di Montevergine Ris. '13	🍷🍷🍷 6
● Taurasi Piano di Montevergine Ris. '07	🍷🍷🍷 6

Francesca Fiasco

loc. Campanaro, km 32.100
84055 Felitto [SA]
(《》 +39 3381563628
☞ www.francescafiasco.com

CELLAR SALES
PRE-BOOKED VISITS
ANNUAL PRODUCTION 20,000 bottles
HECTARES UNDER VINE 7.00

We are pleased to once again feature Francesca Fiasco's winery in the main section of our guide. This young woman has taken on the viticultural work begun by her grandfather Luigi around the 1960s, and the vineyard now spans 7 hectares (both owned and leased parcels) in Felitto, where the winery is based, as well as in Castel San Lorenzo and Roccadaspide. The region's traditional grapes are grown: aglianico, aglianicone, barbera, fiano, falanghina, and coda di volpe, along with small amounts of sangiovese and cabernet sauvignon. Theirs is a Mediterranean range with slightly rustic traits, reflecting Francesca's craftsmanship without compromising taste or pleasure. The earthy Ersa '21 boasts crunchy dark fruit; its palate is fleshy and close-knit, yet fragrant and layered with a mineral undertone reminiscent of graphite. In the Principe Diphesa, aromas of crusco pepper, tobacco leaves, and blueberry open the way to a dynamic palate that finishes on notes of bitter orange.

● Ersa '21	♟♟ 4
● Mèrcori '20	♟♟ 8
● Principe Diphesa '20	♟♟ 5
● Difesa '18	♟♟ 5
● Difesa '17	♟♟ 5
● Difesa Rosso '16	♟♟ 5
● Ersa '20	♟♟ 4
● Ersa '19	♟♟ 4
● Ersa Rosso '17	♟♟ 4
○ Lapazio '22	♟♟ 5
○ Lapazio '21	♟♟ 5
● Mèrcori '18	♟♟ 8
● Mèrcori '17	♟♟ 8
● Mèrcuri Rosso '16	♟♟ 8

Fiorentino

c.da Barbassano
83052 Paternopoli [AV]
(《》 +39 082771463
☞ www.fiorentinovini.it

CELLAR SALES
PRE-BOOKED VISITS
ANNUAL PRODUCTION 15,000 bottles
HECTARES UNDER VINE 5.00
SUSTAINABLE WINERY

Gianni Fiorentino's winery is a model of bioarchitecture, constructed entirely from wood. This modern touch complements a long family tradition: it was Gianni's grandfather, Luigi, who purchased the land in Paternopoli after returning from the United States. The vineyard spans five hectares, with aglianico taking center stage. Indeed, the district is one of the most important and prestigious within the Taurasi appellation, where the volcanic soils bring out the best of the varietal. This is evident in the two 2019s tasted this year. The Taurasi sees sensations of medicinal herbs alternate with wild black fruits, with a touch of spice sweetening the aromatic spectrum. A juicy, smooth palate follows, despite its dense tannins, with a balsamic, mouthfilling finish to top things off. The Riserva is also delicious?a sapid, full-bodied, and mineral drink.

● Taurasi '19	♟♟ 5
● Taurasi Ris. '19	♟♟ 6
○ Irpinia Coda di Volpe Zirpoli '23	♟ 4
● Taurasi '15	♟♟♟ 5
● Irpinia Aglianico Celsì '18	♟♟ 3
● Irpinia Aglianico Celsì '16	♟♟ 3
● Irpinia Aglianico Celsì '14	♟♟ 3
○ Irpinia Coda di Volpe Zirpoli '22	♟♟ 4
◉ Irpinia Rosato Flavia '22	♟♟ 3
● Taurasi '16	♟♟ 5
● Taurasi '14	♟♟ 5
● Taurasi Ris. '18	♟♟ 6
● Taurasi Ris. '17	♟♟ 5

★Fontanavecchia
via Fontanavecchia, 7
82030 Torrecuso [BN]
☎ +39 0824876275
⌨ www.fontanavecchia.info

Fonzone
loc. Scorzagalline
83052 Paternopoli [AV]
☎ +39 08271730100
⌨ www.fonzone.it

CELLAR SALES
PRE-BOOKED VISITS
ACCOMMODATION AND RESTAURANT SERVICE
ANNUAL PRODUCTION 175,000 bottles
HECTARES UNDER VINE 20.00

PRE-BOOKED VISITS
ANNUAL PRODUCTION 100,000 bottles
HECTARES UNDER VINE 37.00
SUSTAINABLE WINERY

It's hard to imagine Sannio viticulture without Fontanavecchia and the contributions of the Rillo family. Founded by Orazio in the early 1990s, the winery has been successfully managed by his sons Libero and Giuseppe for some time now. The pair have diligently worked to develop the resources that the territory has to offer, particularly falanghina. Their latest project includes a study of vineyard zoning, leading to the creation of three different versions of their Falanghina Vendemmia Tardiva Libero. The T031 '20 hails from their Torrecuso vineyards, while the B148 '20 comes from Bonea: the former is elegantly citrusy, with a vaguely smoky touch on the finish; the latter has a mineral-structured palate characterized by notable sapidity and tension. You'll find the third, from Foglianise, reviewed in the "Rare Wines" section. Don't underestimate the delicious Falanghina BjondoRe '23, classic in its nuances of hay and green citrus, made delectable by a delicate hint of white peach. On the palate, it's a lively, energetic, and dynamically flavorful drink.

Fonzone draws on three different territories: San Potito Ultra for fiano, Altavilla Irpina and Tufo for greco, and Paternopoli, the winery's base, for aglianico. 37 hectares of vineyards are cultivated by Lorenzo Fonzone Caccese, a surgeon with a passion for wine, according to a strict code of environmental sustainability. The parcels produce excellent grapes that are then vinified in a modern, underground winery perfectly integrated into the landscape. Excellent performance for the Fiano and Greco reserves. The Sequoia '22 features aromas of candied lemon, citron, sage, and basil, accented by a subtle toasty note; on the palate, it proves dynamic and layered, with sweet citrus following through on a sapid background. The Oikos '22 features mountain meadow scents, toasted hazelnut, and green citrus peels; on the palate, it's precise and elegant, driven by an acidic strength that carries its flavor to a long finish. The Fiano '23 also impressed.

○ Falanghina del Sannio Taburno BjondoRe '23	♟♟♟ 3*
○ Falanghina del Sannio Taburno V.T. Libero B148 '20	♟♟ 6
○ Falanghina del Sannio Taburno V.T. Libero T031 '20	♟♟ 6
○ Falanghina del Sannio Taburno V.T. Libero F190 '20	♟♟ 6
● Aglianico del Taburno TabaRosso '20	♟♟ 3
● Sannio Piedirosso '22	♟♟ 3
● Aglianico del Taburno V. Cataratte Ris. '19	♟ 6
● Aglianico del Taburno '18	♟♟♟ 3*
○ Falanghina del Sannio Taburno '20	♟♟♟ 3*
○ Falanghina del Sannio Taburno '19	♟♟♟ 3
○ Falanghina del Sannio Taburno '18	♟♟♟ 3*
○ Falanghina del Sannio Taburno V.T. Libero '19	♟♟♟ 6

○ Fiano di Avellino Sequoia Ris. '22	♟♟ 5
○ Greco di Tufo Oikos Ris. '22	♟♟ 5
○ Fiano di Avellino '23	♟♟ 3
○ Greco di Tufo '23	♟♟ 3
● Irpinia Campi Taurasini Mattodà '20	♟♟ 4
○ Irpinia Falanghina Le Mattine '22	♟♟ 4
● Taurasi Scorzagalline Ris. '19	♟♟ 6
○ Fiano di Avellino '16	♟♟♟ 3*
○ Greco di Tufo '19	♟♟♟ 3*
○ Greco di Tufo '13	♟♟♟ 3*
○ Greco di Tufo Oikos Ris. '21	♟♟♟ 5
○ Fiano di Avellino '21	♟♟ 3*
○ Greco di Tufo '22	♟♟ 3*
○ Greco di Tufo '21	♟♟ 3
○ Greco di Tufo '20	♟♟ 3
● Irpinia Campi Taurasini Mattodà '19	♟♟ 4

Masseria Frattasi

loc. San Biagio
via Guide, 2
82013 Bonea [BN]
(» +39 0824834392
⊕ www.masseriafrattasi.it

★La Guardiense - Janare

c.da Santa Lucia, 104/106
82034 Guardia Sanframondi [BN]
(» +39 0824864034
⊕ www.janare.it

CAMPANIA

CELLAR SALES
PRE-BOOKED VISITS
ANNUAL PRODUCTION 120,000 bottles
HECTARES UNDER VINE 30.00

CELLAR SALES
PRE-BOOKED VISITS
RESTAURANT SERVICE
ANNUAL PRODUCTION 5,500,000 bottles
HECTARES UNDER VINE 1500.00
VITICULTURE METHOD Certified Organic

The Cecere Clemente family has certainly written important chapters in the history of Campania and Sannio's viticulture, with a legacy of winemaking dating back to the late 16th century. This tradition has now been passed down to Pasquale Clemente, who leads Masseria Frattasi today. In his cellar, housed in an ancient building from 1779, he produces a range of local wines, drawing on the vineyards of Bonea, Montesarchio, Tocco Claudio, and Baselice. Among the wines proposed, the Falanghina Bonea stands out for its clear aromatic definition: notes of yellow and green citrus chase hints of aromatic herbs before solidifying into a taut and linear palate, offering drinking pleasure and freshness without ever becoming banal. The Donnalaura is an intense and structured but light late-harvest wine, with lovely fruity suggestions of pear and white peach. The Kapnios features aromas of ripe black fruits and sweet spices, and is quite full-bodied and dense on the palate.

With over 60 years of history, around 1,000 members, 5.5 million bottles annually, and 1,500 hectares of estate land, La Guardiense stands out as one of southern Italy's most important cooperatives. Under careful and forward-looking management, it has risen to the elite of Sannio producers, achieving notable results across various lines, especially their Janare selections. The range covers all Sannio's main traditional grape varieties, with a focus on falanghina and aglianico, as well as sparkling wines. The Falanghina Anima Lavica boasts an excellent aromatic profile with notes of acacia flowers meeting white rose and peach; hay notes refresh the bouquet, leading to an elegant and subtle palate, balanced in flavor and acidity. The Lucchero '20 is an aglianico where wild berries meet rain-soaked earth, with abundant, taut tannins. The mid-palate shows nice fruity pulp and juice; balsamic and spicy on the finish.

○ Falanghina del Sannio Taburno Bonea '23	♟♟♟ 5
○ Chardonnay '23	♟♟ 5
○ Coda di Volpe '23	♟♟ 6
○ Falanghina del Sannio Taburno '23	♟♟ 6
○ Falanghina del Sannio Taburno V.T. Donnalaura '23	♟♟ 6
● Kapnios Aglianico '19	♟♟ 8
○ Falanghina del Sannio Taburno Bonea '20	♟♟♟ 4*
○ Falanghina del Sannio Taburno '22	♟♟ 4
○ Falanghina del Sannio Taburno Bonea '21	♟♟ 4
○ Falanghina del Sannio Taburno V.T. Donnalaura '22	♟♟ 6
○ Falanghina del Sannio Taburno V.T. Donnalaura '21	♟♟ 5
● Kapnios Aglianico '20	♟♟ 8

○ Falanghina del Sannio Janare Anima Lavica '23	♟♟ 3*
○ Falanghina del Sannio Janare Senete '23	♟♟ 3
○ Falanghina del Sannio Mirata '23	♟♟ 2*
○ Janare Anima Lavica Brut	♟♟ 3
● Sannio Aglianico Janare '21	♟♟ 2*
● Sannio Aglianico Janare Lucchero '20	♟♟ 3
○ Sannio Aglianico Rosato Janare Nafris '23	♟♟ 3
○ Falanghina del Sannio Janare Anima Lavica '21	♟♟♟ 3*
○ Falanghina del Sannio Janare Anima Lavica '20	♟♟♟ 3*
○ Falanghina del Sannio Janare Senete '22	♟♟♟ 3*
○ Falanghina del Sannio Janare Senete '19	♟♟♟ 3*

911

Macchie Santa Maria

c.da Caponi
83038 Montemiletto [AV]
📞 +39 0825963476
🌐 www.macchiesantamaria.it

CELLAR SALES
PRE-BOOKED VISITS
ANNUAL PRODUCTION 50,000 bottles
HECTARES UNDER VINE 14.00
SUSTAINABLE WINERY

Founded in 2010, Oreste De Santis's young winery is based in Montemiletto, on the hills overlooking the Calore river valley. Here, aglianico is primarily cultivated, but the 14 hectares of vineyards, which includes both owned and leased plots, are located in some of Irpinia's best areas for wine-growing. Their greco is sourced from Montefusco and Santa Paolina, while their fiano hails from Lapio. The resulting range, which centers on local wines, naturally, has shown consistent qualitative growth in recent years. Once again their entire range put in a strong performance, with peaks of absolute excellence among both their whites and reds. The Contrada Epitaffio '22 is redolent of fresh hazelnut, lemon zest, basil, and smoky tones. Great character on the palate, clear and very flavorful. The Boschi a Lapio is a bit more original, almost earthy, very herbaceous, and nicely expansive. Mediterranean scrub, tobacco leaves, blackberry, and licorice feature in the Taurasi Piana delle Macchie '18, a sapid drink that unfolds superbly.

○ Fiano di Avellino Boschi a Lapio Ris. '22	♟♟ 6
○ Greco di Tufo Contrada Epitaffio Ris. '22	♟♟ 6
● Taurasi Piana Delle Macchie '18	♟♟ 5
○ Greco di Tufo Triarii '23	♟♟ 3
○ Irpinia Rosato Ophelia '23	♟♟ 3
● Taurasi Evocatus Ris. '18	♟♟ 7
● Irpinia Aglianico Optio '19	♟ 3
○ Fiano di Avellino Boschi a Lapio Ris. '21	♟♟ 5
○ Greco di Tufo Contrada Epitaffio Ris. '21	♟♟ 5
○ Greco di Tufo Triarii '22	♟♟ 4
○ Greco di Tufo Triarii '16	♟♟ 3
● Taurasi Evocatus Ris. '11	♟♟ 5

Salvatore Molettieri

c.da Musanni, 19b
83040 Montemarano [AV]
📞 +39 082763722
🌐 www.salvatoremolettieri.com

CELLAR SALES
PRE-BOOKED VISITS
ANNUAL PRODUCTION 67,000 bottles
HECTARES UNDER VINE 15.00

Salvatore Molettieri was among the first of a group of Irpinian winemakers who, after operating as grape suppliers, began creating their own wineries. Today, the estate is run by his sons Giuseppe, Luigi, Paolo, and Giovanni. About 15 hectares feature two standout aglianico crus, Cinque Querce and Ischa Piana, which form a solid base for producing Taurasi wines of great character. Take, for example, the Renonno. Attractive oak and slightly smoky notes meet leather and dried aromatic herbs on the nose; a solid palate follows with close-knit tannins yet to fully integrate. The Riserva Cinque Querce '16 shows more gustatory range, releasing hints of Mediterranean scrub, with toasted notes in the background. On the palate, it's voluminous, with firm structure and freshness on the finish, lending harmony and dynamism. The Cinque Querce '17 opts for notes of chocolate and alcohol-steeped fruit; tannins are abundant, somewhat overpowering.

● Irpinia Aglianico Ischa Piana '20	♟♟ 4
○ Irpinia Coda di Volpe '22	♟♟ 3
○ Irpinia Rosato '22	♟♟ 3
● Taurasi Renonno '18	♟♟ 6
● Taurasi V. Cinque Querce '17	♟♟ 7
● Taurasi V. Cinque Querce Ris. '16	♟♟ 8
● Irpinia Aglianico Cinque Querce '20	♟ 4
● Taurasi Renonno '08	♟♟♟ 5
● Taurasi V. Cinque Querce '13	♟♟♟ 6
● Taurasi V. Cinque Querce '05	♟♟♟ 6
● Taurasi V. Cinque Querce '04	♟♟♟ 6
● Taurasi V. Cinque Querce Ris. '05	♟♟♟ 7
● Taurasi V. Cinque Querce Ris. '04	♟♟♟ 7
○ Greco di Tufo '20	♟♟ 4
● Taurasi Renonno '17	♟♟ 6
● Taurasi V. Cinque Querce '16	♟♟ 7

★★Montevetrano

fraz. Campigliano
via Montevetrano, 3
84099 San Cipriano Picentino [SA]
📞 +39 089882285
🌐 www.montevetrano.it

CELLAR SALES
PRE-BOOKED VISITS
ANNUAL PRODUCTION 60,000 bottles
HECTARES UNDER VINE 5.00

Silvia Imparato's winemaking journey began almost as a hobby in 1991 when she produced the first, very few bottles of Montevetrano. Over the years, San Cipriano Picentino has become a key destination for Campanian wine, thanks to this unique blend of aglianico, merlot, and cabernet sauvignon, which gained worldwide recognition. Today, the legendary wine is joined by two companions: Core Aglianico and Core Bianco, made from greco and fiano grapes. It's not the first time this wine has topped our preferences. This year, it once again proves a superb Mediterranean white. The 2023 combines lime and green grapefruit with white rose and linden, all seasoned with iodized nuances. On the palate, it's supple and nimble, streaked with a fresh herbaceous flavor. Blueberry, blackberry, black currant, and red flower sensations characterize the Core Aglianico '21, a wine whose firm tannic framework proves balanced by nice, fruity pulp. The Montevetrano sees Mediterranean scrub blend with ripe plum. We expect its boisterous tannins to evolve well.

○ Core Bianco '23	♟♟ 4
● Core Aglianico '21	♟♟ 4
● Montevetrano '22	♟♟ 8
○ Core Bianco '20	♟♟♟ 4*
○ Core Bianco '19	♟♟♟ 4
● Montevetrano '20	♟♟♟ 8
● Montevetrano '17	♟♟♟ 8
● Montevetrano '16	♟♟♟ 8
● Montevetrano '14	♟♟♟ 7
● Montevetrano '12	♟♟♟ 7
● Montevetrano '11	♟♟♟ 7
● Montevetrano '10	♟♟♟ 7
● Montevetrano '09	♟♟♟ 7
● Montevetrano '08	♟♟♟ 7
● Montevetrano '07	♟♟♟ 7
● Montevetrano '06	♟♟♟ 7

Mustilli

via Caudina, 10
82019 Sant'Agata de' Goti [BN]
📞 +39 0823718142
🌐 www.mustilli.com

CELLAR SALES
PRE-BOOKED VISITS
ACCOMMODATION AND RESTAURANT SERVICE
ANNUAL PRODUCTION 100,000 bottles
HECTARES UNDER VINE 15.00

The Mustilli name is an important one here in Campania, as the winery is known for its important work in rediscovering and promoting falanghina. It was engineer Leonardo Mustilli who first believed in the variety, bottling an unblended version as early as 1979. Today, his daughters Paola and Anna Chiara manage the 15 hectares of vineyards, producing a reliable and solid range of wines. An outstanding performance from the Falanghina Vigna Segreta '22. The nose reveals an aromatic mosaic of citron and lemons, cut grass and sage, gooseberry and white plum, the prelude to a tonic drink, elegant and fine, reactive and lively, infiltrating and deep. The Artus also impressed with its procession of smoky hints, blueberries, and bramble blackberries, a bouquet echoed on a firm, fleshy, and rhythmic palate. The other wines tasted prove well crafted and faithful to the varietals used.

○ Falanghina del Sannio Sant'Agata dei Goti V. Segreta '22	♟♟♟ 5
○ Falanghina del Sannio '23	♟♟ 3
○ Sannio Greco '23	♟♟ 4
● Sannio Sant'Agata dei Goti Aglianico Cesco di Nece '21	♟♟ 5
● Sannio Sant'Agata dei Goti Piedirosso Artus '21	♟♟ 5
● Sannio Aglianico '22	♟ 3
○ Falanghina del Sannio Sant'Agata dei Goti V. Segreta '18	♟♟♟ 4*
● Sannio Sant'Agata dei Goti Piedirosso Artus '17	♟♟♟ 5
● Sannio Sant'Agata dei Goti Piedirosso Artus '16	♟♟♟ 5
● Sannio Sant'Agata dei Goti Piedirosso Artus '15	♟♟♟ 4*

Cantine Olivella

via Zazzera, 28
80048 Sant'Anastasia [NA]
📞 +39 0815311388
🌐 www.cantineolivella.wine

CELLAR SALES
PRE-BOOKED VISITS
ANNUAL PRODUCTION 110,000 bottles
HECTARES UNDER VINE 15.00
VITICULTURE METHOD Certified Organic
SUSTAINABLE WINERY

Cantine Olivella was founded in 2004 when the three founding partners, Andrea Cozzolino, Ciro Giordano, and Domenico Ceriello, decided to create a winery, betting firmly on the potential of the Vesuvian territory and its grape varieties. The central hub of operations is the winery in Santa Anastasia, at the foot of Monte Somma, in the Vesuvius National Park. The winery is named after the Olivella spring, which also supplied water to the Royal Palace of the Bourbons in Portici. While piedirosso and caprettone are the stars of the vineyard, catalanesca also holds a prominent place, with the winery heavily investing in the varietal. We tasted two versions this year. The Summa '22 reveals aromas of yellow peaches, basil, and Mediterranean scrub, offering a complex aromatic profile with citrus notes on the palate. Similarly, the Kat? is characterized by citrus nuances, with a fragrant and rather taut palate. Among the reds, we enjoyed the Vesuvio Rosso '22, a volcanic and fragrant wine redolent of black stone fruits? dynamic and well-paced.

○ Katà Catalanesca '23	♟♟ 4
○ Summa Catalanesca '22	♟♟ 5
● Vesuvio Rosso '22	♟♟ 6
○ Vesuvio Caprettone Emblema '23	♟ 3
● Vesuvio Lacryma Christi Rosso Lacrimanero '23	♟ 3
☉ Vesuvio Rosato Ereo '23	♟ 4
○ Katà Catalanesca '22	♟♟ 4
○ Katà Catalanesca '19	♟♟ 3
○ Lacryma Christi del Vesuvio Bianco Lacrimabianco '22	♟♟ 3
○ Lacryma Christi del Vesuvio Bianco Lacrimabianco '19	♟♟ 3
○ Vesuvio Caprettone Emblema '22	♟♟ 3
☉ Vesuvio Rosato Ereo '22	♟♟ 4
● Vesuvio Rosso '17	♟♟ 5

Passo delle Tortore

c.da Vertecchia
83030 Pietradefusi [AV]
📞 +39 3355946330
🌐 www.passodelletortore.it

CELLAR SALES
PRE-BOOKED VISITS
ANNUAL PRODUCTION 35,000 bottles
HECTARES UNDER VINE 5.50

A few years ago, we saw potential in Passo delle Tortore and have closely followed its evolution. Year after year, it has proven to be a project dedicated to quality. Based in Pietradefusi, where Irpinia almost gives way to Benevento, Passo delle Tortore was founded by four young entrepreneurs, who availed themselves of a young winemaker with international experience. Their vineyard spans just over five hectares and is dedicated solely to native grapes. This year, only whites were submitted for tasting. The Greco Riserva Le Arcaie di San Pio is detailed in the "Rare Wines" section. Here, we focus on the exciting Le Arcaie: one of the most clear and fragrant Grecos tasted this year. Aromas of rain-washed stones give way to ferns, lemon leaves, and green hazelnut. On the palate, it's lively and energetic, with perfectly balanced acidity and a notable, mineral structure. We don't have space to describe the drive and tension of the Fiano, but we encourage you to seek it out and taste it.

○ Fiano di Avellino Bacio delle Tortore '23	♟♟ 5
○ Greco di Tufo Le Arcaie '23	♟♟ 4
○ Fiano di Avellino Bacio delle Tortore '21	♟♟♟ 4*
○ Greco di Tufo Le Arcaie '20	♟♟♟ 4*
○ Fiano di Avellino Bacio delle Tortore '22	♟♟ 5
○ Fiano di Avellino Bacio delle Tortore '20	♟♟ 4
○ Fiano di Avellino Bacio delle Tortore '19	♟♟ 4
○ Greco di Tufo Le Arcaie '22	♟♟ 4
○ Greco di Tufo Le Arcaie '21	♟♟ 4
○ Greco di Tufo Le Arcaie '19	♟♟ 4
● Irpinia Aglianico Sassoserra '21	♟♟ 4
● Irpinia Campi Taurasini Pietrarubra '19	♟♟ 5
○ Irpinia Falanghina Piano del Cardo '22	♟♟ 4
○ Irpinia Falanghina Piano del Cardo '20	♟♟ 4
○ Irpinia Falanghina Piano del Cardo '19	♟♟ 4

Perillo

c.da Valle, 19
83040 Castelfranci [AV]
(call) +39 082772252
cantinaperillo@libero.it

CELLAR SALES
PRE-BOOKED VISITS
ANNUAL PRODUCTION 20,000 bottles
HECTARES UNDER VINE 5.00

In 1999, Michele Perillo decided to trade in his blue collar for a role as a winemaker, focusing entirely on the small family property. This modest winery quickly gained recognition, becoming a touchstone in the Castelfranci and Montemarano areas. The light clay and limestone soils, century-old pergolas, and the "coda di cavallo" clone of aglianico are the ingredients for austere and long-lived Taurasi wines, which age at length before being released to the market. Today, Michele is not alone in the venture: he is joined by his sons Felice, a winemaker, and Nicola, an agronomist. It's our first time tasting their Irpinia Aglianico, a warm and juicy 2019. However, our main focus is the Taurasi '13. It reveals aromatic layers of humus, undergrowth, resins, dark chocolate, and pipe tobacco. The mystery remains how a wine over 10 years old can still be so vibrant on the palate. We may never know the answer, but we're more than happy to acknowledge it.

• Taurasi '13	♟♟ 8
• Irpinia Aglianico '19	♟♟ 6
• Taurasi Ris. '12	♟♟ 8
• Taurasi '07	♟♟♟ 6
• Taurasi '05	♟♟♟ 4
• Taurasi Ris. '06	♟♟♟ 6
• Taurasi '12	♟♟ 8
• Taurasi '09	♟♟ 6
• Taurasi '08	♟♟ 6
• Taurasi '06	♟♟ 4
• Taurasi '04	♟♟ 4*
• Taurasi '03	♟♟ 5
• Taurasi Ris. '08	♟♟ 6
• Taurasi Ris. '07	♟♟ 6
• Taurasi Ris. '05	♟♟ 5

Ciro Picariello

via Campo di Maio
83010 Summonte [AV]
(call) +39 3478885625
www.ciropicariello.it

CELLAR SALES
PRE-BOOKED VISITS
ACCOMMODATION AND RESTAURANT SERVICE
ANNUAL PRODUCTION 8,000 bottles
HECTARES UNDER VINE 16.00
SUSTAINABLE WINERY

This year marks the 20th anniversary of Ciro Picariello's winery—a relatively short period in the wine world but enough to carve out a significant space in the crowded and competitive Irpinia area. Supported by his wife Rita and children Emma and Bruno, he manages a vineyard that now covers 16 hectares, divided between the Montefredane and Summonte areas, two grand crus for the production of Fiano di Avellino. An unbreakable bond has formed between Ciro Picariello and the fiano grape, thanks to sustainable practices and artisanal expressiveness in the winery. We only tasted the Fiano Ciro 906 '21 and were captivated. This quintessential fiano, almost paradigmatic, releases hay and fresh hazelnut aromas alongside iodine whiffs and smoky tones, sensations that translate to a sapid, taut, clear, and stony palate, lively and vibrant.

○ Fiano di Avellino Ciro 906 '21	♟♟♟ 6
○ Fiano di Avellino '14	♟♟♟ 4*
○ Fiano di Avellino '10	♟♟♟ 3*
○ Fiano di Avellino '21	♟♟ 4
○ Fiano di Avellino '19	♟♟ 4
○ Fiano di Avellino '18	♟♟ 4
○ Fiano di Avellino '17	♟♟ 4
○ Fiano di Avellino '15	♟♟ 4
○ Fiano di Avellino '13	♟♟ 4
○ Fiano di Avellino '11	♟♟ 3*
○ Fiano di Avellino '09	♟♟ 3
○ Fiano di Avellino '07	♟♟ 3*
○ Fiano di Avellino Ciro 906 '20	♟♟ 5
○ Fiano di Avellino Ciro 906 '19	♟♟ 4
○ Fiano di Avellino Ciro 906 '13	♟♟ 4
○ Fiano di Avellino Ciro 906 '12	♟♟ 4

★★Pietracupa
c.da Vadiaperti, 17
83030 Montefredane [AV]
☎ +39 0825607418
pietracupa@email.it

★Rocca del Principe
via Arianiello, 9
83030 Lapio [AV]
☎ +39 08251728013
⊛ www.roccadelprincipe.it

CELLAR SALES
PRE-BOOKED VISITS
ANNUAL PRODUCTION 50,000 bottles
HECTARES UNDER VINE 7.50

CELLAR SALES
PRE-BOOKED VISITS
ANNUAL PRODUCTION 40,000 bottles
HECTARES UNDER VINE 7.00

In 1990, Peppino Loffredo decided to enter the winemaking business, though the winery, which is based in Contrada Vadiaperti, Montefredane, has long been managed his son Sabino, a recognized top producer of Italian whites. Recently, he chose to forgo the DOCG designation for Fiano di Avellino and Greco di Tufo, focusing solely on the fruits of his vineyards in Montefredane and Prata. His aglianico, on the other hand, is cultivated in the prime Campoceraso growing area in Torre Le Nocelle. Unfortunately, there was no standout this year; the wines seemed slightly less precise than usual, perhaps not fully ready and somewhat backward. The Fiano '22 offers an intricate nose, with aromas of freshly cut grass, fresh almond, and white-fleshed fruit. The palate is intense and well-structured but needs more time to fully develop. The same holds for the Greco, with a power that's still a bit restrained. We made note of the deep and layered Taurasi.

Campania, Irpinia, Lapio, Arianiello. It's clear that we're in the heart of Fiano di Avellino wine country, a territory characterized by its mountainous terrain and tense wines, a bit hard at the outset but appreciated by those with patience. Rocca del Principe's story began here in 2004, when Ercole Zarella, his wife Aurelia Fabrizio, and his brother Antonio decided to go independent after years spent as suppliers to other wineries. The seven-hectare property is divided into the Lenze and Monticelli parcels on the west side, Tognano on the northern side, and finally Campore, where they cultivate the grapes for their Taurasi. The excellence of their Tognano is no longer a surprise. Yet every year, we are amazed by how this white manages to combine intensity and elegance, flavor and finesse, dynamic depth, and linear progression. We're convinced that the 2021 still has much to tell and will reveal even more to those patient enough to wait a few years. The Taurasi Aurelia '20 is also worthy of a standing ovation.

○ Fiano '22	♟♟ 5
○ Greco '22	♟♟ 4
● Taurasi '18	♟♟ 6
○ Cupo '10	♟♟♟ 5
○ Fiano '21	♟♟♟ 5
○ Fiano di Avellino '13	♟♟♟ 3*
○ Fiano di Avellino '12	♟♟♟ 3*
○ Greco '20	♟♟♟ 4*
○ Greco '19	♟♟♟ 4*
○ Greco '18	♟♟♟ 4*
○ Greco di Tufo '17	♟♟♟ 3*
○ Greco di Tufo '16	♟♟♟ 3*
○ Greco di Tufo '15	♟♟♟ 3*
○ Greco di Tufo '14	♟♟♟ 3*
○ Greco di Tufo '10	♟♟♟ 3*
● Taurasi '10	♟♟♟ 5

○ Fiano di Avellino Tognano Ris. '21	♟♟♟ 5
● Taurasi Aurelia '20	♟♟ 6
○ Fiano di Avellino '22	♟♟ 5
○ Fiano di Avellino '14	♟♟♟ 3*
○ Fiano di Avellino '13	♟♟♟ 3*
○ Fiano di Avellino '12	♟♟♟ 3*
○ Fiano di Avellino '10	♟♟♟ 3*
○ Fiano di Avellino '08	♟♟♟ 2*
○ Fiano di Avellino '07	♟♟♟ 2*
○ Fiano di Avellino Tognano '18	♟♟♟ 5
○ Fiano di Avellino Tognano '17	♟♟♟ 5
○ Fiano di Avellino Tognano '16	♟♟♟ 5
○ Fiano di Avellino Tognano '15	♟♟♟ 5
○ Fiano di Avellino Tognano Ris. '20	♟♟♟ 5
○ Fiano di Avellino Tognano Ris. '19	♟♟♟ 5

Ettore Sammarco

via Civita, 9
84010 Ravello [SA]
☎ +39 089872774
✆ www.ettoresammarco.it

CELLAR SALES
PRE-BOOKED VISITS
ACCOMMODATION AND RESTAURANT SERVICE
ANNUAL PRODUCTION 50,000 bottles
HECTARES UNDER VINE 15.00

With over 60 years of activity, the winery founded by Ettore Sammarco in 1962 is a historic name on the Amalfi Coast. Based in Ravello, one of the area's most important districts, the vineyard now spans about 15 hectares, some difficult to cultivate due to the terrain's morphology. The estate, which is today led by Bartolo (though under the constant guidance of Ettore), preserves and promotes native grapes like ginestrella, biancazita, biancatenera, per' e' palummo, and olivella through its wines. This year's lineup seemed a bit below expectations. Nevertheless, a fragrant Ravello Bianco Vigna Grotta Piana 2023 stood out. Very intense with fruity aromas of white peach and linden flowers, the palate turns towards green citrus sensations like lime and grapefruit, and aromatic herbs. The very juicy Selva delle Monache '23 also made its mark.

○ Costa d'Amalfi Ravello V. Grotta Piana '23	♀♀ 6
○ Costa d'Amalfi Ravello Bianco Selva delle Monache '23	♀♀ 4
○ Costa d'Amalfi Bianco Terre Saracene '23	♀ 4
⊙ Costa d'Amalfi Ravello Rosato Selva delle Monache '23	♀ 4
⊙ Costa d'Amalfi Rosato Terre Saracene '23	♀ 4
◐ Costa d'Amalfi Ravello Bianco Selva delle Monache '22	♀♀♀ 4*
○ Costa d'Amalfi Ravello Bianco Selva delle Monache '20	♀♀♀ 3*
○ Costa d'Amalfi Ravello Bianco Selva delle Monache '17	♀♀♀ 3*

Tenuta San Francesco

fraz. Corsano
via Sofilciano, 19
84010 Tramonti [SA]
☎ +39 089876434
✆ www.vinitenutasanfrancesco.com

CELLAR SALES
PRE-BOOKED VISITS
ACCOMMODATION
ANNUAL PRODUCTION 50,000 bottles
HECTARES UNDER VINE 16.00

Nestled between cliffs and the rugged Chiunzi Pass gorge, Tenuta San Francesco is a key name in the challenging Tramonti subzone. The winery's 4 founders, Vincenzo D'Avino, Luigi Giordano, Gaetano, and Generoso Bove, were fully aware of the challenge ahead. Though they didn't back down and worked to develop their highly fragmented 16-hectare vineyard, a treasure trove of various grape varieties, including pepella, ginestra, biancazita, biancatenera, aglianico, piedirosso, and tintore, all brilliantly showcased in a consistently impressive range. The Eva '22 is one of the most intriguing wines tasted this year. A blend of falanghina, ginestra, and pepella, all vinified in stainless steel, it boasts a sweet, enticing aromatic profile of linden flowers and white roses, elegant with saline and white fruit nuances, streaked with fine herbal suggestions. On the palate, it harmoniously reveals its flavor, unfolding smoothly thanks to balanced acidity, finishing juicy and sapid.

○ Costa d'Amalfi Bianco Per Eva '22	♀♀ 5
● Costa d'Amalfi Tramonti Rosso '21	♀♀ 3
● È Iss Tintore Prephilloxera '19	♀♀ 6
⊙ Costa d'Amalfi Rosato Ed '23	♀ 3
○ Costa d'Amalfi Tramonti Bianco '23	♀ 3
○ Costa d'Amalfi Bianco Per Eva '13	♀♀♀ 4*
● È Iss Tintore Prephilloxera '16	♀♀♀ 5
○ Costa d'Amalfi Bianco Per Eva '21	♀♀ 5
○ Costa d'Amalfi Bianco Per Eva '20	♀♀ 4
○ Costa d'Amalfi Bianco Per Eva '19	♀♀ 4
○ Costa d'Amalfi Bianco Per Eva '18	♀♀ 4
○ Costa d'Amalfi Tramonti Bianco '22	♀♀ 3
○ Costa d'Amalfi Tramonti Bianco '21	♀♀ 3
● Costa d'Amalfi Tramonti Rosso '20	♀♀ 3
● Costa d'Amalfi Tramonti Rosso '19	♀♀ 3
● È Iss Tintore Prephilloxera '18	♀♀ 6

★San Salvatore 1988

via Dioniso, 12
84050 Giungano [SA]
☎ +39 08281990900
✉ www.sansalvatore1988.it

CELLAR SALES
ACCOMMODATION AND RESTAURANT SERVICE
ANNUAL PRODUCTION 500,000 bottles
HECTARES UNDER VINE 42.00
VITICULTURE METHOD Certified Organic
SUSTAINABLE WINERY

Founded by Giuseppe Pagano, San Salvatore has over 40 hectares of organic vineyards spread across the hills overlooking Paestum, Stio, and Giungano in the Cilento National Park. The estate focuses on wine production but also includes olive groves, orchards, and buffalo farms, and their products are used in Pagano's prestigious hotels and restaurants. Their range, which maintains similarly high standards, is characterized by aromatic whites and richer reds. Due to an unfavorable vintage, the winery decided not to produce the Pian di Stio, one of its flagships. We consoled ourselves with the Calpazio, a fragrant and floral Greco, clean, decisive, smooth, and very pleasant. The Pinot Nero Pino di Stio is intriguing, revealing sweet red fruit sensations alongside balsamic notes and rich nuances. The Aglianico Jungano proves broad and multifaceted?a juicy, Mediterranean wine.

Sanpaolo
Claudio Quarta Vignaiolo

fraz. c.da San Paolo
via Aufieri, 25
83010 Torrioni [AV]
☎ +39 0832704398
✉ www.claudioquarta.it

CELLAR SALES
PRE-BOOKED VISITS
ANNUAL PRODUCTION 250,000 bottles
HECTARES UNDER VINE 20.00
SUSTAINABLE WINERY

Claudio Quarta and his daughter Alessandra offer contemporary-style wines here at Sanpaolo (named after one of Tufo's best areas for cultivating Greco). The project began in 2005 when Claudio left his international biotechnology career to invest in viticulture in Irpinia and Salento. In addition to the vineyards in Tufo and Torrioni, the grapes are also sourced from parcels in Lapio and Candida (fiano) and Taurasi and Castelfranci (aglianico). The Puddinghe '23 showcases an original aromatic profile: very fragrant with fruity sensations of white melon and pear, slightly backgrounding the mineral, smoky component we loved in the previous vintage. The palate is graceful and flavorful, linear in its progression, with a lovely fleshiness that echoes the nose. The Taurasi '18 performs well, with candied cherries, licorice, and a slight toastiness on the nose; the palate features nice tannic extraction.

○ Calpazio Greco '23	▼▼ 4
○ Elea Greco '22	▼▼ 5
● Jungano Aglianico '21	▼▼ 4
● Pino di Stio Pinot Nero '21	▼▼ 5
○ Trentenare '22	▼▼ 4
◉ Vetere Rosato '23	▼▼ 3
○ Pian di Stio '22	♀♀♀ 5
○ Pian di Stio '21	♀♀♀ 5
○ Pian di Stio '20	♀♀♀ 5
○ Pian di Stio '19	♀♀♀ 5
○ Pian di Stio '18	♀♀♀ 4*
○ Pian di Stio '17	♀♀♀ 4*
○ Pian di Stio '14	♀♀♀ 4*
○ Pian di Stio '13	♀♀♀ 4*
○ Trentenare '16	♀♀♀ 3*
○ Trentenare '15	♀♀♀ 3*

○ Greco di Tufo Puddinghe '23	▼▼ 5
○ Fiano di Avellino '23	▼▼ 3
○ Greco di Tufo '23	▼▼ 3
◉ Jacarando Pas Dosé Rosé M. Cl.	▼▼ 4
● Taurasi '18	▼▼ 5
○ Falanghina '23	▼ 3
○ Jacarando Blanc de Blancs Pas Dosé M. Cl.	▼ 4
○ Greco di Tufo Claudio Quarta '13	♀♀♀ 6
○ Greco di Tufo Claudio Quarta '12	♀♀♀ 6
○ Greco di Tufo Claudio Quarta Special Edition '19	♀♀♀ 4*
○ Greco di Tufo Puddinghe '22	♀♀♀ 5
○ Fiano di Avellino '22	♀♀ 3
○ Fiano di Avellino '21	♀♀ 3*
○ Greco di Tufo '22	♀♀ 3
● Taurasi '16	♀♀ 5

Sclavia

loc. Marianello
via Case Sparse
81040 Liberi [CE]
(☎ +39 3357406773
⊕ www.sclavia.com

CELLAR SALES
PRE-BOOKED VISITS
ANNUAL PRODUCTION 30,000 bottles
HECTARES UNDER VINE 17.00
VITICULTURE METHOD Certified Organic
SUSTAINABLE WINERY

Situated in the province of Caserta, nestled between the Middle Volturno Valley and the Trebulani Mountains, the small town of Liberi was once known as Sclavia. Hence the name chosen by Andrea Granito, a doctor by profession, for the winery that he founded here, in the Marianello area, in the early 2000s. Over the years, the estate has expanded, with major acquisitions of new, prestigious plots. Today, some 17 hectares are cultivated organically, primarily with rediscovered native varieties of Caserta, especially pallagrello bianco and nero. Thanks in part to Lucia Ferrara and Maurizio Alongi, Andrea submitted a solid range this year, led by the Lucia a Monticelli. This unblended pallagrello nero opens with a balsamic profile streaked with hints of licorice, which meld into a brackish note before transitioning to black fruits?morello cherry and blueberry. On the palate, it's quite elegant, featuring a close-knit but velvety tannic structure. The Montecardillo also impresses, with cherry and Mediterranean scrub on the nose, and a sapid, compact palate.

● Lucia a Monticelli '21	♟♟	5
● Montecardillo Pallagrello Nero '22	♟♟	3
○ Calù Pallagrello Bianco '23	♟	4
○ Calù Pallagrello Bianco '22	♟♟	4
○ Calù Pallagrello Bianco '21	♟♟	3
○ Calù Pallagrello Bianco '20	♟♟	3
○ Calù Pallagrello Bianco '18	♟♟	3
○ Calù Pallagrello Bianco '17	♟♟	3*
● Casavecchia di Pontelatone Liberi '15	♟♟	5
● Granito '19	♟♟	3
● Lucia a Monticelli '20	♟♟	5
● Lucia a Monticelli '19	♟♟	5
● Montecardillo Pallagrello Nero '20	♟♟	3
● Pallagrello Nero Montecardillo '19	♟♟	3
◐ Sciròcco Rosato '21	♟♟	3
◐ Sciròcco Rosato '20	♟♟	3

Tenuta Scuotto

c.da Campomarino, 2/3
83030 Lapio [AV]
(☎ +39 08251851965
⊕ www.tenutascuotto.it

CELLAR SALES
PRE-BOOKED VISITS
ANNUAL PRODUCTION 70,000 bottles
HECTARES UNDER VINE 10.00

After achieving success as an entrepreneur in the graphic design industry, Eduardo Scotto decided in 2009 to invest in a long-held passion by purchasing a wine estate. Today, he is joined by his son Adolfo, and together they care for a vineyard of about 10 hectares in Campomarino di Lapio, one of 2 municipalities where both Taurasi and Fiano di Avellino can be produced. Indeed these 2 wines are the focus of their range, though the estate also produces other traditional classics using greco and falanghina grapes. Oi N? is a sunny, pervasive monovarietal fiano. On the nose it offers up aromas of orange blossom, freshly cut grass, chamomile, pollen, and yellow peach. The palate begins with a soft attack that avoids sweetness, gradually unfolding warmth over a fragrant trail of ripe citrus. The Fiano '23 plays on aromatic notes of yellow-fleshed fruits and herbs; on the palate, lemon and a nicely calibrated herbaceous sensation make their encore. The Taurasi '20 showcases chocolate and ripe blackberry sensations on a soft, alluring palate.

○ Fiano di Avellino '23	♟♟	4
○ Greco di Tufo '23	♟♟	3
○ Oi Nì '21	♟♟	5
● Taurasi '20	♟♟	6
○ Fiano di Avellino '21	♟♟♟	3*
○ Fiano di Avellino '20	♟♟♟	3*
○ Fiano di Avellino '19	♟♟♟	3*
○ Fiano di Avellino '22	♟♟	4
○ Fiano di Avellino '18	♟♟	3*
○ Greco di Tufo '17	♟♟	3*
○ Greco di Tufo '16	♟♟	3*
○ Greco di Tufo Kuris Ris. '21	♟♟	5
○ Oi Nì '20	♟♟	5
○ Oi Nì '19	♟♟	5
● Taurasi '19	♟♟	5
● Taurasi '18	♟♟	5

CAMPANIA

919

La Sibilla

fraz. Baia
via Ottaviano Augusto, 19
80070 Bacoli [NA]
☎ +39 0818688778
✉ www.sibillavini.com

CELLAR SALES
PRE-BOOKED VISITS
ANNUAL PRODUCTION 70,000 bottles
HECTARES UNDER VINE 9.50
SUSTAINABLE WINERY

Vincenzo, Salvatore, and Mattia carry forward the winery created by their father Luigi and mother Restituta in 1997. It's a venture deeply tied to the Phlegraean fields (as the name, which celebrates Virgil's Cumaean Sibyl, suggests). Indeed, Sibilla has become a cornerstone of the region thanks to its uncommon ability to combine the untamed character of the terroir—volcanic soil composed of ash and lapilli, proximity to the sea and the presence of many ungrafted vines—with a clear, juicy style, especially their premium selections. The Vigna Madre truly represents the Phlegraean fields: the volcanic influence translates into sensations of burnt embers and graphite, which, when combined with the grape's trademark floral and spicy notes , create an intriguing and fascinating olfactory layering. The palate then looks to the Tyrrhenian coast for a briny touch that challenges its fine, flavorful tannins. The finish surprises with the juiciness of wild black berries.

● Campi Flegrei Piedirosso V. Madre '22	▼▼▼ 5
● Campi Flegrei Piedirosso '23	▼▼ 3*
○ Campi Flegrei Falanghina '23	▼▼ 3
○ Campi Flegrei Falanghina Cruna deLago '22	▼▼ 5
● Marsiliano '20	▼▼ 5
○ Domus Giulii Falanghina '22	▼ 5
○ Campi Flegrei Falanghina '13	♀♀♀ 2*
○ Campi Flegrei Falanghina Cruna deLago '19	♀♀♀ 5
○ Campi Flegrei Falanghina Cruna deLago '18	♀♀♀ 5
○ Campi Flegrei Falanghina Cruna deLago '15	♀♀♀ 4*
○ Campi Flegrei Falanghina '22	♀♀ 3*
● Campi Flegrei Piedirosso V. Madre '21	♀♀ 5

Tenuta del Meriggio

c.da Serra, 79/81a
83038 Montemiletto [AV]
☎ +39 0825962282
✉ www.tenutadelmeriggio.it

CELLAR SALES
PRE-BOOKED VISITS
ANNUAL PRODUCTION 80,000 bottles
HECTARES UNDER VINE 23.00
SUSTAINABLE WINERY

Founded by Bruno Pizza and Nunzia Guerriero in 2010, Tenuta del Meriggio is, like many other Irpinian wineries, a composite puzzle of vineyards. To produce the solid range that the producer has accustomed us to, they source the grapes from some of the most prestigious municipalities in the province's main appellations. Thus their aglianico is cultivated in the ridge of Serra di Montemiletto (their production headquarters), Paternopoli, Taurasi and Pietradefusi. Their greco is grown in Santa Paolina and Tufo, and their fiano comes from Montefalcione and Candida. The lineup of wines tasted once again demonstrates the extremely high level of quality achieved. The Colle delle Ginestre Riserva '22 stands out. It's a fiano with pronounced sensations of mountain meadow, flint, green citrus, anise, and fresh almond, suggestions that flow into a palate of extreme clarity, taut and vibrant, with a solid mineral structure. The Colle dei Lauri Riserva '20 is also delicious?rousing and powerful, energetic, radiant, and sapid.

○ Fiano di Avellino Colle delle Ginestre Ris. '22	▼▼▼ 5
○ Greco di Tufo Colle dei Lauri Ris. '20	▼▼ 5
○ Fiano di Avellino '22	▼▼ 4
○ Greco di Tufo '22	▼▼ 4
● Taurasi '18	▼▼ 5
○ Irpinia Coda di Volpe '23	▼ 3
○ Fiano di Avellino '17	♀♀♀ 3*
○ Fiano di Avellino '21	♀♀ 3
○ Fiano di Avellino '20	♀♀ 3*
○ Fiano di Avellino Colle delle Ginestre Ris. '19	♀♀ 5
○ Greco di Tufo '21	♀♀ 3
○ Greco di Tufo '20	♀♀ 3*
○ Greco di Tufo Colle dei Lauri Ris. '21	♀♀ 5
● Irpinia Aglianico '17	♀♀ 3

CAMPANIA

★Terre Stregate

loc. Santa Lucia
82034 Guardia Sanframondi [BN]
📞 +39 0824817857
🌐 www.terrestregate.it

CELLAR SALES
PRE-BOOKED VISITS
ANNUAL PRODUCTION 140,000 bottles
HECTARES UNDER VINE 25.00

Terre Stregate was founded in 2004 when Armando Iacobucci, determined to revive a time-honored family tradition, decided to make wine-growing part of the estate's activities (alongside olive oil). He restored the cellar that belonged to his grandfather and formally established the winery, now led by his children Carlo, who oversees the vineyard, and Filomena, who manages the commercial side. The vineyards are located among the gentle hills overlooking the Calore River, between the Telesina Valley and the Matese foothills, in one of Sannio Beneventano's most renowned production areas, between Guardia Sanframondi, Castelvenere, and Puglianello. The Falanghina Svelato remains the driving force behind the winery's lineup, which is solid and convincing across both whites and reds. It needs some time in the class before fully expressing itself, revealing a bouquet of clear herbaceous sensations, a slightly almond-like touch, and fresh citrus streaks. The palate is straightforward but not trivial?juicy, fleshy, and marked by a refreshing acidity. The full-bodied Arcano Riserva '18 also caught our attention.

○ Falanghina del Sannio Svelato '23	♟♟♟	3*
○ Cara Cara Falanghina '19	♟♟	6
● Sannio Aglianico Arcano Ris. '18	♟♟	4
○ Sannio Greco Aurora '23	♟♟	3
○ Trama Falanghina '23	♟♟	3
● Idillio Aglianico '22	♟	3
○ Sannio Fiano Genius Loci '23	♟	3
○ Falanghina del Sannio Svelato '22	♟♟♟	3*
○ Falanghina del Sannio Svelato '21	♟♟♟	3*
○ Falanghina del Sannio Svelato '20	♟♟♟	3*
○ Falanghina del Sannio Svelato '19	♟♟♟	3*
○ Falanghina del Sannio Svelato '18	♟♟♟	3*
○ Falanghina del Sannio Svelato '17	♟♟♟	2*
○ Falanghina del Sannio Svelato '16	♟♟♟	2*
○ Falanghina del Sannio Svelato '15	♟♟♟	2*
● Falanghina del Sannio Svelato '14	♟♟♟	2*

★Villa Matilde Avallone

s.da st.le Domitiana, 18
81030 Cellole [CE]
📞 +39 0823932088
🌐 www.villamatilde.it

CELLAR SALES
PRE-BOOKED VISITS
ACCOMMODATION AND RESTAURANT SERVICE
ANNUAL PRODUCTION 700,000 bottles
HECTARES UNDER VINE 130.00
SUSTAINABLE WINERY

Once praised by the poet Horace, the territory of Falerno lives on, revised and improved, in the range offered by Villa Matilde Avallone. The project, founded by Francesco Paolo Avallone in the 1960s in an area that the Romans called "ager falernus" (hence the name), has grown over time. The vineyards in Cellole and Sessa Aurunca have been joined by properties in Sannio Beneventano and Irpinia, where the wines for their Pietrafusa line are produced. Today, the estate, which now boasts 130 hectares of vineyards, is carried on by Maria Ida and Salvatore, the children of Francesco Paolo. Their Tenuta di Pietrafusa spawned a Fiano Montelapio that's generous in its aromas of wildflowers, lemon flesh, and fresh almond. A luscious hint of white peach opens the way to a substantive palate with excellent gustatory clarity. The Falerno Vigna Caracci also delivers: citron, peach, hay, sweet spices?an intense yet smooth drink, still very fresh and taut. The Mata, a Metodo Classico of superb cleanness, should not be underestimated.

○ Falerno del Massico Bianco V. Caracci '21	♟♟	7
○ Fiano di Avellino Montelapio '23	♟♟	4
○ Greco di Tufo Daltavilla '23	♟♟	4
○ Mata Cuvée de la Famille Extra Brut M. Cl.	♟♟	5
○ Sinuessa Falanghina '23	♟♟	3
○ Falerno del Massico Bianco Colle Castrese '23	♟	4
● Roccaleoni Aglianico '21	♟	3
○ Falerno del Massico Bianco V. Caracci '08	♟♟♟	3
○ Falerno del Massico Bianco V. Caracci '05	♟♟♟	3
● Falerno del Massico Camarato '05	♟♟♟	6
● Falerno del Massico Camarato '04	♟♟♟	5
○ Greco di Tufo Daltavilla '22	♟♟♟	3*

Villa Raiano

loc. Cerreto
via Bosco Satrano, 1
83020 San Michele di Serino [AV]
📞 +39 0825595663
🌐 www.villaraiano.com

CELLAR SALES
PRE-BOOKED VISITS
RESTAURANT SERVICE
ANNUAL PRODUCTION 270,000 bottles
HECTARES UNDER VINE 27.00
VITICULTURE METHOD Certified Organic

Villa Raiano takes its name from an ancient hamlet in the municipality of Serino, where the family's olive oil business once stood. In 1996, Sabino and Simone Basso founded the winery, deciding in 2009 to move the entire cellar to San Michele di Serino, in a dominant position overlooking the Sabato River valley. Today, their children Federico and Brunella have joined the winery. Together with their parents, they manage a 27-hectare estate in some of Irpinia's best growing areas. The grapes for the Alimata come from Montefredane. The 2022 showcases a trademark smoky note perfectly integrated with an elegant floral and herbaceous sensation; on the palate, a fresh balsamic suggestion intertwines with a solid mineral structure, before giving way to a long, deep finish. The Costa Baiano is one of the region's most precise reds?taut, rich in rocky, mineral sensations, sapid, juicy, and energetic. The Greco Ponte dei Santi proves flavoursome and powerful. The other wines submitted also performed well.

Vinosia

c.da Nocelleto
83052 Paternopoli [AV]
📞 +39 082771754
🌐 www.vinosia.it

CELLAR SALES
PRE-BOOKED VISITS
RESTAURANT SERVICE
ANNUAL PRODUCTION 800,000 bottles
HECTARES UNDER VINE 50.00
VITICULTURE METHOD Certified Organic
SUSTAINABLE WINERY

In 2004, Luciano Ercolino founded his winery in Paternopoli, building on a long family heritage. Located in one of Irpinia's most renowned and historic production zones, his 50 hectares are cultivated with native varieties, fiano, greco, and aglianico. These form the solid foundation for a project aimed at shining a light on Irpinian winemaking traditions interpreted through a contemporary lens. As seen in the Fiano di Avellino Le Grade '23: lovely herbaceous sensations, wildflowers, white peach, basil?an aromatic profile that reverberates in a highly flavorful, precise, harmonious palate where everything is in its right place. The Greco L'Ariella follows a similar pattern: lemon pulp, rain-washed stone, fresh hazelnut, flint nuances, and laurel overlap on a lively, sapid, and energetic palate. In terms of their reds, we enjoyed the juicy San Michele '20: ripe red fruit, sweet spicy notes, dark chocolate; an orderly palate, fine tannins.

○ Fiano di Avellino Alimata '22	🍷🍷🍷 5
○ Greco di Tufo Ponte dei Santi '22	🍷🍷 5
● Irpinia Campi Taurasini Costa Baiano '20	🍷🍷 4
○ Fiano di Avellino '23	🍷🍷 4
○ Greco di Tufo '23	🍷🍷 4
● Taurasi '19	🍷🍷 5
○ Fiano di Avellino Alimata '21	♀♀♀ 5
○ Fiano di Avellino Alimata '18	♀♀♀ 5
○ Fiano di Avellino Alimata '15	♀♀♀ 4*
○ Fiano di Avellino Alimata '10	♀♀♀ 4
○ Fiano di Avellino Bosco Satrano '17	♀♀♀ 4*
○ Fiano di Avellino Ventidue '20	♀♀♀ 5
○ Fiano di Avellino Ventidue '16	♀♀♀ 4*
○ Fiano di Avellino Ventidue '13	♀♀♀ 4*

○ Fiano di Avellino Le Grade '23	🍷🍷🍷 4*
○ Greco di Tufo L'Ariella '23	🍷🍷 4
● Irpinia Campi Taurasini San Michele '20	🍷🍷 4
○ Irpinia Falanghina Fontana della Loggia '23	🍷🍷 3
● Taurasi Rajamagra Ris. '17	🍷 6
○ Fiano di Avellino Le Grade '22	♀♀♀ 4*
○ Fiano di Avellino Le Grade '21	♀♀ 4
○ Fiano di Avellino Le Grade '15	♀♀ 3
○ Greco di Tufo L'Ariella '22	♀♀ 4
○ Greco di Tufo L'Ariella '21	♀♀ 4
○ Greco di Tufo L'Ariella '15	♀♀ 3
● Irpinia Aglianico Sesto a Quinconce '12	♀♀ 8
● Taurasi Santandrea '17	♀♀ 5
● Taurasi Santandrea '16	♀♀ 5

OTHER WINERIES

Cantine Barone

via Giardino, 2
84070 Rutino [SA]
+39 0974830463
www.cantinebarone.it

CELLAR SALES
PRE-BOOKED VISITS
ACCOMMODATION
ANNUAL PRODUCTION 100,000 bottles
HECTARES UNDER VINE 16.00
VITICULTURE METHOD Certified Organic

● Cilento Aglianico Pietralena '21	🍷🍷 4
○ Cilento Fiano Mater '20	🍷🍷 4
● Cilento Aglianico Miles Ris. '20	🍷 5
○ Cilento Fiano Vignolella '22	🍷 3

Cantina dei Monaci

fraz. Santa Lucia, 266
83030 Santa Paolina [AV]
+39 0825964350
www.cantinadeimonaci.it

CELLAR SALES
PRE-BOOKED VISITS
ACCOMMODATION
ANNUAL PRODUCTION 10,000 bottles
HECTARES UNDER VINE 6.50
SUSTAINABLE WINERY

○ Greco di Tufo '23	🍷🍷 4
○ Greco di Tufo Decimo Sesto Ris. '22	🍷🍷 5
● Irpinia Aglianico Santa Lucia '20	🍷🍷 5

Cantina di Lisandro

fraz. Squille
s.da prov.le 325, 30
81100 Castel Campagnano [CE]
+39 0823867228
www.cantinadilisandro.it

CELLAR SALES
PRE-BOOKED VISITS
ACCOMMODATION AND RESTAURANT SERVICE
ANNUAL PRODUCTION 75,000 bottles
HECTARES UNDER VINE 12.00
VITICULTURE METHOD Certified Organic
SUSTAINABLE WINERY

● Cimmarino Casavecchia '21	🍷🍷 4
○ Lancella Pallagrello Bianco '23	🍷🍷 3

Cantine del Mare

via Cappella IV, trav. 6
80070 Monte di Procida [NA]
+39 0815233040
www.cantinedelmare.it

CELLAR SALES
PRE-BOOKED VISITS
ANNUAL PRODUCTION 45,000 bottles
HECTARES UNDER VINE 11.00

○ Campi Flegrei Falanghina Luce Flegrea '23	🍷🍷 4
● Campi Flegrei Piedirosso '21	🍷🍷 4
● Campi Flegrei Piedirosso Terrazze Romane '21	🍷🍷 5

Casa di Baal

fraz. Macchia
via Tiziano, 14
84096 Montecorvino Rovella [SA]
+39 089981143
www.casadibaal.it

CELLAR SALES
PRE-BOOKED VISITS
ANNUAL PRODUCTION 28,000 bottles
HECTARES UNDER VINE 5.00
VITICULTURE METHOD Certified Organic
SUSTAINABLE WINERY

○ Bianco di Baal '23	🍷🍷 4
○ Fiano di Baal '22	🍷🍷 4
○ Il Tocco di Baal '23	🍷🍷 4
○ La Mossa di Baal '23	🍷🍷 4

Cantine Cennerazzo

c.da Casale Bosco, 10
83010 Torrioni [AV]
+39 3395955515
www.cantinecennerazzo.com

CELLAR SALES
PRE-BOOKED VISITS
ANNUAL PRODUCTION 9,000 bottles
HECTARES UNDER VINE 4.00

○ Greco di Tufo Sphera '21	🍷🍷 4
○ Audere Pas Dosé M. Cl. '16	🍷🍷 6

OTHER WINERIES

Donna Elvira

loc. Grottoni
c.da Isca delle Noci
83038 Montemiletto [AV]
+39 3282988289
www.donnaelvira.com

CELLAR SALES
ANNUAL PRODUCTION 40,000 bottles
HECTARES UNDER VINE 9.50
SUSTAINABLE WINERY

- ○ Fiano di Avellino Fink '21 🍷🍷 7
- ○ Greco di Tufo Aegidius '21 🍷🍷 7
- ● Irpinia Campi Taurasini Entonos '19 🍷🍷 6
- ○ Irpinia Falanghina Fringilla '21 🍷🍷 6

Guerritore

loc. Nocelleto
84081 Baronissi [SA]
+39 0892880445
info@viniguerritore.it

CELLAR SALES
PRE-BOOKED VISITS
ACCOMMODATION AND RESTAURANT SERVICE
ANNUAL PRODUCTION 18,000 bottles
HECTARES UNDER VINE 5.00
SUSTAINABLE WINERY

- ○ Acquamela Fiano '22 🍷🍷 5
- ● Cariti '21 🍷🍷 6
- ● Fusara Aglianico '21 🍷 5

Tenuta Madre

via Stazione, area industriale
83010 Tufo [AV]
+39 3338008884
www.tenutamadre.it

CELLAR SALES
PRE-BOOKED VISITS
ACCOMMODATION
ANNUAL PRODUCTION 13,000 bottles
HECTARES UNDER VINE 4.50
SUSTAINABLE WINERY

- ● Taurasi V. Carrani '20 🍷🍷 6
- ○ Fiano di Avellino I Sognatori '22 🍷 5

Raffaele Guastaferro

via A. Gramsci, 2
83030 Taurasi [AV]
+39 3341551543
info@guastaferro.it

CELLAR SALES
ANNUAL PRODUCTION 10,000 bottles
HECTARES UNDER VINE 7.00

- ● Irpinia Aglianico Memini '20 🍷🍷 4
- ● Taurasi Primum '18 🍷🍷 8

Antonio Iovino

via San Gennaro Agnano, 63
80078 Pozzuoli [NA]
+39 0815206719
www.vitivinicolaiovano.com

CELLAR SALES
ANNUAL PRODUCTION 19,000 bottles
HECTARES UNDER VINE 3.00

- ● Campi Flegrei Piedirosso Gruccione '22 🍷🍷 3
- ● Campi Flegrei Piedirosso V. Solfatara '21 🍷🍷 5
- ○ Campi Flegrei Falanghina Grande Farnia '22 🍷 3
- ○ Campi Flegrei Falanghina V. Solfatara '21 🍷 5

Salvatore Martusciello

c.so della Repubblica, 138
80078 Pozzuoli [NA]
+39 3497896111
www.salvatoremartusciello.it

PRE-BOOKED VISITS
ANNUAL PRODUCTION 70,000 bottles
HECTARES UNDER VINE 2.00

- ○ Aversa Asprinio Brut Trentapioli 🍷🍷 4
- ● Campi Flegrei Piedirosso Settevulcani '23 🍷🍷 3
- ● Penisola Sorrentina Gragnano Ottouve '23 🍷🍷 3
- ● Penisola Sorrentina Lettere Ottouve '23 🍷🍷 4

OTHER WINERIES

Monserrato 1973

c.da La Francesca
82100 Benevento
☎ +39 0824565041
✹ www.monserrato1973.it

CELLAR SALES
PRE-BOOKED VISITS
ACCOMMODATION
ANNUAL PRODUCTION 24,000 bottles
HECTARES UNDER VINE 13.00
VITICULTURE METHOD Certified Organic

● Barbera '22	♟♟ 3
○ Murate di Sopra '23	♟♟ 4
● Rintocco '22	♟♟ 3
○ Scuotiterra Rosato Frizzante '23	♟♟ 3

Fattoria La Rivolta

c.da Rivolta
82030 Torrecuso [BN]
☎ +39 0824872921
✹ www.fattorialarivolta.com

CELLAR SALES
PRE-BOOKED VISITS
ACCOMMODATION
ANNUAL PRODUCTION 230,000 bottles
HECTARES UNDER VINE 30.00
VITICULTURE METHOD Certified Organic

○ Aglianico del Taburno Rosato Le Mongolfiere a San Bruno '22	♟♟ 3
● Aglianico del Taburno Terra di Rivolta Ris. '20	♟♟ 6

Tenuta Sarno 1860

c.da Serroni, 4b
83100 Avellino
☎ +39 335431812
✹ www.tenutasarno1860.it

ANNUAL PRODUCTION 15,000 bottles
HECTARES UNDER VINE 6.00

Fiano di Avellino '22	♟♟ 4
Fiano di Avellino Erre Ris. '21	♟♟ 5

La Pietra di Tommasone

s.da prov.le Lacco-Fango, 144
80076 Lacco Ameno [NA]
☎ +39 0813330330
✹ www.tommasonevini.it

CELLAR SALES
PRE-BOOKED VISITS
ANNUAL PRODUCTION 100,000 bottles
HECTARES UNDER VINE 12.00
SUSTAINABLE WINERY

○ Ischia Biancolella '23	♟♟ 5
● Pignanera '21	♟♟ 6
○ Ischia Forastera '23	♟ 5
● Pithecusa Rosso '22	♟ 4

Tenuta Sant'Agostino

via Cupa, 8
82036 Solopaca [BN]
☎ +39 3935051862
✹ www.tenutasantagostino.it

CELLAR SALES
PRE-BOOKED VISITS
ANNUAL PRODUCTION 10,000 bottles
HECTARES UNDER VINE 5.00
VITICULTURE METHOD Certified Organic
SUSTAINABLE WINERY

○ Scomposto '21	♟♟ 4
○ Ventiventi '21	♟♟ 4

Tempa di Zoè

via San Pietro
84043 Agropoli [SA]
☎ +39 09749135796
✹ www.tempadizoe.it

CELLAR SALES
ANNUAL PRODUCTION 30,000 bottles
HECTARES UNDER VINE 13.00
SUSTAINABLE WINERY

○ 3 Rosé '23	♟♟ 3
○ Asterìas Fiano '23	♟♟ 4
○ Xa Fiano '22	♟♟ 6
● Xenos '22	♟♟ 5

OTHER WINERIES

Traerte - Vadiaperti

loc. Vadiaperti
83030 Montefredane [AV]
☎ +39 0825607013
info@traerte.it

CELLAR SALES
PRE-BOOKED VISITS
ANNUAL PRODUCTION 81,000 bottles
HECTARES UNDER VINE 6.00

○ Fuori Limite Greco '22	♥♥ 4
○ Irpinia Coda di Volpe Torama '23	♥♥ 5
○ Fiano di Avellino Vadiaperti '23	♥ 3

VentitréFilari

loc. Alimata
via Piante, 43
83030 Montefredane [AV]
☎ +39 0825672482
⊕ www.ventitrefilari.com

CELLAR SALES
PRE-BOOKED VISITS
ANNUAL PRODUCTION 4,000 bottles
HECTARES UNDER VINE 0.80
SUSTAINABLE WINERY

○ Fiano di Avellino Numero Primo Ris. '22	♥♥ 6
○ Fiano di Avellino Elemento '22	♥♥ 6

Vigne Guadagno

via Amerigo Vespucci
83030 Taurasi [AV]
☎ +39 08251686379
⊕ www.vigneguadagno.it

CELLAR SALES
PRE-BOOKED VISITS
ANNUAL PRODUCTION 20,000 bottles
HECTARES UNDER VINE 7.00

○ Fiano di Avellino '22	♥♥ 4
○ Greco di Tufo '21	♥♥ 4
● Irpinia Aglianico '20	♥ 4

Vallisassoli

via Tufara Scautieri, 47
83018 San Martino Valle Caudina [AV]
☎ +39 3339942832
⊕ www.vallisassoli.it

CELLAR SALES
PRE-BOOKED VISITS
ANNUAL PRODUCTION 3,000 bottles
HECTARES UNDER VINE 2.50
VITICULTURE METHOD Certified Biodynamic
SUSTAINABLE WINERY

○ 33/33/33 '21	♥♥ 6

Vestini Campagnano

fraz. Santi Giovanni e Paolo
via Baraccone, 5
81013 Caiazzo [CE]
☎ +39 0823679087
⊕ www.vestinicampagnano.it

CELLAR SALES
PRE-BOOKED VISITS
ACCOMMODATION
ANNUAL PRODUCTION 100,000 bottles
HECTARES UNDER VINE 4.00
VITICULTURE METHOD Certified Organic
SUSTAINABLE WINERY

● Connubio '19	♥♥ 7
○ Pallagrello Bianco '23	♥♥ 4
● Pallagrello Nero '22	♥♥ 5
● Casavecchia di Pontelatone Ris. '20	♥ 5

Villa Dora

s.da prov.le Zabatta, 252
80040 Terzigno [NA]
☎ +39 0815295016
⊕ www.cantinevilladora.com

CELLAR SALES
PRE-BOOKED VISITS
ANNUAL PRODUCTION 70,000 bottles
HECTARES UNDER VINE 16.00
VITICULTURE METHOD Certified Organic

○ Lacryma Christi del Vesuvio Bianco V. del Vulcano '22	♥♥
● Lacryma Christi del Vesuvio Rosso Forgiato '21	♥♥

BASILICATA

Once again, Basilicata delighted us with some remarkable expressions. This region remains one of Italy's most captivating terroirs, despite being among the least known. The Vulture appellation, with its renowned aglianico, is naturally the most familiar name for wine lovers. It accounts for the majority of wineries, the highest volume of wine produced, and those names that have the most visibility both in Italy and abroad. Nevertheless, there are other appellations showing modest signs of growth, such as the Matera DOC, which benefits from having one of Italy's most enchanting cities as its capital. Additionally, the Grottino di Roccanova and Terre dell'Alta Val d'Agri appellations hold potential that remains partially untapped.

We shouldn't forget, however, that the current moment is far from ideal. Both the domestic and international markets are shrinking, and large-scale buyers are increasingly seeking lower prices, making it difficult for local winemakers to thrive. Growth, both in quality and in terms of market presence, depends on significant investments—whether in the vineyard, the cellar, or in promotional efforts. Unfortunately, the impact of the 2023 vintage was devastating for many producers, with some seeing almost no harvest at all. This places the livelihoods of many small artisanal wineries at serious risk, let alone their ability to invest. While resources are limited, lowering prices and reducing margins is not the answer. On the contrary, such a strategy would be a threat to the future.

Having said that, we must commend the producers who earned our highest ratings. They presented aglianico del Vulture wines that skillfully interpreted the volcanic territory and its signature grape with creativity, sensitivity, and intelligence. The stories of Terra dei Re, Donato D'Angelo, Cantine del Notaio, and Elena Fucci exemplify success; they possess all the necessary ingredients, starting with the professionalism of their teams, and they continually reinvest—something that's evident in their wines. The only issue is that these names have long featured in our rankings. It's time to bring in new names and expand this list. That said, the number of wines making it to our finals is growing, and this gives us real hope for the future.

Basilisco

via delle Cantine, 20
85022 Barile [PZ]
(☎) +39 0972771033
⊕ www.basiliscovini.it

CELLAR SALES
PRE-BOOKED VISITS
ANNUAL PRODUCTION 70,000 bottles
HECTARES UNDER VINE 30.00
VITICULTURE METHOD Certified Organic
SUSTAINABLE WINERY

Founded in the 1990s, the winery embarked on a restoration project in 2011, when it was acquired by Feudi di San Gregorio. The effort aimed to revive the historic Parco delle Cantine di Barile, a site with ancient cellars carved into lava rock, underscoring the area's rich heritage. The estate spans 25 hectares, including some of the most renowned vineyards in Barile, highlighted by a historic plot over 80 years old, cultivated in the traditional Lucanian "capanno" method. The Superiore Fontanelle '17 easily earned its place in our final round with its deep ruby color and elegant, complex aromas of ripe red fruit, particularly morello cherry, complemented by a touch of spice and aromatic herbs. On the palate, it unfolds harmoniously, showcasing tannins of notable finesse. The Teodosio '21, the winery's flagship, offers meaty tones of ripe cherry and chocolate, supported by a fresh acidic vein that carries it to a convincing, fruit-driven finish. The Superiori Cru? and Fiordimarna (the latter more evolved), both 2017s, are also worth noting.

Battifarano

c.da Cerrolongo, 1
75020 Nova Siri [MT]
(☎) +39 0835536174
⊕ www.battifarano.com

CELLAR SALES
PRE-BOOKED VISITS
ACCOMMODATION
ANNUAL PRODUCTION 100,000 bottles
HECTARES UNDER VINE 35.00
SUSTAINABLE WINERY

The Battifarano family has been connected to this land for 5 centuries. Their winery operates across 3 estates: Cerrolongo, a 70-hectare plot situated on a plateau; Torre Bollita, 12 hectares located in the valley below Nova Siri Marina; and Santa Lania, an 18-hectare estate near the Calabrian border. The soils here are predominantly clay-sandy with a notable presence of gravel. The Akratos '21 upheld the prestige of the Matera DOC appellation in our final tastings. Made from primitivo, it pours rich and opulent, with a deep ruby hue. The nose reveals tones of well-ripened cherry and morello, accented by spicy notes, particularly white pepper, which transition into delicate wood nuances on the finish. On the palate, it's powerful, smooth, and warm, with excellent balance, closing energetically on red fruit notes and balsamic hints. The Toccaculo '21 (named after a local stream) is a characterful Petit Verdot with rich structure?matured in new oak, it exhibits balance and a pleasant drinkability.

Wine	Rating
● Aglianico del Vulture Sup. Fontanelle '17	▼▼ 6
● Aglianico del Vulture Sup. Cruà '21	▼▼ 6
● Aglianico del Vulture Teodosio '21	▼▼ 3
● Aglianico del Vulture Sup. Fiordimarna '21	▼ 6
● Aglianico del Vulture Basilisco '09	▼▼▼ 5
● Aglianico del Vulture Basilisco '08	▼▼▼ 5
● Aglianico del Vulture Basilisco '07	▼▼▼ 5
● Aglianico del Vulture Basilisco '06	▼▼▼ 5
● Aglianico del Vulture Basilisco '04	▼▼▼ 5
● Aglianico del Vulture Basilisco '01	▼▼▼ 5
● Aglianico del Vulture Sup. Cruà '13	▼▼▼ 5
● Aglianico del Vulture Sup. Fiordimarna '16	▼▼ 6
● Aglianico del Vulture Sup. Storico '13	▼▼ 8
● Aglianico del Vulture Teodosio '19	▼▼ 3*
● Aglianico del Vulture Teodosio '17	▼▼ 3*
● Aglianico del Vulture Teodosio '16	▼▼ 3*

Wine	Rating
● Matera Primitivo Akratos '21	▼▼ 3*
○ Matera Greco Le Paglie '23	▼▼ 3
○ Toccacielo Fiano '23	▼▼ 2*
● Toccaculo '21	▼▼ 4
○ Matera Primitivo Rosato Akratos '23	▼ 3
○ Matera Greco Bianco Le Paglie '21	▼▼ 2
○ Matera Greco Le Paglie '22	▼▼ 3
● Matera Moro Curaffanni Ris. '18	▼▼ 5
● Matera Moro Curaffanni Ris. '17	▼▼ 5
● Matera Moro Torre Bollita '20	▼▼ 2
● Matera Primitivo Akratos '19	▼▼ 2
○ Toccacielo Bianco '20	▼▼ 2
● Toccacielo Rosso '20	▼▼ 2
● Toccaculo '20	▼▼ 4
● Toccaculo '19	▼▼ 2

Cantina di Venosa

loc. Vignali
via Appia
85029 Venosa [PZ]
☎ +39 097236702
✆ www.cantinadivenosa.it

★Cantine del Notaio

via Roma, 159
85028 Rionero in Vulture [PZ]
☎ +39 0972723689
✆ www.cantinedelnotaio.it

CELLAR SALES
PRE-BOOKED VISITS
ANNUAL PRODUCTION 1,500,000 bottles
HECTARES UNDER VINE 800.00
SUSTAINABLE WINERY

CELLAR SALES
PRE-BOOKED VISITS
ANNUAL PRODUCTION 590,000 bottles
HECTARES UNDER VINE 52.00

Established in 1957, Cantina di Venosa Vignali ranks among southern Italy's most important cooperatives. Today, the producer boasts 350 members who cultivate 800 hectares of vines, primarily in the municipality of Venosa, the leading producer of aglianico grapes in the Vulture area. With state-of-the-art facilities and meticulous management by the members, from harvest to grape selection and aging, the cooperative delivers a consistently high-quality range, a faithful reflection of the terroir. The Aglianico Gesualdo '21, a structured and rich wine aged in new oak, deserved its place in the finals. It offers fleshy, ripe fruit and exceptionally fine-grained tannins. The Verbo Rosato '23 impressed us with its pleasing consistency and rich tones of cherry and Mediterranean scrub, as did the Verbo Bianco '23, made from malvasia bianca, which displays a lovely floral bouquet and delicate aromatic nuances. The Aglianico Verbo '21 proves structured but slightly dried out by oak. The Matematico '21 is rich and close-knit, though still seeking balance.

Gerardo Giuratrabocchetti, together with his wife Marcella Libutti, embarked on a successful venture in 1998 to elevate the status of Aglianico del Vulture. Backed by the family's 7 generations of commitment to winemaking, the estate now covers 52 hectares, spread across 7 main plots situated at elevations spanning 430-600 meters. Some vines are over 100 years old, thriving in the volcanic soils here. For some time, among the portfolio crafted by Gerardo and oenologist Saverio Vernucci, 2 reds have vied for attention: the Aglianico Repertorio and the La Firma. In our final round, the Repertorio '22 edged out the competition. It's a red with character, supple and well-structured, rich in tones of small fruits and Mediterranean scrub, revealing smooth tannins and lovely aromatic persistence. La Firma, in one of its best editions in recent years, is more powerful and concentrated, offering ripe fruit and distinct sensations of oak. The other wines tasted are also excellent.

● Aglianico del Vulture Gesualdo '21	🍷🍷 4
● Aglianico del Vulture Verbo '21	🍷🍷 3
○ Verbo Malvasia '23	🍷🍷 3
◉ Verbo Rosato '23	🍷🍷 3
● Matematico '21	🍷 7
● Aglianico del Vulture Baliaggio '21	🍷🍷 2*
● Aglianico del Vulture Gesualdo da Venosa '19	🍷🍷 4
● Aglianico del Vulture Terre di Orazio '20	🍷🍷 3*
● Aglianico del Vulture Verbo '20	🍷🍷 3
● Aglianico del Vulture Verbo '19	🍷🍷 3
○ Greco d'Avalos di Gesualdo '21	🍷🍷 3
○ Verbo Malvasia '20	🍷🍷 3
◉ Verbo Rosato '22	🍷🍷 3
● Verbo Rosso '21	🍷🍷 3

● Aglianico del Vulture Il Repertorio '22	🍷🍷🍷 4*
● Aglianico del Vulture La Firma '21	🍷🍷 6
● Aglianico del Vulture Il Sigillo '18	🍷🍷 6
● Il Protesto	🍷🍷 2*
○ L'Autentica '22	🍷🍷 6
○ La Parcella '23	🍷🍷 7
○ La Postilla Moscato Spumante Dolce	🍷🍷 2*
○ La Raccolta '23	🍷🍷 3
◉ La Stipula Brut Rosé M. Cl. '17	🍷🍷 5
○ Il Preliminare '23	🍷 3
● L'Atto '23	🍷 3
● La Procura '22	🍷 5
● Aglianico del Vulture Il Repertorio '21	🍷🍷🍷 4*
● Aglianico del Vulture Il Repertorio '20	🍷🍷🍷 4*
● Aglianico del Vulture Il Repertorio '19	🍷🍷🍷 4*

Carbone Vini

via Nitti, 48
85025 Melfi [PZ]
☏ +39 3282814344
✉ www.carbonevini.it

CELLAR SALES
PRE-BOOKED VISITS
ANNUAL PRODUCTION 30,000 bottles
HECTARES UNDER VINE 8.00
VITICULTURE METHOD Certified Organic

The Carbone family's journey began in the 1970s with brothers Vittorio and Enzo Carbone. Although interrupted in the late 1980s, the business was revitalized in 2005 thanks to the passion of Vittorio's children, Luca and Sara, who proudly carried forward a project of renewal. The estate now dedicates eight hectares to aglianico, fiano, and moscato. The modern winery is located in Contrada Braide, while the heart of production lies in a striking underground cellar carved from volcanic tuff in the historic center of Melfi. Stupor Mundi is an Aglianico dedicated, as the name suggests, to Emperor Frederick II, who left an indelible mark on the region. It's a structured and characterful red, rich in notes of ripe plum, marasca cherry, and blackberry, with lovely Mediterranean hues on the nose. On the palate, it opens broad and assertive, echoing fruity notes, revealing velvety tannins, and closing long. We preferred it over the still commendable 400 Some '21, which, though rich on the palate, is less supple. The Nero '20 is warm, pervasive, and of good quality, though its tannins are still a bit rough.

● Aglianico del Vulture Stupor Mundi '20	♟♟ 5
● Aglianico del Vulture 400 Some '20	♟♟ 4
● Nero Carbone '20	♟ 3
● Aglianico del Vulture 400 Some '19	♟♟ 4
● Aglianico del Vulture 400 Some '18	♟♟ 4
● Aglianico del Vulture 400 Some '14	♟♟ 4
● Aglianico del Vulture 400 Some '13	♟♟ 4
● Aglianico del Vulture Stupor Mundi '19	♟♟ 5
● Aglianico del Vulture Stupor Mundi '18	♟♟ 5
● Aglianico del Vulture Stupor Mundi '17	♟♟ 5
● Aglianico del Vulture Stupor Mundi '13	♟♟ 5
● Aglianico del Vulture Stupor Mundi '12	♟♟ 5
● Aglianico del Vulture Sup. Stupor Mundi '15	♟♟ 5

Donato D'Angelo
di Filomena Ruppi

loc. Le Querce
85028 Barile [PZ]
☏ +39 0972724602
✉ www.donatodangelo.it

PRE-BOOKED VISITS
ANNUAL PRODUCTION 150,000 bottles
HECTARES UNDER VINE 20.00

Donato D'Angelo has devoted his professional life to Aglianico del Vulture. Today, his winery encompasses 20 hectares spread across Barile, Ripacandida, and Maschito, in the heart of the territory. Alongside him are his wife Filomena Ruppi, also a winemaker, and their daughter Emiliana, while their other daughter, Erminia, manages administration. Their wines are classically styled, elegant, and among the finest expressions of the appellation. Donato D'Angelo offers few labels, but they are of excellent quality. Once again, the Calice '22 secures our highest honor. It has a beautiful deep ruby color, and the nose opens complex with notes of ripe cherry, spices, and Mediterranean herbs, forming a bouquet of rare finesse. On the palate, it reveals a slender body with great depth, combining extraordinary drinkability with a remarkable overall harmony. The Donato D'Angelo '21 is also excellent, with pleasant balsamic and mentholated tones, slightly more subtle but with great sapidity and freshness. The rosato Ede '23 is also enjoyable.

● Aglianico del Vulture Calice '22	♟♟♟ 3*
● Aglianico del Vulture Donato D'Angelo '21	♟♟ 5
⊙ Ede '23	♟ 3
● Aglianico del Vulture Calice '21	♟♟♟ 3*
● Aglianico del Vulture Calice '20	♟♟♟ 3*
● Aglianico del Vulture Calice '19	♟♟♟ 3*
● Aglianico del Vulture Donato D'Angelo '17	♟♟♟ 4*
● Balconara '09	♟♟♟ 4*
● Aglianico del Vulture Donato D'Angelo '14	♟♟ 3*
● Aglianico del Vulture Donato D'Angelo '13	♟♟ 3*
● Aglianico del Vulture Donato D'Angelo '12	♟♟ 3*
● Aglianico del Vulture Donato D'Angelo '11	♟♟ 4
● Balconara '19	♟♟ 4

★Elena Fucci

c.da Solagna del Titolo
85022 Barile [PZ]
📞 +39 3204879945
🌐 www.elenafuccivini.com

CELLAR SALES
PRE-BOOKED VISITS
ANNUAL PRODUCTION 30,000 bottles
HECTARES UNDER VINE 9.00
VITICULTURE METHOD Certified Organic
SUSTAINABLE WINERY

Elena Fucci made a passionate choice, one rooted in courage and determination, that upended her plans and life trajectory. In 2000, she decided that the handful of hectares her grandfather Generoso had purchased in the 1960s, in the Solagna del Titolo area, would define her future. She earned a degree in oenology and transformed the winery into a small gem of technology and sustainability. Today, the estate spans 9 hectares, with some vineyards over 70 years old. Here?s another excellent interpretation of aglianico that Elena crafts with the collaboration of her husband, Andrea Manzani. The '22 seamlessly combines the robust structure typical of aglianico with a slender, elegant profile. It?s rich with hints of spices and Mediterranean scrub that enhance a fleshy and vivid fruit, supported by a lovely fresh vein and smooth tannins. The By Amphora version from the same vintage shows a more austere and mineral character but is equally compelling. The Aglianico Sceg and the red Verha from the same vintage are also outstanding.

● Aglianico del Vulture Titolo '22	♟♟♟ 6
● Aglianico del Vulture Titolo by Amphora '22	♟♟ 8
● Aglianico del Vulture Sceg '22	♟♟ 5
● Verha '22	♟♟ 3
⊙ Titolo Pink Edition '23	♟ 5
● Aglianico del Vulture Titolo '21	♟♟♟ 6
● Aglianico del Vulture Titolo '20	♟♟♟ 6
● Aglianico del Vulture Titolo '19	♟♟♟ 6
● Aglianico del Vulture Titolo '18	♟♟♟ 8
● Aglianico del Vulture Titolo '17	♟♟♟ 8
● Aglianico del Vulture Titolo '16	♟♟♟ 6
● Aglianico del Vulture Titolo '15	♟♟♟ 6
● Aglianico del Vulture Titolo '14	♟♟♟ 6
● Aglianico del Vulture Titolo '13	♟♟♟ 6
● Aglianico del Vulture Titolo '12	♟♟♟ 5
● Aglianico del Vulture Titolo '11	♟♟♟ 5

Grifalco

loc. Pian di Camera
85029 Venosa [PZ]
📞 +39 097231002
🌐 www.grifalcovini.com

CELLAR SALES
PRE-BOOKED VISITS
ANNUAL PRODUCTION 80,000 bottles
HECTARES UNDER VINE 16.00
VITICULTURE METHOD Certified Organic
SUSTAINABLE WINERY

After two decades of experience in Tuscany, Cecilia and Fabrizio Piccin moved to Basilicata in 2004 to focus on producing Aglianico del Vulture. Spread out across Maschito, Venosa, Rapolla, and Ginestra, the winery's 16 hectares occupy some of the appellation's best positions. Today, the estate is led by their sons: Lorenzo, who oversees the vineyards and cellar, and Andrea, who manages the business side. In the final round, the Gricos '22 stands out with its beautiful ruby color with violet highlights. On the nose, it reveals an intriguing bouquet of blackberry, marasca cherry, and ripe plum, accompanied by Mediterranean and balsamic undertones. The palate is firm and solid, showcasing smooth tannins. The DaMaschito '21 (from Maschito grapes) offers a touch more finesse and depth, closing with persistent notes of scrub, wild mint, and rosemary. The DaGinestra '21 has a strong structure and still needs time to evolve, while the Grifalco '22 offers a more approachable and immediately enjoyable experience.

● Aglianico del Vulture DaMaschito '21	♟♟ 6
● Aglianico del Vulture Gricos '22	♟♟ 4
● Aglianico del Vulture DaGinestra '21	♟♟ 6
● Aglianico del Vulture Grifalco '22	♟♟ 4
● Aglianico del Vulture Gricos '18	♟♟♟ 3*
● Aglianico del Vulture Gricos '17	♟♟♟ 3*
● Aglianico del Vulture Gricos '14	♟♟♟ 3*
● Aglianico del Vulture Gricos '21	♟♟ 4
● Aglianico del Vulture Gricos '20	♟♟ 4
● Aglianico del Vulture Gricos '16	♟♟ 3*
● Aglianico del Vulture Gricos '15	♟♟ 3*
● Aglianico del Vulture Grifalco '21	♟♟ 4
● Aglianico del Vulture Grifalco '20	♟♟ 4
● Aglianico del Vulture Sup. DaGinestra '19	♟♟ 6
● Aglianico del Vulture Sup. DaGinestra '18	♟♟ 6
● Aglianico del Vulture Sup. DaGinestra '17	♟♟ 6

Musto Carmelitano
via Pietro Nenni, 23
85020 Maschito [PZ]
☎ +39 097233312
🖰 www.mustocarmelitano.it

CELLAR SALES
PRE-BOOKED VISITS
ANNUAL PRODUCTION 25,000 bottles
HECTARES UNDER VINE 6.50
VITICULTURE METHOD Certified Organic

Musto Carmelitano has been a family-run winery for over 3 generations. Since 2005, siblings Elisabetta and Luigi, alongside their father Francesco, have been committed to a high-quality, artisanal approach. The estate consists of 3 vineyards, totaling nearly 7 hectares: Pian del Moro, Serra del Prete, and Vernavà, all situated on soils of red clay rich in minerals. The crown jewels are the old vines, some of which are up to 80 years old. The Serra del Prete '21 secured a place in our final round and solidifies its reputation as one of the most captivating labels in the appellation. It displays a lovely ruby color, with elegant aromas of red fruits (marasca cherry and blackberry in the forefront) accented by a pleasing hint of spice and aromatic herbs. On the palate, it opens fleshy, rich, with good tension, freshness, and dynamism. The Maschitano Rosso '21 is slightly more rustic and immediate in character but wins over with its vitality, pleasantness, and typicity. We appreciated the greater complexity of the Superiore Pian del Moro '20, with its more evolved and mature tones.

Wine	Rating
● Aglianico del Vulture Serra del Prete '21	♛♛ 4
● Aglianico del Vulture Sup. Pian del Moro '20	♛♛ 5
● Aglianico del Vulture Maschitano Rosso '21	♛♛ 3
● Aglianico del Vulture Serra del Prete '09	♛♛♛ 2
● Aglianico del Vulture '19	♛♛ 3
● Aglianico del Vulture '17	♛♛ 6
● Aglianico del Vulture Maschitano Rosso '20	♛♛ 3
● Aglianico del Vulture Maschitano Rosso '19	♛♛ 3*
● Aglianico del Vulture Pian del Moro '19	♛♛ 5
● Aglianico del Vulture Pian del Moro '18	♛♛ 4
● Aglianico del Vulture Serra del Prete '20	♛♛ 4
● Aglianico del Vulture Serra del Prete '19	♛♛ 4
● Aglianico del Vulture Serra del Prete '17	♛♛ 4
● Aglianico del Vulture Serra del Prete '16	♛♛ 4

★Paternoster
c.da Valle del Titolo
85022 Barile [PZ]
☎ +39 0972770224
🖰 www.paternostervini.it

CELLAR SALES
PRE-BOOKED VISITS
ANNUAL PRODUCTION 150,000 bottles
HECTARES UNDER VINE 20.00
VITICULTURE METHOD Certified Organic

The story of Paternoster begins in 1925 with Anselmo, its founder and a pioneer of Italian viticulture. It continued with his son Giuseppe, who brought innovation to the producer with new winemaking methods and was a trailblazer in the use of barriques. Today, Paternoster boasts 20 hectares of vineyards, primarily scattered across the various districts of the Barile municipality. The Synthesi '20 marks, in our view, a turning point in the stylistic evolution of this historic estate, now part of the Tommasi group. This winery?s flagship wine made it to our finals and is appreciated for its clarity, typicity, and stylistic purity, offering a refined expression of aglianico. It?s creamy in its fruit, elegant and subtle, with well-integrated notes of wood and balsamic hints, and tannins of good maturity, creating a harmonious and enjoyable experience. We hope this approach will extend to future vintages of the estate's other labels, like the Don Anselmo, which in the '20 vintage, does not exhibit the same vital freshness.

Wine	Rating
● Aglianico del Vulture Synthesi '20	♛♛ 3*
● Aglianico del Vulture Don Anselmo '20	♛♛ 7
○ Vulcanico Falanghina '23	♛ 3
● Aglianico del Vulture Don Anselmo '16	♛♛♛ 6
● Aglianico del Vulture Don Anselmo '15	♛♛♛ 6
● Aglianico del Vulture Don Anselmo '13	♛♛♛ 6
● Aglianico del Vulture Don Anselmo '09	♛♛♛ 6
● Aglianico del Vulture Don Anselmo '94	♛♛♛ 6
● Aglianico del Vulture Don Anselmo Ris. '05	♛♛♛ 6
● Aglianico del Vulture Rotondo '11	♛♛♛ 5
● Aglianico del Vulture Rotondo '01	♛♛♛ 5
● Aglianico del Vulture Rotondo '00	♛♛♛ 5
● Aglianico del Vulture Rotondo '98	♛♛♛ 5
● Aglianico del Vulture Bariliòtt '21	♛♛ 2*
● Aglianico del Vulture Rotondo '18	♛♛ 6
● Aglianico del Vulture Synthesi '19	♛♛ 3*

★Re Manfredi

loc. Pian di Camera
85029 Venosa [PZ]
☏ +39 097231263
✉ www.cantineremanfredi.it

Terra dei Re

via Monticchio km 2,700
85028 Rionero in Vulture [PZ]
☏ +39 0972725116
✉ www.terradeire.com

CELLAR SALES
PRE-BOOKED VISITS
RESTAURANT SERVICE
ANNUAL PRODUCTION 200,000 bottles
HECTARES UNDER VINE 110.00

CELLAR SALES
PRE-BOOKED VISITS
ACCOMMODATION AND RESTAURANT SERVICE
ANNUAL PRODUCTION 70,000 bottles
HECTARES UNDER VINE 11.00
VITICULTURE METHOD Certified Organic
SUSTAINABLE WINERY

Part of the Gruppo Italiano Vini, Re Manfredi was established in 1998. Over the years, the winery has expanded significantly and now oversees about 110 hectares of vineyards, primarily in Venosa but also in Barile and Maschito. The crown jewel is the Serpara vineyard, which produces their most prestigious wine. The constantly updated and renovated production space is a technological marvel. While the Serpara '19 (from the vineyard of the same name in Maschito) matures in the cellar, winemaker Morgan McCrum presented us with an excellent Re Manfredi '22. It pours a lovely, intense ruby red, releasing complex aromas in which red fruit blends with elegant notes of spices, Mediterranean scrub, and a delicate balsamic hint. On the palate, it's full, rich, and already enjoyable. The Aglianico Taglio del Tralcio '22, from a late harvest, is also impressive, standing out for its dynamic profile, pleasant minty notes, and opulent creaminess.

Founded in 2000, this beautiful estate reflects the passion of the Leone and Rabasco families, who meticulously cultivate 11 hectares of vineyards spread across Rionero, Barile, Melfi, and Rapolla. In their modern Rionero cellar, a carefully curated range of local wines comes to life, with a unique feature: 2 vineyards are dedicated to pinot noir, which has found an ideal habitat on the high slopes of the volcano. Once again, the labels reaching our finals this year are exceptional. The Nocte '20 confirms its class: a modern, rich, balanced, and elegant aglianico that highlights the integrity of the fruit and the finesse of its tannic structure, with an elegant nose featuring mountain herbs, spices, floral nuances, and a delicate touch of oak. The Pinot Nero Calata delle Brecce '21 is also elegant, refined, complex, and varietal, offering tones of small fruits, from red and black currants to blueberries, with delicate Mediterranean notes and clear smoky hints that evoke the volcano.

● Aglianico del Vulture Re Manfredi '22	♟♟ 5
● Aglianico del Vulture Taglio del Tralcio '22	♟♟ 3
○ Flordelis '23	♟♟ 3
○ Bianco degli Svevi '23	♟ 3
● Aglianico del Vulture Re Manfredi '19	♟♟♟ 5
● Aglianico del Vulture Re Manfredi '18	♟♟♟ 5
● Aglianico del Vulture Re Manfredi '16	♟♟♟ 5
● Aglianico del Vulture Re Manfredi '15	♟♟♟ 5
● Aglianico del Vulture Re Manfredi '13	♟♟♟ 6
● Aglianico del Vulture Re Manfredi '11	♟♟♟ 4*
● Aglianico del Vulture Re Manfredi '10	♟♟♟ 4*
● Aglianico del Vulture Serpara '10	♟♟♟ 5
● Aglianico del Vulture Sup. Serpara '17	♟♟♟ 6
● Aglianico del Vulture Sup. Serpara '16	♟♟♟ 5
● Aglianico del Vulture Sup. Serpara '12	♟♟♟ 5

● Aglianico del Vulture Nocte '20	♟♟♟ 5
● Calata delle Brecce Pinot Nero '21	♟♟ 6
○ Lerà Malvasia '23	♟♟ 2*
● Lerà Rosso '19	♟ 3
● Aglianico del Vulture Nocte '19	♟♟♟ 5
● Aglianico del Vulture Nocte '18	♟♟♟ 5
● Aglianico del Vulture Nocte '17	♟♟♟ 5
● Aglianico del Vulture Nocte '16	♟♟♟ 4*
● Aglianico del Vulture Nocte '15	♟♟ 4
● Calata delle Brecce Pinot Nero '20	♟♟ 6
○ Lerà Malvasia '21	♟♟ 2*
● Pinot Nero Calata delle Brecce '19	♟♟ 6
● Vulcano 800 '20	♟♟ 5
● Vulcano 800 '19	♟♟ 5
● Vulcano 800 Pinot Nero '21	♟♟ 5

OTHER WINERIES

Arteteke

Corso Alcide De Gasperi, 84
85025 Melfi [PZ]
+39 0972641 6608
www.artetekewines.it

SUSTAINABLE WINERY

● Aglianico del Vulture Franco '19	🍷🍷 6
● Aglianico del Vulture Russe '20	🍷🍷 4
⊙ Ancestrale Rosé '22	🍷🍷 4
○ lànghë '22	🍷 4

Francesco Bonifacio

c.da Piani di Camera
85029 Venosa [PZ]
+39 097231436
www.cantinebonifacio.it

CELLAR SALES
PRE-BOOKED VISITS
ANNUAL PRODUCTION 110,000 bottles
HECTARES UNDER VINE 15.00

● Aglianico del Vulture Certamen '20	🍷🍷 2*
● Aglianico del Vulture La Sfida '18	🍷🍷 4

Cantina del Vulture

via San Francesco
85028 Rionero in Vulture [PZ]
+39 0972721062
www.cantinadelvulture.it

CELLAR SALES
PRE-BOOKED VISITS
ANNUAL PRODUCTION 45,000 bottles
HECTARES UNDER VINE 100.00

● Aglianico del Vulture Carteggio '20	🍷🍷 2*

D'Angelo

via Padre Pio, 8
85028 Rionero in Vulture [PZ]
+39 0972721517
www.dangelowine.com

CELLAR SALES
PRE-BOOKED VISITS
ANNUAL PRODUCTION 300,000 bottles
HECTARES UNDER VINE 30.00
VITICULTURE METHOD Certified Organic

● Aglianico del Vulture '20	🍷🍷 3
● Aglianico del Vulture Tecum '19	🍷🍷 8
● Canneto '22	🍷🍷 5
⊙ Villa dei Pini '23	🍷🍷 3

Cantine De Biase

c.da Calvello, s.da prov.le 89 Km 2+800
85036 Roccanova [PZ]
+39 3489580264
www.cantinedebiase.it

CELLAR SALES
PRE-BOOKED VISITS
ACCOMMODATION
ANNUAL PRODUCTION 30,000 bottles
HECTARES UNDER VINE 5.00
VITICULTURE METHOD Certified Organic
SUSTAINABLE WINERY

● Grottino di Roccanova Rosso L'Essenza '20	🍷🍷 5
● Grottino di Roccanova Rosso Collevivo '22	🍷 4

Agricola Di Fuccio

via Foresta
85059 Viggiano [PZ]
+39 3382274900
www.aziendaagricoladifuccio.it

CELLAR SALES
PRE-BOOKED VISITS
ANNUAL PRODUCTION 35,000 bottles
HECTARES UNDER VINE 3.00

⊙ Terre dell'Alta Val d'Agri Antifonario '22	🍷🍷 5
○ Eremo '22	🍷 5
● Terre dell'Alta Val d'Agri La Preta '19	🍷 6

OTHER WINERIES

Cantine Graziano

via Ponte, 25
85036 Roccanova [PZ]
📞 +39 3486951612
🌐 www.cantinegraziano.com

CELLAR SALES
PRE-BOOKED VISITS
ANNUAL PRODUCTION 25,000 bottles
HECTARES UNDER VINE 6.00
VITICULTURE METHOD Certified Organic

● Grottino di Roccanova Rosso Norce '20	🍷🍷 5
● Grottino di Roccanova Rosso Terre di Norce '21	🍷🍷 3

Tenuta I Gelsi

fraz. Monticchio Bagni
c.da Paduli
85028 Rionero in Vulture [PZ]
📞 +39 0972080289
🌐 www.tenutaigelsi.com

CELLAR SALES
PRE-BOOKED VISITS
ANNUAL PRODUCTION 60,000 bottles
HECTARES UNDER VINE 10.00
SUSTAINABLE WINERY

● Aglianico del Vulture Casello 105 '21	🍷🍷 4
● Aglianico del Vulture Il Rosso di Carmine '22	🍷🍷 3

Tenuta Lagala

c.da La Maddalena
85029 Venosa [PZ]
📞 +39 097232735
🌐 www.lagala.it

CELLAR SALES
PRE-BOOKED VISITS
ACCOMMODATION AND RESTAURANT SERVICE
ANNUAL PRODUCTION 50,000 bottles
HECTARES UNDER VINE 7.00

● Aglianico del Vulture Aquila del Vulture '19	🍷🍷 5
⊙ Angelica Rosato '22	🍷🍷 4
○ Spiralis '22	🍷 4

Macarico Vini

via Roma, 159
85028 Rionero in Vulture [PZ]
📞 +39 0972723689
🌐 www.macaricovini.it

CELLAR SALES
PRE-BOOKED VISITS
ANNUAL PRODUCTION 46,000 bottles
HECTARES UNDER VINE 3.00

● Aglianico del Vulture '22	🍷🍷 7
● Aglianico del Vulture Macarì '22	🍷🍷 3
● Rosso del Vulcano '23	🍷🍷 2*
○ Xjnestra '23	🍷 4

Cantine Madonna delle Grazie

loc. Vignali
via Appia
85029 Venosa [PZ]
📞 +39 097235704
🌐 www.cantinemadonnadellegrazie.it

CELLAR SALES
PRE-BOOKED VISITS
ANNUAL PRODUCTION 18,000 bottles
HECTARES UNDER VINE 8.00
VITICULTURE METHOD Certified Organic

● Aglianico del Vulture Liscone '19	🍷🍷 3
○ Leuconoe '23	🍷🍷 3
● Aglianico del Vulture Bauccio '17	🍷 4

Martino

via La Vista, 2a
85028 Rionero in Vulture [PZ]
📞 +39 0972721422
🌐 www.martinovini.com

CELLAR SALES
PRE-BOOKED VISITS
ANNUAL PRODUCTION 250,000 bottles
HECTARES UNDER VINE 30.00

● Aglianico del Vulture Pretoriano Anniversario '13	🍷🍷 6

OTHER WINERIES

Quarta Generazione

c.da Macarico
85022 Barile [PZ]
(+39 3342039805
⊛ www.quartagenerazione.com

ANNUAL PRODUCTION 20,000 bottles
HECTARES UNDER VINE 3.00
VITICULTURE METHOD Certified Organic

● Aglianico del Vulture '22	♟♟ 5

Regio Cantina

loc. Piano Regio
85029 Venosa [PZ]
(+39 0577540 I I
⊛ www.piccini1882.it

CELLAR SALES
PRE-BOOKED VISITS
ANNUAL PRODUCTION 90,000 bottles
HECTARES UNDER VINE 15.00
VITICULTURE METHOD Certified Organic

● Aglianico del Vulture Genesi '22	♟♟ 3
● Aglianico del Vulture Sup. Campo Melograno Ris. '19	♟ 5

Troilo

via A. Diaz, 43
85029 Venosa [PZ]
(+39 097236900
⊛ www.troilo.it

Tenuta Le Querce

via delle Cantine, 10
85022 Barile [PZ]
(+39 3892422972
⊛ www.tenutalequerce.eu

CELLAR SALES
PRE-BOOKED VISITS
ANNUAL PRODUCTION 350,000 bottles
HECTARES UNDER VINE 70.00

○ Costanza '23	♟♟ 5
○ Valentina '23	♟♟ 4
● Aglianico del Vulture Angelina '21	♟ 3

Tenuta del Portale

s.da Padre Pio , 10
85028 Rionero in Vulture [PZ]
(+39 3899141559
tenutadelportale@gmail.com

CELLAR SALES
PRE-BOOKED VISITS
ANNUAL PRODUCTION 150,000 bottles
HECTARES UNDER VINE 15.00

● Aglianico del Vulture Le Vigne a Capanno '21	♟♟ 5
● Aglianico del Vulture '22	♟♟ 3
● Starsa '23	♟ 2

Vitis in Vulture

c.so Giustino Fortunato, 159
85024 Lavello [PZ]
(+39 097283983
⊛ www.vitisinvulture.com

ANNUAL PRODUCTION 50,000 bottles
HECTARES UNDER VINE 100.00

● Aglianico del Vulture Caveto '18	♟♟ 5
● Aglianico del Vulture Leukanos '20	♟♟ 2*
○ Gran Cuvée Brut	♟ 2

⊙ Forentum Rosato '23	♟♟ 3
○ Riseca Bianco '23	♟♟ 3

PUGLIA

The years roll on, each with its own character. If 2023 was especially challenging due to climate issues and plant health concerns, 2024 has proven to be another hot year, prompting harvests to begin at least a week earlier. This trend, given the century's climate trajectory, may now be the new normal, requiring adjustments. The drought led to a significant drop in yields, but producers with well-positioned vineyards, older vines, and strong vineyard management have achieved results ranging from satisfactory to excellent in terms of quality. The real issue taking shape, however, revolves around the identity the Puglian wine sector wants to project and which market it aims to target.

The grape market is struggling, with prices now below sustainable levels. In our view, the region's future lies in a focus on quality production and an increase in bottled wine output rather than chasing volume and selling bulk or grapes. Highlighting premium terroirs—a trend increasingly visible in the number of wines awarded by our guide compared to a few years ago—seems the only viable way to maintain the prestige and value of Puglia's vineyards. Other strategies must also be explored, from boosting direct sales at wineries to promoting agritourism, all while working to expand in increasingly important foreign markets.

In our guide, primitivo-based wines continue to take center stage, with 16 out of the 26 Tre Bicchieri awarded going to the varietal. Joining them are classic negroamaro wines, and, for the first time, two Malvasia Nera and a Castel del Monte Bombino Nero. Another first: two new wineries have entered our Tre Bicchieri "club": Masseria Borgo dei Trulli, with their Primitivo di Manduria Mirea, and Masseria Cuturi with their Zacinto, a monovarietal negroamaro. Despite the limited impact of our past observations, we can't help but note, yet again, the baffling number of "ultra-heavy" bottles crowding our tasting tables, making any talk of sustainability and environmental responsibility appear, at best, ambiguous.

Amastuola

via Appia, km 632,200
74016 Massafra [TA]
☎ +39 0998856984
⊛ www.amastuola.it

CELLAR SALES
PRE-BOOKED VISITS
ACCOMMODATION AND RESTAURANT SERVICE
ANNUAL PRODUCTION 360,000 bottles
HECTARES UNDER VINE 109.00
VITICULTURE METHOD Certified Organic

Amastuola is nestled in the heart of the Terra delle Gravine Regional Natural Park, where the Montanaro family renovated a 15th-century farmhouse with a closed courtyard. The estate spans over 100 hectares of vineyards, home to both traditional and international grape varieties. Their wines, all sealed with screw caps, are characterized by quality, a focus on expressing the terroir and enhancing drinkability. This year, we were particularly impressed by the Bialento '23, a blend of aromatic grapes—75% malvasia bianca and the rest minutolo. It reveals fragrances of white flowers, aromatic herbs, and plum, with a properly aromatic palate, free from excessive bitterness—a fresh, enjoyable quaff. Two other wines prove well-crafted: the fresh and pleasant Calaprice '23, a complex blend of sauvignon, chardonnay, and fiano, and the Centosassi Primitivo '21, which features tones of Mediterranean scrub and wild black fruits.

Apollonio

via San Pietro in Lama, 7
73047 Monteroni di Lecce [LE]
☎ +39 0832327182
⊛ www.apolloniovini.it

CELLAR SALES
PRE-BOOKED VISITS
ANNUAL PRODUCTION 1,500,000 bottles
HECTARES UNDER VINE 20.00

Brothers Marcello and Massimiliano Apollonio, fourth-generation winemakers, have been leading their family winery for the past 30 years. Established in 1870, today the estate unfolds primarily on calcareous clay soils, where traditional varieties such as negroamaro and primitivo dominate, alongside malvasia nera, susumaniello, and bianco d'Alessano. Production is rooted in tradition, showcasing the essence of these local grapes. Among the various wines offered, the 150 Susumaniello Rosato '23 stands out, with its floral notes and hints of small red fruits on the nose, while the palate proves fresh, flavorful and pleasing to drink. The Valle Cupa '20 is also well-made, with its notes of Mediterranean scrub and blackberry, nice freshness, and well-managed tannins. It's worth noting two traditional, "Apollonio-style" wines: the Diciotto Fanali '19, a negroamaro rosé with oxidative tones of nuts (but still holding up well), and the Copertino Rosso Divoto Riserva '13, long and, despite its eleven years, still fresh.

○ Bialento '23	♟♟♟ 3*
○ Calaprice '23	♟♟ 2*
● Centosassi Primitivo '21	♟♟ 5
● Aglianico '20	♟ 3
○ Ondarosa '23	♟ 2
● Aglianico '17	♟♟ 3
○ Calaprice '19	♟♟ 2*
● Capocanale '17	♟♟ 3
● Centosassi Primitivo '20	♟♟ 5
○ Dolce Vitae '21	♟♟ 4
● Lamarossa '17	♟♟ 3
● Lamarossa '15	♟♟ 2*
● Negroamaro '19	♟♟ 3
● Onda del Tempo '21	♟♟ 3
● Onda del Tempo '19	♟♟ 3
○ Ondarosa '21	♟♟ 2*
○ Ondarosa '19	♟♟ 2*

○ Il 150 Susumaniello Rosato '23	♟♟ 3*
● Copertino Rosso Divoto Ris. '13	♟♟ 6
○ Diciotto Fanali '19	♟♟ 4
● Valle Cupa '20	♟♟ 5
● Il 150 Susumaniello Rosso '22	♟ 3
○ Il 150 Verdeca '23	♟ 3
● Salice Salentino Rosso Mani de Sud '22	♟ 4
● Terragnolo Primitivo '21	♟ 5
● Primitivo di Manduria Mani del Sud '18	♟♟ 4
○ Salice Salentino Bianco Mani del Sud '21	♟♟ 4
● Salice Salentino Rosso Mani del Sud '21	♟♟ 4
● Salice Salentino Rosso Mani del Sud '20	♟♟ 4
● Terragnolo Negroamaro '17	♟♟ 5
● Terragnolo Primitivo '20	♟♟ 5
● Valle Cupa '17	♟♟ 5

Masseria Borgo dei Trulli

loc. Roselle
s.da prov.le 130
74020 Maruggio [TA]
☎ +39 0461247135
✉ www.masseriaborgodeitrulli.com

CELLAR SALES
ANNUAL PRODUCTION 500,000 bottles
HECTARES UNDER VINE 45.50
SUSTAINABLE WINERY

Masseria Borgo dei Trulli acquired vineyards less than a decade ago in the Primitivo di Manduria area, specifically in the towns of Sava, Manduria, and Maruggio, where the winery is located, and in the Salice Salentino area, in the town of Guagnano. The estate comprises three main vineyard holdings: Roselle, a 12-hectare plot surrounding the winery on sandy red soils, where mostly primitivo and negroamaro are cultivated; Pasano, another 12 hectares on more clay-rich red soils, supporting both white and red grape varieties; and 4 hectares in Salice Salentino. The Primitivo di Manduria Mirea '22 stands out, conjuring up aromas of blackberry, black cherry, and undergrowth on the nose, while the palate proves consistent, with nice body and acidity, long, finishing on rich fruit. The Liala '22, a negroamaro, is also well-crafted, opting for tones of wild black fruits and rain-soaked earth on the nose, and a palate of fine body, always fruit-driven, with a finish of nice tension and length.

I Buongiorno

c.so Vittorio Emanuele, 73
72012 Carovigno [BR]
☎ +39 0831996286
✉ ibuongiorno.com

CELLAR SALES
RESTAURANT SERVICE
ANNUAL PRODUCTION 37,000 bottles
HECTARES UNDER VINE 10.00
SUSTAINABLE WINERY

The Buongiorno family, long known for running one of Puglia's most renowned restaurants, ventured into winemaking about 15 years ago. Their vineyards, located in the Carovigno area, host the region's traditional varieties, including primitivo, negroamaro, aleatico, and fiano. They produce a small range of modern wines, with a focus on expressing the distinct characteristics of the grapes and the terroir. The Nicolaus '22 is excellent—a blend of primitivo and negroamaro redolent of wild berries and spicy notes on the nose, and a fresh palate, with nice body and length. The entire range is well-made: the Negroamaro '23 proves balanced, rich in fruit and smooth, with elegant tannins; the Primitivo '22 offers hints of blackberry and Mediterranean scrub, with freshness and juiciness; the Rosalento '23 is a sapid and floral rosé; the Susumaniello '23 drinks easily, with tones of figs and black plum; while the Nerisco '21 is a juicy, highly approachable negroamaro.

● Primitivo di Manduria Mirea '22	♛♛♛ 4*
● Liala '22	♛♛ 5
● Primitivo di Manduria '22	♛ 3
● Primitivo di Manduria Duna Mirante '22	♛ 8
● Salice Salentino Ris. '20	♛ 3

● Nicolaus '22	♛♛ 3*
● Negroamaro '23	♛♛ 3
● Nerisco '21	♛♛ 4
● Primitivo '22	♛♛ 3
⊙ Rosalento '23	♛♛ 3
● Susumaniello '23	♛♛ 3
○ Fiano '21	♕♕ 3
○ Fiano '20	♕♕ 3
● Negroamaro '21	♕♕ 3
● Negroamaro '17	♕♕ 3
● Nicolaus '18	♕♕ 4
● Nicolaus '17	♕♕ 4
● Primitivo '21	♕♕ 3
● Primitivo '19	♕♕ 3
● Susumaniello '22	♕♕ 3
● Susumaniello '21	♕♕ 2*

Francesco Candido

via Lombardia, 27
72025 San Donaci [BR]
℡ +39 0831635674
⊕ www.candidowines.it

CELLAR SALES
PRE-BOOKED VISITS
ANNUAL PRODUCTION 800,000 bottles
HECTARES UNDER VINE 110.00
VITICULTURE METHOD Certified Organic

The Candido family's nearly century-old winery spans a vast vineyard area between Guagnano and San Donaci, benefiting from the breezes of both the Ionian and Adriatic seas. The estate hosts negroamaro, primitivo, and aleatico, cultivated using the traditional Pugliese bush-training method, while montepulciano, syrah, and chardonnay are trained on trellises. Their range is technically precise and deeply rooted in tradition. The Duca d'Aragona '19, made from 80% negroamaro with a touch of montepulciano, reveals scents of ripe black stone fruits on the nose, leading to a palate of great depth and body, fresh, with beautiful length. Other well-made wines include the juicy Salice Salentino Negroamaro Immensum Riserva '21, with its spicy tones, notes of white pepper and tobacco, and well-managed tannins, and the Salice Salentino Negroamaro Rosato Le Pozzelle '23, with its aromas of rose petals and wild berries—a smooth and immediately gratifying drink.

● Duca d'Aragona '19	♟♟ 5
⊙ Salice Salentino Negroamaro Rosato Le Pozzelle '23	♟♟ 2*
● Salice Salentino Rosso Immensum Ris. '21	♟♟ 3
● Cappello di Prete '20	♟ 3
○ Luminosia Chardonnay '23	♟ 3
⊙ Piccoli Passi '23	♟ 3
○ Piccoli Passi Verdeca '23	♟ 3
● Cappello di Prete '19	♟♟ 3
● Cappello di Prete '18	♟♟ 3*
● Duca d'Aragona '18	♟♟ 5
● Primitivo di Manduria Cassio Dione Ris. '19	♟♟ 5
● Salice Salentino Negroamaro Immensum Ris. '20	♟♟ 3
⊙ Salice Salentino Negroamaro Rosato Le Pozzelle '22	♟♟ 2*

Cantele

s.da prov.le 365, km 1
73010 Guagnano [LE]
℡ +39 0832507010
⊕ www.cantele.it

CELLAR SALES
PRE-BOOKED VISITS
ANNUAL PRODUCTION 1,500,000 bottles
HECTARES UNDER VINE 48.00
SUSTAINABLE WINERY

Since 2001, cousins Luisa, Gianni, Paolo, and Umberto have managed Cantele, a property with about 50 hectares of privately-owned vineyards in Guagnano, Montemesola, and San Pietro Vernotico. The estate vineyards, which are situated on calcareous-clay soils dominated by red earth, are complemented by another 150 hectares overseen by the winery staff. Alongside chardonnay, which produces some of the winery's historic wines, traditional grape varieties take center stage, yielding modern-styled wines with superb typicity and appeal. The Amativo '22, a blend of primitivo and negroamaro, showcases aromas of black fruits and Mediterranean scrub with hints of cinchona, leading to a palate with fine balance and freshness. The Primitivo '23 is also excellent, playing on floral tones and black fruits, and a long palate, with beautiful acidity and sapidity. The rest of their range is always reliable and well-made, with special mentions for the Susumaniello '23, which goes all in on spicy notes and black cherry, and the Fanòi '21, a fresh and elegant primitivo.

● Amativo '22	♟♟♟ 4*
● Primitivo '23	♟♟ 3*
● Fanòi '21	♟♟ 6
● Salice Salentino Negroamaro Teresa Manara Ris. '21	♟♟ 4
● Susumaniello '23	♟♟ 2*
⊙ Rohesia Negroamaro Rosato '23	♟ 3
○ Teresa Manara Chardonnay '23	♟ 3
● Teresa Manara Primitivo '22	♟ 4
○ Verdeca '23	♟ 2
● Amativo '21	♟♟♟ 4*
● Amativo '07	♟♟♟ 4*
● Amativo '03	♟♟♟ 3*
● Salice Salentino Rosso Ris. '19	♟♟♟ 2*
● Salice Salentino Rosso Ris. '09	♟♟♟ 2*
● Salice Salentino Negroamaro Teresa Manara Ris. '20	♟♟ 4

Tenute Capovaccaio

v.le 7 Liberatori della Selva, 10/3
70011 Alberobello [BA]
☎ +39 3773929828
🌐 www.tenutecapovaccaio.com

★Carvinea

loc. Pezza d'Arena
via per Serranova
72012 Carovigno [BR]
☎ +39 3483738581
🌐 www.carvinea.com

CELLAR SALES
PRE-BOOKED VISITS
ACCOMMODATION
ANNUAL PRODUCTION 20,000 bottles
HECTARES UNDER VINE 4.00
SUSTAINABLE WINERY

CELLAR SALES
PRE-BOOKED VISITS
ACCOMMODATION AND RESTAURANT SERVICE
ANNUAL PRODUCTION 70,000 bottles
HECTARES UNDER VINE 10.00
VITICULTURE METHOD Certified Organic

Founded just two years ago, Francesco Pezzolla's winery is a small operation that follows biodynamic principles. The vineyards are split between two estates, located in the Valle d'Itria at about 300 meters in elevation, and in the Murgia region, between Alberobello and Noci, at elevations spanning 450-500 meters. The region's classic grape varieties are grown, including verdeca, minutolo, fiano, susumaniello, and primitivo. The wines are crafted to express the unique characteristics of both the grapes and their origins. Leading their lineup is the Sinjari '23, a fresh and sapid minutolo with floral tones, exotic fruit fragrances, and aromatic herbs. Other excellent wines include the long and energetic Gioia del Colle Primitivo Gipeto '23, with its balsamic notes and black cherry; the Tagarote '23, a well-structured and tense primitivo redolent of wild black fruits and blood orange; the Feldeggii '23, a rich and pleasant susumaniello; and the Verdeca Timoniera '22, which plays on yellow fruit tones, and a sapid, smooth, long palate.

Beppe Di Maria's winery is housed in a 16th-century farmhouse in the Carovigno area, near the Torre Guaceto nature reserve. The estate's vineyards, situated around the winery on calcareous tuff soils and cooled by the salty air blowing on off both the Ionian and Adriatic seas, are home to traditional Salentine grape varieties, with ottavianello playing a leading role. The Otto '22, a monovarietal ottavianello, conjures up aromas of black stone fruits and aromatic herbs on the nose, while the palate is juicy, with good fruit and length. Other well-made wines include the Frugifero '21, a pleasant and fresh primitivo redolent of Mediterranean scrub; the original Metodo Classico Ottorosé Brut '19, from ottavianello grapes, a creamy and persistent drink characterized by pastry aromas and wild strawberry; and another ottavianello, the Ottorosa '23, which offers up notes of rose petals and wild red berries on the nose, with a smooth, approachable palate.

○ Sinjari '23	⚟⚟ 3*
⊙ Feldeggii '23	⚟⚟ 5
● Gioia del Colle Primitivo Gipeto '20	⚟⚟ 5
● Tagarote '23	⚟⚟ 5
○ Timoniera '22	⚟⚟ 4
○ Albidus '23	⚟ 5
○ Araeus '23	⚟ 3
● Gioia del Colle Primitivo Remigante Ris. '21	⚟ 5
● Ulula '23	⚟ 3

● Otto '22	⚟⚟ 5
● Frugifero Primitivo '21	⚟⚟ 4
⊙ Ottorosa '23	⚟⚟ 4
⊙ Ottorosé Brut M. Cl. '19	⚟⚟ 5
○ Lucerna Fiano '23	⚟ 3
● Frugifero '19	⚟⚟⚟ 4*
● Merula '11	⚟⚟⚟ 3*
● Negroamaro '17	⚟⚟⚟ 5
● Negroamaro '14	⚟⚟⚟ 5
● Negroamaro '13	⚟⚟⚟ 5
● Negroamaro '11	⚟⚟⚟ 3*
● Otto '18	⚟⚟⚟ 5
● Otto '16	⚟⚟⚟ 4*
⊙ Ottorosa '20	⚟⚟⚟ 3*
● Primitivo '15	⚟⚟⚟ 5
● Sierma '09	⚟⚟⚟ 5

Castello Monaci

via Case Sparse
73015 Salice Salentino [LE]
☏ +39 0831665700
✉ castellomonaci.it

CELLAR SALES
PRE-BOOKED VISITS
RESTAURANT SERVICE
ANNUAL PRODUCTION 1,500,000 bottles
HECTARES UNDER VINE 210.00

Castello Monaci oversees an extensive estate divided into three properties, each on different soils: sandy terrain near the sea at Masseria Flaminio in Brindisi, where primarily white varieties are cultivated; iron-rich red earth at Masseria Vittorio in Trepuzzi, Lecce, mainly for primitivo; and clay and tuff soils at the Salice Salentino estate, where both indigenous red grapes and international varieties are grown. As always, Castello Monaci's wines put in a strong overall performance. The Kreos '23 is a rosé from negroamaro grapes, highly enjoyable with its floral tones and sweet citrus; the Maru '23 is a negroamaro where fruity notes and Mediterranean scrub stand out; the Pilùna '23 is a primitivo redolent of plum and wild black fruits, offering a pleasant, fresh, and taut palate. The Salice Salentino Aiace Riserva '21 highlights notes of ripe black fruit and sweet spices across a body of considerable volume.

Giancarlo Ceci

c.da Sant'Agostino
76123 Andria [BT]
☏ +39 0883565220
✉ www.giancarloceci.com

CELLAR SALES
PRE-BOOKED VISITS
ANNUAL PRODUCTION 350,000 bottles
HECTARES UNDER VINE 70.00
VITICULTURE METHOD Certified Biodynamic
SUSTAINABLE WINERY

Giancarlo Ceci's winery is based on a single, 70-hectare vineyard situated within a nearly 250-hectare biodynamically farmed estate. Located between Andria and Castel del Monte, about 20 kilometers from the sea, in the lower hills of the Murge plateau, the property features stony, calcareous soils. Mostly traditional regional grapes are grown: nero di Troia alongside montepulciano, bombino nero, bombino bianco, and fiano. Among the various wines offered this year, the standout is the Castel del Monte Nero di Troia Parco Marano '19. Aromas of bramble, ripe fruit, and licorice rise from the glass, while the palate is slightly marked by oak but has decent length and a pleasant, sapid and spicy finish. The Castel del Monte Rosso Parco Grande '22 is also well-made, with its tones of black fruits and sweet spices, offering good body and depth. The other wines tasted are also on point.

⊙ Kreos '23	♟♟ 3*
● Maru '23	♟♟ 3
● Pilùna '23	♟♟ 3
● Salice Salentino Aiace Ris. '21	♟♟ 4
○ Acante Fiano '23	♟ 3
● Artas '21	♟ 6
○ Petraluce '23	♟ 3
● Artas '07	♟♟♟ 5
● Artas '06	♟♟♟ 4
● Artas '05	♟♟♟ 4*
● Artas '04	♟♟♟ 3*
● Artas '20	♟♟ 5
● Artas '13	♟♟ 5
⊙ Kreos '22	♟♟ 3*
● Salice Salentino Aiace Ris. '19	♟♟ 3*
● Salice Salentino Aiace Ris. '13	♟♟ 3*

● Castel del Monte Nero di Troia Parco Marano '19	♟♟ 4
● Castel del Monte Rosso Parco Grande '22	♟♟ 3
○ Castel del Monte Bombino Bianco Brut M. Cl. Apnea '19	♟ 5
⊙ Castel del Monte Bombino Bianco Brut M. Cl. Rosé Apnea '19	♟ 5
○ Castel del Monte Bombino Bianco Panascio '23	♟ 3
○ Castel del Monte Bombino Nero Parchitello '23	♟ 3
○ Clara Fiano '22	♟ 4
● Castel del Monte Nero di Troia Parco Marano '18	♟♟ 3*
● Castel del Monte Rosso Parco Grande '21	♟♟ 3*

★Tenute Chiaromonte

loc. c.da Scapparagno
s.da prov.le 178, km 2.800
70021 Acquaviva delle Fonti [BA]
+39 0805127551
tenutechiaromonte.com

CELLAR SALES
PRE-BOOKED VISITS
ACCOMMODATION AND RESTAURANT SERVICE
ANNUAL PRODUCTION 300,000 bottles
HECTARES UNDER VINE 60.00
VITICULTURE METHOD Certified Organic

Tenute Chiaromonte, a leading player in the Gioia del Colle appellation's success over the past decade, offers a range of wines primarily based on primitivo. These come from vineyards located over 300 meters above sea level on the karstic soils of the Murge, including more than ten hectares of 60-year-old primitivo bush vines. The wines, captivating and complex, fully express the character of the territory. The splendid Gioia del Colle Primitivo Muro Sant'Angelo Contrada Barbatto '21 offers up aromas of black berries, aromatic herbs, and sweet spices. It boasts a rich texture, vibrant energy, and impressive length and freshness. The Gioia del Colle Primitivo Riserva '17 is marked by a mouthfilling, full-bodied profile, with tones of black figs, leather, and plum jam, lengthening into a long, sapid finish. The Ancestrale Brut Rosé '19, one of the region's best Metodo Classicos, stands out with its floral tones, balancing freshness and creaminess.

● Gioia del Colle Primitivo Muro Sant'Angelo Contrada Barbatto '21	TTT	7
⊙ Chiaromonte Ancestrale Brut Nature M. Cl. Rosé '19	TT	8
● Gioia del Colle Primitivo Ris. '17	TT	8
● Gioia del Colle Primitivo Muro Sant'Angelo '21	TT	5
○ Kimìa Moscato '23	TT	3
● Donna Carlotta Primitivo '21	T	3
○ Kimìa Fiano '23	T	4
⊙ Kimìa Susumaniello Rosato '23	T	4
● Gioia del Colle Primitivo Muro Sant'Angelo Contrada Barbatto '20	YYY	7
● Gioia del Colle Primitivo Muro Sant'Angelo Contrada Barbatto '19	YYY	7

★Conti Zecca

via Cesarea
73045 Leverano [LE]
+39 0832925613
www.contizecca.it

CELLAR SALES
PRE-BOOKED VISITS
ANNUAL PRODUCTION 2,500,000 bottles
HECTARES UNDER VINE 250.00
SUSTAINABLE WINERY

The Conti Zecca family has been present in Leverano for over 400 years and now manages a vast estate divided into four properties in Leverano and Salice Salentino. The wide range offered, divided into various production lines, includes both traditional Salentine grape varieties and international ones. A modern production style features nice freshness and fruit richness, while always maintaining a strong sense of territorial identity. The Salice Salentino Rosso Cantalupi Riserva '22 shines with its aromas of plum, cinnamon, and wild berries, followed by a palate of good substance, freshness, and juiciness, with a taut and austere finish. Other well-crafted wines include the Leverano Negroamaro Rosso Superiore Liranu '22, which features blackberry and Mediterranean scrub on the nose, leading to a palate with good length and freshness; and the plum and cherry-scented Terra '20, an Aglianico with lovely structure and depth. The Nero '21 falls a bit short, still overly marked by oak.

● Salice Salentino Rosso Cantalupi Ris. '22	TTT	3*
● Leverano Negroamaro Sup. Liranu '22	TT	3
● Terra '20	TT	4
● Cantalupi Primitivo '23	T	2
○ Mendola '23	T	3
● Nero '21	T	6
⊙ Venus '23	T	3
● Nero '09	YYY	5
● Nero '08	YYY	5
● Nero '07	YYY	5
● Nero '06	YYY	5
● Nero '03	YYY	5
● Nero '02	YYY	5
● Nero '01	YYY	5
● Salice Salentino Cantalupi Ris. '20	YYY	3*

Coppi

s.da prov.le Turi - Gioia del Colle
70010 Turi [BA]
☎ +39 0808915049
✉ www.vinicoppi.it

CELLAR SALES
PRE-BOOKED VISITS
RESTAURANT SERVICE
ANNUAL PRODUCTION 900,000 bottles
HECTARES UNDER VINE 100.00
VITICULTURE METHOD Certified Organic

The Coppi family's private estate spans about 100 hectares of vineyards, mainly in the Gioia del Colle appellation, with about half composed of bush-trained vines. These are flanked by another 100 hectares managed separately in Brindisi's Salento area. Their wines, made exclusively with indigenous grape varieties, are modern, territorially expressive, and notably aromatic. Once again, the Gioia del Colle Primitivo Senatore leads the winery's lineup. The 2021 version opens on floral notes accompanied by fruity hints of figs and black plums, with a palate that's sapid, nicely textured and supple. The Serralto Malvasia Bianca '23 is also well-crafted, with citrus and white fruit aromas, pleasant freshness, and a finish with nice energy and persistence. The Cantonovo Primitivo Rosato '23 proves true to type in its floral whiffs and hints of aromatic herbs—an immediately gratifying, easy drink.

d'Araprì

via Michele Zannotti, 30
71016 San Severo [FG]
☎ +39 0882227643
✉ www.darapri.it

CELLAR SALES
PRE-BOOKED VISITS
ANNUAL PRODUCTION 180,000 bottles
HECTARES UNDER VINE 18.00
SUSTAINABLE WINERY

It has been 45 years since three friends decided to create a winery in San Severo dedicated to producing Metodo Classico wines, and today, the second generation is taking the reins. The estate's vineyards are all located in the San Severo area and are mostly trained in the Pugliese pergola system to avoid excessive sun exposure. The main grape is bombino bianco, complemented by pinot nero, montepulciano, and nero di Troia. Only Metodo Classico is made here. The Gran Cuvée XXI Secolo Brut '17, made from bombino bianco, pinot nero, and montepulciano, reveals scents of white fruit and pastry, with notes of almond brittle and raspberry. The palate is rich, with good structure and persistence, yet also energetic and sapid. The Pas Dosé, crafted from bombino bianco and pinot nero, offers up aromas of toasted hazelnuts, honey, and walnuts. A fresh, long, and elegant wine. The Brut R.N. '19, exclusively from bombino bianco, showcases acacia honey tones, along with structure and persistence.

● Gioia del Colle Primitivo Senatore '21	▼▼▼ 5
⊙ Cantonovo Primitivo Rosato '23	▼▼ 3
○ Serralto Malvasia Bianca '23	▼▼ 3
● Cantonovo Primitivo '21	▼ 3
⊙ Corè Negroamaro Rosato '23	▼ 3
● Don Antonio Primitivo '17	♉♉♉ 3*
● Gioia del Colle Primitivo Senatore '20	♉♉♉ 5
● Gioia del Colle Primitivo Senatore '19	♉♉♉ 5
● Gioia del Colle Primitivo Senatore '18	♉♉♉ 5
● Gioia del Colle Primitivo Senatore '17	♉♉♉ 5
● Gioia del Colle Primitivo Senatore '15	♉♉♉ 5
● Gioia del Colle Primitivo Senatore '11	♉♉♉ 5
● Gioia del Colle Primitivo Senatore '10	♉♉♉ 3*
● Don Antonio Primitivo '19	♉♉ 3*
● Gioia del Colle Primitivo Senatore '16	♉♉ 5

○ Gran Cuvée XXI Secolo Brut M. Cl. '17	▼▼ 8
○ Pas Dosé M. Cl.	▼▼ 7
○ RN Brut M. Cl. '19	▼▼ 8
○ d'Araprì Gran Cuvée XXI Secolo '09	♉♉ 6
○ d'Araprì Nobile Ris. '04	♉♉ 5

Cantine De Falco

via Milano, 25
73051 Novoli [LE]
☎ +39 0832711597
✐ www.cantinedefalco.it

★Cantine Due Palme

via San Marco, 130
72020 Cellino San Marco [BR]
☎ +39 0831617865
✐ www.cantineduepalme.it

CELLAR SALES
PRE-BOOKED VISITS
ACCOMMODATION
ANNUAL PRODUCTION 300,000 bottles
HECTARES UNDER VINE 20.00

CELLAR SALES
PRE-BOOKED VISITS
ACCOMMODATION
ANNUAL PRODUCTION 17,000,000 bottles
HECTARES UNDER VINE 2500.00
VITICULTURE METHOD Certified Organic
SUSTAINABLE WINERY

Established in 1949, the De Falco family's winery boasts vineyards located in the heart of Salento, particularly in the Salice Salentino and Squinzano appellations. The vineyards, mostly trained in the traditional Pugliese bush method, primarily host the region's classic varieties, such as negroamaro, malvasia nera, and primitivo. The wines are crafted with a modern approach, yet remain faithful to expressing the characteristics of the terroir. At the top of the winery's range is the Salice Salentino Falco Nero Riserva '21, with its aromas of black fruits, sweet spices, and Mediterranean scrub. Lon, and pleasant, the palate shows nice stuffing and volume. The rest of the lineup is equally well-crafted, with highlights including the Bocca della Verità '22, a soft and pervasive Primitivo with tones of black cherry and licorice, and the Salice Salentino Negroamaro Salore '22, where the nose is still somewhat marked by oak in its spicy notes but reveals good substance and length.

Cantina Due Palme relies on about 1,000 members who cultivate a sizable area across the provinces of Brindisi, Taranto, and Lecce. 40% of the vines are bush trained and 90% are red grape varieties. The wide range offered is primarily produced with local grape varieties, while the production style yields a traditional, Mediterranean profile where time-honored viticultural approaches combines with modern winemaking methods. The Salice Salentino Rosso Selvarossa Riserva '21 opens with scents of ripe black fruits, Mediterranean scrub, and underbrush, followed by a palate with crisp fruit tones, good body, juiciness, and a pleasant, fresh finish. The Primitivo di Manduria San Gaetano '23 features notes of black fruit jam and cinnamon against a backdrop of aromatic herbs, with a long, well-sustained acidic finish. The Seraia '23, a blend of equal parts negroamaro and primitivo, offers floral aromas with spicy and fresh plum nuances, resulting in a smooth and energetic palate.

● Salice Salentino Rosso Falco Nero Ris. '21	♟♟ 4
● Bocca della Verità '22	♟♟ 3
● Salice Salentino Negroamaro Salore '22	♟♟ 3
○ Artiglio Bianco Verdeca '23	♟ 3
● Artiglio Susumaniello '23	♟ 3
⊙ Artiglio Susumaniello Rosato '23	♟ 3
○ Caolino '23	♟ 3
○ Etesio '23	♟ 3
● Primitivo di Manduria Ottante '22	♟ 5
⊙ Salice Salentino Negroamaro Rosato Stelle di Lorenzo '23	♟ 3
● Bocca della Verità '21	♟♟ 3
● Bocca della Verità '20	♟♟ 2*
● Salice Salentino Negroamaro Salore '19	♟♟ 2*
● Salice Salentino Rosso Falco Nero Ris. '20	♟♟ 4

● Salice Salentino Rosso Selvarossa Ris. '21	♟♟♟ 6
● 1943 del Fondatore '21	♟♟ 8
● Primitivo di Manduria San Gaetano '23	♟♟ 4
● Seraia '23	♟♟ 2*
⊙ Cuntamè Susumaniello Rosato '23	♟ 5
● Ettamiano '21	♟ 4
○ Salice Salentino Bianco Tinaia '23	♟ 4
● Selvamara Negroamaro '23	♟ 4
● Serre Susumaniello '23	♟ 4
○ Veramore Verdeca '23	♟ 5
● 1943 del Presidente '19	♟♟♟ 6
● 1943 del Presidente '18	♟♟♟ 8
● Salice Salentino Rosso Selvarossa Ris. '20	♟♟♟ 4*
● Salice Salentino Rosso Selvarossa Ris. '19	♟♟♟ 5

Tenute Eméra
Claudio Quarta Vignaiolo

c.da Provica
s.da prov.le 124
74123 Lizzano [TA]
☎ +39 0832704398
✉ www.claudioquarta.it

CELLAR SALES
PRE-BOOKED VISITS
ACCOMMODATION
ANNUAL PRODUCTION 600,000 bottles
HECTARES UNDER VINE 55.00
SUSTAINABLE WINERY

Led by Claudio Quarta and his daughter Alessandra, Tenute Eméra comprises over fifty hectares of vineyards on mineral and fossil-rich soils near the Ionian coast, close to Lizzano. There's also an old, bush-trained vineyard of just over a hectare in Guagnano (where the grapes for their Salice Salentino are cultivated), and the Sanpaolo winery in Irpinia. The wines are traditionally styled but notable for their precision and aromatic clarity. In the absence of the winery's more important reds (still aging in the cellar), the Lizzano Negroamaro Superiore Anima di Negroamaro '20 put in a noteworthy performance. It opens with aromas of stone fruits and Mediterranean scrub, with a palate that's fruity and fresh despite a noticeable alcohol presence. The Negroamaro rosato La Vigne En Rose '23 features floral tones and fresh red cherry, with a sapid and refreshing palate, avoiding excessive sweetness.

★Felline

s.da comunale Santo Stasi I, 42b
74024 Manduria [TA]
☎ +39 0999711660
✉ www.agricolafelline.it

CELLAR SALES
PRE-BOOKED VISITS
ACCOMMODATION
ANNUAL PRODUCTION 800,000 bottles
HECTARES UNDER VINE 110.00
VITICULTURE METHOD Certified Organic
SUSTAINABLE WINERY

Gregory Perrucci's winery spans various zones within the Primitivo di Manduria appellation. The result is a range that reflect the different soils, thanks in part to major zoning work and the preservation of old, Pugliese bush-trained vines. It's a range where a more modern profile based on fresh fruit and elegance harmonizes with a more traditional focus on depth and volume. The Primitivo di Manduria Terra Bianca Giravolta '20 put in another strong performance. Its complex and multifaceted nose reveals notes of ripe plum, underbrush, and cloves, while the palate proves fresh, taut, extending into a long, austere finish, with no excessive sweetness. The Edmond Dantes Pas Dosé, made from vermentino grapes, ranks among the region's best Metodo Classicos, elegant and enjoyable with floral and tropical fruit tones. The rest of the lineup is well-crafted, with a special mention for the sapid and fresh Susumaniello Polignano '23.

Wine	Rating
⊙ Là Vigne en Rose '23	♟♟ 3
● Lizzano Sup. Anima di Negroamaro '20	♟♟ 3
○ Amure '23	♟ 3
○ Anima di Chardonnay (R)evolution '23	♟ 3
● Primitivo di Manduria Oro di Eméra '20	♟♟♟ 5
● Primitivo di Manduria Anima di Primitivo '21	♟♟ 3*
● Primitivo di Manduria Anima di Primitivo '19	♟♟ 3*
● Primitivo di Manduria Anima di Primitivo '16	♟♟ 3*
● Primitivo di Manduria Oro di Eméra '21	♟♟ 5
● Primitivo di Manduria Oro di Eméra '18	♟♟ 5
● Salice Salentino Rosso Moros Ris. '17	♟♟ 4

Wine	Rating
● Primitivo di Manduria Terra Bianca Giravolta '20	♟♟♟ 4*
○ Edmond Dantes Pas Dosé M. Cl.	♟♟ 6
⊙ Polignano Rosé '23	♟♟ 2*
● Primitivo di Manduria Terra Nera Sinfarosa Zinfandel '20	♟♟ 5
⊙ Cicala Rosé '23	♟ 2
● Trullari Nero di Troia '22	♟ 2
○ Verdeca '23	♟ 2
○ Vermentino '23	♟ 2
● Primitivo di Manduria Sinfarosa Zinfandel '18	♟♟♟ 4*
● Primitivo di Manduria Sinfarosa Zinfandel Terra Nera '19	♟♟♟ 5
● Primitivo di Manduria Terra Bianca Giravolta '19	♟♟♟ 4*

★Gianfranco Fino

c.da Reni
74024 Manduria [TA]
☎ +39 0997773970
🌐 www.gianfrancofino.it

CELLAR SALES
PRE-BOOKED VISITS
RESTAURANT SERVICE
ANNUAL PRODUCTION 30,000 bottles
HECTARES UNDER VINE 23.00
SUSTAINABLE WINERY

Gianfranco Fino and Simona Natale's winery, which is celebrating its 20th anniversary this year, mainly draws on bush-trained primitivo vines that go back anywhere from 50-100 years. The property's calcareous-clay red earth also hosts small quantities of negroamaro. Since 2021, the winery has featured a new cellar and a wine resort as well. The wines produced are both complex and vigorous, with impressive density and freshness. Once again, the Es proves to be one of the best Primitivos out there. The 2022 vintage opens on vibrant aromas of stone fruits, carob, black olives, and spices, while the palate is consistent, close-knit, slightly extractive, yet rich in fruit, sapid, juicy, with impressive length and persistence. The Jo '21, a monovarietal negroamaro, is also excellent, though still somewhat marked by oak on the nose, with notes of dried fruit and Mediterranean scrub—yet the palate is pervasive, with considerable substance and volume.

Cantine Paolo Leo

via Tuturano, 21
72025 San Donaci [BR]
☎ +39 3357036811
🌐 www.paololeo.it

CELLAR SALES
PRE-BOOKED VISITS
ACCOMMODATION
ANNUAL PRODUCTION 5,000,000 bottles
HECTARES UNDER VINE 70.00
VITICULTURE METHOD Certified Organic
SUSTAINABLE WINERY

The Leo family's winery boasts two cellars: one in San Donaci, within the Salice Salentino appellation, and the other in Monteparano, near Primitivo di Manduria. Some 40 wines are offered, sourced from estate vineyards cultivated using the traditional Puglian bush training system, and from trusted growers overseen by their technicians. The wines exhibit a modern structure, focusing on a pleasant and fruity profile. This year, the Moramora Malvasia Nera '23 beat out the rest of their range. One of the few monovarietal versions of the grape in Puglia (it's traditionally blended with negroamaro), it conjures up pronounced black berry aromas, accompanied by floral and aromatic herb nuances, while the palate is immediately expressive, fresh, and pleasantly drinkable. The Primitivo di Manduria Passo del Cardinale '23 is also well-made, with good concentration and rich fruit.

● Es '22	♟♟♟ 8
● Jo '21	♟♟ 8
● Es '21	♟♟♟ 8
● Es '19	♟♟♟ 7
● Primitivo di Manduria Es '12	♟♟♟ 7
● Primitivo di Manduria Es '11	♟♟♟ 7
● Primitivo di Manduria Es '10	♟♟♟ 6
● Primitivo di Manduria Es '09	♟♟♟ 6
● Primitivo di Manduria Es '08	♟♟♟ 6
● Primitivo di Manduria Es '07	♟♟♟ 6
● Primitivo di Manduria Es '06	♟♟♟ 5
● Es '20	♟♟ 8
● Es '18	♟♟ 7
● Es '17	♟♟ 7
● Es '16	♟♟ 7
● Jo '20	♟♟ 7

● Moramora Malvasia Nera '23	♟♟♟ 3*
● Primitivo di Manduria Passo del Cardinale '23	♟♟ 3
● Fiore di Vigna Primitivo '21	♟ 5
● Orfeo Negroamaro '22	♟ 5
⊙ Rosamora '23	♟ 3
● Orfeo Negroamaro '18	♟♟♟ 5
● Orfeo Negroamaro '16	♟♟♟ 5
● Orfeo Negroamaro '15	♟♟♟ 4*
● Primitivo di Manduria Passo del Cardinale '22	♟♟♟ 3*
● Primitivo di Manduria Passo del Cardinale '21	♟♟♟ 3*
● Primitivo di Manduria Passo del Cardinale '20	♟♟♟ 3*
● Taccorosso Negroamaro '15	♟♟♟ 6

★Leone de Castris

via Senatore de Castris, 26
73015 Salice Salentino [LE]
📞 +39 0832731112
🌐 www.leonedecastris.com

CELLAR SALES
PRE-BOOKED VISITS
ACCOMMODATION AND RESTAURANT SERVICE
ANNUAL PRODUCTION 2,000,000 bottles
HECTARES UNDER VINE 300.00
SUSTAINABLE WINERY

Leone de Castris owns several properties in the towns of Salice Salentino, Campi, Guagnano, and Gioia del Colle. About half of the vineyards use the bush training system, with both traditional and international grape varietals cultivated. Their extensive range draws on a modern approach, resulting in everything from immediately expressive, fruit-rich offerings to more complex and age-worthy wines. This Gioia del Colle estate's flagship wine put in an impressive performance this year. The Gioia del Colle Primitivo Colpo di Zappa '21 opens on aromas of black fruits and Mediterranean scrub, followed by a touch of spice. On the palate, it's fresh, long, and juicy. The Five Roses Anniversario '23, with its floral notes and wild red berries, is equally pleasant and sapid. The Salice Salentino Negroamaro Per Lui Riserva '19 stands out for its clarity, rich fruit, and impressive volume. The rest of the range is also well-crafted.

Masca del Tacco

via Tripoli, 7
72020 Erchie [BR]
📞 +39 069426980
🌐 www.mascadeltacco.com

ANNUAL PRODUCTION 800,000 bottles
HECTARES UNDER VINE 140.00

Felice Mergè, who also owns Poggio Le Volpi in the Castelli Romani, is the man behind Puglia's Masca del Tacco. The vineyards, located in Erchie, Veglie, and Torricella, feature a variety of soils and host both traditional and international grape varietals. The wines are distinctly modern, aiming for fullness and volume while maintaining notable aromatic precision. Without their flagship, the Primitivo di Manduria Piano Chiuso, the estate's top wine this year is the Primitivo di Manduria Li Filitti Riserva '20. It offers up red fruit aromas, quinine, white pepper, and underbrush on the nose, while the palate is structured, with good length and persistence. The Primitivo di Manduria Lu Rappaio '22 follows with black cherry, figs, and carob aromas, leading to a sweet, fruit-driven palate. The Susumaniello Rosato '23 proves pleasant and balanced, with floral and yellow fruit notes.

● Gioia del Colle Primitivo Colpo di Zappa '21	▼▼▼ 5
⊙ Five Roses Anniversario '23	▼▼ 4
● Salice Salentino Negroamaro Per lui Ris. '19	▼▼ 7
● Gioia del Colle Primitivo Saliscendi Ris. '20	▼▼ 7
○ Messapia Verdeca '23	▼▼ 3
● Primitivo di Manduria Villa Santera '23	▼▼ 4
● Salice Salentino Negroamaro Donna Lisa Ris. '20	▼▼ 6
● Il Lemos '23	▼ 3
⊙ Marisa '23	▼ 5
⊙ Five Roses 74° Anniversario '17	▽▽▽ 3*
⊙ Five Roses 77° Anniversario '20	▽▽▽ 3*
⊙ Five Roses 78° Anniversario '21	▽▽▽ 3*
⊙ Five Roses 79° Anniversario '22	▽▽▽ 4*

● Primitivo di Manduria Li Filitti Ris. '20	▼▼ 4
● Primitivo di Manduria Lu Rappaio '22	▼▼ 3
⊙ Susumaniello Rosato '23	▼▼ 3
○ L'Uetta Fiano '23	▼ 4
● Susumaniello '23	▼ 3
● Primitivo di Manduria Piano Chiuso 26 27 63 Ris. '19	▽▽▽ 6
● Primitivo di Manduria Piano Chiuso 26 27 63 Ris. '18	▽▽▽ 6
● Primitivo di Manduria Piano Chiuso 26 27 63 Ris. '17	▽▽▽ 5
● Primitivo di Manduria Piano Chiuso 26 27 63 Ris. '16	▽▽▽ 5
● Primitivo di Manduria Lu Rappaio '15	▽▽ 4
● Primitivo di Manduria Piano Chiuso 26 27 63 Ris. '15	▽▽ 4

Masseria Cuturi

s.da prov.le 137
74024 Manduria [TA]
📞 +39 0999711660
🌐 www.masseriacuturi.com

Menhir Salento

via Salvatore Negro
73020 Bagnolo del Salento [LE]
📞 +39 0836818199
🌐 www.menhirsalento.it

CELLAR SALES
PRE-BOOKED VISITS
ACCOMMODATION AND RESTAURANT SERVICE
ANNUAL PRODUCTION 60,000 bottles
HECTARES UNDER VINE 40.00
VITICULTURE METHOD Certified Organic
SUSTAINABLE WINERY

CELLAR SALES
PRE-BOOKED VISITS
RESTAURANT SERVICE
ANNUAL PRODUCTION 1,500,000 bottles
HECTARES UNDER VINE 50.00
SUSTAINABLE WINERY

Although the origins of this winery date back to the late 19th century, it was only about 20 years ago that the vineyards were replanted on a single estate, located near the sea and the oaks of the Bosco dei Cuturi nature reserve. Situated in the Manduria area, the vineyard's flagship grape is, unsurprisingly, primitivo, accompanied by negroamaro and fiano. The wines are technically precise and dedicated to expressing the terroir. The Zacinto '23, a monovarietal negroamaro, is splendid, revealing ripe black fruit aromas, plum in particular, along with hints of underbrush. A rich, juicy, and immediately gratifying drink. The two Primitivo di Manduria wines presented, the Monte Diavoli '20 and Chidro '21, are both well-crafted. The Monte Diavoli '20 plays on Mediterranean scrub and plum jam aromas, with a sapid and substantive palate. The Chidro '21 is fresher and more supple, although the finish is slightly marked by alcohol.

The Marangelli family's winery is a benchmark for Terra d'Otranto. The vineyards are located in Minervino, Palmariggi, and Bagnolo, supplemented by grapes purchased from trusted growers who are monitored year-round by the winery's staff. The focus is on traditional Salento varietals, making for a range that emphasizes fruit richness and aromatic precision. This year, the spotlight is on the Negroamaro di Terra d'Otranto Rosso Filo Riserva '22, which offers plum, mulberry, quinine, and underbrush aromas. The palate is well-structured, juicy, and pleasant. Though not as brilliant as last year's, the Terra d'Otranto Rosso Vega Riserva '22 is still well-made, with a soft and fruity profile. The Pietra Susumaniello '23 proves fresh, with firm tannins—a balanced drink, with good length. The Primitivo CalaMuri '22 stands out for its underbrush and plum tones, with a pervasive and fruit-rich palate. Finally, we also appreciated the delicious Menhir Rosato.

● Zacinto '23	♟♟♟ 3*
● Primitivo di Manduria Chidro '21	♟♟ 4
● Primitivo di Manduria Monte Diavoli '20	♟♟ 6
⊙ Rosa dei Cuturi '23	♟ 3
○ Segreto di Bianca '23	♟ 3
● Tumà '22	♟ 3
● Primitivo di Manduria Il 1° '12	♟♟ 4
● Primitivo di Manduria Monte Diavoli '19	♟♟ 6
⊙ Rosa dei Cuturi '22	♟♟ 3
⊙ Rosa dei Cuturi '21	♟♟ 3
⊙ Rosa dei Cuturi '19	♟♟ 3
○ Segreto di Bianca '22	♟♟ 3
○ Segreto di Bianca '20	♟♟ 3
● Tumà Primitivo '17	♟♟ 4
● Zacinto '21	♟♟ 3
● Zacinto '17	♟♟ 2*

● Negroamaro di Terra d'Otranto Rosso Filo Ris. '22	♟♟♟ 5
⊙ Menhir Rosato '23	♟♟ 2*
● Calamuri '22	♟♟ 3
● Pietra Susumaniello '23	♟♟ 3
● Terra d'Otranto Rosso Vega Ris. '22	♟♟ 5
● Negroamaro di Terra d'Otranto Rosso Pepe '22	♟ 3
● Primitivo di Terra d'Otranto Rosso Vola '22	♟ 3
⊙ Terra d'Otranto Rosato Nina '23	♟ 4
● Terra d'Otranto Rosso Vega Ris. '21	♟♟♟ 5
⊙ Pietra Rosato '17	♟♟ 3
● Quota 29 Primitivo '21	♟♟ 2*
● Quota 29 Primitivo '20	♟♟ 2
● Terra d'Otranto Primitivo Vola '21	♟♟ 3*

Morella

c.da Marroco
74024 Manduria [TA]
📞 +39 0999791482
🌐 www.morellavini.com

CELLAR SALES
PRE-BOOKED VISITS
ANNUAL PRODUCTION 30,000 bottles
HECTARES UNDER VINE 20.00
VITICULTURE METHOD Certified Biodynamic

Lisa Gilbee and Gaetano Morella manage a small but prized heritage of old bush-trained vines, which go back anywhere from 35 to +80 years, in the Manduria area. Their vineyards, located about two kilometers from the sea on red soils, primarily host primitivo, alongside negroamaro, malbek, and fiano. The wines are designed to showcase the authentic qualities and true expression of the territory. The Primitivo Old Vines '20 showcases cherry, blackberry, and Mediterranean scrub on the nose. The palate is fruit-driven, long, sapid, and highly enjoyable. The Primitivo La Signora '20 impresses with its iodine notes of black fruits and aromatic herbs, while the palate is energetic, taut, slightly austere, yet fresh, with licorice and blueberry emerging on the finish. The Mezzanotte '22, an easy-drinking, fresh, and sapid Primitivo, and the Malbek Primitivo '22, with its gentian and wild berry tones, are also well-made.

Mottura Vini del Salento

p.zza Melica, 4
73058 Tuglie [LE]
📞 +39 0833596601
🌐 www.motturavini.it

CELLAR SALES
PRE-BOOKED VISITS
ANNUAL PRODUCTION 1,800,000 bottles
HECTARES UNDER VINE 120.00

Barbara Mottura passionately and competently manages her family's winery. The cellar in Tuglie is supported by a sizable set of vineyards in Cellino San Marco, Campi Salentina, Salice Salentino, and Squinzano. The plots, which feature calcareous and clay soils covered by a thin layer of red earth, host bush-trained vines that go back around 60 years. The area's native grapes are cultivated, making for traditionally styled wines that highlight their terroir. The Rosone '22, a negroamaro, impresses with its balsamic hints, plum nuances, quinine, and Mediterranean scrub. The palate is substantive, fresh, balanced, and long. The Salice Salentino Le Pitre '21 stands out with its underbrush and sour cherry tones, juicy palate, and a finish well-supported by acidity. The Primitivo di Manduria Stilio '22, with its mature black fruit and aromatic herb notes, and the I Classici Negroamaro '23, which offers pleasant black berry tones, are also well-made.

• Primitivo Old Vines '20	♟♟♟ 7
• La Signora Primitivo '20	♟♟ 7
• Malbek Primitivo '22	♟♟ 4
• Mezzanotte Primitivo '22	♟♟ 3
• Mezzarosa '23	♟ 3
• La Signora Primitivo '10	♟♟♟ 6
• La Signora Primitivo '07	♟♟♟ 5
• Old Vines Primitivo '18	♟♟♟ 7
• Old Vines Primitivo '09	♟♟♟ 5
• Old Vines Primitivo '08	♟♟♟ 5
• Old Vines Primitivo '07	♟♟♟ 5
• La Signora Primitivo '19	♟♟ 7
• La Signora Primitivo '18	♟♟ 7
• Negroamaro Primitivo '21	♟♟ 4
• Negroamaro Primitivo '20	♟♟ 4
• Old Vines Primitivo '19	♟♟ 7

• Rosone '22	♟♟ 4
• Salice Salentino Le Pitre '22	♟♟ 3*
• I Classici Negroamaro '23	♟♟ 2*
• Primitivo di Manduria Stilio '22	♟♟ 4
• I Classici Primitivo '23	♟ 3
• Primitivo di Manduria Le Pitre '22	♟ 3
• Salice Salentino Le Pitre '19	♟♟♟ 3*
○ Fiano del Salento '22	♟♟ 2*
• Negroamaro del Salento '22	♟♟ 2*
• Primitivo di Manduria Stilio '21	♟♟ 4
• Primitivo di Manduria Villa Mottura '19	♟♟ 3*
⊙ Rosato del Salento '22	♟♟ 2*
• Rosone '20	♟♟ 4
• Salice Salentino Le Pitre '21	♟♟ 3
• Salice Salentino Le Pitre '20	♟♟ 3*

Palamà

via Armando Diaz, 6
73020 Cutrofiano [LE]
☎ +39 0836542865
🌐 www.vinicolapalama.com

CELLAR SALES
PRE-BOOKED VISITS
ANNUAL PRODUCTION 200,000 bottles
HECTARES UNDER VINE 14.00
VITICULTURE METHOD Certified Organic
SUSTAINABLE WINERY

For nearly 90 years, the Palamà family has been producing quality wines in the heart of Salento. Their vineyards are spread out across various properties in Cutrofiano and Matino, where medium-textured soils host primarily bush-trained vines. All their wines come from indigenous varietals, aiming to showcase the quality and characteristics of both the grapes and their terroir. This year's lineup is commendable, with the Patrunale '21 standing out. A Primitivo, it releases classic black fruit aromas alongside Mediterranean scrub, all followed by a fresh and enjoyable palate. The Metiusco Rosato '23 is among the best rosés in the region, a floral and iodine-rich negroamaro, sapid and highly enjoyable. The Metiusco Anniversario '22, another monovarietal negroamaro, reveals black cherry and sweet spice notes, with a juicy palate and still prominent tannins.

Tenuta Patruno Perniola

c.da Marzagaglia
70023 Gioia del Colle [BA]
☎ +39 3383940830
🌐 www.tenutapatrunoperniola.it

CELLAR SALES
PRE-BOOKED VISITS
ACCOMMODATION AND RESTAURANT SERVICE
ANNUAL PRODUCTION 16,000 bottles
HECTARES UNDER VINE 3.60
VITICULTURE METHOD Certified Organic
SUSTAINABLE WINERY

Paolo Patruno's Patruno Perniola includes a small vineyard on a hillside, part of a 30-hectare property on mineral-rich rocky red soil. Apart from a small amount of verdeca, the winery focuses on primitivo, producing half a dozen Mediterranean-style bottles that highlight fruit richness and pleasantness. In the absence of the Riserva, the Gioia del Colle Primitivo Marzagaglia '21 takes the lead for the estate. It opens with black fruit and aromatic herb aromas, followed by a substantive and fruit-rich palate, juicy with a sapid finish. The Lenos Primitivo '22, with its plum and mulberry aromas, proves pervasive and taut, while the Ghirigori Rosato '23, made from primitivo grapes, is floral, with rosehip and red fruit tones—pleasant drinking, with good persistence and freshness.

⊙ Metiusco Rosato '23	♥♥ 3*
● Patrunale '21	♥♥ 5
● Metiusco Anniversario '22	♥♥ 4
● 75 Vendemmie '21	♥ 5
● D'Arcangelo Il Vino '22	♥ 5
● 75 Vendemmie '11	♥♥♥ 4*
● 75 Vendemmie '19	♥♥ 5
● Il Vino d'Arcangelo '21	♥♥ 5
● Mavro '17	♥♥ 4
● Metiusco Anniversario '21	♥♥ 4
⊙ Metiusco Rosato '21	♥♥ 3*
⊙ Metiusco Rosato '19	♥♥ 3*
⊙ Metiusco Rosato '18	♥♥ 3*
● Metiusco Rosso '20	♥♥ 3*
● Patrunale '16	♥♥ 5

● Gioia del Colle Primitivo Marzagaglia '21	♥♥ 4
⊙ Ghirigori Rosato '23	♥♥ 3
● Lenos Primitivo '22	♥♥ 3
○ Striale Verdeca '23	♥ 3
● Gioia del Colle Primitivo 1821 Ris. '19	♥♥♥ 5
● Gioia del Colle Primitivo Marzagaglia '20	♥♥ 4
● Gioia del Colle Primitivo Marzagaglia '19	♥♥ 4
● Gioia del Colle Primitivo Marzagaglia '17	♥♥ 4
● Gioia del Colle Primitivo Marzagaglia '12	♥♥ 4
● Lenos Primitivo '21	♥♥ 3

Pietraventosa

loc. Parco Largo
s.da vic.le Latta Latta, 248
70023 Gioia del Colle [BA]
℡ +39 3355730274
🖳 www.pietraventosa.it

ANNUAL PRODUCTION 35,000 bottles
HECTARES UNDER VINE 7.40
VITICULTURE METHOD Certified Organic
SUSTAINABLE WINERY

For 20 years, Marianna Annio and Raffaele Leo have managed this winery within the Gioia del Colle appellation. Their vineyards, including a notable hectare of 70-year-old bush-trained primitivo, are planted on calcareous and clay soils rich in minerals, at elevations of about 380 meters. The wines exhibit a modern style, aptly expressing the varietals and their origin. This year, the Gioia del Colle Primitivo Riserva is back at the top. The 2019 vintage stands out with its ripe black fruit, Mediterranean scrub, sweet spices, and coffee aromas, followed by a palate that's well-structured and voluminous, with fruity tones, freshness, juiciness, and a clear finish. The Primitivo rosato EstRosa '23 is excellent, with floral, sapid, and iodine-rich notes—highly enjoyable yet with good backbone. Finally, the Ossimoro '20, a blend of primitivo and aglianico, proves austere yet rich in fruit, with good length and structure.

Plantamura

via V. Bodini, 9a
70023 Gioia del Colle [BA]
℡ +39 3474711027
🖳 www.viniplantamura.it

CELLAR SALES
PRE-BOOKED VISITS
ANNUAL PRODUCTION 50,000 bottles
HECTARES UNDER VINE 10.00
VITICULTURE METHOD Certified Organic
SUSTAINABLE WINERY

The Plantamura family's winery has been organically run since its founding in 2002. Their vineyards, at about 350 meters above sea level, feature both old bush-trained vines and newer trellised vines on calcareous karst soils, with a thin layer of red clay. The wines, all from primitivo grapes, are distinctive and strongly tied to their terroir. Once again, the Gioia del Colle Primitivo Riserva ranks among the best wines of the Gioia appellation. The 2021 version reveals aromatic herbs, underbrush, and cherry aromas, with a spirited, fruit-rich, fresh palate that's particularly approachable for its type. The Gioia del Colle Primitivo Contrada San Pietro '22 is also well-crafted, with ripe black cherry and blackberry aromas, a spirited and fluid palate, and nice persistence.

● Gioia del Colle Primitivo Ris. '19	▼▼▼ 6
⊙ EstRosa '23	▼▼ 4
● Ossimoro '20	▼▼ 5
⊙ EstRosa '22	♈♈ 4*
● Gioia del Colle Primitivo Ris. '06	♈♈ 4
⊙ EstRosa '17	♈ 3*
● Gioia del Colle Primitivo Allegoria '21	♈ 4
● Gioia del Colle Primitivo Allegoria '19	♈ 4
● Gioia del Colle Primitivo Allegoria '17	♈ 3
● Gioia del Colle Primitivo Ris. '17	♈ 6
● Gioia del Colle Primitivo Ris. '16	♈ 6
● Gioia del Colle Primitivo Ris. '15	♈ 5
● Gioia del Colle Primitivo Ris. '13	♈ 6
● Volere Volare Primitivo '21	♈ 3*
● Volere Volare Primitivo '19	♈ 3
● Volere Volare Primitivo '18	♈ 3

● Gioia del Colle Primitivo Ris. '21	▼▼ 5
● Gioia del Colle Primitivo Et. Nera Contrada San Pietro '22	▼▼ 4
● Gioia del Colle Primitivo Et. Nera Contrada San Pietro '13	♈♈ 3*
● Gioia del Colle Primitivo Et. Nera Contrada San Pietro '12	♈♈ 3*
● Gioia del Colle Primitivo Et. Rossa '11	♈♈ 4*
● Gioia del Colle Primitivo Parco Largo '22	♈♈ 3*
● Gioia del Colle Primitivo Ris. '17	♈♈ 4*
● Gioia del Colle Primitivo Contrada San Pietro '19	♈ 3*
● Gioia del Colle Primitivo Parco Largo '17	♈ 3*
● Gioia del Colle Primitivo Ris. '20	♈ 5
● Gioia del Colle Primitivo Ris. '19	♈ 4

Podere 29

fraz. Tressanti
s.da prov.le 544 Trinitapoli-Foggia
76016 Cerignola [FG]
☏ +39 08831926995
🌐 www.podere29.it

CELLAR SALES
PRE-BOOKED VISITS
ACCOMMODATION
ANNUAL PRODUCTION 130,000 bottles
HECTARES UNDER VINE 20.00
VITICULTURE METHOD Certified Organic

Giuseppe Marrano's winery is situated about 10 kilometers from the Margherita di Savoia salt pans, an area heavily influenced by the sea. The vineyards, planted in 2003, host primarily the indigenous nero di Troia grape. The wines, with their Mediterranean character and modern profile, prove enjoyable, beautifully expressing their varietal traits. Among the best rosé wines of the region, the Gelso Rosa '23 is a Nero di Troia with pronounced floral and wild red berry aromas. The palate is fresh, approachable, and easy-drinking. The rest of the range is also well-crafted, particularly the Unio '23, a blend of primitivo (60%) and nero di Troia that schowcases crisp dark fruit tones and Mediterranean herbs—good length. The Gelso d'Oro '22, a monovarietal Nero di Troia, also caught our attention for its juicy, immediately gratifying, and full-bodied profile.

⊙ Gelso Rosa '23	▼▼	3*
● Gelso d'Oro '22	▼▼	6
● Unio '23	▼▼	4
● Avia Pervia Primitivo '23	▼	3
● Duna Susumaniello '22	▼	7
○ Gelso Bianco Fiano '23	▼	4
○ Salina Chardonnay '23	▼	3
● Gelso d'Oro '15	▽▽	5
● Gelso d'Oro '14	▽▽	5
● Gelso d'Oro Nero di Troia '20	▽▽	5
● Gelso d'Oro Nero di Troia '19	▽▽	5
● Gelso d'Oro Nero di Troia '18	▽▽	5
● Gelso d'Oro Nero di Troia '16	▽▽	5
● Gelso Nero '20	▽▽	2*
⊙ Gelso Rosa '21	▽▽	2*
⊙ Gelso Rosa '20	▽▽	2*

★Polvanera

s.da Vicinale Lamie Marchesana, 601
70023 Gioia del Colle [BA]
☏ +39 080758900
🌐 www.cantinepolvanera.it

CELLAR SALES
RESTAURANT SERVICE
ANNUAL PRODUCTION 750,000 bottles
HECTARES UNDER VINE 120.00
VITICULTURE METHOD Certified Organic

In just over 20 years, the Cassano family has elevated Polvanera to the pinnacle of Gioia del Colle wine production. The estate's vineyards are located at elevations spanning 300-450 meters, with calcareous rock covered by a thin layer of red soil. The flagship grape is primitivo, though other traditional varieties are also grown, making for a range of modern wines that showcases the best qualities of both the grape and the region. The splendid Gioia del Colle Primitivo 17 Montevella '21 offers up mulberry and rosemary notes accompanied by mineral nuances. The palate is fruity, full, energetic, and long, with a pleasant finish, despite its alcoholic richness. Other excellent pours include the Gioia del Colle Primitivo Riserva '19, which features ripe dark fruit and sweet spice tones, yet remains fresh, smooth, and energetic with good length, and the Minutolo '23, with its aromas of wood resin, moss, and white fruit, and a sapid, well-defined palate. The rest of the wines offered are also of a high standard.

● Gioia del Colle Primitivo 17 Vign. Montevella '21	▼▼▼	5
● Gioia del Colle Primitivo Ris. '19	▼▼	7
○ Minutolo '23	▼▼	3*
○ Gioia del Colle Bianco '23	▼▼	4
● Gioia del Colle Primitivo 14 Marchesana '22	▼▼	3
● Gioia del Colle Primitivo 16 Vign. San Benedetto '21	▼▼	5
⊙ Gioia del Colle Rosato '23	▼▼	4
● Gioia del Colle Rosso '23	▼▼	4
● Gioia del Colle Primitivo 17 Vign. Montevella '20	▽▽▽	5
● Gioia del Colle Primitivo 17 Vign. Montevella '19	▽▽▽	5
● Gioia del Colle Primitivo 17 Vign. Montevella '18	▽▽▽	5

Produttori di Manduria

via Fabio Massimo, 19
74024 Manduria [TA]
☎ +39 0999735332
✉ www.produttoridimanduria.it

Rivera

loc. c.da Rivera
s.da prov.le 231, km 60,500
76123 Andria [BT]
☎ +39 0883569510
✉ www.rivera.it

CELLAR SALES
PRE-BOOKED VISITS
ANNUAL PRODUCTION 2,300,000 bottles
HECTARES UNDER VINE 900.00
SUSTAINABLE WINERY

CELLAR SALES
PRE-BOOKED VISITS
ACCOMMODATION
ANNUAL PRODUCTION 1,200,000 bottles
HECTARES UNDER VINE 75.00

Produttori di Manduria is a historic cooperative winery with 400 members. The growers' vineyards are all within the Primitivo di Manduria appellation, where a bush-trained vines dominate (over half are dedicated to primitivo). The extensive range is modern in style, making for wines rich in fruit and true to the attributes of the varietals used. The Primitivo di Manduria Sonetto Riserva '19 confirms its place at the top, with its spicy notes, aromatic herbs, and black cherry aromas. The palate is marked by juicy, dark berry fruits and finishes with a sapid, highly pleasant note. The Primitivo di Manduria Elegia Riserva '21 proves well-crafted, though still slightly marked by wood, with pleasant black plum notes and nice length. The Primitivo di Manduria Lirica '22 proves brooding on the nose, with tones of jammy dark fruits, tanned leather, and rain-soaked earth. Good volume and fullness on the palate.

For over 70 years, the De Corato family has offered some of Castel del Monte's best wines. Recently, they've added a small selection from other districts through agreements with trusted growers. Their vineyards are situated between 200-350 meters in conditions that are particularly cool for the area, making for wines with bold flavors and lovely aromatic clarity. The Castel del Monte Aglianico Cappellaccio Riserva '19 is excellent, revealing aromas of Mediterranean scrub, rain-soaked earth, and black plum. The palate is full-bodied, with nice volume and a sapid fruit finish. Other well-made wines include the Castel del Monte Nero di Troia Violante '22, with its ripe fruit aromas, smooth, fresh, and long palate, and the Castel del Monte Rosso Il Falcone Riserva '19, a charming and notably deep wine that still needs time to achieve its full potential. The Castel del Monte Nero di Troia Puer Apuliae Riserva was negatively impacted by the challenging 2018 vintage.

● Primitivo di Manduria Sonetto Ris. '19	♛♛♛ 6
● Primitivo di Manduria Elegia Ris. '21	♛♛ 5
● Primitivo di Manduria Lirica '22	♛♛ 3
● Abatemasi Negroamaro '21	♛ 5
○ Alice Verdeca '23	♛ 3
● Electric Bee Unconventional Primitivo '23	♛ 2
⊙ Garnet '23	♛ 3
○ Zin Fiano '23	♛ 3
● Primitivo di Manduria Lirica '21	♕♕♕ 3*
● Primitivo di Manduria Lirica '20	♕♕♕ 3*
● Primitivo di Manduria Lirica '19	♕♕♕ 2*
● Primitivo di Manduria Lirica '18	♕♕♕ 2*
● Primitivo di Manduria Lirica '17	♕♕♕ 2*
● Primitivo di Manduria Dolce Naturale Madrigale '20	♕♕ 4
● Primitivo di Manduria Memoria '22	♕♕ 3*

● Castel del Monte Aglianico Cappellaccio Ris. '19	♛♛ 3*
● Castel del Monte Nero di Troia Violante '22	♛♛ 3
● Castel del Monte Rosso Il Falcone Ris. '19	♛♛ 4
○ Castel del Monte Bombino Bianco Marese '23	♛ 2
⊙ Castel del Monte Bombino Nero Pungirosa '23	♛ 3
○ Castel del Monte Chardonnay Lama dei Corvi '23	♛ 4
● Castel del Monte Nero di Troia Puer Apuliae Ris. '18	♛ 5
● Castel del Monte Nero di Troia Puer Apuliae '04	♕♕♕ 6
● Castel del Monte Rosso Il Falcone Ris. '17	♕♕ 4

★Tenute Rubino

via E. Fermi, 50
72100 Brindisi
(》 +39 0831571955
⊚ www.tenuterubino.com

San Marzano Vini

via Monsignor A. Bello, 9
74020 San Marzano di San Giuseppe
[TA]
(》 +39 0999574181
⊚ www.sanmarzano.wine

CELLAR SALES
PRE-BOOKED VISITS
ACCOMMODATION AND RESTAURANT SERVICE
ANNUAL PRODUCTION 800,000 bottles
HECTARES UNDER VINE 180.00
SUSTAINABLE WINERY

CELLAR SALES
ANNUAL PRODUCTION 12,000,000 bottles
HECTARES UNDER VINE 1500.00
VITICULTURE METHOD Certified Organic
SUSTAINABLE WINERY

The Rubino family's winery boasts an extensive area under vines, spread out across five estates between the Adriatic coast and the inland province of Brindisi, reaching close to the Ionian Sea. Among the local grapes cultivated, susumaniello stands out, with the winery focusing on enhancing the varietal to create both modern and strongly terroir-driven wines. The Torre Testa Rosato '23, a bright Susumaniello rosé, takes center stage in the absence of the Oltremé. It reveals floral notes, cherry, and aromatic herbs on the nose, while the palate is fresh, sapid, crisp, and highly enjoyable. The Brindisi Negroamaro Rosato Saturnino '23 drinks smooth and easy with its tones of wild red berries and sweet citrus, while the Brindisi Rosso Riserva Jaddico '19 opts for aromas of black olives, plums, and cola, with a palate of nice structure and volume.

San Marzano boasts some 1200 grower members. Their vineyards are situated primarily in the municipalities of San Marzano, Sava, and Francavilla Fontana, on red soils and calcareous substrates. Mostly traditional varieties are cultivated on old bush-trained vines. The wines aim to balance traditional alcoholic richness with a modern profile and drinkability. Despite the absence of their two flagship Primitivo di Mandurias, the Sessantanni and Anniversario 62 Riserva, the winery's range remains consistently high in quality. The Talò Malvasia Nera '23 is immediately expressive, revealing pleasant fruity and floral tones—a fresh and elegant pour. The Edda '23, a chardonnay-based white, has butter and vanilla scents with hints of sage and white fruit, creamy, rich, and full-bodied. The Sessantanni Rosé '21, more golden in color than rosé, proves full-bodied, conjuring up aromas of yellow plum.

⊙ Torre Testa Rosato '23	♈♈ 4
⊙ Brindisi Negroamaro Rosato Saturnino '23	♈♈ 3
● Brindisi Rosso Jaddico Ris. '19	♈♈ 5
○ Giancòla Malvasia Bianca '22	♈ 4
○ Salende Vermentino '23	♈ 3
● Visellio '21	♈ 5
● Brindisi Rosso Susumaniello Oltremé '21	♈♈♈ 3*
● Brindisi Rosso Susumaniello Oltremé '20	♈♈♈ 3*
● Brindisi Rosso Susumaniello Oltremé '19	♈♈♈ 3*
● Brindisi Rosso Susumaniello Oltremé '18	♈♈♈ 4*
● Oltremé Susumaniello '18	♈♈♈ 3*

● Talò Malvasia Nera '23	♈♈♈ 3*
○ Edda '23	♈♈ 4
⊙ Sessantanni Rosé '21	♈♈ 5
⊙ Amai Susumaniello Rosé '23	♈♈ 3
● Primitivo di Manduria Talò '23	♈♈ 3
○ M. Cl. Brut Rosé Calce '20	♈ 6
○ M. Cl. Brut Calce '20	♈ 5
○ Talò Verdeca '23	♈ 3
● F Negroamaro '20	♈♈♈ 5
● Primitivo di Manduria Sessantanni '19	♈♈♈ 5
● Primitivo di Manduria Sessantanni '18	♈♈♈ 5
● Primitivo di Manduria Sessantanni '17	♈♈♈ 5
● Primitivo di Manduria Sessantanni '16	♈♈♈ 5
● Primitivo di Manduria Anniversario 62 Ris. '19	♈♈ 6

Schola Sarmenti

via Generale Cantore, 37
73048 Nardò [LE]
☎ +39 0833567247
🖳 www.scholasarmenti.it

CELLAR SALES
PRE-BOOKED VISITS
RESTAURANT SERVICE
ANNUAL PRODUCTION 730,000 bottles
HECTARES UNDER VINE 82.00
VITICULTURE METHOD Certified Organic
SUSTAINABLE WINERY

Schola Sarmenti, with 85% of its vines bush-trained (and some going back as many as 80 years), is one of the most important wineries in the Nardò area. The vineyards are predominantly planted with traditional grape varieties, including negroamaro, malvasia nera, primitivo, susumaniello, and fiano. The wines are known for their rich fruit and high concentration, aimed at fully expressing the qualities of both the territory and the region's traditional grape varieties. At the top of the lineup this year is the Nardò Nerìo Riserva '21, with its ripe cherry and rosemary scents on the nose, followed by a fresh, juicy palate and a soft finish on sweet dark fruit tones. Other well-crafted wines include the Primitivo di Manduria Chiacchierino '19, with its pronounced aromas of underbrush and black plum—a smooth drink with a pleasant finish—and the Cubardi '22, a monovarietal Primitivo with jammy dark fruit tones and balsamic nuances, all followed by a crisp and austere palate.

Cosimo Taurino

s.da prov.le 365, km 1,400
73010 Guagnano [LE]
☎ +39 0832706490
🖳 www.taurinovini.it

CELLAR SALES
PRE-BOOKED VISITS
ANNUAL PRODUCTION 900,000 bottles
HECTARES UNDER VINE 90.00

The Taurino family's vineyards are located on sandy, calcareous soils between Guagnano, Salice Salentino, and San Donaci, in the heart of Salento. With vines over 80 years old, the dominant varieties are negroamaro and malvasia nera, which are flanked by smaller quantities of other local and international grapes. Their wines are traditionally styled, aiming for longevity and full expression of the terroir. Another testament to this style is the 2019 version of the historic Patriglione Negroamaro, with its licorice and truffle aromas, sweet spices, and Mediterranean scrub notes. The palate is multifaceted, complex, with good length and balance. We also appreciated the excellent passito Le Ricordanze '21, a blend of riesling and semillon, where nuts, chestnut honey, and caramel aromas are followed by a palate that aptly balances sweetness and sapidity. The rest of the range is also well-made.

● Nardò Nerìo Ris. '21	♟♟ 4
● Cubardi '22	♟♟ 5
● Primitivo di Manduria Chiacchierino '19	♟♟ 5
○ Ambace Fiano Chardonnay '23	♟ 4
⊙ Antieri Susumaniello Rosé '23	♟ 5
○ Cortices Fiano Orange '23	♟ 4
⊙ Nardò Rosato Opra '23	♟ 4
● Nauna '22	♟ 5
● Viginti '20	♟ 8
● Cubardi '17	♟♟ 4
● Diciotto Primitivo '19	♟♟ 8
● Nardò Rosso Nerìo Ris. '17	♟♟ 3
● Nauna '19	♟♟ 5
● Nauna '16	♟♟ 5

● Patriglione '19	♟♟♟ 8
○ Le Ricordanze '21	♟♟ 5
● Kompà '21	♟♟ 2*
● Settimo Ceppo '21	♟♟ 3
● Salice Salentino Rosso Ris. '18	♟ 3
⊙ Scaloti '23	♟ 2
● Notarpanaro '18	♟♟♟ 4*
● Notarpanaro '17	♟♟♟ 3*
● Notarpanaro '16	♟♟♟ 3*
● Patriglione '94	♟♟♟ 7
● Patriglione '88	♟♟♟ 7
● Patriglione '85	♟♟♟ 5
● Notarpanaro '15	♟♟ 3*
● Patriglione '18	♟♟ 8
● Patriglione '17	♟♟ 8
● Patriglione '16	♟♟ 7

Teanum

via Croce Santa, 48
71016 San Severo [FG]
☎ +39 0882336332
● www.teanum.com

CELLAR SALES
PRE-BOOKED VISITS
ANNUAL PRODUCTION 1,500,000 bottles
HECTARES UNDER VINE 200.00

Teanum operates seven estates, all located in the province of Foggia, totaling 200 hectares of vineyards (with 150 hectares owned and another 50 leased). The soils here, which range from calcareous to sandy, host traditional varieties, including nero di Troia, aglianico, montepulciano, primitivo, susumaniello, and falanghina, along with international varieties like chardonnay. The wines have a modern style. This year, the spotlight is on the Sumarello Nero di Troia '21, with its tones of Mediterranean scrub, ripe dark fruits, and underbrush on the nose. The palate is full-bodied, with well-managed tannins and a long, fresh finish. Other well-made wines include the energetic, juicy, and enjoyable Black Primitivo '21, with its tapenade and mulberry aromas, the Otre Primitivo Rosato '23, a smooth and immediately expressive drink redolent of wild red berries and aromatic herbs, and finally, the Otre Aglianico '21, a bit unpolished but with good progression, playing on sensations of dark stone fruit and herbs.

Terre di Sava

s.da st.le 7ter, km 16
74028 Sava [TA]
☎ +39 0999576100
● www.terredisava.it

ANNUAL PRODUCTION 6,000,000 bottles
HECTARES UNDER VINE 500.00
SUSTAINABLE WINERY

Terre di Sava manages several vineyards on the Salento peninsula, particularly within the Primitivo di Manduria appellation, where old bush-trained vines dominate. Over twenty different wines are produced, with the the focus mainly on primitivo, though other local and international varieties are used as well. The result is a modern range that emphasize freshness and rich fruit. The Terra d'Otranto Negroamaro Notte Rossa '22 is excellent, evoking aromas of fresh red fruits, aromatic herbs, and cinchona notes on the nose, leading to a fresh, enjoyable, and juicy palate. The Notte Rossa Primitivo Rosato '23 proves floral scented, with wild strawberry and white currant notes, and a full-bodied palate, finishing on sweet fruit tones, while the Primitivo di Manduria Notte Rossa '23 is characterized by black cherry sensations, blueberry, and hints of tanned leather. Immediately enjoyable, clean and clear.

● Sumarello Nero di Troia '21	♀♀ 3*
● Black Primitivo '21	♀♀ 3
● Otre Aglianico '21	♀♀ 2*
⊙ Otre Primitivo Rosato '23	♀♀ 2*
● Collezione del Fondatore Vincenzo De Matteo '19	♀ 5
○ Otre Falanghina '23	♀ 2
○ Otre Fiano '23	♀ 2
● Otre Nero di Troia '21	♀ 2
⊙ Sumarello Nero di Troia Rosato '23	♀ 3
● Gran Tiati '13	♀♀ 5
○ Otre Falanghina '22	♀♀ 2*
● Otre Primitivo '19	♀♀ 2*
⊙ Otre Primitivo Rosato '22	♀♀ 2*
⊙ Sumarello Nero di Troia Rosato '22	♀♀ 3
● Tiati Black Primitivo '19	♀♀ 3*

● Terra d'Otranto Negroamaro Notte Rossa '22	♀♀ 3*
⊙ Notte Rossa Primitivo Rosato '23	♀♀ 3
● Primitivo di Manduria Notte Rossa '23	♀♀ 3
● Notte Rossa Malvasia Nera '23	♀ 2
● Notte Rossa Primitivo '22	♀ 3
● Notte Rossa Susumaniello '21	♀ 3
● Primitivo di Manduria Notte Rossa Ris. '19	♀♀♀ 4*
● Notte Rossa Bascià Rosso '21	♀♀ 4
● Notte Rossa Nero di Troia '20	♀♀ 3
⊙ Notte Rossa Primitivo Rosato '22	♀♀ 2*
● Primitivo di Manduria Notte Rossa '20	♀♀ 3
● Primitivo di Manduria Notte Rossa Ris. '18	♀♀ 5

Terrecarsiche 1939

via Maestri del Lavoro, 6/8
70013 Castellana Grotte [BA]
(+39 0804962309
@ www.terrecarsiche.it

★Torrevento

s.da prov.le 234, Km 10.600
70033 Corato [BA]
(+39 0808980923
@ www.torrevento.it

CELLAR SALES
PRE-BOOKED VISITS
ACCOMMODATION
ANNUAL PRODUCTION 800,000 bottles
HECTARES UNDER VINE 40.00

PRE-BOOKED VISITS
ANNUAL PRODUCTION 2,500,000 bottles
HECTARES UNDER VINE 450.00
SUSTAINABLE WINERY

Founded in 2011, but rooted in a family tradition dating back to 1939, this winery's vineyards are located in the Murge region, mainly in the Gioia del Colle and Valle d'Itria appellations. They also source a selection of grapes from collaborating growers throughout the year. Theirs is a decidedly modern range with bold flavors and notable freshness. Leading the way this year is the Gioia del Colle Primitivo Fanova Riserva. The 2020 reveals notes of dark fruits, cinchona, and sweet spices, while the palate is more fruit-driven, with a pervasive and lingering finish. The rest of the range is also well-made, particularly the Gioia Rosa '23, a rosé made from primitivo (80%) and aleatico, offering pleasant and fresh aromas of wild strawberries and roses, and the Gioia del Colle Primitivo Fanova '22, a notably full-bodied and mouthfilling drink, though slightly lacking in the energy of previous vintages.

Francesco Liantonio's Torrevento is a stylistic benchmark for the Castel del Monte appellation. 250 hectares of estate vineyards on the calcareous-rocky soil of the Alta Murgia National Park are complemented by another 200 hectares of rented vineyards in the Valle d'Itria and Salento. Their wines reflect a low-intervention approach, prioritizing freshness, balance, and expression of territorial identity. In the absence of the historic Vigna Pedale, the spotlight falls on the Castel del Monte Bombino Nero Veritas '23 a rosé redolent of red fruit aromas, hints of humus and jasmine, and a fresh, sapid palate with great length and pleasure. Other well-crafted wines include the Kebir '22, a blend of nero di Troia, cabernet sauvignon, and aglianico, with its floral notes, energetic profile, and a long, austere finish; the Salice Salentino Sine Nomine Riserva '21, rich in fruit with evident but well-textured tannins; and the Moscato di Trani Dolce Naturale Dulcis in Fundo '22, a sweet sip, though never cloying.

● Gioia del Colle Primitivo Fanova Ris. '20	♥♥♥ 5
● Gioia del Colle Primitivo Fanova '22	♥♥ 3
⊙ Gioia Rosa '23	♥♥ 3
○ Passaturi Minutolo '23	♥♥ 3
○ Cava Bianca '22	♥ 5
● Gioia del Colle Primitivo Fanova '21	♀♀♀ 3*
● Gioia del Colle Primitivo Fanova '20	♀♀♀ 3*
● Gioia del Colle Primitivo Fanova '16	♀♀ 3*
● Gioia del Colle Primitivo Fanova Ris. '16	♀♀ 3*
● Nero di Troia '15	♀♀ 3

⊙ Castel del Monte Bombino Nero Rosato Veritas '23	♥♥♥ 2*
● Kebir '22	♥♥ 4
○ Moscato di Trani Dolce Naturale Dulcis In Fundo '22	♥♥ 3
● Salice Salentino Rosso Sine Nomine Ris. '21	♥♥ 3
○ Bacca Rara '23	♥ 3
○ Torre del Falco Fiano '23	♥ 2
● Castel del Monte Rosso Bolonero '19	♀♀♀ 2*
● Castel del Monte Rosso V. Pedale Ris. '19	♀♀♀ 3*
● Castel del Monte Rosso V. Pedale Ris. '16	♀♀♀ 3*
● Torre del Falco Nero di Troia '21	♀♀♀ 2*

Cantine Tre Pini

s.da prov.le 79, km 16 - via Vecchia
per Altamura
70020 Cassano delle Murge [BA]
☎ +39 3807274124
🌐 www.cantinetrepini.com

CELLAR SALES
PRE-BOOKED VISITS
ACCOMMODATION AND RESTAURANT SERVICE
ANNUAL PRODUCTION 100,000 bottles
HECTARES UNDER VINE 10.00
VITICULTURE METHOD Certified Organic
SUSTAINABLE WINERY

For over 30 years, the Plantamura family has operated an agriturismo on their estate in the Alta Murgia park, and for the past dozen years, they have produced a small range of wines exclusively from local grape varieties. Their vineyards are located in the municipalities of Cassano delle Murge and Acquaviva delle Fonti, at elevations spanning 400-450 meters. The wines focus on aromatic clarity, fresh fruit, and drinkability. The splendid Gioia del Colle Primitivo Riserva '21 consistently confirms this approach: a fresh, energetic wine, bordering on austerity, it evokes notes of wild blackberries, Mediterranean scrub, cloves, and nutmeg, offering great length and persistence on the palate. Other notable wines include the Crae Primitivo '23, with its mulberry and fresh red fruit aromas, and a pleasant, immediately expressive palate, and the Trullo di Carnevale '22, also made from primitivo, which leans more toward spicy and herbal tones.

Agricole Vallone

via XXV Luglio, 7
73100 Lecce
☎ +39 0832308041
🌐 www.agricolevallone.com

ANNUAL PRODUCTION 500,000 bottles
HECTARES UNDER VINE 180.00
SUSTAINABLE WINERY

One of Salento's historic wineries, the Vallone family estate produces about 15 wines, mainly from traditional local grapes, with a particular focus on negroamaro. The estate comprises three distinct sections: one in the Brindisi appellation, another in Salice Salentino, and the third in the Torre Guaceto nature reserve. The wines offered are an authentic expression of the grapes and the territory from which they originate. The Graticciaia, a historic wine not only for the producer but for the entire region, continues to lead the way. The 2019 version of this monovarietal negroamaro opens on notes of undergrowth, dried flowers, and black stone fruits, while the palate shows good structure and volume, with its signature evolved tones well-supported and refreshed by sapidity and acidic tension. The Castel Serranova '23, with its notes of white fruit and raspberry, proves fresh and supple. The Desidera '21 a sweet, soft, and pervasive wine, also stood out.

● Gioia del Colle Primitivo Ris. '21	🍷🍷🍷 5
● Crae Primitivo '23	🍷🍷 2*
● Trullo di Carnevale '22	🍷🍷 3
○ Donna Johanna Malvasia Bianca '23	🍷 2
⊙ Ventifile '23	🍷 2
● Gioia del Colle Primitivo Piscina delle Monache '20	🍷🍷🍷 4*
● Gioia del Colle Primitivo Ris. '14	🍷🍷🍷 5
● Gioia del Colle Primitivo Ris. '13	🍷🍷🍷 4*
● Gioia del Colle Primitivo Piscina delle Monache '21	🍷🍷 4
● Gioia del Colle Primitivo Piscina delle Monache '18	🍷🍷 3*
● Gioia del Colle Primitivo Ris. '20	🍷🍷 5
● Gioia del Colle Primitivo Ris. '18	🍷🍷 5
● Gioia del Colle Primitivo Ris. '17	🍷🍷 5

● Graticciaia '19	🍷🍷 7
● Castel Serranova '23	🍷🍷 4
○ Desidera '21	🍷🍷 3
● Graticciaia '18	🍷🍷🍷 7
● Graticciaia '17	🍷🍷🍷 7
● Graticciaia '16	🍷🍷🍷 7
● Graticciaia '03	🍷🍷🍷 6
● Graticciaia '01	🍷🍷🍷 6
⊙ Brindisi Rosato V. Flaminio '13	🍷🍷 2*
● Graticciaia '15	🍷🍷 7
● Graticciaia '13	🍷🍷 7
● Graticciaia '12	🍷🍷 7
● Graticciaia '10	🍷🍷 7
● Salice Salentino Negroamaro Vereto Ris. '21	🍷🍷 2*
● Vigna Castello '11	🍷🍷 5

Varvaglione 1921

c.da Santa Lucia
74020 Leporano [TA]
📞 +39 0995315370
🌐 www.varvaglione.com

CELLAR SALES
PRE-BOOKED VISITS
ACCOMMODATION
ANNUAL PRODUCTION 4,000,000 bottles
HECTARES UNDER VINE 400.00
SUSTAINABLE WINERY

Now under the leadership of the fourth generation of family, Varvaglione 1921 boasts an extensive estate of mainly native grape varieties. They also source grapes from associated growers overseen by the winery's staff. This combination allows them to produce a wide range of classic wines that aim to express both varietal characteristics and the attributes of the terroir. One of Puglia's finest wines, the Primitivo di Manduria Collezione Privata Cosimo Varvaglione Old Vines, reaffirms its standing. The 2021 highlights notes of black stone fruits and sweet spices on the nose, with nuances of Mediterranean scrub, followed by a balanced palate, offering good substance and volume, with a long, energetic, and pleasing finish. The 12 e Mezzo '22, a negroamaro characterized by woody notes and undergrowth, shows good structure and drive, while the Tatu '22, a primitivo redolent of aromatic herbs, plum, and pomegranate, reveals a fresh and enjoyable palate.

Masseria Li Veli

s.da prov.le Cellino - Campi, km 1
72020 Cellino San Marco [BR]
📞 +39 0831618259
🌐 www.liveli.it

CELLAR SALES
PRE-BOOKED VISITS
ANNUAL PRODUCTION 700,000 bottles
HECTARES UNDER VINE 59.00
SUSTAINABLE WINERY

The Falvo family vineyards are located between Cellino San Marco and the Valle d'Itria. In the former, red grapes are cultivated on bush-trained vines in red, sandy soils, while in the latter white grapes dominate. The grape varieties are almost exclusively traditional, making for a modern production style that skillfully balances territorial identity and varietal character. The Askos Verdeca reaffirms its place among Puglia's best whites. The 2023 exudes aromas of citrus, lychee, and white flowers, accompanied by iodized and Mediterranean scrub nuances, while the palate is fresh, sapid, with good structure and a gritty finish that leaves a slight bitterness. We also appreciated the Primitivo di Manduria Le Cerrate '22, with its tones of figs and dates, and the juicy, long and fresh Salice Salentino Rosso Pezzo Morgana Riserva '21, which features sensations of licorice, tar, and ripe black plum.

● Primitivo di Manduria Collezione Privata Cosimo Varvaglione Old Vines '21	♈♈♈ 6
● 12 e Mezzo Negroamaro '22	♈♈ 2*
● Tatu '22	♈♈ 3
○ Primadonna '23	♈ 3
⊙ Susumaniello Rosè '23	♈ 3
● Collezione Privata Cosimo Varvaglione Old Vines Negroamaro '19	♈♈♈ 6
● Collezione Privata Cosimo Varvaglione Old Vines Negroamaro '17	♈♈♈ 6
● Primitivo di Manduria Collezione Privata Cosimo Varvaglione Old Vines '20	♈♈♈ 6
● Primitivo di Manduria Collezione Privata Cosimo Varvaglione Old Vines '19	♈♈♈ 6

○ Askos Verdeca '23	♈♈♈ 4*
● Primitivo di Manduria Le Cerrate '22	♈♈ 4
● Salice Salentino Rosso Pezzo Morgana Ris. '21	♈♈ 5
● Askos Susumaniello '23	♈ 4
● MLV '21	♈ 5
● Askos Susumaniello '22	♈♈♈ 4*
○ Askos Verdeca '21	♈♈♈ 4*
○ Askos Verdeca '20	♈♈♈ 4*
○ Askos Verdeca '19	♈♈♈ 4*
○ Askos Verdeca '18	♈♈♈ 4*
○ Askos Verdeca '17	♈♈♈ 4*
● Masseria Li Veli '10	♈♈♈ 5
○ Askos Verdeca '22	♈♈ 4
● Salice Salentino Rosso Pezzo Morgana Ris. '18	♈♈ 5

★Vespa Vignaioli per Passione

c.da Reni
via Manduria - Avetrana km 3,8
74024 Manduria [TA]
☎ +39 063722120
✉ www.vespavignaioli.it

CELLAR SALES
PRE-BOOKED VISITS
ACCOMMODATION AND RESTAURANT SERVICE
ANNUAL PRODUCTION 250,000 bottles
HECTARES UNDER VINE 34.00
SUSTAINABLE WINERY

Located in the Masseria Li Reni, the Vespa family winery has various vineyards in Manduria and Salice Salentino, primarily on clay and clay-sandy soils. The main grape here is primitivo, accompanied by other local varieties like aleatico, fiano, and negroamaro. Their wines are modern in style, with a particular focus on freshness and drinkability. The Primitivo di Manduria Raccontami '22 reveals notes of sweet spices and black plum on the nose, followed by a balanced, pervasive palate with good structure and a long, energetic finish. The Primitivo di Manduria Il Rosso '23, with its balsamic hints and nuances of wild black fruits, proves fruity and pleasant, with a long sapid finish. The Primitivo Bruno '23 highlights spicy and black olive tapenade notes, offering a consistent, fruit-forward palate with immediate appeal.

Tenuta Viglione

s.da prov.le 140 km 4,500
70029 Santeramo in Colle [BA]
☎ +39 0802123661
✉ www.tenutaviglione.com

CELLAR SALES
PRE-BOOKED VISITS
ACCOMMODATION
ANNUAL PRODUCTION 1,000,000 bottles
HECTARES UNDER VINE 200.00
VITICULTURE METHOD Certified Organic

The Zullo family winery boasts a large estate between Gioia del Colle and Santeramo in Colle, at elevations of around 450 meters, on clay and limestone soils rich in minerals, topped with thin layers of red earth. Both traditional grapes, especially primitivo and aleatico, and international varieties are cultivated, making for a range of wines that aptly expresses the territory, with a focus on freshness and fullness of fruit. The Gioia del Colle Primitivo Marpione Riserva continues to lead the way. The 2021 showcases mulberry and Mediterranean scrub notes on the nose, while the palate is substantive, energetic, juicy, and sapid, making it truly enjoyable and flavorful. The highly convincing Maioliche Negroamaro '22, with its red fruit aromas and herbal nuances, proves smooth and fresh. The Gioia del Colle Primitivo Sellato '22 also delivers, with its tones of juniper, wood resin and wild berries, and its immediately enjoyable, tasty palate.

● Primitivo di Manduria Raccontami '22	▼▼▼ 6
● Bruno dei Vespa '23	▼▼ 3
● Primitivo di Manduria Il Rosso '23	▼▼ 4
○ Donna Augusta '22	▼ 7
⊙ Flarò '23	▼ 3
● Primitivo di Manduria Raccontami '21	♈♈♈ 6
● Primitivo di Manduria Raccontami '20	♈♈♈ 5
● Primitivo di Manduria Raccontami '19	♈♈♈ 5
● Primitivo di Manduria Raccontami '18	♈♈♈ 5

● Gioia del Colle Primitivo Marpione Ris. '21	▼▼▼ 5
● Gioia del Colle Primitivo Sellato Ris. '22	▼▼ 3
● Maioliche Negroamaro '22	▼▼ 3
○ Herba '23	▼ 3
○ Maidomo Negroamaro Bianco '23	▼ 3
○ Maioliche Fiano '23	▼ 2
⊙ Maioliche Primitivo Rosato '23	▼ 2
⊙ Maioliche Primitivo Rosato '22	▼ 2
● Gioia del Colle Primitivo Marpione Ris. '20	♈♈♈ 5
● Gioia del Colle Primitivo Marpione Ris. '19	♈♈♈ 5
● Gioia del Colle Primitivo Marpione Ris. '18	♈♈♈ 5
● Gioia del Colle Primitivo Marpione Ris. '15	♈♈♈ 3*
● Gioia del Colle Primitivo Marpione Ris. '13	♈♈♈ 3*
● Gioia del Colle Primitivo Marpione Ris. '11	♈♈♈ 3*
● Gioia del Colle Primitivo Sellato '18	♈♈♈ 3*

OTHER WINERIES

A Mano Wine

via San Giovanni, 41
70015 Noci [BA]
📞 +39 0803434872
🌐 www.amanowine.com

CELLAR SALES
PRE-BOOKED VISITS
ANNUAL PRODUCTION 200,000 bottles
HECTARES UNDER VINE 31.00
SUSTAINABLE WINERY

● A Mano Primitivo '22	🍷🍷 3
⊙ Imprint of Mark Shannon Susumaniello Rosato '23	🍷🍷 3
● Prima Mano Negroamaro '20	🍷🍷 5

Antica Enotria

loc. c.da Risicata
s.da prov.le 65, km 7
71042 Cerignola [FG]
📞 +39 0885418462
🌐 anticaenotria.it

CELLAR SALES
PRE-BOOKED VISITS
ANNUAL PRODUCTION 100,000 bottles
HECTARES UNDER VINE 20.00
VITICULTURE METHOD Certified Organic

⊙ Falanghina '23	🍷🍷 3
● Nero di Troia '21	🍷🍷 4
● Dieci Ottobre '18	🍷 5
⊙ Fiano '23	🍷 3

Cantine Bonsegna

via A. Volta, 17
73048 Nardò [LE]
📞 +39 0833561483
🌐 www.vinibonsegna.it

CELLAR SALES
PRE-BOOKED VISITS
ANNUAL PRODUCTION 150,000 bottles
HECTARES UNDER VINE 25.00

⊙ Nardò Rosato Narthos '23	🍷🍷 3
● Nardò Rosso Danze della Contessa Et. Nera '22	🍷🍷 3
● Nardò Rosso Danze della Contessa '22	🍷 2

Donato Angiuli

fraz. Montrone
via Principe Umberto, 27
70010 Adelfia [BA]
📞 +39 0804597130
🌐 www.angiulidonato.com

CELLAR SALES
PRE-BOOKED VISITS
ANNUAL PRODUCTION 200,000 bottles
HECTARES UNDER VINE 9.00

● Gioia del Colle Primitivo Adelphòs '22	🍷🍷 3*
● Maccone Nero di Troia Passito '22	🍷🍷 4
⊙ Maccone Notardomenico Rosato '23	🍷🍷 3
⊙ Maccone Moscato Secco '23	🍷 2

Cantine Barsento

c.da San Giacomo
70015 Noci [BA]
📞 +39 0804979657
🌐 www.cantinebarsento.com

CELLAR SALES
PRE-BOOKED VISITS
RESTAURANT SERVICE
ANNUAL PRODUCTION 150,000 bottles
HECTARES UNDER VINE 20.00
SUSTAINABLE WINERY

● Gioia del Colle Primitivo Casaboli Ris. '21	🍷🍷 5
● Ladislao '21	🍷🍷 4
● Malicchia Mapicchia '21	🍷 5
⊙ Pàndaro '23	🍷 3

Caiaffa

via dei Gerani, 2
71042 Cerignola [FG]
📞 +39 3293449555
🌐 www.caiaffavini.it

⊙ Mantis '23	🍷🍷 3
● Primitivo '22	🍷🍷 2*
⊙ Carabus '23	🍷 3
⊙ Nero di Troia Rosato '23	🍷 3

OTHER WINERIES

Vigneti Calitro

c.da Papacaniello, 18/19
74028 Sava [TA]
☎ +39 0999721127
✉ www.vigneticalitro.it

CELLAR SALES
PRE-BOOKED VISITS
ACCOMMODATION AND RESTAURANT SERVICE
ANNUAL PRODUCTION 70,000 bottles
HECTARES UNDER VINE 100.00

● Ausilio Susumaniello '22	♟♟ 3
⊙ Negroamaro Rosato '23	♟♟ 3
● Primitivo di Manduria Ausilio '22	♟♟ 3
● Ausilio Negroamaro '22	♟ 3

Erminio Campa

s.da prov.le 129 Torricella Monacizzo
74020 Torricella [TA]
☎ +39 3383940636
✉ www.erminiocampa.it

CELLAR SALES
PRE-BOOKED VISITS
ACCOMMODATION
ANNUAL PRODUCTION 50,000 bottles
HECTARES UNDER VINE 25.00

● Primitivo di Manduria Li Cameli Ris. '21	♟♟ 5
● Primitivo di Manduria Li Janni '23	♟♟ 3
● Primitivo di Manduria Li Cameli '22	♟ 4

Cannito

c.da Parco Bizzarro - s.da vicinale
Macerano, 13
70025 Grumo Appula [BA]
☎ +39 080623529
✉ www.agricolacannito.it

CELLAR SALES
PRE-BOOKED VISITS
ACCOMMODATION
ANNUAL PRODUCTION 100,000 bottles
HECTARES UNDER VINE 20.00
VITICULTURE METHOD Certified Organic
SUSTAINABLE WINERY

● Gioia del Colle Primitivo Drùmon Ris. '19	♟♟ 7
● Gioia del Colle Primitivo Drùmon S '20	♟♟ 6
● Gioia del Colle Primitivo Dùmon '20	♟♟ 5
● Gioia del Colle Primitivo Centrum '18	♟ 8

Centovignali

p.zza Aldo Moro, 10
70010 Sammichele di Bari [BA]
☎ +39 0805768215
✉ www.centovignali.it

CELLAR SALES
PRE-BOOKED VISITS
ANNUAL PRODUCTION 35,000 bottles
HECTARES UNDER VINE 25.00
VITICULTURE METHOD Certified Organic

● Gioia del Colle Primitivo Pentimone Ris. '21	♟♟ 6
● Gioia del Colle Primitivo Indellicato '22	♟♟ 5
⊙ Frassinito '23	♟ 3
⊙ Susumaniello Rosato '23	♟ 3

Cantina Coppola 1489

loc. Tenuta Patitari
via Sansonetti
73014 Gallipoli [LE]
☎ +39 0883201425
✉ www.cantinacoppola.it

CELLAR SALES
PRE-BOOKED VISITS
ACCOMMODATION AND RESTAURANT SERVICE
ANNUAL PRODUCTION 90,000 bottles
HECTARES UNDER VINE 18.00
SUSTAINABLE WINERY

● Alezio Rosso Li Cuti '20	♟♟ 3
○ Rocci '22	♟♟ 5
● Alezio Rosso Doxi Ris. '17	♟ 5

Cupertinum

via Martiri del Risorgimento, 6
73043 Copertino [LE]
☎ +39 0832947031
✉ www.cupertinum.it

CELLAR SALES
PRE-BOOKED VISITS
ANNUAL PRODUCTION 900,000 bottles
HECTARES UNDER VINE 320.00
SUSTAINABLE WINERY

● Copertino Rosso '20	♟♟ 2*
⊙ Spinello dei Falconi '23	♟♟ 3
● Copertino Rosso Ris. '15	♟ 3
● Glykòs '21	♟ 4

OTHER WINERIES

Feudo Croce

c.da Civitella
74021 Carosino [TA]
📞 +39 0995924445
🌐 www.tinazzi.it

CELLAR SALES
PRE-BOOKED VISITS
ANNUAL PRODUCTION 600,000 bottles
HECTARES UNDER VINE 32.00
SUSTAINABLE WINERY

● Malnera '23	♟♟ 5
● Nyktòs '23	♟♟ 5
● Primitivo '23	♟♟ 5
● Megale '23	♟ 5

Giustini

via Pietro Germi
74027 San Giorgio Jonico [TA]
📞 +39 0995330411
🌐 www.giustini.wine

CELLAR SALES
PRE-BOOKED VISITS
ANNUAL PRODUCTION 400,000 bottles
HECTARES UNDER VINE 60.00

● Primitivo di Manduria Acinorè Limited Edition '22	♟♟ 5
● Primitivo di Manduria Acinorè Old Vines '22	♟♟ 5
● Vecchio Sogno Negroamaro '23	♟♟ 3

Lucio Leuci

via Villa Baldassarri, km 1
73010 Guagnano [LE]
📞 +39 0832706500
🌐 www.vinileuci.it

CELLAR SALES
PRE-BOOKED VISITS
ANNUAL PRODUCTION 200,000 bottles
HECTARES UNDER VINE 30.00

● Primile '20	♟♟ 3
● Salice Salentino Rosso Idume '19	♟♟ 3
⊙ Cisaria '23	♟ 2
● Primitivo di Manduria Brunese '21	♟ 4

Tenute Girolamo

via Noci, 314
74015 Martina Franca [TA]
📞 +39 0804402141
🌐 www.tenutegirolamo.it

CELLAR SALES
PRE-BOOKED VISITS
ANNUAL PRODUCTION 300,000 bottles
HECTARES UNDER VINE 45.00

● Monte dei Cocci Negroamaro '22	♟♟ 4
● Conte Giangirolamo Et. Oro '18	♟♟ 6
● Monte dei Cocci Susumaniello '22	♟ 3
○ Monte dei Cocci Verdeca '23	♟ 3

Antica Masseria Jorche

c.da Palermo
74020 Torricella [TA]
📞 +39 0999573232
🌐 www.jorche.it

CELLAR SALES
PRE-BOOKED VISITS
ACCOMMODATION AND RESTAURANT SERVICE
ANNUAL PRODUCTION 130,000 bottles
HECTARES UNDER VINE 40.00
SUSTAINABLE WINERY

● Primitivo di Manduria Dolce Naturale Lo Apu '22	♟♟ 8
● Primitivo di Manduria Ris. '20	♟♟ 7
○ Sosò '23	♟ 3

Masso Antico

via Chiurlia
39040 Cellino San Marco [BR]
📞 +39 0471803311
🌐 www.schenkitalia.it

● I Clasti '23	♟♟ 3
● Primitivo di Manduria '23	♟♟ 3
● Ice Primitivo '23	♟ 3
● Primitivo Single Estate '23	♟ 2

OTHER WINERIES

Mocavero
via Mallacca-Zummari
73010 Arnesano [LE]
☏ +39 0832327194
✉ www.mocaverovini.it

CELLAR SALES
PRE-BOOKED VISITS
RESTAURANT SERVICE
ANNUAL PRODUCTION 600,000 bottles
HECTARES UNDER VINE 65.00
SUSTAINABLE WINERY

● Salice Salentino Rosso Puteus Ris. '19	♟♟ 3*
◉ Sire Negroamaro Rosato '23	♟♟ 2*
○ Curtirussi Verdeca '23	♟ 3
● Santufili Primitivo '19	♟ 4

La Pruina Vini
s.da prov.le 56, 21
72021 Francavilla Fontana [BR]
☏ +39 3441937783
✉ www.lapruinavini.com

CELLAR SALES
ANNUAL PRODUCTION 100,000 bottles
HECTARES UNDER VINE 25.00
VITICULTURE METHOD Certified Organic

● ADz Rosso '23	♟♟ 3*
● Non t'Aspetti Negroamaro Rosso '22	♟♟ 3
○ Melesco Malvasia Bianca '22	♟ 5
● Primitivo di Manduria '22	♟ 3

Cantina San Donaci
via Mesagne, 62
72025 San Donaci [BR]
☏ +39 0831681085
✉ www.cantinasandonaci.eu

CELLAR SALES
PRE-BOOKED VISITS
ANNUAL PRODUCTION 800,000 bottles
HECTARES UNDER VINE 320.00

● Salice Salentino Rosso Anticaia Ris. '20	♟♟ 3*
● Posta Vecchia '20	♟♟ 3
○ Assina Bianco Negroamaro '23	♟ 2
● Fulgeo '20	♟ 5

Cantine Paradiso
via Manfredonia, 39
71042 Cerignola [FG]
☏ +39 0885428720
✉ www.cantineparadiso.it

ANNUAL PRODUCTION 400,000 bottles
HECTARES UNDER VINE 40.00

● Darione '22	♟♟ 3
● Posta Piana Nero di Troia '22	♟♟ 3
● Stizzato '22	♟♟ 3
● Salice Salentino Rosso Posta Piana '21	♟ 3

Rosa del Golfo
via Garibaldi, 18
73011 Alezio [LE]
☏ +39 0833281045
✉ www.rosadelgolfo.com

CELLAR SALES
PRE-BOOKED VISITS
ANNUAL PRODUCTION 300,000 bottles
HECTARES UNDER VINE 40.00

◉ Hype Limited Edition '23	♟♟ 3
◉ Rosato '23	♟♟ 3
◉ Mazzì '22	♟ 3
● Portulano '21	♟ 3

Cantine Santa Barbara
via Maternità e Infanzia, 23
72027 San Pietro Vernotico [BR]
☏ +39 0831652749
✉ www.cantinesantabarbara.it

CELLAR SALES
PRE-BOOKED VISITS
ANNUAL PRODUCTION 2,000,000 bottles
HECTARES UNDER VINE 150.00
VITICULTURE METHOD Certified Organic
SUSTAINABLE WINERY

● Capirussu Negroamaro Rosso '23	♟♟ 3
● Capirussu Primitivo '23	♟♟ 3
● Capirussu Susumaniello '23	♟ 3
● Sumanero '22	♟ 3

OTHER WINERIES

Santa Lucia

loc. Castel del Monte
s.da Comunale San Vittore, I
70033 Corato [BA]
(+39 0817642888
@ www.vinisantalucia.com

CELLAR SALES
PRE-BOOKED VISITS
ANNUAL PRODUCTION 50,000 bottles
HECTARES UNDER VINE 14.00
VITICULTURE METHOD Certified Organic
SUSTAINABLE WINERY

● Castel del Monte Nero di Troia Le More Ris. '20	♥♥ 6
☉ Castel del Monte Bombino Nero Fior di Ribes '23	♥♥ 4

Masseria Trullo di Pezza

c.da Trullo di Pezza
74020 Torricella [TA]
(+39 0999872011
@ www.trullodipezza.com

CELLAR SALES
PRE-BOOKED VISITS
ACCOMMODATION AND RESTAURANT SERVICE
ANNUAL PRODUCTION 100,000 bottles
HECTARES UNDER VINE 50.00
VITICULTURE METHOD Certified Organic

● Primitivo di Manduria Pezzale Ris. '18	♥♥ 5
● Scarfoglio '22	♥♥ 3
● Arlati Susumaniello '23	♥ 3
● Mezza Pezza Primitivo '22	♥ 3

Vigneti Reale

via Egidio Reale, 55
73100 Lecce
(+39 0832248433
@ www.vignetireale.it

PRE-BOOKED VISITS
ACCOMMODATION AND RESTAURANT SERVICE
ANNUAL PRODUCTION 180,000 bottles
HECTARES UNDER VINE 85.00
SUSTAINABLE WINERY

● Primitivo di Manduria Gloria '22	♥♥ 5
● Rudiae Primitivo '22	♥♥ 3
○ Blasi Chardonnay '23	♥ 3
☉ Vivia Susumaniello Rosato '23	♥ 3

Cantine Spelonga

via Menola
71047 Stornara [FG]
(+39 0885431048
@ www.cantinespelonga.com

CELLAR SALES
PRE-BOOKED VISITS
ANNUAL PRODUCTION 70,000 bottles
HECTARES UNDER VINE 15.00

☉ Marilina Rosé '23	♥♥ 3*
● Primitivo '22	♥♥ 4
☉ Ninù Nero di Troia Rosato '23	♥ 2
● Tyron '21	♥ 4

Vecchia Torre

via Marche, I
73045 Leverano [LE]
(+39 0832925053
@ www.cantinavecchiatorre.it

CELLAR SALES
PRE-BOOKED VISITS
ANNUAL PRODUCTION 3,500,000 bottles
HECTARES UNDER VINE 1500.00
SUSTAINABLE WINERY

● Negroamaro '22	♥♥ 3*
● A Passo Lento '21	♥♥ 3
● Leverano Rosso Ris. '20	♥ 3
● Primitivo di Manduria Auro '18	♥ 3

Vinicola Mediterranea

via Maternità e Infanzia, 22
72027 San Pietro Vernotico [BR]
(+39 0831676323
@ www.vinicolamediterranea.it

CELLAR SALES
PRE-BOOKED VISITS
RESTAURANT SERVICE
ANNUAL PRODUCTION 500,000 bottles

● Primitivo di Manduria Empirio '22	♥♥ 3
● Soraya Appassimento '23	♥♥ 2*
● Susumaniello '23	♥♥ 3
● Primitivo di Manduria Primoduca '22	♥ 4

PUGLIA

CALABRIA

A closer look at the promising results coming out of Calabria's wine sector reveals several noteworthy trends. First and foremost is the region's success with sweet wines, often referred to as "vini da meditazione" in a nod to the great Veronelli. This is an area where Calabria stands apart from the rest of Italy: production here is increasing, and with great success. Even when aged for extended periods, as in the case of the Moscato di Saracena from the Bisconte brothers' Feudo di San Severino or, staying in the same area, the version from Biagio Diana, these wines excel. Another point of note is the strong comeback of Cirò. Thanks to the skill and passion of both established and newer producers, this wine is reasserting itself as a southern classic with undeniable elegance.

Beyond the statistics, never before have we had such a strong sense that this historic Calabrian wine is poised for an international renaissance, standing alongside other iconic southern DOC wines. We've covered the evolution of southern Calabria's wines in the past, and the shift we identified back then is proving to be more than a temporary trend. The quality and consistency continue to solidify, often driven by first-generation or returning winemakers who are dedicated to reviving local and family wine traditions, sometimes after pursuing other careers. This renewed commitment is evident in the dry vinification of zibibbo and greco di Bianco, as well as the increasingly widespread use of pecorello, also known as "greco di Rogliano", which produces distinctive and authoritative whites.

Overall, it's clear that Calabria is experiencing a remarkable moment, steadily closing the gap with other regions as it finds its own path toward growth and recognition. This year, four wines from Calabria were awarded top honors: the Ciròs from Librandi and Brigante, Ceraudo's Pecorello Grisara, and Lombardo's Greco Particella 58. These familiar names provide continuity, while three other standout expressions also earned acclaim: Tenuta del Travale's Eleuteria Special Edition in Anfora and the Moscato di Saracena wines from Luigi Viola's Feudo dei Sanseverino, which made it into our "Rare Wines" section, a highlight of this year's guide. But for us, Feudo dei Sanseverino's Moscato Passito al Governo di Saracena '15 is also our Meditation Wine of the Year.

'A Vita

s.s. Statale 106 Jonica
88811 Cirò Marina [KR]
☎ +39 3290732473
🌐 www.avitavini.it

CELLAR SALES
PRE-BOOKED VISITS
ANNUAL PRODUCTION 15,000 bottles
HECTARES UNDER VINE 8.00

Francesco de Franco's winery was born from a
deep desire to return to Calabria. Like many of
his peers, he had pursued a career far from
home after completing his law studies. But in
2008, he left his profession and returned to Cirò
to dedicate himself, alongside his partner Laura
Violino, to his family's vineyards. Their firm
intention was to produce wines that honored
the region, emphasizing local grape varieties and
working in harmony with nature. It was a
transitional year for Francesco and Laura: their
Cirò wines are still aging, so they presented a
new creation, Il Rosso '22, made from gaglioppo
grapes with a touch of magliocco. It offers
elegant tones of fruit and spice on the nose, and
is austere and well-balanced on the palate. The
grapes are sourced from an old vineyard now in
"complantation," and even if Francesco could
have bottled it as a Cirò (as permitted by
regulations), he chose not to, emphasizing
that for him, Cirò Rosso should only be made
from gaglioppo.

Cantine Benvenuto

c.da Ziopà
89815 Francavilla Angitola [VV]
☎ +39 3317292517
🌐 www.cantinebenvenuto.it

CELLAR SALES
PRE-BOOKED VISITS
RESTAURANT SERVICE
ANNUAL PRODUCTION 50,000 bottles
HECTARES UNDER VINE 16.50
VITICULTURE METHOD Certified Organic

In just a few years, Giovanni Benvenuto
transformed his family's land into a winery
producing distinctive and well-crafted wines
from native grapes grown organically. His work
has also brought attention to a heritage grape
variety, the zibibbo of Pizzo. The winery and its
surrounding vineyards are situated in the hills, at
an elevation of about 300 meters, in the
Francavilla Angitola area of Vibo Valentia's
hinterland. In addition to zibibbo, Giovanni
cultivates malvasia, greco nero, and magliocco.
The entire range is of excellent quality, starting
with the Benvenuto Zibibbo Orange '23. A
refined and complex nose of exotic fruit and
Mediterranean herbs emerges, echoed on a
long-lasting palate driven by acidity. The dry
version is also superb. Indeed, the Benvenuto
Zibibbo '23 reached our finals, thanks to its clear
and multifaceted citrus, floral, and yellow fruit
notes. The palate is consistent with the nose,
sapid, offering a dynamic tasting experience.

● Il Rosso '22	♟♟♟ 4	
⊙ 'A Vita Rosato '23	♟♟♟ 4	
● Cirò Rosso Cl. Sup. Ris. '17	♟♟♟ 6	
● Cirò Rosso Cl. Sup. Ris. '15	♟♟♟ 6	
⊙ 'A Vita Rosato '18	♟♟ 3	
⊙ Cirò Rosato '22	♟♟ 4	
⊙ Cirò Rosato '21	♟♟ 2*	
● Cirò Rosso Cl. '09	♟♟ 3*	
● Cirò Rosso Cl. Ris. '10	♟♟ 4	
● Cirò Rosso Cl. Sup. '15	♟♟ 2*	
● Cirò Rosso Cl. Sup. '09	♟♟ 3*	
● Cirò Rosso Cl. Sup. Ris. '18	♟♟ 6	
● Cirò Rosso Cl. Sup. Ris. '16	♟♟ 6	
● Cirò Rosso Cl. Sup. Ris. '13	♟♟ 4	
● Cirò Rosso Cl. Sup. Ris. '11	♟♟ 4	
○ Leukò '17	♟♟ 2*	

○ Benvenuto Zibibbo '23	♟♟ 5	
○ Benvenuto Zibibbo Orange '23	♟♟ 5	
○ Bianco di Falco '23	♟♟ 8	
● Terra '23	♟♟ 3	
⊙ Celeste '23	♟ 3	
○ Mare '23	♟ 3	
○ Sughero Storto Brut M. Cl. '21	♟ 7	
○ Benvenuto Orange Zibibbo '22	♟♟♟ 5	
○ Benvenuto Orange Zibibbo '21	♟♟ 4	
○ Benvenuto Orange Zibibbo '20	♟♟ 4	
○ Benvenuto Orange Zibibbo '19	♟♟ 3*	
○ Benvenuto Zibibbo '22	♟♟ 4	
○ Benvenuto Zibibbo '21	♟♟ 3*	
⊙ Celeste Rosato '21	♟♟ 3	
○ Mare '21	♟♟ 3	
● Terra '21	♟♟ 3	

Brigante Vigneti & Cantina

via Sant'Elia, 31
88813 Cirò [KR]
📞 +39 3334135843
🖰 www.vinocirobrigante.it

CELLAR SALES
PRE-BOOKED VISITS
ANNUAL PRODUCTION 54,000 bottles
HECTARES UNDER VINE 11.00
VITICULTURE METHOD Certified Organic
SUSTAINABLE WINERY

Despite coming from families with generations of viticulture experience, Stefania Carè and her husband Enzo Sestito initially envisioned a future outside agriculture. They succeeded in their endeavors, but passion ultimately led them back to winemaking, just like their ancestors, in the historic Cirò district. Today, they run their winery with dedication and expertise, pioneering innovative projects like the Essenzo and Zero lines. Their production approach calls for spontaneous fermentation, without the use of added yeasts, sulfites, or chemicals. The Cirò 0727 Riserva took home Tre Bicchieri, fully convincing with its elegant bouquet of floral notes, citrus, and fresh red fruits, shifting to aromatic herbs and tobacco. The palate is sapid with close-knit, silky tannins, culminating in a persistent and characterful finish. The Cirò '20 Etefe, authentic and representative of its terroir, showcases tones of black fruits and underbrush on the nose, with a rich and enticing palate.

Caparra & Siciliani

s.da st.le 106
88811 Cirò Marina [KR]
📞 +39 0962373319
🖰 www.caparraesiciliani.com

CELLAR SALES
PRE-BOOKED VISITS
ANNUAL PRODUCTION 800,000 bottles
HECTARES UNDER VINE 180.00
VITICULTURE METHOD Certified Organic

The visionary agreement between the Caparra and Siciliani families dates back to 1963. Combining their generational experience as vintners, they founded a winery that remains one of the most reliable in Cirò. For several years now, technical management has been in the hands of young winemaker Jacopo Vagaggini. His impressive results showcase his ability to expertly manage a winery that includes 20 contributing members and 180 hectares of vineyards, spread out across 12 farms that now work synergistically under his guidance. The Lice '21, one of the finest Cirò wines tasted this year, advanced to the finals. It impressed us with its complex and pleasing bouquet of wild berries, aromatic herbs, licorice, and spices, providing a fitting prelude to a sapid and dynamic palate. Its harmonious synthesis of fruit and well-extracted tannins is remarkable.

● Cirò Rosso Cl. Sup. Ris. 0727 '19	♟♟♟ 5
● Cirò Rosso Cl. Sup. Etefe '20	♟♟ 3
○ Essenzo Bianco '21	♟♟ 5
○ Zero Gaglioppo Bianco '23	♟♟ 5
○ Cirò Bianco Phemina '23	♟ 3
⊙ Cirò Rosato Manyarì '23	♟ 3
⊙ Zero Gaglioppo Rosato '20	♟♟♟ 6
⊙ Cirò Rosato Manyarì '21	♟♟ 3
● Cirò Rosso Cl. Sup. 0727 Ris. '18	♟♟ 5
○ Essenzo '18	♟♟ 6
○ Essenzo Bianco '20	♟♟ 5
● Essenzo Rosso '21	♟♟ 5
● Essenzo Rosso '20	♟♟ 5
● Gaglioppo Zero '18	♟♟ 3*
⊙ Zero Gaglioppo Rosato '21	♟♟ 5
● Zero Gaglioppo Rosso '22	♟♟ 5
● Zero Gaglioppo Rosso '21	♟♟ 5

● Cirò Rosso Cl. Sup. Lice Ris. '21	♟♟ 5
○ Cirò Bianco Curiale '23	♟♟ 3
⊙ Cirò Rosato Le Formelle '23	♟♟ 3
● Cirò Rosso Cl. Sup. Timpagrande Ris. '21	♟♟ 3
● Cirò Rosso Cl. Sup. Volvito Ris. '21	♟♟ 4
● Cirò Rosso Cl. Solagi '22	♟ 3
⊙ Cirò Rosato Le Formelle '22	♟♟ 3
⊙ Cirò Rosato Le Formelle '19	♟♟ 2*
⊙ Cirò Rosato Le Formelle '18	♟♟ 2*
● Cirò Rosso Cl. Solagi '17	♟♟ 2*
● Cirò Rosso Cl. Sup. '20	♟♟ 3
● Cirò Rosso Cl. Sup. Ris. '16	♟♟ 2*
● Cirò Rosso Cl. Sup. Volvito Ris. '20	♟♟ 4
● Cirò Rosso Cl. Sup. Volvito Ris. '17	♟♟ 2*
● Cirò Rosso Cl. Sup. Volvito Ris. '12	♟♟ 2*
● Cirò Rosso Cl. Sup. Volvito Ris. '11	♟♟ 3*
● Mastrogiurato '10	♟♟ 3*

Casa Comerci

fraz. Badia di Nicotera
c.da Comerci, 6
89844 Nicotera [VV]
☎ +39 3495313133
✉ www.casacomerci.it

CELLAR SALES
PRE-BOOKED VISITS
ACCOMMODATION AND RESTAURANT SERVICE
ANNUAL PRODUCTION 45,000 bottles
HECTARES UNDER VINE 15.00
VITICULTURE METHOD Certified Organic

This young winery from Badia di Nicotera, in the Vibo Valentia area, continues to impress. Despite its recent founding, it boasts deep roots in local viticulture. The ancestors of lawyer Domenicoantonio Silipo Jr. were winemakers as early as the 1800s and were also the master coopers of the town. Even though he practices law and lives in Emilia Romagna, Domenicoantonio was determined to revive his family's agricultural roots, cultivating about 30 hectares of land, mostly planted with native varieties like magliocco, greco, and nerello, all under organic farming methods. The Magliocco 'A Batia '22 reached our finals, offering inviting tones of red berries, aromatic herbs, potpourri, and spices. The palate is pervasive, refreshed by a lively acidity that supports close-knit and vibrant tannins. The Greco Bianco Sogno '22, a méthode ancestrale, is delightful with aromas of hops, quince, flowers, citrus, and bay leaf. The palate is fresh, with elegant effervescence, closing with a long, minty finish.

★Roberto Ceraudo

c.da Dattilo
88815 Strongoli [KR]
☎ +39 0962865613
✉ www.dattilo.it

CELLAR SALES
PRE-BOOKED VISITS
ACCOMMODATION AND RESTAURANT SERVICE
ANNUAL PRODUCTION 70,000 bottles
HECTARES UNDER VINE 20.00
VITICULTURE METHOD Certified Organic
SUSTAINABLE WINERY

A simple wooden gate at the end of a dirt road marks the entrance to the verdant estate overseen by Roberto Ceraudo and his family. Tenuta Dattilo is a meticulously tended property where citrus, olives, vineyards, and a vegetable garden have been free of chemicals for nearly 40 years (the estate has been organic since the 1980s, converting to biodynamic methods some time ago). Completing this idyllic setting are an elegant agriturismo and a restaurant. Among the most acclaimed in southern Italy, they're run by Roberto's daughter Caterina. His other children, Giuseppe and Susy, are also part of the business. Once again, the Pecorello Grisara '23 took home Tre Bicchieri with its superb and persistent aromatic suite, opening with tones of yellow fruits and flowers, lime, bergamot, iodine, anise, and Mediterranean herbs. Incredibly fresh on the palate, it boasts a charming balance between fruit and sapidity, leading to a long, citrus-inflected finish.

● 'A Batia '22	▼▼5
○ Rèfulu '23	▼▼4
○ Sogno Greco Bianco Frizzante '22	▼▼4
⊙ Granàtu '23	▼3
○ Jancu '22	▼5
● 'A Batia '21	♀♀5
● 'A Batia '20	♀♀5
● 'A Batia '19	♀♀5
○ Fantasia Greco Bianco '21	♀♀3
○ Fantasia Metodo Ancestrale '22	♀♀4
⊙ Granàtu '21	♀♀3
○ Jancu '21	♀♀5
● Libìci '17	♀♀4
● Libìci '15	♀♀3*
● Libìci '12	♀♀3*
○ Rèfulu '22	♀♀4

○ Grisara Pecorello '23	▼▼▼5
⊙ Grayasusi Et. Rame '23	▼▼5
● Nanà '23	▼▼5
○ Petelia '23	▼▼5
⊙ Grayasusi Et. Argento '23	▼6
○ Imyr '23	▼6
○ Grisara '17	♀♀♀4*
○ Grisara '16	♀♀♀4*
○ Grisara '15	♀♀♀4*
○ Grisara '14	♀♀♀3*
○ Grisara '13	♀♀♀3*
○ Grisara '12	♀♀♀3*
○ Grisara Pecorello '22	♀♀♀5
○ Grisara Pecorello '21	♀♀♀5
○ Grisara Pecorello '20	♀♀♀5
○ Grisara Pecorello '19	♀♀♀5
○ Grisara Pecorello '18	♀♀♀4*

Ferrocinto

fraz. Vigne
c.da Ferrocinto
87012 Castrovillari [CS]
(•) +39 0981415122
✎ www.ferrocinto.it

CELLAR SALES
PRE-BOOKED VISITS
ANNUAL PRODUCTION 700,000 bottles
HECTARES UNDER VINE 45.00
VITICULTURE METHOD Certified Organic

The Nola family's estate, which occupies more
than 150 hectares (all organically farmed), takes
its name from the district in Castrovillari. A third
of the area is planted with vines, primarily native
varieties like magliocco, mantonico, and greco
bianco. The winery's operations are led by
Stefano Coppola, a seasoned technician who
personally oversees the work in the vineyard as
well. The wines tasted this year were decidedly
impressive, marked by an elegant stylistic profile
that blends varietal character with terroir. The
Pollino Magliocco '22 stood out with its intense,
fruity nose, complemented by aromatic herbs
and a lovely spicy background that highlights the
seamless integration of oak. The palate is broad
and pervasive, closing with a fresh note of dark
citrus. The Pollino Bianco '23, a Mantonico, also
reached the finals, showcasing exotic fruit,
jasmine, and Mediterranean scrub tones—a
generous and long drink.

Feudo dei Sanseverino

via Vittorio Emanuele, 108/110
87010 Saracena [CS]
(•) +39 098121461
✎ www.feudodeisanseverino.it

CELLAR SALES
PRE-BOOKED VISITS
ANNUAL PRODUCTION 20,000 bottles
HECTARES UNDER VINE 6.00
VITICULTURE METHOD Certified Organic
SUSTAINABLE WINERY

We take pride in having helped introduce wine
enthusiasts to meditation wines, especially by
preserving Moscato di Saracena, which faced the
threat of extinction just 20 years ago despite a
history dating back to the 16th century (when
Cardinal Sirleto sent it to the papal court).
Credit also goes to Roberto Bisconte for
envisioning a second life for this noble wine type.
His brilliant idea was to allow it to mature for as
long as 10 years before bottling, giving it the
time to reach an extraordinary aromatic profile.
You'll find the Moscato Passito al Governo di
Saracena '15 in our "rare wines" section. It
features an extraordinarily elegant and complex
bouquet, with aromas of citrus meeting ginger,
candied yellow fruits, saffron, chocolate-covered
figs, honey, green tea, and spices. It's sweet but
well-balanced by sapidity and incredible
freshness. The palate is broad, velvety, and...
practically never-ending! It's our Meditation
Wine of the Year.

○ Terre di Cosenza Pollino Bianco '23	♟♟ 4
● Terre di Cosenza Pollino Magliocco '22	♟♟ 3*
● Terre di Cosenza Pollino Magliocco Ris. '16	♟♟ 4
⊙ Terre di Cosenza Pollino Rosato '23	♟ 3
○ Il Macerato Pecorello '21	♟♟ 3*
○ Pecorello '21	♟♟ 3
○ Terre di Cosenza Pollino Bianco '22	♟♟ 4
○ Terre di Cosenza Pollino Bianco '21	♟♟ 3
○ Terre di Cosenza Pollino Bianco '20	♟♟ 3
● Terre di Cosenza Pollino Magliocco '22	♟♟ 3
● Terre di Cosenza Pollino Magliocco 24 Ris. '14	♟♟ 4
● Terre di Cosenza Pollino Magliocco 24 Ris. '13	♟♟ 4
● Terre di Cosenza Pollino Magliocco 24 Ris. '11	♟♟ 4
● Terre di Cosenza Pollino Magliocco Ris. '15	♟♟ 4

○ Terre di Cosenza Pollino Bianco Sestito '23	♟♟ 4
○ Terre di Cosenza Pollino Moscato Passito Mastro Terenzio '14	♟♟♟ 5
● Lacrima Nera Ris. '13	♟♟ 3
○ Mastro Terenzio '09	♟♟ 5
○ Moscato Passito al Governo di Saracena '14	♟♟ 5
○ Moscato Passito al Governo di Saracena '13	♟♟ 5
○ Moscato Passito Mastro Terenzio '13	♟♟ 5
○ Terre di Cosenza Pollino Moscato Passito Mastro Terenzio '16	♟♟ 5
○ Terre di Cosenza Pollino Moscato Passito Mastro Terenzio '15	♟♟ 5

Ippolito 1845

via Tirone, 132
88811 Cirò Marina [KR]
📞 +39 096231106
🌐 www.ippolito1845.it

CELLAR SALES
PRE-BOOKED VISITS
ANNUAL PRODUCTION 1,000,000 bottles
HECTARES UNDER VINE 100.00
SUSTAINABLE WINERY

This solid, Cirò-based producer, whose wines have consistently been of excellent quality, has been owned by the same family for five generations. Today Vincenzo, Gianluca, and Paolo Ippolito are at the helm, having skillfully navigated the latest generational transition while making investments to transform the winery's image. Indeed, the large cellar has been modernized with the latest technology, packaging completely revamped, and significant efforts made in both the vineyard and winery to produce clear, elegant, and regionally expressive wines. The Cirò Rosso Colli del Mancuso '21, a gaglioppo, reached our final round with aromas of blackberry, dried violet, medicinal herbs, and spices. It offers a solid, well-structured palate with its noble tannic expression. The Pecorello '23 is a noteworthy white, showcasing crystalline citrus and exotic fruit tones, with sapid freshness and nice aromatic persistence.

Tenuta Iuzzolini

loc. Frassà
88811 Cirò Marina [KR]
📞 +39 0962373893
🌐 www.tenutaiuzzolini.it

CELLAR SALES
PRE-BOOKED VISITS
ANNUAL PRODUCTION 3,000,000 bottles
HECTARES UNDER VINE 110.00

Pasquale Iuzzolini, a visionary agricultural entrepreneur, has skillfully blended innovation with tradition in his winery, starting with a modern underground cellar that extends deep beneath what appears to be a traditional stone and brick farmhouse in Cirò. The estate includes 100 hectares of vineyards, another 150 hectares of arable land and olive groves, as well as a free-range cattle farm for the podolica breed. Among this year's standouts is the Cirò Rosso Riserva '21 Maradea, which displays an expansive bouquet of elegant red fruits, dog rose, and Mediterranean scrub. On the palate, it's juicy, well-balanced by acidity, leading to a long, spicy finish. The Magliocco Paternum '18 proves complex and elegant, with a nose rich in fruit and spices, and a close-knit, round palate of great persistence. The blend of greco and chardonnay, Madre Goccia '23, is a pleasant quaff, with clear notes of fruit and yellow flowers, offering freshness and a long finish.

Wine	Rating
● Cirò Rosso Cl. Sup. Colli del Mancuso Ris. '21	♟♟ 4
○ Pecorello '23	♟♟ 3*
● 160 Anni '21	♟♟ 5
● Calabrise '23	♟♟ 2*
○ Cirò Bianco Mare Chiaro '23	♟♟ 2*
⊙ Cirò Rosato Mabilia '23	♟ 2
● Cirò Rosso Cl. Liber Pater '23	♟ 2
⊙ Pescanera '23	♟ 3
○ Pecorello '21	♟♟♟ 3*
○ Pecorello '17	♟♟♟ 2*
● 160 Anni '13	♟♟ 5
○ Ciro Bianco Mare Chiaro '19	♟♟ 2*
● Cirò Rosso Cl. Sup. Colli del Mancuso Ris. '20	♟♟ 4
○ Pecorello '16	♟♟ 2*

Wine	Rating
● Cirò Rosso Cl. Sup. Maradea Ris. '21	♟♟ 5
⊙ Cirò Rosato '23	♟♟ 2*
○ Madre Goccia '23	♟♟ 3
● Paternum '18	♟♟ 4
○ Prima Fila Pecorello '23	♟♟ 3
⊙ Lumare '23	♟ 3
● Muranera '22	♟ 4
● Principe Spinelli '23	♟ 3
● Belfresco '21	♟♟ 3
○ Cirò Bianco '21	♟♟ 2*
⊙ Cirò Rosato '22	♟♟ 2*
● Cirò Rosso Cl. Sup. Maradea Ris. '19	♟♟ 5
● Cirò Rosso Cl. Sup. Maradea Ris. '18	♟♟ 5
⊙ Lumare '22	♟♟ 3
● Muranera '21	♟♟ 4
● Muranera '20	♟♟ 4
● Paternum '17	♟♟ 8

Cantine Lento

via del Progresso, 1
88040 Amato [CZ]
☎ +39 096828028
✉ www.cantinelento.it

CELLAR SALES
PRE-BOOKED VISITS
ANNUAL PRODUCTION 500,000 bottles
HECTARES UNDER VINE 70.00

The historic Lento family estate boasts three distinct production areas. Over the years, the vines best suited to each microclimate and soil type have been planted. For example, the Romeo estate, situated in the hills with a maritime exposure, is dedicated to greco bianco. At the Caracciolo property, where the soils are sandier and more calcareous, they cultivate magliocco. Finally, at the Amato estate—the largest, a south-facing natural amphitheater—we find the remaining plots, including a few hectares of international varietals. This is also where their large, modern winery is located. The Magliocco '20 proves vibrant and deep on the nose, with tones of small black fruits, eucalyptus, and spices. The palate is round and velvety, supported by acidity, leading to a long, fruit-driven finish. The Lamezia Greco '23 is a delightful wine, with a complex nose of apricot, elderberry, and wild fennel. On the palate, it's sapid and fresh, shining with its pleasant drinkability.

★★Librandi

loc. San Gennaro
s.s. Jonica, 106
88811 Cirò Marina [KR]
☎ +39 096231518
✉ www.librandi.it

CELLAR SALES
PRE-BOOKED VISITS
ANNUAL PRODUCTION 2,200,000 bottles
HECTARES UNDER VINE 232.00
SUSTAINABLE WINERY

Consistency in quality: this succinctly captures the philosophy of this historic and award-winning Ciro-based winery, now firmly in the hands of the Librandi family. Following the path set by founders Antonio and Nicodemo, who believed that quality wines start with careful vineyard management, the second generation continues to produce modern, well-crafted wines that remain true to the local terroir. The Cirò Duca Sanfelice '22, a wine of rare complexity and elegance, deservedly earns Tre Bicchieri. It opens on the nose with fresh black and red fruits, Mediterranean scrub, dark flowers and citrus, and a delicate balsamic vegetal note. Refined and well-extracted tannins, combined with round, juicy fruit, characterize a palate with notable aromatic persistence. The Magliocco Megonio '22 is also excellent, offering blackberry, dried rose, and underbrush aromas, with a pervasive, juicy palate and a long, spicy finish.

● Magliocco '20	♟♟ 5
○ Contessa Emburga '23	♟♟ 3
○ Lamezia Greco '23	♟♟ 3
○ Dragone Bianco '23	♟ 3
⊙ Dragone Rosato '23	♟ 3
○ Zì di Lento '23	♟ 4
○ Dragone Bianco '21	♟♟ 3
⊙ Dragone Rosato '21	♟♟ 3
● Dragone Rosso '21	♟♟ 4
● Dragone Rosso '20	♟♟ 3
● Federico II '20	♟♟ 4
● Federico II '19	♟♟ 4
○ Lamezia Greco '22	♟♟ 3
○ Lamezia Greco '21	♟♟ 3
● Lamezia Ris. '19	♟♟ 5
● Lamezia Rosso Salvatore Lento Ris. '15	♟♟ 4
● Magliocco '19	♟♟ 5

● Cirò Rosso Cl. Sup. Duca Sanfelice Ris. '22	♟♟♟ 3*
● Megonio '22	♟♟ 4
○ Almaneti Brut M. Cl. '20	♟♟ 4
⊙ Cirò Rosato Segno '23	♟♟ 2*
○ Critone '23	♟♟ 3
○ Efeso '23	♟♟ 4
● Gravello '22	♟♟ 5
● Calaonda '23	♟ 3
○ Cirò Bianco Segno '23	♟ 2
● Cirò Rosso Cl. Segno '23	♟ 2
○ Melissa Bianco Asylia '23	♟ 2
● Melissa Rosso Asylia '23	♟ 2
⊙ Terre Lontane Rosato '23	♟ 3
● Cirò Rosso Cl. Sup. Duca Sanfelice Ris. '21	♟♟♟ 3*
● Gravello '16	♟♟♟ 5

CALABRIA

Antonella Lombardo

c.da Chiusi
89032 Bianco [RC]
(') +39 09641901835
⊗ www.antonellalombardo.com

ANNUAL PRODUCTION 5,220 bottles
HECTARES UNDER VINE 5.00

Founded in 2019, this producer could have been overwhelmed by the pandemic that struck the following year. Instead, Antonella Lombardo, with pragmatism, turned adversity into opportunity. During the long lockdown, she honed her already solid manual skills in the vineyard and winery, working closely with her team. Her philosophy was clear from the start: to revive the cultivation of local indigenous grapes with full respect for nature and biodiversity. Antonella's wines are organic, original, and full of character, reflecting her determined personality and far-sighted vision. The Greco Particella Cinquantotto '23 took home Tre Bicchieri, proving close-knit and complex, opening with notes of citrus, mint, and fresh yellow flowers and fruits. Its vibrant acidity extends through a sapid and pervasive palate towards a long finish. The Greco '23 is similarly impressive, with expansive, persistent aromas of peach, citron, and anise, combining complexity and freshness on the palate.

Masseria Falvo 1727

loc. Garga
s.da prov.le Piana
87010 Saracena [CS]
(') +39 098138127
⊗ www.masseriafalvo.com

CELLAR SALES
ANNUAL PRODUCTION 80,000 bottles
HECTARES UNDER VINE 26.00
VITICULTURE METHOD Certified Organic
SUSTAINABLE WINERY

The date 1727, carved above the main entrance, marks the year the noble Falvo family from Cosenza began building this impressive estate, which functioned as a farm until the post-war era. About 20 years ago, brothers Ermanno and Pier Giorgio, the latest generation of the Falvo family, took it upon themselves to retore the property, preserving its architectural integrity while transforming it into a winery. Today, it boasts 26 hectares of organic vineyards on the slopes of Mount Pollino. The entire range, rooted in the local terroir, shows consistent quality, producing elegant and well-crafted wines. A standout is the refined Moscato passito Milirosu '22, which conveys vibrant aromas of ripe yellow fruit, verbena, lavender, citrus, and baked figs. On the palate, it's harmonious, with a sweet fruitiness balanced by lively acidity. We also appreciated the Spart '23, a dry malvasia with an enticing aromatic profile—fresh, citrusy, and expansive on the palate.

○ Particella 58 '23	▼▼▼ 5
⊙ Charà '23	▼▼ 5
○ Cheiras '20	▼▼ 6
○ Greco '23	▼▼ 5
○ Autoritratto Mantonico '23	▼ 6
○ Cheiras '19	♀♀♀ 6
○ Greco '22	♀♀♀ 5
○ Pi Greco '19	♀♀♀ 5
● Aoristo '21	♀♀ 6
● Aoristo '20	♀♀ 6
⊙ Charà '22	♀♀ 5
⊙ Charà '20	♀♀ 5
○ Cheiras '21	♀♀ 6
● Ichò '21	♀♀ 5
● Ichò '20	♀♀ 5
○ Particella 58 '21	♀♀ 4
○ Pi greco '20	♀♀ 5

⊙ Milirosu Moscato Passito '22	▼▼ 4
○ Terre di Cosenza Pollino Bianco Pircoca '23	▼▼ 3
○ Terre di Cosenza Pollino Bianco Spart '23	▼▼ 3
● Terre di Cosenza Pollino Don Rosario '19	▼▼ 5
● Terre di Cosenza Pollino Magliocco Cires '23	▼ 3
⊙ Terre di Cosenza Pollino Rosato Cjviz '23	▼ 3
○ Terre di Cosenza Bianco Ejà '14	♀♀ 5
○ Terre di Cosenza Bianco Pircoca '19	♀♀ 3
○ Terre di Cosenza Bianco Spart '18	♀♀ 3
● Terre di Cosenza Pollino Magliocco Graneta Ris. '18	♀♀ 3*

974

Santa Venere

loc. Tenuta Volta Grande
s.da prov.le 4, km 10.00
88813 Cirò [KR]
☎ +39 096238519
✉ www.santavenere.com

Statti

c.da Lenti
88046 Lamezia Terme [CZ]
☎ +39 0968456138
✉ www.statti.com

CELLAR SALES
PRE-BOOKED VISITS
ANNUAL PRODUCTION 150,000 bottles
HECTARES UNDER VINE 35.00
VITICULTURE METHOD Certified Organic

CELLAR SALES
PRE-BOOKED VISITS
RESTAURANT SERVICE
ANNUAL PRODUCTION 500,000 bottles
HECTARES UNDER VINE 100.00
SUSTAINABLE WINERY

The Santa Venere estate, named after the river that runs through it, has belonged to the noble Scala family since the 1600s. Even then, in addition to olives, vines were cultivated here. The transformation into a full-fledged farm is much more recent, dating back to the early 1960s when Federico Scala began producing wines under his own label, laying the foundation for what is today one of the most reliable wineries in the Ciro area. All the wines tasted this year were of good quality, with peaks of excellence. They are stylistically modern, elegant, and showcase the characteristics of the local varietals. This year we appreciated the Cirò Riserva Federico Scala '22, with its broad, dense nose of ripe fruit accompanied by fresher balsamic notes, and a juicy palate supported by close-knit, pleasantly rough tannins. Among the whites, the elegant Vescovado '23 stands out. It's made from guardavalle grapes, a nearly forgotten native variety revived by the Scala family, along with marsigliana nera.

The estate of Barons Antonio and Alberto Statti covers over 500 hectares in the Lamezia plains, in the southern part of Calabria. For more than 200 years, the family has produced wine, olive oil, citrus, and raised livestock. With a strong commitment to environmental sustainability, the Stattis process all waste from their operations using a large biogas plant, making the estate completely off the grid. Their range is extensive, spanning everything from easy-drinking wines to more complex and intriguing interpretations of both native and international grape varieties. A highlight is the Bordeaux-style blend 25° Anniversario '21, a wine rich in fruity and balsamic aromas, along with hints of undergrowth and spices. The palate is vibrant, full-bodied, and pervasive, energized by a nervy acidity before a long, balsamic finish. Among those expressions that draw on native varietals, the Mantonico '22 stands out for its bouquet rich in citrus, balsamic herbs, peach, and anise. On the palate, it's bold and dynamic, with a juicy finish.

● Cirò Rosso Cl. Sup. Federico Scala Ris. '22	▼▼ 6
○ Cirò Bianco '23	▼▼ 3
○ Vescovado '23	▼▼ 4
● Vurgadà '22	▼▼ 5
○ Calamacca Zibibbo '23	▼ 5
⊙ Cirò Rosato '23	▼ 3
⊙ Scassabarile '23	▼ 4
● Cirò Rosso Cl. Sup. Federico Scala Ris. '21	♀♀ 6
● Cirò Rosso Cl. Sup. Federico Scala Ris. '20	♀♀ 5
● Cirò Rosso Cl. Sup. Federico Scala Ris. '19	♀♀ 5
● Cirò Rosso Cl. Sup. Federico Scala Ris. '18	♀♀ 5

● 25° Anniversario '21	▼▼ 5
○ Greco '23	▼▼ 3
○ Mantonico '22	▼▼ 6
⊙ Greco Nero Rosato '23	▼ 3
○ Lamezia Bianco '23	▼ 4
● Arvino '20	♀♀ 3
● Cauro '19	♀♀ 5
● Gaglioppo '22	♀♀ 3
● Gaglioppo '21	♀♀ 3
● Lamezia Batasarro Ris. '20	♀♀ 4
● Lamezia Batasarro Ris. '17	♀♀ 4
○ Lamezia Bianco '21	♀♀ 4
⊙ Lamezia Rosato '21	♀♀ 2*
○ Mantonico '21	♀♀ 6
○ Mantonico '20	♀♀ 6
○ Mantonico '19	♀♀ 6

Tenuta del Conte

via Tirone, 131
88811 Cirò Marina [KR]
☎ +39 096236239
✇ www.tenutadelconte.it

PRE-BOOKED VISITS
ANNUAL PRODUCTION 30,000 bottles
HECTARES UNDER VINE 15.00
VITICULTURE METHOD Certified Organic

The arrival of the fourth generation of
winemakers—Mariangela, Giuseppe, and
Caterina—completely revolutionized the
approach to production at this winery, founded
in the 1960s by Francesco Parilla. The family first
transitioned to organic farming, then became
completely self-sufficient in production, using
only grapes from their four estate vineyards.
Finally, they returned to vinifying without the use
of selected yeasts, aiming to fully preserve the
varietal characteristics of the local grapes in
their wines. Aged for two years on fine lees, the
Cirò Bianco DiversaMente '20 is outstanding
and original. Its complex nose reveals citrus
tones, exotic fruit, stony beach, and almond. The
palate is sapid and slender, with a long citrusy
finish. The Cirò Rosso '20 is also excellent, with
a broad nose conjuring up black fruits and violet,
and a velvety, gentle palate with a vital
acidic-tannic component.

Tenuta del Travale

c.da Travale, 13
87050 Rovito [CS]
☎ +39 3937150240
✇ www.tenutadeltravale.it

CELLAR SALES
PRE-BOOKED VISITS
ANNUAL PRODUCTION 14,000 bottles
HECTARES UNDER VINE 2.00
SUSTAINABLE WINERY

When Raffaella Ciardullo purchased and
established Tenuta del Travale, it's likely she was
inspired by the ecological microeconomic
theories of Ernst Schumacher, particularly his
famous work "Small is Beautiful." Her winery is
indeed a tiny operation, managed by the family
with her husband and two daughters, cultivating
just a couple of hectares of vines—organically, of
course. Raffaella produces only a few thousand
bottles, each distinguished by elegant labels that
feature miniatures from an ancient medieval
manuscript. The Nerello Mascalese Eleuterìa '21
proves original and elegant, with its aromas of
raspberry, blood peach, bay leaf, wild olive, sweet
spices, and tobacco. An austere, fine palate
follows, where acidity, tannins, and fruit vie for
prominence in a harmonious and pleasing profile.
The Epicarma '23, a rosé from nerello cappuccio,
is also delicious, revealing hints of almond,
citrus, and roses, offering freshness and sapidity
on the palate.

○ Cirò Bianco DiversaMente '20	♀♀ 4
● Cirò Rosso Cl. Sup. '20	♀♀ 5
○ Cirò Bianco '23	♀♀ 4
⊙ Cirò Rosato Mani Contadine '23	♀ 4
○ Cirò Bianco '22	♀♀ 4
⊙ Cirò Rosato Mani Contadine '22	♀♀ 4
● Cirò Rosso Cl. Dagò '13	♀♀ 2*
● Cirò Rosso Cl. Sup. Dalla Terra Ris. '16	♀♀ 5

● Eleuteria '21	♀♀ 8
⊙ Epicarma '23	♀♀ 5
● Esmen Tetra '18	♀♀♀ 4*
● Eleuteria '20	♀♀ 8
● Eleuteria '18	♀♀ 7
● Eleuteria '17	♀♀ 6
● Eleuteria '16	♀♀ 6
● Eleuteria '15	♀♀ 6
● Eleuteria '14	♀♀ 6
⊙ Epicarma '22	♀♀ 5
● Esmen Tetra '21	♀♀ 6
● Esmen Tetra '20	♀♀ 5
● Esmen Tetra '19	♀♀ 5

OTHER WINERIES

Acroneo

fraz. La Mucone
c.da Serricella, 28
87041 Acri [CS]
+39 3291646040
www.acroneo.it

CELLAR SALES
PRE-BOOKED VISITS
ANNUAL PRODUCTION 17,000 bottles
HECTARES UNDER VINE 2.50
SUSTAINABLE WINERY

● Arkaios '21	🍷🍷 8
● Arkon '22	🍷 8
○ Elektron '23	🍷 5

Antiche Vigne

c.da Vallelonga
87050 Marzi [CS]
+39 3493695254
www.antichevigne.com

CELLAR SALES
PRE-BOOKED VISITS
ACCOMMODATION
ANNUAL PRODUCTION 60,000 bottles
HECTARES UNDER VINE 14.00
SUSTAINABLE WINERY

● Terre di Cosenza Savuto Sup. Succo di Pietra '15	🍷🍷 6
● Terre di Cosenza Savuto Cl. '22	🍷🍷 3

Cantine Artese

fraz. Porto Salvo
via Roma, 26
89900 Vibo Valentia
+39 3482406829
www.viniartese.it

○ Aurum Dei '22	🍷🍷 5
○ Aramoni '23	🍷🍷 3
● Limani '20	🍷 3

Cerminara

loc. Flandina
88813 Cirò [KR]
+39 096235956
www.cerminaravini.it

PRE-BOOKED VISITS
ANNUAL PRODUCTION 9,000 bottles
HECTARES UNDER VINE 6.50
SUSTAINABLE WINERY

● Cirò Rosso Cl. '22	🍷🍷 4
⊙ Cirò Rosato '22	🍷🍷 4

Colacino Wines

c.da Colle Manco
87050 Marzi [CS]
+39 09841900252
www.colacino.it

PRE-BOOKED VISITS
ACCOMMODATION
ANNUAL PRODUCTION 99,000 bottles
HECTARES UNDER VINE 21.00
SUSTAINABLE WINERY

○ Quarto '23	🍷🍷 3
● Savuto Rosso Britto '19	🍷🍷 5
● Savuto Rosso Si '23	🍷🍷 2*
○ Savuto Bianco Si '23	🍷 2

Cantine De Luca

s.da st.le 106
88814 Melissa [KR]
+39 0962935802
www.vinideluca.it

ANNUAL PRODUCTION 250,000 bottles
HECTARES UNDER VINE 27.00
VITICULTURE METHOD Certified Organic
SUSTAINABLE WINERY

● 1949 '21	🍷🍷 4
○ Cirò Bianco '23	🍷🍷 2*
⊙ Cirò Rosato '23	🍷 2
● Cirò Rosso Sup. Melisseo '20	🍷 2

Cantine De Mare

via Saffo
88811 Cirò Marina [KR]
☏ +39 3393768853
☻ www.cantinedemare.it

CELLAR SALES
PRE-BOOKED VISITS
ANNUAL PRODUCTION 100,000 bottles
HECTARES UNDER VINE 33.00

○ Cirò Rosato Prima Luce '23	♥♥ 3
● Cirò Rosso Amarillo '22	♥♥ 2*
● Cirò Rosso Cl. Sup. Altura '22	♥♥ 3
○ Cirò Bianco Sant'Angelo '23	♥ 3

Diana

c.da Mileo
87010 Saracena [CS]
☏ +39 3473892928
☻ www.aziendaagricoladiana.it

○ Moscato Passito '19	♥♥ 6
● Mileo '21	♥ 3

Barone Macrì

c.da Modi, 01
89040 Gerace [RC]
☏ +39 0964356497
☻ www.baronemacri.it

CELLAR SALES
PRE-BOOKED VISITS
ACCOMMODATION AND RESTAURANT SERVICE
ANNUAL PRODUCTION 30,000 bottles
HECTARES UNDER VINE 11.00
VITICULTURE METHOD Certified Organic
SUSTAINABLE WINERY

○ Centocamere Brut M. Cl. '20	♥♥ 5
● Pozzello Rosso '19	♥♥ 5
◉ Centocamere Brut M. Cl. Rosé '20	♥ 5
○ Pozzello Bianco '22	♥ 5

Dell'Aera

c.da Grandine
88050 Soveria Simeri [CZ]
☏ +39 3292021807
☻ www.dellaeravini.it

CELLAR SALES
PRE-BOOKED VISITS
ACCOMMODATION
ANNUAL PRODUCTION 15,000 bottles
HECTARES UNDER VINE 18.00
SUSTAINABLE WINERY

○ Vanitas '21	♥♥ 4
○ Kometes '23	♥♥ 3
● Krio '23	♥ 3

Enotria

loc. San Gennaro
s.da st.le Jonica, 106
88811 Cirò Marina [KR]
☏ +39 0962371181
☻ www.cantinaenotria.wine

CELLAR SALES
PRE-BOOKED VISITS
ANNUAL PRODUCTION 300,000 bottles
HECTARES UNDER VINE 45.00

○ Cirò Bianco '23	♥♥ 2*
● Cirò Rosso Cl. Sup. '22	♥♥ 3
○ Pecorello '23	♥♥ 2*
◉ Cirò Rosato '23	♥ 2

Nesci

via Marina, 1
89038 Palizzi [RC]
☏ +39 3209785653
☻ www.aziendanesci.it

ANNUAL PRODUCTION 45,000 bottles
HECTARES UNDER VINE 12.00

● Frasanè '22	♥♥ 5
○ Olimpia '22	♥♥ 4
● Chapeaux '22	♥ 5
● Fra Antonio '16	♥ 8

OTHER WINERIES

OI - Origine & Identità

via Solis
89866 Ricadi [VV]
📞 +39 3391965700
🌐 www.origineidentita.it/

○ OI Zibibbo Evoluzione '23	🍷🍷 4
○ OI Zibibbo Dosaggio Zero M. Cl. '21	🍷🍷 5

Tenute Pacelli

fraz. Pauciuri
c.da Rose
87010 Malvito [CS]
📞 +39 3384783678
🌐 www.tenutepacelli.it

CELLAR SALES
PRE-BOOKED VISITS
ACCOMMODATION
ANNUAL PRODUCTION 25,000 bottles
HECTARES UNDER VINE 11.00
VITICULTURE METHOD Certified Organic
SUSTAINABLE WINERY

● Terra Rossa '21	🍷🍷 3
○ Zoe Brut M. Cl. '18	🍷 5

La Peschiera

c.da Peschiera
87040 San Lorenzo del Vallo [CS]
📞 +39 0981950841
🌐 www.lapeschiera.net

CELLAR SALES
PRE-BOOKED VISITS
ACCOMMODATION
ANNUAL PRODUCTION 15,000 bottles
HECTARES UNDER VINE 13.00

⊙ Terre di Cosenza Rosato Abbaruna '23	🍷🍷 3
○ Terre di Cosenza Bianco Il Pecorello del Casello '23	🍷 3

Rocca Brettia

fraz. Donnici Inferiore
c.da Verzano
87100 Cosenza
📞 +39 3476722630
🌐 www.roccabrettia.com

CELLAR SALES
PRE-BOOKED VISITS
ANNUAL PRODUCTION 13,000 bottles
HECTARES UNDER VINE 4.00

○ Svevo '23	🍷🍷 4
⊙ Terre di Cosenza Donnici Rosato Peuce '23	🍷🍷 4

Fattoria San Francesco

loc. Quattromani
88813 Cirò [KR]
📞 +39 096232228
🌐 www.fattoriasanfrancesco.it

CELLAR SALES
PRE-BOOKED VISITS
ANNUAL PRODUCTION 224,000 bottles
HECTARES UNDER VINE 70.00

○ Bianco di Sale '23	🍷🍷 3
○ Cirò Bianco '23	🍷🍷 2*
● Cirò Rosso Cl. Sup. Duca dell'Argillone Ris. '19	🍷🍷 4

Scala

loc. Torricella di San Biagio
88811 Cirò Marina [KR]
📞 +39 096232716
🌐 www.cantinascala.it

CELLAR SALES
PRE-BOOKED VISITS
ANNUAL PRODUCTION 90,000 bottles
HECTARES UNDER VINE 15.00
VITICULTURE METHOD Certified Organic
SUSTAINABLE WINERY

○ Cirò Bianco '23	🍷🍷 4
● Cirò Rosso Cl. Sup. '22	🍷🍷 4
⊙ Cirò Rosato '23	🍷 4
● Cirò Rosso Cl. Sup. Ris. '21	🍷 6

OTHER WINERIES

Serracavallo

c.da Serracavallo
87043 Bisignano [CS]
☎ +39 09841758235
✆ www.viniserracavallo.com

CELLAR SALES
PRE-BOOKED VISITS
ACCOMMODATION AND RESTAURANT SERVICE
ANNUAL PRODUCTION 100,000 bottles
HECTARES UNDER VINE 30.00
VITICULTURE METHOD Certified Organic

○ Filovento '22	♟♟ 4
○ Petramola '23	♟♟ 3
● Terre di Cosenza Colline del Crati Magliocco V. Savuco Ris. '19	♟♟ 7

Tenuta Sposato

c.da Ciriaco
87012 Castrovillari [CS]
☎ +39 3928897107
✆ www.sposatovineyard.it

CELLAR SALES
ANNUAL PRODUCTION 15,000 bottles
HECTARES UNDER VINE 13.00

○ Terre di Cosenza Pecorello '23	♟♟ 3*
● Terre di Cosenza Aglianico '21	♟♟ 4

Vigneti Vumbaca

c.so Lilio
88811 Cirò [KR]
☎ +39 3889320696
✆ www.vignetivumbaca.it

CELLAR SALES
PRE-BOOKED VISITS
ANNUAL PRODUCTION 28,000 bottles
HECTARES UNDER VINE 7.00
VITICULTURE METHOD Certified Organic
SUSTAINABLE WINERY

○ Cirò Bianco '23	♟♟ 3
● Cirò Rosso Cl. Sup. Ris. '21	♟♟ 6
● Cirò Rosso Cl. Sup. '22	♟ 4

Spiriti Ebbri

via Roma, 96
87050 Spezzano Piccolo [CS]
☎ +39 0984408992
✆ www.spiritiebbri.it

CELLAR SALES
PRE-BOOKED VISITS
ANNUAL PRODUCTION 20,000 bottles
HECTARES UNDER VINE 2.50

● Appianum Rosso '21	♟♟ 5
○ Neostòs Bianco '23	♟♟ 4
● Neostòs Rosso '21	♟♟ 5
○ Cotidie Bianco '23	♟ 3

Cantine Vulcano

loc. Fego
via Piciara, 1a
88811 Cirò Marina [KR]
☎ +39 09621876736
✆ www.vulcanowine.com

CELLAR SALES
ANNUAL PRODUCTION 250,000 bottles
HECTARES UNDER VINE 4.00

○ Cirò Bianco Capo a Frutto '22	♟♟ 4
○ Cirò Rosato Mavile '23	♟♟ 3

Zito

loc. Punta Alice
via Scalaretto
88811 Cirò Marina [KR]
☎ +39 096231853
✆ www.zito.it

CELLAR SALES
PRE-BOOKED VISITS
ANNUAL PRODUCTION 800,000 bottles
HECTARES UNDER VINE 80.00
VITICULTURE METHOD Certified Organic

● Cirò Rosso Cl. Sup. Krimisa '21	♟♟ 3
○ Ginestra Bianca Pecorello '23	♟♟ 2*
○ Cirò Bianco Nosside '23	♟ 2
● Cirò Rosso Cl. Alceo '22	♟ 2

SICILY

This year's tastings saw the major issue of the 2023 vintage, a severe downy mildew attack on Sicilian vineyards, come to the fore. This, coupled with the effects of climate change (though to a far lesser extent), led to a 40% drop in production compared to 2022, with some areas experiencing even steeper declines. In some cases, producers were forced to release only very limited quantities of certain wines, or not produce them at all. With that important quantitative detail noted, let's get to the essence of things.

Once again, Etna has shown the character and personality of its wines—nearly all from vintages prior to 2023 and predominantly from red grape varieties. These wines are elegant, deep, complex, and unmistakably tied to their terroir, embodying the very qualities that have made them a global sensation. It's also finally time for catarratto to shine. Long undervalued, perhaps due to a lack of awareness of its potential, the grape is now thriving in western Sicily. Many wines captivated our tasting panels with their richness of flavor, longevity, and distinct character. This variety, long associated with the Alcamo area, has also been central to a movement—active for several decades—of so-called natural wines, championed by the "Catarratto boys." This group, led by Aldo Viola, draws on the region's traditions, focusing on sustainability, ethics, precision winemaking, and respect for nature. These values are strengthened by a deep sense of personal responsibility, and the wines they produce range from organic to biodynamic and even orange wines—all equally commendable.

A quick side note: we sense (almost with certainty) a renewed interest in high-end wines made from nero d'Avola, a historic variety that several wineries are betting on once again. Time will tell. As we wrap up this edition of the guide, we celebrate a total of 28 award-winning wines, along with five prestigious expressions featured in the new Rare Wines section.

Alessandro di Camporeale

c.da Mandranova
90043 Camporeale [PA]
📞 +39 092437038
🌐 www.alessandrodicamporeale.it

CELLAR SALES
PRE-BOOKED VISITS
ANNUAL PRODUCTION 260,000 bottles
HECTARES UNDER VINE 40.00
VITICULTURE METHOD Certified Organic

The winery was established in 2000 by the
Natale brothers, Nino and Rosolino, so as to
vinify the grapes that the Alessandro family had
been cultivating for over a century. The fourth
generation includes cousins Anna, responsible
for administration and hospitality, Benedetto "Il
Rosso," the winemaker, and Benedetto "Il Nero,"
who manages marketing. The vineyards,
organically farmed in Camporeale, host
catarratto, grillo, nero d'Avola, syrah, and
sauvignon blanc grapes. The Catarratto Monreale
Vigna di Mandranova '22 took home a gold: its
exceptionally refined nose of floral and
herbaceous notes is mirrored in the wine's
pervasive texture, fresh, sapid, and with
long-lasting persistence. The Sicilia Grillo Vigna di
Mandranova '23 also reached the final round,
with its intense, well-defined tropical fruit and
citrus blossom aromas, and a pulpy, elegant
palate. The Syrah Kaid '22 proves highly
enjoyable, featuring spicy and balsamic notes,
clear and consistent fruit.

Alta Mora

fraz. Pietramarina
c.da Verzella
95012 Castiglione di Sicilia [CT]
📞 +39 0918908713
🌐 www.altamora.it

PRE-BOOKED VISITS
ANNUAL PRODUCTION 134,000 bottles
HECTARES UNDER VINE 44.00
SUSTAINABLE WINERY

In 2013, Diego and Alberto Cusumano made a
significant contribution to the Etna terroir with
their independent winery. They focus on the
unique characteristics of individual vineyards,
selecting the best sites. In their underground
winery in Verzella, seamlessly integrated into the
surrounding landscape, they vinify only native
grapes from the same district, including
Guardiola, Pietramarina, Feudo di Mezzo, and
Solicchiata. Tre Bicchieri for the Etna Bianco Alta
Mora '23, with its intense and elegant notes of
white peach and citrus blossom. The palate
shines with its vibrant tension, minerality, and
long persistence. The Etna Rosso Feudo di
Mezzo '20 also made it to our finals—it's rich on
the nose with black forest fruits and sorb apple,
with fine, close-knit tannins to follow. The Rosso
Guardiola '20 opens on a floral bouquet
enriched with distinct smoky nuances,
developing on the palate with nice balance.
The fresh, fragrant, and sapid Rosato '23 is also
highly enjoyable.

○ Monreale Bianco V. di Mandranova '22	🍷🍷🍷 5
○ Sicilia Grillo V. di Mandranova '23	🍷🍷 3*
● Sicilia Kaid Vendemmia Tardiva '23	🍷🍷 5
○ Sicilia M. Cl. Extra Brut '20	🍷🍷 6
○ Sicilia M. Cl. Sboccatura Tardiva '17	🍷🍷 8
● Sicilia Syrah Kaid '22	🍷🍷 4
○ Siclia Catarratto Benedè '23	🍷🍷 3
○ Monreale Bianco V. di Mandranova '20	🏆🏆🏆 4*
○ Sicilia Catarrato V. di Mandranova '18	🏆🏆🏆 4*
○ Sicilia Grillo V. di Mandranova '18	🏆🏆🏆 3*
● Sicilia Syrah Kaid '19	🏆🏆🏆 4*

○ Etna Bianco Alta Mora '23	🍷🍷🍷 5
● Etna Rosso Alta Mora Feudo di Mezzo '20	🍷🍷 8
⊙ Etna Rosato Alta Mora '23	🍷🍷 5
● Etna Rosso Alta Mora '21	🍷🍷 5
● Etna Rosso Alta Mora Guardiola '20	🍷🍷 8
○ Etna Bianco Alta Mora '20	🏆🏆🏆 4*
○ Etna Bianco Alta Mora '19	🏆🏆🏆 4*
○ Etna Bianco Alta Mora '18	🏆🏆🏆 4*
○ Etna Bianco Alta Mora '17	🏆🏆🏆 4*
○ Etna Bianco Alta Mora '16	🏆🏆🏆 4*
○ Etna Bianco Alta Mora '14	🏆🏆🏆 3*
● Etna Rosso Alta Mora '19	🏆🏆🏆 5
● Etna Rosso Alta Mora Guardiola '19	🏆🏆🏆 8
○ Etna Bianco Alta Mora '22	🍷🍷 5
○ Etna Bianco Alta Mora '21	🍷🍷 5

Assuli

c.da Carcitella
91026 Mazara del Vallo [TP]
☎ +39 3516857240
✉ www.assuli.it

CELLAR SALES
ANNUAL PRODUCTION 190,000 bottles
HECTARES UNDER VINE 130.00
VITICULTURE METHOD Certified Organic
SUSTAINABLE WINERY

Based between Mazara del Vallo and Trapani, the winery is firmly in the hands of the Caruso family, now in its third generation with Roberto, Nicoletta, and Michele. Assuli, a word that derives from Sicilian dialect and means "under the sun," is comprised of five properties at elevations spanning 100-600 meters. The plots benefit from a Mediterranean climate with breezy summers and mild winters. Classic Sicilian varieties, as well as some syrah, are all grown and vinified locally. The Inzolia Carinda '23 delivers, conjuring up a highly pleasant bouquet of citrus and orange blossom. On the palate, it's in line with its aromatic sensations, fresh, sapid, and mineral. The rosé version of the Perricone Fiordispina '22 showcases vibrant aromas of cherries and wild strawberries, accompanied by citrus notes. In the mouth, it's juicy and well-balanced. The deep, terroir-driven Furioso '21 is a perricone with expressive tones of black plum and a lovely balsamic finish.

Barone di Villagrande

via del Bosco, 25
95010 Milo [CT]
☎ +39 0957082175
✉ www.villagrande.it

CELLAR SALES
PRE-BOOKED VISITS
ACCOMMODATION AND RESTAURANT SERVICE
ANNUAL PRODUCTION 90,000 bottles
HECTARES UNDER VINE 38.00
VITICULTURE METHOD Certified Organic
SUSTAINABLE WINERY

The first wine labeled Barone di Villagrande dates back to 1727, and the winery has always been in the capable hands of the Nicolosi Asmundo family. Today, the talented Marco continues this legacy. The estate is based in Contrada Villagrande, a unique area for producing Etna Bianco Superiore. A small relais with a charming view of the first, historic carricante vineyard has been added, and the venture has expanded to the island of Salina. The Etna Rosso Contrada Monte Ilice '22, made from nerello mascalese and other local varieties, perfectly expresses its volcanic terroir. It alternates floral scents, red fruits, balsamic notes, and smoky hints, offering elegance and balance on the palate, with persistent cherry notes and velvety tannins, all rounded out by delightful freshness. The Etna Bianco Superiore '23 is equally excellent, a harmonious and refined blend of carricante, minnella, and visparola, multifaceted on the nose and elegant on the palate.

○ Sicilia Insolia Carinda '23	♟♟ 3*
○ Sicilia Lucido Donna Angelica '23	♟♟ 3
● Sicilia Perricone Furioso '21	♟♟ 5
◉ Sicilia Perricone Rosato Fiordispina '22	♟♟ 4
● Sicilia Perricone Arcodace '23	♟ 3
○ Sicilia Zibibbo Dardinello '23	♟ 3
○ Astolfo '15	♟♟♟ 4*
● Lorlando '15	♟♟♟ 2*
● Lorlando '14	♟♟♟ 2*
● Sicilia Nero d'Avola Lorlando '17	♟♟♟ 3*
● Sicilia Perricone Furioso '18	♟♟♟ 5
● Sicilia Nero d'Avola Lorlando '22	♟♟ 5
○ Sicilia Zibibbo Dardinello '22	♟♟ 4

● Etna Rosso Contrada Monte Ilice '22	♟♟♟ 7
○ Etna Bianco Sup. '23	♟♟ 6
○ Etna Bianco Sup. Contrada Villagrande '21	♟♟ 8
◉ Etna Rosato '23	♟♟ 5
● Etna Rosso '21	♟♟ 6
● Etna Rosso Contrada Monte Arso '22	♟♟ 7
○ Salina Bianco '23	♟♟ 8
○ Etna Bianco Sup. Contrada Villagrande '19	♟♟♟ 8
○ Etna Bianco '19	♟♟ 4
○ Etna Bianco Sup. Contrada Villagrande '17	♟♟ 8
● Etna Rosso Contrada Villagrande '18	♟♟ 8
○ Salina Bianco '21	♟♟ 8

Tenuta Bastonaca

c.da Bastonaca
97019 Vittoria [RG]
📞 +39 0932686480
🌐 www.tenutabastonaca.it

CELLAR SALES
PRE-BOOKED VISITS
ACCOMMODATION
ANNUAL PRODUCTION 75,000 bottles
HECTARES UNDER VINE 19.00
VITICULTURE METHOD Certified Organic

Silvana Raniolo and Giovanni Calcaterra's young winery has gained a cult following for its distinctive range, which fully expresses the terroirs and grape varieties represented. With the valuable assistance of skilled winemaker Benedetto Alessandro, the producer has expanded beyond Ragusa, acquiring several hectares on Etna and Pantelleria. These new sites have already produced noteworthy bottles, all while maintaining a commitment to respect the environmental and authenticity. Hailing from a high-quality line that exemplifies the three key areas of the estate, the elegant Cerasuolo di Vittoria Classico '22 stands out with its deep ruby color and refined tones of sour cherry, plum, black spices, and cherry, sensations that return on the palate alongside fresh hints of conifer and medicinal herbs. The finish is juicy, with silky, exemplary tannins. The Frappato '23 is also excellent, recalling rose petals and wild strawberries—highly drinkable.

● Cerasuolo di Vittoria Cl. '22	♟♟ 3*
● Cerasuolo di Vittoria Classico Tonneaux '22	♟♟ 4
○ Etna Bianco '23	♟♟ 5
● Etna Rosso Piano dei Daini '22	♟♟ 5
○ Pantelleria '23	♟♟ 5
○ Sicilia Grillo '23	♟♟ 3
○ Sicilia Un Grillo...al Sole Passito '23	♟♟ 8
● Sud Nero d'Avola '22	♟♟ 5
● Vittoria Frappato '23	♟♟ 3
● Cerasuolo di Vittoria Cl. '21	♟♟♟ 3*
● Etna Rosso '20	♟♟ 5
○ Sicilia Grillo '22	♟♟ 3
● Sicilia Nero d'Avola '22	♟♟ 3
● Sud '19	♟♟ 5
● Vittoria Frappato '22	♟♟ 3

★Benanti

via Giuseppe Garibaldi, 361
95029 Viagrande [CT]
📞 +39 0957893399
🌐 www.benanti.it

CELLAR SALES
PRE-BOOKED VISITS
RESTAURANT SERVICE
ANNUAL PRODUCTION 170,000 bottles
HECTARES UNDER VINE 28.00
VITICULTURE METHOD Certified Organic
SUSTAINABLE WINERY

Founded by the visionary Giuseppe Benanti in the late 1990s, the Benanti winery on Etna has long been a symbol of focused work on specific cultivars. As a pioneer in a region now highly regarded, both nationally and internationally, Benanti was the first to label his wines with the name of the district. After his passing, his sons Antonio and Salvino have continued his work, making significant commercial decisions, including a partnership with well-known entrepreneur Rosso. The Etna Bianco Superiore Pietra Marina '19 reached our final round, enchanting with its elegant aromas of smoked salt, thyme, lavender, and orange blossom, along with smoky hints, peach, and almond notes. On the palate, its sapidity and freshness make for a long, persistent, citrusy, and satisfying finish. We also appreciated the Etna Rosso Rovittello, Particella 341 '18, an elegant and pervasive wine on the nose, with fruit notes of currant and peach and pronounced minerality, offering vibrancy and dynamism on the palate, thanks to still-vivid tannins.

○ Etna Bianco Sup. Pietra Marina '19	♟♟ 8
● Etna Rosso Rovittello Particella No. 341 '18	♟♟ 8
○ Etna Bianco Contrada Cavaliere '22	♟♟ 6
○ Etna Bianco Sup. Contrada Rinazzo '22	♟♟ 7
● Etna Rosso Contrada Calderara Sottana '22	♟♟ 6
● Etna Rosso Contrada Cavaliere '22	♟♟ 6
● Etna Rosso Contrada Dafara Galluzzo '22	♟♟ 6
● Etna Rosso Contrada Monte Serra '22	♟♟ 6
● Etna Rosso Serra della Contessa Particella No. 587 '18	♟♟ 8
○ Etna Bianco Sup. Contrada Rinazzo '19	♟♟♟ 7
○ Etna Bianco Sup. Pietramarina '09	♟♟♟ 5
● Etna Rosso Contrada Monte Serra '17	♟♟♟ 6
● Etna Rosso Serra della Contessa '06	♟♟♟ 7

Bonavita

loc. Faro Superiore
c.da Corso
98158 Messina
(+39 3471754683
⊕ www.bonavitafaro.com

PRE-BOOKED VISITS
ANNUAL PRODUCTION 15,000 bottles
HECTARES UNDER VINE 2.50
VITICULTURE METHOD Certified Organic

Giovanni Scarfone's passion and commitment
are unmistakable to anyone familiar with his
work—though calling it "work" might be
inaccurate. For Giovanni, winemaking has always
been a true calling, something he felt destined
for since he was a child. He even chose to
attend an agricultural high school, giving up
summer vacations to work alongside his
grandfather in the vineyards. His approach is
marked by dedication and a strict adherence to
natural methods, working personally both in the
vineyard and the cellar, and refusing to use
chemicals. Only estate grapes are used, even in
difficult years, like when a fire destroyed part of
a vineyard two years ago. The Faro '21 proves
impeccably fresh and aromatic, with nuances of
cherry giving way to red citrus, nutmeg, and
spices. On the palate, it's vibrant and long-lasting.
The Nocera Ilnò '22 also shows great character,
with its noble nose of wild cherry aromas and
Mediterranean scrub, and a soft palate with a
supple progression of flavor.

Tenuta Calamoni

c.da Calamoni
91023 Favignana [TP]
(+39 0923882755
⊕ www.firriato.it

CELLAR SALES
PRE-BOOKED VISITS
ANNUAL PRODUCTION 12,000 bottles
HECTARES UNDER VINE 5.50
SUSTAINABLE WINERY

Owned by Irene and Salvatore Di Gaetano, who
revived vine cultivation in the Egadi Islands after
over a century, this small estate is characterized
by spectacular maritime viticulture. The unique
setting, with grapes caressed by the waves and
cooled by sea breezes, is brought out by
increased salinity, made possible thanks to the
use of posidonia for fertilization. The result of
this meticulous work is wines that are original
and indomitable in character, made exclusively
from Trapani's native cultivars. One of the best
versions to date, the Passulè '20 is an elegant
zibibbo passito with a bright light-orange color,
the prelude to a refined aromatic profile of
peach, candied orange, apricot, lavender, thyme,
and rosemary. On the palate, it's sweet and
pulpy, with an alluring balance between acidity
and softness. La Muciara '22, made from
catarratto, grillo, and zibibbo, is citrusy and
delicately herbaceous—a fresh, mineral, and
highly sapid drink.

● Faro '21	♟♟ 5
● Ilnò '22	♟♟ 6
⊙ Il Rosato '23	♟ 4
● Faro '18	♟♟♟ 5
● Faro '20	♟♟ 5
● Faro '17	♟♟ 5
● Faro '16	♟♟ 5
● Faro '14	♟♟ 5
⊙ Il Rosato '22	♟♟ 4
● Ilnò '21	♟♟ 6
● Ilnò '19	♟♟ 5
⊙ Rosato '21	♟♟ 2*
⊙ Rosato '20	♟♟ 2*
⊙ Rosato '18	♟♟ 2*
⊙ Rosato '17	♟♟ 2*
● Rosso '19	♟♟ 5

○ Favinia Passulè '20	♟♟ 6
○ Favinia La Muciara '22	♟♟ 6
● Favinia Le Sciabiche '20	♟♟ 6
○ Favinia La Muciara '21	♟♟ 6
○ Favinia La Muciara '20	♟♟ 5
● Favinia Le Sciabiche '19	♟♟ 6
● Favinia Le Sciabiche '18	♟♟ 6
○ Favinia Passulè '19	♟♟ 6
○ Favinia Passulè '16	♟♟ 6

Calcagno

fraz. Passopisciaro
via Regina Margherita, 153
95012 Castiglione di Sicilia [CT]
(☏) +39 3387772780
⊚ www.vinicalcagno.it

CELLAR SALES
PRE-BOOKED VISITS
ANNUAL PRODUCTION 13,000 bottles
HECTARES UNDER VINE 3.00

The Calcagno brothers' winery, managed by Gianni, Franco and Franco's daughter Giusy, is still relatively young. Although their family has been growing grapes for generations, it wasn't until 2006 that they began bottling their own wines, having previously sold their grapes to other producers. Initially, they used a friend's cellar, but a few years later, they moved to their own facility. The winery and vineyards are located in Passopisciaro, on Mount Etna's northern slope. The old bush-trained vineyards, primarily planted with nerello mascalese and carricante, are situated in Arcuria, Calderara, and Feudo di Mezzo. The Etna Bianco Superiore Primazappa '22 is beautifully crafted, with its brilliant straw-yellow color. The nose reveals characteristic mineral notes, followed by yellow citrus and more mature fruit nuances. The palate is consistent, fine and sapid, with a fresh, citrusy finish. The Etna Bianco Ginestra '23 expresses its varietal character with ripe yellow fruit, brackish notes, and an acidity that adds a lively rhythm.

○ Etna Bianco Sup. Primazappa '22	🍷🍷 6
○ Etna Bianco Ginestra '23	🍷🍷 5
⊙ Etna Rosato Romice delle Sciare '23	🍷🍷 5
● Etna Rosso Feudo di Mezzo '22	🍷🍷 5
● Etna Rosso Calderara '21	🍷 6
○ Etna Bianco Ginestra '22	🍷🍷 5
○ Etna Bianco Sup. Primazappa '21	🍷🍷 6
⊙ Etna Rosato Romice delle Sciare '22	🍷🍷 5
● Etna Rosso Arcuria '21	🍷🍷 5
● Etna Rosso Arcuria '20	🍷🍷 5
● Etna Rosso Arcuria '13	🍷🍷 4
● Etna Rosso Calderara '20	🍷🍷 6
● Etna Rosso Feudo di Mezzo '21	🍷🍷 5
● Etna Rosso Feudo di Mezzo '20	🍷🍷 5

Caravaglio

via Gelso, 2
98050 Malfa [ME]
(☏) +39 3398115953
⊚ www.caravaglio.it

+PRE-BOOKED VISITS
ACCOMMODATION
ANNUAL PRODUCTION 50,000 bottles
HECTARES UNDER VINE 15.00
VITICULTURE METHOD Certified Organic
SUSTAINABLE WINERY

Over the past decade, Nino Caravaglio's journey has been marked by consistent quality. An authentic and passionate winemaker, Caravaglio has become a key figure in Sicilian wine. Supported by his wife Elisa and daughter Alda, Nino has made significant investments in vineyards across three different islands—Vulcano, Stromboli, and his native Salina—despite economic sacrifices. The new underground winery is almost ready. The Malvasia Infatata '23 excels with its enticing aromatic notes that gradually give way to exotic fruit, lavender, jasmine, and coastal scents. The palate is exceptionally fresh and elegant, with delicate, juicy, and enticing fruit. The Corinto Nero Palmento di Salina '23 is a pleasure, conjuring up beguiling nuances of blueberries, wild strawberries, laurel, and licorice, offering a harmonious balance of fruit and tannins.

○ Infatata '23	🍷🍷🍷 5
● Palmento di Salina '23	🍷🍷 4
○ Occhio di Terra Malvasia '23	🍷🍷 5
● Scampato '21	🍷🍷 8
○ Infatata '22	🍷🍷🍷 4*
○ Infatata '21	🍷🍷🍷 4*
○ Malvasia delle Lipari Passito '19	🍷🍷🍷 5
○ Malvasia delle Lipari Passito '18	🍷🍷🍷 5
○ Malvasia delle Lipari Passito '17	🍷🍷🍷 5
○ Malvasia delle Lipari Passito '16	🍷🍷🍷 5
○ Occhio di Terra Malvasia '20	🍷🍷🍷 5
○ Infatata '19	🍷🍷 3*
○ Malvasia delle Lipari Passito '22	🍷🍷 5
○ Malvasia delle Lipari Passito '21	🍷🍷 5
○ Malvasia delle Lipari Passito '20	🍷🍷 5

★Le Casematte

loc. Faro Superiore
c.da Corso
98163 Messina
☎ +39 0906409427
✉ www.lecasematte.it

CELLAR SALES
ANNUAL PRODUCTION 40,000 bottles
HECTARES UNDER VINE 11.00
VITICULTURE METHOD Certified Organic
SUSTAINABLE WINERY

In just a few short years, the winery of
Gianfranco Sabatino and Andrea Barzagli has
become a benchmark for the small but
prestigious Doc Faro. After building a new aging
cellar, they have begun constructing a facility that
will include offices, guest accommodations, and a
large tasting room overlooking the Strait of
Messina. Meanwhile, with new plantings and
acquisitions, the two partners have nearly
doubled the estate's vineyard area. This dynamic
operation continues to grow not only in quantity
but, as our tastings confirm, especially in quality.
The refined Faro '22 delivers with its
sophisticated bouquet, opening on elegant floral
notes, wild herbs, fresh red fruit, and spices. In
the mouth, it's well balanced, with a subtle use of
oak, offering a harmonious palate where fruit
melds beautifully with close-knit, smooth tannins.
We also appreciated the Grillo Pharis '22, which
hails from a vineyard overlooking the Strait. It
combines yellow fruit and flowers with dynamic
notes of citrus and iodine; on the palate it
proves highly enjoyable, with delicate sapidity.

● Faro '22	♟♟♟ 5
○ Sicilia Grillo Pharis '22	♟♟ 5
● Nanuci '22	♟♟ 5
● Peloro Rosso '22	♟♟ 3
⊙ Rosematte Nerello Mascalese '23	♟♟ 3
○ Sicilia Peloro Bianco '23	♟♟ 4
● Faro '21	♟♟♟ 5
● Faro '20	♟♟♟ 5
● Faro '19	♟♟♟ 5
● Faro '18	♟♟♟ 5
● Faro '17	♟♟♟ 5
● Faro '16	♟♟♟ 5
● Faro '15	♟♟♟ 5
● Faro '14	♟♟♟ 5
● Faro '13	♟♟♟ 5
● Nanuci '21	♟♟ 5

Centopassi

c.da Don Tommaso
90048 San Cipirello [PA]
☎ +39 0918577655
✉ www.centopassisicilia.it

CELLAR SALES
PRE-BOOKED VISITS
ACCOMMODATION AND RESTAURANT SERVICE
ANNUAL PRODUCTION 500,000 bottles
HECTARES UNDER VINE 75.00
VITICULTURE METHOD Certified Organic
SUSTAINABLE WINERY

This winery, which honors anti-mafia activist
Peppino Impastato, is associated with the Libera
Terra cooperative. Libera Terra cultivates land
confiscated from organized crime outfits and
turns it into socially productive businesses. The
vineyards, spread across the provinces of
Palermo and Agrigento, span 12 districts, from
calcareous soils where grillo is grown to
sandstone and clay terrain where catarratto is
cultivated and the parent rock itself, which hosts
nocera and nerello mascalese. Each wine
highlights individual parcels and symbolizes the
region's revival. The refined Giato '23, a blend of
grillo and catarratto, is highly convincing,
revealing a bouquet of vibrant fruit aromas like
peach and ripe pear, intertwined with floral
hints of jasmine, wisteria, and yellow daisies.
On the palate, it's fresh and sapid, with pleasant
persistence and a fruity encore. The Teatro
Cajjo '22, made from carricante grapes grown in
the San Giuseppe Jato area, delivers tropical fruit
and citrus aromas, developing lively and elegant
on the palate. A highly gratifying drink.

○ Sicilia Giato '23	♟♟ 3*
○ Sicilia Catarratto Terre Rosse di Giabbascio '23	♟♟ 3
● Sicilia Cimento di Perricone '23	♟♟ 3
○ Sicilia Teatro Cajjo Carricante '22	♟♟ 3
● Sicilia Argille di Tagghia Via Nero d'Avola '23	♟ 3
● Sicilia Pietre a Purtedda da Ginestra '22	♟ 5
○ Sicilia Rocce di Pietralonga Grillo '23	♟ 3
○ Sicilia Catarratto Terre Rosse di Giabbascio '18	♟♟♟ 3*
● Argille di Tagghia Via '13	♟♟ 3*
● Argille di Tagghia Via di Sutta '20	♟♟ 5
○ Sicilia Grillo Rocce di Pietra Longa '22	♟♟ 3
● Sicilia Nero d'Avola Perricone Giato '22	♟♟ 2*
● Sicilia Perricone Cimento di Perricone '22	♟♟ 3

Frank Cornelissen

fraz. Solicchiata
via Nazionale, 297
95012 Castiglione di Sicilia [CT]
(+39 0942986315
www.frankcornelissen.it

CELLAR SALES
PRE-BOOKED VISITS
ANNUAL PRODUCTION 70,000 bottles
HECTARES UNDER VINE 18.00
VITICULTURE METHOD Certified Organic

Frank is an authentic character, renowned for his early discovery of the Etna wine region in 2001 and for his ability to transcend conventions and dogmas, exploring and experimenting with the area like a modern-day dowser. His internationally acclaimed wines interpret the volcanic area with originality and impeccable technique, captivating with their strong character and authenticity. The Munjebel Rosso Monte Colla '21, from old nerelle mascalese vines planted at nearly 800 meters elevation, took home Tre Bicchieri. It's a deep and elegant wine, evoking medicinal herbs, flat peach compote, bay leaf, and pomegranate. On the palate, it's complex, with a mineral base that recalls slate and graphite, all supported by soft, silky tannins. Equally noteworthy are the Munjebel Rosso CR and the Munjebel Rosso Calderara Sottana, both 2021s and made from old, prized vineyards of nerello mascalese.

★Cottanera

loc. Iannazzo
s.da prov.le 89
95030 Castiglione di Sicilia [CT]
(+39 0942963601
www.cottanera.it

CELLAR SALES
PRE-BOOKED VISITS
ANNUAL PRODUCTION 350,000 bottles
HECTARES UNDER VINE 65.00

Founded by Guglielmo and Enzo Cambria, Cottanera quickly became a key player in Etna's wine renaissance. Initially, they focused on international varietals like syrah, merlot, and mondeuse, which integrated exceptionally well into the region. Over time, they shifted their attention to native varietals and the potential of their individual vineyards, supported by notable holdings in prestigious districts. The Zottorinoto Riserva '20 continues its winning streak, displaying remarkable aromatic elegance, with a complex, well-defined bouquet of black forest fruits, mineral suggestions, and smoky notes. On the palate, it's invigorating, with notable length. The outstanding Feudo di Mezzo '21 also made it to our finals, with its lovely ferrous tones and Mediterranean brush—lively and refined. The Etna Rosato '23 proves vibrant in its fruity and floral tones, while the Syrah Sole di Sesta '21 is spicy, pleasantly green, and juicy.

• Munjebel Rosso MC '21	▼▼▼ 8
• Sicilia Rosso Magma '21	▼▼ 8
○ Munjebel Bianco '22	▼▼ 8
○ Munjebel Bianco VA '21	▼▼ 8
• Munjebel Rosso CD '21	▼▼ 8
• Munjebel Rosso CR '21	▼▼ 8
• Munjebel Rosso CS '21	▼▼ 8
• Munjebel Rosso FM '21	▼▼ 8
• Munjebel Rosso PA '21	▼▼ 8
⊙ Susucaru '23	▼▼ 6
• Sicilia Rosso Magma '20	♈♈♈ 8
• Magma Barbabecchi '10	♈♈ 8
• Magma Decima Edizione '12	♈♈ 8
• Magma Dodicesima Edizione '14	♈♈ 8
○ Munjebel Bianco VA '20	♈♈ 8
• Munjebel Vigne Alte 9 '12	♈♈ 7

• Etna Rosso Contrada Zottorinoto Ris. '20	▼▼▼ 8
• Etna Rosso Feudo di Mezzo '21	▼▼ 6
○ Etna Bianco '23	▼▼ 4
○ Etna Bianco Calderara '22	▼▼ 5
⊙ Etna Rosato '23	▼▼ 3
• Etna Rosso '22	▼▼ 4
• Sicilia Rosso L'Ardenza '22	▼▼ 4
• Sicilia Syrah Sole di Sesta '21	▼▼ 4
• Etna Rosso Contrada Zottorinoto Ris. '19	♈♈♈ 8
• Etna Rosso Feudo di Mezzo '19	♈♈♈ 6
• Etna Rosso Feudo di Mezzo '16	♈♈♈ 6
• Etna Rosso Zottorinoto Ris. '17	♈♈♈ 8
• Etna Rosso Zottorinoto Ris. '16	♈♈♈ 8
• Etna Rosso Zottorinoto Ris. '14	♈♈♈ 8

Cristo di Campobello

loc. c.da Favarotta
s.da st.le 123 km 19,200
92023 Campobello di Licata [AG]
+39 0922 877709
www.cristodicampobello.it

PRE-BOOKED VISITS
ANNUAL PRODUCTION 300,000 bottles
HECTARES UNDER VINE 35.00

This esteemed winery, owned by the Bonetta family, was established in 2000 in Campobello di Licata, adjacent to a revered statue of Christ, a site of frequent local pilgrimages. The vineyards are situated on limestone-gypsum hills at 300 meters elevation. The winery's philosophy emphasizes low yields, optimal harvest timing, handpicking into small crates, and meticulous vinification using cutting-edge equipment and computerized controls. The consistently high-quality Nero d'Avola Lu Patri '22 offers up balsamic notes and aromatic herbs accompanied by blackberry and black cherry. It's a round and soft wine, with remarkable persistence of flavor, complex, warm, pervasive, and spicy, with a hint of licorice on the finish. The Grillo Metodo Classico Extra Brut '19, which spent more than 36 months on the lees, is also delicious, revealing fragrant aromas of bread crust and floral notes of broom, shifting toward fruity hints of peach, pear, and citrus. On the palate, it's creamy, with a lovely almond finish.

● Sicilia Nero d'Avola Lu Patri '22	🍷🍷 5
⊙ C'D'C' Cristo di Campobello Rosato '23	🍷🍷 3
● C'D'C' Cristo di Campobello Rosso '23	🍷🍷 3
○ Extra Brut M. Cl. '19	🍷🍷 6
○ Sicilia Bianco Adènzia '23	🍷🍷 4
● Sicilia Syrah Lusirà '22	🍷🍷 5
○ Sicilia Chardonnay Laudàri '22	🍷 5
● Lu Patri '09	YYY 5
○ Sicila Bianco Adènzia '19	YY 3*
○ Sicilia Grillo Lalùci '20	YY 3*
○ Sicilia Grillo Lalùci '17	YY 3*
● Sicilia Nero d'Avola Lu Patri '21	YY 5
● Sicilia Syrah Lusirà '20	YY 5
● Sicilia Syrah Lusirà '17	YY 5

I Custodi delle Vigne dell'Etna

loc. Solicchiata
c.da Moganazzi
95012 Castiglione di Sicilia [CT]
+39 3931898430
www.icustodi.it

CELLAR SALES
PRE-BOOKED VISITS
ANNUAL PRODUCTION 80,000 bottles
HECTARES UNDER VINE 20.00
VITICULTURE METHOD Certified Organic
SUSTAINABLE WINERY

This winery represents a love story between a Roman, Mario Paoluzi, and Europe's highest volcano, Mount Etna. His passion, nurtured district by district, bush vine by bush vine, has borne fruit in the wines produced here. The unique soil and climate conditions, with elevations ranging from 650 to 900 meters and significant temperature variations, impart distinctive characteristics to the wines. The process follows nature's course, starting with the use of indigenous yeasts. The Etna Rosso Aetneus '20 put in a worthy performance, just falling short. It pours a ruby-garnet color, revealing a nose that's both intense and complex, with notes of red fruits, particularly currant and blackberry, and a touch of minerality that reemerges on its long and pleasant palate. The Etna Bianco Ante '21, with its bright straw-yellow hue, stands out for its fruit notes, from peach to citrus; in the mouth it's elegant and dynamic. We also enjoyed the Etna Bianco Superiore Imbris '20 by virtue of its exuberant minerality.

○ Etna Bianco Ante '21	🍷🍷 6
● Etna Rosso Aetneus '20	🍷🍷 6
○ Etna Bianco Aedes '23	🍷🍷 4
○ Etna Bianco Sup. Imbris '20	🍷🍷 7
● Etna Rosso Pistus '22	🍷🍷 4
● Etna Rosso Saeculare Ris. '15	🍷🍷 8
○ Etna Bianco Aedes '21	YYY 4*
○ Etna Bianco Ante '20	YY 6
○ Etna Bianco Ante '19	YY 6
○ Etna Bianco Sup. Imbris '19	YY 7
● Etna Rosso Aetneus '17	YY 6
● Etna Rosso Pistus '21	YY 4
● Etna Rosso Pistus '20	YY 4
● Etna Rosso Saeculare Ris. '14	YY 8
● Nerello Cappuccio '22	YY 5
● Nerello Cappuccio '21	YY 5

★★Cusumano

c.da San Carlo
s.da st.le 113, km 307
90047 Partinico [PA]
(☎) +39 0918908713
⊛ www.cusumano.it

CELLAR SALES
PRE-BOOKED VISITS
ANNUAL PRODUCTION 2,500,000 bottles
HECTARES UNDER VINE 520.00
SUSTAINABLE WINERY

In the early 2000s, brothers Alberto and Diego Cusumano embarked on an adventure that has since become a well-established winery, known both nationally and internationally. Their goal is to narrate Sicily through its various territories and grapes. Each wine represents a project, a varietal, a terroir, revealed in ways that are at times immediately expressive and enjoyable, and at others rich in nuance. Today, the Cusumano brand is known worldwide for its unmistakable style. The Grillo Shamaris '22, with its deep straw-yellow color, impresses with its great complexity and intense aromas of yellow fruit and flowers. On the palate, it's harmonious, pleasant, and vibrant, with a truly long finish. The Rosato Ramusa '23, made from pinot nero, also stands out for its freshness and fine fruit. The Salealto Tenuta Ficuzza '22, a blend of grillo, insolia, and zibibbo, is right up there, revealing refined citrus and plum notes and an intriguing sapidity.

⊙ Ramusa Tenuta Ficuzza '23	♟♟ 3*
○ Sicilia Shamaris Tenuta Monte Pietroso '22	♟♟ 3*
○ Angimbè Tenuta Ficuzza '23	♟♟ 3
● Fosnuri Tenuta San Giacomo '21	♟♟ 8
○ Jalè Tenuta Ficuzza Vigneto del Ventaglio '22	♟♟ 5
○ Moscato dello Zucco '14	♟♟ 6
○ Salealto Tenuta Ficuzza '22	♟♟ 7
● Sicilia Benuara Tenuta Presti e Pegni '23	♟♟ 4
● Sicilia Nero d'Avola Disueri Tenuta San Giacomo '23	♟♟ 3
○ Salealto Tenuta Ficuzza '21	♟♟♟ 6
○ Salealto Tenuta Ficuzza '20	♟♟♟ 6
○ Salealto Tenuta Ficuzza '19	♟♟♟ 6

★★Donnafugata

via S. Lipari, 18
91025 Marsala [TP]
(☎) +39 0923724200
⊛ www.donnafugata.it

CELLAR SALES
PRE-BOOKED VISITS
ANNUAL PRODUCTION 3,650,000 bottles
HECTARES UNDER VINE 488.00
SUSTAINABLE WINERY

The Rallo family's Donnafugata continues its impressive trajectory of growth, boasting a presence in four renowned Sicilian terroirs: Contessa Entellina, the island of Pantelleria, Cerasuolo di Vittoria, and Etna. The operational heart remains the historic Marsala winery. Their fruitful collaboration with Dolce & Gabbana continues, which has led to the Isolano, Cuordilava, Etna Bianco, Etna Rosso and Rosa (a blend of nerello and nocera designated as part of the Doc Sicilia appellation). Once again, the Passito di Pantelleria Ben Ryé triumphs, reaffirming its status in the 2021 vintage. The nose is breathtaking, with intense and multifaceted notes of lavender, rosemary, and dried apricot, which carry over to an invigorating palate, rich with sumptuous pleasure and an incredibly long finish. We also found the complex and fleshy Etna Bianco Sul Vulcano '21 in our finals, with its sapid character, as well as the Vittoria Contesa dei Venti '22, a Nero d'Avola with a sunny Mediterranean bouquet, and an elegant, profile of plump, silky fruit.

○ Passito di Pantelleria Ben Ryé '21	♟♟♟ 8*
○ Etna Bianco Sul Vulcano '21	♟♟ 5
● Vittoria Nero d'Avola Contesa dei Venti '22	♟♟ 4
● Cerasuolo di Vittoria Floramundi '22	♟♟ 4
○ Etna Bianco Isolano Dolce & Gabbana '21	♟♟ 5
⊙ Etna Rosato Sul Vulcano '23	♟♟ 5
● Etna Rosso Contrada Marchesa '20	♟♟ 8
● Etna Rosso Fragore C.da Montelaguardia '20	♟♟ 8
○ Sicilia Bianco Vigna di Gabri '22	♟♟ 4
○ Sicilia Contessa Entellina Chardonnay Chiarandà '21	♟♟ 6
⊙ Sicilia Rosato Rosa Dolce & Gabbana '23	♟♟ 5

SICILY

★Duca di Salaparuta

via Nazionale, s.da. st.le. 113
90014 Casteldaccia [PA]
(·)) +39 091945201
● www.duca.it

Eolia

via Roma, 17
98050 Malfa [ME]
(·)) +39 3939631166
● www.eoliasalina.it

CELLAR SALES
PRE-BOOKED VISITS
ANNUAL PRODUCTION 1,000,000 bottles
HECTARES UNDER VINE 171.00
SUSTAINABLE WINERY

PRE-BOOKED VISITS
ANNUAL PRODUCTION 10,000 bottles
HECTARES UNDER VINE 7.00

Duca di Salaparuta, a key player in Sicily's oenological history, is celebrating its 200th anniversary. Since 2001, the producer has been partnered with the storied Florio winery, under the ownership of Saronno's ILLVA group (led by the Reina family). This winning synergy spans various territories, adding new estates like Risignolo in Trapani, Vajasindi on Etna, and Suomarchesa in Riesi, to the historic properties in Casteldaccia and Marsala. Their flagship lines are Corvo, Duca, and Florio. Tre Bicchieri for the refined Duca Enrico '20, a wine that encapsulates Sicily's richness in the bottle. The bouquet features small red fruits tinged with citrus and spices, thanks to long aging, making for an elegant wine with great aging potential. The Triskelè '21, a top-drawer Nero d'Avola, boasts a strong personality with pervasive nuances of rose petals, cherry, and black pepper. Silky tannins pave the way for an authoritative, balsamic finish—a gratifying drink.

Luca Caruso and Natascia Santandrea's ambitious project is taking shape after three years. With a well-equipped winery, six hectares of vineyards, and ongoing acquisitions, they aim to produce dry wines from indigenous grapes, highlighting the attributes of the island's diverse terroirs. Situated on an extinct volcano, where soil composition varies according to ancient lava flows, they vinify and bottle each parcel separately according to its origin. We were truly impressed by the Malvasia Eolia V '22 ("V" stands for Valdichiesa, the Malfa hamlet where it's produced). Vibrant on the nose with aromas of apricot, aromatic herbs, and iodized mineral tones, it stands out in the glass for its fragrant fruit and lovely saline finish. The Corinto Nero CN '22 is also delightful, offering aromas of cherries, violets, and samphire, with a soft texture and irresistibly pleasing drinkability.

● Sicilia Nero d'Avola Duca Enrico '20	♥♥♥ 8
○ Bianca di Valguarnera '21	♥♥ 6
○ Sicilia Kados Grillo '23	♥♥ 4
● Sicilia Passo delle Mule Nero d'Avola '22	♥♥ 4
● Sicilia Triskelè '21	♥♥ 5
● Duca Enrico '03	♥♥♥ 6
● Duca Enrico '01	♥♥♥ 6
● Duca Enrico '84	♥♥♥ 6
○ Marsala Vergine Ris. '11	♥♥♥ 7
● Duca Enrico '18	♥♥ 8
● Duca Enrico '17	♥♥ 8
○ Marsala Sup. Targa 1840 Ris. '07	♥♥ 4
○ Passito di Pantelleria Florio '14	♥♥ 6
● Sicilia Nero d'Avola Duca Enrico '19	♥♥ 8

○ Eolia V '22	♥♥ 7
◉ Eolia Rosa '23	♥♥ 5
● Rosso CN '21	♥♥ 7
○ Bianco M '22	♥♥ 5
○ Bianco M '21	♥♥ 6
○ Bianco V '21	♥♥ 7
○ Bianco V '20	♥♥ 6

★Feudi del Pisciotto

c.da Pisciotto
93015 Niscemi [CL]
(») +39 09331930280
⊛ www.castellare.it

CELLAR SALES
PRE-BOOKED VISITS
ACCOMMODATION
ANNUAL PRODUCTION 200,000 bottles
HECTARES UNDER VINE 45.00

The winery's owner is also a shareholder of Gambero Rosso spa. To avoid any conflict of interest, Paolo Panerai has subordinated the possible awarding of Tre Bicchieri—which, in any case, only occurs through a blind tasting—to the attainment of the same rating of excellence, upwards of 90/100, by an independent, international panel. This was the case. Indeed, this year the Domini di Castellare group's Sicilian winery submitted a selection of elegant and terroir-driven wines for tasting. The wines presented this year prove highly elegant and deeply reflective of their terroir. The standout is the Moro di Testa '21, a Syrah with a Mediterranean soul that perfectly balances the sunny quality of ripe red fruit with fresh herbal notes of rosemary and mint, underpinned by a refined, spicy finish. On the palate, it's propelled by the interplay of acidity and tannins, gliding elegantly toward a long finish marked by green pepper. We were also impressed by the Nero d'Avola Versace '22, which reached the final round. Its close-knit, fruity nose leads into a taut, supple, and persistent palate.

● Moro di Testa '21	♈♈♈	6
○ Sicilia Grillo Carolina Marengo Kisa '23	♈♈	4
● Sicilia Nero d'Avola Versace '22	♈♈	4
● Carolina Marengo Kisa Frappato '22	♈♈	4
● Cerasuolo di Vittoria Giambattista Valli Paris '22	♈♈	4
○ Gianfranco Ferré Passito '22	♈♈	5
○ Gurra di Mare Tirsat '22	♈♈	4
● L'Eterno '22	♈♈	7
● Cerasuolo di Vittoria Giambattista Valli '18	♉♉♉	4*
● Moro di Testa '20	♉♉♉	6
○ Sicilia Grillo Carolina Marengo Kisa '20	♉♉♉	4*
● Sicilia Nero d'Avola Versace '19	♉♉♉	4*

Feudo Arancio

c.da Portella Misilbesi
92017 Sambuca di Sicilia [AG]
(») +39 0925579000
⊛ www.feudoarancio.it

CELLAR SALES
PRE-BOOKED VISITS
ACCOMMODATION
ANNUAL PRODUCTION 6,000,000 bottles
HECTARES UNDER VINE 700.00
SUSTAINABLE WINERY

Feudo Arancio's main property is situated near Lake Arancio, the operational heart of the Mezzacorona Group, an international wine powerhouse whose significant investments in Sicily have made it a prominent player in the island's wine scene. The vineyards along the breezy coasts of Sambuca and Acate yield intense and expressive wines. Drawing on both indigenous and international varietals, their range is well-known and appreciated in all markets. Both the whites and reds presented this year were excellent. The standout among them is the Dalila Riserva '22, a harmonious blend of grillo and viognier that showcases a rich, straw-yellow hue. Its aromas recall jasmine and tropical fruits, especially mango. On the palate, it's broad, pervasive, and fresh, with a fine, citrus-tinged finish. We were even more impressed with the Hedonis, a close-knit, pervasive Nero d'Avola with Mediterranean tones of black fruit and spices. It offers a creamy, smooth, sapid, and deep drinkability.

● Sicilia Hedonis Ris. '22	♈♈♈	6
○ Sicilia Bianco Dalila Ris. '22	♈♈	4
○ Sicilia Bianco Tinchitè '23	♈♈	3
○ Sicilia Quèto Grillo '23	♈♈	3
● Sicilia Rosso Cantodoro Ris. '21	♈	5
○ Hekate Passito '18	♉♉	5
○ Sicilia Bianco Dalila Ris. '21	♉♉	4
○ Sicilia Bianco Dalila Ris. '19	♉♉	4
● Sicilia Cantodoro Ris. '20	♉♉	4
○ Sicilia Grillo '21	♉♉	3
○ Sicilia Grillo Quèto '21	♉♉	3*
● Sicilia Hedonis Ris. '21	♉♉	6
● Sicilia Hedonis Ris. '18	♉♉	6
● Sicilia Hedonis Ris. '16	♉♉	4
● Sicilia Hedonis Ris. '15	♉♉	4
● Sicilia Nero d'Avola Quèto '21	♉♉	3
● Sicilia Rosso Cantodoro Ris. '17	♉♉	4

★Feudo Maccari

c.da Maccari
s.da prov.le Noto-Pachino km 13,5
96017 Noto [SR]
(☎ +39 3456925843
⊛ www.feudomaccari.it

CELLAR SALES
PRE-BOOKED VISITS
ANNUAL PRODUCTION 300,000 bottles
HECTARES UNDER VINE 60.00
VITICULTURE METHOD Certified Organic
SUSTAINABLE WINERY

25 years have passed since Antonio Moretti
Cuseri, a multifaceted Tuscan entrepreneur and
owner of Tenuta Setteponti in Arezzo, bought
Feudo Maccari. This 265-hectare estate includes
olive groves, fruit trees, and 60 hectares of
vineyards, predominantly planted with nero
d'Avola and grillo in the bush-trained style.
Antonio was one of the first to believe that
grillo could produce a great Sicilian white
capable of aging well, and today, judging by the
results, he has succeeded magnificently. The
Saia '22 is the finest Nero d'Avola tasted this
year. Rich and varietal, it boasts aromas of
bramble fruits, carob, capers, bay leaf, and red
citrus. On the palate, it's refined, sunny, and
pervasive, with a persistent finish that enhances
its fruity sweetness. The Grillo Family and
Friends '23 is also excellent, fragrant with
notes of peach, grapefruit, and orange blossom.
Its vibrant citrus aromas are complemented
by a slightly brackish palate with a crisp,
refreshing progression.

Feudo Montoni

c.da Montoni Vecchi
92022 Cammarata [AG]
(☎ +39 091513106
⊛ www.feudomontoni.it

PRE-BOOKED VISITS
ANNUAL PRODUCTION 250,000 bottles
HECTARES UNDER VINE 44.00
VITICULTURE METHOD Certified Organic
SUSTAINABLE WINERY

This splendid haven of biodiversity, based on a
1469 estate owned for over a century by the
Sireci family, draws on native varietals and a
tailor-made production style. Fabio and Melissa
live year-round in the superb 15th-century
farmhouse, lovingly tending the extensive
property, which also hosts grains, olive trees, and
vegetables. An appealing sense of place combined
with the technical precision of each wine have
made this prestigious maison a "must" for
enthusiasts and connoisseurs. The 2020 version
of the Vrucara, a monovarietal Nero d'Avola, put
in a performance for the ages. It captivated us
with its nuances of caper, rose petals, sweet
spices, myrtle berries, and forest floor. On the
palate, it's fine and elegant, offering pronounced
mineral and balsamic notes with tannins that are
already vital, round, and pervasive. The rest of
the lineup is also strong, particularly the fresh
and traditionally-styled Inzolia Fornelli '23, and
the refined Catarratto Masso '23, which
showcases flavors of white plum and peach.

● Sicilia Nero d'Avola Saia '22	￥￥￥ 5
○ Family and Friends Grillo '23	￥￥ 5
○ Familiy and Friends Firraru '22	￥￥ 8
⊙ Rosé di Neré '23	￥￥ 3
○ Sicilia Grillo Olli '23	￥￥ 3
○ Familiy and Friends Firraru '21	￥￥￥ 8
○ Family and Friends Grillo '21	￥￥￥ 5
● Saia '14	￥￥￥ 4*
● Saia '13	￥￥￥ 4*
● Saia '12	￥￥￥ 4*
● Saia '11	￥￥￥ 4*
● Sicilia Nero d'Avola Saia '19	￥￥￥ 5
● Sicilia Nero d'Avola Saia '18	￥￥￥ 4*
● Sicilia Nero d'Avola Saia '17	￥￥￥ 4*
● Sicilia Nero d'Avola Saia '16	￥￥￥ 4*
● Sicilia Saia '15	￥￥￥ 4*

● Sicilia Nero d'Avola Vrucara '20	￥￥ 5
○ Passito Bianco	￥￥ 5
● Passito Rosso	￥￥ 5
○ Sicilia Catarratto V. del Masso '23	￥￥ 4
○ Sicilia Grillo V. della Timpa '23	￥￥ 3
○ Sicilia Inzolia dei Fornelli '23	￥￥ 3
● Sicilia Nero d'Avola V. Lagnusa '22	￥￥ 4
⊙ Sicilia Nerello Mascalese Rose di Adele '23	￥ 4
○ Sicilia Catarratto V. del Masso '22	￥￥ 4
○ Sicilia Grillo V. della Timpa '20	￥￥ 3*
○ Sicilia Inzolia dei Fornelli '22	￥￥ 3
○ Sicilia Inzolia dei Fornelli '21	￥￥ 3*
● Sicilia Nero d'Avola V. Lagnusa '21	￥￥ 4
● Sicilia Nero d'Avola Vrucara '19	￥￥ 5
● Sicilia Perricone V. del Core '21	￥￥ 4
● Sicilia Perricone V. del Core '18	￥￥ 4

★★Firriato

via Trapani, 4
91027 Paceco [TP]
☎ +39 0923882755
✉ www.firriato.it

CELLAR SALES
PRE-BOOKED VISITS
ACCOMMODATION AND RESTAURANT SERVICE
ANNUAL PRODUCTION 4,500,000 bottles
HECTARES UNDER VINE 490.00
VITICULTURE METHOD Certified Organic
SUSTAINABLE WINERY

Salvatore Di Gaetano and his wife Vinzia Novara elevated their beautiful family winery to international prominence with a high-quality range. Now, their young daughter Irene, who has significant academic credentials, leads this prestigious winery. She continues the family vision: elegant wines that reflect their territories—Trapani, the island of Favignana, and Etna—crafted with meticulous attention to sustainability and carbon neutrality. The estate's iconic wine, Ribeca '19, a Perricone with strong personality and sense of place, takes the top spot on the podium. Its intense, brilliant ruby color opens to refined nuances of pomegranate, black mulberry, plum, and violet, enriched by elegant notes of Mediterranean herbs and conifers. Sapid and incredibly long, it reveals silky tannins and fine minty tones. The Etna Bianco Cavanera Verzella '23 is also excellent, showcasing citrus and mineral notes with a captivating and satisfying drinkability.

Vini Franchetti Passopisciaro

loc. Passopisciaro
c.da Guardiola
95012 Castiglione di Sicilia [CT]
☎ +39 0942395449
✉ www.vinifranchetti.com

CELLAR SALES
ANNUAL PRODUCTION 75,000 bottles
HECTARES UNDER VINE 26.00

The journey that Andrea Franchetti began 25 years ago continues, with a focus on Etna's terroir and its diverse expressions, meticulously identified in distinctive crus known for their personality and elegance. Chiappemacine, Porcaria, Guardiola, Sciaranuova, and Rampante host old, bush-trained nerello mascalese vineyards at elevations ranging from 550 to 1,000-plus meters above seal level on the northeast slopes of the volcano. The Passorosso '22, an Etna of great character, proves vibrant and expressive on the nose, passing from aromas of currant to blueberry and Mediterranean scrub, alongside elegant mineral hints of hydrocarbons. On the palate, it's juicy, round, and persistent in its fruitiness. The Passobianco '22, a Chardonnay from Contrada Guardiola, also reached the finals. It's strongly marked by the terroir, with citrus and floral aromas, and a fresh, deep and long palate. Another standout cru is the Contrada C '21, with its fine notes of aromatic herbs.

● Sicilia Perricone Ribeca '19	♟♟♟ 5
○ Etna Bianco Cavanera Ripa di Scorciavacca Verzella '23	♟♟ 5
○ Etna Bianco Cavanera Contrada Zottorinotto '22	♟♟ 5
○ Etna Brut M. Cl. Gaudensius Blanc de Noir	♟♟ 5
○ Etna Brut M. Cl. Gaudensius Vintage '13	♟♟ 8
● Etna Rosso Cavanera Contrada Zucconero '20	♟♟ 6
○ Gaudensius Pas Dosé M. Cl.	♟♟ 6
● Sicilia Nero d'Avola Harmonium '19	♟♟ 6
● Sicilia Rosso Camelot '20	♟♟ 6
● Sicilia Rosso Quater Vitis '20	♟♟ 5
○ Etna Bianco Cavanera Ripa di Scorciavacca '22	♟♟♟ 6

● Etna Rosso Passorosso '22	♟♟ 5
○ Passobianco '22	♟♟ 5
● Contrada C '22	♟♟ 8
● Contrada G '22	♟♟ 8
● Contrada P '22	♟♟ 8
○ Contrada PC '22	♟♟ 8
● Contrada R '22	♟♟ 8
● Contrada S '22	♟♟ 8
● Franchetti '22	♟♟ 8
● Contrada C '17	♟♟♟ 6
● Contrada G '11	♟♟♟ 8
● Contrada P '10	♟♟♟ 7
● Contrada R '19	♟♟♟ 8
● Contrada S '20	♟♟♟ 8
● Contrada Sciaranuova '15	♟♟♟ 6
● Etna Rosso Passorosso '18	♟♟♟ 5

Generazione Alessandro

c.da Borriglione
95015 Linguaglossa [CT]
☎ +39 3773633065
✉ www.generazionealessandro.it

Tenuta Gorghi Tondi

c.da San Nicola
91026 Mazara del Vallo [TP]
☎ +39 0923719741
✉ www.gorghitondi.it

CELLAR SALES
PRE-BOOKED VISITS
ANNUAL PRODUCTION 35,000 bottles
HECTARES UNDER VINE 10.00

CELLAR SALES
PRE-BOOKED VISITS
ANNUAL PRODUCTION 800,000 bottles
HECTARES UNDER VINE 130.00
VITICULTURE METHOD Certified Organic
SUSTAINABLE WINERY

A desire to break out on their own led three cousins, the fourth generation of the Alessandro family (from the winery of the same name in Camporeale), to create this remarkable, strongly territorial venture. Of the three, all with specialized degrees and international experience, Anna, a jurist, handles administration and wine tourism, Benedetto, a famous winemaker, oversees production, and the other Benedetto, an industry expert, oversees marketing and promotion. The Etna Rosso Croceferro '22 handily took home Tre Bicchieri. Elegant right from its intense, brilliant ruby color, it offers up clear aromas of wild strawberry, blueberry, black plum, and nutmeg. On the palate, it's sumptuous, ranging from tones of graphite to peppermint, and mountain herbs, unfolding gracefully with soft, seductive tannins. The Etna Bianco Trainara '22, with its smoky notes and nuances of white fruit and wisteria, offers superb drinkability and a remarkably long, refined aromatic persistence.

Two sisters, Annamaria and Clara Sala, are the driving forces behind Gorghi Tondi, located in a unique spot near the sea and two lakes, a WWF natural reserve. The winery's history dates back to the late 1800s when their family acquired the estate. Their desire to develop and promote the territory comes in the wake of the work initiated by the late Michele Sala. Experimentation and the continuous search for new products is guided by the skilled hand of winemaker Tonino Guzzo. The Ziller 47, made from prized grillo grapes, earned top honors with its bright, intense amber color and complex, sophisticated aromas of oxidation, sumac, and dried flowers. On the palate, it's soft, rich, fresh, and elegant. The Grillo d'Oro Vendemmia Tardiva '18 is also well-made, with its golden tones, pervasive sweetness, and softness. The Catarratto Midor '23 is fragrant and forthright, marked by citrus and apple aromas, with a fresh, gratifying palate.

● Etna Rosso Croceferro '22	♟♟ 5
○ Etna Bianco Trainara '22	♟♟ 5
⊙ Etna Rosato Vignazza '22	♟♟ 6
● Etna Rosso V.V. Sciaramanico '21	♟♟ 5
○ Etna Bianco Trainara '18	♟♟♟ 4*
● Etna Rosso Croceferro '19	♟♟♟ 4*
○ Etna Bianco Trainara '21	♟♟ 5
○ Etna Bianco Trainara '20	♟♟ 5
○ Etna Bianco Trainara '19	♟♟ 4
⊙ Etna Rosato Vignazza '21	♟♟ 5
● Etna Rosso Croceferro '21	♟♟ 5
● Etna Rosso Croceferro '20	♟♟ 4
● Etna Rosso Croceferro '18	♟♟ 4
● Etna Rosso V. Vecchia '21	♟♟ 5

○ Ziller 47	♟♟♟ 8
○ Sicilia Catarratto Midor '23	♟♟ 4
○ Sicilia Grillo d'Oro V.T. '18	♟♟ 7
○ Sicilia Grillo Kheirè '23	♟♟ 5
⊙ Sicilia Brut Nature Rosé M. Cl '20	♟ 6
● Sicilia Frappato Dumè '23	♟ 4
○ Sicilia Grillo Kheirè '22	♟♟♟ 5
○ Sicilia Grillo Kheirè '21	♟♟♟ 4*
○ Sicilia Catarratto Midor '22	♟♟ 3
○ Sicilia Catarratto Midor '21	♟♟ 3
● Sicilia Frappato Dumè '22	♟♟ 3*
● Sicilia Frappato Dumè '21	♟♟ 3
○ Sicilia Grillo d'Oro Passito '17	♟♟ 7
○ Sicilia Grillo Kheirè '20	♟♟ 4
○ SIcilia Zibibbo Rajàh '22	♟♟ 5
○ Sicilia Zibibbo Rajàh '21	♟♟ 5

★Graci

loc. Passopisciaro
c.da Feudo di Mezzo
95012 Castiglione di Sicilia [CT]
☎ +39 3487016773
◉ www.graci.eu

CELLAR SALES
PRE-BOOKED VISITS
ANNUAL PRODUCTION 65,000 bottles
HECTARES UNDER VINE 18.00
VITICULTURE METHOD Certified Organic

Alberto Aiello Graci's range embodies elegance and finesse, capturing the volcanic terroir's essence through wines from different contradas, where local grape varieties respond uniquely to various exposures, soils, and vineyard ages. This meticulous pursuit of diversity is complemented by the use of concrete vats and large conical barrels. The producer's distinctive style has made it a benchmark for critics and wine lovers alike. The Etna Bianco Muganazzi '22, which mistakenly appeared in the 2024 version of the guide under the same vintage, earned Tre Bicchieri for its finesse and elegance. On the nose, it evokes broom, saturn peach, wisteria, jasmine, and medicinal herbs on a backdrop of graphite. The palate offers a linear acidity tempered by surprising texture and a drinkability that proves exceptionally gratifying. The Etna Bianco '23 exudes class, with its seductive smoky nuances from which delicate aromas of white peach and citron peel emerge.

Hibiscus

c.da Tramontana
90010 Ustica [PA]
☎ +39 0918449543
◉ www.agriturismohibiscus.com

CELLAR SALES
PRE-BOOKED VISITS
ACCOMMODATION
ANNUAL PRODUCTION 10,000 bottles
HECTARES UNDER VINE 4.00

Margherita Longo and Vito Barbera have brought specific expertise and youthful energy to their family's deep agricultural roots, quickly earning international acclaim for Ustica's only winery. The wines themselves, born from unique volcanic soils and constant marine breezes, are technically precise and remarkably flavorful, appreciated for their distinct personalities and seductive nuances of flavor. The Grotta dell'Oro '23, a monovarietal zibibbo, is a fine wine redolent of lavender, lemon blossom, willow flowers, and Mediterranean herbs. On the palate, it's elegant and seductive, developing with pleasant persistence and finishing beautifully on fresh almond notes. The rest of the lineup is also high quality, starting with the delicious L'Isola Rosato '23, which pours a brilliant peach blossom color, releasing fruity and mineral tones. The delicate zibibbo passito Zhabib '23 is equally notable.

○ Etna Bianco Muganazzi '22	♟♟♟ 6
○ Etna Bianco '23	♟♟ 5
○ Etna Bianco Arcuria '22	♟♟ 6
◉ Etna Rosato '23	♟♟ 3
● Etna Rosso '22	♟♟ 4
● Etna Rosso Arcurìa '22	♟♟ 6
● Etna Rosso Feudo di Mezzo '22	♟♟ 6
○ Etna Bianco Arcuria '21	♟♟♟ 6
○ Etna Bianco Arcuria '19	♟♟♟ 6
○ Etna Bianco Arcuria '18	♟♟♟ 6
○ Etna Bianco Arcuria '11	♟♟♟ 5
● Etna Rosso '16	♟♟♟ 3*
● Etna Rosso Arcurìa '20	♟♟♟ 6
● Etna Rosso Arcurìa '17	♟♟♟ 6
● Etna Rosso Arcurìa '13	♟♟♟ 6
● Etna Rosso Arcurìa '12	♟♟♟ 6

○ Grotta dell'Oro '23	♟♟ 5
○ L'Isola Bianco '23	♟♟ 4
◉ L'Isola Rosato '22	♟♟ 5
○ Onde di Sole '23	♟♟ 4
○ Zhabib Passito '23	♟♟ 6
○ Grotta dell'Oro '21	♟♟♟ 5
○ Zhabib Passito '20	♟♟♟ 6
○ Grotta dell'Oro '22	♟♟ 5
○ L'Isola Bianco '22	♟♟ 4
○ L'Isola Bianco '21	♟♟ 4
○ L'Isola Bianco '20	♟♟ 3
○ Onde di Sole '22	♟♟ 4
○ Onde di Sole '21	♟♟ 4
○ Onde di Sole '20	♟♟ 4
○ Onde di Sole '19	♟♟ 4
○ Zhabib Passito '22	♟♟ 6

Francesco Intorcia Heritage

via Mazara, 10
91025 Trapani
(☎) +39 0923999133
✆ https://www.heritagewines.it

CELLAR SALES
PRE-BOOKED VISITS
ACCOMMODATION
ANNUAL PRODUCTION 1,000,000 bottles
HECTARES UNDER VINE 10.00

Sometimes, crises become opportunities for those who persevere, like the challenges that have affected Marsala, one of Sicily's most famous wines. Francesco Intorcia is one such case. Having survived the tough times of the 1980s, he now has dozens of historic vintages of Marsala aging perfectly in wooden barrels. This led to the creation of the Heritage project, aimed at reintroducing these aged Marsala wines to enthusiasts, including a unique version that, after bottling, continues to mature underwater at a depth of 40 meters. From Vat No. 8, an extraordinary 2004 Marsala Vergine Secco emerged, captivating us with its brilliant amber color and broad, complex bouquet. On the nose it spans everything from candied citrus to spices and aged wood, then shifts to strawberry tree honey and vanilla, adorned by delicious notes of "rancio". The palate reveals aromatic herb sensations, citrus essential oils, and an endless finish on hazelnut, almond, and walnut husk. But the rest of the lineup is noteworthy as well.

○ Marsala Vergine Secco Tino n. 8 '04	♔♔♔	6
○ Marsala Vergine Secco Under Water Wine Ris. '80	♔♔	8
● Marsala Rubino Sup. Tino n. 6 Ris. '14	♔♔	6
○ Marsala Sup. Ambra Dolce Tino n. 9 '04	♔♔	8
○ Marsala Vergine Secco Tino 43 '15	♔♔	6
○ Pre British Metodo Perpetuo Tradizionale	♔♔	5
● Marsala Rubino Sup. Tino n. 31 Ris. '16	♔	6
○ Grillo Perpetuo '16	♔♔	7
○ Marsala Sup. Ambra Dolce Tino 2 Ris. '80	♔♔	8
○ Marsala Sup. Oro Tino 22 Five Y.O. Ris. '14	♔♔	5
○ Marsala Superiore Oro Tino 42 Ris. '15	♔♔	6
○ Sicilia Grillo Vignemie '22	♔♔	3

Lisciandrello

via Case Nuove, 31
90048 San Giuseppe Jato [PA]
(☎) +39 3395917618
✆ www.cantinalisciandrello.com

ANNUAL PRODUCTION 30,000 bottles
HECTARES UNDER VINE 6.00

Giuseppe Lisciandrello ventured into winemaking after 25 successful years running wine shops in Palermo. He partnered with Luciano Tocco, who has over 30 years of vineyard experience, and renowned oenologist Benedetto Alessandro. The winery, located in San Giuseppe Jato on clay and limestone soils at 550 meters, cultivates catarratto and perricone grapes, with additional plots in Segesta and on Mount Etna. All the wines boast vigorous personality, exceptional class, and longevity. Once again, the winery submitted a stellar lineup. The Iàto '22, a catarratto cultivated on high, stands out for its personality and style, earning it a place in the final round. Its nose reveals notes of peach, grapefruit, and citrus, while the palate showcases a clear acidic vein, with hints of almond and aromatic herbs, leading to a long, lingering finish. The Chardonnay Templum '22 is also notable, with its varietal aromas of hazelnut, butter, and lemon. On the palate, it's incredibly fresh and sapid, lively and pervasive.

○ Monreale Bianco Iàto '22	♔♔	3*
○ Sicilia Carricante Lapis '22	♔♔	4
○ Sicilia Chardonnay Templum '22	♔♔	4
● Sicilia Nerello Mascalese Terrae '21	♔♔	3
● Sicilia Rosso Iàto '21	♔♔	4
○ Etna Bianco Carricante '18	♔♔	4
○ Etna Bianco Lapis '18	♔♔	4
○ Monreale Bianco Iàto '21	♔♔	3*
○ Monreale Iàto '19	♔♔	4
○ Monreale Iàto '18	♔♔	4
● Nerello Mascalese '16	♔♔	3*
○ Sicilia Carricante Lapis '20	♔♔	4
○ Sicilia Carricante Lapis '20	♔♔	4
● Sicilia Nerello Mascalese Terrae '20	♔♔	3*
● Sicilia Rosso Radicato '19	♔♔	4

Maugeri

via Mazzini, 50
95010 Milo [CT]
(☎ +39 3289220154
☺ www.cantinamaugeri.it

ANNUAL PRODUCTION 15,000 bottles
HECTARES UNDER VINE 7.00
VITICULTURE METHOD Certified Organic

Renato Maugeri and his daughters run this winery in Contrada Volpare, in the municipality of Milo. Situated at 700 meters elevation on the eastern slope of the volcano, the vineyards overlook the Ionian Sea. Encircling the 19th-century "palmento" and bordered by characteristic dry stone lava walls, the five hectares of terraced vineyards are primarily planted with carricante, with some catarratto. The vineyard area will soon double, and the Maugeris have recently acquired 2 more hectares of old vines in nearby Contrada Rinazzo. Tre Bicchieri for the Contrada Volpare '23, which expresses the refined complexity of the carricante grape. It's harmonious and vibrant on the palate, supported by a perfect balance between acidity and sapidity. We also appreciated the cru Contrada Praino Frontemare '23, which offers exotic fruit tones refreshed by Mediterranean herb notes, followed by a superb mineral nuance; the palate is crystalline, with a still sharp acidity. The Contrada Volpare Frontebosco '23 shows notable depth, with clear citrus notes still shining through.

Wine	Rating
○ Etna Bianco Sup. Contrada Volpare '23	♛♛♛ 6
○ Etna Bianco Sup. Contrada Praino Frontemare '23	♛♛ 8
○ Catarratto '23	♛♛ 5
○ Etna Bianco Sup. Contrada Volpare Frontebosco '23	♛♛ 8
⊚ Etna Rosato Contrada Volpare '23	♛♛ 4
○ Etna Bianco Sup. Contrada Volpare Frontebosco '22	♛♛♛ 8
○ Etna Bianco Sup. Contrada Volpare Frontebosco '21	♛♛♛ 8
○ Catarratto '22	♛♛ 5
○ Etna Bianco Sup. Contrada Praino Frontemare '22	♛♛ 8
○ Etna Bianco Sup. Contrada Volpare '22	♛♛ 4
⊚ Etna Rosato Contrada Volpare '22	♛♛ 4

Monteleone

c.da Cuba
95012 Castiglione di Sicilia [CT]
(☎ +39 334 5772422
☺ www.monteleonetna.com

ANNUAL PRODUCTION 15,000 bottles
HECTARES UNDER VINE 5.00

In just five years, Giulia Monteleone's winery has established itself as a prominent representative of Etna DOC, a crowded and competitive appellation. Her success is primarily due to meticulous vineyard management, personally overseen by Giulia and her husband, Benedetto Alessandro, one of Sicily's most talented oenologists. Together, they manage all stages of production, both in the vineyard and the winery. The entire range is flawless—theirs are elegant, terroir-driven Etna wines, foremost the Etna Rosso Qubba '22. It features elegant floral tones and black fruits, with balsamic and tobacco hints. On the palate, it's supremely elegant—voluptuous yet racy. The Anthemis '22, a white, is already delightful now, but promises even more for the future, with a broad bouquet of lavender, anise, yellow fruit, citrus, and smoked salt. It's slender and incredibly fresh on the palate, unfolding with sapidity and juiciness.

Wine	Rating
● Etna Rosso Qubba '22	♛♛♛ 7
● Etna Bianco Anthemis '22	♛♛ 8
● Etna Bianco '23	♛♛ 5
● Etna Rosso '22	♛♛ 5
● Etna Rosso Rumex '22	♛♛ 8
● Etna Bianco '22	♛♛♛ 5
● Etna Bianco Anthemis '19	♛♛♛ 7
● Etna Rosso Qubba '18	♛♛♛ 7
● Etna Rosso Rumex '20	♛♛♛ 8
● Etna Bianco '19	♛♛ 5
● Etna Bianco Anthemis '21	♛♛ 8
● Etna Rosso Cuba '17	♛♛ 6
● Etna Rosso Qubba '21	♛♛ 7
● Etna Rosso Qubba '20	♛♛ 8
● Etna Rosso Qubba '19	♛♛ 7
● Etna Rosso Rumex '21	♛♛ 8

Cantine Nicosia

via Luigi Capuana, 65
95039 Trecastagni [CT]
(+39 0957806767
www.cantinenicosia.it

CELLAR SALES
PRE-BOOKED VISITS
RESTAURANT SERVICE
ANNUAL PRODUCTION 1,800,000 bottles
HECTARES UNDER VINE 240.00
VITICULTURE METHOD Certified Organic
SUSTAINABLE WINERY

Today led by forward-thinking Carmelo Nicosia and his sons Francesco and Graziano, this distinguished winery has been in the same family's hands since 1898. Their wines, known for their distinctive personalities and strong identity, have driven significant acquisitions on the volcano and in esteemed areas like Noto and Vittoria, all with a focus on sustainability. The contributions of Maria Carella, a sensitive and skilled winemaker, are noteworthy. The Lenza di Munti 720 slm '21 earned our highest accolades. It's an exemplary wine that perfectly reflects the Etna typology and terroir—refined and deep, with beautiful fruit notes of mulberry, blackberry, and blackcurrant, laced with nuances of slate, violet, and black spices. Authoritative on the palate, it showcases a close-knit texture, underscored by soft yet vibrant tannins. The Etna Bianco Contrada Monte San Nicolò '23 is on par, subtle and charming, with flavors of citrus, star anise, peach, and aromatic herbs.

Arianna Occhipinti

fraz. Pedalino
s.da prov.le 68 Vittoria-Pedalino km 3,3
97019 Vittoria [RG]
(+39 09321865519
www.agricolaocchipinti.it

CELLAR SALES
PRE-BOOKED VISITS
ANNUAL PRODUCTION 130,000 bottles
HECTARES UNDER VINE 22.00
VITICULTURE METHOD Certified Organic
SUSTAINABLE WINERY

The vineyards are located along the road connecting the ancient city-states of Gela and Kamarina, in the heart of Cerasuolo di Vittoria. 30 hectares spread out across Fossa di Lupo (also home to the cellar), Bombolieri, Bastonaca, Pettineo, Santa Teresa, Serra d'Elia, and Santa Margherita. Arianna's wines are always personal and moving, offering a pure expression of the vineyard in any given year, without oenological compromises or artifice. The Grotte Alte '19 and the Frappato '22 both earned a place in our finals. The former showcases great character, with an elegant and intense nose of spices, caper, myrtle, and a palate of impressive texture and persistence. The latter is earthy and rich, with vibrant fruit and a clean, long finish. The SP 68 Rosso '23, a blend of nero d'avola and frappato, proves quite pleasant, clearly defined in its profile and plump, with fragrant, fleshy cherry fruit. The fresh and sapid Grillo SM Vino di Contrada '22 is also delicious, revealing a lovely bay leaf note on the nose.

• Etna Rosso Lenza di Munti 720 slm '21	🍷🍷🍷 3*
○ Etna Bianco Contrada Monte San Nicolò '23	🍷🍷 4
• Cerasuolo di Vittoria Hybla '22	🍷🍷 3
○ Etna Carricante Brut M. Cl. Sosta Tre Santi '20	🍷🍷 4
• Etna Rosso Contrada Monte Gorna '21	🍷🍷 6
• Etna Rosso Contrada Monte San Nicolò '20	🍷🍷 4
• Etna Rosso Vulkà '22	🍷🍷 3
• Sicilia Frappato Fondo Filara '23	🍷🍷 3
○ Etna Bianco Fondo Filara Contrada Monte Gorna '16	🍷🍷🍷 4*
○ Etna Bianco Lenza di Munti 720 slm '22	🍷🍷🍷 3*
• Etna Rosso Lenza di Munti 720 slm '18	🍷🍷🍷 3*
• Etna Rosso Lenza di Munti 720 slm '17	🍷🍷🍷 3*
• Etna Rosso Vign. Monte Gorna Ris. '13	🍷🍷🍷 6
• Etna Rosso Vign. Monte Gorna Ris. '12	🍷🍷🍷 6
• Etna Rosso Vulkà '20	🍷🍷🍷 3*

• Cerasuolo di Vittoria Cl. Grotte Alte '19	🍷🍷 8
• Il Frappato '22	🍷🍷 6
○ SM Vino di Contrada '22	🍷🍷 7
• SP 68 Rosso '23	🍷🍷 4
• SP 68 Rosso '15	🍷🍷🍷 3*
• Cerasuolo di Vittoria Cl. Grotte Alte '16	🍷🍷 7
• Cerasuolo di Vittoria Cl. Grotte Alte '13	🍷🍷 7
• Cerasuolo di Vittoria Cl. Grotte Alte '10	🍷🍷 7
• Il Frappato '20	🍷🍷 5
• Il Frappato '18	🍷🍷 5
○ SM Vino di Contrada '21	🍷🍷 7
• SP 68 '09	🍷🍷 3*

Tenute Orestiadi

v.le Santa Ninfa
91024 Gibellina [TP]
(») +39 092469124
⊕ www.tenuteorestiadi.it

CELLAR SALES
PRE-BOOKED VISITS
ANNUAL PRODUCTION 1,400,000 bottles
HECTARES UNDER VINE 140.00
VITICULTURE METHOD Certified Organic
SUSTAINABLE WINERY

Tenute Orestiadi is an ambitious project in which territory and wine are intimately bound. Based in Gibellina, the winery merges the well-known Orestiadi Foundation, established in 2008, with a group of growers from the Belice Valley. Indeed, this isn't just a winemaking project—it's a true gift to the region, with wines that have become emblematic of the area, showcasing the terroir and its cultural and artistic aspects. The winery also has a small presence on Etna, La Gelsomina, located in Piedimonte Etneo. The Sicilia Orange Insolia Bio '22 intrigues right from its bright, pale golden color and scents of yellow flowers, dried apricot, and sorb apple. In the mouth it's crisp, showcasing liveliness and pleasantness. The Moscato Passito La Gelsomina '18 is also good, with a lightly orange-tinted golden hue anticipating aromas of candied orange, figs, dates, and honey of the loquat; on the palate it stands out for its balance. The Petramater Metodo Classico '22 plays on clearly defined nuances of pineapple, citron zest, and vanilla.

★★Palari

loc. Santo Stefano Briga
c.da Barna
98137 Messina
(») +39 090630194
⊕ www.palari.it

ANNUAL PRODUCTION 50,000 bottles
HECTARES UNDER VINE 7.00

A sophisticated world traveler and renowned architect, Salvatore Geraci has linked his name to one of Sicily's most famous wines, an icon of high oenology. For many years, with his brother Giampiero managing the practical aspects of the winery (housed in their 18th-century family villa), he led a "solo operation", while also encouraging other producers in the Faro appellation to step up. The successful establishment of the Faro brand rightfully fills him with pride. The Palari '19 returns to the podium with its vibrant nuances of bramble blackberry, blackcurrant, and cherry preserved in alcohol, all intertwined with hints of mint, spices, myrtle berries, and conifer tones. On the palate, it's vibrant, elegant, very complex, and balanced, with silky tannins. The Rosso del Soprano '20 is equally captivating, a delightful wine with elegant Mediterranean scents of caper, scrubland, and rose petals, sensations mirrored on the palate.

○ Etna Bianco La Gelsomina '22	♼♼ 3
○ Moscato Passito La Gelsomina '18	♼♼ 5
○ Pacènzia Zibibbo V.T.	♼♼ 4
○ Petramater Metodo Classico '22	♼♼ 4
○ Sicilia Orange Insolia Bio '22	♼♼ 4
● Sicilia Perricone Adeni '22	♼♼ 3
● Sicilia Rosso di Ludovico Ris. '19	♼♼ 4
○ Etna M. Cl. Blanc de Noir Brut La Gelsomina	♼ 5
⊙ Etna M. Cl. Brut Rosè	♼ 5
● Etna Rosso La Gelsomina '21	♼ 4
○ Etna Bianco La Gelsomina '20	♼♼ 3
● Etna Rosso La Gelsomina '18	♼♼ 4
○ La Gelsomina Moscato Passito '17	♼♼ 5
○ Sicilia Il Bianco di Ludovico Ris. '18	♼♼ 4
● Sicilia Rosso di Ludovico Ris. '18	♼♼ 4

● Faro Palari '19	♼♼♼ 6
● Rosso del Soprano '20	♼♼ 5
● Faro Palari '14	♼♼♼ 6
● Faro Palari '12	♼♼♼ 6
● Faro Palari '11	♼♼♼ 6
● Faro Palari '09	♼♼♼ 6
● Faro Palari '08	♼♼♼ 6
● Faro Palari '07	♼♼♼ 6
● Faro Palari '06	♼♼♼ 6
● Faro Palari '05	♼♼♼ 6*
● Faro Palari '04	♼♼♼ 7
● Faro Palari '03	♼♼♼ 6
● Rosso del Soprano '15	♼♼♼ 4*
● Rosso del Soprano '11	♼♼♼ 4*
● Rosso del Soprano '10	♼♼♼ 4*
● Rosso del Soprano '07	♼♼♼ 4

Palmento Costanzo

loc. Passopisciaro
c.da Santo Spirito
95012 Castiglione di Sicilia [CT]
📞 +39 0942983239
🖥 www.palmentocostanzo.com

CELLAR SALES
PRE-BOOKED VISITS
RESTAURANT SERVICE
ANNUAL PRODUCTION 90,000 bottles
HECTARES UNDER VINE 18.00
VITICULTURE METHOD Certified Organic
SUSTAINABLE WINERY

Fifteen years ago, Mimmo and Valeria Costanzo restored an ancient "palmento" (traditional Sicilian wine press) in Santo Spirito. Their exemplary renovations preserved the original operational logic, including the use of gravity to move liquids without mechanical intervention. The organically grown grapes come from prestigious crus, distinguished by lineage and age, located in Santo Spirito, Feudi di Mezzo, Zottorinoto, and Bragaseggi on the northern slopes of Etna, and Cavaliere on the southwest slopes of the volcano. The Etna Rosso Mofete '21 performed impressively, earning Tre Bicchieri with its vibrant, defined nose of peach, red rose, and violet, alongside a highly elegant mineral character and plump, juicy fruit. A well-structured and persistent pour. The Nero di Sei '21 is also very enjoyable, with its mature jammy tones, round tannins, and a juicy palate. Maturity of fruit is also evident in the Rosato Mofete '23, which opens on distinct notes of mountain herbs and a nice smoky tone before revealing its sapid, fresh pulp.

● Etna Rosso Mofete '21	🍷🍷🍷 4*
☉ Etna Rosato Mofete '23	🍷🍷 4
● Etna Rosso Nero di Sei '21	🍷🍷 5
○ Etna Bianco Mofete '23	🍷 4
○ Etna Spumante Brut	🍷 5
○ Etna Bianco di Sei '17	🍷🍷🍷 5
☉ Etna Rosato Mofete '18	🍷🍷🍷 3*
● Etna Rosso Contrada Santo Spirito Part. 468 '16	🍷🍷🍷 6
○ Etna Bianco Contrada Santo Spirito '20	🍷🍷 5
● Etna Rosso Contrada Santo Spirito '19	🍷🍷 6
● Etna Rosso Mofete '20	🍷🍷 4
● Etna Rosso Mofete '18	🍷🍷 4
● Etna Rosso Nero di Sei '19	🍷🍷 5
● Etna Rosso Nero di Sei '16	🍷🍷 5
● Etna Rosso Prefillossera '17	🍷🍷 8

Pellegrino

via Battaglia delle Egadi, 10
91025 Marsala [TP]
📞 +39 0923719911
🖥 www.carlopellegrino.it

CELLAR SALES
PRE-BOOKED VISITS
RESTAURANT SERVICE
ANNUAL PRODUCTION 5,000,000 bottles
HECTARES UNDER VINE 150.00
VITICULTURE METHOD Certified Organic
SUSTAINABLE WINERY

Pellegrino, a historic brand rooted in 1880 and now in its seventh generation, stands out among Marsala wineries. Indeed, while Marsala is a focal point, the winery has diversified over the years, significantly expanding its brand. Recently, the estate underwent a comprehensive restyling of both packaging and production, and new spaces have been created within the beautiful winery. The Pantelleria Bianco Isesi '22 (from moscato d'Alessandria) landed a place in our final round. It pours a pale straw color with greenish reflections and a marked aromatic note where fine nuances of rose, lavender, and citrus emerge. These flavors return pleasantly on the palate, which proves fresh and delightfully sapid, with a long finish. We were also impressed with the Grillo Il Salinaro '23, a wine that's focused in its aromas of asparagus, helichrysum, pear, and fresh almond, and equally vibrant on the palate, where it develops pleasing and exuberant.

○ Pantelleria Bianco Isesi '22	🍷🍷 4
○ Sicilia Grillo Il Salinaro '23	🍷🍷 3
● Sicilia Perricone Capoarso '22	🍷 4
○ Marsala Sup. Ambra Semisecco Ris. '85	🍷🍷🍷 4*
○ Marsala Vergine Ris. '81	🍷🍷🍷 6
○ Passito di Pantelleria Nes '09	🍷🍷🍷 5
● Tripudium Rosso Duca di Castelmonte '13	🍷🍷🍷 5
● Tripudium Rosso Duca di Castelmonte '09	🍷🍷🍷 4*
● Marsala Sup. Rubino Dolce	🍷🍷 3*
○ Marsala Vergine Single Barrel n. 167 Ris. '01	🍷🍷 8
○ Passito di Pantelleria Nes '21	🍷🍷 6
○ Passito di Pantelleria Nes '17	🍷🍷 7

SICILY

★Pietradolce

fraz. Solicchiata
c.da Rampante
95012 Castiglione di Sicilia [CT]
(》 +39 3484037792
◈ www.pietradolce.it

ANNUAL PRODUCTION 50,000 bottles
HECTARES UNDER VINE 38.00

SICILY

In 2008, the Faro brothers made a striking debut in our guide, winning its first Tre Bicchieri with its inaugural wine, the 2007 Etna Rosso Archineri. Since then, much has changed. Riding a wave of critical and commercial success, the Faro brothers invested heavily, building a state-of-the-art winery seamlessly integrated into the landscape, while also quadrupling their vineyard, which now spans nearly 40 hectares across 7 different districts. The range submitted by this Solicchiata producer remains commendable as always, starting with one of the best versions of the Etna Rosso Vigna Barbagalli '21, a wine of rare elegance and complexity, that we've yet tasted. It reveals clear tones of bramble fruit, graphite, underbrush, and scrub, while offering a close-knit, vibrant palate with refined tannins. The exemplary Etna Rosso '23 stands out for its rich and multifaceted nose, and a dynamic, juicy drinkability.

★★★Planeta

c.da Dispensa
92013 Menfi [AG]
(》 +39 091327965
◈ www.planeta.it

PRE-BOOKED VISITS
ACCOMMODATION AND RESTAURANT SERVICE
ANNUAL PRODUCTION 2,500,000 bottles
HECTARES UNDER VINE 371.00
VITICULTURE METHOD Certified Organic
SUSTAINABLE WINERY

"Viaggio in Sicilia," which began 40 years ago with the planting of the first vines at Ulmo, continued in Menfi, Noto, Vittoria, on Etna, and at Capo Milazzo. It's a journey that's been marked by successes and international recognition for Alessio, Francesca, and Santi Planeta's winery. The most recent accolade is the "Wine Family of the Year" award from the Meininger Awards in Wine and Spirits. This family, proud of their heritage, views entrepreneurship as a driving force for progress and shared values. 2022 made for an outstanding Chardonnay. It's marked by finesse and harmony on the nose, where oak is beautifully integrated into a floral and elegant, fruit-driven bouquet. On the palate, this richness is mirrored with soft, fleshy fruit. The Noto Moscato Allemanda '23 also impressed our tasters, charming with its weave of yellow flowers, aromatic herbs, and spices. Finally, the Cerasuolo di Vittoria '22 proves delightful, playing on whiffs of violet, rose, and geranium before fading into notes of watermelon and cherry for a clean, linear, and highly drinkable palate.

● Etna Rosso V. Barbagalli '21	♟♟♟ 8
● Etna Rosso '23	♟♟ 5
● Etna Rosso Contrada Rampante '22	♟♟ 6
○ Etna Bianco Archineri '23	♟♟ 6
○ Etna Bianco Pietradolce '23	♟♟ 5
⊙ Etna Rosato Pietradolce '23	♟♟ 3
● Etna Rosso Archineri '22	♟♟ 6
● Etna Rosso Contrada Santo Spirito '22	♟♟ 6
● Etna Rosso Feudo di Mezzo '22	♟♟ 6
○ Vigna Sant'Andrea Carricante '21	♟♟ 8
● Etna Rosso Archineri '20	♟♟♟ 6
● Etna Rosso Barbagalli '18	♟♟♟ 8
● Etna Rosso Barbagalli '17	♟♟♟ 8
● Etna Rosso V. Barbagalli '20	♟♟♟ 8
● Etna Rosso V. Barbagalli '16	♟♟♟ 8

● Cerasuolo di Vittoria '22	♟♟♟ 3*
○ Etna Bianco Contrada Taccione '22	♟♟ 5
○ Noto Moscato Allemanda '23	♟♟ 3*
○ Sicilia Menfi Chardonnay '22	♟♟ 5
○ Passito di Noto '22	♟♟ 5
○ Sicilia Eruzione 1614 Carricante '20	♟♟ 5
○ Sicilia Menfi Didacus Chardonnay '22	♟♟ 8
○ Sicilia Menfi Fiano Cometa '23	♟♟ 5
● Sicilia Menfi Merlot Sito dell'Ulmo '19	♟♟ 5
● Sicilia Menfi Rosso Burdese '19	♟♟ 5
● Sicilia Menfi Rosso Didacus '20	♟♟ 8
● Sicilia Menfi Syrah Maroccoli '20	♟♟ 5
○ Sicilia Menfi Terebinto '23	♟♟ 3
● Sicilia Nerello Mascalese Eruzione 1614 '21	♟♟ 5
● Vittoria Frappato '23	♟♟ 3

Poggio di Bortolone

fraz. Roccazzo
via Bortolone, 19
97010 Chiaramonte Gulfi [RG]
(☎) +39 0932921161
☞ www.poggiodibortolone.it

CELLAR SALES
PRE-BOOKED VISITS
RESTAURANT SERVICE
ANNUAL PRODUCTION 70,000 bottles
HECTARES UNDER VINE 15.00
SUSTAINABLE WINERY

Pigi Cosenza has inherited a family tradition in viticulture dating back to the late 18th century. His 15 hectares of vineyards are located in the best growing areas of his 60-hectare estate, near the Mazzarronello and Para Para rivers. On the stony bed of the latter lies a Cerasuolo di Vittoria Classico cru (named Para Para) that's among the most expressive and elegant of the appellation. The focus is mainly on red grapes and wines, with a new addition: a blend of chenin blanc and vermentino. The Pigi '22, a blend of syrah and cabernet sauvignon, landed a place in our finals with its lovely nose of red fruit jam, fine spicy notes, and clay-like mineral hints. On the palate, it shows character and fullness. The Vittoria Frappato '23 proves highly enjoyable, with well-expressed vegetal and fruity aromas, while the Cerasuolo Poggio di Bortolone '22 delivers balsamic notes and fine, ripe cherry fruit. The Addamanera '23, also a syrah and cabernet sauvignon blend, pleases with its green pepper notes and a vibrant, fleshy fruit core.

Possente

c.da Bifarelle - Pergola
91020 Salaparuta [TP]
(☎) +39 0924502706
☞ www.possente.it

ANNUAL PRODUCTION 80,000 bottles
HECTARES UNDER VINE 37.00
VITICULTURE METHOD Certified Organic
SUSTAINABLE WINERY

Founded in 1982, this winery is now managed by three siblings: Antonio, who also serves as the winemaker, Maria, and Stefania. The estate includes land and a cellar in the Salaparuta area, situated at elevations spanning 250-400 meters in a hilly, breezy region. New plantings of catarratto are located in Alcamo. Their work follows a simple principle: care for the land, respect it, and listen to it in order to create wines that authentically reflect the beauty of the terroir. Once again the Acini di Grillo '23 put in a brilliant performance. This lightly macerated white unveils pervasive notes of peach, citrus, aromatic herbs, and Mediterranean scrub. On the palate, its freshness and personality are accompanied by a subtle and refined tannic note, making for a very dynamic taste. The elegant Abir '23 (zibibbo) is equally charming. Exuberant and persistent, it plays on nuances of exotic fruit, white melon, rosemary, and thyme.

SICILY

● Sicilia Rosso Pigi '22	♟♟ 5
● Addamanera '23	♟♟ 3
● Cerasuolo di Vittoria Cl. Poggio di Bortolone '22	♟♟ 3
● Cerasuolo di Vittoria Cl. V. Para Para '21	♟♟ 5
● Vittoria Frappato '23	♟♟ 3
● Cerasuolo di Vittoria Cl. Contessa Costanza '22	♟ 3
○ Chenin Blanc - Vermentino '23	♟ 3
● Cerasuolo di Vittoria Il Para Para '17	♟♟♟ 5
● Cerasuolo di Vittoria V. Para Para '05	♟♟♟ 4
● Sicilia Rosso Pigi '17	♟♟ 5

○ Sicilia Acini di Grillo '23	♟♟ 4
○ Abir '23	♟♟ 3
○ Kima Catarratto '22	♟♟ 3
○ Sicilia Grillo '23	♟♟ 3
● Sicilia Nero d'Avola '22	♟♟ 3
○ Abir '22	♟♟ 3*
○ Cinque Inverni Catarratto '15	♟♟ 5
○ Kima Catarratto '21	♟♟ 3
○ Sicilia Acini di Grillo '22	♟♟ 4
○ Sicilia Acini di Grillo '21	♟♟ 4
○ Sicilia Grillo '22	♟♟ 3

Principi di Butera

c.da Deliella
93011 Butera [CL]
☎ +39 0934347726
⊕ www.principidibutera.it

CELLAR SALES
PRE-BOOKED VISITS
ANNUAL PRODUCTION 800,000 bottles
HECTARES UNDER VINE 100.00
SUSTAINABLE WINERY

One of Sicily's most renowned wineries, Principi di Butera was founded by the Zonin family over two decades ago, and has since come to epitomize an innovative and intrepid renaissance for the island. Located in Caltanissetta province, the estate benefits from sunny weather and sea breezes, as well as white limestone soils at elevations spanning 250-350 meters. The meticulously cultivated grapes include nero d'Avola and international varieties for reds, and chardonnay, grillo, and insolia for whites. The lineup submitted remains consistently pleasant, with the Nero d'Avola Amìra '22 standing out for its complexity. Intense aromas of cherry meet blueberry, violet, and myrtle, all followed by delicate spices and pleasant balsamic notes; in the mouth it's dry, fine and well-structured with nice persistence. The Metodo Classico Pas Dosè '19, made from nero d'Avola vinified off-the-skins, is an intriguing wine—taut and linear in its profile, supported by pronounced minerality.

● Sicilia Nero d'Avola Amira '22	♟♟ 4
○ Sicilia Metodo Classico Pas Dosè '19	♟♟ 7
○ Sicilia Diamanti Grillo '23	♟ 3
○ Sicilia Inzolia Carizza '23	♟ 3
● Deliella '12	♟♟♟ 6
● Deliella '05	♟♟♟ 6
● Deliella '02	♟♟♟ 7
● Deliella '00	♟♟♟ 6
● Sicilia Deliella '13	♟♟♟ 6
● Sicilia Nero d'Avola Deliella '16	♟♟♟ 6
● Sicilia Syrah '15	♟♟♟ 3*
● Symposio '15	♟♟ 5
● Symposio '14	♟♟ 5
● Symposio '13	♟♟ 5
● Symposio '12	♟♟ 5

Rallo

via Vincenzo Florio, 2
91025 Marsala [TP]
☎ +39 0923721633
⊕ www.aziendaagricolarallo.it

ANNUAL PRODUCTION 500,000 bottles
HECTARES UNDER VINE 79.00
VITICULTURE METHOD Certified Organic

The Vesco family acquired this historic estate in the late 1990s. Their vineyards span three areas: Pattipiccolo, 68 hectares between Monreale and Alcamo; Piane Liquide, a 10-hectare plot of grillo set in the Stagnone Natural Reserve; and two hectares of zibibbo in Bugeber, on the island of Pantelleria. In 2007, Andrea Vesco began converting the vineyards to organic farming and, through a series of initiatives, has helped revitalize Marsala over the years. The Zibibbo Al Qasar '23 reached our finals with its pale straw color tinged with gold, offering alluring scents of chamomile, lavender, and orange blossom. On the palate, it explodes with intense citrus, particularly grapefruit. You'll find the AV01 Catarratto Orange '22 in our "rare wines" section: it pours a golden hue with notes of chamomile, honey, and apricot rising from the glass. On the palate, it delivers freshness and sapidity, with a pleasant and persistent encore of fruit. The Inzolia Evrò '23 is notable for its fine minerality.

○ Sicilia Zibibbo Al Qasar '23	♟♟ 3*
○ Sicilia Grillo Bianco Maggiore '23	♟♟ 3
○ Sicilia Grillo La Cuba '21	♟♟ 5
○ Sicilia Inzolia Evrò '23	♟♟ 3
● Sicilia Syrah La Clarissa '23	♟♟ 3
⊙ Sicilia Alba Rosea '23	♟ 3
● Sicilia Perricone '22	♟ 3
○ Alcamo Beleda '17	♟♟♟ 4*
○ Alcamo Beleda '15	♟♟♟ 4*
○ Alcamo Beleda '13	♟♟♟ 2*
○ AV 01 Catarratto Orange '21	♟♟♟ 5
○ Sicilia Bianco Maggiore '18	♟♟♟ 3*
○ Sicilia Bianco Maggiore '16	♟♟♟ 3*
○ Sicilia Bianco Maggiore '14	♟♟♟ 3*
○ Sicilia Zibibbo Al Qasar '19	♟♟♟ 3*

Tenute Rapitalà

c.da Rapitalà
90043 Camporeale [PA]
📞 +39 092437233
🌐 www.rapitala.it

CELLAR SALES
PRE-BOOKED VISITS
ANNUAL PRODUCTION 600,000 bottles
HECTARES UNDER VINE 176.00

The meeting of Count Hugues Bernard de la Gatinais and Gigi Guarrasi was not just a love story between a man and a woman, France and Sicily, but also the creation of one of the most renowned wineries in the regional and national wine scene. Based in Camporeale and Alcamo, the estate has been cherished and maintained by the couple since 1968. Today it's being managed exceptionally well by their son Laurent. The Chardonnay Conte Hugues Bernard de La Gatinais '22 made it to our finals. It pours a bright straw color, the prelude to a complex nose where aromatic herbs mix with hints of oregano, basil, and vanilla, all followed by citrus notes that return on the palate—here oak is well integrated, with a fresh, pervasive, and persistent finish. The Nero d'Avola Alto Reale '23, with its deep ruby color and violet reflections, also stood out, featuring aromas of ripe fruit with a touch of balsamic notes. It's a lively, long quaff.

○ Sicilia Chardonnay Conte Hugues Bernard de La Gatinais '22	🍷🍷 5
○ Alcamo Cl.V. Casalj '23	🍷🍷 3
● Sicilia Nero d'Avola Alto Reale '23	🍷🍷 3
○ Sicilia Grillo Vivirì '23	🍷 3
● Sicilia Syrah Nadir '22	🍷 3
○ Conte Hugues Bernard de la Gatinais Grand Cru '10	🍷🍷🍷 4*
● Hugonis '01	🍷🍷🍷 6
● Solinero '03	🍷🍷🍷 5
● Solinero '00	🍷🍷🍷 5
○ Conte Hugues Bernard De La Gatinais Grand Cru '18	🍷🍷 5
○ Sicilia Chardonnay Conte Hugues '21	🍷🍷 5
● Sicilia Hugonis '19	🍷🍷 5
● Sicilia Hugonis '18	🍷🍷 5

★Girolamo Russo

loc. Passopisciaro
via Regina Margherita, 78
95012 Castiglione di Sicilia [CT]
📞 +39 3283840247
🌐 www.girolamorusso.it

CELLAR SALES
PRE-BOOKED VISITS
ANNUAL PRODUCTION 65,000 bottles
HECTARES UNDER VINE 15.00
VITICULTURE METHOD Certified Organic

Giuseppe Russo is undoubtedly one of the finest interpreters of Etna. His wines consistently reflect the vintage, varietal and terroir, free of trends and technical gimmicks. Tasting wines from neighboring contradas like Calderara Sottana and Feudo reveals Giuseppe's skill in drawing out the soul of two terroirs, where not only soils and exposures differ, but also biotypes of nerello mascalese, a topic that, like soils, would require further exploration. The Etna Rosso Feudo di Mezzo '21 impresses, conjuring up a complex and elegant nose of volcanic notes, rain-soaked earth, underbrush, red flowers, herbs, and juniper. The palate holds together well, with flavors of red fruits and citrus supported by authoritative yet refined tannins. The Etna Rosso 'A Rina '22 is also impressive, emanating lovely smoky nuances followed by peach, dog rose, and Mediterranean scrub, then delivering a spirited, taut palate with clear and juicy fruit.

● Etna Rosso 'A Rina '22	🍷🍷 5
● Etna Rosso Feudo di Mezzo '21	🍷🍷 8
● Etna Rosso San Lorenzo '22	🍷🍷 6
○ Etna Bianco Nerina '23	🍷🍷 6
○ Etna Bianco San Lorenzo '23	🍷🍷 7
● Etna Rosso Feudo '23	🍷🍷 6
● Etna Rosso Feudo '22	🍷🍷 6
○ Etna Bianco Nerina '20	🍷🍷🍷 6
● Etna Rosso 'A Rina '15	🍷🍷🍷 4*
● Etna Rosso Feudo di Mezzo '16	🍷🍷🍷 6
● Etna Rosso San Lorenzo '18	🍷🍷🍷 6
● Etna Rosso San Lorenzo '14	🍷🍷🍷 6
● Etna Rosso San Lorenzo '13	🍷🍷🍷 5
● Etna Rosso San Lorenzo Piano delle Colombe '20	🍷🍷🍷 8

★Cantine Settesoli

s.da st.le 115
92013 Menfi [AG]
☎ +39 092577111
⊛ www.cantinesettesoli.it

Spadafora

c.da Virzì
90144 Monreale [PA]
☎ +39 091514952
⊛ www.spadafora.com

CELLAR SALES
PRE-BOOKED VISITS
ANNUAL PRODUCTION 20,000,000 bottles
HECTARES UNDER VINE 6000.00

CELLAR SALES
PRE-BOOKED VISITS
RESTAURANT SERVICE
ANNUAL PRODUCTION 200,000 bottles
HECTARES UNDER VINE 100.00
VITICULTURE METHOD Certified Organic
SUSTAINABLE WINERY

The winery spans over 6,000 hectares of vineyards, 1,000 of which are organically farmed, scattered throughout Sicily. The system is a cooperative of 2,000 members—small family farms that cultivate an average of 3-4 hectares each. The heart of the operation is in Terre Sicane and the Menfi area. The winery is composed of 3 brands: Settesoli, Inycon, and the flagship line Mandrarossa, which brings together selections of the finest grapes, the result of meticulous traceability work. Yet another gold for the Cavadiserpe '22, a merlot and alicante bouschet blend. A vibrant, refined nose opens with aromas of wild berries, black mulberry, and plum, all followed by spicy hints. The palate is well-structured and pleasant, aided by a fine tannic weave, with a persistent finish. The Petit Verdot Timperosse '23 is also excellent, unveiling elegant and intense notes of red fruits and aromatic herbs. On the palate, it's youthful and lively, with soft, gentle tannins.

Like a fairy tale, there's a magical place, a country estate that unfolds between Monreale and Alcamo, and a prince, Francesco Spadafora. Today, his vision of making wine in a pristine and unique place, one that has always belonged to the family, is being carried forward by his daughter Enrica, who has brought a feminine touch to a producer rooted in passion, dreams, and above all, commitment and dedication. The careful selection of grapes ensures that the final product is highly representative of the territory. The Siriki Orange '17 landed a place in our finals, standing out for its brilliant golden-orange hue. A complex nose highlights scents of resin, dried citrus peel, tea, ginger, and dried apricot. On the palate, all these aromas return in a pleasant, sapid texture, with a clean, persistent finish. The Schietto Nero d'Avola '16 is also appealing, with its ruby color and aromas of ripe fruit and jam, offering a pervasive palate with soft, velvety tannins.

● Cavadiserpe Mandrarossa '22	♈♈♈ 4*
○ Passito di Pantelleria Serapias Mandrarossa '21	♈♈ 7
● Sicilia Bonera Mandrarossa '23	♈♈ 3
● Sicilia Mandrarossa Cartagho '21	♈♈ 3
● Timperosse Mandrarossa '23	♈♈ 3
○ Sicilia Bianco Bertolino Soprano Mandrarossa '23	♈ 5
● Cavadiserpe Mandrarossa '21	♈♈♈ 4*
● Cavadiserpe Mandrarossa '16	♈♈♈ 3*
○ Santannella Mandrarossa '20	♈♈♈ 3*
● Sicilia Mandrarossa Cartagho '18	♈♈♈ 3*
● Sicilia Mandrarossa Cartagho '17	♈♈♈ 3*
● Sicilia Mandrarossa Cartagho '16	♈♈♈ 3*
● Sicilia Mandrarossa Cartagho '14	♈♈♈ 3*
● Timperosse Mandrarossa '14	♈♈♈ 3*

○ Siriki Orange '17	♈♈ 6
○ Catarratto '23	♈♈ 3
● Schietto Nero d'Avola '16	♈♈ 6
○ Don Pietro Bianco '23	♈ 3
● Don Pietro Rosso '20	♈ 4
☉ Il Nostro Rosato '22	♈ 3
○ Principe G '21	♈ 4
○ Catarratto '22	♈♈ 3*
○ Don Pietro Bianco '22	♈♈ 3
● Don Pietro Rosso '19	♈♈ 3
○ Enrica Spadafora Brut Nature M. Cl. '18	♈♈ 5
☉ Il Nostro Rosato '20	♈♈ 2*
○ Principe G '20	♈♈ 3
○ Principe G '19	♈♈ 3
● Principe N '20	♈♈ 2*
● Syrah '21	♈♈ 3

★★★Tasca d'Almerita

c.da Regaleali
90020 Sclafani Bagni [PA]
📞 +39 0916459711
🌐 www.tascadalmerita.it

CELLAR SALES
PRE-BOOKED VISITS
ACCOMMODATION AND RESTAURANT SERVICE
ANNUAL PRODUCTION 2,159,548 bottles
HECTARES UNDER VINE 376.80
SUSTAINABLE WINERY

After the passing of Count Lucio, governance of this historic Sicilian winery is now firmly in the hands of his son Alberto, who had already been captaining it for years. Recently, with determination and conviction, Alberto invested significantly in environmental sustainability, rendering the estates, from Etna to Mozia, Regaleali and Salina, among the greenest in Italy. The most notable developments are from Etna, where alongside the contrada reds, a promising new white will be released this year. A range of outstanding quality emerges from the Tasca family's five estates, scattered throughout Italy, with all the wines submitted performing exceptionally well. The refined and sunny catarratto Buonsenso '23 took home Tre Bicchieri, evoking island beaches with aromas of seaweed and seashells, shifting to melon, apricot, and aromatic herbs. On the palate, it's fresh and rich with juicy fruit, showing a pleasant sapidity and a very long finish.

Tenuta di Castellaro

loc. Quattropani
fraz. Castellaro
via Caolino
98055 Lipari [ME]
📞 +39 090 9587713
🌐 www.tenutadicastellaro.it

CELLAR SALES
PRE-BOOKED VISITS
ACCOMMODATION
ANNUAL PRODUCTION 75,000 bottles
HECTARES UNDER VINE 20.00
VITICULTURE METHOD Certified Organic

Twenty years ago, Massimo Lentsch and Stefania Frattolillo realized their dream of cultivating grapes and producing wine on Lipari, a volcanic terroir with a millennia-old winemaking tradition. The entire production process harmonizes with the island's nature and traditions, from the vineyards on the Castellaro plain, where the alberello (bush) training system is preserved, to the cellar, a fascinating structure that uses sunlight and wind for lighting and thermal regulation. The Bianco Pomice '23, a blend of malvasia and carricante, reached our finals with its elegant bouquet of fresh herbs, wild scrub, and citrus flowers. The fruit is solid and full on the palate, with a long, grapefruit finish. The Eùxenos '22, a macerated malvasia, offers intriguing aromas of citron zest and ginger. In the mouth it's round and sapid, with impressive persistence. Among the Massimo Lentsch Etna wines, we particularly appreciated the fruity and linear Rosso '21 and the refined, mineral Rosato '23.

○ Sicilia Bianco Catarratto Buonsenso '23	🍷🍷🍷 3*
● Etna Rosso Tascante Ghiaia Nera '22	🍷🍷 5
○ Sicilia Bianco Grillo Cavallo delle Fate '23	🍷🍷 3*
○ Contea di Sclafani Almerita Extra Brut Contessa Franca '16	🍷🍷 8
● Contea di Sclafani Rosso del Conte '19	🍷🍷 7
○ Didyme '23	🍷🍷 3
○ Etna Bianco Tascante Contrada Sciaranuova '22	🍷🍷 7
● Etna Rosso Tascante Contrada Sciaranuova V.V. '20	🍷🍷 8
○ Sicilia Bianco Nozze d'Oro '22	🍷🍷 4
○ Sicilia Chardonnay V. San Francesco '22	🍷🍷 6
○ Sicilia Grillo Tasca d'Almerita Whitaker '23	🍷🍷 5
● Sicilia Rosso Cygnus '20	🍷🍷 4
● Sicilia Rosso Perricone Guarnaccio '22	🍷🍷 3
○ V. di Paola Tenuta Capofaro '23	🍷🍷 6

○ Bianco Pomice '23	🍷🍷 5
⊙ Etna Rosato Massimo Lentsch '23	🍷🍷 5
● Etna Rosso Massimo Lentsch '21	🍷🍷 5
○ Eùxenos '22	🍷🍷 8
● Nero Ossidiana '21	🍷🍷 6
● Corinto '21	🍷 7
○ Etna Bianco Massimo Lentsch '23	🍷 5
● Etna Rosso Feudo di Mezzo Massimo Lentsch '21	🍷 6
○ Bianco Pomice '22	🍷🍷 5
○ Bianco Pomice '20	🍷🍷 5
● Corinto '20	🍷🍷 7
● Etna Rosso Massimo Lentsch '20	🍷🍷 5
○ Malvasia delle Lipari Passito '18	🍷🍷 6
● Nero Ossidiana '19	🍷🍷 5
● Nero Ossidiana '17	🍷🍷 5

★Tenuta di Fessina

fraz. Rovittello
via Nazionale 120, km 22
95012 Castiglione di Sicilia [CT]
(+39 3458346477
www.tenutadifessina.com

CELLAR SALES
PRE-BOOKED VISITS
ACCOMMODATION AND RESTAURANT SERVICE
ANNUAL PRODUCTION 80,000 bottles
HECTARES UNDER VINE 15.00
VITICULTURE METHOD Certified Organic
SUSTAINABLE WINERY

An ancient "baglio" (an enclosed Sicilian farmstead), tastefully restored, and a beautiful surrounding vineyard immortalize Silvia Maestrelli's love for Etna and her keen sense of beauty. Silvia, a passionate Tuscan producer who is no longer with us, passed her spirit and inspiration on to her daughter Lavinia Silva, who's supported by talented winemaker Benedetto Alessandro. The hallmark of the maison remains the same: classy, complex, and territorial wines that bring out the best of local varietals. The most coveted prize goes to the Erse 1911 Contrada Moscamento '20, a wine of great stature and personality. It pours a deep ruby tone edging towards garnet, opening with nuances of wormwood, red peach, black fruits, pink pepper, and tobacco. Elegant and refined on the palate, it reveals velvety tannins and a juicy, captivating drinkability. We were also captivated by the Etna Bianco A' Puddara '22, with its notes of pear, almond, verbena, and everlasting flower—an iodized, mineral, and persistent wine on the palate.

● Etna Rosso Erse 1911 Contrada Moscamento '20	♟♟♟ 5
○ Etna Bianco A' Puddara SM Vigne Alte '21	♟♟ 8
○ Etna Bianco A'Puddara '22	♟♟ 6
○ Etna Bianco Superiore Il Musmeci '21	♟♟ 8
● Etna Rosso Erse '22	♟♟ 5
● Etna Rosso Prephilloxera Il Musmeci '22	♟♟ 7
○ Etna Bianco A' Puddara '20	♟♟♟ 6
○ Etna Bianco A' Puddara '19	♟♟♟ 6
○ Etna Bianco A' Puddara '17	♟♟♟ 5
○ Etna Bianco A' Puddara '16	♟♟♟ 5
○ Etna Bianco A' Puddara '13	♟♟♟ 5
○ Etna Bianco A' Puddara '12	♟♟♟ 5
○ Etna Bianco A' Puddara '11	♟♟♟ 5
○ Etna Bianco A'Puddara '21	♟♟♟ 6
● Etna Rosso Erse 1911 Contrada Moscamento '17	♟♟♟ 5

Terra Costantino

via Garibaldi, 417
95029 Viagrande [CT]
(+39 095434288
www.terracostantino.it

CELLAR SALES
PRE-BOOKED VISITS
ACCOMMODATION
ANNUAL PRODUCTION 76,000 bottles
HECTARES UNDER VINE 12.00
VITICULTURE METHOD Certified Organic
SUSTAINABLE WINERY

Fabio Costantino's winery is one of the oldest on Etna, with records testifying to its existence as far back as 1699. Today, the estate boasts 10 hectares of vineyards in Contrada Blandano and 2 in Contrada Praino, in Milo. Fabio, attentive to sustainability, was the first to obtain organic certification on Etna (in the year 2000). To respect biodiversity, the vineyards, where green manure is practiced, are surrounded by 20 different types of fruit trees. To reduce pollution, most operations, including harvesting, are carried out by hand. Despite a challenging vintage, the Etna Rosato de Aetna '23 impresses, opening with clear aromas of flowers and red fruits, peach, and Mediterranean herbs. The palate is fresh, sapid, and marked by a precise encore of fruit. The Etna Bianco Contrada Blandano '20 is deeply tied to its terroir, emanating aromas of yellow fruit, citron, broom, and pumice stone, offering a brackish palate, well-balanced between acidity and fruit.

☉ Etna Rosato De Aetna '23	♟♟ 4
○ Etna Bianco Contrada Blandano '20	♟♟ 6
○ Etna Bianco Sup. Contrada Praino '22	♟♟ 5
● Etna Rosso De Aetna '22	♟♟ 5
☉ Etna Rosato de Aetna '22	♟♟♟ 4*
○ Etna Bianco Contrada Blandano '19	♟♟ 6
○ Etna Bianco de Aetna '21	♟♟ 4
○ Etna Bianco de Aetna '19	♟♟ 5
○ Etna Bianco de Aetna '18	♟♟ 5
● Etna Rosso Contrada Blandano '16	♟♟ 5
● Etna Rosso Contrada Blandano Ris. '18	♟♟ 6
● Etna Rosso de Aetna '17	♟♟ 3*
● Etna Rosso de Aetna '16	♟♟ 3*

Terrazze dell'Etna

c.da Bocca d'Orzo
95036 Randazzo [CT]
📞 +39 0916236343
🌐 www.terrazzedelletna.it

CELLAR SALES
PRE-BOOKED VISITS
ANNUAL PRODUCTION 120,000 bottles
HECTARES UNDER VINE 38.00

Founded thanks to engineer Nino Bevilacqua's attention to the environment and to the restoration of stone terraces and "palmentos" (traditional Sicilian wine presses), Terrazze dell'Etna is a delightful vineyard paradise. The amphitheater of terraced parcels host the volcano's native grape varieties: from nerello mascalese to nerello cappuccio and carricante. International varieties like chardonnay and pinot nero are also present. Today, this charming estate is diligently run by Nino's daughter Alessia. Their range is excellent, with the Metodo Classico sparkling wines standing out in particular. The Rosé Brut 50 mesi '19 (pinot nero with a touch of nerello mascalese) is superb, revealing an intense and long bouquet of bread crust, orange blossom, peach, plum, and yeasts. The palate is mineral, full-bodied, with pleasant sapidity and a fruity finish. The velvety, alluring Blanc Brut 50 mesi '19 (chardonnay) proves complex, playing on citrus and minty notes.

⊙ Cuvée Brut 50 Mesi M. Cl. Rosé '19	♟♟ 5	
○ Cuvée Brut 50 Mesi M. Cl. '19	♟♟ 5	
⊙ Cuvée Brut M. Cl. Rosé '21	♟♟ 5	
● Etna Rosso Carusu '22	♟♟ 4	
○ Cuvée Brut M. Cl. '21	♟ 5	
● Etna Rosso Cirneco '09	♟♟♟ 6	
● Etna Rosso Cirneco '08	♟♟♟ 5	
○ Cuvée Blanc Brut M. Cl. '20	♟♟ 5	
○ Cuvée Brut 50 Mesi M. Cl. '17	♟♟ 5	
○ Cuvée Brut 50 Mesi M. Cl. '15	♟♟ 5	
○ Cuvée Brut 50 Mesi M. Cl. '14	♟♟ 5	
⊙ Cuvée Brut 50 Mesi M. Cl. Rosé '16	♟♟ 5	
● Etna Rosso Cirneco '12	♟♟ 6	
● Etna Rosso Cirneco '11	♟♟ 6	
● Etna Rosso Cirneco '10	♟♟ 6	
⊙ Rosé Brut '08	♟♟ 5	

Girolamo Tola

c.da Grassuri Airoldi
90047 Partinico [PA]
📞 +39 3356629801
🌐 www.vinitola.com

CELLAR SALES
PRE-BOOKED VISITS
ANNUAL PRODUCTION 400,000 bottles
HECTARES UNDER VINE 30.00
VITICULTURE METHOD Certified Organic
SUSTAINABLE WINERY

SICILY

The winery extends in the northwestern part of Sicily, in the province of Palermo, between the town of Alcamo, the small village of Grisì, and the town of Partinico. Tola was made possible thanks to the passion and instincts of Girolamo Tola, known as "Mimmo," who inherited from his father a love for the land, especially for sustainable and low-impact viticulture. Today, the maison is experiencing a period of strong growth and product innovation thanks to the input of Mimmo's children, Domiziana and Francesco. The Nero d'Avola Chimaera '22 earned a well-deserved place in our finals. A brilliant ruby color anticipates aromas of Mediterranean scrub, alongside rich sensations of ripe red and black fruits, balsamic hints of thyme and dark spices. The palate is fresh and fragrant, perfectly balanced between acidity, sapidity, and fine, delicate tannins. The Granduca '19, also made from nero d'Avola, is very elegant, with flavors of black currant and blueberries meeting licorice and tobacco—it's a vigorous and highly enjoyable wine.

⊙ Costarosa '22	♟♟ 3	
○ Granduca Chardonnay '22	♟♟ 3	
○ Sicilia Chimaera Catarratto '23	♟♟ 2*	
○ Sicilia Chimaera Grillo '23	♟♟ 2*	
● Sicilia Chimaera Nero d'Avola '23	♟♟ 2*	
● Sicilia Chimaera Syrah '23	♟♟ 2*	
● Sicilia Granduca Nero d'Avola '19	♟♟ 4	
● Sicilia Lavinaro Ris. '21	♟♟ 3	
● Sicilia Nero d'Avola Black Label '21	♟♟ 3	
○ White Label '23	♟♟ 3	
● Sicilia Nero d'Avola '22	♟♟ 3	
● Sicilia Nero d'Avola Black Label '19	♟♟ 3	
○ White Label '21	♟♟ 3	

Francesco Tornatore

fraz. Verzella
via Pietramarina, 8a
95012 Castiglione di Sicilia [CT]
☎ +39 3662641380
🌐 www.tornatorewine.com

CELLAR SALES
PRE-BOOKED VISITS
ANNUAL PRODUCTION 120,000 bottles
HECTARES UNDER VINE 74.00

For dynamic entrepreneur Francesco Tornatore, the substantial investment made on the northern slope of Etna, where his more than 70 hectares of vineyards and 2 wineries can be found, marks a return to his roots. Francesco's successful career began in Castiglione di Sicilia, working alongside his father on the family farm. It's no surprise that the wine produced in Contrada Trimarchisa, in the vineyard surrounding his father's palmento, is now the producer's flagship. The Etna Rosso Pietrarizzo '21, which repeated the success of the 2020 vintage, wins Tre Bicchieri for its exemplary varietal expression, offering up aromas of peach, blood orange, licorice, and smoky notes. On the palate, it's austere yet clear and elegant. No less impressive, the Carricante Pietrarizzo '23 proves close-knit and complex on the nose, featuring floral and balsamic tones, while the palate is fresh, brackish, and long.

● Etna Rosso Contrada Pietrarizzo '21	♈♈♈ 5
○ Etna Bianco Contrada Pietrarizzo '23	♈♈ 5
● Etna Rosso '21	♈♈ 4
○ Etna Bianco '23	♈♈ 4
● Etna Rosso Contrada Trimarchisa '19	♈♈ 6
○ Etna Bianco Pietrarizzo '20	♈♈♈ 5
○ Etna Bianco Pietrarizzo '19	♈♈♈ 5
● Etna Rosso '17	♈♈♈ 4*
● Etna Rosso '15	♈♈♈ 4*
● Etna Rosso Contrada Calderara '19	♈♈♈ 6
● Etna Rosso Contrada Pietrarizzo '20	♈♈♈ 5
● Etna Rosso Trimarchisa '16	♈♈♈ 6
○ Etna Bianco Contrada Zottorinotto '21	♈♈ 5
● Etna Rosso Contrada Pietrarizzo '19	♈♈ 5
● Etna Rosso Ris. '17	♈♈ 5

Aldo Viola

via per Camporeale, 18c
91011 Alcamo [TP]
☎ +39 3396969889
violaaldo69@yahoo.it

ANNUAL PRODUCTION 40,000 bottles

Aldo Viola epitomizes the aristan winemaker. His persistence has driven him to experiment with wines that truly express who he is. His methods include long macerations, the absence of fining and stabilizations, and the minimal use of sulfur dioxide, all hallmarks of his winemaking philosophy. His vineyards, located in the Feudo Guarini area near Alcamo in the province of Trapani, are entirely his own. His near-religious devotion to the catarratto grape has yielded impressive results, as have his experiments with syrah and perricone. The Krimiso '19 is excellent. An appealingly brackish, Mediterranean wine made from catarratto, it macerates on the skins for about 5 months in stainless steel tanks. Its aromatic profile reveals citrus, yellow fruit, and aromatic herbs, while the palate is sapid and mineral, with delicate tannins on the finish. Catarratto also stars in the Shiva '17, an orange wine of great character, with a broad aromatic profile and a sumptuous palate, balanced and fresh, revealing a compelling Sicilian soul.

○ Krimiso '19	♈♈♈ 5
○ Shiva '17	♈♈ 7
● Moretto '21	♈♈ 5
● Saignee Rosso '21	♈♈ 4
○ Biancoviola '22	♈♈ 4
● Moretto '20	♈♈ 5
● Syrah Guarini Plus '19	♈♈ 5

OTHER WINERIES

Abbazia Santa Anastasia

c.da Santa Anastasia
90013 Castelbuono [PA]
+39 0921671959
www.abbaziasantanastasia.com

CELLAR SALES
PRE-BOOKED VISITS
ACCOMMODATION AND RESTAURANT SERVICE
ANNUAL PRODUCTION 470,000 bottles
HECTARES UNDER VINE 69.50
VITICULTURE METHOD Certified Organic
SUSTAINABLE WINERY

● Sicilia Montenero '22	🍷🍷 4
● Sicilia Nero d'Avola Sensinverso '22	🍷🍷 5
○ Sicilia Sauvignon Sinestesìa '23	🍷🍷 4
○ Sicilia Grillo '23	🍷 3

Abraxas

c.da Kuddia Randazzo
90139 Pantelleria [TP]
+39 0916116832
www.abraxasvini.com

CELLAR SALES
PRE-BOOKED VISITS
ACCOMMODATION
ANNUAL PRODUCTION 95,000 bottles
HECTARES UNDER VINE 26.00
VITICULTURE METHOD Certified Organic

○ Pantelleria Passito Sentivento '17	🍷🍷 5
○ Pantelleria Bianco Alsine '23	🍷🍷 4
⊙ Sicilia Rosato Reseda '23	🍷 3

Alberelli di Giodo

loc. Solicchiata
95012 Castiglione di Sicilia [CT]
+39 3516220372
carlo.ferrini27@gmail.com

ANNUAL PRODUCTION 6,000 bottles
HECTARES UNDER VINE 1.50
SUSTAINABLE WINERY

○ Sicilia Bianco Alberelli di Giodo '22	🍷🍷 7
● Sicilia Alberelli di Giodo '21	🍷🍷 7

Ansaldi - Donnafranca

fraz. Bufalata
c.da Florio, 1
91025 Marsala [TP]
+39 3317984324
www.ansaldi.donnafranca.it

CELLAR SALES
PRE-BOOKED VISITS
ACCOMMODATION AND RESTAURANT SERVICE
ANNUAL PRODUCTION 50,000 bottles
HECTARES UNDER VINE 44.00
VITICULTURE METHOD Certified Organic
SUSTAINABLE WINERY

● Sicilia Rosso Cipponeri Ris. '17	🍷🍷 5
○ Abbadessa Zibibbo V.T. '13	🍷🍷 5
○ Sicilia Grillo Bianco di Abbadessa '21	🍷🍷 3
● Sicilia Rosso di Cipponeri '19	🍷🍷 3

Baglio di Pianetto

loc. Pianetto
via Francia
90030 Santa Cristina Gela [PA]
+39 0918570002
www.bagliodipianetto.it

CELLAR SALES
PRE-BOOKED VISITS
ACCOMMODATION
ANNUAL PRODUCTION 900,000 bottles
HECTARES UNDER VINE 106.00
VITICULTURE METHOD Certified Organic
SUSTAINABLE WINERY

○ Sicilia Grillo '23	🍷🍷 3
⊙ Viafrancia Rosato '23	🍷🍷 4
○ Sicilia Insolia '23	🍷 3
● Sicilia Syrah '22	🍷 3

Barone Sergio

loc. Noto
s.da prov.le 26 Pachino-Rosolini
96018 Pachino [SR]
+39 0902927878
www.baronesergio.it

CELLAR SALES
PRE-BOOKED VISITS
RESTAURANT SERVICE
ANNUAL PRODUCTION 80,000 bottles
HECTARES UNDER VINE 130.00
VITICULTURE METHOD Certified Organic

○ Alluccà '23	🍷🍷 3
● Eloro Nero d'Avola Sergio '22	🍷🍷 3
● Reliquia '21	🍷🍷 5
⊙ Sicilia Rosato Luigia '23	🍷🍷 3

OTHER WINERIES

Biscaris

via Maresciallo Giudice, 52
97011 Acate [RG]
📞 +39 0932990762
🌐 biscaris.it

CELLAR SALES
ANNUAL PRODUCTION 50,000 bottles
HECTARES UNDER VINE 10.00
VITICULTURE METHOD Certified Biodynamic

● Vittoria Nero d'Avola '23	🍷🍷 2*
● Cerasuolo di Vittoria '23	🍷🍷 3
● Frappato '23	🍷 2

Tenute Bosco

s.da prov.le 64 Solicchiata
95012 Castiglione di Sicilia [CT]
📞 +39 3494543911
🌐 www.tenutebosco.com

CELLAR SALES
PRE-BOOKED VISITS
ANNUAL PRODUCTION 50,000 bottles
HECTARES UNDER VINE 12.00
VITICULTURE METHOD Certified Organic
SUSTAINABLE WINERY

○ Etna Bianco '23	🍷🍷 4
● Etna Rosso '22	🍷🍷 4

Brugnano

loc. c.da San Carlo
s.da st.le 113, km 307
90047 Partinico [PA]
📞 +39 0918783360
🌐 www.brugnano.it

CELLAR SALES
PRE-BOOKED VISITS
ANNUAL PRODUCTION 120,000 bottles
HECTARES UNDER VINE 45.00

○ Ammaru Zibibbo '23	🍷🍷 3
○ Kuè Inzolia Viognier '23	🍷🍷 3
○ Sicilia Grillo Lunario '23	🍷🍷 4
● Sicilia Rosso Naisi '22	🍷 3

Mirella Buscemi

c.da Tartaraci
95034 Bronte [CT]
📞 +39 3421845630
🌐 www.mirellabuscemi.it

○ Sicilia Bianco Il Bianco '23	🍷🍷 6
● Sicilia Rosso Tartaraci '21	🍷🍷 6

Caruso & Minini

via Salemi, 3
91025 Marsala [TP]
📞 +39 0923982356
🌐 www.carusoeminini.com

CELLAR SALES
PRE-BOOKED VISITS
ANNUAL PRODUCTION 650,000 bottles
HECTARES UNDER VINE 120.00
VITICULTURE METHOD Certified Organic
SUSTAINABLE WINERY

● Delia Nivolelli Syrah Ris. '17	🍷🍷 5
⊙ Frappo Rosé '23	🍷🍷 3
● Sicilia Perricone Perripò '21	🍷🍷 4
○ Sicilia Catarratto Catalù '23	🍷 3

Casa Grazia

c.da Passo di Piazza
93012 Gela [CL]
📞 +39 0933919465
🌐 www.casagrazia.com

CELLAR SALES
ANNUAL PRODUCTION 90,000 bottles
HECTARES UNDER VINE 30.00
VITICULTURE METHOD Certified Organic
SUSTAINABLE WINERY

● Sicilia Cabernet Sauvignon Vi Veri '21	🍷🍷 5
○ Sicilia Grillo Per Mari '23	🍷🍷 3
● Cerasuolo di Vittoria Cl. Brunetti d'Opera '21	🍷 6

OTHER WINERIES

Case Alte
loc. Macellarotto
via Pisciotta, 27
90043 Camporeale [PA]
(+39 3297130750
www.casealte.it

ACCOMMODATION
ANNUAL PRODUCTION 33,000 bottles
HECTARES UNDER VINE 12.00
VITICULTURE METHOD Certified Organic

● Sicilia Nero d'Avola 16 Filari '22	♈♈ 4
○ Monreale Catarratto 12 Filari '23	♈♈ 4
● Monreale Syrah di Macellarotto '22	♈♈ 5
○ Sicilia Grillo 4 Filari '23	♈♈ 4

Cantine Colosi
loc. Pace del Mela
fraz. Giammoro
98042 Messina
(+39 0909385549
www.cantinecolosi.it

CELLAR SALES
PRE-BOOKED VISITS
ANNUAL PRODUCTION 700,000 bottles
HECTARES UNDER VINE 13.00
VITICULTURE METHOD Certified Organic

○ Malvasia delle Lipari Passito Na'jm '22	♈♈ 5
○ Passito '20	♈♈ 3
● Salina Guardiano del Faro '21	♈♈ 6
○ Sicilia Grillo Acacia '23	♈ 3

Feudo Disisa
loc. Grisì
fraz. c.da Disisa
s.da prov.le 30, Km 6
90040 Monreale [PA]
(+39 0916127109
www.feudodisisa.it

CELLAR SALES
PRE-BOOKED VISITS
ANNUAL PRODUCTION 220,000 bottles
HECTARES UNDER VINE 150.00
VITICULTURE METHOD Certified Organic

● Monreale Rosso Vuaria '20	♈♈ 4
○ Sicilia Pas Dosé M. Cl. Renè '17	♈♈ 6
● Sicilia Roano '20	♈♈ 4
○ Sicilia Chara '23	♈ 4

Castellucci Miano
via Sicilia, 1
90029 Valledolmo [PA]
(+39 0921542385
www.castelluccimiano.it

CELLAR SALES
PRE-BOOKED VISITS
ANNUAL PRODUCTION 150,000 bottles
HECTARES UNDER VINE 125.00

○ Contea di Sclafani Miano Valledolmo '23	♈♈ 3
○ Contea di Sclafani Shiarà Valledolmo '22	♈♈ 6
○ Miano Brut	♈ 3
● Sicilia PerricOne '22	♈ 4

Contrada Santo Spirito di Passopisciaro
loc. Passopisciaro
c.da Santo Spirito
95012 Castiglione di Sicilia [CT]
(+39 0575477857
www.contradasantospiritodipassopisciaro.it

ANNUAL PRODUCTION 6,800 bottles
HECTARES UNDER VINE 9.00

● Etna Rosso Animardente C.da Santo Spirito '21	♈♈ 6
● Etna Rosso Animantica '22	♈♈ 6
● Etna Rosso Animavulcano '22	♈♈ 4

Elios
via G. Lipari, 40
91011 Alcamo [TP]
(+39 3334095994
www.eliosfood.it

CELLAR SALES
PRE-BOOKED VISITS
ACCOMMODATION
ANNUAL PRODUCTION 25,000 bottles
HECTARES UNDER VINE 15.00
VITICULTURE METHOD Certified Organic
SUSTAINABLE WINERY

○ Sicilia Bianco Modus Bibendi Macerato '21	♈♈ 5
○ Blanc de Blancs M. Cl. Brut Nature '21	♈♈ 6
○ Sicilia Bianco Modus Bibendi '23	♈♈ 4

SICILY

OTHER WINERIES

Ferreri e Bianco

c.da Salinella
91029 Santa Ninfa [TP]
+39 3332143255
www.ferrerivini.it

CELLAR SALES
PRE-BOOKED VISITS
ACCOMMODATION AND RESTAURANT SERVICE
ANNUAL PRODUCTION 80,000 bottles
HECTARES UNDER VINE 36.00
SUSTAINABLE WINERY

○ Sicilia Catarratto '23	🍷🍷 3
● Sicilia Perricone Pignatello '20	🍷🍷 3
⊙ Sicilia Perricone Pignatello Rosé '23	🍷🍷 3
○ Sicilia Grillo '23	🍷 3

Cantine Fina

c.da Bausa
91025 Marsala [TP]
+39 3200868387
www.cantinefina.it

CELLAR SALES
PRE-BOOKED VISITS
ACCOMMODATION
ANNUAL PRODUCTION 1,000,000 bottles
HECTARES UNDER VINE 30.00
VITICULTURE METHOD Certified Organic
SUSTAINABLE WINERY

⊙ Hanami '23	🍷🍷 3
○ La Stanza del Re '22	🍷🍷 4
● Caro Maestro '19	🍷 5
○ Kikè '23	🍷 3

Fondo Antico

s.da Fiorame, 54a
91031 Misiliscemi [TP]
+39 0923864339
www.fondoantico.it

CELLAR SALES
PRE-BOOKED VISITS
ANNUAL PRODUCTION 500,000 bottles
HECTARES UNDER VINE 80.00

○ Sicilia Grillo Parlante '23	🍷🍷 3*
○ Baccadoro	🍷🍷 4
○ Bello Mio '23	🍷 3
● Sicilia Nero d'Avola Nenè '22	🍷 3

Gambino

c.da Petto Dragone
95015 Linguaglossa [CT]
+39 3488220130
www.vinigambino.it

● Etna Rosso Petto Dragone '20	🍷🍷 5
● Etna Rosso Tifeo '20	🍷🍷 4
○ Etna Bianco Tifeo '23	🍷 4
⊙ Etna Rosato Tifeo '23	🍷 4

Nino Gandolfo

via Marsala, 57
91018 Salemi [TP]
+39 3669753000
www.ninogandolfo.com

CELLAR SALES
PRE-BOOKED VISITS
ACCOMMODATION
ANNUAL PRODUCTION 120,000 bottles
HECTARES UNDER VINE 50.00
SUSTAINABLE WINERY

○ Catarratto '23	🍷🍷 3
● Nerello Mascalese '22	🍷🍷 3
○ Sicilia Grillo '23	🍷🍷 4
○ Sicilia Grillo Passito Pietro '22	🍷🍷 8

Giovinco

c.da Anguilla, s.da st.le 188
92017 Sambuca di Sicilia [AG]
+39 3455948625
www.giovincowines.it

CELLAR SALES
PRE-BOOKED VISITS
ACCOMMODATION
ANNUAL PRODUCTION 30,000 bottles
HECTARES UNDER VINE 50.00
VITICULTURE METHOD Certified Organic
SUSTAINABLE WINERY

○ Etna Bianco '23	🍷🍷 5
○ Giovinco Extra Brut M. Cl. '20	🍷🍷 7
● Sambuca di Sicilia Nero d'Avola Sgarretta '22	🍷🍷 3

OTHER WINERIES

Iuppa
c.da Salice, 22
95010 Milo [CT]
📞 +39 3389146668
🌐 www.cantineiuppa.it

CELLAR SALES
PRE-BOOKED VISITS
ACCOMMODATION
ANNUAL PRODUCTION 35,000 bottles
HECTARES UNDER VINE 7.00
VITICULTURE METHOD Certified Organic

○ Etna Bianco Dosaggio Zero M. Cl. Piccolot '19	♈♈ 7
○ Etna Bianco Sup. Lindo Contrada Salice '22	♈♈ 5
● Etna Rosso Clo '21	♈♈ 5

Domenico Lombardo Vivignato
c.da Mezzatesta
s.da prov.le 33
91013 Calatafimi [TP]
📞 +39 3338658580
🌐 www.domenicolombardovini.com

○ Mezzatesta Catarratto '22	♈♈ 4
● Alcamo Nero d'Avola Scarlata '22	♈♈ 5

Maggio Vini
via Filippo Bonetta, 35
97019 Vittoria [RG]
📞 +39 0932984771
🌐 www.maggiovini.it

CELLAR SALES
PRE-BOOKED VISITS
ACCOMMODATION
ANNUAL PRODUCTION 400,000 bottles
HECTARES UNDER VINE 55.00
VITICULTURE METHOD Certified Organic
SUSTAINABLE WINERY

● Cerasuolo di Vittoria V. di Pettineo '22	♈♈ 3
● Sicilia Nero d'Avola V. di Pettineo '20	♈♈ 3
● Vittoria Frappato Vigna di Pettineo '23	♈♈ 3
◐ Luna Nascente Frappato Spumante	♈ 3

Tenute Lombardo
c.da Cusatino, km 50
93100 Caltanissetta
📞 +39 09341935148
🌐 www.tenutelombardo.it

CELLAR SALES
PRE-BOOKED VISITS
ANNUAL PRODUCTION 120,000 bottles
HECTARES UNDER VINE 35.00

○ Fiore di Nero '23	♈♈ 3
● Passadinero '21	♈♈ 5
○ Sicilia Bianco d'Altura '23	♈ 4
○ Sicilia Grillo Sup. Grillo d'Altura '23	♈ 4

Longarico
via Pietro Scaglione, 4
91011 Alcamo [TP]
📞 +39 3932280171
longarico@libero.it

CELLAR SALES
PRE-BOOKED VISITS
ANNUAL PRODUCTION 12,500 bottles
HECTARES UNDER VINE 2.00
VITICULTURE METHOD Certified Organic

○ All'Ombra dei Pini Catarratto M. Cl. '22	♈♈ 5
○ Catartico Catarratto Macerato '21	♈♈ 5
● Insolito '22	♈♈ 4
○ Nostrale Catarratto '23	♈ 3

Tenute Mokarta
c.da S. Ciro, 487
91018 Salemi [TP]
📞 +39 3343633792
🌐 www.tenutemokarta.com

CELLAR SALES
PRE-BOOKED VISITS
ANNUAL PRODUCTION 240,000 bottles
HECTARES UNDER VINE 45.00
VITICULTURE METHOD Certified Organic
SUSTAINABLE WINERY

● Sicilia Nero d'Avola Talìa '21	♈♈ 3
○ Sicilia Sauvignon Blanc Talìa '23	♈♈ 3
● Sicilia Syrah Talìa '22	♈♈ 3
○ Sicilia Zibibbo Talìa '23	♈♈ 4

Montecarrubo
Peter Vinding-Diers
c.da Case Nuove
96010 Melilli [SR]
📞 +39 3355950018
🌐 www.montecarrubo.com

Morgante
c.da Racalmare
92020 Grotte [AG]
📞 +39 0922945579
🌐 www.morgantevini.it

CELLAR SALES
ANNUAL PRODUCTION 215,000 bottles
HECTARES UNDER VINE 52.00

● Vigna Grande Syrah '20	♟♟ 6
● Quant a Soi '21	♟♟ 8
● Vignolo Bianco '22	♟♟ 8
● Vignolo Rosso '22	♟♟ 8

● Sicilia Nero d'Avola Don Antonio Ris. '21	♟♟ 7
○ Bianco di Morgante '23	♟♟ 3
● Sicilia Nero d'Avola '22	♟♟ 3
⊙ Sicilia Nero d'Avola Rosé di Morgante '23	♟ 3

Neri
c.da Arrigo
95015 Linguaglossa [CT]
📞 +39 3760343468
🌐 www.nerietna.com

Agricola Ottoventi
c.da Torrebianca - Fico
91019 Valderice [TP]
📞 +39 3474936661
🌐 www.cantinaottoventi.wine

CELLAR SALES
PRE-BOOKED VISITS
ACCOMMODATION
ANNUAL PRODUCTION 250,000 bottles
HECTARES UNDER VINE 60.00
VITICULTURE METHOD Certified Organic

● Etna Rosso Contrada Arrigo '22	♟♟ 5
○ Etna Bianco Contrada Arrigo '22	♟♟ 5

○ Sicilia Catarratto '23	♟♟ 3
○ Venti Eloquenti Catarratto Zibibbo '23	♟♟ 3
● Venti Eloquenti Syrah '22	♟♟ 3
○ Sicilia Zibibbo '23	♟ 3

Cantine Paolini
c.da Gurgo, 168a
91025 Marsala [TP]
📞 +39 0923967042
🌐 www.cantinapaolini.com

Cantine Patrì
via Lombardia, 1
93016 Butera [CL]
📞 +39 3204473563
🌐 www.cantinepatri.it

ANNUAL PRODUCTION 4,000,000 bottles
HECTARES UNDER VINE 2739.00
VITICULTURE METHOD Certified Organic

ANNUAL PRODUCTION 100,000 bottles
HECTARES UNDER VINE 40.00
SUSTAINABLE WINERY

○ 72 Filara Lucido '23	♟♟ 2*
● 72 Filara Nero d'Avola Frappato '22	♟♟ 2*
○ Sicilia Grillo Maleka '23	♟♟ 2*
○ Sicilia Zibibbo Di Siu '23	♟♟ 3

● Sicilia Frappato '21	♟♟ 4
○ Sicilia Inzolia '23	♟♟ 4
○ Sicilia Rosato Frappato Sikelia '23	♟♟ 3
○ Sicilia Chardonnay Solitario '23	♟ 3

Poggio Graffetta

c.da Graffetta
Ispica [RG]
📞 +39 0577731004
🌐 www.poggiograffetta.it

HECTARES UNDER VINE 22.00

○ Sicilia Grillo '23	🍷🍷 3
● Sicilia Nero d'Avola '22	🍷🍷 5
● Sicilia Syrah '22	🍷 5

Pupillo

c.da La Targia
96100 Siracusa
📞 +39 0931494029
🌐 www.pupillowines.com

CELLAR SALES
PRE-BOOKED VISITS
ACCOMMODATION AND RESTAURANT SERVICE
ANNUAL PRODUCTION 60,000 bottles
HECTARES UNDER VINE 20.00
SUSTAINABLE WINERY

○ Sicilia Brut Nature M.Cl. Podere 27 '22	🍷🍷 5
○ Siracusa Moscato Cyane '23	🍷🍷 3
○ Siracusa Moscato Passito Solacium '23	🍷🍷 4
● Sicilia Rosso Baronessa di Canseria '23	🍷 4

Restivo

loc. Passopisciaro
fraz. c.da Arcuria
95012 Castiglione di Sicilia [CT]
📞 +39 095388557
🌐 www-restivowine.it

⊙ Etna Rosato '23	🍷🍷 5
⊙ Etna Bianco Contrada Arcuria '23	🍷🍷 5

Porta del Vento

c.da Valdibella
90043 Camporeale [PA]
📞 +39 0916116531
🌐 www.portadelvento.it

ANNUAL PRODUCTION 40,000 bottles
HECTARES UNDER VINE 12.00
VITICULTURE METHOD Certified Organic

○ Monreale Cataratto '23	🍷🍷 4
○ Sicilia Grillo '23	🍷🍷 5
○ Trebbì '22	🍷🍷 4
○ Mira Brut Nature M.Cl.	🍷 5

Ramaddini

fraz. Marzamemi
c.da Lettiera
96018 Pachino [SR]
📞 +39 09311847100
🌐 www.ramaddini.com

CELLAR SALES
PRE-BOOKED VISITS
ACCOMMODATION
ANNUAL PRODUCTION 100,000 bottles
HECTARES UNDER VINE 25.00
VITICULTURE METHOD Certified Organic

○ Perla Marina Brut	🍷🍷 4
○ Sicilia Passito di Noto Al Hamen '23	🍷🍷 5

Riofavara

fraz. Rio Favara
s.da prov.le 49 Ispica-Pachino
97014 Ispica [RG]
📞 +39 0932705130
🌐 www.riofavara.it

CELLAR SALES
PRE-BOOKED VISITS
ACCOMMODATION
ANNUAL PRODUCTION 45,000 bottles
HECTARES UNDER VINE 14.00
VITICULTURE METHOD Certified Organic
SUSTAINABLE WINERY

○ Sicilia Moscato Bianco Notissimo '23	🍷🍷 3*
○ Marzaiolo '23	🍷🍷 3
● San Basilio '21	🍷 3
○ Sicilia Bianco Nsajàr '22	🍷 6

OTHER WINERIES

Tenuta Sallier de La Tour

loc. Camporeale
c.da Pernice
90046 Monreale [PA]
(+39 0916459711
☻ www.tascadalmerita.it

PRE-BOOKED VISITS
ANNUAL PRODUCTION 250,000 bottles
HECTARES UNDER VINE 50.58
SUSTAINABLE WINERY

● Monreale Syrah La Monaca '21	♟♟ 5
⊙ Sicilia Rosato Madamarosé '23	♟♟ 3

Valle dell'Acate

c.da Biddine Soprana
97011 Acate [RG]
(+39 0932874166
☻ www.valledellacate.com

CELLAR SALES
PRE-BOOKED VISITS
ACCOMMODATION
ANNUAL PRODUCTION 300,000 bottles
HECTARES UNDER VINE 70.00
VITICULTURE METHOD Certified Organic
SUSTAINABLE WINERY

● Sicilia Il Moro Nero d'Avola '21	♟♟ 4
⊙ Sicilia Zagra Grillo '23	♟♟ 3
⊙ Thymbra Vermentino '23	♟♟ 3
● Vittoria Frappato Gaetana Jacono '23	♟♟ 5

Wiegner

fraz. Passopisciaro
c.da Marchesa, 1
95012 Castiglione di Sicilia [CT]
(+39 3489046391
☻ www.wiegnerwine.com

⊙ Etna Bianco Contrada Rampante '22	♟♟ 5
● Etna Rosso Contrada Rampante '19	♟♟ 6
● Etna Rosso Tre Terre '22	♟♟ 4
● Etna Rosato Tre Terre '22	♟ 4

Vaccaro

c.da Comune
91020 Salaparuta [TP]
(+39 092475151
☻ www.vinivaccaro.it

CELLAR SALES
ACCOMMODATION
ANNUAL PRODUCTION 800,000 bottles
HECTARES UNDER VINE 300.00
VITICULTURE METHOD Certified Organic
SUSTAINABLE WINERY

⊙ Salaparuta Bianco Timè '22	♟♟ 4
⊙ Sicilia Metodo Classico Pas Dosé '21	♟♟ 5
⊙ Sicilia Rosato di Nero d'Avola Liddàli '23	♟♟ 3
⊙ Liciumi Catarratto '23	♟ 3

Alessandro Viola

via per Camporeale, 18c
91011 Alcamo [TP]
(+39 3395046839

⊙ Le Mie Origini '21	♟♟ 5
⊙ Blanc de Blancs Pas Dosé M. Cl. '21	♟♟ 6
⊙ Note di Bianco '23	♟♟ 4
● Note di Rosso '22	♟♟ 5

Zisola

c.da Zisola
96017 Noto [SR]
(+39 0931839288
☻ www.mazzei.it

CELLAR SALES
PRE-BOOKED VISITS
ANNUAL PRODUCTION 120,000 bottles
HECTARES UNDER VINE 24.00
VITICULTURE METHOD Certified Organic
SUSTAINABLE WINERY

⊙ Contrada Zisola '22	♟♟ 7
● Noto Nero d'Avola Doppiozeta '21	♟♟ 6
● Noto Rosso Zisola '22	♟ 4
⊙ Sicilia Grillo Azisa '23	♟ 4

SARDINIA

"Sardinia is almost a continent, despite its small size. Its geological structure is one of the most complex in the world, its landscape shifting with endless variety, much like the veins of minerals that run beneath its surface." We borrow these words from writer Marcello Serra, who penned them in 1959 to describe the region you'll read about in the following pages. We do so because we firmly believe this definition perfectly fits Sardinian viticulture.

The sheer variety of grape varietals, mostly indigenous or those that have adapted seamlessly to the island's soils, is astonishing. But what's even more remarkable is the diversity of soils, elevations, and microclimates you encounter as you travel through the region, from the granite of Gallura to the limestone of Coros, the clays of Ogliastra to the sands of Sulcis—just to name a few. Add to this significant climatic differences: in Barbagia and Mandrolisai, some vineyards sit at over 700 meters above sea level, representing true mountain viticulture, while others, as one might expect, grow just steps from the sea. There's also the value of old vines—still abundant despite the reckless uprootings of a few decades ago. This entire heritage, this biodiversity, is consistently found in the glass. Sardinian wines today aren't just good; they are increasingly distinctive, authentic, and capable of expressing their terroir of origin. This is why we'll never tire of insisting on a comprehensive overhaul of the appellations, particularly the regional ones, which are generic, outdated, and no longer represent what's happening in the region.

Now, let's turn to the latest award winners. For the first time, Giovanna Chessa's Cagnulari, Sella & Mosca's Cannonau Mustazzo, Pusole's Case Sparse Cannonau and Tenute Gregu's Pietraia Vermentino di Gallura, a white released three years after harvest, have reached the podium. Another new development (for the entire guide) is the "Rare Wines" section: 50 expressions of extraordinary quality produced in limited quantities. Here, the island earned six recognitions, spanning reds, whites, and two unmissable meditation wines: Malvasia di Bosa and Vernaccia di Oristano, two unique, precious wines that are highly regarded across the globe.

★★★Argiolas

via Roma, 28/30
09040 Serdiana [SU]
📞 +39 070740606
🌐 www.argiolas.it

CELLAR SALES
PRE-BOOKED VISITS
ANNUAL PRODUCTION 2,200,000 bottles
HECTARES UNDER VINE 250.00

With over 80 years of history, this winery has become a benchmark and one of the most representative estates in Sardinia's winemaking landscape. Cannonau, carignano, malvasia, nasco, bovale, and vermentino are the grapes cultivated in southern Sardinia, between Serdiana and Sulcis, highlighting a focus on indigenous varieties. The winery's range spans everything from daily drinking wines to more prestigious selections, all produced using sustainable methods that respect the land. A vast range of exceptional quality was presented. While the Turriga '20 once again affirms its status as a purebred classic, with notes of myrtle, ripe cherries, cinchona, and sweet spices, we were truly taken aback by the Angialis '19, a nasco from overripe grapes harvested in the Valli di Porto Pino. Ginger and candied orange join apricot sensations, the palate is supple, sweetness is measured, and its freshness undeniable. This year, it took the top spot. The Korem and Senes are also outstanding.

○ Angialis '19	♀♀♀ 7
● Turriga '20	♀♀ 8
● Cannonau di Sardegna Senes Ris. '20	♀♀ 5
● Is Solinas Carignano '21	♀♀ 5
● Korem Bovale '21	♀♀ 6
● Monica di Sardegna Sup. Iselis '21	♀♀ 4
○ Nasco di Cagliari Iselis '23	♀♀ 5
○ Vermentino di Sardegna Merì '23	♀♀ 4
● Cardanera Carignano '23	♀ 4
○ Nuragus di Cagliari S'Elegas '23	♀ 2
○ Vermentino di Sardegna Cerdena '21	♀ 7
○ Vermentino di Sardegna Is Argiolas '23	♀ 5
● Turriga '19	♀♀♀ 8
● Turriga '18	♀♀♀ 8
● Turriga '17	♀♀♀ 8
● Turriga '16	♀♀♀ 8
● Turriga '15	♀♀♀ 8

Audarya

loc. Sa Perdera
s.s. 466, km 10,100
09040 Serdiana [SU]
📞 +39 070 740437
🌐 www.audarya.it

CELLAR SALES
PRE-BOOKED VISITS
ANNUAL PRODUCTION 400,000 bottles
HECTARES UNDER VINE 50.00

Salvatore and Nicoletta Pala, with the help of their father Enrico, continue to run this winery nestled in the Serdiana area. In just a few years, Audarya has gained significant recognition both in Italy and abroad thanks to a range of wines that embodies the character of the territory. The estate covers over 30 hectares, where traditional Sardinian varieties like cannonau, vermentino, malvasia, nuragus, bovale, and monica are grown on clay-limestone soils. Several wines stood out in our tastings. The whites, in particular, excel, thanks to certain varietals, vinified dry, that deliver plenty of satisfaction, complementing their more well-known vermentino. We're talking about nasco, nuragus, and malvasia, with the latter offering the most delight. The Estissa is a wine of great aromatic complexity, with fruit standing out alongside floral and herbal sensations. Dry on the palate, it's fresh, exhibiting the right level of aromatic intensity. The Camminera '22 is also notable, as is the Kiobu '20, the latest addition to the lineup.

○ Cagliari Malvasia Estissa '22	♀♀ 5
○ Vermentino di Sardegna Camminera '22	♀♀ 3*
● Cannonau di Sardegna '22	♀♀ 3
● Kiobu '20	♀♀ 7
○ Nasco di Cagliari Bessiu '22	♀♀ 4
○ Nuragus di Cagliari '23	♀♀ 3
○ Bisai '22	♀ 5
⊘ Cannonau di Sardegna Rosato '23	♀ 3
○ Vermentino di Sardegna '23	♀ 3
○ Nasco di Cagliari Bessiu '21	♀♀♀ 4*
● Nuracada '19	♀♀♀ 5
● Nuracada Bovale '18	♀♀♀ 5
● Nuracada Bovale '17	♀♀♀ 5
○ Vermentino di Sardegna Camminera '20	♀♀♀ 5
● Cannonau di Sardegna '21	♀♀ 3*
● Nuracada '21	♀♀ 5
○ Vermentino di Sardegna Camminera '21	♀♀ 3*

Bentu Luna

via Meriaga, 1
09080 Neoneli [OR]
📞 +39 3470919610
emanuela.flore@bentuluna.com

CELLAR SALES
ANNUAL PRODUCTION 70,000 bottles
HECTARES UNDER VINE 25.00
SUSTAINABLE WINERY

Bentu Lunta is dedicated to telling the story of the land while preserving a heritage of old vineyards. Owned by Castello di Cicognola, the winery is located in the heart of Sardinia, near the town of Neoneli, adjacent to the Mandrolisai DOC appellation. Surrounded by woods, Mediterranean scrub, and mountains, the estate is home to century-old bush vines. The vineyards and production are overseen by winemaker Emanuela Fiore, whose character and passion help create wines with a strong sense of identity. The reds have long been the most convincing, and this year's range saw cannonau, bovale, and monica shine. The Sobi once again proves why it's a champion. It's the wine that best represents the estate, as it comes from old vines planted with a mix of varieties, as was done traditionally. The nose reveals hints of scrubland and red fruit, while the palate is voluminous yet sapid. Clean and deep, it has character in spades. The Mari, a 2022 Mandrolisai, is also delicious.

● Sobi '22	♥♥ 5
● Mandrolisai Rosso Mari '21	♥♥ 5
○ Vermentino di Sardegna Unda '23	♥♥ 4
● Cannonau di Sardegna Susu '22	♥ 5
○ V Vernaccia '23	♥ 6
● Sobi '21	♀♀♀ 5
● Sobi '20	♀♀♀ 5
● Sobi '19	♀♀♀ 5
● Cannonau di Sardegna Susu '21	♀♀ 5
● Mandrolisai Rosso Mari '21	♀♀ 5
● Mandrolisai Rosso Mari '20	♀♀ 5
● Mandrolisai Sup. Mari '19	♀♀ 5
● Susu '20	♀♀ 5
● Susu '19	♀♀ 5
○ V Vernaccia '22	♀♀ 6

Cantina Berritta

via Kennedy, 108
08022 Dorgali [NU]
📞 +39 3773256459
🌐 www.cantinaberritta.it

CELLAR SALES
PRE-BOOKED VISITS
ANNUAL PRODUCTION 40,000 bottles
HECTARES UNDER VINE 20.00
VITICULTURE METHOD Certified Organic
SUSTAINABLE WINERY

The area around Dorgali is characterized by vineyards and Mediterranean scrub, with the Oddoene Valley being particularly well-suited for cannonau. Here, the winery operates according to the principles of sustainable and artisanal agriculture. Cannonau, the star of their range, is cultivated alongside other indigenous varieties, but their portfolio also includes white wines, such as a vermentino and a white made from the unique panzale grape, a rare local variety. In recent years, multiple versions of Cannonau di Sardegna has been produced, depending on the age of the vines and the location of the vineyards. This year, we tasted reds from three different vintages, with the Bailanu '21 impressing us the most, even though the overall quality was excellent. It offers aromas of scrubland, blackberries, and spices, with a hint of iron. The palate is slender, elegant, and linear in its structure. The Montetondu and Nostranu, fresher and more immediately expressive versions, were also very good.

● Cannonau di Sardegna Baillanu '21	♥♥ 5
● Cannonau di Sardegna Cl. Montetundu '20	♥♥ 4
● Cannonau di Sardegna Nostranu '22	♥♥ 4
○ Vermentino di Sardegna Tziu Martine '23	♥ 4
● Cannonau di Sardegna Baillanu '19	♀♀ 6
● Cannonau di Sardegna Cl. Monte Tundu '19	♀♀ 4
● Cannonau di Sardegna Cl. Monte Tundu '17	♀♀ 4
● Cannonau di Sardegna Cl. Monte Tundu '16	♀♀ 4
● Cannonau di Sardegna Monte Tundu '20	♀♀ 6
● Cannonau di Sardegna Nostranu '21	♀♀ 4
● Cannonau di Sardegna Nostranu '20	♀♀ 4
● Cannonau di Sardegna Thurcalesu '20	♀♀ 4
● Cannonau di Sardegna Thurcalesu V. di Oddone '21	♀♀ 5
○ Panzale '22	♀♀ 5

SARDINIA

Francesco Cadinu

via Vittorio Emanuele II, 37
08024 Mamoiada [NU]
📞 +39 3290906997
🌐 www.francescocadinu.it

CELLAR SALES
PRE-BOOKED VISITS
ANNUAL PRODUCTION 12,000 bottles
HECTARES UNDER VINE 8.00
VITICULTURE METHOD Certified Organic

Francesco Cadinu embodies the spirit of the
vigneron. In Mamoiada, he dedicates himself,
along with his wife, to cultivating a few hectares
and producing artisanal wines. The vineyards,
nestled on the hills of Barbagia, reach notable
elevations in some areas and are home to very
old vines. Their wines reflect a production
philosophy that follows a cru system, aimed at
preserving the diverse nuances of the land and
its identity. All the single-vineyard wines
(Ghiradas) were impressive, starting with the
Fittiloghe, a red redolent of tobacco, thyme, and
bay leaf, with a lively, flavorful palate. The Elisi and
Loreto follow closely behind, but another
standout is the Perdas Longas, not a cru but a
blend from multiple vineyards. Despite lacking
the complexity of other Cannonau wines, it
reveals great balance, freshness, and elegance,
with juicy, energetic drinkability. The white and
rosé are also pleasant.

Cantina del Rimedio

loc. Rimedio
via Oristano, 6a
09170 Oristano
📞 +39 078333383
🌐 www.vinovernaccia.com

CELLAR SALES
PRE-BOOKED VISITS
ANNUAL PRODUCTION 260,000 bottles
HECTARES UNDER VINE 120.00

Known in recent years as Cantina della
Vernaccia, the cooperative is now reverting to
its original name, Cantina del Rimedio, reflecting
the winery's location. Founded in 1953, it has
developed production to perfection, particularly
excelling in Vernaccia di Oristano in all its forms,
including a Metodo Classico sparkling wine.
However, their range is not limited to Vernaccia;
it also includes various indigenous grapes like
cannonau, vermentino, monica, and especially the
hyper-local nieddera. The biggest surprise is the
Corbesa. This Vernaccia, though released under
the IGT rather than DOC designation, aptly
represents the characteristics of this famous
Sardinian wine, with an easy-drinking, pleasing
quality. Dry, with notes of nuts and sweet spices,
it also has significant sapidity and a light tannic
sensation that enlivens the palate. The Terresinis,
another vernaccia, is a classic white, fresh and
fragrant. Among the reds, the Cannonau di
Sardegna Maimone is very good.

● Cannonau di Sardegna Ghirada Fittiloghe '22	♈♈ 8
● Cannonau di Sardegna Perdas Longas '22	♈♈ 5
● Cannanau di Sardegna Ghirada Loreto '22	♈♈ 8
● Cannonau di Sardegna Ghirada Elisi '22	♈♈ 6
○ Mattio '23	♈ 5
☉ Tziu Simone '23	♈ 5
● Cannonau d Sardegna Ghirada Elisi '20	♈♈ 6
● Cannonau di Sardegna Ghirada Elisi '21	♈♈ 6
● Cannonau di Sardegna Ghirada Elisi '19	♈♈ 6
● Cannonau di Sardegna Ghirada Fittiloghe '20	♈♈ 8
● Cannonau di Sardegna Ghirada Fittiloghe '19	♈♈ 7
● Cannonau di Sardegna Pedras Longas '21	♈♈ 5
● Cannonau di Sardegna Perdas Longas '20	♈♈ 5
● Cannonau di Sardegna Perdas Longas '19	♈♈ 4

○ Corbesa Vernaccia	♈♈ 3
● Cannonau di Sardegna Maiomone '22	♈♈ 2*
● Montiprama Nieddera '21	♈♈ 3
○ Terresinis Vernaccia '23	♈♈ 3
○ Vermentino di Sardegna Is Arutas '23	♈♈ 2*
○ Aristanis M. Cl. Brut	♈ 3
● Cannonau di Sardegna Corash Ris. '20	♈ 3
☉ Seu '22	♈ 2
○ Vernaccia di Oristano Sup. Jughissa '08	♈♈♈ 3*
● Cannonau di Sardegna Corash Ris. '18	♈♈ 3
● Cannonau di Sardegna Corash Ris. '16	♈♈ 3
● Cannonau di Sardegna Corash Ris. '15	♈♈ 3
● Cannonau di Sardegna Corash Ris. '12	♈♈ 3
● Cannonau di Sardegna Corash Ris. '11	♈♈ 3*
● Cannonau di Sardegna Maimone '17	♈♈ 2*
● Cannonau di Sardegna Maiomone '15	♈♈ 2*
○ Terresinis '12	♈♈ 2*

Cantina di Calasetta

via Roma, 134
09011 Calasetta [SU]
☎ +39 078188413
✉ www.cantinadicalasetta.it

CELLAR SALES
PRE-BOOKED VISITS
ANNUAL PRODUCTION 450,000 bottles
HECTARES UNDER VINE 120.00

Cantine di Dolianova

loc. Sant'Esu
s.s. 387 km 17,150
09041 Dolianova [SU]
☎ +39 070744101
✉ www.cantinedidolianova.it

CELLAR SALES
PRE-BOOKED VISITS
ANNUAL PRODUCTION 4,000,000 bottles
HECTARES UNDER VINE 1200.00

From the 13 growers who started in 1932, the cooperative has grown to over 300 contributors today. Supported by a team of skilled technicians and managers, the winery maintains high-quality production. The grapes hail from southeast Sardinia, specifically from the island of Sant'Antioco, an area characterized by sandy soils, which allows for the cultivation of century-old vines on their own, ungrafted rootstocks. Carignano, the leading variety, is produced in different styles here, while vermentino and moscato serve as the basis for their line of white wines. Two wines made it to our final round, confirming the respectability of their range. Both are Carignano del Sulcis, but they differ greatly. The Dèsea is a fresh, approachable, light, and vibrant version. Despite its simplicity, it's true to its varietal and terroir. The Bricco delle Piane is a selection that offers ripe red fruit, sweet spices, and light hints of oak. The two 932s, a white and a red, also rank among the best. The rest of the range is solid, with remarkably fair pricing.

This winery has managed to pair quantity with quality for over 70 years, producing a range of well-crafted, daily drinking wines alongside notable selections. Southern Sardinia's classic varieties are cultivated, from barbera sarda to cannonau, nasco, nuragus, monica, and vermentino. The numbers speak for themselves: 300 cooperative members and an annual production of 4 million bottles. It's an example of how producing a lot can still mean producing something very good. The lineup presented proves its worth, with no fewer than nine wines of high quality, particularly some premium selections. We start with the whites. The Perlas is a delightful Nuragus di Cagliari, elegant and sapid. The Montesicci excels in complexity and flavor, with an extra year of aging adding further depth. Among the reds, we appreciated the Terresicci, made from barbera sarda grapes, and the Blasio, a Cannonau Riserva from 2017.

● Carignano del Sulcis Bricco delle Piane - Cala di Seta Ris. '21	♟♟ 5
● Carignano del Sulcis Desèa - Cala di Seta '22	♟♟ 3*
● Cannonau di Sardegna Desàia - Cala di Seta '22	♟♟ 3
● Carignano del Sulcis Sup. 932 - Cala di Seta '21	♟♟ 6
○ Vermentino di Sardegna 932 - Cala di Seta '23	♟♟ 5
● Carignano del Sulcis Inrigo '22	♟ 4
⊙ Carignano del Sulcis Rosato Destè - Cala di Seta '23	♟ 3
○ Vermentino di Sardegna Demà - Cala di Seta '23	♟ 3
● Carignano del Sulcis Tupei '10	♟♟♟ 2*
● Carignano del Sulcis Bricco delle Piane - Cala di Seta Ris. '19	♟♟ 4

● Cannonau di Sardegna Blasio Ris. '17	♟♟ 3
● Monica di Sardegna Arenada '21	♟♟ 2*
○ Nasco di Cagliari Montesicci '22	♟♟ 3
○ Nuragus di Cagliari Perlas '23	♟♟ 2*
● Terresicci '19	♟♟ 5
○ Vermentino di Sardegna Prendas '23	♟♟ 2*
● Cannonau di Sardegna Anzenas '21	♟ 2
⊙ Cannonau di Sardegna Rosato Rosada '23	♟ 3
● Falconaro '22	♟ 3
● Falconaro '11	♟♟♟ 3*
● Terresicci '14	♟♟♟ 5
● Falconaro '21	♟♟ 3
○ Moscato di Sardegna Passito '15	♟♟ 5
○ Nuragus di Cagliari Perlas '21	♟♟ 2*
○ Vermentino di Sardegna Prendas '22	♟♟ 2*

Canu

loc. Balaiana
07020 Luogosanto [SS]
(») +39 3511633419
⊛ www.cantinacanu.com

CELLAR SALES
PRE-BOOKED VISITS
ANNUAL PRODUCTION 35,000 bottles
HECTARES UNDER VINE 8.00

Canu is a young operation with deep roots in the past. Its name comes from a traditional 19th-century farmstead that's been carefully restored to house a modern winery. The estate covers 230 hectares in the Luogosanto area, with eight hectares under vine. Located in the heart of Gallura, the vineyards are planted on granite soils, influenced by the nearby sea and benefiting from the area's signature day-night temperature swings. Three wines are offered: a red, a rosé, and a white. In terms of the wines themselves, we begin with this last: the Deispanta is an excellent Vermentino di Gallura, redolent of aromatic herbs, white fruit, and hints of anise and almond. The palate is sapid, with a slightly bitter finish.

○ Vermentino di Gallura Sup. Deispanta '23	♥♥	4
○ Vermentino di Gallura Sup. Deispanta '22	♀♀	4
○ Vermentino di Gallura Sup. Deispanta '21	♀♀	4

Cantina Castiadas

loc. Olia Speciosa
via della Cantina, 2/4
09040 Castiadas [CA]
(») +39 0709949004
⊛ www.cantinacastiadas.com

CELLAR SALES
PRE-BOOKED VISITS
ANNUAL PRODUCTION 200,000 bottles
HECTARES UNDER VINE 150.00
SUSTAINABLE WINERY

The cooperative takes its name from the inland town that sits on the coast, marking the subzone of Cannonau di Sardegna Capo Ferrato. Vermentino, carignano, and other indigenous grapes are used to create a range of wines that reflect the area's identity, with a focus on quality. However, cannonau is the true star here, available in various versions and styles (including a Metodo Classico sparkling version) that showcase the nuances this grape variety develops in the local terroir. Their work reflects the evolution of the winery's efforts in recent years. The range produced is extensive, with several wines ranking among the top in our tastings. Among the whites, the two Vermentino di Sardegnas stood out, with the Praidis being simpler and the Notteri more complex. The already mentioned Saeprus, a Metodo Classico Pas Dosé Cannonau, performed superbly. The best of all, however, was the Cannonau Riserva '19, an authentic and characterful Capo Ferrato. Minty and eucalyptus notes complement ever-present red fruit, with a truly exemplary balance of sapidity and tannins.

● Cannonau di Sardegna Capo Ferrato Ris. '19	♥♥	4
○ Spumante M. Cl. Pas Dosé Saeprus '21	♥♥	5
○ Vermentino di Sardegna Notteri '23	♥♥	3
○ Vermentino di Sardegna Praidis '23	♥♥	2*
● Cannonau di Sardegna Capo Ferrato Rei '21	♥	3
Cannonau di Sardegna Capo Ferrato Rosato '23	♥	2
● Monica di Sardegna Genis '22	♥	2
● Parolto '19	♥	4
○ Vermentino di Sardegna Notte '22	♥	4
● Cannonau di Sardegna Capo Ferrato Rei '20	♀♀	3*
● Cannonau di Sardegna Capo Ferrato Rei '09	♀♀	2*

Giovanni Maria Cherchi

loc. Sa Pala e Sa Chessa
07049 Usini [SS]
☎ +39 079380273
✉ www.vinicolacherchi.it

Chessa

via San Giorgio
07049 Usini [SS]
☎ +39 3283747069
✉ www.cantinechessa.it

SARDINIA

CELLAR SALES
PRE-BOOKED VISITS
ANNUAL PRODUCTION 180,000 bottles
HECTARES UNDER VINE 30.00

CELLAR SALES
PRE-BOOKED VISITS
ANNUAL PRODUCTION 43,000 bottles
HECTARES UNDER VINE 15.00

In establishing the winery, its founder aimed to tell the story of Usini and its clay-limestone soils, an ambitious vision that continues to shape production to this day. The estate's 30 hectares under vines benefit from the influence of the sea and elevations of 200 meters above sea level, factors that contribute to the freshness and aromatic complexity of the various wines produced here. The cagnulari, vermentino, and cannonau grapes cultivated are featured across three lines (Classici, Billia, and Speciali), with additional offerings that include a passito and a Metodo Classico. Salvatore Cherchi presented a top-tier range for tasting. The iconic Tuvaoes, a hallmark of Vermentino di Sardegna, stands out. Aromas of white flowers and fruit blend with hints of mint, almond, and aromatic herbs. On the palate, it's elegant, fresh, and sapid. The Cagnulari '22 is also excellent, with notes of plum and black pepper. The close-knit, full-bodied Luzzana impresses, while the two Billia wines, a Cagnulari and a Vermentino, prove simple but impeccable.

Giovanna Chessa has bet on the potential of vermentino and cagnulari to showcase the potential of Usini wine country. As a passionate producer, she excels in preserving the distinct characteristics of vines rooted in the area's clay-limestone soils, which are situated on hillsides caressed by breezes. The range produced is marked by great finesse and drinkability, offering freshness and elegance, with an ability to age gracefully. In addition to whites and reds, there's also a Moscato Passito. The 2022 version of the Cagnulari is the most elegant, multifaceted, and complex ever presented. Plum aromas are joined by a touch of vanilla and spice, while the palate is pervasive yet fine and deep. The tannins are soft and well-integrated with the wine's structure, and the palate reveals vibrant acidity. The two Vermentinos are also very good, each distinct. The Mattariga is an emblem of Usini's soils, while the C'era Una Volta is the result of time-honored production methods that skillfully showcase the varietal.

○ Vermentino di Sardegna Tuvaoes '23	♟♟♟ 4*
● Cagnulari '22	♟♟ 3*
● Luzzana '22	♟♟ 5
● Billia Cagnulari '23	♟ 2
○ Vermentino di Sardegna Billia '23	♟ 2
○ Vermentino di Sardegna Tuvaoes '20	♟♟♟ 3*
○ Vermentino di Sardegna Tuvaoes '16	♟♟♟ 3*
○ Vermentino di Sardegna Tuvaoes '88	♟♟♟ 4*
● Cagnulari '21	♟♟ 3*
● Cannonau di Sardegna '20	♟♟ 3*
● Cannonau di Sardegna '16	♟♟ 3*
● Luzzana '18	♟♟ 4
○ Vermentino di Sardegna Tuvaoes '22	♟♟ 4
○ Vermentino di Sardegna Tuvaoes '21	♟♟ 4
○ Vermentino di Sardegna Tuvaoes '17	♟♟ 3*

● Cagnulari '22	♟♟♟ 4*
○ Vermentino di Sardegna C'era Una Volta '20	♟♟ 7
○ Vermentino di Sardegna Mattariga '23	♟♟ 3
● Cannonau di Sardegna Gemmanera '20	♟ 4
● Lugherra '19	♟ 5
● Cagnulari '21	♟♟ 3*
● Cagnulari '19	♟♟ 3*
● Cagnulari '18	♟♟ 3*
● Cannonau di Sardegna Gemmanera '19	♟♟ 4
○ Moscato di Sardegna Passito Kentàales '21	♟♟ 5
○ Moscato di Sardegna Passito Kentàales '18	♟♟ 5
○ Vermentino di Sardegna Mattariga '22	♟♟ 3
○ Vermentino di Sardegna Mattariga '19	♟♟ 3

Attilio Contini

via Genova, 48/50
09072 Cabras [OR]
(+39 0783290806
www.vinicontini.com

CELLAR SALES
PRE-BOOKED VISITS
ANNUAL PRODUCTION 2,000,000 bottles
HECTARES UNDER VINE 200.00
VITICULTURE METHOD Certified Organic
SUSTAINABLE WINERY

The winemaking history of Oristano is intimately bound up with this producer, founded in 1898 by Salvatore Contini. Over the years, the winery grew under the leadership of Salvatore's son, Attilio, while today the fourth generation, represented by cousins Alessandro and Mauro, keeps the legacy alive as a beacon of Sardinian excellence. A standout in the winery's portfolio is the Vernaccia di Oristano, one of the island's oenological gems. A wide range was presented, with several wines at the top of our tastings. We start with the Flor, the one that earned a place in our final round. This younger wine, as its name suggests, is made with an oxidative method, allowing the development of a "flor" yeast layer. Complex on the nose with notes of nuts and candied orange, it has a sapid, pervasive palate. Two other Vernaccia-based wines were also very good: the Pontis, a passito, and the Karmis, a dry, flavorful wine.

La Contralta

loc. Enas
via Giovanni Pascoli
07020 Loiri Porto San Paolo [SS]
(+39 3496806547
www.lacontralta.it

CELLAR SALES
PRE-BOOKED VISITS
ACCOMMODATION
ANNUAL PRODUCTION 30,000 bottles
HECTARES UNDER VINE 11.00
SUSTAINABLE WINERY

The winery gets its name from the small beach of Palau in northern Sardinia, situated beneath the famous "Bear Rock". Here, the vines thrive in a landscape dominated by granite and Mediterranean scrub, close to the sea. The main grape varieties cultivated are cannonau, carignano, and vermentino. The estate is overseen by Roberto Gariup, who is also active at Enas, in Porto San Paolo, where the producer has additional vineyards and a brand-new production facility. Despite being a young winery, the quality is very high. Three wines reached the final round in three different categories. The M'Illumino is a Carignano that captures the energy of Gallura's granite-rich terrain. The Le Ultime Cose is a complex passito, where sweetness is nicely balanced by freshness. The Sicut Erat is a standout in its category: skin maceration brings out aromas of candied lemon, ginger, and dried orange. The palate is refined, deep, and impeccably clean, without any bitterness or clenching: you'll find it in our "rare wines" section.

○ Vernaccia di Oristano Flor '20	♟♟ 4
⊙ I Giganti Rosato '23	♟♟ 3
○ Karmis Cuvée '23	♟♟ 3
○ Pontis '22	♟♟ 5
○ Vermentino di Sardegna Mamaioa '23	♟♟ 3
● Cannonau di Sardegna 'Inu Ris. '19	♟ 4
○ I Giganti Bianco '22	♟ 4
● I Giganti Rosso '21	♟ 5
○ Vermentino di Gallura Elibaria '23	♟ 3
● Barrile '13	♟♟♟ 7
● Barrile '11	♟♟♟ 6
○ Pontis '00	♟♟♟ 4
○ Vernaccia di Oristano Antico Gregori '76	♟♟♟ 8
○ Vernaccia di Oristano Antico Gregori	♟♟♟ 7
○ Vernaccia di Oristano Ris. '88	♟♟♟ 4*
○ Vernaccia di Oristano Ris. '71	♟♟♟ 5

○ Le Ultime Cose '22	♟♟ 5
● M'Illumino Carignano '22	♟♟ 8
● Cannonau di Sardegna L'Ora Grande '22	♟♟ 5
○ Vermentino di Gallura Sup. Fiore Del Sasso '22	♟♟ 5
○ Tu Enas Vermentino '23	♟ 5
● Cannonau di Sardegna L'Ora Grande '20	♟♟♟ 5
● Cannonau di Sardegna L'Ora Grande '19	♟♟♟ 5
● Cannonau di Sardegna L'Ora Grande '21	♟♟ 5
○ Sicut Erat Vermentino '21	♟♟ 6
○ Vermentino di Gallura Sup. Fiore del Sasso '21	♟♟ 5
○ Vermentino di Gallura Sup. Fiore del Sasso '20	♟♟ 5

Antonella Corda

loc. Pranu Raimondo
s.s. 466 km 6,800
09040 Serdiana [SU]
(》 +39 0707966300
❀ www.antonellacorda.it

CELLAR SALES
PRE-BOOKED VISITS
ACCOMMODATION
ANNUAL PRODUCTION 85,500 bottles
HECTARES UNDER VINE 18.00
VITICULTURE METHOD Certified Organic

The young agronomist Antonella Corda is
crafting wines of rare elegance with great skill,
effectively charting a new course for cannonau
and beyond. Bold and visionary, she has made
her mark on Sardinia with wines sourced from
the island's southern regions. Her range is a true
expression of her homeland, focusing on
cannonau, as well as nuragus and vermentino,
vinified with meticulous care using stainless
steel, wood, and amphorae. This year saw an
outstanding performance, with several wines
reaching the heights of regional excellence. The
Cannonau Riserva stands out as truly
exemplary—complex, multifaceted, and yet
light and fresh, as only a great Cannonau can be.
Bay leaf, myrtle, and blackberry on the nose
lead to a spirited palate with velvety tannins.
The Cannonau '22 is also excellent. Among the
whites, we particularly appreciated the Nuragus
di Cagliari. Both Vermentinos are remarkable,
especially the 2023 and the unique Ziru, aged
in amphora.

Cantina Dorgali

via Piemonte, 11
08022 Dorgali [NU]
(》 +39 078496143
❀ www.cantinadorgali.it

CELLAR SALES
PRE-BOOKED VISITS
ANNUAL PRODUCTION 1,500,000 bottles
HECTARES UNDER VINE 550.00
SUSTAINABLE WINERY

Dorgali's members manage more than 600
hectares of vineyards between the Tyrrhenian
coast of the Gulf of Orosei and Supramonte, an
area renowned for producing cannonau, the
island's most iconic grape. The winery's approach
is rooted in traditional bush-trained vines,
single-varietal vinification, and innovative
offerings such as rosé and sparkling cannonau.
Their portfolio also includes vermentino whites
and sweet wines made from traditional aromatic
grapes. A respectable lineup, though we expected
more from certain wines, given the producer's
past glory. That said, we particularly enjoyed the
Icorè '22, a delightful Cannonau di Sardegna with
cherry aromas and a sapid palate. The Fùili '21
and Hortos '20 are also good, both products of
one of the best cannonau parcels cultivated by
their grower members.

● Cannonau di Sardegna Ris. '21	♟♟♟ 7
● Cannonau di Sardegna '22	♟♟ 4
○ Nuragus di Cagliari '23	♟♟ 3*
○ Vermentino di Sardegna '23	♟♟ 3
○ Ziru '21	♟♟ 6
● Cannonau di Sardegna '19	♟♟♟ 4*
● Cannonau di Sardegna '17	♟♟♟ 3*
● Cannonau di Sardegna '16	♟♟♟ 3*
● Cannonau di Sardegna Ris. '19	♟♟♟ 7
● Cannonau di Sardegna '21	♟♟ 4
● Cannonau di Sardegna '20	♟♟ 4
● Cannonau di Sardegna '18	♟♟ 5
○ Nuragus di Cagliari '22	♟♟ 3*
○ Vermentino di Sardegna '20	♟♟ 3*
○ Ziru '18	♟♟ 6

● Cannonau di Sardegna Icorè '22	♟♟ 3
● Fùili '21	♟♟ 5
● Hortos '20	♟♟ 6
● Cannonau di Sardegna Cl. D53 '13	♟♟♟ 4*
● Cannonau di Sardegna Cl. D53 '12	♟♟♟ 4*
● Cannonau di Sardegna Vinìola Ris. '10	♟♟♟ 4*
● Cannonau di Sardegna Vinìola Ris. '07	♟♟♟ 3*
● Cannonau di Sardegna Vinìola Ris. '06	♟♟♟ 3*
● Hortos '08	♟♟♟ 6
● Cannonau di Sardegna Cl. D53 '19	♟♟ 5
● Cannonau di Sardegna Cl. D53 '18	♟♟ 5
○ Cannonau di Sardegna Rosato Filieri '21	♟♟ 2*
● Hortos '16	♟♟ 6
● Hortos '15	♟♟ 6
○ Vermentino di Sardegna Filine '22	♟♟ 3
○ Vermentino di Sardegna Filine '21	♟♟ 3

SARDINIA

Li Duni

loc. Alza Longa
07030 Badesi [SS]
C +39 0799144480
www.cantinaliduni.it

CELLAR SALES
PRE-BOOKED VISITS
ANNUAL PRODUCTION 70,000 bottles
HECTARES UNDER VINE 22.00
SUSTAINABLE WINERY

In Gallura dialect, "Li Duni" means "the dunes," referring to the sandy slopes where the area's vineyards are situated. Located in the far north of Sardinia, along the coast facing Corsica to the west, the village of Badesi lies near the border of the Vermentino di Gallura DOCG appellation. The sandy soils allow for many ungrafted vines to thrive here. Li Duni jealously oversees a significant portion of them, drawing on their grapes to produce its flagship wines. An authentic example is the Nozzinnà, a unique wine distinguished by its slight residual sugar, perfectly balanced by sapidity and freshness. Ripe yellow fruit and curry plant dominate the nose, while the palate is pervasive and pleasantly soft. Another wine from ungrafted vines is the Tajanu, a blend of native Sardinian grapes. The 2021 vintage made for a distinctly Mediterranean red. The Cannonau Nalboni is excellent, and the two Extra Dry sparkling wines are delightful.

Fradiles

loc. Creccherì
via S. Pertini, 2
08030 Atzara [NU]
C +39 3331761683
paolo.savoldo@fradiles.it

CELLAR SALES
PRE-BOOKED VISITS
ANNUAL PRODUCTION 20,000 bottles
HECTARES UNDER VINE 12.00
SUSTAINABLE WINERY

In Atzara, within the historic Mandrolisai district (and DOC production zone), at elevations spanning 500-700 meters, lie 12 hectares of vineyards, some of which are ancient and bush-trained. Paolo Savoldo, together with his uncles and cousins, runs a winery where family bonds are intertwined with a shared passion. The focus is on cannonau, bovale, and monica grapes, varieties represented with an artisanal and authentic production style. The lineup presented put in an outstanding performance, with three selections reaching our finals. Regardless of the results, we can confidently say that these are three great wines, traditionally-styled and Mediterranean. At the top is the Istentu '21, a red of great complexity, with cherry and underbrush tones, an energetic, fleshy palate, and impressive depth. The Azzàra from the Domos de Pedra line is also excellent, embodying what Mandrolisai is all about. Finally, the younger version, the Fradiles '22, proves a simple but highly characterful wine.

• Tajanu '21	♟♟ 4
○ Vermentino di Gallura Sup. Nozzinnà '22	♟♟ 5
• Cannonau di Sardegna Nalboni '22	♟♟ 3
⊙ Li Junchi Extra Dry Rosé '23	♟♟ 4
○ Vermentino di Sardegna Extra Dry Li Junchi '23	♟♟ 4
⊙ Cannonau di Sardegna Rosato Minnammentu '23	♟ 3
○ Vermentino di Gallura Nou '23	♟ 3
○ Vermentino di Gallura Sup. Renabianca '23	♟ 4
• Cannonau di Sardegna Nalboni '20	♟♟ 3*
○ Vermentino di Gallura Nou '22	♟♟ 3
○ Vermentino di Gallura Sup. Nozzinnà '21	♟♟ 5
○ Vermentino di Gallura Sup. Renabianca '22	♟♟ 4
○ Vermentino di Gallura Sup. Renabianca '21	♟♟ 3

• Mandrolisai Fradiles '22	♟♟♟ 3*
• Istentu '21	♟♟ 5
• Mandrolisai Azzàra Domos de Pedra '22	♟♟ 3*
• Bagadiu Bovale '22	♟♟ 3
• Mandrolisai Memorias Creccherie '22	♟♟ 7
• Mandrolisai Sup. Angraris '20	♟♟ 8
• Mandrolisai Sup. Antiogu '21	♟♟ 4
○ Bianco Dolce	♟ 4
○ Funtanafrisca Domos De Pedra '23	♟ 4
• Mandrolisai Fradiles '20	♟♟♟ 3*
• Mandrolisai Rosso Fradiles '21	♟♟♟ 3*
• Mandrolisai Sup. Antiogu '11	♟♟♟ 5
• Bagadiu '21	♟♟ 3*
• Mandrolisai Sup. Antiogu '17	♟♟ 4

★Giuseppe Gabbas

via Trieste, 59
08100 Nuoro
(☎) +39 078433745
⊛ www.gabbas.it

Cantina Giba

via Principe di Piemonte, 16
09010 Giba [SU]
(☎) +39 0781689718
⊛ www.cantinagiba.it

CELLAR SALES
PRE-BOOKED VISITS
ANNUAL PRODUCTION 70,000 bottles
HECTARES UNDER VINE 20.00

CELLAR SALES
ANNUAL PRODUCTION 80,000 bottles
HECTARES UNDER VINE 11.20
SUSTAINABLE WINERY

Giuseppe Gabbas is undoubtedly one of the most noteworthy and influential interpreters of cannonau. His work has elevated the grape's status while also honoring the land of Barbagia. Since 1974, his meticulous vineyard practices, with low yields and careful attention during production, have resulted in wines of rare complexity and craftsmanship. Alongside cannonau, he cultivates bovale and vermentino with the same dedication. This last grape shines in the only white produced, the Manzanile, a quintessential example of Vermentino di Sardegna in Barbagia, skillfully expressing the breakdown of granitic rock and elevation. Among the reds, there is an abundance of choices: the Lillové is approachable and fresh, the Arbòre soft and pervasive. The Dule is the purebred classic: close-knit and elegant, with aromas of red fruit and scrubland, velvety tannins, and an exceptional sapidity.

Established in 2013 following the renovation of the 6Mura winery, the estate had a clear goal from the outset: to represent its territory as authentically as possible through its wines. Based in Sulcis, the estate's flagship grape is carignano, grown as bush-trained vines on their own roots, with vermentino also cultivated. Both are bottled under the estate's premium line, 6Mura, as well as the more accessible Giba line. Additionally, the estate has pursued an intriguing project with a Metodo Classico made from carignano grapes. The Carignano del Sulcis Riserva '21 6Mura is a true standout, taking home a gold with its complex and captivating nose, where red fruit and spice merge with hints of scrubland and myrtle. The palate is warm and pervasive, with a pronounced sapidity. The Vermentino from the same line is also excellent—flavorful and satisfying. The two Giba wines are delightful, particularly the Carignano '22.

● Cannonau di Sardegna Cl. Dule '21	♥♥♥ 5
● Cannonau di Sardegna Cl. Arbòre '21	♥♥ 4
● Cannonau di Sardegna Lillové '23	♥♥ 3*
○ Vermentino di Sardegna Manzanile '23	♥♥ 3
● Cannonau di Sardegna Cl. Dule '20	♀♀♀ 5
● Cannonau di Sardegna Cl. Dule '19	♀♀♀ 5
● Cannonau di Sardegna Cl. Dule '18	♀♀♀ 5
● Cannonau di Sardegna Cl. Dule '17	♀♀♀ 4*
● Cannonau di Sardegna Cl. Dule '16	♀♀♀ 4*
● Cannonau di Sardegna Cl. Dule '15	♀♀♀ 4*
● Cannonau di Sardegna Cl. Dule '13	♀♀♀ 4*
● Cannonau di Sardegna Cl. Dule '12	♀♀♀ 4*
● Cannonau di Sardegna Cl. Dule '11	♀♀♀ 4*
● Cannonau di Sardegna Dule Ris. '10	♀♀♀ 4*
● Cannonau di Sardegna Dule Ris. '09	♀♀♀ 3*

● Carignano del Sulcis 6Mura Ris. '21	♥♥♥ 6
○ Cagliari Vermentino Sup. 6Mura '23	♥♥ 4
● Carignano del Sulcis Giba '22	♥♥ 3
○ Cagliari Vermentino Sup. Giba '23	♥ 3
⊙ Carignano del Sulcis Rosato 6Mura '19	♥ 2
● Carignano del Sulcis 6Mura '12	♀♀♀ 5
● Carignano del Sulcis 6Mura '11	♀♀♀ 5
● Carignano del Sulcis 6Mura '10	♀♀♀ 5
● Carignano del Sulcis 6Mura '09	♀♀♀ 5
● Carignano del Sulcis 6Mura Ris. '18	♀♀♀ 5
● Carignano del Sulcis 6Mura Ris. '17	♀♀♀ 5
● Carignano del Sulcis 6Mura Ris. '16	♀♀♀ 5
● Carignano del Sulcis 6Mura Ris. '15	♀♀♀ 5
● Carignano del Sulcis 6Mura Ris. '19	♀♀ 5
● Carignano del Sulcis 6Mura Rosso Ris. '20	♀♀ 6

Tenute Gregu

loc. Giuncheddu, 2
07023 Calangianus [SS]
☎ +39 3519156527
✆ www.tenutegregu.com

Luca Gungui

c.so Vittorio Emanuele, 21
08024 Mamoiada [NU]
☎ +39 3473320735
cantinagungui@tiscali.it

CELLAR SALES
PRE-BOOKED VISITS
ACCOMMODATION
ANNUAL PRODUCTION 90,000 bottles
HECTARES UNDER VINE 30.00
SUSTAINABLE WINERY

ANNUAL PRODUCTION 9,000 bottles
HECTARES UNDER VINE 2.30

For about 20 years, the Gregu family has invested in one of the most beautiful estates in the Gallura region. Here, vermentino finds one of its natural habitats, flourishing in granite soils surrounded by Mediterranean scrub, olive trees, and rocks. The white wines produced reflect the character of their birthplace, with vermentino revealing unexpected longevity. There is also space for a few cannonaus. Every wine is vinified with deep respect for the varieties and the land. The entire range demonstrates the quality achieved here, with some wines standing as true emblems of their type. The Pitraia is one example. Part of the newly launched Monogram line, it's released three years after harvest. Aromas strike a balance between primary fruit and subtle tertiary notes, while the palate is energetic and dynamic, showing that aging only enhances certain bottles. The Grehos, a red from the same line, is also outstanding, but there's also room for younger, more approachable wines like the Rìas '23. The rest of the range is impeccable.

Luca Gungui, a young and passionate winemaker, is the face behind this small yet remarkable producer based in Mamoiada. Their cannonau is cultivated on bush vines at elevations ranging from 500 to 850 meters, rooted in granite soils low in clay and rich in minerals. The winery's offerings are limited but all exhibit a sapid, balanced character, successfully highlighting the precise interplay between the terroir and the grape variety. Three Cannonaus were presented, all of exceptional quality. Two are single-vineyard wines from historic vines that proudly bear the name of their plot. Both are youthful, embodying a fresh, lively, elegant expression of the grape, but also plenty of character. The third is a Riserva, meticulously selected from the finest vineyards. It's a standout, offering aromas of blackberry, cherries, currants, underbrush, spices, and resins that introduce a complex, sapid, and well-balanced palate with impressive depth and finesse.

○ Vermentino di Gallura Sup. Pitraia Monogram '21	♀♀♀ 8
● Grehos Monogram '19	♀♀ 8
○ Vermentino di Gallura Rias '23	♀♀ 3*
● Cala Granis Carignano '22	♀♀ 8
◉ Cannonau di Sardegna Rosato Siré '23	♀♀ 3
○ Vermentino di Gallura Sup. Selenu '22	♀♀ 4
● Cannonau di Sardegna Raighinas '21	♀♀ 3
○ Vermentino di Gallura Rias '22	♀♀ 3
○ Vermentino di Gallura Rias '21	♀♀ 3
○ Vermentino di Gallura Rias '19	♀♀ 3
○ Vermentino di Gallura Sup. Selenu '21	♀♀ 3*
○ Vermentino di Gallura Sup. Selenu '20	♀♀ 3*
○ Vermentino di Gallura Sup. Selenu '19	♀♀ 3

● Cannonau di Sardegna Berteru Ris. '22	♀♀ 6
● Cannonau di Sardegna Nuraghe Sas de Melas '23	♀♀ 6
● Cannonau di Sardegna Sa Cava de Pulenaria '23	♀♀ 6
● Cannonau di Sardegna Berteru '20	♀♀ 6
● Cannonau di Sardegna Berteru '19	♀♀ 6
● Cannonau di Sardegna Berteru '18	♀♀ 6
◉ Cannonau di Sardegna Berteru En Rose '19	♀♀ 8
● Cannonau di Sardegna Berteru Nuraghe Sas de Melas '21	♀♀ 6
● Cannonau di Sardegna Berteru Ris. '21	♀♀ 8
● Cannonau di Sardegna Berteru Ris. '20	♀♀ 8
● Cannonau di Sardegna Berteru Ris. '19	♀♀ 8
● Cannonau di Sardegna Sa Cava de Pulenaria '22	♀♀ 6

Antichi Poderi Jerzu

via Umberto I, 1
08044 Jerzu [OG]
📞 +39 078270028
🌐 www.jerzuantichipoderi.it

CELLAR SALES
PRE-BOOKED VISITS
ANNUAL PRODUCTION 1,500,000 bottles
HECTARES UNDER VINE 750.00

In the landscape of Sardinian cooperatives, this historic winery stands out on the island's eastern coast. Located in Jerzu, one of the three subzones of the Cannonau di Sardegna DOC, this Ogliastra-based producer has evolved significantly over the years without losing its identity. It has also undertaken important initiatives, such as dividing the grapes delivered according to a zoning program, which results in various cannonau wines based on the different soils where the vines are cultivated. The lineup presented showcases a clear expression of single-vineyard winemaking, with their Cannonaus, all vinified identically, highlighting the differences between the vineyards. The two Baccu wines, the S'Alinu and Is Baus, prove to be elegant, marked by masterful drinkability and a focus on depth rather than power. The former is more sapid and close-knit, while the latter is finer and more delicate. The Cinquesse is a fuller-bodied Cannonau, but still maintains its drinkability. The Filare, a delightful Vermentino di Sardegna, features notes of Mediterranean herbs.

● Cannonau di Sardegna Baccu Is Baus Ris. '19	♟♟ 5
● Cannonau di Sardegna Baccu S'Alinu Ris. '19	♟♟ 5
● Cannonau di Sardegna Cinquesse '20	♟♟ 4
● Cannonau di Sardegna J osto Miglior Ris. '09	♟♟♟ 4*
● Cannonau di Sardegna Josto Miglior Ris. '05	♟♟♟ 4
● Radames '01	♟♟♟ 5
● Cannonau di Sardegna Jerzu Bantu '20	♟♟ 2*
● Cannonau di Sardegna Jerzu Marghia '19	♟♟ 4
○ Vermentino di Sardegna Telavè '20	♟♟ 2*

Tenuta Masone Mannu

loc. Su Canale
07020 Monti [SS]
📞 +39 078947140
🌐 www.tenutamasonemannu.it

CELLAR SALES
PRE-BOOKED VISITS
ACCOMMODATION
ANNUAL PRODUCTION 90,000 bottles
HECTARES UNDER VINE 30.00
SUSTAINABLE WINERY

The 2018 purchase of Masone Mannu by Tenuta Mara brought with it a decisive push toward environmental sustainability. The goal was to eliminate the use of herbicides and chemical fertilizers to achieve healthy grapes, working according to biodynamic principles. The estate, located just a few kilometers from Olbia, spans 60 hectares. Among the vineyards, you'll find vermentino, cannonau, bovale, and carignano, as well as merlot and cabernet sauvignon, which have acclimatized very well here. Theirs is a highly drinkable range that possess a distinctive personality. Three Vermentino wines were presented, two from Gallura and the third labeled IGT. Among them, the Roccaia stands out as the most complex, with aromas of anise and green tea, accompanied by a pleasant fruity touch. The palate is sapid and fleshy. It's surprising that two years after harvest, it remains so vibrant, a quality also found in the Funtana Manna, an intriguing and captivating white. Among the reds, the Bovale '22 impresses with its creamy texture and fresh yet dense character.

○ Vermentino di Gallura Roccaia '22	♟♟ 5
● Bovale '22	♟♟
● Entu '20	♟♟ 5
○ Funtana Manna '22	♟♟ 4
○ Vermentino di Gallura Petrizza '23	♟♟ 4
● Cannonau di Sardegna Zojosu '22	♟ 3
⊘ Gran Rosé	♟ 3
● Zurrìa Carignano '22	♟ 3
○ Vermentino di Gallura Petrizza '21	♟♟♟ 3*
○ Vermentino di Gallura Petrizza '20	♟♟♟ 3*
○ Vermentino di Gallura Sup. Costarenas '18	♟♟♟ 4*
○ Vermentino di Gallura Sup. Costarenas '16	♟♟♟ 3*
○ Vermentino di Gallura Sup. Costarenas '22	♟♟ 5
○ Vermentino di Gallura Sup. Roccaìa '20	♟♟ 5

Cantina Mesa

loc. Su Baroni
09010 Sant'Anna Arresi [CA]
(» +39 0781965057
⊕ www.cantinamesa.com

CELLAR SALES
PRE-BOOKED VISITS
ANNUAL PRODUCTION 726,000 bottles
HECTARES UNDER VINE 74.00

It's been just two decades since Gavino Sanna, a renowned global advertising executive, founded the winery. In recent times, the estate was acquired by the Santa Margherita wine group, but their approach remains largely the same, with Sanna serving as honorary president. Carignano, cannonau, vermentino, and syrah are cultivated across more than 70 hectares (66 of which are owned), primarily in sandy soils. The winery produces a range of precise and authentic wines that express the history of Sardinia. At the top of our tastings is the Buio Buio, a true and authentic Carignano that showcases its power without ever feeling heavy. Sweet spices, underbrush, and wild herbs define the nose, while the palate proves close-knit and creamy, with soft tannins and a pleasant, acid-saline finish. The simpler but equally delicious Buio also impresses, while among the whites, the Opale stands out as a Vermentino with great character and distinct iodine notes.

Mura

loc. Azzanidò, 1
07020 Loiri Porto San Paolo [SS]
(» +39 3402602507
⊕ www.vinimura.it

CELLAR SALES
PRE-BOOKED VISITS
RESTAURANT SERVICE
ANNUAL PRODUCTION 50,000 bottles
HECTARES UNDER VINE 12.00

With over 40 years of activity, this winery, located in Loiri Porto San Paolo, just a short distance from Olbia, is now managed by siblings Salvatore (sales) and Marianna (winemaker), the children of the winery's founder, Filippo. The estate spans 20 hectares and focuses on vermentino, though it also produces using bovale and cannonau grapes. The sandy, clay, and granite soils in which the vines are rooted confer character, minerality, and typicity to the wines, while the climate tempers their structure and lends finesse, elements that are evident with every sip. Three wines were presented, with two versions of Vermentino standing out. Beyond their excellence, they offer an incredible sense of place. At the top is the Sienda, the Superiore, which in the 2023 vintage delivers intense floral and fruity sensations, with a hint of fresh almond preceding an elegant, sapid palate. The Cheremi '23 is simpler but refined, making for a gratifying drink, while the Cortes '22 is a well-made, enjoyable pour.

● Carignano del Sulcis Buio Buio Ris. '21	♟♟7
● Carignano del Sulcis Buio '22	♟♟5
○ Vermentino di Sardegna Opale '23	♟♟6
⊘ Rosa Grande '23	♟5
○ Vermentino di Sardegna Giunco '23	♟5
● Buio Buio '10	♟♟♟4*
● Carignano del Sulcis Buio Buio Ris. '20	♟♟♟5
● Carignano del Sulcis Buio Buio Ris. '13	♟♟♟5
● Carignano del Sulcis Buio Buio Ris. '12	♟♟♟5
● Carignano del Sulcis Buio Buio Ris. '19	♟♟5
● Carignano del Sulcis Buio Buio Ris. '18	♟♟5
● Carignano del Sulcis Passito Forterosso '21	♟♟5
○ Vermentino di Sardegna Opale '22	♟♟5

○ Vermentino di Gallura Sup. Sienda '23	♟♟♟5
○ Vermentino di Gallura Cheremi '23	♟♟4
● Cannonau di Sardegna Cortes '22	♟4
○ Vermentino di Gallura Sup. Sienda '22	♟♟♟4*
● Baja '19	♟♟5
● Cannonau di Sardegna Cortes '20	♟♟4
⊘ Jara '22	♟♟3
○ Sienda Il Decennio '21	♟♟6
○ Sienda Il Decennio '20	♟♟6
○ Sienda Il Decennio '19	♟♟6
○ Sienda il Decennio '18	♟♟6
○ Vermentino di Gallura Cheremi '22	♟♟4
○ Vermentino di Gallura Cheremi '20	♟♟3
○ Vermentino di Sardegna Prisma '22	♟♟3

Olianas

loc. Porruddu
09055 Gergei [CA]
(☏) +39 3442369837
⊕ www.olianas.it

★Pala

via Verdi, 7
09040 Serdiana [SU]
(☏) +39 070740284
⊕ www.pala.it

CELLAR SALES
PRE-BOOKED VISITS
ANNUAL PRODUCTION 170,000 bottles
HECTARES UNDER VINE 25.00
VITICULTURE METHOD Certified Organic
SUSTAINABLE WINERY

CELLAR SALES
PRE-BOOKED VISITS
ANNUAL PRODUCTION 490,000 bottles
HECTARES UNDER VINE 99.00

The winery was born out of a vision shared by the Olianas family and Stefano Casadei, a winemaker involved in several Tuscan estates. Located in Sarcidano, in the island's interior, the winery boasts 25 hectares of vines and benefits from a great diversity of soils that impart unique characteristics to the varieties cultivated: cannonau, semidano, bovale, nasco, and malvasia. Their production philosophy is rooted in respect for the environment and sustainability, following a strict internal protocol known as "biointegral". Over the years, there has been extensive research into the use of amphorae for maturation and aging. The Cannonau di Sardegna Le Anfore '22 proves to be a model of elegance and finesse. Small wild berries are joined by hints of rose, while the palate envelops and caresses with a juicy, light drinkability. The finish is deep and clean. The Perdixi, a monovarietal bovale that's more structured and full-bodied, plays on brackish nuances, while both the Cannonau Riserva and Vermentino stand out as enjoyable and balanced. The original Migiu '21 also caught our attention.

The family name is now synonymous with the winery, which has been operating for 60 years. Mario, along with his children Elisabetta and Massimiliano, who have inherited the knowledge and passion that are the foundation of the venture, leads the estate. The family owns eight different properties, starting from Serdiana and extending to the Oristano area, covering a total of about 100 hectares of vineyards. Their extensive range represents different zones, focusing primarily on cannonau, bovale, vermentino, and nuragus, each with its own distinct nuances. A highly respectable range was presented, with three wines making it to our final round, confirming the good progress being made. The Stellato '23 is one of Southern Sardinia's great Vermentinos, offering a sapid, iodine character with a nose that spans everything from wildflowers to yellow fruit, alongside touches of aromatic herbs. Only a few bottles of the Nature version, an even more fascinating and fleshy wine, are produced. The Cannonau di Sardegna Riserva, aged in large barrels, is also excellent, showcasing elegance and finesse—a highly characterful red.

● Cannonau di Sardegna Le Anfore '22	♟♟♟	5
● Perdixi Bovale '22	♟♟	5
● Cannonau di Sardegna Ris. '21	♟♟	5
○ Vermentino di Sardegna '23	♟♟	3
○ Migiu Le Anfore '22	♟	5
● Cannonau di Sardegna Le Anfore '21	♟♟♟	5
● Cannonau di Sardegna '22	♟♟	3
● Cannonau di Sardegna '21	♟♟	3
● Cannonau di Sardegna Ris. '19	♟♟	4
● Cannonau di Sardegna Ris. '16	♟♟	4
● Cannonau di Sardegna Ris. '15	♟♟	4
● Perdixi '21	♟♟	5
● Perdixi '20	♟♟	4
● Perdixi '19	♟♟	4
⊙ Rosato '22	♟♟	3
○ Vermentino di Sardegna '21	♟♟	3

○ Stellato Vermentino '23	♟♟♟	5
● Cannonau di Sardegna Ris. '22	♟♟	5
○ Stellato Nature '23	♟♟	8
⊙ Chiaro di Stelle '23	♟♟	3
○ Entemari Bianco '22	♟♟	5
● Monica di Sardegna Oltreluna '22	♟♟	3
○ Nuragus di Cagliari Milleluci '23	♟♟	3
● Silenzi Rosso '21	♟♟	2*
○ Silenzi Bianco '23	♟	2
○ Vermentino di Sardegna Soprasole '23	♟	3
○ Stellato Vermentino '22	♟♟♟	5
○ Stellato Vermentino '21	♟♟♟	5
○ Vermentino di Sardegna Stellato '20	♟♟♟	4*
○ Vermentino di Sardegna Stellato '19	♟♟♟	4
○ Vermentino di Sardegna Stellato '18	♟♟♟	4*
○ Vermentino di Sardegna Stellato '17	♟♟♟	4*
○ Vermentino di Sardegna Stellato '16	♟♟♟	4*

Cantina Pedres

via Mincio, 42
07026 Olbia [SS]
☎ +39 0789595075
🌐 www.cantinapedres.it

Tenute Perda Rubia

loc. Pranu Mannu
s.da prov.le 56, km 7,1
08040 Talana [NU]
☎ +39 3884250995
🌐 www.tenuteperdarubia.com

CELLAR SALES
PRE-BOOKED VISITS
ANNUAL PRODUCTION 500,000 bottles
HECTARES UNDER VINE 80.00
SUSTAINABLE WINERY

CELLAR SALES
PRE-BOOKED VISITS
ANNUAL PRODUCTION 20,000 bottles
HECTARES UNDER VINE 20.00
VITICULTURE METHOD Certified Organic

The winery's 80 hectares are spread out across the Gallura area, at elevations of about 300 meters above sea level. The emblem of their diverse and multifaceted range is vermentino, the region's flagship variety. It's complemented by moscato, cannonau, sangiovese, merlot, and syrah, which are crafted into both reds and sparkling wines, both dry and sweet. All the wines benefit from the area's viticultural prowess and a climate moderated by sea breezes, resulting in a portfolio of exceptional quality. An expansive range was presented this year, with several wines making their first appearance in our tastings. The Thilibas is the standout, a Vermentino di Gallura Superiore redolent of white flowers and citrus, accented by anise and almond, while the palate is subtle, sapid, with a linear structure. Among the whites, the Brino and Prexio (respectively Vermentino di Sardegna and Gallura) also impress, while the reds shine with the Cerasio '22 and Cagnulari '21.

When Mario Mereu founded his winery in 1949, he made a bold bet on Ogliastra's native grape, cannonau. Today, the founder's grandchildren manage 20 hectares of vines with the same passion and enthusiasm. The estate's vines are own-rooted, and the resulting wines are of extraordinary quality, capturing the essence of the terroir in every glass. In addition to vineyards, the property is also dedicated to forestry, olive growing, and the cultivation of ancient grains. A small but impressive range was submitted for tasting. The two Cannonau wines are true emblems of the style. The Nahia '22 is juicy and spicy, with great elegance and deep, gratifying drinkability. The more complex and multifaceted Perda Rubia hails from the estate's oldest vines, conjuring up aromas of wild berries, dried roses, and black pepper; the palate is smooth and fresh, with a clean, deep finish marked by sapidity. Finally, the Lanùra '23, the only white produced, proves to be a pleasant wine.

○ Vermentino di Gallura Sup. Thilibas '23	🍷🍷 4
● Antonella Collection Cagnulari '21	🍷🍷 5
● Cannonau di Sardegna Cerasio '22	🍷🍷 4
○ Mon Ami Bianco Antonella Collection '22	🍷🍷 5
● Muros Rosso '22	🍷🍷 4
○ Vermentino di Gallura Brino '23	🍷🍷 3
○ Vermentino di Sardegna Desigio '23	🍷🍷 3
● Cannonau di Sardegna Desigio '22	🍷 3
☉ Cannonau di Sardegna Rosato Brino Rosé '23	🍷 3
○ Vermentino di Gallura 0789 '23	🍷 3
○ Vermentino di Gallura Sup. Antonella Collection '23	🍷 5
○ Vermentino di Sardegna Prexio '23	🍷 3
○ Vermentino di Gallura Sup. Thilibas '10	🍷🍷🍷 3*
○ Vermentino di Gallura Sup. Thilibas '09	🍷🍷🍷 3*

● Cannonau di Sardegna Perda Rubia '21	🍷🍷🍷 6
● Cannonau di Sardegna Nahia '22	🍷🍷 4
○ Vermentino di Sardegna Lanùra '23	🍷 3
● Cannonau di Sardegna Naniha '18	🍷🍷🍷 4*
● Cannonau di Sardegna Perda Rubia '20	🍷🍷🍷 5
● Cannonau di Sardegna Cl. Perdarubia '17	🍷🍷 5
● Cannonau di Sardegna Naniha '21	🍷🍷 4
● Cannonau di Sardegna Perda Rubia '19	🍷🍷 5
● Cannonau di Sardegna Perda Rubia '18	🍷🍷 5
● Naniha '19	🍷🍷 3*
○ Vermentino di Sardegna Lanùra '22	🍷🍷 3
○ Vermentino di Sardegna Lanùra '21	🍷🍷 5

F.lli Puddu

loc. Orbuddai
08025 Oliena [NU]
+39 0784288457
info@aziendapuddu.it

ANNUAL PRODUCTION 70,000 bottles
HECTARES UNDER VINE 30.00
VITICULTURE METHOD Certified Organic

The winery is located in Barbagia, within the Nepente di Oliena subzone of the Cannonau di Sardegna DOC appellation. Since its founding in 1976, the estate has gradually become a benchmark in the Sardinian wine scene. Success has been driven by modernizing machinery and production processes, as well as diversifying activities, with 15 hectares of olive groves. Reds, whites, rosés, and an "Italian method" (cuve close method) sparkling wine are produced, all using cannonau grapes. The four red wines presented, all Cannonau di Sardegna, are of exceptional quality. The producer's latest creation, a Nepente di Oliena dedicated to 30 vintages of the famous Sardinian red, is especially noteworthy. Its nose reveals red fruit and spice, while the palate proves close-knit, creamy, and brimming with sapidity. Equally impressive are the Tiscali '21 and Pro Vois '19, two refined Cannonau wines with a focus on body and structure.

● Cannonau di Sardegna Cl. Nepente di Oliena Carros '20	🍷🍷 3
● Cannonau di Sardegna Nepente di Oliena Tiscali '21	🍷🍷 3
● Cannonau di Sardegna Nepente di Oliena Pro Vois Ris. '15	🍷🍷🍷 5
● Cannonau di Sardegna Nepente di Oliena Pro Vois Ris. '14	🍷🍷🍷 5
● Cannonau di Sardegna Cl. Nepente di Oliena Carros '18	🍷🍷 3*
● Cannonau di Sardegna Nepente di Oliena Pro Vois Ris. '19	🍷🍷 5
● Cannonau di Sardegna Nepente di Oliena Tiscali '20	🍷🍷 3*
● Cannonau di Sardegna Nepente di Oliena Tiscali '19	🍷🍷 3*
● Cannonau di Sardegna Nepente di Oliena Trenta Vendemmie '22	🍷🍷 3

Pusole

loc. Perda 'e Cuba
08040 Lotzorai [OG]
+39 3334047219
budana.robby@gmail.com

CELLAR SALES
PRE-BOOKED VISITS
ACCOMMODATION
ANNUAL PRODUCTION 10,000 bottles
HECTARES UNDER VINE 7.50
SUSTAINABLE WINERY

Pusole is the family name of two brothers, Lorenzo and Roberto, who passionately continue their family's agricultural legacy. Wine remains their greatest passion, with extensive work in the vineyard and minimal intervention in the winery. The result is a range that embodies the essence of Ogliastra, with a distinct saline character that reflects the proximity to the sea. Several wines are produced, with cannonau leading the way, followed by vermentino and a rare white cannonau, an unusual grape variety in the area. One of the best reds we've tasted in Sardinia this year is the Casesparse, an IGT Ogliastra made from cannonau. Its nose bursts with red fruit, especially blackberry, currant, and cherry, complemented by hints of scrub and myrtle. On the palate, it's juicy, smooth, dynamic, and remarkably deep. The Cannonau di Sardegna '22 is a simple but reliable choice, while the Pusole Bianco, made from vermentino grapes, stands out with its sapid and slightly tannic notes. Sa Scala '19 is a bit more cropped and extracted.

● Casesparse Ogliastra '22	🍷🍷🍷 5
● Cannonau di Sardegna '22	🍷🍷 4
○ Vermentino di Sardegna Pusole Bianco '23	🍷🍷 5
● Cannonau di Sardegna Cl. Sa Scala '19	🍷 6
● Cannonau di Sardegna '15	🍷🍷 3*
● Cannonau di Sardegna '14	🍷🍷 3*
● Cannonau di Sardegna Cl. Sa Scala '14	🍷🍷 3*

Quartomoro di Sardegna

loc. Is Bangius

09094 Marrubiu [OR]
✆ +39 3467643522
🌐 www.quartomoro.it

Santa Maria la Palma

loc. **Santa Maria la Palma**
07040 Alghero [SS]
✆ +39 079999008
🌐 www.santamarialapalma.it

CELLAR SALES
PRE-BOOKED VISITS
ANNUAL PRODUCTION 50,000 bottles
HECTARES UNDER VINE 13.00

CELLAR SALES
PRE-BOOKED VISITS
ANNUAL PRODUCTION 5,000,000 bottles
HECTARES UNDER VINE 700.00

Piero Cella, an oenologist and vine grower, founded the winery in 2009 with his wife, Luciana. Its 13 hectares of vineyards are located in Arborea, in the province of Oristano. The main varieties grown include vermentino, cannonau, bovale, nuragus, and semidano. Piero and Luciana favor minimal intervention both in the vineyard and the winery, allowing the grapes to shine at their best. The wines are highly representative of their origin, with numerous selections divided into different lines, each telling its own unique story. From the Memorie di Vite line, our attention was caught by the Bovale '22 (labeled BVL), a close-knit, full-bodied wine, but also fresh and sapid. We also appreciated the Terralba Superiore DOC '21. The Vernaccia Sulle Bucce is a traditionally-styled wine of great charm, while the NRG proves to be an outstanding Nuragus di Cagliari. The CNS Cannonau di Sardegna '21 also delivered excellent results. The other wines tasted are pleasant and consistently well-made.

The vineyards of this cooperative winery stretch from the Gulf of Alghero to the Bay of Porto Conte—in all, its members cultivate some 700 hectares. Founded in 1956, the producer has continually renewed and improved itself. Today, it offers a quality range, from everyday drinking wines to premium vermentino, cannonau, and cagnulari, as well as some sparkling wines. This year, we tasted four wines from their premium production line. The Vermentino di Sardegna Ràfia '22, which we tried last year, once again proves to be a great Mediterranean white, best enjoyed a year after harvest. Among the reds, both the Cagnulari '20 and Cannonau '19 were excellent. The Recònta, with its aromas of dark fruit and spice, features a sapid, tannic palate. The Cannonau, on the other hand, is more pervasive, creamy, and fresh. The Akenta Extra Dry sparkling wine is also delightful.

● BVL Bovale Memorie di Vite '22	♈♈ 4
● Cannonau di Sardegna CNS Memorie di Vite '21	♈♈ 4
○ Nuragus di Cagliari NRG Memorie di Vite '23	♈♈ 4
○ Orriu Sulle Bucce Vernaccia '23	♈♈ 3
● Terralba Sup. BVL Superiore Memorie di Vite '21	♈♈ 6
○ Nasco di Cagliari NSC Memorie di Vite '23	♈ 5
○ Semidano di Mogoro SMD Memorie di Vite '22	♈ 4
○ Spumante M. Cl. Pas Dosé Q	♈ 5
● BVL Memorie di Vite '18	♈♈ 4
● MAI Intrecci di Vite '17	♈♈ 6
● Memorie di Vite BVL Bovale '21	♈♈ 4

● Cannonau di Sardegna Redìt Ris. '19	♈♈ 5
● Alghero Cagnulari Recònta Ris. '20	♈♈ 5
○ Vermentino di Sardegna Extra Dry Akènta Cuvée '22	♈ 3
● Cannonau di Sardegna R Ris. '15	♈♈♈ 3*
● Alghero Cagnulari Recònta Ris. '16	♈♈ 4
● Cannonau di Sardegna '18	♈♈ 3
● Cannonau di Sardegna Naramae Ris. '18	♈♈ 3
● Cannonau di Sardegna Redìt Ris. '18	♈♈ 5
● Cannonau di Sardegna Redit Ris. '16	♈♈ 3*
● Cannonau di Sardegna Ris. '06	♈♈ 3
○ Vermentino di Sardegna Ràfia '22	♈♈ 4

SARDINIA

★★Cantina Santadi

via Giacomo Tachis, 14
09010 Santadi [SU]
(+39 0781950127
@ www.cantinadisantadi.it

CELLAR SALES
PRE-BOOKED VISITS
ANNUAL PRODUCTION 1,800,000 bottles
HECTARES UNDER VINE 650.00

Antonello Pilloni, the winery's president, brought
about major improvements to the estate nearly
50 years ago. In addition to renewing the winery
with a laboratory, and selecting the best grape
suppliers, he enlisted the exceptional winemaker
Giacomo Tachis. Tasked with elevating carignano,
the region's most emblematic grape, Tachis
helped the winery achieve national recognition.
The other grapes vinified include vermentino,
cannonau, nasco, and nuragus. A broad range was
presented, but it's the Terre Brune that once
again shines, cementing its place as an icon of
Sardinian wine on the global stage. The 2020
vintage proved exceptional for the grape, making
for a profile that's close-knit, complex, sapid, and
deep. The Shardana, another standout from the
same year, is an IGT with carignano as the star.
The Latinia, a passito nasco, is another top
performer. The rest of the range, particularly the
Rocca Rubia, Araja, Villa di Chiesa, and Pedraia,
also stood out.

Saraja

via Sa Raja
07020 Telti [SS]
(+39 3458080429
@ www.saraja.it

PRE-BOOKED VISITS
ANNUAL PRODUCTION 86,000 bottles
HECTARES UNDER VINE 49.00

A project launched by friends who became
business partners, all already involved in the
industry, this winery has experienced steady
growth both in the vineyard and in terms of
winemaking. Their non-interventionist
philosophy supports the character of the various
terroirs, starting with Gallura. The vineyards
span three distinct regions: primarily Gallura,
along with Romangia and Sulcis, with some
selected grapes sourced from the island's most
renowned areas. Gallura continues to impress us
with its offerings: two Vermentinos made it to
the final round, both from a rigorous selection of
grapes grown in the island's northeast. The
Kramori '23 is an energetic white, redolent of
white flowers and citrus, while its freshness
balances a broad palate. The complex,
multifaceted, and sapid Kari di Pètra is a
late-harvest Vermentino (though dry) that's
released three years after the vintage. Across the
board, their range shows a consistently high level
of quality.

● Carignano del Sulcis Sup. Terre Brune '20	♛♛♛ 8
○ Latinia	♛♛ 5
● Shardana '20	♛♛ 5
● Araja '21	♛♛ 3
● Carignano del Sulcis Grotta Rossa '22	♛♛ 3
● Carignano del Sulcis Rocca Rubia Ris. '21	♛♛ 5
● Monica di Sardegna Antigua '23	♛♛ 2*
○ Nuragus di Cagliari Pedraia '23	♛♛ 3
○ Vermentino di Sardegna Cala Silente '23	♛♛ 4
○ Villa di Chiesa '22	♛♛ 6
● Cannonau di Sardegna Noras '21	♛ 4
⊙ Carignano del Sulcis Rosato Tre Torri '23	♛ 2
○ Spumante Brut M. Cl. Solais 19a cuvee	♛ 5
○ Vermentino di Sardegna Villa Solais '23	♛ 3
● Carignano del Sulcis Sup. Terre Brune '18	♛♛♛ 8
● Carignano del Sulcis Sup. Terre Brune '17	♛♛♛ 8
● Carignano del Sulcis Sup. Terre Brune '16	♛♛♛ 7

○ Vermentino di Gallura Sup. Kramori '23	♛♛ 4
○ Vermentino di Gallura V. T. Kari di Pétra '21	♛♛ 5
● Cannonau di Sardegna Aisittà Ris. '21	♛♛ 4
● Cannonau di Sardegna Inkibi '22	♛♛ 3
⊙ M. Cl. Pas Dosé Istade '23	♛♛ 3
○ Vermentino di Gallura Kintari '23	♛♛ 3
○ Vermentino di Sardegna Tarra Noa '23	♛♛ 3
● Libaltai '22	♛ 3
○ Vermentino di Gallura Sup. Kramori '22	♛♛♛ 4*
○ Vermentino di Gallura Sup. Kramori '21	♛♛♛ 4*
● Cannonau di Sardegna Aisittà Ris. '20	♛♛ 4
● Carignano del Sulcis '20	♛♛ 3
● Libaltai '21	♛♛ 3
○ Vermentino di Gallura '20	♛♛ 3*
○ Vermentino di Gallura Kintari '22	♛♛ 3*
○ Vermentino di Gallura Kintari '21	♛♛ 3*
○ Vermentino di Gallura Sup. '20	♛♛ 3*

SARDINIA

Giuseppe Sedilesu

via Vittorio Emanuele II, 64
08024 Mamoiada [NU]
(☎ +39 078456791
🖥 www.giuseppesedilesu.com

★★Tenute Sella & Mosca

loc. I Piani
07041 Alghero [SS]
(☎ +39 079997700
🖥 www.sellaemosca.com

CELLAR SALES
PRE-BOOKED VISITS
ANNUAL PRODUCTION 120,000 bottles
HECTARES UNDER VINE 20.00
VITICULTURE METHOD Certified Organic
SUSTAINABLE WINERY

CELLAR SALES
PRE-BOOKED VISITS
ANNUAL PRODUCTION 4,500,000 bottles
HECTARES UNDER VINE 542.00

Giuseppe Sedilesu purchased his first hectare in the 1970s, in Mamoiada. It was the beginning of a long journey that led the producer to start bottling its own wines, rather than sell them in bulk, in 2000. Today Salvatore and his family oversee 15 hectares of vineyards and winemaking itself, with a strong commitment to environmental balance and biodiversity. Their Sedilesu wines, made from cannonau, often display a wild, robust character, highlighting their authenticity. In addition to cannonau, they produce Granazza, a captivating and unique wine made from the grape of the same name. The Granazza captivated our tasting panel. This distinctive white delights with its tones of candied orange and lime, while the palate is energetic, lively, and dominated by sapidity, leading to a clean, citrus-driven finish. Among the cru wines, the Ghirada Murruzzone stood out as a magnificent example of mamoiadino Cannonau. The Carnevale Riserva '21 remains a dependable choice.

Sella & Mosca's founders, engineer Erminio Sella and lawyer Edgardo Mosca (both from Piedmont), established the winery in the late 19th century. Originally, it was a prestigious nursery, but after several changes in ownership, it was acquired by the Terra Moretti group. The estate now boasts a wide and varied range, including sparkling wines, whites, rosés, reds, and fortified wines. Their 500 hectares of vineyards are managed as a single organic entity, the largest of its kind in Europe, with additional plots sourced from the island's most renowned regions. Three wines in the final round alone testifies to the quality of their range, but for the first time, the Mustazzo Cannonau di Sardegna '20 hit peaks of excellence. Made from a rigorous selection of grapes from the classic growing area for this renowned Sardinian variety, it reveals aromas of blackberry, cherry, and dried rose, with a dense but incredibly fresh palate. Also at the top are the Marchese di Villamarina, a celebrated Mediterranean cabernet sauvignon, and Ambat, a delightful Vermentino di Sardegna.

● Cannonau di Sardegna Ghirada Murruzzone '19	♟♟ 7
○ Granazza '23	♟♟ 4
● Cannonau di Sardegna Carnevale Ris. '21	♟♟ 5
● Popassa '21	♟ 5
● Cannonau di Sardegna Mamuthone '20	♟♟♟ 4*
● Cannonau di Sardegna Mamuthone '17	♟♟♟ 4*
● Cannonau di Sardegna Mamuthone '15	♟♟♟ 3*
● Cannonau di Sardegna Mamuthone '12	♟♟♟ 3*
● Cannonau di Sardegna Mamuthone '11	♟♟♟ 3*
● Cannonau di Sardegna Mamuthone '08	♟♟♟ 3*
○ Perda Pintà '09	♟♟♟ 4
○ Perda Pintà '07	♟♟♟ 5
● Cannonau di Sardegna Carnevale Ris. '19	♟♟ 5
● Cannonau di Sardegna Mamuthone '21	♟♟ 4
● Cannonau di Sardegna Sartiu '21	♟♟ 3*
○ Granazza '22	♟♟ 4

● Cannonau di Sardegna Mustazzo '20	♟♟♟ 5
● Alghero Cabernet Marchese di Villamarina Ris. '20	♟♟ 7
○ Vermentino di Sardegna Ambat '22	♟♟ 5
● Alghero Rosso Tanca Farrà '21	♟♟ 5
○ Alghero Torbato Catore '22	♟♟ 5
○ Alghero Torbato Terre Bianche Cuvée 161 '23	♟♟ 4
○ Vermentino di Gallura Sup. Monteoro '23	♟♟ 4
○ Vermentino di Sardegna Cala Reale '23	♟♟ 3
● Alghero Cabernet Marchese di Villamarina Ris. '17	♟♟♟ 6
○ Alghero Torbato Catore '20	♟♟♟ 5
○ Alghero Torbato Catore '18	♟♟♟ 5
○ Alghero Torbato Terre Bianche Cuvée 161 '18	♟♟♟ 3*

Siddùra

loc. Siddùra
07020 Luogosanto [SS]
📞 +39 0796513027
🌐 www.siddura.com

Su'Entu

s.da prov.le 48, km. 1,8
09025 Sanluri [SU]
📞 +39 0707050410
🌐 www.cantinesuentu.com

CELLAR SALES
PRE-BOOKED VISITS
ACCOMMODATION AND RESTAURANT SERVICE
ANNUAL PRODUCTION 300,000 bottles
HECTARES UNDER VINE 40.00
SUSTAINABLE WINERY

CELLAR SALES
PRE-BOOKED VISITS
ANNUAL PRODUCTION 300,000 bottles
HECTARES UNDER VINE 36.50
SUSTAINABLE WINERY

Luca Vitaletti and Dino Dini, an agronomist and a winemaker, expertly showcase the best of Luogosanto, a granite-rich terroir in Gallura, gently caressed by sea breezes. The winery was founded by Nathan Gottesdiener, a German entrepreneur who fell in love with the area. Here they produce wines that are refined, elegant, and impeccably crafted. The grape varieties most cultivated include vermentino, cannonau and moscato, alongside carignano, cagnulari, and sangiovese. As usual, the range presented didn't disappoint. While precision is never lacking, it sometimes detracts from the wines' charm. The Maìa, however, continues to stand out as a true champion: it's fragrant with citrus, aromatic herbs, and white flowers, while the palate proves remarkably fresh and deep. Tasted two years after the harvest, it's impressive, hinting at good aging potential. The Spèra, a fresher and more approachable version, is also excellent, while the Béru shows the influence of wood aging. Among the reds, we appreciated the characterful Cannonau di Sardegna Fòla Riserva '20.

Located just a few kilometers from Sanluri, this winery spans 36 hectares. The vines take root in poor soils, yet the grapes mature beautifully in this stunning area known as Marmilla, a region with a strong agricultural tradition. The winery has a deep respect for the land, with sustainability at the core of its cultivation approach. Their whites are made from vermentino, nasco, moscato, and chardonnay, while the reds feature cannonau, monica, syrah, and especially bovale. Each wine captures the essence of the territory and a passion for these gentle hills, a true showcase of viticultural excellence. Two new wines enriched a lineup where quality is the common denominator. The Terruas wines, a Cannonau and a Vermentino, are notable additions. The Vermentino is a superb white, with textbook sapidity, while the Cannonau is a true standout: aromas of rose, cherry, and blackberry lead to a palate of great elegance and finesse, as expected of a true Cannonau. The two Bovale wines also deliver: the Su'Diterra is simpler and more approachable, while the Su'Nico proves more close-knit and complex.

○ Vermentino di Gallura Sup. Maìa '22	♟♟ 5	
● Bàcco Carignano '22	♟♟ 5	
● Cannonau di Sardegna Érema '22	♟♟ 4	
● Cannonau di Sardegna Fòla Ris. '20	♟♟ 6	
○ Vermentino di Gallura Spéra '23	♟♟ 4	
○ Vermentino di Gallura Sup. Béru '22	♟♟ 7	
◉ Cannonau di Sardegna Rosato Nudo '23	♟ 5	
○ Vermentino di Gallura Sup. Maìa '21	♟♟♟ 4*	
○ Vermentino di Gallura Sup. Maìa '19	♟♟♟ 4*	
○ Vermentino di Gallura Sup. Maìa '15	♟♟♟ 4*	
○ Vermentino di Gallura Sup. Maìa '14	♟♟♟ 4*	
● Bàcco Cagnulari '21	♟♟ 5	
● Cannonau di Sardegna Fòla Ris. '19	♟♟ 5	
○ Vermentino di Gallura Spèra '20	♟♟ 3*	
○ Vermentino di Gallura Sup. Maìa '20	♟♟ 4	
○ Vermentino di Gallura Sup. Maìa '18	♟♟ 4	

● Su'Nico Bovale '22	♟♟♟ 5	
● Cannonau di Sardegna Terruas '22	♟♟ 6	
● Su'Diterra Bovale '23	♟♟ 4	
● Cannonau di Sardegna Su'Anima '22	♟♟ 4	
○ Su'aro '23	♟♟ 4	
○ Vermentino di Sardegna Terruas '23	♟♟ 6	
● Bovale '16	♟♟♟ 5	
● Su' Nico '18	♟♟♟ 5	
● Su' Nico Bovale '21	♟♟♟ 5	
● Su' Nico Bovale '20	♟♟♟ 5	
● Cannonau di Sardegna Su'Anima '19	♟♟ 3*	
● Su'Diterra '21	♟♟ 3*	
● Su'Diterra Bovale '22	♟♟ 4	
● Su'Nico Bovale '19	♟♟ 5	
● Su'Oltre '16	♟♟ 3*	
○ Vermentino di Sardegna Su'Orma '17	♟♟ 3*	

★Surrau

s.da prov.le Arzachena - Porto Cervo
07021 Arzachena [SS]
📞 +39 078982933
🌐 www.vignesurrau.it

CELLAR SALES
PRE-BOOKED VISITS
ANNUAL PRODUCTION 300,000 bottles
HECTARES UNDER VINE 50.00
SUSTAINABLE WINERY

The estate's more than 50 hectares are spread across the rolling hills of Arzachena, deep in the heart of Gallura. The vineyards are divided into seven distinct areas, ranging from 50 to 150 meters in elevation. The sandy, granite-rich soils imbue the wines with unique characteristics, especially vermentino, which thrives in this ideal habitat in northeastern Sardinia. Red grape varieties are also present, including cannonau (from which a Metodo Classico is produced), muristellu, carignano, and caricagiola. The lineup is broad and impressive, featuring several standouts. One of the stars is undoubtedly the Sciala, an exceptional Vermentino di Gallura, among the finest of its kind. Sapid and bright with acidity, it offers iodized notes and aromatic herbs, with remarkable depth of flavor. The Branu, a simpler and more approachable wine, is also very good. As for the reds, the Sincaru is an excellent Cannonau that embodies all the essence of Gallura, while the Barriu is a red with great body. The Giola is a delightful rosé.

VikeVike

via Marsala, 19/21
08024 Mamoiada [NU]
📞 +39 3482290179
🌐 www.cantinavikevike.com

PRE-BOOKED VISITS
ACCOMMODATION
ANNUAL PRODUCTION 25,000 bottles
HECTARES UNDER VINE 5.00
VITICULTURE METHOD Certified Organic

Simone Sedilesu, the son and grandson of two prominent interpreters of cannonau from Mamoiada, upholds the family legacy with his own ambitious project. While it might be considered "artisanal" in scale, his work is anything but small in vision. Indeed, he's dedicated to exploring and conveying the essence of the local terroir through his wines. From indigenous grapes, he crafts elegant, highly drinkable wines that embody a contemporary style without losing their distinctive character and identity. Four wines were presented: three reds and a white made from granazza. The reds are all Cannonau, though labeled as IGT Barbagia. At the top is the Ghirada Istevene '21, with its aromas of myrtle and scrub, and a palate that's both subtle and incredibly fresh. The white also impressed, with its notes of candied citron and wildflowers, and an energetic palate. The other two cru wines, the Gurguruò and Fittiloghe, were excellent, with the Fittiloghe standing out for its elegance and finesse.

○ Vermentino di Gallura Sup. Sciala '23	♟♟♟ 5	
○ Vermentino di Gallura Branu '23	♟♟ 3*	
● Barriu '21	♟♟ 5	
● Cannonau di Sardegna Sincaru '22	♟♟ 5	
⊙ Gjola Caricagiola '23	♟♟ 4	
○ Spumante M. Cl. Pas Dosé	♟♟ 5	
○ Vermentino di Gallura Montidimola V.T. '22	♟♟ 6	
● Cannonau di Sardegna Pentima Ris. '21	♟ 6	
○ Vermentino di Gallura Passito Sole di Surrau '23	♟ 4	
○ Vermentino di Gallura Sup. Sciala '22	♛♛♛ 5	
○ Vermentino di Gallura Sup. Sciala '21	♛♛♛ 5	
○ Vermentino di Gallura Sup. Sciala '20	♛♛♛ 5	
○ Vermentino di Gallura Sup. Sciala '19	♛♛♛ 5	
○ Vermentino di Gallura Sup. Sciala '18	♛♛♛ 5	

● Ghirada Istevene '21	♟♟ 8	
○ Granazza '23	♟♟ 5	
● Ghirada Fittiloghe '21	♟♟ 5	
● Ghirada Gurguruò '21	♟♟ 6	
● Ghirada Fittiloghe '20	♛♛♛ 5	
○ Barbagia Bianco '21	♛♛ 4	
○ Barbagia Bianco '19	♛♛ 5	
● Cannonanu di Sardegna Ghirada Fittiloghe '19	♛♛ 4	
● Cannonanu di Sardegna Ghirada Gurguruò '19	♛♛ 5	
● Ghirada Gurguruò '20	♛♛ 6	
● Ghirada Istevene '20	♛♛ 8	

OTHER WINERIES

Atlantis
via Torino, 3
07022 Berchidda [SS]
📞 +39 3398952020
🕸 www.atlantiswine.it

CELLAR SALES
PRE-BOOKED VISITS
ANNUAL PRODUCTION 50,000 bottles
HECTARES UNDER VINE 16.00
SUSTAINABLE WINERY

○ Vermentino di Gallura Sup. Clos '22	♟♟ 5
● Cannonau di Sardegna Demiurgo '23	♟ 5

Carpante
via Garibaldi, 151
07049 Usini [SS]
📞 +39 079380614
🕸 www.carpante.it

CELLAR SALES
PRE-BOOKED VISITS
ANNUAL PRODUCTION 30,000 bottles
HECTARES UNDER VINE 8.00

● Cagnulari '22	♟♟ 3
● Carignano del Sulcis '22	♟♟ 4
● Carpante Rosso '19	♟♟ 4
○ Vermentino di Sardegna Longhera '23	♟ 2

Famiglia Demelas
loc. S'Ulimu
08030 Atzara [NU]
📞 +39 3470993307
🕸 www.famigliademelas.com

CELLAR SALES
PRE-BOOKED VISITS
ACCOMMODATION AND RESTAURANT SERVICE
ANNUAL PRODUCTION 17,000 bottles
HECTARES UNDER VINE 8.00
SUSTAINABLE WINERY

● Cannonau di Sardegna Giogu '22	♟♟ 4
○ Frore '23	♟♟ 4

Carboni
via Umberto, 163
08036 Ortueri [NU]
📞 +39 078466213
🕸 www.vinicarboni.it

CELLAR SALES
PRE-BOOKED VISITS
ANNUAL PRODUCTION 25,000 bottles
HECTARES UNDER VINE 13.00
SUSTAINABLE WINERY

● Balente '23	♟♟ 4
○ Helios '23	♟♟ 4
● Pin8	♟♟ 5

Ferruccio Deiana
loc. Su Leunaxi
via Gialeto, 7
09060 Settimo San Pietro [CA]
📞 +39 070749117
🕸 www.ferrucciodeiana.it

CELLAR SALES
PRE-BOOKED VISITS
ANNUAL PRODUCTION 430,000 bottles
HECTARES UNDER VINE 120.00

● Cannonau di Sardegna Sileno '22	♟♟ 3*
● Monica di Sardegna Karel '22	♟♟ 2*
○ Pluminus '22	♟♟ 6
● Girò di Cagliari '21	♟ 4

Dessena
loc. Luise Secchi
07010 Benetutti [SS]
📞 +39 3475935155
🕸 www.cantinadessena.com

○ Fàula '22	♟♟ 6
○ Fàuledda '22	♟♟ 3
● Cannonau di Sardegna Balentia Ris. '18	♟ 5

OTHER WINERIES

Tenute Faragò

loc. Su Niau
09040 Serdiana [SU]
℡ +39 3357780494
🌐 www.tenutefarago.it

○ Cagliari Vermentino Sup. '23	🍷🍷 4
● Bovale '23	🍷🍷 4
● Cannonau di Sardegna Ris. '21	🍷🍷 5
○ Malvasia Macerato '22	🍷🍷 5

Cantina Gallura

via Val di Cossu, 9
07029 Tempio Pausania
℡ +39 079631241
🌐 www.cantinagallura.com

CELLAR SALES
PRE-BOOKED VISITS
ANNUAL PRODUCTION 1,300,000 bottles
HECTARES UNDER VINE 350.00

○ Vermentino di Gallura Sup. Canayli '23	🍷🍷 3*
○ Balajana '20	🍷🍷 3
○ Vermentino di Gallura Piras '23	🍷 2

Cantina Agricola Giacu

via Veneto, 20a
08038 Sorgono [NU]
℡ +39 3931948566
🌐 www.agricolagiacu.it

CELLAR SALES
PRE-BOOKED VISITS
ACCOMMODATION
ANNUAL PRODUCTION 10,000 bottles
HECTARES UNDER VINE 1.00

● Galanzette Monte 'e Pischina '22	🍷🍷 4
● Mandrolisai G '21	🍷🍷 4
● Mandrolisai Sup. Baiore Monte e' Pischina '20	🍷🍷 5

Tenute Fois Accademia Olearia

loc. Ungias Galantè, Lotto E1, Zona D2
07041 Alghero [SS]
℡ +39 079980394
🌐 www.accademiaolearia.com

CELLAR SALES
PRE-BOOKED VISITS
ANNUAL PRODUCTION 10,000 bottles
HECTARES UNDER VINE 11.00

○ Vermentino di Sardegna Chlamys '23	🍷🍷 3*

I Garagisti di Sorgono

via Emilia, 10
08038 Sorgono [NU]
℡ +39 3288714316
🌐 www.garagistidisorgono.com

CELLAR SALES
PRE-BOOKED VISITS
ANNUAL PRODUCTION 40,000 bottles
HECTARES UNDER VINE 9.00
VITICULTURE METHOD Certified Organic

● Mandrolisai Rosso Uraas '21	🍷🍷 5
● Mandrolisai Sup. Sa Sedda '20	🍷🍷 5
● Cannonau di Sardegna Manca '21	🍷 5
● Monica di Sardegna Murru '22	🍷 4

Podere Guardia Grande

via Punta Cristallo
07041 Alghero [SS]
℡ +39 3473457757
🌐 www.podereguardiagrande.it

● Cannonau di Sardegna Nascimento '23	🍷🍷 4
○ Vermentino di Sardegna Saldenya '23	🍷🍷 5
● Alghero Cagnulari L'Alghè '23	🍷 5

OTHER WINERIES

Iolei

via Nuoro, 47
08025 Oliena [NU]
(») +39 3488863219
☞ www.iolei.it

CELLAR SALES
PRE-BOOKED VISITS
ANNUAL PRODUCTION 50,000 bottles
HECTARES UNDER VINE 4.00
SUSTAINABLE WINERY

● Cannonau di Sardegna Nepente di Oliena Hospes Ris. '21	♟♟ 6
○ Vermentino di Sardegna Majga '23	♟♟ 3

Pietro Lilliu

via Sardegna, 13
09020 Ussaramanna [SU]
(») +39 3407591144
☞ www.cantinalilliu.it

CELLAR SALES
PRE-BOOKED VISITS
ANNUAL PRODUCTION 20,000 bottles
HECTARES UNDER VINE 4.00
SUSTAINABLE WINERY

○ Cagliari Malvasia Mendula '22	♟♟ 5
● Prexu Syrah '19	♟♟ 5
● Biatzu Bovale '21	♟ 4

Mora&Memo

via Giuseppe Verdi, 9
09040 Serdiana [SU]
(») +39 3311972266
☞ www.moraememo.it

CELLAR SALES
PRE-BOOKED VISITS
ANNUAL PRODUCTION 80,000 bottles
HECTARES UNDER VINE 40.00

○ Tino Sur Lie '22	♟♟ 4
● Bo&Co '22	♟♟ 3
● Monica di Sardegna Ica '21	♟♟ 4
○ Vermentino di Sardegna Tino '23	♟♟ 4

Tenuta L'Ariosa

loc. Predda Niedda Sud
s.da 15
07100 Sassari
(») +39 079261905
☞ www.lariosa.it

CELLAR SALES
ANNUAL PRODUCTION 100,000 bottles
HECTARES UNDER VINE 16.00
VITICULTURE METHOD Certified Organic

● Sass'antico Cagnulari '21	♟♟ 3*
○ Vermentino di Sardegna Arenu '23	♟♟ 3
● Cannonau di Sardegna Assolo '21	♟ 3
○ Vermentino di Sardegna Galatea '23	♟ 4

Alberto Loi

s.s. 125 Km124,1
08040 Cardedu [OG]
(») +39 070240866
☞ www.albertoloi.it

PRE-BOOKED VISITS
ANNUAL PRODUCTION 250,000 bottles
HECTARES UNDER VINE 51.00
SUSTAINABLE WINERY

● C Carignano '22	♟♟ 3
● Cannonau di Sardegna Jerzu AL '23	♟♟ 3
○ Leila '20	♟ 5
○ Vermentino di Sardegna Theria '23	♟ 3

Murales

loc. Piliezzu, 1
07026 Olbia [SS]
(») +39 078953174
☞ www.vinimurales.com

CELLAR SALES
PRE-BOOKED VISITS
ACCOMMODATION AND RESTAURANT SERVICE
ANNUAL PRODUCTION 80,000 bottles
HECTARES UNDER VINE 20.00

○ Vermentina di Gallura Miradas '23	♟♟ 4
● Cannonau di Sardegna Arcanos '20	♟♟ 4
○ Vermentino di Gallura Lumenera '23	♟ 5

OTHER WINERIES

Nuraghe Crabioni

loc. Su Crabioni
07037 Sorso [SS]
☎ +39 3468292457
✉ www.nuraghecrabioni.com

CELLAR SALES
PRE-BOOKED VISITS
ANNUAL PRODUCTION 60,000 bottles
HECTARES UNDER VINE 35.00
SUSTAINABLE WINERY

○ Sussinku Cagnulari '22	♥♥ 4
○ Vermentino di Sardegna Kanimari '23	♥♥ 4
● Cannonau di Sardegna Crabioni '20	♥ 3
○ Sussinku Bianco '22	♥ 3

Poderi Parpinello

loc. Janna de Mare
s.da st.le 91
07100 Sassari
☎ +39 3465915194
✉ www.poderiparpinello.it

ANNUAL PRODUCTION 250,000 bottles
HECTARES UNDER VINE 32.00

● Cannonau di Sardegna Ris. '21	♥♥ 4
● Kressia Cagnulari '23	♥♥ 4
○ Vermentino di Sardegna Ala Blanca '23	♥♥ 3
○ Alghero Torbato Centogemme '23	♥ 3

Rigàtteri

loc. Santa Maria La Palma
reg. Flumelongu, 56
07041 Alghero [SS]
☎ +39 3408636375
✉ www.rigatteri.com

CELLAR SALES
PRE-BOOKED VISITS
ANNUAL PRODUCTION 15,000 bottles
HECTARES UNDER VINE 10.00
SUSTAINABLE WINERY

● Cannonau di Sardegna Mirau '22	♥♥ 3
● Sirbone '22	♥♥ 3
○ Vermentino di Sardegna Yiòs '23	♥♥ 2*

Cantina Oliena

via Nuoro, 112
08025 Oliena [NU]
☎ +39 0784287509
✉ www.cantinasocialeoliena.it

ANNUAL PRODUCTION 300,000 bottles
HECTARES UNDER VINE 180.00

● Cannonau di Sardegna Nepente di Oliena '22	♥♥ 3
● Cannonau di Sardegna Nepente di Oliena Corrasi Ris. '18	♥♥ 4

Giuliana Puligheddu

p.zza Collegio, 5
08025 Oliena [NU]
☎ +39 3470820346
✉ www.giulianapuligheddu.it

PRE-BOOKED VISITS
ANNUAL PRODUCTION 5,000 bottles
HECTARES UNDER VINE 3.00
VITICULTURE METHOD Certified Organic

● Cannonau di Sardegna Cupanera Ris. '22	♥♥ 6
● Cannonau di Sardegna Cupanera '23	♥♥ 5

Tenute Rossini

s.da st.le 127 Settentrionale Sarda, 4
07030 Laerru [SS]
☎ +39 3405363814

ANNUAL PRODUCTION 14,000 bottles
HECTARES UNDER VINE 3.00

● Cannonau di Sardegna Bodale Ris. '16	♥♥ 5
● Rossini Rosso '18	♥♥ 5
● Uttiu Syrah '17	♥♥ 5
○ Vermentino di Sardegna Aria '22	♥♥ 3

OTHER WINERIES

Sardus Pater
via Rinascita, 46
09017 Sant'Antioco [SU]
(+39 3758799713
www.cantinesarduspater.it

CELLAR SALES
PRE-BOOKED VISITS
ANNUAL PRODUCTION 600,000 bottles
HECTARES UNDER VINE 300.00

● Carignano del Sulcis Is Arenas Ris. '21	♟♟ 5
● Carignano del Sulcis Nur '22	♟♟ 3
○ Elat '23	♟ 3
○ Vermentino di Sardegna Lugore '23	♟ 4

Agricola Soi
via Cucchesì, 1
08030 Nuragus [CA]
(+39 3488140084
www.agricolasoi.it

CELLAR SALES
PRE-BOOKED VISITS
ANNUAL PRODUCTION 16,000 bottles
HECTARES UNDER VINE 4.00

☉ Cannonau di Sardegna Rosato Nèa '23	♟♟ 4
○ Nuragus di Cagliari Nurà '23	♟♟ 4
● Cannonau di Sardegna Soi '19	♟ 4

Tenute Soletta
loc. Signor'Anna
07040 Codrongianos [SS]
(+39 079435067
www.tenutesoletta.it

CELLAR SALES
PRE-BOOKED VISITS
ACCOMMODATION AND RESTAURANT SERVICE
ANNUAL PRODUCTION 100,000 bottles
HECTARES UNDER VINE 15.00
VITICULTURE METHOD Certified Organic
SUSTAINABLE WINERY

● Cannonau di Sardegna Corona Majore Ris. '19	♟♟ 4
○ Kyanos Limited Edition '22	♟♟ 4
○ Vermentino di Sardegna Chimera '23	♟♟ 3

Tenuta Teo d'Oro
loc. Li Scapizzati
07052 San Teodoro [SS]
(+39 3356650552
www.tenutateodoro.it

○ Vermentino di Sardegna Origina '23	♟♟ 5
● Gaspà '21	♟ 5
○ Vermentino di Sardegna Theo '23	♟ 6

Cantina Trexenta
v.le Piemonte, 40
09040 Senorbì [CA]
(+39 0709808863
www.cantinatrexenta.it

CELLAR SALES
ANNUAL PRODUCTION 1,000,000 bottles
HECTARES UNDER VINE 150.00

● Cannonau di Sardegna Tanca su Conti Ris. '20	♟♟ 4
● Monica di Sardegna Bingias '22	♟♟ 2*
○ Nasco di Cagliari Sant'Efis '22	♟♟ 4

Cantina Vinzas Artas
via San Cosimo, 2
08024 Mamoiada [NU]
(+39 3203754341
vinzasartas@gmail.com

CELLAR SALES
PRE-BOOKED VISITS
ACCOMMODATION
ANNUAL PRODUCTION 6,000 bottles
HECTARES UNDER VINE 5.00

● Garaunele 1920 '22	♟♟ 8
● Nigheddu '22	♟♟ 5
● Sa Lahana '22	♟ 6

SARDINIA

INDEX
**wineries
in alphabetical order**

'A Vita	968
1701	250
Abate Nero	312
Abbadia Ardenga	741
Abbazia di Novacella	332
Abbona	62
Abbona, Anna Maria	62
Abrigo, F.lli	63
Abrigo, Giovanni	63
Abrigo, Orlando	64
Accordini, Stefano	370
Accornero Giulio e Figli	64
Acquabona	741
Ada Nada	161
Adami	370
Adanti	820
Adriano Marco e Vittorio	65
Agnes, F.lli	250
Agnoletti, Ida	371
Agostina Pieri	695
Agostino Pavia e Figli	169
Agostino Vicentini	442
Agricola Vallecamonica	293
Agricole Vallone	959
Agricosimo	884
Agriverde	866
Aia dei Colombi	894
Alario, Claudio	65
Alberto Paltrinieri	573
Albinea Canali	554
Albino Rocca	186
Aldeno, Cantina	312
Aldo Clerico	113
Aldo Rainoldi	285
Aldo Viola	1010
Alessandri, Massimo	232
Alessandria, F.lli	66
Alessandria, Gianfranco	66
Alessandro di Camporeale	982
Alessandro Moroder	796
Alessandro Pascolo	500
Alessio Brandolini	257
Alessio Komjanc	493
Alfieri, Marchesi	67
Alfredo Bertolani	556
Alice Bel Colle, Cantina	67
Allegrini	371
Allevi, Maria Letizia	772
Almondo, Giovanni	68
Alois	894
Alongi, Maurizio	594
Alta Mora	982
Altare, Elio	68
Amalia Cascina in Langa	69
Amastuola	938
Ambra, Fattoria	594
Amerighi, Stefano	595
Amorotti	866
André Pellissier	57
Andrea Felici	786
Andrea Picchioni	283
Andrea Visintini	533
Andreola	372
Anfosso, Tenuta	232
Angelini, Paolo	69
Angelo Negro	162
Anna Maria Abbona	62
Anselmet, Maison	54
Anselmi	372
Ansitz Waldgries, Tenuta	332
Antica Fattoria La Parrina	690
Antiche Cantine Migliaccio	848
Antichi Poderi Jerzu	1031
Antichi Vigneti di Cantalupo	70
Antinori, Marchesi	595
Antonella Corda	1027
Antonella Lombardo	974
Antonella Pacchiarotti	854
Antonelli - San Marco	820
Antonello Coletti Conti	851
Antonio Caggiano	897
Antonio Camillo	611
Antonio Costantini - Fattoria Colline Verdi	885
Antoniolo	70
Antoniotti, Odilio	71
Antonutti	466
Apollonio	938
Aquila del Torre	466
AR.PE.PE	251
Arcangelo, Poderi	741
Aresca, F.lli	71

Argentaia	741	Barollo	373
Argentiera	596	Baron Longo	364
Argiano	596	Barone Cornacchia	867
Argillae	821	Barone di Valforte,	
Argiolas	1020	Tenute	884
Arianna Occhipinti	999	Barone di Villagrande	983
Arillo in Terrabianca	597	Barone Pizzini	253
Armangia, L'	72	Barone Ricasoli	708
Armilla	741	Basile	601
Arnaldo Caprai	824	Basilisco	928
Arnaldo Rivera	72	Bastianich	468
Arno, Vinicola	73	Bastonaca, Tenuta	984
Arrighi	597	Batasiolo	74
Arrigoni	233	Battaglino, Fabrizio	74
Arunda	364	Battegazzore, Vignaioli	75
Aschero, Laura	233	Battifarano	928
Assirelli	554	Battista Cola	264
Assolati	741	Battistelle, Le	374
Assuli	983	Bava - Cocchi	75
Assunta, Podere L'	742	Beconcini, Pietro	742
Astroni, Cantine	895	Begali, Lorenzo	374
Attems	467	Begnardi	742
Attilio Contini	1026	Bel Colle	76
Audarya	1020	Belguardo	602
Aurora	772	Belisario	773
Ausonia	884	Bellafonte, Tenuta	822
Avanzi, Giovanni	251	Bellaria	896
Avignonesi	598	Bellaveder	313
Azelia	73	Bellavista	253
		Bellei & C., Francesco	555
Baciate Me	598	Bellini, Cantine	602
Badia a Coltibuono	599	Benanti	984
Badia di Morrona	599	Benito Favaro	127
Baia del Sole - Federici, La	234	Benito Ferrara	908
Bajta - Fattoria Carsica	467	Bentu Luna	1021
Baldetti	600	Benvenuto, Cantine	968
Balestri Valda	373	Bera	76
Ballabio	252	Bergaglio, Cinzia	77
Balter, Nicola	313	Bergaglio, Nicola	77
Balzo, Il	742	Berlucchi Franciacorta,	
Bambinuto	895	Guido	254
Baracchi	742	Berritta, Cantina	1021
Baraldo, Giacomo	600	Bersano	78
Barba, F.lli	867	Bersi Serlini	254
Barberani	821	Bertani	375
Barbicaia	742	Bertè & Cordini -	
Baricci	601	Francesco Montagna	255
Barisei, I	252	Berti, Stefano	555

Bertille, Le	743	Bosio	256	
Bertinga	743	Bossanova	884	
Bertolani, Alfredo	556	Bove	884	
Bessererhof - Otmar Mair	364	Boveri, Giacomo	82	
BiancaVigna	375	Boveri, Luigi	83	
Bianchi, Maria Donata	234	Bovio, Gianfranco	83	
Bindella - Tenuta Vallocaia	603	Bozen, Cantina	333	
Biondi - Santi		Braida	84	
Tenuta Greppo	603	Brancaia	607	
BioVio	235	Branchini	556	
Bisci	773	Brandolini, Alessio	257	
Bisi	255	Branko	472	
Bisol1542	376	Brezza Giacomo e Figli	84	
Boasso - Gabutti	78	Bric Castelvej -		
Bocale	822	Gallino Domenico	85	
Boglietti, Enzo	79	Bric Cenciurio	85	
Bolla	376	Bricco dei Guazzi	86	
Bollina, La	79	Bricco Maiolica	86	
Bolzicco	468	Brigaldara	379	
Bonacchi, Cantine	604	Brigante Vigneti & Cantina	969	
Bonavita	985	Brigatti, Francesco	87	
Bonfante, Marco	80	Brigl, Josef	333	
Boniperti, Gilberto	80	Briziarelli	823	
Bonomi, Castello	256	Broccardo	87	
Bonotto delle Tezze	377	Broglia -		
Bonsalto, Fattoria	604	Tenuta La Meirana	88	
Borgo Conventi, Tenuta	469	Bronca, Sorelle	380	
Borgo dei Trulli, Masseria	939	Brovia	88	
Borgo delle Oche	469	Bruna	235	
Borgo La Stella	766	Bruna Grimaldi	141	
Borgo Macereto	605	Brunelli - Le Chiuse		
Borgo Maragliano	81	di Sotto, Gianni	607	
Borgo Paglianetto	774	Brunelli, Luigi	380	
Borgo Salcetino	605	Bruni	608	
Borgo San Daniele	470	Brunnenhof -		
Borgo Savaian	470	Kurt Rottensteiner	334	
Borgo Stajnbech	377	Bruno Giacosa	137	
Borgogno & Figli, Giacomo	81	Bruno Rocca	186	
Borgoluce	378	Bruno Verdi	294	
Borin Vini & Vigne	378	Brunori	774	
Boroli	82	Bucci	775	
Borro, Il	606	Buglioni	381	
Bortolomiol	379	Buiatti, Livio e Claudio	472	
Bortolusso, Cav. Emiro	471	Bulichella	608	
Boscarelli	606	Buongiorno, I	939	
Bosco de' Medici	896	Burlotto, G. B.	89	
Bosco del Merlo	471	Buse dal Lôf, La	473	
Bosco, Nestore	868	Busso, Piero	89	

Bussoletti, Leonardo	823	Campo al Mare, Tenuta	743
Butussi, Valentino	473	Campo al Noce	743
Buzzinelli, Maurizio	474	Campo al Pero	744
Cà du Ferrà	236	Campo al Signore, Tenuta	744
Cà Maiol	257	Campo alla Sughera	611
Cà Tessitori	258	Canà, Le	777
Ca' Bianca	90	Canaio, Cantina	612
Ca' Bolani	474	Canalicchio - Franco Pacenti	744
Ca' d' Gal	90	
Ca' del Baio	91	Canalicchio di Sopra	612
Ca' del Bosco	258	Candido, Francesco	940
Ca' del Gè	259	Canevel Spumanti	384
Ca' di Frara	259	Caniette, Le	777
Ca' di Sopra	557	Canoso	385
Ca' La Bionda	381	Cantalici	744
Ca' Liptra	775	Cantele	940
Ca' Lojera	260	Cantina Cinque Terre	237
Ca' Lustra - Zanovello	382	Cantina Mesa	1032
Ca' Marcanda	609	Cantina Aldeno	312
Ca' Romé	91	Cantina Alice Bel Colle	67
Ca' Rugate	382	Cantina Berritta	1021
Ca' Tullio	475	Cantina Bozen	333
Ca' Viola	92	Cantina Canaio	612
Caccia al Piano	609	Cantina Castiadas	1024
Cacciagalli, I	897	Cantina Chiacchiera	749
Cacciagrande	743	Cantina Colterenzio	335
Cadibon	475	Cantina d'Isera	314
Cadinu, Francesco	1022	Cantina Dainelli	751
Caggiano, Antonio	897	Cantina dei Colli Ripani	778
Caiarossa	610	Cantina del Giusto	744
Calamoni, Tenuta	985	Cantina del Nebbiolo	93
Calatroni	260	Cantina del Pino	93
Calcagno	986	Cantina del Rimedio	1022
Calcinara, La	776	Cantina della Volta	557
Caldera, Fabrizia	92	Cantina di Calasetta	1023
Calepino, Il	261	Cantina di Carpi e Sorbara	558
Calle, Le	743	Cantina di Montalcino	744
Calleri, Cantine	236	Cantina di Pitigliano	745
Camerani - Corte Sant'Alda	383	Cantina di Solopaca	898
Camigliano	610	Cantina di Tortona	94
Camillo Montori	875	Cantina di Venosa	929
Camillo, Antonio	611	Cantina Dorgali	1027
Camossi	261	Cantina Giba	1029
Campagnola, Giuseppe	383	Cantina Girlan	338
Campanelli	776	Cantina Kaltern	342
Campi, I	384	Cantina Kurtatsch	345

Cantina Merano 349
Cantina Pedres 1034
Cantina Peppucci 835
Cantina Produttori Cormòns 482
Cantina Produttori del Gavi 180
Cantina Produttori San Michele Appiano 354
Cantina Produttori Valle Isarco 361
Cantina Rotaliana 314
Cantina San Paolo 354
Cantina Sant'Andrea 856
Cantina Santa Croce 577
Cantina Santadi 1037
Cantina Settecani 578
Cantina Sociale di Monteforte d'Alpone 414
Cantina Terlano 358
Cantina Toblino 327
Cantina Tollo 881
Cantina Tramin 359
Cantina Valpolicella Negrar 440
Cantina Valtidone 580
Cantine Astroni 895
Cantine Sant'Agata 191
Cantine Bellini 602
Cantine Benvenuto 968
Cantine Bonacchi 604
Cantine Calleri 236
Cantine De Falco 945
Cantine del Notaio 929
Cantine di Dolianova 1023
Cantine di Marzo 905
Cantine di Verona 385
Cantine Due Palme 945
Cantine Garrone 136
Cantine Lento 973
Cantine Lombardini 565
Cantine Lunae Bosoni 240
Cantine Monrubio 833
Cantine Nicosia 999
Cantine Olivella 914
Cantine Paolo Leo 947
Cantine Romagnoli 575
Cantine Settesoli 1006
Cantine Tre Pini 959

Cantrina 262
Canu 1024
Canus 476
Capaccia, Podere 745
Capanna 613
Capannelle 745
Caparra & Siciliani 969
Caparsa 745
Capitano, Fattoria il 745
Capitoni, Marco 745
Caplana, La 94
Capovaccaio, Tenute 941
Cappellasantandrea 613
Cappello, Fernanda 476
Cappuccina, La 386
Caprai, Arnaldo 824
Caprera 884
Caprili 614
Caravaglio 986
Carbone Vini 930
Cardinali, Podere Vito 778
Careglio, Pierangelo 95
Carga 546
Carline, Le 386
Carlo & Figli Revello 183
Carlo Giacosa 138
Carlone, Davide 95
Carmignani, Enzo 746
Carolina Jakončič Winery 548
Carpi e Sorbara, Cantina di 558
Carpineta Fontalpino, Fattoria 614
Carpineti, Marco 848
Carpineto 615
Carretta, Tenuta 96
Carvinea 941
Casa alle Vacche 615
Casa Cecchin 387
Casa Comerci 970
Casa di Terra, Fattoria 746
Casa E. di Mirafiore 96
Casa Emma 746
Casa Lucii 746
Casa Setaro 898
Casaccia di Franceschi, La 616
Casaccia, La 97

Casadei, Tenuta	616		Castello del Trebbio	621
Casal Thaulero	885		Castello della Paneretta	747
Casale del Giglio	849		Castello della Sala	824
Casale Marchese	849		Castello di Albola	622
CasalFarneto	779		Castello di Ama	622
Casali, Tenuta	558		Castello di Bolgheri	623
Casanova di Neri	617		Castello di Buttrio	477
Cascina Barisél	97		Castello di Cacchiano	747
Cascina Bongiovanni	98		Castello di Cigognola	263
Cascina Ca' Rossa	98		Castello di Corbara	825
Cascina Chicco	99		Castello di Fonterutoli	623
Cascina Corte	99		Castello di Gabbiano	624
Cascina del Colle	885		Castello di Gabiano	106
Cascina delle Rose	100		Castello di Gussago -	
Cascina Faletta	100		La Santissima	263
Cascina Fonda	101		Castello di Meleto	624
Cascina Fontana	101		Castello di Monsanto	625
Cascina Gilli	102		Castello di Montepò	625
Cascina Guido Berta	102		Castello di Monterinaldi	626
Cascina La Barbatella	103		Castello di Querceto	626
Cascina Lanzarotti	103		Castello di Radda	627
Cascina Lo Zoccolaio	146		Castello di Spessa	477
Cascina Luisin	104		Castello di Verduno	107
Cascina Morassino	104		Castello di Vicarello	747
Cascina Salicetti	105		Castello di Volpaia	627
Cascina Val del Prete	105		Castello La Leccia	747
Case Paolin	387		Castello Monaci	942
Casebianche	899		Castello Romitorio	628
Casematte, Le	987		Castello Sonnino	748
Casenuove, Tenute	617		Castello Tricerchi	748
Casina, Podere	746		Castello Vicchiomaggio	628
Casisano	618		Castelsina	748
Castel de Paolis	850		Castelvecchio	748
Castel Sallegg	334		Castelvecchio	478
CastelFaglia - Monogram	262		Castelvecchio	629
Castelfalfi	618		Castiadas, Cantina	1024
Castelfeder	335		Castiglion del Bosco	629
CastelGiocondo, Tenuta	619		Castignano -	
Castell'in Villa	619		Cantine dal 1960	779
Castellaccio, Podere Il	620		Castorani	868
Castellani, Michele	388		Catabbo	890
Castellare di Castellina	620		Cataldi Madonna	869
Castellari Bergaglio	106		Caudrina	107
Castellina, La	746		Cautiero	899
Castellinuzza e Piuca	747		Cav. Emiro Bortolusso	471
Castellinuzza, Podere	747		Cavalchina	388
Castello Bonomi	256		Cavalier Pepe, Tenuta	900
Castello del Terriccio	621		Cavallini, I	748

Cavallotto -
Tenuta Bricco Boschis 108
Cavazza 389
Cave Gargantua 55
Cavelli, Davide 108
Cavicchioli 559
Cavit 315
Cecchetto, Giorgio 389
Cecchi, Famiglia 630
Ceci, Giancarlo 942
Celestino Pecci 759
Celli 559
Cenatiempo 900
Cencioni, Patrizia 630
Centolani 631
Centopassi 987
Centorame 885
Ceraudo, Roberto 970
Ceretto 109
Ceri, Tenuta 748
Cerulli Spinozzi 869
Cerutti 109
Cesani, Vincenzo 631
Cesari, Gerardo 390
Cesari, Umberto 560
Cescon, Italo 390
Cheo 237
Cherchi, Giovanni Maria 1025
Chessa 1025
Chiacchiera, Cantina 749
Chiappini, Giovanni 632
Chiara Condello 562
Chiara Ziliani 295
Chiara, La 110
Chiarli Tenute Agricole,
Cleto 560
Chiarlo, Michele 110
Chiaromonte, Tenute 943
Chiesina di Lacona 749
Chionetti 111
Chiuse, Le 632
Chiusure, Le 264
Ciabot Berton 111
Ciacci - Poggio Nardone,
Tiziano 633
Ciacci Piccolomini
D'Aragona 633
Ciavolich 870

Cieck 112
Cigliano di Sopra,
Fattoria 749
Cigliuti, F.lli 112
Cimarelli 780
Cinciano 749
Cincinelli 634
Cincinnato 850
Cinciole, Le 634
Cinelli Colombini,
Donatella 635
Cingilia 870
Cinque Terre, Cantina 237
Cinti, Floriano 561
Cinzia Bergaglio 77
Ciolli, Damiano 851
Cipressi, Claudio 890
Cirelli, Francesco 885
Ciro Picariello 915
Cisa Asinari
dei Marchesi di Grésy,
Tenute 113
Citra Vini 871
Civa, Tenimenti 478
Clara Marcelli 792
Claudio Alario 65
Claudio Cipressi 890
Claudio Mariotto 152
Clerico, Aldo 113
Clerico, Domenico 114
Cleto Chiarli
Tenute Agricole 560
Cocci Grifoni, Tenuta 780
Cocco 826
Coffele 391
Cogno, Elvio 114
Col d'Orcia, Tenuta 635
Col di Bacche 636
Col di Corte 781
Col di Lamo 636
Cola, Battista 264
Coletti Conti, Antonello 851
Colla, Poderi 115
Collalto, Conte 391
Collavini, Eugenio 479
Colle Bereto 749
Colle Ciocco 826
Colle di Bordocheo 637

Colle Duga	479	Contralta, La	1026
Colle Santa Mustiola	637	Contucci	750
Colle Verde, Fattoria	749	Conventino, Il	750
Collelceto -		Convento Cappuccini - B8	118
Elia Palazzesi	638	Coos, Dario	481
ColleMassari	638	Coppi	944
Collemattoni	750	Coppi, Vigne Marina	118
Collestefano	781	Coppo	119
Collevite	782	Corda, Antonella	1027
Colli di Castelfranci	901	Cordero San Giorgio	266
Colli di Lapio	901	Cordero, Gabriele	119
Collina dei Ciliegi, La	392	Corino, Giovanni	120
Collina Serragrilli	115	Corino, Renato	120
Colline Albelle	750	Cormòns,	
Colline della Stella -		Cantina Produttori	482
Arici	265	Cornarea	121
Colline di Sopra	750	Cornelia Tessari	436
Colognole	639	Cornelissen, Frank	988
Colombaio di Cencio	639	Corte dei Venti	641
Colombaio		Corte Fusia	267
di Santa Chiara, Il	640	Corte Gardoni	393
Colombera, La	116	Corte Moschina	393
Colombo	116	Corte Pavone	641
Colonnara	782	Corte Rugolin	394
ColSanto, Fattoria	827	Corte Scaletta	394
Colterenzio, Cantina	335	Cortese, Giuseppe	121
Colture, Le	392	Cortonesi	642
Colutta, Gianpaolo	480	Corvée	316
Colutta, Giorgio	480	Corzano e Paterno,	
Comai	315	Fattoria	642
Comelli, Paolino	481	Cosimo Taurino	956
Condé	561	Cossetti 1891	122
Condello, Chiara	562	Costa Arente	395
Contadi Castaldi	265	Costa, La	267
Conte Collalto	391	Costa, Stefanino	122
Conte d'Attimis-Maniago	483	Costantini - Fattoria	
Conte Emo Capodilista -		Colline Verdi, Antonio	885
La Montecchia	398	Costaripa	268
Conte Guicciardini -		Cotarella, Famiglia	852
Castello di Poppiano	640	Cottanera	988
Conte Villa Prandone, Il	783	Crastin	482
Conte Vistarino	266	Crespaia	783
Conterno, Giacomo	117	Crêtes, Les	54
Conterno, Paolo	117	Cristo di Campobello	989
Contesa	871	Crotta di Vegneron, La	55
Conti Zecca	943	Cuomo, Marisa	902
Contini, Attilio	1026	Cura, La	750
Contrada Salandra	902	Custodi	827

Custodi delle Vigne dell'Etna, I	989
Cusumano	990
D'Alesio - Sciarr	872
D'Ambra - Vini d'Ischia	903
d'Amico, Paolo e Noemia	852
D'Angelo di Filomena Ruppi, Donato	930
d'Aprì	944
d'Attimis-Maniago, Conte	483
Daglio, Giovanni	123
Dainelli, Cantina	751
Dal Cero - Tenuta Corte Giacobbe	395
Dal Maso	396
Dama, La	396
Damiano Ciolli	851
Damijan Podversic	505
Dario Coos	481
Dario Di Vaira	644
David Sterza	433
Davide Cavelli	108
Davide Carlone	95
Davide Fregonese	132
Davino Meroi	497
De Angelis Corvi	885
De Angelis, Tenuta	784
De Falco Vini	903
De Falco, Cantine	945
De Stefani	397
De Vescovi Ulzbach	316
De Vigili	317
De Vito, Laura	904
De' Ricci	643
Decugnano dei Barbi	828
Dei, Maria Caterina	643
Della Porta, Masseria	904
Deltetto 1953	123
Denis Pizzulin	505
Dezi, Fattoria	784
Dezzani	124
Di Filippo	828
di Lenardo	483
Di Majo Norante	891
di Marzo, Cantine	905
Di Meo	905
Di Vaira, Dario	644
Diadema	751
Dianella	644
Dianetti, Emanuele	785
Diego Morra	159
Diego Pressenda	178
Dievole	645
Dino Illuminati	874
Dionisio, Fabrizio	645
Dirupi	268
Doglia, Gianni	124
Domaine Marjan Simčič	549
Domenico Clerico	114
Donà, Hartmann	364
Donà, Tenuta	364
Donatella Cinelli Colombini	635
Donati, Marco	317
Donato D'Angelo di Filomena Ruppi	930
Donato Giangirolami	853
Donna Olimpia 1898	646
Donnachiara	906
Donnafugata	990
Donne Fittipaldi	751
Dorfmann, Weingut Thomas	364
Dorgali, Cantina	1027
Dorigo	484
Doro Princic	508
Dosio Vigneti	125
Dottori, Edoardo	785
Draga - Miklus	484
Drius	485
Drusian	397
Dryas	906
Duca della Corgna - Cantina del Trasimeno	829
Duca di Salaparuta	991
Due Palme, Cantine	945
Duemani	646
Duni, Li	1028
Durio	125
Ebner - Florian Unterthiner, Tenuta	336
Edi Keber	492
Edi Skok	520

Edoardo Dottori	785	F.lli Tedeschi	435
Eichenstein	336	F.lli Turina	292
Einaudi, Poderi Luigi	126	F.lli Vagnoni	769
Elena Fucci	931	Fabbri - Susanna Grassi, I	647
Elena Walch	362	Fabbrica Pienza	648
Elio Altare	68	Fabio Motta	682
Elio Grasso	140	Fabrizia Caldera	92
Elio Ottin	57	Fabrizio Battaglino	74
Elvio Cogno	114	Fabrizio Dionisio	645
Emanuele Dianetti	785	Fabrizio Pratesi	704
Eméra - Claudio Quarta Vignaiolo, Tenute	946	Facchino, F.lli	126
Emidio Pepe	877	Falchetto, Tenuta Il	127
Emiliano Falsini	649	Falene, Le	648
Emo Capodilista - La Montecchia, Conte	398	Falkenstein - Franz Pratzner	337
Endrizzi	318	Falsini, Emiliano	649
Englar, Schloss	337	Famiglia Cecchi	630
Enio Ottaviani	572	Famiglia Cotarella	852
Enrico Gatti	271	Fanti, Tenuta	649
Enrico Neri	844	Fantinel	486
Enrico Serafino	195	Fappiano	907
Enzo Boglietti	79	Farina	398
Enzo Carmignani	746	Farnete - Cantagallo, Tenuta Le	650
Eolia	991	Fattoi	650
Erbhof Unterganzner - Josephus Mayr	360	Fattoria Mancini	792
Ermacora	485	Fattoria Ambra	594
Erta di Radda, L'	647	Fattoria Bonsalto	604
Erzetič	546	Fattoria Carpineta Fontalpino	614
Ettore Germano	137	Fattoria Casa di Terra	746
Ettore Sammarco	917	Fattoria Carsica - Bajta	467
Etyssa	318	Fattoria Cigliano di Sopra	749
Eugenio Collavini	479	Fattoria Colle Verde	749
Ezio Poggio	176	Fattoria ColSanto	827
		Fattoria Corzano e Paterno	642
F.lli Facchino	126	Fattoria dei Barbi	651
F.lli Abrigo	63	Fattoria del Pino	651
F.lli Agnes	250	Fattoria Dezi	784
F.lli Alessandria	66	Fattoria di Doccia	751
F.lli Aresca	71	Fattoria di Fugnano e Bombereto	751
F.lli Barba	867	Fattoria di Grignano - Tenuta Inghirami	753
F.lli Cigliuti	112	Fattoria di Magliano	652
F.lli Giacosa	138	Fattoria di Montechiari	751
F.lli Monchiero	156	Fattoria di Montemaggio	757
F.lli Pardi	835	Fattoria Fibbiano	653
F.lli Puddu	1035		
F.lli Revello	184		

Fattoria il Capitano	745	Ferraris Agricola	129
Fattoria Kappa	753	Ferraris, Roberto	129
Fattoria La Torre	768	Ferrocinto	971
Fattoria La Torre	769	Ferruccio Sgubin	518
Fattoria Lavacchio	754	Feudi del Pisciotto	992
Fattoria Le Ginestre	752	Feudi di Romans	487
Fattoria Le Pupille	705	Feudi di San Gregorio	908
Fattoria Le Terrazze	810	Feudo Antico	873
Fattoria Mantellassi	671	Feudo Arancio	992
Fattoria Montecchio	757	Feudo dei Sanseverino	971
Fattoria Montellori	677	Feudo Maccari	993
Fattoria Monticino Rosso	569	Feudo Montoni	993
Fattoria Moretto	570	Feuduccio	
Fattoria Nannì	797	di Santa Maria D'Orni, Il	886
Fattoria Nicodemi	876	Fiamberti	270
Fattoria Nicolucci	571	Fiasco, Francesca	909
Fattoria Ormanni	758	Fibbiano, Fattoria	653
Fattoria Petrolo	692	Fiegl	488
Fattoria Poggio Capponi	700	Figli Luigi Oddero -	
Fattoria San Donato	715	Tenuta Parà	165
Fattoria San Felo	764	Filippo Gallino	135
Fattoria San Lorenzo	803	Filò delle Vigne, Il	399
Fattoria		Filodivino	786
San Michele a Torri	765	Finigeto	270
Fattoria Santo Stefano	766	Fino, Gianfranco	947
Fattoria Selvapiana	719	Fiorano	787
Fattoria Svetoni	767	Fiorentino	909
Fattoria		Fiorenzo Nada	161
Terre del Marchesato	729	Fiorita, La	654
Fattoria Villa Saletta	739	Firriato	994
Fattoria Zerbina	583	Fitto, Il	752
Fauri, Tenuta I	872	Fliederhof -	
Favaro, Benito	127	Stefan Ramoser	365
Favati, I	907	Floriano Cinti	561
Fay, Sandro	269	Folonari, Tenute	
Felici, Andrea	786	Ambrogio e Giovanni	654
Felline	946	Fongaro Spumanti	399
Felluga, Livio	486	Fontana, Livia	130
Felluga, Marco	487	Fontanabianca	130
Fèlsina	652	Fontanacota	238
Fendi, Guido F.	653	Fontanafredda	131
Fenocchio, Giacomo	128	Fontanavecchia	910
Ferdinand	547	Fontefico	873
Ferghettina	269	Fontezoppa	787
Fernanda Cappello	476	Fonti, Le	752
Ferrando	128	Fontodi	655
Ferrara, Benito	908	Fontuccia	655
Ferrari	319	Fonzone	910

Fornacelle	656
Fornacelle, Le	752
Forte, Podere	656
Fortemasso	131
Fortuna, Tenuta La	752
Fradiles	1028
Fraghe, Le	400
Fralluca, La	657
Francesca Fiasco	909
Francesco Bellei & C.	555
Francesco Brigatti	87
Francesco Cadinu	1022
Francesco Candido	940
Francesco Cirelli	885
Francesco Intorcia Heritage	997
Francesco Sobrero	196
Francesco Tornatore	1010
Francesco Vosca	534
Franchetti - Passopisciaro, Vini	994
Franchetto	400
Franco Ivaldi	145
Franco M. Martinetti	152
Franco Toros	525
Frank Cornelissen	988
Franz Haas	341
Frasca - La Guaragna	132
Frascole	657
Fratelli Grimaldi - Ca' du Sindic	142
Frattasi, Masseria	911
Freccianera - F.lli Berlucchi	271
Fregonese, Davide	132
Frescobaldi, Marchesi	658
Fucci, Elena	931
Fuligni	658
Fusina, La	133
G. B. Burlotto	89
G. D. Vajra	204
Gabbas, Giuseppe	1029
Gabriele Cordero	119
Gaggino	133
Gaggioli	562
Gagliardo, Poderi Gianni	134
Gaja	134

Gallegati	563
Gallino, Filippo	135
Galliussi	489
Gamba	401
Garesio	135
Gargantua, Cave	55
Garlider - Christian Kerschbaumer	338
Garofoli, Gioacchino	788
Garrone, Cantine	136
Gatti, Enrico	271
Gatti, Marco	788
Gatto, Pierfrancesco	136
Generazione Alessandro	995
Gennaro Pigliacampo	887
Gentili	401
Gerardo Cesari	390
Gerla - Aisna, La	659
Germano, Ettore	137
Giacomelli	238
Giacomo Baraldo	600
Giacomo Borgogno & Figli	81
Giacomo Boveri	82
Giacomo Conterno	117
Giacomo Fenocchio	128
Giacomo Grimaldi	142
Giacomo Montresor	416
Giacomo Mori	757
Giacosa, Bruno	137
Giacosa, Carlo	138
Giacosa, F.lli	138
Giampaolo Tabarrini	838
Giancarlo Ceci	942
Giancarlo Travaglini	203
Gianfranco Alessandria	66
Gianfranco Bovio	83
Gianfranco Fino	947
Giangirolami, Donato	853
Gianni Brunelli - Le Chiuse di Sotto	607
Gianni Doglia	124
Gianni Moscardini	757
Giannitessari	402
Gianpaolo Colutta	480
Giba, Cantina	1029
Gigante	489
Gilberto Boniperti	80
Ginestraia, La	239

Ginestre, Fattoria Le	752
Gini	402
Gioacchino Garofoli	788
Giodo	659
Giorgi	272
Giorgio Colutta	480
Giorgio Cecchetto	389
Giorgio Meletti Cavallari	756
Giorgio Scarzello e Figli	193
Giovanna Madonia	566
Giovanna Tantini	434
Giovanni Abrigo	63
Giovanni Almondo	68
Giovanni Avanzi	251
Giovanni Chiappini	632
Giovanni Corino	120
Giovanni Daglio	123
Giovanni Manzone	149
Giovanni Maria Cherchi	1025
Giovanni Rosso	188
Giovanni Sordo	197
Giovanni Terenzi	858
Girlan, Cantina	338
Girolamo Russo	1005
Girolamo Tola	1009
Gironda, La	139
Giuliano Pettinella	878
Giuseppe Campagnola	383
Giuseppe Cortese	121
Giuseppe Gabbas	1029
Giuseppe Gorelli	661
Giuseppe Mascarello e Figlio	153
Giuseppe Quintarelli	424
Giuseppe Sedilesu	1038
Giuseppe Stella	199
Giusti & Zanza, I	660
Giusti Wine	403
Giusti, Luigi	789
Giustiniana, Tenuta La	139
Giuva, La	403
Glögglhof - Franz Gojer	339
Godiolo	752
Gondi - Tenuta Bossi, Marchesi	660
Gorelli, Giuseppe	661
Goretti	829
Gorghi Tondi, Tenuta	995
Gorgo	404
Gori Agricola	490
Gottardi	339
Gozzelino	140
Gracciano della Seta, Tenuta di	753
Graci	996
Gradis'ciutta	490
Grasso, Elio	140
Grasso, Silvio	141
Grattamacco	661
Graziano Merotto	411
Graziano Prà	423
Gregoletto	404
Gregu, Tenute	1030
Grieco, Tenimenti	891
Griesbauerhof - Georg Mumelter	340
Griesserhof	365
Grifalco	931
Grignano - Tenuta Inghirami, Fattoria di	753
Grillo Iole	491
Grimaldi - Ca' du Sindic, Fratelli	142
Grimaldi, Bruna	141
Grimaldi, Giacomo	142
Grosjean	56
Grosskemat	365
Guado al Melo	662
Guado al Tasso, Tenuta	662
Gualdo del Re	753
Guardiense - Janare, La	911
Guerrieri Rizzardi	405
Guicciardini Strozzi	663
Guido Berlucchi Franciacorta	254
Guido F. Fendi	653
Guido Platinetti	175
Guido Porro	177
Gummerhof - Malojer	340
Gump Hof - Markus Prackwieser	341
Gungui, Luca	1030
Haas, Franz	341
Haderburg	342
Hartmann Donà	364

WINERIES IN ALPHABETICAL ORDER

Hibiscus	996
Hilberg - Pasquero	143
Himmelreichhof	365
Hof Gandberg - Thomas Niedermayr	365
I Veroni	737
I Barisei	252
I Buongiorno	939
I Cacciagalli	897
I Campi	384
I Cavallini	748
I Custodi delle Vigne dell'Etna	989
I Fabbri - Susanna Grassi	647
I Favati	907
I Giusti & Zanza	660
I Vitari	295
Iaquin	547
Ida Agnoletti	371
Il Calepino	261
Il Palazzone	688
Il Poggiolino	762
Il Rocchin	187
Il Roncat - Giovanni Dri	512
Il Balzo	742
Il Borro	606
Il Colombaio di Santa Chiara	640
Il Conte Villa Prandone	783
Il Conventino	750
Il Feuduccio di Santa Maria D'Orni	886
Il Filò delle Vigne	399
Il Fitto	752
Il Molinaccio di Montepulciano	675
Il Mottolo	418
Il Palagione	687
Il Palazzo	759
Il Pignetto	422
Il Roncal	511
Il Sassolo	766
Illuminati, Dino	874
Inalto Vini d'Altura	874
Inama	405
Incisa della Rocchetta, Marchesi	143
Innocenti	753
Intorcia Heritage, Francesco	997
Ioppa	144
Ippolito 1845	972
Isidoro Polencic	506
Isimbarda	272
Isola	563
Isola delle Falcole	753
Isolabella della Croce	144
Isole e Olena	663
Istine	664
Italo Cescon	390
Iuzzolini, Tenuta	972
Ivaldi, Franco	145
Jacùss	491
Jakončič Winery, Carolina	548
Jermann	492
Jerzu, Antichi Poderi	1031
Josef Brigl	333
Josef Weger	368
Josetta Saffirio	189
Josmoar Hof - Sebastian Tonner	365
K. Martini & Sohn	348
Ka' Manciné	239
Kaltern, Cantina	342
Kappa, Fattoria	753
Keber, Edi	492
Kettmeir	343
Klaus Lentsch	346
Klet Brda	548
Klosterhof - Oskar Andergassen	343
Köfererhof - Günther Kerschbaumer	344
Komjanc, Alessio	493
Kornell, Tenuta	344
Kränzelhof - Graf Franz Pfeil, Tenuta	366
Kuenhof - Peter Pliger	345
Kurtatsch, Cantina	345
Kurtin	493
L'Armangia	72
L'Erta di Radda	647
L'Infinito, Podere	789

La Caplana	94	La Plantze	58
La Castellina	746	La Raia	181
La Gerla - Aisna	659	La Rajade	509
La Lastra	754	La Roncaia	511
La Lecciaia	666	La Sala del Torriano	713
La Monacesca	795	La Sibilla	920
La Poderina	698	La Togata	731
La Querce	706	La Toledana	202
La Rasina	707	La Tordera	439
La Sclusa	517	La Tosa	579
La Smilla	196	La Valle del Sole	811
La Staffa	807	La Viarte	528
La Valentina	882	La Vis - Cembra	319
La Baia del Sole - Federici	234	La Vrille	59
La Berta, Podere	564	Laimburg	346
La Bollina	79	Lambardi, Maurizio	754
La Buse dal Lôf	473	Lambruschi, Ottaviano	240
La Calcinara	776	Lamole di Lamole	665
La Cappuccina	386	Lanciola	754
La Casaccia	97	Langasco, Tenuta	145
La Casaccia di Franceschi	616	Lantieri de Paratico	273
La Chiara	110	Lapone	830
La Chiesa, Podere	664	Larcherhof - Spögler	366
La Collina dei Ciliegi	392	LaSelva	754
La Colombera	116	Lastra, La	754
La Contralta	1026	Laura Aschero	233
La Costa	267	Laura De Vito	904
La Crotta di Vegneron	55	Lavacchio, Fattoria	754
La Cura	750	Lavandaro, Podere	247
La Dama	396	Lazzari	273
La Fiorita	654	Le Canà	777
La Fralluca	657	Le Chiuse	632
La Fusina	133	Le Chiusure	264
La Ginestraia	239	Le Cinciole	634
La Gironda	139	Le Colture	392
La Giuva	403	Le Fonti	752
La Guardiense - Janare	911	Le Marchesine	275
La Leccia	666	Le Battistelle	374
La Madeleine	831	Le Bèrne, Podere	665
La Madonnina	670	Le Bertille	743
La Magia	670	Le Calle	743
La Mesma	155	Le Caniette	777
La Montagnetta	157	Le Carline	386
La Montanina	675	Le Casematte	987
La Morandina	159	Le Falene	648
La Nascosta	758	Le Fornacelle	752
La Palazzetta	687	Le Fraghe	400
La Pietra del Focolare	242	Le Macchiole	669

Le Macioche	669
Le Marognole	407
Le Miccine	674
Le Monde	497
Le Morette	417
Le Novelire	758
Le Piane	173
Le Pianore	760
Le Ragose	425
Le Rocche Malatestiane	574
Le Salette	428
Le Strette	199
Le Tende	435
Le Vigne di San Pietro	444
Le Vigne di Zamò	531
Leccia, La	666
Lecciaia, La	666
Lehengut	366
Lento, Cantine	973
Lentsch, Klaus	346
Lentsch, Tenuta H.	366
Lenzini, Tenuta	667
Leo, Cantine Paolo	947
Leonardo Bussoletti	823
Leonardo da Vinci	754
Leone de Castris	948
Lequio, Ugo	146
Les Crêtes	54
Letrari	320
Leuta	755
LeVide	320
Li Duni	1028
Librandi	973
Licinia, Tenuta	667
Lini 910	564
Lis Fadis	494
Lis Neris	494
Lisciandrello	997
Livia Fontana	130
Livio e Claudio Buiatti	472
Livio Felluga	486
Livon	495
Lo Sparviere	289
Lo Triolet	56
Lo Zoccolaio, Cascina	146
Loacker Schwarhof	347
Lodali	147
Lombardini, Cantine	565
Lombardo, Antonella	974
Loredan Gasparini	406
Lorenz Martini	348
Lorenzo Begali	374
Lorenzo Negro	163
Lu.Va.	565
Luca Gungui	1030
Lucarelli, Roberto	790
Lucchetti, Mario	790
Luce, Tenuta	755
Luciano Sandrone	190
Luigi Boveri	83
Luigi Brunelli	380
Luigi Giusti	789
Luigi Pira	174
Luigi Spertino	198
Luisa, Tenuta	495
Lunadoro	668
Lunae Bosoni, Cantine	240
Lunelli - Castelbuono, Tenute	830
Lunelli - Podernovo, Tenute	668
Lungarotti	831
Luretta	566
Maccario Dringenberg	241
Macchie Santa Maria	912
Macchiole, Le	669
Macinatico	755
Macioche, Le	669
Maculan	406
Madeleine, La	831
Madonia, Giovanna	566
Madonna del Latte	832
Madonnabruna	791
Madonnina, La	670
Madrevite	832
Maestà della Formica	755
Magda Pedrini	170
Magia, La	670
Maison Anselmet	54
Maixei	241
Malabaila di Canale	147
Malenchini	671
Malgiacca	755
Malvirà	148
Mamete Prevostini	274

Man Spumanti	321	Marisa Cuomo	902	
Manara	407	Marognole, Le	407	
Mancini	791	Marotti Campi	793	
Mancini, Fattoria	792	Martinetti, Franco M.	152	
Mandirola	148	Martini & Sohn, K.	348	
Manincor	347	Martini, Lorenz	348	
Mantellassi, Fattoria	671	Martoccia, Podere	672	
Manuelina	274	Mas dei Chini	321	
Manzone, Giovanni	149	Masari	408	
Manzone, Paolo	149	Masca del Tacco	948	
Mara, Tenuta Biodinamica	567	Mascarello e Figlio, Giuseppe	153	
Marangona	275			
Marcalberto	150	Masciantonio, Tommaso	886	
Marcampo, Podere	755	Masciarelli	875	
Marcarini, Poderi	150	Masi	408	
Marcelli, Clara	792	Maso Cantanghel	322	
Marchesi Alfieri	67	Maso Martis	322	
Marchesi Antinori	595	Masone Mannu, Tenuta	1031	
Marchesi di Barolo	151	Masottina	409	
Marchesi Frescobaldi	658	Massa, Vigneti	153	
Marchesi Gondi - Tenuta Bossi	660	Masseria Borgo dei Trulli	939	
		Masseria Cuturi	949	
Marchesi Incisa della Rocchetta	143	Masseria Della Porta	904	
		Masseria Frattasi	911	
Marchesi Pancrazi - Villa di Bagnolo	688	Masseria Li Veli	960	
		Masseto	672	
Marchesine, Le	275	Massimago	409	
Marchetti, Maurizio	793	Massimo Alessandri	232	
Marco Bonfante	80	Massolino - Vigna Rionda	154	
Marco Capitoni	745			
Marco Carpineti	848	Mastrojanni	673	
Marco Donati	317	Masùt da Rive	496	
Marco Felluga	487	Máté	673	
Marco Gatti	788	Matijaz Tercic	524	
Marco Mosconi	417	Mattioli, Poderi	794	
Marco Porello	176	Mattoni, Valter	794	
Marco Sara	516	Maugeri	998	
Marco Scolaris	517	Maurizio Alongi	594	
Mareli, Tenuta	756	Maurizio Buzzinelli	474	
Marengo, Mario	151	Maurizio Lambardi	754	
Maria Caterina Dei	643	Maurizio Marchetti	793	
Maria Donata Bianchi	234	Mauro Molino	155	
Maria Letizia Allevi	772	Mauro Sebaste	194	
Marina Romin	764	Mauro Veglio	205	
Marinig	496	Mazzarosa	886	
Mario Lucchetti	790	Mazzi e Figli, Roberto	410	
Mario Marengo	151	Mazzolino, Tenuta	276	
Mariotto, Claudio	152	Mazzoni, Tiziano	154	

Medici Ermete	567	Monte Rossa	277
Meletti Cavallari, Giorgio	756	Monte Santoccio	413
Melini - Vigneti		Monte Solaio	676
La Selvanella	674	Monte Tondo	413
Menegotti	410	Monte Zovo -	
Menhir Salento	949	Famiglia Cottini	414
Menta e Rosmarino	568	Montecappone - Mirizzi	795
Merano, Cantina	349	Montecchio, Fattoria	757
Meraviglia - Tenuta		Monteforte d'Alpone,	
Le Colonne, Tenuta	756	Cantina Sociale di	414
Merlotta	568	Montegrande -	
Meroi, Davino	497	Cristofanon	415
Merotto, Graziano	411	Monteleone	998
Mesa, Cantina	1032	Montellori, Fattoria	677
Mesma, La	155	Montelvini	415
Mezzacorona	323	Montemaggio, Fattoria di	757
Miccine, Le	674	Montemagno, Tenuta	158
Michael Puff	367	Montenidoli	677
Michele Castellani	388	Montepepe	757
Michele Chiarlo	110	Monteraponi	678
Michele Reverdito	184	Monterò	678
Michele Satta	718	MonteRosola	679
Mirabella	276	Monterotondo	757
Molettieri, Salvatore	912	Monteti, Tenuta	679
Molinaccio		Monteverro	680
di Montepulciano, Il	675	Monteversa	416
Molino, Mauro	155	Montevertine	680
Molon, Ornella	411	Montevetrano	913
Monacesca, La	795	Monticino Rosso, Fattoria	569
Monastero		Montina Franciacorta	278
dei Frati Bianchi	756	Montori, Camillo	875
Monastero, Podere	756	Montresor, Giacomo	416
Monchiero Carbone	156	Monviert	498
Monchiero, F.lli	156	Monzio Compagnoni	278
Monde, Le	497	Morandina, La	159
Monrubio, Cantine	833	Morella	950
Monsupello	277	Morette, Le	417
Montagnetta, La	157	Moretti Omero	834
Montalbera	157	Moretto, Fattoria	570
Montalbino	756	Mori, Giacomo	757
Montali - Quercia		Morisfarms	681
d'Arabona, Patrizio	886	Mormoraia	681
Montanina, La	675	Moroder, Alessandro	796
Montaribaldi	158	Morra Stefanino	160
Montauto	676	Morra, Diego	159
Monte dall'Ora	412	Moscardini, Gianni	757
Monte del Frà	412	Moschioni	498
Monte delle Vigne	569	Mosconi, Marco	417

Moser	323		Noah	164
Moser, Tenuta	349		Nododivino	876
Mosnel	279		Noelia Ricci	571
Mosole	418		Norina Pez	503
Motta, Fabio	682		Noüe Marinič, Vini	549
Mottolo, Il	418		Novaia	420
Mottura Vini del Salento	950		Novaripa	886
Mottura, Sergio	853		Novelire, Le	758
Mulin di Mezzo, Tenuta	419		Noventa Botticino	280
Mulini di Segalari	758		Numa	797
Mura	1032			
Mura Mura	160		Oasi degli Angeli	798
Muralia	682		Oberstein	366
Muratori	279		Occhipinti, Arianna	999
Muri-Gries	350		Oddero - Tenuta Parà,	
Murva	499		Figli Luigi	165
Musico	758		Oddero, Poderi e Cantine	165
Musone, Tenuta	796		Odilio Antoniotti	71
Mustilli	913		Odino Vaona	441
Musto Carmelitano	932		Olianas	1033
Mutiliana	570		Olim Bauda, Tenuta	166
Muzic	499		Olivastri, Tommaso	886
			Olivella, Cantine	914
Nada, Ada	161		Olivini	281
Nada, Fiorenzo	161		Oltrenero	281
Nals Margreid	350		Ômina Romana	854
Nannì, Fattoria	797		Opera Roses	282
Nardello	419		Orestiadi, Tenute	1000
Nardi, Tenute Silvio	683		Orlandi Contucci Ponno	877
Nascosta, La	758		Orlando Abrigo	64
Negretti	162		Orma	684
Negri, Nino	280		Ormanni, Fattoria	758
Negro, Angelo	162		Ornella Molon	411
Negro, Lorenzo	163		Ornellaia	684
Neri, Enrico	844		Orsolani	166
Nervi Conterno	163		Orsumella	758
Nestore Bosco	868		Orzan	540
Nicodemi, Fattoria	876		Ottaviani, Enio	572
Nicola Balter	313		Ottaviano Lambruschi	240
Nicola Bergaglio	77		Ottella	421
Nicolis	420		Ottin, Elio	57
Nicolucci, Fattoria	571			
Nicolussi-Leck, Tenuta	351		Pacchiarotti, Antonella	854
Nicosia, Cantine	999		Pace	167
Niklaserhof - Dieter Sölva	351		Pacenti, Siro	685
Nino Negri	280		Pagani de Marchi	685
Nittardi	683		Paitin	167
Nizza, Silvano	164		Pakravan-Papi, Tenuta	686

Pala	1033
Palagetto, Tenute	686
Palagione, Il	687
Palamà	951
Palari	1000
Palazzetta, La	687
Palazzo	759
Palazzo Vecchio	759
Palazzo, Il	759
Palazzo, Podere	572
Palazzone	834
Palazzone, Il	688
Palladino	168
Palmento Costanzo	1001
Paltrinieri, Alberto	573
Pancrazi - Villa di Bagnolo, Marchesi	688
Panizzi	689
Pantaleone	798
Paolino Comelli	481
Paolo Angelini	69
Paolo Conterno	117
Paolo e Noemia d'Amico	852
Paolo Manzone	149
Paolo Rodaro	510
Paolo Scavino	194
Paradiso di Cacuci	759
Paraschos	500
Pardi, F.lli	835
Parmoleto	689
Parrina, Antica Fattoria La	690
Parusso	168
Pascolo, Alessandro	500
Pasetti	887
Pasini San Giovanni	282
Pasqua	421
Passo delle Tortore	914
Paternoster	932
Patrizia Cencioni	630
Patrizio Montali - Quercia d'Arabona	886
Patruno Perniola, Tenuta	951
Pavia e Figli, Agostino	169
Pazzaglia, Tenuta La	855
Pecchenino	169
Pecci, Celestino	759
Pecorari, Pierpaolo	501
Pedemontis	170
Pedres, Cantina	1034
Pedrini, Magda	170
Pelassa	171
Pelissero	171
Pellegrino	1001
Pellissier, André	57
Pepe, Emidio	877
Pepi Lignana - Fattoria Il Casalone	759
Peppucci, Cantina	835
Peq Agri	242
Perano, Tenuta	690
Perda Rubia, Tenute	1034
Perillo	915
Perla del Garda	283
Pertinace	172
Perusini	501
Pescaja	172
Pesolillo	887
Peteglia	760
Peter Sölva & Söhne	355
Peter Zemmer	363
Petra	691
Petricci e Del Pianta	691
Petrolo, Fattoria	692
Petrucco	502
Petrussa	502
Pettinella, Giuliano	878
Pez, Norina	503
Pezzuoli	573
Pfannenstielhof - Johannes Pfeifer	352
Pfitscher, Tenuta	352
Pföstl, Weingut	366
Piaggia	692
Pian delle Querci	760
Piancornello	693
Piandaccoli	693
Piane, Le	173
Pianirossi	694
Piano di Rustano, Tenuta	799
Pianore, Le	760
Pianta Grossa	58
Picariello, Ciro	915
Picchioni, Andrea	283
Piccini 1882	694
Picech, Roberto	503

Pichler, Thomas	367	Podere Forte	656
Pico Maccario	173	Podere Il Castellaccio	620
Piemaggio	760	Podere Il Saliceto	576
Pieralisi, Tenute	799	Podere L' Assunta	742
Pierangelo Careglio	95	Podere L'Infinito	789
Pierfrancesco Gatto	136	Podere La Berta	564
Pieri, Agostina	695	Podere La Chiesa	664
Piero Busso	89	Podere La Regola	707
Pieropan	422	Podere Lavandaro	247
Pierpaolo Pecorari	501	Podere Le Bèrne	665
Pietra del Focolare, La	242	Podere Le Poggiarelle	761
Pietracupa	916	Podere Marcampo	755
Pietradolce	1002	Podere Martoccia	672
Pietraserena	760	Podere Monastero	756
Pietraventosa	952	Podere Palazzo	572
Pietro 17	800	Podere Poggio Scalette	762
Pietro Beconcini	742	Podere San Cristoforo	714
Pietro Torti	291	Podere Sapaio	717
Pietro Zanoni	447	Podere Vito Cardinali	778
Pietro Zardini	448	Poderi Marcarini	150
Pietroso	695	Poderi Arcangelo	741
Pievalta	800	Poderi Colla	115
Pieve di Santo Stefano	696	Poderi e Cantine Oddero	165
Pieve Santa Restituta	760	Poderi Gianni Gagliardo	134
Pighin	504	Poderi Luigi Einaudi	126
Pigliacampo, Gennaro	887	Poderi Mattioli	794
Pignetto, Il	422	Poderi Rosso Giovanni	188
Pinino	761	Poderi San Lazzaro	803
Pio Cesare	174	Poderi Vaiot	175
Piovene Porto Godi	423	Poderina, La	698
Pira, Luigi	174	Podernuovo a Palazzone	698
Pisoni Spumanti	324	Podversic, Damijan	505
Pittaro, Vigneti	504	Poggiarelle, Podere Le	761
Pizzulin, Denis	505	Poggio al Tesoro	699
Planeta	1002	Poggio alla Sala, Tenuta	761
Plantamura	952	Poggio Antico	699
Plantze, La	58	Poggio Brigante	761
Platinetti, Guido	175	Poggio Capponi, Fattoria	700
Podere Capaccia	745	Poggio di Bortolone	1003
Podere Terreno		Poggio di Sotto	700
alla Via della Volpaia	768	Poggio Grande	761
Podere 29	953	Poggio Il Castellare	761
Podere 414	696	Poggio La Noce	762
Podere Casina	746	Poggio Landi -	
Podere Castellinuzza	747	Podere Brizio	701
Podere dell'Angelo	574	Poggio Le Volpi	855
Podere della Civettaja	697	Poggio Rosso, Tenuta	701
Podere Erica	697	Poggio Salvi, Villa	702

WINERIES IN ALPHABETICAL ORDER

Poggio Scalette, Podere	762
Poggio Sorbello	762
Poggio, Ezio	176
Poggiolino, Il	762
Poggione, Tenuta II	702
Pojer & Sandri	324
Polencic, Isidoro	506
Poliziano	703
Polje	506
Polvanera	953
Pomario	836
Pomona	703
Porello, Marco	176
Porro, Guido	177
Possente	1003
Post dal Vin - Terre del Barbera	177
Potazzine, Tenuta Le	704
Prà, Graziano	423
Prackfolerhof	367
Pradio	507
Pratesi, Fabrizio	704
Pravis	325
Prediomagno	178
Pressenda, Diego	178
Primaia	705
PrimaLuce	762
Prime Alture	284
Primosic	507
Princic, Doro	508
Principi di Butera	1004
Prinsi	179
Priorino	762
Produttori del Barbaresco	179
Produttori del Gavi, Cantina	180
Produttori di Manduria	954
Provveditore	763
Prunotto	180
Pucciarella	845
Puddu, F.lli	1035
Puff, Michael	367
Puiatti	508
Pupille, Fattoria Le	705
Pusole	1035
Quadra Franciacorta	284
Quartomoro di Sardegna	1036
Querce, La	706
Querceto di Castellina	706
Quercia al Poggio	763
Querciamatta, Tenuta	763
Quintarelli, Giuseppe	424
Quntì	801
Quota 101	424
Rabissi	763
Radica, Vigneti	887
Ragose, Le	425
Raia, La	181
Raineri	181
Rainoldi, Aldo	285
Raiz, Teresa	509
Rajade, La	509
Rallo	1004
Rametz	367
Rapitalà, Tenute	1005
Rascioni e Cecconello	763
Rasina, La	707
Ratti, Renato	182
Re Manfredi	933
Reassi	425
Regola, Podere La	707
Renato Corino	120
Renato Ratti	182
Repetto, Vigneti	182
Resistenti Nicola Biasi	325
Réva	183
Revello, Carlo & Figli	183
Revello, F.lli	184
Reverdito, Michele	184
Revì	326
Ricasoli, Barone	708
Ricci Curbastro	285
Ridolfi	708
Riecine	709
Rigoli	709
Ritterhof, Tenuta	353
Rivera	954
Rizzi	185
Roagna	185
Roberto Ceraudo	970
Roberto Ferraris	129
Roberto Lucarelli	790
Roberto Mazzi e Figli	410
Roberto Picech	503

Roberto Sarotto	192
Roberto Scubla	518
Roberto Venturi	812
Rocca Bernarda	510
Rocca del Principe	916
Rocca delle Macìe - Famiglia Zingarelli	710
Rocca di Castagnoli - Tenute Calì	710
Rocca di Frassinello	711
Rocca di Montegrossi	763
Rocca di Montemassi	711
Rocca, Albino	186
Rocca, Bruno	186
Roccafiore	836
Roccapesta	712
Rocche Costamagna	187
Rocche Malatestiane, Le	574
Rocchin, Il	187
Roccolo Grassi	426
Rodaro, Paolo	510
Roeno	426
Rohregger, Weingut	367
Romagnoli, Cantine	575
Romanelli	837
Romen, Tenuta	367
Romin, Marina	764
Roncaia, La	511
Roncal, Il	511
Roncat - Giovanni Dri, Il	512
Ronchi di Castelluccio	575
Ronchi di Manzano	512
Ronco Blanchis	513
Ronco Calino	286
Ronco dei Tassi	513
Ronco Margherita	514
Ronco Scagnèt	514
Rosset Terroir	59
Rosso Giovanni, Poderi	188
Rosso, Giovanni	188
Rotari	326
Rottensteiner, Tenuta Hans	353
Rubinelli Vajol	427
Rubino, Tenute	955
Ruffino	712
Ruggeri & C.	427
Russiz Superiore	515
Russo, Girolamo	1005
Sabbionare	801
Saffirio, Josetta	189
Sala del Torriano, La	713
Saladini Pilastri	802
Salcheto	713
Salette, Le	428
Saliceto, Podere Il	576
Salvatore Molettieri	912
Salvioni	714
Sammarco, Ettore	917
San Benedetto	764
San Cristoforo	286
San Cristoforo, Podere	714
San Donato, Fattoria	715
San Fabiano, Tenute	764
San Felice	715
San Felo, Fattoria	764
San Fereolo	189
San Filippo	802
San Filippo	764
San Francesco, Tenuta	917
San Giacomo	878
San Giovenale	856
San Guglielmo	764
San Guido, Tenuta	716
San Jacopo in Castiglioni, Tenuta	765
San Lazzaro, Poderi	803
San Leonardo	327
San Leonino	716
San Lorenzo Vini	879
San Lorenzo, Fattoria	803
San Marzano Vini	955
San Michele	287
San Michele a Torri, Fattoria	765
San Michele Appiano, Cantina Produttori	354
San Paolo, Cantina	354
San Patrignano	576
San Polo Montalcino	717
San Salvatore 1988	918
San Sebastiano, Tenuta	190
San Sisto, Tenute	804
San Valentino	577

San Vito in Fior di Selva, Tenuta	765
Sandro Fay	269
Sandrone, Luciano	190
Sanoner, Tenuta	765
Sanpaolo - Claudio Quarta Vignaiolo	918
Sansonina	428
Sant'Agata, Cantine	191
Sant'Agnese	765
Sant'Andrea, Cantina	856
Sant'Antonio, Tenuta	429
Sant'Elena	515
Sant'Isidoro, Tenuta	857
Santa Barbara	804
Santa Caterina, Tenuta	191
Santa Croce, Cantina	577
Santa Lucia	765
Santa Lucia, Tenuta	578
Santa Margherita	429
Santa Maria la Palma	1036
Santa Sofia	430
Santa Venere	975
Santadi, Cantina	1037
Santi	430
Santo Stefano, Fattoria	766
Santori, Tenuta	805
Sapaio, Podere	717
Sara & Sara	516
Sara, Marco	516
Saraja	1037
Sarotto, Roberto	192
Sartarelli	805
Sartori	431
SassodiSole	766
Sassolo, Il	766
Sassotondo	718
Satta, Michele	718
Scacciadiavoli	837
Scagliola - Sansì	192
Scarpa	193
Scarzello e Figli, Giorgio	193
Scavino, Paolo	194
Scerscé, Tenuta	287
Schloss Englar	337
Schola Sarmenti	956
Sclavia	919
Sclusa, La	517
Scolaris, Marco	517
Scubla, Roberto	518
Scuotto, Tenuta	919
Scuropasso - Roccapietra	288
Sebaste, Mauro	194
Secondo Marco	431
Sedilesu, Giuseppe	1038
Seeperle, Tenuta	355
Sella & Mosca, Tenute	1038
Sella, Tenute	195
Selva Capuzza	288
Selvapiana, Fattoria	719
Sensi - Fattoria Calappiano	719
Sequerciani	766
Serafini & Vidotto	432
Serafino, Enrico	195
Sergio Mottura	853
Sesti - Castello di Argiano	720
Sette Cieli, Tenuta	766
Sette Ponti, Tenuta	720
Settecani, Cantina	578
Settesoli, Cantine	1006
Sgubin, Ferruccio	518
Sibilla, La	920
Siddùra	1039
Silvano Nizza	164
Silvio Grasso	141
Simčič, Domaine Marjan	549
Simon di Brazzan	519
Sincette	289
Sirch	519
Sirk, Valter	550
Siro Pacenti	685
Skerk	520
Skok, Edi	520
Smilla, La	196
Sobrero, Francesco	196
Socré	197
Sölva & Söhne, Peter	355
Sordo, Giovanni	197
Sorelle Bronca	380
Sottimano	198
Spadafora	1006
Sparapani - Frati Bianchi	806
Sparviere, Lo	289
Specogna	521

Speri	432	Tende, Le	435
Spertino, Luigi	198	Tenimenti Civa	478
Spinelli	879	Tenimenti Grieco	891
Spinelli, Tenuta	806	Tenuta Cavalier Pepe	900
Spitalerhof -		Tenuta Cocci Grifoni	780
Günther Oberpertinger,		Tenuta Kornell	344
Tenuta	368	Tenuta Anfosso	232
St. Quirinus - Robert Sinn	356	Tenuta Ansitz Waldgries	332
Staffa, La	807	Tenuta Bastonaca	984
Stanig	543	Tenuta Bellafonte	822
Stefanino Costa	122	Tenuta Biodinamica Mara	567
Stefano Accordini	370	Tenuta Borgo Conventi	469
Stefano Amerighi	595	Tenuta Calamoni	985
Stefano Berti	555	Tenuta Campo al Mare	743
Steinhaus	356	Tenuta Campo al Signore	744
Stella, Borgo La	766	Tenuta Carretta	96
Stella, Giuseppe	199	Tenuta Casadei	616
Stella, Tenuta	521	Tenuta Casali	558
Sterza, David	433	Tenuta CastelGiocondo	619
Stocco	522	Tenuta Ceri	748
Stomennano	767	Tenuta Col d'Orcia	635
Strappelli	887	Tenuta De Angelis	784
Strasserhof -		Tenuta del Buonamico	767
Hannes Baumgartner	357	Tenuta del Conte	976
Strette, Le	199	Tenuta del Meriggio	920
Stroblhof	357	Tenuta del Priore -	
Sturm	522	Col del Mondo	887
Su'Entu	1039	Tenuta del Travale	976
Suavia	433	Tenuta dell'Ugolino	807
Subida di Monte	523	Tenuta delle Ripalte	722
Sulin	200	Tenuta di Angoris	523
Surrau	1040	Tenuta di Arceno	723
Sutto	434	Tenuta di Artimino	723
Svetoni, Fattoria	767	Tenuta di Bibbiano	724
		Tenuta di Capezzana	724
Tabarrini, Giampaolo	838	Tenuta di Carleone	725
Tacchino	200	Tenuta di Castellaro	1007
Talenti	721	Tenuta di Fessina	1008
Talosa	721	Tenuta di Fiorano	857
Tantini, Giovanna	434	Tenuta di Frà	808
Tasca d'Almerita	1007	Tenuta di Ghizzano	725
Taschlerhof -		Tenuta di Gracciano	
Peter Wachtler	358	della Seta	753
Tassi	722	Tenuta di Lilliano	726
Taurino, Cosimo	956	Tenuta di Sesta	726
Teanum	957	Tenuta di Tavignano	808
Tedeschi, F.lli	435	Tenuta di Trinoro	727
Tenaglia, Tenuta	201	Tenuta di Valgiano	727

Tenuta Donà	364	Tenuta Ritterhof	353
Tenuta Ebner - Florian Unterthiner	336	Tenuta Romen	367
Tenuta Fanti	649	Tenuta San Francesco	917
Tenuta Gorghi Tondi	995	Tenuta San Guido	716
Tenuta Guado al Tasso	662	Tenuta San Jacopo in Castiglioni	765
Tenuta H. Lentsch	366	Tenuta San Sebastiano	190
Tenuta Hans Rottensteiner	353	Tenuta San Vito in Fior di Selva	765
Tenuta I Fauri	872	Tenuta Sanoner	765
Tenuta Il Falchetto	127	Tenuta Sant'Antonio	429
Tenuta Il Poggione	702	Tenuta Sant'Isidoro	857
Tenuta Iuzzolini	972	Tenuta Santa Caterina	191
Tenuta Kränzelhof - Graf Franz Pfeil	366	Tenuta Santa Lucia	578
Tenuta La Fortuna	752	Tenuta Santori	805
Tenuta La Giustiniana	139	Tenuta Scerscé	287
Tenuta La Pazzaglia	855	Tenuta Scuotto	919
Tenuta La Vigna	769	Tenuta Seeperle	355
Tenuta La Viola	582	Tenuta Sette Cieli	766
Tenuta Langasco	145	Tenuta Sette Ponti	720
Tenuta Le Farnete - Cantagallo	650	Tenuta Spinelli	806
Tenuta Le Potazzine	704	Tenuta Spitalerhof - Günther Oberpertinger	368
Tenuta Lenzini	667	Tenuta Stella	521
Tenuta Licinia	667	Tenuta Tenaglia	201
Tenuta Luce	755	Tenuta Terraviva	880
Tenuta Luisa	495	Tenuta Travaglino	291
Tenuta Mareli	756	Tenuta Trerose	733
Tenuta Masone Mannu	1031	Tenuta Unterortl - Castel Juval	361
Tenuta Mazzolino	276	Tenuta Valdipiatta	735
Tenuta Meraviglia - Tenuta Le Colonne	756	Tenuta Viglione	961
Tenuta Montemagno	158	Tenuta Villanova	532
Tenuta Monteti	679	Tenute Ambrogio e Giovanni Folonari	654
Tenuta Moser	349	Tenute Barone di Valforte	884
Tenuta Mulin di Mezzo	419	Tenute Capovaccaio	941
Tenuta Musone	796	Tenute Casenuove	617
Tenuta Nicolussi-Leck	351	Tenute Chiaromonte	943
Tenuta Olim Bauda	166	Tenute Cisa Asinari dei Marchesi di Grésy	113
Tenuta Pakravan-Papi	686	Tenute del Cerro	728
Tenuta Patruno Perniola	951	Tenute del Garda	290
Tenuta Perano	690	Tenute Eméra - Claudio Quarta Vignaiolo	946
Tenuta Pfitscher	352	Tenute Gregu	1030
Tenuta Piano di Rustano	799	Tenute Lunelli - Castelbuono	830
Tenuta Poggio alla Sala	761		
Tenuta Poggio Rosso	701		
Tenuta Querciamatta	763		

Tenute Lunelli - Podernovo	668	Tezza	437
Tenute Orestiadi	1000	Thomas Pichler	367
Tenute Palagetto	686	Thomas Unterhofer	368
Tenute Perda Rubia	1034	Thurnhof - Andreas Berger	368
Tenute Pieralisi	799	Tiare - Roberto Snidarcig	524
Tenute RaDe	201	Tiberini	768
Tenute Rapitalà	1005	Tiberio	768
Tenute Rubino	955	Tiberio	880
Tenute San Fabiano	764	Tiefenbrunner	359
Tenute San Sisto	804	Tiezzi	768
Tenute Sella	195	Tiziano Ciacci - Poggio Nardone	633
Tenute Sella & Mosca	1038	Tiziano Mazzoni	154
Tenute Silvio Nardi	683	Toblino, Cantina	327
Tenute Tomasella	437	Tocco	888
Tercic, Matijaz	524	Todini	839
Terenzi	728	Togata, La	731
Terenzi, Giovanni	858	Tola, Girolamo	1009
Terenzuola	243	Tolaini	731
Teresa Raiz	509	Toledana, La	202
Terlano, Cantina	358	Tollena	768
Terra Costantino	1008	Tollo, Cantina	881
Terra dei Re	933	Tomasella, Tenute	437
Terra Fageto	809	Tomassetti	810
Terradonnà	729	Tommasi Viticoltori	438
Terrapremiata	809	Tommaso Masciantonio	886
Terraviva, Tenuta	880	Tommaso Olivastri	886
Terrazze dell'Etna	1009	Tonello	438
Terrazze, Fattoria Le	810	Tordera, La	439
Terre Astesane	202	Tornatore, Francesco	1010
Terre Bianche	243	Toros, Franco	525
Terre d'Aenòr	290	Torraccia del Piantavigna	203
Terre de La Custodia	838	Torre a Cona	732
Terre del Marchesato, Fattoria	729	Torre dei Beati	881
Terre dell'Etruria	730	Torre Raone	888
Terre di Leone	436	Torre Rosazza	525
Terre di Sava	957	Torre Zambra	882
Terre di Sovernaja	767	Torre, Fattoria La	768
Terre Margaritelli	839	Torre, Fattoria La	769
Terre Nere	767	Torrevento	958
Terre Stregate	921	Torti, Pietro	291
Terrecarsiche 1939	958	Tosa, La	579
Terreno	767	Toscani	732
Terreno alla Via della Volpaia, Podere	768	Tramin, Cantina	359
Teruzzi	730	Travaglini, Giancarlo	203
Tessari, Cornelia	436	Travaglino, Tenuta	291
		Tre Monti	579
		Tre Pini, Cantine	959

Trerè	580	Varramista	736
Trerose, Tenuta	733	Varvaglione 1921	960
Tua Rita	733	Vecchia Cantina	
Tudernum	840	di Montepulciano	737
Tunella	526	Veglio, Mauro	205
Turetta Ca' Bianca	439	Velenosi	812
Turina, F.lli	292	Veli, Masseria Li	960
		Venica & Venica	527
Uberti	292	Ventolaio	769
Uccelliera - Voliero	734	Venturi, Roberto	812
Ugo Lequio	146	Venturini	441
Umani Ronchi	811	Venturini Baldini	581
Umberto Cesari	560	Verdi, Bruno	294
Unterganzner -		Veroni, I	737
Josephus Mayr, Erbhof	360	Vespa - Vignaioli	
Unterhofer, Thomas	368	per Passione	961
Untermoserhof -		Viarte, La	528
Georg Ramoser	360	Viberti	205
Unterortl - Castel Juval,		Vicara	206
Tenuta	361	Vicari	813
Usiglian Del Vescovo	769	Vicentini, Agostino	442
		Vie di Romans	528
Vagnoni, F.lli	769	Vietti	206
Vajra, G. D.	204	Viglione, Tenuta	961
Val delle Corti	734	Vigna del Lauro	529
Val di Suga	735	Vigna Petrussa	529
Valchiarò	526	Vigna Ròda	442
Valdipiatta, Tenuta	735	Vigna Traverso	530
Valdo Spumanti	440	Vigna, Tenuta La	769
Valentina, La	882	Vignaioli Battegazzore	75
Valentino Butussi	473	Vignaioli del Morellino	
Valfaccenda	204	di Scansano	738
Valle del Sole, La	811	Vignale di Cecilia	443
Valle Isarco,		Vignalta	443
Cantina Produttori	361	VignaMadre -	
Valle Reale	883	Famiglia Di Carlo	883
Vallecamonica, Agricola	293	Vignamaggio	738
Vallepicciola	736	Vignamato	813
Vallone, Agricole	959	Vigne del Malina	530
Valori	888	Vigne di San Pietro, Le	444
Valpanera	527	Vigne di Zamò, Le	531
Valpolicella Negrar,		Vigne Marina Coppi	118
Cantina	440	Vigneti Cenci	294
Valter Mattoni	794	Vigneti Massa	153
Valter Sirk	550	Vigneti Pittaro	504
Valtidone, Cantina	580	Vigneti Radica	887
Vanzini	293	Vigneti Repetto	182
Vaona, Odino	441	Vigneti Villabella	446

Vigneto Due Santi	444	Voerzio Martini	209	
VikeVike	1040	Von Blumen	362	
Villa Poggio Salvi	702	Vosca, Francesco	534	
Villa a Sesta	769	Vrille, La	59	
Villa Cafaggio	770			
Villa Calcinaia -		Walch, Elena	362	
Conti Capponi	770	Wassererhof	363	
Villa de Puppi	531	Weger, Josef	368	
Villa di Corlo	581	Weinberghof -		
Villa Guelpa	207	Christian Bellutti	368	
Villa La Ripa	770	Weingut Pföstl	366	
Villa Le Corti	739	Weingut Rohregger	367	
Villa Matilde Avallone	921	Weingut Thomas		
Villa Mongalli	840	Dorfmann	364	
Villa Papiano	582			
Villa Patrizia	770	Zaccagnini	888	
Villa Raiano	922	Zambon Vulcano	447	
Villa Russiz	532	Zangani	244	
Villa Saletta, Fattoria	739	Zanoni, Pietro	447	
Villa Sandi	445	Zanut	550	
Villa Santo Stefano	740	Zappacosta	888	
Villa Simone	858	Zardini, Pietro	448	
Villa Sparina	207	Zemmer, Peter	363	
Villa Spinosa	445	Zenato	448	
Villa Vallacchio	770	Zeni 1870	449	
Villabella, Vigneti	446	Zerbina, Fattoria	583	
Villanova, Tenuta	532	Zidarich	534	
Villanoviana	770	Ziliani, Chiara	295	
Villscheiderhof -		Zorzettig	535	
Florian Hilpold	368	Zuani	535	
Vinae Montae	740	Zucchi	583	
Vincenzo Cesani	631	Zymè	449	
Vinchio Vaglio	208			
Vinco	888			
Vini Franchetti -				
Passopisciaro	994			
Vini Noüe Marinič	549			
Vinicola Arno	73			
Vinosia	922			
Viola, Aldo	1010			
Viola, Tenuta La	582			
Virna Borgogno	208			
Vis Amoris	244			
Visintini, Andrea	533			
Vistorta	533			
Vitari, I	295			
Vite Colte	209			
Viviani	446			

WINERIES IN ALPHABETICAL ORDER